D1156344

For our students,
with thanks for permitting us to take the journey with you

For Clyde Stickney and Paul Brown,
with thanks for allowing us the privilege to carry on their legacy of teaching through this book

For our families, with love,
Debbie, Jessica, Jaymie, Lynn, Drew, Marie, Kim, Ben, and Lucy

Preface

The process of financial reporting, financial statement analysis, and valuation is intended to help investors and analysts to deeply understand a firm's profitability and risk and to use that information to forecast future profitability and risk and ultimately value the firm, enabling intelligent investment decisions. This process lies at the heart of the role of accounting, financial reporting, capital markets, investments, portfolio management, and corporate management in the world economy. When conducted with care and integrity, thorough and thoughtful financial statement analysis and valuation is a fascinating and potentially rewarding activity that can create tremendous value for society. However, as the recent financial crises in our capital markets reveal, when financial statement analysis and valuation is conducted carelessly and without integrity, it can create enormous loss of value in our capital markets and trigger deep recession in even the most powerful economies in the world. The stakes are high.

In addition, the game is changing. The world is shifting toward a new approach to financial reporting, and expectations for high quality and high integrity financial analysis and valuation are increasing among investors and securities regulators. Many of the world's most powerful economies, including the European Union, Canada, and Japan, have already shifted or will soon shift to International Financial Reporting Standards (IFRS). The U.S. Securities and Exchange Commission (SEC) has already begun to accept financial statement filings based on IFRS from non-U.S. registrants, and is seriously considering whether to converge financial reporting from U.S. Generally Accepted Accounting Principles (GAAP) to IFRS for U.S. registrants. Given the pace and breadth of financial reform legislation, it is clear that it is no longer "business as usual" on Wall Street and around the world for financial statement analysis and valuation.

Given the profound importance of financial reporting, financial statement analysis, and valuation, and given our rapidly changing world in accounting and the capital markets, this textbook provides a principled and disciplined approach to analysis and valuation. This textbook demonstrates and explains a thoughtful and thorough six-step framework for financial statement analysis and valuation. The effective analysis of a set of financial statements begins with an evaluation of **(1)** the economic characteristics and current conditions of the industries in which a firm competes, and **(2)** the particular strategies the firm executes to compete in each of these industries. It then moves to **(3)** assessing how well the firm's financial statements reflect the economic effects of the firm's strategic decisions and actions. This assessment requires an understanding of the accounting principles and methods used to create the financial statements, the relevant and reliable information that the financial statements provide, and the appropriate adjustments that the analyst should make to improve the quality of the information the financial statements provide. In this text we embrace financial reporting and financial statement analysis based on U.S. GAAP and IFRS—new for the seventh edition. Next, the analyst **(4)** assesses the profitability and risk of the firm using financial statement ratios and other analytical tools, and then **(5)** forecasts the firm's future profitability and risk, incorporating information about expected changes in the economics of the industry and the firm's strategies. Finally, the analyst **(6)** values the firm using various valuation methods, making an investment decision by comparing likely ranges of the value of the share to the share price observed in the capital market. This six-step process forms the conceptual and pedagogical framework for this book, and it is a principled and disciplined approach to intelligent analysis and valuation.

All textbooks on financial statement analysis include step (4), assessing the profitability and risk of a company. Textbooks differ, however, with respect to their emphases on the other five steps. Consider the following depiction of these steps.

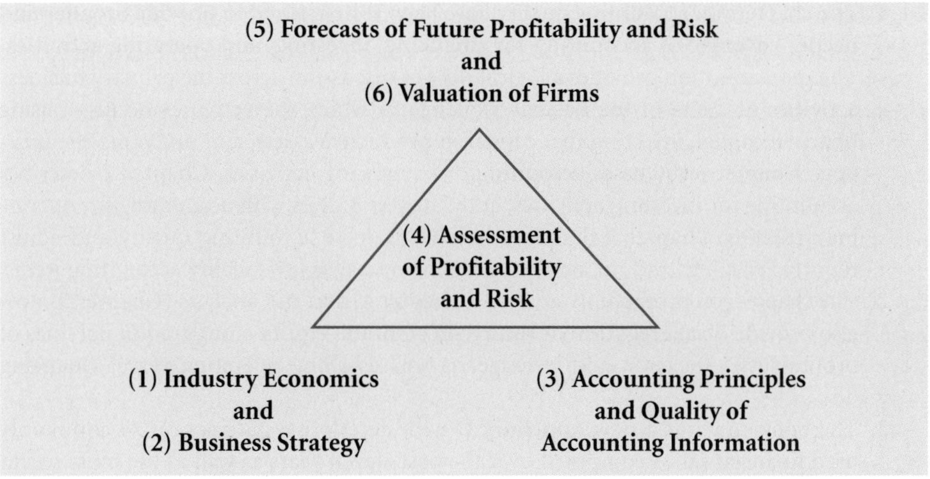

Our view is that these six steps must form an integrated endeavor for effective and complete financial statement analysis. We have therefore structured and developed this book to provide balanced, integrated coverage of all six elements. We sequence our study by beginning with industry economics and firm strategy, moving to a general consideration of GAAP and IFRS and the quality of accounting information, and providing a structure and tools for the analysis of profitability and risk. We then delve more deeply into specific accounting issues and the determinants of accounting quality, and then conclude with forecasting and valuation. We anchor each step in the sequence on the firm's profitability and risk, which are the fundamental drivers of value. We continually relate each part to those preceding and following it to maintain this balanced, integrated perspective.

The premise of this book is that you will learn financial statement analysis most effectively by performing the analysis on actual companies. The book's narrative sets forth the important concepts and analytical tools and demonstrates their application using the financial statements of PepsiCo. Each chapter contains a set of questions, exercises, problems, and cases based primarily on financial statement data of actual companies. Each chapter also contains an integrative case involving Starbucks so you can apply the tools and methods throughout the text. A financial statement analysis package (FSAP) is available to aid in the analytical tasks (discussed later).

MAJOR CHANGES IN THIS EDITION

The most significant change in this edition is the addition of two excellent new coauthors, Stephen Baginski and Mark Bradshaw, to replace Clyde Stickney and Paul Brown. Clyde Stickney, the original author of the first three editions of this book and coauthor of the fourth, fifth, and sixth editions, is enjoying his well-earned retirement. Paul Brown, a coauthor of the fourth, fifth, and sixth editions, is now the Dean of the College of Business and Economics at Lehigh University. Mark and Steve are both outstanding research scholars and award-winning teachers in accounting, financial statement analysis, and valuation. They bring many fresh new ideas and insights to produce a new edition with a strong focus on thoughtful and disciplined fundamental analysis, a broad and deep coverage of accounting issues including IFRS, and expanded analysis of companies within a global economic environment.

The next section discusses the content of each chapter and the changes made in this edition. Listed below are the major changes made in this edition that impact all chapters or groups of chapters.

1. The chapters on accounting quality have been **restructured to provide broader and deeper coverage of accounting for financing, investing, and operating activities.** The reorganization provides a logical flow of discussion across the primary business activities of firms in the natural sequence in which the activities occur—raising financial capital, investing that capital in productive assets, and operating the business. **Chapter 6** discusses accounting for financing activities. **Chapter 7** describes accounting for investing activities, and **Chapter 8** deals with accounting for operating activities. **Chapter 9** describes how to evaluate accounting quality and adjust reported earnings and financial statements to cleanse low-quality accounting items.
2. The chapters on profitability analysis (**Chapter 4**) and risk analysis (**Chapter 5**) now also provide **disaggregation of return on common equity** along traditional lines of profitability, efficiency, and leverage, as well as along operating versus financing lines.
3. The book contains a **new Appendix D** with descriptive statistics on 24 commonly used financial ratios computed over the past eleven years as well as the most recent three years for 48 industries. These ratios data enable you to benchmark your analyses and forecasts against industry averages.
4. Each chapter includes **relevant new discussion of how U.S. GAAP compares to IFRS**, and how analysts should deal with such differences in financial statement analysis. End-of-chapter materials contain many problems and cases involving non-U.S. companies, with **application of financial statement analysis techniques to IFRS-based financial statements.**
5. Each chapter provides references to specific standards in U.S. GAAP using the traditional citations (such as SFAS numbers) as well as the **new FASB Codification system.**
6. The chapters provide a number of **relevant new insights from empirical accounting research**, added because they are pertinent to financial statement analysis and valuation.
7. The end-of-chapter material for each chapter contains portions of an updated, integrative case applying the concepts and tools discussed in that chapter to Starbucks. This series of cases builds on the illustrations in the chapter in which the concepts and tools are applied to PepsiCo.
8. Each chapter contains approximately **50 percent new or substantially revised and updated end-of-chapter material, including new problems and cases.** This is a doubling of the amount of new or revised material that appeared in the sixth edition, and this material is relevant, real-world, and written for maximum learning value.
9. The Financial Statement Analysis Package (**FSAP**) available with this book has been **substantially revised and made more user-friendly**.

OVERVIEW OF THE TEXT

This section describes briefly the content of each chapter, indicating the major changes made since the previous edition.

Chapter 1—Overview of Financial Reporting, Financial Statement Analysis, and Valuation. This chapter introduces the six interrelated sequential steps in financial statement analysis that serve as the organization structure for this book. It presents several frameworks for understanding the industry economics and business strategy of a firm and applies them to PepsiCo. It also reviews the purpose, underlying concepts, and content of each of the three principal financial statements, including those of non-U.S. companies appearing in a different format. It also contains a section with key provisions of the Sarbanes-Oxley Act of 2002 that are of particular relevance to the analyst. Another new section provides the rationale for analyzing financial statements in capital market settings, including showing the results from an empirical study of the association between unexpected earnings and market-adjusted stock returns as well as various empirical results showing that fundamental analysis can help investors generate above-market returns. The appendix presents an extensive discussion to help students do a term project involving the analysis of one or more companies. Our examination of the course syllabi of users of the previous edition indicated that most courses require students to engage in such a project. This appendix should guide students in how to proceed, where to get information, and so on.

In addition to the new integrative case involving Starbucks, the chapter includes an updated version of a case involving Nike.

Chapter 2—Asset and Liability Valuation and Income Recognition. This chapter covers three topics we believe our students need to review from previous courses before delving into the more complex topics in this book.

- First, we discuss the link between the valuation of assets and liabilities on the balance sheet and the measurement of income. We believe that students understand topics such as revenue recognition and accounting for marketable securities, derivatives, pensions, and other topics more easily when they examine them with an apprecia-tion for the inherent trade-off of a balance sheet versus income statement perspective. A new aspect of this chapter to the seventh edition is that it reviews the trade-offs faced by accounting standard setters, regulators, and corporate managers who attempt to simultaneously provide both reliable and relevant financial statement information. We also examine whether firms should recognize value changes imme-diately in net income or delay their recognition, sending them temporarily through other comprehensive income.
- Second, we present a framework for analyzing the dual effects of economic transac-tions and other events on the financial statements. This framework relies on the bal-ance sheet equation to trace these effects through the financial statements:

A_{BEG} =	L_{BEG}	+	CC_{BEG}	+	$AOCI_{BEG}$	+	RE_{BEG}
$+\Delta A$	$+\Delta L$		$+\Delta Stock$		$+OCI$		$+NI$ $-D$
A_{END} =	L_{END}	+	CC_{END}	+	$AOCI_{END}$	+	RE_{END}

This framework manifests itself in how we present transactions in the text; for example:

	Assets		=	Liabilities	+	Shareholders' Equity			
						CC	AOCI	RE	
1.	Cash	+300,000						Gain on Sale of Land	+90,000
	Land	−210,000							

Cash	300,000		
Land		210,000	
Gain on Sale of Land		90,000	

	Assets		=	Liabilities	+	Shareholders' Equity			
						CC	AOCI	RE	
2.	Cash	−36,000						Income Tax Expense	−36,000

Income Tax Expense	36,000		(0.40 × [300,000 − 210,000])
Cash		36,000	

Even students who are well grounded in double-entry accounting find this framework helpful in visually identifying the effects of various complex business transactions, such as corporate acquisitions, derivatives, and leases. We use this framework in subsequent chapters as we discuss various GAAP topics.

- Third, we discuss the measurement of income tax expense, particularly with regard to the treatment of temporary differences between book income and taxable income. Virtually every business transaction has income tax consequences, and it is crucial that analysts grasp the information conveyed in income tax disclosures. Delaying consideration of the income tax consequences until later in the text hinders effective coverage of such topics as restructuring charges, asset impairments, depreciation, and leases.

The end-of-chapter materials include various new asset and liability valuation problems involving Walmart, Biosante Pharmaceuticals, Prepaid Legal Services, and Nike, as well as an integrative case involving Starbucks.

Chapter 3—Income Flows Versus Cash Flows: Understanding the Statement of Cash Flows. Chapter 3 reviews the statement of cash flows and presents a model for relating the cash flows from operating, investing, and financing activities to a firm's position in its product life cycle. The chapter demonstrates procedures for preparing the statement of cash flows when a firm provides no cash flow information. The chapter also addresses EBITDA (earnings before interest, taxes, depreciation, and amortization), which is becoming increasingly widely used by analysts of financial statements. We describe the differences between EBITDA and cash flow from operations. The chapter also provides new insights that place particular emphasis on how to use information in the statement of cash flows to assess earnings quality.

The end-of-chapter materials utilize cash flow and earnings data for a number of companies including eBay, Amazon, The Walt Disney Company, Fedex, Kroger, Coca-Cola, Texas Instruments, Sirius XM Radio, Sunbeam, AerLingus, and Fuso Pharmaceuticals. A case (Prime Contractors) illustrates the relation between earnings and cash flows as a firm experiences profitable and unprofitable operations and changes its business strategy. The classic W. T. Grant case illustrates the use of earnings and cash flow information to assess solvency risk and avoid bankruptcy.

Chapter 4—Profitability Analysis. This chapter discusses the concepts and tools for analyzing a firm's profitability, integrating industry economic and strategic factors that affect the interpretation of financial ratios. It then applies these concepts and tools to the analysis of the profitability of PepsiCo. The analysis of profitability centers on the rate of return on assets and its disaggregated components, the rate of return on common shareholders' equity and its disaggregated components, and earnings per share. The chapter contains a section on the well-publicized measurement of EVA (economic value added) and shows its relation to net income under GAAP. This chapter also considers analytical tools unique to certain industries, such as airlines, service firms, and financial institutions.

A number of new problems and exercises at the end of the chapter cover profitability analyses for companies such as Nucor Steel, Boston Scientific, Valero Energy, Microsoft, Oracle, Dell, Sun Microsystems, Texas Instruments, Hewlett Packard, Georgia Pacific, General Mills, Abercrombie & Fitch, Hasbro, Coca-Cola and many others. The integrative case on Starbucks involves analysis of Starbucks in both a time-series setting and in a cross-sectional setting in comparison to Panera Bread Company. Another case involves the time-series analysis of Walmart Stores and the cross-sectional analysis of its profitability versus Target and Carrefour.

Chapter 5—Risk Analysis. This chapter begins with a discussion of recently required disclosures on the extent to which firms are subject to various types of risk, including unexpected changes in commodity prices, exchange rates, and interest rates and how firms manage these risks. The chapter provides new insights and discussion about the benefits and dangers associated with financial flexibility and the use of leverage. New in this edition is the articulation of how to decompose return on common equity into components that highlight the contribution of the inherent profitability of the firm's assets and the contribution from the strategic use of leverage to enhance the returns to common equity investors. The chapter provides a new approach to in-depth financial statement analysis of various risks associated with leverage, including short-term liquidity risk, long-term solvency risk, credit risk, bankruptcy risk, systematic and firm-specific market risk, and fraudulent financial reporting risk. This chapter also describes and illustrates the calculation and interpretation of risk ratios and applies them to the financial statements of PepsiCo, focusing on both short-term liquidity risk and long-term solvency risk. We also explore credit risk and bankruptcy risk in greater depth. An important section examines the risk of financial reporting manipulation, illustrating Beneish's multivariate model for identifying potential manipulators.

A unique feature of the problems in Chapters 4 and 5 is the linking of the analysis of several companies across the two chapters, including problems involving Hasbro, Abercrombie & Fitch, Coca-Cola, Starbucks, and Walmart. Chapter-ending cases involve risk analysis for Starbucks, classic cases on credit risk analysis (Massachusetts Stove Company) and bankruptcy prediction (Fly-By-Night International Group), and financial reporting manipulation (Millennial Technologies).

Chapter 6—Financing Activities. This chapter has been completely restructured along with Chapters 7 and 8 to discuss accounting issues in their natural sequence—raising financial capital, then investing the capital in productive assets, and then managing the operations of the business. Chapter 6 discusses the accounting principles and practices under U.S. GAAP and IFRS associated with firms' financing activities. The chapter begins by describing the financial statement reporting of capital investments by owners (equity issues) and distributions to owners (dividends and share repurchases). The chapter then describes the accounting for equity issued to compensate employees (stock options, stock appreciation rights, and restricted stock). In this discussion, the chapter reviews the provisions of FASB *Statement No. 123* and *123(Revised 2004)*, addressing accounting for stock options and their impact on both financial statement amounts and firm value. The chapter demonstrates how shareholders' equity reflects the effects of transactions with non-owners which flow through the income statement (net income) and those which do not (other comprehensive income). The chapter also describes the principles of liability recognition in financial statements and applies the liability recognition principles to various types of long-term debt (bonds, notes payable, lease liabilities, and troubled debt) as well as hybrid securities (convertible bonds, preferred stock). The chapter also presents financial reporting for off-balance sheet financing. The chapter then describes the effects of accounting for operating and capital leases on the financial statements and demonstrates the adjustments required to convert operating leases to capital leases. Throughout the chapter we highlight the differences between U.S. GAAP and IFRS in the area of equity and debt financing.

In addition to various questions and exercises, the end-of-chapter material includes problems probing accounting for various financing alternatives, Ford Motor Credit's securitization of receivables, off-balance sheet financing at International Paper, operating versus capital leases of various retail chains including The Gap and Limited Brands and airlines such as Northwest Airlines, and stock-based compensation at Coca-Cola, General Electric, and Eli Lilly. End-of-chapter cases include the integrative case involving Starbucks, a case on stock compensation at Oracle, and long-term financing and solvency risk at Southwest Airlines versus Lufthansa.

Chapter 7—Investing Activities. This chapter has been thoroughly restructured and discusses various accounting principles and methods under U.S. GAAP and IFRS associated with a firm's investments in long-lived tangible assets, intangible assets, and financial investments. The chapter demonstrates the accounting for a firm's investments in tangible productive assets including property, plant, and equipment, covering the initial decision to capitalize or expense and the use of choices and estimates to allocate costs through the depreciation process. The chapter also demonstrates and explains alternative ways that firms account for intangible assets, highlighting research and development expenditures, software development expenditures, and goodwill, including the exercise of judgment in the allocation of costs through the amortization process. The chapter also reviews and applies the rules for evaluating the impairment of different categories of long-lived assets, including goodwill. The chapter also describes accounting and financial reporting of intercorporate investments in securities (trading securities, available-for-sale securities, held-to-maturity securities, and noncontrolled affiliates) and corporate acquisitions (including the market value, equity, proportionate consolidation, and full consolidation methods). The discussion of corporate acquisitions incorporates the provisions of FASB *Statements No. 141R, 142,* and *160.* The discussion of consolidation policy includes the treatment of variable-interest entities, including special-purpose entities and the provisions of FASB *Interpretation No. 46R* and *Statements No. 166* and *167.* The chapter reviews accounting for variable-interest entities, including the requirement to consolidate them with the firm identified as the primary beneficiary. Finally, the chapter prepares a set of translated financial statements using the all-current method and the monetary/nonmonetary method and describes the conditions under which each method best portrays the operating relationship between a U.S. parent firm and its foreign subsidiary.

The end-of-chapter questions, exercises, problems, and cases include a problem involving Molson Coors Brewing Company and its variable interest entities, an integrative application of the chapter topics to Starbucks, and a case involving Disney's acquisition of Marvel Entertainment.

Chapter 8—Operating Activities. Chapter 8 has been reorganized to discuss how financial statements prepared under U.S. GAAP or IFRS capture and report the firm's operating activities. The chapter opens with discussion of how financial accounting measures and reports the revenues and expenses generated by a firm's operating activities, as well as the related assets, liabilities, and cash flows. This discussion reviews the criteria for recognizing revenue and expenses under the accrual basis of accounting and applies these criteria to various types of businesses. The chapter evaluates the financial statement effects of recognizing income prior to the point of sale, at the time of sale, and subsequent to sale. The chapter also analyzes and interprets the effects of FIFO versus LIFO on financial statements and demonstrates how to convert the statements of a firm from a LIFO to a FIFO basis. The chapter identifies the working capital investments created by operating activities, and the financial statement effects of credit policy and credit risk. The chapter also shows how to use the financial statement and footnote information for corporate income taxes to analyze the firm's tax strategies. The chapter also describes how to utilize the financial statement and note disclosures to evaluate pensions and other post-employment benefits obligations, as well how a firm is using derivative instruments to take or to hedge risk.

The end-of-chapter problems and exercises examine revenue and expense recognition for a wide variety of operating activities, including revenues for software, consulting, transportation, construction, manufacturing, and others. End-of-chapter problems also involve Coca-Cola's derivatives and tax notes, and include an integrative case involving Starbucks, a case on alternative revenue recognition timing for the Arizona Land Development Company, and a case involving Coca-Cola's pension disclosures.

Chapter 9—Accounting Quality. This chapter, previously Chapter 6, begins with a new expanded discussion of the quality of accounting information, emphasizing substantive economic content and earnings persistence as the key characteristics, and how accounting quality can differ across U.S. GAAP and IFRS. This discussion draws heavily on the discussions of various accounting issues in Chapters 6 to 8. We then consider several financial reporting topics that primarily affect the persistence of earnings, including gains and losses from discontinued operations, extraordinary gains and losses, changes in accounting principles, other comprehensive income items, impairment losses, restructuring charges, changes in estimates, and gains and losses from peripheral activities. The chapter concludes with a discussion of the conditions under which managers might likely engage in earnings management, contrasting it with earnings manipulation and fraud discussed in Chapter 5.

Chapter-ending materials include problems involving Nestlé, H.J. Heinz, Vulcan Materials, Northrop Grumman, Intel, and General Dynamics. End-of-chapter materials also include an integrative case involving the analysis of the earnings quality of Starbucks in light of the inclusion of several potentially nonrecurring items in earnings, as well as a new case on the earnings quality of Citigroup.

Chapter 10—Forecasting Financial Statements. This chapter describes and illustrates the procedures for preparing forecasted financial statements. This material plays a central role in the valuation of companies, a topic discussed in Chapters 11 to 14. The chapter begins with an overview of forecasting and the importance of creating integrated and articulated financial statement forecasts. It then illustrates the preparation of projected financial statements for PepsiCo. The chapter also demonstrates how to get forecasted balance sheets to balance and how to compute implied statements of cash flows from forecasts of balance sheets and income statements. The chapter also discusses forecast shortcuts analysts sometimes take, and when such forecasts are reliable and when they are not. The Forecast and Forecast Development spreadsheets within FSAP provide templates students can use to develop and build their own financial statement forecasts.

Short end-of-chapter problems illustrate techniques for projecting key accounts for firms like Home Depot, Intel, Hasbro, and Barnes and Noble, determining the cost structure of firms like Nucor Steel and Sony, and dealing with irregular changes in accounts. Longer problems and cases require the preparation of financial statements for cases discussed in earlier chapters involving Walmart and Starbucks. The end-of-chapter material also includes a classic case involving the projection of financial statements to assist the Massachusetts Stove Company in its strategic decision to add gas stoves to its wood stove line. The problems and cases specify the assumptions students should make to illustrate the preparation procedure. We link and use these longer problems and cases in later chapters that rely on these financial statement forecasts in determining share value estimates for these firms.

Chapter 11—Risk-Adjusted Expected Rates of Return and the Dividends Valuation Approach. Chapters 11 to 14 form a unit in which we explore various approaches to valuing a firm. Chapter 11 focuses on fundamental issues of valuation that apply to all of the valuation chapters. This chapter provides an extensive discussion of the measurement of the cost of debt and equity capital and the weighted average cost of capital, as well as the dividends-based valuation approach. The chapter also discusses various issues of valuation, including forecasting horizons, projecting long-run continuing dividends, and computing continuing (sometimes called terminal) value. The chapter describes and illustrates the internal consistency in valuing firms using dividends, free cash flows, or earnings. Particular emphasis is placed on helping you understand that the different approaches to valuation are simply differences in perspective (dividends capture wealth distribution, free cash flows capture wealth realization in cash, and earning represent wealth creation), and that these approaches should produce internally consistent estimates of value. In this chapter we demonstrate the cost-of-capital measurements and the dividends-based valuation approach for PepsiCo, using the forecasted amounts from PepsiCo's financial statements discussed in Chapter 10. The chapter also presents techniques for assessing the sensitivity of value estimates, varying key assumptions such as the costs of capital and long-term growth rates. The chapter also discusses and illustrates the cost-of-capital computations and dividends valuation model computations within the Valuation spreadsheet in FSAP. This spreadsheet takes the forecast amounts from the Forecast spreadsheet and other relevant information and values the firm using the various valuation methods discussed in Chapters 11 to 14.

End-of-chapter material includes the computation of costs of capital across different industries and companies, including Whirlpool, IBM, and Target Stores, as well as short dividends valuation problems for companies like Royal Dutch Shell. Longer problems and cases involve computing costs of capital and dividends-based valuation of Walmart, Starbucks, and Massachusetts Stove Company from financial statement forecasts developed in Chapter 10's problems and cases.

Chapter 12—Valuation: Cash-Flow Based Approaches. Chapter 12 focuses on valuation using the present value of free cash flows. This chapter distinguishes free cash flows to all debt and equity stakeholders and free cash flows to common equity shareholders and the settings where one or the other measure of free cash flows is appropriate for valuation. The chapter develops and demonstrates valuation using free cash flows for common equity shareholders, and valuation using free cash flows to all debt and equity stakeholders. The chapter also considers and applies techniques for projecting free cash flows and measuring the continuing value after the forecast horizon. The chapter applies both of the discounted free cash flows valuation methods to PepsiCo, demonstrating how to measure the free cash flows to all debt and equity stakeholders, as well as the free cash flows to common equity. The valuations for PepsiCo use the forecasted amounts from PepsiCo's projected financial statements discussed in Chapter 10. The chapter also presents techniques for assessing the sensitivity of value estimates, varying key assumptions such as the costs of capital and long-term growth rates. The chapter also explains and demonstrates the consistency of valuation estimates across different approaches and shows that the dividends approach in Chapter 11 and the free cash flows approaches in Chapter 12 should and do lead to identical value estimates for PepsiCo. The Valuation spreadsheet in FSAP uses projected amounts from the Forecast spreadsheet and other relevant information and values the firm using both of the free cash flows valuation approaches.

Updated shorter problem material asks you to compute free cash flows from financial statement data for companies like 3M and Dick's Sporting Goods. Problem material also includes using free cash flows to value firms in leveraged buyout transactions, such as May Department Stores, Experian Information Solutions, and Wedgewood Products. Longer problem material includes the valuation of Walmart, Coca-Cola, Starbucks, and Massachusetts Stove Company. The chapter also introduces the Holmes Corporation case, which is an integrated case relevant for Chapters 10 to 13 in which students select forecast assumptions, prepare projected financial statements, and value the firm using the various methods discussed in Chapters 10 to 13. This case can be assigned piecemeal with each chapter or as an integrated case after Chapter 13.

Chapter 13—Valuation: Earnings-Based Approaches. Chapter 13 emphasizes the role of accounting earnings in valuation, focusing on valuation methods using the residual income approach. The residual income approach uses the ability of a firm to generate income in excess of the cost of capital as the principal driver of a firm's value in excess of its book value. We apply the residual income valuation method to the forecasted amounts for PepsiCo from Chapter 10. The chapter also demonstrates that the dividends valuation methods, the free cash flows valuation methods, and the residual income valuation methods are consistent with a fundamental valuation approach. In the chapter we explain and demonstrate that these approaches yield identical estimates of value for PepsiCo. The Valuation spreadsheet in FSAP includes valuation models that use the residual income valuation method.

End-of-chapter materials include various problems involving computing residual income across different firms, including Abbott Labs, IBM, Target Stores, Microsoft, Intel, Dell, Southwest Airlines, Kroger, and Yum! Brands. Longer problems also involve the valuation of other firms such as Steak 'n Shake in which the needed financial statement information is given. Longer problems and cases apply the residual income approach to Coca-Cola as well as to Walmart, Starbucks, and Massachusetts Stove Company, considered in Chapters 10, 11, and 12.

Chapter 14—Valuation: Market-Based Approaches. Chapter 14 demonstrates how to analyze and use the information in market value. In particular, the chapter describes and applies market-based valuation multiples, including the market-to-book ratio and the price-to-earnings ratio. The chapter describes and illustrates the theoretical and conceptual approaches to market multiples, and contrasts them with the practical approaches to market multiples. The chapter demonstrates how the market-to-book ratio is consistent with residual ROCE valuation and the residual income model discussed in Chapter 13. The chapter also describes the factors that drive market multiples, so analysts can adjust multiples appropriately to reflect differences in profitability, growth, and risk across comparable firms. An applied analysis demonstrates how to reverse engineer a firm's stock price to infer the valuation assumptions that the stock market appears to be making. We apply all of these valuation methods to PepsiCo. The chapter concludes with a new discussion of the role of market efficiency, as well as striking evidence on using earnings surprises to pick stocks and form portfolios (the Bernard-Thomas post-earnings announcement drift anomaly) as well as using value-to-price ratios to form portfolios (the Frankel-Lee strategy), both of which appear to help investors generate significant above-market returns.

End-of-chapter materials include problems involving computing and interpreting market-to-book ratios for pharmaceutical companies, Enron, Coca-Cola, Walmart, and Steak 'n Shake and the integrative case involving Starbucks.

Appendices. Appendix A includes the financial statements and notes for PepsiCo used in the illustrations throughout the book. Appendix B is PepsiCo's letter to the shareholders and the management discussion and analysis of operations, which we use when interpreting PepsiCo's financial ratios and in our financial statement projections. Appendix C presents the output from FSAP for PepsiCo, including the Data worksheet, the Analysis worksheet (profitability and risk ratio analyses), the Forecasts and Forecast Development worksheets, and the Valuations worksheet. A new Appendix D provides descriptive statistics on 24 financial statement ratios across 48 industries over the past eleven years as well as the most recent three years.

CHAPTER SEQUENCE AND STRUCTURE

Our own experience and our discussions with other professors suggest that there are various approaches to teaching the financial statement analysis course, each of which works well in particular settings. We have therefore designed this book for flexibility with respect to the sequence of chapter assignments. The following diagram sets forth the overall structure of the book.

<table>
<tr><td colspan="6">Chapter 1: Overview of Financial Reporting, Financial Statement Analysis, and Valuation</td></tr>
<tr><td colspan="3">Chapter 2: Asset and Liability Valuation and Income Recognition</td><td colspan="3">Chapter 3: Income Flows Versus Cash Flows</td></tr>
<tr><td colspan="3">Chapter 4: Profitability Analysis</td><td colspan="3">Chapter 5: Risk Analysis</td></tr>
<tr><td colspan="2">Chapter 6:
Financing Activities</td><td colspan="2">Chapter 7:
Investing Activities</td><td colspan="2">Chapter 8:
Operating Activities</td></tr>
<tr><td colspan="6">Chapter 9: Accounting Quality</td></tr>
<tr><td colspan="6">Chapter 10: Forecasting Financial Statements</td></tr>
<tr><td colspan="6">Chapter 11: Risk-Adjusted Expected Rates of Return and the Dividends Valuation Approach</td></tr>
<tr><td colspan="3">Chapter 12: Valuation: Cash-Flow-Based Approaches</td><td colspan="3">Chapter 13: Valuation: Earnings-Based Approaches</td></tr>
<tr><td colspan="6">Chapter 14: Valuation: Market-Based Approaches</td></tr>
</table>

The chapter sequence follows the six steps in financial statement analysis discussed in Chapter 1. Chapters 2 and 3 provide the conceptual foundation for the three financial statements. Chapters 4 and 5 present tools for analyzing the financial statements. Chapters 6 to 9 examine the accounting for financing, investing, and operating activities, and assessing the quality of accounting information under U.S. GAAP and IFRS. Chapters 10 to 14 focus primarily on forecasting financial statements and valuation.

Some schools teach U.S. GAAP and IFRS topics and financial statement analysis in separate courses. Chapters 6 to 9 are an integrated unit and sufficiently rich for the U.S. GAAP and IFRS course. The remaining chapters will then work well in the financial statement analysis course. Some schools leave the topic of valuation to finance courses. Chapters 1 to 9 (or, alternatively, Chapters 1 to 10) will then work well for the accounting prelude to the finance course. Some instructors may wish to begin with valuation (Chapters 11 to 14) and then examine data issues that might affect the numbers used in the valuations (Chapters 6 to 9). This textbook is adaptable to other sequences of the various topics.

OVERVIEW OF THE ANCILLARY PACKAGE

The Financial Statement Analysis Package (FSAP) is available on the website for this book (www.cengage.com/accounting/wahlen) to all purchasers of the text. The package performs various analytical tasks (common-size and rate of change financial statements, ratio computations, risk indicators such as the Altman-Z score and the Beneish manipulation index), provides a worksheet template for preparing financial statements forecasts, and applies amounts from the financial statement forecasts to valuing a firm using various valuation methods. A user manual for FSAP is embedded within FSAP.

Packaged with this book is Thomson ONE Business School Edition for the purpose of supplementary financial research beyond the problems and cases in the book. Thomson

ONE Business School Edition is an educational version of the same financial data provided by Thomson Reuters that experts use on a daily basis. For 500 companies, this online resource provides:

- Worldscope®, which includes company profiles, financials and accounting results, market per-share data, annual information, and monthly prices going back to 1980.
- I/B/E/S Consensus Estimates, which provides consensus estimates, analyst-by-analyst earnings coverage, and analysts' forecasts.
- Disclosure SEC Database, which includes company profiles, annual and quarterly company financials, pricing information and earnings.
- An Instructor's Manual is also available to faculty who adopt this book. It contains suggestions for using the textbook, solutions to all problems and cases, and teaching notes to cases.

ACKNOWLEDGMENTS

Many individuals provided invaluable assistance in the preparation of this book and we wish to acknowledge their help in a formal manner here.

We wish to especially acknowledge many helpful comments and suggestions from Susan Eldridge at the University of Nebraska—Omaha. We also appreciate the help of Betsy Laydon, at Indiana University, for helpful comments and suggestions for chapters and for assistance in updating and creating end of chapter problem material. We are also grateful for the research assistance of Julia Yu and Drew Baginski, both of the University of Georgia. Julia helped create the financial ratios appendix and Drew helped create problems and cases for end of chapter materials. We also appreciate the assistance of Matthew Diamond of PepsiCo, who reviewed textual material related to PepsiCo and provided other helpful comments.

The following professional colleagues have assisted in the development of this edition by reviewing or providing helpful comments on previous editions:

Kristian Allee, Michigan State University
Messod Daniel Beneish, Indiana University
Aaron Hipscher, New York University
Robert Howell, Dartmouth College
Amy Hutton, Boston College
Prem Jain, Georgetown University
Ross Jennings, University of Texas at Austin
April Klein, New York University
Yuri Loktionov, New York University
D. Craig Nichols, Cornell University
Virginia Soybel, Babson College
Christine Wiedman, University of Waterloo
Matthew Wieland, University of Georgia
Michael Williamson, University of Texas at Austin

Additional reviewers whose thoughts on the new Seventh Edition deserve our thanks:

Murad Antia, University of South Florida
Michael Clement, University of Texas, Austin
Ellen Engel, University of Chicago
Robert A. Howell, Dartmouth College
J. William Kamas, University of Texas, Austin
Michael Keane, University of Southern California

We wish to thank the following individuals at South-Western, who provided guidance, encouragement, or assistance in various phases of the revision: Craig Avery, Matt

Filimonov, Kim Kusnerak, and Erin Shelton. Katherine Rybowiak did an outstanding job assisting with preparation of the solutions/instructor's manual.

Finally, we wish to acknowledge the role played by former students in our financial statement analysis classes for being challenging partners in our learning endeavors. We also acknowledge and thank Clyde Stickney and Paul Brown for allowing us to carry on their legacy by teaching financial statement analysis and valuation through this book. Lastly, and most importantly, we are deeply grateful for our families for being encouraging and patient partners in this work. We dedicate this book to each of you.

James M. Wahlen
Stephen P. Baginski
Mark T. Bradshaw

About the Authors

James M. Wahlen is the James R. Hodge Chair, Professor of Accounting, and the former Chairman of the MBA Program at the Kelley School of Business at Indiana University. He received his Ph.D. from the University of Michigan and has served on the faculties of the University of North Carolina at Chapel Hill, INSEAD, the University of Washington, and Pacific Lutheran University. Professor Wahlen's teaching and research interests focus on financial accounting, financial statement analysis, and the capital markets. His research investigates earnings quality and earnings management, earnings volatility as an indicator of risk, fair value accounting for financial instruments, accounting for loss reserve estimates by banks and insurers, stock market efficiency with respect to accounting information, and testing the extent to which future stock returns can be predicted with earnings and other financial statement information. His research has been published in a wide array of academic and practitioner journals in accounting and finance. He has had public accounting experience in both Milwaukee and Seattle and is a member of the American Accounting Association. He has received numerous teaching awards during his career. In his free time Jim loves outdoor sports (biking, hiking, skiing, golf), cooking (and, of course, eating), and listening to rock music (especially if it is loud and live).

Stephen P. Baginski is the Herbert E. Miller Chair in Financial Accounting at the University of Georgia's J.M. Tull School of Accounting. He received his Ph.D. from the University of Illinois in 1986, and he has taught a variety of financial and managerial undergraduate, MBA, and executive education courses at Indiana University, Illinois State University, the University of Illinois, Northeastern University, Florida State University, Washington University in St. Louis, the University of St. Galen, the Swiss Banking Institute at the University of Zurich, and INSEAD. Professor Baginski has published articles in a variety of journals including *The Accounting Review, Journal of Accounting Research, Contemporary Accounting Research, The Journal of Risk and Insurance, Quarterly Review of Finance and Economics,* and *Review of Quantitative Finance and Accounting.* His research primarily deals with the causes and consequences of voluntary management disclosures of earnings forecasts, and he also investigates the usefulness of financial accounting information in security pricing and risk assessment. Professor Baginski has served on several editorial boards and as an associate editor at *Accounting Horizons* and *The Review of Quantitative Finance and Accounting.* He has won numerous undergraduate and graduate teaching awards at the department, college, and university level during his career, including receipt of the Doctoral Student Inspiration Award from students at Indiana University. Professor Baginski loves to watch college football, play golf, and run (very slowly) in his spare time.

Mark T. Bradshaw is an Associate Professor of Accounting at the Carroll School of Management of Boston College. Bradshaw received a Ph.D. from the University of Michigan Business School, and earned a BBA summa cum laude with highest honors in accounting and master's degree in financial accounting from the University of Georgia. He previously taught at University of Chicago, Harvard Business School, and University of Georgia. He has been a Certified Public Accountant since 1991 and was an auditor for Arthur Andersen & Co. in Atlanta. Bradshaw conducts research on capital markets, specializing in the examination of securities analysts and financial reporting issues. His research has been published in a variety of academic and practitioner journals, and he currently serves as Associate Editor for both *Journal of Accounting and Economics* and *Journal of Accounting Research*, is on the Editorial Board of *The Accounting Review*, and is a reviewer for numerous other accounting and finance journals. He has also authored a book with Brian Bruce, *Analysts, Lies, and Statistics—Cutting through the Hype in Corporate Earnings Announcements.* Approximately twenty pounds ago, Bradshaw was an accomplished cyclist. Currently focused on other pursuits (including the co-administration of the lives of two toddlers), he still routinely passes younger and thinner cyclists.

BRIEF CONTENTS

CONTENTS

Chapter 1

Overview of Financial Reporting, Financial Statement Analysis, and Valuation

Learning Objectives

1. **Understand the six-step analytical framework that is the logical structure for financial statement analysis and valuation, and establishes the foundation for this book. This framework enables the analyst to link the economic characteristics and strategies of a firm, its financial statements and notes, assessments of its current and forecasted profitability and risk, and its market value.**
2. **Apply three tools for assessing the economic characteristics and dynamics that drive competition in an industry: (a) value chain analysis, (b) Porter's five forces framework, and (c) an economic attributes framework.**
3. **Review the purpose, underlying concepts, and format of the balance sheet, income statement, and statement of cash flows.**
4. **Become familiar with PepsiCo, the firm analyzed throughout the book, obtaining an overview of its economics, strategy, and financial statements.**
5. **Examine the provisions of the Sarbanes-Oxley Act of 2002 that relate to financial statement information.**
6. **Obtain an introduction to the tools used to analyze a firm's profitability and risk, including financial ratios, common-size financial statements, and percentage change financial statements.**
7. **Obtain an overview of how to use financial statement information to forecast the future business activities of a firm and to value a firm.**
8. **Examine the role of financial statement analysis in an efficient capital market.**
9. **Review sources of financial information available for publicly held firms.**
10. **Obtain guidance and direction for conducting a financial statement analysis project (Appendix 1.1).**

The principal activity of security analysts is to value firms. Security analysts collect and analyze a wide array of information from financial statements and other sources to evaluate a firm's current and past performance and to predict its future performance. Then they use the expected future performance to measure the value of the firm's shares. Comparisons of the analysts' estimates of the firm's share value with the market price for the shares provide the basis for making good investment decisions.

This book has three principal purposes, each designed to help you gain important knowledge and skills necessary for financial statement analysis and valuation:

1. To demonstrate how you can link the economics of an industry, a firm's strategy, and its financial statements, gaining important insights about the firm's profitability and its risk. Chapters 1–5 discuss the principal financial statements and tools for analyzing profitability and risk.
2. To enhance your understanding of the accounting principles and methods under U.S. GAAP (Generally Accepted Accounting Principles) and IFRS (International Financial Reporting Standards) that firms use to measure and report their financing, investing, and operating activities in a set of financial statements and the adjustments the analyst may make to reported amounts to increase their relevance and reliability. Chapters 6–9 explore accounting principles in depth.
3. To demonstrate how you can use financial statement data to build forecasts of future financial statements and then use the expected future amounts of earnings, cash flows, and dividends in the valuation of firms. Chapters 10–14 focus on forecasting and valuation.

Financial analysis is an exciting and rewarding activity, particularly when the objective is to assess whether the market is pricing a firm's shares fairly. Studying the intrinsic characteristics of a firm (for example, its business model; product and service market share; and operating, investing, and financing decisions) and using this information to make informed judgments can be a very satisfying endeavor. Financial statements play a central role in the study and analysis of a firm.

Besides being used to measure firm value, the tools of effective financial statement analysis can be applied in many different decision-making settings, including the following:

- Assigning credit ratings or extending credit for a short-term period (for example, a bank loan used to finance accounts receivable or inventories) or a long-term period (for example, a bank loan or public bond issue used to finance the acquisition of property, plant, or equipment)
- Assessing the operating performance and financial health of a supplier, customer, competitor, or potential employer
- Managing a firm and communicating results to investors, creditors, employees, and other stakeholders
- Consulting with a firm and offering helpful strategic advice
- Evaluating firms for potential acquisitions or mergers or divestitures
- Valuing a firm in the initial public offering of its stock
- Forming a judgment about damages sustained in a lawsuit
- Assessing the extent of auditing needed to form an opinion about a client's financial statements

OVERVIEW OF FINANCIAL STATEMENT ANALYSIS

We view effective financial statement analysis as a three-legged stool, as Exhibit 1.1 depicts. The three legs of the stool in the figure represent effective analysis based on the following:

1. Identifying the economic characteristics of the industries in which a firm participates and the relation of those economic characteristics to various financial statement ratios
2. Describing the strategies that a firm pursues to differentiate itself from competitors as a basis for evaluating a firm's competitive advantages, the sustainability of a firm's earnings, and its risks

EXHIBIT 1.1

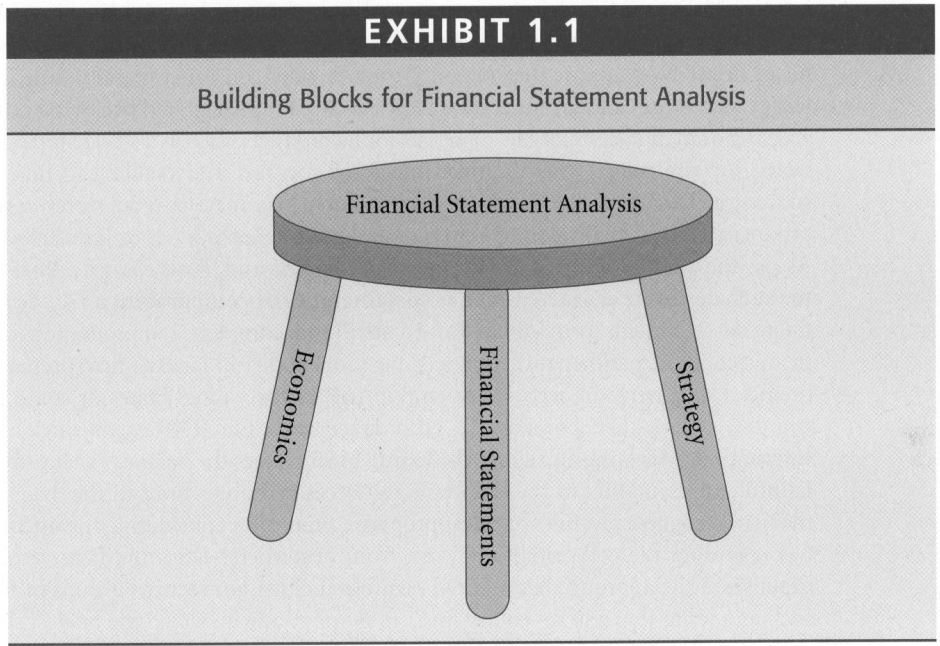

Building Blocks for Financial Statement Analysis

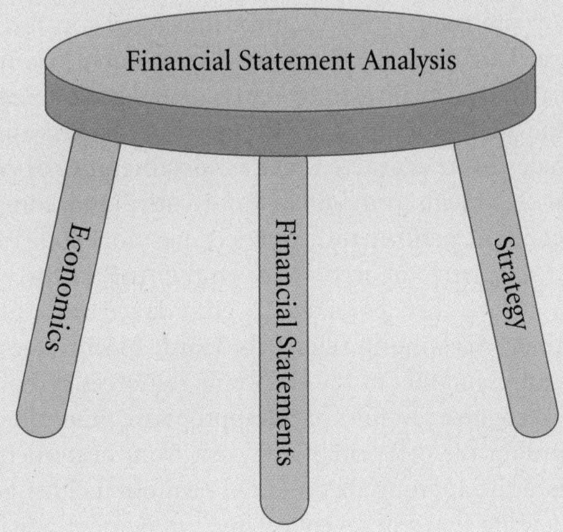

3. Evaluating the financial statements, including the accounting concepts and methods that underlie them and the quality of the information they provide

Our approach to effective analysis of financial statements for valuation and many other decisions involves six interrelated sequential steps, depicted in Exhibit 1.2.

1. **Identify the economic characteristics and competitive dynamics of the industry in which a particular firm participates.** What dynamic forces drive competition in the industry? For example, does the industry include a large number of firms selling similar products, such as grocery stores, or only a small number of competitors selling unique products, such as pharmaceutical companies? Does technological change play an important role in maintaining a competitive advantage, as in computer software? Are industry sales growing rapidly or slowly?
2. **Identify the strategies the firm pursues to gain and sustain a competitive advantage.** What business model is the firm executing to be different and successful in its

EXHIBIT 1.2

The Six Interrelated Sequential Steps in Financial Statement Analysis

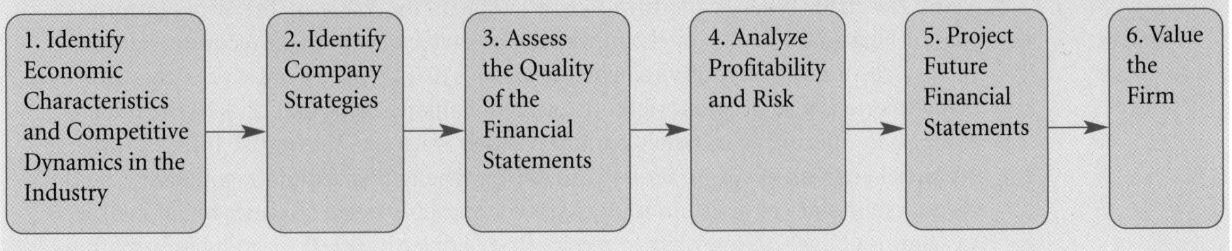

industry? Does the firm have competitive advantages? If so, how sustainable are they? Are its products designed to meet the needs of specific market segments, such as ethnic or health foods, or are they intended for a broader consumer market, such as typical grocery stores and family restaurants? Has the firm integrated backward into the growing or manufacture of raw materials for its products, such as a steel company that owns iron ore mines? Has the firm integrated forward into retailing to final consumers, such as an athletic footwear manufacturer that operates retail stores to sell its products? Is the firm diversified across several geographic markets or industries?

3. **Assess the quality of the firm's financial statements and, if necessary, adjust them for such desirable characteristics as sustainability or comparability.** Do the firm's financial statements provide an informative and complete representation of the firm's economic performance, financial position, and risk? Has the firm prepared its financial statements in accordance with GAAP in the United States or some other country, or are they prepared in accordance with the IFRS established by the International Accounting Standards Board (IASB)? Does the balance sheet provide a faithful representation of the economic resources and obligations of the firm? Does the firm recognize revenues at the appropriate time, after considering the uncertainties regarding the collectibility of cash from customers? Does the firm recognize expenses at the appropriate time? Do earnings include nonrecurring gains or losses, such as a write-down of an equity investment or goodwill, which the analyst should evaluate differently from recurring components of earnings? Has the firm structured transactions or commercial arrangements or has it selected accounting principles to appear more profitable or less risky than economic conditions otherwise suggest?
4. **Analyze the current profitability and risk of the firm using information in the financial statements.** Most financial analysts assess the profitability of a firm relative to the risks involved. What rate of return is the firm generating from the use of its assets? How much return is the firm generating for the equity capital invested? Is the firm's profit margin increasing or decreasing over time? Are returns and profit margins higher or lower than those of its key competitors? How much leverage does the firm have in its capital structure? How much of the leverage consists of debt financing that will come due in the short-term versus the long-term? Ratios that reflect relations among particular items in the financial statements are the tools used to analyze profitability and risk.
5. **Prepare forecasted financial statements.** What will be the firm's future resources, obligations, investments, cash flows, revenues, and expenses? What will be the likely future profitability and risk and, in turn, the likely future returns from investing in the company? Forecasts of a firm's ability to manage risks, particularly those elements of risk with measurable financial consequences, permit the analyst to estimate the likelihood that the firm will experience financial difficulties in the future. Forecasted financial statements that rely on the analyst's projections of the firm's future operating, investing, and financing activities provide the basis for projecting future profitability and risk.
6. **Value the firm.** What is the firm worth? What is the value of the firm's common shares? Financial analysts use their estimates of share value to make recommendations to buy, sell, or hold the equity securities of various firms whose market price they think is too low, too high, or about right. Investment banking firms that underwrite the initial public offering of a firm's common stock must set the initial offering price. Financial analysts in corporations considering whether to acquire a company (or to divest a subsidiary or division) must assess a reasonable range of values to bid in order to acquire a target (or to expect to receive from a divestiture). Translating information

from the financial statements into reliable estimates of firm value (and therefore into intelligent investment decisions) is the principal activity of financial analysts.

These six interrelated steps represent the subject matter of this book. We use these six steps as the analytical framework for analysts to follow in their efforts to analyze and value a company. This chapter briefly explores each step. Subsequent chapters develop the important concepts and tools in considerably more depth.

Throughout this book, we use financial statements, notes, and other information provided by PepsiCo, Inc. and Subsidiaries (PepsiCo) to illustrate the various topics discussed. Appendix A at the end of the book includes the fiscal year 2008 financial statements and notes for PepsiCo, as well as statements by management and the opinion of the independent accountant regarding these financial statements. Appendix B includes excerpts from a financial review provided by management that discusses the business strategy of PepsiCo; it also offers explanations for changes in PepsiCo's profitability and risk over time. Appendix C presents the output of the FSAP (Financial Statements Analysis Package), which is the financial statement analysis software that accompanies this book. The FSAP model is an Excel add-in that enables analysts to enter financial statement data, after which the model computes a wide array of profitability and risk ratios and creates templates for forecasting future financial statements and estimating a variety of valuation models. Appendix C presents the use of FSAP for PepsiCo for recent years, including PepsiCo's profitability and risk ratios, projected future financial statements, and valuation. FSAP is available at www.cengage.com/accounting/wahlen. You can use FSAP for many of the problems and cases in this book to aid in your analysis (FSAP applications are highlighted with the FSAP icon in the margin of the text). FSAP contains a user manual with guides to assist you. Appendix D presents tables of descriptive statistics on a wide array of financial ratios across 48 industries.

FSAP

STEP 1: IDENTIFY THE INDUSTRY ECONOMIC CHARACTERISTICS

The economic characteristics and competitive dynamics of an industry play a key role in influencing the strategies firms in the industry will employ and therefore the types of financial statement relationships the analyst should expect to observe when analyzing a set of financial statements. Consider, for example, the financial statement data for firms in four different industries shown in Exhibit 1.3. This exhibit expresses all items on the balance sheets and income statements as percentages of revenue. Consider how the economic characteristics of these industries affect their financial statements.

Grocery Store Chain

The products of a particular grocery store chain are difficult to differentiate from similar products of other grocery store chains, a trait that characterizes such products as *commodities*. In addition, low barriers to entry exist in the grocery store industry; an entrant needs primarily retail space and access to food products distributors. Thus, extensive competition and nondifferentiated products result in a relatively low net income to sales, or profit margin, percentage (3.5 percent in this case). Grocery stores, however, need relatively few assets to generate sales (34.2 cents in assets for each dollar of sales in this case). The assets are described as turning over 2.9 times (= 100.0%/34.2%) per year. (Each dollar invested in assets generated, on average, \$2.90 of revenues.) Each time the assets of this grocery store chain turn over, or generate one dollar of revenue, it generates a profit of 3.5 cents. Thus, during a one-year period, the grocery store earns 10.15 cents (= 3.5% × 2.9) for each dollar invested in assets.

EXHIBIT 1.3

Common-Size Financial Statement Data for Four Firms

	Grocery Store Chain	Pharmaceutical Company	Electric Utility	Commercial Bank
BALANCE SHEET				
Cash and marketable securities	0.7%	11.0%	1.5%	261.9%
Accounts and notes receivable	0.7	18.0	7.8	733.5
Inventories	8.7	17.0	4.5	—
Property, plant, and equipment, net	22.2	28.7	159.0	18.1
Other assets	1.9	72.8	29.2	122.6
Total Assets	34.2%	147.5%	202.0%	1,136.1%
Current liabilities	7.7%	30.8%	14.9%	936.9%
Long-term debt	7.6	12.7	130.8	71.5
Other noncurrent liabilities	2.6	24.6	1.8	27.2
Shareholders' equity	16.3	79.4	54.5	100.5
Total Liabilities and Shareholders' Equity	34.2%	147.5%	202.0%	1,136.1%
INCOME STATEMENT				
Revenue	100.0%	100.0%	100.0%	100.0%
Cost of goods sold	(74.1)	(31.6)	(79.7)	—
Operating expenses	(19.7)	(37.1)	—	(41.8)
Research and development	—	(10.1)	—	—
Interest	(0.5)	(3.1)	(4.6)	(36.6)
Income taxes	(2.2)	(6.0)	(5.2)	(8.6)
Net Income	3.5%	12.1%	10.5%	13.0%

Pharmaceutical Company

The barriers to entry in the pharmaceutical industry are much higher than for grocery stores. Pharmaceutical firms must invest considerable amounts in research and development to create new drugs. The research and development process is lengthy with highly uncertain outcomes. Very few projects result in successful development of new drugs. Once new drugs have been developed, they must undergo a lengthy government testing and approval process. If the drugs are approved, firms receive patents that give them exclusive rights to manufacture and sell the drugs for an extended period. These high entry barriers (research and development expenditures, government approval process, patent protection) permit pharmaceutical firms to realize much higher profit margins on approved patent-protected products compared to the profit margins of grocery stores. Exhibit 1.3 indicates that the pharmaceutical firm generated a profit margin of 12.1 percent, more than three times that reported by the grocery store chain. Pharmaceutical firms, however, face product liability risks as well as the risk that competitors will develop superior drugs that make a particular firm's drug offerings obsolete. Because of these business risks, pharmaceutical firms tend to take on relatively small amounts of debt financing as compared to firms in industries such as electric utilities and commercial banks.

Electric Utility

The principal assets of an electric utility are its capital-intensive generating plants. Thus, property, plant, and equipment dominate the balance sheet. Because of the large investments required in such assets, in the past, electric utility firms generally demanded a monopoly position in a particular locale. Government regulators permitted this monopoly position but set the rates that utilities charged customers for electric services. Thus, electric utilities have traditionally realized relatively high profit margins (10.5 percent in this case) to offset their relatively low total asset turnovers (.495 = 100.0%/202.0% in this case). The monopoly position and regulatory protection reduced the risk of financial failure and permitted electric utilities to invest large amounts of capital in long-lived assets and take on relatively high proportions of debt in their capital structures. The economic characteristics of electric utilities have changed dramatically in recent years. The gradual elimination of monopoly positions and the introduction of competition that affects rates are reducing profit margins considerably.

Commercial Bank

Through their borrowing and lending activities, commercial banks serve as intermediaries in the supply and demand for financial capital. The principal assets of commercial banks are investments in financial securities and loans to businesses and consumers. The principal financing for commercial banks comes from customers' deposits and short-term borrowings. Because customers can generally withdraw deposits at any time, commercial banks invest in securities that they can quickly convert into cash if necessary. Money is a commodity: money borrowed from one bank is similar to money borrowed from another bank. Thus, one would expect a commercial bank to realize a small profit margin on the revenue it earns from lending (interest revenue) over the price it pays for its borrowed funds (interest expense). The profit margins on lending are indeed relatively small. The 13.0 percent margin for the commercial bank shown in Exhibit 1.3 reflects the much higher profit margins it generates from offering fee-based financial services such as structuring financing packages for businesses, guaranteeing financial commitments of business customers, and arranging mergers and acquisitions. Note that the assets of this commercial bank turn over just .09 (= 100.0%/1,136.1%) times per year, reflecting the net effect of interest revenues from investments and loans of 6–8 percent per year, which requires a large investment in financial assets, and fee-based revenues, which require relatively few assets.

TOOLS FOR STUDYING INDUSTRY ECONOMICS

Three tools for studying the economic characteristics of an industry are (1) value chain analysis, (2) Porter's five forces classification framework, and (3) an economic attributes framework. The microeconomics literature suggests other analytical frameworks as well.

Value Chain Analysis

The value chain for an industry sets forth the sequence or chain of activities involved in the creation, manufacture, and distribution of its products and services. Exhibit 1.4 portrays a value chain for the pharmaceutical industry. Pharmaceutical companies invest in research and development to discover and develop new drugs. When promising drugs emerge, a lengthy drug approval process begins. Estimates suggest that it takes seven to ten years and almost $1 billion to discover and obtain approval of new drugs. To expedite the approval process, reduce costs, and permit their scientists to devote energies to the more creative

EXHIBIT 1.4

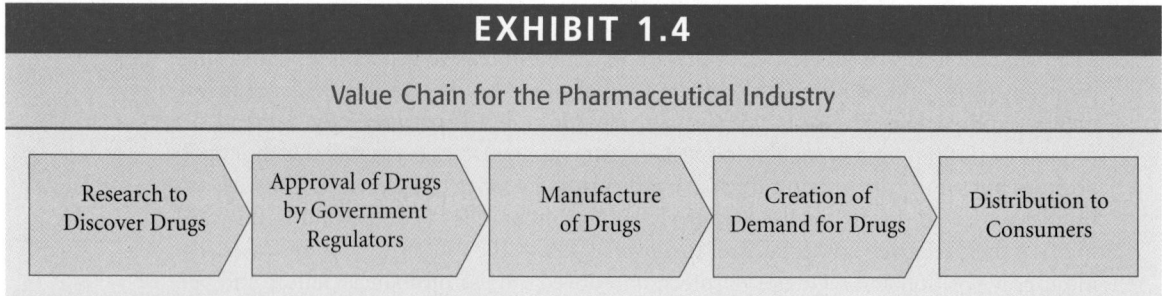

Value Chain for the Pharmaceutical Industry

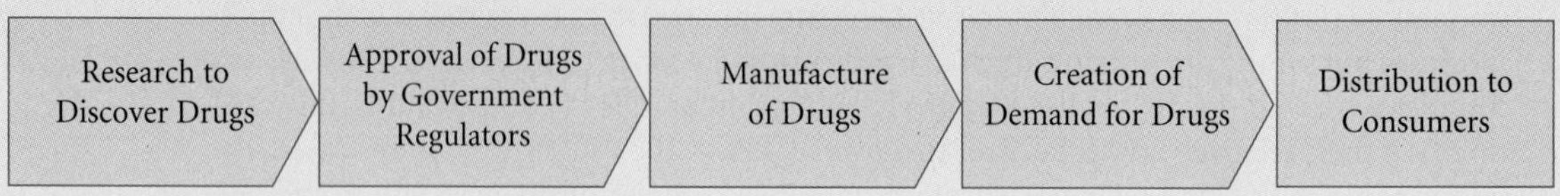

drug discovery phase, pharmaceutical companies often contract with clinical research firms to conduct the testing and shepherding of new drugs through the approval process.

The manufacture of drugs involves combining various chemicals and other elements. For quality control and product purity reasons, pharmaceutical companies use highly automated manufacturing processes. Pharmaceutical companies employ sales forces to market drugs to doctors, hospitals, and health maintenance organizations. In an effort to create demand, these companies have increasingly advertised new products through multiple advertising media, suggesting that consumers ask their doctors about the drug. Drug distribution typically channels through pharmacies, although bulk mail-order and Internet purchases are increasingly common (and encouraged by health insurers).

To the extent prices are available for products or services at each stage in the value chain, the analyst can study where value is added within an industry. For example, the analyst can look at the prices paid to acquire firms with promising or newly discovered drugs to ascertain the value of the drug discovery phase. The prices that clinical research firms charge to test and obtain approval of new drugs signal the value added by this activity. The higher the value added from any activity, the higher the profitability should be from engaging in that phase.

The analyst also can use the value chain to identify the strategic positioning of a particular firm within the industry. Traditionally, pharmaceutical firms have maintained a presence in the discovery through demand creation phases, leaving distribution to pharmacies and increasingly contracting out the drug testing and approval phase.

Refer to Note 1, "Basis of Presentation and Our Divisions," to the financial statements of PepsiCo (Appendix A) for an organizational chart of PepsiCo's divisions and segments. PepsiCo operates three business units: PepsiCo Americas Foods (PAF), PepsiCo Americas Beverages (PAB), and PepsiCo International (PI). PepsiCo Americas Foods is organized into three divisions: Frito-Lay North America (FLNA; branded snacks, chips, and other food products), Quaker Foods North America (QFNA; cereal and related products), and Latin America Foods (LAF; branded snacks, chips, and other food products). PepsiCo Americas Beverages operates as a single-segment division, and it manufactures and distributes soft drinks and other beverages throughout North America. PepsiCo International operates in markets outside North America and manufactures and sells branded snack foods, breakfast foods, soft drinks, and other beverages. The PepsiCo International unit is organized into two geographic divisions: the United Kingdom and Europe (UKEU) and the Middle East, Africa & Asia (MEAA). Exhibit 1.5 shows the amounts taken from Note 1 to PepsiCo's financial statements in Appendix A, the proportions of revenues and operating profit that PepsiCo derived from each division, and the operating profit margin (operating profit divided by revenues) of each division for 2008.

Exhibit 1.6 illustrates a value chain for one of PepsiCo's principal businesses, the soft drink/beverage industry. Note that this is PepsiCo's legacy business, so for completeness an

EXHIBIT 1.5

Division Revenues and Operating Profits for PepsiCo for 2008
(Dollar amounts in millions)

	Revenues		Operating Profits		Operating Profit Margin
PepsiCo Americas Foods					
Frito-Lay North America	$12,507	28.9%	$2,959	37.3%	23.7%
Quaker Foods North America	1,902	4.4%	582	7.3%	30.6%
Latin America Foods	5,895	13.6%	897	11.3%	15.2%
PepsiCo Americas Beverages	10,937	25.3%	2,026	25.5%	18.5%
PepsiCo International					
United Kingdom & Europe	6,435	14.9%	811	10.2%	12.6%
Middle East, Africa & Asia	5,575	12.9%	667	8.4%	12.0%
Total	$43,251	100.0%	$7,942	100.0%	18.4%

analyst should also evaluate PepsiCo's other principal businesses, particularly in the snack food and breakfast food industries.

Although the classic PepsiCo soft drinks (for example, Pepsi, Diet Pepsi, Mountain Dew®, and Slice™) have not changed for many years, the company continually engages in new product development. Once a product appears to have commercial feasibility, PepsiCo combines raw materials into a concentrate or syrup base. The ingredients and their mixes are highly confidential. PepsiCo ships the concentrate to its franchise bottlers (or, in the case of syrup, to its national fountain accounts), which combine it with water and sweeteners to produce the finished soft drink.

PepsiCo relies on noncontrolled affiliates to bottle and distribute a large percentage of its beverages. That is, PepsiCo contracts out the bottling operation. (We discuss the rationale for this arrangement in the strategy section later in this chapter.) The bottlers transport the bottled beverages and syrups to independent distributors and retail establishments.

Because the analyst can obtain separate financial statements for PepsiCo and its bottlers, one can observe where value is added along the value chain. We examine the profitability and risk of PepsiCo and its bottlers in greater depth in Chapters 4, 5, 8, and 9.

EXHIBIT 1.6

Value Chain for the Soft Drink/Beverage Industry

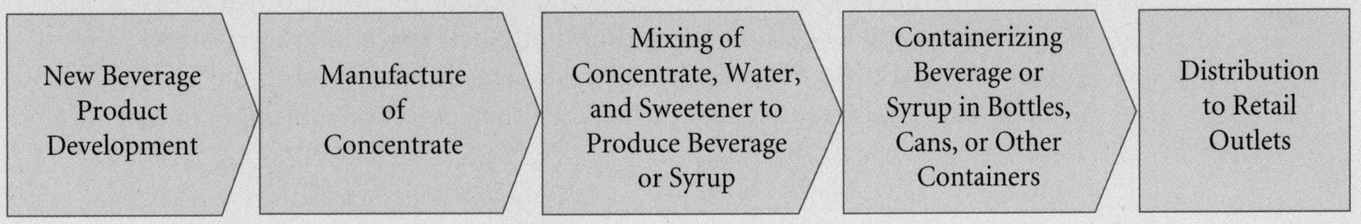

Porter's Five Forces Classification Framework

Porter suggests that five forces influence the level of competition and the profitability of firms in an industry.[1] Three of the forces—rivalry among existing firms, potential entry, and substitutes—represent horizontal competition among current or potential future firms in the industry and closely related products and services. The other two forces—buyer power and supplier power—depict vertical competition in the value chain, from the suppliers through the existing rivals to the buyers. We discuss each of these forces next and illustrate them within the soft drink/beverage industry. Exhibit 1.7 depicts Porter's five forces in the soft drink/beverage industry.

1. **Rivalry among Existing Firms.** Direct rivalry among existing firms is often the first order of competition in an industry. Some industries can be characterized by concentrated rivalry (such as a monopoly, a duopoly, or an oligopoly), whereas others have diffuse rivalry across many firms. Economists often assess the level of competition with industry concentration ratios, such as a four-firm concentration index that measures the proportion of industry sales controlled by the four largest competitors. Economics teaches that in general, the greater the industry concentration, the lower the competition between existing rivals and thus the more profitable the firms will be.

   PepsiCo and Coca-Cola dominate the soft drink/beverage industry in the United States. Because some consumers view the two companies' products as being similar, intense competition based on price could develop. Also, the soft drink market in the United States is mature (that is, not growing rapidly), so price cutting could become a strategy to gain market share. Although intense rivalries have a tendency to reduce profitability, in this case, PepsiCo and Coca-Cola appear to tacitly avoid competing based on price and compete instead on brand image, access to key distribution channels (for example, fast-food chains and grocery store shelf space), and other attributes. Growth opportunities do exist in other countries, which these companies pursue aggressively. Thus, we characterize industry rivalry as moderate.
2. **Threat of New Entrants.** How easily can new firms enter a market? Are there entry barriers such as large capital investment, technological expertise, patents, or regulations that inhibit new entrants? Do the existing rivals have distinct competitive advantages (such as brand names) that will make it difficult for other firms to enter and compete successfully? If so, firms in the industry will likely generate higher profits than if new entrants can enter the market easily and compete away the excess profits.

   The soft drink/beverage industry has no barriers to entry. This is evident by the numerous small juice, sports drink, water, and soft drink companies that exist; the frequency with which new firms enter the industry; and the availability of generic and no-name beverage products. However, the existing major players in the soft drink/beverage industry have competitive advantages that reduce the threat of new entrants. Brand recognition by PepsiCo and Coca-Cola serves as a very powerful deterrent to potential new competitors. Another deterrent is these two firms' domination of distribution channels. Most restaurant chains sign exclusive contracts to serve the beverages of one or the other of these two firms. Also, PepsiCo and Coca-Cola often dominate shelf space in grocery stores.
3. **Threat of Substitutes.** How easily can customers switch to substitute products or services? How likely are they to switch? When there are close substitutes in a market,

---

[1]Michael E. Porter, *Competitive Strategy: Techniques for Analyzing Industries and Competitors* (New York: Free Press), 1998.

EXHIBIT 1.7

Porter's Five Forces in the Soft Drink/Beverage Industry

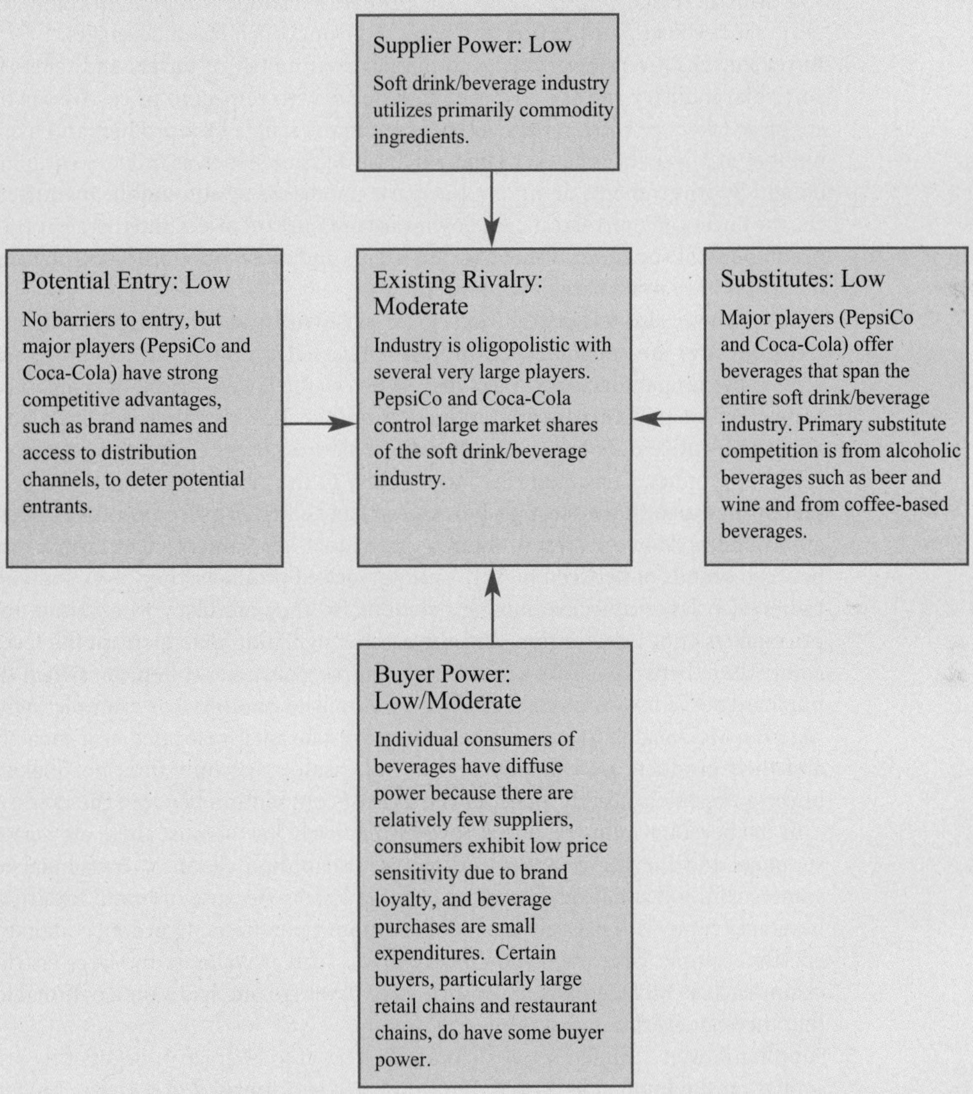
Supplier Power: Low
Soft drink/beverage industry utilizes primarily commodity ingredients.
Potential Entry: Low
No barriers to entry, but major players (PepsiCo and Coca-Cola) have strong competitive advantages, such as brand names and access to distribution channels, to deter potential entrants.
Existing Rivalry: Moderate
Industry is oligopolistic with several very large players. PepsiCo and Coca-Cola control large market shares of the soft drink/beverage industry.
Substitutes: Low
Major players (PepsiCo and Coca-Cola) offer beverages that span the entire soft drink/beverage industry. Primary substitute competition is from alcoholic beverages such as beer and wine and from coffee-based beverages.
Buyer Power: Low/Moderate
Individual consumers of beverages have diffuse power because there are relatively few suppliers, consumers exhibit low price sensitivity due to brand loyalty, and beverage purchases are small expenditures. Certain buyers, particularly large retail chains and restaurant chains, do have some buyer power.

competition increases and profitability diminishes (for example, between restaurants and grocery stores for certain types of prepared foods and between airlines, automobiles, and other means of transportation for traveling short distances). Unique products with few substitutes, such as certain prescription medications, enhance profitability.

The carbonated soft drink industry faces substitute competition from an array of other beverages that consumers can substitute to quench their thirst. Fruit juices, bottled waters, sports drinks, teas, coffees, milk, beers, and wines serve a similar thirst-quenching function to that of soft drinks. Over the years, Coca-Cola and PepsiCo have expanded their beverage portfolios to encompass virtually all nonalcoholic beverages except coffee. For example, PepsiCo purchased Tropicana and Gatorade to enhance its product offerings in juices, sports drinks, and bottled water. Because of the wide range of beverage products offered by PepsiCo and Coca-Cola and because of consumer buying habits, brand loyalty, and channel availability, the threat of substitutes in the soft drink/beverage industry is low. The primary substitute competition comes from alcoholic beverages such as beer and wine and from coffee-based beverages.

4. **Buyer Power.** Buyer power relates to the relative number of buyers and sellers in a particular industry and the leverage buyers have with respect to price. Are the buyers price takers or price setters? If there are many sellers of a product and a small number of buyers making very large purchase decisions, such as military equipment bought by governments or automobile parts purchased by automobile manufacturers, the buyer can exert significant downward pressure on prices and therefore on the profitability of suppliers. If there are few sellers and many buyers, as with beverages, the sellers have more bargaining power.

   Buyer power also relates to buyers' price sensitivity and the elasticity of demand. How sensitive are consumers to product prices? If products are similar to those offered by competitors, consumers may switch to the lowest-priced offering. If consumers view a particular firm's products as unique, however, they will likely be less sensitive to price differences. Another dimension of price sensitivity is the relative cost of a product. Consumers are less sensitive to the prices of products that represent small expenditures, such as beverages, than to higher-priced products, such as automobiles. However, even though individual consumers may switch easily between brands or between higher- or lower-priced products, they make individual rather than large collective buying decisions; so they are likely to continue to be price takers (not price setters) and the ease of switching may increase the level of competition between existing rivals. For example, consumers often can switch their purchase decisions from one fast-food restaurant to another (for example, switching from McDonald's to Subway) because the restaurants are located near each other and their products are similarly priced. But ease of switching does not make the buyer powerful; instead it increases the level of competition between the rivals.

   In the beverage industry, buyer power is relatively low because there are very few suppliers and they have access to essential distribution channels. Individual consumers tend to exhibit relatively low price sensitivity because of brand loyalty, and beverages comprise relatively small dollar amount purchases. However, certain buyers (for example, large retail and grocery chains such as Walmart and large fast-food chains such as McDonald's) make such large beverage purchases on a national level that they can exert significant buyer power.

5. **Supplier Power.** A similar set of factors with respect to leverage in negotiating prices applies on the input side as well. If an industry is comprised of a large number of potential buyers of inputs that are produced by relatively few suppliers, the suppliers will have greater power in setting prices and generating profits. For example, many firms assemble and sell personal computers and laptops, but these firms face significant supplier power because Microsoft is a dominant supplier of operating systems and application software and Intel is a dominant supplier of microprocessors.

   Beverage companies produce their concentrates and syrups with raw materials that are commodities. Although PepsiCo does not disclose every ingredient, PepsiCo is not likely to be dependent on one supplier (or even a few suppliers) for its raw materials. It also is unlikely that any of these ingredients are sufficiently unique that the suppliers could exert much power over PepsiCo. Given PepsiCo's size, the power more likely resides with PepsiCo than with its suppliers.

In sum, competition in the soft drink/beverage industry rates low on supplier power, threat of new entrants, and threat of substitutes; the industry rates low on buyer power of consumers but moderate on buyer power of fast-food chains and large retail and grocery chains; and the industry rates moderate on rivalry within the industry. Unless PepsiCo or Coca-Cola decides to compete on the basis of low price, the analyst might expect these firms to continue to generate relatively high profitability.

Economic Attributes Framework

We find the following framework useful in studying the economic attributes of a business, in part because it ties in with items reported in the financial statements.

1. **Demand**
   - Are customers highly price-sensitive, as in the case of automobiles, or are they relatively insensitive, as in the case of soft drinks?
   - Is demand growing rapidly, as in the case of long-term health care, or is the industry relatively mature, as in the case of grocery stores?
   - Does demand move with the economic cycle, as in the case of construction of new homes and offices, or is demand insensitive to business cycles, as in the case of food products and medical care?
   - Does demand vary with the seasons, as in the case of summer clothing and ski equipment, or is demand relatively stable throughout the year, as in the case of most grocery store products?
2. **Supply**
   - Are many suppliers offering similar products, or are few suppliers offering unique products?
   - Are there high barriers to entry, or can new entrants gain easy access?
   - Are there high barriers to exit, as in the case of firms that face substantial environment cleanup costs?
3. **Manufacturing**
   - Is the manufacturing process capital-intensive, as in the case of electric power generation; labor-intensive, as in the case of advertising, investment banking, auditing, and other professional services; or a combination of the two, as in the case of automobile manufacturing and airline transportation?
   - Is the manufacturing process complex with low tolerance for error, as in the case of heart pacemakers and microchips, or relatively simple with ranges of products that are of acceptable quality, as in the case of apparel and nonmechanized toys?
4. **Marketing**
   - Is the product promoted to other businesses, in which case a sales staff plays a key role, or is it marketed to consumers, so that advertising, location, and coupons serve as principal promotion mechanisms?
   - Does steady demand pull products through distribution channels, or must firms continually create demand?
5. **Investing and Financing**
   - Are the assets of firms in the industry relatively short-term, as in the case of commercial banks, which require short-term sources of funds to finance them? Or are assets relatively long-term, as in the case of electric utilities, which require primarily long-term financing?

- Is there relatively little risk in the assets of firms in the industry, such as from technological obsolescence, so that firms can carry high proportions of debt financing? Alternatively, are there high risks resulting from short product life cycles or product liability concerns that dictate low debt and high shareholders' equity financing?
- Is the industry relatively profitable and mature, generating more cash flow from operations than is needed for acquisitions of property, plant, and equipment? Alternatively, is the industry growing rapidly and in need of external financing?

Exhibit 1.8 summarizes the economic attributes of the soft drink/beverage industry.

EXHIBIT 1.8

Economic Attributes of the Soft Drink/Beverage Industry

Demand

- Demand is relatively insensitive to price.
- There is low growth in the United States, but more rapid growth opportunities are available in other countries.
- Demand is not cyclical.
- Demand is higher during warmer weather.

Supply

- Two principal suppliers (PepsiCo and Coca-Cola) sell branded products.
- Branded products and domination of distribution channels by two principal suppliers create significant competitive advantages.

Manufacturing

- Manufacturing process for concentrate and syrup is not capital-intensive.
- Bottling and distribution of final product is capital-intensive.
- Manufacturing process is simple (essentially a mixing operation) with some tolerance for quality variation.

Marketing

- Brand recognition and established demand pull products through distribution channels, but advertising can stimulate demand to some extent.

Investing and Financing

- Bottling operations and transportation of products to retailers require long-term financing.
- Profitability is relatively high and growth is slow in the United States, leading to excess cash flow generation. Growth markets in other countries require financing from internal domestic cash flow or from external sources.

STEP 2: IDENTIFY THE COMPANY STRATEGIES

Firms establish business strategies to differentiate themselves from competitors, but an industry's economic characteristics affect the flexibility that firms have in designing these strategies. In some cases, firms can create sustainable competitive advantages. PepsiCo's size, brand name, and access to distribution channels give it sustainable competitive advantages over smaller, less well-known beverage companies. Coca-Cola enjoys similar advantages. The reputation for quality family entertainment provides Disney with a sustainable advantage. A reputation for low prices generates advantages in high customer traffic and high sales volume for Walmart.

In many industries, however, products and ideas quickly get copied. Consider, for example, computer hardware; chicken, pizza, and hamburger restaurant chains; and financial services. In these cases, firms may achieve competitive advantage by being the first with new concepts or ideas (referred to as *first mover advantage*) or by continually investing in product development to remain on the leading edge of change in an industry. Such competitive advantages are difficult (but not impossible) to sustain for long periods of time.

Framework for Strategy Analysis

The set of strategic choices confronting a particular firm varies across industries. The following framework dealing with product and firm characteristics helps the analyst identify and structure the set of trade-offs and choices a firm must face.

1. **Nature of Product or Service.** Is a firm attempting to create unique products or services for particular market niches, thereby achieving relatively high profit margins (referred to as a *product differentiation strategy*)? Or is it offering nondifferentiated products at low prices, accepting a lower profit margin in return for a higher sales volume and market share (referred to as a *low-cost leadership strategy*)? Is a firm attempting to achieve both objectives by differentiating (perhaps by creating brand loyalty or technological innovation) and being price competitive by maintaining tight control over costs?
2. **Degree of Integration in Value Chain.** Is the firm pursuing a vertical integration strategy, participating in all phases of the value chain, or selecting just certain phases in the chain? With respect to manufacturing, is the firm conducting all manufacturing operations itself (as usually occurs in steel manufacturing), outsourcing all manufacturing (common in athletic shoes), or outsourcing the manufacturing of components but conducting the assembly operation in-house (common in automobile and computer hardware manufacturing)?

   With respect to distribution, is the firm maintaining control over the distribution function or outsourcing it? Some restaurant chains, for example, own all of their restaurants, while other chains operate through independently owned franchises. Computer hardware firms have recently shifted from selling through their own sales staffs to using various indirect sellers, such as value-added resellers and systems integrators—in effect shifting from in-house sourcing to outsourcing of the distribution function.
3. **Degree of Geographical Diversification.** Is the firm targeting its products to its domestic market or integrating horizontally across many countries? Operating in other countries creates opportunities for growth but exposes firms to risks from changes in exchange rates, political uncertainties, and additional competitors.
4. **Degree of Industry Diversification.** Is the firm operating in a single industry or diversifying across multiple industries? Operating in multiple industries permits

firms to diversify product, cyclical, regulatory, and other risks encountered when operating in a single industry but raises questions about management's ability to understand and manage multiple and different businesses effectively.

Application of Strategy Framework to PepsiCo's Beverage Division

To apply this strategy framework to PepsiCo's beverage division, we rely on the description provided by PepsiCo's management (Appendix B). Most U.S. firms include this type of management discussion and analysis in their Form 10-K filing with the Securities and Exchange Commission (SEC).

1. **Nature of Product or Service.** PepsiCo's beverage division competes broadly in the beverage industry, with offerings in soft drinks, fruit juices, bottled waters, sports drinks, teas, and coffees. However, its principal beverage products are soft drinks. Although one might debate whether its products differ from similar products offered by Coca-Cola and other competitors (a debate that invariably involves taste), brand recognition and domination of distribution channels permit PepsiCo to sell a somewhat differentiated product.
2. **Degree of Integration in Value Chain.** PepsiCo engages in new product development, manufactures concentrates and syrups, and promotes its products while it allows its bottlers to manufacture and distribute soft drink products. This arrangement exists because PepsiCo realizes that the principal value added comprises the secret formulas that make up the concentrates and syrups as well as the product and brand promotion that maintain its brand name and brand loyalty. Maintaining product quality and efficient and effective distribution channels are critical to PepsiCo's success, so PepsiCo emphasizes the important role that bottlers play and the oversight role PepsiCo plays to ensure its financial strength and efficient operation. Thus, a close operational relationship exists between PepsiCo and its bottlers. However, bottling operations are relatively simple, yet capital-intensive; require long-term financing, typically debt; and are not particularly value-enhancing. By not owning a majority interest in the bottling and distribution operations, PepsiCo reports greater profitability. The company also appears less risky because it does not include the debt of the bottling operations on its balance sheet.

   Because of its heavy influence (supplier power) over its bottlers, PepsiCo is able to price its concentrate sales to these bottlers to garner a significant portion of the profit margin for itself. The bottlers are willing to accept a lower margin because of the control PepsiCo gives them in a particular locale and the strong demand for the PepsiCo products they produce. (Subsequent chapters consider PepsiCo's strategy with respect to its bottlers when assessing the company's profitability, quality of financial information, and risk.)

   Interestingly, PepsiCo's main competitor in the soft drink industry, Coca-Cola, structures its operations similar to PepsiCo's. As with PepsiCo, Coca-Cola's principal products are the concentrates it sells to bottlers, which are responsible for bottling and distributing the final Coca-Cola soft drinks.
3. **Degree of Geographical Diversification.** Note 1, "Basis of Presentation and Our Divisions," to PepsiCo's financial statements (Appendix A) and Exhibit 1.5 indicate that the PepsiCo Americas Beverages division generated 25.3 percent of the firm's revenues during 2008 from beverage sales in North America, South America, and Central America. PepsiCo derived 27.8 percent of its revenues during 2008 from the

PepsiCo International division, but PepsiCo does not disclose the proportion of international revenues it derived from beverages alone. Overall, PepsiCo derived about two-thirds of its revenues from the Americas and one-third from other parts of the world.

4. **Degree of Industry Diversification.** To focus and streamline the presentation of industry analysis and strategic analysis techniques, our discussion thus far has focused on PepsiCo's beverages business. However, PepsiCo generates greater revenues and higher operating profit margins from the snack food and breakfast foods divisions than from the beverage division. Exhibit 1.5 indicates that during 2008, PepsiCo generated 28.9 percent of its revenues from the Frito-Lay North America snack food division, 13.6 percent from the Latin America Foods division, and 4.4 percent from the Quaker Foods North America division selling breakfast foods and cereal products. Because PepsiCo does not disclose the proportions of PepsiCo International revenues that derive from sales of snack foods, soft drinks and beverages, and cereal and related products, we cannot measure PepsiCo's worldwide mix of product sales.

   Although PepsiCo is more industry-diverse than Coca-Cola, many economic characteristics of the beverage, snack food, and cereal industries are similar in nature, involving the selling of branded consumer products. These industries can be characterized as having low barriers to entry but a small number of powerful rivals with brand recognition and access to key distribution channels. These industries rely on commodity raw materials for inputs, facing low supplier power, and relatively price-insensitive buyers because of brand loyalty and distribution channels. As a result, PepsiCo's strategies are similar between the beverage and foods divisions, focusing on product development and promotion to leverage the brand recognition and maintaining access to important distribution channels.

STEP 3: ASSESS THE QUALITY OF THE FINANCIAL STATEMENTS

Business firms prepare three principal financial statements to report the results of their activities: (1) balance sheet, (2) income statement, and (3) statement of cash flows. Many firms prepare a fourth statement, the statement of shareholders' equity, which provides further detail of the shareholders' equity section of the balance sheet. Firms also include a set of notes that elaborate on items included in these statements. Together, the financial statements and notes provide an extensive set of information about the firm's financial position, performance, and cash flows. The statements provide insights to an analyst about the firm's profitability, risk, and growth.

Using the financial statements and notes for PepsiCo in Appendix A as examples, this section presents a brief overview of the purpose and content of each of these three financial statements. Understanding accounting concepts and methods and evaluating the quality of a firm's financial statements is a central element of effective financial statement analysis and therefore one of the three central purposes of this book. Chapters 2 and 3 describe the fundamental accounting concepts and methods for measuring and reporting:

- Assets, liabilities, and shareholders' equity
- Revenues, expenses, and income
- Cash flows associated with operating, investing, and financing activities

Chapters 6–9 describe specific accounting principles and methods in depth. The sequencing of these chapters is powerful and intuitive because it follows the natural sequencing of firms' economic activities. Chapter 6 begins the sequence by describing accounting for financing activities because firms initiate business activities by raising capital. Chapter 7 then describes accounting for investing activities, which occur after the firm has raised capital. Once capital has been raised and invested in productive resources, the firm commences operating activities by producing products and services for customers and incurring costs of conducting those operations, which are discussed in Chapter 8. Chapter 9 concludes the sequence by demonstrating how to evaluate the quality of a firm's accounting and discussing the faithfulness with which the financial statements represent the firm's economic resources, obligations, and performance.

Accounting Principles

Firms produce financial statements and notes based on accounting standards and principles established by the accounting profession. For U.S. firms, GAAP determines the valuation and measurement methods used in preparing financial statements. Official rule-making bodies set these principles. The SEC (Securities and Exchange Commission), an agency of the federal government, has the legal authority to specify acceptable accounting principles in the United States (http://www.sec.gov). The SEC has, for the most part, delegated the responsibility for setting GAAP to the FASB (Financial Accounting Standards Board), a private-sector body within the accounting profession (http://www.fasb.org). The FASB is an independent board comprising five members and a full-time professional staff. The FASB specifies acceptable accounting principles only after receiving extensive comments on proposed accounting standards from various preparers, auditors, and users of financial statements.

The IASB is an independent entity comprising 15 members (to be expanded to 16 members in 2012) and a full-time professional staff (http://www.iasb.org). The IASB specifies acceptable accounting principles known as IFRS. Many countries have dropped their own country-specific accounting rules, formally accepting IFRS as the applicable accounting standards. Beginning in 2005, the financial statements of firms in the European Community were required to conform to the pronouncements of the IASB.

The SEC accepts financial statement filings prepared under IFRS from non-U.S. registrants, although it has not yet accepted IFRS-based financial statement filings from U.S. firms. In 2008, the SEC pronounced a road map for convergence, providing a timetable under which it would be willing to accept filings from U.S. companies using IFRS instead of U.S. GAAP. The road map projected acceptance of such filings beginning as early as 2011 for large firms and as late as 2014 for small firms. Since publicizing the road map, the SEC has had to deal with some major crises in the U.S. capital markets, including the subprime crisis, the credit crunch, the failure and bailout of many large banks and insurers, and several major frauds. As a result, in February of 2010 the SEC issued a Work Plan for the SEC staff to determine by the end of 2011 whether, and if so, when and how to incorporate IFRS into the U.S. financial reporting system. The SEC's Work Plan indicates that, if IFRS-based filings are approved, the soonest U.S. companies would report financial statements under IFRS would be no earlier than 2015.

The FASB and IASB are working together closely to harmonize financial reporting worldwide. Although substantial differences must be resolved between the two sets of standards (we will highlight existing differences throughout this book), the two Boards have managed to find common ground on most major principles. Now when the two Boards propose a new principle or a revision of an existing principle, they typically work jointly to develop the proposed principle and to collect and evaluate comments from various constituencies. They then agree on the final principle, which becomes part of U.S. GAAP and IFRS. Working together, the IASB and FASB are reducing diversity in accounting principles across countries to encourage greater standardization. Global harmonization in accounting standards will simplify financial statements analysis, enabling analysts to evaluate and compare financial statements from firms across many countries, prepared under similar accounting principles. This should make allocation of capital more efficient worldwide.

Balance Sheet—Measuring Financial Position

The balance sheet, or statement of financial position, presents a snapshot of the resources of a firm (assets) and the claims on those resources (liabilities and shareholders' equity) as of a specific date. The balance sheet derives its name from the fact that it reports the following balance, or equality:

$$\text{Assets} = \text{Liabilities} + \text{Shareholders' Equity}$$

That is, a firm's assets are in balance with, or equal to, the claims on those assets by creditors (liabilities) and owners (shareholders' equity). The balance sheet views resources from two perspectives: a list of the specific resources the firm holds (for example, cash, inventory, and equipment) and a list of the persons or entities that provided the funds to finance the business and therefore have claims on the assets (for example, suppliers, employees, governments, financial institutions, and shareholders).

The assets portion of the balance sheet reports the effects of a firm's operating decisions (principally those involving assets used in day-to-day activities to produce and deliver products and services to customers) and investing decisions (principally those involving financial assets to generate interest income, dividends, and other returns on investment). Refer to the balance sheets for PepsiCo as of fiscal year-end 2004 through 2008 in Exhibit 1.9. PepsiCo's principal operating assets are cash and cash equivalents; accounts and notes receivable; inventories; prepaid expenses; property, plant, and equipment; and goodwill and intangible assets. PepsiCo's principal financial assets from investing activities include short-term investment securities and investments in the equity securities of noncontrolled affiliates.

The liabilities and shareholders' equity portion of the balance sheet reports obligations that arise from a firm's operating decisions (involving obligations to pay employees and suppliers of goods and services) and financing decisions (raising debt capital from banks and other lenders as well as raising equity capital from investors in common stock). PepsiCo obtains financing from suppliers of goods and services (reported as accounts payable, other current liabilities, and other long-term liabilities), banks and other lenders (reported as both short- and long-term obligations), preferred equity investors (reported as preferred stock, offset by repurchased preferred stock), and common equity investors (reported as common shareholders' equity).

For sake of comparison, also refer to the balance sheets for The Coca-Cola Company as of fiscal year-end 2004 through 2008 in Exhibit 1.10. Notice that Coca-Cola's principal assets, liabilities, and financing from banks, lenders, and common equity investors are similar to those of PepsiCo.

Under U.S. GAAP, firms are required to report assets and liabilities in descending order of liquidity; so the assets that are closest to cash are listed first while the assets that are hardest to convert to cash are reported last. Similarly, the liabilities that are likely to be settled soonest are listed first while the liabilities likely to be settled furthest in the future are shown last.

Formats of balance sheets in some countries can differ from the format used in the United States. Under IFRS, for example, firms can choose to report the balance sheet with assets and liabilities listed in descending order of liquidity or they can report the balance

EXHIBIT 1.9

PepsiCo, Inc. and Subsidiaries
Consolidated Balance Sheets (in millions)

As of Fiscal Year-End:	2008	2007	2006	2005	2004
ASSETS					
Cash and cash equivalents	$ 2,064	$ 910	$ 1,651	$ 1,716	$ 1,280
Short-term investments	213	1,571	1,171	3,166	2,165
Accounts and notes receivable, net	4,683	4,389	3,725	3,261	2,999
Inventories	2,522	2,290	1,926	1,693	1,541
Prepaid expenses and other current assets	1,324	991	657	618	654
Total Current Assets	$10,806	$10,151	$ 9,130	$10,454	$ 8,639
Property, plant, and equipment, net	11,663	11,228	9,687	8,681	8,149
Amortizable intangible assets, net	732	796	637	530	598
Goodwill	5,124	5,169	4,594	4,088	3,909
Other nonamortizable intangible assets	1,128	1,248	1,212	1,086	933
Investments in noncontrolled affiliates	3,883	4,354	3,690	3,485	3,284
Other assets	2,658	1,682	980	3,403	2,475
Total Assets	$35,994	$34,628	$29,930	$31,727	$27,987
LIABILITIES AND SHAREHOLDERS' EQUITY					
Short-term obligations	$ 369	$ —	$ 274	$ 2,889	$ 1,054
Accounts payable and other current liabilities	8,273	7,602	6,496	5,971	5,599
Income taxes payable	145	151	90	546	99
Total Current Liabilities	$ 8,787	$ 7,753	$ 6,860	$ 9,406	$ 6,752
Long-term debt obligations	7,858	4,203	2,550	2,313	2,397
Other liabilities	7,017	4,792	4,624	4,323	4,099
Deferred income taxes	226	646	528	1,434	1,216
Total Liabilities	$23,888	$17,394	$14,562	$17,476	$14,464
Preferred stock, no par value	$ 41	$ 41	$ 41	$ 41	$ 41
Repurchased preferred stock	(138)	(132)	(120)	(110)	(90)
Common stock, par value	30	30	30	30	30
Capital in excess of par value	351	450	584	614	618
Retained earnings	30,638	28,184	24,837	21,116	18,730
Accumulated other comprehensive loss	(4,694)	(952)	(2,246)	(1,053)	(886)
Treasury stock	(14,122)	(10,387)	(7,758)	(6,387)	(4,920)
Total Common Shareholders' Equity	$12,203	$17,325	$15,447	$14,320	$13,572
Total Liabilities and Shareholders' Equity	$35,994	$34,628	$29,930	$31,727	$27,987

EXHIBIT 1.10

The Coca-Cola Company
Consolidated Balance Sheets (in millions)

As of Fiscal Year-End:	2008	2007	2006	2005	2004
ASSETS					
Cash and cash equivalents	$ 4,701	$ 4,093	$ 2,440	$ 4,701	$ 6,707
Short-term investments	278	215	150	66	61
Accounts and notes receivable, net	3,090	3,317	2,587	2,281	2,244
Inventories	2,187	2,220	1,641	1,424	1,420
Prepaid expenses and other current assets	1,920	2,260	1,623	1,778	1,849
Total Current Assets	$12,176	$12,105	$ 8,441	$10,250	$12,281
Property, plant, and equipment, net	8,326	8,493	6,903	5,786	6,091
Amortizable intangible assets, net	2,417	5,153	2,045	1,946	2,037
Goodwill	4,029	4,256	1,403	1,047	1,097
Other nonamortizable intangible assets	6,059	2,810	1,687	828	702
Investments in noncontrolled affiliates	5,779	7,777	6,783	6,922	6,252
Other assets	1,733	2,675	2,701	2,648	2,981
Total Assets	$40,519	$43,269	$29,963	$29,427	$31,441
LIABILITIES AND SHAREHOLDERS' EQUITY					
Short-term obligations	$ 6,066	$ 6,915	$ 3,235	$ 4,518	$ 4,531
Accounts payable and other current liabilities	6,205	5,919	5,055	4,493	4,403
Current maturities of long-term debt	465	133	33	28	1,490
Income taxes payable	252	258	567	797	709
Total Current Liabilities	$12,988	$13,225	$ 8,890	$ 9,836	$11,133
Long-term debt obligations	2,781	3,277	1,314	1,154	1,157
Other liabilities	3,401	3,133	2,231	1,730	2,814
Deferred income taxes	877	1,890	608	352	402
Total Liabilities	$20,047	$21,525	$13,043	$13,072	$15,506
Common stock, par value	$ 880	$ 880	$ 878	$ 877	$ 875
Capital in excess of par value	7,966	7,378	5,983	5,492	4,928
Retained earnings	38,513	36,235	33,468	31,299	29,105
Accumulated other comprehensive loss	(2,674)	626	(1,291)	(1,669)	(1,348)
Treasury stock	(24,213)	(23,375)	(22,118)	(19,644)	(17,625)
Total Shareholders' Equity	$20,472	$21,744	$16,920	$16,355	$15,935
Total Liabilities and Shareholders' Equity	$40,519	$43,269	$29,963	$29,427	$31,441

sheet with long-term assets such as property, plant, and equipment and other noncurrent assets appearing first, followed by current assets. On the financing side, balance sheets prepared under IFRS may list shareholders' equity first, followed by noncurrent liabilities and current liabilities. Both formats under IFRS maintain the balance sheet equality but present accounts in a different sequence.

In the United Kingdom, for example, the balance sheet equation commonly takes the following form:

$$\text{Noncurrent Assets} + [\text{Current Assets} - \text{Current Liabilities}] - \text{Noncurrent Liabilities} = \text{Shareholders' Equity}$$

This format takes the perspective of shareholders by reporting the net assets available for shareholders after subtracting claims by creditors. Financial analysts can rearrange the components of published balance sheets to the format they consider most informative, although ambiguity may exist for some balance sheet categories.

Assets—Recognition, Valuation, and Classification

Which of its resources should a firm recognize as assets? At what amount should the firm report these assets? How should it classify them in the assets portion of the balance sheet? U.S. GAAP and IFRS establish the principles that firms must use to determine responses to those questions.

Defining what resources firms should recognize as assets is one of the most important definitions among all of the principles established by U.S. GAAP and IFRS:[2]

> **Assets are probable future economic benefits obtained or controlled by a particular entity as a result of past transactions or events.**

Assets are resources that have the potential to provide a firm with future economic benefits: the ability to generate future cash inflows (as with accounts receivable, inventories, and investment securities) or to reduce future cash outflows (as with prepayments) or to provide future service potential for operating activities (as with property and equipment and intangibles). Therefore, asset recognition depends on managers' expectations for future economic benefits. A firm can recognize as assets only those resources (1) for which it has the rights to future economic benefits as a result of a past transaction or event and (2) for which the firm can predict and measure, or quantify, the future benefits with a reasonable degree of precision and reliability. If an expenditure does not meet both criteria, it cannot be capitalized and must be expensed. A firm should derecognize assets (that is, write off assets from the balance sheet) that it determines no longer represent future economic benefits (such as writing off not uncollectible receivables or unsalable inventory). Resources that firms do not normally recognize as assets because they fail to meet one or both of the criteria include purchase orders received from customers; employment contracts with corporate officers and employees; and a quality reputation with employees, customers, or citizens of the community.

Most assets on the balance sheet are either *monetary* or *nonmonetary*. (We will define these categories more specifically in the discussion of foreign currency translation in Chapter 7.) Monetary assets include cash and claims to future payments of cash (such as receivables). PepsiCo's monetary assets include cash, accounts and notes receivable, and investments in debt and equity securities of other firms. Under U.S. GAAP and IFRS,

---

[2]Financial Accounting Standards Board, *Statement of Financial Accounting Concepts No. 6*, "Elements of Financial Statements" (1985), par. 25.

balance sheets report monetary assets using a variety of measurement attributes intended to enhance the relevance and reliability of reported asset values. Some monetary assets such as cash are reported at current value. Others, such as accounts receivable, are reported at net realizable value (the amounts the firm expects to collect). For other assets, such as notes receivable and loans with cash receipts that extend beyond one year, the firm reports the monetary asset at the present value of the future cash flows using a discount rate that reflects the underlying uncertainty of collecting the cash as assessed at the time the claim initially arose. Still other assets, such as debt and equity investment securities, are typically reported at fair value, which represents those cash amounts the firm could expect to realize if it sold the securities. Chapter 2 provides more discussion on the various measurement attributes that accounting principles employ to achieve relevant and reliable asset valuations.

Nonmonetary assets include assets that are *tangible,* such as inventories, buildings, and equipment, and assets that are *intangible,* including brand names, patents, trademarks, licenses, and goodwill. In contrast to monetary assets, nonmonetary assets do not represent claims to fixed amounts of cash. The amount of cash firms receive from using or selling nonmonetary assets depends on market conditions at the time of their use or sale. Under U.S. GAAP and IFRS, firms might report nonmonetary assets at the amounts initially paid to acquire them (acquisition, or historical, cost), at the original acquisition cost adjusted for the use of the asset over time (acquisition cost net of accumulated depreciation or amortization), at the amounts currently required to replace them (replacement cost), at the amounts for which firms could currently sell the asset (net realizable value), or at the present values of the amounts firms expect to receive in the future from selling or using the assets (present value of future cash flows). The valuation attribute used typically depends on the nature of the asset. U.S. GAAP and IFRS generally require the reporting of most nonmonetary assets on the balance sheet at their acquisition cost amounts (adjusted for accumulated depreciation or amortization if long-lived) because cost-based valuation is usually more objective and verifiable than other valuation bases. IFRS also permits periodic revaluation of certain types of nonmonetary assets to current values (such as real estate held for investment purposes rather than for operating use). Chapter 2 discusses alternative valuation methods and their implications for measuring earnings.

Perhaps PepsiCo's most valuable resources are its brand names (for example, Pepsi, Frito-Lay®, and Quaker® Oats). PepsiCo and its subsidiaries created and developed these brand names through past expenditures on advertising, event sponsorships, product development, and quality control. Yet ascertaining the portion of these expenditures that creates reliably predictable future economic benefits and the portion that simply stimulates sales during the current period is too uncertain to justify recognizing an asset. The amounts that PepsiCo does report for amortizable intangible assets, goodwill, and other nonamortizable intangible assets (see Note 4, "Property, Plant, and Equipment and Intangible Assets," to PepsiCo's financial statements in Appendix A) result from PepsiCo's purchases of other companies, transaction-based events that provide market evidence of the value of acquired intangibles. PepsiCo's balance sheet reports $732 million of amortizable intangible assets and $1,128 million of nonamortizable intangibles, principally brand names. The remaining $5,124 million of intangible assets is goodwill, which represents the portion of the purchase price of other businesses that PepsiCo could not allocate to identifiable assets and liabilities. Every year PepsiCo tests the value of all of its intangible assets for impairment, and if the evaluation indicates impairment, the intangible asset is written down to its estimated fair value. Chapter 7 discusses the accounting for goodwill and intangibles.

The classification of assets in the balance sheet varies widely in published annual reports. The principal asset categories are as follows:

Current Assets. Current assets include cash and other assets that a firm expects to collect, sell, or consume during the normal operating cycle of a business, usually one year. Cash; short-term investments; accounts and notes receivable; inventories; and prepayments for rent, insurance, and advertising appear as current assets for PepsiCo.

Investments. This category includes short-term and long-term investments in the debt and equity securities of other entities. If a firm makes such investments for short-term purposes, it classifies them under current assets. A principal asset for PepsiCo is the investments in noncontrolled affiliates, which are primarily its bottlers (Pepsi Bottling Group, PepsiAmericas, and other bottlers). Note 8, "Noncontrolled Bottling Affiliates," to PepsiCo's financial statements (Appendix A) indicates that it owns very substantial proportions but less than 50 percent of the common stock of these bottlers. Therefore, PepsiCo does not prepare consolidated financial statements with these bottlers; instead, it reports the investments on the balance sheet using the equity method (discussed in Chapter 7).

Property, Plant, and Equipment. This category includes the tangible, long-lived assets that a firm uses in operations over a period of years. Note 4, "Property, Plant, and Equipment and Intangible Assets," to PepsiCo's financial statements (Appendix A) indicates that property, plant, and equipment includes land and improvements, buildings and improvements, machinery and equipment, and construction in progress. It reports property, plant, and equipment at acquisition cost and then subtracts the accumulated depreciation recognized on these assets since acquisition.

Intangibles. Intangibles include the rights established by law or contract to the future use of property. Patents, trademarks, licenses, and franchises are intangible assets. The most troublesome asset recognition questions revolve around which rights satisfy the criteria for an asset. As Chapter 7 discusses in more depth, firms generally recognize as assets intangibles acquired in external market transactions with other entities (as is the case for brand names and goodwill included in PepsiCo's balance sheet under the categories of amortizable and nonamortizable intangible assets, which it details in Note 4, "Property, Plant, and Equipment and Intangible Assets," in Appendix A), but do not recognize as assets intangibles developed internally by the firm (the Pepsi and Frito-Lay® brand names, for example). The rationale for the different accounting treatment is that the value of intangibles acquired in external market transactions is more reliable than the value of internally developed intangibles.

Liabilities—Recognition, Valuation, and Classification

Under U.S. GAAP and IFRS, firms must report obligations as liabilities if they meet the **definition** of a liability:[3]

> **Liabilities are probable future sacrifices of economic benefits arising from present obligations of a particular entity to transfer assets or provide services to other entities in the future as a result of past transactions or events.**

Therefore, liabilities represent a firm's existing obligations to make payments of cash, goods, or services in a reasonably predictable amount at a reasonably predictable future time as a result of a past transaction or event. Liabilities reflect managers' expectations of future sacrifices of resources to satisfy existing obligations. Liabilities for PepsiCo include obligations to suppliers of goods and services (accounts payable and other current liabilities), governments (income taxes payable), and banks and other lenders (short-term and long-term debt obligations).

---

[3] *Ibid.*, par. 35.

Most troublesome questions regarding liability recognition relate to *executory contracts* and *contingent obligations.* Under U.S. GAAP and IFRS, firms do not recognize executory contracts for labor, purchase order commitments, and some lease agreements as liabilities because the firm has not yet received the benefits from these items and is not yet obligated to pay for them. For example, a firm should not recognize a liability when it places an order to purchase inventory, which is a contingent obligation; the obligation arises only when the firm receives the inventory. Likewise, the firms should not recognize a liability for future wages to employees; instead, it should recognize the liability once the employees have earned the wages. Notes to the financial statements disclose material executory contracts and other contingent claims. For example, refer to PepsiCo's long-term contractual commitments in Note 9, "Debt Obligations and Commitments" (Appendix A). PepsiCo lists noncancelable operating leases, purchasing commitments, and marketing commitments among its executory contracts. The note also describes $2.3 billion of guarantees it has issued for long-term debt of Bottling Group, LLC. Chapters 6 and 8 discuss these claims more fully.

Most liabilities are monetary, requiring future payments of cash. U.S. GAAP and IFRS report those due within one year at the amount of cash the firm expects to pay to discharge the obligation. If the payment dates extend beyond one year, U.S. GAAP and IFRS state the liability at the present value of the required future cash flows (discounted at an interest rate that reflects the underlying uncertainty of paying the cash as assessed at the time the obligation initially arose). Some liabilities, such as warranties, require delivery of goods or services instead of payment of cash, and the balance sheet states those liabilities at the expected future cost of providing these goods and services. Other liabilities also involve obligations to deliver goods or services when customers prepay, giving rise to deferred revenue liabilities. For example, such obligations can arise from the sale of gift cards redeemable for products or services, insurance premia, airfares, subscriptions, and memberships. The balance sheet reports these liabilities at the amount of revenues that have been received from customers and not yet earned.

Published balance sheets classify liabilities in various ways. Virtually all firms (except banks) use a current liabilities category, which includes obligations a firm expects to settle within one year. Balance sheets report the remaining liabilities in a section labeled "noncurrent liabilities" or "long-term debt." PepsiCo uses three noncurrent liability categories: long-term debt obligations, other liabilities, and deferred income taxes. Chapters 2 and 8 discuss deferred income taxes.

Shareholders' Equity Valuation and Disclosure

The shareholders' equity in a firm is a residual interest or claim. That is, the owners have a claim on all assets not required to meet the claims of creditors. Therefore, the valuation of assets and liabilities in the balance sheet determines the valuation of total shareholders' equity.[4]

Balance sheets separate total shareholders' equity into (1) amounts initially contributed by shareholders for an interest in a firm (PepsiCo uses the accounts common stock and capital in excess of par value), (2) cumulative net income in excess of dividends declared (PepsiCo's account is retained earnings), (3) shareholders' equity effects of the recognition or valuation of certain assets or liabilities (PepsiCo includes items related to available-for-sale investment securities, foreign currency translation, derivatives, and pensions in accumulated other comprehensive loss), and (4) treasury stock (PepsiCo

[4]The issuance of bonds with equity characteristics (such as convertible bonds), the issuance of equity claims with debt characteristics (such as redeemable preferred or common stock), and the issuance of obligations to be settled with the issuance of equity shares (such as stock options) cloud the distinction between liabilities and shareholders' equity.

shares repurchased by PepsiCo). PepsiCo also reports a small amount of contributed capital as preferred stock (which had been issued by Quaker prior to PepsiCo's acquisition of Quaker) less the amount of repurchased preferred stock.

Changes in Balance Sheet Accounts

The total assets of a firm and the claims on assets change over time because of investing and financing activities. For example, a firm may issue common stock for cash, acquire a building by mortgaging a portion of the purchase price, or issue common stock in exchange for convertible bonds. These investing and financing activities affect the amount and structure of a firm's assets, liabilities, and shareholders' equity.

The total assets of a firm and the claims on assets also change every day because of operating activities. The firm engages in daily business operations to generate revenues and create assets, but to do so, the firm must consume resources and incur obligations. Ideally, the firm sells goods or services to customers for an amount larger than the firm's cost to acquire or produce the goods and services. Creditors and owners provide capital to a firm with the expectation that the firm will use the capital to conduct profitable business operations and provide an adequate return to the suppliers of capital for the level of risk involved. The balance sheet is the summary of the firm's financial position at the end of each period; therefore, it summarizes the results of the operating, investing, and financing activities.

Assessing the Quality of the Balance Sheet as a Complete Representation of Economic Position

Analysts frequently examine the relation between items in the balance sheet when assessing a firm's financial position and credit risk. For example, an excess of current assets over current liabilities suggests that a firm has sufficient liquid resources to pay short-term creditors. A relatively low percentage of long-term debt to shareholders' equity suggests that a firm likely has sufficient long-term assets to repay the long-term debt at maturity, or at least an ability to take on new debt financing using the long-term assets as collateral to repay debt coming due.

However, when using the balance sheet for these purposes, the analyst must recognize the following:

1. Certain valuable resources of a firm that generate future cash flows, such as a patent for a pharmaceutical firm or a brand name for a consumer products firm such as PepsiCo, appear as assets only if they were acquired from another firm and therefore have a measurable acquisition cost.
2. Nonmonetary assets are reported at acquisition cost, net of accumulated depreciation or amortization, even though some of these assets may have current market values that exceed their recorded amounts. An example is the market value versus recorded value of land on the balance sheets of railroads and many urban department stores.
3. Certain rights to use resources and commitments to make future payments may not appear as assets and liabilities. On the balance sheet of airlines, you generally do not see, for example, leased aircraft or commitments to make future lease payments on those aircraft. Also, on the balance sheets of steel, tire, and automobile companies, you do not see the rights to receive labor services or the commitments to make future payments for labor services under labor union contracts.
4. Noncurrent liabilities appear at the present value of expected cash flows discounted at an interest rate determined at the time the liability initially arose instead of at a current market interest rate.

For certain firms under these circumstances, the balance sheet reporting may provide incomplete measures of the economic position of the firms. When using the balance sheet, the analyst should consider making adjustments for items that impact balance sheet quality. Chapters 6–9 discuss these issues more fully.

Income Statement—Measuring Operating Performance

The second principal financial statement, the income statement, provides information about the profitability of a firm for a period of time. As is common among analysts and investors, we use the terms *net income, earnings,* and *profit* interchangeably when referring to the bottom-line amount in the income statement. Exhibit 1.11 presents the income statements for PepsiCo for the five years 2004 through 2008.

Net income equals revenues and gains minus expenses and losses. Revenues measure the inflows of assets and the settlements of obligations from selling goods and providing services

EXHIBIT 1.11

PepsiCo, Inc. and Subsidiaries
Consolidated Statements of Income (in millions except per share amounts)

For Fiscal Year:	**2008**	**2007**	**2006**	**2005**	**2004**
Net revenue	$43,251	$39,474	$35,137	$32,562	$29,261
Cost of sales	20,351	18,038	15,762	14,176	12,674
Gross Profit	$22,900	$21,436	$19,375	$18,386	$16,587
Selling, general, and administrative expenses	15,901	14,208	12,711	12,314	11,031
Other operating charges	64	58	162	150	147
Restructuring charges	0	0	0	0	150
Operating Profit	$ 6,935	$ 7,170	$ 6,502	$ 5,922	$ 5,259
Bottling equity income	374	560	553	557	380
Interest expense	(329)	(224)	(239)	(256)	(167)
Interest income	41	125	173	159	74
Income before Income Taxes	$ 7,021	$ 7,631	$ 6,989	$ 6,382	$ 5,546
Provision for income taxes	1,879	1,973	1,347	2,304	1,372
Income from Continuing Operations	$ 5,142	$ 5,658	$ 5,642	$ 4,078	$ 4,174
Tax benefit from discontinued operations	0	0	0	0	38
Net Income	$ 5,142	$ 5,658	$ 5,642	$ 4,078	$ 4,212
Net income per common share:					
Basic	$ 3.26	$ 3.48	$ 3.42	$ 2.43	$ 2.45
Diluted	$ 3.21	$ 3.41	$ 3.34	$ 2.39	$ 2.41

to customers. Expenses measure the outflows of assets that a firm consumes and the incurrence of obligations in the process of operating the business to generate revenues. As a measure of performance, revenues report the resources generated by a firm and expenses report the resources consumed. Gains and losses result from selling assets or settling liabilities for more or less than their book values in transactions that are only peripherally related to a firm's central operations. For example, the sale of a building by PepsiCo for more than its book value would appear as a gain on the income statement. Chapter 2 describes income measurement in detail, and Chapter 3 contrasts income measurement with cash flows. Chapter 8 describes accounting for operating activities, particularly recognizing revenues and expenses.

PepsiCo generates revenues from selling goods in three principal product categories: snack foods; various soft drink concentrates, syrups, and bottled beverages; and cereals and related items. Revenues also include interest income from investments in debt instruments and equity method income from investments in affiliated but noncontrolled bottlers.

Costs of sales include the cost of manufacturing snack foods; the cost of producing concentrates, syrups, and bottled beverages; and the cost of manufacturing cereals and related items. Expenses also include selling, general, and administrative expenses (including advertising and other promotion costs) and interest expense on short- and long-term borrowing. PepsiCo reports amortization of intangible assets as a separate expense.

Compare PepsiCo's income statements to those of its closest rival, Coca-Cola. Exhibit 1.12 presents the income statements for Coca-Cola for the five years 2004 through 2008. Although PepsiCo is larger than Coca-Cola in terms of annual revenues, Coca-Cola is generally more

EXHIBIT 1.12

The Coca-Cola Company
Consolidated Statements of Income (in millions except per share amounts)

For Fiscal Year:	**2008**	**2007**	**2006**	**2005**	**2004**
Net revenue	$31,944	$28,857	$24,088	$23,104	$21,742
Cost of sales	11,374	10,406	8,164	8,195	7,674
Gross Profit	$20,570	$18,451	$15,924	$14,909	$14,068
Selling, general, and administrative expenses	11,774	10,945	9,431	8,739	7,890
Other operating charges	350	254	185	85	480
Operating Profit	$ 8,446	$ 7,252	$ 6,308	$ 6,085	$ 5,698
Bottling equity income	(874)	668	102	680	621
Interest expense	(438)	(456)	(220)	(240)	(196)
Interest income	333	236	193	235	157
Other income (loss) net	(28)	173	195	(70)	(58)
Income before Income Taxes	$ 7,439	$ 7,873	$ 6,578	$ 6,690	$ 6,222
Provision for income taxes	1,632	1,892	1,498	1,818	1,375
Net Income	$ 5,807	$ 5,981	$ 5,080	$ 4,872	$ 4,847
Net income per common share:					
Basic	$ 2.51	$ 2.59	$ 2.16	$ 2.04	$ 2.00
Diluted	$ 2.49	$ 2.57	$ 2.16	$ 2.04	$ 2.00

profitable in terms of annual net income. For example, in 2008, PepsiCo generated total revenues of $43,251 million and net income of $5,142 million; during the same year, Coca-Cola generated total revenues of $31,944 and net income of $5,807.

When using the income statement to assess a firm's profitability, the analyst is interested not only in its current and past profitability, but also in the likely level of sustainable earnings in the future (Step 5 in our six-step framework). When forecasting future earnings, the analyst must project whether past levels of revenues and expenses will likely continue and grow. Chapters 4 and 9 discuss some of the factors the analyst should consider before making these judgments. Chapter 10 provides an extensive discussion of building forecasts of future financial statements.

Accrual Basis of Accounting

Exhibit 1.13 depicts the operating, or earnings, cycle for a manufacturing firm. Net income from this series of activities equals the amount of cash received from customers minus the amount of cash paid for raw materials, labor, and the services of production facilities. If the entire operating cycle occurred in one accounting period, few difficulties would arise in measuring operating performance. Net income would equal cash inflows minus cash outflows related to these operating activities. However, firms acquire raw materials in one accounting period and use them in several future accounting periods. They acquire buildings and equipment in one accounting period and use them during many future accounting periods. Firms commonly sell goods or services in an earlier period than the one in which customers pay. Firms often consume resources or incur obligations in one accounting period and pay for those resources or settle those obligations in subsequent periods.

Under a cash basis of accounting, a firm recognizes revenue when it receives cash from customers and recognizes expenses when it pays cash to suppliers, employees, and other providers of goods and services. Because a firm's operating cycle usually extends over several accounting periods, the cash basis of accounting provides a poor measure of economic performance for specific periods of time because it provides a poor matching of resources earned (revenues) with resources used (expenses). To overcome this deficiency of the cash basis, both U.S. GAAP and IFRS require that firms use the accrual basis of accounting in measuring performance.

Under the accrual basis of accounting, a firm recognizes revenue when it meets the following two criteria:

- **It has completed all (or substantially all) of the revenue-generating process by delivering products or services to customers.**
- **It is reasonably certain it has satisfied a liability or generated an asset that it can measure reliably.**

Most firms recognize revenue during the period in which they sell goods or render services. Consider the accrual basis of accounting applied to a manufacturing firm. The cost

EXHIBIT 1.13

Operating Cycle for a Manufacturing Firm

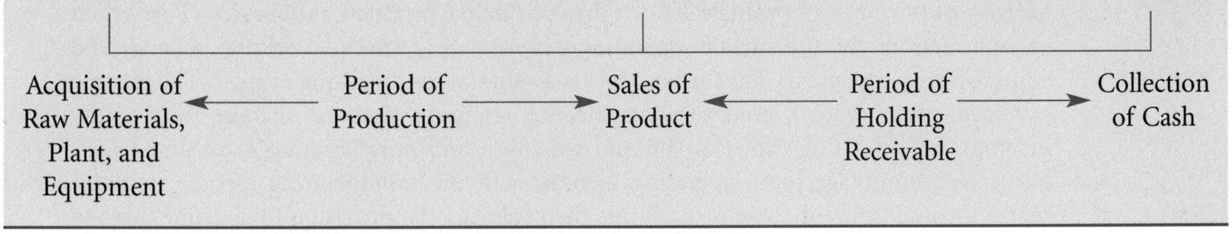

of manufacturing a product remains on the balance sheet as an asset (inventory) until the time of sale. At the time of sale, the firm recognizes revenue in the amount of cash it expects to collect. It recognizes the cost of manufacturing the product as a cost of the goods sold. Most costs cannot be matched to particular revenues because they are costs of operating the business for a particular period of time (for example, the salary of the chief executive officer and rent on corporate offices.). Therefore, the firm recognizes such costs as expenses on the income statement in the period in which it consumes those resources (that is, matching expenses to a period rather than to specific revenues).

Note that under accrual accounting a firm should not delay revenue recognition until it receives cash from customers as long as the firm can estimate with reasonable precision the amount of cash it will ultimately receive. The amount will appear in accounts receivable prior to the receipt of cash. The accrual basis provides a better measure of operating performance than the cash basis because it matches inputs with outputs more accurately.

Classification and Format in the Income Statement

Investors commonly assess a firm's value based on the firm's expected future sustainable earnings stream. As Chapter 10 discusses more fully, analysts predict the future earnings, or net income, of a firm by projecting future business activities that will drive future revenues, expenses, and profits. To inform analysts and other financial statement users about sustainable earnings, firms often report income from recurring business activities separately from income effects from unusual or nonrecurring activities (such as asset impairments, restructuring, discontinued business segments, and extraordinary events). To provide more useful information for prediction, U.S. GAAP requires that the income statement include some or all of the following sections or categories depending on the nature of the firm's income for a period:

- Income from continuing operations
- Income, gains, and losses from discontinued operations
- Extraordinary gains and losses

Income from Continuing Operations. The first section, Income from Continuing Operations, reports the revenues and expenses of activities in which a firm anticipates an ongoing involvement. When a firm does not have items in the second and third categories of income in a particular year, all of its income items are related to continuing operations; so it does not need to use the continuing operations label.

Firms report their expenses in various ways. Most firms in the United States report expenses by their function: cost of goods sold for manufacturing, selling expenses for marketing, administrative expenses for administrative management, and interest expense for financing. Other firms, particularly those in the European Community, tend to report expenses by their nature: raw materials, compensation, advertising, and research and development.

Many variations in income statement format appear in corporate annual reports. Most commonly, firms list various sources of revenues from selling their goods and services and then list the cost of goods sold. Some firms (Coca-Cola but not PepsiCo) choose to report a subtotal of gross profit (sales revenues minus cost of goods sold), which is an important measure of the inherent profitability of a firm's principal products and services. Firms then list subtractions for the various operating expenses (for example, selling, general, and administrative expenses). This format reports a subtotal for operating income. The income statement then reports nonoperating income amounts (interest income and equity income), nonoperating expenses (interest expense), and nonoperating gains and losses. Firms commonly aggregate operating income with the nonoperating income items to report income before income taxes. Firms then subtract the provision for income taxes to compute and report the bottom-line net income. As shown in Exhibit 1.11 and Appendix A, PepsiCo uses this multistep format to report its income statement.

Income from Discontinued Operations. A firm that intends to remain in a line of business but decides to sell or close down some portion of that line (such as closing a single plant or dropping a line of products) generally will report any income, gain, or loss from such an action under continuing operations. On the other hand, if a firm decides to terminate its involvement in a line of business (such as selling or shuttering an entire division or subsidiary), it will report the income, gain, or loss in the second section of the income statement, labeled "Income, Gains, and Losses from Discontinued Operations."

For example, on August 14, 1997, PepsiCo announced that it would spin off its restaurant businesses (which included Pizza Hut, Taco Bell, and KFC), forming a new restaurant company named Tricon Global Restaurants, Inc. (now known as Yum! Brands, Inc.). For 1997, PepsiCo reported income from continuing operations separately from discontinued operations. In that year, PepsiCo reported a total of $1,491 million of income (net of tax) from continuing operations and $651 million of income (net of tax) associated with the discontinued restaurants segment.

Extraordinary Gains and Losses. Extraordinary gains and losses arise from events that are (1) unusual given the nature of a firm's activities, (2) nonrecurring, and (3) material in amount. Corporate annual reports rarely disclose such items.

Many firms, including PepsiCo, have reported restructuring charges and impairment losses in their income statements in recent years. Such items often reflect the write-down of assets or the recognition of liabilities arising from changes in economic conditions and corporate strategies. Because restructuring charges and impairment losses do not usually satisfy the criteria for discontinued operations or extraordinary items, firms report them in the continuing operations section of the income statement. If the amounts are material, they appear on a separate line to distinguish them from recurring income items. Chapters 4 and 9 discuss the benefits and possible pitfalls of segregating such amounts when analyzing profitability.

Income, gains, and losses from discontinued operations and extraordinary gains and losses appear in the income statement net of any income tax effects. The majority of published income statements include only the first section because discontinued operations and extraordinary gains and losses occur infrequently.

Comprehensive Income

The FASB and IASB have determined that the balance sheet is the cornerstone of accounting and that income should be measured by changes in the values of assets and liabilities. To provide relevant and reliable measures of assets and liabilities, U.S. GAAP and IFRS use a variety of measurement attributes, some of which require firms to adjust asset or liability values to reflect changes in net realizable values, fair values, or present values. Valuation adjustments to assets and liabilities usually give rise to revenues (or gains) or to expenses (or losses). For example, if a firm determines that it will not collect some of its accounts receivable or will not be able to sell some items of inventory, it should adjust receivables and inventory to their net realizable values and recognize those adjustments as expenses or losses in net income.

The FASB and IASB have determined that four particular types of valuation adjustments represent unrealized gains or losses that should be classified as "other comprehensive income" items. Other comprehensive income items are accumulated over time in a special account in shareholders' equity titled Accumulated Other Comprehensive Income or Loss (similar to how net income is accumulated over time in the shareholders' equity account titled Retained Earnings). These other comprehensive income items are not recognized in net income until they are realized in an economic transaction, such as when the related assets are sold or the liabilities are settled.

Review the Consolidated Statement of Common Shareholders' Equity for PepsiCo in Appendix A. It details the four types of unrealized gain/loss items that are triggered by the valuation of assets and liabilities and are recognized as other comprehensive income items. It also reports the components of Accumulated Other Comprehensive Loss: (1) currency translation adjustments; (2) cash flow hedges, net of tax; (3) certain changes in pension and retiree medical plan obligations, net of tax; and (4) unrealized losses/gains on securities, net of tax. Later chapters discuss the accounting for each of these items.

The FASB and IASB are aware that unrealized gains and losses of this nature affect the market value of firms, but users of financial statements might overlook them because they do not yet appear in net income. Therefore, firms must report an amount in one of their financial statements that the FASB refers to as *Comprehensive Income.*[5] Comprehensive income equals *all* revenues, expenses, gains, and losses for a period. Comprehensive income includes net income plus or minus the other comprehensive income items. Refer again to PepsiCo's consolidated statement of common shareholders' equity in Appendix A. The bottom portion of the statement shows the computation of PepsiCo's comprehensive income each year. Comprehensive income for PepsiCo for 2008 is as follows (in millions):

Net income	$5,142
Currency translation adjustment	(2,484)
Cash flow hedges, net of tax	21
Pension and retiree medical plan liability adjustments, net of tax	(1,303)
Unrealized losses on securities, net of tax	(21)
Other	(6)
Comprehensive income	$1,349

Firms have considerable flexibility as to where they report comprehensive income in the financial statements. It may appear in the income statement, in a separate statement of comprehensive income, or as part of the analysis of changes in shareholders' equity accounts. PepsiCo uses this last method of disclosure.

Firms also have flexibility as to how they label disclosures related to comprehensive income. That is, firms need not use the term *comprehensive income,* but instead may label the amount as, for example, net income plus or minus changes in other non-owner equity accounts. The balance sheet disclosure might use the term *accumulated other comprehensive income/loss* for the portions of comprehensive income not related to reported earnings or use a term such as *accumulated non-owner equity account changes.*

Appendix A indicates that PepsiCo uses the term *Accumulated Other Comprehensive Loss* in its Consolidated Balance Sheet. In addition, PepsiCo reports the accumulated balances for each component of its other comprehensive income in Note 13, "Accumulated Other Comprehensive Loss," to the financial statements.

Assessing the Quality of Earnings as a Complete Representation of Economic Performance

Common stock prices in the capital markets usually react quickly when firms announce new earnings information, indicating that earnings play an important role in the valuation

[5]Financial Accounting Standards Board, *Statement of Financial Accounting Standards Statement No. 130,* "Reporting Comprehensive Income" (1997).

of firms. We provide some striking empirical evidence of the association between earnings and stock returns later in this chapter. In using earnings information for valuation, however, the analyst needs to be alert to the possibility that reported earnings for a particular period represent an incomplete measure of current period profitability or are a poor predictor of ongoing sustainable profitability. For example, reported net income may include amounts that are not likely to recur in the future, such as restructuring or impairment charges; income, gains, and losses from discontinued operations; or extraordinary gains or losses. The analyst may want to eliminate the effects of nonrecurring items when assessing operating performance for purposes of forecasting future earnings. (Chapters 9 and 10 discuss these ideas more fully.)

In some circumstances managers use subtle means to manage earnings. For example, a firm might accelerate recognition of revenues, understate its estimate of bad-debt expense or warranty expense, cut back on advertising or research and development expenditures, or delay maintenance expenditures as a means of increasing earnings in a particular period. Chapter 9 discusses the quality of accounting information and illustrates adjustments the analyst might make to improve the quality of earnings.

Statement of Cash Flows

The third principal financial statement is the statement of cash flows. This statement reports for a period of time the net cash flows (inflows minus outflows) from three principal business activities: operating, investing, and financing. The purpose of the statement of cash flows is important but simple: to inform analysts about the sources and uses of cash. The statement provides useful information to complement the income statement, demonstrating how cash flows differ from accrual-based income. Because the cash flows statement reveals how a firm is generating and using cash, it also is a useful tool for gauging how the firm is executing its strategy.

Rationale for the Statement of Cash Flows

The statement of cash flows provides information on the sources and uses of cash. Even profitable firms—especially those growing rapidly—sometimes find themselves strapped for cash and unable to pay suppliers, employees, and other creditors. This can occur for two principal reasons:

- The timing of cash receipts from customers does not necessarily coincide with the recognition of revenue, and the timing of cash expenditures does not necessarily coincide with the recognition of expenses under the accrual basis of accounting. In the usual case, cash expenditures precede the recognition of expenses and cash receipts follow the recognition of revenue. Thus, a firm might have positive net income for a period but a negative net cash flow from operations.
- The firm may need to acquire new property, plant, and equipment; retire outstanding debt; or reacquire shares of its common stock when sufficient cash is not available.

In many cases, a profitable firm finding itself short of cash can obtain the needed funds from short- or long-term creditors or from equity investors. The firm must repay with interest the funds borrowed from creditors. Owners may require that the firm pay periodic dividends as an inducement to invest in the firm. Eventually, the firm must generate sufficient cash from operations if it is to survive.

Sometimes firms are flush with cash. In such cases, the analyst should determine why the firm has excess cash, which can occur for two principal reasons:

- Firm operations may be profitable, with cash flows from operations equal to or greater than profits. This can occur, for example, when the firm is mature, stable, and profitable and does not need to invest excess cash flows in capital or growth opportunities (sometimes referred to as cash-cow firms).

- The firm may have engaged in cash-raising transactions by selling assets or divesting subsidiaries, issuing short-term or long-term debt, or issuing equity shares.

The analyst will find it useful to know which of the two reasons explain the firm's excess cash because they have different implications for the firm's strategy and are likely to influence how the analyst values the firm.

Classification of Cash Flows

Cash flows are the connecting link between operating, investing, and financing activities. They permit each of these three principal business activities to continue functioning smoothly and effectively. The statement of cash flows also can be helpful in assessing a firm's past ability to generate free cash flows and for predicting future free cash flows. The concept of free cash flows is first introduced in Chapter 3. As discussed in Chapter 12, free cash flows are central to cash-flow-based valuation models.

The statement of cash flows classifies cash flows as relating to operating, investing, or financing activities.

Operating. Selling goods and providing services are among the most important ways a financially healthy company generates cash. Assessing cash flow from operations over several years indicates the extent to which operating activities have provided the necessary cash to maintain operating capabilities (and the extent to which firms have had to rely on other sources of cash).

Investing. The acquisition of long-lived productive assets, particularly property, plant, and equipment, usually represents major ongoing uses of cash. Firms must replace such assets as they wear out. If firms are to grow, they must acquire additional long-lived productive assets. Firms obtain a portion of the cash needed to acquire long-lived productive assets from sales of existing assets. However, such cash inflows are seldom sufficient to cover the cost of new acquisitions.

Financing. A firm obtains cash from short- and long-term borrowing and from issuing preferred and common stock. It uses cash to repay short- and long-term borrowing, to pay dividends, and to reacquire shares of outstanding preferred and common stock.

Exhibit 1.14 presents the statement of cash flows for PepsiCo for 2004 through 2008. The statement reveals that cash flow from operating activities exceeded the net cash outflow for investing activities in each of the three years. In 2006, PepsiCo used a portion of the excess cash flow for financing activities, reducing short-term and long-term debt. But PepsiCo shifted its financing strategy in 2007 and 2008, generating large amounts of net cash inflows from proceeds of short-term and long-term borrowings. In all three years, PepsiCo used large amounts of cash to pay dividends to shareholders and to repurchase shares of its common stock. For comparative purposes, Exhibit 1.15 (see page 37) presents the statement of cash flows for Coca-Cola for 2004 through 2008.

Firms sometimes engage in investing and financing transactions that do not directly involve cash. For example, a firm might acquire a building by assuming a mortgage obligation. It might issue common stock upon conversion of long-term debt. Firms disclose these transactions in a supplementary schedule or note to the statement of cash flows in a way that clearly indicates that the transactions are investing and financing activities that do not affect cash. In Note 14, "Supplemental Financial Information," (Appendix A), PepsiCo reports the portion of its acquisitions in recent years that did not directly involve the use of cash.

EXHIBIT 1.14

PepsiCo, Inc. and Subsidiaries
Consolidated Statements of Cash Flows (in millions)

For Fiscal Year:	2008	2007	2006	2005	2004
OPERATING ACTIVITIES					
Net income	$ 5,142	$ 5,658	$ 5,642	$ 4,078	$ 4,212
Adjustments to reconcile net income to net cash provided by operating activities					
Depreciation and amortization	1,543	1,426	1,406	1,308	1,264
Stock-based compensation expense	238	260	270	311	368
Restructuring and impairment charges	543	102	67	—	150
Excess tax benefits from share-based payment arrangements	(107)	(208)	(134)	—	—
Cash payments for restructuring charges	(180)	(22)	(56)	(22)	(92)
Pension and retiree medical plan contributions	(219)	(310)	(131)	(877)	(534)
Pension and retiree medical plan expenses	459	535	544	464	395
Bottling equity income, net of dividends	(202)	(441)	(442)	(411)	(297)
Deferred income taxes and other tax charges and credits	573	118	(510)	585	(75)
Change in accounts and notes receivable	(549)	(405)	(330)	(272)	(130)
Change in inventories	(345)	(204)	(186)	(132)	(100)
Change in prepaid expenses and other current assets	(68)	(16)	(37)	(56)	(31)
Change in accounts payable and other current liabilities	718	522	279	188	216
Change in income taxes payable	(180)	128	(295)	609	(268)
Other, net	(367)	(209)	(3)	79	(24)
Net Cash Provided by Operating Activities	$ 6,999	$ 6,934	$ 6,084	$ 5,852	$ 5,054
INVESTING ACTIVITIES					
Capital spending	$(2,446)	$(2,430)	$(2,068)	$(1,736)	$(1,387)
Sales of property, plant, and equipment	98	47	49	88	38
Acquisitions and investments in noncontrolled affiliates	(1,925)	(1,293)	(547)	(1,095)	(64)
Cash restricted for pending acquisitions	(40)	—	—	—	—
Cash proceeds from sale of PBG and PAS stock	358	315	318	214	—
Divestitures	6	—	37	3	52
Short-term investments, by original maturity					
More than three months—purchases	(156)	(83)	(29)	(83)	(44)
More than three months—maturities	62	113	25	84	38
Three months or less, net	1,376	(413)	2,021	(992)	(963)
Net Cash Used for Investing Activities	$(2,667)	$(3,744)	$ (194)	$(3,517)	$(2,330)

(Continued)

EXHIBIT 1.14 (Continued)

For Fiscal Year:	2008	2007	2006	2005	2004
FINANCING ACTIVITIES					
Proceeds from issuances of long-term debt	$ 3,719	$ 2,168	$ 51	$ 25	$ 504
Payments of long-term debt	(649)	(579)	(157)	(177)	(512)
Short-term borrowings, by original maturity					
More than three months—proceeds	89	83	185	332	153
More than three months—payments	(269)	(133)	(358)	(85)	(160)
Three months or less, net	625	(345)	(2,168)	1,601	1,119
Cash dividends paid	(2,541)	(2,204)	(1,854)	(1,642)	(1,329)
Share repurchases—common	(4,720)	(4,300)	(3,000)	(3,012)	(3,028)
Share repurchases—preferred	(6)	(12)	(10)	(19)	(27)
Proceeds from exercises of stock options	620	1,108	1,194	1,099	965
Excess tax benefits from share-based payment arrangements	107	208	134	—	—
Net Cash Used for Financing Activities	$(3,025)	$(4,006)	$(5,983)	$(1,878)	$(2,315)
Effect of exchange rate changes on cash and cash equivalents	$ (153)	$ 75	$ 28	$ (21)	$ 51
Net Increase (Decrease) in Cash and Cash Equivalents	$ 1,154	$ (741)	$ (65)	$ 436	$ 460
Cash and Cash Equivalents, Beginning of Year	910	1,651	1,716	1,280	820
Cash and Cash Equivalents, End of Year	$ 2,064	$ 910	$ 1,651	$ 1,716	$ 1,280

The statement of cash flows is required under both U.S. GAAP and IFRS, but it is not a required financial statement in some countries. Increasingly, however, most large international firms are providing the statement on a voluntary basis. Chapter 3 describes and illustrates analytical procedures for preparing a statement of cash flows in situations where firms provide only a balance sheet and income statement. Chapter 10 demonstrates techniques for projecting future statements of cash flows from projected balance sheets and income statements.

Important Information with the Financial Statements

A firm's accounting system records the results of transactions, events, and commercial arrangements and generates the financial statements, but the financial statements do not stand alone. To provide more relevant and reliable information for financial statement users, firms typically provide a substantial amount of important additional information with the financial statements. This section briefly introduces three important additional elements of information: (a) Notes, (b) Management Discussion and Analysis, and (c) Managers' and Independent Auditors' Attestations.

Notes

The financial statements report the accounts and amounts that comprise the balance sheet, income statement, and statement of cash flows, but they do not explain how those accounts

EXHIBIT 1.15

The Coca-Cola Company
Consolidated Statements of Cash Flows
(in millions)

For Fiscal Year:	2008	2007	2006	2005	2004
OPERATING ACTIVITIES					
Net income	$ 5,807	$ 5,981	$ 5,080	$ 4,872	$ 4,847
Adjustments to reconcile net income to net cash provided by operating activities					
Depreciation and amortization	1,228	1,163	938	932	893
Stock-based compensation expense	266	313	324	324	345
Deferred income taxes	(360)	109	(35)	(88)	162
Bottling equity income, net of dividends	1,128	(452)	124	(446)	(476)
Foreign currency adjustments	(42)	9	52	47	(59)
Gains on sales of assets	(130)	(244)	(303)	(32)	(44)
Other operating charges	209	166	159	85	480
Other items	153	99	233	299	437
Net change in operating assets and liabilities	(688)	6	(615)	430	(617)
Net Cash Provided by Operating Activities	$ 7,571	$ 7,150	$ 5,957	$ 6,423	$ 5,968
INVESTING ACTIVITIES					
Acquisitions and investments	$ (759)	$(5,653)	$ (901)	$ (637)	$ (267)
Purchases of other investments	(240)	(99)	(82)	(53)	(46)
Proceeds from disposals of acquisition and investments	479	448	640	33	161
Purchases of property, plant, and equipment	(1,968)	(1,648)	(1,407)	(899)	(755)
Proceeds from disposals of property, plant, and equipment	129	239	112	88	341
Other investing activities	(4)	(6)	(62)	(28)	63
Net Cash Used for Investing Activities	$(2,363)	$(6,719)	$(1,700)	$(1,496)	$ (503)
FINANCING ACTIVITIES					
Issuances of debt	$ 4,337	$ 9,979	$ 617	$ 178	$ 3,030
Payments of debt	(4,308)	(5,638)	(2,021)	(2,460)	(1,316)
Issuances of stock	586	1,619	148	230	193
Purchases of stock for treasury	(1,079)	(1,838)	(2,416)	(2,055)	(1,739)
Dividends	(3,521)	(3,149)	(2,911)	(2,678)	(2,429)
Net Cash Used for Financing Activities	$(3,985)	$ 973	$(6,583)	$(6,785)	$(2,261)
Effect of exchange rate changes on cash and cash equivalents	$ (615)	$ 249	$ 65	$ (148)	$ 141
Net Increase (Decrease) in Cash and Cash Equivalents	$ 608	$ 1,653	$(2,261)	$(2,006)	$ 3,345
Cash and Cash Equivalents, Beginning of Year	4,093	2,440	4,701	6,707	3,362
Cash and Cash Equivalents, End of Year	$ 4,701	$ 4,093	$ 2,440	$ 4,701	$ 6,707

and amounts have been determined. The notes to financial statements provide important details about the accounting methods and principles the firm has used to measure assets, liabilities, revenues, expenses, gains, and losses. The first note typically provides a summary of the key accounting principles the firm has used. Because each account in the financial statements requires application of judgments, estimates, and accounting principles, the notes typically describe and explain how each account has been determined (except accounts that are deemed not to be material). For example, the notes explain how the firm is accounting for inventory and what cost methods the firm used to value inventory on hand as well as cost of goods sold. The notes explain how property, plant, and equipment are valued; how they are being depreciated; how much depreciation has been accumulated to date; and what the expected useful lives of the underlying assets are. Notes also provide important details about key financial statement estimates, such as fair values of investment securities, pension and postemployment benefit liabilities, income taxes, and intangible assets.

In the 2008 Annual Report (Appendix A), PepsiCo provides a total of 14 notes to explain the accounting principles, methods, and estimates used to prepare the financial statements. Immediately following the financial statements, the notes comprise an additional 21 pages of the annual report. You should read the notes carefully because they provide important information that is useful for understanding the firm's accounting and assessing its accounting quality.

Management Discussion and Analysis

Many firms accompany the financial statements and notes with extensive narrative and quantitative discussion and analysis from the managers. The MD&A (Management Discussion and Analysis) section of the financial statements provides insights into managers' strategies and their assessments and evaluation of the firm's performance. In some cases, MD&A disclosures provide glimpses into managers' expectations about the future of the company.

In the 2008 Annual Report, PepsiCo provides a total of 24 pages of MD&A (Appendix B). In the MD&A, PepsiCo describes the business as a whole, as well as the operations of the business in each of the six divisions. In addition to qualitative descriptions, the MD&A section provides valuable details about the financial performance of each division, with managers' analysis comparing results of 2008 to 2007 and 2007 to 2006. In addition, PepsiCo's MD&A section provides important insights into the firm's business risks and the way PepsiCo is managing them, critical accounting policies PepsiCo has applied, and PepsiCo's liquidity and capital resource situation. The MD&A section also provides valuable glimpses into a few of PepsiCo's plans for the future, such as its intention in 2009 to repurchase up to $2.5 billion in common shares. Because the MD&A section provides insight into the company from the managers' point of view, you should read it carefully to obtain all of the information available. But you also should read it with a bit of skepticism because managers tend to be optimistic when evaluating the strategies and performance of their firms.

Managers' and Independent Auditors' Attestations

The design and operation of the accounting system are the responsibility of a firm's managers. However, the SEC and most stock exchanges require firms with publicly traded common stock to have their accounting records and financial statements audited by independent auditors. The independent auditor's attestation as to the fairness and reliability of a firm's financial statements relative to U.S. GAAP or IFRS is an essential element in the efficiency of the capital markets. Investors and other users of the financial statements can rely on financial statements for essential information about a firm only if they are confident that the independent auditor has examined the accounting records and has concluded that the financial statements are fair and reliable according to U.S. GAAP or IFRS.

In response to some managers' misrepresenting their financial statements and audit breakdowns in now infamous cases involving Enron, Global Crossing, Qwest Communications, and other firms, Congress passed the Sarbanes-Oxley Act of 2002. This act more clearly defines the explicit responsibility of managers for financial statements, the relation between the independent auditor and the firm audited, and the kinds of services permitted and not permitted. Exhibit 1.16 summarizes some of the more important provisions of the Sarbanes-Oxley Act as they relate to financial statements.

For many years, firms have included with their financial statements a report by management that states its responsibility for the financial statements. The Sarbanes-Oxley Act of 2002 now requires that the management report include an attestation that managers assume responsibility for establishing and maintaining adequate internal control structure and procedures (referred to as the *Management Assessment*). This new requirement now makes explicit management's responsibility not only for the financial statements, but also

EXHIBIT 1.16

Summary of the Principal Provisions of the Sarbanes-Oxley Act of 2002

1. Violation of the provisions of the Sarbanes-Oxley Act of 2002 is a violation of the Securities Exchange Act of 1934. The Securities Exchange Act of 1934 governs the public trading of securities.
2. The Sarbanes-Oxley Act of 2002 created the Public Company Accounting Oversight Board (PCAOB), which has responsibility for setting generally accepted auditing standards, ethics standards, and quality-control standards for audits.
3. The SEC has oversight and enforcement authority over the PCAOB.
4. The act precludes a registered public accounting firm from performing non-audit services contemporaneously with the audit. Certain services, such as tax work, are allowed if they are preapproved by the firm's audit committee or constitute less than 5 percent of the billing price for audit and other services.
5. The lead audit or coordinating partner and the reviewing partner of the public accounting firm must rotate, or change, every five years.
6. Members of the audit committee of a firm's board of directors will have primary responsibility for appointment, oversight, and compensation of the registered public accounting firm.
7. At least one member of the audit committee of the board of directors must be a "financial expert."
8. The firm's chief executive officer and the chief financial officer must issue a statement along with the audit report stating that the financial statements and notes fairly present the operations and financial position of the firm.
9. Each annual report must contain an "internal control report" that states management's responsibility for establishing and maintaining an adequate internal control structure and procedures (Management Assessment Report). The annual report must also contain an assessment of the effectiveness of the internal control structure and procedures by the firm's auditor (Assurance Opinion). The assurance opinion can be unqualified, qualified, adverse, or a disclaimer, the same as the independent accountant's opinion on the financial statements and notes.

for the underlying accounting and control system that generates the financial statements. The chief executive officer and the chief financial officer must sign this management report. PepsiCo's management report appears in Appendix A.

The independent auditor also assesses a firm's internal control system, designs its audit tests in light of the quality of these internal controls, and then forms an opinion about the fairness of the amounts reported in the financial statements based on its audit tests. The independent auditor must now include opinions on the effectiveness of the internal control system (referred to as the *Assurance Opinion*) and the fairness of the amounts reported in the financial statements. This dual opinion makes explicit the independent auditor's responsibility for testing the effectiveness of the internal control system and judging the fairness of the amounts reported. The report of PepsiCo's independent auditor (KPMG, LLP) appears in Appendix A after Note 14, "Supplemental Financial Information." Note that the last paragraph includes opinions on both the internal control system and the financial statements and reads as follows:

> In our opinion, the consolidated financial statements referred to above present fairly, in all material respects, the financial position of PepsiCo, Inc. as of December 27, 2008 and December 29, 2007, and the results of their operations and their cash flows for each of the fiscal years in the three-year period ended December 27, 2008, in conformity with U.S. generally accepted accounting principles. Also, in our opinion, PepsiCo, Inc. maintained, in all material respects, effective internal control over financial reporting as of December 27, 2008, based on criteria established in *Internal Control-Integrated Framework* issued by COSO.

Summary of Financial Statements, Notes, MD&A, and Managers' and Auditors' Attestations

The three principal financial statements, the notes, the MD&A section, and managers' and auditors' attestations provide analysts with an immense amount of useful information for understanding various aspects of a firm's operating, investing, and financing activities.

- The balance sheet reports the results of firms' decisions to acquire assets and the financing of those assets. Most assets result from decisions about operating activities (for example, credit policies for customers, production and control systems for inventories, and plant and productive capacity), yet other assets result from investing decisions (for example, holding investment securities and investing in noncontrolled affiliates). Many liabilities of firms also result from decisions about operating activities (such as policies for paying suppliers of good and services and compensation and benefits plans for employees) or from claims from government tax authorities. Financing decisions also determine many liabilities, including the firm's decisions about the use of short-term and long-term borrowings and common stock to finance assets.
- The income statement primarily reflects the results of operating decisions (for example, product mix and pricing, sourcing of production and marketing, and use of plant and equipment). The income statement also reports amounts related to investing decisions (for example, interest and dividend income) and financing decisions (for example, interest expense). The other comprehensive income items, which are reported as part of comprehensive income in the statement of shareholders' equity, reflect gains and losses from changes in values of certain assets and liabilities that are not reported in net income until such gains and losses are realized.

- The statement of cash flows reflects the sources of uses of cash during a period. The statement of cash flows classifies cash changes during a period into operating, investing, and financing categories.
- The notes to the financial statements explain and describe the accounting methods, assumptions, estimates, and judgments used to prepare the statements.
- The MD&A section provides managers' insights and evaluation of the firm's performance and risks.
- The managers' attestation and the independent auditor's attestation provide statements about (and take responsibility for) the quality and effectiveness of the firm's internal control system and the fairness of its financial statements and notes in reporting a firm's financial position, performance, and cash flows. The independent audit adds credibility and reliability to the financial statements and notes prepared by management.

STEP 4: ANALYZE PROFITABILITY AND RISK

The first three steps of the six-step analytical framework establish three key building blocks:

- An understanding of the economics of the industry in which a firm competes
- An understanding of the particular strategies that the firm has chosen to compete in its industry
- An understanding of the information contained in the financial statements and notes that report the results of a firm's operating, investing, and financing activities and an assessment of the quality of the financial statements

The analyst is now ready to conduct a financial statement analysis.

Most financial statement analysis aims to evaluate a firm's profitability and risk. This twofold focus stems from the emphasis of investment decisions on returns and risk. Investors acquire shares of common stock in a company because of the return they expect from such investments. This return includes any dividends received plus the change in the market price of the shares of stock while the investor holds them. A rational investor will not be indifferent between two investments that are expected to yield, for example, a 20 percent return if there are differences in the uncertainty, or risk, of earning that 20 percent return. The investor will demand a higher expected return from higher-risk investments to compensate for the additional risk assumed.

The income statement reports a firm's net income during the current year and prior years. Assessing the profitability of the firm during these periods, after adjusting as appropriate for nonrecurring or unsustainable items, permits the analyst to evaluate the firm's current and past profitability and to begin forecasting its likely future profitability. Empirical research has shown an association between earnings and market rates of return on common stock, a point discussed in the next section in this chapter and in greater depth in Chapters 13 and 14.

Financial statements also are useful for assessing the risk of a firm. Empirical research has shown that volatility in reported earnings over time is correlated with stock market-based measures of firm risk, such as market equity beta. In addition, firms that cannot generate sufficient cash flow from operations will likely encounter financial difficulties and perhaps even bankruptcy. Firms that have high proportions of debt in their capital structures will experience financial difficulties if they are unable to repay the debt at maturity or replace maturing debt with new debt. Assessing the financial risk of a firm assists the investor in identifying the level of risk incurred when investing in the firm's common stock.

Tools of Profitability and Risk Analysis

Most of this book describes and illustrates tools for analyzing financial statements. The purpose here is simply to introduce several of these tools as a broad overview.

Common-Size Financial Statements

One simple but powerful analytical tool is common-size financial statements, a tool that is helpful in highlighting relations in a financial statement. Common-size income statements and balance sheets express all items in the statement as a percentage of a common base. Common-size balance sheets often use total assets as the base. Sales revenue is a common base in a common-size income statement.

The first five columns of Exhibit 1.17 present common-size balance sheets for PepsiCo for 2004 through 2008. Note that various common-size percentages for PepsiCo remain quite stable while others change over this period. For example, PepsiCo experienced a significant increase in the proportion of assets comprising cash, but a sharp drop in the short-term investments during 2008. To better understand the reasons for the increased proportion of cash and marketable securities, refer to PepsiCo's statement of cash flows in Exhibit 1.14. It shows that significant amounts of short-term investments matured or were sold, explaining the drop in short-term investments. In addition, Exhibit 1.14 shows that the cash flow from operations was more than sufficient to finance expenditures on property, plant, and equipment. In addition, PepsiCo raised more cash by issuing a significant amount of long-term debt. PepsiCo used a large amount of cash to pay dividends and repurchase shares of its own stock. PepsiCo invested the remaining excess cash in cash and cash equivalents, leading to the increased common-size percentage.

The common-size balance sheets also show that the proportion of financing from liabilities rose from 51.7 percent in 2004 to 66.4 percent in 2008. In particular, the long-term debt obligations grew from 8.6 percent of assets in 2004 to 21.8 percent in 2008. This is consistent with the prior observation from the statement of cash flows that PepsiCo increased its long-term borrowing. The common-size balance sheet also reveals that large increase in treasury stock. Again, PepsiCo's statement of cash flows in Exhibit 1.14 reports repurchases of common shares totaled $4,720 million in 2008. The common-size balance sheets for Coca-Cola for 2004 through 2008, presented in the first five columns of Exhibit 1.19 (see pages 46–47), do not reveal the same trends: Coca-Cola's proportions of liabilities and common shareholders' equity remained relatively constant over the same period.

The first five columns of Exhibit 1.18 (see page 45) present common-size income statements for PepsiCo for 2004 through 2008. Note that net income as a percentage of sales (also known as the *profit margin*) decreased from 16.1 percent in 2006 to 11.9 percent in 2008. The common-size income statements show that most expenses as a percentage of sales revenue increased during this period. The decreasing profit margin results primarily from cost of sales increasing by 2.2 percent of sales and selling general and administrative expenses increasing by 0.6 percent of sales from 2006 through 2008. Management's discussion and analysis of operations presented in Appendix B explains some of these changes. The task of the financial analyst is to delve into the reasons for such changes, taking into consideration industry economics, company strategies, management's explanations, and the operating results for competitors. Chapter 4 explores the reasons for PepsiCo's decreased profit margin.

The common-size income statements for Coca-Cola for 2004 through 2008, presented in the first five columns of Exhibit 1.20 (see page 48), reveal a decline in profit margin over the same period of time. Coca-Cola's profit margin was 22.3 percent of revenues in 2004 and dropped to 18.2 percent of revenues in 2008.

EXHIBIT 1.17

Common-Size and Percentage Change Balance Sheets for PepsiCo (allow for rounding)

	Common-Size Balance Sheets:					Percentage Change Balance Sheets:			
	2008	2007	2006	2005	2004	2008	2007	2006	2005
ASSETS									
Cash and cash equivalents	5.7%	2.6%	5.5%	5.4%	4.6%	126.8%	(44.9%)	(3.8%)	34.1%
Short-term investments	0.6%	4.5%	3.9%	10.0%	7.7%	(86.4%)	34.2%	(63.0%)	46.2%
Accounts and notes receivable, net	13.0%	12.7%	12.4%	10.3%	10.7%	6.7%	17.8%	14.2%	8.7%
Inventories	7.0%	6.6%	6.4%	5.3%	5.5%	10.1%	18.9%	13.8%	9.9%
Prepaid expenses and other current assets	3.7%	2.9%	2.2%	1.9%	2.3%	33.6%	50.8%	6.3%	(5.5%)
Total Current Assets	30.0%	29.3%	30.5%	32.9%	30.9%	6.5%	11.2%	(12.7%)	21.0%
Property, plant, and equipment, net	32.4%	32.4%	32.4%	27.4%	29.1%	3.9%	15.9%	11.6%	6.5%
Amortizable intangible assets, net	2.0%	2.3%	2.1%	1.7%	2.1%	(8.0%)	25.0%	20.2%	(11.4%)
Goodwill	14.2%	14.9%	15.3%	12.9%	14.0%	(0.9%)	12.5%	12.4%	4.6%
Other nonamortizable intangible assets	3.1%	3.6%	4.0%	3.4%	3.3%	(9.6%)	3.0%	11.6%	16.4%
Investments in noncontrolled affiliates	10.8%	12.6%	12.3%	11.0%	11.7%	(10.8%)	18.0%	5.9%	6.1%
Other assets	7.4%	4.9%	3.3%	10.7%	8.8%	58.0%	71.6%	(71.2%)	37.5%
Total Assets	100.0%	100.0%	100.0%	100.0%	100.0%	3.9%	15.7%	(5.7%)	13.4%
LIABILITIES AND SHAREHOLDERS' EQUITY									
Short-term obligations	1.0%	0.0%	0.9%	9.1%	3.8%	n.m.	(100.0%)	(90.5%)	174.1%
Accounts payable and other current liabilities	23.0%	22.0%	21.7%	18.8%	20.0%	8.8%	17.0%	8.8%	6.6%
Income taxes payable	0.4%	0.4%	0.3%	1.7%	0.4%	(4.0%)	67.8%	(83.5%)	451.5%
Total Current Liabilities	24.4%	22.4%	22.9%	29.6%	24.1%	13.3%	13.0%	(27.1%)	39.3%
Long-term debt obligations	21.8%	12.1%	8.5%	7.3%	8.6%	87.0%	64.8%	10.2%	(3.5%)
Other liabilities	19.5%	13.8%	15.4%	13.6%	14.6%	46.4%	3.6%	7.0%	5.5%
Deferred income taxes	0.6%	1.9%	1.8%	4.5%	4.3%	(65.0%)	22.3%	(63.2%)	17.9%
Total Liabilities	66.4%	50.2%	48.7%	55.1%	51.7%	37.3%	19.4%	(16.7%)	20.8%

(Continued)

EXHIBIT 1.17 (Continued)

	Common-Size Balance Sheets:					Percentage Change Balance Sheets:			
	2008	**2007**	**2006**	**2005**	**2004**	**2008**	**2007**	**2006**	**2005**
Preferred stock, no par value	0.1%	0.1%	0.1%	0.1%	0.1%	0.0%	0.0%	0.0%	0.0%
Repurchased preferred stock	(0.4%)	(0.4%)	(0.4%)	(0.3%)	(0.3%)	4.5%	10.0%	9.1%	22.2%
Common stock, par value	0.1%	0.1%	0.1%	0.1%	0.1%	0.0%	0.0%	0.0%	0.0%
Capital in excess of par value	1.0%	1.3%	2.0%	1.9%	2.2%	(22.0%)	(22.9%)	(4.9%)	(0.6%)
Retained earnings	85.1%	81.4%	83.0%	66.6%	66.9%	8.7%	13.5%	17.6%	12.7%
Accumulated other comprehensive loss	(13.0%)	(2.7%)	(7.5%)	(3.3%)	(3.2%)	393.1%	(57.6%)	113.3%	18.8%
Treasury stock	(39.2%)	(30.0%)	(25.9%)	(20.1%)	(17.6%)	36.0%	33.9%	21.5%	29.8%
Total Common Shareholders' Equity	33.9%	50.0%	51.6%	45.1%	48.5%	(29.6%)	12.2%	7.9%	5.5%
Total Liabilities and Shareholders' Equity	100.0%	100.0%	100.0%	100.0%	100.0%	3.9%	15.7%	(5.7%)	13.4%

EXHIBIT 1.18

Common-Size and Percentage Change Income Statements for PepsiCo (allow for rounding)

	Common-Size Income Statements					Percentage Change Income Statements			
	2008	2007	2006	2005	2004	2008	2007	2006	2005
Net revenue	100.0%	100.0%	100.0%	100.0%	100.0%	9.6%	12.3%	7.9%	11.3%
Cost of sales	47.1%	45.7%	44.9%	43.5%	43.3%	12.8%	14.4%	11.2%	11.9%
Gross Profit	52.9%	54.3%	55.1%	56.5%	56.7%	6.8%	10.6%	5.4%	10.8%
Selling, general, and administrative expenses	36.8%	36.0%	36.2%	37.8%	37.7%	11.9%	11.8%	3.2%	11.6%
Other operating charges	0.1%	0.1%	0.5%	0.5%	0.5%	10.3%	(64.2%)	8.0%	2.0%
Restructuring charges	0.0%	0.0%	0.0%	0.0%	0.5%	n.m.	n.m.	n.m.	n.m.
Operating Profit	16.0%	18.2%	18.5%	18.2%	18.0%	(3.3%)	10.3%	9.8%	12.6%
Bottling equity income	0.9%	1.4%	1.6%	1.7%	1.3%	(33.2%)	1.3%	(0.7%)	46.6%
Interest expense	(0.8%)	(0.6%)	(0.7%)	(0.8%)	(0.6%)	46.9%	(6.3%)	(6.6%)	53.3%
Interest income	0.1%	0.3%	0.5%	0.5%	0.3%	(67.2%)	(27.7%)	8.8%	114.9%
Income before Income Taxes	16.2%	19.3%	19.9%	19.6%	19.0%	(8.0%)	9.2%	9.5%	15.1%
Provision for income taxes	4.3%	5.0%	3.8%	7.1%	4.7%	(4.8%)	46.5%	(41.5%)	67.9%
Income from Continuing Operations	11.9%	14.3%	16.1%	12.5%	14.3%	(9.1%)	0.3%	38.4%	(2.3%)
Tax benefit from discontinued operations	0.0%	0.0%	0.0%	0.0%	0.1%	n.m.	n.m.	n.m.	n.m.
Net Income	11.9%	14.3%	16.1%	12.5%	14.4%	(9.1%)	0.3%	38.4%	(3.2%)

EXHIBIT 1.19

Common-Size and Percentage Change Balance Sheets for Coca-Cola (allow for rounding)

	Common-Size Balance Sheets:					Percentage Change Balance Sheets:			
	2008	**2007**	**2006**	**2005**	**2004**	**2008**	**2007**	**2006**	**2005**
ASSETS									
Cash and cash equivalents	11.6%	9.5%	8.1%	16.0%	21.3%	14.9%	67.7%	(48.1%)	(29.9%)
Short-term investments	0.7%	0.5%	0.5%	0.2%	0.2%	29.3%	43.3%	127.3%	8.2%
Accounts and notes receivable, net	7.6%	7.7%	8.6%	7.8%	7.1%	(6.8%)	28.2%	13.4%	1.6%
Inventories	5.4%	5.1%	5.5%	4.8%	4.5%	(1.5%)	35.3%	15.2%	0.3%
Prepaid expenses and other current assets	4.7%	5.2%	5.4%	6.0%	5.9%	(15.0%)	39.2%	(8.7%)	(3.8%)
Total Current Assets	30.1%	28.0%	28.2%	34.8%	39.1%	0.6%	43.4%	(17.6%)	(16.5%)
Property, plant, and equipment, net	20.5%	19.6%	23.0%	19.7%	19.4%	(2.0%)	23.0%	19.3%	(5.0%)
Amortizable intangible assets, net	6.0%	11.9%	6.8%	6.6%	6.5%	(53.1%)	152.0%	5.1%	(4.5%)
Goodwill	9.9%	9.8%	4.7%	3.6%	3.5%	(5.3%)	203.3%	34.0%	(4.6%)
Other nonamortizable intangible assets	15.0%	6.5%	5.6%	2.8%	2.2%	115.6%	66.6%	103.7%	17.9%
Investments in noncontrolled affiliates	14.3%	18.0%	22.6%	23.5%	19.9%	(25.7%)	14.7%	(2.0%)	10.7%
Other assets	4.3%	6.2%	9.0%	9.0%	9.5%	(35.2%)	(1.0%)	2.0%	(11.2%)
Total Assets	100.0%	100.0%	100.0%	100.0%	100.0%	(6.4%)	44.4%	1.8%	(6.4%)
LIABILITIES AND SHAREHOLDERS' EQUITY									
Short-term obligations	15.0%	16.0%	10.8%	15.4%	14.4%	(12.3%)	113.8%	(28.4%)	(0.3%)
Accounts payable and other current liabilities	15.3%	13.7%	16.9%	15.3%	14.0%	4.8%	17.1%	12.5%	2.0%
Current maturities of long-term debt	1.1%	0.3%	0.1%	0.1%	4.7%	249.6%	303.0%	17.9%	(98.1%)
Income taxes payable	0.6%	0.6%	1.9%	2.7%	2.3%	(2.3%)	(54.5%)	(28.9%)	12.4%
Total Current Liabilities	32.1%	30.6%	29.7%	33.4%	35.4%	(1.8%)	48.8%	(9.6%)	(11.7%)
Long-term debt obligations	6.9%	7.6%	4.4%	3.9%	3.7%	(15.1%)	149.4%	13.9%	(0.3%)
Other liabilities	8.4%	7.2%	7.4%	5.9%	9.0%	8.6%	40.4%	29.0%	(38.5%)
Deferred income taxes	2.2%	4.4%	2.0%	1.2%	1.3%	(53.6%)	210.9%	72.7%	(12.4%)
Total Liabilities	49.5%	49.7%	43.5%	44.4%	49.3%	(6.9%)	65.0%	(0.2%)	(15.7%)

Common stock, par value	2.2%	2.0%	2.9%	3.0%	2.8%	0.0%	0.2%	0.1%	0.2%
Capital in excess of par value	19.7%	17.1%	20.0%	18.7%	15.7%	8.0%	23.3%	8.9%	11.4%
Retained earnings	95.0%	83.7%	111.7%	106.4%	92.6%	6.3%	8.3%	6.9%	7.5%
Accumulated other comprehensive loss	(6.6%)	1.4%	(4.3%)	(5.7%)	(4.3%)	(527.2%)	(148.5%)	(22.6%)	23.8%
Treasury stock	(59.8%)	(54.0%)	(73.8%)	(66.8%)	(56.1%)	3.6%	5.7%	12.6%	11.5%
Total Common Shareholders' Equity	50.5%	50.3%	56.5%	55.6%	50.7%	(5.8%)	28.5%	3.5%	2.6%
Total Liabilities and Shareholders' Equity	100.0%	100.0%	100.0%	100.0%	100.0%	(6.4%)	44.4%	1.8%	(6.4%)

EXHIBIT 1.20

Common-Size and Percentage Change Income Statements for Coca-Cola (allow for rounding)

	Common-Size Income Statements					Percentage Change Income Statements			
	2008	2007	2006	2005	2004	2008	2007	2006	2005
Net revenue	100.0%	100.0%	100.0%	100.0%	100.0%	10.7%	19.8%	4.3%	6.3%
Cost of sales	35.6%	36.1%	33.9%	35.5%	35.3%	9.3%	27.5%	(0.4%)	6.8%
Gross Profit	64.4%	63.9%	66.1%	64.5%	64.7%	11.5%	15.9%	6.8%	6.0%
Selling, general, and administrative expenses	36.9%	37.9%	39.2%	37.8%	36.3%	7.6%	16.1%	7.9%	10.8%
Other operating charges	1.1%	0.9%	0.8%	0.4%	2.2%	37.8%	37.3%	117.6%	(82.3%)
Operating Profit	26.4%	25.1%	26.2%	26.3%	26.2%	16.5%	15.0%	3.7%	6.8%
Bottling equity income	(2.7%)	2.3%	0.4%	2.9%	2.9%	(230.8%)	554.9%	(85.0%)	9.5%
Interest expense	(1.4%)	(1.6%)	(0.9%)	(1.0%)	(0.9%)	(3.9%)	107.3%	(8.3%)	22.4%
Interest income	1.0%	0.8%	0.8%	1.0%	0.7%	41.1%	22.3%	(17.9%)	49.7%
Other income (loss), net	(0.1%)	0.6%	0.8%	(0.3%)	(0.3%)	(116.2%)	(11.3%)	(378.6%)	20.7%
Income before Income Taxes	23.3%	27.3%	27.3%	29.0%	28.6%	(5.5%)	19.7%	(1.7%)	7.5%
Provision for income taxes	5.1%	6.6%	6.2%	7.9%	6.3%	(13.7%)	26.3%	(17.6%)	32.2%
Net Income	18.2%	20.7%	21.1%	21.1%	22.3%	(2.9%)	17.7%	4.3%	0.5%

The analyst must interpret common-size financial statements carefully. The amount for any one item in these statements is not independent of all other items. The dollar amount for an item might increase between two periods, but its relative percentage in the common-size statement would decrease (or remain the same) if the dollar amount increased at a slower (or the same) rate as total assets. For example, PepsiCo's dollar amounts for property, plant, and equipment increased between 2007 and 2008, but the common-size percentages remained the same because they increased at the same rate as total assets. Common-size percentages provide a general overview of financial position and operating performance, but the analyst must supplement them with other analytical tools.

Percentage Change Financial Statements

Another powerful analytical tool is percentage change financial statements, a tool that is helpful in highlighting the relative rates of growth in financial statement amounts from year to year and over longer periods of time. These statements present the percentage change in the amount of an item relative to its amount in the previous period or the compounded average percentage change over several prior periods.

The four rightmost columns of Exhibit 1.17 present percentage changes in balance sheet items during 2005 through 2008 for PepsiCo. Note that the increase in cash and the decrease in short-term investment securities are the largest percentage changes in assets between 2007 and 2008, consistent with the preceding observations with respect to changes in the common-size balance sheet. Another large percentage change between 2007 and 2008 occurred for long-term obligations, consistent with the prior observation from the statement of cash flows that PepsiCo issued a large amount of long-term debt in 2008. Also note that the huge percentage increase in accumulated other comprehensive loss for 2008 was 393 percent. This change reflects an increase in the accumulated loss from a negative $952 million in 2007 to a negative $4,694 million in 2008. This is an example in which a large percentage change in an account corresponds with a large dollar amount of change. For comparison, the four rightmost columns of Exhibit 1.19 present the percentage changes in balance sheet items for Coca-Cola during 2005 through 2008.

The analyst must exert particular caution when interpreting percentage change balance sheets for a particular year. If the amount for the preceding year that serves as the base is relatively small, even a small change in dollar amount can result in a large percentage change. This is the case, for example, with PepsiCo's deferred tax liability. The liability declined by 65.0 percent in 2008, but it amounted to only a drop from $646 million in 2007 to $226 million in 2008. However, note that the deferred tax liability comprises only 0.6 percent of total assets at the end of 2008. A large percentage change in an account that makes up a smaller portion of total financing is not as meaningful as a smaller percentage change in an account that makes up a larger portion of total assets or total financing.

The four rightmost columns of Exhibit 1.18 present percentage change income statement amounts for PepsiCo. Note that during 2008, 2007, and 2005, net income growth did not keep pace with revenue growth. An analyst might direct particular concern to the rapid growth rates in cost of sales, which have exceeded the growth rates in sales each of the four years. This implies a lower degree of cost control, a loss of pricing power, or a shift in product mix to lower margin products, leading to shrinking gross profit margins. The analyst should carefully investigate the reasons for this deterioration in PepsiCo's profitability. By comparison, the four rightmost columns of Exhibit 1.20 present the percentage change income statement amounts for Coca-Cola during the same span of years, and they reveal that (with the exception of 2007) Coca-Cola exhibited stronger control over cost of sales as a percentage of revenues.

Financial Statement Ratios

Perhaps the most useful analytical tools for assessing profitability and risk are financial statement ratios. Financial statement ratios express relations among various items from the three financial statements. Researchers and analysts have found that such ratios are effective indicators of various dimensions of profitability and risk and serve as useful signals of future profitability and risk. Chapters 4 and 5 discuss these financial ratios in depth. The discussion here merely introduces several of them. Appendix D presents descriptive statistics for many of the most commonly used financial ratios across 48 industries over the past eleven years.

Profitability Ratios. Perhaps the most commonly encountered financial ratio is EPS (earnings per share). Basic EPS equals net income available to the common shareholders (that is, net income minus dividends on preferred stock) divided by the weighted average number of common shares outstanding. For 2008, basic EPS for PepsiCo (see Exhibit 1.11 and Note 11, "Net Income per Common Share," in Appendix A) is $3.26 [(= $5,142 – $8)/1,573 shares]. Firms typically report both basic and diluted EPS in their income statements, with per share amounts for continuing operations, discontinued operations, and extraordinary gains and losses shown separately. Chapter 4 discusses the computation of EPS. Furthermore, as Chapter 14 makes clear, financial analysts often use a multiple of EPS to derive what they consider an appropriate price for a firm's common stock.

Another profitability ratio is the ROCE (rate of return on common shareholders' equity). ROCE equals net income available to the common shareholders divided by average common shareholders' equity for the year. ROCE for PepsiCo for 2008 is 34.8 percent [= ($5,142 – $8)/(0.5{$12,203 + $17,325})]. This ROCE is large relative to those of many firms. However, we should expect PepsiCo to generate a high rate of return for its shareholders because it has developed an effective and sustainable strategy as one of only two major players in the soft drink industry and one of the global leaders in the snack food industry, which we assessed to have relatively favorable competitive conditions. This example illustrates that it is difficult to interpret ROCE and other financial ratios without a frame of reference, which the analyst builds by conducting the industry analysis, the strategic analysis, and the accounting quality analysis. Analysts compare ratios to corresponding ratios of earlier periods (time-series analysis), to corresponding ratios of other firms in the same industry (cross-sectional analysis), and to industry averages in order to interpret the ratios. Chapter 4 provides an in-depth analysis of PepsiCo's ROCE and other profitability ratios.

Risk Ratios. To assess the volatility in a firm's earnings over time and to gauge the uncertainty inherent in the firm's future earnings, analysts can calculate the standard deviation in ROCE over time.

To assess the ability of firms to repay short-term obligations, analysts frequently calculate various short-term liquidity ratios such as the current ratio, which equals current assets divided by current liabilities. The current ratio for PepsiCo at the end of 2008 is 1.23 (= $10,806/$8,787). As with profitability ratios, this ratio is meaningful only when the analyst performs a time-series and cross-sectional analysis. Like most firms, PepsiCo's current ratio has exceeded 1.0 in each of the past five years; so PepsiCo appears to have minimal short-term liquidity risk.

To assess the ability of firms to continue operating for a longer term (that is, to avoid bankruptcy), the analyst looks at various long-term solvency ratios, such the relative amount of long-term debt in the capital structure. The ratio of long-term debt to common shareholders' equity for PepsiCo at the end of 2008 is 0.644 (= $7,858/$12,203). This ratio for PepsiCo jumped significantly in 2008, from 0.244 in 2007, because PepsiCo issued large amounts of long-term debt and paid large amounts of cash to common shareholders through common stock dividends and repurchases. Clearly, PepsiCo is increasing its leverage, but given PepsiCo's level of profitability, strong cash flows, and solid short-term liquidity position, bankruptcy risk is low. Chapter 5 provides an in-depth analysis of PepsiCo's debt-to-equity ratio and other risk ratios.

STEP 5: PREPARE FORECASTED FINANCIAL STATEMENTS

Each of the steps in our six-step analysis and valuation framework is important, but the crucial (and most difficult) step is forecasting future financial statements. Such forecasts are the inputs into valuation models or other financial decisions, and the quality of the decisions rests on the reliability of the forecasts. Thus, the analyst uses a thorough understanding of the firm's industry, strategy, accounting quality, and financial statement ratios, including common-size and percentage change statements and other analytical tools, to evaluate the profitability and risk of the firm in the current and recent past and to provide useful information to begin forecasting future financial statements. Forecasted financial statements rely on assumptions the analyst makes about the future: Will the firm's strategy remain the same or change? At what rate will the firm generate revenue growth? Will the firm likely gain or lose market share relative to competitors? Will revenues grow because of increases in sales volume, prices, or both? How will its costs change? How much will the firm need to increase operating assets (inventory, plant, and equipment) to achieve its growth strategies? How much capital will the firm need to raise to finance growth in assets? Will it change the mix of debt versus equity financing? How will a change in the debt-equity mix change the risk of the firm? Responses to these and other questions provide the basis for preparing forecasted income statements, balance sheets, and statements of cash flows. The analyst can compare financial ratios of forecasted financial statement items with the corresponding ratios from the reported financial statements to judge the reasonableness of the assumptions made. Amounts from the forecasted financial statements serve as the basis for the valuation models in Step 6, discussed next. Chapter 10 describes and illustrates the techniques to project future financial statements and applies the techniques to build financial statement projections for PepsiCo for the next five years.

STEP 6: VALUE THE FIRM

Capital market participants most commonly use financial statement analysis to value firms, which is the culmination of the previous five steps of the framework incorporated into a valuation model. Financial statements—specifically, key metrics from the statements such as earnings, dividends, and cash flows—play a central role in firm valuation. Thus, the emphasis of this book is to arm the analyst with the knowledge necessary to apply sophisticated and comprehensive valuation models.

To develop reliable estimates of firm value, and therefore to make intelligent investment decisions, the analyst must rely on well-reasoned and objective forecasts of the firm's future profitability and risk. Forecasts of future dividends, earnings, and cash flows form the basis for the most frequently used valuation models.

In some cases, analysts prefer to assess firm value using the classical dividends-based approach, which takes the perspective of valuing the firm from the standpoint of the cash that investors can expect to receive through dividends (or the sale of their shares). It also is common for analysts to assess firm value using measures of the firm's expected future free cash flows—cash flows that are available to be paid as dividends after necessary payments are made to reinvest in productive assets and meet required debt payments. An equivalent approach to valuation involves computing firm value based on the book value of equity and the earnings of the firm the analyst expects to exceed the firm's cost of capital (similar in logic to "economic value-added" computations). In many circumstances, analysts find it necessary or desirable to estimate firm value quickly using valuation heuristics such as price-earnings ratios and market-to-book value ratios. Chapters 11–14 describe the theory and demonstrate the practical applications of each of these approaches to valuation using PepsiCo.

ROLE OF FINANCIAL STATEMENT ANALYSIS IN AN EFFICIENT CAPITAL MARKET

Market efficiency describes the degree to which the market impounds information into security prices. The larger the set of information that is priced and the greater the speed with which security prices reflect new information, the higher the degree of market efficiency. A highly efficient capital market would impound all publicly available value-relevant information (such as an announcement of surprisingly good or poor earnings in a particular period) quickly and completely and without bias into share prices. In a less efficient market, share prices would react more slowly to value-relevant information. In the U.S. capital markets, for example, share prices of the largest market capital firms, which tend to have a wide following by buy-side and sell-side analysts, many institutional investors, and frequent coverage in the financial press tend to be more efficient than share prices for small market capital stocks, which have no analyst following, no institutional investors, and rare press coverage.

There are differing views as to the benefits of analyzing a set of financial statements in the context of market efficiency. One view is that stock market prices react with a high degree of efficiency to published information about a firm. That is, market participants react intelligently and quickly to information they receive so that market prices continually reflect underlying economic values. One implication of a highly efficient capital market is that analysts and investors have more difficulty finding "undervalued" or "overvalued" securities by analyzing financial statements because the capital market quickly impounds new financial statement information into security prices.

Opposing views include the following:

- For markets to be efficient, analysts and investors must do the analysis to bring about the appropriate prices. With their expertise and access to information about firms, financial analysts do the analysis quickly and engage in the trading necessary to achieve efficient pricing. They are agents of market efficiency.
- Research on capital market efficiency aggregates financial data for individual firms and studies the average reaction of the market to earnings and other financial statement information. A finding that the market is efficient on average does not preclude temporary mispricing of individual firms' shares. A principal task of the financial analyst is to identify and buy/sell mispriced securities of particular firms.
- Research has shown that equity markets are not perfectly efficient. Anomalies include the tendency for market prices to adjust with a lag to new earnings information, systematic underreaction to the information contained in earnings announcements, and the ability to use a combination of financial ratios to detect under- and overpriced securities.[6]

---

[6] For a summary of the issues and related research, see Ray Ball, "The Theory of Stock Market Efficiency: Accomplishments and Limitations," *Journal of Applied Corporate Finance* (Spring 1995), pp. 4–17.

- Management has incentives related to job security and compensation to report as favorable a picture as possible in the financial statements within the constraints of GAAP. Therefore, these reports may represent biased indicators of the economic performance and financial position of firms. Analysts must analyze and adjust these financial statements to remove such biases if market prices are to reflect underlying economic values.

Financial statement analysis is valuable in numerous settings outside equity capital markets, including credit analysis by a bank to support corporate lending, competitor analysis to identify competitive advantages, and merger and acquisition analysis to identify buyout candidates.

THE ASSOCIATION BETWEEN EARNINGS AND SHARE PRICES

As discussed earlier in this chapter, performing financial analysis that relies on analysis, forecasting, and valuation of key accounting measures (such as earnings) from a firm's financial statements can be very rewarding. To illustrate the striking relation between accounting earnings and stock returns and to foreshadow the potential to generate positive excess returns through analysis and forecasting, consider the results from empirical research by D. Craig Nichols and James Wahlen.[7] They studied the average cumulative market-adjusted returns generated by firms during the 12 months leading up to and including the month in which each firm announced annual earnings numbers. For a sample of 31,923 firm-years between 1988 and 2001, they found that the average firm that announced an increase in earnings (over the prior year's earnings) experienced stock returns that exceeded market average returns by roughly 19.2 percent. On the other hand, the average firm that announced a decrease in earnings experienced stock returns that were roughly 16.4 percent lower than the market average. Their results suggest that merely the sign of the change in earnings was associated with a 35.6 percent stock return differential in one year, on average, over their sample period. Exhibit 1.21 presents a graph of their results.

To an analyst, the results of the Nichols and Wahlen study indicate how informative accounting earnings are to the capital markets and emphasize the importance of forecasting the changes in earnings one year ahead. Analysts should view the Nichols and Wahlen results as encouraging and intriguing because they imply that if analysts can forecast earnings changes correctly more often than not, they should be able to earn some portion of the excess returns documented in this study. To be sure, analysts will not be able to beat the market consistently by 35 percent per year—Nichols and Wahlen's research had the advantage of perfect foresight, which analysts do not have. Using historical earnings data, Nichols and Wahlen knew with certainty which firms would announce earnings increases or decreases one year ahead. Analysts must forecast earnings changes and take positions in stocks on the basis of their earnings expectations.

Note in the graph of the Nichols and Wahlen results in Exhibit 1.21 that their study also examined the relation between changes in cash flows from operations and cumulative market-adjusted stock returns. Using the same firm-years and study period, Nichols and Wahlen documented that firms experiencing positive changes in cash from operations

[7] D. Craig Nichols and James Wahlen, "How Do Earnings Numbers Relate to Stock Returns? A Review of Classic Accounting Research with Updated Evidence," *Accounting Horizons* (December 2004), pp. 263–286. The portion of the Nichols and Wahlen study described here is a replication of path-breaking research in accounting by Ray Ball and Philip Brown, "An Evaluation of Accounting Income Numbers," *Journal of Accounting Research* (Autumn 1968), pp. 159–178.

EXHIBIT 1.21

The Association between Changes in Annual Earnings and Cumulative Abnormal Returns

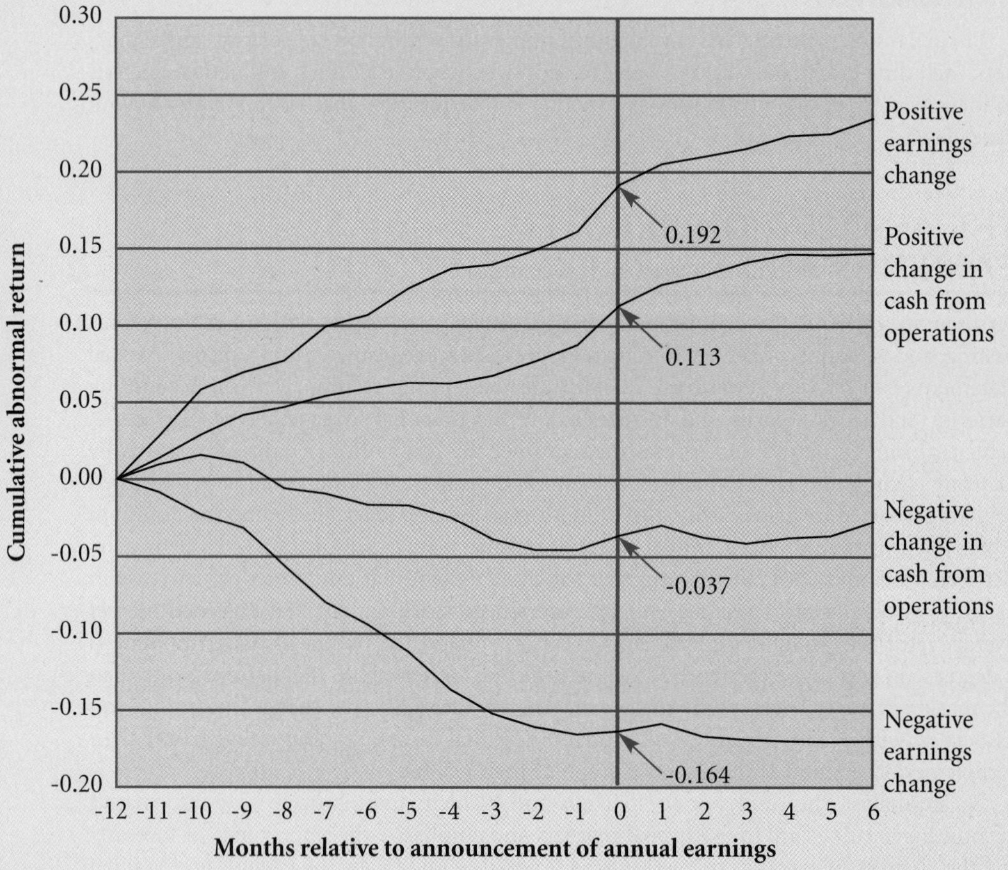

Source: D. Craig Nichols and James Wahlen, "How Do Earnings Numbers Relate to Stock Returns? A Review of Classic Accounting Research with Updated Evidence," *Accounting Horizons* (December 2004), pp. 263–286. Reprinted with permission from American Accounting Association.

experienced stock returns that beat the market by an average of 11.3 percent, whereas firms experiencing decreases in cash from operations experienced stock returns that were lower than the market by an average of 3.7 percent. These results suggest that the sign of the change in cash from operations was associated with a 15.0 percent stock return differential in one year, on average, during the study period. This implies that changes in cash flows also are strongly related to stock returns, but they are not as informative for the capital markets as are changes in earnings. This should not be surprising because changes in cash flow are less indicative of a firm's performance in one period than are changes in earnings. For example, a firm experiencing a negative change in cash from operations could be attributable to cash flow distress (bad news) or a large investment of cash in growth opportunities (good news). A negative change in earnings, on the other hand, is almost always bad news. This explains, in part, why analysts, firm managers, the financial press, boards of directors, auditors, and therefore financial statement analysis textbook writers focus so much attention on analyzing and forecasting earnings numbers.

Empirical research in accounting has deepened our understanding of the many dimensions of the role of accounting numbers in the capital market by documenting that share prices react strongly to the magnitude of the change in earnings and the persistence of the change in earnings for future periods and that financial statement ratios are useful for predicting future earnings changes. We will refer to important research results such as these throughout this book.

SOURCES OF FINANCIAL STATEMENT INFORMATION

Firms whose bonds or common shares trade in public capital markets in the United States typically make the following information available:

- **Annual Report to Shareholders.** The glossy annual report includes balance sheets for the most recent two years and income statements and statements of cash flows for the most recent three years, along with various notes and supporting schedules. The annual report also includes a letter from the chairperson of the board of directors and from the chief executive officer summarizing the activities of the most recent year. The report typically includes management's discussion and analysis of the firm's operating performance, financial position, and liquidity. Firms vary with respect to the information provided in this Management Discussion and Analysis of operations. Some firms, such as PepsiCo, give helpful information about the firm's strategy and reasons for the changes in profitability, financial position, and risk. (See Appendix B.) Other firms merely repeat amounts presented in the financial statements without providing helpful explanations for operating results.
- **Form 10-K Annual Report.** The Form 10-K annual report filed with the SEC includes the same financial statements and notes as the corporate annual report in addition to supporting schedules required by the SEC. For example, compared to the corporate annual report, Form 10-K often includes more detailed information on changes in the allowance for uncollectible accounts and other valuation accounts. Firms are required by the SEC to report several key items in the Form 10-K that are necessary reading for the analyst. These include a description of the business (Item 1); risk factors (Item 1A); a description of company properties (Item 2); the management discussion and analysis (Item 7); and, of course, the financial statements, notes, and supplemental schedules (Item 8). Large firms must file their annual reports with the SEC within 60 days after the end of their annual accounting period.
- **Form 10-Q Quarterly Report.** The Form 10-Q quarterly report filed with the SEC includes condensed balance sheet and income statement information for the most recent three months, as well as comparative data for earlier quarters. Unlike the annual filing of Form 10-K, the financial statements included in Forms 10-Q are not audited.
- **Prospectus or Registration Statement.** Firms intending to issue new bonds or capital stock file a prospectus with the SEC that describes the offering (amount and intended uses of proceeds). The prospectus includes much of the financial information found in the Form 10-K annual report.

A large number of firms include all or a portion of their annual reports and SEC filings on their corporate websites. For example, PepsiCo provides all of the financial data and analysis provided in Appendices A and B on its website (http://www.pepsico.com). In addition, many firms provide additional financial data on their sites that is not published in the annual reports. For example, Gap Inc., consisting of Gap, Banana Republic, and Old

Navy clothing store chains, provides monthly sales data for each chain and information on the opening and closing of stores. Firms also provide other useful information in the investor relations section of their corporate websites, such as (1) presentations made to analysts; (2) press releases pertaining to new products, customer acquisitions, and earnings announcements; and (3) transcripts or archived webcasts of conference calls with analysts.

Firms are required to file reports electronically with the SEC, and filings for recent years are available at the SEC website (http://www.sec.gov). Numerous commercial online and CD-ROM services also provide financial statement information (for example, Thomson One Analytics, Bloomberg, Standard & Poor's, and Moody's).

Appendix 1.1 discusses sources of financial information more fully.

SUMMARY

The purpose of this chapter is to provide a broad overview of the six-step analysis and valuation framework that is the focus of this book and is a logical process for analyzing and valuing companies:

1. Identify the economic characteristics of the industry in which a firm participates.
2. Identify the corporate strategy that a firm pursues to compete in its industry.
3. Read the information in a set of financial statements and notes carefully and assess the quality of a firm's financial statements, adjusting them, if necessary, for items lacking sustainability or comparability.
4. Analyze and interpret the profitability and risk of a firm, assessing the firm's performance and the strength of its financial position.
5. Prepare forecasted financial statements.
6. Value the firm.

You should not expect to fully understand these six steps at this stage of your studies. The remaining chapters discuss each step in greater depth. Chapter 2 discusses the important links between the valuation of assets and liabilities on the balance sheet and revenues and expenses on the income statement. Chapter 3 details the preparation and interpretation of the statement of cash flows for firms in different industries at various stages of growth. Chapter 4 describes common financial statement ratios used to assess profitability and illustrates their calculation and interpretation for PepsiCo. Chapter 5 parallels the preceding chapter by describing common financial statement ratios used to assess risk. Chapters 6–9 examine U.S. GAAP and IFRS for financing, investing, and operating activities and address concerns that affect the quality of earnings and financial position. Chapters 10–14 shift the focus to valuation. Chapter 10 demonstrates the preparation of forecasted financial statements. Chapters 11–14 examine various valuation models based on dividends, cash flows, earnings, and amounts for comparable firms. With firm valuation being the most frequent objective of financial statement analysis, these chapters represent a fitting culmination to the book.

Appendix 1.1

Preparing a Term Project

Our reading of the course syllabi by various users of previous editions of this book indicates that many instructors require their students to apply the concepts and tools of analysis in this book to the financial statements of one or more companies. This appendix provides helpful hints for you in conducting such a project. Our students find it useful to complete each part of the project as the topic is covered in class. For example, soon after completing Chapter 1, you should select the companies you intend to study and complete the industry economics and company strategy portion of the project. Obtaining financial statement data and performing a first pass on profitability and risk ratios follows coverage of Chapters 4 and 5. Assessments of the quality of the financial statements should coincide with coverage of Chapters 6–9. Forecasts of future financial statement amounts follow coverage of Chapter 10. Applying various valuation models must await coverage of Chapters 11–14. Based on our experience, we can assure you that by following this approach, your learning experience will be much richer and more rewarding than if you wait until the last few weeks of the course to do the major work on the project. For this reason, we ask our students to submit progress reports throughout the term. These progress reports help students stay on schedule and permit us to provide suggestions to assist them going forward.

SELECTING COMPANIES FOR THE TERM PROJECT

Some instructors ask students to analyze a single company over time (a time-series analysis), while other instructors ask students to compare two or more companies over time (a cross-sectional analysis). We have found that comparing companies in the same industry over time provides the most interesting insights.

When selecting companies to analyze, select an industry and firms in which you have an interest. You will likely spend considerable time on the project. Selecting firms of interest enhances motivation. Some students select firms for which they hope or expect to work. The in-depth analysis of the firm often enhances the job interview and early work experience once the student is hired. Our students find that selecting firms with somewhat different strategies usually provides better insights than selecting firms with similar strategies. Some students' richest term projects have involved analyzing firms in the same industry but headquartered in different countries. However, such projects involve additional work to learn U.S. GAAP as well as IFRS and institutional and cultural differences in each country that might affect interpretation of the financial analyses.

Various online databases list firms in the United States and worldwide in various industries. Your library may or may not subscribe to all of the databases discussed in this appendix. Packaged with this book is access to the Gale Business & Company Resource Center. This site provides information about particular industries and companies. Information includes company overviews and histories, newspaper and magazine articles, financial data, and investment reports. A similar online information service is OneSource, published by Global Business Browser (http://www.onesource.com).

UNDERSTANDING INDUSTRY ECONOMICS AND COMPANY STRATEGIES

The Form 10-K report the firm filed with the SEC (http://www.sec.gov) may be the best place to begin learning about the economics of an industry and the particular strategy a firm has selected for competing in the industry. The first section of Form 10-K is a descriptive narrative entitled "Item 1. Business." This section usually describes the firm's principal businesses and provides information about suppliers, competitors, regulation, and other items. Reading this section of Form 10-K for the other firms selected for study usually provides sufficient information so that you can summarize the economics of the industry using a value chain, Porter's five forces framework, or the economics attributes framework discussed in the chapter. These sources will not likely set forth precise economics to fit any of the industry economics frameworks, so some interpretation and synthesis on your part will be necessary.

Reading the Business description section of the Form 10-K report should provide you with information on the strategy of each firm studied. We find it useful to search the notes to the financial statements to find the segment data by products or services and by geographical location. We convert the reported numbers to mix percentages, as we did for PepsiCo in Exhibit 1.5, to obtain an overview of the firm's principal involvements.

Another source for industry information is Standard & Poor's Industry Surveys. These surveys describe the most important factors affecting the industry, key firms in the industry, and key financial ratios for each firm. The Gale Business & Company Resource Center and OneSource resources, described previously, also provide helpful information about the industry.

ASSESSING THE QUALITY OF THE FINANCIAL STATEMENTS

Two steps are necessary: (1) reading the financial statements carefully and thoroughly and creating a data file with the amounts from the financial statements and (2) adjusting the reported financial statement amounts to improve the quality of the financial statement data.

Reading the Financial Statements and Creating a Data File

Our experience, and that of our students, is that careful and thorough reading of the financial statements yields a great deal of information about the firm. The financial statements, the notes, and management's discussion and analysis provide valuable insights into the business strategies, profitability, and risk of the firm. Many firms explicitly disclose elements of the business that are performing well or poorly, also providing explanations about the performance. Many firms explicitly disclose (or one can infer) projections of future business activities, such as expected future sales growth rates or capital expenditures, which is helpful information for projecting future financial statements. Analysts who do not carefully read the financial statements stand to miss this valuable information.

After careful reading, the analyst should enter the financial statement data into a data file. One initial choice in creating a data file is whether to use the accounts and amounts that the firm provides in its Form 10-K or annual report to shareholders or to download and use amounts from various online sources or databases that format the amounts into a standardized template. One advantage of following the first approach is that you rely on the primary source of the financial statements, not on a secondary source about which you may not know all of the reclassifications and adjustments made to conform the reported amounts to the standardized template. Another advantage of following the first approach is that the financial statement data will be classified into accounts consistent with the notes to the financial statements, the main source of information for assessing the quality of the reported amounts, a topic discussed shortly. The principal advantages of using amounts in a standardized template are that use of the template can save time and the financial statement amounts are reasonably comparable across firms.

The next decision to be made is whether to input the financial statement data into FSAP, a financial statement analysis package that accompanies this text, or to create a new spreadsheet file. The principal advantages of FSAP are that it provides spreadsheets that have embedded formulas for the various profitability and risk ratios, it provides a template for preparing forecasted financial statements using the previously reported actual amounts as a base, and it inputs the forecasted amounts into several valuation models to arrive at equity values. (Appendix C illustrates the use of FSAP to analyze and value PepsiCo. FSAP contains a user manual that explains how to create a data file.) The disadvantage of using FSAP from a learning perspective is that much of the work is done for you. The advantage of creating a new spreadsheet file is that you must program the spreadsheets to compute the financial ratios, prepare forecasted financial statements, and apply the various valuation models. To enhance learning, many instructors prefer that students program the spreadsheet themselves.

Downloading financial statement data from online sources means that the data are already in a standard format. You can program the spreadsheet for this format and use it for all firms analyzed. Downloading financial statement data from a firm's Form 10-K requires that, at least initially, the spreadsheet use the firm's specific categories and grouping of accounts. The other firms analyzed are not likely to use precisely the same accounts. Thus, you must transform the reported amounts to a standard format or program each firm's spreadsheet to conform to its specific accounts and categories.

It is a good idea to program various mathematical checks into the spreadsheet. For example, check whether the sum of the individual assets equals the sum of the individual liability and shareholders' equity accounts. The net of individual revenues and expenses must equal net income. The cash flow from operating, investing, and financing activities must equal the change in cash. The latter should agree with the change in cash on the balance sheet from the beginning to the end of the year.

One issue you must face is how many years of financial statement data to obtain. We recommend using at least three years of income statements and statements of cash flows and four years of balance sheets (although this many years of data may not be available for very young firms or for initial public offering firms). We recommend using an extra year of balance sheet data because computing certain ratios requires average amounts for certain accounts on the balance sheet. FSAP permits the inputting of six years of balance sheet, income statement, and cash flow data. The longer historical time frame is useful when deciding on appropriate growth rates for forecasting financial statements, particularly when the recent past was unusual (for example, because of a recession).

Another issue you must face is whether to use the originally reported amounts for each year or to use amounts as retroactively restated for discontinued operations, acquisitions, divestitures, or for other factors. The advantage of using restated numbers is that the financial statements amounts may be more consistent with amounts that might be expected going forward. The disadvantage is that firms seldom provide restated data beyond the three income statements and statements of cash flows and the two balance sheets commonly found in annual reports. Thus, using restated data is not likely to yield financial statements that are fully consistent over time. Chapter 9 discusses this issue more fully.

Assessing the Quality of the Reported Amounts

One of the most important steps in financial statement analysis is to assess the quality of the reported amounts and make appropriate adjustments before proceeding to the analysis of profitability and risk. The saying "garbage in, garbage out" applies with particular importance to financial statements. To assess quality, you must read the financial statements and notes. Chapters 6–9 describe the most important factors to look for in this quality assessment. Material nonrecurring or unusual income items are candidates for adjustment. Significant off-balance-sheet assets or liabilities also are candidates. Some adjustments may be needed to increase the comparability of the financial statement amounts for each of the firms analyzed in the term project. You might consider keeping a log of adjustments made to refer to later when interpreting profitability and risk ratios and forecasting future financial statements.

ANALYZING PROFITABILITY AND RISK

If you use FSAP to create data files, FSAP will automatically calculate the profitability and risk ratios discussed in Chapters 4 and 5. If you create your own spreadsheet file for the financial statement data, you should include a separate worksheet within that file to compute the financial statement ratios. This worksheet should contain the formulas for the financial ratios, referring back to the worksheets with the financial statement data to obtain the amounts for the numerator and denominator of each ratio. If you change any of the amounts in the financial statements portion of the worksheet later in the project (for example, making adjustments to improve the quality of the data), the financial ratios will automatically update.

When analyzing profitability and risk using the financial statement ratios, you may find it helpful to do a time-series analysis for each firm and then do cross-sectional comparisons across firms. As a first pass, look for financial ratios that have changed significantly over time or that differ significantly across firms. Then relate the changes and differences to the economics of the industry and strategies of the firms. You will find it helpful to read the MD&A section of the annual report to shareholders or the Form 10-K (Item 7) to find explanations for the time-series changes. A useful sequence is as follows:

- Time-series analysis of profitability for each firm using (1) common-size and percentage change financial statements, (2) rate of return on assets and its components, and (3) ROCE and its components
- Cross-sectional profitability analysis of profitability for all firms using (1) common-size and percentage change financial statements, (2) rate of return on assets and its components, and (3) ROCE and its components
- Time-series and cross-sectional comparisons of short-term liquidity risk
- Time-series and cross-sectional comparisons of long-term liquidity risk

PREPARING FORECASTED FINANCIAL STATEMENTS

Having analyzed the profitability and risk of each firm in the recent past, you are ready to project the financial statement amounts into the future. As Chapter 10 discusses, you should identify any important factors that are likely to change, such as a major divestiture or acquisition, changes in the economic or regulatory environment, or a change in business strategy.

Spreadsheets are particularly powerful tools for preparing forecasted financial statements. It is desirable to link the forecasted financial statements with the financial statement data and related ratios from the recent past. FSAP does this automatically. If you program your own spreadsheet file with the financial statement data, you can program additional worksheets in this file for the forecasted amounts. We suggest that you build the same kind of mathematical data checks into the forecasted amounts that you included for the reported amounts. We also find it useful to include a spreadsheet that computes the same financial ratios for the forecasted amounts as it does for the reported amounts. Then you can study the financial ratios to see if the assumptions underlying the forecasted amounts make sense relative to the past and to expected changes going forward.

VALUE THE FIRMS

You should program the spreadsheet to use the projected financial statements to compute the amounts used in valuation models. Chapters 11–14 describe and illustrate various models to value firms, including the following:

- Present value of projected dividends (Chapter 11)
- Present value of expected free cash flows (Chapter 12)
- Residual income valuation (Chapter 13)
- Market-based comparables (Chapter 14)

All of these valuation models rely on data from the forecasted financial statements. Your instructor may ask you to follow one or more than one of these approaches in your valuations. We have programmed FSAP to compute all of these valuation approaches and to conduct analysis to determine the sensitivity of the value estimate to different assumptions about the discount rate and the long-run growth rate.

Good luck and enjoy!

QUESTIONS, EXERCISES, PROBLEMS, AND CASES

Questions and Exercises

1.1 VALUE CHAIN ANALYSIS APPLIED TO THE TIMBER AND TIMBER PRODUCTS INDUSTRY. Create a value chain for the timber and timber products industry, beginning with the growing of timber and ending with the retailing of timber and paper products. Briefly describe each link in the value chain and list the name of one U.S. company involved in each link. (Hint: Access Gale's Business & Company Resource Center, Global Business Browser, or Standard & Poor's Industry Surveys to obtain the needed information.)

1.2 PORTER'S FIVE FORCES APPLIED TO THE AIR COURIER INDUSTRY. Apply Porter's five forces to the air courier industry. Industry participants include such firms as FedEx, UPS, and DHL. (Hint: Access Gale's Business & Company Resource Center, Global Business Browser, or Standard & Poor's Industry Surveys to obtain the needed information.)

1.3 ECONOMIC ATTRIBUTES FRAMEWORK APPLIED TO THE SPECIALTY RETAILING APPAREL INDUSTRY. Apply the economic attributes framework discussed in the chapter to the specialty retailing apparel industry, which includes such firms as Gap, Limited Brands, and Abercrombie & Fitch. (Hint: Access Gale's Business & Company Resource Center, Global Business Browser, or Standard & Poor's Industry Surveys to obtain the needed information.)

1.4 IDENTIFICATION OF COMMODITY BUSINESSES. A recent article in *Fortune* magazine listed the following firms among the top ten most admired companies in the United States: Dell, Southwest Airlines, Microsoft, and Johnson & Johnson. Access the websites of these four companies or read the Business section of their Form 10-K reports (http://www.sec.gov). Describe whether you would view their products or services as commodities. Explain your reasoning.

1.5 IDENTIFICATION OF COMPANY STRATEGIES. Refer to the websites and the Form 10-K reports of Home Depot (http://www.homedepot.com) and Lowe's (http://www.lowes.com). Compare and contrast their business strategies.

1.6 RESEARCHING THE FASB WEBSITE. Go to the website of the Financial Accounting Standards Board (http://www.fasb.org). Identify the most recently issued financial reporting standard and summarize briefly (in one paragraph) its principal provisions. Also search under Project Activities to identify the reporting issue with the most recent update. Describe the issue briefly and the nature of the action taken by the FASB.

1.7 RESEARCHING THE IASB WEBSITE. Go to the website of the International Accounting Standards Board (http://www.iasb.org). Search for the International Financial Reporting Standards (IFRS) summaries. Identify the most recently issued international financial reporting standard and summarize briefly (in one paragraph) its principal provisions.

1.8 EFFECT OF INDUSTRY ECONOMICS ON BALANCE SHEET. Access the investor relations or corporate information section of the websites of American Airlines (http://www.aa.com), Intel (http://www.intel.com), and Disney (http://disney.go.com). Study the business strategies of each firm. Examine the financial ratios below and indicate which firm is likely to be American Airlines, Intel, and Disney. Explain your reasoning.

	Firm A	Firm B	Firm C
Property, Plant, and Equipment/Assets	27.9%	34.6%	62.5%
Long-Term Debt/Assets	18.2%	3.7%	35.7%

1.9 EFFECT OF BUSINESS STRATEGY ON COMMON-SIZE INCOME STATEMENT. Access the investor relations or corporate information section of the websites of Apple Computer (http://www.apple.com) and Dell (http://www.dell.com). Study the strategies of each firm. Examine the following common-size income statements and indicate which firm is likely to be Apple Computer and which is likely to be Dell. Explain your reasoning. Indicate any percentages that seem inconsistent with their strategies.

	Firm A	Firm B
Sales	100.0%	100.0%
Cost of Goods Sold	(82.1)	(59.9)
Selling and Administrative	(11.6)	(9.7)
Research and Development	(1.1)	(3.1)
Income Taxes	(1.4)	(8.9)
All Other Items	0.2	0.8
Net Income	4.1%	19.2%

1.10 EFFECT OF BUSINESS STRATEGY ON COMMON-SIZE INCOME STATEMENT. Access the investor relations or corporate information section of the websites of Dollar General (http://www.dollargeneral.com) and Macy's Inc. (http://www.macysinc.com). Study the strategies of each firm. Examine the following common-size income statements and indicate which firm is likely to be Dollar General and which is likely to be Macy's. Explain your reasoning. Indicate any percentages that seem inconsistent with their strategies.

Firm A	Firm A	Firm B
Sales	100.0%	100.0%
Cost of Goods Sold	(70.7)	(60.3)
Selling and Administrative	(23.4)	(34.1)
Income Taxes	(0.8)	(0.5)
All Other Items	(4.0)	(0.1)
Net Income	1.0%	5.2%

Problems and Cases

1.11 EFFECT OF INDUSTRY CHARACTERISTICS ON FINANCIAL STATEMENT RELATIONSHIPS. Effective financial statement analysis requires an understanding of a firm's economic characteristics. The relations between various financial statement items provide evidence of many of these economic characteristics. Exhibit 1.22 (see pages 66–67) presents common-size condensed balance sheets and income statements for 12 firms in different industries. These common-size balance sheets and income statements express various items as a percentage of operating revenues. (That is, the statement divides all amounts by operating revenues for the year.) Exhibit 1.22 also shows the ratio of cash flow from operations to capital expenditures. A dash for a particular financial statement item does not necessarily mean the amount is zero. It merely indicates that the amount is not sufficiently large for the firm to disclose it. Amounts that are not meaningful are shown as *n.m.* A list of the 12 companies and a brief description of their activities follow.

A. Amazon.com: Operates websites to sell a wide variety of products online. The firm operated at a net loss in all years prior to that reported in Exhibit 1.22.

B. Carnival Corporation: Owns and operates cruise ships.

C. Cisco Systems: Manufactures and sells computer networking and communications products.

D. Citigroup: Offers a wide range of financial services in the commercial banking, insurance, and securities business. Operating expenses represent the compensation of employees.

E. eBay: Operates an online trading platform for buyers to purchase and sellers to sell a variety of goods. The firm has grown in part by acquiring other companies to enhance or support its online trading platform.

F. Goldman Sachs: Offers brokerage and investment banking services. Operating expenses represent the compensation of employees.

G. Johnson & Johnson: Develops, manufactures, and sells pharmaceutical products, medical equipment, and branded over-the-counter consumer personal care products.

H. Kellogg's: Manufactures and distributes cereal and other food products. The firm acquired other branded food companies in recent years.

I. MGM Mirage: Owns and operates hotels, casinos, and golf courses.

J. Molson Coors: Manufactures and distributes beer. Molson Coors has made minority ownership investments in other beer manufacturers in recent years.

K. Verizon: Maintains a telecommunications network and offers telecommunications services. Operating expenses represent the compensation of employees. Verizon has made minority investments in other cellular and wireless providers.

L. Yum! Brands: Operates chains of name-brand restaurants, including Taco Bell, KFC, and Pizza Hut.

Required

Use the ratios to match the companies in Exhibit 1.22 with the firms listed above.

1.12 EFFECT OF INDUSTRY CHARACTERISTICS ON FINANCIAL STATEMENT RELATIONSHIPS. Effective financial statement analysis requires an understanding of a firm's economic characteristics. The relations between various financial statement items provide evidence of many of these economic characteristics. Exhibit 1.23 (see pages 68–69) presents common-size condensed balance sheets and income statements for 12 firms in different industries. These common-size balance sheets and income statements express various items as a percentage of operating revenues. (That is, the statement divides all amounts by operating revenues for the year.) Exhibit 1.23 also shows the ratio of cash flow from operations to capital expenditures. A dash for a particular financial statement item does not necessarily mean the amount is zero. It merely indicates that the amount is not sufficiently large for the firm to disclose it. A list of the 12 companies and a brief description of their activities follow.

A. Abercrombie & Fitch: Sells retail apparel primarily through stores to the fashion-conscious young adult and has established itself as a trendy, popular player in the specialty retailing apparel industry.

B. Allstate Insurance: Sells property and casualty insurance, primarily on buildings and automobiles. Operating revenues include insurance premiums from customers and revenues earned from investments made with cash received from customers before Allstate pays customers' claims. Operating expenses include amounts actually paid or expected to be paid in the future on insurance coverage outstanding during the year.

C. Best Buy: Operates a chain of retail stores selling consumer electronic and entertainment equipment at competitively low prices.

D. E. I. du Pont de Nemours: Manufactures chemical and electronics products.

E. Hewlett-Packard: Develops, manufactures, and sells computer hardware. The firm outsources manufacturing of many of its computer components.

F. HSBC Finance: Lends money to consumers for periods ranging from several months to several years. Operating expenses include provisions for estimated uncollectible loans (bad debts expense).

G. Kelly Services: Provides temporary office services to businesses and other firms. Operating revenues represent amounts billed to customers for temporary help services, and operating expenses include amounts paid to the temporary help employees of Kelly.

H. McDonald's: Operates fast-food restaurants worldwide. A large percentage of McDonald's restaurants are owned and operated by franchisees. McDonald's frequently owns the restaurant buildings of franchisees and leases them to franchisees under long-term leases.

I. Merck: A leading research-driven pharmaceutical products and services company. Merck discovers, develops, manufactures, and markets a broad range of products to improve human and animal health directly and through its joint ventures.

J. Omnicom Group: Creates advertising copy for clients and is the largest marketing services firm in the world. Omnicom purchases advertising time and space from various media and sells it to clients. Operating revenues represent commissions and fees earned by creating advertising copy and selling media time and space. Operating expenses includes employee compensation.

K. Pacific Gas & Electric: Generates and sells power to customers in the western United States.

L. Procter & Gamble: Manufactures and markets a broad line of branded consumer products.

EXHIBIT 1.22

Common-Size Financial Statement Data for Firms in 12 Industries (Problem 1.11)

	1	2	3
BALANCE SHEET			
Cash and marketable securities	2,256.1%	4.1%	20.1%
Receivables	352.8%	2.8%	15.2%
Inventories	0.0%	2.4%	7.9%
Property, plant, and equipment, at cost	0.0%	286.8%	43.0%
Accumulated depreciation	(0.0%)	(59.8%)	(20.4%)
Property, plant, and equipment, net	0.0%	227.0%	22.5%
Intangibles	0.0%	36.5%	43.4%
Other assets	57.3%	7.2%	24.0%
Total Assets	2,666.2%	280.0%	133.2%
Current liabilities	2,080.8%	37.8%	32.7%
Long-term debt	390.9%	69.1%	12.7%
Other long-term liabilities	92.6%	5.6%	21.1%
Shareholders' equity	101.9%	167.5%	66.7%
Total Liabilities and Shareholders' Equity	2,666.2%	280.0%	133.2%
INCOME STATEMENT			
Operating revenues	100.0%	100.0%	100.0%
Cost of sales (excluding depreciation) or operating expenses[a]	(54.6%)	(61.6%)	(29.0%)
Depreciation and amortization	(2.0%)	(9.9%)	(4.4%)
Selling and administrative	(1.4%)	(12.1%)	(29.3%)
Research and development	(1.6%)	0.0%	(12.2%)
Interest (expense)/income	9.5%	(2.8%)	(0.1%)
Income taxes	(14.3%)	(0.1%)	(6.2%)
All other items, net	(8.0%)	0.1%	1.6%
Net Income	27.6%	13.6%	20.3%
Cash flow from operations/capital expenditures	n.m.	1.0	4.9

[a] See the problem narrative for items included in operating expenses.

EXHIBIT 1.22 (Continued)

4	5	6	7	8	9	10	11	12
2.0%	10.6%	96.9%	4.1%	2,198.0%	26.0%	4.5%	1.9%	39.3%
8.9%	12.0%	8.8%	4.2%	1,384.8%	4.0%	13.3%	2.0%	5.1%
7.0%	2.1%	3.0%	1.5%	0.0%	8.9%	4.0%	1.3%	0.0%
55.4%	221.5%	33.8%	278.8%	0.0%	7.8%	41.4%	61.1%	32.9%
(32.5%)	(132.6%)	(22.6%)	(52.8%)	(0.0%)	(2.6%)	(14.1%)	(28.3%)	(18.9%)
22.9%	88.9%	11.2%	226.0%	0.0%	5.3%	27.3%	32.9%	14.0%
39.8%	75.2%	40.5%	6.0%	101.9%	5.0%	109.4%	8.3%	90.9%
4.8%	19.0%	28.3%	81.0%	208.5%	7.2%	59.7%	11.4%	33.3%
85.4%	207.9%	188.6%	322.9%	3,893.3%	56.4%	218.2%	57.9%	182.6%
27.7%	26.6%	37.8%	41.7%	2,878.4%	30.0%	20.7%	15.3%	43.4%
31.7%	48.2%	28.5%	172.2%	596.1%	0.4%	38.4%	31.6%	0.0%
14.6%	90.2%	15.3%	53.8%	171.3%	4.4%	33.9%	12.0%	9.4%
11.3%	42.8%	107.0%	55.1%	247.5%	21.4%	125.3%	(1.0%)	129.8%
85.4%	207.9%	188.6%	322.9%	3,893.3%	56.4%	218.2%	57.9%	182.6%
100.0%	100.0%	100.0%	100.0%	100.0%	100.0%	100.0%	100.0%	100.0%
(58.1%)	(40.1%)	(36.1%)	(56.0%)	(73.4%)	(85.8%)	(59.5%)	(75.1%)	(26.1%)
(2.9%)	(15.0%)	(1.5%)	(10.8%)	(5.0%)	(1.5%)	(5.7%)	(4.9%)	(2.8%)
(23.7%)	(27.6%)	(27.6%)	(19.3%)	(5.1%)	(2.6%)	(27.9%)	(7.6%)	(33.7%)
0.0%	0.0%	(14.6%)	0.0%	(7.7%)	(5.1%)	0.0%	0.0%	(8.5%)
(2.5%)	(1.9%)	1.0%	(8.5%)	78.4%	0.0%	(1.8%)	(2.0%)	1.3%
(3.8%)	(3.4%)	(4.3%)	(2.6%)	(16.0%)	(1.0%)	(2.2%)	(2.8%)	(4.7%)
0.0%	(5.5%)	0.0%	2.3%	(28.8%)	(0.3%)	5.2%	0.4%	0.0%
9.0%	6.6%	17.0%	5.3%	42.3%	3.7%	8.0%	8.0%	25.5%
2.7	1.5	9.8	1.0	n.m.	8.8	1.8	1.6	5.1

Required

Use the ratios to match the companies in Exhibit 1.23 with the firms listed above.

1.13 EFFECT OF INDUSTRY CHARACTERISTICS ON FINANCIAL STATEMENT RELATIONSHIPS: A GLOBAL PERSPECTIVE. Effective financial statement analysis requires an understanding of a firm's economic characteristics. The relations between various financial statement items provide evidence of many of these economic characteristics. Exhibit 1.24 (see pages 70–71) presents common-size condensed balance sheets and income statements for 12 firms in different industries. These common-size balance sheets and income statements express various items as a percentage of operating revenues. (That is, the statement divides all amounts by operating revenues for the year.) A dash for a particular

EXHIBIT 1.23

Common-Size Financial Statement Data for Firms in 12 Industries (Problem 1.12)

	1	2	3
BALANCE SHEET			
Cash and marketable securities	11.6%	23.0%	9.2%
Receivables	18.2%	48.4%	25.0%
Inventories	17.8%	9.6%	2.9%
Property, plant, and equipment, at cost	87.8%	101.2%	272.3%
Accumulated depreciation	(52.8%)	(50.9%)	(92.8%)
Property, plant, and equipment, net	35.0%	50.3%	179.5%
Intangibles	15.2%	8.2%	0.0%
Other assets	15.8%	58.4%	60.5%
Total Assets	113.7%	197.9%	277.1%
Current liabilities	30.5%	60.0%	51.2%
Long-term debt	24.0%	16.5%	70.1%
Other long-term liabilities	36.9%	42.7%	88.9%
Shareholders' equity	22.4%	78.7%	66.9%
Total Liabilities and Shareholders' Equity	113.7%	197.9%	277.1%
INCOME STATEMENT			
Operating revenues	100.0%	100.0%	100.0%
Cost of sales (excluding depreciation) or operating expenses[a]	(75.6%)	(23.4%)	(60.7%)
Depreciation and amortization	(4.5%)	(6.8%)	(12.6%)
Selling and administrative	(6.8%)	(24.1%)	0.0%
Research and development	(4.4%)	(20.1%)	0.0%
Interest (expense)/income	(1.2%)	(1.1%)	(4.8%)
Income taxes	(1.2%)	(8.4%)	(3.3%)
All other items, net	0.0%	16.7%	(10.6%)
Net Income	6.3%	32.7%	8.1%
Cash flow from operations/capital expenditures	1.6	5.1	0.8

[a] See the problem narrative for items included in operating expenses.

financial statement item does not necessarily mean the amount is zero. It merely indicates that the amount is not sufficiently large for the firm to disclose it. A list of the 12 companies, the country of their headquarters, and a brief description of their activities follow.

A. Accor (France): World's largest hotel group, operating hotels under the names of Sofitel, Novotel, Motel 6, and others. Accor has grown in recent years by acquiring established hotel chains.

B. Carrefour (France): Operates grocery supermarkets and hypermarkets in Europe, Latin America, and Asia.

C. Deutsche Telekom (Germany): Europe's largest provider of wired and wireless telecommunication services. The telecommunications industry has experienced increased deregulation in recent years.

EXHIBIT 1.23 (Continued)

4	5	6	7	8	9	10	11	12
362.6%	6.0%	1.1%	1.6%	14.7%	8.3%	27.3%	8.8%	11.6%
47.7%	8.9%	4.1%	15.7%	2.7%	43.2%	697.5%	4.0%	16.8%
0.0%	8.7%	10.6%	0.0%	10.5%	5.0%	0.0%	0.5%	5.3%
10.3%	46.4%	15.4%	6.9%	66.1%	13.1%	3.2%	132.4%	18.3%
(6.7%)	(21.8%)	(6.1%)	(3.7%)	(26.6%)	(7.7%)	(1.3%)	(46.3%)	(8.5%)
3.6%	24.6%	9.3%	3.1%	39.5%	5.4%	1.9%	86.1%	9.8%
2.8%	112.8%	6.0%	2.6%	0.0%	55.7%	40.9%	9.5%	34.7%
120.7%	9.5%	4.1%	4.7%	12.9%	12.0%	26.7%	12.2%	22.0%
537.5%	170.6%	35.2%	27.8%	80.5%	129.6%	794.3%	121.0%	100.2%
391.7%	39.1%	18.7%	10.3%	12.7%	73.0%	122.1%	10.8%	37.5%
19.4%	26.1%	2.5%	0.9%	2.8%	22.9%	565.5%	43.3%	12.2%
51.3%	25.5%	3.6%	2.7%	12.8%	7.4%	20.2%	10.0%	15.1%
75.1%	79.8%	10.3%	13.9%	52.1%	26.4%	86.5%	56.9%	35.4%
537.5%	170.6%	35.2%	27.8%	80.5%	129.6%	794.3%	121.0%	100.2%
100.0%	100.0%	100.0%	100.0%	100.0%	100.0%	100.0%	100.0%	100.0%
(91.6%)	(49.2%)	(75.6%)	(82.5%)	(33.3%)	(87.4%)	(29.1%)	(63.3%)	(76.4%)
(0.9%)	(3.9%)	(1.8%)	(0.8%)	(5.1%)	(1.8%)	(1.7%)	(5.1%)	(4.2%)
(10.7%)	(23.9%)	(18.2%)	(15.3%)	(49.4%)	0.0%	(25.0%)	(4.9%)	(6.0%)
0.0%	(2.6%)	0.0%	0.0%	0.0%	0.0%	0.0%	0.0%	(2.5%)
21.0%	(1.7%)	(0.2%)	0.0%	0.3%	(0.6%)	(32.7%)	(2.2%)	(0.6%)
(6.9%)	(5.1%)	(1.5%)	(0.5%)	(5.0%)	(4.1%)	(3.7%)	(7.8%)	(1.5%)
4.2%	0.7%	(0.5%)	(0.1%)	0.0%	1.2%	(3.3%)	1.7%	(2.1%)
15.2%	14.3%	2.2%	0.8%	7.4%	7.5%	4.5%	18.3%	6.7%
18.7	4.6	1.4	1.6	1.3	6.6	100.9	2.8	3.6

D. E.ON AG (Germany): One of the major public utility companies in Europe and the world's largest privately owned energy service provider.

E. Fortis (Netherlands): Offers insurance and banking services. Operating revenues include insurance premiums received, investment income, and interest revenue on loans. Operating expenses include amounts actually paid or amounts it expects to pay in the future on insurance coverage outstanding during the year.

F. Interpublic Group (U.S.): Creates advertising copy for clients. Interpublic purchases advertising time and space from various media and sells it to clients. Operating revenues represent the commissions or fees earned for creating advertising copy and selling media time and space. Operating expenses include employee compensation.

EXHIBIT 1.24

Common-Size Financial Statement Data for Firms in 12 Industries
(Problem 1.13)

	1	2	3
BALANCE SHEET			
Cash and marketable securities	313.7%	2.2%	21.8%
Receivables	412.9%	8.4%	48.8%
Inventories	0.0%	27.7%	6.9%
Property, plant, and equipment, at cost	6.6%	186.9%	66.2%
Accumulated depreciation	(2.8%)	(125.4%)	(36.5%)
Property, plant, and equipment, net	3.8%	61.4%	29.7%
Intangibles	2.4%	0.0%	0.0%
Other assets	66.2%	33.2%	16.2%
Total Assets	829.8%	133.0%	123.5%
Current liabilities	120.3%	18.3%	45.4%
Long-term debt	630.8%	40.9%	22.8%
Other long-term liabilities	55.6%	24.7%	10.1%
Shareholders' equity	23.1%	49.0%	45.1%
Total Liabilities and Shareholders' Equity	829.8%	133.0%	123.5%
INCOME STATEMENT			
Operating revenues	100.0%	100.0%	100.0%
Cost of sales (excluding depreciation) or operating expenses[a]	(18.7%)	(80.3%)	(76.2%)
Depreciation and amortization	(0.6%)	(6.0%)	(5.7%)
Selling and administrative	(4.8%)	(1.4%)	(5.9%)
Research and development	0.0%	0.0%	(3.6%)
Interest (expense)/income	(69.7%)	(0.3%)	0.5%
Income taxes	(1.1%)	(5.1%)	(3.5%)
All other items, net	(0.4%)	0.0%	0.9%
Net Income	4.7%	6.8%	6.5%
Cash flow from operations/capital expenditures	(5.5)	1.1	2.1

[a] See the problem narrative for items included in operating expenses.

G. Marks & Spencer (U.K.): Operates department stores in England and other retail stores in Europe and the United States. Offers its own credit card for customers' purchases.

H. Nestlé (Switzerland): World's largest food processor, offering prepared foods, coffees, milk-based products, and mineral waters.

I. Roche Holding (Switzerland): Creates, manufactures, and distributes a wide variety of prescription drugs.

J. Sumitomo Metal (Japan): Manufacturer and seller of steel sheets and plates and other construction materials.

K. Sun Microsystems (U.S.): Designs, manufactures, and sells workstations and servers used to maintain integrated computer networks. Sun outsources the manufacture of many of its computer components.

EXHIBIT 1.24 (Continued)

4	5	6	7	8	9	10	11	12
4.9%	16.2%	32.7%	19.5%	17.9%	43.4%	4.7%	6.0%	6.5%
12.0%	17.0%	69.6%	21.8%	38.8%	20.4%	6.9%	6.6%	12.2%
2.1%	1.3%	0.0%	4.9%	5.8%	12.2%	5.9%	7.8%	8.5%
195.3%	92.8%	23.2%	35.2%	134.7%	62.9%	82.6%	34.5%	42.0%
(127.9%)	(36.9%)	(15.2%)	(23.6%)	(76.0%)	(24.9%)	(29.3%)	(17.7%)	(22.8%)
67.4%	55.9%	8.1%	11.6%	58.7%	38.0%	53.3%	16.8%	19.2%
87.5%	31.6%	46.3%	27.2%	26.5%	32.3%	4.4%	14.1%	34.1%
25.9%	25.5%	17.5%	18.4%	28.5%	12.7%	4.9%	7.7%	16.1%
199.7%	147.5%	174.1%	103.3%	176.2%	158.8%	80.1%	59.0%	96.6%
40.3%	70.2%	98.8%	40.8%	40.6%	25.3%	25.5%	32.2%	30.2%
8.8%	24.9%	25.7%	9.1%	21.3%	6.2%	23.4%	10.8%	5.8%
80.7%	6.3%	14.2%	13.1%	43.5%	15.0%	8.1%	3.6%	10.7%
69.9%	46.0%	35.6%	40.3%	70.8%	112.4%	23.2%	12.4%	50.0%
199.7%	147.5%	174.1%	103.3%	176.2%	158.8%	80.1%	59.0%	96.6%
100.0%	100.0%	100.0%	100.0%	100.0%	100.0%	100.0%	100.0%	100.0%
(56.1%)	(70.4%)	(62.4%)	(53.5%)	(64.5%)	(28.5%)	(62.8%)	(77.9%)	(51.3%)
(17.8%)	(5.8%)	(2.5%)	(3.4%)	(5.1%)	(3.5%)	(4.5%)	(2.1%)	(2.4%)
(15.9%)	0.0%	(26.4%)	(25.1%)	(22.7%)	(20.5%)	(24.7%)	(16.3%)	(30.2%)
0.0%	0.0%	0.0%	(13.4%)	0.0%	(18.5%)	0.0%	0.0%	(1.8%)
(4.0%)	(1.1%)	(1.7%)	1.2%	(1.4%)	0.5%	(1.8%)	(0.6%)	(1.0%)
(2.3%)	(3.5%)	(2.2%)	(1.5%)	(0.1%)	(6.9%)	(2.2%)	(0.8%)	(3.4%)
(0.1%)	(11.3%)	(0.5%)	0.2%	1.1%	0.1%	1.6%	0.1%	7.6%
3.8%	7.9%	4.2%	4.5%	7.3%	22.6%	5.6%	2.3%	17.3%
2.3	2.0	6.3	3.0	1.7	4.0	2.7	1.8	2.2

L. Toyota Motor (Japan): Manufactures automobiles and offers financing services to its customers.

Required

Use the ratios to match the companies in Exhibit 1.24 with the firms listed above.

1.14 VALUE CHAIN ANALYSIS AND FINANCIAL STATEMENT RELATIONSHIPS. Exhibit 1.25 (see page 74) presents common-size income statements and balance sheets for seven firms that operate at various stages in the value chain for the pharmaceutical industry. These common-size statements express all amounts as a percentage of sales revenue. Exhibit 1.25 also shows the cash flow from operations to capital expenditures ratios for each firm. A dash for a particular financial statement item does not necessarily mean the amount is zero. It merely indicates that the amount is not sufficiently large for the firm to disclose it. A list of the seven companies and a brief description of their activities follow.

A. Wyeth: Engages in the development, manufacture, and sale of ethical drugs (that is, drugs requiring a prescription). Wyeth's drugs represent primarily mixtures of chemical compounds. Ethical-drug companies must obtain approval of new drugs from the U.S. Food and Drug Administration (FDA). Patents protect such drugs from competition until other drug companies develop more effective substitutes or the patent expires.

B. Amgen: Engages in the development, manufacture, and sale of drugs based on biotechnology research. Biotechnology drugs must obtain approval from the FDA and enjoy patent protection similar to that for chemical-based drugs. The biotechnology segment is less mature than the ethical-drug industry, with relatively few products having received FDA approval.

C. Mylan Laboratories: Engages in the development, manufacture, and sale of generic drugs. Generic drugs have the same chemical compositions as drugs that had previously benefited from patent protection but for which the patent has expired. Generic-drug companies have benefited in recent years from the patent expiration of several major ethical drugs. However, the major ethical-drug companies have increasingly offered generic versions of their ethical drugs to compete against the generic-drug companies.

D. Johnson & Johnson: Engages in the development, manufacture, and sale of over-the-counter health care products. Such products do not require a prescription and often benefit from brand recognition.

E. Covance: Offers product development and laboratory testing services for biotechnology and pharmaceutical drugs. It also offers commercialization services and market access services. Cost of goods sold for this company represents the salaries of personnel conducting the laboratory testing and drug approval services.

F. Cardinal Health: Distributes drugs as a wholesaler to drugstores, hospitals, and mass merchandisers. Also offers pharmaceutical benefit management services in which it provides customized databases designed to help customers order more efficiently, contain costs, and monitor their purchases. Cost of goods sold for Cardinal Health includes the cost of drugs sold plus the salaries of personnel providing pharmaceutical benefit management services.

G. Walgreens: Operates a chain of drugstores nationwide. The data in Exhibit 1.25 for Walgreens include the recognition of operating lease commitments for retail space.

Required

Use the ratios to match the companies in Exhibit 1.25 with the firms listed above.

INTEGRATIVE CASE 1.1

STARBUCKS

The first case at the end of this chapter and each of the remaining chapters is a series of integrative cases involving Starbucks. The series of cases applies the concepts and analytical tools discussed in each chapter to Starbucks' financial statements and notes. The preparation of responses to the questions in these cases results in an integrated illustration of the six sequential steps in financial statement analysis discussed in this chapter and throughout the book.

Introduction

"They don't just sell coffee; they sell the *Starbucks Experience*," remarked Deb Mills while sitting down to enjoy a cup of Starbucks cappuccino with her friend Kim Shannon. Kim, an investment fund manager for a large insurance firm, reflected on that observation and what it might mean for Starbucks as a potential investment opportunity. Glancing around the store, Kim saw a number of people sitting alone or in groups, lingering over their drinks while chatting, reading, or checking e-mail and surfing the Internet through the store's Wi-Fi network. Kim noted that in addition to the wide selection of hot coffees, French and Italian style espressos, teas, and cold coffee-blended drinks, Starbucks also offered food items and baked goods, packages of roasted coffee beans, coffee-related accessories and equipment, and even its own line of CDs. Intrigued, Kim made a mental note to do a full-blown valuation analysis of Starbucks to evaluate whether its business model and common equity shares were as good as their coffee.

Growth Strategy

Kim's research quickly confirmed her friend's observation that Starbucks is about the *experience* of enjoying a good cup of coffee. The Starbucks 2008 Form 10-K (page 2) boldly asserts that

> "The Company's retail goal is to become the leading retailer and brand of coffee in each of its target markets by selling the finest quality coffee and related products, and by providing each customer a unique *Starbucks Experience.* The *Starbucks Experience*, or third place beyond home and work, is built upon superior service as well as clean and well-maintained Company-operated retail stores that reflect the personalities of the communities in which they operate, thereby building a high degree of customer loyalty."

The *Starbucks Experience* strives to create a "third place"—somewhere besides home and work where a customer can feel comfortable and welcome—through friendly and skilled customer service in clean and personable retail store environments. This approach enabled Starbucks to grow rapidly from just a single coffee shop near Pike's Place Market in Seattle to a global company with 16,680 locations worldwide at the end of fiscal 2008. Of that total, Starbucks owns and operates 9,217 stores (7,238 U.S. stores and 1,979 international stores), while licensees own and operate 7,463 stores (4,329 U.S. stores and 3,134 international stores).

Most of Starbucks' stores at the end of fiscal 2008 were located in the United States (11,567 stores), amounting to one Starbucks retail location for every 27,000 U.S. residents. However, Starbucks was clearly not a company content to focus simply on the U.S. market, as it was extending the reach of its stores globally, with 5,113 stores outside the United States. At the end of fiscal 2008, Starbucks owned and operated stores in a number of countries around the world, including 731 stores in Canada, 664 stores in the United Kingdom, and 178 stores in China. In addition, by the end of 2008, Starbucks' licensees operated 1,933 stores in the Asia-Pacific region; 685 stores in Europe, the Middle East, and Africa; and 472 stores in Canada and Mexico.

Starbucks' success can be attributed in part to its successful development and expansion of a European idea—enjoying a fine coffee-based beverage and sharing that experience with others in a comfortable, friendly environment with pleasant, competent service. Starbucks imported the idea of the French and Italian café into the busy North American lifestyle. Ironically, Starbucks successfully extended its brand and style of café into the European continent. On January 16, 2004, Starbucks opened its first coffeehouse in

EXHIBIT 1.25

Common-Size Financial Statement Data for Seven Firms in the Pharmaceutical Industry (Problem 1.14)

	1	2	3	4	5	6	7
BALANCE SHEET							
Cash and marketable securities	12.5%	1.9%	63.7%	63.7%	12.1%	4.1%	20.1%
Receivables	22.7%	5.7%	13.8%	16.0%	18.7%	3.9%	15.2%
Inventories	20.7%	7.2%	13.8%	13.1%	3.7%	10.7%	7.9%
Property, plant, and equipment, at cost	34.2%	3.9%	66.6%	73.9%	74.2%	22.6%	43.0%
Accumulated depreciation	(13.5%)	(2.0%)	(27.4%)	(24.9%)	(27.1%)	(5.5%)	(20.4%)
Property, plant, and equipment, net	20.7%	1.9%	39.2%	49.0%	47.1%	17.1%	22.5%
Intangibles	109.3%	6.1%	95.5%	20.5%	5.8%	2.3%	43.4%
Other assets	16.8%	2.5%	16.9%	30.5%	8.5%	1.6%	24.0%
Total Assets	202.6%	25.2%	242.9%	192.8%	96.0%	39.7%	133.2%
Current liabilities	30.1%	11.5%	32.6%	30.0%	25.2%	10.7%	32.7%
Long-term debt	100.5%	3.3%	61.2%	47.4%	0.0%	3.7%	12.7%
Other long-term liabilities	19.4%	1.7%	13.3%	31.5%	5.4%	2.6%	21.1%
Shareholders' equity	52.6%	8.8%	135.9%	84.0%	65.4%	22.7%	66.7%
Total Liabilities and Shareholders' Equity	202.6%	25.2%	242.9%	192.8%	96.0%	39.7%	133.2%
INCOME STATEMENT							
Operating revenues	100.0%	100.0%	100.0%	100.0%	100.0%	100.0%	100.0%
Cost of sales (excluding depreciation) or operating expenses	(59.7%)	(94.4%)	(15.3%)	(27.4%)	(62.5%)	(72.2%)	(29.0%)
Depreciation and amortization	(8.3%)	(0.4%)	(7.2%)	(4.1%)	(3.9%)	(1.5%)	(4.4%)
Selling and administrative	(12.2%)	(3.1%)	(20.1%)	(25.9%)	(13.7%)	(21.1%)	(29.3%)
Research and development	(6.2%)	0.0%	(20.2%)	(14.8%)	0.0%	0.0%	(12.2%)
Interest (expense)/income	(6.9%)	(0.2%)	0.2%	(0.1%)	0.4%	(0.1%)	(0.1%)
Income taxes	(2.7%)	(0.5%)	(7.0%)	(8.4%)	(4.3%)	(1.8%)	(6.2%)
All other items, net	0.1%	0.0%	(2.5%)	(0.1%)	(5.3%)	0.0%	1.6%
Net Income	4.1%	1.3%	28.0%	19.3%	10.5%	3.2%	20.3%
Cash flow from operations/ capital expenditures	2.3	3.0	8.9	4.4	4.0	2.2	4.9

France—in the heart of Paris at 26 Avenue de l'Opera—and had a total of 46 stores in France by the end of 2008. The success of Starbucks' retail coffeehouse concept is illustrated by the fact that by the end of 2008, Starbucks had opened over 1,000 company-operated and licensed locations in Europe, with the majority of them in the United Kingdom.

Not long ago Starbucks' CEO Howard Schultz stated that his vision and ultimate goal for Starbucks was to have 20,000 Starbucks retail locations in the United States, to have another 20,000 retail locations in international markets worldwide, and to have Starbucks recognized among the world's leading brands. Kim Shannon wondered whether Starbucks could ultimately achieve that level of global penetration because she could name only a few such worldwide companies. Among those that came to mind were McDonald's, with 31,677 retail locations in 119 countries; Subway, with 32,191 locations in 90 countries (of which, 21,995 were in the United States); and Yum! Brands, with 36,000 restaurants in 110 countries under brand names such as KFC, Pizza Hut, and Taco Bell.

Until 2009, growth in the number of retail stores had been one of the primary drivers of Starbucks' growth in revenues. The most significant area of expansion of the Starbucks model in recent years has been the rapid growth in the number of licensed retail stores. At the end of fiscal 1999, Starbucks had only 363 licensed stores, but by the end of fiscal 2008, the number of licensed stores had mushroomed to 7,463.

Recent Performance

Starbucks' performance in 2008 caused Kim to question whether Starbucks had already reached (or perhaps exceeded) its full potential. She wondered whether it could generate the impressive growth in new stores and revenues it had created in the past.

In fiscal year 2008, Starbucks opened 1,669 net new retail locations (681 net new company-owned stores and 988 new licensed stores), but this number was well below the initial target (2,500 new stores) and well below the 2,571 new stores opened in 2007. Late in 2008, Starbucks announced a plan to close approximately 600 underperforming stores in the United States as well as 64 underperforming stores in Australia. Early in fiscal 2009, it increased the restructuring plan to close a total of approximately 800 U.S. stores (an increase of 200) and announced a plan to close 100 additional stores in various international markets during 2009. During fiscal 2008, Starbucks managed to close 205 U.S. stores and the 64 underperforming stores in Australia. The restructuring plans called for closing 595 stores in the United States and 100 international stores during fiscal 2009. The store closings triggered restructuring charges that reduced Starbucks' operating income by $267 million in 2008. Similar charges would likely reduce 2009 operating income by $360 million. Overall in fiscal 2009, for the first time in company history, Starbucks' projected that net store growth in the United States would be negative, with company-operated store closings outnumbering new store openings. Growth in U.S.-licensed stores also was expected to be slow, with less than 100 new stores planned. Internationally, Starbucks' plans for store opening for 2009 were conservative, owing in part to the difficult economic conditions in its primary markets. Starbucks planned to open 100 new company-operated international stores in 2009 and 300 new licensed stores.

In fiscal 2008, total revenues grew to $10.383 billion from $9.411 billion in fiscal 2007, a growth rate of 10.3 percent. Prior to 2008, Starbucks had generated impressive revenue growth rates of 20.9 percent in fiscal 2007 and 22.2 percent in fiscal 2006.

Starbucks' revenue growth was driven not only by the opening of new stores, but also by sales growth among existing stores. Through 2007, Starbucks could boast of a streak of 16 consecutive years in which it achieved comparable store sales growth rates equal to or greater than 5 percent, but that string was broken with –3 percent comparable store sales growth in 2008. Unfortunately, given the economic conditions in Starbucks' primary markets, it was not clear whether same store sales growth rates would improve in 2009.

In January 2008, Howard Schultz returned from retirement and resumed his role as president and CEO of Starbucks to restructure the business and its potential for growth. Focal points of his transformation plan included overseeing the restructuring efforts, taking a more disciplined approach to opening new stores, reinvigorating the *Starbucks Experience*, and developing and implementing even better service and quality while cutting operating and overhead costs. In addition, the transformation plans included introducing new beverage and food offerings, including baked goods, breakfast items, and chilled foods. A key to Starbucks profit growth lies in increasing same store sales growth via new products. Starbucks regularly introduces new specialty coffee-based drinks and coffee flavors as well as iced coffee-based drinks, such as the successful line of Frappuccino® and Iced Shaken Refreshment drinks.

Starbucks also planned to continue to expand the scope of its business model through new channel development in order to "reach customers where they work, travel, shop, and dine." To further expand the business model, Starbucks entered into a licensing agreement with Kraft Foods to market and distribute Starbucks whole bean and ground coffee to grocery stores and warehouse club stores. By the end of fiscal 2008, Starbucks whole bean and ground coffees were available throughout the United States in approximately 39,000 grocery and warehouse club stores. In addition, Starbucks sells whole bean and ground coffee through institutional foodservice companies that service business, education, office, hotel, restaurant, airline, and other foodservice accounts. For example, in 2008, Starbucks (and its subsidiary Seattle's Best Coffee) was the only superpremium national brand of coffee promoted by Sysco Corporation to such foodservice accounts. Finally, Starbucks had formed partnerships to produce and distribute bottled Frappuccino® and Doubleshot® drinks with PepsiCo and premium ice creams with Dreyer's Grand Ice Cream, Inc.

Despite Starbucks' difficulties with store closings, restructuring charges, and negative comparable store sales growth rates, Kim could see positive aspects of Starbucks' financial performance and condition. She noted that Starbucks had been profitable in 2008 despite the restructuring charges and falling revenues. The restructuring plan was expected to help Starbucks reduce costs, even during these difficult times. Further, she noted that Starbucks' operating cash flows had remained fairly strong throughout this period, amounting to $1,259 million in fiscal 2008. Starbucks had a cash balance of nearly $270 million. Perhaps Starbucks could weather the economic recession and its restructuring and look to better days ahead.

Product Supply

Starbucks purchases green coffee beans from coffee-producing regions around the world and custom roasts and blends them to its exacting standards. Although coffee beans trade in commodity markets and experience volatile prices, Starbucks purchases higher-quality coffee beans that sell at a premium to commodity coffees. Starbucks purchases its coffee beans under fixed-price purchase contracts with various suppliers, with purchase prices reset annually. Starbucks also purchases significant amounts of dairy products from suppliers located near its retail stores. Starbucks purchases paper and plastic products from several suppliers, the prices of which vary with changes in the prices of commodity paper and plastic resin.

Competition in the Specialty Coffee Industry

After some reflection, Kim realized that Starbucks faced intense direct competition. Kim could think of a wide array of convenient retail locations where a person can purchase a cup of coffee. Kim reasoned that Starbucks competes with a broad scope of coffee beverage retailers, including fast-food chains (for example, McDonald's), doughnut chains (for example, Krispy Kreme, Dunkin' Donuts, and Tim Hortons), and convenience stores associated with many gas stations, but that these types of outlets offer an experience that is very different from what Starbucks offers. In particular, Kim was aware that McDonald's had started to expand development of its McCafé shops, which sold premium coffee drinks (lattes, cappuccinos, and mochas) in McDonald's restaurants. It appeared to Kim that the McCafé initiative was intended to be a direct competitive challenge to Starbucks' business.

Kim also identified a number of companies that were growing chains of retail coffee shops that could be compared to Starbucks, including firms such as Panera Bread Company; Diedrich Coffee; New World Restaurant Group, Inc.; and Caribou Coffee Company, Inc. (a privately-held firm). However, these firms were much smaller than Starbucks, with the largest among them being the Panera Bread Company, with 1,325 bakery-cafés systemwide (763 franchised and 562 company-owned) as of the end of fiscal 2008. On the other end of the spectrum, Kim was aware that Starbucks faced competition from local mom-and-pop coffee shops and cafés.

Kim recognized that despite facing extensive competition, Starbucks had some distinct competitive advantages. Very few companies were implementing a business strategy comparable to that of Starbucks, with emphasis on the quality of the experience, the products, and the service. In addition, only the fast-food chains and the doughnut chains operated on the same scale as Starbucks. Finally, Starbucks had developed a global brand that was synonymous with the quality of the *Starbucks Experience.* Recently, Interbrand ranked the Starbucks brand as one of the world's top 100 most valuable brand names, estimating it to be worth in excess of $3 billion.

Financial Statements

Exhibit 1.26 presents comparative balance sheets, Exhibit 1.27 presents comparative income statements, and Exhibit 1.28 (see page 80) presents comparative statements of cash flows for Starbucks for the four fiscal years ending September 28, 2008.

Required

Respond to the following questions relating to Starbucks.

Industry and Strategy Analysis

a. Apply Porter's five forces framework to the specialty coffee retail industry.

b. How would you characterize the strategy of Starbucks? How does Starbucks create value for its customers? What critical risk and success factors must Starbucks manage?

Balance Sheet

c. Describe how Cash differs from Cash Equivalents.

d. Why do investments appear on the balance sheet under both current and noncurrent assets?

e. Accounts receivable are reported net of allowance for uncollectible accounts. Why? Identify the events or transactions that cause accounts receivable to increases and

EXHIBIT 1.26

Starbucks Corporation Comparative Balance Sheets
(amounts in millions)
(Integrative Case 1.1)

As of Fiscal Year End September:	2005	2006	2007	2008
ASSETS				
Current Assets				
Cash and equivalents	$ 173.8	$ 312.6	$ 281.3	$ 269.8
Short-term investments	133.2	141.0	157.4	52.5
Receivables	190.8	224.3	287.9	329.5
Inventories	546.3	636.2	691.7	692.8
Prepaid expenses and other assets	94.4	126.9	148.8	169.2
Deferred income taxes, net	70.8	88.8	129.5	234.2
Total Current Assets	**$1,209.3**	**$1,529.8**	**$1,696.5**	**$1,748.0**
Long-term investments	60.5	5.8	21.0	71.4
Equity and other investments	201.1	219.1	258.8	302.6
Property and equipment, gross	$3,467.6	$4,257.7	$5,306.6	$5,717.3
Accumulated depreciation	(1,625.6)	(1,969.8)	(2,416.1)	(2,760.9)
Property and equipment, net	$1,842.0	$2,287.9	$2,890.4	$2,956.4
Other assets	72.9	186.9	219.4	261.1
Other intangible assets	35.4	38.0	42.0	66.6
Goodwill	92.5	161.5	215.6	266.5
Total Assets	**$3,513.7**	**$4,428.9**	**$5,343.9**	**$5,672.6**
LIABILITIES AND STOCKHOLDERS' EQUITY				
Current Liabilities				
Accounts payable	$ 221.0	$ 340.9	$ 390.8	$ 324.9
Short-term borrowings	277.0	700.0	710.2	713.0
Accrued compensation and related costs	232.4	289.0	292.4	253.6
Accrued occupancy costs	44.5	54.9	74.6	136.1
Accrued taxes	78.3	94.0	92.5	76.1
Insurance reserves	–	–	137.0	152.5
Other accrued expenses	198.1	224.2	160.3	164.4
Deferred revenue	175.0	231.9	296.9	368.4
Current portion of long-term debt	0.7	0.8	0.8	0.7
Total Current Liabilities	**$1,227.0**	**$1,935.6**	**$2,155.6**	**$2,189.7**
Long-term debt	2.9	2.0	550.1	549.6
Other long-term liabilities	193.6	262.9	354.1	442.4
Total Liabilities	**$1,423.4**	**$2,200.4**	**$3,059.8**	**$3,181.7**
Shareholders' Equity				
Common stock	91.0	0.8	0.7	0.7
Paid-in capital	39.4	39.4	39.4	39.4
Retained earnings	1,939.0	2,151.1	2,189.4	2,402.4
Accum. other comprehensive income	20.9	37.3	54.6	48.4
Total Shareholders' Equity	**$2,090.3**	**$2,228.5**	**$2,284.1**	**$2,490.9**
Total Liabilities and Shareholders' Equity	**$3,513.7**	**$4,428.9**	**$5,343.9**	**$5,672.6**

EXHIBIT 1.27

Starbucks Corporation Comparative Income Statements
(amounts in millions except per share figures)
(Integrative Case 1.1)

Fiscal Years Ended September:	2005	2006	2007	2008
Company-operated retail stores	$5,391.9	$6,583.1	$7,998.3	$ 8,771.9
Specialty:				
Licensing	673.0	860.7	1,026.3	1,171.6
Foodservice and other	304.4	343.2	386.9	439.5
Total Specialty	977.4	1,203.9	1,413.2	1,611.1
Net Revenues	**$6,369.3**	**$7,787.0**	**$9,411.5**	**$10,383.0**
Cost of sales including occupancy costs	(2,605.2)	(3,178.8)	(3,999.1)	(4,645.3)
Gross Profit	**$3,764.1**	**$4,608.2**	**$5,412.4**	**$ 5,737.7**
Store operating expenses	(2,165.9)	(2,687.8)	(3,215.9)	(3,745.1)
Other operating expenses	(192.5)	(253.7)	(294.1)	(330.1)
Depreciation and amortization	340.2	387.2)	467.2	549.3
General and administrative expenses	(361.6)	(479.4)	(489.2)	(456.0)
Restructuring charges	—	—	—	266.9
Income from equity investees	(76.6)	(93.9)	(108.0)	(113.6)
Operating Income	**$ 780.5**	**$ 894.0**	**$1,054.0**	**$ 503.9**
Interest and other income	17.1	20.7	40.6	9.0
Interest expense	(1.3)	(8.4)	(38.2)	(53.4)
Income Before Income Taxes	$ 796.3	$ 906.3	$1,056.4	$ 459.5
Provision for income taxes	(302.0)	(324.8)	(383.7)	(144.0)
Cumulative effect of an accounting change	—	(17.2)	—	—
Net Income	**$ 494.3**	**$ 564.3**	**$ 672.7**	**$ 315.5**
Net Income Per Share				
Basic	$ 0.63	$ 0.76	$ 0.90	$ 0.43
Diluted	$ 0.61	$ 0.73	$ 0.87	$ 0.43

decrease. Also identify the events or transactions that cause the allowance account to increase and decrease.

f. How does the account Accumulated Depreciation on the balance sheet differ from Depreciation Expense on the income statement?

g. Deferred income taxes appear as a current asset on the balance sheet. Under what circumstances will deferred income taxes give rise to an asset?

h. Accumulated Other Comprehensive Income includes unrealized gains and losses from marketable securities and investments in securities as well as unrealized gains and losses from translating the financial statements of foreign subsidiaries into U.S. dollars. Why are these gains and losses not included in net income on the income statement? When, if ever, will these gains and losses appear in net income?

EXHIBIT 1.28

Starbucks Corporation Comparative Statements of Cash Flows
(amounts in millions)
(Integrative Case 1.1)

Fiscal Years Ended September:	2005	2006	2007	2008
OPERATING ACTIVITIES:				
Net income	$ 494.5	$ 564.3	$ 672.6	$ 315.5
Depreciation and amortization	367.2	412.6	491.2	604.5
Provisions for impairments and disposals	20.2	19.6	26.0	325.0
Deferred income taxes, net	(31.3)	(84.3)	(37.3)	(117.1)
Equity in income of investees	(49.6)	(60.6)	(65.7)	(61.3)
Distributions of income from equity investees	30.9	49.2	65.9	52.6
Stock-based compensation	110.0	105.7	103.9	75.0
Other non-cash items in net income	10.1	(96.9)	(84.7)	(11.0)
Changes in operating assets and liabilities:				
Inventories	(121.6)	(85.5)	(48.6)	(0.6)
Accounts payable	9.7	105.0	36.1	(63.9)
Accrued expenses and taxes	22.7	132.7	86.4	7.3
Deferred revenues	53.3	56.6	63.2	72.4
Other operating assets and liabilities	7.6	13.2	22.2	60.3
Cash Flow from Operating Activities	**$ 923.7**	**$1,131.6**	**$ 1,331.2**	**$ 1,258.7**
INVESTING ACTIVITIES:				
Purchases, sales, maturities of investment securities	$ 452.2	$ 61.1	$ (11.7)	$ 24.1
Net additions to property, plant, and equipment	(644.0)	(771.2)	(1,080.3)	(984.5)
Acquisitions and other investments	(29.5)	(130.9)	(109.9)	(126.2)
Cash Flow Used in Investing Activities	**$(221.3)**	**$ (841.0)**	**$(1,201.9)**	**$(1,086.6)**
FINANCING ACTIVITIES:				
Net (payments on) proceeds from short-term borrowings	$ 277.0	$ 423.0	$ 10.2	$ 2.2
Net (payments on) proceeds from long-term debt	(0.7)	(0.9)	548.2	(0.6)
Net (repurchases of) issues of common equity shares	(950.1)	(694.8)	(819.9)	(199.1)
Excess tax benefit from exercise of stock options	—	117.4	89.6	13.0
Cash Flow Used in Financing Activities	**$(673.8)**	**$ (155.3)**	**$ (171.9)**	**$ (184.5)**
Effects of exchange rate changes on cash	$ 0.1	$ 3.5	$ 11.3	$ 0.9
Net Change in Cash and Cash Equivalents	**$ 28.7**	**$ 138.8**	**$ (31.3)**	**$ (11.5)**
Beginning Cash and Cash Equivalents	**145.1**	**173.8**	**312.6**	**281.3**
Ending Cash and Cash Equivalents	**$ 173.8**	**$ 312.6**	**$ 281.3**	**$ 269.8**

Income Statement

i. Starbucks reports three principal sources of revenues: company-operated stores, licensing, and foodservice and other consumer products. Using the narrative information provided in this case, describe the nature of each of these three sources of revenue.

j. What types of expenses does Starbucks likely include in (1) Cost of Sales, (2) Occupancy Costs, and (3) Store Operating Expenses?

k. Starbucks reports Income from Equity Investees in its income statement. Using the narrative information provided in this case, describe the nature of this type of income.

Statement of Cash Flows

l. Why does net income differ from the amount of cash flow from operating activities?

m. Why does Starbucks add the amount of depreciation and amortization expense to net income when computing cash flow from operating activities?

n. Why does Starbucks show an increase in inventory as a subtraction when computing cash flow from operations?

o. Why does Starbucks show a decrease in accounts payable as a subtraction when computing cash flow from operations?

p. Starbucks includes short-term investments in current assets on the balance sheet, yet it reports purchases and sales of investment securities as investing activities on the statement of cash flows. Explain why changes in investment securities are investing activities while changes in most other current assets (such as accounts receivable and inventories) are operating activities.

q. Starbucks includes changes in Short-Term Borrowings as a financing activity on the statement of cash flows. Explain why changes in Short-Term Borrowings are a financing activity when most other changes in current liabilities (such as accounts payable and other current liabilities) are operating activities.

Relations between Financial Statements

r. Prepare an analysis that explains the change in Retained Earnings from $2,189.4 at the end of fiscal 2007 to $2,402.4 at the end of fiscal 2008.

s. Prepare an analysis that explains the changes in Property, Plant, and Equipment from $5,306.5 at the end of fiscal 2007 to $5,717.3 at the end of fiscal 2008 and Accumulated Depreciation from $2,416.1 at the end of fiscal 2007 to $2,760.9 at the end of fiscal 2008. You may need to deduce certain amounts that Starbucks does not disclose. For simplicity, assume that all of the depreciation and amortization expense is depreciation.

Interpreting Financial Statement Relations

Exhibit 1.29 presents common-size and percentage change balance sheets and Exhibit 1.30 (see page 84) presents common-size and percentage change income statements for Starbucks for 2005–2008. The percentage change statements report the annual percentage change in each account as well as the compound annual growth rate from 2005 through 2008. Respond to the following questions.

t. The dollar amount shown for property and equipment net of accumulated depreciation (see Exhibit 1.26) increased between the end of fiscal 2007 and the end of fiscal 2008, yet the percentage of total assets comprising these assets declined (see Exhibit 1.29). Explain.

EXHIBIT 1.29

Starbucks Corporation Common-Size and Percentage Change Balance Sheets (allow for rounding)
(Integrative Case 1.1)

	Common-Size Balance Sheets				Percentage Change Balance Sheets			
As of Fiscal Year-End September:	**2005**	**2006**	**2007**	**2008**	**2006**	**2007**	**2008**	**Compound Growth**
ASSETS								
Current Assets								
Cash and equivalents	4.9%	7.1%	5.3%	4.8%	79.9%	(10.0%)	(4.1%)	15.8%
Short-term investments	3.8%	3.2%	2.9%	0.9%	5.9%	11.6%	(66.7%)	(26.7%)
Receivables	5.4%	5.0%	5.4%	5.8%	17.6%	28.4%	14.4%	20.0%
Inventories	15.6%	14.4%	12.9%	12.2%	16.5%	8.7%	0.2%	8.2%
Prepaid expenses and other assets	2.7%	2.8%	2.8%	3.0%	34.4%	17.2%	13.7%	21.5%
Deferred income taxes, net	2.0%	2.0%	2.4%	4.1%	25.4%	45.8%	80.9%	49.0%
Total Current Assets	**34.4%**	**34.5%**	**31.7%**	**30.8%**	**26.5%**	**10.9%**	**3.0%**	**13.1%**
Long-term investments	1.7%	0.1%	0.4%	1.3%	(90.4%)	261.8%	239.6%	5.7%
Equity and other investments	5.7%	4.9%	4.9%	5.3%	9.0%	18.1%	16.9%	14.6%
Property and equipment, gross	98.7%	96.1%	99.3%	100.8%	22.8%	24.6%	7.7%	18.1%
Accumulated depreciation	(46.3%)	(44.5%)	(45.2%)	(48.7%)	21.2%	22.7%	14.3%	19.3%
Property and equipment, net	52.4%	51.7%	54.1%	52.1%	24.2%	26.3%	2.3%	17.1%
Other assets	2.1%	4.2%	4.1%	4.6%	156.4%	17.4%	19.0%	53.0%
Other intangible assets	1.0%	0.9%	0.8%	1.2%	7.2%	10.8%	58.4%	23.4%
Goodwill	2.7%	3.7%	4.0%	4.7%	74.6%	33.5%	23.6%	42.3%
Total Assets	**100.0%**	**100.0%**	**100.0%**	**100.0%**	**26.0%**	**20.7%**	**6.2%**	**17.3%**

LIABILITIES AND STOCKHOLDERS' EQUITY								
Current Liabilities								
Accounts payable	6.3%	7.7%	7.3%	5.7%	54.3%	14.6%	(16.9%)	13.7%
Short-term borrowings	7.9%	15.8%	13.3%	12.6%	152.7%	1.5%	0.4%	37.0%
Accrued compensation and related costs	6.6%	6.5%	5.5%	4.5%	24.4%	1.2%	(13.3%)	3.0%
Accrued occupancy costs	1.3%	1.3%	1.4%	2.4%	23.3%	35.9%	82.5%	45.2%
Accrued taxes	2.2%	2.1%	1.7%	1.3%	20.1%	(1.6%)	(17.7%)	(0.9%)
Insurance reserves	0.0%	0.0%	2.6%	2.7%	n.m.	n.m.	11.3%	n.m.
Other accrued expenses	5.6%	5.1%	3.0%	2.9%	13.2%	(28.5%)	2.6%	(6.0%)
Deferred revenue	5.0%	5.2%	5.6%	6.5%	32.5%	28.0%	24.1%	28.2%
Current portion of long-term debt	0.0%	0.0%	0.0%	0.0%	1.9%	1.7%	(9.7%)	(2.2%)
Total Current Liabilities	**34.9%**	**43.7%**	**40.4%**	**38.6%**	**57.8%**	**11.4%**	**1.6%**	**21.3%**
Long-term debt	0.1%	0.1%	10.3%	9.7%	(31.8%)	27,996.1%	(0.1%)	476.4%
Other long-term liabilities	5.5%	5.9%	6.6%	7.8%	35.8%	34.7%	24.9%	31.7%
Total Liabilities	**40.5%**	**49.7%**	**57.3%**	**56.1%**	**54.6%**	**39.1%**	**4.0%**	**30.7%**
Shareholders' Equity								
Common stock	2.6%	0.0%	0.0%	0.0%	(99.2%)	(2.4%)	0.0%	(79.9%)
Paid-in capital	1.1%	0.9%	0.7%	0.7%	0.0%	0.0%	0.0%	0.0%
Retained earnings	55.2%	48.6%	41.0%	42.4%	10.9%	1.8%	9.7%	7.4%
Accumulated other comprehensive income	0.6%	0.8%	1.0%	0.9%	78.2%	46.5%	(11.4%)	32.3%
Total Shareholders' Equity	**59.5%**	**50.3%**	**42.7%**	**43.9%**	**6.6%**	**2.5%**	**9.1%**	**6.0%**
Total Liabilities and Shareholders' Equity	**100.0%**	**100.0%**	**100.0%**	**100.0%**	**26.0%**	**20.7%**	**6.2%**	**17.3%**

EXHIBIT 1.30

Starbucks Corporation Common-Size and Percentage Change Income Statements (allow for rounding)
(Integrative Case 1.1)

	Common-Size Income Statements				Percentage Change Income Statements			
Fiscal Year End September:	**2005**	**2006**	**2007**	**2008**	**2006**	**2007**	**2008**	**Compound Growth**
Company-operated retail stores	84.7%	84.5%	85.0%	84.5%	22.1%	21.5%	9.7%	17.6%
Specialty:								
Licensing	10.5%	11.1%	10.9%	11.3%	27.9%	19.2%	14.2%	20.3%
Foodservice and other	4.8%	4.4%	4.1%	4.2%	12.8%	12.7%	13.6%	13.0%
Total specialty	15.3%	15.5%	15.0%	15.5%	23.2%	17.4%	14.0%	18.1%
Net Revenues	**100.0%**	**100.0%**	**100.0%**	**100.0%**	**22.3%**	**20.9%**	**10.3%**	**17.7%**
Cost of sales including occupancy costs	(40.9)	(40.8)	(42.5)	(44.7)	22.0%	25.8%	16.2%	21.3%
Gross Profit	**59.1%**	**59.2%**	**57.5%**	**55.3%**	**22.4%**	**17.5%**	**6.0%**	**15.1%**
Store operating expenses	34.0%	34.5%	34.2%	36.1%	24.1%	19.6%	16.5%	20.0%
Other operating expenses	3.0%	3.3%	3.1%	3.2%	31.8%	15.9%	12.2%	19.7%
Depreciation and amortization	5.3%	5.0%	5.0%	5.3%	13.8%	20.6%	17.6%	17.3%
General and administrative expenses	5.7%	6.2%	5.2%	4.4%	32.6%	2.1%	(6.8%)	8.0%
Restructuring charges	0.0%	0.0%	0.0%	2.6%	n.m.	n.m.	n.m.	n.m.
Income from equity investees	1.2%	1.2%	1.2%	1.1%	22.6%	15.0%	5.2%	14.0%
Operating Income	**12.3%**	**11.4%**	**11.2%**	**4.8%**	**14.5%**	**17.9%**	**(52.2%)**	**(13.6%)**
Interest and other income	0.2%	0.3%	0.4%	0.1%	20.8%	96.3%	(77.8%)	(19.3%)
Interest expense	0.0%	(0.1%)	(0.4%)	(0.5%)	546.2%	354.8%	39.8%	245.0%
Income before income taxes	12.5%	11.6%	11.2%	4.4%	13.8%	16.6%	(56.5%)	(16.7%)
Provision for income taxes	4.7%	4.2%	4.1%	1.4%	7.5%	18.2%	(62.5%)	(21.9%)
Net Income	**7.8%**	**7.2%**	**7.1%**	**3.0%**	**14.1%**	**19.2%**	**(53.1%)**	**(13.9%)**

u. From 2005 through 2008, the proportion of total liabilities increased while the proportion of shareholders' equity declined. What are the likely explanations for these changes?

v. How has the revenue mix of Starbucks changed from 2005 to 2008? Relate these changes to Starbucks' business strategy.

w. Net income as a percentage of total revenues increased from 7.8 percent in fiscal 2005 to 3.0 percent in fiscal 2008. Identify the most important reasons for this change.

CASE 1.2

NIKE: SOMEWHERE BETWEEN A SWOOSH AND A SLAM DUNK

Nike's principal business activity involves the design, development, and worldwide marketing of high-quality footwear, apparel, equipment, and accessory products for serious and recreational athletes. Almost 25,000 employees work for the firm. Nike boasts the largest worldwide market share in the athletic-footwear industry and a leading market share in sports and athletic apparel.

This case uses Nike's financial statements and excerpts from its notes to review important concepts underlying the three principal financial statements (balance sheet, income statement, and statement of cash flows) and relationships among them. The case also introduces tools for analyzing financial statements.

Industry Economics

Product Lines

Industry analysts debate whether the athletic footwear and apparel industry is a performance-driven industry or a fashion-driven industry. Proponents of the performance view point to Nike's dominant market position, which results in part from continual innovation in product development. Proponents of the fashion view point to the difficulty of protecting technological improvements from competitor imitation, the large portion of total expenses comprising advertising, the role of sports and other personalities in promoting athletic shoes, and the fact that a high percentage of athletic footwear and apparel consumers use the products for casual wear rather than the intended athletic purposes (such as playing basketball or running).

Growth

There are only modest growth opportunities for footwear and apparel in the United States. Concern exists with respect to volume increases (how many pairs of athletic shoes will consumers tolerate in their closets) and price increases (will consumers continue to pay prices for innovative athletic footwear that is often twice as costly as other footwear).

Athletic footwear companies have diversified their revenue sources in two directions in recent years. One direction involves increased emphasis on international sales. With dress codes becoming more casual in Europe and East Asia and interest in American sports such as basketball becoming more widespread, industry analysts view international markets as the major growth markets during the next several years. Increased emphasis on soccer (European football) in the United States aids companies such as Adidas that have reputations for quality soccer footwear.

The second direction for diversification is sports and athletic apparel. The three leading athletic footwear companies capitalize on their brand name recognition and distribution channels to create a line of sportswear that coordinates with their footwear. Team uniforms and matching apparel for coaching staffs and fans have become a major growth avenue recently. For example, to complement Nike's footwear sales, Nike recently acquired Umbro, a major brand-name line of jerseys, shorts, jackets, and other apparel in the soccer market.

Production

Essentially all athletic footwear and most apparel are produced in factories in Asia, primarily China (40 percent), Indonesia (31 percent), Vietnam, South Korea, Taiwan, and Thailand. The footwear companies do not own any of these manufacturing facilities. They typically hire manufacturing representatives to source and oversee the manufacturing process, helping to ensure quality control and serving as a link between the design and the manufacture of products. The manufacturing process is labor-intensive, with sewing machines used as the primary equipment. Footwear companies typically price their purchases from these factories in U.S. dollars.

Marketing

Athletic footwear and sportswear companies sell their products to consumers through various independent department, specialty, and discount stores. Their sales forces educate retailers on new product innovations, store display design, and similar activities. The market shares of Nike and the other major brand-name producers dominate retailers' shelf space, and slower growth in sales makes it increasingly difficult for the remaining athletic footwear companies to gain market share. The slower growth also has led the major companies to increase significantly their advertising and payments for celebrity endorsements. Many footwear companies, including Nike, have opened their own retail stores, as well as factory outlet stores for discounted sales of excess inventory.

Athletic footwear and sportswear companies have typically used independent distributors to market their products in other countries. With increasing brand recognition and anticipated growth in international sales, these companies have recently acquired an increasing number of their distributors to capture more of the profits generated in other countries and maintain better control of international marketing.

Finance

Compared to other apparel firms, the athletic footwear firms generate higher profit margins and rates of return. These firms use cash flow generated from this superior profitability to finance needed working capital investments (receivables and inventories). Long-term debt tends to be relatively low, reflecting the absence of significant investments in manufacturing facilities.

Nike

Nike targets the serious athlete with performance-driven footwear and athletic wear, as well as the recreational athlete. The firm has steadily expanded the scope of its product portfolio from its primary products of high-quality athletic footwear for running, training, basketball, soccer, and casual wear to encompass related product lines such as sports apparel, bags, equipment, balls, eyewear, timepieces, and other athletic accessories. In addition, Nike has expanded its scope of sports, now offering products for swimming, baseball, cheerleading, football, golf, lacrosse, tennis, volleyball, skateboarding, and other leisure activities. In recent years, the firm has emphasized growth outside the United States. Nike also has grown by acquiring other apparel companies, including Cole Haan (dress and casual footwear),

Converse (athletic and casual footwear and apparel), Hurley (apparel for action sports such as surfing, skateboarding, and snowboarding), and Umbro (footwear, apparel, and equipment for soccer). The firm sums up the company's philosophy and driving force behind its success as follows: "Nike designs, develops, and markets high quality footwear, apparel, equipment and accessory products worldwide. We are the largest seller of athletic footwear and apparel in the world. Our strategy is to achieve long-term revenue growth by creating innovative, 'must-have' products; building deep, personal consumer connections with our brands; and delivering compelling retail presentation and experiences."

To maintain its technological edge, Nike engages in extensive research at its research facilities in Beaverton, Oregon. It continually alters its product line to introduce new footwear, apparel, equipment, and evolutionary improvements in existing products.

Nike maintains a reputation for timely delivery of footwear products to its customers, primarily as a result of its "Futures" ordering program. Under this program, retailers book orders five to six months in advance. Nike guarantees delivery of the order within a set time period at the agreed price at the time of ordering. Approximately 89 percent of the U.S. footwear orders received by Nike during 2009 came though its Futures program. This program allows the company to improve production scheduling, thereby reducing inventory risk. However, the program locks in selling prices and increases Nike's risk of increased raw materials and labor costs.

Independent contractors manufacture virtually all of Nike's products. Nike sources all of its footwear and approximately 95 percent of its apparel from other countries.

The following exhibits present information for Nike:

Exhibit 1.31: Consolidated balance sheets for 2007, 2008, and 2009
Exhibit 1.32: Consolidated income statements for 2007, 2008, and 2009
Exhibit 1.33: Consolidated statements of cash flows 2007, 2008, and 2009
Exhibit 1.34: Excerpts from the notes to Nike's financial statements
Exhibit 1.35: Common-size and percentage change income statements
Exhibit 1.36: Common-size and percentage change balance sheets

Required

Study the financial statements and notes for Nike and respond to the following questions.

Income Statement

a. Identify the time at which Nike recognizes revenues. Does this timing of revenue recognition seem appropriate? Explain.

b. Identify the cost-flow assumption(s) that Nike uses to measure cost of goods sold. Does Nike's choice of cost-flow assumption(s) seem appropriate? Explain.

c. Nike reports property, plant, and equipment on its balance sheet and discloses the amount of depreciation for each year in its statement of cash flows. Why doesn't depreciation expense appear among its expenses on the income statement?

d. Identify the portion of Nike's income tax expense of $469.8 million for 2009 that is currently payable to governmental entities and the portion that is deferred to future years. Why is the amount currently payable to governmental entities in 2009 greater than the income tax expense?

Balance Sheet

e. Why do accounts receivable appear net of allowance for doubtful accounts? Identify the events or transactions that cause the allowance account to increase or decrease.

f. Identify the depreciation method(s) that Nike uses for its buildings and equipment. Does Nike's choice of depreciation method(s) seem appropriate?

EXHIBIT 1.31

Consolidated Balance Sheet for Nike
(amounts in millions)
(Case 1.2)

As of Fiscal Year-End May 31	2007	2008	2009
ASSETS			
Current Assets			
Cash and equivalents	$ 1,856.7	$ 2,133.9	$ 2,291.1
Short-term investments	990.3	642.2	1,164.0
Accounts receivable	2,494.7	2,795.3	2,883.9
Inventories	2,121.9	2,438.4	2,357.0
Prepaid expenses and other assets	393.2	602.3	765.6
Deferred income taxes, net	219.7	227.2	272.4
Total Current Assets	$ 8,076.5	$ 8,839.3	$ 9,734.0
Property and equipment, gross	3,619.1	4,103.0	4,255.7
Accumulated depreciation	(1,940.8)	(2,211.9)	(2,298.0)
Property and equipment, net	$ 1,678.3	$ 1,891.1	$ 1,957.7
Identifiable intangible assets	409.9	743.1	467.4
Goodwill	130.8	448.8	193.5
Deferred income taxes and other assets	392.8	520.4	897.0
Total Assets	$10,688.3	$12,442.7	$13,249.6
LIABILITIES AND STOCKHOLDERS' EQUITY			
Current Liabilities			
Current portion of long-term debt	$ 30.5	$ 6.3	$ 32.0
Notes payable	100.8	177.7	342.9
Accounts payable	1,040.3	1,287.6	1,031.9
Accrued liabilities	1,303.4	1,761.9	1,783.9
Income taxes payable	109.0	88.0	86.3
Total Current Liabilities	$ 2,584.0	$ 3,321.5	$ 3,277.0
Long-term debt	409.9	441.1	437.2
Deferred taxes and other long-term liabilities	668.7	854.5	842.0
Total Liabilities	$ 3,662.6	$ 4,617.1	$ 4,556.2
Redeemable preferred stock	$ 0.3	$ 0.3	$ 0.3
Common Shareholders' Equity			
Common stock	2.8	2.8	2.8
Capital in excess of stated value	1,960.0	2,497.8	2,871.4
Retained earnings	4,885.2	5,073.3	5,451.4
Accumulated other comprehensive income	177.4	251.4	367.5
Total Common Shareholders' Equity	$ 7,025.4	$ 7,825.3	$ 8,693.1
Total Liabilities and Shareholders' Equity	$10,688.3	$12,442.7	$13,249.6

EXHIBIT 1.32

Consolidated Income Statement for Nike
(amounts in millions except per share figures)
(Case 1.2)

Fiscal Years Ended May 31:	2007	2008	2009
Revenues	$16,325.9	$ 18,627.0	$ 19,176.1
Cost of sales	(9,165.4)	(10,239.6)	(10,571.7)
Gross Profit	$ 7,160.5	$ 8,387.4	$ 8,604.4
Selling and administrative expenses	(5,028.7)	(5,953.7)	(6,149.6)
Restructuring charges	—	—	(195.0)
Goodwill impairment	—	—	(199.3)
Intangible and other asset impairment	—	—	(202.0)
Other income (expenses)	0.9	(7.9)	88.5
Operating Income	$ 2,132.7	$ 2,425.8	$ 1,947.0
Interest and other income	116.9	115.8	49.7
Interest expense	(49.7)	(38.7)	(40.2)
Income before income taxes	$ 2,199.9	$ 2,502.9	$ 1,956.5
Provision for income taxes	(708.4)	(619.5)	(469.8)
Net Income	$ 1,491.5	$ 1,883.4	$ 1,486.7
Net income per share			
Basic	$ 2.96	$ 3.80	$ 3.07
Diluted	$ 2.93	$ 3.74	$ 3.03

g. Nike includes identifiable intangible assets on its balance sheet as an asset. Does this account include the value of the Nike name and Nike's "swoosh" trademark? Explain.

h. Nike includes deferred income taxes among current assets, noncurrent assets, and noncurrent liabilities. Under what circumstances will deferred income taxes give rise to an asset? To a liability?

i. Nike reports accumulated other comprehensive income of $367.5 million at the end of 2009 and $251.4 million at the end of 2008, implying that other comprehensive income items amounted to $116.1 million during 2009. Why is this "income" reported as part of shareholders' equity and not part of net income in the income statement?

Statement of Cash Flows

j. Why does the amount of net income differ from the amount of cash flow from operations?

k. Why does Nike add depreciation expense back to net income when calculating cash flow from operations?

l. Why does Nike subtract deferred income taxes from net income when calculating cash flow from operations for 2009?

m. Why does Nike subtract increases in accounts receivable to net income when calculating cash flow from operations for 2009?

EXHIBIT 1.33

Consolidated Statement of Cash Flows for Nike
(amounts in millions)
(Case 1.2)

Fiscal Years Ended May 31:	2007	2008	2009
OPERATING ACTIVITIES:			
Net income	$ 1,491.5	$ 1,883.4	$1,486.7
Depreciation	269.7	303.6	335.0
Deferred income taxes, net	34.1	(300.6)	(294.1)
Stock-based compensation	147.7	141.0	170.6
Impairments of goodwill, intangibles and other assets	—	—	401.3
Gain on divestiture	—	(60.6)	—
Amortization and other	0.5	17.9	48.3
Changes in operating assets and liabilities:			
Increase in accounts receivable	(39.6)	(118.3)	(238.0)
Decrease (increase) in inventories	(49.5)	(249.8)	32.2
Decrease (increase) in prepaid expenses	(60.8)	(11.2)	14.1
(Decrease) increase in payables and accrued liabilities	85.1	330.9	(220.0)
Cash Provided by Operations	$ 1,878.7	$ 1,936.3	$1,736.1
INVESTING ACTIVITIES:			
Purchases, sales, maturities of investment securities	$ 382.4	$ 380.4	$ (518.7)
Net additions to property, plant, and equipment	(285.2)	(447.3)	(423.7)
Acquisition of subsidiary, net of cash acquired	—	(571.1)	—
Proceeds from divestiture	—	246.0	—
Other investing activities	(4.3)	(97.8)	144.3
Cash Used in (Provided by) Investing Activities	$ 92.9	$ (489.8)	$ (798.1)
FINANCING ACTIVITIES:			
Proceeds from notes payable	$ 52.6	$ 63.7	$ 177.1
Net (payments on) proceeds from long-term debt	(213.9)	(35.2)	(6.8)
Proceeds from exercise of stock options	322.9	343.3	186.6
Excess tax benefit from exercise of stock options	55.8	63.0	25.1
Repurchases of common equity shares	(985.2)	(1,248.0)	(649.2)
Dividends—common and preferred	(343.7)	(412.9)	(466.7)
Cash Used by Financing Activities	$(1,111.5)	$(1,226.1)	$ (733.9)
Effects of exchange rate changes on cash	$ 42.4	$ 56.8	$ (46.9)
Net Change in Cash and Cash Equivalents	$ 902.5	$ 277.2	$ 157.2
Beginning Cash and Cash Equivalents	954.2	1,856.7	2,133.9
Ending Cash and Cash Equivalents	$ 1,856.7	$ 2,133.9	$2,291.1

EXHIBIT 1.34

Excerpts from Notes to Consolidated Financial Statements for Nike
(amounts in millions)
(Case 1.2)

Summary of Significant Accounting Policies

Recognition of Revenues: Nike recognizes wholesale revenues when the risks and rewards of ownership have passed to the customer, based on the terms of sale. This occurs upon shipment or upon receipt by the customer depending on the country of the sale and the agreement with the customer. Nike recognizes revenue at time of retail sales to its customers. Provisions for sales discounts and returns are made at the time of sale.

Allowance for Uncollectible Accounts Receivable: Accounts receivable consists principally of amounts receivable from customers. Nike makes ongoing estimates relating to the collectability of our accounts receivable and maintains an allowance for estimated losses resulting from the inability of our customers to make required payments. The allowance for uncollectible accounts receivable was $110.8 million and $78.4 million at May 31, 2009 and 2008, respectively.

Inventory Valuation: Inventories appear at lower of cost or market. Nike determines cost using the first-in, first-out (FIFO) method.

Property, Plant, and Equipment and Depreciation: Property, plant, and equipment are recorded at acquisition cost. Nike computes depreciation using the straight-line method. Estimated useful lives are over 2 to 40 years for buildings and leasehold improvements; over 2 to 15 years for machinery and equipment; and over 3 to 10 years for computer software.

Identifiable Intangible Assets and Goodwill: This account represents the excess of the purchase price of acquired businesses over the market values of identifiable net assets, net of amortization to date on assets with limited lives.

Foreign Currency Translation: Adjustments resulting from translating foreign functional currency financial statements into U.S. dollars and gains and losses from derivatives that Nike uses to hedge changes in exchange rate are included in accumulated other comprehensive income.

Income Taxes: Nike provides deferred income taxes for temporary differences between income before taxes for financial reporting and tax reporting. Income tax expense includes the following:

	2007	2008	2009
Currently Payable	$674.1	$920.1	$763.9
Deferred	34.3	(300.6)	(294.1)
Income Tax Expense	$708.4	$619.5	$469.8

Stock Repurchases: Nike repurchases outstanding shares of its common stock each year and retires them. Any difference between the price paid and the book value of the shares appears as an adjustment of retained earnings.

n. Why does Nike adjust net income by subtracting increases in inventory and adding decreases in inventory when calculating cash flow from operations?

o. When calculating cash flow from operations, why does Nike adjust net income by adding increases and subtracting decreases in accounts payable and other current liabilities?

p. Nike recognized a gain from the divestiture of the subsidiary for the Bauer line of hockey apparel and equipment in 2008. Why does Nike subtract the gain on the

EXHIBIT 1.35

Common-Size and Percentage Change Income Statements for Nike (Case 1.2)

	Common-Size Income Statements			Percentage Change Income Statements		
Fiscal Years Ended May 31:	**2007**	**2008**	**2009**	**2008**	**2009**	**Compound Growth**
Revenues	100.0%	100.0%	100.0%	14.1%	2.9%	8.4%
Cost of sales	(56.1%)	(55.0%)	(55.1%)	11.7%	3.2%	7.4%
Gross Profit	43.9%	45.0%	44.9%	17.1%	2.6%	9.6%
Selling and administrative expenses	(30.8%)	(32.0%)	(32.1%)	18.4%	3.3%	10.6%
Restructuring charges	0.0%	0.0%	(1.0%)	n.m.	n.m.	n.m.
Goodwill impairment	0.0%	0.0%	(1.0%)	n.m.	n.m.	n.m.
Intangible and other asset impairment	0.0%	0.0%	(1.1%)	n.m.	n.m.	n.m.
Other income (expenses)	0.0%	0.0%	0.5%	n.m.	n.m.	n.m.
Operating Income	13.1%	13.0%	10.2%	13.7%	(19.7%)	(4.5%)
Interest and other income	0.7%	0.6%	0.3%	(0.9%)	(57.1%)	(34.8%)
Interest expense	(0.3%)	(0.2%)	(0.2%)	(22.1%)	3.9%	(10.1%)
Income before income taxes	13.5%	13.4%	10.3%	13.8%	(21.8%)	(5.7%)
Provision for income taxes	(4.4%)	(3.3%)	(2.5%)	(12.5%)	(24.2%)	(18.6%)
Net Income	9.1%	10.1%	7.8%	26.3%	(21.1%)	(0.2%)

EXHIBIT 1.36

Common-Size and Percentage Change Balance Sheets for Nike
(Case 1.2)

	Common-Size Balance Sheets			Percentage Change Balance Sheets		
As of Fiscal Year End May 31	**2007**	**2008**	**2009**	**2008**	**2009**	**Compound Growth**
ASSETS						
Current Assets						
Cash and equivalents	17.4%	17.1%	17.3%	14.9%	7.4%	11.1%
Short-term investments	9.3%	5.2%	8.8%	(35.2%)	81.3%	8.4%
Accounts receivable	23.3%	22.5%	21.8%	12.0%	3.2%	7.5%
Inventories	19.9%	19.6%	17.8%	14.9%	(3.3%)	5.4%
Prepaid expenses and other assets	3.7%	4.8%	5.8%	53.2%	27.1%	39.5%
Deferred income taxes, net	2.0%	1.8%	2.0%	3.4%	19.9%	11.3%
Total Current Assets	75.6%	71.0%	73.5%	9.4%	10.1%	9.8%
Property and equipment, gross	33.9%	33.0%	32.1%	13.4%	3.7%	8.4%
Accumulated depreciation	(18.2%)	(17.8%)	(17.3%)	14.0%	3.9%	8.8%
Property and equipment, net	15.7%	15.2%	14.8%	12.7%	3.5%	8.0%
Identifiable intangible assets	3.8%	6.0%	3.5%	81.3%	(37.1%)	6.8%
Goodwill	1.2%	3.6%	1.4%	243.1%	(56.9%)	21.6%
Deferred income taxes and other assets	3.7%	4.2%	6.8%	32.5%	72.4%	51.1%
Total Assets	100.0%	100.0%	100.0%	16.4%	6.5%	11.3%

(*Continued*)

EXHIBIT 1.36 (Continued)

	Common-Size Balance Sheets			Percentage Change Balance Sheets		
As of Fiscal Year End May 31	**2007**	**2008**	**2009**	**2008**	**2009**	**Compound Growth**
LIABILITIES AND STOCKHOLDERS' EQUITY						
Current Liabilities						
Current portion of long-term debt	0.3%	0.1%	0.2%	(79.3%)	407.9%	2.4%
Notes payable	1.0%	1.4%	2.6%	76.3%	93.0%	84.4%
Accounts payable	9.7%	10.3%	7.8%	23.8%	(19.9%)	(0.4%)
Accrued liabilities	12.2%	14.2%	13.4%	35.2%	1.2%	17.0%
Income taxes payable	1.0%	0.7%	0.7%	(19.3%)	(1.9%)	(11.0%)
Total Current Liabilities	24.2%	26.7%	24.7%	28.5%	(1.3%)	12.6%
Long-term debt	3.8%	3.5%	3.3%	7.6%	(0.9%)	3.3%
Deferred taxes and other long-term liabilities	6.3%	6.9%	6.4%	27.8%	(1.5%)	12.2%
Total Liabilities	34.3%	37.1%	34.4%	26.1%	(1.3%)	11.5%
Redeemable preferred stock	0.0%	0.0%	0.0%	0.0%	0.0%	0.0%
Common Shareholders' Equity						
Common stock	0.0%	0.0%	0.0%	0.0%	0.0%	0.0%
Capital in excess of stated value	18.3%	20.1%	21.7%	27.4%	15.0%	21.0%
Retained earnings	45.7%	40.8%	41.1%	3.9%	7.5%	5.6%
Accumulated other comprehensive income	1.7%	2.0%	2.8%	41.7%	46.2%	43.9%
Total Common Shareholders' Equity	65.7%	62.9%	65.6%	11.4%	11.1%	11.2%
Total Liabilities and Shareholders' Equity	100.0%	100.0%	100.0%	16.4%	6.5%	11.3%

divestiture from the operating activities? Why does Nike include the proceeds from the divestiture as an investing activity?

q. Given that notes payable appear on the balance sheet as a current liability, why does Nike include increases in this liability as a financing activity rather than as an operating activity?

Relations between Financial Statement Items

r. Compute the amount of cash collected from customers during 2009.

s. Compute the amount of cash payments made to suppliers of merchandise during 2009.

t. Prepare an analysis that accounts for the change in the property, plant, and equipment account and the accumulated depreciation account during 2009. You will have to plug certain amounts if Nike does not disclose them.

u. Identify the reasons for the change in retained earnings during 2009.

Interpreting Financial Statement Relationships

v. Exhibit 1.35 presents common-size and percentage change income statements for Nike for 2007, 2008, and 2009. What are the likely reasons for the higher net income/sales revenue percentages for Nike between 2007 and 2008? What are the likely reasons for the lower net income/sales revenue percentages for Nike between 2008 and 2009?

w. What are the likely reasons for the decrease in the cost of goods sold to sales percentages between 2007 and 2009?

x. What are the likely reasons for the increase in the selling and administrative expenses to sales percentages between 2007 and 2009?

y. Exhibit 1.36 presents common-size and percentage change balance sheets for Nike at the end of 2007, 2008, and 2009. What is the likely explanation for the relatively small percentages for property, plant, and equipment?

z. What is the likely explanation for the relatively small percentages for notes payable and long-term debt?

aa. What is the likely explanation for the small decreases in property, plant, and equipment for Nike for 2008 and 2009?

bb. Refer to the statement of cash flows for Nike in Exhibit 1.33. Cash flow from operations exceeded net income during all three years. Why?

cc. How has Nike primarily financed its acquisitions of property, plant, and equipment during the three years?

dd. What are the likely reasons for the repurchases of common stock during the three years?

ee. The dividends paid by Nike increased each year ($343.7 million in 2007, $412.9 million in 2008, and $466.7 million in 2009). Given that Nike repurchased its stock each year, what is the likely explanation for the increasing amount of dividends?

Chapter 2

Asset and Liability Valuation and Income Recognition

Learning Objectives

1. **Understand that U.S. GAAP and IFRS financial statements rely on a mixed attribute accounting model that measures different assets and liabilities using a combination of various historical and current values.**
2. **Understand how changes in asset and liability valuations on the balance sheet impact the measurement of net income on the income statement.**
3. **Obtain an overview of the pervasive importance of income tax effects on reported financial statements and appreciate the use of deferred tax assets and liabilities to reconcile financial reporting with tax reporting.**
4. **Apply an analytical framework for mapping the effects of various business events and transactions on the balance sheet and the income statement.**

Chapter 1 provided a broad overview of financial statement analysis, introducing the six-step framework for financial statement analysis used throughout this text. The chapter also described tools used to analyze industry economics and firm strategies and the effects of economic and strategic factors on profitability and risk. In addition, Chapter 1 described the purpose and content of the three principal financial statements, some tools for analyzing them, and links between financial statement information and valuation. The remainder of the text develops all of these ideas more completely and provides tools for each step of the framework.

To lay the groundwork for many of the tools used for the effective analysis of financial statements, we must first understand fundamental elements of financial statements, such as how to identify transactions that need to be reflected in the financial statements, how to measure them, and how their recognition is subsequently accounted for in the financial statements. To effectively analyze financial statements, you must clearly understand how they are prepared and what economic events and transactions they represent. To provide this understanding and set a solid foundation to develop financial statement analysis skills, this chapter provides a review of basic financial accounting concepts using various examples of specific transactions. The chapter also develops a powerful analytical framework for the effects of various transactions and events on balance sheets and income statements.

You might legitimately wonder whether it is necessary to understand individual transactions if the primary concern is to learn how to analyze financial statements as a whole. After all, firms engage in millions of transactions during the year. The reasons for the need to understand how specific events and transactions affect the financial statements are twofold.

First, to be able to make appropriate interpretations about a firm's profitability and risk, you must understand the effects of numerous similar, repetitive transactions that balance sheet and income statement amounts represent. Second, given the increased complexity of many nonrecurring transactions in recent years, effective financial statement analysis requires an ability to deduce how discrete events impact each of the financial statements.

As noted in Chapter 1, the primary financial statements include the balance sheet and income statement, with the statement of cash flows providing a link between the information in these two statements. This chapter will discuss the building blocks underlying the balance sheet and income statement, and the next chapter will take up a joint analysis of the income statement and statement of cash flows. Of course, it is difficult to discuss a line item on one financial statement without referencing another line item or another financial statement. For example, any full discussion of accounts receivable necessarily includes a discussion of recognizing the revenues that give rise to the accounts receivable and collecting the cash flows that derive from the receivables. The approach in this chapter is to discuss both, but the order follows the natural sequence of transactions that a firm experiences.

To provide a foundation for analysis and valuation discussed later in the text, this chapter highlights (1) the principles that underlie the measurement and reporting of assets, liabilities, and income; (2) the pervasive role of income taxes; and (3) analysis of the impact of business events and transactions on each of the financial statements. Note that the chapter does not specifically focus on the statement of cash flows. Because this statement reconciles the balance sheet and income statement under accrual accounting, we defer its discussion until the next chapter, where we incorporate the building blocks from this chapter.

INTRODUCTION TO THE MIXED ATTRIBUTE ACCOUNTING MODEL

Consider the fundamental accounting identity:

$$\text{Assets} = \text{Liabilities} + \text{Shareholders' Equity}$$

At the instant a firm is formed and receives financing (typically through equity investment by owners or shareholders, but perhaps through debt financing from banks), the balance sheet of a company is simple and the valuation of the assets and liabilities is straightforward. For example, suppose an entrepreneur starts a consulting company by borrowing $1,000,000 from a bank. Initially, the value of the cash assets would be $1,000,000, equal to the entrepreneur's liability to the bank. However, valuing the company's assets and the liability gets less clear (but becomes more interesting) as the company begins deploying that cash, time progresses, and operating activities commence. Following are a number of simple but challenging examples that might arise (which you will learn to account for and analyze throughout this chapter and the remainder of this text):

1. The entrepreneur purchases an automobile for use in the business. Is the value of the automobile what the entrepreneur paid for it or what the entrepreneur could sell it for in the want ads? If the company also had to pay registration and certain legal fees as part of the acquisition of the automobile, are those fees a part of the value of the automobile?
2. Should the company have to periodically reduce the value of the automobile to reflect the wear and tear and associated decline in the value? If so, how should the company compute the amount of the decline in value each period?

3. If the company acquires a building in which the entrepreneur will work, should the company periodically adjust the value of the building, as it does with the automobile? Unlike an automobile that clearly declines in value over time, the value of a building might increase. If so, should the amount at which the company values the building on the balance sheet be increased? Absent a sale of the building, how would someone estimate the value of the building?
4. The entrepreneur performs consulting services for ten clients and bills each client $5,000. The company now has an asset reflecting the amount due from each client, totaling $50,000. However, suppose one of the clients is likely to end up not being able to pay the entire bill. Should the company adjust the value of the $50,000 asset to reflect this fact? If so, how much should the value of the asset be adjusted? Is the reason for reflecting this amount in the financial statements to value the accounts receivable on the balance sheet appropriately or is it to ensure that a cost of doing business (that is, selling to people who do not pay) is properly reflected in the income statement or is it both?
5. Suppose the entrepreneur finds bill collecting stressful. He or she knows of companies that specialize in the collection of bills and that agree to pay for these assets, but at an amount less than the total $50,000 due. Should the company reduce the value of the $50,000 assets for accounts receivable from clients to the amount the collection company would pay to assume collection of the accounts receivable?
6. When should the company record the consulting revenues—when it performs the work, when it bills the clients, or when the clients pay? Suppose that as part of the consulting services, the entrepreneur promises to be available for subsequent questions that might (but are unlikely to) arise in the months subsequent to the consulting engagement. Would this change when the company should record the revenues from the clients?
7. The entrepreneur invests some of the remaining cash from the bank loan into a mutual fund. After several months, the value of the mutual fund investment has increased. Should the company adjust the value of this investment on the balance sheet? What should the company do if the investment falls back to the initial amount invested? What if the value falls below the initial amount invested? Should the company record each of these adjustments to the balance sheet as a gain or a loss on the income statement?
8. The bank loan is subject to a charge for interest. Knowing that, in general, changes in interest rates affect the value of financial assets and liabilities, does the value of the company's liability for the bank loan change if interest rates subsequently change? If so, should the company reflect this change in value on its balance sheet? Its income statement?

Although these hypothetical questions are prompted by an example of a company with limited assets and liabilities, the questions raise a variety of ways to measure this simple company's assets and liabilities. Clearly, the valuation of assets and liabilities becomes increasingly complex when real companies engage in numerous and diverse activities. One way to approach this complexity is to apply a standardized framework to analyze the impact of events and transactions on the financial statements; we present this framework at the end of this chapter. Prior to that, the chapter outlines the many different approaches that companies use to value assets and liabilities in financial statements under U.S. GAAP and IFRS, which reflect the use of a *mixed attribute accounting model*.

An important thing to keep in mind is that whether you are concerned with the valuation of assets and liabilities or in the income effects of events, it is difficult to view them separately. Double-entry bookkeeping views transactions as having two equal sides (what is given and what is gotten; resources equal claims on resources), which requires that at least two accounts be affected when transactions and events occur that should be reflected in the financial statements.[1] For example, the incorporation of the hypothetical business above led to an increase in an asset (what is gotten; the resource: cash) and an increase in a liability (what is given; the claim on the resource: the bank loan and promise to repay). Thus, this event affected an asset and a liability. When the entrepreneur performed consulting services and the clients were billed, double-entry bookkeeping affected an asset (accounts receivable increased) and a revenue (consulting revenues increased). Numerous other combinations are common as well, and Exhibit 2.1 provides additional examples. After a

EXHIBIT 2.1

Examples of Combined Financial Statement Impacts of Various Events and Transactions

Combined Financial Statement Impacts[a, b]	**Examples**
Asset and Asset	A customer pays an account receivable. *Cash increases, Accounts Receivable decreases*
Asset and Liability	A customer prepays for services. *Cash increases, Unearned Revenue increases*
Liability and Liability	A company refinances a short-term loan. *Short-Term Debt decreases, Long-Term Debt increases*
Asset and Revenue	A sale is made. *Accounts Receivable increases, Revenue increases*
Asset and Expense	Current month equipment leases are paid. *Cash decreases, Rent Expense increases*
Liability and Revenue	Service is provided to a customer who prepaid. *Unearned Revenue decreases, Revenue increases*
Liability and Expense	Salaries accrued but not paid at month end are recorded. *Salaries Payable increases, Salaries Expense increases*

[a]No combinations are listed for "Revenue and Revenue," "Expense and Expense," and "Revenue and Expense," as any event that affects only Revenues and/or Expenses is most likely a reclassification rather than a primitive economic event. Also note that these examples do not include a separate treatment of Shareholders' Equity. Other Comprehensive Income, which is an important account that affects Shareholders' Equity, will be discussed later in the chapter.

[b]It is helpful to recall the definitions of revenues and expenses to better understand the links among income statement and balance sheet items in this exhibit. Revenues are defined as "inflows or other enhancements of assets of an entity or settlements of its liabilities (or a combination of both) from delivering or producing goods, rendering services, or other activities that constitute the entity's ongoing major or central operations." Similarly, expenses are defined as "outflows or other using up of assets or incurrences of liabilities (or a combination of both) from delivering or producing goods, rendering services, or carrying out other activities that constitute the entity's ongoing major or central operations." *Statement of Financial Accounting Concepts No. 6,* "Elements of Financial Statements."

[1]The "double" in double-entry bookkeeping refers to the fact that there must be at least one debit and one credit.

discussion of asset and liability valuation, the chapter will turn to income recognition. Keep in mind the discussion from Chapter 1 regarding the important difference between *net* income and *comprehensive* income; comprehensive income exists to accommodate various fair value adjustments.

The intent of the accounting system is to provide relevant information about both the balance sheet and the income statement, but emphasizing the usefulness of one sometimes affects the usefulness of the other. The two statements are obviously complementary as the balance sheet presents information *as of* a point in time, whereas the income statement presents information about flows *between* two points in time. Further, the preparation of the balance sheet and income statement is simultaneous, but one has to measure either the balance sheet first, and then indirectly derive the income statement line items, or vice versa. Thus, measurement of different accounts is affected by what perspective the preparer has regarding which financial statement should receive more measurement emphasis. As a result, there are two possible perspectives with regard to the relevance of financial statements for valuation. The first perspective is that the balance sheet should be prepared first, and the income statement then reflects changes in the balance sheet amounts from period to period. The second perspective is that the income statement should be prepared first, and the balance sheet reflects accounting accruals necessary to recognize revenues and expenses. There is an inherent tension between the two perspectives.

To illustrate this tension, consider the financial reporting of fixed assets and depreciation expense. A balance sheet emphasis would require an accountant to estimate the value of fixed assets as of the end of each reporting period and would allow for adjustments to the valuation of fixed assets in both down and up directions. On the other hand, an emphasis on the income statement would require the accountant to "match" the amount of the fixed asset consumed to generate revenues in a reporting period. Thus, the periodic recording of depreciation fits the income statement perspective, as depreciation expense is an estimate of the fixed assets consumed to generate revenues. With a balance sheet emphasis, depreciation expense would not be recognized; instead, the firm would recognize a gain or loss for the change in the fair value of the fixed assets during a period.

Academic research has examined the relative usefulness of the balance sheet and income statement to explain common stock prices. The evidence supports the notion that during the past 20 years, financial statements appear to have become more in line with the balance sheet emphasis than the income statement emphasis. Based on data from a study by Collins, Maydew, and Weiss (1997), Exhibit 2.2 shows the incremental explanatory power of earnings (income statement emphasis) and book value of equity (balance sheet emphasis) to explain common stock prices over four decades. Exhibit 2.2 plots the incremental explanatory power of book value relative to earnings, and earnings relative to book values. A decreasing trend line suggests a decline in the ability of that measure to explain security prices relative to the other. Consistent with the claims of many observers, the incremental explanatory power of book values increased relative to earnings over that period. Moreover, the study documented that the overall ability of both book value and earnings has increased over this four-decade period, consistent with increasing usefulness of financial statements.[2]

[2]Observers of accounting regulators (for example, the FASB and IASB) have argued that the recent trend in accounting rules reflects gravitation away from an income statement emphasis to a balance sheet emphasis.

EXHIBIT 2.2

Relative Explanatory Power of Book Value and Net Income to Explain Market Value from 1953–1993

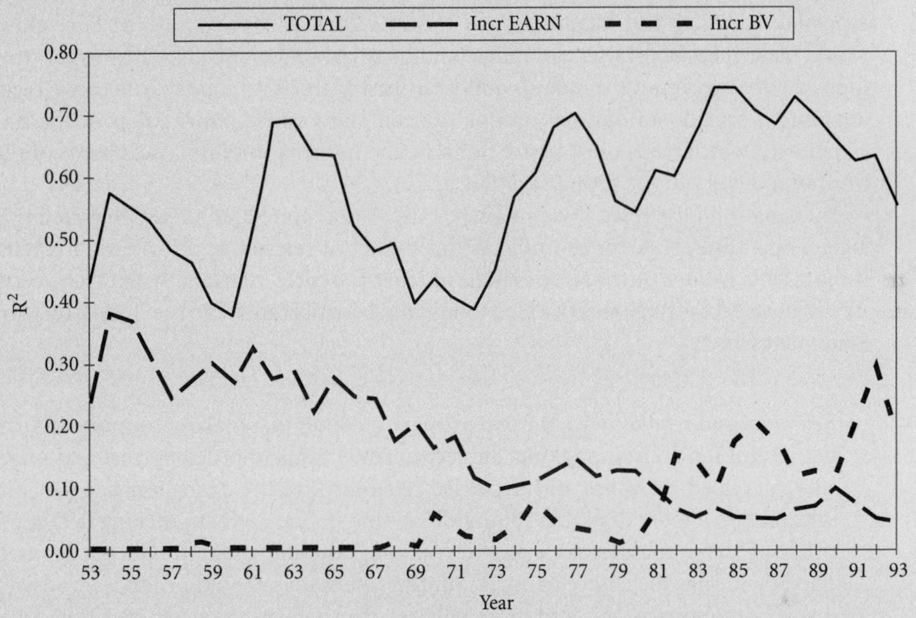

Source: Daniel W. Collins, Edward L. Maydew, and Ira S. Weiss, "Changes in the Value-Relevance of Earnings and Book Values over the Past Forty Years," *Journal of Accounting & Economics* (1997), pp. 39–67. Reprinted with permission from Elsevier.

ASSET AND LIABILITY VALUATION

As described in Chapter 1, the balance sheet reports the assets of a firm and the claims on those assets by creditors (liabilities) and owners (shareholders' equity) at a moment in time. A useful way to think about assets, liabilities, and shareholders' equity is that liabilities and shareholders' equity represent the capital contributed by suppliers, lending institutions, and shareholders so that the company can acquire operating assets to use in profit-generating activities. Within this framework, Chapter 6 discusses accounting for the sources of capital, Chapter 7 discusses accounting for the investment of that capital, and Chapter 8 discusses accounting for the operations using those investments. Chapter 9 discusses issues of accounting quality, covering assets, liabilities, and reported profitability. The concern in this section is the valuation of assets and liabilities that are recognized in the financial statements, and the focus is on a conceptual understanding of how such assets and liabilities should be valued and reported in the financial statements. Do not become anxious about mastering procedures for analyzing specific assets or liabilities; they are addressed in these subsequent chapters.

Assets provide economic benefits to a firm in the future and liabilities require firms to sacrifice economic resources in the future. Although assets and liabilities clearly have a future orientation, balance sheet accounting for assets and liabilities under U.S. GAAP and IFRS follows a *mixed attribute accounting model.* What this means is that some assets are reported based on original cost, some are based on current fair values, and others are based on a hybrid approach; for liabilities, some are measured at the initial amount of the incurred liability, whereas others are measured at the current value of the liability based on prevailing interest rates and other factors.

An obvious question is why aren't all assets and liabilities recorded similarly? Wouldn't that greatly simplify financial statement analysis? For example, it might seem obvious that reporting all assets and liabilities at historical values only or at current fair values only would make it easier for users to understand financial statements. The answer for why most high-quality accounting standards follow a mixed attribute model is because regulators attempt to provide an optimal mix of *relevant* and *reliable* information in the financial statements, which helps users better translate the information into assessments of the risk, timing, and amounts of future cash flows.

Information is relevant if it can affect a user's decision based on the reported financial statements; timeliness, for example, is one aspect of relevance. Information is reliable if it represents what it purports to represent (that is, representationally faithful); verifiability is an aspect of reliability. The following is articulated by the FASB in Concepts Statement No. 2:

> *Relevance* and *reliability* are the two primary qualities that make accounting information useful for decision making. Subject to constraints imposed by cost and materiality, increased relevance and increased reliability are the characteristics that make information a more desirable commodity—that is, one useful in making decisions. If either of those qualities is completely missing, the information will not be useful. Though, ideally, the choice of an accounting alternative should produce information that is both more reliable and more relevant, it may be necessary to sacrifice some of one quality for a gain in another.[3]

As a consequence of this balancing act to make the overall financial statements as useful as possible to external users, accounting standards require that some assets and liabilities must be valued based on more reliable information and others must be based on more relevant information.

Therefore, valuations of assets and liabilities reflect various combinations of historical data, current information, and expectations of future outcomes. The astute analyst draws advantage from the information available in the mixed attributes of asset and liability valuation. The remainder of this section provides brief descriptions and numerous examples of the primary valuation alternatives that are most common for balance sheet accounts. This discussion sets the stage for a more detailed understanding of financial statement line items in later chapters.

Historical value is based on the cost of an asset when a firm acquired it or the nominal amount of a liability when a firm initially incurred it. Current value, on the other hand, updates historical value with information about the fair value of an asset and a liability at the date of the current balance sheet. Valuation methods that reflect *historical values* include the following:

- Acquisition cost (assets)
- Adjusted acquisition cost (assets)
- Initial present value (assets and liabilities)

---

[3]Financial Accounting Standards Board, *Statement of Financial Accounting Concepts No. 2*, "Qualitative Characteristics of Accounting Information" (May 1980).

Valuation methods that reflect *current values* or a *combination of historical and current values* include the following:

- Fair value (assets and liabilities), which also includes
  - Current replacement cost (assets)
  - Net realizable value (assets)

Historical Value: Acquisition Cost

The acquisition cost of an asset is the amount paid initially to acquire the asset. Acquisition cost includes all costs required to prepare the asset for its intended use, but does not include costs to operate the asset. At the time assets are obtained, acquisition cost valuations are ideal because they are *relevant* insofar as they measure the amounts that firms actually paid to acquire resources; they are *reliable* in the sense that they are unbiased, objective, and verifiable through invoices, canceled checks, and other documents that provide clear support for the valuation.

Example 1

At a cost of $200,000, In-N-Out Burger acquired a tract of land for a restaurant site. It paid attorneys $7,500 to conduct a title search and to prepare the required legal documents for the purchase, and it paid a state real estate transfer tax of $2,500. The acquisition cost of the land is $210,000 (= $200,000 + $7,500 + $2,500).

Example 2

Mollydooker Wines paid employees $700,000 to oversee the growing of grapes in its vineyards, to harvest the grapes, and to process the grapes into wine. Depreciation on buildings and equipment pertaining to wine production totaled $250,000. Mollydooker incurred insurance, taxes, and other operating costs of $150,000 related to wine production. The acquisition cost of the wine in inventory prior to commencement of aging totaled $1,100,000 (= $700,000 + $250,000 + $150,000). Mollydooker Wines will increase the inventory account in later periods by capitalizing additional costs incurred during the aging process, eventually recording all costs of producing the wine as inventory prior to eventual sale.

One valuation question that often arises concerns the costs to include in the asset amount. Should the acquisition cost of the land in Example 1 include the salaries of In-N-Out Burger personnel engaged in selecting the site? Should the acquisition cost of the wine in Example 2 include interest on funds that Mollydooker borrowed to finance production of the wine? Variation in practice exists, and accounting procedures for material amounts should be present in the financial statement footnote disclosures.

A second valuation question concerns the relevance of acquisition cost valuations to financial statement users. At the time a firm acquires an asset, acquisition cost valuations are timely and objectively measured, so are both *reliable* and *relevant* to financial statement users. As time passes, however, the acquisition cost valuation retains reliability but can lose relevance if the valuation becomes dated and does not reflect current values. Acquisition costs are one explanation for why market-to-book ratios (which equal market value of common equity divided by book value of common shareholders' equity) are typically greater than 1; whereas accountants use acquisition costs, investors and capital market participants can attempt to estimate (with error) fair values of various assets and liabilities as part of the collective price setting of securities prices.

Historical Value: Adjusted Acquisition Cost

For some assets, the service potential is consumed gradually (like machinery that has a limited life) or immediately (like inventory, which provides all of its benefits when it is sold). As the service potential of an asset is consumed, the consumed portion is expensed (that is, the asset is reduced and an expense is increased). For machinery, the expense is depreciation; for inventory, the expense is cost of goods sold. Over the life during which a firm enjoys the benefits of an asset, the firm should either derecognize the asset when its value has been consumed (for example, inventory) or ratably adjust the acquisition cost downward through systematic depreciation or amortization (for example, machinery).

Example 3

JPMorgan Chase, a financial services firm, acquires a computer from IBM for $5 million, expects to use the computer for five years, and then plans to sell it for $1 million. JPMorgan Chase depreciates $4 million over the computer's expected five-year useful life. At the end of the five-year useful life, the remaining $1 million of adjusted acquisition cost reflects the expected sales proceeds, with differences between this and any actual sales proceeds recorded as a gain or loss.

Example 4

American Airlines acquires a regional airline in the midwestern United States for $450 million. American Airlines allocates $150 million of the purchase price to landing rights at various airports. The landing rights expire in five years. American Airlines amortizes the $150 million over the five years of use. Accordingly, the acquisition cost of the landing rights ratably declines $30 million each year, to a final adjusted acquisition cost of zero at the end of five years.

The difficulty of physically observing the consumption of service potential that results from use of an asset makes measuring the amount of depreciation or amortization or the estimate of impairment subjective. To apply adjusted acquisition cost valuations, managers must estimate the expected useful life and salvage value of fixed assets. Furthermore, U.S. GAAP and IFRS permit firms to select from among several time-series patterns for measuring depreciation and amortization expenses (for example, straight line or accelerated patterns). Finally, many economic events are sufficiently firm-specific in nature that there is limited specific accounting guidance, which requires additional judgment by managers.

Like acquisition cost valuations, adjusted acquisition cost valuations involve a trade-off between *reliability* and *relevance.* In Example 3, the valuation of the computer equipment at $1 million at the end of the five-year estimated life is based on a combination of a reliable acquisition cost ($5 million) and a good faith estimate of the portion that eventually will be realized through a sale ($1 million). In Example 4, the acquisition cost of the landing rights is estimated to be a portion ($150 million) of the reliable $450 million total acquisition cost of the regional airline. In both examples, the estimates attempt to provide valuations that are relevant. Even though the estimates are expected to be made in good faith, they are of uncertain amounts and may turn out to be incorrect. Moreover, because of the measurement error inherent in good faith estimates, self-interested managers might intentionally bias such estimates, detracting from reliability. Analysts can minimize such distortions by understanding how estimates are used in asset and liability valuation.

Historical Value: Initial Present Value

Firms use acquisition cost valuations and adjusted acquisition cost valuations for assets that are not characterized by fixed and determinable amounts of future cash flows (that is, nonmonetary assets). For example, inventories; land; buildings; equipment; legal rights to use another entity's technologies, facilities, name, or distribution channels; and goodwill are examples of nonmonetary assets. When the future economic benefits of an asset are sufficiently uncertain, firms use acquisition cost and adjusted acquisition cost as a reliable measure of the asset's value.

Monetary assets and liabilities, on the other hand, represent amounts of cash the firm can expect to receive or pay in the future. Cash, accounts receivable, and notes receivable are monetary assets; accounts, notes, and bonds payable are monetary liabilities. Firms typically value monetary assets and liabilities using present values, although U.S. GAAP and IFRS permit firms to ignore the discounting process for monetary assets and liabilities due within one year. In certain circumstances, firms also might value certain nonmonetary assets (for example, goodwill) at the present value of expected future cash flows.

Selling goods or services on account to customers or lending funds to others creates either an account receivable or a note receivable for the selling or lending firm. Purchasing goods or services on account from a supplier or borrowing funds from others creates a liability (for example, accounts payable, notes payable, and bonds payable). Discounting the expected future cash flows under such arrangements to a present value expresses those cash flows in terms of a current cash-equivalent value. When the monetary asset or liability is first entered in the financial statements, the present value computation (if the cash flows span more than one year) uses interest rates appropriate for the particular financing arrangement at that time.

Example 5

Sun Microsystems sells computer equipment to Petroleo Brasileiro, which requires payments to Sun Microsystems of $250,000 at the end of each of the next five years and pledges the equipment as collateral for the loan. An assessment of the credit standing of Petroleo Brasileiro at the time of the sale and of the value of the collateral suggests that 8 percent is an appropriate interest rate for this loan. The present value of $250,000 per year for five years when discounted at 8 percent is $998,178. Sun Microsystems records a note receivable and Petroleo Brasileiro records a note payable in the amount of $998,178. During the first year, interest on the note of $79,854 (= 0.08 × $998,178) increases the book value of the note and the cash payment of $250,000 reduces the book value of the note to $828,032 (= $998,178 + $79,854 − $250,000). The book value of the note of $828,032 equals the present value of the four remaining annual cash flows of $250,000 when discounted at the historical interest rate of 8 percent.

Example 6

The Home Depot sells a refrigerator to a customer on July 1, permitting the customer to delay payment of the $500 selling price until December 31. An assessment of the customer's credit standing suggests that 6 percent per year is an appropriate interest rate for this extension of credit. The present value of $500, when discounted back for one-half year at 6 percent, is $485.44. A strict application of the present value of cash flows valuation method results in reporting sales revenue of $485.44 on July 1 and interest revenue of $14.56 (= 0.06 × 0.5 × $485.44) for the six-month period from July 1 to December 31. However, as indicated earlier, U.S. GAAP and IFRS permit firms to ignore the discounting process for monetary assets and liabilities due within one year on the grounds that the financial statement effects of discounting or not discounting are not materially different.

Because financing arrangements between sellers and buyers usually specify the timing and amounts of future cash flows, valuing monetary assets and liabilities at the present value of cash flows using historical interest rates is relevant and reasonably reliable. Moreover, for multi-year collection periods, the relevance of the present values (versus nominal values) justifies the extra efforts to discount assets or liabilities to the present value of future cash flows. Some subjectivity may exist in establishing an appropriate interest rate at the time of the transaction. The borrower, for example, might choose to use the interest rate at which it could borrow on similar terms from a bank, whereas the seller might use the interest rate that would discount the cash flows to a present value equal to the cash selling price of the good or service sold. These small differences in interest rates usually do not result in material differences in valuation between the entities involved in the transaction.

Note that laying out the different historical cost-based approaches to assets and liabilities in three distinct categories is somewhat artificial. This is because these categories are neither authoritative nor strictly separable from each other and because practical applications often involve a hybrid of approaches, as the following example highlights.

Example 7

Massey Ferguson sells agricultural machinery to farmers and large agribusiness companies. At the end of the first fiscal quarter, it has $3 billion in receivables. Based on the age of various receivables, historical bad debt experience, and recent economic activity, Massey Ferguson estimates that $150 million will ultimately become uncollectible. The initial present value of the receivables is offset by $150 million to better reflect the adjusted value, which the firm believes is $2.85 billion.

In Example 7, the receivables are monetary assets and the valuation approach for them best fits into the third category of historical valuation based on initial present values. Alternatively, you could make a compelling argument that the initial valuation of receivables simply reflects the acquisition cost of that asset, which is certainly true for receivables expected to be collected within a year or less. Accordingly, recording a valuation allowance that offsets the historical acquisition cost of the receivables is similar to using an adjusted acquisition cost valuation for the receivables. Moreover, you also could view the downward valuation of accounts receivable triggered by the estimate of uncollectible accounts as an attempt to reflect the receivables at their current value (discussed in the next section). The point to take away here is that there are numerous approaches to valuation and the attempt to distinctly categorize approaches is to provide a helpful exposition rather than to define fixed categories. The next section discusses current value approaches, which can sometimes overlap with historical value approaches.

Current Values: Fair Value

Whereas historical value approaches to valuing assets and liabilities provide relevant and reliable information, they may lose relevance as valuations become old and outdated and do not reflect current economic conditions. As a consequence, the FASB and IASB increasingly develop accounting standards that value assets and liabilities using current value approaches, which emphasize relevance while at the same time are sufficiently reliable. Nevertheless, defining fair value has proved difficult to implement. The FASB defines fair value as "the price that would be received to sell an asset or paid to transfer a liability in an orderly transaction between market participants at the measurement date."[4] This definition explicitly characterizes fair value as a measure of "exit price," which is the amount for which

[4]Financial Accounting Standards Board, *Statement of Financial Accounting Standards No. 157,* "Fair Value Measurements" (September 2006). *FASB Codification Topic 820.*

a firm could sell an asset or pay to settle or transfer a liability. The IASB defines fair value slightly differently, as "the amount for which an asset could be exchanged, or a liability settled, between knowledgeable, willing parties in an arm's length transaction."[5] This definition allows for the use of an exit price or an entry price (the amount for which a firm could buy an asset or incur a liability). Differences could arise between entry and exit price approaches, for example, when the market in which a purchase takes place is different from the one in which a sale takes place (such as a securities firm that transacts with retail customers, institutional investors, or other securities firms). In addition to the use of quoted market prices as inputs into current values, accountants sometimes use present value techniques to estimate certain current values (for example, Level 3 assets, discussed below).

Clearly, fair values are of interest to financial statement users, particularly in settings where fair values have diverged greatly from acquisition costs of assets or initial present values of liabilities (for example, financial institutions). Obtaining "the price" at which assets and liabilities can be exchanged can provide extremely reliable and relevant measurements when they are based on observable prices in orderly markets for stocks, bonds, securities, commodities, derivatives, and other items. However, obtaining "the price" can require management estimates when there is no quoted price in an active market for an asset or a liability. Generally, prices are more readily available for financial assets (and commodities) and liabilities than for nonmonetary assets or liabilities.

Even among financial assets and liabilities, however, there is wide variation in the availability of quoted market prices. Accordingly, there is a three-tiered hierarchy within U.S. GAAP and IFRS (specified in SFAS No. 157 and IFRS No. 7) that distinguishes among different sources of fair value estimates.[6] Level 1 inputs for estimating fair values are based on inputs that are readily available via prices for identical assets or liabilities in actively traded markets such as securities exchanges. Level 2 inputs for estimating fair values include quoted prices for similar assets or liabilities in active or inactive markets, other *observable* information such as yield curves and price indexes, and other *observable* data such as market-based correlation estimates. Finally, Level 3 inputs for estimating fair values include a firm's own assumptions about the fair value of an asset or a liability, such as using various data about future cash flows and discount rates to estimate present values. As of 2009, it is estimated that the S&P 500 companies report over $6 trillion of assets under fair value (the vast majority of which are financial assets); of those, approximately 10 percent incorporate Level 3 inputs for fair value estimation.

Fair value approaches to valuation for financial assets and liabilities is becoming commonplace within U.S. GAAP and IFRS. Reporting financial assets and liabilities at fair values also is referred to as "mark-to-market" accounting. Although the relevance of fair values is obvious, given the subjective nature of current value estimation along the continuum of reliability from Level 1 to Level 3 inputs for assets and liabilities, the reliability of such valuations is sometimes questioned. For example, Level 1 inputs are applicable for most assets traded on active exchanges with published market quotes, whereas Level 3 inputs relate primarily to illiquid investments such as mortgaged-backed securities. Recent rules released by the FASB and IASB allow firms to make a one-time election to report certain financial instruments at fair value (with subsequent changes to flow through earnings) and will be

[5]International Accounting Standards Board, *International Accounting Standards No. 39,* "Financial Instruments: Recognition and Measurement" (December 1998). At the time of publication of this text, the IASB was considering a change to the definition of fair value, which matched the exit price notion explicit in the FASB definition.

[6]The International Accounting Standards Board amended IFRS No. 7 to incorporate the Level 1, Level 2, and Level 3 disclosures as well.

[7]Financial Accounting Standards Board, *Statement of Financial Accounting Standards No. 159,* "The Fair Value Option for Financial Assets and Financial Liabilities" (February 2007). *FASB Codification Topic 825;* International Accounting Standards Committee, *International Accounting Standards No. 39,* "Financial Instruments: Recognition and Measurement" (revised June 2005); International Accounting Standards Committee, *International Accounting Standards No. 40,* "Investment Properties" (revised December 2003).

most applicable for financial institutions.[7] Nevertheless, valuations of numerous nonmonetary assets also rely on fair value estimates, either of the asset itself or of the current present value of cash flows expected to be generated by an asset.

Example 8

Smithfield Foods is the world's largest producer of pork. Almost half of Smithfield Foods' inventories are live hogs. There is an actively traded market in hogs and hog futures on the Chicago Mercantile Exchange, which enables a straightforward fair valuation of the live hog portion of inventories (assuming Smithfield intends to sell these hogs in open markets).

Example 9

In Example 5, at the end of the first year, both the note receivable on the books of Sun Microsystems and the note payable on the books of Petroleo Brasileiro are reflected at a book value of $828,032 (which equals the present value of the remaining four payments of $250,000 when discounted at the historical interest rate of 8 percent). Assume that the market interest rate appropriate for this note declines to 6 percent. The present value of these payments at 6 percent is $866,276. Accounting rules could require the firms to revalue the receivables and payables to $866,276 to reflect the change in value caused by the change in the discount rate. Recent accounting rules issued by the FASB and IASB include requirements that certain assets and liabilities be marked to market values, but these are applicable primarily to financial institutions; thus, the nonfinancial firms of Sun Microsystems and Petroleo Brasileiro would not be *required* to adjust the values of the receivable and payable, but under some circumstances could choose to do so.

Example 10

Kimpton Hotels owns numerous boutique hotels throughout North America. It reports these hotels at adjusted acquisition cost. With no actively traded market in individual hotels upon which to determine the fair value of each property, one alternative for determining fair value would require Kimpton Hotels to forecast the net cash flows it anticipates from each hotel in the future and discount them to a present value using current interest rates.

Using the present value of cash flows to value a monetary asset or liability with preset cash flows is relatively reliable. Selecting the appropriate current interest rate to revalue the monetary item each period entails a degree of subjectivity. Valuing nonmonetary assets, such as the hotels of Kimpton Hotels in Example 10, entails considerable subjectivity. Unlike the case for a monetary asset, the cash flows for a nonmonetary asset are not predetermined. Consequently, a current valuation requires forecasts of the timing and amount of the expected cash flows for years into the future. Revaluations of the asset each period reflect changes in expected cash flows, changes in the discount (interest) rate, or both. Thus, the reliability of such estimates can become questionable depending on the method of forecasting cash flows and estimating discount rates.

Current Values: Fair Value Based on Current Replacement Cost

Current replacement cost is the amount a firm would have to pay currently to acquire or produce an asset it now holds. By virtue of the term's reference to an external market, this is special case of applying the fair value approach discussed previously. However, whereas straightforward fair values generally pertain to financial assets and commodities, current replacement cost generally applies to nonmonetary assets. The most common use of current replacement cost is through application of lower of cost or market valuation of inventories. Current replacement cost should reflect normal purchases and sales between unrelated parties, not distressed purchases and sales in which one party holds a major advantage in setting prices. Furthermore, whereas the FASB advocates "exit prices" for fair valuation in general, the concept of current replacement cost references an "entry price."

Example 11

Graybar Electric Company is a distributor of electrical equipment and maintains inventory at various distribution facilities. Graybar holds a large inventory of gas tube surge protectors for use in residential telephone lines (1,000,000 units at a cost of $0.75 each). Due to the rise of low-cost producers and the decreased demand due to decreasing deployment of wired telephone lines, the cost of these protectors has fallen to $0.25 per unit. Thus, Graybar has an unrealized holding loss for this inventory of $500,000 (= 1,000,000 × [$0.75 − $0.25]), so must reduce the value of the gas tube protector inventory from $750,000 to $250,000.[8]

Example 12

Although current replacement cost accounting is most applicable in a lower of cost or market inventory setting (as in Example 11), the principles are also applicable to valuations of other long-lived or intangible assets. In Example 4, American Airlines amortizes the landing rights during the first year for $30 million (= $150 million/5 years), resulting in a book value of $120 million. Assume that a curtailment of air travel results in a decline in the replacement cost of these landing rights. A study of recent sales of landing rights suggests that the current replacement cost of landing rights with a four-year remaining life is $55 million, which would trigger a write-down in the valuation of the landing rights if a replacement cost valuation approach was used.

Current replacement cost valuations generally reflect greater subjectivity than acquisition cost valuations, but they are least subjective and most reliable when based on observable market prices from recent transactions in which similar assets or liabilities have been exchanged in active markets. For example, you could obtain reliable measures of current replacement costs of raw commodities by referencing spot prices in commodities markets. When active markets do not exist, as is often the case for equipment designed specifically for a particular firm's needs, the degree of subjectivity increases. Thus, although replacement cost values are more relevant, subjectivity in estimating them in most markets reduces the reliability of such values. Nevertheless, users of financial statements may find current replacement cost valuations used occasionally and more relevant than out-of-date acquisition cost valuations.

Current Values: Fair Value Based on Net Realizable Value

Net realizable value is the net amount a firm would receive if it sold an asset (for example, inventory for which current value has declined below cost). Just as with current replacement cost valuation, net realizable value is another special case of a fair value approach. However, it also shares features of adjusted historical cost valuation approaches, because historical cost

[8]The application of current replacement cost is actually a bit more complex, with limitations placed on the valuation of the gas tube protectors that depend on net realizable value (that is, normal sales price less costs necessary to sell the units, and sometimes less normal gross profit). Depending on where current replacement cost falls relative to net realized value, Graybar might use a net realizable value for valuing the inventory rather than current replacement cost.

provides a reference point to determine whether net realizable valuation is applicable. Thus, this is a hybrid approach and the examples below exhibit similarities with other valuation approaches (both historical cost and current cost). We include net realizable value within our discussion of current value approaches because of the reference to exit prices. The difference is that rather than estimating the cost of acquiring a similar asset in a hypothetical transaction, the net realizable value approach focuses on the amount a firm is likely to realize given prevailing market conditions, offset by any pertinent selling costs.

Example 13

Google holds approximately $8 billion of investments in various short-term securities. The net realizable value of these investments could be computed based on the closing price of each security minus costs to sale, such as trading commissions.

Example 14

Inventory for Pulte Homes is approximately two-thirds of total assets and reflects primarily house and land inventory. The recent recession caused a reduction in the demand for new homes and land, which results in the net realizable value of Pulte Homes' inventory being below acquisition cost. Certain land held by Pulte was written down to its net realizable value, reflecting estimated fair value less costs to sell. The outcome is similar to an application of the lower of cost or market approach discussed in the previous section.

Using net realizable values to value assets has the same advantages and disadvantages as using current replacement costs. Net realizable values may provide more relevant information to financial statements users but result in greater subjectivity when active markets for the assets do not exist. In Example 13, because the net realizable value of Google's short-term investments is based on prices quoted in actively traded markets, this amount is both relevant and reliable. In contrast, the valuation of Pulte Homes' land inventory in Example 14 is more difficult to value given the less liquid markets for land; thus, although relevant, the estimated net realizable value of this inventory is subject to greater concerns over reliability.

Summary of U.S. GAAP and IFRS Valuations

U.S. GAAP and IFRS do not utilize a single valuation method for all assets and liabilities. Instead, they use numerous valuation approaches for different assets and liabilities. U.S. GAAP and IFRS, for example, stipulate that firms use historical values for some assets and liabilities and current, or fair, values for other assets and liabilities. For this reason, U.S. GAAP and IFRS are mixed attribute accounting models. Revisions to U.S. GAAP increasingly require use of fair values in the valuation of certain assets and liabilities, and this trend continues with IFRS. When accounting rules require firms to use fair value for an asset, firms might measure fair value using quoted market prices, current replacement cost, or net realizable value. If markets are not sufficiently active to provide reliable evidence of fair value, firms can use the present value of expected cash flows to approximate fair value.[9] For liabilities, the fair value approach is generally more straightforward than for assets because most liabilities are denominated in monetary and contractual terms, which are more amenable to fair value approaches. Exhibit 2.3 summarizes the use of these valuation methods for various assets and liabilities, which later chapters discuss more fully.

---

[9]For a conceptual discussion of present value approaches, see Financial Accounting Standards Board, *Statement of Financial Accounting Concepts No. 7,* "Using Cash Flow Information and Present Value Accounting Measurement" (February 2000). For the authoritative literature on fair value measurement approaches, see *FASB Codification Topic 820,* "Fair Value Measurements and Disclosures."

EXHIBIT 2.3

Examples of Valuation Methods for Various Assets and Liabilities

Historical Values

- Acquisition cost: Land; intangibles with indefinite lives; goodwill; prepayments
- Adjusted acquisition cost: Buildings; equipment and other depreciable assets; intangibles with limited lives
- Initial present value: Investments in bonds held to maturity; long-term receivables and payables; noncurrent unearned revenue; current receivables and payables (but U.S. GAAP and IFRS ignore the discounting process on the grounds that discounted and undiscounted cash flows do not result in materially different valuations)

Current Values

- Fair value: Investments in marketable equity securities; investments in debt securities classified as either trading securities or securities available for sale; financial instruments and derivative instruments subject to hedging activities; assets and liabilities of a business acquired using the acquisition method; assets and liabilities of a business to be discontinued

Combination of Historical and Current Values

- Current replacement cost of long-lived assets relative to acquisition cost
- Lower of cost or fair value for inventory; net realizable value of inventory; accounts receivable net of an allowance for uncollectible accounts

INCOME RECOGNITION

Recognition simply means that the accountant makes an entry to record a transaction or an event. Recognized net income equals revenues and gains minus expenses and losses. The income statement reports the earnings from a firm's operating activities for a period of time (as the difference between revenues and expenses), but also reports gains or losses realized from investing activities (for example, sale of marketable securities at a gain or loss) and financing activities (for example, retirement of debt before maturity at a gain or loss).[10] In an ideal world, net income for a period would equal all changes in the economic value of the net assets and liabilities of a firm during that period. However, financial statement users must wrestle with the mixed attribute accounting model (discussed in the previous section), whereby assets and liabilities appear in the balance sheet under different valuation approaches. It is exactly for this reason that income recognition sometimes does not reflect "all changes in the economic value of a firm." The relevance versus reliability trade-off shows up on the income statement as well.

Recall that valuation of assets and liabilities falls within a continuum from historical value to current (fair) value approaches. Similarly, we can relate approaches to reporting changes in value on the income statement by appealing to the same continuum, as shown in Exhibit 2.4.

[10]The terms *earnings* and *income* are generally used interchangeably in this text and among analysts, managers, and investors. However, note earnings and income refer to *net income,* which is different from *comprehensive income,* which includes both net income and other comprehensive income,

EXHIBIT 2.4

How Changes in Economic Value Can Be Recognized on the Balance Sheet and Income Statement

	Maximum Reliability (and Verifiability)		**Maximum Relevance (and Timeliness)**
Asset and Liability Valuation Approaches:	*Historical Value*	↔	*Current Value*
Income Recognition of Changes in Economic Value	*Approach 1:* Recognize value changes on the balance sheet and the income statement when they are realized in a market transaction (that is, when a firm sells an asset or pays a liability)	*Approach 2:* Recognize value changes on the balance sheet when the value changes occur over time but recognize them in net income when they are realized in a market transaction.	*Approach 3:* Recognize value changes on the balance sheet and the income statement when they occur, even though they are not yet realized in a market transaction.

The next three sections discuss these alternative approaches. Before that discussion, however, the following point highlights the fundamental reason for the existence of accrual accounting:

> *Over sufficiently long time periods, net income equals cash inflows minus cash outflows, other than cash flows with owners (for example, issuing or repurchasing common stock, and paying dividends). Asset and liability valuation and income measurement merely affect when and how the financial statements report these value changes. All value changes eventually affect net income and retained earnings.*

The ultimate goal of a firm is to generate more cash inflows than it incurs cash outflows. Thus, one option for reporting financial performance would be simply to report cash inflows and outflows. However, simply reporting cash inflows and outflows would suffer from timing issues as a measure of firm performance and financial condition. To review this basic premise, consider a stylized example of three transactions under accrual accounting versus cash flow reporting approaches, as presented in Exhibit 2.5.

In this stylized example, a firm purchases supplies (December 31, 2009), uses the supplies to provide services to a customer, and collects cash for the billed services. Under cash inflow and outflow reporting, income from this transaction appears in three reporting periods in the following pattern: −\$100, \$0, and \$1,000, whereas under accrual accounting, the net of \$900 appears in a single period (the period in which the activity occurs). In this example, we see that reporting cash inflows and outflows yields a series of performance measures that vary from negative to zero to positive, whereas accrual accounting measures and reports when and how the value changes are generated. The accrual accounting approach moves the timing of income and expenses to the period in which the real activity occurs (2010). The investment in supplies in 2009 and the collection of the account receivable in 2011 are handled by accruals, which can be thought of as "placeholders" on the balance sheet (assets in this example). Under accrual accounting, the supplies are classified as

EXHIBIT 2.5

Stylized Example to Demonstrate the Advantages of Accrual Accounting Relative to Reporting Cash Inflows and Outflows

Date	Transaction
December 31, 2009	Firm purchases supplies for $100
August 17, 2010	Firm uses supplies to provide services, billed at $1,000
January 1, 2011	Customer pays $1,000 for services billed

	2009	2010	2011
Net cash inflow and outflow reporting	– $100	$0	$1,000
Accrual accounting	$0	$900 (= $1,000 billed – $100 supplies)	$0

inventory, which, like many nonmonetary assets, is "an expense waiting to happen." The amounts billed for services is classified as a receivable (with the offset being the revenue recorded), which, like many monetary assets, is a "cash flow waiting to happen."

Although stylized, this example is symbolic of real-world evidence. Dechow (1994) examined the relative ability of cash flows and accounting earnings to capture firm performance. She predicts and finds that

> "... for firms in steady state (that is, firms with cash requirements for working capital, investments, and financing that are relatively stable), cash flows have few timing and matching problems and are a relatively useful measure of firm performance. However, for firms operating in volatile environments with large changes in their working capital and investment and financing activities, cash flows ... have more severe timing and matching problems. Thus, cash flows' ability to reflect firm performance will decline as the firms' working capital requirements and investment and financing activities increase. Accruals ... mitigate timing and matching problems in cash flows. As a consequence, earnings ... better reflect firm performance than cash flows, in firms with more volatile operating, investment and financing activities.... [Finally], cash flows and earnings ... [are] equally useful in industries with short operating cycles. However, in industries with long operating cycles, cash flows are ... relatively poor measure of firm performance."[11]

In summary, reporting cash inflows and outflows is reliable but is often not relevant for predicting future cash flows. On the other hand, reporting income under accrual accounting procedures provides a measure of financial performance that is more relevant for users interested in predicting the ultimate payoff of cash flows, albeit with a

---

[11] Patricia M. Dechow, "Accounting Earnings and Cash Flows as Measures of Firm Performance: The Role of Accounting Accruals," *Journal of Accounting & Economics* (July 1994), pp. 3–42.

potential for information to be less reliable (because it is based on estimates and other reporting judgments). The FASB's Conceptual Framework, which is the foundation for U.S. GAAP, is based on observations similar to those documented by Dechow. In *Statement of Financial Accounting Concepts No. 1*, the FASB states "Information about enterprise earnings and its components measured by accrual accounting generally provides a better indication of enterprise performance than does information about current cash receipts and payments." This will be discussed in more detail in Chapter 3. Next, we discuss the three alternative approaches to income measurement. Please note that because Approach 2 is a hybrid of Approach 1 and Approach 3, the discussion of Approach 2 follows the discussion of Approach 3.

Approach 1: Economic Value Changes Recognized on the Balance Sheet and Income Statement *When Realized*

Just as the conventional method of asset and liability valuation leans on historical value approaches (but with a decreasing emphasis), the conventional approach to income measurement relies on *realization* as the trigger for recognizing components of income. "Realization" for revenues occurs when firms receive cash, a receivable, or some other asset subject to reasonably reliable measurement from a customer for goods sold or services performed. The receipt of this asset validates the amount of the value change, and accountants characterize the firm as having *realized* the value change. This ensures that the amounts recorded as revenue are both relevant and reliable.

For expenses, the concept of "realization" is somewhat different because expenses frequently reflect the consumption of assets or incurrence of liabilities, which often is not as directly observable as an event like a sale to a customer. The conventional way of thinking about recognizing expenses is that they are *matched* to the revenues they are used up to generate, but this convention applies only to certain expenses that can be clearly linked to realization of revenues (for example, product costs such as costs of good sold).[12] For example, a sale of lumber by The Home Depot indicates that revenues have been realized, which then triggers derecognition of the inventory and the accompanying recognition of an expense for cost of goods sold. More commonly, expenses are realized by the consumption of resources (such as paying salaries to employees) or the passage of time (such as rent or interest).

As presented in the discussion of asset and liability valuation, delaying the recognition of value changes for assets and liabilities until triggered by some realization (such as a sale) means that the balance sheet reports assets and liabilities at historical values. When historical values are used, valuation changes in assets and liabilities are not recognized until they are realized, meaning that some event (such as a sale) establishes a reliable basis for adjusting the financial statements. In this case, realization affects the balance sheet and the income statement simultaneously, which characterizes Approach 1. An intuitive way to think about Approach 1 is that the accountant takes a "wait-and-see" approach, waiting for the realization of some change in economic value of assets or liabilities before adjusting the value of the asset or liability and recording the adjustment as a revenue, expense, gain, or loss. Note that the receipt or disbursement of cash is *not* a requirement for realization. Because cash flows may precede, coincide with, or follow the value change, the balance sheet utilizes various *accruals* as placeholders for cash flows (such as accounts receivable, accounts payable, or prepayments). The following examples help clarify Approach 1.

[12]As regulators gravitate away from the historical value approaches to assets and liabilities (toward current value approaches), the emphasis and popularity of the matching objective is becoming diminished. However, it remains useful when considering when and how to recognize certain expenses (for example, depreciation).

Example 15

In Example 1, In-N-Out Burger reports land on the balance sheet at $210,000, its acquisition cost, as long as the firm continues to hold the land and regardless of whether the land rises in value. Suppose In-N-Out Burger decides to sell the land two years after acquiring it for $300,000 in cash. The sale of the land triggers the firm to recognize the economic value increase of $90,000, reflected as a $300,000 increase in cash, offset by the $210,000 derecognition of the land. The accompanying effect on the income statement is a gain on the sale of the land of $90,000. Incidentally, firms typically report the income from sales of assets peripheral to their main business as a net amount, $90,000, rather than showing the selling price of $300,000 as "revenue" and the cost of the asset sold of $210,000 as an expense. In contrast, income from a firm's principal business activities appears as gross amounts, as in the next example.

Example 16

In Example 2, Mollydooker Wines accumulates various costs of producing the wine in its inventory account while the aging occurs. When Mollydooker Wines completes the aging and sells the wine, it recognizes the value increase in both its assets and net income. Assume that Mollydooker Wines incurs total costs of processing and aging the wine of $1,300,000 (= $1,100,000 for the initial processing and $200,000 for aging) and sells the wine at the completion of the aging for $2,000,000 on account. During each year of the aging process, the inventory balance accumulates various acquisition costs. By the end of the aging process, however, the economic value of the inventory (the price for which Mollydooker Wines can sell it) likely exceeds the accumulated acquisition costs in the inventory balance. Not until realization of the sale to a customer does Mollydooker Wines recognize the economic value change on the income statement. At that time, revenue of $2,000,000 is recognized (along with an account receivable of $2,000,000). This then triggers the firm to derecognize the $1,300,000 of inventory and increase cost of goods sold in the same amount. Thus, using Approach 1 delays the income recognition of the $700,000 economic change in the value of inventory until the sale actually takes place (that is, realization).

Approach 3: Economic Value Changes Recognized on the Balance Sheet and the Income Statement *When They Occur*

We will skip Approach 2 for the time being, as it is a hybrid of Approaches 1 and 3. Approach 3 to recognizing income entails firms revaluing assets and liabilities to fair value each period and recognizing these *unrealized* gains and losses in net income in that same period. As shown in Exhibit 2.4, this approach to income recognition aligns with the current value approach for assets and liabilities. With exceptions discussed next for Approach 2, U.S. GAAP generally does not permit firms to revalue assets upward for value increases, which would recognize the unrealized gain as part of net income. The reason for this is that the combination of reliability concerns for the estimated increases in economic value and managers' self-interested incentives to report higher book values and income might lead to poorer quality financial statements (despite the potential for greater relevance). Instead, firms must await the validation of such increases in value through a market transaction (that is, realization) to provide a sound, reliable basis for recognizing the gain.

As you have seen, however, U.S. GAAP is not symmetric regarding recognition of value increases and decreases. Firms must generally write down assets whose fair values decrease below their book values and flow through the decline in economic value immediately to income. Given the judgments often required in measuring fair values and inherent manager incentives to report higher asset valuations and higher income, U.S. GAAP does not permit upward revaluations of assets. It is more concerned with the reliability of positive unrealized value changes relative to negative changes. In contrast, IFRS allows for a number of situations where firms are permitted to increase asset valuations. For example, upon initial adoption of IFRS, firms may elect to value property and equipment at fair value. In addition, firms can record investment property (such as rental property), intangible assets, and some financial assets at fair values even when those fair values rise above carrying values. Therefore, IFRS may not seem to be as concerned about reliability of positive unrealized value changes relative to negative ones. Note, however, that when firms report unrealized changes in economic value in current earnings under IFRS, additional disclosures must accompany the use of fair values, including the methodology of determining fair value. These additional disclosures are an attempt to increase the transparency of the fair values and therefore the reliability of amounts that could be deemed less reliable. Also note that under IFRS, if a firm elects to recognize increased valuations of assets, it must do so for entire classes of similar assets (for example, all real estate, not just single properties) and it must continue to revalue such classes of assets thereafter (even if fair values decline). These requirements are meant to discourage firms from cherry-picking which assets to revalue upward and when.

Example 17

In Example 8, suppose Smithfield Foods has live hog inventory valued at $882 million. Despite the fact that swine flu is not spread by eating properly cooked pork, the swine flu epidemic sends the market price of live hogs down approximately 5 percent on the Chicago Mercantile Exchange. As a consequence, Smithfield Foods' inventory is overstated by $44 million. This decline in inventory value is recognized on both the balance sheet and income statement based on the new market prices. The new value of live hog inventory is $838 million, and this decline in economic value is recognized in income as a lower of cost or market adjustment for the decline in live hog inventory of $44 million.

Example 18

In Examples 5 and 9, recall that the present value of the note payable on the books of Petroleo Brasileiro is $828,032 based on the historical interest rate of 8 percent. The decrease in interest rates to 6 percent results in an increase in the fair value of the note to $866,276. Traditionally, U.S. GAAP has not required firms to revalue such financial instruments to market value to reflect changes in interest rates. However, Petroleo Brasileiro may want to repay the note prior to maturity and refinance the note at the new lower rates. However, in anticipation of this, Sun Microsystems, the holder of the note, may have contracted a price for early repayment that incorporates any change in market interest rates at the time of repayment. For example, Sun Microsystems could require Petroleo Brasileiro to pay $866,276 to repay the note at this time if interest rates have declined to 6 percent.

Petroleo Brasileiro may obtain a hedging contract, referred to as a derivative, from another entity that protects the net amount Petroleo Brasileiro must pay to retire the debt prior to maturity. When firms acquire derivatives to hedge changes in value of a financial instrument, U.S. GAAP requires the firms to revalue both the financial instrument and the derivative to fair value each period and recognize unrealized gains and losses in net income immediately. In this example, Petroleo Brasileiro would increase the valuation of the note payable from $828,032 to $866,276 and recognize a loss in net income for the difference, $38,244. It also would revalue the derivative, which in this case is an asset. If the derivative perfectly hedged the change in interest rates, it would increase in value by $38,244 as well. Accordingly, Petroleo Brasileiro would increase the valuation of the derivative asset and recognize a gain of $38,244. If the hedge is not perfectly effective, the gain and loss will not precisely offset and net income will increase or decrease for the difference. The accounting for financial instruments and derivatives is complex and is discussed in Chapter 8.

Example 19

In Example 10, Kimpton Hotels was interested in determining the fair value of each of its hotels. In response to a sharp decrease in occupancy and revenues per available room due to a recession, the management team of Kimpton Hotels engages an appraisal firm to perform an analysis of its hotels for any valuation impairment. Based on projected cash flows for each hotel, the analysis indicates that the present value of expected future cash flows for a hotel located in Cambridge, Massachusetts is $8 million below the adjusted acquisition cost of that hotel on Kimpton's balance sheet. This decline in economic value, although not realized, may be recognized on both the balance sheet (by decreasing the adjusted acquisition cost) and the income statement (by recording an impairment charge). Chapter 7 discusses impairment charges in more detail.

In Examples 17–19, the valuation of assets and liabilities followed the use of fair values. This contrasts with the use of initial historical values under Approach 1. The traditional accounting model follows Approach 1 and delays the recognition of value changes of assets and liabilities until a market transaction validates their amounts (that is, realization occurs). At the other end of the spectrum, Approach 3 permits changes in economic value to be recognized on both the balance sheet and income statement when they occur, but such adjustments are usually for declines in economic value rather than increases.

Approach 2: Economic Value Changes Recognized on the Balance Sheet *When They Occur* but Recognized on the Income Statement *When Realized*

The value changes of some assets and liabilities are of particular interest to users and are measurable with a sufficiently high degree of reliability that U.S. GAAP and IFRS requires firms to revalue them to fair value each period. U.S. GAAP and IFRS recognize, however, that the value change is *unrealized* until the firm sells the asset or settles the liability. The ultimate *realized* gain or loss will likely differ from the unrealized gain or loss each period, particularly if the market values of the underlying assets or liabilities are volatile. Therefore, U.S. GAAP and IFRS require firms to delay including the gain or loss in *net* income until realization of the gain or loss occurs. However, such gains or losses do appear as part of *comprehensive* income (as discussed in Chapter 1). The most common types of unrealized gains and losses that receive treatment under Approach 2 include foreign currency translation effects, remeasurements of financial assets classified as available-for-sale investments, and other general asset revaluations. In addition, other amounts bypass the income statement and statement of comprehensive income, and are recorded directly to equity. Examples include corrections of errors and retroactive adjustments required under certain changes in accounting principles.[13]

To put this in context, consider the actual share price of Walmart during calendar year 2007, shown in Exhibit 2.6. Walmart's common stock is one of the most widely held investments. Consider how the fluctuations in Walmart's stock price would have affected

---

[13]Accounting Principles Board Opinion No. 9, "Reporting the Results of Operations" (December 1966). *FASB Codification Topic 250;* International Accounting Standards Board, *International Accounting Standards No. 8,* "Accounting Policies, Changes in Accounting Estimates and Errors" (revised January 2008).

EXHIBIT 2.6

Walmart Stock Price, January–December 2007

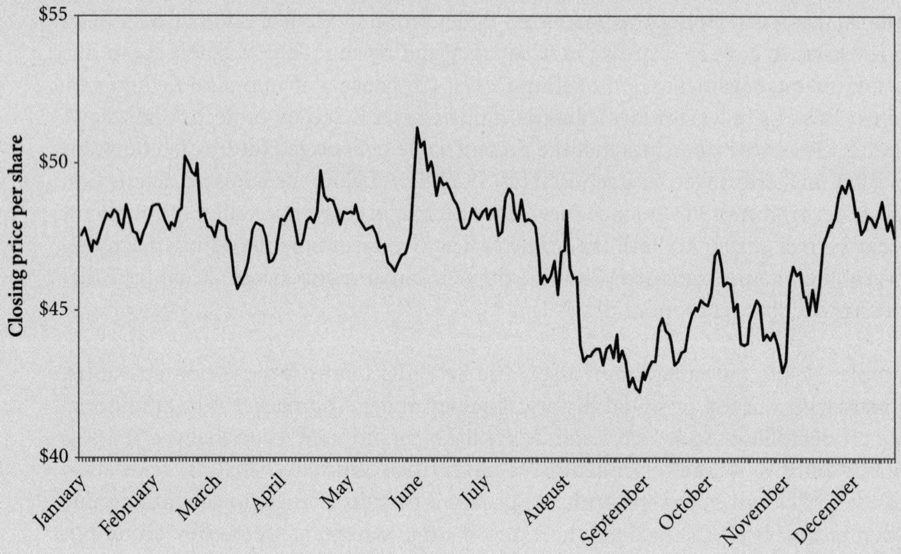

the financial statements of firms holding an investment in Walmart common stock during 2007. The stock price ended the year at $47.53, virtually unchanged from its price at the beginning of the year, $47.55. Thus, any investment would have changed in value only trivially over this period. However, keep in mind that firms report results quarterly so that a firm with a December fiscal year-end would have seen the value of an investment in Walmart drop only 1.3 percent to $46.95 at the end of first quarter; increase 2.5 percent from the first-quarter close to $48.11 at the end of the second quarter; decrease 9.3 percent from there to $43.65 during the third quarter; and finally increase to 8.9 percent to $47.55, very close to where it was at the beginning of the year. If applied to each quarter's financial statements, Approach 3 would have resulted in volatile seesaw net income recognition across the four quarters as down, up, down, up, although the year-over-year valuation of the investment was essentially flat. The intent here is not to argue that either approach is superior to the other, but just to highlight their differences.

Thus, as a compromise between Approach 1 and Approach 3 to income recognition, U.S. GAAP and IFRS require firms to recognize unrealized gains and losses of certain assets and liabilities on the balance sheet, but delay their recognition in net income (reporting such effects on the statement of comprehensive income). This is an attempt to incorporate the benefits of relevant and timely fair values on the balance sheet while minimizing net income volatility. In the meantime, both U.S. GAAP and IFRS require firms to include unrealized gains or losses arising each period as other comprehensive income (not part of determining net income) and the cumulative unrealized gain or loss as accumulated other comprehensive income (in shareholders' equity on the balance sheet). Accumulated other comprehensive income changes each period by the amount of other comprehensive income for the period. Only at the time of realization of the economic value change will the firm include the realized gain or loss in net income. The firm simultaneously removes any related amounts from accumulated other comprehensive income.

Approach 2 is a hybrid of Approaches 1 and 3. The primary characteristic is that it attempts to capture the relevance of economic value changes recognized for assets and liabilities under Approach 3 (which uses the current value approach for asset and liability valuation). However, Approach 2 stops short of flowing through such unrealized economic value changes immediately to the income statement because they may be temporary and reverse. Instead, Approach 2 incorporates the reliability feature of Approach 1 by delaying recognition of the economic value change in net income until the change is realized in a market transaction, but requires such changes to appear as part of other comprehensive income on the statement of comprehensive income.

Note that the practice of stopping short of flowing fair value changes through net income under Approach 2 presumes that the investors perceive *net income* as the summary of income for a firm, but view amounts disclosed as *other comprehensive income* as mere disclosures, not necessarily part of what most investors consider "income." Indeed, in a study of comprehensive income disclosures shortly after they were first required, Dhaliwal, Subramanyam, and Trezevant (1998) concluded that investors do not perceive other comprehensive income to be important components of a firm's performance, given net income.[14] However, numerous other studies demonstrate a strong association between security prices and underlying fair value estimates. For example, Carroll, Linsmeier, and Petroni (2003) examine closed-end mutual funds and show a strong association between stock prices and the fair value of investment securities and between the changes in fair values and stock returns.[15] In addition, Hodder, Hopkins, and Wahlen (2006) show that the volatility of fair value changes reflected in comprehensive income explain numerous measures of risk for commercial banks.[16] Thus, overall it is clear that investors view fair value amounts as relevant despite the risk that such amounts might be less reliable than historical valuations. The net effect of Approach 2 is that asset and liability valuations reflect current values, but the net income effect is temporarily held as accumulated other comprehensive income in shareholders' equity until realization of the gain or loss occurs.

Example 20

Assume that Microsoft has cash well in excess of its near-term needs. Rather than allow the cash to remain in its bank account, Microsoft purchases marketable equity securities costing $4,500,000. The fair value of these securities on December 31 is $4,900,000. Microsoft intends to sell these securities when it needs cash. The current fair value of these securities is likely of more interest to users of the firm's financial statements than is acquisition cost. Moreover, the ready market for these securities provides reliable evidence of their fair value. Thus, U.S. GAAP requires Microsoft to revalue the securities upward $400,000 to fair value and recognize an unrealized holding gain of $400,000. The holding gain appears on the statement of comprehensive income within other comprehensive income, which is included in accumulated other comprehensive income in shareholders' equity. Thus, assets increase by $400,000 and shareholders' equity increases by $400,000. No income statement effect is recognized at this point.

---

[14]See, for example, Dan Dhaliwal, K. R. Subramanyam, and Robert Trezevant, "Is Comprehensive Income Superior to Net Income as a Measure of Firm Performance?" *Journal of Accounting & Economics* (1999), pp. 1–3, 43–67.

[15]Thomas J. Carroll, Thomas J. Linsmeier, and Kathy R. Petroni, "The Reliability of Fair Value versus Historical Cost Information: Evidence from Closed-End Mutual Funds," *Journal of Accounting, Auditing and Finance* (2003), pp. 1–23.

[16]Leslie D. Hodder, Patrick E. Hopkins, and James M. Wahlen, "Risk-Relevance of Fair Value Income Measures for Commercial Banks," *The Accounting Review* (April 2006).

Next, suppose Microsoft sells the securities in early June of the following year for $5,000,000. The firm then recognizes a *realized* gain on sale in net income of $500,000 ($5,000,000 − $4,500,000). Microsoft also must eliminate the $400,000 unrealized gain from accumulated other comprehensive income. Thus, assets increase by $100,000 (cash increases by $5,000,000, and marketable securities decrease by $4,900,000) and shareholders' equity increases by $100,000 (net income causes retained earnings to increase by $500,000, and other comprehensive income of ($400,000) causes accumulated other comprehensive income on the balance sheet to decrease by $400,000. Chapter 7 discusses the accounting for marketable securities more fully.

Example 21

Ford Motor Company operates in Europe through its subsidiary, Ford Europe. Ford Europe keeps its accounts in euros each period. Ford Motor Company must translate these euro amounts into their U.S. dollar equivalent amounts each period in order to prepare consolidated financial statements for the two entities. As the exchange rate between the U.S. dollar and the euro changes each period, the U.S. dollar equivalent of the euro-measured assets and liabilities of Ford Europe changes.

U.S. GAAP requires firms in most circumstances to use the current exchange rate on the date of the balance sheet to translate the assets and liabilities of foreign entities into U.S. dollars. The U.S. parent company will not realize the economic effect of the value change, however, until the foreign unit remits cash to the parent and the parent converts the euro cash into U.S. dollars. Therefore, U.S. GAAP does not permit firms to immediately flow through the unrealized foreign currency translation gain or loss to net income. Instead, firms must include the unrealized gain or loss as other comprehensive income on the statement of comprehensive income, and then close this amount to accumulated other comprehensive income (in shareholders' equity). Later, when Ford Motor Company makes a currency conversion with the cash received, it realizes an exchange gain or loss and includes it in net income. It simultaneously reduces accumulated other comprehensive income for the applicable unrealized gain or loss recognized in earlier periods. Chapter 7 discusses the accounting for foreign entities more fully.

Summary of Asset and Liability Valuation and Income Recognition

The traditional accounting model relies mostly on historical values for assets and liabilities and delays income recognition until realization (Approach 1). Under this approach, asset and liability valuation directly link to income recognition; in other words, recognition of changes in the economic value of assets and liabilities is delayed until the income is recognized (which occurs only when some market transaction triggers realization of the economic value changes). However, the FASB and IASB are more often requiring the use of fair values in the valuation of certain assets and liabilities. Using the fair value approach for assets and liabilities generally translates into Approach 3, which recognizes such economic value changes in income immediately. Between these approaches, some economic value changes are recognized on the balance sheet before they are recognized on the income statement (Approach 2). In the intervening time, firms use accumulated other comprehensive income (in shareholders' equity) as a temporary "holding tank" for unrealized gains and losses for which the assets and liabilities have been marked to fair value but the gains and losses are yet to be realized in a market transaction. When the change in economic value is realized, the firm formally recognizes the previously unrealized gains and losses by removing them from accumulated other comprehensive income and reporting them within net income.

This mixed attribute accounting model does a fairly good job of capturing economic events and transactions in a way that maintains the reliability of the overall financial statements. (Recall the increasing usefulness of financial statements indicated in Exhibit 2.2.) The FASB, and now the IASB, are constantly monitoring the needs of financial statement users and adapt financial reporting rules to those needs. Currently, the FASB and IASB are attempting to overhaul the conceptual frameworks upon which the accounting model is based with the goal of making the accounting for similar events and transactions consistent across firms and across time. However, because of the trade-off between relevance and reliability, it is unlikely that financial reporting will move toward any extreme, such as full historical values or full fair values. Instead, the evolution of the mixed attribute accounting model reflects a continuous improvement in financial reporting that adapts to the evolving needs of financial statement users. Also, an important fact to keep in mind is that the quality of financial reporting can be enhanced (or offset) by other features of the economic environment, such as corporate governance practices, shareholder protection, regulation, and enforcement. For example, Hung (2000) demonstrates that the usefulness of accrual accounting is higher in countries that have institutional features that protect shareholders (such as common law legal systems and shareholders' rights provisions).[17]

INCOME TAXES

In this chapter, the discussion thus far has considered the measurement of assets, liabilities, revenues, gains, expenses, and losses before considering any income tax effects. Everyone is aware that taxes are a significant aspect of doing business, but few understand how taxes impact financial statements. The objective of the brief discussion in this section is to familiarize you with the basic concepts underlying the treatment of income taxes in the financial statements. A more detailed discussion appears in Chapter 8.

The fundamental reason for the difficulty in understanding the financial reporting of income taxes is that financial reporting of income uses one set of rules (U.S. GAAP, for example), while taxable income uses another set of rules (the Internal Revenue Code, for example). Reconciling the differences between these sets of rules necessitates the use of various accruals such as deferred income tax assets and liabilities. These differences are analogous to differences between financial reporting rules and cash basis accounting, which necessitate the use of various accruals such as accounts receivable and accounts payable. Thus, an understanding of financial statement analysis requires the appreciation that there are (at least) three primary alternatives by which financial performance can be measured, as shown in Exhibit 2.7.

Income taxes affect virtually every transaction in which a firm engages. All of the previous examples face some tax exposure. For example:

- Smithfield Foods (in Example 17) writes down its live hog inventory \$44 million due to a decline in the market price for live hogs. However, for tax reporting, Smithfield Foods cannot deduct this write-down immediately, but must wait until the loss is realized through an actual sale of the live hogs. Should Smithfield Foods record the presumed tax benefit that will arise from this write-down now or wait until the loss is realized?
- Kimpton Hotels (in Example 19) recognizes an \$8 million impairment loss on one of its hotels. However, Kimpton Hotels will not be permitted to deduct this impairment for tax reporting immediately, but instead must continue to depreciate or amortize it over time. Thus, U.S. GAAP and the income tax law treat the value of the building and the depreciation expense on it differently. Do these differences matter for financial reporting?

---

[17]Mingyi Hung, "Accounting Standards and Value Relevance of Financial Statements: An International Analysis," *Journal of Accounting & Economics* (December 2000).

EXHIBIT 2.7

Alternative Sets of Rules for Determining Financial Performance

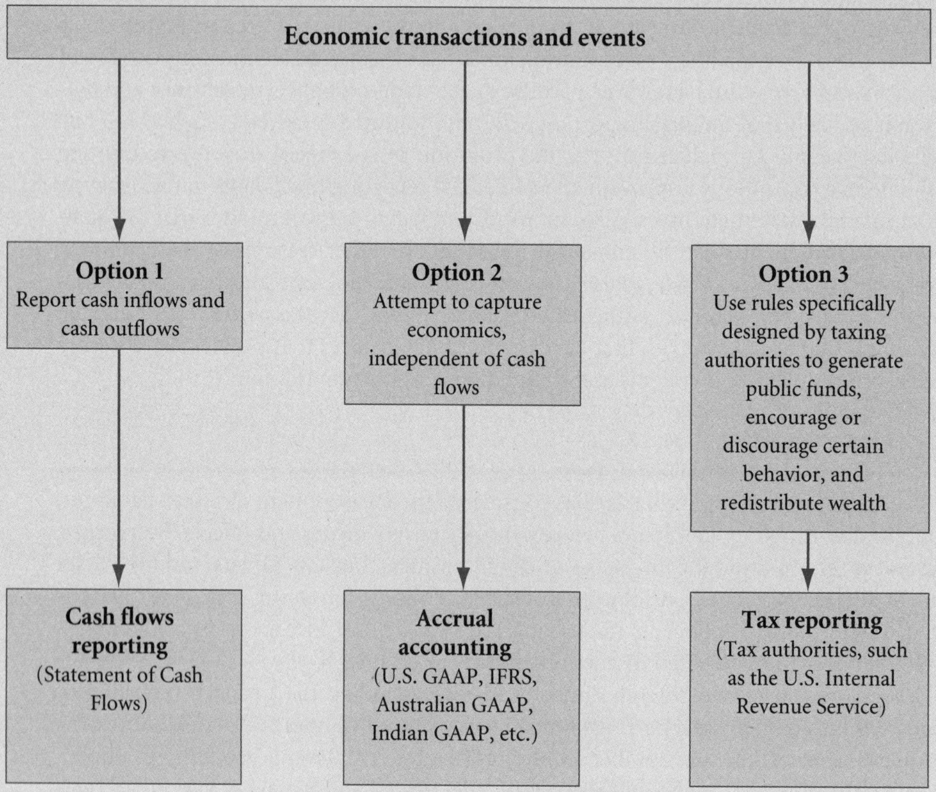

- Microsoft (in Example 20) includes a $400,000 increase in the fair value of marketable equity securities in other comprehensive income. Microsoft will report the effect of any gains or losses in taxable income only when it sells the securities. Should Microsoft recognize any income tax liability or expense now on the $400,000 of other comprehensive income?

To fully understand business transactions, you need to understand their income tax effects. Thus, before specific financial reporting topics are discussed in Chapters 6–9, an overview of the required accounting for income taxes under U.S. GAAP and IFRS is necessary.

Overview of Financial Reporting of Income Taxes[18]

Income taxes significantly affect the analysis of a firm's reported profitability (income tax expense is a subtraction in computing net income), cash flows (income taxes paid are an operating use of cash), and assets and liabilities (for accrued taxes payable and deferred tax

[18]Our discussion proceeds as if accounting for income taxes follows an income statement perspective. However, this is not technically correct, as accounting standards require a balance sheet perspective. We have found that exposition using the income statement perspective is more intuitive for students than the technically correct balance sheet perspective,

EXHIBIT 2.8

Differences in Nomenclature for Financial Reporting and Tax Reporting

Financial Reporting	Tax Reporting
"Revenues" (GAAP) – "Expenses"	"Revenues" (tax rules) – "Deductions"
= "Income before taxes" (or "Pretax income") – "Income tax expense"	= Taxable income ⇒ Taxes owed
= Net income	*[no counterpart]*

assets or liabilities). Income tax expense under accrual accounting for a period does not necessarily equal income taxes owed under the tax laws for that period (for which the firm must remit cash). The discussion first helps you clarify nomenclature that differs between financial reporting of income taxes (in financial statements) and elements of income taxes for tax reporting (on income tax returns). Exhibit 2.8 demonstrates the primary differences that will help with the exposition of these differences.

Both financial reporting and tax reporting begin with revenues, but revenue recognition rules for financial reporting do not necessarily lead to the same figure for revenues as reported for tax reporting. From there, it is helpful to distinguish between summary items for financial and tax reporting. Under tax reporting, firms report "deductions" rather than "expenses." Revenues less deductions equal "taxable income" (rather than "income before taxes," or "pretax income"). Finally, taxable income determines "taxes owed," which can be substantially different from "tax expense" on the income statement, as highlighted later in this section. The balance sheet recognizes the difference between the two amounts as deferred tax assets or deferred tax liabilities. The balance sheet also recognizes any taxes owed at year-end (beyond the estimated tax payments firms may have made throughout the year) as a current liability for income taxes payable.

A simple example illustrates the issues in accounting for income taxes. Exhibit 2.9 sets forth information for the first two years of a firm's operations. The first column for each year shows the financial reporting amounts (referred to as "book amounts" or "financial reporting"). The second column shows the amounts reported to income tax authorities (referred to as "tax amounts" or "tax reporting"). To clarify some of the differences between book and tax effects in the first two columns, the third column indicates the effect of each item on cash flows. Assume for this example and those throughout this chapter that the income tax rate is 40 percent. Additional information on each item is as follows:

- Sales Revenue: The firm reports sales of $500 each year for both book and tax reporting. Assume that it collects the full amount each year in cash (that is, the firm has no accounts receivable).
- Interest Income on Municipal Bonds: The firm earns $25 of interest on municipal bonds. The firm includes this amount in its book income. The federal government does not tax interest on state and municipal bonds, so this amount is excluded from taxable income.
- Depreciation Expense: The firm has equipment costing $120 with a two-year life. It depreciates the equipment using the straight-line method for financial reporting, recognizing $60 of depreciation expense on its books each year. Income taxing authorities permit the firm to write off a larger portion of the asset's cost in the first year, $80, than

EXHIBIT 2.9

Illustration of the Effects of Income Taxes on Net Income, Taxable Income, and Cash Flows

	First Year			Second Year		
	Book Amounts	Tax Amounts	Cash Flow Amounts	Book Amounts	Tax Amounts	Cash Flow Amounts
Sales revenue	$500	$500	$500	$500	$500	$500
Interest on municipal bonds	25	—	25	25	—	25
Depreciation expense	(60)	(80)	—	(60)	(40)	—
Warranty expense	(10)	(4)	(4)	(10)	(12)	(12)
Other expenses	(300)	(300)	(300)	(300)	(300)	(300)
Net Income before Taxes or Taxable Income	$155	$116		$155	$148	
Income tax expense or payable	(52)	$(46.4)	(46.4)	(52)	$(59.2)	(59.2)
Net Income	$103			$103		
Net Cash Flows			$174.6			$153.8

can be done using the straight-line method. Because total depreciation over the life of an asset cannot exceed acquisition cost, the firm recognizes only $40 of depreciation for tax reporting in the second year.

- Warranty Expense: The firm estimates that the cost of providing warranty services on products sold equals 2 percent of sales. It recognizes warranty expense of $10 (= 0.02 × $500) each year for financial reporting, which matches the estimated cost of warranties against the revenue from the sale of products subject to warranty. Income tax laws do not permit firms to claim a deduction for warranties in computing taxable income until they make cash expenditures to provide warranty services. Assume that the firm incurs cash costs of $4 in the first year and $12 in the second year.
- Other Expenses: The firm incurs and pays other expenses of $300 each year.
- Income before Taxes and Taxable Income: Based on the preceding assumptions, income before taxes for financial reporting is $155 each year. Taxable income is $116 in the first year and $148 in the second year.
- Taxes Payable: Assume that the firm pays all income taxes payable at each year-end.

Income before taxes for financial reporting differs from taxable income for the following principal reasons:

1. **Permanent Differences:** Revenues and expenses that firms include in net income for financial reporting but that never appear in the income tax return. Interest revenue on the municipal bond is a permanent revenue difference. Examples of expenses that would be disallowed as deductions include executive compensation above a specified cap, certain entertainment expenses, political and lobbying expenses, and some fees and penalties.

2. **Temporary Differences:** Revenues and expenses that firms include in both net income and taxable income but in different periods. Thus, the differences are "temporary" until they "reverse." Depreciation expense is a temporary difference. The firm recognizes total depreciation of $120 over the life of the equipment for both financial and tax reporting but in a different pattern over time. Similarly, warranty expense is also a temporary difference. The firm recognizes a total of $20 of warranty expense over the two-year period for financial reporting. It deducts only $16 over the two-year period for tax reporting. If the firm's estimate of total warranty costs turns out to be correct, the firm will deduct the remaining $4 of warranty expense for tax reporting in future years when it provides warranty services.

A central conceptual question in accounting for income taxes concerns the measurement of income tax expense on the income statement for financial reporting.

1. Should the firm compute income tax expense based on book income before taxes ($155 for each year in Exhibit 2.9)?
2. Should the firm compute income tax expense based on book income before taxes but excluding permanent differences ([$130 = $155 − $25] for each year in Exhibit 2.9)?
3. Should the firm compute income tax expense based on taxable income ($116 in the first year and $148 in the second year in Exhibit 2.9)?

U.S. GAAP and IFRS require firms to follow the second approach, which complicates an understanding of income tax accounting because the amount upon which tax expense is based does not necessarily appear on the income statement (that is, income before taxes minus permanent differences). For this reason, U.S. GAAP and IFRS require a footnote that shows how the firm calculates income tax expense. This should clear up a misconception that income tax expense is the amount of income taxes currently owed (the third approach). If a firm does not have any permanent differences, there is no difference between the first and second approaches.

The rationale behind basing income tax expense on income before taxes (minus permanent differences) is that it aligns the recognition of *all* tax consequences of items and events already recognized in the financial statements or on tax returns in the period they occur. Thus, firms must recognize the expected benefits of future tax deductions and the obligations related to future taxable income that arise because of temporary differences each year. Permanent differences do not affect taxable income or income taxes paid in any year, and firms do not recognize income tax expense or income tax savings on permanent differences.

Thus, under the second approach, income tax expense is $52 (= 0.40 × $130) in each year. The journal entry to recognize income tax expense for the first year is as follows:

Income Tax Expense	52.0		(0.40 × 130)
Deferred Tax Asset—Warranty	2.4		(0.40 × 6)
Deferred Tax Liability—Depreciation		8.0	(0.40 × 20)
Cash		46.4	(0.40 × 116)

Income tax expense of 52.0 is recognized, which reduces net income, whereas the firm only pays cash taxes of 46.4. The deferred tax asset measures the future tax saving that the firm will realize when it provides warranty services in future years and claims a tax deduction for the realization of expenses that are estimated in the first year. The firm expects to incur $6 (= $10 − $4) of warranty costs in the second year and later years. When it incurs these costs, it will reduce its taxable income, which will result in lower taxes owed for the year, all else equal. Hence, the deferred tax asset of \$2.4 (= 0.40 × \$6) reflects this future deductibility of amounts already expensed for financial reporting but not yet deducted for tax reporting. The \$8 (= 0.40 × \$20) deferred tax liability measures taxes that the firm must pay in the second year when it recognizes \$20 less depreciation for tax reporting than for financial reporting.

The following summarizes the differences between book and tax amounts and the underlying cash flows. The \$25 of interest on municipal bonds is a cash flow, but it is not reported on the tax return. (It is a permanent difference.) Depreciation is an expense that is a temporary difference between tax reporting and financial reporting but does not use cash. The firm recognized warranty expense of \$10 in measuring net income but used only \$4 of cash in satisfying warranty claims, which is the amount allowed to be deducted on the tax return. Finally, the firm recognized \$52 of income tax expense in measuring net income but used only \$46.4 cash for income taxes due to permanent and temporary differences. Overall, net income is \$103, taxable income is \$116, and cash flows are \$174.6. The largest discrepancy between net income and cash flows is depreciation, which is true generally.

In the second year, the journal entry to recognize the income tax effects is as follows:

Income Tax Expense	52.0		(0.40 × 130)
Deferred Tax Liability—Depreciation	8.0		(0.40 × 20)
Deferred Tax Asset—Warranty		0.8	(0.40 × 2)
Cash		59.2	(0.40 × 148)

As in the first year, income tax is recognized as the effective tax rate times the pretax income, and cash paid for taxes equals the tax rate times taxable income. The temporary difference related to depreciation completely reverses in the second year, so the firm reduces the deferred tax liability to zero, which increases income taxes currently payable by \$8. The temporary difference related to the warranty partially reversed during the second year, but the firm created additional temporary differences in that year by making another estimate of future warranty expense. For the two years as a whole, warranty expense for financial reporting of \$20 (= \$10 + \$10) exceeds the amount recognized for tax reporting of \$16 (= \$4 + \$12). Thus, the firm will recognize tax savings of \$1.6 (= 0.40 × \$4) in future years (a deferred tax asset). The deferred tax asset had a balance of \$2.4 at the end of the first year, so the adjustment in the second year reduces the balance of the deferred tax asset by \$0.8 (= \$2.4 − \$1.6).

Now consider the cash flow effects for the second year. Cash flow from operations is \$153.8. Again, depreciation expense is a non-cash expense of \$60. The firm recognized warranty expense of \$10 for financial reporting but used \$12 of cash to satisfy warranty claims. The \$2 subtraction also equals the net reduction in the warranty liability accounting during the second year, as the following analysis shows:

Warranty Liability, beginning of second year	\$ 6
Warranty Expense, second year	10
Warranty Claims, second year	(12)
Warranty Liability, end of second year	\$ 4

The firm recognized \$52 of income tax expense but used \$59.2 of cash for income taxes. The additional \$7.2 of cash used to pay taxes in excess of the tax expense reduces the net deferred tax liability position. The \$7.2 subtraction also equals the net change in the

Deferred Tax Asset ($0.8 decrease) and Deferred Tax Liability ($8 decrease) during the second year, as the following analysis shows:

Net Deferred Tax *Liability*,[19] beginning of second year ($8 liability − $2.4 asset)	$ 5.6
Income Tax Expense, second year	52.0
Income Taxes Paid, second year	(59.2)
Net Deferred Tax *Asset*, end of second year ($0 liability − $1.6 asset)	$ (1.6)

Measuring Income Tax Expense: A Bit More to the Story (to Be Technically Correct)

The preceding illustration followed what might be termed an *income statement approach* to measuring income tax expense. It compared revenues and expenses recognized for book and tax purposes, eliminated permanent differences, and computed income tax expense based on book income before taxes excluding permanent differences. However, FASB Statement No. 109 and IAS 12[20] require firms to follow a *balance sheet approach* when computing income tax expense. For example, Statement No. 109 states the following: "a difference between the tax basis of an asset or a liability and its reported amount in the [balance sheet] will result in taxable or deductible amounts in some future year(s) when the reported amounts of assets are recovered and the reported amounts of liabilities are settled" (para. 11). Similarly, IAS 12 states "It is inherent in the recognition of an asset or liability that the reporting entity expects to recover or settle the carrying amount of that asset or liability. If it is probable that recovery or settlement of that carrying amount will make future tax payments larger (smaller) than they would be if such recovery or settlement were to have no tax consequences, this Standard requires an entity to recognize a deferred tax liability (deferred tax asset), with certain limited exceptions." Thus, in the context of the preceding example, the perspective under the *balance sheet approach* is as follows:

Step 1. In the illustration, the book basis (that is, the amount on the balance sheet) of the equipment at the end of the first year is $60 (= $120 − $60) and the tax basis (that is, what would appear if the firm prepared a tax reporting balance sheet) is $40 (= $120 − $80). Both the book and tax basis are zero at the end of the second year. The book basis of the warranty liability at the end of the first year is $6 (= $10 − $4), and the tax basis is zero. That is, the firm recognizes a deduction for tax purposes when it pays warranty claims and would therefore show no liability if it were to prepare a tax balance sheet.) The book basis of the warranty liability at the end of the second year is $4 (= $6 + $10 − $12), and the tax basis remains zero.

Step 2. After identifying book and tax differences, eliminate those that will not have a future tax consequence (that is, permanent differences). There are no permanent

[19] We are presenting the *net* change in deferred tax balances for ease of presentation. However, note that the deferred tax liability for the equipment would be classified as noncurrent and the deferred tax asset for the warranties is (usually) classified as current, so in practice deferred taxes do not appear net.

[20] Financial Accounting Standards Board, *Statement of Financial Accounting Standards No. 109*, "Accounting for Income Taxes" (1992). *FASB Codification Topic 740;* International Accounting Standards Committee, *International Accounting Standards No. 12*, "Income Taxes" (October 1996).

differences in the book and tax bases of assets and liabilities in the example. However, suppose the firm had not yet received the $25 of interest on the municipal bond investment by the end of the first year. It would show an interest receivable on its financial reporting balance sheet of $25, but no receivable would appear on its tax balance sheet. Because the tax law does not tax such interest, the difference between the book and tax basis is a permanent difference. The firm would eliminate this book-tax difference before moving to the next step.

Step 3. Next, separate the remaining differences into those that give rise to future tax *deductions* and those that give rise to future taxable *income*. Exhibit 2.10 summarizes the possibilities and gives several examples of these temporary differences, as later chapters discuss. The difference between the book basis ($6) and the tax basis ($0) of the warranty liability at the end of the first year means that the firm will have future tax deductions (assuming that the book basis of the estimate is accurate). The difference between the book basis ($60) and the tax basis ($40) of the equipment at the end of the first year gives rise to future taxable income (meaning that depreciation deductions will be lower, which will increase taxable income, all else equal). We multiply these differences by the marginal tax rate expected to apply *in those future periods*. In the example, the future tax deduction for the warranties results in a deferred tax asset at the end of the first year of $2.4 (= 0.40 × [$6 book basis − $0 tax basis]). The future taxable income (due to the lower future depreciation of the equipment) results in a deferred tax liability at the end of the first year of $8 (= 0.40 × [$60 book basis − $40 tax basis]).

EXHIBIT 2.10

Examples of Temporary Differences

	Assets	Liabilities
Future Tax Deduction *(results in deferred tax assets)*	Tax basis of assets exceeds financial reporting basis. *Example:* Accounts receivable using the direct charge-off method for uncollectible accounts for tax purposes exceeds accounts receivable (net) using the allowance method for financial reporting.	Tax basis of liabilities is less than financial reporting basis. *Example:* Tax reporting does not recognize an estimated liability for warranty claims (firms can deduct only actual expenditures on warranty claims), whereas firms must recognize such a liability for financial reporting to match warranty expense with sales revenue in the period of sale.
Future Taxable Income *(results in deferred tax liabilities)*	Tax basis of assets is less than financial reporting basis. *Example:* Depreciation is computed using accelerated depreciation for tax purposes and the straight-line method for financial reporting.	Tax basis of liabilities exceeds financial reporting basis. *Example:* Leases are recognized by a lessee, the user of the leased assets, as a capital lease for tax reporting and an operating lease for financial reporting.

Step 4. Finally, the rules for income tax accounting require managers to assess the likelihood that the firm will realize the future benefits of any recognized deferred tax assets. This assessment should consider the nature (whether cyclical or non-cyclical, for example) and characteristics (growing, mature, or declining, for example) of a firm's business and its tax planning strategies for the future. If realization of the benefits of deferred tax assets is "more likely than not" (that is, exceeds 50 percent), then deferred tax assets equal the amounts computed in Step 3. However, if it is "more likely than not" that the firm will *not* realize some or all of the deferred tax assets, then the firm must reduce the deferred tax asset using a valuation allowance (similar in concept to the allowance for uncollectible accounts receivable). The valuation allowance reduces the deferred tax assets to the amounts the firm expects to realize in the form of lower tax payments in the future (similar to a net realizable value approach). For purposes here, assume that the firm in the preceding illustration considers it more likely than not that it will realize the tax benefits of the deferred tax assets related to warranties and therefore recognizes no valuation allowance.

The result of this four-step procedure for the example is a deferred tax asset and a deferred tax liability at each balance sheet date. The amounts in the preceding illustration are as follows:

	January 1, First Year	December 31, First Year	December 31, Second Year
Deferred Tax Asset—Warranties	$0.0	$2.4	$1.6
Deferred Tax Liability—Equipment	0.0	8.0	0.0

Income tax expense for each period equals:

1. Income taxes currently payable on taxable income
2. Plus (minus) any increases (decreases) in deferred tax liabilities
3. Plus (minus) any decreases (increases) in deferred tax assets.

Thus, income tax expense in the preceding illustration is as follows:

	First Year	Second Year
Income Taxes Currently Payable on Taxable Income	$46.4	$59.2
Plus (Minus) Increase (Decrease) in Deferred Liability	8.0	(8.0)
Minus (Plus) Increase (Decrease) in Deferred Tax Asset	(2.4)	0.8
Income Tax Expense	$52.0	$52.0

The income statement approach illustrated in the first section and the balance sheet approach illustrated in this section yield identical results whenever (1) enacted tax rates applicable to future periods do not change and (2) the firm recognizes no valuation allowance on deferred tax assets. Legislated changes in tax rates applicable to future periods will cause the tax effects of previously recognized temporary differences to differ from the amounts in the deferred tax asset and deferred tax liability accounts. The firm revalues the deferred tax assets and liabilities for the change in tax rates and flows through the effect of the change to income tax expense in the year of the legislated change. A change in the valuation allowance for deferred tax assets likewise flows through immediately to income tax expense.

Reporting Income Taxes in the Financial Statements

Understanding income tax accounting becomes difficult because firms may not include all income taxes for a period on the line for income tax expense in the income statement. Some amounts may appear elsewhere:

- Discontinued Operations and Extraordinary Items: Under U.S. GAAP, firms with either of these categories of income for a particular period report them in separate sections of the income statement, each net of their income tax effects. Thus, income tax expense reflects income taxes on income from continuing operations only. IFRS does not permit extraordinary item categorizations, but exceptional or material items may be disclosed separately, including income tax effects.
- Other Comprehensive Income: Unrealized changes in the market value of marketable securities classified as "available for sale," unrealized changes in the market value of hedged financial instruments and derivatives classified as cash flow hedges, unrealized foreign currency translation adjustments, and certain changes in pension and other post-employment benefit assets and liabilities appear in other comprehensive income, net of their tax effects. These items usually give rise to deferred tax assets or deferred tax liabilities because the income tax law includes such gains and losses in taxable income when realized. Thus, a portion of the change in deferred tax assets and liabilities on the balance sheet does not flow through income tax expense on the income statement.

PepsiCo's Reporting of Income Taxes

PepsiCo reports information on income taxes in Note 5, "Income Taxes," to its financial statements (Appendix A), excerpts of which appear in Exhibit 2.11. Income tax expense for 2008 of $1,879 million includes $1,634 million currently owed and $245 million deferred. Thus, excluding permanent differences, PepsiCo's income for financial reporting exceeded its taxable income for 2008 (as evidenced by the $245 of deferred tax expense, reflecting income tax liabilities that will be due in the future). In contrast, for 2007, income taxes currently owed exceeds total income tax expense, suggesting that PepsiCo's taxable income exceeded its income for financial reporting (consistent with the reversal of previously deferred income tax liabilities).

At the end of 2008, PepsiCo's deferred tax assets exceeded its deferred tax liabilities, for a net deferred tax asset of $168 million. In the previous year, PepsiCo ended with deferred tax liabilities in excess of deferred tax assets, for a net deferred tax liability of $321 million. The $489 million change from a net deferred tax liability to a net deferred tax asset differs substantially from the amount of deferred tax expense of $245 million (a combined discrepancy of $734 million = $489 million deferred tax *benefit* minus $245 million *expense*). This difference reflects a number of items, but a large explanation for the difference between the change in the deferred tax amounts on the balance sheet and deferred tax expense relates to the components of other comprehensive income shown in the Statement of Shareholders' Equity and accumulated other comprehensive loss, shown in Note 13, "Accumulated Other Comprehensive Loss" (Appendix A). For example, the large adjustment for "Unamortized pension and retiree medical, net of tax" includes approximately $643 million of tax adjustments for 2008 other comprehensive income (= $1,288 tax effect for 2008 minus the $645 tax effect for 2007), which offset declines in the fair value of pension and retiree medical assets during 2008 of approximately $2.2 billion (= $5,782 + $1,595 − $3,974 − $1,165), as reported in Note 7, "Pension, Retiree Medical and Savings Plans" (Appendix A). The complexity of accounting for deferred taxes makes it difficult to fully reconcile deferred tax expense to changes in the balance sheet accounts.

EXHIBIT 2.11

Excerpts from PepsiCo's Note 5 on Income Taxes (amounts in millions)

Income Statement for Year:	**2008**	**2007**	**2006**
Provision for income taxes—continuing operations:			
Current	$1,634	$2,015	$1,401
Deferred	245	(42)	(54)
Total	$1,879	$1,973	$1,347

Balance Sheet at End of Year:	**2008**	**2007**
Gross deferred tax liabilities (details omitted)	$2,442	$2,555
Gross deferred tax assets (details omitted)	$3,267	$2,929
Valuation allowances	(657)	(695)
Deferred tax assets, net	$2,610	$2,234
Net Deferred Tax (Assets) Liabilities	$ (168)	$ 321

	2008	**2007**
Deferred taxes included within:		
ASSETS:		
Prepaid expenses and other current assets	$ 372	$ 325
Other assets	22	—
LIABILITIES:		
Deferred income taxes	226	646
Analysis of valuation allowances:		
Balance, beginning of year	695	624
(Benefit) / Provision	(5)	39
Other (deductions) / additions	(33)	32
Balance, end of year	$ 657	$ 695

Note that Exhibit 2.11 also indicates that PepsiCo's gross deferred tax assets in both 2007 and 2008 were accompanied by valuation allowances. For 2008, the valuation allowance was $657 million on the gross deferred tax assets of $3,267 million. The valuation allowance likely relates to $7.2 billion of operating loss carryforwards (which create large deferred tax assets) that have various expiration dates. (See Note 5 to PepsiCo's financial statements in Appendix A.) If PepsiCo's management determines that it is more likely than not that some portion of these carryforwards will not be able to be used, a valuation allowance must be established.

Finally, the last table in Exhibit 2.11 indicates that PepsiCo's deferred tax assets and liabilities appear in three locations on the balance sheet—current assets ("Prepaid expenses and other current assets"), noncurrent assets ("Other assets"), and noncurrent liabilities ("Deferred income taxes").

You will return to the study of income taxes in Chapter 8 to explore in greater depth the concepts and procedures of accounting for income taxes, which you may find challenging.

FRAMEWORK FOR ANALYZING THE EFFECTS OF TRANSACTIONS ON THE FINANCIAL STATEMENTS

In each period, firms prepare financial statements that aggregate and summarize the results of numerous transactions. This section presents and illustrates an analytical framework for understanding the effects of various transactions on the financial statements. The beginning of this chapter noted that understanding the impact of individual transactions is important because financial statement analysis requires an understanding of the composition of current financial statements. Understanding the composition of the current financial statements is necessary for analyzing cash flows (Chapter 3), profitability (Chapter 4), and risk (Chapter 5), which help the analyst project future results (Chapter 10) so that the analyst can estimate the value of a firm (Chapters 11–14). With this in mind, consider the following examples of publicly traded corporations and how the business descriptions generate questions about the effect of various transactions on the financial statements, which an analyst interested in projecting future earnings and cash flows for valuation purposes must know.

Example 22

PepsiCo combines various ingredients to produce syrup for its soft drinks for its beverages unit. It sells the syrup to its bottlers, who add water and other ingredients to manufacture the finished soft drink and then bottle it. PepsiCo owns approximately 40 percent of the common stock of its bottlers, with individuals and other entities owning the remainder. When PepsiCo sells syrup to the bottlers, how should it recognize this income? Should it recognize revenue immediately in an amount equal to the selling price of the syrup, just like it would if it sold the syrup to nonaffiliated bottlers? Or should PepsiCo delay the recognition of revenue until the bottlers manufacture and sell soft drinks to end customers? What assets and liabilities of the bottlers, if any, should PepsiCo recognize in its balance sheets? Should PepsiCo include all of the assets and liabilities of the bottlers in its balance sheet; a proportion of the assets and liabilities equal to its ownership percentage; or none of these assets and liabilities, merely showing its ownership of the bottlers as an investment? How would the analysis of PepsiCo's profitability and risk differ depending on PepsiCo's accounting methods for transactions with and investments in its bottlers?

Example 23

Xerox Corporation sells photocopying machines, photographic paper, and after-sale maintenance services in bundled packages to customers on multiyear installment payment plans. Xerox generates four types of income from this activity: (1) income from manufacturing and selling the machines for more than their cost, (2) income from selling photographic paper for more than the cost of that paper, (3) maintenance income from providing services over the life of the maintenance contract, and (4) interest income from providing financing services over the life of the installment sales contract. What is the impact on total assets and net income each year if Xerox attributes too much of the cash it will receive to the manufacturing activity and too little to the maintenance services? What is the impact on total assets and net income each year if Xerox uses a discount rate of 7 percent instead of 8 percent to discount the cash flows to their present value? What amount, if any, will appear among liabilities related to Xerox's obligation under the maintenance agreement?

Example 24

Majesco Entertainment Company develops and markets video game software for use on platforms such as the Wii™, Game Boy™, Xbox®, and PlayStation®. The company makes periodic milestone payments to independent software developers during the development stage. Occasionally, software requires the use of licensed intellectual property, which requires Majesco to pay license fees, and sometimes such arrangements stipulate minimum royalty payments if the intellectual property is part of a video game. The company distributes video games through outlets such as Best Buy, Walmart, Target, and Toys"R"Us. Not all software development projects lead to a marketable video game. How should Majesco Entertainment account for the milestone payments made to the independent software developers? Are these payments assets, expenses, or deferred expenses? Do intellectual property licensing agreements trigger recognition of an asset or a liability? How does the accounting for software development costs and licensing agreements affect the analysis of Majesco Entertainment's profitability?

Example 25

Tyco International engaged in extensive restructuring of its operations, closing down or selling manufacturing facilities and severing employees. U.S. GAAP and IFRS require firms to recognize restructuring expenses when they commit to a restructuring plan, even though several years may elapse before completing the plan. Will the recognition of restructuring expense result in an immediate decrease in assets, an increase in liabilities, or both? What is the effect on the income statement when the firm actually closes or sells a manufacturing facility or severs employees? What is the effect on subsequent balance sheet and income statement amounts if the firm discovers later that its initial restructuring expense was too small or too large? Might managers be able to manipulate earnings through the use of these estimates?

Example 26

Nortel Networks made numerous corporate acquisitions in recent years totaling \$33.5 billion. It allocated \$14.5 billion of the purchase price to identifiable assets such as accounts receivable, inventories, plant, and equipment and to identifiable liabilities such as accounts payable and long-term debt. Nortel allocated the remaining \$19 billion to goodwill. What would be the effect on net income of subsequent years if Nortel had allocated more of the purchase price to identifiable assets and liabilities and less to goodwill? Nortel subsequently recognized a \$12.3 billion goodwill impairment loss because the fair value of the acquired firms had declined since the acquisitions. What is the impact of the goodwill impairment loss on total assets, total liabilities, and shareholders' equity?

At this point, you likely experienced some difficulty understanding the effects of each of these transactions on the financial statements. This is expected. Chapters 6–9 discuss important transactions like these in greater depth. These examples should help you see the need for an analytical framework to structure your thinking about business transactions and their effects on the financial statements.

Overview of the Analytical Framework

The analytical framework relies on the balance sheet equation:

$$\text{Assets (A)} = \text{Liabilities (L)} + \text{Total Shareholders' Equity (TSE)}$$

We can expand Total Shareholders' Equity (TSE) into its component parts, which will help identify the sources of changes in shareholders' net investment in a firm:

$$\begin{array}{c}\text{Total Shareholders'}\\ \text{Equity}\end{array} = \begin{array}{c}\text{Contributed}\\ \text{Capital (CC)}\end{array} + \begin{array}{c}\text{Accumulated Other}\\ \text{Comprehensive Income (AOCI)}\end{array} + \begin{array}{c}\text{Retained}\\ \text{Earnings (RE)}\end{array}$$

Contributed Capital (CC) accumulates net stock transactions with shareholders and includes accounts such as par value of common stock, additional paid-in-capital, treasury stock, and other paid-in-capital accounts. Accumulated Other Comprehensive Income (AOCI) is the "holding tank" discussed in Chapter 1 and earlier in this chapter, where unrealized gains or losses on certain assets and liabilities are held until realization occurs. Finally, Retained Earnings (RE) is simply the accumulation of all net income minus dividends (and occasionally other transactions).

Firms prepare balance sheets at the beginning and end of a period. Thus, for each component of the balance sheet equation, the following equations hold:

$$A_{BEG} + \Delta A = A_{END}$$
$$L_{BEG} + \Delta L = L_{END}$$
$$TSE_{BEG} + \Delta TSE = TSE_{END}$$

where *BEG* and *END* subscripts refer to beginning-of-period and end-of-period balances, respectively, and Δ indicates changes in balances. Changes in assets, liabilities, and total shareholders' equity over a period reflect the net effect of all individual transactions during the period, which is why it is important to understand how individual transactions affect the financial statements. Changes in total shareholders' equity have multiple components, so it reflects the net of stock transactions with owners, the "holding tank" of unrealized gains and losses on certain assets and liabilities, and the accumulation of net income minus dividends. Because of this mix of elements in TSE, it is helpful to partition the change in total shareholders' equity into these components:

$$\Delta TSE = \begin{matrix}\text{Stock transactions}\\(\Delta\text{Stock})\end{matrix} + \begin{matrix}\text{Other Comprehensive}\\\text{Income (OCI)}\end{matrix} + \text{Net Income (NI)} - \text{Dividends (D)}$$

Thus, as a working framework for capturing beginning-of-period and end-of-period balance sheets as well as changes during the period (which include changes due to net income recognized on the income statement), we use the following framework to summarize transactions and events throughout this book:

A_{BEG} =	L_{BEG}	+	CC_{BEG}	+	$AOCI_{BEG}$	+	RE_{BEG}
+ΔA	+ΔL		+ΔStock		+OCI		+NI − D
A_{END} =	L_{END}	+	CC_{END}	+	$AOCI_{END}$	+	RE_{END}

To demonstrate this analytical framework, which will be used extensively throughout this book, the following examples illustrate how to apply this framework to several of the transactions described earlier in this chapter. For the transactions we analyze, we present the analytical framework showing how the transaction affects (increases or decreases shown by +/− signs and amounts) the categories of the balance sheet. We also present the journal entries to show how each transaction will affect specific financial statement accounts.

Example 27

In Examples 1 and 15, In-N-Out Burger sold land with an acquisition cost of $210,000 for $300,000 in cash. For simplicity, assume that In-N-Out Burger pays taxes immediately at a 40 percent rate.

	Assets		=	Liabilities	+	Shareholders' Equity: CC	AOCI	RE	
1.	Cash	+300,000						Gain on Sale of Land	+90,000
	Land	−210,000							

Cash	300,000	
Land		210,000
Gain on Sale of Land		90,000

	Assets		=	Liabilities	+	Shareholders' Equity: CC	AOCI	RE	
2.	Cash	−36,000						Income Tax Expense	−36,000

Income Tax Expense	36,000		(0.40 × [300,000 − 210,000])
Cash		36,000	

Note that if you wanted to compute overall changes in balance sheet accounts across a set of transactions, you need only sum the amounts within any partition. For example, the overall impact on assets of the above transactions is a net increase of $54,000, equal to the aggregation of +$300,000, −$210,000, and −$36,000. Similarly, to compute the net impact on income, sum the amounts in the Retained Earnings column. In the above transactions, the impact on *net income* is +$90,000 and −$36,000, or net income of $54,000. Not surprisingly, the change in assets in this example exactly equals the change in retained earnings (because there were no effects on liabilities, contributed capital, or accumulated other comprehensive income).

Example 28

In Examples 2 and 16, we discussed the accumulation of costs into inventory and subsequent sale of wine by Mollydooker Wines. The following three events affect the financial statements:

1. The sale of wine for $2,000,000 on account (Accounts Receivable)
2. The derecognition of the wine inventory with an accumulated cost of $1,600,000
3. The immediate payment of income taxes at a 40 percent rate

	Assets	=	Liabilities	+	Shareholders' Equity: CC	AOCI	RE
1.	Accounts Receivable +2,000,000						Sales +2,000,000

Accounts Receivable	2,000,000	
Sales		2,000,000

	Assets	=	Liabilities	+	Shareholders' Equity: CC	AOCI	RE
2.	Inventory −1,600,000						Cost of Goods Sold −1,600,000

Cost of Goods Sold	1,600,000	
Inventory		1,600,000

	Assets	=	Liabilities	+	Shareholders' Equity: CC	AOCI	RE
3.	Cash −160,000						Income Tax Expense −160,000

Income Tax Expense	160,000		(0.40 × [2,000,000 − 1,600,000])
Cash		160,000	

Summing the increases and decreases in any column indicates the net effect of the wine sale (after taxes). For example, the change in assets as a result of this transaction is +$2,000,000 − $1,600,000 − $160,000 = $240,000. Similarly, shareholders' equity increased by the same amount. This transaction has no other effect on Mollydooker's balance sheet. The income effects of this transaction are the sum of any effects reflected under RE that would appear on the income statement, which for this transaction would be +$2,000,000 (Sales), –$1,600,000 (Cost of Goods Sold), and –$160,000 (Tax Expense), for a net impact on income of +$240,000.

Example 29

In Examples 8 and 17, Smithfield Foods records an inventory write-down for live hog inventory, driven by the drop in market prices of live hogs. The live hog inventory with a book value of $882 million was written down by approximately 5 percent, or $44 million. Income tax law would not permit Smithfield Foods to deduct the write-down on the live hog inventory until the loss is realized. Thus, the 40 percent tax effect of the write-down becomes a deferred tax asset until that time. This leads to the recording of the following two effects:

	Assets	=	Liabilities	+	Shareholders' Equity CC	AOCI	RE
1.	Inventory −44,000,000						Inventory Write-Down Loss −44,000,000

Inventory Write-Down Loss	44,000,000	
Inventory		44,000,000

	Assets	=	Liabilities	+	Shareholders' Equity CC	AOCI	RE
2.	Deferred Tax Asset +17,600,000						Income Tax Expense +17,600,000

Deferred Tax Asset	17,600,000		(0.40 × 44,000,000)
Income Tax Expense		17,600,000	

The overall impact of the $44 million write-down is to decrease assets by $26.4 million (= $44 million write-down offset by $17.6 million deferred tax effect). The same amount flows through to net income as well, reducing retained earnings.

Example 30

In Examples 5 and 9, Petroleo Brasileiro purchases computer equipment from Sun Microsystems and signs a five-year note payable in the amount of $998,178 (= present value of $250,000 a year for five years at 8 percent). The purchase, use of the equipment, and first-year principal and interest payment trigger that the following events be recognized (ignoring income taxes):

1. Purchase of the computer equipment and signing of the note payable
2. Depreciation of $199,636 (= $998,178/5) on the computer for the first year based on a five-year useful life
3. Interest expense for the first year of $79,854 (= 0.08 × $998,178), the cash payment of $250,000, and the reduction in principal of $170,146 (= $250,000 − $79,854)

	Assets	=	Liabilities	+	Shareholders' Equity CC	AOCI	RE
1.	Computer Equipment +998,178		Note Payable +998,178				

Computer Equipment	998,178	
Note Payable		998,178

	Assets	=	Liabilities	+	Shareholders' Equity CC	AOCI	RE
2.	Accumulated Depreciation −199,636						Depreciation Expense −199,636

Depreciation Expense	199,636	
Accumulated Depreciation		199,636

	Assets	=	Liabilities	+	Shareholders' Equity CC	AOCI	RE
3.	Cash −250,000		Note Payable −170,146				Interest Expense −79,854

Interest Expense	79,854	
Note Payable	170,146	
Cash		250,000

Example 31

Example 20 discussed Microsoft's investment in marketable equity securities. The following events occurred:

1. Initial $4,500,000 investment in marketable equity securities
2. Increase in fair value as of December 31 to $4,900,000
3. Deferred tax effect of the unrealized gain (assume 40 percent)
4. Sale of marketable equity securities in June for $5,000,000
5. Settlement of the tax liability (assume taxes paid immediately after the sale)

	Assets	=	Liabilities	+	Shareholders' Equity		
					CC	AOCI	RE
1.	Marketable Equity Securities +4,500,000 Cash −4,500,000						

Marketable Equity Securities	4,500,000		
Cash		4,500,000	

	Assets	=	Liabilities	+	Shareholders' Equity		
					CC	AOCI	RE
2.	Marketable Equity Securities +400,000					Unrealized Holding Gain +400,000	

Marketable Equity Securities	400,000		
Unrealized Holding Gain		400,000	

	Assets	=	Liabilities	+	Shareholders' Equity		
					CC	AOCI	RE
3.			Deferred Tax Liability +160,000			Unrealized Holding Gain −160,000	

Unrealized Holding Gain	160,000		
Deferred Tax Liability		160,000	

	Assets	=	Liabilities	+	Shareholders' Equity		
					CC	AOCI	RE
4.	Cash +5,000,000 Marketable Equity Securities −4,900,000					Unrealized Holding Gain −400,000	Gain on Sale of Marketable Equity Securities +500,000

Cash	5,000,000		
Unrealized Holding Gain	400,000		
Marketable Equity Securities		4,900,000	
Gain on Sale of Marketable Equity Securities		500,000	

	Assets	=	Liabilities	+	Shareholders' Equity		
					CC	AOCI	RE
5.	Cash −200,000		Deferred Tax Liability −160,000			Unrealized Holding Gain +160,000	Income Tax Expense −200,000

Income Tax Expense	200,000		(0.40 × 500,000)
Deferred Tax Liability	160,000		
Unrealized Holding Gain		160,000	
Cash		200,000	

This example demonstrates the mechanics of how other comprehensive income affects the financial statements. At the end of the year, when Microsoft has an unrealized gain of $400,000, the value of the marketable equity securities is written up to its fair value of $4,900,000. Because this increase has not been realized in a market transaction (such as a sale), Microsoft puts this gain in the accumulated other comprehensive income "holding tank" rather than recognize it as part of net income. However, note that Microsoft will be required to present this amount as part of other comprehensive income on the statement of comprehensive income. The amount recognized as other comprehensive income is then closed out to the accumulated other comprehensive income account and labeled as unrealized holding gain or loss. When Microsoft sells the marketable equity securities in June, the $400,000 is removed from the "holding tank" of accumulated other comprehensive income and recognized in income as gain on sale, along with an additional $100,000 that occurred subsequent to December. Of course, the associated tax effects are accumulated and reversed from accumulated other comprehensive income as well. The overall net effect is that Microsoft realizes a $500,000 gain, offset by $200,000 of income tax expense, for an increase in net assets of $300,000.

Summary of the Analytical Framework

This analytical framework may seem a bit unfamiliar at this stage in your study. Repeated use in later chapters will not only increase your comfort, but also demonstrate the framework's value in your gaining an understanding of the effects of a variety of complex business transactions on financial statements. You may find it useful to use the framework with other examples. To that end, several problems at the end of the chapter require the use of this analytical framework. The importance of understanding this framework cannot be overemphasized, as you can rest assured that one of the first questions managers or investors will ask about a prospective event (such as a large sale or an investment) is "How will this affect our financials?"

SUMMARY

This chapter provides a conceptual foundation for understanding the balance sheet and the income statement. U.S. GAAP, IFRS, and other major sets of accounting standards are best characterized as mixed attribute accounting models. Different assets and liabilities on the balance sheet are valued using various methods based on historical values and current values. The conventional accounting model uses historical, or acquisition, costs to value assets and liabilities and delays the recognition of value changes until external market transactions validate their amounts. Use of acquisition costs generally results in more reliable asset and liability valuations than do current values, but such valuation can lose relevance for users wanting to value the firm, especially as the time from the initial transaction passes and historical values diverge from current values. Recognizing value changes for assets and liabilities still leaves open the question of when the value change should affect net income. Such value changes may affect net income immediately or may affect it later, initially being temporarily held as accumulated other comprehensive income (in shareholders' equity) until validated through an external market transaction. Over sufficiently long time periods, net income equals cash inflows minus cash outflows (excluding cash transactions with owners). Different approaches to asset and liability valuation and to income measurement affect the pattern of net income over time, but not its ultimate amount.

Almost every transaction affecting net income has an income tax effect. The financial reporting issue is whether firms should recognize the income tax effect when the related revenue or expense affects net income or when it affects taxable income. U.S. GAAP requires firms to measure income tax expense each period based on the pretax income for financial reporting, excluding permanent differences. When income tax expense differs from income taxes currently owed on taxable income, firms recognize deferred tax assets and deferred tax liabilities. Deferred tax assets arise when taxable income exceeds book income. Firms prepay taxes now but reduce taxes paid later when the temporary difference reverses and book income exceeds taxable income. Deferred tax liabilities are the opposite, arising when book income exceeds taxable income. Firms delay paying taxes now, but will pay the taxes later when the temporary differences reverse and taxable income exceeds book income.

Later chapters discuss the specific accounting procedures for various assets, liabilities, revenues, and expenses. The analytical framework discussed in this chapter provides a valuable tool for analyzing business transactions and understanding their effects on the financial statements. The analytical framework uses the balance sheet equation and captures changes in balance sheet amounts, including changes in shareholders' equity reflecting income effects. Repeated application of this framework in later chapters will demonstrate its value as a tool of analysis.

QUESTIONS, EXERCISES, PROBLEMS, AND CASES

Questions and Exercises

2.1 ASSET VALUATION AND INCOME RECOGNITION. "Asset valuation and recognition of net income closely relate." Explain, including conditions when they do not.

2.2 RELIABILITY VERSUS RELEVANCE. "Some asset valuations using historical costs are highly relevant and very reliable, whereas others may be reliable but lack relevance. Some asset valuations based on fair values are highly relevant and very reliable, whereas others may be relevant but lack reliability." Explain and provide examples of each.

2.3 INCOME FLOWS VERSUS CASH FLOWS. The text states, "Over sufficiently long time periods, net income equals cash inflows minus cash outflows, other than cash flows with owners." Demonstrate the accuracy of this statement in the following scenario: Two friends contributed $50,000 each to form a new business. The owners used the amounts contributed to purchase a machine for $100,000 cash. They estimated that the useful life of the machine was five years and the salvage value was $20,000. They rented out the machine to a customer for an annual rental of $25,000 a year for five years. Annual cash operating costs for insurance, taxes, and other items totaled $6,000 annually. At the end of the fifth year, the owners sold the equipment for $22,000, instead of the $20,000 salvage value initially estimated. *(Hint: Compute the total net income and the total cash flows other than cash flows with owners for the five-year period as a whole.)*

2.4 MEASUREMENT OF ACQUISITION COST. United Van Lines purchased a truck with a list price of $250,000 subject to a 6 percent discount if paid within 30 days. United Van Lines paid within the discount period. It paid $4,000 to obtain title to the truck with the state and an $800 license fee for the first year of operation. It paid $1,500 to paint the firm's name on the truck and $2,500 for property and liability insurance for the first year of operation. What acquisition cost of this truck should United Van Lines record in its accounting records? Indicate the appropriate accounting treatment of any amount not included in acquisition cost.

2.5 MEASUREMENT OF A MONETARY ASSET. Boeing sold a 767 aircraft to American Airlines on January 1, 2009. The sales agreement required American Airlines to pay $10 million immediately and $10 million on December 31 of each year for 20 years, beginning on December 31, 2009. Boeing and American Airlines judge that 8 percent is an appropriate interest rate for this arrangement.

a. Compute the present value of the receivable on Boeing's books on January 1, 2009, immediately after receiving the $10 million down payment.
b. Compute the present value of the receivable on Boeing's books on December 31, 2009.
c. Compute the present value of the receivable on Boeing's books on December 31, 2010.

2.6 FAIR VALUE MEASUREMENTS. The text discusses inputs managers might use to determine fair values of assets and liabilities and identifies different classifications of assets identified in SFAS No. 157. Suppose a major university endowment has investments in a wide array of assets, including (a) common stocks; (b) bonds; (c) real estate; (d) timber investments, which receive cash flows from sales of timber; (e) private equity funds; and (f) illiquid asset-backed securities. Consider how the portfolio manager would estimate the fair values of each of those classes of assets, and characterize the inputs you identify as Level 1, Level 2, or Level 3.

2.7 COMPUTATION OF INCOME TAX EXPENSE. A firm's income tax return shows $50,000 of income taxes owed for 2009. For financial reporting, the firm reports deferred tax assets of $42,900 at the beginning of 2009 and $38,700 at the end of 2009. It reports deferred tax liabilities of $28,600 at the beginning of 2009 and $34,200 at the end of 2009.

- **a.** Compute the amount of income tax expense for 2009.
- **b.** Assume for this part that the firm's deferred tax assets are as stated above for 2009 but that its deferred tax liabilities were $58,600 at the beginning of 2009 and $47,100 at the end of 2009. Compute the amount of income tax expense for 2009.
- **c.** Explain contextually why income tax expense is higher than taxes owed in Part a and lower than taxes owed in Part b.

2.8 COMPUTATION OF INCOME TAX EXPENSE. A firm's income tax return shows income taxes for 2009 of $35,000. The firm reports deferred tax assets before any valuation allowance of $24,600 at the beginning of 2009 and $27,200 at the end of 2009. It reports deferred tax liabilities of $18,900 at the beginning of 2009 and $16,300 at the end of 2009.

- **a.** Assume for this part that the valuation allowance on the deferred tax assets totaled $6,400 at the beginning of 2009 and $7,200 at the end of 2009. Compute the amount of income tax expense for 2009.
- **b.** Assume for this part that the valuation allowance on the deferred tax assets totaled $6,400 at the beginning of 2009 and $4,800 at the end of 2009. Compute the amount of income tax expense for 2009.

Problems and Cases

2.9 EFFECT OF VALUATION METHOD FOR NONMONETARY ASSET ON BALANCE SHEET AND INCOME STATEMENT. Walmart (WMT) acquires a tract of land on January 1, 2009, for $100,000 cash. On December 31, 2009, the current market value of the land is $150,000. On December 31, 2010, the current market value of the land is $120,000. The firm sells the land on December 31, 2011, for $180,000 cash.

Required

Ignore income taxes. Using the analytical framework discussed in the chapter, indicate the effect of the preceding information for 2009, 2010, and 2011 under each of the following valuation methods (Parts a–c).

- **a.** Valuation of the land at acquisition cost until sale of the land.
- **b.** Valuation of the land at current market value but including unrealized gains and losses in accumulated other comprehensive income until sale of the land.

c. Valuation of the land at current market value and including market value changes each year in net income.

d. Why is retained earnings on December 31, 2011, equal to $80,000 in all three cases despite the reporting of different amounts of net income each year?

2.10 EFFECT OF VALUATION METHOD FOR MONETARY ASSET ON BALANCE SHEET AND INCOME STATEMENT. Refer to Problem 2.9. Assume that Walmart (WMT) has accounted for the value of the land at acquisition cost and sells the land on December 31, 2011, for a two-year note receivable with a present value of $180,000 instead of for cash. The note bears interest at 8 percent and requires cash payments of $100,939 on December 31, 2012 and 2013. Interest rates for notes of this risk level increase to 10 percent on December 31, 2012, resulting in a market value for the note on this date of $91,762.

Required

Ignore income taxes. Using the analytical framework discussed in the chapter, indicate the effect of the preceding information for 2011, 2012, and 2013 under each of the following valuation methods.

a. Valuation of the note at the present value of future cash flows using the historical market interest rate of 8 percent (Approach 1).

b. Valuation of the note at the present value of future cash flows, adjusting the note to fair value upon changes in market interest rates and including unrealized gains and losses in net income (Approach 3).

c. Why is retained earnings on December 31, 2013, equal to $101,878 in both cases despite the reporting of different amounts of net income each year?

2.11 EFFECT OF VALUATION METHOD FOR NONMONETARY ASSET ON BALANCE SHEET AND INCOME STATEMENT. Southern Copper Corporation (PCU) acquired mining equipment for $100,000 cash on January 1, 2009. The equipment had an expected useful life of four years and zero salvage value. PCU calculates depreciation using the straight-line method over the remaining expected useful life in all cases. On December 31, 2009, after recognizing depreciation for the year, PCU learns that new equipment now offered on the market makes the purchased equipment partially obsolete. The market value of PCU's equipment on December 31, 2009, reflecting this obsolescence, is $60,000. The expected useful life does not change. On December 31, 2010, the market value of the equipment is $48,000. PCU sells the equipment on January 1, 2012, for $26,000.

Required

Ignore income taxes.

a. Assume for this part that PCU accounts for the equipment using acquisition cost adjusted for depreciation and impairment losses. Using the analytical framework discussed in the chapter, indicate the effects of the following events on the balance sheet and income statement.

(1) Acquisition of the equipment for cash on January 1, 2009.
(2) Depreciation for 2009.
(3) Impairment loss for 2009.
(4) Depreciation for 2010.
(5) Depreciation for 2011.
(6) Sale of the equipment on January 1, 2012.

b. Assume that PCU accounts for the equipment using current fair market values adjusted for depreciation and impairment losses (with changes in fair market values recognized in net income). Using the analytical framework discussed in the chapter, indicate the effect of the following events on the balance sheet and income statement.

(1) Acquisition of the equipment for cash on January 1, 2009.
(2) Depreciation for 2009.
(3) Impairment loss for 2009.
(4) Depreciation for 2010.
(5) Recognition of unrealized holding gain or loss for 2010.
(6) Depreciation for 2011.
(7) Recognition of unrealized holding gain or loss for 2011.
(8) Sale of the equipment on January 1, 2012.

c. After the equipment is sold, why is retained earnings on January 1, 2012, equal to a negative $74,000 in both cases despite having shown a different pattern of expenses, gains, and losses over time?

2.12 EFFECT OF VALUATION METHOD FOR MONETARY ASSET ON BALANCE SHEET AND INCOME STATEMENT. Alfa Romeo incurs costs of $30,000 in manufacturing a red convertible automobile during 2009. Assume that it incurs all of these costs in cash. Alfa Romeo sells this automobile to you on January 1, 2010, for $45,000. You pay $5,000 immediately and agree to pay $14,414 on December 31, 2010, 2011, and 2012. Based on the interest rate appropriate for this note of 4 percent on January 1, 2012, the present value of the note is $40,000. The interest rate appropriate for this note is 5 percent on December 31, 2010, resulting in a present value of the remaining cash flows of $26,802. The interest rate appropriate for this note is 8 percent on December 31, 2011, resulting in a present value of the remaining cash flows of $13,346.

Required

Ignore income taxes.

a. Assume that Alfa Romeo accounts for this note throughout the three years using its initial present value and the historical interest rate (Approach 1). Using the analytical framework discussed in the chapter, indicate the effects of the following events on the balance sheet and income statement.

(1) Manufacture of the automobile during 2009.
(2) Sale of the automobile on January 1, 2010.
(3) Cash received and interest revenue recognized on December 31, 2010.
(4) Cash received and interest revenue recognized on December 31, 2011.
(5) Cash received and interest revenue recognized on December 31, 2012.

b. Assume that Alfa Romeo values this note receivable at fair value each year with fair value changes recognized in net income (Approach 3). Changes in market interest rates affect the valuation of the note on the balance sheet immediately and the computation of interest revenue for the next year.

(1) Manufacture of the automobile during 2009.
(2) Sale of the automobile on January 1, 2010.
(3) Cash received and interest revenue recognized on December 31, 2010.
(4) Note receivable revalued and an unrealized holding gain or loss recognized on December 31, 2010.
(5) Cash received and interest revenue recognized on December 31, 2011.

(6) Note receivable revalued and an unrealized holding gain or loss recognized on December 31, 2011.
(7) Cash received and interest revenue recognized on December 31, 2012.

c. Why is retained earnings on December 31, 2012, equal to $18,242 in both cases despite having shown a different pattern of income over time?

d. Discuss the trade-off in financial reporting when moving from Approach 1 in Part a to Approach 3 in Part b.

2.13 DEFERRED TAX ASSETS. Components of the deferred tax asset of Biosante Pharmaceuticals are shown in Exhibit 2.12. The company had no deferred tax liabilities.

Required

a. At the end of 2008, the largest deferred tax asset is for net operating loss carryforwards. (Net operating loss carryforwards [also referred to as tax loss carryforwards] are amounts reported as taxable losses on tax filings. Because the tax authorities generally do not "pay" corporations for incurring losses, companies are allowed to "carry forward" taxable losses to future years to offset taxable income. These future tax benefits give rise to deferred tax assets.) As of the end of 2008, what is the dollar amount of the company's net operating loss carryforwards? What is the dollar amount of the deferred tax asset for the net operating loss carryforwards? Describe how these two amounts are related.

EXHIBIT 2.12

Income Tax Disclosures for Biosante Pharmaceuticals
(Problem 2.13)

	2008	2007
Net operating loss carryforwards	$23,609,594	$17,588,392
Tax basis in intangible assets	403,498	538,819
Research and development credits	3,415,143	2,569,848
Stock option expense	1,462,065	1,017,790
Other	56,063	103,235
Gross Deferred Tax Asset	$28,946,363	$21,818,084
Valuation allowance	(28,946,363)	(21,818,084)
Net Deferred Tax Asset	$ 0	$ 0

At December 31, 2008, the company had approximately $62,542,000 of net operating loss carryforwards available to reduce future taxable income for a period of up to 20 years. The net operating loss carryforwards expire in 2018–2028. The net operating loss carryforwards as well as amortization of various intangibles, principally acquired in-process research and development, generate deferred tax benefits that have been recorded as deferred tax assets and are entirely offset by a tax valuation allowance. The valuation allowance has been provided at 100 percent to reduce the deferred tax assets to zero, the amount management believes is more likely than not to be realized. In addition, the company has provided a full valuation allowance against $3,415,143 of research and development credits, which are available to reduce future income taxes, if any, through 2028.

b. Biosante has gross deferred tax assets of $28,946,363. However, the net deferred tax assets balance is zero. Explain.

c. The valuation allowance for the deferred tax asset increased from $21,818,084 to $28,946,363 between 2007 and 2008. How did this change affect the company's net income?

2.14 INTERPRETING INCOME TAX DISCLOSURES. The financial statements of ABC Corporation, a retail chain, reveal the information for income taxes shown in Exhibit 2.13.

EXHIBIT 2.13

Income Tax Disclosures for ABC Corporation (amounts in millions) (Problem 2.14)

For the Year Ended January 31:	2008	2007
Income before income taxes		
United States	$ 3,031	$ 2,603
Income tax expense		
Current:		
Federal	$ 908	$ 669
State and local	144	107
Total Current	$ 1,052	$ 776
Deferred:		
Federal	$ 83	$ 184
State and local	11	24
Total Deferred	$ 94	$ 208
Total	$ 1,146	$ 984

January 31:	2008	2007	2006
Components of deferred tax			
Assets and liabilities			
Deferred tax assets:			
Self-insured benefits	$ 179	$ 143	$ 188
Deferred compensation	332	297	184
Inventory	47	44	56
Postretirement health care obligation	38	42	41
Uncollectible accounts	147	133	113
Other	128	53	166
Total Deferred Tax Assets	$ 871	$ 712	$ 748
Deferred tax liabilities:			
Depreciation	$(1,136)	$ (945)	$ (826)
Pensions	(268)	(218)	(190)
Other	(96)	(84)	(59)
Total Deferred Tax Liabilities	$(1,500)	$(1,247)	$(1,075)
Net Deferred Tax Liability	$ (629)	$ (535)	$ (327)

Required

a. Assuming that ABC had no significant permanent differences between book income and taxable income, did income before taxes for financial reporting exceed or fall short of taxable income for 2007? Explain.

b. Did income before taxes for financial reporting exceed or fall short of taxable income for 2008? Explain.

c. Will the adjustment to net income for deferred taxes to compute cash flow from operations in the statement of cash flows result in an addition or a subtraction for 2007? For 2008?

d. ABC does not contract with an insurance agency for property and liability insurance; instead, it self-insures. ABC recognizes an expense and a liability each year for financial reporting to reflect its average expected long-term property and liability losses. When it experiences an actual loss, it charges that loss against the liability. The income tax law permits self-insured firms to deduct such losses only in the year sustained. Why are deferred taxes related to self-insurance disclosed as a deferred tax asset instead of a deferred tax liability? Suggest reasons for the direction of the change in amounts for this deferred tax asset between 2006 and 2008.

e. ABC treats certain storage and other inventory costs as expenses in the year incurred for financial reporting but must include these in inventory for tax reporting. Why are deferred taxes related to inventory disclosed as a deferred tax asset? Suggest reasons for the direction of the change in amounts for this deferred tax asset between 2006 and 2008.

f. Firms must recognize expenses related to postretirement health care and pension obligations as employees provide services, but claim an income tax deduction only when they make cash payments under the benefit plan. Why are deferred taxes related to health care obligation disclosed as a deferred tax asset? Why are deferred taxes related to pensions disclosed as a deferred tax liability? Suggest reasons for the direction of the change in amounts for these deferred tax items between 2006 and 2008.

g. Firms must recognize expenses related to uncollectible accounts when they recognize sales revenues, but claim an income tax deduction when they deem a particular customer's accounts uncollectible. Why are deferred taxes related to this item disclosed as a deferred tax asset? Suggest reasons for the direction of the change in amounts for this deferred tax asset between 2006 and 2008.

h. ABC uses the straight-line depreciation method for financial reporting and accelerated depreciation methods for income tax purposes. Why are deferred taxes related to depreciation disclosed as a deferred tax liability? Suggest reasons for the direction of the change in amounts for this deferred tax liability between 2006 and 2008.

2.15 INTERPRETING INCOME TAX DISCLOSURES. Prepaid Legal Services (PPD) is a company that sells insurance for legal expenses. Customers pay premiums in advance for coverage over some specified period. Thus, PPD obtains cash but has unearned revenue until the passage of time over the specified period of coverage. Also, the company pays various costs to acquire customers (such as sales materials, commissions, and prepayments to legal firms who provide services to customers). These upfront payments are expensed over the specified period that customers' contracts span. Exhibit 2.14 provides information from Prepaid Legal's income tax footnote.

EXHIBIT 2.14

Income Tax Disclosures for Prepaid Legal Services (Problem 2.15)

The provision for income taxes consists of the following:

	2008	2007	2006
Current	$36,840	$33,864	$27,116
Deferred	385	(552)	774
Total Provision for Income Taxes	$37,225	$33,312	$27,890

Deferred tax liabilities and assets at December 31, 2008 and 2007, are comprised of the following:

	2008	2007
Deferred tax liabilities relating to:		
Deferred member and associate service costs	$ 6,919	$ 7,367
Property and equipment	8,693	7,829
Unrealized investment gains	159	131
Total Deferred Tax Liabilities	$15,771	$15,327
Deferred tax assets relating to:		
Expenses not yet deducted for tax purposes	$ 4,028	$ 3,552
Deferred revenue and fees	11,138	11,564
Other	110	101
Total Deferred Tax Assets	$15,276	$15,217
Net Deferred Tax Liability	$ (495)	$ (110)

Required

a. Assuming that PPD had no significant permanent differences between book income and taxable income, did income before taxes for financial reporting exceed or fall short of taxable income for 2007? For 2008? Explain.

b. Will the adjustment to net income for deferred taxes to compute cash flow from operations in the statement of cash flows result in an addition or a subtraction for 2007? For 2008?

c. PPD must report as taxable income premiums collected from customers, although the company defers recognizing them as income for financial reporting purposes until they are earned over the contract period. Why are deferred taxes related to deferred revenue disclosed as a deferred tax asset instead of a deferred tax liability? Suggest reasons for the direction of the change in amounts for this deferred tax asset between 2007 and 2008.

d. Firms are generally allowed to deduct cash costs on their tax returns, although they might defer some of these costs for financial reporting purposes. As noted above, PPD defers various costs associated with obtaining customers. Why are deferred taxes related to this item disclosed as a deferred tax liability? Suggest reasons for the direction of the change in amounts for this deferred tax asset between 2007 and 2008.

e. Like most companies, PPD uses the straight-line depreciation method for financial reporting and accelerated depreciation methods for income tax purposes. Why are deferred taxes related to depreciation disclosed as a deferred tax liability? Suggest reasons for the direction of the change in amounts for this deferred tax liability between 2007 and 2008.

f. Based only on the selected disclosures from the income tax footnote provided in Exhibit 2.14 and your responses to Parts d and e above, do you believe that PPD reported growing or declining revenue and profitability in 2008 relative to 2007? Explain.

2.16 INTERPRETING INCOME TAX DISCLOSURES. The financial statements of Nike Corporation reveal the information regarding income taxes shown in Exhibit 2.15.

Required

a. Assuming that Nike had no significant permanent differences between book income and taxable income, did income before taxes for financial reporting exceed or fall short of taxable income for 2007? Explain.

b. Did book income before taxes for financial reporting exceed or fall short of taxable income for 2008? Explain.

c. Will the adjustment to net income for deferred taxes to compute cash flow from operations in the statement of cash flows result in an addition or a subtraction for 2008?

d. Nike recognizes provisions for sales returns and doubtful accounts each year in computing income for financial reporting. Nike cannot claim an income tax deduction for these returns and doubtful accounts until customers return goods or accounts receivable become uncollectible. Why do the deferred taxes for returns and doubtful accounts appear as deferred tax assets instead of deferred tax liabilities? Suggest possible reasons why the deferred tax asset for sales returns and doubtful accounts increased between 2007 and 2008.

e. Nike recognizes an expense related to deferred compensation as employees render services but cannot claim an income tax deduction until it pays cash to a retirement fund. Why do the deferred taxes for deferred compensation appear as a deferred tax asset? Suggest possible reasons why the deferred tax asset increased between 2007 and 2008.

f. Nike states that it recognizes a valuation allowance on deferred tax assets related to foreign loss carryforwards because the benefits of some of these losses will expire before the firm realizes the benefits. Why might the valuation allowance have decreased slightly between 2007 and 2008?

g. Nike reports a large deferred tax liability for Intangibles. In another footnote, Nike states, "During the fourth quarter ended May 31, 2008 the Company completed the acquisition of Umbro Plc ("Umbro"). As a result, $378.4 million was allocated to unamortized trademarks, $319.2 million was allocated to goodwill and $41.1 million was allocated to other amortized intangible assets consisting of Umbro's sourcing network, established customer relationships and the United Soccer League Franchise." Why would Nike report a deferred tax liability associated with this increase in intangible assets on the balance sheet?

h. Nike recognizes its share of the earnings of foreign subsidiaries each year for financial reporting but recognizes income from these investments for income tax reporting only when it receives a dividend. Why do the deferred taxes related to these investments appear as a deferred tax liability?

i. Why does Nike recognize both deferred tax assets and deferred tax liabilities related to investments in foreign operations?

EXHIBIT 2.15

Income Tax Disclosures for Nike Corporation (amounts in millions)
(Problem 2.16)

Income before income taxes is as follows:	2008	2007	2006
Income before income taxes:			
United States	$ 713.0	$ 805.1	$ 838.6
Foreign	1,789.9	1,394.8	1,303.0
	$2,502.9	$2,199.9	$2,414.6

The provision for income taxes consists of the following:	2008	2007	2006
Current:			
United States			
Federal	$ 469.9	$ 352.6	$ 359.0
State	58.4	59.6	60.6
Foreign	391.8	261.9	356.0
	$ 920.1	$ 674.1	$ 775.6
Deferred:			
United States			
Federal	$ (273.0)	$ 38.7	$ (4.2)
State	(5.0)	(4.8)	(6.8)
Foreign	(22.6)	0.4	(15.0)
	$ (300.6)	$ 34.3	$ (26.0)
Total Provision for Income Taxes	$ 619.5	$ 708.4	$ 749.6

Deferred tax assets and (liabilities) are comprised of the following:	2008	2007
Deferred tax assets:		
Allowance for doubtful accounts	$ 13.1	$ 12.4
Inventories	49.2	45.8
Sales returns reserves	49.2	42.1
Deferred compensation	158.4	132.5
Stock-based compensation	55.2	30.3
Reserves and accrued liabilities	57.0	46.2
Property, plant, and equipment	7.9	16.3
Foreign loss carry-forwards	40.1	37.5
Foreign tax credit carry-forwards	91.9	3.4
Hedges	42.9	26.2
Other	40.5	33.0
Total Deferred Tax Assets	$605.4	$425.7
Valuation allowance	(40.7)	(42.3)
Total Deferred Tax Assets after Valuation Allowance	$564.7	$383.4

EXHIBIT 2.15 (Continued)

	2008	2007
Deferred tax liabilities:		
Undistributed earnings of foreign subsidiaries	$(113.2)	$(232.6)
Property, plant, and equipment	(67.4)	(66.1)
Intangibles	(214.2)	(97.2)
Hedges	(1.3)	(2.5)
Other	(0.7)	(17.8)
Total Deferred Tax Liability	$(396.8)	$(416.2)
Net Deferred Tax Asset (Liability)	$ 167.9	$ (32.8)

2.17 ANALYZING TRANSACTIONS. Using the analytical framework illustrated in the chapter, indicate the effect of the following related transactions of a firm.

- **a.** January 1: Issued 10,000 shares of common stock for $50,000.
- **b.** January 1: Acquired a building costing $35,000, paying $5,000 in cash and borrowing the remainder from a bank.
- **c.** During the year: Acquired inventory costing $40,000 on account from various suppliers.
- **d.** During the year: Sold inventory costing $30,000 for $65,000 on account.
- **e.** During the year: Paid employees $15,000 as compensation for services rendered during the year.
- **f.** During the year: Collected $45,000 from customers related to sales on account.
- **g.** During the year: Paid merchandise suppliers $28,000 related to purchases on account.
- **h.** December 31: Recognized depreciation on the building of $7,000 for financial reporting. Depreciation expense for income tax purposes was $10,000.
- **i.** December 31: Recognized compensation for services rendered during the last week in December but not paid by year-end of $4,000.
- **j.** December 31: Recognized and paid interest on the bank loan in Part b of $2,400 for the year.
- **k.** Recognized income taxes on the net effect of the preceding transactions at an income tax rate of 40 percent. Assume that the firm pays cash immediately for any taxes currently due to the government.

2.18 ANALYZING TRANSACTIONS. Using the analytical framework illustrated in the chapter, indicate the effect of each of the three independent sets of transactions described next.

(1) **a.** January 15, 2009: Purchased marketable equity securities for $100,000.
b. December 31, 2009: Revalued the marketable securities to their market value of $90,000. Unrealized changes in the market value of marketable equity securities appear in accumulated other comprehensive income.

c. December 31, 2009: Recognized income tax effects of the revaluation in Part b at an income tax rate of 40 percent. The income tax law includes changes in the market value of equity securities in taxable income only when the investor sells the securities.

d. January 5, 2010: Sold the marketable equity securities for $94,000.

e. January 5, 2010: Recognized the tax effect of the sale of the securities in Part (d). Assume that the tax is paid in cash immediately.

(2) **a.** During 2010: Sells inventory on account for $500,000.

b. During 2010: The cost of the goods sold in Part (b) is $400,000.

c. During 2010: Estimated that uncollectible accounts on the goods sold in Part (a) will equal 2 percent of the selling price.

d. During 2010: Estimated that warranty claims on the goods sold in Part (a) will equal 4 percent of the selling price.

e. During 2010: Actual accounts written off as uncollectible totaled $3,000.

f. During 2010: Actual cash expenditures on warranty claims totaled $8,000.

g. December 31, 2010: Recognized income tax effects of the preceding six transactions. The income tax rate is 40 percent. The income tax law permits a deduction for uncollectible accounts when a firm writes off accounts as uncollectible and for warranty claims when a firm makes warranty expenditures. Assume that any tax is paid in cash immediately.

(3) **a.** January 1, 2010: Purchased $100,000 face value of zero-coupon bonds for $68,058. These bonds mature on December 31, 2014, and are priced on the market at the time of issuance to yield 8 percent compounded annually. Zero-coupon bonds earn interest as time passes for financial and tax reporting, but the issuer does not pay interest until maturity. Assume that any tax owed on taxable income is paid in cash immediately.

b. December 31, 2010: Recognized interest revenue on the bonds for 2010.

c. December 31, 2010: Recognized income tax effect of the interest revenue for 2010. The income tax law taxes interest on zero-coupon bonds as it accrues each year.

d. December 31, 2011: Recognized interest revenue on the bonds for 2011.

e. December 31, 2011: Recognized income tax effect of the interest revenue for 2011.

f. January 2, 2012: Sold the zero-coupon bonds for $83,683.

g. January 2, 2012: Recognized the income tax effect of the gain or loss on the sale. The applicable income tax rate is 40 percent, which affects cash immediately.

INTEGRATIVE CASE 2.1

STARBUCKS

The financial statements of Starbucks Corporation are presented in Exhibits 1.26–1.28 (see pages 78–80). The income tax note to those financial statements reveals the information regarding income taxes shown in Exhibit 2.16.

Required

a. Assuming that Starbucks had no significant permanent differences between book income and taxable income, did income before taxes for financial reporting exceed or fall short of taxable income for 2007? Explain.

b. Did book income before taxes for financial reporting exceed or fall short of taxable income for 2008? Explain.

EXHIBIT 2.16

Income Tax Disclosures for Starbucks (amounts in millions)
(Integrative Case 2.1)

For the Year Ended September 28 and September 30, respectively:	2008	2007
Income Tax Expense		
Current:		
Federal	$180.4	$326.7
Foreign	40.4	65.3
State	34.3	31.2
Deferred	(111.1)	(39.5)
Total	$144.0	$383.7

As of the Year Ended September 28 and September 30, respectively:	2008	2007
Components of Deferred Tax Assets and Liabilities		
Deferred tax assets:		
Accrued occupancy costs	$ 54.8	$ 47.6
Accrued compensation and related costs	56.2	65.1
Other accrued expenses	25.2	9.4
FIN 47 asset	13.3	14.3
Deferred revenue	36.0	18.3
Asset impairments	80.8	14.9
Foreign tax credits	26.1	11.1
Stock-based compensation	79.6	66.8
Other	49.6	29.2
Total Deferred Tax Assets	$421.6	$276.7
Valuation allowance	(20.0)	(13.7)
Net Deferred Tax Assets	$401.6	$263.0
Deferred tax liabilities:		
Property, plant, and equipment	$(18.1)	$(22.9)
Other	(21.4)	(23.9)
Total Deferred Tax Liabilities	$(39.5)	$(46.8)
Net Deferred Tax Asset	$362.1	$216.2

c. Will the adjustment to net income for deferred taxes to compute cash flow from operations in the statement of cash flows result in an addition or subtraction for 2007? For 2008?

d. Starbucks rents retail space for its coffee shops. It must recognize rent expense as it uses rental facilities but cannot claim an income tax deduction until it pays cash to the landlord. Suggest the scenario that would give rise to a deferred tax asset instead of a deferred tax liability related to occupancy cost.

e. Starbucks recognizes an expense related to retirement benefits as employees rendered services but cannot claim an income tax deduction until it pays cash to a retirement fund. Why do the deferred taxes for deferred compensation appear as a deferred tax asset? Suggest possible reasons why the deferred tax asset decreased between the end of 2007 and the end of 2008.

f. Starbucks reports deferred revenue for sales of stored value cards, such as the Starbucks Card and gift certificates. These amounts are taxed when collected, but not recognized in financial reporting income until tendered at a store. Why does the tax effect of deferred revenue appear as a deferred tax asset? Why might the value of this deferred tax asset doubled from 2007 to 2008?

g. Starbucks recognizes a valuation allowance on its deferred tax assets to reflect "net operating losses of consolidated foreign subsidiaries." Presumably, these are included in "Other" deferred tax assets. Why might the valuation allowance have increased between 2007 and 2008?

h. Starbucks uses the straight-line depreciation method for financial reporting and accelerated depreciation for income tax reporting. Why do the deferred taxes related to depreciation appear as deferred tax liabilities? Suggest possible reasons why the amount of the deferred tax liability related to depreciation decreased between 2007 and 2008.

Chapter 3

Income Flows versus Cash Flows: Understanding the Statement of Cash Flows

Learning Objectives

1. **Understand the relation between net income and cash flow from operations and how the cash flow statement articulates information in the income statement and balance sheet.**
2. **Become comfortable with the structure and interpretation of operating, investing, and financing cash flow activities on the statement of cash flows.**
3. **Appreciate how the statement of cash flows reflects cash flows for firms in various stages of their life cycles.**
4. **Prepare a statement of cash flows from balance sheet and income statement data.**
5. **Understand how to use the statement of cash flows to evaluate earnings quality.**

The previous chapter discussed general principles for the valuation of assets and liabilities on the balance sheet and the recognition of components of income on the income statement. The focus of this chapter is on the statement of cash flows. In addition to a balance sheet and an income statement, U.S. GAAP and IFRS require firms to include a statement of cash flows in their published financial statements each period.[1] Most other sets of accounting standards require a similar statement as well. Smaller privately held firms often prepare just a balance sheet and an income statement. The objective of providing a statement of cash flows is to assist users in understanding the cash flows of a firm's primary activities, which is difficult to obtain from the balance sheet and income statement.

Under the indirect method for both U.S. GAAP and IFRS, the first line of the statement of cash flows is net income, which is reconciled to the net change in cash during the period. An oversimplification of the statement of cash flows is that it reports all of the sources and

---

[1]An interesting fact is that the statement of cash flows was not required until 1988. Previously, firms reported a statement of changes in financial position, which provided some similar information but focused on "funds" and did not require firms to report cash flows during a period. See Financial Accounting Standards Board, *Statement of Financial Accounting Standards No. 95*, "Statement of Cash Flows," November 1987. *FASB Codification Topic 230.* The statement of cash flows required under IFRS is similar to that required under U.S. GAAP in all material respects; International Accounting Standards Board, *International Accounting Standard 7*, "Statement of Cash Flows" (1992). There are only two substantive differences in statements of cash flows between U.S. GAAP and IFRS. First, IFRS defines cash and cash equivalents to include a net for bank overdrafts, whereas these are treated as working capital under U.S. GAAP. Second, IFRS allows interest and dividends paid to be classified as either operating or financing cash flows; interest and dividends received can be classified as either operating or investing. Under U.S. GAAP, interest paid, interest received, and dividends received are classified as operating activities, whereas dividends paid are classified as a financing activity.

uses of cash during a period. However, the statement of cash flows provides at least three key insights not available from either the balance sheet or the income statement. First, the statement of cash flows is logically organized in three sections, which correspond to the primary pursuits necessary to generate profits. These sections include operating activities, investing activities, and financing activities. Second, the statement of cash flows provides information about cash flows to and from entities with which the firm conducts business, such as employees, customers, suppliers, creditors, and investors. Third, an analyst can combine information from the statement of cash flows, balance sheet, and income statement to assess the overall "quality" of the financial statements, particularly the quality of earnings.

A firm's cash flows will differ from net income each period because (1) cash receipts from customers do not necessarily occur in the same period in which a firm recognizes revenues; (2) cash expenditures to employees, suppliers, and governments do not necessarily occur in the same period in which a firm recognizes expenses; and (3) cash inflows and outflows that pertain to investing and financing activities do not immediately flow through the income statement. A primary objective in preparing an income statement is to obtain a measure of operating performance that matches economic resources used, or consumed, as expenses, with the associated economic resources earned as revenues. When the accountant cannot directly match economic resources earned and consumed, accrual accounting matches the economic resources consumed with the period in which they are consumed. The accrual basis of accounting ignores the timing of cash receipts when recognizing revenues and gains and the timing of cash expenditures when recognizing expenses and losses. However, cash is a necessary ingredient for operating, investing, and financing activities. This fact means that firms must provide another financial statement that reports the flows of cash in and out of a firm: the statement of cash flows.

An understanding of a firm's cash flows is an integral part of each of the six steps in financial statement analysis discussed in Chapter 1:

- **Identify the Economic Characteristics of a Business:** The pattern of cash flows from operating, investing, and financing activities differs among various types of businesses as well as within a firm throughout various stages of the firm's life cycle. For example, high-growth, capital-intensive firms generally experience insufficient cash flow from operations to finance capital expenditures (investing activities); thus, they require external sources of capital (financing activities). In contrast, mature companies usually can finance their needs for capital expenditures through cash flow from operations and use excess cash flow to repay debt, pay dividends, or repurchase common stock (financing activities).
- **Identify the Strategy of the Firm:** The analyst should expect the statement of cash flows to reflect the overall strategy of a firm, especially the trajectory of growth. For example, a rapidly growing capital-intensive firm will show large investments in fixed assets. A firm opting for organic growth will exhibit large positive cash flows from operations, which are funneled into investing activities. On the other hand, a firm pursuing a strategy of growth by acquiring other firms will report significant cash outflows for corporate acquisitions (investing activities). A diversified firm that is refocusing and divesting itself of noncore businesses will report cash inflows from disposal of these businesses (investing activities).
- **Adjust the Financial Statements for Nonrecurring, Unusual Items:** The cash flow statement contains insights into the cash versus non-cash components of unusual items, such as one-time gains or losses and discontinued operations. In addition, an analyst who chooses to eliminate nonrecurring or unusual items from net income to more clearly assess operating profitability also should adjust the relevant parts of the cash flow statement.

- **Analyze Profitability and Risk:** Chapter 2 clearly states that over sufficiently long periods, net income equals the net cash flow from operating, investing, and non-owner financing activities. Thus, a reality check on net income is that it should converge to operating cash flows as a firm matures, although they still will fluctuate relative to each other. Also, the ability of a firm to generate sufficient cash flow from operations to finance capital expenditures and adequately service debt obligations is a key signal of the financial health of the firm.
- **Prepare Forecasted Financial Statements:** As Chapter 10 will show, forecasting may be the most important part of firm valuation. Forecasting profitability is incomplete without forecasts of all balance sheet items. In turn, a forecasted cash flow statement is a necessary part of forecasting future profitability and balance sheets. For example, driven by continued investment in productive assets, an analyst may forecast continued growth in net income. However, a key determinant of such forecasts is how the firm will generate the cash necessary to finance future growth. Will operations generate sufficient cash flow? Or will external financing be required?
- **Value the Firm:** Chapter 12 discusses firm valuation based on "free cash flows" to equity shareholders, which is cash flow available for distribution to investors after necessary reinvestments in operating assets or required payments to debtholders are made. Discounting these cash flows at an appropriate discount rate yields an estimate of the total value of a firm's equity.

This chapter explores the statement of cash flows in greater depth than the overview presented in Chapter 1. First, the chapter explores the partitioning of cash flows into operating, investing, and financing activities; then it examines hypotheses about what cash flows analysts should expect for firms in various stages of their life cycles. Next, the chapter examines the relation between net income and cash flow from operations for various types of businesses, primarily through the discussion of several examples. Finally, the chapter walks through the nuts and bolts of preparing the statement of cash flows using information from the balance sheet and income statement. An understanding of how to prepare a basic cash flow statement is necessary for the ultimate goal of firm valuation based on forecasted financial statements. The last part of the chapter introduces how an analyst can integrate an understanding of the relations between net income and cash flows to draw inferences about earnings quality.

UNDERSTANDING THE RELATIONS AMONG NET INCOME, BALANCE SHEETS, AND CASH FLOWS

Cash flows are cash transactions that a firm realizes during a period of time. As noted in Chapter 2, one alternative to reporting financial performance under accrual accounting is simply to report cash inflows and outflows. If an analyst takes a "cash is king" perspective, the statement of cash flows provides fundamental information on the flows of cash in and out of a firm. However, over short horizons such as a fiscal quarter or year, cash inflows and outflows are not very informative with regard to a firm's profitability now or in the future. As a simple example, consider the decision to pay a supplier for goods received on December 31 versus January 1 of the following year. This decision affects cash flows, but it should not affect any useful or predictive measure of the firm's performance during either year. Thus, with the objective of accrual accounting being to better reflect the economic substance of firm performance and financial position, an accrual of a liability to a supplier at December 31 is recorded. Accrual accounting goes beyond measurement of cash flows to measure economic inflows and outflows. Economic resources and obligations generate assets and liabilities constituting a balance sheet, which in turn allows for an improved measure of performance based on economic resources generated and consumed, constituting an income statement.

The statement of cash flows is closely tied to net income, but serves several additional roles. First, it partitions a firm's activities into categories that provide insight beyond that obtained from the balance sheet or income statement. Second, the statement of cash flows reconciles the beginning and ending cash balance (from the balance sheet). Finally, the statement of cash flows highlights non-cash components of reported net income, which enable an analyst to penetrate the drivers of reported performance to assess current and future profitability. Keeping those features of the statement of cash flows in mind, you need an understanding of the following three relations to be able to interpret the information completely:

- The overall relation among the net cash flows from operating, investing, and financing activities.
- The relation between the change in the cash balance on the balance sheet and the net changes reflected on the statement of cash flows.
- The specific relation between net income and cash flow from operations.

These topics are discussed next. Because the third relation is most important, it is addressed in two parts. First, the discussion focuses specifically on the operating section of the statement of cash flows, highlighting the types of adjustments necessary to reconcile net income to cash flows from operations; then a more general discussion covers the relation between net income and cash flows from operations.

The Relations among Cash Flows from Operating, Investing, and Financing Activities

See PepsiCo's Consolidated Statement of Cash Flows in Appendix A. The first feature to note is the organization of the statement into three groups of cash flows related to operating activities, investing activities, and financing activities. For all years presented, PepsiCo generates positive cash flows from operating activities and negative cash flows for both investing and financing activities. For example, in 2008, PepsiCo generated $6,999 million from operating activities and used $2,667 million and $3,025 million for investing and financing activities, respectively. Thus, PepsiCo generates a great deal of cash from its core operations and uses much of it to invest in productive assets and to return cash to capital providers. Operating activities include all activities directly involving the production and delivery of goods or services; for PepsiCo, examples include cash received from customers and cash used to purchase raw materials and to compensate employees. Investing activities include expenditures for (and proceeds from dispositions of) assets intended to be used to generate cash flows; examples include cash payments to acquire property, plant, and equipment and to invest in joint ventures, as well as cash receipts from the sale, or liquidation, of such assets or investments. Finally, financing activities include cash received from (or returned to) capital providers such as banks, other lending institutions, and shareholders. The subtotals for net operating, investing, and financing cash flows provide the net increase or decrease in cash and cash equivalents. For PepsiCo, the net of operating, investing, and financing activities is an increase in cash and cash equivalents of $1,154 million (which includes an adjustment for the effects of exchange rate changes on cash balances).

Note several important line items in PepsiCo's statement of cash flows for 2008. First, the largest adjustment in the operating section is for the addback of depreciation and amortization, which adds $1,543 million to PepsiCo's $5,142 million of net income. The sum of other non-working capital adjustments (from "Stock-based compensation expense" through "Deferred income taxes and other tax charges and credits") is $1,105 million, indicating a net positive adjustment to net income due to these items. The large depreciation and amortization adjustment and net positive adjustment for the other non-working capital items is typical of a large, mature company such as PepsiCo. Second, the net of the working capital adjustments (from "Change in accounts and notes receivable" through "Other, net") is −$791 million, indicating a net increase of investments in working capital during 2008. Third, investing cash flows primarily reflects capital spending ($2,446 million) and acquisitions and investments in affiliates ($1,925 million), offset by the sale of short-term investments ($1,376 million). Finally, the financing section suggests that PepsiCo is rebalancing its capital structure because it raised $3,070 million in *net* long-term debt and used $2,541 million to pay dividends and $4,720 million to repurchase common shares.

A helpful framework for intuitively grasping the information conveyed through this organization of cash flows incorporates the product life cycle concept from economics and marketing. Individual products (goods or services) move through four phases: (1) introduction, (2) growth, (3) maturity, and (4) decline. These phases are graphically depicted in Exhibit 3.1, which shows stylized patterns for revenues, net income, and cash flows over a product life cycle. The top graph shows the pattern of revenues throughout the four phases, which typically follows a period of growth, peaking during maturity, and subsequent decline as customers switch to alternatives. Obviously, the length of these phases and the steepness of the revenue curve vary by the type and success of a product. Products subject to rapid technological change, such as semiconductors and computer software, or driven by fads, such as clothing fashions, move through these four phases in just a few years. Other products, such as venerable staple products like PepsiCo's beverages, McDonald's fast foods, and Campbell's soup, can remain in the maturity phase for many years. Although the analyst will experience difficulty pinpointing the precise location of a product on its life cycle curve at any particular time, he or she usually can identify the phase and whether the product is in the early or later portion of that phase. Moreover, most firms provide numerous products, so the applicability of the theory and evidence for single products is more difficult when firms are diversified across numerous products at different stages of their life cycle. Nevertheless, an understanding of these patterns is useful in understanding changes in firm performance over time as the firm introduces new products and discontinues older ones.

The middle panel of Exhibit 3.1 shows the trend of net income over the product life cycle. Net losses usually occur in the introduction and early growth phases because revenues do not cover the cost of designing and launching new products. Net income peaks during the maturity phase and then begins to decline. The lower panel of Exhibit 3.1 shows the cash flows from operating, investing, and financing activities during the four life cycle phases. As with revenues, the length of phases and steepness of the net income and cash flow curves vary depending on the success of a product and the sustainability of the firm's product strategy. PepsiCo's systematically large positive net income and cash flows from operations are consistent with PepsiCo's products (in aggregate) being both mature and profitable.

During the initial introduction of a product, revenues are minimal; therefore, net income and net cash flows are typically low or negative. As the growth phase accelerates, operations become profitable and begin to generate cash. However, firms must use the cash generated to finance activities such as selling products on credit (that is, accounts receivable) and building up inventory in anticipation of higher sales levels in the future. Thus, because these expenditures are accounted for as assets on the balance sheet rather than being expensed immediately, compared to cash flow from operations, net income usually turns positive earlier. The extent of the negative cash flow from investing activities depends on the rate of growth and the degree of capital expenditure needs and asset intensity. As in

EXHIBIT 3.1

Stylized Patterns of Revenues, Net Income Flows, and Cash Flows from Operations, Investing, and Financing at Various Stages of Product Life Cycle

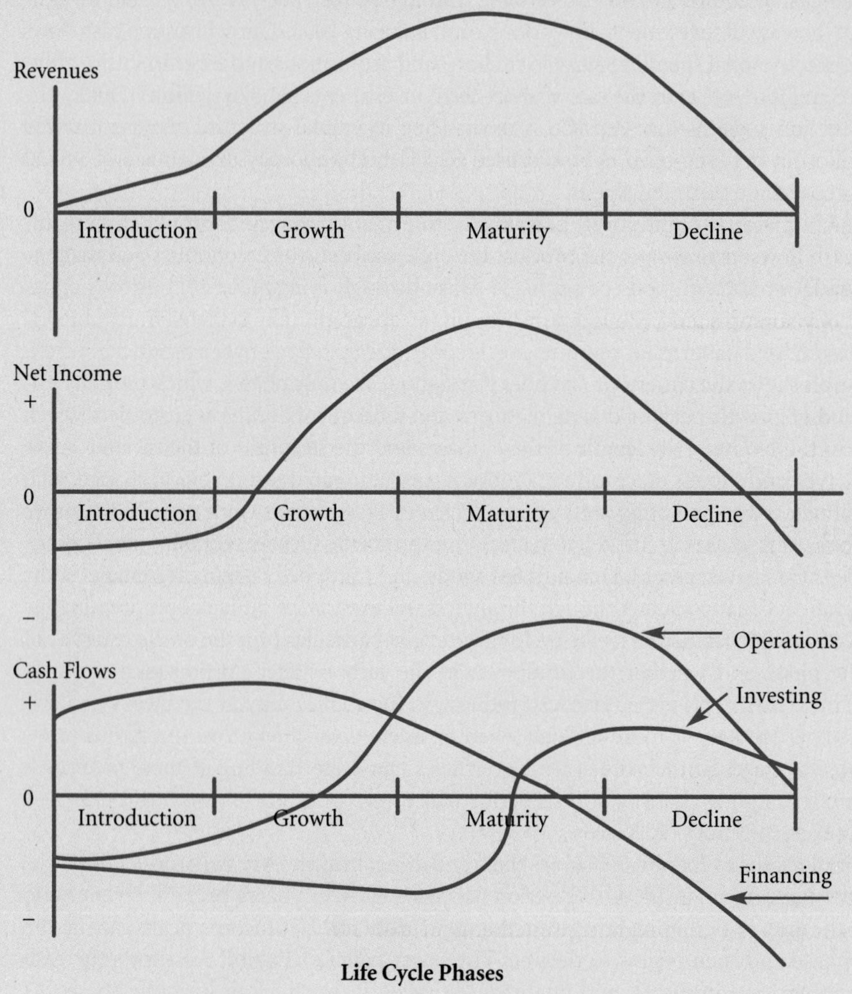

the introduction phase, firms obtain most of the cash they need during the growth phase by borrowing and issuing stock from external financing sources.

As products move through the maturity phase, the cash flow pattern changes dramatically. Operations become profitable and generate substantial positive cash flows because of market acceptance of the product and a leveling off of working capital needs and asset acquisitions. Also, with revenues leveling off, firms invest to *maintain* rather than *increase* productive capacity. During the later stages of the maturity phase, net cash flows from sales of unneeded plant assets sometimes result in a net positive cash flow from investing activities. Firms can use the excess cash flow from operations and, to a lesser extent, from the sale of investments to repay debt incurred during the introduction and growth phases, to pay dividends, and to repurchase their common stock. During the decline phase, cash flows from operations and investing activities taper off as customers become satiated or switch to alternative products, thus decreasing sales. At this point, firms use cash flows to repay associated debt required during the introduction and growth phases and can pay dividends or repurchase common stock from equity investors.

The product life cycle model discussed previously provides helpful insights about the relation between sales, net income, and cash flows from operating, investing, and financing activities for a single product. The discussion, however, relates to a single product. Few business firms rely on a single product; most have a range of products at different stages of the life cycle. A multiproduct firm such as PepsiCo can use cash generated from products in the maturity phase of their life cycle to finance products in the introduction and growth phases and therefore not need as much external financing. Furthermore, the statement of cash flows discussed in this chapter reports amounts for a firm as a whole and not for each product. If the life cycle concept is to assist in interpreting published statements of cash flows, the analyst must understand how individual products aggregate at the firm level.

Clearly, developing such a multiproduct view is difficult. However, knowledge of industry dynamics and trends can help guide an overall assessment of firm-level cash flows. For example, investor excitement in technology-driven industries such as biotechnology most often peaks during the growth phase. Although such firms may have some products at various stages of the product life cycle, the interest is in forecasting the emergence of new technologies that translate into new products that might generate large cash flows. In contrast, many consumer food companies are characterized as being well into the maturity phase of overall product life cycles. Branded consumer food products can remain in their maturity phase for many years with proper product quality control and promotion, such as PepsiCo's portfolio of soft drink offerings. Such companies continually bring new products to the market that replace similar products that are out of favor, but the life cycle of these products tends to be more like products in the maturity phase than introductory products in the growth phase. Certain industries in developed countries, such as textiles, old-line steel, and automotive, are probably in the early decline phase because of foreign competition and/or outdated technology. Some companies in these industries have built technologically advanced production facilities to compete more effectively on a worldwide basis and have, therefore, essentially reentered the maturity phase. Other firms have diversified geographically to realize the benefits of shifts to foreign production, which also prolongs their ability to enjoy the maturity phase of their portfolio of products.

This section ends by highlighting statements of cash flows for three firms to contrast how these statements capture various stages of the product life cycle (that is, introduction, growth, maturity, and decline).

Arise Technologies Corporation

Arise Technologies Corporation is a Canadian company that manufactures and markets solar technologies. Its primary products include photovoltaic cells, applications to produce silicon for use in solar products, and rooftop and solar farm installations. Arise is a small firm competing in a highly competitive industry with rapidly evolving technologies. Exhibit 3.2 provides its statements of cash flows for 2008 and 2007, which show the typical pattern of a firm in the introduction phase, with negative cash flows from both operating and investing activities, funded by large positive cash flows from financing activities. As is typical of a start-up business, Arise is reporting large net losses, increasing from a loss of CDN$11.6 million in 2007 to a loss of CDN$42.3 million in 2008. Similarly, the cash flows from operating activities are large and negative. For 2008, cash used in operating activities is CDN$32.5 million. The source of the cash flows is primarily financing activities, also typical of a firm with products in the

EXHIBIT 3.2

Arise Technologies Corporation
Statement of Cash Flows

	Year ended December 31,	
	2008	**2007**
CASH FLOWS FROM OPERATING ACTIVITIES		
Net loss for the year	$CDN(42,308,873)	$CDN(11,607,037)
Items which do not involve cash:		
Valuation write-down of inventory related assets	8,978,726	—
Depreciation and amortization	2,458,352	34,667
Issuance of capital stock for services	—	214,488
Employee stock option compensation	4,552,531	2,078,289
Non-employee stock option compensation	276,091	152,361
	$CDN(26,043,173)	$CDN (9,127,232)
Changes in working capital items from operations		
Increase in accounts receivable	(7,337,713)	(74,098)
Increase in inventories	(16,372,428)	(481,326)
Decrease in other receivables	948,251	—
Increase in prepaid expenses	(8,977,057)	(1,853,207)
Increase in accounts payable and accrued liabilities	12,330,507	8,094,988
Increase (Decrease) in deferred revenue	12,903,715	(18,765)
Net Cash Provided by Operating Activities	$CDN(32,547,898)	$CDN (3,459,640)
CASH FLOWS FROM FINANCING ACTIVITIES		
Issuance of capital stock for cash	$CDN 45,280,904	$CDN 63,088,696
Share issuance costs	(2,520,608)	(4,435,432)
Exercise of warrants and options	2,625,622	4,386,424
Proceeds from bank loans	21,530,447	1,087,835
Issuance of long-term debt	14,100,844	—
Net Cash Used in Financing Activities	$CDN 81,017,209	$CDN 64,127,523
CASH FLOWS FROM INVESTING ACTIVITIES		
Increase in restricted cash	$CDN (1,508,671)	$CDN —
Purchase of capital assets	(45,954,392)	(26,708,880)
Purchase of intangible assets	(135,412)	(49,137)
Change in long-term deposits	(28,490,426)	(5,181,347)
Government assistance	10,830,312	8,981,689
Net Cash Used in Investing Activities	$CDN(65,258,589)	$CDN(22,957,675)
Net Cash Flow	$CDN(16,789,278)	$CDN 37,710,208
Cash and cash equivalents, beginning of year	37,908,430	198,222
Cash and Cash Equivalents, End of Year	$CDN 21,119,152	$CDN 37,908,430

introduction and growth phases. Arise obtained substantial capital from financing activities in both 2007 and 2008 (CDN$64.1 and CDN$81.0 million, respectively). In addition to plowing these proceeds into operations, Arise also used substantial cash in investing activities, rising from CDN$23.0 million in 2007 to CDN$65.3 million in 2008. The overall impact on cash and cash equivalents across these two years is a growth in balance from CDN$198 thousand at the beginning of 2007 to CDN$37.9 million at the end of 2007 (reflecting large inflows from financing activities) and a subsequent decline to CDN$21.1 million at the end of 2008 (reflecting large uses of cash for investing activities and operations).

Exxon Mobil Corporation

As of 2008, Exxon Mobil was the world's largest publicly traded company as measured by market capitalization, which was in excess of $500 billion. The company explores, produces, and sells natural gas, crude oil, and petroleum-based products. Clearly, a corporation as large as Exxon Mobil has entered the maturity phase of its overall product life cycle. The statement of cash flows for Exxon Mobil is shown in Exhibit 3.3. It exhibits the typically large positive cash flows from operating activities and negative cash flows for both investing and financing

EXHIBIT 3.3

ExxonMobil Corporation
Statement of Cash Flows
(amounts in millions)

	2008	2007	2006
CASH FLOWS FROM OPERATING ACTIVITIES			
Net income			
Accruing to ExxonMobil shareholders	$ 45,220	$ 40,610	$ 39,500
Accruing to minority interests	1,647	1,005	1,051
Adjustments for noncash transactions:			
Depreciation and depletion	12,379	12,250	11,416
Deferred income tax charges	1,399	124	1,717
Postretirement benefits expense in excess of (less than) payments	57	(1,314)	(1,787)
Other long-term obligation provisions in excess of (less than) payments	(63)	1,065	(666)
Dividends received greater than (less than) equity in current earnings of equity companies	921	(714)	(579)
Changes in operational working capital, excluding cash and debt:			
Reduction (Increase) in notes and accounts receivable	8,641	(5,441)	(181)
Reduction (Increase) in inventories	(1,285)	72	(1,057)
Reduction (Increase) in other current assets	(509)	280	(385)
Increase (Reduction) in accounts and other payables	(5,415)	6,228	1,160
Net (gain) on asset sales	(3,757)	(2,217)	(1,531)
All other items net	490	54	628
Net Cash Provided by Operating Activities	$ 59,725	$ 52,002	$ 49,286

(Continued)

EXHIBIT 3.3 (Continued)

	2008	2007	2006
CASH FLOWS FROM INVESTING ACTIVITIES			
Additions to property, plant, and equipment	$(19,318)	$(15,387)	$(15,462)
Sales of subsidiaries, investments, and property, plant, and equipment	5,985	4,204	3,080
Decrease in restricted cash and cash equivalents	—	4,604	—
Additional investments and advances	(2,495)	(3,038)	(2,604)
Collection of advances	574	391	756
Additions to marketable securities	(2,113)	(646)	—
Sales of marketable securities	1,868	144	—
Net Cash Used in Investing Activities	$(15,499)	$ (9,728)	$(14,230)
CASH FLOWS FROM FINANCING ACTIVITIES			
Additions to long-term debt	$ 79	$ 592	$ 318
Reductions in long-term debt	(192)	(209)	(33)
Additions to short-term debt	1,067	1,211	334
Reductions in short-term debt	(1,624)	(809)	(451)
Additions (Reductions) in debt with three months or less maturity	143	(187)	(95)
Cash dividends to ExxonMobil shareholders	(8,058)	(7,621)	(7,628)
Cash dividends to minority interests	(375)	(289)	(239)
Changes in minority interests and sales (purchases) of affiliate stock	(419)	(659)	(493)
Tax benefits related to stock-based awards	333	369	462
Common stock acquired	(35,734)	(31,822)	(29,558)
Common stock sold	753	1,079	1,173
Net Cash Used in Financing Activities	$(44,027)	$(38,345)	$(36,210)
Effects of exchange rate changes on cash	$ (2,743)	$ 1,808	$ 727
Increase (Decrease) in Cash and Cash Equivalents	$ (2,544)	$ 5,737	$ (427)
Cash and cash equivalents at beginning of year	33,981	28,244	28,671
Cash and Cash Equivalents at End of Year	$ 31,437	$ 33,981	$ 28,244

activities. The company was generating large and persistent net income, reporting $45 billion in 2008 (relative to total assets of approximately $200 billion). Similarly, Exxon Mobil generated enormous cash flows from operating activities, which reached $59.7 billion in 2008. With such large amounts generated by cash flows from operating activities, the company relied very little on external financing; instead, it tended to pay large dividends and reacquire common stock, contributing to $44.0 billion used for financing activities. Also, Exxon Mobil continued to use cash for investing activities, which totaled $15.5 billion in 2008. The net of these activities from year to year resulted in Exxon Mobil maintaining a cash and cash equivalents balance that averaged around $30 billion.

General Motors

As an example of a firm in the decline phase of its product life cycle, Exhibit 3.4 shows the statement of cash flows for General Motors during its final years before being nationalized

EXHIBIT 3.4

General Motors
Statement of Cash Flows
(amounts in millions)

	2007	2006	2005
CASH FLOWS FROM OPERATING ACTIVITIES			
Net loss from continuing operations	$(43,297)	$ (2,423)	$(10,621)
Adjustments to reconcile loss from continuing operations to net cash provided by (used in) continuing operating activities:			
Depreciation, impairments, and amortization expense	9,513	10,885	15,732
Mortgage servicing rights and premium amortization		1,021	1,142
Goodwill impairment GMAC and Delphi charge	1,547	1,328	6,212
Loss on sale of 51% interest in GMAC	—	2,910	—
Provision for credit financing losses	—	1,799	1,074
Net gains on sale of credit receivables and investment securities	—	(2,262)	(1,845)
Other postretirement employee benefit (OPEB) expense	2,362	3,567	5,650
OPEB payments	(3,751)	(24,953)	(34,358)
VEBA/401(h) withdrawals	1,694	3,061	3,168
Net pension expense (contributions)	862	3,879	1,662
Provisions for deferred taxes	36,977	(4,166)	(6,731)
Change in other investments and miscellaneous assets	663	(477)	(690)
Change in other operating assets and liabilities, net of acquisitions and disposals	(3,412)	(8,512)	20
Other	4,573	2,584	2,729
Net Cash Provided by (Used in) Operating Activities	$ 7,731	$(11,759)	$(16,856)
CASH FLOWS FROM INVESTING ACTIVITIES			
Expenditures for property	$ (7,542)	$ (7,902)	$ (8,141)
Investments in marketable securities, net (acquisitions) liquidations	(2,036)	3,019	737
Net change in mortgage servicing rights and finance receivables	—	(1,221)	(6,849)
Proceeds from sale of finance receivables, equity interest in GMAC, and other discontinued operations	5,354	36,233	32,498
Operating leases, net (acquisitions) liquidations	3,165	(10,031)	(10,134)
Capital contribution to GMAC LLC	(1,022)	—	—
Investments in companies, net of cash acquired	(46)	(357)	1,355
Other	367	(46)	(901)
Net Cash Provided by (Used in) Investing Activities	$ (1,760)	$ 19,695	$ 8,565
CASH FLOWS FROM FINANCING ACTIVITIES			
Net increase (decrease) in short-term borrowings	$ (5,749)	$ 7,030	$(10,125)
Borrowings of long-term debt	2,131	79,566	78,276
Payments made on long-term debt	(1,403)	(92,290)	(69,566)
Cash dividends paid to stockholders	(567)	(563)	(1,134)
Other	(5)	2,490	6,029
Net Cash Provided by (Used in) Financing Activities	$ (5,593)	$ (3,767)	$ 3,480

(*Continued*)

EXHIBIT 3.4 (Continued)

	2007	2006	2005
Effect of exchange rate changes on cash and cash equivalents	$ 316	$ 365	$ (85)
Net Increase (Decrease) in Cash and Cash Equivalents	$ 694	$ 4,534	$(4,896)
Cash and cash equivalents retained by GMAC LLC upon disposal	—	(11,137)	—
Cash and cash equivalents of held for sale operations	—	—	(371)
Cash and cash equivalents at beginning of the year	24,123	30,726	35,993
Cash and Cash Equivalents at End of the Year	$24,817	$24,123	$30,726

by the U.S. government. As is typical of a firm in decline, General Motors reported a string of net losses that were associated with generally negative cash flows from operations (in 2005 and 2006). Further, as assets and various operations were sold or disposed of, General Motors realized positive cash flows from investing activities (in 2005 and 2006). Within the investing activities section of the statement of cash flows, there are numerous asset dispositions and sales that led to cash inflows from the liquidation of various investments. Finally, as assets were sold or liquidated, General Motors used available proceeds to repay short-term borrowings and long-term debt. Subsequently, the company delisted from the New York Stock Exchange and was renamed Motors Liquidation Company.

The Relation between Cash Balances and Net Cash Flows

The primary purpose of the statement of cash flows is to provide financial statement users with information about a firm's cash receipts and payments. Implicit in this objective of providing information on the net cash flows of a period is reporting the sources and uses of cash that cause the change in the cash balance on the balance sheet. This is accounting in its simplest form:

$$\text{Beginning Cash} + \text{Cash Receipts} - \text{Cash Expenditures} = \text{Ending Cash Balance}$$

Net cash flows for a period should equal the change in cash for the period. FASB *Statement No. 95* and IASB *International Accounting Standard 7* define cash flows in terms of their effect on the balance of *cash and cash equivalents*. Cash equivalents include highly liquid investments that are readily convertible into cash and so near to maturity that changes in interest rates present an insignificant risk to their market value. Cash equivalents usually include very short-term Treasury bills, commercial paper, and money market funds. Both U.S. GAAP and IFRS indicate that a maturity date of three months or less would generally qualify short-term investments as cash equivalents. A subtle difference between U.S. GAAP and IFRS is that IFRS permits bank overdrafts to be netted in cash and cash equivalents in countries where these overdrafts are payable on demand and are part of the cash management function. Throughout this book, the term *cash* is used to mean cash and cash equivalents as defined under both U.S. GAAP and IFRS.

On the statement of cash flows, the net cash flows equal the (net) sum of cash flows provided by or used for operating, investing, and financing activities. Refer again to PepsiCo's statement of cash flows in Appendix A. The net cash flow for PepsiCo during 2008 is the sum of \$6,999 million (operations), −\$2,667 million (investing), and −\$3,025 million (financing), a net positive change in cash of $1,307 million. The balance sheet indicates that cash and cash equivalents rose from $910 million to $2,064 million during 2008, an increase of $1,154 million. The difference between net cash flows of $1,307 million and the actual increase in cash and cash equivalents of $1,154 million is −$153 million. This reconciling amount is highlighted at the bottom of the statement of cash flows as the effect of exchange rate changes on the measurement of cash and cash equivalents (which is done using the fair value approach described in Chapter 2). This difference shows that PepsiCo's cash and cash equivalents suffered negative effects from exchange rate changes, which slightly offset the positive net cash flows realized during 2008.

Also note that the reconciling adjustments throughout the statement of cash flows relate to non-cash accounts on the balance sheet, but it is rare that changes in the balance sheet accounts equal the reconciling adjustments on the statement of cash flows. For example, the amounts of the adjustments for changes in operating working capital accounts in the statement of cash flows do not always equal the difference in amounts on the comparative balance sheets at the beginning and end of the year. For example, in 2008, PepsiCo's subtraction of $549 million for the change in accounts and notes receivable indicates that this account increased during the year. However, the comparative balance sheet for PepsiCo in Appendix A indicates that accounts and notes receivable increased from $4,389 million at the end of 2007 to $4,683 million at the end of 2008, an increase of only $294 million. Thus, $294 million of the $549 million increase in accounts and notes receivable relates to operating activities. The remaining $255 million of the increase results from the net change in this account from acquisitions and divestitures during the year.[2] Although it is not possible to reconcile this amount in the statement of cash flows perfectly, PepsiCo reports the amounts of cash used for acquisitions and the cash received from divestitures in the investing section of its statement of cash flows in Appendix A. During 2008, PepsiCo made large acquisitions and investments in noncontrolled affiliates of $1,925 million. This amount includes the cash invested in noncontrolled affiliates (PepsiCo bottlers) and the cash used to acquire the assets and liabilities of other businesses, and one of the assets likely acquired is accounts and notes receivable. Both U.S. GAAP and IFRS require firms to report the amount of cash used to acquire other businesses, which implicitly includes the net amount of individual assets and liabilities acquired with that cash, in the investing section. On occasion, some firms alert readers of the financial statements that changes in working capital in the operating section of the statement of cash flows do not equal changes in the corresponding accounts on the comparative balance sheet by phrasings in the operating section such as "changes in operating working capital, *excluding effects of acquisitions and dispositions.*" The inability to reconcile balance sheet changes perfectly also applies to non-working capital accounts such as property, plant, and equipment; long-term investments; long-term debt; and other liabilities.

The Operating Section of the Statement of Cash Flows

Many would argue that the first section of the statement of cash flows—operating activities—is most important because it provides information on the core activities that generate profits. These activities include cash received from selling goods and services to customers offset by cash paid to suppliers, employees, governments, and other providers of goods and services. In addition to providing insights into core operations, the operating section also is important because it is where an analyst can gather information about the quality of earnings. As discussed in the previous chapter (and throughout this book), the accounting entries that aggregate into the financial statements depend on the estimates and judgments that alter the

[2]This difference also may include the effects of fluctuations in foreign currencies in which PepsiCo conducts business worldwide.

recognition of revenues and expenses from the simple timing of the cash flows. Because accounting estimates are based on imperfect estimates, managers can strategically use this uncertainty to inject bias into accounting numbers. For example, when the timing of revenue recognition is unclear, managers may tend to opt for earlier recognition, which optimistically biases revenues. An understanding of the operating section of the statement of cash flows can help users see into drivers of reported profitability on the income statement and can sometimes raise red flags for cash flow manipulation. Analysis of earnings quality will be discussed fully in Chapter 9, but that discussion is introduced later in this chapter in the limited context of the statement of cash flows.

Given the importance of the operating section of the statement of cash flows, this section discusses several important aspects of the structure and information available to the analyst from an understanding of the reconciliation of net income to cash flows from operations. First, we highlight the two formats allowable under U.S. GAAP and IFRS. Second, we examine the different types of adjustments to net income that appear in the operating section. Finally, we provide several illustrative examples of these adjustments.

The Operating Section: Format Alternatives

Under U.S. GAAP and IFRS, firms may present cash flow from operations in one of two formats: the direct method or the indirect method. The *direct method,* which is preferred by both the FASB and IASB, lists individual classes of cash receipts and cash payments, such as cash collected from customers, cash paid to suppliers, and cash paid to employees. In contrast, the *indirect method* reconciles reported net income to cash flows from operations by "undoing" non-cash (accrual) components of earnings. Despite a preference for the direct method by standard setters, almost all companies report cash flows using the indirect method. In 2008, the AICPA surveyed 600 firms and identified only 6 that used the direct method.[3] The reluctance to report under the direct method seems to be based on practicality because the FASB and IASB require that firms using the direct method also provide a separate schedule for the reconciliation between net income and operating cash flows (in other words, an indirect method operating section). Exhibit 3.5 is a rare example of the direct method for the operating cash flows, for the drugstore chain CVS Caremark. Note that the total operating cash flows are

EXHIBIT 3.5

Cash Flow from Operations
Presented in Direct and Indirect Methods for CVS Caremark
(amounts in millions)

	Dec. 31, 2008	Dec. 29, 2007	Dec. 30, 2006
CASH FLOWS FROM OPERATING ACTIVITIES			
Cash receipts from revenues	$69,493.70	$61,986.30	$43,273.70
Cash paid for inventory	(51,374.70)	(45,772.60)	(31,422.10)
Cash paid to other suppliers and employees	(11,832.00)	(10,768.60)	(9,065.30)
Interest and dividends received	20.30	33.60	15.90
Interest paid	(573.70)	(468.20)	(228.10)
Income taxes paid	(1,786.50)	(1,780.80)	(831.70)
Net Cash Provided by Operating Activities	$ 3,947.10	$ 3,229.70	$ 1,742.40

[3] AICPA, *Accounting Trends & Techniques* (2008).

EXHIBIT 3.5 (Continued)

	Dec. 31, 2008	Dec. 29, 2007	Dec. 30, 2006
CASH FLOWS FROM INVESTING ACTIVITIES			
Additions to property and equipment	$ (2,179.90)	$ (1,805.30)	$ (1,768.90)
Proceeds from sale-leaseback transactions	203.80	601.30	1,375.60
Acquisitions (net of cash acquired) and other investments	(2,650.70)	(1,983.30)	(4,224.20)
Cash outflow from hedging activities	—	—	(5.30)
Sale of short-term investments	27.50	—	—
Proceeds from sale or disposal of assets	18.70	105.60	29.60
Net Cash Used in Investing Activities	$ (4,580.60)	$ (3,081.70)	$ (4,593.20)
CASH FLOWS FROM FINANCING ACTIVITIES			
Net additions to short-term debt	$ 959.00	$ 242.30	$ 1,589.30
Repayment of debt assumed in acquisition	(352.80)	—	—
Additions to long-term debt	350.00	6,000.00	1,500.00
Reductions in long-term debt	(1.80)	(821.80)	(310.50)
Dividends paid	(383.00)	(322.40)	(140.90)
Proceeds from exercise of stock options	327.80	552.40	187.60
Excess tax benefits from stock-based compensation	53.10	97.80	42.60
Repurchase of common stock	(23.00)	(5,370.40)	—
Net Cash Provided by Financing Activities	$ 929.30	$ 377.90	$ 2,868.10
Net Increase in Cash and Cash Equivalents	$ 295.80	$ 525.90	$ 17.30
Cash and cash equivalents at beginning of year	1,056.60	530.70	513.40
Cash and Cash Equivalents at End of Year	$ 1,352.40	$ 1,056.60	$ 530.70
RECONCILIATION OF NET EARNINGS TO NET CASH PROVIDED BY OPERATING ACTIVITIES			
Net earnings	$ 3,212.10	$ 2,637.00	$ 1,368.90
Adjustments required to reconcile net earnings to net cash provided by operating activities:			
Depreciation and amortization	1,274.20	1,094.60	733.30
Stock-based compensation	92.50	78.00	69.90
Deferred income taxes and other non-cash items	(3.40)	40.10	98.20
Change in operating assets and liabilities providing (requiring) cash, net of effects from acquisitions:			
Accounts receivable, net	(291.00)	279.70	(540.10)
Inventories	(488.10)	(448.00)	(624.10)
Other current assets	12.50	(59.20)	(21.40)
Other assets	19.10	(26.40)	(17.20)
Accounts payable	(63.90)	(181.40)	396.70
Accrued expenses	182.50	(168.20)	328.90
Other long-term liabilities	0.60	(16.50)	(50.70)
Net Cash Provided by Operating Activities	$ 3,947.10	$ 3,229.70	$ 1,742.40

$3,947.1 million for 2008, which is shown in the top part of the statement of cash flows and is shown as an addendum for the reconciliation of net income at the bottom of the statement of cash flows. The line item descriptions in the direct method are more intuitive than those in the indirect method. For example, "Cash paid for inventory" is more straightforward than the change in inventories (net of effects from acquisitions) shown as a reconciling item in the indirect method (at the bottom of Exhibit 3.5). Nevertheless, the chapter later describes how analysts can compute the more intuitive figures such as cash paid for inventory from information in the balance sheet and income statement.

Under the *indirect method,* firms begin with net income to calculate cash flow from operations. The provisional assumption implicit in starting with net income is that revenues increased cash and expenses decreased cash. However, as was discussed in Chapter 2, in accrual accounting not all revenues result in simultaneous cash receipts and not all expenses result in simultaneous cash expenditures; likewise, not all cash receipts result in simultaneous revenues and not all cash expenditures result in simultaneous expenses. Because of this mix in the timing of cash flow and income statement recognition, net income must be reconciled to cash flows by adjusting for non-cash effects. As noted previously, even though CVS Caremark reports a direct method operating section, an indirect method of presentation is required, as shown at the bottom of Exhibit 3.5.

Most firms use the indirect method because it reconciles net income for a period with the net amount of cash received or paid for operations, which provides a direct link to the income statement. Critics of the indirect method suggest that the rationale for some of the reconciling items is difficult for less sophisticated users to understand. These are discussed in more detail in the next section, but a simple example is the change in accounts receivable adjustment. A decrease in receivables is an increase in cash flow (because cash is collected from customers); however, this increase in cash appears on the statement of cash flows under the indirect method and is labeled as "Decrease in Accounts Receivable." Although only a moderate amount of effort is required to understand the reconciliation adjustments, certain peculiarities challenge even the most seasoned analysts. We use the indirect method throughout this text because of its dominance among financial reports.

The Operating Section: Adjustments for the Indirect Method

The calculation of cash flow from operations under the indirect method involves two types of adjustments to net income, each of which will be discussed in this section—working capital and non-working capital adjustments. Both of these adjustments, explained below, are necessary because of timing differences between income recognition and cash flow realization. Adjustments to net income for revenues, expenses, gains, and losses that are recognized in income and are associated with changes in noncurrent assets, noncurrent liabilities, and shareholders' equity accounts that do not affect cash by the same amounts that period. These items are thus referred to as non-working capital adjustments. Common adjustments include depreciation, amortization, deferred taxes, and gains/losses on asset dispositions. As an example, consider depreciation expense. Depreciation expense reduces net income, but it is a non-cash expense. Thus, in reconciling net income to cash flows from operations, net income must be adjusted upward for non-cash expenses such as depreciation. Working capital adjustments, on the other hand, are adjustments for changes in operating working capital accounts during the period.[4] Common adjustments include increases and decreases in accounts receivable, inventories, and accounts payable.

[4]Working capital means current assets minus current liabilities. Operating working capital accounts generally include all current assets except marketable securities and all current liabilities except short-term loans and the current portion of long-term debt. A later section of this chapter explains the rationale for excluding these items from operating working capital.

We now discuss adjustments under the indirect method of preparing the operating section of the statement of cash flows. In accordance with the typical format of the operating section, we first discuss non-working capital adjustments, and then working capital adjustments. Certain revenues and expenses are associated with changes in a noncurrent asset, a noncurrent liability, or a shareholders' equity account and affect cash flow differently from net income. For these items, firms must add amounts to or subtract amounts from net income to convert net income to cash flow from operations. There are numerous such adjustments due to the wide variety of long-term transactions that firms experience. Rather than attempting to be comprehensive, this section highlights the most common non-working capital adjustments.

Depreciation and amortization expense.[5] Depreciation expense reduces *net* property, plant, and equipment and net income. However, depreciation expense does not require an *operating* cash outflow in the period of the expense. Cash flows that are paid out for depreciable assets are classified as *investing* activities in the year of acquisition. PepsiCo, for example, lists such acquisitions as "Capital spending" in the investing section of its statement of cash flows (in Appendix A). The addback of depreciation expense to net income when computing cash flow from operations reverses the effect of the subtraction of depreciation expense when computing net income (that is, the addback ensures that depreciation does not affect the cash flow from operations). Similarly, amortization expense reflects the consumption of intangible assets, and its effects on net income must be removed in computing operating cash flows. PepsiCo includes depreciation on buildings and equipment and amortization of intangibles on a single line as an addback to net income in computing cash flow from operations, which is a common practice. PepsiCo's "Depreciation and amortization" adjustment, which is $1,543 million, is the single largest non-working capital adjustment to net income. Thus, the net income of $5,142 million is adjusted upward by $1,543 million to add back the non-cash expenses of depreciation and amortization.

Deferred tax expense. Chapter 2 points out that firms recognize deferred tax assets and/or deferred tax liabilities on the balance sheet when they use different methods of accounting for financial reporting and income tax reporting; on the income statement, they recognize income tax expense that contains a component for deferred income taxes. The total amount of income tax expense, including both current and deferred components, will differ from the amount of income taxes owed or payable for the fiscal year (from the tax return). Thus, firms must add back the excess of income tax expense over income taxes owed for the year (that is, current tax expense). PepsiCo shows an addback for deferred income taxes of $573 million in 2008, suggesting that income tax expense exceeds income taxes owed for the year. In contrast, PepsiCo shows a subtraction for deferred taxes of $510 million in 2006, indicating that taxes payable in 2006 exceeded income tax expense. Note that these adjustments for deferred taxes adjust income tax expense to the amount of income tax currently owed for the year. The next section describes adjustments to convert taxes currently payable to the actual amount of cash paid for taxes.

---

[5]Adjustments for depreciation and amortization on the statement of cash flows are more complex than implied in this discussion because depreciation is often allocated to the cost of inventory. If the balance of inventory changes during a period, the change may include allocated depreciation to the cost basis of inventory. Thus, the allocation of depreciation (and amortization) to inventory creates a discrepancy between amounts expensed and the addback on the statement of cash flows. Firms handle this discrepancy a variety of ways, which makes it rare that depreciation expense on the income statement equals the depreciation adjustment on the statement of cash flows. (Similarly, the change in inventory balances on the balance sheet rarely equals the working capital adjustment for increases or decreases in inventory on the statement of cash flows.) This is one of the compelling motivations for requiring a statement of cash flows to be provided by management, which has the information to prepare cash flow statements more precisely than external users can by using approximations from the other financial statements. We will discuss the technical aspects of preparing a cash flow statement towards the end of the chapter.

Employee stock options. Chapter 6 discusses the required recognition of an expense for the cost of employee stock options, which permit employees to purchase shares of the firm's common stock for less than their market value. This expense reduces net income and increases a shareholders' equity account, but it does not affect cash flows. Because the expense does not use cash, firms add back stock option expense to net income when computing cash flow from operations. In 2008, PepsiCo lists an addback of $238 million for "Stock-based compensation expense" in the operating section of its statement of cash flows. Incidentally, when employees exercise stock options, it is common that they pay the strike price to the firm, and this resulting cash inflow to the company appears in the financing section of the statement of cash flows. In 2008, PepsiCo lists $620 million from such stock issuances as "Proceeds from exercises of stock options" in the financing section of its statement of cash flows in Appendix A.

Gains and losses. Companies that sell an item of property, plant, or equipment report the full cash proceeds in investing activities on the statement of cash flows. For example, refer to the line for $98 million of "Sales of property, plant, and equipment" for PepsiCo in 2008 (in Appendix A). Because assets are rarely sold for their book value (which would result in no gain or loss), net income includes gains and losses on these sales (that is, sale proceeds minus book value of the item sold). Therefore, the operating section of the statement of cash flows shows an addback for a loss and a subtraction for a gain to offset their inclusion in net income (and to avoid double-counting the gain or loss, given that the investing section includes the full cash proceeds from the asset sale). The absence of a line item for gains or losses on PepsiCo's statement of cash flows suggests that these amounts are sufficiently small and likely included in the line "Other, net." Because these gains and losses are related to investing activities, the adjustment for gains and losses appears in the operating section to remove their effect from net income.

Equity method income. As Chapter 7 describes, firms holding investments of 20–50 percent of the common shares in another entity generally use the equity method to account for the investment (a noncurrent asset). As an investor, the firm recognizes in net income its share of the investee's earnings each period and increases the balance of the investment account and reduces the investment account for any cash dividends received. Therefore, net income reflects the investor's share of the investee's earnings, not the cash received. The statement of cash flows usually shows a subtraction from net income for the excess of the investor's share of the investee's earnings over dividends received. For example, PepsiCo reports "Bottling equity income, net of dividends" as a $202 million subtraction when converting net income to cash flow from operations. The income statement shows $374 million for Bottling equity income. Thus, we infer that PepsiCo received $172 million in cash dividends from bottling investments. The inclusion of $374 income recognized is included in net income, the starting point for the indirect cash flow statement. The $202 million adjustment converts the Bottling equity income to the cash flows actually received of $172 million.

Employee-related costs such as pensions. As Chapter 8 illustrates, the accounting for pensions and other postretirement benefits is complex due to the number of estimates involved (for example, the length of time an employee will work, the length of time an employee will realize benefits postretirement, the growth in the cost of those benefits, and the return on investments set aside to cover those future costs). As a result, expenses generally differ from the cash paid for these benefits each period. Companies with such benefit plans adjust net income for the net difference between the expense and cash transactions. Alternatively, companies such as PepsiCo separately add back the pension expense and deduct the actual cash contributed to fund pension assets and postretirement benefits. For example, in 2008, PepsiCo reports an addback of "Pension and retiree medical plan expenses" of $459 million and a deduction for "Pension and retiree medical plan contributions" of $219 million, for a net positive adjustment to net income of $240 million.

This indicates that PepsiCo funded less than half the amount recognized as expense, which means cash flows will be higher than net income, all else equal.

Tax benefits from share-based compensation plans. As noted previously, employee stock-based compensation expense appears as an adjustment in the operating section and the cash inflows from employee exercises appears in the financing section. Generally, when employees exercise stock options, they owe taxes on the difference between the stock price at the time of exercise and the amount they have to pay to exercise the option (the strike price). At this time, the company is entitled to a tax deduction equal to the amounts the employees realize as taxable income. This tax benefit reduces taxes owed for the current fiscal year and reduces tax expense on the income statement. Because the cash flows pertaining to stock options are classified as a financing activity, the cash savings for tax deductions derived from employee stock option exercises also are classified as a financing activity. To achieve this, companies must subtract the tax benefit (that increased net income) in the operating section and show it instead in the financing section. This can easily be seen in PepsiCo's statement of cash flows, where the 2008 adjustment in the operating section is a *deduction* of $107 million ("Excess tax benefits from share-based payment arrangements"), and this same $107 million adjustment appears in the financing section as a *positive* cash flow. Note that this separate treatment of taxes associated with a certain class of transactions is unique because the general requirement under both U.S. GAAP and IFRS is for all tax payments to be included as part of operating cash flows; this is the reason the adjustment for stock-based compensation tax savings is labeled "excess."

Impairment- and restructuring-related charges. Write-offs and write-downs of assets reduce net income through impairment charges, but there are usually no associated cash transactions. Thus, impairment charges must be added back to net income in the computation of operating cash flows. Similarly, restructuring charges are estimated and the associated cash flows generally follow later. Thus, restructuring charges appear as addbacks to income and cash payments for restructuring appear as subtractions from income in the operating section.

The second type of adjustment used to reconcile net income to cash flow from operations involves changes in operating current asset and current liability accounts. Similar to the objective of removing non-cash effects for non-working capital, non-cash components of changes in current asset and liability accounts need to be removed from net income to compute operating cash flows. Again, we discuss each of the most common working capital adjustments reported in the operating section of the statement of cash flows. For example, Appendix A presents PepsiCo's working capital adjustments at the bottom of the operating section.

Accounts receivable. As discussed in the previous chapter, revenue recognition is based on the economics of a sale rather than the realization of cash. An increase in accounts receivable for a period indicates that a firm did not collect as much cash as the amount of revenues included in net income, and a decrease indicates that a firm collected more cash than it recognized as revenues. Thus, increases in accounts receivable require subtractions from net income to reconcile cash flows from operations; decreases in accounts receivable require additions to net income.

Inventories. Two features of inventory accounting lead to adjustments to net income in computing operating cash flows. First, when inventory balances increase, the cash flow statement includes a negative adjustment because this increase has not been expensed as cost of goods sold, but does involve a cash outlay. Second, when inventory balances decrease, the cash flow statement includes a positive adjustment because the decrease is expensed as cost of goods sold, but some of this amount relates to inventory that was paid for in a prior reporting period. It also is important to understand how non-cash allocations of depreciation and amortization are adjusted on the cash flow statement, as highlighted previously in the discussion of depreciation and amortization.

Prepaid expenses. Prepaid expenses are simply cash payments that have yet to be expensed. Increases in prepaid expenses indicate cash payments in excess of amounts recognized as expenses in computing net income; decreases in prepaid expenses represent amounts that were expensed but for which there was no equivalent simultaneous cash flow. Thus, the cash flow statement must show an adjustment to net income for increases in prepaid expenses (through a deduction from net income) or decreases in prepaid expenses (through an addback to net income).

Accounts payable and accrued expenses. An increase in current liabilities for operating expenses means that a firm did not use as much cash for operating expenses as the amounts appearing on the income statement. For example, suppose a firm was invoiced for goods and services received at the end of the fiscal year but did not pay the invoices until the following fiscal year. The firm would recognize the goods received in inventory and recognize the service expense at the end of the year. The offsetting entries would recognize the associated liabilities. These amounts do not reduce cash flows (until the period in which they are paid), so they need to be added back to net income in computing operating cash flows.

Income taxes payable. Recall from the earlier discussion about non-working capital adjustments that the addition to or subtraction from net income for deferred income tax expense or benefit converts income tax expense to income taxes currently payable. The adjustment for the changes in income taxes payable converts income taxes currently payable as indicated on the income tax return for the year to the income taxes actually paid. Firms typically do not pay all taxes due for a particular year during that year. Some taxes that a firm pays within a year relate to taxes due for the preceding year; some taxes due for the current year are paid by the firm the following year.

In addition to the working capital accounts discussed previously, there are other current accounts such as marketable equity securities, short-term investments, commercial paper, and other short-term borrowings. The cash flows pertaining to these items are shown in investing (marketable equity securities, short-term investments) or financing activities (commercial paper, short-term borrowings).

The Operating Section: Illustrations of Adjustments for the Indirect Method

The operating section of the statement of cash flows is the first section presented on a statement of cash flows. The investing section generally follows the operating section, and the financing section appears last, although there is slight variation in practice. The presentation of the investing and financing sections is essentially a "direct method" presentation, with intuitive labels such as "Capital expenditures," "Sales of property, plant, and equipment," "Proceeds from short-term borrowings," and "Cash dividends paid." In contrast, the indirect presentation of the operating section favored by most firms is less intuitive and the organization and line item descriptions vary across firms. This variability in the organization and descriptions is partially attributed to the simple fact that firms vary significantly in their operations (along dimensions such as technology, product markets, and customers) but investing and financing activities are fairly standard. Thus, this section focuses on several examples of the operating section to illustrate the variety of presentations that firms use.

Hitachi Ltd. Hitachi is a large Japanese conglomerate engaged in telecommunications, information systems, consumer digital media and information products, and financial services. The operating section for Hitachi is shown in Exhibit 3.6. The most striking aspect of Hitachi's operating activities is that the company has reported large net losses for all years presented but simultaneously reports large positive operating cash flows. For example, in 2009, Hitachi reported a ¥787 billion net loss but positive cash flows of ¥559 billion. Hitachi does not categorize working capital and non-working capital adjustments separately, labeling all

EXHIBIT 3.6

Hitachi Ltd.
Statement of Cash Flows: Operating Section
(amounts in millions)

	2009	2008	2007
CASH FLOWS FROM OPERATING ACTIVITIES			
Net loss	¥(787,337)	¥ (58,125)	¥ (32,799)
Adjustments to reconcile net loss to net cash provided by operating activities:			
Depreciation	478,759	541,470	472,175
Amortization	178,164	146,136	149,823
Impairment losses for long-lived assets	128,400	87,549	9,918
Deferred income taxes	403,968	84,587	20,514
Equity in net (earnings) loss of affiliated companies	162,205	(22,586)	(11,289)
Gain on sale of investments and subsidiaries' common stock	(1,353)	(94,798)	(53,240)
Impairment of investments in securities	45,016	14,411	8,309
Loss on disposal of rental assets and other property	24,483	13,424	31,590
Income (loss) applicable to minority interests	(7,783)	110,744	72,323
Decrease in receivables	342,008	47,843	52,599
Increase in inventories	(57,206)	(107,546)	(212,028)
(Increase) Decrease in prepaid expenses and other current assets	12,772	(32,763)	(80,172)
Increase (Decrease) in payables	(359,230)	42,453	104,987
Decrease in accrued expenses and retirement and severance benefits	(27,050)	(38,303)	(21,166)
Increase (Decrease) in accrued income taxes	(76,343)	12,841	18,623
Increase in other liabilities	39,711	61,041	38,470
Net change in inventory-related receivables from financial services	2,117	(11,392)	(9,819)
Other	57,646	(5,149)	56,224
Net Cash Provided by Operating Activities	¥ 558,947	¥791,837	¥615,042

adjustments as simply "Adjustments to reconcile net loss to net cash provided by operating activities." Within these adjustments, the largest ones are positive non-working capital adjustments such as depreciation (¥479 billion), amortization (¥178 billion), impairment losses (¥128 billion), deferred income taxes (¥404 billion), and equity in net earnings of affiliated companies (¥162 billion). As described earlier in the chapter, all of these adjustments are non-cash items that reduced net income, thus appearing as positive adjustments. The only other large adjustments are for receivables (¥342 billion) and payables (−¥359 billion). Receivables decreased, which generated cash that was not associated with any current period income; so the receivables decrease is added to net income. Payables also decreased, indicating that Hitachi paid out cash in excess of associated expense recognition in the current period; so the payables decrease is subtracted from net income. The overall effect of these adjustments is a dramatic swing between reported net losses and large positive cash flows.

PetroQuest Energy, Inc. PetroQuest Energy manages oil and natural gas reserves in and around the Gulf of Mexico. The operating section of PetroQuest's statement of cash flows is shown in Exhibit 3.7. Similar to Hitachi, which lumped all reconciling adjustments together, PetroQuest also labels all adjustments as "Adjustments to reconcile net income (loss) to net cash

EXHIBIT 3.7

PetroQuest Energy Inc.
Statement of Cash Flows: Operation Section
(amounts in thousands)

	Year Ended December 31,		
	2008	2007	2006
CASH FLOWS FROM OPERATING ACTIVITIES			
Net income (loss)	$(96,960)	$ 40,619	$ 23,986
Adjustments to reconcile net income (loss) to net cash provided by operating activities:			
Deferred tax expense (benefit)	(55,581)	23,664	14,604
Gain on sale of gas-gathering assets	(26,812)	—	—
Depreciation, depletion, and amortization	134,340	119,969	85,858
Ceiling test write-down	266,156	—	—
Share-based compensation expense	9,582	9,818	5,651
Accretion of asset retirement obligation	1,317	923	1,513
Amortization expense and other	1,492	1,187	1,140
Payments to settle asset retirement obligations	(19,377)	(6,058)	(252)
Changes in working capital accounts:			
Revenue receivable	2,746	(1,053)	725
Joint interest billing receivable	(1,323)	(2,864)	(2,505)
Prepaid drilling costs	(10,075)	3,438	(3,630)
Drilling pipe inventory	(25,898)	—	—
Accounts payable and accrued liabilities	(4,567)	37,050	(13,552)
Advances from co-owners	(7,521)	(521)	7,517
Other	1,542	(2,443)	(1,685)
Net Cash Provided by Operating Activities	$169,061	$223,729	$119,370

provided by operating activities." However, PetroQuest groups working capital adjustments separately under "Changes in working capital accounts." Also similar to Hitachi, PetroQuest reports cash flows in excess of the reported net income (or loss) each year. Several items are noteworthy. First, a negative adjustment for deferred taxes of $55.6 million in 2008 indicates that PetroQuest recognized a deferred tax benefit (rather than expense) in 2008; the deferred tax benefit increased income (or more accurately, mitigated the reported loss) but is not associated with current cash inflow, so it appears as deduction. Second, the company reports an addback of $266.2 million for an asset writedown ("Ceiling test writedown"). Because asset writedowns reduce net income but are not necessarily associated with current cash outflows, the adjustment is positive. In contrast, PetroQuest also reports a negative adjustment for "Payments to settle asset retirement obligations." This reflects actual cash paid for asset retirement obligations (such as actual dismantling and disposal costs) that had been accrued periodically over many prior years but for which the expense appeared in periods prior to the current year. For example, as PetroQuest operated assets, part of the annual cost was the eventual cost to retire the asset attributable to its use in that year, so the company recognized annually an incremental expense for the estimated costs of eventual retirement; the initiating adjustment appears as a non-working capital adjustment labeled "Accretion of asset retirement obligation." Finally, consider the working capital adjustments for "Prepaid drilling costs" and "Drilling pipe inventory." The balance sheet indicates the following balances under current assets (amounts in thousands):

	2008	2007	Change
Prepaid drilling costs	$11,523	$1,448	↑$10,075
Drilling pipe inventory	$25,898	0	↑$25,898

These increases correspond to increases in current assets that required an outlay of cash, necessitating the negative adjustments on the statement of cash flows. The prepaid drilling costs and drilling pipe inventory will be consumed in future years and will reduce income at that time, and they will appear as positive adjustments because there is no cash outflows associated with the recognized expenses.

Blackboard Inc. Blackboard Inc., a company based in Washington, D.C., provides software applications used in education, such as course website management and mobile applications. The operating section of the 2008 statement of cash flows is provided in Exhibit 3.8.

EXHIBIT 3.8

Blackboard Inc.
Statement of Cash Flows: Operating Activities
(amounts in thousands)

	Year Ended December 31,		
	2008	2007	2006
CASH FLOWS FROM OPERATING ACTIVITIES			
Net (loss) income	$ 2,820	$12,865	$(10,737)
Adjustments to reconcile net (loss) income to net cash provided by operating activities:			
Deferred tax benefit	(8,113)	(2,830)	(5,075)
Excess tax benefits from exercise of stock options	(2,107)	(6,845)	(3,317)
Amortization of debt discount	1,653	1,840	1,701
Depreciation and amortization	15,703	10,681	8,980
Amortization of intangibles resulting from acquisitions	37,866	22,122	17,969
Change in allowance for doubtful accounts	161	(2)	(109)
Stock-based compensation	15,127	12,043	8,056
Gain on investment in common stock warrants	(3,980)	—	—
Changes in operating assets and liabilities, net of effect of acquisitions:			
Accounts receivable	(31,721)	(225)	(21,780)
Inventories	306	288	(571)
Prepaid expenses and other current assets	(2,594)	(1,233)	(42)
Deferred cost of revenues	(394)	372	(5,129)
Accounts payable	(4,018)	952	133
Accrued expenses	4,227	9,394	(5,588)
Deferred rent	9,675	1,101	(245)
Deferred revenues	45,224	8,834	38,640
Net Cash Provided by Operating Activities	$79,835	$69,357	$ 22,886

Blackboard shows an enormous difference between net income and operating cash flows for 2008 ($2.8 million net income versus $79.8 million operating cash flows). The largest non-working capital adjustments are typical and include depreciation and amortization ($15.7 million), amortization of acquired intangibles ($37.9 million), and stock-based compensation ($15.1 million). For working capital adjustments, note that Blackboard provides the useful description "net of effect of acquisitions," which, as discussed, notifies the reader that simple changes in balance sheet amounts are unlikely to correspond to the reconciling amounts on the statement of cash flows because acquisitions are reported under investing activities and include working capital accounts acquired. For example, Blackboard shows a $31.7 million negative adjustment for accounts receivable, indicating that accounts receivable increased, which was associated with recognized revenues. Because these amounts have not been collected, they are deducted from net income to compute operating cash flows. Also, the large positive adjustment for deferred revenues of $45.2 million indicates that cash was received in advance from customers, and these amounts have yet to be recognized in income; so net income must be increased for these cash flows. These adjustments, however, contrast with information on the balance sheet (amounts in millions), as follows:

	2008	2007	Change
Accounts receivable	$ 93.4	$ 53.6	↑$39.8
Deferred revenue	$184.7	$129.5	↑$55.2

As noted in the previous discussion of working capital adjustments, changes in balance sheet accounts will not equal adjustment amounts in the operating section of the statement of cash flows if there are acquisitions. This is why Blackboard qualifies the description of the working capital adjustments ("net of effect of acquisitions"). Indeed, the financial statement footnotes for Blackboard indicate an acquisition of NTI Group, Inc., on January 31, 2008, for $187.8 million, reflecting the following (amounts in thousands):

Cash and cash equivalents	$ 1,592	
Accounts receivable	8,123	←
Prepaid expenses and other current assets	1,143	
Restricted cash	888	
Property and equipment	2,304	
Accounts payable	(650)	
Other accrued liabilities	(2,142)	
Deferred tax liabilities, net	(16,806)	
Deferred revenue	(10,045)	←
Net tangible liabilities to be acquired	$ (15,593)	
Definite-lived intangible assets acquired	60,325	
Goodwill	143,089	
Total estimated purchase price	$ 187,821[6]	

[6]Incidentally, the $187.8 million purchase price will not be the amount presented in the investing section, which shows an acquisition cash outflow of $133.0 million, for two reasons. First, the purchase was made through a combination of cash and stock, so only the cash portion of the purchase price appears in the investing section. Second, the cash and cash equivalents acquired in the acquisition ($1.6 million) are netted against the cash paid in the investing section.

The discrepancy between the actual change in accounts receivable of $39.8 million and the $31.7 million reconciling adjustment on the statement of cash flows ($8.1 million) reflects accounts receivable assumed through acquisitions during 2008. Similarly, deferred revenue increased $55.2 million on the balance sheet, but the statement of cash flows shows an adjustment of only $45.2 million, indicating that the difference ($10.0 million) reflects deferred revenues assumed as part of acquisitions.

Cephalon, Inc. All of the examples discussed thus far have shown operating cash flows that exceed reported net income. This is generally true due to large non-cash addbacks for non-working capital items such as depreciation, amortization, deferred taxes, stock-based compensation, and impairment charges. Exhibit 3.9 shows the operating section of the statement of cash flows for Cephalon, which reports net income substantially above operating cash flows for 2008. Although there are numerous

EXHIBIT 3.9

Cephalon Inc.
Statement of Cash Flows: Operating Activities
(amounts in thousands)

	Year Ended December 31,		
	2008	2007	2006
CASH FLOWS FROM OPERATING ACTIVITIES			
Net income (loss)	$222,548	$(194,125)	$146,509
Adjustments to reconcile net income (loss) to net cash provided by operating activities:			
Deferred income tax expense (benefit)	(50,889)	(2,361)	29,045
Shortfall tax benefits from stock-based compensation	(511)	(360)	—
Debt exchange expense	—	—	48,122
Depreciation and amortization	172,457	141,358	128,927
Write-off of debt issuance costs associated with convertible subordinated notes	—	—	13,105
Stock-based compensation expense	43,975	46,695	42,807
Gain on forgiveness of debt	—	(5,319)	—
Gain on sale of investment	—	(5,791)	—
Loss on sale of property and equipment	17,178	1,022	—
Impairment charges	99,719	—	12,417
Acquired in-process research and development	16,955	—	—
Minority interest in variable interest entity	(21,073)	—	—
Changes in operating assets and liabilities, net of effect from acquisitions:			
Receivables	(144,975)	(601)	(63,932)
Inventory	(37,397)	(2,328)	21,015
Other assets	11,792	(54,838)	(8,082)
Accounts payable and accrued expenses	(376,232)	385,463	(18,375)
Other liabilities	44,576	76,041	(31,641)
Net Cash Provided by (Used for) Operating Activities	$ (1,877)	$ 384,856	$319,917

adjustments for non-working capital and working capital accounts that are large, the explanation for the discrepancy between net income ($222.5 million) and operating cash flows (−$1.9 million) is the working capital adjustment for "Accounts payable and accrued expenses," totaling −$376.2 million. As with the Blackboard illustration, the analyst must look elsewhere in the financial statements to obtain an understanding of the large adjustment. The footnotes of Cephalon's financial statements describe a 2007 settlement agreement entered into with the U.S. General Attorney's Office for making false claims with respect to several pharmaceutical drugs marketed by the company. The settlement required Cephalon to pay a penalty of $375 million. This amount was accrued (and expensed) during 2007, but not paid until 2008. Note the large positive adjustment of $385.5 million for accounts payable and accrued expenses in 2007, which added back this amount to net income because the settlement amount had been expensed but not yet paid. In 2008, when the settlement was paid, there was no associated expense recognized in 2008 net income, so the operating section shows this decrease in the accrued settlement liability as a deduction in computing cash flows from operations.

Research in Motion Limited. The final illustration of the operating section of the statement of cash flows appears in Exhibit 3.10. Research in Motion is a Canadian company that manages e-mail, phone, and text communications as well as providing consumer hardware, most prominently for the popular BlackBerry® wireless platform. Net income and operating cash flows track each other fairly closely for the three years presented. However, what is most noticeable about the operating section for Research in Motion is how simple it is, showing just five non-working capital adjustments and one working capital adjustment. This simplicity is due to Research in Motion's decision to net all working capital adjustments into a single line item ($769.1 million for the year ended February 28, 2009).

EXHIBIT 3.10

Research in Motion Limited
Statement of Cash Flows: Operating Activities
(amounts in thousands)

	For the Year Ended:		
	February 28, 2009	**March 1, 2008**	**March 3, 2007**
CASH FLOWS FROM OPERATING ACTIVITIES			
Net income	$CDN 1,892,616	$CDN 1,293,867	$CDN 631,572
Items not requiring an outlay of cash:			
Amortization	327,896	177,366	126,355
Deferred income taxes	(36,623)	(67,244)	101,576
Income taxes payable	(6,897)	4,973	—
Stock-based compensation	38,100	33,700	19,063
Other	5,867	3,303	(315)
Net changes in working capital items (note 16(a))	(769,114)	130,794	(142,582)
Net Cash Provided by Operating Activities	$CDN 1,451,845	$CDN 1,576,759	$CDN 735,669

A footnote reference on the face of the statement of cash flows directs the reader to a footnote, which includes the following excerpt (amounts in thousands):

Footnote 16 SUPPLEMENTAL INFORMATION
(a) Cash flows resulting from net changes in working capital items are as follows:

	For the Year Ended:		
	February 28, 2009	**March 1, 2008**	**March 3, 2007**
Trade receivables	$(936,514)	$(602,055)	$(254,370)
Other receivables	(83,039)	(34,515)	(8,300)
Inventory	(286,133)	(140,360)	(121,238)
Other current assets	(50,280)	(26,161)	(16,827)
Accounts payable	177,263	140,806	47,625
Accrued liabilities	506,859	383,020	119,997
Income taxes payable	(113,868)	401,270	83,310
Deferred revenue	16,598	8,789	7,221
	$(769,114)	$ 130,794	$(142,582)

This illustration, as well as each of the four presented previously, indicates that while certain information must be presented to enable financial statement users to reconcile net income to operating cash flows, the formats can vary significantly. Thus, it is important to understand the substance of how accountants reconcile reported income to cash flows, not necessarily to memorize the format or sign of adjusting items.

The Relation between Net Income and Cash Flow from Operations

What is the general relation between net income and cash flow from operations? When should one exceed the other? Should they be approximately the same over a long time period, and, if so, how long? As you saw in the previous examples, net income tended to be primarily below cash flows from operations, although there were exceptions. Not surprisingly, the relation between net income and cash flows depends on numerous factors, including economic characteristics of the industry, the firm, its rate of growth, and even discretionary reporting choices made by managers. However, in recent years, operating cash flows exceed net income approximately 80 percent of the time.

The tendency for operating cash flows to exceed net income is not surprising for several reasons. First, the largest adjustments to net income in the operating section are generally non-working capital adjustments for changes in noncurrent assets, noncurrent liabilities, and shareholders' equity accounts, and these are primarily addbacks to net income rather than subtractions. For example, these addbacks include depreciation expense (noncurrent assets), deferred tax expense (noncurrent liability), and share-based compensation (shareholders' equity). Almost all firms report depreciation, but primary cash flows pertaining to capital expenditures for the underlying assets are negative and appear in the investing section (as opposed to the operating section). Similarly (and related to property, plant, and equipment), a majority of firms report deferred tax liabilities, which reflect negative cash flows that are deferred to future years, although an expense is recognized currently. This contributes to current cash flows exceeding net income for many firms. Also, stock-based compensation remains a popular form of paying employees, and the relatively small amounts of cash flows associated with these arrangements appear in the financing section (primarily cash inflows from employees who pay the exercise price on options and the contemporaneous tax savings). Finally, recent years are characterized by a large number of asset write-downs and restructuring charges, which reduce net income but not operating cash flows.

Firms that are growing rapidly can reflect various relations between operating cash flows and net income. Growth firms often report substantial adjustments for changes in accounts receivable, inventories, and current operating liabilities. For example, when a firm increases its sales, its working capital accounts tend to increase as well. Suppose a firm doubles its sales over several years. It is likely that the company also would increase its sales made on credit (accounts receivable), increase products available for sale (inventory), and increase its own credit with vendors (payables). Most growing firms expand their accounts receivable and inventories (that is, uses of cash) more rapidly than their current operating liabilities (that is, sources of cash) and find that the net effect of changes in operating working capital is a subtraction from net income when computing cash flow from operations, which can make cash flows from operations less than net income. Alternatively, if expansions of working capital assets are accompanied by approximately equal increases in working capital liabilities, cash used in the expansion of receivables and inventory can be offset by cash provided by increasing payables. As a result, the primarily positive non-working capital adjustments discussed previously will dominate, leading to operating cash flows greater than net income.

Another factor that may cause cash flow from operations to differ from net income is the length of the operating cycle (as discussed in Chapter 1). The operating cycle encompasses the period of time from when a firm commences production until it receives cash from customers for the sale of the products. Firms such as construction companies and aerospace manufacturers with relatively long operating cycles often experience a long lag between the expenditures of cash for design, development, raw materials, and labor and the receipt of cash from customers. Unless such firms receive cash advances from their customers prior to completion and delivery of the products or delay payments to their suppliers, the net effect of changes in operating working capital accounts is a subtraction from net income when computing cash flow from operations. The longer the operating cycle and the more rapid the growth of a firm, the larger the difference between net income and cash flow from operations. Consider a winery, which must plant vines, cultivate them for years, harvest grapes, ferment them, age wine in barrels for months or years, bottle the wine, ship it, and sell it; significant cash outflows are required years before the winery will realize any cash inflows. Firms with short operating cycles, such as restaurants and service firms, experience less of a lag between the creation and delivery of their products and the collection of cash from customers. Thus, for these firms, changes in operating working capital accounts play a relatively minor role in creating a wedge between net income and cash flow from operations.

For an example of the relation between various cash flows and net income, Exhibit 3.11 shows graphically the relation between net income and cash flows for PepsiCo from 2004–2008. First, note that cash flows from operations are positive every year but cash flows from both investing and financing activities are negative each year. This is consistent with the typical pattern for a mature, profitable firm. Second, cash flow from operations exceeds net income each year, consistent with the previous discussion. The question arises as to why cash flows from operations exceed net income for PepsiCo every year. Is it due to non-working capital or working capital adjustments? The plots for non-working capital and working capital adjustments indicate that the non-working capital adjustments are always (net) positive but the working capital adjustments are both positive and negative. Thus, the excess of cash flows from operations over net income is clearly due to the large positive non-working capital adjustments. Third, the most volatile pattern for the components of

EXHIBIT 3.11

Relation among PepsiCo's Net Income, Cash Flows from Operations, Cash Flows from Investing Activities, and Cash Flows from Financing Activities

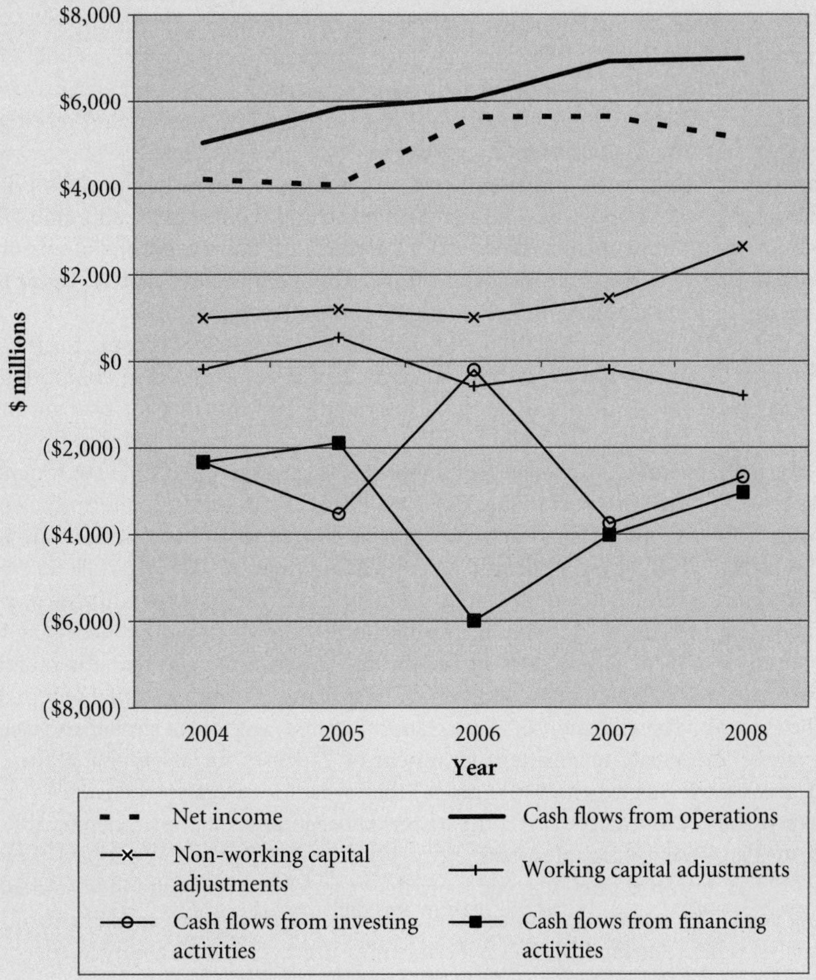

cash flows from operations is for working capital adjustments, which increase and decrease across years and are sometimes positive and sometimes negative. Therefore, even though working capital adjustments are relatively smaller in magnitude than non-working capital adjustments in each year, the significant variation in these adjustments contributes directly to the variation in net income and the computation of cash flows from operations. For example, during 2008, when the net working capital adjustments grew to −$791 million, net income revealed the first decline in several years and the large investment in working capital offset what would otherwise be a significant increase in cash flows from operations. The key takeaway is that working capital adjustments, which reflect standard accounting accruals, are associated directly with the level and variability of net income. The introduction of earnings quality will discuss this observation in the next section.

Aside: Earnings before Interest, Taxes, Depreciation and Amortization (EBITDA)

Before proceeding, note that analysts often discuss a metric related to net income, non-working capital adjustments, and cash flows from operations: *earnings before interest, taxes, depreciation and amortization* (EBITDA). In using this measure, analysts presumably believe that an evaluation of the profitability and ultimate valuation of a firm rests on a measure of profitability that excludes four significant non-working capital adjustments. The theoretical rationale of using a measure that excludes these four expenses is unclear. It is not clear what economic performance construct EBITDA measures. A reading of analyst reports and the financial literature suggests that analysts view EBITDA as an approximation of a cash-based measure of pretax operating earnings. Its "quick and dirty" calculation adds to its popularity. The analyst can generally compute its amount easily by using information on the income statement. However, cash flows from operations or operating income are more complete measures of operating performance that are easier to calculate because they are reported directly in the financial statements.

The exclusion of depreciation and amortization adjusts net income for the items that, for most firms, are the largest non-working capital adjustments in computing cash flow from operations. If a firm is not growing rapidly, adjustments for changes in operating working capital accounts should be relatively small and vary around zero from year to year (as is the case for PepsiCo). The presumption in such cases is that EBITDA roughly approximates cash flow from operations. However, EBITDA can differ significantly depending on other activities of the firm. For PepsiCo, 2008 cash flows from operations are $6,999 million and EBITDA (from Appendix A) is $8,852 million ($7,021 − $41 + $329 + $1,543). For PepsiCo, EBITDA ignores large investments in capital expenditures in addition to increasing investments in its noncontrolled affiliates, which appear necessary to generate continued and increasing sales in the future. This is especially true for rapidly growing firms, where EBITDA ignores additional investments in working capital required to sustain that growth. The exclusion of depreciation expense, without a similar exclusion for rent expense, can create inconsistent treatment of expenses for assets that a firm owns and depreciates versus expenses for "assets" that a firm leases. The exclusion of depreciation expense also can lead to false comparisons between firms that own depreciable assets and firms that lease depreciable assets.

The exclusion of interest expense provides a measure of earnings independent of financing costs. The exclusion of interest in computing EBITDA has an element of logic if the analyst is interested in EBITDA as a crude measure of the firm's ability to cover the costs of leverage or if the analyst uses EBITDA for enterprise valuation using a discount rate or earnings multiple that incorporates the cost of both debt and equity capital. However, the rationale for the exclusion of income taxes is not at all clear. Firms that generate positive earnings must pay income taxes just as they must pay suppliers, employees, and other providers of goods and services.

Academic research has examined the correlation between market rates of return on common stock and (1) net income, (2) cash flow from operations, and (3) EBITDA.[7] The results of these studies indicate that stock returns are more highly correlated with net income than with either cash flow from operations or EBITDA. This finding is not surprising given that net income is a bottom-line measure of profitability. The finding that

[7]Mary E. Barth, Donald P. Cram, and Karen K. Nelson, "Accruals and the Prediction of Future Cash Flows," *Accounting Review* (January 2001), pp. 27–58.

cash flow from operations has less information content for equity valuation than does net income results from the omission of working capital adjustments (also referred to as accruals), which, as noted, have information content for future cash flows, and from the omission of cash flows related to investing and financing activities. Cash flow from operations is an incomplete measure of cash flows for valuation purposes. Cash flow from operations omits important elements of performance, which net income does not omit. For example, if net income is negative in a given period, it is generally indicative of poor performance and value destruction. On the other hand, if cash flow from operations is negative, it is ambiguous and may reflect very good performance and value creation (for example, start-up and growth firms). Refer again to Exhibit 1.14 in Chapter 1, which shows that results in Nichols and Wahlen (2004) indicate the spread in abnormal returns between increases and decreases in earnings averages 35.6 percent, whereas the spread between positive and negative changes in cash flows from operations is only 15.0 percent. In the same manner that operating cash flows omits important elements of performance, EBITDA excludes expenses that are value-relevant for profitable, capital-intensive, or leveraged firms.

Given that operating income, net income, and cash flow from operations are required disclosures, you might wonder why analysts often use EBITDA as an approximation of these measures. As noted, EBITDA not only ignores four important costs of conducting business, but also ignores changes in operating working capital accounts that can fluctuate depending on growth, operating cycles, and managerial discretion, all crucial to the assessment of firm profitability and valuation.

PREPARING THE STATEMENT OF CASH FLOWS

This section illustrates a procedure for preparing an implied statement of cash flows using information from the balance sheet and income statement. The implied statement of cash flows assumes that all of the changes in non-cash assets, liabilities, and shareholders' equity accounts imply cash flows. (For example, an increase in a liability implies borrowing, while a decrease implies payment.) The implied statement of cash flows that you prepare merely approximates the amounts the statement of cash flows would report if the analyst had full access to a firm's accounting records. For example, you can assume that all changes in operating working capital accounts are operating transactions even though some of these changes might arise from a corporate acquisition or divestiture, which are investing activities. As a second example, consider a firm that acquires another firm by paying cash and assuming its liabilities (like the Blackboard illustration earlier in the chapter). Only the cash outflow appears in the investing section of the statement of cash flows. Acquiring assets by assuming liabilities is a non-cash acquisition of assets; that is, assets increase and liabilities increase. Such non-cash exchanges do not appear in the statement of cash flows because they do not affect cash. However, firms must report them in a supplemental note to the financial statements. PepsiCo includes the disclosures as the last part of Note 14, "Supplemental Financial Information" (Appendix A). In 2008, PepsiCo made acquisitions totaling \$2.9 billion, but paid only \$1.9 billion in cash, which is the amount appearing in the investing section of the statement of cash flows (Appendix A). Absent information about non-cash exchanges, the preparation procedure described in this section assumes that all of the change in each account involves a cash flow that relates to one of the three activities reported in the statement of cash flows. Despite these concerns, the estimated amounts should approximate the actual amounts closely enough for the analyst to make meaningful interpretations.

Algebraic Formulation

You know from the accounting equation that

$$\text{Assets} = \text{Liabilities} + \text{Shareholders' Equity}$$

This equality holds for balance sheets at the beginning and end of each period. If you subtract the amounts on the balance sheet at the beginning of the period from the corresponding amounts on the balance sheet at the end of the period, you obtain the following equality for changes (Δ) in balance sheet amounts:

$$\Delta\ \text{Assets} = \Delta\ \text{Liabilities} + \Delta\ \text{Shareholders' Equity}$$

You can now expand the change in assets as follows:

$$\Delta\ \text{Cash} + \Delta\ \text{Non-Cash Assets} = \Delta\ \text{Liabilities} + \Delta\ \text{Shareholders' Equity},$$

where Cash represents cash and cash equivalents as defined by the FASB and IASB. Rearranging terms,

$$\Delta\ \text{Cash} = \Delta\ \text{Liabilities} + \Delta\ \text{Shareholders' Equity} - \Delta\ \text{Non-Cash Assets}$$

The statement of cash flows explains the reasons for the change in cash during a period. You can see that the change in cash equals the change in all other (non-cash) balance sheet amounts.

Refer to Exhibit 3.12, which shows the comparative balance sheet of Logue Shoe Store for the years ending December 31, Year 4, Year 3, and Year 2. The balance sheets at the end of Year 2 and Year 3 report the following equalities:

	Cash	+	Non-Cash Assets	=	Liabilities	+	Shareholders' Equity
Year 2	$13,698	+	$132,136	=	$105,394	+	$40,440
Year 3	$12,595	+	$129,511	=	$ 85,032	+	$57,074
Changes	$(1,103)	+	$ (2,625)	=	$(20,362)	+	$16,634

Subtracting the amounts at the end of Year 2 from the amounts at the end of Year 3, you obtain the following:

$$\begin{array}{llllll} \Delta\ \text{Cash} + & \Delta\ \text{Non-Cash Assets} & = & \Delta\ \text{Liabilities} & + & \Delta\ \text{Shareholders' Equity} \\ \$(1{,}103) + & \$(2{,}625) & = & \$(20{,}362) & + & \$16{,}634 \end{array}$$

Rearranging terms.

$$\begin{array}{llllll} \Delta\ \text{Cash} = & \Delta\ \text{Liabilities} & + & \Delta\ \text{Shareholders' Equity} & - & \Delta\ \text{Non-Cash Assets} \\ \$(1{,}103) = & \$(20{,}362) & + & \$16{,}634 & - & \$(2{,}625) \end{array}$$

The decrease in cash of $1,103 equals the decrease in liabilities plus the increase in shareholders' equity minus the decrease in non-cash assets.

To link the above decomposition of the balance sheet equation into the format of the statement of cash flows, partition non-cash assets and liabilities into working capital and non-working capital components. Also assume that all non-working capital liabilities

EXHIBIT 3.12

Logue Shoe Store
Balance Sheet

	December 31, Year 4	December 31, Year 3	December 31, Year 2
ASSETS			
Cash	$ 5,815	$ 12,595	$ 13,698
Accounts receivable	1,816	1,978	1,876
Inventories	123,636	106,022	98,824
Other current assets	1,560	—	3,591
Total Current Assets	$132,827	$120,595	$117,989
Property, plant, and equipment, at cost	$ 64,455	$ 65,285	$ 63,634
Less accumulated depreciation	(54,617)	(45,958)	(37,973)
Net property, plant, and equipment	$ 9,838	$ 19,327	$ 25,661
Intangible assets	2,184	2,184	2,184
Total Assets	$144,849	$142,106	$145,834
LIABILITIES AND SHAREHOLDERS' EQUITY			
Accounts payable	$ 13,954	$ 15,642	$ 21,768
Notes payable	10,814	—	—
Current portion of long-term debt	7,288	10,997	18,256
Other current liabilities	5,489	6,912	4,353
Total Current Liabilities	$ 37,545	$ 33,551	$ 44,377
Long-term debt	43,788	51,481	61,017
Total Liabilities	$ 81,333	$ 85,032	$105,394
Common stock	$ 1,000	$ 1,000	$ 1,000
Additional paid-in capital	124,000	124,000	124,000
Retained earnings	(61,484)	(67,926)	(84,560)
Total Shareholders' Equity	$ 63,516	$ 57,074	$ 40,440
Total Liabilities and Shareholders' Equity	$144,849	$142,106	$145,834

reflect debt financing. Indicating the components with "WC" and "NWC" subscripts, the changes equation becomes

$$\begin{aligned}\Delta \text{ Cash} = {} & \Delta \text{ Liabilities}_{WC} + \Delta \text{ Liabilities}_{NWC} + \Delta \text{ Shareholders' Equity} \\ & - \Delta \text{ Non-Cash Assets}_{WC} - \Delta \text{ Non-Cash Assets}_{NWC}.\end{aligned}$$

Rearranging terms,

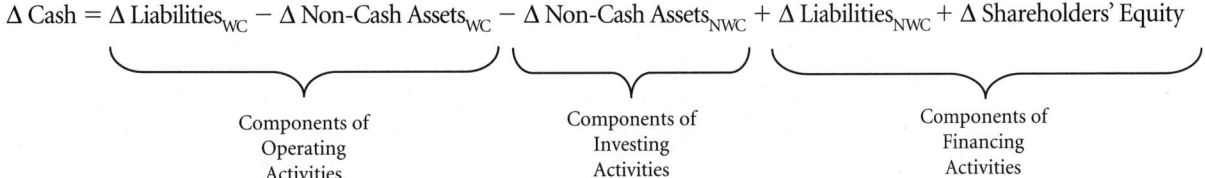

$$\Delta \text{ Cash} = \underbrace{\Delta \text{ Liabilities}_{WC} - \Delta \text{ Non-Cash Assets}_{WC}}_{\substack{\text{Components of}\\ \text{Operating}\\ \text{Activities}}} - \underbrace{\Delta \text{ Non-Cash Assets}_{NWC}}_{\substack{\text{Components of}\\ \text{Investing}\\ \text{Activities}}} + \underbrace{\Delta \text{ Liabilities}_{NWC} + \Delta \text{ Shareholders' Equity}}_{\substack{\text{Components of}\\ \text{Financing}\\ \text{Activities}}}$$

The rearrangement of the familiar balance sheet equation (and use of simplifying assumptions) yields the intuitive equation above, which *figuratively* maps into the information on the statement of cash flows. The mapping is figurative and is not technically representative, however, because net income is included in Δ Shareholders' Equity above and is an operating activity.

Classifying Changes in Balance Sheet Accounts

The statement of cash flows classifies the reasons for the change in cash as being an operating, investing, or financing activity. Converting the balance sheet and income statement into a statement of cash flows requires the analyst to classify the change in each non-cash balance sheet account (right-hand side of the preceding equation) into one of these three categories. Some of the analyst's classifications in this step will necessarily be approximations. Some of the changes in balance sheet accounts clearly fit into one of the three categories. (For example, the change in long-term debt is usually a financing transaction.) However, some balance sheet changes (for example, retained earnings) result from the netting of several changes, some of which relate to operations (net income) and some of which relate to financing activities (dividends). The analyst should use whatever information the financial statements and notes provide about changes in balance sheet accounts to classify the net change properly in each account each period.

Exhibit 3.13 classifies the changes in the non-cash balance sheet accounts and provides a schematic worksheet for the preparation of the statement of cash flows. The text will refer to this exhibit in walking through the preparation of a statement of cash flows for Logue Shoe Store and in several exercises at the end of the chapter. The classification of each of these changes is discussed next.

1. Accounts Receivable

Cash collections from customers during a period equal sales for the period plus accounts receivable at the beginning of the period minus accounts receivable at the end of the period, or alternatively, sales minus the change in accounts receivable.

$$\text{Cash Collected from Customers} = \text{Sales} - \Delta\ \text{Accounts Receivable}$$

Recall that an increase in accounts receivable indicates that less cash was collected than was recognized in revenues, so the adjustment is a subtraction, and vice versa for decreases in accounts receivable. Thus, the change in accounts receivable clearly relates to operations. Cash collected from customers is a line item in a cash flow statement prepared under the direct method. However, under the indirect method that most firms use and that we are describing, we use the change in accounts receivable to accomplish the same computation. Line (18) of Exhibit 3.13 shows net income as a source of cash from operations. Sales revenue is included in the starting point of the indirect cash flow statement. Thus, the amount for sales revenue included in the amount on line (18) adjusted for the change in accounts receivable on line (1) results in the amount of cash received from customers.

2. Marketable Securities

Firms typically acquire marketable securities when they temporarily have excess cash and sell these securities when they need cash. The holding of marketable securities for a relatively short period might make their purchases and sales appear as operating activities. Indeed, many firms with seasonal business hold marketable securities to smooth the amounts of readily available cash throughout the year. However, the temporarily excess cash could result from selling fixed assets, from issuing bonds or common stock, or from

EXHIBIT 3.13

Worksheet for Preparation of Statement of Cash Flows

Balance Sheet Accounts	Amount of Balance Sheet Changes	Operating	Investing	Financing
(INCREASE) DECREASE IN ASSETS				
(1) Accounts receivable		x		
(2) Marketable securities			x	
(3) Inventories		x		
(4) Other current assets		x		
(5) Investments in securities			x	
(6) Property, plant, and equipment cost			x	
(7) Accumulated depreciation		x		
(8) Intangible assets		x	x	
INCREASE (DECREASE) IN LIABILITIES AND SHAREHOLDERS' EQUITIES				
(9) Accounts payable		x		
(10) Notes payable				x
(11) Current portion of long-term debt				x
(12) Other current liabilities		x		
(13) Long-term debt				x
(14) Deferred income taxes		x		
(15) Other noncurrent liabilities		x		
(16) Common stock				x
(17) Additional paid-in capital				x
(18) Retained earnings		x (net income)		x (dividends)
(19) Treasury stock				x
(20) Other accumulated comprehensive income				
(21) Cash				

operating activities. Likewise, firms might use the cash inflow from the sale of marketable securities to purchase fixed assets, retire debt, repurchase common or preferred stock, or finance operating activities. U.S. GAAP and IFRS ignore the reason for the excess cash (with which firms purchase marketable securities) and the use of the cash proceeds (from the sale of marketable securities) and classify the cash flows associated with purchases and sales of marketable securities as investing activities. (You may reclassify purchases and sales of marketable securities as operating or financing activities if deemed appropriate for purposes of analysis.) Because net income includes gains or losses on sales of marketable securities, you must subtract gains and add back losses to net income in deriving cash flow from operations if purchases and sales are viewed as investing activities. Failure to offset the gain or loss included in earnings results in reporting too much (sales of marketable securities at a gain) or too little (sales of marketable securities at a loss) cash flow from operations. Cash flow from operations should include none of the cash flows associated with sales of marketable securities if such transactions are viewed as investing activities.

3. Inventories

Purchases of inventory during a period equal cost of goods sold for the period plus inventories at the end of the period minus inventories at the beginning of the period, or alternatively, cost of goods sold plus the change in inventory.

$$\text{Purchases of Inventory} = \text{Cost of Goods Sold} + \Delta \text{ Inventory}$$

Line (18) includes cost of goods sold as an expense in measuring net income. The change in inventories on line (3) coupled with cost of goods sold included in net income on line (18) results in the amount of purchases for the period. Cash paid to suppliers for inventory is a line item in a direct method cash flow statement. However, for the indirect method we must adjust reported net income, which includes cost of goods sold, for the change in inventory balances to compute cash paid for inventory (that is, purchases). The presumption is that the firm made a cash outflow equal to the amount of purchases. If the firm does not pay cash for all of these purchases, accounts payable will change. You adjust for the change in accounts payable on line (9), discussed later.

4. Other Current Assets

Other current assets typically include prepayments for various operating costs such as insurance and rent. Unless the financial statements and notes present information to the contrary, the presumption is that the change in other current assets relates to operations. Under this presumption, the related expenses are included in net income, so we must adjust these amounts for any changes in other current assets to convert those expenses into the cash amounts. The logic is the same as that for inventory.

5. Investments in Securities

The investments in securities account can change for the following reasons:

Source of Change	Classification in Statement of Cash Flows
Recognition of income or loss using equity method	Operating (subtraction or addition)
Acquisition of new investments	Investing (outflow)
Receipt of dividend from investee	Operating (inflow)
Sale of investments	Investing (inflow)
Purchases or sales of securities classified as "trading" securities	Operating (inflow or outflow)

We discussed the adjustment for equity method income for PepsiCo earlier in the chapter. These types of investments are generally separately disclosed. If a firm's balance sheet, income statement, or notes provide information that permits the disaggregation of the net change in investments in securities into these separate components, you can make appropriate classifications of the components. Absent such information, however, it is natural to classify the change in investment securities other than trading securities as an investing activity. Required disclosures for the valuation of financial instruments provides detailed information on the components of securities, which can assist the analyst in identifying the different categories of investment securities.

6. Property, Plant, and Equipment

Cash flows related to purchases and sales of fixed assets are classified as investing activities. Because net income includes any gains or losses from sales of fixed assets, you offset their effect on earnings by adding back losses and subtracting gains from net income when computing cash flow from operations. You then include the full amount of the proceeds from sales of fixed assets as an investing activity.

7. Accumulated Depreciation

The amount of depreciation expense recognized each period reduces net income but does not use cash. Thus, you add back depreciation expense as an operating item with a positive sign on line (7). When you add the amount for depreciation expense included under operations on line (7) to depreciation expense included as a negative element in net income on line (18), you eliminate the effect of depreciation expense on the Operations column. This treatment is appropriate because depreciation expense is not a cash flow (ignoring income tax consequences). If a firm sells depreciable assets during a period, the net change in accumulated depreciation includes both the accumulated depreciation removed from the account for assets sold and depreciation expense for the period. Thus, you cannot assume that the change in the accumulated depreciation account relates only to depreciation expense unless disclosures indicate that the firm did not sell depreciable assets during the year.

8. Intangible Assets

Intangible assets on the balance sheet include patents, copyrights, goodwill, and similar assets. A portion of the change in these accounts represents amortization, which requires an addback to net income when computing cash flow from operations. Unless the financial statements and notes provide contrary information, the presumption is that the remaining change in these accounts is an investing activity.

Many firms include another line item on their balance sheets labeled "Other Noncurrent Assets." You should use whatever information firms disclose to determine the appropriate classification of the change in this account.

9. Accounts Payable

Under the assumption that all accounts payable are due to suppliers from which the firm makes purchases, the cash outflow for accounts payable equals inventory purchases during the period plus accounts payable at the beginning of the period minus accounts payable at the end of the period, or equivalently, purchases minus change in accounts payable.

$$\text{Cash Paid to Suppliers} = \text{Purchases of Inventory} - \Delta\ \text{Accounts Payable}$$

The amount for inventory purchases of the period was derived as part of the calculations in line (3) for inventories. The adjustment on line (9) for the change in accounts payable converts cost of goods sold that is included within net income to cash payments for purchases and, like inventories, is an operating activity.

10. Notes Payable

Notes payable is the account generally used when a firm engages in short-term borrowing from a bank or another financial institution. The typical classification of such borrowings is as a financing activity on the statement of cash flows even though the firm might use the proceeds to finance accounts receivable, inventories, or other working capital needs. The presumption underlying the classification of bank borrowing as a financing activity is that firms derive operating cash inflows from their customers, not by borrowing from banks.

11. Current Portion of Long-Term Debt

The change in the current portion of long-term debt during a period equals (a) the reclassification of long-term debt from a noncurrent liability to a current liability (that is, debt that the firm expects to repay within one year as of the end-of-the-period balance sheet) minus (b) the current portion of long-term debt actually repaid during the period. The latter amount represents the cash outflow from this financing transaction. The amount arising from the reclassification in connection with line (13) will be considered shortly.

12. Other Current Liabilities

Firms generally use this account for obligations related to goods and services used in operations other than purchases of inventories. Thus, changes in other current liabilities appear as operating activities.

13. Long-Term Debt

This account changes for the following reasons:

- Issuance of new long-term debt
- Reclassification of long-term debt from a noncurrent to a current liability
- Retirement of long-term debt
- Conversion of long-term debt to preferred or common stock

These items are clearly financing transactions, but all of them do not affect cash. The issuance of new debt and the retirement of old debt do affect cash flows. The reclassification of long-term debt included in the amount on line (13) offsets the corresponding amount included in the change on line (11), and they effectively cancel each other. This is appropriate because the reclassification does not affect cash flow. Likewise, any portion of the change in long-term debt on line (13) due to a conversion of debt into common stock offsets a similar change on lines (16) and (17). You enter reclassifications and conversions of debt, such as those described previously, on the worksheet for the preparation of a statement of cash flows because such transactions help explain changes in balance sheet accounts. However, these transactions do not appear on the formal statement of cash flows because they do not involve actual cash flows.

14. Deferred Income Taxes

Income taxes currently payable equal income tax expense [included on line (18) as a negative element of net income] plus or minus the change in deferred taxes during the period. Thus, changes in deferred income taxes appear as an operating activity.

15. Other Noncurrent Liabilities

This account includes unfunded pension and retirement benefit obligations, long-term deposits received, and other miscellaneous long-term liabilities. Changes in these types of obligations are operating activities. Absent information to the contrary (for example, a footnote stating other noncurrent liabilities contain long-term financing obligations, which is uncommon), you classify the change in other noncurrent liability accounts as operating activities.

16 and 17. Common Stock and Additional Paid-in Capital

These accounts change when a firm issues new common stock or repurchases and retires outstanding common stock, and they appear as financing activities. The additional paid-in capital account also changes when firms recognize compensation expense related to stock options (discussed in Chapter 6). This is a non-cash expense that, like depreciation, requires an addback to net income to compute cash flow from operations.

18. Retained Earnings

Retained earnings increase by the amount of net income and decrease with the declaration of dividends each period.

$$\text{Ending Retained Earnings} = \text{Beginning Retained Earnings} + \text{Net Income} - \text{Dividends}$$
$$\Rightarrow \Delta \text{ Retained Earnings} = \text{Net Income} - \text{Dividends}$$

Net income is an operating activity, and dividends are a financing activity.

19. Treasury Stock

Repurchasing a firm's outstanding capital stock is a financing activity.

20. Accumulated Other Comprehensive Income

Recall that accumulated other comprehensive income is a component of shareholders' equity and includes various gains and losses that have not been realized. Examples include gains and losses on foreign currency hedges, certain investment securities, derivative instruments, and certain pension items. The change in accumulated other comprehensive income on the balance sheet represents the amount of other comprehensive income for the period, net of any accumulated other comprehensive income items that were realized in cash and therefore recognized in net income during the period. Also recall that

$$\text{Net income} + \text{Other Comprehensive Income} = \text{Comprehensive Income.}$$

Other comprehensive income represents only non-cash adjustments (that is, gains and losses that have not been realized). Accumulated other comprehensive income items that are realized in cash are already recognized in net income for the period. Therefore, the change in accumulated other comprehensive income on the balance sheet needs no further recognition on the statement of cash flows, because the statement of cash flows starts with net income, not comprehensive income.

Illustration of the Preparation Procedure

Based on the data for Logue Shoe Store, the procedure for preparing the statement of cash flows is illustrated in Exhibits 3.14 (Year 3) and 3.15 (Year 4). In addition to the balance sheet data shown there, net income was $16,634 for Year 3 and $6,442 for Year 4. The first column of Exhibit 3.14 shows the change in each non-cash balance sheet account that nets to the $1,103 decrease in cash for the period. You should observe with particular care the direction of the change. Recall the earlier decomposition of the balance sheet equation. Possible combinations of net changes in cash, liabilities, shareholders' equity, and non-cash assets can be described as follows:

Δ Cash	=	Δ Liabilities	+	Δ Shareholders' Equity	−	Δ Non-Cash Assets
Increase	=	Increase				
Decrease	=	Decrease				
Increase	=			Increase		
Decrease	=			Decrease		
Decrease	=					Increase
Increase	=					Decrease

EXHIBIT 3.14

Worksheet for Statement of Cash Flows for Logue Shoe Store
Year 3

Balance Sheet Accounts	**Amount of Balance Sheet Changes**	**Operating**	**Investing**	**Financing**	**Cross-Reference to Statement of Cash Flows in Exhibit 3.16**
(INCREASE) DECREASE IN ASSETS					
Accounts receivable	$ (102)	$ (102)	—	—	❶
Inventories	(7,198)	(7,198)	—	—	❷
Other current assets	3,591	3,591	—	—	❸
Property, plant, and equipment	(1,651)	—	$(1,651)	—	❹
Accumulated depreciation	7,985	7,985	—	—	❺
Intangible assets	—	—	—	—	
INCREASE (DECREASE) IN LIABILITIES AND SHAREHOLDERS' EQUITIES					
Accounts payable	$(6,126)	$(6,126)	—	—	❻
Notes payable	—	—	—	—	❼
Current portion of long-term debt	(7,259)	—	—	$ (7,259)	❽
Other current liabilities	2,559	2,559	—	—	❾
Long-term debt	(9,536)	—	—	(9,536)	❽
Common stock	—	—	—	—	
Additional paid-in capital	—	—	—	—	
Retained earnings	16,634	16,634	—	—	
Cash	$(1,103)	$17,343	$(1,651)	$(16,795)	❿

Thus, changes in liabilities and shareholders' equity have the same directional effect on cash, whereas changes in non-cash assets have the opposite directional effect. Bank borrowings increase liabilities and cash; debt repayments decrease liabilities and cash. Issuing common stock increases shareholders' equity and cash; paying dividends or repurchasing outstanding common stock reduces shareholders' equity and cash. Purchasing equipment increases non-cash assets and reduces cash; selling equipment reduces non-cash assets and increases cash.

You classify the change in each account as an operating, investing, or financing activity because you have no information that more than one activity caused the change in the account. Observe the following inferences for Year 3:

1. Operating activities were a net source of cash for the period. Cash flow from operations approximately equaled net income. Logue Shoe Store increased its inventories but reduced accounts payable. Most firms attempt to increase accounts payable to finance increases in inventories. The reduced accounts payable suggests a desire to pay suppliers more quickly, perhaps to take advantage of cash discounts, or pressure from suppliers to pay more quickly.

2. Cash flow from operations was more than sufficient to finance the increase in property, plant, and equipment. Note that capital expenditures were small relative to the amount of depreciation for the year, suggesting that the firm is not increasing its capacity.
3. Logue Shoe Store used the cash derived from operations in excess of capital expenditures to repay long-term debt.

Exhibit 3.15 presents a worksheet for Year 4. The preparation procedure is identical to that in Exhibit 3.14. Note in this year that operations were a net user of cash. Accounts payable did not increase with the substantial increase in inventories. Instead, accounts payable decreased, so Logue was either unable or chose not to use supplier financing for the increase in inventories. Long-term debt was again redeemed in Year 4, but it appears that the firm used short-term bank borrowing to finance the redemption. The negative cash flow from operations coupled with the use of short-term debt to redeem long-term debt suggests an increase in short-term liquidity risk.

Exhibit 3.16 presents the statement of cash flows for Logue Shoe Store for Year 3 and Year 4 using the amounts taken from the worksheets in Exhibits 3.14 and 3.15. The farthest right columns of Exhibits 3.14 and 3.16 provide cross-references for clarifying how the worksheets are used to prepare the statement of cash flows.

EXHIBIT 3.15

Worksheet for Statement of Cash Flows for Logue Shoe Store
Year 4

Balance Sheet Accounts	Amount of Balance Sheet Changes	Operating	Investing	Financing
(INCREASE) DECREASE IN ASSETS				
Accounts receivable	$ 162	$ 162	—	—
Inventories	(17,614)	(17,614)	—	—
Other current assets	(1,560)	(1,560)	—	—
Property, plant, and equipment	830	—	$830	—
Accumulated depreciation	8,659	8,659	—	—
Intangible assets	—	—	—	—
INCREASE (DECREASE) IN LIABILITIES AND SHAREHOLDERS' EQUITIES				
Accounts payable	$(1,688)	$(1,688)	—	—
Notes payable	10,814	—	—	$10,814
Current portion of long-term debt	(3,709)	—	—	(3,709)
Other current liabilities	(1,423)	(1,423)	—	—
Long-term debt	(7,693)	—	—	(7,693)
Common stock	—	—	—	—
Additional paid-in capital	—	—	—	—
Retained earnings	6,442	6,442	—	—
Cash	$(6,780)	$(7,022)	$830	$ (588)

EXHIBIT 3.16

Statement of Cash Flows for Logue Shoe Store

	Year 4	Year 3	Cross-Reference of Year 3 Amounts to Exhibit 3.14
OPERATING			
Net Income	$ 6,442	$ 16,634	
Depreciation	8,659	7,985	❺
(Increase) Decrease in accounts receivable	162	(102)	❶
(Increase) Decrease in inventories	(17,614)	(7,198)	❷
(Increase) Decrease in other current assets	(1,560)	3,591	❸
Increase (Decrease) in accounts payable	(1,688)	(6,126)	❻
Increase (Decrease) in other current liabilities	(1,423)	2,559	❾
Cash Flow from Operating	$ (7,022)	$ 17,343	❿
INVESTING			
Sale (acquisition) of property, plant, and equipment	$ 830	$ (1,651)	❹
Cash Flow from Investing	$ 830	$ (1,651)	❿
FINANCING			
Increase in notes payable	$ 10,814	—	❼
Repayment of long-term debt	(11,402)	(16,795)	❽
Cash Flow from Financing	$ (588)	$(16,795)	❿
Net Change in Cash	$ (6,780)	$ (1,103)	❿
Cash at beginning of year	12,595	13,698	
Cash at End of Year	$ 5,815	$ 12,595	

Using the Statement of Cash Flows to Assess Earnings Quality

Having discussed general relations between net income and cash flows and having walked through the preparation of the statement of cash flows, the chapter closes by describing how information on differences between net income and cash flows can be useful to analysts interested in assessing the "quality of earnings" for a company. The notion of earnings quality is ill-defined, but analysts often try to gauge whether reported net income reflects the underlying economics of the business. The characterization of earnings quality is thus the closeness of reported earnings to economic earnings (which are unobservable). Net income can figuratively be viewed as reflecting a combination of underlying *economics*, *measurement error*, and intentional *bias*. Procedures such as allocating depreciation across the periods over which a machine is utilized, recognizing sales when the firm is entitled to payment and has no remaining performance obligations, and recognizing pension expenses during the period in which workers earn future benefits are attempts to capture the economics of underlying operating activities. However, all of these transactions require judgment and estimation to implement. For example, to record depreciation, managers must make estimates of salvage values and service life and choose a depreciation method (such as straight-line or accelerated). Inevitably, estimates will differ from actual results; the firm may end up using a depreciable asset for a period that differs from that initially estimated as useful life or the amount realized as salvage value will differ from that originally estimated. These measurement errors are unintentional and, it is hoped, small and perhaps offsetting across the many estimates a firm must make. Unfortunately, because of the flexibility inherent in estimates, managers can abuse their available discretion and intentionally bias estimates to affect the financial reporting outcome. For example, a manager wanting to report higher income could base depreciation expense on depreciable lives that are longer than what is truthfully expected (lowering the annual amount of depreciation) or can presume a higher salvage value than is realistic (decreasing the amount of the asset to be depreciated).

Financial accounting appears to work well at achieving the goal of capturing economic transactions when they occur, not necessarily when the associated cash flows are realized, thus mapping economics into net income. For example, Chapter 2 discussed research by Dechow (1994), who examined the relative ability of cash flows and net income to explain stock returns. Her study confirms that as the measurement window increases (she aggregated firm performance measures over several years), cash flows and net income become similar in their association with stock returns. Dechow showed that over long windows such as five years, both aggregate cash flows and aggregate earnings capture economics well and are closely associated with changes in stock prices. It is over short horizons (such as a quarter or a year) that net income is more closely associated with changes in stock price. Moreover, the primary conclusion supported by many studies, including Dechow's, is that "earnings better reflect firm performance than cash flows, in firms with more volatile operating, investment and financing activities."[8]

Financial accounting also enables analysts to understand implications of currently reported earnings for future earnings and cash flows. In the figurative description of net income, the goal of assessing earnings quality is to determine how well net income reflects economics, as opposed to measurement error or management bias. As it turns out, if managers introduce bias into the accounting system, it typically will occur in their discretionary estimates with respect to accounting choices such as recognition of accounts receivable (and revenues), depreciation expense, inventory (and cost of goods sold), and various accrued liabilities (and expenses). Even if managers do not introduce bias into the financial statements, components of income such as accounting accruals will have different properties than other components of net income, which generates a slightly different version of earnings quality—earnings persistence—discussed below. Collectively, accounting accruals can be succinctly identified as the adjustments in the operating section of the statement of cash flows (as for PepsiCo in Exhibit 3.11). Accruals have been examined extensively in academic research, and the results of these studies have been insightful for analysts and investment managers because the research indicates that stock prices reflect only the information in the components of net income with a lag. This allows analysts and investors who understand financial statements to gain an edge over those who do not.

To clarify what is meant by "accruals," Exhibit 3.17 provides a schematic of a statement of cash flows and identifies accruals. Accruals are the adjustments that reconcile net income to cash flows from operations. They are components of earnings because they map underlying economics into reported profitability. As you saw with PepsiCo, the level of cash flows from

[8]Patricia M. Dechow, "Accounting Earnings and Cash Flows as Measures of Firm Performance: The Role of Accounting Accruals," *Journal of Accounting and Economics* (1994), p. 7.

EXHIBIT 3.17

Simplified Schematic of the Computation of Accruals from the Operating Section of the Statement of Cash Flows

Statement of Cash Flows		
Net income	NI	
Accruals: + Depreciation		
+ Amortization		
+ Deferred taxes		$\frac{\text{NI} - \text{OCF}}{\text{Avg.Total Assets}}$
Adjustments for working capital		↓
+/– Accounts receivable		
+/– Prepaid expenses		
+/– Inventory		
+/– Other assets		
+/– Accounts payable		Possibly low earnings quality if this is large and positive [i.e., when income-increasing accruals are big]
+/– Accrued liabilities		
+/– Other liabilities		
Operating cash flows	OCF	
Cash flows from investing activities	I	
Cash flows from financing activities	F	
Net change in cash	CHANGE	

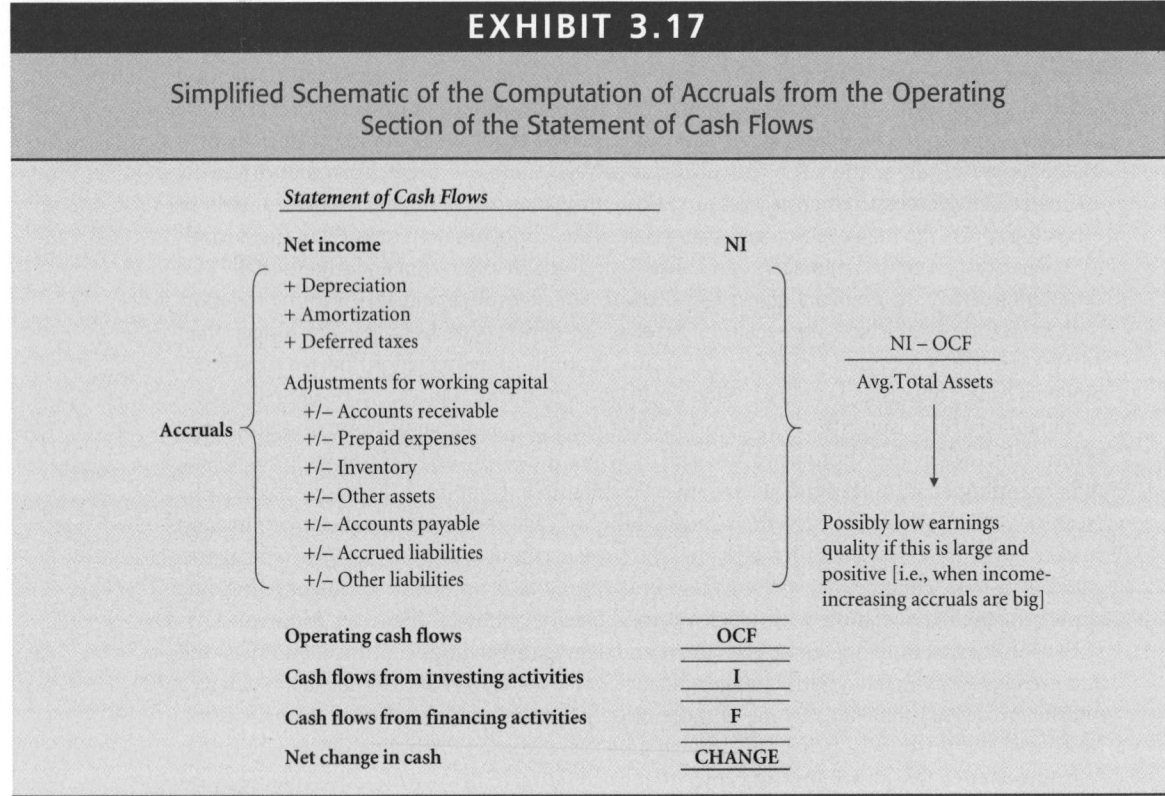

operations tends to be more stable than net income. Investors who fixate on net income or operating cash flows without understanding the relation between the two may make erroneous inferences regarding the persistence of cash flows or earnings. Sloan (1996) examined the relation between net income and operating cash flows by focusing on the behavior of net income conditional on the magnitude of the accruals.[9] First, note that accruals are computed as net income minus operating cash flows, and this amount is scaled by average beginning and ending total assets so that firms can be compared regardless of their size. Then all firms are ranked based on this measure of accruals, and net income (scaled by average total assets) is plotted for five years before and after the year in which accruals are measured.

Exhibit 3.18 provides the plots for the decile of firms with the lowest (most negative) and the decile of firms with the highest (most positive) accruals. The top line on the graph indicates that in the ranking year, firms with the highest accruals have very high income. Moreover, this high income represents a spike relative to the previous five years; more importantly, it represents a spike that dissipates almost entirely in the next year. On the other side, firms with the most negative accruals report net income that is extremely low relative to prior years, but this decline turns around over the following years. When net income is high relative to operating cash flows, we describe the firm as having recorded "*income-increasing*" accruals; when net income is low relative to operating cash flows, we describe the firm as having recorded "*income-decreasing*" accruals. Also recall from the previous discussion that non-working capital accruals tend to be more persistent than working capital accruals, which tend to go up and down and generally fluctuate around zero for mature firms.

[9]Richard G. Sloan, "Do Stock Prices Fully Reflect Information in Accruals and Cash Flows About Future Earnings?" *The Accounting Review* (1996), pp. 289–315.

EXHIBIT 3.18

Patterns of Earnings Surrounding High and Low Accruals

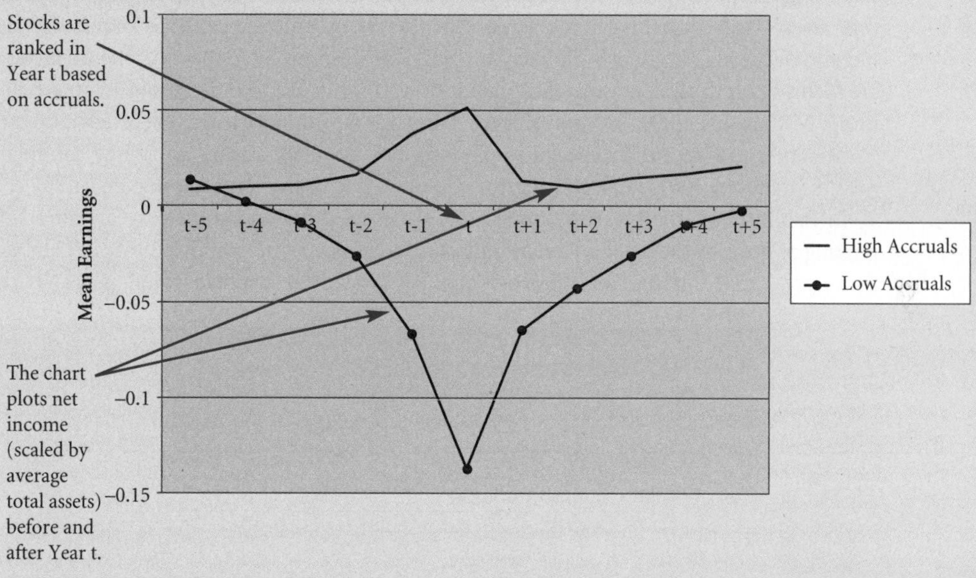

Source: Sloan (1996) op cit.

The patterns of net income in Exhibit 3.18 indicate that when net income is high because of large income-increasing accruals (such as increases in accounts receivable and decreases in payables), the reversal of these accruals generates predictable decreases in the level of earnings in future years. The same is true for income-decreasing accruals (such as decreases in receivables and increases in payables). This should be intuitive given a basic understanding of accounting. For example, if a firm generates a spike in sales made on credit, this increases accounts receivable and recognized sales. In the following year, the firm will have to generate incremental sales to maintain the level (or growth) in sales, which is difficult to do if the prior year's high levels were unusual or transitory. The statement of cash flows highlights the evolution of receivables by quantifying period-to-period changes in the balance. If a firm with a high increase in sales made on credit does not replenish these with more sales, the statement of cash flows in the following period will indicate a decrease in receivables. Although the collection of cash will contribute to cash flows from operations, net income will tend to fall because of the relative reduction in sales due to the nonreplenishment of prior-period credit sales. As discussed in this book, declines in earnings are strongly associated with declines in security prices.

If investors neglect to examine the components of net income, they may fail to appreciate the fact that large earnings that are driven by large *income-increasing* accruals are less persistent. Similarly, they might fail to appreciate that low earnings driven by large *income-decreasing* accruals also are less persistent and generally reverse with improved earnings in future periods. If enough investors fail to fully appreciate the relation between components of current earnings and future earnings, the result may be mispricing of shares. Indeed, this describes the pattern of stock returns for the firms shown in Exhibit 3.18.

Total accruals divided by average total assets can be thought of as an inverse measure of earnings quality: the higher the measure, the lower the earnings quality in the sense that reported earnings may not be as economically sustainable in the future and will likely decline.

As noted above, the lack of sustainability might be due to low earnings quality in the sense that managers introduced undue bias into accruals, which will have to reverse under double entry accounting, or it might be due to the tyranny of mean reversion whereby shocks like large increases in credit sales or big decreases in expenses are not sustainable. Similarly, lower measures (that is, more income-decreasing accruals) are associated with current reported earnings that are of higher quality in the sense that the earnings level, which is dampened due to income-decreasing accruals, will likely increase. Increasingly, investors and the financial press are focusing on the link between accruals and earnings quality. For example, in an article profiling Microsoft's 2009 second-quarter earnings announcement, TheStreet.com stated, "Companies that report lukewarm results on poor earnings quality are prime candidates to miss estimates by a wide margin in future quarters due to the reversal of accruals."[10]

In Exhibit 3.19, the future stock returns are plotted for one and two years ahead of the ranking of firms by the sign and magnitude of accruals shown in Exhibit 3.18. As in Exhibit 3.18, firms are ranked based on reported accruals scaled by average total assets. With the

EXHIBIT 3.19

One- and Two-Year Ahead Stock Returns to an Accruals Investment Strategy

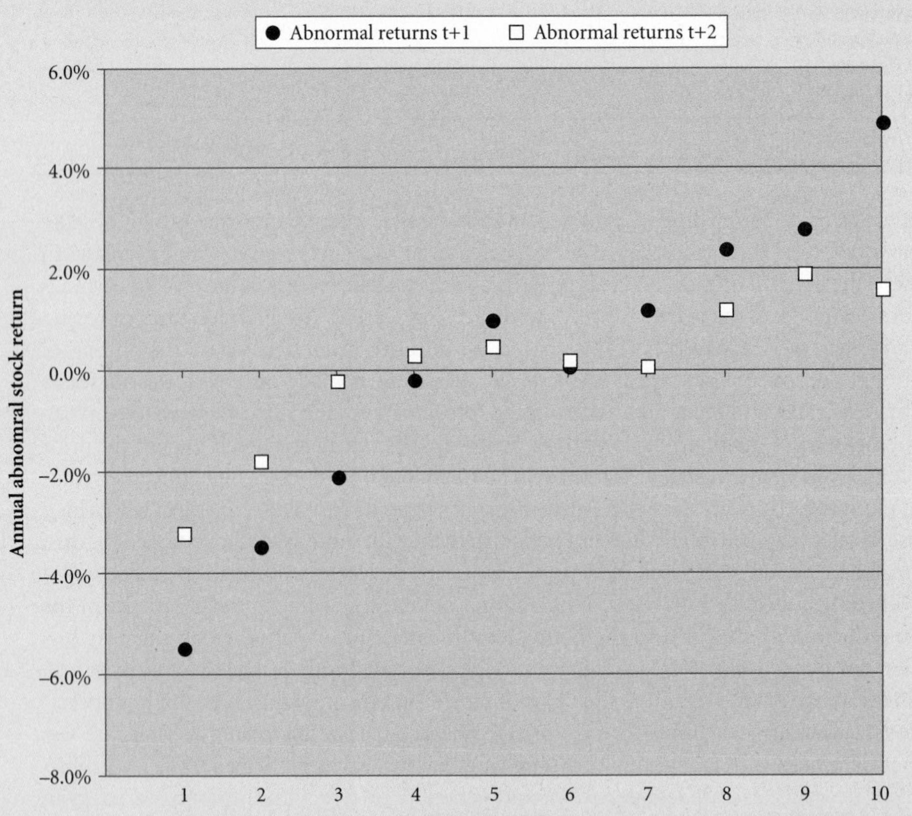

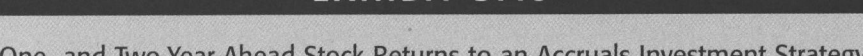

Decile 1 = largest income-increasing accruals; potentially low earnings quality
Decile 10 = largest income-decreasing accruals; potentially high earnings quality

Source: Sloan (1996) op cit.

[10]David MacDougall, "Analyst's Toolkit: Don't Hate on Microsoft," *TheStreet.com* (July 29, 2009).

characterization of income-increasing accruals being of potential low quality, decile 1 consists of the 10 percent of firms with the highest income-increasing accruals. Decile 10 consists of the 10 percent of firms with the largest income-decreasing accruals. The stock returns plotted in Exhibit 3.19 are the average stock return for all firms in the decile, where each firm's return is first adjusted for the return of a portfolio of similarly sized firms. Thus, the returns are referred to as "abnormal" returns. Positive abnormal returns indicate that the firm's stock price performed much better than similar-sized firms, and negative abnormal returns indicate worse performance than similar-sized firms. Exhibit 3.19 indicates that in the first year after firms are ranked based on the magnitude of their accruals, the firms with the lowest earnings quality (that is, highest income-increasing accruals) experience the worst stock returns and firms with the highest earnings quality (that is, highest income-decreasing accruals) experience the best stock returns. The plots show a similar ranking of stock returns in the second year after stocks are ranked based on accruals, but the effect diminishes somewhat. Overall, these patterns of returns, on average, are consistent with investors, on average, not realizing how important the components of reported earnings are in helping them form expectations of future earnings and, as a consequence, in mispricing stocks. As firms report quarterly results in years subsequent to large income-increasing or income-decreasing accruals, investors gradually see the turnaround in earnings that is shown in Exhibit 3.18. As this occurs, stock prices gradually adjust to the investors' revised expectations of future earnings.

Another way to examine how well investors understand the implications of accruals for future earnings is to examine analysts who forecast earnings. Analysts ought to be familiar with financial statements and be adept at understanding when earnings are temporarily high or low due to large income-increasing or income-decreasing accruals. Exhibit 3.20 provides

EXHIBIT 3.20

Analyst EPS Forecast Errors Subsequent to Low and High Accruals

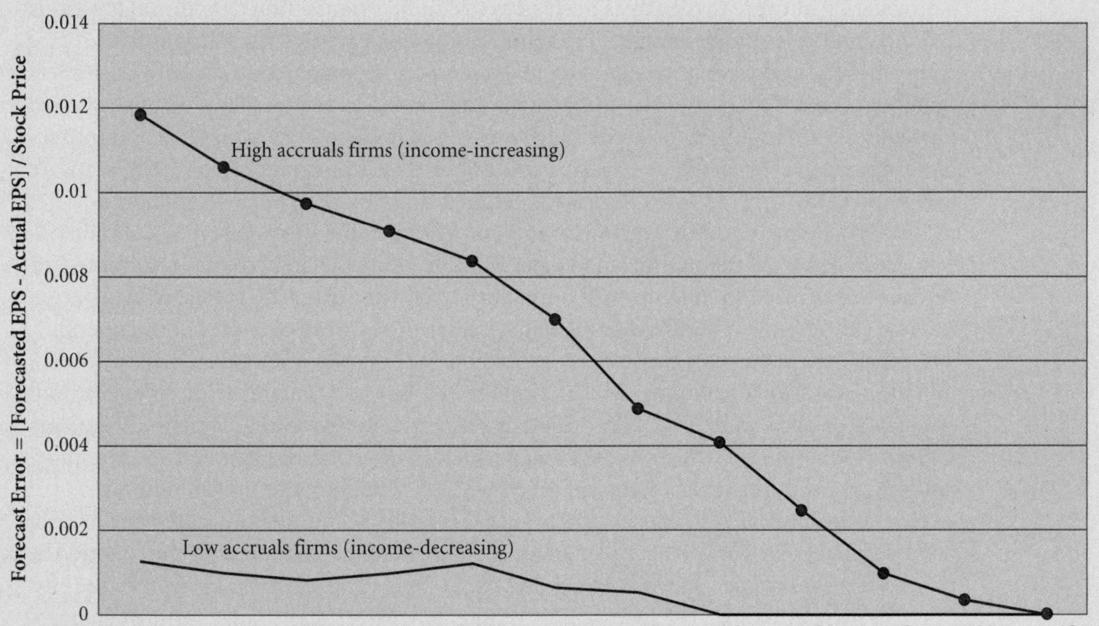

Source: Bradshaw, Richardson, and Sloan (2001)

evidence from a study by Bradshaw, Richardson, and Sloan (2001) consistent with analysts failing to understand the patterns of earnings shown in Exhibit 3.18[11]. The plot shows analysts' forecast errors for the 12 months subsequent to the ranking of firms based on accruals (as shown in Exhibit 3.18). Forecast errors are computed as the analysts' forecast of earnings per share (EPS) for a firm minus the actual EPS that is eventually reported, and this measure is scaled by stock price per share so that forecast errors can be averaged across firms. The exhibit displays the average forecast errors for the highest decile of income-increasing and income-decreasing accrual firms. It is clear that for firms with the highest income-increasing accruals (and hence, high earnings driven by the accruals), analysts tend to extrapolate those high earnings into the future (in the first several months) but gradually realize that the high earnings reported in the previous year are not repeating in the subsequent year. Eventually, the analysts walk down their forecasts to the amount reported, but it takes the entire 12-month period subsequent to the announcement of the previous year's earnings for them to get it right. As was shown in Exhibit 3.19, during this time, the firms' stock prices are falling as well due to the same phenomenon whereby investors are "walking down" their expectations and valuations from elevated levels driven by the high earnings composed of income-increasing accruals in the previous year. It bears noting that analysts are typically optimistic in their forecasts early in a year. This optimistic bias early in a fiscal year results in the forecasts for the firms with the lowest earnings (driven by large income-decreasing accruals) being optimistic, but not nearly to the extent that they are for the income-increasing accrual firms.

Overall, the patterns of earnings, stock returns, and analysts' forecasts shown in Exhibits 3.18−3.20 suggest that investors who utilize the statement of cash flows to identify circumstances in which earnings are supported by accruals that tend to reverse will have an advantage over other investors, including professional analysts. Later chapters explore more deeply the analysis of accruals as part of assessing earnings and overall accounting quality. As a final prelude to that discussion, refer to Exhibit 3.21, which shows two versions of the 1998 statement of cash flows for MicroStrategy, Inc.—one as originally reported and the other as subsequently restated for changes in the accounting for revenues. MicroStrategy is a provider of software that enables businesses to conduct transaction data through various channels and to examine information about customers, partners, and supply chains. The company was aggressive at recognizing revenue upon signing a contract with customers (and often before that), and the restatement announced in March 2000 included revised procedures for recognizing revenues only after sales contracts were completed and for recognizing revenues over the contract period rather than immediately. For 1998, software license revenues of $72.721 million were restated downward to $61.635 million and net income was restated downward from a *profit* of $6.178 million to a *loss* of $2.255 million. The restatement affected the balance sheet through decreases in accounts receivable (for revenues recognized premature to the finalization of the contract), increases in deferred revenue (for revenue recognized immediately rather than spread over the contract period), and other miscellaneous adjustments. As Exhibit 3.21 shows, MicroStrategy used $2.548 million of cash for operations, which is unaffected by the restatement of revenues (and associated balance sheet data). As originally reported, non-working capital adjustments totaled $4.183 million, which totaled $5.185 million after the restatement; more importantly, working capital adjustments fell from −$12.909 million to −$5.478 million.

Several features of MicroStrategy's original operating section of the statement of cash flows stand out. First, as you have seen in other examples discussed earlier in the chapter, the typical relation of net income being less than operating cash flows is reversed for MicroStrategy. Although net income can legitimately exceed cash flows from operations,

[11]Mark T. Bradshaw, Scott A. Richardson, and Richard G. Sloan, "Do Analysts and Auditors Use Information in Accruals?" *Journal of Accounting Research* (June 2001), pp. 45–74.

EXHIBIT 3.21

MicroStrategy, Inc.
Statement of Cash Flows for 1998
(amounts in thousands)

	As Reported	Restated
OPERATING ACTIVITIES		
Net income (loss)	$ 6,178	$(2,255)
Adjustments to reconcile net income (loss) to net cash from operating activities:		
Depreciation and amortization	3,250	3,250
Provision for doubtful accounts, net of write-offs and recoveries	815	815
Net change in deferred taxes	(45)	0
Other	163	1,120
Changes in operating assets and liabilities, net of effect of foreign exchange rate changes:		
Accounts receivable	(17,525)	(10,835)
Prepaid expenses and other current assets	(711)	(3,758)
Accounts payable and accrued expenses, compensation, and benefits	5,948	5,508
Deferred revenue	2,267	3,795
Deposits and other assets	(188)	(188)
Long-term accounts receivable	(2,700)	0
Net Cash Used in Operating Activities	$ (2,548)	$(2,548)
INVESTING ACTIVITIES		
Acquisition of property and equipment	$ (9,295)	$(9,295)
Net Cash Used in Investing Activities	$ (9,295)	$(9,295)
FINANCING ACTIVITIES		
Proceeds from sale of Class A common stock and exercise of stock options, net of offering costs	$48,539	$48,539
Repayments on short-term line of credit, net	(4,508)	(4,508)
Repayments of dividend notes payable	(5,000)	(5,000)
Proceeds from issuance of note payable	862	862
Principal payments on notes payable	(4,190)	(4,190)
Net Cash Provided by Financing Activities	$35,703	$35,703
Effect of foreign exchange rate changes on cash	$ 125	$ 125
Net Increase in Cash and Cash Equivalents	$23,985	$23,985
Cash and cash equivalents, beginning of year	3,506	3,506
Cash and Cash Equivalents, End of Period	$27,491	$27,491

especially for growth firms, it is a red flag for accounting quality issues because of managerial discretion necessary in the reporting of non-working capital and working capital adjustments. Second, the existence of negative cash flows from operations but positive net income represents a situation in which managers may be keenly interested in reporting profits rather than losses, increasing incentives to adopt aggressive accounting practices.

Third, the magnitude of the working capital adjustments exceeds that of non-working capital adjustments, which indicates that the accounting for working capital accounts has an elevated importance for the level of reported earnings. For example, accounts receivable and deferred revenues are directly associated with the recognition of revenues.

As originally reported, MicroStrategy showed a negative adjustment for accounts receivable of $17.525 million, indicating that accounts receivable increased (and revenue was recognized); on the other hand, the originally reported change in deferred revenue was relatively smaller, increasing cash flows by $2.267 million (as customers prepaid and MicroStrategy actually deferred revenue). After the restatement, however, the increase in receivables declined to $10.835 million (pushing revenue recognition to future years) and the increase in deferred revenue increased to $3.795 million (deferring even more of the revenues for which customers had prepaid). Both of these changes reflect less aggressive accounting practice in terms of revenue recognition. Finally, the average total assets of MicroStrategy for 1998 was $56.377 million (not shown in Exhibit 3.21), so the quality of earnings metric discussed above (that is, total accruals ÷ average total assets) would be 0.1548 [= (6.178 − (2.548)) ÷ 56.377]. The median value of scaled total accruals for all firms is approximately −0.04, with a lower quartile of −0.10 and upper quartile of +0.008.[12] Thus, a value of +0.15 is remarkably high, and as mentioned earlier in the chapter, higher values of this metric are suggestive of lower earnings quality, which certainly characterized MicroStrategy's originally reported 1998 financial statements. The restatement was costly to the company's shareholders as the price of MicroStrategy common shares fell from $227 to $113 within five days of the announcement of the restatement.[13] Clearly, the financial statements as originally reported contained clues investors could have used to raise concerns about the quality of earnings possibly being low.

SUMMARY

As a complement to the balance sheet and the income statement, the statement of cash flows is an informative statement for analysts for the following reasons:

- Analysts who understand the types of information this statement presents and the kinds of interpretations that are appropriate find that the statement of cash flows reveals information about the economic characteristics of a firm's industry, its strategy, and the stage in its life cycle.
- The statement of cash flows provides information to assess the financial health of a firm. Analysts increasingly recognize that cash flows do not necessarily track income flows. A firm with a healthy income statement is not necessarily financially healthy, and vice versa. Cash requirements to service debt, for example, may outstrip the ability of operations to generate cash.
- The statement of cash flows highlights accounting accruals, which can provide insight into the overall sustainability and quality of a firm's reported earnings.

QUESTIONS, EXERCISES, PROBLEMS, AND CASES

Questions and Exercises

3.1 NEED FOR A STATEMENT OF CASH FLOWS. "The accrual basis of accounting creates the need for a statement of cash flows." Explain.

[12] Bradshaw, Richardson, and Sloan (2001) op cit.

[13] Susan Scholz, "The Changing Nature and Consequences of Public Company Financial Restatements." The Department of the Treasury (April 2008).

3.2 ARTICULATION OF THE STATEMENT OF CASH FLOWS WITH OTHER FINANCIAL STATEMENTS. Describe how the statement of cash flows is linked to each of the other financial statements (income statement and balance sheet). Also review how the other financial statements are linked with each other.

3.3 CLASSIFICATION OF INTEREST EXPENSE. Under U.S. GAAP, the statement of cash flows classifies cash expenditures for interest expense as an operating activity but classifies cash expenditures to redeem debt as a financing activity. Explain this apparent paradox.

3.4 CLASSIFICATION OF CASH FLOWS RELATED TO THE COST OF FINANCING. Under U.S. GAAP, the statement of cash flows classifies cash expenditures for interest expense on debt as an operating activity but classifies cash expenditures for dividends to shareholders as a financing activity. Explain this apparent paradox.

3.5 CLASSIFICATION OF CHANGES IN SHORT-TERM FINANCING. The statement of cash flows classifies changes in accounts payable as an operating activity but classifies changes in short-term borrowing as a financing activity. Explain this apparent paradox.

3.6 TREATMENT OF NON-CASH EXCHANGES. The acquisition of equipment by assuming a mortgage is a transaction that firms cannot report in their statement of cash flows but must report in a supplemental schedule or note. Of what value is information about this type of transaction? What is the reason for its exclusion from the statement of cash flows?

3.7 COMPUTING CASH COLLECTIONS FROM CUSTOMERS. Caterpillar manufactures heavy machinery and equipment and provides financing for purchases by its customers. Caterpillar reported sales and interest revenues of $51,324 million for 2008. The balance sheet showed current and noncurrent receivables of $15,752 million at the beginning of 2008 and $18,448 million at the end of 2008. Compute the amount of cash collected from customers during 2008.

3.8 COMPUTING CASH PAYMENTS TO SUPPLIERS. Lowe's Companies, a retailer of home improvement products, reported cost of goods sold of $31,729 million for the fiscal year ended January 30, 2009. It reported merchandise inventories of $7,611 million at the beginning of fiscal 2009 and $8,209 million at the end of fiscal 2009. It reported accounts payable to suppliers of $3,713 million at the beginning of fiscal 2009 and $4,109 million at the end of fiscal 2009. Compute the amount of cash paid to merchandise suppliers during fiscal 2009.

3.9 COMPUTING CASH PAYMENTS FOR INCOME TAXES. Visa Inc., the credit card company, reported income tax expense of $1,648 million for 2008, comprising $1,346 million of current taxes and $302 million of deferred taxes. The balance sheet showed income taxes payable of $122 million at the beginning of 2008 and $327 million at the end of 2008. Compute the amount of income taxes paid in cash during 2008.

3.10 INTERPRETING RELATIONS BETWEEN NET INCOME AND CASH FLOW FROM OPERATIONS. Combined data for three years for two firms appear below (in millions).

	Firm A	Firm B
Net income	$2,381	$2,825
Cash flow from operations	$1,133	$7,728

One of these firms is Amazon.com, a rapidly growing internet retailer, and the other is Kroger, a retail grocery store chain growing at approximately the same rate as the population. Identify each firm and explain your reasoning.

3.11 INTERPRETING RELATIONS BETWEEN NET INCOME AND CASH FLOW FROM OPERATIONS. Three years of combined data for two firms appear below (in millions).

	Firm A	Firm B
Net income	$ 996	$2,846
Cash flow from operations	$3,013	$3,401

The two firms experienced similar growth rates in revenues during the three-year period. One of these firms is Accenture Ltd., a management consulting firm, and the other is Southwest Airlines, a provider of airline transportation services. Identify each firm and explain your reasoning.

3.12 INTERPRETING RELATIONS BETWEEN CASH FLOWS FROM OPERATING, INVESTING, AND FINANCING ACTIVITIES. Three years of combined data for two firms appear below (in millions).

	Firm A	Firm B
Net income	$ 2,378	$ 2,399
Cash flow from operations	$ 7,199	$ 3,400
Cash flow from investing	$(6,764)	$ (678)
Cash flow from financing	$ 570	$(2,600)

One of these firms is FedEx, a relatively high-growth firm that provides courier services, and the other is Kellogg Company, a more mature consumer foods processor. Identify each firm and explain your reasoning.

3.13 INTERPRETING RELATIONS BETWEEN CASH FLOWS FROM OPERATING, INVESTING, AND FINANCING ACTIVITIES. Three years of combined data for two firms appear below (in millions).

	Firm A	Firm B
Cash flow from operations	$ 2,639	$ 2,759
Cash flow from investing	$(3,491)	$(1,281)
Cash flow from financing	$ 1,657	$(1,654)

One of these firms is eBay, an online retailer with a three-year growth in sales of 337.3 percent, and the other is TJX Companies, Inc., a specialty retail store with a three-year growth in sales of 39.3 percent. Identify each firm and explain your reasoning.

3.14 RELATION BETWEEN NET INCOME, EBITDA, AND CASH FLOW FROM OPERATIONS. Selected data for The Walt Disney Company appear below (in millions).

	Year 4	Year 3	Year 2	Year 1
Net income	$2,345	$1,267	$1,236	$1,169
Conversion of net income to cash flow from operations:				
Non-working capital adjustments	2,076	1,370	1,077	2,124
Working capital adjustments	(51)	264	(27)	(245)
Cash flow from operations	$4,370	$2,901	$2,286	$3,048
EBITDA	$5,554	$4,106	$3,919	$3,759
Growth rate in revenues	13.6%	6.8%	0.6%	(0.6%)

Examine the differences between net income, cash flow from operations, and EBITDA for The Walt Disney Company. Comment on the relations among these series over time. Why does cash flow from operations exceed net income? What adjustments contribute to this pattern? Is this typical or unusual? Why is EBITDA so much higher than both net income and cash flow from operations?

Problems and Cases

3.15 INTERPRETING THE STATEMENT OF CASH FLOWS. The Coca-Cola Company (Coca-Cola), like PepsiCo, manufactures and markets a variety of beverages. Exhibit 3.22 presents a statement of cash flows for Coca-Cola for 2006 to 2008.

Required

Discuss the relationship between net income and cash flow from operations and between cash flows from operating, investing, and financing activities for the firm over the three-year period. Identify characteristics of Coca-Cola's cash flows that you would expect for a mature company.

3.16 INTERPRETING THE STATEMENT OF CASH FLOWS. Texas Instruments primarily develops and manufactures semiconductors for use in technology-based products for various industries. The manufacturing process is capital-intensive and subject to cyclical swings in the economy. Because of overcapacity in the industry and a cutback on spending for technology products due to a recession, semiconductor prices collapsed in Year 1 and commenced a steady comeback between Year 2 and Year 4. Exhibit 3.23 presents a statement of cash flows for Texas Instruments for Year 0 to Year 4.

Required

Discuss the relationship between net income and cash flows from operations and between cash flows from operating, investing, and financing activities for the firm over the five-year period.

EXHIBIT 3.22

The Coca-Cola Company
Statement of Cash Flows
(amounts in millions)
(Problem 3.15)

Year Ended December 31,	2008	2007	2006
OPERATING ACTIVITIES			
Net income	$ 5,807	$ 5,981	$ 5,080
Depreciation and amortization	1,228	1,163	938
Stock-based compensation expense	266	313	324
Deferred income taxes	(360)	109	(35)
Equity income or loss, net of dividends	1,128	(452)	124
Foreign currency adjustments	(42)	9	52
Gains on sales of assets, including bottling interests	(130)	(244)	(303)
Other operating charges	209	166	159
Other items	153	99	233
Net change in operating assets and liabilities	(688)	6	(615)
Net Cash Provided by Operating Activities	$ 7,571	$ 7,150	$ 5,957
INVESTING ACTIVITIES			
Acquisitions and investments, principally beverage and bottling companies and trademarks	$ (759)	$(5,653)	$ (901)
Purchases of other investments	(240)	(99)	(82)
Proceeds from disposals of bottling companies and other investments	479	448	640
Purchases of property, plant, and equipment	(1,968)	(1,648)	(1,407)
Proceeds from disposals of property, plant, and equipment	129	239	112
Other investing activities	(4)	(6)	(62)
Net Cash Used in Investing Activities	$(2,363)	$(6,719)	$(1,700)
FINANCING ACTIVITIES			
Issuances of debt	$ 4,337	$ 9,979	$ 617
Payments of debt	(4,308)	(5,638)	(2,021)
Issuances of stock	586	1,619	148
Purchases of stock for treasury	(1,079)	(1,838)	(2,416)
Dividends	(3,521)	(3,149)	(2,911)
Net Cash Provided by (Used in) Financing Activities	$(3,985)	$ 973	$(6,583)
Effect of exchange rate changes on cash and cash equivalents	$ (615)	$ 249	$ 65
CASH AND CASH EQUIVALENTS			
Net Increase (Decrease) During the Year	$ 608	$ 1,653	$(2,261)
Balance at beginning of year	4,093	2,440	4,701
Balance at End of Year	$ 4,701	$ 4,093	$ 2,440

EXHIBIT 3.23

Texas Instruments
Statement of Cash Flows
(amounts in millions)
(Problem 3.16)

	Year 4	Year 3	Year 2	Year 1	Year 0
OPERATIONS					
Net income (loss)	$ 1,861	$1,198	$ (344)	$ (201)	$ 3,087
Depreciation and amortization	1,549	1,528	1,689	1,828	1,376
Deferred income taxes	68	75	13	19	1
Other additions (Subtractions)	(179)	(469)	709	(68)	(2,141)
(Increase) Decrease in accounts receivable	(238)	(197)	(114)	958	(377)
(Increase) Decrease in inventories	(272)	(194)	(39)	482	(372)
(Increase) Decrease in prepayments	134	(183)	191	(235)	56
Increase (Decrease) in accounts payable	(71)	264	(81)	(687)	246
Increase (Decrease) in other current liabilities	294	129	(32)	(277)	309
Cash Flow from Operations	$ 3,146	$2,151	$ 1,992	$ 1,819	$ 2,185
INVESTING					
Fixed assets acquired	$(1,298)	$ (800)	$ (802)	$(1,790)	$(2,762)
Change in marketable securities	145	86	(238)	164	834
Acquisition of businesses	(8)	(128)	(69)	—	(3)
Other investing transactions	—	—	—	—	107
Cash Flow from Investing	$(1,161)	$ (842)	$(1,109)	$(1,626)	$(1,824)
FINANCING					
Increase in short-term borrowing	$ —	$ —	$ 9	$ —	$ 23
Increase in long-term borrowing	—	—	—	3	250
Issue of common stock	192	157	167	183	242
Decrease in short-term borrowing	(6)	(8)	(16)	(3)	(19)
Decrease in long-term borrowing	(429)	(418)	(22)	(132)	(307)
Acquisition of common stock	(753)	(284)	(370)	(395)	(155)
Dividends	(154)	(147)	(147)	(147)	(141)
Other financing transactions	15	260	14	(16)	(290)
Cash Flow from Financing	$(1,135)	$ (440)	$ (365)	$ (507)	$ (397)
Change in Cash	$ 850	$ 869	$ 518	$ (314)	$ (36)
Cash—Beginning of year	1,818	949	431	745	781
Cash—End of Year	$ 2,668	$1,818	$ 949	$ 431	$ 745
Change in sales from previous year	+27.9%	+17.3%	+2.2%	−30.9%	−1.9%

3.17 INTERPRETING THE STATEMENT OF CASH FLOWS. Gap Inc. operates chains of retail clothing stores under the names of Gap, Banana Republic, and Old Navy. Exhibit 3.24 presents the statement of cash flows for Gap for Year 0 to Year 4.

EXHIBIT 3.24

Gap
Statement of Cash Flows
(amounts in millions)
(Problem 3.17)

	Year 4	Year 3	Year 2	Year 1	Year 0
OPERATIONS					
Net income (loss)	$ 1,150	$ 1,031	$ 478	$ (8)	$ 877
Depreciation	620	675	706	811	590
Other additions and subtractions	(28)	180	166	30	92
(Increase) Decrease in inventories	(90)	385	(258)	213	(455)
(Increase) Decrease in prepayments	(18)	5	33	(13)	(61)
Increase (Decrease) in accounts payable	42	(10)	(47)	42	250
Increase (Decrease) in other current liabilities	(56)	(106)	165	243	(3)
Cash Flow from Operations	$ 1,620	$ 2,160	$1,243	$1,318	$ 1,290
INVESTING					
Fixed assets acquired	$ (442)	$ (261)	$ (308)	$ (940)	$(1,859)
Changes in marketable securities	259	(2,063)	(313)	—	—
Other investing transactions	343	6	(8)	(11)	(16)
Cash Flow from Investing	$ 160	$(2,318)	$ (629)	$ (951)	$(1,875)
FINANCING					
Increase in short-term borrowing	$ —	$ —	$ —	$ —	$ 621
Increase in long-term borrowing	—	85	1,346	1,194	250
Issue of capital stock	130	26	153	139	152
Decrease in short-term borrowing	—	0	(42)	(735)	—
Decrease in long-term borrowing	(871)	(668)	—	(250)	—
Acquisition of capital stock	(976)	—	—	(1)	(393)
Dividends	(79)	(79)	(78)	(76)	(75)
Other financing transactions	—	28	27	(11)	(11)
Cash Flow from Financing	$(1,796)	$ (608)	$1,406	$ 260	$ 544
Change in Cash	$ (16)	$ (766)	$2,020	$ 627	$ (41)
Cash—Beginning of year	2,261	3,027	1,007	380	421
Cash—End of Year	$ 2,245	$ 2,261	$3,0.27	$1,007	$ 380
Change in sales from previous year	+2.6%	+9.7%	+4.4%	+1.3%	+17.5%

Required

Discuss the relationship between net income and cash flow from operations and between cash flows from operating, investing, and financing activities for the firm over the five-year period.

3.18 INTERPRETING THE STATEMENT OF CASH FLOWS. Sirius XM Radio Inc. is a satellite radio company, formed from the merger of Sirius and XM in 2008. Exhibit 3.25 presents a statement of cash flows for Sirius XM Radio for 2006, 2007, and 2008. Sirius XM and its predecessor, Sirius, realized revenue growth of 49 percent in 2007 and 81 percent in 2008. The merger was a stock-for-stock merger.

Required

Discuss the relation between net loss and cash flow from operations and the pattern of cash flows from operating, investing, and financing activities during the three years.

EXHIBIT 3.25

Sirius XM Radio Inc.
Statement of Cash Flows
(amounts in thousands)
(Problem 3.18)

	2008	2007	2006
CASH FLOWS FROM OPERATING ACTIVITIES			
Net loss	$(5,313,288)	$(565,252)	$(1,104,867)
Adjustments to reconcile net loss to net cash used in operating activities:			
Depreciation and amortization	203,752	106,780	105,749
Impairment loss	4,766,190	—	10,917
Non-cash interest expense, net of amortization of premium	(6,311)	4,269	3,107
Provision for doubtful accounts	21,589	9,002	9,370
Non-cash loss from redemption of debt	98,203	—	—
Loss on disposal of assets	4,879	(428)	1,661
Loss on investments, net	28,999	—	4,445
Share-based payment expense	87,405	78,900	437,918
Deferred income taxes	2,476	2,435	2,065
Other non-cash purchase price adjustments	(67,843)	—	—
Changes in operating assets and liabilities, net of assets and liabilities acquired:			
Accounts receivable	(32,121)	(28,881)	(1,871)
Inventory	8,291	4,965	(20,246)
Prepaid expenses and other current assets	(19,953)	11,118	(42,132)
Other long-term assets	(13,338)	(729)	(39,878)
Accounts payable and accrued expenses	(65,481)	66,169	26,366
Accrued interest	23,081	(8,920)	1,239
Deferred revenue	55,778	169,905	181,003
Other long-term liabilities	64,895	1,901	3,452
Net Cash Used in Operating Activities	$ (152,797)	$(148,766)	$ (421,702)

(Continued)

EXHIBIT 3.25 (Continued)

	2008	2007	2006
CASH FLOWS FROM INVESTING ACTIVITIES			
Additions to property and equipment	$ (130,551)	$ (65,264)	$ (92,674)
Sales of property and equipment	105	641	127
Purchases of restricted and other investments	(3,000)	(310)	(12,339)
Acquisition of acquired entity cash	819,521	—	—
Merger-related costs	(23,519)	(29,444)	—
Purchase of available-for-sale securities	—	—	(123,500)
Sale of restricted and other investments	65,869	40,191	255,715
Net Cash Provided by (Used in) Investing Activities	$ 728,425	$ (54,186)	$ 27,329
CASH FLOWS FROM FINANCING ACTIVITIES			
Proceeds from exercise of warrants and stock options and from share/borrow arrangement	$ 471	$ 4,097	$ 25,787
Long-term borrowings, net of related costs	531,743	244,879	—
Payment of premiums on redemption of debt and payments to minority interest holder	(20,172)	—	—
Repayment of long-term borrowings	(1,146,044)	(625)	—
Net Cash (Used in) Provided by Financing Activities	$ (634,002)	$248,351	$ 25,787
Net (Decrease) Increase in Cash and Cash Equivalents	$ (58,374)	$ 45,399	$(368,586)
Cash and cash equivalents at beginning of period	438,820	393,421	762,007
Cash and Cash Equivalents at End of Period	$ 380,446	$438,820	$ 393,421

3.19 INTERPRETING THE STATEMENT OF CASH FLOWS. Sunbeam Corporation manufactures and sells a variety of small household appliances, including toasters, food processors, and waffle grills. Exhibit 3.26 presents a statement of cash flows for Sunbeam for Year 5, Year 6, and Year 7. After experiencing decreased sales in Year 5, Sunbeam hired Albert Dunlap in Year 6 to turn the company around. Albert Dunlap, known in the industry as "Chainsaw Al," had previously directed restructuring efforts at Scott Paper Company. The restructuring effort at Sunbeam generally involved firing employees and cutting costs aggressively. Most of these restructuring efforts took place during Year 6. The market expected significantly improved results in Year 7. Reported sales increased 18.7 percent between Year 6 and Year 7, and net income improved. However, subsequent revelations showed that almost half of the sales increase resulted from fraudulent early recognition of revenues in the fourth quarter of Year 7 that the firm should have recognized in the first quarter of Year 8. Growth in revenues for Years 5, 6, and 7 was −2.6 percent, −3.2 percent, and 18.7 percent, respectively.

Required

a. Using the information provided and the statement of cash flows for Year 5 in Exhibit 3.26, identify any signals before the turnaround effort that Sunbeam was experiencing operating difficulties and was in need of restructuring.

b. Using information in the statement of cash flows for Year 6, identify indicators of the turnaround efforts and any relations between cash flows that trouble you.

c. Using information in the statement of cash flows for Year 7, indicate any signals that the firm might have engaged in aggressive revenue recognition and had not yet fixed its general operating problems.

EXHIBIT 3.26

Sunbeam Corporation
Statement of Cash Flows
(amounts in millions)
(Problem 3.19)

	Year 7	Year 6	Year 5
OPERATIONS			
Net income (loss)	$109.4	$(228.3)	$ 50.5
Depreciation and amortization	38.6	47.4	44.2
Restructuring and asset impairment charges	—	283.7	—
Deferred income taxes	57.8	(77.8)	25.1
Other additions	13.7	46.2	10.8
Other subtractions	(84.6)	(27.1)	(21.7)
(Increase) Decrease in accounts receivable	(84.6)	(13.8)	(4.5)
(Increase) Decrease in inventories	(100.8)	(11.6)	(4.9)
(Increase) Decrease in prepayments	(9.0)	2.7	(8.8)
Increase (Decrease) in accounts payable	(1.6)	14.7	9.2
Increase (Decrease) in other current liabilities	52.8	(21.9)	(18.4)
Cash Flow from Operations	$ (8.3)	$ 14.2	$ 81.5
INVESTING			
Fixed assets acquired	$(58.3)	$ (75.3)	$(140.1)
Sale of businesses	91.0	—	65.3
Acquisitions of businesses	—	(.9)	(33.0)
Cash Flow from Investing	$ 32.7	$ (76.2)	$(107.4)
FINANCING			
Increase (Decrease) in short-term borrowing	$ 5.0	$ 30.0	$ 40.0
Increase in long-term debt	—	11.5	—
Issue of common stock	26.6	9.2	9.8
Decrease in long-term debt	(12.2)	(1.8)	(5.4)
Acquisition of common stock	—	—	(13.0)
Dividends	(3.4)	(3.3)	(3.3)
Other financing transactions	.5	(.4)	(.2)
Cash Flow from Financing	$ 16.5	$ 45.2	$ 27.9
Change in Cash	$ 40.9	$ (16.8)	$ 2.0
Cash—Beginning of year	11.5	28.3	26.3
Cash—End of Year	$ 52.4	$ 11.5	$ 28.3

3.20 INTERPRETING THE STATEMENT OF CASH FLOWS. Montgomery Ward operates a retail department store chain. It filed for bankruptcy during the first quarter of Year 12. Exhibit 3.27 presents a statement of cash flows for Montgomery Ward for Year 7 to Year 11. The firm acquired Lechmere, a discount retailer of sporting goods

EXHIBIT 3.27

Montgomery Ward
Statement of Cash Flows
(amounts in millions)
(Problem 3.20)

	Year 11	Year 10	Year 9	Year 8	Year 7
OPERATIONS					
Net income	$(237)	$ (9)	$ 109	$ 101	$ 100
Depreciation	122	115	109	98	97
Other addbacks	13	8	24	25	32
Other subtractions	(197)	(119)	(29)	—	—
(Increase) Decrease in accounts receivable	(32)	(54)	(38)	(9)	9
(Increase) Decrease in inventories	225	(112)	(229)	(204)	(38)
(Increase) Decrease in prepayments	27	(32)	(39)	(58)	36
Increase (Decrease) in accounts payable	(222)	85	291	148	(17)
Increase (Decrease) in other current liabilities	(55)	(64)	(45)	28	(64)
Cash Flow from Operations	$(356)	$(182)	$ 153	$ 129	$ 155
INVESTING					
Fixed assets acquired	$ (75)	$(122)	$(184)	$(142)	$(146)
Change in marketable securities	20	(14)	(4)	(27)	137
Other investing transactions	(93)	27	(113)	6	9
Cash Flow from Investing	$(148)	$(109)	$(301)	$(163)	$ —
FINANCING					
Increase in short-term borrowing	$ 588	$ 16	$ 144	$ —	$ —
Increase in long-term borrowing	—	205	168	100	—
Issue of capital stock	3	193	78	1	1
Decrease in short-term borrowing	—	—	—	—	—
Decrease in long-term borrowing	(63)	(17)	(275)	(18)	(403)
Acquisition of capital stock	(20)	(98)	(9)	(11)	(97)
Dividends	(9)	(4)	(24)	(23)	(19)
Other	—	—	1	2	2
Cash Flow from Financing	$ 499	$ 295	$ 83	$ 51	$(516)
Change in Cash	$ (5)	$ 4	$ (65)	$ 17	$(361)
Cash—Beginning of year	37	33	98	81	442
Cash—End of Year	$ 32	$ 37	$ 33	$ 98	$ 81
Change in sales from previous year	−10.0%	−.5%	+17.2%	+3.7%	+2.0%

and electronic products, during Year 9. It acquired Amoco Enterprises, an automobile club, during Year 11. During Year 10, it issued a new series of preferred stock and used part of the cash proceeds to repurchase a series of outstanding preferred stock. The "other subtractions" in the operating section for Year 10 and Year 11 represent reversals of deferred tax liabilities.

Required

Discuss the relationship between net income and cash flow from operations and between cash flows from operating, investing, and financing activities for the firm over the five-year period. Identify signals of Montgomery Ward's difficulties that might have led to its filing for bankruptcy.

3.21 INTERPRETING A DIRECT METHOD STATEMENT OF CASH FLOWS. Aer Lingus is an international airline based in Ireland. Exhibit 3.28 provides the statement of cash flows for 2007 and 2008, which includes a footnote from the financial statements. 2008 was characterized by weakening consumer demand for air travel due to a recession and record high fuel prices. In addition, 2008 includes exceptional items totaling €141 million, which reflects a staff restructuring program for early retirement (€118 million), takeover defense costs due to a bid by Ryanair (€18 million), and other costs (€5 million).

EXHIBIT 3.28

Aer Lingus
Statement of Cash Flows
(Problem 3.21)

	2008	2007
CASH FLOWS FROM OPERATING ACTIVITIES		
Cash (used in) generated from operations (see Note 27)	€ (8,627)	€ 59,122
Interest paid	(17,684)	(22,437)
Income tax received (paid)	5,046	(4,002)
Net Cash (Used in) Generated from Operating Activities	€ (21,265)	€ 32,683
CASH FLOWS FROM INVESTING ACTIVITIES		
Purchases of property, plant, and equipment	€(114,490)	€(200,604)
Purchases of intangible assets	(5,619)	(4,294)
Proceeds from sale of investment	—	11,374
Disposal of available-for-sale financial assets	—	9,031
(Increase) Decrease in deposits and restricted cash with maturity greater than 3 months	(44,099)	138,066
Dividends received	—	2,998
Interest received	46,766	60,008
Net Cash (Used in) Generated from Investing Activities	€(117,442)	€ 16,579
CASH FLOWS FROM FINANCING ACTIVITIES		
Costs arising from issuance of ordinary shares	€ —	€ (3,720)
Proceeds from borrowings	186,135	2,090
Repayments of borrowings	(38,695)	(61,104)
Net Cash Generated from (Used in) Financing Activities	€ 147,440	€ (62,734)
Net Increase (Decrease) in Cash, Cash Equivalents and Bank Overdrafts	€ 8,733	€ (13,472)

(Continued)

EXHIBIT 3.28 (Continued)

	2008	2007
Cash, cash equivalents, and bank overdrafts at beginning of year	€ (12,185)	€ (1,226)
Exchange gains on cash, cash equivalents, and bank overdrafts	9,533	2,513
Cash, Cash Equivalents, and Bank Overdrafts at End of Year	€ 6,081	€ (12,185)
NOTE 27 CASH GENERATED FROM OPERATIONS		
(Loss) Profit before tax	€(119,696)	€ 124,726
Adjustments for:		
Depreciation	69,558	63,664
Amortisation	2,307	5,635
Net movements in provisions for liabilities and charges	(13,084)	(14,690)
Net fair value losses on derivative financial instruments	945	40
Finance income	(60,860)	(65,143)
Finance cost	22,018	22,572
Net exceptional items	140,888	(3,517)
Other (gains) losses	(8,796)	8,880
Changes in working capital		
Inventories	360	(140)
Trade and other receivables	(16,329)	181
Trade and other payables	(25,938)	20,914
Payment to supplemental pension arrangements	—	(104,000)
Cash Generated from Operations	€ (8,627)	€ 59,122

Required

a. Based on information in the statement of cash flows, compare and contrast the cash flows for 2007 with 2008. Explain significant differences in individual reconciling items and direct cash flows.

b. The format of Aer Lingus' statement of cash flows is the direct method, as evidenced by the straightforward titles used in the operating section (for example, "Interest paid"). How is this statement different from the presentation that Aer Lingus would report using the indirect method?

3.22 IDENTIFYING INDUSTRY DIFFERENCES IN STATEMENT OF CASH FLOWS. Exhibit 3.29 presents common-size statements of cash flows for eight firms in various industries. All amounts in the common-size statements of cash flows are expressed as a percentage of cash flow from operations. In constructing the common-size percentages for each firm, reported amounts for each firm for three consecutive years were summed and the common-size percentages are based on the summed amounts. This procedure reduces the effects of a nonrecurring item in a particular year, such as a major

EXHIBIT 3.29

Common-Size Statements of Cash Flows for Selected Companies (Problem 3.22)

	1	2	3	4	5	6	7	8
OPERATIONS								
Net income	34.9%	38.6%	40.9%	45.4%	61.2%	62.4%	76.5%	97.6%
Depreciation	47.9	55.2	62.9	37.7	46.0	22.3	38.0	23.3
Other	3.1	24.3	5.1	(5.0)	9.4	11.6	2.3	3.9
(Increase) Decrease in accounts receivable	6.5	(4.8)	(.6)	(12.4)	(34.2)	(7.8)	(6.8)	(8.5)
(Increase) Decrease in inventories	1.5	(15.1)	(1.2)	(14.4)	(11.9)	(3.1)	(7.4)	(58.4)
Increase (Decrease) in accounts payable	1.5	3.1	(5.6)	12.4	3.0	2.9	12.6	39.9
Increase (Decrease) in other current liabilities	4.6	(1.3)	(1.5)	36.3	26.5	11.7	(15.2)	2.2
Cash Flow from Operations	100.0%	100.0%	100.0%	100.0%	100.0%	100.0%	100.0%	100.0%
INVESTING								
Fixed assets acquired	(37.1%)	(64.0%)	(81.1%)	(165.7%)	(44.7%)	(13.4%)	(39.3%)	(153.4%)
Change in marketable securities	—	—	(2.8)	(75.1)	(14.8)	(3.5)	5.9	(17.5)
Other investing transactions	(7.7)	8.5	16.4	(28.4)	(15.9)	(17.3)	(40.6)	23.2
Cash Flow from Investing	(44.8%)	(55.5%)	(67.5%)	(269.2%)	(75.4%)	(34.2%)	(74.0%)	(147.7%)
FINANCING								
Change in short-term debt	(0.6%)	—	(7.4%)	—	(2.4%)	—	7.9%	—
Increase in long-term debt	19.5	41.4%	8.4	75.7%	—	33.1%	24.0	46.9%
Issue of capital stock	11.2	9.9	—	82.5	17.7	1.7	6.7	13.5
Decrease in long-term debt	(36.0)	(85.0)	(9.1)	(2.7)	(7.0)	(27.6)	(3.1)	(1.2)
Repurchase of capital stock	(18.9)	(1.5)	(0.1)	—	(50.7)	(21.4)	(26.9)	—
Dividends	(29.5)	(10.9)	(29.9)	—	—	(46.1)	(43.5)	(11.5)
Other financing transactions	—	—	(0.2)	—	—	0.6	9.8	1.9
Cash Flow from Financing	(54.3%)	(46.1%)	(38.3%)	155.5%	(42.4%)	(59.7%)	(25.1%)	49.6%
Net Change in Cash	0.9%	(1.6%)	(5.8%)	13.7%	(17.8%)	6.1%	0.9%	1.9%
Growth in Revenues	(3.6%)	5.7%	5.7%	23.0%	18.2%	7.7%	8.6%	28.3%

debt or a common stock issue. Exhibit 3.29 also shows the compound annual rate of growth in revenues over the three-year period. The eight companies are as follows:

- Biogen creates and manufactures biotechnology drugs. Many drugs are still in the development phase in this high-growth, relatively young industry. Research and manufacturing facilities are capital-intensive, although the research process requires skilled scientists.
- ChevronTexaco explores, extracts, refines, and markets petroleum products. Extraction and refining activities are capital-intensive. Petroleum products are in the mature phase of their product life cycle.
- H. J. Heinz manufactures and markets branded consumer food products. Heinz has acquired several other branded food products companies in recent years.
- Home Depot sells home improvement products. Home Depot competes in a new retail category known as "category killer" stores. Such stores offer a wide selection of products in a particular product category (for example, books, pet products, or office products). In recent years, these stores have taken away significant market share from more diversified department and discount stores.
- Inland Steel manufactures steel products. Although steel plants are capital-intensive, they also use unionized workers to process iron into steel products. Demand for steel products follows cyclical trends in the economy. Steel manufacturing in the United States is in the mature phase of its life cycle.
- Pacific Gas & Electric provides electric and gas utility services. The electric utility industry in the United States has excess capacity. Increased competition from less regulated, more open markets has forced down prices and led some utilities to reduce their capacity.
- ServiceMaster provides home cleaning and restoration services. ServiceMaster has recently acquired firms offering cleaning services for health care facilities and has broadened its home services to include termite protection, garden care, and other services. ServiceMaster operates as a partnership. Partnerships do not pay income taxes on their earnings each year. Instead, partners (owners) include their share of the earnings of ServiceMaster in their taxable income.
- Sun Microsystems creates, manufactures, and markets computers, primarily to the scientific and engineering markets and to network applications. Sun follows an assembly strategy in manufacturing computers, outsourcing the components from other firms worldwide. In recent years, Sun has been rumored to be a takeover target by larger technology companies, and during January 2010, Oracle Corporation acquired Sun Microsystems.

Required

Use the clues in the common-size statements of cash flows to match the companies in Exhibit 3.29 with the companies listed here. Discuss the reasoning for your selection in each case.

3.23 PREPARING A STATEMENT OF CASH FLOWS FROM BALANCE SHEETS AND INCOME STATEMENTS. Fuso Pharmaceutical Industries develops, manufactures, and markets pharmaceutical products in Japan. Its main product is a solution used by individuals with artificial kidneys. Most individuals in Japan are covered by a national health insurance system. The Japanese government sets the policies for the proportion of health care costs covered by the government versus the proportion that is the responsibility of the individual. The government also establishes the prices for prescription drugs. The Japanese economy experienced recessionary conditions in recent years. In response to these conditions, the Japanese government increased the proportion of medical costs that is the patient's responsibility and lowered the prices for prescription drugs. Exhibit 3.30 presents the firm's balance sheets on March 31 of Year 1 to Year 4, and Exhibit 3.31 presents the firm's income statements for the years ending March 31, Year 2 to Year 4.

EXHIBIT 3.30

Fuso Pharmaceutical Industries
Balance Sheets
(amounts in millions)
(Problem 3.23)

March 31:	Year 4	Year 3	Year 2	Year 1
ASSETS				
Cash	¥ 6,233	¥ 4,569	¥ 4,513	¥ 5,008
Accounts and notes receivable—Trade	19,003	17,828	19,703	19,457
Inventories	7,693	7,948	8,706	8,607
Deferred income taxes	1,355	1,192	948	824
Prepayments	432	325	640	634
Total Current Assets	¥34,716	¥31,862	¥34,510	¥34,530
Investments	3,309	2,356	3,204	4,997
Property, plant, and equipment, at cost	71,792	71,510	71,326	71,018
Less accumulated depreciation	(40,689)	(38,912)	(36,854)	(35,797)
Deferred income taxes	236	1,608	1,481	494
Other assets	4,551	3,904	3,312	3,463
Total Assets	¥73,915	¥72,328	¥76,979	¥78,705
LIABILITIES AND SHAREHOLDERS' EQUITY				
Accounts and notes payable—Trade	¥10,087	¥ 9,629	¥10,851	¥10,804
Notes payable to banks	10,360	10,328	9,779	10,023
Current portion of long-term debt	100	200	—	—
Other current liabilities	7,200	6,170	9,779	7,565
Total Current Liabilities	¥27,747	¥26,327	¥30,409	¥28,392
Long-term debt	8,140	7,889	6,487	8,147
Deferred income taxes	3,361	—	—	—
Employee retirement benefits	809	905	1,087	1,166
Other noncurrent liabilities	175	174	200	216
Total Liabilities	¥40,232	¥35,295	¥38,183	¥37,921
Common stock	¥10,758	¥10,758	¥10,758	¥10,758
Additional paid-in capital	15,012	15,012	15,012	15,012
Retained earnings	9,179	11,838	13,697	15,014
Accumulated other comprehensive income	(342)	(490)	(659)	—
Treasury stock	(924)	(85)	(12)	—
Total Shareholders' Equity	¥33,683	¥37,033	¥38,796	¥40,784
Total Liabilities and Shareholders' Equity	¥73,915	¥72,328	¥76,979	¥78,705

EXHIBIT 3.31

Fuso Pharmaceutical Industries
Income Statements
(amounts in millions)
(Problem 3.23)

Year Ended March 31:	Year 4	Year 3	Year 2
Sales	¥41,352	¥41,926	¥44,226
Cost of goods sold	(27,667)	(27,850)	(28,966)
Selling and administrative expenses	(13,396)	(15,243)	(15,283)
Interest expense	(338)	(364)	(368)
Income tax expense	(1,823)	443	34
Net Income	¥(1,872)	¥(1,088)	¥ (357)

Required

a. Prepare a worksheet for the preparation of a statement of cash flows for Fuso Pharmaceutical Industries for each of the years ending March 31, Year 2 to Year 4. Follow the format of Exhibit 3.13 in the text. Notes to the financial statements indicate the following:

(1) The changes in Accumulated Other Comprehensive Income relate to revaluations of Investments in Securities to market value. The remaining changes in Investments in Securities result from purchases and sales. Assume that the sales occurred at no gain or loss.

(2) No sales of property, plant, and equipment took place during the three-year period.

(3) The changes in Other Noncurrent Assets are investing activities.

(4) The changes in Employee Retirement Benefits relate to provisions made for retirement benefits net of payments made to retired employees, both of which the statement of cash flows classifies as operating activities.

(5) The changes in Other Noncurrent Liabilities are financing activities.

b. Prepare a comparative statement of cash flows for Year 2, Year 3, and Year 4.

c. Discuss the relation between net income and cash flow from operations and the pattern of cash flows from operating, investing, and financing transactions for Year 2, Year 3, and Year 4.

3.24 PREPARING A STATEMENT OF CASH FLOWS FROM BALANCE SHEETS AND INCOME STATEMENTS. Flight Training Corporation is a privately held firm that provides fighter pilot training under contracts with the U.S. Air Force and the U.S. Navy. The firm owns approximately 100 Lear jets that it equips with radar jammers and other sophisticated electronic devices to mimic enemy aircraft. The company recently experienced cash shortages to pay its bills. The owner and manager of Flight Training Corporation stated, "I was just dumbfounded. I never had an inkling that there was a problem with cash."

Exhibit 3.32 presents comparative balance sheets for Flight Training Corporation on December 31, Year 1 through Year 4, and Exhibit 3.33 presents income statements for Year 2 through Year 4.

EXHIBIT 3.32

Flight Training Corporation
Balance Sheets
(amounts in thousands)
(Problem 3.24)

December 31:	Year 4	Year 3	Year 2	Year 1
CURRENT ASSETS				
Cash	$ 159	$ 583	$ 313	$ 142
Accounts receivable	6,545	4,874	2,675	2,490
Inventories	5,106	2,514	1,552	602
Prepayments	665	829	469	57
Total Current Assets	$ 12,475	$ 8,800	$ 5,009	$ 3,291
NONCURRENT ASSETS				
Property, plant, and equipment	$106,529	$76,975	$24,039	$17,809
Less accumulated depreciation	(17,231)	(8,843)	(5,713)	(4,288)
Net property, plant, and equipment	$ 89,298	$68,132	$18,326	$13,521
Other assets	$ 470	$ 665	$ 641	$ 1,112
Total Assets	$102,243	$77,597	$23,976	$17,924
CURRENT LIABILITIES				
Accounts payable	$ 12,428	$ 6,279	$ 993	$ 939
Notes payable	—	945	140	1,021
Current portion of long-term debt	60,590	7,018	1,789	1,104
Other current liabilities	12,903	12,124	2,423	1,310
Total Current Liabilities	$ 85,921	$26,366	$ 5,345	$ 4,374
NONCURRENT LIABILITIES				
Long-term debt	$ —	$41,021	$ 9,804	$ 6,738
Deferred income taxes	—	900	803	—
Other noncurrent liabilities	—	—	226	—
Total Liabilities	$ 85,921	$68,287	$16,178	$11,112
SHAREHOLDERS' EQUITY				
Common stock	$ 34	$ 22	$ 21	$ 20
Additional paid-in capital	16,516	5,685	4,569	4,323
Retained earnings	(29)	3,802	3,208	2,469
Treasury stock	(199)	(199)	—	—
Total Shareholders' Equity	$ 16,322	$ 9,310	$ 7,798	$ 6,812
Total Liabilities and Shareholders' Equity	$102,243	$77,597	$23,976	$17,924

EXHIBIT 3.33

Flight Training Corporation
Income Statements
(amounts in thousands)
(Problem 3.24)

Year Ended December 31:	Year 4	Year 3	Year 2
Sales	$54,988	$36,597	$20,758
Cost of services	$47,997	$29,594	$14,247
Selling and administrative	5,881	2,972	3,868
Interest	5,841	3,058	1,101
Income taxes	(900)	379	803
Total Expenses	$58,819	$36,003	$20,019
Net Income	$(3,831)	$ 594	$ 739

Required

a. Prepare a worksheet for the preparation of a statement of cash flows for Flight Training Corporation for each of the years ending December 31, Year 2 through Year 4. Follow the format of Exhibit 3.13 in the text. Notes to the financial statements indicate the following:

(1) The firm did not sell any aircraft during the three-year period.

(2) Changes in other noncurrent assets are investing transactions.

(3) Changes in deferred income taxes are operating transactions.

(4) Changes in other noncurrent liabilities and treasury stock are financing transactions.

(5) The firm violated covenants in its borrowing agreements during Year 4. Therefore, the lenders can require Flight Training Corporation to repay its long-term debt immediately. Although the banks have not yet demanded payment, the firm reclassified its long-term debt as a current liability.

b. Prepare a comparative statement of cash flows for Flight Training Corporation for each of the years ending December 31, Year 2 through Year 4.

c. Comment on the relation between net income and cash flow from operations and the pattern of cash flows from operating, investing, and financing activities for each of the three years.

d. Describe the likely reasons for the cash flow difficulties of Flight Training Corporation.

3.25 PREPARING A STATEMENT OF CASH FLOWS FROM BALANCE SHEETS AND INCOME STATEMENTS. GTI, Inc., manufactures parts, components, and processing equipment for electronics and semiconductor applications in the communications, computer, automotive, and appliance industries. Its sales tend to vary with changes in the business cycle because the sales of most of its customers are cyclical. Exhibit 3.34 presents balance sheets for GTI as of December 31, Year 7 through Year 9, and Exhibit 3.35 presents income statements for Year 8 and Year 9.

EXHIBIT 3.34

GTI, Inc.
Balance Sheets
(amounts in thousands)
(Problem 3.25)

December 31:	Year 9	Year 8	Year 7
ASSETS			
Cash	$ 367	$ 475	$ 430
Accounts receivable	2,545	3,936	3,768
Inventories	2,094	2,966	2,334
Prepayments	122	270	116
Total Current Assets	$5,128	$ 7,647	$ 6,648
Property, plant, and equipment, net	4,027	4,598	3,806
Other assets	456	559	193
Total Assets	$9,611	$12,804	$10,647
LIABILITIES AND SHAREHOLDERS' EQUITY			
Accounts payable	$ 796	$ 809	$ 1,578
Notes payable to banks	2,413	231	11
Other current liabilities	695	777	1,076
Total Current Liabilities	$3,904	$ 1,817	$ 2,665
Long-term debt	2,084	4,692	2,353
Deferred income taxes	113	89	126
Total Liabilities	$6,101	$ 6,598	$ 5,144
Preferred stock	$ 289	$ 289	$ —
Common stock	85	85	83
Additional paid-in capital	4,395	4,392	4,385
Retained earnings	(1,259)	1,440	1,035
Total Shareholders' Equity	$3,510	$ 6,206	$ 5,503
Total Liabilities and Shareholders' Equity	$9,611	$12,804	$10,647

Required

a. Prepare a worksheet for the preparation of a statement of cash flows for GTI, Inc., for Year 8 and Year 9. Follow the format of Exhibit 3.13 in the text. Notes to the firm's financial statements reveal the following (amounts in thousands):

(1) Depreciation expense was $641 in Year 8 and $625 in Year 9. GTI, Inc., did not sell any fixed assets during Year 8 and Year 9.

(2) Other Assets represents patents. Patent amortization was $25 in Year 8 and $40 in Year 9. GTI, Inc., sold a patent during Year 9 at no gain or loss.

(3) Changes in Deferred Income Taxes are operating activities.

b. Discuss the relation between net income and cash flow from operations and the pattern of cash flows from operating, investing, and financing activities.

EXHIBIT 3.35

GTI, Inc.
Income Statements
(amounts in thousands)
(Problem 3.25)

Year Ended December 31:	Year 9	Year 8
Sales	$11,960	$22,833
Cost of goods sold	(11,031)	(16,518)
Selling and administrative expenses	(3,496)	(4,849)
Interest expense	(452)	(459)
Income tax expense	328	(590)
Net Income	$(2,691)	$ 417
Dividends on preferred stock	(8)	(12)
Net Income Available to Common	$(2,699)	$ 405

INTEGRATIVE CASE 3.1

STARBUCKS

Exhibit 3.36 presents a statement of cash flows for Starbucks for 2006, 2007, and 2008. This statement is an expanded version of the statement of cash flows for Starbucks shown in Exhibit 1.28.

Required

a. Explain why equity in income of investees appears as a subtraction when net income is converted to cash flow from operations.

b. Compute the amount of cash received from investees as dividends each year. To answer this question, you need to refer to the income statement of Starbucks in Exhibit 1.27 in Chapter 1 (Integrative Case 1.1).

c. Explain why stock-based compensation appears as an addition to net income to compute cash flow from operations.

d. Discuss the relation between net income and cash flow from operations for each of the three years.

e. Discuss the relation between cash flows from operating, investing, and financing activities for each of the three years.

f. Refer to the income statement for Starbucks in Exhibit 1.27 in Chapter 1 (Integrative Case 1.1). Compute the amount of EBITDA for 2006, 2007, and 2008.

g. Discuss the relationships among net income, non-working capital adjustments, working capital adjustments, operating cash flows, and EBITDA for the three years. Are the patterns similar or different? What are the primary determinants of the differences between the summary measures net income, operating cash flows, and EBITDA?

EXHIBIT 3.36

Starbucks Corporation
Comparative Statements of Cash Flows
(amounts in millions)
(Case 3.1)

Fiscal Year Ended:	Sept. 28, 2008	Sept. 30, 2007	Oct. 1, 2006
OPERATING ACTIVITIES			
Net earnings	$ 315.5	$ 672.6	$ 564.3
Adjustments to reconcile net earnings to net cash provided by operating activities:			
Cumulative effect of accounting change for FIN 47, net of taxes	—	—	17.2
Depreciation and amortization	604.5	491.2	412.6
Provision for impairments and asset disposals	325.0	26.0	19.6
Deferred income taxes, net	(117.1)	(37.3)	(84.3)
Equity in income of investees	(61.3)	(65.7)	(60.6)
Distributions of income from equity investees	52.6	65.9	49.2
Stock-based compensation	75.0	103.9	105.7
Tax benefit from exercise of stock options	3.8	7.7	1.3
Excess tax benefit from exercise of stock options	(14.7)	(93.1)	(117.4)
Other	(0.1)	0.7	2.0
Cash provided (used) by changes in operating assets and liabilities:			
Inventories	(0.6)	(48.6)	(85.5)
Accounts payable	(63.9)	36.1	105.0
Accrued taxes	7.3	86.4	132.7
Deferred revenue	72.4	63.2	56.6
Other operating assets and liabilities	60.3	22.2	13.2
Net Cash Provided by Operating Activities	$ 1,258.7	$ 1,331.2	$1,131.6
INVESTING ACTIVITIES			
Purchase of available-for-sale securities	$ (71.8)	$ (237.4)	$ (639.2)
Maturity of available-for-sale securities	20.0	178.2	269.1
Sale of available-for-sale securities	75.9	47.5	431.2
Acquisitions, net of cash acquired	(74.2)	(53.3)	(91.7)
Net purchases of equity, other investments, and other assets	(52.0)	(56.6)	(39.2)
Net additions to property, plant, and equipment	(984.5)	(1,080.3)	(771.2)
Net Cash Used by Investing Activities	$ (1,086.6)	$ (1,201.9)	$ (841.0)
FINANCING ACTIVITIES			
Repayments of commercial paper	$(66,068.0)	$(16,600.9)	—
Proceeds from issuance of commercial paper	65,770.8	17,311.1	—
Repayments of short-term borrowings	(228.8)	(1,470.0)	$ (993.1)
Proceeds from short-term borrowings	528.2	770.0	1,416.1
Proceeds from issuance of common stock	112.3	176.9	159.2

(Continued)

EXHIBIT 3.36 (Continued)

Fiscal Year Ended:	Sept. 28, 2008	Sept. 30, 2007	Oct. 1, 2006
Excess tax benefit from exercise of stock options	14.7	93.1	117.4
Principal payments on long-term debt	(0.6)	(0.8)	(0.9)
Proceeds from issuance of long-term debt	—	549.0	—
Repurchase of common stock	(311.4)	(996.8)	(854.0)
Other	(1.7)	(3.5)	—
Net Cash Used by Financing Activities	$(184.5)	$(171.9)	$(155.3)
Effect of exchange rate changes on cash and cash equivalents	0.9	11.3	3.5
Net increase (decrease) in cash and cash equivalents	$ (11.5)	$ (31.3)	$ 138.8
CASH AND CASH EQUIVALENTS			
Beginning of period	281.3	312.6	173.8
End of the Period	$ 269.8	$ 281.3	$ 312.6

h. The income statement in Exhibit 1.27 in Chapter 1 (Integrative Case 1.1) shows depreciation and amortization expense as follows:

2006	2007	2008
$387.2	$467.2	$549.3

However, the statement of cash flows shows addbacks for depreciation and amortization as follows:

2006	2007	2008
$412.6	$491.2	$604.5

Explain why the amount on the income statement differs from the amount on the statement of cash flows each year.

CASE 3.2

PRIME CONTRACTORS

Prime Contractors (Prime) is a privately owned company that contracts with the U.S. government to provide various services under multiyear (usually five-year) contracts. Its principal services are as follows:

Refuse: Picks up and disposes of refuse from military bases.

Shuttle: Provides parking and shuttle services on government-sponsored research campuses.

Animal Care: Provides feeding and veterinary care for animals used in research at government-sponsored facilities.

Prime's sales mix for the years ending September 30, Year 6 to Year 10, is as follows:

	Refuse Services	Shuttle Services	Animal Care Services
Year 6	59.9%	40.1%	—
Year 7	48.5%	31.2%	20.3%
Year 8	20.7%	22.0%	57.3%
Year 9	11.4%	26.9%	61.7%
Year 10	7.1%	22.5%	70.4%

As the sales mix data indicate, Prime engaged in a strategic shift beginning in Year 7. It began to exit the refuse services business and geared up its animal care services business. Exhibit 3.37 presents a statement of cash flows for Prime for Year 6 to Year 10.

EXHIBIT 3.37

Prime Contractors
Statement of Cash Flows
(amounts in thousands)
(Case 3.2)

	Year 10	Year 9	Year 8	Year 7	Year 6
OPERATIONS					
Net income	$ 568	$ 474	$ 47	$ 249	$ 261
Depreciation	595	665	827	616	306
Deferred income taxes	(139)	(110)	55	180	159
Loss (Gain) on disposition of fixed assets	(82)	(178)	—	—	20
Other additions and subtractions	(4)	(19)	(52)	(7)	2
(Increase) Decrease in accounts receivable	62	(865)	(263)	(647)	(1,421)
(Increase) Decrease in other current assets	19	(9)	(40)	(26)	(38)
Increase (Decrease) in accounts payable	(174)	(272)	(33)	(177)	507
Increase (Decrease) in other current liabilities	(310)	926	423	100	268
Cash Flow from Operations	$ 535	$ 612	$ 964	$ 288	$ 64
INVESTING					
Fixed assets sold	$ 146	$ 118	$ —	$ —	$ 80
Fixed assets acquired	(15)	(19)	(56)	(911)	(2,003)
Other investing transactions	37	—	—	62	(17)
Cash Flow from Investing	$ 168	$ 99	$ (56)	$(849)	$(1,940)
FINANCING					
Increase (Decrease) in short-term borrowing	$ 324	$ 12	$(127)	$ 276	$ 204
Increase in long-term borrowing	—	—	208	911	1,987
Decrease in long-term borrowing	(960)	(742)	(1,011)	(658)	(423)
Cash Flow from Financing	$(634)	$(730)	$(930)	$ 529	$ 1,768
Change in Cash	$ 69	$ (19)	$ (22)	$ (32)	$ (108)
Cash—Beginning of year	6	25	47	79	187
Cash—End of Year	$ 75	$ 6	$ 25	$ 47	$ 79
Change in sales from previous year	+15.5%	+18.0%	+38.5%	+47.1%	+53.5%

Required

a. What evidence do you see in Exhibit 3.37 of Prime's strategic shift from refuse services to animal care services?

b. Discuss how Prime's net income could decline between Year 6 and Year 8 while its cash flow from operations increased.

c. Discuss how Prime's net income could increase between Year 8 and Year 10 while its cash flow from operations decreased.

d. What is the likely reason that the adjustment for deferred income taxes when converting net income to cash flow from operations was an addition in Year 6 to Year 8 but a subtraction in Year 9 and Year 10?

e. Explain why gains on the disposition of fixed assets appear as a subtraction from net income when cash flow from operations is computed.

f. Prime increased its long-term debt net in Year 6 and Year 7 but decreased it net in Year 8 to Year 10. What is the likely reason for this shift in financing?

CASE 3.3

W. T. GRANT COMPANY[13]

When it filed for bankruptcy in October 1975, W. T. Grant (Grant) was the seventeenth largest retailer in the United States, with almost 1,200 stores, more than 82,000 employees, and sales of $1.7 billion. It had paid dividends consistently since 1906. The collapse of Grant came largely as a surprise to the capital markets, particularly to the banks that provided short-term working capital loans. Grant had altered its business strategy in the mid-1960s to transform itself from an urban discount store chain to a suburban house goods store chain. Its failure serves as a classic study of poor implementation of what seemed like a sound business strategy. What happened to Grant and why did it happen are questions that, with some analysis, can be answered. On the other hand, why the symptoms of Grant's prolonged illness were not diagnosed and treated earlier is difficult to understand.

The Strategic Shift

Prior to the mid-1960s, Grant built its reputation on sales of low-priced soft goods (clothing, linens, and sewing fabrics). It placed its stores in large urban locations and appealed primarily to lower-income consumers.

However, the mid-1960s marked the beginning of urban unrest and movement to the suburbs. To service the needs of these new homeowners, suburban shopping centers experienced rapid growth. Sears led the way in this movement, establishing itself as the anchor store in many of the more upscale locations. Montgomery Ward and JCPenney followed

[14]This case was coauthored with Professor James A. Largay.

suit. At this time, Sears held a dominant market share in the middle-income consumer market. However, it saw an opportunity to change its product line, becoming more upscale, to compete with the established department stores (for example, Macy's and Marshall Field's), which had not yet begun their move to the suburbs. To implement this new strategy, Sears introduced its Sears Best line of products.

The outward population move to the suburbs and increased competition from growing discount chains such as Kmart caused Grant to alter its strategy as well. One aspect of this strategic shift was rapid expansion of new stores into suburban shopping centers. Between 1963 and 1973, Grant opened 612 new stores and expanded 91 others. It concentrated most of that expansion in the 1969–1973 period when it opened 369 new stores, 15 on one particularly busy day. Because Grant's reputation had been built on sales to lower-income consumers, it was often unable to locate its new stores in the choicest shopping centers. Louis C. Lustenberger, president of Grant from 1959 to 1968, started the expansion program, although later, as a director, he became concerned over dimensions of the growth and the problems it generated. After Lustenberger stepped down, the pace of expansion accelerated under the leadership of Chairman Edward Staley and President Richard W. Mayer.

A second aspect of Grant's strategy involved a change in its product line. Grant perceived a vacuum in the middle-income consumer market when Sears moved more upscale. Grant introduced a higher-quality, medium-priced line of products into its new shopping center stores to fill this vacuum. In addition, it added furniture and private-brand appliances to its product line and implemented a credit card system. With much of the move to the suburbs representing middle-income consumers, Grant attempted to position itself as a primary supplier to outfit the new homes being constructed.

To implement this new strategy, Grant chose a decentralized organizational structure. Each store manager controlled credit extension and credit terms. At most stores, Grant permitted customers 36 months to pay for their purchases; the minimum monthly payment was $1 regardless of total purchases. Bad debt expenses averaged 1.2 percent of sales each year until fiscal 1975, when a provision of $155.7 million was made. Local store managers also made inventory and pricing decisions. Merchandise was acquired from regional Grant warehouses or ordered directly from the manufacturer. At this time, Grant did not have an information system in place that permitted one store to check the availability of a needed product from another store. Compensation of employees was considered among the most generous in the industry, with most employees owning shares of Grant's common stock acquired under employee stock option plans. Compensation of store managers included salary plus stated percentages of the store's sales and profits.

To finance the expansion of receivables and inventory, Grant used commercial paper, bank loans, and trade credit. To finance the expansion of store space, Grant entered into leasing arrangements. Because Grant was liquidated before the FASB issued *Statement of Financial Accounting Standards No. 13,* requiring the capitalization of capital leases on the balance sheet and the disclosure of information on operating leases in the notes to the financial statements, it did not disclose its long-term leasing arrangements. Property, plant, and equipment reported on its balance sheet consisted mostly of store fixtures. Grant's long-term debt included debentures totaling $200 million issued in 1971 and 1973. Based on per-square-foot rental rates at the time, Grant's disclosures of total square footage of space, and an 8 percent discount rate, the estimated present values of Grant's leases are as follows (in thousands):

January 31	Present Value of Lease Commitments	January 31	Present Value of Lease Commitments
1966	$394,291	1971	$496,041
1967	$400,090	1972	$626,052
1968	$393,566	1973	$708,666
1969	$457,111	1974	$805,785
1970	$486,837	1975	$821,565

Advance and Retreat—The Attempt to Save Grant

By 1974, it became clear that Grant's problems were not of a short-term operating nature. In the spring of 1974, both Moody's and Standard & Poor's eliminated their credit rating for Grant's commercial paper. Banks entered the picture in a big way in the summer of 1974. To provide financing, a group of 143 banks agreed to offer lines of credit totaling $525 million. Grant obtained a short-term loan of $600 million in September 1974, with three New York money center banks absorbing approximately $230 million of the total. These three banks also loaned $50 million out of a total of $100 million provided to Grant's finance subsidiary.

Support of the banks during the summer of 1974 was accompanied by a top management change. Staley and Mayer stepped down in the spring and were replaced in August 1974 by James G. Kendrick, brought in from Zeller's Ltd., Grant's Canadian subsidiary. As chief executive officer, Kendrick moved to cut Grant's losses. He slashed payroll significantly, closed 126 unprofitable stores, and phased out the big-ticket furniture and appliance lines. New store space opened in 1975 was 75 percent less than in 1974.

The positive effects of these moves could not overcome the disastrous events of early 1975. In January, Grant defaulted on about $75 million in interest payments, and in February, results of operations for the year ended January 31, 1975, were released. Grant reported a loss of $177 million, with substantial losses from credit operations accounting for 60 percent of the total.

The banks now assumed a more active role in what was becoming a struggle to save Grant. Robert H. Anderson, a vice president of Sears, was offered a lucrative $2.5 million contract. He decided to accept the challenge to turn the company around, joining Grant as its new president in April 1975. Kendrick remained as chairman of the board. The banks holding 90 percent of Grant's debt extended their loans from June 2, 1975, to March 31, 1976. The balance of about $56 million was repaid on June 2. A major problem confronting Anderson was how to maintain the continued flow of merchandise to Grant stores. Suppliers became skeptical of Grant's ability to pay for merchandise, and in August 1975, the banks agreed to subordinate $300 million of debt to the suppliers' claims for merchandise shipped. With the approach of the Christmas shopping season, the need for merchandise became critical. Despite the banks' subordination of their claims to those of suppliers and the intensive cultivation of suppliers by Anderson, Grant did not receive sufficient quantities of merchandise in the stores.

During this period, Grant reported a $111.3 million net loss for the six months ended on July 31, 1975. Sales had declined 15 percent from the comparable period in 1974. Kendrick observed that a return to profitability before the fourth quarter was unlikely.

On October 2, 1975, Grant filed a Chapter 11 bankruptcy petition. The rehabilitation effort was formally underway, and the protection provided by Chapter 11 permitted a continuation of the reorganization and rehabilitation activities for the next four months. On February 6, 1976, after store closings and liquidations of inventories had generated $320 million in cash, the creditors committee overseeing the bankruptcy voted for liquidation and W. T. Grant ceased to exist.

Financial Statements for Grant

Two changes in accounting principles affect Grant's financial statements. Prior to fiscal 1970, Grant accounted for the investment in its wholly owned finance subsidiary using the equity method. Beginning with the year ending January 31, 1970, Grant consolidated the finance subsidiary. Prior to fiscal 1975, Grant recorded the total finance charge on credit sales as income in the year of the sale. Therefore, accounts receivable included the full amount to be received from customers, not the present value of such amount. Beginning with the fiscal year ending January 31, 1975, Grant recognized finance changes on credit sales over the life of the installment contract.

Exhibit 3.38 presents comparative balance sheets and Exhibit 3.39 (see page 232) presents statements of income and retained earnings for Grant based on the amounts originally reported for each year. Exhibits 3.40, 3.41, and 3.42 (see pages 233–237) present balance sheets, income statements, and statements of cash flow, respectively, based on revised amounts reflecting retroactive restatement for the two changes in accounting principles described earlier. These three statements consolidate the finance subsidiary for all years. Grant provided the necessary data to restate for the change in income recognition of finance charges for the 1971 to 1975 fiscal years only. Exhibit 3.43 (see pages 238–239) presents selected other data for Grant, the variety chain store industry, and the aggregate economy.

Required

Using the narrative information and the financial data provided in Exhibits 3.38−3.43, your mission is to apply tools of financial analysis to determine the major causes of Grant's financial problems. If you had been performing this analysis contemporaneously with the release of publicly reported information, when would you have become skeptical of the ability of Grant to continue as a viable going concern? To assist in this analysis, Exhibits 3.44−3.46 (see pages 240–245) present selected ratio and growth rate information based on the following assumptions:

Exhibit 3.44: Based on the amounts as originally reported for each year (Exhibits 3.38 and 3.39)

Exhibit 3.45: Based on the amounts as retroactively restated for changes in accounting principles (Exhibits 3.40−3.42)

Exhibit 3.46: Same as Exhibit 3.45 except that assets and liabilities reflect the capitalization of leases using the amounts presented in the case

EXHIBIT 3.38

W. T. Grant Company
Comparative Balance Sheets
(as originally reported in thousands)
(Case 3.3)

January 31:	1966	1967	1968
ASSETS			
Cash and marketable securities	$ 22,559	$ 37,507	$ 25,047
Accounts receivable[c]	110,943	110,305	133,406
Inventories	151,365	174,631	183,722
Other current assets	—	—	—
Total Current Assets	$284,867	$322,443	$342,175
Investments	38,419	40,800	56,609
Property, plant, and equipment, net	40,367	48,071	47,572
Other assets	1,222	1,664	1,980
Total Assets	$364,875	$412,978	$448,336
LIABILITIES AND SHAREHOLDERS' EQUITY			
Short-term debt	$ —	$ —	$ 300
Accounts payable—Trade	58,252	75,885	79,673
Current deferred taxes	37,590	47,248	57,518
Total Current Liabilities	$ 95,842	$123,133	$137,491
Long-term debt	70,000	70,000	62,622
Noncurrent deferred taxes	6,269	7,034	7,551
Other long-term liabilities	4,784	4,949	4,858
Total Liabilities	$176,895	$205,116	$212,522
Preferred stock	$ 15,000	$ 15,000	$ 14,750
Common stock	15,375	15,636	16,191
Additional paid-in capital	25,543	27,977	37,428
Retained earnings	132,062	149,249	167,445
Total	$187,980	$207,862	$235,814
Less cost of treasury stock	—	—	—
Total Stockholders' Equity	$187,980	$207,862	$235,814
Total Liabilities and Shareholders' Equity	$364,875	$412,978	$448,336

[a] In the year ending January 31, 1970, W. T. Grant changed its consolidation policy and commenced consolidating its wholly owned finance subsidiary.
[b] In the year ending January 31, 1975, W. T. Grant changed its method of recognizing finance income on installment sales. In prior years, Grant recognized all finance income in the year of the sale. Beginning in the 1975 fiscal period, it recognized finance income over the time the installment receivable was outstanding.
[c] Accounts receivable comprises the following:

January 31:	1966	1967	1968
Customer installment receivables	$114,470	$114,928	$140,507
Less allowances for uncollectible accounts	(7,065)	(9,383)	(11,307)
Unearned credit insurance	—	—	—
Unearned finance income	—	—	—
Net	$107,405	$105,545	$129,200
Other receivables	3,538	4,760	4,206
Total receivables	$110,943	$110,305	$133,406

EXHIBIT 3.38 (Continued)

1969	1970[a]	1971	1972	1973	1974	1975[b]
$ 28,460	$ 32,977	$ 34,009	$ 49,851	$ 30,943	$ 45,951	$ 79,642
154,829	368,267	419,731	477,324	542,751	598,799	431,201
208,623	222,128	260,492	298,676	399,533	450,637	407,357
—	5,037	5,246	5,378	6,649	7,299	6,581
$391,912	$628,409	$719,478	$831,229	$ 979,876	$1,102,686	$ 924,781
62,854	20,694	23,936	32,367	35,581	44,251	49,764
49,213	55,311	61,832	77,173	91,420	100,984	101,932
2,157	2,381	2,678	3,901	3,821	5,063	5,790
$506,136	$706,795	$807,924	$944,670	$1,110,698	$1,252,984	$1,082,267
$ 180	$182,132	$246,420	$237,741	$ 390,034	$ 453,097	$ 600,695
102,080	104,144	118,091	124,990	112,896	104,883	147,211
64,113	80,443	94,785	112,846	130,137	132,085	2,000
$166,373	$366,719	$459,296	$475,577	$ 633,067	$ 690,065	$ 749,906
43,251	35,402	32,301	128,432	126,672	220,336	216,341
7,941	8,286	8,518	9,664	11,926	14,649	—
5,519	5,700	5,773	5,252	4,694	4,196	2,183
$223,084	$416,107	$505,888	$618,925	$ 776,359	$ 929,246	$ 968,430
$ 13,250	$ 11,450	$ 9,600	$ 9,053	$ 8,600	$ 7,465	$ 7,465
17,318	17,883	18,180	18,529	18,588	18,599	18,599
59,945	71,555	78,116	85,195	86,146	85,909	83,914
192,539	211,679	230,435	244,508	261,154	248,461	37,674
$283,052	$312,567	$336,331	$357,285	$ 374,488	$ 360,434	$ 147,652
—	(21,879)	(34,295)	(31,540)	(40,149)	(36,696)	(33,815)
$283,052	$290,688	$302,036	$325,745	$ 334,339	$ 323,738	$ 113,837
$506,136	$706,795	$807,924	$944,670	$1,110,698	$1,252,984	$1,082,267

1969	1970[a]	1971	1972	1973	1974	1975[b]
$162,219	$381,757	$433,730	$493,859	$ 556,091	$ 602,305	$ 518,387
(13,074)	(15,270)	(15,527)	(15,750)	(15,770)	(18,067)	(79,510)
—	(5,774)	(9,553)	(12,413)	(8,768)	(4,923)	(1,386)
—	—	—	—	—	—	(37,523)
$149,145	$360,713	$408,650	$465,696	$ 531,553	$ 579,315	$ 399,968
5,684	7,554	11,081	11,628	11,198	19,484	31,233
$154,829	$368,267	$419,731	$477,324	$ 542,751	$ 598,799	$ 431,201

EXHIBIT 3.39

W. T. Grant Company
Statements of Income and Retained Earnings
(as originally reported in thousands)
(Case 3.3)

Year Ended January 31:	1967	1968	1969	1970	1971	1972	1973	1974	1975
Sales	$920,797	$979,458	$1,096,152	$1,210,918	$1,254,131	$1,374,811	$1,644,747	$1,849,802	$1,761,952
Concessions	2,249	2,786	3,425	3,748	4,986	3,439	3,753	3,971	4,238
Equity in earnings	2,072	2,987	3,537	2,084	2,777	2,383	5,116	4,651	3,086
Finance charges	—	—	—	—	—	—	—	—	91,141
Other income	1,049	2,010	2,205	2,864	2,874	3,102	1,188	3,063	3,376
Total Revenues	$926,167	$987,241	$1,105,319	$1,219,614	$1,264,768	$1,383,735	$1,654,804	$1,861,487	$1,863,793
Cost of goods sold	$631,585	$669,560	$ 741,181	$ 817,671	$ 843,192	$ 931,237	$1,125,261	$1,282,945	$1,303,267
Selling, general, and administration	233,134	253,561	287,883	307,215	330,325	374,334	444,879	491,287	769,253
Interest	4,970	4,907	4,360	14,919	18,874	16,452	21,127	78,040	86,079
Taxes:									
Current	13,541	17,530	25,600	24,900	21,140	13,487	9,588	(6,021)	(19,439)
Deferred	11,659	9,120	8,400	13,100	11,660	13,013	16,162	6,807	(98,027)
Total Expenses	$894,889	$954,678	$1,067,424	$1,177,805	$1,225,191	$1,348,523	$1,617,017	$1,853,058	$2,041,133
Net income	$ 31,278	$ 32,563	$ 37,895	$ 41,809	$ 39,577	$ 35,212	$ 37,787	$ 8,429	$ (177,340)
Dividends	(14,091)	(14,367)	(17,686)	(19,737)	(20,821)	(21,139)	(21,141)	(21,122)	(4,457)
Change in accounting **principles:**									
Consolidation of finance subsidiary	—	—	4,885	(2,932)	—	—	—	—	—
Recognition of financing charges	—	—	—	—	—	—	—	—	(28,990)
Change in retained earnings	$ 17,187	$ 18,196	$ 25,094	$ 19,140	$ 18,756	$ 14,073	$ 16,646	$ (12,693)	$ (210,787)
Retained earnings— Beginning of period	132,062	149,249	167,445	192,539	211,679	230,435	244,508	261,154	248,461
Retained Earnings— End of Period	$149,249	$167,445	$ 192,539	$ 211,679	$ 230,435	$ 244,508	$ 261,154	$ 248,461	$ 37,674

EXHIBIT 3.40

W. T. Grant Company
Comparative Balance Sheets
(as retroactively reported for changes in accounting principles in thousands)
(Case 3.3)

January 31:	1966	1967	1968	1969	1970[a]	1971	1972	1973	1974	1975[b]
ASSETS										
Cash and marketable securities	$ 22,638	$ 39,040	$ 25,141	$ 25,639	$ 32,977	$ 34,009	$ 49,851	$ 30,943	$ 45,951	$ 79,642
Accounts receivable[c]	172,706	230,427	272,450	312,776	368,267	358,428	408,301	468,582	540,802	431,201
Inventories	151,365	174,631	183,722	208,623	222,128	260,492	298,676	399,533	450,637	407,357
Other current assets	3,630	4,079	3,982	4,402	5,037	5,246	5,378	6,649	7,299	6,581
Total Current Assets	$350,339	$448,177	$485,295	$551,440	$628,409	$658,175	$762,206	$ 905,707	$1,044,689	$ 924,781
Investments	13,405	14,791	16,754	18,581	20,694	23,936	32,367	35,581	44,251	49,764
Property, plant, and equipment, net	40,372	48,076	47,578	49,931	55,311	61,832	77,173	91,420	100,984	101,932
Other assets	1,222	1,664	1,980	2,157	2,381	2,678	3,901	3,821	5,063	5,790
Total Assets	$405,338	$512,708	$551,607	$622,109	$706,795	$746,621	$875,647	$1,036,529	$1,194,987	$1,082,267
LIABILITIES AND SHAREHOLDERS' EQUITY										
Short-term debt	$ 37,314	$ 97,647	$ 99,230	$118,125	$182,132	$246,420	$237,741	$ 390,034	$ 453,097	$ 600,695
Accounts payable	58,252	75,885	79,673	102,080	104,144	118,091	124,990	112,896	104,883	147,211
Current deferred taxes	36,574	44,667	56,545	65,073	80,443	58,536	72,464	87,431	103,078	2,000
Total Current Liabilities	$132,140	$218,199	$235,448	$285,278	$366,719	$423,047	$435,195	$ 590,361	$ 661,058	$ 749,906
Long-term debt	70,000	70,000	62,622	43,251	35,402	32,301	128,432	126,672	220,336	216,341
Noncurrent deferred taxes	6,269	7,034	7,551	7,941	8,286	8,518	9,664	11,926	14,649	—
Other long-term liabilities	4,785	5,159	5,288	5,519	5,700	5,773	5,252	4,694	4,196	2,183
Total Liabilities	$213,194	$300,392	$310,909	$341,989	$416,107	$469,639	$578,543	$ 733,653	$ 900,239	$ 968,430
Preferred stock	$ 15,000	$ 15,000	$ 14,750	$ 13,250	$ 11,450	$ 9,600	$ 9,053	$ 8,600	$ 7,465	$ 7,465

(Continued)

EXHIBIT 3.40 (Continued)

January 31:	1966	1967	1968	1969	1970[a]	1971	1972	1973	1974	1975[b]
Common stock	15,375	15,636	16,191	17,318	17,883	18,180	18,529	18,588	18,599	18,599
Additional paid-in capital	25,543	27,977	37,428	59,945	71,555	78,116	85,195	86,146	85,909	83,914
Retained earnings	136,226	153,703	172,329	189,607	211,679	205,381	215,867	229,691	219,471	37,674
Total	$192,144	$212,316	$240,698	$280,120	$312,567	$311,277	$328,644	$ 343,025	$ 331,444	$ 147,652
Less cost of treasury stock	—	—	—	—	(21,879)	(34,295)	(31,540)	(40,149)	(36,696)	(33,815)
Total Stockholders' Equity	$192,144	$212,316	$240,698	$280,120	$290,688	$276,982	$297,104	$ 302,876	$ 294,748	$ 113,837
Total Liabilities and Shareholders' Equity	$405,338	$512,708	$551,607	$622,109	$706,795	$746,621	$875,647	$1,036,529	$1,194,987	$1,082,267

[a]See note (a) to Exhibit 3.38.

[b]See note (b) to Exhibit 3.38.

[c]Accounts receivable comprises the following:

	1966	1967	1968	1969	1970[a]	1971	1972	1973	1974	1975[b]
Customer installment receivables		*NOT DISCLOSED ON A FULLY CONSOLIDATED BASIS WITH FINANCE SUBSIDIARY*		$381,757	$433,730	$493,859	$556,091	$ 602,305	$ 518,387	
Less allowances for uncollectible Accounts				(15,270)	(15,527)	(15,750)	(15,770)	(18,067)	(79,510)	
				(5,774)	(9,553)	(12,413)	(8,768)	(4,923)	(1,386)	
Unearned credit insurance				—	(61,303)	(69,023)	(74,169)	(57,997)	(37,523)	
Unearned finance income				$360,713	$347,347	$396,073	$457,384	$ 521,318	$ 399,968	
Net other Receivables				7,554	11,081	11,628	11,198	19,484	31,233	
Total Receivables	$172,706	$230,427	$272,450	$312,776	$368,267	$358,428	$408,301	$ 468,582	$ 540,802	$ 431,201

EXHIBIT 3.41

W. T. Grant Company
Statements of Income and Retained Earnings
(as retroactively revised for changes in accounting principles in thousands)
(Case 3.3)

Year Ended January 31:	1967	1968	1969	1970	1971	1972	1973	1974	1975
Sales	$920,797	$979,458	$1,096,152	$1,210,918	$1,254,131	$1,374,812	$1,644,747	$1,849,802	$1,761,952
Concessions	2,249	2,786	3,425	3,748	4,986	3,439	3,753	3,971	4,238
Equity in earnings	1,073	1,503	1,761	2,084	2,777	2,383	5,116	4,651	3,086
Finance charges	—	—	—	—	63,194	66,567	84,817	114,920	91,141
Other income	1,315	2,038	2,525	2,864	2,874	3,102	1,188	3,063	3,376
Total Revenues	$925,434	$985,785	$1,103,311	$1,219,614	$1,327,962	$1,450,303	$1,739,621	$1,976,407	$1,863,793
Cost of goods sold	$631,585	$669,560	$ 741,181	$ 817,671	$ 843,192	$ 931,237	$1,125,261	$1,282,945	$1,303,267
Selling, general, and administration	229,130	247,093	278,031	307,215	396,877	445,244	532,604	601,231	769,253
Interest	7,319	8,549	9,636	14,919	18,874	16,452	21,127	78,040	86,079
Taxes:									
Current	14,463	18,470	27,880	24,900	22,866	13,579	11,256	(6,021)	(19,439)
Deferred	11,369	9,120	8,400	13,100	9,738	12,166	14,408	9,310	(98,027)
Total Expenses	$893,866	$952,792	$1,065,128	$1,177,805	$1,291,547	$1,418,678	$1,704,656	$1,965,505	$2,041,133
Net income	$ 31,568	$ 32,993	$ 38,183	$ 41,809	$ 36,415	$ 31,625	$ 34,965	$ 10,902	$ (177,340)
Dividends	(14,091)	(14,367)	(17,686)	(19,737)	(20,821)	(21,139)	(21,141)	(21,122)	(4,457)
Change in accounting principles:									
Consolidation of finance subsidiary	—	—	(3,219)	—	—	—	—	—	—
Recognition of financing charges	—	—	—	—	(21,892)	—	—	—	—
Change in retained earnings	$ 17,477	$ 18,626	$ 17,278	$ 22,072	$ (6,298)	$ 10,486	$ 13,824	$ (10,220)	$ (181,797)
Retained earnings— Beginning of period	136,226	153,703	172,329	189,607	211,679	205,381	215,867	229,691	219,471
Retained Earnings— End of Period	$153,703	$172,329	$ 189,607	$ 211,679	$ 205,381	$ 215,867	$ 229,691	$ 219,471	$ 37,674

EXHIBIT 3.42

W. T. Grant Company
Statement of Cash Flows
(as retroactively revised for changes in accounting principles)
(Case 3.3)

Year Ended January 31:	1967	1968	1969	1970	1971	1972	1973	1974	1975
OPERATIONS									
Net income	$ 31,568	$ 32,993	$ 38,183	$ 41,809	$ 36,415	$ 31,625	$ 34,965	$ 10,902	$(177,340)
Depreciation	7,524	8,203	8,388	8,972	9,619	10,577	12,004	13,579	14,587
Other	66	(856)	(1,140)	(1,559)	(2,470)	(1,758)	(1,699)	(1,345)	(16,993)
(Increase) Decrease in receivables	(57,721)	(42,023)	(40,326)	(55,491)	(11,981)	(49,873)	(60,281)	(72,220)	109,601
(Increase) Decrease in inventories	(23,266)	(9,091)	(24,901)	(13,505)	(38,364)	(38,184)	(100,857)	(51,104)	43,280
(Increase) Decrease in prepayments	(449)	97	(420)	(635)	(209)	(132)	(1,271)	(650)	718
Increase (Decrease) in accounts payable	17,633	3,788	22,407	2,064	13,947	6,899	(12,094)	(8,013)	42,328
Increase (Decrease) in other current liabilities	8,093	11,878	8,528	15,370	(21,907)	13,928	14,967	15,647	(101,078)
Cash Flow from Operations	$(16,552)	$ 4,989	$ 10,719	$ (2,975)	$(14,950)	$(26,918)	$(114,266)	$(93,204)	$ (84,897)
INVESTING									
Acquisition of property, plant, and equipment	$(15,257)	$ (7,763)	$(10,626)	$(14,352)	$(16,141)	$(25,918)	$ (26,251)	$(23,143)	$ (15,535)
Acquisition of investments	(269)	(418)	(35)	—	(436)	(5,951)	(2,216)	(5,700)	(5,282)
Cash Flow from Investing	$(15,526)	$ (8,181)	$(10,661)	$(14,352)	$(16,577)	$(31,869)	$ (28,467)	$(28,843)	$ (20,817)

FINANCING									
Increase (Decrease) in short-term borrowing	$ 60,333	$ 1,583	$ 18,895	$ 64,007	$ 64,288	$ (8,679)	$ 152,293	$ 63,063	$ 147,598
Increase (Decrease) in long-term borrowing	—	(1,500)	(1,500)	(1,687)	(1,538)	98,385	(1,584)	93,926	(3,995)
Increase (Decrease) in capital stock	2,695	3,958	844	(17,860)	(8,954)	7,407	(8,227)	1,833	886
Dividends	(14,091)	(14,367)	(17,686)	(19,737)	(20,821)	(21,139)	(21,141)	(21,122)	(4,457)
Cash Flow from Financing	$ 48,937	$(10,326)	$ 553	$ 24,723	$ 32,975	$ 75,974	$ 121,341	$137,700	$ 140,032
Other	$ (457)	$ (381)	$ (113)	$ (58)	$ (416)	$ (1,345)	$ 2,484	$ (645)	$ (627)
Change in Cash	$ 16,402	$(13,899)	$ 498	$ 7,338	$ 1,032	$ 15,842	$ (18,908)	$ 15,008	$ 33,691

EXHIBIT 3.43

W. T. Grant Company
Other Data
(Case 3.3)

December 31:	**1965**	**1966**	**1967**	**1968**	**1969**	**1970**	**1971**	**1972**	**1973**	**1974**
W. T. Grant Co.										
Sales (millions)[a]	$ 839.7	$ 920.8	$ 979.5	$ 1,096.1	$ 1,210.9	$ 1,254.1	$1,374.8	$1,644.7	$1,849.8	$1,762.0
Number of stores	1,088	1,104	1,086	1,092	1,095	1,116	1,168	1,208	1,189	1,152
Store area (thousands of square feet)		[a]Data Not Available			—	38,157	44,718	50,619	53,719	54,770
Dividends per share[a]	$ 0.80	$ 1.10	$ 1.10	$ 1.30	$ 1.40	$ 1.40	$ 1.50	$ 1.50	$ 1.50	$ 0.30
Stock Price										
—High	31⅛	35⅛	37⅜	45⅛	59	52	70⅝	48¾	44⅜	12
—Low	18	20½	20¾	30	39¼	26⅞	41⅞	38¾	9⅞	1½
—Close (12/31)	31⅛	20¾	34⅜	42⅝	47	47⅛	47¾	43⅞	10⅞	1⅞
Variety Chain Store Industry										
Sales (millions)	$5,320.0	$ 5,727.0	$ 6,078.0	$ 6,152.0	$ 6,426.0	$ 6,959.0	$6,972.0	$7,498.0	$8,212.0	$8,714.0
Standard & Poor's Variety Chain Stock Price Index										
—High	31.0	31.2	38.4	53.6	66.1	61.4	92.2	107.4	107.3	73.7
—Low	24.3	22.4	22.3	34.7	48.8	40.9	60.2	82.1	60.0	39.0
—Close (12/31)	31.0	22.4	37.8	50.5	59.6	60.4	88.0	106.8	66.2	41.9

AGGREGATE ECONOMY										
Gross national product (billions)	$ 684.9	$ 747.6	$ 789.7	$ 865.7	$ 932.1	$1,075.3	$1,107.5	$1,171.1	$1,233.4	$1,210.0
Average bank short-term lending rate	4.99%	5.69%	5.99%	6.68%	8.21%	8.48%	6.32%	5.82%	8.30%	11.28%
Standard & Poor's 500 Stock Price Index										
—High	92.6	94.1	97.6	108.4	106.2	93.5	104.8	119.1	120.2	99.8
—Low	81.6	73.2	80.4	87.7	89.2	69.3	90.2	101.7	92.2	62.3
—Close (12/31)	92.4	80.3	96.5	103.9	92.1	92.2	102.1	118.1	97.6	68.6

[a]These amounts are for the fiscal year ending January 31 of the year after the year indicated in the column. For example, sales for W. T. Grant of $839.7 in the 1965 column are for the fiscal year ending January 31, 1966.

EXHIBIT 3.44

W. T. Grant Company
Financial Ratios and Growth Rates Based on Amounts as Originally Reported
(Case 3.3)

Financial Ratios	1967	1968	1969	1970	1971	1972	1973	1974	1975
PROFITABILITY ANALYSIS									
Profit margin for ROA	3.7%	3.6%	3.7%	4.1%	3.9%	3.2%	3.0%	2.6%	(7.5%)
Assets turnover	2.4	2.3	2.3	2.0	1.7	1.6	1.6	1.6	1.5
Return on assets (ROA)	8.7%	8.2%	8.4%	8.2%	6.5%	5.0%	4.7%	4.1%	(11.4%)
Return on common shareholders' equity (ROCE)	16.8%	15.5%	15.2%	15.1%	13.7%	11.4%	11.7%	2.5%	(84.1%)
OPERATING PERFORMANCE									
Cost of goods sold/sales	68.6%	68.4%	67.6%	67.5%	67.2%	67.7%	68.4%	69.4%	74.0%
Selling and administrative expenses/sales	25.3%	25.9%	26.3%	25.4%	26.3%	27.2%	27.0%	26.6%	43.7%
ASSET TURNOVERS									
Accounts receivable	8.3	8.0	7.6	4.6	3.2	3.1	3.2	3.2	3.4
Inventory	3.9	3.7	3.8	3.8	3.5	3.3	3.2	3.0	3.0
Fixed asset	20.8	20.5	22.7	23.2	21.4	19.8	19.5	19.2	17.4
SHORT-TERM LIQUIDITY RISK									
Current ratio	2.62	2.49	2.36	1.71	1.57	1.75	1.55	1.60	1.23
Quick ratio	1.20	1.15	1.10	1.09	0.99	1.11	0.91	0.93	0.68
Days receivables	44	45	48	79	115	119	113	113	107
Days inventory	94	98	97	96	104	110	113	121	120
Days payables	37	42	43	45	46	46	35	30	37
Operating cash flow/current liabilities	(15.1%)	3.8%	7.1%	(1.1%)	(3.6%)	(5.8%)	(20.6%)	(14.1%)	(11.8%)

LONG-TERM LIQUIDITY RISK

Liabilities/Assets	49.7%	47.4%	44.1%	58.9%	62.6%	65.5%	69.9%	74.2%	85.9%
Long-term debt/assets	17.0%	14.0%	8.5%	5.0%	4.0%	13.6%	11.4%	17.6%	20.0%
Operating cash flow/ total liabilities	(8.7%)	2.4%	4.9%	(0.9%)	(3.2%)	(4.8%)	(16.4%)	(10.9%)	(9.0%)
Interest coverage ratio	12.4	13.1	17.5	6.4	4.8	4.8	4.0	1.1	(2.4)

Growth Rates	**1968**	**1969**	**1970**	**1971**	**1972**	**1973**	**1974**	**1975**
Accounts receivable	20.9%	16.1%	137.9%	14.0%	13.7%	13.7%	10.3%	(28.0%)
Inventories	5.2%	13.6%	6.5%	17.3%	14.7%	33.8%	12.8%	(9.6%)
Fixed assets	(1.0%)	3.4%	12.4%	11.8%	24.8%	18.5%	10.5%	0.9%
Total Assets	8.6%	12.9%	39.6%	14.3%	17.0%	17.6%	12.8%	(13.6%)
Accounts payable	5.0%	28.1%	2.0%	13.4%	5.8%	(9.7%)	(7.1%)	40.4%
Bank loans	—	(40.0%)	N/A	35.3%	(3.5%)	64.1%	16.2%	32.6%
Long-term debt	(10.5%)	(30.9%)	(18.1%)	(8.8%)	297.6%	(1.4%)	73.9%	(1.8%)
Shareholders' equity	13.4%	20.0%	2.7%	3.9%	7.8%	2.6%	(3.2%)	(64.8%)
Sales	6.4%	11.9%	10.5%	3.6%	9.6%	19.6%	12.5%	(4.7%)
Cost of goods sold	6.0%	10.7%	10.3%	3.1%	10.4%	20.8%	14.0%	1.6%
Selling and administrative expenses	8.8%	13.5%	6.7%	7.5%	13.3%	18.8%	10.4%	56.6%
Net Income	4.1%	16.4%	10.3%	(5.3%)	(11.0%)	7.3%	(77.7%)	(2,203.9%)

EXHIBIT 3.45

W. T. Grant Company
Financial Ratios and Growth Rates Based on Amounts Retroactively Restated for Changes in Accounting Principles
(Leases Not Capitalized)
(Case 3.3)

Financial Ratios	1967	1968	1969	1970	1971	1972	1973	1974	1975
PROFITABILITY ANALYSIS									
Profit margin for ROA	3.8%	3.8%	3.9%	4.1%	3.7%	2.9%	2.8%	2.8%	(7.5%)
Assets turnover	2.0	1.8	1.9	1.8	1.7	1.7	1.7	1.7	1.5
Return on assets (ROA)	7.7%	7.0%	7.4%	7.5%	6.4%	5.0%	4.8%	4.6%	(11.6%)
Return on common shareholders' equity (ROCE)	16.6%	15.3%	15.3%	15.1%	13.2%	11.3%	11.9%	3.6%	(90.2%)
OPERATING PERFORMANCE									
Cost of goods sold/sales	68.6%	68.4%	67.6%	67.5%	67.2%	67.7%	68.4%	69.4%	74.0%
Selling and administrative expenses/sales	24.9%	25.2%	25.4%	25.4%	31.6%	32.4%	32.4%	32.5%	43.7%
ASSET TURNOVERS									
Accounts receivable	4.6	3.9	3.7	3.6	3.5	3.6	3.8	3.7	3.6
Inventory	3.9	3.7	3.8	3.8	3.5	3.3	3.2	3.0	3.0
Fixed asset	20.8	20.5	22.5	23.0	21.4	19.8	19.5	19.2	17.4
SHORT-TERM LIQUIDITY RISK									
Current ratio	2.05	2.06	1.93	1.71	1.56	1.75	1.53	1.58	1.23
Quick ratio	1.23	1.26	1.19	1.09	0.93	1.05	0.85	0.89	0.68
Days receivables	80	94	97	103	106	102	97	100	101
Days inventory	94	98	97	96	104	110	113	121	120
Days payables	37	42	43	45	46	46	35	30	37
Operating cash flow/current liabilities	(9.4%)	2.2%	4.1%	(0.9%)	(3.8%)	(6.3%)	(22.3%)	(14.9%)	(12.0%)

LONG-TERM LIQUIDITY RISK									
Liabilities/Assets	58.6%	56.4%	55.0%	58.9%	62.9%	66.1%	70.8%	75.3%	89.5%
Long-term debt/assets	13.7%	11.4%	7.0%	5.0%	4.3%	14.7%	12.2%	18.4%	20.0%
Operating cash flow/ liabilities	(6.4%)	1.6%	3.3%	(0.8%)	(3.4%)	(5.1%)	(17.4%)	(11.4%)	(9.1%)
Interest coverage ratio	8.8	8.1	8.7	6.4	4.7	4.5	3.9	1.2	(2.4)

Growth Rates	**1968**	**1969**	**1970**	**1971**	**1972**	**1973**	**1974**	**1975**
Accounts receivable	18.2%	14.8%	17.7%	(2.7%)	13.9%	14.8%	15.4%	(20.3%)
Inventories	5.2%	13.6%	6.5%	17.3%	14.7%	33.8%	12.8%	(9.6%)
Fixed assets	(1.0%)	4.9%	10.8%	11.8%	24.8%	18.5%	10.5%	0.9%
Total assets	7.6%	12.8%	13.6%	5.6%	17.3%	18.4%	15.3%	(9.4%)
Accounts payable	5.0%	28.1%	2.0%	13.4%	5.8%	(9.7%)	(7.1%)	40.4%
Bank loans	1.6%	19.0%	54.2%	35.3%	(3.5%)	64.1%	16.2%	32.6%
Long-term debt	(10.5%)	(30.9%)	(18.1%)	(8.8%)	297.6%	(1.4%)	73.9%	(1.8%)
Shareholders' equity	13.4%	16.4%	3.8%	(4.7%)	7.3%	1.9%	(2.7%)	(61.4%)
Sales	6.4%	11.9%	10.5%	3.6%	9.6%	19.6%	12.5%	(4.7%)
Cost of goods sold	6.0%	10.7%	10.3%	3.1%	10.4%	20.8%	14.0%	1.6%
Selling and administrative expenses	7.8%	12.5%	10.5%	29.2%	12.2%	19.6%	12.9%	27.9%
Net Income	4.5%	15.7%	9.5%	(12.9%)	(13.2%)	10.6%	(68.8%)	(1,726.7%)

EXHIBIT 3.46

W. T. Grant Company
Financial Ratios and Growth Rates Based on Amounts Retroactively Restated for Changes in Accounting Principles
(Leases Capitalized)
(Case 3.3)

Financial Ratios	1967	1968	1969	1970	1971	1972	1973	1974	1975
PROFITABILITY ANALYSIS									
Profit margin for ROA	3.8%	3.8%	3.9%	4.1%	3.7%	2.9%	2.8%	2.8%	(7.5%)
Assets turnover	1.1	1.1	1.1	1.1	1.0	1.0	1.0	1.0	0.9
Return on assets (ROA)	4.1%	4.0%	4.3%	4.4%	3.8%	2.9%	2.8%	2.7%	(6.8%)
Return on common Shareholders' equity (ROCE)	16.6%	15.3%	15.3%	15.1%	13.2%	11.3%	11.9%	3.6%	(90.2%)
OPERATING PERFORMANCE									
Cost of goods sold/sales	68.6%	68.4%	67.6%	67.5%	67.2%	67.7%	68.4%	69.4%	74.0%
Selling and administrative expenses/sales	24.9%	25.2%	25.4%	25.4%	31.6%	32.4%	32.4%	32.5%	43.7%
ASSET TURNOVERS									
Accounts receivable	4.6	3.9	3.7	3.6	3.5	3.6	3.8	3.7	3.6
Inventory	3.9	3.7	3.8	3.8	3.5	3.3	3.2	3.0	3.0
Fixed Asset	2.1	2.2	2.3	2.3	2.3	2.2	2.2	2.2	1.9
SHORT-TERM LIQUIDITY RISK									
Current ratio	2.05	2.06	1.93	1.71	1.56	1.75	1.53	1.58	1.23
Quick ratio	1.23	1.26	1.19	1.09	0.93	1.05	0.85	0.89	0.68
Days receivables	80	94	97	103	106	102	97	100	101
Days inventory	94	98	97	96	104	110	113	121	120
Days payables	37	42	43	45	46	46	35	30	37
Operating cash flow/ current liabilities	(9.4%)	2.2%	4.1%	(0.9%)	(3.8%)	(6.3%)	(22.3%)	(14.9%)	(12.0%)

LONG-TERM LIQUIDITY RISK

Liabilities/Assets	76.7%	74.5%	74.0%	75.6%	77.7%	80.2%	82.6%	85.3%	94.0%
Long-term debt/assets	51.5%	48.3%	46.4%	43.8%	42.5%	50.2%	47.9%	51.3%	54.5%
Operating cash flow/liabilities	(2.5%)	0.7%	1.4%	(0.3%)	(1.6%)	(2.5%)	(8.6%)	(5.9%)	(4.9%)
Interest coverage	8.8	8.1	8.7	6.4	4.7	4.5	3.9	1.2	(2.4)

Growth Rates	**1968**	**1969**	**1970**	**1971**	**1972**	**1973**	**1974**	**1975**
Accounts receivable	18.2%	14.8%	17.7%	(2.7%)	13.9%	14.8%	15.4%	(20.3%)
Inventories	5.2%	13.6%	6.5%	17.3%	14.7%	33.8%	12.8%	(9.6%)
Fixed assets	1.6%	14.9%	6.9%	2.9%	26.1%	13.8%	13.3%	1.8%
Total assets	3.5%	14.2%	10.6%	4.1%	20.8%	16.2%	14.6%	(4.8%)
Accounts payable	5.0%	28.1%	2.0%	13.4%	5.8%	(9.7%)	(7.1%)	40.4%
Bank loans	1.6%	19.0%	54.2%	35.3%	(3.5%)	64.1%	16.2%	32.6%
Long-term debt	(3.0%)	9.7%	4.4%	1.2%	42.8%	10.7%	22.8%	1.1%
Shareholders' equity	13.4%	16.4%	3.8%	(4.7%)	7.3%	1.9%	(2.7%)	(61.4%)
Sales	6.4%	11.9%	10.5%	3.6%	9.6%	19.6%	12.5%	(4.7%)
Cost of goods sold	6.0%	10.7%	10.3%	3.1%	10.4%	20.8%	14.0%	1.6%
Selling and administrative expenses	7.8%	12.5%	10.5%	29.2%	12.2%	19.6%	12.9%	27.9%
Net Income	4.5%	15.7%	9.5%	(12.9%)	(13.2%)	10.6%	(68.8%)	(1,726.7%)

Chapter 4

Profitability Analysis

Learning Objectives

1. Evaluate firm profitability using the primary measure of firm performance—net income—as well as profitability analysis techniques including per share analysis, common-size analysis, percentage change analysis, and alternative measures of income.
2. Analyze and interpret levels of and changes in the profitability of a firm using the rate of return on assets and its components: profit margin and total assets turnover.
3. Become comfortable linking the effects of economic and strategic factors to the interpretation of the rate of return on assets and its components.
4. Examine other measures of operating performance that supplement the rate of return on assets in assessing profitability, including the integration of nonfinancial and financial measures.
5. Analyze and interpret levels of and changes in the rate of return on common shareholders' equity, including the conditions when a firm uses financial leverage successfully to increase the return to common shareholders.

The primary objective in most financial statement analysis is to value a firm's equity securities. As Chapters 10–14 make clear, the value of an equity security relates to the future *profitability* an investor anticipates relative to the *risk* involved. However, even if the objective is not valuation, but simply performance assessment, financial statement analysis examines aspects of a firm's *profitability* and its *risk.* Examining the profitability of a firm in the recent past provides information that helps the analyst project the firm's future profitability and the expected return from investing in the firm's equity securities. Evaluations of risk involve judgments about a firm's success in managing various dimensions of risk in the past and its ability to manage risks in the future.

This chapter describes several commonly used financial statement analysis techniques for analyzing profitability. Chapter 5 explores the use of financial statements in assessing risk. Both chapters apply these tools of analysis to the financial statements of PepsiCo, which appear in Appendix A. These financial statements also appear as Exhibits 1.9 (balance sheet), Exhibit 1.11 (income statement), and Exhibit 1.14 (statement of cash flows) in Chapter 1. We recommend that you trace the calculation of each financial ratio discussed in this chapter and the next chapter to these financial statements to ensure that you understand the source of the amounts used. The analytical tools discussed in Chapters 4 and 5 provide the framework for the discussion of alternative accounting principles and other data issues in Chapters 6–9 and the valuation of firms in Chapters 10–14. Although we will make some preliminary interpretations of the analytical results for PepsiCo in Chapters 4 and 5, a deeper understanding requires consideration of accounting issues relating to PepsiCo's financial statements, discussed in later chapters.

Our analysis examines changes in the financial ratios for PepsiCo over time, a process referred to as *time-series analysis,* which allows the analyst to address questions about changes over time. Is PepsiCo becoming more or less profitable over time? Is it becoming more or less risky? Are changes in PepsiCo's strategy, economic conditions, competition, or other factors causing its profitability and risk to change? How is management responding to external economic forces? Time-series analysis helps answer these questions.

It also is useful to compare the financial ratios for PepsiCo with those of its competitors, a process referred to as *cross-sectional analysis.* PepsiCo's principal competitor is The Coca-Cola Company (Coca-Cola). We might compare our analysis of PepsiCo with the corresponding financial ratios for Coca-Cola to gain a cross-sectional perspective on the profitability of the two firms. Profitability sometimes appears similar for two firms, but cross-sectional analysis of components of profitability may reveal that similar profitability is driven by different factors across firms. Similarly, we also might compare the results for PepsiCo with average industry ratios, such as those published by Moody's, Robert Morris Associates, Dun & Bradstreet, and others. Appendix D contains averages and other descriptive statistics for the most common ratios across time for 48 industries.

As discussed in Chapter 1, we view financial statement analysis as a three-legged stool (see Exhibit 1.1), which requires the analyst to understand the economics of a firm's industry and markets, the firm's specific strategy within its industry, and the information captured in its financial statements. The analysis of profitability includes, among other things, the analysis of various financial ratios based on numbers from the financial statements. We will discuss many ratios in this chapter. An important concept at this point is that ratios are not metrics to be memorized, but are useful tools that analysts may construct in different ways to capture information relevant to their particular task. Although in this text we demonstrate the most common and theoretically sound approaches to computing and interpreting ratios, some analysts use these ratios somewhat differently. (For example, analysts may vary whether they include gross or net sales or beginning or average asset balances in a ratio.) In particular, ratios differ across industries, especially as analysts following specific industries create and use specialized ratios designed to capture important elements of profitability and risk within that industry (such as revenues per passenger seat mile for airlines and loan loss allowances over total loans among banks). When confronted with ratios prepared by others, you need to understand how those ratios were defined and computed. Although differences in ratio definitions do not always generate substantive differences, sometimes they do.

Chapter 1 introduced the economic characteristics of the beverage industry and the strategy of PepsiCo to compete in this industry. We incorporate this information and other information provided by PepsiCo in its management discussion and analysis, or MD&A (Appendix B), into our interpretations of PepsiCo's financial ratios. Appendix C provides a printout for PepsiCo of FSAP (Financial Statement Analysis Package) available with this book, containing financial ratios computed for PepsiCo. Finally, Appendix D provides descriptive data for the distribution of commonly used financial rations, which provides a useful benchmark for many of the ratios we discuss in this chapter.

OVERVIEW OF PROFITABILITY ANALYSIS

Profitability analysis evaluates whether managers are effectively executing a firm's strategy. With this in mind, we view financial statement analysis as a form of hypothesis testing. For example, knowing that PepsiCo is a leading manufacturer of beverages, snack foods and breakfast foods with well-recognized brands and an international presence, we might hypothesize that PepsiCo is more profitable than the average firm. We can obtain data from the financial statements for PepsiCo and comparable firms to see if this hypothesis is descriptive of PepsiCo's performance. Because there are numerous ways to measure profitability, it is important to approach the many tools for analyzing profitability in an organized manner. In this chapter, using PepsiCo as an example, we discuss the analysis of profitability as a step-by-step examination of different layers of financial information.

Although firms must report comprehensive income, net income, or earnings, remains the key measure of profitability. Dhaliwal, Subramanyam, and Trezevant (1999) examined the association between stock returns and comprehensive income and its components.[1] With the exception of firms in the financial industry, net income is more strongly associated with stock returns than comprehensive income. Our purpose in analyzing profitability is to generate an understanding of a firm's performance to enable forecasts of future performance. Other comprehensive income amounts exhibit a very low level of persistence. Thus, we focus on net income as our primary measure of profitability, with the caveat that components of other comprehensive income for certain firms should not be automatically dismissed.[2] Different approaches to analyzing a firm's profitability are aimed at generating a deeper understanding of net income. The emphasis in this chapter is on the conceptual framework for analyzing net income in the context of a firm's overall financial statements. Obviously, Chapters 2 and 3 have laid important foundations of understanding how assets and liabilities and income are measured and how net income and cash flows differ. In addition, accounting method choices will affect the financial statements and the measurement of net income, topics discussed in Chapters 6–9. This chapter will address some accounting measurement effects on profitability, with later chapters providing more comprehensive discussion of these effects.

Exhibit 4.1 provides a diagram of the approaches to analyzing net income. The diagram begins with net income, which is the summary measure of profits from the income statement. From net income, two branches represent alternative approaches to better understanding firms' net income. On the left, the approach is to analyze alternative transformations of measured net income. The next four sections discuss the following approaches: earnings per share analysis, common-size analysis, percentage change analysis, and alternative definitions of profits. These are straightforward approaches to understand, so the majority of this chapter will focus on the right side of the diagram, which frames profitability in terms of rate of return metrics. Rates of return integrate information from the income statement and the balance sheet to compute various profitability metrics, the most common being ROA (return on total assets) and ROCE (return on common equity). Most of this chapter will focus on understanding how to interpret ROCE and ROA, as these are key metrics in the discussions of accounting quality in Chapters 6–9 and forecasting and valuation in Chapters 10–14. As Exhibit 4.1 shows, ROA and ROCE can be decomposed into measures of margin, turnover,

[1]Dan Dhaliwal, K. R. Subramanyam, and Robert Trezevant, "Is Comprehensive Income Superior to Net Income as a Measure of Firm Performance?" *Journal of Accounting and Economics* Vol. 26, Issues 1–3 (January 1999) pp. 43–67.

[2]For example, one possibility for the findings that components of other comprehensive income do not correlate strongly with stock prices is that investors are inappropriately downplaying the importance of these components. Indeed, a subsequent study confirmed that items of other comprehensive income are treated as transitory by investors, which leads to investors pricing the value of other comprehensive income on a dollar-for-dollar basis. See Dennis Chambers, Thomas J. Linsmeier, Catherine Shakespeare, and Theodore Sougiannis, "An Evaluation of SFAS No. 130 Comprehensive Income Disclosures." *Review of Accounting Studies* Vol. 12, No. 4 (December 2007).

EXHIBIT 4.1

Diagram of Alternative Approaches to Analyzing Net Income

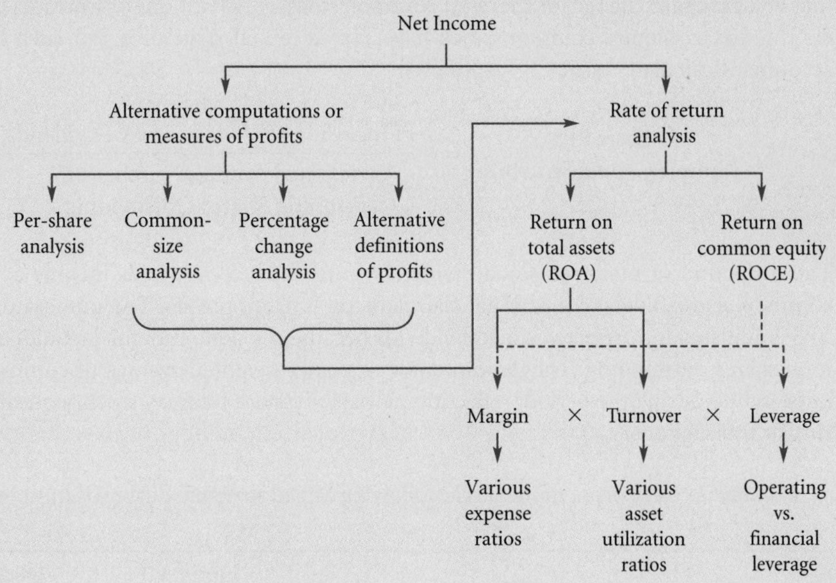

and leverage, which facilitate a deeper understanding of how a firm is generating wealth for its shareholders. The dashed lines for the decomposition of ROCE into margin (and leverage) highlight that there are differences in the decompositions for ROA and ROCE, as will be discussed later (under the section "Relating ROA to ROCE"). The primary difference is that profit margins for ROA and ROCE are computed based on different measures of income in the numerator. Finally, the measures of margin, turnover, and leverage can be further dissected by means of various financial ratios prepared from different line items in the financial statements. Later sections in the chapter discuss ROA and ROCE, including the decomposition into components and various explanatory ratios. However, note that the two branches of analysis of net income displayed in Exhibit 4.1 are interrelated, especially the use of common-size analysis and alternative definitions of profits. Both of these can be incorporated into rate of return analysis, as we will do later in the chapter.

EARNINGS PER SHARE (EPS)

One of the most frequently used measures of profitability is EPS (earnings per common share). As Chapter 14 discusses more fully, analysts and investors frequently use multiples of EPS, referred to as *price-earnings ratios,* to value firms. EPS is the only financial ratio that GAAP requires firms to disclose on the face of the income statement and is covered explicitly by the opinion of the independent auditor.[3] This section briefly describes the calculation of EPS and discusses some of its uses and limitations.

[3]Financial Accounting Standards Board, *Statement of Financial Accounting Standards No. 128,* "Earnings per Share" (1997), *FASB Codification Topic 260.* International Accounting Standards Board, *International Accounting Standard No. 33,* "Earnings Per Share" (2003).

Calculating EPS

Simple Capital Structure: Basic EPS

Firms that do not have (1) outstanding convertible bonds or convertible preferred stock that holders can exchange for shares of common stock or (2) options or warrants that holders can use to acquire common stock have *simple* capital structures. For such firms, the accountant calculates basic EPS as follows:

$$\frac{\text{Basic EPS}}{\text{(Simple Capital Structure)}} = \frac{\text{Net Income} - \text{Preferred Stock Dividends}}{\text{Weighted Average Number of Common Shares Outstanding}}$$

The deduction of preferred stock dividends from net income yields income available to common shareholders, the residual claimants on a firm's profits. The numerator of basic EPS is adjusted for preferred stock dividends because the denominator includes only common shares outstanding. The denominator is a daily weighted average of common shares outstanding during the period, reflecting new stock issues, treasury stock acquisitions, and similar transactions.

Example 1. Cat Corporation had the following capital structure during its most recent year:

	January 1	December 31
Preferred Stock, $20 Par Value, 500 Shares Issued and Outstanding	$ 10,000	$ 10,000
Common Stock, $10 Par Value, 4,000 Shares Issued	40,000	40,000
Additional Paid-In Capital	50,000	50,000
Retained Earnings	80,000	85,600
Treasury Shares—Common (1,000 shares)	—	(30,000)
Total Shareholders' Equity	$180,000	$155,600

Retained earnings changed during the year as follows:

Retained Earnings, January 1	$ 80,000
Plus Net Income	7,500
Less Dividends:	
Preferred Stock	(500)
Common Stock	(1,400)
Retained Earnings, December 31	$ 85,600

The preferred stock is not convertible into common stock. The firm acquired 1,000 shares of treasury stock on July 1. No stock options or warrants are outstanding. The calculation of basic earnings per share for Cat Corporation follows:

$$\text{Basic EPS} = \frac{\$7{,}500 - \$500}{(0.5 \times 4{,}000) + (0.5 \times 3{,}000)} = \frac{\$7{,}000}{3{,}500} = \$2 \text{ per share}$$

Complex Capital Structure: Diluted EPS

Firms that have convertible securities and/or stock options or warrants outstanding have *complex* capital structures. Such firms must present two EPS amounts: basic EPS and diluted EPS. Diluted EPS reflects the dilution potential of convertible securities, options, and warrants. Dilution refers to the reduction in basic EPS that would result if holders of convertible securities exchanged them for shares of common stock or if holders of stock options or warrants exercised them. Firms include in diluted EPS calculations only those securities, options, and warrants that would reduce EPS; income and share dilution effects of equity instruments are excluded from both the numerator and denominator if their conversion would increase EPS (such securities would be referred to as "out of the money" and their effect on EPS as "antidilutive"). Accordingly, diluted EPS will always be less than (or equal to) basic EPS. This section describes the calculation of diluted EPS in general terms.

$$\begin{array}{c}\text{Diluted EPS}\\ \text{(Complex Capital Structure)}\end{array} = \frac{\begin{array}{c}\text{Net Income} - \text{Preferred}\\ \text{Stock Dividends}\end{array} + \begin{array}{c}\text{Adjustments for}\\ \text{Dilutive Securities}\end{array}}{\begin{array}{c}\text{Weighted Average}\\ \text{Number of Common}\\ \text{Shares Outstanding}\end{array} + \begin{array}{c}\text{Weighted Average Number}\\ \text{of Shares Issuable from}\\ \text{Dilutive Securities}\end{array}}$$

Adjustments for dilutive securities and the adjustment to weighted average number of shares outstanding presumes that the dilutive securities are converted to common shares *as of the beginning of the year.* To calculate diluted EPS, the accountant assumes the conversion of convertible bonds and convertible preferred stock and the exercise of stock options and warrants if their effect would be dilutive. The accountant adds back any interest expense (net of taxes) on convertible bonds and dividends on convertible preferred stock the firm subtracted in computing net income to common shareholders. Consistency would suggest that the accountant also add back to net income any compensation expense recognized on the employee stock options. However, U.S. GAAP and IFRS do not stipulate such an addback, but instead require firms to incorporate any unamortized compensation expense on those options into the calculation of the denominator of diluted EPS, as discussed next.

The diluted EPS computation adds common shares issuable on conversion of bonds and preferred stock and exercise of stock options and warrants to the denominator. The computation of the additional shares to be issued on the exercise of stock options assumes that the firm would repurchase common shares on the open market using an amount equal to the sum of (1) any cash proceeds from such exercise, (2) any unamortized compensation expense on those options, and (3) any tax benefits that would be credited to additional paid-in capital.[4] Only the net incremental shares issued (shares issued under options minus assumed shares repurchased) enter the computation of diluted EPS.

---

[4]Understanding the rationale for including unamortized compensation expense in the computation of the incremental shares issuable requires an understanding of the accounting for stock options, which is discussed in Chapter 6. In general terms, U.S. GAAP and IFRS view the value of stock options as a substitute for cash compensation. Firms expense this value over the expected period of benefit, which usually begins in the year firms grant the options and continues until the vesting date. The assumption underlying diluted EPS is that employees have exercised the options and the firm realizes a pseudo cash savings equal to the value of options not yet recognized, or amortized.

Example 2. Assume that Dawg Corporation has the same capital structure as Cat Corporation, except the preferred stock of Dawg Corporation is convertible into 1,000 shares of common stock. Also assume that Dawg Corporation has stock options outstanding that holders can currently exchange for 300 incremental shares of common stock.[5] The calculation of diluted EPS is as follows:

$$\text{Diluted EPS} = \frac{\$7{,}500 - \$500 + \$500}{(0.5 \times 4{,}000) + (0.5 \times 3{,}000) + (1.0 \times 1{,}000) + (1.0 \times 300)} = \frac{\$7{,}500}{4{,}800}$$

$$= \$1.56$$

The calculation assumes the conversion of the convertible preferred stock into common stock as of January 1. If conversion had taken place, the firm would not have paid preferred dividends during the year. Thus, the accountant adds back to the numerator of fully diluted earnings per share the $500 of preferred dividends, which the accountant subtracted in computing net income available to common stock when calculating basic earnings per share. The weighted average number of shares in the denominator increases for the 1,000 common shares the firm would issue on conversion of the preferred stock. The weighted average number of shares in the denominator also increases for the incremental shares issuable under stock option plans.

Refer to the income statement of PepsiCo in Appendix A. PepsiCo reports basic EPS of $3.26 and diluted EPS of $3.21 for 2008. PepsiCo's Note 11, "Net Income per Common Share" (Appendix A), shows the calculation of its EPS amounts. Basic EPS shows a subtraction from net income for preferred dividends. It also shows a subtraction for the redemption premium that PepsiCo paid when it redeemed some of the outstanding preferred stock.[6] Note 11 also indicates that the numerator of diluted EPS shows an addition for ESOP convertible preferred stock, which is dilutive; so the preferred dividends and redemption premium are added back to the numerator before calculating diluted EPS (based on the beginning-of-year conversion assumption). PepsiCo also reports the additional common shares issuable under stock option plans and from the convertible ESOP convertible preferred stock.

Criticisms of EPS

Critics of EPS as a measure of profitability point out that it does not consider the amount of assets or capital required to generate a particular level of earnings. Two firms with the same earnings and EPS are not equally profitable if one firm requires twice the amount of assets or capital to generate those earnings compared to the other firm. Also, the number of shares of common stock outstanding serves as a poor measure of the amount of capital in use. The number of shares outstanding usually relates to a firm's attempts to achieve a desirable trading range for its common stock. Suppose a firm has an aggregate market value for its common shares of $10 million. If the firm has 500,000 shares outstanding, the shares will sell for $20 per share. If the firm has 1 million shares outstanding, the shares will sell for $10 per share. The amount of capital in place is the same in both instances, but the number of shares outstanding (and therefore EPS) are different. A comparison of the EPS of PepsiCo and Coca-Cola is an example of how different EPS figures are not comparable. For 2008, Coca-Cola

[5]We are simplifying this example with the assumption of 300 *incremental* shares. An actual calculation would require separate computation of the proceeds from exercise, unamortized compensation expense, and associated tax benefits.

[6]The treatment of redemption premia in calculating basic EPS occurs infrequently and is beyond the scope of this book.

reported net income of $5.8 billion, higher than PepsiCo's $5.1 billion; however, PepsiCo reported higher basic EPS of $3.26 versus $2.51 for Coca-Cola because the two firms have very different numbers of shares outstanding. The comparison of EPS is not definitive about the relative performance of these two companies. Two firms can have identical earnings, common shareholders' equities, and ROCEs, but their EPSs will differ if they have different numbers of shares outstanding. Also, EPS is an ambiguous measure of changes in profitability over time because changes in shares outstanding over time can have disproportionate effects on the numerator and denominator. For example, a firm can experience reduced earnings during the year but report a higher EPS than it did the previous year if it repurchased sufficient shares during the period. When assessing earnings performance, the analyst must separate the impact of these two factors on EPS.

Despite these criticisms of EPS as a measure of profitability, it remains one of the focal points of the quarterly earnings announcement season and analysts frequently use it in valuing firms. The reason for its ubiquity is the direct comparability to firms' share prices. Chapter 14 discusses the use of EPS in valuation.

COMMON-SIZE ANALYSIS

A simple way of creating greater comparability across firms and for the same firm through time is common-size analysis. Common-size analysis is most frequently utilized in the analysis of profitability (the income statement), but it also can be used in the analysis of financial position (the balance sheet). Common-size income statements express all line items scaled by revenues (generally the largest line item on the income statement and the driver of many expenses); common-size balance sheets express all line items scaled by total assets (generally the largest line item on the balance sheet and reflective of resources used to generate returns to all providers of capital). Through the use of a common denominator, the common scaling enables figures across firms and across time (for the same firm) to be more comparable. For example, suppose a firm has ten times the sales of a competitor. The profitability of the two firms can be compared more meaningfully by scaling net income and the individual expense line items to a common denominator (each firm's total revenues) to remove the large discrepancy in the size of the two firms' operations.

Chapter 1 introduced common-size financial statements and examined PepsiCo and Coca-Cola (both a cross-sectional and a time-series analysis) for 2004–2008. Refer to Exhibits 1.18 and 1.20. The 2008 common-size figures scaled by revenues suggest that Coca-Cola shows a more favorable gross profit of 64 percent of revenues, relative to 53 percent for PepsiCo. Selling, general, and administrative expenses are similar for both companies, both being approximately 37 percent of revenues. Other line items contribute relatively limited differences, and the substantial difference in gross profits contributes to higher common-size net income for Coca-Cola relative to PepsiCo. Common-size analysis is a simple but powerful approach to understanding profitability. For example, the analyses in Exhibits 1.18 and 1.20 suggest that Coca-Cola realizes substantially higher profitability per dollar of sales than PepsiCo. However, to more deeply understand this comparison, an analyst must perform additional analysis to understand that a primary explanation for the higher gross profit at Coca-Cola is substantially greater presence and profitability in international beverage markets, despite PepsiCo's domestic operations being more profitable than those of Coca-Cola.

The common-size analysis of profitability across firms can be extended to time-series analysis as well. For example, Exhibits 1.18 and 1.20 show income statement data for five years for PepsiCo and Coca-Cola, respectively. Examining the time series for each company may suggest the direction in which various expenses are going. As noted previously, the primary difference between PepsiCo's and Coca-Cola's profitability in 2008 is due to the higher gross profit margins for Coca-Cola. Examining the trend in gross profit over the period 2004–2008 indicates that Coca-Cola's gross profit has varied from 64–66 percent, with no apparent trend. In contrast, PepsiCo's gross profit has ranged between 53 and 57 percent, with a monotonic downward trend. This suggests that PepsiCo's input costs are rising at a higher rate than increases in sales revenue or that the prices it is charging for products is declining or that it is shifting its revenue mix to lower margin products and markets. The MD&A suggests that pricing is generally increasing, so input prices must be the explanation. As discussed later in the chapter, PepsiCo reports that a primary driver of the decreased gross profit margin is higher commodity costs that could not be passed through to customers via price increases (for example, cooking oil and fuel).

Common-size analysis requires the analyst to be aware that percentages can change because of:

- changes in expenses in the numerator independent of changes in sales (for example, an increase in employee compensation levels),
- changes in sales independent of changes in expenses (for example, because the expense being examined is fixed for the period),
- interaction effects between the numerator and denominator (an increase in advertising expenses leads to an increase in sales), or
- coincident but independent changes in the numerator and denominator (that is, combinations of the other three possibilities).

Thus, although common-size analysis is useful, to fully understand patterns it reveals, the analyst must dig deeper into the economics of the firm's environment and the firm's strategy during the period being analyzed, as well as conduct further financial analysis using finer partitions of data. **That is why the six-step analytical framework of this book begins with an analysis of the firm's economic environment and strategy.** Note that FSAP performs the task of computing common-size financial statements automatically.

PERCENTAGE CHANGE ANALYSIS

Another way to analyze financial data is to compute percentage changes in individual line items, which also can be compared across firms or across time. Common-size analysis is useful because the process of dividing all line items on a financial statement by a common measure standardizes financial data such that the analyst can then compare different firms or the same firm across time. Percentage change analysis also permits the analyst to compare financial data because the transformations into percentage changes are comparable across firms or across time as well. However, the focus is not on the financial data themselves, but on the changes in individual line items through time. Percentage change analysis was introduced briefly in Chapter 1 along with common-size analysis. In addition to common-size figures, Exhibits 1.17 and 1.19 (balance sheets) and Exhibits 1.18 and 1.20 (income statements) also provide percentage change figures for PepsiCo and Coca-Cola, respectively, over 2005–2008. Note the loss of one year of data relative to common-size analysis, which simply reflects that financial data for 2004–2008 are required for computing changes; thus, five years of data yields four changes.

In the common-size analysis discussed above, we noted significant differences in the gross profit percentages between PepsiCo and Coca-Cola. The analyst might be further interested in whether there are trends in gross profits as a percentage of sales for PepsiCo relative to Coca-Cola. An increasing difference between the two companies would indicate that PepsiCo's performance is declining relative to Coca-Cola's; a decreasing difference would indicate the opposite. Examining percentage change analysis is helpful in further understanding differences revealed in common-size analysis. Refer to Exhibits 1.18 and 1.20, which show four-year percentage change analyses for PepsiCo and Coca-Cola, respectively. During 2005–2006, PepsiCo's revenue growth exceeded that of Coca-Cola, but this reversed in 2007–2008. More importantly, the percentage change of PepsiCo's cost of sales exceeds the percentage change in revenues for each year, which results in the decreased gross profits highlighted in the common-size analysis above. In addition, PepsiCo shows double-digit increases in SG&A expenses in every year except 2006. Chapter 10 discusses forecasting, and a helpful starting point is to examine prior percentage changes (and common-size data) to identify trends that may persist in the future. However, a limitation of percentage change analysis is that nonrecurring items or changes in "other" categories can be associated with extreme percentage changes. This can be seen for PepsiCo and Coca-Cola for a number of line items, including "Other operating charges," "Restructuring and impairment," and "Other income (loss)."

ALTERNATIVE DEFINITIONS OF PROFITS

When the analyst assesses the profitability of a firm in the recent past, the concern is with all revenues, expenses, gains, and losses that affected the economic value of the firm. However, when the analyst uses measures of past profitability to forecast the firm's future profitability, the emphasis is on those revenues, expenses, gains, and losses that are expected to persist. If net income in the recent past includes nonrecurring gains from sales of assets or nonrecurring losses from unusual asset impairment or restructuring charges, the analyst might decide to eliminate those items from past earnings when using past earnings to forecast future earnings. For purposes of valuation, the analyst strives to forecast the sustainable earnings of a firm. The famous investment text by Benjamin Graham and David Dodd refers to this concept as "earnings power."[7] Sustainable earnings, or earnings power, is the level of earnings and the growth in the level of earnings expected to persist in the future. Nonrecurring gains and losses may occur in future periods, but the analyst cannot anticipate their occurrence, their timing, or their amount with sufficient precision to include them in sustainable earnings. Thus, a key to developing forecasts that are useful for valuation is to identify components of bottom-line earnings that are recurring.

Comprehensive Income

Most financial statement users analyze net income as a summary bottom-line measure of performance. However, both U.S. GAAP and IFRS require presentation of comprehensive income, which is defined as "The change in equity (net assets) of a business entity during a period from transactions and other events and circumstances from nonowner sources. It includes all changes in equity during a period except those resulting from investments by owners and distributions to owners."[8] Thus, items included as part of "other comprehensive income" are added to or deducted from net income. Under U.S. GAAP, presentation of comprehensive income can be at the bottom of the income statement, can be a separate statement, or can be included in the statement of changes in shareholders' equity; IFRS permits all alternatives except the statement of changes in shareholders' equity. The presentation of comprehensive income is required only if the company has items that qualify as other comprehensive income. Such items include certain foreign currency translation items, defined benefit pension plan and other postretirement plan adjustments, certain unrealized gains and losses on investment securities and derivatives, and other adjustments.

[7] Benjamin Graham and David Dodd, *Security Analysis* (New York: McGraw-Hill), 1934.

[8] *FASB Codification 220-10-20.*

The overriding objective of reporting items of other comprehensive income is to present an *all-inclusive* picture of a company's economic events during a period, where items included as other comprehensive income are generally more likely to be *temporary* in nature and may likely reverse prior to ultimate realization of the currently recognized gains and losses. As with net income, reliance on comprehensive income as a summary measure of performance is not emphasized as much as an understanding of the components. The primary interest in examining the components is to assess situations in which certain components are likely to persist.

Operating Income, EBIT, EBITDA, and Other Profit Measures

Another factor driving the analysis of different aggregations of income statement line items is that firms have different organizational and capital structures. As a consequence, it is sometimes helpful to examine profitability prior to considering a variety of expenses that vary depending on different organizational or capital structures. Thus, analysts are sometimes interested in analyzing different levels of profitability. Examples include gross profit, operating income, EBIT, EBITDA, EBITDAR, NOPAT, EBIAT, and earnings excluding any number of recognized expenses.[9] For example, gross profit for manufacturing firms (revenues less cost of goods sold) is a key measure of profitability because it captures the amount of profits generated by the sale of primary products that are available to cover other firm costs, such as salaries, general and administrative expenses, interest payments, and taxes. Larger gross profits may reflect a price premium advantage due to brand assets or patents or may be due cost efficiencies due to low-cost supplier relationships or technological advantages. Thus, analysts frequently start with an income statement as reported by a firm and selectively create measures of profits that aggregate various components of revenues and expenses. As we saw in the common-size income statement analysis in Exhibits 1.18 and 1.20, gross profits is a key component of profitability when comparing PepsiCo and Coca-Cola, but PepsiCo's income statement (in Appendix A) does not report a separate line item for gross profit. Thus, the analyst should be adept at reconfiguring income statements to suit different purposes, especially cross-sectional comparisons. Similarly, measures of profitability farther down the income statement are also common, especially EBITDA. Unfortunately, many analysts and investors confuse EBITDA as a proxy for a firm's cash flows, as discussed in Chapter 3. If the objective of analyzing EBITDA is that it is a proxy for a firm's cash flows, it does not make sense to use EBITDA in lieu of operating cash flows, which are easily found on the statement of cash flows. Each metric identified above can be informative, but none should be viewed as the single indicator of financial performance.

Segment Profitability

Many firms consist of more than one operating segment. Both U.S. GAAP and IFRS require that companies provide measures of profitability and certain additional information for each segment. The definition of segments follows the "management approach," which leaves the identification of operating segments up to managers based on how they manage the operations of the company. For example, PepsiCo discloses three operating segments

---

[9]The acronyms mentioned are as follows: EBIT = earnings before interest and taxes; EBITDA = earnings before interest, taxes, depreciation, and amortization; EBITDAR = earnings before interest, taxes, depreciation, amortization, and rent; NOPAT = net operating profits after tax; EBIAT = earnings before interest after tax.

(Americas foods, Americas beverages, and international) and PepsiCo further partitions the foods and international segments into smaller segments determined by geography (see discussion later in this chapter). Most often, disclosure of segment profitability data is presented in the footnotes to the financial statements. Given the open-ended management approach to these required disclosures, there is generally wide variation in the details provided across firms, which makes cross-sectional comparisons of segments challenging. However, firms are required to reconcile revenues and other disclosed items presented for segments to the corresponding totals for the firm. Firms often do not allocate all general and administrative expenses to individual segments, so it also is challenging to compare performance of a segment within a multisegment firm to that of a pure-play firm, for which such costs are included on the income statement.

Pro Forma, Adjusted, or Street Earnings

Although it is useful to examine alternative levels and sources of profits in the income statement, the analyst should know that managers of firms have incentives to classify certain expenses as one-time or nonrecurring because the managers are aware that analysts are most interested in sustainable earnings. This is frequently accomplished with the earnings release disclosures that accompany earnings announcements. Managers frequently discuss specific computations of "earnings" that exclude certain line items and refer to such earnings as "pro forma" or "adjusted" earnings; collectively, such presentations of earnings, which are widely followed on Wall Street, are called "Street" earnings. Research Director Chuck Hill commented on the practice, "What companies are trying to do is entice analysts into excluding certain charges and value them only on that basis."[10] Exhibit 4.2 shows a hypothetical approach to computing pro forma earnings by sequentially arguing that certain line items on the income statement are nonrecurring or are not relevant to the assessment of current profitability. The example shows revenues of \$100, total expenses of \$50, and net income of \$50. Consider a manager who argues that Expense 5 is a one-time expense, such as severance payments to workers from a closed plant. The manager would report pro forma earnings of \$60 after

EXHIBIT 4.2

Pro Forma Earnings Example

		GAAP	Pro Forma 1	Pro Forma 2	Pro Forma 3	Pro Forma 4	Pro Forma 5
Revenues		\$100	\$100	\$100	\$100	\$100	\$100
– Expenses:	*Expense 1*	(10)	(10)	(10)	(10)	(10)	—
	Expense 2	(10)	(10)	(10)	(10)	—	—
	Expense 3	(10)	(10)	(10)	—	—	—
	Expense 4	(10)	(10)	—	—	—	—
	Expense 5	(10)	—	—	—	—	—
= Earnings		\$ 50	\$ 60	\$ 70	\$ 80	\$ 90	\$100

[10]Elizabeth MacDonald, "Varied Profit Reports by Firms Create Confusion," *The Wall Street Journal* (August 24, 1999), p. C1.

excluding this charge (Pro Forma 1 in Exhibit 4.2). Expense 4 might be for an expenditure such as advertising or R&D (research and development); so a manager might claim that these expenditures generate assets and are not relevant for assessing current performance. Excluding Expense 4 yields pro forma earnings of $70 (Pro Forma 2 in Exhibit 4.2). The manager also might claim that expenses such as depreciation and amortization should be ignored and not deducted in the measurement of "earnings" simply because such expenses do not involve cash outflows in the current period. If Expense 3 in Exhibit 4.2 represents depreciation and amortization, the manager might report and discuss Pro Forma 3, which reports earnings of $80. A scheming manager even might be inclined to argue against including *all* expenses, ending up reporting pro forma earnings equal to revenues without including any expenses (Pro Forma 5 in Exhibit 4.2). This may seem far-fetched, but it is what Internet firms did during the growth of this sector in the late 1990s. Managers of such firms argued that the key to assessing performance was the level of and growth in revenues, which reflected first-mover advantages to gain market share and growth in customers who would secure the firm's profitability in the future. Needless to say, most market observers agree that the valuation of such firms reached irrational levels and resulted in a subsequent stock market crash, partially attributable to the temporary disregard for profitability measured to include operating expenses.

An empirical research study by Bradshaw and Sloan (2002) revealed a significant increase in the trend of managers reporting pro forma earnings higher than bottom-line net income, primarily by excluding certain charges and expenses from reported "pro forma" earnings.[11] Exhibit 4.3 shows results from the study. The widening gap between plots in the graph makes it clear that firms increasingly excluded expenses from reported pro forma earnings beginning as far back as the late 1980s. In a study of how managers highlight nonrecurring gains

EXHIBIT 4.3

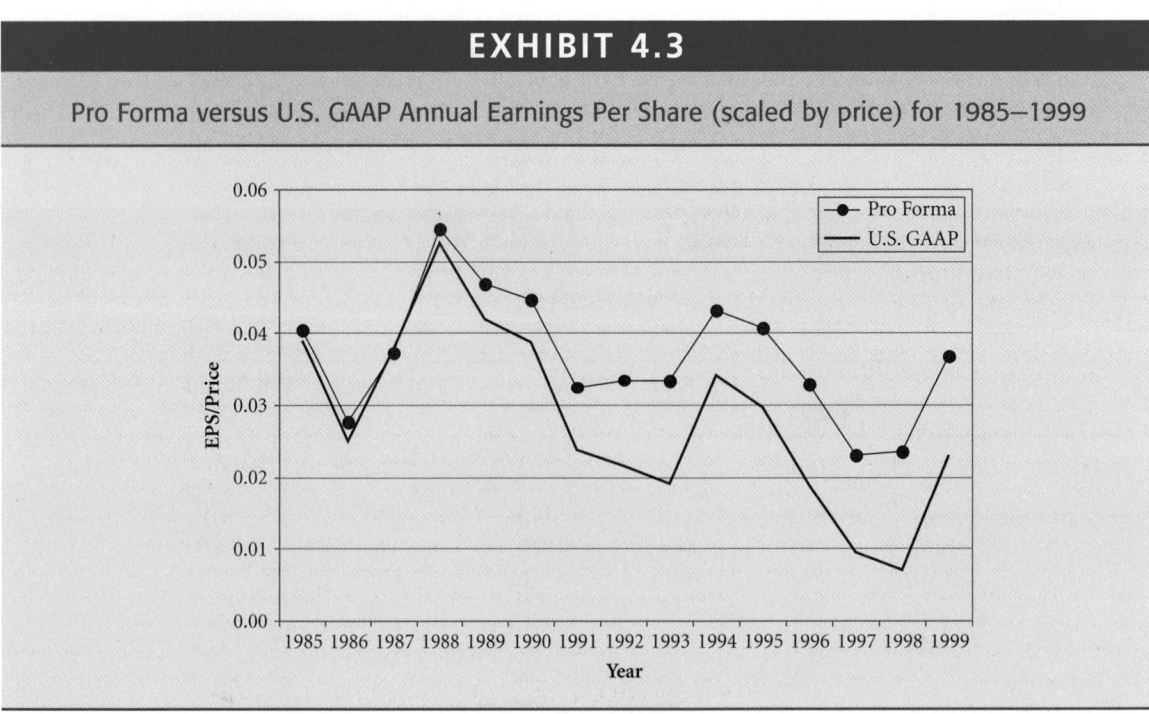

Pro Forma versus U.S. GAAP Annual Earnings Per Share (scaled by price) for 1985–1999

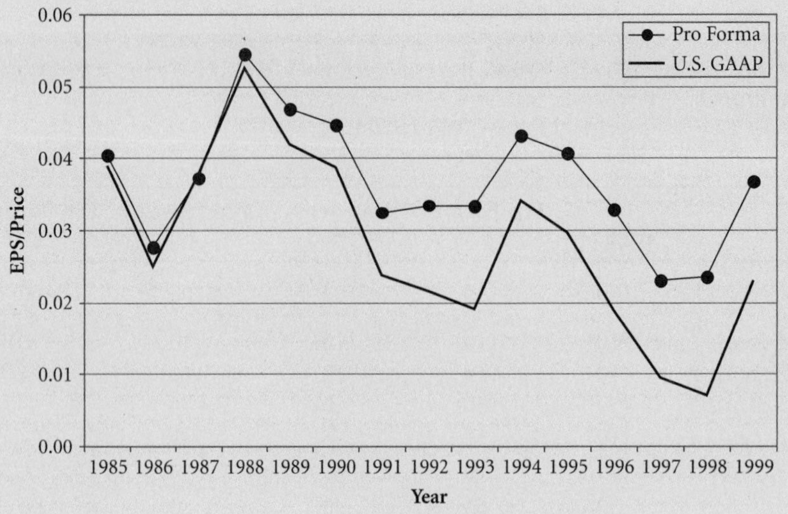

[11]Mark T. Bradshaw and Richard G. Sloan, "GAAP versus the Street: An Empirical Assessment of Two Alternative Definitions of Earnings," *Journal of Accounting Research*, Vol. 40, No. 1 (March 2002), pp. 41–66.

and losses, Schrand and Walther (2000) discovered that managers tend to highlight unusual or one-time expenses or losses during the quarter in which they occur.[12] However, when that quarter is used as a benchmark for the announcement of the same quarter's earnings in the next year, managers tend not to remind investors that the previous year included an unusual or one-time expense or loss. This makes the earnings announcement at that time appear more favorable in terms of year-to-year improvement in profitability.

In reaction to perceived abuses in the reporting of profits, the U.S. Securities and Exchange Commission (SEC) became concerned that the emphasis placed on pro forma earnings by managers risked misleading the average investor. The SEC issued Regulation G in 2003, which deals with what the SEC calls "non-GAAP" earnings, otherwise known in the investment community as pro forma earnings. Regulation G prohibits firms from placing more emphasis on pro forma earnings relative to bottom-line GAAP earnings or from identifying an amount as nonrecurring or unusual when such amounts have occurred in the past or are likely to recur in the future. Nevertheless, the reporting of non-GAAP (or pro forma) earnings is not prohibited outright, so investors must be diligent in understanding the composition of alternative measures of profits. For example, firms often include financial highlights in their annual reports but use small fonts for footnotes indicating that certain charges have been excluded from the figures presented. However, many firms now make it easier for investors to understand how management views nonrecurring or unusual charges with separate disclosures. For example, in PepsiCo's MD&A (Appendix B), the company includes a section titled "Reconciliation of GAAP and Non-GAAP Information," which shows various measures of profitability for PepsiCo, after excluding various charges such as mark-to-market losses and restructuring and impairment charges. The next section discusses whether and how to adjust measures of profitability such as ROA for nonrecurring or unusual charges.

RATE OF RETURN ON ASSETS (ROA)

The right-hand branch of Exhibit 4.1 relates to analysis of profitability using rate of return measures. Rate of return measures presume that a certain amount of investment generates economic profits. A simple example is interest earned on a savings account. A straightforward computation of the rate of return on such an investment is the interest income earned divided by the amount deposited. Conceptually, the analysis of returns to creditors and equity shareholders is similar. In the analysis of financial statements, the two most common measures of rate of return are ROA (return on assets) and ROCE. Our discussion of rate of return analysis begins with ROA. The next section builds on this discussion, transitioning to an examination of ROCE.

The rate of ROA measures a firm's success in using assets to generate earnings independent of the financing of those assets. ROA takes as given the particular set of environmental factors and strategic choices that a firm makes (such as product markets, operating decisions, and financing policies) and focuses on how well a firm has used its assets to generate earnings in a particular period. Most importantly, ROA ignores the means and costs of financing the firm's net assets (that is, the proportion of debt versus equity financing and the costs of those forms of capital).

The analyst calculates ROA as follows:

$$\text{ROA} = \frac{\text{Net Income} + (1 - \text{Tax Rate})(\text{Interest Expense}) + \text{Minority Interest in Earnings}}{\text{Average Total Assets}}$$

[12]Catherine M. Schrand and Beverly R. Walther, "Strategic Benchmarks in Earnings Announcements: The Selective Disclosure of Prior-Period Earnings Components," *The Accounting Review*, Vol. 75, No. 2 (April 2000), pp. 151–177.

The numerator of ROA adjusts net income to exclude the effects of any financing costs. Thus, as discussed in the previous section on alternative definitions of profitability, the measure of profits pertinent to ROA is net income *before* financing costs. If a firm has income from discontinued operations or extraordinary gains or losses, the analyst might exclude those items and start with net income from continuing operations instead of net income if the objective is to measure a firm's sustainable profitability.

Because accountants subtract interest expense when computing net income, the analyst must add it back when computing ROA. However, firms can deduct interest expense in measuring taxable income. Therefore, the *incremental* effect of interest expense on net income equals one minus the marginal tax rate times interest expense.[13] That is, the analyst adds back the full amount of interest expense to net income and then subtracts, or eliminates, the tax savings from that interest expense.

The tax savings from interest expense depends on the statutory tax rate in the tax jurisdiction where the firm raises its debt. As of the date this text was written, the statutory federal tax rate is 35 percent in the United States. Firms must disclose in a note to the financial statements why the average income tax rate (defined as income tax expense divided by net income before income taxes) differs from the federal statutory tax rate of 35 percent. The statutory federal rate will differ from a firm's average tax rate because of (1) state, local, and foreign tax rates that differ from 35 percent (Chapter 8 provides a discussion of these effects) and (2) revenues and expenses that firms include in accounting income but that do not impact taxable income (that is, permanent differences as described in Chapter 2). The analyst can approximate the combined statutory federal, state, local, and foreign tax rate applicable to tax savings from interest expense using 35 percent plus or minus the amounts disclosed related to (1) above. Permanent differences in (2) usually do not relate to interest expense and therefore should not affect the statutory tax rate applicable to interest expense deductions. To simplify the calculations, we will follow the common practice of using the *statutory* federal tax rate of 35 percent in the computations of the tax savings from interest in the numerator of ROA throughout this book. Because accountants do not subtract dividends on preferred and common stocks in measuring net income, calculating the numerator of ROA requires no adjustment for dividends.[14]

The rationale for adding back the minority interest in earnings relates to attaining consistency in the numerator and the denominator of ROA. The denominator of ROA includes all assets of the consolidated entity, not just the parent company's share. Net income in the numerator, however, represents the parent's earnings plus the parent's share of the earnings of consolidated subsidiaries. The accountant computes consolidated earnings by combining the earnings of the parent and consolidated subsidiaries and then subtracting the minority interest's claim on the earnings of consolidated subsidiaries. Consistency with the inclusion of all of the assets of the consolidated entity in the denominator of ROA requires that the numerator include all of the earnings of the consolidated entity, not just the parent's share. The addback of the minority interest in earnings accomplishes this objective. Most publicly traded corporations, including PepsiCo, do not disclose the minority interest in earnings because its amount, if any, is usually immaterial. Thus, the analyst makes this adjustment only for significant minority interests.

---

[13]The marginal tax rate times interest expense is the *interest tax shield.* An interest tax shield is the reduction in taxes payable for firms that deduct interest expense in the computation of income tax liability.

[14]One could argue that the analyst should exclude returns from short-term investments of excess cash (that is, interest revenue) from the numerator of ROA and the short-term investments from the denominator of ROA under the view that such investments are negative financings (that is, savings rather than borrowings). We do not make this adjustment when computing ROA, although we consider the effect of such short-term investments in the discussion of valuation in Chapters 10–14.

Calculating the numerator is usually accomplished most easily by starting with net income, as listed above, and that will be our approach. Equivalently, however, one could start with earnings before interest and taxes and deduct taxes applicable to pretax profits. For example, the numerator could also be stated as follows:

$$\text{Revenues} - \text{Cost of Goods Sold} - \text{All Other Expenses (Excluding Interest Expense)} \\ - \text{Adjusted Taxes}$$

The difficulty with this specification is that "adjusted taxes" means taxes on the profits of the firm before deducting interest expense, which is not equal to income tax expense on the income statement. The difference is the tax savings associated with the interest deductible on tax returns, which is approximated as the marginal tax rate times interest expense. We label the numerator as in the first equation above, but analysts occasionally refer to this construct by acronyms such as NOPAT (net operating profit after taxes) or EBIAT (earnings before interest after taxes).[15]

Because net income before financing costs in the numerator of ROA reports the results for a period of time, the optimal denominator uses a measure of average assets in use during that same period. This computation aligns the income measure in the numerator with the average assets in place during the period. Using average total assets is not mandatory, however, in the sense that using beginning total assets is not necessarily wrong. (In fact, if total assets have not changed significantly during the period, there will be little difference between the beginning amount and the average.) The use of average total assets is a simple way to account for the changing level of investments in total assets upon which profits are judged. Thus, for a nonseasonal business, an average of assets at the beginning and end of the year is usually satisfactory. For a seasonal business, the analyst might use an average of assets at the end of each quarter.

Refer to the financial statements for PepsiCo in Appendix A. Also refer to the ROA and other ratio computations in the Analysis worksheet in FSAP, which are presented in Appendix C. The calculation of ROA for 2008 is as follows:

$$\text{ROA} = \frac{\begin{matrix}\text{Net Income from} \\ \text{Continuing Operations}\end{matrix} + \begin{matrix}(1 - \text{Tax Rate}) \times \\ (\text{Interest Expense})\end{matrix} + \begin{matrix}\text{Minority Interest} \\ \text{in Earnings}\end{matrix}}{\text{Average Total Assets}}$$

$$15.2\% = \frac{\$5{,}142 + (1 - 0.35)(\$329) + \$0}{0.5(\$35{,}994 + \$34{,}628)}$$

As noted earlier in the chapter, the analyst should consider whether reported net income includes any unusual or nonrecurring items that might affect assessments of a firm's ongoing profitability. The notes to the financial statements and the MD&A provide information for making these assessments. PepsiCo includes a section in its MD&A (Appendix B) labeled "Items Affecting Comparability." PepsiCo lists several items affecting net income that the analyst might consider unusual or nonrecurring (such as mark-to-market fair value adjustments and restructuring and impairment charges). If the objective is to measure the sustainable profitability of PepsiCo, the analyst might decide to adjust the reported amounts for such items. Chapter 9 discusses and illustrates these adjustments more fully.

[15]Often analysts calculate EBIAT by deducting tax expense from the income statement, not including the adjustment for taxes on interest. For firms with limited amounts of interest-bearing debt, usually this is not a material omission. However, as with any ratio or financial computation, analysts should know whether trade-offs are being made for computational ease but at the expense of deviating from a theoretically correct construct.

In preparing a time-series analysis of ROA for 2006–2008, analysts should consider adjusting PepsiCo's reported net income for the following five items, all highlighted by PepsiCo in its MD&A. The following subsections discuss adjustments for each of these items in more detail.

1. For 2008, PepsiCo reports $543 million of pretax impairment and restructuring charges ($408 million after taxes) related to the closure of six plants under the company's Productivity for Growth program. For 2007, restructuring and impairment charges are $102 million ($70 million after tax); for 2006, such charges are $67 million ($43 million after tax).
2. For 2008, PepsiCo reports negative $346 million of mark-to-market adjustments (negative $223 million after taxes) related to commodity derivatives, for which gains and losses must be recognized immediately in income. For 2007, the mark-to-market adjustment is a positive $19 million ($12 million after tax); for 2006, the mark-to-market adjustment is negative $18 million (negative $12 million after tax).
3. For 2007, PepsiCo reports $129 million of tax benefits relative to favorable resolution of certain foreign tax matters; for 2006, PepsiCo recognized tax benefits of $602 million from favorable resolution of domestic tax matters.
4. For 2008, PepsiCo reports an after-tax charge of $114 million in bottling equity income ($138 million pre-tax charge), representing PepsiCo's share of Pepsi Bottling Group's (PBG's) impairment charges related to business in Mexico.
5. For 2006 only, PepsiCo reports an after-tax benefit of $18 million ($21 million pre-tax bottling equity income) related to PepsiCo's share of a favorable tax settlement from the conclusion of an audit by the Internal Revenue Service (IRS) of PBG's income tax returns for 1999–2000.

Impairment and Restructuring Charges

The first and fourth items in the preceding list of possible adjustments result from the closing of plants or impairment charges. PepsiCo closed manufacturing plants and other facilities, which required the firm to write off or write down the amounts appearing on the balance sheet for these plants and other facilities and to provide severance payments to employees; similarly, PBG began a restructuring initiative, triggering charges in 2008 related to operations in Mexico. PepsiCo recognized restructuring or impairment charges for the three recent years, and such charges are common going further back in time. When deciding whether to eliminate these charges as part of assessing sustainable profitability, the analyst will likely consider whether the plant closures are complete or will likely continue. PepsiCo does not disclose specific information about its plans in this regard, so the analyst must predict based on events of the recent past and knowledge of the firm's strategy and industry. The existence of PepsiCo's Productivity for Growth Program and recent history suggest that such charges will continue, supporting an analyst's decision to leave them in earnings when assessing profitability. Moreover, one could argue that "if it is not one thing, it will be another" and implicitly acknowledge that nonrecurring or unusual charges are more common than the nomenclature implies.

On the other hand, PepsiCo will not likely continue to close manufacturing facilities indefinitely. Also, closing such plants is not central to PepsiCo's ongoing activities, which include manufacturing and distributing foods and beverages. Thus, the analyst could decide in this case to eliminate such charges. A third approach is to leave the charges in earnings but de-emphasize them when contextually analyzing ongoing profitability, which is a fairly common approach.

We follow the second approach and eliminate the charges in 2006–2008 based on their peripheral nature to PepsiCo's central operations and the assumption that the closing of manufacturing facilities is largely complete. (We view the decision whether to eliminate the charges in this case as very close to call and could easily have concluded not to eliminate them based on their recurring nature in the recent past. In Chapter 10, we project future financial statements for PepsiCo based on the assumption that these charges will not be recurring.) Our decision to eliminate the charges is also due in part to the benefits of describing the elimination procedure, which we demonstrate later in this section.

Mark-to-Market Accounting Adjustments

The second item results from fluctuations in commodity derivatives, which PepsiCo's corporate finance group manages on behalf of all divisions. Prices of commodity derivatives are notoriously volatile, so it is not surprising that PepsiCo realizes adjustments in all three years. The question for the analyst is whether to cleanse reported earnings of such charges when analyzing profitability. The argument to exclude them is that they are tangential to core operations and that price movements of commodities are unpredictable. However, because the commodity derivatives cover "energy, fruit and other raw materials," it seems compelling that these are primary inputs into PepsiCo's core operations and hence not tangential. Thus, we do *not* exclude these charges from reported income during 2006–2008.

Tax Benefits

The third and fifth items are for the settlement of income taxes for PepsiCo and PBG for ongoing businesses in 2006 and 2007. The tax benefits do not appear to relate to earnings of current years, but to those of earlier years (for example, the $602 million benefit recognized in 2006 related to tax returns for 1998–2002 and the $18 million benefit related to PBG's tax returns for 1999–2000). Because PepsiCo continues to operate these businesses, we eliminate the tax benefits realized in 2006 and 2007 because the amounts are part of a negotiated settlement with taxing authorities, which is inherently unpredictable.

In summary, we adjust net income for all items listed above, except for the second item relating to mark-to-market adjustments of commodity derivative contracts. All adjustments should be net of income tax effects. If firms disclose the income tax effect, we use the reported amounts. Otherwise, we assume that the current marginal federal tax rate applies. PepsiCo discloses the pretax and after-tax amounts for each of these items in the section of the MD&A labeled "Items Affecting Comparability." The adjustments to net income appear in Exhibit 4.4. It is important to carefully consider the sign of the adjustments in Exhibit 4.4. Income-reducing charges such as impairments and restructuring charges are *added back* to income before income taxes, which is intuitive. The adjustment for tax effects is less intuitive, however. For example, because impairments and restructuring charges are associated with reduced income tax expense (to the extent that such amounts are tax deductible), removing these charges from the computation of income before taxes requires an adjustment to *increase* the level of tax expense; hence, the adjustments in Exhibit 4.4 must be added back to income tax expense. Similarly, tax benefits from settlements with taxing authorities reduced reported income tax expense, so adjusting net income to remove the effects of these settlements requires that such amounts also be added back to income tax expense.

The adjusted ROA for PepsiCo for 2008 is as follows:

$$16.7\% = \frac{\$5{,}664 + (1 - 0.35)(\$329) + \$0}{0.5(\$35{,}994 + \$34{,}628)} = \frac{\$5{,}878}{\$35{,}311}$$

We make similar adjustments for impairment and restructuring charges in 2007 and 2006 and the tax benefits in 2007 and 2006. As shown in Exhibit 4.4, adjusted net income is

EXHIBIT 4.4

Adjustments to Reported Net Income for Unusual and Nonrecurring Items for PepsiCo (amounts in millions)

	2008	2007	2006
Reported Income before Income Taxes	$7,021	$7,631	$6,989
Impairment and Restructuring Charges: (PepsiCo + PBG)	681	102	67
Adjusted Income from Continuing Operations before Income Taxes	$7,702	$7,733	$7,056
Reported Income Tax Expense	$1,879	$1,973	$1,347
Tax Effects of Impairment and Restructuring Charges:			
2008: $681 − $408 − $114	159	—	—
2007: $102 − $70	—	32	—
2006: $67 − $43	—	—	24
Tax Benefits from Settlements with Taxing Authorities:	—	129	602
	—	—	18
Adjusted Income Tax Expense	$2,038	$2,134	$1,991
Adjusted Net Income	$5,664	$5,599	$5,065
Reported Net Income	$5,142	$5,658	$5,642

higher than reported net income for 2008, but in 2007 and 2006, adjusted income is lower than reported net income.

Calculations for both unadjusted and adjusted ROA are shown for all three years in Exhibit 4.5. Note that the numerator of ROA based on as-reported net income declines from $5,804 million in 2007 to $5,356 million in 2008, but the numerator based on adjusted net income increases in 2008 relative to 2007 (from $5,745 million to $5,878 million), largely due to the purging of large restructuring and impairment charges in 2008. ROA based on reported net income is 15.2 percent, 18.0 percent, and 18.8 percent in 2008, 2007, and 2006, respectively. Analyzing the time series of PepsiCo's ROA based on reported net income, performance in 2008 appears well below that in previous years. However, adjusting net income for nonrecurring items that we hypothesize affect comparability across years, ROA for 2008 appears more in line with recent ROA (16.7 percent versus 16.9–17.8 percent). Refer to the Analysis worksheet in the FSAP model for a five-year time series of these and other ratios computed based on as-reported and adjusted figures (also presented in Appendix C).

FSAP

Two Comments on the Calculation of ROA

First, some analysts subtract average non-interest-bearing liabilities (such as accounts payable and accrued liabilities) from average total assets in the denominator of ROA, the argument being that these items are sources of indirect financing. An alternative argument for reducing total assets by non-interest-bearing liabilities is that ROA is better characterized as a return on invested capital when items that are not directly invested capital (such

EXHIBIT 4.5

Calculations of Unadjusted and Adjusted ROA for PepsiCo
(Data for total assets from Appendix C
and adjusted net income data from Exhibit 4.4.)

	2008	2007	2006
Total assets—Beginning of year	$34,628	$29,930	$31,727
Total assets—End of year	$35,994	$34,628	$29,930
Average total assets	$35,311	$32,279	$30,829
Net income	$ 5,142	$ 5,658	$ 5,642
Adjusted net income	$ 5,664	$ 5,599	$ 5,065
Interest expense	$ 329	$ 224	$ 239
Net income + (1 − 0.35) × Interest expense	$ 5,356	$ 5,804	$ 5,797
Adjusted net income + (1 − 0.35) × Interest expense	$ 5,878	$ 5,745	$ 5,220
ROA (unadjusted)	15.2%	18.0%	18.8%
ROA (adjusted)	16.7%	17.8%	16.9%

as accounts payable) are purged from total assets. Economics suggests that when liabilities do not provide for *explicit* interest charges, the creditor charges *implicit* interest by adjusting the terms of the contract, such as offering discounts for those who do pay immediately or setting higher prices for those who do not pay immediately. The numerator of the ROA calculation is a measure of income before deducting financing costs; therefore, an alternative approach would be to adjust net income for both explicit and implicit financing costs. Unfortunately, it is difficult to reliably estimate the implicit interest charges associated with non-interest-bearing liabilities such as accounts payable and accrued liabilities and to reclassify the implicit increments for financing charges in cost of goods sold and selling, general and administrative expenses to interest expense (which is added back to net income). Adjusting prefinancing income this way would increase the measure of operating income in the numerator, increasing calculated ROA. (An alternative of reducing the denominator by subtracting non-interest-bearing liabilities from total assets also would increase calculated ROA.) Despite the logic of adjusting income in the ROA calculation to account for implicit interest or adjusting total assets for indirectly invested capital, in all but extreme cases, the materiality of such theoretically correct adjustments is questionable and the degree of precision in estimating such amounts is low. Consequently, the examples and problems in this book follow the conventional practice of using average total assets in the denominator of ROA, making no adjustment for non-interest-bearing liabilities.

Second, it is important to note that although we adjusted the numerator of ROA for unusual or nonrecurring items, we did not adjust the denominator. This implicitly states that the effects of the unusual or nonrecurring items on profits are not persistent but that their effects on total assets are persistent. For example, consider the non-cash impairment charges that were added back to net income. These impairment charges reduced the carrying value of assets. Thus, our adjustment added back to net income the effect of the write-down but included the effect in the ending balance of total assets, which will be lower because of the write-down. Thus, our adjustment to the numerator (increase) paired with the impact of the unadjusted balance sheet write-down in the denominator (decrease) leads to an upward bias in current period ROA. The logic behind this seemingly inconsistent treatment is motivated by a desire to compute sustainable ROA. The current period restructuring charges will not persist in future periods, but the asset write-downs are permanent (those assets are worthless); thus, the adjusted ROA provides a better indicator of the ROA we might expect to observe next period even though it is a biased measured of the current period's ROA. Again, our approach reflects conventional practice, but the astute analyst should understand that blindly ignoring negative charges on the income statement but allowing them to affect the balance sheet can affect adjusted performance. This caveat echoes the cautionary discussion earlier in the chapter regarding the potentially misleading practice of managers emphasizing pro forma earnings.

Disaggregating ROA

The analyst obtains further insight into the behavior of ROA by disaggregating it into profit margin for ROA and total assets turnover (also simply referred to as *assets turnover*) components as follows:

$$\textbf{ROA} = \textbf{Profit Margin for ROA} \times \textbf{Assets Turnover}$$

$$\frac{\text{Net Income + Interest Expense (net of taxes) + Minority Interest in Earnings}}{\text{Average Total Assets}} = \frac{\text{Net Income + Interest Expense (net of taxes) + Minority Interest in Earnings}}{\text{Sales}} \times \frac{\text{Sales}}{\text{Average Total Assets}}$$

The profit margin for ROA indicates the ability of a firm to generate earnings for a particular level of sales.[16] Assets turnover indicates the ability to manage the level of investment in assets for a particular level of sales or, to put it another way, the ability to generate sales from a particular level of investment in assets. The assets turnover ratio indicates the firm's ability to use assets to generate sales, and the profit margin for ROA indicates the firm's ability to use sales to generate profits.

The disaggregation of ROA for PepsiCo for 2008, after adjusting for nonrecurring items, is as follows:

$$\textbf{ROA} = \textbf{Profit Margin for ROA} \times \textbf{Assets Turnover}$$

$$\frac{\$\ 5{,}878}{\$35{,}311} = \frac{\$\ 5{,}878}{\$43{,}251} \times \frac{\$43{,}251}{\$35{,}311}$$

$$16.7\% = 13.6\% \times 1.22$$

Exhibit 4.6 summarizes ROA, profit margin for ROA, and assets turnover for PepsiCo for 2006–2008. PepsiCo's profit margin for ROA has been declining steadily. However, PepsiCo has increased assets turnover. After exploring economic and strategic factors underlying ROA and its components in the next section, we return to analyzing the profit margin for ROA and assets turnover of PepsiCo in greater depth.

---

[16]One might argue that the analyst should use total *revenues*, not just *sales*, in the denominator because assets generate returns in forms other than sales (for example, interest revenue and equity in earnings of affiliates). However, interpretations of various expense ratios (discussed later in this chapter) are usually easier when we use sales in the denominator.

EXHIBIT 4.6

ROA, Profit Margin, and Assets Turnover
for PepsiCo: 2006–2008 (adjusted data)

	2008	2007	2006
ROA	16.7%	17.8%	16.9%
Profit Margin for ROA	13.6%	14.6%	14.9%
Assets Turnover	1.22	1.22	1.14

Economic and Strategic Factors in the Interpretation of ROA[17]

ROA and its components differ across industries depending on their economic characteristics and across firms within an industry depending on the design and implementation of their strategies. This section explores economic and strategic factors that impact the interpretation of ROA and its components.

Exhibit 4.7 depicts graphically the 15-year average of the median annual ROAs, profit margins for ROA, and assets turnovers of 23 industries for 1990–2004. The two isoquants

EXHIBIT 4.7

Median ROA, Profit Margin for ROA, and Assets Turnover
for 23 Industries for 1990–2004

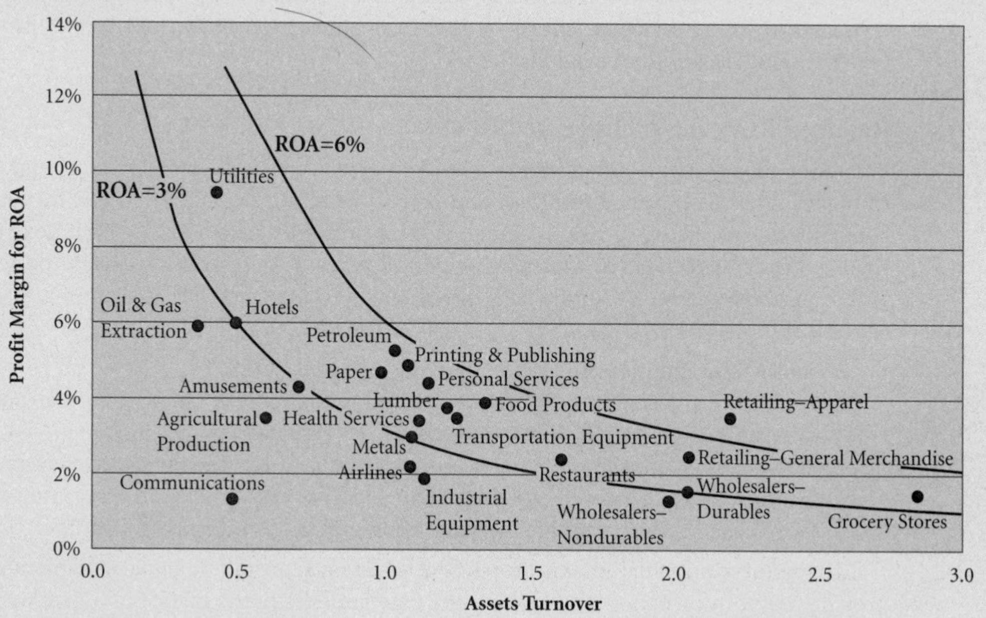

[17]The material in this section draws heavily from Thomas I. Selling and Clyde P. Stickney, "The Effects of Business Environments and Strategy on a Firm's Rate of Return on Assets," *Financial Analysts Journal* (January/February 1989), pp. 43–52.

reflect ROAs of 3 percent and 6 percent. The isoquants show the various combinations of profit margin for ROA and assets turnover that yield an ROA of 3 percent and 6 percent. For instance, an ROA of 6 percent results from any of the following profit margins for ROA × assets turnover combinations: 6% × 1.0, 3% × 2.0, 2% × 3.0, 1% × 6.0.

The data for ROA, profit margin for ROA, and assets turnover underlying the plots in Exhibit 4.7 reflect aggregated amounts across firms and across years. Financial statement analysis focuses on the ROAs of specific firms (or even segments of specific firms) for particular years (or even quarters). However, we can obtain useful insights about the behavior of ROA at the segment or firm level by examining the average industry-level data, particularly the following:

1. What factors explain the consistently high or consistently low ROAs of some industries relative to the average of all industries? (That is, what are the reasons for differences in the distribution of industries in the inner left area versus the outer right area of Exhibit 4.7?)
2. What factors explain the fact that certain industries have high profit margins and low assets turnovers while other industries experience low profit margins and high assets turnovers? (That is, what are the reasons for differences in the distribution of industries in the upper left area versus the lower right area of Exhibit 4.7?)

The microeconomics and business strategy literature provides useful background for interpreting the behavior of ROA, profit margin, and assets turnover. As a prelude to the discussion that follows, consider the two extreme industries in Exhibit 4.7. Utilities show the highest profit margins in Exhibit 4.7, which can be explained by significant barriers to entry (both regulatory and enormous fixed costs). Barriers to entry permit existing firms to realize higher profit margins due to limited competition. On the other hand, grocery stores show the highest assets turnover in Exhibit 4.7. Given lower barriers to entry and significant competition, this industry survives not based on profit margins, but on the ability of firms in the industry to run efficient operations and generate substantial asset turnover, consistent with the perpetual efforts by such companies to generate foot traffic through ever-changing sales and promotions.

Realized ROA versus Expected ROA

Economic theory suggests that higher levels of perceived risk in any activity should lead to higher levels of expected return if that activity is to attract capital. The extra return compensates for the extra risk assumed. Realized rates of return (ROAs) derived from financial statement data for a particular period will not necessarily correlate perfectly with expected returns or with the level of risk involved in an activity as economic theory suggests if

1. Faulty assumptions were used in deriving expected ROAs.
2. Changes in the environment after expectations are formed (such as an unexpected recession) cause realized ROAs to deviate from expectations.
3. ROA is an incomplete measure of economic rates of return (that is, rates of return that include all changes in economic value) because GAAP relies on acquisition costs for reliable measurement of assets and conservatism in measuring income.

Despite these potential weaknesses, ROAs based on reported financial statement data provide useful information for tracking the past periodic performance of a firm and its segments and for developing expectations about future earnings potential. Three elements of risk help in understanding differences across firms and changes over time in ROAs: (1) operating leverage, (2) cyclicality of sales, and (3) product life cycles.

Operating Leverage. Firms operate with different mixtures of fixed and variable costs in their cost structures. Firms in the utilities, communications, hotel, petroleum, and chemical industries are capital-intensive. Depreciation and many operating costs are more or less fixed for any given period. Most retailers and wholesalers, on the other hand, have high proportions of variable costs in their cost structures. Firms with high proportions of fixed costs experience significant increases in operating income as sales increase, a phenomenon known as *economies of scale.* The increased income occurs because the firms spread fixed costs over a larger number of units sold, resulting in a decrease in average unit cost. Likewise, when sales decrease, these firms experience sharp decreases in operating income, the result of *diseconomies of scale.* Economists refer to this process of operating with high proportions of fixed costs as *operating leverage.* Firms with high levels of operating leverage experience greater variability in their ROAs than firms with low levels of operating leverage. All else being equal (see the discussion of cyclicality of sales in the next section), firms with high levels of operating leverage incur more risk in their operations and should earn higher rates of return.

Measuring the degree of operating leverage of a firm or its segments requires information about the fixed and variable cost structure. The top panel of Exhibit 4.8 shows the total revenue and total cost functions of two stylized firms, A and B. The graphs assume that the two firms are the same size and have the same total revenue functions (the line labeled "Total Revenue: A or B") and the same break-even points (the point where the total revenue line intersects with each firm's cost function line). These assumptions simplify the discussion of operating leverage but are not necessary when comparing actual companies.

Firm B has a higher level of fixed costs than Firm A does, as indicated by the intersection of the firm's total cost line on the y-axis above that for Firm A in the top panel of

EXHIBIT 4.8

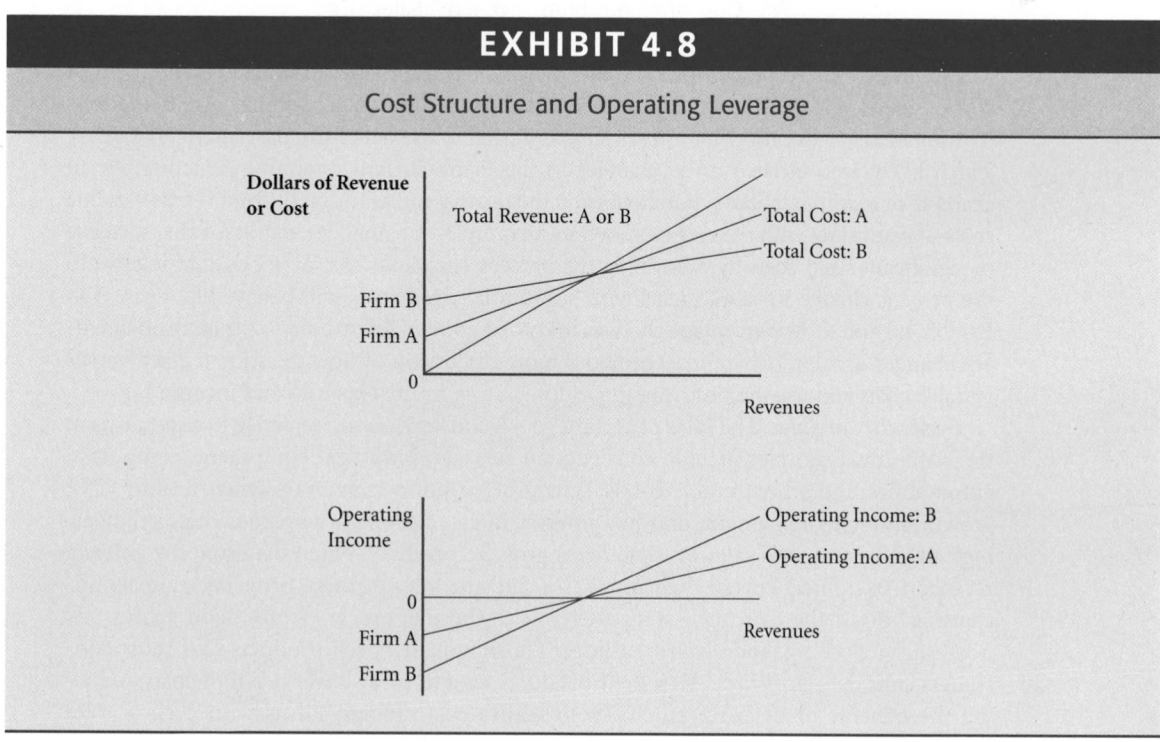

Cost Structure and Operating Leverage

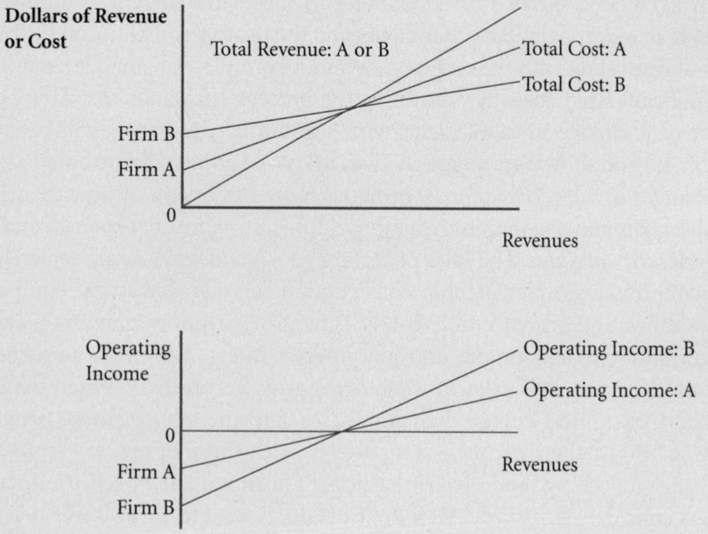

Exhibit 4.8. Firm A has a higher level of variable costs than Firm B does, as indicated by the steeper slope of Firm A's total cost function as revenues increase above zero. The lower panel nets the total revenue and total cost functions to derive the operating income function (that is, revenue minus cost). Operating income is negative in an amount equal to fixed costs when revenues are zero and operating income is zero at break-even revenues. We use the slope of the operating income line as a measure of the extent of operating leverage. Firm B, with its higher fixed-cost and lower variable-cost mix, has more operating leverage. As revenues increase, its operating income increases more sharply than that of Firm A. On the downside, however, income decreases more sharply for Firm B as revenues decrease.

Unfortunately, firms do not publicly disclose information about their fixed and variable cost structures. To examine the influence of operating leverage on the behavior of ROA for a particular firm or its segments, the analyst must estimate the fixed versus variable cost structure. One approach to such estimation is to study the various cost items of a firm and attempt to identify items that are likely to behave as fixed costs. Firms incur some costs in particular amounts, referred to as *committed fixed costs,* regardless of the actual level of activity during the period. Examples include depreciation, amortization, and rent. Firms can alter the amount of other costs, referred to as *discretionary fixed costs,* in the short run in response to operating conditions, but in general, these costs do not vary directly with the level of activity. Examples include research and development, maintenance, advertising, and central corporate staff expenses. Whether the analyst should classify these latter costs as fixed costs or as variable costs in measuring operating leverage depends on their behavior in a particular firm. Given sufficient time-series data, an analyst also could estimate the level of fixed costs by estimating a regression of an operating expense on a variable that drives the variable component of the operating expense. For example, to estimate the fixed component of cost of goods sold, the analyst could estimate the following regression:

$$\text{Cost of Goods Sold}_t = \alpha + \beta * \text{Sales}_t + \varepsilon_t$$

The estimated intercept, α, would be the analyst's best estimate of the fixed component of cost of goods sold. Although ideal in theory, to obtain a sufficient number of observations to estimate the above model, the analyst would need to use data from past quarters or years, which likely are outdated given changes in the firm's current operating structure. As an example of a simpler approach for assessing the relative contribution of fixed versus variable costs—continuing with the cost of goods sold example—an analyst can test for the existence of significant fixed costs by examining the percent change in cost of goods sold relative to the percent change in sales. Firms with substantial fixed costs will behave like Firm B in Exhibit 4.8 and show percentage changes in cost of goods sold that are less than the percentage changes in sales. (Chapter 10 provides more discussion of how to estimate fixed versus variable costs and use that information in forecasting future expenses and income.)

Cyclicality of Sales. The sales of certain goods and services are sensitive to conditions in the economy. Examples include construction services, industrial equipment, computers, automobiles, and other durable goods. When the economy is in an upswing (healthy GNP growth, low unemployment, and low interest rates), customers purchase these relatively high-priced items, and sales of these firms grow accordingly. When the economy enters a recession, customers curtail their purchases, and the sales of these firms decrease significantly. Contrast these cyclical sales patterns with those of grocery stores, food processors, nonfashion clothing, and electric utilities. Those industries sell products that most consumers consider necessities. Also, their products tend to carry lower per-unit costs, reducing the benefits of delaying purchases to realize cost savings. Firms with cyclical sales patterns incur more risk than firms with noncyclical sales.

One means of reducing the risk inherent in cyclical sales is to strive for a high proportion of variable cost in the cost structure. Examples of variable-cost strategies include paying employees an hourly wage instead of a fixed salary and renting buildings and equipment under short-term cancelable leases instead of purchasing them. Cost levels should change proportionally with sales, thereby maintaining stable profit margin percentages and reducing risk. Of course, this depends on whether the firm can make timely adjustments to cost structures in response to changes in demand, such as the ability to furlough workers or return leased equipment to lessors.

The nature of the activities of some firms is such that they must carry high levels of fixed costs (that is, operating leverage). Examples include capital-intensive service firms such as airlines and railroads. Firms in these industries may attempt to transform the cost of their physical capacity from a fixed cost to a variable cost by engaging in short-term leases. However, lessors then bear the risk of cyclical sales and demand higher returns (that is, rents). Thus, some firms are especially risky because they bear a combination of operating leverage and cyclical sales risks.

A noncyclical sales pattern can compensate for high operating leverage and effectively neutralize this element of risk. Electric utilities, for example, carry high levels of fixed costs. However, their dominant positions in most service areas reduce their operating risks and permit them to achieve stable profitability.

Product Life Cycle. A third element of risk that affects ROA relates to the stage and length of a firm's product life cycle, a concept discussed in Chapter 3 with regard to relations between cash flows from operating, investing, and financing activities. Products move through four identifiable phases: introduction, growth, maturity, and decline. During the introduction and growth phases, a firm focuses on product development (product R&D spending) and capacity enlargement (capital spending). The objective is to gain market acceptance and market share. Considerable uncertainty may exist during these phases regarding the market viability of a firm's products. Products that have survived into the maturity phase have gained market acceptance. Also, firms have probably been able to cut back capital expenditures on new operating capacity. During the maturity phase, however, competition becomes more intense and the emphasis shifts to reducing costs through improved capacity utilization (economies of scale) and more efficient production (process R&D spending aimed at reducing manufacturing costs through better utilization of labor and materials). During the decline phase, firms exit the industry as sales decline and profit opportunities diminish.

Exhibit 4.9 depicts the behavior of revenues, operating income, investment, and ROA that corresponds to the four phases of the product life cycle. During the introduction and early growth phases, expenditures on product development and marketing, coupled with relatively low sales levels, lead to operating losses and negative ROAs. As sales accelerate during the high-growth phase, operating income and ROAs turn positive. Extensive product development, marketing, and depreciation expenses during this phase moderate operating income, while heavy capital expenditures to build capacity for expected higher future sales increase the denominator of ROA. Thus, ROA does not grow as rapidly as sales. ROA increases significantly during the maturity phase due to benefits of economies of scale and learning curve phenomena and to curtailments of capital expenditures. ROA deteriorates during the decline phase as operating income decreases, but ROA may remain positive or even increase for some time into this phase (particularly if the depreciable assets have been largely depreciated). Thus, as products move through their life cycles, their ROAs should move to the upper right area in Exhibit 4.9, peak during the maturity stage, and then move to the lower left area as the decline phase sets in. This movement in ROA appears negatively correlated with the level of risk. Risks are probably greatest in the introduction and growth stages, when ROA is low or negative, and least in the maturity phase, when ROA is high.

EXHIBIT 4.9

Relation between Sales, Operating Income, Investment, and ROA during Product Life Cycle

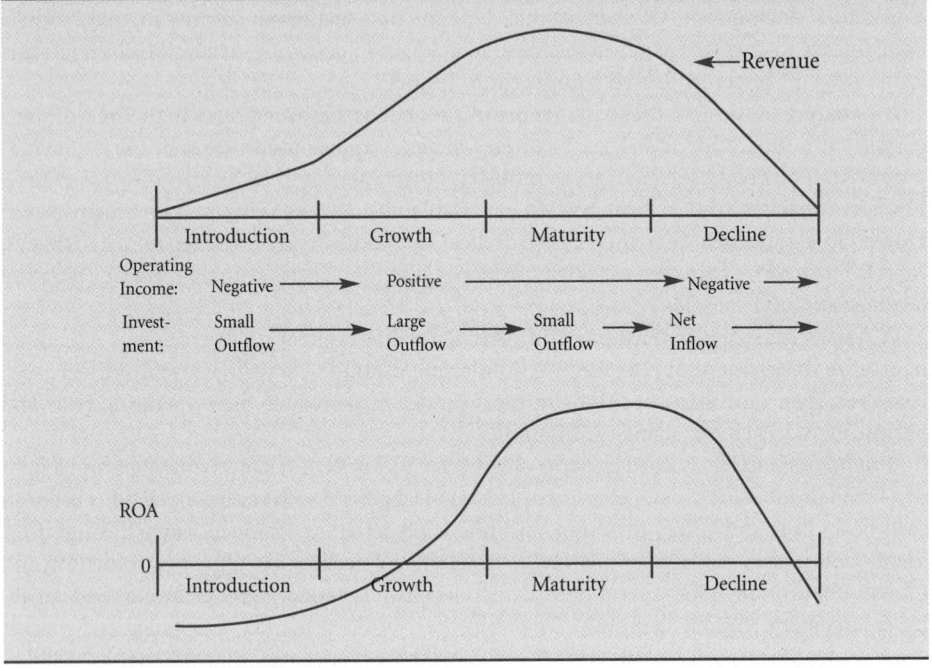

Recall, though, that ROA measures realized accounting returns in a given period, whereas the usual risk-return trade-off refers to expected returns and expected risks. Taking a weighted average of ROAs over several years will reflect more accurately the economic returns generated by high-growth firms.

Note that the product life cycle theory focuses on individual products. We can extend the theory to an industry level by examining the average stage in the product life cycle of all products in that industry. For instance, products in the computer industry range from the introduction to the decline phases, but the overall industry is probably in the latter part of the high-growth phase. The beverage and food-processing industries, the primary markets of PepsiCo, are mature, although PepsiCo and its competitors continually introduce new products. We might view the steel industry, at least in the United States, as in the early decline phase, although some companies have modernized production sufficiently to stave off the decline.[18]

In addition to the stage in the product life cycle, the length of the product life cycle also is an element of risk. Products with short product life cycles require more frequent expenditures to develop replacement or new products, thereby increasing risks. The product life cycles of most computer products run one to two years. Most pharmaceutical products experience product life cycles of approximately seven years. In contrast, the life cycles of PepsiCo's soft drinks, branded food products, and some toys (for example, Barbie® dolls and Matchbox® cars) are much longer.

---

[18]Empirical support for a link between life cycle stage, sales growth, capital expenditure growth, and stock market reaction appears in Joseph H. Anthony and K. Ramesh, "Association between Accounting Performance Measures and Stock Prices: A Test of the Life Cycle Hypothesis," *Journal of Accounting and Economics* 15 (1992), pp. 203–227.

Refer again to the average industry ROAs in Exhibit 4.7. The location of several industries is consistent with their incurring one or more of these elements of risk. The relatively high ROAs of the utilities and petroleum industries are consistent with high operating leverage. Paper, petroleum, and transportation equipment experience cyclical sales, and apparel retailers face the risk of their products becoming obsolete.

Some of the industry locations in Exhibit 4.7 appear inconsistent with these elements of risk. Oil and gas extraction, agricultural production, and communications are capital-intensive, yet their ROAs are the lowest of the 23 industries. One might view these positions as disequilibrium situations. Generating such low ROAs will not likely attract capital over the longer term.

The ROA locations of several industries appear to be affected by GAAP. A principal resource of food products firms such as General Mills and Campbell's Soup is the value of their brand names. Yet GAAP requires these firms to immediately expense advertising and other costs incurred to develop these brand names. Thus, their asset bases are understated and their ROAs are overstated.[19] Likewise, the publishing industry does not recognize the value of copyrights or authors' contracts as assets, resulting in an overstatement of ROAs. A similar overstatement problem occurs for service firms, for which the value of their employees does not appear as an asset.

Trade-Offs between Profit Margin and Assets Turnover

In addition to the differences in ROA depicted in Exhibit 4.7, we also must examine reasons for differences in the relative mix of profit margin and assets turnover. Explanations come from the microeconomics and business strategy literature.

Microeconomic Theory. Exhibit 4.10 sets out some important economic factors that constrain certain firms and industries to operate with particular combinations of profit

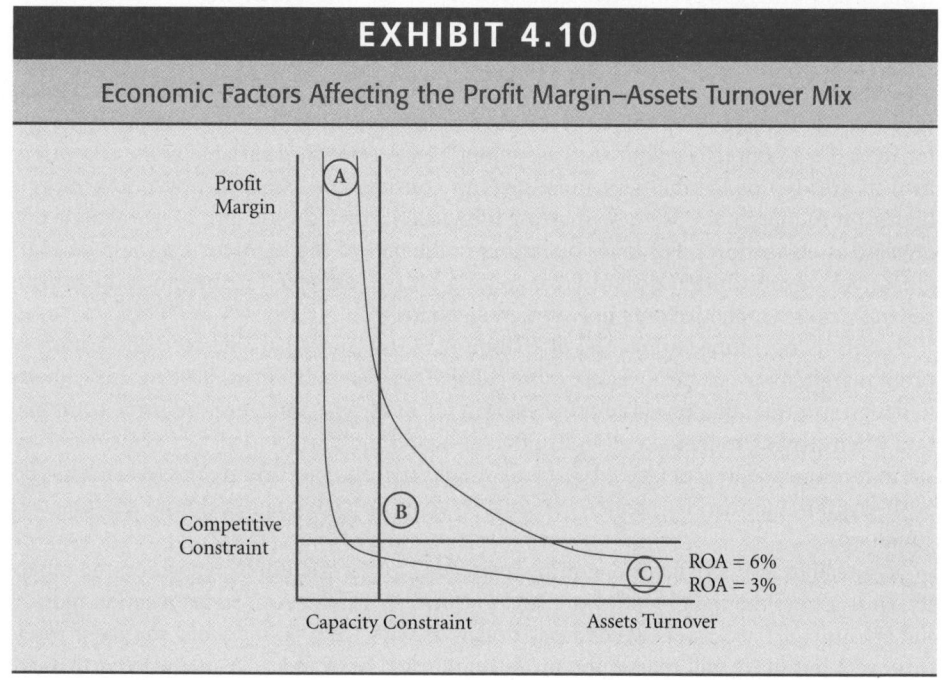

EXHIBIT 4.10

Economic Factors Affecting the Profit Margin–Assets Turnover Mix

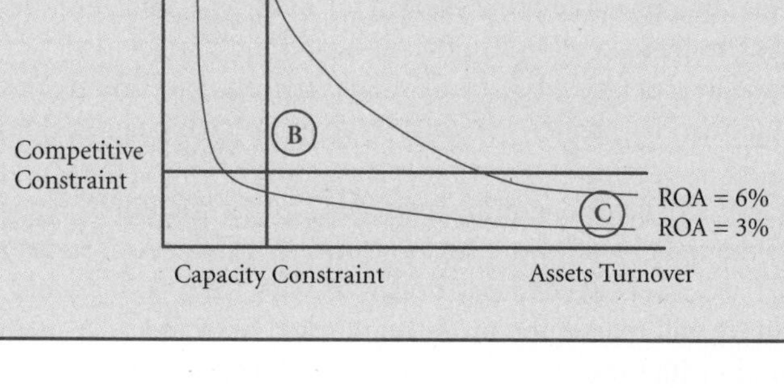

[19]The immediate expensing of advertising costs understates net income as well, but the difference between the amount expensed and amortization of amounts from the current and prior periods that perhaps should have been capitalized results in less distortion of net income than of total assets.

margins and assets turnovers. Firms and industries characterized by heavy fixed capacity costs and lengthy periods required to add new capacity operate under a capacity constraint. There is an upper limit on the size of assets turnover achievable. To attract sufficient capital, these firms must generate a relatively high profit margin. Therefore, such firms operate in the area of Exhibit 4.10 marked Ⓐ. The firms usually achieve the high profit margin through some form of entry barrier. The entry barrier may take the form of large required capital outlays, high risks, or regulation. Such factors help explain the profit margin–assets turnover mix of utilities, oil and gas extraction, communications, hotels, and amusements in Exhibit 4.7.

Firms whose products are commodity-like where there are few entry barriers and where competition is intense operate under a competitive constraint. There is an upper limit on the achievable level of profit margin for ROA. To attract sufficient capital, these firms must strive for high assets turnovers. Therefore, such firms will operate in the area of Exhibit 4.10 marked Ⓒ. Firms achieve the high assets turnovers by keeping costs as low as possible (for example, minimizing fixed overhead costs, purchasing in sufficient quantities to realize discounts, and integrating vertically or horizontally to obtain cost savings). These firms match such actions to control costs with aggressively low prices to gain market share and drive out marginal firms. Most retailers and wholesalers operate in the low profit margin–high assets turnover area of Exhibit 4.7.

Firms that operate in the area of Exhibit 4.10 marked Ⓑ are not as subject to capacity or competitive constraints as severe as those that operate in the tails of the ROA curves. Therefore, they have more flexibility to take actions that will increase profit margin for ROA, assets turnover, or both to achieve a higher ROA.

The notion of flexibility in trading off profit margin for assets turnover (or vice versa) is important when a firm considers strategic alternatives. The underlying economic concept is the marginal rate of substitution. First, consider a firm with a profit margin–assets turnover combination that puts it in area Ⓐ of Exhibit 4.10. Such a firm will have to give up a significant amount of profit margin for ROA to obtain a meaningful increase in assets turnover. To increase ROA, this firm should emphasize actions that increase profit margin for ROA; for example, it might increase selling prices or reduce variable costs. Likewise, a firm in area Ⓒ of Exhibit 4.10 must give up considerable assets turnover to achieve a higher profit margin for ROA. To increase ROA, such a firm should emphasize actions that increase assets turnover. For firms operating in the tails of the ROA curves, the poor marginal rates of substitution do not favor trading off one variable for the other. Such firms generally must emphasize only one of these factors.

For firms operating in area Ⓑ of Exhibit 4.10, the marginal rates of substitution of profit margin for assets turnover are more equal. Therefore, such firms have more flexibility to design strategies that promote profit margin for ROA, assets turnover, or some combination when striving to increase ROA. Unless the economic characteristics of a business constrain it to operate in area Ⓐ or Ⓒ, firms should strive to position themselves in area Ⓑ. Such positioning provides greater potential to adapt to changing economic and business conditions.

As already suggested, firms operating in area Ⓐ might attempt to reposition the capacity constraint to the right by outsourcing some of their production. Such an action reduces the amount of fixed assets needed per dollar of sales (that is, increases the fixed assets turnover) but likely will reduce the profit margin for ROA (because of the need to share some of the margin with the outsourcing company). Firms operating in area Ⓒ might add products with a higher profit margin for ROA. Grocery stores, for example, have added fresh flowers, salad bars, fresh bakery products, and pharmaceutical prescription services to their product offerings in recent years in an effort to increase their profit margin for ROA and advance beyond the competitive constraint common for grocery products.

In summary, the economic concepts underlying the profit margin–assets turnover mix are as follows:

Area in Exhibit 4.10	Capital Intensity	Competition	Likely Strategic Focus
A	High	Monopoly	Profit Margin for ROA
B	Medium	Oligopolistic or Monopolistic Competition	Profit Margin for ROA, Assets Turnover, or some combination
C	Low	Pure Competition	Assets Turnover

Business Strategy. Hall[20] and Porter[21] suggest that firms have two generic alternative strategies for a particular product: product differentiation and low-cost leadership. The thrust of the product differentiation strategy is to differentiate a product in such a way as to obtain market power over revenues and, therefore, profit margins. The differentiation could relate to product capabilities, product quality, service, channels of distribution, or some other factor. The thrust of the low-cost leadership strategy is to become the lowest-cost producer, thereby enabling the firm to charge the lowest prices and to achieve higher sales volumes. Such firms can achieve the low-cost position through economies of scale, production efficiencies, outsourcing, or similar factors or by asset parsimony (maintaining strict controls on investments in receivables, inventories, and capital expenditures).[22]

In terms of Exhibit 4.10, movements in the direction of area Ⓐ from any point along the ROA curves focus on product differentiation. Likewise, movements in the direction of area Ⓒ from any point along the ROA curves focus on low-cost leadership. For an example, look at the average profit margins for ROA and assets turnovers for three types of retailers.

	Profit Margin for ROA	Assets Turnover
Specialty Retailers	2.97%	2.21
General Merchandise Stores	2.38%	2.02
Grocery Stores	1.43%	2.82

In the retailing industry, specialty retailers have differentiated themselves by following a niche strategy and have achieved a higher profit margin for ROA than the other two segments. Competition severely constrains the profit margin for ROA of grocery stores, and they must pursue more low-cost leadership strategies. Thus, a firm does not have to be in the tails of the ROA curves to be described as a product differentiator or a low-cost leader. The appropriate basis of comparison is not other industries, but other firms in the same industry. Remember, however, that the relative location along the ROA curve affects a firm's flexibility to trade off

[20]W. K. Hall, "Survival Strategies in a Hostile Environment," *Harvard Business Review* (September–October 1980), pp. 78–85.

[21]M. E. Porter, *Competitive Strategy: Techniques for Analyzing Industries and Competitors* (New York: Free Press), 1998. Porter suggests that firms also might pursue a niche strategy. Because a niche strategy essentially represents differentiation within a market segment, we include it here under product differentiation strategy.

[22]Research in business strategy suggests that firms can simultaneously pursue product differentiation and low-cost leadership because product differentiation is revenue-oriented (output) and low-cost leadership is more expense-oriented (input).

profit margin (product differentiation) for assets turnover (low-cost leadership). More importantly, note that in any industry, firms are dispersed among the profit margin and asset turnover dimensions. For example, within grocery stores, Kroger has higher asset turnover and lower profit margin, whereas Whole Foods has higher profit margin but lower asset turnover.

Summarizing, differences in the profit margin for ROA–assets turnover mix relate to economic factors external to a firm (such as degree of competition, extent of regulation, entry barriers, and similar factors) and to internal strategic choices (such as product differentiation and low-cost leadership). The external and internal factors are, of course, interdependent and dynamic.

PepsiCo's Positioning Relative to the Consumer Foods Industry

PepsiCo is part of the consumer foods industry. The median ROA, profit margin for ROA, and assets turnover for the consumer foods industry and the average amounts for PepsiCo for 2006–2008 are as follows:

	Consumer Foods Industry	PepsiCo
ROA	8.4%	17.1%
Profit Margin for ROA	6.8%	14.3%
Assets Turnover	1.4	1.2

Note that the average ROA of PepsiCo significantly exceeds that for the consumer foods industry because of higher profit margins for ROA earned by PepsiCo. Possible economic or strategic explanations for the higher profit margin for ROA include (1) more value to PepsiCo's brand names than to other food products companies, (2) greater pricing power because of PepsiCo's and Coca-Cola's domination of the beverage industry, (3) greater pricing power because of PepsiCo's influence over its bottlers, and (4) greater efficiencies due to PepsiCo's size or quality of management. The next section explores this higher profit margin for ROA more fully.

Analyzing the Profit Margin for ROA

Profit margin for ROA captures the overall profitability of a firm's operations and is measured as the amount of after-tax profit generated (before financing costs) as a percentage of sales. Thus, the analysis of profit margin focuses on all expenses (other than interest expense) that reduce sales to after-tax profit. Using unadjusted income, ROA for PepsiCo declined steadily from 2006–2008, but adjusted ROA fluctuated somewhat, rising from 16.9 percent in 2006 to 17.8 percent in 2007 and then dropping back to 16.7 percent in 2008. The disaggregation of ROA into the profit margin for ROA and assets turnover components in Exhibit 4.6 (using adjusted ROA) reveals that the fluctuation in ROA results from steadily declining profit margins for ROA offset by a significant increase in assets turnover in 2007, followed by a small increase in 2008. One might liken this disaggregation to peeling an onion. ROA is the outer layer. Peeling away that layer reveals the profit margin for ROA and assets turnover. We can peel the onion an additional layer by examining the components of the profit margin for ROA and the components of assets turnover.

Appealing to the usefulness of common-size analysis discussed earlier in the chapter, we express each revenue and expense amount as a percentage of sales to identify reasons for changes in the profit margin for ROA. Exhibit 4.11 presents these revenue and expense percentages for PepsiCo. We maintain consistency with our earlier decision to adjust reported income for various items and show these effects separately in Exhibit 4.11.

EXHIBIT 4.11

Analysis of the Profit Margin for PepsiCo: 2006–2008

	2008	2007	2006
Net Revenue	100.0%	100.0%	100.0%
Bottling equity income	0.9%	1.4%	1.6%
Interest income	0.1%	0.3%	0.5%
Cost of sales	(47.1%)	(45.7%)	(44.9%)
Selling, general, and administrative expenses	(36.8%)	(36.0%)	(36.2%)
Amortization of intangible assets	(0.1%)	(0.1%)	(0.5%)
Adjustments (from Exhibit 4.6)	1.6%	0.3%	0.2%
Provision for income taxes (adjusted)	(5.0%)	(5.6%)	(5.9%)
Profit margin for ROA	13.6%	14.6%	14.9%

Note from Exhibit 4.11 that PepsiCo's profit margin for ROA decreases because of the following factors:

- Decreases in bottling equity income relative to sales
- Decreases in interest income relative to sales
- Increases in the cost of sales as a percentage of sales
- Increases in selling, general, and administrative expenses relative to sales
- Decreases in the provision for income taxes relative to sales, which offsets the effects of the above items

The above summary contains a degree of measurement error relating to the adjustments made earlier because the restructuring and impairment charges that we added back to reported income are scattered across several of the line items in Exhibit 4.11, including cost of sales and selling, general, and administrative expenses. As discussed in Note 3, "Restructuring and Impairment Charges" (Appendix A), of PepsiCo's $543 million restructuring charge, $455 million is included in selling, general, and administrative expenses and $88 million is included in cost of sales. Thus, unfavorable trends in both of these line items are not quite as negative as suggested if we adjust individual line items rather than the aggregate restructuring and impairment charges.

The task for the financial analyst is to identify reasons for the changes in these revenue and expense percentages. The MD&A provides information for interpreting the changes in these profitability percentages. Firms vary with respect to the informativeness of these discussions. Some firms give specific reasons for changes in various financial ratios. Other firms simply indicate the amount or rate of increase or decrease without providing explanations for the changes. Even when firms provide explanations, the analyst should assess their reasonableness in light of conditions in the economy and the industry, as well as the firm's stated strategy and the results for the firms' competitors. The analyst also should be cautious when a firm does not provide discussion or an explanation for a significant shift in a financial ratio; it implies that the firm is not being forthcoming with useful information.

We use information provided by PepsiCo in its MD&A (Appendix B) to identify reasons for changes in the profit margin for ROA.

Bottling Equity Income

Note 8, "Noncontrolled Bottling Affiliates" (Appendix A), indicates that PepsiCo owns approximately 40 percent of the common stock of some of its bottlers. Because PepsiCo does not own more than 50 percent of the common stock of these bottlers, it does not consolidate the financial statements of the bottlers. Instead, PepsiCo accounts for these investments using the equity method, which Chapter 7 discusses more fully. Firms using the equity method recognize as income each period their share of the net income or net loss of the investees. Thus, bottling equity income for PepsiCo represents its share of the net income of its noncontrolled bottling companies. PepsiCo discloses in its MD&A (Appendix B) that bottling equity income also includes gains and losses from selling shares of its bottlers. Bottling equity income as a percent of sales is as follows (in millions):

2006: $553/$35,137 = 1.57%
2007: $560/$39,474 = 1.42%
2008: $374/$43,251 = 0.86%

The above percentages are not very meaningful because the bottling equity income is not directly related to PepsiCo's sales revenue. Thus, a better ratio to use to evaluate the bottling investments' profitability is bottling equity income as a percentage of the average investments balance. Bottling equity income as a percentage of the average balance in Investments in Noncontrolled Affiliates is as follows (in millions)[23]:

2006: $553/$3,588 = 15.4%
2007: $560/$4,022 = 13.9%
2008: $374/$4,119 = 9.1%

PepsiCo discloses that it sold 8.8 million shares of PBG stock in 2008 and 9.5 million shares in 2007. Thus, PepsiCo has been decreasing its ownership stake in PBG. Over the same period, the profitability of the PBG investments have been decreasing as well, as a percentage of PepsiCo's sales and as a percentage of the investments in noncontrolled affiliates balance. PepsiCo does not provide sufficient information to determine how much of the bottling equity income represents its share of the income of the bottlers and how much represents gains or losses on sales of common stock in the bottlers. However, as discussed earlier, PepsiCo does highlight the fact that the decline in bottling equity income during 2008 is due primarily to PepsiCo's share of PBG's restructuring and impairment charges. PepsiCo's pretax share of this charge is $138 million, or $114 million after tax; thus, adjusting the numerator of the above computations for 2008 results in bottling equity income as a percentage of sales of 1.18% [($374 + $138)/$43,251] and 12.4 percent as a percentage of the average balance in Investments in Noncontrolled Affiliates [($374 + $138)/$4,119]. Even with this adjustment, the profitability of these investments is declining. Thus, we might infer that PepsiCo's decision to decrease investments in PBG is related to the declining profitability of these affiliates.

Bottling equity income is more central to PepsiCo's core operations. The analyst should evaluate with caution the increases in profitability of these bottlers. These bottlers derive most of their income by purchasing concentrate or syrup from PepsiCo, processing it into consumable beverages, placing it in bottles or other containers, and then selling and shipping the product. A principal cost to these bottlers is the amount it pays PepsiCo for the concentrate or syrup. Thus, PepsiCo's pricing policies in selling to the bottlers directly impacts the profitability of the bottlers. In addition, large brand-name consumer goods

---

[23]PepsiCo's current annual report has only two balance sheets but Exhibit 1.9 includes balance sheets for the previous five years. We need more balance sheets than income statements for this ratio because we are using an average balance in the denominator.

companies such as PepsiCo typically provide substantial amounts of marketing, advertising, and administrative support to key noncontrolled affiliates such as PepsiCo's bottlers. Also affecting the income of the bottlers is their control over other manufacturing, selling, and administrative costs. Firms seldom provide the information necessary for the analyst to identify how much of any changes in profitability results from pricing actions by the investor company (change in the investor company's share of marketing and support costs) and how much results from the affiliate's better management of other costs.

Interest Revenue

PepsiCo earns interest on cash balances and short-term investments. Interest revenue as a percentage of the average balance in cash and short-term investments during 2006–2008 are as follows (in millions):

2006: \$173/\$3,852 = 4.5%
2007: \$125/\$2,652 = 4.7%
2008: \$41/\$2,379 = 1.7%

Thus, the decreased interest revenue to sales percentage results from declining average balances in cash and short-term investments and decreases in the yield.

Firms with temporarily excess cash should invest the cash in income-yielding securities, as PepsiCo has done, instead of allowing the cash to remain idle. However, analysts generally do not view interest revenue as an important source of profitability for most manufacturing and retailing firms (except retailing or other firms that offer their own credit cards). To have the greatest impact on share value, firms should derive most of the increases in profitability from their core operations, which in PepsiCo's case is manufacturing and selling consumer foods and beverages. A buildup of excess cash and marketable securities may suggest that a firm has few opportunities to invest in its core operations. The proportion of assets comprising cash and short-term investments for PepsiCo averaged approximately 6–9 percent of total assets during the most recent three years.

Cost of Goods Sold

Interpreting changes in the cost of goods sold to sales percentage is often difficult because explanations might relate to sales revenue only, to cost of goods sold only, or to common factors affecting both the numerator and the denominator. Consider, for example, the following possible explanations for a decrease in the cost of goods sold to sales percentage for a firm:

1. An increase in demand for products in excess of available capacity in an industry will likely result in an increase in selling prices. Even though the cost of manufacturing the product does not change, the cost of goods sold percentage will decrease.
2. As a result of product improvements or effective advertising, a firm's market share for its product increases. The firm allocates the fixed cost of manufacturing the product over a larger volume of production, thereby lowering its per-unit cost. Even though selling prices do not change, the cost of goods sold to sales percentage will decrease.
3. A firm lowers the price for its product to gain a larger market share. It lowers its manufacturing cost per unit by purchasing raw materials in larger quantities to take advantage of quantity discounts. Cost of goods sold per unit declines more than selling price per unit, causing the cost of goods sold to sales percentage to decline.
4. A firm sells multiple products with different cost of goods sold to sales percentages. The product mix shifts toward products with higher profit margins, thereby lowering the overall cost of goods sold to sales percentage.

Thus, the analyst must consider changes in selling prices, manufacturing costs, and product mix when interpreting changes in the cost of goods sold percentage.

Exhibit 4.11 indicates that PepsiCo's cost of goods sold to sales percentage has increased steadily during the three-year period, from 44.9 percent in 2006 to 47.1 percent in 2008. Management's discussion of the results of operations (Appendix B) indicates that PepsiCo encountered higher commodity costs, particularly for cooking oil and fuel in both 2007 and 2008.

Selling, General, and Administrative Expenses

Most firms combine selling, general, and administrative expenses on the income statement. Combining these expense items is unfortunate from an analysis perspective because different factors tend to drive these expenses. Selling expenses include sales commissions, advertising, and promotion materials, which usually vary with the level of sales. General expenses include overhead expenses such as rent, utilities, communications, and insurance, whereas administrative expenses include top management's salaries and the cost of operating staff departments such as information systems, legal services, and R&D. These costs tend not to vary with the level of sales.

PepsiCo's selling, general, and administrative expenses to sales percentages were level between 2006 and 2007 (36.2 percent to 36.0 percent), but they increased to 36.8 percent in 2008. Sales increased 12.3 percent between 2006 and 2007, so the spreading of relatively fixed administrative costs over a larger sales base might explain the decrease from 36.2 percent to 36.0 percent in 2007. Sales increased during 2008, but at a lower rate of 9.6 percent, while selling, general, and administrative expense increased 11.9 percent. Management's discussion of operations (Appendix B) does not give sufficient information to ensure an understanding of the detailed breakdown of selling, general, and administrative expenses, but management does discuss that "other corporate unallocated expenses decreased." However, this decrease was more than offset by the $346 million mark-to-market adjustment discussed earlier, which is classified as a separate corporate unallocated expense. Additionally, Note 3, "Restructuring and Impairment Charges," indicates that $455 million of the $543 million restructuring and impairment charges discussed earlier is included within selling, general, and administrative expenses (with the remainder affecting cost of goods sold). The impact of these two amounts on selling, general, and administrative expenses in Exhibit 4.11 is 1.85 percent [= ($346 + $455 million)/$43,251 million]. Adjusting selling, general and administrative expenses in Exhibit 4.11 for these effects results in a lower percentage of sales (34.95 percent), which is an improvement relative to the levels in 2006 and 2007.

Income Taxes

Exhibit 4.11 indicates that income taxes as a percentage of sales declined from 5.9 percent in 2006 to 5.0 percent in 2008. Note that the computations for the provision for income taxes are adjusted for the tax impact of the adjustments made to the numerator of the adjusted ROA calculation. As discussed earlier, the income tax adjustments include increases for the restructuring and impairment charges and adjustments for tax benefits from settlements with taxing authorities. Further, tax expense is not based on sales (the denominator in Exhibit 4.11), but on pretax profits. A more relevant computation of common-size income taxes is income tax expense as a percentage of pretax operating profit (in millions):

As reported:	**Adjusted income tax expense (from Exhibit 4.4):**
2006: $1,347/$6,989 = 19.3%	$1,991/$7,056 = 28.2%
2007: $1,973/$7,631 = 25.9%	$2,134/$7,733 = 27.6%
2008: $1,879/$7,021 = 26.8%	$2,038/$7,702 = 26.5%

The comparison of as-reported figures suggests an increasing tax rate, with a marked jump in tax rates in 2007 relative to 2006. Again, the explanation pertains to "unusual" adjustments.

The adjustments to compute adjusted ROA shown in Exhibit 4.4 include tax adjustments totaling $620 million in 2006, reflecting (1) a settlement with the IRS of $602 million of tax filings for 1998–2002 and (2) PepsiCo's portion of PBG's $18 million settlement for 1999–2000. Excluding only these adjustments, the tax rate in 2006 is 28.1 percent [($1,347 + $620)/$6,989]. The adjusted income tax rate, based on adjusted tax expense from Exhibit 4.4, suggests a more stable tax rate of between 28 and 29 percent. Thus, income taxes play a minor role in explaining the overall decrease in the profit margin for ROA.

Firms must disclose in notes to the financial statements their average tax rate and the reasons this rate differs from the statutory federal tax rate. Note 5, "Income Taxes," to PepsiCo's financial statements (Appendix A) presents this information. The figures disclosed under "Tax rate reconciliation" correspond to those based on as-reported figures above. Although the adjusted income tax rate calculations above show a relatively stable tax rate, the reconciliation suggests that one item that is affecting PepsiCo's net income tax rate positively is a favorable decrease in the taxes of foreign results. This suggests an analysis of foreign versus U.S. results, which is discussed next.

Segment Data

The aggregate results in the common-size income statements for PepsiCo examined in Exhibit 4.11 mask potentially important differences in profitability in different product lines or geographic markets. Fortunately, as highlighted earlier in the chapter, both U.S. GAAP and IFRS require firms to provide financial data for their operating segments, products and services, and major customers.[24] Note 1, "Basis of Presentation and Our Divisions," to PepsiCo's financial statements (Appendix A) presents these segment data for 2006–2008. PepsiCo reports product segment data for three large divisions: PepsiCo Americas Foods, PepsiCo Americas Beverages, and PepsiCo International. Within these divisions, PepsiCo further partitions the first and third divisions into segments, with PepsiCo Americas Foods broken out by Frito-Lay North America, Quaker Foods North America, and Latin American Foods, and PepsiCo International broken out into two geographic segments, the United Kingdom & Europe, and the Middle East, Africa, & Asia. Geographic segment data also are reported for the United States, Mexico, Canada, the United Kingdom, and all other countries combined.

The segment disclosures permit the analyst to examine ROA, profit margin, and assets turnover at an additional level of depth, in effect peeling the onion one more layer. Firms such as PepsiCo report revenues, operating profits, and other aggregate information by segment, but to avoid disclosure of sensitive information, firms, unfortunately, do not generally report cost of goods sold and selling, general, and administrative expenses for each segment. That means we cannot reconcile changes in segment profit margins to changes in the overall levels of these two expense percentages. Firms also report segment data pretax, meaning that the segment ROAs and profit margins exceed those for the overall company to a considerable extent.

Exhibit 4.12 presents sales mix data for PepsiCo. PepsiCo's sales mix has shifted during the three years from its North America food and beverage segments to international segments, with international growth in Latin America Foods, United Kingdom & Europe, and All Other Countries segments. (Chapter 10 also utilizes this information data to develop financial statement forecasts.) An important insight that is conveyed by the common-size analysis in Exhibit 4.12 is that the three segments comprising PepsiCo Americas Foods

---

[24]Financial Accounting Standards Board, *Statement of Financial Accounting Standards No. 131*, "Disclosures about Segments of an Enterprise and Related Information" (1997); *FASB Codification No. 280*; International Accounting Standards Board, *International Financial Reporting Standards No. 8*, "Operating Segments" (November 2006).

EXHIBIT 4.12

Sales Mix Data for PepsiCo

	2008	2007	2006
Product/Geographic Segments			
PepsiCo Americas Foods			
Frito-Lay North America	28.9%	29.4%	30.9%
Quaker Foods North America	4.4%	4.7%	5.0%
Latin America Foods	13.6%	12.3%	11.3%
PepsiCo Americas Beverages	25.3%	28.1%	29.5%
PepsiCo International			
United Kingdom & Europe	14.9%	13.9%	13.5%
Middle East, Africa, & Asia	12.9%	11.6%	9.8%
Total	100.0%	100.0%	100.0%
Country-Level Sales Mix			
United States	52.1%	55.7%	59.2%
Mexico	8.6%	8.9%	9.2%
Canada	4.9%	5.0%	4.8%
United Kingdom	4.9%	5.0%	5.2%
All other countries	29.5%	25.4%	21.6%
	100.0%	100.0%	100.0%

account for almost half of PepsiCo's total sales. Food sales also are included in the PepsiCo International segments. Together, these data suggest that, contrary to the popular belief that PepsiCo is a beverage company, for those determined to categorize the company along a product line, PepsiCo may more accurately be deemed to be a food company than a beverage company (especially because the highest profit margins and asset turnovers reside in the foods segments, as we will see next).

Exhibit 4.13 presents ROAs, profit margins, and assets turnovers for each of PepsiCo's segments. Note that our methods of computation here differ from those we performed previously for PepsiCo consolidated. First, we compute segment ROAs and assets turnover using assets at the *end of the period* to simplify the calculations. The difficulty the analyst often encounters with using average segment assets is that firms frequently change their definition of segments over time and firms report the three most recent years of segment asset data in their current annual report. The analyst would need to access asset data for the fourth year back in order to compute average assets for the three years and hope that the firm maintained its definition of segments. Firms that have changed their segment definitions within the last year will not consistently show assets with current segment definitions. For a stable, mature company such as PepsiCo, the use of assets at the end of the period instead of the average for the period will affect the level of the ROAs and the asset turnover ratios but will not likely have a material effect on the trend of these segment ratios over time unless the firm made a significant corporate acquisition or divestiture during one of the years. Second, note that the numerator of our profitability calculations is based on pretax operating profits rather than net income adjusted for after-tax interest expense. This decision also is made for

EXHIBIT 4.13

Product Segment Pretax Profitability Analysis for PepsiCo

ROA

	2008	2007	2006
PepsiCo Americas Foods			
Frito–Lay North America	47.1%	45.4%	43.8%
Quaker Foods North America	56.2%	56.7%	55.2%
Latin America Foods	29.7%	23.2%	30.2%
PepsiCo Americas Beverages	26.4%	32.0%	32.5%
PepsiCo International			
United Kingdom & Europe	9.4%	10.9%	11.9%
Middle East, Africa, & Asia	16.8%	13.7%	13.5%

	Profit Margin for ROA			Assets Turnover		
	2008	2007	2006	2008	2007	2006
PepsiCo Americas Foods						
Frito–Lay North America	23.7%	24.6%	24.1%	1.99	1.85	1.82
Quaker Foods North America	30.6%	30.5%	31.3%	1.84	1.86	1.76
Latin America Foods	15.2%	14.7%	16.5%	1.95	1.58	1.83
PepsiCo Americas Beverages	18.5%	22.4%	22.3%	1.43	1.43	1.45
PepsiCo International						
United Kingdom & Europe	12.6%	14.1%	14.7%	0.75	0.77	0.81
Middle East, Africa, & Asia	12.0%	11.7%	11.7%	1.41	1.17	1.16

simplicity. Financing policies and activities frequently reside with the corporate division; thus, they are not allocated to operating segments. As with our use of end-of-period total assets, this simplifying procedure is not likely to prevent an analyst from gaining objective insight into the relative profitability and efficiency of the segments being analyzed. The primary limitation of these assumptions is that we cannot precisely reconcile the segment calculations with those for the consolidated results of PepsiCo. Data availability and practicality frequently drive financial analysis decisions and techniques, which further emphasizes our earlier cautionary note that the astute analyst does not memorize ratios, but understands the rationale for how to interpret various measures.

The top portion of Exhibit 4.13 indicates that the segments with the highest ROAs are Frito-Lay North America and Quaker Foods North America. Overall, the foods division is more profitable than the beverages or international division. The lower portion of Exhibit 4.13 shows the decomposition of ROA into profit margin and assets turnover. The profit margins generally mirror the distribution of ROA in the upper portion of Exhibit 4.13, with PepsiCo Americas Foods showing the highest profit margins. Similarly, this division also has the highest assets turnover, followed by PepsiCo Americas Beverages and PepsiCo International. The overall higher level of profitability and asset utilization for PepsiCo Americas Foods and PepsiCo Americas Beverages is consistent with our discussions of life cycle theory in Chapter 3 (Exhibit 3.1) and earlier in this chapter (Exhibit 4.9). The Americas segments are older and more mature than the International segments, so it is understandable that the Americas divisions are more profitable and efficient. Growth segments such as PepsiCo International are not as profitable due to required investments in growing sales volume and refining production and distribution operations to levels comparable to more mature segments. If PepsiCo proves as successful internationally as it has been in the Americas, profit margin and asset turnover for these segments should improve in the future. Because of this regularity, segment disclosures are frequently most helpful in the forecasting part of financial statement analysis and valuation, which we will return to in Chapter 10.

A caveat of segment reporting analysis relates to the data used. Note that the information in Note 1 of PepsiCo's footnotes is the basis of calculations for Exhibits 4.12 and 4.13. Exhibit 4.12 is based on sales that reconcile to the total for consolidated results for PepsiCo; that is, the total sales of all six segments adds up to the total sales for PepsiCo consolidated. However, Exhibit 4.13 is based on operating profits that do not reconcile with consolidated total operating profit for PepsiCo. As indicated in Note 1 of PepsiCo's footnotes, the difference between total operating profit of $6,935 million in 2008 and the $7,942 million sum of the operating profits of the individual operating segments is caused by corporate unallocated expenses of $1,007 million. Total corporate unallocated expenses increased 33.7 percent from $753 million in 2007, while total sales increased only 9.6 percent. PepsiCo includes these expenses in selling, general, and administrative expenses in its income statement but does not allocate them to its operating segments when disclosing segment data. Following are the corporate unallocated expenses as a percentage of sales for the three years (in millions):

2006: $738/$35,137 = 2.1%
2007: $753/$39,474 = 1.9%
2008: $1,007/$43,251 = 2.3%

The analyst must exert caution when interpreting segment profit margins and ROAs. Changes in the amount of expenses allocated versus not allocated to segments, a choice made by management, affect these ratios. PepsiCo discloses that the increase in corporate unallocated expenses in 2008 relates primarily to $346 million in mark-to-market adjustments for commodity derivative hedges, which we discussed above and chose not to adjust in our analyses.

Summary of Profit Margin Analysis

We noted at the beginning of this section that PepsiCo's profit margin for ROA fluctuated between 16.7 and 17.8 percent during 2006 through 2008. This reflected a declining profit margin for ROA (from 14.9 percent in 2006 to 13.6 percent in 2008) and increasing assets turnover. We used common-size analysis to identify the primary contributions to the observed profit margins and analyzed each item to better understand the factors contributing to the overall profit margin. The summary of our findings for the analysis of profit margins is as follows:

- Bottling equity income decreased in 2008, due primarily to PepsiCo's pretax share of a $138 million restructuring charge by PBG.

- Interest revenue declined due to declining balances of cash and short-term investments and declining yields.
- Cost of sales increased due to higher commodity costs, including cooking oil and fuel.
- Selling, general, and administrative expenses increased in 2008, due primarily to a $346 million mark-to-market adjustment for derivative hedges.
- Income tax expense increased relative to sales, but this was due primarily to a large favorable settlement in the benchmark year of 2006.
- Segment analysis suggested that the growth in sales is occurring in international markets, where margins are lower than in more mature markets such as the Americas.

Having examined the first component of ROA—profit margin—we examine next the other component—total assets turnover.

Analyzing Total Assets Turnover

Total assets turnover captures how efficiently assets are being utilized to generate revenues. Higher sales generated with a given level of assets indicates more efficient use of those assets. Exhibit 4.6 showed that PepsiCo's total assets turnover increased between 2006 and 2007 from 1.14 to 1.22 and stayed at that level for 2008. Unlike the analysis of profit margin, where we decomposed the numerator by examining different expenses that determined operating profit, the analysis of total assets turnover can best be achieved by decomposing the denominator. We can gain greater insight into changes in the total assets turnover by examining turnover ratios for particular classes of assets. Analysts frequently calculate the following three turnover ratios:

- Accounts receivable turnover
- Inventory turnover
- Fixed assets turnover

Management's discussion and analysis of operations usually provides detailed explanations for operating profits, but it does not include explanations for changes in asset turnovers; so the analyst must search for possible clues. This is unfortunate because small changes in assets turnover can have enormous effects on the overall profitability of a firm (that is, ROA and ROCE).

Accounts Receivable Turnover

The rate at which accounts receivable turn over indicates the average time until firms collect them in cash. The analyst calculates accounts receivable turnover by dividing net sales on account by average accounts receivable. Most sales transactions between businesses are on account, not for cash. Except for retailers and restaurants that deal directly with consumers, the assumption that all sales are on account is usually reasonable. The calculation of the accounts receivable turnover for 2008 for PepsiCo, assuming that it makes all sales on account, is as follows (in millions):

$$\text{Accounts Receivable Turnover} = \frac{\text{Net Sales on Account}}{\text{Average Accounts Receivable}}$$

$$9.5 = \frac{\$43{,}251}{0.5\ (\$4{,}683 + \$4{,}389)}$$

PepsiCo's accounts receivable turnover was 9.7 in 2007 and 10.1 in 2006.

The analyst often expresses the accounts receivable turnover in terms of the average number of days receivables are outstanding before firms collect them in cash. The calculation divides 365 days by the accounts receivable turnover.[25] The average number of days that accounts receivable were outstanding was 38.4 days (= 365/9.5) during 2008, 37.6 days (= 365/9.7) during 2007, and 36.1 days (= 365/10.1) during 2006. One also could calculate the days sales included in the *ending* accounts receivable balance, in which case the calculation would be ending accounts receivable divided by average daily sales (= sales/365). Given an increased accounts receivable balance during 2008, this computation would yield slightly higher days sales for the ending receivables [$4,683/($43,251/365) = 39.5].

The interpretation of the average collection period depends on the terms of sale. These computations clearly indicate that PepsiCo is collecting accounts receivable more slowly. Assuming that customers must pay within 45 days, it appears that although they are paying more slowly, most of PepsiCo's customers pay within the required period. If the terms of sale are, for example, 15 days, on average, PepsiCo does not collect within the required period. Many firms transact business with credit sales terms of 30 days.

The interpretation of changes in the accounts receivable turnover and average collection period also relates to a firm's credit extension policies. Firms often use credit terms as a means of stimulating sales. For example, in an effort to stimulate sales, firms might permit customers to delay making payments on purchases of lawn mowers until after the summer and on snowmobiles until after the winter. Such actions would lead to a decrease in the accounts receivable turnover and an increase in the number of days receivables are outstanding. The changes in these accounts receivable ratios would not necessarily signal negative news if the increase in net income from the additional sales exceeded the cost of carrying accounts receivable for the extra time. Firms also can use credit policy to provide implicit financing to support affiliated companies, such as credit extended by automobile manufacturers to dealerships, producers to closely related distributors (such as PepsiCo and Coca-Cola to affiliated bottlers), and restaurant chains to franchisees or licensees (such as McDonald's to franchisees and Starbucks to licensees).

Retailing firms, particularly department store chains such as Sears and JCPenney, offer their own credit cards to customers. They use credit cards to stimulate sales and to earn interest revenue from customers' installment payments. Interpreting an increase in the number of days accounts receivable are outstanding involves two conflicting signals. The increase might suggest greater risk of uncollectibility, but it also provides additional interest revenues. Some firms price their products to obtain a relatively low gross margin from the sale and depend on interest revenue as a principal source of earnings. Thus, the analyst must consider a firm's credit strategy and policies when interpreting the accounts receivable turnover and days receivable outstanding ratios.

PepsiCo does not explain the slower accounts receivable turnover. A significant proportion of PepsiCo's accounts receivable likely relates to amounts owed PepsiCo by its bottlers and grocery retailers. PepsiCo might have intentionally granted more favorable repayment terms to support its bottlers and grocery retailers during the recessionary economy in 2007 and 2008. Another possibility is that repayment terms in other countries may differ from those in the United States. An increased percentage of sales from countries with longer repayment times might account for the slower accounts receivable turnover. In any case, the increase in the number of days it takes to collect accounts receivable from 36.1 days in 2006 to 38.4 days in 2008 does not seem to be a major concern. However, the trend has been increasing for several years going back prior to 2006. Assuming that PepsiCo borrowed

[25]Some analysts use 360 days in calculations like this. Although this choice introduces slight measurement error biasing toward faster turnover, as long as it is used consistently in all calculations, it is unlikely to have a significant effect on inferences.

short-term debt at 4 percent interest to finance the greater number of days receivables were outstanding, it would have cost PepsiCo approximately $1.1 million [= ({38.4 − 36.1}/365) × 0.04 × 0.5($4,683 + $4,389)] during 2008. PepsiCo's interest expense for 2008 was $329 million. Under these assumptions, the increase in collection period increased interest expense only 0.3 percent (= $1.1/$329).

Inventory Turnover

The rate at which inventories turn over indicates the length of time needed to produce, hold, and sell inventories. The analyst calculates the inventory turnover by dividing cost of goods sold by the average inventory during the period. The calculation of inventory turnover for PepsiCo for 2008 is as follows (in millions):

$$\text{Inventory Turnover} = \frac{\text{Cost of Goods Sold}}{\text{Average Inventories}}$$

$$8.5 = \frac{\$20{,}351}{0.5(\$2{,}522 + \$2{,}290)}$$

Thus, PepsiCo's inventory was on hand for an average of 42.9 days (= 365/8.5) during 2008. PepsiCo's inventory turnover was 8.6 (42.4 days) in 2007 and 8.7 (42.0 days) in 2006. Thus, the inventory turnover slowed by 0.9 days during the three-year period.

PepsiCo does not explain the slower inventory turnover. One possibility is that worldwide economic conditions led to reduced purchases of premium snacks or beverages, which could have led to reduced inventory turnover. The CEO's letter to shareholders (Appendix B) attributes sales declines for PepsiCo Americas Beverages to weakness in the U.S. economy. The MD&A (Appendix B) provides more details on the effect of the U.S. economy on beverage sales, indicating that carbonated soft drink volume declined 4 percent, largely due to lower sales of Pepsi and Sierra Mist, offset by increases in sales of Mountain Dew. Another possibility is that PepsiCo experienced a shift in sales mix due to its expansion in international markets with different consumer preferences. Unfortunately, the analyst cannot assess the latter possibility without a breakout of the various products by segment.

The interpretation of the inventory turnover figure involves two opposing considerations. A firm would like to sell as many goods as possible with a minimum of capital tied up in inventories. Moreover, inventory is subject to obsolescence or spoilage, especially in the case of food products. An increase in the rate of inventory turnover between periods would seem to indicate more profitable use of the investment in inventory and lowering costs for financing and carrying inventory. On the other hand, a firm does not want to have so little inventory on hand that shortages result and the firm misses sales opportunities. An increase in the rate of inventory turnover in this case may mean a loss of sales opportunities, thereby offsetting any cost savings achieved by a decreased investment in inventory. Firms must make trade-offs in deciding the optimum level of inventory and thus the desirable rate of inventory turnover.

The analyst often gains insight into changes in the inventory turnover by simultaneously examining changes in the inventory turnover and the cost of goods sold to sales percentage. Consider the following scenarios and possible interpretations:

- **Increasing cost of goods sold to sales percentage, coupled with an increasing inventory turnover.** The firm lowers prices to sell inventory more quickly. The firm shifts its product mix toward lower-margin, faster-moving products. The firm outsources the production of a higher proportion of its products, requiring it to share profit margin with the outsourcer but reducing the amount of raw materials and work-in-process inventories.

- **Decreasing cost of goods sold to sales percentage, coupled with a decreasing inventory turnover.** The firm raises prices to increase its gross margin, but inventory sells more slowly. The firm shifts its product mix toward higher-margin, slower-moving products. The firm produces a higher proportion of its products instead of outsourcing, thereby capturing more of the gross margin but requiring the firm to carry raw materials and work-in-process inventories.
- **Increasing cost of goods sold to sales percentage, coupled with a decreasing inventory turnover.** Weak economic conditions lead to reduced demand for the firm's products, necessitating price reductions to move goods. Despite price reductions, inventory builds up.
- **Decreasing cost of goods sold to sales percentage, coupled with an increasing inventory turnover.** Strong economic conditions lead to increased demand for the firm's products, allowing price increases. An inability to replace inventory as fast as the firm sells it leads to an increased inventory turnover. The firm implements a just-in-time inventory system, reducing storage costs, product obsolescence, and the amount of inventory held.

Some analysts calculate the inventory turnover ratio by dividing sales, rather than cost of goods sold, by the average inventory. As long as there is a reasonably constant relation between selling prices and cost of goods sold, the analyst can identify changes in the trend of the inventory turnover using either measure. It is inappropriate to use sales in the numerator if the analyst wants to use the inventory turnover ratio to calculate the average number of days inventory is on hand until sale or if the analyst wants to compare inventory turnover across firms with different markups and gross profit margins.

The cost-flow assumption (FIFO, LIFO, or weighted average) for inventories and cost of goods sold can significantly affect both the inventory turnover ratio and the cost of goods sold to sales percentage. Chapter 8 discusses the impact of the cost-flow assumption and illustrates adjustments the analyst might make to deal with these effects.

Fixed Assets Turnover

The fixed assets turnover ratio measures the relation between sales and the investment in property, plant, and equipment. The analyst calculates the fixed assets turnover by dividing sales by average fixed assets (net of accumulated depreciation) during the year. The fixed assets turnover ratio for PepsiCo for 2008 is as follows:

$$\text{Fixed Assets Turnover} = \frac{\text{Sales}}{\text{Average Fixed Assets}}$$

$$3.8 = \frac{\$43{,}251}{0.5(\$11{,}663 + \$11{,}228)}$$

The fixed assets turnover for PepsiCo also was 3.8 in 2007 and 2006. Increasing the fixed assets turnover ratio generally indicates greater efficiency in the use of existing fixed assets, but if a firm has excess capacity, it can indicate increasing utilization of that capacity. With this information in mind, the analyst must carefully interpret changes in the fixed assets turnover ratio. Firms invest in fixed assets in anticipation of higher production and sales in future periods. Thus, a temporarily low or decreasing rate of fixed assets turnover may signal an expanding firm preparing for future growth. On the other hand, a firm may reduce its capital expenditures if the near-term outlook for its products is poor. Such an action could lead to an increase in the fixed assets turnover ratio.

In recent years, many firms have increased the proportion of production outsourced to other manufacturers. This action allows firms to achieve the same (or increasing) sales levels with less fixed assets, thereby increasing the fixed assets turnover.

Other Asset Turnover Ratios

Although turnover ratios are most common for the assets discussed above (receivables, inventory, and fixed assets), any asset can be examined as a turnover ratio as long as the appropriate numerator is used in the calculation. For example, firms maintain varying levels of cash and analysts are often interested in the efficiency with which cash is managed. Thus, an investor can gauge the strategic maintenance of cash balances by a cash turnover ratio. The cash turnover ratio is computed by dividing sales by the average cash balance during the year. The cash turnover ratio for PepsiCo for 2008 is as follows:

$$\text{Cash Turnover} = \frac{\text{Sales}}{\text{Average Cash and Cash Equivalents}}$$

$$29.1 = \frac{\$43{,}251}{0.5(\$2{,}064 + \$910)}$$

Thus, PepsiCo turns over its cash balance approximately 29 times per year; equivalently, PepsiCo maintains a cash balance of approximately 12.5 days sales (= 365/29.1). Calculated with *sales* in the numerator, this implies that PepsiCo replenishes its cash balance every 12.5 days, which assumes that all sales are in cash. Alternatively, an analyst could view cash as a means of funding other working capital (inventory, for example). With this perspective, the analyst might calculate the cash turnover ratio with cost of goods sold in the numerator. The computations are similar to those above, but the interpretation is different.

Similarly, the analyst might want an overall metric for the efficiency with which all current assets are managed (rather than individually). Accordingly, the analyst would compute a current asset turnover ratio by dividing sales by the average current assets during the year. The current assets turnover ratio for PepsiCo for 2008 is as follows:

$$\text{Current Assets Turnover} = \frac{\text{Sales}}{\text{Average Current Assets}}$$

$$4.1 = \frac{\$43{,}251}{0.5(\$10{,}806 + \$10{,}151)}$$

Thus, PepsiCo turns over its current assets approximately every fiscal quarter. The current assets turnover ratio conveys information similar to that for individual asset turnover ratios for cash, receivables, or inventory. However, the current assets turnover ratio is often more representative because the volatility of total current assets is less than the volatility of an individual current asset. For example, stronger-than-expected end-of-year sales might result in ending receivables being temporarily above normal levels and inventory being temporarily below current levels. This would cause the receivables turnover ratio to be deflated but the inventory turnover ratio to be inflated. All else equal, however, the current assets turnover ratio would be less likely to be affected because the volatilities in receivables balances and inventory levels tend to offset each other.

The analysis of working capital turnovers also will be important in Chapter 5 when we discuss the use of financial analysis to assess short-term liquidity risks.

Summary of Assets Turnover Analysis

PepsiCo's total assets turnover was steady between 2007 and 2008. We examined the three primary asset turnover ratios: accounts receivable, inventory, and fixed assets. Both accounts receivable turnover and inventory turnover decreased slightly, while fixed assets turnover held constant. Accounts receivable make up approximately 13 percent of total assets, and inventories make up approximately 7 percent of total assets. (See the common-size balance sheet percentages in Exhibit 1.17.) However, fixed assets make up 32 percent of total assets. Thus, one would expect that the pattern in fixed assets turnover would dominate among these three, especially given only small changes in accounts receivable and inventory turnovers. However, other assets beside receivables, inventories, and fixed assets affect the total assets turnover computation with which we began our analysis. The utilization of other assets could be examined to supplement our analysis of only three asset classes that collectively account for just over half of total assets. For example, the percentage of total assets represented by intangible assets fell from 20.8 percent in 2007 to 19.3 percent in 2008. Note 4, "Property, Plant, and Equipment and Intangible Assets," in PepsiCo's 2008 Annual Report (Appendix A) indicates that the relative decrease in intangibles is due to scheduled amortization of amortizable intangible assets combined with negative currency translation adjustments for goodwill and brands at PepsiCo's various non-U.S. segments. In addition, Investments in Noncontrolled Affiliates fell from 12.6 percent of total assets to 10.8 percent in 2008. As discussed under "Bottling Equity Income" in our analysis of profit margin earlier in the chapter, PepsiCo has been reducing its level of investments in PBG, which explains the decrease.

Summary of ROA Analysis

Recalling the analogy of decomposing profitability to peeling back layers of an onion, our analysis of operating profitability involves four levels of depth:

- Level 1: ROA for the firm as a whole
- Level 2: Disaggregation of ROA into profit margin for ROA and assets turnover for the firm as a whole
- Level 3a: Disaggregation of profit margin into expense ratios for various cost items
- Level 3b: Disaggregation of assets turnover into turnovers for individual assets
- Level 4: Analysis of profit margins and asset turnovers for the segments of a firm

Exhibit 4.14 summarizes this analysis in a format used throughout the remainder of this book. **This layered approach to analyzing financial statements provides a disciplined approach that can be applied to any firm.**

Supplementing ROA in Profitability Analysis

ROA uses average total assets as a base for assessing a firm's effectiveness in using resources to generate earnings. For some firms and industries, total assets may not serve an informative role for this purpose because, as Chapter 2 discusses, accounting practices (1) do not assign asset values to certain valuable resources (technological knowledge and human capital) and (2) report assets at acquisition costs instead of current market values (forests for forest products companies and land for railroads). To supplement straightforward financial statement analysis, analysts often supplement ROA by relating sales, expenses, and earnings to *nonfinancial* attributes when evaluating profitability. This section discusses techniques for assessing profitability unique to several industries. The discussion is not intended to be exhaustive of all industries, but to provide a flavor for the types of supplemental measures used.

EXHIBIT 4.14

Profitability Analysis for PepsiCo at Levels 1, 2, and 3

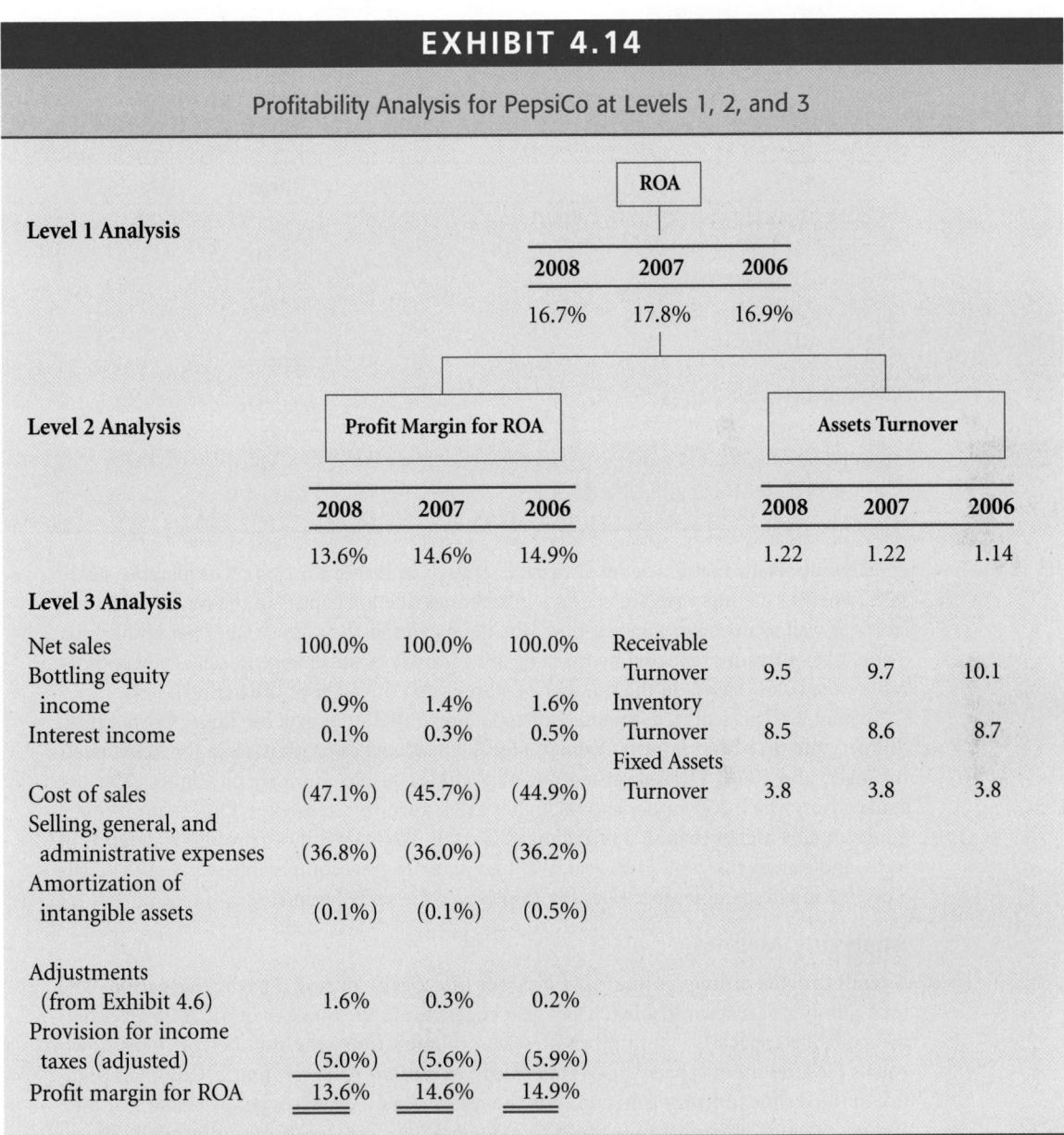

Level 1 Analysis

ROA

2008	2007	2006
16.7%	17.8%	16.9%

Level 2 Analysis

Profit Margin for ROA

2008	2007	2006
13.6%	14.6%	14.9%

Assets Turnover

2008	2007	2006
1.22	1.22	1.14

Level 3 Analysis

	2008	2007	2006
Net sales	100.0%	100.0%	100.0%
Bottling equity income	0.9%	1.4%	1.6%
Interest income	0.1%	0.3%	0.5%
Cost of sales	(47.1%)	(45.7%)	(44.9%)
Selling, general, and administrative expenses	(36.8%)	(36.0%)	(36.2%)
Amortization of intangible assets	(0.1%)	(0.1%)	(0.5%)
Adjustments (from Exhibit 4.6)	1.6%	0.3%	0.2%
Provision for income taxes (adjusted)	(5.0%)	(5.6%)	(5.9%)
Profit margin for ROA	13.6%	14.6%	14.9%

	2008	2007	2006
Receivable Turnover	9.5	9.7	10.1
Inventory Turnover	8.5	8.6	8.7
Fixed Assets Turnover	3.8	3.8	3.8

Analyzing Retailers

A key resource of retailers is their retail space. Some retailers own their stores, while others lease their space. The analyst can constructively capitalize the present value of operating lease commitments to ensure that total assets include store buildings under operating leases. (Chapter 6 discusses this adjustment.) An alternative approach when analyzing retailers is to express sales, operating expenses, and operating income on a per-store basis or per square foot of retail selling space. This supplemental base for evaluating profitability circumvents the issue of whether firms own or lease their space. It also eliminates the effects on the denominator of ROA of using different depreciation methods and depreciable lives and having fixed assets with different ages. However, it does not eliminate the effect of different depreciation methods or depreciable lives on income in the numerator. An

EXHIBIT 4.15

Profitability Ratios for Target and Walmart

	Target	Walmart
Per Square Foot:		
Sales	$ 302	$ 454
Cost of Goods Sold	(205)	(342)
Selling and Administrative	(76)	(86)
Operating Income	$ 21	$ 26
Profit Margin for ROA	4.30%	3.82%
Assets Turnover	1.47	2.45
ROA	6.3%	9.4%
Comparable Store Sales Change	(2.9)%	3.5%

equally important metric for retail firms is growth in "same store" or "comparable store" sales. Analysts are interested in changes in revenues due to changes in the number of retail stores as well as in changes in revenues due to changes in the average sales per retail store. Thus, a key measure reported by firms in this industry is the change in sales on a comparable store basis (based on the number of stores open throughout the period).

Exhibit 4.15 presents per-square-foot and comparable store data for Target Corporation (Target) and Wal-Mart Stores (Walmart) for 2008, as well as profit margin for ROA, assets turnover, and ROA. The superior ROA of Walmart results from much higher sales per square foot, which corresponds to its higher assets turnover. However, Target's profit margin is actually higher than that of Walmart. Overall, Walmart is more profitable in terms of ROA, and during the 2008 fiscal year, Walmart actually grew comparable stores sales versus a decline in comparable store sales for Target over the same period.

Analyzing Airlines

Aircraft provide airlines with a fixed amount of capacity during a particular period. The total number of seats available to carry passengers times the number of miles flown equals the available capacity. The number of seats occupied times the number of miles flown equals the amount of capacity used (referred to as *revenue passenger miles*). Common practice in the airline industry is to compute the revenues and expenses per available seat mile and per revenue passenger mile flown to judge pricing, cost structure, and profitability.

Exhibit 4.16 presents selected profitability data for American Airlines, JetBlue, and Airtran for 2008. American operates both domestic and international routes, while JetBlue and Airtran provide primarily domestic services. The employees of American and Airtran are unionized, while those of JetBlue are not. All three airlines are publicly owned. The first three columns present revenues, expenses, and operating income before income taxes per available seat mile, and the last three columns present the same income items per revenue passenger mile flown.

The costs of an airline (such as depreciation and compensation) are largely fixed for a particular year. Thus, the operating expenses per available seat mile indicate the costs of operating each airline. Fuel costs were significant for all airlines, but JetBlue had the lowest cost; American had the highest. Compensation costs also were highest at American, as were all other operating expenses. This resulted in a significant operating loss for American in

EXHIBIT 4.16

Profitability Ratios for American, JetBlue, and Airtran

	Per Available Seat Mile			Per Revenue Passenger Mile		
	American	JetBlue	Airtran	American	JetBlue	Airtran
Operating Revenues	14.53¢	10.44¢	10.72¢	18.04¢	13.00¢	13.47¢
Fuel	(5.51)	(4.17)	(5.02)	(6.84)	(5.19)	(6.30)
Compensation	(4.07)	(2.14)	(1.99)	(5.05)	(2.66)	(2.51)
Other Operating Expenses	(6.11)	(3.79)	(4.01)	(7.58)	(4.73)	(5.04)
Operating Income	(1.16¢)	0.34¢	(0.30¢)	(1.43¢)	0.42¢	(0.38¢)
Profitability Decomposition:						
Profit Margin for ROA				(8.7%)	2.2%	(8.7%)
Assets Turnover				0.68	0.58	1.24
ROA				(5.9%)	1.3%	(10.8%)

2008, despite also having the highest revenue per seat mile. Airtran had lower costs than American, but because operating revenues on a per-mile basis were lower, it also realized an operating loss in 2008. In contrast, JetBlue had the lowest operating revenue on a per-mile basis, but due to low fuel, compensation, and other costs, it was profitable in 2008. The profit margins were similar (and negative) for American and Airtran but were positive for JetBlue. The assets turnover for Airtran was highest, which combined with the negative profit margin to yield Airtran's negative ROA. Given similar profit margins, the difference in ROA between Airtran and American is driven by assets turnover differences. The explanation for the higher assets turnover for Airtran relative to American is that Airtran leases 100 of 136 aircraft, versus 220 out of 892 for American (not shown in Exhibit 4.16). JetBlue had the lowest assets turnover, but it had a positive profit margin, which produced a positive but low ROA.

The analyst can apply similar metrics to other firms with fixed capacity. The analysis of hospitals often focuses on income data per available bed or per patient day. The analysis of hotels uses income data per room. The analysis of cable and telecommunications companies examines income data per subscriber or customer. For-profit education firms are judged based on income data per student.

Analyzing Service Firms

Using ROA to analyze the profitability of firms that provide services can result in misleading conclusions because their most important resources, their employees who deliver the services, do not appear on the balance sheet as assets under GAAP. One approach to deal with this omission is to express income on a per-employee basis. However, the analyst must use these data cautiously because of differences among firms in their use of full- versus part-time employees and their mix of direct service providers versus support personnel.

Exhibit 4.17 presents profitability data for three service firms. VisionChina Media is one of China's largest mobile TV advertising networks, with extensive coverage in public transportation facilities (<500 employees). Monster Worldwide is an online recruitment firm that links employers with people seeking employment (approximately 7,000 employees). Accenture is a multinational management consulting firm (>175,000 employees). VisionChina has the highest operating revenues per employee, followed by Monster, then Accenture. This is due to

EXHIBIT 4.17

Profitability Data for VisionChina Media, Monster Worldwide, and Accenture

Per Employee:	VisionChina Media	Monster Worldwide	Accenture
Operating Revenues	$ 220,044	$193,328	$130,909
Compensation	(5,619)	(78,168)	(92,259)
Administrative and Other Expenses	(126,293)	(90,706)	(23,713)
Operating Income before Income Taxes	$ 88,132	$ 24,454	$ 14,937
Profitability Decomposition:			
Profit Margin for ROA	45.1%	9.4%	7.5%
Assets Turnover	0.44	0.67	1.88
ROA	19.8%	6.3%	14.1%

the combined exclusivity of VisionChina's network throughout China and the fact that the service it provides—advertising via mobile video terminals—does not rely on people to provide the service. In sharp contrast, Accenture's services are provided almost exclusively by employees. Also, compensation expense is highest for Accenture, followed by Monster and VisionChina, with VisionChina having the lowest compensation costs per employee.[26] Administrative and other expenses are highest for VisionChina, which incurs substantial costs for media equipment (essentially cost of sales) and other media under certain agreements, which Monster and Accenture do not report. This difference in business models can be seen with the significantly lower assets turnover for VisionChina, which actually maintains substantial investments in assets, as it is not purely a "service" firm. Assets turnover is highest for Accenture, which maintains limited fixed assets and possesses brand recognition and an extensive professional network. Operating revenues and operating income before taxes per employee are lowest at Accenture (with the largest workforce), but Accenture generates a very high ROA due to the high assets turnover. Monster's operating revenues and operating income before taxes per employee are between those of Accenture and VisionChina, but its ROA is lowest.

Per-employee data might usefully supplement traditional financial ratios for numerous other industries, including investment banking, temporary help firms, engineering firms, advertising firms, professional sports teams, information technology, and other service firms. The use of per-employee data also might supplement the analysis of firms that use fixed assets in the provision of services, such as airlines, health care providers, and hotels.

Analyzing Technology-Based Firms

ROA can be an even more misleading ratio for analyzing technology-based firms than for analyzing service firms if the two most important resources of technology firms do not appear in their assets: (1) their people and (2) their technologies. Employees contribute to the creation of technologies, but the most important resource not recognized is the value of the

[26]The individual line items require judgment, as neither company separately discloses an income statement line item for salaries and benefits. So the analyst must examine additional disclosures when available to best prepare cross-sectionally comparable expense classifications.

technologies (when those technologies have been internally generated rather than acquired). GAAP requires firms to expense R&D costs in the year incurred. Thus, both assets and net income are understated during periods in which firms invest heavily in R&D. Subsequently, after R&D has led to the introduction of successful, profitable new products, assets are understated but income is overstated because the firms have already expensed investments in R&D.

Research by Lev and Sougiannis documents the value of technologies that might provide a basis for recognizing a technology asset on the balance sheet and recomputing net income each year.[27] The authors propose a methodology that involves studying the relationship between R&D expenditures in a particular year and revenues of subsequent years. The technology "asset" equals the present value of the future revenue stream net of the R&D expenditure during the year. The analyst would then amortize this "asset" over the future periods of benefit based on the projected stream of revenues. Traditional financial ratio analysis works reasonably well for established technology firms that have products in all stages of their life cycles. Traditional financial ratio analysis does not work as well for start-up firms and firms with most of their products in the early high-growth stages of their life cycles. Thus, many analysts take as-reported income statement and balance sheets for such companies and recast them to allow for the capitalization of technology assets (and subsequent amortization), similar to the study by Lev and Sougiannis. This further emphasizes the need for analysts to understand financial statements and business operations rather than memorize ratio formulas or scripted analysis techniques.

RATE OF RETURN ON COMMON SHAREHOLDERS' EQUITY

ROA measures the profitability of operations before considering the effects of financing. That is, ROA ignores the proportion of debt versus equity financing that a firm uses to finance the assets and the cost of debt financing. ROA is important for analysts interested in the profitability and efficiency of the firm's core operations. ROCE, on the other hand, measures the return to common shareholders after subtracting from revenues not only operating expenses (such as cost of goods sold, selling and administration expenses, and income taxes), but also the costs of financing debt and preferred stock that are senior to the common stock. The latter includes interest expense on debt and dividends on preferred stock (if any). Thus, ROCE incorporates the results of a firm's operating, investing, and financing decisions.

The analyst calculates ROCE as follows:

$$\text{ROCE} = \frac{\text{Net Income} - \text{Preferred Stock Dividends}}{\text{Average Common Shareholders' Equity}}$$

The numerator measures the amount of net income for the period available to the common shareholders after subtracting all amounts allocable to senior claimants. The accountant subtracts interest expense on debt in measuring net income, so the calculation of the numerator of ROCE requires no adjustment for creditors' claims on earnings. However, the analyst must subtract dividends paid or payable on preferred stock from net income to obtain income attributable to the common shareholders.[28]

---

[27] Baruch Lev and Theodore Sougiannis, "The Capitalization, Amortization and Value-Relevance of R&D," *Journal of Accounting and Economics* (1996), pp. 107–138.

[28] Chapter 14 indicates that for purposes of valuation, the analyst might compute ROCE using comprehensive income available to common shareholders, not net income available to common shareholders. Recall from Chapter 2 that comprehensive income equals net income plus or minus changes in the value of certain assets and liabilities that GAAP requires firms to include in Other Comprehensive Income until realized.

The denominator of ROCE measures the average amount of total common shareholders' equity in use during the period. An average of the total common shareholders' equity at the beginning and end of the year is appropriate unless a firm made a significant new common stock issue or buyback during the year. If the latter occurred, the analyst should use an average of the common shareholders' equity at the end of each quarter to better reflect the outstanding common shareholders' equity during the year.

Common shareholders' equity equals total shareholders' equity minus the minority interest in the net assets of consolidated subsidiaries minus the par value of preferred stock. Because net income to common shareholders in the numerator reflects a subtraction for the minority interest in earnings of consolidated subsidiaries, the denominator should exclude the minority interest in net assets (if any). Firms seldom issue preferred stock significantly above par value, so the analyst can assume that the amount in the additional paid-in capital account relates to common stock.[29]

FSAP

PepsiCo reports no minority interest in its income statement or balance sheet, although it does have preferred stock outstanding. The calculation of the ROCE of PepsiCo for 2008, using the *reported* amounts of net income, which is shown on the "Analysis" worksheet of FSAP, is as follows (in millions):

$$\text{ROCE} = \frac{\text{Net Income} - \text{Preferred Stock Dividends}}{\text{Average Common Shareholders' Equity}}$$

$$34.8\% = \frac{\$5{,}142 - \$8}{0.5(\$12{,}203 + \$17{,}325)}$$

The calculation of the ROCE of PepsiCo for 2008, using the *adjusted* amounts of net income discussed previously and displayed in Exhibit 4.4, is as follows (in millions):

$$\text{ROCE} = \frac{\text{Adjusted Net Income} - \text{Preferred Stock Dividends}}{\text{Average Common Shareholders' Equity}}$$

$$38.3\% = \frac{\$5{,}664 - \$8}{0.5(\$12{,}203 + \$17{,}325)}$$

The amount for the preferred stock dividends appears in Note 11, "Net Income per Common Share from Continuing Operations" (Appendix A).[30] For purposes of our analysis of PepsiCo in this chapter, we demonstrate how to calculate net income available to common shareholders using the full preferred stock dividends, including a redemption premium.[31] Adjusting net

[29]Some analysts use the acronym ROCE to refer to "return on capital employed." The numerator of return on capital employed is net income before interest expense (net of tax savings) on long-term debt. The denominator is the average amount of long-term debt and shareholders' equity during the year. The rate of return on capital employed generally falls between ROA and ROCE as we have defined these ratios. We do not use return on capital employed in this book, but it is important to realize the confusion that blind adherence to acronyms can cause. Indeed, ROE is probably more common than ROCE, but we use the latter to emphasize that the construct we want is return on *common* shareholders' equity, not to be confused with total equity, which includes preferred equity for firms that issue preferred stock.

[30]The $8 million amount for preferred dividends in the numerator is actually a preferred dividend of $2 million and a redemption premium on preferred stock of $6 million. The SEC requires firms that redeem preferred stock for more than its book, or carrying, value to subtract the excess from net income when computing net income available to common shareholders in the computation of earnings per share. See Securities and Exchange Commission, *EITF Abstracts,* Topic No. D 42, "The Effect on the Calculation of Earnings per Share for the Redemption or Induced Conversion of Preferred Stock" (1994); *FASB Codification Topic 260.* To maintain consistency in the calculation of ROCE and earnings per share, we subtract the redemption premium in the numerator of both ratios. Analysts will likely encounter such redemption premiums infrequently.

[31]However, users of FSAP should note that due to the rarity of this item and its relative immateriality, FSAP follows the standard approach of adjusting only for the preferred stock dividend and treats the redemption premium as other expense. The alternative exposition in the chapter is intended to highlight the judgment required when analyzing financial statements, particularly when firms engage in unusual or nonrecurring transactions.

income for the preferred stock dividends and redemption premium, the ROCE of PepsiCo was 34.1 percent in 2007 and 34.0 percent in 2006, consistent with an upward trend in ROCE, in contrast to the fluctuating trend in ROA discussed earlier in the chapter.

Benchmarks for ROCE

Having computed (adjusted) ROCE for PepsiCo of 38.3 percent in 2008, the question arises as to whether this is "good" or "bad." One benchmark is the average ROCE of other firms. The average ROCE for the cross-section of publicly traded firms in the United States is approximately 10–12 percent, so PepsiCo is well above the average ROCE; hence, 38.3 percent is certainly "good."[32] Also, the ROCE of a similar firm such as Coca-Cola also can serve as a benchmark. For 2008, Coca-Cola had an ROCE of 27.5 percent, which also supports the inference that PepsiCo generates a substantially above average ROCE.

A more direct benchmark against which to judge ROCE is the return demanded by common shareholders for a firm's use of their capital. Because common shareholders are the residual claimants of the firm, accountants do not treat the cost of common shareholders' equity capital as an expense when computing net income. On the other hand, a firm that earns less than the cost of common equity capital destroys value for shareholders, whereas a firm that generates ROCE that exceeds the cost of capital creates value. ROCE measures the return to the common shareholders but does not indicate whether this rate of return exceeds or falls short of the cost of common equity capital.

To illustrate, PepsiCo's ROCE for 2008 as computed above is 38.3 percent. If the cost of common equity capital of PepsiCo is, for example, 8 percent, PepsiCo generated an excess return of 30.3 percent (= 38.3% − 8.0%). If the cost of common equity capital is, for example, 40 percent, PepsiCo did not generate a return sufficient to cover the cost of common equity capital.[33]

Conceptually, the cost of common equity capital is the rate of return the common shareholders demand as compensation for forgoing consumption and bearing the risk of investing in a firm. Measuring the cost of common equity capital is more difficult than measuring the cost of debt because debt instruments typically specify an interest rate, which occasionally differs from the effective rate, but typically by only small amounts. The dividend on common stock is not an accurate measure of the cost of common equity capital because managers and boards of directors determine dividend payout policies, whereas equity investors determine the cost of equity capital. Chapter 11 discusses the computation of the cost of equity capital, and Chapters 11–14 incorporate it into various valuation methods.

Chapter 13 describes a measure known as *residual income* (also called *abnormal earnings*). The principal difference between net income available to common shareholders, the numerator of ROCE, and residual income is that residual income includes a subtraction for the cost of common shareholders' equity capital, as follows:

$$\text{Residual Income} = \text{Net Income Available to Common Shareholders} - (\text{Cost of Equity Capital} \times \text{Beginning Common Shareholders' Equity})$$

The analyst might view residual income as a measure of the wealth a firm generates for its common shareholders in a period beyond the required return on their investment in the

---

[32]Average ROCEs depend on many factors, including the period of measurement, samples of firms used, and definitions of accounting data used in the numerator and denominator of the ROCE calculation.

[33]PepsiCo's cost of common equity capital is likely closer to 8 percent than to 40 percent. Chapter 11 discusses PepsiCo's cost of equity capital more fully, where we estimate it to be 8.5 percent.

firm. In recent years, the financial press and some corporate managers have given considerable attention to a measure called *economic value added* (EVA)®. Stern Stewart & Co., a management consulting firm, has taken the lead in promoting this measure.[34] Similar to but not identical to residual income, EVA likewise includes a subtraction for the cost of common shareholders' equity capital.[35] The concept behind EVA is that a firm does not create value unless it earns more than the cost of all of its capital, including common shareholders' equity capital. Chapter 13 describes how forecasts of residual income can be used to value a firm, equivalent to values obtained from using dividends or free cash flows as valuation model inputs. The intuition under this approach is that valuations are higher as firms generate future ROCE higher than the cost of equity capital. This same intuition is relevant in any analysis of ROCE.

As will be discussed further on the topic of the implications of market-based ratios in Chapter 14, ROCE is subject to the same life cycle and competitive pressures discussed earlier in the chapter. For example, Bernard (1994) examined the behavior of ROCE across time, conditional on the base year ROCE.[36] Exhibit 4.18 plots results from his study, which

EXHIBIT 4.18

Evolution of Future ROCE Conditional on Current ROCE

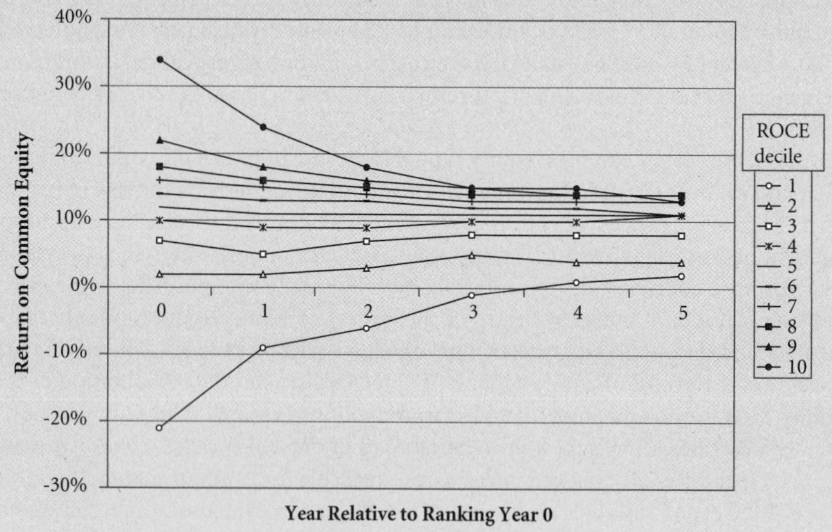

---

[34]Other consulting firms promote similar measures, such as HOLT Value Associates' *cash flow return on investment* (CFROI), L.E.K. Consulting's *shareholder value added* (SVA), Marakon's *discounted economic profits* (EP), and KPMG's *economic value management* (EVM).

[35]The precise computation of EVA involves other accounting adjustments to net income that we do not consider here. See G. Bennett Stewart, III, *The Quest for Value* (New York: HarperCollins Publishers), 1999. Young and O'Bryne (2001) discuss that although close to 200 accounting adjustments have been discussed, most applications involve around ten adjustments. See David S. Young and Stephen F. O'Byrne, *EVA and Value-Based Management—A Practical Guide to Implementation* (New York: McGraw-Hill), 2001.

[36]See Victor L. Bernard, "Accounting-Based Valuation Methods, Determinants of Market-to-Book Ratios, and Implications for Financial Statement Analysis." Unpublished manuscript, University of Michigan Business School, Kresge Library (January 1994).

partitioned firms into deciles based on beginning ROCE and then tracked the average ROCE for each decile over subsequent years. The graph indicates that the initial spread in ROCE is very large, with the most profitable firms generating ROCEs in excess of 30 percent and the least profitable firms generating returns below negative 20 percent. However, competitive pressures erode the abnormally high ROCEs of the most profitable firms, and survival (or bankruptcy or an acquisition) results in the poorest performing firms increasing ROCE to positive levels. This does not imply that all firms with above-average ROCEs will realize lower ROCEs in the future, but it is the dominant pattern. A few companies with sustainable strategic advantages and/or substantial off-balance assets and equity (such as PepsiCo's valuable brand names) can generate ROCEs well above the average for extended numbers of years.

Relating ROA to ROCE

ROA measures operating performance independent of financing, while ROCE explicitly considers the cost of debt and preferred stock financing. Exhibit 4.1 diagrams the relation between ROA and ROCE and shows that both can be decomposed into margin, turnover, and leverage (although differences are highlighted with dashed lines). An expanded diagram of the relation between ROA and ROCE is as follows:[37]

Return on Assets	→	**Return to Creditors**	**Return to Preferred Shareholders**	**Return to Common Shareholders**
Net Income + Interest Expense Net of Taxes	→	Interest Expense Net of Taxes	Preferred Dividends	Net Income to Common
Average Total Assets		Average Total Liabilities	Average Preferred Shareholders' Equity	Average Common Shareholders' Equity

The analyst allocates each dollar of return generated from using assets to the various providers of capital. Creditors receive their return first in the form of interest payments. The cost of this capital to the firm is interest expense net of the income tax benefit derived from deducting interest in calculating taxable income. Many other liabilities, such as accounts payable and salaries payable, carry no explicit interest cost.

The preferred stock carries a cost equal to the preferred dividend amount. Historically, firms could not deduct preferred dividends when calculating taxable income, but in recent years, firms have been successful in structuring preferred stock issues so that they qualify for tax deductibility of dividends paid. In those cases, the analyst should adjust preferred dividends for the related tax savings.

The portion of net income that is *not* allocated to creditors or preferred shareholders is available for the common shareholders as the residual claimants. Likewise, the portion of a firm's assets not financed with capital provided by creditors or preferred shareholders represents the capital provided by the common shareholders.[38]

[37] Note that the relation does not appear as an equation. We use an arrow instead of an equal sign to indicate that the return on assets gets allocated to the various suppliers of capital. To express the relation as an equality requires that we weight each rate by the proportion of each type of capital in the capital structure.

[38] If a firm does not own 100 percent of the common stock of a consolidated subsidiary, the accountant must allocate a portion of the ROA to the minority shareholders. Thus, a fourth term would appear on the right-hand side of the arrow: minority interest in earnings/average minority interest in net assets.

Now consider the relation between ROA and ROCE. Under what circumstances will ROCE exceed ROA? Under what circumstances will ROCE be less than ROA? The key to answering those questions lies in understanding how the use of financing from sources other than common shareholders can harm or benefit common shareholders.

ROCE will exceed ROA whenever ROA exceeds the cost of capital provided by creditors and preferred shareholders. If a firm can generate a higher return on capital provided by creditors and preferred shareholders than the cost of those sources of capital, the excess return belongs to the common shareholders.

To illustrate, recall that PepsiCo generated an ROA of 16.7 percent during 2008 (adjusted for unusual items). The after-tax cost of capital provided by creditors during 2008 was 1.04 percent [= (1−0.35)($329)/0.5($23,888 + $17,394)].[39] The difference between the 1.04 percent cost of creditor capital and the 16.7 percent ROA generated on assets financed with debt capital belongs to the common shareholders. The preferred shareholders received a dividend of $2 million and PepsiCo paid a redemption premium of $6 million when it redeemed preferred stock during 2008. PepsiCo paid this dividend on the $41 million of outstanding preferred stock. However, PepsiCo repurchased preferred stock for more than it initially issued the stock, resulting in a negative net amount for preferred stock on the balance sheet. The average amount of preferred stock equity is a negative $94 million [= 0.5($41 − $138 + $41 − $132)]. Therefore, the calculated cost of preferred equity capital is negative 8.5 percent (= $8/−$94). Although showing a negative preferred shareholders' equity is mathematically correct, it is not conceptually sound. The excess in an economic sense reduces *common* shareholders' equity. However, we follow PepsiCo's treatment of the repurchased preferred stock as an element of preferred stock equity, not common stock equity.

The common shareholders also have a full claim on the 16.7 percent ROA generated on the assets financed with the equity capital they provided. Thus, the ROCE of PepsiCo for 2008 comprises the following. (Calculations use rates of return taken to more decimal points than the three shown, such as ROA = 0.1665.)

Excess Return on Capital Provided by Creditors:	
[0.167 − 0.010][0.5($23,888 + $17,394)]	$3,222
Deficient Return on Negative Capital Provided by Preferred Shareholders:	
[0.167 − (–0.085)][0.5($41 − $138 + $41 − $132)]	(24)
Return on Capital Provided by Common Shareholders:	
[0.167][0.5($12,203 + $17,325)]	2,458
Total Return to Common Shareholders	$5,656
ROCE: $5,656/[0.5($12,203 +$17,325)]	38.3%

Common business terminology refers to the practice of using lower-cost creditor and preferred stock capital to increase the return to common shareholders as *financial leverage* or *capital structure leverage.* To clarify the concept, consider the following simple example: Suppose a firm has one common equity investor who invests $100 to fund a firm that generates an ROA of 10 percent. At the end of the year, income available to the common equity investor is $10, reflecting the ROA of 10 percent (= $10 income ÷ $100 investment). Alternatively, the single equity investor could have invested only $10 and borrowed $90 to

[39] The amounts in the denominator for PepsiCo equal total assets minus total shareholders' equity, or equivalently, total liabilities. The after-tax cost of creditor capital seems low, but recall that many liabilities do not carry an explicit interest cost.

have the same amount to invest ($100) and generate the same return (10 percent). Suppose creditors provide the $90 loan at an after-tax interest cost to the firm of 5 percent. At the end of the year, the firm would have generated the same income of $10, but the after-tax cost of financing would be $4.50 (= $90 debt × 5 percent), leaving income available to the common shareholder of $5.50. Thus, a much smaller investment of $10 (rather than $100) combined with debt financing of $90 enables the common equity investor to realize a substantially higher rate of return. In this case, rather than a 10 percent return on equity, the equity investor would have realized a 55 percent return on equity (= $5.50 income ÷ $10 investment). This example demonstrates the advantages of the strategic use of financial leverage to increase returns to equity investors: deploying assets that generate 10 percent but partially financing through capital that costs only 5 percent generates "abnormal" returns. Of course, increased leverage triggers greater risk, which we will discuss in Chapter 5.

Regarding debt and preferred shareholders' equity combined, PepsiCo's financial leverage worked to the advantage of its common shareholders in 2006–2008 because its ROA exceeded the cost of all non-common equity financing. This resulted in ROCE exceeding ROA. We can measure the incremental effect of financial leverage beyond ROA by computing the ratio of ROCE divided by ROA. The ratios for PepsiCo are as follows:

2008: 38.3%/16.7% = 2.29
2007: 34.1%/17.8% = 1.92
2006: 34.0%/16.9% = 2.01

Thus, financial leverage worked very well during 2008 relative to the previous two years. Next, we explore the possible reasons for this increased effectiveness.

Disaggregating ROCE

We can disaggregate ROCE into several components to aid in its interpretation, much as we did with ROA. The disaggregated components of ROCE are profit margin for ROCE, assets turnover, and capital structure leverage. Note the distinction between profit margin for ROA and profit margin for ROCE is simply the different numerator used. The numerator of profit margin for ROCE is net income available to common shareholders, and the numerator for profit margin for ROA is net income with after tax interest expense and minority interest added back, which yields a measure of profits before deduction of financing costs.

ROCE	=	**Profit Margin for ROCE**	×	**Assets Turnover**	×	**Capital Structure Leverage**

$$\frac{\text{Net Income to Common}}{\text{Average Common Shareholders' Equity}} = \frac{\text{Net Income to Common}}{\text{Sales}} \times \frac{\text{Sales}}{\text{Average Total Assets}} \times \frac{\text{Average Total Assets}}{\text{Average Common Shareholders' Equity}}$$

The profit margin for ROCE indicates the earnings allocable to the common shareholders after subtracting from revenues all operating expenses and all financing costs of capital senior to the common shareholders. Note that the profit margin for ROA, used in the disaggregation of ROA, is measured *before* financing costs. The profit margin for ROCE is measured *after* financing costs for debt and preferred stock capital. Assets turnover is identical to that used to disaggregate ROA. The capital structure leverage ratio measures the degree to which a firm utilizes financial leverage to finance assets. The difference between the numerator and the denominator of the capital structure leverage ratio is the amount of liabilities (and preferred shareholders' equity, if any) in the capital structure. The larger the amount of capital obtained from these sources, the smaller the amount of capital obtained from common shareholders and therefore the larger the capital structure leverage ratio. Another way to interpret the capital structure leverage ratio is as follows:

$$\frac{\text{Total Assets}}{\text{Common Shareholders' Equity}} = \frac{\text{Debt} + \text{Preferred Equity} + \text{Common Shareholders' Equity}}{\text{Common Shareholders' Equity}} = 1 + \frac{\text{Debt} + \text{Preferred Equity}}{\text{Common Shareholders' Equity}}$$

Thus, capital structure leverage is simply one plus the debt-to-equity ratio for a firm with no preferred stock or one plus the ratio of debt plus preferred equity to common shareholder equity for a firm with preferred stock.

Before proceeding with a disaggregation of PepsiCo's ROCE, we note that there are many more ways to disaggregate ROA or ROCE than are discussed in this chapter. We will explore one alternative method of decomposing ROCE in the next chapter, which will highlight the importance of benchmarking the returns generated by the firm's assets against the cost of borrowing from creditors. The decomposition of ROCE to be discussed in Chapter 5 requires the analyst to partition the income statement and balance sheet into operating and financing components. Then the analyst computes ROCE as follows:

$$\text{ROCE} = \text{RNOA} + \text{Leverage} \times (\text{RNOA} - \text{Net Borrowing Cost}),$$

where RNOA is "return on net operating assets." As will be discussed in Chapter 5, RNOA captures the returns generated by the operating activities of the firm, Leverage captures the extent to which the firm uses creditor financing, and the term (RNOA − Net Borrowing Cost) is the relative spread between the operating returns and the effective cost of creditor financing. The intuition is that when the firm's assets generate sufficiently high returns to cover the cost of borrowing (that is, the last term in the preceding equation), financial leverage can be strategically used to boost returns to common shareholders.

The disaggregation of ROCE for PepsiCo for 2008 under the basic decomposition discussed in this chapter is as follows:

$$\textbf{ROCE} = \textbf{Profit Margin for ROCE} \times \textbf{Assets Turnover} \times \textbf{Capital Structure Leverage}$$

$$\frac{\$5{,}664 - \$8}{0.5(\$12{,}203 + \$17{,}325)} = \frac{\$5{,}664 - \$8}{\$43{,}251} \times \frac{\$43{,}251}{0.5(\$35{,}994 + \$34{,}628)} \times \frac{0.5(\$35{,}994 + \$34{,}628)}{0.5(\$12{,}203 + \$17{,}325)}$$

$$38.3\% = 13.1\% \times 1.22 \times 2.39$$

Exhibit 4.19 presents the disaggregation of ROCE of PepsiCo for 2006–2008. The increasing ROCE of PepsiCo results from the net effect of (1) decreasing profit margins over 2006–2008, (2) an increase in assets turnover in 2007, and (3) a marked increase in capital structure leverage in 2008. The decreasing profit margin for ROCE mirrors that discussed previously for ROA. The calculation of assets turnover is the same in the decomposition of ROA and ROCE, so it also mirrors the previous discussion about the decomposition of

EXHIBIT 4.19

Disaggregation of ROCE of PepsiCo: 2006–2008

	ROCE	=	Profit Margin for ROCE	×	Total Assets Turnover	×	Capital Structure Leverage
2008	38.3%	=	13.1%	×	1.22	×	2.39
2007	34.1%	=	14.2%	×	1.22	×	1.97
2006	34.0%	=	14.4%	×	1.14	×	2.07

ROA. The primary difference between the ROA and ROCE decompositions is the capital structure leverage component. We must examine changes in PepsiCo's capital structure by examining changes in each source of financing. The change in preferred equity on the balance sheet is minimal, so it cannot explain the increased leverage. (See Appendix A.) The balance sheet does indicate changes in liabilities (which increased from $17,394 million to $23,888 million) and common shareholders' equity (which decreased from $17,325 million to $12,203 million).

The statement of cash flows and Note 9, "Debt Obligations and Commitments," indicate that PepsiCo issued $1,750 million and $2,000 million of senior unsecured notes in the second and fourth quarters of 2008, respectively, accounting for an additional $3,750 million of long-term debt obligations, netted by scheduled payments of long-term debt and other activity for short-term borrowings. Also, other liabilities increased from $4,792 million to $7,017 million. PepsiCo does not specifically discuss this change in other liabilities, but Note 7, "Pension, Retiree Medical, and Savings Plans," shows that PepsiCo's U.S. pension plan assets declined in value $1,434 billion during 2008, resulting in an underfunded status of the pension plans in the United States of $2,243 million, of which $2,183 million was included in other liabilities (relative to only $672 million at the end of 2007). The decline in value of pension fund assets is consistent with the sharp decline in the financial markets during 2008.

The statement of common shareholders' equity (see Appendix A) provides an explanation for why common shareholders' equity declined, with components summarized as follows (in millions):

	2008	2007	Change
Common stock	$ 30	$ 30	$ 0
Paid-in capital	351	450	(99)
Retained earnings	30,638	28,184	2,454
Accumulated other comprehensive loss	(4,694)	(952)	(3,742)
Treasury stock	(14,122)	(10,387)	(3,735)
Common Shareholders' Equity	$12,203	$17,325	$(5,122)

The net decrease in common shareholders' equity reflects the net of three large changes. First, retained earnings increased, reflecting primarily net income of $5,142 million less common dividends of $2,589 million, preferred dividends of $2 million, and restricted stock unit (RSU) dividends of $8 million. Second, PepsiCo's accumulated other comprehensive loss increased $3,742 million. This reflects primarily two changes. Currency translation adjustments turned unfavorable, reducing common shareholders' equity by $2,484 million, and net pension plan assets suffered declines of $1,376 million. Both amounts are commensurate with the global economic crisis during 2008 and sharp declines in the financial markets.

A moderate increase in liabilities—along with a significant decrease in shareholders' equity—caused PepsiCo's common shareholder leverage to increase from 1.97 to 2.39 in 2008. The $5,122 million net decrease in common shareholders' equity includes a large amount of other comprehensive loss, one can view the net of changes in retained earnings and treasury stock as net changes in common shareholders' equity due to management's decisions regarding capital structure. This change equates to a net decrease in the net of shareholders' equity and treasury stock of $1,281 million (= $2,454 − $3,735) reflecting a return of capital to shareholders in excess of what was generated during 2008. In addition, PepsiCo issued $3,750 million in debt during the year. The combination of the $1,281 decrease in common equity (exclusive of accumulated other comprehensive income) and $3,750 million increase in debt results in a deliberate net increase in leverage by PepsiCo management. During periods when equity prices fall, managers of profitable firms often repurchase common shares on the open market and seek needed financing through the debt markets (rather than issue shares at potentially deflated prices). The adjustments of $3,742 million for accumulated other comprehensive loss further reduced common shareholders' equity at the end of 2008, making a significant contribution to the overall increased leverage. The rationale for allowing adjustments for accumulated other comprehensive income to reside temporarily in shareholders' equity is that such adjustments are expected to be temporary. If the adjustments reverse and PepsiCo makes no further capital structure changes, PepsiCo's leverage will decline from current levels. The analyst will want to better understand these adjustments to gauge the likelihood and timing of any such adjustments. For example, losses in pension plan assets that are more likely to be permanent indicate a substantial future drag on shareholders' income to remedy the underfunded pension fund status. We will discuss pension plans in more detail in Chapter 8.

INTERPRETING FINANCIAL STATEMENT RATIOS

Financial ratios are easy to compute, and there are many sources of financial data that do the computing for investors, including free websites such as Yahoo! Finance and Smartmoney.com. The most important and valuable step, however, is *interpreting and gleaning key insights from a financial ratio.* To do this successfully, the analyst must know how a ratio was computed. For example, was ROA computed correctly such that the numerator includes net profits after taxes but before interest, or is the analyst using someone else's calculation that simply uses EBIT in the numerator? Differences in computations do not always create significant differences in ratio calculations, but the astute analyst must be aware of the underlying data embedded in ratios. The second, and most crucial, aspect of interpreting ratios is doing so with an understanding of the firm's economic environment and business strategy. As noted earlier in the chapter, an analyst must understand a firm's industry, organizational structure, and strategy to develop hypotheses about what to expect in terms of financial position, profitability, risk, and growth.

Analyzing financial statement ratios is the forensic part of the process of investigating for insights and answers to questions about how the firm is performing. In this step, the analyst must dig deep to understand why ratios are what they are. How do the ratios reflect the economics of the industry and the specific strategy of the firm? Do the ratios suggest that a firm is performing better or worse compared to its peers or is performing better or worse through time? Are there accounting choices that hinder the ability to productively use ratios to better understand the firm? In summary, the first three steps of the six-step process discussed in Chapter 1 (that is, (1) identify economic characteristics of the industry, (2) identify company strategies, and (3) assess the quality of the financial statements) link directly to the use of ratios to validate an analyst's understanding of the profitability and risk of a firm and to generate new insights not discovered in the first three steps.

The analyst can compare financial ratios for a particular firm with similar ratios for the same firm for earlier periods (time-series analysis), as we did in this chapter for PepsiCo, or with those of other firms for the same period (cross-sectional analysis), as we did for PepsiCo versus Coca-Cola and several other sets of firms in this chapter. The next section discusses some of the general issues involved in making such comparisons.

Comparisons with Earlier Periods

A time-series analysis of a particular firm's financial statement ratios permits a historical tracking of the trends and variability in the ratios over time. A firm's past financial ratios serve as a benchmark for interpreting its financial ratios during the current period. The analyst can draw useful insights by comparing a firm with itself over time. The analyst can study the impact of economic conditions (recession and inflation), industry conditions (shift in regulatory status and new technology), and firm-specific conditions (shift in corporate strategy and new management) on the time-series pattern of these ratios.

Some questions the analyst should raise before using ratios of past financial statement data as a basis for interpreting ratios for the current period are as follows:

1. Has the firm made a significant change in its product, geographic, or customer mix that affects the comparability of financial statement ratios over time?
2. Has the firm made a major acquisition or divestiture?
3. Has the firm changed its methods of accounting over time? For example, does the firm now consolidate a previously unconsolidated entity?
4. Are there any unusual or nonrecurring amounts that impair a comparable analysis of financial results across years?

Analysts should not use past performance as a basis for comparison without considering the level of past and current performance. For example, prior performance might have been at an unsatisfactory level. Improvement during the current year may still leave the firm at an undesirable level. An improved profitability ratio may mean little if the firm still ranks last in its industry in terms of profitability in all years. Similarly, if the firm's prior performance was exceptional but declined in the current period, the firm still may have performed well in the current period. An analyst may be less concerned about a decline in profitability if the firm ranks as the most profitable firm in its industry.

Another concern involves interpreting the relative rate of change in a ratio over time. The analyst's interpretation of a 10 percent increase in profit margin for ROA differs depending on whether other firms in the industry experienced a 15 percent versus a 5 percent increase. Comparing a particular firm's ratios with those of similar firms lessens the concerns discussed here.

Careful time-series analyses of a firm's financial ratios will not only yield key insights about how and why the firm's profitability has been changing over time, but also will provide valuable information about trends. Chapter 10 discusses techniques for building detailed and careful forecasts of financial statements, and we rely heavily on the information and trends gathered from time-series analysis of ratios. In that chapter, we project future financial statements for PepsiCo for the next five years, and the information in the current and past financial ratios provides valuable insights to help us make more reliable forecasts.

Comparisons with Other Firms

The major task confronting the analyst in performing a cross-sectional analysis is identifying the other firms to use for comparison. The objective is to select firms with similar products and strategies and similar size and age. Few firms may meet these criteria, and no firms will meet these criteria perfectly. Coca-Cola, for example, is a logical comparison firm for PepsiCo. However, Coca-Cola derives virtually all of its revenues from beverages, whereas PepsiCo derives revenues from beverages and food products, which makes the comparison less than perfect. However, comparable firms are never perfectly comparable. Even the comparison of similar firms such as Target and Walmart (discussed earlier in the chapter) gets complicated because Target's operations include a segment for its branded credit card and Walmart's operations include the Sam's Club warehouse store chain. The analyst must accept the fact that cross-sectional comparisons of ratios between firms will require subjective judgment about how the differences across firms in business model, strategy, and accounting affect the ratios.

An alternative approach uses average industry ratios, such as those published by Moody's, Dun & Bradstreet, and Robert Morris Associates, or ratios derived from computerized databases such as Compustat. These average industry ratios provide an overview of the performance of an industry, aiming to capture the commonalities across many firms.

The analyst should consider the following issues when using industry ratios:

1. **Definition of the industry:** Publishers of industry average ratios generally classify diversified firms into the industry of their major product. PepsiCo, for example, appears as a "beverage" company even though it generates a large percentage of its revenues from consumer foods. The industry may also exclude privately held and foreign firms if data are not available for those firms. If these types of firms are significant for a particular industry, the analyst should recognize the possible impact of their absence from the published data.
2. **Calculation of industry average:** Is the published ratio a simple (unweighted) average of the ratios of the included firms, or is it weighted by size of firm? Is the weighting based on sales, assets, market value, or some other factor? Is the median of the distribution used instead of the mean?
3. **Distribution of ratios around the mean:** To interpret a deviation of a particular firm's ratio from the industry average requires information on the distribution around the mean. The analyst interprets a ratio that is 10 percent larger than the industry mean differently depending on whether the standard deviation is 5 percent versus 15 percent greater or less than the mean. Useful sources of industry ratios give either the quartiles or the range of the distribution.
4. **Definition of financial statement ratios:** The analyst should examine the definition of each published ratio to ensure that it is consistent with that calculated by the analyst. For instance, is the rate of ROCE based on average or beginning-of-the-period common shareholders' equity? Are any adjustments made to reported net income, such as for nonrecurring or unusual charges?

Average industry ratios serve as a useful basis of comparison as long as the analyst recognizes their possible limitations. To assist the reader, Appendix D presents data on the distribution of the most common financial statement ratios across time for 48 industries.

SUMMARY

This chapter introduces the fourth step of the six-step process of financial statement analysis, which is to analyze profitability and risk. (See Exhibit 1.2.) We examined various financial statement ratios useful for assessing profitability in this chapter; analysis of risk is covered in Chapter 5. The large number of financial ratios discussed may be overwhelming at this point. Enhanced understanding of these financial ratios results from using and interpreting the ratios, *not from memorizing them.* The FSAP software available with this book facilitates calculation of the ratios and permits the analyst to devote more time to interpretations. As noted in the chapter, however, it cannot be emphasized enough how important the *interpretation* of financial statement ratios is. This is a necessarily qualitative and intellectual process, which requires the analyst to have understood the firm's specific strategy in the context of the industry *and* to be aware of any underlying accounting choices that affect the data used in the computation of the financial ratios being examined.

In this chapter, we highlighted alternative methods for examining profitability. The first part of the chapter focused on simple approaches, such as earnings-per-share, common-size, and percentage change analysis, as well as subjective redefinition of profits. However, the majority of the chapter focused on how to interpret different levels of profitability ratios. Exhibit 4.20 summarizes many of the key profitability ratios discussed in this chapter. Profitability analysis proceeds through four levels of depth. Level 1 involves measures of profitability for a firm as a whole: the rate of ROA and the rate of ROCE. Level 2 disaggregates ROA and ROCE into important components. ROA disaggregates into profit margin for ROA and assets turnover. ROCE disaggregates into profit margin for ROCE, assets turnover,

EXHIBIT 4.20

Summary of Profitability Ratios

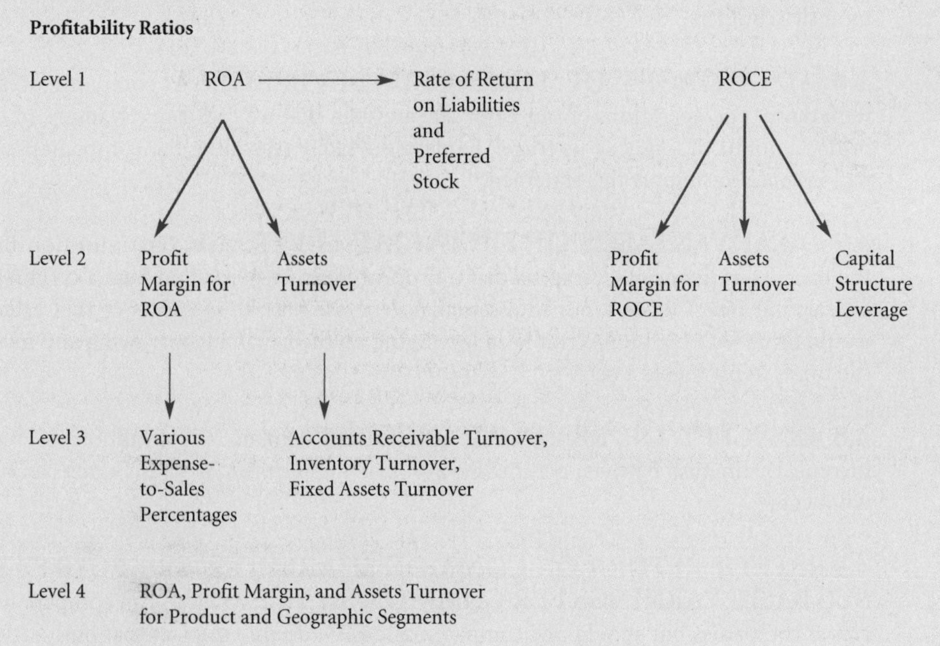

and capital structure leverage components. Level 3 disaggregates the profit margin into various expense-to-sales percentages and disaggregates assets turnover into individual asset turnovers. Level 4 uses product and geographic segment data to study ROA, profit margin, and assets turnover more fully.

QUESTIONS, EXERCISES, PROBLEMS, AND CASES

Questions and Exercises

4.1 COMMON-SIZE ANALYSIS. Common-size analysis is a simple way to make financial statements of different firms comparable. What are possible shortcomings of comparing two different firms using common-size analysis?

4.2 EARNINGS PER SHARE. Firm A reports an increase in earnings per share; Firm B reports a decrease in earnings per share. Is this unconditionally informative about each firm's performance? If not, why is earnings per share so commonly discussed in the financial press?

4.3 PRO FORMA EARNINGS. Firms often provide supplemental disclosures that report and discuss income figures that do not necessarily equal bottom-line net income from the income statement. Discuss the merits and shortcomings of this managerial practice.

4.4 PROFIT MARGIN FOR ROA VERSUS ROCE. Describe the difference between the profit margin for ROA and the profit margin for ROCE. Explain why each profit margin is appropriate for measuring the rate of ROA and the rate of ROCE, respectively.

4.5 CONCEPT AND MEASUREMENT OF FINANCIAL LEVERAGE. Define financial leverage. Explain how financial leverage works to the benefit of the common shareholders.

4.6 ADVANTAGES OF FINANCIAL LEVERAGE. A company president remarked, "The operations of our company are such that we can take advantage of only a minor amount of financial leverage." Explain the likely reasoning the company president had in mind to support this statement.

4.7 DISADVANTAGES OF FINANCIAL LEVERAGE. The intuition behind the benefits of financial leverage is that a firm can borrow funds that bear a certain interest rate but invest those funds in assets that generate returns in excess of that rate. Why would firms with high ROAs not keep leveraging up their firm by borrowing and investing the funds in profitable assets?

4.8 CONCEPT OF RESIDUAL INCOME. Explain the intuition of residual income. Distinguish between net income available to the common shareholders and residual income.

4.9 RATE OF RETURN ON COMMON SHAREHOLDERS' EQUITY VERSUS BASIC EARNINGS PER COMMON SHARE. Analysts can compare ROCEs across companies but should not compare basic EPSs despite the fact that both ratios use net income to the common shareholders in the numerator. Explain.

4.10 CALCULATING ROA AND ITS COMPONENTS. Nucor, a steel manufacturer, reported net income for 2008 of $1,831 million on sales of $23,663 million. Interest expense for 2008 was $135 million, and minority interest was $314 million for 2008. The income tax rate is 35 percent. Total assets were $9,826 million at the beginning of 2008 and $13,874 million at the end of 2008. Compute the rate of ROA for 2008 and disaggregate ROA into profit margin for ROA and asset turnover components.

4.11 CALCULATING ROCE AND ITS COMPONENTS. Phillips-Van Heusen, an apparel manufacturer, reported net income (amounts in thousands) for Year 4 of $58,615 on sales of $1,460,235. It declared preferred dividends of $21,122. Preferred shareholders' equity totaled $264,746 at both the beginning and end of Year 4. Common shareholders' equity totaled $296,157 at the beginning of Year 4 and $364,026 at the end of Year 4. Phillips-Van Heusen had no minority interest in its equity. Total assets were $1,439,283 at the beginning of Year 4 and $1,549,582 at the end of Year 4. Compute the rate of ROCE for Year 4 and disaggregate it into profit margin for ROCE, assets turnover, and capital structure leverage ratio components.

4.12 CALCULATING BASIC AND DILUTED EPS. TJX, Inc., an apparel retailer, reported net income (amounts in thousands) of $609,699 for Year 4. The weighted average of common shares outstanding during Year 4 was 488,809 shares. TJX, Inc., subtracted interest expense net of tax saving on convertible debt of $4,482. If the convertible debt had been converted into common stock, it would have increased the weighted average common shares outstanding by 16,905 shares. TJX, Inc., has outstanding stock options that, if exercised, would increase the weighted average of common shares outstanding by 6,935 shares. Compute basic and diluted earnings per share for Year 4, showing supporting computations.

4.13 RELATING ROA AND ROCE. Boston Scientific, a medical device manufacturer, reported net income (amounts in millions) of $1,062 on sales of $5,624 during Year 4. Interest expense totaled $64. The income tax rate was 35 percent. Average total assets were $6,934.5, and average common shareholders' equity was $3,443.5. The firm did not have preferred stock outstanding or minority interest in its equity.

a. Compute the rate of ROA. Disaggregate ROA into profit margin for ROA and assets turnover components.

b. Compute the rate of ROCE. Disaggregate ROCE into profit margin for ROCE, assets turnover, and capital structure leverage ratio components.

c. Calculate the amount of net income to common shareholders derived from the excess return on creditors' capital and the amount from the return on common shareholders' capital.

4.14 RELATING ROA AND ROCE. Valero Energy, a petroleum company, reported net income of $1,803.8 on revenues of $54,618.6 for Year 4. Interest expense totaled $359.7, and preferred dividends totaled $12.5. Average total assets for Year 4 were $17,527.9. The income tax rate is 35 percent. Average preferred shareholders' equity totaled $204.3, and average common shareholders' equity totaled $6,562.3. All amounts are in millions.

a. Compute the rate of ROA. Disaggregate ROA into profit margin for ROA and assets turnover components.

b. Compute the rate of ROCE. Disaggregate ROCE into profit margin for ROCE, assets turnover, and capital leverage ratio components.

c. Calculate the amount of net income to common shareholders derived from the excess return on creditors' capital, the excess return on preferred shareholders' capital, and the return on common shareholders' capital.

Problems and Cases

4.15 ANALYZING OPERATING PROFITABILITY. Exhibit 4.21 presents selected operating data for three retailers for a recent year. Macy's operates several department store chains selling consumer products such as brand-name clothing, china, cosmetics, and bedding and has a large presence in the bridal and formalwear markets (under store names Macy's and Bloomingdale's). Home Depot sells a wide range of building materials and home improvement products, which includes lumber and tools, riding lawn mowers, lighting fixtures, and kitchen cabinets and appliances. Supervalu operates grocery stores under numerous brands (including Albertsons, Cub Foods, Jewel-Osco, Shaw's, and Star Market).

a. Compute the rate of ROA for each firm. Disaggregate the rate of ROA into profit margin for ROA and assets turnover components. Assume that the income tax rate is 35 percent for all companies.

b. Based on your knowledge of the three retail stores and their respective industry concentrations, describe the likely reasons for the differences in the profit margins for ROA and assets turnovers.

4.16 CALCULATING AND INTERPRETING ACCOUNTS RECEIVABLE TURNOVER RATIOS. Microsoft Corporation (Microsoft) and Oracle Corporation (Oracle) engage in the design, manufacture, and sale of computer software. Microsoft sells and licenses a wide range of systems and application software to businesses, computer hardware manufacturers, and consumer retailers. Oracle sells software for information management almost exclusively to businesses. Exhibit 4.22 presents selected data for the two firms for 2006–2008.

Required

a. Calculate the accounts receivable turnover ratio for Microsoft and Oracle for 2006, 2007, and 2008.

b. Suggest possible reasons for the differences in the accounts receivable turnovers of Microsoft and Oracle during the three-year period.

c. Suggest possible reasons for the changes in the accounts receivable turnover for the two firms over the three-year period.

EXHIBIT 4.21

Selected Data for Three Retailers
(amounts in millions)
(Problem 4.15)

	Macy's	Home Depot	Supervalu
Sales	$24,892	$71,288	$44,564
Cost of Goods Sold	15,009	47,298	34,451
Interest Expense	588	624	633
Net Income	(4,803)	2,260	(2,855)
Average Inventory	4,915	11,202	2,743
Average Fixed Assets	10,717	26,855	7,531
Average Total Assets	24,967	42,744	19,333

EXHIBIT 4.22

Selected Data for Microsoft and Oracle
(amounts in millions)
(Problem 4.16)

	2008	2007	2006
Microsoft			
Sales	$58,437	$60,420	$51,122
Average Accounts Receivable	12,391	12,464	10,327
Change in Sales from Previous Year	−3.3%	+18.2%	+15.5%
Oracle			
Sales	$23,252	$22,430	$17,996
Average Accounts Receivable	4,430	5,799	4,589
Change in Sales from Previous Year	+3.7%	+24.6%	+25.2%

4.17 CALCULATING AND INTERPRETING INVENTORY TURNOVER RATIOS. Dell produces computers and related equipment on a made-to-order basis for consumers and businesses. Sun Microsystems designs and manufactures higher-end computers that function as servers and for use in computer-aided design. Sun Microsystems sells primarily to businesses. It also provides services to business customers in addition to product sales of computers. Selected data for each firm for 2007–2009 appear in Exhibit 4.23. (Dell's fiscal year-end is in January; Sun's fiscal year-end is in June. As of the writing of this text, an acquisition of Sun by Oracle is pending.)

EXHIBIT 4.23

Selected Data for Dell and Sun Microsystems
(amounts in millions)
(Problem 4.17)

	2009	2008	2007
Dell			
Cost of Goods Sold	$49,375	$48,855	$47,433
Average Inventories	1,024	920	618
Change in Sales from Previous Year	+1.1%	+3.0%	+4.1%
Sun Microsystems			
Cost of Goods Sold	$ 5,948	$ 6,639	$ 6,778
Average Inventories	623	602	532
Change in Sales from Previous Year	−10.4%	−2.1%	+3.7%

Required

a. Calculate the inventory turnover ratio for each firm for 2007–2009.
b. Suggest reasons for the differences in the inventory turnover ratios of these two firms.
c. Suggest reasons for the changes in the inventory turnover ratios during the three-year period.

4.18 CALCULATING AND INTERPRETING ACCOUNTS RECEIVABLE AND INVENTORY TURNOVER RATIOS. Nucor and AK Steel are steel manufacturers. Nucor produces steel in mini-mills. Mini-mills transform scrap ferrous metals into standard sizes of rolled steel, which Nucor then sells to steel service centers and distributors. Its steel falls on the lower end in terms of quality (strength and durability). AK Steel is an integrated steel producer, transforming ferrous metals into rolled steel and then into various steel products for the automobile, appliance, construction, and other industries. Its steel falls on the higher end in terms of quality. Exhibit 4.24 sets forth various data for these two companies for 2007 and 2008.

Required

a. Calculate the accounts receivable turnovers for Nucor and AK Steel for 2007 and 2008.
b. Describe the likely reasons for the differences in the accounts receivable turnovers for these two firms.
c. Describe the likely reasons for the trend in the accounts receivable turnovers of these two firms during the two-year period.
d. Calculate the inventory turnovers for Nucor and AK Steel for 2007 and 2008.

EXHIBIT 4.24

Selected Data for Nucor and AK Steel
(amounts in millions)
(Problem 4.18)

	2008	2007
Nucor		
Sales	$23,663	$16,593
Cost of Goods Sold	19,612	13,035
Average Accounts Receivable	1,420	1,340
Average Inventories	2,005	1,371
Change in Sales from Previous Year	+42.6%	+12.5%
AK Steel		
Sales	$ 7,644	$ 7,003
Cost of Goods Sold	6,479	5,904
Average Accounts Receivable	572	686
Average Inventories	607	752
Change in Sales from Previous Year	+9.2%	+15.3%

e. Describe the likely reasons for the differences in the inventory turnovers of these two firms.
f. Describe the likely reasons for the trend in the inventory turnovers of these two firms during the two-year period.

4.19 CALCULATING AND INTERPRETING FIXED ASSETS TURNOVER RATIOS. Texas Instruments (TI) designs and manufactures semiconductor products for use in computers, telecommunications equipment, automobiles, and other electronics-based products. The manufacturing of semiconductors is highly capital-intensive. Hewlett-Packard Corporation (HP) manufactures computer hardware and various imaging products, such as printers and fax machines. Exhibit 4.25 presents selected data for TI and HP for 2006–2008.

Required

a. Compute the fixed assets turnover for each firm for 2006, 2007, and 2008.
b. Suggest reasons for the differences in the fixed assets turnovers of TI and HP.
c. Suggest reasons for the changes in the fixed assets turnovers of TI and HP during the three-year period.

4.20 CALCULATING AND INTERPRETING THE RATE OF RETURN ON COMMON SHAREHOLDERS' EQUITY AND ITS COMPONENTS. JCPenney operates a chain of retail department stores, selling apparel, shoes, jewelry, and home furnishings. It also offers most of its products through catalog distribution. During fiscal Year 5, it sold Eckerd Drugs, a chain of retail drugstores, and used the cash proceeds,

EXHIBIT 4.25

Selected Data for Texas Instruments and Hewlett-Packard
(amounts in millions)
(Problem 4.19)

	2008	2007	2006
Texas Instruments			
Sales	$ 12,501	$ 13,835	$ 14,255
Cost of Goods Sold	6,256	5,432	5,775
Capital Expenditures	763	686	1,272
Average Fixed Assets	3,457	3,780	3,925
Percentage Fixed Assets Depreciated	54.9%	52.3%	49.0%
Percentage Change in Sales	−9.6%	−3.0%	+6.4%
Hewlett-Packard			
Sales	$114,552	$118,364	$104,286
Cost of Goods Sold	86,351	87,065	76,965
Capital Expenditures	3,695	2,990	3,040
Average Fixed Assets	11,050	9,318	7,331
Percentage Fixed Assets Depreciated	74.7%	72.4%	87.0%
Percentage Change in Sales	−3.2%	+13.5%	+13.8%

EXHIBIT 4.26

Selected Data for JCPenney
(amounts in millions)
(Problem 4.20)

	Year Ended January 31:		
	Year 5	Year 4	Year 3
Sales	$18,424	$17,786	$17,633
Net Income (Loss)	524	(928)	405
Interest Expense	279	271	245
Preferred Stock Dividend	12	25	27
Income Tax Rate	35%	35%	35%

January 31:	Year 5	Year 4	Year 3	Year 2
Total Assets	$14,127	$18,300	$17,787	$18,048
Preferred Stock	0	304	333	363
Total Common Shareholders' Equity	4,856	5,121	6,037	5,766

in part, to repurchase shares of its common stock. Exhibit 4.26 presents selected data for JCPenney for fiscal Year 3, Year 4, and Year 5.

Required

a. Calculate the rate of ROA for fiscal Year 3, Year 4, and Year 5. Disaggregate ROA into the profit margin for ROA and total assets turnover components. The income tax rate is 35 percent.

b. Calculate the rate of ROCE for fiscal Year 3, Year 4, and Year 5. Disaggregate ROCE into the profit margin for ROCE, assets turnover, and capital structure leverage components.

c. Suggest reasons for the changes in ROCE over the three years.

d. Compute the ratio of ROCE to ROA for each year.

e. Calculate the amount of net income available to common stockholders derived from the use of financial leverage with respect to creditors' capital, the amount derived from the use of preferred shareholders' capital, and the amount derived from common shareholders' capital for each year.

f. Did financial leverage work to the advantage of the common shareholders in each of the three years? Explain.

4.21 INTERPRETING THE RATE OF RETURN ON COMMON SHAREHOLDERS' EQUITY AND ITS COMPONENTS. Selected financial data for Georgia-Pacific Corporation, a forest products and paper firm, appear in Exhibit 4.27.

EXHIBIT 4.27

Selected Data for Georgia-Pacific Corporation
(Problem 4.22)

	Year 4	Year 3	Year 2	Year 1	Year 0
ROCE	10.8%	6.5%	(4.2%)	(9.1%)	7.4%
ROA	4.8%	3.7%	1.5%	0.8%	3.3%
Profit Margin for ROA	5.8%	4.6%	1.7%	0.9%	3.3%
Profit Margin for ROCE	3.2%	1.6%	(0.9%)	(1.9%)	1.6%
Assets Turnover	0.8	0.8	0.9	0.9	1.0
Capital Structure Leverage	4.1	4.9	5.4	5.3	4.8
Growth Rate in Sales	0.0%	(13.5%)	(9.2%)	13.4%	24.1%

Required

a. In which years did financial leverage work to the advantage of the common shareholders? In which years did it work to their disadvantage? Explain.

b. Identify possible reasons for the changes in the capital structure leverage ratio during the five-year period.

4.22 CALCULATING AND INTERPRETING THE RATE OF RETURN ON COMMON SHAREHOLDERS' EQUITY AND EARNINGS PER COMMON SHARE. Selected data for General Mills for 2007, 2008, and 2009 appear below (amounts in millions).

	2009	2008	2007
Net Income	$1,304.4	$1,294.7	$1,144.0
Weighted Average Number of Common Shares Outstanding	331.9	333.0	346.5
Average Common Shareholders' Equity	$5,695.3	$5,767.4	$5,545.5

Required

a. Compute the rate of ROCE for 2007, 2008, and 2009.

b. Compute basic EPS for 2007, 2008, and 2009.

c. Interpret the changes in ROCE versus EPS over the three-year period.

4.23 CALCULATING AND INTERPRETING PROFITABILITY RATIOS. Hasbro is a leading firm in the toy, game, and amusement industry. Its promoted brands group includes products from Playskool, Tonka, Milton Bradley, Parker Brothers, Tiger, and Wizards of the Coast. Sales of toys and games are highly variable from year to year depending on whether the latest products meet consumer interests. Hasbro also faces increasing competition from electronic and online games. Hasbro develops and promotes its core brands and manufactures and distributes products created by others under license arrangements. Hasbro pays a royalty to the creator of such products. In recent years, Hasbro has attempted to reduce its reliance on license arrangements, placing more emphasis on its core brands. Hasbro also has embarked on a strategy of reducing fixed selling and administrative costs in an effort to offset the negative effects on earnings of highly variable sales. Exhibit 4.28 presents the balance sheets for Hasbro for the years ended December 31, Year 1 through Year 4. Exhibit 4.29 presents the income statements and Exhibit 4.30 presents the statements of cash flows for Year 2 through Year 4.

EXHIBIT 4.28

Hasbro
Balance Sheets
(amounts in millions)
(Problem 4.23)

	December 31:			
	Year 4	Year 3	Year 2	Year 1
ASSETS				
Cash	$ 725	$ 521	$ 496	$ 233
Accounts receivable	579	607	555	572
Inventories	195	169	190	217
Prepayments	219	212	191	346
Total Current Assets	$1,718	$1,509	$1,432	$1,368
Property, plant, and equipment, net	207	200	213	236
Other assets	1,316	1,454	1,498	1,765
Total Assets	$3,241	$3,163	$3,143	$3,369
LIABILITIES AND SHAREHOLDERS' EQUITY				
Accounts payable	$ 168	$ 159	$ 166	$ 123
Short-term borrowing	342	24	223	36
Other current liabilities	639	747	578	599
Total Current Liabilities	$1,149	$ 930	$ 967	$ 758
Long-term debt	303	687	857	1,166
Other noncurrent liabilities	149	141	128	92
Total Liabilities	$1,601	$1,758	$1,952	$2,016
Common stock	$ 105	$ 105	$ 105	$ 105
Additional paid-in capital	381	398	458	455
Retained earnings	1,721	1,567	1,430	1,622
Accumulated other comprehensive income (loss)	82	30	(47)	(68)
Treasury stock	(649)	(695)	(755)	(761)
Total Shareholders' Equity	$1,640	$1,405	$1,191	$1,353
Total Liabilities and Shareholders' Equity	$3,241	$3,163	$3,143	$3,369

EXHIBIT 4.29

Hasbro
Income Statements
(amounts in millions)
(Problem 4.23)

	For the Year Ended December 31:		
	Year 4	Year 3	Year 2
Sales	$ 2,998	$ 3,139	$ 2,816
Cost of goods sold	(1,252)	(1,288)	(1,099)
Selling and administrative expenses:			
Advertising	(387)	(364)	(297)
Research and development	(157)	(143)	(154)
Royalty expense	(223)	(248)	(296)
Other selling and administrative	(687)	(799)	(788)
Interest expense	(32)	(53)	(78)
Income tax expense	(64)	(69)	(29)
Net Income	$ 196	$ 175	$ 75

EXHIBIT 4.30

Hasbro
Statements of Cash Flows
(amounts in millions)
(Problem 4.23)

	For the Year Ended December 31:		
	Year 4	Year 3	Year 2
OPERATIONS			
Net income	$196	$ 175	$ 75
Depreciation and amortization	146	164	184
Addbacks and subtractions, net	17	68	(67)
(Increase) Decrease in accounts receivable	76	(13)	34
(Increase) Decrease in inventories	(16)	35	39
(Increase) Decrease in prepayments	29	8	185
Increase (Decrease) in accounts payable and other current liabilities	(90)	17	23
Cash Flow from Operations	$358	$ 454	$ 473
INVESTING			
Property, plant, and equipment acquired	$(79)	$ (63)	$ (59)
Other investing transactions	(6)	(2)	(3)
Cash Flow from Investing	$(85)	$ (65)	$ (62)

(Continued)

EXHIBIT 4.30 (Continued)

	For the Year Ended December 31:		
	Year 4	Year 3	Year 2
FINANCING			
Increase in common stock	$ 3	$ 40	$ 3
Decrease in short-term borrowing	(7)	—	(15)
Decrease in long-term borrowing	(58)	(389)	(127)
Acquisition of common stock	—	(3)	—
Dividends	(37)	(21)	(21)
Other financing transactions	7	9	12
Cash Flow from Financing	$(69)	$(364)	$(148)
Change in Cash	$204	$ 25	$ 263
Cash—Beginning of year	521	496	233
Cash—End of Year	$725	$ 521	$ 496

Required

a. Exhibit 4.31 presents profitability ratios for Hasbro for Year 2 and Year 3. Calculate each of these financial ratios for Year 4. The income tax rate is 35 percent.

EXHIBIT 4.31

Hasbro
Financial Statement Ratio Analysis
(Problem 4.23)

	Year 4	Year 3	Year 2
Profit Margin for ROA		6.7%	4.5%
Assets Turnover		1.0	0.9
ROA		6.6%	3.9%
Profit Margin for ROCE		5.6%	2.7%
Capital Structure Leverage		2.4	2.6
ROCE		13.5%	5.9%
Cost of Goods Sold/Sales		41.0%	39.0%
Advertising Expense/Sales		11.6%	10.5%
Research and Development Expense/Sales		4.6%	5.5%
Royalty Expense/Sales		7.9%	10.5%
Other Selling and Administrative Expense/Sales		25.4%	28.0%
Income Tax Expense (excluding tax effects of interest expense)/Sales		2.8%	2.0%
Accounts Receivable Turnover		5.4	5.0
Inventory Turnover		7.2	5.4
Fixed Assets Turnover		15.2	12.5

b. Analyze the changes in ROA and its components for Hasbro over the three-year period, suggesting reasons for the changes observed.
c. Analyze the changes in ROCE and its components for Hasbro over the three-year period, suggesting reasons for the changes observed.

4.24 CALCULATING AND INTERPRETING PROFITABILITY RATIOS. Abercrombie & Fitch sells casual apparel and personal care products for men, women, and children through retail stores located primarily in shopping malls. Its fiscal year ends January 31 of each year. Financial statements for Abercrombie & Fitch for fiscal years ending January 31, Year 3, Year 4, and Year 5 appear in Exhibit 4.32 (balance sheets), Exhibit 4.33

EXHIBIT 4.32

Abercrombie & Fitch
Balance Sheets
(amounts in millions)
(Problem 4.24)

	January 31:			
	Year 5	Year 4	Year 3	Year 2
ASSETS				
Cash	$ 350	$ 56	$ 43	$ 188
Marketable securities	—	465	387	51
Accounts receivable	26	7	10	21
Inventories	248	201	169	130
Prepayments	28	24	20	15
Total Current Assets	$ 652	$ 753	$ 629	$ 405
Property, plant, and equipment, net	1,560	1,342	1,172	947
Other assets	8	1	1	—
Total Assets	$2,220	$2,096	$1,802	$1,352
LIABILITIES AND SHAREHOLDERS' EQUITY				
Accounts payable	$ 84	$ 58	$ 79	$ 32
Short-term borrowing	54	33	—	—
Other current liabilities	276	220	193	132
Total Current Liabilities	$ 414	$ 311	$ 272	$ 164
Long-term debt	872	713	629	581
Other noncurrent liabilities	265	214	165	12
Total Liabilities	$1,551	$1,238	$1,066	$ 757
Common stock	$ 1	$ 1	$ 1	$ 1
Additional paid-in capital	140	139	143	141
Retained earnings	1,076	906	701	520
Treasury stock	(548)	(188)	(109)	(67)
Total Shareholders' Equity	$ 669	$ 858	$ 736	$ 595
Total Liabilities and Shareholders' Equity	$2,220	$2,096	$1,802	$1,352

EXHIBIT 4.33

Abercrombie & Fitch
Income Statements
(amounts in millions)
(Problem 4.24)

	For the Year Ended January 31:		
	Year 5	Year 4	Year 3
Sales	$2,021	$1,708	$1,596
Cost of goods sold	(1,048)	(936)	(893)
Selling and administrative expenses	(562)	(386)	(343)
Interest expense	(63)	(54)	(48)
Interest income	5	4	4
Income tax expense	(137)	(131)	(121)
Net Income	$ 216	$ 205	$ 195

(income statements), and Exhibit 4.34 (statements of cash flows). These financial statements reflect the capitalization of operating leases in property, plant, and equipment and long-term debt, a topic discussed in Chapter 6. Exhibit 4.35 (see page 322) presents financial statement ratios for Abercrombie & Fitch for Year 3 and Year 4. Selected data for Abercrombie & Fitch appear here.

	Year 5	Year 4	Year 3
Number of Stores	788	700	597
Square Feet of Retail Space (in thousands)	5,590	5,016	4,358
Number of Employees	48,500	30,200	22,000
Growth Rate in Sales	18.3%	7.0%	16.9%
Comparable Store Sales Increase	2.0%	(9.0%)	5.0%

Required

a. Calculate the ratios in Exhibit 4.35 for Year 5. The income tax rate is 35 percent.
b. Analyze the changes in ROA for Abercrombie & Fitch during the three-year period, suggesting possible reasons for the changes observed.
c. Analyze the changes in ROCE for Abercrombie & Fitch during the three-year period, suggesting possible reasons for the changes observed.

4.25 INTERPRETING PROFITABILITY RATIOS IN A CROSS-SECTIONAL SETTING. Coca-Cola Company is the principal competitor of PepsiCo in the soft drink beverage business. Coca-Cola engages almost exclusively in beverages, whereas, in addition to beverages, PepsiCo also engages in the manufacture and distribution of packaged foods such as chips, salsas, and cereals.

EXHIBIT 4.34

Abercrombie & Fitch
Statements of Cash Flows
(amounts in millions)
(Problem 4.24)

	For the Year Ended January 31:		
	Year 5	Year 4	Year 3
OPERATIONS			
Net income	$ 216	$ 205	$ 195
Depreciation and amortization	106	90	76
Addbacks and subtractions, net	13	56	49
(Increase) Decrease in inventories	(34)	(27)	(34)
Increase (Decrease) in current liabilities	125	19	60
Cash Flow from Operations	$ 426	$ 343	$ 346
INVESTING			
Property, plant, and equipment acquired	$ (185)	$ (160)	$ (146)
Marketable securities sold	4,779	3,771	2,419
Marketable securities purchased	(4,314)	(3,849)	(2,729)
Other investing transactions	—	—	5
Cash Flow from Investing	$ (280)	$ (238)	$ (451)
FINANCING			
Increase in short-term borrowing	$ 20	$ 4	$ 4
Increase in common stock	49	20	—
Acquisition of common stock	(435)	(116)	(43)
Dividends	(46)	—	—
Cash Flow from Financing	$ (412)	$ (92)	$ (39)
Change in Cash	$ 294	$ 13	$ (144)
Cash—Beginning of year	56	43	188
Cash—End of Year	$ 350	$ 56	$ 43

The value chain for beverages involves the following steps:

1. Manufacturing concentrate and syrup to be used in the beverages
2. Mixing syrup, water, and other ingredients and placing the finished beverage in a container (can or bottle), a relatively capital-intensive process
3. Distributing packaged beverages to food distributors, retail establishments, and restaurant chains, also a capital-intensive process

Coca-Cola and PepsiCo are engaged primarily in the manufacture of concentrate and syrup (Step 1). They both rely heavily on other entities to perform Steps 2 and 3.

EXHIBIT 4.35

Abercrombie & Fitch
Financial Statement Ratio Analysis
(Problem 4.24)

	Year 5	Year 4	Year 3
Profit Margin for ROA		14.1%	14.2%
Assets Turnover		0.9	1.0
ROA		12.3%	14.3%
Profit Margin for ROCE		12.0%	12.2%
Capital Structure Leverage		2.4	2.4
ROCE		25.7%	29.3%
Cost of Goods Sold/Sales		54.8%	56.0%
Selling and Administrative Expense/Sales		22.6%	21.5%
Interest Revenue/Sales		0.2%	0.3%
Income Tax Expense (excluding tax effects of interest expense)/Sales		8.8%	8.6%
Accounts Receivable Turnover		200.9	103.0
Inventory Turnover		5.1	6.0
Fixed Assets Turnover		1.4	1.5
Sales per Store		$2,440,000	$2,673,367
Sales per Square Foot		$ 340.51	$ 366.22
Sales per Employee		$ 56,556	$ 72,545

The value chain for packaged foods involves the following steps:

1. Combining ingredients, cooking as appropriate, and packaging the finished food products
2. Distributing packaged food products to food distributors and retail establishments

Exhibit 4.36 presents ROA and its disaggregated components for Coca-Cola and PepsiCo for 2006–2008. Exhibit 4.37 (see page 324) presents ROCE and its disaggregated components, and Exhibit 4.38 (see page 324) presents segment data for these two companies. The ratio amounts for PepsiCo correspond to those discussed in the chapter but appear next to those for Coca-Cola to ease interpretation. No adjustments for unusual or nonrecurring items have been made for Coca-Cola. To ease computations, the segment computations of ROA and asset turnover use asset amounts at the end of the year instead of average assets during the year. (See the discussion under "Segment Data" in the chapter for an explanation of the use of end-of-year assets.) The segment profit margins and ROA are based on operating income before interest and income taxes. Thus, the aggregate profit margins and ROAs for the segments exceed those for the companies as a whole because the segment data do not subtract corporate-level overhead expenses. The segment data disclosed by each company have been categorized in three geographic segments, but there may be slight deviations from the actual segment data because of differences in the way each company defines its segments.

EXHIBIT 4.36

ROA and Its Disaggregated Components for Coca-Cola and PepsiCo (Problem 4.25)

ROA

	2008	2007	2006
Coca-Cola	14.5%	17.1%	17.6%
PepsiCo	16.7%	17.8%	16.9%

	Profit Margin for ROA			Assets Turnover		
	2008	2007	2006	2008	2007	2006
Coca-Cola	19.1%	21.8%	21.7%	0.76	0.79	0.81
PepsiCo	13.6%	14.6%	14.9%	1.22	1.22	1.14

	Coca-Cola			PepsiCo		
	2008	2007	2006	2008	2007	2006
Net Revenue	100.0%	100.0%	100.0%	100.0%	100.0%	100.0%
Bottling equity income	(2.7)	2.3	0.4	0.9	1.4	1.6
Interest income	1.0	0.8	0.8	0.1	0.3	0.5
Cost of sales	(35.6)	(36.1)	(33.9)	(47.1)	(45.7)	(44.9)
Selling, general, and administrative expenses	(36.9)	(37.9)	(39.2)	(36.8)	(36.0)	(36.2)
Amortization of intangible assets, other charges	(1.2)	(0.3)	0.0	(0.1)	(0.1)	(0.5)
Adjustments (from Exhibit 4.6)	—	—	—	1.6	0.3	0.2
Provision for income taxes (adjusted for PepsiCo)	(5.1)	(6.6)	(6.2)	(4.7)	(5.4)	(5.7)
Less: 0.35 × interest expense	(0.5)	(0.6)	(0.3)	(0.3)	(0.2)	(0.2)
Profit margin for ROA	19.1%	21.8%	21.7%	13.6%	14.6%	14.9%
Receivables turnover	10.0	9.8	9.9	9.5	9.7	10.1
Inventory turnover	5.2	5.4	5.4	8.5	8.6	8.7
Fixed assets turnover	3.8	3.7	3.8	3.8	3.8	3.8

Required

a. PepsiCo has shown a higher ROA than Coca-Cola for the last two years, but Coca-Cola has historically generated higher ROA than PepsiCo. Explain the current differences in ROA between PepsiCo and Coca-Cola.

b. Why might PepsiCo have a higher cost of sales than Coca-Cola?

EXHIBIT 4.37

ROCE and Its Disaggregated Components for Coca-Cola and PepsiCo
(Problem 4.25)

ROCE

	2008	2007	2006
Coca-Cola	27.5%	30.9%	30.5%
PepsiCo	38.3%	34.1%	34.0%

	Profit Margin for ROCE			Asset Turnover			Capital Structure Leverage		
	2008	2007	2006	2008	2007	2006	2008	2007	2006
Coca-Cola	18.2%	20.7%	21.1%	0.76	0.79	0.81	2.0	1.9	1.8
PepsiCo	13.1%	14.2%	14.4%	1.22	1.22	1.14	2.4	2.0	2.1

EXHIBIT 4.38

Geographic Segment Data for Coca-Cola and PepsiCo
(Problem 4.25)

	Coca-Cola			PepsiCo		
	2008	2007	2006	2008	2007	2006
Sales Mix						
Americas	59.8%	59.1%	56.4%	72.2%	74.5%	76.7%
UK & Europe	18.2%	18.3%	19.0%	14.9%	13.9%	13.5%
Middle East, Africa & Asia	22.0%	22.6%	24.6%	12.9%	11.6%	9.8%
	100.0%	100.0%	100.0%	100.0%	100.0%	100.0%
Profit Margin						
Americas	8.4%	15.9%	14.3%	20.7%	22.5%	22.8%
UK & Europe	54.9%	52.8%	52.0%	12.6%	14.1%	14.7%
Middle East, Africa & Asia	37.7%	36.2%	38.0%	12.0%	11.7%	11.7%
Assets Turnover						
Americas	0.65	0.57	0.73	1.73	1.62	1.66
UK & Europe	1.93	1.77	1.77	0.75	0.77	0.81
Middle East, Africa & Asia	2.93	2.62	3.00	1.41	1.17	1.16
ROA						
Americas	5.5%	9.1%	10.5%	35.9%	36.5%	37.7%
UK & Europe	105.6%	93.3%	91.9%	9.4%	10.9%	11.9%
Middle East, Africa & Asia	110.3%	94.8%	114.1%	16.8%	13.7%	13.5%

c. What are the likely reasons PepsiCo's inventory turnover ratio exceeds that for Coca-Cola? (Hint: Incorporate information from Exhibit 4.13 regarding PepsiCo's disclosed segments.)

d. For which firm is financial leverage helping the common shareholders more? Explain in such a way as to demonstrate your understanding of financial leverage.

4.26 ANALYZING THE PROFITABILITY OF A SERVICE FIRM. Kelly Services (Kelly) places employees at clients' businesses on a temporary basis. It segments its services into (1) commercial, (2) professional and technical, and (3) international. Kelly recognizes revenues for the amount billed to clients. Kelly includes the amount it pays to temporary employees in cost of services sold. It includes the compensation paid to permanent employees that administer its offices in selling and administrative expenses. The latter expense also includes data processing costs relating to payroll records for all employees, rent, taxes, and insurance on office space. Amounts receivable from clients appear in accounts receivable, and amounts payable to permanent and temporary employees appear in current liabilities.

The temporary personnel business offers clients flexibility in adjusting the number of workers to meet changing capacity needs. Temporary employees are typically less costly than permanent workers because they have fewer fringe benefits. However, temporary workers generally are not as well trained as permanent workers and have less loyalty to clients.

Barriers to entry in the personnel supply business are low. This business does not require capital for physical facilities (most space is rented), does not need specialized assets (most temporary employees do not possess unique skills; needed data processing technology is readily available), and operates with little government regulation. Thus, competition is intense and margins tend to be thin.

Exhibit 4.39 presents selected profitability ratios and other data for Kelly Services, the largest temporary personnel supply firm in the United States. Note that the data in Exhibit 4.39 reflect the capitalization of operating leases in property, plant, and equipment and long-term debt, a topic discussed in Chapter 6.

Required

Analyze the changes in the profitability of Kelly Services during the three-year period in as much depth as permitted by the data provided.

4.27 ANALYZING THE PROFITABILITY OF TWO HOTELS. Starwood Hotels (Starwood) owns and operates many hotel properties under well-known brand names, including Sheraton, W, Westin, and St. Regis. Starwood focuses on the upper end of the lodging industry. Choice Hotels (Choice) is a primarily a franchisor of several hotel chains, including Comfort Inn, Sleep Inn, Clarion, EconoLodge, and Rodeway Inn. Choice properties represent primarily the midscale and economy segments of the lodging industry. Exhibit 4.40 (see page 327) presents selected profitability ratios and other data for Starwood, and Exhibit 4.41 (see page 327) presents data for Choice. (Note that ROCE is not meaningful for Choice because of negative common shareholders' equity due to open market share repurchases, not accumulated deficits. As of the end of 2008, Choice had repurchased over one-third of all common shares issued: 34,640,510 out of 95,345,362 shares.) One of the closely followed metrics in the lodging industry is occupancy rate, which gives an indication of the capacity utilization of available hotel rooms. A second measure is the ADR (average daily rate), which measures the amount actually collected for an average room per night. Finally, REVPAR (revenue per available room) also is an important measure, which measures period-to-period growth in revenues per room for comparable properties (adjusted for properties sold or closed or otherwise not comparable across years). The interaction of occupancy rate and ADR is REVPAR.

EXHIBIT 4.39

Profitability Ratios and Other Data for Kelly Services
(Problem 4.26)

	Year 4	Year 3	Year 2
Profit Margin for ROA	0.6%	0.3%	0.6%
Assets Turnover	3.8	3.5	3.5
ROA	2.2%	0.9%	2.1%
Profit Margin for ROCE	0.4%	0.1%	0.4%
Capital Structure Leverage	2.1	2.0	1.9
ROCE	3.3%	0.8%	2.9%
Revenues	100.0%	100.0%	100.0%
Compensation of Temporary Employees/Revenues	84.0%	83.9%	82.9%
Selling and Administrative Expense/Revenues	15.1%	15.7%	16.1%
Income Tax Expense/Revenues	0.3%	0.2%	0.4%
Accounts Receivable Turnover	7.2	7.1	7.3
Fixed Assets Turnover	16.0	14.0	12.9
Sales Mix Data:			
Commercial	46.7%	49.3%	51.9%
Professional and Technical	20.7	20.7	21.4
International	32.6	30.0	26.7
Total	100.0%	100.0%	100.0%
Segment Profit Margin:			
Commercial	5.1%	4.4%	5.6%
Professional and Technical	6.0%	5.9%	5.8%
International	0.8%	0.0%	0.5%
Number of Offices	2,600	2,500	2,400
Number of Permanent Employees	8,400	7,900	8,200
Number of Temporary Employees, approximate	700,000	700,000	700,000
Growth Rate in Revenues	15.2%	6.9%	(4.7%)
Per-Office Data:			
Revenues	$1,916,923	$1,730,000	$1,690,417
Net Income	$ 8,077	$ 2,000	$ 7,500
Permanent Employees	3.2	3.2	3.4
Temporary Employees	269	280	292
Per-Permanent-Employee Data:			
Revenues	$ 593,333	$ 547,468	$ 494,756
Net Income	$ 2,500	$ 633	$ 2,195
Temporary Employees	83.3	88.6	85.4
Per-Temporary-Employee Data:			
Revenues	$ 7,120	$ 6,177	$ 5,796
Net Income	$ 30	$ 7	$ 26

EXHIBIT 4.40

Profitability Ratios and Other Data for Starwood Hotels
(Problem 4.27)

	2008	2007	2006
Sales Growth	(4.0%)	2.9%	0.0%
Profit Margin for ROA	7.8%	10.4%	19.8%
Assets Turnover	0.61	0.65	0.55
ROA	4.8%	6.8%	10.9%
Profit Margin for ROCE	5.6%	8.8%	17.4%
Capital Structure Leverage	5.23	3.72	2.65
ROCE	17.8%	21.3%	25.4%
Number of Hotels	942	925	871
Number of Rooms	285,000	282,000	266,000
Rooms/Hotel	303	305	305
Occupancy Rate	71.1%	72.7%	71.2%
Revenue/Available Room Night	$168.93	$171.01	$136.33
Average Daily Rate	$237.45	$235.18	$191.56

EXHIBIT 4.41

Profitability Ratios and Other Data for Choice Hotels
(Problem 4.27)

	2008	2007	2006
Sales Growth	4.2%	14.0%	13.1%
Profit Margin for ROA	16.7%	19.6%	22.6%
Assets Turnover	1.95	1.95	1.90
ROA	32.6%	38.2%	42.9%
Profit Margin for ROCE	15.6%	18.1%	20.9%
Capital Structure Leverage	(2.23)	(2.88)	(2.48)
ROCE	n.m.	n.m.	n.m.
Number of Hotels	4,716	4,445	4,211
Number of Rooms	373,884	354,139	$339,441
Rooms/Hotel	79	80	81
Occupancy Rate	55.3%	57.9%	58.4%
Revenue/Available Room Night	$ 40.98	$ 41.75	$ 40.13
Average Daily Rate	$ 74.11	$ 72.07	$ 68.71

n.m.: not meaningful due to negative common shareholders' equity

Required

Analyze the changes and the differences in the profitability of these two hotel chains to the deepest levels available given the data provided. Compare and contrast the ROAs and ROCEs of both companies. Do the results match your prior expectations given the type of lodging for which each company specializes?

4.28 ANALYZING THE PROFITABILITY OF TWO RESTAURANT CHAINS. Analyzing the profitability of restaurants requires consideration of their strategies with respect to ownership of restaurants versus franchising. Firms that own and operate their restaurants report the assets and financing of those restaurants on their balance sheets and the revenues and operating expenses of the restaurants on their income statements. Firms that franchise their restaurants to others (that is, franchisees) often own the land and buildings of franchised restaurants and lease them to the franchisees. The income statement includes fees received from franchisees in the form of license fees for using the franchiser's name; rent for facilities and equipment; and various fees for advertising, menu planning, and food and paper products used by the franchisee. The revenues and operating expenses of the franchised restaurants appear on the financial statements of the franchisees.

Exhibit 4.42 presents profitability ratios and other data for Brinker International, and Exhibit 4.43 presents similar data for McDonald's. Brinker operates chains of specialty

EXHIBIT 4.42

Profitability Ratios and Other Data for Brinker International (Problem 4.28)

	Year 4	Year 3	Year 2
Profit Margin for ROA	5.1%	6.2%	6.5%
Assets Turnover	1.4	1.3	1.3
ROA	7.1%	8.4%	8.8%
Profit Margin for ROCE	4.1%	5.1%	5.2%
Capital Structure Leverage	2.5	2.3	2.3
ROCE	14.1%	15.8%	16.1%
Cost of Goods Sold/Revenues	81.2%	80.9%	81.0%
Selling and Administrative Expenses/Revenues	10.9%	9.8%	9.1%
Income Tax Expense (excluding tax effects of interest expense)/ Revenues	2.8%	3.1%	3.4%
Accounts Receivable Turnover	100.2	106.0	101.3
Inventory Turnover	97.1	115.5	95.5
Fixed Assets Turnover	1.7	1.6	1.6
Revenues per Restaurant (000's)	$ 2,516	$ 2,343	$ 2,277
Operating Income per Restaurant (000's)	$ 129	$ 145	$ 148
Fixed Assets per Restaurant (000's)	$ 1,476	$ 1,493	$ 1,506
Percentage of Restaurants Owned and Operated	80.1%	81.7%	81.9%
Growth in Revenues	12.8%	13.8%	16.7%
Growth in Number of Restaurants	5.3%	10.6%	10.9%

EXHIBIT 4.43

Profitability Ratios and Other Data for McDonald's
(Problem 4.28)

	Year 4	Year 3	Year 2
Profit Margin for ROA	15.1%	12.2%	10.0%
Assets Turnover	0.6	0.5	0.5
ROA	8.5%	6.7%	5.3%
Profit Margin for ROCE	12.0%	8.8%	6.4%
Capital Structure Leverage	2.6	2.8	2.9
ROCE	17.4%	13.5%	9.8%
Cost of Goods Sold/Revenues	65.8%	66.7%	66.7%
Selling and Administrative Expenses/Revenues	12.6%	14.4%	17.0%
Income Tax Expense (excluding tax effects of interest expense)/Revenues	6.5%	6.7%	6.3%
Accounts Receivable Turnover	25.7	21.6	17.7
Inventory Turnover	90.9	94.8	94.2
Fixed Assets Turnover	0.7	0.6	0.6
Revenues per Restaurant (000's)	$ 605	$ 551	$ 495
Operating Income per Restaurant (000's)	$ 91	$ 67	$ 50
Fixed Assets per Restaurant (000's)	$ 881	$ 856	$ 795
Percentage of Restaurants Owned and Operated	29.2%	28.8%	28.9%
Growth in Revenues	11.2%	11.3%	3.6%
Growth in Number of Restaurants	1.4%	0.1%	3.4%

sit-down restaurants in the United States under the names of Chili's, Romano's Macaroni Grill, On the Border, Maggiano's Little Italy, and Corner Bakery Cafe. Its restaurants average approximately 7,000 square feet. Brinker owns and operates approximately 81 percent of its restaurants. McDonald's operates chains of fast-food restaurants in the United States and other countries under the names of McDonald's, Boston Market, Chipotle Mexican Grill, and Donatos Pizza. Its restaurants average approximately 2,800 square feet. McDonald's owns and operates approximately 29 percent of its restaurants. It also owns approximately 25 percent of the restaurant land and buildings of franchisees. The financial ratios and other data in Exhibits 4.42 and 4.43 reflect the capitalization of operating leases in property, plant, and equipment and long-term debt, a topic discussed in Chapter 6.

Required

a. Suggest reasons for the changes in the profitability of Brinker during the three-year period.

b. Suggest reasons for the changes in the profitability of McDonald's during the three-year period.

c. Suggest reasons for differences in the profitability of Brinker and McDonald's during the three-year period.

INTEGRATIVE CASE 4.1

STARBUCKS

Part A

Integrative Case 1.1 introduced the industry economics of coffee shops and the business strategy of Starbucks to compete in this industry. Exhibit 1.26 presents balance sheets for Starbucks for the years ending 2005–2008. Exhibit 1.27 presents its income statements and Exhibit 1.28 presents the statement of cash flows for fiscals 2005, 2006, 2007, and 2008. Exhibit 1.29 presents common-size balance sheets and Exhibit 1.30 presents common-size income statements for Starbucks. Before beginning preparation of Integrative Case 4.1, we recommend that you review Integrative Case 1.1 in Chapter 1.

Part A of Integrative Case 4.1 analyzes changes in the profitability of Starbucks for fiscal 2006–2008.

Required

a. Exhibit 4.44 presents profitability ratios for Starbucks for fiscals 2006 and 2007. Using the financial statement data in Exhibits 1.26 and 1.27, compute the values of these ratios for fiscal 2008. The income tax rate is 35 percent. For accounts receivable turnover, use only specialty revenues for the numerator, because the accounts

EXHIBIT 4.44

Starbucks
Financial Statement Ratio Analysis
(Integrative Case 4.1, Part A)

	2008	2007	2006
Profit Margin for ROA		7.4%	7.3%
Assets Turnover		1.93	1.96
ROA		14.3%	14.3%
Profit Margin for ROCE		7.1%	7.2%
Capital Structure Leverage		2.17	1.84
ROCE		29.8%	26.1%
Cost of Sales/Revenues		42.5%	40.8%
Store Operating Expenses/Revenues		34.2%	34.5%
Nonretail Operating Expenses/Revenues		3.1%	3.3%
Depreciation and Amortization Expense/Revenues		5.0%	5.0%
General and Administrative Expense/Revenues		5.2%	6.2%
Restructuring Charge/Revenues		0.0%	0.0%
Income from Equity Investees/Revenues		1.1%	1.2%
Interest Revenue/Revenues		0.4%	0.3%
Income Tax Expense (excluding tax effects of interest expense)/ Revenues		4.2%	4.2%
Accounts Receivable Turnover		5.5	5.8
Inventory Turnover		6.0	5.4
Fixed Assets Turnover		3.6	3.8

receivable are primarily related to licensing and food service operations, not the retail operations. Use cost of sales, including occupancy costs, for the numerator of the inventory turnover because Starbucks does not disclose separately the cost of products sold (the appropriate numerator) and occupancy costs.

b. What are the most important reasons Starbucks' ROA decreased during the three-year period? Analyze the financial ratios to the maximum depth possible with the information given. Using the nomenclature from the schematic in Exhibit 4.20, Exhibit 4.45 provides information for analyzing profitability at Level 1, Level 2, and Level 3. Exhibit 4.45 presents additional information for Starbucks at a business segment level to permit analysis at Level 4. Corporate-level expenses not allocated to domestic or international operations, which include depreciation, amortization, general, and administrative expenses, as a percentage of total revenues were 3.3 percent for fiscal 2008, 3.6 percent for fiscal 2007, and 4.3 percent for fiscal 2006.

c. What are the most important reasons Starbucks' ROCE decreased during the three-year period?

Part B

Part B of Integrative Case 4.1 compares the profitability of Starbucks with Panera Bread Company. Although Starbucks and Panera Bread Company are not direct competitors in terms of the principal food products offered, they compete in the sense of offering a relaxed café experience. Whereas the products of Starbucks center on coffee and related beverages, Panera Bread Company emphasizes freshly baked bread and pastries. Panera Bread Company also sells sandwiches, soups, and similar lunch and light dinner products that build on their bread offerings, as well as coffee and other beverages. The average size of a Panera Bread Company retail outlet is typically larger than that of Starbucks. Both Starbucks and Panera Bread Company own some of their retail stores and franchise or license rights to use their names and products to other parties that own and operate other retail stores. Panera Bread Company prepares fresh dough daily in various regional facilities to use in company-owned stores and to sell to franchisees. Unlike Starbucks, it has not expanded beyond the United States.

Exhibit 4.46 (see page 333) presents profitability ratios for Panera Bread Company for 2006–2008, and Exhibit 4.47 (see pages 333–334) presents segment profitability and other data. The format of Exhibit 4.46 is similar to that of Exhibit 4.44. However, due to less detailed disclosures by Panera, Exhibit 4.47 does not contain specific cost structures for Panera's operating segments, similar to what was available from Starbucks and presented in Exhibit 4.45. The proportions of general and administrative expenses not allocated to divisions for Panera Bread Company are similar to the corresponding percentages for Starbucks (suggesting they are not material enough to specifically factor into the analysis).

Required

a. Panera's ROA has typically been below that of Starbucks prior to 2008. What are the likely reasons for the relative levels of ROA between Panera and Starbucks? Analyze the data to the maximum depth permitted by the information given and speculate on economic explanations for what the analysis indicates.

b. Panera's ROCE also has typically been below that of Starbucks, but by a large margin. Why?

EXHIBIT 4.45

Starbucks Segment Profitability Data
(Integrative Case 4.1, Parts A and B)

	United States			International			Global Consumer Products Group		
	2008	2007	2006	2008	2007	2006	2008	2007	2006
Total Revenue Mix	76.0%	78.1%	79.3%	20.3%	18.0%	16.7%	3.8%	3.9%	3.9%
Net Revenues:									
Company-operated retail	88.7%	89.3%	88.9%	84.3%	84.7%	83.5%	0.0%	0.0%	0.0%
Licensing	6.4%	6.0%	6.0%	13.1%	13.0%	14.3%	0.0%	0.0%	0.0%
Foodservice and other	4.9%	4.7%	5.1%	2.6%	2.2%	2.2%	100.0%	100.0%	100.0%
Total net revenues	100.0%	100.0%	100.0%	100.0%	100.0%	100.0%	100.0%	100.0%	100.0%
Cost of sales including occupancy costs	42.8%	40.2%	38.4%	50.1%	48.6%	48.0%	55.9%	59.6%	58.7%
Store operating expenses	39.1%	36.5%	36.9%	31.6%	31.3%	31.3%	0.0%	0.0%	0.0%
Other operating expenses	2.8%	2.8%	3.1%	4.2%	4.1%	3.9%	5.6%	5.3%	4.0%
Depreciation and amortization	5.1%	4.7%	4.6%	5.2%	5.0%	5.1%	0.0%	0.0%	0.0%
General and administrative expenses	0.9%	1.2%	1.5%	5.4%	5.5%	6.0%	1.6%	1.7%	2.1%
Restructuring charges	2.7%	0.0%	0.0%	0.9%	0.0%	0.0%	0.0%	0.0%	0.0%
Total operating expense	93.3%	85.4%	84.5%	97.3%	94.6%	94.3%	63.2%	66.7%	64.8%
Income (loss) from equity investees	0.0%	0.0%	0.0%	2.6%	2.7%	2.6%	15.5%	16.8%	19.4%
Segment Profit Margin	6.7%	14.6%	15.5%	5.2%	8.1%	8.3%	52.3%	50.1%	54.6%
Segment Asset Turnover	2.5	2.5	2.5	2.6	2.5	2.9			
Segment ROA	17.0%	35.8%	39.0%	13.3%	20.6%	24.0%			
Stores Owned	7,238	6,793	5,728	1,979	1,743	1,435			
Stores Licensed	4,329	3,891	3,168	3,134	2,615	2,170			
Total Stores	11,567	10,684	8,896	5,113	4,358	3,605			
Revenues[a]/Stores Owned	$966,800	$965,832	$959,358	$896,513	$824,670	$758,118			
Revenues[b]/Stores Licensed	$116,470	$112,850	$116,509	$ 87,683	$ 84,474	$ 85,714			
Total Revenues/Total Stores	$681,854	$687,851	$694,526	$411,383	$389,215	$361,415			
Operating Income/Total Stores	$ 45,656	$100,197	$107,374	$ 21,514	$ 31,597	$ 30,097			
Assets/Total Stores	$267,995	$279,914	$274,966	$161,314	$153,258	$125,659			
Total Revenues Increase	7.3%	18.9%	21.2%	24.0%	30.2%	27.4%			
Comparable Stores Sales Increase[c]	(5.0%)	4.0%	7.0%	2.0%	7.0%	8.0%			

[a] Revenues represent sales from company-operated retail stores.
[b] Revenues represent fees and other revenues from licensees.
[c] Comparable stores represent stores open at least two full years.

EXHIBIT 4.46

Panera Bread Company
Financial Statement Ratio Analysis
(Integrative Case 4.1, Part B)

	2008	2007	2006
Sales growth	21.8%	28.7%	29.5%
Profit Margin for ROA	5.4%	5.4%	7.1%
Assets Turnover	1.89	1.72	1.69
ROA	10.2%	9.2%	12.0%
Profit Margin for ROCE	5.2%	5.4%	7.1%
Capital Structure Leverage	1.46	1.47	1.37
ROCE	14.3%	13.6%	16.5%
Cost of Sales/Revenues	34.0%	34.2%	34.1%
Store Operating Expenses/Revenues	34.4%	34.2%	31.3%
Nonretail Operating Expenses/Revenues	11.3%	11.4%	11.1%
Depreciation and Amortization Expense/Revenues	5.2%	5.4%	5.3%
General and Administrative Expense/Revenues	6.5%	6.5%	7.2%
Income Tax Expense (excluding tax effects of interest expense)/Revenues	3.2%	3.0%	4.1%
Accounts Receivable Turnover	64.4	48.3	44.5
Inventory Turnover	37.8	36.2	35.2
Fixed Assets Turnover	3.1	2.7	2.7

EXHIBIT 4.47

Panera Bread Company
Segment Profitability Data
(Integrative Case 4.1, Part B)

	2008	2007	2006
Net Revenues:			
Company-operated retail	85.2%	83.9%	80.4%
Franchising	5.8%	6.3%	7.4%
Foodservice and other	9.1%	9.8%	12.2%
Total net revenues	100.0%	100.0%	100.0%
Operating profit:			
Company-operated retail	14.1%	13.6%	14.9%
Franchising	5.0%	5.5%	6.5%
Foodservice and other	0.7%	1.1%	1.9%
Segment Asset Turnover:			
Company-operated retail	2.2	1.7	1.8
Franchising	12.6	10.9	16.5
Foodservice and other	4.2	3.2	2.7

(*Continued*)

EXHIBIT 4.47 (Continued)

	2008	2007	2006
Segment ROA:			
Company-operated retail	36.5%	28.3%	33.0%
Franchising	1,092.3%	955.0%	1,448.1%
Foodservice and other	18.1%	21.2%	25.6%
Stores Owned	562	532	391
Stores Franchised	763	698	636
Total Stores	1,325	1,230	1,027
Revenues/Stores Owned	$1,968,496	$1,682,147	$1,703,685
Revenues/Stores Franchised	$ 98,034	$ 96,258	$ 96,747
Total Revenues/Total Stores	$ 980,266	$ 867,228	$ 807,177
Operating Income/Total Stores	$ 82,044	$ 72,268	$ 90,240
Assets/Total Stores	$ 508,617	$ 568,091	$ 528,344
Total Revenues Increase	21.8%	28.7%	29.5%
Comparable Stores Sales Increase	5.8%	1.9%	3.9%

CASE 4.2

PROFITABILITY AND RISK ANALYSIS OF WAL-MART STORES

Part A

Wal-Mart Stores (Walmart) is the world's largest retailer. It employs an "everyday low price" strategy and operates stores as three business segments: Wal-Mart Stores U.S., International, and Sam's Club.

1. **Wal-Mart Stores U.S.:** This segment represented 63.7 percent of all 2008 sales and operates stores in three different formats: Discount stores (approximately 108,000 square feet), Supercenters (approximately 186,000 square feet), and Neighborhood Markets (approximately 42,000 square feet). Each format carries a variety of clothing, housewares, electronic equipment, pharmaceuticals, health and beauty products, sporting goods, and similar items, and Supercenters including a full-line supermarket.[40] Wal-Mart U.S. Stores are in all 50 states, Discount stores are in 47 states, Supercenters are in 48 states, and Neighborhood Markets are in 16 states. Customers also can purchase many items through the company's website at http://www.walmart.com.
2. **International:** The International segment includes wholly owned subsidiaries in Argentina, Brazil, Canada, Japan, Puerto Rico, and the United Kingdom; majority-owned subsidiaries in five countries in Central America, Chile, and Mexico; and joint ventures in India and China. The merchandising strategy for the International segment is similar to that of the Walmart U.S. segment.
3. **Sam's Clubs:** Sam's Clubs are membership club warehouses that operate in 48 states. The average Sam's Club is approximately 133,000 square feet, and customers can purchase

[40] Walmart's fiscal year ends at the end of January of each year. Despite Walmart's convention of referring to its year ending January 31, 2009, as its fiscal 2009, we follow the common practice of referring to it as 2008 because 11 of the 12 months fall within 2008. This same convention holds true for Carrefour and Target in Part B of this case.

many items through the company's website at http://www.samsclub.com. These warehouses offer bulk displays of brand name merchandise, including hardgoods, some softgoods, institutional-size grocery items, and certain private-label items. Gross margins for Sam's Clubs stores are lower than those of the U.S. and International segments.

Walmart uses centralized purchasing through its home office for substantially all of its merchandise. It distributes products to its stores through regional distribution centers. During fiscal 2008, the proportion of merchandise channeled through its regional distribution centers was as follows:

Walmart Stores, Supercenters, and Neighborhood Markets	81%
Sam's Club (non-fuel)	65%
International	74%

Exhibit 4.48 sets out various operating data for Walmart for its most recent three years. Exhibit 4.49 presents segment data. Exhibit 4.50 presents comparative balance sheets for Walmart for 2005–2008 (an extra year to enable average balance computations when necessary), Exhibit 4.51 (see page 338) presents comparative income statements for 2006–2008, and Exhibit 4.52 (see page 339) presents comparative statements of cash flows for 2006–2008. Exhibit 4.53 (see page 340) presents selected financial statement ratios for Walmart for 2006–2008. The statutory income tax rate is 35 percent.

EXHIBIT 4.48

Operating Data for Wal-Mart Stores (Case 4.2, Part A)

	Fiscal Year:		
	2008	**2007**	**2006**
Walmart Discount Stores, Supercenters, and Neighborhood Markets (U.S.)			
Number	3,656	3,550	3,443
Square Footage (millions)	589.3	566.6	540.4
Sales per Square Foot	$ 433.98	$ 422.75	$ 418.75
Operating Income per Square Foot	$ 31.84	$ 30.91	$ 30.76
International			
Number	3,615	3,098	2,734
Square Footage (millions)	251.8	222.6	188.4
Sales per Square Foot	$ 391.76	$ 406.20	$ 383.04
Operating Income per Square Foot	$ 19.62	$ 21.23	$ 18.76
Sam's Club (Domestic)			
Number	602	591	579
Square Footage (millions)	79.9	78.2	76.3
Sales per Square Foot	$ 586.41	$ 567.23	$ 544.98
Operating Income per Square Foot	$ 20.15	$ 20.69	$ 19.40
Domestic Comparable Store Sales Increase	3.5%	1.6%	2.0%

EXHIBIT 4.49

Segment Profitability Analysis for Wal-Mart Stores (Case 4.2, Part A)

	Fiscal Year:		
	2008	2007	2006
Sales Mix			
Walmart Discount Stores, Supercenters, and Neighborhood Markets	63.7%	64.0%	65.6%
International	24.6	24.1	22.3
Sam's Club	11.7	11.9	12.1
	100.0%	100.0%	100.0%
Walmart Discount Stores, Supercenters, and Neighborhood Markets			
Operating Profit Margin	7.3%	7.3%	7.3%
Assets Turnover	3.0	2.8	2.9
ROA	22.2%	20.8%	21.0%
International			
Operating Profit Margin	5.0%	5.2%	5.5%
Assets Turnover	1.6	1.5	1.4
ROA	8.2%	7.6%	7.8%
Sam's Club			
Operating Profit Margin	3.4%	3.6%	3.6%
Assets Turnover	3.8	3.8	3.6
ROA	13.0%	13.8%	12.9%

EXHIBIT 4.50

Wal-Mart Stores Balance Sheets (amounts in millions) (Case 4.2, Part A)

	2008	2007	2006	2005
ASSETS				
Cash and cash equivalents	$ 7,275	$ 5,492	$ 7,373	$ 6,193
Marketable securities				
Accounts receivable—Net	3,905	3,642	2,840	2,575
Inventories	34,511	35,159	33,685	31,910
Prepaid expenses and other current assets	3,063	2,760	2,690	2,468
Current assets of discontinued segments	195	967	—	679
Current Assets	$ 48,949	$ 48,020	$ 46,588	$ 43,825

EXHIBIT 4.50 (Continued)

	2008	2007	2006	2005
Long-term investments	—	—	—	1,884
Property, plant, & equipment—At cost	131,161	127,992	115,190	100,929
Accumulated depreciation	(35,508)	(31,125)	(26,750)	(23,064)
Goodwill and nonamortizable intangibles	18,827	18,627	16,165	14,613
Total Assets	$163,429	$163,514	$151,193	$138,187
LIABILITIES AND EQUITIES				
Accounts payable—Trade	$ 28,849	$ 30,344	$ 28,090	$ 25,101
Current accrued liabilities	18,112	15,725	14,675	13,274
Notes payable and short-term debt	1,506	5,040	2,570	3,754
Current maturities of long-term debt	6,163	6,229	5,713	4,879
Income taxes payable	760	1,140	706	1,817
Current Liabilities	$ 55,390	$ 58,478	$ 51,754	$ 48,825
Long-term debt	34,549	33,402	30,735	30,096
Deferred tax liabilities—Noncurrent	6,014	5,087	4,971	4,630
Total Liabilities	$ 95,953	$ 96,967	$ 87,460	$ 83,551
Minority interest	$ 2,191	$ 1,939	$ 2,160	$ 1,465
Common stock + paid-in capital	4,313	3,425	3,247	3,013
Retained earnings	63,660	57,319	55,818	49,105
Accum. other comprehensive income (loss)	(2,688)	3,864	2,508	1,053
Common Shareholders' Equity	$ 65,285	$ 64,608	$ 61,573	$ 53,171
Total Liabilities and Equities	$163,429	$163,514	$151,193	$138,187

Required

a. What are the likely reasons for the changes in Walmart's rate of ROA during the three-year period? Analyze the financial ratios to the maximum depth possible.

b. What are the likely reasons for the changes in Walmart's rate of ROCE during the three-year period?

Note: Parts c and d require coverage of material from Chapter 5.

c. How has the short-term liquidity risk of Walmart changed during the three-year period?

d. How has the long-term solvency risk of Walmart changed during the three-year period?

Part B

Part A of Case 4.2 analyzed the profitability and risk of Wal-Mart Stores for its fiscals 2006, 2007, and 2008. Part B of this case compares the profitability and risk ratios of Walmart and two other leading discount retailers, Carrefour and Target, for their 2006–2008 fiscal years.

Carrefour

Carrefour, headquartered in France, is Europe's largest retailer and the second-largest retailer in the world. Sales in 2008 totaled €86,967 million (approximately $118,000 million).

EXHIBIT 4.51

Wal-Mart Stores
Income Statements
(amounts in millions)
(Case 4.2, Part A)

	2008	2007	2006
Revenues	$ 405,607	$ 378,476	$ 348,368
Cost of goods sold	(306,158)	(286,350)	(263,979)
Gross Profit	$ 99,449	$ 92,126	$ 84,389
Selling, general, and administrative expenses	(76,651)	(70,174)	(63,892)
Operating Profit	$ 22,798	$ 21,952	$ 20,497
Interest income	284	309	280
Interest expense	(2,184)	(2,103)	(1,809)
Income Before Tax	$ 20,898	$ 20,158	$ 18,968
Income tax expense	(7,145)	(6,889)	(6,354)
Minority interest in earnings	(499)	(406)	(425)
Income (loss) from discontinued operations	146	(132)	(905)
Net Income (Computed)	$ 13,400	$ 12,731	$ 11,284
Other comprehensive income items	(6,552)	1,356	1,575
Comprehensive Income	$ 6,848	$ 14,087	$ 12,859

Carrefour is organized by geographic region (France, Europe excluding France, Asia, and Latin America). Each segment is organized according to store formats, which include the following (2008 number of stores and sales mix percentages in parentheses):

Hypermarkets (203; 62%): Offer a wide variety of household and food products at competitively low prices under the Carrefour store brand

Supermarkets (590; 22%): Sell traditional grocery products under the Champion, Norte, GS, and GB supermarkets and other store brands

Hard Discount Stores (842; 11%): Offer a limited variety of food products in smaller stores than those of hypermarkets and supermarkets at aggressively low prices under the Dia, Ed, and Minipreco store brands

Other activities (9; 5%): Includes convenience stores and wholesale stores, the latter targeted at business customers, under the SHOPI, Marche Plus, 8 A Huit, express, Contact, and Proxi store brands

Carrefour derived approximately 44 percent of its 2008 sales in France, 37 percent in Europe excluding France, 12 percent in Latin America, and 7 percent in Asia.

Target

Target Corporation, headquartered in the United States, operates two reportable segments: retail and credit card. The retail segment includes all merchandising operations, including large-format general merchandise and food discount stores as well as an online business at

EXHIBIT 4.52

Wal-Mart Stores
Statements of Cash Flows
(amounts in millions)
(Case 4.2, Part A)

STATEMENT OF CASH FLOWS	2008	2007	2006
Net income	$ 13,400	$ 12,731	$ 11,284
Add back depreciation and amortization expenses	6,739	6,317	5,459
Deferred income taxes	581	(8)	89
(Increase) Decrease in accounts receivable	(101)	(564)	(214)
(Increase) Decrease in inventories	(220)	(775)	(1,274)
Increase (Decrease) in accounts payable	(410)	865	2,132
Increase (Decrease) in other current liabilities	2,036	1,034	588
Other addbacks to net income			
Other subtractions from net income	(146)	132	860
Other operating cash flows	1,268	910	1,311
Net Cash Flows from Operations	$ 23,147	$ 20,642	$ 20,235
Proceeds from sales of property, plant, and equipment	$ 714	$ 957	$ 394
Property, plant, and equipment acquired	(11,499)	(14,937)	(15,666)
Investments sold	781		267
Investments acquired		(95)	
Other investment transactions	(1,576)	(1,338)	(68)
Other	838	(257)	610
Net Cash Flows from Investing Activities	$(10,742)	$(15,670)	$(14,463)
Increase in short-term borrowing		$ 2,376	
Decrease in short-term borrowing	$ (3,745)		$ (1,193)
Increase in long-term borrowing	6,566	11,167	7,199
Decrease in long-term borrowing	(5,739)	(9,066)	(6,098)
Share repurchases—Treasury stock	(3,521)	(7,691)	(1,718)
Dividend payments	(3,746)	(3,586)	(2,802)
Other financing transactions	267	(622)	(510)
Net Cash Flows from Financing Activities	$ (9,918)	$ (7,422)	$ (5,122)
Effects of exchange rate changes on cash	(781)	252	97
Net Change in Cash	$ 1,706	$ (2,198)	$ 747
Cash and Cash Equivalents, Beginning of Year *	$ 5,492	$ 7,373	$ 6193

* The amounts do not reconcile with the balance sheet presentation because Walmart reclassified cash and equivalents applicable to discontinued operations.

http://www.target.com. Target stores offer a wide variety of clothing, household, electronics, sports, toys, and entertainment products at discount prices. Target stores attempt to differentiate themselves from Walmart's discount stores by pushing trendy merchandising with more brand-name products. Target emphasizes customer service, referring to its customers as "guests" and focusing on the theme of "Expect More, Pay Less." Target Corporation

EXHIBIT 4.53

Wal-Mart Stores
Financial Ratio Analysis
(Case 4.2, Part A)

	Fiscal Year:		
	2008	2007	2006
Profitability Ratios			
ROA	9.3%	9.3%	9.5%
Profit Margin for ROA	3.7%	3.9%	4.0%
Assets Turnover	2.5	2.4	2.4
Cost of Goods Sold/Sales	75.5%	75.7%	75.8%
Selling and Administrative Expense/Sales	18.9%	18.5%	18.3%
Interest Expense (net of taxes)/Sales	0.3%	0.4%	0.3%
Income Tax Expense (excluding tax effects of interest expense)/Sales	2.0%	2.0%	2.0%
Accounts Receivable Turnover	107.5	116.8	128.7
Inventory Turnover	8.8	8.3	8.0
Fixed Assets Turnover	4.2	4.1	4.2
ROCE	20.4%	20.4%	21.2%
Profit Margin for ROCE	3.3%	3.4%	3.5%
Capital Structure Leverage	2.5	2.4	2.4
Risk Ratios			
Current Ratio	0.88	0.82	0.90
Quick Ratio	0.20	0.16	0.20
Accounts Payable Turnover	10.3	9.9	10.0
Cash Flow from Operations to Current Liabilities Ratio	40.7%	37.5%	40.2%
Long-Term Debt Ratio	34.6%	34.1%	33.3%
Total Liabilities/Total Assets Ratio	58.7%	59.3%	57.8%
Cash Flow from Operations to Total Liabilities Ratio	24.0%	22.4%	23.7%
Interest Coverage Ratio	10.6	10.5	11.0

attempts to differentiate itself from competitors by providing wider aisles and a less cluttered store appearance. At the end of fiscal 2008, Target Corporation operated 1,682 stores and 34 distribution centers. The credit card segment offers branded proprietary credit cards under the names Target Visa and the Target Card. For 2008, total revenues were $64,948, consisting of retail sales of 62,884 and credit card revenues of $2,064.

Exhibits 4.54 and 4.55 (see page 342) present profitability ratios for Carrefour, Target, and Walmart for their 2006–2008 fiscal years. Exhibit 4.56 (see page 343) presents risk ratios for the three firms. Exhibit 4.57 (see page 344) presents selected other data for these firms. The financial statements include the present value of commitments under all leases in property, plant, and equipment and in long-term debt.

EXHIBIT 4.54

Cross-Section ROA Profitability Analysis for Carrefour, Target, and Walmart (Case 4.2, Part B)

ROA

	2008	2007	2006
Carrefour	3.0%	4.4%	4.5%
Target	6.0%	7.8%	8.6%
Walmart	9.3%	9.3%	9.5%

	Profit Margin for ROA			Assets Turnover		
	2008	**2007**	**2006**	**2008**	**2007**	**2006**
Carrefour	1.8%	2.6%	2.8%	1.7	1.7	1.6
Target	4.2%	5.2%	5.4%	1.4	1.5	1.6
Walmart	3.7%	3.9%	4.0%	2.5	2.4	2.4

	Carrefour			Target			Walmart		
	2008	**2007**	**2006**	**2008**	**2007**	**2006**	**2008**	**2007**	**2006**
Sales	100.0%	100.0%	100.0%	100.0%	100.0%	100.0%	100.0%	100.0%	100.0%
Other Revenues	1.4	1.4	1.3	3.3	2.1	2.8	1.1	1.1	1.0
Cost of Goods Sold	(79.0)	(78.6)	(78.6)	(70.2)	(69.8)	(69.7)	(76.3)	(76.5)	(76.6)
Selling and Administrative	(19.2)	(18.7)	(18.6)	(26.1)	(24.7)	(24.3)	(19.1)	(18.7)	(18.5)
Income Taxes	(0.9)	(1.0)	(1.1)	(2.1)	(2.9)	(3.0)	(1.8)	(1.8)	(1.8)
Profit Margin for ROA*	1.8%	2.6%	2.8%	4.2%	5.2%	5.4%	3.7%	3.9%	4.0%
Receivable Turnover	27.4	23.3	21.7	7.8	8.6	9.8	107.5	116.8	128.7
Inventory Turnover	10.0	10.0	9.9	6.5	6.6	6.7	8.8	8.3	8.0
Fixed Assets Turnover	5.9	5.8	5.7	2.5	2.7	2.9	4.2	4.1	4.2

*Amounts do not sum because Profit Margin for ROA is reduced by taxes on operating profits, which do not equal total taxes reported on the income statement.

EXHIBIT 4.55

Cross-Section ROCE Profitability Analysis for Carrefour, Target, and Walmart (Case 4.2, Part B)

ROCE

	2008	2007	2006
Carrefour	14.8%	24.6%	27.2%
Target	15.3%	18.4%	18.7%
Walmart	20.4%	20.4%	21.2%

	Profit Margin for ROCE			Assets Turnover			Capital Structure Leverage		
	2008	**2007**	**2006**	**2008**	**2007**	**2006**	**2008**	**2007**	**2006**
Carrefour	1.8%	3.0%	3.2%	1.7	1.7	1.6	5.0	4.9	5.2
Target	3.5%	4.6%	4.8%	1.4	1.5	1.6	3.1	2.6	2.4
Walmart	3.3%	3.4%	3.5%	2.5	2.4	2.4	2.5	2.5	2.5

Required

a. Walmart and Target follow somewhat different strategies. Walmart consistently has a higher ROA compared to Target. Using information in Exhibits 4.54 and 4.57, suggest reasons for these differences in operating profitability.

b. Walmart and Carrefour follow similar strategies. Walmart consistently outperforms Carrefour on ROA. Using information in Exhibits 4.54 and 4.57, suggest reasons for these differences in operating profitability.

c. Refer to Exhibit 4.55. Which firm appears to have used financial leverage most effectively in enhancing the rate of ROCE? Explain your reasoning.
Note: Parts d and e require coverage of material from Chapter 5.

d. Refer to Exhibit 4.56. Rank-order these firms in terms of their short-term liquidity risk. Do any of these firms appear unduly risky as of the end of fiscal 2008? Explain.

e. Refer to Exhibit 4.56. Rank-order these firms in terms of their long-term liquidity risk. Do any of these firms appear unduly risky as of the end of fiscal Year 4? Explain.

EXHIBIT 4.56

Cross-Section Risk Analysis for Carrefour, Target, and Walmart
(Case 4.2, Part B)

	Carrefour			Target			Walmart		
	2008	**2007**	**2006**	**2008**	**2007**	**2006**	**2008**	**2007**	**2006**
Short-Term Liquidity									
Current Ratio	0.70	0.65	0.66	1.66	1.60	1.32	0.88	0.82	0.90
Quick Ratio	0.39	0.36	0.37	0.85	0.89	0.63	0.20	0.16	0.20
Cash Flow from Operations/ Average Current Liabilities	14.1%	14.2%	13.1%	39.7%	36.0%	47.0%	40.7%	37.5%	40.2%
Days Receivable	24	27	29	47	48	49	3	3	3
Days Inventory	37	39	37	55	58	57	42	44	45
Days Payable	92	95	99	52	56	59	35	37	37
Long-Term Solvency									
Long-Term Debt Ratio	46.5%	41.3%	41.8%	56.1%	49.7%	35.7%	34.6%	34.1%	33.3%
Total Liabilities/ Total Assets Ratio	79.0%	77.3%	77.9%	68.9%	65.6%	58.1%	58.7%	59.3%	57.8%
Cash Flow from Operations/ Average Total Liabilities	9.9%	10.2%	9.4%	14.9%	16.2%	22.9%	24.0%	22.4%	23.7%
Interest Coverage Ratio	6.4	8.4	9.1	5.9	9.6	10.0	10.6	10.5	11.0

EXHIBIT 4.57

Selected Other Financial Data
for Carrefour, Target, and Walmart
(Case 4.2, Part B)

	2008	2007	2006
Growth Rate in Sales			
Carrefour	5.9%	6.8%	5.2%
Target	2.3%	6.2%	12.9%
Walmart	9.4%	7.2%	8.6%
Number of Stores			
Carrefour	15,430	14,991	12,547
Target	1,682	1,591	1,488
Walmart	7,873	7,239	6,756
Square Footage (000's)			
Carrefour	192,801	181,900	164,350
Target	222,588	207,945	192,064
Walmart	921,000	867,400	805,100
Sales per Square Foot			
Carrefour	€451	€452	€468
Target	$283	$296	$301
Walmart	$440	$436	$433
Sales per Store			
Carrefour	€5,636,215	€5,479,855	€6,127,919
Target	$37,386,445	$38,636,706	$38,896,505
Walmart	$51,518,735	$52,282,912	$51,564,239
Square Feet per Store			
Carrefour	12,495	12,134	13,099
Target	132,335	130,701	129,075
Walmart	116,982	119,823	119,168
Fixed Assets per Square Foot			
Carrefour	€77	€81	€84
Target	$116	$116	$112
Walmart	$104	$112	$110
Sales per Employee			
Carrefour	€175,589	€167,636	€168,503
Target	$179,157	$167,954	$164,426
Walmart	$193,146	$180,227	$183,352
Exchange Rate:			
U.S. Dollars per Euro (€)	$1.4097	$1.4728	$1.3200

Chapter 5

Risk Analysis

Learning Objectives

1. Utilize the information that U.S. GAAP and IFRS require firms to disclose about their risk exposures and risk management activities.
2. Understand the concept of *financial flexibility* and use an innovative decomposition of return on common equity to assess financial flexibility.
3. Apply analytical tools to assess working capital management and *short-term liquidity risk*.
4. Evaluate the benefits and risks of financial leverage and apply analytical tools for assessing *long-term solvency risk*.
5. Use risk analysis tools in assessing *credit risk*.
6. Apply predictive statistical models to assess *bankruptcy risk*.
7. Understand the distinction between *firm-specific risks*, as measured by various financial statement ratios, and *systematic risk*, as measured by market equity beta, and relationships between these types of risks.
8. Examine factors that may lead firms to manipulate reported financial statement amounts and apply tools for analyzing the *fraudulent financial reporting risk*.

Equity investors make investment decisions based on the *expected return* from equity investments relative to the *risks* of realizing those returns. Similarly, lenders make lending decisions based on the *expected return* in the form of interest revenue relative to the *risks* of the borrower defaulting on repayments. The analysis of risk is central to any decision to commit economic resources to a project or an investment. This chapter describes disclosures required by U.S. GAAP and IFRS to inform financial statement users about how certain risks can affect a firm and how the firm manages those risks. The chapter also explores the analysis of various types of risk using financial statement ratios, predictive statistical models, and other analytical tools.

DISCLOSURES REGARDING RISK AND RISK MANAGEMENT

The sources and types of risk a firm faces are numerous and often interrelated. They include the following:

Source	Type or Nature
Firm-Specific	Ability to attract, retain, and motivate employees Dependence on one or few customers Dependence on one or few suppliers Employee relations Litigation Environmental or political scrutiny
Industry	Technology Competition Regulation Availability and price of raw materials or other production inputs Labor wages and supply
Domestic	Recessions Inflation or deflation Interest rate volatility Demographic shifts Political environment
International	Exchange rate changes Host government regulations and posturing Political unrest or asset expropriation

Most of these risks are inevitable, and firms must continually monitor each one to ensure that appropriate actions are taken to minimize the impact of detrimental events or changes in circumstances. The focus in this chapter, however, is on how to assess the financial consequences of these types of risk using disclosures and data from financial reports. Various financial reporting standards and financial market regulations require firms to discuss in notes to the financial statements or in regulatory filings how important elements of risk affect a particular firm and the actions the firm takes to manage these risks. Some of the more important disclosures are discussed below. Later chapters discuss more fully the accounting procedures for more complex and risky assets and liabilities. We use the disclosures available in PepsiCo's 10-K under "Item 1A. Risk Factors," a required disclosure for all companies under the purview of the SEC. We also use disclosures in Note 10, "Risk Management" (Appendix A), and the discussion under the heading "Market Risks" in PepsiCo's MD&A (Appendix B) to illustrate information that firms provide about risk.

Firm-Specific Risks

Like all companies, PepsiCo is subject to numerous firm-specific risks that are driven by the nature of the business, competition, supplier relationships, customers, and overall firm strategy. For Forms 10-K filed with the SEC, a candid discussion of such risks is required as Item 1A. For non-U.S. companies that list securities in the United States, a required

Form 20-F includes "Item 3D. Risk Factors." Capital market regulators generally require companies around the world to file similar reports in their local jurisdictions. For example, in France, companies file a Registration Document annually with the Autorité des Marchés Financiers (AMF) and in Singapore, companies file an Annual Return and Audited Accounts with the Accounting and Corporate Regulatory Authority (ACRA).

Within Item 1A of Form 10-K, PepsiCo identifies the following risks related to its business:

- *Demand for our products may be adversely affected by changes in consumer preferences and tastes or if we are unable to innovate or market our products effectively.*
- *Our operating results may be adversely affected by increased costs, disruption of supply or shortages of raw materials and other supplies.*
- *If we are not able to build and sustain proper information technology infrastructure, successfully implement our ongoing business transformation initiative or outsource certain functions effectively our business could suffer.*
- *Any damage to our reputation could have an adverse effect on our business, financial condition and results of operations.*
- *Trade consolidation, the loss of any key customer, or failure to maintain good relationships with our bottling partners could adversely affect our financial performance.*
- *If we are unable to hire or retain key employees or a highly skilled and diverse workforce, it could have a negative impact on our business.*
- *Changes in the legal and regulatory environment could limit our business activities, increase our operating costs, reduce demand for our products or result in litigation.*
- *Disruption of our supply chain could have an adverse impact on our business, financial condition and results of operations.*
- *Unstable political conditions, civil unrest or other developments and risks in the countries where we operate may adversely impact our business.*

Although many of the disclosures PepsiCo provides are general and applicable to any company, each is discussed in more detail in the company's Form 10-K. For example, PepsiCo gives more detail on the second risk factor, listed above, relating to input prices with the following discussion:

> We and our business partners use various raw materials and other supplies in our business, including aspartame, cocoa, corn, corn sweeteners, flavorings, flour, grapefruits and other fruits, juice and juice concentrates, oats, oranges, potatoes, rice, seasonings, sucralose, sugar, vegetable and essential oils, and wheat. Our key packaging materials include PET resin used for plastic bottles, film packaging used for snack foods, aluminum used for cans, glass bottles and cardboard. Fuel and natural gas are also important commodities due to their use in our plants and in the trucks delivering our products.

The identification and discussion of firm-specific risks provides a useful bridge between understanding a company's industry, business strategy, and profitability and identifying specific risks that may have an impact on the company's ability to grow, be profitable, and ultimately create value for debt and equity stakeholders. Of the firm-specific risks identified above, some are quantifiable and subject to required disclosures in the footnotes to financial statements. The remaining discussion in this section focuses on examples of such disclosures.

Commodity Prices

Firms purchase raw materials to use in manufacturing products. Changes in the prices of those raw materials affect future profitability unless the firm can pass along price increases to customers, engage in fixed-price contractual arrangements with suppliers, or purchase commodity futures contracts. For example, some firms manage this risk by engaging in a purchase commitment with suppliers to purchase certain quantities at a specified price over a particular period of time. Alternatively, the firm might acquire a futures contract or another hedging instrument to neutralize the risk of changes in prices. Chapter 8 discusses the accounting for such hedging instruments.

PepsiCo discloses the following with respect to commodity price risk in Note 10, "Risk Management" (Appendix A):

> We are subject to commodity price risk because our ability to recover increased costs through higher pricing may be limited in the competitive environment in which we operate. This risk is managed through the use of fixed-price purchase orders, pricing agreements, geographic diversity and derivatives. We use derivatives, with terms of no more than three years, to economically hedge price fluctuations related to a portion of our anticipated commodity purchases, primarily for natural gas and diesel fuel. For those derivatives that qualify for hedge accounting, any ineffectiveness is recorded immediately. However, such commodity cash flow hedges have not had any significant ineffectiveness for all periods presented. We classify both the earnings and cash flow impact from these derivatives consistent with the underlying hedged item. During the next 12 months, we expect to reclassify net losses of $64 million related to cash flow hedges from accumulated other comprehensive loss into net income. Derivatives used to hedge commodity price risks that do not qualify for hedge accounting are marked to market each period and reflected in our income statement.

In the MD&A section (Appendix B) and Note 10, "Financial Instruments" (Appendix A), PepsiCo provides the following information about the extent of hedging on commodity prices and the effect on pretax earnings if commodity prices declined:

> Our open commodity derivative contracts that qualify for hedge accounting had a face value of $303 million at December 27, 2008 and $5 million at December 29, 2007. These contracts resulted in net unrealized losses of $117 million at December 27, 2008 and net unrealized gains of less than $1 million at December 29, 2007. At the end of 2008, the potential change in fair value of commodity derivative instruments, assuming a 10% decrease in the underlying commodity price, would have increased our net unrealized losses in 2008 by $19 million.

It is unclear whether the $303 million of open derivative contracts at the end of 2008 relate to accounts payable and other current liabilities of $8,273 million or to purchasing commitments of $3,273 million. (See the balance sheet and Note 9, "Debt Obligations and Commitments," in Appendix A.) Regardless, the amount of open contracts is small compared to either base. PepsiCo uses a 10 percent decline in commodity prices to illustrate the sensitivity of earnings to hedged commodity price changes, which would be a loss on these contracts of $19 million. This amount is 0.3 percent of income before income taxes for 2008 (= $19/$7,021).

In addition to the above derivative contracts that qualify for hedge accounting, Note 10 also discloses a greater exposure for contracts that do not qualify for hedge accounting. These totaled $626 million at December 27, 2008 (relative to $105 million at December 29, 2007). Because these contracts did not qualify for hedge accounting, losses on these contracts of $343 million in 2008 are included in net income. This amount constitutes the bulk of the $346 million of mark-to-market impacts discussed in Chapter 4 as part of making adjustments to rate of return on assets calculations.

Foreign Exchange

Changes in foreign exchange rates can affect a firm in multiple ways:

- The prices a firm pays to acquire raw materials from suppliers abroad
- The prices a firm charges for products sold to customers abroad
- The amount of cash a firm receives when it collects an account receivable, a loan receivable, or another receivable denominated in a currency other than its own
- The amount of cash a firm pays when it settles an account payable, a loan payable, or another payable denominated in a currency other than its own
- The amount of cash a firm collects when it receives remittances from a foreign branch or dividends from a foreign subsidiary
- The cash-equivalent value of assets invested abroad and liabilities borrowed abroad in the event the firm liquidates the foreign unit

Firms often use foreign exchange contracts to hedge some or all of these risks. Chapter 7 discusses the effect of exchange rate changes on reporting the operations of foreign units, and Chapter 8 discusses forward contracts used to hedge such risks.

PepsiCo states the following in Note 10, "Financial Instruments" (Appendix A):

> Our operations outside of the U.S. generate 48% of our net revenue, with Mexico, Canada and the United Kingdom comprising 19% of our net revenue. As a result, we are exposed to foreign currency risks. On occasion, we enter into hedges, primarily forward contracts with terms of no more than two years, to reduce the effect of foreign exchange rates. Ineffectiveness of these hedges has not been material.

In its MD&A (Appendix B), PepsiCo discloses that foreign currency derivatives had a face value of $1.4 billion at the end of 2008, considerably more than the amount of commodity derivatives. A 10 percent unfavorable change in exchange rates would have resulted in a pretax loss of $70 million for 2008. This amount is 1.0 percent of income before income taxes (= $70/$7,021), a larger amount than for commodity derivatives and a larger amount than that for 2007.

Interest Rates

Changes in interest rates can affect firms in various ways:

- The value of investments in bonds or other investment securities with fixed interest rates
- The value of liabilities with fixed interest rates
- The returns a firm generates from pension fund investments

Firms often use interest rate swaps to hedge, or neutralize, the risk of interest rate changes. As Chapter 8 discusses, locking in a fixed rate insulates the principal amount from interest rate changes, but it exposes the fair value of the principal. Locking in a variable rate protects the fair value of the principal but induces risk (volatility) in the cash flows for interest payments. Firms, particularly financial institutions, also hedge some interest rate risk by matching investments in fixed-interest-rate assets with fixed-rate liabilities of equivalent amounts and duration.

PepsiCo discloses the following in Note 10, "Financial Instruments" (Appendix A):

> We centrally manage our debt and investment portfolios considering investment opportunities and risks, tax consequences and overall financing strategies. We may use interest rate and cross currency interest rate swaps to manage our overall interest expense and foreign exchange risk. These instruments effectively change the interest rate and currency of specific debt issuances. Our 2008 and 2007 interest rate swaps

were entered into concurrently with the issuance of the debt that they modified. The notional amount, interest payment and maturity date of the swaps match the principal, interest payment and maturity date of the related debt.

The MD&A (Appendix B) indicates that an increase in interest rates of 1-percentage-point would have increased net interest expense by $21 million for 2008, which is approximately 6.4 percent of realized interest expense (= $21/$329).

Other Risk-Related Disclosures

The particular elements of risk that firms include in their risk management disclosures depend on the types of risks to which a firm is exposed, and many of the financial statement footnotes include qualitative discussions or quantitative indicators of such risks. For example, PepsiCo discloses in Note 7, "Pension, Retiree Medical and Savings Plans," the effect that a 1-percentage-point change in the assumed health care cost trend rate would have on service cost and interest cost components of retiree medical expense and the associated benefit liability. The required disclosures in Note 6, "Stock-Based Compensation," enable financial statement users to assess the impact of different assumptions underlying the valuation of stock options. Similarly, information in Note 5, "Income Taxes," indicates that in determining the income tax provision, the company assesses the risk of a tax position being sustained on audit based on the technical merits of the position. Finally, Note 9, "Debt Obligations and Commitments," indicates that PepsiCo is the guarantor on $2.3 billion of long-term debt of Bottling Group, LLC, which highlights that the company is exposed not only to its own firm-specific financial risks, but also to those of affiliated companies.

Firms now disclose considerably more information for the analyst to use in assessing the effect of various risks on a firm. Increasingly, standard setters and regulators have required firms to disclose the sensitivity of reported amounts to changes in various variables and assumptions. One would expect the information value of these disclosures to increase even more as analysts and other users of financial statements become more familiar with them.

FINANCIAL STATEMENT ANALYSIS OF RISK

In addition to using information about risk disclosed in the notes to the financial statements and in the MD&A, analysts typically assess many dimensions of risk using ratios of various items in the financial statements. In addition to the balance sheet and income statement, the statement of cash flows (discussed in Chapter 3), which reports the net amount of cash generated or used by operating, investing, and financing activities, also is an important source of information for studying risk. In this chapter, we discuss how to use the collective information in the three primary financial statements to examine risk. We demonstrate financial statement analysis techniques to assess the following types of risk:

- Financial flexibility
- Short-term liquidity risk
- Long-term solvency risk
- Credit risk
- Bankruptcy risk
- Market equity risk
- Financial reporting manipulation risk

Many firms use financial leverage to increase returns to equity shareholders. When firms obtain funds from borrowing and invest those funds in assets that generate a higher return than the after-tax cost of the borrowing, the common shareholders benefit. Therefore, capital structure leverage enhances the return to the common shareholders, but it involves risk.

The impact of leverage on returns to common shareholders is part of the disaggregation of ROCE (return on common equity) discussed in Chapter 4. Therefore, the analysis of profitability discussed in that chapter is linked to the analysis of risk discussed in this chapter by an examination of *financial flexibility.* Financial flexibility is the ability of a firm to obtain debt financing conditional on its current leverage and profitability of its operating assets.

The risk associated with leverage arises because satisfying future debt retirements requires cash payments. Exhibit 5.1 relates the factors affecting a firm's ability to generate cash with its need to use cash. Many financial statement analysis techniques designed to assess risk focus on a comparison of the supply of cash and the demand for cash. For example, risk analysis using financial statement information can examine *short-term liquidity risk,* which is the near-term ability to generate cash to meet working capital needs and debt service requirements, as well as *long-term solvency risk,* which is the longer-term ability to generate cash internally or externally to satisfy plant capacity and debt repayment needs.

The field of finance identifies two closely related types of firm-specific risk: *credit risk* and *bankruptcy risk,* both of which can be evaluated using financial statement information. Credit risk concerns a firm's ability to make ongoing interest and principal payments on borrowings as they come due. Bankruptcy risk, on the other hand, relates to the likelihood that a firm will ultimately be forced to file for bankruptcy and perhaps subsequently liquidate due to a combination of insufficient profitability and cash flows and high debt service costs. Analysts view these two types of risk as states of financial distress that fall along a continuum of increasing gravity from (1) failing to make a required interest payment on time to (2) restructuring debt to (3) defaulting on a principal payment on debt to (4) filing for bankruptcy to (5) liquidating a firm. Analysts concerned with the economic loss of a portion of or the entire amount lent to or invested in a firm would examine a firm's position on this financial distress continuum. We demonstrate how analysts can use tools of short-term liquidity and long-term solvency risk in assessing credit risk and bankruptcy risk.

Less than 5 percent of publicly traded firms experience financial distress as defined by one of the five states listed previously. The other 95 percent of firms that are reasonably financially healthy utilize borrowings to finance future expansion or unforeseen investment opportunities, which is captured by the notion of financial flexibility described earlier. Thus, while examination of liquidity, solvency, credit, and bankruptcy risk is sometimes very important, analysts are more often interested in the financial flexibility of a firm to strategically utilize leverage through borrowing to enhance the returns to the firm's common equity investors.

EXHIBIT 5.1

Framework for Financial Statement Analysis of Risk

Activity	Ability to Generate Cash	Need to Use Cash	Financial Statement Analysis Performed
Operations	Profitability of goods and services sold	Working capital requirements	Short-term liquidity risk
Investing	Sales of existing plant assets or investments	Plant capacity requirements	Long-term solvency risk
Financing	Borrowing capacity	Debt service requirements	

The preceding types of risk do not encompass the full range of risks that equity investors must consider as the residual risk bearers of firms. Therefore, to value firms, investors also assess elements of risk inherent in investing in common shares of a firm relative to the risks that are common to all firms. For example, investors consider systematic (nondiversifiable) risk and use it to explain differences in expected rates of return on common stocks. Economic theory teaches that differences in risk relate to differences in expected returns. Studies of this risk/return relation use market equity beta as one measure of *market equity risk.* Market equity beta measures the covariability of a firm's returns with an index of returns of all securities in the equity capital market. Research and practice show that market equity betas are increasing in financial leverage. We briefly discuss the research relating financial statement data and market equity beta later in this chapter but elaborate on it more fully in Chapters 11–14. The discussion included in this chapter is intended to emphasize that market risk is related to the other risks discussed.

In conducting financial statement analysis, the presumption is that a firm adheres to its designated accounting standards in preparing its financial statements, which permits the analyst to use the reported amounts to assess each type of risk. In some cases, however, firms intentionally manipulate the financial statements in an effort to portray a more profitable or less risky profile than is appropriate. If the financial statements are manipulated, they are not useful—or worse, are misleading—as the basis for analyzing various risks. Thus, assessing *financial reporting manipulation risk* is an integral part of using financial statement data as the basis of risk analysis.

As will become clear, all seven of these elements of risk are interrelated. Firms use financial flexibility and leverage to achieve higher returns for equity investors, but doing so involves financial risk. Analysts evaluate short-term liquidity and long-term solvency risk and assess both credit risk and bankruptcy risk. Some of the factors affecting long-term solvency risk and financial flexibility also affect market equity risk. Financial reporting manipulation risk affects all of the other risks because such risk detracts from the usefulness of the financial statements as a basis for risk assessment.

We illustrate the analyses of various dimensions of risk using the financial statements of PepsiCo in Appendix A. As we did in Chapter 4, we compare financial ratios for PepsiCo for 2008 with the corresponding ratios for 2006 and 2007. Additional insights are often attained through comparison of the ratios for PepsiCo with average industry ratios or with those of PepsiCo's competitors (for example, Coca-Cola).

ANALYZING FINANCIAL FLEXIBILITY: ALTERNATIVE APPROACHES TO DISAGGREGATE ROCE

Firms that borrow funds and invest those funds in assets that generate a higher return than the after-tax cost of the borrowing create value for the common shareholders. Common shareholders benefit with increasing proportions of debt in the capital structure as long as the firm maintains an excess rate of return on assets over the after-tax cost of the debt. Therefore, financial leverage can enhance the return to common shareholders. The impact of leverage on returns to common shareholders is part of the disaggregation of ROCE discussed in Chapter 4. The disaggregation of ROCE into components of profit margin for ROCE (assets turnover and capital structure leverage) is as follows:

$$\text{ROCE} = \frac{\text{Net Income to Common}}{\text{Average Common Equity}}$$

$$= \frac{\text{Net Income to Common}}{\text{Sales}} \times \frac{\text{Sales}}{\text{Average Total Assets}} \times \frac{\text{Average Total Assets}}{\text{Average Common Equity}}$$

$$= \text{Profit Margin for ROCE} \times \text{Assets Turnover} \times \text{Capital Structure Leverage}$$

The disaggregation of ROCE provides insight about the degree to which common equity shareholders benefit from using leverage. Higher leverage generally suggests greater financial risk, as discussed in the following sections on short-term liquidity risk, long-term solvency risk, credit risk, and bankruptcy risk. The risk is primarily attributable to the costs of borrowing, reflected by interest expense for long-term debt and the requirement to make debt payments in cash when they come due. The disaggregation of ROCE suggests that common equity shareholders benefit from increasing leverage (that is, the third term in the ROCE disaggregation). However, there are two offsetting effects of increasing leverage. First, increasing leverage assumes that the firm can deploy the financing proceeds into assets that maintain the current levels of profitability and turnover (that is, the first and second terms), which depends on the firm's ability to scale up operations without experiencing diminishing returns, market saturation, and other strategic roadblocks. Second, increasing leverage increases interest expense, which reduces profit margins (that is, the first term in the disaggregation). Thus, increasing leverage has potential benefits and risks.

A shortcoming of the standard disaggregation of ROCE is the inability to directly gauge the extent to which a firm can strategically increase leverage to increase returns to common shareholders without offsetting profitability. We refer to this as *financial flexibility*. A better way to represent a firm's financial flexibility is to disaggregate ROCE to capture operating and financing impacts separately on returns to common shareholders. The alternative disaggregation discussed next requires that we reformulate the balance sheet and income statement into operating and financing components.[1]

Exhibit 5.2 presents the standard balance sheet equation in which assets are equal to liabilities plus equity. Each of these amounts is decomposed into primary components.

- Assets = Current Assets + Noncurrent Assets
- Liabilities = Current Liabilities + Noncurrent Liabilities + Short-Term Debt + Long-Term Debt + Preferred Equity + Minority Interest
- Equity = Common Equity

EXHIBIT 5.2

Reformulation of Standard Balance Sheet into Net Operating Assets, Financing Obligations, and Common Equity Components

Assets = Liabilities + Equity

Current Assets (CA) + Noncurrent Assets (NCA) = Current Liabilities (CL) + Noncurrent Liabilities (NCL) + S.T. Debt + L.T. Debt + Preferred Equity + Minority Interest + Common Equity

CA − CL + NCA − NCL = S.T. Debt + L.T. Debt + Preferred Equity + Minority Interest + Common Equity

(S.T. Debt + L.T. Debt + Preferred Equity + Minority Interest + Common Equity): Sources of Debt and Equity Financing that Generate Financing Costs

(CA − CL + NCA − NCL): **Net Operating Assets**

(S.T. Debt + L.T. Debt + Preferred Equity + Minority Interest): **Financing Obligations**

(Common Equity): **Common Equity**

---

[1] This alternative disaggregation of ROCE is sometimes referred to as the "Penman decomposition," following pioneering work by Stephen H. Penman in articulating the operating and financing activities of firms. For a more detailed discussion, see Chapter 11 of Stephen H. Penman, *Financial Statement Analysis and Security Valuation* (New York: McGraw-Hill Irwin), 2004.

These components are rearranged to group operating components together and financing components separately, which are then aggregated back into a reformulated balance sheet equation. We treat minority interest as preferred equity (that is, a financing obligation), consistent with the treatment of minority interest in accounting standards for business combinations. However, some analysts make the argument that minority interest should be netted against operating assets. Either approach can be justified so long as consistent treatment is used for minority interest on the income statement (discussed below).

The reformulated balance sheet equation is as follows:

$$\text{Net Operating Assets} = \text{Financing Obligations} + \text{Common Equity}$$

The primary change of this financial statement reformulation is that operating liabilities—both current and noncurrent—are netted against operating assets, leaving pure financing obligations and common equity on the right-hand side of the equation. Also, minority interest and preferred equity are included in financing obligations to be distinct from common equity. The equation still balances, but the totals differ from the standard balance sheet equation.

For ease of exposition, we assume that firms have no financial assets. However, most firms maintain some financial assets, which include cash, marketable equity securities, and short-term investments. Such financial assets should be netted against financing obligations, which yield net financing obligations (similar to how operating liabilities are netted against operating assets to yield net operating assets). This necessarily involves making judgments based on the purpose of the financial assets. Some financial assets are held for liquidity (marketable securities), strategic purposes (investments in noncontrolling interests of other firms), or financing (bond sinking funds). A more challenging determination is how to treat cash. Some cash is necessary as part of working capital, but firms can hold *excess cash*. There is no magic formula for computing excess cash, and any estimation of excess cash must consider possible reasons a firm holds what appears to be excess cash.

For example, in 2004, investors criticized Microsoft for holding excess cash. At the end of 2004, cash and short-term investments amounted to over $60 billion, relative to total assets of $94 billion. Microsoft subsequently paid a $3 per share special dividend, totaling $33 billion, and announced a plan to buy back up to $30 billion of outstanding common stock. It was difficult to quantify how much excess cash Microsoft held in 2004, but any approximation would have resulted in negative net financing obligations for Microsoft (which had no short- or long-term debt). Negative net financing obligations does not present a problem as long as the partition of the income statement, discussed below, is done consistently with the allocation of assets and liabilities to operating and financing components.

The reformulated balance sheet for PepsiCo is shown in Exhibit 5.3. Assuming that PepsiCo holds no financial assets intended for financing purposes (such as a bond sinking fund), we classify PepsiCo's cash and cash equivalents and short-term investments as operating assets. Thus, PepsiCo's operating assets are the same as total assets. Current and noncurrent liabilities are netted against operating assets, resulting in net operating assets of $20,333 million for 2008. Note that total assets as reported (Appendix A) are $35,994 million for 2008.

The reformulated balance sheet isolates operating assets (net of operating liabilities) and direct sources of financing.[2] To be consistent, we do the same for the income statement.

[2] As discussed in the previous section, we can view accounts payable as a source of financing. However, the objective here is to classify as financing only those obligations that have direct costs of capital associated with them.

EXHIBIT 5.3

Reformulated Balance Sheets for PepsiCo
(amounts in millions)

	2008	2007	2006	2005
OPERATING ASSETS				
Cash and cash equivalents	$ 2,064	$ 910	$ 1,651	$ 1,716
Short-term investments	213	1,571	1,171	3,166
Accounts and notes receivable, net	4,683	4,389	3,725	3,261
Inventories	2,522	2,290	1,926	1,693
Prepaid expenses and other current assets	1,324	991	657	618
Property, plant, and equipment, net	11,663	11,228	9,687	8,681
Amortizable intangible assets, net	732	796	637	530
Goodwill	5,124	5,169	4,594	4,088
Other nonamortizable intangible assets	1,128	1,248	1,212	1,086
Investments in noncontrolled affiliates	3,883	4,354	3,690	3,485
Other assets	2,658	1,682	980	3,403
LESS: OPERATING LIABILITIES				
Accounts payable and other current liabilities	(8,273)	(7,602)	(6,496)	(5,971)
Income taxes payable	(145)	(151)	(90)	(546)
Other liabilities	(7,017)	(4,792)	(4,624)	(4,323)
Deferred income taxes	(226)	(646)	(528)	(1,434)
Net Operating Assets	$20,333	$21,437	$18,192	$19,453
FINANCING OBLIGATIONS				
Short-term obligations	$ 369	$ 0	$ 274	$ 2,889
Current maturities of long-term debt	0	0	0	0
Long-term debt obligations	7,858	4,203	2,550	2,313
Preferred stock, no par value	41	41	41	41
Repurchased preferred stock	(138)	(132)	(120)	(110)
Financing Obligations	$ 8,130	$ 4,112	$ 2,745	$ 5,133
COMMON EQUITY				
Common stock, par value	$ 30	$ 30	$ 30	$ 30
Capital in excess of par value	351	450	584	614
Retained earnings	30,638	28,184	24,837	21,116
Accumulated other comprehensive loss	(4,694)	(952)	(2,246)	(1,053)
Treasury stock	(14,122)	(10,387)	(7,758)	(6,387)
Common Equity	$12,203	$17,325	$15,447	$14,320
Total Financing Obligations and Common Equity	$20,333	$21,437	$18,192	$19,453

EXHIBIT 5.4

Reformulated Income Statements for PepsiCo
(amounts in millions)

	2008	2007	2006
Net revenue	$43,251	$39,474	$35,137
Cost of sales	(20,351)	(18,038)	(15,762)
Selling, general, and administrative expenses	(15,901)	(14,208)	(12,711)
Other operating charges	(64)	(58)	(162)
Operating Profit	$ 6,935	$ 7,170	$ 6,502
Bottling equity income	374	560	553
Interest income	41	125	173
Adjusted Income Before Income Taxes	$ 7,350	$ 7,855	$ 7,228
Provision for income taxes at effective rate	(1,967)	(2,031)	(1,393)
Net Operating Profit After Tax (NOPAT)	$ 5,383	$ 5,824	$ 5,835
FINANCING EXPENSE			
Interest expense × (1 – Effective tax rate)	$ (241)	$ (166)	$ (193)
Preferred dividends	(8)	(12)	(11)
Net Financing Expense (After Tax)	$ (249)	$ (178)	$ (204)
Net Income to Common	$ 5,134	$ 5,646	$ 5,631
Effective Tax Rate	26.8%	25.9%	19.3%

Exhibit 5.4 demonstrates the straightforward identification of costs associated with financing for PepsiCo, including primarily interest expense and preferred dividends. All other amounts are elements of operating profit.[3] Operating profits are reduced by a provision for income taxes, generating the revised measure of profitability—NOPAT (Net Operating Profit After Taxes). Finance texts sometimes refer to this construct as EBIAT (Earnings Before Interest After Tax), which is the same as NOPAT with consistent treatment of operating and financing activities and proper treatment of taxes (discussed next).[4]

Note how the provision for income taxes from PepsiCo's as-reported income statement (Appendix A) is allocated to operating and financing activities. For 2008, PepsiCo's provision was $1,879 million (Appendix A), but Exhibit 5.4 indicates a provision on adjusted income before income taxes of $1,967 million. The higher provision in Exhibit 5.4 is due to the removal of financing expense from income before income taxes. The tax benefit of interest expense reduces the effective interest expense from $329 million (Appendix A) to $241 million, as shown in Exhibit 5.4. Preferred dividends are not tax-deductible, so no tax adjustment is necessary. The difference in the provision for income taxes on adjusted income before

[3] Chapter 4 emphasized that judgment could be exercised in the preparation of profitability ratios. The exposition there used adjusted net income based on a subjective assessment of nonrecurring components of reported profitability. For purposes here, we revert to the amounts reported in the 2008 financial statements. Further, we deliberately use net income available to common, which requires that preferred dividends be deducted from net income as shown on the income statement in Appendix A.

[4] NOPAT is more common than EBIAT. A simple online search of each term indicates approximately four times as many results for NOPAT. Further, many search results for EBIAT relate to last names, not the profitability construct.

income taxes in Exhibit 5.4 and the provision for income taxes as reported (Appendix A) equals the difference between gross interest expense as reported (Appendix A) and the after-tax interest expense shown in Exhibit 5.4 ($1,967 − $1,879 = $329 − $241 = $88). This difference of $88 million is equal to interest expense of $329 million times the effective tax rate of 26.8 percent (= $1,879/$7,021 from the income statement).

Also note the following:

NOPAT
− Net Financing Expense (after tax)
= Net Income Available to Common

If we had categorized PepsiCo's short-term investments as a financing asset, this asset would have been netted against PepsiCo's financing obligations in Exhibit 5.3. Accordingly, to be consistent with the treatment on the balance sheet, interest revenues (after tax) pertaining to the short-term investments would have been netted against interest expense (after tax) to compute net financing expense (after tax) in Exhibit 5.5. The reformulated balance sheets would still balance, with different totals, and the reformulated income statements would still reflect the same net income available to common. The same argument holds true for the treatment of minority interest for applicable companies. If the analyst treats minority interest as part of financing obligations (as we do in Exhibit 5.2), minority interest from the income statement would be included in net financing expense.

With these new financial statement classifications, Exhibit 5.5 demonstrates the algebraic disaggregation of ROCE into operating and financing components. The algebra is simple and easy to follow. The result is an alternative disaggregation of ROCE:

$$\text{ROCE} = \text{Operating ROA} + (\text{Leverage} \times \text{Spread})$$

Operating ROA is the rate of return the firm generates on its *net* operating assets. Operating ROA is the rate of return available to *all* sources of financing, including debt, preferred equity, and common equity. It is different from the definition of ROA discussed in Chapter 4, primarily because the denominator is net operating assets (as opposed to total assets).[5]

In addition to operating ROA, the right-hand side of the new ROCE equation consists of two other factors: leverage and spread. As noted in Exhibit 5.5, leverage is simply the total financial obligations divided by common equity, which is commensurate with the standard debt-to-equity ratio, except that preferred equity and minority interest are included in financial obligations. Spread is the difference between operating ROA and the net borrowing rate, which is the combined effective rate of interest and preferred dividends. Thus, the intuition of the new ROCE equation is that returns to common equity shareholders increase by the following:

- Increases in the rate of return on the firm's net operating assets
- Increases in leverage
- Decreases in the after-tax cost of debt and preferred equity

[5] An easy way to understand how the classification of financial statement amounts can vary while still resulting in components that combine mathematically to ROCE is to consider reformulated financial statements where all assets and all liabilities are categorized as operating. Thus, short- and long-term debt, preferred stock (if any), and minority interest are netted against assets to compute net operating assets. By definition, this equals common equity. Then to be consistent with this treatment in reformulation of the income statement, all interest expense, preferred dividends, and minority interest would be categorized as operating items. The result would be net income available to common. The alternative disaggregation of ROCE into Operating ROA + (Leverage × Spread) would reduce to ROCE = Operating ROA, where Operating ROA = Net Income Available to Common/Common Equity. This would not accomplish much, but the point of the exercise is to emphasize the mathematical equivalence of this ROCE decomposition regardless of how assets or liabilities are reformulated.

EXHIBIT 5.5

Algebra Demonstrating the Disaggregation of Return on Common Equity (ROCE)

$$
\begin{aligned}
\text{ROCE} &= \frac{\text{Net Income Available to Common}}{\text{Common Equity}} \\
&= \frac{\text{NOPAT} - \text{Net Financing Expense (after tax)}}{\text{Common Equity}} \\
&= \frac{\text{NOPAT}}{\text{Net Operating Assets}} \times \frac{\text{Net Operating Assets}}{\text{Common Equity}} - \frac{\text{Net Financing Expense (after tax)}}{\text{Financing Obligations}} \times \frac{\text{Financing Obligations}}{\text{Common Equity}} \\
&= \frac{\text{NOPAT}}{\text{Net Operating Assets}} \times \frac{\text{Common Equity} + \text{Financing Obligations}}{\text{Common Equity}} - \frac{\text{Net Financing Expense (after tax)}}{\text{Financing Obligations}} \times \frac{\text{Financing Obligations}}{\text{Common Equity}} \\
&= \frac{\text{NOPAT}}{\text{Net Operating Assets}} \times \left(1 + \frac{\text{Financing Obligations}}{\text{Common Equity}}\right) - \frac{\text{Net Financing Expense (after tax)}}{\text{Financing Obligations}} \times \frac{\text{Financing Obligations}}{\text{Common Equity}} \\
&= \text{Operating ROA} \times \left(1 + \frac{\text{Financing Obligations}}{\text{Common Equity}}\right) - \frac{\text{Net Financing Expense (after tax)}}{\text{Financing Obligations}} \times \frac{\text{Financing Obligations}}{\text{Common Equity}} \\
&= \text{Operating ROA} + \left[\text{Operating ROA} \times \frac{\text{Financing Obligations}}{\text{Common Equity}}\right] - \left[\frac{\text{Net Financing Expense (after tax)}}{\text{Financing Obligations}} \times \frac{\text{Financing Obligations}}{\text{Common Equity}}\right] \\
&= \text{Operating ROA} + \frac{\text{Financing Obligations}}{\text{Common Equity}} \times \left[\text{Operating ROA} - \frac{\text{Net Financing Expense (after tax)}}{\text{Financing Obligations}}\right] \\
&= \text{Operating ROA} + \left[\text{Leverage} \times (\text{Operating ROA} - \text{Net Borrowing Rate})\right] \\
&= \text{Operating ROA} + \text{Leverage} \times \text{Spread}
\end{aligned}
$$

Incidentally, note that similar to ROA, operating ROA can be further disaggregated simply by dividing and multiplying by sales:

$$\text{Operating ROA} = \frac{\text{NOPAT}}{\text{Average Net Operating Assets}}$$

$$= \frac{\text{NOPAT}}{\text{Sales}} \times \frac{\text{Sales}}{\text{Average Net Operating Assets}}$$

Operating ROA is thus the product of profit margin for operating ROA and net operating asset turnover in the same way that ROA is the product of profit margin for ROA and total assets turnover.

Spread is the key to understanding financial flexibility. As stated, incremental increases in leverage are likely associated with increased borrowing costs. For example, second mortgages on properties generally carry higher interest rates than first mortgages. Increases in the cost of debt or preferred equity increase the net borrowing rate, which decreases spread, lowering the incremental benefits of increasing leverage. Nevertheless, firms with a large spread probably face strategic roadblocks in deploying capital that leads to diminishing rates of return, which dominates any increasing cost of debt or preferred equity. Thus, firms that generate very high operating ROA relative to the cost of borrowing can likely increase the level of borrowings—with either debt or preferred equity—and thus are characterized as having greater financial flexibility. Financial flexibility also is associated with lower short-term and long-term solvency risk, discussed in the next two sections.

To illustrate the disaggregation of ROCE into operating ROA, leverage, and spread, Exhibit 5.6 uses the amounts from the financial statements in Exhibits 5.3 and 5.4 to compute ROCE. For comparison, Exhibit 5.6 presents the standard and alternative decompositions of ROCE. Of course, both computations produce the same ROCE.

The alternative ROCE decomposition reveals that PepsiCo generates a significant spread between operating ROA and the net borrowing rate. For 2006, 2007, and 2008, Operating ROA is 31.0, 29.4, and 25.8 percent, respectively. PepsiCo's operations clearly utilize the operating assets very profitably. The net borrowing rates were 4.1 percent in 2008 and 5.1 percent in both 2007 and 2006 (not tabulated in Exhibit 5.6). Therefore, PepsiCo's spread was 21.7 percent in 2008 (= 25.8 percent operating ROA − 4.1 percent net borrowing rate), 24.2 percent in 2007, and 25.8 percent in 2006. An interpretation of PepsiCo's spread in 2008 is that for every dollar PepsiCo currently borrows and deploys in operating assets, it generates 25.8¢ in operating profit, whereas the borrowing triggers only 4.1¢ in net borrowing costs (after tax), resulting in 21.7¢ accruing to common equity shareholders. This is the essence of strategic use of leverage by equity investors.

The large spread generated by PepsiCo indicates that the company enjoys a high level of financial flexibility. Creditors are relatively comfortable lending money to companies that generate rates of returns on assets that far exceed debt service costs. However, the trends shown in Exhibit 5.6 suggest that PepsiCo is increasing its leverage significantly. PepsiCo's leverage was only 0.26 in 2006 and 0.21 in 2007, but it jumped to 0.41 in 2008.

Therefore, the alternative ROCE decomposition reveals that PepsiCo's ROCE in 2008 of 34.8 percent is the result of an operating ROA of 25.8 percent plus leverage of 0.41 times the spread of 21.7 percent [34.8% = 25.8% + (0.41 × 21.7%)]. In comparison to 2007, this decomposition reveals that PepsiCo's operating ROA and spread fell dramatically in 2008, but ROCE increased slightly because of a dramatic increase in leverage.

Both approaches to the decomposition of ROCE indicate decreases in margins, increases in turnover, and increases in leverage from 2006 to 2008. However, the alternative ROCE decomposition provides additional insights about the nature of the change in leverage that

EXHIBIT 5.6

Computations of ROCE Decomposition Using Standard and Alternative Approaches for PepsiCo 2006–2008
(dollar amounts in millions)

Standard ROCE decomposition		Calculation for 2008	2008	2007	2006
Profit Margin for ROCE	Net Income to Common/Sales	$5,134/$43,251	11.9%	14.3%	16.0%
× Assets Turnover	Sales/Average Total Assets	$43,251/ 0.5($35,994 + $34,628)	1.22	1.22	1.14
× Capital Structure Leverage	Average Total Assets/ Average Common Equity	0.5($35,994 + $34,628)/ 0.5($12,203 + $17,325)	2.39	1.97	2.07
= ROCE	Net Income to Common/ Average Common Equity	$5,134/ 0.5($12,203 + $17,325)	34.8%	34.5%	37.8%

Alternative ROCE decomposition			2008	2007	2006
Net Margin for Operating ROA	NOPAT/Sales	$5,383/$43,251	12.4%	14.8%	16.6%
× Net Operating Assets Turnover	Sales/Average Net Operating Assets	$43,251/ 0.5($20,333 + $21,437)	2.07	1.99	1.87
= Operating ROA	NOPAT/Average Net Operating Assets	$5,383/ 0.5($20,333 + $21,437)	25.8%	29.4%	31.0%
+ Leverage	Average Financing Obligations/ Average Common Equity	0.5($8,130 + $4,112)/ 0.5($12,203 + $17,325)	0.41	0.21	0.26
× Spread	Operating ROA – Net Borrowing Rate (=Net Financing Expense (after tax)/Average Financing Obligations	25.8% – 4.1%	21.7%	24.2%	25.8%
= ROCE	Operating ROA + (Leverage × Spread)	25.8% + (0.41 × 21.7%)	34.8%	34.5%	37.8%
Net Borrowing Rate	Net Financing Expense (after tax)/ Average Financing Obligations	[$249/ 0.5($8,130 + $4,112)]	4.1%	5.2%	5.2%

are masked in the traditional ROCE decomposition at the top of Exhibit 5.6. For the alternative ROCE decomposition in the bottom part of Exhibit 5.6, the increase in leverage is more dramatic, especially between 2007 and 2008 when it nearly doubled from 0.21 to 0.41; under the standard ROE decomposition, capital structure leverage increases from 1.97 to 2.39 between 2007 and 2008. Recall that under the standard approach to disaggregating ROCE, leverage is defined as follows:

$$\text{Capital Structure Leverage} = \frac{\text{Total Assets}}{\text{Common Equity}}$$

$$= \frac{\text{Total Liabilities} + \text{Common Equity}}{\text{Common Equity}}$$

$$= 1 + \frac{\text{Total Liabilities}}{\text{Common Equity}}$$

Thus, the standard approach treats *all* liabilities as leverage, not just those that generate borrowing costs. If non-interest-bearing liabilities are significant, including such amounts can mask the true leverage attributable to interest-bearing debt. Indeed, Appendix A shows that total liabilities are $23,888 million at the end of 2008, but only $8,227 million are actually interest-bearing financing obligations (= $369 million short-term obligations + $7,858 million long-term debt obligations). The other liabilities treated as leverage in the standard decomposition of ROCE include accounts payable of $8,273 million and other liabilities of $7,017 million, neither of which are leverage in the sense that matters in terms of long-term solvency risk.

Summary of Financial Flexibility

Financial flexibility represents the ability of a firm to strategically use creditor financing to increase the returns to common shareholders. We discussed an alternative decomposition of ROCE that requires the analyst to reformulate financial statements into operating and financing components, which highlights the benefits available to common shareholders through the use of leverage. Firms with large spreads—return on net operating assets minus the net after-tax borrowing rate—stand to benefit from leverage. PepsiCo generates large returns on net operating assets and has a large degree of financial flexibility. The analysis of financial flexibility provides a natural link between profitability analysis discussed in the previous chapter and the analysis of numerous risks, discussed next.

ANALYZING SHORT-TERM LIQUIDITY RISK

The analysis of short-term liquidity risk requires an understanding of the operating cycle of a firm, introduced in Chapter 1. Consider a typical manufacturing firm. It acquires raw materials on account, promising to pay suppliers within 30–60 days. The firm then combines the raw materials, labor services, and other inputs to produce a product. It pays for some of these costs at the time of incurrence and delays payment of other costs. At some point, the firm sells the product to a customer, probably on account. It then collects the customer's account and pays suppliers and others for purchases on account.

If a firm (1) can delay all cash outflows to suppliers, employees, and others until it receives cash from customers and (2) receives more cash than it must disburse, the firm will not likely encounter short-term liquidity problems. Most firms, however, cannot time their cash inflows and outflows precisely, especially firms in the start-up or growth phase. Employees may require weekly or semimonthly payments, whereas customers may delay payments for 30 days or more. Firms may experience rapid growth and need to produce more units of product than they sell during a period. Even if perfectly timed, the cash outflows to support the higher level of production in this period can exceed customers' cash inflows this period from the lower level of sales of prior periods. Firms that operate at a net loss for a period often find that the completion of the operating cycle results in a net cash outflow instead of a net cash inflow. As an extreme example, consider a Scotch whiskey distillery that incurs significant cash outflows for grains and other ingredients, distills the whiskey, and then ages it in wooden barrels for many years before finally generating cash inflows from sales to customers.

Short-term liquidity problems also can arise from a high degree of longer-term leverage. For example, a firm may assume a relatively high percentage of debt in its capital structure. This level of debt usually requires periodic interest payments and may require repayments of principal as well. For some firms, especially financial, real estate, and energy firms, interest expense is one of the largest single costs. The operating cycle must generate sufficient cash not only to supply operating working capital needs, but also to service debt.

Financially healthy firms frequently close temporary cash flow gaps in their operating cycles with short-term borrowing. Such firms may issue commercial paper on the market or obtain three- to six-month bank loans. Most firms maintain lines of credit with their banks so they can obtain cash quickly for working capital needs. The notes to the financial statements usually disclose the amount of the line of credit and the level of borrowing used on that line during the year, as well as any financial covenant restrictions imposed by the line of credit agreements. PepsiCo, for example, discloses the following in Note 9, "Debt Obligations and Commitments" (Appendix A):

> Additionally, in the fourth quarter of 2008, we entered into a new 364-day unsecured revolving credit agreement which enables us to borrow up to $1.8 billion, subject to customary terms and conditions, and expires in December 2009. This agreement replaced a $1 billion 364-day unsecured revolving credit agreement we entered into during the third quarter of 2008. Funds borrowed under this agreement may be used to repay outstanding commercial paper issued by us or our subsidiaries and for other general corporate purposes, including working capital, capital investments and acquisitions. This line of credit remained unused as of December 27, 2008.
>
> This 364-day credit agreement is in addition to our $2 billion unsecured revolving credit agreement. Funds borrowed under this agreement may be used for general corporate purposes, including supporting our outstanding commercial paper issuances. This agreement expires in 2012. This line of credit remains unused as of December 27, 2008.

Note 9 indicates that PepsiCo's outstanding short-term debt totaled $369 million and its long-term debt totaled $7,858 million at the end of 2008. Thus, PepsiCo has the ability to increase borrowing approximately 46.2 percent [= ($1,800 + $2,000)/($369 + $7,858)] at the end of 2008 by drawing on its existing lines of credit. It is important to note available but untapped borrowing capacity when assessing the overall financial risk profile of a firm. These amounts represent potential increases in financial risk, but at the same time, they provide the firm with beneficial financial flexibility (as discussed in the previous section).

A simple way to quickly grasp short-term liquidity issues is to examine common-size balance sheets, as discussed in Chapter 1. Common-size balance sheets provide a basic quantification of the relative amount of cash tied up in non-cash assets, and the relative amount of liabilities across several categories. We discuss seven financial statement ratios for assessing short-term liquidity risk: (1) current ratio, (2) quick ratio, (3) operating cash flow to current liabilities ratio, (4) accounts receivable turnover, (5) inventory turnover, (6) accounts payable turnover, and (7) revenues to cash ratio.

Current Ratio

The current ratio equals current assets divided by current liabilities. It indicates the amount of cash available at the balance sheet date plus the amount of other current assets the firm expects to turn into cash within one year of the balance sheet date (from collection of receivables and sale of inventory) relative to obligations coming due during that period. Large current ratios indicate the substantial amounts of cash and near-cash assets available to repay obligations coming due within the next year. Small ratios, on the other hand, indicate that current levels of cash and near-cash assets may not be sufficient to repay short-term obligations.

The current ratio for PepsiCo at the end of 2008 is as follows:

$$\text{Current Ratio} = \frac{\text{Current Assets}}{\text{Current Liabilities}}$$

$$1.23 = \frac{\$10{,}806}{\$8{,}787}$$

The current ratio for PepsiCo was 1.31 at the end of 2007 and 1.33 at the end of 2006. Thus, PepsiCo experienced a decreasing current ratio during the three years.

Banks, suppliers, and others that extend short-term credit to a firm generally prefer a current ratio in excess of 1.0. They typically evaluate the appropriate level of a firm's current ratio based on the length of the firm's operating cycle, the expected cash flows from operations, the extent to which the firm has noncurrent assets that could be used for liquidity if necessary, the extent to which the firm's current liabilities do not require cash outflows (such as liabilities for deferred revenues), and similar factors. Prior to the 1980s, the average current ratios for most industries exceeded 2.0. As interest rates increased in the early 1980s, firms attempted to stretch their accounts payable and use suppliers to finance a greater portion of their working capital needs (that is, receivables and inventories). Also, firms increasingly instituted just-in-time inventory systems that reduced the amount of raw materials and finished goods inventories. As a consequence of these two factors, current ratios began moving in the direction of 1.0. Current ratios hovering around this level, or even just below 1.0, are now common. Although this directional movement suggests an increase in short-term liquidity risk, most investors view this level of risk as tolerable. Recall that accountants report inventories, a major component of current assets for many firms, at acquisition cost. The cash that firms expect to generate from selling inventories is larger than the amount used in calculating the current ratio. PepsiCo, for example, has a cost of goods sold to sales percentage of approximately 47 percent. Thus, inventories have selling prices of 2.1 (= 1.00/.47) times the amount appearing on the balance sheet. Therefore, a current ratio slightly greater than 1.0 at the end of 2006 through 2008 is not a major concern for PepsiCo.

Analysts should consider several additional interpretive issues when evaluating the current ratio:

- An increase of equal amounts in current assets and current liabilities (for example, purchasing inventory on account) results in a decrease in the current ratio when the ratio is greater than 1.0 before the transaction but an increase in the current ratio when it is less than 1.0 before the transaction. Similar interpretive difficulties arise when current assets and current liabilities decrease by equal amounts. With current ratios for many firms now in the neighborhood of 1.0, this concern with the current ratio has greater significance.

- A very high current ratio may accompany poor business conditions, whereas a low or decreasing ratio may accompany profitable operations. For example, during a recession, firms may encounter difficulties in selling inventories and collecting receivables, causing the current ratio to increase to higher levels due to the growth in receivables and inventory. In a boom period, just the reverse can occur.
- The current ratio is susceptible to window dressing; that is, management can take deliberate steps leading up to the balance sheet date to produce a better current ratio than is the normal or average ratio for the period. For instance, toward the end of the period, a firm may accelerate purchases of inventory on account (if the current ratio is less than 1.0) or delay such purchases (if the current ratio is greater than 1.0) in an effort to improve the current ratio. Alternatively, a firm may collect loans previously made to officers, classified as noncurrent assets, and use the proceeds to reduce current liabilities.

Despite these interpretive issues with the current ratio, the analyst will find widespread use of the current ratio as a measure of short-term liquidity risk. Empirical studies of bond default, bankruptcy, and other conditions of financial distress have found that the current ratio has strong predictive power for costly financial outcomes. A later section of this chapter discusses this empirical research more fully.

Quick Ratio

A variation of the current ratio is the quick ratio, also called the acid test ratio. The analyst computes the quick ratio by including in the numerator only those current assets the firm could convert *quickly* into cash, often interpreted as within 90 days. The numerator customarily includes cash, marketable securities, and receivables. However, the analyst should study the facts in each case before deciding whether to include receivables and exclude inventories. Some businesses can convert their inventory of merchandise into cash more quickly (for example, a retail chain such as Walmart) than other businesses can collect their receivables (for example, an equipment manufacturer such as John Deere that provides long-term financing for its customers' purchases).

Assuming that we include accounts receivable but exclude inventories, the quick ratio of PepsiCo at the end of 2008 is as follows:

$$\text{Quick Ratio} = \frac{\text{Cash} + \text{Marketable Securities} + \text{Accounts Receivable}}{\text{Current Liabilities}}$$

$$0.79 = \frac{\$2{,}064 + \$213 + \$4{,}683}{\$8{,}787}$$

The quick ratio for PepsiCo was 0.89 at the end of 2007 and 0.95 at the end of 2006. Unless inventory turnovers have changed dramatically, the comparative trends in the quick ratio and the current ratio correlate highly. That is, the analyst obtains similar information about improving or deteriorating short-term liquidity risk by examining either ratio. Note that the current and quick ratios for PepsiCo follow the same downward trend. However, the decline in the quick ratio is more pronounced. In 2008, current assets increased 6 percent, whereas current liabilities increased 13 percent. On the other hand, the sum of cash, marketable securities, and accounts receivable increased only 1 percent in 2008, leading to the decline in these amounts relative to current liabilities. Thus, the discrepancy between the current ratio and quick ratio for PepsiCo is due to changes in less liquid current assets. The balance sheet indicates that PepsiCo increased prepaid expenses and other current assets by 34 percent in 2008.

The quick ratio is subject to some of the same interpretive issues as the current ratio. With quick ratios typically less than 1.0, equal increases in the numerator and denominator increase the ratio and equal decreases in the numerator and denominator decrease the ratio. The quick ratio also is susceptible to year-end window dressing or temporary increases in cash on hand.

Operating Cash Flow to Current Liabilities Ratio

In addition to using current assets measured at a point in time as an indicator of a firm's ability to generate cash in the near term, the analyst also can use cash flow from operations. Cash flow from operations, reported on the statement of cash flows, indicates the amount of cash the firm derived from (or used in) operations after funding working capital needs. Because the numerator of this ratio uses amounts for a period of time, the denominator typically uses an average of current liabilities for the same period. This ratio for PepsiCo for 2008 is as follows:

$$\text{Operating Cash Flow to Current Liabilities Ratio} = \frac{\text{Cash Flow from Operations}}{\text{Average Current Liabilities}}$$

$$0.85 = \frac{\$6{,}999}{0.5(\$8{,}787 + \$7{,}753)}$$

The ratio was 0.95 for 2007 and 0.75 for 2006. An empirical study utilizing the operating cash flow to current liabilities ratio found that a ratio of 0.40 or more was common for a typical healthy manufacturing or retailing firm.[6] PepsiCo consistently has an operating cash flow to current liabilities ratio well in excess of 0.40. Thus, PepsiCo does not display much short-term liquidity risk in terms of operating cash flows relative to current liabilities.

Working Capital Turnover Ratios

The analyst uses three measures of the rate of activity in working capital accounts to study the cash-generating ability of operations and the short-term liquidity risk of a firm:

$$\text{Accounts Receivable Turnover} = \frac{\text{Sales}}{\text{Average Accounts Receivable}}$$

$$\text{Inventory Turnover} = \frac{\text{Cost of Goods Sold}}{\text{Average Inventories}}$$

$$\text{Accounts Payable Turnover} = \frac{\text{Purchases}}{\text{Average Accounts Payable}}$$

Chapter 4 discussed the accounts receivable and inventory turnovers, which are components of *total* assets turnover, as measures of profitability. These same ratios are used here as measures of the speed with which firms sell inventories and turn accounts receivable into cash. The accounts payable turnover indicates the speed at which a manufacturing or retailing firm pays for purchases of raw materials or inventories on account. Firms typically do not disclose the amount of raw materials or inventory purchases, but

[6] Cornelius Casey and Norman Bartczak, "Cash Flow—It's Not the Bottom Line," *Harvard Business Review* (July–August 1984), pp. 61–66.

this amount can be easily computed. Recall that the inventory account primarily reflects the following:

$$\text{Ending Inventory} = \text{Beginning Inventory} + \text{Purchases} - \text{Cost of Goods Sold.}$$

The analyst can approximate purchases as follows:[7]

$$\text{Purchases} = \text{Cost of Goods Sold} + \text{Ending Inventory} - \text{Beginning Inventory.}$$

Note that Purchases is used to generically capture retailing firms' purchase of inventory or manufacturing firms' purchase of raw materials and production costs.

The analyst often expresses the preceding three ratios in terms of the number of days each balance sheet item (that is, receivables, inventories, and accounts payable) is outstanding. To do so, divide 365 days by the turnover metrics. More intuitively stated, divide the balance sheet item by the appropriate flow variable converted to a daily average amount (that is, divided by 365). For example, the days sales outstanding in accounts receivable can be calculated equivalently as 365/Accounts Receivable Turnover or, more intuitively, as Accounts Receivable/(Sales/365).

Exhibit 5.7 presents the calculation of these three turnover ratios and the related number of days for PepsiCo for 2008. PepsiCo combines accounts payable and other current liabilities on its balance sheet. Note 14, "Supplemental Financial Information" (Appendix A), disaggregates this combined amount into its various elements and reports the amounts for accounts payable separately. We use the amounts for accounts payable from Note 14 to compute the accounts payable turnover. For example, of the $8,273 million total accounts payable and other current liabilities at the end of 2008, only $2,846 million relate to accounts payable; the remainder includes accrued marketplace spending, accrued compensation, dividends payable, and other current liabilities.

EXHIBIT 5.7

Working Capital Activity Ratios for PepsiCo for 2008

Accounts Receivable Turnover

$$\frac{\$43{,}251}{0.5(\$4{,}683 + \$4{,}389)} = 9.5 \text{ times per year}$$

Days Receivables Outstanding

$$\frac{365}{9.5} = 38 \text{ days}$$

Inventory Turnover

$$\frac{\$20{,}351}{0.5(\$2{,}522 + \$2{,}290)} = 8.5 \text{ times per year}$$

Days Inventory Held

$$\frac{365}{8.5} = 43 \text{ days}$$

Accounts Payable Turnover

$$\frac{\$20{,}351 + \$2{,}522 - \$2{,}290}{0.5(\$2{,}846 + \$2{,}562)} = 7.6 \text{ times per year}$$

Days Accounts Payable Outstanding

$$\frac{365}{7.6} = 48 \text{ days}$$

[7] The accounts payable turnover ratio will be skewed upward if cost of goods sold includes a high proportion of costs (such as depreciation and labor) that do not flow through accounts payable. This bias is more of a concern for manufacturing firms than for retailing firms and is more of an issue in cross-sectional comparisons than in time-series analyses.

The number of days firms hold inventory until sale plus the number of days firms hold accounts receivable until collection indicates the total number of days from the production or purchase of inventory until collection of cash from the sale of inventory to customers. This combined number of days indicates the length of time for which the firm must obtain financing for its primary working capital assets. The number of days accounts payable are outstanding indicates the working capital financing the firm obtained from suppliers. The difference between the total number of days for which the firm requires financing for its working capital and the number of days for which it obtained financing from suppliers indicates the additional days for which it must obtain financing. This difference is known as the cash-to-cash cycle (also known as the cash operating cycle), and it quantifies the length of time between cash outlays that ultimately result in cash collections. The offset for the days outstanding in accounts payable reflects the benefit of suppliers delaying the time before the firm is required to remit cash. We depict these relations here.

Days of Working Capital Financing Required:

Days Inventory Held	Days Accounts Receivable Outstanding

Days of Working Capital Financing Provided:

Days Account Payable Outstanding	Days of Working Capital Financing Needed from Other Sources

Exhibit 5.8 shows the net number of days of financing needed from other sources for PepsiCo for 2006, 2007, and 2008. PepsiCo's days accounts payable is slightly higher than its days inventory, indicating that it has strategically utilized supplier financing for its inventory. The net days financed from other sources approximates the days accounts receivable were outstanding. Like most companies, PepsiCo used short-term borrowing to finance part of the net days of needed financing.

In general, the shorter the number of days of needed financing, the larger the cash flow from operations to average current liabilities ratio. A small number of net days indicates

EXHIBIT 5.8

Net Number of Days of Working Capital Financing Needed from Other Sources for PepsiCo

Year	Days Accounts Receivable Outstanding	+	Days Inventory Held	−	Days Accounts Payable Outstanding	=	Days Other Financing Required
2006	36		42		(45)		33
2007	38		43		(46)		35
2008	38		43		(48)		33

relatively little need to finance accounts receivable and inventories (that is, the firm sells inventory quickly and receives cash from customers soon after sale) or aggressive use of suppliers to finance these current assets (that is, the firm delays paying cash to suppliers). Both scenarios enhance cash flow from operations in the numerator of this ratio. Furthermore, firms with a shorter number of days of financing required from other sources need not engage in as much short-term borrowing from banks and other financing institutions. Such borrowing increases current liabilities in the denominator of the operating cash flow to current liabilities ratio, thereby lowering this ratio.

As an example of a company with extreme favorable working capital requirements, Exhibit 5.9 shows the working capital financing investments for Amazon, a well-known large online retailer of books, electronic media, and numerous other products. Due to low levels of accounts receivable and inventory and extended accounts payable, Amazon has a *negative* value for days of other financing required. Not surprisingly, Amazon does not require any short-term debt financing. The only other liabilities Amazon has at the end of 2009 are (1) accrued expenses of $1,759 million, (2) long-term debt of $109 million, and (3) other long-term liabilities of $1,083 million (relative to total assets of $13,813 million).

Revenues to Cash Ratio

Firms ultimately collect revenues in cash and pay operating costs and current liabilities with cash. The amount of cash on the balance sheet reflects the net effect of operating, investing, and financing activities on cash, as well as management's judgments about the desired level of cash. A ratio that incorporates the amount of cash on the balance sheet helps the analyst evaluate short-term liquidity. To aid comparability across time and across firms, we must relate the amount of cash to some measure of operating activity.

EXHIBIT 5.9

Net Number of Days of Working Capital Financing Needed from Other Sources for Amazon, 2005–2009
(amounts in millions)

	2005	2006	2007	2008	2009
Sales	$8,490	$10,711	$14,835	$19,166	$24,509
Cost of Goods Sold	$6,451	$ 8,255	$18,978	$14,896	$11,482
Purchases	$6,537	$ 8,566	$19,301	$15,095	$12,254
Accounts Receivable	$ 274	$ 399	$ 705	$ 827	$ 988
Inventory	$ 566	$ 877	$ 1,200	$ 1,399	$ 2,171
Accounts Payable	$1,366	$ 1,816	$ 2,795	$ 3,594	$ 5,605
Days Receivables Outstanding	10.2	11.5	13.6	14.6	13.5
Days Inventory Held	29.6	31.9	20.0	31.8	56.7
Days Accounts Payable Outstanding	(70.0)	(67.8)	(43.6)	(77.2)	(137.0)
Days Other Financing Required	(30.2)	(24.4)	(10.0)	(30.8)	(66.8)

Either revenues or cash operating expenses may serve as the measure of activity, but we use revenues. The revenues to cash ratio for PepsiCo for 2008 is as follows:

$$\text{Revenues to Cash Ratio} = \frac{\text{Revenues}}{\text{Average Cash Balance}}$$

$$29.1 = \frac{\$43{,}251}{0.5(\$2{,}064 + \$910)}$$

The revenues to cash flow ratio was 30.8 for 2007 and 20.9 for 2006. Interpreting the revenues to cash ratio requires caution. From the viewpoint of short-term liquidity risk, lenders prefer a smaller revenues to cash ratio (that is, more cash in the denominator) and a larger number of days revenue available as cash on hand. However, management may prefer to avoid maintaining excess idle cash. Further, unless managers focus on window-dressing the balance sheet, the amount of cash on hand is expected to fluctuate with the timing of cash receipts and outflows.

Days Revenues Held in Cash

One can view the revenues to cash ratio as a cash turnover ratio, analogous to the accounts receivable turnover ratio described previously. We can express the revenues to cash ratio in terms of the number of days of revenue held in cash by dividing 365 days by the revenues to cash ratio. That ratio for PepsiCo is as follows:

2006: 365/20.9 = 17.5 days
2007: 365/30.8 = 11.9 days
2008: 365/29.1 = 12.5 days

The intuition of the days revenues held in cash measure is that it quantifies the number of days sales the firm has on hand as available cash. This measure will prove useful when analysts forecast financial statements because the forecast of the cash balance can be defined as a function of revenues. Furthermore, as the number of days revenues held in cash becomes high, this ratio may identify firms that are carrying excess cash and thus are more vulnerable to agency problems or takeover.

One variation in this ratio is to include not only the amount of cash, but also the amount of marketable securities. Firms typically invest in marketable securities when they have temporary excess cash, then sell the securities when they need cash. The classification of marketable securities as a current asset suggests that firms could easily sell the securities if they needed cash. Including cash and marketable securities in the denominator results in a revenues to cash and marketable securities ratio of 18.2 [= \$43,251/0.5(\$2,064 + \$213 + \$910 + \$1,571)] for 2008 and 20.1 days (= 365/18.2) of revenues held in cash and marketable securities.

Another variation of this ratio uses cash operating expenses instead of revenues in the numerator. The rationale is that firms generally need cash to pay operating expenses. The analyst can approximate cash operating expenses by summing cost of goods sold and selling and administrative expenses and subtracting depreciation and amortization. Refer to the income statement of PepsiCo in Appendix A. PepsiCo reports amortization expense separately. However, it includes depreciation expense in cost of sales and selling, general, and administrative expenses. Note 4, "Property, Plant, and Equipment and Intangible Assets" (Appendix A), indicates that depreciation expense for 2008 is \$1,422 million. Thus, cash operating expenses, excluding impairment and restructuring charges, total \$34,830 million

(= \$20,351 + \$15,901 − \$1,422). The ratio of cash operating expenses to average cash and marketable securities for 2008 is 14.6 [= \$34,830/(.5{\$2,064 \$213 + \$910 + \$1,571})], and the days of cash and marketable securities held for paying operating expenses is 25.0 days (= 365/14.6). This ratio is a variant of the *defensive interval*[8] or *run rate*, which indicates the number of days a firm could continue to operate without injections of additional cash. The defensive interval has intuitive merit, but note that we use the ratio of revenues to cash in this book instead of these variations in the ratio.

Summary of Short-Term Liquidity Risk

The short-term liquidity risk ratios suggest that PepsiCo has relatively little short-term liquidity risk. Although the current ratio is slightly above 1, the quick ratio is just below 1; in addition, the operating cash flow to current liabilities ratio equals or exceeds 0.75 in all years. PepsiCo has an established brand name and dominates (along with Coca-Cola) the soft drink beverage industry, generating substantial amounts of positive cash flow from operating activities. Chapter 4 discussed PepsiCo's healthy profitability profile, suggesting that it could obtain short-term financing if needed. Moreover, it maintains two revolving credit agreements that totaled \$3.8 billion at the end of 2008. Neither revolving credit agreement had been used as of the end of the year. The availability of such revolving credit agreements is consistent with PepsiCo enjoying financial flexibility, which was discussed in the preceding section. We turn to long-term solvency risk next.

ANALYZING LONG-TERM SOLVENCY RISK

As described in the section on financial flexibility, financial leverage enhances the return to common shareholders when firms borrow funds and invest those funds in assets that generate a higher return than the after-tax cost of borrowing. Common shareholders benefit with increasing proportions of debt in the capital structure as long as the firm maintains an excess rate of return on assets over the after-tax cost of the debt. However, increasing the proportion of debt in the capital structure increases the risk that the firm cannot pay interest and repay the principal on the amount borrowed. That is, credit and bankruptcy risk increases, and the incremental cost of borrowing also is likely to increase. Analysts use measures of long-term solvency risk to examine a firm's ability to make interest and principal payments on long-term debt and similar obligations as they come due.

Perhaps the best indicator for assessing long-term solvency risk is a firm's ability to generate earnings over a period of years. Profitable firms generate sufficient cash from operations or obtain needed cash from creditors or owners. Therefore, the measures of profitability discussed in Chapter 4 apply to this purpose as well. Also, firms must survive in the short term if they are to survive in the long term. Thus, analysis of long-term solvency risk must begin with an assessment of the level of and trends in financial flexibility and with an analysis of short-term liquidity risk. Having discussed these analyses, we turn to three measures used in examining long-term solvency risk: (1) debt ratios, (2) interest coverage ratios, and (3) the operating cash flow to total liabilities ratio.

[8] See George H. Sorter and George Benston, "Appraising the Defensive Position of a Firm: The Interval Measure," *Accounting Review* 35 (October 1960), pp. 633–640. The denominator of their defensive interval measure included marketable securities and accounts receivable in addition to cash. See the discussion of bankruptcy risk later in this chapter.

Debt Ratios

Analysts use debt ratios to measure the amount of liabilities, particularly long-term debt, in a firm's capital structure. The higher this proportion, the greater the long-term solvency risk. The capital structure leverage ratio discussed in Chapter 4, one of the disaggregated components of ROCE, is one version of a debt ratio, as is the alternative computation of leverage used in the alternative decomposition of ROCE discussed earlier in this chapter. Several additional variations in debt ratios exist. Four commonly encountered measures are as follows:

$$\text{Liabilities to Assets Ratio} = \frac{\text{Total Liabilities}}{\text{Total Assets}}$$

$$\text{Liabilities to Shareholders' Equity Ratio} = \frac{\text{Total Liabilities}}{\text{Total Shareholders' Equity}}$$

$$\begin{array}{r}\text{Long-Term Debt to}\\ \text{Long-Term Capital Ratio}\end{array} = \frac{\text{Long-Term Debt}}{\text{Long-Term Debt} + \text{Total Shareholders' Equity}}$$

$$\text{Long-Term Debt to Shareholders' Equity Ratio} = \frac{\text{Long-Term Debt}}{\text{Total Shareholders' Equity}}$$

The debt ratios for PepsiCo at the end of 2008 are as follows:

$$\text{Liabilities to Assets Ratio} = \frac{\$23{,}888}{\$35{,}994} = 0.664$$

$$\text{Liabilities to Shareholders' Equity Ratio} = \frac{\$23{,}888}{\$12{,}106} = 1.973$$

$$\text{Long-Term Debt to Long-Term Capital Ratio} = \frac{\$7{,}858}{\$7{,}858 + \$12{,}106} = 0.394$$

$$\text{Long-Term Debt to Shareholders' Equity Ratio} = \frac{\$7{,}858}{\$12{,}106} = 0.649$$

Exhibit 5.10 shows the debt ratios for PepsiCo at the end of 2006, 2007, and 2008. The debt ratios involving total liabilities increased during the three-year period, but not as significantly as the long-term debt ratios over the same period. This is consistent with the insights generated in the previous discussion of trends in financial flexibility for PepsiCo.

EXHIBIT 5.10

Debt Ratios for PepsiCo at the End of 2006–2008

	2006	2007	2008
Liabilities to Assets Ratio	0.487	0.502	0.664
Liabilities to Shareholders' Equity Ratio	0.948	1.009	1.973
Long-Term Debt to Long-Term Capital Ratio	0.142	0.196	0.394
Long-Term Debt to Shareholders' Equity Ratio	0.166	0.244	0.649

Note the high correlations between changes in the two debt ratios involving total liabilities over time and in the two long-term debt ratios over time. These results are not surprising because they use overlapping financial statement data. Generally, the analyst can select one of these ratios and use it consistently over time. Because different debt ratios exist, the analyst should use caution when reading financial periodicals and discussing debt ratios with others to be sure of the particular version of the debt ratio used. A liabilities to shareholders' equity ratio greater than 1.0 (that is, more liabilities than shareholders' equity) is not unusual, but a liabilities to assets ratio or a long-term debt to long-term capital ratio greater than 1.0 is highly unusual (because it requires a negative shareholders' equity).

In addition to computing debt ratios, the analyst should study the note to the financial statements on long-term debt. The note includes information on the types of debt a firm has issued and the interest rates and maturity dates of the debt. The analyst also should examine the debt contract for each debt issue to assess whether the firm is nearing violation of any debt covenants.

Refer to Note 9, "Debt Obligations and Commitments" (Appendix A), for PepsiCo. PepsiCo indicates that it classifies a portion of its short-term borrowing as a noncurrent liability even though the amounts are due within the next year. PepsiCo states the following:

> As of December 27, 2008, we have reclassified $1.3 billion of short-term debt to long-term based on our intent and ability to refinance on a long-term basis.

GAAP permits PepsiCo and other firms to reclassify short-term debt in this way. PepsiCo's reclassification of $1.3 billion in additional short-term borrowing is similar to a reclassification at the end of 2007 totaling $1.4 billion.

Note 9 also provides information about the increase in long-term debt from $4.2 billion to $7.9 billion between 2007 and 2008. PepsiCo issued two tranches of senior unsecured 10-year notes during the year, which totaled $3.75 billion, accounting for almost all of the change in long-term obligations. For both issuances, PepsiCo indicates that the proceeds were used for "general corporate purposes, including the repayment of outstanding short-term indebtedness." Further, as discussed in the previous section, the interest rate on the incremental debt issuances is higher. The $1.75 billion issued in the second quarter of 2008 carried a 5 percent fixed rate, while the $2.0 billion issued in the fourth quarter carried a 7.9 percent rate. PepsiCo entered into an interest rate swap to convert the 5 percent fixed rate on the $1.75 billion of debt to a variable rate based on LIBOR. This is relevant for solvency risk analysis because swaps like this hedge the fair value of the debt but create cash flows risk.

In an effort to appear less risky and to lower their cost of financing or perhaps to avoid violating debt covenants in existing borrowing arrangements, firms often attempt to structure financing in a manner that keeps debt off the balance sheet. Chapter 6 discusses some of the avenues available under GAAP (for example, accounting for leases as operating leases instead of capital leases) to minimize reported long-term debt. The analyst should recognize the possibility of such actions when interpreting debt ratios and perhaps adjust the reported amounts, as illustrated for leases in Chapter 6.

Interest Coverage Ratios

Interest coverage ratios indicate the number of times a firm's income or cash flows could cover interest charges. For example, one common approach to the interest coverage ratio divides net income before interest expense and income taxes by interest expense. This income-based interest coverage ratio for PepsiCo, using the amounts reported for net income and income tax expense for 2008, is as follows:[9]

$$\text{Interest Coverage Ratio (Net Income Basis)} = \frac{\text{Net Income + Interest Expense + Income Tax Expense + Minority Interest in Earnings}}{\text{Interest Expense}}$$

$$22.3 = \frac{\$5{,}142 + \$329 + \$1{,}879 + \$0}{\$329}$$

The interest coverage ratio for PepsiCo was 35.1 in 2007 and 30.2 in 2006. PepsiCo's reported profitability decreased slightly during the three-year period (see the discussion in Chapter 4) while its debt levels increased, resulting in a decreasing interest coverage ratio. Analysts typically view coverage ratios of less than approximately 2.0 as risky situations. Thus, by this measure, PepsiCo exhibits very low long-term solvency risk. Sometimes firms are able to capitalize interest as part of the cost basis of tangible assets. The analyst should be aware of significant interest capitalization when examining net borrowing costs.

If a firm must make other required periodic payments (such as pensions or leases), the analyst could include these amounts in the calculation as well. If so, the ratio is referred to as the *fixed charges coverage ratio.*

One criticism of the interest and the fixed charges coverage ratios as measures of long-term solvency risk is that they use earnings rather than cash flows in the numerator. Firms pay interest and other fixed charges with cash, not earnings. The analyst can create cash-flow-based variations of these coverage ratios by using cash flow from operations (before interest and income taxes) in the numerator. When the value of the ratio based on earnings in the numerator is relatively low (that is, less than approximately 2.0), the analyst should use cash flow from operations before interest and income taxes in the numerator to calculate coverage ratios.

To illustrate, cash flow from operations for PepsiCo for 2008 was $6,999 million. Note 14, "Supplemental Financial Information" (Appendix A), indicates that PepsiCo paid $359 million for interest and $1,477 million for income taxes during 2008. The calculation of the interest coverage ratio using cash flows is as follows:

$$\text{Interest Coverage Ratio (Cash Flow Basis)} = \frac{\text{Cash Flow from Operations + Payments for Interest and Income Taxes}}{\text{Cash Payments for Interest}}$$

$$24.6 = \frac{\$6{,}999 + \$359 + \$1{,}477}{\$359}$$

Operating Cash Flow to Total Liabilities Ratio

Standard debt ratios such as the Liabilities to Assets Ratio give no recognition to the ability of a firm to generate cash flow from operations to service debt. The ratio of cash flow from operations to average total liabilities overcomes this deficiency. This cash flow ratio is similar to the one used in assessing short-term liquidity, but here the denominator includes all liabilities (current and noncurrent).

---

[9] Increased precision suggests that the denominator include total interest cost for the year, not just the amount recognized as interest expense. If a firm self-constructs fixed assets, it must capitalize a portion of its interest cost each year and add it to the cost of the self-constructed assets. The analyst probably should apply this refinement of the interest coverage ratio only to electric utilities, which engage in heavy borrowing to construct their capital-intensive plants.

The operating cash flow to total liabilities ratio for 2008 for PepsiCo is as follows:

$$\frac{\text{Operating Cash Flow to}}{\text{Total Liabilities Ratio}} = \frac{\text{Cash Flow from Operations}}{\text{Average Total Liabilities}}$$

$$0.34 = \frac{\$6{,}999}{0.5(\$23{,}888 + \$17{,}394)}$$

The ratio for PepsiCo was 0.43 in 2007 and 0.38 in 2006. A ratio of 0.20 or more is common for a financially healthy company.[10] Thus, by this measure, PepsiCo appears to have low long-term solvency risk.

Summary of Long-Term Solvency Risk

The debt, interest coverage, and cash flow ratios indicate that PepsiCo has low long-term solvency risk. PepsiCo is profitable and generates the needed cash flow to service its debt. However, the trends indicate increasing use of leverage, which calls for the analyst to monitor future changes to ensure that PepsiCo's current low solvency risk persists. Similarly, decreases in financial flexibility (discussed earlier in the chapter) could be an early indicator of potential liquidity and solvency problems.

ANALYZING CREDIT RISK

Potential lenders to a firm, whether short- or long-term, assess the likelihood that the firm will pay periodic interest and repay the principal amount lent. To assess credit risk, lenders use the short-term liquidity and long-term solvency ratios already presented in the chapter. Lenders also consider other factors when deciding whether to extend credit. Common practice uses the following checklist as factors a creditor might consider when making lending decisions. The list is neither an exhaustive catalog of the factors that lenders consider in assessing credit risk nor a mandatory list of factors that must be examined.

1. Circumstances Leading to Need for the Loan

The reason a firm needs to borrow affects the riskiness of the loan and the likelihood of repayment. Consider the following examples.

Example 1

W. T. Grant Company, a discount retail chain, filed for bankruptcy in 1975. Its bankruptcy has become a classic example of how poorly designed and implemented controls can lead a firm into financial distress. (See Case 3.3 in Chapter 3.) Between 1968 and 1975, Grant experienced increasing difficulty collecting accounts receivable from credit card customers. To finance the buildup of its accounts receivable, Grant borrowed short-term funds from commercial banks. However, Grant failed to fix the credit extension and cash collection problems with its receivables. The bank loans simply kept Grant in business in an ever-worsening credit situation. Lending to satisfy cash-flow needs related to an unsolved problem or difficulty can be highly risky.

[10] Casey and Bartczak, *op. cit.*

Example 2

Toys"R"Us purchases toys, games, and other entertainment products in September and October in anticipation of heavy demand during the end-of-the-year holiday season. It typically pays its suppliers within 30 days for these purchases but does not collect cash from customers until December, January, or later. To finance its inventory, Toys"R"Us borrows short term from its banks. It repays these loans with cash collected from customers. Lending to satisfy cash-flow needs related to ongoing seasonal business operations is generally relatively low risk. Toys"R"Us has an established brand name and predictable demand. Although some risk exists that the products offered will not meet customer preferences in a particular year, Toys"R"Us offers a sufficiently diverse product line that failure to collect sufficient cash to repay the bank loan is low. Despite being profitable, Toys"R"Us suffered declines in market share relative to rivals such as Walmart. As a result, Toys"R"Us was acquired by an investment group formed by Bain Capital, LLC; Kohlberg Kravis Roberts & Co.; and Vornado Realty Trust. The company continues to follow the same seasonal purchasing pattern.

Example 3

Wal-Mart Stores has grown the number of its stores during each of the last five years. (See Case 4.2 in Chapter 4.) The fastest growth is in its international segment, which now represents approximately 25 percent of total sales. Walmart borrows a large portion of the funds needed to construct new stores using 20- to 25-year loans. (Walmart also enters into leases for a portion of the space needed for its new stores.) Such loans are relatively low-risk given the operating success of Walmart in the past and the existence of land and buildings that serve as collateral for the loans.

Example 4

National Semiconductor designs and manufactures semiconductors for use in computers and other electronic products. Its principal competitors include well-known companies such as Intel, Analog Devices, Linear Technology, Maxim Integrated Products, and Texas Instruments. National Semiconductor has continued to lose market share in recent years. Assume that National Semiconductor wants to develop new semiconductors and needs to borrow funds to finance the design and development effort. Such a loan would likely be relatively high-risk. Technological change occurs rapidly in semiconductors, which would make obsolete any semiconductors developed by National Semiconductor. In addition, expenditures on design and development of semiconductors would not likely result in assets that could serve as collateral for the loan.

In sum, lending to established firms for ongoing operating needs and capital expenditures presents the lowest credit risk. Lending to firms experiencing operating problems, lending to emerging businesses, and lending to support investments in intangible assets typically carry higher risks. Lenders should be wary of borrowers that are unclear as to how they intend to use the proceeds of a loan.

2. Credit History

Lenders like to see that a firm has borrowed in the past and successfully repaid the loans. Young firms sometimes shy away from borrowing to avoid constraints that such borrowing may impose. However, such firms often find that an inadequate credit history precludes them from borrowing later when they need to do so. On the other hand, developing a poor credit history early on can doom a firm to failure because of the difficulty of overcoming initial impressions.

3. Cash Flows

Lenders prefer that firms generate sufficient cash flows to pay interest and repay principal (collectively referred to as *debt service)* on a loan rather than having to rely on selling the collateral. Tools for studying the cash-generating ability of a firm include examining the statement of cash flows for recent years, computing various cash flow financial ratios, and studying cash flows in projected financial statements.

Statement of Cash Flows

An examination of a firm's statement of cash flows for the most recent three or four years will indicate whether a firm is experiencing potential cash flow problems. We discussed cash flows in detail in Chapter 3. Some of the indicators of potential cash flow problems, if observed for several years in a row, include:

- Growth in accounts receivable and inventories that exceeds the growth rate in sales.
- Increases in accounts payable or other liabilities that routinely exceed the increase in inventories or sales.
- Persistent negative cash flow from operations because of net losses or substantial increases in net working capital (current assets minus current liabilities).
- Capital expenditures that substantially exceed cash flow from operations. Although the analyst should expect such an excess for a rapidly growing, capital-intensive firm, the negative excess cash flow (cash flow from operations minus capital expenditures) indicates a firm's continuing need for external financing to sustain that growth.
- Reductions in capital expenditures over time. Although such reductions conserve cash in the near term, they might signal that a firm expects declines in future sales, earnings, and operating cash flows.
- Sales of marketable securities in excess of purchases of marketable securities. Such sales provide cash immediately but might signal the inability of a firm's operations to provide adequate cash flow to finance working capital and long-term investments. Firms sell the marketable securities to obtain the cash needed for these purposes. Such sales, however, may not indicate cash flow problems if the firm temporarily invested excess cash that it now plans to use to make a corporate acquisition or to acquire fixed assets.
- A reduction or elimination of dividend payments or stock repurchases. Although such actions conserve cash in the near term, dividend reductions or omissions and cessation of share repurchase plans can provide a negative signal about a firm's future prospects.
- A full use of available revolving lines of credit. Full utilization of letters of credit might suggest that a firm's cash flows have become insufficient for operating purposes.

Although none of these indicators by themselves represents conclusive evidence of cash flow problems, they do signal the need to obtain explanations from management to see whether an emerging cash flow problem does exist. Just as analysts must understand a firm's industry and strategy to effectively analyze profitability, lenders must follow the same analysis steps.

Cash Flow Financial Ratios

Previous sections of this chapter discussed two cash flow ratios that may signal a cash flow problem: (1) operating cash flow to current liabilities ratio and (2) operating cash flow to total liabilities ratio.

Cash Flows in Projected Financial Statements

Projected financial statements represent forecasted income statements, balance sheets, and statements of cash flows for some number of years in the future. Lenders may require potential borrowers to prepare such statements (which are rarely made publicly available) to demonstrate the borrower's ability to repay the loan with interest as it comes due. The credit analyst should question each of the important assumptions (such as sales growth, cost structure, or capital expenditures plans) underlying these projected financial statements. The credit analyst also should assess the sensitivity of the projected cash flows to changes in key assumptions. For example, suppose sales grow by 4 percent instead of the 6 percent projected. Suppose raw materials costs increase 5 percent instead of the 3 percent projected. Suppose additional plant expenditures are necessary because a firm reaches capacity limits with a higher-than-expected sales increase. What impact will each of these changed assumptions have on cash flow from operations? Chapter 10 illustrates the preparation of projected, or forecasted, financial statements.

4. Collateral

A fourth consideration when assessing credit risk is the availability and value of collateral for a loan. If a company's cash flows are insufficient to pay interest and repay the principal on a loan, the lender has the right to take possession of any collateral pledged in support of the loan. Depending on the nature of the collateral pledged, the analyst might examine the following:

Marketable Securities

Chapter 7 discusses the accounting for marketable securities. Marketable equity securities representing less than a 20 percent ownership appear on the balance sheet at market value. The analyst can assess whether the market value of securities pledged as collateral exceeds the unpaid balance of a loan. Marketable securities representing 20 percent or more of another entity generally appear on the balance sheet using the equity method. Determining whether the market value of such securities adequately covers the unpaid balance of a loan is more difficult. The analyst might examine the amount reported as equity in earnings of affiliates in recent years to assess the level and changes in profitability of the investee.

Accounts Receivable

A lender should assess whether the current value of accounts receivable is sufficient to cover the unpaid portion of a loan collateralized by accounts receivable. Determining whether the book value of accounts receivable accurately reflects their market value involves an examination of changes in the provision for uncollectible accounts relative to sales, the balance in allowance for uncollectible accounts relative to gross accounts receivable, the amount of accounts written off as uncollectible relative to gross accounts receivable, and the number of days receivables that are outstanding. Deterioration in the days receivables outstanding can suggest decreasing collectability or lowering of customer credit standards.

Inventories

Inventory represents valuable collateral to a lender only if it is salable for sufficient cash flows in the event of the borrower's distress. The analyst should examine changes in the inventory turnover ratio; in the cost of goods sold to sales percentage; and in the mix of raw materials, work-in-process, and finished goods inventories to identify possible inventory obsolescence problems. The analyst should remember that the market value of inventories are likely to differ more from their book value for a firm using LIFO than for a firm using FIFO. Firms using LIFO must report the excess of market or FIFO value over LIFO cost, permitting the analyst to assess the adequacy of LIFO inventories to cover the unpaid balance on a loan collateralized by inventories. (See the discussion of inventories in Chapter 8.)

Property, Plant, and Equipment

Firms often pledge fixed assets as collateral for long-term borrowing. Determining the market values of such assets is difficult using reported financial statement information because of the use of acquisition cost valuations. Market values of unique firm-specific assets are particularly difficult to ascertain. Clues indicating market value declines include restructuring charges, asset impairment charges, and recent sales of such assets at a loss. (See the discussion of property, plant, and equipment in Chapter 7.)

Intangibles

Intangibles generally do not serve well as collateral for borrowing because lenders cannot easily repossess the intangible (that is, sever it from all other assets or capabilities of the firm) in the event of a loan default. For example, the value of a newspaper or magazine publisher's customer list is closely tied to its writers and reporters and its production and distribution capability. The value of a brand name of a consumer foods product is closely tied to the firm's manufacturing quality control and marketing expertise. On the other hand, in some limited situations, intangibles can serve as collateral for borrowing. Rights owned by airlines to landing and gate slots at airports can be transferred to lenders in the event of loan default and resold to cover unpaid balances on a loan.

Some lending occurs on a nonsecured basis; that is, the borrower pledges no specific collateral in support of the loan. In these cases, the lender should study the notes to the financial statements to ascertain how much of the borrower's assets, if any, are not already pledged or otherwise restricted. The liquidation value of such assets represents the available resources of a firm to repay unsecured creditors. For smaller family-owned businesses, an additional source of collateral may be the personal assets of management or major shareholders. Has management or the shareholders pledged their personal residence, debt or equity securities owned, or other assets to serve as additional collateral for a business loan?

5. Capacity for Debt

Closely related to a firm's cash-generating ability and available collateral is a firm's capacity to assume additional debt. The cash flows and the collateral represent the means to repay the debt. Most firms do not borrow up to the limit of their debt capacity. Lenders want to make sure a margin of safety exists. Although no precise methodology exists to measure debt capacity, the analyst can study various financial statement ratios when assessing debt capacity. Capacity for debt is related to the discussion earlier in the chapter for financial flexibility. Moreover, footnote disclosures highlight the amount of unused credit lines, which provide additional, direct evidence of capacity for debt, especially if the firm exhibits a history of maintaining unused lines of credit.

Debt Ratios

An earlier section described several ratios that relate the amount of long-term debt or total liabilities to shareholders' equity or total assets as measures of the proportion of liabilities in the capital structure. In general, the higher the debt ratios, the higher the credit risk and the lower the unused debt capacity of the firm. When measuring debt ratios, the analyst must be careful to consider possible off-balance-sheet obligations (such as operating lease commitments or underfunded pension or health care benefit obligations). The analyst can compare a particular firm's debt ratios with those of similar firms in the same industry.

Interest Coverage Ratio

As discussed earlier, the number of times interest payments are covered by operating income before interest and income taxes serves as a gauge of the margin of safety provided by operations to service debt. When firms make heavy use of operating leases for their fixed assets, as is common for airlines and retail stores, the analyst might convert the operating leases to capital leases for the purpose of computing the interest coverage ratio. (See the discussion of leases in Chapter 6.) When computing cash flows from operations, the analyst adds back the lease payments (that is, rent expense) to net income in the numerator of this ratio and includes the lease payments in the denominator. When the interest coverage ratio falls below approximately 2, the credit risk is generally considered high. Interest coverage ratios that exceed 4 or 5 usually suggest a capacity to carry additional debt.

6. Contingencies

The credit standing of a firm could change abruptly in the future if current uncertainties turn out negatively for the firm. Questions the analyst might ask include the following:

- Is the firm a defendant in a major lawsuit involving its principal products, its technological advantages, its income tax returns, or other core endeavors that could change its profitability and cash flows in the future? Consider, for example, the uncertainty currently confronting the tobacco and asbestos industries with the unsettled status of lawsuits in the United States. Most large firms are continually engaged in lawsuits as a normal part of their business. Most of their losses are insured. Negative legal judgments are likely to have a more pronounced effect on smaller firms, however, because they have less of a resource base with which to defend themselves and to sustain such losses and may not carry adequate insurance.
- Has the firm sold receivables with recourse or served as guarantor on a loan by a subsidiary, joint venture, special-purpose entity, or corporate officer that, if payment is required, will consume cash flows otherwise available to service other debt obligations?
- Is the firm exposed to making payments related to derivative financial instruments that could adversely affect future cash flows if interest rates, exchange rates, or other prices change significantly in an unexpected direction? (See the discussion of derivatives in Chapter 8.)
- Is the firm dependent on one or a few key employees, contracts or license agreements, or technologies, the loss of which could substantially affect the viability of the business?

Obtaining answers to such questions require the analyst to read the notes to the financial statement carefully and to ask astute questions of management, attorneys, and others.

7. Character of Management

An intangible that can offset to some extent otherwise weak signals about the creditworthiness of a firm is the character of its management. Has the management team successively weathered previous operating problems and challenges that could have bankrupted most firms? Has the management team delivered in the past on projections regarding sales levels, cost reductions, new product development, and similar operating targets? Does the firm have a reputation for honest and fair dealings with suppliers, customers, bankers, and others? Lenders also are more comfortable lending to firms in which management has a substantial portion of its personal wealth invested in the firm's common equity. Managers wanting to increase the value of their equity holdings have incentives to operate the firm profitably and avoid defaulting on debt.

8. Communication

Developing relations with lenders requires effective communication at the outset and on an ongoing basis. If lenders are unfamiliar with the business or its managers, efforts must be directed at communicating the nature of the firm's products and services and the strategies the firm pursues to gain competitive advantage. The firm's managers must demonstrate their knowledge of the business, including principal competitors, role of technological change, extent of government regulation, and similar factors. Inviting lenders to an office or plant visit provides visual evidence of an ongoing business.

Throughout the term of a loan, the borrowing firm should communicate regularly with lenders. If lenders required projected financial statements at the outset, communicating the extent to which the firm meets its projections is desirable. Alerting lenders to unexpected problems that may arise demonstrates that the firm's managers are on top of the problem and are dealing with it. Lenders do not like surprises and need to receive transparent information throughout the term of the loan.

9. Conditions or Covenants

Lenders often place restrictions, or constraints, on a firm to protect their interests. Such restrictions might include minimum or maximum levels of certain financial ratios. For example, the current ratio cannot fall below 1.2 and the long-term debt to shareholders' equity ratio cannot exceed 75 percent. Firms also may be precluded from paying dividends, repurchasing common stock, or taking on new financing with rights senior to existing lenders in the event of bankruptcy. Violation of these debt constraints, or covenants, could result in the need to repay loans immediately, higher interest rates, or other burdensome restrictions. Although these covenants can protect the interest of senior collateralized lenders, they can place less senior lenders in jeopardy if the firm must quickly liquidate assets to repay debt. Thus, debt covenants are a double-edged sword from the viewpoint of credit risk. They provide protection against undue deterioration in the financial condition of a firm but increase the likelihood of default or bankruptcy if the constraints are too tight.

Summary of Credit Risk Analysis

The analysis of credit risk is a multifaceted endeavor. The financial statements and notes provide evidence of a firm's cash-generating ability, extent of collateralized assets, amount of unused debt capacity, and constraints imposed by existing borrowing agreements. Although the financial statements might provide some clues, the credit analyst must search beyond the financial statements for information on the credit history of the borrower, the market value of collateral, contingencies confronting the firm, and the character of management. Existing lenders should monitor a firm's credit risk on an ongoing basis, maintaining communications throughout the process. New lenders should assess how their loan will incrementally affect the firm's credit risk.

ANALYZING BANKRUPTCY RISK

This section discusses the analysis of bankruptcy risk by using information in the financial statements.

The Bankruptcy Process

During the recession of 2008–2009, a staggering number of large, well-known firms filed for bankruptcy, including IndyMac Bancorp (July 2008), Lehman Brothers (September 2008),

Washington Mutual (September 2008), Circuit City (November 2008), Tribune Group (December 2008), Saab Automobile (February 2009), Chrysler (April 2009), General Motors (June 2009), Eddie Bauer (June 2009), The Jolt Company (September 2009), and Simmons Bedding (November 2009). Most firms that file for bankruptcy in the United States file under Chapter 11 of the National Bankruptcy Code. Under Chapter 11, firms have six months in which to present a plan of reorganization to the court. After that period elapses, creditors, employees, and others can file their plans of reorganization. One such plan might include immediately selling the assets of the business and paying creditors the amounts due. The court decides which plan provides the fairest treatment for all parties concerned. While the firm is in bankruptcy, creditors cannot demand payment of their claims. The court oversees the execution of the reorganization. When the court determines that the firm has executed the plan of reorganization successfully and appears to be a viable entity, the firm is released from bankruptcy.

A Chapter 7 filing entails an immediate sale, or liquidation, of the firm's assets and a distribution of the proceeds to the various claimants in order of priority.

Firms typically file for bankruptcy when they have insufficient cash to pay creditors' claims coming due. If such firms did not file for bankruptcy, creditors could exercise their right to take possession of any collateral pledged to secure their lending and effectively begin liquidation of the firm. In an effort to keep assets intact and operating activities functioning and to allow time for the firm to reorganize, the firm files for bankruptcy. In recent years, some firms have filed for bankruptcy for reasons other than insufficient liquid resources to pay creditors. Some firms have filed for bankruptcy to avoid labor contracts or retirement obligations because the firms considered them too costly. Other firms facing potentially costly litigation have filed for bankruptcy as a means of forcing the contending party to negotiate a settlement.

Models of Bankruptcy Prediction

Empirical studies of bankruptcy attempt to distinguish the financial characteristics of firms that file for bankruptcy from those that do not, a dichotomous outcome. The objective is to develop a model that predicts which firms will likely file for bankruptcy one or more years before the filing. These models use financial statement ratios and other data.

Univariate Bankruptcy Prediction Models

Early research on bankruptcy prediction in the mid-1960s used univariate analysis. Univariate models examine the relation between a particular financial statement ratio and bankruptcy. Multivariate models, discussed next, combine several financial statement ratios to determine whether the set of ratios together can improve bankruptcy prediction. Beaver[11] studied 29 financial statement ratios for the five years preceding bankruptcy using a sample of 79 bankrupt and 79 nonbankrupt firms. The objective was to identify the ratios that best differentiated between these two groups of firms and to determine how many years prior to bankruptcy the differences in the ratios emerged. The six ratios with the best discriminating power (and the nature of the risk that each ratio measures) were as follows:

1. Net Income plus Depreciation, Depletion, and Amortization/Total Liabilities (long-term solvency risk)[12]
2. Net Income/Total Assets (profitability)

[11] William Beaver, "Financial Ratios as Predictors of Failure," *Empirical Research in Accounting: Selected Studies, 1966,* supplement to *Journal of Accounting Research* (1966), pp. 71–102.

[12] This ratio is similar to the operating cash flow to total liabilities ratio discussed earlier in this chapter except that the numerator of Beaver's ratio does not include changes in working capital accounts. Published "funds flow" statements at the time of Beaver's study defined funds as working capital (instead of cash).

3. Total Debt/Total Assets (long-term solvency risk)
4. Net Working Capital/Total Assets (short-term liquidity risk)
5. Current Assets/Current Liabilities (short-term liquidity risk)
6. Cash, Marketable Securities, Accounts Receivable/Operating Expenses Excluding Depreciation, Depletion, and Amortization (short-term liquidity risk)[13]

Note that this list includes profitability, short-term liquidity risk, and long-term solvency risk ratios. Beaver's best predictor was net income before depreciation, depletion, and amortization divided by total liabilities. Exhibit 5.11 summarizes for each of the five years preceding bankruptcy the success of this ratio in correctly predicting firms that go bankrupt. The predictive accuracy increased as bankruptcy approached, but was close to 80 percent for as early as five years preceding bankruptcy.

The error rates deserve particular attention, however. A Type I error is classifying a firm as nonbankrupt when it ultimately goes bankrupt. A Type II error occurs when a firm is classified as bankrupt and ultimately survives. A Type I error is more costly to an investor because of the likelihood of losing the full amount invested. A Type II error costs the investor the opportunity cost of funds invested. Note in Exhibit 5.11 that the Type I error rates are much higher than the Type II error rates in Beaver's study. When the net income before depreciation, depletion, and amortization to total liabilities ratio is used to predict bankruptcy four years prior to bankruptcy, 47 percent of the predictions that firms would be nonbankrupt turned out to be incorrect, whereas only 3 percent of the predictions that firms would be bankrupt turned out to be incorrect.

Because univariate analysis helps identify factors related to bankruptcy, it is a useful step in the initial development of predictors of bankruptcy risk. However, in the assessment of risk, univariate analysis does not provide a means of measuring the relative importance of individual financial statement ratios or of combining them. For example, does a firm with a high current ratio and a high debt-to-assets ratio have more bankruptcy risk than a firm with a low current ratio and a low debt-to-assets ratio? The analyst also must subjectively judge the level of each financial ratio that signals a high probability of bankruptcy.

EXHIBIT 5.11

Classification Accuracy and Error Rates for Bankruptcy Prediction based on Net Income before Depreciation, Depletion, and Amortization/Total Liabilities

Years Prior to Bankruptcy	Proportion Correctly Classified	Error Rate	
		Type I	Type II
5	78%	42%	4%
4	76%	47%	3%
3	77%	37%	8%
2	79%	34%	8%
1	87%	22%	5%

Source: William Beaver, "Financial Ratios as Predictors of Failure," *Empirical Research in Accounting: Selected Studies*, 1966, supplement to *Journal of Accounting Research* (1966), p. 90. Reprinted by permission of Wiley-Blackwell.

[13] This ratio, referred to as the *defensive interval*, indicates the proportion of a year that a firm could continue to operate by paying cash operating expenses with cash and near-cash assets. See the discussion earlier in this chapter in the section on the revenues to cash ratio.

Bankruptcy Prediction Models Using Multiple Discriminant Analysis (MDA)

During the late 1960s and throughout the 1970s, deficiencies of univariate analysis led researchers to use MDA, a multivariate statistical technique, to develop bankruptcy prediction models. Researchers typically selected a sample of bankrupt firms and matched them with healthy firms of approximately the same size in the same industry. This matching procedure attempts to control factors for size and industry so the researcher can examine the impact of other factors that might explain bankruptcy. The researcher then calculates a large number of financial statement ratios expected a priori to explain bankruptcy. Using these financial ratios as inputs, an MDA model selects the subset (usually four to six ratios) that best discriminates between bankrupt and nonbankrupt firms. The resulting MDA model includes a set of coefficients that, when multiplied by the particular financial statement ratios and then summed, yields a multivariate score that is the basis of predicting the likelihood of a firm going bankrupt. The researcher then examines the pattern of Type I and Type II errors and chooses a cutoff that distinguishes firms with a high probability of bankruptcy from those with a low probability. Researchers usually develop the MDA model on an estimation sample and apply the resulting model to a separate holdout, or prediction, sample to check on the general applicability and predictability of the model.

Perhaps the best-known MDA bankruptcy prediction model is Altman's Z-score.[14] Altman used data for manufacturing firms to develop the model. Following is the calculation of the Z-score:

$$\begin{aligned}\text{Z-score} = {} & 1.2\left[\frac{\text{Net Working Capital}}{\text{Total Assets}}\right] + 1.4\left[\frac{\text{Retained Earnings}}{\text{Total Assets}}\right] \\ & + 3.3\left[\frac{\text{Earnings before Interest and Taxes}}{\text{Total Assets}}\right] + 0.6\left[\frac{\text{Market Value of Equity}}{\text{Book Value of Liabilities}}\right] \\ & + 1.0\left[\frac{\text{Sales}}{\text{Total Assets}}\right]\end{aligned}$$

Each ratio captures a different dimension of profitability or risk as follows:

1. Net Working Capital/Total Assets: The proportion of total assets comprising relatively liquid net current assets (current assets minus current liabilities). This ratio serves as a measure of short-term liquidity risk.
2. Retained Earnings/Total Assets: Accumulated profitability and relative age of a firm.
3. Earnings before Interest and Taxes/Total Assets: A variant of ROA. This ratio measures current profitability.
4. Market Value of Equity/Book Value of Liabilities: A form of the debt-to-equity ratio but it incorporates the market's assessment of the value of the firm's shareholders' equity. Therefore, this ratio measures long-term solvency risk and the market's overall assessment of the profitability and risk of the firm.
5. Sales/Total Assets: Similar to the total assets turnover ratio discussed in Chapter 4. This ratio indicates the ability of a firm to use assets to generate sales.

In applying this model, Altman found that Z-scores of less than 1.81 indicated a high probability of bankruptcy, while Z-scores higher than 3.00 indicated a low probability of bankruptcy. Scores between 1.81 and 3.00 were in the gray area.

---

[14] Edward Altman, "Financial Ratios, Discriminant Analysis, and the Prediction of Corporate Bankruptcy," *Journal of Finance* (September 1968), pp. 589–609.

We can convert the Z-score into a more intuitive probability of bankruptcy using the normal density function in Excel.[15] A Z-score of 3.00 translates into a probability of bankruptcy of 2.75 percent. A Z-score of 1.81 translates into a probability of bankruptcy of 20.90 percent. Thus, Z-scores that correspond to probabilities of less than 2.75 percent indicate low probability of bankruptcy, probabilities between 2.75 percent and 20.90 percent are in the gray area, and probabilities above 20.90 percent are in the high probability area. These probabilities levels cannot be interpreted in the usual way. Altman had to trade off Type I and Type II errors when specifying the cutoff points for ranges of low probability, gray area, and high probability.

Altman obtained a 95 percent correct prediction accuracy rate one year prior to bankruptcy, with a Type I error rate of 6 percent and a Type II error rate of 3 percent. The correct prediction rate two years before bankruptcy was 83 percent, with a Type I error rate of 28 percent and a Type II error rate of 6 percent. As with Beaver's study, the more costly Type I error rate is larger than the Type II error rate.

Exhibit 5.12 shows the calculation of Altman's Z-score for PepsiCo for 2008. We use the originally reported amounts for PepsiCo instead of the adjusted amounts that eliminate nonrecurring items because Altman developed his model using originally reported amounts. If Altman had adjusted the earnings numbers to eliminate nonrecurring items, the coefficients would likely have been different; the financial ratios with the most discriminating power might have been different as well. Not surprisingly, PepsiCo's Z-score of 5.2709 clearly indicates a low probability of bankruptcy. FSAP computes Altman's Z-scores and the corresponding probabilities of bankruptcy (Appendix C).

FSAP

The principal strengths of MDA are as follows:

1. It incorporates multiple financial ratios simultaneously.
2. It provides the appropriate coefficients for combining the independent variables.
3. It is easy to apply once the initial model has been developed.

EXHIBIT 5.12

Altman's Z-Score for PepsiCo

Net Working Capital/Total Assets	
1.2[($10,806 – $8,787)/$35,994]	0.0673
Retained Earnings/Total Assets	
1.4[$30,638/$35,994]	1.1917
Earnings before Interest and Taxes/Total Assets	
3.3[($5,142 + $329 + $1,879)/$35,994]	0.6739
Market Value of Equity/Book Value of Liabilities	
0.6[($54.77 × 1,553)/$23,888]	2.1364
Sales/Total Assets	
1.0[$43,251/$35,994]	1.2016
Z-Score	5.2709

[15] The formula in Excel is =NORMSDIST(1–Z score). Altman developed his model so that higher positive Z-scores mean lower probability of bankruptcy; thus, computing the probability of bankruptcy requires that the normal density function be applied to 1 minus the Z-score. The website for this book (www.cengage.com/accounting/wahlen) contains an Excel spreadsheet for computing Altman's Z-score and the probability of bankruptcy. FSAP also computes these values.

The principal criticisms of MDA are as follows:

1. As in univariate applications, the researcher cannot be sure that the MDA model includes all relevant discriminating financial ratios. Most early studies, for example, used only accrual-basis income statement and balance sheet data and did not augment those data with cash flow data. MDA selects the best ratios from those provided, but that set does not necessarily provide the best explanatory power.
2. As in univariate applications, the researcher must subjectively judge the value of the cutoff score that best distinguishes bankrupt from nonbankrupt firms, taking into consideration the levels and costs of Type I and Type II errors.
3. The development and application of the MDA model requires firms to disclose the information needed to compute each financial ratio. Firms excluded because they do not provide the necessary data may bias the MDA model.
4. MDA assumes that each of the financial ratios for bankrupt and nonbankrupt firms is normally distributed. Firms experiencing financial distress often display unusually large or small ratios that can skew the distribution away from normal. In addition, the researcher cannot include dummy variables (for example, 0 if financial statements are audited and 1 if they are not audited). Dummy variables are not normally distributed.
5. MDA requires that the variance-covariance matrix of the explanatory variables be the same for bankrupt and nonbankrupt firms.[16]

Bankruptcy Prediction Models Using Logit Analysis

A third stage in the methodological development of bankruptcy prediction research was the move during the 1980s and early 1990s to using logit analysis instead of MDA. Logit does not require that the data display the underlying statistical properties described previously for MDA.

The use of logit analysis to develop a bankruptcy prediction model follows a procedure that is similar to that of MDA: (1) initial calculation of a large set of financial ratios, (2) reduction of the set of financial ratios to a subset that best predicts bankrupt and nonbankrupt firms, and (3) estimation of coefficients for each included variable.

The logit model defines the probability of bankruptcy as follows:

$$\text{Probability of Bankruptcy for a Firm} = \frac{1}{1 + e^{-y}}$$

where e equals approximately 2.718282. The exponent y is a multivariate function that includes a constant and coefficients for a set of explanatory variables (that is, financial statement ratios that discriminate bankrupt and nonbankrupt firms).

Ohlson[17] and Zavgren[18] used logit analysis to develop bankruptcy prediction models. Their models use different financial statement ratios than Altman's model does, and they are somewhat more complex to apply. We do not discuss their models in depth here, but interested readers can consult the research cited. Despite the shortcomings of discriminant models, Altman's Z-score model is still the most widely referenced and the one emphasized in this chapter.

---

[16] For an elaboration of these criticisms, see James A. Ohlson, "Financial Ratios and the Probabilistic Prediction of Bankruptcy," *Journal of Accounting Research* (Spring 1980), pp. 109–131, and Mark E. Zmijewski, "Methodological Issues Related to the Estimation of Financial Distress Prediction Models," *Journal of Accounting Research,* Supplement (1984), pp. 59–82.

[17] Ohlson, *op. cit.*.

[18] Christine V. Zavgren, "Assessing the Vulnerability to Failure of American Industrial Firms: A Logistic Analysis," *Journal of Business Finance and Accounting* (Spring 1985), pp. 19–45.

Application of Altman's Bankruptcy Prediction Model to W. T. Grant Company

W. T. Grant Company (Grant), one of the largest retailers in the United States at the time, filed for bankruptcy in October 1975. Case 3.3 in Chapter 3 includes financial statement data for Grant for its fiscal years ended January 31, 1967 through 1975. Exhibit 5.13 shows the calculation of Altman's Z-score for each of these fiscal years using amounts from Exhibits 3.38 and 3.39 of Case 3.3.

Altman's model shows a low probability of bankruptcy prior to the 1973 fiscal year, a move into the gray area in 1973 and 1974, and a high probability of bankruptcy in 1975. The absolute levels of these Z-scores are inflated because Grant was a retailer, whereas Altman developed the model using manufacturing firms. Retailing firms typically have a faster assets turnover than do manufacturing firms. In this case, the trend of the Z-score is more meaningful than its absolute level. Note that the Z-score declined steadily beginning in the 1970 fiscal year. With a few exceptions in individual years, each of the five components also declined steadily.[19]

Other Methodological Issues in Bankruptcy Prediction Research

Bankruptcy prediction research has addressed several other methodological issues.

1. **Equal Sample Sizes of Bankrupt and Nonbankrupt Firms.** The proportion of bankrupt firms in the economy is substantially smaller than the proportion of nonbankrupt firms. The matched-pairs research design common in most studies overfits the MDA and logit models toward the characteristics of bankrupt firms. This overfitting is not necessarily a problem if the objective is to identify characteristics of bankrupt firms. However, it will likely result in classifying too many nonbankrupt firms as bankrupt (a Type II error) when the model is applied to the broader population of firms. Researchers (such as Ohlson in the study cited previously) have addressed this criticism by using a proportion of nonbankrupt firms that more closely reflects the population of firms.
2. **Matching Bankrupt and Nonbankrupt Firms on Size and Industry Characteristics.** This matching precludes consideration of either of these factors as possible explanatory variables for bankruptcy. Yet compared to larger firms, small firms may experience greater difficulty obtaining needed funds. Industry membership, particularly for cyclical industries, may be an important factor in explaining bankruptcy. Some researchers select a random sample of nonbankrupt firms. Another approach is to develop the MDA or logit models for each industry. Platt,[20] for example, developed models for 16 two-digit SIC industries. The explanatory variables and their coefficients varied across the industries. Platt and Platt[21] normalized the financial ratios of each firm by relating them to the corresponding average industry ratio of the firm's industry. They found that normalized financial ratios increased the classification accuracy of their sample to 90 percent, versus 78 percent based on a model of non-normalized ratios.
3. **Use of Accrual versus Cash Flow Variables.** Until the mid-1980s, most bankruptcy research used accrual-basis balance sheet and income statement ratios or ratios from

[19] The solution to the Grant case indicates that prior to its 1975 fiscal year, Grant failed to provide adequately for uncollectible accounts. The effect of this action was to overstate the net working capital/assets, retained earnings/assets, and EBIT/assets components of the Z-score; understate the sales/assets component; and probably overstate the overall Z-score.

[20] Harlan D. Platt, "The Determinants of Interindustry Failure," *Journal of Economics and Business* (1989), pp. 107–126.

[21] Harlan D. Platt and Marjorie B. Platt, "Development of a Class of Stable Predictive Variables: The Case of Bankruptcy Prediction," *Journal of Business, Finance, and Accounting* (Spring 1990), pp. 31–51.

EXHIBIT 5.13

Application of Altman's Bankruptcy Prediction Models to W. T. Grant

Fiscal Year:	**1968**	**1969**	**1970**	**1971**	**1972**	**1973**	**1974**	**1975**
Altman's Z-Score Model								
Net Working Capital/Assets	0.54353	0.51341	0.44430	0.37791	0.44814	0.36508	0.38524	0.19390
Retained Earnings/Assets	0.43738	0.42669	0.41929	0.38511	0.34513	0.31023	0.25712	0.04873
EBIT/Assets	0.41358	0.44611	0.44228	0.38848	0.27820	0.26029	0.25470	(0.63644)
Market Value Equity/Book Value Liabilities	0.86643	1.01740	0.95543	0.89539	0.69788	0.50578	0.10211	0.01730
Sales/Assets	1.77564	1.76199	1.71325	1.67974	1.57005	1.58678	1.54797	1.62802
Z-Score	4.03656	4.16560	3.97455	3.72663	3.33940	3.02816	2.54714	1.25151
Probability of Bankruptcy Range	Low	Low	Low	Low	Low	Gray	Gray	High
Probability of Bankruptcy	0.12%	0.07%	0.15%	0.32%	0.97%	2.13%	6.09%	40.07%

the "funds flow" statement, which defined funds as working capital. The transition to a cash definition of funds in the statement of cash flows led researchers to add cash flow variables to bankruptcy prediction models. Casey and Bartczak,[22] among others, found that adding cash flow from operations/current liabilities and cash flow from operations/total liabilities did not significantly add explanatory power to models based on accrual basis amounts. However, other researchers have found contrary results, suggesting that the use of cash flow variables may enhance bankruptcy prediction.[23]

4. **Stability in Bankruptcy Prediction Models over Time.** A final methodological issue in bankruptcy prediction research concerns the stability of the bankruptcy prediction models over time with regard to the explanatory variables included and their coefficients. Bankruptcy laws and their judicial interpretation change over time. The frequency of bankruptcy filings changes as economic conditions change. Changes occur in the mix of industry concentration of firms. New financing vehicles emerge (for example, redeemable preferred stock or debt and equity securities with various option rights) that previous MDA or logit models did not consider in their formulation. To apply these models in practical settings, the analyst should update them periodically.

Begley, Ming, and Watts[24] applied Altman's MDA model and Ohlson's logit model to a sample of bankrupt and nonbankrupt firms in the 1980s, a later period than that used by Altman and Ohlson. Begley, Ming, and Watts found that the Type I and Type II error rates increased substantially relative to those in the original studies. They then reestimated the coefficients for each model using data for a portion of their 1980s sample. The coefficients on the liquidity ratios increased and the coefficients on the debt ratio decreased relative to those in the original studies. When they applied the original and reestimated coefficients to the 1980s sample, they observed a reduction in Type II errors but no improvement in Type I errors for the Altman model. For the Ohlson model, they found that a reduction in Type II errors was offset by an equal increase in Type I errors. Thus, the revised coefficients result in fewer errors in classifying nonbankrupt firms as bankrupt, but similar or worse errors occur in classifying bankrupt firms as nonbankrupt.

Synthesis of Bankruptcy Prediction Research

The preceding sections of this chapter discussed bankruptcy prediction models. Similar streams of research relate to commercial bank lending,[25] bond ratings,[26] corporate restructurings,[27] corporate liquidations,[28] and earnings management.[29] Although the statistical models and relevant financial statement ratios vary among the numerous studies,

---

[22] Casey and Bartczak, *op. cit.*

[23] For a summary of this research, see Michael J. Gombola, Mark E. Haskins, J. Edward Ketz, and David D. Williams, "Cash Flow in Bankruptcy Prediction," *Financial Management* (Winter 1987), pp. 55–65.

[24] Joy Begley, Jin Ming, and Susan Watts, "Bankruptcy Classification Errors in the 1980s: An Empirical Analysis of Altman's and Ohlson's Models," *Review of Accounting Studies* 1, No. 4 (1996), pp. 267–284.

[25] Edward Altman, *Corporate Financial Distress and Bankruptcy,* 2nd ed., (New York: John Wiley & Sons, 1993), pp. 245–266.

[26] George E. Pinches and Kent A. Mingo, "A Multivariate Analysis of Industrial Bond Ratings," *Journal of Finance* (March 1973), pp. 1–18.

[27] James E. Seward, "Corporate Restructuring and Reorganization" in *Handbook of Modern Finance,* ed. Dennis Logue, (New York: Warren, Gorham & Lamont, 1993), pp. E8–1 to E8–36.

[28] Cornelius J. Casey, Victor McGee, and Clyde P. Stickney, "Discriminating between Reorganized and Liquidated Firms in Bankruptcy," *Accounting Review* (April 1986), pp. 249–262.

[29] Messod D. Beneish, "Detecting GAAP Violation: Implications for Assessing Earnings Management among Firms with Extreme Financial Performance," *Journal of Accounting and Public Policy* (1997), pp. 271–309.

certain commonalities do appear. This section summarizes the factors that explain bankruptcy most consistently across various studies.

Investment Factors

The following two factors relate to the asset side of the balance sheet:

1. Relative Liquidity of a Firm's Assets. The probability of financial distress decreases as the relative liquidity of a firm's assets increases. Firms with relatively large proportions of current assets tend to experience less financial distress than firms with fixed assets or intangible assets as the dominant assets. Greater asset liquidity means that the firm has or will soon generate the necessary cash to meet creditors' claims. Note that the expected return from more liquid assets (for example, cash, marketable securities, and accounts receivable) is usually less (reflecting lower risk) than the expected return from fixed and intangible assets. Thus, firms must balance their mix of assets to obtain the desired return/risk profile. This chapter has described a number of ratios that analysts typically use to measure relative liquidity—cash/total assets, current assets/total assets, and net working capital/total assets; analysts use ratios such as fixed assets/total assets to measure relative illiquidity.

2. Rate of Asset Turnover. The returns from investment of funds in any asset are ultimately realized in cash. Firms acquire fixed assets or create intangibles to produce a salable product (inventory) or to create a desired service. Goods or services are often sold on account (accounts receivable) and later collected in cash. The faster assets turn over, the more quickly they generate cash. Thus, a retailer may have the same proportion of fixed assets to total assets as a manufacturing firm. The other assets of the retailer (that is, accounts receivable and inventories) likely turn over more quickly and thus are more liquid. Commonly used financial ratios for this factor are total assets turnover, accounts receivable turnover, and inventory turnover. The working capital turnover ratio [= sales/(current assets minus current liabilities)] and fixed assets turnover ratio (= sales/fixed assets) have not generally shown statistical significance in studies of financial distress.

Financing Factors

The following two factors relate to the liability side of the balance sheet:

1. Relative Proportion of Total Debt in the Capital Structure. Firms experience bankruptcy because they are unable to pay liabilities as they come due. The higher the proportion of total liabilities in the capital structure, the higher the probability that firms will experience bankruptcy. Firms with lower proportions of debt tend to have unused borrowing capacity that they can use in times of difficulty. Some measure of the proportion of debt in the capital structure appears in virtually all bankruptcy prediction models. Commonly used ratios include total liabilities/total assets and total liabilities/shareholders' equity.

2. Relative Proportion of Short-Term Debt in the Capital Structure. This factor has a similar rationale to that described previously except that the earlier maturity of short-term debt increases the risk of bankruptcy. Thus, considering only the financing side of the balance sheet, a retailer using extensive short-term bank and creditor financing will likely have a greater risk of bankruptcy than a manufacturer with a similar proportion of total liabilities but whose liabilities are primarily long-term debt. A commonly used ratio for this factor is current liabilities/total assets.

Operating Factors

The following two factors relate to the operating activities of a firm:

1. Relative Level of Profitability. Profitable firms ultimately generate positive cash flows. Also, compared to unprofitable firms, profitable firms are usually able to borrow funds more easily. Firms with low or negative profitability must often rely on available cash or additional borrowing to meet financial commitments as they come due. Research has demonstrated that most bankruptcies initiate with one or several consecutive years of poor operating performance. Firms with unused debt capacity can often borrow for a year or two until the operating difficulties reverse. A combination of weak profitability and high debt ratios usually triggers financial distress. Commonly used financial ratios for profitability are net income/assets, income before interest and taxes/assets, net income/sales, and cash flow from operations/assets. The second profitability measure (income before interest and taxes/assets) identifies profitability problems in the core input/output markets of a firm before debt service costs and income taxes are considered. The third measure (net income/sales) appears in bankruptcy distress prediction models because profit margin, not assets turnover, is usually the driving force behind return on assets. The fourth measure (cash flow from operations/assets) substitutes cash flow from operations for net income in measuring profitability on the premise that cash pays the bills, not earnings.

2. Variability of Operations. Firms that experience variability in their operations (for example, from cyclical sales patterns) exhibit a greater likelihood of bankruptcy than do firms with low variability. During the down times in the cycle, such firms often struggle to obtain financing to meet financial commitments and maintain operating levels. The risk of bankruptcy in these cases relates to the unknown length of the down portion of the cycle. For how many years can a firm hold on until the cycle reverses? Researchers typically use the change in sales or the change in net income from the previous year to measure variability, although a longer period seems more reasonable.

Other Possible Explanatory Variables

Three other factors examined in bankruptcy research warrant discussion.

1. Size. Studies of bankruptcy, particularly since the early 1980s, have increasingly identified size as an important explanatory variable. Larger firms generally have access to a wider range of financing sources and more flexibility to redeploy assets than do smaller firms. Until recently, larger firms experienced very low probabilities of bankruptcy. Most studies measure size using total assets.

2. Growth. Studies of bankruptcy often include some measure of growth (for example, growth in sales, assets, or net income) as a possible explanatory variable. The statistical significance of growth as an independent variable has varied considerably across studies. Therefore, it is difficult to conclude much about its relative importance. The mixed results may relate in part to ambiguity in how growth relates to bankruptcy. Rapidly growing firms often need external financing to cover cash shortfalls from operations and to permit acquisitions of fixed assets. These firms often display financial ratios typical of a firm in financial difficulty (that is, high debt ratios and weak profitability). Yet their growth potential provides access to capital that allows them to survive. Firms in the late maturity or early decline phase of their life cycle may experience slow (or negative) growth and display healthy financial ratios, but prospects are sufficiently poor that the probability of future financial difficulty is high.

3. Qualified Audit Opinion. Several studies have examined the information value of a qualified audit opinion in predicting bankruptcy. Hopwood, McKeown, and Mutchler compared the predictive accuracy of a qualified audit opinion versus models that include only financial ratios in predicting bankruptcy.[30] They found that the qualified audit opinion had similar predictive accuracy to that of the models based on financial ratios. This

---

[30] William Hopwood, James C. McKeown, and Jane F. Mutchler, "A Reexamination of Auditor versus Model Accuracy within the Context of the Going-Concern Opinion Decision," *Contemporary Accounting Research* (Spring 1994), pp. 409–431.

result is not surprising if auditors use bankruptcy prediction models in deciding whether to issue a qualified opinion. Chen and Church found that the negative stock price reaction at the time of a bankruptcy filing was less for firms that had previously had a qualified audit opinion than for firms that had only clean audit opinions, suggesting that the audit opinion had information content.[31]

Some Final Thoughts

Bankruptcy prediction research represents an effort to integrate traditional financial statement analysis with statistical modeling. This area of research evolved between the mid-1960s and mid-1980s from relatively simple univariate models to multivariate models. The models developed by Altman, Ohlson, and Zavgren rely on data that are decades old and are based on business activities and bankruptcy laws that differ from those currently encountered. Nevertheless, security analysts and academic researchers continue to use these models and they appear relatively robust despite the numerous limitations discussed previously.[32]

MARKET EQUITY BETA RISK

Firms face additional risks besides credit and bankruptcy risk. Recessions, inflation, changes in interest rates, foreign currency fluctuations, rising unemployment, and similar economic factors affect all firms, but in varying degrees depending on the nature of their operation. The investor in a firm's common stock must consider these dimensions of risk when making investment decisions. Economic theory teaches that differences in expected rates of return between investment alternatives should relate to differences in risk. Thus, we can turn to equity markets to obtain a broader measure of risk. Then we will relate this market measure of risk to financial statement information.

Studies of market rates of return have traditionally used the CAPM (capital asset pricing model). The research typically regresses the rate of returns on a particular firm's common shares [dividends plus (minus) capital gains (losses)/beginning-of-period share price] over some period of time on the excess of the returns of all common stocks over the risk-free rate. The regression takes the following form:

$$\begin{matrix}\text{Returns on Common Stock}\\ \text{of a Particular Firm}\end{matrix} = \begin{matrix}\text{Risk-Free}\\ \text{Interest Rate}\end{matrix} + \begin{matrix}\text{Market}\\ \text{Beta}\end{matrix} \times \begin{bmatrix}\begin{matrix}\text{Market}\\ \text{Return}\end{matrix} - \begin{matrix}\text{Risk-Free}\\ \text{Interest Rate}\end{matrix}\end{bmatrix} + \text{Error}$$

The beta coefficient measures the covariability of a firm's returns with the returns of a diversified portfolio of all shares traded on the market (in excess of the risk-free interest rate). Firms with a market beta of 1.0 experience covariability in returns equal to the average covariability of the stock market as a whole. Firms with a beta greater than 1.0 experience greater covariability than the average. Firms with a beta less than 1.0 experience less covariability than the average firm. A beta of 1.20 suggests 20 percent greater covariability. A beta of .80 suggests 20 percent less covariability.

---

[31] Kevin C. W. Chen and Bryan K. Church, "Going Concern Opinions and the Market's Reaction to Bankruptcy Filings," *Accounting Review* (January 1996), pp. 117–128.

[32] A recent study models bankruptcy prediction as an option pricing valuation using market values. The authors compare the prediction accuracy of this market-based model with the Altman and Ohlson models and find that their model has better prediction accuracy. However, using either the Altman or Ohlson model in addition to the option pricing model adds to the prediction accuracy. See Stephen A. Hillegeist, Donald P. Cram, Elizabeth K. Keating, and Kyle G. Lundstedt, "Assessing the Probability of Bankruptcy," *Review of Accounting Studies* (March 2004), pp. 5–34.

Beta is a measure of the *systematic* (or *nondiversifiable*) *risk* of the firm. The market, through the pricing of a firm's shares, rewards shareholders for bearing systematic risk. Elements of risk that are not systematic are referred to as nonsystematic risk. Nonsystematic risk factors include firm-specific risks such as product obsolescence; labor strike; loss of a product liability lawsuit; and damages from fire, weather, or natural disaster. By constructing a diversified portfolio of securities, the investor can eliminate the effects of nonsystematic risk on the returns to the portfolio as a whole. Thus, market pricing should provide no returns for the assumption of nonsystematic risk.

Studies of the determinants of market beta have identified the following three principal explanatory variables:[33]

1. Degree of operating leverage
2. Degree of financial leverage
3. Variability of sales

Each of these factors causes the earnings of a particular firm to vary over time.

Operating leverage refers to the extent of fixed operating costs in the cost structure. Costs such as depreciation and amortization do not vary with the level of sales. Other costs, such as insurance and executive and administrative salaries and benefits, may vary somewhat with the level of sales, but they remain relatively fixed for any particular period. The presence of fixed operating costs leads to variations in operating earnings as sales increase and decrease. Likewise, the presence of debt in the capital structure adds a fixed cost for interest and creates the potential for causing earnings to increase or decrease as sales vary.

The presence of these fixed costs does not necessarily lead to earnings fluctuations over time. A firm with stable or growing sales may be able to adjust the level of fixed assets and related financing (for example, through leasing) to the level of sales, in effect converting fixed costs into variable costs. Firms with high fixed costs from operating and financial leverage, such as electric utilities, historically have had a regulated form of monopoly power to price their services to cover costs regardless of demand. Such firms likewise have not experienced wide variations in earnings. Operating and financial leverage create variations in earnings when sales vary and firms cannot alter their level of fixed costs. Thus, we would expect capital-intensive firms in cyclical industries to experience wide variations in earnings over the business cycle.

Research has shown a link between changes in earnings and changes in stock prices.[34] Thus, operating leverage, financial leverage, and variability of sales should result in fluctuations in the market returns for a particular firm's common shares. The average returns for all firms in the market should reflect the average level of operating leverage, financial leverage, and sales variability of these firms. Therefore, the market beta for a particular firm reflects its degree of variability relative to the average firm. Chapters 11 and 14 discuss more fully the relation between financial statement information and market beta and the use of market beta in the valuation of firms.

---

[33] Robert S. Hamada, "The Effect of a Firm's Capital Structure on the Systematic Risk of Common Stocks," *Journal of Finance* (May 1972), pp. 435–452; Barr Rosenberg and Walt McKibben, "The Prediction of Systematic and Specific Risk in Common Stocks," *Journal of Financial and Quantitative Analysis* (March 1973), pp. 317–333; James M. Gahlon and James A. Gentry, "On the Relationship between Systematic Risk and Degrees of Operating and Financial Leverage," *Financial Management* (Summer 1982), pp. 15–23.

[34] Ray Ball and Philip Brown, "An Empirical Evaluation of Accounting Income Numbers," *Journal of Accounting Research* (Autumn 1968), pp. 159–178.

FINANCIAL REPORTING MANIPULATION RISK

Enron, Parmalat, WorldCom, Global Crossing, Ahold, Sunbeam, AIG, Fannie Mae, Tyco, Societe General, Allied Irish, Satyam, and other companies have been the subject of SEC and other government regulatory investigations and negative media coverage in recent years for allegedly preparing financial statements outside the limits of permissible accounting standards. The firms violated accounting standards in an effort to portray themselves in a more favorable light. As a consequence, because they cannot rely on misleading financial statements when assessing profitability and risk, analysts must be vigilant in order to gain comfort that financial statements are not misleading. This section explores the characteristics of firms accused of falsifying their financial statements and describes tools for assessing this type of risk.

At the outset, we need to recognize a distinction between earnings manipulation and earnings management. *Earnings manipulation,* which refers to reporting amounts outside the limits of U.S. GAAP or IFRS, is the subject of this section. *Earnings management* refers to choices made within the limits of U.S. GAAP or IFRS or may refer to actual operating decisions that affect reported earnings. Not all financial economists or accountants agree with this distinction between earnings manipulation and earnings management, but it is important to at least appreciate the continuum from innocuous attempts to window-dress earnings to flagrant disregard for financial reporting rules. Chapter 9 discusses less egregious forms of earnings management. The focus of this discussion is on the more flagrant violations of accounting standards and regulations promulgated by oversight bodies such as the FASB, IASB, and SEC.

Motivations for Earnings Manipulation

A firm might manipulate earnings for the following reasons:

1. To influence stock prices positively (or delay stock price declines) by meeting or beating the market's expectations for earnings
2. To increase management bonuses based on earnings or stock prices
3. To obtain debt financing at a lower cost by appearing more profitable or less risky
4. To avoid violation of debt covenants or influence the effects of other binding constraints from accounting-based contracts
5. To influence the outcomes of transactions that affect corporate control, such as proxy fights, takeovers, initial public offerings, seasoned equity offerings, and share repurchases
6. To avoid regulatory intervention or adverse political consequences

Empirical Research on Earnings Manipulation

Dechow, Sloan, and Sweeney[35] examined the governance characteristics of firms subject to accounting and auditing enforcement actions by the SEC. They found that such firms have weak corporate governance structures, including the absence of an audit committee within their board of directors, the appointment of the founder of the company as the CEO (chief executive officer), the appointment of the CEO as chairperson of the board, and the domination of the board by insiders (employees, consultants, or individuals otherwise closely associated with the firm). The SEC enforcement actions led to a 9 percent reduction in

[35] Patricia M. Dechow, Richard G. Sloan, and Amy P. Sweeney, "Causes and Consequences of Earnings Manipulation: An Analysis of Firms Subject to Enforcement Actions by the SEC," *Contemporary Accounting Research* (Spring 1996), pp. 1–36.

stock price on average, an increase in the bid-ask spread, less analyst consensus on earnings forecasts, and increased short interest, each of which likely increases the firm's cost of capital. Nevertheless, governance is neither a solution nor a well-defined concept. For example, the World Council for Corporate Governance awarded Satyam its Golden Peacock Award for Corporate Governance in 2008, shortly before it was uncovered in January 2009 that the company had perpetrated one of the largest financial reporting frauds in corporate history.

Given the importance of identifying financial reporting risk, Beneish developed a probit model to identify the financial characteristics of firms likely to engage in earnings manipulation. Beneish developed both a twelve-factor model[36] and an eight-factor model.[37] The twelve-factor model relies on a combination of financial statement items and changes in stock prices for a firm's shares. The eight-factor model uses only financial statement items. Beneish developed the models using data for firms subject to SEC enforcement actions related to fraudulent accounting reports.

Developing these models involves identifying characteristics of firms likely to manipulate earnings, selecting financial statement ratios or other measures of these characteristics, and then using probit regressions to select the significant factors and the appropriate coefficient for each factor (similar to the MDA and logit approaches for identifying predictors of bankruptcy, described earlier in this chapter). Applying the coefficient to the value of each factor for a particular firm yields a score that becomes the value of y.

Unlike logit models, which convert the value of y into a probability based on a logistical distribution using the somewhat nonintuitive metric, $\frac{1}{1 + e^{-y}}$, probit converts y into a probability using a standardized normal distribution and a specified prior probability of earnings manipulation. The command NORMSDIST in Excel, when applied to a particular value of y, converts it to the appropriate probability value.[38] Positive coefficients increase the probability of earnings manipulation.

Beneish's eight factors and the rationale for their inclusion are as follows:

1. ***Days Sales in Receivables Index (DSRI).*** This index relates the ratio of accounts receivable at the end of the current year as a percentage of sales for the current year to the corresponding amounts for the preceding year. A large increase in accounts receivable as a percentage of sales might indicate an overstatement of accounts receivable and sales during the current year to boost earnings. Such an increase also might result from a change in the firm's credit policy (for example, liberalizing credit terms).
2. ***Gross Margin Index (GMI).*** This index relates gross margin (that is, sales minus cost of goods sold) as a percentage of sales last year to the gross margin as a percentage of sales for the current year. A decline in the gross margin percentage will result in an index greater than 1.0. Firms with weaker profitability this year are more likely to engage in earnings manipulation.
3. ***Asset Quality Index (AQI).*** Asset quality refers to the proportion of total assets comprising assets other than (1) current assets; (2) property, plant, and equipment; and (3) investments in securities. The remaining assets include intangibles for which future

[36] Beneish, *op. cit.* For an instructional case applying this model to an actual company, see Christine I. Wiedman, "Instructional Case: Detecting Earnings Manipulation," *Issues in Accounting Education* (February 1999), pp. 145–176. Also see Messod D. Beneish, "A Note on Wiedman's (1999) Instructional Case: Detecting Earnings Manipulation," *Issues in Accounting Education* (May 1999), pp. 369–370.

[37] Messod D. Beneish, "The Detection of Earnings Manipulation," *Financial Analyst Journal* (September/October 1999), pp. 24–36.

[38] In contrast to Altman's Z-score model, Beneish set up his model so that larger positive values increase the probability of earnings manipulation. Thus, one can simply apply the normal density function directly to the value of y to compute the probability of earnings manipulation.

benefits are less certain than for current assets and property, plant, and equipment. The AQI equals the proportion of these potentially lower-quality assets during the current year relative to the preceding year. An increase in the proportion might suggest an increased effort to capitalize and defer costs the firm should have expensed.

4. ***Sales Growth Index (SGI).*** This index equals sales of the current year relative to sales of the preceding year. Growth does not necessarily imply manipulation. However, growing companies usually rely on external financing more than mature companies do. The need for low-cost external financing might motivate managers to manipulate sales and earnings. Growing companies are often young and tend to have less developed governance practices to monitor managers' manipulation efforts.
5. ***Depreciation Index (DEPI).*** This index equals depreciation expense as a percentage of net property, plant, and equipment before depreciation for the preceding year relative to the corresponding percentage for the current year. A ratio greater than 1.0 indicates that the firm has slowed the rate of depreciation, perhaps by lengthening depreciable lives, thereby increasing earnings.
6. ***Selling and Administrative Expense Index (SAI).*** This index equals selling and administrative expenses as a percentage of sales for the current year to the corresponding percentage for the preceding year. An index greater than 1.0 might suggest increased marketing expenditures that would lead to increased sales in future periods. Firms not able to sustain the sales growth might be induced to engage in earnings manipulation. An alternative interpretation is that an index greater than 1.0 suggests that the firm has not taken advantage of capitalizing various costs; instead, it has expensed them. Firms attempting to manipulate earnings would defer costs, and the index value would be less than 1.0. If this latter explanation is descriptive, the coefficient on this variable will be negative. Thus, the interpretation of this component of Beneish's fraud model is conditional.
7. ***Leverage Index (LVGI).*** This index equals the proportion of total financing comprising current liabilities and long-term debt for the current year relative to the proportion for the preceding year. An increase in the proportion of debt likely subjects a firm to a greater risk of violating debt covenants and the need to manipulate earnings to avoid the violation.
8. ***Total Accruals to Total Assets (TATA).*** Total accruals equals the difference between income from continuing operations and cash flow from operations. Dividing total accruals by total assets at the end of the year scales total accruals across firms and across time. Beneish used this variable as an indicator of the extent to which earnings result from accruals instead of from cash flows. A large excess of income from continuing operations over cash flow from operations indicates that accruals play a large part in measuring income. Accruals can serve as a means of manipulating earnings.

Beneish developed a weighted probit model that takes the proportion of earnings manipulations into account and an unweighted probit model. We illustrate the unweighted model in this section and FSAP uses the unweighted model to compute Beneish's Manipulation Index and the corresponding probabilities of earnings manipulation. The unweighted model tends to classify more nonmanipulating firms as manipulators (higher Type II error), but lowers the most costly Type I error rate. The value of y is as follows:

FSAP

$$y = -4.840 + 0.920\,(\text{DSRI}) + 0.528\,(\text{GMI}) + 0.404\,(\text{AQI}) + 0.892\,(\text{SGI}) + 0.115\,(\text{DEPI}) - 0.172\,(\text{SAI}) - 0.327\,(\text{LVGI}) + 4.670\,(\text{TATA})$$

The coefficient on SAI is negative, suggesting that a lower selling and administrative expense to sales percentage in the current year relative to the preceding year increases the likelihood that the firm engaged in earnings manipulation to boost earnings. The coefficient on the leverage variable also is negative. A decrease in the proportion of debt in the capital structure may suggest decreased ability to obtain funds from borrowing and the need to engage in earnings manipulation to portray a healthier firm. The coefficients on the SAI and LVGI variables were not statistically significant. However, one cannot interpret the sign or statistical significance of a coefficient in a multivariate model independent of the other variables in the model; so these factors must be included.

Application of Beneish's Model to Sunbeam Corporation

We illustrate the application of Beneish's probit model to the financial statements of Sunbeam Corporation (Sunbeam). Sunbeam manufactures countertop kitchen appliances and barbecue grills. Its sales growth and profitability slowed considerably in the mid-1990s, and the firm experienced market price declines for its common stock. The firm hired Al Dunlap in mid-1996 as CEO. Known as "Chainsaw Al," he had developed a reputation for dispassionately cutting costs and strategically redirecting troubled companies. Dunlap laid off half the workforce, closed or consolidated more than half of Sunbeam's factories, and divested several businesses in 1996 and 1997. He also announced major growth initiatives centering on new products and corporate acquisitions.

The reported results for 1997 showed significant improvement over 1996. Sales increased 18.7 percent while gross margin increased from 8.5 percent to 28.3 percent. The stock price more than doubled between the announcement of Dunlap's hiring in mid-1996 and the end of 1997.

The turnaround appeared to proceed according to plan until the firm announced earnings for the first quarter of 1998, seven quarters into the turnaround effort. To the surprise of analysts and the stock market, Sunbeam reported a net loss for the quarter. Close scrutiny by analysts and the media suggested that Sunbeam might have manipulated earnings in 1997. The SEC instituted a formal investigation into this possibility in mid-1997. Sunbeam responded in October 1998 by restating its financial statements from the fourth quarter of 1996 to the first quarter of 1998. The restatements revealed that Sunbeam had engaged in various actions that boosted earnings for 1997. The actions included the following:

- Sunbeam instituted "early buy" and "bill and hold" programs in 1997 to encourage retailers to purchase inventory from Sunbeam during the last few months of 1997. Sunbeam did not adequately provide for returns and canceled transactions, resulting in an overstatement of sales and net income for 1997.
- Sunbeam overstated a restructuring charge in the fourth quarter of 1996 for expenses that should have appeared in the income statement for 1997.
- Sunbeam understated bad debt expense for 1997.

Exhibit 5.14 shows the application of Beneish's earnings manipulation model to the originally reported financial statement amounts and the restated amounts for 1996 and 1997.[39]

Selecting the cutoff probability that signals earnings manipulation involves trade-offs between Type I and Type II errors, in a manner similar to that of Beaver's bankruptcy prediction tests discussed earlier. A Type I error involves failing to identify a firm as an income

[39] The website for this book (www.cengage.com/accounting/wahlen) contains an Excel spreadsheet called Beneish's Manipulation Index for use in calculating the probability of earnings manipulation using Beneish's probit model. This spreadsheet is adapted from one prepared by Professor Christine I. Wiedman (see Wiedman 1999, *op. cit.*). FSAP also computes Beneish's Manipulation Index and the corresponding probability of earnings manipulation.

EXHIBIT 5.14

Application of Beneish's Earnings Manipulation Model to Sunbeam Corporation

	Originally Reported		Restated	
Value of Variable before Applying Coefficient	**1996**	**1997**	**1996**	**1997**
Days in Receivables Index	1.020	1.167	1.020	0.982
Gross Margin Index	2.403	0.300	2.303	0.393
Asset Quality Index	0.912	0.928	0.912	0.919
Sales Growth Index	0.968	1.187	0.968	1.090
Depreciation Index	0.752	1.284	0.752	1.290
Selling and Administrative Expense Index	1.608	0.516	1.665	0.632
Leverage Index	1.457	0.795	1.457	0.917
Total Accruals/Total Assets	(0.196)	0.117	(0.208)	0.055
Beneish's Manipulation *y* Value	(2.983)	(1.827)	(3.101)	(2.388)
Probability of Manipulation	0.143%	3.386%	0.096%	0.848%

Note: The amounts in this table are rounded to three decimal places.

manipulator when it turns out to be one. A Type II error involves identifying a firm as an income manipulator when it turns out not to be one. The Type I error is more costly to the investor than a Type II error is. The cutoff probability depends on the analyst's view of the relative cost of the Type I error compared to a Type II error. That is, how much more costly is it to classify an actual earnings manipulator as a nonmanipulator than to classify an actual nonmanipulator as a manipulator? A Type I error can result in an investor losing *all* of the investment in a firm when the manipulation comes to light. In contrast, misclassifying an actual nonmanipulator results only in a forgone investment opportunity, the amount being the return that could have been earned had an investment been made in the firm. However, the investor presumably invested the funds in another firm. Thus, as with bankruptcy prediction, the Type I error is more costly. If a particular investment makes up a small proportion of an investor's diversified portfolio of investments, a Type I error is less costly than if the investment comprises a more significant proportion of a less diversified portfolio of investments. The cutoff probabilities for various relative mixtures of Type I and Type II error costs follow.

Cost of Type I Error Relative to Type II Error	Cutoff Probability
10:1	6.85%
20:1	3.76%
30:1	3.76%
40:1 or higher	2.94%

Exhibit 5.14 indicates that the probability of manipulation for Sunbeam for 1996 is 0.143 percent based on its originally reported amounts. This probability level falls well below the cutoff probabilities listed previously for all mixtures of Type I and Type II errors;

therefore, it does not suggest earnings manipulation. On the other hand, the probability for 1997 jumps to 3.386 percent. (See Exhibit 5.14.) Under the assumption of a 40:1 Type I to Type II cost relation, you would conclude that Sunbeam is a manipulator. An examination of changes in the individual variables between 1996 and 1997 signals the nature of the manipulation that might have occurred. TATA increased significantly. Sunbeam reported a significant increase in income from continuing operations from a net loss of $196.7 million in 1996 to a net profit of $123.1 million 1997, but cash flow from operations turned from $13.3 million in 1996 to a negative $8.2 million in 1997. Buildups of accounts receivable and inventories are major reasons for the negative cash flow from operations in 1997. The days receivable index increased between these two years, consistent with the buildup of receivables related to the early buy-and-bill and hold programs. The SGI also increased, consistent with the aggressive recognition of revenues. The depreciation index variable increased between the two years, but the firm's financial statements and notes provide no obvious explanation to suggest manipulation. The gross margin improved significantly between the two years, moderating the increased probability of earnings manipulation. However, this improvement is misleading because of failure to provide adequately for returns and canceled transactions.

Exhibit 5.14 indicates that the probabilities of manipulation based on the restated data are below the cutoff points for 1996 and 1997. The most important difference between the reported and restated probabilities arises for 1997. The downward restatement of income from continuing operations results in fewer accruals, moderating the influence of this variable on the manipulation index. Interestingly, the model would not indicate that Sunbeam was an earnings manipulator if it had reported accurately to begin with (that is, reported the restated data). Initially reporting the restated data, however, would likely have decreased Sunbeam's stock price, which Dunlap presumably wanted to avoid.

Summary of Earnings Manipulation Risk

The recent revelations of corporate reporting abuses add to the importance of assessing whether firms have intentionally manipulated earnings. Academic research on earnings manipulation is at an early stage of development. The data in the studies discussed previously deal with reporting violations prior to the mid-1990s. The business environment since that time has changed dramatically, particularly for technology-based companies. Additional research in this area might be expected in coming years. Also, the analyst should note that the assessment of earnings manipulation risk is not restricted to the construction of financial ratios. Also relevant are qualitative factors that might change the incentives of managers to incur the potential costs of manipulating earnings, such as an increase in compensation based on stock options, an expectation of growth, or extensive related party transactions.

SUMMARY

An effective analysis of risk requires the analyst to consider a wide range of factors (for example, government regulatory status, industry competition, technological change, management's health, competitors' actions, profitability, and financial reporting risk). This chapter examines those dimensions of risk that have financial consequences and impact the financial statements.

This chapter began with a discussion of financial flexibility, which is an extension of profitability analysis, but with an emphasis on partitioning the firm's financial statements into operating and financing components. With an understanding of how leverage can be strategically used to increase returns available to shareholders, we then examined the analysis of financial risk associated with the use of leverage along the following four dimensions:

1. *With respect to time frame:* We examined the analysis of a firm's ability to pay liabilities coming due the next year (short-term liquidity risk analysis) and its ability to pay liabilities coming due over a longer term (long-term solvency risk analysis). The financial ratios examined a firm's need for cash and other liquid resources relative to amounts coming due within various time frames.
2. *With respect to the degree of financial distress:* We emphasized the need to consider risk as falling along a continuum from low risk to high risk of financial distress. Firms with a great deal of financial flexibility fall on the low side of this continuum. Most credit analysis occurs on the low- to medium-risk side of this continuum. Most bankruptcy risk analysis occurs on the medium- to high-risk side of this continuum.
3. *With respect to covariability of returns with other securities in the market:* We briefly highlighted the use of market equity beta as an indicator of systematic risk with the market, which is affected by the types of risk analyzed in this chapter.
4. *With respect to financial reporting:* We described various motives that induce managers to manipulate and report earnings numbers and other accounting data outside the bounds of GAAP and illustrated a model that estimates the likelihood of financial reporting manipulation.

Analysts and academic researchers refer to the first two dimensions of risk as nonsystematic, or firm-specific, risk. They refer to the third dimension of risk as systematic risk. They sometimes refer to the fourth dimension of risk as information risk. Common factors come into play in all four settings of risk analysis. Fixed costs related to operations or to financing constrain the flexibility of a firm to adapt to changing economic, business, and firm-specific conditions. The profitability and cash-generating ability of a firm allow it to operate within its constraints or to change the constraints in some desirable direction. If the constraints are too high or the capabilities to adapt are too low, a firm faces the risk of financial distress. Firms facing potential financial distress are more likely to manipulate earnings and accounting information.

QUESTIONS, EXERCISES, PROBLEMS, AND CASES

Questions and Exercises

5.1 INTERPRETING THE ALTERNATIVE DECOMPOSITION OF ROCE WITH NEGATIVE NET FINANCIAL OBLIGATIONS. Suppose an analyst reformulates financial statements to prepare the alternative decomposition of ROCE for a firm with no debt. The analyst determines that the company holds excess cash as large marketable equity securities. The result will be net financial obligations that are negative. Assume that operating ROA is positive and large. How will this affect the decomposition of ROCE = Operating ROA + (Leverage × Spread)? How do you interpret the net borrowing rate for this firm?

5.2 RELATION BETWEEN CURRENT RATIO AND OPERATING CASH FLOW TO CURRENT LIABILITIES RATIO. A firm has experienced an increasing current ratio but a decreasing operating cash flow to current liabilities ratio during the last three years. What is the likely explanation for these results?

5.3 RELATION BETWEEN CURRENT RATIO AND QUICK RATIO. A firm has experienced a decrease in its current ratio but an increase in its quick ratio during the last three years. What is the likely explanation for these results?

5.4 RELATION BETWEEN WORKING CAPITAL TURNOVER RATIOS AND CASH FLOW FROM OPERATIONS. While a firm's sales and net income have been steady during the last three years, the firm has experienced a decrease in its accounts receivable and inventory turnovers and an increase in its accounts payable turnover. What is the likely direction of change in cash flow from operations? How would your answer be different if sales and net income were increasing?

5.5 EFFECT OF TRANSACTIONS ON DEBT RATIOS. A firm had the following values for the four debt ratios discussed in the chapter:

Liabilities to Assets Ratio: less than 1.0
Liabilities to Shareholders' Equity Ratio: equal to 1.0
Long-Term Debt to Long-Term Capital Ratio: less than 1.0
Long-Term Debt to Shareholders' Equity Ratio: less than 1.0

a. Indicate whether each of the following independent transactions increases, decreases, or has no effect on each of the four debt ratios.
   (1) The firm issued long-term debt for cash.
   (2) The firm issued short-term debt and used the cash proceeds to redeem long-term debt (treat as a unified transaction).
   (3) The firm redeemed short-term debt with cash.
   (4) The firm issued long-term debt and used the cash proceeds to repurchase shares of its common stock (treat as a unified transaction).

b. The text states that analyst need not compute all four debt ratios each year because the debt ratios are highly correlated. Does your analysis in Part a support this statement? Explain.

5.6 INTEREST COVERAGE RATIO AS A MEASURE OF LONG-TERM SOLVENCY RISK. Identify the assumptions underlying the interest coverage ratio needed to make it an appropriate measure for analyzing long-term solvency risk.

5.7 INTEREST COVERAGE RATIO AS A MEASURE OF SHORT-TERM LIQUIDITY RISK. In what sense is the interest coverage ratio more a measure for assessing short-term liquidity risk than it is a measure for assessing long-term solvency risk?

5.8 INTERPRETING OPERATING CASH FLOW TO CURRENT AND TOTAL LIABILITIES RATIOS. Empirical research cited in the text indicates that firms with an operating cash flow to current liabilities ratio exceeding 0.40 portray low short-term liquidity risk. Similarly, firms with an operating cash flow to total liabilities ratio exceeding 20 percent portray low long-term solvency risk. What do these empirical results suggest about the mix of current and noncurrent liabilities for a financially healthy firm? What do they suggest about the mix of liabilities versus shareholders' equity financing?

5.9 INTERPRETING ALTMAN'S Z-SCORE BANKRUPTCY PREDICTION MODEL. Altman's bankruptcy prediction model places a coefficient of 3.3 on the earnings before interest and taxes divided by total assets variable but a coefficient of only 1.0 on the sales to total assets variable. Does this mean that the earnings variable is 3.3 times as important in predicting bankruptcy as the asset turnover variable? Explain.

5.10 MARKET EQUITY BETA IN RELATION TO SYSTEMATIC AND NONSYSTEMATIC RISK. Market equity beta measures the covariability of a firm's returns with all shares traded on the market (in excess of the risk-free interest rate). We refer to the degree of covariability as systematic risk. The market prices securities so that the expected returns should compensate the investor for the systematic risk of a particular stock. Stocks carrying a market equity beta of 1.20 should generate a higher return than stocks carrying a market equity beta of 0.90. Nonsystematic risk is any source of risk that does not affect the covariability of a firm's returns with the market. Some writers refer to nonsystematic risk as firm-specific risk. Why is the characterization of nonsystematic risk as firm-specific risk a misnomer?

5.11 COMPARISON OF ALTMAN'S BANKRUPTCY PREDICTION MODEL AND BENEISH'S EARNINGS MANIPULATION RISK MODEL. Altman's bankruptcy risk model utilizes the values of the variables at a particular point in time (balance sheet variables) or for a period of time (income statement values). For the most part, Beneish's earnings manipulation risk model utilizes changes in variables from one period to the next. Why might the levels of values in Altman's model be more appropriate for predicting bankruptcy and changes in values in Beneish's model be more appropriate for identifying earnings manipulation?

Problems and Cases

5.12 CALCULATING AND INTERPRETING RISK RATIOS. Refer to the financial statement data for Hasbro in Problem 4.23 in Chapter 4. Exhibit 5.15 presents risk ratios for Hasbro for Year 2 and Year 3.

EXHIBIT 5.15

Risk Ratios for Hasbro
(Problem 5.12)

	Year 4	Year 3	Year 2
Revenues to Cash Ratio		6.2	7.7
Days Revenues Held in Cash		59	47
Current Ratio		1.6	1.5
Quick Ratio		1.2	1.1
Operating Cash Flow to Average Current Liabilities Ratio		0.479	0.548
Days Accounts Receivable		68	73
Days Inventory		51	68
Days Accounts Payable		47	49
Net Days Working Capital		72	91
Liabilities to Assets Ratio		0.556	0.621
Liabilities to Shareholders' Equity Ratio		1.251	1.639
Long-Term Debt to Long-Term Capital Ratio		0.328	0.418
Long-Term Debt to Shareholders' Equity Ratio		0.489	0.720
Operating Cash Flow to Total Liabilities Ratio		0.245	0.238
Interest Coverage Ratio		5.6	2.3

Required

a. Calculate the amounts of these ratios for Year 4.
b. Assess the changes in the short-term liquidity risk of Hasbro between Year 2 and Year 4 and the level of that risk at the end of Year 4.
c. Assess the changes in the long-term solvency risk of Hasbro between Year 2 and Year 4 and the level of that risk at the end of Year 4.

5.13 CALCULATING AND INTERPRETING RISK RATIOS. Refer to the financial statement data for Abercrombie & Fitch in Problem 4.24 in Chapter 4. Exhibit 5.16 presents risk ratios for Abercrombie & Fitch for fiscal Year 3 and Year 4.

Required

a. Compute the amounts of these ratios for fiscal Year 5.
b. Assess the changes in the short-term liquidity risk of Abercrombie & Fitch between fiscal Year 3 and fiscal Year 5 and the level of that risk at the end of fiscal Year 5.
c. Assess the changes in the long-term solvency risk of Abercrombie & Fitch between fiscal Year 3 and fiscal Year 5 and the level of that risk at the end of fiscal Year 5.

EXHIBIT 5.16

Risk Ratios for Abercrombie & Fitch
(Problem 5.13)

	Year 5	Year 4	Year 3
Revenues to Cash Ratio		34.5	13.8
Days Revenues in Cash		11	26
Current Ratio		2.4	2.3
Quick Ratio		1.7	1.6
Operating Cash Flow to Current Liabilities Ratio		1.177	1.587
Days Accounts Receivable		2	4
Days Inventory		72	61
Days Accounts Payable		26	22
Net Days Working Capital		48	43
Liabilities to Assets Ratio		0.591	0.592
Liabilities to Shareholders' Equity Ratio		1.443	1.448
Long-Term Debt to Long-Term Capital Ratio		0.454	0.461
Long-Term Debt to Shareholders' Equity Ratio		0.831	0.855
Operating Cash Flow to Total Liabilities Ratio		0.298	0.380
Interest Coverage Ratio		7.2	7.6

5.14 INTERPRETING RISK RATIOS. Refer to the profitability ratios of Coca-Cola in Problem 4.25 in Chapter 4. Exhibit 5.17 presents risk ratios for Coca-Cola for 2006-2008. As we did within the chapter for PepsiCo, we utilize Coca-Cola's footnote disclosures

EXHIBIT 5.17

Risk Ratios for Coca-Cola
(Problem 5.14)

	2008	2007	2006
Revenues to Cash Ratio	6.9	8.4	6.5
Days Revenues in Cash	53	44	56
Current Ratio	0.9	0.9	0.9
Quick Ratio	0.6	0.6	0.6
Operating Cash Flow to Average Current Liabilities Ratio	0.578	0.647	0.636
Days Accounts Receivable	37	37	37
Days Inventory	71	68	68
Days Accounts Payable	44	38	40
Net Days Working Capital	64	67	65
Liabilities to Assets Ratio	0.495	0.497	0.435
Liabilities to Shareholders' Equity Ratio	0.979	0.990	0.771
Long-Term Debt to Long-Term Capital Ratio	0.120	0.131	0.072
Long-Term Debt to Shareholders' Equity Ratio	0.136	0.151	0.078
Operating Cash Flow to Average Total Liabilities Ratio	0.364	0.414	0.456
Interest Coverage Ratio	17.0	17.3	29.9

to extract the amount of trade accounts payable included within the line item accounts payable and accrued expenses.

Required

a. Assess the changes in the short-term liquidity risk of Coca-Cola between 2006 and 2008.

b. Assess the changes in the long-term solvency risk of Coca-Cola between 2006 and 2008.

c. Compare the short-term liquidity ratios of Coca-Cola with those of PepsiCo discussed in the chapter. Which firm appears to have more short-term liquidity risk? Explain.

d. Compare the long-term solvency ratios of Coca-Cola with those of PepsiCo discussed in the chapter. Which firm appears to have more long-term solvency risk? Explain.

5.15 COMPUTING AND INTERPRETING RISK AND BANKRUPTCY PREDICTION RATIOS FOR A FIRM THAT DECLARED BANKRUPTCY. Delta Air Lines is one of the largest airlines in the United States. It has operated on the verge of bankruptcy for several years. Exhibit 5.18 presents selected financial data for Delta Air Lines for each of the five years ending December 31, 2000, to December 31, 2004. Delta Air Lines filed for bankruptcy on September 14, 2005. We recommend that you create an Excel spreadsheet to compute the values of the ratios and the Altman's Z-score in Parts a and b, respectively.

EXHIBIT 5.18

Financial Data for Delta Air Lines
(amounts in millions except per share amounts)
(Problem 5.15)

Year Ended December 31:	2004	2003	2002	2001	2000
Sales	$15,002	$14,087	$13,866	$13,879	$15,657
Net Income (Loss) before Interest and Taxes	$(3,168)	$ (432)	$(1,337)	$(1,365)	$ 1,829
Interest Expense	$ 824	$ 757	$ 665	$ 499	$ 380
Net Income (Loss)	$(5,198)	$ (773)	$(1,272)	$(1,216)	$ 828
Current Assets	$ 3,606	$ 4,550	$ 3,902	$ 3,567	$ 3,205
Total Assets	$21,801	$25,939	$24,720	$23,605	$21,931
Current Liabilities	$ 5,941	$ 6,157	$ 6,455	$ 6,403	$ 5,245
Long-Term Debt	$12,507	$11,040	$ 9,576	$ 7,781	$ 5,797
Total Liabilities	$27,320	$26,323	$23,563	$19,581	$16,354
Retained Earnings (Deficit)	$(4,373)	$ 844	$ 1,639	$ 2,930	$ 4,176
Shareholders' Equity	$(5,519)	$ (384)	$ 1,157	$ 4,024	$ 5,577
Cash Flow Provided by Operations	$(1,123)	$ 142	$ 225	$ 236	$ 2,898
Common Shares Outstanding	139.8	123.5	123.4	123.2	123.0
Market Price per Share	$ 7.48	$ 11.81	$ 12.10	$ 29.26	$ 50.18

Required

a. Compute the value of each the following risk ratios.
   (1) Current Ratio (at the end of 2000–2004)
   (2) Operating Cash Flow to Current Liabilities Ratio (for 2001–2004)
   (3) Liabilities to Assets Ratio (at the end of 2000–2004)
   (4) Long-Term Debt to Long-Term Capital Ratio (at the end of 2000–2004)
   (5) Operating Cash Flow to Total Liabilities Ratio (for 2001–2004)
   (6) Interest Coverage Ratio (for 2000–2004)

b. Compute the value of Altman's Z-score for Delta Air Lines for each year from 2000–2004.

c. Using the analyses in Parts a and b, discuss the most important factors that signaled the likelihood of bankruptcy of Delta Air Lines in 2005.

5.16 COMPUTING AND INTERPRETING RISK AND BANKRUPTCY PREDICTION RATIOS FOR A FIRM THAT WAS ACQUIRED. Sun Microsystems develops, manufactures, and sells computers for network systems. Exhibit 5.19 presents selected financial data for Sun Microsystems for each of the five years ending June 30, 2005, to June 30, 2009. The company did not go bankrupt, but instead was acquired in 2010 by Oracle. We recommend that you create an Excel spreadsheet to compute the values of the ratios and the Altman's Z-score in Parts a and b, respectively.

EXHIBIT 5.19

Financial Data for Sun Microsystems
(amounts in millions except per share amounts)
(Problem 5.16)

Year Ended June 30:	2009	2008	2007	2006	2005
Sales	$11,449	$13,880	$13,873	$13,086	$11,070
Net Income (Loss) before Interest and Taxes	$(2,166)	$ 640	$ 622	$ (620)	$ (150)
Interest Expense	$ 17	$ 30	$ 39	$ 55	$ 34
Net Income (Loss)	$(2,234)	$ 403	$ 473	$ (864)	$ (107)
Current Assets	$ 6,864	$ 7,834	$ 9,328	$ 8,460	$ 7,191
Total Assets	$11,232	$14,340	$15,838	$15,082	$14,190
Current Liabilities	$ 5,621	$ 5,668	$ 5,451	$ 6,165	$ 4,766
Long-Term Debt	$ 695	$ 1,265	$ 1,264	$ 575	$ 1,123
Total Liabilities	$ 7,927	$ 8,752	$ 8,659	$ 8,738	$ 7,516
Retained Earnings	$(2,055)	$ 430	$ 189	$ (257)	$ 1,387
Shareholders' Equity	$ 3,305	$ 5,588	$ 7,179	$ 6,344	$ 6,674
Cash Flow Provided by Operations	$ 457	$ 1,329	$ 958	$ 567	$ 279
Common Shares Outstanding	752	752	884	876	$ 852
Market Price per Share	$ 9.22	$ 10.88	$ 20.76	$ 16.60	$ 14.92

Required

a. Compute the value of each of the following risk ratios.
  (1) Current Ratio (at the end of 2005–2009)
  (2) Operating Cash Flow to Current Liabilities Ratio (for 2006–2009)
  (3) Liabilities to Assets Ratio (at the end of 2005–2009)
  (4) Long-Term Debt to Long-Term Capital Ratio (at the end of 2005–2009)
  (5) Operating Cash Flow to Total Liabilities Ratio (for 2006–2009)
  (6) Interest Coverage Ratio (for 2005–2009)

b. Compute the value of Altman's Z-score for Sun Microsystems for each year from 2005–2009.

c. Using the analyses in Parts a and b, discuss the most important factors that signal the likelihood of bankruptcy of Sun Microsystems in 2010.

5.17 COMPUTING AND INTERPRETING BANKRUPTCY PREDICTION RATIOS. Exhibit 5.20 presents selected financial data for Best Buy and Circuit City for fiscal 2008 and 2007. Best Buy and Circuit City operate as specialty retailers offering a wide range of consumer electronics, service contracts, product repairs, and home installation. Competition from Walmart, Costco, and Internet retailers has put downward pressure on prices and margins. In November 2008, Circuit City filed Chapter 7 bankruptcy. In the media, Circuit City's bankruptcy is largely blamed on its poor treatment of employees. In early 2007, Circuit City laid off 3,400 high-paid salespersons, or approximately 8 percent of its workforce, which left inexperienced, low-paid workers in charge of customer service. Customer service plummeted, which was especially harmful for the

EXHIBIT 5.20

Financial Data for Best Buy and Circuit City
(amounts in thousands except per share amounts)
(Problem 5.17)

	Best Buy		Circuit City	
	Year-End 3/1		Year-End 2/28	
	2008	2007	2008	2007
Sales	$40,023	$35,934	$11,744	$12,430
Net Income (Loss) before Interest and Taxes	$ 2,290	$ 2,161	$ (352)	$ 22
Net Income (Loss)	$ 1,407	$ 1,377	$ (321)	$ (10)
Current Assets	$ 7,342	$ 9,081	$ 2,440	$ 2,884
Total Assets	$12,758	$13,570	$ 3,746	$ 4,007
Current Liabilities	$ 6,769	$ 6,301	$ 1,606	$ 1,714
Total Liabilities	$ 8,274	$ 7,369	$ 2,243	$ 2,216
Retained Earnings	$ 3,933	$ 5,507	$ 981	$ 1,336
Common Shares Outstanding	411	481	169	171
Market Price per Share	$ 42.00	$ 44.97	$ 4.38	$ 18.47

company that previously provided higher levels of customer satisfaction for their expensive electronic items, warranty products, and installation services.

Required

a. Compute Altman's Z-score for Best Buy and Circuit City for 2007 and 2008.
b. How did the bankruptcy risk of Best Buy change between 2007 and 2008? Explain.
c. How did the bankruptcy risk of Circuit City change between 2007 and 2008? Explain.
d. As noted, Circuit City filed Chapter 7 bankruptcy in November 2008. Using the analysis from Parts b and c, would you have predicted Circuit City or Best Buy to file bankruptcy in 2008? Explain.

5.18 APPLYING AND INTERPRETING BANKRUPTCY PREDICTION MODELS. Exhibit 5.21 presents selected financial data for Harvard Industries and Marvel Entertainment for fiscal Year 5 and Year 6. Harvard Industries manufactures automobile components that it sells to automobile manufacturers. Competitive conditions in the automobile industry in recent years have led automobile manufacturers to put pressure on suppliers such as Harvard Industries to reduce costs and selling prices. Marvel Entertainment creates and sells comic books, trading cards, and other youth entertainment products and licenses others to use fictional characters created by Marvel Entertainment in their products. Youth readership of comic books and interest in trading cards have been declining steadily in recent years. Marvel Entertainment recognized a significant asset impairment charge in fiscal Year 6.

Required

a. Compute Altman's Z-score for Harvard Industries and Marvel Entertainment for fiscal Year 5 and Year 6.

EXHIBIT 5.21

Financial Data for Harvard Industries and Marvel Entertainment
(amounts in thousands except per share amounts)
(Problem 5.18)

	Harvard Industries		Marvel Entertainment	
	Year 6	Year 5	Year 6	Year 5
Sales	$ 824,835	$ 631,832	$ 745,400	$ 828,900
Net Income (Loss) before Interest and Taxes	$ (11,012)	$ 40,258	$(370,200)	$ 25,100
Net Income (Loss)	$ (68,712)	$ 6,921	$(464,400)	$ (48,400)
Current Assets	$ 156,226	$ 195,417	$ 399,500	$ 490,600
Total Assets	$ 617,705	$ 662,262	$ 844,000	$1,226,310
Current Liabilities	$ 163,384	$ 176,000	$ 345,800	$ 318,100
Total Liabilities	$ 648,934	$ 624,817	$ 999,700	$ 948,100
Retained Earnings	$(184,308)	$(115,596)	$(350,300)	$ 114,100
Common Shares Outstanding	7,014	6,995	101,810	101,703
Market Price per Share	$ 85.00	$ 100.50	$ 1.625	$ 10.625

b. How did the bankruptcy risk of Harvard Industries change between fiscal Year 5 and Year 6? Explain.

c. How did the bankruptcy risk of Marvel Entertainment change between Year 5 and Year 6? Explain.

d. Which firm is more likely to file for bankruptcy during fiscal Year 7? Explain using the analyses from Part b.

5.19 APPLYING AND INTERPRETING BANKRUPTCY PREDICTION MODELS. Exhibit 5.22 presents selected financial data for Tribune Company and Washington Post for fiscal 2006 and 2007. The Washington Post Company is an education and media company. It owns, among others, Kaplan, Inc.; Cable ONE Inc.; *Newsweek* magazine; and Washington Post Media. The Tribune Company is a media and entertainment company, which also is diversified, owning the *Chicago Tribune*, the *Los Angeles Times*, television and radio affiliates such as The CW Network and WGN, and the Chicago Cubs. The Tribune Company filed for bankruptcy in December 2008.

Required

a. Compute Altman's Z-score for Tribune Company and Washington Post for fiscal 2006 and 2007.

b. How did the bankruptcy risk of Tribune Company change between fiscal 2006 and 2007? Explain.

c. How did the bankruptcy risk of Washington Post change between fiscal 2006 and 2007? Explain.

d. The Tribune Company filed Chapter 7 bankruptcy in December 2008. Using the analysis from Parts b and c, would you have predicted the Tribune Company or the Washington Post Company to file bankruptcy? Explain.

EXHIBIT 5.22

Financial Data for Tribune Company and Washington Post
(amounts in millions except per share amounts)
(Problem 5.19)

	Tribune Company		Washington Post	
	2007	2006	2007	2006
Sales	$ 5,063	$ 5,444	$ 4,180	$ 3,905
Net Income (Loss) before Interest and Taxes	$ 619	$ 1,085	$ 505	$ 544
Net Income (Loss)	$ 87	$ 594	$ 289	$ 324
Current Assets	$ 1,385	$ 1,346	$ 995	$ 935
Total Assets	$13,150	$13,401	$ 6,005	$ 5,381
Current Liabilities	$ 2,190	$ 2,549	$ 1,013	$ 812
Total Liabilities	$16,664	$ 9,081	$ 2,543	$ 2,222
Retained Earnings (Deficit)	$(3,474)	$ 3,138	$ 4,330	$ 4,120
Common Shares Outstanding	239	307	10	10
Market Price per Share	$ 45.04	$ 58.69	$759.25	$711.53

EXHIBIT 5.23

Financial Statement Data for Enron Corporation
(amounts in millions)
(Problem 5.20)

	2000	1999	1998	1997
Accounts Receivable	$ 10,396	$ 3,030	$ 2,060	$ 1,697
Current Assets	30,381	7,255	5,933	4,669
Property, Plant, and Equipment, net	11,743	10,681	10,657	9,170
Total Assets	65,503	33,381	29,350	23,422
Current Liabilities	28,406	6,759	6,107	4,412
Long-Term Debt	8,550	7,151	7,357	6,254
Sales	100,789	40,112	31,260	20,273
Cost of Goods Sold	94,517	34,761	26,381	17,311
Selling and Administrative Expenses	3,184	3,045	2,473	1,406
Income from Continuing Operations	979	1,024	703	105
Cash Flow from Operations	4,779	1,228	1,640	501
Depreciation Expense	485	565	563	480

5.20 APPLYING AND INTERPRETING THE EARNINGS MANIPULATION MODEL. Exhibit 5.23 presents selected financial statement data for Enron Corporation for 1997, 1998, 1999, and 2000. These data reflect amounts from the financial statements as originally reported for each year. In 2001, Enron restated its financial statements for earlier years because it reported several items beyond the limits of GAAP.

Required

a. Use Beneish's earnings manipulation model to compute the probability that Enron engaged in earnings manipulation for 1998, 1999, and 2000.

b. Identify the major reasons for the changes in the probability of earnings manipulation during the three-year period.

5.21 REFORMULATING FINANCIAL STATEMENTS, PREPARING AN ALTERNATIVE DECOMPOSITION OF ROCE, AND ASSESSING FINANCIAL FLEXIBILITY. Exhibit 5.24 presents balance sheets for 2007 and 2008 for Whole Foods; Exhibit 5.25 presents income statements for 2006–2008.

Required

a. Prepare the standard Dupont decomposition of ROCE. Use average balances for balance sheet amounts.

b. Assume that all cash is operating cash (that is, no excess cash). Also assume that deferred lease liabilities are operating. Prepare the alternative decomposition of ROCE by computing NOPAT, Net Financing Expense (after tax), Operating Profit

EXHIBIT 5.24

Balance Sheets for Whole Foods
(amounts in thousands)
(Problem 5.21)

	2008	2007
ASSETS		
Cash and cash equivalents	$ 31,151	$ 2,310
Accounts receivable and other receivables	115,424	270,263
Merchandise inventories	327,452	288,112
Prepaid expenses and other current assets	68,150	40,402
Deferred income taxes	80,429	66,899
Total Current Assets	$ 622,606	$ 667,986
Property and equipment, net of accumulated depreciation and amortization	1, 900,117	1, 666,559
Goodwill	659,559	668,850
Intangible assets, net of accumulated amortization	78,499	97,683
Deferred income taxes	109,002	104,877
Other assets	10,953	7,173
Total Assets	$3,380,736	$3,213,128
LIABILITIES AND SHAREHOLDERS' EQUITY		
Current installments of long-term debt and capital lease obligations	$ 380	$ 24,781
Accounts payable	183,134	225,728
Accrued payroll, bonus and other benefits due team members	196,233	181,290
Other current liabilities	286,430	340,551
Total Current Liabilities	$ 666,177	$ 772,350

(Continued)

EXHIBIT 5.24 (Continued)

	2008	2007
Long-term debt and capital lease obligations, less current installments	$ 928,790	$ 736,087
Deferred lease liabilities	199,635	152,552
Other long-term liabilities	80,110	93,335
Total Liabilities	$1,874,712	$1,754,324
Common stock, no par value, 300,000 shares authorized; 140,286 and 143,787 shares issued, 140,286 and 139,240 shares outstanding in 2008 and 2007, respectively	$1,066,180	$1,232,845
Common stock in treasury, at cost	—	(199,961)
Accumulated other comprehensive income	422	15,722
Retained earnings	439,422	410,198
Total Shareholders' Equity	$1,506,024	$1,458,804
Total Liabilities and Shareholders' Equity	$3,380,736	$3,213,128

EXHIBIT 5.25

Income Statements for Whole Foods
(amounts in thousands)
(Problem 5.21)

	2008	2007	2006
Sales	$7,953,912	$6,591,773	$5,607,376
Cost of goods sold and occupancy costs	5,247,207	4,295,170	3,647,734
Gross Profit	$2,706,705	$2,296,603	$1,959,642
Direct store expenses	2,107,940	1,711,229	1,421,968
General and administrative expenses	270,428	217,743	181,244
Pre-opening expenses	55,554	59,319	32,058
Relocation, store closure and lease termination	36,545	10,861	5,363
Operating Income	$ 236,238	$ 297,451	$ 319,009
Interest expense	(36,416)	(4,208)	(32)
Investment and other income	6,697	11,324	20,736
Income before income taxes	$ 206,519	$ 304,567	$ 339,713
Provision for income taxes	91,995	121,827	135,885
Net Income	$ 114,524	$ 182,740	$ 203,828

Margin, Net Operating Assets Turnover, Operating ROA, Leverage, and Spread for 2008. Use average balances for balance sheet amounts.

c. Use the same assumptions as in Part b, except that all cash is a financing asset (that is, all cash is excess cash) and deferred lease liabilities are a financing obligation. Prepare the alternative decomposition of ROCE by computing NOPAT, Net Financing Expense (after tax), Operating Profit Margin, Net Operating Assets Turnover, Operating ROA, Leverage, and Spread for 2008. Use average balances for balance sheet amounts.

d. Does the different treatment of financial assets and liabilities affect inferences you draw from the decomposition of ROCE? Explain.

INTEGRATIVE CASE 5.1

STARBUCKS

Exhibit 5.26 presents risk ratios for Starbucks for 2006 and 2007. Exhibits 1.26, 1.27, and 1.28 in Chapter 1 present the financial statements for Starbucks.

EXHIBIT 5.26

Risk Ratios for Starbucks
(Integrative Case 5.1)

	2008	2007	2006
Revenues to Cash Ratio		31.7	32.0
Days Revenues Held in Cash		11.5	11.4
Current Ratio		0.79	0.79
Quick Ratio		0.34	0.35
Operating Cash Flow to Average Current Liabilities Ratio		65.1%	71.6%
Days Accounts Receivable		66	63
Days Inventory		61	68
Days Accounts Payable		33	31
Net Days Working Capital		94	100
Liabilities to Assets Ratio		0.573	0.497
Liabilities to Shareholders' Equity Ratio		1.340	0.987
Long-Term Debt to Long-Term Capital Ratio		0.194	0.001
Long-Term Debt to Shareholders' Equity Ratio		0.241	0.001
Operating Cash Flow to Average Total Liabilities Ratio		0.506	0.625
Interest Coverage Ratio		28.7	106.8
Altman's Z-Score		6.72	9.95
Probability of Bankruptcy		0.0%	0.0%
Beneish's Earnings Manipulation Score		−2.84	−2.89
Probability of Earnings Manipulation		0.23%	0.19%

Required

a. Compute the values of each of the ratios in Exhibit 5.26 for Starbucks for 2008. Starbucks had 735.5 million common shares outstanding at the end of 2008, and the market price per share was $14.17. For days accounts receivable, use only specialty revenues in your calculations, because accounts receivable are primarily related to licensing and food service operations, not the retail operations. Use cost of sales, including occupancy costs, in the numerator of the GMI in the Beneish earnings manipulation model.

b. Interpret the changes in Starbucks risk ratios during the three-year period, indicating areas of concern.

CASE 5.2

MASSACHUSETTS STOVE COMPANY—BANK LENDING DECISION

Massachusetts Stove Company manufactures wood-burning stoves for the heating of homes and businesses. The company has approached you, as chief lending officer for the Massachusetts Regional Bank, seeking to increase its loan from the current level of $93,091 as of January 15, Year 12, to $143,091. Jane O'Neil, chief executive officer and majority stockholder of the company, indicates that the company needs the loan to finance the working capital required for an expected 25 percent annual increase in sales during the next two years, to repay suppliers, and to provide funds for expected nonrecurring legal and retooling costs.

The company's woodstoves have two distinguishing characteristics: (1) the metal frame of the stoves includes inlaid soapstone, which increases the intensity and duration of the heat provided by the stoves and enhances their appearance as an attractive piece of furniture, and (2) a catalytic combuster, which adds heating potential to the stoves and reduces air pollution.

The company manufactures wood-burning stoves in a single plant in Greenfield, Massachusetts. It purchases metal castings for the stoves from foundries in Germany and Belgium. The soapstone comes from a supplier in Canada. These purchases are denominated in U.S. dollars. The catalytic combuster is purchased from a supplier in the United States. The manufacturing process is essentially an assembly operation. The plant employs an average of eight workers. The two keys to quality control are structural airtightness and effective operation of the catalytic combuster.

The company rents approximately 60 percent of the 25,000-square-foot building it uses for manufacturing and administrative activities. This building also houses the company's factory showroom. The remaining 40 percent of the building is not currently rented.

The company's marketing of woodstoves follows three channels:

1. Wholesaling of stoves to retail hardware stores. This channel represents approximately 20 percent of the company's sales in units.
2. Retail direct marketing to individuals in all 50 states. This channel utilizes (a) national advertising in construction and design magazines and (b) the sending of brochures to potential customers identified from personal inquiries. This channel represents approximately 70 percent of the company's sales in units. The company is the only firm in the industry with a strategic emphasis on retail direct marketing.
3. Retailing from the company's showroom. This channel represents approximately 10 percent of the company's sales in units.

The company offers three payment options to retail purchasers of its stoves:

1. Full payment: Check, money order, or charge to a third-party credit card is used to pay in full.
2. Layaway plan: Monthly payments are made over a period not exceeding one year. The company ships the stove after receiving the final payment.
3. Installment financing plan: The company has a financing arrangement with a local bank to finance the purchase of stoves by credit-approved customers. The company is liable if customers fail to repay their installment bank loans.

The imposition of strict air emission standards by the Environmental Protection Agency (EPA) has resulted in a major change in the woodstove industry. By December 31, Year 9, firms were required by EPA regulations to demonstrate that their woodstoves met or surpassed specified air emission standards. Besides these standards being stricter than industry practices at the time, firms had to engage in numerous company-sponsored and independent testing of their stoves to satisfy EPA regulators. As a consequence, the number of firms in the woodstove industry decreased from more than 200 in the years prior to Year 10 to approximately 35 by December 31, Year 11.

The company received approval for its Soapstone Stove I in Year 11, after incurring retooling and testing costs of $63,001. It capitalized these costs in the Property, Plant, and Equipment account. It depreciates these costs over the five-year EPA approval period. A second stove, Soapstone Stove II, is currently undergoing retooling and testing. For this stove, the company incurred costs of $19,311 in Year 10 and $8,548 in Year and has received preliminary EPA approval. It anticipates additional design, tooling, and testing costs of approximately $55,000 in Year 12 and $33,000 in Year 13 to obtain final EPA approval.

The company holds an option to purchase the building in which it is located for $608,400. The option also permits the company to assume the unpaid balance on a low-interest-rate loan on the building from the New England Regional Industrial Development Authority. The interest rate on this loan is adjusted annually and equals 80 percent of the bank prime interest rate. The unpaid balance on the loan exceeds the option price and will result in a cash transfer to the company from the owner of the building at the time of transfer. The company exercised its option in Year 9, but the owner of the building refused to comply with the option provisions. The company sued the owner. The case has gone through the lower court system in Massachusetts and is currently under review by the Massachusetts Supreme Court. The company incurred legal costs totaling $68,465 through Year 11 and anticipates additional costs of approximately $45,000 in Year 12. The lower courts have ruled in favor of the company's position on all of the major issues in the case. The company expects the Massachusetts Supreme Court to concur with the decisions of the lower courts when it renders its final decision in the spring of Year 12. The company has held discussions with two prospective tenants for the building's 10,000 square feet that Massachusetts Stove Company does not use in its operations.

Jane O'Neil owns 51 percent of the company's common stock. The remaining stockholders include John O'Neil (chief financial officer and father of Jane O'Neil), Mark Forest (vice president of manufacturing), and four independent local investors.

To assist in the loan decision, the company provides you with financial statements (see the first three columns of Exhibits 5.27–5.29 on pages 414–416) and notes for the three years ending December 31, Year 9, Year 10, and Year 11. These financial statements were prepared by John O'Neil, chief financial officer, and are not audited. The company also provides you with projected financial statements for Year 12 and Year 13 (see the last two columns of Exhibits 5.27–5.29) to demonstrate its need for the loan and its ability to repay. The loan requested involves an increase in the current loan amount from

EXHIBIT 5.27

Massachusetts Stove Company
Income Statements
(Case 5.2)

	Actual			Projected	
	Year 9	**Year 10**	**Year 11**	**Year 12**	**Year 13**
Sales	$ 665,771	$ 783,754	$ 955,629	$1,194,535	$1,493,170
Cost of goods sold	(460,797)	(474,156)	(514,907)	(609,213)	(731,653)
Selling and administrative	(177,631)	(290,719)	(390,503)	(489,760)	(612,200)
Legal (Note 1)	(28,577)	(30,092)	(9,796)	(45,000)	—
Interest	(25,948)	(24,122)	(23,974)	(26,510)	(26,510)
Income tax (Note 2)	—	—	—	—	—
Net Income (Loss)	$ (27,182)	$ (35,335)	$ 16,449	$ 24,052	$ 122,807

$93,091 to $143,091. The company will pay monthly interest and repay the $50,000 additional amount borrowed by December 31, Year 13. Exhibit 5.30 (see page 417) presents financial statement ratios for the company.

The assumptions underlying the projected financial statements are as follows:

Sales: Sales are projected to increase 25 percent annually during the next two years, after increasing 17.7 percent in Year 10 and 21.9 percent in Year 11. The increase reflects continuing market opportunities related to the company's strategic emphasis on retail direct marketing and to the expected continuing contraction in the number of competitors in the industry.

Cost of Goods Sold: Most manufacturing costs vary with sales. The company projects cost of goods sold to equal 51 percent of sales in Year 12 and 49 percent of sales in Year 13, having declined from 69.2 percent of sales in Year 9 to 53.9 percent of sales in Year 11. The reductions resulted from a higher proportion of retail sales in the sales mix (which have a higher gross margin than wholesale sales), a more favorable pricing environment in the industry (fewer competitors), a switch to lower-cost suppliers, and more efficient production.

Selling and Administrative Expenses: The company projects these costs to equal 41 percent of sales, having increased from 26.7 percent of sales in Year 9 to 40.9 percent of sales in Year 11. The increases resulted from a heavier emphasis on retail sales, which require more aggressive marketing than wholesale sales.

Legal Expenses: The additional $45,000 of legal costs represents the best estimate by the company's attorneys.

Interest Expense: Interest expense has averaged approximately 6 percent of short- and long-term borrowing during the last three years. The projected income statement assumes a continuation of the 6 percent average rate.

Income Tax Expense: The company has elected to be taxed as a Subchapter S corporation, which means that the net income of the firm is taxed at the level of the individual shareholders, not at the corporate level. Thus, the pro forma financial statements include no income tax expense. The firm has operated at a net loss for tax purposes for several years

EXHIBIT 5.28

Massachusetts Stove Company
Balance Sheets
(Case 5.2)

	Actual				Projected	
December 31:	**Year 8**	**Year 9**	**Year 10**	**Year 11**	**Year 12**	**Year 13**
ASSETS						
Cash	$ 3,925	$ 11,707	$ 8,344	$ 37,726	$ 11,289	$ 6,512
Accounts receivable	94,606	54,772	44,397	31,964	40,035	49,964
Inventories	239,458	208,260	209,004	225,490	291,924	329,480
Total Current Assets	$ 337,989	$ 274,739	$ 261,745	$ 295,180	$ 343,248	$ 385,956
Property, plant, and equipment, at cost	$ 258,870	$ 316,854	$ 362,399	$ 377,784	$ 440,284	$ 487,784
Accumulated depreciation	(205,338)	(228,985)	(250,189)	(274,347)	(302,502)	(333,694)
Property, plant, and equipment, net	$ 53,532	$ 87,869	$ 112,210	$ 103,437	$ 137,782	$ 154,090
Other assets	$ 17,888	$ 17,888	$ 17,594	$ 17,006	$ 17,006	$ 17,006
Total Assets	$ 409,409	$ 380,496	$ 391,549	$ 415,623	$ 498,036	$ 557,052
LIABILITIES AND SHAREHOLDERS' EQUITY						
Accounts payable	$ 148,579	$ 139,879	$ 189,889	$ 160,905	$ 198,206	$ 176,915
Notes payable—Banks (Note 3)	152,985	140,854	125,256	93,091	143,091	93,091
Other current liabilities (Note 4)	13,340	11,440	23,466	62,440	33,500	41,000
Total Current Liabilities	$ 314,904	$ 292,173	$ 338,611	$ 316,436	$ 374,797	$ 311,006
Long-term debt (Note 3)	248,000	269,000	268,950	298,750	298,750	298,750
Total Liabilities	$ 562,904	$ 561,173	$ 607,561	$ 615,186	$ 673,547	$ 609,756
Common stock	$ 2,000	$ 2,000	$ 2,000	$ 2,000	$ 2,000	$ 2,000
Additional paid-in capital	435,630	435,630	435,630	435,630	435,630	435,630
Accumulated deficit	(591,125)	(618,307)	(653,642)	(637,193)	(613,141)	(490,334)
Total Shareholders' Equity	$(153,495)	$(180,677)	$(216,012)	$(199,563)	$(175,511)	$ (52,704)
Total Liabilities and Shareholders' Equity	$ 409,409	$ 380,496	$ 391,549	$ 415,623	$ 498,036	$ 557,052

EXHIBIT 5.29

Massachusetts Stove Company
Statements of Cash Flows
(Case 5.2)

	Actual			Projected	
	Year 9	Year 10	Year 11	Year 12	Year 13
OPERATIONS					
Net income (loss)	$(27,182)	$(35,335)	$ 16,449	$ 24,052	$122,807
Depreciation and amortization	23,647	21,204	24,158	28,155	31,192
(Increase) Decrease in accounts receivable	39,834	10,375	12,433	(8,071)	(9,929)
(Increase) Decrease in inventories	31,198	(744)	(16,486)	(66,434)	(37,556)
Increase (Decrease) in accounts payable	(8,700)	50,010	(28,984)	37,301	(21,291)
Increase (Decrease) in other current liabilities	(1,900)	12,026	38,974	(28,940)	7,500
Cash Flow from Operations	$ 56,897	$ 57,536	$ 46,544	$(13,937)	$ 92,723
INVESTING					
Fixed assets acquired	$(57,984)	$(45,545)	$(15,385)	$(62,500)	$(47,500)
Other investing	—	294	588	—	—
Cash Flow from Investing	$(57,984)	$(45,251)	$(14,797)	$(62,500)	$(47,500)
FINANCING					
Increase (Decrease) in short-term borrowing	$(12,131)	$(15,598)	$(32,165)	$ 50,000	$(50,000)
Increase (Decrease) in long-term borrowing	21,000	(50)	29,800	—	—
Cash Flow from Financing	$ 8,869	$(15,648)	$ (2,365)	$ 50,000	$(50,000)
Change in Cash	$ 7,782	$ (3,363)	$ 29,382	$(26,437)	$ (4,777)
Cash—Beginning of year	3,925	11,707	8,344	37,726	11,289
Cash—End of Year	$ 11,707	$ 8,344	$ 37,726	$ 11,289	$ 6,512

prior to Year 11, primarily because of losses of a lawn products business that it acquired ten years ago. The company discontinued the lawn products business in Year 10.

Cash: The projected amounts for cash represent a plug to equate projected assets with projected liabilities and shareholders' equity. Projected liabilities include the requested loan during Year 12 and its repayment at the end of Year 13.

Accounts Receivable: Days accounts receivable outstanding, calculated on the average accounts receivable balances, will be 11 days in Year 12 and Year 13.

Inventories: Days inventory held, calculated on the average inventory balances, will be 155 days in Year 12 and Year 13.

EXHIBIT 5.30

Massachusetts Stove Company
Profitability and Risk Ratios
(Case 5.2)

	Actual			Projected	
	Year 9	**Year 10**	**Year 11**	**Year 12**	**Year 13**
Profit Margin for ROA	(0.2%)	(1.4%)	4.2%	4.2%	10.0%
Assets Turnover	1.7	2.0	2.4	2.6	2.8
Return on Assets	(0.3%)	(2.9%)	10.0%	11.1%	28.3%
Cost of Goods Sold/Sales	69.2%	60.5%	53.9%	51.0%	49.0%
Selling and Administrative/Sales	26.7%	37.1%	40.9%	41.0%	41.0%
Legal Expense/Sales	4.3%	3.8%	1.0%	3.8%	—
Interest Expense/Sales	3.9%	3.1%	2.5%	2.2%	1.8%
Days Accounts Receivable	41	23	15	11	11
Days Inventory	177	161	154	155	155
Days Accounts Payable	122	127	122	96	89
Fixed Assets Turnover	9.4	7.8	8.9	9.9	10.2
Current Ratio	0.9	0.8	0.9	0.9	1.2
Quick Ratio	0.2	0.2	0.2	0.1	0.2
Operating Cash Flow to Current Liabilities Ratio	0.187	0.182	0.142	(0.040)	0.270
Liabilities to Assets Ratio	1.475	1.552	1.480	1.352	1.095
Long-Term Debt to Total Assets Ratio	0.707	0.687	0.719	0.600	0.536
Operating Cash Flow to Total Liabilities Ratio	0.101	0.098	0.076	(0.022)	0.145
Interest Coverage Ratio	0.0	(0.5)	1.7	1.9	5.6

Property, Plant, and Equipment: Capital expenditures for Year 12 include a $55,000 cost for retooling the Soapstone Stove II and $7,500 for other equipment; for Year 13, they include $33,000 for retooling the Soapstone Stove II and $14,500 for other equipment. The projected balance excludes the cost of acquiring the building, its related debt, the cash received at the time of transfer, and rental revenues from leasing the unused 40 percent of the building to other businesses.

Accumulated Depreciation: This is continuation of the historical relation between depreciation expense and the cost of property, plant, and equipment.

Other Assets: A new financial reporting standard no longer requires amortization of intangibles after Year 11.

Accounts Payable: Days accounts payable outstanding, based on the average accounts payable balances, will be 97 days in Year 12 and 89 days in Year 13. The decrease in days payable reflects the ability to pay suppliers more quickly with the proceeds of the increased bank loan.

Notes Payable: Notes payable is projected to increase by the amount of the bank loan in Year 12 and to decrease by the loan repayment at the end of Year 13.

Other Current Liabilities: The large increase at the end of Year 11 resulted from a major promotional offer in the fall of Year 11, which increased the amount of deposits by customers. The projected amounts for Year 12 and Year 13 represent more normal expected levels of deposits.

Long-Term Debt: Long-term borrowing represents loans from shareholders to the company. The company does not plan to repay any of these loans in the near future.

Retained Earnings: The change each year represents net income or net loss from operations. The company does not pay dividends.

Statement of Cash Flows: Amounts are taken from the changes in various accounts on the actual and projected balance sheets.

Notes to Financial Statements

Note 1: The company has incurred legal costs to enforce its option to purchase the building used in its manufacturing and administrative activities. The case is under review by the Massachusetts Supreme Court, with a decision expected in the spring of Year 12.

Note 2: The company is not subject to income tax because it has elected Subchapter S tax status.

Note 3: The notes payable to banks are secured by machinery and equipment, shares of common stock of companies traded on the New York Stock Exchange owned by two shareholders, and personal guarantees of three shareholders. The long-term debt consists of unsecured loans from three shareholders.

Note 4: Other current liabilities include the following:

	Year 8	Year 9	Year 10	Year 11
Customer Deposits	$11,278	$ 9,132	$20,236	$59,072
Employee Taxes Withheld	2,062	2,308	3,230	3,368
	$13,340	$11,440	$23,466	$62,440

Required

Would you make the loan to the company in accordance with the stated terms? Explain. In responding, consider the reasonableness of the company's projections, positive and negative factors affecting the industry and the company, and the likely ability of the company to repay the loan. (Excel spreadsheet for this case is available at www.cengage.com/accounting/wahlen.)

Case 5.3

FLY-BY-NIGHT INTERNATIONAL GROUP: CAN THIS COMPANY BE SAVED?

Douglas C. Mather, founder, chair, and chief executive of Fly-by-Night International Group (FBN), lived the fast-paced, risk-seeking life that he tried to inject into his company. Flying the company's Learjets, he logged 28 world speed records. Once he throttled a company plane to the top of Mount Everest in three and a half minutes.

These activities seemed perfectly appropriate at the time. Mather was a Navy fighter pilot in Vietnam and then flew commercial airlines. In the mid-1970s, he started FBN as a pilot training school. With the defense buildup beginning in the early 1980s, Mather branched out into government contracting. He equipped the company's Learjets with radar jammers and other sophisticated electronic devices to mimic enemy aircraft. He then contracted his "rent-an-enemy" fleet to the Navy and Air Force for use in fighter pilot training. The Pentagon liked the idea, and FBN's revenues grew to $55 million in the fiscal year ending April 30, Year 14. Its common stock, issued to the public in Year 9 at $8.50 a share, reached a high of $16.50 in mid-Year 13. Mather and FBN received glowing write-ups in *Business Week* and *Fortune*.

EXHIBIT 5.31

Fly-by-Night International Group
Comparative Balance Sheets
(amounts in thousands)
(Case 5.3)

April 30:	Year 14	Year 13	Year 12	Year 11	Year 10	Year 9
ASSETS						
Cash	$ 159	$ 583	$ 313	$ 142	$ 753	$ 192
Notes receivable	—	—	—	1,000	—	—
Accounts receivable	6,545	4,874	2,675	1,490	1,083	2,036
Inventories	5,106	2,514	1,552	602	642	686
Prepayments	665	829	469	57	303	387
Net assets of discontinued businesses	—	—	—	—	1,926	—
Total Current Assets	$ 12,475	$ 8,800	$ 5,009	$ 3,291	$ 4,707	$ 3,301
Property, plant, and equipment	$106,529	$76,975	$24,039	$17,809	$37,250	$17,471
Less accumulated depreciation	(17,231)	(8,843)	(5,713)	(4,288)	(4,462)	(2,593)
Net	$ 89,298	$68,132	$18,326	$13,521	$32,788	$14,878
Other assets	$ 470	$ 665	$ 641	$ 1,112	$ 1,566	$ 1,278
Total Assets	$102,243	$77,597	$23,976	$17,924	$39,061	$19,457
LIABILITIES AND SHAREHOLDERS' EQUITY						
Accounts payable	$ 12,428	$ 6,279	$ 993	$ 939	$ 2,285	$ 1,436
Notes payable	—	945	140	1,021	4,766	—
Current portion of long-term debt	60,590	7,018	1,789	1,104	2,774	1,239
Other current liabilities	12,903	12,124	2,423	1,310	1,845	435
Total Current Liabilities	$ 85,921	$26,366	$ 5,345	$ 4,374	$11,670	$ 3,110
Long-term debt	—	41,021	9,804	6,738	20,041	9,060
Deferred income taxes	—	900	803	—	1,322	1,412
Other noncurrent liabilities	—	—	226	—	248	—
Total Liabilities	$ 85,921	$68,287	$16,178	$11,112	$33,281	$13,582
Common stock	$ 34	$ 22	$ 21	$ 20	$ 20	$ 20
Additional paid-in capital	16,516	5,685	4,569	4,323	3,611	3,611
Retained earnings	(29)	3,802	3,208	2,469	2,149	2,244
Treasury stock	(199)	(199)	—	—	—	—
Total Shareholders' Equity	$ 16,322	$ 9,310	$ 7,798	$ 6,812	$ 5,780	$ 5,875
Total Liabilities and Shareholders' Equity	$102,243	$77,597	$23,976	$17,924	$39,061	$19,457

In mid-Year 14, however, FBN began a rapid descent. Although still growing rapidly, its cash flow was inadequate to service its debt. According to Mather, he was "just dumbfounded. There was never an inkling of a problem with cash."

In the fall of Year 14, the board of directors withdrew the company's financial statements for the year ending April 30, Year 14, stating that there appeared to be material misstatements that needed investigation. In December of Year 14, Mather was asked to step aside as manager and director of the company pending completion of an investigation of certain transactions between Mather and the company. On December 29, Year 14, NASDAQ (over-the-counter stock market) discontinued quoting the company's common shares. In February, Year 15, following its investigation, the board of directors terminated Mather's employment and membership on the board.

Exhibits 5.31–5.33 present the financial statements and related notes of FBN for the five years ending April, Year 10, through April, Year 14. The financial statements for Year 10 to Year 12 use the amounts originally reported for each year. The amounts reported on the statement of cash flows for Year 10 (for example, the change in accounts receivable) do not precisely reconcile to the amounts on the balance sheet at the beginning and end of the year because certain items classified as relating to continuing operations on the balance sheet at the end of Year 9 were reclassified as relating to discontinued operations on the balance sheet at the end of Year 10. The financial statements for Year 13 and Year 14 represent the restated financial statements for those years after the board of directors completed its investigation of suspected material misstatements that caused it to withdraw the originally issued financial statements for fiscal Year 14. Exhibit 5.34 (see page 422) lists the members of the board of directors. Exhibit 5.35 (see page 422) presents profitability and risk ratios for FBN.

EXHIBIT 5.32

Fly-by-Night International Group
Comparative Income Statements
(amounts in thousands)
(Case 5.3)

For the Year Ended April 30:	Year 14	Year 13	Year 12	Year 11	Year 10
CONTINUING OPERATIONS					
Sales	$54,988	$36,597	$20,758	$19,266	$31,992
EXPENSES					
Cost of services	$38,187	$26,444	$12,544	$ 9,087	$22,003
Selling and administrative	5,880	3,020	3,467	2,989	4,236
Depreciation	9,810	3,150	1,703	2,798	3,003
Interest	5,841	3,058	1,101	2,743	2,600
Income taxes	(900)	379	803	671	74
Total Expenses	$58,818	$36,051	$19,618	$18,288	$31,916
Income—Continuing operations	$(3,830)	$ 546	$ 1,140	$ 978	$ 76
Income—Discontinued Operations	—	47	(400)	(659)	(171)
Net Income	$(3,830)	$ 593	$ 740	$ 319	$ (95)

EXHIBIT 5.33

Fly-by-Night International Group
Comparative Statements of Cash Flows
(amounts in thousands)
(Case 5.3)

For the Year Ended April 30:	Year 14	Year 13	Year 12	Year 11	Year 10
OPERATIONS					
Income—Continuing operations	$ (3,830)	$ 546	$ 1,140	$ 978	$ 76
Depreciation	9,810	3,150	1,703	2,798	3,003
Other adjustments	1,074	1,817	1,119	671	74
Changes in Working Capital:					
(Increase) Decrease in receivables	(1,671)	(2,199)	(1,185)	(407)	403
(Increase) Decrease in inventories	(2,592)	(962)	(950)	40	19
(Increase) Decrease in prepayments	164	(360)	(412)	246	36
Increase (Decrease) in accounts payable	6,149	5,286	54	(1,346)	359
Increase (Decrease) in other current liabilities	779	9,701	1,113	(535)	596
Cash Flow from Continuing Operations	$ 9,883	$ 16,979	$ 2,582	$ 2,445	$ 4,566
Cash flow from discontinued operations	—	(77)	(472)	(752)	(335)
Net Cash Flow from Operations	$ 9,883	$ 16,902	$ 2,110	$ 1,693	$ 4,231
INVESTING					
Sale of property, plant, and equipment	$ 259	$ 3	$ 119	$ 18,387	$ 12
Acquisition of property, plant, and equipment	(33,035)	(52,960)	(6,573)	(2,424)	(20,953)
Other	(1,484)	78	1,017	(679)	30
Net Cash Flow from Investing	$(34,260)	$(52,879)	$(5,437)	$ 15,284	$(20,911)
FINANCING					
Increase in short-term borrowing	$ —	$ 805	$ —	$ —	$ 4,766
Increase in long-term borrowing	43,279	42,152	5,397	5,869	14,739
Issue of common stock	12,266	191	428	—	—
Decrease in short-term borrowing	(945)	—	(881)	(3,745)	—
Decrease in long-term borrowing	(30,522)	(7,024)	(1,647)	(19,712)	(2,264)
Acquisition of common stock	—	(198)	—	—	—
Other	(125)	321	201	—	—
Net Cash Flow from Financing	$ 23,953	$ 36,247	$ 3,498	$(17,588)	$ 17,241
Change in Cash	$ (424)	$ 270	$ 171	$ (611)	$ 561
Cash—Beginning of year	583	313	142	753	192
Cash—End of Year	$ 159	$ 583	$ 313	$ 142	$ 753

EXHIBIT 5.34

Fly-by-Night International Group
Members of the Board of Directors
(Case 5.3)

Charles A. Barry, USAF (Ret.), Executive Vice President of Wicks and Associates, Inc., a management consulting firm
Thomas P. Gilkey, Vice President, Marketing
Lawrence G. Hicks, Secretary and General Counsel
Michael S. Holt, Vice President, Finance, and Chief Financial Officer
Gordon K. John, Executive Vice President and Chief Operating Officer
Douglas C. Mather, Chair of the Board, President and Chief Executive Officer
Edward F. O'Hara, President of the O'Hara Companies, which manufactures aircraft products
E. William Shapiro, Professor of Law, Emory University

EXHIBIT 5.35

Profitability and Risk Ratios for FBN
(Case 5.3)

	Year 14	Year 13	Year 12	Year 11	Year 10
Profit Margin for ROA	(0.1%)	6.9%	9.0%	14.5	5.6%
Assets Turnover	0.6	0.7	1.0	0.7	1.1
ROA	0.0%	5.0%	8.9%	9.8%	6.1%
Cost of Goods and Services/Sales	69.4%	72.3%	60.4%	47.2%	68.8%
Selling and Administrative/Sales	10.7%	8.3%	16.7%	15.5%	13.2%
Depreciation Expense/Sales	17.8%	8.6%	8.2%	14.5%	9.4%
Income Tax Expense (excluding tax effects of interest)/Sales	2.1%	4.0%	5.7%	8.3%	3.0%
Interest Expense/Sales	10.6%	8.4%	5.3%	14.2%	8.1%
Days Accounts Receivable	38	38	37	24	18
Days Accounts Payable	84	48	26	65	31
Fixed Assets Turnover	0.7	0.8	1.3	0.8	1.3
Profit Margin for ROCE	(7.0%)	1.5%	5.5%	5.1%	0.2%
Capital Structure Leverage	7.0	5.9	2.9	4.5	5.0
ROCE	(29.9%)	6.4%	15.6%	15.5%	1.3%
Current Ratio	0.2	0.3	0.9	0.8	0.4
Quick Ratio	0.1	0.2	0.6	0.6	0.2
Operating Cash Flow to Current Liabilities Ratio	0.176	1.071	0.531	0.305	0.618
Liabilities to Assets Ratio	0.840	0.880	0.675	0.620	0.852
Long-Term Debt to Long-Term Capital Ratio	0.000	0.815	0.557	0.497	0.776
Operating Cash Flow to Total Liabilities Ratio	0.128	0.402	0.189	0.112	0.195
Interest Coverage Ratio	0.2	1.3	2.8	1.6	1.1

Required

Study these financial statements and notes and respond to the following questions:

a. What evidence do you observe from analyzing the financial statements that might signal the cash flow problems experienced in mid-Year 14?

b. Can FBN avoid bankruptcy during Year 15? What changes in the design or implementation of FBN's strategy would you recommend? To compute Altman's Z-score, use the low-bid market price for the year to determine the market value of common shareholders' equity.

Notes to Financial Statements

1. Summary of Significant Accounting Policies

Consolidation. The consolidated financial statements include the accounts of the company and its wholly owned subsidiaries. The company uses the equity method for subsidiaries that are not majority owned (50 percent or less) and eliminates significant intercompany transactions and balances.

Inventories. Inventories, which consist of aircraft fuel, spare parts, and supplies, appear at lower of FIFO cost or market.

Property and Equipment. Property and equipment appear at acquisition cost. The company capitalizes major inspections, renewals, and improvements, while it expenses replacements, maintenance, and repairs that do not improve or extend the life of the respective assets. The company computes depreciation of property and equipment using the straight-line method.

Contract Income Recognition. Contractual specifications (such as revenue rates, reimbursement terms, and functional considerations) vary among contracts; accordingly, the company recognizes guaranteed contract income (guaranteed revenue less related direct costs) as it logs flight hours or on a straight-line monthly basis over the contract year, whichever method better reflects the economics of the contract. The company recognizes income from discretionary hours flown in excess of the minimum guaranteed amount each month as it logs such discretionary hours.

Income Taxes. The company recognizes deferred income taxes for temporary differences between financial and tax reporting amounts.

2. Transactions with Major Customers

The company provides contract flight services to three major customers: the U.S. Air Force, the U.S. Navy, and the Federal Reserve Bank System. These contracts have termination dates in Year 16 or Year 17. Revenues from all government contracts as a percentage of total revenues were as follows: Year 14, 62 percent; Year 13, 72 percent; Year 12, 73 percent; Year 11, 68 percent; and Year 10, 31 percent.

3. Segment Data

During Year 10, the company operated in the following five business segments:

Flight Operations—Business. Provides combat readiness training to the military and nightly transfer of negotiable instruments for the Federal Reserve Bank System, both under multiyear contracts.

Flight Operations—Transport. Provides charter transport services to a variety of customers.

Fixed-Base Operations. Provides ground support operations (fuel and maintenance) to commercial airlines at several major airports.

Education and Training. Provides training for nonmilitary pilots.

Aircraft Sales and Leasing. Acquires aircraft that the company then resells or leases to various firms.

The company discontinued the Flight Operations—Transport and Education and Training segments in Year 11. It sold most of the assets of the Aircraft Sales and Leasing segment in Year 11.

Segment revenue, operating profit, and asset data for the various segments are as follows (amounts in thousands):

April 30:	Year 14	Year 13	Year 12	Year 11	Year 10
Revenues					
Flight Operations—Business	$ 44,062	$31,297	$16,026	$11,236	$10,803
Flight Operations—Transport	—	—	—	—	13,805
Fixed-Base Operations	9,597	4,832	4,651	3,911	3,647
Education and Training	—	—	—	—	542
Aircraft Sales and Leasing	1,329	468	81	4,119	3,195
Total	$ 54,988	$36,597	$20,758	$19,266	$31,992
Operating Profit					
Flight Operations—Business	$ 5,707	$ 4,863	$ 3,455	$ 2,463	$ 849
Flight Operations—Transport	—	—	—	—	(994)
Fixed-Base Operations	(2,041)	1,362	1,038	174	332
Education and Training	—	—	—	—	12
Aircraft Sales and Leasing	1,175	378	(15)	1,217[b]	2,726[a]
Total	$ 4,841	$ 6,603	$ 4,478	$ 3,854	$ 2,925
Assets					
Flight Operations—Business	$ 85,263	$64,162	$17,738	$11,130	$13,684
Flight Operations—Transport	—	—	—	—	1,771
Fixed-Base Operations	16,544	13,209	5,754	5,011	4,784
Education and Training	—	—	—	—	1,789
Aircraft Sales and Leasing	436	226	438	1,262	18,524
Total	$102,243	$77,597	$23,930	$17,403	$40,552

[a]Includes a gain of $2.6 million on the sale of aircraft
[b]Includes a gain of $1.2 million on the sale of aircraft

4. Discontinued Operations

Income from discontinued operations consists of the following (amounts in thousands):

Year 13	
Income from operations of Flight Operations—Transport ($78), net of income taxes of $31	$ 47
Year 12	
Loss from write-off of airline operations certificates in Flight Operations—Transport business	$(400)
Year 11	
Loss from operations of Flight Operations—Transport ($1,261) and Education and Training ($172) segments, net of income tax benefits of $685	$(748)
Gain on disposal of Education and Training business, net of income taxes of $85	89
Total	$(659)
Year 10	
Loss from operations of Charter Tour business, net of income tax benefits of $164	$(171)

5. Related-Party Transactions

On April 30, Year 11, the company sold most of the net assets of the Aircraft Sales and Leasing segment to Interlease, Inc., a Georgia corporation wholly owned by the company's majority stockholder, whose personal holdings at that time represented approximately 75 percent of the company.

Under the terms of the sale, the sales price was $1,368,000, of which the buyer paid $368,000 in cash and gave a promissory note for the remaining $1,000,000. The company treated the proceeds received in excess of the book value of the net assets sold of $712,367 as a capital contribution due to the related-party nature of the transaction. FBN originally acquired the assets of the Aircraft Sales and Leasing segment during Year 10.

On September 29, Year 14, FBN's board of directors established a Transaction Committee to examine certain transactions between the company and Douglas Mather, FBN's chair, president, and majority stockholder. These transactions appear here.

Certain Loans to Mather. In early September, Year 13, the board of directors authorized a $1 million loan to Mather at the company's cost of borrowing plus $^1/_8$ percent. On September 19, Year 13, Mather tendered a $1 million check to the company in repayment of the loan. On September 22, Year 13, at Mather's direction, the company made an additional $1 million loan to him, the proceeds of which Mather apparently used to cover his check in repayment of the first $1 million loan. The Transaction Committee concluded that the board of directors did not authorize the September 22, Year 13, loan to Mather, nor was any director other than Mather aware of the loan at the time. The company's Year 13 Proxy Statement, dated September 27, Year 13, incorrectly stated that "as of September 19, Year 13, Mather had repaid the principal amount of his indebtedness to the company." Mather's $1 million loan remained outstanding until it was canceled in connection with the ESOP (employee stock ownership plan) transaction discussed next.

ESOP Transaction. On February 28, Year 14, the company's ESOP acquired 100,000 shares of the company's common stock from Mather at $14.25 per share. FBN financed the purchase. The ESOP gave the company a $1,425,000 unsecured demand note. To complete the transaction, the company canceled a $1,000,000 promissory note from Mather and paid the remaining $425,000 in cash. The Transaction Committee determined that the board of directors did not authorize the $1,425,000 loan to the ESOP, the cancellation of Mather's $1,000,000 note, or the payment of $425,000 in cash.

Eastwind Transaction. On April 27, Year 14, the company acquired four Eastwind aircraft from a German company. FBN subsequently sold these aircraft to Transreco, a corporation owned by Douglas Mather, for a profit of $1,600,000. In late September and early October, Transreco sold these four aircraft at a profit of $780,000 to unaffiliated third parties. The Transactions Committee determined that none of the officers or directors of the company were aware of the Eastwind transaction until late September, Year 14.

On December 12, Year 14, the company announced that Mather had agreed to step aside as chair and director and take no part in management of the company pending resolution of the matters presented to the board by the Transactions Committee. On February 13, Year 15, the company announced that it had entered into a settlement agreement with Mather and Transreco resolving certain of the issues addressed by the Transactions Committee. Pursuant to the agreement, the company will receive $211,000, the bonus paid to Mather for fiscal Year 14, and $780,000, the gain recognized by Transreco on the sale of the Eastwind aircraft. Also pursuant to the settlement, Mather will resign all positions with the company and waive his rights under his employment agreement to any future compensation or benefits to which he might otherwise have a claim.

6. Long-Term Debt

Long-term debt consists of the following (amounts in thousands):

April 30:	Year 14	Year 13	Year 12	Year 11	Year 10
Notes Payable to Banks:					
Variable Rate	$44,702	$30,495	$ 2,086	$2,504	$ 3,497
Fixed Rate	13,555	14,679	6,292	3,562	1,228
Notes Payable to Finance Companies:					
Variable Rate	—	—	1,320	1,667	10,808
Fixed Rate	—	—	—	—	325
Capitalized Lease Obligations	2,333	2,865	1,295	—	5,297
Other	—	—	600	39	1,660
Total	$60,590	$48,039	$11,593	$7,842	$22,815
Less Current Portion	(60,590)	(7,018)	(1,789)	(1,104)	(2,774)
Net	$ —	$41,021	$ 9,804	$6,738	$20,041

Substantially all of the company's property, plant, and equipment serve as collateral for this debt. The borrowings from bank and finance companies contain restrictive covenants, the most restrictive of which appear in the following table:

	Year 14	Year 13	Year 12	Year 11	Year 10
Liabilities/Tangible Net Worth	<2.5	<3.0	<4.2	<5.5	<6.7
Tangible Net Worth	>$20,000	>$5,800	>$5,400	>$5,300	>$5,100
Working Capital	>$5,000	—	—	—	—
Interest Coverage Ratio	>1.15	—	—	—	—

As of April 30, Year 14, the company is in default of its debt covenants. It is also in default with respect to covenants underlying its capitalized lease obligations. As a result, lenders have the right to accelerate repayment of their loans. Accordingly, the company has classified all of its long-term debt as a current liability.

The company has entered into operating leases for aircraft and other equipment. The estimated present value of the minimum lease payments under these operating leases as of April 30 of each year is as follows:

Year 14:	$2,706
Year 13:	$3,142
Year 12:	$3,594
Year 11:	$3,971
Year 10:	$4,083

7. Income Taxes

Income tax expense consists of the following:

	Year Ended April 30				
	Year 14	Year 13	Year 12	Year 11	Year 10
Current					
Federal	$ —	$ —	$ —	$—	$ —
State	—	—	—	—	—
Deferred					
Federal	$(845)	$380	$685	$67	$(85)
State	(55)	30	118	4	(5)
Total	$(900)	$410	$803	$71	$(90)

The cumulative tax loss and tax credit carryovers as of April 30 of each year are as follows:

April 30:	Tax Loss	Tax Credit
Year 14	$10,300	$250
Year 13	5,200	280
Year 12	1,400	300
Year 11	2,100	450
Year 10	4,500	750

The deferred tax provision results from temporary differences in the recognition of revenues and expenses for income tax and financial reporting. The sources and amounts of these differences for each year are as follows:

	Year 14	Year 13	Year 12	Year 11	Year 10
Depreciation	$ —	$ 503	$ 336	$(770)	$ 778
Aircraft Modification Costs	—	1,218	382	982	703
Net Operating Losses	(900)	(1,384)	290	—	(1,729)
Other	—	73	(205)	(141)	158
Total	$(900)	$ 410	$ 803	$ 71	$ (90)

A reconciliation of the effective tax rate with the statutory tax rate is as follows:

	Year 14	Year 13	Year 12	Year 11	Year 10
Federal Taxes at Statutory Rate	(35.0)%	35.0%	34.0%	34.0%	(34.0)%
State Income Taxes	(2.5)	3.0	3.0	3.0	(3.0)
Effect of Net Operating Loss and Investment Credits	16.5	—	(7.2)	(29.9)	—
Other	2.0	2.9	22.2	11.1	(12.0)
Effect Tax Rate	(19.0)%	40.9%	52.0%	18.2%	(49.0)%

8. Market Price Information

The company's common stock trades on the NASDAQ National Market System under the symbol FBN. Trading in the company common stock commenced on January 10, Year 10. High- and low-bid prices during each fiscal year are as follows:

Fiscal Year	High Bid	Low Bid
Year 14	$16.50	$9.50
Year 13	$14.63	$6.25
Year 12	$11.25	$3.25
Year 11	$ 4.63	$3.00
Year 10	$ 5.25	$3.25

On December 29, Year 14, the company announced that NASDAQ had decided to discontinue quoting the company's common stock because of the company's failure to comply with NASDAQ's filing requirements.

Ownership of the company's stock at various dates appears here.

April 30:	Year 14	Year 13	Year 12	Year 11	Year 10
Douglas Mather	42%	68%	72%	75%	75%
Public	48	23	24	25	25
Company ESOP	10	9	4	—	—
	100%	100%	100%	100%	100%
Common Shares Outstanding (000's)	3,357.5	2,222.8	2,095.0	2,000.0	2,000.0

CASE 5.4

MILLENNIAL TECHNOLOGIES: APOCALYPSE NOW

Millennial Technologies, a designer, manufacturer, and marketer of PC cards for portable computers, printers, telecommunications equipment, and equipment diagnostic systems, was the darling of Wall Street during Year 6. Its common stock price was the leading gainer for the year on the New York Stock Exchange. Its bubble burst during the third quarter of Year 7 when revelations about seriously misstated financial statements for prior years became known. This case seeks to identify signals of the financial shenanigans and to assess the likelihood of the firm's future survival.

Industry and Products

Digital computing and processing have expanded beyond desktop computing systems in recent years to include a broad array of more mobile applications, including portable computers, cell phones, digital cameras, and medical and automobile diagnostic equipment. A PC card is a rugged, lightweight, credit-card-sized device inserted into a dedicated slot in these products that provides programming, processing, and storage capabilities normally provided on hard drives and floppy disks in conventional desktop computers. The PC card has a high shock and vibration tolerance, low power consumption, a small size, and a high access speed. The market for PC cards is one of the fastest-growing segments of the electronics industry.

Millennial Technologies designs PC cards for four principal industries: (1) communications (routers, cell phones, and local-area networks), (2) transportation (vehicle diagnostics and navigation), (3) mobile computing (handheld data collection terminals and notebook computers), and (4) medical (blood gas analysis systems and defibrillators). The firm targets its engineering and product development, all of which it conducts in-house, to these four industry groups. It works closely with original equipment manufacturers (OEMs) to design PC cards that meet specific needs of products aimed at these four industries. Its customers include Lucent Technologies, Philips Electronics, 3Com Corporation, and Bay Networks. Millennial Technologies also conducts its manufacturing in-house, which allows it to respond quickly to changing requirements and schedules of these OEMs. The firm markets its products using its own sales force.

In Year 4, Millennial Technologies was incorporated in Delaware as the successor of M. Millennial, a Massachusetts corporation. The firm made its initial public offering of common stock (1 million shares) on April 19, Year 4, at a price of $5.625 per share. Each common share issued included a redeemable common stock purchase warrant that permitted the holder to purchase one share of the firm's common stock for $7.20. Prior to its initial public offering, Millennial Technologies obtained a $550,000 bridge loan during Year 4, which it repaid with proceeds from the initial public offering. Holders of the stock purchase warrants exercised their options during Year 5 and Year 6. The firm obtained equity capital during Year 5 as a result of a private placement of its common stock at $5.83 a share. It issued additional shares to the public during Year 6 at $18 a share. Its stock price was $5.25 on June 30, Year 4; $22.625 on June 30, Year 5; $29.875 on June 30, Year 6; and $52 on December 31, Year 7.

Millennial Technologies maintained a line of credit throughout Year 4 to Year 6 with a major Boston bank to finance its accounts receivables and inventories. The borrowing was at the bank's prime lending rate. Substantially all of the assets of the firm collateralized this borrowing.

The firm's chief executive officer, Manuel Pinoza, also is its major shareholder. The firm maintains an employment agreement with Pinoza under which it pays his compensation to a Swiss executive search firm, which then pays Pinoza.

Beginning in Year 6, Millennial Technologies made minority investments in five corporations engaged in technology development, four of which the firm accounts for using the cost method and one of which it accounts for using the equity method. Products developed by these companies could conceivably use PC cards. Millennial Technologies also advanced amounts to some of these companies using interest-bearing notes.

Exhibits 5.36–5.38 (see pages 430–432) present the financial statements for the fiscal years ended June 30, Year 4, Year 5, and Year 6, for Millennial Technologies based on the amounts originally reported for each year. Exhibit 5.39 (see page 433) presents selected financial statement ratios based on these reported amounts.

Financial Statement Irregularities

On February 10, Year 7, after receiving information regarding various accounting and reporting irregularities, the board of directors fired Pinoza and relieved the chief financial officer of his duties. The board formed a special committee of outside directors to investigate the purported irregularities, obtaining the assistance of legal counsel and the firm's independent accountants. On February 21, Year 7, the New York Stock Exchange

EXHIBIT 5.36

Balance Sheets for Millennial Technologies
As Originally Reported
(amounts in thousands)
(Case 5.4)

Year Ended June 30:	Year 6	Year 5	Year 4	Year 3
ASSETS				
Cash	$ 6,182	$ 970	$ 981	$ —
Marketable securities	4,932	—	—	—
Accounts receivable	12,592	3,932	1,662	730
Inventories	18,229	8,609	3,371	2,257
Other current assets	6,256	1,932	306	234
Total Current Assets	$48,191	$15,443	$6,320	$3,221
Investments in securities	2,472	—	—	—
Property, plant, and equipment, net	4,698	1,323	669	208
Other assets	421	1,433	601	666
Total Assets	$55,782	$18,199	$7,590	$4,095
LIABILITIES AND SHAREHOLDERS' EQUITY				
Accounts payable	$ 3,494	$ 3,571	$ 616	$1,590
Notes payable	4,684	1,153	—	980
Current portion of long-term debt	336	103	—	—
Other current liabilities	614	765	516	457
Total Current Liabilities	$ 9,128	$ 5,592	$1,132	$3,027
Long-term debt	367	162	—	—
Deferred tax liability	242	—	39	24
Total Liabilities	$ 9,737	$ 5,754	$1,171	$3,051
Common stock	$ 165	$ 110	$ 90	$ 60
Additional paid-in capital	38,802	10,159	5,027	146
Retained earnings	7,078	2,176	1,302	838
Total Shareholders' Equity	$46,045	$12,445	$6,419	$1,044
Total Liabilities and Shareholders' Equity	$55,782	$18,199	$7,590	$4,095

announced the suspension of trading in the firm's common stock. The stock was delisted on April 25, Year 7. On February 14, Year 7, the major Boston bank providing working capital financing notified the firm that the firm had defaulted on its line of credit agreement. Although this bank subsequently extended the line of credit through July 31, Year 7, it increased the interest rate significantly above prime. Millennial Technologies decided to seek a new lender.

The investigation by the board's special committee revealed the following accounting and reporting irregularities:

- Recording of invalid sales transactions: The firm created fictitious purchase orders from regular customers using purchase order forms from legitimate purchase transactions.

EXHIBIT 5.37

Income Statements for Millennial Technologies
As Originally Reported
(amounts in thousands)
(Case 5.4)

For the Year Ended June 30:	Year 6	Year 5	Year 4
Sales	$ 37,848	$12,445	$ 8,213
Other revenues	353	10	9
Cost of goods sold	(23,636)	(6,833)	(4,523)
Selling and administrative	(4,591)	(3,366)	(1,889)
Research and development	(1,434)	(752)	(567)
Interest	(370)	(74)	(495)[a]
Income taxes	(3,268)	(556)	(284)
Net Income	$ 4,902	$ 874	$ 464

[a]Includes the cost of factoring receivables and interest on bridge financing obtained and repaid during the year.

The firm then purportedly shipped empty PC card housings to these customers at bogus addresses. Pinoza apparently paid the accounts receivable underlying these sales with his personal funds.

- Recording of revenues from bill and hold transactions: The firm kept its books open beyond June 30 each year and recorded as sales of each year products that were shipped in July and should have been recorded as revenues of the next fiscal year.
- Manipulation of physical counts of inventory balances and inclusion of empty PC card housings in finished goods inventories.
- Failure to write down inventories adequately for product obsolescence.
- Inclusion of certain costs in property, plant, and equipment that the firm should have expensed in the period incurred.
- Inclusion in advances to other technology companies of amounts that represented prepaid license fees. The firm should have amortized these fees over the license period.
- Failure to provide adequately for uncollectible amounts related to advances to other technology companies.
- Failure to write down or write off investments in other technology companies when their market value was less than the cost of the investment.

Exhibits 5.40–5.42 (see pages 434–436) present the restated financial statements for Millennial Technologies for the fiscal years ending June 30, Year 4, Year 5, and Year 6, after correcting for the irregularities described previously. These exhibits also present the financial statements for the nine months ended March 30, Year 7. The firm decided during February of Year 7 to change its fiscal year to a March year-end. Exhibit 5.43 presents (see page 437) selected financial ratios based on the restated financial statements.

Required

a. Using information in the financial statements as originally reported in Exhibits 5.36–5.38, compute the value of Beneish's manipulation index for fiscal Year 5 and Year 6.

EXHIBIT 5.38

Statements of Cash Flows for Millennial Technologies
As Originally Reported
(amounts in thousands)
(Case 5.4)

For the Year Ended June 30:	Year 6	Year 5	Year 4
OPERATIONS			
Net income	$ 4,902	$ 874	$ 464
Depreciation	645	337	193
Other addbacks and subtractions, net	1,159	(5)	219
Working capital provided by operations	$ 6,706	$ 1,206	$ 876
(Increase) Decrease in accounts receivables	(8,940)	(2,433)	(981)
(Increase) Decrease in inventories	(9,620)	(5,238)	(1,115)
(Increase) Decrease in other current assets	(836)	(2,406)	(71)
Increase (Decrease) in accounts payable	(76)	2,955	(974)
Increase (Decrease) in other current liabilities	(152)	251	87
Cash Flow from Operations	$(12,918)	$(5,665)	$(2,178)
INVESTING			
Sale of investments	$ 3,981	$ —	$ —
Acquisition of fixed assets	(3,899)	(862)	(525)
Acquisitions of investments	(11,186)	—	—
Other investing transactions	(2,800)	—	—
Cash Flow from Investing	$(13,904)	$ (862)	$ (525)
FINANCING			
Increase in short-term borrowing	$ 3,531	$ 1,153	$ 550
Increase in long-term borrowing	691	320	—
Increase in common stock	28,064	5,099	4,663
Decrease in short-term borrowing	—	—	(1,529)
Decrease in long-term borrowing	(252)	(56)	—
Cash Flow from Financing	$ 32,034	$ 6,516	$ 3,684
Net Change in Cash	$ 5,212	$ (11)	$ 981
Cash—Beginning of year	970	981	—
Cash—End of Year	$ 6,182	$ 970	$ 981

b. Using information from Part a and the financial ratios in Exhibit 5.39, indicate possible signals that Millennial Technologies might have been manipulating its financial statements.

c. Describe the effect of each of the eight accounting irregularities on the balance sheet, income statement, and statement of cash flows.

EXHIBIT 5.39

Financial Ratios for Millennial Technologies Based on Originally Reported Amounts (Case 5.4)

	Year 6	Year 5	Year 4
Profit Margin for ROA	13.6%	7.4%	9.6%
Assets Turnover	1.0	1.0	1.4
ROA	13.9%	7.2%	13.5%
Profit Margin for ROCE	13.0%	7.0%	5.6%
Capital Structure Leverage	1.3	1.4	1.6
ROCE	16.8%	9.3%	12.4%
Cost of Goods Sold/Sales	62.4%	54.9%	55.1%
Selling and Administrative/Sales	12.1%	27.0%	23.0%
Research and Development/Sales	3.8%	6.0%	6.9%
Income Tax Expense (excluding tax effects of interest expense)/Sales	9.0%	4.7%	5.5%
Accounts Receivable Turnover	4.6	4.4	6.9
Inventory Turnover	1.8	1.1	1.6
Fixed Assets Turnover	12.6	12.5	18.7
Current Ratio	5.3	2.8	5.6
Quick Ratio	2.6	0.9	2.3
Days Accounts Payable	39	63	71
Operating Cash Flow to Current Liabilities Ratio	(1.755)	(1.685)	(1.047)
Long-Term Debt to Long-Term Capital Ratio	0.008	0.013	—
Liabilities to Assets Ratio	0.175	0.316	0.154
Operating Cash Flow to Total Liabilities Ratio	(1.668)	(1.636)	(1.032)
Interest Coverage Ratio	23.1	20.3	2.5

d. Using information in the restated financial statements in Exhibits 5.40–5.42, the financial ratios in Exhibit 5.43, and the information provided in this case, as a commercial banker, would you be willing to offer Millennial Technologies a line of credit as of July 31, Year 7? If so, provide the conditions that would induce you to offer such a line of credit.

e. Exhibit 5.44 (see page 438) presents the values of Altman's Z-score for fiscal Year 4, Year 5, and Year 6 based on the originally reported amounts and the restated amounts. Compute the value of Altman's Z-score for the fiscal year ended March 31, Year 7. Although this is not technically correct, use the income amounts for the nine-month period ending March 31, Year 7. Based on the amounts in the proposed settlement of the class-action lawsuits, the value of the common equity on March 31, Year 7, is $50,068,568.

f. Can Millennial Technologies avoid bankruptcy as of mid-Year 7? Explain. Why doesn't the Altman model signal the financial difficulties earlier?

EXHIBIT 5.40

Balance Sheets for Millennial Technologies
Using Restated Data
(amounts in thousands)
(Case 5.4)

	March 31:	June 30:			
	Year 7	Year 6	Year 5	Year 4	Year 3
ASSETS					
Cash	$ 57	$ 6,182	$ 970	$ 981	$ —
Marketable securities	—	4,932	—	—	—
Accounts receivable	5,571	11,260	2,802	1,280	730
Inventories	7,356	8,248	2,181	1,581	2,257
Other current assets	14,229	6,395	2,284	839	669
Total Current Assets	$ 27,213	$ 37,017	$ 8,237	$4,681	$3,656
Investments in securities	20,332	1,783	—	—	—
Property, plant, and equipment, net	3,087	2,033	923	399	243
Other assets	566	299	390	123	172
Total Assets	$ 51,198	$ 41,132	$ 9,550	$5,203	$4,071
LIABILITIES AND SHAREHOLDERS' EQUITY					
Accounts payable	$ 4,766	$ 3,025	$ 3,303	$ 772	$1,590
Notes payable	10,090	4,684	1,153	—	980
Current portion of long-term debt	671	336	103	—	—
Other current liabilities	7,117	811	562	116	457
Total Current Liabilities	$ 22,644	$ 8,856	$ 5,121	$ 888	$3,027
Long-term debt	—	367	162	—	—
Total Liabilities	$ 22,644	$ 9,223	$ 5,283	$ 888	$3,027
Common stock	$ 177	$ 165	$ 110	$ 90	$ 60
Additional paid-in capital	82,240	42,712	10,843	5,059	146
Retained earnings	(53,630)	(10,968)	(6,686)	(834)	838
Foreign currency adjustment	(233)	—	—	—	—
Total Shareholders' Equity	$ 28,554	$ 31,909	$ 4,267	$4,315	$1,044
Total Liabilities and Shareholders' Equity	$ 51,198	$ 41,132	$ 9,550	$5,203	$4,071

EXHIBIT 5.41

Income Statements for Millennial Technologies
Using Restated Data
(amounts in thousands)
(Case 5.4)

	Nine Months Ended March 31:	Year Ended June 30:		
	Year 7	**Year 6**	**Year 5**	**Year 4**
Sales	$ 28,263	$ 33,412	$ 8,982	$ 7,801
Other revenues	67	353	10	9
Cost of goods sold	(24,453)	(29,778)	(11,575)	(6,508)
Selling and administrative	(7,318)	(3,803)	(2,442)	(2,083)
Research and development	(1,061)	(1,434)	(753)	(567)
Loss on investments	(14,096)[a]	(2,662)[a]	—	—
Investigation costs	(3,673)[b]	—	—	—
Provision for settlement of shareholder litigation	(20,000)[c]	—	—	—
Interest	(391)	(370)	(74)	(495)
Income taxes	—[d]	—[d]	—[d]	171
Net Income (Loss)	$(42,662)	$ (4,282)	$ (5,852)	$(1,672)

[a]Write-offs of advances (and write-downs or write-offs of investments) in technology companies.

[b]Legal, accounting, and related costs of investigating misstatements of financial statements.

[c]Estimated cost of class-action lawsuits arising from misstatements of financial statements. Millennial Technologies reached an agreement on June 18, Year 7, to pay the plaintiffs $1,475,000 in cash (included in accounts payable on the March 31, Year 7 balance sheet) and common stock of $18,525,000 (included in additional paid-in capital on the March 31, Year 7 balance sheet). The common stock portion of the settlement represents 37 percent of the common stock of Millennial Technologies.

[d]Millennial Technologies incurred net losses for income tax purposes and maintains a valuation allowance equal to the balance in deferred tax assets.

EXHIBIT 5.42

Statements of Cash Flows for Millennial Technologies
Using Restated Data
(amounts in thousands)
(Case 5.4)

	Nine Months Ended March 31:	Year Ended June 30:		
	Year 7	Year 6	Year 5	Year 4
OPERATIONS				
Net loss	$(42,662)	$ (4,282)	$(5,852)	$(1,672)
Depreciation and amortization	831	471	281	176
Other addbacks and subtractions, net	28,812	2,005	224	352
Working capital provided by operations	$(13,019)	$ (1,806)	$(5,347)	$(1,144)
(Increase) Decrease in accounts receivable	5,289	(8,883)	(1,693)	(599)
Increase (Decrease) in inventories	454	(6,067)	(600)	676
(Increase) Decrease in other current assets	(8,092)	(5,213)	(1,932)	(176)
Increase (Decrease) in accounts payable	6,572	(9)	3,072	(818)
Increase (Decrease) in other current liabilities	—	(20)	(96)	(340)
Cash Flow from Operations	$ (8,796)	$(21,998)	$(6,596)	$(2,401)
INVESTING				
Sale of investments	$ 32,182	$ 3,981	$ —	$ —
Acquisition of fixed assets	(2,074)	(1,459)	(583)	(332)
Acquisition of investments	(38,892)	(11,186)	—	—
Cash Flow from Investing	$ (8,784)	$ (8,664)	$ (583)	$ (332)
FINANCING				
Increase in short-term borrowing	$ 5,406	$ 3,531	$ 1,153	$ 550
Increase in long-term borrowing	250	691	320	—
Increase in capital stock	4,060	28,813	5,099	4,663
Decrease in short-term borrowing	—	—	—	(1,529)
Decrease in long-term borrowing	(282)	(252)	(56)	—
Proceeds from related-party transaction	2,021	3,091	652	30
Cash Flow from Financing	$ 11,455	$ 35,874	$ 7,168	$ 3,714
Change in Cash	$ (6,125)	$ 5,212	$ (11)	$ 981
Cash—Beginning of year	6,182	970	981	—
Cash—End of Year	$ 57	$ 6,182	$ 970	$ 981

EXHIBIT 5.43

Financial Ratios for Millennial Technologies
Based on Restated Data
(Case 5.4)

	Year 7[a]	Year 6	Year 5	Year 4
Profit Margin for ROA	(150.0%)	(12.1%)	(64.6%)	(17.2%)
Assets Turnover	0.6	1.3	1.2	1.7
ROA	(91.9%)	(15.9%)	(78.7%)	(29.0%)
Profit Margin for ROCE	(150.9%)	(12.8%)	(65.2%)	(21.4%)
Capital Structure Leverage	1.5	1.4	1.7	1.7
ROCE	(141.1%)	(23.7%)	(136.4%)	(62.4%)
Cost of Goods Sold/Sales	86.5%	89.1%	128.9%	83.4%
Selling and Administrative/Sales	25.9%	11.4%	27.2%	26.7%
Research and Development/Sales	3.8%	4.3%	8.4%	7.3%
Special Provisions/Sales	133.6%	8.0%	—	—
Accounts Receivable Turnover	3.4	4.8	4.4	7.8
Inventory Turnover	3.1	5.7	6.2	3.4
Fixed Assets Turnover	11.0	22.6	13.6	24.3
Current Ratio	1.2	4.2	1.6	5.3
Quick Ratio	0.3	2.5	0.7	2.6
Days Accounts Payable	60	32	61	74
Operating Cash Flow to Current Liabilities Ratio	(0.558)	(3.148)	(2.195)	(1.227)
Long-Term Debt to Long-Term Capital Ratio	—	0.011	0.037	—
Liabilities to Assets Ratio	0.442	0.224	0.553	0.171
Operating Cash Flow to Total Liabilities Ratio	(0.552)	(3.033)	(2.138)	(1.227)
Interest Coverage Ratio	(108.1)	(10.6)	(78.1)	(2.7)

[a]Amounts based on a nine-month fiscal year

EXHIBIT 5.44

Altman's Z-Score for Millennial Technologies (Case 5.4)

	Originally Reported Data			Restated Data		
	Year 6	Year 5	Year 4	Year 6	Year 5	Year 4
Net Working Capital/Total Assets	0.8403	0.6496	0.8203	0.8216	0.3915	0.8748
Retained Earnings/Total Assets	0.1776	0.1674	0.2402	(0.3733)	(0.9801)	(0.2244)
Income Before Interest and Taxes/Total Assets	0.5052	0.2727	0.5404	(0.3139)	(1.9966)	(0.8550)
Market Value of Equity/Book Value of Liabilities	15.3089	13.1911	8.0700	16.1620	14.3672	10.6419
Sales/Total Assets	0.6785	0.6838	1.0821	0.8123	0.9405	1.4993
Z-Score	17.5105	14.9646	10.7530	17.1088	12.7225	11.9366

Chapter 6

Financing Activities

Learning Objectives

1. Describe the financial statement reporting of investments by owners (equity issuances) and distributions to owners (dividends and share repurchases).
2. Explain the accounting for equity issued to compensate employees (stock options, stock appreciation rights, and restricted stock).
3. Separate financial reporting effects of transactions with non-owners into those that flow through the current income statement (net income) and those that do not (other comprehensive income).
4. Apply financial statement recognition principles to long-term and short-term debt (bonds, notes payable, leases, and troubled debt).
5. Explain the accounting for and financial reporting of hybrid securities.
6. Identify forms of off-balance-sheet financing and, when necessary, how to adjust the financial statements to recognize this financing.
7. Understand the effects of the accounting methods for operating and capital leases on the financial statements and make the adjustments required to convert operating leases to capital leases.
8. Identify the differences between U.S. GAAP and International Financial Reporting Standards in the area of equity and debt financing.

The previous five chapters demonstrated how to analyze a firm's strategy, performance, and financial position using financial statement ratios and analytical tools. This chapter and the next three describe the principles and practices of how the financial statements are prepared so that the analyst can more deeply understand the accounting procedures used by management to, hopefully, best represent the economics of the business. In this chapter, we examine the accounting issues related to financing activities—the right-hand side of the balance sheet. We focus on the financial statement information that conveys the results of raising capital from investors (equity capital) and creditors (debt capital). If the growth opportunities of a business cannot be satisfied using cash flows from current operations or if the terms of external capital are favorable, firms engage in financing activities to raise the capital necessary to engage in investing activities (the acquisition of productive and investment assets), which we cover in Chapter 7. Having deployed external capital into productive assets, firms engage in their primary operating activities, which we discuss in Chapter 8. Throughout Chapters 6–9, we identify the choices made by management and the rules promulgated by standard setters that lead to published financial statements. Because of the rapid pace with which accounting is moving toward common standards for financial reporting, we cover both U.S. generally accepted accounting principles (U.S. GAAP) and standards issued by the International Accounting Standards Board (International Financial Reporting Standards, or IFRS). Many of the accounting principles are similar under U.S. GAAP and IFRS. If a difference exists, we discuss U.S. GAAP and then IFRS differences.[1] Chapter 9 discusses how to evaluate the quality of financial statements and the implications of financial statement quality for forecasting future earnings. The final five chapters, Chapters 10–14, utilize the information derived from the financial ratios analyses and the firm's accounting to forecast future financial statements and to estimate firm value.

To preview the focus in this chapter on financing activities, refer to PepsiCo's December 27, 2008 Consolidated Balance Sheet (Appendix A). PepsiCo reports $35,994 million of total assets, virtually all of it used in operations. The primary claims against these assets are $23,888 million of creditor claims (that is, Total Liabilities), of which $7,858 million and $369 million are classified as Long-Term and Short-Term Debt Obligations, respectively, and $12,203 million in equity claims (that is, total common shareholders' equity). This chapter focuses on the balance sheet claims represented by Long-Term and Short-Term Debt Obligations, as well as residual claims represented by Shareholders' Equity. Chapter 8 covers all of the creditor claims that arise from operating activities such as transactions with suppliers, employees, and tax authorities, as opposed to transactions with shareholders, bondholders, banks, and other financial institutions.

We begin with equity financing activities, which include raising capital by issuing common stock and preferred stock, the return of capital to shareholders via dividends and share repurchases, and the use of equity (and equity appreciation) to compensate employees via stock options, stock appreciation rights, and restricted stock plans. Then we discuss the shareholders' equity effects of net income and other comprehensive income. The second section of the chapter deals with debt financing activities. After a review of the financial statement recognition principles relating to liabilities in general, we examine the specific accounting for and reporting of notes payable and bonds, troubled debt, and hybrid securities. The chapter concludes with a focus on risk analysis when potential liabilities are not reflected in financial statements (off-balance-sheet financing), including operating leases and their effective capitalization for cross-sectional comparability and risk analysis purposes.

EQUITY FINANCING

Corporations raise a substantial amount of cash by issuing shares of common stock and by deploying the funds received into profitable operations. The amount of shareholders' equity reported in the balance sheet (the *book value* of shareholders' equity) is the investment base for return on equity calculations used in profitability analysis (Chapter 4), the measure of owner financing in risk analysis (Chapter 5), and the measure of the value of net assets in place used in residual income-based equity valuation (Chapter 13). The three primary events that lead to changes in the book value of shareholders' equity are:

- Investments by shareholders, usually net cash received by the company at equity issue date.
- Distributions to shareholders, usually in the form of periodic cash dividend payments to investors and sometimes in the form of share repurchases.

[1]We refer to specific accounting standards by the FASB and IASB. Also, we provide codification numbers from the FASB's Codification Project, which represents authoritative guidance in the United States as of July 1, 2009.

- Profitable operating and investing activities. Net income is a large component of this increase. Chapters 6–9 will show that another part of this increase is designated as "other comprehensive income."

The following sections discuss the accounting and financial statement disclosures related to these events.[2]

Investments by Shareholders: Common Equity Issuance

The general rule of accounting for common equity issues is to record the equity claim on the balance sheet at the *fair value* of what the corporation initially receives from the investor. If the issuing firm cannot reliably measure fair value of what it receives, it will use the fair value of the equity issued to record the transaction. As long as the fair value of one side of the exchange is determinable, the fair value of the other side of the transaction is implied under the assumption that unrelated parties exchange equal fair values in arm's-length transactions.

Most commonly, an equity investor transfers cash to the corporation to secure an equity interest. However, the investor could transfer property to the corporation or perform services for the corporation in return for an equity interest. Instead of issuing common stock, the corporation could issue other types of equity interests: preferred stock, stock subscriptions, options to purchase common stock, or stock rights to the investor.[3] In any event, the fair value rule applies. The fair value received is split between two contributed capital accounts: common stock (par value) and additional paid-in capital (amount of fair value received that exceeds par value). Additional paid-in capital is generally referred to as *share premium* in many non-U.S. jurisdictions. The partition of proceeds into the par and additional paid-in capital accounts is not significant from an analysis viewpoint because par value is declared by the board of directors and has no economic meaning. In fact, some firms issue "no par" common stock.[4]

Common shareholders' equity is the residual interest in the corporation, which equals the assets remaining after all liabilities are paid. Because common shareholders bear both residual upside and downside risk, they generally have control as evidenced by the right to vote. However, contractual relationships between the firm and other parties can limit common shareholder control. For example, effective control can be obtained through contracts to acquire all of a firm's output or to use all of a firm's productive capacity or through rights

---

[2]*FASB Codification Topic 505* describes applicable U.S. GAAP on shareholders' equity accounting, and Financial Accounting Standards Board, *Statement of Financial Accounting Standards No. 129*, "Disclosure of Information about Capital Structure," (1979) describes U.S.GAAP relating to capital structure disclosure. Equity financing is a prime example of the scarcity of formal IFRS guidance. Other than standards on disclosure (International Accounting Standards Board, *International Accounting Standards 1*, "Presentation of Financial Statements," amended 2005) and share-based payment (International Accounting Standards Board, *International Financial Reporting Standard 2*, "Share-Based Payment"), international standards are basically silent on how to account for shareholders' equity transactions.

[3]Common shareholders normally possess a preemptive right that enables them to maintain a proportional ownership when the corporation issues additional stock. When a corporation issues stock rights, it receives nothing from investors in return (no effect on financial statements). The issuance of rights is nothing more than a formal recognition of a right that already existed. When investors exercise their stock rights, the resulting issuance of common stock is reported as an issue of stock for cash. Another type of stock right sometimes issued by a company as a takeover defense, stock purchase rights, allows current shareholders to purchase an additional number of shares in the event that an outside party acquires or attempts to acquire a substantial equity stake in the company.

[4]Generally, fair value is measured at the date on which common shares are issued. Under some circumstances (discussed in this and later chapters), the fair value might be measured at an earlier date when the first part of a two-part transaction occurs (for example, date of issue of warrants, convertible preferred stock, and stock options). Also, on occasion, individuals and governments donate assets to a corporation. Although the corporation issues nothing in return, existing shareholders have greater equity because of the donation. The basis for recording a donation is the fair value of the donated asset.

to obtain control of productive capacity through purchase at a later date. These types of contracts are common in the area of SPEs (special purpose entities), which are discussed in more detail later in this chapter and in Chapter 7. Also, to protect their claims on assets, debtholders often require firms to enter into debt covenants, which are contracts to restrict common shareholder control of certain operating and financing decisions such as expansion, dividend payment, and additional borrowings.

Corporations also issue *preferred stock*. Issuing preferred stock involves a trade-off between maintaining corporate control (preferred stock does not have voting rights) and creating a class of shareholders with preference in all asset distributions, including dividends. Accounting for the initial issue of preferred stock is no different than accounting for the issue of common stock. The fair value rule applies when a firm issues preferred stock. Preferred stock (at par) is normally reported before common stock in the shareholders' equity section because preferred shareholders have priority over common shareholders in corporate liquidations. Any additional paid-in capital on preferred stock usually is listed with additional paid-in capital amounts on common stock so that only one amount appears for additional paid-in capital. In addition to the preference in dividends and distribution, preferred stock dividends may accumulate if not declared and paid (the cumulative right). These *dividends in arrears* must be declared and paid before common stock dividends are declared and paid and must be disclosed in the notes to the financial statements. Preferred stock may be convertible into common shares (a positive feature for investors) or callable at scheduled dates or at the firm's discretion (a negative feature for investors). The call options that can exist on preferred stock raise the larger issue (discussed in a later section) of whether certain types of preferred stock should be designated as debt rather than equity.

Finally, to market shares in initial (and, less often, seasoned) public offerings, firms sometimes enter into agreements whereby the companies agree to issue shares in the future and potential buyers agree to pay for the shares in the future. The transaction, called a *subscription agreement*, results in a subscriptions receivable to the extent that cash is not collected when the subscription agreement is reached. The SEC (Securities and Exchange Commission) and IFRS (in IAS 1) require reporting of the fair value of the subscribed shares as common equity and the subscriptions receivable as contra-equity (an account that is subtracted in determining total shareholders' equity). Therefore, only the cash received from investors at subscription increases owners equity.

Example 1

Assume that a company raises capital through the following series of equity issues:

1. Issues 100,000 shares of $1 par value common stock for $5 per share.
2. Receives land in exchange for 28,000 shares of $1 par common stock. The equity investor purchased the land for $85,000. Similar land has recently sold for $150,000.
3. Issues 5,000 shares of $10 par value preferred stock for $75,000.
4. Receives subscriptions for the issue of 40,000 shares of $1 par value common stock. The share issue price is $6, of which 30 percent is received as a down payment. Subsequently, the remaining 70 percent is received.

Exhibit 6.1 summarizes the financial statement effects of the transactions. (Let APIC = Additional paid-in capital.) Dollar amounts indicate the effects of each transaction on the financial statement elements (that is, Assets; Liabilities; or sub-element of Shareholders' Equity: Contributed capital = CC; Accumulated other comprehensive income = AOCI; and Retained earnings = RE). The applicable journal entry follows each financial statement effect template entry and shows the effects of each transaction on specific accounts.

EXHIBIT 6.1: EXAMPLE 1 SOLUTION

	Assets	=	Liabilities	+	Shareholders' Equity		
					CC	AOCI	RE
1	Cash +500,000				Common Stock +100,000 APIC +400,000		

Cash	500,000	
Common Stock		100,000
APIC		400,000

	Assets	=	Liabilities	+	Shareholders' Equity		
					CC	AOCI	RE
2	Land +150,000				Common Stock +28,000 APIC +122,000		

Land	150,000	
Common Stock		28,000
APIC		122,000

	Assets	=	Liabilities	+	Shareholders' Equity		
					CC	AOCI	RE
3	Cash +75,000				Preferred Stock +50,000 APIC +25,000		

Cash	75,000	
Preferred Stock		50,000
APIC		25,000

Down Payment

	Assets	=	Liabilities	+	Shareholders' Equity		
					CC	AOCI	RE
4	Cash +72,000				Common Stock +40,000 APIC +200,000 Subscriptions Receivable −168,000		

Cash	72,000	
Subscriptions Receivable	168,000	
Common Stock		40,000
APIC		200,000

Receipt of Remaining Cash

	Assets	=	Liabilities	+	Shareholders' Equity		
					CC	AOCI	RE
4	Cash +168,000				Subscriptions Receivable +168,000		

Cash	168,000	
Subscriptions Receivable		168,000

Shareholders' equity is increased by the fair value of the asset (cash) contributed to the corporation in Transaction 1. In Transaction 2, the fair value of the land contributed to the company is a readily determinable $150,000 (cash price of similar land), and this amount becomes the basis for measurement of the transaction. However, often non-cash asset (for example, land) fair values are harder to obtain and may require the corporation to rely on an estimate of the fair value of common shares issued (for example, share price in an active market if available). Note that contributed capital is divided into par value and additional paid-in capital amounts when preferred or common shares are issued (Transactions 1–3). In Transaction 4, the contra-equity account, Subscriptions Receivable, is used to set the net equity interest equal to the cash received as down payment. Because a down payment of only $72,000 is received, contributed capital increases only $72,000 (= $40,000 par value + $200,000 APIC – $168,000 subscription receivable contra-equity). When the remainder of the cash is received, the contra-equity account is reduced, which increases total contributed capital by the amount of cash received.

Cash flow effects of these financing activities are reported in the financing section of the statement of cash flows as sources of cash. The issue of stock for land is reported in a separate schedule of "significant investing and financing activities that do not affect cash" that accompanies the statement of cash flows.

Example 2

Refer to PepsiCo's Consolidated Balance Sheet (Appendix A). PepsiCo has issued 1,782 million shares of common stock (out of 3,600 million shares authorized for issue by the board of directors) with a par value of 1 2/3¢ per share. (1,782 million × 1 2/3¢ per share is approximately equal to $30 million.) The December 27, 2008 balance in capital in excess of par (that is, additional paid-in capital) implies that issue prices over time have exceeded par value by $351 million. PepsiCo reports $41 in preferred stock, but does not use a separate additional paid-in capital account because the preferred stock has no par value. PepsiCo reports in Note 12 that the preferred stock was issued for an employee stock ownership program established by its Quaker subsidiary. Each of the 266,253 shares outstanding as of December 27, 2008, is convertible into 4.9625 shares of PepsiCo common stock at the option of the holder. PepsiCo also may call the preferred shares at $78 per share plus accrued and unpaid dividends. We examine the financial statement effects of conversions and calls later in this chapter.

Distributions to Shareholders: Dividends

Net income is accumulated through time in retained earnings, which is reported as part of shareholders' equity in the balance sheet. Total shareholders' equity, which represents the shareholders' claims on assets, equals original capital contributed by shareholders plus the accumulation of net income (in retained earnings) and other comprehensive income (in accumulated other comprehensive income) less treasury stock. Dividend distributions are simply a transfer (usually in cash) to shareholders of a portion of what they already own: namely, the net assets of the firm. As a consequence, dividends reduce retained earnings. The portion of net income not paid out in dividends represents reinvestments by shareholders. As discussed in Chapter 12, retention of earnings by corporations effectively reflects additional equity investment by shareholders, which increases the earnings hurdle for the company.

The declaration of dividends is formalized by three important dates because of the administrative complexity of identifying shareholders of record at any given point in time. On the date on which the board of directors declares a dividend, the *date of declaration*, the firm incurs a legal liability to distribute the dividend to owners of the stock on a specific future date, the *date of record.* On the *date of payment*, the dividend distribution occurs. Typically, these three dates are several weeks apart.

Corporations generally pay dividends in cash. However, corporations can pay dividends with an interest-bearing promise to pay dividends (scrip dividends), investments in other corporations' stock (property dividends), or additional shares of the corporation's own stock

(stock dividends). For cash, scrip, and property dividends, the retained earnings component of shareholders' equity is reduced by the fair value of the item distributed on the date of declaration and a liability is recorded. Dividends decrease the net assets of a corporation, and this decrease is reported in the statement of shareholders' equity. The date of record has no impact on the corporation's accounting. No change in equity occurs on the date of payment because both assets (cash or property) and liabilities (dividends payable) decrease (that is, no change in *net* assets). If dividends are declared but not paid by year-end, a (non-operating) liability for dividends payable appears in the current liabilities section of the balance sheet.[5]

In many jurisdictions (especially non-U.S. countries), the balance of retained earnings represents the limit for dividend payments.[6] However, *liquidating dividends*, payments to shareholders that exceed the balance in retained earnings, can occur. Recall that the two primary components of shareholders' equity are contributed capital (common and preferred shares at par value plus additional paid-in capital accounts) and retained earnings. When equity capital is issued, the contributed capital accounts increase. As income is earned, retained earnings increases. Finally, when dividends are paid, retained earnings decreases. If the dividend is greater than the retained earnings balance, in most jurisdictions, the increment must be used to decrease contributed capital. A liquidating dividend is a return of the original investment by shareholders (that is, their original contribution to the firm when they purchased common shares).

Stock Dividends and Stock Splits

On occasion, corporations distribute shares of their own stock to investors. A *stock dividend* does not involve a transfer of assets to investors. Thus, unlike other dividends, stock dividends result in no change in total shareholders' equity. Also, because no change occurs in the assets of the corporation and proportional ownership is retained, investor wealth is unchanged by stock dividends, per se.

The effects of stock dividends and splits on retained earnings and contributed capital are determined by accounting rules and jurisdictional legal requirements.[7] In small stock dividends (distributions of less than 20–25 percent of common shares), the fair value of shares issued is transferred out of retained earnings and into contributed capital. U.S. GAAP is ambiguous with respect to midrange dividends (20–100 percent), and frequently, laws of the state of incorporation determine the accounting treatment. However, in most cases (and consistent with SEC guidance), midrange stock dividends are treated as a transfer of the par value of shares among shareholders' equity accounts (that is, from retained earnings to contributed capital or within contributed capital accounts).

Most large distributions that are greater than or equal to 100 percent are in the form of a *stock split*. Suppose a company wanted to double the number of shares outstanding and therefore halve the price of its stock. This could be accomplished by issuing a 100 percent stock dividend or a 2-for-1 stock split. Similar to midrange stock dividends, accounting for a large stock dividend depends on appropriate state law. Most of the time, the par value of the shares is transferred to common stock from either retained earnings or additional paid-in capital.

---

[5]IFRS (*IAS* 1) requires disclosure of proposed but not yet approved dividends and post-year-end declared dividends.

[6]Dividends also are often based on earnings calculated under statutory financial statements of a given country. For example, SAP reports in its 2008 Annual Report that "Under the German Stock Corporation Act (Aktiengesetz), the total amount of dividends available for distribution to SAP AG's shareholders is based on the earnings of SAP AG as reported in its statutory financial statements which are determined under the accounting rules stipulated by the German Commercial Code (Handelsgesetzbuch)."

[7]Committee on Accounting Procedure, *Accounting Research Bulletin No. 43*, "Restatement and Revision of Accounting Research Bulletins No. 1–42" (1953); *FASB Codification Topic 505.*

In a stock split, U.S. GAAP does not require an amount to be shifted from retained earnings to contributed capital, but state laws may allow an amount to be shifted from either retained earnings or additional paid-in capital to common stock. Accounting rules require that the par value of individual shares be adjusted so that the total par value after the stock split is the same as the total par value before the split. Therefore, in a 2-for-1 split of 50,000 shares of $10 par value stock, a company issues an additional 50,000 shares and reduces par value to $5 on all 100,000 shares.

From an analysis viewpoint, it is important to remember that the accounting for stock dividends and splits simply reallocates amounts *within* shareholders' equity. The total amount of shareholders' equity remains unchanged because assets have not been disbursed from the corporation (that is, cash has not been paid out), although increasing the number of shares outstanding does proportionately decrease per-share amounts for earnings, book value, and cash flow.

Example 3

Motorola, Inc., reports the following in its 2007 financial statements: common stock, $3 par, 2,263.1 million shares outstanding; average share price during 2007 was approximately $20; common dividends paid during 2007 were $.20 per share. Exhibit 6.2 shows the financial statement effects of the following events. (Assume the events are independent.)

1. Motorola's dividend declaration and payment (2,263.1 million shares × $.20 per share = $452.6 million). Assume that the dividends are declared and then paid at a later date.
2. Motorola distributes a property dividend by giving common shareholders common shares of another company that it carries as a short-term investment in marketable securities. The securities have a fair value of $2,000,000 and an original cost of $1,800,000. Motorola uses mark-to-market accounting for these securities and declares the dividend at some time after the securities have been marked to market.
3. Motorola distributes a 10 percent stock dividend (10% × 2,263.1 million shares outstanding = 226.3 million shares; 226.3 million shares × $3 = $678.9 million par value; 226.3 million shares × $20 market price = $4,526 million fair value).
4. Motorola distributes a 100 percent stock dividend (2,263.1 million additional shares; 2,263.1 × $3 = $6,789.3 million par value).
5. Motorola declares a 2-for-1 stock split.
6. Motorola declares a 1-for-2 reverse stock split.

All amounts in Exhibit 6.2 are in millions of dollars:

Exhibit 6.2: Example 3 Solution

Declaration

	Assets	=	Liabilities	+	Shareholders' Equity: CC	Shareholders' Equity: AOCI	Shareholders' Equity: RE
1			Dividends Payable +452.6				Retained Earnings −452.6

Retained Earnings	452.6	
Dividends Payable		452.6

Payment

	Assets	=	Liabilities	+	Shareholders' Equity: CC	Shareholders' Equity: AOCI	Shareholders' Equity: RE
1	Cash −452.6		Dividends Payable −452.6				

Dividends Payable	452.6	
Cash		452.6

(Continued)

EXHIBIT 6.2 (CONTINUED)

	Assets	=	Liabilities	+	Shareholders' Equity		
					CC	AOCI	RE
2	Investments −2.0						Retained Earnings −2.0

Retained Earnings	2.0	
Investments		2.0

	Assets	=	Liabilities	+	Shareholders' Equity		
					CC	AOCI	RE
3					Common Stock +678.9 APIC +3,847.1		Retained Earnings −4,526.0

Retained Earnings	4,526.0	
Common Stock		678.9
APIC		3,847.1

	Assets	=	Liabilities	+	Shareholders' Equity		
					CC	AOCI	RE
4					Common Stock +6,789.3		Retained Earnings −6,789.3

Retained Earnings	6,789.3	
Common Stock		6,789.3

5. Memorandum entry only to note number of shares outstanding doubles to 4,526.2 million, and par value decreases to $1.50 per share.
6. Memorandum entry only to note number of shares outstanding falls in half to 1,131.6 million, and par value doubles to $6 per share.

Note that dividends distributed in the form of assets (that is, cash and property; Transactions 1 and 2) decrease shareholders' equity (the sum of the last three columns). Dividends distributed in the form of common stock (Transactions 3 and 4) generate a rearrangement of shareholders' equity but no change in total shareholders' equity. Likewise, stock splits (Transactions 5 and 6) have no effect on total shareholders' equity or the balance of any account in shareholders' equity. Cash outflow for cash dividends is reported in the financing section of the statement of cash flows.[8]

Example 4

Refer to PepsiCo's 2008 Consolidated Statement of Common Shareholders' Equity. In the reconciliation from beginning to ending retained earnings, PepsiCo reports cash dividends declared in 2008 on common stock ($2,589 million), on preferred stock ($2 million), and on RSUs, restricted stock units ($8 million), yielding total reduction of retained earnings due to a dividend declaration of $2,599 million. PepsiCo's Consolidated Statement of Cash Flows reports $2,541 million cash dividends paid in the Financing Activities section. The excess of dividends declared over dividends paid as of the balance sheet date ($58 million) is reflected as an increase in the non-operating liability "Dividends payable." (See Example 3, Transaction 1.) Note 14, "Supplemental Financial Information" (Appendix A), disaggregates current liabilities and confirms the $58 million increase in dividends payable from $602 million at the end of 2007 to $660 million at the end of 2008.

[8]Transactions 3 and 4 in Example 3 assume that Motorola declares a stock dividend and distributes the dividend in the same period. If a financial statement reporting date intervenes, "Stock dividend distributable" will be reported as a contra-equity account instead of a reduction in retained earnings as shown in the template.

Distributions to Shareholders: Share Repurchases

For several reasons, corporations may distribute cash to shareholders and reduce shareholders' equity via *share repurchases*. For example, employee compensation plans often grant options to acquire common stock. To service the possible exercise of options, companies may repurchase shares to have a supply of their own stock on hand or, alternatively, to offset the dilution of existing shareholders' proportional ownership from share issuances under the option exercises. Corporations also might repurchase stock simply to shift the mix of debt and equity financing or to signal to investors that corporate management believes the stock is undervalued because investors have underestimated potential future earnings or cash flows. Finally, fewer shares outstanding means less dilution of voting power. This may be particularly important if the firm is facing a takeover attempt.

When a firm engages in transactions like those above that reduce equity, the effects on the statement of cash flows are simple. Using cash to reduce equity is a cash outflow reported as a financing activity. Similarly, the effects on the income statement are simple: there are no effects. The reduction of equity is a distribution to owners, a transaction that does not affect income. Balance sheet effects of share repurchases depend on whether the shares of stock are retired or held as treasury stock for eventual reissue. If the shares are retired, the amounts originally recorded in the common stock (that is, par value) and the additional paid-in capital accounts are removed. The typical case is that the cash paid to retire the shares exceeds the amount at which the shares were originally issued. This excess is treated as a dividend, and like regular cash dividends, it is removed from retained earnings. Less typical is the case in which the amount paid to buy back the shares is less than the original issue price. In this case, additional paid-in capital is increased as if the shareholders left amounts in the firm as a permanent capital contribution.

If firms repurchase stock for reissue at a later date, the stock is referred to as *treasury stock*. Two acceptable methods are used to account for treasury stock: the cost method and the par method. Because the par method is rarely used, we focus our discussion on the cost method. The cost method was designed under the assumption that any treasury stock acquired would be reissued.

A cash disbursement to acquire stock to be held in the treasury decreases shareholders' equity. The treasury stock acquired is not an asset of the corporation. A corporation cannot own itself. The payment of cash to owners is a distribution to owners. Under the cost method, this distribution is shown as an increase in a contra-equity account called treasury stock. The increase in contra-equity is equivalent to a decrease in equity. Under the cost method, the treasury stock account is usually shown at the bottom of the shareholders' equity section. Subsequent treasury share reissues increase (or decrease) additional paid-in capital if the subsequent reissue price is greater than (less than) the cost of the treasury stock. No gain or loss is recorded because the reissue of treasury stock is, in concept, identical to the original issue of common stock (cash invested, common stock issued).[9]

---

[9]The main difference between the cost and rarely used par methods is in how treasury stock is disclosed in the shareholders' equity section of the balance sheet. The amount of cash paid by a corporation to reacquire a share and hold it as treasury stock is intended to compensate the shareholder for his or her original contribution (par value of stock plus additional paid-in capital) plus his or her share of earnings not paid out in dividends (retained earnings). Therefore, the cost method discloses treasury stock as a subtraction from the totality of shareholders' equity. Under the par method, the cost of treasury stock would be broken up and allocated as reductions of the individual accounts in owners' equity. The portion of treasury stock cost related to par value would be subtracted from the common stock account. The portion related to originally contributed capital over par would be subtracted from the additional paid-in capital account. The portion related to earnings not paid out in dividends would be subtracted from retained earnings. Thus, the accounts in shareholders' equity would be reported net of the allocated portion of the treasury share purchase. The sole exception to this "netting" is that common stock would be reported at par value of shares issued and a contra-equity account, treasury stock, would be reported as a subtraction from common stock at an amount equal to par value as a means of disclosing the existence of treasury stock.

Example 5

Refer to the Common Shareholders' Equity section of PepsiCo's Consolidated Balance Sheet (Appendix A). PepsiCo reports a subtraction in the equity section for (in millions) "Repurchased common stock, at cost (229 and 177 shares, respectively)" of $14,122 million and $10,387 million at the ends of 2008 and 2007, respectively. Therefore, PepsiCo uses the cost method. PepsiCo's Consolidated Statement of Common Shareholders' Equity explains the change between years. Additional share repurchases total $4,720 million. This amount is a cash outflow to reduce equity capital, so it also is reported in the Financing Activities section of PepsiCo's Consolidated Statement of Cash Flows. In fact, it is the largest single cash flow for 2008. Treasury stock is often reissued when stock options are exercised, a topic discussed in the next section.

Equity Issued as Compensation: Stock Options

Firms develop compensation plans to attract, retain, and motivate employees. Many of these plans include cash compensation that is fixed or that varies with levels of employee performance, with performance defined by an accounting-based income measure (such as return on equity) or stock returns. In a typical compensation arrangement, firms give employees the right, or option, to acquire shares of common stock at a fixed price. If share prices increase over time, employees can exercise their option to purchase shares at a price that is less than the market price of the shares. These arrangements are referred to as *stock options*, and their use skyrocketed in the last 20 years. Firms in the technology sector, especially since the Internet boom of the 1990s, have used options as a dominant component of their employee compensation packages.[10]

Stock options permit employees to purchase shares of common stock at a price usually equal to the market price of the stock at the time the firm grants the stock option. Employees exercise these stock options at a later time if the stock price increases above the stock option exercise price. Corporations grant stock options because options have characteristics that align the interests of the employee with those of shareholders. Clearly, an increase in stock price benefits shareholders, which is the same way stock options reward employees. Unlike compensation in the form of salaries, however, stock options do not require firms to use cash during the period when they grant stock options to employees. In addition to the incentive feature of stock options, they also can be used to attract or retain employees. The ability of a corporation to attract employees is enhanced when firms offer equity incentives such as stock options as part of a sign-on or retention package. Likewise, corporations benefit by reduced employee turnover, as employees with unvested stock options face incentives to continue their employment with the company to realize the financial upside as the company's stock price appreciates.

Fair Value Method and Required Disclosures

An understanding of the accounting for stock-based compensation requires understanding several key parameters. The *grant date* is the date a firm gives a stock option to employees. The *vesting date* is the first date employees can exercise their stock options. Employees cannot exercise options before the vesting date or after the end of the option's life. To enhance employee retention and increase motivation during the vesting period, firms usually structure stock

---

[10]Due to more recent concerns about excessive executive compensation, the use of stock options has declined to some degree. However, many companies still use stock option plans for incentive compensation.

option plans so that a period of time elapses between the grant date and the vesting date. Firms may preclude employees from exercising the option for one or more years, or they may set an exercise price so high that employees would not want to exercise the option until the stock price increases. The *exercise date* is the date employees elect to exchange the option plus cash for shares of common stock. The *exercise price* is the price specified in the stock option contract for purchasing the common stock. The *market price* is the price of the stock as it trades in the market. In theory, the value of a stock option has two elements: (1) the benefit realized on the exercise date because the market price of the stock exceeds the exercise price (the *benefit element*) and (2) the length of the period during which the holder can exercise the option (the *time-value element*).

The amount of the benefit element is not known until the exercise date. In general, stock options with exercise prices less than the current market price of the stock (described as *in the money*) have a higher value than stock options with exercise prices exceeding the current market price of the stock (described as *out of the money*). The time-value element of an option results from the benefit it provides its holder if the market price of the stock increases during the exercise period. The greater the market price of the stock exceeds the exercise price during the exercise period, the greater the benefit to the option holder. This time-value element of an option will have more value the longer the exercise period, the more volatile the market price of the stock, the lower the dividend yield, and the lower the discount rate. Note that a stock option may have an exercise price that exceeds the current market price (zero value for the benefit element) but still have value because of the possibility that the market price will exceed the exercise price on the exercise date (positive value for the time-value element). As the expiration date of the option approaches, the value of the time-value element approaches zero.[11]

Statements No. 123 and *No. 123 (Revised 2004)* address accounting for stock options, and both were extremely controversial and followed decades of tumultuous arguments about how to reflect the cost of granting stock options to employees.[12] Before these standards, APB *Opinion No. 25* (released in 1972) accounted for stock-based compensation expense using the *intrinsic value method.* Under this method, the amount to be expensed under any option grant was deemed to be the intrinsic value of the option when it was granted, equal to the market value of the underlying share minus the exercise price of the option. Perhaps not surprisingly, companies converged to a practice whereby they granted options with the exercise price equal to the market price per share on the date of grant. Under the intrinsic value method of computing the value of a stock option, setting the exercise price equal to the market price on the date of grant yields an intrinsic value of zero. So stock-based compensation expense was zero, allowing firms to report higher earnings numbers.[13] The FASB revisited the topic in the 1990s, culminating in the board's issuing an exposure draft of a new reporting standard that would have required firms to recognize the cost of stock options as compensation expense on the date of the grant based on measurement of the option's fair value based on an option pricing model. This proposal was never adopted, however, because the business community lobbied various congressional interests so vigorously that some U.S. senators pressured the FASB to withdraw its proposal. The FASB eventually issued *Statement No. 123* in 1995, which reaffirmed the conclusions of *Opinion No. 25* but required only pro

---

[11]For an elaboration on the history of options pricing, see Fischer Black and Myron Scholes, "The Pricing of Options and Corporate Liabilities," *Journal of Political Economy* (May/June 1973), pp. 637–654.

[12]Financial Accounting Standards Board, *Statement No. 123,* "Accounting for Stock-Based Compensation" (1995); Financial Accounting Standards Board, *Statement No 123 (Revised 2004),* "Accounting for Share-Based Payment" (2004). *FASB Codification Topic 718.*

[13]Accounting Principles Board *Opinion No. 25,* "Accounting for Stock Issued to Employees" (1972). *Statements No. 123* and *123 (Revised 2004)* supersede *Opinion No. 25.*

forma *disclosures* in the notes to the financial statements about the impact of stock option grants on earnings if the company utilized the fair value method instead of the intrinsic value method. In contrast to the intrinsic value method, the fair value method of accounting for stock options computes the value of an option grant based on various option pricing models, all of which attach a positive value to stock options with exercise prices equal to or greater than the share price on the date of grant.

Subsequent to issuance of *Statement No. 123* in 1995 and, importantly, after the financial reporting and accounting scandals of the early 2000s, some firms began to voluntarily treat the cost of stock options given to employees as compensation expense based on an assessment of the option's fair value. These firms decided that the fair value approach is theoretically superior or that investors would view these firms more favorably for taking this voluntary action. Riding the growing movement of stock options being recognized as a form of compensation expense, as well as the view of many that the accounting scandals were partially the result of poor corporate governance and reporting, including reporting for stock options, the FASB revisited the topic. The result was *Statement No. 123 (Revised 2004)*, which requires firms to use the fair value method to value stock options and report the amounts as compensation expense in the income statement.[14]

As noted previously, under the fair value method, firms must measure the value of stock options on the date of grant. Because the value of employee stock options typically cannot be measured with an observable value established by trading in an active market, *Statement No. 123 (Revised 2004)* recognizes that most firms will use an option pricing model to estimate the value of the options. *Statement No. 123 (Revised 2004)* does not require a specific option pricing model, although the Black-Scholes model [15] or a lattice model (for example, the binomial model) are most commonly used. A detailed discussion of option valuation models can be found in the finance literature and is beyond the scope of this text. However, any model employed must incorporate a variety of factors, including the exercise price of the option, the term of the option, the current market price of each share of underlying stock, expected stock volatility, dividends, and the risk-free interest rate.[16]

Once the value of stock options is estimated using an acceptable option pricing model, firms must recognize this amount as compensation expense ratably over the period in which an employee provides services. This is commonly the vesting period of the stock options. *Statement No. 123 (Revised 2004)* requires disclosures regarding stock option grants, their effect on total compensation expense, the methodology (model) used to value the stock options, and the key assumptions made to estimate the value of the stock options.

Example 6

Assume that an Internet-based company decides to conserve cash and align upper management incentives with shareholders' incentives by compensating managers with 9,000 options to purchase $1 par value common stock any time during the next seven years for $10 per share. The current stock price is $10 per share. The vesting period is three years. Using an appropriate options pricing model, the company values the options at $2 each.

---

[14]The promulgation of FASB *Statement No. 123 (Revised 2004)* represents a convergence with international standards. International Accounting Standards Board, *International Financial Reporting Standard 2*, "Share-Based Payment."

[15]See footnote 9.

[16]A critique of the reliability of various valuation models can be found in American Accounting Association's Financial Accounting Standards Committee, "Response to the FASB's Exposure Draft on Share-Based Payment: An Amendment of FASB *Statements No. 123* and *No. 95*," *Accounting Horizons* (June 2005), pp. 101–114.

Exhibit 6.3 illustrates the financial statement effects of these transactions:

1. Grant date (the date options are granted to management)
2. Recognition of compensation expense for each of the three years in the vesting period
3. Exercise of a single option when a share of common stock is trading at $18
4. Expiration of a single option
5. Revocation of a single option early in the third year of the vesting period when a manager leaves the firm

The options' fair value is $2 per option × 9,000 options = $18,000. No financial statement effects occur at the grant date because the manager has yet to provide service to the firm. The $18,000 fair value is allocated over the three-year vesting period, $6,000 per year, as an increase in compensation expense (a decrease in net income, which is also a decrease in retained earnings). Rather than accepting cash compensation, the manager accepts an option to acquire an equity interest as evidenced by the stock options. APIC from stock options increases shareholders' equity. In Transaction 2, note that shareholders' equity in total (the sum of the last three columns) is not affected by the compensation allocation process because assets and liabilities do not change.[17]

Exercise of a single option (Transaction 3) involves a transfer of the stock option plus a $10 exercise price from the manager to the corporation. Through the effects on three shareholders' equity accounts, total shareholders' equity increases by $10, the fair value of the cash received. Note that the cash received is not equal to the fair value of the common equity, which is trading at $18. The amount reflected in the equity accounts after this transaction is posted is $1 in common stock and $11 in additional paid-in capital. Thus, common stock issued is recorded at $12, which equals the fair value of the cash surrendered ($10) plus the grant date estimate of the fair value of the option ($2).[18]

In a stock option expiration (Transaction 4), the capital contributed to the firm by the manager's employment is reclassified as a permanent contribution to shareholders' equity. If a manager fails to perform the three years of service, the option is revoked (Transaction 5). The amount of the compensation expense related to revoked options is removed from compensation expense of the current period. This treatment is an example of a change in estimate handled prospectively. The firm estimated that compensation expense was $6,000 per year based on the expected three-year service of employees. If an employee leaves the firm and an option is revoked, estimates must be revised *going forward.* Prior period adjustments to expenses are not made.[19]

Option events create two cash flows. The exercise of an option increases cash from equity issues and is reported as a financing activity. Although not shown in the preceding template, the corporation will receive a tax deduction at the date the manager exercises the option, equal to the market price at the exercise date minus the exercise price. (The manager will be taxed on this same amount because it is compensation.) Under a recent FASB rule, the tax savings is treated as a financing cash inflow.[20]

---

[17]The no longer accepted intrinsic value method assumes the options have no intrinsic value at the grant date because the exercise price equals the stock price. This approach ignored the time value of money element and assumed that managers are indifferent about using the option to acquire at $10 per share or just going out into the open market and acquiring the share for $10. Compensation expense under the intrinsic value method would have been zero.

[18]If previously acquired treasury shares rather than new shares are issued, treasury stock is reduced by the amount of the original acquisition cost and APIC is used to record the remainder of the equity increase.

[19]We assume that the forfeiture was unexpected. If forfeitures are expected, then the original estimate of compensation expense should be lower, and the treatment we show should be used for additional unexpected forfeitures. Also, we reduced compensation expense by the entire amount of the option (instead of the two-thirds already recognized as compensation expense) assuming that the last year's worth of the compensation expense allocation would be unaffected. An alternative would be to reduce compensation expense by $2 × 2/3 and reduce the $6,000 compensation expense for Year 3 by the same amount.

[20]Financial Accounting Standards Board, *Statement No 123 (Revised 2004),* "Accounting for Share-Based Payment" (2004).

Exhibit 6.3: Example 6 Solution

1. No entry at grant date. (The contract is executory.) However, the fair value of the options is measured at the grant date. Fair value = 9,000 options × $2 per option = $18,000.

Year 1

	Assets	=	Liabilities	+	Shareholders' Equity: CC	Shareholders' Equity: AOCI	Shareholders' Equity: RE
2					APIC—Stock Options +6,000		Compensation Expense −6,000

Year 2

	Assets	=	Liabilities	+	Shareholders' Equity: CC	Shareholders' Equity: AOCI	Shareholders' Equity: RE
2					APIC—Stock Options +6,000		Compensation Expense −6,000

Year 3

	Assets	=	Liabilities	+	Shareholders' Equity: CC	Shareholders' Equity: AOCI	Shareholders' Equity: RE
2					APIC—Stock Options +6,000		Compensation Expense −6,000

Each year:

Compensation Expense	6,000	
APIC—Stock Options		6,000

Exercise

	Assets	=	Liabilities	+	Shareholders' Equity: CC	Shareholders' Equity: AOCI	Shareholders' Equity: RE
3	Cash +10				Common Stock +1 APIC +11 APIC—Stock Options −2		

Cash	10	
APIC—Stock Options	2	
Common Stock		1
APIC		11

Expiration

	Assets	=	Liabilities	+	Shareholders' Equity: CC	Shareholders' Equity: AOCI	Shareholders' Equity: RE
4					APIC—Expired Options +2 APIC—Stock Options −2		

APIC—Stock Options	2	
APIC—Expired Options		2

Revocation

	Assets	=	Liabilities	+	Shareholders' Equity: CC	Shareholders' Equity: AOCI	Shareholders' Equity: RE
5					APIC—Stock Options −2		Compensation Expense +2

APIC—Stock Options	2	
Compensation Expense		2

Alternative Share-Based Compensation: Restricted Stock and RSUs

Exercising stock options can create a cash flow problem for managers at the exercise date. The manager must pay the exercise price and may have to pay taxes on compensation in order to acquire the stock, which he or she may want to hold rather than sell. An alternative share-based compensation program eliminates a manager's need to pay the exercise price. At the grant date, the manager could be given shares of stock rather than options (far fewer shares than options because the fair value of a share is usually greater than the fair value of an option to purchase the stock), which cannot be traded until the vesting period is completed (*restricted stock*).[21] Or the manager could receive non-tradable rights for a number of shares of stock once the vesting period is completed (called *restricted stock units*, or RSUs). In concept, the accounting for stock options, restricted stock, and RSUs is similar except for the fact that stock is issued (or restrictions placed on trading already issued stock will be removed) once the vesting period ends. Accordingly, financial statements reflect the existence of the restricted stock or RSU at the grant date as illustrated in the following example.

Example 7

Assume that an Internet-based company decides to compensate managers by giving them 1,000 shares of $1 par value common stock when the stock price is $10 per share. The vesting period is two years, and the stock cannot be traded until the vesting period is over. Exhibit 6.4 illustrates the financial statement effects of the following transactions:

1. Grant date (the date restricted stock is granted to management)
2. Recognition of compensation expense at the end of each of the two years in the vesting period

Recall that no entry occurs at the grant date in the case of stock options. However, in the case of restricted stock (Transaction 1), the common stock has been issued, so an entry recognizes the existence of the common stock. Note that no change in net assets occurred, so total shareholders' equity does not change. During the vesting period, as managers earn the compensation under the restricted stock plan (Transaction 2), retained earnings is decreased by the net income effect of compensation expense and deferred compensation, a contra-equity account, is decreased. The net effect of the second transaction is a shift of amounts out of retained earnings in to contributed capital. Again, no change in assets or liabilities occurred, so no change in total shareholders' equity is recognized.

The decrease in stock option use in recent years has been offset by an increase in the use of restricted stock plans and cash settlement plans. Once the FASB disallowed the use of the intrinsic value method to value stock options (usually at $0), the primary benefit of using stock options for compensation—no expense on the income statement—disappeared. As a consequence, the use of restricted stock became more common, and although there are some tax ramifications to the employee, a primary benefit to the employee of restricted stock grants relative to option grants is that options can expire worthless but restricted stock almost always has a nonzero value.

[21]The descriptor *restricted* simply means that the stock granted is generally restricted from being traded until it vests. Generally, the shares are common shares approved by shareholders for such purposes.

Exhibit 6.4: Example 7 Solution

Grant Date

	Assets	=	Liabilities	+	Shareholders' Equity: CC	Shareholders' Equity: AOCI	Shareholders' Equity: RE
1					Common Stock +1,000 APIC +9,000 Deferred Compensation +10,000		

Deferred Compensation	10,000	
Common Stock		1,000
APIC		9,000

Year 1

	Assets	=	Liabilities	+	Shareholders' Equity: CC	Shareholders' Equity: AOCI	Shareholders' Equity: RE
2					Deferred Compensation +5,000		Compensation Expense −5,000

Year 2

	Assets	=	Liabilities	+	Shareholders' Equity: CC	Shareholders' Equity: AOCI	Shareholders' Equity: RE
2					Deferred Compensation +5,000		Compensation Expense −5,000

Each Year:

Compensation Expense	5,000	
Deferred Compensation		5,000

Alternative Share-Based Compensation: Cash-Settled Share-Based Plans

The number, complexity, and diversity of share-based compensation plans do not permit a comprehensive treatment in any given textbook. However, the stock option, restricted stock, and RSU plans illustrated in this chapter represent the large majority of compensation plans settled by the conveyance of common stock to an employee.

In recent years, a number of firms have created compensation plans that provide cash compensation to employees based on share-price appreciation. These plans, often called *stock appreciation rights* plans, are cash-settled plans and, accordingly, do not result in increases in the contributed capital portion of shareholders' equity pursuant to a distribution of an option or a share of common stock. Conceptually, cash-settled share appreciation plans are similar to compensating employees with cash bonuses for output (for example, exceeding sales quotes or earnings targets). The key difference is that the firm relies on the stock market's assessment of the value of the firm to determine the amount of the cash payment.

The essence of the accounting for cash-settled compensation plans is an increase in an operating liability for the estimated cash payments to the employee and a corresponding increase in compensation expense. For example, SAP AG's IFRS-based financial statements describe the workings of its STAR plan and note that "As our STAR plans are settled in cash, rather than by issuing equity instruments, a liability is recorded for such plans based on the current fair value of the STAR awards at the reporting date."

Example 8

Note 6, "Stock-Based Compensation" (Appendix A), describes the stock options PepsiCo granted to employees and members of the company's board of directors. The PepsiCo LTIP (long-term incentive plan) is typical of plans offered by many firms. PepsiCo options generally have ten-year terms and three-year vesting periods. In a subsection of Note 6, "Stock-Based Compensation—Method of Accounting and Our Assumptions" (Appendix A), PepsiCo states, "We account for our employee stock options . . . under the fair value method of accounting using a Black-Scholes valuation model to measure stock option expense at the date of grant." The subsection describes the assumptions used in the Black-Scholes model. PepsiCo also uses RSUs to compensate executives. Stock-based compensation for 2008 ($238 million) is relatively small for PepsiCo when compared to its total expenses for 2008 of more than $36 billion, as shown on its Consolidated Income Statement. However, this is not the case for some firms, particularly technology-based firms.

PepsiCo reports four line items in its 2008 Consolidated Statement of Cash Flows that relate to share-based compensation arrangements. In the Financing Activities section, cash proceeds from the exercise of stock options totaled $620 million, which by any measure is a substantial increase in equity financing. The Financing Activities section also includes the tax benefits from the deduction afforded PepsiCo when employees exercise their options, $107 million in 2008. Because stock option-based compensation is an operating expense that reduces net income (and the tax savings increases net income), two line items exist in the Operating Activities section as well. Under the indirect method of preparing this section, stock-based compensation expense is a non-cash expense; thus, $238 million is added back to net income. Also, although the excess tax benefits are a source of cash, the source is not considered an operating activity by rule; thus, the $107 million tax benefits are deducted to arrive at operating cash flows.

Net Income, Retained Earnings, Accumulated Other Comprehensive Income, and Reserves

In addition to contributed capital, earned capital not distributed in dividends is available to finance investing and operating activities. The following sections describe the reporting of earned capital.

Net Income and Retained Earnings

The financing events examined so far—equity issues, share buybacks, and dividends—are transactions with shareholders in which net assets (that is, shareholders' equity) either increase or decrease. The use of capital obtained from financing activities to support profitable investing and operating activities also leads to increases in shareholders' equity via increases in net assets reported as net income on the income statement. Then, through the accounting closing process, net income is reflected as an increase in retained earnings on the statement of shareholders' equity, which supports the final balance in retained earnings reported on the balance sheet.

PepsiCo's 2008 Consolidated Statement of Shareholders' Equity reconciles the balance of retained earnings at the beginning of 2008 ($28,184 million) to its balance at the balance sheet date, December 27, 2008 ($30,638 million). Net income of $5,142 million causes retained earnings (and thus, shareholders' equity) to increase. Dividends declared on common stock, preferred stock, and RSUs decrease retained earnings. Note that PepsiCo adjusts the beginning balance of retained earnings in two of the years before performing the reconciliation. We address these "prior period adjustments" in Chapter 9.

Accumulated Other Comprehensive Income

Another component of shareholders' equity, *AOCI (accumulated other comprehensive income),* is a consequence of standard setters allowing certain asset and liability revaluations (called *other comprehensive income*) to bypass the income statement and be reported directly in shareholders' equity (as opposed to the treatment of items in net income, which first appear on the income statement and then are reflected as an increase in shareholders' equity via an increase in retained earnings).[22] Chapter 3 introduced the comprehensive income concept. This chapter provides brief examples, with subsequent chapters discussing the detailed accounting and reporting.

For example, other comprehensive income arises when firms experience unrealized fair value gains or losses on securities deemed available for sale (described in detail in Chapter 7). Each year, a firm will recognize in comprehensive income the net change in unrealized gains or losses on available-for-sale securities, which are reported cumulatively in AOCI. When the firm sells the securities, it eliminates the unrealized gain or loss account and recognizes a realized gain or loss in measuring net income.

Another example relates to foreign currency translation (discussed in Chapter 7). U.S. firms with foreign operations usually translate the financial statements of their foreign entities into U.S. dollars each period using the exchange rate at the end of the period. Changes in the exchange rate cause an unrealized foreign currency gain or loss. Firms do not recognize this gain or loss in measuring net income each period; instead, they increase or decrease accumulated other comprehensive income (through the Statement of Comprehensive Income). Presumably, using accumulated other comprehensive income to capture such unrealized gains and losses minimizes the impact of the volatility of foreign currency exchange rates on reported profits while reflecting current values of assets and liabilities. If exchange rates reverse or the firm disposes of the foreign unit, it eliminates the unrealized foreign currency adjustment from accumulated other comprehensive income and, in the case of a disposal, recognizes a gain or loss in net income.

IFRS permits periodic revaluations of fixed assets and intangible assets to their current market value (discussed in Chapter 7). Increased valuation of assets leads to an increase in a revaluation reserve account included in the shareholders' equity section of the balance sheet (similar to accumulated other comprehensive income). Depreciation or amortization of the revalued assets may appear fully on the income statement each period as an expense or may be split between the income statement (depreciation or amortization based on acquisition cost) and a reduction in the revaluation reserve (depreciation or amortization based on the excess of current market value over acquisition cost).

The analyst's concern with other comprehensive income is the appropriateness of revaluing the asset and delaying recognition of its income effect. Are the revaluations the free choice of the company's managers, or are they under the purview of the board of directors, the auditors, or other external parties? Total shareholders' equity is the same regardless of whether the unrealized gain or loss immediately affects net income or affects another shareholders' equity account and later affects net income. Because this treatment does not result in an effect on net income of the current period, the analyst may want to restate reported net income of the current period to incorporate other comprehensive income. We revisit this issue in Chapter 9.

---

[22]Financial Accounting Standards Board, *Statement of Accounting Standards No. 130,* "Reporting Comprehensive Income" (1997); *FASB Codification Topic 220*; International Accounting Standards Board, *International Accounting Standard 1,* "Presentation of Financial Statements."

Reserves

In the United States, major revenues, gains, expenses, and losses flow through the income statement. In some countries outside the United States, local country GAAP permits certain income items to bypass the income statement and, instead, increase or decrease a shareholders' equity account directly. A practice in some countries is to create a reserve account by reducing retained earnings. For example, a firm might decrease retained earnings and increase an account titled reserve for contingencies or retained earnings appropriated for contingencies. These reserve accounts appear among the shareholders' equity accounts. When firms later resolve the contingency, they charge the cost against the reserve account rather than include it in expenses. Therefore, these costs bypass the income statement and usually result in an overstatement of earnings. Note that this use of reserves does not misstate total shareholders' equity because all of the affected accounts (retained earnings, reserve accounts, and expense accounts) are components of shareholders' equity. Thus, the analyst's primary concern with these reserves is assessing whether the reported net income that excludes these items is an appropriate base for estimating future earnings. The analyst can study the shareholders' equity portion of the balance sheet to ascertain whether firms have used reserve accounts to avoid sending legitimate expenses through the income statement. Reserves of this type had been particularly common in the German home-country standards-based reporting system prior to the adoption of IFRS.[23]

Example 9

Refer to the Common Shareholders' Equity section of PepsiCo's Consolidated Balance Sheet (Appendix A). At December 27, 2008, PepsiCo reports retained earnings of $30,638 million and an accumulated other comprehensive loss of $4,694 million. The retained earnings balance represents accumulated (over the life of PepsiCo) increases in net assets of the company, *which were reported in net income*, minus dividends declared. The accumulated other comprehensive loss represents decreases in net assets of the company from asset and liability revaluations, *which were not reported in net income*. PepsiCo's Consolidated Statement of Common Shareholders' Equity describes how accumulated other comprehensive loss changed during 2008 from a beginning accumulated loss of $952 million to an ending accumulated loss of $4,694 million. This *change* in accumulated other comprehensive loss (that is, the current year's portion) is the difference between 2008 net income ($5,142 million) and 2008 comprehensive income ($1,349 million). PepsiCo shows this reconciliation in a statement of comprehensive income appearing at the bottom of the Consolidated Statement of Common Shareholders' Equity.[24] The losses that PepsiCo recognize in comprehensive income in 2008 are largely a consequence of a negative currency translation adjustment ($2,484 million) and net losses associated with pensions ($1,358 million). During 2007, comprehensive income was larger than net income because of a positive foreign currency translation adjustment and gains associated with pensions. One argument for recognizing such gains and losses in other comprehensive income and in the accumulated

---

[23]Also found in financial statements prepared under home-country GAAP is the use of a reserve account to designate that a portion of shareholders' equity is not available for dividends. Local laws or practices may dictate that firms transfer an amount from retained earnings, which is available for dividends, to a more permanent account that is not available for dividends. U.S. firms typically "capitalize" a portion of retained earnings when they issue a stock dividend. Several other countries require firms to report a certain amount of legal capital on the balance sheet. Such firms reduce retained earnings and increase an account titled Legal Capital or Legal Reserve. The implication of such disclosures is that assets equal to the amount of this legal capital are not available for dividends. This use of reserves has no effect on net income of the current period or future periods.

[24]IFRS (IAS 1) requires a separate schedule of other comprehensive income included in a note disclosure or included with net income in a statement of comprehensive income. U.S. GAAP also permits these two approaches.

other comprehensive income/loss account is that these types of revaluations of assets and liabilities tend to be transitory; that is, they have the potential to reverse over time. The analyst should examine the behavior of accumulated other comprehensive income through time to see whether including elements of other comprehensive income in current income would aid in the assessment of the risk of the firm and in the prediction of future income.

Summary and Interpretation of Equity

Common shareholders' equity represents the book value of equity investor claims. Dividing common shareholders' equity by the number of common shares outstanding yields *book value per share.* The economic meaning of this number is not clear because owners' equity is the difference between assets and liabilities, each measured using different attributes (for example, historical cost, present value, fair market value, or net realizable value). Reference to equity securities markets provides a *market price per share* of common stock that is created by the interaction of supply and demand for shares. This market price is the dollar amount that a common shareholder would receive from selling a share of owners' equity. The ratio of book and market value, called the *market-to-book ratio,* is as follows:

$$\text{Market-to-Book Ratio} = \text{Market Price per Share/Book Value per Share}$$

Market-to-book ratios are commonly greater than one for two primary reasons. First, the conservatism of accounting (as a result of accounting standards themselves or management's application of accounting standards) leads to book values of individual assets that are typically equal to or less than their fair values (but not greater than their fair values). For example, if a company's operations include a great deal of R&D (research and development) (expensed immediately under U.S. GAAP), the unrecorded economic assets created by such expenditures causes book value per share to be lower than fair value. Second, future growth opportunities increase market price per share but have not been reflected in accounting measurements of book value.

For book value to be recognized in financial statements, U.S. GAAP and IFRS require that transactions have taken place or that unresolved future events can be estimated reliably. Therefore, book value of shareholders' equity tends to lag market value. Chapter 13 describes a valuation approach that relates book value to market value through the expectations of future accounting earnings not yet embedded in book value.

Changes in shareholders' equity result from transactions with owners (issuances of stock and distributions such as dividends and share buybacks) and transactions with non-owners, which are reflected in one of the two parts of comprehensive income, either net income or other comprehensive income. Financing strategy drives the changes in shareholders' equity from transactions with owners. Operating strategies drive the changes in shareholders' equity from transactions with non-owners.

DEBT FINANCING

As discussed in Chapter 5, the use of debt to finance investments and operations levers up the return on common equity, which can benefit common shareholders. However, the use of debt also has its costs. The required return to common shareholders (that is, the cost of equity capital) is increasing in the amount of debt in a corporation's capital structure. Further, net income is reduced by the amount of interest charges on debt and long-term solvency risk is increasing in the amount of debt. Accordingly, the financial reporting and analysis of debt is critical to understanding the profitability and risk of a firm.

This section addresses the accounting for debt financing. Our discussion begins with the principles of liability recognition and the measurement and application of those principles. Liabilities arise from both operating and financing activities. Therefore, this chapter pertains to debt financing; operating liabilities (both short- and long-term) that arise from operating activities are discussed in Chapter 8. Then this chapter considers how financial statements report traditional financing activities, which receive balance sheet recognition (for example, the issue of long-term notes and bonds, debt reduction, accounting for troubled debt, and the issue and conversion of hybrid securities). The final part of the chapter discusses off-balance-sheet financing, giving special attention to lease financing and how an analyst can adjust financial statements to incorporate off-balance-sheet lease financing in the assessment of financial risk.

Principles of Liability Recognition

Financial reporting recognizes an obligation as a liability if it satisfies the following three criteria:

- The obligation involves a probable future sacrifice of economic benefits—a future transfer of cash, goods, or services; the forgoing of a future cash receipt; or the transfer of equity shares—at a specified or determinable date. The firm can measure with reasonable precision the cash-equivalent value of the resources needed to satisfy the obligation.
- The firm has a present obligation (not a possible future obligation) and little or no discretion to avoid the transfer.
- The transaction or event that gave rise to the obligation has already occurred. [25]

Principles of Liability Valuation

The general principles underlying the valuation of liabilities are as follows:

- Liabilities requiring future cash payments (such as the debt financing provided by bonds payable) appear at the present value of the required future cash flows discounted at an interest rate that reflects the uncertainty that the firm will be able to make the cash payments. The firm establishes the discount rate at the time it initially records a liability in the accounts (often referred to as the *historical interest rate*) and generally uses this interest rate in accounting for the liability in all future periods.
- Liabilities requiring the future delivery of goods or services (such as the operating liability for warranties) appear at the estimated cost of those goods and services.
- Liabilities representing cash advances from customers (such as the operating liabilities Rental Fees Received in Advance or Subscription Fees Received in Advance) appear at the amount of the cash advance.

The fair value of a liability may differ from the amount appearing on the balance sheet, particularly for long-term debt. Fair value reflects current interest rates and assessments of the firm's ability to make the required payments as opposed to historical rates in effect when the debt contracts were originally written. U.S. GAAP requires firms to disclose the fair values of financial instruments, whether or not these financial instruments appear as liabilities (or assets) in the notes to the financial statements. Also, recent standards issued

[25]Financial Accounting Standards Board, *Statement of Financial Accounting Concepts No. 6*, "Elements of Financial Statements" (1985). Financial Accounting Standards Board, *Statement of Financial Accounting Standards No. 150*, "Accounting for Certain Financial Instruments with Characteristics of both Liabilities and Equity," (2008) requires certain obligations settled in equity shares to be classified as liabilities; *FASB Codification Topic 480.*

by the FASB and IASB allow firms the option of valuing financial liabilities (and assets) at fair value in the financial statements.[26] Firms may choose to exercise this option on an instrument-by-instrument basis, but the choice, once made, is irrevocable for the life of the financial instrument. The choice is made upon first adoption of FASB *Statement No. 159* or IASB *IAS 39* or at the initial acquisition of a financial asset instrument or incurrence of a financial liability instrument.

Several exceptions exist with regard to the general rule of using the historical interest rate to report long-term liabilities on the balance sheet. For example, firms that have hedged the interest rate or foreign exchange risk in liabilities (discussed in Chapter 8) must report them at the present value of the cash flows using the current market interest rate. Also, for some liabilities due within the next year (such as the operating liabilities accounts payable, income taxes payable, and salaries payable), the difference between the amount of the future cash flows and their present value is sufficiently small that accounting ignores the discounting process and reports the liabilities at the amounts ultimately payable.

Application of Criteria for Liability Recognition

The criteria for liability recognition may appear straightforward and subject to unambiguous interpretation. Unfortunately, this is often not the case. Various obligations of an enterprise fall along a continuum with respect to how well they satisfy these criteria. Exhibit 6.5 classifies obligations into six groups.

Obligations with Fixed Payment Dates and Amounts

The obligations that most clearly satisfy the liability recognition criteria are those with fixed payment dates and amounts (typically set by contract). Most obligations arising from borrowing arrangements (classified as financing activities) fall into this category. A firm receives the benefit of having funds available for use. The borrowing agreement specifies the timing and amount of interest and principal payments.

Obligations with Fixed Payment Amounts but Estimated Payment Dates

Most current (operating) liabilities fall into this category. Oral agreements, written agreements, or legal statutes fix the amounts payable to suppliers, employees, and government agencies. Firms normally settle these obligations within a few months after incurring them. The firm can estimate the settlement date with sufficient accuracy to warrant recognizing a liability.

Obligations with Estimated Payment Dates and Amounts

Obligations in this group require estimation because the firm cannot identify the specific future recipients of cash, goods, or services at the time the obligation becomes a liability. In addition, the firm cannot precisely compute what amount of resources it will transfer in the future or when the transfer will occur. For example, when a firm sells products under a warranty agreement, it promises to replace defective parts or perform certain repair services for a specified period of time. At the time of sale, the firm can neither identify the specific customers who will receive warranty benefits nor ascertain the timing or amounts of customers' claims. Past experience, however, often provides the necessary information for

[26]Financial Accounting Standards Board, *Statement of Financial Accounting Standards No. 107,* "Disclosures about Fair Values of Financial Instruments" (1991); Financial Accounting Standards Board, *Statement of Financial Accounting Standards No. 159,* "The Fair Value Option for Financial Assets and Financial Liabilities" (2008); *FASB Codification Topic 825*; International Accounting Standards Board, *International Accounting Standard 39,* "Financial Instruments: Recognition and Measurement."

EXHIBIT 6.5

Classification of Accounting Liabilities by Degree of Uncertainty

Obligations with Fixed Payment Dates and Amounts	Obligations with Fixed Payment Amounts but Estimated Payment Dates	Obligations for which the Firm Must Estimate Both Timing and Amount of Payment	Obligations Arising from Advances from Customers on Unexecuted Contracts and Agreements	Obligations under Mutually Unexecuted Contracts	Contingent Obligations[a]
• Notes Payable • Interest Payable • Bonds Payable	• Accounts Payable • Salaries Payable • Taxes Payable	• Warranties Payable • Insurance Claims	• Rental Fees Received in Advance • Subscription Fees Received in Advance	• Purchase Commitments • Employment Commitments	• Unsettled Lawsuits • Financial Instruments with Off-Balance-Sheet Risk • Loan Guarantees

Most Certain ←——————————————————→ Least Certain

←—— Recognized as Accounting Liabilities ——→ ←—— Not Generally Recognized as Accounting Liabilities ——→

[a]If an obligation meets certain criteria for a loss contingency, firms must recognize this obligation as a liability. See the discussion later in this chapter.

estimating the likely proportion of customers who will make claims and the probable average amount of their claims. As long as the firm can reasonably estimate the probable amount of the obligation, it satisfies the first criterion for a liability. The selling price of goods sold under warranty includes an explicit or implicit charge for the warranty services. Thus, the receipt of cash or the right to receive cash in the sales transaction benefits the firm and creates the warranty liability.

Obligations Arising from Advances from Customers on Unexecuted Contracts and Agreements

A firm sometimes receives cash from customers in advance for goods or services it will provide at a future time. For example, a rental firm may receive cash in advance of the rental period for rented property. A magazine publisher may receive subscription fees in advance of the subscription period. Organizations and associations may receive membership dues prior to the membership period. Airlines may receive cash for tickets prior to passenger travel. Retailers and restaurant chains may sell cash gift cards or certificates that are redeemable for future products and services. These firms generally cannot recognize revenue upon receipt of cash because revenue recognition usually requires that the firm deliver the goods or provide the services. In the case of advances from customers, all of the required transfer of resources (goods or services) will occur in the future. Thus, the receipt of cash in advance from customers creates a liability equal to the cash received. The firm might conceivably recognize a liability equal to the expected cost of delivering the promised goods or services, but doing so would result in recognizing the profit from the transaction before substantial performance had occurred.

Obligations under Mutually Unexecuted Contracts

Mutually unexecuted contracts arise when two entities agree to transfer resources but *neither* entity has yet made a transfer. For example, a firm may agree to purchase from its suppliers specified amounts of merchandise over the next two years. A baseball organization may agree to pay its "franchise" player a certain sum as compensation for services the player will render over the next five years. A bank may agree to provide lines of credit to its business customers in the event these firms need funds in the future. Both parties have exchanged promises, but neither party has transferred resources. Thus, no accounting liability arises at the time of the exchange of promises. A liability arises only when one party or the other transfers resources in the future. This category of obligation, called *executory contracts*, differs from the preceding two, in which the contracts or agreements are partially executed. With warranty agreements, a firm receives cash but has not fulfilled its warranty obligation. With advances from customers, a firm receives cash but has not provided the required goods or services.

GAAP generally does not require firms to recognize as accounting liabilities obligations under mutually unexecuted contracts. (Exceptions do occur for some leasing arrangements, discussed later in this chapter, and for derivatives, discussed in Chapter 8.) If the amounts involved are material, the firm must disclose the nature of the obligation and its amount in notes to the financial statements. The analyst might conclude, however, that these obligations create sufficient risk for the firm to justify adjusting the reported financial statements to include such obligations.

Contingent Obligations

An event whose future outcome is unknown may create an obligation for the future transfer of resources. For example, a firm may be a defendant in a lawsuit, the outcome of which depends on the results of legal proceedings. Or a firm may guarantee loans of a subsidiary, the outcome of which depends on the future solvency of the subsidiary. Or an insurer may promise to pay certain amounts or reimburse certain expenses if particular future events occur. Obligations such as these are *contingent* on future events.

Contingent obligations may or may not give rise to accounting liabilities. Financial reporting requires firms to recognize an estimated loss from a contingency (called a *loss contingency*) and a related liability only if both of the following conditions are met:

- Information available prior to the issuance of the financial statements indicates that it is probable that an asset has been impaired or that a liability has been incurred.
- The firm can estimate the amount of the loss with reasonable precision.[27]

The first criterion for recognition of a loss contingency rests on the probability, or likelihood, that an asset has been impaired or a liability has been incurred. Financial reporting does not

[27]Financial Accounting Standards Board, *Statement of Financial Accounting Standards No. 5*, "Accounting for Contingencies" (1975); *FASB Codification Topic 450.*

provide clear guidance as to what probability cutoff defines *likely* or *probable*. The FASB has stated that "probable is used with its usual general meaning, rather than in a specific accounting or technical sense, and refers to that which can be expected or believed on the basis of available evidence or logic but is neither certain or proved."[28]

The second criterion requires reasonable estimation of the amount of the loss. Again, financial reporting does not define *reasonably estimable* in precise terms. Instead, if the firm can narrow the amount of the loss to a reasonable range, however large, financial reporting presumes that the firm has achieved sufficient precision to justify recognition of a liability. The amount of the loss is the most likely estimate within the range. If no amount within the range is more likely than another, the firm should use the amount at the lower end of the range. As might be suspected, the estimates of contingent liabilities is fraught with measurement error, and possibly managerial bias.

Financial reporting refers to obligations meeting both of these criteria as loss contingencies. One example suggested by the FASB relates to a toy manufacturer that sold toys that were later found to present a safety hazard. The toy manufacturer concludes that the likelihood of having to pay damages is high. The firm meets the second criterion if experience or other information enables the manufacturer to make a reasonable estimate of the loss. The toy manufacturer recognizes a loss and a liability in this case. As another example, firms in the tobacco industry and in environmentally sensitive industries grapple with measuring loss contingencies related to litigation and draw on lawyers and others to facilitate quantifying the loss.

Closely related to the concept of a loss contingency is a *guarantee*. For example, one firm may guarantee the repayment of another entity's borrowing in the event the other entity cannot repay the loan at maturity. As another example, a firm may sell a portion of its accounts receivable to another entity, promising to reimburse the other entity if uncollectible accounts exceed a specified amount. The need to make a future cash payment is contingent on future events. U.S. GAAP requires firms to recognize the fair value of the guarantee as a liability.[29] Measuring this fair value involves estimating the likelihood, timing, and amount that might be payable. However, a guarantee can have a fair value even when the likelihood of making a future payment is low. A guarantee by a financially strong firm of a financially weaker firm's debt will reduce the weaker firm's cost of borrowing. The guarantor recognizes a receivable and a liability for the fair value of the benefit granted to the borrower by the grantor. The obligation to reimburse a purchaser of accounts receivable for excess uncollectibles likely increases the amount the buyer pays the seller for the receivables. Recognizing the fair value of this guarantee as a liability affects the amount of gain or loss the seller recognizes on the sale of the receivables. In addition to recognizing the fair value of guarantees as liabilities, firms must disclose the maximum amount that could become payable and any available collateral that the guarantor could recover in the event it must execute the guarantee. Note 9, "Debt Obligations and Commitments," of PepsiCo's 2008 financial statements (Appendix A) indicates that PepsiCo guarantees $2.3 billion of Bottling Group, LLC's long-term debt.

Financing with Long-Term Debt

As illustrated in Chapters 4 and 5, firms are able to use leverage to increase the rate of return on common equity. The primary source of leverage for most firms is the issuance of

[28]*Statement of Financial Accounting Concepts No. 6* (1985). Although the FASB has not defined *probable*, practice demands that firms and auditors define it. Currently, most firms and auditors appear to use *probable* to mean 80–85 percent or larger.

[29]Financial Accounting Standards Board, *Interpretation No. 45*, "Guarantor's Accounting and Disclosure Requirements for Guarantees, Including Indirect Indebtedness of Others" (2002); *FASB Codification Topic 460.*

long-term debt in the form of notes payable (primarily to banks and other financial institutions), bonds payable (to any type of bondholder, including open-market debt investors), and leases (entered into with property owners, equipment dealers, or finance companies). Debt issuance is evidenced by a bond indenture, promissory note, or lease agreement. These documents will specify promises to pay maturity amounts at specified dates; promises to pay cash interest (or in the case of leases, lease payments) of specified amounts at specified dates; call provisions; descriptions of property pledged as security; whether the debt is convertible to another claim and at what rate the conversion will occur; and covenants and restrictions that specify sinking fund requirements, working capital restrictions, dividend payment restrictions, restrictions on the issuance of new debt, and other restrictions. Bonds are issued almost exclusively for cash consideration. Notes also are issued for cash consideration, but they may be issued for non-cash consideration as well. Lease agreements result in a lessee receiving non-cash consideration, the use of property, plant, and equipment.

This section illustrates the accounting for long-term debt using notes payable. Accounting for bonds payable is similar except for the possibility that bonds may be traded in more active markets, thus having more readily determinable fair values. As discussed in the following sections, fair value of financial instruments is a required disclosure in the notes to the financial statements and an optional measurement for recognition in the financial statements. Lease accounting is discussed in a subsequent section about off-balance-sheet financing.

Example 10

Note 9, "Debt Obligations and Commitments" (Appendix A), indicates that PepsiCo uses both long-term interest-bearing and long-term non-interest-bearing (that is, "zero coupon") notes to raise capital. Assume that on January 1, 2010, PepsiCo borrows money from a bank by issuing a $100 million promissory note to the bank. The note matures in five years on January 1, 2015, and pays 5 percent interest once a year on January 1. The bank transfers $95.79 million (rounded) to PepsiCo.

PepsiCo's cash flows over the life of the note are as follows (in millions):

Cash inflow at issue		$ 95.79
Annual cash outflows (interest payments):		
Face amount of note	$100.00	
Coupon or stated interest rate	× 5%	
Annual cash interest payment	$ 5.00	
Years	× 5	
Total Interest Payments		(25.00)
Cash outflow at retirement date		(100.00)
Net cash outflow		$ (29.21)

The $29.21 net cash outflow represents the total interest cost on the note. Accrual accounting's goal is to recognize the interest cost on the note over the five-year period in an economically meaningful way.

By paying less than $100 million for the note, the bank will earn a return that is greater than the 5 percent stated interest rate. That is, this investment is sufficiently risky such that a yield or an effective rate of interest should be higher than 5 percent, and therefore, the bank "discounts" the note. For a bond or note, the *cash interest* is determined by the *coupon rate* or *stated rate* of interest, which may be negotiated in a note or private bond placement or simply presented to potential buyers in a public bond issuance, multiplied by the face value of the debt. Cash interest may or may not be a function of the risk characteristics of the transaction. *Effective interest*, also known as the *yield, yield-to-maturity,* or *rate of return,* is a function of the risk characteristics of the transaction. It is the economic return on the transaction to creditors and the economic cost to debtors.[30]

A number of factors determine the effective interest rate. A portion of any effective interest rate contains compensation for the use of the lender's funds. While the funds are on loan, alternative, possibly more profitable opportunities for lending may become available. Also, the effective interest rate will reflect expected inflation, which causes future dollars to have less purchasing power. In addition, if the loan is denominated in a foreign currency, relative changes in economic conditions across countries could result in an unfavorable transformation of foreign currency into the dollar. Finally, firm-specific liquidity and solvency risk (as discussed in Chapter 5) explains differences in effective interest rates.

Analysts solve for a loan's effective rate of return (i) using the following formula:

$$\text{Present Value} = \sum_{n=1}^{t} \frac{\text{Cash Interest}}{(1+i)^n} + \frac{\text{Maturity Value}}{(1+i)^t}$$

$$\$95.79 \text{ million} = \sum_{n=1}^{5} \frac{\$5 \text{ million}}{(1+i)^n} + \frac{\$100 \text{ million}}{(1+i)^5}$$

Solving for i results in a yield of 6 percent.[31]

PepsiCo must use the effective interest method to account for the note. The method can be best understood by referring to the effective interest amortization table in Exhibit 6.6, in which the cash interest column is obtained by multiplying the face value of the debt by the stated interest rate of 5 percent and the effective interest column is obtained by multiplying the beginning of the period book value of debt (previous row) by the 6 percent effective interest rate charged by the bank.

EXHIBIT 6.6

Example 10. Effective Interest Amortization Table (amounts in millions)

Date	5% Cash Interest	6% Effective Interest Expense	Amortization	Book Value of Note
1/1/10				\$ 95.79
12/31/10	\$ 5.00	\$ 5.75	\$0.75	\$ 96.54
12/31/11	\$ 5.00	\$ 5.79	\$0.79	\$ 97.33
12/31/12	\$ 5.00	\$ 5.84	\$0.84	\$ 98.17
12/31/13	\$ 5.00	\$ 5.89	\$0.89	\$ 99.06
12/31/14	\$ 5.00	\$ 5.94	\$0.94	\$100.00
	\$25.00	\$29.21		

[30]If the effective rate of interest and the stated rate of interest are equal, computing the present value of the note will yield a present value equal to the face value of the note. When the debtholder pays the face value to acquire a bond or note, the bond or note is said to be "issued at par."

[31]Using a financial calculator to solve for i involves setting n (number of annual interest payments) = 5, payment (annual cash interest payment) = \$5 million, present value = \$95.79 million, and future value = \$100 million.

The beginning book value of $95.79 million represents the amount lent to PepsiCo on 1/1/10. In 2010, PepsiCo incurs a 6 percent interest charge on its $95.79 million initial borrowing, $5.75 million of effective interest expense. Essentially, the debt has grown by $5.75 million. Because PepsiCo pays only $5 million in cash interest to the bank, the difference between the effective interest expense and cash interest paid [shown in the amortization column ($0.75 million)] increases the book value of the debt. Note that the amount of effective interest expense increases each period. This occurs because the amount borrowed increases each period and PepsiCo incurs a constant 6 percent economic interest charge on the debt. The annual increase in the debt is paid off as part of the $100 million maturity payment.

Financial Reporting of Long-Term Debt

In the balance sheet, notes payable are reported at the present value of future cash flows using the historical effective rate of interest at the issue date. Note that the effective interest amortization table provides the book values of the note at each year-end. At December 31, 2014, the $100 million maturity value must be reclassified as a current liability because funds will be disbursed within one year of the balance sheet date (actually, the next day). A reclassification of a large note payable from long-term to current may have a material adverse impact on working capital (current assets minus current liabilities) and the current ratio (current assets divided by current liabilities). In practice, this potential adverse impact is alleviated two ways. First, a firm may set up a sinking fund in liquid assets (because of debt covenants or as part of the firm's cash management policy) to be used to repay the debt. The sinking fund and debt classifications will have countervailing effects on working capital.[32]

Another means of avoiding the reclassification of long-term debt to a current liability is to enter into a refinancing agreement. If management intends to refinance the debt on a long-term basis and the corporation demonstrates the ability to refinance the debt, GAAP allows the obligation to remain in the long-term classification at the balance sheet date. Auditors will investigate whether the ability to refinance is present by searching for a refinancing agreement with a lender or for evidence that actual refinancing has taken place before the financial statements are issued.[33] In Note 9, "Debt Obligations and Commitments" (Appendix A), PepsiCo reports $1,259 million reclassified from short-term to long-term debt. In the note, PepsiCo describes entering into two long-term borrowing agreements, part of which will be used to repay short-term debt.

The statement of cash flows reports the net proceeds of debt issues, interest payments, and maturity payments. Under both U.S. GAAP and IFRS, cash flows relating to principal amounts of debt are reported as financing activities. Under U.S. GAAP, interest expense is included as an operating cash outflow because interest expense reduces net income, which is reported as a source of cash flow from operating activities under the indirect method. Additional adjustments in the operating cash flow section include changes in interest payable and amortizations of bond discounts and premiums. (Although due to the use of the indirect method, which does not directly disclose cash payments for interest, many companies disclose cash interest payments in the notes to the financial statements or in a supplementary schedule provided with the cash flow statement. PepsiCo discloses cash paid for interest in Note 14.) Under IFRS, cash payments for interest can be reported as an operating or financing cash outflow. Under both U.S. GAAP and IFRS, the income statement reports interest expense as a non-operating charge.

---

[32]FASB No. 47 requires note disclosure of sinking fund and bond retirement payments for each of the next five years after the balance sheet date.

[33]Balance sheet classification intricacies of long-term debt are addressed in FASB *Statement of Financial Accounting Standards No. 6*, "Balance Sheet Classification of Short-Term Obligations Expected to Be Refinanced" (Stamford, CT: FASB 1975*); No. 47*, "Disclosure of Long-Term Obligations" (1981); and *No. 129*, "Disclosure of Information about Capital Structure" (1997).

Fair Value Disclosure and the Fair Value Option

Long-term notes and bonds are financial instruments; therefore, firms must disclose the fair values of such debt in the notes to the financial statements.[34] In referring back to Exhibit 6.6, the December 31, 2012, book value of the note payable is $98.17 million. This amount is referred to as *amortized cost* because it represents the original "cost" of the debt, $95.79 million, adjusted for the amortization of the bank's discount for 2010–2012. The amount also represents the present value of the remaining cash flows (two more $5 million interest payments and one final $100 million principal payment) at the historical 6 percent effective rate of interest.

$$\$98.17 \text{ million} = \sum_{n=1}^{2} \frac{\$5 \text{ million}}{(1 + 0.06)^n} + \frac{\$100 \text{ million}}{(1 + 0.06)^2}$$

If the market's required rate of interest has changed since the original signing date of the note, the fair value of the debt will change as well. Suppose the market requires a 7 percent return on PepsiCo's note at December 31, 2012.

$$\$96.38 \text{ million} = \sum_{n=1}^{2} \frac{\$5 \text{ million}}{(1 + 0.07)^n} + \frac{\$100 \text{ million}}{(1 + 0.07)^2}$$

PepsiCo would report the amortized cost of $98.17 million on the face of the balance sheet (probably in a group with other long-term debt) and the fair value of $96.38 million in the notes to the financial statements.

Recently, both the FASB and IASB passed a rule allowing firms the option of using fair value as the basis for balance sheet reporting of financial liabilities (and financial assets) instead of amortized cost.[35] If PepsiCo were to adopt the *fair value option* for this debt, it would report $96.38 million of notes payable on the face of the balance sheet and an unrealized gain on remeasurement of long-term debt equal to $98.17 million − $96.38 million = $1.79 million on the income statement. The standards are silent on how to recognize interest expense on this new long-term-debt basis. However, using the effective interest method (as described previously) with the new market rate and new book value would be consistent with current practice.

Example 11

Using the data in Example 10 and the remeasurement under the fair value option in the preceding paragraphs, Exhibit 6.7 summarizes the accounting for the long-term note payable through the remeasurement at December 31, 2012 (all amounts in millions of dollars).

Measuring Fair Value

The challenge that companies face in providing fair value disclosures is obtaining reliable data. Historically, standard setters have eschewed fair value measurement in favor

[34]Financial Accounting Standards Board, *Statement of Financial Accounting Standards No.107*, "Disclosures about Fair Value of Financial Instruments" (1991); *FASB Codification Topic 825*; International Accounting Standards Board, *International Financial Reporting Standard 7*, "Financial Instruments: Disclosures."

[35]Financial Accounting Standards Board, *Statement of Financial Accounting Standards No.159*, "The Fair Value Option for Financial Assets and Financial Liabilities" (2008); *FASB Codification Topic 825;* International Accounting Standards Board, *International Financial Reporting Standard 39*, "Financial Instruments: Recognition and Measurement."

EXHIBIT 6.7: EXAMPLE 11 SOLUTION

1/1/10 Signing

Assets	=	Liabilities	+	Shareholders' Equity CC	AOCI	RE
Cash +95.79		Note Payable +95.79				

Cash	95.79	
Note Payable		95.79

12/31/10 Year-End Interest Accrual

Assets	=	Liabilities	+	Shareholders' Equity CC	AOCI	RE
		Note Payable +0.75 Interest Payable +5.00				Interest Expense −5.75

Interest Expense	5.75	
Note Payable		0.75
Interest Payable		5.00

1/1/11 Interest Payment Date

Assets	=	Liabilities	+	Shareholders' Equity CC	AOCI	RE
Cash +5.00		Interest Payable −5.00				

Interest Payable	5.00	
Cash		5.00

12/31/11 Year-End Interest Accrual

Assets	=	Liabilities	+	Shareholders' Equity CC	AOCI	RE
		Note Payable +0.79 Interest Payable +5.00				Interest Expense −5.79

Interest Expense	5.79	
Note Payable		0.79
Interest Payable		5.00

1/1/12 Interest Payment Date

Assets	=	Liabilities	+	Shareholders' Equity CC	AOCI	RE
Cash +5.00		Interest Payable −5.00				

Interest Payable	5.00	
Cash		5.00

12/31/12 Year-End Interest Accrual

Assets	=	Liabilities	+	Shareholders' Equity CC	AOCI	RE
		Note Payable +0.84 Interest Payable +5.00				Interest Expense −5.84

Interest Expense	5.84	
Note Payable		0.84
Interest Payable		5.00

(Continued)

EXHIBIT 6.7 (CONTINUED)

12/31/12 Year-End Remeasurement at Fair Value

Assets	=	Liabilities	+	Shareholders' Equity		
				CC	AOCI	RE
		Note Payable −1.79				Unrealized Gain +1.79

Note Payable	1.79	
Unrealized Gain		1.79

of reliable historical data obtained from arm's-length transactions between the company and outside parties. Recently, however, the alleged relevance of fair value data in decision making has been judged to outweigh potential measurement reliability issues, especially when the item being measured is a financial asset or financial liability and the company can provide information on the level of likely data reliability.

Authoritative guidance for fair value measurement (SFAS No. 157) identifies a hierarchy of inputs for fair value measurements, which were introduced in the discussion of fair value in Chapter 2.[36] Level 1 inputs provide the most reliable measure and should be used if possible, followed by Level 2 and then Level 3. The level used for each asset or liability measurement must be disclosed. If multiple levels are used for a measurement, the least reliable level having a significant influence on the measurement must be disclosed. The levels are as follows:

Level 1: Observable quoted market prices in active markets for identical assets or liabilities

Level 2: Observable market data (other than Level 1 market prices) serving as inputs into estimates of the market value of the asset or liability in question, including quoted market prices of similar assets or liabilities in active markets, quoted market prices of identical assets or liabilities in inactive markets, and inputs into present value-based measurements of fair value such as interest rates, foreign exchange rates, and default rates

Level 3: Unobservable inputs used by the reporting entity when modeling how the market would determine the fair value of the asset or liability in question

Exhibit 6.8 summarizes information in PepsiCo's Note 10 about fair value measurement. Notice that PepsiCo uses a Level 2 basis for determining the fair value of its long-term debt.

EXHIBIT 6.8

An Excerpt from PepsiCo's Note 10, "Financial Instruments," from Its December 27, 2008 Annual Report (Appendix A)

We adopted SFAS 157 at the beginning of our 2008 fiscal year and our adoption did not have a material impact on our financial statements. The fair value framework requires the categorization of assets and liabilities into three levels based on the assumptions (inputs) used to price the assets or liabilities. Level 1 provides the most reliable measure of fair value, whereas Level 3 generally requires significant management judgment. . . . Under SFAS 157, the fair value of our debt obligations as of December 27, 2008 was $8.8 billion, based upon prices of similar instruments in the market place. The fair value of our debt obligations as of December 29, 2007 was $4.4 billion.

[36] As of the writing of this text, the IASB is deliberating on guidance for fair value measurement.

While few question the relevance of fair value measurement, many worry about the reliability of Level 2 and Level 3 estimates of fair values. While the quoted market prices of Level 1 valuations have intuitive appeal, the reliability of a Level 1 valuation is compromised if the market from which it comes is not "orderly." The market for mortgage-backed securities in 2008–2009 exhibited a volatility that caused some to question its orderliness.

Reducing Debt

Outstanding debt can be reduced by waiting until maturity to pay off the maturity value. Alternatively, debt can be retired earlier through engagement in open-market purchase of traded debt, exercising call options if available, or through a forced conversion (if available). The difference between the amounts used to extinguish the debt and the book value of the debt at the time of extinguishment is reported as a realized gain or loss on the income statement. Cash flows used to reduce debt are reported as cash outflows from financing activities in the statement of cash flows. *In-substance defeasance* of debt, transferring or pledging assets to an irrevocable trust to satisfy debt while remaining contingently obligated, used to be another popular way of removing debt from the balance sheet. U.S. GAAP and IFRS (IAS 39) now prohibit de-recognition of debt via in-substance defeasance.

Accounting for Troubled Debt

The financial crisis of the late 2000s found many firms struggling to make debt payments. Many firms ended up declaring bankruptcy or renegotiating the terms of outstanding debt obligations. This section examines how the debtor accounts for the restructuring of troubled debt.[37] From the debtor's perspective, two situations exist for handling troubled debt: settlement and modification of terms.

The *settlement* of troubled debt results in an economic gain to the debtor because the creditor accepts less than the book value of the debt to settle the debt. If a non-cash asset is transferred to settle the debt (for example, a collateral asset), the non-cash asset must be adjusted to fair value prior to its transfer, with the resulting gain or loss reported in income. A gain on debt settlement is recognized as the difference between the book value of the debt settled (principal plus any accrued interest) and the fair market value of the non-cash asset or cash transferred to retire the debt. Alternatively, debt could be settled by issuing capital stock. In this case, the stock issue is recorded at its fair market value and the gain to the debtor is the excess of the book value of the debt relative to the fair value of the stock issued to settle the debt.

Instead of accepting an asset or common stock (a right of net asset ownership) to retire the debt, a creditor might *modify the terms* of the debt, hoping a debtor will be able to perform under less stringent debt service requirements. Under U.S. GAAP, if terms are modified, the debtor must compare the total (undiscounted) future cash flows of the restructured debt to the current book value of the debt. If the total restructured future cash flows remain greater than the book value of the debt, the debtor will make no adjustment to book value (that is, record no gain). Future recognition of interest expense will follow the effective interest method using a new interest rate that discounts the total restructured future cash flows to the current book value.

Alternatively, if the total undiscounted restructured future cash flows are less than the book value of the debt, the debtor will reduce the book value of the debt to equal the total of the new restructured future cash flows, recording a gain in the process. Future interest expense will not be recognized because all future cash flows represent the repayment of

---

[37]U.S. GAAP for the debtor is found in "Accounting by Debtors and Creditors for Troubled Debt Restructurings," FASB No. 15 (Norwalk, CT: FASB, 1977); *FASB Codification Topic 470.* We address creditor accounting for troubled debt in Chapter 7.

principal; that is, the discount rate is zero. This accounting is conservative because future cash flows must fall fairly far before the debtor can recognize a gain. The result of the conservative accounting is to minimize any gains recognized by debtors who experience difficulty and must restructure debt agreements. The existing conservative accounting rules for troubled debt are subject to frequent (and deserved) criticism because they ignore the present value of future restructured cash flows for determining book values of troubled debt and gains from debt restructuring, and they often result in subsequent recognition of interest expense based on an unrealistic interest rate assumption.

Under IFRS (IAS 39), the measurement and recognition rules are quite different from those under U.S. GAAP. The following example contrasts U.S. GAAP and IFRS treatment of troubled debt from the debtor's perspective.

Example 12

Assume that Tribune Co. owes Bank of America $2,000,000 on a 5-year, 8% note originally issued at par. After one year of making scheduled payments, the firm faces financial difficulty. At the end of the second year, Tribune owes Bank of America $2,000,000 plus $160,000 of accrued but unpaid interest. Bank of America restructures the note by forgiving the $160,000 interest payable, reducing the note principal to $1,800,000, and reducing the interest rate to 7 percent.

Under U.S. GAAP, Tribune compares the gross (that is, undiscounted) future cash outflows under the restructured debt to the current book value of the debt as follows:

Undiscounted future cash flows of restructured debt:		
New principal	$1,800,000	
New interest ($1,800,000 × 7% × 3 remaining years)	378,000	$2,178,000
Current book value of debt:		
Old principal	$2,000,000	
Old accrued interest	160,000	$2,160,000

Because undiscounted future cash flows exceed the current book value of the debt, Tribune does not record a gain. Future interest expense is accounted for using the effective interest method and an effective interest rate that equates the future cash flows with the present value (that is, current book value) of the debt.

$$\$2{,}160{,}000 = \sum_{n=1}^{3} \frac{\$126{,}000}{(1+i)^n} + \frac{\$1{,}800{,}000}{(1+i)^3}$$

Solving for i yields a very small interest rate of 0.0029 percent.

Instead, if Bank of America reduced the principle to $1,700,000, Tribune would make the following comparison:

Undiscounted future cash flows of restructured debt:		
New principal	$1,700,000	
New interest ($1,700,000 × 7% × 3 remaining years)	357,000	$2,057,000
Current book value of debt:		
Old principal	$2,000,000	
Old accrued interest	160,000	$2,160,000

Because undiscounted future cash flows are less than the current book value of debt, Tribune reduces the book value of the debt to $2,057,000 and records a gain of

$2,160,000 − 2,057,000 = $103,000. Future interest expense does not exist (that is, the effective rate is set equal to zero) because the future cash flows are now equal to the present value (that is, the reduced book value).

Under IFRS, Tribune would compare the present value of future cash flows under the restructured debt (instead of the undiscounted cash flows as under U.S. GAAP) to the book value of the debt. Return to the original example where Bank of America reduced the principal to $1,800,000. The present value calculation uses the historical effective interest rate of 8 percent as follows:

Present value of future cash flows (using a financial calculator: FV = $1,800,000, PMNT = $1,800,000 × 7% = $126,000, i = 8%, n = 3):		$1,753,612
Current book value of debt:		
Old principal	$2,000,000	
Old accrued interest	160,000	$2,160,000

IFRS uses a "10 percent rule" to determine whether a gain is recognized. Because the present value of $1,753,612 is 23.2 percent below the book value of $2,160,000 (that is, greater than 10 percent below book value), Tribune recognizes a gain. The *amount* of the gain is equal to the amount by which the *fair value* of the debt is below the current book value. Computing fair value of the restructured debt's cash flows requires the use of a current market rate of interest instead of the historical rate of 8 percent. For example, because of Tribune's financial difficulties, assume that a more appropriate current rate of interest for Tribune is 12 percent. Discounting the same cash flows using a 12 percent rate yields a present value of $1,583,835. Therefore, Tribune would record a gain of $2,160,000 − 1,583,835 = $576,165. Future interest expense would be recognized using the 12 percent effective interest rate so that the new book value (computed using the 12 percent rate) is correctly amortized to the new maturity value by the maturity date.

If the present value of the restructured cash flows at the historical rate is within 10 percent of the book value of the debt, Tribune does not recognize a gain. Income effects are similar to the effects under U.S. GAAP when no gain is recognized. Because IFRS uses the economically sound present value approach to determine the magnitude of the settlement and U.S. GAAP uses the more conservative undiscounted future cash flows approach, the magnitude of the new book value of the restructured debt will be lower and the gain recognition will be larger under IFRS.

Example 13

PepsiCo's Consolidated Balance Sheet (Appendix A) shows Long-Term Debt Obligations of $7,858 and $4,203 million at the end of 2008 and 2007, respectively. Note that PepsiCo reports Short-term Obligations (usually the currently due portion of long-term obligations) of $369 million at the end of 2008. Both of these liabilities are financing instead of operating liabilities. The financing activities section in the Consolidated Statement of Cash Flows shows that $3,719 million of long-term debt capital was raised in 2008 and $649 million was paid off. Also, short-term borrowings increased. Note 9, "Debt Obligations and Commitments" (Appendix A), reports the detail on the short- and long-term obligations. Note 9 also reports interest rate swaps, which we cover in Chapter 8.

ADDITIONAL ISSUES IN LIABILITY RECOGNITION AND DEBT FINANCING

In the following sections, we examine two additional issues in long-term liability reporting, the use of hybrid securities to obtain financing and the structure of financing arrangements to keep debt off of the balance sheet.

Hybrid Securities

Ambiguities arise in the measurement and classification of certain securities issued to raise capital because the securities have both debt and equity characteristics. These securities are referred to as *hybrid securities* or *compound financing instruments.* For example, firms often issue preferred stock that is subject to certain rights of redemption in either cash or common shares after some period of time.[38] The classification of preferred stock as debt or equity depends on who holds the power to trigger redemption and whether the firm reports under U.S. GAAP or IFRS. If redemption will occur at a specific time or upon a specific event (for example, death of the holder), both U.S. GAAP and IFRS treat the preferred stock as a liability. This situation is typically referred to as *mandatorily redeemable preferred stock.* If the redemption is at the option of the issuing firm (that is, the preferred stock is callable), U.S. GAAP and IFRS will treat the preferred stock as equity. If redemption is at the holder's discretion (that is, the preferred stock is "putable"), U.S. GAAP will require that the stock be disclosed between debt and equity (the so-called "mezzanine" disclosure) and IFRS will require disclosure as a liability.

Convertible preferred stock is similar to preferred stock except that the holder has the option to exchange the convertible preferred stock for common stock under some pre-agreed exchange ratio. For example, a holder of 1,000 shares of $100 par, 7% convertible preferred stock may have the right to exchange each share of convertible preferred for five shares of $10 par common stock. Convertible preferred stock is treated as preferred stock at the date of issue. (Equity increases by the fair value of the consideration received at the issue date.) If converted to common stock, the recorded amounts are simply shifted from preferred stock to common stock.

Convertible debt may, at the creditor's option, be converted into common shares at a prespecified exchange rate. The creditor holds (1) debt with a stated interest rate and maturity date and (2) an option to exchange the debt for equity. However, the debt and option features do not trade separately in secondary markets. While holding the convertible debt, the creditor receives interest payments, a feature of debt. Also, the debtholder has the ability to exchange the debt for equity, an equity-like feature. Under U.S. GAAP, accountants have historically recorded convertible debt as a financial liability and recorded interest expense. The option to exchange the debt for equity is not valued and recorded. IFRS differs in that the debt and equity features are recorded separately to the extent that the separate components can be reliably estimated at fair value.

---

[38]The following discussion is based on Financial Accounting Standards Board, *Statement No. 150,* "Accounting for Certain Financial Instruments with Characteristics of Both Liabilities and Equity" (2003); Accounting Principles Board, *Opinion No. 14,* "Accounting for Convertible Debt and Debt Issued with Stock Purchase Warrants" (1969); *FASB Codification Topic 480*; Securities and Exchange Commission *Accounting Series Release No. 268,* "Presentation in Financial Statements of Redeemable Preferred Stock"; And International Accounting Standards Board, *International Accounting Standard 32,* "Financial Instruments: Presentation" (revised 2003).

Under both U.S. GAAP and IFRS, most companies use the *book value method* to record conversion. The book value method is based on the idea that the conversion is a culmination of the original transaction. Whatever amounts are recorded in debt (and in equity under IFRS) are simply shifted to shareholders' equity when the debt is converted into equity. Both U.S. GAAP and IFRS allow the use of the *market value method,* under which the market value of the common stock determines the basis of the conversion transaction. This approach is rarely used because it generates potentially large losses.

Example 14

The December 31, 2008, Consolidated Balance Sheet of Digital River, Inc., reports 1.25%, 20-year convertible senior notes originally issued in 2004 at a par value of $195 million. Each $1,000 of note principal may be converted into 22.6948 shares of Digital River $0.01 par value common stock, a conversion price of $44.063 per share. Exhibit 6.9

Exhibit 6.9: Example 14 Solution

U.S. GAAP

	Assets	=	Liabilities	+	Shareholders' Equity		
					CC	**AOCI**	**RE**
1	Cash +195.00		Notes Payable +195.00				

Cash	195.00	
Notes Payable		195.00

IFRS

	Assets	=	Liabilities	+	Shareholders' Equity		
					CC	**AOCI**	**RE**
1	Cash +195.00		Notes Payable +122.12		APIC—Notes Payable +72.88		

Cash	195.00	
Notes Payable		122.12
APIC—Notes Payable		72.88

U.S. GAAP

	Assets	=	Liabilities	+	Shareholders' Equity		
					CC	**AOCI**	**RE**
2	Cash −2.4375						Interest Expense −2.4375

Interest Expense	2.4375	
Cash		2.4375

IFRS

	Assets	=	Liabilities	+	Shareholders' Equity		
					CC	**AOCI**	**RE**
2	Cash −2.4375		Notes Payable +2.4073				Interest Expense −4.8848

Interest Expense	4.8848	
Notes Payable		2.4073
Cash		2.4375

(Continued)

EXHIBIT 6.9 (CONTINUED)

U.S. GAAP

	Assets	=	Liabilities	+	Shareholders' Equity: CC	Shareholders' Equity: AOCI	Shareholders' Equity: RE
3a			Notes Payable −195.0000		Common Stock +0.0443 APIC +194.9557		

Notes Payable	195.0000	
Common Stock		0.0443
APIC		194.9557

IFRS

	Assets	=	Liabilities	+	Shareholders' Equity: CC	Shareholders' Equity: AOCI	Shareholders' Equity: RE
3a			Notes Payable −124.5273		APIC—Notes Payable −72.8800 Common Stock +0.0443 APIC +197.3630		

Notes Payable	124.5273	
APIC—Notes Payable	72.8800	
Common Stock		0.0443
APIC		197.3630

U.S. GAAP

	Assets	=	Liabilities	+	Shareholders' Equity: CC	Shareholders' Equity: AOCI	Shareholders' Equity: RE
3b			Notes Payable −195.0000		Common Stock +0.0443 APIC +221.2300		Loss on Conversion −26.2743

Notes Payable	195.0000	
Loss on Conversion	26.2743	
Common Stock		0.0443
APIC		221.2300

IFRS

	Assets	=	Liabilities	+	Shareholders' Equity: CC	Shareholders' Equity: AOCI	Shareholders' Equity: RE
3b			Notes Payable −124.5273		APIC—Notes Payable −72.8800 Common Stock +0.0443 APIC +221.2300		Loss on Conversion −23.8670

Notes Payable	124.5273	
APIC—Notes Payable	72.8800	
Loss on Conversion	23.8670	
Common Stock		0.0443
APIC		221.2300

shows the financial statement effects under both U.S. GAAP and IFRS of the following transactions:

1. Recording of the original issue. For the IFRS treatment, assume that Digital River would have borrowed at 4 percent if it did not offer a conversion privilege.
2. Recognition of one year's interest effect.
3. Conversion of the notes assuming a share of Digital River trades at $50
   a. Using the "book value method."
   b. Using the "market value method."

U.S. GAAP treats the entire convertible note issue proceeds of Transaction 1 as debt. Under IFRS, the proceeds are allocated between the fair values of the notes and the conversion options on the notes. If Digital would have paid 4 percent interest on the notes issued without the conversion option, the fair value of the notes could be approximated by discounting the notes' contractual cash flows at 4 percent. The present value of $195 million received 20 years hence and a contractual cash interest payment of $2.4375 million ($195 million × 1.25%) each period for 20 years equals $122.12 million. Thus, the note payable is recorded at $122.12 million and the remainder of the proceeds ($195 million − $122.12 million = $72.88 million) is classified as equity. The account Additional paid-in capital—Note payable would be reported in the shareholders' equity section as part of additional paid-in capital.

U.S. GAAP records the $2.4375 million annual payment as interest expense in Transaction 2. The cash interest and effective interest are equal because Digital River issued the notes payable at par. Under IFRS treatment, the notes were discounted at the effective interest rate of 4 percent. Therefore, the effective interest of $4.8848 million ($122.12 million beginning note book value times 4% effective interest rate) does not equal the contractual cash interest, and the note payable discount ($2.4073 million) is amortized.[39]

The book value method (Transaction 3a) is based on the idea that the conversion is a culmination of the original transaction. Whatever amounts recorded in debt are simply shifted to shareholders' equity when the debt is converted into equity. Under U.S. GAAP, the original issue was recorded as debt. Therefore, the $195 million is removed from notes payable. The common shares issued at conversion total 4,425,486, which is computed by multiplying the 22.6948 contractual conversion rate per $1,000 of note principal by $195 million divided by $1,000. The common stock account is increased by the par value of those shares ($0.01 × 4,425,486 shares), and the rest is treated as additional paid-in capital. Under IFRS, the original issue was treated as part debt (recorded in notes payable) and part equity (recorded in additional paid-in capital—notes payable). Upon conversion, amounts are shifted from these two accounts into common stock (at par) and additional paid-in capital. The amount shifted out of notes payable is equal to its original issue price from Transaction 1 plus the increase in notes payable from the amortization of the note in Transaction 2.

Transaction 3b shows how the market value method affects financial statements. Basically, the equity issued is recorded at the $50 current market value, split between common stock at par and additional paid-in capital. Because the increase in equity (what the corporation is giving) is greater than the decrease in debt (debt and equity under IFRS) surrendered by the claimholders, a loss on conversion is recorded. This loss would reduce net income and retained earnings.

Bonds issued with detachable warrants provide a good example of where debt and equity features may be more easily separated (and are separated under both U.S. GAAP and IFRS). Typically, after issuance, the bonds and detachable warrants are traded separately in secondary markets. When purchasing bonds with detachable warrants, an investor is buying a debt instrument (the bond) and the option to acquire equity at a fixed price (the stock warrants). Because the debt and equity features trade separately after issuance, accountants allocate the purchase price of the bond with detachable warrants between the bond and the stock warrants on the basis of the two instruments' relative fair market values. As a simple example, assume that bonds with a face value of $1,000,000 plus detachable warrants are issued for $975,000. Assume that immediately

[39]As is the case with any long-term debt, accrual of interest expense at the effective rate increases the amount owed by Digital River and contractual cash payments decrease the amount owed. Given that the effective interest is greater than the cash payment, Digital River's debt has increased as evidenced by the increase in notes payable.

after issue, the bonds trade for $900,000 and the warrants trade for $100,000. Accountants would allocate 90 percent ($900,000 value of the bonds/$1,000,000 value of bonds plus warrants) of the $975,000 value received to the bonds ($975,000 × 90% = $877,500) and 10 percent to the warrants ($975,000 × 10% = $97,500).

Off-Balance-Sheet Financing Arrangements

Investors and lenders often use the proportion of debt in a firm's capital structure as a measure of risk and therefore as a factor in establishing the cost of funds. (Chapter 5 discusses various ratios for measuring risk, and Chapter 11 describes techniques for using a firm's capital structure to compute the weighted average cost of capital.) Other things being equal, firms prefer to obtain funds without showing a liability on the balance sheet in the hope that future lenders or investors will ignore the risks associated with such financing. Firms sometimes structure innovative financing arrangements in ways that may not satisfy the criteria for the recognition of a liability. That is, firms structure financing in such a way that GAAP treats the obligation (if any) as an executory contract or a contingency. The principal aim of such arrangements is to reduce the amount shown as liabilities on the balance sheet. Although there is little empirical evidence to support the notion that lenders and investors ignore such financing in assessing a firm's risk, some firms act as if they do overlook such borrowing. Firms usually accomplish off-balance-sheet financing using one or a combination of two approaches: (1) sale of an existing asset and (2) use of another entity to obtain the financing.

Sale of an Existing Asset

A firm may use accounts receivable; inventories; property, plant, and equipment; and other assets as collateral for a loan. If the firm borrowed funds using the assets as collateral, The selling firm would increase cash and increase a liability. The notes to its financial statements would disclose that certain assets serve as collateral for the loan. Structuring the transaction in this way places debt on the balance sheet.

If, on the other hand, the firm sold the same asset to the provider of the funds, it would increase cash, reduce the asset transferred, and recognize a gain or loss for the difference. The selling firm would show cash but would not show a liability on the balance sheet. This is appropriate as long as the sale did not expose the selling firm to the risk of having to make payments to the purchaser in the future (for example, if the selling firm had to guarantee that the purchaser could resell the asset for a certain minimum amount). A similar transaction is a sale-leaseback. The firm sells a long-lived asset to a lessor, using the cash received from the sale to reduce any liabilities originally used to finance the asset purchase. The firm then leases the asset from the lessor under an operating lease that is not shown as a long-term liability. Later in this chapter, lease accounting is illustrated in more detail.

Use of Another Entity to Obtain Financing

The general theme of this approach to off-balance-sheet financing is that the firm obtains access to the asset that the funds finance, but neither the asset nor its financing appear on the firm's balance sheet. Instead, they appear on the balance sheet of another entity.

Suppose, for example, a firm needs additional manufacturing capacity but does not want to borrow funds to build the extra plant assets. Instead, it commits to purchase a certain amount of output from an unaffiliated company at a specified cost that covers operating and debt-service costs. The unaffiliated company takes the purchase commitment to a financial institution and obtains a loan. The unaffiliated company uses the loan proceeds to construct the needed capacity. The new plant assets and the loan appear on the balance sheet of the unaffiliated company. The purchase commitment is a mutually unexecuted contract of the firm initially needing the additional manufacturing capacity. Recall from the earlier discussion and Exhibit 6.5 that firms do not recognize mutually unexecuted contracts as liabilities.

Alternatively, the firm can accomplish the same result using an affiliated company, one over which the firm has a greater degree of influence than an unaffiliated one. The key to keeping debt off the balance sheet in this case is to ensure that the firm is not required to prepare consolidated financial statements with the affiliated company. Consolidated statements aggregate the separate financial statements of two or more entities under the control of one of the entities. The debt will appear on the consolidated balance sheet as long as it appears on the balance sheet of any one entity in the consolidated group. (Chapter 7 discusses consolidated financial statements more fully.) To avoid consolidation, the firm needing the financing must not effectively *control* the entity obtaining the financing.

One means of avoiding consolidation is to set up a joint venture with another entity, with each entity owning 50 percent of the common stock. In this case, neither firm controls the joint venture. GAAP currently does not require either firm to prepare consolidated financial statements with the joint venture.

Another means of avoiding consolidation is to set up an *SPE (special-purpose entity)*, also known as a *VIE (variable interest entity)*. The SPE obtains financing and either (1) constructs or acquires the asset desired by the firm attempting to keep debt off its balance sheet or (2) purchases the particular asset from this firm. In both cases, the asset held by the SPE serves as collateral for the loan. The lender to the SPE will likely require some commitment from the firm that sets up the SPE to ensure repayment of the loan. The commitment may take the form of a noncancelable purchase commitment or a loan guarantee. The key to avoiding consolidation is that effective control of the SPE must not reside primarily with the firm setting it up. The SPE must have economic substance of its own and other parties—the lender or other equity owners—must be the primary beneficiary of the SPE.

Central to the early 2000's bankruptcy of Enron was the misuse of SPEs to hold off-balance-sheet derivative instruments, securities, and other assets such as power plants in India and Nigeria initially acquired by Enron and to keep the related financing for these instruments and securities off the balance sheet. Enron did not consolidate these SPEs, maintaining that it did not control them. Later revelations showed that Enron had effective control, requiring Enron to restate its previously issued financial statements. The restatements increased assets and liabilities on the balance sheet and eliminated gains that Enron recognized on the "sale" of the assets to the SPEs. Chapter 7 discusses the accounting for SPEs.

The following sections describe several off-balance-sheet financing arrangements. In several cases, the FASB or IASB have issued an accounting standard that specifies how firms should treat such transactions for financial reporting purposes. In other cases, the standard-setting bodies have not issued a specific financial reporting standard and the accountant must apply the general criteria for liability recognition.

Sale of Receivables

Firms sometimes sell their receivables as a means of obtaining financing or use an SPE to issue securities backed by the receivables (for example, mortgage-backed securities issued by financial institutions or their SPEs). If collections from customers are not sufficient to repay the amount borrowed plus interest, the transferring firm may have to pay the difference; that is, the lender has recourse against the borrowing firm.

The question arises as to whether the recourse provision creates an accounting liability. Some argue that the arrangement is similar to a collateralized loan. The firm should leave the receivables on its books and recognize a liability in the amount of the cash received. Others argue that the firm has sold an asset; it should recognize a liability only if it is probable that collections from customers will be insufficient and the firm will be required to repay some portion of the amount received.

The FASB and IASB provide accounting rules to guide the decision of whether to classify a transfer of receivables as a sale or a loan.[40] For example, Statement of Financial Accounting Standards No. 140, "Accounting for Transfers and Servicing of Financial Assets and Extinguishments of Liabilities," requires that firms recognize transfers of receivables as sales only if the transferor surrenders control of the receivables. Firms surrender control only if all of the following conditions are met:

- The assets transferred (that is, receivables) have been isolated from the selling ("transferor") firm; that is, neither the transferor nor a creditor of the selling firm could access the receivables in the event of the seller's bankruptcy.
- The buying ("transferee") firm obtains the right to pledge or exchange the transferred assets, and no condition both constrains the transferee from taking advantage of its right and provides more than a trivial benefit to the transferor.
- The selling firm does not maintain effective control over the assets transferred through (a) an agreement that both entitles and obligates it to repurchase the assets or (b) the ability to unilaterally cause the transferee to return specific assets.

The principal refinement to the concept of an accounting liability brought out by Statement No. 140 relates to identifying the party involved in the transaction that controls the determination of which party enjoys the economic benefits and sustains the economic risk of the assets (receivables in this case). If the selling (borrowing) firm controls the economic benefits/risks, the transaction is a collateralized loan. If the arrangement transfers these benefits/risks to the buying (lending) firm, the transaction is a sale.

Example 15

Assume that Sears transfers $1,000,000 of installment receivables to a bank in exchange for $950,000. Sears is liable to the bank for uncollectible receivables (a "with recourse" transfer), and the estimated fair value of the recourse obligation is $20,000. Exhibit 6.10 shows the financial statement effects if reported as a borrowing and if reported as a sale.

EXHIBIT 6.10: EXAMPLE 15 SOLUTION

Borrowing

Assets	=	Liabilities	+	Shareholders' Equity: CC	Shareholders' Equity: AOCI	Shareholders' Equity: RE
Cash +950,000		Loan Payable +950,000				

Cash	950,000	
Loan Payable		950,000

Sale

Assets	=	Liabilities	+	Shareholders' Equity: CC	Shareholders' Equity: AOCI	Shareholders' Equity: RE
Cash +950,000 Accounts Receivable −1,000,000		Recourse Liability +20,000				Loss on Sale −70,000

Cash	950,000	
Loss on Sale	70,000	
Accounts Receivable		1,000,000
Recourse Liability		20,000

[40] Financial Accounting Standards Board, *Statement of Financial Accounting Standards No. 140*, "Accounting for Transfers and Servicing of Financial Assets and Extinguishments of Liabilities" (2000); *FASB Codification Topic 860;* Financial Accounting Standards Board, *Statement of Financial Accounting Standards No. 156*, "Accounting for Servicing of Financial Assets" (2006); International Accounting Standards Board, *International Accounting Standard No. 39*, "Financial Instruments: Recognition and Measurement" (revised 2003).

In the "borrowing" transaction, Sears does not surrender control of the receivables (that is, does not meet the FASB's three conditions to record a sale). Therefore, Sears keeps the accounts receivable on its books and records the receipt of cash and the incurrence of a liability (loan payable). In the "sale" transaction, the accounts receivable are removed from Sears' balance sheet because Sears no longer controls the accounts receivable. Sears also records the expected cash outflow to satisfy the recourse provisions of the agreement should customers fail to pay. Because assets decrease in the net by $50,000 and liabilities increase by $20,000, Sears records a loss on sale of $70,000, which is reported on the income statement and reduces retained earnings.

Product Financing Arrangements

Product financing arrangements occur when a firm (sponsor) does either of the following:

- Sells inventory to another entity and, in a related transaction, agrees to repurchase the inventory at specified prices over specified times
- Arranges for another entity to purchase inventory items on the firm's behalf and, in a related transaction, agrees to purchase the inventory items from the other entity

The first arrangement is similar to the sale of receivables with recourse except that greater certainty exists that the inventory transaction will require a future cash outflow. The second arrangement is structured to appear as a purchase commitment. In this case, however, the sponsoring firm usually creates an SPE for the sole purpose of acquiring the inventory. The sponsoring firm usually guarantees the debt incurred by the SPE in acquiring the inventory.

Financial reporting requires that firms recognize product financing arrangements as liabilities if they meet two conditions:

- The arrangement requires the sponsoring firm to purchase the inventory, substantially identical inventory, or processed goods of which the inventory is a component at specified prices.
- The payments made to the other entity cover all acquisition, holding, and financing costs.[41]

The second criterion requires that the sponsoring firm recognize a liability whenever it incurs the economic risks (such as changing costs or interest rates) of purchasing and holding inventory, even though it may not physically control the inventory or have a legal obligation to the supplier of the inventory. Thus, as with sales of receivables with recourse, a firm recognizes a liability when it controls the determination of which party enjoys the economic benefits and incurs the economic risks of the asset involved. It also recognizes an asset of equal amount, usually inventory.

Research and Development Financing Arrangements

When a firm borrows funds to conduct R&D, it recognizes a liability at the time of borrowing and recognizes expenses as it incurs R&D costs. As the next example demonstrates, firms have engaged in innovative means of financing aimed at keeping liabilities off the balance sheet and effectively excluding R&D expenses from the income statement.

Example 16

Merck, a pharmaceutical company, forms joint ventures with another pharmaceutical company to develop, manufacture, and market new products. Because joint ventures are owned equally by the two entities in each case, Merck does not consolidate the financial statements

[41]Financial Accounting Standards Board, *Statement of Financial Accounting Standards No. 49*, "Accounting for Product Financing Arrangements" (1981); *FASB Codification Topic 470.*

of the joint ventures with its own financial statements; instead, it reports its share of ownership in the joint venture as an investment. Any liabilities of the joint ventures appear on the financial statements of the joint ventures, not on Merck's balance sheet. Likewise, the R&D expense of the joint ventures appears on the income statement issued by the joint ventures, not on Merck's income statement.

Firms can also use other arrangements besides joint ventures. Although the structures vary somewhat across firms, they generally operate as follows:

1. The sponsoring firm contributes either preliminary development work or rights to future products to a partnership in exchange for a general interest in the partnership. It obtains limited partners (often corporate directors or officers) who contribute cash for their partnership interests.
2. The sponsoring firm conducts R&D work for the partnership for a fee. The sponsoring firm usually performs the R&D on a best-efforts basis, with no guarantee of success. The sponsoring firm recognizes amounts received from the partnership for R&D services as revenues. The amount of revenue generally equals or exceeds the R&D costs it incurs.
3. The rights to any resulting products usually reside in the partnership. However, the partnership agreement usually constrains the returns and risks of the limited partners. The sponsoring firm can often acquire the limited partners' interests in the partnership if valuable products emerge. The sponsoring firm may have to guarantee certain minimum royalty payments to the partnership or agree to purchase the partnership's rights to the product.

In arrangements such as these, a primary objective of the sponsoring firm involves obtaining financing for its R&D work without having to recognize a liability. Criteria exist for when firms must recognize such financing arrangements as liabilities.[42] The sponsoring firm recognizes a liability under the following conditions:

- If the contractual agreement requires the sponsoring firm to repay any of the funds provided by the other parties regardless of the outcome of the R&D.
- If surrounding conditions indicate that the sponsoring firm bears the risk of failure of the R&D work even though the contractual agreement does not obligate it to repay the other parties. For example, if a sponsoring firm guarantees the debt of the partnership, must make minimum royalty payments to the partnership, or must acquire the partnership's interest in any product, the sponsoring firm will bear the risk of the R&D work.

The criteria require that, as with the off-balance-sheet financing arrangements involving receivables and inventories discussed previously, firms recognize liabilities when they bear the risk associated with the asset or product involved in the financing of a joint venture for R&D.[43]

The joint ventures formed by Merck and the other pharmaceutical company operate as independent entities, with broad oversight by the joint owners. The joint ventures retain the rights to products developed. Neither joint owner guarantees any debt of the joint ventures. Neither joint owner must pay the other joint owner any amounts if the research effort is nonproductive. Although the two joint owners ultimately bear the risk of failure of the

[42]Financial Accounting Standards Board, *Statement of Financial Accounting Standards No. 68*, "Research and Development Arrangements" (1982); *FASB Codification Topic 730.*

[43]A study of firms that conduct their research and development through limited partnerships found that the stock market appears to consider the call option that firms have on research findings in the valuation of the firm. The author calls for improved disclosure of these arrangements instead of recognition of a liability in the balance sheet. See Terry Shevlin, "The Valuation of R&D Firms with R&D Limited Partnerships," *Accounting Review* (January 1991), pp. 1–21.

joint venture, GAAP accounting for the Merck joint ventures requires only that the joint owners recognize their equity investment in the joint venture on the balance sheet.

Take-or-Pay or Throughput Contracts

A take-or-pay contract is an agreement in which a purchaser agrees to pay specified amounts periodically to a seller for products or services. A throughput contract is similar to a take-or-pay contract except that the "product" purchased is transportation or processing services.

To understand the rationale for such arrangements, consider the following case. Suppose two petroleum companies need additional refining capacity. If either company builds a refinery, it will record an asset and any related financing on its balance sheet. Suppose instead the two companies form a joint venture to construct a refinery. The joint venture, an entity separate from the two petroleum companies, obtains financing and constructs the refinery. To secure financing for the joint venture, the two petroleum companies sign take-or-pay contracts agreeing to make certain payments to the joint venture each period for refining services. The payments are sufficient to cover all of the refinery's operating and financing costs. The joint owners must make the payments even if they acquire no refinery services.

The economic substance of this arrangement is that each petroleum company owns half of the refinery and is obligated to the extent of half of the financing. The legal status of the arrangement is that the two firms have simply signed noncancelable purchase commitments (that is, executory contracts). Accounting likewise treats these arrangements as executory contracts. At the time of signing the contract, the firms have not yet received any benefits that obligate them to pay. As they receive benefits or incur obligations over time, a liability arises. If one or the other entity guarantees the debt of the partnership, the guarantee is a contingent obligation, which is not recognized as a liability until future events indicate that payment is probable.

Financial reporting requires firms to disclose take-or-pay and throughput commitments in the notes.[44] The analyst should examine disclosures of these commitments in notes to the financial statements to assess whether the firm incurs the risks and rewards of the arrangement and should therefore recognize a liability.

Example 17

Refer to Note 9, "Debt Obligations and Commitments," to PepsiCo's Consolidated Financial Statements (Appendix A). PepsiCo presents a subsection entitled "Long-Term Contractual Commitments" in which it lists cash payments due under noncancelable contracts, some of which are reflected in the balance sheet as liabilities and some that are not. Long-term debt payments totaling $6,599 million are reflected in the balance sheet at the present value of those payments. Interest on debt obligations is reflected as interest payable in the balance sheet to the extent incurred (as time passes) and not yet paid. Operating leases are not treated as liabilities, as you will learn in a later section of this chapter. Purchase commitments and marketing commitments are executory contracts not reflected as liabilities (hence, their required supplemental disclosure in Note 9). In a section entitled "Off-Balance-Sheet Arrangements," PepsiCo discloses that it guarantees $2.3 billion of Bottling Group, LLC's long-term debt and that its " . . . payment obligation would be triggered if Bottling Group, LLC failed to perform under these debt obligations. . . . "

---

[44]Financial Accounting Standards Board, *Statement of Financial Accounting Standards No. 47*, "Disclosure of Long-Term Obligations," 1981.

Summary of Off-Balance-Sheet Financing

The conventional accounting model based on historical cost is exchange or transaction oriented. Accounting recognizes events when an exchange takes place. The criteria for liability recognition discussed earlier in this chapter and in Exhibit 6.5 illustrate this exchange orientation. Accounting recognizes liabilities when a firm incurs an obligation to sacrifice resources in the future for benefits already received. Financial reporting has typically not recognized mutually unexecuted contracts as liabilities because the parties have merely exchanged promises to perform in the future. Financial reporting also does not generally require the recognition of contingent obligations as liabilities because some future obligating event must occur to establish the existence of a liability.

The evolving concept of an accounting liability recognizes that exchanges of promises can have economic substance even though a legal obligation to pay does not immediately arise. When a firm controls the determination of which party enjoys the economic benefits and/or incurs the economic risks from an asset, the firm should recognize the asset and its related financial obligations.

The FASB and IASB closely monitor reporting issues related to off-balance-sheet commitments of firms, but both boards continue to be challenged because of the ever-changing nature of business financing arrangements and the flexible and fluid organizational arrangements that firms create.[45]

LEASES

Many firms acquire rights to use assets through leases. For example, a company might agree to lease computer equipment for 3 years, an office suite for 5 years, or an entire building for 40 years, promising to pay a fixed periodic fee for the duration of the lease. Leasing provides benefits to lessees, the users of the leased assets, such as the following:

- Ability to shift the tax benefits from depreciation and other deductions from a lessee that has little or no taxable income (such as an airline) to a lessor, or owner of the asset, that has substantial taxable income. The lessee expects the lessor to share some of the benefits of these tax deductions by allowing lower lease payments.
- Flexibility to change capacity as needed without having to purchase or sell assets.
- Ability to reduce the risk of technological obsolescence, relative to outright ownership, by maintaining the flexibility to shift to technologically more advanced assets.
- Ability to finance the "acquisition" of an asset using lessor financing when alternative sources of financing are unavailable or more costly.

These potential benefits of leasing to lessees do not come without a cost. When the lessor assumes the risks of ownership, it requires the lessee to make larger lease payments than if the lessee faces these risks. Which party bears the risks is a matter of negotiation between lessor and lessee.

Promising to make an irrevocable series of lease payments commits the firm just as surely as a bond indenture or mortgage, and the accounting is similar in many cases.[46] This section examines two methods of accounting for long-term leases: the operating lease method and the capital (sometimes called finance) lease method.[47] The illustrations show

---

[45]Specific IFRS rules relating to off-balance-sheet financing are rare. However, guidelines may be found in IASB, *SIC Interpretation 12*, "Consolidating Special Purpose Entities" (1998).

[46]Lease disclosures often use the term *noncancelable leases* to capture the contractual lease commitments of the lessee. Under noncancelable leases, the lessee typically can cancel the lease only after incurring a severe penalty.

[47]Financial Accounting Standards Board, *Statement of Financial Accounting Standards No. 13*, "Accounting for Leases," (1975); *FASB Codification Topic 840*; International Accounting Standards Board, *International Accounting Standard 17*, "Leases" (revised 2003).

the accounting by the lessee, the user of the leased asset. Chapter 7 illustrates the accounting for the lessor, the owner of the asset.

Example 18

To illustrate these two methods, suppose Myers Company wants to acquire a computer that has a three-year life and could be purchased for $45,000. Also assume that Myers Company must pay 10 percent per year to borrow money for three years. The computer manufacturer is willing to sell the equipment for $45,000 or to lease it for three years. Myers Company is responsible for property taxes, maintenance, and repairs of the computer whether it leases or purchases the computer.

Assume that Myers Company signs a lease on January 1, Year 1, and must make payments on the lease on December 31, Year 1, Year 2, and Year 3. (In practice, lessees usually make lease payments in advance, but the assumption of year-end payments simplifies the computations.) The lessor sets the lease payments to return the $45,000 principal and 10 percent interest in three equal end-of-year payments. Similar to bond and note calculations, the payment is the amount that solves the following equation:

$$\$45{,}000 = \sum_{n=1}^{3} \frac{\text{Payment}}{(1 + 0.10)^n}$$

Solving this equation for the payment using a financial calculator ($i = .10$, $n = 3$, future value = 0, present value = $45,000) yields an annual payment of $18,095.

Operating Lease Method

In an operating lease, the owner, or lessor, transfers only the rights to use the property to the lessee for specified periods of time. At the end of the lease period, the lessee returns the property to the lessor. For example, car rental companies lease cars by the day or week on an operating basis. In leasing arrangements in which the lessee neither assumes the risks nor enjoys the rewards of ownership, the lessee should treat the lease as an operating lease. Accounting gives no recognition to the signing of an operating lease. (That is, the lessee reports neither the leased asset nor a lease liability on its balance sheet; the lease is simply a mutually unexecuted contract). Over the life of the lease, the lessee recognizes rent expense in measuring net income each year. The effect on the financial statements of Myers Company each year (ignoring income taxes) if it treats the lease as an operating lease appears in Exhibit 6.11.

EXHIBIT 6.11: EXAMPLE 18 SOLUTION FOR OPERATING LEASES

12/31/Year 1

Assets		=	Liabilities	+	Shareholders' Equity: CC	AOCI	RE	
Cash	−18,095						Rent Expense	−18,095

Rent Expense	18,095	
Cash		18,095

12/31/Year 2

Assets		=	Liabilities	+	Shareholders' Equity: CC	AOCI	RE	
Cash	−18,095						Rent Expense	−18,095

Rent Expense	18,095	
Cash		18,095

(*Continued*)

EXHIBIT 6.11 (CONTINUED)

12/31/Year 3

Assets		=	Liabilities	+	Shareholders' Equity CC	AOCI	RE
Cash	−18,095						Rent Expense −18,095

Rent Expense	18,095	
Cash		18,095

Total income effect over three years = $54,285 decrease

The total income statement effect over the three years is the sum of the rent expense ($54,285), which also equals the total cash outflow from lease payments.

Capital Lease Method

In leasing arrangements in which the lessee assumes the risks and enjoys the rewards of ownership, the lease contract is considered a capital lease. In a capital lease, the lessee recognizes the signing of the lease as the simultaneous acquisition of a long-term asset and the incurring of a long-term liability for lease payments. Lessees recognize two expense items each year on capital leases. First, the lessee must depreciate the leased asset over the time period it uses the asset (that is, the least term or the asset's economic useful life if the asset is expected to remain with the lessee after the lease term expires). Assuming that Myers Company uses straight-line depreciation, it recognizes depreciation expense of $15,000 (= $45,000/3) each year. Second, as shown in the amortization schedule in Exhibit 6.12, the lease payment made each year is part interest expense on the lease liability and part reduction in the liability itself.

The effects of (1) the signing of the capital lease on January 1, Year 1, and the recognition of (2) depreciation and (3) interest for each year appear in Exhibit 6.13.

EXHIBIT 6.12

Example 18 Lease Amortization Table

Date	Payment	10% Effective Interest Expense	Amortization	Book Value of Lease Liability
1/1/Year 1				$45,000
12/31/Year 1	$18,095	$4,500	$13,595	$31,405
12/31/Year 2	$18,095	$3,141	$14,954	$16,451
12/31/Year 3	$18,095	$1,644	$16,451	$ 0
	$54,285	$9,285	$45,000	

EXHIBIT 6.13: EXAMPLE 18 SOLUTION FOR CAPITAL LEASES

1/1/Year 1 Signing

Assets	=	Liabilities	+	Shareholders' Equity CC	AOCI	RE
Leased Asset +45,000		Lease Liability +45,000				

Leased Asset	45,000	
Lease Liability		45,000

(Continued)

Exhibit 6.13 (Continued)

12/31/Year 1 Payment

Assets	=	Liabilities	+	Shareholders' Equity		
				CC	AOCI	RE
Cash −18,095		Lease Liability −13,595				Interest Expense −4,500

Interest Expense	4,500	
Lease Liability	13,595	
Cash		18,095

12/31/Year 1 Depreciation

Assets	=	Liabilities	+	Shareholders' Equity		
				CC	AOCI	RE
Leased Asset (Net) −15,000						Depreciation Expense −15,000

Depreciation Expense	15,000	
Leased Asset (Net)		15,000

12/31/Year 2 Payment

Assets	=	Liabilities	+	Shareholders' Equity		
				CC	AOCI	RE
Cash −18,095		Lease Liability −14,954				Interest Expense −3,141

Interest Expense	3,141	
Lease Liability	14,954	
Cash		18,095

12/31/Year 2 Depreciation

Assets	=	Liabilities	+	Shareholders' Equity		
				CC	AOCI	RE
Leased Asset (Net) −15,000						Depreciation Expense −15,000

Depreciation Expense	15,000	
Leased Asset (Net)		15,000

12/31/Year 3 Payment

Assets	=	Liabilities	+	Shareholders' Equity		
				CC	AOCI	RE
Cash −18,095		Lease Liability −16,451				Interest Expense −1,644

Interest Expense	1,544	
Lease Liability	16,451	
Cash		18,095

12/31/Year 3 Depreciation

Assets	=	Liabilities	+	Shareholders' Equity		
				CC	AOCI	RE
Leased Asset (Net) −15,000						Depreciation Expense −15,000

Depreciation Expense	15,000	
Leased Asset (Net)		15,000

The leased asset and liability are shown on the balance sheet as of the signing of the lease. Then in each year, the effective interest method is used to account for the lease liability as was illustrated earlier for a note payable, and the leased asset is depreciated each year. Notice that in the capital lease method, the total expense over the three years is $54,285, comprising $45,000 (= $15,000 + $15,000 + $15,000) for depreciation expense and $9,285 (= $4,500 + $3,141 + $1,644) for interest expense. This total expense is the same as that recognized under the operating lease method described previously ($18,095 × 3 = $54,285). The capital lease method recognizes expenses sooner than the operating lease method does. But over sufficiently long time periods, total expense equals the cash expenditure. One difference between the operating lease method and the capital lease method is the timing of the expense recognition. The other difference is that the capital lease method recognizes both the asset and the liability on the balance sheet.[48]

Choosing the Accounting Method

When a lessee treats a lease as a capital lease, it recognizes both an asset and a liability, thereby increasing total liabilities and making the company appear riskier. Given a choice, most lessees prefer not to show the asset and a related liability on the balance sheet. Lessees prefer an operating lease to an installment purchase or a capital lease, for which both the asset and liability appear on the balance sheet. Lessees also prefer to recognize expenses for financial reporting later rather than sooner. These preferences have led a number of lessees to structure asset acquisitions so that the financing takes the form of an operating lease, thereby achieving off-balance-sheet financing.

U.S. GAAP provides detailed rules of accounting for long-term leases. The lessor and lessee must account for a lease as a capital lease if the lease meets any one of four conditions.[49] These conditions attempt to identify which party, the lessor or the lessee, bears most of the risk related to the asset under lease. When the lessor bears most of the risk, the lease is an operating lease. When the lessee bears most of the risk, the lease is a capital lease.

A lease is a capital lease if it meets any one of the following conditions:

- If it extends for at least 75 percent of the asset's total expected economic life (that is, the lessee uses the asset for most of its life).
- If it transfers ownership to the lessee at the end of the lease term (that is, the lessee bears the risk of changes in the residual value of the asset at the end of the lease term).
- If it seems likely the lessor will transfer ownership to the lessee because of a "bargain purchase" option (that is, the lessee again bears the residual value risk; a bargain purchase option gives the lessee the right to purchase the asset for a price less than the expected fair market value of the asset when the lessee exercises its option).
- The present value of the contractual minimum lease payments equals or exceeds 90 percent of the fair market value of the asset at the time of signing.[50]

The first three conditions are relatively easy to avoid in lease contracts if lessors and lessees prefer to treat a lease as an operating lease instead of a capital lease. The most difficult

---

[48]The fair value option is not allowed for assets and liabilities reported under capital leases.

[49]Financial Accounting Standards Board, *Statement of Financial Accounting Standards No. 13*, "Accounting for Leases" (1976); *FASB Codification Topic 840.*

[50]IFRS criteria are similar, although as is often the case with IFRS, the criteria do not provide "bright-line" percentages such as 75 or 90 percent. Instead, judgment is relied upon to implement the following: (1) Does ownership transfer from the lessor to the lessee at the end of the lease? (2) Is there a bargain purchase option? (3) Does the lease extend for the major portion of the asset's useful life? (4) Does the present value of the minimum lease payments equal substantially all of the asset's fair value? (5) Is the leased asset specialized for use by the lessee?

of the four conditions to avoid is the fourth. When the present value of the contractual minimum lease payments equal or exceed 90 percent of the fair market value of the asset at the time of signing, the lessor has less than or equal to 10 percent of the asset's value at risk to an uncertain residual value at the end of the lease term. Therefore, the lease transfers the major risks and rewards of ownership from the lessor (landlord) to the lessee. In economic substance, the lessee has acquired an asset and has agreed to pay for it under a long-term contract, which the lessee recognizes as a liability. When the present value of the minimum lease payments is less than 90 percent of the fair market value of the asset at the time of signing, the lessor bears the major risks and rewards of ownership and the lease is an operating lease.

Firms often report both operating and capital leases because certain lease agreements meet one or more of these conditions; other lease agreements meet none of the conditions.

Example 19

Airtran leases many of its aircraft and ground facilities. In the notes to its December 31, 2008 financial statements, Airtran Holdings, Inc., provides a schedule of capital and operating lease commitments, as reported in Exhibit 6.14 (in thousands). The firm also reports the present value of its capital lease commitments ($16,866 thousand on December 31, 2008, of which $16,031 thousand is long-term). Airtran reports other long-term debt of $940,569 thousand. Thus, the capitalized lease payments are not a large portion of Airtran's total long-term debt at the end of 2008. Airtran's commitments under operating leases (gross future cash flows of $3,125,518 thousand) are more substantial, representing an important off-balance-sheet cash flow commitment of the firm.

EXHIBIT 6.14

Excerpt from Airtran Holdings, Inc.'s December 31, 2008 Annual Report

Note 6 (partial). Total rental expense charged to operations for aircraft, facilities and office space for the years ended December 31, 2008, 2007 and 2006 was approximately $326.0 million, $315.6 million and $287.5 million, respectively. . . . The following schedule outlines the future minimum lease payments at December 31, 2008, under non-cancelable operating leases and capital leases with initial terms in excess of one year (in thousands):

	Capital leases	Operating leases
2009	$ 2,328	$ 288,031
2010	2,328	275,985
2011	2,328	263,684
2012	2,328	262,020
2013	2,328	256,901
Thereafter	15,904	1,778,897
Total minimum lease payments	$ 27,544	$3,125,518
Less: amounts representing interest	(10,678)	
Present value of future payments	$ 16,866	
Less: current obligations	(835)	
Long-term obligations	$ 16,031	

Converting Operating Leases to Capital Leases

Lease commitments by lessees accounted for as operating leases do not appear as assets or liabilities on the balance sheet and, if one believes these obligations are essentially financial commitments, can cause the analyst to understate the short-term liquidity or long-term solvency risk of the firm. In cross-sectional comparisons of different firms, the analyst also may want to treat all leases as capital leases with the objective of making all firms more comparable in terms of assets and liabilities. For this reason, the analyst may want to restate the financial statements of lessees to convert all operating leases into capital leases. Such a restatement provides a more conservative measure of total liabilities.

Example 20

To illustrate the procedure, refer to PepsiCo's operating lease disclosures in Note 9, "Debt Obligations and Commitments" (Appendix A). Exhibit 6.15 summarizes PepsiCo's information on operating lease commitments. The second column shows PepsiCo's commitments on noncancelable operating leases net of sublease revenues at December 27, 2008. PepsiCo reports aggregate payments for 2010–2011 and 2012–2013. We assume the payments are evenly distributed. To convert these operating lease cash payments to a capital lease, the analyst must express the lease commitments in present value terms. The discount rate the analyst should use is the lessee's incremental borrowing rate for secured debt with similar risk to that of the leasing arrangement. PepsiCo's interest expense (see the income statement) as a percentage of average short- and long-term borrowing for 2008 (see the balance sheet) is 5.3 percent [= $329/(0.5{$0 + $4,203 + $369 + $7,858})]. A 6 percent rate is assumed in this case to compute the present value of operating lease commitments.

Exhibit 6.15 illustrates the lease capitalization process. The present value of each cash flow equals the cash flow times a present value factor. Each factor in the column is obtained from a present value table or by the formula $1/(1 + i)^n$. For example, 2010's factor of $0.89000 = 1/(1 + 0.06)^2$. To select a present value factor for payments in 2014 and beyond, you need to know the years and amounts in which PepsiCo will pay the $268 million.

EXHIBIT 6.15

PepsiCo., Inc. Operating Lease Disclosures; Summarized from PepsiCo, Inc. December 27, 2008 Annual Report (amounts in millions)

Year	Operating Lease Commitments	Present Value Factor at 6%	Present Value
2009	$ 262.0	0.94340	$247.2
2010	179.5	0.89000	159.8
2011	179.5	0.83962	150.7
2012	99.5	0.79209	78.8
2013	99.5	0.74726	74.4
2014 and beyond	268.0	—	178.4*
	$1,088.0		$889.3

*Present value of an annuity of $89.3 million for three periods at 6 percent, then that present value discounted back five periods at 6 percent.

Presume that payments will continue at the same amount as the \$99.5 million payment in 2013, in which case PepsiCo will pay the remaining \$268 million in less than three periods (\$268/\$99.5 < 3). Given the decline in payments over the years shown in Exhibit 6.15, the remainder is spread over an assumed three periods, yielding a payment of \$89.3 million per year (\$268 million/3 years). The \$178.4 million present value is obtained by computing the present value of an annuity of \$89.3 million for three periods at 6 percent to yield a present value at the end of 2013 and then discounting that amount five additional periods at 6 percent. The present value of all of PepsiCo's operating lease payments is \$889.3 million.

To approximate what leased asset and liability would have existed if capital lease treatment had been used, the analyst adds the \$889.3 million lease to property, plant, and equipment; the \$247.2 million present value of the 2009 lease payments to short-term debt; and the \$652.1 million present value of lease payments in 2010 and beyond to long-term debt on the December 27, 2008 balance sheet. Certain ratios could be affected substantially by the operating lease capitalization. For example, PepsiCo's ratio of long-term debt to shareholders' equity based on reported amounts is \$7,858/\$12,203 = 64.4%. Adding the long-term portion of the capital lease liability of \$652.1 million to the numerator of the ratio changes the ratio to (\$7,858 + \$652.1)/\$12,203 = 69.7%. While this increase is substantial, greater increases are often found when the adjustment is made for retailers, restaurant chains, and airlines. For time-series analysis of PepsiCo, similar calculations would be necessary for at least two previous years.

If the analyst views the economic substance of this lease more as a means of financing the acquisition of long-term assets (that is, as a capital lease) than as a right to use such assets for a short period of time, the analyst also should convert the income statement from the operating to the capital lease method by eliminating rent expense but including depreciation expense on the capitalized asset and interest expense on the lease obligation. In general, if the average lease is in the first half of its life, total expenses under the capital lease method tend to exceed total expenses under the operating lease method; so adjusted income will tend to be less than reported income. If the average lease is in the last half of its life, total expenses under the capital lease method tend to be less than under the operating lease method; so adjusted income tends to be greater than reported income. The two expense amounts are approximately equal at the midlife point. The average operating lease for PepsiCo appears to be near the midpoint of its life. You reach this conclusion by comparing the operating lease payment in 2009 (\$262 million), which would be treated as rent expense if the lease were operating, to the following rough approximations for expenses if the lease were capital:

$$\text{Depreciation Expense} = \$889.3 \text{ million asset}/6.27 \text{ years remaining lease life}^{51}$$
$$= \$141.83 \text{ million}$$

$$\text{Interest Expense} = \$889.3 \text{ million lease liability} \times 6\% = \$53.36 \text{ million}$$

The sum of depreciation expense and interest expense (capital lease treatment) is \$195.19 million, which is less than but relatively close to the \$262.0 million in rent

[51]We calculated the 6.27 years as a weighted average. If the rent payments are equal over the 2009–2016 period, it would be reasonable to assume that all leased assets are going to be used over the eight-year period. However, the rent payments decline, implying that some assets are used up and, thus, off-lease. Working backwards in the schedule, \$89.3 million of cash flow appears in each year, \$10.2 million additional cash flow (\$89.3 + \$10.2 = \$99.5) in cash flow appears in the first five years, \$80 million additional cash flow appears for the first three years (\$99.5 + \$80 = \$179.5), and \$82.5 million additional cash flow (\$179.5 + \$82.5 = \$262) appears in 2009. Therefore 66 percent of the cash flows related to assets in use for eight years (\$89.3 per year × 8 years = \$714.4 out of a total of \$1,087.9), 5 percent of the cash flows related to assets in use for five years (\$10.2 per year × 5 years = \$51 out of a total of \$1,087.9), and so on. Weighting an eight-year life by 66 percent, a five-year life by 5 percent, and so on, yields an average useful life of 6.27 years.

expense (operating lease treatment). PepsiCo's Note 4, "Property, Plant, and Equipment and Intangible Assets" (Appendix A), shows that accumulated depreciation on depreciable property, plant, and equipment is about one-half of property, plant, and equipment, confirming the estimate that remaining asset lives are approximately at the midpoint of total useful life.

Therefore, constructive capitalization of the operating leases would increase net income by the difference between these two expenses ($66.81 million) times one minus the statutory tax rate, or $66.81 million × (1 – 0.35) = $43.42 million. This amount is less than 1 percent of PepsiCo's 2008 net income of $5,142 million.

Often, balance sheet restatements are more significant than income statement restatements. Consequently, the analyst usually can ignore restatements of the income statement, particularly if the analyst's emphasis is assessment of a firm's credit risk, as discussed in Chapter 5. However, note that even for firms with leases at the midlife point, where the income statement effect may be immaterial, the effect on the balance sheet can be substantial.[52]

The analyst could restate the statement of cash flows for the capitalization of operating leases. Under the operating lease method, the lease payment for the year is an operating use of cash. Its inclusion as a subtraction in computing net income results in reporting its negative cash flow effect in the operating section of the statement of cash flows. Under the capital lease method, a portion of the cash payment represents a repayment of the lease liability, a financing use of cash instead of an operating use of cash. The analyst should reclassify this portion of the cash payment from the operating section to the financing section of the statement of cash flows. The analyst also could reduce net income for depreciation expense on the capitalized lease assets, but this amount appears as an addback to net income for a non-cash expense. Thus, the net effect of depreciation expense on operating cash flows is zero.

It is clear from the discussion that note disclosures allow the financial analyst to capitalize operating leases effectively, but with error. A number of assumptions and estimates (sometimes rough) must be employed, and these assumptions may not be valid for all firms in all industries. As a result, credit rating agencies such as Moody's and Fitch have developed methodologies with the objectives of standardization and simplicity. For example, some analysts estimate the lease liability and leased asset to be capitalized simply using an "8X" rule. That is, a simple method of computing the capitalized liability and asset is to multiply the amount of annual rent expense times eight. Because this "8X" heuristic is based on specific assumptions (a 6 percent interest rate and an asset life of 15 years), Moody's uses a modified approach that takes into account industry differences in useful lives and the "seasoning" (that is, age) of the leased assets. Thus, for any given firm, a factor of 5X, 6X, 8X, or greater might be applied, with firms with long-lived assets such as airlines, shipping, and public utilities receiving the highest factor. Fitch also uses the 8X heuristic, a present value approach if sufficient data exists, and individual analysis about the validity of the approach for a given firm.[53]

---

[52]For an alternative procedure for converting operating leases into capital leases, see Eugene A. Imhoff, Jr., Robert C. Lipe, and David W. Wright, "Operating Leases: Impact of Constructive Capitalization," *Accounting Horizons* (March 1991), pp. 51–63. In this study, the authors found that capitalizing operating leases decreased the rate of return on assets 34 percent for high-lease firms and 10 percent for low-lease firms and increased the debt-to-equity ratio 191 percent for high-lease firms and 47 percent for firms.

[53]Moody's Approach to Global Standard Adjustments in the Analysis of Financial Statements for Non-Financial Corporations—Part I, *Standardized Adjustments to Enable Global Consistency for US and Canadian GAAP Issuers* (March 2005); "Capitalization of Operating Leases by Credit Rating Agencies," *ELT* (February 2007).

Impact of Accounting for Operating Leases as Capital Leases

Virtually all firms have some amount of commitment under operating leases. The change in debt ratios for some firms is relatively minor, as is the case for PepsiCo. For other firms, particularly airlines and retail stores, the effect can be significant. Even for firms for which the effect is relatively small, adding the effect of capitalizing operating leases to the effect of other off-balance-sheet obligations can result in a combined material effect. Thus, the analyst should examine the effect of leases when assessing the risk and accounting quality of a firm's financial statements. The analyst should also consider the effects of off-balance-sheet leases when determining capital structure weights and debt costs for the weighted average cost of capital calculations used in enterprise valuation.

SUMMARY

This chapter explores various accounting issues related to measuring the financing activities of the firm. Both profitability analysis and risk analysis are affected by management's choice between interest-bearing debt and shareholders' equity to finance the acquisition of operating capacity. The proper measurement and reporting of liabilities enables the analyst to understand the risk of investing in the firm's debt and equity instruments, and the existence of off-balance-sheet arrangements complicates the analysis.

Although we provide a broad description of liability recognition, this chapter focuses primarily on the set of liabilities arising from transactions with lending institutions that generate notes and bonds payable. Typically, these liabilities are generated to raise funds for investments in long-term assets used in operations. The next chapter (Chapter 7) examines the accounting issues surrounding these long-term assets. Chapter 8 returns to measuring and reporting liabilities generated from operating activities, such as accounts payable, provisions, deferred tax liabilities, and pension liabilities.

QUESTIONS, EXERCISES, PROBLEMS, AND CASES

Questions and Exercises

6.1 COMMON EQUITY TRANSACTIONS. Describe the directional effect (increase, decrease, or no effect) of each transaction on the components of the book value of common shareholders' equity shown in the chart on the next page.

- **a.** Issuance of $1 par value common stock at an amount greater than par value
- **b.** Donation of land by a governmental unit to a corporation
- **c.** Cash dividend declared
- **d.** Previously declared cash dividend paid
- **e.** Property dividend declared and paid
- **f.** Large stock dividend declared and issued
- **g.** Small stock dividend declared and issued
- **h.** 2-for-1 stock split announced and issue
- **i.** Stock options granted
- **j.** Recognition of compensation expense on stock options
- **k.** Stock options exercised
- **l.** Stock options expired
- **m.** Treasury stock acquired (company uses the cost method)

n. Treasury stock in Transaction m reissued at an amount greater than original acquisition price
o. Treasury stock in Transaction m reissued at an amount less than the original acquisition price
p. Restricted stock issued (grant date)
q. Recognition of compensation expense related to restricted stock
r. Granting of stock appreciation rights to be settled with cash
s. Recognition of compensation expense on stock appreciation rights
t. Reacquisition and retirement of common stock at an amount greater than original issue price

Item	Common Stock	Additional Paid-in Capital	Deferred Compensation	Retained Earnings (use * to indicate income statement effect)	Treasury Stock at Cost	Total Common Shareholders' Equity
a						
b						
c						
...						

6.2 COMMON EQUITY ISSUE. Assume that a start-up manufacturing company raises capital through a series of equity issues.

a. Using the financial statement template below, summarize the financial statement effects of the following transactions. Identify the account affected and use plus and minus signs to indicate the increases and decreases in the specific element of the balance sheet (assets, liabilities, components of shareholders' equity).
(1) Issues 100,000 shares of $1 par value common stock for $10 per share.
(2) Receives land in exchange for 10,000 shares of $1 par common stock when the common stock is trading in the market at $15 per share. The land has no readily determinable market value.
(3) Receives subscriptions for the issue of 40,000 shares of $1 par value common. The share issue price is $20, of which 30 percent is received as a down payment. Subsequently, the remaining 70 percent is received.

	Assets	=	Liabilities	+	Shareholders' Equity: CC	Shareholders' Equity: AOCI	Shareholders' Equity: RE
Journal entry:							

b. In each case, how does the company measure the transaction? What measurement attribute is used?

6.3 DIVIDENDS. Following is the shareholders' equity section of All-Wood Doors on a day its common stock is trading at $130 per share.

Common stock ($2 par value, 40,000 shares issued and outstanding)	$ 80,000
Additional paid-in capital on common stock	1,600,000
Retained earnings	3,000,000

a. Use the financial statement template below to show the financial statement effects of the following dividend events. (Assume that the events are independent.)

(1) Cash dividend declaration and payment of $1 per share
(2) Property dividend declaration and payment of shares representing a short-term investment in Screen Products, Ltd., with a fair value of $10,000
(3) 10 percent stock dividend
(4) 100 percent stock dividend
(5) 3-for-1 stock split
(6) 1-for-2 reverse stock split

	Assets	=	Liabilities	+	Shareholders' Equity		
					CC	AOCI	RE
Journal entry:							

b. Which events changed the book value of common equity? Under what conditions will these events lead to future increases and decreases in ROE?

6.4 CASH FLOW EFFECTS OF EQUITY AND DEBT FINANCING. Identify where the cash flow effect of each of the following transactions is reported in the statement of cash flows: operating, investing, or financing section. State the direction of each change. State *None* if there is no cash flow effect.

a. Issuance of stock for cash
b. Issuance of stock for land
c. Acquisition of treasury stock
d. Reissuance of treasury stock
e. Declaration of a cash dividend
f. Payment of a cash dividend previously declared
g. Declaration and issuance of a large stock dividend
h. Declaration and issuance of a small stock dividend
i. Granting of stock options
j. Exercise of stock options
k. Granting of RSUs
l. Issuance of long-term notes payable
m. Issuance of convertible bonds
n. Conversion of convertible bonds to common stock
o. Payment of interest on bonds
p. Retirement of bonds at book value
q. Retirement of bonds at a gain
r. Retirement of bonds at a loss

6.5 ACCOUNTING FOR A NOTE PAYABLE. Assume that on December 31, 2010, The Coca-Cola Company borrows money from a consortium of banks by issuing a

$900 million promissory note. The note matures in four years on December 31, 2014, and pays 3 percent interest once a year on December 31. The consortium transfers $867.331 million (rounded) to Coca-Cola, implying that the bank expects a 4 percent return on the note.

a. Use the template below to show the financial statement effects of (1) the December 31, 2010 issue, (2) the December 31, 2011 interest payment and interest expense accrual, and (3) the December 31, 2012 interest payment and interest expense accrual.

	Assets	=	Liabilities	+	Shareholders' Equity		
					CC	AOCI	RE
Journal entry:							

b. Assume that events involving foreign operations have increased the risk of The Coca-Cola Company to the point where creditors expect a 5 percent return on the note as of December 31, 2012. What amounts would Coca-Cola report for long-term debt (1) on the face of its December 31, 2012 balance sheet and (2) in the notes to the financial statements?

c. In addition to the information in Part b, assume that The Coca-Cola Company has chosen the fair value option for the reporting of this note. What amounts would Coca-Cola report for long-term debt (1) on the face of its December 31, 2012 balance sheet and (2) and on the income statement with respect to the note's fair value change?

6.6 ACCOUNTING FOR TROUBLED DEBT: SETTLEMENT. Assume that Circuit City owes Synovus Bank $1,000,000 on a 4-year, 7% note originally issued at par. After one year of making scheduled payments, Circuit City faces financial difficulty. At the end of the second year, Circuit City owes Synovus $1,000,000 plus $70,000 of accrued but unpaid interest. Circuit City settles the debt by paying $700,000 in cash and transferring investments to Synovus. Circuit City recently purchased the investments for $120,000 and carried them on the books at that amount. The investments are worth $135,000 at the date of the debt settlement. Use the template below to show the financial statement effects of the debt settlement.

	Assets	=	Liabilities	+	Shareholders' Equity		
					CC	AOCI	RE
Journal entry:							

6.7 ACCOUNTING FOR TROUBLED DEBT: MODIFICATION OF TERMS. Assume that Great Beef Co. owes Bank of America $5,000,000 on a 3-year, 9% note originally issued at par. After one year of making scheduled payments, the firm faces financial difficulty. At the end of the second year, Great Beef owes Bank of America

$5,000,000 plus $450,000 of accrued but unpaid interest. (Assume that the financial difficulty has increased the riskiness of Great Beef Co. to the point where it would have to pay 15 percent to borrow money.)

a. Assume that Bank of America restructures the note by forgiving the $450,000 interest payable, reducing the note principal to $4,500,000, and reducing the interest rate to 6 percent. Show the financial statement effects at the date of restructuring using the template below assuming that Great Beef Co. uses
(1) U.S. GAAP.
(2) IFRS.

	Assets	=	Liabilities	+	Shareholders' Equity		
					CC	AOCI	RE
Journal entry:							

b. Assume that Bank of America restructures the note by forgiving the $450,000 interest payable, reducing the note principal to $4,800,000, and reducing the interest rate to 7 percent. Show the financial statement effects at the date of restructuring using the template below assuming that Great Beef Co. uses
(1) U.S. GAAP.
(2) IFRS.

	Assets	=	Liabilities	+	Shareholders' Equity		
					CC	AOCI	RE
Journal entry:							

c. Comment on the differences between the two systems. Which reporting system better represents the underlying economics of the debt restructuring? Will U.S. GAAP supplemental disclosures provide similar information? Explain.

6.8 REDEEMABLE PREFERRED STOCK. Determine and compare the financial reporting (debt versus equity classification) of redeemable preferred stock with the following characteristics under U.S. GAAP and IFRS.

a. Redemption will occur at a specific time or upon a specific event (for example, death of the holder).
b. Redemption is at the option of the issuing firm; that is, the preferred stock is "callable."
c. Redemption is at the holder's discretion; that is, the preferred stock is "putable."

6.9 CONVERTIBLE PREFERRED STOCK. Assume that John Deere Co. issues 2,000 shares of $100 par, 6% convertible preferred stock for $105 per share. Shareholders have the right to exchange each share of convertible preferred stock for five shares of

$10 par common stock. Use the template below to show the financial statement effects of the following events.

a. Issuance of the preferred stock.

b. Declaration and payment of the cash dividend on the preferred stock.

c. Conversion of the preferred stock to common stock when the market value of the common stock is $29 per share.

	Assets	=	Liabilities	+	Shareholders' Equity		
					CC	AOCI	RE

Journal entry:

6.10 CONVERTIBLE DEBT UNDER IFRS AND U.S. GAAP ARTL Company issued 3%, 10-year convertible bonds on January 1, 2010, at their par value of $500 million. Each $1,000 bond is convertible into 40 shares of ARTL's $1 par value common stock. Use the template below to show the financial statement effects under U.S. GAAP and IFRS of the following transactions.

a. Original issue. For the IFRS treatment, assume that ARTL would have borrowed at 8 percent if it did not offer a conversion privilege.

b. Recognition of one year's interest effect.

c. Conversion of the bonds when a share of ARTL common stock trades at $30.

(1) Using the "book value method"
(2) Using the "market value method"

	Assets	=	Liabilities	+	Shareholders' Equity		
					CC	AOCI	RE

Journal entry:

6.11 BONDS ISSUED WITH DETACHABLE WARRANTS. Assume that Motorola, Inc., issues bonds with a face value of $10,000,000 for $9,200,000. The bonds have detachable warrants that may be traded in for shares of common stock. Assume that immediately after issue, bonds with warrants detached trade for $9,000,000; the warrants, for $400,000. Use the template below to show the financial statement effects at the date of issue.

	Assets	=	Liabilities	+	Shareholders' Equity		
					CC	AOCI	RE

Journal entry:

6.12 ACCOUNTING FOR LOSS CONTINGENCIES. The text states that loss contingencies may or may not give rise to accounting liabilities. Financial reporting requires firms to recognize a loss contingency when two criteria are met. Describe the two criteria and provide an example in which applying the criteria would trigger booking the loss contingency as an accounting liability.

6.13 SECURITIZATION OF RECEIVABLES. Firms such as Deere & Company and Macy's, Inc., often sell their receivables as a means of obtaining financing. Should firms selling receivables remove the receivables from the balance sheet, or should the receivables remain on the balance sheet? Should the firms recognize a liability in the amount of the cash received for the receivables? Describe the applicable criteria to determine whether the transfer of receivables can be recorded as a sale.

6.14 EFFECT OF CAPITAL AND OPERATING LEASES ON THE FINANCIAL STATEMENTS. All leases for financial reporting purposes are treated as either capital (finance) leases or operating leases. The effects of the two reporting techniques on the financial statements differ substantially. From the perspective of the lessee, prepare a chart that lists the line items reported on the (a) income statement, (b) balance sheet, and (c) statement of cash flows under each reporting technique.

6.15 NATURE OF RESERVE ACCOUNTS. The use of the term *reserve* in the title of a financial statement account is not acceptable in the United States, primarily because its purpose is often too vague. However, informal use of the term by chief financial officers, analysts, and the media is common when they are discussing various aspects of *acceptable* accrual accounting techniques employed by U.S. firms. Provide several examples of financial statement accounts that are often loosely referred to as reserves. What is typically common about all financial statement accounts that are informally referred to as reserves?

6.16 ACCOUNTING FOR STOCK-BASED COMPENSATION. Historically, technology firms have been the most aggressive users of stock-based compensation in the form of stock options granted to almost all employees of the firms. What is the rationale for offering stock options as compensation? Why has this form of compensation been particularly popular with technology firms in the past?

Problems and Cases

6.17 ACHIEVING OFF-BALANCE-SHEET FINANCING (ADAPTED FROM MATERIALS BY R. DIETER, D. LANDSITTEL, J. STEWART, AND A. WYATT). Patrick Company wants to raise $50 million cash but for various reasons does not want to do so in a way that results in a newly recorded liability. The firm is sufficiently solvent and profitable, so its bank is willing to lend up to $50 million at the prime interest rate. Patrick Company's financial executives have devised six different plans, described in the following sections.

Transfer of Receivables with Recourse

Patrick Company will transfer to Credit Company its long-term accounts receivable, which call for payments over the next two years. Credit Company will pay an amount equal to the present value of the receivables, less an allowance for uncollectibles, as well as a discount, because it is paying now but will collect cash later. Patrick Company must repurchase from Credit Company at face value any receivables that become uncollectible in excess of the allowance. In addition, Patrick Company may repurchase any of the receivables not yet due at face value less a discount specified by formula and based on the prime rate at the time of the initial transfer. (This option permits Patrick Company to benefit if an unexpected drop in interest rates occurs after the transfer.) The accounting issue is whether the transfer is a sale (in which Patrick Company increases Cash, reduces Accounts Receivable, and recognizes expense or loss on transfer) or merely a loan collateralized by the receivables (in which Patrick Company increases Cash and increases Notes Payable at the time of transfer).

Product Financing Arrangement

Patrick Company will transfer inventory to Credit Company, which will store the inventory in a public warehouse. Credit Company may use the inventory as collateral for its own borrowings, whose proceeds will be used to pay Patrick Company. Patrick Company will pay storage costs and will repurchase the entire inventory within the next four years at contractually fixed prices plus interest accrued for the time elapsed between the transfer and later repurchase. The accounting issue is whether the inventory is sold to Credit Company, with later repurchases treated as new acquisitions for Patrick's inventory, or whether the transaction is merely a loan, with the inventory remaining on Patrick's balance sheet.

Throughput Contract

Patrick Company wants a branch line of a railroad built from the main rail line to carry raw material directly to its plant. It could, of course, borrow the funds and build the branch line itself. Instead, it will sign an agreement with the railroad to ship specified amounts of material each month for ten years. Even if Patrick Company does not ship the specified amounts of material, it will pay the agreed shipping costs. The railroad will take the contract to its bank and, using it as collateral, borrow the funds to build the branch line. The accounting issue is whether Patrick Company would increase an asset for future rail services and increase a liability for payments to the railroad. The alternative is to make no accounting entry except when Patrick makes payments to the railroad.

Construction Partnership

Patrick Company and Mission Company will jointly build a plant to manufacture chemicals that both need in their production processes. Each will contribute $5 million to the project, called Chemical. Chemical will borrow another $40 million from a bank, with Patrick being the only guarantor of the debt. Patrick and Mission are each to contribute equally to future operating expenses and debt service payments of Chemical, but in return for its guaranteeing the debt, Patrick will have an option to purchase Mission's interest for $20 million four years hence. The accounting issue is whether Patrick Company should recognize a liability for the funds borrowed by Chemical. Because of the debt guarantee, debt service payments ultimately will be Patrick Company's responsibility. Alternatively, the debt guarantee is a commitment merely to be disclosed in notes to Patrick Company's financial statements.

Research and Development Partnership

Patrick Company will contribute a laboratory and preliminary findings about a potentially profitable gene-splicing discovery to a partnership, called Venture. Venture will raise funds by selling the remaining interest in the partnership to outside investors for $2 million and borrowing $48 million from a bank, with Patrick Company guaranteeing the debt.

Although Venture will operate under the management of Patrick Company, it will be free to sell the results of its further discoveries and development efforts to anyone, including Patrick Company. Patrick Company is not obligated to purchase any of Venture's output. The accounting issue is whether Patrick Company would recognize the liability.

Hotel Financing

Patrick Company owns and operates a profitable hotel. It could use the hotel as collateral for a conventional mortgage loan. Instead, it considers selling the hotel to a partnership for \$50 million cash. The partnership will sell ownership interests to outside investors for \$5 million and borrow \$45 million from a bank on a conventional mortgage loan, using the hotel as collateral. Patrick Company guarantees the debt. The accounting issue is whether Patrick Company would record the liability for the guaranteed debt of the partnership.

Required

Discuss the appropriate treatment of each proposed arrangement from the viewpoint of the auditor, who must apply GAAP in deciding whether the transaction will result in a liability to be recorded or whether footnote disclosure will suffice. Does GAAP reporting result in an accurate portrayal of the economics of the arrangement in each case? Explain.

6.18 ACCOUNTING FOR SECURITIZATION OF RECEIVABLES. Ford Motor Credit Company discloses the following information with respect to finance receivables (amounts in millions).

December 31:	Year 4	Year 3
Finance Receivables	\$146,451	\$152,276
Securitized Receivables Sold	\$(35,600)	\$(46,900)
Finance Receivables on Balance Sheet	\$110,851	\$105,376
Retained Interest in Securitized Receivables Sold	\$ 9,166	\$ 12,569

Notes to Financial Statements

The Company periodically sells finance receivables in securitization transactions to fund operations and to maintain liquidity. The securitization process involves the sale of interest-bearing securities to investors, the payment of which is secured by a pool of receivables. In many securitization transactions, the Company surrenders control over certain of its finance receivables by selling these assets to SPEs. SPEs then securitize the receivables by issuing certificates representing undivided interests in the SPEs' assets to outside investors and to the Company (retained interest). These certificates entitle the holder to a series of scheduled cash flows under present terms and conditions, the receipt of which is dependent upon cash flows generated by the related SPEs' assets. The cash flows on the underlying receivables are used to pay principal and interest on the debt securities as well as transaction expenses.

In each securitization transaction, the Company retains certain subordinated interests in the SPE, which are the first to absorb credit losses on the sold receivables. As a result, the credit quality of certificates held by outside investors is enhanced. However, the investors and the trusts have no recourse against the Company beyond the trust assets. The Company also retains the servicing rights to the sold receivables and receives a servicing fee. While servicing the sold receivables for the SPE, the Company applies the same servicing policies and procedures that it applies to its own receivables and maintains a normal relationship with its financing customers.

Required

a. Applying the criteria for the sale of receivables from FASB *Statement No. 140,* justify Ford Motor Credit's treatment of the securitization of finance receivables on December 31, Year 3 and Year 4, as a sale instead of a collateralized loan.

b. Assume that the receivables disclosed as securitized on December 31, Year 3, had been initially securitized on that day. Give the journal entry that Ford Motor Credit would have made to securitize these receivables, assuming that it securitized the receivables at no gain or loss.

c. Assume that Ford Motor Credit decided to consolidate its receivables securitization structure in Year 4 and to start accounting for it as secured borrowings. Give the journal entry that the company would make on December 31, Year 4, to account for this change, assuming that it recognized no gain or loss on this event.

d. Most firms prefer to report the securitization of receivables as a sale. The alternative is to view the arrangement as a collateralized loan with the receivables remaining on the firm's balance sheet. Speculate on why firms prefer to report the securitization of receivables as a sale.

6.19 ACCOUNTING FOR ATTEMPTED OFF-BALANCE-SHEET FINANCING ARRANGEMENTS.

a. International Paper Company (IP) needs $100 million of additional financing, but because of restrictions in existing debt covenants, it cannot place any more debt on its balance sheet. To obtain the needed funds, it plans to transfer cutting rights to a mature timber tract to a newly created trust as of January 1, Year 8. The trust will use the cutting rights to obtain a $100 million, 5-year, 10% interest rate bank loan due in five equal installments, with interest on December 31 of each year.

The timber will be harvested each year and sold to obtain funds to service the loan and pay operating costs. Based on current prices, 10 percent more standing wood is available for cutting than should be needed to service the loan and pay ongoing operating costs of the tract (including wind, fire, and erosion insurance). If the selling price of timber decreases in the future, the volume of timber harvested will be increased sufficiently to service the debt. If the selling price of timber increases in the future, the volume harvested will remain as originally anticipated, but any cash left over after debt service and coverage of operating costs will be invested by the trust to provide a cushion for possible future price decreases. The value of any cash or uncut timber at the end of five years will revert to IP.

IP will not guarantee the debt. The bank, however, has the right to inspect the tract at any time and to replace IP's forest management personnel with managers of its own choosing if it believes the tract is being mismanaged.

Required

Discuss the appropriate accounting for this transaction by IP in light of other FASB pronouncements on off-balance-sheet financing.

b. On June 24, Year 4, Delta Air Lines entered into a revolving accounts receivable facility (Facility) providing for the sale of $489 million of a defined pool of accounts receivable (Receivables) through a wholly owned subsidiary to a trust in exchange for a senior certificate in the principal amount of $300 million (Senior Certificate) and a subordinate certificate in the principal amount of $189 million (Subordinate Certificate). The subsidiary retained the Subordinate Certificate, and the company received $300 million in cash from the sale of the Senior Certificate to a third party. The principal amount of the Subordinate Certificate fluctuates daily depending on the volume of Receivables sold and is payable to the subsidiary only to the extent that the collections received on the Receivables exceed amounts due on the Senior Certificate. The full amount of the allowance for doubtful accounts related to the Receivables sold has been retained, as the company has substantially the same credit risk as if the Receivables had not been sold. Under the terms of the Facility, the company is obligated to pay fees that approximate the purchaser's cost of issuing a like amount of commercial paper plus certain administrative costs.

Required

Delta requests your advice on the appropriate accounting for this transaction. How would you respond?

c. In Year 2, a wholly owned subsidiary of Sun Company became a one-third partner in Belvieu Environmental Fuels (BEF), a joint venture formed for the purpose of constructing, owning, and operating a $220 million methyl tertiary butyl ether (MTBE) production facility in Mont Belvieu, Texas. As of December 31, Year 3, BEF had borrowed $128 million against a construction loan facility of which the company guarantees one-third, or $43 million. The plant, which has a designed daily capacity of 12,600 barrels of MTBE, is expected to begin production in mid-Year 4. When production commences, the construction loan will be converted into a five-year, nonrecourse term loan with a first priority lien on all project assets.

To obtain a secure supply of oxygenates for the manufacture of reformulated fuels, Sun has entered into a ten-year take-or-pay agreement with BEF, which commences when the plant becomes operational. Pursuant to this agreement, Sun will purchase all MTBE production from the plant. The minimum per-unit price to be paid for the MTBE production while the nonrecourse term loan is outstanding will equal BEF's annual raw material and operating costs and debt service payments divided by the plant's annual designed capacity. Notwithstanding this minimum price, during the first three years of the off-take agreement, Sun has agreed to pay BEF a price that approximates prices included in current MTBE long-term sales agreements in the marketplace. This price is expected to exceed the minimum price required by the loan agreement. Sun will negotiate a new pricing arrangement with BEF for the remaining years the take-or-pay agreement is in effect. That pricing arrangement will be based on the expected market conditions existing at the time.

Required

How should Sun account for this transaction?

6.20 EFFECT OF CAPITALIZING OPERATING LEASES ON BALANCE SHEET RATIOS. Some retailing companies own their own stores or acquire their premises under capital leases. Other retailing companies acquire the use of store facilities under operating leases, contracting to make future payments. An analyst comparing the capital structure risks of retailing companies may want to adjust reported financial statement data to put all firms on a comparable basis.

Certain data from the financial statements of Gap Inc. and Limited Brands follow (amounts in millions).

Balance Sheet as of January 31, 2009	Gap Inc.	Limited Brands
Current liabilities	$2,158	$1,255
Long-term debt	0	2,897
Other noncurrent liabilities	1,019	946
Shareholders' equity	4,387	1,874
Total	$7,564	$6,972

Minimum Payments under Operating Leases		
2009	$1,069	$ 478
2010	927	455
2011	712	416
2012	520	373
2013	386	341
After 2013	1,080	1,334
Total	$4,694	$3,397

Required

a. Compute the present value of operating lease obligations using an 8 percent discount rate for Gap Inc. and Limited Brands as of January 31, 2009. Assume that all cash flows occur at the end of each year. Also assume that the minimum lease payment each year after 2013 equals $360 million per year for three years for Gap Inc. and $333.5 million for four years for Limited Brands. (This payment scheduling assumption can be obtained by assuming that the payment amount for 2013 continues until the aggregate payments after 2013 have been made, rounding the number of years upward, and then assuming level payments for that number of years. For Gap Inc.: $1,080/$386 = 2.8 years. Rounding up to three years creates a three-year annuity of $1,080/3 years = $360 million per year.)

b. Compute each of the following ratios for Gap, Inc. and Limited Brands as of January 31, 2009, using the amounts originally reported in their balance sheets for the year.

(1) Liabilities to Assets Ratio = Total Liabilities/Total Assets

(2) Long-Term Debt to Long-Term Capital Ratio = Long-Term Debt/(Long-Term Debt + Shareholders' Equity)

c. Repeat Part b but assume that these firms capitalize operating leases.

d. Comment on the results from Parts b and c.

6.21 STOCK-BASED COMPENSATION. Exhibit 6.16 includes a footnote excerpt from the annual report of The Coca-Cola Company for Year 4. The beverage company offers stock options to key employees under plans approved by stockholders.

Required

Review Exhibit 6.16 and answer the following questions.

a. Coca-Cola reports both pretax and after-tax stock-based compensation in its notes to the financial statements. What is the tax savings for Year 2, Year 3, and Year 4 that Coca-Cola generates from the stock-based compensation provided to its employees? Speculate on what income statement line item includes this tax savings as well as what income statement line item includes the stock-based compensation expense. (The income statement is not provided in this problem.)

b. The average option price per share and market price per share at time of grant is equal each year ($44.69 for Year 2, $49.67 for Year 3, and $41.63 for Year 4). Discuss why Coca-Cola structured the stock option grants this way each year.

EXHIBIT 6.16

The Coca-Cola Company
Stock Option Disclosures
(Problem 6.21)

Note—Stock-Based Compensation (partial footnote disclosure)

Our Company currently sponsors stock option plans. Effective January 1, Year 2, our Company adopted the preferable fair value recognition provisions of Statement of Financial Accounting Standards ("SFAS") No. 123, "Accounting for Stock-Based Compensation." The fair values of the stock awards are determined using a single estimated expected life. The compensation expense is recognized on a straight-line basis over the vesting period. The total stock-based compensation expense, net of related tax effects, was $254 million in Year 4, $308 million in Year 3 and $267 million in Year 2.

	Year 4	Year 3	Year 2
Stock-Based Compensation Expense, pretax[a]	$ 345	$ 422	$ 365
Number of Options Granted[b]	31	24	29
Average Option Price per Share	$41.63	$49.67	$44.69
Average Market Price per Share at Time of Grant	$41.63	$49.67	$44.69
Fair Value of Option Granted per Share	$ 8.84	$13.49	$13.10
Vesting Period of Options Granted, years	1–4	1–4	1–4
Life of Options, years	10	10	10
Option Valuation Assumptions for Black-Scholes Model[b]			
Risk-Free Interest Rate	3.8%	3.5%	3.4%
Dividend Yield	2.5%	1.9%	1.7%
Stock Volatility	23.0%	28.1%	30.2%
Expected Option Life, years	6.0	6.0	6.0
Number of Options Exercised[a]	5	4	3
Average Option Exercise Price	$35.54	$26.96	$31.09

[a]Amounts in millions.
[b]Weighted averages.

c. What are the likely reasons that the fair value of options granted per share increased from Year 2 to Year 3 and then decreased from Year 3 to Year 4?

d. Coca-Cola does not report the market price of its stock at the time employees exercised options (3 million in Year 2, 4 million in Year 3, and 5 million in Year 4), but in each year the end-of-year market price is substantially higher than the average option exercise price reported in Exhibit 6.16 ($31.09 for Year 2, $26.96 for Year 3, and $35.54 for Year 4). Discuss why Coca-Cola is willing to sell shares of its stock to employees at a price (option exercise price) much lower than the firm could obtain for shares sold on the market (market price at time of exercise).

e. Coca-Cola employs the Black-Scholes valuation model for valuing stock option grants. Speculate on the directional effects of the key assumptions made in applying the Black-Scholes options pricing model. That is, which assumptions will result in a higher fair value for stock options and which will result in a lower fair value? Why?

6.22 STOCK-BASED COMPENSATION. Eli Lilly and Company produces pharmaceutical products for humans and animals. Exhibit 6.17 includes a footnote excerpt from the quarterly report of Lilly for the period ending March 31, Year 5. The firm first adopted *Statement No. 123 (Revised 2004)* reporting in this quarter.

Required

Review Exhibit 6.17 and answer the following questions.

a. Lilly's statement of cash flows (not provided in this problem) includes an addback for stock-based compensation in calculating cash flows from operations of $108.2 million for Year 5 and $25.2 million for Year 4. Why does Lilly add stock-based compensation back to net income?

EXHIBIT 6.17

Eli Lilly and Company
Stock Option Disclosures
(Problem 6.22)

Note—Stock-Based Compensation (partial footnote disclosure)

We adopted Statement of Financial Accounting Standards No. 123 (revised 2004), Share-Based Payment (SFAS 123R), effective January 1, Year 5. SFAS 123R requires the recognition of the fair value of stock-based compensation in net income. Stock options are granted to employees at exercise prices equal to the fair market value of our stock at the dates of grant. Generally, options fully vest three years from the grant date and have a term of 10 years. We recognize the stock-based compensation expense over the requisite service period of the individual grantees, which generally equals the vesting period.

We recognized compensation cost in the amount of $108.2 million and $25.2 million in the first quarter of Year 5 and Year 4, respectively, as well as related tax benefits of $32.8 million and $8.8 million, respectively.

Beginning with the Year 5 stock option grant, we utilized a lattice-based option valuation model for estimating the fair value of the stock options. The lattice model allows the use of a range of assumptions related to volatility, risk-free interest rate, and employee exercise behavior. Expected volatilities utilized in the lattice model are based on implied volatilities from traded options on our stock, historical volatility of our stock price, and other factors. Similarly, the dividend yield is based on historical experience and our estimate of future dividend yields. The risk-free interest rate is derived from the U.S. Treasury yield curve in effect at the time of grant. The model incorporates exercise and post-vesting forfeiture assumptions based on an analysis of historical data. The expected life of the Year 5 grants is derived from the output of the lattice model.

The weighted-average fair values of the options granted in the first quarter of Year 5 were $16.06 per option, determined using the following assumptions:

Dividend Yield	2.0%
Weighted-Average Volatility	27.8%
Range of Volatilities	27.6%–30.7%
Risk-Free Interest Rate	2.5%– 4.5%
Weighted-Average Expected Life	7.2 years

As of March 31, Year 5, the total remaining unrecognized compensation cost related to non-vested stock options amounted to $397.5 million which will be amortized over the weighted-average remaining requisite service period of 2 years.

b. Refer to Part a. Lilly's statement of cash flows includes a cash inflow in the section on cash flows from financing activities of $12.5 million for Year 5 and $46.5 million for Year 4. The amounts are labeled "Issuance of common stock under stock plans." Who provided these cash inflows to Lilly? In general terms, how are the amounts determined?

c. Lilly states in the note: "Stock options are granted to employees at exercise prices equal to the fair market value of our stock at the dates of grant." Discuss why Lilly structured the stock option grants this way.

d. The note reports $397.5 million of remaining unrecognized compensation cost related to nonvested stock options. What portion of this amount will be reported as compensation expense in the second quarter ending June 30, Year 5? Does this amount represent total stock-based compensation expense for the quarter?

e. Prior to *Statement No. 123 (Revised 2004),* firms were required to report pro forma earnings per share, taking into consideration stock-based compensation. As discussed in the chapter, *Statement No. 123 (Revised 2004)* requires stock-based compensation to be reported in the income statement, and thus included in the calculations of reported earnings per share. In addition to properly following GAAP (that is, *Statement No. 123 Revised 2004*), many firms present non-GAAP earnings numbers before deducting the effects of stock compensation as a supplemental disclosure in their annual reports (which is comparable to the old reported earnings number before 123R). Why do companies do this? Which earnings number is more meaningful, net income or this non-GAAP measure?

6.23 STOCK-BASED COMPENSATION–VESTING AND VALUATION MODELS. Exhibits 6.16 and 6.17 provide footnote excerpts to the financial reports of The Coca-Cola Company and Eli Lilly and Company that discuss the stock option grants given to the employees of the two firms. Each firm uses options extensively to reward employees for their performance.

Required

Review Exhibits 6.16 and 6.17 and answer the following questions.

a. Explain the concept of vesting. Discuss why firms typically include a vesting feature in the stock-based compensation plans that they offer to their employees.

b. What are the vesting characteristics of the two plans discussed in the exhibits? What effect do they have on stock-based compensation expense using the fair value method as required by *Statement No. 123 (Revised 2004)?*

c. For each firm, (1) what is the life of the options granted, (2) how does option life relate to the vesting period, and (3) why might the weighted-average *expected* life of the options be less than the full life of the options?

d. The Coca-Cola Company uses the Black-Scholes valuation model for estimating the fair value of the stock options, whereas Eli Lilly and Company utilizes a lattice-based option valuation model. Both valuation techniques are permitted by GAAP. Perform an Internet search to determine which valuation model is more commonly used by the largest publicly held firms. Speculate on why this is the case.

6.24 INTERPRETING STOCK OPTION DISCLOSURES. Exhibit 6.18 summarizes the information disclosed by General Electric Company (GE) regarding its stock option plans for Year 2 to Year 4. Assume an income tax rate of 35 percent.

EXHIBIT 6.18

General Electric Company
Stock Option Disclosures
(Problem 6.24)

	Year 4	Year 3	Year 2
Number of Options Granted[a]	27.141	8.261	46.928
Average Option Price per Share	\$32.26	\$31.19	\$27.37
Average Market Price per Share at Time of Grant	\$32.26	\$31.19	\$27.37
Fair Value of Option Granted per Share	\$ 8.33	\$ 9.44	\$ 7.73
Vesting Period of Options Granted, years	1–5	1–5	1–5
Option Valuation Assumptions:			
Discount Rate	4.0%	3.5%	3.5%
Volatility	27.7%	34.7%	33.7%
Dividend Yield	2.5%	2.5%	2.7%
Expected Option Life, years	6.0	6.0	6.0
Number of Options Exercised[a]	43.110	43.829	29.146
Average Option Exercise Price	\$10.54	\$ 9.45	\$ 9.45
Average Market Price at Time of Exercise	\$32.68	\$27.59	\$31.86

[a]Amounts in millions.

Required

a. The average option price per share and market price per share at time of grant is equal in each year (\$27.37 for Year 2, \$31.19 for Year 3, and \$32.26 for Year 4). Speculate on why GE structured the stock option grants this way in each year.

b. What are the likely reasons that the fair value of options granted per share increased from Year 2 to Year 3?

c. Compute the amount that GE received from the exercise of stock options each year versus the amount it would have received if it had issued the same number of shares on the market.

d. Refer to your answer to Part c. Discuss why GE is willing to sell shares of its stock to employees at a price (average option exercise price) much lower than the firm could obtain for shares sold on the market (average market price at time of exercise).

e. Refer again to your answer to Part c. Compute the effect of stock-based compensation on net income for each year, assuming that stock option compensation expense equaled the difference between the market price and the exercise price of options exercised.

f. Discuss the strengths and weaknesses of each of the following approaches to recognizing the cost of stock options: (1) no expense as long as the option price equals the market price on the date stock options are granted, (2) expense in the year of the grant equal to value of options granted, and (3) expense in the year of exercise equal to the benefit realized by employees from purchasing shares for less than market value.

INTEGRATIVE CASE 6.1

STARBUCKS

A common practice of fast-food and retail coffee shop chains such as Starbucks is to lease some or all of their retail space. Starbucks' Form 10-K filing states that the firm "leases retail store, roasting and distribution facilities and office space under operating leases."

Note 12 to Starbuck's Consolidated Financial Statements for the fiscal year ending September 28, 2008, provides the following future operating lease commitments of Starbucks as of the end of the fiscal year (amounts in millions).

Fiscal Year Ending in:	
2009	$ 741.0
2010	706.6
2011	660.7
2012	604.6
2013	546.4
Thereafter	1,838.8
Total Lease Payments	$5,098.1

Required

a. Compute the present value of operating lease obligations using a 6 percent discount rate for Starbucks at September 28, 2008. Assume that all cash flows occur at the end of each year. Also assume that the minimum lease payments after 2013 occur evenly over a four-year period.

b. Refer to Exhibit 1.26 (Chapter 1), which reports the fiscal 2008 comparative balance sheet for Starbucks. Compute each of the following ratios for Starbucks as of September 28, 2008, using the amounts as originally reported in its balance sheets for the year.

(1) Liabilities to Assets Ratio = Total Liabilities/Total Assets

(2) Long-Term Debt to Long-Term Capital Ratio = Long-Term Debt/(Long-Term Debt + Shareholders' Equity)

c. Repeat Part b but assume that Starbucks capitalizes operating leases and reports them as part of long-term debt.

d. Comment on the results from Parts b and c. To what extent does the capitalization of operating lease obligations affect your assessment of Starbucks' risk?

e. Refer to Exhibit 1.27 (Chapter 1), which reports the comparative income statement for Starbucks for Year 4. Note that the firm reports an expense labeled "Cost of Sales including Occupancy Costs." Speculate why Starbucks reports cost of sales and occupancy (operating lease payments) costs as a combined amount on the income statement.

Note: See Integrative Case 2.1 (Chapter 2), which addresses Starbucks' accounting for income taxes.

CASE 6.2

ORACLE CORPORATION: SHARE-BASED COMPENSATION EFFECTS/STATEMENT OF SHAREHOLDERS' EQUITY

A sales-based ranking of software companies provided by Yahoo! Finance on November 5, 2008, places Oracle Corporation third behind sales leaders Microsoft Corporation and IBM Software. Typical of high-tech companies in the software industry, Oracle Corporation uses share-based compensation plans extensively to motivate its employees. In Note 11 of its May 31, 2008 annual report, Oracle states that it settles employee stock options exercises primarily with newly issued common shares.

As indicated by the selected data from Oracle's May 31, 2008 Consolidated Balance Sheet in Exhibit 6.19, Oracle finances operations using substantially more common shareholder's equity than it does long-term debt. However, Oracle's long-term debt to shareholders' equity ratio of 44.5 percent is substantially larger than major U.S. competitor Microsoft Corporation and major foreign competitor SAP AG, both of which report almost no long-term financial debt. Exhibit 6.20 presents the most current year of the multiyear Consolidated Statement of Shareholders' Equity for Oracle. Exhibit 6.21 (see page 512) presents portions of financial statement notes 10 and 11 from Oracle's May 31, 2008 annual report.

Required

a. Compute Oracle's long-term debt to shareholders' equity ratio for May 31, 2008 and 2007. Identify the increases in shareholders' equity in 2008 from share-based compensation plans. Calculate the long-term debt to shareholders' equity ratio that would have occurred had Oracle not implemented the stock repurchase plan. Comment on the potential effect on future ROE of Oracle's financing strategy.

b. Retained earnings increases because of net income and decreases because of dividends declared. Why, then, did Oracle decrease retained earnings when it repurchased common stock?

EXHIBIT 6.19

Oracle Corporation May 31, 2008 Consolidated Balance Sheet
(in millions of dollars)

	May 31,	
	2008	2007
Non-current notes payable and other non-current borrowings	$10,235	$ 6,235
Stockholders' equity		
Common stock, $0.01 par value and additional paid-in capital—authorized: 11,000 shares; outstanding: 5,150 shares and 5,107 shares as of May 31, 2008 and 2007	$12,446	$10,293
Retained earnings	9,961	6,223
Accumulated other comprehensive income	618	403
Total stockholders' equity	$23,025	$16,919

EXHIBIT 6.20

Oracle Corporation Consolidated Statements of Stockholders' Equity at May 31, 2008 (in millions of dollars)

	Comprehensive Income	Common Stock and Additional Paid-in Capital: Number of Shares	Common Stock and Additional Paid-in Capital: Amount	Retained Earnings	Accumulated Other Comprehensive Income	Total
Balances as of May 31, 2007		5,107	$10,293	$6,223	$403	$16,919
Common stock issued under stock award plans		137	1,229			1,229
Common stock issued under stock purchase plans		3	59			59
Assumption of stock award in conjunction with acquisitions			240			240
Stock-based compensation			367			367
Repurchase of common stock		(97)	(214)	(1,786)		(2,000)
Tax benefits from stock plans			472			472
Adjustment to retained earnings upon adoption of FIN 48				3		3
Net unrealized loss on defined benefit plan assets, net of tax	$ (9)				(9)	(9)
Foreign currency translation	300				300	300
Net unrealized losses on derivative financial instruments, net of tax	(77)				(77)	(77)
Net unrealized gain on marketable securities, net of tax	1				1	1
Net income	5,521			5,521		5,521
Comprehensive income	$5,736					
Balances as of May 31, 2008		5,150	$12,446	$9,961	$618	$23,025

c. Of the first five changes listed in the shareholders' equity section, one of them, the common stock repurchase, clearly represents a cash outflow. Identify the cash flow effects of the other four items. Where will each cash flow effect be reported in the statement of cash flows?

d. Oracle engages in many transactions with non-owners (that is, customers, suppliers, and the government) that increase net assets. For example, Oracle's foreign subsidiaries perform services on credit with unrelated third-party customers. The

EXHIBIT 6.21

10. STOCKHOLDERS' EQUITY (partial)

Stock Repurchases

Our Board of Directors has approved a program for Oracle to repurchase shares of our common stock to reduce the dilutive effect of our stock option and stock purchase plans. In April 2007, our Board of Directors expanded our repurchase program by $4.0 billion and as of May 31, 2008, $2.2 billion was available for share repurchases pursuant to our stock repurchase program. We repurchased 97.3 million shares for $2.0 billion (including 1.1 million shares for $24 million that were repurchased but not settled), 233.5 million shares for $4.0 billion and 146.9 million shares for $2.1 billion in fiscal 2008, 2007 and 2006, respectively.

Our stock repurchase authorization does not have an expiration date and the pace of our repurchase activity will depend on factors such as our working capital needs, our cash requirements for acquisitions, our debt repayment obligations (as described above), our stock price, and economic and market conditions. Our stock repurchases may be affected from time to time through open market purchases or pursuant to a Rule 10b5-1 plan. Our stock repurchase program may be accelerated, suspended, delayed or discontinued at any time.

11. EMPLOYEE BENEFIT PLANS (partial)

Stock-based Compensation Plans

Stock Option Plans

. . . In connection with certain of our acquisitions, including PeopleSoft, BEA, Siebel and Hyperion, we assumed all of the outstanding stock options and other stock awards of each acquiree's respective stock plans. These stock options and other stock awards generally retain all of the rights, terms and conditions of the respective plans under which they were originally granted. As of May 31, 2008, options to purchase 77 million shares of common stock and 1 million shares of restricted stock were outstanding under these plans.

Tax Benefits from Option Exercises

We settle employee stock option exercises primarily with newly issued common shares and may, on occasion, settle employee stock option exercises with our treasury shares. Total cash received as a result of option exercises was approximately $1.2 billion, $873 million and $573 million for fiscal 2008, 2007 and 2006, respectively. The aggregate intrinsic value of options exercised was $2.0 billion, $986 million and $594 million for fiscal 2008, 2007 and 2006, respectively. In connection with these exercises, the tax benefits realized by us were $588 million, $338 million and $169 million for fiscal 2008, 2007 and 2006, respectively. The adoption of Statement 123(R) required us to change our cash flow classification of certain tax benefits received from stock option exercises beginning in fiscal 2007. Of the total tax benefits received, we classified excess tax benefits from stock-based compensation of $454 million and $259 million as cash flows from financing activities rather than cash flows from operating activities for fiscal 2008 and 2007, respectively.

Employee Stock Purchase Plan

We have an Employee Stock Purchase Plan (Purchase Plan). Starting with the April 1, 2005 semi-annual option period, we amended the Purchase Plan such that employees can purchase shares of common stock at a price per share that is 95% of the fair value of Oracle stock as of the end of the semi-annual option period. As of May 31, 2008, 81 million shares were reserved for future issuances under the Purchase Plan. During fiscal 2008, 2007 and 2006, we issued 3 million, 3 million and 6 million shares, respectively, under the Purchase Plan.

accounts receivable generated by the transactions are denominated in a foreign currency and thus are reported on the foreign subsidiaries balance sheet in that foreign currency. The consolidation process causes the subsidiary's accounts receivable to be added to the parent company's (Oracle's) accounts receivable and reported on Oracle's Consolidated Balance Sheet. Assuming that the foreign currency strengthens relative to the U.S. dollar, how does Oracle's Consolidated Statement of Shareholders' Equity capture the increases in accounts receivable described in this example transaction?

e. Using the foreign currency translation gain of $300 million as a context, present an argument for including the gain on Oracle's income statement and an argument for excluding the gain as Oracle does under GAAP.

f. Under Oracle's Employee Stock Purchase Plan, employees can purchase common shares at 95 percent of their fair values. Will Oracle report a loss on this transaction? Why or why not?

CASE 6.3

LONG-TERM SOLVENCY RISK: SOUTHWEST AND LUFTHANSA AIRLINES

The first decade of the 21st century witnessed a flurry of losses, bankruptcies, acquisitions, and strategic partnerships in the airline industry. The heavily levered firms in the industry are particularly susceptible to increases in fuel prices, economic changes that affect travel, and safety concerns. These conditions require the analyst to have a strong understanding of the long-term solvency risk of firms in the airline industry.

Two of the larger liabilities of airlines relate to promises to provide free flights to customers (frequent-flyer programs) and promises to make cash payments under flight equipment and ground facilities agreements. The former liability is captured in the total liabilities to assets ratio. The latter promise is captured in the total liabilities to assets ratio and in the long-term debt to shareholders' equity ratio, but only if the promises are treated as long-term debt.

Exhibits 6.22–6.27 (see pages 514–521) present the income statements, balance sheets, and other key information for U.S. airline Southwest, which prepares financial statements under U.S. GAAP, and German airline Lufthansa, which prepares financial statements under IFRS.

Required

a. Using the information in the exhibits, provide a comprehensive and detailed comparison of the long-term solvency risk of Southwest to Lufthansa as of December 31, 2008, and as of December 31, 2007. (Ignore tax effects. Deferred taxes are covered in Chapter 8 on operating activities.)

(1) Consider the following ratios in your analysis:
Liabilities to assets ratio = Total Liabilities/Total Assets
Long-term debt to shareholders' equity ratio = Long-Term Debt/Total Shareholders' Equity
Operating cash flow to average total liabilities ratio = Operating Cash Flow/Average Total Liabilities
Interest coverage ratio (cash basis) = (Operating Cash Flow + Interest Paid + Taxes Paid)/Interest Paid

(2) Compute the ratios using financial information (a) as reported and (b) after capitalization of operating leases. (Hint: Adjusting operating cash flow for assumed lease capitalization requires the removal of rent paid from operating cash flows

EXHIBIT 6.22

SOUTHWEST AIRLINES CO.
CONSOLIDATED BALANCE SHEET

	December 31	
	2008	**2007**
	(In millions, except share data)	
ASSETS		
Current assets:		
Cash and cash equivalents	**$ 1,368**	$ 2,213
Short-term investments	**435**	566
Accounts and other receivables	**209**	279
Inventories of parts and supplies, at cost	**203**	259
Fuel derivative contracts	**—**	1,069
Deferred income taxes	**365**	—
Prepaid expenses and other current assets	**313**	57
Total current assets	**2,893**	4,443
Property and equipment, at cost:		
Flight equipment	**13,722**	13,019
Ground property and equipment	**1,769**	1,515
Deposits on flight equipment purchase contracts	**380**	626
	15,871	15,160
Less allowance for depreciation and amortization	**4,831**	4,286
	11,040	10,874
Other assets	**375**	1,455
	$14,308	$16,772
LIABILITIES AND STOCKHOLDERS' EQUITY		
Current liabilities:		
Accounts payable	**$ 668**	$ 759
Accrued liabilities	**1,012**	3,107
Air traffic liability	**963**	931
Current maturities of long-term debt	**163**	41
Total current liabilities	**2,806**	4,838
Long-term debt less current maturities	**3,498**	2,050
Deferred income taxes	**1,904**	2,535
Deferred gains from sale and leaseback of aircraft	**105**	106
Other deferred liabilities	**1,042**	302
Commitments and contingencies		
Stockholders' equity:		
Common stock, $1.00 par value: 2,000,000,000 shares authorized; 807,611,634 shares issued in 2008 and 2007	**808**	808
Capital in excess of par value	**1,215**	1,207
Retained earnings	**4,919**	4,788
Accumulated other comprehensive income (loss)	**(984)**	1,241

EXHIBIT 6.22 (Continued)

	December 31	
	2008	2007
	(In millions, except share data)	
Treasury stock, at cost: 67,619,062 and 72,814,104 shares in 2008 and 2007, respectively	(1,005)	(1,103)
Total stockholders' equity	4,953	6,941
	$14,308	$16,772

See accompanying notes.

EXHIBIT 6.23

SOUTHWEST AIRLINES CO.
CONSOLIDATED STATEMENT OF INCOME

	Years Ended December 31,		
	2008	2007	2006
	(In millions, except per share amounts)		
OPERATING REVENUES:			
Passenger	**$10,549**	$9,457	$8,750
Freight	**145**	130	134
Other	**329**	274	202
Total operating revenues	**11,023**	9,861	9,086
OPERATING EXPENSES:			
Salaries, wages, and benefits	**3,340**	3,213	3,052
Fuel and oil	**3,713**	2,690	2,284
Maintenance materials and repairs	**721**	616	468
Aircraft rentals	**154**	156	158
Landing fees and other rentals	**662**	560	495
Depreciation and amortization	**599**	555	515
Other operating expenses	**1,385**	1,280	1,180
Total operating expenses	**10,574**	9,070	8,152
OPERATING INCOME	**449**	791	934
OTHER EXPENSES (INCOME):			
Interest expense	**10**	119	128
Capitalized interest	**(25)**	(50)	(51)
Interest income	**(26)**	(44)	(84)
Other (gains) losses, net	**92**	(292)	151
Total other expenses (income)	**171**	(267)	144
INCOME BEFORE INCOME TAXES	**278**	1,058	790
PROVISION FOR INCOME TAXES	**100**	413	291
NET INCOME	**$ 178**	$ 645	$ 499
NET INCOME PER SHARE, BASIC	**$ .24**	$ .85	$ .63
NET INCOME PER SHARE, DILUTED	**$ .24**	$ .84	$ .61

EXHIBIT 6.24

Additional Data from Southwest Airlines Co. December 31, 2008 10K Filing

From Consolidated Statement of Cash Flows (in millions):	2008	2007
Net cash provided by (used in) operating activities	$(1,521)	$2,845
Interest paid	$ 100	$ 63
Income taxes	$ 71	$ 94

From 2008 Note 8 (Leases)

. . . Total rental expense for operating leases, both aircraft and other, charged to operations in 2008, 2007, and 2006 was $527 million, $469 million, and $433 million, respectively. The majority of the Company's terminal operations space as well as 82 aircraft were under operating leases at December 31, 2008. Future minimum lease payments under capital leases and noncancelable operating leases with initial or remaining terms in excess of one year at December 31, 2008, are provided in the following table.

In millions	Capital Leases	Operating Leases
2009	$16	$ 376
2010	15	324
2011	12	249
2012	—	203
2013	—	152
After 2013	—	728
Total minimum lease payments	43	$2,032
Less amount representing interest	4	
Present value of minimum lease payments	39	
Less current portion	14	
Long-term portion	$25	

From 2007 Note 8 (Leases)

. . . Total rental expense for operating leases, both aircraft and other, charged to operations in 2007, 2006, and 2005 was $469 million, $433 million, and $409 million, respectively. The majority of the Company's terminal operations space as well as 86 aircraft were under operating leases at December 31, 2007. Future minimum lease payments under capital leases and noncancelable operating leases with initial or remaining terms in excess of one year at December 31, 2007, are provided in the following table.

In millions	Capital Leases	Operating Leases
2008	$16	$ 400
2009	17	335
2010	15	298
2011	12	235
2012	—	195
After 2012	—	876
Total minimum lease payments	60	$2,339
Less amount representing interest	8	
Present value of minimum lease payments	52	
Less current portion	13	
Long-term portion	$39	

and the inclusion of interest paid in operating cash flows. Use rent expense and interest expense to approximate rent paid and interest paid, respectively.

b. An analyst who compares the debt ratios of firms under U.S. GAAP and IFRS must consider key differences in the two sets of standards related to convertible debt and troubled debt restructurings. In general, which system would most likely yield lower debt and higher equity? Explain.

EXHIBIT 6.25

Lufthansa
Consolidated Balance Sheet as of 31 December 2008

Assets

in €m	**Notes**	**31.12.2008**	**31.12.2007**
Intangible assets with indefinite useful life*	17)	821	797
Other intangible assets	18)	261	252
Aircraft and reserve engines	19) 22)	8,764	8,380
Repairable spare parts for aircraft		669	586
Property, plant and other equipment	20) 22)	1,931	1,773
Investment property	21)	3	3
Investments accounted for using the equity method	23)	298	323
Other equity investments	24) 25)	790	777
Non-current securities	24) 25)	509	298
Loans and receivables	24) 26)	475	399
Derivative financial instruments	24) 27)	339	368
Accrued income and advance payments	30)	15	22
Effective income tax receivables	14)	72	79
Deferred claims for income tax rebates	14)	28	19
Non-current assets		**14,975**	**14,076**
Inventories	28)	581	511
Trade receivables and other receivables	24) 29)	3,015	3,448
Derivative financial instruments	24) 27)	213	481
Accrued income and advance payments	30)	119	110
Effective income tax receivables		130	62
Securities	24) 31)	1,834	1,528
Cash and cash equivalents	24) 32)	1,444	2,079
Assets held for sale	33)	97	25
Current assets		**7,433**	**8,244**
Total assets		**22,408**	**22,320**

*Incl. goodwill.

(Continued)

EXHIBIT 6.25 (Continued)

Shareholders' equity and liabilities

in €m	**Notes**	**31.12.2008**	**31.12.2007**
Issued capital	34) 35)	1,172	1,172
Capital reserve	36)	1,366	1,366
Retained earnings	36)	3,140	2,063
Other neutral reserves	36)	579	589
Net profit for the period		599	1,655
Equity attributable to shareholders of Deutsche Lufthansa AG		6,856	6,845
Minority interests		63	55
Shareholders' equity		**6,919**	**6,900**
Pension provisions	37)	2,400	2,461
Other provisions	38)	291	349
Borrowings	39) 40)	3,161	3,098
Other financial liabilities	41)	51	55
Advance payments received, accruals and deferrals and other non-financial liabilities	42)	64	66
Derivative financial instruments	27) 39)	118	371
Deferred income tax liabilities	14)	813	749
Non-current provisions and liabilities		**6,898**	**7,149**
Other provisions	38)	1,873	1,686
Borrowings	39) 40)	420	247
Trade payables and other financial liabilities	39) 43)	3,626	3,959
Liabilities from unused flight documents		1,693	1,546
Advance payments received, accruals and deferrals and other non-financial liabilities	44)	388	289
Derivative financial instruments	27) 39)	492	481
Actual income tax liabilities		99	51
Provisions and liabilities included in disposal groups	45)	—	12
Current provisions and liabilities		**8,591**	**8,271**
Total shareholders' equity and liabilities		**22,408**	**22,320**

EXHIBIT 6.26

Lufthansa
Consolidated Income Statement for the 2008 Financial Year

in €m	Notes	2008	2007
Traffic revenue	3)	19,998	17,568
Other revenue	4)	4,872	4,852
Total revenue		**24,870**	**22,420**
Changes in inventories and work performed by the enterprise and capitalised	5)	178	119
Other operating income	6)	1,969	1,571
Cost of materials and services	7)	−13,707	−11,553
Staff costs	8)	−5,692	−5,498
Depreciation, amortisation and impairment	9)	−1,289	−1,204
Other operating expenses	10)	−4,946	−4,269
Profit from operating activities		**+1,383**	**+1,586**
Result of equity investments accounted for using the equity method	11)	−22	+223
Result from other equity investments	11)	+42	+131
Interest income	12)	202	177
Interest expense	12)	−374	−371
Other financial items	13)	−427	−133
Financial result		**−579**	**+27**
Profit before income taxes		**+804**	**+1,613**
Income taxes	14)	−195	−356
Profit from continuing operations		**+609**	**+1,257**
Profit from the discontinued Leisure Travel segment	15)	—	**+503**
Profit after income taxes		**+609**	**+1,760**
Minority interests		−10	−105
Net profit attributable to shareholders of Lufthansa AG		**+599**	**+1,655**
Basic earnings per share in €	16)	1.31	+3.61
Diluted earnings per share in €	16)	1.30	+3.60

EXHIBIT 6.27

Additional Data from Lufthansa December 31, 2008 Annual Report

From Consolidated Statement of Cash Flows (In €m):	2008	2007
Net cash provided by (used in) operating activities	2,473	2,862
Net interest paid	172	194
Income taxes	123	274

12) Net interest

Net Interest

In €m	2008	2007
Income from other securities and financial loans	11	13
Other interest and similar income	191	164
Interest income	**202**	**177**
Interest expenses on pensions obligations	−119	−154
Interest expense on other provisions	−16	−9
Interest and other similar expenses	−239	−208
Interest expenses	**−374**	**−371**
	−172	**−194**

Operating leases

In addition to the finance leases, a large number of leases have been signed which, on the basis of their economic parameters, are qualified as operating leases, i.e. the leased asset is deemed to belong to the lessor. As well as 106 additional aircraft on operating leases, these are mainly aircraft leased as part of the Lufthansa Regional concept and leases for buildings.

The operating leases for aircraft have a term of between one and nine years. These agreements generally end automatically after the term has expired, but there is sometimes an option for extending the agreement.

The leases for buildings generaly run for up to 25 years. The fixtures at the airports in Frankfurt and Munich are leased for 30 years.

The following payments are due in the years ahead (amounts in millions; p.a. denotes per annum):

in €m	2009	2010–2013	from 2014
Aircraft	209	343	—
Various buildings	213	872	215 p.a.
Other leases	70	273	56 p.a.
	492	**1,488**	**271 p.a.**
Payments from sub-leasing	9	13	1 p.a.

EXHIBIT 6.27 (Continued)

In the previous year the following figures were given for operating leases:

in €m	2008	2009–2012	from 2013
Aircraft	196	418	—
Various buildings	236	920	227 p.a.
Other leases	80	306	65 p.a.
	512	**1,644**	**292 p.a.**
Payments from sub-leasing	14	13	2 p.a.

Chapter 7

Investing Activities

Learning Objectives

1. Describe the accounting for a firm's investments in tangible productive assets, including the initial decision to capitalize or expense and the use of choices and estimates to allocate costs through the depreciation process.
2. Describe the alternative ways that firms account for intangible assets, highlighting research and development expenditures, software development expenditures, and goodwill, including the exercise of judgment in the allocation of costs through the amortization process.
3. Review and apply the rules for testing the impairment of different categories of long-lived assets, including goodwill.
4. Describe the accounting and reporting of investments in securities, including the market value, equity, proportionate consolidation, and full consolidation methods.
5. Explain the accounting for variable-interest entities, commonly referred to as special-purpose entities, including the requirement to consolidate them with the firm identified as the primary beneficiary.
6. Prepare a set of translated financial statements using the all-current method and the monetary/nonmonetary method and describe the conditions under which each method best portrays the operating relationship between a U.S. parent firm and its foreign subsidiary.

In Chapter 6 we discussed the financial reporting for financing activities, which are the primary source of capital for investing and operating activities. In this chapter, we discuss the accounting, reporting, and analysis of investing activities. Once a firm obtains financing, it must invest the proceeds effectively to generate returns that cover the costs of the financing.

Investing activities include (1) the acquisition of long-term tangible and intangible assets in the operations of the business or financial assets for investment purposes and (2) the dispositions of those assets. The accounting for investing activities directly affects the analysis of the profitability of the firm. Investing activities significantly impact the denominator (assets) for ROA (return on assets) computations discussed in Chapters 4 and 5. Also, the profits that arise from using assets and the gains and losses that arise from holding assets create the numerator (net income before financing costs, adjusted for tax) used in the ROA computation. Finally, forecasted future financial statements depend heavily on forecasted investing activities, especially investments in operating assets such as property, plant, and equipment.

This chapter addresses accounting and reporting topics related to asset investments, which fall into two broad categories as follows:

- Investments in long-lived operating assets (which include long-lived tangible fixed assets such as land, building, and equipment; intangible assets such as patents, brand names, customer lists, and goodwill; and natural resources such as oil reserves and timberlands).
- Investments in the securities of other firms (including stock and bond investments). (Because a significant subset of stock investments are controlling investments in foreign subsidiaries, a third major section of the chapter deals with the translation of foreign subsidiary financial statements denominated in a foreign currency.)

Firms also make tactical and operating investments in net working capital. Because working capital assets (for example, accounts receivable and inventory) and working capital liabilities (for example, accounts payable and other current liabilities) are generated by and used in day-to-day normal revenue-generating activities, we consider these investments in working capital in the chapter about operating activities (Chapter 8).

For an illustration of the scope of this chapter, refer to the Assets section of PepsiCo's 2008 Consolidated Balance Sheet in Appendix A. This chapter focuses on the types of assets that PepsiCo shows as Short-term investments (in the Current Assets section) and all of the assets listed as noncurrent apart from other assets (that is, property, plant, and equipment, net; amortizable intangible assets, net; goodwill; other nonamortizable intangible assets; and investments in noncontrolled affiliates). Collectively, these assets sum to $22,743 million, or more than 63 percent of PepsiCo's $35,994 million total assets at December 27, 2008. Also, the fact the PepsiCo's statements are "consolidated" means that in all of its financial statements, PepsiCo includes the assets, liabilities, revenues, expenses, and cash flows of its subsidiaries.

Because this chapter is about a major portion of a company's assets, it is useful to revisit the definition of *assets* discussed in Chapter 1 prior to consideration of the two major classifications of assets created by investing activities. Currently, the FASB's *Statements of Accounting Concepts* (*Nos. 5* and *6*) define an asset as having four characteristics (the first three form the definition of an asset and the fourth is a key characteristic for measurement): (1) probable future benefits, (2) obtained/controlled by the entity, (3) as a result of a past transactions and events, and (4) reliably measured (essentially at acquisition cost or fair value).[1] Practical application of the definition of an *asset* is guided by management's judgment and by rule. Remember that costs not judged to be assets are expensed in the current period and thus immediately reduce net income. Consideration given to acquire financial assets with contractual and other legal rights, such as investments in bonds or common stock of another company, clearly yields assets. Also, for many acquisitions of long-lived productive assets, such as a simple acquisition of a piece of machinery by sacrifice

[1] Financial Accounting Standards Board, *Statement of Financial Accounting Concepts No. 5*, "Recognition and Measurement in Financial Statements of a Business Enterprise," (1984); Financial Accounting Standards Board, *Statement of Financial Accounting Concepts No. 6*, "Elements of Financial Statements," (1985). Currently, the IFRS definition of an asset is very similar to the U.S. GAAP definition. As of the writing of this text, the FASB and IASB are in discussions about a new definition of assets that de-emphasizes past transactions and events and expected future benefits in favor of determining whether the entity has, at present, an economic resource that (a) is separable from the entity by sale, license, or another potential type of exchange or (b) is arising from a contractual or legal right. This definition is consistent with standard-setters' beliefs that more assets and liabilities should be measured at fair value. The separability of the asset and the contractual or legal right definitions directly permit or enhance the ability to measure an asset's fair value.

of cash or creation of a liability (for example, issuance of a note payable), determining whether the item acquired is an asset and measuring its cost are not difficult. However, some transactions are not as clear-cut. For example, as you will see in the following subsections relating to long-lived operating assets, certain costs might fail the probable future benefits test, such as certain costs related to research and development, marketing and brand-building activities, and exploration for natural resources. Also, as discussed in the second major part of the chapter, the control criterion will determine which assets are reported on the books of the investor in an intercompany investment and availability of reliable fair value information will drive the measurement for many financial assets.

INVESTMENTS IN LONG-LIVED OPERATING ASSETS

Example 1

Refer to PepsiCo's Note 4, "Property, Plant and Equipment and Intangible Assets" in Appendix A in which PepsiCo provides the detail to support the following long-lived operating assets reported in its Consolidated Balance Sheet at December 27, 2008:

- $11,663 million in property, plant and equipment, net
- $732 million in amortizable intangible assets, net
- $6,252 million in nonamortizable intangible assets (including goodwill)

The individual amounts in Note 4 provide a good summary of the accounting issues of interest to a financial statement analyst, as follows:

1. PepsiCo uses the first part of the note to explain the $11,663 million reported as its *tangible asset* property, plant and equipment. PepsiCo reports $22,552 million as the cost of acquiring the property, plant, and equipment, and accumulated depreciation is $10,889 million to date. The difference, the $11,663 million *net book value of the asset*, is reported on the balance sheet. The annual depreciation expenses (that sum over time to equal accumulated depreciation) are reflected each year in PepsiCo's net income. For 2008, PepsiCo reports $1,422 million of depreciation expense.
2. In the second part of the note, PepsiCo repeats this description of acquisition cost and accumulated amortization for a second type of long-lived operating asset, *amortizable intangible assets* with definite useful lives. PepsiCo recognizes amortization expense of $64 million in 2008 net income.
3. In the last part of the note, PepsiCo reconciles from the beginning to the ending balances of the components of a third type of long-lived operating asset, its *nonamortizable intangible assets*—perpetual brands and goodwill. Because these assets have been judged to have indefinite lives, they are not amortized, but instead are assessed annually for impairment. If impaired, the carrying amounts are written down to fair value. As a result, PepsiCo recognizes no amortization expense for these assets in net income in 2008.

Each of the following sections identifies an important issue in financial statement analysis and refers back to Note 4. The section headings are in the form of analysts' questions. It is important to understand that the answers to these questions are prescribed by accounting rule, are the result of managers' choice and judgment, or are some combination of rules and judgments. The answers determine accounting quality in the long-lived asset investments area. The chapter discusses how the answers affect an analyst's ability to conduct profitability and risk analysis and to forecast future financial statements.

Are the Acquisition Costs "Assets"?

The following subsections examine the practical application of rules and judgments to determine whether the costs of acquiring property, plant, and equipment; research and development costs; software development costs; subsequent expenditures to enhance or maintain property, plant, and equipment; costs of self-construction; costs of acquiring intangible assets; and costs of acquiring natural resources can be recognized as assets or whether they should receive expense treatment. The financial statement effects of the capitalization (asset treatment) versus immediate expensing decision are shown in Exhibit 7.1.

EXHIBIT 7.1: FINANCIAL STATEMENT EFFECTS OF CAPITALIZATION VERSUS EXPENSING

Assets	=	Liabilities	+	Total Shareholders' Equity: CC	AOCI	RE
Capitalization (initial acquisition costs):						
Cash consideration:						
Long-Lived Asset (net) +xx						
Cash −xx						
Liability incurred:						
Long-Lived Asset (net) +xx		Liability +xx				
Common stock consideration:						
Long-Lived Asset (net) +xx				Common Stock +xx		
				APIC +xx		
Subsequent cost allocation to periods benefitted via depreciation, amortization, and depletion:						
Long-Lived Asset (net) −xx						Expense −xx

Capitalization (initial acquisition costs):

Cash consideration:		
Long-Lived Asset (net)	xx	
Cash		xx
Liability incurred:		
Long-Lived Asset (net)	xx	
Liability		xx
Common stock consideration:		
Long-Lived Asset (net)	xx	
Common Stock		xx
APIC		xx
Subsequent cost allocation to periods benefitted via depreciation, amortization, and depletion:		
Expense	xx	
Long-Lived Asset (net)		xx

Assets	=	Liabilities	+	CC	AOCI	RE
Expense treatment:						
Cash consideration:						
Cash −xx						Expense −xx
Liability incurred:		Liability +xx				Expense −xx
Common stock consideration:				Common Stock +xx		Expense −xx
				APIC +xx		

(Continued)

EXHIBIT 7.1 (CONTINUED)

Expense treatment:		
Cash consideration:		
Expense	xx	
Cash		xx
Liability incurred:		
Expense	xx	
Liability		xx
Common stock consideration:		
Expense	xx	
Common Stock		xx
APIC		xx

Note: We use Long-Lived Asset (net) in all entries to link to the balance sheet presentation. However, most accountants use Long-Lived Asset for all acquisition and disposal entries to account for the original acquisition cost and the contra-asset account Accumulated Depreciation as the credit in the depreciation entry.

The effects on financial statements of the capitalization of initial acquisition costs depends on the consideration given (cash paid, liability incurred, or shares of stock issued). Subsequent cost allocation decreases the long-lived asset over its useful life, and the consumption of the cost is treated as an expense. The remaining book value of the asset (its *adjusted acquisition cost*) is reported on the balance sheet. If a cost is deemed to be an expense, the amount of consideration given will be expensed immediately and no balance sheet asset will exist. Therefore, the key difference between the capitalization and expense treatment is the timing of expense recognition.

Accounting for the Acquisition of Property, Plant, and Equipment: General Rule

In many cases, it is clear that costs have been incurred to acquire a piece of property, plant, and equipment that will yield future benefits; thus, asset recognition is warranted. The general rule for recording the acquisition of an asset is that it should be recorded at the fair value of what has been sacrificed to acquire and prepare the asset for its intended use. This sacrifice includes cash paid, the fair value of debt incurred, the fair value of lease payments under capital leases (as illustrated in Chapter 6), or the fair value of stock issued to acquire the asset, in addition to costs to ship, temporarily store, insure, set up, test, and calibrate (as in the case of machinery) an asset as it is prepared for operational use.

Cash used to acquire property, plant, and equipment is reported as a cash outflow in the investing activities section of the statement of cash flows. If property, plant, and equipment are acquired using long-term debt or equity (both of which are non-cash transactions), the investing activity will be reported as a significant non-cash investing and financing activity in a separate schedule accompanying the statement of cash flows. PepsiCo reports capital spending of more than $2 billion per year over the 2006–2008 period in its Consolidated Statement of Cash Flows (Appendix A), which represents a use of more than one-third of the more than $6 billion annually of net cash provided by operating activities.

In many other cases, it is less clear whether cost incurrence yields probable future benefits. The following sections address these cases.

Accounting for Research and Development Costs

R&D (research and development) is an important activity for many firms. However, U.S. GAAP requires firms to expense immediately all R&D costs incurred *internally* because of the inherent uncertainty in determining whether R&D activities will produce sufficient future economic benefits to warrant being capitalized as an asset.[2] Externally acquired R&D from purchasing patents or licenses can be capitalized because the arm's-length transaction between two market participants provides a reliable measure of acquisition cost and is an indicator of the existence of future economic benefits. For industries with high R&D expenditures, such as the research-intensive biotechnology industry, the U.S. GAAP requirement to expense rather than capitalize is especially troublesome because a major asset never appears on the balance sheet because standard-setters question whether expected future benefits will exist or are reliably measurable.

Consider the following three examples for biotechnology firms.

Example 2

Biogen Idec (formerly Biogen) is a biotech company with leading products and capabilities in oncology and immunology. Revenues for 2008 exceed $2.8 billion. Biogen Idec principally develops drug-related products *internally* in its research laboratories and is engaged in discovering and developing drugs for human health care through genetic engineering. Its two highest revenue-producing drugs on the market as of December 31, 2008, were Avonex® to treat multiple sclerosis and Rituxan® to treat rheumatoid arthritis and non-Hodgkin's lymphoma. In describing its accounting policy on R&D costs, Biogen Idec states that "research and development expenses consist of upfront fees and milestones paid to collaborators and expenses incurred in performing research and development activities including salaries and benefits, facilities expenses, overhead expenses, clinical trial and related clinical manufacturing expenses, contract services and other outside expenses. Research and development expenses are expensed as incurred."

The firm's R&D expense averaged slightly more than 40 percent of sales during the 2006–2008 period. In accordance with U.S. GAAP, the firm showed no asset on its balance sheet related to this in-house research activity.[3]

Example 3

Genzyme Corporation is a biotechnology and health care products firm engaged in the development of medical products and services. For 2008, revenues totaled $4.6 billion, with the firm's top products including Cerezyme® (Gaucher disease), Renagel® (end-stage renal disease), and Fabrazyme® (Fabry disease). The company follows a strategy of *internal* development of technology and *acquisition of other companies* involved in biotechnology research. Genzyme *expenses* the portion of the acquisition price of companies related to *in-process* technology, but it *capitalizes and subsequently amortizes* any portion of the price related to *completed* technologies.

Several years ago Genzyme made a large acquisition and, as a result, expensed a large amount of in-process R&D related to the acquisition. The R&D expense for internal R&D costs for the year was slightly more than 20 percent of sales. However, because of the acquisition, Genzyme also expensed the portion of the purchase price related to in-process technology. As a result, the total R&D expense/sales percentage for the year was almost 50 percent. A year later the total R&D expense/sales percentage was less than 25 percent because only a small portion of in-process technology was purchased and expensed.

[2] Financial Accounting Standards Board, *Statement of Financial Accounting Standards No. 2*, "Accounting for Research and Development Costs" (1974); *FASB Codification Topic 730*. Long-lived assets used in multiple R&D projects are initially capitalized; then the depreciation of the assets is assigned to R&D expense.

[3] Biogen Idec does report an intangible asset on its balance sheet for established core technologies and patent rights acquired in acquisitions.

Example 4

Amgen Inc. is a leading human therapeutics company in the biotechnology industry, generating over $15 billion in revenues in 2008 from a number of top-selling products, including Epogen® (Epoetin alfa), a recombinant version of a human protein that stimulates the production of red blood cells, and Aranesp®, which also stimulates red blood cell production and is used to treat anemia associated with chronic renal failure. The firm follows a strategy of *internal* development of biotechnology and *external* development through a series of joint ventures and partnerships. Amgen contributes preliminary research findings to obtain its interest in these joint ventures and partnerships. The other participants provide funding to continue development of this preliminary research.

In some cases, Amgen contracts with the joint venture or partnership to perform the continued development in its own laboratories. In this case, Amgen receives a fee each period in an amount approximately equal to the R&D costs incurred in conducting the research (resulting in no net R&D cost). In other cases, the joint venture or partnership entity conducts the research, in which case Amgen may show no R&D expense on its books. Amgen generally maintains a right of first refusal for any products developed, in which case it must pay the owners of the joint venture a periodic royalty.

Amgen's R&D expense for 2008 was 20.2 percent of sales, the lowest of the three firms for the most recent year. The company shows only minor amounts on its balance sheet for investments in joint ventures and partnerships, relating to cash advances. Because Amgen must expense initial development costs when incurred, its contribution of preliminary research findings for an interest in these joint ventures and partnerships does not increase an asset.

Summary of Examples 2–4

Examples 2–4 illustrate three different strategies that firms pursue in developing biotechnologies and highlight the problem with current R&D reporting rules. The different strategies that firms follow, especially when combined with the required accounting for R&D costs, complicate any cross-sectional analysis of firms' financial data. To the extent that the economic substance of these arrangements differ, different accounting treatments may be appropriate.

The economic characteristics of R&D arrangements suggest the following twofold approach that an analyst might use:

1. Modify as-reported financial statements by capitalizing and subsequently amortizing all expenditures on R&D that have future service potential, whether a firm incurs the R&D cost internally or purchases in-process or completed technology externally. Immediately expense all R&D costs that have no future service potential.
2. Consolidate the firm's share of the assets, liabilities, revenues, and expenses of R&D joint ventures or partnerships.

Unfortunately, the inherent uncertainty about future benefits that led accounting standard setters to require all R&D expenditures to be expensed creates difficulties for an analyst to judge future service potential from financial statement disclosures alone. Reliance on firm disclosures of scientific and other information outside the financial reporting model is necessary. Also, only some R&D joint venture data will be present in notes to the financial statements. Therefore, the consolidation of joint ventures also might prove to be difficult.

The analyst must be aware of the effects of the R&D expensing rule on profitability analysis. The effects on ROA are countervailing between numerator and denominator. Missing assets understate the denominator. The numerator of ROA, net income, is understated when all R&D is classified as current expense and is overstated when the amortization of an R&D asset is excluded. In the typical case of growing R&D expenditures, the numerator will be understated because current R&D expenses exceed the amortizations. A maturing firm may reach a steady state where current R&D expense equals the amortizations, which would have taken place if R&D had been capitalized. If that happens, the ROA numerator would be unaffected, but the denominator would still be understated due to the omission of the R&D asset.

In general, capitalization and amortization (relative to immediate expensing) results in a smoother income series and thus is an easier prediction of future net income. To yield improved predictions of future income and cash flows (illustrated in Chapter 10), the analyst should examine the past time series of R&D expenditures, looking for volatility and growth. Dealing with the potential effects of asset understatement and income understatement in valuation is addressed in Chapters 11–13.

IFRS rules on R&D mitigate the likely overstatement of ROA because research costs are expensed and product development costs (the costs incurred after the research yields a product or process that is technologically feasible) are capitalized.[4] Also, recent standards have changed the accounting for *in-process R&D* acquired as part of an acquisition. If the in-process R&D meets the criterion of separability discussed later in this chapter, it is capitalized at an amount equal to its fair value.[5]

Although managers and others view R&D as a necessary investing activity, statement of cash flow reporting treats R&D as an operating activity because it does not result in a balance sheet asset. R&D reduces current period net income and thus reduces current period cash flows from operating activities.

Accounting for Software Development Costs

U.S. GAAP treats the cost of developing computer software somewhat differently from R&D costs. Similar to IFRS treatment, firms must expense as incurred all costs incurred internally in developing computer software until such development achieves the "technological feasibility" of a product. Thereafter, the firm must capitalize and subsequently amortize additional development costs.[6] The FASB defines technological feasibility as "completion of a detailed program design or, in its absence, completion of a working model." Clearly, determining when a software development project achieves technological feasibility requires significant judgment by managers and other personnel. Another key issue in capitalizing software development costs is the treatment of costs to improve an existing product.

Example 5

Consider the software accounting policies of IBM, Adobe Systems, and Microsoft.

IBM is a world leader in providing software and consulting services. The firm includes the following note on its accounting for software development costs in a recent Form 10-K filing:

> **Software Costs.** Costs that are related to the conceptual formulation and design of licensed programs are expensed as incurred to R&D expense. Also for licensed programs, the company capitalizes costs that are incurred to produce the finished product

---

[4] International Accounting Standards Board, *International Accounting Standard 38*, "Intangible Assets" (1998).

[5] Financial Accounting Standards Board, *Statement of Financial Accounting Standards No. 141 (revised 2007)*, "Business Combinations"; *FASB Codification Topic 805*; International Accounting Standards Board, *International Financial Reporting Standard 3*, "Business Combinations" (2007).

[6] Financial Accounting Standards Board, *Statement of Financial Accounting Standards No. 86*, "Accounting for the Costs of Computer Software to Be Sold, Leased, or Otherwise Marketed" (1985); *FASB Codification Topic 985*. This standard does not apply to software created for internal use that is capitalized and amortized, similar to the treatment of long-lived tangible assets.

> after technological feasibility has been established. Capitalized amounts are amortized using the straight-line method, which is applied over periods ranging up to three years. The company performs periodic reviews to ensure that unamortized program costs remain recoverable from future revenue. Costs to support or service licensed programs are charged to software cost as incurred.

As indicated here, IBM's R&D expense includes costs for conceptual formulation of software products as well as amortization of software costs previously capitalized for products that had reached the technological feasibility stage.

Adobe Systems also is a leading developer of graphics software. Its Acrobat® and Reader® products are well known because of their extensive use in the financial community. Adobe develops new software internally and through aggressive external acquisitions of other software companies. Adobe expenses initial software development costs incurred internally as R&D. Adobe capitalizes software development costs once the firm deems a graphics software program to have achieved technological feasibility. It also capitalizes the cost of software acquired in corporate acquisitions if the software has achieved technological feasibility. In both scenarios, however, Adobe indicates that the amount of software costs capitalized is immaterial to the financial statements. The firm states in a recent Form 10-K:

> Capitalization of software development costs begins upon the establishment of technological feasibility, which is generally the completion of a working prototype that has been certified as having no critical bugs and is a release candidate or when alternative future use exists. To date, software development costs incurred between completion of a working prototype and general availability of the related product have not been material and have not been capitalized.

Microsoft appears to capitalize a very small portion of the development costs of subsequent generations of Windows® or Office because of the lateness of the point at which it believes that technological feasibility has been reached. The following policy is taken from the notes to Microsoft's 2008 annual report:

> Research and development expenses include payroll, employee benefits, stock-based compensation, and other headcount-related expenses associated with product development. Research and development expenses also include third-party development and programming costs, localization costs incurred to translate software for international markets, the amortization of purchased software code and services content, and in-process research and development. We have determined that technological feasibility for our software products is reached shortly before the products are released to manufacturing. The amortization of these costs is included in cost of revenue over the estimated lives of the products.

Interpretation of the meaning of *technological feasibility* has created diversity in practice. The Software Publishers Association, a trade association for firms in the software development industry, has advocated expensing all software development costs when incurred, suggesting that expensing these costs eliminates the concerns of extremely shortened software product lives and uncertainty over realization of software assets. On the other hand, a study addressing this intriguing position of the association shows that in recent years, enhancing reported earnings through software capitalization schemes has diminished.[7] The researchers conclude that because software capitalization no longer provides an opportunity

[7] David Aboody and Baruch Lev, "The Value-Relevance of Intangibles: The Case of Software Capitalization," *Journal of Accounting Research* supplement (1998), pp. 161–191.

for earnings management, nothing is lost by restricting software producers to only one allowable reporting technique. In addition, the study addresses the more substantive issue of whether software capitalization is value-relevant to investors. For firms that capitalize software development costs (that is, report a cumulative software intangible asset on the balance sheet), the researchers find a significant association between these costs and future earnings, concluding that this finding supports capitalizing and amortizing product development costs, as permitted by U.S. GAAP and IFRS.

The flexibility available to firms applying software accounting standards should cause the analyst to proceed cautiously when analyzing computer software development companies. An added concern in this regard is the small size of many such companies and the rapid pace of technological change in this industry. The information technology industry, and particularly the software segment of the industry, has experienced an even greater rate of change over the past decade due to the surge of interest in the Internet and related services. The crash that many information technology industry stocks experienced several years ago is further reason to practice a healthy level of skepticism when analyzing firms in the industry.

Subsequent Expenditures for Enhancement or Improvements

Subsequent to acquiring long-lived operating assets, firms make additional expenditures to add to or improve them. Proper accounting is to capitalize (that is, add to the asset's book value) expenditures that increase the service life or potential (in either quantity or quality) of an asset beyond that originally anticipated. Firms should expense immediately expenditures for repairs and maintenance that merely maintain the originally expected service potential. For example, replacing tires on a delivery truck does not qualify as a capital expenditure because the original useful life was determined with the assumption that tires would be replaced regularly. However, if a refrigeration unit was added to the cargo area of the truck to add the capability to transport perishable cargo, the expenditure would be capitalized because the quality of service was improved beyond original estimates.

Example 6

American Airlines, one of the largest airlines in the world, follows a rigorous maintenance program for all of its aircraft. In a recent annual report, the firm provides the following information about its maintenance and repair costs:

> **Maintenance and Repair Costs.** Maintenance and repair costs for owned and leased flight equipment are charged to operating expense as incurred, except costs incurred for maintenance and repair under flight hour maintenance contract agreements, which are accrued based on contractual terms when an obligation exists.

Management judgment in the subsequent expenditures area creates ample opportunity for earnings management. Remember that the capitalization versus expensing choice has immediate effects on the income statement. One way to increase earnings is to (incorrectly) classify routine maintenance and repair costs as capital expenditures. Thus, investors must rely on management integrity and auditor monitoring as protection against self-interested managers manipulating earnings through biased application of the judgment necessary in many settings. Strong corporate governance and auditor reporting of internal control weaknesses assist the assessment of accounting quality.

Costs of Self-Construction

A company might choose to self-construct plant and equipment because it wants to save costs or because no external supplier is available. Wal-Mart Stores, Inc., for example, might construct its own stores. The cost of a self-constructed asset equals the fair value of all necessary costs incurred to produce it, including materials, labor, and overhead, both variable (that is, varies directly with production activity) and fixed. For example, self-construction projects frequently use existing equipment and do not create the need for additional expenditures on equipment, plant management supervision, and property taxes. But these fixed costs are necessary for the construction to occur, and both U.S. GAAP and IFRS require an allocation of part of the fixed overhead cost to self-construction costs. If internal expenditures exceed the cost of acquiring the asset externally, the amount recorded in the self-constructed asset's account will be limited to the cost of external purchase and the excess of costs incurred over the external fair value is recorded as a loss of the period under the conservatism principle. This process ensures that an asset is not recorded initially at an amount greater than its fair value.

Interest Incurred to Self-Construct Assets

As a general rule, interest costs on debt are treated as an expense of the period, as illustrated in Chapter 6. However, both U.S. GAAP and IFRS have an exception to this rule for interest cost incurred during the self-construction of a long-lived productive asset intended for the company's own use.[8] Interest on debt used to finance asset construction is a valid and often necessary cost of constructing an asset. By capitalizing interest on self-constructed assets, the firm better captures the fair value sacrificed to acquire the asset. The capitalized interest cost becomes part of the asset's historical cost (depreciation basis) and, hence, annual depreciation expense.

Avoidable interest is the term used to describe the amount of a company's annual interest cost that should be capitalized. To compute avoidable interest, expenditures linked to the self-construction project are weighted by the amount of time the expenditures were outstanding during the year. The weighted expenditures, called *average accumulated expenditures,* are multiplied by the interest rate on specific borrowings to fund the construction. If accumulated expenditures exceed specific construction borrowings, the excess average accumulated expenditures are multiplied by the weighted average interest cost of the company's other interest-bearing debt.[9] If the company has no debt, it has no avoidable interest.[10]

Example 7

Assume that Target Corporation obtained a $10,000,000 construction loan bearing a 5 percent interest rate and began construction of several warehousing facilities for a regional distribution center on January 1, 2010 (interest paid at the end of each year). Materials, labor, and overhead expenditures on the project are as follows:

January 1, 2010	$ 6,000,000
July 1, 2010	6,000,000
October 1, 2010	10,000,000
Total through December 31, 2010	$22,000,000

[8] Interest costs also may be capitalized on construction of certain types of inventory (discussed in Chapter 8). Financial Accounting Standards Board, *Statement of Financial Accounting Concepts No. 34*, "Capitalization of Interest Cost," (1979); *FASB Codification Topic 835*; International Accounting Standards Board, *International Accounting Standard 23 (revised 2007)*, "Borrowing Costs."

[9] Alternatives exist in the application of SFAS No. 34 with respect to the assignment of interest rates to average accumulated expenditures other than the method provided in this text. For an analysis of these alternatives, see Kathryn Means and Paul Kazenski, "SFAS 34: Recipe for Diversity," *Accounting Horizons* (September 1998).

[10] Public utilities are an exception, however, because they are permitted by public utility commissions and specific industry accounting rules to impute interest on *equity* when capitalizing interest costs.

On December 31, 2010, the project was completed. In addition to the construction note, two other interest-bearing debts were outstanding during the construction period:

Bond payable (4%)	$20,000,000
Note payable (8%)	$40,000,000

The amount of avoidable interest to be capitalized in 2010 is computed as follows:

Average accumulated expenditures:

$ 6,000,000 × 12 months/12 months =	$ 6,000,000
6,000,000 × 6 months/12 months =	3,000,000
10,000,000 × 3 months/12 months =	2,500,000
$22,000,000	$11,500,000

Avoidable interest:

The average accumulated expenditures of $11,500,000 are greater than the $10,000,000 specific construction borrowing. Therefore, to compute avoidable interest, the specific borrowing's 5 percent interest rate is used for the first $10,000,000 of average accumulated expenditures and a weighted average interest rate on other borrowings is used for the excess accumulated expenditures:

$10,000,000 × 5.0% =	$500,000
1,500,000 × 6.7%* =	100,500
$11,500,000	$600,500

* The weighted interest rate on other interest bearing borrowings is as follows:
[$20 million/($20 million + $40 million) × 4%] + [$40 million/($20 million + $40 million) × 8%] = 6.7%

Avoidable interest cannot exceed actual interest:

Construction note	$10,000,000 × 5% =	$ 500,000
Bond payable	$20,000,000 × 4% =	800,000
Note payable	$40,000,000 × 8% =	3,200,000
Total actual interest		$4,500,000

The total recorded amount for the regional distribution center is obtained by adding the $22,000,000 expenditures to the $600,500 capitalized interest, yielding a depreciable fixed asset acquisition cost of $22,600,500.[11] The remainder of the $4,500,000 interest ($4,500,000 − 600,500 capitalized = $3,899,500) is charged to interest expense of the current period. The capitalized interest becomes an expense through the annual depreciation process.

[11] Temporary investments of funds not used in construction generate interest revenue and are not to be treated as offsets to capitalizable interest (Financial Accounting Standards Board *Statement of Financial Accounting Standards No. 62*, "Capitalization of Interest Cost in Situations Involving Certain Tax-Exempt Borrowings and Certain Gifts and Grants—an amendment of FASB Statement No. 34"). FASB Codification Topic 835. Under IFRS, the revenue is treated as an offset to borrowing costs. International Accounting Standards Board, *International Accounting Standard 23(Revised 2007)*, "Borrowing Costs."

Costs of Acquiring Natural Resources

Oil fields, timber tracts, and mineral deposits are examples of natural resources. Three types of costs incurred in connection with natural resources are as follows:

- Acquisition costs
- Exploration costs
- Development costs[12]

Acquisition Costs. Acquisition costs include the costs of acquiring the natural resources and the costs associated with returning the resource site to an acceptable condition after the resources have been obtained. Often, the natural resource is attached to land that is salvageable at the end of production. If that is the case, the initial cost is separated into two accounts, with the portion of cost attributable to land reported separately in a "land" or "property" account. All other costs of acquisition are capitalized as part of the "natural resources" account and reported in the property, plant, and equipment section with the other productive, operational assets.

Frequently, a natural resource asset is subject to *reclamation cost* or *restoration costs* at the end of the life of a project. For example, at the end of coal strip mine's productive life, the mine operator incurs substantial costs to fill in the mine and return the land to its original contour. The need to incur costs to reclaim a natural resource is an example of an *ARO (asset retirement obligation)*. The fair value of the obligation (usually determined by discounting expected future reclamation costs) is capitalized and amortized over the life of the related natural resource asset.[13]

Exploration Costs. Exploration costs are incurred to discover the existence and exact location of the natural resource. For example, a petroleum manufacturer acquires an oil field (acquisition cost) and then drills to discover oil. The costs of engaging in drilling activity, including supplies, labor, and machinery depreciation charges, are exploration costs. The accounting for exploration costs has emerged as one of the most controversial topics in accounting history. At the center of the controversy is the determination of whether the costs of unsuccessful exploration activities are assets or expenses. The following two schools of thought on that issue have emerged:

- *Successful efforts* (exploration costs of successful wells are capitalized as assets, but unsuccessful wells are expensed)
- *Full costing* (exploration costs of successful and unsuccessful wells are assets)

The *successful efforts* argument maintains that if six wells are drilled and only two strike oil, the exploration costs of the two successful wells are capitalized in the natural resources

[12] Financial Accounting Standards Board, *Statement of Financial Accounting Standards No. 19*, "Financial Accounting and Reporting by Oil and Gas Companies" (1977); *FASB Codification Topics 930 and 932;* International Accounting Standards Board, *International Financial Reporting Standard 6*, "Exploration for and Evaluation of Mineral Resources" (2004). IFRS cost classifications are slightly different from U.S. GAAP classifications. IFRS requires a clear and consistent accounting policy in the natural resource area involving judgment as to whether costs are capitalized or expensed. As of the writing of this text, the International Accounting Standards Board continues to consider natural resource accounting issues. Given that the U.S. GAAP rules described in this section yield asset measurements that can be justified by reasonable judgment and permit some choice in the capitalization versus expensing decision, one can conclude that U.S. GAAP and IFRS treatments are not likely to yield variations in natural resource valuations that are greater than the variations in valuations that occur in U.S. GAAP.

[13] Financial Accounting Standards Board, *Statement of Financial Accounting Standards No. 141*, "Accounting for Asset Retirement Obligations" (2001); *FASB Codification Topic 410;* International Accounting Standards Board, *International Accounting Standard 16*, "Property, Plant and Equipment" (1998).

account and the costs of the four unsuccessful wells are expensed. This argument is rational because only the successful wells yield probable future economic benefits (that is, the sale of oil) and, hence, should be called assets.

The *full costing* approach capitalizes exploration costs for all six wells as part of the natural resources account. The argument is that it was necessary to drill all of the wells in order to discover oil. The cost of exploring all six locations is deemed a necessary investment to generate future economic benefits. Therefore, all costs are capitalizable. This argument also is rational, and it has precedence in other areas of accounting. The costs of producing defective or spoiled output, for example, are included as part of the cost of producing good output if it is necessary to destroy or spoil some goods in the production of good output. For example, the rapid filling of beverage bottles involves some waste; however, the cost of the wasted beverage is capitalized as part of beverage inventory. An unexpected machine malfunction causing a material waste of the beverage is not necessary for successful beverage production and thus would be treated as an expense of the period.

Because reasonable arguments can be made to support successful efforts or full costing, both methods are used to account for natural resource exploration costs. Managers choose the method they believe is best for their company. Firms in the same industry frequently choose different approaches, and the resulting financial statements are not comparable across firms.

In the past, many financial statement users complained about the lack of comparability brought about by the availability of two such different accounting methods for the same transaction. At one time, the SEC (Securities and Exchange Commission) urged the accounting profession to decide on one method, and accounting policy makers chose the successful efforts method. Smaller companies then presented economic consequences arguments in favor of full costing for their firms. They argued that smaller companies would be less likely to raise capital with favorable terms because their income was not sufficiently large to absorb the expensing of unsuccessful wells. As an unfavorable consequence, oil exploration would decrease. In response to the political pressure from firms supporting full costing, the SEC rejected both the full costing and the successful efforts method in favor of a value-based measure, *RRA (reserve recognition accounting).* RRA required the company to estimate the value of reserves which, in substance, required estimates of the magnitude of reserves and when the reserves would be extracted, how much it would cost to do so, when the goods would be sold, what the selling price would be, and what an appropriate interest rate would be to discount cash flows. Practical implementation problems eventually led the SEC to abandon RRA. Under intense political pressure, the FASB reversed its earlier position and once again allowed both the full costing and the successful efforts methods. Currently, the successful efforts method tends to be used by larger producers, while full costing tends to be used by smaller producers. Accordingly, the financial analyst should consider the differential treatment of exploration costs when comparing the profitability and risk of small and large firms in the extractive industry. Firms disclose their method choice in the accounting policies note to the financial statements.

Development Costs. Once the natural resource has been acquired and exploration has determined the location of deposits, the natural resource must be developed. Development costs are both tangible (for example, heavy equipment to drill and transport the resource) and intangible (for example, the costs of drilling wells and constructing mine shafts). Tangible development costs are capitalized as part of the equipment (or another property, plant, and equipment) account. Intangible development costs are capitalized as part of the natural resources account because the costs are not separable from the natural resource; for example, the costs associated with drilling a specific oil well cannot be moved to another well site.[14]

In summary, acquisition costs, exploration costs (of successful efforts or all efforts depending on the method used), and intangible development costs are capitalized as part of the natural resource account. Eventually, the costs are expensed as the natural resource is consumed. Depletion expense represents an estimate of the amount of consumption.

Costs of Acquiring Intangible Assets

Intangible assets include trade and brand names, trademarks, patents, copyrights, franchise rights, customer lists, and goodwill. Under both U.S. GAAP and IFRS, firms expense the cost of *internally* developing intangibles in the period incurred. The rationale for immediate expensing of such costs is the difficulty and uncertainty in ascertaining whether a particular expenditure results in a future benefit (that is, an asset) or not (an expense). Thus, although PepsiCo spends millions of dollars each year promoting its products, and brand names such as Pepsi and Frito-Lay® represent valuable economic "assets" of the firm, PepsiCo is not permitted to recognize an asset for the expenditures made to internally develop and maintain its brand names. The rationale for not recognizing the value of intangible assets such as brand names is that the error in estimating such valuations and management incentives to misuse discretion over the capitalization of such costs are so great as to offset the relevance of such estimates in the financial statements.

Firms capitalize as an asset the costs to acquire intangible assets from others because the existence of an external market transaction provides evidence of the existence of the intangible asset as well as a reliable measure of its value. The front matter in PepsiCo's 2008 Annual Report identifies 18 "mega-brands" controlled by PepsiCo, each generating more than $1 billion in annual sales. PepsiCo acquired many of these brands over the years through acquisitions. The third part of Note 4, "Property, Plant and Equipment and Intangible Assets" to PepsiCo's 2008 Financial Statements (Appendix A) shows that total capitalized brands equal $1,128 million. Using the same reasoning, in-process R&D is recorded at its fair value if arising from a corporate acquisition.

Because intangible assets, by definition, involve an inherently high degree of uncertainty regarding future economic benefits, most analysts prefer immediate expensing of all intangible assets.[15] Some analysts remove from the balance sheet any R&D costs, software development costs, and goodwill reported as assets before performing a financial analysis. By doing so, they argue that (1) quality of earnings information improves because the ability to manage earnings is reduced and (2) quality of balance sheet information improves because the balance sheet is cleansed of "soft" assets lacking physical substance. Some analysts also remove the costs of the intangible assets from retained earnings, as if intangible acquisition costs had been expensed over time. (Often the term *tangible equity* is used to describe the remaining shareholders' equity.) The financial analysis must be interpreted carefully, however, because the analyst may understate a firm's asset base by eliminating these assets—as is the case with PepsiCo's asset base because PepsiCo's balance sheet does not recognize brand names such as Pepsi and Frito-Lay® (among other important intangibles owned by the firm). Further, as discussed in more detail later in this chapter, many

[14] The accounting system captures costs incurred with respect to natural resources, including additional costs incurred to protect the environment. Some costs are incurred to minimize the environmental risk. For example, in the aftermath of the Exxon Valdez oil spill, double-hull oil tankers, which are more expensive to produce than single-hull tankers, are now used to transport Alaskan crude oil. The direct cost to Exxon to clean up the oil spill and indirect costs associated with tarnishing Exxon's reputation were substantial.

[15] For a stable or moderate-growth firm, the expense each year from immediate expensing is approximately the same as the expense from capitalizing expenditures and subsequently amortizing them.

intangibles acquired in a business combination receive balance sheet recognition because they have fair values accruing from a contractual right and may be separated and either leased or sold by the firm.

Goodwill

The most common setting for intangible asset recognition is in corporate acquisitions, where acquiring firms must allocate the purchase price to the assets acquired and liabilities assumed. Acquiring firms usually allocate the purchase price to the fair values of identifiable, tangible assets (inventories, land, and equipment) and liabilities first. They then allocate any excess purchase price to the fair values of specifically identifiable intangible assets such as patents, customer lists, and trade names, with the remainder allocated to goodwill. *Goodwill* is a residual and effectively represents all intangibles that are not specifically identifiable.

How should an analyst treat goodwill that appears on a firm's balance sheet? One approach is to follow financial reporting rules and view goodwill like any other productive asset in which the firm has invested (such as property, plant, and equipment). The justification for this approach is that the initial valuation of goodwill arose from an arm's-length investment in another corporate entity and simply represents valuable resources that accountants cannot identify and measure separately. The analyst should include these resources in the asset base on which management is expected to generate a reasonable return. If these valuable resources are not likely to last forever, amortization of their cost over some number of years is appropriate.

Another approach available to the analyst is to eliminate goodwill from assets and to subtract its amount from retained earnings or other common shareholders' equity accounts. The justification for this approach is based on an assumption that the amount allocated to goodwill from a corporate acquisition may occur simply because the firm paid too much and may not necessarily indicate the presence of resources with future service potential. Subtracting the amount allocated to goodwill from retained earnings suggests that the excess purchase price is a loss for the firm. Immediate subtraction of goodwill from retained earnings treats goodwill arising from an acquisition similar to goodwill developed internally. Later in this chapter, we discuss corporate acquisitions, and we address goodwill in more detail at that point.

What Choices Are Managers Making to Allocate Acquisition Costs to the Periods Benefited?

As discussed in the previous sections, some investing-like activities (R&D, pretechnological feasibility software costs, maintenance, and exploration costs) result in immediate recognition of expenses. However, most acquisition costs are capitalized and are subsequently expensed through the cost allocation processes of depreciation (for tangible fixed assets), amortization (for limited-life intangible assets), and depletion (for natural resources).

Managers make three primary choices and estimates when allocating acquisition costs of tangible assets and intangible assets to the periods benefited: they (1) choose an allocation method, (2) estimate useful life, and (3) estimate salvage value. Also, throughout the life of a long-lived asset, the book value must be tested for reasonableness relative to economic values, which may result in revaluing the asset for impairment (U.S. GAAP and IFRS) or appreciation (an option under IFRS). Such assessments often require a significant amount of judgment. Given the magnitude of long-lived assets on most balance sheets and the importance of understanding accounting judgments available to managers, the following subsections discuss these choices and estimates.

Useful Life for Long-Lived Tangible and Limited-Life Intangible Assets

Depreciation (amortization and depletion) is the process of allocating the historical cost of a long-lived asset less the estimate of its salvage value to the periods of its use in a rational and systematic manner. Both physical wear and tear and technological obsolescence affect the projection of the total useful life and salvage value. Because managers estimate expected useful lives, they have an opportunity to convey information to the firm's stakeholders about their expectations of the future usefulness of long-lived assets. However, the estimation process also provides an opportunity to introduce bias into reported earnings. For example, a manager wanting to report higher earnings could bias the estimated useful lives or salvage values of assets upward, which would result in lower annual depreciation expense.

Unfortunately, the disclosures that firms make about depreciable lives are usually not very helpful to the analyst in assessing a firm's aggressiveness in lengthening or shortening depreciable lives to manage earnings. The problems include the aggregated nature of the disclosures, the fact that firms usually disclose ranges of useful lives for asset categories, and the rare disclosure of expected salvage values.

Example 8

In this example, we demonstrate the process of estimating average lives for long-lived assets from note disclosures using PepsiCo financial disclosures. PepsiCo's Note 4, "Property, Plant and Equipment and Intangible Assets" (Appendix A), reports average useful lives of depreciable and amortizable assets, as follows:

Land and improvements	10–34 years
Buildings and improvements	20–44 years
Machinery and equipment, including fleet and software	5–14 years
Brands	5–40 years
Other identifiable intangibles	10–24 years

Because most firms in the U.S. use the straight-line depreciation method for financial reporting purposes, the analyst can estimate the average useful life of depreciable (and amortizable) assets by dividing average depreciable cost (gross, assuming zero salvage value) by depreciation expense for the year. The calculations for PepsiCo are as follows (amounts in millions):

	Property, plant, and equipment (excluding land and construction in progress)	**Amortizable intangible assets**
December 27, 2008	$19,911.0	$1,771.0
December 29, 2007	$19,048.0	$1,820.0
Average cost	$19,479.5	$1,795.5
Depreciation/amortization expense for 2008	$ 1,422.0	$ 64.0
Average total life = Average depreciable cost/ Annual depreciation or amortization expense	13.7 years	28.1 years

Even with such aggregated data, analysts can gain insight by comparing the average useful life of depreciable assets across firms. Firms with similar asset composition should have similar useful lives; if not, the analyst should assess why they differ. Analysts also need to question firms that report dramatic changes in the useful lives of depreciable assets over time.[16] Is the change because of assumption changes in the useful lives of the assets, has the composition of the firm's assets changed over time, or has the firm made the strategic decision to use assets differently? Firms choosing useful lives that accurately (and consistently) represent the period of time they expect to be able to use the assets report the highest-quality accounting data for depreciable assets.

Repeating the analysis for 2007 (using 2006 and 2007 data from PepsiCo's 2007 Annual Report) yields average total life estimates of 13.8 years for property, plant, and equipment and 29.3 years for amortizable intangible assets. Comparing these estimates to the estimates calculated for 2008 (13.7 and 28.1 years) shows the consistency of PepsiCo's total useful lives used in depreciation and amortization computations. The slight change in useful life for intangibles is immaterial. If PepsiCo had used 29.3 years life for the amortization computation in 2008, amortization expenses would have been \$61.3 million (= \$1,795.5/29.3) instead of \$64.0 million reported in 2008. The \$2.7 million pretax difference is less than four one-hundredths of one percent of the \$7,021 million pretax income in 2008. The after-tax effect of this difference would have to be ten times higher to affect earnings per share by one cent.

Both U.S. GAAP and IFRS allow managers to classify certain intangible assets (such as perpetual brands and goodwill reported by PepsiCo in Note 4) as having an indefinite life; therefore, they are not amortized. These nonamortizable intangibles are assessed for impairment (discussed in a later section).

Cost Allocation (Depreciation/Amortization/Depletion) Method

Firms may allocate the acquisition costs over the useful life of the asset using *any* systematic and rational allocation method. The allocation of cost is charged to depreciation expense (for tangible fixed assets), amortization expense (for intangibles), or depletion expense (for natural resources) and is reported on the income statement.[17]

Most firms write off tangible long-lived assets evenly over their useful lives (straight-line method). Some firms write off larger amounts during the early years and smaller amounts in later years (accelerated depreciation methods). Nearly all firms amortize intangible assets using the straight-line method. Firms generally deplete natural resources using the straight-line method or in proportion to the amount of natural resource consumed (for example, number of board feet of lumber harvested relative to an estimate of the total amount of board feet of lumber in a forest). Regardless of the cost allocation method chosen, the total depreciation over an asset's life generally does not exceed acquisition costs (except in rare cases when firms revalue such assets to current fair values). Thus, the various depreciation methods differ only in the timing of expense, not in its total amount over time.

Virtually all firms in the U.S. use accelerated depreciation methods for tax reporting based on depreciable lives specified in the income tax law, which are usually shorter than the depreciable lives that firms use for financial reporting purposes. In countries where tax

---

[16] When a firm changes a useful life or salvage value estimate, it handles the change prospectively. That is, it simply depreciates the remaining book value over the remaining useful life. Financial Accounting Standards Board, *Statement of Financial Accounting Standards No. 154*, "Accounting Changes and Error Corrections" (2005*); FASB Codification Topic 250;* International Accounting Standards Board, *International Accounting Standard 16*, "Property, Plant and Equipment" (1998).

[17] If the long-lived asset is used in production, the depreciation is initially added to inventory as a product cost and then expensed as cost of goods sold when the inventory is sold.

laws heavily influence financial reporting (such as Germany, France, and Japan), many firms use accelerated depreciation methods for both financial and tax reporting. Thus, comparisons of U.S. firms with those of some other countries require the analyst to assess the effect of different depreciation methods and assumptions. To increases the comparability of firms across such different environments, the analyst must restate reported U.S. amounts to an accelerated basis or convert reported amounts for other countries to a straight-line basis.

The analyst can place U.S. firms on an accelerated depreciation basis using information in the income tax note. As Chapter 2 described, *Statement No. 109* requires firms to report in notes to the financial statements the portion of the deferred tax liability that is attributable to book versus tax depreciation timing differences at the beginning and end of the year.[18]

Example 9

In Note 5, "Income Taxes" (Appendix A), PepsiCo reports that the portion of its deferred tax liability attributable to property, plant, and equipment was $828.0 million on December 29, 2007, and $881.0 million on December 27, 2008. An increase in a deferred tax liability relating to differences in expensing procedure for book and tax purposes indicates that PepsiCo depreciated fixed assets faster for tax purposes than for book purposes. As a result, taxes are lower in the current period, but they will be higher in the future when depreciation for tax purposes falls below depreciation for financial reporting purposes (hence, the current period increase in the deferred tax liability). If the analyst wants to compare PepsiCo's profitability and risk to another company (foreign or otherwise) that uses accelerated methods of depreciation, he or she must convert key amounts for PepsiCo, including the asset PP&E (net) and net income, to an accelerated depreciation method basis or convert those amounts for the comparable firm to a straight-line basis. The following computations demonstrate the former approach, converting PepsiCo's amounts to an accelerated depreciation basis. (PepsiCo discloses a 35 percent federal statutory tax rate in Note 5. We use this rate in the computation that follows, which assumes that the depreciation differences arise primarily from U.S. operations.)

Conversion of PP&E (net) to an accelerated basis (amounts in millions):

PP&E (net) as reported at December 27, 2008, using book depreciation method		$11,663.0
Excess accumulated depreciation over time using tax method:		
Deferred tax liability related to excess depreciation (measured originally by multiplying the excess depreciation by the tax rate) ÷ tax rate	$881.0 ÷ 0.35	(2,517.1)
PP&E (net) using tax depreciation method		$ 9,145.9

Because PepsiCo measures the deferred tax liability of $881.0 million by multiplying the excess tax depreciation over time by 35 percent, the excess accumulated tax depreciation over time ($2,517.1 million) can be obtained by dividing the deferred tax liability amount by 35 percent.

[18] Financial Accounting Standards Board, *Statement of Financial Accounting Standards No. 109*, "Accounting for Income Taxes" (1992); *FASB Codification Topic 740*. Chapter 2 provides an initial discussion of this statement.

Excess current depreciation expense using tax method:

Increase in deferred tax liability during the year ($881.0 − $828.0)	$ 53.0	
÷ tax rate	÷ 0.35	$ 151.4
Decrease in tax expense ($151.4 × 0.35)		(53.0)
Decrease in 2008 net income if tax depreciation method is used		$ 98.4

This latter computation relies on the idea that income is affected by the *change* in the deferred tax liability amount ($53.0 million), which, when divided by the tax rate, represents the excess tax depreciation expense if an accelerated method is used. If PepsiCo had used the tax method, it would have had a lower pretax income and, hence, a lower tax expense of $53.0 million. Thus, the effect of changing PepsiCo's book depreciation to a tax-based method is a decrease in 2008 net income of $98.4 million. This would represent an almost 2 percent decrease in 2008 net income.

Depreciation, amortization, and depletion also are reported as addbacks to net income in the operating section of the statement of cash flows because they reduce net income but are not cash outflows. In fact, for many firms, the depreciation addback is the largest single reconciling item between net income and cash flow from operations.

What Is the Relationship between the Book Values and Market Values of Long-Lived Assets?

Companies use the aforementioned depreciation choice and useful life and salvage value estimates to report long-lived operational assets at acquisition costs less the accumulated depreciation to date (adjusted acquisition cost). The use of acquisition-cost-based reporting rests on the presumption that such amounts are more objectively measurable than the fair values of fixed assets. Difficulties encountered in determining fair values include (1) the absence of active markets for many used fixed assets, particularly those specific to a particular firm's needs; (2) the need to identify comparable assets currently available in the market to value assets in place; and (3) the need to make assumptions about the effect of technological and other improvements when using the prices of new assets currently available on the market in the valuation process.

Nevertheless, accounting standards require firms to determine whether the net book values of long-lived assets reflect the economic reality of market values. In particular, accounting standards are concerned with how long-lived asset values must be tested for impairments and written down if impairment losses have occurred. The following sections examine the U.S. GAAP and IFRS standards related to reporting long-lived assets when book values and market values differ. To facilitate the discussion, the next three sections deal, in turn, with three basic types of long-lived operating assets: (1) long-lived assets subject to depreciation and amortization (land is in this category even though it is not depreciated), (2) intangible assets not subject to amortization because of indefinite lives, and (3) goodwill. Then, a fourth section addresses upward revaluations of long-lived assets under IFRS.

Impairment of Long-Lived Assets Subject to Depreciation and Amortization

The development of new technologies by competitors, changes in government regulations, changes in demographic trends, and other external factors may reduce the future benefits originally anticipated from long-lived assets. Firms are required to assess whether conditions exist implying that the carrying amounts of fixed assets are not recoverable, and if they are not, firms are to write down the assets to their fair values and recognize impairment losses in income from continuing operations.[19]

U.S. GAAP defines a carrying amount (that is, the book value at the moment of the impairment test) as not being recoverable if it is greater than the sum of the *undiscounted* cash flows expected from the asset's use and disposal. If an impairment charge is to be recorded because the asset's carrying amount is not recoverable, the charge equals the amount by which the carrying value exceeds the asset's fair value. Recognize that under U.S. GAAP, although the firm uses undiscounted future cash flows to decide whether an impairment charge is necessary, fair value is used to measure the actual impairment charge. Fair value is defined using the three-level FASB designation described in Chapters 2 and 6. Because of the difficulty of observing values of the same or similar assets in organized markets, firms often must estimate fair values by computing the present (*discounted*) value of expected cash flows from using the fixed asset (Level 3 inputs used in a valuation approach applying present value techniques).

In requiring firms to use undiscounted cash flows to test for impairment of long-lived tangible assets, U.S. standard setters reasoned that a loss had not occurred if the firm could recover in future cash flows an amount equal to or larger than the current book value. Accounting theorists and practitioners question the logic of using undiscounted, instead of discounted, cash flows in testing for impairment. In some cases, the economic value of the long-lived asset may decline below its carrying value but the firm would recognize no impairment because the *undiscounted* future cash flows from the asset exceed its carrying value.

IFRS uses rules that are more theoretically defensible. Firms are required to determine whether an impairment has occurred and to measure impairment by comparing the book value of the long-lived asset to the greater of (1) the fair value of the assets less estimated costs to *sell* the asset or (2) the value of the asset *in use* (which is the present value of estimated future cash flows from using the asset).

Example 10

Assume that a real estate company owns an apartment building that originally cost $20 million, with a current carrying amount of $15 million. The company originally expected to collect rents of $1.67 million each year for 30 years before selling the apartment complex for $8 million. Deteriorating neighborhood conditions, however, have caused the company to reassess the future rentals, especially given a recent appraisal that set a fair value for the apartment building at $10 million. The company now estimates that it will receive rentals of $1.35 million per year for 15 years and then will sell the building for $5 million. The company uses an 8 percent discount rate to compute the present value for this investment. Costs to sell are estimated at $300,000.

U.S. GAAP Treatment: Because total undiscounted future cash flows of $25.25 million [= ($1.35 × 15) + $5] exceed the carrying value of $15 million, the real estate company reports no impairment loss. In essence, the firm has suffered an economic loss but will not report any loss for financial reporting. If the total undiscounted future cash flows in this illustration were estimated to fall below the carrying value of $15 million, the real estate

[19] Financial Accounting Standards Board, *Statement of Financial Accounting Standards No. 144*, "Accounting for Impairment of Long-Lived Assets" (2001); *FASB Codification Topic 360;* International Accounting Standards Board, *International Accounting Standard 36*, "Impairment of Assets" (revised 2004).

company would compute an impairment loss as the difference between the carrying value and the fair market value of the apartment building (in this case, $10 million). The company would report the impairment loss of $5 million in income from continuing operations, and the apartment building would be recorded at the new carrying value of $10 million.

IFRS Treatment: Under IFRS, the greater of the asset's value in use and fair value from sale is identified first. Value in use is $13.1 million, obtained by using the 8 percent discount rate to compute the present value of a 15-year annuity of $1.35 million cash inflow plus the present value of $5 million received at the end of Year 15. The value from a sale is $9.7 million, the $10 million fair value less $0.3 million in disposal costs. The larger of the two, $13.1 million, is then compared to the carrying value of $15 million, and a $1.9 million impairment is recorded. The company would report an impairment loss of $1.9 million in income from continuing operations, and the apartment building would be recorded at the new carrying value of $13.1 million.

Impairment of Intangible Assets Not Subject to Amortization

For intangibles *not requiring* amortization (that is, intangible assets with an indefinite life), firms must test for asset impairment annually—or more frequently if events and circumstances indicate that the asset may be impaired. Unlike the impairment test for depreciable assets and amortizable intangible assets, U.S. GAAP defines impairment of intangible assets not subject to amortization as occurring when the fair value of the intangible asset is below its carrying amount. This approach is more defendable from a theoretical viewpoint because fair value is more closely related to discounted cash flows than to the undiscounted cash flows used in the impairment tests for limited-life assets. IFRS impairment tests for intangible assets not subject to amortization mirror its tests for depreciable and amortizable assets.

Impairment of Goodwill

The U.S. GAAP and IFRS goodwill impairment tests are similar. Both sets of standards view goodwill as not being separable from other assets and therefore require the impairment test to be conducted at the unit level, where several assets combine to produce future cash flows. U.S. GAAP (SFAS No. 142, FASB Codification Topic 350) defines a *reporting unit* as a segment or a component of a segment that is a business with separate financial information that management regularly reviews. IFRS (IAS 36) defines a *cash generating unit* as "the smallest identifiable group of assets that generates cash inflows that are largely independent of the cash inflows from other assets or groups of assets." The impairment test is basically a simulation of a transaction between the firm and an outsider in an organized market to reacquire the unit.

Example 11

Woods Co. acquires Golf Tech, Inc., on January 1, 2010, by paying $1,000,000 in cash. At the date of acquisition, the price is allocated as follows:[20]

Price paid	$1,000,000
Fair value of Golf Tech's long-lived tangible assets	(400,000)
Fair value of a brand name with an indefinite useful life	(100,000)
Goodwill	$ 500,000

[20] In an acquisition, the fair value transferred by the acquirer ($1,000,000 in this example) is assigned to the assets acquired, which are recorded at their fair values. The excess is recorded as goodwill. The acquisition process is discussed in greater detail later in the chapter.

One year later on December 31, 2010, Woods estimates the fair value of the Golf Tech unit to be $800,000. The fair value of Golf Tech's long-lived tangible assets is $400,000, and the fair value of the brand name is $70,000.

U.S. GAAP Treatment: Firms following U.S. GAAP would first apply impairment tests to its non-goodwill assets. The fair value of the brand name has declined by $30,000. Therefore, a $30,000 intangible asset impairment charge is reported by reducing the carrying value of the intangible asset to $70,000.

The second step in the process is to compare the carrying amount of the unit to the unit's fair value, as follows:

Fair value of Golf Tech unit at 12/31/09		$800,000
Carrying value of Golf Tech unit at 12/31/09		
Long-lived tangible assets	$400,000	
Brand name (after its reduction to fair value)	70,000	
Goodwill	500,000	$970,000

If the fair value of the unit exceeds the carrying amount, goodwill is deemed not to be impaired. However, in this example, the carrying value exceeds the fair value of the unit, so Wood's must measure the amount of goodwill impairment by simulating a reacquisition. The fair value of the unit is compared to the fair value of the identifiable assets to yield an implied goodwill, as follows:

Fair value of Golf Tech unit at 12/31/09		$800,000
Fair values of Golf Tech's assets other than goodwill at 12/31/09:		
Long-lived tangible assets	$400,000	
Brand name	70,000	(470,000)
Implied goodwill at 12/31/09		$330,000

Goodwill is written down from $500,000 to $330,000, and a $170,000 impairment loss is reflected in operating income. Exhibit 7.2 shows the brand name and goodwill impairment charges, which total $200,000.

EXHIBIT 7.2: SOLUTION TO EXAMPLE 11 ON GOODWILL IMPAIRMENT UNDER U.S. GAAP

Assets		=	Liabilities	+	Total Shareholders' Equity			
					CC	AOCI	RE	
Brand Name	−30,000						Impairment	
Goodwill	−170,000						Losses	−200,000

Impairment Losses	200,000	
Brand Name		30,000
Goodwill		170,000

Note that the new carrying amounts for individual assets are as follows:

Long-lived tangible assets	$400,000
Brand name ($100,000 − $30,000 impairment)	70,000
Goodwill ($500,000 − $170,000 impairment)	330,000
Total new carrying value	$800,000

IFRS Treatment: Under IFRS, the recoverable amount of the assets is compared to their original carrying amounts. For long-lived tangible assets and brand names, the recoverable amount is the higher of fair value in use or from sale (less disposal costs). For goodwill, recoverable amount is the implied goodwill of $330,000 computed in the same way as previously illustrated for the U.S. GAAP treatment.

	Original Carrying Amount	Recoverable Amount
Long-lived tangible assets	$ 400,000	$400,000
Brand name	100,000	70,000
Goodwill	500,000	330,000
Total	$1,000,000	$800,000

The financial statement effects are the same as those shown in Exhibit 7.2. These amounts support the write-down of brand name and goodwill by $30,000 and $170,000, respectively.

It is clear from the example above that managers (and their valuation consultants) make several estimates of future cash flows or fair values to support a goodwill impairment charge. The analyst should consider several issues when assessing current profitability and predicting future earnings. First, the relatively unpredictable and volatile goodwill impairment charge has replaced the inherently certain and constant goodwill amortization charge. The analyst should examine a firm's past time series of goodwill impairment charges as well as the reasonableness of prices paid in recent acquisitions to forecast whether additional impairments are likely. Second, the analyst should attempt to determine whether the goodwill impairment charge is indicative of management performance or is due to uncontrollable external factors. Finally, the substantial estimation involved in goodwill impairments permits earnings management.

Example 12

The impairment of goodwill can occur shortly after an acquisition. In 2008, Nike acquired Umbro. Nike reports the following in its June 2009 10K:

> ***Umbro Impairment***
> In accordance with FAS 142 "Goodwill and Other Intangible Assets," the Company performs annual impairment tests on goodwill and intangible assets with indefinite lives in the fourth quarter of each fiscal year, or when events occur or circumstances change that would, more likely than not, reduce the fair value of a reporting unit or intangible assets with an indefinite life below its carrying value. As a result of a significant decline in global consumer demand and continued weakness in the macroeconomic environment, as well as decisions by Company management to adjust planned investment in the Umbro brand, the Company concluded that sufficient indicators of impairment existed to require the performance of an interim assessment of Umbro's goodwill and indefinite lived intangible assets as of February 1, 2009. Accordingly, the Company performed the first step of the goodwill impairment assessment for Umbro by comparing the estimated fair value of Umbro to its carrying amount, and determined there was a potential impairment of goodwill as the carrying amount exceeded the estimated fair value. Therefore, the Company performed the second step of the assessment which compared the implied fair value of Umbro's goodwill to the book value of goodwill. The implied fair value of goodwill is

> determined by allocating the estimated fair value of Umbro to all of its assets and liabilities, including both recognized and unrecognized intangibles, in the same manner as goodwill was determined in the original business combination.
>
> The Company measured the fair value of Umbro by using an equal weighting of the fair value implied by a discounted cash flow analysis and by comparisons with the market values of similar publicly traded companies. The Company believes the blended use of both models compensates for the inherent risk associated with either model if used on a stand-alone basis, and this combination is indicative of the factors a market participant would consider when performing a similar valuation. The fair value of Umbro's indefinite-lived trademark was estimated using the relief from royalty method, which assumes that the trademark has value to the extent that Umbro is relieved of the obligation to pay royalties for the benefits received from the trademark. The assessments of the Company resulted in the recognition of impairment charges of $199.3 million and $181.3 million related to Umbro's goodwill and trademark, respectively, during the third quarter ended February 28, 2009. A deferred tax benefit of $54.5 million was recognized as a result of the trademark impairment charge. In addition to the above impairment analysis, the Company determined an equity investment held by Umbro was impaired, and recognized a charge of $20.7 million related to the impairment of this investment. These charges are included in the Company's "Other" category for segment reporting purposes.
>
> The discounted cash flow analysis calculated the fair value of Umbro using management's business plans and projections as the basis for expected cash flows for the next twelve years and a 3% residual growth rate thereafter. The Company used a weighted average discount rate of 14% in its analysis, which was derived primarily from published sources as well as our adjustment for increased market risk given current market conditions. Other significant estimates used in the discounted cash flow analysis include the rates of projected growth and profitability of Umbro's business and working capital effects. The market valuation approach indicates the fair value of Umbro based on a comparison of Umbro to publicly traded companies in similar lines of business. Significant estimates in the market valuation approach include identifying similar companies with comparable business factors such as size, growth, profitability, mix of revenue generated from licensed and direct distribution and risk of return on investment.
>
> Holding all other assumptions constant at the test date, a 100 basis point increase in the discount rate would reduce the adjusted carrying value of Umbro's net assets by 12%.

Note that Nike uses a combination of models (discounted cash flow analysis and market comparables) because it argues that these models are used by market participants. Also note the assumptions to develop the projections used in the discounted cash flow analysis, the use of a weighted average discount rate, and the sensitivity analysis performed. Return to this example after studying financial statement forecasts and valuation covered in Chapters 10–14.

If a company reports an impairment of any kind, net income is reduced. However, impairments are not cash outflows. Accordingly, impairments, if any, are added back to net income in the operating section of the statement of cash flows.

IFRS Treatment of Upward Asset Revaluations

Under U.S. GAAP, upward revaluations of long-lived assets are not permitted. However, IFRS gives firms the option to revalue upward both intangible and tangible long-lived assets.[21] When fair value remains above original acquisition cost, upward and downward revaluations are reported as other comprehensive income and are accumulated in the shareholders' equity section of the balance sheet. The account typically used in the other comprehensive income classification is "Revaluation Surplus." If fair value is less than or equal to cost, reversals of previous downward revaluations (that were reported as losses on the income statement) are treated as gains on the income statement.

Example 13

Assume that a French company following IFRS has land originally costing €2,000,000. At the end of the next four years, the land is worth the following:

2009:	€2,500,000
2010:	€2,300,000
2011:	€1,900,000
2012:	€2,000,000

Exhibit 7.3 shows the effects of upward and downward revaluations of the asset.

Fair value increases above original acquisition cost in 2009, causing an upward revaluation of the land and an increase in comprehensive income (OCI) but not net income. The increase is recognized in accumulated other comprehensive income in the shareholders'

EXHIBIT 7.3: SOLUTION TO EXAMPLE 13 ON UPWARD ASSET REVALUATIONS UNDER IFRS

Assets		=	Liabilities	+	Total Shareholders' Equity				
					CC	AOCI		RE	
2009:									
Land	+500,000					Unrealized Gains	+500,000		
2010:									
Land	−200,000					Unrealized Gains	−200,000		
2011:									
Land	−400,000					Unrealized Gains	−300,000	Unrealized Losses	−100,000
2012:									
Land	+100,000							Unrealized Gains	+100,000

2009:		
Land	500,000	
Unrealized Gains (OCI)		500,000
2010:		
Unrealized Gains (OCI)	200,000	
Land		200,000
2011:		
Unrealized Gains (OCI)	300,000	
Unrealized Losses (NI)	100,000	
Land		400,000
2012:		
Land	100,000	
Unrealized Gains (NI)		100,000

[21] International Accounting Standards Board, *International Accounting Standard 16*, "Property, Plant and Equipment" (1998).

equity section. In 2010, the land is revalued downward, causing a partial reversal in the accumulated unrealized gains. Such reversals of previously unrealized gains are reported as losses in other comprehensive income and reduce accumulated other comprehensive income on the balance sheet as long as fair value is greater than original acquisition cost. In 2011, fair value falls below original acquisition cost, causing a reversal of the remainder of the accumulated unrealized gains in accumulated other comprehensive income via the recognition in other comprehensive income of €300,000 unrealized loss and recognition in net income of €100,000 unrealized loss. The land recovers its value in 2012, and the reversal of the 2011 unrealized loss reported in net income is reported in 2012 net income as an unrealized gain.

Firms must choose the class of asset to which revaluations will apply and then perform the revaluations on a regular basis. The choice is irrevocable, and as mentioned previously, the fair value of nonfinancial assets in active markets is difficult to obtain and the process takes a great deal of time and effort. As a result, few firms choose the upward revaluation option.[22]

When Will the Long-Lived Assets Be Replaced?

Forecasting future financial statements requires expectations of future tangible asset acquisitions for both replacement of existing production or service capacity and growth in capacity. Although the analyst must rely on knowledge of industry conditions and firm strategy to estimate capital expenditure growth, he or she can make two computations to gain a better understanding of when existing long-lived assets must be replaced. Because the amount of accumulated depreciation depends on the number of years for which depreciation has been taken, the *average age of depreciable assets* equals the average amount of accumulated depreciation divided by depreciation expense. Based on PepsiCo's Note 4, "Property, Plant and Equipment and Intangible Assets" (Appendix A), disclosures, 0.5 × ($10,889 + $10,668)/$1,422 equals 7.6 years average age. Also, the *proportion of depreciable assets consumed* equals total accumulated depreciation divided by acquisition cost. For PepsiCo, $10,889/$19,911 = 54.7%. In the same vein, the analyst also can estimate the *remaining useful life* by dividing net depreciable PP&E by annual depreciation expense. For PepsiCo, ($19,911 − $10,889)/$1,422 = 6.3 years average remaining life. The analyst can track average age and proportion consumed through time and compare them to competitors' numbers to ascertain whether assets are getting older on average and whether they are at a point where large capital expenditures are necessary to replace them. Also, older assets and high proportion consumed provides an indication that the firm is in a later stage of average product life cycle.

When older assets are taken out of service and scrapped, any remaining book value must be removed from the accounts and reported as a realized loss on disposal in operating income. Cash inflow from a sale of long-lived assets reduces the loss or causes a gain to be reported. These cash inflows are reported in the investing section of the statement of cash flows. Gains and losses on the sale must be adjusted out of operating income so that the total amount of cash inflow from the sale can be reported as an investing cash flow.

Assets also may be traded in for newer assets. Both U.S. GAAP and IFRS require firms to record the new asset acquired at fair value with resulting gains and losses on trade-ins reported in net income. An exception to this rule occurs if the transaction lacks commercial

[22] A final category of long-lived assets exists that is unique to IFRS. Biological assets are living plants and animals that will be transformed into items for sale, agricultural produce, or additional biological assets. For example, in the production of wine, the vintner has vines that produce grapes that ultimately produce wine. The vines are the biological asset. Unless fair value is clearly unreliable, biological assets are reported at fair value less estimated disposal costs at each balance sheet date, with all value changes reflected in current net income. International Accounting Standards Board, *International Accounting Standard 41*, "Agriculture" (2001).

substance, in which case the acquired asset is recorded at the book value of the assets surrendered (including the traded-in asset) and liabilities assumed with no recognition of gain or loss.[23]

Because most gains and losses on asset dispositions are reported in net income of the period, analysts must be aware of the earnings management opportunity afforded by disposal timing. Analysts must decide whether these gains and losses are persistent by looking at the past history of the firm's gain and loss reporting.

Summary

The preceding discussion suggests that an assessment of accounting quality in the area of investments in long-lived assets is determined by answering the following questions:

1. Are capitalized acquisition costs justified? Were assets created, or should the costs be expensed? Are the firm's capitalization policies clear and in line with competitors and economic reality? Were some economic assets created even though accounting rules require expense treatement?
2. Are useful lives and salvage values reasonable given the economic service and value of the assets? Are they in line with competitors? Can changes in average useful lives be explained by strategy or economic reality, or do the useful life changes appear to be opportunistic?
3. Are depreciation methods consistent with the expected economic lives of the assets? Are they similar to useful lives used by competitors with similar assets? Are methods frequently changed?
4. Are asset impairment charges consistent with the firm's economic environment? Are the charges transitory or do they occur frequently? Are asset impairment charges or IFRS upward revaluations based on reliable fair value estimates?

The analyst should understand the firm's accounting policy in the long-lived asset area. The choices that managers make can convey a wealth of information to financial statement users, but this freedom also permits managers to bias or manipulate the financial statements through manipulated accounting choices. The analyst should pay particular attention to changes in estimates used in the depreciation and amortization process and the reasons for and timing of asset impairment charges.

INVESTMENTS IN SECURITIES

Investments in a firm's own operational assets generate profits reflected in operating revenues, expenses, gains, and losses. Firms also may invest in the securities underlying the operations of other firms, such as common stock and long-term debt, thus acquiring claims to the returns from other firms' operations. In either case, the investment assets acquired increase the ROA denominator and profits from the investments increase both the denominator (assets) and numerator (net income) in computations of ROA. This section examines the accounting, reporting, and analysis issues surrounding investments in securities.

[23] Financial Accounting Standards Board, *Statement of Financial Accounting Standards No. 153*, "Exchanges of Nonmonetary Assets" (2004); *FASB Codification Topic 845;* International Accounting Standards Board, *International Accounting Standard 16*, "Property, Plant and Equipment" (revised 1998). A lack of commercial substance is evidenced by relatively little change in the cash flows to the firm after it replaces the asset. This provision exists to remove the past abuse of asset trading rules in which two firms trade nearly identical assets with book values below their fair values simply to record the gain on the difference between fair and book value rather than for any commercial reason.

Firms invest in the securities of governments, corporations, variable-interest entities, joint ventures, and partnerships for a variety of reasons: to earn interest or dividends; to speculate on potential price appreciation of the securities; to lock in high yields on longer-term debt securities; to exert significant influence or gain control of an important raw materials supplier, customer, technological innovator, or other valued entity; or to achieve other strategic purposes. The appropriate accounting for investments depends on the level of "controlling financial interest" by the firm making the investment, determined by the following:

1. What percentage of ownership one firm has in another entity
2. Whether the reporting firm is deemed the primary beneficiary of the investment it has made in a VIE (variable-interest entity), as defined in FASB *Interpretation No. 46R*.

The following sections discuss each criterion in turn.

Percentage of Ownership

Exhibit 7.4 identifies three types of investments based on percentage of voting stock ownership, and Exhibit 7.5 summarizes the accounting and reporting for each type of investment. The types of investments are (1) minority, passive; (2) minority, active; and (3) majority, active.

Minority, Passive Investments

Firms often acquire some stake in the debt securities or shares of capital stock of another corporation for the anticipated interest or dividends and capital gains. The percentage that a firm owns of another corporation's voting shares is not so large that the acquiring company can control or exert significant influence over the other company, and the investing firm is not deemed the VIE's primary beneficiary as defined by *Interpretation No. 46R* (discussed in a later section). Investments in debt securities, preferred stock, or common stock when the firm holds less than 20 percent of the voting stock are minority, passive investments.

EXHIBIT 7.4

Types of Intercorporate Investments in Capital Stock

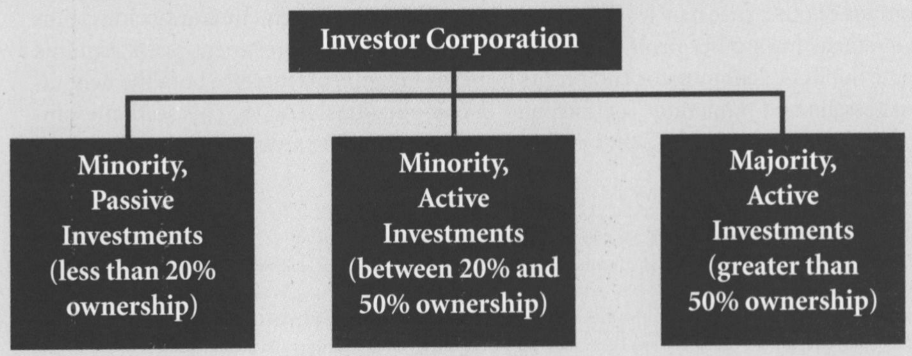

EXHIBIT 7.5

Reporting Investments in Securities in the Financial Statements

Financial Statement	Minority, Passive Investments*	Minority, Active Investments*	Majority, Active Investments
Income Statement	Interest and dividend revenue Unrealized increases and decreases in the market value of securities classified as trading securities Realized gains and losses on sales of securities	Investor's share of investee's net income	Individual revenues and expenses of investee minus the noncontrolling (that is, minority) interest's share of investee's net income included in consolidated net income
Balance Sheet	Marketable securities and investments in securities reported at market value (except debt securities held to maturity reported at amortized acquisition cost) Unrealized increases and decreases in market value of securities classified as available for sale included in Accumulated Other Comprehensive Income in the shareholders' equity section of the balance sheet	Investments reported at acquisition cost plus investor's cumulative share of investee's net income minus dividends received from investee since acquisition	Investment in securities account eliminated and replaced by investee's individual assets and liabilities in preparing consolidated balance sheet Noncontrolling interest's claim on investee's net assets shown in the shareholders' equity section of consolidated balance sheet
Statement of Cash Flows	Cash received from interest and dividends included in cash flow from operations; cash flows associated with purchases and sales included in cash flows from investing	Cash received from interest and dividends included in cash flow from operations. Cash flows associated with purchases and sales included in cash flows from investing	Individual cash flows from operating, investing, and financing activities of investee included in consolidated statement of cash flows

*The accounting for minority, passive and minority, active investments illustrated in the exhibit assumes that the investing firm is not a VIE primary beneficiary as defined by FASB Interpretation No. 46R. If the investing firm is a VIE primary beneficiary, the firm must follow the reporting for investments in securities categorized as majority, active investments.

A summary of the accounting for minority, passive investments follows:[24]

1. Firms initially record investments at acquisition cost.
2. Revenues each period equal interest and dividends received or receivable.
3. The accounting at the end of each period depends on the type of security and the firm's ability and intent to hold it. The three classifications of securities are:
   a. Debt securities for which a firm has a positive intent and ability to *hold to maturity*.
   b. Debt and equity securities held as *trading* securities.
   c. Debt and equity securities held as *available for sale*.
4. Firms must account for debt securities they expect to hold until maturity at amortized acquisition cost. That is, the firm must amortize any difference between the acquisition cost and maturity value of these debt securities as an adjustment to interest revenue over the life of the debt. This accounting is equivalent to the effective interest method demonstrated in Chapter 6. While the creditor shows bonds payable and interest expense in its financial records, the investor shows an investment in bonds and interest revenue. Firms report all other debt and equity securities at fair value at the end of each period. The reporting of any unrealized holding gain or loss depends on the purpose of holding the securities. If a firm actively buys and sells securities to take advantage of short-term differences or changes in market values, the firm will classify the securities as trading securities, a current asset on the balance sheet. Commercial banks, for example, often trade securities in different capital markets worldwide to take advantage of temporary differences in market prices. Manufacturers, retailers, and other nonfinancial firms occasionally invest funds for trading purposes, but such situations are unusual. Firms include unrealized holding gains and losses on trading securities in net income each period. Firms classify debt and equity securities that do not fit one of these first two categories (debt securities held to maturity and trading securities) as securities available for sale, including them as either current or noncurrent assets depending on the expected holding period. Unrealized holding gains or losses on securities available for sale are not included in net income each period; instead, they appear as a component of other comprehensive income, labeled Unrealized Holding Gain or Loss on Securities Available for Sale. The cumulative unrealized holding gain or loss on securities available for sale appears in the shareholders' equity section of the balance sheet as part of accumulated other comprehensive income.
5. When a firm sells a trading security, it recognizes the difference between the selling price and the book value (that is, the market value at the end of the most recent accounting period prior to sale) as a gain or loss in measuring net income. When a firm sells a security classified as available-for-sale, it recognizes the difference between the selling price and the acquisition cost of the security (or amortized cost if the available-for-sale security is a bond) as a realized gain or loss on the income

[24] U.S. GAAP and IFRS are consistent in the accounting and reporting of minority, passive investments. Relevant standards of investments representing passive investment (minority, passive investments) are *Statement of Financial Accounting Standards No. 115*, "Accounting for Certain Investments in Debt and Equity Securities" (1993) (referred to as *Statement No. 115*); *FASB Codification Topic 320;* International Accounting Standards Board, *International Accounting Standard 39*, "Financial Instruments: Recognition and Measurement" (revised 2003); International Accounting Standards Board, *International Financial Reporting Standard 7*, "Financial Instruments: Disclosure" (2005). Two key differences exist: (1) Under U.S. GAAP, unless the firm is a broker/dealer, an investment company, an insurance company, or a defined benefit plan, *unlisted* equity securities are generally carried at cost unless impaired or the fair value option is chosen, while IFRS simply requires reliably measurable fair value. (2) U.S. GAAP distinguishes between a debt securities (for example, a bond) and a loan (for example, a promissory note) and limits SFAS 115 treatment to securities, while IFRS makes no such distinction.

statement. At the time of sale, the firm must remove any amount in the shareholders' equity account, accumulated other comprehensive income, for the unrealized holding gain or loss related to that security by recognizing it in current period other comprehensive income; the realized gain or loss is then recognized in retained earnings through its net income effect.

Example 14

To understand these concepts, consider the following illustration of the accounting for investments by James Company. James had no equity investments prior to the transactions indicated below.

During 2010, James Company purchased the following common stocks:

Andrew Company	10,000 shares @ $5/sh.	$50,000	
Ball Company	5,000 shares @ $4/sh.	20,000	
Edwards Company	2,000 shares @ $6/sh.	12,000	
Watts Company	3,000 shares @ $20/sh.	60,000	$142,000
Porter Company	10,000 shares @ $3/sh.	$30,000	
Moore Company	10,000 shares @ $2/sh.	20,000	50,000
			$192,000

James intends to hold the Andrew, Ball, Edwards, and Watts shares as trading securities while holding the Porter and Moore shares as available-for-sale for an indefinite period. James does not have significant influence with any of the companies. During 2010 and 2011, James received $25,000 and $20,000, respectively, in dividends from the stock investments. James sold the investment in Watts Company in 2011 for $62,000. At the end of 2010 and 2011, market values were as follows:[25]

	2010	2011
Andrew	$ 30,000	$55,000
Ball	20,000	23,000
Edwards	10,000	10,000
Watts	63,000	0
Total	$123,000	$88,000
Porter	$ 25,000	$20,000
Moore	30,000	22,000
Total	$ 55,000	$42,000

Because James has no significant influence with the investee companies, James records these investments using the market method. In the statement of cash flows (see Exhibit 7.6), purchases and sales of investments in available-for-sale securities ($50,000 purchase in this

[25] Note that in this example, James holds three of the trading securities over a two-year period. By definition, a trading security is held for a short period of time (for example, 90 days). A security that is held for two years should not be classified as trading. However, the purpose of this problem is to compare and contrast the accounting for trading and available-for-sale equity security investments. Accordingly, the trading securities are artificially held over two periods so that you can compare and contrast the accounting for trading and available-for-sale equity security investments.

EXHIBIT 7.6

James Company Statement of Cash Flows (cash outflows in parentheses)

	2010	2011
OPERATING ACTIVITIES (DIRECT METHOD)		
Dividends received	$ 25,000	$20,000
Investments in trading securities	(142,000)	
Sales of trading securities		62,000
INVESTING ACTIVITIES		
Investments in available-for-sale securities	(50,000)	
Net Change in Cash	$(167,000)	$82,000

example) are listed in the investing activities section and purchases and sales of investments in trading securities ($142,000 purchase in this example) are listed in the operating activities section. Dividends received on investments accounted for under the market method are reported as revenues on the income statement, and U.S. GAAP requires that cash receipts from dividends ($25,000 and $20,000 in the two years) are reported in the operating activities section.[26]

The balance sheet (see Exhibit 7.7) shows the effects of the investments under alternative classifications. Because the available-for-sale securities are held for an indefinite period, they are classified as long-term assets. Alternatively, they could be classified as current assets if management's intent was to hold them for only a short period or to sell them whenever needed. The trading securities are classified as current. The cash balance reflects the cumulative effect of the change in cash reported in the statement of cash flows.

The investment in equity securities amounts reported in the balance sheet are determined by an analysis of the costs and fair values of the two portfolios of investments in trading and available-for-sale securities at each balance sheet date, as follows:

Trading Securities:	**Costs and Fair Values in Thousands**			
	December 31, 2010		**December 31, 2011**	
	Cost	**Fair Value**	**New Basis**	**Fair Value**
Andrew	$ 50	$ 30	$30	$55
Ball	20	20	20	23
Edwards	12	10	10	10
Watts	60	63	—	—
Totals	$142	$123	$60	$88
(Loss) gain reported on income statement as unrealized	$(19)		$28	

[26] IFRS permits reporting dividend receipts in the investing section of the statement of cash flows.

Available-for-Sale Securities:	Costs and Fair Values in Thousands			
	December 31, 2010		December 31, 2011	
	Cost	Fair Value	New Basis	Fair Value
Porter	$30	$25	$ 30	$20
Moore	20	30	20	22
Totals	$50	$55	$ 50	$42
Unrealized gain (loss) reported on balance sheet in shareholders' equity as accumulated other comprehensive income	$ 5		$ (8)	
Change from prior year reported in other comprehensive income as unrealized gain (loss)	$ 5		$(13)	

In the current assets section of the balance sheet, investments in trading equity securities are reported at their December 31, 2010, and December 31, 2011, fair values of $123,000 and $88,000, respectively. In the long-term ivestments section, the investments in available-for-sale equity securities also are reported at fair values as of December 31, 2010, and December 31, 2011, at $55,000 and $42,000, respectively.

The year-to-year fluctuations in the trading security fair values, a $19,000 unrealized loss in 2010 and a $28,000 unrealized gain in 2011, are reported in the income statement

EXHIBIT 7.7

James Company End-of-Period Balance Sheet (Effects of Investments Only)

	2010	2011
CURRENT ASSETS		
Cash	$(167,000)	$(85,000)
Investments in trading securities at fair value	123,000	88,000
LONG-TERM INVESTMENTS		
Investments in available-for-sale securities at fair value	55,000	42,000
Net effect on assets	$ 11,000	$ 45,000
SHAREHOLDERS' EQUITY		
Retained earnings (net effect in income of equity investments, ignoring income taxes)*	$ 6,000	$ 53,000
Accumulated other comprehensive income		
Cumulative unrealized gain (loss) on available-for-sale securities at fair value	5,000	(8,000)
Net Effect on Shareholders' Equity	$ 11,000	$ 45,000

*See income statement in Exhibit 7.8.

EXHIBIT 7.8

James Company Income Statement Effects

	2010	2011
Other Revenues, (Expenses), Gains, and (Losses)		
Dividend revenue	$ 25,000	$ 20,000
Unrealized gain (loss) on trading securities at fair value	(19,000)	28,000
Realized loss on sale of trading securities		(1,000)
Net Income Effect	$ 6,000	$ 47,000

James Company Statement of Comprehensive Income Effects

(Ignoring income tax effects)	**2010**	**2011**
Effect on net income (see income statement effects above)	$ 6,000	$ 47,000
Other comprehensive income		
Unrealized gain (loss) on available-for-sale securities	5,000	(13,000)
Comprehensive Income Effect	$ 11,000	$ 34,000

(Exhibit 7.8). Available-for-sale securities have a cumulative adjustment from cost to fair value reported in the accumulated other comprehensive income section of the owners' equity section (instead of in net income and retained earnings) because the current year's change is reported as other comprehensive income.

Dividend income is reported in each of the two years. A realized loss on sale of the Watts Company trading equity securities also is reported in 2011. The gain is computed by comparing the new basis (that is, the fair value at the end of 2010) to the selling price, as follows:

Sales price	$ 62,000
December 31, 2010 basis of Watts Company securities	(63,000)
Realized loss on sale	$ (1,000)

The reporting of unrealized gains and losses on available-for-sale securities in owners' equity rather than income has the advantage of deferring short-term value fluctuations on longer-term transactions. Keeping these gains and losses out of current income is a reasonable approach because the intent is not to liquidate in the short run. However, earnings management opportunities are created by the special treatment afforded available-for-sale securities: "winners" can be sold, and "losers" can be held in the portfolio. This allows realized gains to be reported as income while unrealized losses as a component of owners' equity are deferred. For example, suppose a company made two recent investments in equity securities classified as available-for-sale. Both were purchased for $10,000. Investment A has appreciated to $11,000 during the current period, and Investment B has declined in fair value to $9,500. If the company wanted to report more income during the current period, Investment A could be sold at a gain of $1,000. Otherwise, the $1,000 would be disclosed as an unrealized gain in the shareholder's equity section. Similar discretion to generate a loss exists with respect to Investment B. Comprehensive income would not be affected by the discretion indicated in this example. Available-for-sale gains and losses, realized or unrealized, are part of comprehensive income.

Exhibit 7.9 presents journal entries.

EXHIBIT 7.9: JOURNAL ENTRIES

2010 purchase of investments		
Investments in Trading Securities	142,000	
Investments in Available-for-Sale Securities	50,000	
Cash		192,000
2010 dividend receipts		
Cash	25,000	
Dividend Revenue		25,000
12/31/10 adjustments to fair value		
Unrealized Loss on Adjustment of Trading Securities to Fair Value	19,000	
Investments in Trading Securities		19,000
Investments in Available-for-Sale Securities	5,000	
Cumulative Unrealized Loss/Gain on Adjustment of Available-for-Sale Securities to Fair Value (OCI)		5,000
2011 dividend receipts		
Cash	20,000	
Dividend Revenue		20,000
2011 sale of Watts Company securities		
Cash	62,000	
Realized Loss on Sale of Trading Securities	1,000	
Investment in Trading Securities		63,000
12/31/11 adjustments to fair value		
Investments in Trading Securities	28,000	
Unrealized Gain on Adjustment of Trading Securities to Fair Value		28,000
Unrealized Loss/Gain on Adjustments of Available-for-Sale Securities to Fair Value (OCI)	13,000	
Investments in Available-for-Sale Securities		13,000

The different treatment given to unrealized gains and losses on available-for-sale securities in net income versus other comprehensive income creates the need to *recycle* realized gains and losses through net income when an available-for-sale security is sold. Extending Example 14, assume that the portfolio of available-for-sale securities was sold during 2012 for $42,000, the portfolio's fair value at December 31, 2011. At that date, the portfolio had a cost of $50,000 and the accumulated comprehensive loss reported in shareholders' equity was $8,000 to reflect the downward valuation of the portfolio. When the portfolio is sold, the loss of $8,000 is realized and reported in (recycled through) net income and then included in retained earnings. The accumulated other comprehensive loss of $8,000 is removed from shareholders' equity by being recognized as a gain in 2012 other comprehensive income. Therefore, the unrealized fair value gains and losses flow through accumulated other comprehensive income (described in Chapter 2 as a temporary "holding tank") until they are realized in cash, at which time they flow through net income and ultimately into retained earnings. Because the realized loss is reported in net income and the decrease in the accumulated other comprehensive loss also is reported in other comprehensive income, the two income effects cancel each other, avoiding double counting in comprehensive income. In other words, comprehensive income reflects fair value gains and losses in the available-for-sale portfolio when they occur during the first two years, not when the securities are sold.

Held-to-Maturity Investments in Debt Securities

Debt securities do not convey voting rights, so controlling influence is not an issue. Therefore, accounting for debt securities classified as trading and available-for-sale parallels the rules for investments in equity securities. Interest revenue determined using the effective interest method illustrated in Chapter 6 is reported on the income statement, and debt amortization is added back to net income in the case of a discount in the operating section of the statement of cash flows (amortization of a premium is deducted from net income in the operating section). At each reporting date, the debt securities are marked-to-market (that is, reported at fair value).

Held-to-maturity debt securities are investments for which managers have the intent and ability to hold to maturity. (Note that "maturity" does not necessarily imply a long-term holding period. If a held-to-maturity debt security is due to mature within one year, it is reported as a current asset.) While intent is quite subjective, ability is less subjective. If, for example, a company has a large liability coming due before the debt investment matures, the investment may have to be liquidated in order to extinguish the liability. Thus, the matching of maturities of assets and liabilities central to financial management is important in documenting the ability to hold to maturity. Held-to-maturity debt investments are reported at amortized cost at each balance sheet date. Standard setters have concluded that short-run fluctuations in market value are less relevant in predicting the level and riskiness of cash flows because the debt security will not be sold before it matures and, hence, will not be subject to the risk of short-run market fluctuations. Accordingly, held-to-maturity debt securities are *not* marked-to-market on the balance sheet, but fair values are *disclosed* in the notes.

Example 15

PepsiCo reports $213 million of short-term investments in the Current Assets section of its December 27, 2008 Consolidated Balance Sheet (Appendix A). In the MD&A discussion titled "Our Liquidity and Capital Resources" (Appendix B), PepsiCo discusses short-term investment activity, and PepsiCo's Statement of Cash Flows (Appendix A) confirms the discussion by reporting that net sales of short-term investments generated more than $1 billion in 2008. Note 10, "Financial Instruments" (Appendix A), provides a list of all of PepsiCo's financial assets, but it does not provide a direct explanation of the composition of the $213 million included in short-term investments. The $98 million relates to short-term investments in index funds that, due to very short maturities, approximate market value. The $41 million is classified as available-for-sale securities. The market values of these securities fell during 2008. The Comprehensive Income Statement provided as part of the Consolidated Statement of Shareholders' Equity reports a $21 million unrealized loss on these securities, net of tax.

Example 16

Qualcomm Incorporated develops, manufactures, and markets digital wireless telecommunications products and services. Qualcomm describes its accounting policy for marketable securities in the notes accompanying its 2008 Form 10-K, which follows. (Exhibit 7.10 provides a portion of the note disclosure.)

> ***Marketable Securities.*** The appropriate classification of marketable securities is determined at the time of purchase, and such designation is reevaluated as of each balance sheet date. Available-for-sale securities are stated at fair value as determined by the most recently traded price of each security at the balance sheet date. For securities that may not have been actively traded in a given period, fair value is determined using matrix pricing and other valuation techniques. The net unrealized gains or losses on available-for-sale securities are reported as a component of other comprehensive income (loss), net of tax. The specific identification method is used to compute the realized gains and losses on debt and equity securities.

EXHIBIT 7.10

Qualcomm Incorporated Marketable Securities Note from 2008 Form 10-K
Available-for-sale securities were comprised as follows (in millions):

	Cost	Unrealized Gains	Unrealized Losses	Fair Value
September 28, 2008				
Equity securities	$2,810	$ 90	$(283)	$2,617
Debt securities	6,966	12	(166)	6,812
	$9,776	$ 102	$(449)	$9,429
September 30, 2007				
Equity securities	$2,941	$ 492	$ (43)	$3,390
Debt securities	6,042	18	(46)	6,014
	$8,983	$ 510	$ (89)	$9,404

The following table shows the gross unrealized losses and fair values of the Company's investments in individual securities that have been in a continuous unrealized loss position deemed to be temporary for less than 12 months and for more than 12 months, aggregated by investment category, at September 28, 2008 (in millions):

	Less than 12 months		More than 12 months	
	Fair Value	Unrealized Losses	Fair Value	Unrealized Losses
Corporate bonds and notes	$1,524	$ (46)	$219	$ (9)
Mortgage- and asset-backed securities	457	(18)	8	—
Non-investment grade debt securities	864	(78)	87	(9)
Government-sponsored enterprise bonds	353	(2)	—	—
Debt mutual funds	86	(4)	—	—
Equity securities	784	(115)	6	(1)
Equity mutual funds and exchange-traded funds	1,229	(167)	—	—
	$5,297	$(430)	$320	$(19)

The unrealized losses on the Company's investments in marketable securities were caused primarily by a major disruption in U.S. and foreign credit and financial markets affecting consumers and the banking, finance and housing industries. This disruption is evidenced by a deterioration of confidence in financial markets and a severe decline in the availability of capital and demand for debt and equity securities. The result has been depressed securities values in most types of investment- and non-investment-grade bonds and debt obligations, mortgage- and asset-backed securities and equity securities. At October 31, 2008, gross unrealized gains were approximately $75 million and gross unrealized losses were approximately $1.3 billion. When assessing marketable securities for other-than-temporary declines in value, the Company considers factors including: how significant the decline in value is as a percentage of the original cost, the underlying factors contributing to a decline in the prices of securities in a single asset class, how long the market value of the investment has been less than its original cost, the performance of the investee's stock price in relation to the stock price of its competitors in the industry, expected market volatility and the market in general, analyst recommendations, the views of external investment managers, any news or financial information that has been released specific to the investee and

(*Continued*)

EXHIBIT 7.10 (Continued)

the outlook for the overall industry in which the investee operates. The Company's analyses of the severity and duration of price declines, market research, industry reports, economic forecasts and the specific circumstances of issuers indicate that it is reasonable to expect marketable securities with unrealized losses to recover in fair value up to the Company's cost bases within a reasonable period of time. Further, the Company has the ability and the intent to hold such securities until they recover. Accordingly, the Company considers the unrealized losses to be temporary at September 28, 2008.

Qualcomm has investments in both debt and equity securities classified as available-for-sale. Qualcomm uses the note disclosure to indicate the unrealized gains and losses on these securities. If these gains and losses are temporary, they will reverse. Qualcomm divides the securities into two groups based on the amount of time for which losses they consider temporary have persisted for more than 12 months. Also note that Qualcomm links the losses to the downward turn in prices in the mortgage-backed securities markets of 2007 and 2008.

In assessing the quality of accounting information, analysts must decide whether to include any change in the unrealized holding gain or loss on securities classified as available-for-sale in earnings for the period. The principal argument for excluding such amounts is that the unrealized gain or loss may likely reverse or may not be realized for many years, if ever. The principal argument for including the change in earnings relates to the fact that regardless of whether it is realized, the gain or loss has economic significance and therefore has a bearing on evaluation of the firm's investment performance. The various disclosures of investment gains and losses are particularly important for financial services firms such as banks and insurers because performance and management of the investment portfolio is critically important to the profitability and risk of financial services firms and because of the sheer magnitude of the numbers. For example, Citigroup, Inc.'s 2008 annual report discloses 2008 unrealized losses on available-for-sale securities totaling $10,118 million. Although this amount appears in Citigroup's comprehensive income, it is not part of its $27,684 million net loss for 2008. Insurance giant AIG also reported a 2008 net unrealized loss on available-for-sale securities of $8,722 million.

"Other than Temporarily Impaired Securities"

As you have learned in the preceding sections, declines in fair values of available-for-sale and held-to-maturity investments are not reflected in net income until they are realized through the sale or maturity of the security. This accounting is driven by the assumption that for available-for-sale securities, the fair value declines might reverse and for held-to-maturity securities, the investor will hold the securities to maturity and collect the interest and maturity value.

If managers of the firm determine that the securities are "other than temporarily impaired," the securities must be written down to fair value, with the unrealized loss reported in net income of the period. For this reason, in each period, managers must test whether securities that have experienced unrealized losses are "other than temporarily impaired." Note that disclosures will show how long "temporarily" impaired securities have remained impaired and that discussions often will describe the reasons for management's belief that interest and maturity values of debt securities will be collected.

Minority, Active Investments

Firms often acquire shares of another corporation to exert significant influence over that company's activities. This significant influence is usually at a broad policy-making level through representation on the other corporation's board of directors. Because of wide dispersion of ownership of most publicly held corporations, and the fact that many shareholders do not vote their shares, firms can exert significant influence over another corporation with ownership of less than a majority of the voting stock. Investments of between 20 and 50 percent of the voting stock of another company are minority, active investments unless evidence indicates that the acquiring firm cannot exert significant influence or the investing firm is deemed the VIE's primary beneficiary as defined by *Interpretation No. 46R* (discussed in a later section).

U.S. GAAP and IFRS require firms to account for minority, active investments, generally those for which ownership is between 20 and 50 percent, using the *equity method.*[27] Under the equity method, the firm owning shares in another firm recognizes as income (loss) each period its share of the net income (loss) of the other firm. See, for example, the income statement of PepsiCo (Appendix A). "Bottling equity income" of $374 million in 2008 represents PepsiCo's share of the earnings from 20–50 percent-owned bottling affiliates. The investor treats dividends received from the investee as a return of investment, not as income. Therefore, PepsiCo's balance sheet reporting of "Investments in Noncontrolled Affiliates" of $3,883 million at December 27, 2008, represents its original investment plus the accumulated amount of bottling equity income it has recognized over time minus the dividends it has received from its noncontrolled affiliates.

The rationale for using the equity method when significant influence is present is best understood by considering the financial statement effects of using the (alternative) fair value method for securities classified as available-for-sale in these circumstances. Under the fair value method, the investor recognizes income or loss on the income statement only when it receives a dividend or sells all or part of the investment. Suppose, as often happens, that the investee finances its own growing operations through retention of earnings and consistently declares dividends that are significantly less than its net income. The market price of the investee's shares will probably increase to reflect the retention of assets generated by earnings. Under the fair value method, the investor's only reported income from the investment will be the modest dividends received because the investment will likely be classified as available-for-sale, and the unrealized gains from fair value changes in the investment are reported in other comprehensive income.

Because of its ownership percentage, the investor can influence the dividend policy of the investee and thereby influence the amount of income recognized under the fair value method. Under these conditions, the fair value method may not reasonably reflect the earnings of the investee generated under the investor's influence. The equity method provides a better measure of a firm's earnings and of its investment when, because of its ownership interest, it can significantly influence the operations and dividend policy of another firm.

Under the equity method, the investor reports its investment in the investee on the balance sheet at acquisition cost plus (minus) the investor's share of the investee's net income (loss) each period. In deriving cash flow from operations on the statement of cash flows,

[27] Relevant standards for investments representing significant influence (minority, active investments) are as follows: Accounting Principles Board, *Opinion No. 18*, "The Equity Method of Accounting for Investments in Common Stock" (1971); Financial Accounting Standards Board, *Interpretation No. 35*, "Criteria for Applying the Equity Method of Accounting for Investments in Common Stock" (1981); *FASB Codification Topic 323;* and International Accounting Standards Board, *International Accounting Standard 28*, "Investments in Associates" (1989).

the investor subtracts its share of the investee's earnings from net income and adds any cash dividends received from the investee. Many firms net these two adjustments on the statement of cash flows, in which the investor would subtract its share of the investee's *undistributed* earnings (equity income minus dividends).

Example 17

On January 1, 2010, Lake Co. bought 40 percent of Pond Co. common stock at a cost of $500,000. Pond Co.'s net assets have a book value of $1,000,000. Assume that the individual fair values of identifiable net assets are equal to the book values of Pond's assets except for a building that has a fair value that is $150,000 above book value. The building has an estimated remaining useful life of ten years. During 2010, Pond's net income is $50,000 and it pays $30,000 in dividends.

Lake Co. paid $500,000 to acquire 40 percent of Pond Co., which implies that $460,000 was paid for identifiable net assets and $40,000 for unidentifiable assets, as follows:

Price paid	$ 500,000
Fair value of identifiable net assets acquired ($1,150,000 × 40%)	(460,000)
Unidentifiable asset acquired (implied goodwill)	$ 40,000

If Lake were to use the market method, the investment in Pond Co. would be market-to-market at year-end. Further, $12,000 in dividend revenue ($30,000 × 40 percent) would be reported in the income statement. Under the equity method, however, the investee's income triggers the investor's income recognition rather than the distribution of dividends. Lake's investment income is determined as follows:

Investee earnings ($50,000 × 40%)	$20,000
Excess building depreciation ($150,000 × 40%/10 years)	(6,000)
Investment revenue	$14,000

The investee (Pond Co.) calculated its $50,000 income by basing depreciation charges on the book values of its assets. Under the equity method, the investor (Lake) records its pro rata share of investee income of $20,000 ($50,000 × 40 percent). However, from Lake's point of view, the resources committed to generating 40 percent of Pond's revenues are greater than 40 percent of Pond's costs because Lake paid $60,000 extra for the appreciated building when it purchased the 40 percent interest. Allocation of the cost of that extra investment also must be reflected in income measurement (hence, the $6,000 additional depreciation expense).

The Investment in Pond Co. account is reported in the long-term investments section of the balance sheet at the original cost plus increases in the investment from the investee's income less decreases in the investment from dividend distribution, as follows:

Investment in Pond (original cost) at January 1, 2010	$500,000
Lake's adjusted share of Pond's earnings	14,000
Lake's share of Pond's dividends ($30,000 × 40%)	(12,000)
Investment in Pond reported at December 31, 2010	$502,000

Exhibit 7.11 summarizes the financial statement effects for Lake Company of its equity method investment in Pond.

EXHIBIT 7.11: FINANCIAL STATEMENT EFFECTS FOR LAKE COMPANY (EQUITY METHOD OF ACCOUNTING FOR ACTIVE MINORITY INVESTMENTS)

Assets	=	Liabilities	+	Total Shareholders' Equity CC	AOCI	RE
Acquisition of investment Investment in Pond +500,000 Cash −500,000						
Dividends received Investment in Pond −12,000 Cash +12,000						
Recognition of Pond's earnings Investment in Pond +14,000						Equity in Affiliate Earnings +14,000

Acquisition of investment		
Investment in Pond	500,000	
Cash		500,000
Dividends received		
Cash	12,000	
Investment in Pond		12,000
Recognition of share of Pond's earnings		
Investment in Pond	14,000	
Equity in Affiliate Earnings		14,000

Although Lake's net income includes an increment of $14,000 from investment revenue, it received only $12,000 of cash dividends. Therefore, Lake's statement of cash flows will report a $2,000 deduction in the operating activities section for undistributed earnings of affiliates.

Minority, active investments are *related parties.* Sales to and purchases from related parties, including any receivable and payable relationships, must be disclosed in the notes to the financial statements.[28] Related-party transactions with minority, active investments are not eliminated from the investor's financial statements. However, profit lodged in inventory from intercompany sales or purchases must be eliminated by reducing both equity in net income of the affiliate and the Investment in Affiliate account. Assume that Lake sold inventory costing $75 to Pond for $100. Pond holds $10 of the inventory at year-end. Lake must eliminate $1 profit because, based on the gross margin percentage of 25 percent (= $25 profit/$100 selling price), the $10 inventory contains $2.50 in profit and Lake owns 40 percent of Pond ($2.50 × 40% = $1).

The analyst also should be cautious when examining the financial statements of firms in other countries that do not prepare under IFRS. Firms commonly use the equity method for minority, active investments in Canada, France, and Great Britain and in certain filings with the Ministry of Finance in Japan. Countries that follow a strict legal definition of the entity, such as Germany, tend to report these intercorporate investments at acquisition cost, even when significant influence is present.

[28] Detailed related-party disclosures can be found in Financial Accounting Standards Board, *Statement of Financial Accounting Standards No. 57*, "Related Party Disclosures" (1982); *FASB Codification Topic 850;* International Accounting Standards Board, *International Accounting Standard 24*, "Related Party Disclosures" (revised 2003); and International Accounting Standards Board, *International Accounting Standard 1*, "Presentation of Financial Statements" (revised 2007).

Example 18

PepsiCo owns less than a majority interest in its major affiliated bottling operations, but it still exerts significant influence over its affiliates' operations, for strategic reasons, which we discussed in Chapter 1 and which PepsiCo discusses throughout its 2008 Annual Report (Appendix B). The assets and liabilities of these bottlers do not appear on PepsiCo's balance sheet, but summary financial information for Pepsi Bottling Group (PBG) and PepsiAmericas (PAS) appears in Note 8, "Noncontrolled Bottling Affiliates" (Appendix A). A later section demonstrates the procedure an analyst might follow to incorporate amounts for such investments on the balance sheet. PepsiCo reports "Bottling equity income" of $374 million on its income statement for 2008 (Appendix A). To compute cash flow from operations, PepsiCo's statement of cash flows shows a subtraction from net income of $202 million for "Bottling equity income, net of dividends," suggesting that PepsiCo received dividends of $172 million from these intercorporate investments during 2008. PepsiCo derived less than 10 percent of its pretax earnings from equity method investees during 2006–2008. Companies must disclose partial balance sheet and income statement information for significant intercorporate investments, as well as the fair value of the investments.[29] PepsiCo states in Note 8 that for its two most significant affiliates, PBG and PAS, investment fair values exceed book values by $567 million and $143 million, respectively.

Majority, Active Investments

When one investor firm owns more than 50 percent of the voting stock of another company, the investor firm generally has control. This control may occur at both a broad policy-making level and a day-to-day operational level. The majority investor in this case is the *parent,* and the majority-owned company is the *subsidiary.* Financial reporting requires combining, or *consolidating,* the financial statements of majority-owned companies with those of the parent (unless for legal or other reasons the parent cannot exercise control).[30]

Reasons for Legally Separate Corporations

For several reasons, a parent company may prefer to operate as a group of legally separate corporations rather than as a single legal entity. For example, separate operations reduce financial risk. Separate corporations may mine raw materials, transport them to a manufacturing plant, produce the product, and sell the finished product to the public. If any part of the total process proves to be unprofitable or inefficient, losses from insolvency fall only on the owners and creditors of the one subsidiary corporation. Furthermore, creditors have a claim on the assets of the subsidiary corporation only, not on the assets of the

---

[29] Companies also may choose the fair value option to report minority active investments, recording all gains and losses from revaluation in operating income.

[30] Accounting for investments that represent control (majority, active investments) is governed by Committee on Accounting Procedure, *Accounting Research Bulletin No. 51,* "Consolidated Financial Statements," as amended by *Statement of Financial Accounting Standards No. 94,* "Consolidation of Majority-Owned Subsidiaries" (1987); Financial Accounting Standards Board, *Interpretation No. 46R,* "Consolidation of Variable Interest Entities" (2003) (referred to as *Interpretation No. 46R*); Financial Accounting Standards Board, *Statement of Financial Accounting Standards No. 167,* "Amendments for FASB Interpretation No. 46(R)" (2009); Financial Accounting Standards Board, *Statement of Financial Accounting Standards No. 166,* "Accounting for Transfers of Financial Assets—an amendment of FASB Statement No. 140" (2009); *FASB Codification Topic 810;* International Accounting Standards Board, *International Accounting Standard 28,* "Investments in Associates" (1989); International Accounting Standards Board, *International Accounting Standard 27,* "Consolidated and Separate Financial Statements" (revised 2003); International Accounting Standards Board, *International Financial Reporting Standard 3,* "Business Combinations" (revised 2008); and International Accounting Standards Board, *Standing Interpretations Committee Interpretation 12,* "Special Purpose Entities" (1998).

parent company. For corporations with potential environmental and product liabilities, legal separation through the use of subsidiaries can be especially advantageous. Also, if a firm does business in many states and countries, often it must contend with overlapping and inconsistent taxation, regulations, and legal requirements. Organizing separate corporations to conduct the operations in the various jurisdictions may reduce administrative costs. Control can be achieved with less than 100 percent ownership of the common shares, which can reduce the amount of capital needed for the investment, and that can make strategic expansion easier. Finally, sometimes there are organizational benefits to operating separate entities, such as incentive alignment between managers and investors when stock in a focused firm can be part of compensation.

Purpose of Consolidated Statements

For a variety of reasons then, a parent and several legally separate subsidiaries may exist as a single economic entity. A consolidation of the financial statements of the parent and each of its subsidiaries presents the results of operations, financial position, and changes in cash flows of an affiliated group of companies under the control of a parent, essentially as if the group of companies were a single entity. The parent and each subsidiary are legally separate entities, but they operate as one centrally controlled economic entity. Consolidated financial statements generally provide more useful information to the shareholders of the parent corporation than do separate financial statements of the parent and each subsidiary.

In general, consolidated financial statements also provide more useful information than does the equity method used to account for minority, active investments. The parent, because of its voting interest, can effectively control the use of the subsidiary's individual assets. Consolidation of the individual assets, liabilities, revenues, and expenses of both the parent and the subsidiary provides a more realistic picture of the operations and financial position of the whole economic entity.

In a legal sense, consolidated statements merely supplement, and do not replace, the separate statements of the individual corporations, although it is common practice in the U.S. to present only the consolidated statements in published annual reports. In some cases, firms do report separate financial statements for consolidated subsidiaries (for example, large conglomerates such as General Electric and Ford reporting separate financial statements for their finance subsidiaries).

Corporate Acquisitions and Consolidated Financial Statements Illustrated

Corporate acquisitions occur when one corporation acquires a majority ownership interest and control in another corporation. Accounting for corporate acquisitions is governed by SFAS 141, 141R, 160 (FASB codification topics 805 and 810) and IFRS 3.[31] Current standards are the result of a joint project between the FASB and IASB on business combinations. This section deals with two types of business combinations: (1) *statutory*

[31] Financial Accounting Standards Board, *Statement No. 141R* (which requires the acquisition method for business combinations) replaces *Statement No. 141*, which required firms to account for all corporate acquisitions using the purchase method. For many years prior to the issuance of *Statement No. 141*, U.S. GAAP required firms to use one of two methods to account for corporate acquisitions: a version of the purchase method or the pooling-of-interests method. The pooling-of-interests method viewed a corporate acquisition as a uniting of the ownership interests of two entities that, while legally combined, continued to operate as they did as separate entities prior to the acquisition. To qualify for the pooling-of-interests method under the rules when it was an allowable reporting technique, the "acquiring" firm had to exchange shares of its common stock for the common stock of the "acquired" company. Most firms preferred to account for corporate acquisitions as pooling of interests rather than as purchases because of the positive effect on earnings subsequent to the acquisition. Pooling, however, has not been an allowable method for some time.

mergers that result when one entity acquires all of the assets and liabilities of another entity and places the acquired assets and liabilities on its books and (2) *acquisitions* of between 51 and 100 percent of the common stock of an acquired entity, where the acquired entity continues to operate as a separate legal entity with separate financial records. Both types of business combinations use the *acquisition method* as laid out in *SFAS 141R* and have the same financial statement effects. However, acquisitions of over 50 percent are active, majority investments as described in the preceding section and thus require the preparation of consolidation worksheets to support consolidated financial statements.

Example 19

On December 31, 2009, Parker issues 100,000 shares of its common stock to acquire 100 percent of the common stock of Smith Company. In addition, Parker agrees to pay former Smith Company shareholders an additional $500,000 in cash if certain earnings projections are achieved over the next two years. Based on probabilities of achieving the earnings projections, Parker estimates the fair value of this promise to be $300,000. Parker pays $20,000 in legal fees and $25,000 in stock issue costs to effect the acquisition. Parker also incurs $10,000 in internal costs related to management's time to complete the transaction. Parker's shares have a fair value of $30 per share at the date of acquisition. Exhibit 7.12 provides the book values of Parker Company and the book and fair values of Smith Company at the date of acquisition.

Assuming a Statutory Merger. To record the acquisition assuming that Smith Company is dissolved (a statutory merger), the acquisition method is applied to this business combination using the following three steps:

1. *Measure the fair value of the consideration transferred to acquire Smith.* A key concept underlying the acquisition method is measurement of the transaction at the fair value transferred by Parker. Parker chose to issue common stock with a fair value of $3,000,000 (10,000 shares × $30 fair value per share) and to incur a liability (the contingent consideration obligation) with a fair value of $300,000. Parker also incurred $55,000 in related legal costs, internal costs, and stock issue costs. Because *SFAS No. 157* defines fair value as the price received to sell an asset or the price paid to transfer a liability in an orderly transaction between market participants at the measurement date, standard setters concluded that the fair value of the transaction is the net proceeds from the stock issue, $2,975,000 (= $3,000,000 − $25,000 costs to issue), plus the fair value of the stock issue costs, $25,000, plus the fair value of the liability assumed, $300,000, which sum to $3,300,000. (Alternatively, just add the fair value of the stock issued to the fair value of the liability assumed because stock issue costs appear as an addition to and subtraction from fair value.) The legal costs of $20,000 and the internal costs of $10,000 are expenses of the period and are not considered part of the acquisition price.
2. *Measure the fair values of the identifiable assets acquired, liabilities assumed, and noncontrolling interests (if any).* In arriving at the $3,300,000 acquisition price, Parker estimated the value of the net assets of Smith Company whether or not they were recorded on Smith's books. The information provided in Exhibit 7.12 indicates that cash, accounts payable, and notes payable had acquisition date fair values equal to their book values. The equality of book and fair values for short-term monetary assets and liabilities (that is, assets and liabilities with fixed cash flows set by contract) is common. Also, with the advent of the fair value option, the likelihood that book values and fair values will be identical increases. Parker estimates

EXHIBIT 7.12

Date of Acquisition Book and Fair Values for Parker Company and Smith Company

	Parker Company **Book Values** at 12/31/09	Smith Company **Book Values** at 12/31/09	Smith Company **Fair Values** at 12/31/09
Cash	$ 900,000	$ 400,000	$ 400,000
Receivables	1,400,000	500,000	450,000
Inventory	1,700,000	1,200,000	1,400,000
PP&E (net)	14,000,000	1,600,000	2,000,000
Customer lists	0	0	100,000
Unpatented technology	0	0	200,000
In-process R&D	0	0	300,000
Total Assets	$ 18,000,000	$ 3,700,000	$ 4,850,000
Accounts payable	$ (600,000)	$ (400,000)	$ (400,000)
Notes payable	(5,100,000)	(2,100,000)	(2,100,000)
Total Liabilities	$ (5,700,000)	$(2,500,000)	$(2,500,000)
Common stock ($1 par)	$ (200,000)	$ (100,000)	
Additional paid-in capital	(4,400,000)	(500,000)	
Retained earnings, 1/1/09	(3,700,000)	(300,000)	
Revenues	(9,000,000)	(2,000,000)	
Expenses	5,000,000	1,700,000	
Total Shareholders' Equity	$(12,300,000)	$(1,200,000)	

Revenues, gains, and net income are in parentheses to indicate that their signs are opposite those of expenses and losses; that is, they are credits for those interpreting the worksheet from the accountant's traditional debit/credit approach. Liabilities and shareholders' equity accounts are in parentheses to indicate that they are claims against assets; again, they are credits in the traditional debit/credit framework.

the fair value of receivables to be $450,000, which is $50,000 less than book value, an indication that Parker believes that Smith has under-reserved for potential uncollectible accounts. Parker estimates that Smith's nonmonetary assets, inventory and property, plant, and equipment, have fair values that are greater than their book values. Under SFAS 141R, an acquirer must recognize separately from goodwill any intangible assets that arise from legal or contractual rights or that can be sold or otherwise separated from the acquired enterprise. SFAS 141 and 141R identify a nonexhaustive list of possible identifiable intangible assets other than goodwill that meet the criteria for recognition as assets. (See Exhibit 7.13.) Parker identifies three such intangible assets that are not recorded on Smith's books. Smith has customer lists with fair values of $100,000, unpatented technology that has a fair value of $200,000, and in-process R&D that has a fair value of $300,000. These assets have no book value because Smith engaged in internal marketing, advertising, and R&D activities to create them. By rule, these costs must be expensed as incurred by Smith.

EXHIBIT 7.13

Examples of Intangible Assets that Meet the Criteria of Recognition Separately from Goodwill

Marketing-related intangible assets

Trademarks, trade names[CL]
Service marks, collective marks, certification marks[CL]
Trade dress (unique color, shape, or package design)[CL]
Newspaper mastheads[CL]
Internet domain names[CL]
Noncompetition agreements[CL]

Customer-related intangible assets

Customer lists[S]
Order or production backlog[S]
Customer contracts and related customer relationships[S]
Noncontractual customer relationships[S]

Artistic-related intangible assets

Plays, operas, and ballets[CL]
Books, magazines, newspapers, and other literary works[CL]
Musical works such as compositions, song lyrics, advertising jingles[CL]
Pictures and photographs[CL]
Video and audiovisual material, including motion pictures, music videos, television programs[CL]

Contract-based intangible assets

Licensing, royalty, standstill agreements[CL]
Advertising, construction, management, service, or supply contracts[CL]
Lease agreements[CL]
Construction permits[CL]
Franchise agreements[CL]
Operating and broadcast rights[CL]
Use rights such as landing, drilling, water, air, mineral, timber cutting, and route authorities[CL]
Servicing contracts such as mortgage servicing contracts[CL]
Employment contracts[CL]

Technology-based intangible assets

Patented technology[CL]
Computer software and mask works[CL]
Unpatented technology[S]
Databases, including title plants[S]
Trade secrets, including secret formulas, processes, recipes[CL]

(Source: SFAS 141 and SFAS 141R)

[CL]indicates that the assets meet the *Contractual/Legal* criterion. (The asset also might meet the separability criterion, but that is not necessary for recognition.)

[S]indicates that the asset does not meet the contractual/legal criterion, but does meet the *Separability* criterion.

3. *Assign any excess consideration to goodwill or record a gain from a bargain purchase.* The difference between the fair value given by the acquirer and the fair values of the individual identifiable assets is goodwill. In this example, Parker gave $3,300,000 to acquire net assets of Smith that had a fair value of $2,350,000 (= $4,850,000 fair value assets − $2,500,000 fair value liabilities). Therefore, goodwill is the difference, $950,000 (= $3,300,000 − $2,350,000). The parties, in their negotiation, assign an enterprise value to Smith that exceeds the sum of the fair values of identifiable assets. Goodwill represents the superior expected profitability of Smith's operations that exceeds what one would expect from Smith's assets.

   If Parker acquired Smith at a bargain, the fair value given would have been less than the fair values of the individual identifiable assets. Bargain purchases rarely occur given the rational behavior of owners. However, they do exist, often because of some unusual circumstance that requires a quick liquidation of a company, such as the death of an owner or forced liquidation due to bankruptcy or other financial distress. If a bargain purchase occurs, the acquirer has an economic gain equal to the fair value received less the fair value given. The gain is reported on the acquirer's income statement.

Exhibit 7.14 shows the effects of the acquisition and the journal entry to record the acquisition on Parker's books at December 31, 2009.

Parker records the fair value of assets and liabilities received from Smith and the fair values of consideration given to Smith's shareholders (the contingent performance obligation and the common stock issued). Note that identifiable intangible assets, in-process

EXHIBIT 7.14: FINANCIAL STATEMENT EFFECTS OF A MERGER (ACQUISITION DATE)

Assets		=	Liabilities		+	Total Shareholders' Equity				
						CC		AOCI	RE	
Cash	+400,000		Accounts Payable	+400,000		Common Stock	+100,000			
Receivables	+450,000		Notes Payable	+2,100,000		APIC	+2,900,000			
Inventory	+1,400,000		Contingent Performance Obligation	+300,000						
PP&E	+2,000,000									
Customer Lists	+100,000									
Unpatented Technology	+200,000									
In-Process R&D	+300,000									
Goodwill	+950,000									
Legal and management costs:										
Cash	−30,000								Operating expenses	−30,000
Stock issue costs:										
Cash	−25,000					APIC	−25,000			

Cash	400,000	
Receivables	450,000	
Inventory	1,400,000	
PP&E	2,000,000	
Customer Lists	100,000	
Unpatented Technology	200,000	
In-Process R&D	300,000	
Goodwill	950,000	
Accounts Payable		400,000
Notes Payable		2,100,000
Contingent Performance Obligation		300,000
Common Stock		100,000
APIC		2,900,000
(to record fair values paid and received)		
Operating Expenses	30,000	
Cash		30,000
(to record legal fees and management time)		
APIC	25,000	
Cash		25,000
(to record stock issue costs)		

R&D, and goodwill are recorded at their fair values even though their original book values on Smith's books were zero. Given that many firms expensed in-process R&D in the past, the change in U.S. GAAP and IFRS to the current acquisition accounting standards is a significant change for firms acquiring technology-intensive firms. Legal costs and management time related to the combination are expensed as part of operating expenses. Stock issue costs reduce the proceeds of the issue and thus are treated as a reduction of additional paid-in capital.

Because Smith's assets and liabilities now appear on Parker's books and Smith no longer exists as a separate legal entity, Parker does not have to prepare consolidated financial statements.

Assuming an Acquisition. If the terms of the business combination cause Smith to continue as a separate legal entity (an acquisition), the date of acquisition journal entry differs from the entry used to record a statutory merger. Exhibit 7.15 shows the effects of the acquisition and the journal entry to record the acquisition on Parker's books if Smith continues as a separate legal entity. In an acquisition, Parker records a single account, "Investment in Smith," to represent its interest in the fair values of Smith. The remaining entries are identical to the entries for a merger.

Because Smith's assets and liabilities do not appear on Parker's books and Parker controls Smith, Parker must prepare consolidated financial statements to reflect the substance of the entity over its legal form. The following schedule is a review of why Parker paid $3,300,000 to acquire Smith's shares. The fair value allocation schedule shows three components present in the $3,300,000 acquisition price. The first two are (1) the book value of Smith and (2) the amounts by which individual identifiable assets exceed their book values. The sum of the first two components equals the fair value of the identifiable assets of Smith. The third component is goodwill.

EXHIBIT 7.15: FINANCIAL STATEMENT EFFECTS OF AN ACQUISITION (ACQUISITION DATE)

Assets		=	Liabilities		+	Total Shareholders' Equity				
						CC		AOCI	RE	
Investment in Smith	+3,300,000		Contingent Performance Obligation	+300,000		Common Stock	+100,000			
						APIC	+2,900,000			
Legal and management costs: Cash	−30,000								Operating Expenses	−30,000
Stock issue costs: Cash	−25,000					APIC	−25,000			

Investment in Smith	3,300,000	
Contingent Performance Obligation		300,000
Common Stock		100,000
APIC		2,900,000
(to record fair values paid and received)		
Operating Expenses	30,000	
Cash		30,000
(to record legal fees and management time)		
APIC	25,000	
Cash		25,000
(to record stock issue costs)		

Fair value allocation schedule (date of acquisition):		
Fair value of consideration transferred by Parker		$ 3,300,000
Book value of Smith (total shareholders' equity from Exhibit 7.12)		(1,200,000)
Excess		$ 2,100,000
Allocation to differences between fair value and book value at acquisition:		
Receivables ($450,000 − $500,000)	$(50,000)	
Inventory ($1,400,000 − $1,200,000)	200,000	
PP&E ($2,000,000 − $1,600,000)	400,000	
Customer Lists ($100,000 − $0)	100,000	
Unpatented Technology ($200,000 − $0)	200,000	
In-Process R&D ($300,000 − $0)	300,000	(1,150,000)
Allocated to goodwill		$ 950,000

Preparing Consolidated Statements at the Date of Acquisition

Exhibit 7.16 presents the worksheet necessary to consolidate Parker and Smith at the date of acquisition. The primary objective of the worksheet is to replace the Investment in Smith account with the aforementioned three components in the account.

1. In the Eliminations column, "Investment in Smith" is removed so that, after the row is summed, the account does not appear in the Consolidated column. From a consolidated viewpoint, the combined Parker and Smith entity does not have an investment in Smith separate from the entity's ownership of all of Smith's assets. Because Parker will add the individual assets and liabilities of Smith into the consolidated totals, maintaining the Investment in Smith account would be double-counting.
2. All of the individual assets and liabilities from Smith Company's own financial statements are added to Parker's individual assets and liabilities by summing each row to obtain the consolidated total. Smith's shareholders' equity accounts are eliminated because no outside ownership of Smith's shares exists. These steps accomplish the objective of having the first component of the acquisition price, *book value of Smith*, appear in the consolidated totals.
3. The remainder of the eliminations add the second (*differences between fair and book values of Smith's identifiable net assets*) and third (*goodwill*) components of acquisition price into the consolidated totals.

The consolidated assets and liabilities appearing in Parker's consolidated financial statements are equal to the sum of Parker's book values and Smith's fair values as remeasured at the acquisition date. Smith's income statement amounts are not part of the consolidation process because the consolidated entity has not yet engaged in operations. Of course, prior year's incomes of Smith Company are reflected in its asset and liability levels. The elimination entries are worksheet entries only. They are not entered in the financial records of Parker or Smith. Therefore, the consolidation worksheet must be prepared each reporting period.

A Note on Acquisition "Reserves"

Use of the acquisition method often entails establishing specific "acquisition reserves" at the time one company acquires another company because the acquiring company may not know the potential losses inherent in the acquired assets or the potential liabilities of the acquired

EXHIBIT 7.16

Date of Acquisition Consolidation Worksheet (December 31, 2009)

	Parker (adjusted for the acquisition) effects)	Smith	Eliminations	Consolidated
INCOME STATEMENT				
Revenues	$ (9,000,000)	—	—	$ (9,000,000)
Expenses	5,030,000	—	—	5,030,000
Net Income	$ (3,970,000)	—	—	$ (3,970,000)
BALANCE SHEET				
Cash	$ 845,000	$ 400,000		$ 1,245,000
Receivables	1,400,000	500,000	$ (50,000)	1,850,000
Inventory	1,700,000	1,200,000	200,000	3,100,000
PP&E (net)	14,000,000	1,600,000	400,000	16,000,000
Investment in Smith	3,300,000	—	(3,300,000)	—
Customer lists	—	—	100,000	100,000
Unpatented technology	—	—	200,000	200,000
In-process R&D	—	—	300,000	300,000
Goodwill	—	—	950,000	950,000
Total Assets	$ 21,245,000	$ 3,700,000	$(1,200,000)	$ 23,745,000
Accounts payable	$ (600,000)	$ (400,000)	—	$ (1,000,000)
Notes payable	(5,100,000)	(2,100,000)	—	(7,200,000)
Contingent performance obligation	(300,000)	—	—	(300,000)
Common stock	(300,000)	(100,000)	$ 100,000	(300,000)
Additional paid-in capital	(7,275,000)	(500,000)	500,000	(7,275,000)
Retained earnings, Dec. 31, 2008	(7,670,000)	(600,000)	600,000	(7,670,000)
Total Liabilities and Shareholders' Equity	$(21,245,000)	$(3,700,000)	$ 1,200,000	$(23,745,000)

Revenues, gains, and net income are in parentheses to indicate that their signs are opposite those of expenses and losses; that is, they are credits for those interpreting the worksheet from the accountant's traditional debit/credit approach. Liabilities and shareholders' equity accounts are in parentheses to indicate that they are claims against assets; again, they are credits in the traditional debit/credit framework.

company.[32] Acquisition reserve accounts increase a liability or reduce an asset. The acquiring company will allocate a portion of the purchase price to various types of acquisition reserves (for example, estimated losses on long-term contracts and estimated liabilities for unsettled lawsuits). An acquiring company has up to one year after the date of acquisition to revalue these acquisition reserves as new information becomes available. After that, the acquisition reserve amounts remain in the accounts and absorb losses as they occur. That is, the acquiring firm charges actual losses against the specific acquisition reserves established, instead of against income, to measure the expected loss.

[32] Chapter 6 discusses the various types of reserve accounts that appear in financial statements. In the title of an account in the U.S. the term *reserve* is generally unacceptable unless it includes a descriptor as to its purpose. U.S. firms generally use more precise titles for reserve accounts, such as allowance for uncollectible accounts and estimated warranty liability.

To illustrate, assume that an acquired company has an unsettled lawsuit for which the acquiring company anticipates that a $10 million pretax loss will ultimately result. It allocates $10 million to an acquisition reserve (estimated liability from lawsuit). The acquiring firm would presumably pay less for this company because of the potential liability. Assume that settlement of the lawsuit occurs three years after the date of the acquisition for $8 million (pretax). The accountant charges the $8 million loss against the $10 million reserve instead of against net income for the year. Furthermore, the accountant reverses the $2 million remaining in the acquisition reserve, increasing net income in the year of the settlement.

Acquisition reserves can affect assessments of the quality of accounting information, and regulators carefully monitor their use (and abuse). When used properly, acquisition reserves are an accounting mechanism that helps ensure that the assets and liabilities of an acquired company reflect market values. However, given the estimates required in establishing such reserves, management has some latitude in managing earnings.

Consolidated Financial Statements Subsequent to Date of Acquisition

For an illustration of the consolidation process after the date of acquisition, consider the Parker acquisition of Smith one year later.

Example 20

Referring to the original data in Example 19 that listed differences between Smith's fair values and book values at the date of acquisition, assume that PP&E, customer lists, unpatented technology, and in-process R&D have remaining useful lives of ten years. Exhibit 7.17 presents the consolidated worksheet one year later on December 31, 2010. To

EXHIBIT 7.17

Consolidation Worksheet One Year after Date of Acquisition

	Parker 12/31/10	Smith 12/31/10	Eliminations	Consolidated 12/31/10
INCOME STATEMENT				
Revenues	(P)	(S)		(P) + (S)
Cost of goods sold	P	S	$200,000	P + S + $200,000
Bad debts expense	P	S	($50,000)	P + S – $50,000
Depreciation expense	P	S	$40,000	P + S + $40,000
Amortization expense	P	S	10,000	
			20,000	P + S + $60,000
			30,000	
Equity in Smith's earnings	(P)		P (to eliminate S's net income adjusted for amortizations of the excesses of fair values over book values)	$0
Net Income	(P)	(S)	S	(P)

(*Continued*)

EXHIBIT 7.17 (Continued)

	Parker 12/31/10	Smith 12/31/10	Eliminations	Consolidated 12/31/10
BALANCE SHEET				
Cash	P	S		P + S
Receivables	P	S		P + S
Inventory	P	S		P + S
PP&E (net)	P	S	$360,000	P + S + $360,000
Investment in Smith	P		(P) (to eliminate equity method balance equal to original investment + S's net income adjusted for amortizations of the excesses of fair values over book values) – S's dividends paid	$0
Customer lists	P		$90,000	P + S + $90,000
Unpatented technology	P		$180,000	P + S + $180,000
In-process R&D	P		$270,000	P + S + $270,000
Goodwill			$950,000	$950,000
Total Assets	P	S	$1,850,000	P + S + $1,850,000
Accounts payable	(P)	(S)		(P) + (S)
Notes payable	(P)	(S)		(P) + (S)
Contingent performance obligation	(P)	(S)		(P) + (S)
Common stock	(P)	(S)	S to eliminate S's shareholders' equity	(P)
Additional paid-in capital	(P)	(S)	S to eliminate S's shareholders' equity	(P)
Retained earnings, 12/31/09	(P)	(S)	S to eliminate S's shareholders' equity	(P)
Total Liabilities and Shareholders' Equity	(P)	(S)	S	(P) + (S's liabilities)

Revenues, gains, and net income are in parentheses to indicate that their signs are opposite those of expenses and losses; that is, they are credits for those interpreting the worksheet from the accountant's traditional debit/credit approach. Liabilities and shareholders' equity accounts are in parentheses to indicate that they are claims against assets; again, they are credits in the traditional debit/credit framework.

focus on eliminations and the meaning of the resulting consolidated numbers, we use P and S for Parker and Smith's own financial statement amounts, respectively. Italicized passages describe the differences between consolidation at acquisition and consolidation subsequent to acquisition.

1. In the Eliminations column, "Investment in Smith" is removed so that, after the row is summed, it does not appear in the Consolidated column. *"Investment in Smith" includes the original investment plus Parker's equity in Smith's earnings for the period (all of Smith's earnings because of 100 percent ownership adjusted for amortizations of the differences between fair and book value) minus Parker's share of Smith's dividends (again, all of Smith's dividends because of 100 percent ownership).*
2. Parker adds all of the individual assets and liabilities from Smith's financial statements to Parker's individual assets and liabilities by summing each row to obtain the consolidated total. Parker eliminates Smith's shareholders' equity accounts because no outside ownership of Smith's shares exists. These steps accomplish the objective of having the first component of the acquisition price, book value of Smith, appear in the consolidated totals. *Smith's assets, liabilities, and owners' equity reflect the book value of Smith at the date of acquisition plus the changes in assets and liabilities from Smith's activities during the year. The changes in assets and liabilities reflected in Smith's income are based on the* book value *of Smith's assets and liabilities. For example, Smith charges cost of goods sold for the book value of inventory when inventory is sold, not the fair value established at the date of acquisition.*
3. A set of adjustments adds the second component (differences between fair and book values of Smith's identifiable net assets) and the third component (goodwill) of acquisition price into the consolidated totals. Exhibit 7.18 supports the entries in the Elimination column. *At the date of acquisition, we deducted $50,000 from receivables in the consolidated worksheet to reflect the lower receivable fair value. Assuming that Parker was correct in believing that the receivables would not be collected (that*

EXHIBIT 7.18

Date of Acquisition Differences	Charged (Credited) to Expense	Balance One Year Later
Receivables: ($50,000)	($50,000) reduction of bad debt expense	$ 0
Inventory: $200,000	$200,000 increase in cost of goods sold	$ 0
PP&E: $400,000	$400,000/10 years = $40,000 increase in depreciation expense	$ 360,000
Customer lists: $100,000	$100,000/10 years = $10,000 increase in amortization expense	$ 90,000
Unpatented technology: $200,000	$200,000/10 years = $20,000 increase in amortization expense	$ 180,000
In-process R&D: $300,000	$300,000/10 years = $30,000 increase in amortization expense	$ 270,000
Allocated to goodwill: $950,000	$0 unless impaired	$ 950,000
Net effects	Decrease income by $250,000	Increase assets by $1,850,000

is, customers defaulted), Smith has shown a larger bad debt expense on its own financial statements due to the unexpected (from its viewpoint) customer defaults in the current year. As Exhibit 7.18 shows, the consolidated worksheet in Exhibit 7.17 reduces bad debts expense by $50,000 and makes no adjustment to accounts receivable. The allocation of all of the fair value/book value acquisition date differences to expenses and none to the asset will occur when an item (accounts receivable in this case) is a current asset. Given that inventory also is a current asset (that is, the inventory is sold in less than a year), Exhibit 7.18 allocates all of the acquisition date $200,000 fair value excess to cost of goods sold and none to inventory. As noted in Item 2 above, Smith based cost of goods sold on book value when it sold the inventory. Parker uses the worksheet to adjust cost of goods sold to the consolidated point of view. The remaining items in Exhibit 7.18 are long-term; therefore, if the items are depreciable or amortizable, a portion of the acquisition date excess fair value will be allocated to expense based on the item's estimated remaining useful life, with the remainder allocated to the asset. Goodwill is not amortized; so the full amount is reflected in the Elimination column as an adjustment to the asset.

4. *Equity in Smith's earnings is eliminated. The one-line consolidation of Smith has been converted to an item-by-item income statement consolidation through addition of revenues and expenses of Parker and Smith across columns.*

We use the letters *P* and *S* instead of numbers in the financial statements of Parker and Smith, respectively, one year later to concentrate on what appears in the Consolidated column subsequent to the date of acquisitions. "Investment in Smith" and "Equity in Smith's earnings" do not appear. The consolidated assets and liabilities appearing in Parker's consolidated financial statements are equal to the sum of Parker's book values and Smith's fair values as measured at the acquisition date and are adjusted for Parker's expensing of a portion of the fair value/book value differences to calculate net income on a consolidated basis. Note that in the case of 100 percent ownership, consolidated net income is simply P's net income under the equity method. Individual revenues and expenses replace the summary of S's income in the Equity in Smith's earnings account, which is already in Parker's net income because of its use of the equity method.

Related-Party Transactions

Several additional transactions must be considered in the preparation of consolidated financial statements. Transactions between the parent and the subsidiary affect their individual financial statements but should not affect the consolidated financial statements. Additional eliminations should be made for:

- Intercompany loans and receivables and the interest expense and revenues from those arrangements. Parents often provide loans to subsidiaries, and the subsidiary's accounting system will show a payable and accrued interest expense on its own books. Similarly, the parent will show a receivable and accrued interest revenue.
- Intercompany sales and purchases and the profits lodged in ending inventory. An earlier section of this chapter discussed investments in affiliates (minority, active investments). Recall that intercompany sales and purchases are disclosed as related-party transactions but are not eliminated. An example also was provided of how profits lodged in inventory on such sales must be eliminated. In the preparation of consolidated financial statements, the intercompany sales and purchases also must be eliminated because the purchases and sales were not with a party outside the consolidated entity. PepsiCo does not eliminate sales to its noncontrolled bottling affiliates. If the affiliates are consolidated, however, PepsiCo eliminates the intercompany sales.

- Intercompany payables and receivables as a result of intercompany sales and purchases. For example, if the parent company purchases inventory from the subsidiary company on credit, the subsidiary will recognize receivables that include payables from the parent.

Other extremely complex transactions that occur between parents and subsidiaries are beyond the scope of this text. However, the guiding principle in the preparation of consolidated financial statements is the need to view the substance of transactions from the consolidated entity's point of view.

What are Noncontrolling Interests?

If an investing firm acquires less than 100 percent of another firm, a *noncontrolling interest* will exist. Many companies use the term *minority interest* to describe the noncontrolling interest in their financial statements. The noncontrolling interest, which may be widely held, has its right to a pro rata portion of net assets, earnings, and dividends. Recent accounting standards have drastically changed accounting for the noncontrolling interest. In the past, an acquisition of less than 100 percent resulted in only a partial remeasurement of the acquired firm's assets and liabilities to fair value. For example, in a 70 percent acquisition, land with a book value of \$100 and fair value of \$110 would be remeasured and reported at \$107 in the consolidated financial statements. The parent's interest in the land would be based on fair value, \$77 (= \$110 × 70%), and the noncontrolling interest would be based on book value, \$30 (= \$100 × 30%). Under current standards (the acquisition method), the basis for recording the acquisition transaction is the fair value of the acquired firm. Therefore, land is remeasured to its fair value of \$110, with a pro rata share allocated to parent and noncontrolling interests. The measurement of noncontrolling interests also extends to goodwill, which puts both controlling and noncontrolling interests at full fair value. However, under IFRS, firms have an option (on a transaction-by-transaction basis) to assign to noncontrolling interests only their pro rata share of differences between fair value and book value of identifiable assets and liabilities, but not goodwill.

Prior to the issuance of the current accounting standards, noncontrolling interests received disclosure on the balance sheet between liabilities and shareholders' equity ("mezzanine" disclosure). Under current accounting standards, noncontrolling interests are a component of shareholders' equity.

Example 21

Exhibit 7.19 presents the separate financial statements at December 31, 2011, of Power Company and its 80 percent owned subsidiary Small Technologies. Two years earlier, on January 1, 2009, Power acquired 80 percent of the common shares of Small for \$3,900 in cash (all amounts in millions). Small's 2010 net income was \$350, but Small paid no dividends in that year. Small's 2011 income was \$450, and it paid \$250 dividends on common stock during 2011.

Shortly after the date of acquisition, Small common stock traded at a share price that was close to the share price Power paid in the acquisition. Because this condition indicated the lack of a control premium, the fair value of Small Technologies was computed as \$4,875 (= \$3,900 acquisition price ÷ 80%). Recording the acquisition at \$4,875 (the acquisition method based on fair value) rather than \$3,900 (the purchase method) causes the noncontrolling interest to reflect fair value as well.[33]

[33] If Small common stock trades at a lower amount than the per share price paid by Power, a control premium exists. The fair value of the acquisition (and, hence, the fair value assigned to the noncontrolling interest) would be based on the price paid by Power plus the lower fair value of the remaining noncontrolling shares.

EXHIBIT 7.19

Power Company and Small Technologies Financial Statements at December 31, 2011

	Power Company	Small Technologies
Revenues	$ (4,550)	$(2,150)
Cost of goods sold	1,720	1,000
Depreciation expense	300	100
Amortization expense	500	375
Interest expense	350	225
Equity in subsidiary earnings	(320)	0
Net Income	$ (2,000)	$ (450)
Cash	$ 2,600	$ 2,000
Short-term investments	1,030	225
Land	1,520	1,475
Equipment (net)	1,950	800
Investment in Small Technologies	4,260	0
Patented technologies	4,400	2,700
Total Assets	$ 15,760	$ 7,200
Long-term liabilities	$ (5,410)	$(2,950)
Common stock	(4,350)	(1,150)
Retained earnings	(6,000)	(3,100)
Total Liabilities and Shareholders' Equity	$(15,760)	$(7,200)

Revenues, gains, and net income are in parentheses to indicate that their signs are opposite those of expenses and losses; that is, they are credits for those interpreting the worksheet from the accountant's traditional debit/credit approach. Liabilities and shareholders' equity accounts are in parentheses to indicate that they are claims against assets; again, they are credits in the traditional debit/credit framework.

Exhibit 7.20 presents Power's allocation of Small's fair value at the date of acquisition, updated through the current balance sheet date, December 31, 2011. One year of excess fair value amortization must be reflected in consolidated net income each year, and the balance sheet amounts have accumulated two years of amortization as of December 31, 2011. For example, patented technologies had a fair value that exceeded Small's book value by $600. If the estimated life is 20 years, patent amortization expense on a consolidated basis must be increased by $30 in a given year. After two years have passed, the consolidated balance sheet reports the excess fair value at $540.

Exhibit 7.21 traces Power Company's equity method accounting for Small. Power paid $3,900 at the acquisition date, increased the investment account to recognize its equity in Small's earnings (percent ownership times Small's earnings, adjusted for the excess amortizations from Exhibit 7.20), and decreased the investment when it received its share of Small's dividends. The $320 equity in Small's earnings for 2011 appears in Power's own income statement, and the $4,260 investment in Small Technologies appears on Power's own December 31, 2011 balance sheet. The noncontrolling interest computations follow the same process, yielding

EXHIBIT 7.20

Power Company's Fair Value Allocation at the Date of Acquisition of Small Technologies

	Allocation of Fair Values	Estimated Life	Charged (Credited) to Expense Each Year	Balance on December 31, 2011
Small fair value at acquisition date	$4,875			
Small book value at acquisition date	(3,700)			
Fair value in excess of book value	$1,175			
Land (not depreciated)	300	NA	$ 0	$300
Equipment	(50)	10	(5)	(40)
Patented technologies	600	20	30	540
Long-term liabilities (lower fair value)	200	8	25	150
Goodwill	$ 125	Indefinite	0	125
			$50	

EXHIBIT 7.21

Investor Interests in Small Technologies (in millions)

	Power Company Controlling Interest (80%)		Noncontrolling Interest (20%)	
Acquisition date fair value (1/1/10) = $4,875		$3,900		$ 975
2010 net income of Small = $350	$280		$70	
Annual excess amortizations = $50 (Exhibit 7.20)	(40)		(10)	
Equity in Small's earnings for 2010		240		60
Investment in Small Technologies (12/31/10)		$4,140		$1,035
2011 net income of Small = $450	$360		$90	
Annual excess amortizations = $50 (Exhibit 7.20)	(40)		(10)	
Equity in Small's earnings for 2011		320		80
Dividends paid by Small in 2011 = $250		(200)		(50)
Investment in Small Technologies (12/31/11)		$4,260		$1,065

a noncontrolling interest in 2011 net income of $80 and a noncontrolling interest in the net assets of Small of $1,065 at December 31, 2011.

Exhibit 7.22 presents the consolidation worksheet at December 31, 2011. The eliminations have been coded to facilitate the explanation. The consolidation process for less than 100 percent ownership follows the same process as illustrated for 100 percent ownership,

EXHIBIT 7.22

Consolidation Worksheet at December 31, 2011 (in millions)

	Power	Small	Eliminations		Consolidated
Revenues	$ (4,550)	$(2,150)			$ (6,700)
Cost of goods sold	1,720	1,000			2,720
Depreciation expense	300	100	C	$ (5)	395
Amortization expense	500	375	C	30	905
Interest expense	350	225	C	25	600
Equity in subsidiary earnings	(320)	0	D	320	0
Net Income	$ (2,000)	$ (450)			
Consolidated net income					$ (2,080)
Noncontrolling interest in net income			E	80	80
Net income to controlling interest					$ (2,000)
Cash	$ 2,600	$ 2,000			$ 4,600
Short-term investments	1,030	225			1,255
Land	1,520	1,475	C	300	3,295
Equipment (net)	1,950	800	C	(40)	2,710
Investment in Small Technologies	4,260	0	A	(4,260)	0
Patented technologies	4,400	2,700	C	540	7,640
Goodwill			C	125	125
Total Assets	$ 15,760	$ 7,200			$ 19,625
Long-term liabilities	$ (5,410)	$(2,950)		150	$ (8,210)
Common stock	(4,350)	(1,150)	B	1,150	(4,350)
Noncontrolling interests			E	(1,065)	(1,065)
Retained earnings	(6,000)	(3,100)	B	3,100	(6,000)
Total Liabilities and Shareholders' Equity	$(15,760)	$ 7,200		$ 0	$(19,625)

Revenues, gains, and net income are in parentheses to indicate that their signs are opposite those of expenses and losses; that is, they are credits for those interpreting the worksheet from the accountant's traditional debit/credit approach. Liabilities and shareholders' equity accounts are in parentheses to indicate that they are claims against assets; again, they are credits in the traditional debit/credit framework.

with the addition of recognizing the noncontrolling interest in net income and net assets computed in Exhibit 7.21. The eliminations are as follows:

- A = Elimination of the Investment in Small Technologies account
- B = Elimination of Small's shareholders' equity accounts
- C = Allocation of excess fair value amounts at the date of acquisition to expenses and to the balance sheet as computed in Exhibit 7.20
- D = Elimination of the Equity in subsidiary earnings account
- E = Recognition of an $80 noncontrolling claim on consolidated net income and of noncontrolling equity of $1,065

The noncontrolling equity interest of $1,065 should be reported as a component of shareholders' equity. As noted in Chapter 4, if the denominator of the ROA computation includes all assets (as it typically does), the numerator should be calculated *before* the allocation of consolidated net income to the noncontrolling interest. A tax effect adjustment is not necessary because the noncontrolling interest is in after-tax net income.

Corporate Acquisitions and Income Taxes

Most corporate acquisitions involve a transaction between the acquiring corporation and the *shareholders* of the acquired corporation. Although the board of directors and management of the acquired company are usually deeply involved in discussions and negotiations, the acquisition usually takes place with the acquiring corporation giving some type of consideration to the shareholders of the acquired corporation in exchange for their stock. From a legal viewpoint, the acquired corporation remains a legally separate entity that has simply had a change in the makeup of its shareholder group.

The income tax treatment of corporate acquisitions follows these legal entity notions. In many acquisitions, the acquired company does not restate its assets and liabilities for tax purposes to reflect the amount that it paid for the shares of common stock. Instead, the tax basis of assets and liabilities of the acquired company before the acquisition carries over after the acquisition (termed a *nontaxable reorganization* by the Internal Revenue Code).

The preceding examples ignored the tax effects to focus on the acquisition and consolidation process. However, the following illustrates how deferred taxes would be recognized on a given difference between fair and book values. Assume that inventory had a book value of $70 and a fair value of $80; the tax rate is 35 percent. In the fair value allocation at the date of acquisition (and in the elimination entries during consolidation) inventory is increased by $10 and a deferred tax liability is increased by $3.50 (= $10 × 35 percent). The deferred tax liability is accrued at the date of acquisition to recognize the increase in tax liability when the inventory is sold in the future. If during the next year the subsidiary sells the inventory at its $80 fair value, the subsidiary will have a pretax profit (for book purposes) and a taxable income (for tax purposes) of $10. However, the consolidated financial statements recognize no profit on the sale because of two counterbalancing effects: the subsidiary shows a $10 pretax profit, but the $10 additional cost of goods sold (the $10 extra paid by the parent to acquire the inventory) is recognized through the elimination process. Accordingly, consolidated pretax profit on the transaction is zero; thus, consolidated income tax expense is zero. However, the tax basis of the inventory has not been "stepped up" to $80 at the date of acquisition. Therefore, the subsidiary must pay taxes of $3.50 when the inventory is sold (the reversal of the deferred tax liability).

Consolidation of Unconsolidated Subsidiaries and Affiliates

In some cases, firms have joint ventures or minority-owned affiliates that comprise strategically important components integral to the operations of the firm but that are not consolidated. To get a more complete picture of the economic position and performance of the firm, the analyst may want to assess the firm after consolidating all important minority-owned affiliates. For example, firms frequently work together in joint ventures to carry out their business activities. These companies do not consolidate the financial statements of the joint ventures with their financial statements, but instead use the equity method to account for the joint ventures because they are not majority-owned by the firm.

As discussed in this chapter and Chapter 1, PepsiCo has significant investments in bottlers that are integral to its operations. PepsiCo does not consolidate the bottlers because they are less than majority-owned. However, consolidation of the financial statements of these affiliates with those of PepsiCo provides a glimpse of the firm from a more fully integrated, *operational* perspective.

Example 22

Exhibit 7.23 presents a consolidation worksheet for PepsiCo and its two primary bottlers, PBG and PAS, based on Note 8, "Noncontrolled Bottling Affiliates" to PepsiCo's financial

EXHIBIT 7.23 (in millions)

Consolidation of PepsiCo and Significant Affiliates

				Eliminations		
December 27, 2008	**PepsiCo**	**PBG**	**PAS**	**PBG**	**PAS**	**Consolidated**
Current assets	$ 10,806	$ 3,141	$ 906			$ 14,853
Investments in noncontrolled affiliates	3,883			$(1,457)	$ (972)	1,454
Remainder of noncurrent assets	21,305	9,841	4,148	536	318	36,148
Total Assets	$ 35,994	$ 12,982	$ 5,054	$ (921)	$ (654)	$ 52,455
Current liabilities	$ (8,787)	$ (3,083)	$(1,048)			$(12,918)
Noncurrent liabilities	(15,101)	(7,408)	(2,175)			(24,684)
Preferred stock	97					97
External interests		(1,148)	(307)	$ (422)	$ (870)	(2,747)
Common shareholders' equity	(12,203)	(1,343)	(1,524)	1,343	1,524	(12,203)
Total Liabilities and Shareholders' Equity	$(35,994)	$(12,982)	$(5,054)	$ 921	$ 654	$(52,455)
PepsiCo's Investment Balance		$ 1,457	$ 972			

				Eliminations		
December 29, 2007	**PepsiCo**	**PBG**	**PAS**	**PBG**	**PAS**	**Consolidated**
Current assets	$ 10,151	$ 3,086	$ 922			$ 14,159
Investments in noncontrolled affiliates	4,354			$(2,022)	$(1,118)	1,214
Remainder of noncurrent assets	20,123	10,029	4,386	507	303	35,348
Total Assets	$ 34,628	$ 13,115	$ 5,308	$(1,515)	$ (815)	$ 50,721
Current liabilities	$ (7,753)	$ (2,215)	$ (903)			$(10,871)
Noncurrent liabilities	(9,641)	(7,312)	(2,274)			(19,227)
Preferred stock	91					91
External interests		(973)	(273)	$(1,100)	$(1,043)	(3,389)
Common shareholders' equity	(17,325)	(2,615)	(1,858)	2,615	1,858	(17,325)
Total Liabilities and Shareholders' Equity	$(34,628)	$(13,115)	$(5,308)	$ 1,515	$ 815	$(50,721)
PepsiCo's Investment Balance		$ 2,022	$ 1,118			

Revenues, gains, and net income are in parentheses to indicate that their signs are opposite those of expenses and losses; that is, they are credits for those interpreting the worksheet from the accountant's traditional debit/credit approach. Liabilities and shareholders' equity accounts are in parentheses to indicate that they are claims against assets; again, they are credits in the traditional debit/credit framework.

statements (Appendix A). The top and bottom halves of the exhibit consolidate the group as of December 27, 2008, and December 29, 2007, respectively. In Note 8, PepsiCo indicates that PBG and PAS are the firm's most significant noncontrolled bottling affiliates but does not disclose additional information about its other affiliates. Therefore, we can prepare a consolidation of PepsiCo with only PBG and PAS.

The first four columns of Exhibit 7.23 present the separate summary balance sheets of PepsiCo, PBG, and PAS. The Eliminations columns show the worksheet adjustments necessary to consolidate the affiliates. The final column presents PepsiCo's balance sheet if the affiliates had been consolidated. The worksheet consolidates two affiliates in each of two years.

According to Note 8, PepsiCo has an investment in PBG of $1,457 million at December 27, 2008. PepsiCo owns 33 percent of PBG common stock, 100 percent of PBG's class B common stock, and 7 percent of the common stock of PBG's primary operating subsidiary. PepsiCo's investment in PBG common stock was 2 percent higher in 2007. PepsiCo also reports that "our investment in PBG, which includes the related goodwill, was $536 million and $507 million higher than our ownership interest in their net assets at year-end 2008 and 2007, respectively." These disclosures imply that PepsiCo's interest in the net assets is as follows (in millions):

	2008	2007
Investment in PBG	$ 1,457	$ 2,022
Excess of investment over book value of PBG net assets	(536)	(507)
Ownership interest in book value of PBG net assets	$ 921	$ 1,515
Combined PBG minority interest and common shareholders' equity	÷2,491	÷3,588
Effective interest in net assets implied by PepsiCo's disclosures	37.0%	42.2%

The combined minority interest and common shareholders' equity equals the book value of PBG's net assets.

Repeating the computations for PAS:

	2008	2007
Investment in PAS	$ 972	$ 1,118
Excess of investment over book value of PAS net assets	(318)	(303)
Ownership interest in book value of PAS net assets	$ 654	$ 815
Combined PAS minority interest and common shareholders' equity	÷1,831	÷2,131
Effective interest in net assets implied by PepsiCo's disclosures	35.7%	38.5%

The 2008 portion of the worksheet for PBG accomplishes the following:

1. We eliminate the $1,457 million of investment in PBG. In Items 2 and 3 below, we replace the single investment line with the individual assets and liabilities in which PepsiCo invested with (a) the individual assets and liabilities of PBG (which are measured at a book value of $921 million shown in the schedule above) and (b) the amount PepsiCo paid for PBG in excess of its book value, $536 million.
2. We add the individual assets and liabilities across columns to yield consolidated numbers. PBG's assets and liabilities are carried at book value.

3. We add \$536 million to assets because it represents the portion of PepsiCo's investment that is not reflected in the book values of PBG's net assets.
4. As explained earlier in the chapter, the purpose of preparing a consolidated worksheet is to simulate the balance sheet that would have occurred if PepsiCo had acquired the assets and liabilities of PBG and PBG's shares no longer existed. Therefore, we eliminate the common equity of PBG.
5. The noncontrolling interest in PBG's net assets from a consolidated (PepsiCo's) viewpoint is 100% − 37.0% (PepsiCo's interest) = 63.0% × PBG's net assets of \$2,491million = \$1,569 million. Given that PBG has minority interest at \$1,148 million, we add \$422 million to minority interest. The remainder of Exhibit 7.23 repeats the process for PBG in 2007 and PAS in 2008 and 2007.

Consider now the effect of consolidating PepsiCo's bottlers on its ROA. For 2008, Chapter 4 calculates an ROA (adjusted for the nonrecurring items discussed in that chapter) as follows:

$$\frac{\$5{,}142 + (1 - 0.35)(\$329) + \$0}{0.5\ (\$35{,}994 + \$34{,}628)} = 15.2\%$$

To exclude the effect of financing from the numerator of ROA, the interest expense (net of taxes) recognized by PepsiCo's bottlers must be added back. Note 8 does not provide the amount of interest expense for those entities, so we estimate the amount by assuming that the noncurrent liabilities of the bottlers represent interest-bearing debt. Based on disclosures in PepsiCo's Note 9, "Debt Obligations and Commitments" (Appendix A), we assume an average interest rate of 5.8 percent on long-term debt. The debt of PepsiCo's investees and amounts for noncurrent liabilities from Note 8 yield interest expense of \$555 million [= 0.058 × 0.5(\$7,408 + \$7,312 + \$2,175 + \$2,247)] for 2008. Obviously the calculation of ROA will be slightly in error if some of the current liabilities of these entities bear interest, if some of the noncurrent liabilities do not bear interest, or if 5.8 percent is not a reasonable interest rate for PBG and PAS debt.

The final adjustment to the numerator of ROA to consolidate these bottlers is to add the minority interest in earnings. This adjustment permits the numerator to include 100 percent of the operating income of PepsiCo and its bottlers and the denominator to include 100 percent of the assets of these entities. PepsiCo's Note 8 shows that the total income for PBG and PAS bottlers for 2008 is \$162 million and \$226 million, respectively. Applying the noncontrolling interest percentages yields the share of income attributable to the external interests in these two subsidiaries of \$247 million (= \$162 × 63.0% + \$226 × 64.3%). Consolidating PepsiCo's bottlers results in the following recomputed ROA for 2008:

$$\frac{\$5{,}142 + (1 - 0.35)(\$329 + \$555) + \$247}{0.5\ (\$52{,}455 + \$50{,}720)} = 11.6\%$$

Thus, PepsiCo's ROA for 2008 drops significantly, from 15.2 percent to 11.6 percent—a 24 percent decline. The capital-intensive nature of bottling reveals itself in this pro forma ratio analysis in that the asset base for PepsiCo increases substantially when the bottling companies are consolidated. The consolidation of majority-owned subsidiaries is a relatively recent phenomenon in some countries (for example, Germany and Japan). These countries tended to follow strict legal definitions of the reporting entity. Non-IFRS financial reporting in these countries now generally requires the preparation of consolidated financial statements, although the requirement in Japan applies only to filings with the Ministry of Finance.

Joint Ventures: Proportionate Consolidation of Unconsolidated Subsidiaries and Affiliates

An alternative to full consolidation of PepsiCo's bottlers is proportionate consolidation. Under proportionate consolidation, the investor's share of the affiliate's assets and liabilities appears in separate sections on the asset and liabilities sides of the balance sheet, with the equity investment account eliminated. (Recall that PepsiCo currently accounts for its investments using the equity method.)

This alternative is particularly appealing for firms that enter into joint ventures in which ownership of the venture is split equally between two firms. Under U.S. GAAP, firms account for investments in joint ventures using the equity method (unless FASB *Interpretation No. 46R* applies) because these investments fall between minority, active investments and majority, active investments. IFRS permits use of proportionate consolidation for joint ventures, arguing that proportionate consolidation better captures the economics of transactions in which joint control is present.

Primary Beneficiary of a Variable-Interest Entity

Control achieved by ownership of more than 50 percent of voting shares justifies the preparation of consolidated financial statements. However, firms can have far less than 50 percent ownership in an entity but still be the primary beneficiary of the entity's operations and achieve control over the entity's decision-making process by contractual relationships. Special-purpose or variable-interest entities (VIEs) were part of the massive fraud infamously perpetrated by Enron, and such arrangements now tend to conjure up images of corporate malfeasance. However, companies may establish VIEs for legitimate business purposes. VIEs can take the form of a corporation, partnership, trust, or any other legal structure used for business purposes. Examples include entities that administer real estate leases, R&D agreements, and energy-related foreign exchange contracts. Often VIEs hold financial assets (such as accounts or loans receivable), real estate, or other property. The VIE may be passive and simply carry out a function on behalf of one or more firms (administering a commercial real estate lease, for example), or it may actively engage in some activity on behalf of one or more firms (such as conducting R&D activities). VIEs can be quite large and significant relative to the sponsoring firms. For example, in 2004, The Walt Disney Company announced that it would consolidate VIEs Euro Disney and Hong Kong Disneyland. The Walt Disney Company owned slightly more than 40 percent of each affiliate.

One of the primary benefits of the VIE is low-cost financing of asset purchases. For example, a sponsoring firm can create a VIE by using minimal amounts of equity investment, some debt investment, and probably some guarantee of VIE debt or other loss protection to outside investors. The VIE could acquire an asset and lease it to the sponsoring firm. Isolation of the asset from the sponsor's operations, the collateral presented by the asset, and sponsor debt guarantees motivate lenders to provide a lower interest rate loan to the VIE to acquire the asset.

Because of the low level of equity investment, the sponsoring firm would not consolidate a VIE under the percentage of ownership criterion. However, the sponsoring firm might possess the rights of a typical equity investor via contractual control of a VIE's operating, investing, and financing activities and may bear losses and reap profits as if it were an equity investor.

When is an Entity Classified as a VIE?

A firm's investment in another entity is classified as a VIE investment, and thus is subject to *Interpretation No. 46R,* if either of the following conditions exist: [34]

- The total equity investment at risk is not sufficient to permit the entity to finance its activities without additional subordinated financial support from other parties, including equity holders. The presumption is that an equity investment of less than 10 percent of the entity's total assets is not sufficient to permit the entity to finance its activities without additional support. However, entities that are holding high-risk assets or are engaging in high-risk activities or that are exposed to risks beyond their reported assets and liabilities may be required to have more than a 10 percent investment.
- The equity investing firms lack any one of the following three characteristics of a controlling financial interest:
  - The direct or indirect ability to make decisions about the entity's activities through voting rights or similar rights. Contractual arrangements with the subordinated providers of funds usually restrict the ability of the equity-investing firms to make decisions about the entity's activities.
  - The obligation to absorb the expected losses of the entity if they occur. The subordinated providers of funds absorb some of the expected losses.
  - The right to receive the expected residual returns of the entity if they occur. The subordinated providers of funds have a claim on some of the expected residual returns.

Which Entity Should Consolidate the VIE?

If a firm has a relationship with an entity deemed to be a VIE, the firm must apply the criteria of FIN 46R to determine whether it is the primary beneficiary of the VIE. If it is, it must consolidate the VIE's assets, liabilities, revenues, expenses, and noncontrolling interests. The firm is the primary beneficiary if it has:

- The direct or indirect ability to make decisions about the entity' activities.
- The obligation to absorb the entity's expected losses if they occur.
- The right to receive the entity's expected residual returns if they occur.

The aforementioned criteria recognize that contractual rights can cause a sponsoring firm to have *variable interests* similar to those possessed by traditional equity owners. FIN 46R provides examples of variable interests, explaining how the variable interests link to potential losses and returns as follows:

- Participation rights (entitling holders to the VIE's residual profits)
- Asset purchase options (entitles holders to benefit from increases in fair values, often versus bargain repurchase rights)
- Guarantees of debt (the maker of the guarantee must stand ready to repay a VIE's liabilities if the VIE cannot)
- Subordinated debt instruments (the subordinated creditor provides the cash flow to pay senior debt when the VIE cannot)
- Lease residual value guarantees (the maker of the guarantee covers losses when a leased assets value falls below its expected residual value)

---

[34] Financial Accounting Standards Board, *Statement No. 140,* discussed in Chapter 8, addresses the accounting for the sale of receivables. In the past, entities formed by the transferor for the sale of receivables, often referred to as *qualifying special-purpose entities,* were excluded from the scope of *Interpretation No. 46R* and thus were not classified as variable-interest entities. As of the June 2009 issue of Financial Accounting Standards Board, *Statement of Financial Accounting Standards No. 166,* "Accounting for Transfers of Financial Assets, an amendment of FASB Statement No. 140," 2009, effective for reporting periods beginning November 15, 2009, the notion of a qualifying special purpose-entity is terminated. Therefore, entities formed by the transferor for the sale of receivables fall under the provision of *Interpretation No. 46R* (*FASB Codification Topics 810 and 860*).

The presence of these variable interests leads to control in the absence of equity ownership. Therefore, consolidation of the VIE is appropriate because the primary beneficiary controls the net assets of the VIE. Consolidation of a VIE follows the same process as that illustrated for majority, active investments.

Disclosure Requirements of Interpretation No. 46R. Both the primary beneficiary firm and the firms holding significant variable interests in a VIE are subject to *Interpretation No. 46R* disclosure rules. If material to the financial statements, the primary beneficiary must disclose (1) the nature, purpose, size, and activities of the VIE; (2) the carrying amount and classification of the consolidated assets that represent collateral for the VIE's obligations; and (3) the status of VIE creditors' recourse (if any) to the assets of the primary beneficiary. Firms holding significant variable interest in a VIE must disclose (1) the nature of its involvement with the VIE and the start of that involvement; (2) the nature, purpose, size, and activities of the VIE; and (3) the investing firm's maximum exposure to loss given its involvement with the VIE.

Example 23

Ford Motor Company describes its VIEs in Note 11 to its 2008 Consolidated Financial Statements. Ford provides the following opening statement in the note:

> We consolidate VIEs of which we are the primary beneficiary. The liabilities recognized as a result of consolidating these VIEs do not necessarily represent additional claims on our general assets; rather, they represent claims against the specific assets of the consolidated VIEs. Conversely, assets recognized as a result of consolidating these VIEs do not represent additional assets that could be used to satisfy claims against our general assets.

This initial statement illustrates the key business purpose of most VIEs, the isolation of risk. As diagrammed in Exhibit 7.24, Ford Motor Company's finance subsidiary, Ford Credit, sponsors (that is, creates) a VIE with a minimal amount of equity investment. The VIE's balance sheet shows relatively small amounts of cash. The VIE needs to acquire assets of some kind to carry out its operations; therefore, it must attract capital from other parties. When a potential capital provider (for example, bank, insurance company, or equity investor) assesses the risk of the VIE, Ford Motor Company's risk is not an issue. The VIE

EXHIBIT 7.24

Diagram of Ford Motor Company Financial VIE Arrangement

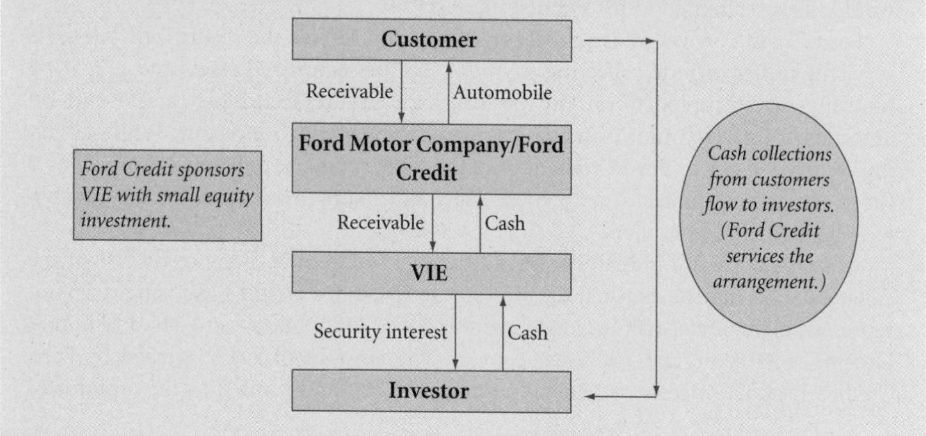

is a legally separate entity from Ford Motor Company. The term used to describe this status is *bankruptcy remote.* Because of bankruptcy remote status, the VIE should be able to obtain better financing terms. The VIE will determine its capital structure based on the risk of cash flows from the assets it acquires to carry on its stated purpose. In the case of Ford's financial services VIEs, the VIEs acquire customer receivables from Ford Credit and securitize the receivables. That is, the VIEs issue rights to investors to the cash flows from receivable collection. The cash it collects from investors upon selling the secured interests is transferred back to Ford Credit as payment for the receivables acquired. Customers pay cash on their receivables to Ford Credit (Note 11 indicates that Ford Credit services the receivables), and Ford Credit delivers scheduled cash payments to the VIEs' investors.

The benefit to Ford Motor Company of this arrangement is clear: Ford quickly converts its receivables to cash, and Ford Credit can offer more financing to stimulate future sales. This benefit comes at a cost. The VIEs' investors demand a return. The bankruptcy remote status of the VIE will help incent VIE investors to accept a lower return, but the VIEs' investors often require more guarantees that Ford Credit will share in the risk that the securitized receivables will not generate sufficient cash flows. Consider the following passages from the same note that describes Ford Credit's risk sharing:

> Ford Credit provides various forms of credit enhancements to reduce the risk of loss for securitization investors. Credit enhancements include over-collaterization (when the principal amount of the securitized assets exceeds the principal amount of related asset-backed securities), segregated cash reserve funds, subordinated securities, and excess spread (when interest collections on the securitized assets exceed the related fees and expenses, including interest payments on the related asset-backed securities). Ford Credit may also provide payment enhancements that increase the likelihood of the timely payment of interest and the payment of principal at maturity. Payment enhancements include yield supplement arrangements, interest rate swaps, liquidity facilities, and certain cash deposits.
>
> Ford Credit retains interests in its securitization transactions, including senior and subordinated securities issued by the VIE, rights to cash held for the benefit of the securitization investors (for example, a reserve fund) and residual interests. Residual interests represent the right to receive collections on the securitized assets in excess of amounts needed to pay securitization investors and pay other transaction participants and expenses. Ford Credit retains credit risk in securitizations because its retained interests include the most subordinated interests in the securitized assets, which are the first to absorb credit losses on the securitized assets. Based on past experience, Ford Credit expects that any credit losses in the pool of securitized assets would likely be limited to its retained interests.
>
> Ford Credit is engaged as servicer to collect and service the securitized assets. Its servicing duties include collecting payments on the securitized assets and preparing monthly investor reports on the performance of the securitized assets and on amounts of interest andor principal payments to be made to investors. While servicing securitized assets, Ford Credit applies the same servicing policies and procedures that Ford Credit applies to its owned assets and maintains its normal relationship with its financing customers.
>
> As residual interest holder, Ford Credit is exposed to underlying credit risk of the collateral, and may be exposed to interest rate risk. Ford Credit's exposure does not represent incremental risk to Ford Credit and was \$18.2 billion and \$16.3 billion at December 31, 2008 and 2007, respectively. The amount of risk absorbed by Ford Credit's residual interests is generally represented by and limited to the amount of

> overcollaterization of its assets securing the debt and any cash reserves funded. For Ford Credit's wholesale transactions, it also includes cash it has contributed to excess funding accounts and its participation interests in the VIE.

Ford Motor Company has applied *FIN 46R* and has concluded that it is the primary beneficiary of the VIEs. Therefore, it consolidates its financial services VIEs. Ford also discloses automotive sector joint ventures for which it is the primary beneficiary. The passage below (from Note 11) illustrates how a company such as Ford controls operations of the VIE through contractual arrangements and how it has variable interests that cause it to be the primary beneficiary (that is, substantially shares in profits and losses based on the VIE's performance).

> Activities with the joint ventures described below include purchasing substantially all of the joint ventures' output under a cost-plus-margin arrangement and/or volume dependent pricing. These contractual arrangements may require us to absorb joint venture losses when production volume targets are not met or allow us, in some cases, to receive bonuses when production volume targets are exceeded.

Income Tax Consequences of Investments in Securities

For income tax purposes, investments fall into the following two categories:

- Investments in debt securities, in preferred stock, and in less than 80 percent of the common stock of another entity. Firms recognize interest or dividends received or receivable each period as taxable income (subject to a partial dividend exclusion), as well as gains or losses when they sell the securities.
- Investments in 80 percent or more of the common stock of another entity. Firms can prepare consolidated tax returns for these investments.

As is evident, the methods of accounting for investments for financial and tax reporting do not overlap precisely. Thus, temporary differences will likely arise for which firms must recognize deferred taxes. PepsiCo, for example, cannot file consolidated tax returns with PBG, PAS, or other equity investments because its ownership percentage is less than 80 percent. In Note 5, "Income Taxes" (Appendix A), PepsiCo reports deferred tax liabilities of $1,193 million on December 27, 2008 ($1,163 million on December 29, 2007), relating to these equity investments because it includes its share of the investees' earnings each year for financial reporting but recognizes dividends received as income on its tax return.

FOREIGN CURRENCY TRANSLATION

Firms headquartered in a particular country often have substantial operations outside of that country. For example, in Note 1, "Basis of Presentation and Our Divisions" (Appendix A), PepsiCo indicates that it generates approximately 48 percent of its net revenues internationally (defined as outside the U.S.).[35] For some firms (such as Coca-Cola), international sales dominate even though the firm is headquartered in the U.S.

---

[35] Financial reporting requires firms to disclose segment data by geographic location (foreign versus domestic) as well as by reportable operating segments and major customers [Financial Accounting Standards Board, *Statement of Financial Accounting Standards No. 131*, "Disclosures about Segments of an Enterprise and Related Information" (1997); *FASB Codification Topic 280*]. PepsiCo reports extensive geographic segment information in Note 1 (Appendix A).

U.S. parent companies must translate the financial statements of foreign branches and subsidiaries into U.S. dollars before preparing consolidated financial statements for shareholders and creditors. This section describes and illustrates the translation methodology and discusses the implications of the methodology for managing international operations and for interpreting financial statement disclosures regarding such operations.[36]

The following general issues arise in translating the financial statements of a foreign branch or subsidiary:

- Should the firm translate individual financial statement items using the exchange rate at the time of the transaction (referred to as the *historical exchange rate*) or the exchange rate during or at the end of the current period (referred to as the *current exchange rate*)? Financial statement items that firms translate using the historical exchange rates appear in the financial statements at the same U.S. dollar equivalent amount each period regardless of changes in the exchange rate. For example, land acquired in France for €10,000 when the exchange rate was $1.05 per euro appears on the balance sheet at $10,500 each period. Financial statement items that firms translate using the current exchange rate appear in the financial statements at a different U.S. dollar amount each period when exchange rates change. Thus, a change in the exchange rate to $1.40 per euro results in reporting the land at $14,000 in the balance sheet. Financial statement items for which firms use the current exchange rate give rise to a *foreign exchange adjustment* each period.
- Should the firm recognize the foreign exchange adjustment as a gain or loss in measuring net income each period as it arises, or should the firm defer its recognition until a future period? The foreign exchange adjustment represents an unrealized gain or loss, much the same as changes in the market value of derivatives, marketable securities, inventories, and other assets. Should financial reporting require realization of the gain or loss through sale of the foreign operation before recognizing it, or should the unrealized gain or loss flow directly to the income statement as the exchange rate changes?

The sections that follow address these two questions.

Functional Currency Concept

Central to the translation of foreign currency items under GAAP is the *functional currency concept.*[37] Determination of the functional currency drives the accounting for translating the financial statements of foreign entities of U.S. firms into U.S. dollars.

Foreign entities (whether branches or subsidiaries) are of two general types:

- A foreign entity operates as a relatively self-contained and integrated unit in a particular foreign country. The functional currency for these operations is the currency of that foreign country. The rationale is that management of the foreign unit likely makes operating, investing, and financing decisions based primarily on economic conditions in that foreign country, with secondary concern for economic conditions, exchange rates, and similar factors in other countries.
- The operations of a foreign entity are a direct and integral component or extension of the parent company's operations. The functional currency for these operations is the U.S. dollar. The rationale is that management of the foreign unit likely makes decisions from the perspective of a U.S. manager concerned with the impact of decisions on U.S. dollar amounts even though day-to-day transactions of the entity are usually conducted in the foreign currency.

---

[36] Other than terminology and other relatively minor implementation differences, IFRS and U.S. GAAP are similar in the foreign currency translation area.

[37] Financial Accounting Standards Board, *Statement of Financial Accounting Standards No. 52* (as amended by *Statement No. 130,* "Reporting Comprehensive Income"), "Foreign Currency Translation" (1981); *FASB Codification Topics 220 and 830.*

The FASB issued *Statement No. 52* prior to the rapid growth in globalization, with firms now sourcing products, services, and capital and selling products and services and investing capital on a global basis. In these settings, no single currency may satisfactorily reflect the global activities of the foreign subsidiary. Nonetheless, U.S. GAAP requires firms to select a single currency—the currency of the foreign unit or the U.S. dollar—as the functional currency.

Statement No. 52 sets out characteristics for determining whether the currency of the foreign unit or the U.S. dollar is the functional currency. Exhibit 7.25 summarizes these characteristics. The operating characteristics of a particular foreign operation may provide mixed signals regarding which currency is the functional currency. Managers must exercise judgment in determining which functional currency best captures the economic effects of a foreign entity's operations and financial position. As a later section discusses, managers may structure certain financing or other transactions to influence the identification of the functional currency. Once a firm determines the functional currency of a foreign entity, it must use that currency consistently over time unless changes in economic circumstances clearly indicate that a change in the functional currency be made.

Statement No. 52 provides for one exception to the guidelines in Exhibit 7.25 for determining the functional currency. If the foreign entity operates in a highly inflationary country, U.S.

EXHIBIT 7.25

Factors for Determining Functional Currency of a Foreign Unit of a U.S.-Based Firm

	Foreign Currency Is Functional Currency	**U.S. Dollar Is Functional Currency**
Cash Flows of Foreign Entity	Receivables and payables denominated in foreign currency and not usually remitted to parent currently	Receivables and payables denominated in U.S. dollars and readily available for remittance to parent
Sales Prices	Influenced primarily by local competitive conditions and not responsive on a short-term basis to exchange rate changes	Influenced by worldwide competitive conditions and responsive on a short-term basis to exchange rate changes
Cost Factors	Foreign unit obtains labor, materials, and other inputs primarily from its own country	Foreign unit obtains labor, materials, and other inputs primarily from the U.S.
Financing	Financing denominated in currency of foreign unit or generated internally by the foreign unit	Financing denominated in U.S. dollars or ongoing fund transfers by the parent
Relations between Parent and Foreign Unit	Low volume of intercompany transactions and little operational interrelations between parent and foreign unit	High volume of intercompany transactions and extensive operational interrelations between parent and foreign unit

GAAP considers its currency too unstable to serve as the functional currency and the firm must use the U.S. dollar instead. A highly inflationary country is one that has experienced cumulative inflation of at least 100 percent over a three-year period. Some developing nations fall within this exception and pose particular problems for U.S. parent companies.

Translation Methodology—Foreign Currency is Functional Currency

When the functional currency is the currency of the foreign unit, U.S. GAAP requires firms to use the *all-current translation method.* The left-hand column of Exhibit 7.26 summarizes the translation procedure under the all-current method.

EXHIBIT 7.26

Summary of Translation Methodology

	Foreign Currency Is the Functional Currency (all-current method)	U.S. Dollar Is the Functional Currency (monetary/ nonmonetary method)
Income Statement	Firms translate revenues and expenses as measured in foreign currency into U.S. dollars using the average exchange rate during the period. Income includes (1) realized and unrealized transaction gains and losses and (2) realized translation gains and losses when the firm sells the foreign unit.	Firms translate revenues and expenses using the exchange rate in effect when the firm made the original measurements underlying the valuations. Firms translate revenues and most operating expenses using the average exchange rate during the period. However, they translate cost of goods sold and depreciation using the historical exchange rate appropriate to the related asset (inventory, fixed assets). Net income includes (1) realized and unrealized transaction gains and losses and (2) unrealized translation gains and losses on the net monetary position of the foreign unit each period.
Balance Sheet	Firms translate assets and liabilities as measured in foreign currency into U.S. dollars using the end-of-the-period exchange rate. Use of the end-of-the-period exchange rate gives rise to unrealized transaction gains and losses on receivables and payables requiring currency conversions in the future. Firms include an unrealized translation adjustment on the net asset position of the foreign unit in accumulated other comprehensive income, until the firm sells the foreign unit.	Firms translate monetary assets and liabilities using the end-of-the-period exchange rate. They translate nonmonetary assets and equities using the historical exchange rate.

Firms translate revenues and expenses at the average exchange rate during the period and balance sheet items at the end-of-the-period exchange rate. Net income includes only *transaction* exchange gains and losses of the foreign unit. That is, a foreign unit that has receivables and payables denominated in a currency other than its own must make a currency conversion on settlement of the account. The gain or loss from changes in the exchange rate between the time the account originated and the time of settlement is a transaction gain or loss. Firms recognize this gain or loss during the period the account is outstanding even though it is not yet realized or settled. As Chapter 8 discusses, firms often acquire derivatives to hedge the risk of foreign currency gains and losses. Firms include the offsetting loss or gain on the derivative to the gain or loss on the item hedged in net income each period. Thus, net income increases or decreases only to the extent that the derivative did not perfectly hedge the change in exchange rates.

When a foreign unit operates more or less independently of the U.S. parent, financial reporting assumes that only the parent's equity investment in the foreign unit is subject to exchange rate risk. The firm measures the effect of exchange rate changes on this investment each period but includes the resulting "translation adjustment" as a component of other comprehensive income rather than net income. The rationale for this treatment is that the firm's investment in the foreign unit is for the long term; therefore, short-term changes in exchange rates should not affect periodic net income. Firms recognize the cumulative amount in the translation adjustment account in net income when measuring any gain or loss in the case of a sale or disposal of a foreign unit.

The "translation adjustment" reported by a firm can include a second component in addition to the effect of exchange rate changes on the parent's equity investment in foreign subsidiaries or branches. Firms can hedge their investment in foreign operations using forward contracts, currency swaps, or other derivative instruments. As part of the translation adjustment, firms report the change in fair value of a derivative that qualifies as a hedge of the net investment in a foreign entity.[38] In this sense, the foreign currency hedge is treated similar to a cash flow hedge (discussed and illustrated in Chapter 8) in that the change in the fair value of the hedge appears in other comprehensive income. The difference is that firms do not separately disclose the change in the fair value of the hedge, but rather embed it in the translation adjustment, which also captures the effect of exchange rate changes on the parent's equity investment in the foreign entity.

Example 24

The functional currency for PepsiCo's foreign subsidiaries is the currency of the foreign unit. As a result, PepsiCo reports the currency translation adjustment in other comprehensive income. PepsiCo's total comprehensive income for 2008 is $1,349 million, which includes a *negative* Currency Translation Adjustment of $2,484 million for the year. This adjustment is a loss, and it substantially explains why net income is $5,142 million, but comprehensive income is only $1,349. The Statement of Changes in Common Shareholders' Equity (Appendix A) for PepsiCo includes the $2,484 million currency translation adjustment in reconciling the change in Accumulated Other Comprehensive Loss for 2008. Also, Note 13, "Accumulated Other Comprehensive Loss" (Appendix A), discloses that the December 27, 2008, accumulated other comprehensive income balance is $(4,694) million (a reduction of shareholders' equity). Of this amount, $(2,271) million represents cumulative translation losses through time.

---

[38] Financial Accounting Standards Board, *Statement of Financial Accounting Standards No. 133*, "Accounting for Derivative Instruments and Hedging Activities" (1998); *FASB Codification Topic* 815. However, if the foreign currency hedge does not qualify as a hedge of the net investment, the criteria established in this standard for fair value and cash flow hedges are applied to determine the appropriate accounting. See Chapter 8 for a discussion of the accounting for derivatives used in fair value and cash flow hedging activities.

Illustration—Foreign Currency Is Functional Currency

Exhibit 7.27 illustrates the all-current method for a foreign unit *during its first year of operations.* The exchange rate was $1:1FC on January 1, $2:1FC on December 31, and $1.5:1FC on average during the year. Thus, the foreign currency increased in value relative to the U.S. dollar during the year. That is, it takes fewer foreign currency units to acquire $1 at the end of the year than at the beginning of the year. The firm translates all assets and liabilities on the balance sheet at the exchange rate on December 31. It translates common

EXHIBIT 7.27

Illustration of Transition Methodology When the Foreign Currency Is the Functional Currency

	Foreign Currency	U.S. Dollars	
BALANCE SHEET			
ASSETS			
Cash	FC 10	$2.0:1FC	$ 20.0
Receivables	20	$2.0:1FC	40.0
Inventories	30	$2.0:1FC	60.0
Fixed assets (net)	40	$2.0:1FC	80.0
Total Assets	FC 100		$200.0
LIABILITIES AND SHAREHOLDERS' EQUITY			
Accounts payable	FC 40	$2.0:1FC	$ 80.0
Bonds payable	20	$2.0:1FC	40.0
Total Liabilities	FC 60		$120.0
Common stock	FC 30	$1.0:1FC	$ 30.0
Retained earnings	10		12.5[a]
Accumulated other comprehensive income-unrealized translation adjustment	—		37.5[b]
Total Shareholders' Equity	FC 40		$ 30.0
Total Liabilities and Shareholders' Equity	FC 100		$200.0
INCOME STATEMENT			
Sales	FC 200	$1.5:1FC	$300.0
Realized transaction gain	2[c]	$1.5:1FC	3.0[c]
Unrealized transaction gain	1[d]	$1.5:1FC	1.5[d]
Cost of goods sold	(120)	$1.5:1FC	(180.0)
Selling & administrative expense	(40)	$1.5:1FC	(60.0)
Depreciation expense	(10)	$1.5:1FC	(15.0)
Interest expense	(2)	$1.5:1FC	(3.0)
Income tax expense	(16)	$1.5:1FC	(24.0)
Net Income	FC 15		$ 22.5

EXHIBIT 7.27 (Continued)

	Foreign Currency		U.S. Dollars
[a]**Retained earnings, January 1**	FC 0.0		$ 0.0
Plus net income	15.0		22.5
Less dividends	(5.0)	$2.0:1FC	$ (10.0)
Retained Earnings, December 31	FC 10.0		$ 12.5
[b]**Net Asset Position, January 1**	FC 30.0	$1.0:1FC	$ 30.0
Plus net income	15.0		22.5
Less dividends	(5.0)	$2.0:1FC	$ (10.0)
Net Asset Position, December 31	FC 40.0		$ 42.5
	⟶	$2.0:lFC	80.0
Unrealized Translation "Gain"			$ 37.5

[c]The foreign unit had receivables and payables denominated in a currency other than its own. When it settled these accounts during the period, the foreign unit made a currency conversion and realized a transaction gain of FC2.

[d]The foreign unit has receivables and payables outstanding that will require a currency conversion in a future period when the foreign unit settles the accounts. Because the exchange rate changed while the receivables/payables were outstanding, the foreign unit reports an unrealized transaction gain for financial reporting.

stock at the exchange rate on the date of issuance; the translation adjustment account includes the effects of changes in exchange rates on this investment. The translated amount of retained earnings results from translating the income statement and dividends. Note that the firm translates all revenues and expenses of the foreign unit at the average exchange rate. The foreign unit realized a transaction gain during the year and recorded it on its books. In addition, the translated amounts for the foreign unit include an unrealized transaction gain arising from exposed accounts that are not yet settled. Note (a) to Exhibit 7.27 shows the computation of translated retained earnings. The foreign unit paid the dividend on December 31.

Note b shows the calculation of the translation adjustment. By investing $30 in the foreign unit on January 1 and allowing the $22.5 of earnings to remain in the foreign unit throughout the year while the foreign currency was increasing in value relative to the U.S. dollar, the parent has a potential exchange gain of $37.5. It reports this amount as a component of other comprehensive income.

Translation Methodology—U.S. Dollar Is Functional Currency

When the functional currency is the U.S. dollar, firms must use the *monetary/nonmonetary translation method.* The right-hand column of Exhibit 7.26 summarizes the translation procedure under the monetary/nonmonetary method.

The underlying premise of the monetary/nonmonetary method is that the translated amounts reflect amounts that the firm would have reported if it had originally made all measurements in U.S. dollars. To implement this underlying premise, it is necessary to distinguish between monetary items and nonmonetary items.

A monetary item is an account whose nominal maturity amount does not change as the exchange rate changes. From a U.S. dollar perspective, these accounts give rise to exchange gains and losses because the number of U.S. dollars required to settle the fixed foreign currency amounts fluctuates over time with exchange rate changes. Monetary items include cash, marketable securities, receivables, accounts payable, other accrued liabilities, and short-term and long-term debt. Firms translate these items using the end-of-the-period exchange rate and recognize translation gains and losses. These translation gains and losses increase or decrease net income each period whether or not the foreign unit must make an actual currency conversion to settle the monetary item. The rationale for the recognition of unrealized translation gains and losses in net income is that the foreign unit will likely make a currency conversion in the near future to settle monetary assets and liabilities or to convert foreign currency into U.S. dollars to remit a dividend to the parent, activities consistent with foreign units that operate as extensions of the U.S. parent.

Nonmonetary items include inventories, fixed assets, common stock, revenues, and expenses. Firms translate these accounts using the historical exchange rate in effect when the foreign unit initially made the measurements underlying these accounts. Inventories and cost of goods sold translate at the exchange rate when the foreign unit acquired the inventory items. Fixed assets and depreciation expense translate at the exchange rate when the foreign unit acquired the fixed assets. Most revenues and operating expenses other than cost of goods sold and depreciation translate at the average exchange rate during the period. The objective is to state these accounts at their U.S. dollar-equivalent historical cost amounts. In this way, the translated amounts reflect the U.S. dollar perspective that is appropriate when the U.S. dollar is the functional currency.

Illustration—U.S. Dollar Is Functional Currency

Exhibit 7.28 shows the application of the monetary/nonmonetary method to the data considered in Exhibit 7.27. Net income again includes both realized and unrealized transaction gains and losses. Net income under the monetary/nonmonetary translation method also includes a $22.5 translation loss.

As Note b to Exhibit 7.28 shows, the firm was in a net monetary liability position during a period when the U.S. dollar decreased in value relative to the foreign currency. The translation loss arises because the U.S. dollars required to settle these foreign-denominated net liabilities at the end of the year exceed the U.S. dollar amount required to settle the net liability position before the exchange rate changed.

The organizational structure and operating policies of a particular foreign unit determine its functional currency. The two acceptable choices and the corresponding translation methods were designed to capture the different economic and operational relationships between a parent and its foreign affiliates. However, firms have some latitude in deciding the functional currency (and therefore the translation method) for each foreign unit. In many cases, signals about the appropriate functional currency will be mixed and firms will have latitude to select among them. Actions that management might consider to swing the

EXHIBIT 7.28

Illustration of Translation Methodology When the U.S. Dollar Is the Functional Currency

	Foreign Currency	U.S. Dollars	
BALANCE SHEET			
ASSETS			
Cash	FC 10	$2.0:1FC	$ 20.0
Receivables	20	$2.0:1FC	40.0
Inventories	30	$1.5:1FC	45.0
Fixed assets (net)	40	$1.0:1FC	40.0
Total Assets	FC 100		$145.0
Liabilities and Shareholders' Equity			
Accounts payable	FC 40	$2.0:1FC	$ 80.0
Bonds payable	20	$2.0:1FC	40.0
Total Liabilities	FC 60		$120.0
Common stock	FC 30	$1.0:1FC	$ 30.0
Retained earnings	10		(5.0)[a]
Total Shareholders' Equity	FC 40		$ 25.0
Total Liabilities and Shareholders' Equity	FC 100		$145.0
Income Statement			
Sales	FC 200	$1.5:1FC	$300.0
Realized transaction gain	2	$1.5:1FC	3.0
Unrealized transaction gain	1	$1.5:1FC	1.5
Unrealized translation loss	—		(22.5)[b]
Cost of goods sold	(120)	$1.5:1FC	(180.0)
Selling & administrative expense	(40)	$1.5:1FC	(60.0)
Depreciation expense	(10)	$1.0:1FC	(10.0)
Interest expense	(2)	$1.5:1FC	(3.0)
Income tax expense	(16)	$1.5:1FC	(24.0)
Net Income	FC 15		$ 5.0
[a]**Retained earnings, January 1**	FC 0		$ 0.0
Plus net income	15		5.0
Less dividends	(5)	$2.0:1FC	(10.0)
Retained Earnings, December 31	FC 10		$ (5.0)

[b]Income for financial reporting includes any unrealized translation gain or loss for the period. The net monetary position of a foreign unit during the period serves as the basis for computing the translation gain or loss. The foreign unit was in a net monetary liability position during a period when the U.S. dollar decreased in value relative to the foreign currency. The translation loss arises because the U.S. dollars required to settle the net monetary liability position at the end of the year exceed the U.S. dollars required to settle the obligation at the

(Continued)

EXHIBIT 7.28 (Continued)

time the firm initially recorded the transactions that gave rise to change in net monetary liabilities during the period. The calculations appear below.

	Foreign Currency		U.S. Dollars
Net Monetary Position, January 1	FC 0.0	—	$ 0.0
Plus:			
Issue of common stock	30.0	$1.0:1FC	30.0
Sales for cash and on account	200.0	$1.5:1FC	300.0
Settlement of exposed receivable/payable at a gain	2.0	$1.5:1FC	3.0
Unrealized gain on exposed receivable/payable	1.0	$1.5:1FC	1.5
Less:			
Acquisition of fixed assets	(50.0)	$1.0:1FC	(50.0)
Acquisition of inventory	(150.0)	$1.5:1FC	(225.0)
Selling & administrative costs incurred	(40.0)	$1.5:1FC	(60.0)
Interest cost incurred	(2.0)	$1.5:1FC	(3.0)
Income taxes paid	(16.0)	$1.5:1FC	(24.0)
Dividend paid	(5.0)	$1.5:1FC	(10.0)
Net Monetary Liability Position, December 31	(30.0)		$ (37.5)
	→	$2.0.1FC	–(60.0)
Unrealized Translation Loss			$ 22.5

balance of factors toward use of the foreign currency as the functional currency include the following:

- *Decentralize decision making to the foreign unit.* The greater the degree of autonomy of the foreign unit, the more likely its currency will be the functional currency. The U.S. parent company can design effective control systems to monitor the activities of the foreign unit while permitting the foreign unit to operate with considerable freedom.
- *Minimize remittances/dividends.* The greater the degree of earnings retention by the foreign unit, the more likely its currency will be the functional currency. The parent may obtain cash from a foreign unit indirectly rather than directly through remittances or dividends. For example, a foreign unit with mixed signals about its functional currency might, through loans or transfer prices for goods or services, send cash to another foreign unit whose functional currency is clearly its own currency. This second foreign unit can then remit it to the parent. Other possibilities for interunit transactions are acceptable as well to ensure that *some* foreign currency rather than the U.S. dollar is the functional currency.

Research suggests that approximately 80 percent of U.S. firms with foreign operations use the foreign currency as the functional currency and that the remainder use the U.S. dollar.[39] Few firms select the foreign currency for some operations and the U.S. dollar for other operations

[39] Eli Bartov and Gordon M. Bodnar, "Alternative Accounting Methods, Information Asymmetry and Liquidity: Theory and Evidence," *The Accounting Review* (July 1996), pp. 397–418.

(except for operations in highly inflationary countries, where firms must use the U.S. dollar as the functional currency). Thus, it appears that firms prefer the all-current translation method, in large part because they can exclude unrealized foreign currency "gains and losses" from earnings each period and experience fewer earnings surprises due to exchange rate fluctuations.

The question for the analyst assessing earnings quality is whether to include the change in the foreign currency translation account in earnings or leave it as a component of other comprehensive income. The principal argument for excluding it is that the unrealized gains or losses may well reverse in the long term and, in any case, may not be realized for many years. The principal arguments for including it in earnings are that (1) management has purposely chosen the foreign currency as the functional currency to avoid including such gains or losses in earnings, not because the firm allows its foreign units to operate as independent units, and (2) the change in the foreign currency translation adjustment represents the current period's portion of the eventual net gain or loss that *will* be realized. When using earnings to value a firm, Chapter 13 suggests that earnings should include all recognized value changes regardless of whether GAAP includes them in net income or other comprehensive income.

A study examining the valuation relevance of the translation adjustment regressed market-adjusted returns on (1) earnings excluding exchange gains and losses, (2) transaction exchange gains and losses included in earnings, and (3) changes in the translation adjustment reported as a component of comprehensive income.[40] The study found that the coefficient on the translation adjustment was statistically significant but smaller than that on earnings excluding all exchange gains and losses, suggesting that the market considers the translation adjustment relevant for security valuation but less persistent than earnings excluding gains and losses. Given this finding, the FASB's decision to require firms to report the translation adjustment change as a *separate and distinct* component of comprehensive income appears to be helpful for investors.

Foreign Currency Translation and Income Taxes

Income tax laws distinguish between a foreign branch of a U.S. parent and a subsidiary of a U.S. parent. A subsidiary is a legally separate entity from the parent; a branch is not. The translation procedure of foreign branches is essentially the same as for financial reporting (except that taxable income does not include translation gains and losses until realized). That is, a firm selects a functional currency for each foreign branch and uses the all-current or monetary/nonmonetary translation method as appropriate.

For foreign subsidiaries, taxable income includes only dividends received each period (translated at the exchange rate on the date of remittance). Because parent companies typically consolidate foreign subsidiaries for financial reporting but cannot consolidate them for tax reporting, temporary differences that require the provision of deferred taxes likely arise.

Interpreting the Effects of Exchange Rate Changes on Operating Results

In addition to understanding the effects of the foreign currency translation method on a firm's financial statements, the analyst should consider how changes in exchange rates affect changes in sales levels, sales mix, and net income.

[40] Billy S. Soo and Lisa Gilbert Soo, "Accounting for the Multinational Firm: Is the Translation Process Valued by the Stock Market?" *The Accounting Review* (October 1995), pp. 617–637.

Example 25

Assume that a firm generated sales of $10,000 in the U.S. and FC2,000 in a particular foreign country during Year 1. The exchange rate between the U.S. dollar and the foreign currency was $2:FC1 during Year 1. The FC2,000 of sales translates into $4,000 of foreign sales, resulting in a mix of 71.4 percent domestic sales and 28.6 percent foreign sales. For illustration, assume that domestic sales for Year 2 are $10,000 and foreign sales are FC2,000. Also assume first that the U.S. dollar increases in value relative to the foreign currency during Year 2, with an average exchange rate of $1.8:FC1. The FC2,000 of foreign sales translates into $3,600, resulting in a mix of 73.5 percent domestic sales and 26.5 percent foreign sales. Alternatively, assume that the U.S. dollar decreases in value during Year 2, with an average exchange rate of $2.4:FC1. The FC2,000 of foreign sales translates into $4,800, resulting in a mix of 67.6 percent domestic sales and 32.4 percent foreign sales. Without considering the effects of changes in selling price and volume, changes in exchange rates affect the level and mix of domestic versus foreign sales.

	Exchange Rate	Domestic Sales	Foreign Sales	Total Sales	Sales Domestic	Mix Foreign
Year 1	$2.0:FC1	$10,000	$4,000[a]	$14,000	71.4%	28.6%
Year 2	$1.8:FC1	$10,000	$3,600[b]	$13,600	73.5%	26.5%
Year 2	$2.4:FC1	$10,000	$4,800[c]	$14,800	67.6%	32.4%

[a]FC2,000 × $2:FC1 = $4,000
[b]FC2,000 × $1.8:FC1 = $3,600
[c]FC2,000 × $2.4:FC1 = $4,800

Changes in exchange rates also affect profit margins and rates of return. The profit margin for a firm is a weighted average of the profit margins of its domestic and foreign units, for which the weights are the sales mix percentages. Changes in exchange rates affect the sales mix proportions (in addition to any affects on the amount for foreign-source earnings) and thereby the firm's overall profit margin.

In PepsiCo's MD&A section accompanying its 2008 Annual Report (Appendix B), PepsiCo discusses the effects of exchange rates on the sales of its various divisions. For some of the divisions, foreign exchange rate fluctuations (and acquisitions) explain major portions of the compound growth rate for sales. In Chapter 10, we predict PepsiCo's future sales. To perform this analysis, we analyze the effects of exchange rates on sales.

SUMMARY

Investing activities create the capacity for operations. Firms invest in assets for their own operations. Their balance sheets report the balances of property, plant, and equipment; intangible assets (including goodwill); and natural resources. Firms also invest in the operations of other firms. Their balance sheets report passive investments in marketable debt and equity securities; active equity method investments in affiliates; and because they are the consolidated with entities they control, the individual assets, liabilities, revenues, and expenses of majority investments in subsidiaries and VIEs for which they are the primary beneficiary.

Firms undertake investing activities on behalf of the claimants to the firm's assets—debtholders, preferred shareholders, controlling interests in shareholders' equity, and noncontrolling interests in shareholders' equity. Management's goal is to generate returns on these investments through operating activities. The next chapter examines the operating process and presents the accounting and reporting for operating activities.

QUESTIONS, EXERCISES, PROBLEMS, AND CASES

Questions and Exercises

7.1 CAPITALIZATION VERSUS EXPENSING DECISION. When a firm incurs costs on an item to be used in operations, management must decide whether to treat the cost as an asset or an expense. Assume that a company used cash to acquire machinery expected to contribute to the generation of revenues over a three-year period and the company erroneously expensed the cost to acquire the machine.

a. Describe the effects on ROA of the error over the three-year period.
b. Explain how the error would affect the statement of cash flows.

7.2 SELF-CONSTRUCTED ASSETS. Assume that a company needs to acquire a large special-purpose materials handling facility. Given that no outside vendor exists for this type of facility and that the company has available engineering, management, and productive capacity, the company borrows funds and builds the facility. Identify the costs to construct this facility that should be capitalized as assets.

7.3 NATURAL RESOURCES. The three types of costs incurred in oil production are acquisition costs (costs to acquire the oil fields, minus the cost of the land, plus the present value of future cash flows necessary to restore the site), exploration costs (costs of drilling), and development costs (pipes, roads, and so on, to extract and transport the oil to refineries). Should each of these costs be capitalized or expensed? Explain.

7.4 RESEARCH AND DEVELOPMENT COSTS. U.S. GAAP requires firms to expense immediately all internal expenditures for R&D costs. Alternatively, GAAP could require firms to capitalize and subsequently amortize all internal expenditures on R&D that have future potential. Why have standard setters chosen not to allow the capitalization alternative? How would analysts be better served if GAAP required capitalization of R&D costs?

7.5 CAPITALIZATION OF SOFTWARE DEVELOPMENT COSTS. In practice, very few firms capitalize costs of developing computer software. However, *Statement No. 86* requires that firms capitalize (and subsequently amortize) development costs once the "technological feasibility" stage of a product is reached. Review the Adobe Systems illustration in the chapter (Example 5) and discuss why the firm does not capitalize any software development costs.

7.6 TESTING FOR GOODWILL IMPAIRMENT. Goodwill is an intangible asset that firms report on their balance sheets as a result of acquiring other firms. Goodwill generally has an indefinite life and should not be amortized, but should be tested for impairment at least annually. Describe the procedures prescribed by U.S. GAAP and IFRS to test for goodwill impairment. How do these procedures differ from the procedure followed for testing the impairment of a patent, which is an intangible asset with a definite life?

7.7 EARNINGS MANAGEMENT AND DEPRECIATION MEASUREMENT. Earnings management entails managers using judgment and reporting estimates in such a way as to alter reported earnings to their favor.

a. Discuss the three factors that must be estimated in measuring depreciation.
b. Provide an illustration as to how each of these factors can be employed to manage earnings.

7.8 CORPORATE ACQUISITIONS AND GOODWILL. Not every acquisition results in goodwill reported in the consolidated balance sheet. Describe the valuation procedures followed by the acquiring firms to determine whether any goodwill should be recorded as a result of an acquisition and the circumstances that could lead to no recognition of goodwill in an acquisition.

7.9 CORPORATE ACQUISITIONS AND ACQUISITION RESERVES. Often the application of the acquisitions method entails establishing one or more acquisition reserves. Define an acquisition reserve, provide several examples of such reserves, and discuss how the quality of accounting information can be diminished as a result of misusing acquisition reserves.

7.10 ACCOUNTING FOR AVAILABLE-FOR-SALE AND TRADING MARKETABLE EQUITY SECURITIES. Firms invest in marketable securities for a variety of reasons. One of the most common reasons is to temporarily invest excess cash. Securities that qualify for the available-for-sale reporting classification are accounted for differently from those that qualify for the trading reporting classification. Describe the similarity between the reporting for the two classifications. Also describe the differences in reporting between the two classifications.

7.11 EQUITY METHOD FOR MINORITY, ACTIVE INVESTMENTS. GAAP requires firms to account for equity investments in which ownership is between 20 and 50 percent using the equity method. Ace Corporation owns 35 percent of Spear Corporation during 2010. Spear Corporation reported net income of $100.4 million for 2010 and declared and paid dividends of $25 million during the year.

a. Calculate the equity income that Ace Corporation reports in 2010 related to its ownership in Spear Corporation.

b. What does Ace Corporation report in its statement of cash flows for 2010 related to its ownership in Spear Corporation?

c. Assuming that Ace Corporation's balance sheet account, Investment in Spear Corporation, is $1,100 million at the beginning of 2010, what is the balance in the account at the end of 2010? Support your answers with calculations.

7.12 CONSOLIDATION OF VARIABLE-INTEREST ENTITIES. Some accounting theorists propose that firms should consolidate any entity in which they have a "controlling financial interest." Typically, the percentage of equity ownership that one firm has in another entity determines whether consolidation is appropriate, with greater than 50 percent ownership requiring consolidation. Why is the percentage of ownership criterion often *not* appropriate for judging whether a VIE should be consolidated? What criterion is used to determine whether a VIE should be consolidated?

7.13 CHOICE OF A FUNCTIONAL CURRENCY. Choosing the functional currency is a key decision for translating the financial statements of foreign entities of U.S. firms into U.S. dollars. Qing Corporation, a U.S. firm that sells car batteries, formed a wholly owned subsidiary in Mexico to manufacture components needed in the production of the batteries. Approximately 50 percent of the subsidiary's sales are to Qing Corporation. The subsidiary also sells the components it manufactures to independent third parties, and these sales are denominated in Mexican pesos. Financing for the manufacturing plants in Mexico is denominated in U.S. dollars, but labor contracts are denominated in both dollars and pesos. All material contracts are denominated in Mexican pesos. Senior managers of the subsidiary are employees of Qing Corporation who have been transferred to the subsidiary for a tour of international service. Is the functional currency of the subsidiary the peso or the U.S. dollar? Explain your reasoning.

7.14 FOREIGN CURRENCY AS FUNCTIONAL CURRENCY. Identify the exchange rates used to translate income statement and balance sheet items when the foreign currency is defined as the functional currency. Discuss the logic for the use of the exchange rates you identified.

Problems and Cases

7.15 ANALYZING DISCLOSURES REGARDING FIXED ASSETS. Exhibit 7.29 presents selected financial statement data for three chemical companies: Monsanto Company, Olin Corporation, and NewMarket Corporation. (NewMarket was formed from a merger of Ethyl Corporation and Afton Chemical Corporation.)

Required

a. Compute the average total depreciable life of assets in use for each firm.

b. Compute the average age to date of depreciable assets in use for each firm at the end of the year.

EXHIBIT 7.29

Three Chemical Companies
Selected Financial Statement Data on Depreciable Assets
(amounts in millions)
(Problem 7.15)

	NewMarket Corporation	Monsanto Company	Olin Corporation
Depreciable Assets at Cost:			
Beginning of year	$752	$4,611	$1,796
End of year	777	4,604	1,826
Accumulated Depreciation:			
Beginning of year	584	2,331	1,301
End of year	611	2,517	1,348
Net Income	33	267	55
Depreciation expense	27	328	72
Deferred tax liability relating to depreciable assets:			
Beginning of year	13	267	83
End of year	9	256	96
Income tax rate	35%	35%	35%
Depreciation method for financial reporting	Straight-Line	Straight-Line	Straight-Line
Depreciation method for tax reporting	Accelerated	Accelerated	Accelerated

c. Compute the amount of depreciation expense recognized for tax purposes for each firm for the year using the amount of the deferred taxes liability related to depreciation timing differences.

d. Compute the amount of net income for the year for each firm assuming that depreciation expense for financial reporting equals the amount computed in Part c for tax reporting.

e. Compute the amount each company would report for property, plant, and equipment (net) at the end of the year if it had used accelerated (tax reporting) depreciation instead of straight-line depreciation.

f. What factors might explain the difference in average total life of the assets of NewMarket Corporation and Olin Corporation relative to the assets of Monsanto Company?

g. What factors might explain the older average age for depreciable assets of NewMarket Corporation and Olin Corporation relative to Monsanto Company?

7.16 ASSET IMPAIRMENTS

Hammerhead Paper Company owns a press used in the production of fine paper products. The press originally cost $2,000,000, and it has a current carrying amount of $1,200,000. A decrease in the demand for fine paper products has caused the company to reassess the future cash flows from using the machine. The company now estimates that it will receive cash flows of $160,000 per year for 12 years. The company uses a 10 percent discount rate to compute the present value for this investment. A similar machine recently sold for $1,000,000 in the secondhand market. Hammerhead estimates that it would cost $50,000 to sell the machine.

Required

a. Compute the amount of Hammerhead's press impairment, if any, under U.S. GAAP and IFRS.

Sterling Co. acquires Vineyard Aging, Inc., on January 1, 2010, by paying $2,000,000 in cash. At the date of acquisition, the price is allocated as follows:

Price paid	$ 2,000,000
Fair value of Vineyard's identifiable assets	(1,600,000)
Goodwill	$ 400,000

One year later on December 31, 2010, Sterling estimates the fair value of the unit to be $1,800,000. The carrying value of Vineyard's identifiable assets is $1,500,000 after impairment tests are applied.

Required

b. Compute the amount of Sterling's goodwill impairment, if any.

c. How is the goodwill impairment reflected in the financial statements?

7.17 UPWARD REVALUATIONS UNDER IFRS

Bed and Breakfast (B&B), an Italian company operating in the Tuscany region, follows IFRS and has made the choice to remeasure long-lived assets at fair value. B&B purchased land in 2009 for €150,000. At the end of the next four years, the land is worth €160,000 in 2009, €155,000 in 2010, €140,000 in 2011, and €145,000 in 2012.

Required

a. Describe how B&B will reflect the changes in the land's value in each of its annual financial statements.

b. Assume that the asset was a building with a ten-year remaining useful life as of the end of 2009. After writing the building upward to €160,000, how much should B&B charge to depreciation expense in 2009?

7.18 APPLICATION OF *STATEMENT NO. 115* FOR INVESTMENTS IN MARKETABLE EQUITY SECURITIES. SunTrust Banks owns a large block of Coca-Cola Company (Coke) common stock that it has held for many years. SunTrust indicates in a note to its financial statements that all equity securities held by the bank, including its investment in Coke stock, are classified as available for sale. A recent annual report of SunTrust reports the following information for its Coke investment (amounts in thousands):

Coke common stock investment, market value on December 31, 2006	$2,324,826
Coke common stock investment, market value on December 31, 2005	$1,945,622
Net income for 2006	$2,109,742

Required

a. Calculate the effect of the change in the market value of SunTrust's investment in Coke's common stock on SunTrust's 2006 (1) net income and (2) shareholders' equity. Ignore taxes.

b. How would your answer to Part a differ if SunTrust classified its investment in Coke's common stock as a trading security?

c. Does the value reported on SunTrust's balance sheet for the investment in Coke's stock differ depending on the firm's reason for holding the stock (that is, whether it is classified as available for sale versus trading by management)? Explain.

7.19 EFFECT OF AN ACQUISTION ON THE DATE OF ACQUISITION BALANCE SHEET. Lexington Corporation acquired all of the outstanding common stock of Chalfont, Inc., on January 1, 2009. Lexington gave shares of its no par common stock with a market value of $504 million in exchange for the Chalfont common stock. Chalfont will remain a legally separate entity after the exchange, but Lexington will prepare consolidated financial statements with Chalfont each period. Exhibit 7.30 presents the balance sheets of Lexington and Chalfont on January 1, 2009, just prior to the acquisition. The market value of Chalfont's fixed assets exceeds their book value by $80 million. Chalfont owns a copyright with a market value of $50 million. Chalfont is a defendant in a lawsuit that it expects to settle during 2009 at a cost of $30 million. The firm carries no insurance against such lawsuits. Lexington plans to establish an acquisition reserve for this lawsuit.

Required

a. Prepare a schedule that shows the allocation of the consideration given to individual assets and liabilities under the acquisition method. Ignore deferred tax effects.

b. Prepare a consolidated balance sheet for Lexington and Chalfont on January 1, 2009. Show your supporting calculations for any amount that is not simply the sum of the amounts for Lexington and Chalfont from their separate financial records.

EXHIBIT 7.30

Lexington Corporation and Chalfont, Inc.
Balance Sheets
January 1, 2009
(amounts in millions)
(Problem 7.19)

	Lexington Corporation	Chalfont, Inc.
Cash	$ 100	$ 30
Accounts receivable	240	90
Fixed assets (net)	1,000	360
Copyright	—	—
Deferred tax asset	40	—
Goodwill	—	—
Total Assets	$1,380	$480
Accounts payable and accruals	$ 240	$ 80
Long-term debt	480	100
Deferred tax liability	160	—
Other noncurrent liabilities	120	—
Common stock	320	100
Retained earnings	60	200
Total Liabilities and Shareholders' Equity	$1,380	$480

7.20 EFFECT OF AN ACQUISITION ON THE POSTACQUISITION BALANCE SHEET AND INCOME STATEMENT. Ormond Co. acquired all of the outstanding common stock of Daytona Co. on January 1, 2010. Ormond Co. gave shares of its common stock with a fair value of $312 million in exchange for 100 percent of the Daytona Co. common stock. Daytona Co. will remain a legally separate entity after the exchange, but Ormond Co. will prepare consolidated financial statements with Daytona Co each period. Exhibit 7.31 presents the balance sheets of Ormond Co. and Daytona Co. on January 1, 2010, just after the acquisition. The following information applies to Daytona Co.:

1. The market value of Daytona Co.'s fixed assets exceeds their book value by $50 million.
2. Daytona Co. owns a patent with a market value of $40 million.
3. Daytona Co. is a defendant in a lawsuit that it expects to settle during 2010 at a cost of $25 million. The firm carries no insurance against such lawsuits. If permitted, Ormond Co. wants to establish an acquisition reserve for this lawsuit.
4. Daytona Co. has an unrecognized and unfunded retirement health care benefits obligation totaling $20 million on January 1, 2010.

Required

a. Prepare a consolidated balance sheet for Ormond Co. and Daytona Co. on January 1, 2010. Ignore deferred tax effects. (A consolidated worksheet is not required, but it will be illustrated in the solution.)

EXHIBIT 7.31

Ormond Co. and Daytona Co.
Balance Sheets on January 1, 2010
(amounts in millions)
(Problem 7.20)

	Ormond Co.	Daytona Co.
Cash	$ 25	$ 15
Accounts receivable	60	40
Investment in Daytona	312	—
Fixed assets (net)	250	170
Patent	—	—
Deferred tax asset	10	—
Goodwill	—	—
Total Assets	$657	$225
Accounts payable & accruals	$ 60	$ 40
Long-term debt	120	60
Deferred tax liability	40	—
Other noncurrent liabilities	30	—
Common stock	392	50
Retained earnings	15	75
Total Liabilities and Shareholders' Equity	$657	$225

b. Exhibit 7.32 presents income statements and balance sheets taken from the separate-company books at the end of 2010. The following information applies to these companies:

- The fixed assets of Daytona Co. had an average remaining life of five years on January 1, 2010. The firms use the straight-line depreciation method.
- The patent of Daytona Co. had a remaining life of ten years on January 1, 2010.
- Daytona Co. settled the lawsuit during 2010 and expects no further liability.
- Daytona Co. will amortize and fund its retirement health care benefits obligation over 20 years. It included $1 million in operating expenses during 2010 related to amounts unrecognized and unfunded as of January 1, 2010.
- The test for goodwill impairment indicates that no impairment charge is necessary for 2010.

Prepare a consolidated income statement for 2010 and a consolidated balance sheet on December 31, 2010. (A consolidated worksheet is not required, but it will be illustrated in the solution.)

7.21 VARIABLE-INTEREST ENTITIES. Molson Coors Brewing Company (Molson Coors) is the fifth-largest brewer in the world. It is one of the leading brewers in the U.S. and Canada; the company's brands include Coors, Molson Canadian, Carling, and Killian's Irish Red. Sales exceeded 32 million barrels (1 U.S. barrel equals 31 gallons) for the year ended December 26, 2004. The firm reported $4.3 billion of net sales for 2004.

Molson Coors invests in various entities to carry out its brewing, bottling, and canning activities. The investments take the legal form of partnerships, joint ventures, and limited

EXHIBIT 7.32

Ormond Co. and Daytona Co.
Income Statement and Balance Sheet for 2010
(in millions)
(Problem 7.20)

	Ormond Co.	Daytona Co.
Income Statement for 2010		
Sales	$ 600	$ 450
Equity in earnings of Daytona Co.	30	—
Operating expenses	(550)	(395)
Interest expense	(10)	(5)
Loss on lawsuit	—	(20)
Income tax expense	(28)	(12)
Net Income	$ 42	$ 18
Balance Sheet on December 31, 2010		
Cash	$ 45	$ 25
Accounts receivable	80	50
Investment in Daytona Co.	339	—
Fixed assets	280	195
Patent	—	—
Deferred tax asset	15	—
Goodwill	—	—
Total Assets	$ 759	$ 270
Accounts payable and accruals	$ 90	$ 55
Long-term debt	140	75
Deferred tax liability	50	—
Other noncurrent liabilities	40	—
Common stock	392	50
Retained earnings	47	90
Total Liabilities and Shareholders' Equity	$ 759	$ 270

liability corporations, among other arrangements. The firm states in its 2004 annual report that each of these arrangements has been tested to determine whether it qualifies as a VIE under *Interpretation No. 46*. (*Interpretation No. 46R* supersedes this interpretation by clarifying certain aspects of its predecessor interpretation. However, most of the content is similar, and either interpretation is sufficient to address this problem.)

The following excerpt is taken from the firm's note on VIEs in its 2004 annual report:

> Note 3. Variable-Interest Entities. Once an entity is determined to be a VIE, the party with the controlling financial interest, the primary beneficiary, is required to consolidate it. We have investments in VIEs, of which we are the primary beneficiary. Accordingly, we have consolidated three joint ventures in 2004, effective December 29, 2003, the first day of 2004. These include Rocky Mountain Metal Container (RMMC), Rocky Mountain Bottle Company (RMBC) and Grolsch (UK) Limited (Grolsch). The impacts to our balance sheet include the addition of net fixed assets of RMMC and RMBC totaling approximately $65 million, RMMC debt of approximately $40 million,

and Grolsch net intangibles of approximately $20 million (at current exchange rates). The most significant impact to our cash flow statement for the year ended December 26, 2004, was to increase depreciation expense by approximately $13.2 million and cash recognized on initial consolidation of the entities of $20.8 million. Our partners' share of the operating results of the ventures is eliminated in the minority interests line of the Consolidated Statements of Income.

As required under *Interpretation No. 46,* Molson Coors also provides additional information in its annual report on each of the consolidated joint ventures, as follows:

1. RMBC is a joint venture with Owens-Brockway Glass Container, Inc., in which we hold a 50 percent interest. RMBC produces glass bottles at a glass-manufacturing facility for use at the Golden, Colorado brewery. Under this agreement, RMBC supplies our bottle requirements and Owens-Brockway has a contract to supply the majority of our bottle requirements not met by RMBC. In 2003 and 2002, the firm's share of pretax joint venture profits for the venture, totaling $7.8 million and $13.2 million, respectively, was included in cost of goods sold on the consolidated income statement.
2. RMMC, a Colorado limited liability company, is a joint venture with Ball Corporation in which we hold a 50 percent interest. RMMC supplies the firm with substantially all of the cans for our Golden, Colorado brewery. RMMC manufactures the cans at our manufacturing facilities, which RMMC operates under a use and license agreement. In 2003 and 2002, the firm's share of pretax joint venture profits (losses), totaling $0.1 million and ($0.6) million, respectively, was included in cost of goods sold on the consolidated income statement. As stated previously, on consolidation of RMMC, debt of approximately $40 million was added to the balance sheet. As of December 26, 2004, Coors is the guarantor of this debt.
3. Grolsch is a joint venture between CBL and Royal Grolsch N.V. in which we hold a 49 percent interest. The Grolsch joint venture markets Grolsch branded beer in the United Kingdom and the Republic of Ireland. The majority of the Grolsch branded beer is produced by CBL under a contract brewing arrangement with the joint venture. CBL and Royal Grolsch N.V. sell beer to the joint venture, which sells the beer back to CBL (for onward sale to customers) for a price equal to what it paid plus a marketing and overhead charge and a profit margin. In 2003 and 2002, the firm's share of pretax profits for this venture, totaling $3.6 million and $2.0 million, respectively, was included in cost of goods sold on the consolidated income statement. As stated previously, on consolidation, net fixed assets of approximately $4 million and net intangibles of approximately $20 million were added to our balance sheet.

Required

a. Describe the operational purpose of the three VIEs consolidated by Molson Coors.

b. Molson Coors is the primary beneficiary for three investments that the firm identified as VIEs. What criteria did Molson Coors apply to determine that the firm is the primary beneficiary for these three investments?

c. For each investment, Molson Coors reports the income statement impact as a reduction of cost of goods sold on the consolidated income statement. What is the rationale for reporting the impact this way on the income statement?

d. The firm states, "Our partners" share of the operating results of the ventures is eliminated in the minority interests line of the Consolidated Statements of Income. Define *minority interests* as it appears on the income statement. Discuss why Molson Coors subtracts it to calculate consolidated net income.

e. RMBC, RMMC, and Grolsch are consolidated with the financial statements of Molson Coors because the three investments qualify as VIEs as defined in *Interpretation No. 46* and the firm determined that it is the primary beneficiary for the investments. Explain what reporting technique Molson Coors would use to account for the investments if, in fact, they did not qualify as VIEs. What would be the impact on the balance sheet? What would be the impact on the income statement? What would be the impact on the statement of cash flows?

f. The firm reports that the depreciation expense on the statement of cash flows for 2004 increased by approximately $13.2 million as a result of consolidating the VIEs. Why did consolidating the VIEs increase depreciation expense?

7.22 ACCOUNTING FOR A MERGER UNDER THE ACQUISITION METHOD. On December 31, 2010, Pace Co. paid $3,000,000 to Sanders Corp. shareholders to acquire 100 percent of the net assets of Sanders Corp. Pace Co. also agreed to pay former Sanders shareholders $200,000 in cash if certain earnings projections were achieved over the next two years. Based on probabilities of achieving the earnings projections, Pace estimated the fair value of this promise to be $150,000. Pace paid $10,000 in legal fees and incurred $10,000 in internal cash costs related to management's time to complete the transaction. Exhibit 7.33 provides the book and fair values of Sanders Corp. at the date of acquisition.

EXHIBIT 7.33

Sanders Corp. Book and Fair Values as of December 31, 2010
(Problem 7.22)

	Sanders Corp. Book Values at 12/31/10	Sanders Corp. Fair Values at 12/31/10
Cash	$ 400,000	$ 400,000
Receivables	500,000	500,000
Inventory	1,200,000	1,600,000
PP&E (net)	1,600,000	2,000,000
Unpatented technology	0	300,000
In-process R&D	0	200,000
Total Assets	$ 3,700,000	$ 5,000,000
Accounts payable	$ (400,000)	$ (400,000)
Notes payable	(2,100,000)	(2,200,000)
Total Liabilities	$(2,500,000)	$(2,600,000)
Common stock ($1 par)	$ (100,000)	
Additional paid-in capital	(500,000)	
Retained earnings, 1/1/09	(300,000)	
Revenues	(2,000,000)	
Expenses	1,700,000	
Total Shareholders' Equity	$(1,200,000)	

Revenues, gains, and net income are in parentheses to indicate that their signs are opposite those of expenses and losses; that is, they are credits for those interpreting the worksheet from the accountant's traditional debit/credit approach. Liabilities and shareholders' equity accounts are in parentheses to indicate that they are claims against assets; again, they are credits in the traditional debit/credit framework.

Required

a. Record the merger using the financial statement effects template or journal entries.
b. How would the financial effects *change* if the cash paid was $2,000,000?

7.23 CONSOLIDATION SUBSEQUENT TO THE DATE OF ACQUISITION METHOD. Exhibit 7.34 presents the separate financial statements at December 31, 2011, of Prestige Resorts and its 80 percent-owned subsidiary Booking, Inc. Two years earlier on January 1, 2010, Prestige acquired 80 percent of the common shares of Booking for $1,170 million in cash. Booking's 2010 net income was $105 million, and Booking paid no dividends in 2010. Booking's 2011 income was $135 million, and it paid $75 million dividends on common stock during 2011. Booking's pre- and post-acquisition stock prices do not support the existence of a control premium. Exhibit 7.35 shows the allocation of fair value at the date of acquisition, January 1, 2010. Exhibit 7.36 traces Prestige Resorts' equity method accounting for Booking, Inc. Ignore deferred tax effects.

EXHIBIT 7.34

Prestige Resorts and Booking, Inc. Financial Statements
at December 31, 2011 (in millions)
(Problem 7.23)

	Prestige Resorts	Booking, Inc.
Revenues	$(1,365)	$ (645)
Cost of goods sold	516	300
Depreciation expense	90	30
Amortization expense	150	112.5
Interest expense	105	67.5
Equity in subsidiary earnings	(96)	0
Net Income	$ (600)	$ (135)
Cash	$ 780	$ 600
Short-term investments	309	67.5
Land	456	442.5
Equipment (net)	585	240
Investment in Small Technologies	1,278	0
Customer lists	1,320	810
Total Assets	$ 4,728	$ 2,160
Long-term liabilities	$(1,623)	$ (885)
Common stock	(1,305)	(345)
Retained earnings	(1,800)	(930)
Total Liabilities and Shareholders' Equity	$(4,728)	$(2,160)

Revenues, gains, and net income are in parentheses to indicate that their signs are opposite those of expenses and losses; that is, they are credits for those interpreting the worksheet from the accountant's traditional debit/credit approach. Liabilities and shareholders' equity accounts are in parentheses to indicate that they are claims against assets; again, they are credits in the traditional debit/credit framework.

EXHIBIT 7.35

Allocations of Fair Value (in millions)
(Problem 7.23)

	Allocation of Fair Values	Estimated Life	Charged (Credited) to Expense Each Year	Balance on December 31, 2011
Booking fair value at acquisition date	$ 1,462.5			
Booking book value at acquisition date	(1,110.0)			
Fair value in excess of book value	$ 352.5			
Land (not depreciated)	90	NA		
Equipment	(15)	10		
Customer lists	180	20		
Long-term liabilities (lower fair value)	60	8		
Goodwill	$ 37.5	Indefinite		
			___	

EXHIBIT 7.36

Investor Interests in Booking, Inc. (in millions)
(Problem 7.23)

	Prestige Properties (80% controlling interest)		Noncontrolling Interest (20%)	
Acquisition date fair value (1/1/10) = $1,462.5		$1,170		
2010 net income of Booking = $105	$ 84			
Annual excess amortizations = $15	(12)		___	
Equity in Booking's earnings for 2010		72		___
Investment in Booking, Inc. (12/31/10)		$1,242		
2011 net income of Booking = $135	$108			
Annual excess amortizations = $15	(12)		___	
Equity in Booking's earnings for 2011		96		
Dividends paid by Booking in 2011 = $75		(60)		___
Investment in Booking, Inc. (12/31/11)		$1,278		

Required

a. Complete Exhibit 7.35 to show income effects and balance sheet adjustments to be reflected in the December 31, 2011 Eliminations column of the consolidated worksheet.

b. Complete Exhibit 7.36 to trace the noncontrolling interests in Booking, Inc.'s earnings and net assets.

c. Prepare a worksheet to consolidate Prestige and Booking at December 31, 2011.

7.24 CALCULATING THE TRANSLATION ADJUSTMENT UNDER THE ALL-CURRENT METHOD AND THE MONETARY/NONMONETARY METHOD. Foreign Sub is a wholly owned subsidiary of U.S. Domestic Corporation. U.S. Domestic Corporation acquired the subsidiary several years ago. The financial statements for Foreign Sub for 2010 in its own currency appear in Exhibit 7.37.

The exchange rates between the U.S. dollar and the foreign currency of the subsidiary were as follows:

December 31, 2009	\$10:1FC
Average, 2009	\$ 8:1FC
December 31, 2010	\$ 6:1FC

On January 1, 2010, Foreign Sub issued FC100 of long-term debt and FC100 of common stock in the acquisition of land costing FC200. Operating activities occurred evenly over the year.

EXHIBIT 7.37

Foreign Sub
Financial Statement Data
(Problem 7.24)

	December 31	
	2009	2010
Cash	FC 100	FC 150
Accounts receivable	300	350
Inventories	350	400
Land	500	700
Total Assets	FC 1,250	FC 1,600
Accounts payable	FC 150	FC 250
Long-term debt	200	300
Common stock	500	600
Retained earnings	400	450
Total Liabilities and Equities	FC 1,250	FC 1,600

	For 2010
Sales	FC 4,000
Cost of goods sold	(3,200)
Selling and administrative expenses	(400)
Income taxes	(160)
Net Income	FC 240
Dividend declared and paid on December 31	(190)
Increase in Retained Earnings	FC 50

Required

a. Assume that the currency of Foreign Sub is the functional currency. Compute the change in the cumulative translation adjustment for 2010. Indicate whether the change increases or decreases shareholders' equity.

b. Assume that the U.S. dollar is the functional currency. Compute the amount of the translation gain or loss for 2010. Indicate whether the amount is a gain or loss.

7.25 TRANSLATING THE FINANCIAL STATEMENTS OF A FOREIGN SUBSIDIARY; COMPARISON OF TRANSLATION METHODS. Stebbins Corporation established a wholly owned Canadian subsidiary on January 1, Year 1, by contributing US$500,000 for all of the subsidiary's common stock. The exchange rate on that date was C$1:US$.90 (that is, one Canadian dollar equaled 90 U.S. cents). The Canadian subsidiary invested C$500,000 in a building with an expected life of 20 years and rented it to various tenants for the year. The average exchange rate during Year 1 was C$1:US$.85, and the exchange rate on December 31, Year 1, was C$1:US$.80. Exhibit 7.38 shows the amounts taken from the books of the Canadian subsidiary at the end of Year 1, measured in Canadian dollars.

EXHIBIT 7.38

Canadian Subsidiary
Financial Statements
Year 1
(Problem 7.25)

Balance Sheet as of December 31, Year 1	
ASSETS	
Cash	C$ 77,555
Rent receivable	25,000
Building (net)	475,000
	C$577,555
LIABILITIES AND EQUITY	
Accounts payable	C$ 6,000
Salaries payable	4,000
Common stock	555,555
Retained earnings	12,000
	C$577,555
Income Statement for Year 1	
Rent revenue	C$125,000
Operating expenses	(28,000)
Depreciation expense	(25,000)
Translation exchange loss	—
Net Income	C$ 72,000
Retained Earnings Statement for Year 1	
Balance, January 1, Year 1	C$ —
Net income	72,000
Dividends	(60,000)
Balance, December 31, Year 1	C$ 12,000

Required

a. Prepare a balance sheet, an income statement, and a retained earnings statement for the Canadian subsidiary for Year 1 in U.S. dollars assuming that the Canadian dollar is the functional currency. Include a separate schedule showing the computation of the translation adjustment account.

b. Repeat Part a assuming that the U.S. dollar is the functional currency. Include a separate schedule showing the computation of the translation gain or loss.

c. Why is the sign of the translation adjustment for Year 1 under the all-current translation method and the translation gain or loss for Year 1 under the monetary/nonmonetary translation method the same? Why do their amounts differ?

d. Assuming that the firm could justify either translation method, which method would management of Stebbins Corporation likely prefer for Year 1? Why?

7.26 TRANSLATING THE FINANCIAL STATEMENTS OF A FOREIGN SUBSIDIARY; SECOND YEAR OF OPERATIONS. Refer to Problem 7.25 for Stebbins Corporation for Year 1, its first year of operations. Exhibit 7.39 shows the amounts

EXHIBIT 7.39

Canadian Subsidiary
Financial Statements
Year 2
(Problem 7.26)

Balance Sheet	
ASSETS	
Cash	C$116,555
Rent receivable	30,000
Building (net)	450,000
	C$596,555
LIABILITIES AND EQUITY	
Accounts payable	C$ 7,500
Salaries payable	5,500
Common stock	555,555
Retained earnings	28,000
	C$596,555
Income Statement	
Rent revenue	C$150,000
Operating expenses	(34,000)
Depreciation expense	(25,000)
Translation exchange gain	—
Net Income	C$ 91,000
Retained Earnings Statement	
Balance, January 1, Year 2	C$ 12,000
Net income	91,000
Dividends	(75,000)
Balance, December 31, Year 2	C$ 28,000

for the Canadian subsidiary for Year 2. The average exchange rate during Year 2 was C\$1:US\$.82, and the exchange rate on December 31, Year 2, was C\$1:US\$.84. The Canadian subsidiary declared and paid dividends on December 31, Year 2.

Required

a. Prepare a balance sheet, an income statement, and a retained earnings statement for the Canadian subsidiary for Year 2 in U.S. dollars, assuming that the Canadian dollar is the functional currency. Include a separate schedule showing the computation of the translation adjustment for Year 2 and the change in the translation adjustment account.

b. Repeat Part a assuming that the U.S. dollar is the functional currency. Include a separate schedule showing the computation of the translation gain or loss.

c. Why is the sign of the translation adjustment for Year 2 under the all-current translation method and the translation gain or loss under the monetary/nonmonetary translation method the same? Why do their amounts differ?

d. Assuming that the firm could justify either translation method, which method would management of Stebbins Corporation likely prefer for Year 2? Why?

7.27 IDENTIFYING THE FUNCTIONAL CURRENCY. Electronic Computer Systems (ECS) designs, manufactures, sells, and services networked computer systems; associated peripheral equipment; and related network, communications, and software products.

Exhibit 7.40 presents geographic segment data. ECS conducts sales and marketing operations outside the U.S. principally through sales subsidiaries in Canada, Europe,

EXHIBIT 7.40

Electronic Computer Systems
Geographic Segment Data
(amounts in thousands)
(Problem 7.27)

	Year 3	Year 4	Year 5
Revenues			
United States Customers	\$ 4,472,195	\$ 5,016,606	\$ 5,810,598
Intercompany	1,354,339	1,921,043	2,017,928
Total	\$ 5,826,534	\$ 6,937,649	\$ 7,828,526
Europe Customers	\$ 2,259,743	\$ 3,252,482	\$ 4,221,631
Intercompany	82,649	114,582	137,669
Total	\$ 2,342,392	\$ 3,367,064	\$ 4,359,300
Canada, Far East, Americas			
Customers	\$ 858,419	\$ 1,120,356	\$ 1,443,217
Intercompany	577,934	659,204	912,786
Total	\$ 1,436,353	\$ 1,779,560	\$ 2,356,003
Eliminations	\$(2,014,922)	\$(2,694,829)	\$(3,068,383)
Net Revenue	\$ 7,590,357	\$ 9,389,444	\$11,475,446

EXHIBIT 7.40 (Continued)

	Year 3	Year 4	Year 5
Income			
United States	$ 342,657	$ 758,795	$ 512,754
Europe	405,636	634,543	770,135
Canada, Far East, Americas	207,187	278,359	390,787
Eliminations	(126,771)	(59,690)	(38,676)
Operating Income	$ 828,709	$ 1,612,007	$ 1,635,000
Interest Income	116,899	122,149	143,665
Interest Expense	(88,079)	(45,203)	(37,820)
Income before Income Taxes	$ 857,529	$ 1,688,953	$ 1,740,845
Assets			
United States	$ 3,911,491	$ 4,627,838	$ 5,245,439
Europe	1,817,584	2,246,333	3,093,818
Canada, Far East, Americas	815,067	843,067	1,293,906
Corporate Assets (temporary cash investments)	2,035,557	1,979,470	2,057,528
Eliminations	(1,406,373)	(1,289,322)	(1,579,135)
Total Assets	$ 7,173,326	$ 8,407,386	$10,111,556

Central and South America, and the Far East; by direct sales from the parent corporation; and through various representative and distributorship arrangements. The company's international manufacturing operations include plants in Canada, the Far East, and Europe. These manufacturing plants sell their output to the company's sales subsidiaries, the parent corporation, or other manufacturing plants for further processing.

ECS accounts for intercompany transfers between geographic areas at prices representative of unaffiliated-party transactions.

Sales to unaffiliated customers outside the United States, including U.S. export sales, were $5,729,879,000 for Year 5, $4,412,527,000 for Year 4, and $3,179,143,000 for Year 3, which represented 50 percent, 47 percent, and 42 percent, respectively, of total operating revenues. The international subsidiaries have reinvested substantially all of their earnings to support operations. These accumulated retained earnings, before elimination of intercompany transactions, aggregated $2,793,239,000 at the end of Year 5, $2,070,337,000 at the end of Year 4, and $1,473,081,000 at the end of Year 3.

The company enters into forward exchange contracts to reduce the impact of foreign currency fluctuations on operations and the asset and liability positions of foreign subsidiaries. The gains and losses on these contracts increase or decrease net income in the same period as the related revenues and expenses; for assets and liabilities, in the period in which the exchange rate changes.

Required

Discuss whether ECS should use the U.S. dollar or the currencies of its foreign subsidiaries as its functional currency.

INTEGRATIVE CASE 7.1

STARBUCKS

Part I—Accounting Policy

Presented below are excerpts from Note 1 to Starbucks' September 28, 2008, Consolidated Financial Statements in which Starbucks describes accounting policy for long-lived assets.

Excerpts from Note 1: "Summary of Significant Accounting Policies"

Property, Plant and Equipment

Property, plant and equipment are carried at cost less accumulated depreciation. Depreciation of property, plant and equipment, which includes assets under capital leases, is provided on the straight-line method over estimated useful lives, generally ranging from two to seven years for equipment and 30 to 40 years for buildings. Leasehold improvements are amortized over the shorter of their estimated useful lives or the related lease life, generally 10 years. For leases with renewal periods at the Company's option, Starbucks generally uses the original lease term, excluding renewal option periods, to determine estimated useful lives. If failure to exercise a renewal option imposes an economic penalty to Starbucks, management may determine at the inception of the lease that renewal is reasonably assured and include the renewal option period in the determination of appropriate estimated useful lives. The portion of depreciation expense related to production and distribution facilities is included in "Cost of sales including occupancy costs" on the consolidated statements of earnings. The costs of repairs and maintenance are expensed when incurred, while expenditures for refurbishments and improvements that significantly add to the productive capacity or extend the useful life of an asset are capitalized. When assets are retired or sold, the asset cost and related accumulated depreciation are eliminated with any remaining gain or loss reflected in net earnings.

Goodwill and Other Intangible Assets

Goodwill and other intangible assets are tested for impairment annually and more frequently if facts and circumstances indicate goodwill carrying values exceed estimated reporting unit fair values and if indefinite useful lives are no longer appropriate for the Company's trademarks. Based on the impairment tests performed, there was no impairment of goodwill or other intangible assets in fiscal 2008, 2007 and 2006. Definite-lived intangibles, which mainly consist of contract-based patents and copyrights, are amortized over their estimated useful lives. For further information on goodwill and other intangible assets, see Note 9.

Long-lived Assets

When facts and circumstances indicate that the carrying values of long-lived assets may be impaired, an evaluation of recoverability is performed by comparing the carrying values of the assets to projected undiscounted future cash flows in addition to other quantitative and qualitative analyses. Upon indication that the carrying values of such assets may not be recoverable, the Company recognizes an impairment loss by a charge to net earnings. The fair value of the assets is estimated using the discounted future cash flows of the assets. Property, plant and equipment assets are grouped at the lowest level for which there are identifiable cash flows when assessing impairment. Cash flows for retail assets are identified at the individual store level. Long-lived assets to be disposed of are reported at the lower of their carrying amount, or fair value less estimated costs to sell.

The Company recognized net impairment and disposition losses of $325.0 million, $26.0 million and $19.6 million in fiscal 2008, 2007 and 2006, respectively, due to underperforming Company-operated retail stores, as well as renovation and remodeling activity in the normal course of business. The net losses in fiscal 2008 include $201.6 million of asset impairments related to the US and Australia store closures and charges incurred for office facilities no longer occupied by the Company due to the reduction in positions within Starbucks leadership structure and non-store organization. See Note 3 for further details. Depending on the underlying asset that is impaired, these losses may be recorded in any one of the operating expense lines on the consolidated statements of earnings: for retail operations, these losses are recorded in "Restructuring charges" and "Store operating expenses"; for specialty operations, these losses are recorded in "Other operating expenses"; and for all other operations, these losses are recorded in "Cost of sales including occupancy costs," "General and administrative expenses," or "Restructuring charges."

Research and Development

Starbucks expenses research and development costs as they are incurred. The Company spent approximately $7.2 million, $7.0 million and $6.5 million during fiscal 2008, 2007 and 2006, respectively, on technical research and development activities, in addition to customary product testing and product and process improvements in all areas of its business.

Asset Retirement Obligations

Starbucks accounts for asset retirement obligations under FASB Interpretation No. 47 ("FIN 47"), "Accounting for Conditional Asset Retirement Obligations—an interpretation of FASB Statement No. 143," which it adopted at the end of fiscal 2006. FIN 47 requires recognition of a liability for the fair value of a required asset retirement obligation ("ARO") when such obligation is incurred. The Company's AROs are primarily associated with leasehold improvements which, at the end of a lease, the Company is contractually obligated to remove in order to comply with the lease agreement. At the inception of a lease with such conditions, the Company records an ARO liability and a corresponding capital asset in an amount equal to the estimated fair value of the obligation. The liability is estimated based on a number of assumptions requiring management's judgment, including store closing costs, cost inflation rates and discount rates, and is accredited to its projected future value over time. The capitalized asset is depreciated using the convention for depreciation of leasehold improvement assets. Upon satisfaction of the ARO conditions, any difference between the recorded ARO liability and the actual retirement costs incurred is recognized as an operating gain or loss in the consolidated statements of earnings. ARO expense was $6.5 million and $4.2 million, in fiscal 2008 and 2007, respectively, with components included in "Costs of sales including occupancy costs," and "Depreciation and amortization expenses". The initial impact of adopting FIN 47 at the end of fiscal year 2006 was a charge of $27.1 million, with a related tax benefit of $9.9 million, for a net expense of $17.2 million, with the net amount recorded as a cumulative effect of a change in accounting principle on the consolidated statement of earnings for fiscal year 2006. As of September 28, 2008 and September 30, 2007, the Company's net ARO asset included in "Property, plant and equipment, net" was $18.5 million and $20.2 million, respectively, while the Company's net ARO liability included in "Other longterm liabilities" was $44.6 million and $43.7 million, as of the same respective dates.

Required

a. Leasehold improvements are substantial costs incurred by Starbucks to outfit, remodel, and improve leased retail outlets. Why does Starbucks capitalize and amortize leasehold improvements? Does its policy for determining useful lives in the presence of a lease renewal option yield high-quality accounting numbers? How would Starbucks account for the leasehold improvement costs remaining at the end of a lease it had expected to renew but did not?

b. Starbucks has an ARO related to the leasehold improvements. Describe how Starbucks recognizes the ARO initially in the balance sheet. Then describe how Starbucks recognizes changes in the ARO-related asset and ARO liability in the income statement over time. How is income affected when Starbucks actually spends cash to return a leased property to its original condition? If Starbucks spends more cash than reflected in the ARO liability, how will it account for the difference?

c. How would the first sentence of the Long-lived Assets section of Note 1 appear if Starbucks followed IFRS? Which system do you believe provides the best quality accounting for long-lived asset impairment?

d. The second paragraph of the long-lived assets section of the note describes how Starbucks reflects impairment charges in the income statement. Which line item would you prefer that Starbucks use to report the charges? Why?

e. How would the first sentence of Starbucks R&D accounting policy appear if Starbucks followed IFRS? Do you prefer the IFRS or U.S. GAAP approach to R&D accounting? Why?

Part II—Business Combinations (Majority, Active Investments)

Starbucks prepares consolidated financial statements. Presented below are excerpts from Note 1 describing accounting policy, Note 2, and a major portion of Note 9 from Starbucks' fiscal 2008 Consolidated Financial Statements.

Excerpts from Note 1: Recent Accounting Pronouncements

In December 2007, the FASB issued SFAS No. 141 (revised 2007), "Business Combinations" ("SFAS 141R"), which replaces SFAS 141. SFAS 141R establishes principles and requirements for how an acquirer recognizes and measures in its financial statements the identifiable assets acquired, the liabilities assumed, any resulting goodwill, and any noncontrolling interest in the acquiree. SFAS 141R also provides for disclosures to enable users of the financial statements to evaluate the nature and financial effects of the business combination. SFAS 141R will be effective for Starbucks first fiscal quarter of 2010 and must be applied prospectively to business combinations completed on or after that date.

In December 2007, the FASB issued SFAS No. 160, "Noncontrolling Interests in Consolidated Financial Statements—an amendment of Accounting Research Bulletin No. 51" ("SFAS 160"), which establishes accounting and reporting standards for noncontrolling interests ("minority interests") in subsidiaries. SFAS 160 clarifies that a noncontrolling interest in a subsidiary should be accounted for as a component of equity separate from the parent's equity. SFAS 160 will be effective for Starbucks first fiscal quarter of 2010 and must be applied prospectively, except for the presentation and disclosure requirements, which will apply retrospectively. The Company is currently evaluating the potential impact that adoption of SFAS 160 may have on its consolidated financial statements.

Note 2: Business Acquisitions

In the fourth quarter of fiscal 2008, the Company acquired substantially all of the assets, including development and operating rights, of Coffee Vision, Inc. ("CVI") and Coffee Vision Atlantic, Inc. ("CVAI"), its licensee in Quebec and Atlantic Canada. In addition, Starbucks acquired full development and operation rights for the retail stores in these provinces. In the third quarter of fiscal 2008, Starbucks purchased 100% equity ownership in Coffee Equipment Company ("CEC"), a Seattle-based manufacturer and seller of a single cup, commercial grade coffee brewer called the CloverTM. In the second quarter of fiscal 2008, the Company purchased the remaining 10% equity ownership in its operations in Beijing, China. Starbucks has applied the consolidation method of accounting since the first quarter of fiscal 2007, when it acquired 90% of these previously-licensed operations.

Note 9: Other Intangible Assets and Goodwill

Other intangible assets consisted of the following *(in millions)*:

Fiscal Year Ended	Sept. 28, 2008	Sept. 30, 2007
Indefinite-lived intangibles	$58.3	$36.9
Definite-lived intangibles	14.2	9.5
Accumulated amortization	(5.9)	(4.3)
Definite-lived intangibles, net	8.3	5.2
Total other intangible assets	$66.6	$42.1
Definite-lived intangibles approximate remaining weighted average useful life in years	8	8

The increase in indefinite-lived intangibles was primarily due to the purchase of distribution rights for Seattle Best Coffee products in Canada as well as the CEC acquisition (see Note 2). The increase in definite-lived intangibles was primarily due to patents acquired in the CEC acquisition. Amortization expense for definite-lived intangibles was $1.5 million, $1.0 million and $1.2 million during fiscal 2008, 2007 and 2006, respectively.

The changes in the carrying amount of goodwill by reportable operating segment for the fiscal year ended September 28, 2008 were as follows *(in millions)*:

	United States	International	Global CPG	Total
Balance as of September 30, 2007	$127.6	$ 78.3	$9.7	$215.6
Business Acquisitions	11.8	39.3	—	51.1
Other	—	(0.2)	—	(0.2)
Balance as of September 28, 2008	$139.4	$117.4	$9.7	$266.5

United States

The $11.8 million increase in goodwill was due to the acquisition of CEC.

International

The increase in goodwill was due to the acquisition of CVI and CVAI, as well as the remaining equity interest in Beijing during the fiscal year, which increased goodwill by $33.0 million and $6.3 million, respectively (see Note 2). The decrease related to "Other" was due to foreign currency fluctuations.

Required

a. How will the concept of fair value drive the accounting for future acquisitions?

b. Starbucks indicates that it will account for the change in standards relating to non-controlling (minority) interests "prospectively." What does that mean?

c. What caused the change in goodwill during 2008? What, if any, impairments were recorded?

Part III—Minority, Passive Investments

Presented below is a major portion of Starbucks' Note 4 to its fiscal 2008 Consolidated Financial Statements in which it describes its minority passive investments.

Excerpt from Note 4: Short-term and Long-term Investments
The Company's short-term and long-term investments consisted of the following *(in millions)*:

	Amortized Cost	Gross Unrealized Holding Losses	Fair Value
September 28, 2008			
Short-term investments—available-for-sale securities:			
Corporate debt securities	$ 3.0	$ —	$ 3.0
Total	3.0	$ —	3.0
Short-term investments—trading securities	58.2		49.5
Total short-term investments	$ 61.2		$ 52.5
Long-term investments—available-for-sale securities:			
State and local government obligations	$ 65.8	$(6.0)	$ 59.8
Corporate debt securities	12.1	(0.5)	11.6
Total long-term investments	$ 77.9	$(6.5)	$ 71.4
September 30, 2007			
Short-term investments—available-for-sale securities:			
State and local government obligations	$ 81.4	$(0.1)	$ 81.3
US government agency obligations	2.5	—	2.5
Total	83.9	$(0.1)	83.8
Short-term investments—trading securities	67.8		73.6
Total short-term investments	$151.7		$157.4
Long-term investments—available-for-sale securities:			
US government agency obligations	$ 21.0	$ —	$ 21.0

For available-for-sale securities, proceeds from sales were $75.9 million, $47.5 million and $431.2 million, in fiscal years 2008, 2007 and 2006, respectively. Gross realized gains from sales were $3.8 million in fiscal year 2006. Gross realized losses from sales were $0.1 million in fiscal year 2006. For fiscal years 2008 and 2007, there were no realized losses and immaterial amounts of realized gains from sales.

As of September 28, 2008, the Company's long-term available-for-sale securities of $71.4 million included $59.8 million invested in auction rate securities ("ARS"). As of September 30, 2007, the Company held $75.6 million of ARS, which were all classified as short-term available-for-sale securities. ARS have long-dated maturities but provide liquidity through a Dutch auction process that resets the applicable interest rate at predetermined calendar intervals. Due to the auction failures that began in mid-February 2008, these securities became illiquid and were classified as long-term investments. The investment principal associated with the failed auctions will not be accessible until:

- successful auctions resume;
- an active secondary market for these securities develops;
- the issuers replace these securities with another form of financing; or
- final payments are made according to the contractual maturities of the debt issues which range from 22 to 37 years.

The Company intends to hold the ARS until it can recover the full principal amount and has the ability to do so based on other sources of liquidity. The Company expects such recoveries to occur prior to the contractual maturities. In July 2008, one of the Company's ARS was called at its par value of $4.7 million. The Company recorded $6.0 million of unrealized losses on ARS in fiscal 2008, determined to be temporary, which is included in accumulated other comprehensive income as a reduction in shareholders' equity. The Company's ARS are collateralized by portfolios of student loans, substantially all of which are guaranteed by the United States Department of Education. As of September 28, 2008, approximately $4.4 million in ARS was rated AA/Aa3 by Standard & Poor's and Moody's, respectively. All of the remaining securities were rated AAA by two or more of the following major rating agencies: Moody's, Standard & Poor's and Fitch Ratings.

Gross unrealized holding losses on the state and local obligations consist of unrealized losses on the Company's twelve ARS. Gross unrealized holding losses on the corporate debt pertain to five fixed income securities and were primarily caused by interest rate increases subsequent to the date of purchase. The contractual terms of the non-ARS fixed income securities do not permit the issuer to settle at a price less than the par value of the investment, which is the equivalent of the amount due at maturity. As Starbucks has the ability and intent to hold its available-for-sale securities until a recovery of fair value, which may be at maturity, the Company does not consider these securities to be other-than-temporarily impaired. Long-term corporate debt securities generally mature in less than five years. There were no realized losses recorded for other than temporary impairments during fiscal years 2008, 2007 or 2006.

Trading securities are comprised mainly of marketable equity mutual funds that approximate a portion of the Company's liability under the Management Deferred Compensation Plan ("MDCP"), a defined contribution plan. The corresponding deferred compensation liability of $68.0 million in fiscal 2008 and $86.4 million in fiscal 2007 is included in "Accrued compensation and related costs" on the consolidated balance sheets. In fiscal years 2008 and 2007, the changes in net unrealized holding gains/losses in the trading portfolio included in earnings were a net loss of $14.5 million and a net gain of $7.5 million, respectively.

Required

a. As of its September 28, 2008 fiscal year-end, Starbucks reports short-term investments in trading securities having an amortized cost of $58.2 million and a fair value of $49.5 million. Calculate (and explain) the amounts Starbucks shows in the following financial statement accounts as of September 28, 2008. Assume a 35 percent tax rate.

(i) September 28, 2008 Short-term investments—trading securities

(ii) 2008 net income effect of the trading securities transactions

(iii) September 28, 2008 retained earnings effect of the trading securities transactions
(iv) 2008 comprehensive income effect of the trading securities transactions
(v) September 28, 2008 accumulated other comprehensive income effect of the trading securities transactions

b. Repeat Requirement 1 assuming that the securities are available for sale instead of trading.

c. Starbucks' available-for-sale securities are primarily ARS. The ARS have been shifted from short- to long-term investments due to liquidity problems in the auction market. At September 28, 2008, the securities had an amortized cost of $65.8 million and a fair value of $59.8 million; thus, they are reported at $59.8 million in the balance sheet. What caused the fair value change? Could Starbucks justify a reclassification of the securities to keep fair value changes out of comprehensive income?

Part IV—Minority Active Investments

Note 7 to Starbucks' 2008 Consolidated Financial Statements presents information about equity method (minority, active) investments.

Note 7: Equity and Cost Investments

The Company's equity and cost investments consisted of the following (*in millions*):

Fiscal Year Ended	Sept. 28, 2008	Sept. 30, 2007
Equity method investments	$267.9	$234.5
Cost method investments	34.7	24.4
Total	$302.6	$258.9

Equity Method

The Company's equity investees and ownership interests by reportable operating segment are as follows:

Fiscal Year Ended	Sept. 28, 2008	Sept. 30, 2007
United States		
StarCon, LLC	50.0%	50.0%
International		
Starbucks Coffee Korea Co., Ltd	50.0	50.0
Starbucks Coffee Austria GmbH	50.0	50.0
Starbucks Coffee Switzerland AG	50.0	50.0
Starbucks Coffee España, S.L.	50.0	50.0
President Starbucks Coffee Taiwan Ltd.	50.0	50.0
Shanghai President Coffee Co.	50.0	50.0
Starbucks Coffee France SAS	50.0	50.0
Berjaya Starbucks Coffee Company Sdn. Bhd. (Malaysia)	50.0	49.9
Starbucks Brasil Comercio de Cafes Ltda.	49.0	49.0
Starbucks Coffee Japan, Ltd.	40.1	40.1
Starbucks Coffee Portugal Lda.	50.0	—
CPG		
The North American Coffee Partnership	50.0	50.0
Starbucks Ice Cream Partnership	50.0	50.0

StarCon, LLC is a joint venture formed in March 2007 with Concord Music Group, Inc. that is engaged in the recorded music business. The International entities operate licensed Starbucks retail stores. The Company also has licensed the rights to produce and distribute Starbucks branded products to two partnerships in which the Company holds 50% equity interests: The North American Coffee Partnership with the Pepsi-Cola Company develops and distributes bottled Frappuccino® beverages and Starbucks DoubleShot® espresso drinks, and Starbucks Ice Cream Partnership with Dreyer's Grand Ice Cream, Inc. develops and distributes superpremium ice creams. Prior to fiscal 2005, Starbucks acquired equity interest in its licensed operations of Malaysia, Austria, Shanghai, Spain, Switzerland and Taiwan. The carrying amount of these investments was $24.3 million more than the underlying equity in net assets due to acquired goodwill, which is evaluated for impairment annually. No impairment was recorded during fiscal years 2008, 2007 or 2006.

The Company's share of income and losses is included in "Income from equity investees" on the consolidated statements of earnings. Also included is the Company's proportionate share of gross margin resulting from coffee and other product sales to, and royalty and license fee revenues generated from, equity investees. Revenues generated from these related parties, net of eliminations, were $128.1 million, $107.9 million and $94.2 million in fiscal years 2008, 2007 and 2006, respectively. Related costs of sales, net of eliminations, were $66.2 million, $57.1 million and $47.5 million in fiscal years 2008, 2007 and 2006, respectively. As of September 28, 2008 and September 30, 2007, there were $40.6 million and $30.6 million of accounts receivable, respectively, on the consolidated balance sheets from equity investees primarily related to product sales and store license fees.

As of September 28, 2008, the aggregate market value of the Company's investment in Starbucks Japan was approximately $214 million, based on its available quoted market price.

Summarized combined financial information of the Company's equity method investees, that represent 100% of the investees' financial information, was as follows (*in millions*):

Financial Position as of	**Sept. 28, 2008**	**Sept. 30, 2007**
Current assets	$ 247.2	$ 183.1
Noncurrent assets	604.9	408.6
Current liabilities	273.5	166.4
Noncurrent liabilities	59.8	56.8

Results of Operations for Fiscal Year Ended	**Sept. 28, 2008**	**Sept. 30, 2007**	**Oct. 1, 2006**
Net revenues	$1,961.0	$1452.9	$1,303.5
Operating income	171.3	186.2	152.3
Earnings before cumulative effect of change in accounting principle	136.9	159.5	136.4
Net earnings	136.9	159.5	124.0

Cost Method

The Company has equity interests in entities to develop and operate Starbucks licensed retail stores in several global markets, including Mexico, Hong Kong and Greece. Additionally, Starbucks has investments in privately held equity securities unrelated to Starbucks licensed retail stores of $2.8 million at September 28, 2008 and September 30, 2007. As of September 28, 2008 and September 30, 2007, management determined that the estimated fair values of each cost method investment exceeded the related carrying values.

There were no realized losses recorded for other-than-temporary impairment of the Company's cost method investments during fiscal years 2008, 2007 or 2006.

Starbucks has the ability to acquire additional interests in some of these cost method investees at certain intervals. Depending on the Company's total percentage of ownership interest and its ability to exercise significant influence over financial and operating policies, additional investments may require the retroactive application of the equity method of accounting.

Required

a. Starbucks' 2008 net income is $315.5 million, and its interest expense is $53.4 million. Assuming a tax rate of 35 percent and the information presented in the worksheet below the requirements, compute Starbucks' 2008 ROA.

b. Using the worksheet below and the note information, consolidate the unconsolidated equity method affiliates using a full consolidation approach. Recompute ROA and explain the change in ROA.

c. Using the information from the full consolidation worksheet, describe how you would change your computation of ROA if you followed a proportionate consolidation approach. Recompute ROA under that approach.

Full Consolidation of Equity Method Affiliates

September 28, 2008	Starbucks	Affiliates	Eliminations	Consolidated
Current assets	$ 1,748.0			
Equity and cost investments	302.6			
Remainder of noncurrent assets	3,622.0			
Total Assets	$ 5,672.6			
Current liabilities	$(2,189.7)			
Noncurrent liabilities	(992.0)			
Shareholders' equity (noncontrolling interest)				
Shareholders' equity (controlling interest)	(2,490.9)			
Total Liabilities and Shareholders' Equity	$(5,672.6)			

September 30, 2007	Starbucks	Affiliates	Eliminations	Consolidated
Current assets	$ 1,696.5			
Equity and cost investments	258.9			
Remainder of noncurrent assets	3,388.5			
Total Assets	$ 5,343.9			
Current liabilities	$(2,155.6)			
Noncurrent liabilities	(904.2)			
Shareholders' equity (noncontrolling interest)				
Shareholders' equity (controlling interest)	(2,284.1)			
Total Liabilities and Shareholders' Equity	$(5,343.9)			

Part V—Investments in Long-Lived Assets

Presented below is a portion of Note 8 to Starbucks' 2008 Consolidated Financial Statements.

Note 8: Property, Plant and Equipment
Property, plant and equipment consisted of the following *(in millions)*:

Fiscal Year Ended	Sep 28, 2008	Sep 30, 2007
Land	$ 59.1	$ 56.2
Buildings	217.7	161.7
Leasehold improvements	3,363.1	3,179.6
Store equipment	1,045.3	1,007.0
Roasting equipment	220.7	208.8
Furniture, fixtures and other	517.8	477.9
Work in progress	293.6	215.3
	$ 5,717.3	$ 5,306.5
Less accumulated depreciation and amortization	(2,760.9)	(2,416.1)
Property, plant and equipment, net	$ 2,956.4	$ 2,890.4

Required

a. Estimate the average total estimated useful life of depreciable property, plant, and equipment. Starbucks reports $604.5 million of depreciation and amortization in the statement of cash flows, of which $1.5 million relates to amortization of limited-life intangible assets. Does the estimate reconcile with stated accounting policy on useful lives for property, plant, and equipment? Explain.

b. How should an analyst interpret fluctuations in this estimate for a given company over time? How should an analyst interpret differences in this estimate between a company and its competitors?

c. Estimate the average age of depreciable assets, the percentage of PP&E that has been used up, and the remaining useful life. How might an analyst use this information?

Part VI—Brand Name

In 2008, Interbrand listed Starbucks as having the 85th most valuable brand name in the world and estimated brand value to be $3.9 billion. Examine the disclosures for intangible long-lived assets in Part II and tangible long-lived assets in Part V. Where in the financial statements does Starbucks disclose brand value?

Case 7.2

DISNEY ACQUISITION OF MARVEL ENTERTAINMENT

In September 2009, The Walt Disney Company announced that it would acquire Marvel Entertainment in a $4 billion cash and common stock deal. On a per-share basis, the consideration given by Disney to Marvel shareholders represents a 29 percent premium over Marvel's share price at the date of acquisition. Disney acquires the more than 5,000 characters in Marvel's library, including Iron Man, Spider-Man, X-Men, Captain America, and the Fantastic Four. Exhibit 7.41 presents the Condensed Consolidated Balance Sheet of Marvel at the end of its June 30, 2009 second quarter.

EXHIBIT 7.41

Marvel Entertainment, Inc.
Condensed Consolidated Balance Sheets
(unaudited)

	June 30, 2009	December 31, 2008
	(in thousands, except per share amounts)	
ASSETS		
Current assets:		
Cash and cash equivalents	$ 81,039	$105,335
Restricted cash	38,220	12,272
Short-term investments	—	32,975
Accounts receivable, net	29,471	144,487
Inventories, net	13,473	11,362
Income tax receivable	206	2,029
Deferred income taxes, net	25,497	34,072
Prepaid expenses and other current assets	9,164	5,135
Total current assets	$197,070	$347,667
Fixed assets, net	4,194	3,432
Film inventory, net	192,068	181,564
Goodwill	346,152	346,152
Accounts receivable, non-current portion	7,010	1,321
Income tax receivable, non-current portion	5,906	5,906
Deferred income taxes, net—non-current portion	17,046	13,032
Deferred financing costs	3,320	5,810
Restricted cash, non-current portion	42,274	31,375
Other assets	5,489	455
Total assets	$820,529	$936,714
LIABILITIES AND EQUITY		
Current liabilities:		
Accounts payable	$ 2,860	$ 2,025
Accrued royalties	89,912	76,580
Accrued expenses and other current liabilities	33,826	40,635
Deferred revenue	67,468	81,335
Film facility	—	204,800
Total current liabilities	$194,066	$405,375
Accrued royalties, non-current portion	806	10,499
Deferred revenue, non-current portion	93,696	48,939
Film facility, non-current portion	—	8,201
Income tax payable	66,522	59,267
Other liabilities	10,680	8,612
Total liabilities	$365,770	$540,893

EXHIBIT 7.41 (Continued)

	June 30, 2009	December 31, 2008
	(in thousands, except per share amounts)	
Commitments and contingencies	—	—
Marvel Entertainment, Inc. stockholders' equity:		
Preferred stock, $.01 par value, 100,000,000 shares authorized, none issued	—	—
Common stock, $.01 par value, 250,000,000 shares authorized, 134,681,030 issued and 77,997,619 outstanding in 2009 and 134,397,258 issued and 78,408,082 outstanding in 2008	$ 1,347	$ 1,344
Additional paid-in capital	752,438	750,132
Retained earnings	628,628	555,125
Accumulated other comprehensive loss	(4,574)	(4,617)
Total Marvel Entertainment, Inc. stockholders' equity before treasury stock	$1,377,839	$1,301,984
Treasury stock, at cost, 56,683,411 shares in 2009 and 55,989,176 shares in 2008	(921,700)	(905,293)
Total Marvel Entertainment, Inc. stockholders' equity	$ 456,139	$ 396,691
Noncontrolling interest in consolidated Joint Venture	(1,380)	(870)
Total equity	$ 454,759	$ 395,821
Total liabilities and equity	$ 820,529	$ 936,714

Required

a. From a strategic perspective, discuss why you believe Disney would make this acquisition.

b. Assuming that the assets and liabilities of Marvel approximate their individual fair values at the date of acquisition, compute goodwill.

c. This is a 100 percent acquisition. What role does the 29 percent premium play in the computation of goodwill? If this were a less than 100 percent acquisition, how would the 29 percent premium affect the computation of the noncontrolling interest?

d. Disney will record a decrease in its cash and an increase in its shareholders' equity totaling $4 billion at the date of acquisition. Contrast the rest of the financial statement effects on Disney's own records and on its consolidated balance sheet between two scenarios: Marvel is dissolved (a merger) and Marvel continues to exist as a separate legal entity (an acquisition).

e. It is unlikely that the assets and liabilities of Marvel as shown in the condensed quarterly balance sheet approximate their individual fair values at the date of acquisition. Indeed, some of Marvel's most valuable resources might not be recognized on their balance sheet. As a result, the entire excess acquisition price is not likely to be assigned to goodwill. Identify items that are likely to receive a portion of the allocation based on the differences between their book values and fair values.

Chapter 8

Operating Activities

Learning Objectives

1. Understand how financial accounting measures and reports the revenues and expenses a firm's operating activities generate, as well as the related assets, liabilities, and cash flows.
2. Review the criteria for recognizing revenue and expenses under the accrual basis of accounting and apply these criteria to various types of businesses.
3. Evaluate the financial statement effects of recognizing income prior to the point of sale, at the time of sale, and subsequent to sale.
4. Analyze and interpret the effects of FIFO versus LIFO on financial statements and convert the statements of a firm from a LIFO to a FIFO basis.
5. Identify the working capital investments that are created by operating activities.
6. Understand the financial statement effects of credit policy and credit risk.
7. Use the financial statement and footnote information for corporate income taxes to analyze the firm's tax strategies.
8. Understand the financial statement and note disclosures for pensions and other postemployment benefits.
9. Utilize financial statement and footnote information to assess how a firm is using derivative instruments to take or to hedge risk.

Chapters 6 and 7 discussed the accounting for financing and investing activities. Once a firm obtains financing and makes investments to create productive and service capacity, it commences operations. This chapter focuses on the accounting and reporting for operating activities.

As discussed in Chapters 2 and 3, the success of a firm's operating activities is reported in the operating income section of the income statement (on an accrual basis—success in generating value) and in the operating cash flows section of the statement of cash flows (on a cash basis—success in generating cash). Also, the balance sheet reflects a number of working capital and longer-term assets and liabilities generated for or by operations.

Example 1

PepsiCo's Consolidated Statement of Income reports operating profit for the year ended December 27, 2008, of $6,935 million. That amount is comprised of $43,251 million in net revenue less $20,351 million in cost of sales; $15,901 million in selling, general, and administrative expense (often called SG&A); and $64 million amortization of intangible assets. Because bottling activities are essential for a beverage producer, investments in affiliate bottlers are considered by most analysts to be a part of PepsiCo's operations; so the bottling equity income of $374 million also would be considered part of PepsiCo's operating activities. The income tax expense related to these aforementioned operating revenues and expenses is the largest portion of the provision for income taxes of $1,879 million. The amount by which operating revenues (accomplishments) exceed operating expenses (efforts) is the accrual basis measure of the operating success of the company in the current year.

PepsiCo's Consolidated Statement of Cash Flows shows net cash provided by operating activities of $6,999 million for the year ended December 27, 2008, a measure of current-period operating success on a cash basis. Like most firms, PepsiCo uses the indirect method to derive cash flow from operations and thus begins the section with net income of $5,142 million. PepsiCo then adjusts for all of the non-cash income items (such as depreciation and amortization expenses) as well as cash flows triggered by changes in operating assets and liabilities (that is, working capital). Therefore, the operating activities section prepared using the indirect method reconciles the two measures of operating success: accrual basis net income and cash basis cash flow from operations.

PepsiCo's Consolidated Balance Sheet reports assets and liabilities at December 27, 2008, most of which are used in or generated by operations. Chapter 6 examined the liabilities generated by financing activities: short-term and long-term debt obligations. Chapter 7 examined the operating assets generated by investing activities: short-term investments; property, plant, and equipment; amortizable intangible assets; goodwill; other nonamortizable intangible assets; and investments in noncontrolled affiliates. This chapter examines the remainder of the assets and liabilities generated for or by operations: the working capital assets (other than short-term investments) found in the current assets section; the working capital liabilities (other than short-term obligations) found in the current liabilities section; the income-tax-related liabilities, including income taxes payable and deferred income taxes; and the pension-related and other postemployment-benefits-related liabilities.

This chapter follows the organization of the income statement to explain operating activities. Accrual accounting measures operating success by the extent to which *accomplishments* (revenues) exceed *efforts* (expenses). Thus, we begin the chapter with the important topic of revenue recognition and the related working capital items created by delayed cash receipt (accounts receivable) and accelerated cash receipt (deferred revenues). Then we examine the accounting and reporting for the major income statement expenses, including cost of sales (along with a consideration of the working capital items inventory and accounts payable), SG&A expenses (including working capital accounts such as prepaid and accrued expenses), income tax expenses (and current and deferred taxes payable), and compensation expenses (including pensions and other postemployment benefits obligations). Finally, we conclude with the accounting for derivatives, which are financial instruments that firms use to take or to hedge operating, investing, and financing risks.

ACCOMPLISHMENTS (REVENUE RECOGNITION)

The income statement begins with a listing of revenues from sales and services. As discussed in Chapter 10, financial statement forecasting begins with a projection of future revenues, and many expense, asset, and liability forecasts are conditional on projected revenues. Therefore, understanding how and when firms recognize revenues is a crucial part of accounting analysis. The following sections discuss the criteria for revenue recognition and practical application of the criteria.

Criteria for Revenue Recognition

Revenue recognition is primarily a question of timing. One of the most important financial reporting decisions firms must make is *when* to recognize revenue. IFRS and U.S GAAP criteria for revenue recognition are similar but not identical. Under U.S. GAAP (FASB issued SFAC No. 5 guidance), revenue recognition occurs under the accrual basis of accounting when a firm has done both of the following:

1. Provided all or a substantial portion of the product to be delivered or the services to be performed. The firm has completed what it needs to do to earn the revenue.
2. Received an asset (such as cash, a receivable that the firm is reasonably certain it will collect or some other asset) or satisfied a liability (such as an advance from a customer or a deferred revenue), with a value the firm can measure with reasonable precision.[1]

A typical firm recognizes revenue at the time of sale, when it delivers goods or services to customers. At this point, a firm has completed production of the goods or creation of the services and has delivered them to a customer, satisfying the first criterion. The benefit a firm obtains from providing goods or services is the cash, receivable, or other consideration that the firm expects to receive. If the customer promises to pay cash in the future, the firm examines the credit standing of the customer and assesses the likelihood of receiving the cash. The second criterion is satisfied so long as the firm can reasonably predict the amount of cash it will collect or the value of the asset it has received or the liability it has satisfied.

The SEC (Securities and Exchange Commission) also considers revenue recognition to be critically important to accurate performance reporting and profit measurement. Accordingly, the SEC issued SAB 104, which outlines the following four conditions for revenue recognition:

1. There is pervasive evidence that an arrangement exists.
2. Delivery has occurred or services have been performed.
3. The seller's price to the buyer is fixed or determinable.
4. Collectability is reasonably assured.[2]

Although worded differently, the SAB 104 criteria are only slightly more restrictive than the two criteria provided by the FASB Concepts Statement (SFAC No. 5). The primary difference is in the addition of the first criterion, the pervasive evidence that an arrangement exists. Evidence of such an arrangement includes a formal contract with a customer stating the buyer's and seller's responsibilities and risks, as well as terms and timing of cash flows. However, less formal relations between buyer and seller that imply these conditions also may be judged as pervasive evidence, including prior business dealings and common business practices.

---

[1] Financial Accounting Standards Board, *Statement of Financial Accounting Concepts No. 5*, "Recognition and Measurement in Financial Statements of Business Enterprises" (1984).

[2] Securities and Exchange Commission, *Staff Accounting Bulletin No. 104, 17 CFR Part 211* (December 2003).

U.S. GAAP also has a substantial amount of industry- and transaction-specific guidance (for example, franchise, real estate, and motion picture revenue recognition) that is summarized in the FASB's Codification. On the other hand, IFRS guidance is nearly all general. With respect to the sale of goods, IFRS provides the following five criteria for revenue recognition:

1. The seller has transferred to the buyer the significant risks and rewards of ownership of the goods.
2. The seller has not retained either effective control or the kind of involvement that is associated with ownership.
3. The amount of revenue can be measured reliably.
4. It is probable that the seller will obtain the economic benefits associated with the transaction.
5. The costs incurred or to be incurred can be measured reliably.[3]

With respect to recognizing revenue from services, IFRS replaces the first two criteria with the criterion that the stage of completion of services can be measured reliably. Again, although worded differently, the IFRS criteria are consistent with U.S. GAAP in principle, and revenue recognition is generally consistent under the two sets of standards. However, one must realize that even subtle differences in wording of U.S. GAAP compared with the IFRS's "principles-based approach" could lead to differences in revenue recognition. Consider, for example, the SEC's requirement that "the seller's price to the buyer is fixed or determinable" versus the IFRS requirement that "the amount of revenue can be reasonably measured." Under the SEC's requirement, a sale involving contingent consideration (payments to the seller based on some future event) would not be recognized as revenue until the contingency is removed. Under IFRS, a high probability of contingency removal is considered "reliable" and revenue recognition can occur earlier.

The complexity of today's business environment, particularly the complexity and variety in commercial arrangements between sellers and customers, has heightened the importance of understanding a firm's business model and its relation to the revenue recognition principles chosen for reporting. Although in many cases it is relatively easy to determine when to recognize revenue (such as at the point of retail sales), in many other cases, it is not. Businesses with sales that include future performance obligations, sales that involve a barter exchange of services between firms, and sales that bundle several products and services are just a few examples in which the selection and application of revenue recognition principles can have a dramatic effect on the amount and timing of reported revenue.

Firms identify the significant accounting policies employed for recognizing revenues in notes to the financial statements. Exhibit 8.1 illustrates a recent disclosure by United Technologies describing how it recognizes revenues on long-term construction contracts, a technique discussed later in the chapter. United Technologies provides technology products and services to the building systems and aerospace industries worldwide. United Technologies' operating units include Otis, Carrier, Chubb, UTC First Security, and UTC Power in the commercial and residential property sectors and Pratt & Whitney, Hamilton Sundstrand, and Sikorsky Aircraft in the aerospace sector. Note that United Technologies' operations are sufficiently diverse to cause revenue recognition at different points in time, including "at the time deliveries are made," "on a percentage of completion basis," "as work is performed," and "over the contractual period or as services are performed." The following sections identify the justifications for recognizing revenue at different points in time.

---

[3] International Accounting Standards Board, *International Accounting Standard 18*, "Revenue" (1993). As of the writing of this textbook, the FASB and IASB are working on a revenue recognition project to clarify and converge the principles for revenue recognition.

EXHIBIT 8.1

United Technologies
Excerpt from "Note 1. Summary of Accounting Principles" in December 31, 2008
Consolidated Financial Statements

Revenue Recognition. Sales under government and commercial fixed-price contracts and government fixed-price-incentive contracts are recorded at the time deliveries are made or, in some cases, on a percentage-of-completion basis. Sales under cost reimbursement contracts are recorded as work is performed.

Sales under elevator and escalator sales, installation and modernization contracts are accounted for under the percentage-of-completion method.

Losses, if any, on contracts are provided for when anticipated. Loss provisions on original equipment contracts are recognized to the extent that estimated inventoriable manufacturing, engineering, product warranty and product performance guarantee costs exceed the projected revenue from the products contemplated under the contractual arrangement. For new commitments, we generally record loss provisions at the earlier of contract announcement or contract signing. For existing commitments, anticipated losses on contracts are recognized in the period in which losses become evident. Products contemplated under contractual arrangement include products purchased under contract and, in the large commercial engine business, future highly probable sales of replacement parts required by regulation that are expected to be purchased subsequently for incorporation into the original equipment. Revenue projections used in determining contract loss provisions are based upon estimates of the quantity, pricing and timing of future product deliveries. Losses are recognized on shipment to the extent that inventoriable manufacturing costs, estimated warranty costs and product performance guarantee costs exceed revenue realized. Contract accounting requires estimates of future costs over the performance period of the contract as well as estimates of award fees and other sources of revenue. These estimates are subject to change and result in adjustments to margins on contracts in progress. The extent of progress toward completion on our long-term commercial aerospace equipment and helicopter contracts is measured using units of delivery. In addition, we use the cost-to-cost method for development contracts in the aerospace businesses and for elevator and escalator sales, installation and modernization contracts in the commercial businesses. For long-term aftermarket contracts, revenue is recognized over the contract period in proportion to the costs expected to be incurred in performing services under the contract. We review our cost estimates on significant contracts on a quarterly basis, and for others, no less frequently than annually or when circumstances change and warrant a modification to a previous estimate. Adjustments to contract loss provisions are recorded in earnings upon identification.

Service sales, representing aftermarket repair and maintenance activities, are recognized over the contractual period or as services are performed. In the commercial businesses, revenue is generally recognized on a straight line basis. In the aerospace businesses, revenue is generally recognized in proportion to cost.

Revenues from engine programs under collaboration agreements are recorded as earned and the collaborator share of revenue is recorded as a reduction of revenue at that time. The collaborator share of revenues under Pratt & Whitney's engine programs was approximately $1.1 billion, $.9 billion and $.8 billion for 2008, 2007 and 2006, respectively. Costs associated with engine programs under collaboration agreements are expensed as incurred. The collaborator share of program costs is recorded as a reduction of the related expense item at that time.

PepsiCo discloses its revenue recognition policy in Note 2 to the financial statements, "Our Significant Accounting Policies—Revenue Recognition" (Appendix A), and in the first section of MD&A, "Our Critical Accounting Policies—Revenue Recognition" (Appendix B). Generally, PepsiCo recognizes revenue when it ships its products or delivers them to the customer. The straightforward revenue recognition policies are not surprising given the short-term nature of PepsiCo's products (food and beverages).

Application of Revenue Recognition Criteria

Applying the revenue recognition principles to actual business settings is not always as straightforward as it is for companies such as PepsiCo. The common expression "the devil is in the details" aptly describes the problem of assessing whether the principles are correctly applied in particular circumstances, and firms often must make subjective measurements, estimates, and judgments. Coupling this problem with the complexities of many commercial arrangements between businesses and customers, it is not surprising that appropriate application of revenue and expense recognition criteria is not always obvious. Indeed, revenue-related accounting is the single most frequent source of SEC enforcement actions and accounting restatements. To obtain a flavor for the complexities often involved in applying these principles, consider the five examples that follow.

Example 2

Xerox Corporation typically manufactures copiers and leases them to customers under multiyear leases. The length of the leases often approximates the useful life of the copiers. Thus, the arrangement is equivalent to a sale of the copier, with Xerox providing financing to the customer signing the lease. The accounting becomes complex, however, because the lease contract usually entails a bundled monthly payment that covers not just use of the copier by the customer over the life of the lease, but also maintenance services, photocopying supplies (paper and toner cartridges) up to certain minimum usage, and financing costs. The revenue recognition question is *when* Xerox should recognize revenue from the four services covered in the lease: (1) copier use, (2) maintenance, (3) supplies, and (4) financing.

The question is most easily answered by considering how Xerox accounts for outright sales of copiers. If Xerox sells a copier to a creditworthy customer, it recognizes revenue from the sale of the copier at the time of delivery. For Items (2)–(4), Xerox meets the substantial performance criterion for revenue recognition over time as it provides these goods and services and revenues for these components are recognized as the services are provided.

Often, however, the copier is *not* an outright sale, but rather a lease arrangement that involves a bundled periodic lease payment. Xerox must unbundle the monthly payment to ascertain the proportion of revenue related to each component of this bundled transaction. If the leasing arrangement is equivalent in economic substance to a sale, Xerox must determine (1) how much revenue the firm should recognize up front for manufacturing the copier and providing its use to the customer over its entire life and (2) how much the firm should allocate to the remaining three categories of the arrangement and recognize over time. In fact, Xerox does make these allocations, but the SEC accused Xerox of allocating too much of the monthly payment to the sale of the copiers and too little to maintenance, supplies, and financing. The result was an acceleration of revenues and earnings that authorities contended was too aggressive. Xerox accordingly restated its earnings.

Example 3

Founded in 1810, the Hartford Financial Services Group is one of the largest investment and insurance companies in the United States. Hartford is a leading provider of (1) life insurance and group and employee benefits, (2) automobile and homeowners insurance, and (3) business insurance.

Hartford's automobile insurance unit receives cash from both premiums and investments each period. It invests in readily marketable securities for the most part so it can measure objectively the changes in the market value of its investments. Measuring the amount of revenue each period while the automobile insurance policy is outstanding presents few difficulties because of the (generally) one-year policy coverage period. In contrast,

Harford's life insurance revenue recognition timing is more complex. In a term policy (five years, for example), it makes sense to recognize revenue over the five-year period. In a whole life policy, premium recognition timing depends on the expected life of the policyholder. Further, straight-line revenue recognition over a whole life policy may not make sense because the probability of death increases over time.

Another issue on the revenue side is whether these firms should recognize as revenue the interest and dividend income from investments as well as realized and unrealized gains and losses from changes in the market value of investments. Common practice in the insurance industry is to recognize both interest and dividend income as well as realized and unrealized gains and losses on investments each year in computing net income.

There is usually little question about the total expense associated with selling and underwriting an insurance policy. Other than selling commissions and administrative costs, the primary direct expense is processing and paying a claim. The income recognition issue is how much of this total cost life insurance companies should recognize as an expense each year to match against premium and investment revenues. The objective is to spread these costs over the life of the coverage period. Again, determining the length of this period for auto and term life is specified by the contract (usually one year), but for whole life contracts, the pattern of expense recognition requires actuarial calculations of expected life, investment returns, and similar factors. Note that allocating an equal portion of the total cost to each year of expected life will not necessarily provide an appropriate measure of performance. Although insurance premiums typically (again, not necessarily) remain level over the contract period, investment revenues increase over time as premiums and investment returns accumulate. Life insurance companies increase a liability each period, often called Policyholder Reserves, for the amount of expense recognized. They reduce this account when they pay insurance claims. An analyst examining the financial statements of a life insurance company should study carefully the amount shown for Policyholder Reserves and the change in this account each year. Such an assessment provides information about the adequacy of assets to cover potential claims and the amount of net income each period.

Example 4

MicroStrategy, Inc., is a software and consulting firm in the information technology sector. The firm specializes in tailoring proprietary software to analyze large databases of clients. Clients often sign two- or three-year contracts with the firm that cover customizing the software to the specific needs of the client and then licensing (as opposed to selling) the use of software for the length of the contract. The contracts often require MicroStrategy to train the client's personnel to use the software to mine large databases and to assist the client in designing reports and analyses based on this data mining. The contracts establish key deliverables, together with a schedule for the payment of fees over the life of the contract.

Assuming reasonable assurance of the collectability of fees from the client, the important revenue recognition issue is *when* MicroStrategy meets the substantial performance criterion for revenue recognition. The situation is complicated because MicroStrategy provides (1) a license to use its proprietary software tailored to the client's needs and (2) a consulting service to ensure that client personnel produce value-added reports and analyses. What proportion of the contract relates to the software, and what proportion relates to the consulting services? How precise are the deliverables requirements, which determine when MicroStrategy has completed the process to earn the revenue?

In the past, MicroStrategy recognized approximately 50 percent of the amount of the total contract as revenue at the time the contract was signed. The firm concluded that it had substantially performed about half of what it promised to the customer at the contract signing date. The SEC disagreed with this assessment, however, and concluded that 50 percent was far too aggressive and represented an inappropriate acceleration of revenue. MicroStrategy scaled back the amount of revenue it recognized at the contract signing date to approximately 10 percent and restated past financial statements. The news of the need to restate previously reported earnings led to a substantial drop in MicroStrategy's stock price.

Example 5

AOL, formerly the Internet services division of AOL Time Warner (it was spun off as a separate company in December 2009), generates subscription revenues from subscribers to its online services, as well as advertising revenues for advertisements it places on various websites.

In the past, AOL entered into an advertising arrangement with eBay. Under the arrangement, AOL located firms that wanted to advertise on the eBay website. AOL sold the advertising space to various companies and remitted a portion of this amount to eBay. AOL bore no credit risk if the firms failed to pay for the advertising space. AOL guaranteed the sale of a minimum amount of advertising space each month. Failure to sell the minimum space required AOL to make payments to eBay. AOL booked the amount to be received from the various companies as revenues and the amount paid to eBay as an expense. In turn, eBay booked the net amount received from AOL as revenue.

The accounting issue for this revenue stream is whether AOL is a principal or an agent in purchasing and selling advertising space. The revenue recognition described above considers AOL a principal because it entails booking the full revenue and expense. However, U.S. GAAP requires a firm to assume substantial product risk if it is to be considered a principal, which would not characterize the AOL–eBay arrangement if AOL is highly likely to sell sufficient advertising space each month to cover the minimum obligation to eBay. AOL bears little risk of unsold advertising space. Thus, it serves as an agent, which requires that only the *net* amount be recognized as revenue. The net amount would be the amount collected from purchasers of advertising less the amount AOL remits to eBay. The distinction is an important one because although there is no effect on net income, the magnitude of revenues reported as a principal is substantially higher than that reported as an agent. Revenues often are a driver for assessing firms, particularly technology and Internet firms such as AOL.

Priceline.com's business model, allowing customers to "name their price" when booking hotel rooms, generates similar revenue recognition questions. Should Priceline recognize the price of the hotel room as revenue (a practice known as grossing up) and the cost of the hotel room charged by the hotel to Priceline as cost of goods sold? Or should Priceline record only the difference between the price and the hotel cost as its "fee revenue"? The latter approach is probably the better measure of Priceline's revenue because recording the full revenue and full cost assumes that Priceline consumed an asset (the right to stay in a hotel room for a night) that caused the expense cost of goods sold. However, Priceline did not bear the risk of ownership of this asset. In fact, Priceline's only significant risk is its contention that it is "the merchant of record" in the transaction. The SEC does not permit the grossing up of revenue for agents, but controversy continues to surround revenue recognition in business models such as Priceline's.

Although the revenue-generating models of AOL and Priceline are unique, the grossing up of revenue also can be seen in more traditional situations where efficient inventory management practices exist. For example, if Dell Inc. receives an order and has its supplier ship inventory directly to the customer, as it often does, should Dell record the grossed-up revenue and associated cost of goods sold for the cost of the inventory that it has probably not even purchased at the time the customer's order was received? Should the French retailer Carrefour gross up revenues when it sells items on its floor that it does not purchase until the point of sale? The analyst who wants to compare ratios such as gross margin percentages across firms and forecast sales growth must read the notes to the financial statements carefully to understand the revenue recognition practices of firms and industries.

Example 6

Global Crossing, Qwest Communications, and other telecommunications companies have created worldwide fiber-optics networks in past years. Companies in the industry typically enter into long-term leases for the use of the networks developed by other companies in the industry. For example, Global Crossing might create a fiber-optics network in India, Qwest Communications might create a similar network in China, and each in turn might lease part of the capacity of the networks to each other. The leases often give the lessee an indefeasible right of use to the capacity, essentially a legal transfer of title to the capacity. Each company books the "sale" of the legal rights to the capacity as revenue in the year it signs the leases. The company treats the "purchase" of the legal rights to the capacity as a capital expenditure, much like the purchase of a long-lived asset.

The revenue recognition issue is whether these firms satisfy the revenue recognition criterion that requires receipt of an asset with a measurable cash-equivalent value when they swap legal rights to capacity. Recognize that, as opposed to the manufacture and sale of physical equipment, these situations simply involve the sale of legal rights to use capacity. If the capacity is already in place, the "manufacturing" activity is complete. As long as there are no significant restrictions on the ability of the buyer to use the capacity purchased, the purchaser of the capacity receives an asset: the right to use capacity of the other firm in the future.

The analyst must consider at least two other issues, however. First, is the seller of the capacity likely to exist for the full period of the contract and be in a position to provide the services? Financial difficulties that firms in the telecommunications industry experienced in recent years make this an important consideration. Second, how should the firms establish the value of the contract? Given that contracts often entail the swapping of promises to provide capacity in the future with no cash changing hands, it is difficult to determine their true value. What is the appropriate value to attach to the revenue for the seller at the signing of the contract? What is the appropriate value to attach to the expense recorded by the buyer during the course of the contract? The SEC decided that the capacity swap accounting inflated profits and assets for these telecommunication giants. They were required to restate their balance sheets and income statements to remove the effects of the swap accounting profits.

The five preceding examples illustrate the difficulty of applying general principles for recognizing revenues and expenses to business practices specific to particular industries. The analyst needs to increase the usual degree of healthy skepticism they practice in analyzing reported financial data when the activities of the firms or industries under scrutiny involve the level of uncertainty and subjectivity represented by these five illustrations. In recent years, the SEC has emphasized the importance to investors of understanding revenue recognition practices through an enforcement focus in the description of revenue recognition practices in the discussion of key accounting practices (often the first footnote to financial statements).

Revenue Recognition at the Time of Sale (Delivery)

For most firms (PepsiCo, for example), revenue recognition occurs at the point of product or service delivery. An account receivable (or cash in the case of a retail sale) is increased for the amount of the sale. If returns are allowed and can be reliably estimated, the sales revenue and associated accounts receivable are reported net of the expected returns.[4] The recognition of revenue at the time of sale (delivery) is so common that analysts may neglect to assess whether this timing is appropriate for a particular firm. Firms may attempt to increase reported earnings by accelerating the timing of revenues or estimating the collectible amounts too aggressively. If so, the quality of accounting information suffers because it does not represent a reliable measure of the economic resources the firm earned that period and is probably not sustainable.

Consider the following three conditions, each of which is a signal that revenue recognition at the time of sale may be too early: (1) large and volatile amounts of uncollectible accounts receivable, (2) unusually large amounts of returned goods, and (3) excessive warranty expenditures. Each of these sales-related expenses should bear a reasonably stable relationship to revenues over time. Large percentages of these expenses relative to sales or widely varying percentages from year to year should raise questions about the appropriateness of revenue recognition at the time of sale.

Another possible signal about potential deterioration in the quality of a firm's revenue recognition arises when a firm experiences a substantial increase in the number of days accounts receivable are outstanding. (Chapter 4 provides a discussion of how to calculate and interpret receivable days outstanding.) Customers taking longer to pay their invoices may suggest an overstatement of revenues and earnings. Note that the analyst should assess the receivable days outstanding *and* the stability of bad debt expense to revenue in tandem because either ratio may provide an incomplete signal about the quality of the firm's revenues. A firm that adequately recognizes bad debt expense for an increasing proportion of uncollectible sales will likely show a stable accounts receivable turnover because providing for estimated uncollectible accounts has the same effect on accounts receivable (that is, reduction) as collecting the accounts in cash. Thus, examining only the accounts receivable turnover does not signal the collection problem. The analyst must examine the ratio of bad debt expense to sales to observe the increasing proportion of uncollectible sales. A firm that does not adequately recognize bad debt expense for an increasing proportion of uncollectible sales will experience a buildup of accounts receivable relative to sales and therefore higher accounts receivable days outstanding. Examining only the ratio of bad debt expense to sales does not signal the slow rate at which customers pay.

Recognizing revenues at the time of sale suffers from an even more fundamental problem at times: to accelerate revenue recognition, some firms may alter their definition of *sale.* Does the receipt of firm customer orders for goods held in inventory constitute a sale? Or does the sale depend on physical delivery of the product and transfer of legal title to the customer? Is completion of custom-produced goods sufficient to recognize revenue, or is physical delivery necessary? In an effort to achieve sales targets for a period, firms sometimes record sales earlier than physical delivery. Revenues must not be recognized until the earnings process is substantially complete, which would suggest that revenues should not be recognized until the firm has delivered control and legal title of the products to customers.

Some firms, eager to report higher sales revenues or sales revenue increases, might be inclined to violate revenue recognition rules by recording sales based on merely an indication of interest in a product by a customer. The pressure that sales personnel place on themselves or that senior management places on them can lead to such a violation of the revenue recognition criteria. A related ploy is to accelerate the shipment of product and the recognition of sales revenues to closely related customers (such as dealerships, franchisees, and

[4] Financial Accounting Standards Board, *Statement of Financial Accounting Standards No. 48,* "Revenue Recognition When Right of Return Exists" (1981), *FASB Codification Topic 605,* provides explicit guidance. IFRS does not. If the amount of returns cannot be reliably estimated, revenue recognition is delayed until the return privilege expires.

affiliates) at the end of the year and then understate the likely sales returns by those customers (a practice known as channel-stuffing). Even more aggressively, some firms create artificial sales invoices and ship and store the goods in a remote or independently owned warehouse, hoping the independent auditor will not detect them.

Chapter 5 points out that the distinction between earnings management and management fraud is often a gray area. In the examples described above, however, it is clear that management crosses the line from earnings management to fraud. The actions are fraudulent in nature because they are outside the bounds of GAAP and management acts to intentionally mislead statement users. As stated earlier, the analyst should be vigilant in assessing whether firms are managing their revenues. Revenues are at the core of a firm's ability to generate and report profits and to grow and prosper. Firms that strive to achieve very aggressive sales growth objectives and firms experiencing declining sales growth relative to other firms in the industry are most likely to be tempted to manage earnings by "stretching" the revenue recognition rules. Although this type of earnings management eventually catches up with the firm, it is precisely in these situations that a firm's sustainable earnings are likely to be declining. The analyst needs to take this into account when forecasting future earnings.[5]

Delaying Revenue Recognition When Substantial Performance Remains

Cash is often collected from customers but the revenue recognition criteria have not been met, usually because the selling firm has not met some or all of its obligations to the buyer. The earlier example of insurance premiums being paid in advance, with revenues being recognized over the life of the policy is a case in point. Many other examples exist in which customers pay in advance of receiving goods or services and revenue recognition must be delayed until the revenues have been earned. Delayed revenue recognition typically arises with sales of gift cards redeemable for products (at Starbucks or Nordstrom, for instance), subscriptions, airfares, and memberships. For example, Sam's Club (a division of Walmart that offers discount warehouse shopping) collects an annual membership fee and promises to let customers shop at Sam's Club stores for one year. When it sells an annual membership, Walmart records the increase in cash, but must delay revenue recognition until Sam's Club meets its obligation to members over time. Walmart records a liability (often called deferred revenue, unearned revenue, or advances from customers) for the full amount of the membership fee. Each month of the annual membership period, Walmart removes one-twelfth of the liability and recognizes one-twelfth of the fee as revenue. At year-end, the portion of the membership fee that has not yet been earned is reported as a liability on Walmart's balance sheet; it will be earned as revenue during the next fiscal year.

Software firms such as MicroStrategy (Example 4) and Microsoft bundle product and services. For example, Microsoft bundles Windows® 7 software, telephone support, and future upgrades. U.S. GAAP and IFRS require the selling price to be allocated to the individual elements of the bundle based on their relative fair values.[6] Delivery of each item or performance of each service triggers revenue recognition equal to the fair value of the element in the bundle. Microsoft, for example, uses the straight-line method to recognize revenue on

---

[5] Under IFRS, revenue recognition may be earlier in some cases. An example is the "bill and hold" practice in which the selling firm produces regular stock inventory, receives an order from a customer, bills the customer, but does not deliver the goods. The SEC prohibits the recognition of revenue, but IFRS allows consideration of conditions that indicate a high probability of delivery, such as segregation of the inventory so that it cannot be used to satisfy another customer's order, delivery delay at the buyer's request, and a regular customer relationship. Revenue recognition might be permitted if the probability of delivery is high.

[6] See FASB *Codification Topic 605* for guidance. IFRS guidance is less specific but similar in spirit.

promised services in its software over the time period of the promise, reporting the remainder of the promised but undelivered service as "unearned revenues."

Income Recognition under Long-Term Contracts

This section describes methods that recognize income earlier than the completion of a long-term contract (a common practice among long-term contractors) or upon completion of a long-term contract (a common practice when firms face high uncertainty regarding the future costs of the long-term contract or the collectability of cash).

The operating cycle for a long-term contractor (such as a commercial or industrial building contractor, an aerospace manufacturer, or a ship builder) differs from that of a manufacturing firm in three important respects:

1. The period of construction (production) may span many accounting periods.
2. Contractors identify customers and agree to build customized projects for the customers for a contract price and terms agreed upon in advance of construction (or at least in the early stages).
3. Customers often make periodic payments of the contract price as work progresses.

The operating activities of long-term contractors often satisfy the criteria for the recognition of revenue during the period of construction and prior to completion. As noted earlier, Exhibit 8.1 describes this form of revenue recognition for United Technologies, a provider of technology products to the construction and aerospace industries. The existence of a contract indicates that the contractor has identified a buyer and the contractor and buyer have agreed on the scope of the construction project and a price. The contractor collects cash in advance or concludes, based on an assessment of the customer's credit standing, that it will receive cash equal to the contract price after construction is completed. Although the contract may obligate the contractor to perform substantial future services, the contractor should be able to estimate the cost of these services with reasonable precision. In agreeing to a contract price, the contractor should have some confidence in the estimates of the total costs it will incur on the contract.

Percentage-of-Completion Method

Many long-term contractors meet the criteria for revenue recognition during the construction process, such as when they complete certain construction milestones and are entitled to invoice the customer for payments for partial completion. When contractors meet the criteria for revenue recognition as construction progresses, they can recognize revenue using the percentage-of-completion method. Under this method, contractors recognize a portion of the total contract price, based on the degree of completion of the work during the period, as revenue for the period. They base this proportion on engineers' or architects' estimates of the degree of completion or on the ratio of costs incurred to date to the total expected costs for the contract. The actual schedule of cash collections is *not* a determining factor in measuring the amount of revenue recognized each period under the percentage-of-completion method. Even if a contractor expects to collect the entire contract price at the completion of construction, it still uses the percentage-of-completion method as long as it can make reasonable estimates as construction progresses of the amount of cash it will collect and of the costs it will incur. As contractors recognize portions of the contract price as revenues, they recognize corresponding proportions of the total estimated costs of the contract as expenses.

Example 7

To illustrate the percentage-of-completion method, assume that a firm agrees to construct a bridge for $5,000,000. Estimated costs are as follows: Year 1, $1,500,000; Year 2,

$2,000,000; Year 3, $500,000. Thus, the expected gross margin from the contract is $1,000,000 (= $5,000,000 − $1,500,000 − $2,000,000 − $500,000). The firm bills the customer (and collects) $2,000,000 in Year 1, $2,000,000 in Year 2, and $1,000,000 in Year 3.

Assuming that the contractor bases the degree of completion on the percentage of total costs incurred to date and that it incurs actual costs as anticipated, revenue and expense from the contract are as follows:

Year	Degree of Completion	Revenue	Expense	Gross Margin
1	$1,500,000/$4,000,000 = 37.5%	$1,875,000	$1,500,000	$ 375,000
2	$2,000,000/$4,000,000 = 50.0%	2,500,000	2,000,000	500,000
3	$500,000/$4,000,000 = 12.5%	625,000	500,000	125,000
		$5,000,000	$4,000,000	$1,000,000

The income statement effect is to recognize as profit the pro rata revenues, expenses, and gross margins as the work is completed, thus providing a better measure of the operating success of the contractor each period during the contract. Exhibit 8.2 provides a more detailed look at the financial statement impacts of the following underlying transactions in this example:

Year 1

1. Incur $1,500,000 costs. (Assume that all costs are paid in cash.)
2. Bill customer for $2,000,000. Collect cash in full.
3. Recognize $1,875,000 of revenue and $1,500,000 of expenses using the percentage-of-completion method.

Year 2

4. Incur $2,000,000 costs. (Assume that all costs are paid in cash.)
5. Bill customer for $2,000,000. Collect cash in full.
6. Recognize $2,500,000 of revenue and $2,000,000 of expenses using the percentage-of-completion method.

Year 3

7. Incur $500,000 costs. (Assume that all costs are paid in cash.)
8. Bill customer for $1,000,000. Collect cash in full.
9. Recognize $625,000 of revenue and $500,000 of expenses using the percentage-of-completion method.

The two primary balance sheet accounts that are unique in the long-term contracts area are the liability account *progress billings* and the asset account *contracts in process.* Contractors report actual contract costs on the balance sheet in a contracts in process account (Transactions 1, 4, and 7), which is an asset because it represents future economic benefits (the project being constructed). It is measured as the accumulated costs and gross margin on construction to date, which totals over the life of the contract to the contract price (gross margin added in Transactions 3, 6, and 9). When the contractor invoices the customer for progress payments, the contractor increases accounts receivable and an account called progress billings, which is a liability account (Transactions 2, 5, and 8). Progress billings is a liability because the customer is billed for promised work at the contract price and the contractor is obligated to deliver the asset under construction to the customer upon completion. The net amount of these two accounts (contracts in progress minus progress billings) is disclosed as a net obligation (if more has been billed than work performed) or as a net asset (if

EXHIBIT 8.2: LONG-TERM CONSTRUCTION ACCOUNTING

	Assets	=	Liabilities	+	Total Shareholders' Equity: CC	AOCI	RE
1.	*Year 1:* Cash −1,500,000 Contracts in Progress +1,500,000						
	Contracts in Progress Cash		1,500,000		 1,500,000		
2.	Accounts Receivable +2,000,000 Accounts Receivable −2,000,000 Cash +2,000,000		Progress Billings +2,000,000				
	Accounts Receivable Progress Billings Cash Accounts Receivable		2,000,000 2,000,000 		 2,000,000 2,000,000		
3.	Contracts in Progress +375,000						Contract Revenue +1,875,000 Contract Expense −1,500,000
	Contracts in Progress Contract Expense Contract Revenue		375,000 1,500,000 		 1,875,000		
4.	*Year 2:* Cash −2,000,000 Contracts in Progress +2,000,000						
	Contract in Progress Cash		2,000,000		 2,000,000		
5.	Accounts Receivable +2,000,000 Accounts Receivable −2,000,000 Cash +2,000,000		Progress Billings +2,000,000				
	Accounts Receivable Progress Billings Cash Accounts Receivable		2,000,000 2,000,000 		 2,000,000 2,000,000		
6.	Contracts in Progress +500,000						Contract Revenue +2,500,000 Contract Expense −2,000,000
	Contracts in Progress Contract Expense Contract Revenue		500,000 2,000,000 		 2,500,000		

(*Continued*)

EXHIBIT 8.2 (CONTINUED)

	Assets	=	Liabilities	+	Total Shareholders' Equity CC	AOCI	RE
7.	*Year 3:* Cash −500,000 Contracts in Progress +500,000						
	Contract in Progress Cash		500,000		 500,000		
8.	Accounts Receivable +1,000,000 Accounts Receivable −1,000,000 Cash +1,000,000		Progress Billings +1,000,000				
	Accounts Receivable Progress Billings Cash Accounts Receivable		1,000,000 1,000,000		 1,000,000 1,000,000		
9.	Contracts in Progress +125,000						Contract Revenue +625,000 Contract Expense −500,000
	Contracts in Progress Contract Expense Contract Revenue		125,000 500,000		 625,000		

more work has been performed than billed). For example, at the end of year 2, Contracts in Progress totals \$4,375,000 (= \$1,500,000 + \$375,000 + \$2,000,000 + \$500,000), and Progress Billings totals \$4,000,000 (= \$2,000,000 + \$2,000,000). Therefore, the year 2 balance sheet reports contracts in progress in excess of billings of \$375,000 as an asset. Upon completing the project at the end of year 3, contracts in progress and progress billings will be equal and will be closed out.

Example 8

Actual costs on contracts seldom coincide precisely with expectations. As new information on expected total costs becomes available, contractors must adjust reported income in current and future periods rather than retroactively restating income of prior periods. Refer again to Example 7. Assume that actual costs incurred in Year 2 for the contract were \$2,200,000 instead of \$2,000,000 and that total expected costs on the contract increase to \$4,200,000. Revenue, expense, and gross margin from the contract are as follows:

Year	Cumulative Degree of Completion	Revenue	Expense	Margin
1	\$1,500,000/\$4,000,000 = 37.5%	\$1,875,000	\$1,500,000	\$375,000
2	\$3,700,000/\$4,200,000 = 88.1%	2,530,000[a]	2,200,000	330,000
3	\$4,200,000/\$4,200,000 = 100%	595,000[b]	500,000	95,000
		\$5,000,000	\$4,200,000	\$800,000

[a] (0.881 × \$5,000,000) − \$1,875,000 = \$2,530,000
[b] \$5,000,000 − \$1,875,000 − \$2,530,000 = \$595,000

The unexpected costs are a *change in estimate.* Therefore, Year 2 revenue is cumulative revenue recognized to date based on the new estimate of costs minus past cumulative revenue recognition based on the old cost estimate.

Example 9

If it appears that the contractor will ultimately realize a loss on completion of a contract, the contractor must recognize the loss in full as soon as it becomes evident. For example, if at the end of Year 2 the contractor expects to realize a loss of $200,000 on the total contract, it must recognize a loss of $575,000 in Year 2. The $575,000 amount offsets the income of $375,000 recognized in Year 1 plus a loss of $200,000 anticipated on the overall contract.

Completed-Contract Method

Under U.S. GAAP, when the contract price, costs, or degree of completion are not reasonably estimable, long-term contractors postpone the recognition of revenue until they complete the construction project. Such firms use the completed-contract method of recognizing revenue. If the firm in Example 7 had used the completed-contract method, it would have recognized no revenue or expense from the contract during Year 1 or Year 2. It would recognize contract revenue of $5,000,000 and contract expenses of $4,000,000 in Year 3. Note that total gross margin is $1,000,000 under both the percentage-of-completion and completed-contract methods, equal to cash inflows of $5,000,000 less cash outflows of $4,000,000. If the contractor anticipates a loss on a contract, it recognizes the loss as soon as the loss becomes evident, even if the contract is incomplete.

IFRS does not permit the use of the completed-contract method if the percentage-of-completion method cannot be used for the reasons given above. Instead, firms must use the cost-recovery method, which we illustrate in a subsequent section.

Choice of Reporting Method by Long-Term Contractors

A contractor should not use the percentage-of-completion method when there is substantial uncertainty regarding the total costs it will incur to complete the project. If the contractor cannot estimate the total costs, it cannot estimate the percentage of total costs incurred as of a given date and thereby the percentage of services already rendered and the amount of revenue that can be recognized. It also will be unable to estimate the total income from the contract prior to its completion.

In some cases, contractors use the completed-contract method because the contracts are of such short duration (such as a few months) that earnings reported with the percentage-of-completion method and the completed-contract method are not significantly different. In these cases, the lower costs of implementing the completed-contract method justify its use. Contractors also use the completed-contract method when they have not obtained a specific buyer during the construction phase, as is sometimes the case in the construction of residential housing. These cases require future selling efforts. Substantial uncertainty may exist regarding the ultimate contract price and the amount of cash that the contractor will receive.

Not surprisingly, contractors must use the percentage-of-completion method for income tax purposes. Although most firms would prefer to use the completed-contract method for tax purposes, thereby delaying the recognition of income and payment of income taxes, the Internal Revenue Code does not permit it.

Examples 7–9 illustrate the dramatic level of estimation and uncertainty involved with income recognition for long-term contractors. Sometimes a project can take a number of years to complete. In some cases, contractors work with hundreds of subcontractors. Renegotiating contracts several times during the course of a large contract is commonplace. Analysts estimating persistent earnings using historical data for firms that construct (and sell) long-term projects must consider these and other firm factors, including the volume of projects currently under way, the success in completing projects on time and within budget, the length of typical projects, the types of projects undertaken, and the nature of the customer (if that information is available). Long-term construction firms usually address many of these factors in the analysis of operations found in the annual report and Form 10-K filing. Because (1) the time period between cash inflows and outflows for these firms is so long and (2) a large degree of estimation is needed to measure revenues and expenses, the potential for earnings management is high. The analyst evaluating firms in the construction, aircraft, and defense-related industries, for example, must be particularly sensitive to this fact.

Revenue Recognition When Cash Collectability Is Uncertain

In many cases, the seller firm has completed delivery of the product or service to the customer but allows the customer to pay over a long period of time. Determining a reliable estimate of the amount of cash the firm will ultimately receive from customers can be difficult. This may occur because the future financial condition of the customer is highly uncertain or because the customer may have the right to return the items purchased, thereby avoiding the obligation to make cash payments. This uncertainty regarding future cash inflows may prevent the selling firm from measuring (at the time of sale) the present value of the cash it expects to receive, thereby failing to fulfill the second criterion for revenue recognition: being able to reliably measure the value of the asset received in a revenue transaction.

Given the difficulty in estimating cash inflows in these situations, the opportunity to manage earnings may cloud management's best intentions to measure earnings accurately. The uncertainty of future cash flows also affects assessments of earnings persistence. As an example, in hindsight, it is now very clear that the future cash collections associated with homes that were sold and financed with subprime mortgages were far more uncertain and riskier than expected.

When future cash collections are uncertain and cannot be reliably estimated, the firm must delay revenue recognition and recognize revenue only at the time it collects cash using either the installment method or the cost-recovery method. The installment and cost-recovery methods exist as prudent and conservative approaches to the problem of revenue recognition when cash collection is uncertain. The task for the analyst is twofold: (1) to understand the installment and cost-recovery method accounting and (2) to judge whether a firm recognizing revenue using the time-of-sale method should be using one of these more conservative methods because the level of cash inflow uncertainty is high. We address these tasks next.

Installment Method

Under the installment method, a firm recognizes revenue as it collects portions of the selling price in cash. At the same time, it recognizes proportionate amounts of the cost of the good or service sold as an expense. For example, assume that a firm makes a \$100 sale of merchandise costing \$60. The buyer agrees to pay (ignoring interest) \$20 each month for five months. The firm recognizes revenue of \$20 each month as it receives cash. Likewise, it recognizes cost of goods sold of \$12 (= \$20/\$100 × \$60) each month. By the end of five months, the firm recognizes total income of \$40 [= 5 × (\$20 − \$12)].

Land development companies, which typically sell undeveloped land and promise to develop it over several future years, sometimes use the installment method. The buyer makes a nominal down payment and agrees to pay the remainder of the purchase price in installments over 10, 20, or more years. In these cases, future development of the land is a significant aspect of the earnings process. Also, substantial uncertainty often exists as to the ultimate collectability of the installment notes, particularly those not due until many years in the future. The customer can always elect to stop making payments, losing the right to own the land.

Cost-Recovery Method

When firms experience substantial uncertainty about cash collection (or if they use IFRS and cannot use percentage-of-completion), they also can use the cost-recovery method of income recognition, which is a very conservative method of income recognition up until the point of cost recovery, after which it is an anti-conservative method of income recognition. The cost-recovery method matches the costs of generating revenues dollar for dollar with cash receipts until the firm recovers all such costs. The firm will not recognize revenue until it receives cash, and then it will recognize matching amounts of expenses in each period until full cost recovery occurs. Only when cumulative cash receipts exceed total costs will a firm begin to show profit in the income statement. Once full cost recovery occurs, the firm will recognize further cash receipts from the customer as revenues, with no further costs to match with those revenues.

To illustrate the cost-recovery method, refer to the previous example relating to the sale of merchandise for $100. During the first three months, the firm would recognize revenue of $20 and expense of $20. By the end of the third month, the total costs have been recovered because cumulative cash receipts of $60 exactly equal the cost of the merchandise sold. During the fourth and fifth months, the firm would recognize revenue of $20 each month, but without an offsetting expense. For the five months as a whole, total income is again $40 (equal to cash inflow of $100 less cash outflow of $60) but the income recognition pattern differs from that of the installment method.

Example 10: Comprehensive Illustration of Income Recognition Methods for Installment Sales

Technor Computer Corporation (TCC) sold a computer costing $16,000,000 to the city of Boston for $20,000,000 on January 1, Year 1. The city of Boston agreed to make annual payments of $5,548,195 on December 31, Year 1, to December 31, Year 5 (five payments in total). Panel A of Exhibit 8.3 shows an amortization table for the note receivable underlying this transaction. The five payments of $5,548,195 each when discounted at 12 percent have a present value equal to the $20,000,000 selling price. Thus, 12 percent is the interest rate implicit in the note. TCC recognizes interest revenue using the effective interest method illustrated in Chapter 6.

In addition to interest revenue on the note, TCC recognizes gross margin on the sale. Panel B shows the revenue, expense, and gross margin under three income recognition methods. The time-of-sale method rests on the premise that the city of Boston will pay the amounts due on the note with a high probability. Receiving immediate recognition are $20,000,000 revenue, $16,000,000 costs, and $4,000,000 gross margin.

If substantial uncertainty exists regarding cash collectability of the notes, TCC should use the installment method or the cost-recovery method. The installment method recognizes revenues equal to collections of the $20,000,000 principal amount of the note as shown in Panel A (that is, the portion of each cash payment made by the city that does not represent interest). Each year's expense is 80 percent (= $16,000,000/$20,000,000) of the revenue recognized. Under the cost-recovery method, TCC recognizes no income until Year 5, when cumulative cash receipts exceed the $16,000,000 cost of manufacturing the computer.

Note that at the end of five years, cumulative gross margin is identical for all three income recognition methods. Only the *timing* of revenue recognition differs. The timing is driven by when the note receivable collection has reached a sufficiently high probability of collection.

Choice of Installment and Cost-Recovery Methods

Firms can use the installment method and the cost-recovery method only when substantial uncertainty exists about cash collection. For most sales of goods and services, past

EXHIBIT 8.3

Illustration of Income Recognition Methods from Installment Sales

Panel A: Amortization Schedule for Note Receivable

Year	Note Receivable, January 1	Interest Revenue at 12 Percent	Cash Payment Received	Repayment of Principal	Note Receivable, December 31
1	$20,000,000	$2,400,000	$ 5,548,195	$ 3,148,195	$16,851,805
2	16,851,805	2,022,217	5,548,195	3,525,978	13,325,827
3	13,325,827	1,599,099	5,548,195	3,949,096	9,376,731
4	9,376,731	1,125,208	5,548,195	4,422,987	4,953,744
5	4,953,744	594,451	5,548,195	4,953,744	0
Total		$7,740,975	$27,740,975	$20,000,000	

Panel B: Income Recognition from Sale of Computer

	Time-of-Sale Method			Installment Method			Cost-Recovery Method		
Year	Revenue	Expense	Gross Margin	Revenue	Expense	Gross Margin	Revenue	Expense	Gross Margin
1	$20,000,000	$16,000,000	$4,000,000	$ 3,148,195	$ 2,518,556	$ 629,639	$ 3,148,195	$ 3,148,195	$ 0
2	0	0	0	3,525,978	2,820,782	705,196	3,525,978	3,525,978	0
3	0	0	0	3,949,096	3,159,277	789,819	3,949,096	3,949,096	0
4	0	0	0	4,422,987	3,538,390	884,597	4,422,987	4,422,987	0
5	0	0	0	4,953,744	3,962,995	990,749	4,953,744	953,744	4,000,000
Total	$20,000,000	$16,000,000	$4,000,000	$20,000,000	$16,000,000	$4,000,000	$20,000,000	$16,000,000	$4,000,000

experience and an assessment of the credit standing of customers provide a sufficient basis for estimating the amount of cash firms will receive. In these cases, firms generally must recognize revenue at the time of sale and do not use the installment method or the cost-recovery method.

Income tax laws allow the installment method for income tax reporting under some circumstances, even when no uncertainty exists regarding cash collections. Manufacturing firms selling on extended payment plans often use the installment method for income tax reporting (while recognizing revenue at the time of sale for financial reporting). Firms seldom use the cost-recovery method for tax reporting.

Investment in Working Capital: Accounts Receivable and Deferred Revenues

Revenues typically generate cash inflows, but they are not necessarily equal in a given period. From the examples given previously in this chapter, it is clear that cash inflows often occur after revenue is recognized, resulting in a working capital asset, accounts receivable or, before revenue is recognized, resulting in a working capital liability, deferred revenues (also called unearned revenues or advances from customers). Cash flow from operations is decreasing in accounts receivable but increasing in deferred revenues.

Example 11

PepsiCo reports $4,683 million in accounts receivable at December 27, 2008, in its Consolidated Balance Sheet, an amount greater than 10 percent of total assets. Note 14, "Supplemental Financial Information" (Appendix A), indicates that the majority of the receivables are "trade receivables," which means that they have been generated by sales. Note 14 also describes the composition of current liabilities but shows no separate amount for deferred revenues. Given PepsiCo's operating model, it is unlikely that cash is received before revenue is recorded. Accordingly, PepsiCo's 2008 Consolidated Statement of Cash Flows shows a $549 million deduction for an increase in accounts and notes receivable when reconciling net income to cash flow from operations.

Retail coffee and fast-food franchisers typically have both receivables and deferred revenues. TCBY Enterprises Inc., has point-of-sale revenues (retail sales of yogurt and ice cream products), receivables (royalties from licensees and product sales to affiliates), and deferred revenues (gift cards and up-front license payments from licensees).

EFFORTS (EXPENSE RECOGNITION)

When engaging in operating activities, firms consume assets and incur liabilities and, thus, incur operating expenses. The next several sections discuss the general criteria for expense recognition and apply the criteria to explain how firms recognize the various operating expenses reported in the income statement.

Criteria for Expense Recognition

Both U.S. GAAP and IFRS require the recognition of expenses under the accrual basis of accounting as follows:

1. Costs *directly* associated with revenues must be recognized as expenses in the period when a firm recognizes the revenues.
2. Costs *not directly* associated with revenues must be recognized as expenses in the period when a firm consumes the services or benefits of the costs in operations.

Most of the costs of manufacturing can be directly linked or reliably allocated to particular products. When the products are sold, the firm recognizes revenue and these directly linked expenses, referred to as *product* costs. Other costs (rent; insurance and property taxes on administrative facilities; salaries of corporate officers; and depreciation on property, plant, and equipment that are not part of the manufacturing process) are related to doing business in a particular period and bear only an indirect relation to revenues generated during the period. Such costs become expenses in the period in which the firm consumes the benefits of these types of services. Accountants refer to such costs as *period* costs.

Because a large proportion of the expenses that firms report in the income statement associate directly with revenue recognized and because another large proportion of the expenses relate to doing business in that particular period, income statements provide generally reliable assessments of firms' economic performance each period. However, certain period expenses are more susceptible to management control than others. Expenditures that are somewhat discretionary and reported on the income statement as period costs are prime candidates for managing earnings. The analyst should carefully monitor advertising, R&D, and maintenance expenditures, as examples, to discern whether substantive reasons exist for changes in the levels of these expenditures (especially relative to sales) or whether the changes are intended to manage earnings. For example, if a firm's earnings in a period just barely meet or beat the consensus analyst forecast and discretionary expenses suddenly decrease for no apparent reason, managers might be cutting these expenses to meet or beat that period's earnings target.

Similar to revenue recognition, firms must identify in notes to the financial statements the significant policies employed for recognizing expenses. For example, refer to PepsiCo's Note 2 to the Consolidated Financial Statements (Appendix A). PepsiCo describes its accounting policies for sales incentives and other marketplace spending, distribution costs, software costs, commitments and contingencies, R&D, and other expenses.

Cost of Sales

For most retail and manufacturing firms, cost of sales represents the single largest expense reported on the income statement. The inventory asset is consumed by the sales process, creating the need to recognize the expense. Retailers accumulate the net costs of inventory purchases (invoice cost less purchase discounts and purchase returns plus freight costs paid by the purchaser) in the inventory account. Manufacturers accumulate the same costs in raw materials inventory. Then as the raw materials are used in production, the raw materials costs are assigned to work-in-process inventory along with production-related labor, supplies, and overhead costs (including depreciation on production-related property, plant, and equipment). As products are finished, the costs are transferred to finished goods inventory. Finally, as products are sold, inventory costs are reported as cost of goods sold.

Firms selling relatively high dollar value items such as automobiles, airplanes, and real estate can ascertain from the accounting records the specific cost of each item sold. They recognize revenue when each item is sold and then recognize the specific cost of each item sold as cost of goods sold.

In most cases, however, firms cannot identify the cost of the specific items sold. Sometimes inventory items are so similar and their unit costs so small that firms cannot justify economically the cost of designing an accounting system to keep track of specific unit costs. To measure cost of goods sold in these cases, firms must make some assumption about the flow of costs. Three cost-flow assumptions exist:

- Weighted average
- First-in, first-out (FIFO)
- Last-in, first-out (LIFO)

Weighted average assigns the average cost of all units available for sale during the period (units in beginning inventory plus units purchased) to units sold and units in ending inventory. FIFO assigns the cost of the earliest purchases to the units sold and the cost of the most recent purchases to ending inventory. LIFO assigns the cost of the most recent purchases to the cost of goods sold and the earliest purchases to inventory. Note that these methods make assumptions about cost flows and do not necessarily reflect the physical flows of units. Also note that many firms use a combination of cost-flow assumptions for different items of inventory in different subsidiaries or business segments or in different countries.

With the introduction of cost-flow assumptions into the reporting system, however, comes the possibility of earnings management and varying degrees of earnings quality. Analyzing earnings quality in the context of inventory accounting requires understanding the implications of the reporting options available to management.

Weighted Average

The weighted average cost-flow assumption simply determines the weighted average cost of all inventory units available for sale during the period, then it assigns that cost to each unit sold and to each unit in ending inventory. When inventory turns over rapidly, purchases during the current period receive a heavy weight in the weighted average unit cost.

FIFO

FIFO results in a balance sheet amount for ending inventory that is closest to current replacement cost. The cost of goods sold can be somewhat out of date, however, because FIFO recognizes costs of goods sold based on the costs of beginning inventory and the earliest purchases during the year. When inventory costs are rising, FIFO leads to the highest reported net income (lowest cost of goods sold) and the highest balance sheet value for inventory of the three methods, and when inventory costs fall, FIFO leads to the smallest net income and the lowest balance sheet value of inventory.

LIFO

LIFO results in amounts for cost of goods sold that closely approximate current replacement costs. Balance sheet amounts, however, can contain the cost of inventory acquisitions made many years previously. During periods of rising inventory costs, LIFO generally results in the highest cost of goods sold and the lowest net income of the three cost-flow assumptions. For this reason, firms usually prefer LIFO for income tax purposes. If a firm chooses a LIFO cost-flow assumption for tax purposes, the income tax law requires the firm to use LIFO for financial reporting to shareholders. IFRS does not permit the use of LIFO.

LIFO Liquidation

One exception to the generalization that LIFO produces the lowest net income during periods of rising prices occurs when a firm sells more units during a period than it purchases (referred to as a *LIFO layer liquidation*). In this case, LIFO assigns the cost of all of the current period's purchases plus the costs assigned to the liquidated LIFO layers to the cost of goods sold. During periods of rising prices, the liquidated layers of LIFO inventory may be at much lower costs than current costs, which can cause costs of goods sold to be relatively low and net income to be relatively high. When firms experience LIFO liquidations, two cash flow effects likely occur. First, firms delay purchasing inventory items, thereby delaying a cash outflow. Second, firms increase taxable income and the required cash outflow for taxes. In Note 7, "Inventory," to its December 31, 2008 Consolidated Financial Statements, General Motors Corporation reports a LIFO reserve of $1,233 million. GM also reports a LIFO layer liquidation as follows: "In 2008 and 2007, U.S. LIFO eligible inventory quantities were reduced. This reduction resulting in a liquidation of LIFO inventory quantities carried at lower costs prevailing in prior years as compared with the cost of 2008 and 2007 purchases, the effect of which decreased automotive cost of sales by approximately $355 million and $100 million in 2008 and 2007, respectively." If GM's LIFO layer liquidation is a transitory event, then GM's current period profits are not indicative of future earnings.

Characteristics of LIFO Adopters

Researchers have examined the characteristics of firms that do and do not adopt LIFO. Although these research studies do not always show consistent results, the following factors appear related to the decision to adopt LIFO:[7]

Firms Following U.S. GAAP. IFRS does not permit the use of LIFO, but U.S. and non-U.S. domiciled firms that follow U.S. GAAP for consolidated reporting are permitted to use LIFO. Some of these firms have subsidiaries that are domiciled in countries that follow IFRS, so they may be prohibited from using LIFO for the inventory of those subsidiaries even though they use LIFO for inventory in the subsidiaries in U.S. GAAP jurisdictions.

Direction and Rate of Factor Price Changes for Inventory Items. Firms experiencing rapidly increasing factor prices for raw materials, labor, or other product costs obtain greater tax benefits from LIFO than firms that experience smaller factor price increases or that experience price decreases. Although adopting LIFO implies future tax savings (good news), it also implies higher expected future factor prices for inventory (bad news).

Variability in the Rate of Inventory Growth. LIFO adopters show more variable rates of inventory growth before adopting LIFO than do firms that remain on FIFO. The variability of inventory growth declines after LIFO is adopted. Because LIFO tends to match more recent inventory costs with sales than does FIFO or weighted average (these methods use costs that are 6–15 months old relative to current replacement costs), LIFO tends to result in less variability in the gross margin percentage over the business cycle. Firms with variable rates of inventory growth (perhaps because of cyclicality in their industry) can more easily accomplish an income-smoothing reporting objective using LIFO than if they use FIFO or average cost. Income smoothing is achieved by creating additional LIFO layers to match against sales through additional end-of-period purchases.

Tax Savings Opportunities. LIFO adopters tend not to have tax loss carryforwards available to offset future taxable income. Instead, these firms adopt LIFO to provide future tax savings. LIFO adopters also realize larger tax savings in the year of adoption than in the surrounding years, suggesting that the decision is in part motivated by tax rather than financial reporting considerations.

Industry Membership. Firms in certain industries are more likely to adopt LIFO. Because firms in a particular industry face similar factor price changes and variability in their inventory growth rates, those firms are likely to make similar choices of cost-flow assumptions.

Asset Size. Larger firms are more likely to adopt LIFO than are smaller firms. LIFO increases record-keeping costs relative to FIFO, both in the year of adoption and in subsequent years. To absorb the adoption and ongoing record-keeping costs of LIFO, larger firms realize larger amounts of tax savings than do smaller firms.

One hypothesis examined in this research is the relation between LIFO adoption and managerial compensation. Because LIFO usually results in lower earnings, managerial compensation of LIFO adopters would likely be less than compensation of non-LIFO adopters or include a lower component of compensation based on earnings. Studies have found no difference in managerial compensation of LIFO and non-LIFO adopters, although adopters had a smaller earnings component to their compensation.

---

[7] For a review of these studies, see Frederick W. Lindahl, "Dynamic Analysis of Inventory Accounting Choice," *Journal of Accounting Research* (Autumn 1989), pp. 201–226, and Nicholas Dopuch and Morton Pincus, "Evidence on the Choice of Inventory Accounting Methods: LIFO versus FIFO," *Journal of Accounting Research* (Spring 1988), pp. 28–59.

Conversion from LIFO to FIFO

If a firm reports current costs in the income statement under LIFO, its balance sheet amount for ending inventory might contain some very old costs relative to FIFO which is an approximation of "current cost" inventory. If LIFO inventory valuation results in low out-of-date inventory values, the balance sheet amounts for inventory reflect poor accounting information quality and provide potentially misleading information to users of financial statements (although costs of goods sold under LIFO may more closely reflect replacement cost and reflect high accounting quality). The SEC requires firms using LIFO to disclose in notes to the financial statements the amounts by which LIFO inventories differ from the amounts the firm would recognize for inventories under FIFO or current cost. Analysts sometimes refer to the difference in ending inventory valuation between LIFO and FIFO or current cost as the *LIFO reserve.* From this disclosure, it is possible to restate a LIFO firm's income and inventory to a FIFO basis. In this way, the analyst can place firms using LIFO on a basis more comparable to that of firms using FIFO.

Example 12

Note 14, "Supplemental Financial Information" (Appendix A), indicates that PepsiCo uses a combination of weighted average, FIFO, and LIFO for inventories and costs of goods sold. The firm indicates that the differences between the FIFO and LIFO methods for valuing inventories are immaterial for both 2008 and 2007. The firm reports inventories on the balance sheet (Appendix A) of $2,522 million at the end of 2008 and $2,290 million at the end of 2007.

Because reporting standards do not require the disclosure of the excess of current cost over average cost of inventories, it is not possible to restate inventories and cost of goods sold fully on a FIFO basis. It appears that PepsiCo's use of a combination of FIFO, LIFO, and average costs has no material effect on measures of its operating profitability.

Example 13

Nucor Corporation, a primarily North American steel manufacturer, was incorporated in 1958. Exhibit 8.4 shows annual report data on the firm's inventory at December 31, 2008. Nucor uses the LIFO inventory method for much of its inventory.

EXHIBIT 8.4

Nucor Corporation
Selected Financial Statement Information
(amounts in thousands)

Balance Sheet	December 31, 2008	December 31, 2007
Inventories	$2,408,157	$1,601,600
Current assets (including inventory)	$6,397,486	$5,073,249
Current liabilities	$1,854,192	$1,582,036
Income Statement	**2008**	
Sales	$23,663,324	
Cost of products sold	$19,612,283	
Gross margin	$4,051,041	
Net income	$1,830,990	

To convert Nucor Corporation to FIFO, we use balance sheet amounts based on LIFO for beginning and ending inventory and the income statement amount for cost of sales to infer purchases during the period. Then to convert the beginning inventory, ending inventory, and cost of sales to the FIFO basis, we use the information from the financial statement note that provides the amount by which FIFO beginning and ending inventories would be larger. The notes to Nucor's financial statements indicate that the FIFO basis beginning and ending inventories are $581,500 thousand and $923,400 thousand higher, respectively, than the amounts reported on the balance sheets under LIFO. The conversion to FIFO is as follows:

In thousands	As reported	Adjustments	FIFO basis
Sales (*a*)	$23,663,324		$23,663,324
Beginning inventory	$ 1,601,600	$ 581,500	$ 2,183,100
Purchases	20,418,840		20,418,840
Goods available for sale	$22,020,440		$22,601,940
Ending inventory	(2,408,157)	(923,400)	(3,331,557)
Cost of sales	$19,612,283	$(341,900)	$19,270,383
Gross margin (*b*)	$ 4,051,041		$ 4,392,941

As typical in periods of rising input prices, FIFO yields a lower cost of sales and therefore a higher gross margin percentage (*b*/*a*):

Gross margin percentage as reported under LIFO = 17.12%

Gross margin percentage on a FIFO basis = 18.56%

Net income (as reported under LIFO) is $1,830,990 thousand. To adjust net income to a FIFO basis, add the decrease in cost of sales times one minus the tax rate to obtain a $222,235 thousand increase in net income [= $341,900 × (1 − 0.35)], which is 12% of reported net income.

The calculation of the inventory turnover ratio (cost of sales/average inventory), a measure that indicates the efficiency with which a firm manages its inventory, is as follows:

As reported under LIFO: $19,612,283/0.5($1,601,600 + $2,408,157) = 9.78

On a FIFO basis: $19,270,383/0.5($2,183,100 + $3,331,557) = 6.99

The dramatic difference in the inventory turnover ratio under LIFO and FIFO reflects the many years that have elapsed since Nucor adopted LIFO. The current (FIFO) cost of its inventory is much larger than its book (LIFO) value. The inventory turnover ratio based on LIFO amounts gives a poor indication of the actual turnover of inventory items because it divides a cost of goods sold amount reflecting current costs by an average inventory amount reflecting very old costs. The inventory turnover ratio under FIFO provides a better indication of the turnover of inventory items because it divides a cost of goods sold reflecting relatively current costs by an average inventory reflecting relatively recent costs. Although the trend in the inventory turnover ratio for a particular firm is likely to be similar under LIFO and FIFO, cross-sectional comparisons are inappropriate if one firm uses LIFO that recognizes very old costs on the balance sheet and another firm uses FIFO that recognizes more current costs on the balance sheet. Also, the LIFO measure of the inventory turnover ratio does not accurately portray the number of days inventories are held if LIFO costs are very old.

The inventory cost-flow assumption also affects the current ratio (current assets/current liabilities), a measure commonly used to assess short-term liquidity risk that was introduced in Chapter 5, as follows:

In thousands	2008	2007
Current assets (as reported)	$6,397,486	$5,073,249
Adjust inventory to FIFO	923,400	581,500
Current assets (FIFO)	$7,320,886	$5,654,749
Current liabilities	$1,854,192	$1,582,036
Current ratio (as reported)	3.45	3.21
Current ratio (FIFO)	3.95	3.57

Nucor's current ratio would be higher in each year if it used FIFO.

Reporting Changes in the Fair Market Value of Inventory

FIFO, LIFO, and weighted average are methods for assigning acquisition costs to ending inventory and cost of sales. For many firms, market values of inventory will likely differ from acquisition costs at balance sheet reporting dates. Under both U.S. GAAP and IFRS, firms are required to follow the conservative lower of cost or market method to report inventory at each balance sheet date.[8] Increases in market value are not reflected in the financial statements until the inventory is sold. If market value has increased and firms are able to pass the market value increases on to customers by increasing selling price, higher gross profits and greater amounts of cash or accounts receivable will exist after sale. This effect should occur relatively quickly because inventory is a current asset.

Under U.S. GAAP and IFRS, when inventory market values decline below cost, the losses must be reflected in the financial statements as decreases in inventory and increases in cost of goods sold or, if material, as a separate income statement line item for the loss on decline in inventory market value. Subsequent recoveries in market value are not reflected as an inventory write-up under U. S. GAAP, but may be under IFRS. Write-downs of inventory in the current period due to market decline are intended to appropriately reflect the value of inventory on the balance sheet and to yield a normal gross margin on a subsequent period's sale. That is, sales price in the subsequent period will be lower due to the market decline and cost of goods sold in the subsequent period will be lower by the same amount because cost of goods sold is determined by the (now lower) cost of the inventory.

Accounting Quality: Cost of Sales and Inventory

To assess the quality of accounting information with respect to cost of sales and inventory, the analyst considers the following:

- The inventory cost-flow assumption chosen by management
- Price variation and the speed at which inventory turns over
- Any liquidation of LIFO inventory layers
- Any physical deterioration or obsolescence of inventory
- The financing of inventory acquisitions

[8] American Institute of Certified Public Accounting, Committee on Accounting Procedures, *Accounting Research Bulletin No. 43*, "Inventory Pricing" (1953); *FASB Codification Topic 330*; International Accounting Standards Board, *International Accounting Standard 2*, "Inventories" (revised 2003). One difference between U.S. GAAP and IFRS is the definition of *market*. Under U.S. GAAP, *market* is defined as the cost to replace the inventory (replacement cost), while under IFRS, *market* is defined as the selling price of the inventory less estimated costs of disposal (net realizable value). U.S. GAAP substitutes net realizable value for replacement cost if net realizable value is less than replacement cost. Therefore, under either set of standards, inventory will not be reported at greater than its net realizable value.

Choice of Cost-Flow Assumption

Because LIFO generally matches the most recent acquisition costs against revenues in measuring earnings, LIFO-based earnings generally provide the best measure of sustainable earnings. A firm must replace goods sold if it is to continue operating, and the most recent cost of the items purchased serves as the best predictor of their replacement costs. A FIFO cost-flow assumption matches older acquisition costs with current revenues, and a weighted average cost-flow assumption provides results between LIFO and FIFO. Researchers examining the relation between market returns on equity securities and earnings based on LIFO versus FIFO cost of goods sold found that earnings numbers based on LIFO explain more of the cross-sectional variation in returns than do earnings numbers based on FIFO.[9]

Although LIFO generally provides higher-quality earnings measures, FIFO generally provides higher-quality financial position measures. This is because the inventory values under LIFO can be considerably less than replacement or current costs, which FIFO values approximate. However, a firm cannot use LIFO for measuring cost of goods sold on the income statement and FIFO for measuring inventory on the balance sheet. Firms using LIFO must disclose the difference between the FIFO and LIFO costs of inventories. As illustrated in an earlier section, with this information, the analyst can convert inventory on the balance sheet to an amount more closely approximating current economic value.

Rapid Inventory Turnover and Price Stability

The tax savings-related preference for LIFO is tempered significantly when (1) inventory turns over quickly or (2) acquisition costs of inventory items do not vary much. LIFO, FIFO, and weighted average cost-flow assumptions yield approximately the same amounts for cost of goods sold if inventory turns over roughly four or more times each year or if inventory does not turn over quickly but prices are so stable that the choice of the cost-flow assumption is of little consequence.

Liquidation of LIFO Inventory Layers

When firms dip into LIFO layers, they must report the amount by which cost of goods sold was reduced (the usual case) and earnings were increased. This is a classic example of lower quality of earnings despite higher reported profits. When using earnings of the current period to estimate sustainable earnings, the analyst should eliminate the effect of the dip into old LIFO layers from the current period's earnings. The analyst also should ascertain from management the reason why inventory levels were depleted.

Obsolete or Damaged Inventory

As noted earlier in the discussion of the lower of cost or market rule, when the current value of inventories declines below acquisition cost because of obsolescence or physical deterioration, firms must write down their inventories to reflect the decline. The analyst needs to rely on management and the auditors to determine when inventory is overvalued, but good gauges include whether competitors are taking write-downs and whether new product or technology introductions have occurred to reduce the value of existing inventory. Another signal comes from industry-wide publications addressing the demand for the firm's products.

---

[9] Ross Jennings, Paul J. Simko, and Robert B. Thompson II, "Does LIFO Inventory Accounting Improve the Income Statement at the Expense of the Balance Sheet?" *Journal of Accounting Research* (Spring 1996), pp. 85–109.

Inventory Financing Arrangements

Firms often need substantial amounts of cash early in their operating cycle to finance the purchase of raw materials. Firms may finance these purchases with suppliers through short-term borrowing agreements that appear on the balance sheet as accounts payable. However, firms sometimes obtain financing for their inventories in a manner that avoids reporting a liability on the balance sheet. For example, a firm might create a legal trust with the sole purpose of purchasing raw materials that the firm needs in its operations. The trust purchases the raw materials on account from various suppliers. The firm later purchases the needed raw materials from the trust at agreed-upon prices and reimburses the trust for the cost of carrying the raw materials until the firm needs them. The supplier is willing to sell to the trust on account because of the firm's purchase commitment.

The economic substance of this arrangement is that the firm has purchased raw material on account, yet no accounts payable appear in the financial statements of the firm. Current financial reporting rules sometimes allow the firm to leave the implicit inventory and the accounts payable off the balance sheet, thereby lowering its debt levels and increasing its inventory and accounts payable turnover ratios. The analyst should examine the notes to the financial statements for significant purchase commitments and consider adding them to inventories and accounts payable. Chapter 6 discusses these arrangements more fully.

Investment in Working Capital: Inventory and Accounts Payable

The cost to acquire inventory is a major working capital investment for most firms. For example, in its Consolidated Balance Sheet (Appendix A), PepsiCo reports inventory of \$2,522 million and \$2,290 million at December 27, 2008, and December 29, 2007, respectively. Also, in its Consolidated Statement of Cash Flows, PepsiCo reports a \$345 million cash outflow for increasing its inventories when computing cash flows from operations.[10]

Combining PepsiCo's two key working capital items (accounts and notes receivable, and inventory) yields \$7,205 million of working capital investments at December 27, 2008, roughly 20 percent of total assets. To offset this large delay in cash receipt from operations, firms delay payments to suppliers, employees, and taxing authorities as long as possible. PepsiCo's current liabilities section shows \$8,273 million for the working capital liabilities accounts payable and other current liabilities at the same date. Note 14, "Supplemental Financial Information" (Appendix A), indicates that \$2,846 million (roughly the amount of inventory) is included in the working capital liability, accounts payable. PepsiCo's Consolidated Statement of Cash Flows (Appendix A) reports that the increase in accounts payable and other current liabilities during the year results in an addition of \$718 million to cash flows from operations.

SG&A (Selling, General, and Administrative) Costs

SG&A costs generally bear a less direct relationship with sales. SG&A expenses reported on the income statement as part of operating profit represent the consumption of assets and incurrence of liabilities to carry on corporate functions other than production, such as

---

[10] The net cash outflow of \$345 million is greater than the change in the inventory balance (\$232 million = \$2,522 million – \$2,290 million). This may be because PepsiCo divested a subsidiary with inventory, reducing the ending balance sheet amount. Recall from Chapter 3 that a change in two balance sheet accounts rarely explains the change reported in the statement of cash flows due to acquisition, divestitures, and other reasons.

advertising, marketing, administration, accounting, information systems, and credit functions. The sections that follow describe the accounting and reporting of SG&A expenses.

Advertising and Marketing Costs

Many firms in the consumer products industry spend large sums of money on advertising and marketing. Although these expenditures are undertaken with the expectation that they will create value, whether they do in fact create value is uncertain. Thus, U.S. GAAP and IFRS require immediate expensing of these costs. As discussed in detail in Chapter 7, these costs do not meet the definition of an asset. Prepayments for advertising (such as prepayments for commercial time on broadcast media such as television and radio or prepayments for advertising space in publications such as magazines and newspapers) create working capital assets (usually titled prepaid expenses). Delay in payment to suppliers and service providers for advertising and marketing costs also creates working capital liabilities (usually reported as accrued expenses). PepsiCo's Note 14, "Supplemental Financial Information" (Appendix A), reports a material liability for marketplace (marketing-related) spending that decreased in from 2007 to 2008, thus reducing the addback to obtain cash flows from operations discussed in the prior section.

Although material for a company such as PepsiCo, these expenses are often not disclosed separately on the face of the income statement. However, PepsiCo discloses in Note 2, "Our Significant Accounting Policies" (Appendix A), under the Sales Incentives and Other Marketplace Spending heading that other marketplace spending totaled $2.9 billion in 2008 and 2007 and $2.7 billion in 2006 and is reported as a part of SG&A expenses on the income statement.

Compensation

Wages, salaries, payroll taxes, bonuses (including share-based payments discussed in Chapter 6), commissions, and fringe benefits (including pension plan and health plan costs discussed in a later section) are capitalized as part of inventory if incurred in the production process. If compensation costs are related to the selling, advertising, marketing, or administrative functions, they are reported as expenses in the SG&A category. Again, Note 14, "Supplemental Financial Information" (Appendix A), reports a working capital liability (accrued compensation) for compensation arising from delayed payments to employees. Note 6, "Stock-Based Compensation" (Appendix A), provides detailed information on stock-based compensation.

Depreciation, Depletion, and Amortization

Chapter 7 illustrates depreciation, amortization, and depletion of long-lived productive assets, which are allocations of the costs of assets to the periods benefited. If the long-lived assets are used in production, the allocated costs are capitalized as part of inventory. If not, the allocated costs are expensed as part of SG&A. The materiality of these expenses requires that they be disclosed in the notes to the financial statements. Also, depreciation, depletion, and amortization typically represent the largest addbacks to net income in the operating section of the statement of cash flows.

Credit Policy

In an effort to increase sales, most firms allow customers to delay payment. If cash collection is not highly likely, the sale should not be recorded in the first place. However, even if cash collection is generally likely to occur, experience leads to the expectation that some customers will not pay. Also, customers' ability to pay can change in the period between the initial sale and dates of scheduled cash payments.

Accounts receivable must be reported on the balance sheet at the amount of cash that is expected to be realized (that is, the *net realizable value*). Net realizable value reporting requires an estimate, at each balance sheet date, of the two causes of uncollectible receivables: sales returns and bad debts.

If sales returns are small in dollar amount and infrequent, they are recorded as incurred by simultaneously reducing sales and accounts receivable. If sales returns are material, they should be accounted for using the *allowance method.* Basically, the expected returns are estimated and reported as a subtraction from sales revenue in the income statement and as a subtraction from accounts receivable on the balance sheet. For example, if a company had $1,000 of credit sales of which $200 was collected in the period and the company estimated $50 in sales returns, the company reports $950 in "net sales" ($1,000 credit sales less $50 expected returns) and $750 in accounts receivable ($1,000 credit sales less $200 collections less $50 expected returns). Note that sales returns are a direct reduction in sales, not an SG&A expense.

Bad debts also are accounted for using the allowance method, with the allowance estimating the amount of outstanding receivables that will not be collected. The proper balance in the allowance for doubtful accounts is typically determined by a percentage of ending accounts receivable, or the "aging" of accounts receivable. By determining the allowance using the aging method, the firm uses its historical experience with past bad debts and its expectations going forward to estimate the proportion of accounts receivable that will not be collected based on the length of time receivables have been outstanding (the "age"). The assumption is that the likelihood an account will not be collected is increasing in age. For example, experience may show that bad debts arise from 1 percent of receivables less than 60 days old, from 5 percent of the receivables that are between 61 and 180 days old, and 40 percent of receivables that are more than 180 days old. At the end of each period, the firm estimates the necessary balance in the allowance for doubtful accounts. The necessary adjustment to increase the allowance for doubtful accounts (which, in effect, is the decrease in net accounts receivable) is recorded as bad debts expense (often called provision for bad debts), which is reported as a component of SG&A expenses.

Example 14

Beckham Company recorded the following in 2011 and 2012, its first two years of operations:

	2011	2012
Credit sales	$1,000,000	$1,200,000
Collections on credit sales	800,000	900,000
Specific accounts that will not be collected and should be written off	0	15,000

Beckham uses an aging of accounts receivable to determine that that 10 percent of gross accounts receivable are estimated to be uncollectible at each balance sheet date.

By the end of 2011, Beckham has outstanding accounts receivable of $200,000 ($1,000,000 in credit sales less $800,000 collections of receivables). Because this is the first year of operations, there is no beginning balance of uncollectible accounts. Therefore, the $0 beginning estimated uncollectible balance is increased to a $20,000 ending estimated uncollectible balance ($200,000 gross accounts receivable × 10%). This $20,000 write-down of receivables flows through to the income statement as bad debts expense as follows:

	Balances before Write-Down	Write-Down	Balances after Write-Down
Accounts receivable	$200,000		$200,000
Allowance for doubtful accounts	0	$20,000	(20,000)
Net realizable value	$200,000		$180,000

The allowance for doubtful accounts indicates an expectation that accounts totaling $20,000 will not be collected. In 2012, Beckham identifies the specific customers who will not pay $15,000. The write-off of these uncollectible accounts is achieved by a simultaneous reduction in accounts receivable and the allowance for doubtful accounts in 2012 as follows:

	Balance before Specific Write-Offs	Write-Off of Specific Accounts	Balance after Specific Write-Offs
Accounts receivable	$200,000	$(15,000)	$185,000
Allowance for doubtful accounts	(20,000)	15,000	(5,000)
Net realizable value	$180,000		$180,000

Note that the write-off of specific uncollectible accounts has no effect on the net realizable value of accounts receivable and thus no income statement effect. The income statement effect was recognized in the prior period (2011) when the extension of credit was used to generate sales revenue and the related bad debt expense was estimated.

By the end of 2012, Beckham has outstanding accounts receivable of $485,000 ($2,200,000 in credit sales in 2011 and 2012 less $1,700,000 collections of receivables and $15,000 of write-offs). Uncollectible accounts are estimated at $48,500 (10 percent of the receivables balance). The $5,000 balance in uncollectible accounts is adjusted to the required $48,500 ending estimated uncollectible balance. This $43,500 write-down of receivables flows through to the income statement as bad debts expense as follows:

	Balances before Write-Down	Write-Down	Balances after Write-Down
Accounts receivable	$485,000		$485,000
Allowance for doubtful accounts	(5,000)	$43,500	(48,500)
Net realizable value	$480,000		$436,500

The preceding example deals with a short-term accounts receivable. Under U.S. GAAP, an analogous treatment is given to receivables with maturity dates beyond one year, such as notes receivable. These receivables are reported at their present value initially. Then at each balance sheet date, an allowance for uncollectible notes (often referred to as an *allowance or reserve for loan losses*) is established. Actual loan impairments are written off against the allowance for loan losses, much like the procedure for bad debts. In contrast, under IFRS, notes receivable balance sheet reporting follows the fair value reporting rules for investments illustrated in Chapter 7.

Warranty Expense

Another method of increasing sales is to guarantee the performance of the product sold. Estimated costs under warranties must be accrued in the period in which the guaranteed goods are sold by increasing a warranty obligation and increasing warranty expense (a portion of SG&A expense). Then as warranty claims arise, the costs of servicing the warranty claims reduce the estimated warranty obligation.

Operating Profit

Sales revenue minus cost of sales and SG&A expenses yields operating profit before tax. Financial revenues and expenses (primarily interest income and interest expense) are then disclosed on the income statement along with equity in the earnings of affiliates. Finally, income tax expense is subtracted to obtain net income. The following section continues Chapter 2's examination of income taxes.

INCOME TAXES

Income taxes affect the analysis of a firm's profitability (income tax expense is a subtraction when computing net income) and its cash flows (income tax payments require cash). Deferred tax assets and deferred tax liabilities on the balance sheet affect future cash flows. The note to the financial statements on income taxes contains useful information for assessing a firm's income tax position. Moreover, the reconciliation of statutory to effective tax rates can be useful in highlighting accounting issues that relate to earnings quality. This section reviews the required accounting for income taxes and discusses how the analyst might use income tax disclosures when analyzing a firm's financial statements.[11]

Review of Income Tax Accounting

Book and tax differences are created from application of different asset and liability measurement rules under financial reporting rules and tax rules. FASB Statement No. 109 requires firms to follow a balance sheet approach when computing income tax expense. The following description summarizes the balance sheet approach:

1. Identify at each balance sheet date all differences between the *book basis* of assets, liabilities, and tax loss carryforwards (that is, the book value for financial reporting) and the *tax basis* of assets, liabilities, and tax loss carryforwards (that is, the values used in tax reporting).
2. Eliminate from Step 1 items that are permanent differences between book and tax basis, meaning that they will not have any future tax consequence.
3. Separate the remaining differences after the first two steps into those that give rise to future tax deductions and those that give rise to future taxable income. Financial reporting refers to these differences as *temporary differences*. Multiply differences between the book and tax basis of assets and liabilities that give rise to future tax deductions by the enacted statutory tax rate expected to apply in those future periods. The result is a *deferred tax asset*. Multiply differences between the book and tax basis of assets and liabilities that give rise to future taxable income by the enacted statutory tax rate expected to apply in those future periods. The result is a *deferred tax liability*.

   Firms may have unused NOL (net operating loss) and tax credit carryforwards as of a balance sheet date. These items have the potential to reduce future taxable income (operating loss carryforwards) or future taxes payable (tax credit carryforwards). The firm includes the tax effect of these carryforwards in deferred tax assets at each balance sheet date.

[11] U. S. GAAP and IFRS have roughly similar deferred tax rules. Financial Accounting Standards Board, *Statement of Financial Accounting Standards No. 109*, "Accounting for Income Taxes" (1992); *FASB Codification Topic 740*; International Accounting Standards Board, *International Accounting Standard 12*, "Income Taxes" (revised 1996, 2001).

4. Assess the likelihood that the firm will realize the benefits of deferred tax assets in the future. This assessment should consider the nature (for example, cyclical or non-cyclical) and characteristics (for example, growing, mature, or declining) of the firm's business and its tax planning strategies for the future. If realization of the benefits of deferred tax assets is "more likely than not" (that is, the likelihood exceeds 50 percent), deferred tax assets equal the amounts computed in Step 3. However, if it is more likely than not that a firm will not realize some or all of the deferred tax assets, the firm must reduce the deferred tax assets using a *valuation allowance* (similar in concept to the allowance for uncollectible accounts). The valuation allowance reduces the deferred tax assets to the amounts the firm expects to realize by way of reduced taxes in the future. Increases in the valuation allowance directly increase income tax expense.

The result of following this four-step procedure is a deferred tax asset and a deferred tax liability at each balance sheet date. Income tax expense each period equals:

- Income taxes currently payable on taxable income
- Plus (minus) an increase (a decrease) in deferred tax liabilities between the beginning and the end of the period
- Minus (plus) an increase (a decrease) in deferred tax assets.

Required Income Tax Disclosures

The note to the financial statements on income taxes is a rich source of information not only for understanding a firm's income tax position, but also for understanding much about its operations and accrual accounting choices. This section describes four specific GAAP disclosures using the following amounts for a hypothetical firm:

1. Components of income tax expense
2. Components of income before taxes
3. Reconciliation of income taxes at statutory rate with income tax expense
4. Components of deferred tax assets and liabilities

Components of Income Tax Expense

Firms must disclose the amount of income taxes currently payable and the amount deferred, broken down by governmental entity (federal, foreign, state, and local).

Components of Income Tax Expense

	2009	2008	2007
Current —Federal	$191	$105	$123
—Foreign	128	75	61
—State/Local	18	12	13
Total Current	$337	$192	$197
Deferred —Federal	$ 35	$ 40	$ 70
—Foreign	38	30	19
Total Deferred	$ 73	$ 70	$ 89
Total Income Tax Expense	$410	$262	$286

This disclosure gives users insight into the components of total income tax expense. The first order partition is for current and deferred tax components of income tax expense. For example, in 2009, this firm recognizes income tax expense of $410, which reflected $337 currently payable and $73 that is deferred. The second order partition is each of these components by taxing authority. For example, the $337 current tax expense reflects the $191, $128, and $18 for federal, foreign, and state/local, respectively.

The following template shows the effects on the financial statements in each year. We use the term *net* deferred tax liability to capture changes in the net of deferred tax liabilities and deferred tax assets.

2009

Assets	=	Liabilities	+	Shareholders' Equity		
				CC	AOCI	RE
		Net Deferred Tax Liability +73 Income Tax Payable +337				Income Tax Expense −410

Income Tax Expense	410	
Net Deferred Tax Liability		73
Income Tax Payable		337

2008

Assets	=	Liabilities	+	Shareholders' Equity		
				CC	AOCI	RE
		Net Deferred Tax Liability +70 Income Tax Payable +192				Income Tax Expense −262

Income Tax Expense	262	
Net Deferred Tax Liability		70
Income Tax Payable		192

2007

Assets	=	Liabilities	+	Shareholders' Equity		
				CC	AOCI	RE
		Net Deferred Tax Liability +89 Income Tax Payable +197				Income Tax Expense −286

Income Tax Expense	286	
Net Deferred Tax Liability		89
Income Tax Payable		197

Components of Income before Taxes

Assessing a firm's tax position over time or relative to other firms requires some base for scaling the amount of income tax expense. Income before taxes serves this purpose.

Components of Income before Tax

	2009	2008	2007
United States	$ 700	$450	$600
Foreign	350	250	200
Total	$1,050	$700	$800

The average, or effective, tax rates for the three years on total income before taxes are as follows:

2007:	\$286/\$800 = 35.7%
2008:	\$262/\$700 = 37.4%
2009:	\$410/\$1,050 = 39.0%

Thus, the average tax rate increased over the three-year period. Combining the information in this disclosure with that in the previous one for components of income tax expense, the analyst can determine that effective tax rates on foreign earnings appear higher than in the United States. For example, U.S. tax expense for 2009 is \$244 (= \$191 + \$18 + \$35) on pretax income of \$700, yielding an effective tax rate of 34.9 percent; in contrast, foreign tax expense for 2009 is \$166 (= \$128 + \$38) on pretax income of \$350, an effective tax rate of 47.4 percent.

Reconciliation of Income Taxes at Statutory Rate with Income Tax Expense

The third required disclosure explains why the average tax rates shown previously differ from the statutory federal tax rate on income before taxes. Firms can express reconciling items in dollar amounts or in percentage terms. For example:

Reconciliation of Income Taxes at Statutory Rate with Income Tax Expense

	2009	2008	2007
(1) Income taxes on income before taxes at statutory rate	35.0%	35.0%	35.0%
(2) Foreign tax rates greater (less) than statutory federal rate	4.1	2.5	1.3
(3) State and local taxes	1.1	1.1	1.1
(4) Dividend deduction	(0.6)	(0.5)	(0.7)
(5) Tax-exempt income	(0.4)	(0.4)	(0.5)
(6) Restructuring and impairment charges	0.6	0.4	0.2
(7) Percentage depletion in excess of cost	(0.8)	(0.7)	(0.7)
income tax expense	39.0%	37.4%	35.7%

The statutory federal tax rate was 35 percent in each year. The average tax rates were greater than the statutory rates. The reconciliation includes two types of reconciling items: (1) tax rate differences and (2) permanent differences. The sections that follow discuss each of these reconciling items more fully.

Foreign Rates Greater (Less) Than the Statutory Federal Rate. The denominator of the average tax rate computation combines both U.S.-source and foreign-source income for financial reporting. The initial assumption on line (1) is that all of this income is subject to taxes at a rate equal to the U.S. federal statutory rate. Foreign tax rates are usually different from the U.S. federal rate, however. This line indicates how much the overall average tax rate increased or decreased because of these foreign rate differences.

Refer to the first two types of income tax disclosures discussed earlier. Foreign tax expense for 2009 totaled \$166 (= \$128 + \$38). Pretax book income from foreign sources was \$350. If this income were subject to tax at the federal rate of 35 percent, foreign income tax expense would have been \$123 (= 0.35 × \$350). Foreign tax expense of \$166 exceeded the amount at the federal statutory rate by \$43 (= \$166 − \$123). The excess tax as a percentage of total pretax book income, the denominator of the average tax rate, is 4.1 percent (= \$43/\$1,050). Foreign-source income was taxed at a rate of 47.4 percent (= \$166/\$350).

For firms with significant international operations, it would be desirable to have a breakdown of total foreign income and foreign taxes by individual countries, but firms rarely disclose such information.

State and Local Taxes. The statutory tax rate on line (1) reflects federal taxes only. The reconciliation adds state and local taxes on income for financial reporting because such taxes are part of income tax expense. The amount of the reconciling item is state and local taxes net of their federal tax benefit. State and local taxes are deductible in determining taxable income for federal purposes, so the incremental effect of state and local taxes beyond the federal statutory rate appears on line (3).

Refer to the disclosure of the components of income tax expense discussed previously. State and local taxes for 2009 were \$18. Net of the federal tax benefit of 35 percent, state and local taxes are \$12 [= (1 − 0.35) × \$18]. This \$12 amount increases the average tax rate by 1.1 percent (= \$12/\$1,050).

As with foreign taxes, the income tax note to the financial statements does not give any further detail on the income and taxes by jurisdictional unit within the United States.

Dividends Received Deduction. Depending on the investor's ownership percentage, only 20 or 30 percent of dividends received from unconsolidated domestic subsidiaries and affiliates is subject to federal taxation. The dividend deduction is intended to reduce the effect of triple taxation of the corporate organization form. The full dividend received is included in income for financial reporting. The calculation on line (1) presumes that the dividend is subject to tax at the statutory rate. The reduction on line (4) indicates the tax savings due to the 70 or 80 percent dividends received deduction.

Tax-Exempt Income. Income for financial reporting includes interest revenue on state and municipal obligations. Such interest revenue, however, is never included in taxable income. The income tax savings from this permanent difference appears on line (5).

Restructuring and Impairment Charges. A firm that acquires another firm must record the assets of the acquired firm at fair value in the consolidated financial statements. (Chapter 7 addresses accounting for business acquisitions.) Any subsequent write-down of the acquired assets, as a separate impairment charge or as impairments embedded in a restructuring charge, typically cannot be deducted for tax purposes. Because the assets were not revalued to fair value for tax purposes at the time of the acquisitions (assuming that the purchase was accounted for as a nontaxable reorganization as discussed in Chapter 7), the possibility of an impairment charge for tax purposes does not exist.

Percentage Depletion in Excess of Cost. In the U.S., the Internal Revenue Code permits firms involved in mineral extraction to claim a depletion deduction equal to a specified percentage times the gross income from the property each year. Over the life of a mineral property, total percentage depletion will likely exceed the acquisition cost of the property. For financial reporting purposes, total depletion cannot exceed acquisition cost. The excess of percentage depletion over book depletion represents a permanent difference that reduces the average tax rate.

The forgoing discussion illustrates the reconciling items most commonly encountered in corporate annual reports. Other items reported have characteristics similar to those discussed previously.

Components of Deferred Tax Assets and Liabilities

The fourth disclosure item in the income tax note is a listing of the components of the deferred tax asset and the deferred tax liability at the beginning and the end of each year. The reconciling items in these disclosures often pertain to accrual accounts that reflect discretion over income and expense recognition. Hence, they provide an analyst interested in assessing the quality of earnings with a useful starting point. Exhibit 8.5 presents the required disclosures. The change in deferred tax asset and deferred tax liability each year represents deferred income tax expense for that year. Note that Deferred Tax Assets experienced a decrease of \$34 (= \$240 − \$274) between 2008 and 2009 and Deferred Tax Liabilities experienced an increase of \$39 (= \$819 − \$780). The total credit change in these accounts of \$73 (= \$34 + \$39) equals the deferred component of income tax expense for 2009. (See the first income tax disclosure item.) The following sections discuss the components of deferred taxes.

Uncollectible Accounts Receivable. Firms provide for estimated uncollectible accounts in the year of sale for financial reporting but cannot recognize bad debt expense for tax purposes until an actual customer's account becomes uncollectible. Thus, the book value of accounts receivable will be less than its tax basis. The difference represents the future tax deductions for bad debt expense. These future tax benefits times the tax rate give rise to a deferred tax asset. The deferred tax asset relating to uncollectible accounts increased between 2006 and 2008, suggesting that bad debt expense for financial reporting continued to exceed bad debt expense for tax reporting. Such a relation characterizes a firm with increasing sales. The decrease in the deferred tax asset during 2009 suggests that sales likely declined, causing bad debt expense for tax reporting to exceed the amount for financial reporting.

Warranties. Firms expense estimated warranty costs in the year of sale for financial reporting but cannot deduct warranty expense for tax reporting until the firm makes actual expenditures to provide warranty services. Thus, the book value of the warranty liability (a positive amount) will exceed the tax basis of the warranty liability (zero because the income tax law does not permit recognition of a warranty liability). The difference represents the

EXHIBIT 8.5

Disclosures Related to Deferred Taxes—
Components of Deferred Tax Assets and Liabilities

	December 31,			
	2009	**2008**	**2007**	**2006**
Deferred Tax Assets				
Uncollectible accounts receivable	\$ 16	\$ 19	\$ 17	\$ 15
Warranties	91	105	89	76
Pensions	71	83	67	53
Leases	62	54	42	32
Net operating losses	—	13	—	—
Total Deferred Tax Assets	\$240	\$274	\$215	\$176
Deferred Tax Liabilities				
Depreciable assets	\$476	\$421	\$355	\$275
Inventories	59	58	49	41
Installment receivables	193	205	171	149
Intangible drilling and development costs	91	96	76	58
Total Deferred Tax Liabilities	\$819	\$780	\$651	\$523

future tax deductions for warranty expense. The increase in the deferred tax asset relating to warranties between 2006 and 2008 is consistent with a growing firm, whereas the decrease in 2009 indicates a firm whose sales of product under warranty plans probably declined.

Pensions. Firms recognize pension expense each year as employees render services for financial reporting and when the firm contributes cash to the pension fund for tax reporting. As will be discussed in a later section on pensions, the income tax law limits a firm's ability to claim tax deductions when a pension fund is overfunded. Thus, firms may curtail making pension fund contributions even though they must recognize pension expense each year. The book basis of the pension liability (a positive amount) will exceed the tax basis (not recognized). The future tax deductions for pension expense result in a deferred tax asset. For our illustrative firm, pension expense for financial reporting exceeded the amount for tax reporting during 2007 and 2008 and the deferred tax asset relating to pensions increased. The deferred tax asset decreased in 2009, indicating a larger expense for tax reporting than for financial reporting. (That is, the book basis of the pension liability decreased during the year.) Several explanations might account for such a decrease. First, the firm resumed funding the pension obligation and made a multiyear contribution. Second, the firm curtailed employment during 2009 in light of a decrease in sales, reducing pension expense, but made a pension contribution sufficient to reduce the pension liability. Third, the firm experienced a negative pension expense (that is, pension income) during 2009 because of an overfunded pension plan. The negative pension expense reduces the pension liability and thereby the amount of future tax deductions previously considered available.

Leases. Our illustrative firm leases equipment from other entities (lessors). As discussed in the section on leases in Chapter 6, firms may treat leases as operating leases or capital leases for financial and tax reporting. If the leases qualify as operating leases, the lessor recognizes rent revenue and depreciation expense and the lessee recognizes rent expense. If leases qualify as capital leases, the lessor recognizes a gain on the "sale" of the leased property at the inception of the lease and recognizes interest revenue each year from financing the lessee's "purchase" of the property. The lessee depreciates the assets each period and recognizes interest expense on its borrowing from the lessor.

Leasing arose as an industry in part to shift tax deductions on property from firms that needed the use of property but did not have sufficient taxable income to take advantage of the tax deductions to other entities with higher tax rates that could take advantage of the deductions. If a lease qualifies as an operating lease for tax purposes, the lessor gets the tax deductions for depreciation and may pass along some of these benefits to the lessee in the form of lower lease payments.

The criteria for an operating lease and a capital lease for financial reporting are not identical to those for tax reporting. It is possible to structure leases that are operating leases for tax reporting even though they qualify as capital leases for financial reporting. Our illustrative firm shows a deferred tax asset relating to leases. The likely scenario is that this firm treats leases as capital leases for financial reporting and as operating leases for tax reporting. Thus, the book basis of the leased asset and lease liability (a positive amount) exceeds the tax basis of the asset and liability (not recognized). Depreciation and interest expense recognized for financial reporting exceed rent expense recognized for tax reporting. In later years, rent expense for tax reporting will exceed depreciation and interest expense. These future tax deductions give rise to a deferred tax asset. The deferred tax asset increased each year, suggesting that this firm increased its involvement in leasing during the three-year period. (That is, the firm has more leased assets in the early years of the lease period when the book expenses exceed the tax deduction than in the later years when the tax deduction exceeds the book expenses.)

Net Operating Losses. A firm may operate for both financial and tax reporting at a net loss for the year. The firm can carry back this net loss to offset taxable income of the three preceding years and receive a refund for income taxes paid in those years. The firm recognizes the refund as an income tax credit in the year of the net loss.

If the firm has no positive taxable income in the three preceding years against which to carry back the net loss or if the net loss exceeds the taxable income of those three preceding years, the firm can carry forward the net loss. This carryforward provides future tax benefits in that it can offset positive taxable incomes and thereby reduce income taxes otherwise payable. The benefits of the NOL carryforward give rise to a deferred tax asset.

Our illustrative firm recognized a deferred tax asset during 2008 and realized the benefits of the NOL carryforward during 2009. Referring back to the disclosure of the components of income tax expense, we see that this firm paid taxes to all three governmental units during 2008. Thus, the firm must have been unable to offset the NOL incurred by some subunit during the year against the taxable income of the overall entity. One possibility is that the firm owns a majority interest in a subsidiary and therefore consolidates it for financial reporting. Its ownership percentage, however, is less than the 80 percent required to include the subsidiary in a consolidated tax return. Thus, the net loss of the subsidiary can offset only net income of that subsidiary in a later year. NOLs generally are not transferable between subsidiaries because the tax law treats the subsidiaries as different taxable entities. If a company such as PepsiCo is generally very profitable and paying taxes but the subsidiary is not, both now and in the future, the deferred tax assets associated with NOL carryforwards may go unused and a valuation allowance is appropriate. The firm recognizes this future benefit as a deferred tax asset. This firm shows no valuation allowance related to the deferred tax asset, indicating a greater than 50 percent probability of realizing the tax benefits in the future.

Depreciable Assets. Firms claim depreciation on their tax returns using accelerated methods over periods shorter than the expected useful lives of depreciable assets. Most firms depreciate assets for financial reporting using the straight-line method over the expected useful lives of such assets. Thus, the book bases of depreciable assets will likely exceed their tax bases. Depreciation expense for tax reporting in future years will be less than the amounts for financial reporting, giving rise to a liability for future tax payments. The deferred tax liability relating to depreciable assets increased each year, suggesting that this firm has more assets in their early years when tax depreciation exceeds book depreciation. However, the deferred tax liability increased at a decreasing rate, suggesting a slowdown in the growth rate of capital expenditures.

Inventories. The book value of inventories for our illustrative firm exceeds their tax basis, giving rise to future tax liabilities. Perhaps this firm includes certain elements of cost as part of manufacturing overhead for financial reporting but deducts them when incurred for tax reporting.

Installment Receivables. Firms that sell assets on account and permit customers to pay over two or more years often recognize revenue for financial reporting when the sale is made and for tax reporting when they collect cash using the installment method. The book basis of these receivables exceeds their tax basis and gives rise to deferred tax liabilities. The deferred tax liability relating to installment sales increased between 2006 and 2008, characteristic of a growing firm. (That is, revenues from sales during the current period exceed collections this period from sales made in prior periods.) The deferred tax liability on installment sales decreased during 2009, consistent with the decline in sales noted previously in the discussion of deferred taxes related to uncollectible accounts and warranties.

Intangible Drilling and Development Costs. In the year of the cash expenditure, for tax purposes, firms can deduct certain costs of acquiring rights to drill and for drilling a property to ascertain the existence of mineral resources. These firms must capitalize and amortize such costs for financial reporting. The book basis of the property will exceed the tax basis and give rise to a deferred tax liability. The deferred tax liability for this item increased between 2006 and 2008, indicating a growth in drilling and development activity. The decrease in the liability during 2009 suggests a cutback in such expenditures.

Assessing a Firm's Tax Position

The note to the financial statements on income taxes defines the average tax rate as follows:

Average Tax Rate = Income Tax Expense/Book Income before Income Taxes

Exhibit 8.6 presents an analysis of average tax rates. This analysis separates the amounts for each year into domestic and foreign components. The combined average tax rate based on income tax expense increased each year. The average tax rate on the domestic portion remained relatively steady at a rate close to the 35 percent federal statutory tax rate. Differences in the domestic tax position due to rate differences and permanent differences offset each other. On the other hand, the average tax rate on the foreign portion exceeded 35 percent and that rate increased each year. The analyst should more fully explore with management the reasons for this increase in the foreign average tax rate. Perhaps the portions of the firm's foreign operations in higher-tax-rate countries grew more rapidly than

EXHIBIT 8.6

Analysis of Average Tax Rates

	2009		2008		2007	
	Domestic	Foreign	Domestic	Foreign	Domestic	Foreign
(1) Net income before income taxes	$700	$350	$450	$250	$600	$200
Income taxes at 35% statutory federal rate	$245	$123	$157	$ 87	$210	$ 70
Foreign tax rates greater than 35%	—	43	—	18	—	10
State and local taxes	11	—	8	—	9	—
Dividends deduction	(6)	—	(3)	—	(4)	—
Tax-exempt income	(4)	—	(3)	—	(4)	—
Goodwill amortization	6	—	3	—	1	—
Percentage depletion	(8)	—	(5)	—	(6)	—
(2) Income tax expense	$244	$166	$157	$105	$206	$ 80
Average tax rates: (2) ÷ (1)	34.9%	47.4%	34.9%	42.0%	34.3%	40.0%
Combined average tax rates	39.0%		37.4%		35.7%	

foreign operations in lower-tax-rate countries. The firm may need to search for more tax-effective ways of operating abroad. For example, the firm might do the following:

- Shift some operations (for example, manufacturing or marketing) to the United States, where the average tax rate is lower.
- Assess whether transfer prices or cost allocations can be adjusted to shift income from high-tax-rate to low-tax-rate jurisdictions.
- Shift from domestic to foreign borrowing to increase deductions for interest against foreign-source income.
- Shift from equity to debt financing of foreign operations to increase interest deductions against foreign-source income.

The increasing tax rates abroad and an increasing proportion of income derived from abroad suggest a continuing increase in the combined average tax rate that could hurt future profitability unless the firm takes counteractions.

Analyzing PepsiCo's Income Tax Disclosures

Refer to PepsiCo's income tax disclosures in Note 5, "Income Taxes," to its financial statements (Appendix A). PepsiCo's average tax rate was 19.3 percent in 2006, 25.9 percent in 2007, and 26.8 percent in 2008. In each year, the average tax rate was less than the 35 percent federal statutory tax rate.

PepsiCo's relatively low average tax rates during these three years are primarily a result of lower tax rates on PepsiCo's income from foreign operations. Recall that the denominator of the average tax rate computation combines both U.S.-source and foreign-source income for financial reporting. The initial assumption is that all of this income is subject to taxes at a rate equal to the U.S. federal statutory rate. Foreign tax rates are usually different from the U.S. federal rate, however, and in the case of PepsiCo, the overall average tax rate decreased because of these foreign rate differences.

State and local income taxes generally trigger increases in firms' average tax rates beyond the federal statutory tax rate of 35 percent. For 2008, for example, state and local taxes increased the average tax rate for PepsiCo by 0.8 percent.

For 2006 and 2007, PepsiCo's average tax rate is lower as a result of resolving open tax issues (as discussed in Chapter 4). PepsiCo reached a settlement with tax authorities after tax audits related to prior years resulted in a tax benefit for 2006 and 2007. The percentage reduction in the average tax rate is quite large in 2006 (8.6 percent). PepsiCo provides a discussion of the tax benefits (Appendix B) as part of the firm's MD&A, "Our Financial Results, Items Affecting Comparability."

PepsiCo's disclosures of current and deferred taxes indicate that a large amount of the firm's tax expense each year also is currently payable. We can gain additional insights about the operations of PepsiCo by examining the components of its deferred tax assets and liabilities.

Investment in Noncontrolled Affiliates

PepsiCo owns less than a controlling interest in its bottlers and uses the equity method to account for its investments in these bottlers. As Chapter 7 explains more fully, PepsiCo recognizes its share of the earnings of these bottlers each year and includes it in "bottling equity income" on its income statement. Income before taxes for 2008 includes $374 million of bottling equity income. The income tax law taxes this income only when PepsiCo receives a dividend from the bottlers. Deferred tax liabilities related to the future dividend receipts from these as well as other non-bottler-related investments totaled $1,163 million at the end of 2007 and $1,193 million at the end of 2008, indicating that PepsiCo has deferred a significant amount of income tax payments because of this temporary difference, and the amount is rising.

Property, Plant, and Equipment

PepsiCo indicates in Note 4, "Property, Plant, and Equipment and Intangible Assets" (Appendix A), that it uses principally the straight-line depreciation method for financial reporting. Income tax laws provide for accelerated depreciation. PepsiCo has deferred tax liabilities of $881 million as of the end of 2008 due to depreciating assets faster for tax than for financial reporting. The deferred tax liability increased during 2008, indicating that PepsiCo has more depreciable assets in the early years of their lives, when accelerated depreciation exceeds straight-line depreciation, than they have depreciable assets in the later years, when straight-line depreciation exceeds accelerated depreciation.

Postretirement Benefits—Pension Benefits and Retiree Medical Benefits

PepsiCo reports deferred tax assets relating to pension benefits and retiree medical benefits for 2008. For both pension and retiree medical benefits, PepsiCo reported greater expense for financial reporting than for tax reporting, which generally prevents tax deductions for these benefits until the firm pays them in cash. PepsiCo will have greater tax deductions later when employees receive the benefits.

Intangible Assets Other Than Goodwill

PepsiCo indicates in its Note 4, "Property, Plant, and Equipment and Intangible Assets" (Appendix A), that it amortizes intangibles other than goodwill over periods ranging from 5–40 years. The reporting of a deferred tax liability for these items suggests that PepsiCo writes off these intangibles more quickly for tax purposes.

Net Carryforwards

PepsiCo recognizes deferred tax assets for the future saving in taxes when it can offset NOLs previously incurred against the positive income of future periods. PepsiCo indicates in Note 5, "Income Taxes" (Appendix A), that it has $7.2 billion of NOL carryforwards as of the end of 2008. The deferred tax asset is $682 million related to carryforwards.

Stock-Based Compensation

For financial reporting, PepsiCo records its stock-based compensation expense by determining option values on the date of the grant of stock options and then recognizing the expense over the vesting period (Note 6, "Stock-Based Compensation," in Appendix A). For tax reporting, the expense is recognized later, most often when the stock options are exercised by employees. Upon exercise, U.S. tax law permits firms to deduct the difference between market price and exercise price of the shares being issued. PepsiCo has deferred tax assets of $410 million at the end of 2008, a decrease of $15 million during the year. PepsiCo's Statement of Common Shareholders' Equity (Appendix A) indicates that the firm received tax deductions in 2007 and 2008 for stock option exercises related to stock-based compensation.

Deferred Tax Asset Valuation Allowances

Recall that firms must recognize a valuation allowance if they are not likely to realize the tax benefits of deferred tax assets, so that deferred tax assets will be reported at the most likely net realizable value. PepsiCo's valuation allowance is similar in amount to the deferred tax asset for net carryforwards each year, suggesting that the valuation allowance likely relates to these items. As we discussed earlier, even though PepsiCo is profitable and paying tax, the deferred tax assets associated with NOL carryforwards are not transferable and might be related to subsidiaries with expected poor future performance. The decrease in the valuation allowance for 2008 is similar in amount to the decrease in the deferred tax asset for carryforwards.

Summary of Income Taxes

Income taxes affect each of the principal financial statements as follows:

- The income statement reports the amount of income tax expense. The analyst can compute the relation between income tax expense and income before taxes, a relation referred to as a firm's *average tax rate.* The average tax rate affects analysis of a firm's profitability. The income tax note explains the major reasons why the average tax rate differs from the statutory federal tax rate. Most differences between average and statutory tax rates are transitory and thus do not affect the prediction of future periods' net income. However, shifts between domestic and foreign operations may create permanent tax rate changes.
- The statement of cash flows usually shows an adjustment to net income for the change in deferred taxes (for PepsiCo, $573 million for 2008 and $118 million for 2007), which converts tax expense to tax payable when computing cash flow from operations. The income tax note indicates the mix of currently payable and deferred taxes and the extent to which a firm has delayed or accelerated the payment of income taxes. It also indicates the components of deferred tax assets and liabilities, which the analyst can tie to analysis of various other transactions of the firm (such as intercorporate investments and pension and retiree medical obligations).
- The balance sheet shows the amount of deferred tax assets and deferred tax liabilities. The income tax note indicates the line items on the balance sheet that include deferred taxes. Typically, firms report one net current deferred tax asset or liability and one net noncurrent deferred tax asset or liability. These amounts affect assessments of a firm's financial position (such as the current ratio and debt ratios).

PENSIONS AND OTHER POSTRETIREMENT BENEFITS

In addition to salaries, bonuses, wages, vacation time, and share-based compensation, most employers provide benefits to employees when they retire. The next several sections deal with pension benefits. Once pensions are discussed, we provide a brief summary of similar accounting methods applied to other postretirement benefits.[12]

To provide for retiree pension benefits, employers sponsor *defined contribution plans* or *defined benefit plans.* In a *defined contribution plan,* employers promise to place a certain percentage of an employee's earnings into an investment vehicle as specified by the employee. During the past decade, more employers have begun to offer defined contribution plans, typically 401(k) plans. The employer makes a cash contribution to an investment

[12] The most recent pension and postemployment benefit accounting rules are found in Financial Accounting Standards Board, *Statement of Financial Accounting Standards No.158,* "Employers' Accounting for Defined Benefit Pension and Other Postretirement Plans" (2006) (prior standards: *SFAS No. 87,* issued December 1985, addresses pension plan accounting; *SFAS No. 106,* issued December 1990, deals with postretirement benefits other than pensions; *SFAS No. 132,* issued February 1998, standardizes disclosure requirements for pension plans and other postretirement benefit plans); *Codification Topics 715 and 958*; International Accounting Standards Board, *International Accounting Standard 19,* "Employees Benefits" (revised 1998).

company each year based on a percentage of the employee's salary. The employer's obligation under the plan is satisfied once the funds are placed into the investment account. The employer does not guarantee a given defined benefit payment when the employee retires. Instead, the fund balance at retirement depends on the investing success of the investment company and the employee's allocation of the contribution across different types of investments. The accounting for a defined contribution plan is straightforward. Because of the plan contract, the employee's current service generates the employer's obligation to make periodic payments, and the employer records pension expense for the amount of the defined contribution obligation. The operating section of the statement of cash flows reports the contribution as a cash outflow in the period in which the funds are contributed to the investment company.

In a *defined benefit plan*, employers incur the obligation to provide a definite pension payment to employees throughout the employee's retirement period. The final obligation is determined by the terms of a pension plan, which are negotiated by employers and employees. Normally, many factors affect the determination of the final obligation, including employee longevity, status at retirement, and final pay. The intricacies of determining the obligation and assigning pension cost to particular periods create complex accounting.

Normally, a corporation hires a third-party trustee, usually an insurance company or another financial services company, to administer such plans. Each year the employer makes an annual contribution to the trustee, which is invested in plan assets (usually a portfolio of cash, debt, and equity securities) managed by the trustee. The trustee keeps records of the plan's obligations to individual employees and makes pension payments to eligible employees. The remaining discussion of pensions relates to understanding the accounting for these more complex defined benefit plans.

The Economics of Pension Accounting in a Defined Benefit Plan

The underlying economic explanation of defined benefit pension plans involves understanding and comparing two key amounts: *pension obligation* and *pension assets.*

Pension Obligation (Liability)

In a typical defined benefit arrangement, employees are promised a lump-sum payment or periodic monthly payments when they retire based on some plan formula. A typical plan formula considers the number of years of employee service, a credit for each year of annual service (usually expressed as a percentage), and final salary at retirement date. For example, assume that a pension plan is governed by the following formula:

$$\text{Annual Benefits} = \text{Annual Credit} \times \text{Years of Service} \times \text{Salary at Retirement Date}$$

If the annual credit is 1 percent, the interpretation of the formula is that for each year of service, an employee's annual retirement benefit increases by 1 percent of the salary at retirement date. An employee who worked 30 years under the plan would retire at 30 percent of final salary. The PBO (*projected benefit obligation*) is the actuarially determined present value of estimated retirement payments calculated according to the benefit formula (using expected future salary levels) to be paid to employees because employees have worked and earned benefits until the current date. The discount (interest) rate used for the present value computation is called the settlement rate, which represents the current market rate at which an outside party would effectively settle the obligation.

Pension Assets

To have the funds available to make pension payments when due, employers accumulate pension assets by setting aside funds for that purpose (self-administration of the plan) or by making cash payments to a plan trustee with the expectation that the trustee will invest the cash and increase the fund by generating returns on the investments. If the employer self-administers the plan, it is referred to as an unfunded plan. If a plan trustee is used, the plan is considered a funded plan. Unless otherwise noted, we assume that all plans are administered by a third-party trustee. The employer and third-party trustee, in consultation with an actuary, make decisions about payments to the trustee based on an assumption about the expected long-term rate of return on plan assets.

Pension fund assets are measured at their fair market value (FMV) at the end of each year. Employers use the year-end FMV or an average FMV over a period of time, usually five years (the average is referred to as the *market-related fair value*), in financial reporting. Determining the fair value of the assets in the fund usually is not a problem because prudent investing of fund assets generally yields funds comprised of cash and widely held, often-traded securities.

The Economic Status of the Plan

The economic status of the plan is determined by comparing the two economic amounts: the PBO and the FMV of plan assets:

PBO > FMV of plan assets: Plan is underfunded.	(net obligation)
PBO < FMV of plan assets: Plan is overfunded.	(net asset)

The economic status of the plan is reflected on the balance sheet.

What Changes the Economic Status of the Plan during the Year?

Other than funding (that is, payments to the trustee), changes in the economic status of the plan are reported in comprehensive income.

What Changes PBO (That is, the Pension Plan Liability)? Five events have the potential of changing the PBO during a given period: service cost, interest on PBO, prior service cost, liability (actuarial) gains and losses, and benefit payments to retirees.

1. Employees earn benefits in the current year (*service cost*).
   By working one additional year, employees earn an increase in future benefits. The actuarially determined present value of the increase in future benefits represents an increase in the employer's pension liability as a result of the employee's service that year. This liability increase is called service cost.
2. Time passes (*interest on PBO*).
   PBO represents the present value of future benefits payable to retirees. As time passes without the liability being extinguished, the liability accumulates interest at the settlement interest rate. That is, the long-term liability PBO grows at a rate of interest equal to the settlement interest rate. The liability increase due to the passage of time is called interest cost.
3. Plan amendments grant retroactive benefits (*prior service cost*).
   From time to time, employers and employees negotiate and decide to change the pension plan benefit formula. Usually, the negotiation leads to increased retirement benefits, which are applied retroactively. Recall the pension plan formula example described earlier. Now assume that the employer amends the pension plan agreement

to increase the annual credit from 1 percent to 2 percent. If the amendment is retroactive, the employee now is entitled to an annual benefit equal to 60 percent of final salary. This sudden increase in retirement payments translates into a sudden increase in PBO because PBO is the actuarially determined present value of the estimated future retirement payments. The increase in PBO from amending a pension plan and retroactively granting benefits is defined as prior service cost. Employers often justify the sudden increase in the liability with the argument that the current employee group benefiting from the retroactive amendment represents a more loyal workforce with a higher morale. These conditions translate into a future economic benefit for the employer over the remaining service life of the affected group.

4. Actuarial assumptions about future retirement payments change [*liability (actuarial) gains and losses*].
   Each period the actuary estimates PBO using the most current assumptions about items such as interest rates, mortality, pay increases, and job classifications. If experience during the period indicates that assumptions should be changed, the actuary recomputes the PBO based on the new assumptions. The resulting increase or decrease in PBO is referred to as a liability (actuarial) gain or loss. For example, if new information becomes available that employees are estimated to live longer after retirement than previously thought, increased future retirement payments will occur, and consequently, PBO increases. The unexpected increase in PBO is a liability loss. Other changes in plan assumptions could lead to decreased PBO, which would be classified as a liability gain.
5. Retirement benefits are paid (*benefit payments*).
   Actually paying retirement benefits to retired employees reduces the PBO.

What Changes the FMV of Pension Plan Assets? Three events may change the FMV of pension plan assets during a given period: employer cash payments to the pension plan, actual return on plan assets, and retirement benefits payments.

1. Employer cash payments are made to the plan trustee (*employer contributions*).
   Funding the plan by making a cash contribution to the pension plan increases the FMV of pension plan assets. Within certain boundaries, company management decides how much cash to contribute to the pension plan each year. The U.S. federal government mandates minimum funding amounts for defined benefit pension plans, which become the minimum company contribution amount. Internal Revenue Service regulations allow only a certain amount to be tax deductible, which become the maximum company contribution amount. Therefore, management normally makes a pension plan contribution between the minimum and maximum amounts.
2. There are actual returns on invested plan assets (*return on plan assets*).
   The pension plan trustee invests the cash contributed by the employer in stocks, bonds, and other assets, which earn a return (for example, dividends or interest) and experience changes in market value. The change in the FMV of plan assets during the period, adjusted for employer contributions and benefit payments, leads to the computation of an *actual return* on plan assets. If the return is positive, the FMV of the assets increased during the period. But the return can be negative as well. The actual return on plan assets can be thought of as being comprised of two components: expected return and unexpected return.
   - The *expected return on plan assets*, which is always positive, is based on long-run expected rates of return.
   - The *unexpected return on plan assets* is based on deviations of actual rates of return from expected rates (*asset gains and losses*).

For example, if a company expects a 10 percent return and the actual return is 9 percent, the two components of actual return are an expected return of 10 percent and an asset loss of 1 percent. The PBO increases due to accruing interest at the settlement rate. In an analogous fashion, the FMV of plan assets increases based on the expected return. The PBO increases or decreases if the settlement rate (or other assumptions) turns out to be different than expected. Similarly, the FMV of plan assets increases (a gain) or decreases (a loss) if the actual return turns out to be different than expected.

3. Retirement benefits are paid (*benefit payments*).
   Finally, actually paying retirement benefits to retired employees reduces the FMV of available plan assets. Note that this amount is equal to the reduction of the obligation to retired employees, the PBO.

Reporting the Income Effects in Net Income and Other Comprehensive Income

SFAS 158 specifies how the comprehensive income effects of each change in the pension plan's PBO and FMV of plan assets is to be reflected in the employer's income statement and other comprehensive income. Each non-cash change is given (1) immediate recognition as a part of pension expense of the current period or (2) delayed recognition as part of other comprehensive income. In review, the changes in PBO and FMV of plan assets are as follows:

Changes in PBO	Changes in FMV of Plan Assets
• Service cost	• Employer cash payments to fund trustee
• Interest cost on PBO	• Actual return on plan assets (two components):
• Prior service cost	◦ Expected return on plan assets
• Liability gains/losses on PBO	◦ Asset gains/losses
• Benefit payments to retirees	• Benefit payments to retirees

The last item listed in each column, benefit payments to retirees, affects PBO and FMV equally, so it has no effect on the net of PBO and FMV (that is, does not change net assets or liabilities); thus, it can be ignored. Also, cash payments to the pension plan trustee are determined by financial policy and represent a cash flow rather than an accrual accounting element.

Eliminating all cash benefit payments to retirees and employer cash contributions to the trustee from the columns leaves the following items for consideration, along with their prescribed treatment by the FASB:

Type of Change in Pension Plan	Treatment in Reporting Income
Changes in PBO:	
Service cost	Increase pension expense (decrease net income)
Interest cost on PBO	Increase pension expense (decrease net income)
Prior service cost	Decrease other comprehensive income
Liability gains/losses on PBO	Increase/decrease other comprehensive income
Changes in FMV of plan assets:	
Actual return on plan assets (two components):	
Expected return on plan assets	Decrease pension expense (increase net income)
Asset gains/losses	Increase/decrease other comprehensive income

Items receiving immediate recognition in net income are service cost, interest cost, and expected return on plan assets. Immediate recognition of service cost and interest on PBO increases pension expense because both represent an increase in a liability (the PBO) and increases in liabilities increase expenses. The expected return on plan assets is always positive. Because it represents an increase in an asset (the FMV of plan assets), it decreases pension expense.[13]

The FASB delayed recognition of prior service cost in net income to be consistent with the idea that the granting of prior service cost is done to generate future employee goodwill, with the benefits of such goodwill realized over the remaining service period of the employees to whom the retroactive benefits were granted. Accordingly, prior service cost is reflected in pension expense over time using an amortization process. However, prior service cost is generally an increase in the PBO liability. Therefore, it decreases other comprehensive income.

Recognition of gains and losses on pension liabilities and assets are delayed because of a "smoothing" objective inherent in the accounting for pensions. A primary argument in support of this objective is that most gains and losses are transitory fluctuations and current recognition should not be given to such transitory fluctuations. The rules for the specific delayed recognition given to gains and losses are complex, and we discuss them subsequently in the chapter. The basic idea is that only if transitory gains and losses become very large are they amortized and reflected in net income. However, in the period in which they occur, all liability gains and losses are reflected in other comprehensive income.

The sum of the amounts currently recognized in net income is reported as pension expense in the income statement. To strengthen your understanding of pension expense computation and to illustrate the balance sheet and footnote presentations, we consider the following simplified example.

Example 15: Pension Expense Calculation (with Balance Sheet and Note Disclosures)

On January 1, 2010, Moreno Co. adopted a defined benefit pension plan, at which time both its PBO and FMV of plan assets equaled zero. In early 2011, Moreno granted retroactive benefits of $100,000 to employees who have an average remaining service period of ten years from that date. Moreno decided to fund the plan at the end of each year by sending $60,000 to a plan trustee. Service cost is $50,000 each year. Moreno earns 10 percent on investments and can settle the obligation by purchasing an annuity with a 7 percent interest rate. To simplify this first example, assume (1) that actual and expected returns on plan assets are equal (that is, no asset gains or losses) and (2) that actual and expected PBO are equal (that is, no liability gains or losses). Our goal is to prepare financial statement disclosures for 2010–2012.

[13] We use the terms *pension expense* and *net pension cost* interchangeably. This is not always correct because a cost can be an expense or an asset depending on whether economic benefits are expected to exist beyond the current period. We have abstracted from the idea that pension cost can be part of inventory (for example, if it is the pension of a direct laborer) to make the discussion easier. However, if pension cost is deemed to be part of inventory, it is not reported as pension expense; instead, it is allocated to inventory as a product cost and then becomes part of cost of goods sold when the inventory is sold.

To compute many of the pension disclosures, it is necessary to reconcile PBO and FMV of plan assets. For the Moreno Co., the reconciliations are as follows:

Changes in PBO		**2010**		**2011**		**2012**
PBO, 1/1		$ 0		$ 50,000		$203,500
Service cost		50,000		50,000		50,000
Interest cost on PBO:						
Beginning PBO balance	$0		$50,000		$203,500	
Settlement rate	× 0.07		× 0.07		× 0.07	
Interest cost		0		3,500		14,245
Prior service cost		0		100,000		0
PBO, 12/31		$50,000		$203,500		$267,745

Changes in FMV of Plan Assets		**2010**		**2011**		**2012**
FMV of plan assets, 1/1		$ 0		$ 60,000		$126,000
Expected return on plan assets:						
Beginning balance	$0		$60,000		$126,000	
Long-term expected return on plan assets	× 0.10		× 0.10		× 0.10	
Expected return		0		6,000		12,600
Contributions		60,000		60,000		60,000
FMV of plan assets, 12/31		$60,000		$126,000		$198,600

In 2010, PBO began at $0 and increased $50,000 due to employees' current service. Because there was no beginning PBO, it did not grow due to the passage of time; thus, interest cost on PBO is $0. No other changes in PBO occurred in 2010. (Two possible other changes intentionally not considered in this example are liability gains/losses and payments to retired employees.) The FMV of plan assets began at zero, no return was earned on the $0 investment, and $60,000 was contributed to the plan trustee at the end of the year. (Again, by construction of the example, no payments were made to retirees.) Comparing PBO and FMV of plan assets at 12/31/10, we see that Moreno contributed $10,000 more than the pension plan obligation to employees. Thus, the plan is overfunded by $10,000. That is, the pension plan is in a $10,000 net asset position.

In 2011, the situation changes substantially. Again, service cost of $50,000 increases PBO. But now the $50,000 beginning PBO accrues interest at the 7 percent settlement rate such that PBO goes up by an additional $3,500 (interest cost on PBO). Also, 2011 is the year in which Moreno granted retroactive benefits in a plan amendment causing PBO to increase $100,000 for prior service cost. Therefore, at December 31, 2011, PBO is $203,500. Moreno did not choose to immediately fund the prior service cost PBO increase. The FMV of plan assets increased only by the 10 percent return on the beginning plan assets plus the annual end-of-period payment of $60,000 to the trustee. Therefore, at December 31, 2011, Moreno is in a net liability position of $77,500, which can be found by comparing the $203,500 PBO to the $126,000 FMV of plan assets. Under certain laws, severe underfunding of a plan can trigger a legal requirement to purchase insurance on the plan. Even if underfunding does not trigger legal actions, employee disenchantment is possible.

The events that change PBO and FMV of plan assets in 2012 are similar. An interesting situation is revealed, however, by the 2012 numbers. Interest on PBO ($14,245) now exceeds the actual return on plan assets ($12,600). When this situation occurs, an employer would have to fund at a rate higher than annual service cost to keep the underfunded position (that is, net obligation) from growing.

Income Statement Effects

Service cost, interest on PBO, and expected return on plan assets received immediate recognition as part of pension expense on Moreno's books. Prior service cost and gains and losses receive delayed recognition by initially recognizing the increase in PBO in other comprehensive income and then recycling through net income by amortizing the beginning balances over the average remaining service period of employees.

Computation of Net Pension Expense	**2010**	**2011**	**2012**
Service cost	$ 50,000	$50,000	$50,000
Interest on PBO	0	3,500	14,245
Expected return on assets	0	(6,000)	(12,600)
Amortization of PSC*	0	0	10,000
Amortization of gain/loss	0	0	0
Net pension expense	$ 50,000	$47,500	$61,645

* Assumes that the December 31, 2011 prior service cost is amortized beginning in 2012. The amount is amortized over average remaining service life of the workforce at December 31, 2011, which is assumed to be ten years.

Note that amortization of prior service cost is $0 in 2000, $0 in 2011 (because there was no beginning balance to amortize), and $10,000 in 2012 ($100,000 prior service cost/10 years). The amortization of prior service cost will continue for nine more years.

Net pension expense is reflected in the income statement in each of the three years. For merchandising firms, it appears as an operating expense. For manufacturing firms, the portion that pertains to employees involved in manufacturing inventory is capitalized as part of inventory and then expensed as a portion of cost of goods sold when the inventory is sold.

Exhibit 8.7 presents the previous discussion within the financial statement effects template. In 2010, an increase in the pension liability occurs that causes $50,000 in pension expense. Funding increases the pension asset by $60,000. In 2011, the plan amendment increases the pension liability by the $100,000 prior service cost. Prior service cost receives delayed recognition (that is, is not reflected in current pension expense). Instead, other comprehensive income is reduced. The remainder of the changes in the pension liability (increase of $53,500) and pension asset (increase of $6,000) are from events receiving immediate recognition in pension expense (increase of $47,500). Again, funding increases the pension asset further ($60,000 increase). In 2012, similar events occur to change the pension asset and liability. In addition, the prior service cost is amortized to pension expense by removing $10,000 from other comprehensive income.

The total amount of pension expense reflected in net income is disclosed by Moreno as follows:

Note Disclosure Net Periodic Pension Expense	**2010**	**2011**	**2012**
Service cost	$50,000	$50,000	$50,000
Interest on PBO	0	3,500	14,245
Expected return on plan assets	0	(6,000)	(12,600)
Amortization of prior service cost	0	0	10,000
Amortization of gain/loss	0	0	0
Net pension expense	$50,000	$47,500	$61,645

EXHIBIT 8.7: FINANCIAL STATEMENT EFFECTS OF PENSION ACCOUNTING

Assets	=	Liabilities	+	Total Shareholders' Equity: CC	AOCI	RE
2010						
Record pension expense:		Pension Liability +50,000				Pension Expense −50,000
Record cash payment:						
Cash −60,000						
Pension Asset +60,000						

Pension Expense	50,000	
Pension Liability		50,000
Pension Asset	60,000	
Cash		60,000

Assets	=	Liabilities	+	CC	AOCI	RE
2011						
Record plan amendment:		Pension Liability +100,000			OCI −100,000	
Record pension expense:						
Pension Asset +6,000		Pension Liability +53,500				Pension Expense −47,500
Record cash payment:						
Cash −60,000						
Pension Asset +60,000						

OCI	100,000	
Pension Liability		100,000
Pension Expense	47,500	
Pension Asset	6,000	
Pension Liability		53,500
Pension Asset	60,000	
Cash		60,000

Assets	=	Liabilities	+	CC	AOCI	RE
2012						
Record pension expense:						
Pension Asset +12,600		Pension Liability +64,245			OCI +10,000	Pension Expense −61,645
Record cash payment:						
Cash −60,000						
Pension Asset +60,000						

Pension Expense	61,645	
Pension Asset	12,600	
OCI		10,000
Pension Liability		64,245
Pension Asset	60,000	
Cash		60,000

Additional required disclosures reconcile beginning PBO to ending PBO and beginning FMV of plan assets to ending FMV of plan assets.

Note Disclosures: Reconciliations of PBO and FMV of Plan Assets	2010	2011	2012
January 1, PBO	$ 0	$ 50,000	$203,500
Service cost	50,000	50,000	50,000
Interest cost	0	3,500	14,245
Prior service cost	0	100,000	0
Benefit payments	0	0	0
December 31, PBO	$ 50,000	$203,500	$267,745
January 1, FMV of plan assets	$ 0	$ 60,000	$126,000
Company contributions	60,000	60,000	60,000
Benefit payments	0	0	0
Actual return on plan assets	0	6,000	12,600
December 31, FMV of plan assets	$ 60,000	$126,000	$198,600
Net pension liability (asset)	$(10,000)	$ 77,500	$ 69,145

Gain and Loss Recognition

To this point, we have assumed that all actual and expected amounts are equal. Gains and losses occur when expectations turn out to be different than realizations. That is:

Expected PBO ≠ Actual PBO, which results in liability gains or losses

Expected FMV ≠ Actual FMV, which results in asset gains or losses

Pension plan accounting defers both asset and liability gains and losses. The net deferred gain/loss amount is amortized only if it becomes very large. The FASB set an arbitrary amount, called the *corridor* amount, as the threshold for deferred gain or loss amortization. The *corridor* is defined as 10 percent of the greater of actual PBO or actual FMV. The logic behind this treatment is simple. Gains and losses are deviations from expectations. If expectations are unbiased, gains and losses will offset over time and the net gain or loss should fluctuate around zero. If the gains and losses do not offset over time, the accumulated gains or losses will become large, with *large* defined as exceeding the corridor. The FASB prescribes amortization only if the balance becomes larger than the corridor. The decision to amortize net deferred gains or losses is made each year, and that decision is independent of any decision made in prior years. Also, the decision is made based upon *beginning-of-the-year balances* (that is, using prior year-end balances for net deferred gain or loss, PBO, and FMV). The financial statement effects of amortizing a net loss are identical to the effects of amortizing prior service cost. Amortizing a net gain decreases other comprehensive income and increases net income via a reduction in pension expense.

Impact of Actuarial Assumptions

Firms must disclose in notes to the financial statements the assumptions made with respect to (1) the discount rate used to compute the pension benefit obligation; (2) the expected rate of return on pension investments (including the pension plan investment guidelines that form the basis for establishing the expected rate of return); and (3) the rate of compensation increase, which affects the amount of the PBO.

The amount of the pension benefit obligation is inversely related to the discount rate. U.S. GAAP specifies that firms should use a long-term government bond rate as the discount rate. Thus, firms should not vary significantly with respect to the discount rate used. However, even small differences in the discount rate can materially affect the size of the pension benefit obligation.

Firms use different expected rates of return on pension investments, in part because of different mixtures of investments in their pension portfolios. For example, a firm with equal proportions of debt and equity should have a lower expected return than a firm that invests fully in equities. PepsiCo discloses in Note 7 that the target allocation is for 60 percent equity securities and 40 percent debt securities, but that the actual allocation for 2008 was 38 percent equity securities, 61 percent debt securities, and 1 percent cash.

Firms also may use different expected rates of return in an effort to manage earnings. The assumed long-term rate of return on pension assets impacts the analysis of pensions in several ways. First, if the firm cannot generate returns, on average, equal to this rate, the firm will need to contribute additional assets in the future. Second, the expected return on pension investments reduces pension expense each period and increases earnings. Firms must amortize any combined difference between expected and actual returns and liability gains and losses if the accumulated gains and losses exceed the corridor; so a deficiency in returns because of assuming too high a level of expected returns shows up slowly in pension expense.

The amount of the pension benefit obligation is directly related to the assumed rate of compensation increases. Firms have incentives to use a lower rather than higher assumed rate of compensation increases, both to lower their PBO and to create lower expectations among employees about future compensation increases.

The analyst should compare a firm's assumptions over time with other firms to evaluate the firm's level of aggressiveness in making assumptions.

Other Postretirement Benefits

Employers provide postretirement benefits other than pensions to employees as well as to employees' spouses and dependents. These benefits may include medical and hospitalization coverage, college tuition assistance, and life insurance coverage. As in the case of pensions, current employee service triggers these promises and the expected obligation for these benefits can be computed as the actuarially determined present value of future payments.

A good understanding of postretirement benefit accounting can be obtained by adopting the same framework for expense recognition, balance sheet presentation, and note reconciliation as that discussed for pensions. However, there are two major differences. First, many companies simply pay these benefits when retirees make claims and do not fund a portfolio of plan assets dedicated to pay for other postretirement benefits because government regulations do not specify minimum funding for postretirement benefits other than pensions. As a result, the FMV of postretirement plan assets is zero for the majority of companies. Second, there are two additional required disclosures for postretirement benefits other than pensions: (1) the assumed health care cost trend rate(s) used in actuarial computations and (2) the effect of a one-percentage-point increase and the effect of a one-percentage-point decrease in the assumed health care cost trend rate on accumulated postretirement benefit obligation for heath care benefits and on the aggregate of the service and interest cost components of net periodic postretirement health care benefit cost.

Signals about Earnings Persistence

Sharp swings in the market values of investments can impact pension expense and earnings significantly. Although firms use long-term expected returns on investments to compute the expected return on assets each period, they apply this rate to the market value of assets in the pension portfolio. When market values increase, as they did in the early to late 1990s, many firms found that their pension expenses became pension income. During this period, some firms' pension income was a substantial portion of their increased earnings. During the stock market downturn that followed, the pension income became pension expense, exacerbating the downward pressure on earnings already experienced from weakened economic conditions. When using earnings of the current period to forecast earnings in the future, the analyst should recognize the impact of changing stock prices on the measurement of pension expense.

PepsiCo's Pensions and Other Postemployment Benefits

Note 7 to PepsiCo's Consolidated Financial Statements, "Pension, Retiree Medical and Saving Plans" (Appendix A), presents pension (for U.S. and International) and other postemployment benefits information (amounts in following discussion in millions). The first major schedule shows that projected benefit liability (PBO) on U.S. plans at the beginning of 2008 was $6,048 and increased to $6,217. PBO increased due to service cost ($244), interest cost on the beginning PBO ($371), and an unfavorable change in the actuarial assumptions used to estimate the PBO ($28). PBO decreased due to a plan amendment that reduced the past benefits of employees ($20) and payments to retired employees ($277). Nontypical adjustments to the plan also occurred. SFAS 158 required that firms align the measurement date for key pension amounts with the balance sheet date. PepsiCo shows how this affects the PBO in each of the years presented. This change is nonrecurring. Also, plans will be terminated or curtailed occasionally. PepsiCo reports a settlement/curtailment in 2008 that decreased PBO $9. Note that PepsiCo reports an offsetting $9 decrease in plan assets due to the settlement/curtailment. Also, an employee group occasionally negotiates a special termination benefit when terminating plan coverage. PepsiCo reports a $31 increase in the PBO due to such an event.

PepsiCo provides similar descriptions of PBO changes from international plans and retiree medical plans in the remaining columns. A substantial difference is the large foreign currency adjustment that reduces the PBO liability when the plans are translated to U.S. dollars ($376). Actuarial assumption changes also had a dramatic favorable effect on the international plans' PBO, reducing it by $165.

PepsiCo explains the changes in the fair value of plan assets in the next part of the schedule. Plan assets began 2008 at $5,782, an amount only slightly less than the beginning PBO of $6,048. Then securities market performance tanked in 2008, causing an actual return on plan assets that was in fact a large loss of $1,434. PepsiCo contributed only $48 to the plan assets and used $277 of plan assets to pay benefits. By year-end, PepsiCo is in a large net liability position because plan assets are only $3,974 as compared to a PBO of $6,217. The difference, $2,243, is reported as a part of other noncurrent liabilities on the balance sheet. Note 7 indicates that $2,183 of the $2,243 is reported in noncurrent liabilities with the remainder in current liabilities.

Again, the remaining columns provide similar descriptions of changes in the fair value of plan assets for international plans and retiree medical plans. The large foreign currency adjustment that reduced the PBO liability ($376) also reduced the fair value of plan assets by $341. Also note in the retiree medical area that PepsiCo, like many other firms, does not set aside funds to pay medical benefits for future retirees, choosing instead to "pay as you go." Employer contributions of $70 exactly equal benefit payments of $70.

Pepsi reports near the bottom of the schedule that most of these changes are included in other comprehensive income. The most significant are any changes in the PBO from plan amendments and changes in the PBO and fair value of the plan assets from a host of changes in actuarial assumptions (change in discount rate, employee-related assumption changes, and liability-related experience different from assumptions) and the difference between the actual return and expected return on plan assets (a very large loss of $1,850).

Current recognition in pension expense appears at the top of the next page of PepsiCo's Note 7. Pension expense is increased by service cost ($244) and interest cost ($371). It is decreased by the *expected* return on plan assets ($416), which you will recall was much larger than the actual *loss* on plan assets. Prior service cost, initially reflected in other comprehensive income, is recycled to pension expense via amortization ($19), and the amount of loss initially reflected in other comprehensive income has become so large that it exceeds the corridor and must be recycled to pension expense via amortization ($55). Settlement/curtailments and special termination benefits also receive immediate recognition in pension expense.

PepsiCo's disclosures highlight the income-smoothing nature of pension accounting. Imagine the effect on net income of the period if all of the actual loss on plan assets was included in current net income instead of added to other comprehensive income. The justification for this treatment is the transitory nature of security market movements and the long-run nature of PepsiCo's obligations to retired employees. However, because actuarial gains and losses, unexpected returns on plan assets, and unamortized prior service costs are part of comprehensive income (along with unrealized gains and losses on available-for-sale securities, foreign currency translation gains and losses, and certain derivative gains and losses) and current comprehensive income affects other accumulated comprehensive income, shareholders' equity is not smoothed by pension accounting. PepsiCo's Consolidated Statement of Shareholders' Equity (Appendix A) reports an after-tax charge to other comprehensive income of $1,376 for pension accounting effects in 2008.

DERIVATIVE INSTRUMENTS

Firms engage in numerous transactions that subject them to risks associated with changes in interest rates, foreign currency exchange rates, commodity prices, and others. *Derivative instruments* can help a firm mitigate (or take) such risks. Consider the following scenarios.

Example 16

Firm A, a U.S. firm, orders a machine on June 30, 2010, for delivery on June 30, 2011, from a British supplier for £10,000 (Great Britain pounds, also referred to as *GBP* throughout this section). Assume that the exchange rate between the U.S. dollar and the GBP is currently $1.60 per GBP, indicating a purchase price of $16,000. Firm A is concerned that the value of the U.S. dollar will decline between June 30, 2010, and June 30, 2011, when it must convert U.S. dollars into GBP, requiring it to pay more than $16,000 to purchase the machine.

Example 17

Firm B gives a note payable to a supplier on January 1, 2010, to acquire manufacturing equipment. The note has a face value of $100,000 and bears a fixed interest rate of 8 percent per year. Interest is payable annually on December 31, and the note matures on December 31, 2012. Firm B has the option of repaying the note prior to maturity. It knows, though, that the equipment supplier will value the note at any time prior to maturity based on existing market interest rates. Firm B is concerned that the value of the note will increase if interest rates decrease and that it will have to pay more than $100,000 if it decides to repay the note early.

Example 18

Firm C gives a note payable to a supplier on January 1, 2010, to acquire manufacturing equipment. The note has a face value of $100,000 and bears interest at the prime lending rate. Assume that the prime lending rate is 8 percent on January 1, 2010. The supplier will reset the interest rate each December 31 to establish the interest charge for the next calendar year. Interest is payable on December 31 of each year, and the note matures on December 31, 2012. Firm C is concerned that interest rates will increase to more than 8 percent during the term of the note and negatively affect its cash flows.

Example 19

Firm D holds 10,000 gallons of whiskey in inventory on October 31, 2010. Firm D expects to finish aging this whiskey by March 31, 2011, at which time it intends to sell the whiskey. However, uncertainties about the quality of the aged whiskey and economic conditions at the time make it difficult to predict the selling price of whiskey on March 31, 2011.

Many firms face risks of economic losses from changes in interest rate, foreign exchange rates, or commodity prices. For example, PepsiCo states the following in Note 10, "Financial Instruments" (Appendix A): "We are exposed to market risks arising from adverse changes in:

- Commodity prices, affecting the cost of our raw materials and energy;
- Foreign exchange risks;
- Interest rates"

Firms can purchase derivative financial instruments to mitigate (or take) these business risks. This section discusses the nature, use, accounting, and reporting of derivative instruments. U.S. GAAP and IFRS have similar derivative accounting rules.[14]

Nature and Use of Derivative Instruments

A derivative is a financial instrument that derives its value from some other financial instrument. An option to purchase a share of stock derives its value from the market price of the stock. A commitment to purchase a certain amount of foreign currency in the future derives its value from changes in the exchange rate for that currency. Firms typically use derivative instruments to hedge the risk of losses from changes in interest rates, foreign exchange rates, and commodity prices. The general idea is that changes in the value of the derivative instrument offset changes in the value of an asset or a liability or changes in future cash flows, thereby neutralizing the economic loss. Reconsider the four examples discussed previously.

Example 20

Refer to Example 16. Firm A wants to minimize the effect of changes in the exchange rate between the U.S. dollar and the GBP while it awaits delivery of the equipment. It purchases a forward foreign exchange contract from a bank on June 30, 2010, in which it promises to pay a fixed U.S. dollar amount on June 30, 2011, in exchange for £10,000. The forward foreign exchange rate between U.S. dollars and British pounds on June 30, 2010, for settlement on June 30, 2011, establishes the number of U.S. dollars the firm must deliver. Assume that

---

[14] Financial Accounting Standards Board, *Statement of Financial Accounting Standards No. 133*, "Accounting for Derivative Instruments and Hedging Activities" (1998); Financial Accounting Standards Board, *Statement of Financial Accounting Standards No. 138*, "Accounting for Certain Derivative Instruments and Certain Hedging Activities" (2000); Financial Accounting Standards Board, *Statement of Financial Accounting Standards No. 161*, "Disclosures about Derivative Instruments and Hedging Activities—an amendment of FASB Statement No. 133" (2009); *FASB Codification Topic 815*; Financial Accounting Standards Board, *Statement of Financial Accounting Standards No. 107*, "Disclosures about Fair Value of Financial Instruments" (1991); *FASB Codification Topic 825*; International Accounting Standards Board, *International Accounting Standard 39*, "Financial Instruments: Recognition and Measurement" (revised 2003); International Accounting Standards Board, *International Financial Reporting Standard 7*, "Financial Instruments: Disclosures," (2005).

the forward rate on June 30, 2010, for settlement of the forward contract on June 30, 2011, is $1.64 per GBP. By purchasing the forward contract, Firm A locks in the cost of the equipment at $16,400 (= £10,000 × $1.64). Thus, it achieves the objective of minimizing the risk of foreign currency exchange rate fluctuations impacting the firm's asset costs.

Example 21

Refer to Example 17. Firm B wants to neutralize the effect of changes in the market value of the note payable caused by changes in market interest rates. It engages in a swap contract with its bank. In effect, the swap allows Firm B to swap its fixed-interest-rate obligation for a variable-interest-rate obligation. The market value of the note will remain at $100,000 as long as the variable interest rate in the swap is the same as the variable rate used by the supplier to revalue the note while it is outstanding. The swap causes the interest payments that Firm B will face on the note payable to vary as the variable interest rate changes, but it locks the value of the note payable at $100,000.

Example 22

Refer to Example 18. Firm C wants to protect its future cash flows against increases in the variable interest rate to more than the initial 8 percent rate. It also engages in a swap contract with its bank. In effect, the swap allows Firm C to swap its variable-interest-rate obligation for a fixed-interest-rate obligation. The swap fixes the firm's annual interest expense and cash expenditure to 8 percent of the $100,000 note. By engaging in the swap, Firm C cannot take advantage of decreases in interest rates to less than 8 percent, which it could have done with its variable-rate note. In this example, the swap locks in the interest payments that Firm C will face on the note payable, but the value of the note payable to the supplier will vary as the variable interest rate changes.

Example 23

Refer to Example 19. Firm D would like to fix the price at which it can sell the whiskey in its inventory on March 31, 2011. It acquires a forward commodity contract in which it promises to sell 10,000 gallons of whiskey on March 31, 2011, at a fixed price. The forward price of whiskey on October 31, 2010, for delivery on March 31, 2011, is $320 per gallon. Thus, Firm D locks in a total cash inflow of $3,200,000 from selling the whiskey. The firm has minimized the risk of a decline in whiskey prices, but it forgoes any possible upside from possible increases in whiskey prices.

Forward contracts and swap contracts are only two of many types of derivative instruments. Banks and other financial intermediaries structure derivatives for a fee to suit the needs of their customers. Thus, the nature and complexity of derivatives vary widely. We confine our discussion to forward and swap contracts to illustrate the accounting and reporting of derivatives.

Consider the following elements of a derivative:

1. A derivative has one or more *underlyings*. An underlying is the specified item to which the derivative applies, such as an interest rate, a commodity price, a foreign exchange rate, or another variable. The underlying in Example 20 is the foreign exchange rate; in Examples 21 and 22, it is an interest rate; and in Example 23, it is the price of whiskey.
2. A derivative has one or more *notional amounts*. A notional amount is a number of units (dollar amounts, foreign currency units, bushels, barrels, gallons, shares, or other units) specified in the contract. The notional amount in Example 20 is £10,000; in Examples 21 and 22, it is the $100,000 face value of the note; and in Example 23, it is 10,000 gallons of whiskey.

3. A derivative may or may not require an initial investment. The firm usually acquires a derivative by exchanging promises with a counterparty, such as a commercial or investment bank. The acquisition of a derivative is usually an exchange of promises, a mutually unexecuted contract.
4. Derivatives typically require, or permit, *net settlement.* Firm A in Example 20 will not deliver $16,400 to the counterparty and receive in exchange £10,000. Firm A will actually purchase £10,000 on the market on June 30, 2011, at the exchange rate on that date, when it needs the British pounds to purchase the equipment. Firm A will receive cash from the counterparty to the extent that the exchange rate on June 30, 2011, exceeds $1.64 per GBP and must pay the counterparty on this date to the extent that the exchange rate is less than $1.64 per GBP. Firm B in Example 21 will pay the supplier the 8 percent interest established in the fixed-rate note. If the variable interest rate used in the swap contract decreases to 6 percent, the counterparty bank will pay Firm B an amount equal to 2 percent (= 0.08 − 0.06) of the notional amount of the note, $100,000. Paying interest of 8 percent to the supplier and receiving cash of 2 percent from the counterparty results in net interest cost of 6 percent. If the variable interest rate increases to 10 percent, Firm B still pays the supplier interest of 8 percent as specified in the original note. It would then pay the counterparty bank an additional 2 percent (= 0.10 − 0.08), resulting in total interest expense equal to the variable rate of 10 percent.

Accounting for Derivatives

Derivatives are reported as assets or liabilities depending on the rights and obligations under the contract. The forward contract in Example 20 is an asset or a liability depending on the exchange rate. The swap contracts in Examples 21 and 22 may be assets or liabilities depending on the level of interest rates. The forward contract in Example 23 may be an asset or a liability depending on the price of whiskey. A later section discusses the initial valuation of these assets and liabilities.

Firms must revalue the derivatives to fair value each period. In addition to increasing or decreasing the derivative asset or liability, the revaluation amount also affects net income immediately or other comprehensive income immediately and net income later depending on U.S. GAAP and IFRS requirements discussed shortly. Recall that other comprehensive income is a temporary shareholders' equity account that reports changes during an accounting period in the recorded amounts of certain assets and liabilities, such as derivatives. Firms close the amount of other comprehensive income at the end of the period to the accumulated other comprehensive income account, a permanent shareholders' equity account. Whether the income effect is reported in net income or other comprehensive income depends on the nature of the hedge for which a firm acquires a derivative. U.S. GAAP and IFRS classify derivatives as speculative investments, fair value hedges, or cash flow hedges. Firms typically classify derivatives as fair value hedges or cash flow hedges. Firms must choose to designate each derivative as one or the other depending on their general hedging strategy and purpose in acquiring the particular derivative instrument. If a firm chooses not to designate a particular derivative as a fair value hedge or a cash flow hedge, U.S. GAAP and IFRS require that the firm account for the derivative as a speculative investment.

Speculative Investment

Firms that acquire derivatives for reasons other than hedging a specific risk classify the derivative as a *speculative investment.* Firms must revalue derivatives held as speculative investments to fair value each period and recognize the resulting gain or loss in net income.

Fair Value Hedges

Derivative instruments acquired to hedge exposure to changes in the fair values of assets or liabilities are *fair value hedges.* Fair value hedges are of two general types: hedges of a *recognized* asset or liability and hedges of an *unrecognized* firm commitment. Firm B in Example 21 entered into the interest swap agreement to neutralize the effect of changes in interest rates on the market value of its notes payable, a hedge of a recognized liability. Firm A in Example 20 acquired the forward foreign exchange contract to neutralize the effect of changes in exchange rates on its commitment to purchase the equipment, a hedge of an unrecognized firm commitment. Therefore, these derivative instruments are fair value hedges.

Cash Flow Hedges

Derivative instruments acquired to hedge exposure to variability in expected future cash flows are *cash flow hedges.* Cash flow hedges are of two general types: hedges of cash flows of an *existing* asset or liability and hedges of cash flows of *forecasted* transactions. Firm C in Example 22 entered into the interest swap agreement to neutralize changes in cash flows for interest payments on its variable-rate notes payable, a hedge of an existing liability. Firm D in Example 23 acquired the forward contract on whiskey to protect itself from changes in the selling price of whiskey between October 31, 2010, and March 31, 2011, a hedge involving a forecasted transaction. Therefore, these derivative instruments are cash flow hedges.

A particular derivative could be a fair value hedge or a cash flow hedge depending on the firm's reason for engaging in the hedge. Both the forward foreign exchange contract in Example 20 and the forward whiskey contract in Example 23 fix the firms' cash flows at a specified amount. The firms could conceivably classify both derivative instruments as cash flow hedges. Firm B in Example 21 acquires the derivative to protect the value of equipment acquired and therefore classifies it as a fair value hedge. Firm D in Example 23 acquires the derivative to protect its cash flows from changes in the price of whiskey and therefore classifies it as a cash flow hedge.

The four examples described thus far in this section illustrate the accounting for four possible scenarios:

Examples	Type of Hedge	Derivative Instrument Used
16 and 20	Fair Value—Firm Commitment	Forward Foreign Exchange Contract
17 and 21	Fair Value—Liability	Swap Contract—Variable for Fixed Rate
18 and 22	Cash Flow—Interest Payments	Swap Contract—Fixed for Variable Rate
19 and 23	Cash Flow—Forecasted Transaction	Forward Commodity Contract

Treatment of Hedging Gains and Losses

U.S. GAAP and IFRS require firms to recognize gains and losses from changes in the fair value of derivative financial instruments classified as fair value hedges in net income each period while the firm holds the financial instrument. U.S. GAAP and IFRS also require firms to revalue the asset or liability that is hedged to fair value and recognize a corresponding loss or gain. If the hedge is fully effective, the gain (loss) on the derivative financial instrument will precisely offset the loss (gain) on the asset or liability hedged. The net effect on earnings is zero. If the hedge is not fully effective, the net gain or loss increases or decreases net income.

U.S. GAAP and IFRS require firms to include gains and losses from changes in the fair values of derivative financial instruments classified as cash flow hedges in other comprehensive income each period to the extent that the financial instrument is "highly effective" in neutralizing the risk. Firms must include the ineffective portion currently in net income. FASB Statement No. 133 gives general guidelines but leaves the meaning of "highly effective" to professional judgment. The firm removes the accumulated amount in other comprehensive income related to a particular derivative instrument and transfers it to net income periodically during the life of the derivative instrument or at the time of settlement, depending on the type of derivative instrument used.

The logic for the different treatment of gains and losses from changes in fair value of derivative financial instruments results from applying the matching principle. In a fair value hedge of a recognized asset or liability, both the hedged asset (or liability) and its related derivative generally appear on the balance sheet. The firm revalues the hedged asset (or liability) and its related derivative to fair value each period and reports the gain or loss on the hedged asset (or liability) and the loss or gain on the derivative in net income. The net gain or loss indicates the effectiveness of the hedge in neutralizing the risk. In a cash flow hedge of an anticipated transaction, the hedged cash flow commitment does not appear on the balance sheet but the derivative instrument does. When a gain or loss is recognized on the derivative instrument in net income each period but the loss or gain is recognized on the anticipated transaction at the time an actual transaction occurs, the result is a misalignment of the ultimate cost or benefit of a derivative with the economic item that is being hedged. For this reason, the firm classifies the gain or loss on the derivative instrument in other comprehensive income and later reclassifies the gain or loss to net income when it records the actual transaction.

Illustrations of Accounting for Derivatives

This section illustrates the accounting for the derivatives using the two examples involving interest rate swaps.

Fair Value Hedge: Interest Rate Swap to Convert Fixed-Rate Debt to Variable-Rate Debt

Refer to Examples 17 and 21. Firm B wants to maintain the fair value of its note payable at not more than \$100,000 in the event that it chooses to repay it prior to maturity. Changes in interest rates will change the fair value of its fixed-rate note. It enters into a swap contract to convert the fixed-rate debt to variable-rate debt. The fair value of the debt will remain at \$100,000 as long as the interest rate incorporated into the swap contract is the same as the rate used by the equipment supplier to value the note payable. Firm B designates the swap contract as a fair value hedge.

Exhibit 8.8 presents the financial statement effects and journal entries for transactions from January 1, 2010, to December 31, 2012. The following paragraphs explain the accounting for the note and the associated derivative.

Firm B issues the note to the supplier on January 1, 2010, in exchange for the equipment and enters into the swap contract on the same date. The swap contract is a mutually unexecuted contract on January 1, 2010. The variable interest rate on this date is 8 percent, the same as the fixed rate for the note to the equipment supplier. The swap contract has a fair value of zero on this date. Thus, Firm B makes no entry to record the swap contract.

On December 31, 2010, Firm B makes the required interest payment of \$8,000 (= 0.08 × \$100,000) on the note for 2010 and reduces net income by the amount of the interest expense. Interest rates declined during 2010. On December 31, the counterparty with whom Firm B entered into the swap contract resets the interest rate to 6 percent for 2011. Firm B must restate the note payable to fair value and record the change in the market value

Exhibit 8.8: Fair Value Hedge: Interest Rate Swap to Convert Fixed-Rate Debt to Variable-Rate Debt

Assets	=	Liabilities	+	Total Shareholders' Equity		
				CC	AOCI	RE
January 1, 2010 Equipment +100,000		Notes Payable +100,000				

Equipment	100,000	
Notes Payable		100,000

Assets	=	Liabilities	+	CC	AOCI	RE
December 31, 2010 *Interest expense on note:* Cash −8,000						Interest Expense −8,000
Revaluation of note:		Notes Payable +3,667				Loss on Revaluation of Notes Payable −3,667
Revaluation of swap contract: Swap Contract +3,667						Gain on Revaluation of Swap Contract +3,667

Interest Expense	8,000	
Cash		8,000
Loss on Revaluation of Notes Payable	3,667	
Notes payable		3,667
Swap Contract	3,667	
Gain on Revaluation of Swap Contract		3,667

Assets	=	Liabilities	+	CC	AOCI	RE
December 31, 2011 *Interest expense on note:* Cash −8,000		Notes Payable −1,780				Interest Expense −6,220
Interest revenue on swap contract asset: Swap Contract +220						Interest Revenue +220
Cash receipt from counterparty: Cash +2,000 Swap Contract −2,000						
Revaluation of note:		Notes Payable −3,705				Gain on Revaluation of Notes Payable +3,705
Revaluation of swap contract: Swap Contract −1,887		Swap Contract +1,818				Loss on Revaluation of Swap Contract −3,705

(Continued)

EXHIBIT 8.8 (CONTINUED)

Interest Expense	6,220	
Notes Payable	1,780	
Cash		8,000
Swap Contract	220	
Interest Revenue		220
Cash	2,000	
Swap Contract		2,000
Notes Payable	3,705	
Gain on Revaluation of Notes Payable		3,705
Loss on Revaluation of Swap Contract	3,705	
Swap Contract		3,705

December 31, 2012 Interest expense on note:								
Cash	−8,000		Notes Payable	+1,818			Interest Expense	−9,818
Interest expense on swap contract liability:			Swap Contract	+182			Interest Expense	−182
Cash payment to counterparty:								
Cash	−2,000		Swap Contract	−2,000				
Repayment of the note:								
Cash	−100,000		Notes Payable	−100,000				

Interest Expense	9,818	
Notes Payable		1,818
Cash		8,000
Interest Expense	182	
Swap Contract		182
Swap Contract	2,000	
Cash		2,000
Notes Payable	100,000	
Cash		100,000

of the swap contract caused by the decline in the interest rate. The present value of the remaining cash flows on the note payable (two cash interest payments of $8,000 and one $100,000 maturity value received in two years) when discounted at 6 percent is $103,667. Firm B records the $3,667 increase in the note's fair value and recognizes a Loss on Revaluation of Note Payable on the income statement in the same amount. Unless the fair value option discussed in Chapters 6 and 7 has been chosen, firms typically do not revalue financial instruments, such as this note payable, to market value when interest rates change. They continue to account for the financial instruments using the interest rate at the time of the initial recording of the financial instrument in the accounts. However, when a firm hedges a financial instrument, it must recognize changes in fair values. It must likewise recognize changes in the fair value of the swap contract.

The decline in interest rates to 6 percent means that Firm B will save $2,000 each year in interest payments. The present value of a $2,000 annuity for two periods at 6 percent is $3,667. Thus, the value of the swap contract increased from zero at the beginning of 2010 to $3,667 at the end of the year. Firm B records the increase in the fair value of the swap contract as an asset and recognizes a $3,667 gain on revaluation of swap contract on the income statement. The loss from the revaluation of the note payable exactly offsets the gain from the revaluation of the swap contract, indicating that the swap contract was fully effective (that is, the loss on revaluation of note payable is 100 percent offset by the gain on revaluation of swap contract) in hedging the interest rate risk.

Firm B follows a similar process at December 31, 2011. First, it records interest expense on the note payable. As illustrated in Chapter 6, Firm B uses the effective interest method to compute interest expense for the year. The effective interest rate for 2011 is 6 percent, and the book value of the note payable at the beginning of the year is $103,667. Therefore, interest expense is $6,220 (= 0.06 × $103,667). The cash payment of $8,000 is the amount set forth in the original borrowing arrangement with the equipment supplier. Because more cash than interest expense is paid, notes payable decreases by the difference, $1,780. (This is a premium amortization.)

Second, the firm records an increase in the swap contract asset due to the passage of time ($220 = 0.06 × $3,667) and the associated interest revenue. Recall that the swap contract was originally valued using present value; thus, its present value increases by the amount of interest each year. Interest expense (net) as a result of the two entries is $6,000 (= $6,220 interest expense − $220 interest revenue), which is the variable rate for 2011 of 6 percent times the face value of the note.

Third, Firm B receives $2,000 under the swap contract with its counterparty because the interest rate decreased from 8 percent to 6 percent [$100,000 × (0.08 − 0.06)], which also reduces the swap contract asset by $2,000. In a sense, the $2,000 cash received from the counterparty reimburses Firm B for paying interest at 8 percent on the note, whereas the swap contract provides that the firm benefits when interest rates decline, in this case to 6 percent.

Fourth, Firm B must revalue the note payable and the swap contract for changes in fair value. Interest rates increased during 2011, so the bank resets the interest rate in the swap agreement to 10 percent for 2012. The present value of the remaining payments on the note (one cash interest payment of $8,000 and one maturity payment of $100,000 one year hence) at 10 percent is $98,182. The book value of the note payable before revaluation is $101,887 (= $103,667 − $1,780). The entry to revalue the note payable reduces the note payable by $3,705 (= $101,887 − $98,182), which is shown as a gain on revaluation of note payable in the income statement.

The fair value of the swap contract decreases. Firm A must now pay an additional $2,000 in interest in 2012 because of the swap contract. Thus, the swap contract becomes a liability instead of an asset. When discounted at 10 percent, the present value of $2,000 is a $1,818 swap contract liability. The book value of the swap contract asset before revaluation is $1,887 (= $3,667 + $220 − $2,000). The entry to revalue the swap contract from a $1,887 asset to a $1,818 liability results in a $3,705 loss on revaluation of swap contract reflected in the income statement. The gain on revaluation of the note exactly offsets the loss on revaluation of the swap contract, so the swap contract hedges the change in interest rates.

Following the same effective interest method as in the prior year, at December 31, 2012, Firm B records interest expense of $9,818 (= 0.10 × $98,182), increasing notes payable by $1,818 (a discount amortization), when it pays $8,000 (= 0.08 × $100,000) in cash. Firm B also recognizes interest expense of $182 (= 0.10 × $1,818) due to the passage of time on the swap contract liability. (Recall that when the swap contract was an asset, interest revenue was generated by the passage of time.) Interest expense (net) after these two effects is

$10,000 (= $9,818 interest expense + $182 interest expense), which equals the variable interest rate of 10 percent times the face value of the note.

Firm B must pay the counterparty an extra 2 percent because the variable interest rate of 10 percent exceeds the fixed interest rate of 8 percent. Thus, cash and the swap contract liability decrease by $2,000. Firm B also repays the note and closes out the swap contract. The swap contract account has a zero balance on December 31, 2012, after the preceding entries (= $1,818 + $182 − $2,000) are made, so the firm does not need to make additional entries to close out this account.

In summary, note that net income reflects the variable interest rate each year: 8 percent for 2010, 6 percent for 2011, and 10 percent for 2012. The note payable and the swap contract net to $100,000 at the end of each year.

Summary of Accounting for a Fair Value Hedge of an Existing Asset or Liability

The following summarizes the accounting for a fair value hedge of an existing asset or liability:

- The hedged asset or liability already appears on the books. Its valuation depends on GAAP's required accounting for the particular asset or liability (for example, lower of cost or market for inventories and present value of future cash flows for long-term receivables and payables).
- The firm recognizes the derivative as an asset on the date of acquisition to the extent it makes an initial investment. Otherwise, if the derivative is an exchange of mutually unexecuted promises, no amount appears on the balance sheet for the derivative.
- At the end of each period, the firm revalues the hedged asset or liability to fair value and includes the resulting gain or loss in net income.
- At the end of each period, the firm revalues the derivative instrument to fair value and includes the resulting loss or gain in net income.
- The firm shows the hedged asset and liability and its related derivative separately on the balance sheet.
- The firm removes the hedged asset or liability and its related derivative from the accounts at the time of settlement (for example, at the time of interest payments).

Cash Flow Hedge: Interest Rate Swap to Convert Variable-Rate Debt to Fixed-Rate Debt

Refer to Examples 18 and 22. Firm C wants to hedge the risk of changes in interest rates on its cash payments for interest. It enters into a swap contract with a counterparty to convert its variable-rate note payable to a fixed-rate note. Firm C designates the swap contract as a cash flow hedge. The facts for the case are similar to those for Firm B. The note has a $100,000 face value and an initial variable interest rate of 8 percent, which the counterparty resets to 6 percent for 2011 and 10 percent for 2012. The note matures on December 31, 2012. Exhibit 8.9 presents the financial statement template for this derivative contract.

On January 1, 2010, Firm C records the issue of the note to acquire the equipment as before. On December 31, 2010, Firm C records the $8,000 cash interest outflow and $8,000 interest expense for 2010.

The fair value of the note in this case, unlike that for Firm B, will not change as interest rates change because the note carries a variable interest rate. However, the fair value of the swap contract does change. The fair value on December 31, 2010, after the counterparty resets the interest rate to 6 percent, is $3,667. This amount is the present value of the $2,000 that Firm C will pay the counterparty on December 31, 2011 and 2012, if the interest rate

EXHIBIT 8.9: CASH FLOW HEDGE: INTEREST RATE SWAP TO CONVERT VARIABLE-RATE DEBT TO FIXED-RATE DEBT

Assets	=	Liabilities	+	Total Shareholders' Equity: CC	AOCI	RE
January 1, 2010						
Equipment +100,000		Notes Payable +100,000				

Equipment	100,000	
Notes Payable		100,000

Assets	=	Liabilities	+	CC	AOCI	RE
December 31, 2010						
Interest expense on note:						
Cash −8,000						Interest Expense −8,000
Revaluation of swap contract:		Swap Contract +3,667			OCI—Swap Contract −3,667	

Interest Expense	8,000	
Cash		8,000
Loss on Revaluation of Swap Contract (OCI)	3,667	
Swap Contract		3,667

Assets	=	Liabilities	+	CC	AOCI	RE
December 31, 2011						
Interest expense on note:						
Cash −6,000						Interest Expense −6,000
Interest "expense" (OCI) on swap contract liability:		Swap Contract +220			OCI—Swap Contract −220	
Cash payment to counterparty:						
Cash −2,000		Swap Contract −2,000				
Reclassification of a portion of other comprehensive income:					OCI—Swap Contract +2,000	Interest Expense −2,000
Revaluation of swap contract:						
Swap Contract +1,818		Swap Contract −1,887			OCI—Swap Contract +3,705	

Interest Expense	6,000	
Cash		6,000
OCI—Swap Contract	220	
Swap Contract		220
Swap Contract	2,000	
Cash		2,000
Interest Expense	2,000	
OCI—Swap Contract		2,000
Swap Contract	3,705	
OCI—Swap Contract		3,705

(Continued)

EXHIBIT 8.9 (CONTINUED)

December 31, 2012				
Interest expense on note: Cash −10,000				Interest Expense −10,000
Interest "revenue" (OCI) on swap contract asset: Swap Contract +182			OCI—Swap Contract +182	
Cash receipt from counterparty: Cash +2,000 Swap Contract −2,000				
Reclassification of a portion of other comprehensive income:			OCI—Swap Contract −2,000	Interest Expense +2,000
Repayment of the note: Cash −100,000	Notes payable −100,000			

Interest Expense	10,000	
Cash		10,000
Swap Contract	182	
OCI—Swap Contract		182
Cash	2,000	
Swap Contract		2,000
OCI—Swap Contract	2,000	
Interest Expense		2,000
Notes Payable	100,000	
Cash		100,000

remains at 6 percent. The swap contract (initially valued at $0) is now a liability of $3,667 due to the interest rate change. The loss from the upward revaluation of the swap contract liability does not immediately affect net income on a cash flow hedge. Instead, it reduces other comprehensive income. Other comprehensive income is closed into (and thus, is an element of) accumulated other comprehensive income, a shareholders' equity account.

Note that the book value of the note payable of $100,000 plus the book value of the swap contract of $3,667 is $103,667. This amount is the present value of the expected cash flows under the fixed-rate note and swap contract combined, discounted at 6 percent.

On December 31, 2011, Firm C pays the (now) $6,000 interest on the variable-rate note and recognizes interest expense. Firm C also must increase the book value of the swap contract liability by $220 (= .06 × $3,667) for the passage of time. Note that the interest charge does not immediately affect net income; instead, it decreases other comprehensive income.

Firm C pays the counterparty the $2,000 [= $100,000 × (0.08 − 0.06)] required by the swap contract and reduces the swap contract liability. Because the swap contract hedged cash flows related to interest rate risk during 2011, Firm C reclassifies a portion of other comprehensive income, $2,000 [= $100,000 × (0.08 − 0.06)], to net income. At this point, the swap contract liability account has a balance of $1,887 (= $3,667 + $220 − $2,000). Accumulated other comprehensive income related to this transaction also has been reduced to a debit balance (that is a net subtraction from shareholders' equity) of $1,887. Interest expense on the income statement is $8,000 (= $6,000 + $2,000).

Restating the interest rate on December 31, 2011, for the year 2012 to 10 percent changes the value of the swap contract from a liability to an asset. The present value of the $2,000 that Firm C will receive from the counterparty at the end of 2012 when discounted at 10 percent is \$1,818. Firm C revalues the swap contract by reducing the swap contract liability by \$1,887 and increasing the swap contract asset by \$1,818. Removing the liability and recognizing the asset increases 2011 other comprehensive income by \$3,705. At this point, other comprehensive income for 2011 is \$5,485 (= \$2,000 + \$3,705 − \$220), which increases accumulated other comprehensive income from its \$3,667 debit balance at the end of 2010 to a \$1,818 credit balance at the end of 2011. This credit balance equals the balance in the swap contract asset account.

On December 31, 2012, Firm C pays the (now) 10 percent interest on the loan and recognizes interest expense. Firm C also increases the book value of the swap contract asset and increases other comprehensive income by \$182 (= 0.10 × \$1,818) for the passage of time. The swap contract requires the counterparty to pay the firm \$2,000 under the swap contract, which reduces the swap contract asset by \$2,000.

Because the swap contract hedged cash flows related to interest rate risk during 2012, Firm C reclassifies \$2,000 of other comprehensive income to net income by reducing interest expense. Thus, interest expense (net) for 2012 is \$8,000 (= \$10,000 − \$2,000).

Finally, Firm C repays the note on December 31, 2012, and closes out the swap contract account. This account has a balance of zero on December 31, 2012 (= \$1,818 + \$182 − \$2,000). Thus, Firm C does not need to make an entry. If the swap contract had been highly but not perfectly effective in neutralizing the interest rate risk, accumulated other comprehensive income would have a balance related to the swap contract, which Firm C would reclassify to net income at this point.

In summary, note that interest expense is \$8,000 each year, the fixed rate of 8 percent that Firm C obtained by entering into the swap contract. The amounts in other comprehensive income reflect changes in the fair value of the swap contract. The swap contract begins and ends with a zero value.

Summary of Accounting for a Cash Flow Hedge of an Existing Asset or Liability

The following summarizes the accounting for a cash flow hedge of an existing asset or liability:

- The hedged asset or liability already appears on the books. Its valuation depends on GAAP's required accounting for the particular asset or liability (for example, lower of cost or market for inventories and present value of future cash flows for long-term receivables and payables).
- The firm recognizes the derivative as an asset on the date of acquisition to the extent that it makes an initial investment. Otherwise, if the derivative consists of mutually unexecuted promises, no amount appears on the balance sheet for the derivative.
- At the end of each period, the firm revalues the hedged asset or liability to fair value and includes the resulting gain or loss in other comprehensive income.
- At the end of each period, the firm revalues the derivative instrument to fair value and includes the resulting loss or gain in other comprehensive income.
- The firm reclassifies gains and losses from other comprehensive income to net income when the gain or loss on the hedged item affects net income. If the derivative is not highly effective in neutralizing the gain or loss on the hedged item, the firm must reclassify the ineffective portion to net income immediately and not wait until the gain or loss on the hedged items affects net income.
- The firm shows the hedged asset and liability and its related derivative separately on the balance sheet. Also, it shows the cumulative amount of net value changes for the hedged items and its related derivative in accumulated other comprehensive income.

- The firm removes the hedged asset or liability and its related derivative from the accounts at the time of settlement (for example, at the time of interest payments).

Summary of Derivative Examples

Firms record changes in the market value of all derivatives each reporting period. Changes in the value of derivatives and the related asset, liability, or commitment for fair value hedges flow through to net income immediately. Changes in the value of derivatives related to cash flow hedges initially increase or decrease other comprehensive income. They affect net income at the same time the cash flows they hedge affect net income. Although this section does not illustrate separately the accounting for derivatives held as speculative investments because of their infrequent usage, the accounting is the same as for fair value hedges.

Disclosures Related to Derivative Instruments

Several FASB pronouncements address disclosures for derivatives. FASB Statement No. 107 requires firms to disclose the book value and the fair value of financial instruments. Financial instruments impose on one entity a right to receive cash and an obligation on another entity to pay cash. Financial instruments include accounts receivable, notes receivable, notes payable, bonds payable, forward contracts, swap contracts, and most derivatives. Fair value is the current amount at which two willing parties exchange the instrument for cash.

FASB Statement No. 133 requires the following disclosures (among others) with respect to derivatives:

- Firms must describe their risk management strategy and how particular derivatives help accomplish their hedging objectives. The description should distinguish between derivative instruments designated as fair value hedges, cash flow hedges, and all other derivatives.
- For fair value and cash flow hedges, firms must disclose the net gain or loss recognized in earnings resulting from the hedges' ineffectiveness (that is, not offsetting the risk hedged) and the line item on the income statement that includes this net gain or loss.
- For cash flow hedges, firms must describe the transactions or events that will result in reclassifying gains and losses from other comprehensive income to net income and the estimated amount of such reclassifications during the next 12 months.
- Firms must disclose the net amount of gains and losses recognized in earnings because a hedged firm commitment no longer qualifies as a fair value hedge or a hedged forecasted transaction no longer qualifies as a cash flow hedge.

Recently, the FASB issued Statement of Financial Accounting Standards No. 161, "Disclosures about Derivative Instruments and Hedging Activities," which requires enhanced disclosures about an entity's derivative and hedging activities. The statement amends and expands the disclosure requirements of Statement 133 with the intent to provide users of financial statements with an enhanced understanding of how and why an entity uses derivative instruments; how derivative instruments and related hedged items are accounted for under Statement 133 and its related interpretations; and how derivative instruments and related hedged items affect an entity's financial position, financial performance, and cash flows. To meet those objectives, the statement requires qualitative disclosures about objectives and strategies for using derivatives, quantitative disclosures about fair value amounts of and gains and losses on derivative instruments, and disclosures about credit-risk-related contingent features in derivative agreements.

PepsiCo's Derivatives Disclosures

As discussed at the beginning of this section, PepsiCo uses derivatives to hedge commodity prices, foreign exchange rates, and interest rates. PepsiCo describes its use of derivatives in Note 9, "Debt Obligations and Commitments," and Note 10, "Financial Instruments" (Appendix A). Note 9 focuses on interest rate hedging. PepsiCo issued $1.75 billion and $1.0 billion in notes payable in the second quarter of 2008 and 2007, respectively, and entered into interest rate swaps to effectively convert the interest rate from a fixed 5 percent (5.15 percent for the 2007 issue) to a variable rate based on LIBOR. Note 10 focuses more on hedging commodity price risk and foreign exchange risk, most of which qualifies as fair value or cash flow hedges. The passages related to commodity risk indicate a change in PepsiCo's risk management strategy. Beginning in 2007 and continuing through 2008, PepsiCo expanded commodity hedges to mitigate exposure to price changes associated with fruit purchases, raw materials, and energy costs. Most of these contracts do not qualify for hedge accounting treatment and therefore are marked-to-market with fair value changes reflected in income.

PepsiCo's Statement of Shareholders' Equity (Appendix A) shows the change in accumulated other comprehensive income for 2008. The firm discloses that it incurred net derivative gains of $16 million during 2008 from cash flow hedges (net of tax) and $5 million in reclassifications of losses to net income. This amount is small when compared to reported net income for 2008. The gain or loss for previous years also is immaterial to the firm's net income for the year.

Firms must report the impact on earnings of certain changes in each of the major risk factors to which the earnings are subject. Firms typically disclose this information in their management discussion and analysis of operations. PepsiCo discusses (Appendix B) the effect on earnings of changes in commodity prices, foreign exchange rates, and interest rates. This information permits the analyst to assess the extent and effectiveness of hedging activities on each of these risks. The following information summarizes PepsiCo's disclosures for 2008:

Change	Nature of Effect	Earnings Sensitivity
Commodity Prices	10% Decrease	$53 Million Decrease
Foreign Exchange Rates	10% Unfavorable	$70 Million Decrease
Interest Rates	1-Percentage-Point Increase	$21 Million Decrease

Again, none of these changes would have a material effect on net income, suggesting that PepsiCo's derivatives would be effective in hedging even larger changes than actually occurred.

Many firms use a value-at-risk (VAR) simulation model to estimate the impact of adverse price movements. The VAR model develops a distribution of the changes in relevant interest rates, exchange rates, commodity prices, or other underlying for a particular period of prior years (for example, ten years). Using the distribution of prior adverse changes and the average net position in various financial instruments for the current year, the model simulates with a 95 percent or other confidence level the minimum, maximum, or average amount of loss that a firm would incur.

Accounting Quality Issues and Derivatives

Firms must mark derivatives to fair value each period. Fair values are usually reliable and easy to obtain when active, established markets exist for derivatives, as is the case for many forward contracts and interest and currency swaps. When firms engage in derivative transactions for which active markets do not exist, questions arise about the reliability of the fair values. Enron, for example, purchased and sold derivatives on the price and availability of broadband services. Broadband services were an emerging market at the time, with Enron one of only a few firms engaging in this type of derivative trading. Enron also held billions of dollars of notional value in derivatives for long-forward sales and purchases of various energy commodities, including oil, natural gas, and electricity, with some as far as 25 years in the future. Enron was the largest market maker (and one of the only market makers) for such derivatives, which were not widely traded.

A second accounting quality concern involves the classification of derivatives as fair value hedges versus cash flow hedges. Recall that the firms in Examples 20 and 23 could have classified the exchange and commodity contracts as fair value hedges or cash flow hedges. Gains and losses on cash flow hedges affect earnings later than those on fair value hedges. When gains and losses on cash flow hedges, which GAAP includes in accumulated other comprehensive income, substantially exceed the gains and losses on fair value hedges included in earnings, the analyst must at least question the firm's classification of its hedges.

When firms use derivatives to manage risks effectively, the net gain or loss each period should be relatively small. Large and varying amounts of gains or losses usually signal ineffective use of derivatives.

SUMMARY

Operating profitability is the key driver of enterprise value. This chapter examined the accounting and reporting issues surrounding operating activities. The income statement plays a major role in describing operating profitability. Our discussion of operating profitability followed the generally occurring order of the income statement. We began with a study of revenue recognition and followed with discussions of the major expense categories: cost of sales, SG&A expense, and income tax expense. Finally, we considered the financial statement effects of pensions and derivatives, two areas in which the reporting of profitability is divided between current recognition in the income statement and delayed recognition in other comprehensive income.

Operating activities generate investments in working capital. Accordingly, we examined issues surrounding inventory and accounts receivable reporting and the reporting of many working capital assets and liabilities that arise when accrual measurement and cash flow timing do not coincide.

In the next chapter, we continue the discussion of accounting quality by focusing on earnings quality and the adjustments to financial statements that might be necessary to understand current profitability and risk and use that understanding to predict future financial statement numbers.

QUESTIONS, EXERCISES, PROBLEMS, AND CASES

Questions and Exercises

8.1 DELAYED REVENUE RECOGNITION. Software companies often bundle upgrades and technical support services with their software. Assume that a software company promises to automatically deliver upgrades for two years when a customer purchases software costing $100. Describe how the software company should determine the amount of revenue to recognize at the date of sale and subsequent to the date of sale.

8.2 REVENUE RECOGNITION. Revenues are at the core of a firm's ability to grow and prosper; thus, they are central to the analysis of a firm's profitability. Although the time-of-sale method is the most common technique employed to recognize revenues, in some instances, a strong argument can be made for recognizing revenue before the product has been completed and delivered. Discuss circumstances in which this scenario is appropriate.

8.3 LONG-TERM CONTRACT PROFIT RECOGNITION. Three alternative revenue recognition methods are available to long-term contractors when cash inflows are probable: percentage of completion, completed contract, and cost recovery. Assuming that the contract price is known, discuss the appropriate method under U.S. GAAP and IFRS under two alternative scenarios: (a) the proportion of work performed and the proportion of work remaining until completion can be reliably determined and (b) no reliable basis exists for determining the total amount of work necessary to complete the project. (Note: Because percentage of completion is generally estimated by comparing the costs to date to expected total costs, the inability to estimate the total amount of work to be performed creates the inability to estimate percent complete reliably.)

8.4 WORKING CAPITAL. Identify the working capital accounts related to (a) revenues recognized and deferred, (b) cost of goods sold, (c) employee salary and wages, and (d) income tax expense. For each account, indicate whether an increase in the working capital asset or liability would be an addition or subtraction when reconciling from net income to cash flows from operations.

8.5 EXPENSE RECOGNITION. Provide three examples of expense recognition justified by (a) a direct relationship with revenue (cause and effect) and (b) an indirect relationship with revenue (the consumption of an asset or an increase in a liability during a period in which revenue is recognized).

8.6 ACCOUNTS RECEIVABLE. Using the following key, identify the effects of the following transactions or conditions on the various financial statement elements: I = increases; D = decreases; NE = no effect.

	Assets	Liabilities	Shareholders' Equity	Net Income
A credit sale				
Collection of a portion of accounts receivable				
Estimate of bad debts				
Write-off of a specific uncollectible account				

8.7 INVENTORY COSTING AND VALUATION. The acquisition cost of inventory remaining at the end of a period is measured using LIFO, FIFO, or average cost.

a. Rank cost of goods sold, gross profit, and ending inventory from highest to lowest under the three cost-flow assumptions when input prices are rising.

b. How should differences between acquisition cost and the market value of inventory be reported on the balance sheet under IFRS and U.S. GAAP?

8.8 LIFO LAYER LIQUIDATION. What is a LIFO layer liquidation? How does it affect the prediction of future earnings?

8.9 EFFECT OF WEIGHTED AVERAGE COST-FLOW ASSUMPTION ON INVENTORY. The weighted average cost-flow assumption is a common technique used to value inventory and determine cost of goods sold. It falls between LIFO and FIFO as to the differential effect on inventory and cost of goods sold amounts, although normally it is more like FIFO than LIFO in its effect on the balance sheet. Why?

8.10 VALUATION OF DERIVATIVES. GAAP classifies derivatives as (a) speculative investments, (b) fair value hedges, or (c) cash flow hedges. However, firms revalue all derivatives to market value each period regardless of the firm's reason for acquiring the derivatives. In addition to increasing or decreasing the derivative asset or liability, the revaluation amount affects net income immediately or other comprehensive income immediately and net income later. For each type of derivative, describe where firms report the revaluation amount on the financial statements.

8.11 RECONCILE PBO/FMV OF PLAN ASSETS. Given the following information, compute December 31, 2010 projected benefit obligation (PBO) and fair market value (FMV) of plan assets for Lee Company.

Prior service cost granted in a 2010 plan amendment	$110,000
Interest on PBO	70,000
Actual return on plan assets	100,000
Service cost	80,000
Contribution sent to plan trustee	60,000
Benefit payments to retirees	20,000
Liability loss (gain)	(30,000)
FMV of plan assets, January 1, 2010	750,000
PBO, January 1, 2010	800,000

What amount of asset or liability will be reported on the balance sheet at December 31, 2010?

8.12 FINANCIAL STATEMENT EFFECTS OF PENSION PLAN EVENTS. Using the following key, identify the effects of the following transactions or conditions on the various financial statement elements: I = increases; D = decreases; NE = no effect. Note that the questions pertain to the employer's financial statements, not to the pension plan's financial statements.

Pension plan events or conditions (Analyze effect on current year only.)	Assets	Liabilities	Shareholders' Equity	Net Income
Employees performing current service				
Plan amendment grants retroactive benefits				
Projected benefit obligation accrues interest at the settlement rate				
Unexpected increases in PBO due to changes in actuarial assumptions				
Retired employees are paid benefits				
Contributions made to plan trustee				
Plan assets increase by expected return from investing				
Unexpected decrease in FMV of plan assets due to an asset loss				
Amortization of prior service cost				
Amortization of gain				

8.13 COMPONENTS OF PENSION EXPENSE. Pension expense typically consists of five components. Answer the following questions related to each component.

a. Service cost: Is it possible for the service cost component to *reduce* pension expense for the year? Explain your answer.
b. Interest cost: Is it possible for the interest cost component to *reduce* pension expense for the year? Explain your answer.
c. Expected return on plan assets: GAAP requires firms to reduce pension expense each year by the expected, not the actual, return on investments. What is the logic employed by policymakers in reaching this decision?
d. Amortization of prior service cost: What is a prior service cost? Provide an example of a plan change that would generate an amount labeled prior service cost.
e. Amortization of actuarial gains and losses: What circumstances give rise to actuarial gains and losses?

8.14 POSTRETIREMENT BENEFITS OTHER THAN PENSIONS. The notes to a firm's financial statements reveal that the obligations for postretirement health care benefits at the end of 2010 total $2.1 billion. The fair value of plan assets for these benefits at the end of 2010 is reported at zero, with an unrecognized net actuarial loss of $310 million reported for the same year. Calculate the amount of the postretirement health care benefit obligation reported by the firm at the end of 2010. Discuss what classification category (or categories) on the balance sheet would appropriately include the obligation.

Problems and Cases

8.15 INCOME RECOGNITION FOR VARIOUS TYPES OF BUSINESSES. Discuss when each of the following types of businesses is likely to recognize revenues and expenses.

a. A bank lends money for home mortgages.
b. A travel agency books hotels, transportation, and similar services for customers and earns a commission from the providers of these services.
c. A Major League Baseball team sells season tickets before the season begins and signs its players to multiyear contracts. These contracts typically defer the payment of a significant portion of the compensation provided by the contract until the player retires.
d. A producer of fine whiskey ages the whiskey 12 years before sale.
e. A timber-growing firm contracts to sell all timber in a particular tract when it reaches 20 years of age. Each year it harvests another tract. The price per board foot of timber equals the market price when the customer signs the purchase contract plus 10 percent for each year until harvest.
f. An airline provides transportation services to customers. Each flight grants frequent-flier miles to customers. Customers earn a free flight when they accumulate sufficient frequent-flier miles.

8.16 MEASURING INCOME FOR A SOFTWARE MANUFACTURER. Parametric Technology Corporation (PTC) is a software manufacturer. It develops, markets, and supports software that helps manufacturers improve the competitiveness of their products. PTC provides a detailed description of its revenue streams in a recent SEC filing, excerpts of which are provided in Exhibit 8.10.

EXHIBIT 8.10

Parametric Technology Corporation
Excerpts from Form 10-K Filing, Note A, "Description of Business and Summary of Significant Accounting Policies–Revenue Recognition"
(Problem 8.16)

We derive revenues from three primary sources: (1) software licenses, (2) maintenance services and (3) other services, which include consulting and education services.

While we apply the guidance of Statement of Position (SOP) No. 97-2, *Software Revenue Recognition*, and Statement of Position No. 98-9, *Modification of SOP 97-2, Software Revenue Recognition with Respect to Certain Transactions*, both issued by the American Institute of Certified Public Accountants, as well as SEC Staff Accounting Bulletin 104, *Revenue Recognition in Financial Statements*, we exercise judgment and use estimates in connection with the determination of the amounts of software license and services revenues to be recognized in each accounting period.

For software license arrangements that do not require significant modification or customization of the underlying software, we recognize revenue when: (1) persuasive evidence of an arrangement exists, (2) delivery has occurred (generally, FOB shipping point or electronic distribution), (3) the fee is fixed or determinable, and (4) collection is probable. Substantially all of our license revenues are recognized in this manner.

Our software is distributed primarily through our direct sales force. However, our indirect distribution channel continues to expand through alliances with resellers. Revenue arrangements with resellers are recognized on a sell-through basis; that is, when we receive persuasive evidence that the reseller has sold the products to an end-user customer. We do not offer contractual rights of return, stock balancing, or price protection to our resellers, and actual product returns from them have been insignificant to date. As a result, we do not maintain reserves for product returns and related allowances.

At the time of each sale transaction, we must make an assessment of the collectibility of the amount due from the customer. Revenue is only recognized at that time if management deems that collection is probable. In making this assessment, we consider customer creditworthiness and historical payment experience. At that same time, we assess whether fees are fixed or determinable and free of contingencies or significant uncertainties. If the fee is not fixed or determinable, revenue is recognized only as payments become due from the customer, provided that all other revenue recognition criteria are met. In assessing whether the fee is fixed or determinable, we consider the payment terms of the transaction and our collection experience in similar transactions without making concessions, among other factors. Our software license arrangements generally do not include customer acceptance provisions. However, if an arrangement includes an acceptance provision, we record revenue only upon the earlier of (1) receipt of written acceptance from the customer or (2) expiration of the acceptance period.

Our software arrangements often include implementation and consulting services that are sold separately under consulting engagement contracts or as part of the software license arrangement. When we determine that such services are not essential to the functionality of the licensed software and qualify as "service transactions" under SOP 97-2, we record revenue separately for the license and service elements of these arrangements.

Maintenance services generally include rights to unspecified upgrades (when and if available), telephone and Internet-based support, updates and bug fixes. Maintenance revenue is recognized ratably over the term of the maintenance contract on a straight-line basis. It is uncommon for us to offer a specified upgrade to an existing product; however, in such instances, all revenue of the arrangement is deferred until the future upgrade is delivered.

When consulting qualifies for separate accounting, consulting revenues under time and materials billing arrangements are recognized as the services are performed.

Education services include on-site training, classroom training, and computer-based training and assessment. Education revenues are recognized as the related training services are provided.

Required

a. PTC generates revenues from software licenses as detailed in Exhibit 8.10. Discuss the appropriateness of revenue recognition techniques employed by the firm for software licenses in relation to the two general criteria for revenue recognition presented in the chapter.

b. PTC recognizes maintenance service revenue ratably over the term of the maintenance contract unless a specific software upgrade is promised to the customer as part of the maintenance contract. Describe the revenue recognition policy of PTC for maintenance contracts that include a specific upgrade. Justify the logic for the policy.

c. PTC provides educational services to its clients, such as on-site training and assessment, and recognizes revenue when the services are provided. Speculate on the criteria employed by PTC to justify when the services have been provided.

d. PTC states in Exhibit 8.10 that the firm must "exercise judgment and use estimates in connection with the determination of the amounts of software license and services revenues to be recognized in each accounting period." Provide several illustrations of judgments or estimates that PTC must employ for determining the amount of software license and service revenues to report each accounting period.

8.17 MEASURING INCOME FOR A CONSULTANCY FIRM. Sapient Corporation is a technology consultancy firm. Sapient's disclosures in a recent Form 10-K filing provided an extensive discussion of its revenue recognition policies, excerpts of which follow:

> We recognize revenue from the provision of professional services under written service contracts with our clients. We derive a significant portion of our revenue from fixed-price, fixed-time contracts. Revenue generated from fixed-price contracts, with the exception of support and maintenance contracts, is recognized based on the ratio of labor hours incurred to estimated total labor hours. This method is used because reasonably dependable estimates of the revenues and costs applicable to various stages of a contract can be made, based on historical experience and milestones set in the contract.
>
> Revenue generated from fixed-price support and maintenance contracts is recognized ratably over the contract term.
>
> Certain contracts provide for revenue to be generated based upon the achievement of certain performance standards. Revenue is recognized when such performance standards are achieved, including $956,000 of revenue recognized.
>
> Revenue from multiple element arrangements is accounted for under EITF Issue No. 00-21 (EITF 00-21), "Revenue Arrangements with Multiple Deliverables." For these arrangements, we evaluate all deliverables in the contract to determine whether they represent separate units of accounting. If the deliverables represent separate units of accounting, we then measure and allocate the consideration from the arrangement to the separate units, based on reliable evidence of the fair value of each deliverable. This evaluation is performed at the inception of the arrangement and as each item in the arrangement is delivered, and involves significant judgments regarding the nature of the services and deliverables being provided and whether these services and deliverables can reasonably be divided into the separate units of accounting.

Required

a. Sapient recognizes revenues based on the provisions of the written service contracts generated for each client. The primary types of contracts are (1) fixed-price, fixed-time contracts; (2) support and maintenance contracts; and (3) performance standards contracts. Discuss the criteria used to recognize revenue for each type of contract and the difficulties in applying the criteria.

b. Discuss the appropriateness of the revenue recognition techniques employed by Sapient in relation to the general revenue recognition criterion of "substantial portion of services has been provided" as discussed in the text of this chapter.

c. As detailed earlier, some contracts have multiple-element arrangements with separate deliverable components. Discuss the criteria used to distinguish among multiple components of the contract. Also speculate on how the firm recognizes revenue when the contract cannot be separated into distinct deliverable components.

8.18 MEASURING INCOME FOR A LONG-HAUL TRANSPORT FIRM. Canadian National Railway Company (CN) spans Canada and mid-America and provides freight transport services from the Atlantic Ocean to the Pacific Ocean and to the Gulf of Mexico. It is currently the largest private rail system in Canada and was privatized by the Canadian government when it was considered one of the worst rail transport companies in North America. CN has been a success story since its privatization and is now considered one of the strongest and most efficient rail freight transport companies. Its success is partly due to a fundamental change in the way it offers freight services to customers. CN runs what the firm refers to as a *scheduled railroad.* Similar to rail passenger service, as much as possible CN maintains a fixed operating schedule and a fixed freight-car fleet movement across the continent. Thus, customers know what shipment options are available to them and know with a high degree of accuracy when shipments will arrive at designated locations.

Typically, a customer contracts a fixed fee with CN to ship its freight from the point of origination (for example, the Port of Halifax) to the point of destination (for example, the Port of Vancouver). CN provides the entire transport (that is, CN does not contract out a portion of the shipment to other rail transport companies), and the length of time taken to deliver the freight depends on the distance and the type of service (fast delivery versus normal delivery, for example) purchased by the customer. In a recent annual report, CN succinctly states its policy on recognizing revenue: "Freight revenues are recognized on services performed by the Company, based on the percentage of complete service method. Costs associated with movements are recognized as the service is performed."

Required

Discuss the appropriateness of the revenue recognition techniques employed by CN for recognizing freight revenues.

8.19 MEASURING INCOME FROM LONG-TERM CONTRACTS. On January 1, 2010, Turner Construction Company agreed to construct an observatory for Dartmouth College for $120 million. Dartmouth College must pay $30 million upon signing and $30 million at the end of 2010, 2011, and 2012. Expected construction costs are $10 million for 2010, $60 million for 2011, and $30 million for 2012. Assume that these cash flows occur at the end of each year. Also assume that an appropriate interest rate for this contract is 10 percent. Amortization schedules for the deferred cash flows follow.

Amortization Schedule for Cash Received (amounts in thousands)

Year	Balance Jan. 1	Interest Revenue	Payment	Reduction in Principal	Balance Dec. 31
2010	$74,606	$7,460	$30,000	$22,540	$52,066
2011	52,066	5,207	30,000	24,793	27,273
2012	27,273	2,727	30,000	27,273	0

Amortization Schedule for Cash Disbursed (amounts in thousands)

Year	Balance Jan. 1	Interest Expense	Payment	Reduction in Principal	Balance Dec. 31
2010	$81,217	$8,122	$10,000	$ 1,878	$79,339
2011	79,339	7,934	60,000	52,066	27,273
2012	27,273	2,727	30,000	27,273	0

Required

a. Indicate the amount and nature of income (revenue and expense) that Turner would recognize during 2010, 2011, and 2012 if it uses the completed-contract method. Ignore income taxes.

b. Repeat Part a using the percentage-of-completion method.

c. Repeat Part a using the installment method.

d. Indicate the balance in the construction in process account on December 31, 2010, 2011, and 2012 (just prior to completion of the contract) under the completed-contract and the percentage-of-completion methods.

8.20 INTERPRETING FINANCIAL STATEMENT DISCLOSURES RELATING TO INCOME RECOGNITION. Deere & Company manufactures agricultural and industrial equipment and provides financing services for its independent dealers and their retail customers. In recent notes to the financial statements, Deere discloses the following:

> Note 1: Deere recognizes income from equipment sales for financial reporting at the time of shipment to dealers. Provisions for sales incentives to dealers, returns and allowances, and uncollectible accounts are made at the time of sale. There is a time lag, which varies based on the timing and level of retail demand, between when Deere records sales to dealers and when dealers sell equipment to retail customers. Deere recognizes income from equipment sales using the installment method for tax reporting.
>
> Note 2: Deere provides financing to independent dealers and retail customers for Deere products. Accounts and notes receivable appear net of unearned finance income. Deere recognizes the unearned finance income as finance revenue over the period that dealer and customer notes are outstanding.

Required

a. Using the criteria for revenue recognition, justify Deere's timing of revenue recognition for its equipment sales. Consider why recognition of revenue earlier or later than the time of shipment to dealers would not be more appropriate.

b. Describe briefly how the balance sheet accounts of Deere & Company listed here would change if it recognized revenues during the period of production using the percentage-of-completion method. You do not need to give amounts, but indicate the likely direction of the change and describe the computation of its amount.

- Accounts and Notes Receivable
- Inventories
- Retained Earnings

c. Respond to Part b assuming that Deere & Company recognized revenue using the installment method.

- Accounts and Notes Receivable
- Inventories
- Retained Earnings

8.21 LIFO AND FIFO COST-FLOW ASSUMPTIONS FOR INVENTORY. A large manufacturer of truck and car tires recently changed its cost-flow assumption method for inventories at the beginning of 2010. The manufacturer has been in operation for almost 40 years, and for the last decade, it has reported moderate growth in revenues. The firm changed from the LIFO method to the FIFO method and reported the following information (amounts in millions):

December 31:	2009	2010
Inventories at FIFO cost	$ 788.1	$ 861.7
Excess of FIFO cost over LIFO cost	$(429.0)	$ (452.4)
Cost of goods sold (FIFO)	—	$4,150.8
Cost of goods sold (LIFO)	—	$4,417.1

Calculate the inventory turnover ratio for 2010 using the LIFO and FIFO cost-flow assumption methods. Explain why the costs assigned to inventory under LIFO at the end of 2009 and 2010 are so much less than they are under FIFO.

8.22 RECONCILE PBO/FMV OF PLAN ASSETS; COMPUTE PENSION EXPENSE. Use the information provided below to

a. Compute the December 31, 2010 PBO and FMV of pension assets.
b. Compute 2010 pension expense.
c. Use the financial statements effects template to show the effects on the 2010 financial statements.

Prior service cost due to 2010 amendment	$ 60,000
PBO, January 1, 2010	1,000,000
FMV, January 1, 2010	1,200,000
Settlement interest rate	7%
Expected return on plan assets	9%
Actual return on plan assets	8%
Liability loss (gain)	(40,000)
Contribution to plan trustee (made at end of year)	100,000
Service cost	115,000
Payments to retired employees	30,000

8.23 ACCOUNTING FOR FORWARD FOREIGN EXCHANGE CONTRACT AS A FAIR VALUE HEDGE. Refer to Examples 16 and 20 in the chapter. Firm A places its order for the equipment on June 30, 2010. It simultaneously signs a forward foreign exchange contract for 10,000 GBP. The forward rate on June 30, 2010, for settlement on June 30, 2011, is $1.64 per GBP. Firm A designates the forward foreign exchange contract as a fair value hedge of the firm commitment.

Required

a. GAAP and IFRS do not require Firm A to record the purchase commitment or the forward foreign exchange contract on the balance sheet as a liability and an asset on June 30, 2010. What is the logic for this accounting?
b. On December 31, 2010, the forward foreign exchange rate for settlement on June 30, 2011, is $1.73 per GBP. Using the financial statement effects template, show the

financial statement effects of recording the change in the value of the purchase commitment and the change in the value of the forward contract for 2010. Assume an 8 percent per year interest rate for discounting cash flows to their present values on December 31, 2010.

c. Show the financial statement effects on June 30, 2011, of recording the change in the present value of the purchase commitment and the forward foreign exchange contract for the passage of time.

d. On June 30, 2011, the spot foreign exchange rate is \$1.75 per GBP. Show the financial statement effects of recording the change in the value of the purchase commitment and the change in the value of the forward contract due to changes in the exchange rate during the first six months of 2011.

e. Show the financial statement effects of the June 30, 2011, purchase of 10,000 GBP with U.S. dollars and acquisition of the equipment.

f. Show the financial statement effects on June 30, 2011, to settle the forward foreign exchange contract.

g. How would the effects in Parts b–f differ if Firm A had chosen to designate the forward foreign exchange contract as a cash flow hedge instead of a fair value hedge?

h. Suggest a scenario that would justify Firm A treating the forward foreign exchange contract as a fair value hedge and a scenario that would justify the firm treating the contract as a cash flow hedge.

8.24 ACCOUNTING FOR FORWARD COMMODITY PRICE CONTRACT AS A CASH FLOW HEDGE. Refer to Examples 19 and 23 in the chapter. Firm D holds 10,000 gallons of whiskey in inventory on October 31, 2010, that costs \$225 per gallon. Firm D contemplates selling the whiskey on March 31, 2011, when it completes the aging process. Uncertainty about the selling price of whiskey on March 31, 2011, leads Firm D to acquire a forward contract on whiskey. The forward contract does not require an initial investment of funds. Firm D designates the forward commodity contract as a cash flow hedge of an anticipated transaction. The forward price on October 31, 2010, for delivery on March 31, 2011, is \$320 per gallon.

Required

a. Using the financial statement effects template, show the financial statement effects, if any, that Firm D would have on October 31, 2010, when it acquires the forward commodity price contract.

b. On December 31, 2010, the end of the accounting period for Firm D, the forward price of whiskey for March 31, 2011, delivery is \$310 per gallon. Show the financial statement effects of recording the change in the value of the forward commodity price contract. Ignore the discounting of cash flows in this part and in the remainder of the problem.

c. Show the financial statement effects of the December 31, 2010, decline in value of the whiskey inventory.

d. On March 31, 2011, the price of whiskey declines to \$270 per gallon. Show the financial statement effects of revaluing the forward contract.

e. Show the financial statement effects on March 31, 2011, to reflect the decline in value of the inventory.

f. Show the financial statement effects on March 31, 2011, to settle the forward contract.

g. Assume that Firm D sells the whiskey on March 31, 2011, for \$270 a gallon. Show the financial statement effects of recording the sale and recognizing the cost of goods sold.

h. How would the effects in Parts b–g differ if Firm D had chosen to designate the forward commodity price contract as a fair value hedge instead of a cash flow hedge?

i. Suggest a scenario that would justify treating the forward commodity price contract as a fair value hedge and a scenario that would justify treating it as a cash flow hedge.

8.25 INTERPRETING DERIVATIVES DISCLOSURES. Excerpts from the disclosures on derivatives in a recent year (denoted Year 4) by The Coca-Cola Company (Coke) appear below.

Our Company uses derivative financial instruments primarily to reduce our exposure to adverse fluctuations in interest rates and foreign exchange rates, and, to a lesser extent, in commodity prices and other market risks. When entered into, the Company formally designates and documents the financial instrument as a hedge of a specific underlying exposure, as well as the risk management objectives and strategies for undertaking the hedge transaction. The Company formally assesses, both at the inception and at least quarterly thereafter, whether the financial instruments that are used in hedging transactions are effective at offsetting changes in either the fair value or cash flows of the related underlying exposures. Our Company does not enter into derivative financial instruments for trading purposes.

Our Company monitors our mix of fixed rate and variable-rate debt. This monitoring includes a review of business and other financial risks. We also enter into interest rate swap agreements to manage these risks. These contracts had maturities of less than one year on December 31, Year 4. The fair value of our Company's interest rate swap agreements was approximately $6 million at December 31, Year 4. The Company estimates the fair value of its interest rate management derivatives based on quoted market prices. Interest rate swap agreements are accounted for as fair value hedges. During Year 4, there has been no ineffectiveness related to fair value hedges.

We enter into forward exchange contracts to hedge certain portions of forecasted cash flows denominated in foreign currencies. These contracts had maturities up to one year on December 31, Year 4. The purpose of our foreign currency hedging activities is to reduce the risk that our eventual U.S. dollar net cash inflows resulting from sales outside the U.S. will be adversely affected by changes in exchange rates. We designate these derivatives as cash flow hedges. During Year 4, we decreased accumulated other comprehensive income by $76 million ($46 million after tax) for changes in the fair value of cash flow hedges. The amount recorded in earnings for the ineffective portion of cash flow hedges during Year 4 was not significant. We also reclassified net losses of $86 million ($52 million after tax) from accumulated other comprehensive income to earnings. The accumulated net loss on cash flow derivatives on December 31, Year 4 is $56 million ($34 million after tax). The carrying and fair value of foreign exchange contracts on December 31, Year 4 is $39 million.

We monitor our exposure to financial market risks using value-at-risk models. Our value-at-risk calculations use a historical simulation model to estimate potential future losses in the fair value of our derivatives and other financial instruments that could occur as a result of adverse movements in foreign currency and interest rates. We examined historical weekly returns over the previous 10 years to calculate our value at risk. The average value at risk represents the simple average of quarterly amounts over the past year. According to our interest rate value-at-risk calculations, we estimate with 95 percent confidence that an adverse move in interest rates over a one-week period would not have a material impact on our consolidated financial statements for Year 4. Similar calculations for adverse movements in foreign exchange rates indicate a maximum impact on earnings over a one-week period of $17 million. Net income for Year 4 was $4,847 million.

Required

a. Coke indicates that it "formally specifies the risk management objectives and strategies for undertaking the hedge transactions." Identify the risk management objective and describe how the particular derivative accomplishes this objective with respect to interest rate swap agreements.
b. Repeat Part a for forward exchange contracts.
c. What is the rationale for Coke's designation of the interest rate swaps as fair value hedges and the forward exchange contracts as cash flow hedges?
d. Why does Coke assess both initially and at least quarterly the effectiveness of these hedging instruments?
e. Compute the amount that Coke initially recorded on its books for foreign exchange contracts outstanding on December 31, Year 4. What events will cause the carrying value of these contracts at any later date to differ from the amounts initially recorded?
f. For Year 4, Coke reports a $76 million net loss from changes in the value of cash flow hedges. What does the disclosure that Coke recognized a net loss instead of a net gain suggest about the direction of changes in exchange rates between the U.S. dollar and the foreign currencies underlying the foreign exchange contracts? Will the forward exchange contracts likely appear on Coke's balance sheet as assets or liabilities? Explain.
g. Justify Coke's treatment of the $76 million net loss from changes in the value of cash flow hedges during Year 4 as a decrease in accumulated other comprehensive income instead of an ineffective cash flow hedge that should be included in earnings.
h. The income tax law taxes gains and losses from changes in the fair value of foreign exchange contracts at the time of settlement. Will the tax effects of the $76 million pretax loss for Year 4 affect current taxes payable or deferred taxes? If the answer to the previous question is deferred taxes, will it affect deferred tax assets or deferred tax liabilities? Explain.
i. Describe the likely event that will cause Coke to reclassify amounts from accumulated other comprehensive to earnings.
j. Assess the effectiveness of Coke's management of risk changes from interest and foreign exchange rates for Year 4.

8.26 INTERPRETING INCOME TAX DISCLOSURES. Disclosures related to income taxes for The Coca-Cola Company (Coke) for 2006–2008 appear in Exhibit 8.11.

Required

a. Why are Coke's average tax rates so low?
b. Is it likely that Coke has recognized a net asset or a net liability on its balance sheet for pension and other postretirement benefit plans? Explain your reasoning.
c. Coke discloses that the valuation allowance on deferred tax assets relates primarily to net operating loss carryforwards. Assume for purposes of this question that Coke had recognized a valuation allowance each year exactly equal to the deferred tax assets recognized for net operating loss carryforwards. Indicate the effect on income

EXHIBIT 8.11

Income Tax Reconciliation and Components of Deferred Taxes
for The Coca-Cola Company (amounts in millions)
(Problem 8.26)

	2008	2007	2006
Income Tax Reconciliation			
U.S. Statutory Tax Rate	35.0%	35.0%	35.0%
State Taxes, net of Federal Tax Benefit	0.8	0.6	0.7
Foreign Earnings Taxes at Lower Rates	(14.3)	(10.8)	(11.4)
Equity Income or Loss	(0.2)	(1.3)	(0.6)
Other Operating Charges	(0.7)	(0.5)	0.6
Other	(0.5)	(0.0)	(1.5)
Average Tax Rate	21.9%	24.0%	22.8%

Components of Deferred Taxes on December 31:	**2008**	**2007**
Deferred Tax Assets		
Property, plant and equipment	$ 33	$ 45
Trademarks and Other Intangible Assets	79	76
Equity Method Investments	339	238
Other Liabilities	447	845
Benefit Plans	1,171	881
Net Operating Loss Carryforwards	494	554
Other	532	266
Total Deferred Tax Assets (Gross)	$ 3,095	$ 2,905
Valuation Allowance	(569)	(611)
Total Deferred Tax Assets (Net)	$ 2,526	$ 2,294
Deferred Tax Liabilities		
Property, plant and equipment	$ (667)	$ (670)
Trademarks and Other Intangible Assets	(1,974)	(1,925)
Equity Method Investments	(267)	(841)
Other Liabilities	(101)	(90)
Other	(229)	(383)
Total Deferred Tax Liabilities	$(3,238)	$(3,909)
Net Deferred Tax Assets (Liability)	$ (712)	$(1,615)

tax expense and income tax payable in the year Coke initially recognizes the net operating loss carryforwards.

d. Refer to Part c. Indicate the effect on income tax expense and income tax payable in the year Coke benefits from the net operating loss carryforwards.

e. Interpret Coke's recognition of net deferred tax liabilities, instead of deferred tax assets, for equity investments in 2008.

f. Why does Coke report tax effects of equity income and investments in the income tax reconciliation and in deferred tax liabilities?

g. Interpret Coke's recognition of deferred tax liabilities, instead of deferred tax assets, for intangible assets.

INTEGRATIVE CASE 8.1

STARBUCKS

Presented below is an excerpt from Starbucks' Note 1, "Summary of Significant Accounting Policies," in its September 28, 2008 Annual Report.

Revenue Recognition

Consolidated revenues are presented net of intercompany eliminations for wholly owned subsidiaries and investees controlled by the Company and for licensees accounted for under the equity method, based on the Company's percentage ownership. Additionally, consolidated revenues are recognized net of any discounts, returns, allowances and sales incentives, including coupon redemptions and rebates.

Stored Value Cards

Revenues from the Company's stored value cards, such as the Starbucks Card, and gift certificates are recognized when tendered for payment, or upon redemption. Outstanding customer balances are included in "Deferred revenue" on the consolidated balance sheets. There are no expiration dates on the Company's stored value cards or gift certificates, and Starbucks does not charge any service fees that cause a decrement to customer balances. While the Company will continue to honor all stored value cards and gift certificates presented for payment, management may determine the likelihood of redemption to be remote for certain card and certificate balances due to, among other things, long periods of inactivity. In these circumstances, to the extent management determines there is no requirement for remitting balances to government agencies under unclaimed property laws, card and certificate balances may be recognized in the consolidated statements of earnings in "Interest income and other, net." For the fiscal years ended September 28, 2008, September 30, 2007 and October 1, 2006, income recognized on unredeemed stored value card balances and gift certificates was $13.6 million, $12.9 million and $4.4 million, respectively.

Retail Revenues

Company-operated retail store revenues are recognized when payment is tendered at the point of sale. Starbucks maintains a sales return allowance to reduce retail revenues for estimated future product returns, including brewing equipment, based on historical patterns. Retail store revenues are reported net of sales, use or other transaction taxes that are collected from customers and remitted to taxing authorities.

Specialty Revenues

Specialty revenues consist primarily of product sales to customers other than through Company-operated retail stores, as well as royalties and other fees generated from licensing operations. Sales of coffee, tea and related products are generally recognized upon shipment to customers, depending on contract terms. Shipping charges billed to customers are also recognized as revenue, and the related shipping costs are included in "Cost of sales including occupancy costs" on the consolidated statements of earnings. Specific to retail store licensing arrangements, initial nonrefundable development fees are recognized upon substantial performance of services for new market business development activities, such as initial business, real estate and store development planning, as well as providing operational materials and functional training courses for opening new licensed retail markets. Additional store licensing fees are recognized when new licensed stores are opened. Royalty revenues based upon a percentage of reported sales and other continuing fees, such as marketing and service fees, are recognized on a monthly basis when earned. For certain licensing arrangements, where the Company intends to acquire an ownership interest, the initial nonrefundable development fees are deferred to "Other long-term liabilities" on the consolidated balance sheets until acquisition, at which point the fees are reflected as a reduction of the Company's investment. Other arrangements involving multiple elements and deliverables as well as upfront fees are individually evaluated for revenue recognition. Cash payments received in advance of product or service delivery are recorded in "Deferred revenue" until earned.

Required

a. The above passages indicate that Starbucks generates revenues in several different ways. For each of the following customers, describe how Starbucks should recognize revenue and the working capital accounts that would likely be created by the revenue recognition approach. (For Items 1–6, ignore sales tax.)

1. Cash customer purchasing coffee at a Starbucks-owned retail store
2. Customer adding cash balance to her Starbucks card
3. Customer at Starbucks-owned retail store paying for coffee with a Starbuck's card
4. Customer at Starbucks-owned retail store using the Duetto card (a co-branded Visa/Starbucks credit card) to make a credit purchase of brewing equipment
5. Other businesses that purchase Starbuck's products on credit
6. Licensed stores
7. Customer remitting sales taxes to Starbucks when purchasing coffee

b. Starbucks' "gold-level" customers purchase 15 cups of coffee and then receive a free 16th cup of coffee. How should Starbucks account for this customer loyalty program? (Assume that the selling price for a cup of coffee is \$2.20 and that the direct inventory cost per cup is \$1.50.)

CASE 8.2

ARIZONA LAND DEVELOPMENT COMPANY

Joan Locker and Bill Dasher organized the Arizona Land Development Company (ALDC) on January 2, Year 1. They contributed land with a market value of \$300,000 and \$100,000 cash for all of the common stock of the corporation. The land served as the initial inventory of property sold to customers.

ALDC sells undeveloped land, primarily to individuals approaching retirement. Within nine years from the date of sale, ALDC promises to develop the land so that it is suitable for the construction of residential housing. ALDC makes all sales on an installment basis. Customers pay 10 percent of the selling price at the time of sale and remit the remainder in equal installments over the next nine years.

ALDC estimates that development costs will equal 50 percent of the selling price of the land and that development work will take nine years to complete from the date of sale. Actual development costs have coincided with expectations. The firm incurs 10 percent of the development costs at the time of sale and incurs the remainder evenly over the next nine years.

ALDC remained a privately held firm for its first six years. Exhibits 8.12–8.14 (see pages 714–716) present the firm's income statement, balance sheet, and statement of cash flows, respectively, for Year 1–Year 6. ALDC recognizes income from sales of undeveloped land at the time of sale. The amount shown for sales each year in Exhibit 8.12 represents the gross amount ALDC ultimately expects to collect from customers for land sold in that year. The amount shown for estimated development costs each year is the gross amount

EXHIBIT 8.12

Arizona Land Development Company
Income Statements
Income Recognition at Time of Sale—No Discounting of Cash Flows
(Case 8.2)

	Year 1	Year 2	Year 3	Year 4	Year 5	Year 6
Sales	$650,000	$900,000	$1,500,000	$2,500,000	$1,200,000	$400,000
Less:						
Cost of land inventory sold	(65,000)	(90,000)	(150,000)	(250,000)	(120,000)	(40,000)
Estimated development costs	(325,000)	(450,000)	(750,000)	(1,250,000)	(600,000)	(200,000)
Gross Profit	$260,000	$360,000	$ 600,000	$1,000,000	$ 480,000	$160,000
Selling expenses	(65,000)	(90,000)	(150,000)	(250,000)	(120,000)	(40,000)
Net Income before Taxes	$195,000	$270,000	$ 450,000	$ 750,000	$ 360,000	$120,000
Income taxes:						
Current	—	—	(9,778)	(26,091)	(73,009)	(94,902)
Deferred	(66,300)	(91,800)	(143,222)	(228,909)	(49,391)	54,102
Net Income	$128,700	$178,200	$ 297,000	$ 495,000	$ 237,600	$ 79,200

EXHIBIT 8.13

Arizona Land Development Company
Balance Sheets
Income Recognition at Time of Sale—No Discounting of Cash Flows
(Case 8.2)

	Year 1	Year 2	Year 3	Year 4	Year 5	Year 6
ASSETS						
Cash	$100,000	$ 132,500	$ 100,222	$ 126,631	$ 131,122	$ 273,720
Notes receivable	520,000	1,175,000	2,220,000	3,915,000	4,320,000	3,965,000
Land inventory	235,000	145,000	95,000	45,000	125,000	185,000
Total Assets	$855,000	$1,452,500	$2,415,222	$4,086,631	$4,576,122	$4,423,720
LIABILITIES AND SHAREHOLDERS' EQUITY						
Estimated development cost liability	$260,000	$ 587,500	$1,110,000	$1,957,500	$2,160,000	$1,982,500
Deferred income taxes	66,300	158,100	301,322	530,231	579,622	525,520
Common stock	400,000	400,000	400,000	500,000	500,000	500,000
Retained earnings	128,700	306,900	603,900	1,098,900	1,336,500	1,415,700
Total Liabilities and Shareholders' Equity	$855,000	$1,452,500	$2,415,222	$4,086,631	$4,576,122	$4,423,720

EXHIBIT 8.14

Arizona Land Development Company
Statements of Cash Flows
Income Recognition at Time of Sale—No Discounting of Cash Flows
(Case 8.2)

	Year 1	Year 2	Year 3	Year 4	Year 5	Year 6
OPERATIONS						
Net income	$ 128,700	$ 178,200	$ 297,000	$ 495,000	$ 237,600	$ 79,200
(Increase) Decrease in notes receivable	(520,000)	(655,000)	(1,045,000)	(1,695,000)	(405,000)	355,000
(Increase) Decrease in land inventory	65,000	90,000	50,000	50,000	(80,000)	(60,000)
Increase (Decrease) in estimated development cost liability	260,000	327,500	522,500	847,500	202,500	(177,500)
Increase (Decrease) in deferred income taxes	66,300	91,800	143,222	228,909	49,391	(54,102)
Cash Flow from Operations	$ 0	$ 32,500	$ (32,278)	$ (73,591)	$ 4,491	$ 142,598
FINANCING						
Common stock issued	—	—	—	100,000	—	—
Change in Cash	$ 0	$ 32,500	$ (32,278)	$ 26,409	$ 4,491	$ 142,598

ALDC ultimately expects to disburse to develop land sold in that year. The firm treats selling expenses as a period expense. It is subject to a 34 percent income tax rate. ALDC uses the installment method of income recognition for income tax purposes.

ALDC contemplates making its initial public offering of common stock early in Year 7. The firm asks you to assess whether its income recognition method, as reflected in Exhibits 8.12–8.14, accurately reflects its operating performance and financial position. To assist you, the firm has prepared financial statements following three other income recognition methods as described next.

Income Recognition at Time of Sale but with Discounting of Future Cash Flows to Present Value

Exhibits 8.15–8.17 (see pages 718–720) present the financial statements that use this income recognition method. This method discounts future cash inflows from customers and future cash outflows for development work to their present values. The gross profit recognized at the time of sale equals the present value of cash inflows net of the present value of cash outflows. One might view this gross profit as the current cash-equivalent value of the gross profit the firm will ultimately realize over the nine-year period. This method reports the increase in the present value of cash inflows as time passes as interest revenue each year and the increase in the present value of cash outflows as interest expense. Thus, this income recognition method results in the reporting of two types of income: a gross profit from the selling of land and interest from delayed cash flows. The computations of present values underlying the financial statements in Exhibits 8.15–8.17 rest on the following assumptions:

1. ALDC makes all sales on January 1 of each year. It receives 10 percent of the gross selling price at the time of sale and pays 10 percent of the gross development costs immediately.
2. The firm receives 10 percent of the gross selling price from customers and pays 10 percent of the gross development costs on December 31 of each year, beginning with the year of sale.
3. The interest rates used in discounting are as follows:

Sales In:	Interest Rate
Year 1	12%
Year 2	12%
Year 3	15%
Year 4	15%
Year 5	12%
Year 6	12%

Income Recognition Using the Installment Method—With Discounting of Cash Flows

Exhibits 8.18–8.20 (see pages 721–723) present the financial statements following this income recognition method. ALDC uses this income recognition method for tax reporting.

Income Recognition Using the Percentage-of-Completion Method

Exhibits 8.21–8.23 (see pages 724–726) present the financial statements that use this income recognition method. The presumption underlying this method is that ALDC is

EXHIBIT 8.15

Arizona Land Development Company
Income Statements
Income Recognition at Time of Sale—With Discounting of Cash Flows
(Case 8.2)

	Year 1	Year 2	Year 3	Year 4	Year 5	Year 6
Sales	$ 411,336[a]	$ 569,543	$ 865,737	$1,442,895	$ 759,390	$ 253,130
Less:						
Cost of land inventory sold	(65,000)	(90,000)	(150,000)	(250,000)	(120,000)	(40,000)
Estimated development costs	(205,668)[b]	(284,771)	(432,869)	(721,448)	(379,695)	(126,565)
Gross Profit	$ 140,668	$ 194,772	$ 282,868	$ 471,447	$ 259,695	$ 86,565
Selling expenses	(65,000)	(90,000)	(150,000)	(250,000)	(120,000)	(40,000)
Interest revenue	41,560[c]	96,293	196,609	361,257	411,130	400,899
Interest expense	(20,780)[d]	(48,147)	(98,304)	(180,628)	(205,566)	(200,449)
Net Income before Taxes	$ 96,448	$ 152,918	$ 231,173	$ 402,076	$ 345,259	$ 247,015
Income taxes:						
Current	—	—	(9,778)	(26,091)	(73,009)	(94,902)
Deferred	(32,792)	(51,992)	(68,821)	(110,615)	(44,379)	10,917
Net Income	$ 63,656	$ 100,926	$ 152,574	$ 265,370	$ 227,871	$ 163,030

[a] Represents the present value of $65,000 received on January 1, Year 1, plus the present value of a series of $65,000 cash inflows on December 31, Year 1 to Year 9, discounted at 12 percent.

[b] Represents the present value of $32,500 paid on January 1, Year 1, plus the present value of a series of $32,500 cash outflows on December 31, Year 1 to Year 9, discounted at 12 percent.

[c] $.12(\$411,336 - \$65,000) = \$41,560$.

[d] $.12(\$205,668 - \$32,500) = \$20,780$.

EXHIBIT 8.16

Arizona Land Development Company
Balance Sheets
Income Recognition at Time of Sale—With Discounting of Cash Flows
(Case 8.2)

	Year 1	Year 2	Year 3	Year 4	Year 5	Year 6
ASSETS						
Cash	$100,000	$ 132,500	$ 100,222	$ 126,631	$ 131,122	$ 273,720
Notes receivable	322,896[a]	743,732	1,351,078	2,350,230	2,725,750	2,624,779
Land inventory	235,000	145,000	95,000	45,000	125,000	185,000
Total Assets	$657,896	$1,021,232	$1,546,300	$2,521,861	$2,981,872	$3,083,499
LIABILITIES AND SHAREHOLDERS' EQUITY						
Estimated development cost liability	$161,448[b]	$ 371,866	$ 675,539	$1,175,115	$1,362,876	$1,312,390
Deferred income taxes	32,792	84,784	153,605	264,220	308,599	297,682
Common stock	400,000	400,000	400,000	500,000	500,000	500,000
Retained earnings	63,656	164,582	317,156	582,526	810,397	973,427
Total Liabilities and Shareholders' Equity	$657,896	$1,021,232	$1,546,300	$2,521,861	$2,981,872	$3,083,499

[a]$411,336 − $65,000 + $41,560 − $65,000 = $322,896 (see Notes (a) and (c) to Exhibit 8.15).
[b]$205,668 − $32,500 + $20,780 − $32,500 = $161,448 (see Notes (b) and (d) to Exhibit 8.15).

EXHIBIT 8.17

Arizona Land Development Company
Statements of Cash Flows
Income Recognition at Time of Sale—With Discounting of Cash Flows
(Case 8.2)

	Year 1	Year 2	Year 3	Year 4	Year 5	Year 6
OPERATIONS						
Net income	$ 63,656	$ 100,926	$ 152,574	$ 265,370	$ 227,871	$163,030
(Increase) Decrease in notes receivable	(322,896)	(420,836)	(607,346)	(999,152)	(375,520)	100,971
(Increase) Decrease in land inventory	65,000	90,000	50,000	50,000	(80,000)	(60,000)
Increase (Decrease) in estimated development cost liability	161,448	210,418	303,673	499,576	187,761	(50,486)
Increase (Decrease) in deferred income taxes	32,792	51,992	68,821	110,615	44,379	(10,917)
Cash Flow from Operations	$ 0	$ 32,500	$ (32,278)	$ (73,591)	$ 4,491	$142,598
FINANCING						
Common stock issued	—	—	—	100,000	—	—
Change in Cash	$ 0	$ 32,500	$ (32,278)	$ 26,409	$ 4,491	$142,598

EXHIBIT 8.18

Arizona Land Development Company
Income Statements
Income Recognition Using Installment Method—With Discounting of Cash Flows
(Case 8.2)

	Year 1	Year 2	Year 3	Year 4	Year 5	Year 6
Sales	$ 88,440[a]	$148,707	$ 258,391	$ 443,744	$ 383,868	$ 354,101
Cost of goods sold	(58,195)[a]	(97,852)	(172,963)	(297,634)	(254,699)	(235,427)
Gross Profit	$ 30,245[a]	$ 50,855	$ 85,428	$ 146,110	$ 129,169	$ 118,674
Selling expenses	(65,000)	(90,000)	(150,000)	(250,000)	(120,000)	(40,000)
Interest revenue	41,560[b]	96,293	196,609	361,257	411,130	400,899
Interest expense	(20,780)[c]	(48,147)	(98,304)	(180,628)	(205,566)	(200,449)
Net Income before Taxes	$(13,975)	$ 9,001	$ 33,733	$ 76,739	$ 214,733	$ 279,124
Income taxes:						
Current	—[d]	—[d]	(9,778)[d]	(26,091)	(73,009)	(94,902)
Deferred	4,751	(3,060)	(1,691)	—	—	—
Net Income	$ (9,224)	$ 5,941	$ 22,264	$ 50,648	$ 141,724	$ 184,222

[a]Exhibit 8.15 indicates that the total gross profit from land sold in Year 1 is $140,668. The present value of the amounts that ALDC will receive from customers is $411,336 (see Exhibit 8.15). Thus, for each dollar of the $411,336 collected, the firm recognizes 34.2 cents (= $140,668/$411,336) of gross profit. During Year 1, ALDC collects $130,000 from sales of land made in Year 1 ($65,000 on January 1 and $65,000 on December 31). However, only $23,440 (= $65,000 − $41,560) of the December 31 payment represents payment of a portion of the $411,336 selling price. The remainder ($41,560) represents interest. Thus, the gross profit recognized in Year 1 is $30,245 [= 0.342 × ($65,000 + $23,440)].

[b]See Note (c) to Exhibit 8.15.

[c]See Note (d) to Exhibit 8.15.

[d]ALDC carries forward the $13,975 loss in Year 1 to offset taxable income in future years ($9,001 in Year 2 and $4,974 in Year 3).

EXHIBIT 8.19

Arizona Land Development Company
Balance Sheets
Income Recognition Using Installment Method—With Discounting of Cash Flows
(Case 8.2)

	Year 1	Year 2	Year 3	Year 4	Year 5	Year 6
ASSETS						
Cash	$100,000	$132,500	$ 100,222	$ 126,631	$ 131,122	$ 273,720
Notes receivable	212,473[a]	489,392	899,298	1,573,113	1,818,107	1,749,245
Land inventory	235,000	145,000	95,000	45,000	125,000	185,000
Deferred tax asset	4,751	1,691	—	—	—	—
Total Assets	$552,224	$768,583	$1,094,520	$1,744,744	$2,074,229	$2,207,965
LIABILITIES AND SHAREHOLDERS' EQUITY						
Estimated development cost liability	$161,448[b]	$371,866	$ 675,539	$1,175,115	$1,362,876	$1,312,390
Deferred income taxes	—	—	—	—	—	—
Common stock	400,000	400,000	400,000	500,000	500,000	500,000
Retained earnings	(9,224)	(3,283)	18,981	69,629	211,353	395,575
Total Liabilities and Shareholders' Equity	$552,224	$768,583	$1,094,520	$1,744,744	$2,074,229	$2,207,965

[a]The derivation of this amount is as follows:

	Notes Receivable—Gross	Deferred Gross Profit	Notes Receivable—Net
January 1, Year 1	$411,336	$140,668	$270,668
Less Cash Received, January 1, Year 1	(65,000)	—	(65,000)
Plus Interest Revenue, Year 1	41,560	—	41,560
Less Cash Received, December 31, Year 1	(65,000)	—	(65,000)
Gross Profit Recognized, Year 1	—	(30,245)	30,245
Totals	$322,896	$110,423	$212,473

[b]See Note (b) to Exhibit 8.16.

EXHIBIT 8.20

Arizona Land Development Company
Statements of Cash Flows
Income Recognition Using Installment Method—With Discounting of Cash Flows
(Case 8.2)

	Year 1	Year 2	Year 3	Year 4	Year 5	Year 6
OPERATIONS						
Net income (loss)	$ (9,224)	$ 5,941	$ 22,264	$ 50,648	$ 141,724	$184,222
(Increase) Decrease in notes receivable	(212,473)	(276,919)	(409,906)	(673,815)	(244,994)	68,862
(Increase) Decrease in land inventory	65,000	90,000	50,000	50,000	(80,000)	(60,000)
(Increase) Decrease in deferred tax asset	(4,751)	3,060	1,691	—	—	—
(Increase) Decrease in estimated development cost liability	161,448	210,418	303,673	499,576	187,761	(50,486)
Cash Flow from Operations	$ 0	$ 32,500	$ (32,278)	$ (73,591)	$ 4,491	$142,598
FINANCING						
Common stock issued	—	—	—	100,000	—	—
Change in Cash	$ 0	$ 32,500	$ (32,278)	$ 26,409	$ 4,491	$142,598

EXHIBIT 8.21

Arizona Land Development Company
Income Statements
Income Recognition Using Percentage-of-Completion Method
(Case 8.2)

	Year 1	Year 2	Year 3	Year 4	Year 5	Year 6
Sales	$ 216,667[a]	$ 354,167	$ 629,167	$1,087,500	$ 862,500	$ 695,833
Cost of goods sold	(130,000)[a]	(212,500)	(377,500)	(652,500)	(517,500)	(417,500)
Gross Profit	$ 86,667[a]	$ 141,667	$ 251,667	$ 435,000	$ 345,000	$ 278,333
Selling expenses	(65,000)	(90,000)	(150,000)	(250,000)	(120,000)	(40,000)
Net Income before Taxes	$ 21,667	$ 51,667	$ 101,667	$ 185,000	$ 225,000	$ 238,333
Income taxes:						
Current	—	—	(9,778)	(26,091)	(73,009)	(94,902)
Deferred	(7,367)	(17,567)	(24,789)	(36,809)	(3,491)	13,869
Net Income	$ 14,300	$ 34,100	$ 67,100	$ 122,100	$ 148,500	$ 157,300

[a]Land sold under contract in Year 1 had a contract price of $650,000 and estimated contract cost of $390,000 (= $65,000 + $325,000) (see Exhibit 8.12). ALDC incurred development costs of $130,000 (= $65,000 for land + $32,500 on January 1, Year 1 + $32,500 on December 31, Year 1) during Year 1. Thus, the percentage of completion as of the end of Year 1 is 33.3 percent (= $130,000/$390,000). Sales are 33.3 percent of $650,000 and cost of goods sold is 33.3 percent of $390,000.

EXHIBIT 8.22

Arizona Land Development Company
Balance Sheets
Income Recognition Using Percentage-of-Completion Method
(Case 8.2)

	Year 1	Year 2	Year 3	Year 4	Year 5	Year 6
ASSETS						
Cash	$ 100,000	$ 132,500	$ 100,222	$ 126,631	$ 131,122	$ 273,720
Contracts in process	216,667[a]	570,834	1,200,001	2,287,501	3,150,001	3,845,834
Less progress billings	(130,000)[b]	(375,000)	(830,000)	(1,635,000)	(2,430,000)	(3,185,000)
Contracts in process, net	$ 86,667	$ 195,834	$ 370,001	$ 652,501	$ 720,001	$ 660,834
Land inventory	235,000	145,000	95,000	45,000	125,000	185,000
Total Assets	$ 421,667	$ 473,334	$ 565,223	$ 824,132	$ 976,123	$ 1,119,554
LIABILITIES AND SHAREHOLDERS' EQUITY						
Deferred income taxes	$ 7,367	$ 24,934	$ 49,723	$ 86,532	$ 90,023	$ 76,154
Common stock	400,000	400,000	400,000	500,000	500,000	500,000
Retained earnings	14,300	48,400	115,500	237,600	386,100	543,400
Total Liabilities and Shareholders' Equity	$ 421,667	$ 473,334	$ 565,223	$ 824,132	$ 976,123	$ 1,119,554

[a]Accumulated costs of $130,000 + gross profit recognized in Year 1 of $86,667 (see Note (a) to Exhibit 8.21).

[b]Down payment of $65,000 received on January 1, Year 1, plus $65,000 installment payment received on December 31, Year 1.

EXHIBIT 8.23

Arizona Land Development Company
Statements of Cash Flows
Income Recognition Using Percentage-of-Completion Method
(Case 8.2)

	Year 1	Year 2	Year 3	Year 4	Year 5	Year 6
OPERATIONS						
Net income	$ 14,300	$ 34,100	$ 67,100	$ 122,100	$ 148,500	$ 157,300
(Increase) Decrease in contracts in process	(216,667)	(354,167)	(629,167)	(1,087,500)	(862,500)	(695,833)
Increase (Decrease) in progress billings	130,000	245,000	455,000	805,000	795,000	755,000
(Increase) Decrease in land inventory	65,000	90,000	50,000	50,000	(80,000)	(60,000)
Increase (Decrease) in deferred income taxes	7,367	17,567	24,789	36,809	3,491	(13,869)
Cash Flow from Operations	$ 0	$ 32,500	$ (32,278)	$ (73,591)	$ 4,491	$ 142,598
FINANCING						
Common stock issued	—	—	—	100,000	—	—
Change in Cash	$ 0	$ 32,500	$ (32,278)	$ 26,409	$ 4,491	$ 142,598

primarily a developer of real estate and that its income should reflect its development activity, not its sales activity. The difference between the contract price and the total estimated costs of the land and development work represents the total income from development of the land. The percentage-of-completion method uses actual costs incurred to date as a percentage of estimated total costs to determine the degree of completion each period. Multiplying this percentage times the contract price yields sales revenue each year. Multiplying this percentage times the total expected costs yields cost of goods sold.

Required

a. For each of the four income recognition methods illustrated in Exhibits 8.12–8.23, show the supporting calculations for each of the following items for Year 2:
  (1) Sales for Year 2
  (2) Cost of goods sold for Year 2
  (3) Gross profit for Year 2
  (4) Notes Receivable on December 31, Year 2, under the first three income recognition methods and the contracts in process account on December 31, Year 2, under the fourth income recognition method
  (5) Estimated development costs liability on December 31, Year 2, under the first three income recognition methods and the progress billings account on December 31, Year 2, under the fourth income recognition method

b. Evaluate each of the four income recognition methods described in the case relative to the criteria for revenue and expense recognition. Which method best portrays the operating performance and financial position of ALDC? Discuss your reasoning.

c. Which income recognition method is ALDC likely to prefer when reporting to shareholders?

d. Why did ALDC choose the installment method for tax reporting?

e. With respect to maximizing cumulative reported earnings, the four income recognition methods rank-order as follows:
  1. Income Recognition at Time of Sale—No Discounting of Cash Flows
  2. Income Recognition at Time of Sale—With Discounting of Cash Flows
  3. Income Recognition Using the Percentage-of-Completion Method
  4. Income Recognition Using the Installment Method—With Discounting of Cash Flows

  What is the reason behind this rank ordering?

f. The difference in cumulative reported earnings between any two income recognition methods equals the difference in notes receivable or contracts in process (net) minus the difference in the estimated development cost liability minus the difference in the deferred income taxes liability. What is the rationale behind this relation?

g. Why is the amount shown on the income statement for "current" income taxes the same in each year for all four income recognition methods but the amount of total income tax expenses (current plus deferred) in each year is different across income recognition methods?

h. Given that net income each year differs across the four income recognition methods, why is the amount of cash provided by operations the same? Under what conditions would a firm report different amounts of cash flow from operations for different income recognition methods?

CASE 8.3

COCA-COLA PENSIONS

In its December 31, 2008 Consolidated Financial Statements, Cola-Cola reports a substantial shift in its net pension liability ($1,328 million) relative to December 31, 2007 ($85 million).

a. Given a portion of Coca-Cola's Note 16 reconciliations provided below, write a memorandum explaining the change in the net pension liability. (Do not assume that the reader knows what items such as *service cost* mean.)

(amounts in millions)	2008
Benefit obligation at the beginning of the year	$3,517
Service cost	114
Interest cost	205
Foreign currency exchange rate changes	(141)
Amendments	(13)
Actuarial loss (gain)	125
Benefits paid*	(199)
Settlements/curtailments	(4)
Special termination benefits	11
Other	3
Benefit obligation at the end of the year	$3,618
Fair value of plan assets at beginning of year	$3,428
Actual return on plan assets	(961)
Employer contributions	96
Foreign currency exchange rate changes	(118)
Benefits paid*	(155)
Settlements/curtailments	(3)
Other	3
Fair value of plan assets at the end of the year	$2,290

*Some pension plans are "unfunded," meaning that the company does not hire an independent trustee and send the funds to the trustee for investment, but, instead, pays retirees out of company rather than trustee pension fund assets. Coca-Cola paid $44 million out of company assets to retirees who are covered by unfunded plans.

b. For each item in the reconciliation, explain whether the effect on the PBO and the fair value of plan assets is reflected in current period pension expense or as a change in other comprehensive income.

c. Provide a general justification for keeping some PBO and fair value of plan asset changes out of current period net income.

d. In the same note, Coca-Cola indicates that it changed a key assumption during the period. The expected rate of increase in compensation levels was decreased by 1 percent. What effect does this assumption change have on the pension liability (PBO) and current and future pension expense?

Chapter 9

Accounting Quality

Learning Objectives

1. Describe the concept of quality of accounting information, including the attributes of economic content and earnings sustainability.
2. Adjust assessments of profitability and risk and predictions of future earnings for various items that occur infrequently yet can have a large impact on reported financial statements, including gains and losses from discontinued operations, extraordinary gains and losses, changes in accounting principles, other comprehensive income items, impairment losses, restructuring charges, changes in estimates, and gains and losses from peripheral activities.
3. Analyze restated financial statements and account classification differences.
4. Define earnings management and be aware of the conditions under which managers might be likely to engage in earnings management.

Chapters 4 and 5 provide a framework and tools for analyzing the profitability and risk of a firm using financial statement data. The presumption in using reported financial statement data is that they accurately portray the economic effects of a firm's decisions and actions during the current period, appropriately characterize the firm's financial position at the end of the period, and are informative about the firm's likely future profitability and risk. The last part of Chapter 5 introduced the Beneish model of financial reporting manipulation risk, indicating that the overall ability of the financial statements to be useful in identifying other risks is contingent on the financial statements being representationally faithful. Thus, to make insightful decisions about profitability and risk based on relations among accounting data (such as ratios and time-series trends), we must assess whether the unadjusted, reported data are the appropriate inputs in the profitability and risk measures used. Chapters 6–8 provide the in-depth understanding of accounting methods and principles that is necessary for assessing accounting quality.

This chapter continues discussion of the concept of accounting quality as it relates to analyzing a firm's profitability and risk and forecasting its future financial statements by illustrating financial reporting for a wide array of items (primarily income statement-related) that typically occur infrequently yet can have a large impact on the financial statements. After providing a general discussion of accounting quality, we discuss reporting for discontinued operations, extraordinary gains and losses, changes in accounting principles, other comprehensive income items, impairment losses, restructuring charges, changes in estimates, and gains and losses from peripheral activities. The important objectives in analyzing these items are to assess (1) their economic effect on the current period's performance and (2) the likelihood that they will persist in the future. Thus, this chapter serves as a bridge between the accounting focus in Chapters 6–8 and the forecasting and valuation focus in Chapters 10–14. This chapter also discusses additional accounting and reporting items and events that may require adjustment, including retroactively restated financial statements and account classification differences.

The chapter concludes with a discussion of the definition of earnings management and the conditions that might provide incentives for managers to manipulate financial statements. Chapter 5 defines earnings manipulation and fraud as the reporting of accounting data outside the limits of U.S. GAAP or IFRS. This chapter discusses earnings management within the limits of U.S. GAAP or IFRS. The goal is to be aware of managers' incentives and disincentives for earnings management so that you can assess the likelihood of earnings management and adjust your due diligence accordingly.

ACCOUNTING QUALITY

Numerous financial reporting abuses by companies such as HealthSouth, AIG, Adelphia, Enron, WorldCom, Parmalat, Ahold, Satayam, and Global Crossing have raised questions about the quality of accounting information. Terms such as *earnings quality* and, less frequently, *balance sheet quality* appear in the financial press. However, these terms often are not defined and are used loosely to capture a myriad of reporting and accountability concerns. Although accounting quality has many dimensions, the commonality in the aforementioned (and many other) financial abuses is that accounting was used to misrepresent a firm's underlying economics and earnings potential. Further, even correctly applied accounting rules may, on occasion, fail to indicate future earnings potential. Accordingly, we focus on the following two accounting quality issues that are central to analysis and valuation:

- Accounting information should be a fair and complete representation of the firm's economic performance, financial position, and risk.
- Accounting information should provide relevant information to forecast the firm's expected future earnings and cash flows.

We intend that our notion of *accounting quality* encompass the economic information content of the income statement, the balance sheet, the statement of cash flows, notes to the financial statements, and MD&A (management's discussion and analysis). We define accounting quality broadly because each of these elements of the financial statements integrates and articulates with the others; thus, a firm's accounting quality depends on the quality of all of these elements. We intend to analyze broadly the firm's accounting quality so that our analysis can fully inform our assessment of the firm's reported financial position, performance, and risk.

Our view of accounting quality is broader than, and should not be confused with, accounting conservatism, which is sometimes construed as an attribute of reporting quality. Conservative accounting numbers in their own right are not high quality for purposes of financial statement analysis and valuation, but conservatism is a prudent response by accountants and managers when faced with uncertainty in measuring the economic effects of transactions, events, and commercial arrangements.

In the two sections that follow, we explore these two elements more fully.

High Quality Reflects Economic Information Content

Conceptually, accounting numbers contain three elements:

- A reflection of economics
- Measurement error (or noise)
- Bias

High quality accounting information portrays fairly and completely the economic effects of a firm's decisions and actions. High quality accounting information paints an accurate economic portrait of the firm's financial position, performance, and risk. That is, quality accounting information minimizes measurement error and bias. Measurement errors occur when managers, in good faith, make estimates that turn out not to be true. Good faith, well-informed estimates yield small errors in directions that are not predictable. The errors will cancel out over time and across the many estimates that managers must make in a given year, yielding high-quality accounting numbers. Bias occurs when managers apply biased accounting standards (for example, standards that require asset write-downs and do not permit asset write-ups) and when managers take advantage of the discretion and flexibility in the estimation process to (most commonly) inject optimism into accounting numbers. The discussion in the last part of this chapter identifies the incentives and disincentives to inject optimistic or pessimistic bias in accounting numbers to manage earnings. Neutral application of accounting standards to reduce bias yields high-quality accounting numbers.[1]

A high-quality balance sheet portrays the economic resources that can be reasonably expected to generate future economic benefits (and the claims on those resources) at a point in time. The assets on the balance sheet should reflect resources that the firm controls—cash and investment securities, collectible receivables, sellable inventory, productive plant and equipment, intangible rights—and that the firm expects to use to generate future economic benefits. If measurement of the expected future economic benefits is highly uncertain [as in the case of the benefits from certain R&D (research and development), advertising, or brand management expenditures] or is outside the firm's control (for example, human capital) or if the expected future economic benefits have expired, a high-quality balance sheet should exclude these items.

A high-quality balance sheet also provides a complete and fair portrayal of all of the firm's obligations at a point in time, including the present value of long-term liabilities for future payments (for example, for pensions, leases, and other commitments). High quality also requires proper classification of short and long term so that users know when assets will be realized and obligations will be met. Shareholders' equity on a high-quality balance sheet represents the net asset position of the firm at that point in time—the residual value of the assets of the firm after the obligations of the firm have been deducted. High-quality shareholders' equity informs users of the sources of contributed equity capital, the earnings reinvested in the firm, and the dividends paid to investors.

A high-quality income statement completely and fairly summarizes the firm's income or loss from operations as well as any other gains or losses from other transactions or events during a period. A high-quality income statement includes all revenues the firm earned during the period and can reasonably expect to collect. A high-quality income statement includes the costs of all resources consumed, including resources consumed in the production process to generate revenues (that is, costs directly related to revenues, such as cost of sales), as well as resources consumed during the period as a function of time that indirectly relate to revenues (such as fixed administrative costs and interest expenses). A high-quality

[1] Some level of bias (for example, conservative accounting standards) may be preferred by creditors.

income statement also includes the effects of any gains or losses from other transactions and events of that period. Accounting quality is low if net income includes revenues the firm did not earn during the period or may not be able to collect, if it fails to include expenses or losses of the period, if it includes expenses or losses that are attributable to other periods, or if it misclassifies or disguises key income items.

A high-quality statement of cash flows summarizes the cash flow implications of the firm's performance and changes in the firm's financial position over a period of time. All non-cash exchanges appear in the notes and are not reported in the statement of cash flows. A high-quality statement of cash flows appropriately classifies cash flows into operating, investing, and financing activities in sufficient detail for the analyst to understand why cash flows change each period.

Notes to the financial statements provide additional information that enhances the users' understanding of the accounting methods used and the judgments and estimates the firm's managers made in measuring and reporting accounting amounts and changes in those amounts. In the MD&A section of the annual report and in Form 10-K, managers enhance these disclosures with qualitative discussions of operations and risks. (See Appendix B for PepsiCo's MD&A discussions of key assumptions; critical accounting policies, risks, liquidity, and capital resources; and estimates made by the firm.) High-quality notes should provide a useful quantitative disaggregation and explanation of financial statement amounts, and high-quality MD&A discussions should provide an in-depth qualitative and unbiased context to the quantitative data reported in the financial statements.

Accounting standard setters establish principles to provide firms with guidance and rules for measuring the economic effects of firms' activities, performance, and financial position. Standard setters also establish principles to provide auditors with a common basis for auditing the fairness of firms' reporting and to provide users of financial statements with a comparable and understandable set of principles for firms' accounting. Standard setters recognize, however, that measuring the economic effects of firms' activities, performance, and financial position often requires judgment, estimation, and subjectivity. Managers must estimate, for example, the rate at which a long-lived asset such as a building or machine loses service potential, the point when a particular customer's account becomes uncollectible, and the point when a firm has earned revenues. While the degree of subjectivity in measuring economic effects increases, also increasing is the potential for firms to report accounting information that includes unintentional measurement error or intentional bias to portray the firm in a light most favorable to the firm or its managers. Standard setters often react to this potential for intentional bias or unintentional estimation error when establishing principles by making trade-offs between accurately reflecting economic reality and obtaining reliable accounting information. Thus, quality accounting information maximizes relevance and economic faithfulness, which are subject to the constraints of the reliability of the measurements.

Standard setters recognize that a single accounting method may not portray the economic effects of a particular transaction for all firms. Firms' choices and estimates within U.S. GAAP or IFRS should be determined by firms' underlying economic circumstances, including conditions in their industry, competitive strategy, and technology.

For example, firms use up the services of buildings and equipment at different rates over time, so accounting standards allow firms to estimate useful lives and select either straight-line or accelerated depreciation methods. Similarly, some firms structure leasing arrangements so that the lessor bears most of the economic risk in some cases (such as very short-term leases), whereas the lessee bears most of the economic risk in other cases (such as leases that extend for most of an asset's useful life). As discussed in Chapter 6, U.S. GAAP and IFRS allow two methods of accounting for leases—the operating lease method and the capital lease method—to reflect differences in the economics of these leasing arrangements.

Thus, to obtain quality accounting information, firms should select the accounting principles that best portray the economics of their activities from the set permitted.

Even when firms select the accounting principles or methods that best portray the economics of their activities, firms still must make estimates in applying those accounting principles. Virtually all accounting amounts require some degree of estimation. For example, firms must estimate the period of time during which buildings and equipment will provide benefits. Firms must estimate the amount of cash they will ultimately receive from customers for credit sales. Similarly, firms must estimate the expected future cost of warranty plans on products sold during the period. Firms also must estimate fair values of financial instruments and derivatives for financial statement reporting or note disclosures. Firms also must estimate and project expected returns, employee longevity, and future salary levels to estimate pension assets and liabilities. Thus, obtaining quality accounting information requires firms' judgments and estimates in applying U.S. GAAP or IFRS.

Given that firms have discretion in choosing their accounting principles in some cases and must make estimates in applying those accounting principles in most cases, firms should disclose sufficient information in the financial statements and notes to permit users to assess the economic appropriateness of those choices. Thus, informative disclosures are an essential element of quality accounting information.

Finally, in some cases, standard setters have removed accounting method choice and have created a situation where certain accounting principles do not faithfully portray underlying circumstances for all firms all of the time. For example, PepsiCo cannot recognize its valuable brand name as an asset because GAAP views internally-developed intangible assets as very difficult to value reliably in the absence of a market-based, arms-length transaction. Microsoft and Eli Lilly rely heavily on investments made in R&D and have proven technologies, patents, and intellectual property that can be traced to R&D expenditures. Yet because GAAP is concerned about the lack of reliable measurements for such assets, these companies cannot capitalize these resources that are critical to their economic position and performance.

In summary, users of financial statements should consider the following when evaluating the quality of accounting information:

- Economic faithfulness of accounting measurements and classifications
- Reliability of the measurements
- When accounting choices exist in U.S. GAAP or IFRS, how the firm's choices fit its activities
- Reasonableness of the estimates made in applying GAAP or IFRS
- Adequacy of disclosures and credibility of qualitative discussions
- When accounting choices do not exist in U.S. GAAP or IFRS, how the rules fit the firm's underlying economic conditions

The analyst may conclude that the reported financial statements for a particular firm fall short on accounting quality. In these cases, the analyst might adjust reported amounts to enhance the accounting quality before using them to assess operating performance, financial position, or risk. For example, the analyst might judge that an accelerated depreciation method more accurately reflects the economic decline in service potential of a building or machine. Converting the reported amounts from straight-line to accelerated depreciation enhances accounting quality. Alternatively, the analyst might judge that a bad debt provision of 3 percent of sales (instead of a 2 percent rate used by the firm) more accurately reflects the likely uncollectible accounts. Chapters 6–8 discuss accounting choices and estimates firms must make in applying them; those chapters also discuss the types of adjustments the analyst might make to reported amounts to enhance the quality of accounting information.

The analyst can then use the adjusted financial statement amounts for the current period to evaluate the firm's managers, to measure profitability, to assess risk, and to test for earnings management or fraud. The analyst also can use the adjusted financial statement amounts to evaluate a second element of quality accounting information: persistence of earnings over time.

High Quality Leads to Earnings Persistence over Time

As Chapters 10–14 illustrate, firm value depends on predictions of future payoffs to investors: dividends, free cash flows, or earnings. Therefore, a key quality of financial accounting information is the extent to which it currently captures conditions that will persist into the future versus conditions that are transitory. When using financial statements to value a firm, the analyst should ask this question: What do the reported or restated amounts for the current period suggest about the long-run persistence of income and therefore the economic value of a firm? This question points out the importance of judging the economic content of current period earnings in order to assess historical earnings persistence and to project future earnings persistence.

Quality accounting information should be informative about the economic value implications of the current period's earnings and about the long-run sustainability of profits. For accounting to be deemed of high quality, both components—fair and complete representation of current economic performance and information about expected future earnings and cash flows—are necessary. Consider the following four possibilities:

1. *Earnings could be very informative about current performance and tell you that current performance is sustainable.* This constitutes high quality on both dimensions (for example, a big jump in sales and earnings this period because of new products that will continue to be successful for a long time).
2. *Earnings could be very informative about current performance and tell you that the current level of earnings performance is not sustainable.* Again, this constitutes high quality on both dimensions. For example, the firm realizes an unexpected gain (or loss) this year but clearly classifies and reports it as nonrecurring; there is no ambiguity because the gain is informative in that it will not likely affect future earnings.
3. *Earnings could be informative about current performance but not informative (that is, does not reduce uncertainty) about the future.* In this case, we have high current period information quality but low information quality for the future. For example, a firm experiences a sudden drop in cost of goods sold due to an unexpected reduction in the cost of raw materials inventory. The cost of goods sold measure is relevant and reliable for the current period performance, but this year's greater income does not help the analyst forecast whether the raw material price decrease is relatively permanent and thus whether earnings are sustainable.
4. *Earnings are not informative about current period performance but are informative about sustainability of future earnings.* Here we have low current period information quality but high information quality for the long run. For example, earnings this period include expenses for pre-opening costs for new stores; the new stores are operational and are expected to be profitable in the future.

Chapters 1, 4, 5, and 11 describe the value of an equity security as a function of the returns expected from investing in the equity security relative to the level of risk. Chapters 10–14 discuss and illustrate how the analyst forecasts future financial statement amounts and uses them to derive appropriate equity values. Our concern in this section is with understanding the different signals that quality accounting information might provide about equity values. To link our discussion about current period earnings and expected future earnings to the value implications of earnings, consider the following four scenarios. In each case, we assume that the analyst has adjusted or restated reported earnings amounts to achieve the desired level of economic information content about current period and future period performance as discussed in the previous section.

Scenario 1: Earnings for the current period are high-quality, are in line with previous expectations, and do not suggest any changes in expected future earnings. The analyst should not expect to observe a change in the market price of the equity securities. Market prices likely already reflect the expected earnings levels. Earnings are informative in the sense that they signal the market that its prior expectations have been met and there are no surprises that trigger a change in expectations for the future.

Scenario 2: Earnings for the current period differ from expectations, and the new earnings level is expected to persist. A firm may have introduced a successful new product during the period, and the market had not fully anticipated the success of the new product in pricing the equity security. The new product should enhance earnings for a number of years in the future. The market price of the security should increase for the realized additional earnings of the current period and for the present value of the expected additional earnings in the future. Earnings are informative if they signal the portion of the current period's earnings due to the new product and the additional earnings in the future as a result of the persistence of this new earnings stream.

Consider a second example. A firm unexpectedly loses a patent infringement lawsuit. As a consequence, the firm is enjoined from selling a key line of products that generate substantial profits for the firm and is required to pay immediate damages. The market value of the firm's equity securities should decline as a result of the damages paid. In addition, the level of expected earnings for the future will decline relative to those previously anticipated, which means that the market value of the firm's equity securities also should decline to reflect the present value of the lower expected future profits. Earnings are informative if they signal the amount of the immediate economic loss and the persistent negative effect on future earnings.

Scenario 3: Earnings for the current period differ from expectations, but expected future earnings do not change. Because a local government corrects a processing error, a firm receives an unexpected rebate on property taxes previously paid. The market value of the firm's equity securities should increase as a result of the rebate. Because expected future earnings do not change, there should be no further market price reaction for the equity securities. Earnings are informative if they disclose the amount of the rebate and signal its one-time nature.

Scenario 4: Earnings for the current period do not differ from expectations, but expected future earnings do change. At the end of the current period, a manufacturing firm replaces a piece of equipment with a new piece of equipment that has an identical cost but is more efficient. The new piece of equipment adds to the firm's productive capacity and will reduce manufacturing costs, increasing expected earnings for future periods. The acquisition of the equipment should not materially affect the market value of the firm's equity securities; however, the market value should increase for the present value of the higher expected future earnings. Earnings are informative if they disclose sufficient information for the analyst to forecast the increase in expected future earnings.

SPECIFIC EVENTS AND CONDITIONS THAT AFFECT EARNINGS QUALITY

The remainder of this chapter addresses specific events and conditions that, although infrequent, affect earnings quality, especially as it relates to earnings persistence. The topics discussed are as follows:

- Discontinued operations
- Extraordinary gains and losses

- Changes in accounting principles
- Other comprehensive income items
- Impairment losses on long-lived assets
- Restructuring and other charges
- Changes in estimates
- Gains and losses from peripheral activities

Exhibit 9.1 presents a hypothetical income statement that shows the reporting of the special items if they receive separate line-item treatment in the income statement. (Changes in accounting principles receive separate line-item treatment prior to 2006; changes in accounting estimates do not receive separate line-item treatment.)

Discontinued Operations

When a firm decides to exit a particular component of its business, it classifies that business as a discontinued operation. This classification provides analysts and other financial statements users with information to distinguish the effects of continuing versus discontinuing operations on current period performance and provides a basis for forecasting future income from the continuing operations of the firm. U.S. GAAP stipulates that a discontinued business is either a separable business or a component of the firm with clearly

EXHIBIT 9.1

Statement of Comprehensive Income for a Hypothetical Company

Sales revenue	X
Cost of goods sold	(X)
Selling and administrative expenses	(X)
Operating Income	X
Gains (losses) from peripheral activities	(X)
Restructuring charges	(X)
Impairment losses	(X)
Interest income	X
Interest expense	(X)
Income before Income Taxes	X
Income tax expense	(X)
Income from Continuing Operations	X
Income from discontinued operations, net of taxes	X
Extraordinary gains (losses), net of taxes	(X)
Changes in accounting principles, net of taxes (pre-2006)	X
Net Income	X
Other comprehensive income items, net of taxes	X
Comprehensive Income	X

distinguishable operations and cash flows.[2] The degree to which a particular divested component operationally integrates with ongoing businesses is likely to vary across firms depending on their organizational structures and operating policies. Thus, the gain or loss from the sale of a business might appear in income from continuing operations for one firm (that is, the divested business is operationally integrated) and in discontinued operations for another firm (that is, the divested business is not operationally integrated).

IFRS rules are more restrictive as to what constitutes a discontinued operation.[3] Only disposals of a major line of business or geographic area qualify. For example, if a restaurant chain with a total of 20 restaurants sold three underperforming restaurants with independent cash flows and the chain had no continuing involvement in the operations of the sold restaurants (for example, through franchising agreements), the sale would qualify as a discontinued operation under U.S. GAAP but not under IFRS.[4]

A firm reports the net income or loss from operating the discontinued business between the beginning of the reporting period and the disposal date as a separate item in the discontinued operations section of the income statement (net of tax effects). Firms also report the gain or loss on disposal (net of tax effects) in this same section of the income statement, often labeled "Income, Gains, and Losses from Discontinued Operations." Most U.S. firms include three years of income statement information in their income statements. A firm that decides to divest a business during the current year includes the net income or loss of this business in discontinued operations for the current year and in comparative income statements for the preceding two years even though the firm had previously reported the latter income in continuing operations in the income statements originally prepared for those two years. If final sale has not occurred as of the end of the period, the remaining assets held for sale are assessed for impairment and an impairment loss (net of tax) is included as part of the discontinued operations disclosure. The assets and liabilities of the discontinued operations are isolated and receive separate disclosure on the balance sheet or in notes that support the balance sheet.

Example 1

On August 14, 1997, PepsiCo announced that it would spin off its restaurant businesses (which included Pizza Hut, Taco Bell, and KFC), forming a new restaurant company named TRICON Global Restaurants, Inc. (now known as Yum! Brands, Inc.). For 1997, PepsiCo reported income from continuing operations separately from discontinued operations. In that year, PepsiCo reported a total of $1,491 million of income (net of tax) from continuing operations and $651 million of income (net of tax) associated with the discontinued restaurants segment.

Example 2

Bowne & Co. is one of the largest printers of financial documents in the United States, specializing in the creation and distribution of regulatory and compliance documents. Bowne prints and distributes Form 10-K filings and proxy reports to shareholders, as well as a wide range of other compliance filings required of U.S. firms. During 2004, Bowne decided to sell its document-related outsourcing business to Williams Lea, Inc., to focus on its core

---

[2] The most recent U.S. GAAP ruling on discontinued operations, Financial Accounting Standards Board, *Statement of Financial Accounting Standards No. 144,* "Accounting for the Impairment or Disposal of Long-Lived Assets" (2001), maintained the basic provisions of Accounting Principles Board, *Opinion No. 30,* "Reporting the Results of Operations" (1973) for presenting discontinued operations, but broadened the presentation to include more disposal transactions. *FASB Codification Topic 360.*

[3] International Accounting Standards Board, *International Financial Reporting Standard 5,* "Noncurrent Assets Held for Sale and Discontinued Operations" (2004).

[4] The FASB and IASB are in the process of converging discontinued operations treatment, probably closer to current IFRS standards, as of the writing of this text.

competency of creation and distribution of regulatory documents. Exhibit 9.2 presents selected data from the financial statements related to discontinued operations.

Note that Bowne presents the income from operating the discontinued businesses separately from the gain on disposal, each net of tax effects. The magnitude of discontinued operations in 2004, net of tax, transforms a small loss from continuing operations into a modest positive net income. Bowne reports the amount of assets and liabilities related to discontinued operations on its balance sheet each year.

When assessing Bowne's sustainable profitability, one should exclude income from discontinued operations from the numerator of the return on assets ratio and exclude the related assets from the denominator as well.

Exhibit 9.2 indicates that Bowne eliminated the effect of discontinued operations from the calculation of cash flow from operations and classified all of the cash flows related to discontinued operations in a separate section of the statement of cash flows after financing activities. Because cash flow from operations contains no amounts related to discontinued operations, the analyst can use it when computing cash flow ratios (for example, cash flow from operations to average current liabilities) without making additional adjustments. If the firm had not excluded the cash flow effects of discontinued operations from cash flow from operations, the analyst should do so.

For some firms that regularly pursue a strategy to acquire firms and subsequently sell them, income from discontinued operations is an ongoing source of profitability, and the analyst might decide to include this income in forecasts of future earnings. For most firms, however, income from discontinued operations represents a source of earnings that does not persist.

Thus, in most cases, the analyst should exclude income from discontinued operations from forecasts of future earnings, focusing instead on income from continuing operations. Exclusion of discontinued operations when predicting Bowne's future profitability (2005 and beyond) makes sense because Bowne reports only one discontinued operation in the 2002–2004 income statements. However, if one examines Bowne income statements after the fact (2005–2008), evidence of persistent discontinued operations exists. Bowne reports net losses from further discontinued operations in 2005, 2006, and 2007 and a gain from discontinued operations in 2008. These losses are $754,000 in 2005 (more than 500 percent of a small income from continuing operations, which causes a net loss to be reported); $14,004,000 in 2006 (114 percent of a modest income from continuing operations, which causes a small net loss to be reported); $223,000 in 2007 (less than 1 percent of a large positive income from continuing operations); and $5,719 in 2008 (almost 20 percent of a loss from continuing operations). Given Bowne's recent history of discontinued operations, the analyst should reassess Bowne's strategy of acquisitions and divestitures to predict future net income.[5]

Extraordinary Gains and Losses

The income statement can include extraordinary gains and losses. To be classified as extraordinary, an income item must meet all three of the following criteria:[6]

- Unusual in nature
- Infrequent in occurrence
- Material in amount

---

[5] PepsiCo does not report discontinued items in any of the last seven years.

[6] Financial Accounting Standards Board, *Statement of Financial Accounting Standards No. 144,* "Accounting for the Impairment or Disposal of Long-Lived Assets" (2001); Accounting Principles Board, *Opinion No. 30,* "Reporting the Results of Operations" (1973). *FASB Codification Topic 225.*

EXHIBIT 9.2

Bowne & Co. Selected Information Related to Discontinued Operations
(amounts in thousands)

Year Ended December 31:	2004	2003
INCOME STATEMENT		
Revenue	$899,011	$847,636
Expenses:		
Cost of revenue	(574,264)	(536,166)
Selling and administrative	(266,034)	(247,977)
Depreciation	(32,121)	(35,466)
Amortization	(2,713)	(2,478)
Gain on sale of building	896	—
Restructuring, integration, and asset impairment charges	(14,644)	(23,076)
Operating (Loss) Income	$ 10,131	$ 2,473
Interest expense	(10,709)	(11,389)
Loss on extinguishment of debt	(8,815)	—
Other expense, net	(118)	(1,367)
Loss from Continuing Operations before Income Taxes	$ (9,511)	$(10,283)
Income tax benefit (expense)	1,313	729
Loss from Continuing Operations	$ (8,198)	$ (9,554)
Discontinued Operations:		
Income from discontinued operations, net of tax	$ 4,150	$ 1,805
Gain on sale of discontinued operations, net of tax	31,552	—
Net Income from Discontinued Operations	$ 35,702	$ 1,805
Net Income (Loss)	$ 27,504	$ (7,749)
CONDENSED CONSOLIDATED BALANCE SHEETS		
Assets held for sale, noncurrent	—	$106,898
Other assets (details not provided)	—	620,927
Total Assets	$648,811	$727,825
Liabilities held for sale, noncurrent	—	$ 3,882
Other liabilities and shareholders' equity	—	723,943
Total Liabilities and Shareholders' Equity	$648,811	$727,825
CONDENSED CONSOLIDATED STATEMENTS OF CASH FLOWS		
Cash Flows from Operating Activities:		
Loss from continuing operations	$ (8,198)	$ (9,554)
Depreciation and amortization	34,834	37,944
Asset impairment charges	518	2,198
Gain on sale of building	(896)	—
Loss on extinguishment of debt	8,815	—
Changes in other assets and liabilities, net of non-cash transactions	(2,404)	(10,339)
Net Cash Provided by Operating Activities	$ 32,669	$ 20,249
Cash Flows from Investing Activities (details omitted)	148,200	(21,117)
Cash Used in Financing Activities (details omitted)	(97,784)	(10,872)
Net Cash Used in Discontinued Operations	(20,123)	(4,131)
Net increase (decrease) in cash and cash equivalents	$ 62,962	$(15,871)
Cash and cash equivalents—Beginning of period	17,010	32,881
Cash and cash equivalents—End of period	$ 79,972	$ 17,010

A firm applies these criteria in the context of its own operations and to similar firms in the same industry, taking into consideration the environment in which the entities operate. Thus, an item might be extraordinary for some firms but not for others. Income items that meet all three of these criteria are rarely found in corporate annual reports in the United States.

Example 3

DIMON Inc. was an international dealer of leaf tobacco, with operations in more than 30 countries. Headquartered in Virginia, its major customers included the U.S. cigarette manufacturers. In 2003, DIMON recognized an extraordinary gain of $1.7 million resulting from a claim resolution with the United Nations Compensation Commission. The claim was based on an uncollected trade receivable due from the Iraqi Tobacco Monopoly, generated from transactions that took place with the organization prior to the Iraqi/Kuwait war of 1991.

The income statement for the company reveals the following (amounts in thousands):

	2003
Earnings from Continuing Operations before Extraordinary Items	$26,280
Gain on Settlement of Lawsuit (net of $957 in income taxes)	1,777
Net Earnings	$28,057
Basic Earnings per Share:	
Continuing Operations	$ 0.59
Gain from Lawsuit	0.04
Basic Earnings per Share	$ 0.63

The question for the analyst is whether to include or exclude extraordinary gains and losses in current period earnings when using current earnings to forecast expected future earnings.[7] The response depends on the persistence of these gains and losses for a particular firm. By definition, the analyst can assume that they are infrequent in occurrence and in most cases will exclude them from forecasts of future profitability, focusing instead on income from continuing operations. As with discontinued operations, the income statement reports the amounts net of any tax effects.

In the case of DIMON, the analyst probably should not consider the extraordinary gain on the UN settlement as an ongoing source of earnings because 2003 is the only year in the last three years that DIMON reported such a gain or loss. Furthermore, the claim settlement relates to an event that occurred more than ten years earlier than the period in which the gain is reported.

DIMON includes the cash provided by the settlement in cash flow from operations in the statement of cash flows (not reported here). Consistent with excluding this extraordinary gain from earnings when using it to assess future profitability, the analyst should exclude the cash provided by the settlement when forecasting future cash flow from ongoing operations. However, eliminating the amount from the statement of cash flows entirely results in the change in cash on the cash flow statement not reconciling with the change in cash on the balance sheet. This would be inappropriate. If the company has not done so, as is the case with DIMON, the analyst might create a separate section of operating cash flows for unusual or extraordinary items and reclassify the cash provided by the settlement there. This was the approach that Bowne followed with respect to its discontinued operations in

[7] Note that for DIMON, regardless of the decision to adjust for the extraordinary gain for assessing persistent earnings, the gain has real economic content for 2003. That is, the gain positively affects current period performance, regardless of whether it recurs.

Example 2 (Exhibit 9.2). When calculating financial ratios that use cash flow from operations, the analyst should use cash flow from ongoing operations only.

In 2005, DIMON, Inc., merged with another world leader in tobacco processing, Standard Commercial Corporation, to form Alliance One International. Examination of the consolidated financial statements of Alliance One through its 2009 fiscal year-end indicates no additional extraordinary item disclosures, lending support to the idea that such items are nonrecurring.

Extraordinary item treatment is indeed rare. Losses from the events of September 11 and Hurricane Katrina were not considered extraordinary. In the case of the September 11 events, standard setters believe that a reliable separation of event-related losses and non-event losses was not possible and thus prohibited extraordinary item treatment. Katrina was not considered to be unusual in nature and infrequent in occurrence given that hurricanes occur regularly in the Gulf Coast region. However, extraordinary items are still reported occasionally. The Mount St. Helens eruption (first eruption in 130 years) was considered extraordinary. Verizon Communications Inc. reported a 2007 extraordinary item for Venezuela's nationalization of one of its unconsolidated affiliates.

Firms reporting under IFRS isolate and describe material, unusual items. However, IFRS does not allow the term *extraordinary* to appear on the face of or in the notes to the financial statements.[8]

Changes in Accounting Principles

For various reasons, firms occasionally change the accounting principles used to generate the financial statements. Sometimes standard setters mandate the changes, while in other cases, firms voluntarily change from one acceptable principle to another. Until recently, U.S. GAAP required firms to recognize the cumulative effect of changing to an alternative accounting principle on net income of the period of the change. The firm reported this cumulative difference (net of taxes) in a separate section of the income statement.[9] Reporting the effects of the change in accounting method in the income statement raised the visibility of the change and increased the likelihood that statement users would not overlook it. However, this reporting resulted in amounts for net income that did not provide sufficient information for forecasting future earnings. Under this cumulative reporting approach, net income of periods prior to the current period was not formally restated to reflect the new method (although pro forma disclosures of the effect on earnings were required when practicable). Also, net income of the current period included the cumulative effect of the change even though it applied to prior periods.

Beginning in 2006, firms following U.S. GAAP must generally report amounts for the current and prior years as if the new accounting principle had been applied all along (termed *retrospective treatment*). The rationale for this reporting is that it results in net income amounts for the current and prior periods measured using the same accounting principles the firm intends to use in future periods, thereby enhancing the information content of reported earnings in forecasting future earnings. This new standard brought U.S. GAAP in line with IFRS.[10]

---

[8] International Accounting Standards Board, *International Accounting Standard 1*, "Presentation of Financial Statements" (revised 2003).

[9] Accounting Principles Board, *Opinion No. 20*, "Accounting Changes" (1971).

[10] Financial Accounting Standards Board, *Statement of Financial Accounting Standards No. 154*, "Accounting Changes and Error Corrections—A Replacement of APB Opinion No. 20 and FASB Statement No. 3" (2005); *FASB Codification Topic 250*; International Accounting Standards Board, *International Accounting Standard 8*, "Accounting Policies, Change in Accounting Estimates, and Errors" (revised 2003).

Firms need not restate prior-year earnings retrospectively if it is impracticable to determine the period-specific effects of the change or the cumulative effect of the change. In this case, firms must apply the new accounting policy to the balances of assets and liabilities as of the earliest period for which retrospective application is practicable and to make a corresponding adjustment to retained earnings for that period. When it is impracticable for an entity to determine the cumulative effect of applying a change in accounting principle to *all* prior periods to which it relates, firms must apply the new accounting principle as if it were made prospectively from the start of the year of the change.

For example, if a firm switches from the FIFO cost-flow assumption to the LIFO cost-flow assumption for inventories and cost of goods sold, typically it is impracticable to reconstruct the effects of the accounting change on prior years. In this case, the change to the LIFO cost-flow assumption will be applied prospectively (that is, in current and future years) at the start of the year in which the accounting change takes place.

Note that firms following U.S. GAAP will continue to report on their income statements any cumulative effect of accounting changes that occurred before 2006. In other words, some firms will report on their income statements the cumulative effect of changes in accounting principles because the changes were made in years prior to the effective date of Statement No. 154. The following example illustrates both the old and new reporting of accounting changes.

Example 4

Occidental Petroleum Corporation operates in two industry segments. The oil and gas segment explores for, produces, and markets crude oil and natural gas. The chemical segment manufactures and markets basic chemicals, vinyls, and performance chemicals. Both segments require large capital expenditures on property, plant, and equipment to support their operations. Related to these expenditures, Occidental recognizes a liability for any costs it might have to occur to retire the assets, such as costs to dismantle assets or remediate properties at the end of their useful lives.[11]

In its Form 10-K filing for 2003, Occidental states: "The initial adoption of SFAS No. 143 on January 1, 2003 resulted in an after-tax charge of $50 million, which was recorded as a cumulative effect of a change in accounting principles." Occidental discloses the pro forma effects of the accounting change on previously reported income, indicating that net income for 2002 would have been reduced by approximately $21 million, net of tax, and net income for 2001 would have been reduced by approximately $29 million, net of tax.

The top portion of Exhibit 9.3 illustrates how the change to the new accounting principle required by Statement No. 143 was reported by Occidental Petroleum following the cumulative-effect technique prescribed by Opinion No. 20. The bottom portion of the exhibit illustrates how the firm would have reported the accounting change if the retrospective technique had been applied as required currently under Statement No. 154. Note that Statement No. 154 would require an adjustment to income from continuing operations and retained earnings for each year the effect of the change is known. In addition, Occidental would apply the accounting change to the balances of assets and liabilities of each year the effect of the change is known (not reported in Exhibit 9.3). Retained earnings as of the end of 2003 is the same under both approaches because at that point, the total effect of the change has been captured in income.

The FASB continues to issue new reporting standards, and in most cases, the accounting change will be reported retrospectively, which enhances comparability across reporting

[11] Financial Accounting Standards Board, *Statement of Financial Accounting Standards No. 143*, "Accounting for Asset Retirement Obligations" (2001); *FASB Codification Topic 410*. See Chapter 7 for a discussion of these asset retirement obligations.

EXHIBIT 9.3

Occidental Petroleum Company
Reporting Approaches: Opinion No. 20 and Statement No. 154
(amounts in millions)

	2003	2002	2001
Opinion No. 20 Approach			
Income from Continuing Operations	$1,595.0	$1,163.0	$1,179.0
Cumulative Effect of Change in Accounting Principle:			
Adoption of Statement No. 143	(50.0)		
Income from Continuing Operations after Accounting Change	$1,545.0	$1,163.0	$1,179.0
Retained Earnings, beginning of year	$2,303.0	$1,788.0	$1,007.0
Retained Earnings, end of year	$3,530.0	$2,303.0	$1,788.0
Statement No. 154 Approach			
Pro Forma Restatement of:			
Income from Continuing Operations	$1,595.0	$1,142.0	$1,150.0
Retained Earnings, beginning of year	$2,253.0	$1,759.0	$1,007.0
Retained Earnings, end of year	$3,530.0	$2,253.0	$1,759.0

periods. In its 2008 10-K, Occidental lists all of the new FASB standards issued since 2005 (there are many), describes the basic accounting issue addressed in each new standard, and states that the standards have no material impact on its financial statements. A review of financial statement disclosures for Occidental confirms the absence of material adjustments.

Example 5

In its Note 7, "Pension, Retiree Medical and Savings Plans," to its 2008 Consolidated Financial Statements (see Appendix A), PepsiCo reports a retrospective adjustment to its owners' equity of $39 million, representing the amount by which application of the measurement date provisions of SFAS 158 reduced its shareholders' equity, net of tax. Under SFAS 158, PepsiCo had to change the date when its actuaries determined their assumptions used to measure pension and other postemployment obligations and assets to coincide with the balance sheet date. The financial statement effects of a sudden remeasurement of assets and liabilities might have appeared as a cumulative adjustment in the income statement of the current year under old accounting standards, but under the preferred retrospective treatment of new accounting standards, the cumulative net asset adjustment (net of tax) of the remeasurement is reflected in beginning balances of the equity accounts. Note 7 shows that the $39 million is reflected in the beginning equity balances by reducing retained earnings by $83 million and increasing accumulated other comprehensive income by $44 million. This split adjustment occurs because, as discussed in Chapter 8, some changes in pension and other postemployment benefits-related assets and liabilities are reflected in net income while others are reflected in other comprehensive income. Thus, remeasurement of prior period changes in these assets and liabilities are properly classified in retained earnings and accumulated other comprehensive income. Beginning with the point in time when the accounting change was made and going forward, PepsiCo uses the new pension assumption determination date in its calculations of pension and other postemployment assets and liabilities.[12]

Firms periodically change reporting principles on a voluntary basis as well. Analysts should examine carefully any voluntary changes in accounting principles made by firms. Such changes may have some bearing on assessing management's attempts to manage earnings upward or downward. We discuss earnings management at the conclusion of the chapter. We also discuss the use of restated data in profitability and risk analysis later in the chapter.

Example 6

Exhibit 9.4 presents Apple Inc.'s filing of Form 10-K/A to amend its Annual Report on Form 10-K for the year ended September 26, 2009, which was filed with the SEC (Securities and Exchange Commission) on October 27, 2009. In the amendment, Apple explains the financial statement effects when it applied new required accounting methods to account for iPhone and Apple TV. Prior accounting methods were conservative in that they required Apple to defer at the time of sale all revenues and expenses related to sales of iPhone and Apple TV and to recognize these revenues and expenses on a straight-line basis over the expected product life because Apple had promised the possibility of free

EXHIBIT 9.4

Apple Inc.'s Explanation of Change in Revenue Recognition Method
Form 10-K/A filed January 25, 2010

As amended by this Form 10-K/A, the Form 10-K reflects the Company's retrospective adoption of the Financial Accounting Standards Board's ("FASB") amended accounting standards related to revenue recognition for arrangements with multiple deliverables and arrangements that include software elements ("new accounting principles"). The new accounting principles permit prospective or retrospective adoption, and the Company elected retrospective adoption. The Company adopted the new accounting principles during the first quarter of 2010, as reflected in the Company's financial statements included in its Quarterly Report on Form 10-Q for the quarter ended December 26, 2009, which was filed with the SEC on January 25, 2010. The new accounting principles significantly change how the Company accounts for certain revenue arrangements that include both hardware and software elements as described further below.

Under the historical accounting principles, the Company was required to account for sales of both iPhone and Apple TV using subscription accounting because the Company indicated it might from time-to-time provide future unspecified software upgrades and features for those products free of charge. Under subscription accounting, revenue and associated product cost of sales for iPhone and Apple TV were deferred at the time of sale and recognized on a straight-line basis over each product's estimated economic life. This resulted in the deferral of significant amounts of revenue and cost of sales related to iPhone and Apple TV. Costs incurred by the Company for engineering, sales, marketing and warranty were expensed as incurred. As of September 26, 2009, based on the historical accounting principles, total accumulated deferred revenue and deferred costs associated with past iPhone and Apple TV sales were $12.1 billion and $5.2 billion, respectively.

[12] Most, but not all, new standards are expected to incorporate retrospective application.

EXHIBIT 9.4 (Continued)

The new accounting principles generally require the Company to account for the sale of both iPhone and Apple TV as two deliverables. The first deliverable is the hardware and software delivered at the time of sale, and the second deliverable is the right included with the purchase of iPhone and Apple TV to receive on a when-and-if-available basis future unspecified software upgrades and features relating to the product's software. The new accounting principles result in the recognition of substantially all of the revenue and product costs from sales of iPhone and Apple TV at the time of sale. Additionally, the Company is required to estimate a standalone selling price for the unspecified software upgrade right included with the sale of iPhone and Apple TV and recognizes that amount ratably over the 24-month estimated life of the related hardware device. For all periods presented, the Company's estimated selling price for the software upgrade right included with each iPhone and Apple TV sold is $25 and $10, respectively. The adoption of the new accounting principles increased the Company's net sales by $6.4 billion, $5.0 billion and $572 million for 2009, 2008 and 2007, respectively. As of September 26, 2009, the revised total accumulated deferred revenue associated with iPhone and Apple TV sales to date was $483 million; revised accumulated deferred costs for such sales were zero.

The Company had the option of adopting the new accounting principles on a prospective or retrospective basis. Prospective adoption would have required the Company to apply the new accounting principles to sales beginning in fiscal year 2010 without reflecting the impact of the new accounting principles on iPhone and Apple TV sales made prior to September 2009. Accordingly, the Company's financial results for the two years following adoption would have included the impact of amortizing the significant amounts of deferred revenue and cost of sales related to historical iPhone and Apple TV sales. The Company believes prospective adoption would have resulted in financial information that was not comparable between financial periods because of the significant amount of past iPhone sales; therefore, the Company elected retrospective adoption. Retrospective adoption required the Company to revise its previously issued financial statements as if the new accounting principles had always been applied. The Company believes retrospective adoption provides the most comparable and useful financial information for financial statement users, is more consistent with the information the Company's management uses to evaluate its business, and better reflects the underlying economic performance of the Company. Accordingly, the Company has revised its financial statements for 2009, 2008 and 2007 in this Form 10-K/A to reflect the retrospective adoption of the new accounting principles. There was no impact from the retrospective adoption of the new accounting principles for 2006 and 2005. Those years predated the Company's introduction of iPhone and Apple TV.

future upgrades and features. The justification for deferral is typically that revenue has not been earned. New standards require Apple to recognize revenue and expenses relating to existing delivered hardware and software at the time of sale and to defer the estimated fair value of the right to receive free future upgrades and features. Apple had a choice of applying the new standards prospectively (in current and future periods) or retrospectively (adjust prior years' results and then use the new standard in current and future periods). Apple chose retrospective application to enhance comparability.

Note the huge amounts involved. Adoption of the new standards increased Apple's revenue by $6.4 billion in 2009, $5.0 billion in 2008, and $483 million in 2007.

Other Comprehensive Income Items

U.S. GAAP and IFRS often require firms to restate certain assets and liabilities to fair value each period even though firms have not yet realized the value change in a market transaction.

As discussed in Chapter 2, the recognition and valuation of these assets and liabilities do not immediately affect net income and retained earnings, but may affect them in future periods. For this reason, standard setters do not require the change in value to be reported as part of net income. These unrealized gains and losses are reported as other comprehensive income for the period and are closed into accumulated other comprehensive income or loss in the shareholders' equity section of the balance sheet.

Under current U.S. GAAP, four balance sheet items receive this accounting treatment: investment securities deemed available for sale, derivatives held as cash flow hedges, pensions and other postemployment benefits, and investments in certain foreign operations. IFRS also permits upward revaluations of tangible fixed assets used in operations. Chapters 6–8 discussed the accounting for each of these items in great detail.

The analyst must decide whether to include the unrealized gains and losses when assessing earnings persistence and predicting future profitability. These gains and losses should be considered part of sustainable earnings when the following conditions hold: (1) such gains and losses closely relate to ongoing operating activities and will likely recur, and (2) measuring the amount of the gain or loss on certain assets is relatively objective when active markets exist to indicate the amount of the value changes. The case against including the unrealized losses in assessments of persistent profitability arises under the following conditions: (1) such gains and losses are not directly related to the firm's ongoing operating activities, (2) the amount of gain or loss that firms ultimately realize when they sell the assets or settle the liabilities will likely differ from the amount reported each period and might reverse in future years prior to disposal or settlement, and (3) measuring the amount of the gain or loss on certain types of assets can be subjective if they are not traded in active markets.

Making accurate predictions of the future period earnings implications of other comprehensive income items is a complex task. The implications ultimately depend on industry characteristics and company strategy and thus make the case for the industry and strategy analysis (see Chapter 1) that form the initial steps in financial statement analysis and valuation.

Consider, for example, the foreign exchange translation gains and losses discussed in Chapter 7. For a U.S. parent, a foreign exchange translation gain reported in other comprehensive income indicates that the foreign currency used for the foreign subsidiaries operations rose in value relative to the U.S. dollar. When the higher translation rate is multiplied by the positive net asset position of the foreign subsidiary, net assets measured in U.S. dollars increases, reflecting an unrealized gain. Is this change in exchange rate temporary? Will it reverse, yielding a loss in the near term (or does it reverse a loss that occurred in a recent period)? What is the company's strategy with respect to the subsidiary? Will large portions of the foreign subsidiary's expected cash flows from assets be realized from use or by sale and the amount remitted to the U.S. parent in cash, thus locking in the exchange rate gain? Alternatively, will the subsidiary move operations to countries with more favorable exchange rates or continue operations in its current location and possibly face higher operating costs? Will it be able to pass the higher operating costs to customers because of its market power? Again, for a given firm, knowledge of industry economics and company strategy is critical in assessing the future earnings implications of movements in foreign exchange rates.

Using large samples to predict future income, academics and practitioners in accounting and finance are currently assessing the general usefulness of fair value changes in assets and liabilities reported as unrealized gains and losses in comprehensive income. Financial statement analysis of individual firms requires the analyst to understand how a given firm's past unrealized gains and losses link to current earnings as a basis for predicting how current unrealized gains and losses link to future earnings. Chapter 10 further illustrates prediction of comprehensive income.

Impairment Losses on Long-Lived Assets

When a firm acquires assets such as property, plant, equipment, and intangible assets, it assumes that it will generate future benefits through their use. This does not always turn out to be the case, however. The development of new technologies by competitors, changes in government regulations, changes in demographic trends, and other factors external to a firm may reduce the future benefits originally anticipated from the assets. As discussed in Chapter 7, firms must assess whether the carrying amounts of long-lived assets are recoverable, and if they are not, the firms must write down the assets to their fair values and recognize an impairment loss in income from continuing operations.

The FASB cites the following events or circumstances as examples that may signal recoverability problems for a long-lived asset or group of assets:

- A significant decrease in the market price of a long-lived asset
- A significant adverse change in the extent or manner in which a long-lived asset is being used or in its physical condition
- A significant adverse change in legal factors or in the business climate that could affect the value of a long-lived asset, including an adverse action or assessment by a regulator
- An accumulation of costs significantly in excess of the amount originally expected for the acquisition or construction of a long-lived asset
- A current-period operating or cash flow loss combined with a history of operating or cash flow losses or a projection or forecast that demonstrates continuing losses associated with the use of a long-lived asset
- A current expectation that, more likely than not, a long-lived asset will be sold or otherwise disposed of significantly before the end of its previously estimated useful life. The term *more likely than not* refers to a level of likelihood that is more than 50 percent.[13]

What is particularly noteworthy about this list is that a firm, in effect, must accrue an impairment when it anticipates that assets previously acquired will no longer provide the future benefits initially anticipated. This is a valuable disclosure for the analyst attempting to assess a firm's past strategic decisions.

Firms must include impairment losses in income before taxes from continuing operations. Although asset impairments do not warrant presentation in a separate section of the income statement, such as that given for discontinued operations or extraordinary gains or losses discussed earlier, alternative methods for reporting the losses include a separate line item on the income statement or a detailed note that describes what line item on the income statement includes the impairment losses. Because impairment charges are often reported with restructuring charges, both phenomena are discussed further in the next section.

Restructuring and Other Charges

Firms may decide to remain in a segment of their business but elect to make major changes in the strategic direction or level of operations of that business.[14] In many of these cases,

[13] *FASB Codification Topic 360 (-10-35-21);* Also, see Hugo Nurnberg and Nelson Dittmar, "Reporting Impairments of Long-Lived Assets: New Rules and Disclosures," *Journal of Financial Statement Analysis* (Winter 1997), pp. 37–50. The article includes examples of how these impairment indicators are applied by firms in the oil and gas, restaurant, retail food, and service-related industries.

[14] If the firm decides to abandon a business segment or component altogether, the reporting policies discussed earlier for discontinued operations apply. In many cases, however, firms are not abandoning current areas of business, but are "restructuring" them to improve profitability.

firms record a restructuring charge against earnings for the cost of implementing the decision. Employee-related costs from downsizing or employee retraining and reassignment typically make up a substantial portion of restructuring costs. Restructuring plans also tend to trigger asset impairments.

The treatment of restructuring charges in analyzing profitability and assessing earnings persistence is important because recessionary conditions often induce firms to include restructuring charges in their reported earnings for the current period. Whether the recessionary conditions are expected to persist will have a bearing on forecasting earnings in the future. Further, restructurings are expected to yield operating efficiencies or strategic benefits, and thus, may be associated with lower future expenses and higher future revenues. Consistent with this value-added characteristic of restructurings, announcements of restructurings are typically associated with stock price increases.

Interpreting a particular firm's restructuring charge is difficult because firms vary in their treatment of these items, as follows:

- Some firms apply their accounting principles conservatively (for example, use relatively short lives for depreciable assets, immediately expense expenditures for repairs of equipment, or use shorter amortization lives for intangible assets). Such firms have smaller amounts to write off as restructuring charges than if they had applied their accounting principles less conservatively.
- Some firms spread out restructuring charges in an attempt to minimize the impact of the restructuring charge on annual earnings. Such firms often must take restructuring charges for several years to provide adequately for restructuring costs.
- Some firms attempt to maximize the amount of the restructuring charge in a particular year. This approach communicates the "bad news" all at once (referred to as the "big bath" approach) and reduces or eliminates the need for additional restructuring charges in the future. If the restructuring charge later turns out to have been too large, income from continuing operations in a later period includes a restructuring credit that increases reported earnings. Another related concern is that if firms overstate restructuring charges in early years, they create a "cookie jar" reserve that can be accessed in future years (by revising the restructuring liability downward) to offset future negative financial statement items.

The prevalence of restructuring charges in recent years has prompted standard setters to address the measurement and reporting of restructuring charges. Also, U.S. GAAP and IFRS rules differ on the timing of the charges.[15] Under U.S. GAAP, firms record a *restructuring liability* on the balance sheet and the associated *restructuring charge* (an expense) on the income statement when two conditions are present: management has committed to the restructuring plan, and restructuring costs meet the definition of a liability. Recall that a liability is a present obligation (not a planned obligation) that the firm has little or no discretion to avoid. Under IFRS, firms record a *restructuring provision* (a liability) on the balance sheet and the associated *restructuring charge* (an expense) on the income statement when management has committed to the restructuring plan over which it exercises control, has estimated the timing and costs of the restructuring actions, and has notified employees to be terminated under the plan. Because IFRS does not require restructuring costs to meet the definition of a liability, the costs may not be present costs or costs that might be avoided. Therefore, under IFRS rules, firms can recognize restructuring costs and associated liabilities sooner than they can under U.S. GAAP.

---

[15] Financial Accounting Standards Board, *Statement of Financial Accounting Standards No. 146*, "Accounting for Costs Associated with Exit or Disposal Activities," 2002; *FASB Codification Topic 420*; International Accounting Standards Board, *International Accounting Standard 37*, "Provisions, Contingent Assets and Contingent Liabilities" (1998).

Firms also report "other charges" on the income statement using a variety of different account titles. These other charges have characteristics similar to restructuring charges, but often are not directly related to any strategic decision by the firm or to the level or direction of its operations. The following examples provide illustrations of restructuring and other similar charges.

Example 7

Iomega Corporation (a wholly owned subsidiary of EMC Corporation as of the second quarter of 2008) sells data storage products to consumer and corporate customers. Iomega is a leading manufacturer of portable data storage solutions, including drives and disks, which are used for sharing, transporting, sorting, and backing up critical information.

Employee compensation and associated costs represent one of the largest expenses for Iomega. Other significant expenses include the cost of leased space and depreciation of furniture and fixtures. In its 2004 annual filing, Iomega provided an extensive note on the composition of its restructuring charges for 2003 and 2004, including amounts for employee severance packages, lease termination fees, and furniture write-offs. An excerpt from Note 5, "Restructuring Charges/Reversals," states the following:

> *2004 Restructuring Actions.* During 2004, the Company recorded $3.7 million of restructuring charges for the 2004 restructuring actions, including $2.6 million of cash charges for severance and benefits for 108 regular and temporary personnel worldwide (approximately 19% of the Company's worldwide workforce) who were notified by September 26, 2004 that their positions were being eliminated, $0.7 million of cash charges for lease termination costs and $0.4 million of non-cash charges related to excess furniture. All of the $3.7 million of restructuring charges recorded during 2004 are being shown as restructuring expenses as a component of operating expenses. None of these restructuring charges were allocated to any of the business segments.
>
> *2003 Restructuring Actions.* The $14.5 million of charges for the 2003 restructuring actions included $6.5 million for severance and benefits for 198 regular and temporary personnel worldwide, or approximately 25% of the Company's worldwide workforce, $3.0 million to exit contractual obligations, $2.6 million to reimburse a strategic supplier for its restructuring expenses, $1.8 million for lease termination costs and $0.6 million related to excess furniture.

Note that Iomega does not disclose the tax savings resulting from the charges for either year. These tax savings are deferred tax assets until the related restructuring liabilities are paid and a deduction is taken on the corporate tax return. Also note that the firm discloses the cash component of the charges for 2004 but not for 2003. The restructuring charges for Iomega also appear to be recurring in nature. Although not reported here, Iomega had a restructuring charge in 2002 as well. Thus, when forecasting future profitability, the analyst appears justified in including them (and related estimated tax effects) in income from continuing operations. Iomega continued to show restructuring charges in future years. It reported $5.7 million in 2005 and $3.0 million in 2006. Iomega did not report a restructuring charge in 2007, the year prior to EMC Corporation acquiring it.

Example 8

Refer to Note 3, "Restructuring and Impairment," of PepsiCo's annual report (Appendix A). During 2008, PepsiCo reported a $543 million charge ($408 million after tax) associated with its Productivity for Growth Program. PepsiCo links the charge with specific income statement accounts, a disclosure that benefits analyses such as the common-size income statements illustrated in Chapter 4. PepsiCo reports that the pretax charge is split between selling, general, and administrative expense ($455 million) and cost of sales (the remaining $88 million). A substantial portion of the restructuring charge comes from asset impairments ($149 million). In 2007, PepsiCo reported an additional $102 million restructuring charge ($70 million after tax), of which $57 million came from asset impairments. In 2006, PepsiCo reported a $63 million restructuring charge ($43 million after tax), of which $43 million relates to asset impairments. Finally, PepsiCo reports another $83 million ($55 million after tax) as a 2005 restructuring charge. It appears reasonable to expect that PepsiCo will continue its restructuring activities in the future, although it is likely that the activities will eventually cease. Therefore, it is difficult to reach a definitive conclusion about whether to view PepsiCo's restructuring charges as a part of sustainable earnings. As mentioned earlier, restructuring activities are now common for many firms.

Changes in Estimates

As discussed earlier in this chapter, application of accounting standards requires firms to make many estimates. Examples include the amount of uncollectible accounts receivable; the depreciable lives for fixed assets; the percentage of completion rate for a long-term project; the return rate for warranties; and interest, compensation, and inflation rates for pensions, health care, and other retirement benefits.

Firms periodically change these estimates. The amounts reported in prior years for various revenues and expenses will differ from the amount suggested by the new estimates. Standard setters view making and revising estimates as an integral and ongoing part of applying accounting principles. They are concerned about the credibility of financial statements if firms restate their prior financial statements each time they change an accounting estimate. Therefore, current accounting standards require firms to account for changes in estimates by using the new estimates in the current year and in future years.

Because new estimates alone can change current period income, analysts should attempt to determine whether estimate changes are significant. However, often analysts must infer the impact of changes in estimates. For example, Chapter 7 provided a formula for computing average useful lives of depreciable assets. If an analyst detects an increase in average useful lives in a year in which reported earnings barely exceeded expectations, the analyst could recompute depreciation expense using the prior year's average useful life to detect whether the depreciation difference drove the increase in current period earnings. Likewise, analysts can monitor changes in estimated bad debts expense by reviewing the ratio of bad debts expense to sales. Whenever possible, analysts should compare estimated to realized amounts through time to assess the extent of management's changes in estimates through time and to determine whether trends will continue. For example, the notes to Harley Davidson, Inc.'s financial statements disclose the estimated warranty liability and actual warranty costs for consecutive years.

When engaging in this analysis, the analyst must remember that estimates change over time for legitimate reasons. One of the main determinants of the value of accrual-based financial statements is that the amounts of reported assets and liabilities can reflect management's beliefs. Again, knowledge of a company's industry economics and strategy allows for a more informed judgment of whether an estimate change is warranted.

Gains and Losses from Peripheral Activities

Firms often enter into transactions that are peripheral to their core operations but generate gains and losses that must be reported on the income statement. For example, to create, manufacture, and market products, firms generally need to invest in assets such as buildings and equipment. When a firm decides to sell and replace such assets, the sale usually results in a gain or loss. Similar to restructuring charges, gains and losses from activities peripheral to the primary activities of a firm are included in income from continuing operations. The analyst should search for such items and decide whether to exclude them when assessing current profitability and forecasting future earnings.

Example 9

Bowne & Co., first discussed in Example 2, is one of the largest financial printers in the United States. Note that Bowne's income statement, reported in Exhibit 9.2, includes a "gain on sale of building" for $896,000 in 2004. Bowne provides the following information on the sale in Note 9 of its annual report:

> In May 2004, the Company sold its financial printing facility in Dominguez Hills, California for net proceeds of $6,731,000 recognizing a gain on the sale of $896,000 during the quarter ended June 30, 2004. The Company moved to a new leased facility in Southern California in September of 2004.

Exhibit 9.2 includes excerpts from Bowne's consolidated statement of cash flows as well. The $896,000 gain is eliminated from cash flows from operations (reported as a subtraction from operating cash flows in the exhibit), with the $6,731,000 proceeds reported as part of cash flows from investing activities (included in the total cash flows provided by investing activity of $148,200,000 reported in Exhibit 9.2).

While such gains and losses affect the firm's current period earnings, the analyst must assess whether the gains and losses are sustainable, although peripheral to the firm's operations, and thus whether to include them in income from continuing operations. In many cases, even though the gains and losses do not relate to the sale of the firm's principal products and services, such gains and losses recur and should enter into estimates of future earnings. Of course, firms that rely heavily on such gains and losses for their earnings will not likely survive for long. Thus, a large percentage of reported earnings comprising gains and losses from peripheral activities might signal the need to revise downward the estimates of sustainable earnings.

Similar to impairment and restructuring charges, firms report peripheral gains and losses on a *pretax* basis. Income tax expense includes any tax effects of the gain or loss. If the analyst decides to eliminate the gain or loss from income from continuing operations, he or she also must eliminate the related tax effect from income tax expense using specific information disclosed about the tax effects or using the statutory rate if the firm does not disclose specific information about the tax effects.

Example 10

Gains and losses can be recurring, material, and a part of corporate strategy. Singapore Airlines, for example, reports the following surplus (gains) on disposal of aircraft, spare parts, and spare engines over the 2003–2008 period (dollar amounts in millions):

Fiscal Year	Surplus on Disposal	Pretax Income	Percentage of Pretax Income
2003–2004	$102.7	$ 820.9	12.5%
2004–2005	$215.2	$1,829.4	11.7%
2005–2006	$115.7	$1,662.1	6.9%
2006–2007	$237.9	$2,284.6	10.4%
2007–2008	$ 60.6	$1,198.6	5.0%

Singapore Airlines maintains a reputation for flying newer, technologically advanced aircraft, which results in the use of aircraft for fewer years than other airlines. Thus, the sale of aircraft and spare parts is a significant portion of Singapore Airline's profitability and should be treated as recurring when forecasting future earnings.

Summary of Accounting Data Adjustments

This section discussed the reporting of various types of special events and conditions related to earnings. A large set of factors were identified that may affect the quality of the accounting information as a predictor of future sustainable earnings. The nature and extent of adjustments made to current earnings in order to use it as a predictor requires knowledge of the industry, the firm and its strategy, and the required financial reporting. The process is more art than science and requires considerable judgment on the part of the analyst. The ability to make good judgment is enhanced by understanding the industry economic characteristics and firm strategy.

RESTATED FINANCIAL STATEMENT DATA

High-quality financial statement data enables the analyst to compare financial statement data across years for any firm. Comparability of data is crucial for effective time-series analysis, a technique used by analysts to judge trends over time and forecast future earnings and cash flows. Standard setters also recognize the importance of comparability, and on implementation of Statement No. 154 as discussed earlier in the chapter, firms retroactively apply new accounting principles unless it is impracticable to determine the cumulative effect or the period-specific effects of the change.

A firm also restates the financial statements of prior years when it decides to discontinue a particular line of business, even though the firm had included this income in continuing operations in income statements originally prepared for these years. The firm also may reclassify the net assets of the discontinued business as of the end of the preceding year to a single line, Net Assets of Discontinued Business, even though these net assets appeared among individual assets and liabilities in the balance sheet originally prepared for the preceding year.

The analyst must decide whether to use the financial statement data as originally reported for each year or as restated to reflect the new conditions. Because the objective of most financial statement analysis is to evaluate the past as a guide for projecting the future, the logical response is to use the restated data.

However, the analyst encounters difficulties when using restated data. In their annual reports, most companies include balance sheets for two years and income statements and statements of cash flows for three years. Analysts can calculate ratios and perform other analyses based on balance sheet data (such as current assets/current liabilities or long-term debt to shareholders' equity) on a consistent basis for only two years. Analysts can calculate ratios based on data from the income statement (for example, cost of goods sold/sales) or from the statement of cash flows (for example, cash flow from operations/capital expenditures) for three years at most on a consistent basis. However, many important ratios and other analyses rely on data from the balance sheet and either the income statement or the statement of cash flows. For example, the rate of return on common shareholders' equity equals net income to common shareholders divided by average common shareholders' equity. The denominator of this ratio requires two years of balance sheet data. Thus, it is possible to calculate comparable ratios based on average restated data from the balance sheet and one of the other two financial statements for only one year under the new conditions.

The analysts could obtain balance sheet amounts for prior years from earlier annual reports, but reliance on the earlier reports results in comparing restated income statement or statement of cash flow data with non-restated balance sheet data for those earlier years. The analyst should evaluate the likely magnitude of the effect of the restatement on ratios using prior years' data. In Example 6, Apple Inc.'s 10-K/A restated revenues and net income for the years 2009, 2008, and 2007. Also, Apple disclosed that the restatement effects on earlier years were immaterial due to limited revenues from iPhone sales prior to 2007.

When a firm provides sufficient information so that the analyst can restate prior years' financial statements using reasonable assumptions, the analyst should use retroactively restated financial statement data. When the firm does not provide sufficient information to do the restatements, the analyst should use the amounts as originally reported for each year. To interpret the resulting ratios, the analyst attempts to assess how much of the change in the ratios results from the new reporting condition and how much relates to other factors. Clearly, restatements can create significant interpretation issues when analyzing historical financial data.

ACCOUNTING CLASSIFICATION DIFFERENCES

Accounting classification differences across firms also affect comparability analysis. Firms frequently classify items in their financial statements in different ways. When the analyst is comparing two or more companies, it is important that he or she obtain comparable data sets. If that is not possible, the analyst must understand the significant differences in accounting classifications across firms. A scan of the financial statements should permit the analyst to identify significant differences that might affect the analysis and interpretations.

Example 11

Exhibit 9.5 presents the Consolidated Income Statement from the 2009 Annual Financial Report of the Finnish company Stora Enso, prepared in accordance with IFRS. Stora Enso is a global paper, packaging, and wood products company that produces newsprint and book paper, magazine paper, fine paper, consumer board, industrial packaging, and wood products. Stora Enso's sales totaled EUR 8.9 billion in 2009. The company has approximately 27,000 employees in more than 35 countries worldwide.

Typical of the financial statements for a non-U.S. company, Stora Enso classifies expenses by source instead of function. For example, a U.S. paper company includes as operating expenses cost of goods sold, SG&A (selling, general, and administrative) expenses, possibly some other gains and losses, restructuring charges, and impairments. Wages and salary costs and depreciation costs are allocated to cost of goods sold and SG&A expenses. Cost of goods sold includes the costs allocated to inventory sold that period, such as wages and depreciation (that is, manufacturing overhead) costs, as well as materials costs. Wages, salaries, and depreciation not related to production appear in SG&A. In contrast, Stora Enso does not make those allocations. For example, "Personnel expenses" are listed, but one does not know the portion of those expenses that would be included in inventory and therefore included in cost of goods sold in the U.S. company. Likewise, Stora Enso reports "Depreciation, amortization, and impairment charge," which is different from what is done in the U.S. reporting approach. Instead of cost of goods sold, Stora Enso reports "Materials and services" and "Changes in inventories of finished goods and work in progress." An analyst estimating cost of goods sold would have to include these two accounts, an estimated portion of personnel expenses to be included in inventory, and an estimated portion of depreciation to be included in inventory.

EXHIBIT 9.5

Stora Enso 2009 Annual Report
Consolidated Income Statement

EUR million	Year Ended 31 December 2009	2008	2007
Continuing Operations			
Sales	**8 945.1**	**11 028.8**	**11 848.5**
Other operating income	172.8	120.2	88.4
Change in inventories of finished goods and work in progress	(200.5)	(76.1)	81.0
Change in net value of biological assets	(3.3)	(18.2)	7.5
Materials and services	(5 464.3)	(6 815.7)	(7 051.5)
Freight and sales commissions	(833.6)	(1 127.1)	(1 133.9)
Personnel expenses	(1 349.6)	(1 669.1)	(1 712.9)
Other operating expenses	(833.1)	(752.6)	(761.9)
Share of results in equity accounted investments	111.8	7.6	341.3
Depreciations, amortisation and impairment changes	(1 152.9)	(1 422.4)	(1 529.6)
Operating (Loss)/Profit	**(607.6)**	**(726.6)**	**176.9**
Financial income	209.3	356.7	161.9
Financial expense	(488.5)	(523.9)	(318.6)
(Loss)/Profit before Tax	**(886.8)**	**(893.8)**	**20.2**
Income tax	8.6	214.8	(7.4)
Net (Loss)/Profit for the Year from Continuing Operations	**(878.2)**	**(679.0)**	**12.8**
Discontinued Operations Profit/(Loss) after Tax for the Year	—	**4.3**	**(225.2)**
Net (Loss) for the Year from Total Operations	**(878.2)**	**(674.7)**	**(212.4)**
Attributable to:			
Equity holders of the Parent Company	(879.7)	(673.4)	(214.7)
Non-controlling interests	1.5	(1.3)	2.3
Net (Loss) for the Year	**(878.2)**	**(674.7)**	**(212.4)**
Earnings per Share			
Basic & diluted (loss) per share, Total Operations, EUR	(1.12)	(0.85)	(0.27)
Basic & diluted (loss)/earning per share, Continuing Operations, EUR	(1.12)	(0.86)	(0.01)

When the analyst can easily and unambiguously reclassify accounts, the reclassified data should serve as the basis for analysis. If the reclassifications require numerous assumptions, the analyst should make them as precisely as possible or avoid making them and note the differences in account classification for further reference when interpreting the financial statement analysis.

FINANCIAL REPORTING WORLDWIDE

Thus far, we have identified many accounting quality and comparability issues. The concerns discussed in the chapter to this point apply equally to firms that follow reporting systems employed outside the United States, such as IFRS. However, important additional concerns also exist in comparing financial data for firms that operate in different countries.

Cross-national analysis of firms entails a two-step approach:

1. Achieve comparability of the reporting methods and accounting principles employed by the firms under scrutiny.
2. Understand corporate strategies, institutional structures, and cultural practices unique to the countries in which the firms operate.

Beginning in 2005, the financial statements of firms in the European Community were required to conform to IFRS pronouncements. In addition, the convergence of IFRS and U.S. GAAP will be central to achieving worldwide conformity of financial reporting. The IASB and FASB pledged to use their best efforts to make existing U.S. and IASB standards fully compatible as soon as practicable and to coordinate their future work programs to ensure that once achieved, compatibility is maintained. Statement No. 154, for example, is the result of close collaboration between the IASB and FASB.

In past years, firms headquartered outside the United States that have debt or equity securities traded in U.S. capital markets were required to file a Form 10-K using U.S. GAAP or a Form 20-F report with the SEC each year. The Form 20-F report included a reconciliation of shareholders' equity and net income as reported under IFRS or GAAP of the firm's local country with GAAP in the United States. With this information, the analyst could convert the financial statements of a non-U.S. firm to achieve comparable accounting principles with U.S. firms.

Preparation of the reconciliation—essentially requiring a foreign filer in the United States to maintain two sets of financial records—is a costly endeavor and a potential deterrent to companies interested in listing on U.S. exchanges. Thus, on November 15, 2007, the SEC relaxed the reporting requirements of non-U.S. filers and began to accept financial reports prepared in accordance with IFRS as legislated by the IASB without reconciliation to U.S. GAAP. In effect on March 4, 2008, the new rule (SEC Final Rule No. 33-8879) provides U.S. investors with two sets of accounting principles—IFRS and U.S. GAAP. The elimination of the reconciliation is a controversial issue because research suggests that material differences between IFRS and U.S. GAAP remain, and eliminating the reconciliation could diminish the relevant information set available to investors in the U.S. and around the world.[16]

Example 12

What did a Form 20-F reconciliation look like? Exhibit 9.6 presents the reconciliations for 2001 through 2003 for Ericsson, a Swedish manufacturer of cell phones. Ericsson provides extensive discussion of each reconciling item in its Form 20-F filing in Note 32, "Reconciliation to Accounting Principles Generally Accepted in the United States." In fact, the note is more than five pages long.

Achieving comparability in reporting is important to the analysis of multinational firms, but the data must be carefully interpreted. Analysis of multinational firms is complicated by the fact that the environments in which the firms operate may vary extensively

[16] Not all firms domiciled in non-U.S. locations use IFRS. Many are required to file legal-based financial statements using home-country standards or IFRS modified for local laws or preferences, and thus would be required to reconcile to U.S. GAAP if listed on U.S. exchanges.

EXHIBIT 9.6

Form 20-F Reconciliations for Ericsson
(amounts in millions)

	2003	2002	2001
Adjustments to Shareholders' Equity			
Reported Shareholders' Equity	SEK 60,481	SEK 73,607	SEK 68,587
Capitalization of Software	6,409	11,652	16,502
Capitalization of Interest Expense	133	172	211
Pensions	(299)	440	99
Goodwill	2,700	1,064	—
Hedging	3,509	2,744	(2,196)
Restructuring Costs	1,442	217	1,458
Sale-Leaseback	(1,381)	(2,063)	(2,176)
Deferred Taxes	(3,347)	(4,021)	(4,487)
Other	316	(609)	(197)
Stockholders' Equity According to U.S. GAAP	SEK 69,963	SEK 83,203	SEK 77,801
Adjustments to Net Income			
Reported Net Loss	SEK (10,844)	SEK (19,013)	SEK (21,264)
Restructuring Costs	1,225	(1,240)	(1,642)
Capitalization of Software Development Costs	(5,153)	(4,940)	(2,135)
Goodwill Amortization	1,636	1,064	—
Pensions	(840)	459	1,006
Hedging	1,603	2,884	(2,233)
Sale-Leaseback	682	113	(815)
Deferred Income Taxes	533	966	2,042
Other	561	(211)	638
Net Income According to U.S. GAAP	SEK (10,597)	SEK (19,918)	SEK (24,403)

across countries. A firm may implement operational strategies in its home country that it cannot implement in other countries. Institutional arrangements, such as significant alliances with banks and extensive intercorporate holdings, may be common in one country but not in another. Cultural characteristics may exist in one country that affect how firms do business in that country—with those same characteristics foreign to other business settings.

For example, in a study addressing comparability of Japanese and U.S. financial reporting, Herrmann, Inoue, and Thomas identify the following environmental characteristics that may influence interpretation of the data:

- Profitability ratios often are more conservative in Japan, attributable in part to the close link between tax and financial reporting systems.
- Japanese companies often have higher debt ratios. High debt ratios are sometimes considered a sign of financial strength because debt is the primary source of capital.

- The corporate group is different in Japan in that Japanese grouping is often based on bank dependence, intercompany loans, mutual shareholding, preferred business transactions, and multiple personal ties.[17]

Herrmann, Inoue, and Thomas stress that environmental factors unique to Japan may influence the financial data reported by Japanese firms in such a way that the data, although comparable to data reported by U.S. firms once the necessary adjustments are made, can be effectively interpreted only when taking these unique factors into consideration.

Other countries have their own unique environmental and business practices. When analyzing multinational firms, the analyst needs to incorporate these factors into his or her interpretation of the data and understand that although the data may be comparable from a measurement perspective, they may not be comparable on other dimensions.

EARNINGS MANAGEMENT

The chapter concludes with a discussion of earnings management because the concepts of accounting quality and earnings management often are linked in a discussion of the need to adjust financial data to better reflect the economic information content of financial data.

As with other concepts discussed in this chapter, earnings management connotes different things to different users of the term.[18] Healy and Wahlen (1999) provide the following definition of earnings management:

> Earnings management occurs when managers use judgment in financial reporting and in structuring transactions to alter financial reports to either mislead some stakeholders about the underlying economic performance of the company or to influence contractual outcomes that depend on reporting accounting numbers.[19]

Chapters 6–9 establish that choices, judgments, and estimates are a necessary part of the reporting process. Healy and Wahlen recognize this and define earnings management as the use of these inherent aspects of the reporting model to mask the underlying economic performance of a firm. Any judgments employed by management that result in lower economic information content of the financial reports (and provide a skewed basis for making decisions) are probably the result of a firm practicing earnings management.

Detecting earnings management is difficult because managers can exercise judgment in financial reporting in so many ways. Moreover, earnings management often creates the same financial statement outcome as fundamental economic growth (for example, increasing sales and receivables). One of the objectives in Chapters 6–8 is to illustrate the judgments that firms must make to apply accounting principles so that the analyst can better discern whether a firm is engaging in earnings management.

Incentives to Practice Earnings Management

Incentives to engage in earnings management exist if use of the choices and estimates allowed in U.S. GAAP or IFRS creates degrees of freedom for optimal contracting and

---

[17] Don Herrmann, Tatsuo Inoue, and Wayne Thomas, "Are There Benefits to Restating Japanese Financial Statements According to U.S. GAAP?" *Journal of Financial Statement Analysis* (Fall 1996), pp. 61–73.

[18] As Chapter 5 notes, earnings management also is linked at times with earnings manipulation, a topic discussed in that chapter and defined as "preparing financial reports based on reporting techniques outside the limits of GAAP."

[19] Paul M. Healy and James M. Wahlen, "A Review of the Earnings Management Literature and Its Implications for Standard Setting," *Accounting Horizons* (December 1999), pp. 365–383.

resource allocation for the benefit of the firm and its stakeholders. Examples of such reason for earnings management include the following:

- To create optimal manager compensation payments under compensation contracts
- To create optimal job security for senior management
- To create optimal lending environments and to mitigate potential violation of debt covenants
- To influence short-term stock price performance and wealth resource allocation over time
- To minimize/manage reported earnings to thwart industry-specific actions and antitrust actions against the firm

Disincentives to Practice Earnings Management

Managers may be deterred from engaging in earnings management for the following reasons:

- Earnings and cash flows over the life of the firm agree, so firms cannot manage earnings forever. Eventually, earnings aggressively reported in early years must be offset by lower earnings or even losses in later years to compensate.
- Capital markets and regulators such as the SEC penalize firms identified as flagrant earnings managers.
- Firms and managers who are perceived as practicing aggressive earnings management will lose their reputation for being honest and trustworthy among capital market participants and stakeholders.
- Legal consequences can result from aggressive earnings management as well as from earnings management that reverts to earnings manipulation and fraud.[20]
- Firms and managers can use aggressive earnings management to manipulate contracts and stakeholders' claims that depend on reported earnings numbers, thereby creating inefficient or opportunistic capital allocation. For example, managers can use earnings management to manipulate their compensation.

A review of these conditions indicates that the analyst is best served by increasing his or her effort of accounting quality analysis when these conditions are present.

Boundaries of Earnings Management

It is important to note that earnings management has boundaries. Securities regulations and stock exchanges require annual audits by independent accountants. Auditors can monitor particularly aggressive actions taken by management to influence earnings, although an auditor's power to thwart actions taken within the bounds of GAAP is limited. In addition, the ongoing scrutiny of financial analysts and investors serves as a check on earnings management. Security analysts typically follow several firms in an industry and have a sense of the corporate reporting "personalities" and strategies of various firms. The frequency, timeliness, and quality of management's communications with shareholders and analysts signal the forthrightness of management and the likelihood of earnings being highly managed.[21]

---

[20] Messod D. Beneish, "Detecting GAAP Violation: Implications for Assessing Earnings Management among Firms with Extreme Financial Performance," *Journal of Accounting and Public Policy* (1997), pp. 271–309; "The Detection of Earnings Management," *Financial Analyst Journal* (September/October 1999), pp. 24–36.

[21] Mark H. Lang and Russell J. Lundholm, "Corporate Disclosure Policy and Analyst Behavior," *Accounting Review* (October 1996), pp. 467–492.

The analyst's task is to identify situations in which earnings management is possible and the avenues management might pursue in those situations to carry out earnings management. Understanding when GAAP provides flexibility to manage earnings should permit the analyst to distinguish high economic information content from what some call "cosmetic" (that is, earnings-managed) content of the reported data.

SUMMARY

The financial analysis framework discussed in Chapters 1–5 and the discussion of forecasting and valuation presented in Chapters 10–14 assume that a firm's reported financial statement data accurately reflect the economic effects of a firm's decisions. Another assumption is that the financial data are informative about the firm's likely future profitability and risk. This chapter develops the concept of accounting quality as the basis for assessing the information content of reported financial statement data and for adjusting that data before assessing a firm's profitability and risk or forecasting or valuing the firm.

The illustrations in this chapter identify items that are part of the current period's performance but may not recur in future years. The chapter indicates adjustments the analyst might make to eliminate the effect of such items from forecasts of future earnings.

The chapter concludes with a discussion of earnings management and the conditions that can trigger earnings management. The concepts of accounting quality and earnings management often are linked in discussions of the need to adjust financial data to better reflect the economic information content of financial data.

QUESTIONS, EXERCISES, PROBLEMS, AND CASES

Questions and Exercises

9.1 CONCEPT OF EARNINGS QUALITY. The concept of earnings quality has several dimensions, but two characteristics often dominate: the accounting information should be a fair representation of performance for the reporting period, and it should provide relevant information to forecast expected future earnings. Provide a specific example of poor earnings quality that would hinder the forecasting of expected future earnings.

9.2 RESTATING EARNINGS FOR LITIGATION LOSS. Rock of Ages, Inc., is the largest integrated granite quarrier, manufacturer, and retailer of finished granite memorials and granite blocks for memorial use in North America. The firm reported a net loss for 2004 of $3.2 million. In 2004, the firm reported a pretax litigation settlement loss of $6.5 million, and management stated that, in its opinion, the litigation settlement loss did not reflect the current year's operations because it was the first year in five years that the firm reported such a loss. Calculate pro forma earnings for 2004 excluding the settlement costs and speculate on management's reasoning as to why it believes that pro forma earnings is a better measure of performance for Rock of Ages. State any assumptions you make in your calculations.

9.3 CONCEPT OF EARNINGS MANAGEMENT. The concept of earnings management connotes different things to different users of the term. Define earnings management. Discuss why it is difficult to discern whether a firm does in fact practice earnings management.

9.4 CRITERIA TO IDENTIFY NONRECURRING ITEMS. The chapter discusses eight accounting and disclosure topics that typically occur infrequently but can have a large impact on financial statements. What criteria should an analyst employ to assess whether to include or eliminate items from the financial statements related to these eight topics?

9.5 EFFECT OF ALTERNATIVE GAAP ON FINANCIAL STATEMENT ANALYSIS. Nestlé Group, a multinational food products firm based in Switzerland, recently issued its financial statements. The auditor's opinion attached to the financial statements stated the following: "In our opinion, the Consolidated Accounts give a true and fair view of the financial position, the net profit and cash flows in accordance with International Financial Reporting Standards (IFRS) and comply with Swiss law." Note that Nestlé's financial reports are prepared using IFRS standards. One of Nestlé's competitors is PepsiCo, which prepares financial reports following U.S. GAAP. Describe the necessary steps an analyst should consider to develop comparable accounting data when conducting a profitability and risk analysis of these two firms.

9.6 REPORTING IMPAIRMENT AND RESTRUCTURING CHARGES. Checkpoint Systems is a global leader in shrink management, merchandising visibility, and apparel labeling solutions. The firm is a leading provider of source tagging, handheld labeling systems, retail merchandising systems, and bar-code labeling systems. In a press release, Checkpoint stated the following:

> GAAP reported net loss for the fourth quarter of 2004 was $29.3 million, or $0.78 per diluted share, compared to net earnings of $4.5 million, or $0.13 per diluted share, for the fourth quarter 2003. Excluding impairment and restructuring charges, net of tax, the Company's net income for the fourth quarter 2004 was $0.30 per diluted share, compared to $0.27 per diluted share in the fourth quarter 2003.

Calculate the amount of the impairment and restructuring charges reported by Checkpoint in 2004 and 2003. Discuss why the firm reported earnings both including and excluding impairment and restructuring charges.

9.7 CONCEPT OF A PERIPHERAL ACTIVITY. Firms often enter into transactions that are peripheral to their core operations but generate gains and losses that must be reported on the income statement. A gain labeled "peripheral" by one firm may not be labeled as such for another firm. Provide an example in which a gain generated from the sale of an equity security may be labeled a peripheral activity by one firm but is considered a core activity by another firm.

9.8 REPORTING IMPAIRMENT CHARGES. Statement No. 144 requires firms to assess whether they will recover carrying amounts of long-lived assets and, if not, to write down the assets to their fair value and recognize an impairment loss in income from continuing operations. Impairment charges often appear as a separate line item on the income statement of companies that experience reductions in the future benefits originally anticipated from the long-lived assets. Conduct a search to identify a firm (other than the examples given in this chapter) that has recently reported an impairment charge. Discuss how the firm (a) reported the charge on the income statement, (b) determined the amount of the charge, and (c) used cash related to the charge.

Problems and Cases

9.9 ADJUSTING FOR UNUSUAL INCOME STATEMENT AND CLASSIFICATION ITEMS. H. J. Heinz is one of the world's leading marketers of branded foods to retail and foodservice channels. According to the firm, Heinz holds the number one or two branded products in more than 50 world product markets. Among the company's well-known brands are Heinz®, StarKist®, Kibbles 'n Bits®, and 9Lives®. Exhibit 9.7 presents an income statement for Heinz for Year 10, Year 11, and Year 12. Notes to the financial statements reveal the following information:

1. **Gain on sale of Weight Watchers.** In Year 10, Heinz completed the sale of the Weight Watchers classroom business for $735 million. The transaction resulted in a pretax gain of $464.5 million. The sale did not include Weight Watchers® frozen meals, desserts, and breakfast items. Heinz did not disclose the tax effect of the gain reported in Exhibit 9.7.
2. **Accounting change for revenue recognition.** In Year 11, Heinz changed its method of accounting for revenue recognition to recognizing revenue upon the passage of title, ownership, and risk of loss to the customer. The change was driven by a new SEC ruling on revenue recognition. The cumulative effect of the change on prior years resulted in a charge to income of $17 million, net of income taxes of $10 million. Heinz indicated that the effect on Year 11 and prior years was not material.
3. **Sale and promotion costs.** In Year 11, Heinz changed the classification of certain sale and promotion incentives provided to customers and consumers. In the past, Heinz classified these incentives as selling and administrative expenses (see Exhibit 9.7), with the gross amount of the revenue associated with the incentives reported in sales. Beginning in Year 11, Heinz changed to reporting the incentives as a reduction of revenues. As a result of this change, the firm reduced reported revenues by $693 million in Year 12, $610 million in Year 11, and $469 million in Year 10. The firm stated that selling and administrative expenses were "correspondingly reduced such

EXHIBIT 9.7

H. J. Heinz Company
Income Statement
(amounts in millions)
(Problem 9-9)

	Year 12	Year 11	Year 10
Sales	$ 9,431	$ 8,821	$ 8,939
Gain on sale of weight watchers	—	—	465
Cost of goods sold	(6,094)	(5,884)	(5,789)
Selling and administrative expenses	(1,746)	(1,955)	(1,882)
Interest income	27	23	25
Interest expense	(294)	(333)	(270)
Other income (expense)	(45)	1	(25)
Income before Income Taxes and Cumulative Effect of Accounting Changes	$ 1,279	$ 673	$ 1,463
Income tax expense	(445)	(178)	(573)
Income before Cumulative Effect of Accounting Change	$ 834	$ 495	$ 890
Cumulative effect of accounting change	—	(17)	—
Net Income	$ 834	$ 478	$ 890

that net earnings were not affected." Exhibit 9.7 already reflects the adjustments to sales revenues and selling and administrative expenses for Years 10 through 12.

4. **Tax rate.** The U.S. federal statutory income tax rate was 35 percent for each of the years presented in Exhibit 9.7.

Required

a. Discuss whether you would adjust for each of the following items when using earnings to forecast the future profitability of Heinz:
   (1) Gain on sale of Weight Watchers classroom business
   (2) Accounting change for revenue recognition

b. Indicate the adjustment you would make to Heinz's net income for each item in Part a.

c. Discuss whether you believe the reclassification adjustments made by Heinz for the sale and promotion incentive costs (Item 3) are appropriate.

d. Prepare a common-size income statement for Year 10, Year 11, and Year 12 using the amounts in Exhibit 9.7. Set sales equal to 100 percent.

e. Repeat Part d after making the income statement adjustments in Part b.

f. Assess the changes in the profitability of Heinz during the three-year period.

9.10 UNUSUAL INCOME STATEMENT ITEMS. Vulcan Materials Company, a member of the S&P 500 Index, is the nation's largest producer of construction aggregates, a major producer of asphalt mix and concrete, and a leading producer of cement in Florida. Following is a summarized income statement prepared from Vulcan's Consolidated Statement of Earnings for the years ended December 31, 2008, 2007, and 2006.

In thousands	2008	2007	2006
Total revenues	$3,651,438	$3,327,787	$3,342,475
Cost of revenues	2,901,726	2,376,884	2,410,571
SG&A	342,584	289,604	264,276
Goodwill impairment	252,664	—	—
Loss (gain) on sale of property, plant & equipment and businesses, net	(94,227)	(58,659)	(5,557)
Other operating (income) expense, net	(411)	5,541	(21,904)
Total operating expenses, net	3,402,336	2,613,370	2,647,386
Operating earnings	249,102	714,417	695,089
Other income (expense), net	(4,357)	(5,322)	28,541
Interest income	3,126	6,625	6,171
Interest expense	(172,813)	(48,218)	(26,310)
Earnings from continuing operations before income taxes	75,058	667,502	703,491
Provision for income taxes	(76,724)	(204,416)	(223,313)
Earnings from continuing operations	(1,666)	463,086	480,178
Discontinued operations (Note 2)			
Loss from results of discontinued operations	(4,059)	(19,327)	(16,624)
Income tax benefit	1,610	7,151	6,660
Loss on discontinued operations, net of income taxes	(2,449)	(12,176)	(9,964)
Net earnings (loss)	$ (4,115)	$ 450,910	$ 470,214

In Note 2 to the Consolidated Financial Statements, "Discontinued Operations," Vulcan describes a June 2005 sale of substantially all assets of its Chemicals business, known as Vulcan Chemicals, to Basic Chemicals, a subsidiary of Occidental Chemical Corporation. Basic Chemicals assumed certain liabilities relating to the chemicals business, including the obligation to monitor and remediate all releases of hazardous materials at or from the Wichita, Geismar, and Port Edwards plant facilities. The decision to sell the chemicals business was based on Vulcan's desire to focus its resources on the construction materials business. The amounts reported as discontinued operations are not revenues and expenses from Vulcan operating the discontinued segment. Instead, the amounts represent a continual updating of the amount payable by the segment buyer. The receivable held by Vulcan from the sale is dependent on the levels of gas and chemical prices through the end of 2012. Vulcan classifies this financial instrument as a derivative contract that must be marked to market. The derivative does not hedge an existing transaction; therefore, its value changes are reflected in income as part of discontinued operations. As of 2008, Vulcan reported that final gains on disposal (if any) would occur after December 31, 2008.

Goodwill impairment relates to Vulcan's cement segment. Vulcan explains the need for the impairment as arising from the need to increase discount rates due to disruptions in credit markets as well as weak levels of construction activity.

Required

a. Discuss the appropriate treatment of the following when forecasting future earnings of Vulcan Materials: (1) goodwill impairment; (2) discontinued operations; and (3) loss (gain) on sale of property, plant, and equipment and businesses (net).

b. Prepare common-size income statements for Vulcan Materials. Interpret changes in profit margin over the three-year period in light of the special items.

9.11 IMPLICATIONS OF A GOODWILL IMPAIRMENT CHARGE FOR FUTURE CASH FLOW AND PROFITABILITY. Northrop Grumman Corporation is a leading global security company that provides innovative systems products and solutions in aerospace, electronics, information systems, shipbuilding, and technical services to government and commercial customers worldwide. In an early 2009 press release, Northrop reported that it would record a non-cash, after-tax charge of between \$3.0 billion and \$3.4 billion for impairment of goodwill in its 2008 fourth-quarter income statement. As a result of the charge, Northrop reported net losses for the fourth quarter and all of 2008.

Northrop explained how it determined the impairment as follows: "The company performed its required annual testing of goodwill as of Nov. 30, 2008 using a discounted cash flow analysis supported by comparative market multiples to determine the fair value of its businesses versus their book values. Testing as of Nov. 30, 2008 indicated that book values for Shipbuilding and Space Technology exceeded the fair values of these businesses. . . . This non-cash charge does not impact the company's normal business operations."

Required

a. Explain how a company computes a goodwill impairment. Describe the usefulness of discounted cash flow and comparative market multiples in the computation of an impairment.

b. Explain the consequences of a goodwill impairment for the assessment of (1) current period profitability as measured by ROA, (2) future earnings projections, and (3) future period profitability as measured by ROA.

9.12 RESTRUCTURING CHARGES AT INTEL. Intel Corporation's Consolidated Income Statement from its 2008 Annual Report appears below.

Three Years Ended December 27, 2008 (In Millions, Except Per Share Amounts)	2008	2007	2006
Net revenue	**$37,586**	**$38,334**	**$35,382**
Cost of sales	16,742	18,430	17,164
Gross margin	**20,844**	**19,904**	**18,218**
Research and development	5,722	5,755	5,873
Marketing, general and administrative	5,458	5,417	6,138
Restructuring and asset impairment charges	710	516	555
Operating expenses	**11,890**	**11,688**	**12,566**
Operating income	**8,954**	**8,216**	**5,652**
Gains (losses) on equity method investments, net	(1,380)	3	2
Gains (losses) on other equity investments, net	(376)	154	212
Interest and other, net	488	793	1,202
Income before taxes	**7,686**	**9,166**	**7,068**
Provision for taxes	2,394	2,190	2,024
Net income	**$ 5,292**	**$ 6,976**	**$ 5,044**
Basic earnings per common share	**$ 0.93**	**$ 1.20**	**$ 0.87**

Note 15, which follows, explains the source of the restructuring charges, the breakdown of the charges into employee-related costs and asset impairments, and the balance of the accrued restructuring liability account.

Note 15: Restructuring and Asset Impairment Charges

The following table summarizes restructuring and asset impairment charges by plan for the three years ended December 27, 2008:

(In Millions)	2008	2007	2006
2008 NAND plan	$215	$ —	$ —
2006 efficiency program	495	516	555
Total restructuring and asset impairment charges	**$710**	**$516**	**$555**

We may incur additional restructuring charges in the future for employee severance and benefit arrangements, and facility-related or other exit activities. Subsequent to the end of 2008, management approved plans to restructure some of our manufacturing and assembly and test operations, and align our manufacturing and assembly and test capacity to current market conditions. These actions, which are expected to take place beginning in 2009, include closing two assembly and test facilities in Malaysia, one facility in the Philippines, and one facility in China; stopping production at a 200mm wafer fabrication facility in Oregon; and ending production at our 200mm wafer fabrication facility in California.

2008 NAND Plan

In the fourth quarter of 2008, management approved a plan with Micron to discontinue the supply of NAND flash memory from the 200mm facility within the IMFT manufacturing network. The agreement resulted in a $215 million restructuring charge, primarily related to the IMFT 200mm supply agreement. The restructuring charge resulted in a reduction of our investment in IMFT of $184 million, a cash payment to Micron of $24 million, and other cash payments of $7 million.

2006 Efficiency Program

The following table summarizes charges for the 2006 efficiency program for the three years ended December 27, 2008:

(In Millions)	2008	2007	2006
Employee severance and benefit arrangements	$151	$289	$238
Asset impairments	344	227	317
Total	**$495**	**$516**	**$555**

The following table summarizes the restructuring and asset impairment activity for the 2006 efficiency program during 2007 and 2008:

(In Millions)	Employee Severance and Benefits	Asset Impairments	Total
Accrued restructuring balance as of December 30, 2006	**$ 48**	**$ —**	**$ 48**
Additional accruals	299	227	526
Adjustments	(10)	—	(10)
Cash payments	(210)	—	(210)
Non-cash settlements	—	(227)	(227)
Accrued restructuring balance as of December 29, 2007	**$127**	**$ —**	**$127**
Additional accruals	167	344	511
Adjustments	(16)	—	(16)
Cash payments	(221)	—	(221)
Non-cash settlements	—	(344)	(344)
Accrued restructuring balance as of December 27, 2008	**$ 57**	**$ —**	**$ 57**

We recorded the additional accruals, net of adjustments, as restructuring and asset impairment charges. The remaining accrual as of December 27, 2008 was related to severance benefits that we recorded within accrued compensation and benefits.

From the third quarter of 2006 through the fourth quarter of 2008, we incurred a total of $1.6 billion in restructuring and asset impairment charges related to this program. These charges included a total of $678 million related to employee severance and benefit arrangements for approximately 11,900 employees, and $888 million in asset impairment charges.

Required

a. Based on your reading of the note, how would you treat Intel's restructuring charges in the assessment of current profitability and the prediction of future earnings?

b. Why is the balance of the "accrued restructuring" limited to employee-related costs?

c. Describe the effect on net income of each entry in the "accrued restructuring balance" account reconciliation. (For example, what is the effect of "Additional accruals" on net income?)

d. How do U.S. GAAP and IFRS differ on the rules used to compute the restructuring charge?

EXHIBIT 9.8

General Dynamics Corporation
Balance Sheet
(amounts in millions)
(Problem 9.13)

	Year 9 as Reported	Year 8 as Restated in Year 9 Annual Report	Year 8 as Originally Reported
ASSETS			
Cash and cash equivalents	$ 513	$ 507	$ 513
Marketable securities	432	307	307
Accounts receivable	64	99	444
Contracts in process	1,550	1,474	2,606
Net assets of discontinued businesses	767	1,468	—
Other current assets	329	145	449
Total Current Assets	$3,655	$4,000	$4,319
Property, plant, and equipment, net	322	372	1,029
Other assets	245	300	859
Total Assets	$4,222	$4,672	$6,207
LIABILITIES AND SHAREHOLDERS' EQUITY			
Accounts payable and accruals	$ 553	$ 642	$2,593
Current portion of long-term debt	145	450	516
Other current liabilities	1,250	1,174	—
Total Current Liabilities	$1,948	$2,266	$3,109
Long-term debt	38	163	365
Other noncurrent liabilities	362	263	753
Total Liabilities	$2,348	$2,692	$4,227
Common stock	$ 42	$ 55	$ 55
Additional paid-in capital	—	25	25
Retained earnings	2,474	2,651	2,651
Treasury stock	(642)	(751)	(751)
Total Shareholders' Equity	**$1,874**	**$1,980**	**$1,980**
Total Liabilities and Shareholders' Equity	$4,222	$4,672	$6,207

9.13 USING ORIGINALLY REPORTED VERSUS RESTATED DATA. Prior to Year 8, General Dynamics Corporation engaged in a wide variety of industries, including weapons manufacturing under government contracts, information technologies, commercial aircraft manufacturing, missile systems, coal mining, material service, ship management, and ship financing. During Year 8, General Dynamics sold its information technologies business. During Year 9, General Dynamics sold its commercial aircraft manufacturing business. During Year 9, it also announced its intention to sell its missile systems, coal mining, material service, ship management, and ship financing businesses. These strategic moves left General Dynamics with only its weapons manufacturing business. Financial statements for General Dynamics for Year 9 as reported, Year 8 as restated in the Year 9 annual report for discontinued operations, and Year 8 as originally reported appear in Exhibit 9.8 (balance sheet), Exhibit 9.9 (income statement), and Exhibit 9.10 (statement of cash flows).

Required

a. Refer to the balance sheets of General Dynamics in Exhibit 9.8. Why does the restated amount for total assets for Year 8 of $4,672 million differ from the originally reported amount of $6,207 million?

b. Refer to the income statement for General Dynamics in Exhibit 9.9. Why are the originally reported and restated net income amounts for Year 8 the same (that is, $505 million) when each of the individual revenues and expenses decreased on restatement?

EXHIBIT 9.9

General Dynamics Corporation
Income Statement
(amounts in millions)
(Problem 9.13)

	Year 9 as Reported	Year 8 as Restated in Year 9 Annual Report	Year 8 as Originally Reported
Continuing Operations			
Sales	$ 3,472	$ 3,322	$ 8,751
Operating costs and expenses	(3,297)	(3,207)	(8,359)
Interest income (expense), net	25	4	(34)
Other expense, net	27	(27)	(27)
Earnings before Income Taxes	$ 227	$ 92	$ 331
Income tax credit	21	114	43
Income from Continuing Operations	$ 248	$ 206	$ 374
Discontinued Operations			
Earnings from operations	$ 193	$ 299	$ 131
Gain on disposal	374	—	—
Net Income	$ 815	$ 505	$ 505

EXHIBIT 9.10

General Dynamics Corporation
Statement of Cash Flows
(amounts in millions)
(Problem 9.13)

	Year 9 as Reported	Year 8 as Restated in Year 9 Annual Report	Year 8 as Originally Reported
OPERATIONS			
Income from continuing operations	$ 248	$ 206	$ 374
Depreciation and amortization	56	140	303
(Increase) Decrease in accounts receivable	35	4	(91)
(Increase) Decrease in contracts in process	(76)	(83)	237
(Increase) Decrease in other current assets	(6)	8	13
Increase (Decrease) in accounts payable and accruals	(66)	51	262
Increase (Decrease) in other current liabilities	11	(41)	(469)
Cash flow from continuing operations	$ 202	$ 285	$ 629
Cash flow from discontinued operations	288	324	44
Cash Flow from Operations	$ 490	$ 609	$ 673
INVESTING			
Proceeds from sale of discontinued operations	$ 1,039	$ 184	$ 184
Capital expenditures	(18)	(29)	(82)
Purchase of marketable securities	(125)	(307)	(307)
Other	32	3	56
Cash Flow from Investing	$ 928	$(149)	$(149)
FINANCING			
Issue of common stock	$ 57	$ —	$ —
Repayment of debt	(454)	(11)	(61)
Purchase of common stock	(960)	—	—
Dividends	(55)	(42)	(42)
Other	—	—	(17)
Cash Flow from Financing	$(1,412)	$ (53)	$(120)
Change in Cash	$ 6	$ 407	$ 404
Cash—Beginning of Year	507	100	109
Cash—End of Year	$ 513	$ 507	$ 513

c. Refer to the statement of cash flows for General Dynamics in Exhibit 9.10. Why is the restated amount of cash flow from operations for Year 8 of $609 million less than the originally reported amount of $673 million?

d. If the analyst wanted to analyze changes in the structure of assets and equities between Year 8 and Year 9, which columns and amounts in Exhibit 9.8 would he or she use? Explain.

e. If the analyst wanted to analyze changes in the operating profitability between Year 8 and Year 9, which columns and amounts in Exhibit 9.9 would he or she use? Explain.
f. If the analyst wanted to use cash flow ratios to assess short-term liquidity and long-term solvency risk, which columns and amounts in Exhibit 9.10 would he or she use? Explain.

INTEGRATIVE CASE 9.1

STARBUCKS

Exhibits 1.26–1.28 of Integrative Case 1.1 (Chapter 1) present the financial statements for Starbucks for 2005–2008. Starbucks explains several components of its income during those years in the following notes to the financial statements:

Note 1: Summary of Significant Accounting Policies (selected excerpts)

Long-lived Assets

When facts and circumstances indicate that the carrying values of long-lived assets may be impaired, an evaluation of recoverability is performed by comparing the carrying values of the assets to projected undiscounted future cash flows in addition to other quantitative and qualitative analyses. Upon indication that the carrying values of such assets may not be recoverable, the Company recognizes an impairment loss by a charge to net earnings. The fair value of the assets is estimated using the discounted future cash flows of the assets. Property, plant and equipment assets are grouped at the lowest level for which there are identifiable cash flows when assessing impairment. Cash flows for retail assets are identified at the individual store level. Long-lived assets to be disposed of are reported at the lower of their carrying amount, or fair value less estimated costs to sell. The Company recognized net impairment and disposition losses of \$325.0 million, \$26.0 million and \$19.6 million in fiscal 2008, 2007 and 2006, respectively, due to underperforming Company-operated retail stores, as well as renovation and remodeling activity in the normal course of business. The net losses in fiscal 2008 include \$201.6 million of asset impairments related to the US and Australia store closures and charges incurred for office facilities no longer occupied by the Company due to the reduction in positions within Starbucks leadership structure and non-store organization. See Note 3 for further details. Depending on the underlying asset that is impaired, these losses may be recorded in any one of the operating expense lines on the consolidated statements of earnings: for retail operations, these losses are recorded in "Restructuring charges" and "Store operating expenses"; for specialty operations, these losses are recorded in "Other operating expenses"; and for all other operations, these losses are recorded in "Cost of sales including occupancy costs," "General and administrative expenses," or "Restructuring charges."

Asset Retirement Obligations

Starbucks accounts for asset retirement obligations under FASB Interpretation No. 47 ("FIN 47"), "Accounting for Conditional Asset Retirement Obligations—an interpretation of FASB Statement No. 143," which it adopted at the end of fiscal 2006. FIN 47 requires recognition of a liability for the fair value of a required asset retirement obligation ("ARO") when such obligation is incurred. The Company's AROs are primarily associated with leasehold improvements which, at the end of a lease, the Company is contractually obligated to remove in order to comply with the lease agreement. At the inception of a lease with such conditions, the Company records an ARO liability and a corresponding capital asset in an amount equal to the estimated fair value of the obligation. The liability is estimated based on a number of assumptions requiring management's judgment, including store closing costs, cost inflation rates and discount rates, and is accreted to its projected future value over time. The capitalized asset is depreciated using the convention for depreciation of leasehold improvement assets. Upon satisfaction of the ARO conditions, any difference between the recorded ARO liability and the actual retirement costs incurred is recognized as an operating gain or loss in the consolidated statements of earnings. ARO expense was $6.5 million and $4.2 million, in fiscal 2008 and 2007, respectively, with components included in "Costs of sales including occupancy costs," and "Depreciation and amortization expenses". The initial impact of adopting FIN 47 at the end of fiscal year 2006 was a charge of $27.1 million, with a related tax benefit of $9.9 million, for a net expense of $17.2 million, with the net amount recorded as a cumulative effect of a change in accounting principle on the consolidated statement of earnings for fiscal year 2006. As of September 28, 2008 and September 30, 2007, the Company's net ARO asset included in "Property, plant and equipment, net" was $18.5 million and $20.2 million, respectively, while the Company's net ARO liability included in "Other long-term liabilities" was $44.6 million and $43.7 million, as of the same respective dates.

Insurance Reserves

The Company uses a combination of insurance and self-insurance mechanisms, including a wholly owned captive insurance entity and participation in a reinsurance pool, to provide for the potential liabilities for workers' compensation, healthcare benefits, general liability, property insurance, director and officers' liability insurance and vehicle liability. Liabilities associated with the risks that are retained by the Company are not discounted and are estimated, in part, by considering historical claims experience, demographic factors, severity factors and other actuarial assumptions.

Recent Accounting Pronouncements

In September 2006, the FASB issued SFAS No. 157, "Fair Value Measurements" ("SFAS 157"), which defines fair value, establishes a framework for measuring fair value and expands disclosures about fair value measurements. For financial assets and liabilities, SFAS 157 will be effective for Starbucks first fiscal quarter of 2009. As permitted by FSP-FAS 157-2, SFAS 157 is effective for nonfinancial assets and liabilities for Starbucks first fiscal quarter of 2010. Starbucks believes the adoption of SFAS 157 for its financial assets and liabilities will not have a material impact on the Company's consolidated financial statements and continues to evaluate the potential impact of the adoption of SFAS 157 related to its nonfinancial assets and liabilities.

In February 2007, the FASB issued SFAS No. 159, "The Fair Value Option for Financial Assets and Financial Liabilities" ("SFAS 159"). SFAS 159 permits companies to choose to measure many financial instruments and certain other items at fair value. SFAS 159 will be effective for Starbucks first fiscal quarter of 2009. Starbucks believes the adoption of SFAS 159 will not have a material impact on the Company's consolidated financial statements.

In December 2007, the FASB issued SFAS No. 141 (revised 2007), "Business Combinations" ("SFAS 141R"), which replaces SFAS 141. SFAS 141R establishes principles and requirements for how an acquirer recognizes and measures in its financial statements the identifiable assets acquired, the liabilities assumed, any resulting goodwill, and any non-controlling interest in the acquiree. SFAS 141R also provides for disclosures to enable users of the financial statements to evaluate the nature and financial effects of the business combination. SFAS 141R will be effective for Starbucks first fiscal quarter of 2010 and must be applied prospectively to business combinations completed on or after that date.

In December 2007, the FASB issued SFAS No. 160, "Noncontrolling Interests in Consolidated Financial Statements—an amendment of Accounting Research Bulletin No. 51"

("SFAS 160"), which establishes accounting and reporting standards for noncontrolling interests ("minority interests") in subsidiaries. SFAS 160 clarifies that a noncontrolling interest in a subsidiary should be accounted for as a component of equity separate from the parent's equity. SFAS 160 will be effective for Starbucks first fiscal quarter of 2010 and must be applied prospectively, except for the presentation and disclosure requirements, which will apply retrospectively. The Company is currently evaluating the potential impact that adoption of SFAS 160 may have on its consolidated financial statements.

In March 2008, the FASB issued SFAS No. 161, "Disclosures about Derivative Instruments and Hedging Activities—an amendment of FASB Statement No. 133" ("SFAS 161"), which requires enhanced disclosures about an entity's derivative and hedging activities. SFAS 161 will be effective for Starbucks second fiscal quarter of 2009.

Note 3: Restructuring Charges (selected excerpts)

In January of fiscal 2008, Starbucks began a transformation plan designed to address the deterioration of its US retail business, reduce its global infrastructure costs and position the Company's business for long-term profitable growth. Since the announcement, a number of actions have been initiated, resulting in the recognition of certain exit, impairment and severance costs. The total amount of these restructuring costs recognized in fiscal 2008 was $266.9 million. Certain additional costs from these actions are expected to be recognized in fiscal 2009, nearly all related to US store closures.

US Store Closures—The most significant action was the commitment to close approximately 600 underperforming Company-operated stores in the US market and reduce the number of future store openings. The decision was a result of a rigorous evaluation of the Company-operated store portfolio, and the Company closed the first 205 of these stores during the fourth quarter of fiscal 2008. As a result of the announced store closures and actions taken to date, the Company recognized $206.3 million of restructuring charges in fiscal 2008, comprised of $169.6 million of store asset impairments, lease exit costs of $33.6 million, and severance totaling $3.1 million. The Company expects to complete the remainder of the closures by the end of fiscal 2009, and recognize the total remaining lease exit costs and related severance during that time.

Australia Store Closures—To address the difficulties specific to its Australia market, Starbucks closed 61 Company-operated stores in the fourth quarter of fiscal 2008. As a result of these store closures, the Company recognized $16.9 million of restructuring charges in fiscal 2008, comprised of $1.5 million of store asset impairments, lease exit costs of $11.6 million, and severance totaling $3.8 million. Starbucks continues to have wholly owned operations in Australia but with a more focused presence with 23 Company-operated stores as of September 28, 2008.

Reduction in Force within the Non-store Organization—To address its global cost structure, on July 29, 2008, Starbucks announced the reduction of approximately 1,000 open and filled positions within its leadership structure and its non-store organization. As a result, the Company recognized, in fiscal 2008, $10.7 million in employee termination benefits expense as well as $33.0 million related to consolidation of support facilities, primarily at the corporate headquarters in Seattle.

Note 13: Shareholders' Equity (selected excerpts)

Comprehensive Income

Comprehensive income includes all changes in equity during the period, except those resulting from transactions with shareholders and subsidiaries of the Company. It has two components: net earnings and other comprehensive income. Accumulated other comprehensive income reported on the Company's consolidated balance sheets consists of foreign currency translation adjustments and the unrealized gains and losses, net of applicable taxes, on available-for-sale securities and on derivative instruments designated and qualifying as cash flow and net investment hedges.

Comprehensive income, net of related tax effects, was as follows (in millions):

Fiscal Year Ended	Sep 28, 2008	Sep 30, 2007	Oct 1, 2006
Net earnings	$315.5	$672.6	$564.3
Unrealized holding gains/(losses) on available-for-sale securities, net of tax (provision)/benefit of $2.4, ($0.2) and ($1.3) in 2008, 2007 and 2006, respectively	(4.0)	0.3	2.2
Unrealized holding gains/(losses) on cash flow hedging instruments, net of tax (provision)/benefit of ($0.4), $7.5 and $1.6 in 2008, 2007 and 2006, respectively	0.7	(12.8)	(2.8)
Unrealized holding losses on net investment hedging instruments, net of tax benefit of $0.6 and $5.2 in 2008 and 2007, respectively	(0.9)	(8.8)	—
Reclassification adjustment for net (gains)/losses realized in net earnings for available-for-sale securities, net of tax provision of $1.1 in 2006	—	—	(1.8)
Reclassification adjustment for net losses realized in net earnings for cash flow hedges, net of tax benefit of $3.0, $0.5 and $2.4 in 2008, 2007 and 2006, respectively	5.0	0.9	4.2
Net unrealized gain/(loss)	0.8	(20.4)	1.8
Translation adjustment, net of tax benefit/(provision) of $0.3, $—, and ($1.8) in 2008, 2007, and 2006, respectively	(7.0)	37.7	14.6
Total comprehensive income	$309.3	$689.9	$580.7

The unfavorable translation adjustment change during fiscal 2008 of $7.0 million was primarily due to the strengthening of the US dollar against several currencies including the Australian dollar, Korean won and Canadian dollar. The favorable translation adjustment change during fiscal 2007 of $37.7 million was primarily due to the weakening of the US dollar against several currencies including the euro, Canadian dollar and British pound sterling. The favorable translation adjustment change during fiscal 2006 of $14.6 million was primarily due to the weakening of the US dollar against several currencies including British pound sterling, the euro and Canadian dollar.

The components of accumulated other comprehensive income, net of tax, were as follows (in millions):

Fiscal Year Ended	Sep 28, 2008	Sep 30, 2007
Net unrealized losses on available-for-sale securities	$(4.1)	$ —
Net unrealized losses on hedging instruments	(22.2)	(27.1)
Translation adjustment	74.7	81.7
Accumulated other comprehensive income	$48.4	$54.6

As of September 28, 2008, the translation adjustment of $74.7 million was net of tax provisionsof $7.0 million. As of September 30, 2007, the translation adjustment of $81.7 million was net of tax provisionsof $7.3 million.

Required

a. Starbucks reports "Restructuring Charges" in its 2008 Income Statement. Assuming a tax rate of 35 percent, discuss whether you would eliminate the charge when forecasting the future earnings of Starbucks. If so, what adjustments would you make to the income statement, balance sheet, and statement of cash flows?

b. Starbucks reports a "Cumulative Effect of an Accounting Change" in its 2006 Income Statement, the last year in which such changes were reported as a separate line item on the income statement. What is the reason for the change? Assuming a tax rate of 35 percent, discuss whether you would eliminate the cumulative effect when assessing Starbucks' current profitability. If so, what adjustments would you make to the income statement, balance sheet, and statement of cash flows. How would you treat the cumulative effect when forecasting the future earnings of Starbucks?

c. Starbucks reports a new line item on its balance sheet beginning in 2007 entitled "Insurance Reserves." Do the changes in this account affect the income statement? If so, describe the likely effect of this account on the income statement and discuss whether you would eliminate the charge when forecasting the future earnings of Starbucks.

d. Examine Starbucks' Note 13 description of comprehensive income. How would you treat the comprehensive income items when forecasting Starbucks' future financial statements?

e. Starbucks lists all of the new pronouncements that may or may not affect its current and future financial statements. Read each pronouncement and discuss how each change might affect the analyst's task of forecasting Starbucks' future earnings.

CASE 9.2

CITI: A VERY BAD YEAR

Citigroup Inc. (Citi) is a leading global financial services company with over 200 million customer accounts and operations in more than 140 countries. Its operating units Citicorp and Citi Holdings provide a broad range of financial products and services to consumers, governments, institutions, and corporations. Services include investment banking, consumer and corporate banking and credit, securities brokerage, and wealth management.

For the year ended December 31, 2008, Citi reported a net loss of $27,684 million, or $5.59 per share. Exhibit 9.11 presents the Consolidated Statements of Income for Citigroup Inc. and Subsidiaries for the year ended December 31, 2008, 2007, and 2006. Various selections from the notes to the consolidated financial statements follow the exhibit.

CONSOLIDATED STATEMENT OF INCOME	*Citigroup Inc. and Subsidiaries*		
	Year ended December 31		
in millions of dollars, except per share amounts	**2008**	**2007**	**2006**
Revenues			
Interest revenue	**$106,655**	$121,429	$93,611
Interest expense	**52,963**	76,051	55,683
Net interest revenue	**$ 53,692**	$ 45,378	$37,928
Commissions and fees	**$ 11,227**	$ 20,706	$18,850
Principal transactions	**(22,188)**	(12,086)	7,990
Administration and other fiduciary fees	**8,560**	9,132	6,903
Realised gains (losses) from sales of investments	**(2,061)**	1,168	1,791
Insurance premiums	**3,221**	3,062	2,769
Other revenue	**342**	11,135	10,096
Total non-interest revenues	**$ (899)**	$ 33,117	$48,399
Total revenues, net of interest expense	**$ 52,793**	$ 78,495	$86,327
Provisions, for credit losses and for benefits and claims			
Provision for loan losses	**$ 33,674**	$ 16,832	$ 6,320
Policyholder benefits and claims	**1,403**	935	967
Provision for unfunded lending commitments	**(363)**	150	250
Total provisions for credit losses and for benefits and claims	**$ 34,714**	$ 17,917	$ 7,537
Operating expenses			
Compensation and benefits	**$ 32,440**	$ 33,892	$29,752
Net occupancy	**7,125**	6,648	5,794
Technology/communication	**4,897**	4,511	3,741
Advertising and marketing	**2,292**	2,803	2,471
Restructuring	**1,766**	1,528	—
Other operating	**22,614**	10,420	8,543
Tolal operating expenses	**$ 71,134**	$ 59,802	$50,301
Income (loss) from continuing operations before income taxes and minority interest	**$(53,055)**	$ 776	$28,489
Provision (benefit) for income taxes	**(20,612)**	(2,498)	7,749
Minority interest, net of taxes	**(349)**	285	289
Income (loss) from continuing operations	**$(32,094)**	$ 2,989	$20,451
Discontinued operations			
Income from discontinued operations	**$ 1,478**	$ 925	$ 1,177
Gain on sale	**3,139**	—	219
Provision (benefit) for income taxes and minority interest, net of taxes	**207**	**297**	**309**
Income from discontinued operations, net of taxes	**$ 4,410**	$ 628	$ 1,087

(*Continued*)

CONSOLIDATED STATEMENT OF INCOME	*Citigroup Inc. and Subsidiaries*		
	Year ended December 31		
in millions of dollars, except per share amounts	**2008**	**2007**	**2006**
Net income (loss)	**$(27,684)**	$ 3,617	$21,518
Basic earning per share (1)			
Income (loss) from continuing operations	**$ (6.42)**	$ 0.60	$ 4.17
Income from discontinued operations, net of taxes	**0.83**	0.13	0.22
Net income (loss)	**$ (5.59)**	$ 0.73	$ 4.39
Weighted average common shares outstanding	**5,265.4**	4,905.8	4,887.3
Diluted earnings per share (1)			
Income (loss) from continuing opetations	**$ (6.42)**	$ 0.59	$ 4.09
Income from discontinued operations, net of taxes	**0.83**	0.13	0.22
Net income (loss)	**$ (5.59)**	$ 0.72	$ 4.31
Adjusted weighted average common shares outstanding	**5,795.1**	4,995.3	4,986.1

(1) Diluted shares used in the diluted EPS calculation represent basic shares for 2009 due to the net loss. Using actual diluted shares would result in anti-dilution.

Excerpts from Financial Statement Notes:
The following excerpts were disclosed in the notes to Citigroup's 2008 financial statements:

3. Discontinued Operations

Sale of Citigroup's German Retail Banking Operations

On December 5, 2008, Citigroup sold its German retail banking operations to Credit Mutuel for Euro 5.2 billion, in cash plus the German retail bank's operating net earnings accrued in 2008 through the closing. The sale resulted in an after-tax gain of approximately $3.9 billion including the after-tax gain on the foreign currency hedge of $383 million recognised during the fourth quarter of 2008.

The sale does not include the corporate and investment banking business or the Germany-based European data center.

The German retail banking operations had total assets and total liabilities as of November 30, 2008, of $15.6 billion and $11.8 billion, respectively.

Results for all of the German retail banking businesses sold, as well as the net gain recognized in 2008 from this sale, are reported as *Discontinued Operations* for all periods presented.

Summarized financial information for *Discontinued Operations*, including cash flows, related to the sale of the German retail banking operations is as follows:

in millions of dollars	**2008**	**2007**	**2006**
Total revenues, net of interest expense	**$6,592**	$2,212	$2,126
Income from discontinued operations	**$1,438**	$ 652	$ 837
Gain on sale	**3,695**	—	—
Provision for income taxes and minority interest, net of taxes	**426**	214	266
Income from discontinued operations, net of taxes	**$4,707**	$ 438	$ 571

in millions of dollars	2008	2007	2006
Cash flows from operating activities	**$ (4,719)**	$2,227	$2,246
Cash flows from investing activities	**18,547**	(1,906)	(3,316)
Cash flows from financing activities	**(14,226)**	(213)	1,147
Net cash provided by (used in) discontinued operations	**$ (398)**	$ 108	$ 77

CitiCapital

On July 31, 2008, Citigroup sold substantially all of CitiCapital, the equipment finance unit in *North America.* The total proceeds from the transaction were approximately $12.5 billion and resulted in an after-tax loss to Citigroup of $305 million. This loss is included in *Income from discontinued operations* on the Company's Consolidated Statement of Income for the second quarter of 2008. The assets and liabilities for CitiCapital totaled approximately $12.9 billion and $0.5 billion, respectively, at June 30, 2008.

This transaction encompassed seven CitiCapital equipment finance business lines, including Healthcare Finance, Private Label Equipment Finance, Material Handling Finance, Franchise Finance, Construction Equipment Finance, Bankers Leasing, and CitiCapital Canada. CitiCapital's Tax Exempt Finance business was not part of the transaction and was retained by Citigroup.

CitiCapital had approximately 1,400 employees and 160,000 customers throughout North America.

Results for all of the CitiCapital businesses sold, as well as the net loss recognized in 2008 from this sale, are reported as *Discontinued operations* for all periods presented.

Summarized financial information for *Discontinued operations,* including cash flows, related to the sale of CitiCapital is as follows:

in millions of dollars	2008	2007	2006
Total revenues, net of interest expense	**$ 24**	$ 991	$ 1,162
Income (loss) from discontinued operations	**$ 40**	$ 273	$ 313
Loss on sale	**(506)**	—	—
Provision (benefit) for income taxes and minority interest, net of taxes	**(202)**	83	86
Income (loss) from discontinued operations, net of taxes	**$ (264)**	$ 190	$ 227

in millions of dollars	2008	2007	2006
Cash flows from operating activities	**$ (287)**	$(1,148)	$ 2,596
Cash flows from investing activities	**349**	1,190	(2,664)
Cash flows from financing activities	**(61)**	(43)	3
Net cash provided by (used in) discontinued operations	**$ 1**	$ (1)	$ (65)

Sale of the Asset Management Business

On December 1, 2005, the Company completed the sale of substantially all of its Asset Management business to Legg Mason, Inc. (Legg Mason).

On January 31, 2006, the Company completed the sale of its Asset Management business within Bank Handlowy (an indirect banking subsidiary of Citigroup located in Poland) to Legg Mason. This transaction, which was originally part of the overall Asset Management business sold to Legg Mason on December 1, 2005, was postponed due to delays in obtaining local regulatory approval. A gain from this sale of $18 million after-tax and minority interest ($31 million pretax and minority interest) was recognized in the first quarter of 2006 in *Discontinued operations.*

During March 2006, the Company sold 10.3 million shares of Legg Mason stock through an underwritten public offering. The net sale proceeds of $ 1.258 billion resulted in a pretax gain of $24 million in *ICG.*

In September 2006, the Company received from Legg Mason the final closing adjustment payment related to this sale. This payment resulted in an additional after-tax gain of $51 million ($83 million pretax), recorded in *Discontinued operations.*

Sale of the Life Insurance and Annuities Business

On July 1, 2005, the Company completed the sale of Citigroup's Travelers Life & Annuity and substantially all of Citigroup's international insurance businesses to MetLife, Inc. (MetLife).

During the first quarter of 2006, $15 million of the total $657 million federal tax contingency reserve release was reported in *Discontinued operations* as it related to the Life Insurance and Annuities business sold to MetLife.

In July 2006, Citigroup recognized an $85 million after-tax gain from the sale of MetLife shares. This gain was reported in income from continuing opetations in *ICG.*

In July 2006, the Company received the final closing adjustment payment related to this sale, resulting in an after-tax gain of $75 million ($ 115 million pretax), which was recorded in *Discontinued operations.*

In addition, during the third quarter of 2006, a release of $42 million of deferred tax liabilities was reported in *Discontinued operations* as it related to the Life Insurance & Annuities business sold to MetLife.

In December 2008, the Company fulfilled its previously agreed upon obligations with regard to its remaining 10% economic interest in the long-term care business that it had sold to the predecessor of Genworth Financial in 2000. Under the terms of the 2005 sales agreement of Citi's Life Insurance and Annuities business to MetLife, Citi agreed to reimburse MetLife for certain liabilities related to the sale of the long-term-care business to Genworth's predecessor. The assumption of the final 10% block Genworth at December 31, 2008, resulted in a pretax loss of $50 million ($33 million after-tax), which has been reported in *Discontinued operations.*

Combined Results for Discontinued Operations

The following is summarized financial information for the German retail banking operations, CitiCapital, Life Insurance and Annuities business, Asset Management business, and TPC:

in millions of dollars	2008	2007	2006
Total revenues, net of interest expense	**$6,616**	$3,203	$3,507
Income from discontinued operations	**$1,478**	$ 925	$1,177
Gain on sale	**3,139**	—	219
Provision (benefit) for income taxes, and minority interest, net of taxes	**207**	297	309
Income from discontinued operations, net of taxes	**$4,410**	$ 628	$1,087

Cash Flows from Discontinued Operations

in millions of dollars	2008	2007	2006
Cash flows from operating activities	**$ (5,006)**	$1,079	$ 4,842
Cash flows from investing activities	**18,896**	(716)	(5,871)
Cash flows from financing activities	**(14,287)**	(256)	1,150
Net cash provided by (used in) discontinued operations	**$ (397)**	$ 107	$ 121

5. Interest Revenue and Expense

For the years ended December 31, 2008, 2007 and 2006, respectively, interest revenue and expense consisted of the following:

in millions of dollars	2008	2007	2006
Interest revenue			
Loan interest, including fees	**$ 62,336**	$ 63,201	$52,086
Deposits with banks	**3,119**	3,113	2,240
Federal funds sold and securities purchased under agreements to resell	**9,175**	18,354	14,199
Investments, including dividends	**10,718**	13,423	10,340
Trading account assets[1]	**17,489**	18,507	11,865
Other interest	**3,818**	4,831	2,881
Total interest revenue	**$106,655**	$121,429	$93,611
Interest expense			
Deposits	**$ 20,271**	$ 28,402	$21,336
Federal funds purchased and securities loaned or sold under agreements to repurchase	**11,330**	23,028	17,448
Trading account liabilities[1]	**1,277**	1,440	1,119
Short-term borrowings	**4,039**	7,071	4,632
Long-term debt	**16,046**	16,110	11,148
Total interest expense	**$ 52,963**	$ 76,051	$55,683
Net interest revenue	**$ 53,692**	$ 45,378	$37,928
Provision for loan losses	**33,674**	$ 16,832	$ 6,320
Net interest revenue after provision for loan losses	**$ 20,018**	$ 28,546	$31,608

(1) Interest expense on *Trading account facilities* of *ICG* is reported as a reduction of interest revenue from *Trading account assets.*

6. Commissions and Fees

Commissions and fees revenue includes charges to customers for credit and bank cards, including transaction-processing fees and annual fees; advisory and equity and debt underwriting services; lending and deposit-related transactions, such as loan commitments, standby letters of credit and other deposit and loan servicing activities; investment management-related fees, including brokerage services and custody and trust services; and insurance fees and commissions.

The following table presents commissions and fees revenue for the years ended December 31:

in millions of dollars	2008	2007	2006
Investment banking	**$ 2,284**	$ 5,228	$ 4,093
Credit cards and bank cards	**4,517**	5,036	5,191
Smith Barney	**2,836**	3,265	2,958
ICG trading-related	**2,322**	2,706	2,464
Checking-related	**1,134**	1,108	911
Transaction Services	**1,423**	1,166	859
Other Consumer	**1,211**	649	279
Nikko Cordial-related[1]	**1,086**	834	—
Loan servicing[2]	**(1,731)**	560	660
Primerica	**415**	455	399
Other *ICG*	**747**	295	243
Other	**(141)**	71	58
Corporate finance[3]	**(4,876)**	(667)	735
Total commissions and fees	**$11,227**	$20,706	$18,850

(1) Commissions and fees for Nikko Cordial have not been detailed due to unavailability of the information.

(2) Includes fair value adjustments on mortgage servicing assets. The mark-to-market on the underlying economic hedges of the MSRs is included in *Other revenue.*

(3) Includes write-downs of approximately $4.9 billion in 2008 and $1.5 billion in 2007, net of underwriting fees, on funded and unfunded highly leveraged finance commitments, recorded at fair value and reported as loans held for sale in *Other assets.* Write-downs were recorded on all highly leveraged finance commitments where there was value impairment, regardless of funding date.

7. Principal Transactions

Principal transactions revenue consists of realized and unrealized gains and losses from trading activities. Not included in the table below is the impact of net interest revenue related to trading activities, which is an integral part of trading activities' profitability. The following table presents principal transactions revenue for the years ended December 31:

in millions of dollars	2008	2007	2006[1]
Institutional Clients Group			
Fixed income[2]	**$ (6,455)**	$ 4,053	$5,593
Credit products[3]	**(21,614)**	(21,805)	(744)
Equities[4]	**(394)**	682	866
Foreign exchange[5]	**2,316**	1,222	693
Commodities[6]	**667**	686	487
Total *ICG*	**$(25,480)**	$(15,162)	$6,895
Consumer Banking/Global Cards[7]	**1,616**	1,364	504
Global Wealth Management[7]	**836**	1,315	680
Corporate/Other	**840**	397	(89)
Total principal transactions revenue	**$(22,188)**	$(12,086)	$7,990

(1) Reclassified to conform to the current period's presentation.

(2) Includes revenues from government securities and corporate debt, municipal securities, preferred stock, mortgage securities, and other debt instruments. Also includes spot and forward trading of currencies and exchange-traded and over-the-counter (OTC) currency options, options on fixed income securities, interest rate swaps, currency swaps, swap options, caps and floors, financial futures, OTC options, and forward contracts on fixed income securities. Losses in 2008 reflect the volatility and dislocation in the credit and trading markets.

(Continued)

(3) Includes revenues from structured credit products such as North America and Europe collateralized debt obligations, In 2007 and 2008, losses recorded were related to subprime-related exposures in *ICG's* lending and structuring business and exposures to super senior CDOs.

(4) Includes revenues from common, preferred and convertible preferred stock, convertible corporate debt, equity-linked notes, and exchange-traded and OTC equity options and warrants.

(5) Includes revenues from foreign exchange spot, forward, option and swap contracts, as well as translation gains and losses.

(6) Primarily includes the results of Phibro LLC, which trades crude oil, refined oil products, natural gas, and other commodities.

(7) Includes revenues from various fixed income, equities and foreign exchange transactions.

10. Restructuring

In the fourth quarter of 2008, Citigroup recorded a pretax restructuring expense of $1.797 billion pre-tax related to the implementation of a Company-wide re-engineering plan. This initiative will generate headcount reductions of approximately 20,600. The charges related to the 2008 Re-engineering Projects Restructuring Initiative are reported in the Restructuring line on the Company's Consolidated Statement of Income and are recorded in each segment.

In 2007, the Company completed a review of its structural expense base in a Company-wide effort to create a more streamlined organization, reduce expense growth, and provide investment funds for future growth initiatives. As a result of this review, a pretax restructuring charge of $1.4 billion was recorded in *Corporate/Other* during the first quarter of 2007. Additional net charges of $151 million were recognized in subsequent quarters throughout 2007 and a net release of $31 million in 2008 due to a change in estimates. The charges related to the 2007 Structural Expense Review Restructuring Initiative are reported in the Restructuring line on the Company's Consolidated Statement of Income.

The primary goals of the 2007 Structural Expense Review and Restructuring, and the 2008 Re-engineering Projects and Restructuring Initiatives were:

- eliminate layers of management/improve workforce management;
- consolidate certain back-office, middle-office and corporate functions;
- increase the use of shared services;
- expand centralized procurement; and
- continue to rationalize operational spending on technology.

The implementation cf these restructuring initiatives also caused certain related premises and equipment assets to become redundant. The remaining depreciable lives of these assets were shortened, aid accelerated depreciation charges began in the second quarter of 2007 and fourth quarter of 2008 for the 2007 and 2008 initiatives, respectively, in addition to normal scheduled depreciation.

19. Goodwill and Intangible Assets

Goodwill

The changes in goodwill during 2007 and 2008 were as follows:

in millions of dollars	**Goodwill**
Balance at December 31, 2006	$33,264
Acquisition of GFU	865
Acquisition of Quilter	268
Acquisition of Nikko Cordial[1]	892
Acquisition of Grupo Cuscatlán	921
Acquisition of Egg	1,471
Acquisition of Old Lane	516

(Continued)

in millions of dollars	**Goodwill**
Acquisition of BISYS	872
Acquisition of BOOC	712
Acquisition of ATD	569
Sale of Avantel	(118)
Foreign exchange translation, smaller acquisitions and other	821
Balance at December 31, 2007	$41,053
Sale of German retail bank	$ (1,047)
Sale of CitiCapital	(221)
Sale of Citigroup Global Services Limited	(85)
Purchase accounting adjustments—BISYS	(184)
Purchase of the remaining shares of Nikko Cordial—net of purchase accounting adjustments	287
Acquisition of Legg Mason Private Portfolio Group	98
Foreign exchange translation	(3,116)
Impairment of goodwill	(9,568)
Smaller acquisitions, purchase accounting adjustments and other	(85)
Balance at December 31, 2008	$27,132

In the following press release, Citi further describes the source of the goodwill impairment:

Citi Announces Fourth Quarter Goodwill Impairment of $9.6 Billion[22]

Results in Additional Net Loss of $9.0 Billion for 2008

New York – Citi announced today that it recorded a pre-tax goodwill impairment charge of approximately $9.6 billion ($8.7 billion after-tax) in the fourth quarter of 2008. Citi had previously announced in its fourth quarter earnings press release (January 16, 2009) that it was continuing to review its goodwill to determine whether a goodwill impairment had occurred as of December 31, 2008, and this charge is the result of that review and testing. The goodwill impairment charge was recorded in North America Consumer Banking, Latin America Consumer Banking, and EMEA Consumer Banking, and resulted in a write-off of the entire amount of goodwill allocated to those reporting units. The charge does not result in a cash outflow or negatively affect the Tier 1 or Total Regulatory Capital ratios, Tangible Common Equity or Citi's liquidity position as of December 31, 2008.

In addition, Citi recorded a $374 million pre-tax charge ($242 million after-tax) to reflect further impairment evident in the intangible asset related to Nikko Asset Management at December 31, 2008.

The primary cause for both the goodwill and the intangible asset impairments mentioned above was the rapid deterioration in the financial markets, as well as in the global economic outlook generally, particularly during the period beginning mid-November through year-end 2008. This deterioration further weakened the near term prospects for the financial services industry.

Giving effect to these charges, Net Income (Loss) from Continuing Operations for 2008 was $(32.1) billion and Net Income (Loss) was $(27.7) billion, resulting in Diluted Earnings per Share of $(6.42) and $(5.59) respectively.

[22] Press release found at: http://www.citigroup.com/citi/press/2009/090227b.htm. Reprinted by permission.

A complete description of Citi's goodwill impairment testing as of December 31, 2008 and the related charges will be included in Citi's Form 10-K to be filed with the Securities and Exchange Commission on or before March 2, 2009.

Required

Consider the following items reported in Citi's Consolidated Statement of Income:

- Principal transactions
- Realized (gain) losses from sales of investments
- Provision for loan losses
- Restructuring
- Other operating expenses (which presumably includes the goodwill impairment)
- Discontinued operations

Discuss whether you would eliminate all or part of each item when assessing current profitability and forecasting the future earnings of Citi. If so, what adjustments would you make to the financial statements (assuming a tax rate of 35 percent)?

Chapter 10

Forecasting Financial Statements

Learning Objectives

1. **Develop the skills to build forecasts of future balance sheets, income statements, and statements of cash flows.**
2. **Identify and incorporate important business and strategic factors into expectations of future business activities, which we measure with forecasts of future accounting numbers and financial statements.**
3. **Apply a seven-step forecasting framework for building financial statement forecasts. These seven steps focus on projecting (a) revenue growth; (b) operating expenses; (c) operating assets and liabilities; (d) financial leverage and capital structure; (e) interest, taxes, and dividends; (f) a balance sheet that balances; and (g) cash flows.**
4. **Understand how and when to use shortcut forecasting techniques.**
5. **Develop forecast models that are flexible and comprehensive, allowing the analyst to respond efficiently and appropriately to important new information.**
6. **Test the sensitivity of the forecasts to variations in critical assumptions and parameters.**

Thus far, this text has discussed the first four steps of the six-step analysis and valuation framework. Drawing on the disciplines of accounting, finance, economics, and strategy, the preceding nine chapters of this text have demonstrated the first four steps of this framework, describing how to analyze (1) the economics of a firm's industry, (2) the competitive advantages and risks of the firm's strategy, (3) the information content and quality of the firm's accounting, and (4) the firm's financial performance and risk. The next five chapters cover the two culminating steps of the framework: (5) forecasting the future operating, investing, and financing activities of the firm and then (6) valuing the firm.

In this chapter, we shift our focus to the future. Economics teaches that the value of an economic resource is a function of its expected future payoffs and the risks inherent in those payoffs. Therefore, this chapter demonstrates how to use your knowledge about a firm's industry, strategy, accounting quality, and past and current performance to forecast the firm's future business activities (that is, operating, investing, and financing activities). The chapter will demonstrate how to capture those expectations in forecasts of future financial statements—income statements, balance sheets, and statements of cash flows. The objective in building financial statement forecasts is to develop unbiased expectations for a firm's future earnings, cash flows, and dividends that the analyst can use to estimate the firm's share value. The analyst also can use financial statement forecasts in a wide array of decision contexts, such as strategic planning, credit analysis, corporate management, and mergers and acquisitions.

In subsequent chapters, we will use these financial statement forecasts to derive the future payoffs to the firm's common equity shareholders, including future earnings, cash flows, and dividends, which we will use to estimate firm value, considering its risk. Chapter 11 demonstrates the classical dividends-based valuation model, which is the theoretical foundation for other approaches to firm valuation. Chapter 11 also describes and applies models to incorporate risk into estimates of expected returns on investments and costs of capital. Chapter 12 demonstrates valuation models based on expected future free cash flows. Chapter 13 discusses and implements valuation models that rely on earnings. Chapter 14 demonstrates valuation approaches that rely on comparable companies and market-based multiples, such as price-earnings ratios and market-to-book ratios. Chapter 14 also illustrates some advanced valuation techniques, including computing price differentials and reverse engineering share prices.

INTRODUCTION TO FORECASTING

Analysts must develop realistic expectations for the outcomes of future business activities. To develop these expectations, analysts build a set of *financial statement forecasts*—expected future income statements, balance sheets, and statements of cash flows. Financial statement forecasts represent an integrated portrayal of a firm's future operating, investing, and financing activities. These activities determine the firm's future profitability, growth, financial position, cash flows, and risk. Financial statement forecasts are important tools because the analyst can derive expectations of future payoffs to equity shareholders—earnings, cash flows, and dividends—which are the fundamental bases for share value.

Financial statement forecasts also are important tools in many other decision contexts. Credit decisions require expectations for future cash flows available to make required interest and principal payments. Managers' decisions about firm strategy, potential customer or supplier relationships, potential mergers or acquisitions, and potential carve-outs of divisions or subsidiaries, and even whether a firm presents a good employment opportunity, all depend on their expectations for future payoffs from such decisions and the risks of those payoffs.

Developing forecasts of future payoffs is in many ways the most difficult step of the six-step framework of this text because it requires the analyst to estimate the effects of future activities, which involves a high degree of uncertainty. Forecast errors can prove very costly. Optimistic forecasts can lead the analyst to overestimate future earnings and cash flows or underestimate risk and therefore make poor investment decisions based on an overstated value of the firm. Pessimistic or conservative forecasts can lead the analyst to understate future earnings and cash flows or overstate risk and consequently miss valuable investment opportunities. Analysts need to develop *realistic* (unbiased and objective, not optimistic or conservative) expectations of future earnings and cash flows that will lead to well-informed investment decisions.

Superior forecasting has the potential to help investors pick stocks and earn superior returns. As Chapter 1 discussed, empirical research results from Nichols and Wahlen (2004) suggest the potential to earn abnormal returns by correctly forecasting the *sign* of the change in annual earnings numbers.[1] Their findings indicate that if a person had accurately predicted the sign of the change in earnings one year ahead for each firm in their sample during their 14-year study period (1988–2001), he or she would have earned returns that beat the market by roughly 19 percent per year by investing in those firms that experienced earnings increases and by roughly 16 percent per year by selling short those firms that experienced earnings decreases.

The evidence in Nichols and Wahlen (2004) also suggests that investors have the potential to earn even greater abnormal returns by correctly forecasting the *sign* and *magnitude* of the change in one-year-ahead earnings.[2] Their findings imply that stock returns for the firms that experience the largest percentage increases in earnings (that is, firms among the top 10 percent of all sample firms each year) generate very large positive returns, beating the market by an average of nearly 50 percent per year. Their findings also indicate that stock returns for firms that experience the largest percentage decreases in earnings (firms among the bottom 10 percent of all sample firms each year) tend to earn stock returns that are on average 22 percentage points per year lower than the market as a whole.

Certainly, analysts do not have perfect foresight to predict one year ahead the direction or amount of earnings increases and decreases for all firms. Nonetheless, analysts should consider the Nichols and Wahlen (2004) results encouraging because those results suggest that by increasing one's accuracy in forecasting future changes in earnings, the analyst should have greater potential to distinguish stocks that are future winners versus losers and earn superior returns. It also is important to keep in mind that firms vary in the quality and detail of the information they disclose to help analysts develop forecasts. Some firms provide rich detail that analysts can use to produce more accurate forecasts, but other firms provide only limited disclosures, perhaps due to concerns about revealing too much information to their competitors.

Accounting researchers also have investigated whether financial statement ratios like those described throughout this text can be used to build models that accurately predict future changes in earnings. For example, Ou and Penman (1989) built prediction models based on regressions of future earnings changes on a set of financial statement ratios.[3] Their earnings-change-prediction models estimate the probability of an earnings increase one year ahead. They conduct out-of-sample tests and find that their probability estimates correctly predict whether one-year-ahead earnings will increase or decrease for roughly 67 percent of their firm-year observations. They also show that taking long positions in shares of firms with a high probability of an earnings increase next year and short positions in shares of firms with a very low probability of an earnings increase next year resulted in average market-adjusted returns of roughly 8 percent per year during their study period. This study and subsequent related studies provide encouraging results suggesting that a fundamental

---

[1] D. Craig Nichols and James M. Wahlen, "How Do Earnings Numbers Relate to Stock Returns? A Review of Classic Accounting Research with Updated Evidence," *Accounting Horizons* 18 (December 2004), pp. 263–286. This study uses data from 1988–2001 to replicate the seminal findings in Ray Ball and Philip Brown, "An Evaluation of Accounting Income Numbers," *Journal of Accounting Research* (Autumn 1968), pp. 159–178; Roger Kormendi and Robert Lipe, "Earnings Innovations, Earnings Persistence, and Stock Returns," *Journal of Business* 60 (1987), pp. 323–345; and Victor Bernard and Jacob Thomas, "Post-Earnings Announcement Drift: Delayed Price Response or Risk Premium?," *Journal of Accounting Research* (1989 Supplement), pp. 1–48.

[2] See also William Beaver, Roger Clarke, and William Wright, "The Association between Unsystematic Security Returns and the Magnitude of Earnings Forecast Errors," *Journal of Accounting Research* 17 (Autumn 1979), pp. 316–341.

[3] See Jane Ou and Stephen Penman, "Financial Statement Analysis and the Prediction of Stock Returns," *Journal of Accounting and Economics* (November 1989), pp. 295–330. For examples of other studies in this area, see Baruch Lev and Ramu Thiagarajan, "Fundamental Information Analysis," *Journal of Accounting Research* (Autumn 1993), pp. 190–215; and Jeffery Abarbanell and Brian Bushee, "Abnormal Stock Returns to a Fundamental Analysis Strategy," *The Accounting Review* 73 (January 1998), pp. 19–46.

analysis of financial statement ratios can produce more accurate forecasts of future earnings and profitable investment decisions.

To maximize the analyst's potential to develop reliable forecasts of financial statements and to mitigate the potential for costly forecast errors, the analyst should base forecasts on expectations that reflect the economics of the industry, the competitive advantages and risks of the firm's strategy, the quality of the firm's accounting, and the drivers of the firm's profitability and risk. The first four steps of the analytical framework of this text provide the necessary foundation for forecasting. These four steps inform the analyst about the critical risk and success factors of the firm and the key drivers of the firm's profitability and risk. The critical factors that are the focal points of the firm's strategy, accounting quality, profitability, and risk are the most important building blocks for forecasting a firm's future financial statements.

This chapter first outlines general forecasting principles, describes a seven-step process for forecasting financial statements, and offers several practical coaching tips on implementing the seven-step sequence. The chapter then illustrates each of the steps by applying them to PepsiCo, developing forecasts for income statements, balance sheets, and statements of cash flows for the next five years. The chapter then describes a set of techniques to enhance the reliability of forecasts, including sensitivity analysis, iteration, and validity checks. The chapter also describes some simplifying steps for shortcut forecasts and the conditions under which such shortcuts are more likely to be reliable and less likely to result in forecast errors.

PREPARING FINANCIAL STATEMENT FORECASTS

In this section we describe in general how to prepare financial statement forecasts. We first describe general principles of building forecasts, and then a seven-step forecasting procedure, along with some practical forecasting tips. We also briefly describe how to use FSAP to build financial statement forecasts.

General Forecasting Principles

Several key principles of forecasting deserve mention at the outset.

- **As noted earlier, the objective of forecasting is to produce reliable and realistic expectations of future earnings, cash flows, and dividends, which determine the future payoffs to investment.** To maximize reliability and avoid costly forecast errors, financial statement forecasts should provide unbiased and objective predictions of the firm's future operating, investing, and financing activities and should not be conservative or optimistic. Firm managers have a tendency to be optimistic, and accountants tend to be conservative. Ideally, the analyst's forecasts should be neither optimistic nor conservative; instead they should be accurate and realistic.
- **Forecasts should not manifest wishful thinking.** The analyst should incorporate forecast assumptions that reflect business strategies that management intends to execute and can achieve in the future. The analyst should not build forecasts based on wishful thinking. That is, the analyst should not create forecasts based on strategies the analyst *hopes* the firm will pursue or thinks the firm *should* pursue. Instead, the forecasts should capture the strategies the analyst believes the firm *actually will pursue* in the future.
- **Financial statement forecasts should be comprehensive.** The financial statement forecasts should be complete and include *all* expected future operating, investing, and financing activities. For example, suppose an analyst takes a quick-and-dirty approach and simply extrapolates expected future sales growth and then projects expected future earnings assuming a constant profit margin in the future. This approach fails to consider all of the elements that determine profitability from sales and the ways those

elements may change in the future, which can cause the earnings forecasts to be incomplete, erroneous, and misleading. By assuming a constant profit margin on sales, the analyst ignores important considerations, such as whether the cost of goods sold and selling, general, and administrative expenses will increase more quickly or more slowly than sales.

- **Financial statement forecasts must be internally consistent.** Forecasts of financial statements should rely on the *additivity* within financial statements and the *articulation* across financial statements to avoid internal inconsistencies. The analyst can rely on the internal discipline of accounting across the three primary financial statements to reduce the possibility of errors from inconsistent assumptions. For example, future sales growth will trigger future growth in costs of sales; accounts receivable; inventory; and property, plant, and equipment. In turn, future growth in inventory; receivables; and property, plant, and equipment will drive growth in related operating elements including accounts payable, accrued expenses, and depreciation and perhaps trigger additional financing through short-term and long-term borrowing and equity capital issues. Each of these elements will, in turn, have implications for the firm's cash flows. For example, simply projecting increasing future revenues without considering the future increases in inventory, and property, plant, and equipment necessary to achieve the projected revenue growth could result in substantial errors in expected future profitability and cash flow. To capture the many complex relations among operating, investing, and financing activities, financial statement forecasts should add up and articulate with each other. The income statement should measure profit or loss appropriately for each period by including all of the revenues, expenses, gains, and losses each period. The balance sheet should capture all of the elements of financial position, should reflect profitability each period, and should balance. The statement of cash flows should reflect all of the cash inflows and outflows implied by the income statement and all of the changes in the firm's balance sheet. Forecasts of each of the financial statements should articulate, and each will impact and be impacted by each of the other statements.
- **Financial statement forecasts must rely on assumptions that have external validity.** Forecast assumptions should pass the test of common sense. The analyst should impose reality checks on the forecast assumptions. For example, do the sales growth forecast assumptions appropriately reflect the firm's strategy and the competitive conditions in the industry, including market demand and price elasticity for the firm's products, as well as the firm's productive capacity? Analysts also should benchmark the external validity of forecast assumptions by comparing them to industry averages and to the firm's past performance and strategies.

Seven-Step Forecasting Game Plan

To prepare a set of financial statement forecasts, the analyst must forecast the firm's future operating, investing, and financing activities. This business activity-based forecasting approach enables the analyst to identify the necessary sequence of steps to project the three principal financial statements into the future. The particular sequence of steps may vary depending on the reason for forecasting the financial statements. For most forecasts of financial statements, the following seven-step sequence works well:

1. Project revenues from sales and other operating activities.
2. Project operating expenses (for example, cost of goods sold and selling, general, and administrative expenses) and derive projected operating income.
3. Project the operating assets (for example, cash; marketable securities; receivables; inventory; property, plant, and equipment; investments; and intangible assets) that will be necessary to support the level of operations projected in Steps 1 and 2. Also

project the operating liabilities that will be triggered by normal business operations (for example, accounts payable and accrued expenses).

4. Project the financial leverage, financial assets, and common equity capital (for example, short-term and long-term debt, common shareholders' equity except for retained earnings, and any financial assets available to service debt or equity claims) that will be necessary to finance the net operating assets projected in Step 3. In addition, determine the financing costs (such as interest expense) triggered by the financial liabilities and any investment income from financial assets (such as interest income) in the firm's capital structure. From projected operating income from Step 2, subtract interest expense and add interest income.
5. Project nonrecurring gains or losses (if any) and derive projected income before tax. Subtract the projected provision for income taxes to derive projected net income. Subtract expected dividends from net income to obtain the projected change in retained earnings. Also project any other comprehensive income items.
6. Check whether the projected balance sheet is in balance. If it is not in balance, the projected financial structure may need to be adjusted. For example, if projected assets exceed projected liabilities and equities, the firm may be required to raise capital through additional short- or long-term debt or equity issuances. Alternately, if projected liabilities and equities exceed projected total assets, the firm may be able to pay down debt, increase dividends, or repurchase stock. Steps 4 and 5 must be repeated until the balance sheet is in balance.
7. Derive the projected statement of cash flows from the projected income statement and the changes in the projected balance sheet amounts.

Exhibit 10.1 summarizes this procedure.

Throughout this chapter and throughout the book, we demonstrate how the analyst can gain additional insights about a firm by evaluating the operating, investing, and financing activities of the firm. The economic, strategic, and financial analysis techniques in Chapters 1 through 5 emphasize how to analyze operating, investing, and financing activities as integrated drivers of the profitability and risk of the firm. The accounting analysis techniques in Chapters 6 through 9 demonstrate how to assess the accounting quality of the financing, investing, and operating activities of the firm. We carry this perspective into the forecasting and valuation techniques in Chapters 10 through 14. In this chapter, the seven-step forecasting procedure begins with projecting the operating activities that occur in the normal day-to-day operations of producing and selling goods and services. Those activities involve accounts such as cash, receivables, inventory, payables, accrued expenses, and taxes. Projecting the firm's investing activities involves forecasting the acquisition and use of long-lived productive resources such as property, plant, and equipment and intangible assets, as well as financial resources such as short-term and long-term investment securities. The projected financing activities determine the financial capital structure of the firm. They typically involve financial liabilities such as short-term and long-term debt (notes, mortgages, bonds, and capital leases), in addition to preferred and common stock, and stock issues and repurchases and dividend payments. In some circumstances, projecting financing activities can also include projections of financial assets (for example, short-term and long-term investment securities) that will be used to retire debt or pay dividends.

Practical Tips for Implementing the Seven-Step Forecasting Game Plan

The analyst should consider these seven steps as integrated and interdependent tasks that are not necessarily sequential or linear. The order in which an analyst implements

EXHIBIT 10.1

A Schematic Representation of the Seven-Step Process for Preparing Financial Statement Forecasts

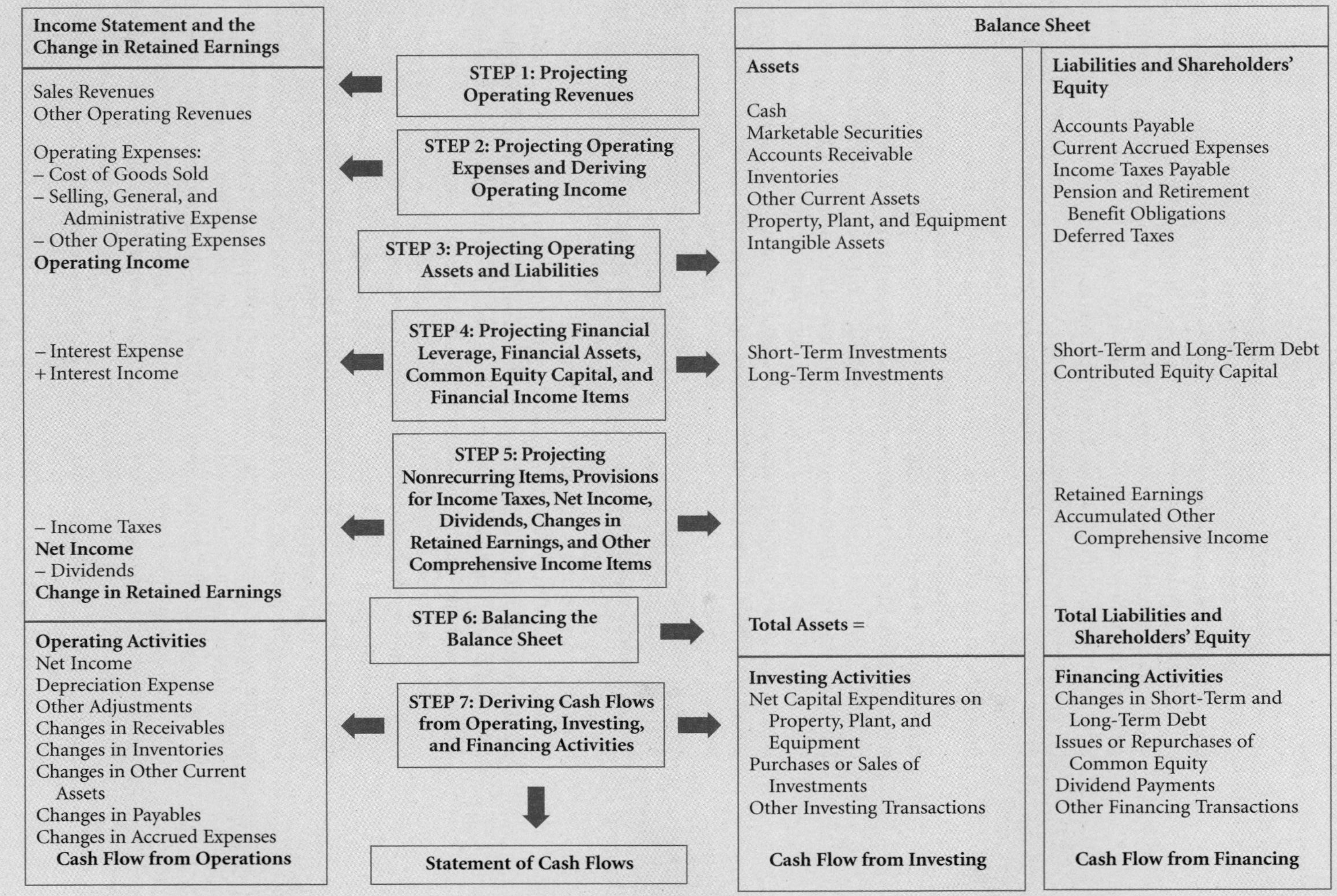
Income Statement and the Change in Retained Earnings
Sales Revenues
Other Operating Revenues
Operating Expenses:
– Cost of Goods Sold
– Selling, General, and Administrative Expense
– Other Operating Expenses
Operating Income
– Interest Expense
+ Interest Income
– Income Taxes
Net Income
– Dividends
Change in Retained Earnings
Operating Activities
Net Income
Depreciation Expense
Other Adjustments
Changes in Receivables
Changes in Inventories
Changes in Other Current Assets
Changes in Payables
Changes in Accrued Expenses
Cash Flow from Operations
STEP 1: Projecting Operating Revenues
STEP 2: Projecting Operating Expenses and Deriving Operating Income
STEP 3: Projecting Operating Assets and Liabilities
STEP 4: Projecting Financial Leverage, Financial Assets, Common Equity Capital, and Financial Income Items
STEP 5: Projecting Nonrecurring Items, Provisions for Income Taxes, Net Income, Dividends, Changes in Retained Earnings, and Other Comprehensive Income Items
STEP 6: Balancing the Balance Sheet
STEP 7: Deriving Cash Flows from Operating, Investing, and Financing Activities
Statement of Cash Flows
Balance Sheet
Assets
Cash
Marketable Securities
Accounts Receivable
Inventories
Other Current Assets
Property, Plant, and Equipment
Intangible Assets
Short-Term Investments
Long-Term Investments
Total Assets =
Liabilities and Shareholders' Equity
Accounts Payable
Current Accrued Expenses
Income Taxes Payable
Pension and Retirement Benefit Obligations
Deferred Taxes
Short-Term and Long-Term Debt
Contributed Equity Capital
Retained Earnings
Accumulated Other Comprehensive Income
Total Liabilities and Shareholders' Equity
Investing Activities
Net Capital Expenditures on Property, Plant, and Equipment
Purchases or Sales of Investments
Other Investing Transactions
Cash Flow from Investing
Financing Activities
Changes in Short-Term and Long-Term Debt
Issues or Repurchases of Common Equity
Dividend Payments
Other Financing Transactions
Cash Flow from Financing

these steps and the amount of emphasis placed on each step will depend on the integration of the firm's operating, investing, and financing activities. For example, forecasts of revenues for a retail or restaurant chain may first require forecasts of the number of new stores that will be open. The sales forecasts for a manufacturer may depend on building a new productive plant capacity, which may depend on obtaining long-term financing.

The forecast amounts must articulate between the three forecasted financial statements. Most forecast amounts affect all three financial statements. For example, sales forecasts will affect the income statement, the balance sheet, and the statement of cash flows. As another example, the ending balance in retained earnings on the balance sheet should reflect the beginning balance plus net income from the income statement minus dividends from the statement of cash flows. Property, plant, and equipment on the balance sheet will be affected by capital expenditures from the statement of cash flows and depreciation expense, which affects the income statement and the statement of cash flows. Net cash flow on the statement of cash flows must equal the change in cash on the balance sheet. The financial statement forecasts represent complex, interrelated business activities.

Preparing financial statement forecasts that balance requires at least one flexible financial account and an iterative and circular process. Firms require financial flexibility. They rely on flexible financial accounts—financial assets, financial liabilities, equity capital, and dividends—that can expand or contract with the firm's supply and demand for capital. For example, a firm with growth opportunities that requires capital to acquire assets may need to raise cash through short-term or long-term borrowing or issuing equity shares. A cash-cow firm may generate substantial amounts of excess cash and deploy it by paying down debt, investing in financial assets, paying dividends, or repurchasing its common shares. Therefore, the analyst must identify what financial flexibility the firm can use. Then the analyst must adjust these flexible financial accounts as necessary to appropriately match the firm's future financial capital structure with the firm's future operations and investments. Thus, producing a set of financial statement forecasts will require several iterations and a degree of circularity. For example, the first pass through a set of financial statement forecasts may reveal to the analyst that the firm must increase long-term debt to finance future capital expenditures. Increased long-term debt, however, will increase interest expense and net income will then fall. As a consequence, retained earnings will fall; so the firm may have to increase long-term debt a bit more. The analyst must repeat this process until the balance sheet balances and articulates with the income statement and the statement of cash flows.[4]

Garbage in, garbage out. The quality of the financial statement forecasts—and the quality of the investment decisions based on these forecasts—will depend on the quality of the forecast assumptions. The analyst should thoughtfully evaluate and justify each assumption, especially the most important assumptions that reflect the critical risk and success factors of the firm's strategy. In addition, the analyst can impose reality checks on the assumptions by analyzing the forecasted financial statements using ratios, common-size, and rate-of-change financial statements. These analytical tools (discussed in Chapters 1, 4, and 5) may reveal that certain assumptions are unrealistic or inconsistent.

Sweat the big stuff. Do not sweat the little stuff. The analyst should devote thoughtful time and analysis developing the most important forecasts, those that reflect the critical business activities that will determine the future growth, success, and risk of the business. For example, for most firms, forecasts of revenues, key operating expenses, important assets (property, plant, and equipment), the debt-equity structure, and a few other items usually

[4] Most computer spreadsheet software facilitates iterative and circular processes. For example, in Excel, under the Tools/Options/Calculation menu, you can check the Iteration box to set the spreadsheet to automatically compute iteratively (for example, 1,000 times) until the computations converge to a specified maximum change.

deserve a good amount of thoughtful attention. However, some of the accounts in a set of financial statements are not critical to the risk or success of the business. As such, the analyst should be efficient, making simple reasonable assumptions about these noncritical accounts, and should not get bogged down in "analysis-paralysis."

The analyst should conduct sensitivity analysis on the financial statement forecasts. The analyst should test, for example, variation in earnings and cash flows across different sales growth scenarios, comparing across the most likely, optimistic, and pessimistic growth rate assumptions. Some assumptions will have more significant consequences than others, and sensitivity analyses will help the analyst assess the extent to which forecast results depend on key assumptions.

The subsequent sections of this chapter illustrate the seven-step forecasting procedure using PepsiCo's 2008 financial statements as a base. In this chapter we analyze and use PepsiCo's financial statement data for 2004 through 2008 to carefully develop forecast assumptions and to compute financial statement forecasts for PepsiCo for 2009 through 2013, which we label Year +1 through Year +5 to denote that they are forecasts of activities we expect to occur one year ahead through five years ahead.[5]

Using FSAP to Prepare Forecasted Financial Statements

FSAP

FSAP, the financial statement analysis package introduced in Chapter 1, contains a Forecast spreadsheet that you can use to prepare financial statement forecasts.[6] If you have not previously designed an Excel spreadsheet to prepare financial statement forecasts, you should do so *before* using the Forecast spreadsheet in FSAP. The proper design of a spreadsheet and the preparation of forecasted financial statements provide excellent learning experiences to enhance and solidify your understanding of the relationships between various financial statement items. Once you become comfortable with using spreadsheets for forecasting financial statements, using the Forecast spreadsheet in FSAP will save you time.

Note that the Forecast spreadsheet in FSAP is a general and adaptable template for forecasting financial statements. In addition, FSAP contains a Forecast Development spreadsheet that provides a scratch pad for the analyst to use in computing various detailed forecast assumptions. To illustrate the use of the Forecast template and the Forecast Development spreadsheet, we incorporate in FSAP the specific forecast assumptions we make for PepsiCo in this chapter. Appendix C presents the output from FSAP for PepsiCo, including printouts of the Forecast spreadsheet for PepsiCo with explicit financial statement forecast assumptions through Year +5, and the Forecast Development spreadsheet with various supporting computations. FSAP also contains useful instructions and user guides for how to use FSAP.

All financial statement amounts throughout this chapter appear in millions. The spreadsheets take all computations to multiple decimal places. Because we express all amounts in this chapter in millions, some minor rounding differences will arise and make it appear as though various subtotals and totals disagree with the sum of the individual items that make up the subtotal or total.

---

[5] Previous chapters have analyzed data from the most recent three years to evaluate PepsiCo's current profitability, risk, and accounting quality. In forecasting financial statements that extend one to five years or more into the future, it is often helpful for the analyst to draw on a longer time series of historical data to evaluate a firm's long-term trends. This is particularly helpful for stable, mature firms such as PepsiCo. For firms in the introduction or growth phase of the life cycle or for firms that have recently experienced significant mergers or divestitures, a long time series of historical data may not be available or may not permit reliable comparisons with current period data.

[6] The website for this text (www.cengage.com/accounting/wahlen) contains a blank FSAP template and the FSAP PepsiCo file for easy downloading and use.

STEP 1: PROJECTING SALES AND OTHER REVENUES

Projecting Revenues from Sales

The principal business activities of most firms involve generating revenues by selling products or delivering services. Therefore, analysts commonly begin the process of forecasting financial statements by projecting revenues from the principal business activities of the firm. For many types of firms, analysts use the expected future level of revenues as a basis for deriving many other amounts in the financial statement forecasts.

Sales volumes and prices determine sales numbers. In the case of sales *volume*, some firms report specific volume figures (for example, automobile manufacturers report numbers of vehicles sold and beverage makers report gallons or cases sold), enabling the analyst to assess volume and price separately as drivers of historical sales growth and to use them for predicting future sales. Some firms report volume-related measures that the analyst can use to forecast sales, such as new stores for retailers and restaurant chains and passengers and revenue seat miles for airlines. For a stable firm in a mature industry (for example, consumer foods), an analyst may conclude that the firm will not significantly increase its market share, in which case he or she might anticipate that sales volume will grow with population growth in the firm's geographic markets. For a firm that has increased its production capacity in an industry with high anticipated growth (for example, biotechnology or cell phones), the analyst can use the industry growth rate coupled with the expansion in the firm's capacity to project sales volume increases.

When projecting *prices*, the analyst should consider factors specific to the firm and its industry that might affect demand and price elasticity, such as excess or constrained capacity, raw material surpluses or shortages, substitute products, and technological changes in products or production methods. Capital-intensive firms such as manufacturers of paper products or computer chips may require several years to add new capacity. If the firm competes in a capital-intensive industry that the analyst expects will operate near capacity for the next few years, price increases will be more likely. On the other hand, if the firm competes in a capital-intensive industry with excess capacity, price increases will be less likely. Further, a capital-intensive firm with excess capacity in a competitive industry may face high exit barriers and thus may experience future price decreases. A firm in transition from the high-growth to the mature phase of its life cycle or a firm with significant technological improvements in its production processes (for example, some portions of the computer industry or cell phone industry) might expect increases in sales volume but decreases in sales prices per unit. If a firm has established a competitive position for its brand name in its markets or has successfully differentiated unique characteristics for its products, it may have a greater potential to increase prices or to avoid price declines than a competitor firm with generic products.

When projecting revenues, the analyst also should consider economy-wide factors such as the expected rate of general price inflation in the economy and the effects of changes in exchange rates on sales denominated in foreign currencies. As discussed in Chapter 7, a parent company adds the revenues and expenses of controlled subsidiaries to its income statement during the consolidation process. If the financial statements of the subsidiary are denominated in a foreign currency that has appreciated relative to the currency used to prepare the parent company's financial statements, the translation and consolidation process will increase reported sales revenues due the foreign exchange rate increase, thus leading to a higher sales revenue growth unrelated to volume or pricing increases. In addition, the analyst also should factor the effects of corporate transactions such as acquisitions and divestitures into sales revenue forecasts. Acquisitions made during the period increase sales growth from firm expansion, whereas divestitures of subsidiaries reduce sales growth due to firm contraction.

If sales have grown at a reasonably steady rate in prior periods and nothing indicates that economic, industry, or firm-specific factors will change significantly, the analyst can project that the historical sales growth rate will persist in the future. If the firm's historical sales growth rate has been affected by changes in foreign exchange rates or by a major acquisition or divestiture, the analyst should adjust for these effects when making projections. Projecting sales for a firm with a cyclical sales pattern (for example, heavy machinery manufacturers, property-casualty insurers, and investment banks) involves an additional degree of difficulty. For cyclical firms, the historical growth rates for sales often exhibit wide variations in both direction and amount over the business cycle. For such firms, the analyst can project a varying sales growth rate that reflects this cyclical pattern, as long as the analyst can identify the current point in the cycle.

This discussion clearly emphasizes how heavily forecasting depends on the first four steps of the analysis process—understanding the economic and competitive forces of the industry, the competitive strategy of the firm, the quality of the accounting, and the drivers of profitability and risk. Projecting the future business activities such as revenues relies heavily on the information available about the industry, strategy, accounting, profitability, and risk of the firm.

Projecting Sales Revenues for PepsiCo

Earlier chapters indicated that the consumer foods industry in the United States is mature. Industry sales have grown recently at the growth rate for the general population, approximately 2 percent per year. Consumer foods companies that have achieved growth rates higher than 2 percent have generated faster growth through corporate acquisitions, expansions into international sales markets, and entry into related markets such as restaurants. PepsiCo has defied these industry averages, generating a compounded rate of growth in net revenues of 10.9 percent between 2006 and 2008. PepsiCo discloses in the MD&A section titled "Results of Operations—Consolidated Review" (Appendix B) information about net sales over these years. Net revenue amounts (in millions) and growth rates for PepsiCo are as follows:

	2006	2007	2008
Total Net Revenue Amounts	$35,137	$39,474	$43,251
Growth Rates		+12.3%	+9.6%
Compound Growth Rate			+10.9%

In PepsiCo's 2008 Annual Report, the MD&A section titled "Results of Operations—Division Review" (Appendix B) discloses information about sales and operating profits for each of PepsiCo's six operating divisions (also called segments), which it organizes into three business units, grouped by product and geography. The largest business unit in terms of sales is PepsiCo Americas Foods, which consists of three divisions: Frito-Lay North America (snack foods), Quaker Foods North America (cereals and breakfast foods), and Latin America Foods. The second-largest business unit in terms of sales is PepsiCo International (snack foods and beverages), which consists of two divisions: United Kingdom & Europe (renamed and reorganized as "Europe" in 2009) and Middle East, Africa & Asia (renamed and reorganized as Asia, Middle East & Africa in 2009). The smallest business unit in sales is PepsiCo Americas Beverages, which is a single-division segment.

For each division, PepsiCo discloses overall growth rates in sales as well as sales growth rates attributable to volume, effective net pricing, foreign exchange rates, and acquisitions. The data for PepsiCo's sales drivers appear in Exhibit 10.2. These data reveal significant differences in these drivers of sales growth across the six segments. For example, these data show

EXHIBIT 10.2

PepsiCo Sales Growth Analysis by Division

Fiscal Years (dollar amounts in millions)	2006	2007	2008
PepsiCo Total Net Revenues	**$35,137**	**$39,474**	**$43,251**
Annual growth rate		12.3%	9.6%
PepsiCo Americas Foods	**$16,585**	**$18,318**	**$20,304**
Annual growth rate		10.4%	10.8%
Compound growth rate			10.6%
Frito-Lay North America	**$10,844**	**$11,586**	**$12,507**
Annual growth rate		6.8%	7.9%
Compound growth rate			7.4%
Compound growth in volume			1.5%
Compound growth in prices			5.6%
Foreign exchange and acquisitions			0.2%
Quaker Foods North America	**$ 1,769**	**$ 1,860**	**$ 1,902**
Annual growth rate		5.1%	2.3%
Compound growth rate			3.7%
Compound growth in volume			0.2%
Compound growth in prices			2.9%
Foreign exchange and acquisitions			0.5%
Latin America Foods	**$ 3,972**	**$ 4,872**	**$ 5,895**
Annual growth rate		22.7%	21.0%
Compound growth rate			21.8%
Compound growth in volume			2.5%
Compound growth in prices			7.0%
Foreign exchange and acquisitions			11.1%
PepsiCo Americas Beverages	**$10,362**	**$11,090**	**$10,937**
Annual growth rate		7.0%	−1.4%
Compound growth rate			2.7%
Compound growth in volume			−2.8%
Compound growth in prices			4.4%
Foreign exchange and acquisitions			1.2%
PepsiCo International	**$ 8,190**	**$10,066**	**$12,010**
Annual growth rate		22.9%	19.3%
Compound growth rate			21.1%

EXHIBIT 10.2 (Continued)

Fiscal Years (dollar amounts in millions)	2006	2007	2008
United Kingdom & Europe	**$ 4,750**	**$ 5,492**	**$ 6,435**
Annual growth rate		15.6%	17.2%
Compound growth rate			16.4%
Compound growth in volume			4.0%
Compound growth in prices			2.1%
Foreign exchange and acquisitions			9.6%
Middle East, Africa & Asia	**$ 3,440**	**$ 4,574**	**$ 5,575**
Annual growth rate		33.0%	21.9%
Compound growth rate			27.3%
Compound growth in volume			12.5%
Compound growth in prices			3.0%
Foreign exchange and acquisitions			9.8%

that all of the divisions have managed to sustain price increases; however, the PepsiCo Americas Beverages division has been experiencing declining sales volumes. Not surprisingly, sales growth rates in the Latin America Foods division and the two PepsiCo International divisions have been favorably affected by foreign exchange rates. Also, the Latin America Foods division has generated the biggest gains in sales growth through acquisitions. By analyzing the drivers of sales growth at the division level, an analyst can develop more accurate forecasts for PepsiCo's sales growth in each division and, in turn, for PepsiCo's total sales.

Frito-Lay North America Sales Growth

The Frito-Lay North America segment generates PepsiCo's revenues from manufacturing and selling snack foods in the United States and Canada. In PepsiCo's 2008 Annual Report, the MD&A section titled "Results of Operations—Division Review" (Appendix B) discloses that this segment generated 8.0 percent sales growth in 2008 and 7.0 percent sales growth in 2007, implying a compound annual sales growth rate of 7.4 percent between 2006 and 2008 (computed as 7.4% = [{(1.08) × (1.07)}^(0.5)] − 1.0). PepsiCo discloses that Frito-Lay North America experienced no growth in unit sales volume in 2008 and 3 percent growth in unit sales volume, implying a 1.5 percent per year compounded growth in unit sales volume during this period. The disclosure also reveals a 0.2 percent compounded sales growth from foreign exchange and acquisitions. This implies that it experienced a 5.6 percent annual compounded growth in prices (1.074/(1.015 × 1.002) = 1.056).[7] The division experienced solid volume growth in key products (Cheetos®, Ruffles®, and dips) but has been hampered a bit by consecutive year volume declines in trademark brand Lays® products. The increase in prices likely reflects overall brand strength of Frito-Lay despite the relatively price-competitive snack foods markets. Based on the underlying strength of Frito-Lay's core brands and its continuing ability to develop and introduce successful new products, an analyst might expect that sales volume will exhibit 3.0 percent growth per year into the future. An analyst also might expect that future price increases will be limited to

[7] In words, 1 + sales growth rate = (1 + price growth rate) × (1 + volume growth rate) × (1 + foreign exchange and acquisitions growth rate). Rearranging to solve for the implied growth rates in prices, (1 + price growth rate) = (1 + sales growth rate) / [(1 + volume growth rate) × (1 + foreign exchange and acquisitions growth rate)].

3.0 percent per year because of the competitive and mature nature of the snack foods industry in North America. Foreign exchange rates or acquisitions are not likely to have a material persistent effect on this division's future sales. These assumptions produce an annual sales growth rate of 6.1 percent (that is, 1.061 = 1.030 × 1.030).

In Year +3, PepsiCo's fiscal year (which ends on the last Saturday of December each year) will contain 53 weeks. To capture this effect in our sales forecasts for Frito-Lay North America in Year +3, we project an overall sales growth rate of 8.1 percent (that is, 1.081 = 1.030 × 1.030 × [53/52]). In Year +4, PepsiCo will revert to a normal 52-week year, so the sales growth rate relative to Year +3 will be only 4.1 percent (that is, 1.041 = 1.030 × 1.030 × [52/53]). PepsiCo will not encounter another 53-week fiscal year for several years in the future, so we ignore the effects on our sales forecasts in Year +5 and beyond.[8]

The sales projections and growth rates for Frito-Lay North America over the first five years of the forecast horizon are as follows (allow for rounding):

2008 actual	$12,507	
Year +1 forecast	$13,269	+6.1%
Year +2 forecast	$14,077	+6.1%
Year +3 forecast	$15,221	+8.1%
Year +4 forecast	$15,843	+4.1%
Year +5 forecast	$16,808	+6.1%

Quaker Foods North America Sales Growth

The Quaker Foods North America division sells cereals and breakfast foods. It is a very stable division in a mature and competitive industry. The Quaker Foods segment experienced a modest compound rate of sales growth over Years 2006 to 2008, 3.7 percent per year. Quaker Foods' sales growth is the result of a 0.2 percent growth in sales volume compounded by an average 2.9 percent increase in prices, further compounded by 0.5 percent sales growth from favorable effects of foreign exchange rates and acquisitions. Looking ahead, an analyst might expect this division to maintain 1.0 percent growth in volume and 3.0 percent price increases. Foreign exchange rates or acquisitions are not likely to have a material affect on this division's future sales. Thus, an analyst might expect the Quaker division to generate 4.0 percent sales growth, on average (that is, 1.040 = 1.010 × 1.030). In Year +3, we expect Quaker to generate a 6.0 percent sales growth due to the 53rd week (that is, 1.060 = 1.010 × 1.030 × [53/52]). In Year +4, after reversing the 53rd-week effect, we expect Quaker to experience only a 2.1 percent growth rate in sales (that is, 1.021 = 1.010 × 1.030 × [52/53]). Sales forecast amounts and growth rates for the Quaker Foods North America division over the five-year forecast horizon are as follows:

2008 actual	$1,902	
Year +1 forecast	$1,979	+4.0%
Year +2 forecast	$2,058	+4.0%
Year +3 forecast	$2,183	+6.0%
Year +4 forecast	$2,228	+2.1%
Year +5 forecast	$2,317	+4.0%

[8] Sales forecasts are particularly important because they have crucial impacts on the projected income statements, balance sheets, and cash flows. Analysts should utilize as much relevant information as possible in developing reliable forecast assumptions (recall the "garbage in, garbage out" discussion earlier in this chapter). Analysts can often find useful information for forecasts in company disclosures, competitors' financial statements and disclosures, industry data, and regional- and country-specific economic data. This chapter seeks to illustrate the techniques of using such information in developing forecasts, while also being concise and efficient for you, the reader.

Latin America Foods Sales Growth

The Latin America Foods division sells snacks, cereals, and breakfast foods throughout Latin America. It grew sales at an impressive compound annual rate of 21.8 percent from 2006 to 2008. This growth rate is the result of an average 2.5 percent growth in sales volume compounded by an average 7.0 percent increase in prices and an average of 11.1 percent growth from acquisitions. Changes in foreign exchange rates have had only a minor impact on sales growth.

An analyst might expect this segment to maintain 2.5 percent growth in volume and 5.0 percent price increases due to the strength of its brands in this region. An analyst also might expect PepsiCo to continue to make acquisitions throughout the Latin America region, which could contribute an additional 5.0 percent growth in sales per year, on average. Therefore, an analyst would expect the Latin America Foods division to generate a 13.0 percent sales growth rate (that is, 1.130 = 1.025 × 1.050 × 1.050) each year. In Year +3, this division would be expected to generate a 15.1 percent sales growth due to the effect of the 53rd week (that is, 1.151 = 1.025 × 1.050 × 1.050 × [53/52]). In Year +4, after reversing the 53rd-week effect, we would expect this division to experience 10.8 percent growth rate in sales (that is, 1.108 = 1.025 × 1.050 × 1.050 × [52/53]). Sales forecast amounts and growth rates for the Latin America Foods division over the five-year forecast horizon are as follows:

2008 actual	$ 5,895	
Year +1 forecast	$ 6,660	+13.0%
Year +2 forecast	$ 7,524	+13.0%
Year +3 forecast	$ 8,663	+15.1%
Year +4 forecast	$ 9,602	+10.8%
Year +5 forecast	$10,848	+13.0%

PepsiCo Americas Beverages Sales Growth

The PepsiCo Americas Beverages manufactures and sells a wide variety of syrups, concentrates, and finished goods beverages including carbonated and noncarbonated soft drinks, juices, water, tea, and coffee in the United States, Canada, and Latin America. This segment experienced only a modest compound annual sales growth rate of 2.7 percent between 2006 and 2008. The segment's sales growth was driven largely by net pricing increases despite declining or flat sales volumes in North America. These declines were partially offset by modest increases in sales volumes in Latin America. Over 2006 to 2008, the PepsiCo Americas Beverages segment generated an average 2.8 percent decline in sales volume, an average 4.4 percent growth from price increases, and an average 1.2 percent growth from foreign exchange and acquisitions. Overall in North America, the liquid refreshment beverage category declined in 2008.

Going forward, an analyst might expect that PepsiCo's beverage segment will bounce back to sustain 3.0 percent growth in sales volume in the future because it has a deep and broad portfolio of branded products that span the beverages market (for example, carbonated soft drinks, sports drinks, juices, waters, coffees, and teas). One may also expect that the 4.4 percent price growth, which exceeded the rate of inflation in North America during that same period, is unsustainable and that PepsiCo will generate and sustain only 3.0 percent growth in prices in the future, closer to the economy-wide inflation rate. One might also expect minimal impact on future sales from foreign exchange and acquisitions. Together, these assumptions create an annual sales growth rate of 6.1 percent.

After including the 53rd-week effect, the sales growth rate in Year +3 should be 8.1 percent (that is, 1.081 = 1.03 × 1.03 × 1.0 × [53/52]). After reversing the 53rd-week effect on sales growth in Year +4, the sales growth rate should be 4.1 percent (that is, 1.041 = 1.03 × 1.03 × 1.0 × [52/53]). In Year +5, the assumption is that sales growth rates will revert to

6.1 percent. Sales forecast amounts and growth rates for the PepsiCo Americas Beverages segment over the five-year forecast horizon are as follows:

2008 actual	$10,937	
Year +1 forecast	$11,603	+6.1%
Year +2 forecast	$12,310	+6.1%
Year +3 forecast	$13,310	+8.1%
Year +4 forecast	$13,855	+4.1%
Year +5 forecast	$14,698	+6.1%

United Kingdom & Europe Sales Growth

The PepsiCo International segment is the fastest-growing segment in the company. In this segment, the United Kingdom & Europe (UKEU) division sells PepsiCo snack food and beverage products throughout the United Kingdom, Europe, Russia, and the former Soviet states. PepsiCo discloses that net revenue growth in the UKEU division was fueled in part by significant growth rates in sales volumes for snack foods and beverages in Russia. The UKEU division experienced an average annual sales growth rate of 16.4 percent for 2006 through 2008, which includes sales volume growth of 4.0 percent, net price growth of 2.1 percent, and growth from acquisitions and foreign exchange of 9.6 percent. Acquisitions contributed 8.0 percent to sales growth in 2008, whereas foreign exchange rate movements contributed nearly 9.0 percent in 2007, particularly because of declines in the value of the British pound and the euro relative to the U.S. dollar. (Therefore, PepsiCo's sales in pounds and euros translate into a greater number of U.S. dollars.)

Based on the track record of PepsiCo's UKEU division, an analyst might expect a 4.0 percent growth in sales volume in the future. An analyst also might expect the division to sustain 2.0 percent growth in prices into the future. The assumption is that favorable foreign currency movements are not likely to persist over the next five years, whereas this division may continue to generate sales growth through acquisitions, perhaps at a rate of 5.0 percent per year. With these assumptions, one would forecast average annual sales growth of 11.4 percent for the UKEU division (that is, $1.114 = 1.040 \times 1.020 \times 1.05$). After including the 53rd-week effect for Year +3, the sales growth rate should be 13.5 percent (that is, $1.135 = 1.040 \times 1.020 \times 1.050 \times [53/52]$). After reversing the 53rd-week effect on projected sales for Year +4, the sales growth rate should be 9.3 percent (that is, $1.093 = 1.04 \times 1.02 \times 1.05 \times [52/53]$). In Year +5, sales growth should be 11.4 percent. Sales amounts and growth rates for PepsiCo's UKEU division over the five-year forecast horizon are as follows:

2008 actual	$ 6,435	
Year +1 forecast	$ 7,168	+11.4%
Year +2 forecast	$ 7,984	+11.4%
Year +3 forecast	$ 9,063	+13.5%
Year +4 forecast	$ 9,905	+9.3%
Year +5 forecast	$11,032	+11.4%

Middle East, Africa & Asia Sales Growth

The single fastest-growing division in PepsiCo is the Middle East, Africa & Asia (MEAA) division, which sells PepsiCo snack food and beverage products throughout these regions. This division experienced a very high average annual sales growth rate of 27.3 percent for 2006 through 2008, which includes sales volume growth of 12.5 percent, net price growth of 3.0 percent, and growth from acquisitions and foreign exchange of 9.8 percent. PepsiCo discloses that net revenue growth in the MEAA division was fueled particularly by significant growth in sales volumes for snack foods and beverages in the Middle East, China, and India. Acquisitions contributed 2.0 percent and 11.0 percent to sales growth of the division in 2008 and 2007, respectively. Foreign exchange rate movements contributed 1.0 percent and 5.5 percent to sales growth in 2008 and 2007, respectively.

The MEAA division clearly has momentum in generating sales growth, which is likely to persist for at least several years. An analyst might expect PepsiCo's MEAA division to sustain 8.0 percent growth in sales volume in the future. An analyst also might expect the division to sustain 3.0 percent growth in prices into the future. It is difficult to envision persistent favorable foreign currency movements over the next five years, but it is plausible for this division to generate 5.0 percent sales growth per year through acquisitions. With these assumptions, one would project average annual sales growth of 16.8 percent for the MEAA division (that is, $1.168 = 1.080 \times 1.030 \times 1.05$). After including the 53rd-week effect for Year +3, the sales growth rate should be 19.1 percent (that is, $1.191 = 1.080 \times 1.030 \times 1.050 \times [53/52]$). After reversing the 53rd-week effect for Year +4, the sales growth rate should be 14.6 percent (that is, $1.146 = 1.08 \times 1.03 \times 1.05 \times [52/53]$). In Year +5, sales growth should revert to 16.8 percent per year. Sales amounts and growth rates for PepsiCo's MEAA division over the five-year forecast horizon are as follows:

2008 actual	$ 5,575	
Year +1 forecast	$ 6,513	+16.8%
Year +2 forecast	$ 7,610	+16.8%
Year +3 forecast	$ 9,061	+19.1%
Year +4 forecast	$10,387	+14.6%
Year +5 forecast	$12,135	+16.8%

Combined Sales Growth

The following table combines the sales forecasts for each of the six divisions of PepsiCo. The table presents the projected sales amount for each segment, segment sales expressed as a percentage of total net sales (in parentheses), PepsiCo's total net sales, and annual sales growth rates for each year through forecast Year +5.

PepsiCo Sales Forecasts by Division

	Actual:	**Forecasts:**				
Division:	**2008**	**Year +1**	**Year +2**	**Year +3**	**Year +4**	**Year +5**
Frito-Lay North America	$ 12,507	$ 13,269	$ 14,077	$ 15,221	$ 15,843	$ 16,808
Percentage of total net sales	(28.9%)	(28.1%)	(27.3%)	(26.5%)	(25.6%)	(24.8%)
Quaker Foods North America	$ 1,902	$ 1,979	$ 2,058	$ 2,183	$ 2,228	$ 2,317
Percentage of total net sales	(4.4%)	(4.2%)	(4.0%)	(3.8%)	(3.6%)	(3.4%)
Latin America Foods	$ 5,895	$ 6,660	$ 7,524	$ 8,663	$ 9,602	$ 10,848
Percentage of total net sales	(13.6%)	(14.1%)	(14.6%)	(15.1%)	(15.5%)	(16.0%)
PepsiCo Americas Beverages	$ 10,937	$ 11,603	$ 12,310	$ 13,310	$ 13,855	$ 14,698
Percentage of total net sales	(25.3%)	(24.6%)	(23.9%)	(23.1%)	(22.4%)	(21.7%)
United Kingdom & Europe	$ 6,435	$ 7,168	$ 7,984	$ 9,063	$ 9,905	$ 11,032
Percentage of total net sales	(14.9%)	(15.2%)	(15.5%)	(15.8%)	(16.0%)	(16.3%)
Middle East, Africa & Asia	$ 5,575	$ 6,513	$ 7,610	$ 9,061	$ 10,387	$ 12,135
Percentage of total net sales	(12.9%)	(13.8%)	(14.8%)	(15.8%)	(16.8%)	(17.9%)
PepsiCo Total Net Sales	**$ 43,251**	**$ 47,191**	**$ 51,562**	**$ 57,502**	**$ 61,820**	**$ 67,839**
Annual growth rate		9.1%	9.3%	11.5%	7.5%	9.7%

The Forecast spreadsheet in FSAP gives the analyst the opportunity to input specific forecast parameters (such as sales growth rates) for Year +1 through Year +5, as well as general forecast parameters for Year +6 and beyond. For Years +1 through +5, we will enter the sales growth rates and amounts shown above. The forecast parameters for Year +6 and beyond represent general forecast assumptions over the long-run horizon. We assume PepsiCo will sustain a 3.0 percent sales growth rate in Year +6 and beyond, consistent with long-run growth in the economy and expected long-run inflation that together will average 3.0 percent per year.[9]

The analyst can use the Forecast Development spreadsheet in FSAP to develop detailed revenues forecasts, capturing the key drivers of the firm's sales growth. That has been done here by analyzing and forecasting PepsiCo's sales growth drivers separately for each division and then aggregating those forecasts into total sales forecasts through Year +5. Appendix C illustrates how we used the Forecast Development spreadsheet in FSAP to develop the sales forecasts for PepsiCo.

STEP 2: PROJECTING OPERATING EXPENSES

The procedure for projecting operating expenses depends on the degree to which they have fixed or variable components. If certain operating expenses vary directly with sales and if the analyst anticipates no changes in the relation between these expenses and sales, the analyst can project these future operating expenses using common-size income statement percentages for such expenses relative to sales. Projected sales are simply multiplied by the appropriate percentage to derive the amounts for operating expenses that vary directly with sales. Equivalently, those operating expenses can be projected to grow at the same rate as sales. Unfortunately, firms rarely disclose the fixed versus variable components of their expense structure. Thus, the analyst must estimate the contribution of fixed versus variable expenses to the total amounts reported.

If the analyst determines that operating expenses reflect cost structures that will not change linearly with sales (for example, the firm may experience economies of scale as sales increase or may face expenses that remain relatively fixed even if sales decrease), using the common-size income statement approach can result in operating expense projections that are too high or too low. A possible clue for the existence of fixed costs is the stability of the ratio of the percentage change in an expense relative to the percentage change in sales. Changes in this ratio over time may be due to the existence of fixed costs. In this case, the analyst should attempt to estimate the variable and fixed cost structure of those particular operating expenses.[10] Capital-intensive manufacturing firms often have high proportions of fixed costs in their cost structures, particularly from depreciation on property, plant, and equipment, and fixed labor charges. When sales increase and the percentage increase in costs of goods sold or selling, general, and administrative expenses is significantly less than

---

[9] Although it is very reasonable and common for analysts to expect that PepsiCo's long-run growth rate will be approximately 3.0 percent, it is unlikely that the revenue growth rate will suddenly and dramatically drop from 9.7 percent in Year +5 to 3.0 percent in Year +6. This somewhat artificial shift in sales growth is a byproduct of using only a five-year forecast horizon for the financial statement projections, which we use to make the exposition of this chapter shorter and more efficient for you. The analyst interested in greater forecast accuracy may want to use longer forecast horizons (for example, ten years), allowing for a more gradual and realistic evolution toward the long-run growth rate.

[10] Many expenses can be viewed as having a fixed portion and a portion that varies with sales. For example, a firm's cost of sales might involve fixed periodic cost such as rent or depreciation on property and equipment and costs for direct labor and materials that vary directly with product sales. Selling, general, and administrative costs often include fixed components for items such as salaries, rent, insurance, and other corporate overhead expenses but variable components that vary directly with sales, such as sales commissions.

the percentage change in sales, it indicates the presence of fixed costs. The analyst can sometimes estimate the variable cost as a percentage of sales for a particular expense (for example, cost of goods sold) by dividing the amount of the change in the expense item between two years by the amount of the change in sales for those two years. The analyst can then multiply the variable-cost percentage times sales to estimate the total variable cost. Subtracting the variable cost from the total cost yields an estimate of the fixed cost for that particular item. Using this approach, one could then project a particular future expense with two components: a fixed component and a component that varies with sales. For a firm that is particularly dependent on property, plant, and equipment, the analyst may need to create a separate schedule to forecast capital expenditures that coincide with or precede projected future sales and depreciation expense amounts that follow property, plant, and equipment (demonstrated later in this chapter).[11]

When projecting operating expenses as a percentage of sales, the analyst should keep in mind that an expense as a percentage of sales can change over time: (1) as expenses change, holding sales constant; (2) as sales change, holding expenses constant; (3) both types of change occurring simultaneously and in the same direction; or (4) both types of change occurring simultaneously but in opposite directions. As an example of case 1, the analyst may expect an expense to become a smaller fraction of sales over time if the firm drives down costs by creating operating efficiencies or new production technologies. As an example of case 2, the analyst may expect that the firm will hold expenses (such as cost of goods sold) relatively steady but will face increased competition for market share and therefore may be forced to lower sales prices, causing the expected expense-to-sales ratio to increase. In case 3, if the analyst expects both sales and operating expenses to increase (or decrease) simultaneously, the net result on the projected expense-to-sales percentage will depend on which of the two effects is proportionally greater. In case 4, if the analyst expects sales to increase while operating expenses decrease (as might occur for a firm in transition from a start-up phase to a growth phase of its life cycle), or vice versa (sales decrease while operating expenses increase, as might occur for a firm in distress), the net result on the projected expense-to-sales percentage will depend on the relative magnitudes of the two effects. In projecting the future relations between revenues and expenses, it is essential to evaluate the firm's strategies with respect to future growth, shifts in product/portfolio mix, changes in the mix of fixed and variable expenses, competitive pressure on pricing, and many other factors that will impact expected future revenues and expenses.

Projecting Cost of Goods Sold

The common-size income statement data discussed in Chapter 1 and 4 (and presented in the Analysis spreadsheet of FSAP presented in Appendix C) indicate that PepsiCo's cost of goods sold as a percent of sales has steadily increased from 43.3 percent in 2004 to 47.1 percent in 2008. In the MD&A section of the annual report (Appendix B), PepsiCo provides very little discussion to explain this negative trend, other than to mention rising raw material commodity costs as a contributing factor. Note 3, "Restructuring and Impairment Charges" (Appendix A), discloses that PepsiCo recognized $543 million of restructuring and impairment charges in 2008 and allocated $88 million of those charges to costs of goods sold.

[11] Sometimes more advanced approaches may be necessary, such as using regression analysis to estimate fixed versus variable components of expenses. For example, an analyst might use time-series data to estimate the relation, $COGS = \alpha + \beta \times Sales + \varepsilon$. The estimated level of fixed costs equals the estimated intercept, α, and the variable component would be reflected by the slope coefficient, β.

Without this restructuring charge, the cost of goods sold percentage in 2008 would have been 46.8 percent (computed as ($20,351 million – $88 million)/$43,251 million).

PepsiCo's cost of goods sold as a percent of sales has been increasing despite the prior observation that PepsiCo's recent sales growth in 2007 and 2008 has been driven more by price increases than sales volume increases. With costs held constant, sales price increases should translate into decreasing cost of goods sold percentages. Given this recent performance, an analyst might question whether PepsiCo will be able to improve its performance and reduce the cost of goods sold percentage in the future by cutting costs, given that it has not been able to do so during periods of rising prices.[12]

In recent years, PepsiCo has generated its fastest rates of sales growth in the Latin America Foods division, the UKEU division, and the MEAA division, which generate the lowest operating profit margins of PepsiCo's six divisions (as disclosed in the 2008 Annual Report MD&A section titled "Results of Operations—Division Review" in Appendix B). Therefore, PepsiCo is generating more of its sales from lower profit margin divisions, which also partially explains why the cost of goods sold has been increasing as a percentage of sales. Given that our sales forecasts project that the Latin America Foods division, the UKEU division, and the MEAA division will become increasingly larger proportions of PepsiCo's total sales, an analyst might expect PepsiCo's future cost of goods sold percentage to increase over the five-year forecast horizon. Ideally, PepsiCo would disclose costs of good sold by division and we could vary projected future costs of goods sold across each division. However, PepsiCo only discloses cost of goods sold aggregated across all divisions.

Given all of this analysis, we predict that PepsiCo's cost of goods sold gradually will increase from 47.3 percent of sales in Year +1 to 48.0 percent in Year +5 and beyond. The cost of goods sold forecasts through Year +5 follow:

	Sales	Percentage of Sales	Cost of Goods Sold
Year +1 Projected	$47,191	47.3%	$22,321
Year +2 Projected	$51,562	47.5%	$24,492
Year +3 Projected	$57,502	47.7%	$27,429
Year +4 Projected	$61,820	47.9%	$29,612
Year +5 Projected	$67,839	48.0%	$32,563

Projecting Selling, General, and Administrative Expenses

The common-size income statement data reveal that PepsiCo's selling, general, and administrative (SG&A) expenses as a percentage of sales varied slightly from 36.2 percent in 2006 down to 36.0 percent in 2007 and then up to 36.8 percent in 2008.[13] As disclosed in the 2008 Annual Report MD&A section titled "Our Financial Results" (Appendix B), in 2008, PepsiCo recognized restructuring and impairment charges amounting to $543 million, of which $455 million was included in SG&A expenses. In addition, PepsiCo included mark-to-market losses on commodity derivatives of $346 million in 2008. Absent these charges

[12] PepsiCo's main competitor in the beverage business, Coca-Cola, exhibits much lower (but also rising) cost of goods sold percentages from 33.9 percent to 35.6 percent over 2006 to 2008. Unlike Coca-Cola, which is primarily a beverage company, PepsiCo's sales include a high proportion of snack foods and breakfast foods, which likely have higher costs as a percentage of sales than do beverages.

[13] On this dimension, PepsiCo outperformed its rival Coca-Cola, which experienced SG&A expenses of 39.2 percent of sales in 2006, 37.9 percent in 2007, and 36.9 percent in 2008.

and losses (which are not likely to persist), SG&A expenses would have been only 34.9 percent of sales in 2008. An analyst might reasonably assume that a firm will achieve incremental efficiencies in future SG&A expenses and reduce this percentage over time, particularly a firm with the potential to generate economies of scale or scope or operating synergies. As disclosed in the 2008 Annual Report MD&A section titled "Our Financial Results" (Appendix B), PepsiCo is implementing a program to control costs and generate significant pretax savings, presumably by creating incremental efficiencies in future SG&A expenses. We therefore project that PepsiCo will maintain SG&A expenses equal to roughly 35.0 percent of sales in the future.

The projected amounts for SG&A expenses are as follows:

	Sales	Percentage of Sales	SG&A Expenses
Year +1 Projected	$47,191	35.0%	$16,517
Year +2 Projected	$51,562	35.0%	$18,047
Year +3 Projected	$57,502	35.0%	$20,126
Year +4 Projected	$61,820	35.0%	$21,637
Year +5 Projected	$67,839	35.0%	$23,744

As the title of this expense account implies, SG&A expenses encompass a wide range of operating expenses. In Note 2, "Our Significant Accounting Policies" (Appendix A), PepsiCo discloses that in 2008, SG&A expenses include $2,900 million in advertising and marketing expenses; $5,300 million in shipping and handling expenses; $388 million in R&D expenses; and amounts for compensation and employee benefits, rent, and various other expenses. If the analyst expects these individual expense items to be driven by factors other than sales growth or if the analyst expects the proportionate composition of these expenses to change relative to future sales, then the analyst should project the items individually and then sum them to obtain total SG&A expense projections.

Projecting Other Operating Expenses

In 2006 through 2008, PepsiCo recognized expenses for amortization of intangible assets amounting to $162 million, $58 million, and $64 million, respectively, which are equivalent to 0.5 percent, 0.1 percent, and 0.1 percent of sales, respectively. These expenses represent amortization of intangibles such as brands and trademarks with limited useful lives (ranging from 5 to 40 years). The net book value of PepsiCo's amortizable intangible assets amounts to $732 million on the 2008 balance sheet. In Note 4, "Property, Plant, and Equipment and Intangible Assets" (Appendix A), PepsiCo provides helpful disclosures indicating that it expects amortization expense for these intangible assets to be $64 million in Year +1, $63 million in Year +2, $62 million in Year +3, $60 million in Year +4, and $56 million in Year +5, based on 2008 foreign exchange rates and the assumption of no additional investments in amortizable intangible assets over that period. Therefore, we use these amounts as our forecasts for PepsiCo's amortization expense over this forecast horizon. We also use these amounts to reduce the net book value of the amortizable intangible asset account balance each year.

U.S. GAAP does not require amortization of goodwill or other intangible assets deemed to have indefinite useful lives. Goodwill ($5,124 million) and other nonamortizable intangible assets ($1,128 million) represent roughly 90 percent of PepsiCo's total intangible assets on the 2008 balance sheet. In our forecasts, we include no amortization expenses or impairment losses for these nonamortizable intangibles.

Projecting Nonrecurring Operating Gains and Losses

As described previously, PepsiCo recognized restructuring and impairment charges in cost of goods sold and SG&A expenses in 2008. We will accept PepsiCo's classification of these items as nonrecurring components of operations, and forecast that these amounts will be zero in the future. It is common for analysts to expect nonrecurring amounts to be zero in future years. The analysts should be cautious, however, because some firms demonstrate a tendency for persistent "nonrecurring" charges.

The sales forecasts, together with the projected costs of goods sold, SG&A expenses, and amortization of intangible assets, lead to the following projected amounts of operating income for PepsiCo for Years +1 through +5:

	Year +1	Year +2	Year +3	Year +4	Year +5
Revenues	$ 47,191	$ 51,562	$ 57,502	$ 61,820	$ 67,839
Cost of Goods Sold	−22,321	−24,492	−27,429	−29,612	−32,563
Gross Profit	$ 24,870	$ 27,070	$ 30,074	$ 32,208	$ 35,277
Gross Profit Margin	(52.7%)	(52.5%)	(52.3%)	(52.1%)	(52.0%)
SG&A Expenses	−16,517	−18,047	−20,126	−21,637	−23,744
Amortization of Intangible Assets	−64	−63	−62	−60	−56
Operating Income	$ 8,289	$ 8,960	$ 9,886	$ 10,511	$ 11,477
Operating Profit Margin	(17.6%)	(17.4%)	(17.2%)	(17.0%)	(16.9%)

Exhibit 10.3 presents the complete forecasts of PepsiCo's income statements, as well as comprehensive income and the change in retained earnings, for Years +1 through +5. The format of this exhibit mirrors the format of the Forecast spreadsheet in FSAP (Appendix C). This chapter will discuss the projections of interest income, interest expense, income tax expense, net income, comprehensive income, and the change in retained earnings after projecting PepsiCo's balance sheet, which we discuss in the next sections.

STEP 3: PROJECTING OPERATING ASSETS AND LIABILITIES ON THE BALANCE SHEET

In this section of the chapter, we forecast how the operating activities projected for the income statement will generate future operating assets and liabilities on the balance sheet. We will demonstrate how to develop forecasts using various drivers of growth in different assets and liabilities, allowing the mix of assets and liabilities to change as the business evolves over time. In the next section of this chapter, we will forecast the financing activities that will be necessary to support the firm's operations.

To develop forecasts of individual operating assets and liabilities, the analyst must first determine, if possible, the underlying operating activities that drive them. For some types of assets, such as inventory and property, plant, and equipment, asset growth typically leads future sales growth. Growth for other types of assets, such as accounts receivable, typically lags sales growth. Certain operating liabilities will be determined by operating assets (such

EXHIBIT 10.3

PepsiCo
Actual and Forecast Statements of Net Income and Comprehensive Income

Actual and forecast amounts in bold; historical common-size and rate of change percentages reported below the actual amounts only; forecast assumptions and brief explanations below forecast amounts. Amounts in millions; allow for rounding.

	Actuals			Forecasts				
Year	**2006**	**2007**	**2008**	**Year +1**	**Year +2**	**Year +3**	**Year +4**	**Year +5**
INCOME STATEMENT								
Revenues	**35,137**	**39,474**	**43,251**	**47,191**	**51,562**	**57,502**	**61,820**	**67,839**
common size	100.0%	100.0%	100.0%	9.1%	9.3%	11.5%	7.5%	9.7%
rate of change		12.3%	9.6%	(See Forecast Development worksheet for details of revenues forecasts.)				
Cost of Goods Sold	**−15,762**	**−18,038**	**−20,351**	**−22,321**	**−24,492**	**−27,429**	**−29,612**	**−32,563**
common size	−44.9%	−45.7%	−47.1%	−47.3%	−47.5%	−47.7%	−47.9%	−48.0%
rate of change		14.4%	12.8%	(Assume slowly increasing cost of goods sold as a percent of sales.)				
Gross Profit	**19,375**	**21,436**	**22,900**	**24,870**	**27,070**	**30,074**	**32,208**	**35,277**
common size	55.1%	54.3%	52.9%	52.7%	52.5%	52.3%	52.1%	52.0%
rate of change		10.6%	6.8%	8.6%	8.8%	11.1%	7.1%	9.5%
Selling, General, and Administrative Expenses	**−12,711**	**−14,208**	**−15,901**	**−16,517**	**−18,047**	**−20,126**	**−21,637**	**−23,744**
common size	−36.2%	−36.0%	−36.8%	−35.0%	−35.0%	−35.0%	−35.0%	−35.0%
rate of change		11.8%	11.9%	(Assume steady SG&A expense as a percent of sales.)				
Amortization of Intangible Assets	**−162**	**−58**	**−64**	**−64**	**−63**	**−62**	**−60**	**−56**
common size	−0.5%	−0.1%	−0.1%	−64.0	−63.0	−62.0	−60.0	−56.0
rate of change		−64.2%	10.3%	(Amounts based on PepsiCo disclosures in Note 4.)				
Operating Profit	**6,502**	**7,170**	**6,935**	**8,289**	**8,960**	**9,886**	**10,511**	**11,477**
common size	18.5%	18.2%	16.0%	17.6%	17.4%	17.2%	17.0%	16.9%
rate of change		10.3%	−3.3%	19.5%	8.1%	10.3%	6.3%	9.2%

(*Continued*)

EXHIBIT 10.3 (Continued)

	Actuals			Forecasts				
Year	**2006**	**2007**	**2008**	**Year +1**	**Year +2**	**Year +3**	**Year +4**	**Year +5**
Interest Income	**173**	**125**	**41**	**73**	**81**	**90**	**98**	**107**
common size	0.5%	0.3%	0.1%	3.0%	3.0%	3.0%	3.0%	3.0%
rate of change		−27.7%	−67.2%	(Interest rate earned on average balance in cash and marketable securities.)				
Interest Expense	**−239**	**−224**	**−329**	**−493**	**−531**	**−579**	**−626**	**−677**
common size	−0.7%	−0.6%	−0.8%	−5.8%	−5.8%	−5.8%	−5.8%	−5.8%
rate of change		−6.3%	46.9%	(Interest rate paid on average balance in financial liabilities.)				
Income from Equity Affiliates	**553**	**560**	**374**	**480**	**509**	**539**	**572**	**606**
common size	1.6%	1.4%	0.9%	12.0%	12.0%	12.0%	12.0%	12.0%
rate of change		1.3%	−33.2%	(Assume expected return of 12% on investments in noncontrolled affilates.)				
Income before Tax	**6,989**	**7,631**	**7,021**	**8,348**	**9,019**	**9,935**	**10,555**	**11,513**
common size	19.9%	19.3%	16.2%	17.7%	17.5%	17.3%	17.1%	17.0%
rate of change		9.2%	−8.0%	18.9%	8.0%	10.2%	6.2%	9.1%
Income Tax Expense	**−1,347**	**−1,973**	**−1,879**	**−2,237**	**−2,417**	**−2,663**	**−2,829**	**−3,085**
common size	−3.8%	−5.0%	−4.3%	−26.8%	−26.8%	−26.8%	−26.8%	−26.8%
rate of change		46.5%	−4.8%	(Effective income tax rate assumptions.)				
Net Income (computed)	**5,642**	**5,658**	**5,142**	**6,111**	**6,602**	**7,273**	**7,726**	**8,427**
common size	16.1%	14.3%	11.9%	12.9%	12.8%	12.6%	12.5%	12.4%
rate of change		0.3%	−9.1%	18.8%	8.0%	10.2%	6.2%	9.1%
Other Comprehensive Income Items	**456**	**1,294**	**−3,793**	**0**	**0**	**0**	**0**	**0**
common size	1.3%	3.3%	−8.8%	0.0	0.0	0.0	0.0	0.0
rate of change		183.8%	−393.1%	(Assume random walk.)				
Comprehensive Income	**6,098**	**6,952**	**1,349**	**6,111**	**6,602**	**7,273**	**7,726**	**8,427**
common size	17.4%	17.6%	3.1%	12.9%	12.8%	12.6%	12.5%	12.4%
rate of change		14.0%	−80.6%	353.0%	8.0%	10.2%	6.2%	9.1%

as inventory purchases driving accounts payable), whereas others will be determined by operating expenses (such as accrued expenses). We project individual operating assets and liabilities for PepsiCo using a combination of forecast drivers, including common-size percentages, growth rates, and assets turnovers. Exhibit 10.4 provides a preview of the projected balance sheets for PepsiCo through Year +5, which we developed using the Forecasts worksheet in FSAP (Appendix C). The following sections discuss the projections of individual operating assets and liabilities.

FSAP

Projecting Cash

The Analysis worksheet in FSAP (Appendix C) computes the average turnover of sales through the average cash balance each year, so we will use those ratios to project PepsiCo's ending cash balances during the forecast horizon. Like all firms, PepsiCo needs a certain amount of cash on hand for day-to-day liquidity.[14] PepsiCo's cash holdings have varied between 2004 and 2008. During 2004 through 2006, PepsiCo had average cash balances that grew from 13.1 days of sales to 17.5 days, whereas in 2007 and 2008, average cash balances were roughly 12.0 days of sales (computed as 365 days divided by the ratio of sales to the average balance in cash; in 2008, 12.5 days = 365/[$43,251/({$2,064 + $910}/2)]. We assume that PepsiCo will maintain average cash balances equivalent to 12 days of sales in the future.

Applying this approach we use our forecasts of sales and the projected number of days of sales in cash to compute the average balance in cash each year. The Year +1 sales forecast is $47,191 million, or an average of $129.3 million per day. We project PepsiCo will hold an average of 12 days of sales in cash during Year +1, for an average cash balance of $1,551 million. The projected cash balances follow:

	Cash			
	Annual Sales Forecasts	**Average Sales per Day**	**Days Sales in Cash**	**Average Cash Balance**
Year +1	$47,191	$129.3	12	$1,551
Year +2	$51,562	$141.3	12	$1,695
Year +3	$57,502	$157.5	12	$1,890
Year +4	$61,820	$169.4	12	$2,032
Year +5	$67,839	$185.9	12	$2,230

The forecasts above project the average cash balances that will be included as the end of year balances for Cash and Cash Equivalents in the projected PepsiCo balance sheets. If more precision is preferred, an analyst can adapt the approach to project year-end balances in cash. Given that the beginning cash balance in Year +1 is $2,064 million and the average balance is projected to be $1,551 million, it implies that the ending balance will be $1,039 million (that is, the implied ending balance equals two times the average

[14] The forecasts assume that PepsiCo uses cash for day-to-day operating liquidity purposes, so cash is treated as an element of working capital. Some firms maintain excess cash balances far beyond what is needed for daily liquidity. For such firms, cash may be forecasted in two separate components: cash necessary for liquidity and excess cash. For these firms, the excess cash can serve as the flexible financial account used to balance the balance sheet and should be considered a financial asset.

EXHIBIT 10.4

PepsiCo Actual and Forecast Balance Sheets

Actual and forecast amounts in bold; historical common-size and rate-of-change percentages reported below the actual amounts only; forecast assumptions and brief explanations below forecast amounts. Amounts in millions; allow for rounding.

	Actuals			Forecasts				
	2006	2007	2008	Year +1	Year +2	Year +3	Year +4	Year +5
BALANCE SHEET								
ASSETS:								
Cash and Cash Equivalents	**1,651**	**910**	**2,064**	**1,551**	**1,695**	**1,890**	**2,032**	**2,230**
common size	5.5%	2.6%	5.7%	12.0	12.0	12.0	12.0	12.0
rate of change		−44.9%	126.8%	(Assume ending cash balances equal to 12 days sales.)				
Marketable Securities	**1,171**	**1,571**	**213**	**1,034**	**1,130**	**1,260**	**1,355**	**1,487**
common size	3.9%	4.5%	0.6%	8.0	8.0	8.0	8.0	8.0
rate of change		34.2%	−86.4%	(Assume ending balances equal to 8 days sales.)				
Accounts Receivable—Net	**3,725**	**4,389**	**4,683**	**5,143**	**5,593**	**6,380**	**6,492**	**7,633**
common size	12.4%	12.7%	13.0%	38.0	38.0	38.0	38.0	38.0
rate of change		17.8%	6.7%	(Assume 38 days to collect sales in accounts receivable.)				
Inventories	**1,926**	**2,290**	**2,522**	**2,730**	**3,033**	**3,421**	**3,546**	**4,116**
common size	6.4%	6.6%	7.0%	8.5	8.5	8.5	8.5	8.5
rate of change		18.9%	10.1%	(Assume average inventory turnover of roughly 8.5 times per year.)				
Prepaid Expenses and Other Current Assets	**657**	**991**	**1,324**	**1,445**	**1,578**	**1,760**	**1,892**	**2,077**
common size	2.2%	2.9%	3.7%	9.1%	9.3%	11.5%	7.5%	9.7%
rate of change		50.8%	33.6%	(Assume growth with sales.)				
Current Assets	**9,130**	**10,151**	**10,806**	**11,904**	**13,029**	**14,712**	**15,318**	**17,543**
common size	30.5%	29.3%	30.0%	30.9%	31.3%	32.1%	31.5%	32.8%
rate of change		11.2%	6.5%	10.2%	9.5%	12.9%	4.1%	14.5%
Long-Term Investments	**3,690**	**4,354**	**3,883**	**4,116**	**4,363**	**4,625**	**4,902**	**5,196**
common size	12.3%	12.6%	10.8%	6%	6%	6%	6%	6%
rate of change		18.0%	−10.8%	(Assume steady growth.)				
Property, Plant & Equipment—at cost	**19,058**	**21,896**	**22,552**	**24,723**	**27,662**	**30,939**	**34,463**	**38,330**
common size	63.7%	63.2%	62.7%					
rate of change		14.9%	3.0%	(PP&E assumptions—see schedule in Forecast Development worksheet.)				
Accumulated Depreciation	**−9,371**	**−10,668**	**−10,889**	**−12,471**	**−14,241**	**−16,220**	**−18,426**	**−20,878**
common size	−31.3%	−30.8%	−30.3%					
rate of change		13.8%	2.1%	(See depreciation schedule in Forecast Development worksheet.)				

Amortizable Intangible Assets (net)	**637**	**796**	**732**	**668**	**605**	**543**	**483**	**427**
common size	2.1%	2.3%	2.0%	−64.0	−63.0	−62.0	−60.0	−56.0
rate of change		25.0%	−8.0%	(Assume amortization per PepsiCo disclosures in Note 4; assume no new investments.)				
Goodwill and Nonamortizable Intangibles	**5,806**	**6,417**	**6,252**	**6,822**	**7,453**	**8,312**	**8,936**	**9,806**
common size	19.4%	18.5%	17.4%	9.1%	9.3%	11.5%	7.5%	9.7%
rate of change		10.5%	−2.6%	(Assume growth with sales.)				
Other Non-Current Assets	**980**	**1,682**	**2,658**	**2,738**	**2,820**	**2,904**	**2,992**	**3,081**
common size	3.3%	4.9%	7.4%	3.0%	3.0%	3.0%	3.0%	3.0%
rate of change		71.6%	58.0%	(Assume steady growth.)				
Total Assets	**29,930**	**34,628**	**35,994**	**38,499**	**41,692**	**45,815**	**48,669**	**53,506**
common size	100.0%	100.0%	100.0%	100.0%	100.0%	100.0%	100.0%	100.0%
rate of change		15.7%	3.9%	7.0%	8.3%	9.9%	6.2%	9.9%
LIABILITIES:								
Accounts Payable—Trade	**2,102**	**2,562**	**2,846**	**3,080**	**3,442**	**3,875**	**3,947**	**4,768**
common size	7.0%	7.4%	7.9%	48.0	48.0	48.0	48.0	48.0
rate of change		21.9%	11.1%	(Assume a steady payment period consistent with recent years.)				
Current Accrued Liabilities	**4,394**	**5,040**	**5,427**	**5,921**	**6,470**	**7,215**	**7,757**	**8,512**
common size	14.7%	14.6%	15.1%	9.1%	9.3%	11.5%	7.5%	9.7%
rate of change		14.7%	7.7%	(Assume growth with SG&A expenses, which grow with sales.)				
Notes Payable and Short-Term Debt	**274**	**0**	**369**	**385**	**417**	**458**	**487**	**535**
common size	0.9%	0.0%	1.0%	1.0%	1.0%	1.0%	1.0%	1.0%
rate of change		−100.0%	na	(Assume 1.0 percent of total assets.)				
Income Taxes Payable	**90**	**151**	**145**	**154**	**167**	**183**	**195**	**214**
common size	0.3%	0.4%	0.4%	0.4%	0.4%	0.4%	0.4%	0.4%
rate of change		67.8%	−4.0%	(Assume steady percent of total assets.)				
Current Liabilities	**6,860**	**7,753**	**8,787**	**9,540**	**10,495**	**11,731**	**12,385**	**14,029**
common size	22.9%	22.4%	24.4%	24.8%	25.2%	25.6%	25.4%	26.2%
rate of change		13.0%	13.3%	8.6%	10.0%	11.8%	5.6%	13.3%
Long-Term Debt	**2,550**	**4,203**	**7,858**	**8,405**	**9,102**	**10,002**	**10,625**	**11,681**
common size	8.5%	12.1%	21.8%	21.8%	21.8%	21.8%	21.8%	21.8%
rate of change		64.8%	87.0%	(Assume steady percent of total assets.)				
Long-Term Accrued Liabilities	**4,624**	**4,792**	**7,017**	**7,656**	**8,365**	**9,329**	**10,030**	**11,006**
common size	15.4%	13.8%	19.5%	9.1%	9.3%	11.5%	7.5%	9.7%
rate of change		3.6%	46.4%	(Assume growth with SG&A expenses, which grow with sales.)				
Deferred Tax Liabilities—Noncurrent	**528**	**646**	**226**	**242**	**262**	**288**	**306**	**336**
common size	1.8%	1.9%	0.6%	0.6%	0.6%	0.6%	0.6%	0.6%
rate of change		22.3%	−65.0%	(Assume steady percent of total assets.)				
Total Liabilities	**14,562**	**17,394**	**23,888**	**25,843**	**28,224**	**31,350**	**33,345**	**37,052**
common size	48.7%	50.2%	66.4%	67.1%	67.7%	68.4%	68.5%	69.2%
rate of change		19.4%	37.3%	8.2%	9.2%	11.1%	6.4%	11.1%

(Continued)

EXHIBIT 10.4 (Continued)

	Actuals			Forecasts				
	2006	2007	2008	Year +1	Year +2	Year +3	Year +4	Year +5
SHAREHOLDERS' EQUITY								
Preferred Stock	**−79**	**−91**	**−97**	**0**	**0**	**0**	**0**	**0**
common size	−0.3%	−0.3%	−0.3%	0.0	0.0	0.0	0.0	0.0
rate of change		15.2%	6.6%	(Preferred stock assumptions.)				
Common Stock + Paid-In Capital	**614**	**480**	**381**	**408**	**441**	**485**	**515**	**566**
common size	2.1%	1.4%	1.1%	1.1%	1.1%	1.1%	1.1%	1.1%
rate of change		−21.8%	−20.6%	(Assume steady percent of total assets.)				
Retained Earnings	**24,837**	**28,184**	**30,638**	**33,565**	**36,842**	**40,296**	**43,624**	**47,203**
common size	83.0%	81.4%	85.1%					
rate of change		13.5%	8.7%	(Add net income and subtract dividends; see dividends forecast box below.)				
Accum. Other Comprehensive Loss	**−2,246**	**−952**	**−4,694**	**−4,694**	**−4,694**	**−4,694**	**−4,694**	**−4,694**
common size	−7.5%	−2.7%	−13.0%	0.0	0.0	0.0	0.0	0.0
rate of change		−57.6%	393.1%	(Add accumulated other comprehensive income items from income statement.)				
Treasury Stock	**−7,758**	**−10,387**	**−14,122**	**−16,622**	**−19,122**	**−21,622**	**−24,122**	**−26,622**
common size	−25.9%	−30.0%	−39.2%	−2500	−2500	−2500	−2500	−2500
rate of change		33.9%	36.0%	(Treasury stock repurchases, net of treasury stock reissues.)				
Common Shareholders' Equity	**15,447**	**17,325**	**12,203**	**12,656**	**13,467**	**14,465**	**15,323**	**16,454**
common size	51.6%	50.0%	33.9%	32.9%	32.3%	31.6%	31.5%	30.8%
rate of change		12.2%	−29.6%	3.7%	6.4%	7.4%	5.9%	7.4%
Total Liabilities and Equities	**29,930**	**34,628**	**35,994**	**38,499**	**41,692**	**45,815**	**48,669**	**53,506**
common size	100.0%	100.0%	100.0%	100.0%	100.0%	100.0%	100.0%	100.0%
rate of change		15.7%	3.9%	7.0%	8.3%	9.9%	6.2%	9.9%

balance minus the beginning balance). Applying this approach, the projected year-end cash balances would be as follows:

	Cash					
	Annual Sales Forecasts	Average Sales per Day	Days Sales in Cash	Average Cash Balance	Beginning Cash Balance	Ending Cash Balance
Year +1	\$47,191	\$129.3	12	\$1,551	\$2,064	\$1,039
Year +2	\$51,562	\$141.3	12	\$1,695	\$1,039	\$2,352
Year +3	\$57,502	\$157.5	12	\$1,890	\$2,352	\$1,428
Year +4	\$61,820	\$169.4	12	\$2,032	\$1,428	\$2,638
Year +5	\$67,839	\$185.9	12	\$2,230	\$2,638	\$1,824

For the three primary financial statement forecasts to articulate with each other, the change in the cash balance on the projected balance sheet each year must agree with the net change in cash on the projected statement of cash flows. We will demonstrate how to compute the implied statement of cash flows later in this chapter.

Operating Asset and Liability Forecasting Techniques

The analyst can use turnover-based techniques to forecast any operating asset and liability accounts that vary reliably with sales, such as accounts receivable; inventories; property, plant, and equipment; and accounts payable. Using turnover rates produces reasonable forecasts of average and year-end account balances if the firm generates sales evenly throughout the year and if the forecasted account varies reliably with sales. However, the analyst should not use a turnover-based forecast technique if the firm will experience substantially different future growth rates in sales and the forecasted account or if the relation between sales and the forecast account varies unpredictably over time.

A less desirable feature of using a sales-turnover forecasting approach is that in some circumstances, it can introduce volatility in ending balances if the firm has exhibited volatility in historical amounts. The preceding illustration using cash is a good example. Notice in the forecasts of PepsiCo's ending cash balances that PepsiCo held a smaller cash balance at the start of 2008 (\$910 million) but a larger cash balance at the end (\$2,064 million). Because the cash balance at the beginning of Year +1 (the end of 2008; \$2,064 million) is larger than the projected average for Year +1 of \$1,551 million, the projected ending cash balance for Year +1 (\$1,039 million) will be relatively small, partially to compensate for the large beginning balance. The relatively small balance in cash at the end of Year +1 then triggers a relatively large balance at the end of Year +2 (\$2,352) to compensate, and so on. Exhibit 10.5 depicts this type of saw-tooth pattern of variability.

In certain contexts, this type of variability is a realistic outcome of volatility in the firm's operating environment (such as seasonality or cyclicality). In other contexts, the analyst may prefer smooth forecasts that mitigate the variability in this pattern.[15] Whether one uses

[15] Volatile forecasts that reflect seasonality or cyclicality are often preferable in contexts in which the analyst is concerned about whether a firm will violate certain minimum or maximum requirements, such as debt covenants or regulatory capital requirements. Smooth forecasts are often preferable in contexts where an analyst expects random variable fluctuations around a generally smooth average growth trend over time. Analysts also often prefer smooth growth forecasts because these forecasts tend to be easier to present and explain to an audience.

EXHIBIT 10.5

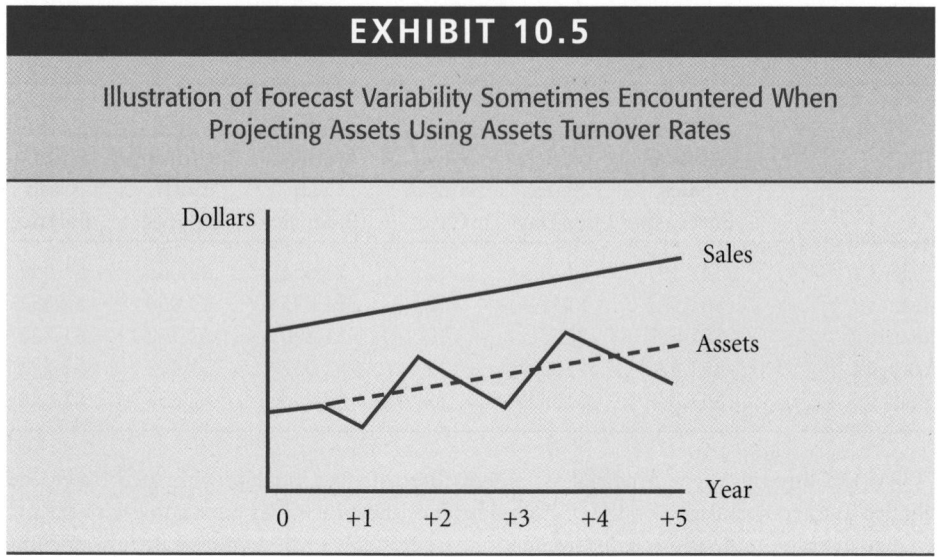

Illustration of Forecast Variability Sometimes Encountered When Projecting Assets Using Assets Turnover Rates

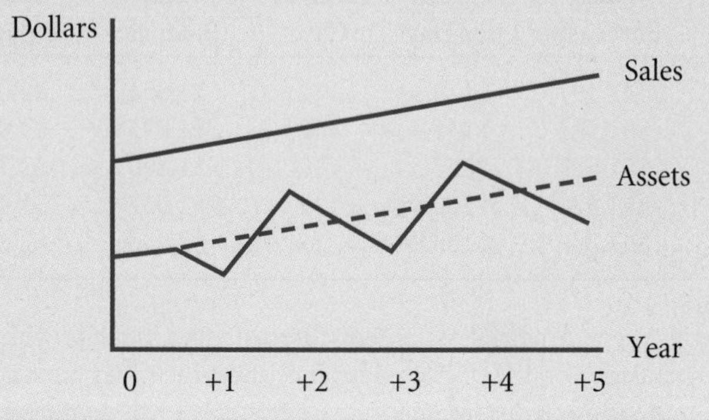

smooth or volatile forecasts for particular accounts such as cash usually has relatively little impact on the valuation of the firm.

A number of techniques exist for the analyst to produce smooth forecasts. One such technique is to project the ending balances to equal the projected average balances. Comparing the average and year-end projections, the averages produce much smoother forecasts, as shown here:

	Average Cash Balance	Ending Cash Balance	Difference: Average Minus Ending Balance	Difference as a Percentage of Ending Cash Balance
Year +1	$1,551	$1,039	+$512	+49.3%
Year +2	$1,695	$2,352	−$656	−27.9%
Year +3	$1,890	$1,428	+$462	+32.4%
Year +4	$2,032	$2,638	−$605	−22.9%
Year +5	$2,230	$1,824	+$407	+22.3%

Smooth forecasts are preferred to simplify the exposition of the chapter, so we will use the average cash balances in our balance sheet projections.

Another technique the analyst can use to produce smooth forecasts involves estimating the average expected rate of growth in cash over a long horizon and then projecting each year-end balance using this growth rate. Alternately, if one expects the ending cash balance to vary directly with sales, then one can simply project growth in cash balances using the expected growth rates in sales. In choosing among forecasting techniques, the analyst must trade off the objectives of achieving forecast precision and minimizing forecast error with avoiding unnecessary computational complexity.

Projecting Marketable Securities

During 2006 through 2008, PepsiCo's marketable securities balances (also commonly referred to as short-term investments) fluctuated inversely with the cash balances, implying that PepsiCo managed marketable securities and cash as complementary sources of liquidity. In years when the cash balance was relatively low, the marketable securities balance was relatively high, and vice versa. Over this period, combined totals of marketable securities and cash have trended down, from 9.4 percent of assets in 2006 to 6.3 percent in 2008.

During 2006, PepsiCo had average marketable securities balances equal to 22.5 days of sales, whereas during 2007 and 2008, average marketable securities balances dropped steadily to 12.7 and then 7.5 days of sales, respectively (computed as 365 days divided by the ratio of sales to the average balance in marketable securities; in 2008, 7.5 days = 365/[$43,251/({$213 + $1,571}/2)]. Going forward, assume that PepsiCo will maintain average marketable securities balances equivalent to eight days of sales.

Following this approach, we use our forecasts of sales to compute the average balance in marketable securities each year, similar to the approach we used to forecast cash. The Year +1 sales forecast is $47,191 million (or an average of $129.3 million per day), and we project that PepsiCo will hold an average of eight days of sales in marketable securities during Year +1, for an average balance of $1,034 million. The projected balances follow:

	Marketable Securities			
	Annual Sales Forecasts	Average Sales per Day	Days in Marketable Securities	Average Marketable Securities Balance
Year +1	$47,191	$129.3	8	$1,034
Year +2	$51,562	$141.3	8	$1,130
Year +3	$57,502	$157.5	8	$1,260
Year +4	$61,820	$169.4	8	$1,355
Year +5	$67,839	$185.9	8	$1,487

Taken together, the forecasts of cash and marketable securities reflect PepsiCo's strategy to manage these accounts as complementary sources of liquidity. By linking both sets of forecasts to future sales activities, the forecasts assume that PepsiCo will continue to manage these accounts jointly and they will maintain a steady, consistent relation with sales. By using average turnover assumptions that are similar to PepsiCo's 2008 holdings of cash and marketable securities (12 and 8 days of sales, respectively), we expect PepsiCo will continue to hold, on average, lower balances in these accounts than it did in 2004–2006. As described shortly, we will also include on the forecasted income statements the future interest income that we expect the cash and marketable securities will generate.

Projecting Accounts Receivable

Chapter 4's analysis of PepsiCo's accounts receivable turnover ratios revealed that PepsiCo's collection period has grown over the last five years, from an average of 36 days during 2004 through 2006 up to 38 days in 2007 and 2008. (In 2008, for example, 38 days = 365/[$43,251/([$4,683 + $4,389]/2)]). We project accounts receivable by assuming that PepsiCo will maintain an average 38-day collection period in the future, turning over accounts receivable approximately 9.6 times a year (= 365/38). As we demonstrated earlier for our projections of cash, we will use the average turnover rate to project PepsiCo's average accounts receivable and then compute the implied year-ending balances. The projected amounts follow:

	Accounts Receivable					
	Annual Sales Forecast	Average Sales per Day	Days Sales in Receivables	Average Balance	Beginning Balance	Ending Balance
Year +1	$47,191	$129.3	38	$4,913	$4,683	$5,143
Year +2	$51,562	$141.3	38	$5,369	$5,143	$5,593
Year +3	$57,502	$157.5	38	$5,985	$5,593	$6,380
Year +4	$61,820	$169.4	38	$6,437	$6,380	$6,492
Year +5	$67,839	$185.9	38	$7,064	$6,492	$7,633

Projecting Inventories

Chapter 4's analysis of PepsiCo's inventory turnover ratios revealed that PepsiCo has experienced steady inventory turnover rates of 43 days in 2004, 42 days in 2005 and 2006, and 43 days in 2007 and 2008. Because of the stability in PepsiCo's inventory management, we project PepsiCo will continue to manage turnover inventory every 43 days, or equivalently, an average turnover rate of 8.5 times per year. The projected year-end inventory amounts follow:

	Inventories				
	Cost of Goods Sold	Average Inventory Turnover Ratio	Average Balance	Beginning Balance	Ending Balance
Year +1	$22,321	8.5	$2,626	$2,522	$2,730
Year +2	$24,492	8.5	$2,881	$2,730	$3,033
Year +3	$27,429	8.5	$3,227	$3,033	$3,421
Year +4	$29,612	8.5	$3,484	$3,421	$3,546
Year +5	$32,563	8.5	$3,831	$3,546	$4,116

For some firms, such as retail chains, inventory is a large proportion of total assets. For such firms, the analyst should link inventory forecasts to projections of the number of stores that will be operating in future years (or even more specifically, to the number of square feet of retail space). For retail firms that operate large big-box stores (Walmart, for example), inventory projections may grow stepwise because each new store will require millions of dollars of additional inventory. Retail chains with seasonal sales will strive to have new stores (and thus new inventory) in place before heavy selling seasons (such as the back-to-school season for casual clothing store chains and the Christmas season for toy store chains); so analysts will link inventory forecasts to projections of new stores in advance of these heavy selling seasons.

Projecting Prepaid Expenses and Other Current Assets

Prepaid expenses and other current assets represent items such as prepaid rent, advertising, and insurance. These items often vary in relation to the level of operating activity, such as sales, advertising, production, new stores or restaurants, and total assets. In the case of PepsiCo, we will simply assume prepaid expenses and other current assets will grow in the future at the same rate as sales. The projected amounts are as follows:

	Prepaid Expenses and Other Current Assets					
	2008	Year +1	Year +2	Year +3	Year +4	Year +5
Projected Amounts	$1,324	$1,445	$1,578	$1,760	$1,892	$2,077
Growth Rates		+9.1%	+9.3%	+11.5%	+7.5%	+9.7%

Projecting Investments in Noncontrolled Affiliates

PepsiCo's long-term investments in securities represent its interests in noncontrolled affiliates, primarily bottlers. These investments grew at a compound annual rate of 5.9 percent over the last five years. The assumption is that investments in noncontrolled affiliates will continue to grow 6 percent per year over the five-year forecast horizon. As we will describe shortly, we will also include on the forecasted income statements the future income that we expect PepsiCo will earn from these investments in noncontrolled affiliates.[16] The projected investment amounts are as follows:

	Investments in Noncontrolled Affiliates					
	2008	Year +1	Year +2	Year +3	Year +4	Year +5
Ending Balance	$3,883	$4,116	$4,363	$4,625	$4,902	$5,196
Growth Rates		+6.0%	+6.0%	+6.0%	+6.0%	+6.0%

Projecting Property, Plant, and Equipment

PepsiCo's fixed-assets turnover ratio remained steady at 3.8 from 2006–2008 (computed for 2008 as 3.8 = $43,251/[($11,663 + $11,228)/2]). This stable fixed-assets turnover is a result of PepsiCo's sales growth varying with capital spending on PP&E (property, plant, and equipment), which averaged roughly 5.7 percent of sales each year. In the 2008 Annual Report, PepsiCo's MD&A section describing "Our Liquidity and Capital Resources" (Appendix B) discloses that management expects "a high single digit *decrease* in net capital spending in 2009." Given this guidance, we will assume that net capital spending in Year +1 will be 4.6 percent of revenues, which amounts to $2,171 (= $47,292 × 0.046). This represents a decrease of 7.5 percent from 2008, which is consistent with PepsiCo's guidance. Given PepsiCo's stable history of capital spending, the assumption is that capital spending in Year +2 and beyond will revert to the historical average of 5.7 percent of revenues. We include these net capital expenditures in our balance sheet projections by increasing PP&E, and we include them as cash outflows in the investing section of our projections of the statement of cash flows. Also, the assumption is that these amounts

[16] For the analyst who wants greater forecast precision, the projections of future balances in Investments in Noncontrolled Affiliates should follow the accounting methods for equity method investments. As such, the balances should grow with the firm's proportionate share of the net income of the affiliate less dividends received from the affiliate each period, and should increase with additional investments and decrease with dispositions of investments in such affiliates.

reflect net capital expenditures, after proceeds from sales of PP&E (which tend to be very minor amounts for PepsiCo).

The projected amounts for capital expenditures follow:

	Property, Plant, and Equipment		
Year	**Annual Sales Forecasts**	**Capital Spending (% of Sales)**	**Capital Spending (millions)**
+1	\$47,191	4.6%	\$2,171
+2	\$51,562	5.7%	\$2,939
+3	\$57,502	5.7%	\$3,278
+4	\$61,820	5.7%	\$3,524
+5	\$67,839	5.7%	\$3,867

PepsiCo's existing PP&E will continue to depreciate as PepsiCo uses these assets in its operations. In addition, PepsiCo's capital expenditures on new PP&E will trigger a new layer of depreciation expense each year. PepsiCo discloses in Note 4, "Property, Plant, and Equipment and Intangible Assets" (Appendix A), that it uses the straight-line depreciation method for financial statement purposes (accelerated depreciation for tax purposes). Note 4 in PepsiCo's financial statements does not disclose information related to salvage values, but an analyst might assume that PepsiCo depreciates PP&E to zero salvage value. Based on this assumption, we can then estimate the average useful life that PepsiCo uses for depreciation by taking the average amount in PP&E at acquisition cost and dividing it by depreciation expense for that year. In 2008, PepsiCo used an average useful life of 15.6 years for depreciation purposes (= [{\$22,552 + \$21,896}/2]/\$1,422). The assumption is that PepsiCo will continue to use a 15.6 year average useful life for depreciation.[17]

In computing depreciation expense for Year +1, we need to forecast two components. The first component is depreciation on the \$22,552 million of existing PP&E as of the beginning of Year +1, which will be \$1,443 million (= \$22,552/15.6 years). The second component is depreciation on the Year +1 capital expenditures of \$2,171 million, which will be \$139 million (= \$2,171/15.6 years). Together, total depreciation expense in Year +1 will be \$1,582 million (= \$1,443 + \$139), and accumulated depreciation will grow to reflect this depreciation. In Year +2, depreciation expense will be \$1,770 million, which will consist of those two components plus a third component to reflect depreciation

[17] PepsiCo discloses that 2008 depreciation expense equals \$1,422 million in Note 4, "Property, Plant, and Equipment and Intangible Assets." In that note, PepsiCo also discloses that PP&E includes land, which is not depreciable (although land improvements are depreciable), and construction in progress, which is not yet depreciable but will be in the future. The analyst interested in slightly greater precision should exclude these amounts from the useful-life computation and the depreciation expense projections. Also note that on PepsiCo's Statement of Cash Flows for 2008 (Appendix A), PepsiCo adds back \$1,543 million in depreciation and amortization expense to net income, which consists of \$1,422 million of depreciation expense and \$121million of amortization expense. We use the depreciation expense disclosed in Note 4 (\$1,422 million) to avoid confounding the estimate of the depreciable useful life with amortization expense. Notice that the total PP&E increased by \$656 million, which is less than the \$2,348 million in net capital expenditures in 2008. Also notice that the increase in accumulated depreciation during 2008 was only \$221 million (from \$10,668 million to \$10,889 million), an amount significantly less than depreciation expense. These differences arise because PepsiCo sold (or wrote off as impaired) PP&E assets that had accumulated depreciation; so the costs of these assets and their respective accumulated depreciation amounts were removed from the accounts.

expense of $188 million (= $2,939/15.6 years) on Year +2 capital expenditures on PP&E, and so on.

The projected amounts for depreciation expense follow:

	Depreciation Expense					
	Depreciable Bases	Depreciation Amounts per Year (assuming 15.6 year life): Year +1	Year +2	Year +3	Year +4	Year +5
Existing PP&E	$22,552	$1,443	$1,443	$1,443	$1,443	$1,443
Capital Spending +1	$ 2,171	$ 139	$ 139	$ 139	$ 139	$ 139
Capital Spending +2	$ 2,939		$ 188	$ 188	$ 188	$ 188
Capital Spending +3	$ 3,278			$ 210	$ 210	$ 210
Capital Spending +4	$ 3,524				$ 225	$ 225
Capital Spending +5	$ 3,867					$ 247
Total Depreciation Expense		$1,582	$1,770	$1,980	$2,205	$2,453

Like most firms, PepsiCo does not report depreciation expense as a separate line item on the income statement, but it allocates depreciation expense to cost of goods sold and SG&A expense based on whether the underlying assets are being used in production or sales and administration. Therefore, in our projections we do not include these amounts of depreciation expense separately in the income statement and assume these amounts are included in our projections of cost of goods sold and SG&A expense. However, we do add depreciation expense back to net income in our projected statement of cash flows, discussed in a later section of the chapter. The projected amounts for capital expenditures; property, plant, and equipment; depreciation expense; and accumulated depreciation follow:

	Property, Plant, and Equipment				
Year	Capital Spending (millions)	Ending Balance (at Cost)	Depreciation Expense	Accumulated Depreciation	Ending Balance (Net)
2008 actual		$22,552		$(10,889)	$11,663
+1	$2,171	$24,723	$1,582	$(12,471)	$12,252
+2	$2,939	$27,662	$1,770	$(14,241)	$13,421
+3	$3,278	$30,939	$1,980	$(16,220)	$14,719
+4	$3,524	$34,463	$2,205	$(18,426)	$16,038
+5	$3,867	$38,330	$2,453	$(20,878)	$17,452

When forecasting fixed assets for capital-intensive firms (such as manufacturing firms or utility companies) or firms for which fixed-asset growth is a critical driver of future sales growth and earnings (for example, new stores for retail chains or restaurant chains), PP&E is typically a large proportion of total assets and has a material impact on the analysts' forecasts of assets, earnings, cash flows, and firm value. For such firms, analysts often invest considerable time and effort in developing detailed forecasts of capital expenditures, PP&E, and depreciation expense. The FSAP Forecast Development spreadsheet for PepsiCo includes a model for forecasting capital expenditures, PP&E, depreciation expense, and accumulated depreciation. The FSAP output (Appendix C) demonstrates the use of this model to compute the preceding forecasts for PepsiCo.

FSAP

Projecting Amortizable Intangible Assets

Amortizable intangible assets for PepsiCo include primarily brands, trademarks, and other identifiable intangible assets with limited useful lives that PepsiCo obtained through acquisitions of other companies. As discussed previously, PepsiCo amortizes these assets ratably over their estimated useful lives (ranging from 5–40 years). The net book value of PepsiCo's amortizable intangible assets amounts to $732 million on the 2008 balance sheet (only 2 percent of total assets). Over the last five years, the balance in amortizable intangible assets has decreased each year because of amortization, but the balance also increased slightly in 2006 and 2007 from certain acquisitions. In Note 4, "Property, Plant, and Equipment and Intangible Assets" (Appendix A), PepsiCo discloses the amount of amortization expense it expects on these intangible assets over the next five years, which we include under the heading "Amortization of Intangible Assets" on the projected income statements. The amortizable intangible asset amounts will continue to decrease by the amounts of amortization expense that PepsiCo disclosed. For simplicity, the assumption is that PepsiCo will not make any additional investments in amortizable intangible assets; instead, it will invest in goodwill and nonamortizable intangible assets, which we discuss next.

Projecting Goodwill and Nonamortizable Intangible Assets

The majority of PepsiCo's intangible assets involve goodwill ($5,124 million) and other nonamortizable intangible assets (primarily brands, $1,128 million) with indefinite lives. These intangible assets arise when PepsiCo acquires other companies. These accounts recognize the portion of the acquisition price that PepsiCo allocates to intangible assets such as goodwill and brands. U.S. GAAP and IFRS do not require firms to amortize these assets because they have indefinite useful lives, but GAAP and IFRS do require firms to test their values annually for impairment and to write the carrying values down to fair value if deemed impaired. Thus far, PepsiCo has not deemed it necessary to recognize any impairment losses on its goodwill or brand assets. Had we forecasted sales declines and negative operating income, this might indicate possibly impaired intangible assets, but the strong sales growth and operating income assumptions imply that future impairment losses are unlikely.

Acquiring other companies with valuable goodwill, brand names, and products is a key element of PepsiCo's strategy. Such acquisitions help PepsiCo create new sales growth, expand its product portfolio, and enter new markets around the world. In 2008 and 2007, PepsiCo invested $1,900 million and $1,300 million in acquisitions, respectively. Of these amounts, Note 4, "Property, Plant and Equipment and Intangible Assets" (Appendix A), discloses that PepsiCo allocated $516 million and $382 million to Goodwill and Nonamortizable Assets (brands) in 2008 and 2007, respectively. It seems clear that PepsiCo will continue to pursue the strategy of making acquisitions, but in the absence of inside information, it is very difficult to forecast specific acquisitions. Thus, the assumption is that PepsiCo's goodwill and nonamortizable intangible assets will grow at the same rate as sales. Another assumption is that no future impairment charges will be necessary for these assets. The projected amounts are as follows:

	Goodwill and Nonamortizable Intangible Assets		
	Beginning Balance	**Sales Growth Rate**	**Ending Balance**
Year +1	$6,252	9.1%	$6,822
Year +2	$6,822	9.3%	$7,453
Year +3	$7,453	11.5%	$8,312
Year +4	$8,312	7.5%	$8,936
Year +5	$8,936	9.7%	$9,806

Projecting Other Noncurrent Assets

In Note 14, "Supplemental Financial Information" (Appendix A), PepsiCo discloses that other noncurrent assets consist of unallocated purchase prices for recent acquisitions, pension assets, noncurrent receivables, and others. For PepsiCo, these amounts have fluctuated widely over the past five years. For example, in 2008, the unallocated purchase price for recent acquisitions jumped by $1,143 million while pension plan assets fell by $607 million. Over the period 2004–2008, other noncurrent assets grew at a compounded annual rate of 3.2 percent despite wide fluctuation in year-to-year growth. During the same period, sales grew at a compounded rate of 9.9 percent. In the absence of more information to forecast other asset amounts specifically, we assume that other noncurrent assets will grow at a 3.0 percent rate each year. The projected amounts are as follows:

	Other Noncurrent Assets		
	Beginning Balance	Growth Rate	Ending Balance
Year +1	$2,658	3.0%	$2,738
Year +2	$2,738	3.0%	$2,820
Year +3	$2,820	3.0%	$2,904
Year +4	$2,904	3.0%	$2,992
Year +5	$2,992	3.0%	$3,081

Projecting Assets That Vary as a Percentage of Total Assets

In some circumstances, analysts may want to project individual asset amounts that will vary as a percentage of total assets, particularly for firms that maintain a steady proportion of total assets invested in specific types of assets. For example, suppose PepsiCo's strategy is to maintain 4.0 percent of total assets in cash for liquidity purposes. Projected amounts for Year +1 for all of the individual assets other than cash are as follows:

Marketable Securities	$ 1,034
Accounts Receivable	5,143
Inventories	2,730
Prepaid Expenses and Other Current Assets	1,445
Long-Term Investments	4,116
Property, Plant, and Equipment, net	12,252
Amortizable Intangible Assets	668
Goodwill and Nonamortizable Intangible Assets	6,822
Other Noncurrent Assets	2,738
Subtotal of Assets	$36,948

The $36,948 subtotal represents 96.0 percent (= 1.00 − 0.04) of total assets. Therefore, projected total assets should equal $38,488 (= $36,948/0.96). Thus, cash should equal $1,540 (= 0.04 × $38,488. This approach to forecasting introduces some circularity into the projected financial statements: the cash balance is a function of total assets, which is a function of the cash balance. This is not unrealistic, nor does it create a problem for the computations. A later subsection of this chapter discusses how to solve for co-determined elements in financial statement forecasts.

Projecting Accounts Payable

PepsiCo reports accounts payable and other current liabilities on a single line on its balance sheet, amounting to $8,273 million at the end of 2008. Note 14, "Supplemental Financial Information" (Appendix A), discloses that $2,846 million of that total is attributable to accounts payable, and the remainder ($5,427 million) is attributable to accrued liabilities for marketing, compensation, dividends, and other expenses. Different factors may drive the future amounts of accounts payable and accrued expenses. Future credit purchases of inventory and PepsiCo's payment policy to its suppliers will likely drive accounts payable, whereas accrued expenses will likely grow with future selling, general, and administrative expenses. Therefore, we forecast accounts payable and accrued expenses separately.

PepsiCo's days payable was 48 days in 2004, but it dropped to 45 days in 2005 and has gradually increased back to 48 days in 2008. Assume that PepsiCo will continue to maintain an accounts payable period of 48 days in the future. To forecast future accounts payable balances, begin by calculating forecasts of inventory purchases on account, as follows:

	Inventory Purchases				
	Year +1	Year +2	Year +3	Year +4	Year +5
Cost of Goods Sold	$22,321	$24,492	$27,429	$29,612	$32,563
Plus Ending Inventory	+2,730	+3,033	+3,421	+3,546	+4,116
Less Beginning Inventory	−2,522	−2,730	−3,033	−3,421	−3,546
Inventory Purchases	$22,529	$24,795	$27,817	$29,737	$33,133

Accounts payable is projected using an average 48 days payable period or, equivalently, an average turnover rate of 7.6 times per year, as follows:

	Accounts Payable				
	Inventory Purchases	Payables Period	Average Balance	Beginning Balance	Ending Balance
Year +1	$22,529	48 days	$2,963	$2,846	$3,080
Year +2	$24,795	48 days	$3,261	$3,080	$3,442
Year +3	$27,817	48 days	$3,658	$3,442	$3,875
Year +4	$29,737	48 days	$3,911	$3,875	$3,947
Year +5	$33,133	48 days	$4,357	$3,947	$4,768

In this case, we rely on our prior forecasts of PepsiCo's cost of goods sold and inventory balances to compute inventory purchases, which will flow through accounts payable, and we assume that the payables period will be a constant 48 days. We then compute the average balance in accounts payable and use it to compute the implied ending balance in accounts payable. Because the accounts payable balance at the start of the forecast period was not unusually high or low relative to cost of goods sold, the forecasts project relatively smooth growth in accounts payable over time, avoiding the sawtooth pattern discussed earlier.

Projecting Other Current Accrued Liabilities

As discussed in the prior section, Note 14, "Supplemental Financial Information" (Appendix A), discloses that at the end of 2008, PepsiCo's accrued liabilities for marketing, compensation, dividends, and other general and administrative expenses amount to $5,427 million. Our forecasts of income for PepsiCo assumed that selling, general, and administrative expenses would remain a steady percentage of sales, and therefore grow proportionately with sales. We therefore forecast that other current accrued liabilities will grow with selling, general, and administrative expenses, which grow with sales.

	Other Current Accrued Liabilities		
	Beginning Balance	SG&A Expense Growth Rate	Ending Balance
Year +1	$5,427	9.1%	$5,921
Year +2	$5,921	9.3%	$6,470
Year +3	$6,470	11.5%	$7,215
Year +4	$7,215	7.5%	$7,757
Year +5	$7,757	9.7%	$8,512

Projecting Current Liabilities: Income Taxes Payable

PepsiCo's current liabilities include a separate line item for income taxes payable. Income taxes payable varies with the income tax provision on the income statement, but income taxes payable also varies with tax payments, settlements of tax disputes, mergers and acquisitions, changes in deferred tax assets and liabilities, and other elements that are difficult to predict with confidence. PepsiCo's income taxes payable has varied within a narrow range between 0.3 percent and 0.4 percent of total assets over 2006–2008. The assumption is that PepsiCo's income taxes payable will average 0.4 percent of total assets in the future. The projected amounts are as follows:

	Income Taxes Payable		
	Total Assets	As a Percentage of Total Assets	Balance
Year +1	$38,499	0.4%	$154
Year +2	$41,692	0.4%	$167
Year +3	$45,815	0.4%	$183
Year +4	$48,669	0.4%	$195
Year +5	$53,506	0.4%	$214

Projecting Other Noncurrent Liabilities

Other noncurrent liabilities are accrued liabilities for expenses that relate to pension obligations, health care obligations, long-term compensation, and other operating and administrative activities. We therefore project other noncurrent liabilities will grow with SG&A expenses, which will grow with sales:

	Other Noncurrent Liabilities		
	Beginning Balance	SG&A Expense Growth Rate	Ending Balance
Year +1	$ 7,017	9.1%	$ 7,656
Year +2	$ 7,656	9.3%	$ 8,365
Year +3	$ 8,365	11.5%	$ 9,329
Year +4	$ 9,329	7.5%	$10,030
Year +5	$10,030	9.7%	$11,006

Projecting Deferred Income Taxes

PepsiCo's Note 5, "Income Taxes" (Appendix A), indicates that deferred taxes relate to a variety of operating items (for example, investments in unconsolidated affiliates; property, plant, and equipment; and pension benefits plans). Over the past three years, deferred income taxes have declined in amount and as a percentage of total assets, from 1.76 percent down to 0.63 percent. We project that deferred tax liabilities will remain at that proportionate level of total assets in future years. The amounts are as follows:

		Deferred Income Taxes	
	Total Assets	As a Percentage of Total Assets	Ending Balance
Year +1	$38,499	0.63%	$242
Year +2	$41,692	0.63%	$262
Year +3	$45,815	0.63%	$288
Year +4	$48,669	0.63%	$306
Year +5	$53,506	0.63%	$336

STEP 4: PROJECTING FINANCIAL ASSETS, FINANCIAL LEVERAGE, COMMON EQUITY CAPITAL, AND FINANCIAL INCOME ITEMS

After completing forecasts of the operating assets and liabilities of the balance sheet, the analyst projects any financial assets the firm will hold, and the financial debt and shareholders' equity capital amounts that will be necessary to finance the firm's operating and investing activities. In addition, the analyst projects the effects of financing on net income, projecting future interest income, interest expense, and other elements of financial income.

For firms that maintain a particular capital structure over time, the analyst can use the common-size balance sheet percentages to project amounts of debt and equity capital. The common-size balance sheet data for PepsiCo (Appendix C) show that the balance sheet percentages for total liabilities climbed fairly dramatically over the last five years, from 51.7 percent of total assets in 2004 to 66.4 percent in 2008. Over the same period, common and preferred shareholders' equity decreased from 48.3 percent of total assets in 2004 to 33.6 percent in 2008. If the analyst predicts that PepsiCo's capital structure will consist of stable proportions of liabilities and equity from this point forward (for instance, the analyst might project that the current structure of 66.4 percent liabilities and 33.6 percent equities will continue into the future), the analyst can use these common-size percentages and the projected amounts of total assets to project future totals of liabilities and equities.

Alternatively, the analyst can project debt capital and shareholders' equity accounts by projecting the financial leverage strategy of the firm. PepsiCo appears to be shifting its financial leverage strategy to recapitalize the firm with greater amounts of short- and long-term debt, while using this debt capital and cash from operations to reduce shareholders' equity through substantial repurchases of common shares and increased dividends. In this section, we forecast debt and equity by projecting the financial leverage strategy of PepsiCo, changing the expected debt and equity amounts over time. Each account is discussed next.

Projecting Financial Assets

In forecasting the firm's future financial capital structure, the analyst must project the future financial assets, such as short-term and long-term investments, that represent financial savings (as opposed to financial liabilities which are borrowings). To do so, the analyst must assess the firm's business and financial strategy to determine whether the firm uses financial assets for operating and liquidity purposes or financial purposes. For example, PepsiCo's 2008 Consolidated Balance Sheet (Appendix A) recognizes short-term investments (marketable securities) and investments in noncontrolled affiliates. As discussed previously, PepsiCo uses short-term investments in conjunction with cash to provide liquidity for operating activities, and the investments in noncontrolled affiliates represent PepsiCo's investments in its affiliated bottlers. As such, we included both of these types of investments in our projections of PepsiCo's operating activities.

By contrast, some firms will hold short-term or long-term investments that are not for operating or liquidity purposes, and are instead intended for future financial purposes, such as corporate acquisitions, debt retirement, repurchasing shares, or paying dividends. Suppose, for example, a firm had issued bonds to finance the purchase of plant and equipment and the bond indenture agreement required the firm to maintain a bond sinking fund (a reserve of cash or securities to be used for future bond retirement). The cash and securities in the sinking fund would represent financial assets for debt retirement, and should be projected with the firm's financial structure rather than as part of the firm's operating activities. As of the 2008 balance sheet, PepsiCo does not have any short-term or long-term investment securities for debt retirement purposes. Because PepsiCo is not likely to need future reserves of investment securities for debt retirement, we will not forecast them.

Projecting Short-Term Debt and Long-Term Debt

PepsiCo's 2008 Consolidated Balance Sheet (Appendix A) recognizes $369 million of short-term obligations. Note 9, "Debt Obligations and Commitments" (Appendix A), reveals that short-term debt obligations actually totaled $1,628 million, which included $273 million of current maturities of long-term debt, $846 million of commercial paper, and $509 million of other short-term borrowings. Of this total, PepsiCo reclassified $1,259 million as long-term debt because of its intent and ability to refinance on a long-term basis. Note 9 also discloses that at the end of 2008, PepsiCo has $7,858 million in long-term debt, including the $1,259 million reclassified as long-term debt, but net of $273 million of long-term debt maturing in 2009.

Note 9 shows that PepsiCo does not rely heavily on short-term debt to meet unexpected cash flow needs. PepsiCo maintains several revolving lines of credit for unexpected cash flow needs; however, PepsiCo draws little on these available lines of credit because it generates substantial amounts of cash from its operations. The Statement of Cash Flows for 2008 for PepsiCo (Appendix A) indicates that the firm generated approximately $7.0 billion of net cash flow from operating activities. PepsiCo used $2.7 billion for investing activities in 2008 and $3.0 billion for financing activities, which primarily involved paying dividends and repurchasing common stock, after raising nearly $3.1 billion (net) from issuing long-term debt. PepsiCo used the remaining $1.2 billion of cash flow from operations to increase the cash account to nearly $2.1 billion. Given that PepsiCo generates so much cash available for financing activities, it is not surprising that short-term borrowings are a minor element of PepsiCo's financial capital structure. The common-size balance sheet data for PepsiCo indicate that short-term debt has ranged from 0.9 percent of total assets in 2006 to 0.0 percent in 2007 to 1.0 percent in 2008. We project that short-term debt will be 1.0 percent of total assets in the future.

With respect to long-term debt, in 2008, PepsiCo shifted its financial leverage strategy to recapitalize using greater amounts of long-term debt instead of common equity. In fact, in the second quarter of 2008, PepsiCo issued $1.75 billion of senior ten-year unsecured notes and in the fourth quarter of 2008 issued another $2.0 billion of senior ten-year unsecured notes for general corporate purposes and for short-term debt retirement. Long-term debt jumped dramatically from $4,203 million at the beginning of 2008 to $7,858 million by the end of 2008. Over the past five years, long-term debt plus current maturities of long-term debt trended down from 9.16 percent of total assets in 2004 to 8.56 percent in 2006, but they have climbed dramatically since then, reaching 21.83 percent of total assets in 2008. We will assume that PepsiCo will maintain long-term debt equal to 21.83 percent of total assets in Year +1 and beyond. The projected amounts for short-term and long-term debt are as follows:

		Short-Term and Long-Term Debt		
	Total Assets	Short-Term Debt (1.00%)	Long-Term Debt (21.83%)	Total Interest-Bearing Debt
Year +1	$38,499	$385	$ 8,405	$ 8,790
Year +2	$41,692	$417	$ 9,102	$ 9,519
Year +3	$45,815	$458	$10,002	$10,460
Year +4	$48,669	$487	$10,625	$11,112
Year +5	$53,506	$535	$11,681	$12,216

In the next section we will use the preceding projected amounts for interest-bearing debt as a basis to project PepsiCo's future interest expense.

PepsiCo's outstanding long-term debt matures at varying dates extending to 2014 and beyond. Note 9 discloses information to enable the analyst to estimate the amounts that mature in Year +1 through Year +5 and beyond. For analysts developing forecasts for firms that are deleveraging and retiring debt or for firms that are highly leveraged and facing a high probability of bankruptcy, the schedule of future long-term debt maturities is very helpful in projecting when the firm will have to retire or refinance mature debt.

Projecting Interest Expense

We can now project our first-iteration estimate of interest expense, based on our projected balances in interest-bearing short-term and long-term debt. Note 9, "Debt Obligations and Commitments" (Appendix A), indicates that at the end of 2008, the interest rates on various short-term borrowings ranged from 0.7 percent on commercial paper up to 10.0 percent on other short-term borrowings. It also discloses that the average interest rate on long-term notes ($6,382 million; roughly 80 percent of the total long-term debt) was 5.8 percent. In addition, Note 9 indicates that PepsiCo's zero-coupon notes carry an implicit interest rate of 13.3 percent and that other forms of long-term debt carry an average interest rate of 5.3 percent. Dividing the 2008 interest expense by the average amount of interest-bearing debt outstanding during 2008 implies that PepsiCo's weighted average interest rate on debt was roughly 5.3 percent [= $329/({$369 + $0 + $4,203 + $7,858}/2)]. This average is likely to be slightly understated, however, because, as noted earlier, PepsiCo issued two very large senior notes in the second and fourth quarters of 2008; so it did not incur interest expense on them for the full year. The assumption is that interest expense will equal 5.8 percent on average interest-bearing debt in Year +1 through Year + 5 to match the average interest rate on the majority of outstanding long-term debt. Using the projected amounts of debt described previously, the projected interest expense amounts follow:

Interest Expense on Interest-Bearing Debt						
	Short-Term Debt	Long-Term Debt	Total Interest-Bearing Debt	Average Interest-Bearing Debt	Interest Rate	Interest Expense
2008	$369	$ 7,858	$ 8,227			$329
Year +1	$385	$ 8,405	$ 8,790	$ 8,508.5	5.8%	$493
Year +2	$417	$ 9,102	$ 9,519	$ 9,154.5	5.8%	$531
Year +3	$458	$10,002	$10,460	$ 9,989.5	5.8%	$579
Year +4	$487	$10,625	$11,112	$10,786.0	5.8%	$626
Year +5	$535	$11,681	$12,216	$11,664.0	5.8%	$677

The interest expense projections are appreciably higher than recent past interest expense amounts for PepsiCo, reflecting PepsiCo's shift in financial strategy in 2008 to much greater reliance on long-term debt capital. We can now enter these "first-pass" interest expense amounts in the projected income statements. If the projected balance sheets imply that PepsiCo will need larger or smaller amounts of long-term debt to finance future asset growth, then we will need to recompute the interest expense projections to reflect different amounts of debt.

Projecting Interest Income

We can also project our first-pass estimates of PepsiCo's interest income on financial assets, such as cash and short-term investments in marketable securities. In 2008, PepsiCo recognized $41 million in interest income. The average amount of cash and marketable securities during 2008 was $2,379 million (= [$910 + $2,064 + $1,571 + $213]/2), for an average return of 1.7 percent (= $41/$2,379). This rate of return reflects the very low interest rate environment present during the 2008 economic recession. It is likely that PepsiCo's cash and marketable securities are very low-risk but highly liquid instruments, and therefore yield very low rates of return. The assumption is that PepsiCo will earn a 3.0 percent return, which is the prevailing risk-free rate on medium-term U.S. Treasury bonds at the beginning of Year +1, on the average balances in cash and marketable securities each year. The projected amounts for interest income follow:

Interest Income					
	Ending Balances:				
Year	Cash	Marketable Securities	Average Balances	Rate of Return	Interest Income
2008	$2,064	$ 213			
+1	$1,551	$1,034	$2,431	3.0%	$ 73
+2	$1,695	$1,130	$2,706	3.0%	$ 81
+3	$1,890	$1,260	$2,988	3.0%	$ 90
+4	$2,032	$1,355	$3,269	3.0%	$ 98
+5	$2,230	$1,487	$3,552	3.0%	$107

If the projected balance sheets imply that PepsiCo will generate larger amounts of cash flow in future years and if we expect that they will retain larger amounts of cash and marketable securities, then we will need to recompute the interest income projections to reflect additional interest-earning assets.

Projecting Bottling Equity Income

PepsiCo generates income from equity investments in noncontrolled affiliates, which are primarily bottlers. To forecast future income from equity investments in bottling affiliates, one can project a normal rate of return and the level of investment in unconsolidated bottling affiliates.[18] During 2008, PepsiCo recognized $374 million in bottling equity income on investments in noncontrolled affiliates with an average book value of $4,119 million [= ($3,883 + 4,354)/2], which implies a rate of return of roughly 9.1 percent.[19] PepsiCo discloses in the MD&A section titled "Results of Operations—Consolidated Review" (Appendix B) that in 2008, one of the bottling affiliates incurred significant restructuring and impairment charges, which reduced PepsiCo's bottling equity income from this affiliate by $138 million. Absent these charges, PepsiCo would have reported bottling equity income of $512 million, which implies a rate of return of 12.2 percent [= ($374 + $138)/{($3,883 +$138 + $4,354)/2}]. In 2007 and 2006, PepsiCo earned considerably higher returns from these affiliates: 13.9 percent and 15.4 percent, respectively. During 2006–2008, PepsiCo earned an average rate of return of 12.8 percent on the book value of these investments. In Note 8, "Noncontrolled Bottling Affiliates" (Appendix A), PepsiCo discloses that its two largest equity investments in unconsolidated bottlers have fair values that exceed their book values by a total of nearly $1 billion. The average rate of return from 2006–2008 relative to the fair value of these investments is roughly 10.1 percent. Bottling companies are relatively low-risk, low-profit-margin businesses, and the income recognized by PepsiCo on these investments has already been adjusted for the income taxes paid by the affiliates. (PepsiCo does not pay taxes on this income until it receives dividends or sells a portion of the investment.) Therefore, it is reasonable to assume that PepsiCo will continue to earn a similar return on these investments. So an analyst can project Bottling Equity Income in future years to be 12.0 percent of the annual average book value of Investments in Noncontrolled Affiliates. We base these forecasts on future book values of the investments (rather than fair values) because the book value amounts are necessary to forecast the balance sheet. We described our projections of book value amounts of Investments in Noncontrolled Affiliates when we projected the assets on the balance sheet. The projected amounts for Bottling Equity Income follow.

	Bottling Equity Income				
	Investments in Noncontrolled Affiliates				
Year	Beginning Balance	Ending Balance	Average Balance	Rate of Return	Bottling Equity Income
+1	$3,883	$4,116	$3,999	12.0%	$480
+2	$4,116	$4,363	$4,239	12.0%	$509
+3	$4,363	$4,625	$4,494	12.0%	$539
+4	$4,625	$4,902	$4,763	12.0%	$572
+5	$4,902	$5,196	$5,049	12.0%	$606

[18] An alternative approach, which would be more time-consuming but potentially more accurate, would be to prepare a full set of financial statement forecasts for PepsiCo's bottling affiliates and estimate PepsiCo's share of expected future income.

[19] This computation assumes that the bottling equity income account on the income statement can be compared directly to the investments in noncontrolled affiliates account on the balance sheet. This is not likely to be strictly true because PepsiCo likely aggregates other nonbottling affiliates in the balance sheet account. In Note 8, "Noncontrolled Bottling Affiliates" (Appendix A), PepsiCo discloses that the most significant noncontrolled affiliates are bottling companies; so the computation is a reasonable estimate of PepsiCo's return on these investments.

Projecting Preferred Stock and Minority Interest

PepsiCo has a negative amount (−\$97 million) in convertible preferred stock at the end of 2008. Note 12, "Preferred Stock" (Appendix A), discloses that Quaker Foods had issued the preferred stock in 2001 as part of an employee stock ownership plan and that the shares can be redeemed by plan participants or repurchased by PepsiCo at a premium. The amount of preferred stock is negative, which is unusual, because PepsiCo raised \$41 million in capital by issuing the stock and to date has paid a total of \$138 million for the shares that employees have redeemed or that PepsiCo has repurchased. In Note 12, PepsiCo also discloses that the roughly 266,000 outstanding preferred shares have a fair value of \$72 million at the end of 2008. We will assume that all of these remaining shares will be repurchased by PepsiCo or redeemed by plan participants in Year +1 at fair value. We assume the payment of \$72 million will be a special one-time liquidating dividend to buy back and retire these preferred shares. Because we forecast that all of the preferred shares will be retired by the end of Year +1, we will then forecast the ending balance in preferred stock to be zero at the end of Year +1. We will record the \$72 million payment to retire the remaining shares and the \$97 million adjustment to zero out the negative balance in the preferred-stock account by reducing retained earnings by \$169 million. (See Chapter 6 for a discussion of accounting for share retirements.)

PepsiCo has no equity capital from minority interest shareholders. We assume that this will remain zero in the future.

Projecting Common Stock and Capital in Excess of Par Value

As Chapter 6 explains, these paid-in common equity capital accounts generally increase as the firm raises capital by issuing common shares to investors in the capital markets or by selling shares to individuals exercising stock options the firm has granted or by issuing shares in a merger or acquisition. These paid-in capital accounts decrease as the firm retires shares. PepsiCo's common stock and capital in excess of par value decreased from 2004 through 2008, dropping from roughly 2.32 percent of total assets to roughly 1.06 percent. PepsiCo has shifted its capital strategy to long-term debt, so we do not expect significant future issues of common equity. We will simply project Common Stock and Capital in Excess of Par Value to grow with total assets, remaining at 1.06 percent of total assets. The projected amounts for Common Stock and Capital in Excess of Par Value are as follows:

	Common Stock and Capital in Excess of Par Value		
	Total Assets	As a Percent of Total Assets	Ending Balance
Year +1	\$38,499	1.06%	\$408
Year +2	\$41,692	1.06%	\$441
Year +3	\$45,815	1.06%	\$485
Year +4	\$48,669	1.06%	\$515
Year +5	\$53,506	1.06%	\$566

Projecting Treasury Stock

The treasury stock account becomes *more* negative when the firm repurchases some of its outstanding common equity shares. The treasury stock account becomes *less* negative when the firm reissues treasury shares on the open market, uses them to meet stock option exercises, issues them in merger or acquisition transactions, or retires them. (See Chapter 6 for more discussion of accounting for treasury stock transactions.) For 2006 through 2008, PepsiCo's Statement of Common Shareholders' Equity (Appendix A) reveals that it has repurchased roughly $12 billion in common shares ($3,000 million in 2006, $4,300 million in 2007, and $4,720 million in 2008) to reduce the equity capital base and increase leverage. In addition, over the same period, PepsiCo reissued treasury shares to meet roughly $4.1 billion in stock option exercises ($1,619 million in 2006, $1,582 million in 2007, and $883 million in 2008).[20]

In PepsiCo's 2008 Annual Report, the MD&A section titled "Our Liquidity, Capital Resources and Financial Position" (Appendix B) discloses that during 2008, PepsiCo completed the $8.5 billion share repurchase program that had been approved by the board of directors in 2006 and had begun repurchasing shares under the $8.0 billion share repurchase program approved in 2007 (expiring in 2010). PepsiCo also disclosed that the repurchase program has approximately $6.4 billion remaining for repurchase. PepsiCo will likely continue to make substantial repurchases. PepsiCo's MD&A disclosures also note that the firm historically repurchases significantly more shares than it issues under stock compensation plans, with average net repurchases amounting to 1.8 percent of outstanding shares over the past five years. In fact, in PepsiCo's MD&A, the firm projects that it expects to make treasury stock purchases of up to $2,500 million in Year +1. We will assume that PepsiCo's treasury stock repurchases, net of treasury stock issued for stock compensation plans, will amount to $2,500 during Year +1 and will persist at this level through Year +5. We may need to reduce this assumption if we determine later in our analysis that PepsiCo will not have sufficient cash flow for these repurchases, or if our equity valuation estimates indicate that the capital market has overpriced PepsiCo stock. Alternately, we may increase this assumption if our analysis reveals that PepsiCo will have excess future cash flow or if our valuation estimates indicate PepsiCo's shares are underpriced.

In projecting stock repurchases net of stock reissues, we implicitly assume that employees will continue to exercise stock options and other stock-based compensation awards in future years. We may need to revise this assumption later in the analysis if our equity valuation estimates indicate that PepsiCo's stock options are not likely to be "in the money." Implicitly included in the income statement forecasts is an expense for the fair value of stock-based compensation in the projections of selling, general, and administrative expense.

The projected amounts for treasury stock are as follows:

	Treasury Stock		
	Beginning Balance	**Share Repurchases, net of Reissues**	**Ending Balance**
2008 actual	−$10,387	−$3,735	−$14,122
Year +1	−$14,122	−$2,500	−$16,622
Year +2	−$16,622	−$2,500	−$19,122
Year +3	−$19,122	−$2,500	−$21,622
Year +4	−$21,622	−$2,500	−$24,122
Year +5	−$24,122	−$2,500	−$26,622

[20] The stock market often interprets share repurchase announcements as "good news," inferring that management, with its in-depth knowledge of the firm, thinks that the capital market is underpricing the firm's stock (although, ironically, most stock repurchase plans are not completed at the announced levels). The stock market typically reacts to this positive signal by bidding up the price of the firm's shares. Stock repurchases also may be perceived favorably by capital markets participants because they represent a form of implicit dividend to individual shareholders that may be taxed at capital gains rates, which may be lower than the ordinary income tax rates on dividends (depending on the shareholders' holding period and tax status).

Projecting Accumulated Other Comprehensive Loss

According to PepsiCo's Statement of Common Shareholders' Equity at the end of 2008 (Appendix A), Accumulated Other Comprehensive Loss was −\$952 million at the beginning of 2008. In 2008, PepsiCo adopted a new accounting standard (SFAS 158) which required PepsiCo to reduce Accumulated Other Comprehensive Loss by \$51 million to −\$901 million. During 2008, PepsiCo's other comprehensive income items took a huge hit. PepsiCo recognized \$3,793 million of losses in comprehensive income for 2008. Consequently, by the end of 2008, Accumulated Other Comprehensive Loss had decreased \$3,793 million to an accumulated loss of −\$4,694 million. Although PepsiCo reported net income of \$5,142 million for 2008, it reported comprehensive income of only \$1,349 million. As described in Chapters 7 and 8, these losses were attributable to primarily two phenomena: foreign currency translation adjustments and net losses on pension and retiree benefit plans. In 2008, the U.S. dollar gained against many other currencies in which PepsiCo holds net assets, which triggered the translation losses. Also in 2008, the capital markets suffered a very difficult year, which partly explains the losses on pension and retiree benefit plans, which contain substantial holdings of investment securities. In addition, interest rates fell in 2008; so the present value of future retirement obligations increased, also partly explaining the losses.

In our previous forecasts of revenues from the PepsiCo's various international divisions, we assumed PepsiCo will continue to expand these international operations. However, even for the most experienced macroeconomic experts, it is difficult to forecast whether the U.S. dollar will increase or decrease in value relative to the foreign currencies PepsiCo uses in its international operations over the next five years. Also, PepsiCo might hedge or limit its exposure to adverse foreign currency movements. Thus, we project that PepsiCo will experience neither persistent negative nor positive foreign currency translation adjustments in the future. This is equivalent to assuming that PepsiCo's future foreign currency translation adjustments are equally likely to be positive or negative in any given year and that, on average, they will be zero over time. In addition, it is logical to assume that PepsiCo's pension and retiree benefit plans are equally likely to generate gains or losses in any given year and that, on average, they will be zero over the next five years. Therefore, we project that Accumulated Other Comprehensive Loss will remain at its current level. Accordingly, Other Comprehensive Income Items included in comprehensive income will also be zero in future years.

The gains and losses that impact other comprehensive income items tend to result from asset and liability revaluations for changes in interest rates and foreign exchange rates (such as fair value gains and losses on available-for-sale securities, foreign currency translation adjustments, certain pension and retiree benefit obligation and asset adjustments, and gains and losses on cash flow hedges; see Chapters 7 and 8 for more discussion). Because economy-wide changes in interest rates and foreign exchange rates tend to be transitory and because many firms tend to hedge or mitigate exposure to such risks, it is often very difficult for an analyst to predict with confidence that a particular firm will consistently generate persistent gains or losses from such changes over long periods of time. As such, analysts commonly forecast gains or losses from other comprehensive income items to be zero, on average.

STEP 5: PROJECTING NONRECURRING ITEMS, PROVISIONS FOR INCOME TAX, AND CHANGES IN RETAINED EARNINGS

Thus far we have developed forecasts of PepsiCo's operating activities, including operating income as well as the operating assets and liabilities. In addition, we have projected PepsiCo's future financial liabilities, common equity capital, and financial income items including interest income, interest expense, and income from noncontrolled affiliates. In Step 5 we complete the forecasting of PepsiCo's net income and dividends, and determine the projection of PepsiCo's retained earnings. This will lead us into Step 6, in which we will determine whether we need to revisit some of our previous forecast assumptions to make our balance sheet forecasts balance.

Projecting Nonrecurring Items

As discussed in prior chapters of this text, it is not uncommon for firms' reported income statements to include other nonrecurring gains or losses that are part of operations, unusual gains or losses that are peripheral to operations, income from discontinued segments, and extraordinary gains or losses. In 2008, for example, PepsiCo included an \$88 million impairment charge in cost of goods sold and an impairment charge of \$455 million as well as \$346 million in mark-to-market losses on commodity derivatives in SG&A expenses. As previous chapters discussed, the analyst must determine whether items such as these are likely to persist in the future and, if so, to include them in the financial statement forecasts. As discussed previously, our projections of future costs of goods sold and SG&A expenses assumed that these charges in 2008 were transitory and will not persist.

Projecting Provisions for Income Taxes

As Chapter 8 discusses, PepsiCo's Note 5, "Income Taxes" (Appendix A), shows the reconciliation between the statutory tax rate and PepsiCo's average, or effective, tax rate. The statutory U.S. federal income tax rate was 35.0 percent during 2006–2008. During 2008, PepsiCo experienced an increase in its average annual tax rate of roughly 0.8 percent from state income taxes and a decrease in its average tax rate of approximately 9.0 percent from lower tax rates in international tax jurisdictions, yielding an average tax rate of approximately 26.8 percent. In 2007 and 2006, PepsiCo experienced even lower effective tax rates of 25.9 percent and 19.3 percent, respectively, from the effects of the favorable settlements of audits of prior years' tax returns.

In PepsiCo's MD&A section titled "Our Critical Accounting Policies," under the heading "Income Tax Expense and Accruals" (Appendix B), PepsiCo discloses that it expects an average tax rate of 26.8 percent in Year +1, equal to the effective rate PepsiCo experienced in 2008. We will rely on that disclosure and assume that the average tax rate for Year +1 will be 26.8 percent. Beyond Year +1, we will assume that PepsiCo's average tax rate will persist at 26.8 percent, which is roughly equivalent to PepsiCo's average combined federal, state, and foreign tax rate of 26.9 percent for 2004 through 2008.

Net Income

All of the elements of the income statement, including first-iteration estimates of interest expense, interest income, and income taxes, are now complete. Recall that Exhibit 10.3 presents these income statement projections. The projected net income amounts, the implied growth rates, and net profit margins are as follows:

Year	Net Income	Implied Percentage Growth	Implied Net Profit Margin
2008 actual	$5,142	−9.1%	11.9%
+1 forecast	$6,111	18.8%	12.9%
+2 forecast	$6,602	8.0%	12.8%
+3 forecast	$7,273	10.2%	12.6%
+4 forecast	$7,726	6.2%	12.5%
+5 forecast	$8,427	9.1%	12.4%

The forecasts of net income for PepsiCo imply more robust growth in net income than PepsiCo has enjoyed in recent years. The forecasts also imply a higher profit margin than in 2008, but lower margins than PepsiCo enjoyed in 2007 and 2006. One contributing factor is the reversion of PepsiCo's earnings growth and profit margins from elimination of the impairment charges and mark-to-market commodity losses that negatively impacted net income in 2008, which should not persist in the future.

Retained Earnings

In general, the retained earnings account typically increases by the amount of net income (or decreases for net loss) and decreases for dividends. During 2004 through 2008, PepsiCo's dividend payout rates varied between 37 percent and 45 percent of prior-year net income. In the 2008 Annual Report, PepsiCo's MD&A section titled "Our Liquidity, Capital Resources and Financial Position" (Appendix B) discloses that PepsiCo's board of directors approved a 13 percent increase in dividend payouts, from $1.50 per share to $1.70 per share.[21] Relying on that disclosure, we project that PepsiCo's dividend payout policy will average 50 percent of prior-year net income from continuing operations in Years +1 through +5. Therefore, forecasts of dividends to common shareholders will vary over time with lagged net income before the effects of discontinued operations. For example, the forecast of dividends to common shareholders in Year +1 is $2,571 million [= 0.50 × ($5,142 − $0)]. This projection is roughly similar to $1.70 per share to each of the 1,553 million outstanding shares as of the beginning of Year +1 ($2,640 million).

Recall that in the discussion of PepsiCo's preferred stock, we projected that PepsiCo would also reduce retained earnings by $169 million to reflect a $72 million payment in Year +1 to retire the remaining outstanding preferred shares and to eliminate the negative $97 million balance in the preferred stock account. The implied changes in retained earnings are as follows (allow for rounding):

21 The capital markets generally react positively when firms announce plans to increase dividend payouts because market participants infer that this is a signal of managers' favorable private information about expectations for future sustainable earnings and cash flows. Moreover, managers are reluctant to cut or omit dividends because the market usually reacts negatively to such announcements. Thus, managers typically do not increase dividends unless they believe the increase can be sustained.

	Retained Earnings				
	Year +1	Year +2	Year +3	Year +4	Year +5
Beginning of Year	$30,638	$34,009	$37,556	$41,528	$45,618
Plus Net Income	6,111	6,602	7,273	7,726	8,427
Less Dividends to Common Shareholders	(2,571)	(3,055)	(3,301)	(3,636)	(3,863)
Less Retirement of Preferred Stock	(169)	(0)	(0)	(0)	(0)
End of Year	$34,009	$37,556	$41,528	$45,618	$50,182

STEP 6: BALANCING THE BALANCE SHEET

Even though the first-pass forecasts of all amounts on the income statement and balance sheet are complete, the balance sheet does not balance because we have projected individual asset and liability accounts to capture their underlying business activities, which do not vary together perfectly. The difference between the initial projected totals of assets minus the projected total liabilities and shareholders' equity each year represents the total amount by which we must adjust a flexible financial account to balance the balance sheet. If the difference is a positive amount, projected assets exceed projected liability and equity claims; so the firm must raise additional debt or equity capital or reduce projected assets by selling financial assets. If the difference is a negative amount, projected assets are less than projected liability and equity claims, in which case the firm can pay down debt, issue larger dividends, repurchase more shares, or increase investments in financial assets. The change in the difference represents the increment by which we must adjust the flexible financial account each year.

The analyst must evaluate the firm's financial flexibility and adjust the balance sheet accordingly. For some firms (for example, start-ups), financial flexibility may be in cash or marketable securities, which represent financial liquidity "safety valves." These firms often keep relatively large amounts of cash or marketable securities on the balance sheet for financial slack, and they use the funds when necessary to meet periodic cash requirements. For these firms, large inflows of cash (such as from a new stock issue) build up the cash and marketable securities accounts and large outflows (such as for the purchase of an asset or R&D expenditures) deplete the accounts. For these firms, analysts can use cash or marketable securities as the financial flexibility account needed to balance the balance sheet after all other balance sheet amounts have been determined.

For profitable growth firms that do not have large reserves of excess cash or marketable securities, financial flexibility may be exercised through short-term or long-term debt or equity. As the firm grows and invests in increasing productive capacity, it must raise the necessary capital through borrowing or issuing equity. As the firm matures and becomes a cash cow, it will shift how it uses its financial flexibility to pay down debt and perhaps initiate or increase dividends and share repurchases. The analyst should consider carefully what financial flexibility the firm has and will use.

Balancing PepsiCo's Balance Sheets

Currently, our projections of PepsiCo's total assets minus our projections of liabilities, shareholders' equity other than retained earnings (which is a negative amount because of treasury stock), and retained earnings, which follow, indicate the amounts by which our balance sheets do not balance (allow for rounding).

Projections:	Year +1	Year +2	Year +3	Year +4	Year +5
Total Assets (A)	$38,499	$41,692	$45,815	$48,669	$53,506
Total Liabilities	$25,843	$28,224	$31,350	$33,345	$37,052
Shareholders' Equity (other than Retained Earnings)	(20,908)	(23,375)	(25,831)	(28,301)	(30,750)
Retained Earnings	34,009	37,556	41,528	45,618	50,182
Total Liabilities and Shareholders' Equity (L + SE)	$38,945	$42,405	$47,047	$50,662	$56,484
Difference [= A − (L + SE)]	−$444	−$713	−$1,232	−$1,993	−$2,978
Change in the Difference	−$444	−$269	−$517	−$762	−$985
Change in the Difference as a Percentage of Total Assets	−1.2%	−0.6%	−1.1%	−1.6%	−1.8%

For PepsiCo, in Year +1, the first-iteration forecasts project that liabilities and equities exceed assets by $444 million (about 1.2 percent of total assets). We need to adjust a flexible financial account by $444 million (by increasing a financial asset account or decreasing a financial liability or shareholders' equity account) to balance the balance sheet. In Year +2, the first-iteration projections indicate that liabilities and equities will exceed assets by a total of $713 million; so we will need an additional adjustment of −$269 million in Year +2 (about 0.6 percent of total assets), and so on.

A number of PepsiCo's flexible financial accounts could be used for this adjustment each year depending on PepsiCo's strategy for investments and capital structure. Consider the following options:

- Increase marketable securities if PepsiCo will retain excess capital in marketable securities for financial flexibility.
- Reduce short-term or long-term debt if PepsiCo will use its financial flexibility to reduce leverage.
- Reduce retained earnings by increasing projected dividends or treasury stock repurchases if PepsiCo will distribute excess capital to common shareholders.

PepsiCo's MD&A section titled "Our Liquidity and Capital Resources" (Appendix B) states that in 2008, "Management operating cash flow was used primarily to repurchase shares and pay dividends. We expect to continue to return approximately all of our management operating cash flow to our shareholders through dividends and share repurchases."[22] Given this disclosure and the fact that PepsiCo has clearly demonstrated its willingness and ability to pay out increasing amounts of capital to shareholders through dividends and share repurchases, we will adjust dividends as the flexible financial account. Therefore, in Year +1, the dividend forecast must be increased by $444 million, the amount necessary to balance the balance sheet. This simply means that if PepsiCo's financial performance and position during Year +1 exactly match our forecasts, then PepsiCo can increase dividend payments slightly to keep assets in balance with liabilities and equity. In Years +2 through +5, we must also adjust our dividends forecasts upward each year by the incremental amount of the necessary adjustment to balance the balance sheet (that is, $269 million in Year +2, $517 million in Year +3, and so on). We refer to these adjustment

[22] "Management operating cash flow" is PepsiCo's measure of cash flows from operating activities less net capital expenditures for property, plant, and equipment.

amounts as *implied dividends*. The projected total amounts of dividends to common shareholders are as follows:

	Year +1	Year +2	Year +3	Year +4	Year +5
Dividends to Common Shareholders (50% of Lagged Net Income from Continuing Operations)	$2,571	$3,055	$3,301	$3,636	$3,863
Implied Dividends	+444	+269	+517	+762	+985
Total Common Dividends	$3,015	$3,324	$3,818	$4,398	$4,848

Equivalently, we can assume that PepsiCo will distribute the excess capital to shareholders through additional treasury stock repurchases rather than implied dividends. In either case, the assumption that PepsiCo will return the excess capital to shareholders through increased dividends or treasury stock repurchases will have equivalent effects on total assets, total liabilities, total shareholders' equity, and net income. After adjusting our dividends projections to include the implied dividends necessary to balance the balance sheet, the changes in retained earnings are as follows (allow for rounding):

	Retained Earnings				
	Year +1	Year +2	Year +3	Year +4	Year +5
Beginning of Year	$30,638	$33,565	$36,842	$40,296	$43,624
Plus Net Income	6,111	6,602	7,273	7,726	8,427
Less Dividends to Common Shareholders	(3,015)	(3,324)	(3,818)	(4,398)	(4,848)
Less Retirement of Preferred Stock	(169)	(0)	(0)	(0)	(0)
End of Year	$33,565	$36,842	$40,296	$43,624	$47,203

The final projections of the balance sheet total amounts, which you should verify by referring back to the projected balance sheets presented in Exhibit 10.4, are as follows (allow for rounding):

Projections:	Year +1	Year +2	Year +3	Year +4	Year +5
Total Assets (A)	$38,499	$41,692	$45,815	$48,669	$53,506
Total Liabilities	$25,843	$28,224	$31,350	$33,345	$37,052
Shareholders' Equity (other than Retained Earnings)	(20,908)	(23,375)	(25,831)	(28,301)	(30,750)
Retained Earnings	33,565	36,842	40,296	43,624	47,203
Total Liabilities and Shareholders' Equity (L + SE)	$38,499	$41,692	$45,815	$48,669	$53,506
Difference (= A − [L + SE])	$ 0	$ 0	$ 0	$ 0	$ 0

Closing the Loop: Solving for Co-determined Variables

If the excess capital had been added to interest-earning asset accounts (for example, marketable securities or cash) or subtracted from interest-bearing liability accounts (for example, short-term or long-term debt), the projected amounts for interest income or interest expense would need to be adjusted on the income statement. This would create an additional set of co-determined variables in the financial statement forecasts. For example, suppose we use long-term debt as the flexible financial account and adjust it to balance assets with liabilities and shareholders' equity. To determine the necessary plug to long-term debt, all of the other asset, liability, and shareholders' equity amounts, including retained earnings, must be known. To forecast retained earnings, net income, which depends on interest expense on long-term debt, must be known. To determine retained earnings, dividends, which depend on net income, also must be known. Thus, it is necessary to simultaneously solve for at least five variables.

This problem might seem intractable, but it is not because of the computational capabilities of computer spreadsheet programs such as Excel. To solve for multiple variables simultaneously in older versions of Excel, first click the Tools menu, then click the Calculations menu, and then click the Iterations box, so that Excel will solve and resolve circular references up to 1,000 times until all calculations fall within the specified tolerance for precision. In newer versions of Excel, click the Office Button, then click the Excel Options menu at the bottom of the drop-down box, and then click the Formulas tab. At the top of that menu, you will see Calculation options; check the box to "Enable iterative calculation" and allow for up to 1,000 iterations. Then you can program each cell to calculate the variables needed, even if they are simultaneously determined with other variables. With FSAP, the default settings allow for iterative simultaneous computations, but some versions of Excel automatically reset the default settings. So you should follow these steps to double-check that the FSAP spreadsheet will compute co-determined variables simultaneously.

STEP 7: PROJECTING THE STATEMENT OF CASH FLOWS

The final step of the seven-step forecasting process involves projecting the statement of cash flows. This is a relatively straightforward task because the statement of cash flows simply characterizes all of the changes in the balance sheet in terms of the implications for cash. Thus, we derive the statement of cash flows directly from the projected income statements and balance sheets. Chapter 3 described the procedures for preparing this statement. We capture all of the changes in the projected balance sheets each year and express these changes in terms of their implied effects on cash. Increases in assets imply uses of cash; decreases in assets imply sources of cash. Increases in liabilities and shareholders' equity imply sources of cash; decreases in liabilities and shareholders' equity imply uses of cash.

Tips for Forecasting Statements of Cash Flows

The analyst should note that the statement of cash flows will not reconcile with the projected income statement and balance sheets if the balance sheets do not balance and if the income statement does not articulate with the balance sheets. (That is, net income should be included in the change in retained earnings.)

An important point is that you *should not* attempt to project future statements of cash flows from historical statements; instead, you should follow the much simpler procedure we describe here in projecting *the implied statement of cash flows.* Unfortunately, unlike historical balance sheets and income statements, historical statements of cash flows *do not* provide good bases for projecting future cash flows because many of the line items on the statement of cash flows are difficult to reconcile with historical changes in balance sheet amounts. The reason is because in preparing the statement of cash flows, the accountant aggregates numerous cash flows on each line item of the statement and the analyst may not be able to determine what amounts have been aggregated. For example, the accountant must report separately the net cash flow implications of a business acquisition on one line of the statement, but the business acquisition causes changes in many asset and liability accounts. In addition, the accountant may choose to disclose details of cash flows that the analyst cannot verify. For example, the accountant might disclose separately in the statement of cash flows the amounts of marketable securities purchased and sold, but the analyst cannot verify those amounts because the analyst can only observe the net change in the marketable securities balance from the beginning to the end of the year. Thus, we recommend simply following the steps below to compute the *implied statement of cash flows* from the projected income statements and balance sheets, which the analyst can observe and verify. The Forecasts worksheet in FSAP (Appendix C) is programmed to use this approach to automatically calculate implied statements of cash flows from the projected income statements and balance sheets.

Specific Steps for Forecasting Implied Statements of Cash Flows

Exhibit 10.6 presents the projected implied statement of cash flows for PepsiCo for Years +1 through +5. We describe the derivation of each of the line items next. You should verify how the projected implied statements of cash flows in Exhibit 10.6 capture the cash inflows and outflows described in each of the following line items.

(1) **Net Income:** Use the amounts in the forecasted income statements (Exhibit 10.3).

(2) **Depreciation Expense:** Add back the projected amount of depreciation expense included in net income and used to compute the net change in accumulated depreciation on property, plant, and equipment. The depreciation expense forecast should reconcile with the change in accumulated depreciation on the projected balance sheet (less the decrease in accumulated depreciation from assets that were sold or retired, if any).

(3) **Amortization Expense:** Add back amortization expense on amortizable intangible assets. The amount of amortization expense to add back to net income should reconcile with the change in amortizable intangible assets balance, adjusted for any new investments in those assets (which should be included as cash outflows in the investing section of this statement).[23] For PepsiCo, we add back amortization expense, which we included as an operating expense on PepsiCo's income statement forecasts. For some firms, if the amount of amortization expense is not large, the analyst can ignore adding it back to net income to compute cash flow from operating activities and simply include the net change in amortizable intangible assets in the investing section. This will slightly understate cash inflows from operations and slightly understate cash outflows for investing activities, but the two effects will offset so that net cash is not affected.

(4) **through (9) Working Capital Accounts:** Adjust net income for changes in various operating current asset and current liability accounts other than cash (such as accounts receivable, inventory, accounts payable, accrued expenses, and others) appearing on the projected balance sheets.

(10) **and (11) Deferred Taxes and Long-Term Accrued Expenses:** Adjust net income for changes in deferred taxes, noncurrent liabilities for accrued expenses, and changes in other noncurrent liabilities. These items include changes in long-term accruals for expenses that are part of operations, including deferred taxes, pension

[23] Note that the analyst should not need to add back any amortization expense for nonamortizable intangible assets such as goodwill and brands with indefinite lives because under U.S. GAAP and IFRS, goodwill and other intangibles with indefinite lives are not amortized. Thus, no amortization expense for these assets was included in the projected income statements.

EXHIBIT 10.6

PepsiCo
Actual and Forecast Statements of Cash Flows

Actual and forecast amounts in bold. Amounts in millions; allow for rounding.

	Actuals		Forecasts				
IMPLIED STATEMENT OF CASH FLOWS	**2007**	**2008**	**Year + 1**	**Year + 2**	**Year + 3**	**Year + 4**	**Year + 5**
(1) Net Income	**5,658**	**5,142**	**6,111**	**6,602**	**7,273**	**7,726**	**8,427**
(2) Add back Depreciation Expense (net)	**1,297**	**221**	**1,582**	**1,770**	**1,980**	**2,205**	**2,453**
(3) Add back Amortization Expense (net)	**58**	**64**	**64**	**63**	**62**	**60**	**56**
(4) (Increase) Decrease in Receivables—Net	**(664)**	**(294)**	**(460)**	**(450)**	**(787)**	**(112)**	**(1,141)**
(5) (Increase) Decrease in Inventories	**(364)**	**(232)**	**(208)**	**(303)**	**(388)**	**(125)**	**(569)**
(6) (Increase) Decrease in Prepaid Expenses	**(334)**	**(333)**	**(121)**	**(134)**	**(182)**	**(132)**	**(184)**
(7) Increase (Decrease) in Accounts Payable—Trade	**460**	**284**	**234**	**362**	**433**	**72**	**821**
(8) Increase (Decrease) in Current Accrued Liabilities	**646**	**387**	**494**	**548**	**745**	**542**	**755**
(9) Increase (Decrease) in Income Taxes Payable	**61**	**(6)**	**9**	**13**	**16**	**11**	**19**
(10) Net Change in Deferred Tax Assets and Liabilities	**118**	**(420)**	**16**	**20**	**26**	**18**	**30**
(11) Increase (Decrease) in Long-Term Accrued Liabilities	**168**	**2,225**	**639**	**709**	**964**	**700**	**977**
Net Cash Flows from Operations	**7,104**	**7,038**	**8,360**	**9,201**	**10,142**	**10,966**	**11,644**
(12) (Increase) Decrease in Prop., Plant, & Equip., at cost	**(2,838)**	**(656)**	**(2,171)**	**(2,939)**	**(3,278)**	**(3,524)**	**(3,867)**
(13) (Increase) Decrease in Marketable Securities	**(400)**	**1,358**	**(821)**	**(96)**	**(130)**	**(95)**	**(132)**
(14) (Increase) Decrease in Investment Securities	**(664)**	**471**	**(233)**	**(247)**	**(262)**	**(277)**	**(294)**
(15) (Increase) Decrease in Amortizable Intangible Assets (net)	**(217)**	**0**	**0**	**0**	**0**	**0**	**0**
(16) (Increase) Decrease in Goodwill and Nonamort. Intang.	**(611)**	**165**	**(570)**	**(632)**	**(859)**	**(624)**	**(870)**
(17) (Increase) Decrease in Other Non-current Assets	**(702)**	**(976)**	**(80)**	**(82)**	**(85)**	**(87)**	**(90)**
Net Cash Flows from Investing Activities	**(5,432)**	**362**	**(3,874)**	**(3,996)**	**(4,613)**	**(4,607)**	**(5,253)**

(*Continued*)

EXHIBIT 10.6 (Continued)

	Actuals		Forecasts				
IMPLIED STATEMENT OF CASH FLOWS	**2007**	**2008**	**Year + 1**	**Year + 2**	**Year + 3**	**Year + 4**	**Year + 5**
(18) Increase (Decrease) in Short-Term Debt	(274)	369	16	32	41	29	48
(19) Increase (Decrease) in Long-Term Debt	1,653	3,655	547	697	900	623	1,056
(20) Increase (Decrease) in Minority Interest and Preferred Stock	(12)	(6)	97	0	0	0	0
(21) Increase (Decrease) in Common Stock + Paid-In Capital	(134)	(99)	27	34	44	30	51
(22) Increase (Decrease) in Accum. OCI and Other Equity Adjs.	1,294	(3,742)	0	0	0	0	0
(23) Increase (Decrease) in Treasury Stock	(2,629)	(3,735)	(2,500)	(2,500)	(2,500)	(2,500)	(2,500)
(24) Dividends	(2,311)	(2,688)	(3,184)	(3,325)	(3,818)	(4,398)	(4,848)
Net Cash Flows from Financing Activities	(2,413)	(6,246)	(4,998)	(5,062)	(5,333)	(6,217)	(6,193)
(25) **Net Change in Cash**	(741)	1,154	(513)	144	195	142	198
Check: Net Change in Cash − Change in Cash Balance	0	0	0	0	0	0	0

NOTE: We label the statements of cash flows and amounts for 2007 and 2008 as "Actuals" because we derive them from the actual balance sheet and income statement amounts in PepsiCo's financial statements rather than from the financial statement forecasts. Appendix A presents PepsiCo's Statements of Cash Flows for 2007 and 2008 as prepared by PepsiCo according to U.S. GAAP.

and retiree benefit obligations, warranties, and other noncurrent liabilities that appear on the projected balance sheets.

Net Cash Flows from Operations: The sum of lines (1) through (11) is the implied amount of net cash flows from operating activities.

(12) **Property, Plant, and Equipment:** The amount on this line captures cash outflows for the projected capital expenditures included in the change in property, plant, and equipment (at cost) on the projected balance sheet in Exhibit 10.4 less any cash proceeds from sales of property, plant, and equipment. As a check, the analyst should make sure the statement of cash flows captures all of the net cash flow implications of property, plant, and equipment. To verify this, the amount of depreciation expense added back to net income *minus* cash outflows for capital expenditures *plus* cash inflows for any asset sales or retirements should equal the change in net property, plant, and equipment on the projected balance sheet.

(13), (14) **Marketable Securities and Investment Securities (net):** The statement of cash flows classifies net purchases and sales of marketable securities (current asset) and investment securities (noncurrent asset) as investing transactions. The net changes in these accounts on the projected balance sheets determine the cash flow amounts for these items on the statement of cash flows. Some error in the implied cash flow amount from investment securities can occur. This change should be increased (become less negative) for the excess (if any) of equity earnings over dividends received from unconsolidated affiliates (which is a non-cash increase in this asset amount). Similarly, the excess of equity earnings over dividends received also should be subtracted from net income in the operating section of the statement of cash flows. Rather than making assumptions about this relatively immaterial item (the effects of which completely offset each other), we simply treat the change in investments fully as an investing transaction. This choice means that cash flows from operating activities are slightly overstated and cash flows from investing activities are slightly understated by an equivalent amount but that the net change in cash each year is not affected.

(15) **Amortizable Intangible Assets:** Enter the net change in amortizable intangible assets on this line. The change in this asset account on the projected balance sheets is the net of cash outflows to acquire amortizable intangible assets plus any cash inflows from sales or retirements of such assets. As discussed in Item (3), amortization expense is added back to income in the operating section of the statement of cash flows. Thus, the adjustment for cash outflows or inflows for amortizable intangible assets in the investing section of the statement should not include the effects of amortization expense. Given that amortizable intangibles are commonly shown on balance sheets net of accumulated amortization, the change in the net amortizable intangible assets account balance will reflect both effects: cash flows from investing activities and amortization expense. To isolate the cash flows from investing, the analyst should add amortization expense back to the net change in this account balance.

(16) **Goodwill and Nonamortizable Intangible Assets:** Enter the changes in goodwill and nonamortizable intangible assets on this line. Given that these assets are not amortized, the net change in the nonamortizable intangible assets balance on the projected balance sheets should reflect cash outflows to acquire new nonamortizable intangible assets less cash inflows from selling or retiring such assets. If the account balance for goodwill or nonamortizable intangible assets has declined because of an impairment charge, the analyst should add this noncash charge

back to net income in the operating section of the statement of cash flows and adjust accordingly the cash flow implications from net changes in goodwill or nonamortizable intangibles in the investing section (similar to adding back amortization expense).

(17) **Other Noncurrent Assets:** Enter the changes in other noncurrent assets on this line. The changes in the other noncurrent asset accounts on the projected balance sheets measure the cash outflows to acquire such assets net of any cash inflows from sales or retirements of such assets.

Net Cash Flows from Investing Activities: The sum of lines (12) through (17) on PepsiCo's projected implied statement of cash flows measures the implied amount of net cash flows from investing activities.

(18), (19) **Short-Term and Long-Term Debt:** Changes in interest-bearing debt (short-term notes payable, current maturities of long-term debt, and long-term debt) on the projected balance sheets are financing activities.

(20) **Minority Interest and Preferred Stock:** The changes in minority interest and preferred stock on the projected balance sheets are financing activities. For PepsiCo in Year +1, the adjustment to zero out the negative balance in preferred stock appears as a cash inflow, but that effect is offset by an equivalent adjustment included as a cash outflow with total dividends on line 24.

(21) **Changes in Common Stock and Additional Paid-In Capital:** These amounts represent the financing cash flows from changes in the common stock and paid-in capital accounts on the projected balance sheets.

(22) **Changes in Accumulated Other Comprehensive Income:** These amounts represent the changes in the accumulated other comprehensive income account that is a component of shareholders' equity on the projected balance sheets.

(23) **Treasury Stock:** The amounts represent the net cash flow implications of treasury stock transactions that are captured in the net change in the treasury stock account on the projected balance sheets.

(24) **Dividends:** Enter the projected amounts for common and preferred dividends each year (discussed earlier in the section on Retained Earnings in the projected balance sheets). For PepsiCo in Year +1, this includes the amounts to retire outstanding preferred stock.

Net Cash Flows from Financing Activities: The sum of lines (18) through (24) measures the implied amount of net cash flows from financing activities.

(25) **Net Change in Cash:** The aggregate of the amounts of cash flows from operations, investing activities, and financing activities. This total should equal the change in cash on the projected balance sheets.

SHORTCUT APPROACHES TO FORECASTING

Thus far, the chapter has emphasized a methodical, detailed approach to forecasting individual accounts on the income statement and balance sheet, allowing the analyst to incorporate drivers of expected future operating, investing, and financing activities related to each account. In some circumstances, however, an analyst may find it necessary to forecast income statement and balance sheet totals directly without carefully considering each account. This shortcut approach has the potential to introduce forecasting error if the shortcut assumptions do not fit each account very well. On the other hand, if the firm is stable and mature in an industry in steady-state equilibrium, shortcut forecasting techniques are efficient approaches to project current steady-state conditions to the future. The next section illustrates shortcut approaches for forecasting PepsiCo's income statements and balance sheets.

Projected Sales and Income Approach

Shortcut projections for total sales and net income can be developed using PepsiCo's recent sales growth rates and net profit margins. Common-size and rate-of-change income statement data reveal that during 2004 through 2008, PepsiCo generated a compound growth rate in sales of 9.9 percent and an average net profit margin of 13.8 percent. If we simply use these ratios to forecast sales and net income over Years +1 to +5, the projected amounts are as follows:

Year	Sales Growth Rate	Projected Sales	Net Profit Margin	Projected Net Income
2008 actual		$43,251		
+1	9.9%	$47,533	13.8%	$6,560
+2	9.9%	$52,239	13.8%	$7,209
+3	9.9%	$57,411	13.8%	$7,923
+4	9.9%	$63,095	13.8%	$8,707
+5	9.9%	$69,341	13.8%	$9,569

These shortcut projections for sales and net income are much higher than the detailed sales and income projections developed for PepsiCo throughout the chapter (particularly those for Years +3 to +5). By forecasting individual expense amounts, the more detailed projections capture expected changes in expenses relative to sales, whereas the shortcut approach assumes that existing relations between sales and expenses will persist linearly into the future.

Projected Total Assets Approach

Total assets can be projected using the recent historical growth rate in total assets. Between the end of 2003 and the end of 2008, PepsiCo's total assets grew at an annual 7.3 percent compound rate. If this growth rate continues through Year +5, total assets will increase as follows:

Year	Asset Growth Rate	Projected Total Assets
2008 actual		$35,994
+1	7.3%	$38,622
+2	7.3%	$41,441
+3	7.3%	$44,466
+4	7.3%	$47,712
+5	7.3%	$51,195

Using historical growth rates to project total assets can result in erroneous projections if the analyst fails to consider the link between sales growth and asset growth. We assumed a sales growth rate for PepsiCo of 9.9 percent in the shortcut approach to sales projections but a 7.3 percent growth in assets, which implies a significant increase in total assets turnover from 1.22 in 2008 to 1.40 in Year +5. If this increase in total asset efficiency is not realistic, the use of these forecast procedures will lead to erroneous projections.

An alternative shortcut approach to projecting total assets uses the total assets turnover ratio, explicitly linking sales growth and asset growth. Like before, the assumption is that

PepsiCo's sales growth will persist at 9.9 percent per year, but now we will also assume total assets turnover will remain at 1.22 over the next five years. The calculation of projected total assets using the assets turnover ratio shortcut follows:

Year	Projected Sales	Average Assets Turnover Ratio	Projected Average Total Assets	Projected Beginning Total Assets	Projected Ending Total Assets	Implied Percent Change in Total Assets
+1	$47,533	1.22	$38,961	$35,994	$41,929	16.5%
+2	$52,239	1.22	$42,819	$41,929	$43,709	4.2%
+3	$57,411	1.22	$47,058	$43,709	$50,407	15.3%
+4	$63,095	1.22	$51,717	$50,407	$53,027	5.2%
+5	$69,341	1.22	$56,837	$53,027	$60,647	14.4%

This approach ties the projections of total assets to projections of sales. One difficulty sometimes encountered with using total assets turnover to project total assets is that it can result in unusual patterns for projected total assets. The total assets turnover uses average total assets in the denominator. If total assets changed by an unusually large (small) percentage in the most recent year preceding the projections, the next year's assets must change by an unusually small (large) proportion to compensate. This sawtooth pattern, which we described earlier in the chapter and illustrated in Exhibit 10.5, makes little intuitive sense, given a smooth growth in sales. We encounter this problem projecting total assets for PepsiCo using its total assets turnover in the preceding data. Note that the forecasts of PepsiCo's total assets increase 16.5 percent during Year +1, 4.2 percent in Year +2, 15.3 percent in Year +3, and so on, whereas we expect PepsiCo's sales to grow smoothly at 9.9 percent per year.

As shown previously in this chapter, the analyst can deal with the sawtooth problem by basing the assets turnover ratio on the ending balance, instead of the average balance, in total assets. Alternately, the analyst can smooth the rate of increase in assets over the forecast horizon. Assuming that assets turnover is stable at 1.22 and sales growth is smooth at 9.9 percent per year, the preceding data indicate that assets will increase from $35,994 million in 2008 to $60,647 million in Year +5, which reflects a compound average annual growth rate of 11.0 percent. The following table shows the revised projected assets following this smoothed approach. Note that total assets equal $60,647 million at the end of Year +5 in both cases (allow for rounding).

Year	Asset Growth Rate	Projected Total Assets
2008 actual		$35,994
+1	11.0%	$39,953
+2	11.0%	$44,348
+3	11.0%	$49,227
+4	11.0%	$54,641
+5	11.0%	$60,647

Once the analyst projects total assets, common-size balance sheet percentages provide a shortcut approach for allocating total assets to individual assets, liabilities, and shareholders' equity. In using these common-size percentages, the analyst assumes that the firm maintains a constant mix of assets, liabilities, and equities regardless of the level of total assets. Equivalently, the analyst assumes that each asset, liability, and equity account grows at the same rate as total assets. For example, the common-size balance sheet for 2008 for PepsiCo (Appendix C) indicates that total liabilities represent 66.4 percent of total assets and equities represent 33.6 percent of total assets. If we assume that PepsiCo will maintain exactly the same proportions of debt and equity in its capital structure in future years, and if we use these proportions and the smoothed projections of total assets, we can project total liabilities and shareholders' equity amounts for Years +1 through +5 as follows:

Year	Projected Total Assets	Projected Total Liabilities (66.4%)	Projected Shareholders' Equity (33.6%)
+1	$39,953	$26,529	$13,424
+2	$44,348	$29,447	$14,901
+3	$49,227	$32,687	$16,540
+4	$54,641	$36,282	$18,359
+5	$60,647	$40,270	$20,377

Using common-size balance sheet percentages to project individual assets, liabilities, and shareholders' equity encounters (at least) two potential shortcomings. First, the common-size percentages for individual assets, liabilities, and shareholders' equity are not independent of each other. For example, a firm such as PepsiCo that acquires and disposes of its bottlers on an ongoing basis may experience a changing proportion for investments in securities among its assets. Other asset categories may show decreasing percentages in some years even though their dollar amounts are increasing. The analyst must interpret these decreasing percentages carefully.

Second, using the common-size percentages does not permit the analyst to easily change the assumptions about the future behavior of an individual asset or liability. For example, assume that PepsiCo intended to implement inventory control systems that should accelerate inventory turnover so that inventory will likely comprise a smaller percentage of total assets in the future than it has in the past. The analyst encounters difficulties adjusting the common-size balance sheet percentages to reflect the changes in inventory policies.

In general, shortcut approaches to forecasting have the virtue of greater efficiency but greater potential for error as compared to a thoughtful and more deliberate approach to forecasting each income statement and balance sheet account. Given that forecast errors can be very costly when they lead to bad investment decisions, we strongly advocate the careful, detailed approach to projecting financial statements by forecasting the firm's future operating, investing, and financing activities using individual income statement and balance sheet accounts.

ANALYZING PROJECTED FINANCIAL STATEMENTS

The reasonableness of the forecast assumptions and their internal consistency can be tested by analyzing the projected financial statements using the same ratios and other analytical tools discussed in previous chapters. Exhibit 10.7 presents a ratio analysis for PepsiCo based on the financial statement forecasts for Year +1 to Year +5. The FSAP Forecasts spreadsheet provides these ratio computations (Appendix C).

FSAP

Forecast growth rates for sales are consistent with PepsiCo's past sales growth performance. The forecasts of net income exhibit growth rates are less volatile than those PepsiCo

EXHIBIT 10.7

PepsiCo
Financial Ratio Analysis Based on Actual and Forecast Financial Statements

	Actuals			Forecasts				
	2006	2007	2008	Year +1	Year +2	Year +3	Year +4	Year +5
FORECAST VALIDITY CHECK DATA:								
GROWTH								
Revenue Growth Rate	7.9%	12.3%	9.6%	9.1%	9.3%	11.5%	7.5%	9.7%
Net Income Growth Rate	38.4%	0.3%	−9.1%	18.8%	8.0%	10.2%	6.2%	9.1%
Total Asset Growth Rate	−5.7%	15.7%	3.9%	7.0%	8.3%	9.9%	6.2%	9.9%
RETURN ON ASSETS								
(based on reported amounts):								
Profit Margin for ROA	16.5%	14.7%	12.4%	13.7%	13.6%	13.4%	13.2%	13.2%
× Assets Turnover	1.1	1.2	1.2	1.3	1.3	1.3	1.3	1.3
= ROA	18.8%	18.0%	15.2%	17.4%	17.4%	17.6%	17.3%	17.5%
RETURN ON ASSETS								
(excluding effects of nonrecurring items):								
Profit Margin for ROA	16.5%	14.7%	12.4%	13.7%	13.6%	13.4%	13.2%	13.2%
× Assets Turnover	1.1	1.2	1.2	1.3	1.3	1.3	1.3	1.3
= ROA	18.8%	18.0%	15.2%	17.4%	17.4%	17.6%	17.3%	17.5%
RETURN ON COMMON EQUITY								
(based on reported amounts):								
Profit Margin for ROCE	16.1%	14.3%	11.9%	12.6%	12.8%	12.6%	12.5%	12.4%
× Assets Turnover	1.1	1.2	1.2	1.3	1.3	1.3	1.3	1.3
× Capital Structure Leverage	2.1	2.0	2.4	3.0	3.1	3.1	3.2	3.2
= ROCE	37.9%	34.5%	34.8%	47.8%	50.5%	52.1%	51.9%	53.0%

RETURN ON COMMON EQUITY (excluding effects of nonrecurring items):								
Profit Margin for ROCE	**16.1%**	**14.3%**	**11.9%**	**12.6%**	**12.8%**	**12.6%**	**12.5%**	**12.4%**
× Assets Turnover	**1.1**	**1.2**	**1.2**	**1.3**	**1.3**	**1.3**	**1.3**	**1.3**
× Capital Structure Leverage	**2.1**	**2.0**	**2.4**	**3.0**	**3.1**	**3.1**	**3.2**	**3.2**
= ROCE	**37.9%**	**34.5%**	**34.8%**	**47.8%**	**50.5%**	**52.1%**	**51.9%**	**53.0%**
OPERATING PERFORMANCE:								
Gross Profit/Revenues	**55.1%**	**54.3%**	**52.9%**	**52.7%**	**52.5%**	**52.3%**	**52.1%**	**52.0%**
Operating Profit Before Taxes/Revenues	**18.5%**	**18.2%**	**16.0%**	**17.6%**	**17.4%**	**17.2%**	**17.0%**	**16.9%**
ASSETS TURNOVER:								
Revenues/Average Accounts Receivable	**10.1**	**9.7**	**9.5**	**9.6**	**9.6**	**9.6**	**9.6**	**9.6**
COGS/Average Inventory	**8.7**	**8.6**	**8.5**	**8.5**	**8.5**	**8.5**	**8.5**	**8.5**
Revenues/Average Fixed Assets	**3.8**	**3.8**	**3.8**	**3.9**	**4.0**	**4.1**	**4.0**	**4.1**
LIQUIDITY:								
Current Ratio	**1.3**	**1.3**	**1.2**	**1.2**	**1.2**	**1.3**	**1.2**	**1.3**
Quick Ratio	**1.0**	**0.9**	**0.8**	**0.8**	**0.8**	**0.8**	**0.8**	**0.8**
SOLVENCY:								
Total Liabilities/Total Assets	**48.7%**	**50.2%**	**66.4%**	**67.1%**	**67.7%**	**68.4%**	**68.5%**	**69.2%**
Total Liabilities/Total Equity	**94.3%**	**100.4%**	**195.8%**	**204.2%**	**209.6%**	**216.7%**	**217.6%**	**225.2%**
Interest Coverage Ratio	**30.2**	**35.1**	**22.3**	**17.9**	**18.0**	**18.1**	**17.9**	**18.0**

experienced in its recent past. The projected rate of ROA (return on assets) varies slightly between 17.4 percent in Year +1 to 17.5 percent in Year +5, consistent with PepsiCo's recent past levels of ROA. The main driver of the increase in projected ROA is the expected slight increase in assets turnover. Similarly, the projected rate of ROCE (return on common equity) increases dramatically from 34.8 percent in 2008 up to 47.8 percent in Year +1 to 53.0 percent in Year +5. This occurs because of the projected shift in financial leverage to increase long-term debt and decrease shareholders' equity, along with slight increases in profit margin and assets turnover.

The projected increase in capital structure leverage over the forecast horizon is the result of PepsiCo's demonstrated shift to increase outstanding long-term debt, a shift that began in 2008 with the net issuance of $3.1 billion in long-term debt. In addition, PepsiCo has returned and will continue to return all excess cash flows to shareholders through increased dividends and share repurchases. PepsiCo is expected to finance the treasury stock repurchases and dividends with cash flow from operations, which will reduce shareholders' equity relative to debt, thereby increasing the capital structure leverage ratio. The net effect of increasing the ratio of long-term debt to assets, while at the same time reducing equity by repurchasing shares and paying dividends, suggests that PepsiCo's capital structure leverage will increase significantly. Given that PepsiCo also is expected to generate healthy profit margins, the increased capital structure leverage will generate increasingly higher returns to common equity shareholders.

The operating performance ratios, liquidity ratios, assets turnover ratios, and solvency ratios confirm that our forecast assumptions are reasonable given PepsiCo's expected future financial performance and position. Unfortunately, these ratios cannot confirm whether our forecast assumptions will turn out to be correct. These ratios do not tell us whether we have accurately and realistically captured PepsiCo's future sales growth, profitability, cash flows, and financial position. For this confirmation, only time will tell.

SENSITIVITY ANALYSIS AND REACTIONS TO ANNOUNCEMENTS

These financial statement forecasts can serve as the base case from which the analyst assesses the impact of various critical forecast assumptions for the firm and from which the analyst reacts to new announcements from the firm. For example, with these financial statement forecasts, the analyst can assess the sensitivity of projected net income and cash flows to key assumptions about the firm's sales growth rates; gross profit margins; control over selling, general, and administrative expenses; and other assumptions. Using the projected financial statements (Exhibits 10.3, 10.4, and 10.6) as the base case, the analyst can easily assess the impact on PepsiCo's profitability from a one-point increase or decrease in sales growth or from a one-point increase or decrease in the gross profit margin.

The analyst also can use the projected financial statements to assess the sensitivity of the firm's liquidity and leverage to changes in key assumptions. For example, the analyst can assess the impact on PepsiCo's liquidity and solvency ratios by varying the long-term debt to assets assumptions and the interest expense assumptions. Lenders and credit analysts can use the projected financial statements to assess the conditions under which the firm's debt covenants may become binding. For example, suppose PepsiCo's long-term debt and revolving line of credit agreements contain covenants that require PepsiCo to maintain liquidity and interest coverage ratios that exceed certain minimum levels. The financial statement forecasts provide the analyst with a structured approach to assess how far net income and cash flows would need to decrease (and how much long-term debt and interest expense would need to increase) before PepsiCo would violate these debt covenants.

The projected financial statements also enable the analyst to react quickly and efficiently to new announcements by the firm. For example, at the time of this writing, PepsiCo has submitted bids to acquire majority equity interests in its two anchor bottlers. The boards of directors and management teams of the two bottlers have rejected these bids, and it is unclear how PepsiCo will respond. Suppose PepsiCo announces new bids to acquire the shares of the two bottlers, their boards deem the bids to be acceptable, and the acquisitions are completed. The projected financial statements enable the analyst to incorporate the effects of acquisitions relatively efficiently into expectations for PepsiCo's future earnings, balance sheets, and cash flows.

As an alternative example, suppose PepsiCo announces that it is reversing its recapitalization strategy, such that it will discontinue purchases of treasury stock in Year +1 (and will reissue previously acquired treasury shares as needed to meet stock options exercises), and that it intends to use this cash to reduce interest-bearing long-term debt. The original projections included $2,500 million in treasury stock repurchases in Year +1, which should now become zero; instead, PepsiCo will use this capital to reduce (rather than increase) long-term borrowings. The analyst can efficiently incorporate the effects of this announcement into the projected financial statements. PepsiCo's original and revised projected ratios for Year +1 follow:

	Year +1 Original Projections	**Year +1 Revised Projections**
Net Profit Margin for ROA	13.7%	13.7%
ROA	17.4%	17.4%
ROCE	47.8%	43.8%
Capital Structure Leverage	3.0	2.7
Total Liabilities/Total Assets	67.1%	60.6%
Interest Coverage Ratio	17.9	21.0

Thus, the assumptions about the growth in treasury stock and long-term debt have significant effects on projected financial statements and ratios for PepsiCo. Various other changes in assumptions are possible. By designing a flexible computer spreadsheet for projecting financial statements, the analyst can quickly and efficiently change any one or a combination of assumptions and observe the effect on the financial statements and ratios. FSAP provides a flexible spreadsheet for forecasting.

SUMMARY

This chapter demonstrates a seven-step procedure for developing financial statement forecasts. The preparation of financial statement forecasts requires numerous assumptions about the future operating, investing, and financing activities of the firm, including future growth rates in sales, cost behavior of various expenses, levels of investments in various working capital and fixed assets, the financial capital structure of the firm, and dividend payouts. The analyst should carefully develop realistic expectations for these activities and capture those expectations in financial statement forecasts that provide an objective and realistic portrait of the firm in the future. The analyst should then study the sensitivity of the financial statements to the assumptions made and to the impact of different assumptions. Spreadsheet software can assist in this sensitivity analysis.

After developing careful and realistic expectations for future earnings, cash flows, and dividends using financial statement projections, the analyst can use the information to make a wide array of decisions about the firm, including evaluating the firm as a potential equity investment. The next four chapters demonstrate how to incorporate expectations for future dividends, cash flows, and earnings into estimates of firm value.

QUESTIONS, EXERCISES, PROBLEMS, AND CASES

Questions and Exercises

10.1 RELYING ON ACCOUNTING TO AVOID FORECAST ERRORS. The chapter states that forecasts of financial statements should rely on the *additivity* within financial statements and the *articulation* across financial statements to avoid internal inconsistencies in forecasts. Explain how the concepts of additivity and articulation apply to financial statement forecasts. Also explain how these concepts can help the analyst avoid potential forecast errors.

10.2 OBJECTIVE AND REALISTIC FORECASTS. The chapter encourages analysts to develop forecasts that are realistic, objective, and unbiased. Some firms' managers tend to be optimistic. Some accounting principles tend to be conservative. Describe the different risks and incentives that managers, accountants, and analysts face. Explain how these different risks and incentives lead managers, accountants, and analysts to different biases when predicting uncertain outcomes.

10.3 PROJECTING REVENUES: THE EFFECTS OF VOLUME VERSUS PRICE. Suppose a firm has generated 10.25 percent revenue growth in the past two years, consisting of 5.0 percent growth in sales volume compounded with 5.0 percent growth in prices. Describe one firm-specific strategic factor, one industry-specific factor, and one economy-wide factor that could help this firm sustain 5.0 percent growth in sales volume next year. Describe one firm-specific strategic factor, one industry-specific factor, and one economy-wide factor that could help this firm sustain 5.0 percent growth in prices next year.

10.4 PROJECTING GROSS PROFIT: THE EFFECTS OF VOLUME VERSUS PRICE. Suppose you are analyzing a firm that is successfully executing a strategy that differentiates its products from those of its competitors. Because of this strategy, you project that next year the firm will generate 6.0 percent revenue growth from price increases and 3.0 percent revenue growth from sales volume increases. Assume that the firm's production cost structure involves strictly variable costs. (That is, the cost to produce each unit of product remains the same.) Should you project that the firm's gross profit will increase next year? If you project that the gross profit will increase, is the increase a result of volume growth, price growth, or both? Should you project that the firm's gross profit margin (gross profit divided by sales) will increase next year? If you project that the gross profit margin will increase, is the increase a result of volume growth, price growth, or both?

10.5 PROJECTING REVENUES, COST OF GOODS SOLD, AND INVENTORY. Walgreens is a leading chain of drugstores in the United States. Use the following data for Walgreens in Years 7 and 8 to project revenues, cost of goods sold, and inventory for Year +1. Assume that Walgreen's Year +1 revenue growth rate, gross profit margin, and inventory turnover will be identical to Year 8. Project the average inventory balance in Year +1 and use it to compute the implied ending inventory balance.

Walgreens (data in millions)	Year 7	Year 8
Sales Revenues	$53,762	$59,034
Cost of Goods Sold	$38,518	$42,391
Ending Inventory	$ 6,791	$ 7,249

10.6 THE FLEXIBLE FINANCIAL ACCOUNT. The chapter describes how firms must use flexible financial accounts to maintain equality between assets and claims on assets from liabilities and equities. Chapter 1 describes how some firms progress through different life-cycle stages—from introduction to growth to maturity to decline—and how firms experience very different cash flows during different stages of the life cycle. For each life-cycle stage, identify the different types of flexible accounts that firms will be more likely to use to balance the balance sheet.

10.7 DIVIDENDS AS A FLEXIBLE FINANCIAL ACCOUNT. The following data for Schwartz Company represent a summary of your first-iteration forecast amounts for Year +1. Schwartz uses dividends as a flexible financial account. Compute the amount of dividends you can assume that Schwartz will pay in order to balance your projected balance sheet. Present the projected balance sheet.

	Year +1
Operating Income	$ 58
Interest Expense	(8)
Income before Tax	$ 50
Tax Provision (20.0 percent effective tax rate)	(10)
Net Income	$ 40
Total Assets	$200
Accrued Liabilities	$ 43
Long-Term Debt	$ 80
Common Stock, at par	$ 20
Retained Earnings (at the beginning of Year +1)	$ 34

10.8 LONG-TERM DEBT AS A FLEXIBLE FINANCIAL ACCOUNT. For this exercise, use the preceding data for Schwartz Company. Now assume that Schwartz pays common shareholders a dividend of $25 in Year +1. Also assume that Schwartz uses long-term debt as a flexible financial account, increasing borrowing when it needs capital and paying down debt when it generates excess capital. For simplicity, assume that Schwartz pays 10.0 percent interest expense on the ending balance in long-term debt for the year and that interest expense is tax deductible at Schwartz's average tax rate of 20.0 percent. Present the projected income statement and balance sheet for Year +1. (Hint: Because of the circularity between interest expense, net income, and debt, several iterations may be needed to balance the projected balance sheet and to have the projected balance sheet articulate with net income. You may find it helpful to program a spreadsheet to work the iterative computations.)

Problems and Cases

10.9 STORE-DRIVEN FORECASTS. The Home Depot is a leading specialty retailer of hardware and home improvement products and is the second-largest retail store chain in the United States. It operates large warehouse-style stores. Despite declining sales and difficult economic conditions in 2007 and 2008, The Home Depot continued to invest in new stores. The following table provides summary data for The Home Depot.

The Home Depot (amounts in millions except number of stores)	2007	2008
Number of Stores	2,234	2,274
Sales Revenues	$77,349	$71,288
Inventory	$11,731	$10,673
Capital Expenditures, net	$ 3,558	$ 1,847

Required

a. Use the preceding data for The Home Depot to compute average revenues per store, capital spending per new store, and ending inventory per store in 2008.

b. Assume that The Home Depot will add 100 new stores by the end of Year +1. Use the data from 2008 to project Year +1 sales revenues, capital spending, and ending inventory. Assume that each new store will be open for business for an average of one-half year in Year +1. For simplicity, assume that in Year +1, Home Depot's sales revenues will grow, but only because it will open new stores.

10.10 PROJECTING PROPERTY, PLANT, AND EQUIPMENT. Intel is a global leader in manufacturing microprocessors, which is very capital-intensive. The production processes in microprocessor manufacturing require sophisticated technology, and the technology changes rapidly, particularly with each new generation of microprocessor. As a consequence, production and manufacturing assets in the microprocessor industry tend to have relatively short useful lives. The following summary information relates to Intel's property, plant, and equipment for 2007 and 2008:

Intel (amounts in millions)	2007	2008
Property, Plant, and Equipment, at cost	$ 46,052	$ 48,088
Accumulated Depreciation	$(29,134)	$(30,544)
Property, Plant, and Equipment, net	$ 16,918	$ 17,544
Depreciation Expense		$ 4,360
Capital Expenditures, net		$ 5,200

Required

Assume that Intel depreciates all property, plant, and equipment using the straight-line depreciation method and zero salvage value. Assume that Intel spends $6,000 on new depreciable assets in Year +1 and does not sell or retire any property, plant, and equipment during Year +1.

a. Compute the average useful life that Intel used for depreciation in 2008.

b. Project total depreciation expense for Year +1 using the following steps: (i) project depreciation expense for Year +1 on existing property, plant, and equipment at the end of 2008; (ii) project depreciation expense on capital expenditures in Year +1 assuming that Intel takes a full year of depreciation in the first year of service; and (iii) sum the results of (i) and (ii) to obtain total depreciation expense for Year +1.

c. Project the Year +1 ending balance in property, plant, and equipment, both at cost and net of accumulated depreciation.

10.11 IDENTIFYING THE COST STRUCTURE AND PROJECTING GROSS MARGINS FOR CAPITAL-INTENSIVE, CYCLICAL BUSINESSES. AK Steel is an integrated manufacturer of high-quality steel and steel products in capital-intensive steel mills. AK Steel produces flat-rolled carbon, stainless and electrical steel products, and carbon and stainless tubular steel products for automotive, appliance, construction, and manufacturing markets. Nucor manufactures more commodity-level steel and steel products at the lower end of the market in less capital-intensive mini-mills. The following data describe sales and cost of products sold for both firms for Years 3 and 4.

($ amounts in millions)	Year 3	Year 4
AK Steel		
Sales	$4,042	$ 5,217
Cost of Products Sold	$3,887	$ 4,554
Gross Profit	$ 155	$ 663
Gross Margin	3.8%	12.7%
Nucor		
Sales	$6,266	$11,377
Cost of Products Sold	$5,997	$ 9,129
Gross Profit	$ 269	$ 2,248
Gross Margin	4.3%	19.8%

Industry analysts anticipate the following annual changes in sales for the next five years: Year +1, 5 percent increase; Year +2, 10 percent increase; Year +3, 20 percent increase; Year +4, 10 percent decrease; Year +5, 20 percent decrease.

Required

a. The analyst can sometimes estimate the variable cost as a percentage of sales for a particular cost (for example, cost of products sold) by dividing the amount of the change in the cost item between two years by the amount of the change in sales for those two years. The analyst can then multiply the variable-cost percentage times sales to estimate the total variable cost. Subtracting the variable cost from the total cost yields an estimate of the fixed cost for that particular cost item. Follow this procedure to estimate the manufacturing cost structure (variable cost as a percentage of sales, total variable costs, and total fixed costs) for cost of products sold for both AK Steel and Nucor in Year 4.

b. Discuss the structure of manufacturing cost (that is, fixed versus variable) for each firm in light of the manufacturing process and type of steel produced.

c. Using the analysts' forecasts of sales growth rates, compute the projected sales, cost of products sold, gross profit, and gross margin (gross profit as a percentage of sales) of each firm for Year +1 through Year +5.

d. Why do the levels and variability of the gross margin percentages differ for these two firms for Year +1 through Year +5?

10.12 IDENTIFYING THE COST STRUCTURE. Sony Corporation manufactures and markets consumer electronics products. Selected income statement data for 2007 and 2008 follow (amounts in billions of yen):

	2007	2008
Sales	¥8,296	¥8,871
Cost of Goods Sold	(5,890)	(6,290)
Selling and Administrative Expenses	(1,788)	(1,714)
Operating Income before Income Taxes	¥618	¥867

Required

a. The analyst can sometimes estimate the variable cost as a percentage of sales for a particular cost (for example, cost of goods sold) by dividing the amount of the change in the cost item between two years by the amount of the change in sales for those two years. The analyst can then multiply total sales by the variable-cost percentage to determine the total variable cost. Subtracting the variable cost from the total cost yields the fixed cost component for that particular cost item. Follow this procedure to determine the cost structure (fixed cost plus variable cost as a percentage of sales) for cost of goods sold for Sony.

b. Repeat Part a for selling and administrative expenses.

c. Sony Corporation discloses that it expects sales to grow at the following percentages in future years: Year +1, 12 percent; Year +2, 10 percent; Year +3, 8 percent; Year +4, 6 percent. Project sales, cost of goods sold, selling and administrative expenses, and operating income before income taxes for Sony for Year +1 to Year +4 using the cost structure amounts derived in Parts a and b.

d. Compute the ratio of operating income before income taxes to sales for Year +1 through Year +4.

e. Interpret the changes in the ratio computed in Part d in light of the expected changes in sales.

10.13 SMOOTHING CHANGES IN ACCOUNTS RECEIVABLE. Hasbro designs, manufactures, and markets toys and games for children and adults in the United States and in international markets. Hasbro's portfolio of brands and products contains some of the most well-known toys and games under famous brands such as Playskool, Tonka Trucks, Milton Bradley, and Parker Brothers and includes such classic games as Scrabble®, Monopoly, and Clue®. Sales during 2008 totaled $4,022 million. Accounts receivable totaled $655 million at the beginning of 2008 and $612 million at the end of 2008.

Required

a. Use the average balance to compute the accounts receivable turnover ratio for Hasbro for 2008.

b. Hasbro generated a compound annual sales growth rate of 13.0 percent over the past two years. Assume that Hasbro's sales will continue to grow at that rate each year for Year +1 through Year +5 and that the accounts receivable turnover ratio each year will equal the ratio computed in Part a for 2008. Project the amount of accounts receivable at year-end through Year +5 based on the accounts receivable turnover computed in Part a. Also compute the percentage change in accounts receivable between each of the year-ends through Year +5.

c. Does the pattern of growth in your projections of Hasbro's accounts receivable seem reasonable considering the assumptions of smooth growth in sales and steady turnover? Explain.

d. The changes in accounts receivable computed in Part b display the sawtooth pattern depicted in Exhibit 10.5. Smooth the changes in accounts receivable by computing the year-end accounts receivable balances for Year +1 through Year +5 using the compound annual growth rate in accounts receivable between the end of 2008 and the end of Year +1 from Part b.

e. Smooth the changes in accounts receivable using the compound annual growth rate in accounts receivable between the end of 2008 and the end of Year +4 from Part b. Apply this growth rate to compute accounts receivable at the end of Year +1 through Year +5. Why do the amounts for ending accounts receivable using the growth rate from Part d differ from those using the growth rate from this part?

f. Compute the accounts receivable turnover for 2008 by dividing sales by the balance in accounts receivable at the end of 2008 (instead of using average accounts receivable as in Part a). Use this accounts receivable turnover ratio to compute the projected balance in accounts receivable at the end of Year +1 through Year +5. Also compute the percentage change in accounts receivable between the year-ends for Year +1 through Year +5.

10.14 SMOOTHING CHANGES IN INVENTORIES. Barnes & Noble sells books, magazines, music, and videos through retail stores and on the Web. For a retailer like Barnes & Noble, inventory is a critical element of the business and it is necessary to carry a wide array of titles. In 2008, sales totaled $5,122 million and cost of sales and occupancy totaled $3,541 million. Inventories constitute the largest asset on Barnes & Noble's balance sheet, totaling $1,203 million at the end of 2008 and $1,358 million at the end of 2007.

Required

a. Compute the inventory turnover ratio for Barnes & Noble for 2008.

b. Over the last two years, the number of Barnes & Noble retail stores has remained fairly steady and sales have grown at a compounded annual rate of 11.6 percent. Assume that the number of stores will remain constant and that sales will continue to grow at an annual rate of 11.6 percent each year between Year +1 and Year +5. Also assume that the future cost of goods sold to sales percentage will equal that realized in 2008 (which is very similar to the cost of goods sold percentage over the past three years). Project the amount of inventory at the end of Year +1 through Year +5 using the inventory turnover ratio computed in Part a. Also compute the percentage change in inventories between each of the year-ends between 2008 and Year +5. Does the pattern of growth in your projections of Barnes & Noble inventory seem reasonable to you considering the assumptions of smooth growth in sales and steady cost of goods sold percentages? Explain.

c. The changes in inventories in Part b display the sawtooth pattern depicted in Exhibit 10.5. Smooth the changes in the inventory forecasts between 2008 and Year +5 using the compound annual growth rate in inventories between the end of 2008 and the end of Year +5 implied by the projections in Part b. Does this pattern of growth seem more reasonable? Explain.

d. Now suppose that instead of following the smoothing approach in Part c, you used the rate of growth in inventory during 2008 to project future inventory balances at the end of Year +1 through Year +5. Use these projections to compute the implied inventory turnover rates. Does this pattern of growth and efficiency in inventory for Barnes & Noble seem reasonable? Explain.

10.15 IDENTIFYING FINANCIAL STATEMENT RELATIONS. Partial forecasts of financial statements for Watson Corporation appear in Exhibit 10.8 (income statement), Exhibit 10.9 (balance sheet), and Exhibit 10.10 (statement of cash flows). Selected amounts have been omitted, as have all totals (indicated by XXXX).

EXHIBIT 10.8

Watson Corporation
Partial Income Statements
(Problem 10.15)

	Year 0 Actual	Year +1 Projected	Year +2 Projected	Year +3 Projected	Year +4 Projected
Sales	$ 46,000	$ 50,600	$ 56,672	$ 64,606	$ 74,943
Cost of goods sold	(29,900)	(32,890)	XXXX	(40,702)	(46,465)
Selling and administrative	(10,580)	(11,638)	(12,468)	(13,567)	(14,989)
Interest expense	(3,907)	(4,298)	d	(3,866)	(5,227)
Income taxes	(565)	(621)	(1,372)	(2,265)	(2,892)
Net Income	$ XXXX	$ XXXX	$ XXXX	$ XXXX	$ XXXX

EXHIBIT 10.9

Watson Corporation
Partial Balance Sheets
(Problem 10.15)

	Year 0 Actual	Year +1 Projected	Year +2 Projected	Year +3 Projected	Year +4 Projected
ASSETS					
Cash	$ 1,200	$ 664	$ 206	$ 416	$ 1,262
Accounts receivable	8,000	8,433	8,855	10,420	12,286
Inventories	7,500	8,223	c	10,711	11,333
Fixed assets:					
Cost	110,400	120,445	126,467	f	169,895
Accumulated depreciation	(33,100)	(36,112)	(37,917)	(45,352)	(50,938)
Total Assets	$XXXX	$XXXX	$XXXX	$XXXX	$XXXX
Liabilities and Shareholders' Equity					
Accounts payable	$ 2,500	$ 2,801	$ 3,107	$ 3,376	$ 3,828
Notes payable	6,500	6,852	7,195	8,467	9,982
Other current liabilities	3,300	3,630	e	4,635	5,376
Long-term debt	45,000	49,094	51,549	h	69,251
Total Liabilities	$XXXX	$XXXX	$XXXX	$XXXX	$XXXX
Common stock	$15,000	$17,233	$17,539	$22,434	$24,319
Retained earnings	21,700	22,043	23,700	g	31,082
Total Shareholders' Equity	$XXXX	$XXXX	$XXXX	$XXXX	$XXXX
Total Liabilities and Shareholders' Equity	$XXXX	$XXXX	$XXXX	$XXXX	$XXXX

EXHIBIT 10.10

Watson Corporation
Partial Statements of Cash Flows
(Problem 10.15)

	Year 0 Actual	Year +1 Projected	Year +2 Projected	Year +3 Projected	Year +4 Projected
OPERATIONS					
Net income	$ 1,048	$ 1,153	$XXXX	$ 4,206	$ 5,370
Depreciation	2,378	b	1,805	7,435	5,586
Change in accounts receivable	(394)	(433)	(422)	(1,565)	(1,866)
Change in inventories	(657)	(723)	(1,322)	(1,166)	(622)
Change in accounts payable	274	301	306	269	452
Change in other current liabilities	300	330	436	569	741
Cash Flow from Operations	$XXXX	$ XXXX	$XXXX	$ XXXX	$ XXXX
INVESTING					
Acquisition of fixed assets	$(9,130)	$(10,045)	$(6,022)	$(24,796)	$(18,632)
FINANCING					
Change in notes payable	$ 320	$ 3352	$ 343	$ 1,272	$ 1,515
Change in long-term debt	3,721	4,094	2,455	10,107	7,595
Change in common stock	2,029	2,233	306	4,895	1,885
Dividends	(750)	a	(891)	(1,016)	(1,178)
Cash Flow from Financing	$XXXX	$ XXXX	$XXXX	$ XXXX	$ XXXX
Change in Cash	$XXXX	$ XXXX	$XXXX	$ XXXX	$ XXXX

Required

Determine the amount of each of the following items.

a. Dividends declared and paid during Year 1
b. Depreciation expense for Year 1 assuming that Watson Corporation neither sold nor retired depreciable assets during Year 1
c. Inventories at the end of Year 2
d. Interest expense on borrowing during Year 2, with an interest rate of 7 percent
e. Other current liabilities at the end of Year 2
f. Property, plant, and equipment at the end of Year 3 assuming that Watson Corporation neither sold nor retired depreciable assets during Year 3
g. Retained earnings at the end of Year 3
h. Long-term debt at the end of Year 3
i. The income tax rate for Year 4
j. Purchases of inventories during Year 4

10.16 PREPARING AND INTERPRETING FINANCIAL STATEMENT FORECASTS. Wal-Mart Stores, Inc. (Walmart) is the largest retailing firm in the world. Building on a base of discount stores, Walmart has expanded into warehouse clubs and Supercenters, which sell traditional discount store items and grocery products.

Exhibits 10.11, 10.12, and 10.13 present the financial statements of Walmart for 2006–2008. Exhibits 4.50–4.52 (Case 4.2 in Chapter 4) also present summary financial statements for Walmart, and Exhibit 4.53 presents selected financial statement ratios for Years 2006–2008. (Note: A few of the amounts presented in Chapter 4 for Walmart differ slightly from the amounts provided here because, for purposes of computing financial analysis ratios, the Chapter 4 data have been adjusted slightly to remove the effects of non-recurring items such as discontinued operations.)

Required (additional requirements follow on page 862)

a. Design a spreadsheet and prepare a set of financial statement forecasts for Walmart for Year +1 to Year +5 using the assumptions that follow. Project the amounts in the order presented (unless indicated otherwise) beginning with the income statement, then the balance sheet, and then the statement of cash flows. For this portion of the problem, assume that Walmart will exercise its financial flexibility with the cash and cash equivalents account to balance the balance sheet.

EXHIBIT 10.11

Balance Sheets for Wal-Mart Stores, Inc.
(Problem 10.16)

	2006	2007	2008
Cash	$ 7,373	$ 5,492	$ 7,275
Receivables	2,840	3,642	3,905
Inventories	33,685	35,159	34,511
Prepaid expenses and other current assets	2,690	2,760	3,063
Current assets of discontinued segments	0	967	195
Current Assets	**$ 46,588**	**$ 48,020**	**$ 48,949**
Property, plant & equipment—At cost	115,190	127,992	131,161
Accumulated depreciation	(26,750)	(31,125)	(35,508)
Goodwill and other non-current assets	16,165	18,627	18,827
Total Assets	**$151,193**	**$163,514**	**$163,429**
Accounts payable—Trade	$ 28,090	$ 30,344	$ 28,849
Accrued liabilities	14,675	15,725	18,112
Accrued income taxes and other current liabilities	706	1,140	760
Notes payable and short term debt	2,570	5,040	1,506
Current maturities of long term debt and leases	5,713	6,229	6,163
Current Liabilities	**$ 51,754**	**$ 58,478**	**$ 55,390**
Long term debt	30,375	33,402	34,549
Deferred taxes and other non-current liabilities	4,971	5,087	6,014
Total Liabilities	**$ 87,460**	**$ 96,967**	**$ 95,953**
Minority interest	2,160	1,939	2,191
Common stock + paid in capital	3,247	3,425	4,313
Retained earnings	55,818	57,319	63,660
Accumulated other comprehensive income	4,971	5,087	(2,688)
Shareholders' Equity	**$ 63,733**	**$ 66,547**	**$ 67,476**
Total Liabilities and Equities	**$151,193**	**$163,514**	**$163,429**

EXHIBIT 10.12

Income Statements for Wal-Mart Stores, Inc.
(Problem 10.16)

	2006	2007	2008
Revenues	$348,368	$378,476	$405,607
Cost of goods sold	(263,979)	(286,350)	(306,158)
Gross Profit	**$ 84,389**	**$ 92,126**	**$ 99,449**
Selling, general, and administrative expense	(63,892)	(70,174)	(76,651)
Operating Profit	**$ 20,497**	**$ 21,952**	**$ 22,798**
Interest income	280	309	284
Interest expense	(1,809)	(2,103)	(2,184)
Income before Tax	**$ 18,968**	**$ 20,158**	**$ 20,898**
Income tax expense	(6,354)	(6,889)	(7,145)
Minority interest in earnings	(425)	(406)	(499)
Income from discontinued operations	(905)	(132)	146
Net Income	**$ 11,284**	**$ 12,731**	**$ 13,400**
Other comprehensive income items	1,575	1,356	(6,552)
Comprehensive Income	**$ 12,859**	**$ 14,087**	**$ 6,848**

EXHIBIT 10.13

Statements of Cash Flows for Wal-Mart Stores, Inc.
(Problem 10.16)

	2006	2007	2008
Net Income	**$ 11,284**	**$ 12,731**	**$ 13,400**
Add back depreciation	5,459	6,317	6,739
Other adjustments to net income	860	132	(146)
Deferred taxes	89	(8)	581
(Increase) Decrease in receivables	(214)	(564)	(101)
(Increase) Decrease in inventories	(1,274)	(775)	(220)
Increase (Decrease) in accounts payable	2,132	865	(410)
Increase (Decrease) in other current liabilities	588	1,034	2,036
Other operating cash flows	1,311	910	1,268
Net Cash Flow From Operations	**$ 20,235**	**$ 20,642**	**$ 23,147**
Proceeds from sales of property, plant, and equipment	394	957	714
Property, plant, and equipment acquired	(15,666)	(14,937)	(11,499)
Investments (acquired) sold	267	(95)	781
Other investment transactions	542	(1,595)	(738)
Net Cash Flow from Investing Activities	**$(14,463)**	**$(15,670)**	**$(10,742)**

(Continued)

EXHIBIT 10.13 (Continued)

	2006	2007	2008
Increase (Decrease) in short-term borrowing	(1,193)	2,376	(3,745)
Increase (Decrease) in long-term borrowing	1,101	2,101	827
Issue of capital stock	—	—	—
Share repurchases—treasury stock	(1,718)	(7,691)	(3,521)
Dividend payments	(2,802)	(3,586)	(3,746)
Other financing transactions	(510)	(622)	267
Net Cash Flow from Financing Activities	**$ (5,122)**	**$ (7,422)**	**$ (9,918)**
Effects of exchange rate changes on cash	97	252	(781)
Net Change in Cash	**$ 747**	**$ (2,198)**	**$ 1,706**

Note: The net changes in cash reported by Walmart do not reconcile exactly with the changes in cash balances each year because Walmart reclassifies prior year amounts of cash associated with discontinued segments.

Income Statement

Sales

Sales grew by 10.4 percent in 2006, 8.6 percent in 2007, and 7.2 percent in 2008. The compound annual sales growth rate during the last five years was 9.4 percent. Walmart generates sales growth primarily through increasing same-store sales, opening new stores, and acquiring other retailers. In the future, Walmart will continue to grow in international markets by opening stores and acquiring other firms and in domestic U.S. markets by converting discount stores to Supercenters. In addition, despite vigorous competition, Walmart will likely continue to generate steady increases in same-store sales, consistent with its experience through 2008. Assume that sales will grow 7.0 percent each year from Year +1 through Year +5.

Cost of Goods Sold

The percentage of costs of goods sold relative to sales decreased slightly from 75.8 percent of sales in 2006 to 75.7 percent in 2007 to 75.5 percent in 2008. Walmart's everyday low-price strategy, its movement into grocery products, and competition will likely prevent Walmart from achieving significant additional decreases in this expense percentage. Assume that the cost of goods sold to sales percentage will remain steady at 75.5 percent for Year +1 to Year +5.

Selling and Administrative Expenses

The selling and administrative expense percentage has steadily increased from 18.3 percent of sales in 2006 to 18.5 percent in 2007 to 18.9 percent of sales in 2008. Identifying and transacting international corporate acquisitions and opening additional Supercenters, together with the slowdown in the sales growth rate, will put upward pressure on this expense percentage. Assume that the selling and administrative expense to sales percentage will be 19.0 percent of sales for Year +1 to Year +5.

Interest Income

Walmart earns some interest income on its cash and cash equivalents accounts. The average interest rate earned on average cash balances was approximately 4.4 percent during 2008, similar to rates earned in 2006 and 2007. Assume that Walmart will earn interest income based on a 4.4 percent interest rate on average cash balances (that is, the sum of beginning and end-of-year cash balances divided by 2) for Year +1 through Year +5. (Note: Projecting the amount of interest income must await projection of cash on the balance sheet.)

Interest Expense

Walmart uses long-term mortgages and capital leases to finance new stores and warehouses and short- and long-term borrowing to finance corporate acquisitions. The average interest rate on all interest-bearing debt and capital leases was approximately 5.0 percent during 2007 and 2008. Assume a 5.0 percent interest rate for all outstanding borrowing (short-term and long-term debt, including capital leases, and the current portion of long-term debt) for Walmart for Year +1 through Year +5. Compute interest expense on the average amount of interest-bearing debt outstanding each year. (Note: Projecting the amount of interest expense must await projection of the interest-bearing debt accounts on the balance sheet.)

Income Tax Expense

Walmart's average income tax rate as a percentage of income before taxes has been a steady 34.2 percent during the last two years. Assume that Walmart's effective income tax rate remains a constant 34.2 percent of income before taxes for Year +1 through Year +5. (Note: Projecting the amount of income tax expense must await computation of income before taxes.)

Minority Interest in Earnings

Minority shareholders in Walmart subsidiaries were entitled to a $499 million share in Walmart's 2008 net income. Assume that the minority interest in earnings for Year +1 through Year +5 will remain a constant $499 million.

Balance Sheet

Cash

We will adjust cash as the flexible financial account to equate total assets with total liabilities plus shareholders' equity. Projecting the amount of cash must await projections of all other balance sheet amounts.

Accounts Receivable

As a retailer, a large portion of Walmart's sales are in cash or for third-party credit card charges, which Walmart can convert into cash within a day or two. Walmart has its own credit card that customers can use for purchases at its Sam's Club warehouse stores, but the total amount of receivables outstanding on these credit cards is relatively minor compared to Walmart's total sales. As a consequence, Walmart's receivables turnover is very steady and fast, averaging roughly three days during each of the past three years. Assume that accounts receivable will increase at the growth rate in sales.

Inventories

Walmart has managed to increase the efficiency of inventory turnover ratio in recent years, in part because of the expanding role of grocery products in Walmart's overall inventory. However, that increase in efficiency has been offset slightly by the stocking of new stores and the distribution of merchandise to stores worldwide. Inventory turns have increased from an average of 45 days in 2006 to 44 days in 2007 to 42 days in 2008. Assume that inventory will continue to turn over, on average, every 42 days, or roughly 8.7 times a year, in Years +1 to +5. Use this turnover rate to compute the average inventories each year and then compute the implied ending inventories each year.

Prepaid Expenses

Current assets include prepayments for ongoing operating costs such as rent and insurance. Assume that prepayments will grow at the growth rate in sales.

Current Assets of Discontinued Segments

Walmart's balance sheets in 2007 and 2008 recognize amounts as current assets that are associated with discontinued segments (subsidiaries that Walmart is divesting). Assume that these amounts will be zero in Year +1 through Year +5.

Property, Plant, and Equipment—At Cost

Property, plant, and equipment (including assets held under capital leases) grew 11.6 percent annually during the most recent five years. The construction of new Supercenters and the acquisition of established retail chains abroad will require additional investments in property, plant, and equipment. Assume that property, plant, and equipment will grow 11.6 percent each year from Year +1 through Year +5.

Accumulated Depreciation

In 2007 and 2008, Walmart depreciated property, plant, and equipment using an average useful life of approximately 19.2 years. For Year +1 through Year +5, assume that accumulated depreciation will increase each year by depreciation expense. For simplicity, compute straight-line depreciation expense based on an average 20-year useful life and zero salvage value. In computing depreciation expense each year, make sure you depreciate the beginning balance in property, plant, and equipment—at cost. Also add a new layer of depreciation expense for the new property, plant, and equipment acquired through capital expenditures. Assume that Walmart recognizes a full year of depreciation on new property, plant, and equipment in the first year of service.

Goodwill and Other Assets

Goodwill and other assets include primarily goodwill arising from corporate acquisitions outside the United States. Such acquisitions increase Walmart sales. Assume that goodwill and other assets will grow at the growth rate in sales. Also assume that goodwill and other assets are not amortizable.

Accounts Payable

Walmart has maintained a steady accounts payable turnover, with payment periods averaging ten times per year (an average turnover of roughly 35–37 days) during the last three years. Assume that accounts payable turnover will continue to turn over every 35 days in Years +1 to +5. Use this turnover rate to compute the average accounts payable each year and then compute the implied ending accounts payable each year. To compute accounts payable turnover, remember to add the change in inventory to the cost of goods sold to obtain the total amount of credit purchases of inventory during the year.

Accrued Liabilities

Accrued liabilities relate to accrued expenses for ongoing operating activities and are expected to grow at the growth rate in selling and administrative expenses, which are expected to grow with sales.

Other Current Liabilities

Other current liabilities include primarily income taxes payable. For simplicity, assume that other current liabilities grow with sales.

Other Noncurrent Liabilities

Other noncurrent liabilities include amounts related to deferred taxes, health care benefits, and accruals for long-term expenses. Since 2006, other noncurrent liabilities have grown at an annual compounded rate of 10 percent per year. Assume that other noncurrent liabilities will continue to grow by 10 percent per year for Year +1 through Year +5.

Short-Term Debt, Current Maturities of Long-Term Debt, Capital Leases, and Long-Term Debt

Walmart uses short-term debt, current maturities of long-term debt, capital leases, and long-term debt to augment cash from operations to finance capital expenditures on property, plant, and equipment and acquisitions of existing retail chains outside the United States. Over the past three years, short-term debt and current maturities of long-term debt have fluctuated considerably from year to year, whereas long-term debt has grown fairly steadily at a compound annual rate of 6.0 percent per year. For simplicity, assume that short-term debt and current maturities of long-term debt will remain constant for Year +1 through Year +5 and that any additional borrowing will be in long-term debt (including capital leases). Assume that Walmart's long-term debt will continue to grow at 6.0 percent per year in Year +1 through Year +5.

Minority Interest

Assume that minority interest will not change.

Common Stock and Additional Paid-In Capital

Over the past three years, Walmart has increased common stock and additional paid-in capital by issuing shares to satisfy stock option exercises by managers, employees, and others. Common stock and additional paid-in capital have increased at a net compounded rate of roughly 15.3 percent per year during this period (net of payments to repurchase company shares on the open market, which Walmart then reissues to satisfy stock option exercises). Assume that common stock and additional paid-in capital will grow at a net rate of 10 percent per year for Year +1 through Year +5.

Retained Earnings

The increase in retained earnings equals net income minus dividends. Walmart paid dividends amounting to $3,746 million to common shareholders in 2008, which amounted to roughly 30 percent of prior year net income. Assume that Walmart will maintain a policy to pay 30 percent of lagged net income in dividends each year in Year +1 through Year +5.

Accumulated Other Comprehensive Income

Assume that accumulated other comprehensive income will not change. Equivalently, assume that future other comprehensive income items will be zero, on average, in Year +1 through Year +5.

Cash

At this point, you can project the amount of cash on Walmart's balance sheet at each year-end from Year +1 to Year +5. Assume that Walmart uses cash as the flexible financial account to balance the balance sheet. The resulting cash balance each year should be the total amount of liabilities and shareholders' equity minus the projected ending balances in all non-cash asset accounts.

Statement of Cash Flows

Depreciation Addback

Include depreciation expense, which should equal the change in accumulated depreciation.

Other Addbacks

Assume that changes in other noncurrent liabilities on the balance sheet are operating activities.

Other Investing Transactions

Assume that changes in other noncurrent assets on the balance sheet are investing activities.

Required (continued from page 856)

b. If you have programmed your spreadsheet correctly, the projected amount of cash grows steadily from Year +1 to Year +5 and the projected cash balance at the end of Year +5 is a whopping $33,511 million (allow for rounding), which is more than 12.5 percent of total assets. Identify one problem that so much cash could create for the financial management of Walmart.

c. Assume that Walmart will augment its dividend policy by paying out 30 percent of lagged net income plus the amount of excess cash each year (if any). Assume that during Year +1 to Year +5, Walmart will maintain a constant cash balance of $7,275 million (the ending cash balance in 2008). Revise your forecast model spreadsheets to change the financial flexibility account from cash to dividends. Determine the total amount of dividends that Walmart could pay each year under this scenario. Identify one potential benefit that increased dividends could create for the financial management of Walmart.

d. Calculate and compare the return on common equity for Walmart using the forecast amounts determined in Parts a and c for Year +1 to Year +5. Why are the two sets of returns different? Which results will Walmart's common shareholders prefer? Why?

INTEGRATIVE CASE 10.1

STARBUCKS

The Starbucks integrative case provides you with an opportunity to apply to Starbucks the entire six-step analysis framework of this textbook. Beginning in Chapter 1 and following each chapter of the book, we use the Starbucks Integrative Case to illustrate and apply all of the tools of financial statements analysis and valuation throughout the book. This chapter illustrates the seven-step forecasting procedure by applying it to PepsiCo to develop complete financial statement forecasts through Year +5. This portion of the integrative case relies on the analysis of Starbucks' financial statements through fiscal year 2008 and applies the seven-step forecasting procedure of this chapter to develop complete forecasts of Starbucks' financial statements through Year +5.

Exhibits 10.14 and 10.15 (see pages 866–869) provide Starbucks' income statements and balance sheets for fiscal years 2006 through 2008 in dollar amounts, common-size format, and rate-of-change format. Exhibit 10.16 (see pages 870–871) presents Starbucks' statements of cash flows for fiscal years 2006 through 2008. These financial statements report the financial performance and position of Starbucks and summarize the results of Starbucks' operating, investing, and financing activities. The common-size and rate-of-change balance sheets and income statements for Starbucks highlight relations among accounts and trends over

EXHIBIT 10.14

Starbucks Income Statements in Amounts, Common-Size Percentages, and Percentage Changes
(Integrative Case 10.1)

Starbucks: Consolidated Statements of Income: Fiscal Years 2003–2008						
(millions except per-share amounts)	2003	2004	2005	2006	2007	2008
Company-operated retail	$3,449.6	$4,457.4	$5,391.9	$6,583.1	$7,998.3	$ 8,771.9
Specialty:						
Licensing	409.6	565.8	673.0	860.7	1,026.3	1,171.6
Foodservice and other	216.3	271.1	304.4	343.2	386.9	439.5
Total Specialty	625.9	836.9	977.4	1,203.8	1,413.2	1,611.1
Net Revenues	**$4,075.5**	**$5,294.2**	**$6,369.3**	**$7,786.9**	**$9,411.5**	**$10,383.0**
Cost of sales (including occupancy costs)	1,681.4	2,191.4	2,605.2	3,178.8	3,999.1	4,645.3
Gross Profit	**2,394.1**	**3,102.8**	**3,764.1**	**4,608.2**	**5,412.4**	**5,737.7**
Store operating expenses	1,379.6	1,790.2	2,165.9	2,687.8	3,215.9	3,745.1
Other operating expenses	141.3	171.6	192.5	253.7	294.1	330.1
Depreciation and amortization	244.7	289.2	340.2	387.2	467.2	549.3
General and administrative expenses	244.6	304.3	361.6	479.4	489.2	456.0
Restructuring charges	—	—	—	—	—	266.9
Income from equity investees	36.7	59.0	76.6	93.9	108.0	113.6
Operating Income	**420.7**	**606.5**	**780.5**	**894.0**	**1,053.9**	**503.9**
Interest and other income	11.9	14.5	17.1	20.7	40.6	9.0
Interest expense	(0.3)	(0.4)	(1.3)	(8.4)	(38.2)	(53.4)
Income Before Income Taxes	**432.3**	**620.6**	**796.3**	**906.2**	**1,056.4**	**459.5**
Provision for income taxes	167.1	231.8	302.0	324.8	383.7	144.0
Cum. effect of an accounting change	—	—	—	(17.2)	—	—
Net Income	**$ 265.2**	**$ 388.9**	**$ 494.4**	**$ 564.3**	**$ 672.6**	**$ 315.5**
Net Income Per Share						
Basic	$ 0.34	$ 0.49	$ 0.63	$ 0.76	$ 0.90	$ 0.43
Diluted	$ 0.33	$ 0.47	$ 0.61	$ 0.73	$ 0.87	$ 0.43

(Continued)

EXHIBIT 10.14 (Continued)

Starbucks: Consolidated Statements of Income: Fiscal Years 2003–2008

	Common-Size						Percentage Change					
	2003	2004	2005	2006	2007	2008	2004	2005	2006	2007	2008	Compound
Company-operated retail	84.6%	84.2%	84.7%	84.5%	85.0%	84.5%	29.2%	21.0%	22.1%	21.5%	9.7%	20.5%
Specialty:												
Licensing	10.0%	10.7%	10.6%	11.1%	10.9%	11.3%	38.2%	18.9%	27.9%	19.2%	14.2%	23.4%
Foodservice and other	5.3%	5.1%	4.8%	4.4%	4.1%	4.2%	25.3%	12.3%	12.8%	12.7%	13.6%	15.2%
Total Specialty	15.4%	15.8%	15.3%	15.5%	15.0%	15.5%	33.7%	16.8%	23.2%	17.4%	14.0%	20.8%
Net Revenues	**100.0%**	**100.0%**	**100.0%**	**100.0%**	**100.0%**	**100.0%**	**29.9%**	**20.3%**	**22.3%**	**20.9%**	**10.3%**	**20.6%**
Cost of sales (including occupancy costs)	41.3%	41.4%	40.9%	40.8%	42.5%	44.7%	30.3%	18.9%	22.0%	25.8%	16.2%	22.5%
Gross Profit	**58.7%**	**58.6%**	**59.1%**	**59.2%**	**57.5%**	**55.3%**	**29.6%**	**21.3%**	**22.4%**	**17.5%**	**6.0%**	**19.1%**
Store operating expenses	33.9%	33.8%	34.0%	34.5%	34.2%	36.1%	29.8%	21.0%	24.1%	19.6%	16.5%	22.1%
Other operating expenses	3.5%	3.2%	3.0%	3.3%	3.1%	3.2%	21.4%	12.2%	31.8%	15.9%	12.2%	18.5%
Depreciation and amortization	6.0%	5.5%	5.3%	5.0%	5.0%	5.3%	18.2%	17.6%	13.8%	20.6%	17.6%	17.6%
General and administrative expenses	6.0%	5.7%	5.7%	6.2%	5.2%	4.4%	24.4%	18.8%	32.6%	2.1%	−6.8%	13.3%
Restructuring charges	0.0%	0.0%	0.0%	0.0%	0.0%	2.6%	na	na	na	na	na	na
Income from equity investees	0.9%	1.1%	1.2%	1.2%	1.1%	1.1%	60.6%	30.0%	22.6%	15.0%	5.2%	25.3%
Operating Income	**10.3%**	**11.5%**	**12.3%**	**11.5%**	**11.2%**	**4.9%**	**44.2%**	**28.7%**	**14.5%**	**17.9%**	**−52.2%**	**3.7%**
Interest and other income	0.3%	0.3%	0.3%	0.3%	0.4%	0.1%	22.0%	17.8%	20.8%	96.3%	−77.8%	−5.5%
Interest expense	0.0%	0.0%	0.0%	−0.1%	−0.4%	−0.5%	33.3%	225.0%	546.2%	354.8%	39.8%	181.9%
Income Before Income Taxes	**10.6%**	**11.7%**	**12.5%**	**11.6%**	**11.2%**	**4.4%**	**43.6%**	**28.3%**	**13.8%**	**16.6%**	**−56.5%**	**1.2%**
Provision for income taxes	4.1%	4.4%	4.7%	4.2%	4.1%	1.4%	38.7%	30.3%	7.5%	18.2%	−62.5%	−2.9%
Cumulative effect of an accounting change	0.0%	0.0%	0.0%	−0.2%	0.0%	0.0%	na	na	na	na	na	na
Net Income	**6.5%**	**7.3%**	**7.8%**	**7.2%**	**7.1%**	**3.0%**	**46.6%**	**27.1%**	**14.1%**	**19.2%**	**−53.1%**	**3.5%**

time. Exhibit 10.17 (see pages 872–873) provides store operating data through fiscal year 2008 for Starbucks, including same-store sales growth rates, new store openings, and total numbers of stores open. Exhibit 10.18 (see page 874) provides a detailed breakdown of Starbucks' revenues and revenue growth by segment and by store. You may want to refer back to Exhibits 1.26–1.30 (Chapter 1) for additional financial statement data. You also may want to refer back to Exhibit 4.44 and 4.45 (Chapter 4) for a ratio analysis of Starbucks' profitability and operating segments. All of the other chapters in the text also have illustrated accounting quality issues and financial statement analysis issues for Starbucks. All of these data and analyses now come into play in this portion of the comprehensive Starbucks case, as you develop forecasts of Starbucks' future financial statements.

Required

Develop complete forecasts of Starbucks' income statements, balance sheets, and statements of cash flows for Years +1 through +5. As illustrated in this chapter, develop objective and unbiased forecast assumptions for all of Starbucks' future operating, investing, and financing activities through Year +5 and capture those expectations using financial statement forecasts.

Specifications

a. Build your own spreadsheets to develop and capture your financial statement forecast assumptions and data for Starbucks. Building your own financial statement forecast spreadsheets is a valuable learning experience. You can use the PepsiCo examples presented throughout this chapter as models to follow in building your spreadsheets. If you have already had the experience of building forecast spreadsheets, you can build your financial statement forecasts using the FSAP template for Starbucks that accompanies this book. If you want to start from scratch, you can download the blank FSAP template from the book's website: www.cengage.com/accounting/wahlen and input the accounting data for Starbucks from Exhibits 10.14–10.16 into the Data Spreadsheet in the blank FSAP template.

FSAP

b. Starbucks' operating, investing, and financing activities involve primarily opening and operating company-owned retail coffee shops in the United States and around the world. Starbucks' annual reports provide useful data on the number of company-operated stores Starbucks owns, the new stores it opens each year, and the same-store sales growth rates. These data reveal that Starbucks' revenues and revenue growth rates differ significantly across different segments and across U.S. versus international stores. Use these data, summarized in Exhibits 10.17 and 10.18, as a basis to forecast (i) Starbucks' future sales from existing stores, (ii) the number of new company-operated stores Starbucks will open, (iii) future sales from new stores, and (iv) capital expenditures for new stores.

c. Starbucks' business also involves generating revenues from licensing Starbucks stores and selling Starbucks coffee and other products through foodservice accounts, grocery stores, warehouse clubs, and so on. Use the data in Exhibits 10.17 and 10.18 to build forecasts of future revenues from licensing activities and foodservice and other activities.

d. Use your forecasts of capital expenditures for new stores together with Starbucks' data on property, plant, and equipment and depreciation to build a schedule to forecast property, plant, and equipment and depreciation expense as described in the chapter and illustrated in Appendix C for PepsiCo.

e. Starbucks appears to use repurchases of common equity shares as the flexible financial account for balancing the balance sheet. Common equity share repurchases are

EXHIBIT 10.15

Starbucks
Balance Sheets in Dollar Amounts, Common-Size Percentages, and Percentage Changes
(Integrative Case 10.1)

Starbucks: Consolidated Balance Sheets: 2003–2008

(dollars in millions)	2003	2004	2005	2006	2007	2008
ASSETS						
Cash and equivalents	$ 200.9	$ 145.1	$ 173.8	$ 312.6	$ 281.3	$ 269.8
Short-term investments	149.1	508.0	133.2	141.0	157.4	52.5
Receivables	114.4	140.2	190.8	224.3	287.9	329.5
Inventories	342.9	422.7	546.3	636.2	691.7	692.8
Prepaid expenses and other assets	55.2	71.3	94.4	126.9	148.8	169.2
Deferred income taxes, net	47.4	63.7	70.8	88.8	129.5	234.2
Total Current Assets	**910.0**	**1,350.9**	**1,209.3**	**1,529.8**	**1,696.5**	**1,748.0**
Long-term investments	136.2	135.2	60.5	5.8	21.0	71.4
Equity and other investments	144.3	167.7	201.1	219.1	258.8	302.6
Property and equipment, gross	2,516.3	2,877.7	3,467.6	4,257.7	5,306.6	5,717.3
Accumulated depreciation	(1,068.6)	(1,326.3)	(1,625.6)	(1,969.8)	(2,416.1)	(2,760.9)
Property and equipment, net	1,447.7	1,551.4	1,842.0	2,287.9	2,890.4	2,956.4
Other assets	52.1	85.6	72.9	186.9	219.4	261.1
Other intangible assets	24.9	26.8	35.4	38.0	42.0	66.6
Goodwill	63.3	69.0	92.5	161.5	215.6	266.5
Total Assets	**$2,778.5**	**$3,386.5**	**$3,513.7**	**$4,428.9**	**$5,343.9**	**$5,672.6**

LIABILITIES AND STOCKHOLDERS' EQUITY						
Accounts payable	$ 169.0	$ 199.3	$ 221.0	$ 340.9	$ 390.8	$ 324.9
Short-term borrowings	—	—	277.0	700.0	710.2	713.0
Accrued compensation and related costs	152.6	208.9	232.4	289.0	292.4	253.6
Accrued occupancy costs	21.7	29.2	44.5	54.9	74.6	136.1
Accrued taxes	54.9	63	78.3	94	92.5	76.1
Insurance reserves	—	—	—	—	137.0	152.5
Other accrued expenses	101.8	123.7	198.1	224.2	160.3	164.4
Deferred revenue	73.5	121.4	175.0	231.9	296.9	368.4
Current portion of long-term debt	0.7	0.7	0.7	0.8	0.8	0.7
Total Current Liabilities	**574.2**	**746.3**	**1,227.0**	**1,935.6**	**2,155.6**	**2,189.7**
Deferred income taxes, net	12.5	21.8	—	—	—	—
Long-term debt	4.4	3.6	2.9	2.0	550.1	549.6
Other long-term liabilities	116.3	144.7	193.6	262.9	354.1	442.4
Total Liabilities	**707.4**	**916.3**	**1,423.4**	**2,200.4**	**3,059.8**	**3,181.7**
Common stock	959.1	956.7	91.0	0.8	0.7	0.7
Paid-in capital	39.4	39.4	39.4	39.4	39.4	39.4
Retained earnings	1,058.3	1,444.9	1,939.0	2,151.1	2,189.4	2,402.4
Accumulated other comp. income	14.3	29.2	20.9	37.3	54.6	48.4
Total Shareholders' Equity	**2,071.1**	**2,470.2**	**2,090.3**	**2,228.5**	**2,284.1**	**2,490.9**
Total Liabilities and Shareholders' Equity	**$2,778.5**	**$3,386.5**	**$3,513.7**	**$4,428.9**	**$5,343.9**	**$5,672.6**

(Continued)

EXHIBIT 10.15 (Continued)

Starbucks: Consolidated Balance Sheets: 2003–2008

	Common-Size						Percentage Change					
	2003	**2004**	**2005**	**2006**	**2007**	**2008**	**2004**	**2005**	**2006**	**2007**	**2008**	**Compound**
Cash and equivalents	7.2%	4.3%	4.9%	7.1%	5.3%	4.8%	−27.8%	19.8%	79.9%	−10.0%	−4.1%	6.1%
Short-term investments	5.4%	15.0%	3.8%	3.2%	2.9%	0.9%	240.7%	−73.8%	5.9%	11.6%	−66.7%	−18.8%
Receivables	4.1%	4.1%	5.4%	5.1%	5.4%	5.8%	22.5%	36.0%	17.6%	28.4%	14.4%	23.6%
Inventories	12.3%	12.5%	15.5%	14.4%	12.9%	12.2%	23.2%	29.3%	16.5%	8.7%	0.2%	15.1%
Prepaid expenses and other assets	2.0%	2.1%	2.7%	2.9%	2.8%	3.0%	29.3%	32.4%	34.4%	17.2%	13.7%	25.1%
Deferred income taxes, net	1.7%	1.9%	2.0%	2.0%	2.4%	4.1%	34.3%	11.2%	25.4%	45.8%	80.9%	37.6%
Total Current Assets	**32.8%**	**39.9%**	**34.4%**	**34.5%**	**31.7%**	**30.8%**	**48.5%**	**−10.5%**	**26.5%**	**10.9%**	**3.0%**	**13.9%**
Long-term investments	4.9%	4.0%	1.7%	0.1%	0.4%	1.3%	na	na	−90.4%	261.8%	239.6%	na
Equity and other investments	5.2%	5.0%	5.7%	4.9%	4.8%	5.3%	16.3%	19.9%	9.0%	18.1%	16.9%	16.0%
PP&E gross	90.6%	85.0%	98.7%	96.1%	99.3%	100.8%	14.4%	20.5%	22.8%	24.6%	7.7%	17.8%
Accum. deprec.	−38.5%	−39.2%	−46.3%	−44.5%	−45.2%	−48.7%	24.1%	22.6%	21.2%	22.7%	14.3%	20.9%
PP&E net	52.1%	45.8%	52.4%	51.7%	54.1%	52.1%	7.2%	18.7%	24.2%	26.3%	2.3%	15.3%
Other assets	1.9%	2.5%	2.1%	4.2%	4.1%	4.6%	64.2%	−14.8%	156.4%	17.4%	19.0%	38.0%
Other intangible assets	0.9%	0.8%	1.0%	0.9%	0.8%	1.2%	7.4%	32.1%	7.2%	10.8%	58.4%	21.7%
Goodwill	2.3%	2.0%	2.6%	3.6%	4.0%	4.7%	8.9%	34.1%	74.6%	33.5%	23.6%	33.3%
Total Assets	**100.0%**	**100.0%**	**100.0%**	**100.0%**	**100.0%**	**100.0%**	**21.9%**	**3.8%**	**26.0%**	**20.7%**	**6.2%**	**15.3%**

Accounts payable	6.1%	5.9%	6.3%	7.7%	7.3%	5.7%	18.0%	10.8%	54.3%	14.6%	−16.9%	14.0%
Short-term borrowings	0.0%	0.0%	7.9%	15.8%	13.3%	12.6%	na	na	152.7%	1.5%	0.4%	na
Accrued compensation	5.5%	6.2%	6.6%	6.5%	5.5%	4.5%	36.9%	11.2%	24.4%	1.2%	−13.3%	10.7%
Accrued occupancy	0.8%	0.9%	1.3%	1.2%	1.4%	2.4%	34.5%	52.2%	23.3%	35.9%	82.5%	44.3%
Accrued taxes	2.0%	1.9%	2.2%	2.1%	1.7%	1.3%	14.7%	24.4%	20.1%	−1.6%	−17.7%	6.8%
Insurance reserves	0.0%	0.0%	0.0%	0.0%	2.6%	2.7%	na	na	na	na	11.3%	na
Other accrued expenses	3.7%	3.7%	5.6%	5.1%	3.0%	2.9%	21.5%	60.2%	13.2%	−28.5%	2.6%	10.1%
Deferred revenue	2.6%	3.6%	5.0%	5.2%	5.6%	6.5%	65.2%	44.2%	32.5%	28.0%	24.1%	38.0%
Current portion of long-term debt	0.0%	0.0%	0.0%	0.0%	0.0%	0.0%	1.8%	1.8%	1.9%	1.7%	−9.7%	−0.6%
Total Current Liabilities	**20.7%**	**22.0%**	**34.9%**	**43.7%**	**40.3%**	**38.6%**	**30.0%**	**64.4%**	**57.8%**	**11.4%**	**1.6%**	**30.7%**
Deferred income taxes, net	0.5%	0.6%	0.0%	0.0%	0.0%	0.0%	73.6%	−100.0%	na	na	na	−100.0%
Long-term debt	0.2%	0.1%	0.1%	0.0%	10.3%	9.7%	−16.9%	−20.7%	−31.8%	27996.1%	−0.1%	163.2%
Other long-term liabilities	4.2%	4.3%	5.5%	5.9%	6.6%	7.8%	24.4%	33.8%	35.8%	34.7%	24.9%	30.6%
Total Liabilities	**25.5%**	**27.1%**	**40.5%**	**49.7%**	**57.3%**	**56.1%**	**29.5%**	**55.3%**	**54.6%**	**39.1%**	**4.0%**	**35.1%**
Common stock	34.5%	28.2%	2.6%	0.0%	0.0%	0.0%	−0.3%	−90.5%	−99.2%	−2.4%	0.0%	−76.2%
Paid-in capital	1.4%	1.2%	1.1%	0.9%	0.7%	0.7%	0.0%	0.0%	0.0%	0.0%	0.0%	0.0%
Retained earnings	38.1%	42.7%	55.2%	48.6%	41.0%	42.4%	36.5%	34.2%	10.9%	1.8%	9.7%	17.8%
Accum. other comp. income	0.5%	0.9%	0.6%	0.8%	1.0%	0.9%	104.9%	−28.5%	78.2%	46.5%	−11.4%	27.7%
Total Shareholders' Equity	**74.5%**	**72.9%**	**59.5%**	**50.3%**	**42.7%**	**43.9%**	**19.3%**	**−15.4%**	**6.6%**	**2.5%**	**9.1%**	**3.8%**
Total Liabilities and Shareholders' Equity	**100.0%**	**100.0%**	**100.0%**	**100.0%**	**100.0%**	**100.0%**	**21.9%**	**3.8%**	**26.0%**	**20.7%**	**6.2%**	**15.3%**

EXHIBIT 10.16

Starbucks
Consolidated Statements of Cash Flows
(Integrative Case 10.1)

	Starbucks: Consolidated Cash Flows: 2003–2008					
(dollars in millions)	**2003**	**2004**	**2005**	**2006**	**2007**	**2008**
OPERATING ACTIVITIES						
Net earnings	$265.4	$389.0	$494.5	$ 564.3	$ 672.6	$ 315.5
Depreciation and amortization	266.3	314.0	367.2	412.6	491.2	604.5
Provisions for impairments and disposals	7.8	13.6	20.2	19.6	26.0	325.0
Deferred income taxes, net	(6.8)	(3.8)	(31.3)	(84.3)	(37.3)	(117.1)
Equity in income of investees	(21.3)	(31.8)	(49.6)	(60.6)	(65.7)	(61.3)
Distributions of income from equity investees	29.0	38.3	30.9	49.2	65.9	52.6
Stock-based compensation	36.6	63.4	110.0	105.7	103.9	75.0
Other non-cash items in net earnings	6.0	11.6	10.1	(96.9)	(84.7)	(11.0)
Operating assets and liabilities:						
Inventories	(64.8)	(77.7)	(121.6)	(85.5)	(48.6)	(0.6)
Accounts payable	25.0	27.9	9.7	105.0	36.1	(63.9)
Accrued expenses and taxes	42.1	54.9	22.7	132.7	86.4	7.3
Deferred revenues	30.7	47.6	53.3	56.6	63.2	72.4
Other operating assets and liabilities	0.2	11.4	7.6	13.2	22.2	60.3
Net Cash Provided by Operating Activities	**$616.1**	**$858.5**	**$923.6**	**$1,131.6**	**$1,331.2**	**$1,258.7**

INVESTING ACTIVITIES						
Purchases, sales, maturities of investment securities	(121.3)	(264.7)	452.2	61.1	(11.7)	24.1
Acquisitions, net of cash acquired	(69.9	(7.5)	(21.6)	(91.7)	(53.3)	(74.2)
Net additions to property, plant, and equipment	(378.0)	(412.5)	(644.0)	(771.2)	(1,080.3)	(984.5)
Other investments	(47.3)	(64.7)	(7.9)	(39.2)	(56.6)	(52.0)
Net Cash Used in Investing Activities	**$(616.4)**	**$(749.5)**	**$(221.3)**	**$(841.0)**	**$(1,201.9)**	**$(1,086.6)**
FINANCING ACTIVITIES						
Net (payments on) proceeds from commercial paper	—	—	—	—	710.2	(297.2)
Net (payments on) proceeds from short-term borrowings	—	—	277.0	423.0	(700.0)	299.4
Net (payments on) proceeds from long-term debt	(0.7)	(0.7)	(0.7)	(0.9)	548.2	(0.6)
Net (repurchases of) issues of common equity shares	31.5	(65.8)	(950.1)	(694.8)	(819.9)	(199.1)
Excess tax benefit from exercise of stock options	—	—	—	117.4	93.1	14.7
Other	—	—	—	—	(3.5)	(1.7)
Net Cash Used by Financing Activities	**$ 30.8**	**$ (66.5)**	**$(673.8)**	**$(155.3)**	**$ (171.9)**	**$ (184.5)**
Effect of exchange rate changes on cash	3.3	3.1	0.3	3.5	11.3	0.9
Net Change in Cash and Cash Equivalents	**$ 33.7**	**$ 45.6**	**$ 28.8**	**$ 138.8**	**$ (31.3)**	**$ (11.5)**
Beginning Cash	65.7	99.5	145.1	173.8	312.6	281.3
Ending Cash	**$ 99.5**	**$ 145.1**	**$ 173.8**	**$ 312.6**	**$ 281.3**	**$ 269.8**

EXHIBIT 10.17

Starbucks
Store Operating Data
(Integrative Case 10.1)

		Starbucks: Store Operating Data: 2003–2008					
		2003	2004	2005	2006	2007	2008
Percentage change in comparable store sales:							
U.S.		9%	11%	9%	7%	4%	−5%
International		7%	6%	6%	8%	7%	2%
Consolidated		8%	10%	8%	7%	5%	−3%
Stores opened during the year:							
U.S.	Company-operated stores	514	521	580	810	1,065	445
	Licensed stores	315	417	596	733	723	438
Int'l.	Company-operated stores	126	144	166	233	277	236
	Licensed stores	246	262	330	423	506	550
Totals	Company-operated stores	640	665	746	1,043	1,342	681
	Licensed stores	561	679	926	1,156	1,229	988
Grand total stores opened		1,201	1,344	1,672	2,199	2,571	1,669
Stores open at year-end:							
U.S.	Company-operated stores	3,817	4,338	4,918	5,728	6,793	7,238
	Licensed stores	1,422	1,839	2,435	3,168	3,891	4,329
Int'l.	Company-operated stores	834	978	1,202	1,435	1,712	1,979
	Licensed stores	1,152	1,414	1,686	2,109	2,615	3,134
Totals	Company-operated stores	4,651	5,316	6,120	7,163	8,505	9,217
	Licensed stores	2,574	3,253	4,121	5,277	6,506	7,463
Grand total stores open at year-end		7,225	8,569	10,241	12,440	15,011	16,680

Stores open at year-end:		Common-Size						Percentage Change					
		2003	2004	2005	2006	2007	2008	2004	2005	2006	2007	2008	Compound
U.S.	Company-operated stores	52.8%	50.6%	48.0%	46.0%	45.3%	43.4%	13.6%	13.4%	16.5%	18.6%	6.6%	13.7%
	Licensed stores	19.7%	21.5%	23.8%	25.5%	25.9%	26.0%	29.3%	32.4%	30.1%	22.8%	11.3%	24.9%
Int'l.	Company-operated stores	11.5%	11.4%	11.7%	11.5%	11.4%	11.9%	17.3%	22.9%	19.4%	19.3%	15.6%	18.9%
	Licensed stores	15.9%	16.5%	16.5%	17.0%	17.4%	18.8%	22.7%	19.2%	25.1%	24.0%	19.8%	22.2%
Totals	Company-operated stores	64.4%	62.0%	59.8%	57.6%	56.7%	55.3%	14.3%	15.1%	17.0%	18.7%	8.4%	14.7%
	Licensed stores	35.6%	38.0%	40.2%	42.4%	43.3%	44.7%	26.4%	26.7%	28.1%	23.3%	14.7%	23.7%
Grand total stores open at year-end		100.0%	100.0%	100.0%	100.0%	100.0%	100.0%	18.6%	19.5%	21.5%	20.7%	11.1%	18.2%

EXHIBIT 10.18

Starbucks
Sales Growth Analysis by Segment
(Integrative Case 10.1)
(amounts in millions)

	2005	2006	2007	2008
Retail Sales	$5,391.9	$6,583.1	$7,998.3	$ 8,771.9
Specialty Revenues	977.4	1,203.8	1,413.2	1,611.1
Net Revenues	**$6,369.3**	**$7,786.9**	**$9,411.5**	**$10,383.0**
Growth rates	20.3%	22.3%	20.9%	10.3%

Sales by Segment and Type:	**2005**	**2006**	**2007**	**2008**
Retail				
U.S.	$4,539.5	$5,495.2	$6,560.9	$6,997.7
International	852.5	1,087.9	1,437.4	1,774.2
Specialty				
U.S. Licensed	278.0	369.2	439.2	504.2
International Licensed	145.7	186.1	220.8	274.8
Foodservice & CPG	553.6	648.6	753.2	832.1
Net Revenues	**$6,369.3**	**$7,786.9**	**$9,411.5**	**$10,383.0**

Sales per Average Store-Year by Segment and Type:	**2005**	**2006**	**2007**	**2008**
Retail				
U.S.	$0.981	$1.032	$1.048	$0.997
Growth rates		5.2%	1.5%	−4.8%
International	$0.782	$0.825	$0.914	$0.961
Growth rates		5.5%	10.7%	5.2%
Specialty				
U.S. Licensed	—	$0.132	$0.124	$0.123
Growth rates			−5.6%	−1.4%
International licensed	—	$0.098	$0.093	$0.096
Growth rates			−4.6%	2.3%
Foodservice & CPG	$553.6	$648.6	$753.2	$832.1
Growth rates		17.2%	16.1%	10.5%

similar to dividends as a mechanism to distribute excess capital to common equity shareholders. Therefore, build your financial statement forecasts using dividends as the flexible financial account.

f. Save your forecast spreadsheets. In subsequent chapters, you will continue to use Starbucks as a comprehensive integrative case. In those chapters, you will apply the valuation models to your forecasts of Starbucks' future earnings, cash flows, and dividends to assess Starbucks' share value.

CASE 10.2

MASSACHUSETTS STOVE COMPANY: ANALYZING STRATEGIC OPTIONS[24]

The Woodstove Market

Since the early 1990s, woodstove sales have declined from 1,200,000 units per year to approximately 100,000 units per year. The decline has occurred because of (1) stringent new federal EPA regulations, which set maximum limits on stove emissions beginning in 1992; (2) stable energy prices, which reduced the incentive to switch to woodstoves to save on heating costs; and (3) changes in consumers' lifestyles, particularly the growth of two-income families.

During this period of decline in industry sales, the market was flooded with woodstoves at distressed prices as companies closed their doors or liquidated inventories made obsolete by the new EPA regulations. Downward pricing pressure forced surviving companies to cut prices, output, or both. Years of contraction and pricing pressure left many of the surviving manufacturers in a precarious position financially, with excessive inventory, high debt, little cash, uncollectible receivables, and low margins.

The shakeout and consolidation among woodstove manufacturers and, to a lesser extent, woodstove specialty retailers have been dramatic. The number of manufacturers selling more than 2,000 units a year (characterized in the industry as "large manufacturers") has declined from approximately 90 to 35 in the last ten years. The number of manufacturers selling less than 2,000 units per year (characterized as "small manufacturers") has declined from approximately 130 to 6. Because the current woodstove market is not large enough to support all of the surviving producers, manufacturers have attempted to diversify in order to stay in business. Seeking relief, virtually all of the survivors have turned to the manufacture of gas appliances.

The Gas Appliance Market

The gas appliance market includes three segments: (1) gas log sets, (2) gas fireplaces, and (3) gas stoves. Gas log sets are "faux fires" that can be installed in an existing fireplace. They are primarily decorative and have little heating value. Gas fireplaces are fully assembled fireboxes that a builder or contractor can install in new construction or in renovated buildings and houses. They are mainly decorative and are less expensive and easier to maintain than a masonry/brick fireplace. Gas stoves are freestanding appliances with a decorative appearance and efficient heating characteristics.

The first two segments of the gas appliance market (log sets and fireplaces) are large, established, stable markets. Established manufacturers control these markets, and distribution

---

[24] The authors acknowledge the assistance of Tom P. Morrissey in the preparation of this case.

is primarily through mass merchandisers. The third segment (gas stoves) is less than five years old. Although it is growing steadily, it has an annual volume of only about 100,000 units (almost identical to the annual volume of the woodstove market). This is the market to which woodstove manufacturers have turned for relief.

The gas stove market is not as heavily regulated as the woodstove market, and there are currently no EPA regulations governing the emissions of gas heating appliances. Gas stoves are perceived as being more appropriate for an aging population because they provide heat and ambiance but require no effort. They can be operated with a wall switch or thermostat or by remote control. Because actual fuel cost (or cost savings) is not an issue for many buyers, a big advantage of heating with wood is no longer a consideration for many consumers. Gas stoves are sold and distributed through mass merchandisers and through natural gas or propane dealers. The gas industry has the financial, promotional, organizational, and lobbying clout to support the development of the gas stove market, attributes that the tiny woodstove industry lacks.

Unfortunately, life has not been rosy for all of the woodstove companies entering this new market. Development costs and selling costs for new products using a different fuel and different distribution system have been substantial. Improvements in gas logs and gas burners have required rapid changes in product design. In contrast, woodstove designs are fairly stable and slow to change. Competition for market share has renewed pricing pressure on gas stove producers. Companies trying to maintain their woodstove sales while introducing gas products must carry large inventories to service both product lines. Failure to forecast demand accurately has left many companies with inventory shortages during the selling season or with large inventories of unsold product at the end of the season.

Many surviving manufacturers who looked to gas stoves for salvation are now quietly looking for suitors to acquire them. A combination of excessive debt and inventory levels, together with high development and distribution costs, has made financial success highly uncertain. Continued consolidation will take place in this difficult market during the next five years.

Massachusetts Stove Company

Massachusetts Stove Company (MSC) is one of the six "small manufacturers" to survive the EPA regulation and industry meltdown. The company has just completed its sixth consecutive year of slow but steady growth in revenue and profit since complying with the EPA regulations. Exhibits 10.19–10.21 (see pages 877–879) present the financial statements of MSC for Year 3–Year 7. Exhibit 10.22 (see page 880) presents selected financial statement ratios.

The success of MSC in recent years is a classic case of a company staying small, marketing in a specific niche, and vigorously applying a "stick-to-your-knitting" policy. MSC is the only woodstove producer that has not developed gas products; 100 percent of its sales currently come from woodstove sales. MSC is the only woodstove producer that sells by mail order directly to consumers. The mail-order market has sheltered MSC from some of the pricing pressure that other manufacturers have had to bear. The combination of high entry costs and high risks make it unlikely that another competitor will enter the mail-order niche.

MSC's other competitive advantages are the high efficiency and unique features of its woodstoves. MSC equips its woodstoves with a catalytic combuster, which reburns gases emitted from burning wood. This reburning not only increases the heat generated by the stoves, but also reduces pollutants in the air. MSC offers a woodstove with inlaid soapstone. This soapstone heats up and provides warmth even after the fire in the stove has dwindled. The soapstone also adds to the attractiveness of the stove as a piece of furniture. MSC's customer base includes many middle- and upper-income individuals.

EXHIBIT 10.19

Massachusetts Stove Company
Income Statements
(Case 10.2)

	Year Ended December 31:				
	Year 3	Year 4	Year 5	Year 6	Year 7
Sales	$1,480,499	$1,637,128	$ 2,225,745	$ 2,376,673	$ 2,734,986
Cost of goods sold	(727,259)	(759,156)	(1,063,135)	(1,159,466)	(1,380,820)
Depreciation	(56,557)	(73,416)	(64,320)	(66,829)	(72,321)
Facilities costs	(59,329)	(47,122)	(66,226)	(48,090)	(45,309)
Facilities rental income	25,856	37,727	38,702	42,142	41,004
Selling expenses	(452,032)	(563,661)	(776,940)	(874,000)	(926,175)
Administrative expenses	(36,967)	(39,057)	(46,444)	(48,046)	(111,199)
Operating Income	$ 174,211	$ 192,443	$ 247,382	$ 222,384	$ 240,166
Interest income	712	2,242	9,541	9,209	16,665
Interest expense	(48,437)	(44,551)	(47,535)	(52,633)	(42,108)
Income Before Income Taxes	$ 126,486	$ 150,134	$ 209,388	$ 178,960	$ 214,723
Income taxes	(35,416)	(42,259)	(64,142)	(45,794)	(60,122)
Net Income	$ 91,070	$ 107,875	$ 145,246	$ 133,166	$ 154,601

MSC believes that profitable growth of woodstove sales beyond gross revenues of $3 million a year in the mail-order niche is unlikely. However, no one is selling gas appliances by mail order. Many of MSC's customers and prospects have asked whether MSC plans to produce a gas stove.

Management of MSC is contemplating the development of several gas appliances to sell by mail order. There are compelling reasons for MSC to do this, as well as some good reasons to be cautious.

Availability of Space

MSC owns a 25,000-square-foot building but occupies only 15,000 square feet. MSC leases the remaining 10,000 square feet to two tenants. The tenants pay rent plus their share of insurance, property taxes, and maintenance costs. The addition of gas appliances to its product line would require MSC to use 5,000 square feet of the space currently rented to one of its tenants. MSC would have to give the tenant six months' notice to cancel its lease.

Availability of Capital

MSC has its own internal funds for product development and inventory, as well as an unused line of credit. But it will lose interest income (or incur interest expense) if it invests these funds in development and increased inventory.

Existing Demand

MSC receives approximately 50,000 requests for catalogs each year and has a mailing list of approximately 220,000 active prospects and 15,000 recent owners of woodstoves. There is anecdotal evidence of sufficient demand so that MSC could introduce its gas stoves with little or no additional marketing expense, other than the cost of printing some catalog pages

EXHIBIT 10.20

Massachusetts Stove Company
Balance Sheets
(Case 10.2)

	December 31:					
	Year 2	Year 3	Year 4	Year 5	Year 6	Year 7
ASSETS						
Cash	$ 50,794	$ 19,687	$ 145,930	$ 104,383	$ 258,148	$ 351,588
Accounts receivable	12,571	56,706	30,934	41,748	30,989	5,997
Inventories	251,112	327,627	347,883	375,258	409,673	452,709
Other current assets	1,368	—	—	—	—	—
Total Current Assets	$ 315,845	$ 404,020	$ 524,747	$ 521,389	$ 698,810	$ 810,294
PP&E, at cost	1,056,157	1,148,806	1,164,884	1,184,132	1,234,752	1,257,673
Accumulated depreciation	(296,683)	(353,240)	(426,656)	(490,975)	(557,804)	(630,125)
Other assets	121,483	94,000	61,500	12,200	—	—
Total Assets	$1,196,802	$1,293,586	$1,324,475	$1,226,746	$1,375,758	$1,437,842
Liabilities and Shareholders' Equity						
Accounts payable	$ 137,104	$ 112,815	$ 43,229	$ 60,036	$ 39,170	$ 47,809
Notes payable	25,000	12,000	—	—	—	—
Current portion of long-term debt	27,600	29,000	21,570	113,257	115,076	27,036
Other current liabilities	39,530	100,088	184,194	189,732	244,241	257,252
Total Current Liabilities	$ 229,234	$ 253,903	$ 248,993	$ 363,025	$ 398,487	$ 332,097
Long-term debt	972,446	953,491	881,415	599,408	574,332	547,296
Deferred income taxes	—	—	—	—	5,460	6,369
Total Liabilities	$1,201,680	$1,207,394	$1,130,408	$ 962,433	$ 978,279	$ 885,762
Common stock	2,000	2,000	2,000	2,000	2,000	2,000
Additional paid-in capital	435,630	435,630	435,630	435,630	435,630	435,630
Retained earnings (deficit)	(442,508)	(351,438)	(243,563)	(98,317)	34,849	189,450
Treasury stock	—	—	—	(75,000)	(75,000)	(75,000)
Total Shareholders' Equity	$ (4,878)	$ 86,192	$ 194,067	$ 264,313	$ 397,479	$ 552,080
Total Liabilities and Shareholders' Equity	$1,196,802	$1,293,586	$1,324,475	$1,226,746	$1,375,758	$1,437,842

EXHIBIT 10.21

Massachusetts Stove Company
Statements of Cash Flows
(Case 10.2)

	Year Ended December 31:				
	Year 3	**Year 4**	**Year 5**	**Year 6**	**Year 7**
OPERATIONS					
Net income	$ 91,070	$107,875	$ 145,246	$133,166	$ 154,601
Depreciation and amortization	56,557	73,416	64,320	66,829	72,321
Other addbacks	27,483	32,500	49,300	17,660	909
(Increase) Decrease in receivables	(44,135)	25,772	(10,814)	10,759	24,992
(Increase) Decrease in inventories	(76,515)	(20,256)	(27,375)	(34,415)	(43,036)
Decrease in other current assets	1,368	—	—	—	—
Increase (Decrease) in payables	(24,289)	(69,586)	16,807	(20,866)	8,639
Increase in other current liabilities	60,558	84,106	5,538	54,509	13,011
Cash Flow from Operations	$ 92,097	$233,827	$ 243,022	$227,642	$ 231,437
INVESTING					
Capital expenditures	$(92,649)	$(16,078)	$ (19,249)	$(50,620)	$ (22,921)
Cash Flow from Investing	$(92,649)	$(16,078)	$ (19,249)	$(50,620)	$ (22,921)
FINANCING					
Increase in long-term debt	$ 10,000	$ —	$ —	$ —	$ —
Decrease in short-term debt	(13,000)	(12,000)	—	—	—
Decrease in long-term debt	(27,555)	(79,506)	(190,320)	(23,257)	(115,076)
Acquisition of common stock	—	—	(75,000)	—	—
Cash Flow from Financing	$(30,555)	$(91,506)	$(265,320)	$(23,257)	$(115,076)
Change in Cash	$(31,107)	$126,243	$ (41,547)	$153,765	$ 93,440
Cash—Beginning of year	50,794	19,687	145,930	104,383	258,148
Cash—End of Year	$ 19,687	$145,930	$ 104,383	$258,148	$ 351,588

each year. MSC's management worries about the risk of the gas stove sales cannibalizing its existing woodstove sales. Also, if the current base of woodstove sales is eroded through mismanagement, inattention, or cannibalization, attempts to grow the business through expansion into gas appliances will be self-defeating.

Vacant Market Niche

No other manufacturer is selling gas stoves by mail order. Because the entry costs are high and the unit volume is small, it is unlikely that another producer will enter the niche. MSC has had the mail-order market for woodstoves to itself for approximately seven years. MSC believes that this lack of existing competition will give it additional time to develop new products. However, management also believes that a timely entry will help solidify its position in this niche.

Suppliers

MSC has existing relationships with many of the suppliers necessary to manufacture new gas products. The foundry that produces MSC's woodstove castings is one of the largest

EXHIBIT 10.22

Massachusetts Stove Company
Financial Statement Ratios
(Case 10.2)

	Year 3	Year 4	Year 5	Year 6	Year 7
Profit Margin for ROA	8.5%	8.5%	8.1%	7.2%	6.8%
Total Assets Turnover	1.2	1.3	1.7	1.8	1.9
ROA	10.1%	10.7%	14.1%	13.1%	13.1%
Profit Margin for ROCE	6.2%	6.6%	6.5%	5.6%	5.7%
Capital Structure Leverage	30.6	9.3	5.6	3.9	3.0
ROCE	224.0%	77.0%	63.4%	40.2%	32.6%
Cost of Goods Sold/Sales	49.1%	46.4%	47.8%	48.8%	50.5%
Depreciation Expense/Sales	3.8%	4.5%	2.9%	2.8%	2.6%
Facilities Costs Net of Rental Income/Sales	2.3%	0.6%	1.2%	0.3%	0.2%
Selling Expense/Sales	30.5%	34.4%	34.9%	36.8%	33.9%
Administrative Expenses/Sales	2.5%	2.4%	2.1%	2.0%	4.0%
Interest Income/Sales	—	0.1%	0.4%	0.4%	0.6%
Interest Expense/Sales	3.3%	2.7%	2.1%	2.2%	1.5%
Income Tax Expense/Income before Taxes	28.0%	28.1%	30.6%	25.6%	28.0%
Accounts Receivable Turnover	42.7	37.4	61.2	65.3	147.9
Inventory Turnover	2.5	2.2	2.9	3.0	3.2
Fixed Assets Turnover	1.9	2.1	3.1	3.5	4.2
Current Ratio	1.59	2.11	1.44	1.75	2.44
Quick Ratio	0.30	0.71	0.40	0.73	1.08
Days Accounts Receivable	9	10	6	6	3
Days Inventory Held	146	166	126	122	114
Days Accounts Payable	51	33	16	14	11
Cash Flow from Operations/ Average Current Liabilities	38.1%	93.0%	79.4%	59.8%	63.4%
Long-Term Debt/ Shareholders' Equity	1,106.2%	454.2%	226.8%	144.5%	99.1%
Cash Flow from Operations/ Average Total Liabilities	7.6%	20.0%	23.2%	23.5%	24.8%
Interest Coverage Ratio	3.6	4.4	5.4	4.4	6.1

suppliers of gas heating appliances in central Europe. On the other hand, MSC would be a small, new customer for the vendors that provide the ceramic logs and gas burners. This could lead to problems with price, delivery, or service for these parts.

Synergies in Marketing and Manufacturing

MSC would sell gas appliances through its existing direct-mail marketing efforts. It would incur additional marketing expenses for photography, printing, and customer service.

MSC's existing plant is capable of manufacturing the shell of the gas units. It would require additional expertise to assemble fireboxes for the gas units (valves, burners, and log sets). MSC would have to increase its space and the number of employees to process and paint the metal parts of the new gas stoves. The gross margin for the gas products should be similar to that of the woodstoves.

Lack of Management Experience

Managing new product development, larger production levels and inventories, and a more complex business would require MSC to hire more management expertise. MSC also would have to institute a new organization structure for its more complex business and define responsibilities and accountability more carefully. Up to now, MSC has operated with a fairly loose organizational philosophy.

Required (additional requirements follow on page 883)

a. Identify clues from the financial statements and financial statement ratios for Year 3– Year 7 that might suggest that Massachusetts Stove Company is in a mature business.

b. Design a spreadsheet for the preparation of projected income statements, balance sheets, and statements of cash flows for MSC for Year 8–Year 12. Also forecast the financial statements for each of these years under three scenarios: (1) best case, (2) most likely, and (3) worst case. The following sections describe the assumptions you can make.

Development Costs

MSC plans to develop two gas stove models, but not concurrently. It will develop the first gas model during Year 8 and begin selling it during Year 9. It will develop the second gas model during Year 9 and begin selling it during Year 10. MSC will capitalize the development costs in the year incurred (Year 8 and Year 9) and amortize them straight line over five years, beginning with the year the particular stove is initially sold (Year 9 and Year 10). Estimated development cost for each stove are as follows:

Best Case: $100,000
Most Likely Case: $120,000
Worst Case: $160,000

Capital Expenditures

Capital expenditures, other than development costs, will be as follows: Year 8, $20,000; Year 9, $30,000; Year 10, $30,000; Year 11, $25,000; Year 12, $25,000. Assume a six-year depreciable life, straight-line depreciation, and a full year of depreciation in the year of acquisition.

Sales Growth

Changes in total sales relative to total sales of the preceding year are as follows:

	Best Case			Most Likely Case			Worst Case		
Year	Wood Stoves	Gas Stoves	Total	Wood Stoves	Gas Stoves	Total	Wood Stoves	Gas Stoves	Total
8	+2%	—	+ 2%	−2%	—	−2%	−4%	—	−4%
9	+2%	+6%	+ 8%	−2%	+4%	+2%	−4%	+2%	−2%
10	+2%	+12%	+14%	−2%	+8%	+6%	−4%	+4%	+0%
11	+2%	+12%	+14%	−2%	+8%	+6%	−4%	+4%	+0%
12	+2%	+12%	+14%	−2%	+8%	+6%	−4%	+4%	+0%

Because sales of gas stoves will start at zero, the projections of sales should *use the preceding growth rates in total sales.* The growth rates shown for woodstove sales and gas stove sales simply indicate the components of the total sales increase.

Cost of Goods Sold

Manufacturing costs of the gas stoves will equal 50 percent of sales, the same as for woodstoves.

Depreciation

Depreciation will increase for the amortization of the product development costs on the gas stoves and depreciation of additional capital expenditures.

Facilities Rental Income and Facilities Costs

Facilities rental income will decrease by 50 percent beginning in Year 9 when MSC takes over 5,000 square feet of its building now rented to another company and will remain at that reduced level for Year 10–Year 12. Facilities costs will increase by $30,000 beginning in Year 9 for facilities costs now paid by a tenant and for additional facilities costs required by gas stove manufacturing. These costs will remain at that increased level for Year 10–Year 12.

Selling Expenses

Selling expenses as a percentage of sales are as follows:

Year	Best Case	Most Likely Case	Worst Case
8	34%	34.0%	34%
9	33%	33.5%	35%
10	32%	33.0%	36%
11	31%	32.5%	37%
12	30%	32.0%	38%

Administrative Expenses

Administrative expenses will increase by $30,000 in Year 8, $30,000 in Year 9, and $20,000 in Year 10 and then remain at the Year 10 level in Years 11 and 12.

Interest Income

MSC will earn 5 percent interest on the average balance in cash each year.

Interest Expense

The interest rate on interest-bearing debt will be 6.8 percent on the average amount of debt outstanding each year.

Income Tax Expense

MSC is subject to an income tax rate of 28 percent.

Accounts Receivable and Inventories

Accounts receivable and inventories will increase at the growth rate in sales.

Property, Plant, and Equipment

Property, plant, and equipment at cost will increase each year by the amounts of capital expenditures and expenditures on development costs. Accumulated depreciation will increase each year by the amount of depreciation and amortization expense.

Accounts Payable and Other Current Liabilities

Accounts payable will increase with the growth rate in inventories. Other current liabilities include primarily advances by customers for stoves manufactured soon after the year-end. Other current liabilities will increase with the growth rate in sales.

Current Portion of Long-Term Debt

Scheduled repayments of long-term debt are as follows: Year 8, $27,036; Year 9, $29,200; Year 10, $31,400; Year 11, $33,900; Year 12, $36,600; Year 13, $39,500.

Deferred Income Taxes

Deferred income taxes relate to the use of accelerated depreciation for tax purposes and the straight-line method for financial reporting. Assume that deferred income taxes will not change.

Shareholders' Equity

Assume that there will be no changes in the contributed capital of MSC. Retained earnings will change each year in the amount of net income.

Required (continued from page 881)

c. Calculate the financial statements ratios listed in Exhibit 10.22 for MSC under each of the three scenarios for Year 8–Year 12.

Note: You should create a fourth spreadsheet as part of your preparation of the projected financial statements that will compute the financial ratios.

d. What advice would you give the management of MSC regarding its decision to enter the gas stove market? Your recommendation should consider the profitability and risks of this action as well as other factors you deem relevant.

Chapter **11**

Risk-Adjusted Expected Rates of Return and the Dividends Valuation Approach

Learning Objectives

1. **Estimate risk-adjusted expected rates of return on equity capital, as well as weighted average costs of capital, which you will use to discount future payoffs to present value.**
2. **Understand the dividends valuation approach and its conceptual and practical strengths and weaknesses.**
3. **Develop practical valuation techniques to deal with the many difficult issues involved in estimating firm value: (a) dividends versus cash flows versus earnings, (b) cash flows to the investor versus cash flows reinvested in the firm, (c) the forecast horizon, and (d) continuing value.**
4. **Apply the dividends valuation techniques to estimate firm value using the present value of future dividends.**
5. **Develop techniques to assess the sensitivity of firm value estimates to key valuation parameters, such as discount rates and expected long-term growth rates.**

INTRODUCTION AND OVERVIEW

Economic theory teaches that the value of an investment equals the present value of the projected future payoffs from the investment discounted at a rate that reflects the time value of money and the risk inherent in those expected payoffs. A general model for the present value of a security at time $t=0$ (denoted as V_0) with an expected life of n future periods is as follows:[1]

$$V_0 = \sum_{t=1}^{n} \frac{\text{Projected Future Payoffs}_t}{(1 + \text{Discount Rate})^t}$$

In securities markets that are less than perfectly efficient, price does not necessarily equal value for every security at all times. Therefore, it can be very fruitful to search for and analyze securities that may have prices that have deviated temporarily from their fundamental

[1] Throughout this chapter, t refers to accounting periods. The valuation process determines an estimate of firm value, denoted V_0, in present value as of today, when $t=0$. The period $t=1$ refers to the first accounting period being discounted to present value. Period $t=n$ is the period of the expected final, or liquidating, payoff.

values. When buying a security, the investor pays the security's price and receives the security's value. When selling a security, the investor receives the selling price and gives up the security's value. Price is observable, but value is not; value must be estimated. Therefore, estimating the value of a security to make intelligent investment decisions is a common objective of financial statement analysis. Investors, analysts, investment bankers, corporate managers, and others engage in financial statement analysis and valuation to determine a reliable appraisal of the value of shares of common equity or the value of whole firms. The questions they typically address include the following:

- What value do I think a share of common stock in a particular company is worth?
- Comparing my estimate of value to the current price in the market, should I buy, sell, or hold a particular firm's common shares?
- What price should I assign to the initial public offering of a firm's common shares?
- What is a reasonable price to accept (or ask) as a seller or pay (or bid) as a buyer for the shares of a firm in a corporate merger or acquisition?

Equity valuation models based on dividends, cash flows, and earnings have been the topic of many theoretical and empirical research studies in recent years. These studies provide many insights into valuation, but two very compelling general conclusions emerge and motivate the discussion and application of valuation models in this text: (1) share prices in the capital markets *generally* correlate closely with share value, but (2) share prices *do not always* equal share values, and temporary deviations of price from value occur. First, many empirical studies demonstrate that dividends, cash flows, and earnings-based valuation models generally provide significant explanatory power for share prices observed in the capital markets.[2] The results show that share value estimates determined from these valuation models exhibit high positive correlations with the stock prices observed in the capital markets. These correlations hold across different types of firms, during different periods of time, and across different countries. In the same vein, many empirical research studies also have shown that unexpected *changes* in earnings, dividends, and cash flows correlate closely with *changes* in stock prices.

Second, a number of empirical research studies show that valuation models also help identify when share prices in the capital markets temporarily deviate from fundamental share values. Research results show that dividends, cash flows, and earnings-based valuation models help identify when shares are temporarily overpriced or underpriced, representing potentially profitable investment opportunities. For example, Exhibit 11.1 is a graphic depiction of results from a study by Frankel and Lee (1998) in which they sorted their sample of firms each year into five portfolios based on quintiles of their estimate of value (V) to share price (P).[3] Their findings show striking differences in the average 36-month stock returns earned by their portfolios. The highest value-to-price quintile portfolio generated significantly greater average returns than the lowest value-to-price portfolio. These results and similar results from a number of related studies should be very encouraging for those interested in developing fundamental forecasting and valuation skills for investment purposes.

The six-step analysis and valuation framework that forms the structure of this book (Exhibit 1.1 in Chapter 1) is a logical sequence of steps for understanding the fundamentals of a business and for determining intelligent estimates of its value. First, we analyze the

[2] For examples, see Stephen Penman and Theodore Sougiannis, "A Comparison of Dividend, Cash Flow, and Earnings Approaches to Equity Valuation," *Contemporary Accounting Research* 15, no. 3 (Fall 1998), pp. 343–383, and Jennifer Francis, Per Olsson, and Dennis Oswald, "Comparing the Accuracy and Explainability of Dividend, Free Cash Flow, and Abnormal Earnings Equity Value Estimates," *Journal of Accounting Research* 38 (Spring 2000), pp. 45–70.

[3] Richard Frankel and Charles Lee, "Accounting Valuation, Market Expectation, and Cross-Sectional Stock Returns," *Journal of Accounting and Economics* 25, Issue 3 (1998), pp. 283–319.

EXHIBIT 11.1

Empirical Evidence on Portfolio Stock Returns Associated with Share Value Relative to Share Price (*V/P*)

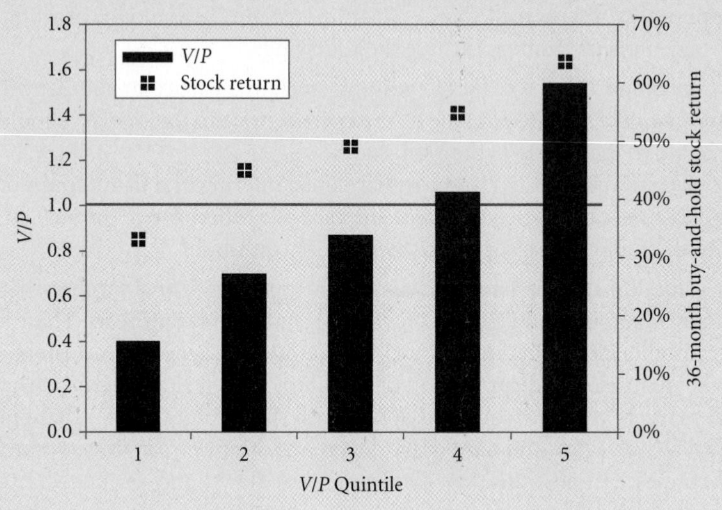

economics and competitive conditions of the industry. Second, we analyze the particular firm's strategy in light of the competitive dynamics of the industry. Third, we assess the quality of the firm's accounting and financial reporting. Fourth, we analyze the firm's profitability and risk with a set of financial ratios. Fifth, we use all of this information to project the firm's future financial statements. Finally, we derive from the projected financial statements our forecasts of future earnings, cash flows, and dividends as measures of projected future payoffs for the firm. We use these projected future payoffs as inputs to valuation models to determine the value of the firm. Reliable projections of future payoffs to the firm (the numerator in the general valuation model presented earlier) depend on unbiased and thorough forecasts of future income statements, balance sheets, and statements of cash flows, all of which depend on reliable projections of the firm's future operating, investing, and financing activities. Assessing an appropriate risk-adjusted discount rate (the denominator in the general valuation model) requires an assessment of the inherent risk in the set of expected future payoffs. Therefore, reliable estimates of firm value depend on unbiased estimates of expected future payoffs and an appropriate risk-adjusted discount rate, all of which depend on all six steps of the framework.

This chapter begins the discussion of the sixth and final step of the analytical framework of this text: valuation. The first portion of this chapter describes and demonstrates computing risk-adjusted expected rates of return on equity capital and weighted average costs of capital, which we use as discount rates in the valuation models. The latter portion of this chapter describes and applies the dividends-based valuation model. Throughout the chapter, we demonstrate these techniques using PepsiCo.

Looking further ahead, Chapter 12 presents and applies cash-flow-based valuation approaches. Chapter 13 describes and applies earnings-based valuation approaches. Chapters 11–13 discuss and illustrate the important issues that determine the conceptual and practical strengths and weaknesses of each approach. All three chapters illustrate the equivalence of these valuation approaches using the theoretical development of the models and applying these approaches to the projected dividends, cash flows, and earnings derived from the financial statements forecasts developed for PepsiCo in Chapter 10. Chapter 14 describes and applies market multiples such as price-earnings ratios and market-to-book ratios that analysts use in some instances to value firms.

EQUIVALENCE AMONG DIVIDENDS, CASH FLOWS, AND EARNINGS VALUATION

As noted earlier, equity valuation models based on dividends, cash flows, and earnings have been the topic of many theoretical and empirical research studies in recent years, which show that, in general, share value estimates determined from these models correlate closely with stock prices observed in the capital markets. However, the valuation models also help identify when stock prices deviate temporarily from share values. Therefore, it is no surprise that analysts, investors, and capital market participants commonly use dividends, cash flows, and earnings to estimate share values. When the analyst derives internally consistent forecasts of future earnings, cash flows, and dividends from a set of financial statement forecasts and uses the same discount rate to compute the present values of those expected future earnings, cash flows, and dividends, the valuation models yield identical estimates of value for a firm. That is, these three valuation models are complementary approaches to valuation that produce equivalent value estimates.

The primary difference between the dividends-, cash-flows-, and earnings-based approaches to valuation are differences in perspective. The dividends-based valuation approach focuses on wealth distribution to shareholders. Essentially, share value is determined by the present value of dividends the shareholder will receive. Cash-flow-based valuation takes an alternative perspective because the analyst forecasts and values the cash flows the firm will generate and use to pay dividends. The cash-flow-based valuation approach measures and values the *free cash flows* that are available for distribution to shareholders after cash is used for necessary investments in operating assets and required payments to debtholders. Free cash flows can be used instead of dividends as the expected future payoffs to the investor in the numerator of the general valuation model. Both approaches, if implemented with consistent assumptions, will lead to identical estimates of value. This equivalence occurs because over the life of the firm, the free cash flows into the firm will be equivalent to the cash flows paid out of the firm in dividends to shareholders.

The earnings-based valuation approach is another alternative valuation perspective, equivalent to both dividends-based and free-cash-flows-based valuation. The earnings-based valuation approach takes the perspective that earnings measures the capital that firms create (or destroy) for common shareholders each period that will ultimately be realized in cash flows and distributed as dividends to shareholders. Thus, the earnings-based valuation approach focuses on the firm's wealth creation for shareholders, the cash-flows-based approach focuses on dividend-paying ability, and the dividends approach focuses on wealth distribution to shareholders. Exhibit 11.2 provides a conceptual illustration of these three approaches to firm valuation.

Analysts who apply these different valuation approaches gain better insights about the value of a firm than analysts who rely on only one approach in all cases. Analysts understand valuation more deeply and thoroughly across a wider array of situations when they can triangulate valuation across the dividends, cash flows, and earnings valuation approaches.

All four valuation chapters (Chapters 11–14) emphasize that the objective of the valuation process is not a single point estimate of value per se; instead, the objective is to determine a reliable distribution of value estimates across the relevant ranges of critical forecast

EXHIBIT 11.2

Conceptual Illustration of Equivalent Approaches to Valuation Using Dividends, Cash Flows, and Earnings

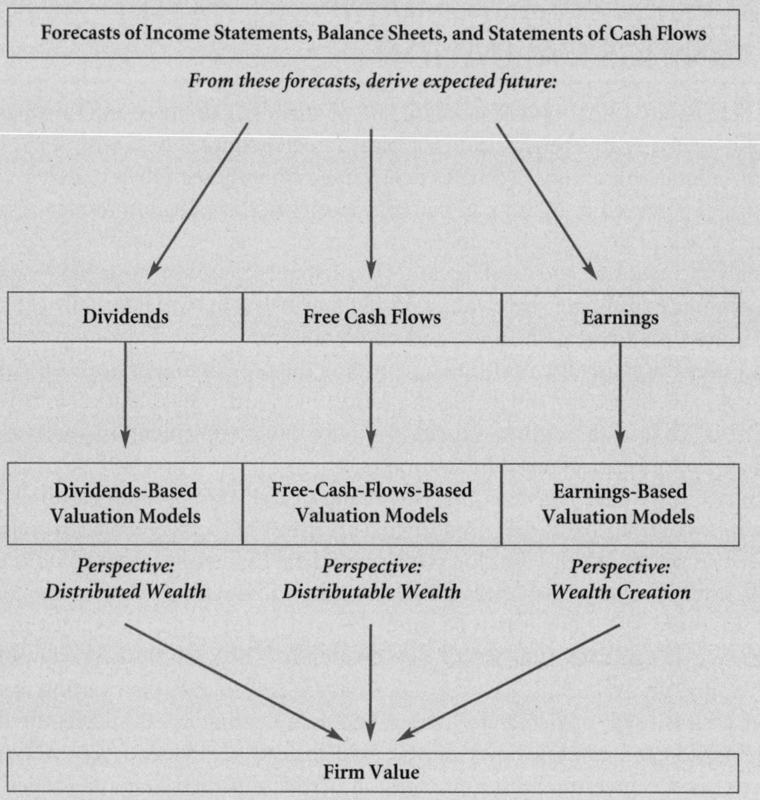

assumptions and valuation parameters. By estimating share value using cash flows, earnings, and dividends and by assessing the sensitivity of these value estimates across a distribution of relevant forecast assumptions and valuation parameters, the goal is to determine the most likely range of values for a share, which are then compared to the share's price in the capital market for an intelligent investment decision.

RISK-ADJUSTED EXPECTED RATES OF RETURN

We base all of the valuation approaches we describe and demonstrate in Chapters 11–14 on the general valuation model set forth at the beginning of this chapter, in which we determine firm value by discounting projected future payoffs to present value. Therefore, for all of the valuation approaches we need a discount rate to compute the present value of all projected future payoffs. To compensate for the time value of money and risk, the discount rate should equal the required rate of return that capital providers demand from the firm to induce them to commit capital. When the analyst computes the present value of payoffs (dividends, free cash flows, or earnings) to *common equity shareholders,* he or she should use a discount rate that reflects the risk-adjusted required rate of return on *common equity* capital.

The discount rate should be a forecast of the required rate of return on the investment and, therefore, should be conditional on the expected future riskiness of the firm and expected future interest rates over the period during which the payoffs will be generated. The historical discount rate of the firm may be a good indicator of the appropriate discount rate to apply to the firm in the future, but only if the following three conditions hold:

- The current risk of the firm is the same as the expected future risk of the firm.
- Expected future interest rates are likely to equal current interest rates.
- The existing capital structure of the firm (that is, the current mix of debt and equity financing) is the same as the expected future capital structure of the firm.

If one or more of these conditions does not hold, the analyst will need to project discount rates that appropriately capture the future risk and capital structure of the firm and future interest rates in the economy over the forecast horizon.

As a starting point to estimate expected rates of return on capital, analysts often compute the prevailing after-tax cost of each type of capital (debt, preferred, and common equity) invested in the firm. Existing costs of capital reflect the required rates of return for the firm's existing capital structure, and they are appropriate discount rates for valuing future payoffs for the firm only if the three preceding conditions hold.

Developing discount rates using costs of capital assumes that the capital markets price capital to reflect the risk-free time value of money plus a premium for risk. The following sections describe and demonstrate techniques to estimate the firm's cost of equity, debt, and preferred stock capital. After these descriptions, the chapter describes and illustrates how to compute a weighted average cost of capital for the firm.

Cost of Common Equity Capital

Analysts commonly estimate the cost of equity capital using the CAPM (capital asset pricing model). The CAPM assumes that the market comprises risk-averse investors holding diversified portfolios of assets. The CAPM assumes that for a given level of expected return, risk-averse investors will seek to bear as little risk as possible and will mitigate risk by diversifying across the types of assets they hold in a portfolio. Therefore, the CAPM hypothesizes that in equilibrium, investors should expect to earn a rate of return on a firm's common equity capital that equals the rate of return the market requires to hold that firm's stock in a diversified portfolio of assets. In theory, the market comprises risk-averse investors who demand a rate of return that (1) compensates them for forgoing the consumption of capital (the time value of money) and (2) compensates them with a risk premium for bearing systematic, marketwide risk that cannot be diversified. Systematic risk arises from economy-wide factors (such as economic growth or recession, unemployment, unexpected inflation, unexpected changes in prices for natural resources such as oil and gas, unexpected changes in exchange rates, and population growth) that affect all firms to varying degrees and therefore cannot be fully diversified. Therefore, the market's required rate of return on equity capital is a function of prevailing risk-free rates of interest in the economy plus a risk premium for bearing risk, all conditional on the level of nondiversifiable risk inherent in the firm's common stock.

Note that the CAPM views nonsystematic risk as factors that are diversifiable by the investor holding a broad portfolio of stocks. Nonsystematic risk factors are industry- and firm-specific, including factors such as the level of competition in an industry, the product portfolio of a particular firm, the sustainability of the firm's strategy, and the firm's ability to generate revenue growth and control expenses. A competitive equilibrium capital market, according to CAPM, does not expect a return for a firm's nonsystematic risk because such risk can be diversified away in a portfolio of stocks.

Analysts measure nondiversifiable or systematic risk as the degree of covariation between a firm's stock returns and a marketwide index of stock returns. Analysts commonly measure systematic risk using the firm's *market beta,* which is estimated as the slope coefficient from regressing the firm's stock returns on an index of returns reflecting a marketwide portfolio of stocks over a relevant period of time.[4] If a firm's market beta from such a regression is equal to 1, it indicates that, on average, the firm's stock returns covary identically with returns to a marketwide portfolio, indicating that the firm has the same degree of systematic risk as the market as a whole. If a firm's market beta is greater than 1, the firm has a greater degree of systematic risk than the market as a whole, whereas a firm with a market beta less than 1 has less systematic risk than the market as a whole.

Exhibit 11.3 reports industry median market betas for a sample of 42 industries over the years 1999–2007. These data depict wide variation in systematic risk across industries during

EXHIBIT 11.3

Relation between Industry and Systematic Risk over 1999–2007

Industry	**Median Beta during 1999–2007**
Forestry	0.17
Utilities	0.32
Depository Institutions	0.39
Tobacco	0.39
Real Estate	0.43
Food Processors	0.47
Grocery Stores	0.50
Insurers	0.55
Restaurants	0.61
Metal Products	0.64
Petroleum Refining	0.65
Printing and Publishing	0.66
Wholesalers—Nondurables	0.66
Personal Services	0.68
Textiles	0.69
Rubber and Plastics	0.70
Hotels	0.74
Health Services	0.75
Amusements and Recreation	0.76
Non-Depository Financial Institutions	0.78
Metal Mining	0.80
Paper	0.81

[4] Researchers and analysts have developed a variety of approaches to estimate market betas. For example, one common approach estimates a firm's market beta by regressing the firm's monthly stock returns on a marketwide index of returns (such as the S&P 500 index) over the last 60 months.

EXHIBIT 11.3 (Continued)

Industry	Median Beta during 1999–2007
Miscellaneous Manufacturing	0.85
Oil and Gas Extraction	0.87
Transportation Equipment	0.89
Retailers—General Merchandise	0.92
Engineering Management	0.95
Lumber	0.96
Motion Pictures	0.97
Wholesalers—Durables	0.97
Miscellaneous Retail	1.01
Instruments and Related Products	1.06
Retailing—Apparel	1.08
Chemicals	1.10
Transportation by Air	1.11
Primary Metals	1.18
Retailing—Home Furniture, Furnishings, and Equipment	1.21
Security and Commodity Brokers	1.24
Industrial and Commercial Machinery and Computer Equipment	1.24
Communications	1.30
Business Services	1.51
Electronic and Electrical Equipment	1.64

this nine-year period, with industry median market betas ranging from a low of 0.17 (Forestry) to a high of 1.64 (Electronic and Electrical Equipment). Various financial reference sources and websites regularly publish market betas for common equity in publicly traded firms. It is not uncommon to find considerable variation in market betas among the various sources. This occurs in part because of differences in the period and methodology used to estimate betas.[5]

The CAPM projects the expected return on common equity capital for Firm j as follows:

$$E[R_{Ej}] = E[R_F] + ß_j \times \{E[R_M] - E[R_F]\}$$

where E denotes that the related variable is an expectation; R_{Ej} denotes required return on common equity in firm j; R_F denotes the risk-free rate of return; $ß_j$ denotes the market beta

[5] Eugene Fama and Kenneth French developed an empirical model that explains realized stock returns using three factors they found to be correlated with returns during their study period. Their model and results indicate that during their sample period (1963–1990), firms' stock returns were related to firms' market betas, market capitalizations (size), and market-to-book ratios [see Eugene F. Fama and Kenneth R. French, "The Cross Section of Expected Stock Returns," *Journal of Finance* (June 1992), pp. 427–465]. Data to implement their model can be obtained from French's website (http://mba.tuck.dartmouth.edu/pages/faculty/ken.french/data_library.html). Although the model deserves and has received a great deal of attention in academics and practice, more research is necessary to determine the theoretical basis for the model and the risk factors and risk premia that constitute the model. In addition, more research is needed to assess the empirical applicability of the model as a predictor of expected stock returns in periods following their sample period.

for firm j; and R_M denotes the required return on a diversified, marketwide portfolio of stocks (such as the S&P 500). According to the CAPM, a common equity security with no systematic risk (that is, a stock with $\beta_j = 0$) should be expected to earn a return equal to the expected rate of return on risk-free securities. Of course, most equity securities are not risk-free. An equity security with systematic risk equal to the average amount of systematic risk of all equity securities in the market has a market beta equal to 1. The subtraction term in brackets in the preceding equation represents the average market risk premium, which is equal to the amount of return above the risk-free rate that equity investors in the capital markets require for bearing the average amount of systematic risk in the market as a whole. Therefore, the cost of common equity capital for a firm with an average level of systematic risk should be equal to the required return on the market portfolio. A firm with a market beta greater than 1 has higher than average systematic risk and faces a higher cost of equity capital because the capital markets expect the firm to yield a commensurately higher return to compensate investors for bearing greater risk. A firm with a market beta less than 1 faces a lower cost of equity capital because the capital markets expect the firm to yield a commensurately lower return to investors for bearing less risk. Exhibit 11.4 depicts the CAPM graphically.

The analyst should use the market return on securities with zero systematic risk as the risk-free interest rate in the CAPM. Returns on such systematic risk-free securities (for example, U. S. Treasury securities) should exhibit no correlation with returns on a diversified marketwide portfolio of stocks. Given that equity securities have indefinitely long lives, it might seem appropriate to use the yield on long-term U.S. Treasury securities as a proxy for a risk-free rate. However, yields on long-term U.S. government securities tend to exhibit greater sensitivity to changes in inflation and interest rates; therefore, they have a greater degree of systematic risk (although the systematic risk is still quite low) compared to short-term U.S. government securities. Common practice uses the yield on short- or intermediate-term U.S. government securities (for example, yields on three-, five-, or ten-year U.S. Treasury securities) as the risk-free rate. Historically, these yields have averaged around 6 percent over the long run, although in recent years, they have averaged roughly 3–4 percent.

The average realized rate of return on the market portfolio depends on the period studied. Historically, the realized rate of return on the market portfolio has varied between 9 and 13 percent. Thus, the excess return of the market portfolio over the risk-free rate has

EXHIBIT 11.4

Relation between Cost of Equity Capital and Systematic Risk

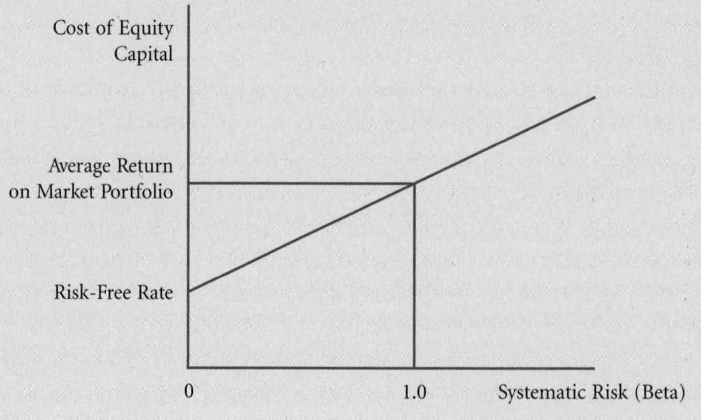

varied between 3 and 7 percent. Some financial economists argue that the market risk premium varies over time with investors' demand for incremental consumption. The economists argue that, on the margin, when the economy is healthy and growing (with low unemployment and high consumer confidence), investors' demand for additional consumption is relatively low; therefore, investors demand relatively low rates of return for postponing incremental consumption and bearing risk. Thus, risk premia tend to be lower (perhaps 3–4 percent) when economic conditions are strong. Conversely, when the economy is weak and investors face a higher degree of uncertainty, investors' demand for additional consumption is relatively high; therefore, they demand relatively high rates of return for postponing consumption and bearing risk. Thus, risk premia tend to be higher (perhaps 6–7 percent) when economic conditions are weak. The theories asserting that risk premia are time-varying (and vary inversely with investors' marginal demand for consumption) seem intuitive and appear to explain risk premia observed in the capital markets quite well, but they require more empirical research.

Example 1: Using the CAPM to Compute Expected Rates of Return

Suppose Firm A has a market beta of 0.60 and Firm B has a market beta of 1.40. Assume that the prevailing yields on three- to five-year U.S. Treasury bonds are roughly 4.0 percent and that the capital markets require a 5.0 percent risk premium for bearing an average amount of systematic risk. Applying the CAPM, we would compute the following expected rates of return for Firm A and Firm B:

$$\text{Firm A: } E[R_A] = 4.0 + (0.60 \times 5.0) = 7.0$$
$$\text{Firm B: } E[R_B] = 4.0 + (1.40 \times 5.0) = 11.0$$

Thus, the CAPM implies that investors require a 7.0 percent rate of return on capital invested in the equity of Firm A and an 11.0 percent rate of return on capital invested in the equity of Firm B. Firm B faces a higher cost of equity capital than Firm A because Firm B has a higher degree of systematic risk. In determining the share values of Firm A and Firm B, investors should discount to present value the expected future payoffs using a 7.0 percent discount rate for Firm A and an 11.0 percent discount rate for Firm B. If investors expect Firm A and Firm B to generate equivalent payoffs (although Firm B's payoffs will be riskier), investors will assign a lower value to (and pay a lower price for) the common shares of Firm B than Firm A. The difference between the value of Firm B's shares and those of Firm A reflects the additional compensation that shareholders demand for holding the riskier Firm B shares relative to shares of Firm A. Shareholders will realize this compensation in the form of the equivalent payoffs, for which shareholders in Firm B paid a lower price than did shareholders in Firm A.

Computing the Required Rate of Return on Equity Capital for PepsiCo

At the end of 2008, different sources provided different estimates of market beta for PepsiCo common stock, ranging from 0.50 to roughly 1.00. Historically, PepsiCo's market beta has varied around 0.75 over time, so we will assume that PepsiCo common stock has a market beta of roughly 0.75 as of the end of 2008. At that time, U.S. Treasury bills with ten years to maturity traded with a yield of just below 4.0 percent, which we use as the risk-free rate. Additionally, economic conditions were in recession, stock market indexes had experienced substantial declines, and investors were more risk-averse than normal; so we will assume investors demanded a 6.0 percent market risk premium. Therefore, the CAPM indicates that PepsiCo has a cost of common equity capital of 8.50 percent [$= 4.0 + (0.75 \times 6.0)$]. At the end of 2008, PepsiCo had 1,553 million shares outstanding and a share price of \$54.77, for a total market capital of common equity of \$85,058 million.

Adjusting Market Equity Beta to Reflect a New Capital Structure

Recall from the discussion in Chapter 5 that market beta reflects operating leverage, financial leverage, variability of sales and earnings, and other firm characteristics. In some settings, such as a leveraged buyout, firms plan to make significant changes in the financial capital structure. The market beta computed using historical market price data reflects the firm's existing capital structure. The analyst can project what market beta is likely to be after the firm changes the capital structure. The analyst can "unlever" the current market beta by adjusting it to remove the effects of leverage and then "relever" it by adjusting it to reflect leverage under the new capital structure. The following formula estimates an unlevered market beta (sometimes referred to as an *asset beta*):

$$\text{Current Levered Market Beta} = \text{Unlevered Market Beta} \times$$
$$\left[1 + (1 - \text{Income Tax Rate}) \times \left(\frac{\text{Current Market Value of Debt}}{\text{Current Market Value of Equity}}\right)\right]$$

The intuition behind this formula is that current market beta reflects two components: (1) the systematic risk of the operations and assets of the firm (the unlevered beta), compounded by (2) the financial leverage of the firm (the debt-equity ratio), net of the tax benefit from using leverage (that is, tax savings from interest expense deductions.) Estimating the new levered beta requires two steps. The first step is to solve for the unlevered beta by rearranging the preceding equation to divide the current levered market beta by the term in square brackets on the right-hand side of the equation, as follows:

$$\text{Unlevered Market Beta} = \text{Current Levered Market Beta}/[1 + (1 - \text{Income Tax Rate}) \times (\text{Current Market Value of Debt}/\text{Current Market Value of Equity})]$$

The second step is to project the new levered market beta by multiplying the unlevered beta by the term in square brackets on the right-hand side of the equation after substituting the projected new ratio of the market value of debt to the market value of equity in place of the current ratio of the market value of debt to the market value of equity, as follows:[6]

$$\text{New Levered Market Beta} = \text{Unlevered Market Beta} \times [1 + (1 - \text{Income Tax Rate}) \times (\text{New Market Value of Debt}/\text{New Market Value of Equity})]$$

Example 2: The Effects of Leverage on Beta and Expected Rates of Return

Suppose a firm has a market beta of 0.9, is subject to an income tax rate of 35 percent, and has a market value of debt to market value of equity ratio of 60 percent. If the risk-free rate is 6 percent and the market risk premium is 7 percent, then according to the CAPM, the

[6] Note that the debt-to-equity ratios used in these computations are based on *market* values of debt and shareholders' equity. These market-value-based ratios will likely differ from the debt to shareholders' equity ratios discussed in Chapter 5 for assessing long-term solvency risk because the ratios in Chapter 5 are based on *book* values of debt and shareholders' equity. As more firms choose the fair value option for recognizing outstanding debt, as discussed in Chapter 6, book and fair values for debt will begin to converge.

market expects this firm to generate equity returns of 12.3 percent $[= 6.0 + (0.9 \times 7.0)]$. The firm intends to adopt a new capital structure that will increase the debt-to-equity ratio to 140 percent. To project the firm's levered beta under the new capital structure, the first step is to solve for the unlevered beta, denoted X, as follows:

$$0.9 = X \times [1 + (1 - 0.35) \times (0.60/1.00)]$$
$$X = 0.9/[1 + (1 - 0.35) \times (0.60/1.00)]$$
$$X = 0.65$$

Because financial leverage is positively related to market beta, removing the effect of financial leverage reduces market beta. The unlevered beta should reflect the effects of the firm's operating risk, sales volatility, and other operating factors, but not risk related to financial leverage. The new market beta is projected to reflect the new debt-to-equity ratio as follows:

$$Y = 0.65 \times [1 + (1 - 0.35) \times (1.40/1.00)] = 1.24$$

The new capital structure will increase the leverage and therefore the systematic risk of the firm. According to the CAPM, this firm will face an equity cost of capital of 14.68 percent $[= 6.0 + (1.24 \times 7.0)]$ under the new capital structure.

Evaluating the Use of the CAPM to Measure the Cost of Equity Capital

The use of the CAPM to calculate the cost of equity capital has been subject to various criticisms, as follows:

- Market betas for a firm should vary over time as the systematic risk of the firm changes; however, market beta estimates are quite sensitive to the time period and methodology used in their computation.
- In theory, the CAPM measures required returns based on the stock's risk relative to a diversified portfolio of assets across the economy, but a return index for a diversified portfolio of assets that spans the entire economy does not exist. Measuring a stock's systematic risk relative to a stock market return index such as the S&P 500 Index fails to consider covariation between the stock's returns and returns on assets outside the stock market, including other financial investments (for example, U.S. government and corporate debt securities and privately held equity), real estate, and human capital.
- The market risk premium is not stable over time and is likewise sensitive to the time period used in its calculation. Considerable uncertainty surrounds the appropriate adjustment for the market risk premium. It is not clear whether the appropriate adjustment should be on the order of 3 percent, 7 percent, or somewhere in between.[7] As noted earlier, some financial economists now argue that the risk premium is lower in periods of economic health and growth and higher in periods of economic weakness and uncertainty, which seems plausible and consistent with observable variation in marketwide stock returns over time. However, this approach requires more research to develop practical models for measuring firm-specific time-varying risk premia.

[7] See, for example, James Claus and Jacob Thomas, "Equity Premia as Low as Three Percent? Empirical Evidence from Analysts' Earnings Forecasts for Domestic and International Stock Markets," *Journal of Finance* 56 (October 2001), pp. 1629–1666. Also see Peter Easton, Gary Taylor, Pervin Shroff, and Theodore Sougiannis, "Using Forecasts of Earnings to Simultaneously Estimate Growth and the Rate of Return on Equity Investment," *Journal of Accounting Research* 40 (June 2000), pp. 657–676.

In light of these criticisms of the CAPM and considering the crucial role of the risk-adjusted discount rate for common equity valuation, it is important to analyze the sensitivity of share value estimates across different discount rates for common equity. For example, the analyst should estimate values for a share of common equity in a particular firm across a relevant range of discount rates for common equity by varying the market risk premium from 3 to 7 percent.

Chapter 14 describes techniques to reverse-engineer the implicit expected rate of return on common equity securities. Chapter 14 also describes an approach to estimate the implicit discount in share price for risk by using risk-free discount rates. These techniques do not require the assumption of an asset pricing model such as the CAPM.

Cost of Debt Capital

The analyst computes the after-tax cost of each component of debt capital, including short-term and long-term notes payable, mortgages, bonds, and capital lease obligations, as the yield to maturity on each type of debt times one minus the statutory tax rate applicable to income tax deductions for interest. The yield to maturity is the rate that discounts the contractual cash flows on the debt to the debt's current fair value. If the fair value of the debt is equal to face value (for example, a \$1,000 debenture trades on an exchange for \$1,000), the yield to maturity equals the stated interest rate on the debt. If the fair value of the debt exceeds the face value of the debt, yield to maturity is lower than the stated rate. This can occur after interest rates fall; previously issued fixed-rate debt will have a stated rate that exceeds current market yields for debt with comparable credit quality and terms. On the other hand, after interest rates rise, existing fixed-rate debt may have a stated rate that is lower than prevailing market rates for comparable debt, in which case the debt will have a fair value that is less than face value and the yield to maturity will be greater than the stated rate.

Firms disclose in notes to their financial statements the stated interest rates on their existing interest-bearing debt capital. Firms also disclose in notes the estimated fair values of their interest-bearing debt, which should reflect the present value of the debt using prevailing market yields to maturity on the debt. Together, these disclosures allow the analyst to estimate prevailing market yields to maturity on the firm's outstanding debt.

In computing costs of debt capital, analysts typically exclude operating liability accounts (such as accounts payable, accrued expenses, deferred income tax liability, and retirement benefit obligations). Instead, analysts typically treat these items as part of the firm's operating activities rather than as part of the firm's financial capital structure.

A capitalized lease obligation will generally have an implicit after-tax cost of capital equal to the after-tax yield to maturity on collateralized borrowing with equivalent risk and maturity. Firms recognize capital lease obligations on the balance sheet as financial liabilities; however, as described in Chapter 6, firms also may have significant off-balance-sheet commitments to make future payments under operating leases. If the firm has significant commitments under operating leases, the analyst may believe it necessary to include them in the computation of the cost of debt capital. If the analyst elects to adjust the firm's balance sheet to capitalize operating lease commitments as debt (as illustrated in Chapter 6), the analyst should make three sets of adjustments to include the effects of operating leases on the total cost of debt capital. First, the analyst should include the present value of operating lease commitments in calculating the fair value of various components of outstanding debt. Second, the analyst should include the discount rate used to compute the present value of the operating lease commitments as the after-tax interest rate on operating leases in the computation of the cost of debt capital. The lessor bears more risk in an operating lease than in a capital lease, so the cost of capital represented by operating leases is likely to be higher than for capital leases. Third, if the analyst treats operating leases as part of debt financing, the cash outflow for rent payments under operating leases should be reclassified as interest and principal payments of debt when computing free cash flows. Chapter 6 discusses techniques for the required adjustments to convert operating leases to capital leases, as well as techniques to adjust for other less common forms of off-balance-sheet financing, including contingent liabilities for receivables sold with recourse and product financing arrangements.

The income tax rate used to compute the tax effects of interest should be the firm's tax rate applicable to interest expense deductions. For most firms, the tax rate applicable to interest expense deductions is the statutory federal tax rate, which is 35 percent in the United States in 2009. However, state and foreign taxes or other special tax factors may increase or decrease the combined statutory tax rate depending on where the firm raises its debt capital. Firms generally do not separately disclose statutory state or foreign tax rates, but do summarize the effect of these taxes in the income tax reconciliation found in the income tax note. To achieve greater precision, the analyst could approximate the combined statutory tax rate applicable to interest expense deductions using the effective tax rate disclosed in the income tax footnote.

Cost of Preferred Equity Capital

The cost of preferred stock capital depends on the preference conditions. Preferred stock that has preference over common shares with respect to dividends and priority in liquidation generally sells near its par value. Therefore, its cost of capital is the dividend rate on the preferred stock. Depending on the attributes of the preferred stock, dividends on preferred stock may give rise to a tax deduction, in which case the after-tax cost of capital will be lower than the pretax cost. Preferred stock that is convertible into common stock has both preferred and common equity attributes. Its cost is a blending of the cost of nonconvertible preferred stock and common equity.

Computing the Weighted Average Cost of Capital

In some circumstances, the analyst may want to determine the present value of payoffs to investment in all of the assets of a firm, not just the equity capital of the firm. Such circumstances might arise, for example, if the analyst is considering acquiring all of the assets of a firm or if the analyst is considering acquiring control of a firm by acquiring all of the financial claims (common equity shares, preferred shares, and debt) on the assets of a firm. If the analyst needs to determine the present value of the payoffs from investing in the total assets of the firm, or, equivalently, acquiring all of the debt, preferred, and common equity claims on the firm, the analyst should use a discount rate that reflects the weighted average required rate of return that encompasses the debt, preferred, and common equity capital used to finance the net operating assets of the firm.

A formula for the weighted average cost of capital (denoted as R_A) is given here:

$$R_A = [w_D \times R_D \times (1 - tax\ rate)] + [w_P \times R_P] + [w_E \times R_E]$$

In this formula, w denotes the weight on each type of capital (D denotes debt capital, P denotes preferred stock capital, and E denotes common equity capital), R denotes the cost of each type of capital, and *tax rate* denotes the tax rate applicable to debt capital costs. The weights used to compute the weighted average cost of capital should be the market values of each type of capital in proportion to the total market value of the financial capital structure of the firm (that is, $w_D + w_P + w_E = 1.0$). On the right-hand side of the equation, the first term in brackets measures the weighted after-tax cost of debt capital, the second term measures the weighted cost of preferred stock capital, and the third term measures the weighted cost of common equity capital.

Example 3: Computing the Weighted Average Cost of Capital

A firm has the following capital structure on its balance sheet:

	Book Value
Long-term bonds, 10 percent annual coupon, issued at par	$20,000,000
Preferred stock, 4 percent dividend, issued at par	5,000,000
Common equity	25,000,000
Total	$50,000,000

The market values of the securities are as follows: bonds, $22,000,000; preferred equity, $5,000,000; common equity, $33,000,000. The market has priced the bonds to yield 8.0 percent. (That is, the interest rate that discounts the annuity of contractual $2,000,000 interest payments and the $20,000,000 maturity value to the bonds' $22,000,000 fair value is 8 percent.) The firm's income tax rate is 35 percent, so the after-tax cost of debt is 5.2 percent [= (1 − 0.35) × 8.0 percent]. Note that this rate is less than the coupon rate of 10 percent and that the market value of the debt is greater than its par value. Use of coupon rates and book values in this case would result in a higher cost of debt capital (6.5 percent = 0.65 × 10.0 percent) but a smaller weight for debt in the weighted average. Assuming that the dividend on the preferred stock is not tax deductible, its cost is the dividend rate of 4.0 percent because it is selling for par value. The equity capital has a market beta of 0.9. Assuming a risk-free interest rate of 6.0 percent and a market premium of 7.0 percent, the cost of equity capital is 12.3 percent [= 6.0 percent + (0.9 × 7.0 percent)]. The calculation of the weighted average cost of capital is as follows:

Security	Market Value	Weight	After-Tax Cost	Weighted Average
Long-Term Debt	$22,000,000	37%	5.2%	1.92%
Preferred Equity	5,000,000	8%	4.0%	0.32%
Common Equity	33,000,000	55%	12.3%	6.77%
Total	$60,000,000	100%		9.01%

Over time, the weights for debt, preferred, and equity capital may change if the analyst expects the firm's capital structure to change over the forecast horizon. In addition, the analyst may expect yields to maturity on debt capital and required rates of return on equity capital to change as interest rates in the economy change, the risk of the firm changes, or the firm's tax status changes. Thus, to capture these changes in the weighted average cost of capital, the analyst may need to project a weighted average cost of capital for each period over the forecast horizon.

To determine the appropriate weights to use in the weighted average cost of capital, the analyst must determine the market values of the debt, preferred, and common equity capital. Market values for debt will be observable only for firms that have issued publicly traded debt; however, U.S. GAAP and IFRS require firms to disclose the fair value of their outstanding debt capital in notes to the financial statements each year. Fair value disclosures may not be available, however, if the firm is privately owned, the firm is not required to follow U.S. GAAP or IFRS, or the firm is a division and does not publish its own financial statements. If market values are not observable and fair values for the firm's debt are not disclosed, the analyst can (1) estimate the fair value of the firm's debt if sufficient data are available about the firm's credit quality and the maturity and terms of the debt or (2) rely on the book value of debt. The book value of debt can be a reliable estimate of fair value if the debt is recently issued, if the debt bears a variable rate of interest, or if the debt bears a fixed rate of interest but interest rates and the firm's credit quality have been stable since the debt was issued. Because the yield to maturity on debt is inversely related to its market value, analysts sometimes approximate the cost of debt by simply using the coupon rate and the book value of debt when computing the weighted average cost of capital, particularly when interest rates are stable and the market value of debt is likely to be close to book value.

If available, market prices for equity securities provide the amounts for determining the market value of equity. Market prices for equity may not be available, however, if the firm is privately owned or if it is a division of a firm. The analyst can then use the book value of equity as a starting point to compute the weight of equity in the capital structure for purposes of estimating a weighted average cost of capital.

The preceding discussion reveals circular reasoning in computing weighted average costs of capital for valuation purposes. Analysts use the market values of debt and equity to compute the weighted average cost of capital, which is used in turn to compute the value of the debt and equity in the firm. This is circular reasoning because the analyst needs to know the market values to determine the weights but needs to know the weights to determine the weighted average cost of capital to use in estimating firm value. In practice, analysts can use two approaches to avoid this circularity. One approach assumes that the firm will maintain a target debt-to-equity structure in the future based on benchmarks such as the firm's past debt-to-equity ratios, the firm's stated strategy with respect to financial leverage, or industry averages. The other approach computes iteratively the weighted average cost of capital and the value of debt and equity capital until the weights and the values converge. Example 4 illustrates this iterative approach.

Example 4: Computing the Weighted Average Cost of Capital Iteratively

Suppose that someone wants to compute the weighted average cost of capital and the market value of equity for a firm for which no market or fair value data are available. Also suppose that the firm has outstanding debt with a book value of $40 million. The firm recently issued this debt, and it carries a stated rate of 8.0 percent; so the analyst can assume that this is a reliable measure of the cost of debt capital. The firm faces a 35 percent tax rate. The book value of equity is $60 million. Similar firms in the same industry with comparable risks have a market beta of 1.2. Using the same risk-free rate and market risk premium as in Example 3, the cost of equity capital is 14.4 percent [= 6.0 percent + (1.2 × 7.0 percent)]. The first estimate of the weighted average cost of capital is as follows:

Security	Amount	Weight	After-Tax Cost	Weighted Average
Debt	$ 40,000,000	40%	5.2%	2.08%
Common Equity	60,000,000	60%	14.4%	8.64%
Total	$100,000,000	100%		10.72%

After using the 10.72 percent weighted average cost of capital to discount the free cash flows to present value, the analyst determines that the firm's equity value is roughly

$120 million (calculations not shown). Therefore, the values and weights used to compute the weighted average cost of capital are inconsistent with value estimates for equity. The first-iteration estimates placed too much weight on debt and too little weight on equity. The analyst should use the revised estimate of the value of equity to recompute the weighted average cost of capital and then recompute the value of the firm. Using the revised estimates produces a weighted average cost of capital estimate as follows:

Security	Amount	Weight	After-Tax Cost	Weighted Average
Debt	$ 40,000,000	25%	5.2%	1.30%
Common Equity	120,000,000	75%	14.4%	10.80%
Total	$160,000,000	100%		12.10%

The analyst should then use the revised estimate of the weighted average cost of capital of 12.10 percent to recompute the value of equity once again and then iterate this process until the values of debt and equity converge with the weights of debt and equity.

Computing the Weighted Average Cost of Capital for PepsiCo

PepsiCo's balance sheet at the end of 2008 shows interest-bearing debt from short-term obligations and long-term debt obligations totaling $8,227 million (= $369 + $7,858, as reported in Appendix A). Recall that Chapter 10 used information disclosed in Note 9, "Debt Obligations and Commitments" (Appendix A), to assess stated interest rates on PepsiCo's interest-bearing debt. In 2008, PepsiCo's outstanding debt carries a weighted average interest rate of approximately 5.8 percent. In Note 10, "Financial Instruments" (Appendix A), PepsiCo discloses that the fair value of outstanding debt obligations at the end of 2008 is $8,800 million. Thus, PepsiCo has experienced an unrealized (and unrecognized) loss of $573 million (= $8,227 million − $8,800 million) on its debt capital. This unrealized loss is surprising because more than half of PepsiCo's outstanding debt obligations were newly issued in 2008 at prevailing market rates. The unrealized loss implies that the firm's outstanding debt carries stated rates of interest that now exceed prevailing market yields, which at the end of 2008 are at relatively low levels given the recession in the U.S. economy. Based on the fact that most of PepsiCo's outstanding debt obligations were recently issued in 2008 and the expectation that prevailing yields to maturity are temporarily low, Chapter 10 projected that PepsiCo's cost of debt capital will continue to approximate 5.8 percent in Year +1 and beyond. We use the current book value (as a proxy for market value) of PepsiCo's debt for weighting purposes. In Note 5, "Income Taxes" (Appendix A), PepsiCo discloses that the combined average federal, state, and foreign tax rate is approximately 26.8 percent in 2008. Chapter 10 projected that PepsiCo will continue to face average tax rates of roughly 26.8 percent in Year +1 and beyond. Therefore, we will assume the tax rate applicable to PepsiCo's interest expense deductions will be the effective 26.8 percent rate rather than the statutory federal rate of 35 percent. Long-run projections imply that PepsiCo faces an after-tax cost of debt capital of 4.25 percent [$4.25 = 5.8 \times (1 - 0.268)$].

PepsiCo also has a net *negative* balance of $97 million in preferred stock on the 2008 balance sheet. Chapter 10 projected that PepsiCo will retire the remaining outstanding preferred stock during Year +1 and that that PepsiCo will not issue any additional preferred stock capital in future years. Therefore, we include no preferred stock in the computation of PepsiCo's weighted average cost of capital.

Recall that earlier in this chapter we used the CAPM to determine that PepsiCo faces an 8.50 percent cost of equity capital. We also computed that at the end of 2008, PepsiCo had

1,553 million shares outstanding and a share price of $54.77, for a total market capital of common equity of $85,058 million.

Bringing these costs of debt and equity capital together, we compute PepsiCo's weighted average cost of capital to be 8.12 percent as follows:

Capital	Value Basis	Amount	Weight	After-Tax Cost of Capital	Weighted-Average Component
Debt	Book	$ 8,227	8.82%	4.25%	0.37%
Common	Market	85,058	91.18%	8.50%	7.75%
Total		$93,285	100.00%		8.12%

This is just an initial estimate of PepsiCo's weighted average cost of capital. As described earlier, the weighted average cost of capital must be computed iteratively until the weights used are consistent with the present values of debt and equity capital.

RATIONALE FOR DIVIDENDS-BASED VALUATION

In theory, the value of a share of common equity is the present value of the expected future dividends the shareholder will receive.[8] Dividends are the most fundamental value-relevant measure of expected future payoffs to use to value shares because they represent the distribution of wealth from the firm to the shareholders. The equity shareholder invests cash to purchase the share and then receives cash in the form of dividends as the payoffs from holding the share, including the final "liquidating" dividend when the investor sells the share. In dividends-based valuation, we define *dividends* broadly to include *all* cash flows between the firm and the common equity shareholders. Therefore, in valuation, "dividends" encompass all cash flows from the firm to shareholders through periodic dividend payments, stock buybacks, and the liquidating dividend, as well as cash flows from the shareholders to the firm when the firm issues shares (in a sense, *negative* dividends).

The rationale for using expected dividends in valuation is twofold:

1. Cash is the primary medium of exchange for consumption, which is the ultimate source of value. When individuals and firms invest in an economic resource, they forgo current consumption in favor of future consumption. Cash is the medium of exchange that will permit them to consume various goods and services in the future. An investment has value because of its ability to provide future cash flows. Dividends measure the cash that investors ultimately receive from investing in an equity share.
2. Dividends are paid in cash, and cash serves as a measurable common denominator for comparing the future benefits of alternative investment opportunities. One might compare investment opportunities involving the holding of a bond, a stock, or an office building, but comparing these alternatives requires a common measuring unit of their future benefits. The future cash flows derived from their future services serve such a function.

As a practical matter, however, quarterly or annual dividend payment amounts are arbitrary, established by a dividend policy set by the firm's managers and board of directors. Periodic dividend payments do not vary closely with firm performance from one period to the next. Some firms do not pay any regular periodic dividends, particularly young, high-growth firms. For most firms, the final liquidating dividend plays an important role,

[8] John Burr Williams, *The Theory of Investment and Value* (Cambridge, Mass.: Harvard University Press), 1938.

usually representing a large proportion of firm value in a dividends-based valuation. The final liquidating dividend arises when the firm liquidates its assets and returns all of the capital to shareholders, when all of the outstanding shares of the firm are acquired by another firm in a merger or an acquisition transaction, or when shareholders elect to liquidate their investment by selling shares. Therefore, to value a firm's shares using dividends, one must forecast dividends over the life of the firm (or the expected length of time the share will be held), including the final liquidating dividend (that is, the future price at which shares will be retired, acquired, or sold). Thus, the analyst faces the challenge of needing to forecast the value of shares in the future at the time of the liquidating dividend in order to value the shares today.

Dividends-Based Valuation Concepts

This section describes and illustrates key concepts in dividends-based valuation, first presenting simple examples involving a single project and then confronting conceptual measurement issues regarding dividends to the investor versus cash flows to the firm and nominal versus real dividends. Later in the chapter, we illustrate this approach with a more complex and realistic example involving the valuation of PepsiCo using dividends derived from the projected financial statements developed in Chapter 10.

Dividends Valuation for a Single-Asset Firm

For the following examples, make these assumptions:

- The firm consists of a single asset that will generate pretax net cash flows of $2 million per year forever.
- The income tax rate is 40 percent.
- After making debt service payments and paying taxes, the firm pays dividends to distribute any remaining cash flows to the equity shareholders each year.

Example 5: Value of Common Equity in an All-Equity Firm

For this example, make the following additional assumptions:

- Equity shareholders have financed the asset entirely with $10 million of equity capital.
- The cost of equity capital is 10 percent.

The value of the common equity investment to the shareholders can be determined using the present value of dividends for common equity shareholders. The dividends to common equity shareholders each year will be as follows:

Net Pretax Cash Flow for All Debt and Equity Capital	$2,000,000
Interest Paid on Debt	(0)
Income Taxes: 0.40 × $2,000,000	(800,000)
Dividends for Common Equity Shareholders	$1,200,000

The value to the shareholders of the common equity in the firm is $12,000,000 (= $1,200,000/0.10). Dividing by the discount rate is appropriate because the $1,200,000 annual dividend for common equity is a perpetuity. This investment is worth $12,000,000 to those shareholders (a gain of $2,000,000 over their initial $10,000,000 investment) because of the present value of the dividends the investment will pay to the shareholders.

Example 6: Value of Common Equity in a Firm with Debt Financing

Assume the same original facts, but now make the following additional assumptions:

- The equity shareholders finance a portion of the investment in the asset with $4 million of equity capital.
- The firm finances the remainder of the asset using $6 million of debt capital.
- This amount of debt in the firm's capital structure does not alter substantially the risk of the firm to the equity investors, so they continue to require a 10 percent rate of return.
- The debt is issued at par, and it is less risky than equity; so the debtholders demand interest of only 6 percent each year, payable at the end of each year.
- Interest expense is deductible for income tax purposes.

Again the value of the common equity investment can be determined using the present value of dividends for common equity shareholders. The dividend to common equity is as follows:

Net Pretax Cash Flow for All Debt and Equity Capital	$2,000,000
Interest Paid on Debt: 0.06 × $6,000,000	(360,000)
Income Taxes: 0.40 × ($2,000,000 − $360,000)	(656,000)
Dividends for Common Equity Shareholders	$ 984,000

Assuming that the firm will pay this amount of dividend each year in perpetuity, the value of the common equity to the shareholders in the firm is $9,840,000 (= $984,000/0.10). Note that in this example, the present value of the gain to the common equity shareholders in excess of their initial investment is $5,840,000 (= $9,840,000 − $4,000,000). In this example, the gain to the shareholders is $3,840,000 (= $5,840,000 − $2,000,000) larger than in the previous example because (1) the debt capital is less expensive than the equity capital (6 percent rather than 10 percent on $6,000,000 of financing), creating $2,400,000 of value for equity shareholders from capital structure leverage [= ($6,000,000 × {0.10 − 0.06})/0.10], and (2) the net tax savings from interest expense creates $1,440,000 of value for equity shareholders [= ($800,000 − $656,000)/0.10, or, alternatively, (= $360,000 interest deduction × 0.40 tax rate)/0.10].

Dividends to the Investor versus Cash Flows to the Firm

The beginning of this chapter asserted that the analyst can use dividends expected to be paid to the investor or the free cash flows expected to be generated by the firm (that will ultimately be paid to the investor) as equivalent approaches to measure value-relevant expected payoffs to shareholders. Will using net cash flows into the firm result in the same estimate of value as using dividends paid out of the firm? Cash flows paid to the investor via dividends and free cash flows to the firm that are available for common equity shareholders will differ each period to the extent that the firm reinvests a portion (or all) of the cash flows generated. However, if the firm generates a rate of return on reinvested free cash flow equal to the discount rate used by the investor (that is, the cost of equity capital), either set of payoffs (dividends or free cash flows) will yield the same valuation of a firm's shares at a point in time. To demonstrate this equivalence, consider the following scenarios.

Example 7: Dividend Policy Irrelevance with 100 Percent Payout

A firm expects to generate free cash flows of 15 percent annually on invested equity capital for the rest of its life, which is likely to continue for an indefinitely long period of time into the future (until $t = n$). Equity investors in this firm require a 15 percent return each year, considering the riskiness of the firm. Assume that the firm pays out 100 percent of the free cash flows each year as dividends to the shareholders. Thus, the free cash flows generated by the firm equal the cash dividends received by the investors each period. Each dollar of capital committed by the investors has a present value of future cash flows equal to one dollar. That is, over an indefinitely long period of time into the future,

$$\$1 = \sum_{t=1}^{n} \frac{\$0.15}{(1.15)^t}$$

Example 8: Dividend Policy Irrelevance with Zero Payout

Assume the same facts as Example 7 except that the firm pays out none of the free cash flows as a dividend. The firm retains the $0.15 free cash flow on each dollar of capital and reinvests it in projects expected to earn 15 percent return per year. In this case, the investor receives no periodic dividends and receives cash only when the investor sells the shares or the firm liquidates at date $t=n$. By the terminal date, n periods in the future, each dollar of capital invested in the firm today will have earned a compound rate of return of 15 percent, equal to the required rate of return. In this case also, each dollar of invested capital has a present value of future cash flows equal to one dollar, exactly the same as in the full payout dividend discount example above. That is,

$$\$1 = \frac{(\$1.15)^n}{(1.15)^n}$$

Example 9: Dividend Policy Irrelevance with Partial Payout

Assume the same facts as Example 8 except that the firm pays out 25 percent of the free cash flow each period as a dividend and reinvests the other 75 percent in projects expected to generate a return of 15 percent. In this case also, each dollar of invested capital has a present value of future cash flows equal to one dollar, the same as in the two preceding examples. That is,

$$V_0 = \sum_{t=1}^{n} \frac{(0.25)(\$0.15)}{(1.15)^t} + \frac{(0.75)(\$1.15)^n}{(1.15)^n}$$

These three examples illustrate the *relevance* of dividends as payoffs that are sufficient for valuation for equity shareholders and the *irrelevance* of the firm's dividend policy in valuation, assuming the firm reinvests cash flows to earn the investors' required rate of return.[9] The same valuation should arise whether the analyst discounts (1) the expected dividends to the investor or (2) the expected free cash flows to the firm that are available to pay future dividends to equity shareholders. Further, the same valuation should arise whether the firm pays all of its cash flows as a dividend, reinvests all cash flows to earn the investors' required rate of return, or pays a portion of cash flows in dividends each period and reinvests the remaining cash flows to earn the investors' required rate of return.

Nominal versus Real Dividends

Changes in general price levels (that is, inflation or deflation) cause the purchasing power of the monetary unit to change over time. Should the valuation use projected nominal dividends,

[9] Merton Miller and Franco Modigliani, "Dividend Policy, Growth and the Valuation of Shares," *Journal of Business* (October 1961), pp. 411–433. Penman and Sougiannis test empirically the replacement property of dividends for future earnings and find support for the irrelevance of dividend policy in valuation. See Stephen H. Penman and Theodore Sougiannis, "The Dividend Displacement Property and the Substitution of Anticipated Earnings for Dividends in Equity Valuation," *The Accounting Review* (January 1997), pp. 1–21.

which include the effects of inflation or deflation, or real dividends, which filter out the effects of changes in general purchasing power?[10] The valuation of an investment in an economic resource should be the same whether nominal or real dividend amounts are used as long as the discount rate used is the nominal or real rate of return that is consistent with the dividend measure. That is, if projected dividends are nominal and include the effects of changes in general purchasing power of the monetary unit, the discount rate should be nominal and include an inflation component. If projected dividends are real amounts that filter out the effects of general price changes, the discount rate should be a real rate of return, excluding the inflation component.

Example 10: Nominal versus Real Dividends

A firm owns an asset that it expects to sell one year from today for \$115.5 million. The firm expects the general price level to increase 10 percent during this period. The real interest rate is 5 percent. The nominal discount rate should be 15.5 percent to measure the compound effects of the real rate of interest and inflation [$0.155 = (1.10 \times 1.05) - 1$]. Discounting nominal or real dividends, the value of the asset to the firm today is \$100 million, as shown:

Nominal Dividends	×	Discount Rate Including Expected Inflation	=	Value
\$115.5 million	×	$1/(1.05 \times 1.10)$	=	\$100 million

Real Dividends	×	Discount Rate Excluding Expected Inflation	=	Value
\$115.5 million/1.10	×	1/1.05	=	\$100 million

Both examples derived the value of the equity of the firm by computing the present value of the dividends to common equity shareholders. As a practical matter, costs of capital and expected returns are typically quoted in nominal terms, so analysts usually find it more straightforward to discount nominal dividends using nominal discount rates than to first adjust nominal dividends to real dividends and then discount real dividends using real interest rates.

THE DIVIDENDS VALUATION MODEL

This section presents the dividends valuation model that determines the value of common shareholders' equity in the firm. The sections following the model demonstrate how to implement the model using PepsiCo.

The dividends valuation model determines the value of common shareholders' equity in the firm (denoted as V_0) as the sum of the present value of all future dividends to shareholders over the life of the firm, which is indefinite. The dividends valuation model includes all-inclusive dividends (denoted as *D*) that encompass all of the net cash flows

[10] Note that the issue here is not with specific price changes of a firm's particular assets, liabilities, revenues, and expenses. These specific price changes affect projections of the firm's dividends, cash flows, and earnings and should enter into the valuation of the firm. The issue is whether some portion, all, or more than all of the specific price changes represent simply an economy-wide change in the purchasing power of the monetary unit, which should not affect the value of a firm.

from the firm to shareholders through periodic dividend payments and stock buybacks and subtracts cash flows from the shareholders to the firm when the firm issues shares. The next section demonstrates how to measure dividends (D). We discount the stream of future dividends to present value using the required return on common equity capital in the firm (denoted as R_E). The following general model expresses the dividends valuation approach:

$$V_0 = \sum_{t=1}^{\infty} \frac{D_t}{(1+R_E)^t} = \frac{D_1}{(1+R_E)^1} + \frac{D_2}{(1+R_E)^2} + \frac{D_3}{(1+R_E)^3} + \ldots$$

Suppose dividend amounts can be reliably forecasted through Year T. At the end of Year T, assume that the continuing value of the common equity of the firm (denoted as V_T) will equal the present value of all expected future continuing dividends in Year T+1 and beyond (a perpetuity of D_{T+1} in every year), which can be expressed as follows:

$$V_T = \sum_{t=1}^{\infty} \frac{D_{T+1}}{(1+R_E)^t}$$

Thus, the value of the firm today can be expressed using periodic dividends over a finite horizon to Year T plus continuing value based on dividends in Year T+1 and beyond as follows:

$$V_0 = \sum_{t=1}^{\infty} \frac{D_t}{(1+R_E)^t} = \frac{D_1}{(1+R_E)^1} + \frac{D_2}{(1+R_E)^2} + \frac{D_3}{(1+R_E)^3} + \ldots + \frac{D_T}{(1+R_E)^T} + \frac{V_T}{(1+R_E)^T}$$

This equation reveals that the estimate of value today (V_0) depends on the estimate of value in the future (V_T).

As described in more detail in an upcoming section, we project the continuing dividends in the continuing value period beyond Year T using the expected, long-run steady state growth of the firm, which we specify as $(1 + g)$. We project the Year T+1 dividend by assuming that each line item on the Year T income statement and balance sheet will grow at rate $(1 + g)$ and then deriving the Year T+1 dividend. As described in an upcoming section, to derive dividends, assume that accounting for the book value of the shareholders' equity (BV) follows the general principle of adding net income (NI) and subtracting dividends to common shareholders each period (that is, $BV_t = BV_{t-1} + NI_t - D_t$). Therefore, the Year T+1 dividend can be derived as follows:

$$D_{T+1} = NI_{T+1} + BV_T - BV_{T+1}$$

The assumption is that growth in net income and book value in Year T+1 equals $(1 + g)$; therefore, $NI_{T+1} = NI_T \times (1 + g)$ and $BV_{T+1} = BV_T \times (1 + g)$. These terms can be substituted, and the D_{T+1} equation can be rewritten as follows:

$$D_{T+1} = [NI_T \times (1 + g)] + BV_T - [BV_T \times (1 + g)]$$

Assuming that D_{T+1} will grow in perpetuity at rate g, the firm can be valued at the end of Year T using the perpetuity-with-growth model as follows:

$$V_T = \sum_{t=1}^{\infty} \frac{D_{T+1}}{(1+R_E)^t} = \frac{D_{T+1}}{(R_E - g)} = \frac{[NI_T \times (1 + g)] + BV_T - [BV_T \times (1 + g)]}{(R_E - g)}$$

Therefore, the present value of common equity today can be expressed using dividends as follows:

$$V_0 = \sum_{t=1}^{\infty} \frac{D_t}{(1 + R_E)^t}$$

$$= \frac{D_1}{(1+R_E)^1} + \frac{D_2}{(1+R_E)^2} + \frac{D_3}{(1+R_E)^3} + \cdots + \frac{D_T}{(1+R_E)^T} + \frac{V_T}{(1+R_E)^T}$$

$$= \frac{D_1}{(1+R_E)^1} + \frac{D_2}{(1+R_E)^2} + \frac{D_3}{(1+R_E)^3} + \cdots + \frac{D_T}{(1+R_E)^T} + \frac{[NI_T \times (1+g)] + BV_T - [BV_T \times (1+g)]}{(R_E - g) \times (1 + R_E)^T}$$

IMPLEMENTING THE DIVIDENDS VALUATION MODEL

Implementing the dividends valuation model to determine the value of the common shareholders' equity in a firm involves measuring the following three elements:

1. The discount rate (denoted as R_E in the valuation model) used to compute the present value of the future dividends
2. The expected future dividends over the forecast horizon (denoted as D_t in periods 1 through T in the valuation model)
3. The expected dividend at the final period of the forecast horizon, which we refer to as the *continuing dividend* (denoted as D_{T+1} in the valuation model) and a forecast of the long-run growth rate (denoted as g in the model) in the continuing dividend beyond the forecast horizon

The first part of this chapter discussed the first element, computing the appropriate discount rate. The following sections discuss measuring the second and third of these elements.

Measuring Dividends

Dividends-based valuation values the common equity in a firm by measuring the present value of all net cash flows from the firm to the equity shareholders. Therefore, the objective in dividends valuation is to measure the present value of *total dividends* for common equity shareholders, including *all* of the cash flows the shareholders will receive from holding the share.

Total dividends encompass cash flows from the firm to common equity shareholders through periodic dividend payments such as quarterly or annual dividends paid to shareholders each period based on the firm's dividend payout policy. Total dividends also include cash flows to common equity shareholders through stock buybacks. Further, cash flows from the shareholders to the firm when the firm issues shares are *negative* dividends. Thus, to measure total value-relevant dividends that encompass all of the cash flows from the firm to common equity shareholders each period, the analyst should include the following three components:

+ Quarterly or annual ordinary dividend payments to common equity shareholders
+ Net cash flows to shareholders from common equity share repurchases
− Net cash flows from shareholders through common equity issues

= Total dividends to common equity shareholders.

Alternatively, accounting for shareholders' equity is a reliable framework for measuring total dividends for valuation. To begin, assume that the accounting for shareholders' equity follows *clean surplus accounting*. Under clean surplus accounting, income must include *all* of the elements of income (all revenues and expenses, all gains and losses) generated by the firm for common equity shareholders. Under U.S. GAAP and IFRS, clean surplus income is measured by comprehensive income (that is, net income plus all of the unrealized gains and losses included in other comprehensive income). Also assume that the effects of all of the direct capital transactions between the firm and the common equity shareholders, such as periodic dividend payments, share issues, and share repurchases, are included in the book value of common shareholders' equity.[11]

Under these simple and general principles of clean surplus accounting, the accounting for common equity is represented as follows:

$$BV_t = BV_{t-1} + I_t - D_t$$

where BV_t denotes the book value of equity at the end of year t, I denotes clean surplus income for year t, and D denotes net direct capital transactions between the firm and common shareholders (dividend payments, stock issues, and stock repurchases) during year t. To isolate all of the net cash flows between the firm and the shareholders during year t, simply rearrange the equation as follows:

$$D_t = I_t + BV_{t-1} - BV_t$$

Therefore, total dividends used in dividends valuation should equal clean surplus income each year, adjusted for the change in the book value of common equity as a result of direct capital transactions.

Measuring Dividends for PepsiCo

This section illustrates the dividends measurement approach using PepsiCo. We derive our dividends expectations from our projected financial statements for PepsiCo in Chapter 10.

In development of the financial statement forecasts for PepsiCo for Year +1, for example, we projected that PepsiCo would pay common equity dividends equal to 50 percent of lagged net income from continuing operations, amounting to $2,571.0 million [= 0.50 × ($5,142.0 − $0)]. We also assumed that PepsiCo would use implied dividends as the flexible financial account to balance the balance sheet, so an additional $444.3 million in capital would be distributed to common equity shareholders through additional dividends or share repurchases. Therefore, we projected that net dividends would amount to $3,015.3 million (= $2,571.0 + $444.3) in Year +1.

We also projected that common stock and additional paid-in capital would remain roughly 1.1 percent of total assets. Because the projections expect total assets to grow by 7.0 percent in Year +1, common stock and additional paid-in capital would also grow by 7.0 percent from $381.0 million to $407.5 million by the end of Year +1, implying new stock issues (in effect, negative dividends) of −$26.5 million. Further, we projected that PepsiCo would engage in direct capital transactions with common equity shareholders through the treasury stock account. We projected that PepsiCo would pay $2,500.0 million to repurchase common shares, net of any shares reissued for stock options exercises. Together, these capital transactions would result in a net cash outflow of $2,473.5 million (= $2,500.0 − $26.5) from PepsiCo to common shareholders.

---

[11] Also assume that direct capital transactions between the firm and common equity shareholders are value-neutral (that is, zero net present value projects) to the existing common shareholders.

Bringing these components together, we projected that total value-relevant dividends to common equity shareholders in Year +1 will be as follows (in millions):

Periodic dividend payments	$3,015.3
Net purchases of treasury stock	2,500.0
Common stock issues	(26.5)
Total dividends to common equity shareholders	$5,488.8

This computation can be reconciled with the clean surplus accounting approach as follows: The Year +1 forecast of comprehensive income is $6,110.9 million. After deducting the forecast of the liquidating dividend to retire the preferred shares, the projected amount of comprehensive income available to common shareholders is as follows (in millions):

$$\$6{,}110.9 - \$169.0 = \$5{,}941.9$$

Total book value of common shareholders' equity is $12,203.0 million at the beginning of Year +1 and $12,656.1 million at the end of Year +1. Using the clean surplus accounting approach, dividends in Year +1 are as follows (in millions):

$$D_t = I_t + BV_{t-1} - BV_t = \$5{,}941.9 + \$12{,}203.0 - \$12{,}656.1 = \$5{,}488.8$$

Exhibit 11.5 demonstrates these computations for Years +1 through +5.

Selecting a Forecast Horizon

For how many future years should the analyst project future payoffs from an investment? The correct answer is the expected life of the investment being valued. This life is a finite number of years for a resource such as a machine, a building, or any resource with limits to its physical existence or a financial instrument with a finite stated maturity (such as a bond, mortgage, or lease). In equity valuation, however, the resource to be valued is an ownership claim on the firm, a resource that has an expected life that is typically indefinite. Therefore, in the case of an equity security, the analyst must project future dividends that, in theory, extend indefinitely.

Of course, as a practical matter, the analyst cannot precisely predict a firm's dividends very many years into the future. Therefore, analysts commonly develop specific projections of all of the elements of the income statements and balance sheets for the firm and use those elements to derive forecasts of dividends over an explicit forecast horizon (for example, five or ten years) depending on the industry, the maturity of the firm, and the expected growth and predictability of the firm's business activities. After the explicit forecast horizon, analysts then typically use general steady-state growth assumptions to project the future income statements and balance sheets and use them to derive the dividends that will persist each period to infinity. Therefore, the analyst will find it desirable to develop specific forecasts of income statements, balance sheets, and cash flows over an explicit forecast horizon that extends until the point at which a firm's growth pattern is expected to settle into steady-state equilibrium, during which time dividends might be expected to grow at a steady, predictable rate.

Selecting a forecast horizon involves trade-offs. Reasonably reliable projections can be developed over longer forecast horizons for stable and mature firms. Projections for such firms, as in the case of PepsiCo demonstrated in Chapter 10, capture relatively steady-state operations. On the other hand, it is more difficult to develop reliable projections over long

EXHIBIT 11.5

Computation of PepsiCo's Total Dividends for the Dividends Valuation Approach

	Computing Total Dividends Using Components				
	Year +1	Year +2	Year +3	Year +4	Year +5
Dividends Paid to Common Shareholders	$ 3,015.3	$ 3,324.5	$ 3,818.5	$ 4,398.5	$ 4,848.3
Less: Common Stock Issues	(26.5)	(33.8)	(43.7)	(30.2)	(51.2)
Plus: Common Stock Repurchases	2,500.0	2,500.0	2,500.0	2,500.0	2,500.0
Total Dividends to Common Equity	$ 5,488.8	$ 5,790.7	$ 6,274.8	$ 6,868.3	$ 7,297.1

	Computing Total Dividends Using Clean Surplus Accounting				
	Year +1	Year +2	Year +3	Year +4	Year +5
Comprehensive Income	$ 6,110.9	$ 6,602.1	$ 7,272.7	$ 7,726.4	$ 8,427.3
Less: Preferred Dividends	(169.0)	(0.0)	(0.0)	(0.0)	(0.0)
Comprehensive Income Available for Common Equity	$ 5,941.9	$ 6,602.1	$ 7,272.7	$ 7,726.4	$ 8,427.3
Plus: Beginning Book Value of Common Equity	12,203.0	12,656.1	13,467.4	14,465.3	15,323.5
Less: Ending Book Value of Common Equity	(12,656.1)	(13,467.4)	(14,465.3)	(15,323.5)	(16,453.6)
Total Dividends to Common Equity	$ 5,488.8	$ 5,790.7	$ 6,274.8	$ 6,868.3	$ 7,297.1

forecast horizons for young high-growth firms because their future operating performance is relatively more uncertain. This difficulty is exacerbated by the fact that a much higher proportion of the value of young growth firms will be achieved in distant future years, after they reach their potential steady-state profitability. Thus, the analyst faces the dilemma of depending most heavily on long-run forecasts for young growth firms for which long-run projections are most uncertain and most difficult to project. The forecasting and valuation process is particularly difficult for growth firms when the near-term dividends are projected to be zero or negative, as is common for rapidly growing firms that finance growth by issuing common stock. In this case, most of the firm's value depends on dividends to be generated in years far into the future.

Unfortunately, there is no way to avoid this dilemma. The predictive accuracy of dividends forecasts many years into the future is likely to be questionable for even the most stable and predictable firms. The analyst must recognize that forecasts and value estimates for all firms, but especially growth firms, have a high degree of uncertainty and estimation risk. To mitigate this uncertainty and estimation risk, the analyst should adhere to the following points:

- Diligently and comprehensively follow all six steps of the analysis framework. By thoroughly analyzing the firm's industry and strategy, the firm's accounting quality, and the firm's financial performance and risk ratios, the analyst will have more information to use to develop long-term forecasts that are as reliable as possible.
- To the extent possible, confront directly the problem of long-term uncertainty by developing specific projections of dividends derived from projected income statements and balance sheets that extend five or ten years into the future, at which point the firm may be projected to reach steady-state growth.
- Assess the sensitivity of the forecast projections and value estimates across the reasonable range of growth assumptions.

Continuing Value of Future Dividends

The previous section described measuring periodic dividends over an explicit forecast horizon. This section describes techniques to project continuing dividends using a steady-state growth rate continuing beyond the explicit forecast horizon and to measure the present value of continuing dividends. We refer to them as *continuing dividends* because they reflect the cash flows from the firm to the common equity shareholders continuing into the long-run future.

In some circumstances, however, the analyst may not find it necessary to forecast dividends continuing beyond the explicit forecast horizon if he or she can reliably predict that the share will receive a future liquidating dividend. In such circumstances, the liquidating dividend is the final cash flow to the shareholder. The liquidating dividend might arise when the firm liquidates its assets at the end of its business life and distributes the proceeds to shareholders to retire their shares. Alternatively, the liquidating dividend might arise when a firm's shares are acquired by another firm in a merger or an acquisition transaction. The liquidating dividend also can arise when the shareholder elects to sell the share, thereby creating a liquidating dividend from the selling price.

Projecting Continuing Dividends

In most circumstances, the analyst will not be able to reliably predict whether or when the share will receive a liquidating dividend. Therefore, analysts commonly forecast dividends over an explicit forecast horizon until the point at which the analyst expects a firm to mature into a steady-state growth pattern, during which time dividends are assumed to grow at a constant steady-state rate. The long-run sustainable growth rate (denoted as g) in future continuing dividends could be positive, negative, or zero. Sustainable growth in dividends could be driven by long-run expectations for inflation, the industry's sales, the economy in general, or the population. The analyst should select a growth rate that captures realistic long-run expectations for Year T+1 and beyond.

Unfortunately, a shortcut analysts sometimes use (and a common error analysts make) in computing the continuing dividends for Year T+1 is to multiply the dividends for Year T by $(1 + g)$ instead of deriving the Year T+1 dividends from the projected Year T+1 income statement and balance sheet. If the analyst wants to compute internally consistent and identical estimates of firm value using dividends, free cash flows, and earnings, he or she should *not* project dividends for Year T+1 by simply multiplying dividends for Year T by $(1 + g)$. Doing so ignores the necessary growth in all of the elements of the balance sheet and the income statement, which can introduce inconsistent forecast assumptions for dividends, cash flows, and earnings. Even if the analyst simply projects Year T+1 dividends, cash flows, and earnings to grow at an identical rate (1 + *g*), doing so may impound inconsistent assumptions and lead to inconsistent value estimates if Year T dividends, cash flows, and earnings are not consistent with their long-run continuing amounts.

Example 11: Projecting Continuing Dividends

Suppose the analyst develops the following forecasts for the firm in Year T−1 and Year T:

	Assets	=	Liabilities	+	Shareholders' Equity
Year T−1 Balances	$100	=	$60	+	$40
+ Net Income	+20				+20
+ New Borrowing	+6		+6		
− Dividends Paid	−10				−10
Year T Balances	$116	=	$66	+	$50

Suppose the analyst projects that the firm will grow at a steady-state rate of 10 percent in Year T+1 and thereafter. If the analyst simply (and erroneously) projects Year T dividends to grow by 10 percent, the Year T+1 projections will be only $11 (= $10 Year T dividends × 1.10), which is not correct because it relies on implicit inconsistent assumptions. This error would force the estimated value of the firm using dividends to be lower than the value estimates using cash flows or earnings.

To project continuing dividends in Year T+1 correctly, the analyst should derive the continuing dividends from the projected Year T+1 income statement and balance sheet. To do so correctly, the analyst should use the expected long-run growth rate (*g*) to project all of the items of the Year T+1 income statement and balance sheet. That is, the analyst should project each item on the Year T+1 income statement and balance sheet by multiplying each item for Year T times (1 + *g*). The analyst can then derive Year T+1 dividends using clean surplus accounting as follows:

$$D_{T+1} = NI_{T+1} + BV_T - BV_{T+1} = [NI_T \times (1 + g)] + BV_T - [BV_T \times (1 + g)]$$

The analyst must impose the long-run growth rate assumption (1 + *g*) uniformly on the Year T+1 income statement and balance sheet projections to derive the dividends for Year T+1 correctly. In the long run, assuming that the firm itself will grow at a steady-state rate, all of the elements of the firm (dividends, revenues, expenses, income, assets, liabilities, shareholders' equity, and cash flows) will grow at the same rate. By applying a uniform growth rate across all of the items of the income statement and balance sheet, the analyst achieves internally consistent steady-state growth across all of the projections of the firm, keeping the balance sheet in balance throughout the continuing forecast horizon and keeping growth in dividends, cash flows, and earnings internally consistent with the long-run growth rate.

Returning to Example 11, to compute continuing dividends in Year T+1 correctly, the analyst should project Year T+1 net income, assets, liabilities, and shareholders' equity to grow by 10 percent each and then compute Year T+1 continuing dividends as follows:

	Assets	=	Liabilities	+	Shareholders' Equity
Year T Balances	$ 116	=	$ 66	+	$50
Growth	×1.10		×1.10		×1.10
Year T+1 Balances	$127.6	=	$72.6	+	$55

The projected net income would be \$22 (= \$20 × 1.10). The Year T+1 dividends projection would be \$17 (= \$22 net income + \$50 beginning shareholders' equity − \$55 ending shareholders' equity). Note that the correct projected Year T+1 dividend amount of \$17 is substantially larger than the erroneous \$11 dividend projection. Also note that the \$17 Year T+1 dividend is substantially larger than the \$10 dividend amount for Year T. The reason the firm can begin to pay larger dividends in Year T+1 and beyond is that the firm's long-run growth rate of 10 percent is lower than the Year T growth rate in assets (16 percent) and shareholders' equity (25 percent); thus, this firm will not need to reinvest as much of its earnings to fund growth and will be able to pay larger dividend amounts in Year T+1 and beyond.

In projecting continuing dividends in Year T+1 and beyond, analysts assume that the firm will settle into a long-run sustainable growth rate. Often analysts assume that the firm's long-run sustainable growth rate will be consistent with long-run growth in the economy, on the order of 3–5 percent. For firms that have been growing faster than that in the years leading up to Year T+1, the long-run sustainable growth rate implies that the firm will maintain a lower growth rate in assets and equity and thus will be able to pay out substantially larger dividends. By projecting Year T+1 net income, assets, and equity using the long-run sustainable growth rate, it is possible to solve for the long-run sustainable dividends the firm can pay. The continuing dividend amount derived for Year T+1 may be significantly larger than the amounts the firm actually paid during its higher-growth-rate years. The Year T+1 dividend amount reflects the firm's transition from a high rate of reinvestment to finance high growth in assets to lower reinvestment for lower growth.

Computing Continuing Value

As was demonstrated earlier in the dividends valuation model, once the analyst has computed continuing dividends for Year T+1, he or she can compute continuing value (sometimes called residual value or terminal value) of continuing dividends in Year T+1 and beyond using the perpetuity-with-growth valuation model, as follows:[12]

$$V_T = \sum_{t=1}^{\infty} \frac{D_{T+1}}{(1+R_E)^t} = \frac{D_{T+1}}{(R_E - g)} = \frac{[NI_T \times (1+g)] + BV_T - [BV_T \times (1+g)]}{(R_E - g)}$$

Example 12: Valuing Continuing Dividends

An analyst forecasts that the dividends of a firm in Year +5 will be \$30 million and that Year +5 earnings and cash flows also will be \$30 million. For simplicity in this example, assume the analyst expects that the firm's income statements and balance sheets will grow uniformly over the long run and, therefore, that cash flows, earnings, and dividends will grow uniformly over the long run. But the analyst is uncertain about the steady-state long-run growth rate in Year +6 and beyond. The analyst believes that the growth rate will most likely be zero but could reasonably fall in the range between +6 and −6 percent per year; so the analyst derived the range of Year +6 dividends shown in the following table. Assuming a 15 percent cost of capital, the table shows the range of possible continuing values (in millions) for the firm in present value at the beginning of the continuing value period (that is, the beginning of Year +6) and in present value as of today; that is, the continuing value is discounted to today using a factor of $1/(1.15)^5$:

[12] This formula is simply the algebraic simplification for the present value of a growing perpetuity.

				Continuing Value in Present Value as of:	
Dividends in Year T	**Long-Run Growth Assumption**	**Dividends in Year T+1**	**Perpetuity with Growth Factor**	**Beginning of Year T+1**	**Today**
$30.00	0%	$30.00	1/(0.15 − 0.0) = 6.67	$200.00	$ 99.44
$30.00	+6%	$31.80	1/(0.15 − 0.06) = 11.11	$353.30	$175.65
$30.00	−6%	$28.20	1/(0.15 + 0.06) = 4.76	$134.23	$ 66.74

Analysts also can estimate continuing value using a multiple of dividends in the first year of the continuing value period. The following table shows the continuing value multiples using $1/(R - g)$ for various costs of equity capital and growth rates. The multiples increase with growth for a given cost of capital, and they decrease as the cost of capital increases for a given level of growth.

Continuing Value Multiples

	Long-Run Growth Rates					
Cost of Equity Capital	**0%**	**2%**	**3%**	**4%**	**5%**	**6%**
6%	16.67	25.00	33.33	50.00	100.00	na
8%	12.50	16.67	20.00	25.00	33.33	50.00
10%	10.00	12.50	14.29	16.67	20.00	25.00
12%	8.33	10.00	11.11	12.50	14.29	16.67
15%	6.67	7.69	8.33	9.09	10.00	11.11
18%	5.56	6.25	6.67	7.14	7.69	8.33
20%	5.00	5.56	5.88	6.25	6.67	7.14

The continuing value computation using the perpetuity-with-growth valuation model does not work when the growth rate equals or exceeds the discount rate (that is, when $g \geq R$) because the denominator in the computation is zero or negative and the resulting continuing value estimate is meaningless. In this case, the analyst cannot use the perpetuity computation illustrated here. Instead, the analyst must forecast dividend amounts for each year beyond the forecast horizon using the terminal period growth rate and then discount each year's dividends to present value using the discount rate. The analyst also should reconsider whether it is realistic to expect the firm's dividends growth rate to exceed the discount rate (the expected rate of return) in perpetuity. This scenario can exist for some years, but is not likely to be sustainable indefinitely. Competition, technological change, new entrants into an industry, and similar dynamic factors eventually reduce growth rates.

An alternative approach for estimating the continuing value is to use the dividends multiples for comparable firms that currently trade in the market. The analyst identifies comparable companies by studying characteristics such as industry, firm size and age, past growth rates in dividends, profitability, risk, and similar factors. Chapter 14 discusses valuation multiples in more depth.

Because of the uncertainty inherent in long-run growth rate forecasts and because continuing value amounts are commonly large proportions of value estimates, analysts should conduct sensitivity analysis to assess how sensitive the firm value estimate is to variations in the long-run growth assumption. For example, suppose an analyst is valuing a young high-growth company and can reliably forecast dividends five years into the future. After that horizon, the analyst expects the firm to grow at 6 percent per year, although this is highly uncertain, and long-run growth could range from −3 percent per year to as much as 9 percent per year. The analyst should conduct sensitivity analysis on the projections and valuation, varying long-run growth across the range from −3 to 9 percent per year.

Using the Dividends Valuation Model to Value PepsiCo

At the end of 2008, trading in PepsiCo shares on the New York Stock Exchange closed at $54.77 per share, which is the price at which an investor can buy or sell PepsiCo shares. But what is the value of these shares? The valuation of PepsiCo shares uses the techniques described in this chapter and the forecasts developed in Chapter 10. The forecasts and valuation estimates are developed using the Forecast and Valuation spreadsheets in FSAP.

We estimate the present value of a share of common equity in PepsiCo at the end of 2008 (equivalently, the start of Year +1) using the risk-adjusted rate of return on PepsiCo's equity capital as the appropriate discount rate. A prior section of this chapter computed the PepsiCo equity cost of capital to be 8.5 percent. Exhibit 11.5 summarizes the computations of PepsiCo's dividends in Years +1 to +5. Discounting these future dividends using a discount rate of 8.50 percent yields a present value estimate of $24,699.3 million. Exhibit 11.6 illustrates these computations, and Exhibit 11.7 (see page 917) presents the dividend valuation model from FSAP.

To compute the present value of continuing value of PepsiCo's dividends in Year +6 and beyond, we project that continuing dividends will grow at a 3 percent rate in perpetuity, consistent with long-run average growth in the economy. We forecast Year +6 dividends as follows:

$$\begin{aligned} D_6 &= [NI_5 \times (1 + g)] + BV_5 - [BV_5 \times (1 + g)] \\ &= [\$8{,}427.3 \text{ million} \times 1.03] + \$16{,}453.6 \text{ million} - [\$16{,}453.6 \text{ million} \times 1.03] \\ &= \$8{,}680.1 \text{ million} + \$16{,}453.6 \text{ million} - \$16{,}947.2 \text{ million} \\ &= \$8{,}186.5 \text{ million} \end{aligned}$$

We use the perpetuity-with-growth model to discount dividends in the continuing value period to present value as of the beginning of Year +6 (the beginning of the continuing value period) using PepsiCo's 8.50 percent cost of equity capital, as follows (allowing for rounding):

$$\begin{aligned} \text{Continuing Value}_0 &= [D_6 \times (1/\{R_E - g\})] \\ &= \$8{,}186.5 \text{ million} \times [1/(0.085 - 0.030)] \\ &= \$8{,}186.5 \text{ million} \times 18.18182 \\ &= \$148{,}845.45 \text{ million} \end{aligned}$$

We then discount the continuing value as of the beginning of Year +6 to present value, as follows (allow for rounding):

$$\begin{aligned} \text{Present Value of Continuing Value}_0 &= \$148{,}845.45 \text{ million} \times [1/\{1 + R_E\}^5] \\ &= \$148{,}845.45 \text{ million} \times [1/\{1 + 0.085\}^5] \\ &= \$148{,}845.45 \text{ million} \times 0.665 \\ &= \$98{,}988.9 \text{ million} \end{aligned}$$

EXHIBIT 11.6

Valuation of PepsiCo
Present Value of Dividends to Common Equity
Year +1 through Year +5 and Beyond

	Valuation of Dividends in Year +1 through Year +5				
	Year +1	**Year +2**	**Year +3**	**Year +4**	**Year +5**
Total Dividends to Common Equity (from Exhibit 11.5)	\$ 5,488.8	\$5,790.7	\$6,274.8	\$6,868.3	\$7,297.1
Present Value Factors (R_E = 8.50%)	0.922	0.849	0.783	0.722	0.665
Present Value of Dividends	\$ 5,058.8	\$4,919.0	\$4,912.6	\$4,956.0	\$4,852.9
Sum of Present Value Dividends, Years +1 through +5	\$24,699.3				

Continuing Value Based on Dividends in Year + 6 and Beyond

Project Year +6 Dividends:

$D_6 = [NI_5 \times (1 + g)] + BV_5 - [BV_5 \times (1 + g)]$

$= [\$8,427.3 \text{ million} \times 1.03] + \$16,453.6 \text{ million} - [\$16,453.6 \text{ million} \times 1.03]$

$= \$8,680.1 \text{ million} + \$16,453.6 \text{ million} - \$16,947.2 \text{ million}$

$= \$8,186.5 \text{ million}$

Present Value of Continuing Value (R_E = 8.50% and g = 3.0%):

Present Value of Continuing Value$_0$ $= D_6 \times [1 / (R_E - g)] \times [1 / (1 + R_E)^5]$

$= \$8,186.5 \text{ million} \times [1 / (0.085 - 0.030)] \times [1 / (1 + 0.085)^5]$

$= \$8,186.5 \text{ million} \times 18.18182 \times 0.665$

$= \$98,988.9 \text{ million}$

Total Value of PepsiCo's Dividends

Present Value of Dividends through Year +5		\$ 24,699.3 million
+ Present Value of Continuing Value	+	98,988.9 million
Present Value of Common Equity		\$123,688.2 million
Adjust for Midyear Discounting (multiply by $1 + [R_E/2]$)	×	1.0425
Total Present Value of Common Equity		\$128,945.0 million
Divide by Number of Shares Outstanding	/	1,553 million
Value per Share of PepsiCo Common Equity	=	\$ 83.03

The total present value of PepsiCo's free cash flows to common equity shareholders is the sum of these two parts:

Present Value of Dividends through Year +5	\$ 24,699.3 million
Present Value of Continuing Value	98,988.9 million
Present Value of Common Equity	\$123,688.2 million

EXHIBIT 11.7

Valuation of PepsiCo
Present Value of Dividends to Common Equity Year +1 through Year +5
and Beyond Using the Dividends Valuation Model in FSAP

Dividends-Based Valuation	Year +1	Year +2	Year +3	Year +4	Year +5	Continuing Value Year +6
Dividends Paid to Common Shareholders	$ 3,015.3	$3,324.5	$3,818.5	$4,398.5	$4,848.3	
Less: Common Stock Issues	(26.5)	(33.8)	(43.7)	(30.2)	(51.2)	
Plus: Common Stock Repurchases	2,500.0	2,500.0	2,500.0	2,500.0	2,500.0	
Dividends to Common Equity	$ 5,488.8	$5,790.7	$6,274.8	$6,868.3	$7,297.1	$8,186.50
Present Value Factors	0.922	0.849	0.783	0.722	0.665	
Present Value of Net Dividends	$ 5,058.8	$4,919.0	$4,912.6	$4,956.0	$4,852.9	
Sum of Present Value Net Dividends	$ 24,699.3					
Present Value of Continuing Value	98,988.9					
Total	$123,688.2					
Adjust to midyear discounting	1.0425					
Total Present Value Dividends	$128,945.0					
Shares Outstanding	1,553.0					
Estimated Value per Share	$ 83.03					
Current Share Price	$ 54.77					
Percent difference	52%					

Midyear Discounting

Present value calculations like those illustrated earlier discount amounts for full periods. Thus, the valuation computations include Year +1 dividends discounted for a full year, Year +2 dividends discounted for two full years, and so on, which is appropriate if the dividends being discounted occur at the end of each year. Dividends often occur throughout the period. If this is the case, present value computations with full-year discounting will overdiscount these flows. To avoid overdiscounting, the analyst can compute the present value discount factors as of the midpoint of each year, thereby effectively discounting the dividends as if they occur, on average, in the middle of each year. Suppose the analyst uses a discount rate of 10 percent ($R = 0.10$). The Year +1 dividends would be discounted from the middle of Year +1 using a factor of $1/(1 + R)^{0.5} = 1/(1.10)^{0.5} = 0.9535$; the Year +2 dividends would be discounted from the middle of Year +2 using a factor of $1/(1 + R)^{1.5} = 1/(1.10)^{1.5} = 0.8668$; and so on. The analyst also can use a shortcut approach to this correction by adjusting the total present value to a midyear approximation by adding back one-half year of discounting. To make this midyear adjustment, the analyst multiplies the total present value of the discounted dividends by a factor of $1 + (R/2)$. For example, if $R = 0.10$, the midyear adjustment is 1.05 [$= 1 + (0.10/2)$]. The Valuation spreadsheet computations in FSAP use this shortcut adjustment.[13]

Applying the midyear discounting adjustment to the computation of the present value of PepsiCo dividends results in the following:

Present Value of Common Equity	$123,688.2 million
Midyear Adjustment Factor [= 1 + (0.085/2)]	× 1.0425
Total Present Value of Common Equity	$128,945.0 million

Computing Common Equity Value per Share

Dividing the total present value of common equity of $128,945.0 million by 1,553 million shares outstanding indicates that PepsiCo's common equity shares have a value of $83.03 per share. We will obtain identical value estimates for PepsiCo when we apply the free cash flows to equity valuation model in Chapter 12 and the residual income valuation model in Chapter 13.

Sensitivity Analysis and Investment Decision Making

One should not place too much confidence in the *precision* of firm value estimates using these (or any) forecasts over the remaining life of any firm, even a mature firm such as PepsiCo. Although we have constructed these forecasts and value estimates with care, the forecasting and valuation process has an inherently high degree of uncertainty and estimation error. Therefore, the analyst should not rely too heavily on any one point estimate of the value of a firm's shares and instead should describe a reasonable range of values for a firm's shares.

[13] The valuation models described in this chapter estimate the present value of the firm as of the first day of the first year of the forecast horizon; for example, January 1 of Year +1 for a firm with an accounting period that matches the calendar year. However, analysts estimate valuations every day of the year. Suppose the analyst values a firm as of June 17 and compares the value estimate to that day's market price. A present value calculation that determines the value of the firm as of January 1 will ignore the value accumulation between January 1 and June 17 of that year. To refine the calculation, the analyst can adjust the present value as of January 1 to a present value as of June 17 by multiplying V_0 by a future value factor that reflects value accumulation for the appropriate number of days (in this case, 168 days). For example, if the valuation date is June 17 and if $R = 0.10$, the analyst can update the January 1 value estimate by multiplying V_0 by $(1 + R)^{(168/365)} = (1 + 0.10)^{(168/365)} = 1.0448$.

Two critical forecasting and valuation parameters in most valuations are the long-run growth rate assumption and the cost of equity capital assumption. Analysts should conduct sensitivity analysis to test the effects of these and other key valuation parameters and forecast assumptions on the share value estimate. Sensitivity analysis tests should allow the analyst to vary these valuation parameters individually and jointly for additional insights into the correlation between share values, growth rates, and discount rate assumptions.

For PepsiCo, the base case assumptions indicate PepsiCo's share value to be roughly $83. The base case valuation assumes a long-run growth rate of 3.0 percent and a cost of equity capital of 8.50 percent. The sensitivity of the estimates of PepsiCo's share value can be assessed by varying these two parameters (or any other key parameters in the valuation) across reasonable ranges. Exhibit 11.8 contains the results of sensitivity analysis varying the long-run growth rate from 0–10 percent and the cost of equity capital from 5–20 percent. The data in Exhibit 11.8 show that as the discount rate increases, holding growth constant, share value estimates of PepsiCo fall. Likewise, value estimates fall as growth rates decrease, holding discount rates constant. Note that we omit value estimates from this analysis when the assumed growth rate equals or exceeds the assumed discount rate because the continuing value computation is meaningless.

Considering the downside possibilities first, sensitivity analysis should consider how sensitive the share value estimate for PepsiCo is to adverse changes in long-run growth and discount rates. For example, by reducing the long-run growth assumption from 3.0 percent to 2.0 percent while holding the discount rate constant at 8.50 percent, PepsiCo share value falls to $73.36, still well above current market price. In fact, reducing the long-run growth assumption to zero, while holding the discount rate constant at 8.50 percent, PepsiCo's

EXHIBIT 11.8

Valuation of PepsiCo
Sensitivity Analysis of Value to Growth and Equity Cost of Capital

		Long-Run Growth Assumptions							
		0%	2%	3%	4%	5%	6%	8%	10%
Discount	5%	105.16	160.50	229.67	437.20				
Rates:	6%	87.18	120.00	152.81	218.45	415.34			
	7%	74.37	95.73	114.41	145.56	207.85	394.72		
	8.50%	60.84	73.36	**83.03**	97.00	118.95	158.47	711.69	
	9%	57.34	68.04	76.06	87.30	104.14	132.22	356.87	
	10%	51.41	59.41	65.13	72.75	83.42	99.42	179.45	
	11%	46.57	52.71	56.94	62.37	69.61	79.75	120.30	323.07
	12%	42.55	47.37	50.58	54.59	59.76	66.64	90.73	163.00
	13%	39.16	43.00	45.50	48.55	52.37	57.28	72.98	109.63
	14%	36.26	39.37	41.35	43.73	46.63	50.26	61.15	82.93
	15%	33.76	36.30	37.90	39.78	42.04	44.80	52.70	66.90
	16%	31.57	33.68	34.98	36.50	38.29	40.44	46.35	56.21
	18%	27.95	29.44	30.33	31.35	32.53	33.90	37.47	42.83
	20%	25.08	26.16	26.79	27.51	28.31	29.24	31.55	34.79

share value estimate falls to $60.84, still above current market price. Similarly, increasing the discount rate from 8.5 percent to 9.0 or 10.0 percent while holding constant the long-run growth assumption at 3.0 percent, PepsiCo shares have a value of roughly $76 or $65, respectively, above current market price. If we revise both assumptions at once, and reduce the long-run growth assumption to 2.0 percent and increase the discount rate assumption to 10.0 percent, PepsiCo's share value falls to roughly $59.

On the upside, reducing the discount rate to 7.0 percent while holding growth constant at 3.0 percent or increasing the long-run growth assumption from 3.0 to 4.0 percent while holding the discount rate constant at 8.50 percent, the value estimates jump to roughly $114 per share or $97 per share, respectively. If we reduce the discount rate assumption further, or increase the long-run growth rate further, the share value estimates for PepsiCo jump dramatically higher. For example, increasing the growth rate assumption to 4.0 percent and decreasing the discount rate assumption to 7.0 percent moves the share value estimate to more than $145.

These data suggest that the value estimate is sensitive to slight variations in the baseline assumptions of 3.0 percent long-run growth and an 8.50 percent discount rate, which yield a share value estimate of $83. Adverse variations in valuation parameters could reduce PepsiCo's share value estimates to $55 or lower, whereas favorable variations could increase PepsiCo's share value to over $100.

If the forecast and valuation assumptions are realistic, the baseline value estimate for PepsiCo is $83 per share at the end of 2008. At that time, the market price of $54.77 per share indicates that PepsiCo shares were underpriced by about 52 percent. Under the forecast assumptions, PepsiCo's share value could vary within a range of a low of $51 per share to a high of $114 per share with only minor perturbations in the growth rate and discount rate assumptions. Given PepsiCo's $54.77 share price, these value estimates would have supported a buy recommendation or perhaps a strong buy recommendation at the end of 2008 because the valuation sensitivity analysis reveals limited downside potential but substantial upside potential for the value of PepsiCo shares.

Evaluation of the Dividends Valuation Method

The principal *advantages* of the dividends valuation method include the following:

- This valuation method focuses on dividends. Economists argue that dividends provide the classical approach to valuing shares. Dividends reflect the payoffs that shareholders can consume.
- Projected amounts of dividends result from projecting expected amounts of revenues, expenses, assets, liabilities, and shareholders' equity. Therefore, they reflect the implications of the analyst's expectations for the future operating, investing, and financing decisions of a firm.

The principal *disadvantages* of the dividends valuation method include the following:

- The continuing value (terminal value) tends to dominate the total value in many cases. For firms that do not pay periodic dividends or repurchase shares, the continuing value can comprise the total value of the firm, which requires the analyst to forecast the future value of the firm in order to compute the present value of the firm. Continuing value estimates are sensitive to assumptions made about growth rates after the forecast horizon and discount rates.
- The projection of dividends can be time-consuming for the analyst, making it costly when the analyst follows many companies and must regularly identify under- and overvalued firms.

SUMMARY

This chapter illustrated the computation of risk-adjusted required rates of return on equity and the weighted average cost of capital, which analysts use as discount rates in valuation models. In valuation, analysts use these discount rates to compute the present value of future dividends, cash flows, or earnings. This chapter also described the dividends valuation model and applied it to value PepsiCo at the end of 2008. As with the preparation of projected financial statements in Chapter 10, the reasonableness of the valuations depends on the reasonableness of the forecast assumptions and the valuation parameters. The analyst should assess the sensitivity of the valuation to alternative long-run growth and discount rate parameters and to other key drivers of value. To validate value estimates using the dividends valuation approach, the analyst also should compute the value of the firm using other approaches, such as the free-cash-flows-based approaches discussed in Chapter 12, the earnings-based approaches discussed in Chapter 13, and the valuation multiples approaches described in Chapter 14.

QUESTIONS, EXERCISES, PROBLEMS, AND CASES

Questions and Exercises

11.1 THE RISK-RETURN TRADE-OFF. Explain why analysts and investors use risk-adjusted expected rates of return as discount rates in valuation. Why do risk-adjusted expected rates of return increase with risk?

11.2 THE COMPONENTS OF THE CAPM. The CAPM computes expected rates of return using the following model (described in the chapter):

$$E[R_{Ej}] = E[R_F] + \beta_j \times \{E[R_M] - E[R_F]\}$$

Explain the role of each of the three components of this model.

11.3 NONDIVERSIFIABLE AND DIVERSIFIABLE RISK FACTORS. Identify the types of firm-specific factors that increase a firm's nondiversifiable risk (systematic risk). Identify the types of firm-specific factors that increase a firm's diversifiable risk (idiosyncratic risk or nonsystematic risk). Why do models of risk-adjusted expected returns include no expected return premia for diversifiable risk?

11.4 DEBT AND THE WEIGHTED AVERAGE COST OF CAPITAL. Why do investors typically accept a lower risk-adjusted rate of return on debt capital than equity capital? Suppose a stable, financially healthy, profitable, tax-paying firm that has been financed with all equity and no debt decides to add a reasonable amount of debt to its capital structure. What effect will that change in capital structure likely have on the firm's weighted average cost of capital?

11.5 THE DIVIDENDS VALUATION APPROACH. Explain the theory behind the dividends valuation approach. Why are dividends value-relevant to common equity shareholders?

11.6 MEASURING VALUE-RELEVANT DIVIDENDS. The chapter describes how the dividends valuation approach measures value-relevant dividends to encompass various transactions between the firm and the common shareholders. What transactions should the analyst include in value-relevant dividends for purposes of implementing the dividends valuation model? Why?

11.7 FIRMS THAT DO NOT PAY PERIODIC DIVIDENDS. Why is the dividends valuation approach applicable to firms that do not pay periodic (quarterly or annual) dividends?

11.8 VALUATION APPROACH EQUIVALENCE. Conceptually, why should an analyst expect the dividends valuation approach to yield equivalent value estimates to the valuation approach that is based on free cash flows available to be distributed to common equity shareholders?

11.9 DIVIDEND POLICY IRRELEVANCE. The chapter asserts that dividends are value-relevant even though the firm's dividend policy is irrelevant. How can that be true? What is the key assumption in the theory of dividend policy irrelevance?

Problems and Cases

11.10 CALCULATING REQUIRED RATES OF RETURN ON EQUITY CAPITAL ACROSS DIFFERENT INDUSTRIES. The data in Exhibit 11.3 on industry median betas suggest that firms in the following three sets of related industries have different degrees of systematic risk.

	Median Beta during 1999–2007
Utilities versus Petroleum Refining	0.32 versus 0.65
Grocery Stores versus Retailing—Apparel	0.50 versus 1.08
Depository Institutions (such as Banks) versus Security and Commodity Brokers	0.39 versus 1.24

Required

a. For each matched pair of industries, describe factors that characterize a typical firm's business model in each industry. Describe how such factors would contribute to differences in systematic risk.

b. For each matched pair of industries, use the CAPM to compute the required rate of return on equity capital for the median firm in each industry. Assume that the risk-free rate of return is 4.0 percent and the market risk premium is 5.0 percent.

c. For each matched pair of industries, compute the present value of a stream of $1 dividends for the median firm in each industry. Use the perpetuity-with-growth model and assume 3.0 percent long-run growth for each industry. What effect does the difference in systematic risk across industries have on the per dollar dividend valuation of the median firm in each industry?

11.11 CALCULATING THE COST OF CAPITAL. Whirlpool manufactures and sells home appliances under various brand names. IBM develops and manufactures computer hardware and offers related technology services. Target Stores operates a chain of general merchandise discount retail stores. Selected data for these companies appear in the following table (dollar amounts in millions). For each firm, assume that the market value of the debt equals its book value.

	Whirlpool	IBM	Target Stores
Total Assets	$13,532	$109,524	$44,106
Interest-Bearing Debt	$ 2,597	$ 33,925	$18,752
Average Pretax Borrowing Cost	6.1%	4.3%	4.9%
Common Equity:			
Book Value	$ 3,006	$ 13,465	$13,712
Market Value	$ 2,959	$110,984	$22,521
Income Tax Rate	35.0%	35.0%	35.0%
Market Equity Beta	2.27	0.78	1.20

Required

a. Assume that the intermediate-term yields on U.S. government Treasury securities are roughly 3.5 percent. Assume that the market risk premium is 5.0 percent. Compute the cost of equity capital for each of the three companies.

b. Compute the weighted average cost of capital for each of the three companies.

c. Compute the unlevered market (asset) beta for each of the three companies.

d. Assume for this part that each company is a candidate for a potential leveraged buyout. The buyers intend to implement a capital structure that has 75 percent debt (with a pretax borrowing cost of 8.0 percent) and 25 percent common equity. Project the weighted average cost of capital for each company based on the new capital structure. To what extent do these revised weighted average costs of capital differ from those computed in Part b?

11.12 CALCULATION OF DIVIDENDS-BASED VALUE. Royal Dutch Shell is a petroleum and petrochemicals company. It engages primarily in the exploration, production, and sale of crude oil and natural gas and the manufacture, transportation, and sale of petroleum and petrochemical products. The company operates in approximately 200 countries worldwide—in countries in North America, Europe, Asia-Pacific, Africa, South America, and the Middle East. During 2006–2008, Royal Dutch Shell generated the following total dividends to common equity shareholders (in USD millions):

	2006	2007	2008
Common Dividend Payments	$ 8,142	$ 9,001	$ 9,516
Stock Repurchases	8,047	4,387	3,573
Total Dividends	$16,189	$13,388	$13,089

Analysts project 5 percent growth in earnings over the next five years. Assuming concurrent 5 percent growth in dividends, the following table provides the amounts that analysts project for Royal Dutch Shell's total dividends for each of the next five years. In Year +6, total dividends are projected for Royal Dutch Shell assuming that its income statement and balance sheet will grow at a long-term growth rate of 3 percent.

	Year +1	Year +2	Year +3	Year +4	Year +5	Year +6
Projected Growth	5%	5%	5%	5%	5%	3%
Projected Total Dividends to Common Equity	$13,743	$14,431	$15,152	$15,910	$16,705	$17,206

At the end of 2008, Royal Dutch Shell had a market beta of 0.71. At that time, yields on intermediate-term U.S. Treasuries were roughly 3.5 percent. Assume that the market required a 5.0 percent risk premium. Royal Dutch Shell had 6,241 million shares outstanding at the end of 2008 that traded at a share price of $24.87.

Required

a. Calculate the required rate of return on equity for Royal Dutch Shell as of the beginning of Year +1.
b. Calculate the sum of the present value of total dividends for Year +1 through +5.
c. Calculate the continuing value of Royal Dutch Shell at the start of Year +6 using the perpetuity-with-growth model with Year +6 total dividends. Also compute the present value of continuing value as of the beginning of Year +1.
d. Compute the total present value of dividends for Royal Dutch Shell as of the beginning of Year +1. Remember to adjust the present value for midyear discounting.
e. Compute the value per share of Royal Dutch Shell as of the beginning of Year +1.
f. Given the share price at the start of Year +1, do Royal Dutch Shell shares appear underpriced, overpriced, or correctly priced?

11.13 VALUING THE EQUITY OF A PRIVATELY HELD FIRM. Refer to the financial statement forecasts for Massachusetts Stove Company (MSC) prepared for Case 10.2. The management of MSC wants to know the equity valuation implications of adding gas stoves under the best, most likely, and worst case scenarios. Under the three scenarios from Case 10.2, the actual amounts of net income and common shareholders' equity for Year 7 and the projected amounts for Year 8–Year 12 are as follows:

	Actual	Projected				
	Year 7	Year 8	Year 9	Year 10	Year 11	Year 12
Best-Case Scenario:						
Net Income	$154,601	$148,422	$123,226	$173,336	$ 271,725	$ 390,639
Common Equity	$552,080	$700,502	$823,728	$997,064	$1,268,789	$1,659,429
Most Likely Scenario:						
Net Income	$154,601	$135,343	$ 74,437	$ 72,899	$ 109,357	$ 149,977
Common Equity	$552,080	$687,423	$761,860	$834,759	$ 944,116	$1,094,093
Worst-Case Scenario:						
Net Income	$154,601	$128,263	$ 18,796	$(39,902)	$ (58,316)	$ (77,156)
Common Equity	$552,080	$680,343	$699,139	$659,238	$ 600,921	$ 523,766

MSC is not publicly traded and therefore does not have a market equity beta. Using the market equity beta of the only publicly traded woodstove and gas stove manufacturing firm and adjusting it for differences in the debt-to-equity ratio, income tax rate, and privately owned status of MSC yields a cost of equity capital for MSC of 13.55 percent.

Required

a. Use the clean surplus accounting approach to derive the projected total amount of MSC's dividends to common equity shareholders in Years 8 through 12.
b. Given that MSC is a privately held company, assume that ending book value of common equity at the end of Year 12 is a reasonable estimate of the value at which the

common shareholders' equity could be liquidated. Calculate the value of the equity of MSC as of the end of Year 7 under each of the three scenarios. Ignore the midyear discounting adjustment.

c. How do these valuations affect your advice to the management of MSC about adding gas stoves to its woodstove line?

11.14 DIVIDENDS-BASED VALUATION OF COMMON EQUITY.

Problem 10.16 projected financial statements for Walmart for Years +1 through +5. The following data for Walmart include the actual amounts for 2008 and the projected amounts for Year +1 to Year +5 for comprehensive income and common shareholders' equity (assuming Walmart will use implied dividends as the financial flexible account to balance the balance sheet; amounts in millions).

	Actual	Projected				
	2008	Year +1	Year +2	Year +3	Year +4	Year +5
Comprehensive Income	$ 6,848	$ 13,995	$ 15,024	$ 16,126	$ 17,306	$ 18,569
Common Shareholders' Equity:						
Paid-In Capital	$ 4,313	$ 4,744	$ 5,219	$ 5,741	$ 6,315	$ 6,946
Retained Earnings	63,660	68,692	77,018	80,957	93,955	97,024
Accumulated Other Comprehensive Income	(2,688)	(2,688)	(2,688)	(2,688)	(2,688)	(2,688)
Total Common Equity	$ 65,285	$ 70,749	$ 79,549	$ 84,010	$ 97,582	$101,282

The market equity beta for Walmart at the end of 2008 was 0.80. Assume that the risk-free interest rate was 3.5 percent and the market risk premium was 5.0 percent. Walmart had 3,925 million shares outstanding at the end of 2008, and share price was $46.06.

Required

a. Use the CAPM to compute the required rate of return on common equity capital for Walmart.

b. Compute the weighted average cost of capital for Walmart as of the start of Year +1. At the end of 2008, Walmart had $42,218 million in outstanding interest-bearing debt on the balance sheet and no preferred stock. Assume that the balance sheet value of Walmart's debt is approximately equal to the market value of the debt. Assume that at the start of Year +1, Walmart will incur interest expense of 5.0 percent on debt capital and that Walmart's average tax rate is 34.2 percent.

c. Use the clean surplus accounting approach to derive the projected dividends for Walmart for Years +1 through +5 based on the projected comprehensive income and shareholders' equity amounts.

d. Use the clean surplus accounting approach to project the continuing dividend in Year +6. Assume that the steady-state long-run growth rate will be 3 percent in Year +6 and beyond.

e. Using the required rate of return on common equity from Part a as a discount rate, compute the sum of the present value of dividends for Walmart for Years +1 through +5.

f. Using the required rate of return on common equity from Part a as a discount rate and the long-run growth rate from Part d, compute the continuing value of Walmart as of the beginning of Year +6 based on Walmart's continuing dividends in Years +6 and beyond. After computing continuing value, bring continuing value back to present value at the start of Year +1.

g. Compute the value of a share of Walmart common stock. (i) Compute the sum of the present value of dividends including the present value of continuing value. (ii) Adjust the sum of the present value using the midyear discounting adjustment factor. (iii) Compute the per-share value estimate.

h. Using the same set of forecast assumptions as before, recompute the value of Walmart shares under two alternative scenarios. Scenario 1: Assume that Walmart's long-run growth will be 2 percent, not 3 percent as before, and assume that Walmart's required rate of return on equity is 1 percentage point higher than the rate you computed using the CAPM in Part a. Scenario 2: Assume that Walmart's long-run growth will be 4 percent, not 3 percent as before, and assume that Walmart's required rate of return on equity is 1 percentage point lower than the rate you computed using the CAPM in Part a. To quantify the sensitivity of your share value estimate for Walmart to these variations in growth and discount rates, compare (in percentage terms) your value estimates under these two scenarios with your value estimate from Part g.

i. What reasonable range of share values would you expect for Walmart common stock? Where is the current price for Walmart shares relative to this range? What do you recommend?

INTEGRATIVE CASE 11.1

STARBUCKS

Dividends-Based Valuation of Starbucks' Common Equity

Integrative Case 10.1 projected financial statements for Starbucks for Years +1 through +5. This portion of the Starbucks Integrative Case applies the techniques in Chapter 11 to compute Starbucks' required rate of return on equity and share value based on the dividends valuation model. This case also compares the value estimate to Starbucks' share price at the time of the case development to provide an investment recommendation.

The market equity beta for Starbucks at the end of 2008 was 0.58. Assume that the risk-free interest rate was 4.0 percent and the market risk premium was 6.0 percent. Starbucks had 735.5 million shares outstanding at the end of 2008, and share price was $14.17.

Required

a. Use the CAPM to compute the required rate of return on equity capital for Starbucks.

b. Compute the weighted average cost of capital for Starbucks as of the start of Year +1. At the start of Year +1, Starbucks had $1,263 million in outstanding interest-bearing debt on the balance sheet and no preferred stock. Assume that the balance sheet value of Starbucks' debt is approximately equal to the market value of the debt. Assume that at the start of Year +1, Starbucks will incur interest expense of 6.25 percent on debt capital and that Starbucks' average tax rate is 36.0 percent.

c. From your forecasts of Starbucks' financial statements for Years +1 through +5, derive the projected dividends using the projected amounts for the plug to dividends less the net amounts of common stock issued each year (if any). Then compute projected dividends for Starbucks for Years +1 through +5 using the clean surplus accounting approach based on projected amounts for comprehensive income and common shareholders' equity. The projected amounts of dividends under the two approaches should be identical.

d. Use the clean surplus accounting approach to project the continuing dividend in Year +6. Assume that the steady-state long-run growth rate will be 3 percent in Year +6 and beyond.

e. Using the required rate of return on common equity capital from Part a as a discount rate, compute the sum of the present value of dividends for Starbucks for Years +1 through +5.

f. Using the required rate of return on common equity capital from Part a as a discount rate and a 3.0 percent long-run growth rate, compute the continuing value of Starbucks as of the beginning of Year +6 based on Starbucks' continuing dividends in Year +6 and beyond. After computing continuing value, bring continuing value back to present value at the start of Year +1.

g. Compute the value of a share of Starbucks' common stock. (i) Compute the sum of the present value of dividends including the present value of continuing value. (ii) Adjust the sum of the present value using the midyear discounting adjustment factor. (iii) Compute the per-share value estimate.

h. Using the same set of forecast assumptions as before, recompute the value of Starbucks shares under two alternative scenarios. Scenario 1: Assume that Starbucks' long-run growth will be 2 percent, not 3 percent as before, and assume that Starbucks' required rate of return on equity is 1 percentage point higher than the rate you computed using the CAPM in Part a. Scenario 2: Assume that Starbucks' long-run growth will be 4 percent, not 3 percent as before, and assume that Starbucks' required rate of return on equity is 1 percentage point lower than the rate you computed using the CAPM in Part a. To quantify the sensitivity of your estimate of share value for Starbucks to variations in long-run growth and discount rates, compare (in percentage terms) your value estimates under these two scenarios with your value estimate from Part f.

i. What reasonable range of share values would you expect for Starbucks' common stock? Where is the current price for Starbucks' shares relative to this range? What do you recommend?

Chapter 12

Valuation: Cash-Flow-Based Approaches

Learning Objectives

1. Understand cash-flow-based valuation models and their conceptual and practical strengths and weaknesses.
2. Apply practical techniques to deal with many of the difficult issues involved in estimating firm value using the present value of expected future free cash flows:
   a. Risk, discount rates, and the cost of capital
   b. Cash flows to the investor versus cash flows to the firm
   c. Nominal versus real cash flows
   d. Pretax versus after-tax cash flows
   e. The forecast horizon
   f. Computation of continuing value
3. Measure free cash flows for all debt and equity capital stakeholders as well as free cash flows for common equity shareholders and understand when each measure is appropriate.
4. Understand the reasons for discounting free cash flows for common equity shareholders using a required rate of return on equity capital and discounting free cash flows for all debt and equity capital stakeholders using a weighted average cost of capital.
5. Apply all of these techniques to estimate firm value using the present value of future free cash flows for common equity shareholders and the present value of future free cash flows for all debt and equity capital stakeholders.
6. Assess the sensitivity of firm value estimates to key valuation parameters such as discount rates and expected long-term growth rates.

INTRODUCTION AND OVERVIEW

This chapter relies heavily on the financial statement forecasts developed for PepsiCo in Chapter 10, as well as the valuation concepts and techniques introduced and applied in Chapter 11. This chapter extends valuation methodology to encompass free-cash-flows-based valuation approaches and applies these valuation approaches to PepsiCo.

As introduced in Chapter 11, economic theory teaches that the value of an investment equals the present value of the expected future payoffs from the investment, discounted at a rate that reflects the risk inherent in those expected payoffs. The general model for estimating the present value of a security (denoted as V_0 with present value denoted at time $t=0$) with an expected life of n future periods is as follows:[1]

$$V_0 = \sum_{t=1}^{n} \frac{\text{Expected Future Payoffs}_t}{(1 + \text{Discount Rate})^t}$$

Valuation methods such as the dividends-based valuation methods demonstrated in the previous chapter, the free-cash-flows-based methods demonstrated in this chapter, and the earnings-based methods demonstrated in the next chapter are all designed to produce reliable estimates of the value of the firm's equity shares. The value estimates that these approaches produce provide the basis for intelligent investment decisions because even in relatively efficient securities markets, price does not necessarily equal value for every security at all times. Price is observable, but value is not; value must be estimated. Therefore, estimating the value of a security is a common objective of financial statement analysis. The financial statement analysis and valuation process enables investors, analysts, portfolio managers, investment bankers, and corporate managers to determine a reliable appraisal of the value of shares of common equity. Comparing value to price then yields a reliable basis to assess whether a firm's equity shares are underpriced, overpriced, or fairly priced in the capital markets.

Whether an analyst will produce reliable estimates of share value as a result of the financial statement analysis and valuation process depends entirely on whether the analyst carefully and thoughtfully applies each step of the process. The six-step analysis framework that forms the structure of this book (Exhibit 1.2 in Chapter 1) is a logical set of steps that enables the analyst to determine reliable estimates of value. Following the first three steps, the analyst should first understand the economics of the industry, then assess the particular firm's strategy, and then carefully evaluate the quality of the firm's accounting, making adjustments if necessary. In the fourth step, the analyst should evaluate the firm's profitability and risk with a set of financial ratios. All of this information should provide the analyst with a solid foundation of information to use in the fifth step, projecting the firm's future financial statements. The analyst can then use those financial statement forecasts to derive expectations of future earnings, cash flows, and dividends, which are the fundamental payoff measures used in valuation. In the sixth and final step, the analyst applies valuation models to these expectations to estimate the value of the firm. Forecasts of expected future payoffs (the numerator in the valuation model) depend on forecasts of future earnings, cash flows, or dividends. Assessing an appropriate risk-adjusted discount rate (the denominator in the valuation model) requires an unbiased assessment of the inherent riskiness in the set of expected future payoffs. Therefore, reliable estimates of firm value depend on unbiased expectations of future payoffs and an appropriate risk-adjusted discount rate, all of which depend on all six steps of the framework.

As explained in the previous chapter, when the analyst derives forecasts of future earnings, cash flows, and dividends from a set of internally consistent financial statement forecasts for a firm and uses the same discount rate in correctly specified models to compute

[1] In this chapter, as in the previous chapter, t refers to accounting periods. The valuation process determines an estimate of firm value, denoted as V_0, in present value as of today, when $t=0$. The period $t=1$ refers to the first accounting period being discounted to present value. Period $t=n$ is the period of the expected final payoff.

present values, the expected earnings, cash flows, and dividends valuation models will yield *identical* estimates of value for a firm. We applied the dividends-based valuation approach to PepsiCo and estimated that, given our forecast assumptions and valuation parameters, PepsiCo's share value should be within a fairly narrow range of around $83 at the time of our analysis. This chapter illustrates the equivalence of the dividends and free cash flows valuation approaches, both in the theoretical development of the models and in their application to the valuation of PepsiCo. The next chapter will describe and apply the earnings-based valuation approach and demonstrate its theoretical and practical equivalence with both the dividends and free cash flows approaches.[2]

It is important that analysts understand the similarities and differences in the dividends, cash flows, and earnings valuation approaches and see their theoretical and practical equivalence. Our experience strongly suggests that applying several different valuation approaches yields better insights about the value of a firm than relying on one approach in all cases. In addition, it is our experience that an analyst is better equipped to work successfully with clients, managers, colleagues, and subordinates in the financial statement analysis and valuation process if the analyst thoroughly understands all three valuation approaches.

All four valuation chapters—Chapters 11–14—emphasize that the objective of the valuation process is not a single point estimate of value per se. Instead, the objective is to determine the distribution of value estimates across the relevant ranges of critical forecast assumptions and valuation parameters. By assessing the sensitivity of value estimates across a distribution of relevant forecast assumptions and valuation parameters, we seek to determine the most likely range of values for a share, which we then compare to the share's current price for an intelligent investment decision.

RATIONALE FOR CASH-FLOW-BASED VALUATION

As we demonstrated in the previous chapter, the value of a share of common equity is the present value of the expected future dividends.[3] Dividends are fundamental expected future payoffs that analysts can use to value shares because they represent the distribution of wealth to shareholders. The equity shareholder invests cash to purchase the share and then receives cash through dividends as the payoffs from holding the share, including the final "liquidating" dividend when the investor sells the share. In dividends-based valuation, we define *dividends* broadly to encompass all cash flows from the firm to the common equity shareholders through periodic dividend payments, stock buybacks, and the liquidating dividend, as well as cash flows from the shareholders to the firm when the firm issues shares (negative dividends).

Cash-flow-based valuation and dividends-based valuation can be considered two sides to the same coin: the analyst can value the firm based on the cash flows into the firm that will be used to pay dividends or, equivalently, value the firm using cash flows the firm pays out in dividends to common shareholders. In the cash flows approach, we focus on the cash that flows *into* the firm; in the dividends approach we focus on the cash that flows *out of* the firm. Instead of focusing on wealth distribution through dividends, the cash-flow-based

---

[2] For examples of research on the complementarity of these approaches, see Stephen Penman and Theodore Sougiannis, "A Comparison of Dividend, Cash Flow, and Earnings Approaches to Equity Valuation," *Contemporary Accounting Research* 15, no. 3 (Fall 1998), pp. 343–383, and Jennifer Francis, Per Olsson, and Dennis Oswald, "Comparing the Accuracy and Explainability of Dividend, Free Cash Flow, and Abnormal Earnings Equity Value Estimates," *Journal of Accounting Research* 38, no. 1 (Spring 2000), pp. 45–70.

[3] John Burr Williams, *The Theory of Investment and Value* (Cambridge, Mass.: Harvard University Press, 1938).

approach focuses on cash flows generated by the firm that create dividend-paying capacity. In any given period, the amount of cash flow into the firm and the amount of dividends paid out of the firm will likely differ; the equivalence of these two valuation approaches arises because over the lifetime of the firm the cash flows into and out of the firm will be equivalent.

The cash-flow-based valuation approach measures and values the cash flows that are "free" to be distributed to shareholders. That is, *free cash flows* are the cash flows each period that are available for distribution to shareholders, unencumbered by necessary reinvestments in operating assets or required payments to debtholders. Free cash flows can be used instead of dividends as the value-relevant measures of expected future payoffs to the investor in the numerator of the general value model set forth at the outset of this chapter. Both approaches, if implemented with consistent assumptions, will lead to identical estimates of value.

The rationale for using expected free cash flows in valuation is twofold and is essentially the same rationale for using dividends, as follows:

- Cash is the ultimate source of value. When individuals and firms invest in an economic resource, they delay current consumption in favor of future consumption. Cash is the medium of exchange that will permit them to consume various goods and services in the future. A resource has value because of its ability to provide future cash flows. The free cash flows approach measures value based on the cash flows that the firm generates that can be distributed to investors.
- Cash is a measurable common denominator for comparing the future benefits of alternative investment opportunities. One might compare investment opportunities involving the holding of a bond, a stock, or an office building, but comparing these alternatives requires a common measuring unit of their future benefits. The future cash flows derived from their future services serve such a function.

FREE-CASH-FLOWS-BASED VALUATION CONCEPTS

The following sections describe and illustrate these key concepts in free-cash-flows-based valuation methods:

- Risk, discount rates, and the cost of capital
- Cash flows to the investor versus cash flows to the firm
- Nominal versus real cash flows
- Pretax versus after-tax cash flows
- The forecast horizon
- Computation of continuing value

These concepts are the same underlying concepts described in the previous chapter in presenting dividends-based valuation methods. Therefore, we will briefly review those concepts here and describe how they apply to free cash flows valuation. Refer back to the previous chapter for more detailed explanations of these concepts.

We first describe computing discount rates to use in free-cash-flows-based valuation, including required rates of return on equity capital and weighted average costs of capital. We then present simple examples involving a single project. Next, we confront conceptual measurement issues regarding cash flows to the investor versus cash flows to the firm, nominal versus real cash flows, and pretax versus after-tax cash flows. We also address forecast horizons and continuing value. A later section of this chapter describes how to compute free cash flows to equity shareholders versus free cash flows to all debt and equity stakeholders. Later in the chapter, we also illustrate the free cash flow valuation approaches by valuing PepsiCo using free cash flows derived from the projected financial statements developed in Chapter 10.

Risk, Discount Rates, and the Cost of Capital

The general valuation model described at the beginning of the chapter is a present value model, so the analyst must determine an appropriate discount rate to use to measure future payoffs in present value. This section briefly reviews the computation of the required rate of return on equity capital and the weighted average cost of capital.

Cost of Common Equity Capital

When discounting the free cash flows available to common equity shareholders, the analyst should use a risk-adjusted required rate of return on equity capital. As described in more depth in the previous chapter, analysts commonly estimate the cost of equity capital using an expected return model such as the CAPM (capital asset pricing model). The CAPM assumes that the market is composed of risk-averse investors who demand a rate of return that (1) compensates them for forgoing the consumption of capital and (2) compensates them with a risk premium for bearing systematic (nondiversifiable) risk. Systematic risk arises from economy-wide factors (such as economic growth or recession, unemployment, unexpected inflation, unexpected changes in prices for natural resources such as oil and gas, unexpected changes in exchange rates, and population growth) that affect all firms to varying degrees and therefore cannot be fully diversified. The amount of the risk premium for a particular stock depends on the level of the firm's systematic risk.

Analysts often measure systematic risk using the firm's market beta, which is estimated as the slope coefficient from regressing the firm's stock returns on an index of returns on a marketwide portfolio of stocks over a relevant period of time.[4] Market beta is an estimate of systematic risk based on the degree of covariation between a firm's stock returns and an index of stock returns for all firms in the market. If a firm's market beta from such a regression is equal to 1, it indicates the firm's stock returns covary identically with returns to a marketwide portfolio, indicating that the firm has the same degree of systematic risk as the market as a whole. If a firm's market beta is greater than or less than 1, the firm has a greater or lesser degree of systematic risk than the market portfolio as a whole.

The CAPM computes the expected return on common equity capital for Firm j as follows:

$$E[R_{Ej}] = E[R_F] + \beta_j \times \{E[R_M] - E[R_F]\}$$

where E denotes that the related variable is an expectation; R_{Ej} denotes return on common equity in Firm j; R_F denotes the risk-free rate of return; β_j denotes the market beta for Firm j; and R_M denotes the return on a diversified, marketwide portfolio of stocks (such as the S&P 500). According to the CAPM, a common equity security with no systematic risk (that is, a stock with $\beta_j = 0$) should be expected to earn a return equal to the expected rate of return on risk-free securities. The subtraction term in brackets in the preceding equation represents the average market risk premium, equal to the return that equity investors in the capital markets require for bearing the average amount of systematic risk in the market portfolio. An equity security with systematic risk equal to the average amount of systematic

[4] Researchers and analysts have developed a variety of approaches to estimate market betas. For example, one common approach estimates a firm's market beta by regressing the firm's monthly stock returns on a marketwide index of returns (such as the S&P 500) over the last 60 months.

risk of all equity securities in the market has a market beta equal to 1 and should expect to earn the same rate of return as the average stock in the market portfolio.

Note that the CAPM views firm-specific nonsystematic risk as diversifiable by the investor. Nonsystematic risk factors would include, for example, the industry and product portfolio of the firm, the sustainability of the firm's strategy, and the firm's ability to generate revenue growth and control expenses. According to CAPM, a competitive equilibrium capital market does not expect a return for a firm's nonsystematic risk because such risk can be diversified away in a portfolio of stocks.

Computing the Weighted Average Cost of Capital

In some circumstances, the analyst may want to value all of the assets of a firm rather than directly value the common equity of the firm. In such circumstances, the analyst should discount to present value the free cash flows that the assets will generate that will be available to satisfy all of the debt and equity claims that finance the assets of the firm. In these circumstances, analysts commonly use a weighted average cost of capital that reflects the relative proportions of debt, preferred, and common equity capital the firm will use to finance the assets and the respective costs of each type of capital. Such circumstances might arise, for example, if the analyst is considering acquiring all of the assets of a firm or acquiring all of the financial claims (common equity shares, preferred shares, and debt) through a merger with the firm. Therefore, the analyst determines the present value of the future free cash flows available to satisfy all of the firm's financing using a discount rate that reflects the weighted average cost of the debt, preferred, and common equity capital the firm uses to finance the net operating assets.

A formula for the weighted average cost of capital (denoted as R_A to indicate that the discount rate is the required rate of return applicable to the net operating *assets* of the firm) is given here:

$$R_A = [w_D \times R_D \times (1 - \textit{tax rate})] + [w_P \times R_P] + [w_E \times R_E]$$

In this formula, the subscripts *D*, *P*, and *E* refer to different types of capital (debt, preferred stock, and common equity, respectively); *w* denotes the weight on each type of capital; *R* denotes the cost of each type of capital; and *tax rate* denotes the tax rate applicable to tax deductions for debt capital costs. The weights used to compute the weighted average cost of capital should be the market values of each type of capital in proportion to the total market value of the capital structure that will be used to finance the firm (that is, $w_D + w_P + w_E = 1.0$). On the right-hand side of this equation, the first term in brackets measures the weighted after-tax cost of debt capital, the second term measures the weighted cost of preferred stock capital, and the third term measures the weighted cost of equity capital. Refer to the previous chapter for more detailed discussions and examples of computing the cost of debt, preferred, and common equity capital.

Free Cash Flows Valuation Examples for a Single-Asset Firm

For the next three examples, make the following assumptions:

- The firm consists of a single asset that will generate net cash flows of $2 million per year forever.
- The income tax rate is 40 percent.

- After making debt service payments and paying taxes, the firm pays dividends to distribute any remaining free cash flows to the equity shareholders each year.
- The cost of equity capital is 10 percent.

Example 1: Value of Common Equity in an All-Equity Firm

Assume that the common equity shareholders have financed the asset entirely with $10 million of equity capital. We can determine the value of the common equity investment to the shareholders using the present value of free cash flows for common equity shareholders. The free cash flow to common equity shareholders each year will be as follows:

Net Cash Flow	$2,000,000
Income Taxes: 0.40 × $2,000,000	(800,000)
Free Cash Flow for Common Equity Shareholders	$1,200,000

The value to the shareholders of the common equity in the firm is $12,000,000 (= $1,200,000/0.10). Dividing by the discount rate is appropriate because the $1.2 million annual free cash flow for common equity is a perpetuity with no growth. This investment is worth $12 million to those shareholders (a gain of $2 million over the original investment of $10 million) because of the present value of the free cash flows the investment will generate and that will in turn be paid out as dividends to the shareholders. Therefore, we would determine the same value for the investment using the dividends-based valuation model as shown in Example 5 in Chapter 11.

Example 2: Value of Common Equity in a Firm with Debt Financing

For this example, we will make the same assumptions as in the preceding example, except we will now make the following additional assumptions to use both debt and equity financing:

- The equity shareholders finance a portion of the investment in the asset with $4 million of equity capital.
- The firm finances the remainder of the asset using $6 million of debt capital.
- This amount of debt in the firm's capital structure does not alter substantially the risk of the firm to the equity investors, so they continue to require a 10 percent rate of return.
- The debt is issued at par, and it is less risky than equity; so the debtholders demand interest of only 6 percent each year, payable at the end of each year.
- Interest expense is deductible for income tax purposes.

We can again determine the value of the common equity investment using the present value of free cash flows for common equity shareholders. Note that this example is essentially the same as Example 6 in Chapter 11, except that the valuation focus changes from dividends to free cash flows. The free cash flow available to common equity shareholders each year is as follows:

Net Cash Flow for All Debt and Equity Capital	$2,000,000
Interest Paid on Debt: 0.06 × $6,000,000	(360,000)
Income Taxes: 0.40 × ($2,000,000 − $360,000)	(656,000)
Free Cash Flow for Common Equity Shareholders	$ 984,000

The value of the common equity to the shareholders in the firm is $9,840,000 (= $984,000/0.10). Dividing by the discount rate is appropriate because the $984,000 annual free cash flow for common equity is a perpetuity with no growth. Note that in this example, the present value of the gain to the common equity shareholders in excess of their initial investment is $5,840,000 (= $9,840,000 − $4,000,000). The gain to the shareholders is $3,840,000 (= $5,840,000 − $2,000,000) larger in this example than in the previous example because (1) the debt capital is less expensive than the equity capital (6 percent rather than 10 percent on $6,000,000 of financing), creating $2,400,000 of value for equity shareholders from capital structure leverage [= ($6,000,000 × {0.10 − 0.06})/0.10], and (2) the net tax savings from interest expense creates $1,440,000 of value for equity shareholders [= ($800,000 − $656,000)/0.10, or, alternatively, = ($360,000 interest deduction × 0.40 tax rate)/0.10].

Example 3: Value of More Risky Common Equity in a Firm with Debt Financing

Now make the same assumptions as the preceding example except now assume that by changing the capital structure to 60 percent debt and 40 percent equity, the firm becomes more risky to the equity investors and they demand a 15 percent rate of return rather than 10 percent. Under these assumptions, the value of the common equity to the investors in the firm will be $6,560,000 (= $984,000/0.15). Note that in this example, the present value of the gain to the common equity investors in excess of their initial investment falls to $2,560,000 (= $6,560,000 − $4,000,000). Because of the increased risk, the investors demand a higher rate of return; so the value for equity investors from the net tax savings from interest expense falls to $960,000 [= ($800,000 − $656,000)/0.15] and the value for equity investors from capital structure leverage falls to $1,600,000 (= $2,560,000 − $960,000).[5]

Cash Flows to the Investor versus Cash Flows to the Firm

The analyst can use expectations of the dividends to be paid to the investor or the free cash flows to be generated by the firm (that will ultimately be paid to the investor) as equivalent approaches to measure the value-relevant expected payoffs to shareholders. Cash flows paid to the investor via dividends and free cash flows that are available for common equity shareholders will differ each period to the extent that the firm reinvests a portion (or all) of the cash flows generated. However, if the firm generates a rate of return on reinvested free cash flow equal to the discount rate used by the investor (that is, the cost of equity capital), either set of payoffs (dividends or free cash flows) will yield the same valuation of a firm's shares. To demonstrate this equivalence, consider the following scenarios.

Example 4: Free Cash Flows with 100 Percent Payout

A firm expects to generate free cash flows of $0.15 for each dollar of invested equity capital for the foreseeable future (until, for example, $t=n$). Considering the riskiness of the

---

[5] The lower value to equity investors from capital structure leverage is the net result of two effects. First, the increased risk of the firm causes the equity investors to increase the discount rate from 10 percent to 15 percent, which would (if considered in isolation) cause the value of the project to fall to $8,000,000 (= $1,200,000/0.15), which would imply a $2,000,000 loss on the investors' $10,000,000 investment. Second, the debt capital is less expensive than the equity capital, creating $3,600,000 of value for equity investors from capital structure leverage [= ($6,000,000 × {0.15 − 0.06})/0.15]. The net result is $1,600,000 of value to equity investors from capital structure leverage, net of the incremental effects of risk.

firm, equity investors in this firm require a 15 percent return each year. We assume that the firm will pay out 100 percent of the free cash flows each year as a dividend. Thus, the free cash flows generated by the firm equal the cash dividends received by the investor each period. Each dollar of capital committed by the investor has a present value of future cash flows equal to one dollar. That is, over an indefinitely long period of time into the future,

$$\$1 = \sum_{t=1}^{n} \frac{\$0.15}{(1.15)^t}$$

Example 5: Free Cash Flows with Zero Payout

Assume the same facts as in Example 4 except that the firm will pay out none of the free cash flows as a dividend. The firm will retain the \$0.15 free cash flow on each dollar of capital and reinvest it in projects expected to earn 15 percent return per year. In this case, the investor receives no periodic dividends and receives cash only when the investor sells the shares or the firm liquidates at date $t=n$. By the terminal date, n periods in the future, each dollar of capital invested in the firm today will have earned a compound rate of return of 15 percent, equal to the required rate of return. Therefore, each dollar of invested capital has a present value of future free cash flows equal to one dollar, as in the preceding example with full payout of free cash flows. That is,

$$\$1 = \frac{(\$1.15)^n}{(1.15)^n}$$

Example 6: Free Cash Flows with Partial Payout

Assume the same facts as in Example 5 except that the firm pays out 25 percent of the free cash flow each period as a dividend and reinvests the other 75 percent in projects expected to generate a return of 15 percent. In this case also, each dollar of invested capital has a present value of future cash flows equal to one dollar. That is,

$$\$1 = \sum_{t=1}^{n} \frac{(0.25)(\$0.15)}{(1.15)^t} + \frac{(0.75)(\$1.15)^n}{(1.15)^n}$$

We used these three examples in the previous chapter to illustrate the *relevance* of dividends as payoffs that are sufficient for valuation for equity shareholders and the *irrelevance* of the firm's dividend policy in valuation.[6] We use the same examples here to illustrate that the assumptions we make about dividend policy are the complementary assumptions we make about free cash flows reinvested in the firm. Therefore, *if the firm can be expected to reinvest cash flows to earn the required rate of return,* the same valuation should arise whether the analyst discounts (1) the expected dividends to the investor, or (2) the expected free cash flows to the firm that are available to pay future dividends to equity shareholders. Further, the same valuation should arise whether the firm pays all of its free cash flows as a dividend, reinvests all free cash flows to earn the investors' required rate of return, or pays

[6] Merton Miller and Franco Modigliani, "Dividend Policy, Growth and the Valuation of Shares," *Journal of Business* (October 1961), pp. 411–433. Penman and Sougiannis test empirically the replacement property of dividends for future earnings and find support for the irrelevance of dividend policy in valuation. See Stephen H. Penman and Theodore Sougiannis, "The Dividend Displacement Property and the Substitution of Anticipated Earnings for Dividends in Equity Valuation," *The Accounting Review* (January 1997), pp. 1–21.

a portion of free cash flows in dividends each period and reinvests the remainder to earn the investors' required rate of return. Note that the crucial assumption is that capital retained in the firm will generate a rate of return exactly equal to the investors' required rate of return.

Nominal versus Real Cash Flows

Changes in general price levels (that is, inflation or deflation) cause the purchasing power of the monetary unit to change over time.[7] The valuation of an investment in an economic resource should be the same whether one uses nominal or real free cash flow amounts as long as the valuation uses a consistent discount rate that is the nominal or real rate of return. That is, if projected free cash flows are nominal and include the effects of changes in general purchasing power of the monetary unit, the discount rate should be nominal and include an inflation component. If projected free cash flows are real amounts that filter out the effects of general price changes, the discount rate should be a real rate of return, excluding the inflation component.

Example 7: Nominal versus Real Free Cash Flows

A firm owns an asset that it expects to sell one year from today for $115.5 million. The firm expects the general price level to increase 10 percent during this period. The real interest rate is 5 percent. The nominal discount rate should be 15.5 percent to measure the compound effects of the real rate of interest and inflation [0.155 = (1.10 × 1.05) − 1]. Discounting nominal or real free cash flows, the present value of the asset to the firm is $100 million, as shown:

Nominal Free Cash Flows	×	Discount Rate Including Expected Inflation	=	Value
$115.5 million	×	1/(1.05 × 1.10)	=	$100 million

Real Free Cash Flows	×	Discount Rate Excluding Expected Inflation	=	Value
$115.5 million/1.10	×	1/1.05	=	$100 million

In both computations, we derived the value of the equity of the firm by computing the present value of the free cash flows to common equity shareholders. As a practical matter, analysts usually find it more straightforward to discount nominal free cash flows using nominal discount rates than to adjust nominal free cash flows to real free cash flows and then discount real free cash flows using real interest rates. Discount rates derived from the CAPM are nominal because the risk-free rate component incorporates expected inflation. Further, stated and effective interest rates on long-term debt also are nominal because they incorporate expected inflation rates. Thus, readily available or easily estimable discount

[7] Note that the issue here is not with specific price changes of a firm's particular assets, liabilities, revenues, and expenses. These specific price changes affect our projections of the firm's dividends, cash flows, and earnings and should enter into the valuation of the firm. The issue is whether some portion, all, or more than all of the specific price changes simply represent an economy-wide change in the purchasing power of the monetary unit, which should not affect the value of a firm.

rates relating to the cost of equity and debt capital are typically nominal rates, as are weighted average costs of capital.

Pretax versus After-Tax Free Cash Flows

Will the same valuation arise if the analyst discounts pretax-free cash flows at a pretax cost of capital and after-tax free cash flows at an after-tax cost of capital? The answer is no if costs of debt and equity capital receive different tax treatments. For tax purposes, firms can typically deduct the costs of debt capital but cannot deduct the costs of equity capital.

Example 8: Tax Effects on Free Cash Flows

Suppose the firm faces the following costs of capital:

	Proportion in Capital Structure	Pretax Cost	Tax Effect	After-Tax Cost	Weighted Average Cost of Capital Pretax	After-Tax
Debt	0.33	10%	0.40	6%	3.33%	2.00%
Equity	0.67	18%	—	18%	12.00%	12.00%
	1.00				15.33%	14.00%

Assume that this firm expects to generate $90 million of pretax-free cash flows and $54 million of after-tax free cash flows [= (1 − 0.40) × $90 million] one year from today. This firm would be valued using pretax and after-tax amounts (assuming a one-year horizon) as follows:

Pretax:	$90 million × 1/1.1533 = $78.04 million
After-tax:	$54 million × 1/1.14 = $47.37 million

These values are not equivalent because cash inflows from assets are taxed at 40 percent and cash outflows to service debt give rise to a tax savings of 40 percent. However, the cost of equity capital does not provide a tax benefit. The appropriate valuation in this case is $47.37 million. Thus, the analyst should use *after-tax* free cash flows and the *after-tax* cost of capital.

Selecting a Forecast Horizon

The analyst will need to project periodic free cash flows over the remaining expected life of the resource to be valued. This life is a finite number of years for a resource with a finite physical life, such as a machine or a building, or a financial instrument with a finite stated maturity, such as a bond, a mortgage, or a lease. But an equity security is a resource that has an indefinite life; therefore, the analyst must project future periodic free cash flows that, in theory, could extend to infinity. As a practical matter, the analyst cannot precisely predict a firm's free cash flows very many years into the future. Therefore, analysts develop specific projections of income statements and balance sheets for the firm and use them to derive forecasts of free cash flows over an explicit forecast horizon (for example, five or ten years) depending on the industry, the maturity of the firm, and the expected growth and predictability of the firm's cash flows. After the explicit forecast horizon, analysts then use general growth assumptions to project the future income statements and balance sheets and use them to derive the free cash flows that will persist each period to infinity. Therefore, the analyst will find it desirable to develop specific forecasts of income statements, balance sheets, and free cash flows over an explicit forecast horizon that extends until the point when the firm's growth can be expected to settle into steady-state equilibrium, during which time free cash flows can be expected to grow at a steady, predictable rate.

Selecting a forecast horizon involves trade-offs. For stable and mature firms such as PepsiCo, one can develop reasonably reliable projections over longer forecast horizons, as demonstrated in Chapter 10. For young high-growth firms, it is more difficult to develop reliable projections of free cash flows over long forecast horizons because their future operating performance is relatively more uncertain. This difficulty is magnified by the fact that these firms will achieve a much higher proportion of their value in distant future years, after they reach their potential steady-state profitability. Ironically, the analyst faces the dilemma of depending most heavily on long-run forecasts for young growth firms for which long-run projections are most uncertain. The forecasting and valuation process is particularly difficult for growth firms when the near-term free cash flows are likely to be negative, as is common for rapidly growing firms that finance growth by issuing common stock. Most of the value of these firms depends on free cash flows they will generate in years far into the future.

Unfortunately, this dilemma is inevitable. The analyst must recognize that forecasts and value estimates for all firms have some degree of uncertainty and estimation risk. To mitigate this uncertainty and estimation risk, we suggest the following:

1. Apply all six steps of the analysis framework. By thoroughly analyzing the firm's industry and strategy, the firm's accounting quality, and the firm's financial performance and risk ratios, the analyst will have more information to use to develop long-term forecasts that are as reliable as possible.
2. To the extent possible, confront directly the problem of long-term uncertainty by developing specific projections of free cash flows derived from projected income statements and balance sheets that extend five or ten years into the future, at which point the firm may be projected to reach steady-state growth.
3. Assess the sensitivity of the forecast projections and value estimates across the reasonable range of long-term growth parameter assumptions.

Computing Continuing Value of Future Free Cash Flows

As described in the previous section, the analyst will find it desirable to forecast free cash flows over an explicit forecast horizon, until the point at which the firm's free cash flows growth will settle into a long-run steady-state growth rate. We refer to these free cash flows as *continuing free cash flows* because they reflect the free cash flows continuing into the long-run future of the firm. The long-run steady-state growth rate in future continuing free cash flows could be positive, negative, or zero. Steady-state growth in free cash flows could be driven by long-run expectations for growth attributable to economy-wide inflation, general economic productivity, the population, or demand for the industry's output. The analyst should select a growth rate that captures realistic expectations for the long run.

Once the analyst projects the firm's long-run steady-state growth rate (denoted as g) continuing after the end of the explicit forecast horizon (for example, after Year T), the analyst can derive the continuing free cash flows from the projected income statements and balance sheets. The same principles demonstrated in the previous chapter for projecting continuing dividends apply here in projecting continuing free cash flows. The analyst should use the expected long-run growth rate (g) to project all of the items of the Year T+1 income statement and balance sheet by multiplying each item on the Year T income statement and balance sheet times $(1 + g)$. The analyst can then derive the Year T+1 statement of cash flows (and thus Year T+1 free cash flows) from the Year T+1 income statement and balance sheet projections. It is necessary to impose the long-run growth rate assumption (1 + *g*) uniformly on the Year T income statement and balance sheet projections in order to derive the free cash flows for Year T+1 correctly. We assume that in steady state, the firm's assets, liabilities, and shareholders' equity (and therefore the firm's earnings, cash flows, and dividends) will all grow at equivalent rates. By applying a uniform growth rate, the analyst achieves internally consistent steady-state growth across all of the projections of the firm, keeping the balance sheet in balance throughout the continuing forecast horizon and keeping the cash flows, earnings, and dividends internally consistent with the assumed long-run growth rate.

In projecting continuing free cash flows in Year T+1 and beyond, analysts often assume that the firm's long-run sustainable growth rate will be consistent with inflation and long-run growth in the economy, on the order of 3–5 percent. For firms that have been growing more quickly than that (for example, at 10 percent) in the years leading up to Year T+1, the long-run sustainable growth rate implies that the firm will maintain a lower growth rate in assets and equity and thus generate substantially larger amounts of free cash flow. By projecting Year T+1 net income, assets, and equity using the long-run sustainable growth rate, we can solve for the long-run sustainable free cash flows the firm will generate. The continuing free cash flow amount we derive for Year T+1 may be significantly larger than the amounts the firm actually generated during its higher-growth-rate years. The Year T+1 free cash flow amount reflects the firm's transition from a high rate of reinvestment of cash flows for growth in assets to reinvestment for a much lower rate of growth, thereby creating the need to solve for the long-run sustainable free cash flows amount.

If the analyst wants to compute internally consistent and identical estimates of firm value using free cash flows, earnings, and dividends, he or she should *not* simply project free cash flows for Year T+1 by multiplying free cash flows for Year T by (1 + *g*). Doing so ignores the necessary growth in all of the elements of the balance sheet and the income statement, which can introduce inconsistent forecast assumptions for cash flows, earnings, and dividends. Even if the analyst simply projects that Year T free cash flows, earnings, and dividends will grow at an identical rate (1 + *g*) in Year T+1, doing so may impound inconsistent assumptions and lead to inconsistent value estimates if Year T cash flows, earnings, and dividends are not consistent with their long-run continuing amounts.

Example 9: Projecting Continuing Value Free Cash Flows

Suppose the analyst develops the following forecasts for the firm in Year T–1 and Year T:

	Assets	=	Liabilities	+	Shareholders' Equity
Year T–1 Balances	$100	=	$60	+	$40
+ Net Income	+20				+20
+ New Borrowing	+ 6		+6		
− Dividends Paid	−10				−10
Year T Balances	$116	=	$66	+	$50

Assume that the entire increase in assets involves growth in assets required for operations, such as inventory and equipment. The analyst would compute Year T free cash flows for common equity shareholders to equal $10 (= $20 net income − $16 increase in assets + $6 increase in liabilities). Now suppose the analyst projects that the firm will grow at a steady-state rate of 10 percent in Year T+1 and thereafter. The analyst should project Year T+1 net income, assets, liabilities, and shareholders' equity to grow by 10 percent each and then compute Year T+1 free cash flows as follows:

	Assets	=	Liabilities	+	Shareholders' Equity
Year T Balances	\$116.0	=	\$66.0	+	\$50.0
Growth	× 1.10		× 1.10		× 1.10
Year T+1 Balances	\$127.6	=	\$72.6	+	\$55.0

The projected net income would be \$22 (= \$20 × 1.10). The Year T+1 free cash flow projection would be \$17 (= \$22 net income − \$11.6 increase in assets + \$6.6 increase in liabilities). However, if the analyst had simply projected Year T free cash flows to grow by 10 percent, the Year T+1 projections would be only \$11 (= \$10 Year T free cash flow × 1.10). By making this simple projection of free cash flows, the analyst is implicitly assuming that the \$16 increase in assets in Year T will grow by 10 percent in Year T+1 (= \$17.6 increase in assets). This is internally inconsistent with our long-run assumption of 10 percent growth in assets, liabilities, equity, and income growth. This will understate free cash flows to equity in Year T+1 by \$6 (= \$11.6 increase in assets − \$17.6 increase in assets). This error will understate the estimated value of the firm using free cash flows, relative to the value estimate using earnings, because of the inconsistent assumptions. Note that the correct projected Year T+1 free cash flow amount of \$17 is substantially larger than the \$10 free cash flow amount for Year T. The reason the firm will generate larger amounts of free cash flow in Year T+1 and beyond is that the firm's long-run growth rate is 10 percent, which is lower than the Year T growth rate in assets (16 percent) and shareholders' equity (25 percent); thus, this firm will not need to reinvest as much of its cash flows to fund growth and will generate larger free cash flow amounts in Year T+1 and beyond.

As demonstrated for dividends in the previous chapter, once the analyst has computed free cash flows for Year T+1, he or she can compute continuing value (sometimes called terminal value) of future free cash flows for Years T+1 and beyond using the perpetuity-with-growth valuation model:[8]

$$\text{Continuing Value at End of Forecast Horizon (Year T)} = \text{Continuing Free Cash Flow Projection for T+1} \times 1/(R-g)$$

where g denotes the projected steady-state growth rate for Years T+1 and beyond and is applied uniformly to project the income statement and balance sheet in Year T+1, which are then used to project the continuing free cash flows in Year T+1; R denotes the appropriate risk-adjusted discount rate. Once the analyst has computed the continuing value at the end of the forecast horizon (Year T), the analyst must discount continuing value from that point in time to present value today by multiplying by the present value factor of $1/(1+R)^T$.

Example 10: Computing Continuing Value

An analyst forecasts that the free cash flow of a firm in Year +5 will be \$30 million and that Year +5 earnings and dividends also will be \$30 million. Assume for the simplicity of this

[8] This formula is simply the algebraic simplification for the present value of a growing perpetuity.

example that the analyst expects that the firm's income statements and balance sheets will grow uniformly over the long run and, therefore, that cash flows, earnings, and dividends will grow uniformly over the long run. But the analyst is uncertain about the steady-state long-run growth rate in Year +6 and beyond. He or she believes that the growth rate will most likely be zero but could reasonably fall between +6 and −6 percent per year. Assuming a 15 percent cost of capital, the following table shows the range of possible continuing values (in millions) for the firm at the beginning of the continuing value period (that is, the beginning of Year +6 or, equivalently, the end of Year +5) and in present value as of today; that is, the continuing value is discounted to today using a factor of $1/(1.15)^5$:

				Continuing Value in Present Value as of:	
Free Cash Flows in Year T	**Long-Run Growth Assumption**	**Free Cash Flows in Year T+1**	**Perpetuity with Growth Factor**	**Beginning of Year T+1**	**Today**
\$30	0%	\$30.00	$\frac{1}{(0.15 - 0.00)} = 6.67$	\$200.00	\$ 99.44
\$30	+6%	\$31.80	$\frac{1}{(0.15 - 0.06)} = 11.11$	\$353.30	\$175.65
\$30	−6%	\$28.20	$\frac{1}{(0.15 + 0.06)} = 4.76$	\$134.23	\$ 66.74

Analysts also can estimate a continuing value using a multiple of free cash flow in the first year of the continuing value period to value the common stock of a firm. The following table shows the cash flow multiples using $1/(R - g)$ for various costs of equity capital and growth rates. The multiples increase with growth for a given cost of capital, and they decrease as cost of capital increases for a given level of growth.

Continuing Value Multiples

	Long-Run Growth Rates					
Cost of Equity Capital	**0%**	**2%**	**3%**	**4%**	**5%**	**6%**
6%	16.67	25.00	33.33	50.00	100.00	na
8%	12.50	16.67	20.00	25.00	33.33	50.00
10%	10.00	12.50	14.29	16.67	20.00	25.00
12%	8.33	10.00	11.11	12.50	14.29	16.67
15%	6.67	7.69	8.33	9.09	10.00	11.11
18%	5.56	6.25	6.67	7.14	7.69	8.33
20%	5.00	5.56	5.88	6.25	6.67	7.14

The continuing value computation using the perpetuity-with-growth valuation model does not work when the growth rate equals or exceeds the discount rate (that is, when $g \geq R$) because the denominator in the computation is zero or negative and the resulting continuing value estimate is meaningless. In this case, the analyst cannot use the perpetuity computation illustrated here. Instead, the analyst must forecast free cash flow amounts for each year beyond the forecast horizon using the terminal period growth rate and then discount each year's cash flows to present value using the discount rate. The analyst also should probably reconsider whether it is realistic to expect the firm's free cash flow growth rate to exceed the discount rate (the expected rate of return) in perpetuity. This scenario can exist for some years, but is not likely to be sustainable indefinitely. Competition, technological change, new entrants into an industry, and similar factors eventually reduce growth rates. Thus, in applying the model, the analyst must attempt to estimate the long-term sustainable growth rate in cash flows. (Refer to the discussion of sustainable earnings in Chapter 9.)

MEASURING PERIODIC FREE CASH FLOWS

This section first presents a conceptual framework for measuring free cash flows. Then it describes specific practical steps to measure free cash flows from two different perspectives—free cash flows to all debt and equity stakeholders and free cash flows to common equity shareholders—and when to use each free cash flow measure.

A Framework for Free Cash Flows

A conceptual framework for free cash flows to the firm emanates from the familiar balance sheet equation in which assets equal liabilities plus shareholders' equity:

$$A = L + SE$$

Recall from Chapter 5 the demonstration of an alternative ROCE decomposition into operating and financial leverage components. Using the same approach, separate all of the assets and liabilities into two categories: operating or financing:

$$OA + FA = OL + FL + SE$$

Operating assets (denoted as *OA*) and operating liabilities (denoted as *OL*) relate to the firm's day-to-day operations in the normal course of business. For most firms, operating assets include cash and short-term investment securities necessary for operating liquidity purposes; accounts receivable; inventory; property, plant, and equipment; intangible assets (for example, licenses, patents, trademarks, and goodwill); and investments in affiliated companies. Operating liabilities typically include accounts payable, accrued expenses, accrued taxes, deferred taxes, pension obligations, and other retirement benefits obligations.

Financial liabilities include interest-bearing liabilities that are part of the financial capital structure of the firm. Financial liabilities (denoted as *FL*) include such interest-bearing items as short-term notes payable; current maturities of long-term debt; and long-term debt in the forms of mortgages, bonds, notes, and capital lease obligations. Insofar as outstanding preferred stock contains features indicating that it is economically similar to debt (features such as limited life, mandatory redemption, and guaranteed dividends), the analyst should include preferred stock with financial liabilities.

In some circumstances, firms may hold financial assets (denoted as *FA*) such as excess cash and short-term or long-term investment securities to provide the firm with liquidity to repay debt, pay dividends, and repurchase common stock. Distinguishing financial assets that the firm will use to change its financial capital structure from cash and marketable securities the firm will use for liquidity for operating purposes requires a judgment call by the analyst. Analysts consider financial assets to be part of the financial structure of the firm if the firm is likely to use the financial assets to offset or retire debt or if the financial assets could be used to pay dividends or repurchase common equity shares. For example, such financial assets may exist if a firm is accumulating cash or investment securities for purposes of retiring debt, if a firm is required to hold certain amounts of restricted cash or investment securities under a loan covenant (such as required compensating cash balances), or if a firm is maintaining and accumulating a sinking fund for bond retirement under the terms of a bond debenture. Analysts typically do not consider financial assets to be part of the financial capital structure of a firm when the financial assets are necessary to manage the liquidity needs of the firm's operating activities across different seasons or business cycles and the assets are held in liquid interest-earning accounts such as cash and cash equivalents, marketable securities, and short-term investment securities. Analysts also typically do not consider financial assets to be part of the financial capital structure of the firm when the financial assets include investment securities that are part of the long-term strategy of the firm, such as investments in affiliated subsidiaries with related operating activities or strategic investments in potential acquisition targets.[9] Capital held in these types of accounts for purposes of operating liquidity or strategic investments in securities of affiliated companies or potential takeover targets should be considered operating assets, not financial assets.

Once the analyst has separated the balance sheet into operating and financing components, he or she should rearrange the balance sheet equation to put operating accounts on one side and financing accounts and shareholders' equity on the other side, as follows:

$$OA - OL = FL - FA + SE,$$

which is equivalent to

$$NetOA = NetFL + SE$$

where $NetOA = OA - OL$ and $NetFL = FL - FA$. For most firms, operating assets are likely to exceed operating liabilities and financial liabilities are likely to exceed financial assets. (Financial borrowing usually exceeds financial assets because the firm uses the funds obtained from borrowing to purchase operating assets.)

This rearrangement of the balance sheet provides a useful basis from which to conceptualize free cash flows to the firm. If we substitute for each term the present values of the expected future net cash flows associated with operating activities, financing activities, and shareholders' equity, we can express the balance sheet in the following cash flow terms:

Present Value of Net Cash Flows from Operations
= Present Value of Net Cash Flows Available for Debt Financing
+ Present Value of Net Cash Flows Available for Shareholders' Equity

This expression indicates that the present value of the expected net cash flows from operations of the firm determines the sum of the values of the debt and equity claims on the firm.[10] Therefore, one can estimate the value of the debt and equity capital of the firm by

---

[9] The calculation of the rate of return on assets, or ROA, in Chapter 4 assumed that all assets were operating assets and that operating income is equal to net income excluding the after-tax cost of financial liabilities. Thus, Chapter 4 made no adjustment to eliminate interest income on financial assets from net income in the numerator of ROA and no adjustment to eliminate financial assets in the denominator. Most manufacturing, retailing, and service firms hold only minor amounts of financial assets, so ignoring adjustments for financial assets does not usually introduce a material amount of bias to the calculation of ROA. A more precise calculation of ROA for firms with a material amount of financial assets in the capital structure adjusts the numerator to eliminate interest income and adjusts the denominator of ROA for the portions of financial assets (cash, marketable securities, and investment securities) that are part of the financial capital structure and are not directly related to operating activities.

[10] The next section explains how our use of Net Cash Flows from Operations in this section differs from Cash Flow from Operations reported in the Statement of Cash Flows.

projecting the net cash flows from operations that are "free" to service debt and equity claims and discounting those free cash flows to present value. We refer to this measure of free cash flows as *the free cash flows for all debt and equity capital stakeholders* because they reflect the cash flows that are available to the debt and equity capital stakeholders in the firm as a whole.

We can rearrange the balance sheet equation slightly further:

$$NetOA - NetFL = SE$$

Using the same present value cash flow terms as before, we can express this form of the balance sheet in terms of present values of expected future cash flows as follows:

Present Value of Net Cash Flows from Operations
− *Present Value of Net Cash Flows Available for Debt Financing*
= *Present Value of Net Cash Flows Available for Shareholders' Equity*

With this expression, we can conceptualize free cash flows specifically attributable to the equity shareholders of the firm. The present value of free cash flows produced by the operations of the firm minus the present value of cash flows necessary to service claims of the net debtholders yields *free cash flows available for common equity shareholders.* This measure captures the net free cash flows available to equity shareholders after debt claims are satisfied.

Free Cash Flows Measurement

The following sections describe how to measure free cash flows from the two perspectives described above—*free cash flows for all debt and equity capital stakeholders* and *free cash flows for common equity shareholders*—and when to use each free cash flow measure. In practice, different analysts compute free cash flows from various starting points: the statement of cash flows, net income, EBITDA (earnings before interest, tax, depreciation, and amortization), and NOPAT (net operating profit adjusted for tax). We describe how to measure free cash flows from each starting point.

Measuring Free Cash Flows: The Statement of Cash Flows as the Starting Point

Under U.S. GAAP and IFRS, firms report the statement of cash flows by decomposing the net change in cash into operating, investing, and financing activity components. These three categories do not match the operating and financing classifications we need for computing free cash flows. Thus, the analyst needs to reclassify some of the components of the statement of cash flows to compute free cash flows for valuation purposes. Exhibit 12.1 describes the computation of each of these two measures of free cash flows.

Cash flow from operations from the projected statement of cash flows is the most direct starting point for computing both measures of free cash flows because it requires the fewest adjustments. Recall from Chapter 3 that the statement of cash flows measures cash flow from operations by beginning with net income, adding back any non-cash expenses or losses (such as depreciation and amortization expenses), subtracting any non-cash income or gains (such as income from equity method affiliates), and then adjusting for net cash flows for operating activities (such as changes in receivables, inventory, accounts payable, and accrued expenses).

EXHIBIT 12.1

Measurement of Free Cash Flows

Free Cash Flows for All Debt and Equity Stakeholders:

Operating Activities:

Cash Flow from Operations
Begin with cash flow from operations on the projected statement of cash flows.

+/− Net Interest after Tax
Add back interest expense and subtract interest income, net of tax effects.

+/− Changes in Cash Requirements for Liquidity
Subtract an increase or add a decrease in cash required for purposes of liquidity for operations.

= Free Cash Flows from Operations for All Debt and Equity

Investing Activities:

+/− Net Capital Expenditures
Subtract cash outflows for capital expenditures and add cash inflows from sales of assets that comprise the productive capacity of the operations of the firm (including property, plant, and equipment; affiliated companies; and intangible assets).

= Free Cash Flows for All Debt and Equity Stakeholders

Free Cash Flows for Common Equity Shareholders:

Operating Activities:

Cash Flow from Operations
Begin with cash flow from operations on the projected statement of cash flows.

+/− Changes in Cash Requirements for Liquidity
Subtract an increase or add a decrease in cash required for purposes of liquidity for operations.

= Free Cash Flows from Operations for Equity

Investing Activities:

+/− Net Capital Expenditures
Subtract cash outflows for capital expenditures and add cash inflows from sales of assets that comprise the productive capacity of the operations of the firm (including property, plant, and equipment; affiliated companies; and intangible assets).

Financing Activities:

+/− Debt Cash Flows

Add cash inflows from new borrowings or subtract cash outflows from repayments of short-term and long-term interest-bearing debt.

+/− Financial Asset Cash Flows

Subtract cash outflows invested in cash, short-term, and long-term investment securities (or add cash inflows from these accounts) if these financial assets are deemed to be part of the financial capital structure of the firm and are not part of the operating activities of the firm.

+/− Preferred Stock Cash Flows

Add cash inflows from new issues of preferred stock or subtract cash outflows from preferred stock retirements and dividend payments.

= *Free Cash Flows for Common Equity Stakeholders*

Free Cash Flows for All Debt and Equity Capital Stakeholders

Free cash flows for all debt and equity capital stakeholders are the cash flows available to make interest and principal payments to debtholders, redeem preferred shares or pay dividends to preferred shareholders, and pay dividends and buy back shares from common equity shareholders. To measure these free cash flows, we begin with cash flow from operations from the projected statement of cash flows, as shown in the left-hand side of Exhibit 12.1. To measure cash flow from operations before the effects of the firm's financial capital structure, the analyst must add back the interest expense on financial liabilities, net of any income tax savings from interest expense. If the analyst makes the judgment call that some or all of the firm's financial assets (such as excess cash holdings or marketable securities) are intended to retire debt and pay dividends and are part of the financial capital structure of the firm (rather than part of the operating liquidity management of the firm), the analyst should subtract the interest income on those financial assets, net of the income taxes paid on that interest income. To adjust interest expense and interest income for tax effects, the analyst typically multiplies interest expense and interest income by one minus the firm's marginal tax rate.[11]

The analyst also should add or subtract any change in the cash balance that the firm will require for operating liquidity. Cash that the firm must maintain for operating liquidity purposes is not available for distribution to debt or equity stakeholders and therefore is not part of free cash flow. For example, suppose an analyst is valuing a retail store chain and the chain must maintain the equivalent of seven days of sales in checking accounts and cash on hand at each store for purposes of conducting retail sales transactions. When the chain opens new stores, it is required to hold additional cash as part of operations (as it would need to hold additional inventory). These additional cash requirements are not available for debt and equity capital providers if the firm intends to maintain its operations. If the firm improves its cash management efficiency and reduces the amount of cash required for operating liquidity, the firm has additional free cash flow that can be distributed to debt or equity stakeholders. Procedurally, the analyst should project the required change in cash for working capital purposes each period and add or subtract that amount to determine free cash flow from operations for debt and equity stakeholders.

Next, the analyst adjusts for cash flows related to capital expenditures on long-lived assets that are a part of the firm's productive capacity (for example, property, plant, and equipment; affiliated companies; intangible assets; and other investing activities). The analyst should subtract cash outflows for purchases and add cash inflows from sales of these types of assets related to the firm's long-term productive activities. The analyst can measure the cash flows for capital expenditures and other investing activities that are part of the long-term productive activities of the firm by using the amounts reported in the investing activities section of the projected statement of cash flows.

As noted earlier, the analyst must make a judgment call about the amounts of the firm's financial assets (for example, in cash and cash equivalents, short-term securities, or long-term investment securities) that are (1) necessary for the liquidity and operating capacity of the firm or (2) part of the financial capital structure of the firm and therefore distributable to debt or equity stakeholders. For example, if the analyst projects that the firm will retain financial assets by saving some portion of its cash flows in a securities account each

[11] Technically, analysts should make these adjustments using the cash amounts of interest paid and interest received rather than the accrual amounts of interest expense and interest income. However, as a practical matter, it is reasonable to assume that forecasted amounts of interest expense will equal interest paid and forecasted amounts of interest income will equal interest received.

period and that this cash can ultimately be used to repay debt, pay dividends, or buy back shares, the analyst should deem these cash flows as free cash flows for debt and equity capital. For instance, the firm may be required by a bond indenture agreement to maintain a sinking fund of cash or liquid securities that will be available to repay the bond when it matures. In this case, the analyst should include the amount of cash added to the bond sinking fund as free cash flows for debt and equity capital.

This adjustment requires a judgment call by the analyst because in some circumstances, firms retain seemingly excess amounts of cash, marketable securities, or investment securities accounts when these assets are in fact not free for potential distribution to capital stakeholders. For example, in some cases, firms with seasonal business need to maintain large balances in cash or securities accounts in order to provide needed liquidity during particular seasons. In other cases, firms may build up large balances in investment securities accounts that represent investments in key affiliates, such as PepsiCo's and Coca-Cola's investments in bottling companies. In scenarios such as these, the analyst should not assess these cash flows as "free" for potential distribution to capital stakeholders, but instead should consider these cash flows necessary investments in the liquidity and productive capacity of the firm.

Together, these computations result in free cash flows for all debt and equity capital stakeholders, which are available to service debt, pay dividends to preferred and common shareholders, and buy back shares or for reinvestment. A later section describes the approach to estimate the present value of the sum of the debt and equity claims on the firm by discounting free cash flows for debt and equity capital using the weighted average cost of capital of the firm.

Free Cash Flows for Common Equity Shareholders

Free cash flows for common equity shareholders are the cash flows specifically available to the common shareholders after all debt service payments have been made to lenders and dividends have been paid to preferred shareholders. Therefore, the free cash flows for common equity shareholders amount to the free cash flows available to all debt and equity capital less any cash flows that are attributable to debt and preferred stock claims.

To measure free cash flows for common equity shareholders, we can again begin with cash flow from operations from the projected statement of cash flows, as presented in the right-hand side of Exhibit 12.1. As in the previous section, the analyst should add or subtract any change in the cash balance that the firm will require for operating liquidity because this cash is not available for distribution to equity shareholders and therefore is not part of free cash flow. Procedurally, the analyst should add or subtract the projected change in cash required for liquidity purposes each period.[12]

Also, as in the previous section, the analyst should adjust for cash flows for capital expenditures on long-lived assets that are a part of the firm's productive capacity (for example, property, plant, and equipment; affiliated companies; intangible assets; and other investing activities). The analyst should subtract cash outflows for purchases and add cash inflows from sales of assets related to the firm's long-term productive activities.

The analyst should incorporate cash flows related to debt claims by adding cash inflows from new borrowing in short- and long-term debt and subtracting cash outflows for repayments of short- and long-term debt. In calculating free cash flows to debt and equity capital, if

---

[12] Note that unlike the computation of free cash flows for all debt and equity stakeholders, we do not adjust for interest expense or interest income after tax when we compute free cash flows for equity. Our measure of free cash flow for equity already reflects net cash flows for interest payments for interest-bearing debt capital because the statement of cash flows starts with net income to compute cash flow from operations and because net income already reflects interest expense after tax.

the analyst made the judgment call that the firm saves financial capital beyond its immediate liquidity needs in a cash or investment securities account, these cash flows reflect financing activities. Therefore, the analyst must (1) subtract the amount of cash outflow used to purchase the securities because this cash obviously was not paid out to equity shareholders or (2) add the amount of cash inflow received from selling such securities because this cash inflow is available for distribution to equity shareholders. For example, if the firm maintains a bond sinking fund to be used for the eventual retirement of bonds when they mature, the cash invested in the sinking fund is clearly not free cash flows available for common equity shareholders. Finally, the analyst also should add cash inflows from new issues of preferred stock and subtract cash outflows from preferred-stock retirements and dividend payments.[13] These computations measure free cash flows for common equity shareholders. These cash flows are available to common equity shareholders for dividends, stock buybacks, or reinvestment. As described in a later section of this chapter, free cash flows for common equity should be discounted at the cost of equity capital to determine the present value of the common equity of the firm.

Measuring Free Cash Flows: Alternative Starting Points

In practice, different analysts use different starting points to compute free cash flows. The approaches described above used cash flow from operations from the projected statement of cash flows because it is the most direct starting point, requiring the fewest adjustments. However, some analysts compute free cash flows by beginning with projected net income, some start with EBITDA, and yet others start with NOPAT. Exhibit 12.2 describes the steps the analyst must take to adjust each of these starting points to determine free cash flows to all debt and equity stakeholders. Exhibit 12.3 (see page 952) describes the steps the analyst must take to adjust each of these starting points to determine free cash flows to common equity shareholders.

If the analyst starts with net income and wants to determine free cash flows for all debt and equity stakeholders, Exhibit 12.2 indicates that the analyst must add back all non-cash expenses (such as depreciation and amortization expenses), subtract all non-cash income items (such as accrued income from equity method affiliates), and adjust for cash flows related to changes in working capital accounts (such as cash flows related to changes in receivables, inventory, and payables). These adjustments bring the analyst up to our starting point, cash flow from operations. The analyst then incorporates the remaining steps by adjusting for net interest expense after tax, changes in cash requirements for liquidity, and capital expenditures.

Other analysts compute free cash flows for all debt and equity by starting with EBITDA, which already adds back non-cash income items for depreciation and amortization, interest expense (but usually not interest income) and *all* of the provision for income taxes. From this starting point, the analyst must adjust further by adding back any other non-cash expenses (apart from depreciation and amortization), adjust for non-cash income items, and adjust for cash flows related to working capital activities. In addition, because EBITDA adds back all of the provision for income taxes, the analyst must subtract cash taxes paid, net of tax saving on interest expense. These adjustments bring the analyst up

[13] It might seem inappropriate to include changes in debt and preferred stock financing, which appear in the financing section of the statement of cash flows, in the valuation of a firm. Economic theory suggests that the capital structure (that is, the proportion of debt versus equity) should not affect the value. Changes in debt and preferred stock, however, affect the amount of cash available to the common shareholders. The analyst includes cash flows related to debt and preferred stock financing in free cash flows for common equity shareholders but adjusts the cost of equity capital to reflect the amounts of such senior financing in the capital structure.

EXHIBIT 12.2

Measurement of Free Cash Flows for All Debt and Equity Stakeholders from Alternative Starting Points

Starting Point:		
Net Income:	**EBITDA:**[a]	**NOPAT:**[b]
Operating Activities:	***Operating Activities:***	***Operating Activities:***
Net income	EBITDA	NOPAT
+ Add back all non-cash expenses	+ Add back all non-cash expenses other than depreciation and amortization	+ Add back all non-cash expenses
− Subtract all non-cash income items	− Subtract all non-cash income items	− Subtract all non-cash income items
+/− Working capital cash flows	+/− Working capital cash flows	+/− Working capital cash flows
+/− Net interest after tax	− Subtract cash taxes paid, net of tax savings on interest expense	
+/− Changes in cash requirements for liquidity	+/− Changes in cash requirements for liquidity	+/− Changes in cash requirements for liquidity
= Free Cash Flows from Operations for All Debt and Equity Stakeholders	***= Free Cash Flows from Operations for All Debt and Equity Stakeholders***	***= Free Cash Flows from Operations for All Debt and Equity Stakeholders***
Investing Activities:	***Investing Activities:***	***Investing Activities:***
+/− Net capital expenditures	+/− Net capital expenditures	+/− Net capital expenditures
= Free Cash Flows for All Debt and Equity Stakeholders	***= Free Cash Flows for All Debt and Equity Stakeholders***	***= Free Cash Flows for All Debt and Equity Stakeholders***

[a] EBITDA denotes earnings before interest, tax, depreciation, and amortization.

[b] NOPAT denotes net operating profit after tax, which equals net income adjusted for net interest expense after tax.

EXHIBIT 12.3

Measurement of Free Cash Flows for Common Equity Shareholders from Alternative Starting Points

Starting Point:		
Net Income:	**EBITDA:**[a]	**NOPAT:**[b]
Operating Activities:	***Operating Activities:***	***Operating Activities:***
Net income	EBITDA	NOPAT
+ Add back all non-cash expenses	+ Add back all non-cash expenses other than depreciation and amortization	+ Add back all non-cash expenses
− Subtract all non-cash income items	− Subtract all non-cash income items	− Subtract all non-cash income items
+/− Working capital cash flows	+/− Working capital cash flows	+/− Working capital cash flows
	− Subtract net interest expense	− Subtract net interest expense after tax
	− Subtract taxes	
+/− Changes in cash requirements for liquidity	+/− Changes in cash requirements for liquidity	+/− Changes in cash requirements for liquidity
= Free Cash Flows from Operations for Equity	***= Free Cash Flows from Operations for Equity***	***= Free Cash Flows from Operations for Equity***
Investing Activities:	***Investing Activities:***	***Investing Activities:***
+/− Net capital expenditures	+/− Net capital expenditures	+/− Net capital expenditures
Financing Activities:	***Financing Activities:***	***Financing Activities:***
+/− Debt cash flows	+/− Debt cash flows	+/− Debt cash flows
+/− Financial asset cash flows	+/− Financial asset cash flows	+/− Financial asset cash flows
+/− Preferred stock cash flows	+/− Preferred stock cash flows	+/− Preferred stock cash flows
= Free Cash Flows for Common Equity Shareholders	***= Free Cash Flows for Common Equity Shareholders***	***= Free Cash Flows for Common Equity Shareholders***

[a] EBITDA denotes earnings before interest, tax, depreciation, and amortization.

[b] NOPAT denotes net operating profit after tax, which equals net income adjusted for net interest expense after tax.

to our starting point, cash flow from operations. The analyst then incorporates the remaining steps by adjusting for changes in cash requirements for operating liquidity and capital expenditures.

Still other analysts begin the computation of free cash flows for all debt and equity stakeholders using NOPAT, which is net income with net interest expense (adjusted for tax savings) added back. From this starting point, the analyst should add back all non-cash expense items (such as depreciation and amortization expenses), subtract all non-cash income items (such as accrued income from equity method affiliates), and adjust for cash flows related to working capital activities. The analyst then incorporates the remaining steps by adjusting for changes in cash requirements for liquidity and capital expenditures.

In practice, some analysts also use net income, EBITDA, and NOPAT as starting points to compute free cash flows for equity shareholders. Exhibit 12.3 shows the steps necessary to adjust each of these starting point amounts to complete measures of free cash flows for common equity. Note that many but not all of the additional adjustments are similar to those demonstrated in Exhibit 12.2. Also note that although it occurs in practice, starting with EBITDA or NOPAT to compute free cash flows for equity is inefficient because it is necessary to subtract interest expense after tax from both EBITDA and NOPAT.

The starting point of the computation of free cash flows is less important than the ending point. The analyst can begin the computation of free cash flows with cash from operating activities on the statement of cash flows, net income, EBITDA, or NOPAT, so long as he or she properly makes all of the necessary adjustments to compute a complete measure of free cash flows as described in Exhibits 12.1–12.3.

Which Free Cash Flow Measure Should Be Used?

The appropriate free cash flow measure to use—free cash flows to all debt and equity stakeholders or free cash flows to equity shareholders—depends on the resource to be valued.

- If the objective is to value operating assets net of operating liabilities or, equivalently, the sum of the debt and equity capital of a firm, the free cash flow for all debt and equity capital is the appropriate cash flow measure and the appropriate discount rate is the weighted average cost of capital.
- If the objective is to value the common shareholders' equity of a firm, the free cash flow for common equity shareholders is the appropriate cash flow measure and the appropriate discount rate is the cost of equity capital.

The difference between these two valuations is the value of total debt financing and preferred stock. To reconcile the two valuations, one could value the debt financing instruments by discounting all future debt service cash flows (including repayments of principal) at the after-tax cost of debt capital and all preferred-stock dividends at the cost of preferred equity. Subtracting the present value of debt financing and preferred stock from the present value of the sum of debt and equity capital yields the present value of common equity. The approach to use depends on the valuation setting.

Example 11: Valuing an Asset Acquisition

One firm wants to acquire the net operating assets of a division of another firm. The acquiring firm will replace the financing structure of the division with a financing structure that matches its own. The relevant cash flows for valuing the division's net operating assets are the free operating cash flows the assets will generate minus the expected capital expenditures in operating assets or, equivalently, the free cash flows for all debt and equity capital. The acquiring firm would then discount these projected free cash flows for all debt and equity capital at the expected future weighted average cost of capital of the division to be acquired, which will match the weighted average cost of capital of the acquiring firm because the acquiring firm will use a similar financing structure for the division.

Example 12: Valuing Equity Shares

An investor wants to value a potential investment in 1,000 shares of common stock in a firm. The relevant cash flows are the free cash flows available for distribution to common equity shareholders. These free cash flows measure the cash flows generated from using the assets of the firm minus the cash required to service the debt. Thus, free cash flows for common equity shareholders should capture the cash generated by operating the assets of the firm plus any beneficial effects of financial leverage on the value of the common equity less the cash flows required to service debt capital. The investor should discount these projected free cash flows at the required return on equity capital.

Example 13: Valuing a Leveraged Buyout

The managers of a firm intend to acquire a target firm through an LBO (leveraged buyout). The managers will offer to purchase the outstanding shares of the target firm by investing their own equity (usually 20–25 percent of the total) and borrowing the remainder from various lenders. The tendered shares serve as collateral for the loan (often called a *bridge loan*) during the transaction. After gaining voting control of the firm, the managers will have the firm engage in sufficient new borrowing to repay the bridge loan. Following an LBO, the firm will likely have a significantly higher debt level in the capital structure from the use of leverage to execute the takeover.

Determining the value of the common shares acquired follows the usual procedure for an equity investment. (See Example 12.) This value should equal the present value of free cash flows for common equity discounted at the cost of common equity capital. The valuation of the equity must reflect the new capital structure and the related increase in debt service costs. Also, the cost of equity capital will likely increase as a result of the higher level of debt in the capital structure; the common shareholders bear more risk as residual claimants on the assets of the firm. Therefore, the valuation must be based on the expected new cost of equity capital.

As an alternative approach that will produce the same value for the common equity, the analyst can treat an LBO as a purchase of assets (similar to Example 11). That is, compute the present value of the free cash flows for all debt and equity capital stakeholders using the expected future weighted average cost of debt and equity capital, using weights that reflect the newly leveraged capital structure of the acquired firm. This amount represents the value of net operating assets. Subtract from the present value of net operating assets the present value of debt raised to execute the LBO.[14] The result is the present value of the common equity.

CASH-FLOW-BASED VALUATION MODELS

Thus far, this chapter has discussed all of the elements of free-cash-flow-based valuation. To bring all of the elements together, we next present equations to describe the free-cash-flow-based valuation models. In each of these equations, all of the variables used to compute firm

[14] It is irrelevant whether any debt on the books of the target firm remains outstanding after the LBO or whether the firm engages in additional borrowing to repay existing debt, as long as the weighted average cost of capital properly includes the costs of each financing arrangement.

value are *expectations* of future free cash flows, future discount rates, and future growth rates. We present the valuation equations with and without explicit terms for continuing values. Recall that Exhibits 12.1–12.3 describe the computations for free cash flows for common equity shareholders and free cash flows for all debt and equity capital stakeholders.

Valuation Models for Free Cash Flows for Common Equity Shareholders

The following equation summarizes the computation of the present value of the common equity of a firm as of time $t=0$ (denoted as V_0) using the present value of free cash flows for common equity shareholders discounted at the required rate of return on equity capital (R_E):

$$V_0 = \sum_{t=1}^{\infty} [\mathit{Free\ Cash\ Flow\ Equity}_t/(1 + R_E)^t]$$

This valuation approach expresses the value of the common equity of the firm as a function of the present value of the free cash flows the firm will generate for the common equity shareholders after the firm has met all other cash requirements for working capital, capital expenditures, principal and interest payments on debt financing, preferred stock dividends, and so on. Given that common equity shareholders are the residual risk-bearers of the firm, this valuation approach estimates common equity value using the residual free cash flows available to them. Therefore, it is appropriate to discount these payoffs to present value using a discount rate that reflects the risk-adjusted required rate of return on common equity capital of the firm.

The following equation summarizes the computation of the present value of common equity as of time $t=0$, but in this equation, the analyst computes the present value of the expected future free cash flows for common equity shareholders over a finite forecast horizon through Year T plus the present value of continuing value of free cash flows for equity shareholders continuing in Year T+1 and beyond.[15] The analyst computes continuing value based on the forecast assumption that the firm will grow indefinitely at rate *g* beginning in Year T+1 and continuing thereafter. The analyst derives free cash flows for common equity shareholders in Year T+1 from the projected income statement and balance sheet for Year T+1, in which the analyst projects all of the elements of the Year T income statement and balance sheet to grow at rate *g* beginning in Year T+1. The equation is as follows:

$$V_0 = \sum_{t=1}^{T} [\mathit{Free\ Cash\ Flow\ Equity}_t/(1 + R_E)^t]$$
$$+ [\mathit{Free\ Cash\ Flow\ Equity}_{T+1}] \times [1/(R_E - g)] \times [1/(1 + R_E)^T]$$

Both of these free-cash-flow-based equations represent the value of the common equity of the firm. The Valuations spreadsheet in FSAP provides a template that calculates V_0 using the present value of free cash flows for common equity shareholders, including the continuing value computation.

FSAP

[15] Note that this valuation model is essentially identical to the dividends valuation model described in Chapter 11 (see page 905). The only difference between the two models is the payoff being valued—dividends versus free cash flows for equity shareholders.

Valuation Models for Free Cash Flows for All Debt and Equity Capital Stakeholders

The following equation determines the present value of the net operating assets of a firm as of time $t=0$ (denoted as $VNOA_0$) by computing the present value of all future free cash flows for all debt and equity capital stakeholders (denoted as *Free Cash Flow All*):

$$VNOA_0 = \sum_{t=1}^{\infty} [Free\ Cash\ Flow\ All_t/(1 + R_A)^t]$$

This equation differs from the models in the previous section in three important ways. First, this valuation approach does not compute the value of common shareholders' equity (V_0); instead, it computes the value of the net operating assets of the firm or, equivalently, the value of all of the debt, preferred, and common equity claims on the net assets of the firm. Second, this model differs from the models of the previous section because it includes the analyst's forecasts (as of time $t = 0$) of future free cash flows to all debt and equity stakeholders. The prior equation focused specifically on the value of common equity capital, measured as the present value of all future free cash flows to common equity shareholders. Third, this equation differs from the prior models because it discounts the free cash flows to present value using R_A, which denotes the expected future weighted average cost of capital (which should reflect the weighted average required rate of return on the net operating assets of the firm). The prior equations relied on a discount rate using the required rate of return to equity (R_E).

This valuation approach expresses the value of the financial claims (debt, preferred, and common equity) on the firm as a function of the present value of the free cash flows the firm's net operating assets will generate that can ultimately be distributed to debtholders, preferred stockholders, and common shareholders. Thus, the value-relevant payoff measure in this approach is the excess cash the firm's operations generate that will be available to satisfy all capital claims. Given that these free cash flows will be distributed to debt, preferred, and common equity stakeholders, it is appropriate to discount these payoffs to present value using a discount rate that reflects the weighted average cost of capital across these different capital claims.

The next equation summarizes the same computation but uses the present value of the analyst's forecasts of free cash flows for all debt and equity capital stakeholders over a finite forecast horizon through Year T (for example, T may be five or ten years in the future) plus the present value of continuing value. The analyst computes continuing value based on the forecast assumption that the firm will grow indefinitely at rate g beginning in Year T+1 and continuing thereafter. The analyst derives free cash flows for all debt and equity capital stakeholders in Year T+1 from the projected income statement and balance sheet for Year T+1, in which the analyst projects all elements of the Year T income statement and balance sheet to grow at rate g beginning in Year T+1. The equation is as follows:

$$VNOA_0 = \sum_{t=1}^{T} [Free\ Cash\ Flow\ All_t/(1 + R_A)^t]$$
$$+ [Free\ Cash\ Flow\ All_{T+1}] \times [1/(R_A - g)] \times [1/(1 + R_A)^T]$$

Both of the prior equations represent estimates of the value of the net operating assets of the firm, which is equivalent to the sum of the values of debt, preferred, and common equity capital. To isolate the value of common equity capital, the analyst must subtract the present value of all interest-bearing debt and preferred stock. The equation to compute the value of equity (denoted as V_0) is as follows:

$$V_0 = VNOA_0 - VDebt_0 - VPreferred_0$$

The Valuations spreadsheet in FSAP provides a template that calculates $VNOA_0$ and V_0 using the present value of free cash flows for all debt and equity capital stakeholders, including the continuing value computation.

In theory, the value of common equity using this valuation approach should be identical to the value of common equity using the free cash flows to equity approach, the dividends valuation approach discussed in the previous chapter, and the earnings-based approaches discussed in the following chapter. As a practical matter, however, it is sometimes difficult to get the equity value estimate from the free cash flows to all debt and equity stakeholders to match the other value estimates. The main reason is the added degrees of circularity in this valuation approach. In this approach, the market-value-based weights for debt, preferred stock, and common equity capital used in computing the weighted average cost of capital must agree with the value estimates for debt, preferred stock, and common equity. Thus, additional degrees of circularity arise because the value estimates depend on the weighted average cost of capital, and the weighted average cost of capital depends on the value estimates. Obtaining an internally consistent set of value estimates for each type of capital and an internally consistent weighted average cost of capital may require a number of iterations until all of the weights and value estimates agree.

FREE CASH FLOWS VALUATION OF PEPSICO

At the end of 2008, trading in PepsiCo shares on the New York Stock Exchange closed at \$54.77 per share. Therefore, we know the *price* at which we can buy or sell PepsiCo shares. The free cash flows valuation methods enable us to estimate the *value* of these shares. This section illustrates the valuation of PepsiCo shares using the free cash flows valuation techniques described in this chapter and the forecasts developed in Chapter 10. We develop these forecasts and value estimates using the Forecast and Valuation spreadsheets in FSAP (see Appendix C).

FSAP

In this section, we estimate the present value of a share of common equity in PepsiCo at the end of 2008 (equivalently, the start of forecast Year +1) two ways by estimating the present value of the following:

1. Free cash flows to common equity shareholders directly, discounted at the required rate of return to common equity
2. Free cash flows to all debt and equity capital stakeholders, discounted using PepsiCo's weighted average cost of capital; then subtract the present value of debt claims.

To proceed with each valuation, we follow four steps:

1. Estimate the appropriate discount rates for PepsiCo.
2. Derive the free cash flows from the projected financial statements for PepsiCo described in Chapter 10 and make assumptions about free cash flows growth in the continuing periods beyond the forecast horizon.
3. Discount the free cash flows to present value, including continuing value.
4. Make the necessary adjustments to convert the present value computation to an estimate of share value for PepsiCo.

Once we have our benchmark estimate of PepsiCo's share value, we conduct sensitivity analysis to determine the reasonable range of values for PepsiCo shares. Finally, we compare this range of reasonable values to PepsiCo's share price in the market and suggest an appropriate investment decision indicated by our analysis.

Recall in the previous chapter that we used the dividends valuation approach to estimate the value of PepsiCo shares to be in a range around $83 per share. This section shows that we obtain equivalent estimates of value using the free cash flows valuation approaches.

PepsiCo Discount Rates

To discount free cash flows to common equity shareholders, we need to compute PepsiCo's required rate of return on equity capital. To discount free cash flows to all debt and equity capital, we need to compute PepsiCo's weighted average cost of capital. The following sections briefly describe the computations. Recall that we briefly explained these computations at the outset of this chapter, and we explained and described these computations in detail in Chapter 11.

Computing the Required Rate of Return on Equity Capital for PepsiCo

At the end of 2008, different sources provided different estimates of market beta for PepsiCo common stock, ranging from 0.50 to roughly 1.00. Historically, PepsiCo's market beta has varied around 0.75 over time, so we will assume that PepsiCo common stock has a market beta of roughly 0.75 as of the end of 2008. At that time, U.S. Treasury bills with one to five years to maturity traded with a yield of approximately 4.0 percent, which we use as the risk-free rate. Assuming a 6.0 percent market risk premium, the CAPM indicates that PepsiCo has a cost of common equity capital of 8.50 percent [$8.50 = 4.0 + (0.75 \times 6.0)$]. At the end of 2008, PepsiCo had 1,553 million shares outstanding and a share price of $54.77 for a total market capital of common equity of $85,058 million.

Computing the Weighted Average Cost of Capital for PepsiCo

PepsiCo's balance sheet at the end of 2008 shows interest-bearing debt from short-term obligations and long-term debt obligations totaling $8,227 million (= $369 + $7,858, as reported in Appendix A). Recall that in Chapter 10, we used information disclosed in Note 9, "Debt Obligations and Commitments" (Appendix A), to assess stated interest rates on PepsiCo's interest-bearing debt. We determined that in 2008, PepsiCo's outstanding debt carries a weighted average interest rate of approximately 5.8 percent. In Note 10, "Financial Instruments" (Appendix A), PepsiCo discloses that the fair value of outstanding debt obligations at the end of 2008 is $8,800 million. Thus, PepsiCo has experienced an unrealized (and unrecognized) loss of $573 million (= $8,227 million − $8,800 million) on its debt capital. This unrealized loss is surprising because more than half of PepsiCo's outstanding debt obligations were newly issued in 2008 at prevailing market rates. The unrealized loss implies that the firm's outstanding debt carries stated rates of interest that now exceed prevailing market yields, which at the end of 2008 are at relatively low levels given the recession in the U.S. economy. Given that most of PepsiCo's outstanding debt obligations were recently issued in 2008 and that prevailing yields to maturity are expected to be temporarily low, we forecast in Chapter 10 that PepsiCo's cost of debt capital will continue to approximate 5.8 percent in Year +1 and beyond. We use the current book value (as a proxy for market value) of PepsiCo's debt for weighting purposes. In Note 5, "Income Taxes" (Appendix A), PepsiCo discloses that the combined average federal, state, and foreign tax rate is approximately 26.8 percent in 2008. In Chapter 10, we forecast that PepsiCo will continue to face average tax rates of roughly 26.8 percent in Year +1 and beyond. Therefore, we assume that the tax rate applicable to PepsiCo's interest expense deductions will be the effective 26.8 percent rate rather than the statutory federal rate of 35 percent. Our long-run projections imply that PepsiCo faces an after-tax cost of debt capital of 4.25 percent [$4.25 = 5.8 \times (1 - 0.268)$].

PepsiCo also has a net *negative* balance of $97 million in preferred stock on the 2008 balance sheet. In Chapter 10, we forecast that PepsiCo will retire the remaining outstanding preferred stock during Year +1. We also forecast that PepsiCo will not issue any additional preferred stock capital in future years. Therefore, we do not include any preferred stock in the computation of PepsiCo's weighted average cost of capital.

Bringing the costs of debt and equity capital together, we compute PepsiCo's weighted average cost of capital to be 8.12 percent as follows:

Capital	Value Basis	Amount	Weight	After-Tax Cost of Capital	Weighted-Average Component
Debt	Book	$ 8,227	8.82%	4.25%	0.37%
Common	Market	85,058	91.18%	8.50%	7.75%
Total		$93,285	100.00%		8.12%

Note that this is just our *initial* estimate of PepsiCo's weighted average cost of capital. As described earlier, the weighted average cost of capital must be computed iteratively until the weights used are consistent with the present values of debt and equity capital.

Computing Free Cash Flows for PepsiCo

This section first describes the computations for PepsiCo's free cash flows for all debt and equity stakeholders, then describes the computations for PepsiCo's free cash flows for common equity shareholders. Recall that Exhibits 12.1–12.3 presented the steps to compute free cash flows.

Chapter 10 described detailed projections of PepsiCo's future statements of cash flows by making specific assumptions regarding each item in the income statement and balance sheet and then deriving the related cash flow effects using a five-year forecast horizon. We use these projections of PepsiCo's statements of cash flows (see Exhibit 10.6) to compute projected free cash flows. We present the projections of free cash flows for all debt and equity stakeholders in Exhibit 12.4 and the projections of free cash flows for common equity shareholders in Exhibit 12.5.

PepsiCo's Free Cash Flows to All Debt and Equity Capital Stakeholders

In Exhibit 12.4, we begin our computation of free cash flows with cash flows from operations from the projected statements of cash flows. In Chapter 10, we developed our projections of PepsiCo's statements of cash flows for Year +1 through Year +5. In Year +1, for example, we project that PepsiCo's cash flows from operations will be $8,359.9 million. We then adjust for net interest, adding back interest expense after tax. Specifically, in Year +1, we add back $361.2 million in interest expense after tax [= $493 million × (1 − 0.268)]. We do not make an adjustment to subtract interest income after tax because we assume that

EXHIBIT 12.4

Projected Free Cash Flows to All Debt and Equity Capital Stakeholders for PepsiCo
Year +1 through Year +6 (dollar amounts in millions)

Free Cash Flows for All Debt and Equity	Year +1	Year +2	Year +3	Year +4	Year +5	Year +6
Net Cash Flow from Operations	$ 8,359.9	$ 9,201.1	$10,141.5	$10,965.8	$11,643.5	$ 9,694.4
Add back: Interest Expense after tax	361.2	388.7	424.1	457.9	495.2	510.1
Subtract: Interest Income after tax	(0.0)	(0.0)	(0.0)	(0.0)	(0.0)	(0.0)
Decrease (Increase) in Cash Required for Operations	512.5	(143.7)	(195.3)	(141.9)	(197.9)	(66.9)
Free Cash Flow from Operations for All Debt and Equity Stakeholders	$ 9,233.6	$ 9,446.1	$10,370.3	$11,281.8	$11,940.8	$10,137.6
Net Cash Flow for Investing Activities	(3,874.4)	(3,995.7)	(4,612.9)	(4,607.1)	(5,252.9)	(1,807.5)
Add back: Net Cash Flows into Financial Assets	0.0	0.0	0.0	0.0	0.0	0.0
Free Cash Flows—All Debt and Equity Stakeholders	$ 5,359.3	$ 5,450.4	$ 5,757.4	$ 6,674.7	$ 6,688.0	$ 8,330.1
Present Value Factors ($R_A = 8.12\%$)	0.925	0.855	0.791	0.732	0.677	
Present Value Free Cash Flows	$ 4,956.5	$ 4,662.1	$ 4,554.6	$ 4,883.5	$ 4,525.5	
Sum of Present Value Free Cash Flows for All Debt and Equity Stakeholders, Year +1 through Year +5	$23,582.3					

EXHIBIT 12.5

Projected Free Cash Flows to Common Equity Shareholders for PepsiCo
Year +1 through Year +6 (dollar amounts in millions)

Free Cash Flows for Common Equity Shareholders	Year +1	Year +2	Year +3	Year +4	Year +5	Year +6
Net Cash Flow from Operations	$ 8,359.9	$ 9,201.1	$10,141.5	$ 10,965.8	$ 11,643.5	$ 9,694.4
Decrease (Increase) in Cash Required for Operations	512.5	(143.7)	(195.3)	(141.9)	(197.9)	(66.9)
Free Cash Flow from Operations for Common Equity Shareholders	$ 8,872.4	$ 9,057.4	$ 9,946.2	$ 10,823.9	$ 11,445.6	$ 9,627.5
Net Cash Flows for Investing	(3,874.4)	(3,995.7)	(4,612.9)	(4,607.1)	(5,252.9)	(1,807.5)
Net Cash Flows from Debt Financing	562.8	729.0	941.5	651.5	1,104.4	366.5
Net Cash Flows into Financial Assets	0.0	0.0	0.0	0.0	0.0	0.0
Net Cash Flows—Preferred Stock and Minority Interests	(72.0)	0.0	0.0	0.0	0.0	0.0
Free Cash Flow for Common Equity Shareholders	$ 5,488.8	$ 5,790.7	$ 6,274.8	$ 6,868.3	$ 7,297.1	$ 8,186.5
Present Value Factors (R_E = 8.50%)	0.922	0.849	0.783	0.722	0.665	
Present Value Free Cash Flows	$ 5,058.8	$ 4,919.0	$ 4,912.6	$ 4,956.0	$ 4,852.9	
Sum of Present Value Free Cash Flows For Common Equity Shareholders Year +1 through Year +5	$24,699.3					

all of PepsiCo's interest income relates to financial assets (cash and short-term investments) that are used for liquidity in operating activities and strategic investments in affiliates such as bottlers and are not part of the capital structure. We also adjust cash flow from operations for required investments in operating cash. In Chapter 10, we projected that PepsiCo would need to maintain roughly 12 days of sales in cash for liquidity purposes; therefore, PepsiCo's required cash balance varies with sales. For example, at the end of Year +1, we project that PepsiCo's cash balance will be $1,551 million, equivalent to 12 days of sales in Year +1. Given that this balance is lower than PepsiCo's 2008 year-end cash balance of $2,064 million, it implies that PepsiCo will reduce its cash by $512.5 million. This increment of cash is available to satisfy debt and equity claims, so we add it to free cash flows. [By contrast, in Year +2, we project that the cash balance will grow by $143.7 million to $1,695 million. This additional increment of cash is required for liquidity in Year +2 and therefore is not a free cash flow; so we subtract it.] As a result of these adjustments, we project that PepsiCo's free cash flows for all debt and equity from operations will be $9,233.6 million in Year +1.

Next, we subtract cash flows for capital expenditures using the amount of net cash flow for investing from PepsiCo's projected statements of cash flows. For example, in Year +1, we projected that net cash flows for investing activities will be $3,874.4 million. These investing cash flows include cash outflows for purchases of property, plant, and equipment; acquisitions of goodwill and other intangible assets; and purchases of marketable securities and investment securities. We consider these to be investing activities because we assumed that these securities are for purposes of operating liquidity and are not financial assets that are part of the financing structure of PepsiCo. Also note that PepsiCo's investing cash flows include cash outflows for long-term investments that relate primarily to affiliated bottling companies, which we deem to be part of PepsiCo's operations and therefore not free cash flows. Therefore, we subtract the full amount of net cash flow for investing activities from the free cash flow from operations. We forecast that PepsiCo's free cash flows for all debt and equity capital stakeholders will be $5,359.3 million (= $9,233.6 million − $3,874.4 million) in Year +1. We repeat these steps each year through Year +5.

To project PepsiCo's free cash flows continuing in Year +6 and beyond, we forecast that PepsiCo will sustain a long-run growth rate of 3.0 percent, consistent with 3.0 percent long-term growth in the economy. To compute continuing free cash flows in Year +6, we project each line item on PepsiCo's Year +5 income statement and balance sheet to grow at 3.0 percent per year in Year +6. We use these Year +6 projected income statement and balance sheet amounts to derive the Year +6 free cash flows for all debt and equity capital, which we project will be $8,330.1 million. We assume that this free cash flow amount is the beginning of a perpetuity of continuing free cash flows that PepsiCo will generate beginning in Year +6, growing at 3 percent each year thereafter. The computations are shown in detail in the Forecast and Valuation spreadsheets in FSAP (Appendix C), which permit specific forecast assumptions to extend as far as Year +5 into the future, with continuing value assumptions thereafter.

FSAP

PepsiCo's Free Cash Flows to Common Equity

Exhibit 12.5 presents estimates of PepsiCo's free cash flows for common equity shareholders through Year +6. The computations begin with the Year +1 projection of $8,359.9 million of cash flows from operations, as described earlier. As in the previous section, we adjust cash flow from operations in Year +1 by adding the increment of $512.5 million of cash no longer required for liquidity. Also as in the previous section, we subtract $3,874.4 million of projected cash outflows for capital expenditures and other investing activities in Year +1. Note that unlike the previous section, we make no adjustment for net interest expense after tax because we need to measure the free cash flows available to equity shareholders net of all debt-related cash flows. Because our starting point, cash flows from operations, is derived from net income and because we measure net income after interest expense, our cash flows amount is net of interest expense.

To further refine these cash flows to free cash flows available to common equity, we need to adjust them for cash flows related to debt and preferred-stock financing. We first add any cash inflows from new borrowing and subtract any cash outflows for debt repayments. For example, in Year +1, we add $562.8 million in cash flows for our projections of PepsiCo's additional short-term and long-term borrowing. Next, we add inflows and subtract outflows related to transactions with preferred stock and minority equity shareholders (if any). In Year +1, we subtract $72.0 million for payments to retire the outstanding preferred stock. We also subtract any cash outflows and add any cash inflows related to financial asset accounts that are part of PepsiCo's capital structure (which we have deemed to be zero). The computations project $5,488.8 million in free cash flows for PepsiCo's common equity shareholders in Year +1. We repeat these steps each year through Year +5.

To project PepsiCo's free cash flows for common equity continuing in Year +6 and beyond, we again forecast that PepsiCo can sustain long-run growth of 3.0 percent. We project the Year +5 income statement and balance sheet amounts to grow at a rate of 3.0 percent in Year +6 and derive free cash flows to common equity from the projected Year +6 statements. Our computations indicate that free cash flows to common equity in Year +6 will be $8,186.5 million (shown in detail in the Forecast and Valuation spreadsheets in FSAP in Appendix C). We assume that these free cash flows will continue to grow at 3.0 percent per year thereafter.

FSAP

Valuation of PepsiCo Using Free Cash Flows to Common Equity Shareholders

We estimate the present value of a share of common equity in PepsiCo at the end of 2008 (equivalently, the start of Year +1) by discounting the free cash flows to equity using PepsiCo's 8.50 percent risk-adjusted required rate of return on equity capital as the appropriate discount rate. Exhibit 12.5 shows that PepsiCo's free cash flows for common equity through Year +5 have a present value of $24,699.3 million. We compute the present value of PepsiCo's continuing value as the present value of a growing perpetuity of free cash flows beginning in Year +6, which we project will be $8,186.5. We project these free cash flows to grow at 3.0 percent and discount them to present value using the 8.50 percent discount rate. The present value of these cash flows is $98,988.9 million. As shown in Exhibit 12.6, the present value of PepsiCo's free cash flows to common equity shareholders is the sum of these two parts:

Present Value Free Cash Flows through Year +5	$ 24,699.3 million
Present Value of Continuing Value in Year +6 and Beyond	98,988.9 million
Present Value of Common Equity	$123,688.2 million

As described in the previous chapter, we need to correct our present value calculations for overdiscounting. To make the correction, we multiply the present value sum by the midyear adjustment factor of 1.0425 [$= 1 + (R_E/2) = 1 + (0.0850/2)$]. The total present value of free cash flows to common equity shareholders should be $128,945.0 million (= $123,688.2 million × 1.0425).

Dividing the total value of common equity of PepsiCo by 1,553 million shares outstanding indicates that PepsiCo's common equity shares have a value of $83.03 per share. This share value estimate is identical to the share value estimate we computed using dividends

EXHIBIT 12.6

Valuation of PepsiCo Using Free Cash Flows to Common Equity Shareholders

Present Value of Free Cash Flows to Common Equity Shareholders in Year +1 through Year +5:

From Exhibit 12.5:	\$ 24,699.3 million

Present Value of Continuing Value of Free Cash Flows to Common Equity in Year +6 and Beyond:

Projected Year +6 Free Cash Flows to
Common Equity (Exhibit 12.5): \$8,186.5 million

Continuing Value in Present Value ($R_E = 8.50\%$ and $g = 3.0\%$):

Continuing Value $= \text{Free Cash Flow}_{\text{Year+6}} \times [1/(R_E - g)]$
$= \$8{,}186.5 \text{ million} \times [1/(0.0850 - 0.0300)]$
$= \$8{,}186.5 \text{ million} \times 18.18182 = \$148{,}845.4 \text{ million}$

Present Value of
Continuing Value $= \text{Continuing Value} \times [1/(1 + R_E)^5]$
$= \$148{,}845.4 \text{ million} \times [1/(1 + 0.0850)^5]$
$= \$148{,}845.4 \text{ million} \times 0.665$ = \$98,988.9 million

Total Value of PepsiCo's Free Cash Flows to Common Equity Shareholders:

Present Value of Free Cash Flows through Year +5	\$ 24,699.3 million
+ Present Value of Continuing Value	+ 98,988.9 million
Present Value of Common Equity	\$123,688.2 million
Adjust for Midyear Discounting (multiply by $1 + [R_E/2]$)	× 1.0425
Total Present Value of Common Equity	\$128,945.0 million
Divide by Number of Shares Outstanding	÷ 1,553 million
Value per Share of PepsiCo Common Equity	= \$ 83.03

FSAP

in the previous chapter. Exhibit 12.7 presents the computations to arrive at PepsiCo's common equity share value using the free cash flows to common equity shareholders approach in the Valuations spreadsheet in FSAP.

Valuation of PepsiCo Using Free Cash Flows to All Debt and Equity Capital Stakeholders

We also estimate the present value of a share of common equity in PepsiCo at the end of 2008 by discounting the free cash flows to all debt and equity stakeholders using PepsiCo's 8.12 percent weighted average cost of capital as the appropriate discount rate. Exhibit 12.4 shows that PepsiCo's free cash flows for all debt and equity stakeholders through Year +5 have a present value of \$23,582.3 million. To compute the present value of PepsiCo's continuing value, we compute the continuing value beyond Year +5 using the perpetuity-with-growth

EXHIBIT 12.7

FSAP Valuation of PepsiCo Using Free Cash Flows to Common Equity Shareholders through Year +5 and Beyond (dollar amounts in millions, except per-share amounts)

Free Cash Flows for Common Equity	Year +1	Year +2	Year +3	Year +4	Year +5	Continuing Value Year +6
Net Cash Flow from Operations	$ 8,359.9	$ 9,201.1	$10,141.5	$10,965.8	$11,643.5	$ 9,694.4
Decrease (Increase) in Cash Required for Operations	512.5	(143.7)	(195.3)	(141.9)	(197.9)	(66.9)
Free Cash Flow from Operations for Common Equity Shareholders	$ 8,872.4	$ 9,057.4	$ 9,946.2	$10,823.9	$11,445.6	$ 9,627.5
Net Cash Flows for Investing	(3,874.4)	(3,995.7)	(4,612.9)	(4,607.1)	(5,252.9)	(1,807.5)
Net Cash Flows from Debt Financing	562.8	729.0	941.5	651.5	1,104.4	366.5
Net Cash Flows into Financial Assets	0.0	0.0	0.0	0.0	0.0	0.0
Net Cash Flows—Preferred Stock and Minority Interests	(72.0)	0.0	0.0	0.0	0.0	0.0
Free Cash Flow for Common Equity Shareholders	$ 5,488.8	$ 5,790.7	$ 6,274.8	$ 6,868.3	$ 7,297.1	$ 8,186.5
Present Value Factors (R_E = 8.50%)	0.922	0.849	0.783	0.722	0.665	
Present Value Free Cash Flows	$ 5,058.8	$ 4,919.0	$ 4,912.6	$ 4,956.0	$ 4,852.9	
Sum of Present Value Free Cash Flows For Common Equity Shareholders Year +1 through Year +5	$ 24,699.3					
Present Value of Continuing Value	98,988.9					
Total	$123,688.2					
Adjust to midyear discounting	1.0425					
Total Present Value Free Cash Flows to Common Equity Shareholders	$128,945.0					
Shares Outstanding	1,553.0					
Estimated Value per Share	$ 83.03					
Current share price	$ 54.77					
Percent difference	52%					

model. First, as described earlier and shown in Exhibit 12.4, we project that PepsiCo will generate free cash flows of $8,330.1 million in Year +6, and that these free cash flows will grow at a rate of 3.0 percent indefinitely. Exhibit 12.8 demonstrates that in present value, PepsiCo's continuing value has a present value of $109,988.1 million.[16] The present value of PepsiCo's free cash flows to all debt and equity capital stakeholders is the sum of these two parts:

Present Value Free Cash Flows through Year +5	$ 23,582.3 million
Present Value of Continuing Value Year +6 and Beyond	109,988.1 million
Present Value of Free Cash Flows for All Debt and Equity Capital	$133,570.4 million

EXHIBIT 12.8

Valuation of PepsiCo Using Free Cash Flows to All Debt and Equity Stakeholders

Present Value of Free Cash Flows to All Debt and Equity Stakeholders in Year +1 through Year +5:

From Exhibit 12.4:	$ 23,582.3 million

Present Value of Continuing Value of Free Cash Flows to All Debt and Equity Stakeholders in Year + 6 and Beyond:

Projected Year +6 Free Cash Flows to All Debt and Equity Stakeholders (Exhibit 12.4): $8,330.1 million

Continuing Value in Present Value ($R_A = 8.12\%$ and $g = 3.0\%$):

Continuing Value = Free Cash $\text{Flow}_{\text{Year+6}} \times [1/(R_A - g)]$
= $8,330.1 million × [1/(0.0812 – 0.0300)]
= $8,330.1 million × 19.5312
= $162,544.5 million

Present Value of Continuing Value = Continuing Value × $[1/(1 + R_A)^5]$
= $162,544.5 million × $[1/(1 + 0.0812)^5]$
= $162,544.5 million × 0.677 = $109,988.1 million

Total Value of PepsiCo's Free Cash Flows to All Debt and Equity Stakeholders:

Present Value of Free Cash Flows through Year +5	$ 23,582.3 million
+ Present Value of Continuing Value	+ 109,988.1 million
Present Value of All Debt and Equity	$133,570.4 million
Subtract Market Value of Debt	– 8,227.0 million
Present Value of Common Equity	$125,343.4 million
Adjust for Midyear Discounting [multiply by $1 + (R_A/2)$]	× 1.0406
Total Present Value of Common Equity	$130,435.3 million
Divide by Number of Shares Outstanding	÷ 1,553 million
Value per Share of PepsiCo Common Equity	= $ 83.99

[16] Because of the effects of rounding, it appears the present value of continuing value computation may be slightly in error. But when computed with greater precision and less rounding the computation is correct, as follows: *Continuing Value* = *Free Cash* $\text{Flow}_{\text{Year+6}} \times [1/(R_A - g)] \times [1/(1 + R_A)^5]$ = $8,330.07 million × [1/(0.08125 – 0.0300)] × $[1/(1 + 0.08125)^5]$ = $8,330.07 million × 19.51298 × 0.67666 = $109,988.1 million.

Necessary Adjustments to Compute Common Equity Share Value

To narrow this computation to the present value of common equity, we need to subtract the market value of interest-bearing debt and preferred stock and add the present value of interest-earning financial assets that are part of the firm's financial capital structure. Relying on PepsiCo's book values of debt, we subtract \$8,227 million for outstanding debt. We assumed that PepsiCo would retire the outstanding preferred stock during Year +1, so our cash outflows already account for the payment to retire that preferred stock. We assumed that PepsiCo's financial assets are not part of the financial capital structure, so we need no adjustments for them. After subtracting the value of debt, the present value of PepsiCo's common equity capital is \$125,343.4 million (= \$133,570.4 million − \$8,227.0 million).

As described earlier, our present value calculations have overdiscounted these cash flows because we have discounted each year's cash flows for a full period when, in fact, PepsiCo generates cash flows throughout each period and we should discount them from the midpoint of the year to the present. Therefore, to make the correction, we multiply the present value sum by the midyear adjustment factor of 1.0406 [$= 1 + (R_A/2) = 1 + (0.0812/2)$]. Therefore, the total present value of free cash flows to common equity capital stakeholders is \$130,435.3 million (= \$125,343.4 million × 1.0406). Dividing by 1,553 million shares outstanding indicates that PepsiCo's common equity shares have a value of \$83.99 per share. Exhibit 12.8 summarizes all of these computations, and Exhibit 12.9 presents the computations to arrive at PepsiCo's common equity share value using the free cash flows to all debt and equity stakeholders approach in the Valuations spreadsheet in FSAP.

Note that our calculation of an \$83.99 value for PepsiCo's common equity shares is slightly different from the value of \$83.03 per share obtained from the free cash flows to common equity approach described previously and the dividends approach in the previous chapter. This is because we used the current market price per share of PepsiCo common stock (\$54.77) in the initial weighted average cost of capital computation. As a consequence, we did not place enough weight on the market value of equity in the initial cost of capital computation. To iterate the valuation approach, we can use the share value estimate of \$83.03 to determine that the total value of PepsiCo common equity in the weighted average cost of capital computation. To further iterate the valuation approach, we can recompute the weighted average cost of equity capital each forecast year because our projections indicate that PepsiCo's common equity in the capital structure will gradually fall in proportion to the debt financing in the capital structure in future years. After a number of iterations, the valuation computations and the weights we use to compute the weighted average cost of capital converge. The equity value estimate of \$128,945.0 million, or \$83.03 per share, is the internally consistent value.

Sensitivity Analysis and Investment Decision Making

As we emphasized in the previous chapter, forecasts of cash flows over the remaining life of any firm, even a mature firm such as PepsiCo, contain a high degree of uncertainty; so one should not place too much confidence in the *precision* of firm value estimates using these forecasts. Although we have constructed these forecasts and value estimates with care, the forecasting and valuation process has an inherently high degree of uncertainty and estimation error. Therefore, the analyst should not rely too heavily on any one point estimate of the value of a firm's shares; instead, the analyst should describe a reasonable range of values for a firm's shares.

EXHIBIT 12.9

FSAP Valuation of PepsiCo Using Free Cash Flows to All Debt and Equity Stakeholders through Year +5 and Beyond (dollar amounts in millions, except per-share amounts)

						Continuing Value
Free Cash Flows for All Debt and Equity	**Year +1**	**Year +2**	**Year +3**	**Year +4**	**Year +5**	**Year +6**
Net Cash Flow from Operations	$ 8,359.9	$ 9,201.1	$10,141.5	$10,965.8	$11,643.5	$ 9,694.4
Add back: Interest Expense after tax	361.2	388.7	424.1	457.9	495.2	510.1
Subtract: Interest Income after tax	0.0	0.0	0.0	0.0	0.0	0.0
Decrease (Increase) in Cash Required for Operations	512.5	(143.7)	(195.3)	(141.9)	(197.9)	(66.9)
Free Cash Flow from Operations for All Debt and Equity Stakeholders	$ 9,233.6	$ 9,446.1	$10,370.3	$11,281.8	$11,940.8	$10,137.6
Net Cash Flow for Investing Activities	(3,874.4)	(3,995.7)	(4,612.9)	(4,607.1)	(5,252.9)	(1,807.5)
Add back: Net Cash Flows into Financial Assets	0.0	0.0	0.0	0.0	0.0	0.0
Free Cash Flows—All Debt and Equity Stakeholders	$ 5,359.3	5,450.4	$ 5,757.4	$ 6,674.7	$ 6,688.0	$ 8,330.1
Present Value Factors (R_A = 8.12%)	0.925	0.855	0.791	0.732	0.677	
Present Value Free Cash Flows	$ 4,956.5	$ 4,662.1	$ 4,554.6	$ 4,883.5	$ 4,525.5	
Sum of Present Value Free Cash Flows for All Debt and Equity Stakeholders, Year +1 through Year +5	$ 23,582.3					
Present Value of Continuing Value	109,988.1					
Total Present Value Free Cash Flows to Debt and Equity Stakeholders	$133,570.4					
Less: Value of Outstanding Debt	(8,227.0)					
Less: Value of Preferred Stock	(0.0)					
Plus: Value of Financial Assets	0.0					
Present Value of Common Equity	$125,343.4					
Adjust to midyear discounting	1.0406					
Total Present Value of Common Equity	$130,435.3					
Shares Outstanding	1,553.0					
Estimated Value per Share	$ 83.99					
Current share price	$ 54.77					
Percent difference	53%					

Two critical forecasting and valuation parameters in most valuations are the long-run growth rate assumption and the cost of equity capital assumption. Analysts should conduct sensitivity analyses to test the effects of these and other key forecast assumptions and valuation parameters on the share value estimate. Sensitivity analysis tests should allow the analyst to vary these assumptions and parameters individually and jointly for additional insights into the correlation between share value, the growth rate, and the discount rate assumptions.

For PepsiCo, our base case assumptions indicate PepsiCo's share value to be roughly $83. Our base case valuation assumptions include a long-run growth rate of 3 percent and a cost of equity capital of 8.50 percent. We can assess the sensitivity of our estimates of PepsiCo's share value by varying these two parameters (or any other key parameters in the valuation) across reasonable ranges. Exhibit 12.10 contains the results of sensitivity analysis varying the long-run growth rate from 0–10 percent and the cost of equity capital from 5–20 percent. The data in Exhibit 12.10 show that as the discount rate increases, holding growth constant, share value estimates of PepsiCo fall. Likewise, value estimates fall as growth rates decrease, holding discount rates constant.

Considering the downside possibilities first, if we reduce the long-run growth assumption to 2.0 percent while holding the discount rate constant at 8.50 percent, PepsiCo's share value falls to $73.36, still well above current market price. In fact, if we drop the long-run growth assumption to zero while holding the discount rate constant at 8.50 percent, PepsiCo's share value estimate falls to $60.84, still above current market price. Similarly, if we increase the discount rate to 9.0 or 10.0 percent while holding the long-run growth assumption constant at 3.0 percent, PepsiCo shares have a value of roughly $76 or $65, respectively. If we revise both assumptions at once and reduce the long-run growth assumption to 0 percent and increase the discount rate assumption to 10.0 percent, PepsiCo's share value falls to roughly $51, which is slightly below market price of $54.77.

On the upside, if we reduce the discount rate to 7.0 percent while holding long-run growth constant at 3.0 percent or if we increase the long-run growth assumption from 3.0 to 4.0 percent while holding the discount rate constant at 8.50 percent, the value estimates jump to roughly $114 per share or $97 per share, respectively. If we reduce the discount rate assumption further or increase the long-run growth rate further, our share value estimates for PepsiCo jump dramatically higher.

These data suggest that our value estimate is sensitive to slight variations of our baseline assumptions of 3.0 percent long-run growth and an 8.50 percent discount rate, which yield a share value estimate of $83. Adverse variations in valuation parameters could reduce PepsiCo's share value estimates to $55 or lower, whereas favorable variations could increase PepsiCo's share value up to or above $100.

If our forecast and valuation assumptions are realistic, our baseline value estimate for PepsiCo is $83 per share at the end of 2008. At that time, the market price of $54.77 per share indicates that PepsiCo shares were underpriced by about 52 percent. Under our forecast assumptions, PepsiCo's share value could vary within a range of a low of $51 per share to a high of $114 per share with only minor perturbations in our growth rate and discount rate assumptions. Given PepsiCo's $54.77 share price, these value estimates would have supported a buy recommendation or perhaps a strong buy recommendation at the end of 2008 because the valuation sensitivity analysis reveals limited downside potential but substantial upside potential for the value of PepsiCo shares.

EXHIBIT 12.10

Valuation of PepsiCo:
Sensitivity Analysis of Value to Growth and Equity Cost of Capital

	Long-Run Growth Assumptions							
	0%	**2%**	**3%**	**4%**	**5%**	**6%**	**8%**	**10%**
Discount Rates:								
5%	105.16	160.50	229.67	437.20				
6%	87.18	120.00	152.81	218.45	415.34			
7%	74.37	95.73	114.41	145.56	207.85	394.72		
8.50%	60.84	73.36	83.03	97.00	118.95	158.47	711.69	
9%	57.34	68.04	76.06	87.30	104.14	132.22	356.87	
10%	51.41	59.41	65.13	72.75	83.42	99.42	179.45	
11%	46.57	52.71	56.94	62.37	69.61	79.75	120.30	323.07
12%	42.55	47.37	50.58	54.59	59.76	66.64	90.73	163.00
13%	39.16	43.00	45.50	48.55	52.37	57.28	72.98	109.63
14%	36.26	39.37	41.35	43.73	46.63	50.26	61.15	82.93
15%	33.76	36.30	37.90	39.78	42.04	44.80	52.70	66.90
16%	31.57	33.68	34.98	36.50	38.29	40.44	46.35	56.21
18%	27.95	29.44	30.33	31.35	32.53	33.90	37.47	42.83
20%	25.08	26.16	26.79	27.51	28.31	29.24	31.55	34.79

EVALUATION OF THE FREE CASH FLOWS VALUATION METHOD

The principal advantages of the present value of future free cash flows valuation method include the following:

- This valuation method focuses on free cash flows, a base that economists would argue has a more basic economic meaning than earnings.
- Projected amounts of free cash flows result from projected amounts of revenues, expenses, assets, liabilities, and shareholders' equities, thereby requiring the analyst to project the future operating, investing, and financing decisions of a firm.
- The free cash flows valuation focuses directly on net cash inflows to the entity that are available to distribute to capital providers, as opposed to focusing on dividends to common equity shareholders. This cash flow perspective is especially pertinent to acquisition decisions.
- The free cash flows valuation approaches are widely used in practice.

The principal disadvantages of the present value of future free cash flows valuation method include the following:

- The projection of free cash flows can be time-consuming for the analyst, making it costly when the analyst follows many companies and must regularly identify under- and overvalued firms.
- The continuing value (terminal value) tends to dominate the total value in many cases. This continuing value is sensitive to assumptions made about growth rates after the forecast horizon and discount rates.
- The analyst must be very careful that free cash flow computations are internally consistent with long-run assumptions regarding growth and payout. Failure to do so can result in unnecessary estimation errors that produce poor valuations that are inconsistent with those derived from expected future dividends and earnings.

SUMMARY

This chapter illustrates valuation using the present value of future free cash flows. As with the preparation of financial statement forecasts in Chapter 10, the reasonableness of the valuations depends on the reasonableness of the assumptions. The analyst should assess the sensitivity of the valuation to alternative assumptions regarding growth and discount rates. To validate value estimates using the free-cash-flows-based approach, the analyst also should compute the value of the common equity of the firm using other approaches, such as the dividends approach described in Chapter 11, the earnings-based approach described in Chapter 13, and the valuation multiples approaches described in Chapter 14.

QUESTIONS, EXERCISES, PROBLEMS, AND CASES

Questions and Exercises

12.1 FREE CASH FLOWS. Explain "free" cash flows. Describe which types of cash flows are *free* and which are not. How do free cash flows available for debt and equity stakeholders differ from free cash flows available for common equity shareholders?

12.2 THE FREE CASH FLOWS VALUATION APPROACH. Explain the theory behind the free cash flows valuation approach. Why are free cash flows value-relevant to common equity shareholders when they are not cash flows to those shareholders, but rather are cash flows into the firm?

12.3 MEASURING VALUE-RELEVANT FREE CASH FLOWS. The chapter describes free cash flows for common equity shareholders. If the firm borrows cash by issuing debt, how does that transaction affect free cash flows for common equity shareholders in that period? If the firm uses cash to repay debt, how does that transaction affect free cash flows for common equity shareholders in that period?

12.4 MEASURING VALUE-RELEVANT FREE CASH FLOWS. The chapter describes free cash flows for common equity shareholders. Suppose a firm has no debt and uses marketable securities to manage operating liquidity. If the firm uses cash to purchase marketable securities, how does that transaction affect free cash flows for common equity shareholders in that period? If the firm sells marketable securities for cash, how does that transaction affect free cash flows for common equity shareholders in that period?

12.5 VALUATION APPROACH EQUIVALENCE. Conceptually, why should an analyst expect valuation based on dividends and valuation based on the free cash flows for common equity shareholders to yield identical value estimates?

12.6 FREE CASH FLOWS VALUATION WHEN FREE CASH FLOWS ARE NEGATIVE. Suppose you are valuing a healthy, growing, profitable firm and you project that the firm will generate negative free cash flows for equity shareholders in each of the next five years. Can you use the free cash flows valuation approach when cash flows are negative? If so, explain how the free cash flows approach can produce positive valuations of firms when they are expected to generate negative free cash flows over the next five years.

12.7 USING DIFFERENT FREE CASH FLOWS MEASURES. The chapter describes free cash flows for all debt and equity stakeholders and free cash flows for equity shareholders. Give examples of valuation settings in which one approach or the other is appropriate.

12.8 APPROPRIATE DISCOUNT RATES. Describe valuation settings in which the appropriate discount rate to use is the required rate of return on equity capital versus settings in which it is appropriate to use a weighted average cost of capital.

12.9 FREE CASH FLOWS AND DISCOUNT RATES. Describe circumstances and give an example of when free cash flows to equity shareholders and free cash flows to all debt and equity stakeholders will be identical. Under those circumstances, will the required rate of return on equity and the weighted average cost of capital be identical too? Explain.

Problems and Cases

12.10 CALCULATING FREE CASH FLOWS. The 3M Company is a global diversified technology company active in the following product markets: consumer and office; display and graphics; electronics and communications; health care; industrial; safety, security, and protection services; and transportation. At the consumer level, 3M is probably most widely known for products such as Scotch® Brand transparent tape and Post-it® notes. Exhibit 12.11 presents information from the statement of cash flows and income

EXHIBIT 12.11

3M Company
Selected Information from the Statement of Cash Flows
(amounts in millions)
(Problem 12.10)

	2008	2007	2006
Cash Flow from Operating Activities	$ 4,118	$ 4,363	$ 3,896
Investing Activities:			
Fixed Assets Acquired, Net	(1,384)	(1,319)	(1,119)
(Acquisition) Sale of Businesses, Net	(1,306)	358	321
(Purchase) Sale of Investments	291	(406)	(662)
Cash Flow from Investing Activities	$(2,399)	$(1,367)	$(1,460)
Financing Activities:			
Increase (Decrease) in Short-Term Borrowing	361	(1,222)	882
Increase (Decrease) in Long-Term Debt	676	2,444	253
Increase (Decrease) in Common Stock	(1,405)	(2,389)	(1,820)
Dividends Paid	(1,398)	(1,380)	(1,376)
Cash Flow from Financing Activities	$(1,766)	$(2,547)	$(2,061)
Net Increase (Decrease) in Cash & Equivalents	$ (47)	$ 449	$ 375
Cash at Beginning of Year	$ 1,896	$ 1,447	$ 1,072
Cash at End of Year	$ 1,849	$ 1,896	$ 1,447
Interest Income	$ 105	$ 132	$ 51
Interest Expense	$ 215	$ 210	$ 122

statement for the 3M Company for 2006–2008. From 2006 through 2008, 3M increased cash and cash equivalents. Assume that 3M considers these increases in cash and cash equivalents to be necessary to sustain operating liquidity. The interest income reported by 3M pertains to interest earned on cash and marketable securities. 3M holds only small amounts of investments in marketable securities. 3M's income tax rate is 35 percent.

Required

a. Beginning with cash flows from operating activities, calculate the amount of free cash flows to all debt and equity capital stakeholders for 3M for 2006, 2007, and 2008.

b. Beginning with cash flows from operating activities, calculate the amount of free cash flows 3M generated for common equity shareholders in 2006, 2007, and 2008.

c. Reconcile the amounts of free cash flows 3M generated for common equity shareholders in 2006, 2007, and 2008 from Part b with 3M's uses of cash flow for equity shareholders, including share repurchases and dividend payments.

12.11 CALCULATING FREE CASH FLOWS. Dick's Sporting Goods is a chain of full-line sporting goods retail stores offering a broad assortment of brand name sporting goods equipment, apparel, and footwear. Dick's Sporting Goods had its initial public offering of shares in fiscal 2003. Since then, Dick's Sporting Goods has grown its chain of retail stores rapidly and has acquired several other chains of retail sporting goods stores, including Golf Galaxy and Chick's Sporting Goods in the fiscal year ending in 2008. As of the end of the fiscal year ending in 2009, Dick's Sporting Goods operated 409 stores in 40 states of the United States. Exhibit 12.12 presents information from the statement of cash flows and income statement for Dick's Sporting Goods for the fiscal years ending in 2007 through 2009. Dick's Sporting Goods requires all of its cash and cash equivalents for operating liquidity and reports no interest income on the income statement. The average income tax rate for Dick's Sporting Goods during 2007 through 2009 is 40 percent.

Required

a. Beginning with cash flows from operating activities, calculate free cash flows to all debt and equity capital stakeholders for Dick's Sporting Goods for fiscal years ending in 2009, 2008, and 2007.

b. Beginning with cash flows from operating activities, calculate free cash flows for common equity shareholders for Dick's Sporting Goods for fiscal years ending in 2009, 2008, and 2007.

c. Reconcile the amounts of free cash flows for common equity shareholders for Dick's Sporting Goods for fiscal years ending in 2009, 2008, and 2007 with Dick's Sporting Goods' sources of cash flow from equity shareholders.

d. Why do the free cash flows to all debt and equity capital stakeholders for Dick's Sporting Goods change so much from 2007 through 2009? In each of these three years, why do the free cash flows to all debt and equity capital stakeholders differ so much from the free cash flows to common equity shareholders?

e. In each of these three years, Dick's Sporting Goods produces negative free cash flows for common shareholders. Does that imply that Dick's Sporting Goods is destroying the value of common equity? Explain.

12.12 VALUING A LEVERAGED BUYOUT CANDIDATE. May Department Stores (May) operates retail department store chains throughout the United States. At the end of Year 12, May reports debt of $4,658 million and common shareholders' equity at book value of $3,923 million. The market value of its common stock is $6,705, and its market equity beta is 0.88.

An equity buyout group is considering an LBO of May as of the beginning of Year 13. The group intends to finance the buyout with 25 percent common equity and 75 percent debt carrying an interest rate of 10 percent. The group projects that the free cash flows to all debt and equity capital stakeholders of May will be as follows: Year 13, $798 million; Year 14, $861 million; Year 15, $904 million; Year 16, $850 million; Year 17, $834 million; Year 18, $884 million; Year 19, $919 million; Year 20, $947 million; Year 21, $985 million; and Year 22, $1,034 million. The group projects free cash flows to grow 3 percent annually after Year 22.

This problem sets forth the steps the analyst might follow in deciding whether to acquire May and the value to place on the firm.

Required

a. Compute the unlevered market equity (asset) beta of May before consideration of the LBO. Assume that the book value of the debt equals its market value. The income tax rate is 35 percent. [See Chapter 11.]

b. Compute the cost of equity capital with the new capital structure that results from the LBO. Assume a risk-free rate of 4.2 percent and a market risk premium of 5.0 percent.

c. Compute the weighted average cost of capital of the new capital structure.

EXHIBIT 12.12

Dick's Sporting Goods
Selected Information from the Statement of Cash Flows
(amounts in thousands)
(Problem 12.11)

	Fiscal year ended:		
	January 31, 2009	February 2, 2008	February 3, 2007
CASH FLOWS FROM OPERATING ACTIVITIES:			
Net (loss) income	$ (35,094)	$ 155,036	$ 112,611
Adjustments to reconcile net (loss) income to net cash provided by operating activities:			
Depreciation and amortization	90,732	75,052	54,929
Impairment of store assets, goodwill and other intangible assets	193,350	—	—
Deferred income taxes	(45,906)	(32,696)	(1,110)
Various addbacks to net income	24,709	2,462	(7,371)
Changes in assets and liabilities, net of acquired assets and liabilities:			
Accounts receivable	3,090	(10,982)	(2,142)
Inventories	29,581	(127,027)	(105,766)
Prepaid expenses and other assets	(10,554)	(4,267)	(29,039)
Accounts payable	(56,709)	12,337	24,444
Accrued expenses	(7,575)	26,222	42,479
Income taxes payable/receivable	(63,089)	114,706	4,750
Deferred construction allowances	19,452	22,256	19,264
Deferred revenue and other liabilities	17,689	29,869	26,560
Net cash provided by operating activities	**$ 159,676**	**$ 262,968**	**$ 139,609**
CASH FLOWS USED IN INVESTING ACTIVITIES:			
Capital expenditures	(191,423)	(172,366)	(162,995)
Purchase of corporate aircraft	(25,107)	—	—
Proceeds from sale of corporate aircraft	27,463	—	—
Proceeds from sale-leaseback transactions	44,873	28,440	32,509
Payment for the purchase of Golf Galaxy, net of $4,859 cash acquired	—	(222,170)	—
Payment for the purchase of Chick's Sporting Goods	—	(69,200)	—
Net cash used in investing activities	**$(144,194)**	**$(435,296)**	**$(130,486)**
CASH FLOWS FROM FINANCING ACTIVITIES:			
Increase (Decrease) Short-term borrowing	(9,927)	4,785	8,829
Long-term borrowing—Construction allowance receipts	11,874	13,282	17,902
Payments on long-term debt and capital leases	(6,793)	(1,058)	(184)
Proceeds from sale of common stock	13,894	69,684	63,708
Net cash provided by financing activities	**$ 9,048**	**$ 86,693**	**$ 90,255**
NET INCREASE (DECREASE) IN CASH	**$ 24,530**	**$ (85,635)**	**$ 99,378**
CASH, BEGINNING OF PERIOD	**50,307**	**135,942**	**36,564**
CASH, END OF PERIOD	**$ 74,837**	**$ 50,307**	**$ 135,942**
Cash paid during the year for interest	$ 8,021	$ 12,314	$ 9,286

d. Compute the present value of the projected free cash flows to all debt and equity capital stakeholders at the weighted average cost of capital. Ignore the midyear adjustment related to the assumption that cash flows occur, on average, over the year. In computing the continuing value, apply the projected growth rate in free cash flows after Year 22 of 3 percent directly to the free cash flows of Year 22.

e. Assume that the buyout group acquires May for the value determined in Part d. Assuming that the realized free cash flows coincide with projections, will May generate sufficient cash flow each year to service the interest on the debt? Explain.

12.13 VALUING A LEVERAGED BUYOUT CANDIDATE. Experian Information Solutions (Experian) is a wholly owned subsidiary of TRW, a publicly traded company. The subsidiary has (in thousands) total assets of $555,443, long-term debt of $1,839, and common equity at book value of $402,759.

An equity buyout group is planning to acquire Experian from TRW in an LBO as of the beginning of Year 6. The group plans to finance the buyout with 60 percent debt that has an interest cost of 10 percent per year and 40 percent common equity. Analysts for the buyout group project free cash flows to all debt and equity capital stakeholders as follows (in thousands): Year 6, $52,300; Year 7, $54,915; Year 8, $57,112; Year 9, $59,396; and Year 10, $62,366. Because Experian is not a publicly traded firm, it does not have a market equity beta. The company most comparable to Experian is Equifax. Equifax has an equity beta of 0.86. The market value of Equifax's debt is $366.5 thousand, and its common equity is $4,436.8 thousand. Assume an income tax rate of 35 percent throughout this problem.

This problem sets forth the steps the analyst might follow in valuing an LBO candidate.

Required

a. Compute the unlevered market equity (asset) beta of Equifax. [See Chapter 11.]

b. Assuming that the unlevered market equity beta of Equifax is appropriate for Experian, compute the equity beta of Experian after the buyout with its new capital structure.

c. Compute the weighted average cost of capital of Experian after the buyout. Assume a risk-free interest rate of 4.2 percent and a market risk premium of 5.0 percent.

d. The analysts at the buyout firm project that free cash flows for all debt and equity capital stakeholders of Experian will increase 5.0 percent each year after Year 10. Compute the present value of the free cash flows at the weighted average cost of capital. Ignore the midyear adjustment related to the assumption that cash flows occur, on average, over the year. In computing the continuing value, apply the 5.0 percent projected growth rate directly to the free cash flows of Year 10.

e. Assume that the buyout group acquires Experian for the value determined in Part d. Assuming that actual free cash flows to all debt and equity capital stakeholders coincide with projections, will Experian generate sufficient cash flow each year to service the debt? Explain.

12.14 APPLYING VARIOUS PRESENT VALUE APPROACHES TO VALUATION. An equity buyout group intends to acquire Wedgewood Products (Wedgewood) as of the beginning of Year 8. The buyout group intends to finance 40 percent of the acquisition price with 10 percent annual coupon debt and 60 percent with common equity. The income tax rate is 40 percent. The cost of equity capital is 14 percent. Analysts at the buyout firm project the following free cash flows for all debt and equity capital stakeholders for Wedgewood (in millions): Year 8, $2,100; Year 9, $2,268; Year 10, $2,449; Year 11, $2,645; and Year 12, $2,857. The analysts project that free cash flows for all debt and equity capital stakeholders will increase 8 percent each year after Year 12.

Required

a. Compute the weighted average cost of capital for Wedgewood based on the proposed capital structure.

b. Compute the total purchase price of Wedgewood (debt plus common equity). To do this, discount the free cash flows for all debt and equity capital stakeholders at the weighted average cost of capital. Ignore the midyear adjustment related to the assumption that cash flows occur, on average, over the year. In computing the continuing value, apply the 8 percent projected growth rate in free cash flows after Year 12 directly to the free cash flows of Year 12.

c. Given the purchase price determined in Part b, compute the total amount of debt, the annual interest cost, and the free cash flows to common equity shareholders for Year 8 to Year 12.

d. The present value of the free cash flows for common equity shareholders when discounted at the 14 percent cost of equity capital should equal the common equity portion of the total purchase price computed in Part b. Determine the growth rate in free cash flows for common equity shareholders after Year 12 that will result in a present value of free cash flows for common equity shareholders equal to 60 percent of the purchase price computed in Part b.

e. Why does the implied growth rate in free cash flows to common equity shareholders determined in Part d differ from the 8 percent assumed growth rate in free cash flows for all debt and equity capital stakeholders?

f. The adjusted present value valuation approach separates the total value of the firm into the value of an all-equity firm and the value of the tax savings from interest deductions. Assume that the cost of unlevered equity is 11.33 percent. Compute the present value of the free cash flows to all debt and equity capital stakeholders at this unlevered equity cost. Compute the present value of the tax savings from interest expense deductions using the pretax cost of debt as the discount rate. Compare the total of these two present values to the purchase price determined in Part b.

12.15 VALUING THE EQUITY OF A PRIVATELY HELD FIRM.

Refer to the projected financial statements for Massachusetts Stove Company (MSC) prepared for Case 10.2. The management of MSC wants to know the equity valuation implications of not adding gas stoves versus adding gas stoves under the best, most likely, and worst scenarios. Under the three scenarios from Case 10.2 and a fourth scenario involving not adding gas stoves, the projected free cash flows to common equity shareholders for Year 8 to Year 12, and assumed growth rates thereafter, are as follows:

Year	Best	Most Likely	Worst	No Gas
8	$ 73,967	$ 47,034	$ 3,027	$162,455
9	$ 52,143	$ (3,120)	$(84,800)	$132,708
10	$213,895	$135,939	$ 48,353	$106,021
11	$315,633	$178,510	$ 36,605	$ 81,840
12	$432,232	$220,010	$ 10,232	$ 60,007
13–17	20% Growth	10% Growth	Zero Growth	Zero Growth
After Year 17	10% Growth	5% Growth	Zero Growth	Zero Growth

MSC is not publicly traded and therefore does not have a market equity beta. Using the market equity beta of the only publicly traded woodstove and gas stove manufacturing firm and adjusting it for differences in the debt-to-equity ratio, income tax rate, and privately owned status of MSC yields a cost of equity capital for MSC of 13.55 percent.

Required

a. Calculate the value of the equity of MSC as of the end of Year 7 under each of the four scenarios. Ignore the midyear adjustment related to the assumption that cash flows occur, on average, over the year. Apply the growth rates in free cash flows to common equity shareholders after Year 12 directly to the free cash flow of the preceding year. (That is, Year 13 free cash flow equals the free cash flow for Year 12 times the given growth rate; Year 18 free cash flow equals the free cash flow for Year 17 times the given growth rate.)

b. How do these valuations affect your advice to the management of MSC regarding the addition of gas stoves to its woodstove line?

12.16 FREE-CASH-FLOWS-BASED VALUATION. The Coca-Cola Company is a global soft drink beverage company (ticker symbol = KO) that is a primary and direct competitor with PepsiCo. The data in Exhibits 12.13–12.15 (see pages 980–983) include the actual amounts for 2006, 2007, and 2008 and projected amounts for Year +1 to Year +6 for the income statements, balance sheets, and statements of cash flows for Coca-Cola (in millions).

The market equity beta for Coca-Cola at the end of 2008 is 0.61. Assume that the risk-free interest rate is 4.0 percent and the market risk premium is 6.0 percent. Coca-Cola has 2,312 million shares outstanding at the end of 2008, when Coca-Cola's share price was $44.42.

Required

Part I—Computing Coca-Cola's Share Value Using Free Cash Flows to Common Equity Shareholders

a. Use the CAPM to compute the required rate of return on common equity capital for Coca-Cola.

b. Derive the projected free cash flows for common equity shareholders for Coca-Cola for Years +1 through +6 based on the projected financial statements. Assume that Coca-Cola's changes in cash each year are necessary for operating liquidity purposes. The financial statement forecasts for Year +6 assume that Coca-Cola will experience a steady-state long-run growth rate of 3 percent in Year +6 and beyond.

c. Using the required rate of return on common equity from Part a as a discount rate, compute the sum of the present value of free cash flows for common equity shareholders for Coca-Cola for Years +1 through +5.

d. Using the required rate of return on common equity from Part a as a discount rate and the long-run growth rate from Part b, compute the continuing value of Coca-Cola as of the start of Year +6 based on Coca-Cola's continuing free cash flows for common equity shareholders in Year +6 and beyond. After computing continuing value as of the start of Year +6, discount it to present value at the start of Year +1.

e. Compute the value of a share of Coca-Cola common stock. (1) Compute the total sum of the present value of all future free cash flows for equity shareholders (from Parts c and d). (2) Adjust the total sum of the present value using the midyear discounting adjustment factor. (3) Compute the per-share value estimate.

Part II—Computing Coca-Cola's Share Value Using Free Cash Flows to All Debt and Equity Stakeholders

f. At the end of 2008, Coca-Cola had $9,312 million in outstanding interest-bearing short-term and long-term debt on the balance sheet and no preferred stock. Assume that the balance sheet value of Coca-Cola's debt is approximately equal to the market value of the debt. The forecasts assume that Coca-Cola will face an interest rate of 4.5 percent on debt capital and that Coca-Cola's average tax rate will be 23.2 percent (based on the past five-year average effective tax rate). Compute the weighted average cost of capital for Coca-Cola as of the start of Year +1.

g. Beginning with projected net cash flows from operations, derive the projected free cash flows for all debt and equity stakeholders for Coca-Cola for Years +1 through +6 based on the projected financial statements. Assume that the change in cash each year is related to operating liquidity needs.

h. Using the weighted average cost of capital from Part f as a discount rate, compute the sum of the present value of free cash flows for all debt and equity stakeholders for Coca-Cola for Years +1 through +5.

i. Using the weighted average cost of capital from Part f as a discount rate and the long-run growth rate from Part b, compute the continuing value of Coca-Cola as of the start of Year +6 based on Coca-Cola's continuing free cash flows for all debt and equity stakeholders in Year +6 and beyond. After computing continuing value as of the start of Year +6, discount it to present value as of the start of Year +1.

j. Compute the value of a share of Coca-Cola common stock. (1) Compute the total value of Coca-Cola's net operating assets using the total sum of the present value of free cash flows for all debt and equity stakeholders (from Parts h and i). (2) Subtract the value of outstanding debt to obtain the value of equity. (3) Adjust the present value of equity using the midyear discounting adjustment factor. (4) Compute the per-share value estimate of Coca-Cola's common equity shares.

Note: Do not be alarmed if your share value estimate from Part e is slightly different from your share value estimate from Part j. The weighted average cost of capital computation in Part f used the weight of equity based on the market price of Coca-Cola's stock at the end of 2008. The share value estimates from Parts e and j likely differ from the market price, so the weights used to compute the weighted average cost of capital are not internally consistent with the estimated share values.

Part III—Sensitivity Analysis and Recommendation

k. Using the free cash flows to common equity shareholders, recompute the value of Coca-Cola shares under two alternative scenarios. Scenario 1: Assume that Coca-Cola's long-run growth will be 2 percent, not 3 percent as before, and assume that Coca-Cola's required rate of return on equity is 1 percent higher than the rate you computed for Part a. Scenario 2: Assume that Coca-Cola's long-run growth will be 4 percent, not 3 percent as before, and assume that Coca-Cola's required rate of return on equity is 1 percent lower than the rate you computed in Part a. To quantify the sensitivity of your share value estimate for Coca-Cola to these variations in growth and discount rates, compare (in percentage terms) your value estimates under these two scenarios with your value estimate from Part e.

l. Using these data at the end of 2008, what reasonable range of share values would you have expected for Coca-Cola common stock? At that time, what was the market price for Coca-Cola shares relative to this range? What investment strategy (buy, hold, or sell) would you have recommended?

12.17 FREE-CASH-FLOWS-BASED VALUATION. In Problem 10.16, we projected financial statements for Wal-Mart Stores, Inc. (Walmart) for Years +1 through +5. The data in Exhibits 12.16–12.18 (see pages 985–987) include the actual amounts for 2008 and the projected amounts for Year +1 to Year +5 for the income statements, balance sheets, and statements of cash flows for Walmart (in millions).

EXHIBIT 12.13

The Coca-Cola Company
Income Statements for 2006 through 2008 (Actual) and Year +1 through +6 (Projected)
(amounts in millions)
(Problem 12.16)

	Actuals			Forecasts					
Year	**2006**	**2007**	**2008**	**Year +1**	**Year +2**	**Year +3**	**Year +4**	**Year +5**	**Year +6**
Revenues	$24,088	$ 28,857	$ 31,944	$ 33,541	$ 35,218	$ 36,979	$ 38,828	$ 40,770	$ 41,993
Cost of goods sold	(8,164)	(10,406)	(11,374)	(11,943)	(12,540)	(13,167)	(13,825)	(14,516)	(14,952)
Gross Profit	$15,924	$ 18,451	$ 20,570	$ 21,599	$ 22,678	$ 23,812	$ 25,003	$ 26,253	$ 27,041
Selling, general, and administrative expenses	(9,431)	(10,945)	(11,774)	(12,363)	(12,981)	(13,630)	(14,311)	(15,027)	(15,478)
Other operating expenses	(185)	(254)	(350)	(368)	(386)	(405)	(425)	(447)	(460)
Operating Profit	$ 6,308	$ 7,252	$ 8,446	$ 8,868	$ 9,312	$ 9,777	$ 10,266	$ 10,779	$ 11,103
Interest income	193	236	333	263	264	264	264	265	273
Interest expense	(220)	(456)	(438)	(425)	(442)	(462)	(482)	(503)	(518)
Income (loss) from equity affiliates	102	668	(874)	469	497	527	559	592	610
Income before Tax	$ 6,578	$ 7,873	$ 7,439	$ 9,175	$ 9,631	$ 10,107	$ 10,607	$ 11,134	$ 11,468
Income tax expense	(1,498)	(1,892)	(1,632)	(2,124)	(2,230)	(2,340)	(2,456)	(2,578)	(2,655)
Net Income	$ 5,080	$ 5,981	$ 5,807	$ 7,051	$ 7,401	$ 7,767	$ 8,151	$ 8,556	$ 8,813
Other comprehensive income items	666	1,917	(3,300)	0	0	0	0	0	0
Comprehensive Income	$ 5,746	$ 7,898	$ 2,507	$ 7,051	$ 7,401	$ 7,767	$ 8,151	$ 8,556	$ 8,813

EXHIBIT 12.14

The Coca-Cola Company
Balance Sheets for 2006 through 2008 (Actual) and Year +1 through +6 (Projected)
(amounts in millions)
(Problem 12.16)

	Actuals			Forecasts					
	2006	2007	2008	Year +1	Year +2	Year +3	Year +4	Year +5	Year +6
ASSETS									
Cash and cash equivalents	$ 2,440	$ 4,093	$ 4,701	$ 4,701	$ 4,701	$ 4,701	$ 4,701	$ 4,701	$ 4,842
Marketable securities	150	215	278	286	295	304	313	322	332
Accounts receivable—Net	2,587	3,317	3,090	3,710	3,430	4,067	3,805	4,461	4,595
Inventories	1,641	2,220	2,187	2,320	2,412	2,556	2,661	2,817	2,902
Prepaid expenses and other current assets	1,623	2,260	1,920	2,016	2,117	2,223	2,334	2,450	2,524
Current Assets	$ 8,441	$12,105	$12,176	$13,033	$12,955	$13,851	$13,813	$14,752	$15,194
Long-term investments in affiliates	6,783	7,777	5,779	6,126	6,493	6,883	7,296	7,734	7,966
Property, plant & equipment—At cost	11,911	14,444	14,400	16,191	18,071	20,045	22,118	24,294	25,023
(Accumulated depreciation)	(5,008)	(5,951)	(6,074)	(7,189)	(8,433)	(9,813)	(11,336)	(13,009)	(13,399)
Amortizable intangible assets (net)	1,687	2,810	2,417	2,417	2,417	2,417	2,417	2,417	2,490
Goodwill and nonamortizable intangibles	3,448	9,409	10,088	10,592	11,122	11,678	12,262	12,875	13,261
Other non-current assets (1)	2,701	2,675	1,733	1,785	1,839	1,894	1,951	2,009	2,069
Total Assets	$29,963	$43,269	$40,519	$42,955	$44,464	$46,954	$48,520	$51,072	$52,604

(Continued)

EXHIBIT 12.14 (Continued)

	Actuals			Forecasts					
	2006	**2007**	**2008**	**Year +1**	**Year +2**	**Year +3**	**Year +4**	**Year +5**	**Year +6**
LIABILITIES									
Accounts payable—Trade	$ 929	$ 1,380	$ 1,370	$ 1,277	$ 1,492	$ 1,425	$ 1,628	$ 1,588	$ 1 ,636
Current accrued liabilities	4,126	5,535	4,835	5,077	5,331	5,597	5,877	6,171	6,356
Notes payable and short-term debt	3,235	5,919	6,066	6,443	6,670	7,043	7,278	7,661	7,891
Current maturities of long-term debt	33	133	465	305	322	333	351	361	372
Income taxes payable	567	258	252	172	178	188	194	204	210
Current Liabilities	$ 8,890	$ 13,225	$ 12,988	$ 13,274	$ 13,992	$ 14,586	$ 15,327	$ 15,985	$ 16,465
Long-term debt	1,314	3,277	2,781	2,948	3,052	3,223	3,330	3,505	3,610
Deferred tax liabilities—Noncurrent	608	1,890	877	930	962	1,016	1,050	1,105	1,139
Other non-current liabilities (1)	2,231	3,133	3,401	3,571	3,750	3,937	4,134	4,341	4,471
Total Liabilities	$ 13,043	$ 21,525	$ 20,047	$ 20,723	$ 21,756	$ 22,762	$ 23,842	$ 24,936	$ 25,685
SHAREHOLDERS' EQUITY:									
Common stock + paid-in capital	$ 6,861	$ 8,258	$ 8,846	$ 9,378	$ 9,707	$ 10,251	$ 10,593	$ 11,150	$ 11,484
Retained earnings	33,468	36,235	38,513	39,742	39,887	40,828	40,973	41,873	43,049
Accum. other comprehensive income (loss)	(1,291)	626	(2,674)	(2,674)	(2,674)	(2,674)	(2,674)	(2,674)	(2,674)
(Treasury stock)	(22,118)	(23,375)	(24,213)	(24,213)	(24,213)	(24,213)	(24,213)	(24,213)	(24,939)
Common Shareholders' Equity	$ 16,920	$ 21,744	$ 20,472	$ 22,232	$ 22,708	$ 24,192	$ 24,679	$ 26,135	$ 26,920
Total Liabilities and Equities	$ 29,963	$ 43,269	$ 40,519	$ 42,955	$ 44,464	$ 46,954	$ 48,520	$ 51,072	$ 52,604

EXHIBIT 12.15

The Coca-Cola Company
Projected Implied Statements of Cash Flows for Year +1 through +6
(amounts in millions)
(Problem 12.16)

	Forecasts					
	Year +1	Year +2	Year +3	Year +4	Year +5	Year +6
IMPLIED STATEMENT OF CASH FLOWS						
Net Income	$ 7,051	$ 7,401	$ 7,767	$ 8,151	$ 8,556	$ 8,813
Add back depreciation expense (net)	1,115	1,244	1,380	1,523	1,673	390
(Increase) Decrease in receivables—Net	(620)	280	(637)	262	(656)	(134)
(Increase) Decrease in inventories	(133)	(93)	(144)	(104)	(156)	(85)
(Increase) Decrease in prepaid expenses	(96)	(101)	(106)	(111)	(117)	(74)
Increase (Decrease) in accounts payable—Trade	(93)	215	(67)	202	(40)	48
Increase (Decrease) in current accrued liabilities	242	254	267	280	294	185
Increase (Decrease) in income taxes payable	(80)	6	10	6	10	6
Net change in deferred tax assets and liabilities	53	33	54	34	55	33
Increase (Decrease) in other non-current liabilities	170	179	187	197	207	130
Net Cash Flows from Operations	**$ 7,608**	**$ 9,419**	**$ 8,711**	**$10,440**	**$ 9,826**	**$ 9,313**
(Increase) Decrease in prop., plant, & equip. at cost	(1,791)	(1,880)	(1,974)	(2,073)	(2,177)	(729)
(Increase) Decrease in marketable securities	(8)	(9)	(9)	(9)	(9)	(10)
(Increase) Decrease in investment securities	(347)	(368)	(390)	(413)	(438)	(232)
(Increase) Decrease in amortizable intangible assets (net)	0	0	0	0	0	(73)
(Increase) Decrease in goodwill and nonamort. intang.	(504)	(530)	(556)	(584)	(613)	(386)
(Increase) Decrease in other non-current assets	(52)	(54)	(55)	(57)	(59)	(60)
Net Cash Flows from Investing	**$(2,702)**	**$(2,839)**	**$(2,984)**	**$(3,136)**	**$(3,295)**	**$(1,490)**
Increase (Decrease) in short-term debt	217	243	384	252	393	241
Increase (Decrease) in long-term debt	167	104	171	107	175	105
Increase (Decrease) in common stock + paid-in capital	532	329	544	342	557	334
Increase (Decrease) in accum. OCI and other equity adjs.	0	0	0	0	0	0
Increase (Decrease) in treasury stock	0	0	0	0	0	(726)
Dividends	(5,822)	(7,255)	(6,826)	(8,006)	(7,656)	(7,637)
Net Cash Flows from Financing	**$(4,906)**	**$(6,579)**	**$(5,727)**	**$(7,305)**	**$(6,531)**	**$(7,683)**
Net Change in Cash	$ —	$ —	$ —	$ —	$ —	**$ 141**

The market equity beta for Walmart at the end of Year 4 was 0.80. Assume that the risk-free interest rate was 3.5 percent and the market risk premium was 5.0 percent. Walmart had 3,925 million shares outstanding at the end of 2008. At the end of 2008, Walmart's share price was $46.06.

Required

Part I—Computing Walmart's Share Value Using Free Cash Flows to Common Equity Shareholders

a. Use the CAPM to compute the required rate of return on common equity capital for Walmart.

b. Beginning with projected net cash flows from operations, derive the projected free cash flows for common equity shareholders for Walmart for Years +1 through +5 based on the projected financial statements. Assume that Walmart uses any change in cash each year for operating liquidity purposes.

c. Project the continuing free cash flow for common equity shareholders in Year +6. Assume that the steady-state long-run growth rate will be 3 percent in Year +6 and beyond. Project that the Year +5 income statement and balance sheet amounts will grow by 3 percent in Year +6; then derive the projected statement of cash flows for Year +6. Derive the projected free cash flow for common equity shareholders in Year +6 from the projected statement of cash flows for Year +6.

d. Using the required rate of return on common equity from Part a as a discount rate, compute the sum of the present value of free cash flows for common equity shareholders for Walmart for Years +1 through +5.

e. Using the required rate of return on common equity from Part a as a discount rate and the long-run growth rate from Part c, compute the continuing value of Walmart as of the start of Year +6 based on Walmart's continuing free cash flows for common equity shareholders in Year +6 and beyond. After computing continuing value as of the start of Year +6, discount it to present value at the start of Year +1.

f. Compute the value of a share of Walmart common stock. (1) Compute the total sum of the present value of all future free cash flows for equity shareholders (from Parts d and e). (2) Adjust the total sum of the present value using the midyear discounting adjustment factor. (3) Compute the per-share value estimate.

Note: If you worked Problem 11.14 in Chapter 11 and computed Walmart's share value using the dividends valuation approach, compare your value estimate from that problem with the value estimate you obtain here. They should be the same.

Part II—Computing Walmart's Share Value Using Free Cash Flows to All Debt and Equity Stakeholders

g. At the end of 2008, Walmart had $42,218 million in outstanding interest-bearing short-term and long-term debt on the balance sheet and no preferred stock. Assume that the balance sheet value of Walmart's debt is approximately equal to the market value of the debt. During 2008, Walmart's income statement included interest expense of $2,184 million. During 2008, Walmart faced an average interest expense of roughly 5.0 percent. Assume that at the start of Year +1, Walmart will continue to incur interest expense of 5.0 percent on debt capital and that Walmart's average tax rate will be 34.2 percent. Compute the weighted average cost of capital for Walmart as of the start of Year +1.

h. Beginning with projected net cash flows from operations, derive the projected free cash flows for all debt and equity stakeholders for Walmart for Years +1 through +5 based on the projected financial statements.

i. Project the continuing free cash flows for all debt and equity stakeholders in Year +6. Use the projected financial statements for Year +6 from Part c to derive the projected free cash flow for all debt and equity stakeholders in Year +6.

EXHIBIT 12.16

Wal-Mart Stores, Inc.
Income Statements for 2008 (Actual) and Year +1 through +5 (Projected)
(amounts in millions)
(Problem 12.17)

	Actual	Projected:				
	2008	**Year +1**	**Year +2**	**Year +3**	**Year +4**	**Year +5**
Revenues	$ 405,607	$ 433,999	$ 464,379	$ 496,886	$ 531,668	$ 568,885
Cost of goods sold	(306,158)	(327,670)	(350,606)	(375,149)	(401,409)	(429,508)
Gross Profit	$ 99,449	$ 106,330	$ 113,773	$ 121,737	$ 130,259	$ 139,377
Selling, general, and administrative expenses	(76,651)	(82,460)	(88,232)	(94,408)	(101,017)	(108,088)
Interest income	284	320	320	320	320	320
Interest expense	(2,184)	(2,163)	(2,269)	(2,383)	(2,503)	(2,630)
Income before tax	$ 20,898	$ 22,027	$ 23,591	$ 25,266	$ 27,059	$ 28,979
Income tax expense	(7,145)	(7,533)	(8,068)	(8,641)	(9,254)	(9,911)
Minority interest in earnings	(499)	(499)	(499)	(499)	(499)	(499)
Net Income	$ 13,400	$ 13,995	$ 15,024	$16,126	$ 17,306	$ 18,569

EXHIBIT 12.17

Wal-Mart Stores, Inc.
Balance Sheets for 2008 (Actual) and Year +1 through +5 (Projected)
(amounts in millions)
(Problem 12.17)

	Actual	Projected				
	2008	Year +1	Year +2	Year +3	Year +4	Year +5
ASSETS						
Cash and cash equivalents	$ 7,275	$ 7,275	$ 7,275	$ 7,275	$ 7,275	$ 7,275
Accounts receivable—Net	3,905	4,178	4,471	4,784	5,119	5,477
Inventories	34,511	40,815	39,784	46,457	45,821	52,917
Prepaid expenses and other current assets	3,063	3,277	3,507	3,752	4,015	4,296
Current assets of discontinued segments	195	0	0	0	0	0
Current Assets	$ 48,949	$ 55,546	$ 55,037	$ 62,268	$ 62,229	$ 69,965
Property, plant & equipment—At cost	131,161	146,376	163,355	182,304	203,452	227,052
(Accumulated depreciation)	(35,508)	(42,827)	(50,995)	(60,110)	(70,282)	(81,635)
Goodwill and nonamortizable intangibles	18,827	20,145	21,555	23,064	24,678	26,406
Total Assets	$163,429	$179,240	$ 188,952	$ 207,527	$ 220,077	$ 241,788
LIABILITIES						
Accounts payable—Trade	$ 28,849	$ 35,201	$ 31,841	$ 41,385	$ 35,475	$ 48,257
Current accrued liabilities	18,112	19,380	20,736	22,188	23,741	25,403
Notes payable and short-term debt	1,506	1,506	1,506	1,506	1,506	1,506
Current maturities of long-term debt	6,163	6,163	6,163	6,163	6,163	6,163
Income taxes payable	760	813	870	931	996	1,066
Current Liabilities	$ 55,390	$ 63,063	$ 61,117	$ 72,173	$ 67,882	$ 82,395
Long-term debt	34,549	36,622	38,819	41,148	43,617	46,234
Deferred tax liabilities—Noncurrent	6,014	6,615	7,277	8,005	8,805	9,686
Total Liabilities	$ 95,953	$106,300	$ 107,213	$ 121,326	$ 120,304	$ 138,315
SHAREHOLDERS' EQUITY						
Minority interest	2,191	2,191	2,191	2,191	2,191	2,191
Common stock + paid-in capital	4,313	4,744	5,219	5,741	6,315	6,946
Retained earnings	63,660	68,692	77,018	80,957	93,955	97,024
Accum. other comprehensive income (loss)	(2,688)	(2,688)	(2,688)	(2,688)	(2,688)	(2,688)
Common Shareholders' Equity	$ 65,285	$ 70,749	$ 79,549	$ 84,010	$ 97,582	$ 101,282
Total Liabilities and Equities	$163,429	$179,240	$ 188,952	$ 207,527	$ 220,077	$ 241,788

EXHIBIT 12.18

Wal-Mart Stores, Inc.
Projected Implied Statements of Cash Flows for Year +1 through +5
(amounts in millions)
(Problem 12.17)

	Projected				
	Year +1	Year +2	Year +3	Year +4	Year +5
IMPLIED STATEMENT OF CASH FLOWS					
Net Income	$ 13,995	$ 15,024	$ 16,126	$ 17,306	$ 18,569
Add back depreciation expense (net)	7,319	8,168	9,115	10,173	11,353
(Increase) Decrease in receivables—Net	(273)	(292)	(313)	(335)	(358)
(Increase) Decrease in inventories	(6,304)	1,032	(6,673)	637	(7,096)
(Increase) Decrease in prepaid expenses	(214)	(229)	(245)	(263)	(281)
(Increase) Decrease in other current assets	195	0	0	0	0
Increase (Decrease) in accounts payable—Trade	6,352	(3,360)	9,544	(5,910)	12,782
Increase (Decrease) in current accrued liabilities	1,268	1,357	1,452	1,553	1,662
Increase (Decrease) in income taxes payable	53	57	61	65	70
Net change in deferred tax assets and liabilities	601	662	728	800	881
Net Cash Flows from Operations	**$ 22,991**	**$ 22,417**	**$ 29,794**	**$ 24,026**	**$ 37,580**
(Increase) Decrease in prop., plant, & equip. at cost	(15,215)	(16,980)	(18,949)	(21,147)	(23,600)
(Increase) Decrease in goodwill and nonamort. intang.	(1,318)	(1,410)	(1,509)	(1,614)	(1,727)
Net Cash Flows from Investing Activities	**$(16,533)**	**$(18,390)**	**$(20,458)**	**$(22,762)**	**$(25,328)**
Increase (Decrease) in short-term debt	0	0	0	0	0
Increase (Decrease) in long-term debt	2,073	2,197	2,329	2,469	2,617
Increase (Decrease) in minority interest and preferred stock	0	0	0	0	0
Increase (Decrease) in common stock + paid-in capital	431	474	522	574	631
Increase (Decrease) in accumulated OCI	0	0	0	0	0
Dividends	(8,963)	(6,699)	(12,187)	(4,308)	(15,501)
Net Cash Flows from Financing Activities	**$ (6,458)**	**$ (4,027)**	**$ (9,336)**	**$ (1,265)**	**$(12,252)**
Net Change in Cash	**$ 0**	**$ 0**	**$ 0**	**$ 0**	**$ 0**

j. Using the weighted average cost of capital from Part g as a discount rate, compute the sum of the present value of free cash flows for all debt and equity stakeholders for Walmart for Years +1 through +5.

k. Using the weighted average cost of capital from Part g as a discount rate and the long-run growth rate from Part c, compute the continuing value of Walmart as of the start of Year +6 based on Walmart's continuing free cash flows for all debt and equity stakeholders in Year +6 and beyond. After computing continuing value as of the start of Year +6, discount it to present value as of the start of Year +1.

l. Compute the value of a share of Walmart common stock. (1) Compute the total value of Walmart's net operating assets using the total sum of the present value of free cash flows for all debt and equity stakeholders (from Parts j and k). (2) Subtract the value of outstanding debt to obtain the value of equity. (3) Adjust the present value of equity using the midyear discounting adjustment factor. (4) Compute the per-share value estimate of Walmart's common equity shares.

Note: Do not be alarmed if your share value estimate from Part f is slightly different from your share value estimate from Part l. The weighted average cost of capital computation in Part g used the weight of equity based on the market price of Walmart's stock at the end of 2008. The share value estimates from Parts f and l likely differ from the market price, so the weights used to compute the weighted average cost of capital are not internally consistent with the estimated share values.

Part III—Sensitivity Analysis and Recommendation

m. Using the free cash flows to common equity shareholders, recompute the value of Walmart shares under two alternative scenarios. Scenario 1: Assume that Walmart's long-run growth will be 2 percent, not 3 percent as before, and assume that Walmart's required rate of return on equity is 1 percentage point higher than the rate you computed using the CAPM in Part a. Scenario 2: Assume that Walmart's long-run growth will be 4 percent, not 3 percent as before, and assume that Walmart's required rate of return on equity is 1 percentage point lower than the rate you computed using the CAPM in Part a. To quantify the sensitivity of your share value estimate for Walmart to these variations in growth and discount rates, compare (in percentage terms) your value estimates under these two scenarios with your value estimate from Part f.

n. Using these data at the end of Year 4, what reasonable range of share values would you have expected for Walmart common stock? At that time, what was the market price for Walmart shares relative to this range? What would you have recommended?

INTEGRATIVE CASE 12.1

STARBUCKS

Free Cash Flows Valuation of Starbucks' Common Equity

In Integrative Case 10.1, we projected financial statements for Starbucks for Years +1 through +5. In this portion of the Starbucks Integrative Case, we use the projected financial statements from Integrative Case 10.1 and apply the techniques in Chapter 12 to compute Starbucks' required rate of return on equity and share value based on the free cash flows valuation model. We also compare our value estimate to Starbucks' share price at the time of the case development to provide an investment recommendation.

The market equity beta for Starbucks at the end of 2008 is 0.58. Assume that the risk-free interest rate is 4.0 percent and the market risk premium is 6.0 percent. Starbucks has

735.5 million shares outstanding at the end of 2008. At the start of Year +1, Starbucks' share price was $14.17.

Required

Part I—Computing Starbucks' Share Value Using Free Cash Flows to Common Equity Shareholders

a. Use the CAPM to compute the required rate of return on common equity capital for Starbucks.

b. Using your projected financial statements from Integrative Case 10.1 for Starbucks, begin with projected net cash flows from operations and derive the projected free cash flows for common equity shareholders for Starbucks for Years +1 through +5. You must determine whether your projected changes in cash are necessary for operating liquidity purposes.

c. Project the continuing free cash flow for common equity shareholders in Year +6. Assume that the steady-state long-run growth rate will be 3 percent in Year +6 and beyond. Project that the Year +5 income statement and balance sheet amounts will grow by 3 percent in Year +6; then derive the projected statement of cash flows for Year +6. Derive the projected free cash flow for common equity shareholders in Year +6 from the projected statement of cash flows for Year +6.

d. Using the required rate of return on common equity from Part a as a discount rate, compute the sum of the present value of free cash flows for common equity shareholders for Starbucks for Years +1 through +5.

e. Using the required rate of return on common equity from Part a as a discount rate and the long-run growth rate from Part c, compute the continuing value of Starbucks as of the start of Year +6 based on Starbucks' continuing free cash flows for common equity shareholders in Year +6 and beyond. After computing continuing value as of the start of Year +6, discount it to present value at the start of Year +1.

f. Compute the value of a share of Starbucks common stock. (1) Compute the total sum of the present value of free cash flows for equity shareholders (from Parts d and e). (2) Adjust the total sum of the present value using the midyear discounting adjustment factor. (3) Compute the per-share value estimate.

Note: If you worked Integrative Case 11.1 from Chapter 11 and computed Starbucks' share value using the dividends valuation approach, compare your value estimate from that case with the value estimate you obtain here. They should be the same.

Part II—Computing Starbucks' Share Value Using Free Cash Flows to All Debt and Equity Stakeholders

g. At the end of 2008, Starbucks had $1,263 million in outstanding interest-bearing short-term and long-term debt on the balance sheet and no preferred stock. Assume that the balance sheet value of Starbucks' debt equals the market value of the debt. Starbucks faces an interest rate of roughly 6.25 percent on its outstanding debt. Assume that Starbucks will continue to face the same interest rate on this outstanding debt capital over the remaining life of the debt. Using the amounts on Starbucks' 2008 income statement in Exhibit 1.27 for Integrative Case 1.1 in Chapter 1, compute Starbucks' average tax rate in 2008. Assume that Starbucks will continue to face the same income tax rate over the forecast horizon. Compute the weighted average cost of capital for Starbucks as of the start of Year +1. Compare your computation of Starbucks' weighted average cost of capital with your estimate of Starbucks' required return on equity from Part a. Why do the two amounts differ?

h. Based on your projections of Starbucks' financial statements, begin with projected net cash flows from operations and derive the projected free cash flows for all debt and equity stakeholders for Years +1 through +5. Compare your forecasts of Starbucks' free cash flows for all debt and equity stakeholders Years +1 through +5 with your forecast of Starbucks' free cash flows for equity shareholders in Part b. Why are the amounts not identical—what causes the difference each year?

i. Project the continuing free cash flows for all debt and equity stakeholders in Year +6. Use the projected financial statements for Year +6 from Part c to derive the projected free cash flow for all debt and equity stakeholders in Year +6.

j. Using the weighted average cost of capital from Part g as a discount rate, compute the sum of the present value of free cash flows for all debt and equity stakeholders for Starbucks for Years +1 through +5.

k. Using the weighted average cost of capital from Part g as a discount rate and the long-run growth rate from Part c, compute the continuing value of Starbucks as of the start of Year +6 based on Starbucks' continuing free cash flows for all debt and equity stakeholders in Year +6 and beyond. After computing continuing value as of the start of Year +6, discount it to present value at the start of Year +1.

l. Compute the value of a share of Starbucks common stock. (1) Compute the value of Starbucks' net operating assets using the total sum of the present value of free cash flows for all debt and equity stakeholders (from Parts j and k). (2) Subtract the value of outstanding debt to obtain the value of equity. (3) Adjust the present value of equity using the midyear discounting adjustment factor. (4) Compute the per-share value estimate.

m. Compare your share value estimate from Part f with your share value estimate from Part l. These values should be similar.

Part III—Sensitivity Analysis and Recommendation

n. Using the free cash flows to common equity shareholders, recompute the value of Starbucks shares under two alternative scenarios. Scenario 1: Assume that Starbucks' long-run growth will be 2 percent, not 3 percent as before, and assume that Starbucks' required rate of return on equity is 1 percentage point higher than the rate you computed using the CAPM in Part a. Scenario 2: Assume that Starbucks' long-run growth will be 4 percent, not 3 percent as before, and assume that Starbucks' required rate of return on equity is 1 percentage point lower than the rate you computed using the CAPM in Part a. To quantify the sensitivity of your share value estimate for Starbucks to these variations in growth and discount rates, compare (in percentage terms) your value estimates under these two scenarios with your value estimate from Part f.

o. At the end of 2008, what reasonable range of share values would you have expected for Starbucks common stock? At that time, where was the market price for Starbucks shares relative to this range? What would you have recommended?

p. If you computed Starbucks' common equity share value using the dividends-valuation approach in Integrative Case 11.1, compare the value estimate you obtained in that case with the estimate you obtained in this case. They should be identical.

CASE 12.2

HOLMES CORPORATION: LBO VALUATION

Holmes Corporation is a leading designer and manufacturer of material handling and process equipment for heavy industry in the United States and abroad. Its sales have more than doubled and its earnings have increased more than sixfold in the past five years. In material handling, Holmes is a major producer of electric overhead and gantry cranes, ranging from 5 tons in capacity to 600-ton giants, the latter used primarily in nuclear and conventional power-generating plants. It also builds underhung cranes and monorail systems for general industrial use carrying loads up to 40 tons, railcar movers, railroad and mass transit shop maintenance equipment, and a broad line of advanced package conveyors. Holmes is a world leader in evaporation and crystallization systems and furnishes dryers, heat exchangers, and filters to complete its line of chemical processing equipment sold internationally to the chemical, fertilizer, food, drug, and paper industries. For the metallurgical industry, it designs and manufactures electric arc and induction furnaces, cupolas, ladles, and hot metal distribution equipment.

The information below and on the following pages appears in the Year 15 annual report of Holmes Corporation.

Highlights

	Year 15	Year 14
Net Sales	$102,698,836	$109,372,718
Net Earnings	6,601,908	6,583,360
Net Earnings per Share	3.62*	3.61*
Cash Dividends Paid	2,241,892	1,426,502
Cash Dividends per Share	1.22*	0.78*
Shareholders' Equity	29,333,803	24,659,214
Shareholders' Equity per Share	16.07*	13.51*
Working Capital	23,100,863	19,029,626
Orders Received	95,436,103	80,707,576
Unfilled Orders at End of Period	77,455,900	84,718,633
Average Number of Common Shares Outstanding during Period	1,824,853*	1,824,754*

*Adjusted for June, Year 15, and June, Year 14, 5-for-4 stock distributions.

Net Sales, Net Earnings, and Net Earnings per Share by Quarter

(adjusted for 5-for-4 stock distribution in June, Year 15, and June, Year 14)

	Year 15			Year 14		
	Net Sales	Net Earnings	Per Share	Net Sales	Net Earnings	Per Share
First Quarter	$ 25,931,457	$1,602,837	$0.88	$ 21,768,077	$1,126,470	$0.62
Second Quarter	24,390,079	1,727,112	0.95	28,514,298	1,716,910	0.94
Third Quarter	25,327,226	1,505,118	0.82	28,798,564	1,510,958	0.82
Fourth Quarter	27,050,074	1,766,841	0.97	30,291,779	2,229,022	1.23
	$102,698,836	$6,601,908	$3.62	$109,372,718	$6,583,360	$3.61

Common Stock Prices and Cash Dividends Paid per Common Share by Quarter

(adjusted for 5-for-4 stock distribution in June, Year 15, and June, Year 14)

	Year 15			Year 14		
	Stock Prices		Cash Dividends	Stock Prices		Cash Dividends
	High	Low	per Share	High	Low	per Share
First Quarter	$\$22\frac{1}{2}$	$\$18\frac{1}{2}$	$0.26	$\$11\frac{1}{4}$	$\$\ 9\frac{1}{2}$	$0.16
Second Quarter	$25\frac{1}{4}$	$19\frac{1}{2}$	0.26	$12\frac{3}{8}$	$8\frac{7}{8}$	0.16
Third Quarter	$26\frac{1}{4}$	$19\frac{3}{4}$	0.325	$15\frac{7}{8}$	$11\frac{5}{8}$	0.20
Fourth Quarter	$28\frac{1}{8}$	$23\frac{1}{4}$	0.375	$20\frac{7}{8}$	$15\frac{7}{8}$	0.26
			$1.22			$0.78

Management's Report to Shareholders

Year 15 was a pleasant surprise for all of us at Holmes Corporation. When the year started, it looked as though Year 15 would be a good year but not up to the record performance of Year 14. However, due to the excellent performance of our employees and the benefit of a favorable acquisition, Year 15 produced both record earnings and the largest cash dividend outlay in the company's 93-year history.

There is no doubt that some of the attractive orders received in late Year 12 and early Year 13 contributed to Year 15 profit. But of major significance was our organization's favorable response to several new management policies instituted to emphasize higher corporate profitability. Year 15 showed a net profit on net sales of 6.4 percent, which not only exceeded the 6.0 percent of last year but represents the highest net margin in several decades.

Net sales for the year were $102,698,836, down 6 percent from the $109,372,718 of a year ago but still the second largest volume in our history. Net earnings, however, set a new record at $6,601,908, or $3.62 per common share, which slightly exceeded the $6,583,360, or $3.61 per common share earned last year.

Cash dividends of $2,241,892 paid in Year 15 were 57 percent above the $1,426,502 paid a year ago. The record total resulted from your Board's approval of two increases during the year. When we implemented the 5-for-4 stock distribution in June, Year 15, we maintained the quarterly dividend rate of $0.325 on the increased number of shares for the January payment. Then, in December, Year 15, we increased the quarterly rate to $0.375 per share.

Year 15 certainly was not the most exuberant year in the capital equipment markets. Fortunately, our heavy involvement in ecology improvement, power generation, and international markets continued to serve us well, with the result that new orders of $95,436,103 were 18 percent over the $80,707,576 of Year 14.

Economists have predicted a substantial capital spending upturn for well over a year, but, so far, our customers have displayed stubborn reluctance to place new orders amid the uncertainty concerning the economy. Confidence is the answer. As soon as potential buyers can see clearly the future direction of the economy, we expect the unleashing of a large latent demand for capital goods, producing a much-expanded market for Holmes' products.

Fortunately, the accelerating pace of international markets continues to yield new business. Year 15 was an excellent year on the international front as our foreign customers continue to recognize our technological leadership in several product lines. Net sales of

Holmes products shipped overseas and fees from foreign licensees amounted to $30,495,041, which represents a 31 percent increase over the $23,351,980 of a year ago.

Management fully recognizes and intends to take maximum advantage of our technological leadership in foreign lands. The latest manifestation of this policy was the acquisition of a controlling interest in Societé Francaise Holmes Fermont, our Swenson process equipment licensee located in Paris. Holmes and a partner started this firm 14 years ago as a sales and engineering organization to function in the Common Market. The company currently operates in the same mode. It owns no physical manufacturing assets, subcontracting all production. Its markets have expanded to include Spain and the East European countries.

Holmes Fermont is experiencing strong demand in Europe. For example, in early May, a $5.5 million order for a large potash crystallization system was received from a French engineering company representing a Russian client. Management estimates that Holmes Fermont will contribute approximately $6 to $8 million of net sales in Year 16.

Holmes' other wholly owned subsidiaries—Holmes Equipment Limited in Canada, Ermanco Incorporated in Michigan, and Holmes International, Inc., our FSC (Foreign Sales Corporation)—again contributed substantially to the success of Year 15. Holmes Equipment Limited registered its second best year. However, capital equipment markets in Canada have virtually come to a standstill in the past two quarters. Ermanco achieved the best year in its history, while Holmes International, Inc. had a truly exceptional year because of the very high level of activity in our international markets.

The financial condition of the company showed further improvement and is now unusually strong as a result of very stringent financial controls. Working capital increased to $23,100,863 from $19,029,626, a 21 percent improvement. Inventories decreased 6 percent from $18,559,231 to $17,491,741. The company currently has no long-term or short-term debt, and has considerable cash in short-term instruments. Much of our cash position, however, results from customers' advance payments which we will absorb as we make shipments on the contracts. Shareholders' equity increased 19 percent to $29,393,803 from $24,690,214 a year ago.

Plant equipment expenditures for the year were $1,172,057, down 18 percent from $1,426,347 of Year 14. Several appropriations approved during the year did not require expenditures because of delayed deliveries beyond Year 15. The major emphasis again was on our continuing program of improving capacity and efficiency through the purchase of numerically controlled machine tools. We expanded the Ermanco plant by 50 percent, but since this is a leasehold arrangement, we made only minor direct investment. We also improved the Canadian operation by adding more manufacturing space and installing energy-saving insulation.

Labor relations were excellent throughout the year. The Harvey plant continues to be nonunion. We negotiated a new labor contract at the Canadian plant, which extends to March 1, Year 17. The Pioneer Division in Alabama has a labor contract that does not expire until April, Year 16. While the union contract at Ermanco expired June 1, Year 15, work continues while negotiation proceeds on a new contract. We anticipate no difficulty in reaching a new agreement.

We exerted considerable effort during the year to improve Holmes' image in the investment community. Management held several informative meetings with security analyst groups to enhance the awareness of our activities and corporate performance.

The outlook for Year 16, while generally favorable, depends in part on the course of capital spending over the next several months. If the spending rate accelerates, the quickening pace of new orders, coupled with present backlogs, will provide the conditions for another fine year. On the other hand, if general industry continues the reluctant spending pattern of the last two years, Year 16 could be a year of maintaining market positions while awaiting better market conditions. Management takes an optimistic view and thus looks for a successful Year 16.

The achievement of record earnings and the highest profit margin in decades demonstrates the capability and the dedication of our employees. Management is most grateful for their efforts throughout the excellent year.

T. R. Varnum	T. L. Fuller
President	Chairman
March 15, Year 16	

Review of Operations

Year 15 was a very active year although the pace was not at the hectic tempo of Year 14. It was a year that showed continued strong demand in some product areas but a dampened rate in others. The product areas that had some special economic circumstances enhancing demand fared well. For example, the continuing effort toward ecological improvement fostered excellent activity in Swenson process equipment. Likewise, the energy concern and the need for more electrical power generation capacity boded well for large overhead cranes. On the other hand, Holmes' products that relate to general industry and depend on the overall capital spending rate for new equipment experienced lesser demand, resulting in lower new orders and reduced backlogs. The affected products were small cranes, underhung cranes, railcar movers, and metallurgical equipment.

Year 15 was the first full year of operations under some major policy changes instituted to improve Holmes' profitability. The two primary revisions were the restructuring of our marketing effort along product division lines, and the conversion of the product division incentive plans to a profit-based formula. The corporate organization adapted extremely well to the new policies. The improved profit margin in Year 15, in substantial part, was a result of the changes.

International activity increased markedly during the year. Surging foreign business and the expressed objective to capitalize on Holmes' technological leadership overseas resulted in the elevation of Mr. R. E. Foster to officer status as Vice President-International. The year involved heavy commitments of the product division staffs, engineering groups, and manufacturing organization to such important contracts as the $14 million Swenson order for Poland, the $8 million Swenson project for Mexico, the $2 million crane order for Venezuela, and several millions of dollars of railcar movers for all areas of the world.

The acquisition of control and commencement of operating responsibility of Societé Francaise Holmes Fermont, the Swenson licensee in Paris, was a major milestone in our international strategy. This organization has the potential of becoming a very substantial contributor in the years immediately ahead. Its long-range market opportunities in Europe and Asia are excellent.

Material Handling Products

Material handling equipment activities portrayed conflicting trends. During the year, when total backlog decreased, the crane division backlog increased. This was a result of several multimillion dollar contracts for power plant cranes. The small crane market, on the other hand, experienced depressed conditions during most of the year as general industry withheld appropriations for new plant and equipment. The underhung crane market experienced similar conditions. However, as Congressional attitudes and policies on investment unfold, we expect capital spending to show a substantial upturn.

The Transportation Equipment Division secured the second order for orbital service bridges, a new product for the containment vessels of nuclear power plants. This design is unique and allows considerable cost savings in erecting and maintaining containment shells.

The Ermanco Conveyor Division completed its best year with the growing acceptance of the unique XenoROL design. We expanded the Grand Haven plant by 50 percent to effect further cost reduction and new concepts of marketing.

The railcar moving line continued to produce more business from international markets. We installed the new 11TM unit in six domestic locations, a product showing signs of exceptional performance. We shipped the first foreign 11TM machine to Sweden.

Process Equipment Products

Process equipment again accounted for slightly more than half of the year's business.

Swenson activity reached an all-time high level with much of the division's effort going into international projects. The large foreign orders required considerable additional work to cover the necessary documentation, metrification when required, and general liaison.

We engaged in considerably more subcontracting during the year to accommodate one-piece shipment of the huge vessels pioneered by Swenson to effect greater equipment economies. The division continued to expand the use of computerization for design work and contract administration. We developed more capability during the year to handle the many additional tasks associated with turnkey projects. Swenson research and development efforts accelerated in search of better technology and new products. We conducted pilot plant test work at our facilities and in the field to convert several sales prospects into new contracts.

The metallurgical business proceeded at a slower pace in Year 15. However, with construction activity showing early signs of improvement, and automotive and farm machinery manufacturers increasing their operating rates, we see intensified interest in metallurgical equipment.

Financial Statements

The financial statements of Holmes Corporation and related notes appear in Exhibits 12.19–12.21 (see pages 996–998). Exhibit 12.22 (see page 999) presents five-year summary operating information for Holmes.

Notes to Consolidated Financial Statements Year 15 and Year 14

Note A—Summary of Significant Accounting Policies. Significant accounting policies consistently applied appear below to assist the reader in reviewing the company's consolidated financial statements contained in this report.

Consolidation—The consolidated financial statements include the accounts of the company and its subsidiaries after eliminating all intercompany transactions and balances.

Inventories—Inventories generally appear at the lower of cost or market, with cost determined principally on a first-in, first-out method.

Property, plant, and equipment—Property, plant, and equipment appear at acquisition cost less accumulated depreciation. When the company retires or disposes of properties, it removes the related costs and accumulated depreciation from the respective accounts and credits, or charges any gain or loss to earnings. The company expenses maintenance and repairs as incurred. It capitalizes major betterments and renewals. Depreciation results from applying the straight-line method over the estimated useful lives of the assets as follows:

Buildings	30 to 45 years
Machinery and equipment	4 to 20 years
Furniture and fixtures	10 years

EXHIBIT 12.19

Holmes Corporation
Balance Sheet
(amounts in thousands)
(Case 12.2)

	Year 10	Year 11	Year 12	Year 13	Year 14	Year 15
Cash	$ 955	$ 962	$ 865	$ 1,247	$ 1,540	$ 3,857
Marketable securities	0	0	0	0	0	2,990
Accounts/Notes receivable	6,545	7,295	9,718	13,307	18,759	14,303
Inventories	7,298	8,685	12,797	20,426	18,559	17,492
Current Assets	$14,798	$16,942	$23,380	$34,980	$38,858	$38,642
Investments	0	0	0	0	0	422
Property, plant, and equipment	12,216	12,445	13,126	13,792	14,903	15,876
Less: Accumulated depreciation	(7,846)	(8,236)	(8,558)	(8,988)	(9,258)	(9,703)
Other assets	470	420	400	299	343	276
Total Assets	$19,638	$21,571	$28,348	$40,083	$44,846	$45,513
Accounts payable—Trade	$ 2,894	$ 4,122	$ 6,496	$ 7,889	$ 6,779	$ 4,400
Notes payable—Nontrade	0	0	700	3,500	0	0
Current portion long-term debt	170	170	170	170	170	0
Other current liabilities	550	1,022	3,888	8,624	12,879	11,142
Current Liabilities	$ 3,614	$ 5,314	$11,254	$20,183	$19,828	$15,542
Long-term debt	680	510	340	170	0	0
Deferred tax	0	0	0	216	328	577
Other noncurrent liabilities	0	0	0	0	0	0
Total Liabilities	$ 4,294	$ 5,824	$11,594	$20,569	$20,156	$16,119
Common stock	$ 2,927	$ 2,927	$ 2,927	$ 5,855	$ 7,303	$ 9,214
Additional paid-in capital	5,075	5,075	5,075	5,075	5,061	5,286
Retained earnings	7,342	7,772	8,774	8,599	12,297	14,834
Accumulated other comprehensive income	0	0	5	12	29	60
Treasury stock	0	(27)	(27)	(27)	0	0
Total Shareholders' Equity	$15,344	$15,747	$16,754	$19,514	$24,690	$29,394
Total Liabilities and Shareholders' Equity	$19,638	$21,571	$28,348	$40,083	$44,846	$45,513

EXHIBIT 12.20

Holmes Corporation
Income Statement
(amounts in thousands)
(Case 12.2)

	Year 11	Year 12	Year 13	Year 14	Year 15
Sales	$ 41,428	$ 53,541	$ 76,328	$109,373	$102,699
Other revenues and gains	0	41	0	0	211
Cost of goods sold	(33,269)	(43,142)	(60,000)	(85,364)	(80,260)
Selling and administrative expense	(6,175)	(7,215)	(9,325)	(13,416)	(12,090)
Other expenses and losses	(2)	0	(11)	(31)	(1)
Operating Income	$ 1,982	$ 3,225	$ 6,992	$ 10,562	$ 10,559
Interest expense	(43)	(21)	(284)	(276)	(13)
Income tax expense	(894)	(1,471)	(2,992)	(3,703)	(3,944)
Net Income	$ 1,045	$ 1,733	$ 3,716	$ 6,583	$ 6,602

Intangible assets—The company has amortized the unallocated excess of cost of a subsidiary over net assets acquired (that is, goodwill) over a 17-year period. Beginning in Year 16, GAAP no longer requires amortization of goodwill.

Research and development costs—The company charges research and development costs to operations as incurred ($479,410 in Year 15, and $467,733 in Year 14).

Pension plans—The company and its subsidiaries have noncontributory pension plans covering substantially all of their employees. The company's policy is to fund accrued pension costs as determined by independent actuaries. Pension costs amounted to $471,826 in Year 15, and $366,802 in Year 14.

Revenue recognition—The company generally recognizes income on a percentage-of-completion basis. It records advance payments as received and reports them as a deduction from billings when earned. The company recognizes royalties, included in net sales, as income when received. Royalties total $656,043 in Year 15, and $723,930 in Year 14.

Income taxes—The company provides no income taxes on unremitted earnings of foreign subsidiaries since it anticipates no significant tax liabilities should foreign units remit such earnings. The company makes provision for deferred income taxes applicable to timing differences between financial statement and income tax accounting, principally on the earnings of a foreign sales subsidiary which existing statutes defer in part from current taxation.

Note B—Foreign Operations. The consolidated financial statements in Year 15 include net assets of $2,120,648 ($1,847,534 in Year 14), undistributed earnings of $2,061,441 ($1,808,752 in Year 14), sales of $7,287,566 ($8,603,225 in Year 14), and net income of $454,999 ($641,454 in Year 14) applicable to the Canadian subsidiary.

The company translates balance sheet accounts of the Canadian subsidiary into U.S. dollars at the exchange rates at the end of the year, and operating results at the average of exchange rates for the year.

EXHIBIT 12.21

Holmes Corporation
Statement of Cash Flows
(amounts in thousands)
(Case 12.2)

	Year 11	Year 12	Year 13	Year 14	Year 15
OPERATIONS					
Net income	$ 1,045	$ 1,733	$ 3,716	$ 6,583	$ 6,602
Depreciation and amortization	491	490	513	586	643
Other addbacks	20	25	243	151	299
Other subtractions	0	0	0	0	(97)
(Increase) Decrease in receivables	(750)	(2,424)	(3,589)	(5,452)	4,456
(Increase) Decrease in inventories	(1,387)	(4,111)	(7,629)	1,867	1,068
Increase (Decrease) accounts payable—Trade	1,228	2,374	1,393	1,496	(2,608)
Increase (Decrease) in other current liabilities	473	2,865	4,737	1,649	(1,509)
Cash Flow from Operations	$ 1,120	$ 952	$ (616)	$ 6,880	$ 8,854
INVESTING					
Fixed assets acquired, net	$ (347)	$ (849)	$ (749)	$(1,426)	$(1,172)
Investments acquired	0	0	0	0	(3,306)
Other investing transactions	45	0	81	(64)	39
Cash Flow from Investing	$ (302)	$ (849)	$ (668)	$(1,490)	$(4,439)
FINANCING					
Increase in short-term borrowing	$ 0	$ 700	$ 2,800	$ 0	$ 0
Decrease in short-term borrowing	0	0	0	(3,500)	0
Increase in long-term borrowing	0	0	0	0	0
Decrease in long-term borrowing	(170)	(170)	(170)	(170)	(170)
Issue of capital stock	0	0	0	0	315
Acquisition of capital stock	(27)	0	0	0	0
Dividends	(614)	(730)	(964)	(1,427)	(2,243)
Other financing transactions	0	0	0	0	0
Cash Flow from Financing	$ (811)	$ (200)	$ 1,666	$(5,097)	$(2,098)
Net Change in Cash	$ 7	$ (97)	$ 382	$ 293	$ 2,317
Cash, beginning of year	955	962	865	1,247	1,540
Cash, End of Year	$ 962	$ 865	$ 1,247	$ 1,540	$ 3,857

EXHIBIT 12.22

Holmes Corporation
Five-Year Summary of Operations
(Case 12.2)

	Year 15	Year 14	Year 13	Year 12	Year 11
Orders Received	$ 95,436,103	$ 80,707,576	$121,445,731	$89,466,793	$55,454,188
Net Sales	102,698,836	109,372,718	76,327,664	53,540,699	41,427,702
Backlog of Unfilled Orders	77,455,900	84,718,633	113,383,775	68,265,708	32,339,614
Earnings before Taxes on Income	$ 10,546,213	$ 10,285,943	$ 6,708,072	$ 3,203,835	$ 1,939,414
Taxes on Income	3,944,305	3,702,583	2,991,947	1,470,489	894,257
Net Earnings	6,601,908	6,583,360	3,716,125	1,733,346	1,045,157
Net Property, Plant, and Equipment	$ 6,173,416	$ 5,644,590	$ 4,803,978	$ 4,568,372	$ 4,209,396
Net Additions to Property	1,172,057	1,426,347	748,791	848,685	346,549
Depreciation and Amortization	643,231	585,735	513,402	490,133	491,217
Cash Dividends Paid	$ 2,242,892	$ 1,426,502	$ 963,935	$ 730,254	$ 614,378
Working Capital	23,100,463	19,029,626	14,796,931	12,126,491	11,627,875
Shareholders' Equity	29,393,803	24,690,214	19,514,358	15,754,166	15,747,116
Earnings per Common Share (1)	$ 3.62	$ 3.61	$ 2.03	$ 0.96	$ 0.57
Dividends per Common Share (1)	1.22	0.78	0.53	0.40	0.34
Book Value per Common Share (1)	16.07	13.51	10.68	9.18	8.62
Number of Shareholders, December 31	2,157	2,024	1,834	1,792	1,787
Number of Employees, December 31	1,549	1,550	1,551	1,425	1,303
Shares of Common Outstanding, December 31 (1)	1,824,853	1,824,754	1,824,754	1,824,941	1,827,515
% Net Sales by Product Line					
Material Handling Equipment	46.1%	43.6%	51.3%	54.4%	63.0%
Processing Equipment	53.9%	56.4%	48.7%	45.6%	37.0%

Note: (1) Based on number of shares outstanding on December 31 adjusted for the 5-for-4 stock distributions in June, Year 13, Year 14, and Year 15.

Note C—Inventories. Inventories used in determining cost of sales appear below:

	Year 15	Year 14	Year 13
Raw materials and supplies	$ 8,889,147	$ 9,720,581	$ 8,900,911
Work in process	8,602,594	8,838,650	11,524,805
Total inventories	$17,491,741	$18,559,231	$20,425,716

Note D—Short-Term Borrowing. The company has short-term credit agreements which principally provide for loans of 90-day periods at varying interest rates. There were no borrowings in Year 15. In Year 14, the maximum borrowing at the end of any calendar month was $4,500,000 and the approximate average loan balance and weighted average interest rate, computed by using the days outstanding method, was $3,435,000 and 7.6 percent. There were no restrictions upon the company during the period of the loans and no compensating bank balance arrangements required by the lending institutions.

Note E—Income Taxes. Provision for income taxes consists of:

	Year 15	Year 14
Current		
Federal	$2,931,152	$2,633,663
State	466,113	483,240
Canadian	260,306	472,450
Total current provision	$3,657,571	$3,589,353
Deferred		
Federal	$ 263,797	$ 91,524
Canadian	22,937	21,706
Total deferred	$ 286,734	$ 113,230
Total provision for income taxes	$3,944,305	$3,702,583

Reconciliation of the total provision for income taxes to the current federal statutory rate of 35 percent is as follows:

	Year 15		Year 14	
	Amount	%	Amount	%
Tax at statutory rate	$3,691,000	35.0%	$3,600,100	35.0%
State taxes, net of U.S. tax credit	302,973	2.9	314,106	3.1
All other items	(49,668)	(.5)	(211,623)	(2.1)
Total provision for income taxes	$3,944,305	37.4%	$3,702,583	36.0%

Note F—Pensions. The components of pension expense appear below:

	Year 15	Year 14
Service cost	$476,490	$429,700
Interest cost	567,159	446,605
Expected return on pension investments	(558,373)	(494,083)
Amortization of actuarial gains and losses	(13,450)	(15,420)
Pension expense	$471,826	$366,802

The funded status of the pension plan appears on the next page.

	December 31:	
	Year 15	Year 14
Accumulated benefit obligation	$5,763,450	$5,325,291
Effect of salary increases	1,031,970	976,480
Projected benefit obligation	$6,795,420	$6,301,771
Pension fund assets	6,247,940	5,583,730
Excess pension obligation	$ 547,480	$ 718,041

Assumptions used in accounting for pensions appear below:

	Year 15	Year 14
Expected return on pension assets	10%	10%
Discount rate for projected benefit obligation	9%	8%
Salary increases	5%	5%

Note G—Common Stock. As of March 20, Year 15, the company increased the authorized number of shares of common stock from 1,800,000 shares to 5,000,000 shares.

On December 29, Year 15, the company increased its equity interest (from 45 percent to 85 percent) in Societé Francaise Holmes Fermont, a French affiliate, in exchange for 18,040 of its common shares in a transaction accounted for as a purchase. The company credited the excess of the fair value ($224,373) of the company's shares issued over their par value ($90,200) to additional contributed capital. The excess of the purchase cost over the underlying value of the assets acquired was insignificant.

The company made a 25 percent common stock distribution on June 15, Year 14, and on June 19, Year 15, resulting in increases of 291,915 shares in Year 14 and 364,433 shares in Year 15, respectively. We capitalized the par value of these additional shares by a transfer of $1,457,575 in Year 14 and $1,822,165 in Year 15 from retained earnings to the common stock account. In Year 14 and Year 15, we paid cash of $2,611 and $15,340, respectively, in lieu of fractional share interests.

In addition, the company retired 2,570 shares of treasury stock in June, Year 14. The earnings and dividends per share for Year 14 and Year 15 in the accompanying consolidated financial statements reflect the 25 percent stock distributions.

Note H—Contingent Liabilities. The company has certain contingent liabilities with respect to litigation and claims arising in the ordinary course of business. The company cannot determine the ultimate disposition of these contingent liabilities but, in the opinion of management, they will not result in any material effect upon the company's consolidated financial position or results of operations.

Note I—Quarterly Data (unaudited). Quarterly sales, gross profit, net earnings, and earnings per share for Year 15 appear below (first quarter results restated for 25 percent stock distribution):

	Net Sales	Gross Profit	Net Earnings	Earnings per Share
First	$ 25,931,457	$ 5,606,013	$1,602,837	$0.88
Second	24,390,079	6,148,725	1,727,112	0.95
Third	25,327,226	5,706,407	1,505,118	0.82
Fourth	27,050,074	4,977,774	1,766,841	0.97
Year	$102,698,836	$22,438,919	$6,601,908	$3.62

Auditors' Report

Board of Directors and Stockholders

Holmes Corporation

We have examined the consolidated balance sheets of Holmes Corporation and Subsidiaries as of December 31, Year 15 and Year 14, and the related consolidated statements of earnings and cash flows for the years then ended. Our examination was made in accordance with generally accepted auditing standards, and accordingly included such tests of the accounting records and such other auditing procedures as we considered necessary in the circumstances.

In our opinion, the financial statements referred to above present fairly the consolidated financial position of Holmes Corporation and Subsidiaries at December 31, Year 15 and Year 14, and the consolidated results of their operations and changes in cash flows for the years then ended, in conformity with generally accepted accounting principles applied on a consistent basis.

SBW, LLP
Chicago, Illinois
March 15, Year 16

Required

A group of Holmes' top management is interested in acquiring Holmes in an LBO.

a. Briefly describe the factors that make Holmes an attractive and, conversely, an unattractive LBO candidate.

b. (This question requires coverage of Chapter 10.) Prepare projected financial statements for Holmes Corporation for Year 16 through Year 20 excluding all financing. That is, project the amount of operating income after taxes, assets, and cash flows from operating and investing activities. State the underlying assumptions made.

c. Ascertain the value of Holmes' common shareholders' equity using the present value of its future cash flows valuation approach. Assume a risk-free interest rate of 4.2 percent and a market premium of 5.0 percent. Note that information in Part e may be helpful in this valuation. Assume the following financing structure for the LBO:

Type	Proportion	Interest Rate	Term
Term debt	50%	8%	7-year amortization[a]
Subordinated debt	25	12%	10-year amortization[a]
Shareholders' equity	25		
	100%		

[a] Holmes must repay principal and interest in equal annual payments.

d. (This question requires coverage of Chapter 13.) Ascertain the value of Holmes' common shareholders' equity using the residual income approach.

e. (This question requires coverage of Chapter 14.) Ascertain the value of Holmes' common shareholders' equity using the residual ROCE model and the price-to-earnings ratio and the market value to book value of comparable companies' approaches. Selected data for similar companies for Year 15 appear in the following table (amounts in millions):

	Agee Robotics	GI Handling Systems	LJG Industries	Gelas Corp.
Industry:	Conveyor Systems	Conveyor Systems	Cranes	Industrial Furnaces
Sales	$4,214	$28,998	$123,034	$75,830
Net Income	$ 309	$ 2,020	$ 9,872	$ 5,117
Assets	$2,634	$15,197	$ 72,518	$41,665
Long-Term Debt	$ 736	$ 5,098	$ 23,745	$ 8,869
Common Shareholders' Equity	$1,551	$ 7,473	$ 38,939	$26,884
Market Value of Common Equity	$6,915	$20,000	$102,667	$41,962
Market Beta	1.12	0.88	0.99	0.93

f. Would you attempt to acquire Holmes Corporation after completing the analyses in Parts a–e? If not, how would you change the analyses to make this an attractive LBO?

Chapter 13

Valuation: Earnings-Based Approaches

Learning Objectives

1. Understand earnings-based valuation, particularly the value-relevance of earnings versus dividends versus cash flows.

2. Evaluate the conceptual and practical strengths and weaknesses of earnings-based valuation using the residual income valuation method.

3. Develop a conceptual understanding and practical techniques to deal with the important issues involved in residual income valuation:

   (a) Utilizing book value of common shareholders' equity, comprehensive income, dividends, and clean surplus accounting in valuation

   (b) Measuring required (or "normal") income by multiplying beginning-of-period book value of equity by the risk-adjusted required rate of return on equity capital

   (c) Measuring residual (or "abnormal") income each period by subtracting required income from expected future income

   (d) Determining the value of common equity as the sum of book value of common shareholders' equity plus the present value of expected future residual income

4. Apply the residual income valuation method by valuing the common shareholders' equity of PepsiCo.

5. Assess the sensitivity of firm value estimates to key valuation parameters such as discount rates and expected long-term growth rates.

6. Identify potential causes of errors if the residual income, free cash flows, and dividend valuations do not determine identical value estimates.

INTRODUCTION AND OVERVIEW

Reported earnings are the single most widely followed measures of firm performance. Accounting standard setters (most notably the FASB and IASB), along with the accounting profession and the community of financial statement users, have designed the accrual accounting process to measure earnings as the bottom line of the firm's profitability each period. As a result, firms' reported earnings play central roles as the primary value-relevant measures of performance used in the capital markets for share pricing and capital allocation.

Because of the demand in the capital markets for earnings information, firms usually release quarterly and annual earnings to the public as soon as accountants have prepared and verified them, often weeks *before* the firms release their detailed quarterly and annual income statements, balance sheets, statements of cash flows, and notes. Firms commonly announce earnings during conference calls and press conferences attended by investors, analysts, managers, board members, and the financial press. Analysts often spend enormous amounts of time and effort building (and when new information arrives, revising) forecasts of firms' upcoming quarterly and annual earnings. Sell-side analysts sell their earnings forecasts to interested investors, brokers, and fund managers. Commercial firms such as I/B/E/S and First Call have built businesses on compiling and distributing daily data on analysts' earnings forecasts. The financial media (broadcast, print, and online) provide daily coverage of firms' earnings announcements. For example, *The Wall Street Journal* provides a summary report of firms' earnings announcements each day in the "Earnings Digest" section. *The Wall Street Journal* also reports daily data on each firm's stock trading activity, including a daily price-earnings ratio. In fact, because of the demand for and attention devoted to earnings among capital markets participants, U.S. GAAP and IFRS require firms to report earnings scaled on a per-share basis in their financial statements. (See the related discussion in Chapter 4.)[1]

Firms' share prices usually react quickly to earnings announcements, and the direction and magnitude of the market's reaction depends on the direction and magnitude of the earnings news relative to the market's expectations. Firms that announce earnings beating the market's expectations ("good news") often experience significant jumps in share price during the day of and the days immediately following the announcement. Likewise, firms that announce earnings falling short of the market's expectations ("bad news") usually experience a decline in share price—and, in some circumstances, severe drops in share price—during the day of and the days immediately following the announcement. As noted in several prior chapters, the seminal Ball and Brown (1968) study[2] and many other research studies, including the Nichols and Wahlen (2004) study described in Chapter 1 and Exhibit 1.21, have shown that firms' stock returns are highly positively correlated with changes in earnings.

Because earnings provide such important information to investors and other external stakeholders, earnings also play key roles in decisions that firms make with regard to internal capital allocation. New project proposals within firms are often evaluated based on the effects they will have on reported earnings. In addition, corporate governance processes commonly reward or punish managers with compensation and bonus plans based on whether firm performance meets certain earnings targets. Managers who meet or exceed specified earnings targets are usually rewarded with substantial bonuses. Managers who consistently fall short of earnings targets do not receive bonuses and typically need to explain why they failed to meet the targets. If the explanations are not satisfactory, they may find themselves being replaced.

The preceding observations establish the important roles of earnings:

- Earnings is the primary measure of firm performance produced by the accrual accounting system.
- Earnings has a direct impact on the capital markets and the pricing of shares.

---

[1] Financial Accounting Standards Board, *Statement of Financial Accounting Standard No. 128*, "Earnings per Share" (1997); *FASB Codification Topic 260*; International Accounting Standards Board, *International Accounting Standard 33*, "Earnings per Share" (revised 2003).

[2] Ray Ball and Philip Brown, "An Evaluation of Accounting Income Numbers," *Journal of Accounting Research* (Autumn 1968), pp. 159–178.

- Corporate managers and boards of directors use earnings for internal capital allocation and for aligning the incentives of managers with shareholders.
- The financial press and the analyst community devote tremendous time and attention to reporting, analyzing, and predicting earnings.

Therefore, it is logical that accounting earnings provide a basis for valuation. This chapter describes the conceptual and practical strengths and weaknesses of the earnings-based valuation model known as the residual income valuation model. The residual income valuation model uses expected future earnings and the book value of common shareholders' equity as the bases for valuation.

To describe, explain, and apply the residual income valuation model, this chapter takes four important steps. Exhibit 13.1 illustrates these steps and some of the key questions we will address in this chapter. First, we describe the rationale behind earnings-based valuation. Second, we explain the theoretical and conceptual foundation for residual income valuation, with a number of illustrations and examples. Third, we demonstrate the residual income

EXHIBIT 13.1

Steps to Understanding Residual Income Valuation

1. ***Rationale***
   - What is the rationale for using earnings as a basis for valuation?
   - What are the practical advantages and concerns associated with using earnings to determine common shareholders' equity value?
2. ***Theoretical and Conceptual Foundations for Residual Income Valuation***
   - What theories and concepts support residual income valuation?
   - How do we measure residual income? What does it represent?
3. ***Practical Applications***
   - What steps do we take to determine value using residual income valuation methods?
   - What implementation issues do we need to understand in order to use the residual income model?
   - What value estimate do we get from this approach for the common shareholders' equity of PepsiCo?
4. ***Linking Residual Income Valuation to Dividends Valuation and Free Cash Flow Valuation***
   - Conceptually, why is the residual income valuation approach equivalent to the valuation approaches that rely on dividends and free cash flows?
   - Practically, does the value estimate we obtain for PepsiCo using the residual income valuation approach agree with the estimate from Chapter 11 using the dividends valuation approach and from Chapter 12 using the free cash flows to equity valuation approach?
   - What if the value estimates do not agree across these three models? How do we find and correct possible valuation errors?

model by applying it to value the common shareholders' equity of PepsiCo. As we apply the model to PepsiCo, we describe the key measurement and implementation issues. Fourth, we come full circle in valuation by demonstrating the internal consistency in dividends, free cash flows, and residual income valuation. We demonstrate that these three valuation approaches yield identical valuations if applied properly. We also help the analyst understand how to identify and correct valuation errors if the three valuation models do not agree.

The residual income valuation model in this chapter provides a powerful approach that is a complementary equivalent to the classical dividends-based valuation approach presented in Chapter 11 and to the free-cash-flows-based valuation approach presented in Chapter 12. The residual income valuation model in this chapter forms the basis for the market-based multiples described in Chapter 14, including the market-to-book ratio and the price-earnings ratio.

RATIONALE FOR EARNINGS-BASED VALUATION

Exhibit 13.1 shows that the first step toward understanding residual income valuation is to establish the theoretical and conceptual rationale for using an earnings-based valuation approach. Economic theory teaches that the value of any resource equals the present value of the expected future payoffs from the resource discounted at a rate that reflects the risk inherent in those expected future payoffs. Like Chapters 11 and 12, we again start with the same general model for the present value of a security (denoted as V_0, with present value denoted as of time $t=0$) with an expected life of n future periods, as follows:[3]

$$V_0 = \sum_{t=1}^{n} \frac{Expected\ Future\ Payoffs_t}{(1 + Discount\ Rate)^t}$$

Chapter 11 demonstrates that the value of a share of common equity should equal the present value of the *expected future dividends* the shareholder will receive.[4] Dividends are the fundamental value-relevant payoffs because they represent the distribution of wealth from the firm to the shareholders. The equity shareholder receives dividends as the payoffs from holding a share, including the final "liquidating" dividend when the firm liquidates the share or the shareholder sells the share. Thus, to value a firm's shares using dividends, one discounts to present value the expected future dividends over the life of the firm (or the expected length of time the share will be held), including the final liquidating dividend. This is a *wealth distribution* (or liquidation) approach to valuation.

Chapter 12 demonstrates that the value of a share of common equity also should equal the present value of the *expected future free cash flows* that the firm will create and ultimately distribute in *dividends* to the common equity shareholders. The free-cash-flows-based valuation approach focuses on the amounts and timing of the cash flows the firm will generate that will eventually be distributed to shareholders in future dividends. Thus, to value a firm's shares using free cash flows, one discounts to present value the expected future free cash flows for common equity shareholders over the life of the firm

---

[3] This chapter uses the same notation as in prior chapters, where t refers to accounting periods. The valuation process determines an estimate of firm value, denoted as V_0, in present value as of today, when $t=0$. The period $t=1$ refers to the first accounting period being discounted to present value. Period $t=n$ is the period of the expected final, or liquidating, payoff.

[4] John Burr Williams, *The Theory of Investment and Value*, Cambridge, Mass.: Harvard University Press (1938).

(or the expected length of time the share will be held), including the final liquidating cash flows. This is a *free cash flow realization* approach to valuation.

The residual income valuation approach presented in this chapter parallels the dividends-based valuation approach and the cash-flow-based valuation approach, except that it uses a different measure of payoffs. The residual income valuation approach uses book value of common shareholders' equity and expected future earnings to determine the value-relevant expected future payoffs to the investor (that is, the numerator of the general value model above) in place of future dividends or future free cash flows. The rationale for the role of book value of shareholders' equity is straightforward: it is the starting point for valuation because it is the balance sheet measure of the common equity shareholders' claim on the net assets of the firm. The rationale for using expected future earnings as a basis for valuation is also straightforward: future earnings measure the net profits or losses the firm will generate for the shareholders. Over the remaining life of the firm, earnings measure the total wealth to be created by the firm for the shareholders. Instead of focusing on wealth distribution through dividends payments and instead of focusing on dividend-paying capacity in free cash flows, residual income valuation focuses on *earnings as a periodic measure of shareholder wealth creation.* Therefore, residual income is a *wealth creation* approach to valuation. In Chapter 11, Exhibit 11.1 showed the differences in valuation approach perspectives between dividends as measures of value distribution, free cash flows as measures of distributable wealth, and earnings as value-relevant measures of wealth creation.

To measure wealth creation, the accrual accounting process measures income for the equity shareholders based on the net amount of economic resources generated and consumed by the firm each period. Accrual accounting also produces periodic statements of financial position—balance sheets that measure assets, liabilities, and shareholders' equity—that report the economic resources (assets) that the firm can control and use to produce expected future economic benefits and the claims on those resources by creditors and investors (liabilities and equities). To produce informative measures of financial performance and position that are relevant and reliable, the accounting profession develops and implements accounting standards through which the accrual accounting process measures income, assets, liabilities, and shareholders' equity using estimates of economic resources earned and consumed each period, rather than just relying on cash inflows and cash outflows, which often do not reflect economic value generated or consumed each period. To measure a firm's economic performance and position in a given period, it makes sense to measure the following:

- *Revenues earned* from operating performance during that period, not just the amounts of cash collected from customers that period
- Expenses incurred for *resources consumed* in that period, not just the amounts of cash paid out of the firm that period
- A portion of the *long-lived resources consumed* during that period, such as periodic depreciation of a building each year of its useful life (rather than recognize the full cost of the building in the year the firm pays for it and ignore the consumption of the building in all other years the firm uses it)
- The cost of *commitments made* during that period to pay retirement benefits to employees in future periods (rather than ignore those commitments and measure their effects only when the firm pays cash)

Accrual accounting earnings are far from perfect performance measures. However, recall the discussion in Chapter 2 (particularly Exhibit 2.4) that described how accounting standards are intended to optimize the relevance and reliability of accrual accounting information (asset and liability valuation and income recognition) for investors and other stakeholders. By virtue of accounting standards, accounting earnings will more closely match the firm's underlying economic performance—the wealth created or destroyed for equity shareholders—in a given period than will the net cash inflows or outflows of that period.

Over the life of a firm, the capital invested in the firm by the shareholders plus the wealth created by the firm for the shareholders will determine the value of the firm to the shareholders. Cash is the ultimate medium of exchange; therefore, over the life of the firm, the cash flows that are distributable to shareholders will equal the shareholders' capital investments in the firm plus the lifetime earnings of the firm. Thus, valuation of shareholders' equity in a firm using the capital invested in the firm plus earnings over the life of the firm is equivalent to valuation using distributable cash flows over the life of the firm, and both are equivalent to valuation using dividends over the life of the firm.[5]

EARNINGS-BASED VALUATION: PRACTICAL ADVANTAGES AND CONCERNS

Although earnings, cash flows, and dividends are equally valid bases for valuation, several practical advantages and concerns arise with earnings-based valuation. One practical advantage arises because the emphasis placed on earnings by firms and the capital markets makes earnings a logical starting point for valuation. Analysts, investors, the capital markets, managers, boards, and the financial press focus on earnings forecasts and earnings reports rather than free cash flow forecasts and free cash flow amounts. Firms usually do not hold press conferences to announce free cash flows. Analysts publish earnings forecasts far more frequently than they publish free cash flow forecasts. *The Wall Street Journal* does not report a "free cash flow digest" every day (but it does track earnings for firms). Boards of directors and compensation committees typically do not establish managers' bonus plans based on achieving free cash flow targets (more often relying on earnings-based measures of performance). The reason for the tendency to rely on earnings is that they align more closely than dividends or free cash flows with the focus of the capital markets and corporate managers and boards of directors on periodic performance measurement.

Another practical advantage arises because it is more direct and efficient for the analyst to go straight from earnings to valuation rather than take a detour to free cash flows.[6]As Exhibit 13.2 depicts, estimating firm value using free cash flows adds an intermediary step to the valuation process. As demonstrated in Chapter 12, our approach to valuing a firm using free cash flows requires that we initially forecast future income statements and balance sheets. Then we derive the implied forecasts of cash flows from those income statements and balance sheets by making adjustments for the accruals in earnings, for the cash flows invested in working capital, and for capital expenditures. We use these cash flows to determine free cash flows, which we then use to compute value. Under the residual income approach, we begin valuation immediately after we forecast future income statements and

---

[5] Over sufficiently long time periods, net income equals free cash flows to common equity. The effect of year-end accruals to convert cash flows to net income lessens as the measurement period lengthens. The correlation between firms' earnings and stock returns increases as the earnings measurement interval increases. The values of R^2 for various intervals are one year, 5 percent; two years, 15 percent; five years, 33 percent; and 10 years, 63 percent. See Peter D. Easton, Trevor S. Harris, and James A. Ohlson, "Aggregate Accounting Earnings Can Explain Most of Security Returns," *Journal of Accounting and Economics* (1992), pp. 119–142.

[6] Researchers have directed considerable attention to the question of whether cash flows or earnings associate more closely with stock returns. This research indicates that earnings and cash flows cumulated over long periods of time are highly positively correlated with stock returns over long periods (for example, five-year periods), but that for shorter periods, earnings show a stronger association with stock returns than cash flows. See Patricia M. Dechow, "Accounting Earnings and Cash Flows as Measures of Firm Performance: The Role of Accounting Accruals," *Journal of Accounting and Economics* (1994), pp. 3–42; C. S. Cheng, Chao-Shin Liu, and Thomas F. Schaefer, "Earnings Permanence and the Incremental Information Content of Cash Flow from Operations," *Journal of Accounting Research* (Spring 1996), pp. 173–181; Richard G. Sloan, "Do Stock Prices Fully Reflect Information in Accruals and Cash Flows about Future Earnings," *The Accounting Review* (July 1996), pp. 289–315.

EXHIBIT 13.2

Residual Income Valuation Requires Fewer Steps Than Free Cash Flows Valuation

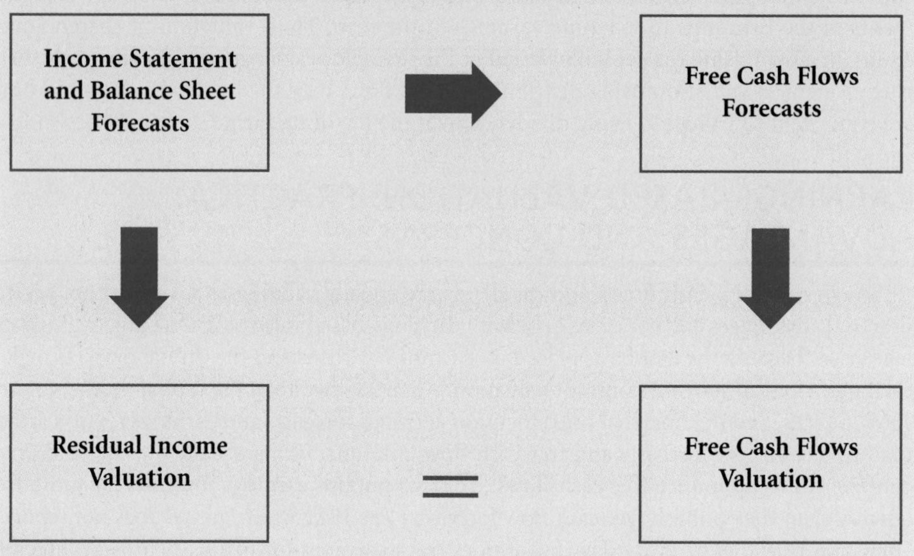

balance sheets. The two valuations should ultimately be the same, but the free cash flows approach requires more computations, which requires more time and effort, and increases the potential for error.

Economists sometimes express concern that earnings are not a value-relevant attribute for valuation because earnings are not as reliable or as meaningful as cash or dividends for valuing investments. When considering earnings, economists sometimes point out that firms pay dividends in cash, not earnings; investors can spend cash but cannot spend earnings for future consumption. This concern is alleviated in valuation, however, by the fact that the differences between earnings, cash flows, and dividends are timing differences: earnings measure when the firm creates wealth, whereas free cash flows measure when the firm realizes wealth in cash, and dividends measure when the firm distributes wealth to shareholders. Over the life of the firm, the present values of future earnings, cash flows, and dividends will be equal.

Some economists worry that accrual accounting earnings reflect accounting methods that no longer capture changes in underlying economic values (for example, depreciation or amortization expenses based on outdated acquisition cost valuations of assets, expenses for research and development that have turned out to be successful, or advertising expenses that have created economically valuable brand equity). Value measurement based on expected earnings over the remaining life of the firm alleviates this concern. Over time, the accrual accounting process will ultimately self-correct measurement errors in accounting numbers. For example, if fixed asset book values are "too high" or "too low" for a company, over time (and it usually does not take long), accrual accounting will naturally correct these measurement errors because the subsequent depreciation expenses will be "too high" or "too low" accordingly. If the current balance sheet does not recognize intellectual capital value created by successful research and development or brand value created by successful marketing, accrual accounting will correct itself over time as the firm generates higher earnings from this intangible capital.[7]

Some economists voice concerns that earnings can be subject to purposeful management or manipulation by a firm. To be sure, analysts should always be alert to the possibility that earnings management (or worse, earnings manipulation and fraudulent reporting) may occur in some periods by some firms. Earlier chapters devoted considerable attention to helping analysts understand how to assess firms' accounting quality. But this is more of a concern about earnings as a measure of current period performance than about a firm's future expected earnings for valuation purposes. In addition, this concern is not a major issue for valuation because residual income valuation relies on the analyst's forecasts of expected future earnings, not on past earnings reports that the firm may have managed (unless, of course, the analyst's forecasts naively project the past managed earnings will persist in future years). Ironically, firms can easily manage cash flows in a given period, but economists rarely voice this concern. Free cash flows each period depend on cash inflows and outflows, which the firm can easily manipulate by accelerating or delaying certain cash payments or cash collections in that particular period. Over the remaining life of the firm, which is the focus of the analyst's forecasting and valuation, the firm's earnings and cash flows will be determined ultimately by the success of the firm's operating, investing, and financing activities, not by the manipulation of past earnings or cash flows.

THEORETICAL AND CONCEPTUAL FOUNDATIONS FOR RESIDUAL INCOME VALUATION[8]

Exhibit 13.1 indicates that the second step toward understanding residual income valuation is to establish the theoretical and conceptual foundation for the residual income valuation approach. The foundation for residual income valuation is the classical dividends-based valuation model from Chapter 11, in which the value of common shareholders' equity is the present value of all future dividends to shareholders over the remaining life of the firm. As described in Chapter 11, we define *dividends* to be all-inclusive measures of the cash flows between the firm and the common equity shareholders, encompassing cash flows from the firm to shareholders through periodic dividend payments, stock buybacks, and the firm's liquidating dividend, as well as cash flows from the shareholders to the firm when the firm issues shares (negative dividends).

Chapter 11 demonstrated how to estimate an appropriate discount rate (using the CAPM or some other risk-based asset-pricing model) based on the rate of return (denoted as R_E) that the capital markets expect for the risk associated with common equity capital in

[7] Indeed, when an analyst asserts that a firm's current balance sheet accounting numbers do not reflect underlying economic values, how does the analyst know that? When an analyst asserts that a firm's balance sheet omits a valuable intangible asset in the form of intellectual property or brand equity, how has the analyst assessed the amount of the omission? Usually, analysts base assertions like these on their assessments that the firm will generate future profits from operations that utilize these economic assets. Earnings-based valuation captures *exactly* the same idea. Firm value depends on expected future earnings over the remaining life of the firm.

[8] Credit for the rigorous development of the residual income valuation model goes to James A. Ohlson, "A Synthesis of Security Valuation Theory and the Role of Dividends, Cash Flows, and Earnings," *Contemporary Accounting Research* (Spring 1990), pp. 648–676; James A. Ohlson, "Earnings, Book Values, and Dividends in Equity Valuation," *Contemporary Accounting Research* (Spring 1995), pp. 661–687; Gerald A. Feltham and James A. Ohlson, "Valuation and Clean Surplus Accounting for Operating and Financial Activities," *Contemporary Accounting Research* (Spring 1995), pp. 216–230. The ideas underlying the earnings-based valuation approach trace to early work by G.A.D. Preinreich, "Annual Survey of Economic Theory: The Theory of Depreciation," *Econometrica* (1938), pp. 219–241, and Edgar O. Edwards and Philip W. Bell, *The Theory and Measurement of Business Income* (Berkeley, CA: University of California Press), 1961.

a firm. That chapter also demonstrated the dividends-based valuation approach, which measures the value of common shareholders' equity (denoted as V_0) as the present value of all expected future dividends (denoted as D) with the following general model:

$$V_0 = \sum_{t=1}^{\infty} \frac{D_t}{(1 + R_E)^t} = \frac{D_1}{(1 + R_E)^1} + \frac{D_2}{(1 + R_E)^2} + \frac{D_3}{(1 + R_E)^3} + \cdots$$

Analysts and investors commonly find it desirable to identify and forecast economic variables that determine the firm's future dividends and can therefore substitute for dividends to yield an equivalent valuation. Accounting numbers provide a solution. Accounting for the book value of common shareholders' equity (denoted as BV) in a firm can be expressed as follows:

$$BV_t = BV_{t-1} + NI_t - D_t$$

In this expression, book value of common shareholders' equity at the end of Year t (BV_t) is equal to book value at the end of Year $t-1$ (BV_{t-1}) plus net income for Year t (NI_t) minus the all-inclusive dividends during Year t (D_t). As in the dividends valuation approach described in Chapter 11, we assume that accounting for net income and book value of shareholders' equity follows *clean surplus accounting.* Clean surplus accounting simply means that net income includes all of the recognized elements of income of the firm for common equity shareholders (that is, all of the amounts in the income statement plus all of the other comprehensive income items) and dividends include all direct capital transactions between the firm and the common equity shareholders (that is, periodic dividend payments, share repurchases, and share issues).

We can rearrange the accounting equation for the book value of common shareholders' equity to isolate dividends as follows:

$$D_t = NI_t + BV_{t-1} - BV_t$$

In this expression, dividends equal net income plus the change in book value from direct capital transactions with common shareholders.

Example 1

Suppose the firm had shareholders' equity on the balance sheet at a book value of \$5,000 at the end of Year $t-1$. Suppose during Year t, the firm earns net income of \$600, pays dividends to shareholders of \$360, issues new stock to raise \$250 of capital, and uses \$50 to repurchase common shares. The book value of shareholders' equity the end of Year t is

$$\begin{aligned} BV_t = BV_{t-1} + NI_t - D_t &= \$5{,}000 + \$600 - \$360 + \$250 - \$50 \\ &= \$5{,}000 + \$600 - \$160 = \$5{,}440. \end{aligned}$$

In this example, all-inclusive dividends (D_t) in Year t amount to \$160. Using the expression for dividends shows that

$$D_t = NI_t + BV_{t-1} - BV_t = \$600 + \$5{,}000 - \$5{,}440 = \$160.$$

One can verify this amount of all-inclusive dividends in this example by recognizing that the dividends paid plus the cash paid for share repurchases minus the cash received from issuing shares equals the total amount of all-inclusive dividends of \$160 (= \$360 + \$50 – \$250).

Because dividends equal net income plus the change in book value of common shareholders' equity, we can substitute net income plus the change in the book value of common shareholders' equity into the classical dividends valuation model, as follows:

$$V_0 = \sum_{t=1}^{\infty} \frac{D_t}{(1+R_E)^t} = \sum_{t=1}^{\infty} \frac{NI_t + BV_{t-1} - BV_t}{(1-R_E)^t}$$

$$= \frac{NI_1 + BV_0 - BV_1}{(1+R_E)^1} + \frac{NI_2 + BV_1 - BV_2}{(1+R_E)^2} + \frac{NI_3 + BV_2 - BV_3}{(1+R_E)^3} + \ldots$$

Algebraically, the present value of BV_{t-1} can be rewritten as follows:

$$\frac{BV_{t-1}}{(1+R_E)^t} = \frac{BV_{t-1}}{(1+R_E)^{t-1}} - \frac{R_E \times BV_{t-1}}{(1+R_E)^t}$$

We substitute the right-hand side expression for the present value of BV_{t-1} into the equation for V_0, rearrange terms, and simplify to obtain the following expression for the *residual income valuation model:*

$$V_0 = BV_0 + \sum_{t=1}^{\infty} \frac{NI_t - (R_E \times BV_{t-1})}{(1+R_E)^t}$$

$$= BV_0 + \frac{NI_1 - (R_E \times BV_0)}{(1+R_E)^1} + \frac{NI_2 - (R_E \times BV_1)}{(1+R_E)^2} + \frac{NI_3 - (R_E \times BV_2)}{(1+R_E)^3} + \ldots$$

The *residual income valuation model* above is a valuation model for common shareholders' equity that is equivalent to dividends-based valuation, yet relies on earnings and book values.[9]

Intuition for Residual Income Measurement and Valuation

The intuition for the residual income valuation model is straightforward. The value of common shareholders' equity is equal to the book value of common equity plus the present value of all expected future *residual income,* which is the amount by which expected future earnings exceed the required earnings, for the remaining life of the firm. The *required earnings* (also known as *normal earnings*) of the firm equals the product of the required rate of return on common equity capital times the book value of common equity capital at the beginning of each period. We compute required earnings for period t as $R_E \times BV_{t-1}$. Required earnings reflect the earnings the firm must earn in period t simply to provide a return to common equity that is equal to the cost of common equity capital. Required earnings are analogous to a charge for the cost of equity capital, similar to interest expense as a charge for the cost of debt capital.

We measure *residual income* (sometimes called *abnormal earnings*) by the subtraction term $NI_t - (R_E \times BV_{t-1})$. Residual income is the difference between the net income the

[9] Chapter 14 demonstrates a version of this residual income approach that determines the intrinsic-value-to-book-value ratio for the firm using the return on common equity (ROCE, described in Chapter 4) and expected growth in the book value of common equity.

analyst expects the firm to generate and the required earnings of the firm. Residual income in period t measures the amount of wealth creation (or destruction) the firm will generate in period t for common equity shareholders above (or below) the earnings required to cover the cost of equity capital. If the analyst expects the firm to generate net income each period in the future that is exactly equal to required earnings (that is, $NI_t - (R_E \times BV_{t-1}) = 0$; zero abnormal earnings for all future periods), the analyst also expects the firm to exactly cover the cost of equity capital, no more, no less. In that case, the value of the firm is exactly equal to the book value of common shareholders' equity. On the other hand, if the analyst expects the firm to create wealth for the shareholders by earning positive amounts of residual income, the value of the firm is equal to book value of common shareholders' equity plus the present value of all expected future residual income.[10]

Illustrations of Residual Income Measurement and Valuation

The following examples illustrate residual income measurement and the residual income valuation model under various assumptions.

Example 2

Suppose investors have invested \$10,000 in common equity in a company. Given the risk of the company, the investors expect to earn a 12 percent return, and they expect the company to pay out 100 percent of income in dividends each year. The required earnings of the company each period are as follows:

$$R_E \times BV_{t-1} = 0.12 \times \$10{,}000 = \$1{,}200$$

Suppose the investors forecast that the company will generate exactly \$1,200 in net income each year. The investors should compute the residual income of the firm as follows:

$$NI_t - (R_E \times BV_{t-1}) = \$1{,}200 - (0.12 \times \$10{,}000) = \$0$$

Using the residual income approach, investors would value this firm based on book value plus expected future residual income as follows:

$$\begin{aligned} V_0 &= BV_0 + \sum_{t=1}^{\infty} \frac{NI_t - (R_E \times BV_{t-1})}{(1 + R_E)^t} \\ &= \$10{,}000 + \sum_{t=1}^{\infty} \frac{\$1{,}200_t - (0.12 \times \$10{,}000_{t-1})}{(1 + 0.12)^t} \\ &= \$10{,}000 + \sum_{t=1}^{\infty} \frac{\$0_t}{(1 + 0.12)^t} = \$10{,}000 \end{aligned}$$

In this case, the firm's expected future income exactly equals the required level of earnings necessary to cover the cost of equity capital. So residual income is zero and the value of the firm is equal to the book value of common equity invested in the firm. The value of the firm

[10] The concept of residual income in the economics literature and the accounting literature predates the commercialization of "Economic Value Added" by decades. Applications of the concept of residual income in valuation and corporate governance practices can be found in G. Bennett Stewart, *The Quest for Value* (New York: Harper Collins), 1991, and in the expanding literature on EVA®.

under the residual income model is identical to the value determined using the dividends valuation model, which would value the company as a stream of dividends in perpetuity with no growth as follows:

$$V_0 = \frac{\$1{,}200}{0.12} = \$10{,}000$$

Example 3

Now assume the same facts as in Example 2, but suppose investors expect the company to pay out no dividends each year and all the earnings will be reinvested in projects that will generate the investors' required 12 percent rate of return.[11] The required earnings of the firm in Year +1 will be

$$R_E \times BV_0 = 0.12 \times \$10{,}000 = \$1{,}200.$$

After retained earnings of \$1,200 are added to book value of equity at the end of Year +1, the required earnings of the company in Year +2 will be

$$R_E \times BV_1 = 0.12 \times [\$10{,}000 + \$1{,}200] = \$1{,}344.$$

After retained earnings of \$1,344 are added to book value of equity at the end of Year +2, the required earnings of the company in Year +3 will be

$$R_E \times BV_2 = 0.12 \times [\$11{,}200 + \$1{,}344] = \$1{,}505.$$

These computations show that the required earnings of the firm will grow as the firm retains and reinvests earnings, on which the investors expect the firm to earn the required rate of return.

Suppose the investors expect the firm to generate future earnings each year that will exactly match required earnings each year; so earnings in Year +1 will be \$1,200, earnings in Year +2 will be \$1,344, and earnings in Year +3 will be \$1,505. Also suppose the investors expect the firm to continue to reinvest all of its earnings and will continue to generate the required level of earnings each year over the remaining life of the firm (that is, continuing in Year +4 and beyond). We can determine the value of equity capital in the firm using the residual income model as follows:

$$
\begin{aligned}
V_0 &= BV_0 + \sum_{t=1}^{\infty} \frac{NI_t - (R_E \times BV_{t-1})}{(1+R_E)^t} \\
&= \$10{,}000 + \frac{\$1{,}200 - (0.12 \times \$10{,}000)}{(1.12)^1} + \frac{\$1{,}344 - (0.12 \times \$11{,}200)}{(1.12)^2} \\
&\quad + \frac{\$1{,}505 - (0.12 \times \$13{,}544)}{(1.12)^3} + \sum_{t=4}^{\infty} \frac{NI_t - (0.12 \times BV_{t-1})}{(1+0.12)^t} \\
&= \$10{,}000 + \frac{\$0}{(1.12)^1} + \frac{\$0}{(1.12)^2} + \frac{\$0}{(1.12)^3} + \sum_{t=4}^{\infty} \frac{\$0_t}{(1+0.12)^t} \\
&= \$10{,}000
\end{aligned}
$$

[11] Although this is simply an illustration, note that this is an important assumption because it presumes that the firm can scale up operations without diminishing future returns.

Example 4

Now assume the same facts as in Example 3, but suppose investors expect the firm simply to reinvest the earnings in cash or other types of assets that will earn no additional return for each of the next three periods. The investors expect the firm to continue to earn $1,200 each year on the original investment of $10,000, but they expect the reinvestment of earnings in the first three years to produce no incremental return. Also assume for simplicity that in Year +4 and beyond, the firm will invest in projects that will earn a total of 12 percent return for equity shareholders.

The required earnings of the firm in Year +1 will be

$$R_E \times BV_0 = 0.12 \times \$10{,}000 = \$1{,}200.$$

After retained earnings of $1,200 are added to book value of equity at the end of Year +1, the required earnings of the company in Year +2 will be

$$R_E \times BV_1 = 0.12 \times [\$10{,}000 + \$1{,}200] = \$1{,}344.$$

After retained earnings of $1,200 are added to book value of equity at the end of Year +2, the required earnings of the company in Year +3 will be

$$R_E \times BV_2 = 0.12 \times [\$11{,}200 + \$1{,}200] = \$1{,}488.$$

We can determine the value of equity capital in the firm using the residual income model as follows:

$$V_0 = BV_0 + \sum_{t=1}^{\infty} \frac{NI_t - (R_E \times BV_{t-1})}{(1 + R_E)^t}$$

$$= \$10{,}000 + \frac{\$1{,}200 - (0.12 \times \$10{,}000)}{(1.12)^1} + \frac{\$1{,}200 - (0.12 \times \$11{,}200)}{(1.12)^2}$$

$$+ \frac{\$1{,}200 - (0.12 \times \$12{,}400)}{(1.12)^3} + \sum_{t=4}^{\infty} \frac{NI_t - (0.12 \times BV_{t-1})}{(1 + 0.12)^t}$$

$$= \$10{,}000 + \frac{\$0}{(1.12)^1} + \frac{\$1{,}200 - \$1{,}344}{(1.12)^2} + \frac{\$1{,}200 - \$1{,}488}{(1.12)^3} + \sum_{t=4}^{\infty} \frac{\$0_t}{(1 + 0.12)^t}$$

$$= \$10{,}000 + \$0 - \$115 - \$205 + \$0$$

$$= \$9{,}680$$

This example shows that by reinvesting earnings to earn zero return rather than the required 12 percent return, the firm's earnings will be $144 less than required earnings in Year +2 and $288 less than required earnings in Year +3. In present value terms, the firm will destroy $115 of shareholder value in Year +2 and $205 of shareholder value in Year +3. Therefore, investors would value the firm at only $9,680 in this example, as compared to $10,000 in the preceding two examples.

Example 5

Now assume the same facts as in Example 2, where investors have invested \$10,000 in common equity in a firm, the investors expect to earn a 12 percent return, and they expect the company to pay out 100 percent of income in dividends each year. Now suppose investors expect the firm to earn net income of \$1,000 in Year +1, \$2,000 in Year +2, \$1,500 in Year +3, and \$1,200 each year thereafter. Investors should compute the residual income valuation as follows:

$$V_0 = BV_0 + \sum_{t=1}^{\infty} \frac{NI_t - (R_E \times BV_{t-1})}{(1 + R_E)^t}$$

$$= \$10{,}000 + \frac{\$1{,}000 - (0.12 \times \$10{,}000)}{(1.12)^1} + \frac{\$2{,}000 - (0.12 \times \$10{,}000)}{(1.12)^2}$$

$$+ \frac{\$1{,}500 - (0.12 \times \$10{,}000)}{(1.12)^3} + \sum_{t=4}^{\infty} \frac{\$1{,}200_t - (0.12 \times \$10{,}000_{t-1})}{(1 + 0.12)^t}$$

$$= \$10{,}000 + \frac{-\$200}{(1.12)^1} + \frac{\$800}{(1.12)^2} + \frac{\$300}{(1.12)^3} + \sum_{t=4}^{\infty} \frac{\$0_t}{(1 + 0.12)^t}$$

$$= \$10{,}000 - \$178 + \$638 + \$214 + \$0$$

$$= \$10{,}674$$

In this example, the firm will generate residual income amounts of −\$200 in Year +1, \$800 in Year +2, \$300 in Year +3, and \$0 each year thereafter. The firm destroys shareholder wealth in Year +1 by failing to earn sufficient income to cover the cost of equity capital, but the firm generates increasing shareholder wealth in Years +2 and +3 and exactly covers the cost of equity capital each year thereafter. Given these assumptions, the present value of the firm under the residual income model is \$10,674.

RESIDUAL INCOME VALUATION MODEL WITH FINITE HORIZON EARNINGS FORECASTS AND CONTINUING VALUE COMPUTATION

Analysts cannot precisely forecast firms' income statements and balance sheets for many years into the future. Therefore, analysts commonly forecast income statements and balance sheets over a foreseeable finite horizon and then make simplifying growth rate assumptions for the years continuing after the forecast horizon. We can modify the residual income valuation model to include explicit forecasts of net income and book value of common equity through Year T [where T is a finite horizon (for example, five or ten years in the future)] and then apply a constant growth rate assumption (denoted as *g*) to project residual income for Year T+1 and all years thereafter. We used similar approaches to forecast and value dividends in Chapter 11 and free cash flows in Chapter 12.

To deal with the uncertainty in long-run forecasts, the analyst must forecast net income, book value of shareholders' equity, and residual income over an explicit forecast horizon until the point at which the analyst expects the firm's growth pattern to settle into steady-state growth, during which time earnings, dividends, and cash flows are expected to grow at a steady, predictable rate. We refer to residual income in this long-run steady-state growth period as *continuing* residual income because it reflects residual income earned by the firm continuing into the long-run future. The long-run steady-state growth rate in future continuing residual income may be positive, negative, or zero. Steady-state growth in residual income may be driven by long-run expectations for inflation, the industry's sales, the economy in general, or the population. In some industries, competitive dynamics eventually drive long-run projections of the future returns earned by the firm (for example, the future ROCE) to an equilibrium level equal to the long-run expected cost of equity capital in the firm. Once a firm reaches that point, the firm can be expected to earn zero residual income in the future. The analyst should select a continuing growth rate in residual income that captures realistic long-run expectations for the firm.

To compute residual income in Year T+1, the analyst should project Year T+1 net income by multiplying Year T net income by the growth factor $(1 + g)$. Year T+1 residual income (denoted as RI_{T+1}) can then be computed as follows:

$$RI_{T+1} = [NI_T \times (1 + g)] - [R_E \times BV_T]$$

By estimating RI_{T+1} this way, the analyst also will be able to apply the same uniform long-run growth factor $(1 + g)$ to estimate Year T+1 income statement and balance sheet amounts and to compute internally consistent projections for Year T+1 free cash flows and dividends, which the analyst can then use in free cash flow value models and dividends value models to determine internally consistent value estimates. Chapters 11 and 12 demonstrate these approaches.

After computing RI_{T+1}, the analyst can treat RI_{T+1} as a growing perpetuity of residual income beginning in Year T+1. The analyst can discount the perpetuity of residual income to present value using the perpetuity-with-growth value model described in Chapters 11 and 12. We include the continuing value computation into the finite horizon residual income model as follows:

$$V_0 = BV_0 + \sum_{t=1}^{\infty} \frac{NI_t - (R_E \times BV_{t-1})}{(1 + R_E)^t}$$

$$= \underset{(1)}{BV_0} + \underset{(2)}{\sum_{t=1}^{T} \frac{NI_t - (R_E \times BV_{t-1})}{(1 + R_E)^t}}$$

$$+ \underset{(3)}{\left[((NI_T \times (1 + g)) - (R_E \times BV_T)) \times \frac{1}{(R_E - g)} \times \frac{1}{(1 + R_E)^T}\right]}$$

This model computes the value of common equity based on three parts: (1) book value of shareholders' equity at time $t=0$ (the BV_0 term), (2) the present value of residual income over the explicit forecast horizon through Year T (the summation term), and (3) the present value of continuing value based on residual income as a perpetuity with growth beginning in Year T+1 (the term in brackets). To compute continuing value, we compute residual income in Year T+1 [the term $NI_T \times (1 + g) - (R_E \times BV_T)$]. We assume that residual income in Year T+1 will grow at constant rate g in perpetuity beginning in Year T+1, so we compute continuing value as of the start of Year T+1 using the perpetuity-with-growth valuation factor [the term $1/(R_E - g)$]. Finally, we discount continuing value to present value at time $t = 0$ using the present value factor [the term $1/(1 + R_E)^T$].

Coaching Tip: Avoid This Crucial But Common Mistake

The preceding subsection demonstrates how to compute residual income in Year T+1, as follows:

$$RI_{T+1} = [NI_T \times (1 + g)] - [R_E \times BV_T]$$

By estimating RI_{T+1} this way, you will effectively apply a uniform long-run growth factor $(1 + g)$ to net income to compute residual income. Recall that Chapters 11 and 12 also demonstrated how to correctly compute free cash flows and dividends in Year T+1 by applying the same long-run growth factor $(1 + g)$ to project all of the Year T+1 income statement and balance sheet amounts and then deriving internally consistent projections for Year T+1 free cash flows and dividends. With this simple but important step, you can use the residual income value model, the free cash flows value model, and the dividends value models to determine internally consistent value estimates. This approach will enable you to avoid the all-too-common mistake of deriving *different* values for the *same* firm using *different* valuation models.

The common mistake analysts make (and you can avoid with the approach shown above) is forecasting RI_{T+1} by simply projecting $RI_{T+1} = RI_T \times (1 + g)$. This (likely erroneous) shortcut projection implicitly assumes that

$$\begin{aligned} RI_T \times (1 + g) &= [NI_T - (R_E \times BV_{T-1})] \times (1+g) \\ &= NI_T \times (1 + g) - [R_E \times BV_{T-1} \times (1 + g)]. \end{aligned}$$

This assumption requires $BV_T = BV_{T-1} \times (1 + g)$, which is not necessarily true. Residual income in Year T+1 depends on book value at the end of Year T. We assume constant growth at rate $(1 + g)$ in residual income beginning in Year T+1. Thus, the only way residual income in Year T+1 will equal residual income in Year T times $(1 + g)$ is if book value in Year T happened to grow (by coincidence) at the same rate $(1 + g)$. This will not likely be the case. The analyst can easily avoid this forecasting and valuation error for RI_{T+1} by correctly computing $RI_{T+1} = [NI_T \times (1 + g)] - [R_E \times BV_T]$.

VALUATION OF PEPSICO USING THE RESIDUAL INCOME MODEL

Step three toward understanding residual income valuation, as Exhibit 13.1 illustrates, is the practical application step. In this step, we apply the residual income valuation approach to value the common shareholders' equity in PepsiCo. As Chapters 11 and 12 described, PepsiCo shares closed trading at \$54.77 on the New York Stock Exchange at the end of 2008. In Chapter 11, we determined our central estimate of the value of PepsiCo shares at the end of 2008 to be roughly \$83.03 using the projected financial statement forecasts developed in Chapter 10 and applying the dividends-based valuation approach. We obtained the same value estimate for PepsiCo shares in Chapter 12 using the same projected financial statement forecasts developed in Chapter 10 and the free cash flow valuation approaches. Next, we illustrate the valuation of PepsiCo shares using the residual income valuation model techniques described in this chapter and the forecasts developed in Chapter 10. The Forecast and Valuation spreadsheets of FSAP (Appendix C) also demonstrate the forecasts and valuation estimates.

FSAP

We value PepsiCo with the residual income approach following these five steps:

1. Estimate the appropriate discount rate using the risk-adjusted required rate of return on equity capital.
2. Determine the book value of common shareholders' equity on PepsiCo's 2008 balance sheet, project expected future residual income from the financial statement forecasts for PepsiCo described in Chapter 10, and project long-run growth in residual income in the continuing periods beyond the forecast horizon.
3. Discount the expected future residual income to present value, including continuing value.
4. Add the book value of equity and the present value of expected future residual income to determine the total value of common shareholders' equity, correct for midyear discounting, and divide by the number of shares outstanding to convert this total to an estimate of share value for PepsiCo.
5. Analyze the sensitivity of the estimate of PepsiCo's share value to determine the reasonable range of values for PepsiCo shares.

After illustrating this five-step valuation process, we will compare the range of reasonable values to PepsiCo's share price in the market and suggest an appropriate investment decision indicated by the analysis.

Discount Rates for Residual Income

To compute the appropriate discount rate for residual income, we again use the CAPM to estimate the market's required rate of return on PepsiCo's common stock, as demonstrated in Chapters 11 and 12. At the end of 2008, PepsiCo's common stock had a market beta of roughly 0.75. At the same time, U.S. Treasury bills with one to five years to maturity traded with a yield of approximately 4.0 percent, which we use as the risk-free rate. Assuming a 6 percent market risk premium, the CAPM indicates that PepsiCo had a cost of common equity capital of 8.50 percent $[R_E = 8.50 = 4.0 + (0.75 \times 6.0)]$ at the end of 2008, the beginning of the valuation period. We used this same cost of common equity capital to value PepsiCo shares in Chapter 11 using the present value of future dividends and in Chapter 12 using the free cash flows to common equity shareholders' valuation model.

Using the residual income valuation model, we do not need to compute the weighted average cost of capital. This does not mean that we ignore debt capital or the costs related to debt capital. Instead, we rely on accounting to capture the effects of debt. We project book value of shareholders' equity after subtracting debt from total assets, and we project net income after subtracting interest expense net of tax effects.

Pepsico's Book Value of Equity and Residual Income

According to PepsiCo's balance sheet (Appendix A), book value of common shareholders' equity is \$12,203.0 million at the end of 2008. This amount is the starting point for the residual income valuation model, the term denoted BV_0 in the valuation equations.

We project residual income each period in the finite forecast horizon using the following four steps:

1. Forecast expected future net income for each period.
2. Forecast expected future book value of common shareholders' equity at the beginning of each period.
3. Compute expected future required income, which is the product of the cost of equity capital times the book value of common shareholders' equity at the beginning of each period ($= R_E \times BV_{t-1}$).
4. Determine expected future residual income by subtracting expected future required income from expected future net income [$= NI_t - (R_E \times BV_{t-1})$].

We completed the first and second steps in Chapter 10. Chapter 10 developed our projections of PepsiCo's future net income by making specific assumptions regarding each line item in the income statement. Chapter 10 also developed specific forecasts of common shareholders' equity on the balance sheet by making specific assumptions about PepsiCo's assets, liabilities, and common equity, including specific forecasts of dividends, stock issues, and stock buybacks. For projections of net income and book value of shareholders' equity beyond Year +5, we assume that PepsiCo will grow in steady state at a rate of 3.0 percent per year in Year + 6 and beyond. Exhibit 13.3 presents projections of PepsiCo's net income, book value of shareholders' equity, required income, and residual income through Year +5 using the forecasts discussed in Chapter 10 and an 8.50 percent cost of equity capital.

In Year +1, for example, we projected PepsiCo's net income to be $6,110.9 million. We forecasted other comprehensive income items to be zero, so projected comprehensive income and net income are equal. (Recall from the earlier discussion that the residual income model requires that we measure income for common equity shareholders comprehensively by using clean surplus accounting.) We projected that preferred stock outstanding would be liquidated, requiring liquidating dividends of $169.0 million in Year +1; so net income available to common shareholders is $5,941.9 million. Given that PepsiCo's

EXHIBIT 13.3

Valuation of PepsiCo: Present Value of Residual Income Year +1 through Year +5 (dollar amounts in millions)

	Year +1	Year +2	Year +3	Year +4	Year +5
Common Shareholders' Equity (at beginning of year; denoted BV_{t-1})	$12,203.0	$12,656.1	$13,467.4	$14,465.3	$15,323.5
Net (Comprehensive) Income Available for Common Shareholders (denoted NI_t)	$ 5,941.9	$ 6,602.1	$ 7,272.7	$ 7,726.4	$ 8,427.3
Required Income ($R_E \times BV_{t-1}$)	(1,037.3)	(1,075.8)	(1,144.7)	(1,229.5)	(1,302.5)
Residual Income [$NI_t - (R_E \times BV_{t-1})$]	$ 4,904.6	$ 5,526.3	$ 6,128.0	$ 6,496.9	$ 7,124.8
Present Value Factors ($R_E = 8.50$ percent)	0.922	0.849	0.783	0.722	0.665
Present Value of Residual Income	$ 4,520.4	$ 4,694.4	$ 4,797.6	$ 4,688.0	$ 4,738.3
Sum of Present Value Residual Income Year +1 through Year +5	**$23,438.7**				

book value of common shareholders' equity at the beginning of Year +1 is $12,203.0 million and PepsiCo's cost of equity capital is 8.50 percent, we project Year +1 required earnings to be $1,037.3 million (= 0.085 × $12,203.0 million). Therefore, we project Year +1 residual income will be $4,904.6 million (= $5,941.9 million − $1,037.3 million).

To project PepsiCo's residual income continuing in Year +6 and beyond, we forecast that PepsiCo can sustain long-run growth of 3.0 percent per year, consistent with long-run average growth in the economy of 3.0 percent. It is the same assumption we made in forecasting long-run growth in Year +6 and beyond for dividends in Chapter 11 and for free cash flows in Chapter 12. We project Year +6 residual income will be $7,281.5 million, computed by projecting Year +5 net income to grow by 3.0 percent and subtracting required earnings, measured as the equity cost of capital times book value at the end of Year +5, as follows:

$$\begin{aligned} RI_6 &= [NI_5 \times (1 + g)] - [R_E \times BV_5] \\ &= (\$8{,}427.3 \text{ million} \times 1.03) - (0.085 \times \$16{,}453.6 \text{ million}) \\ &= \$8{,}680.1 \text{ million} - \$1{,}398.6 \text{ million} = \$7{,}281.5 \text{ million} \end{aligned}$$

Discounting Pepsico's Residual Income to Present Value

We discount residual income to present value using PepsiCo's 8.50 percent cost of equity capital. Exhibit 13.3 shows that the sum of the present value of PepsiCo's residual income from Year +1 through Year +5 is $23,438.7 million.

We compute the present value of PepsiCo's continuing value of residual income as a perpetuity beginning in Year +6 with growth at a 3.0 percent rate. To compute the continuing value estimate, we use the perpetuity-with-growth valuation model, which determines the present value of the growing perpetuity at the start of the perpetuity period. We then discount that value back to present value at time t=0. We compute the present value of the continuing value of PepsiCo's residual income as follows (allowing for rounding):

$$\begin{aligned} &\textit{Present Value of} \\ &\textit{Continuing Value}_0 = [NI_6 \times (1 + g)] - (R_E \times BV_5)] \times [1/(R_E - g)] \times [1/(1 + R_E)^5] \\ &\quad = [(\$8{,}427.3 \text{ million} \times 1.03) - (0.085 \times \$16{,}453.6 \text{ million})] \\ &\quad\quad \times [1/(0.085 - 0.03)] \times [1/(1 + 0.085)^5] \\ &\quad = [\$8{,}680.1 \text{ million} - \$1{,}398.6 \text{ million}] \times 18.18182 \times 0.665 \\ &\quad = \$7{,}281.5 \text{ million} \times 18.18182 \times 0.665 \\ &\quad = \$88{,}046.5 \text{ million} \end{aligned}$$

The total present value of PepsiCo's residual income is the sum of these two parts:

Present Value of Residual Income Year +1 through Year +5 (Exhibit 13.3)	$ 23,438.7 million
Present Value of Continuing Value in Year +6 and beyond	88,046.5 million
Present Value of Residual Income	$111,485.2 million

Computing Pepsico's Common Equity Share Value

To compute the total value of common equity, we add PepsiCo's book value of common equity to the present value of residual income. The total value of common equity of PepsiCo as of the beginning of Year +1 is the sum of these two amounts:

Present Value of Residual Income	\$111,485.2 million
Book Value of Common Shareholders' Equity	12,203.0 million
Present Value of Common Shareholders' Equity Before Mid-Year Discounting	\$123,688.2 million

As Chapter 11 and 12 describe, our present value calculations overdiscount because they discount each year's residual income for full periods when, in fact, residual income is generated throughout each period and should be discounted from the midpoint of each year to the present. Therefore, to make the correction, we multiply the total by the midyear adjustment factor of 1.0425 [$= 1 + (R_E/2) = 1 + (0.085/2)$]. Therefore, the total present value of common shareholders' equity should be computed as follows:

Present Value of Common Shareholders' Equity Before Mid-Year Discounting	\$123,688.2 million
Mid-Year Discounting Adjustment Factor	× 1.0425
Total Present Value of Common Shareholders' Equity	\$128,945.0 million

Dividing the total present value of common shareholders' equity of \$128,945.0 million by 1,553 million shares outstanding indicates that PepsiCo's common equity shares have a value of \$83.03 per share. This value estimate is identical to the value estimate based on dividends in Chapter 11 and free cash flows to common equity shareholders in Chapter 12. Exhibit 13.4 summarizes the computations to arrive at PepsiCo's common equity share value. Exhibit 13.5 presents the residual income model application for PepsiCo from FSAP.

FSAP

EXHIBIT 13.4

Valuation of PepsiCo Using the Residual Income Valuation Model (dollar amounts in millions except per-share amounts)

Valuation Steps	Computations		Amounts
Sum of Present Value of Residual Income, Year +1 through Year +5	See Exhibit 13.3.		\$ 23,438.7
Add Present Value of Continuing Value	Year +6 residual income assumed to grow at 3.0%; discounted at 8.50%	+	88,046.5
Total Present Value of Residual Income		=	\$111,485.2
Add: Beginning Book Value of Equity	Beginning Book Value of Equity from 2008 Balance Sheet	+	12,203.0
Total		=	\$123,688.2
Adjust to Midyear Discounting	Multiply by $1+(R_E/2)$	×	1.0425
Total Present Value of Common Equity		=	\$128,945.0
Divide by Shares Outstanding	1,553 million shares outstanding	÷	1,553.0
Estimated Value per Share		=	\$ 83.03
Current Price per Share			\$ 54.77
Percent Difference	Positive number indicates underpricing		52%

EXHIBIT 13.5

Valuation of PepsiCo: The Residual Income Valuation Approach
(dollar amounts in millions except per-share amounts)

RESIDUAL INCOME VALUATION	Year +1	Year +2	Year +3	Year +4	Year +5	Continuing Value Year +6
Comprehensive Income Available for Common Shareholders	$ 5,941.9	$ 6,602.1	$ 7,272.7	$ 7,726.4	$ 8,427.3	$ 8,680.1
Lagged Book Value of Common Shareholders' Equity (at *t*–1)	$ 12,203.0	$12,656.1	$13,467.4	$14,465.3	$15,323.5	$16,453.6
Required Earnings	$ 1,037.3	$ 1,075.8	$ 1,144.7	$ 1,229.5	$ 1,302.5	$ 1,398.6
Residual Income	$ 4,904.6	$ 5,526.3	$ 6,128.0	$ 6,496.9	$ 7,124.8	$ 7,281.5
Present Value Factors	0.922	0.849	0.783	0.722	0.665	
Present Value of Residual Income	$ 4,520.4	$ 4,694.4	$ 4,797.6	$ 4,688.0	$ 4,738.3	
Sum of Present Value of Residual Income	$ 23,438.7					
Present Value of Continuing Value	88,046.5					
Total	$111,485.2					
Add: Beginning Book Value of Equity	12,203.0					
Present Value of Equity	$123,688.2					
Adjust to Midyear Discounting	1.0425					
Total Present Value of Equity	$128,945.0					
Shares Outstanding	1,553.0					
Estimated Value per Share	$ 83.03					
Current Share Price	$ 54.77					
Percent Difference	52%					

Sensitivity Analysis and Investment Decision Making

We cautioned in Chapters 11 and 12 and we reiterate here that one should not place too much confidence in the precision of a single point estimate of firm value using these (or any) forecasts for residual income over the remaining life of any firm, even a mature firm such as PepsiCo. Although we have constructed these forecasts and value estimates with care, the forecasting and valuation process has an inherently high degree of uncertainty and estimation error. Therefore, the analyst should not rely too heavily on any one point estimate of the value of a firm's shares; instead, the analyst should describe a reasonable range of values for a firm's shares.

Two critical forecasting and valuation parameters are the long-run growth assumption, which we forecast to be 3.0 percent, and the cost of equity capital, which we forecast to be 8.50 percent. With these assumptions, our base case estimate is that PepsiCo common shares should be valued at roughly \$83 per share. As in Chapters 11 and 12, we assess the sensitivity of our estimate of PepsiCo's share value by varying these two parameters across reasonable ranges. Exhibit 13.6 contains the results of sensitivity analysis in FSAP varying the long-run growth assumption from 0–10 percent and the cost of equity capital from 5–20 percent. The data in Exhibit 13.6 show that value estimates of PepsiCo are inversely related to discount rates, holding growth constant. In contrast, share value estimates are positively related to growth rates, holding discount rates constant. We omit value estimates from this analysis when the growth rate equals or exceeds the discount rate because the continuing value computation is meaningless.

As we observed in our sensitivity analyses in Chapters 11 and 12, these data suggest that our value estimate is sensitive to slight variations of our baseline assumptions of 3.0 percent long-run growth and an 8.50 percent discount rate. Slight adverse variations in valuation parameters (such as 0 percent long-run growth and a 10 percent discount rate) reduce PepsiCo's share value to as low as \$51, whereas slightly more favorable variations (such as 4 percent long-run growth and a 7 percent discount rate) increase PepsiCo's share value to \$145. If our forecast and valuation assumptions are realistic, our baseline value estimate for PepsiCo is \$83 per share at the end of 2008. At that time, the market price of \$54.77 per share indicates that PepsiCo shares were underpriced by about 52 percent. Under our forecast assumptions, PepsiCo's share value could vary within a range of a low of \$51 per share to a high of \$145 per share with only minor perturbations in our growth rate and discount rate assumptions. Given PepsiCo's \$54.77 share price, these value estimates would have supported a buy recommendation at the end of 2008.

RESIDUAL INCOME MODEL IMPLEMENTATION ISSUES

The residual income valuation model is a rigorous and straightforward valuation approach, but the analyst should be aware of four important implementation issues: (1) "dirty surplus" accounting items, (2) common stock transactions, (3) portions of net income attributable to equity claimants other than common shareholders, and (4) negative book value of equity. The next four sections describe these issues.

Dirty Surplus Accounting

The first implementation issue arises because the residual income model requires that the analyst follow clean surplus accounting in developing expectations for future earnings, dividends, and book values. This means that the expected future income amounts should

EXHIBIT 13.6

Valuation of PepsiCo:
Sensitivity Analysis of Share Value Estimates to Growth and Equity Cost of Capital

RESIDUAL INCOME VALUATION SENSITIVITY ANALYSIS:

		Long-Run Growth Assumptions							
		0%	**2%**	**3%**	**4%**	**5%**	**6%**	**8%**	**10%**
Discount Rates:	5%	105.16	160.50	229.67	437.20				
	6%	87.18	120.00	152.81	218.45	415.34			
	7%	74.37	95.73	114.41	145.56	207.85	394.72		
	8.50%	60.84	73.36	83.03	97.00	118.95	158.47	711.69	
	9%	57.34	68.04	76.06	87.30	104.14	132.22	356.87	
	10%	51.41	59.41	65.13	72.75	83.42	99.42	179.45	
	11%	46.57	52.71	56.94	62.37	69.61	79.75	120.30	323.07
	12%	42.55	47.37	50.58	54.59	59.76	66.64	90.73	163.00
	13%	39.16	43.00	45.50	48.55	52.37	57.28	72.98	109.63
	14%	36.26	39.37	41.35	43.73	46.63	50.26	61.15	82.93
	15%	33.76	36.30	37.90	39.78	42.04	44.80	52.70	66.90
	16%	31.57	33.68	34.98	36.50	38.29	40.44	46.35	56.21
	18%	27.95	29.44	30.33	31.35	32.53	33.90	37.47	42.83
	20%	25.08	26.16	26.79	27.51	28.31	29.24	31.55	34.79

include all of the income recognized by the firm for the common equity shareholders and that all-inclusive dividends should include all capital transactions with common equity shareholders. Currently, U.S. GAAP and IFRS do *not* follow clean surplus accounting. U.S. GAAP admits four *dirty surplus* items. These items are the other comprehensive income amounts that firms recognize directly in shareholders' equity. The four dirty surplus items are unrealized fair value gains and losses on available-for-sale investment securities, foreign currency translation gains and losses, changes in assets and liabilities related to pensions and postemployment benefits that arise from plan amendments and actuarial experience, and the effects of cash flow hedges. U.S. GAAP requires that firms recognize these items in *comprehensive income* but does not allow firms to recognize them in net income until they are realized (for example, when the firm realizes gains or losses by selling an available-for-sale investment security). Under U.S. GAAP and IFRS, firms usually report comprehensive income in the Statement of Common Shareholders' Equity or in a note to the financial statements.

For example, PepsiCo reported in the Consolidated Statement of Common Shareholders' Equity and again in Note 13, "Accumulated Other Comprehensive Loss" (Appendix A), that in 2008, other comprehensive income items totaled −$3,793 million. As a result of these items, PepsiCo's comprehensive income in 2008 was $1,349 million (= net income of $5,142 million minus other comprehensive income items totaling $3,793 million). By the end of 2008, total accumulated other comprehensive loss (which measures total accumulated other comprehensive income adjustments over the life of PepsiCo and is included as a component of shareholders' equity) declined from −$952 million to −$4,694 million. As Chapters 7 and 10 described, the main two culprits driving other comprehensive income for PepsiCo have been foreign currency translation adjustments, amounting to −$2,484 million in 2008, and a cumulative total of −$2,271 million, as well as pension and retiree benefits adjustments amounting to −$1,303 million in 2008, and a cumulative total of −$2,435 million.

The four dirty surplus items in U.S. GAAP typically arise because of unrealized gains and losses attributable to changes in market prices, such as changes in investment security fair values, foreign currency exchange rates, or interest rates. Thus, in expectation, the analyst may determine that such gains and losses are certain to occur but that it is impossible to predict with precision either the sign or amount of the future unrealized gains and losses. In that case, the analyst would likely forecast the expected future dirty surplus items to be zero, on average, and therefore forecast net income and comprehensive income to be equal. We used this assumption in building forecasts for PepsiCo in Chapter 10.

On the other hand, if the analyst can project the amounts and timing of future unrealized gains and losses from available-for-sale investment securities, gains and losses from foreign currency translations, gains and losses from cash flow hedges, and adjustments to assets and liabilities related to pension and postretirement benefits from plan amendments and actuarial experience, the analyst should incorporate these unrealized gains and losses in comprehensive income forecasts and base the residual income valuation on comprehensive income rather than net income. To allow for either possibility (expectations of zero or nonzero comprehensive income items in the future), the residual income model in the Valuation spreadsheet in FSAP begins with forecasts of future comprehensive income.

FSAP

Common Stock Transactions

Common stock transactions that change the intrinsic value of existing common shareholders' equity also can cause violations of the clean surplus accounting relation and hinder the ability of the residual income model to measure firm value correctly. To illustrate, consider the firm that sells common shares or repurchases common shares at transaction prices that exactly reflect the intrinsic value of the shares (that is, share sales or repurchases that are zero net present value projects for existing shareholders). Such transactions leave the existing shareholders' value unchanged, and clean surplus accounting holds for these transactions. On the other hand, suppose the firm issues common shares at a price that is lower than their intrinsic value. This transaction has a dilutive effect on (that is, reduces the value of) all of the existing common shares. Net income and the all-inclusive dividend do not reflect this loss in value to existing shareholders, so it violates clean surplus accounting.

It is reasonable to assume that clean surplus accounting for most common stock transactions holds, in expectation, because most issues and repurchases of common shares are accounted for at market value. Most of these capital transactions will likely have zero net present value effects on existing shareholders and will conform to clean surplus accounting.

The most prominent exception, however, is the issuance of common equity shares for employee stock options exercises. As Chapter 6 discusses, the exercise of stock options by employees at strike prices below the prevailing market price dilutes the existing shareholders' equity value. If the firm estimates the fair value of the employee stock options at the time it grants them and recognizes the estimated value of the grants as an expense in measuring net income, it mitigates the violation of clean surplus accounting. In this case, the analyst should forecast the fair value of expected future options grants and subtract these estimated expenses when forecasting expected future net income. We followed this approach in Chapter 10 in building our forecasts of net income for PepsiCo because PepsiCo expenses the fair value of stock options at the date of grant. Under Statement No. 123 (Revised 2004) and IAS 2, firms are required to expense the fair value of stock options by amortizing them over the vesting period, beginning at the date of grant.[12]

It is not uncommon for firms to repurchase common equity shares in the open market and then use these shares to fulfill stock option exercises. In that case, the accounting for the stock repurchase at market value and the issue of the treasury share at the option strike price captures the dilutive effect of the option exercise on shareholders' equity. For example, if the firm repurchases a share in the market for $60 and issues it to an employee exercising an option with a strike price of $40, the net effect of the accounting will capture the $20 decrease in shareholders' equity. On the other hand, if the firm fulfills stock option exercises by issuing new shares (or treasury shares repurchased in prior periods at prices that do not reflect the current period market value), the accounting will reflect the issue of the shares at the option's strike price and the dilutive effect on existing shareholders will violate clean surplus accounting.

In 2008, for example, PepsiCo reports in the Consolidated Statement of Common Shareholders' Equity (Appendix A) that it repurchased a total of 68 million shares for $4,720 million, implying an average cost of $69.41 per share. PepsiCo also discloses in that statement that it reissued 15 million treasury shares for options exercises, thereby increasing equity capital by $603 million ($883 million in the Repurchased Common Stock account less $280 million in the Capital in Excess of Par Value account), for an average book value of $40.20 per share issued. The difference between the average cost of $69.41 per share and the average book value of $40.20 per share indicates an average dilution of $29.21 per share issued. Given that PepsiCo issued 15 million shares, the total dilution is $438 million. With 1,553 million shares outstanding, that amounts to $0.282 dilution per outstanding share, which is roughly 0.5 percent of the year-end share price of $54.77.

The analyst should devote particular time and attention to stock-based compensation when valuing a firm with substantial amounts of options outstanding that will likely be

---

[12] The FASB *Statement No. 123 (Revised 2004)* "Accounting for Share-Based Payment," and the IASB *International Financial Reporting Standard 2* "Share-Based Payment" were issued in 2004.

exercised (options that the analyst expects will ultimately expire or be forfeited pose no problems for valuation) or a firm that is likely to grant large numbers of options in the future that will probably be exercised. In cases like these, the analyst should explicitly forecast future stock-based compensation expenses that include the fair values of future options grants. In addition, the analyst should forecast the future dilutive effects of options exercises on the book value of common equity. The analyst should capture both effects (stock-based compensation expense effects on income and stock option exercise effects on book value of equity) in valuation.[13]

Portions of Net Income Attributable to Equity Claimants Other Than Common Shareholders

In some circumstances, a portion of net income is attributable to equity claimants other than common shareholders. For example, preferred stockholders may be entitled to preference in dividends over common shareholders. Also, minority shareholders have a claim on the portion of net income that is attributable to their share of the equity in the subsidiary they own. For purposes of residual income measurement and valuation, these portions of net income do not represent net income available to the common equity shareholders and should be excluded from residual income. Residual income valuation should be based on the net income available for common equity shareholders. In the case of PepsiCo in Year +1, for example, we forecast that PepsiCo will pay a $169 million liquidating dividend to retire outstanding preferred stock; so we measure residual income after subtracting this dividend to determine net income available to common equity shareholders. PepsiCo did not disclose any minority equity shareholders at the end of 2008.

Negative Book Value of Common Shareholders' Equity

Some firms report negative amounts for total common shareholders' equity (liabilities exceed assets). This is not common, but it can arise among firms that are in the start-up phase of the life cycle, when the firm's operations may be generating significant losses. Negative book value of common equity also can arise following a significant releveraging, during which time the firm may use debt capital to repurchase shares or pay dividends, driving total shareholders' equity below zero.

In these uncommon cases, the analyst should not use the residual income valuation approach because the computation of required earnings ($R_E \times BV_{t-1}$) will be negative. The computation of residual income [$NI_t - (R_E \times BV_{t-1})$] will then effectively result in *adding* (subtracting a negative amount) required earnings to net income, which is not correct. In this situation, the analyst should simply rely on the dividends valuation approach and the free cash flows valuation approach.[14]

CONSISTENCY IN RESIDUAL INCOME, DIVIDENDS, AND FREE CASH FLOW VALUE ESTIMATES

As Exhibit 13.1 illustrates, the fourth and final step toward understanding residual income valuation—and valuation in general—is to understand the internal consistency between

[13] For an illustration of stock options and valuation, see Leonard Soffer, "SFAS No. 123 Disclosures and Discounted Cash Flow Valuation," *Accounting Horizons* Vol. 14, No. 2 (June 2000), pp. 169–189.

[14] Note that this implementation issue arises only when total book value of common shareholders' equity is negative. This implementation issue does not arise when retained earnings is a negative amount (in such circumstances, it is termed *retained deficit*), but when total book value of common shareholders' equity is positive. This situation is not uncommon among firms that have generated significant operating losses, particularly during the start-up phase.

the dividends valuation approach, the free cash flows valuation approach, and the earnings-based valuation approach. Throughout Chapters 11–13, we have anchored the discussions of each of the valuation approaches on the common, general valuation model and have conceptually and theoretically linked each valuation approach to that general model. Along the way, we have demonstrated the internal consistency of these approaches through our analysis and valuation of PepsiCo and have demonstrated the equivalence of value estimates based on residual income, free cash flows, and dividends.

The former baseball player and coach Yogi Berra is reported to have said, "In theory, practice and theory are the same. In practice, they're not." In theory, all three valuation models, when correctly implemented with internally consistent assumptions, will produce the same estimates of value. In practice, the analyst may discover that the three models yield different value estimates. If so, the analyst should check the analysis for one or more of the following three common errors (errors that we have experienced ourselves).[15]

1. *Incomplete or inconsistent earnings and cash flow forecasts.* The analyst should make sure that projected earnings, cash flows, and dividends are complete and based on assumptions that are consistent with one another. As Chapter 10 emphasized, the analyst can reduce the chance of incomplete or inconsistent forecasts by forecasting complete financial statements in which the balance sheets balance, the income statements add up, and the statements of cash flows articulate with the income statements and the changes in the balance sheets. The analyst also should ensure that projected shareholders' equity reflects clean surplus accounting. As suggested in Chapter 10, relying on the additivity and articulation of financial statements will help the analyst avoid inconsistent forecasts and valuations.
2. *Inconsistent estimates of weighted average costs of capital.* Suppose the analyst computes the present value of free cash flows to all debt and equity capital using the weighted average cost of capital as a discount rate and then subtracts the present value of debt and preferred stock to determine the present value of common equity value (as shown in Chapter 12). The only way the value estimates from this approach will be identical with value estimates from the residual income approach or the dividends approach is if the weighted average cost of capital uses weights that are perfectly internally consistent with the present values of debt, preferred stock, and common equity. Thus, the analyst may have to iterate the computation of the weighted average cost of capital a number of times until all of the weights and present values are internally consistent.
3. *Incorrect continuing value computations.* Chapters 11–13 have emphasized that the analyst must carefully estimate continuing value, particularly the Year T+1 amount for residual income, free cash flow, and dividends. If the analyst uses inconsistent assumptions to project the beginning amounts used to compute continuing value, the value estimates will not agree. To avoid this problem, the analyst should first project the Year T+1 income statement and balance sheet amounts assuming a uniform rate of growth $(1 + g)$ and then use these projections to derive the Year T+1 amounts for residual income, free cash flow, and dividends. The derived amounts for Year T+1 can then be used as the starting values of the perpetuity to calculate continuing value. A common error that analysts make is simply to assume that all residual income, free cash flows, and dividends in Year T will grow at the same rate g. This

[15] For a more complete description of diagnosing errors that can cause differences in the three value model estimates, see Russell Lundholm and Terry O'Keefe, "Reconciling Value Estimates from the Discounted Cash Flow Model and the Residual Income Model," *Contemporary Accounting Research* (Summer 2001), pp. 1–26.

shortcut will *not* ensure consistent assumptions and valuation. As described in the past three chapters, that shortcut may impound inconsistent assumptions in the Year T+1 amounts and therefore inconsistent value estimates.

SUMMARY COMMENTS ON VALUATION

Chapters 11–13 have described and applied three different but equivalent approaches to valuation using the present value of projected dividends, the present value of projected free cash flows, and the present value of projected residual income. Together these approaches are theoretically sound and practical techniques to convert forecasts of future cash flows, earnings, and dividends into estimates of firm value. Our experience with valuation suggests that using several valuation approaches yields more useful insights than using just one approach in all circumstances. Chapter 14 demonstrates a variety of additional valuation techniques, including the use of market-based valuation multiples, such as market-to-book ratios and price-earnings ratios.

QUESTIONS, EXERCISES, PROBLEMS, AND CASES

Questions and Exercises

13.1 REQUIRED INCOME. Explain required income. What does required income represent? How is required income conceptually analogous to interest expense?

13.2 RESIDUAL INCOME. Explain residual income. What does residual income represent? What does residual income measure?

13.3 INTERPRETING RESIDUAL INCOME. If a firm's residual income for a particular year is positive, does that mean the firm was profitable? Explain. If a firm's residual income for a particular year is negative, does that mean the firm necessarily reported a loss on the income statement? Explain. What does it mean when a firm's residual income is zero?

13.4 THE EFFECTS OF INVESTMENTS ON RESIDUAL INCOME. Assume that the firm's cost of equity capital is 10 percent and that the firm's existing assets and operations generate a 10 percent return on common equity. If the firm raises additional equity capital and invests in assets that will generate a return less than 10 percent, what effect will that investment have on the firm's residual income? If the firm raises additional equity capital and invests in assets that will generate a rate of return that exceeds 10 percent, what effect will that investment have on the firm's residual income?

13.5 THE EFFECTS OF BORROWING ON RESIDUAL INCOME. If the firm borrows capital from a bank and invests it in assets that earn a return greater than the interest rate charged by the bank, what effect will that have on residual income for the firm? How does that effect compare with the effects of capital structure leverage described in Chapters 4 and 5?

13.6 THE EFFECTS OF COMPETITION ON RESIDUAL INCOME. If the firm competes in a very competitive, mature industry, what effect will competitive conditions have on residual income for the firm and others in the industry? Now suppose the firm holds a competitive advantage in an industry, but the advantage is not likely to be sustainable for more than a few years because of the potential for entry in the industry. As the firm's competitive advantage diminishes, what effect will that have on that firm's residual income?

13.7 THE RESIDUAL INCOME VALUATION APPROACH. Explain the theory behind the residual income valuation approach. Why is residual income value-relevant to common equity shareholders?

13.8 THE RESIDUAL INCOME VALUATION APPROACH. Explain the two roles of book value of common shareholders' equity in the residual income valuation approach.

13.9 VALUATION APPROACH EQUIVALENCE. Conceptually, why should an analyst expect valuation based on dividends, valuation based on the free cash flows for common equity shareholders, and valuation based on the residual income approach to yield equivalent value estimates?

13.10 APPROPRIATE DISCOUNT RATES. Why is it appropriate to use the required rate of return on equity capital (rather than the weighted average cost of capital) as the discount rate in the residual income valuation approach?

13.11 THE EFFECTS OF CONSERVATIVE ACCOUNTING ON RESIDUAL INCOME VALUATION. Suppose you are applying the residual income valuation model to value a firm with extremely conservative accounting. Suppose, for example, the firm is following U.S. GAAP or IFRS but the firm does not recognize a substantial intangible asset on the balance sheet. (Perhaps the firm has expensed substantial amounts of research and development expenditures that have lead to valuable intellectual property or substantial amounts of advertising that have created a valuable brand name). As a consequence of this extremely conservative accounting, the firm reports assets and equity at book values that are much lower than their respective economic values. Explain why the residual income value estimates will not be distorted by conservative accounting. How does the residual income valuation model correct for the effects of conservative accounting and understated book values of equity?

13.12 THE EFFECTS OF AGGRESSIVE ACCOUNTING ON RESIDUAL INCOME VALUATION. Suppose you are applying the residual income valuation model to value a firm with extremely aggressive accounting. Suppose, for example, the firm has a substantially overvalued asset on the balance sheet. (Perhaps the firm has a large amount of goodwill on the balance sheet from a prior acquisition and has delayed recording a necessary impairment charge that would write off the value of the goodwill.) As a consequence of this extremely aggressive accounting, the firm reports assets and equity at book values that are much higher than their respective economic values. Explain why the residual income value estimates will not be distorted by aggressive accounting. How does the residual income valuation model correct for the effects of aggressive accounting and overstated book values of equity?

Problems and Cases

13.13 COMPUTING RESIDUAL INCOME. The following data represent total assets, book value, and market value of common shareholders' equity (dollar amounts in millions) for Abbott Labs, IBM, and Target Stores. Abbott Labs manufactures and sells health care products. IBM develops and manufactures computer hardware and offers related technology services. Target Stores operates a chain of general merchandise discount retail stores. In addition, these data include existing market betas for the three firms and analysts' consensus forecasts of net income for Year +1 (in millions). Assume that for each firm, analysts expect other comprehensive income items for Year +1 to be zero; so Year +1 net income and comprehensive income will be identical. Assume that the risk-free rate of return in the economy is 4.0 percent and the market risk premium is 5.0 percent.

	Abbott Labs	IBM	Target Stores
Total Assets	$42,419	$109,524	$44,106
Common Equity:			
Book Value	$17,480	$ 13,466	$13,712
Market Value	$83,050	$166,420	$34,600
Market Equity Beta	0.27	0.73	1.09
Analysts' Consensus Forecasts of Net Income for Year +1	$ 5,750	$ 12,956	$ 2,384

Required

a. Using the CAPM, compute the required rate of return on equity capital for each firm.
b. Project required income for Year +1 for each firm.
c. Project residual income for Year +1 for each firm.
d. What do the different amounts of residual income imply about each firm? Do the projected residual income amounts help explain the differences in market value of equity across these three firms? Explain.

13.14 COMPUTING RESIDUAL INCOME. The following data represent total assets, book value, and market value of common shareholders' equity (dollar amounts in millions) for Microsoft, Intel, and Dell, three firms involved in different aspects of the computer technology industry. Microsoft engages primarily in the development, manufacture, license, and support of software products. Intel develops and manufactures semiconductor chips and microprocessors for the computing and communications industries. Dell designs and manufactures a range of computer hardware systems, such as laptops, desktops, and servers. These data also include existing market betas for these three firms and analysts' consensus forecasts of net income for Year +1 (in millions). Assume that for each firm, analysts expect other comprehensive income items for Year +1 to be zero; so Year +1 net income and comprehensive income will be identical. Assume that the risk-free rate of return in the economy is 4.0 percent and the market risk premium is 5.0 percent.

	Microsoft	Intel	Dell
Total Assets	$ 77,888	$ 50,715	$26,500
Common Equity:			
Book Value	$ 39,558	$ 39,088	$ 4,271
Market Value	$264,510	$112,480	$26,000
Market Equity Beta	0.96	1.12	1.28
Analysts' Consensus Forecasts of Net Income for Year +1	$ 16,250	$ 8,060	$ 1,882

Required

a. Using the CAPM, compute the required rate of return on equity capital for each firm.
b. Project required income for Year +1 for each firm.
c. Project residual income for Year +1 for each firm.
d. Rank the three firms using expected residual income for Year +1 relative to book value of common equity.
e. What do the different amounts of residual income imply about each firm? Do the projected residual income amounts help explain the differences in market value of equity across these three firms? Explain.

13.15 COMPUTING RESIDUAL INCOME. The following data represent total assets, book value, and market value of common shareholders' equity (dollar amounts in millions) for three firms. Each of these firms, Southwest Airlines, Kroger, and Yum! Brands, operates in a different industry, but all of them operate in very competitive industries. Southwest Airlines is a U.S. domestic airline that provides low-cost point-to-point air transportation services. Kroger operates retail supermarkets across the United States. Yum! Brands operates and franchises quick-service restaurants, including KFC, Pizza Hut, Taco Bell, Long John Silver, and A&W All American Food restaurants. These data also include existing market betas for the three firms and analysts' consensus forecasts of net income for Year +1 (in millions). Assume that for each firm, analysts expect other comprehensive income items for Year +1 to be zero; so Year +1 net income and comprehensive income will be identical. Assume that the risk-free rate of return in the economy is 4.0 percent and the market risk premium is 5.0 percent.

	Southwest Airlines	Kroger	Yum! Brands
Total Assets	$14,308	$23,211	$ 7,242
Common Equity:			
Book Value	$ 4,953	$ 5,176	$ 1,139
Market Value	$ 7,490	$14,870	$15,950
Market Equity Beta	1.10	0.35	1.04
Analysts' Consensus Forecasts of Net Income for Year +1	$ 252	$ 1,263	$ 1,010

Required

a. Using the CAPM, compute the required rate of return on equity capital for each firm.
b. Project required income for Year +1 for each firm.
c. Project residual income for Year +1 for each firm.
d. Rank the three firms using expected residual income for Year +1 relative to book value of common equity.
e. What do the different amounts of residual income imply about each firm? Do the projected residual income amounts help explain the differences in market value of equity across these three firms? Explain.

13.16 EQUITY VALUATION USING THE RESIDUAL INCOME MODEL.

Morrissey Tool Company manufactures machine tools for other manufacturing firms. The firm is wholly owned by Kelsey Morrissey. The firm's accountant developed the following long-term forecasts of net income:

Year +1:	$213,948
Year +2:	$192,008
Year +3:	$187,444
Year +4:	$196,442
Year +5:	$206,667

The accountant expects net income to grow 5 percent annually after Year +5. Kelsey withdraws 30 percent of net income each year as a dividend. Total common shareholders' equity on January 1, Year +1, is $1,111,141. Kelsey expects to earn a rate of return on her invested equity capital of 12 percent each year.

Required

a. Using the residual income valuation model, compute the value of Morrissey Tool Company as of January 1, Year +1.

b. What advice would you give Kelsey regarding her ownership of the firm?

13.17 EQUITY VALUATION USING THE RESIDUAL INCOME AND DIVIDEND DISCOUNT MODELS.

Priority Contractors provides maintenance and cleaning services to various corporate clients in New York City. The firm has provided the following forecasts of net income for Year +1 to Year +5:

Year +1:	$478,246
Year +2:	$491,882
Year +3:	$485,568
Year +4:	$515,533
Year +5:	$554,198

Total common shareholders' equity was $2,224,401 on January 1, Year +1. The firm does not expect to pay a dividend during the period of Year +1 to Year +5. The cost of equity capital is 12 percent.

Required

a. Compute the value of Priority Contractors on January 1, Year +1, using the residual income valuation model. The firm expects net income to grow 5 percent annually after Year +5.

b. Compute the value of Priority Contractors on January 1, Year +1, using the dividend discount model. The firm will pay its first dividend in Year +6. (Hint: Solve for the dividend amount using clean surplus accounting and 5 percent growth in earnings and shareholders' equity in Year +6.)

13.18 EQUITY VALUATION USING THE RESIDUAL INCOME, FREE CASH FLOW, AND DIVIDEND DISCOUNT MODELS.

Exhibit 13.7 presents selected data from projected financial statements for Steak 'n Shake for Year +1 to Year +11. The amounts for Year +11 reflect a long-term growth assumption of 3 percent. The cost of equity capital is 9.34 percent.

EXHIBIT 13.7

Steak 'n Shake
Selected Financial Information
(amounts in millions)
(Problem 13.18)

	Year +1	Year +2	Year +3	Year +4	Year +5	Year +6	Year +7	Year +8	Year +9	Year +10	Year +11[a]
Common Equity, Beginning of Year	$165.8	$177.6	$192.0	$206.0	$216.6	$227.7	$234.2	$238.1	$239.4	$255.8	$269.5
Net Income	24.5	25.8	27.6	29.6	31.8	34.2	36.8	39.5	53.9	57.0	58.7
Dividends	(12.7)	(11.4)	(13.6)	(19.0)	(20.8)	(27.7)	(32.9)	(38.2)	(37.4)	(43.3)	(50.6)
Common Equity, End of Year[b]	$177.6	$192.0	$206.0	$216.6	$227.7	$234.2	$238.1	$239.4	$255.8	$269.5	$277.6
Cash Flow from Operations	$ 45.4	$ 51.2	$ 56.3	$ 61.5	$ 67.1	$ 72.9	$ 78.9	$ 85.2	$ 85.6	$ 92.4	$ 73.2
Cash Flow for Investing	(35.2)	(41.1)	(41.9)	(42.7)	(43.5)	(44.4)	(45.2)	(46.0)	(47.3)	(48.1)	(22.1)
Cash Flow for Long-Term Debt	(0.5)	2.0	—	1.0	(2.0)	—	—	—	—	—	—
Cash Flow for Dividends	(12.7)	(11.4)	(13.6)	(19.0)	(20.8)	(27.7)	(32.9)	(38.2)	(37.4)	(43.3)	(50.6)
Net Change in Cash	$ (3.0)	$ 0.7	$ 0.8	$ 0.8	$ 0.8	$ 0.8	$ 0.8	$ 1.0	$ 0.9	$ 1.0	$ 0.5

[a]The amounts for Year +11 result from increasing each income statement and balance sheet amount by the expected long-term growth rate of 3 percent and then deriving the amounts for the statement of cash flows.
[b]Amounts on this line may differ from the amounts above due to rounding of intermediate computations.

Required

a. Compute the value of Steak 'n Shake as of January 1, Year +1, using the residual income model.

b. Repeat Part a using the present value of expected free cash flows to the common equity shareholders.

c. Repeat Part a using the dividend discount model.

d. Identify the reasons for any differences in the valuations in Parts a–c.

e. The market value of Steak 'n Shake on January 1, Year +1, is $309.98 million. Based on your valuations in Parts a–c, what is your assessment of the market value of this firm?

13.19 RESIDUAL INCOME VALUATION. The Coca-Cola Company is a global soft-drink beverage company (ticker: KO) that is a primary and direct competitor with PepsiCo. The data in Chapter 12's Exhibits 12.13, 12.14, and 12.15 include the actual amounts for 2006, 2007, and 2008 and projected amounts for Year +1 to Year +6 for the income statements, balance sheets, and statements of cash flows, respectively, for Coca-Cola (in millions).

The market equity beta for Coca-Cola at the end of 2008 is 0.61. Assume that the risk-free interest rate is 4.0 percent and the market risk premium is 6.0 percent. Coca-Cola has 2,312 million shares outstanding at the end of 2008, when Coca-Cola's share price was $44.42.

Required

Part I—Computing Coca-Cola's Share Value Using the Residual Income Valuation Approach

a. Use the CAPM to compute the required rate of return on common equity capital for Coca-Cola.

b. Derive the projected residual income for Coca-Cola for Years +1 through +6 based on the projected financial statements. The financial statement forecasts for Year +6 assume that Coca-Cola will experience a steady-state long-run growth rate of 3 percent in Year +6 and beyond.

c. Using the required rate of return on common equity from Part a as a discount rate, compute the sum of the present value of residual income for Coca-Cola for Years +1 through +5.

d. Using the required rate of return on common equity from Part a as a discount rate and the long-run growth rate from Part b, compute the continuing value of Coca-Cola as of the start of Year +6 based on Coca-Cola's continuing residual income in Year +6 and beyond. After computing continuing value as of the start of Year +6, discount it to present value at the start of Year +1.

e. Compute the value of a share of Coca-Cola common stock. (1) Compute the total sum of the present value of all residual income (from Parts c and d). (2) Add the book value of equity as of the beginning of the valuation (that is, as of the end of 2008, or the start of Year+1). (3) Adjust the total sum of the present value of residual income plus book value of common equity using the midyear discounting adjustment factor. (4) Compute the per-share value estimate.

Part II—Sensitivity Analysis and Recommendation

f. Using the residual income valuation approach, recompute the value of Coca-Cola shares under two alternative scenarios. Scenario 1: Assume that Coca-Cola's long-run growth will be 2 percent, not 3 percent as above, and that Coca-Cola's required rate of return on equity is 1 percent higher than that calculated in Part a. Scenario 2: Assume that Coca-Cola's long-run growth will be 4 percent, not 3 percent as above, and that Coca-Cola's required rate of return on equity is 1 percent lower than that calculated in Part a. To quantify the sensitivity of your share value estimate for Coca-Cola to these variations in growth and discount rates, compare (in percentage terms) your value estimates under these two scenarios with your value estimate from Part e.

g. Using these data at the end of 2008, what reasonable range of share values would you have expected for Coca-Cola common stock? At that time, what was the market price for Coca-Cola shares relative to this range? What would you have recommended?

h. If you completed Problem 12.16 in Chapter 12, compare the value estimate you obtained in Part e of that problem (using the free cash flows to common equity shareholders valuation approach) with the value estimate you obtain here using the residual income valuation approach. The value estimates should be the same. If you have not completed Problem 12.16, you would benefit from doing so now.

13.20 RESIDUAL INCOME VALUATION. In Problem 10.16, we projected financial statements for Wal-Mart Stores, Inc. (Walmart) for Years +1 through +5. The data in Chapter 12's Exhibits 12.16, 12.17, and 12.18 include the actual amounts for 2008 and the projected amounts for Year +1 to Year +5 for the income statements, balance sheets, and statements of cash flows, respectively, for Walmart (in millions).

The market equity beta for Walmart at the end of 2008 was 0.80. Assume that the risk-free interest rate was 3.5 percent and the market risk premium was 5.0 percent. Walmart had 3,925 million shares outstanding at the end of 2008. At the end of 2008, Walmart's share price was $46.06.

Required

Part I—Computing Walmart's Share Value Using the Residual Income Valuation Approach

a. Use the CAPM to compute the required rate of return on common equity capital for Walmart.

b. Derive the projected residual income for Walmart for Years +1 through +5 based on the projected financial statements.

c. Project the continuing residual income in Year +6. Assume that the steady-state long-run growth rate will be 3 percent in Year +6 and beyond. Project that the Year +5 income statement and balance sheet amounts will grow by 3 percent in Year +6; then derive the projected amount of residual income for Year +6.

d. Using the required rate of return on common equity from Part a as a discount rate, compute the sum of the present value of residual income for Walmart for Years +1 through +5.

e. Using the required rate of return on common equity from Part a as a discount rate and the long-run growth rate from Part c, compute the continuing value of Walmart as of the start of Year +6 based on Walmart's continuing residual income in Year +6 and beyond. After computing continuing value as of the start of Year +6, discount it to present value at the start of Year +1.

f. Compute the value of a share of Walmart common stock. (1) Compute the total sum of the present value of all future residual income (from Parts d and e). (2) Add the book value of equity as of the beginning of the valuation (that is, as of the end of 2008, or the start of Year +1). (3) Adjust the total sum of the present value of residual income plus book value of common equity using the midyear discounting adjustment factor. (4) Compute the per-share value estimate.

Part II—Sensitivity Analysis and Recommendation

g. Using the residual income valuation method, recompute the value of Walmart shares under two alternative scenarios. Scenario 1: Assume that Walmart's long-run growth will be 2 percent, not 3 percent as above, and that Walmart's required rate of return on equity is 1 percentage point higher than the rate you computed using the CAPM in Part a. Scenario 2: Assume that Walmart's long-run growth will be 4 percent, not 3 percent as above, and that Walmart's required rate of return on equity is 1 percentage point lower than the rate you computed using the CAPM in Part a. To quantify the sensitivity of your share value estimate for Walmart to these variations in growth and discount rates, compare (in percentage terms) your value estimates under these two scenarios with your value estimate from Part f.

h. Using these data at the end of 2008, what reasonable range of share values would you have expected for Walmart common stock? At that time, what was the market price for Walmart shares relative to this range? What would you have recommended?

i. If you worked Problem 11.14 from Chapter 11 and computed Walmart's share value using the dividends valuation approach, compare your value estimate from Part g of that problem with the value estimate you obtained here. Similarly, if you worked Problem 12.17 from Chapter 12 and computed Walmart's share value using the free cash flows to common equity shareholders, compare your value estimate from Part f of that problem with the value estimate you obtained here. You should obtain the same value estimates for Walmart shares under all three approaches. If you have not worked both of those problems, you would benefit from doing so now.

INTEGRATIVE CASE 12.1

STARBUCKS

Residual Income Valuation of Starbucks' Common Equity

In Integrative Case 10.1, we projected financial statements for Starbucks for Years +1 through +5. In this portion of the Starbucks Integrative Case, we use the projected financial statements from Integrative Case 10.1 and apply the techniques in Chapter 13 to compute Starbucks' required rate of return on equity and share value based on the residual income valuation model. We also compare our value estimate to Starbucks' share price at the time of the case to provide an investment recommendation.

The market equity beta for Starbucks at the end of 2008 is 0.58. Assume that the risk-free interest rate is 4.0 percent and the market risk premium is 6.0 percent. Starbucks has 735.5 million shares outstanding at the end of 2008. At the start of Year +1, Starbucks' share price was $14.17.

Required

Part I—Computing Starbucks' Share Value Using the Residual Income Valuation Approach

a. Use the CAPM to compute the required rate of return on common equity capital for Starbucks.

b. Using your projected financial statements from Integrative Case 10.1 for Starbucks, derive the projected residual income for Starbucks for Years +1 through +5.

c. Project the continuing residual income in Year +6. Assume that the steady-state long-run growth rate will be 3 percent in Year +6 and beyond. Project that the Year

+5 income statement and balance sheet amounts will grow by 3 percent in Year +6; then derive the projected residual income for Year +6.

d. Using the required rate of return on common equity from Part a as a discount rate, compute the sum of the present value of residual income for Starbucks for Years +1 through +5.

e. Using the required rate of return on common equity from Part a as a discount rate and the long-run growth rate from Part c, compute the continuing value of Starbucks as of the start of Year +6 based on Starbucks' continuing residual income in Year +6 and beyond. After computing continuing value as of the start of Year +6, discount it to present value at the start of Year +1.

f. Compute the value of a share of Starbucks common stock. (1) Compute the total sum of the present value of all future residual income (from Parts d and e). (2) Add the book value of equity as of the beginning of the valuation (that is, as of the end of 2008, or the start of Year +1). (3) Adjust the total sum of the present value of residual income plus book value of common equity using the midyear discounting adjustment factor. (4) Compute the per-share value estimate.

Part II—Sensitivity Analysis and Recommendation

g. Using the residual income valuation approach, recompute the value of Starbucks shares under two alternative scenarios. Scenario 1: Assume that Starbucks' long-run growth will be 2 percent, not 3 percent as above, and that Starbucks' required rate of return on equity is 1 percentage point higher than the rate you computed using the CAPM in Part a. Scenario 2: Assume that Starbucks' long-run growth will be 4 percent, not 3 percent as above, and that Starbucks' required rate of return on equity is 1 percentage point lower than the rate you computed using the CAPM in Part a. To quantify the sensitivity of your share value estimate for Starbucks to these variations in growth and discount rates, compare (in percentage terms) your value estimates under these two scenarios with your value estimate from Part f.

h. At the end of 2008, what reasonable range of share values would you have expected for Starbucks common stock? At that time, where was the market price for Starbucks shares relative to this range? What would you have recommended?

i. If you computed Starbucks' common equity share value using the dividends valuation approach in Integrative Case 11.1 in Chapter 11, compare the value estimate you obtained in that case with the estimate you obtained in this case. Similarly, if you computed Starbucks' common equity share value using the free cash flows to common equity shareholders valuation approach in Integrative Case 12.1 in Chapter 12, compare the value estimate you obtained in that case with the estimate you obtained in this case. You should obtain the same value estimates under all three approaches. If you have not worked both of those cases, you would benefit from doing so now.

Chapter **14**

Valuation: Market-Based Approaches

Learning Objectives

1. Understand how to use market-based valuation multiples such as MB (market-to-book) and PE (price-earnings) ratios to evaluate how the capital markets value a particular stock, along with the practical advantages and disadvantages of using market-based valuation multiples.
2. Apply a version of the residual income valuation model to compute the VB (value-to-book) ratio and understand how to make investment decisions by comparing the VB ratio to the MB ratio.
3. Understand how to compute and use the firm's VE (value-earnings ratio). Understand how to incorporate growth into the VE ratio to compute the VEG (value-earnings-growth) ratio. Make investment decisions by comparing the VE and VEG ratios to the PE ratio and the PEG (price-earnings-growth ratio), respectively. Use VE and VEG ratios and PE and PEG ratios to analyze firm value over time and across firms.
4. Analyze the impact of the following factors on market multiples: (a) risk and the cost of equity capital, (b) growth, (c) differences between current and expected future earnings, and (d) alternative accounting methods and principles. Use these factors to explain how VB, VE, and VEG ratios should differ across firms and why MB, PE, and PEG ratios do differ across firms.
5. Estimate the price differential, which is the difference between market price and "risk-neutral value".
6. Reverse-engineer a firm's stock price to determine the implicit expected return or the implicit expected long-run growth rate.
7. Understand the role of capital market efficiency in valuation and the academic evidence on the degree to which the capital markets efficiently impound earnings information into share prices. Exploit earnings information for investment decisions by forecasting future earnings, reacting when firms announce earnings each quarter and each year, and incorporating earnings into valuation.

INTRODUCTION AND OVERVIEW

Chapters 1–13 focus on using the information in accounting numbers, financial statements, and related notes to analyze firms' fundamental characteristics of profitability, risk, growth, and value. These prior chapters establish a disciplined and effective six-step framework to attack a very difficult but interesting problem—how to analyze and value a business. To use this framework, we must first understand the firm's industry and business strategy and then use that understanding to assess the quality of the firm's accounting, making adjustments as necessary. We then evaluate the firm's profitability, risk, growth, efficiency, liquidity, and leverage, using a set of financial ratios. On the foundation of these steps, we construct forecasts of future financial statements, from which we derive the expected future earnings, cash flows, and dividends that form the bases for valuation. We then apply valuation models based on expected future dividends, free cash flows, and residual income to value the firm and assess the sensitivity of firm value estimates to key valuation parameters such as the cost of capital and the expected long-run growth rate. To culminate this process, we compute the realistic range of firm value estimates and compare this range to the firm's share price in the market in order to make an intelligent investment decision.

Exhibit 14.1 provides a summary representation of this fundamentals-driven valuation process. The top of the exhibit depicts the firm's value drivers, such as expected future earnings, cash flows, growth, and risk, which comprise the economic foundations of valuation. We capture these value drivers in forecasts of future financial statements, and then convert these forecasts into estimates of firm value using the residual income model, the free cash flows model, and the dividends model.

EXHIBIT 14.1

Fundamentals of Valuation

Fundamental Value Drivers over the Remaining Life of the Firm:
Expected Future Earnings, Cash Flows, Growth, Risk

↓

Financial Statement Forecasts

↓

Compute:
Book Value of Common Equity + Present Value of Expected Future Residual Income
= Present Value of Expected Future Free Cash Flows to Common Equity Shareholders
= Present Value of Expected Future Dividends

↓

Firm Value

In this chapter, we continue our focus on fundamental characteristics of profitability, risk, growth, and value, but we augment that analytical approach with techniques that allow us to exploit the information in *market value* and *share price.* We describe and apply a variety of techniques that compare the firm's market value or share price to the firm's fundamentals. The techniques described in this chapter include commonly used market multiples—MB (market-to-book) ratios, PE (price-earnings) ratios, and PEG (price-earnings-growth) ratios—which provide efficient shortcuts in the valuation process. As Exhibit 14.2 depicts, market multiples require an understanding of the same set of value drivers in the valuation process as the valuation models discussed in Chapters 11–13—expected earnings, cash flows, dividends, growth, and risk—but market multiples collapse the valuation process in two important ways:

1. Instead of developing financial statement forecasts, market multiples use just one or two summary accounting numbers (such as earnings or book value of equity) to represent the value drivers.
2. Instead of using extensive present value computations, market multiples summarize value using relatively simple ratios of market value of common equity to summary accounting numbers.

In this chapter, we also demonstrate two additional techniques to infer and exploit the information in share prices. First, we introduce a measure of the impact of risk on share price, which we call the *price differential.* Second, we demonstrate *reverse-engineering* share prices, which enables an analyst to infer the assumptions the capital market appears to be making in pricing a particular share. In the last section of the chapter, we summarize a few

EXHIBIT 14.2

Market Multiples

Fundamental Value Drivers over the Remaining Life of the Firm:
Expected Future Earnings, Cash Flows, Growth, Risk

↓

Summary Accounting Numbers:
Book Value of Common Shareholders' Equity, Earnings, Long-Run Growth

↓

Market Multiples:
Market-to-Book Ratios, Price-Earnings Ratios, Price-Earnings-Growth Ratios

↓

Firm Value

key insights from the last 40 years of accounting and finance research suggesting that the capital markets are highly but not perfectly efficient in using accounting earnings information to price stocks. These research findings are encouraging for those interested in using earnings and accounting information for fundamental analysis and valuation of stocks and for developing trading strategies to exploit accounting information.

MARKET MULTIPLES OF ACCOUNTING NUMBERS

Throughout this text, we have described how to analyze and exploit a wide array of financial information: earnings, financial statements, footnotes, supplemental management disclosures, financial ratios, growth rates, and others. However, we have not analyzed and exploited the information in one very important number: share price. The market price for a share of common equity is a special and informative number: it aggregates the expectations of all of the market participants following that particular stock. The market price is the result of the market's trading activity in that stock. It summarizes the aggregate information the market participants have about the firm and their aggregate expectations for the firm's future profitability, growth, risk, and value.

The market price of a share does not mean that all market participants agree that the price is the correct value for the share. In fact, the prices at which potential buyers or sellers may be willing to trade differ across market participants and over time. Indeed, the market price simply indicates that the equilibrium point at which the forces of supply (market participants potentially willing to sell the stock—the "ask" side of trading) and the forces of demand (market participants potentially willing to buy the stock—the "bid" side of trading) are momentarily in balance. Stock prices are dynamic, constantly changing with the arrival of new information that changes investors' expectations about share value and triggers trading in the firm's shares in the market. We can analyze share price to obtain a wealth of information.

Market participants commonly calibrate firm valuation using market value or share price expressed as a multiple of a fundamental summary accounting number, such as the MB ratio or the PE ratio. These market multiples play two important roles for analysts: as analytical tools and as valuation tools. As analytical tools, market multiples capture *relative* valuation per dollar of book value or per dollar of earnings. In this way, market multiples measure market value (or share price) relative to a key accounting number as a common denominator, thereby enabling analysts to draw inferences about a particular firm's relative market capitalization, to assess changes in a firm's relative valuation over time, to compare values across firms, and to project comparable firms' values. For example, PE ratios allow an analyst to quickly gauge and compare the multiples at which the market is capitalizing different firms' annual earnings. As analytical tools, market multiples enable analysts to conduct time-series and cross-sectional analyses to summarize and compare how the capital markets are valuing stocks (in the same way analysts compare other ratios such as ROA and ROCE across firms and over time).

Market multiples also can serve as useful and efficient fundamental valuation tools, but they must be applied and interpreted carefully, after considering the firm's expected future profitability, growth, and risk. Multiples such as MB ratios and PE ratios are relative value metrics; therefore, by themselves, they are not meaningful as valuation measures. For example, an analyst cannot determine whether a particular firm's PE ratio should be 10, 20, 50, or some other number unless the analyst knows the firm's fundamental characteristics—expected future profitability, growth, and risk. Similarly, an analyst cannot determine whether a particular firm's PE ratio should be higher or lower than some other firm's PE ratio or an industry average PE ratio unless the analyst knows how the firm's expected future profitability, growth, and risk characteristics compare to those characteristics of the other firm or the industry as a whole. For example, a firm may have a very high PE ratio at a particular point in time for very different reasons: perhaps the share price is too high, perhaps the market expects and prices very high future earnings growth, or perhaps the firm experienced temporarily low earnings last period (because of a restructuring charge, for example). If an analyst uses market multiples to draw naive inferences about the firm's market price without carefully researching the firm's fundamentals, the analyst is at risk for badly misinterpreting market multiples.

Market multiples can be very useful shortcut valuation tools. Unfortunately, analysts sometimes apply market multiples as valuation tools to estimate value in ad hoc ways. Valuation using market multiples may be easy (the so-called "quick-and-dirty" approach), but also may be misleading. A naive analyst might be tempted to value a firm simply by using that firm's historical average or the industry average market multiple. The firm's historical average MB ratio, for example, may be an appropriate fit for the valuation of the firm today, but only if the firm's current fundamental characteristics match those of the past. In the same vein, an industry average price-earnings multiple may be an appropriate yardstick for valuing a particular firm, but only if that firm's fundamental characteristics match the industry averages. If the firm's fundamentals are different today than they were in the past or if the firm's fundamentals do not match the industry averages, market multiples must be adjusted to reflect the firm's fundamental characteristics.

This chapter continues to emphasize the distinction between *value* and *price*. The chapter focuses on how to compute *value*-based multiples that properly reflect the firm's fundamentals and that can be reliably compared to market *price*-based multiples. This focus also directs our attention to the factors that drive multiples so that the analyst can avoid being ad hoc and can adjust historical or industry average multiples correctly to reflect the firm's expected profitability, growth, and risk appropriately.

MARKET-TO-BOOK AND VALUE-TO-BOOK RATIOS

The MB ratio can be computed easily by dividing the firm's market value of common equity at a point in time by the book value of common shareholders' equity from the firm's most recent balance sheet. For example, at the end of 2008, PepsiCo's market value was \$85,058 million (= \$54.77 per share × 1,553 million shares) and PepsiCo's 2008 book value of common shareholders' equity was \$12,203.0 million (Appendix A). Thus, PepsiCo was trading at an MB ratio equal to 6.97 (= \$85,058 million/\$12,203 million). The MB ratio measures market value as a multiple of accounting book value at a point in time. The MB ratio reflects what the market value *is*, but it does not tell us what the ratio *should be* given our estimate of intrinsic value.

A Theoretical Model of the Value-to-Book Ratio[1]

We can compute the ratio of the firm's intrinsic value of common shareholders' equity divided by the book value of common shareholders' equity—the VB ratio—using a version

[1] As noted in Chapter 13, credit for the rigorous development of the residual income model and its extension to the value-to-book ratio model goes to James A. Ohlson, "A Synthesis of Security Valuation Theory and the Role of Dividends, Cash Flows, and Earnings," *Contemporary Accounting Research* (Spring 1990), pp. 648–676; James A. Ohlson, "Earnings, Book Values, and Dividends in Equity Valuation," *Contemporary Accounting Research* (Spring 1995), pp. 661–687; Gerald A. Feltham and James A. Ohlson, "Valuation and Clean Surplus Accounting for Operating and Financial Activities," *Contemporary Accounting Research* (Spring 1995), pp. 216–230. The ideas underlying the value-to-book ratio also trace to early work by G.A.D. Preinreich, "Annual Survey of Economic Theory: The Theory of Depreciation," *Econometrica* (1938), pp. 219–241 and Edgar O. Edwards and Philip W. Bell, *The Theory and Measurement of Business Income* (Berkeley, CA: University of California Press), 1961.

of the residual income model developed in Chapter 13. In fact, the VB ratio model is simply the residual income model scaled by book value of common shareholders' equity. The numerator of the VB ratio is the estimated intrinsic value of common equity, which takes into account the book value of common shareholders' equity, expected future profitability, growth, risk, and the time value of money. The analyst can compare the VB ratio to the MB ratio to evaluate share price and make an investment decision the same way previous chapters compared intrinsic value to share price. The analyst also can use the VB ratio of one firm to estimate the value of a comparable firm provided the analyst makes the appropriate and necessary adjustments to the VB ratio so that it reflects the comparable firm's fundamental characteristics. This section demonstrates the theoretical and empirical relation between intrinsic value, book value, and market value.

Using the same notation from prior chapters, we compute the VB ratio using the following model:

$$\frac{V_0}{BV_0} = 1 + \sum_{t=1}^{\infty} \frac{[ROCE_t - R_E] \times \dfrac{BV_{t-1}}{BV_0}}{(1 + R_E)^t}$$

In short, the VB ratio should be equal to 1 plus the present value of expected future residual return on common equity [the $(ROCE_t - R_E)$ term above] times cumulative growth in book value (the BV_{t-1}/BV_0 term above). The growth in book value indicates the increase in net assets on which firms can earn residual income. The growth in book value depends on ROCE, dividend payout, and changes in common stock outstanding from share issues or repurchases. As the model shows, if a firm generates greater positive residual ROCE $[ROCE_t - R_E]$ and generates greater growth in book value (through reinvested earnings and/or stock issues) on which the firm will earn positive residual ROCE, the firm will create greater value for shareholders (the numerator on the right-hand side will increase, so the value-to-book ratio will increase).

To derive this model, recall from Chapter 13 the residual income valuation model:

$$V_0 = BV_0 + \sum_{t=1}^{\infty} \frac{NI_t - (R_E \times BV_{t-1})}{(1 + R_E)^t}$$

The residual income valuation model estimates the value of common shareholders' equity as equal to the book value of common equity plus the present value of all expected future residual income, which is the amount by which expected future earnings exceed required earnings for the remaining life of the firm.[2] We compute the required earnings (or "normal" earnings) of the firm in Year t as the product of the required rate of return on common equity capital times the book value of common equity at the beginning of Year t $(R_E \times BV_{t-1})$. Required earnings captures the amount of net income the firm must generate to provide a return to common equity capital that is equal to the cost of common equity capital. We measure *residual income* (or "abnormal" earnings) by the subtraction term $NI_t - (R_E \times BV_{t-1})$. Residual income is the difference between expected net income in Year t and required earnings of the firm in Year t. Residual income measures the amount of wealth the

[2] Chapter 13 described that the residual income valuation model depends on clean surplus accounting for book value of common shareholders' equity, which requires expected future earnings forecasts to be comprehensive measures of income for the firm's common equity shareholders and expected future dividends to reflect all capital transactions between the firm and common equity shareholders. Throughout this chapter, when we refer to expected future "earnings" or "net income" in the context of residual income valuation, we mean expected future comprehensive income available for common shareholders under clean surplus accounting.

analyst expects the firm to create (or destroy) in Year t for common equity shareholders above (or below) the required return to equity capital.

To convert the residual income model into a model for the VB ratio, we scale both sides of the equation by BV_0, which produces the following equation:

$$\frac{V_0}{BV_0} = \frac{BV_0}{BV_0} + \sum_{t=1}^{\infty} \frac{\frac{NI_t}{BV_0} - \left(R_E \times \frac{BV_{t-1}}{BV_0}\right)}{(1 + R_E)^t}$$

The term BV_0 divided by BV_0 is, of course, equal to 1. We rewrite the NI_t/BV_0 term as follows:

$$\frac{NI_t}{BV_0} = \frac{NI_t}{BV_{t-1}} \times \frac{BV_{t-1}}{BV_0} = ROCE_t \times \frac{BV_{t-1}}{BV_0}$$

To rewrite NI_t/BV_0 this way, we state $ROCE_t = NI_t/BV_{t-1}$. Note that this computation of $ROCE_t$ divides net income in period t by book value of common equity at the *beginning* of period t. This ROCE computation differs slightly from the approach in Chapter 4 in which we compute ROCE as net income divided by the *average* book value of equity during period t.[3]

Also note that BV_{t-1}/BV_0 is the cumulative growth factor in book value of common equity between year 0 (the date of the valuation) and period $t - 1$. As indicated previously, growth in book value is a function of the earnings generated each period plus additional capital contributions by shareholders less equity capital paid out to shareholders through dividends and stock buybacks. The growth in book value indicates growth in net assets, on which a firm can earn residual income.[4]

By decomposing the term NI_t/BV_0 into these two parts, we can restate NI_t/BV_0 as the product of profitability times growth: *ROCE* in Year t times the cumulative growth in book value from year 0 to the start of Year t. Return on common equity is a function of profitability relative to beginning-of-year common equity; beginning-of-year common equity is a function of cumulative growth.

We then substitute these two components of NI_t/BV_0 into the VB equation as follows:

$$\frac{V_0}{BV_0} = 1 + \sum_{t=1}^{\infty} \frac{\left(ROCE_t \times \frac{BV_{t-1}}{BV_0}\right) - \left(R_E \times \frac{BV_{t-1}}{BV_0}\right)}{(1 + R_E)^t}$$

Now both terms in the numerator of the summation term are multiplied by the same cumulative book value growth factor. We rearrange that equation as follows:

$$\frac{V_0}{BV_0} = 1 + \sum_{t=1}^{\infty} \frac{[ROCE_t - R_E] \times \frac{BV_{t-1}}{BV_0}}{(1 + R_E)^t}$$

We now have a useful model for the VB ratio. Let's consider each term.

---

[3] Theoretical and empirical research on the VB ratio defines ROCE as net income to common shareholders for a year divided by common shareholders' equity at the *beginning* of the year. In contrast, in prior chapters (particularly Chapter 4) we used *average* common shareholders' equity in the denominator of ROCE. The theoretical development and application of the VB model in this section uses shareholders' equity at the beginning of the year, although the bias in using average shareholders' equity should not be particularly significant for most firms.

[4] Indeed, as we will discuss in more detail later, if a firm increases common shareholders' equity through retained earnings or common equity issues and it does not generate future earnings increases, the firm will experience a decline in the value-to-book ratio.

First, as a starting point, the VB ratio will equal 1, to reflect the book value of common equity invested in the firm. The summation term indicates how the VB ratio should differ from 1 as a function of the firm's expected future abnormal profitability (the $ROCE_t - R_E$ term) times the firm's cumulative growth in book value (the BV_{t-1}/BV_0 term), all of which is discounted to present value, reflecting the firm's cost of equity capital (R_E) and the time value of money. Thus, the residual income model specifies the firm's VB ratio as a function of the firm's value drivers: capital in place, profitability, growth, cost of equity capital, risk, and the time value of money. The VB model provides a valuation approach in which all of the inputs to valuation can be expressed as forecasts of rates—expected future ROCE, R_E, and growth. The only dollar amount the analyst needs in order to use the VB ratio to compute the dollar value of common shareholders' equity is the book value of common shareholders' equity, which is observable from the shareholders' equity section of the balance sheet.

The expression for the VB ratio provides some insights into valuation:

- Economics teaches that in equilibrium firms should expect to earn a return equal to the cost of capital (that is, ROCE $= R_E$). The VB model indicates that a firm in steady-state equilibrium earning ROCE $= R_E$ will maintain (not create or destroy) shareholder wealth and will be valued at book value (that is, VB $= 1$).
- A firm's value should be greater than its book value of common equity if the firm will generate wealth for common equity shareholders by earning a return (ROCE) that exceeds the cost of capital (R_E). That is, VB > 1 if ROCE $> R_E$. Firms earning a return that is less than the cost of equity capital (that is, ROCE $< R_E$) will destroy shareholder wealth and will be valued below book value (that is, VB < 1).
- By itself, growth does not add value. Growth adds value to shareholders only if the growth creates additional residual income for common equity shareholders. If expected ROCE equals R_E on new projects (that is, zero NPV projects), these new projects will not create (or destroy) common shareholders' equity value. New projects will be abnormally profitable and create new wealth for equity shareholders (that is, will be positive NPV projects) only when expected ROCE exceeds R_E.
- The risk of the firm increases the equity cost of capital. Increasing the equity cost of capital reduces firm value in two ways: (1) by increasing the required ROCE the firm must earn to cover the increased cost of capital R_E (that is, the "hurdle rate" goes up in the numerator) and (2) by increasing the discount rate used to compute the present value of residual income (which increases the denominator).
- If a firm's VB ratio differs from the industry average VB ratio, it should be because the firm's expected future ROCE, R_E, and/or book value growth differ from the industry averages.
- If a firm's VB ratio changes over time, current expectations for the firm's future ROCE, R_E, and/or book value growth should differ from past expectations for the firm's future ROCE, R_E, and/or book value growth, respectively.

Example 1

Suppose an analyst wants to value a firm with $1,000 of book value of common equity and a cost of equity capital equal to 10 percent. Assume that the analyst forecasts the firm will earn ROCE of 15 percent from Year +1 through Year +3 but that after Year +3, the firm will earn ROCE equal to 10 percent. The analyst also expects the firm will reinvest all net income (that is, pay zero dividends) and not issue or repurchase stock. Using the VB ratio approach, the analyst should assign the firm a VB ratio equal to 1 plus the present value of future residual ROCE times growth. The present value of future residual ROCE times growth is determined as follows:

Year	Expected ROCE	Residual ROCE $(ROCE - R_E)$	Cumulative Book Value Growth Factor to Year $t-1$	Residual ROCE × Cumulative Growth	PV Factor	PV of Residual ROCE × Cumulative Growth
+1	0.15	0.05	$1.00 = (1.15)^0$	0.05000	0.9091	0.04545
+2	0.15	0.05	$1.15 = (1.15)^1$	0.05750	0.8264	0.04752
+3	0.15	0.05	$1.3225 = (1.15)^2$	0.06613	0.7513	0.04968
+4	0.10	0.00	$1.52088 = (1.15)^3$	0.00000	0.6830	0.00000
					Total	0.14265

The sum of the present values of residual ROCE times cumulative growth through Year +3 equals 0.14265, and the sum in all years after Year +3 is zero. Adding this present value amount to 1 (to reflect the book value of equity already in place), the VB ratio of this firm is 1.14265. Note that we have determined this VB ratio with all of the inputs expressed in rates. We can multiply the VB ratio by book value of equity to determine that firm value is $1,142.65 (= 1.14265 VB ratio × $1,000 book value of equity). We can confirm this value using dollar amounts and the residual income model approach from Chapter 13 as follows:

Year	Expected ROCE	Expected Earnings	Cumulative Book Value at the end of Year $t-1$ (BV_{t-1})	Required Income $(BV_{t-1} \times R_E)$	Residual Income	PV Factor	PV of Residual Income
+1	0.15	$150.00		$100	$50.00		
		= 0.15 × $1,000	$1,000	= $1,000 × 0.10	= $150 − $100	0.9091	$ 45.45
+2	0.15	$172.50	$1,150	$115	$57.50		
		= 0.15 × $1,150	= $1,000 + $150	= $1,150 × 0.10	= $172.50 − $115	0.8264	$ 47.52
+3	0.15	$198.38	$1,322.5	$132.25	$66.13		
		= 0.15 × $1,322.5	= $1,150 + $172.50	= $1,322.5 × 0.10	= $198.38 − $132.25	0.7513	$ 49.68
+4	0.10	$152.09	$1,520.88	$152.09	$0.00		
		= 0.10 × $1,520.88	= $1,322.50 + $198.38	= $1,520.88 × 0.10	= $152.09 − $152.09	0.6830	$ 0.00
						Total	$142.65

The sum of the present values of residual income through Year +3 equals $142.65, the sum in all years after Year +3 is zero, and book value of equity is $1,000; so the residual income model confirms that firm value is $1,142.65.

The Value-to-Book Model with Finite Horizon Earnings Forecasts and Continuing Value Computation

As we discussed in Chapters 11–13, analysts commonly forecast income statements and balance sheets over a foreseeable, finite horizon and then make simplifying growth rate assumptions for the years continuing after the forecast horizon. We can modify the value-to-book ratio model to include specific forecasts of net income, book value of common equity, and ROCE through Year T (where T is a finite horizon, for example, five or ten years in the future) and then apply a constant growth rate assumption (denoted as *g*) to project ROCE for Year T+1 and all years thereafter. We used similar approaches to forecast and value dividends in Chapter 11, free cash flows in Chapter 12, and residual income in Chapter 13.

To develop the value-to-book model with finite horizon earnings forecasts and continuing value computations, we will follow the same approach used in Chapter 13, with only slight modifications. Recall from Chapter 13 that we used specific forecasts of financial statements for a finite horizon through Year T and then projected Year T+1 net income by multiplying Year T net income by the long-run growth factor $(1 + g)$. We then computed Year T+1 residual income (denoted as RI_{T+1}) as follows:

$$RI_{T+1} = [NI_T \times (1 + g)] - [R_E \times BV_T]$$

By estimating RI_{T+1} this way, we apply the same uniform long-run growth factor $(1 + g)$ to estimate Year T+1 income statement and balance sheet amounts and compute internally consistent projections for Year T+1 free cash flows, dividends, and residual income.

As we discussed in Chapter 13, after computing RI_{T+1}, the analyst can treat RI_{T+1} as a growing perpetuity of residual income beginning in Year T+1. The analyst can compute the present value of the perpetuity of residual income using the perpetuity-with-growth value model as follows:

$$\text{Present Value of Continuing Value}_0 = [NI_T \times (1 + g)] - [R_E \times BV_T] \times [1/(R_E - g)] \times [1/(1+R_E)^T]$$

We can modify this computation to adapt it to the value-to-book model with two steps:

1. Divide the term $[NI_T \times (1 + g)]$ by BV_T to convert it to an ROCE measure for Year T+1.
2. Divide the BV_T term by BV_0 to measure the cumulative growth in book value.

The result of these two steps is a continuing value computation based on projected future residual ROCE and book value growth as follows:

$$\begin{aligned}
&\text{Present Value of Continuing Value}_0\\
&= [\{NI_T \times (1 + g)/BV_T\} - R_E] \times [BV_T/BV_0] \times [1/(R_E - g)] \times [1/(1+R_E)^T]\\
&= [ROCE_{T+1} - R_E] \times [BV_T/BV_0] \times [1/(R_E - g)] \times [1/(1+R_E)^T]\\
&\qquad\quad (1) \qquad\qquad\quad (2) \qquad\qquad\quad (3) \qquad\qquad\quad (4)
\end{aligned}$$

The first term in the computation is projected residual ROCE in Year T+1. The second term is the cumulative growth in book value from present (BV_0) to the beginning of the continuing value period (BV_T). The third term is the familiar perpetuity-with-growth factor, computing the present value of the perpetuity as of the start of the continuing value period. And the fourth term is familiar as the present value factor that discounts continuing value to present value today.

We include the continuing value computation into the finite horizon value-to-book model as follows:

$$\underset{(1)}{\frac{V_0}{BV_0}} = 1 + \underset{(2)}{\sum_{t=1}^{T} \frac{[ROCE_t - R_E] \times \dfrac{BV_{t-1}}{BV_0}}{(1 + R_E)^t}} + \underset{(3)}{[ROCE_{T+1} - R_E] \times [BV_T/BV_0] \times [1/(R_E - g)] \times [1/(1+R_E)^T]}$$

This model computes the value-to-book ratio of common equity based on three parts: (1) book value scaled by book value (equal to 1, which represents BV_0/BV_0), (2) the present value of residual ROCE over the explicit forecast horizon through Year T (the summation term), and (3) the present value of continuing value based on the present value of residual ROCE as a perpetuity with growth beginning in Year T+1.

APPLICATION OF THE VALUE-TO-BOOK MODEL TO PEPSICO

In Chapter 13, we determined that PepsiCo's share value at the end of 2008 should be within a reasonable range centered on $83.03. We determined this amount using the financial statement forecasts developed in Chapter 10 and the residual income valuation model. Next, we illustrate the valuation of PepsiCo shares using the value-to-book model. We rely on the same financial statement forecasts developed in Chapter 10, the same equity cost of capital (8.50 percent), and the same expected long-run growth rate (3.0 percent). We present all of the forecasts and valuation models in the FSAP Forecasts and Valuation spreadsheet in Appendix C.

To compute the VB model for PepsiCo and to use it to make an investment decision with regard to PepsiCo shares, we follow these nine steps:

1. For each forecast year, project the expected ROCE, computed as NI_t/BV_{t-1}.
2. For each forecast year, compute expected residual ROCE by subtracting the equity cost of capital from expected ROCE.
3. Determine the cumulative growth factor in book value of common shareholders' equity to the beginning of each forecast year (computed as BV_{t-1}/BV_0).
4. Multiply the expected residual ROCE by the cumulative growth factor each forecast year.
5. Discount to present value the expected residual ROCE times growth for each forecast year.
6. Compute continuing value based on expected residual ROCE as a perpetuity with growth beginning in Year T+1, and discount continuing value to present value.
7. Add 1 (the ratio of book value over book value) plus the sum of the present values of all expected future residual ROCE times growth plus the present value of continuing value.
8. Compute the implied VB ratio by multiplying the sum by the midyear discounting adjustment factor $[1 + (R_E/2)]$, as described in prior chapters.
9. Compare the implied VB ratio to the MB ratio to determine whether market price is greater than, equal to, or less than the estimate of value. Equivalently, you can multiply the implied VB ratio by book value of equity to determine the value of common shareholders' equity and then divide by the number of shares outstanding to convert this total to an estimate of share value, which you then compare directly to share price.

Next, we illustrate each of these nine steps with PepsiCo. The Year +1 projected ROCE is 48.7 percent, computed as projected comprehensive income available for common shareholders in Year +1 divided by book value of common equity at the start of Year +1 (= $5,941.9 million/$12,203.0 million). The residual ROCE is 40.2 percent after subtracting 8.50 percent for the cost of equity capital. The cumulative growth factor in book value (BV_{t-1}/BV_0) in Year +1 is 1.0 because Year +1 is the first year of the valuation horizon.[5]

[5] We project that PepsiCo's book value of common equity will grow to $12,656.1 million during Year +1. Therefore, the cumulative growth factor in book value of common equity as of the start of Year +2 will be 1.037 (= $12,656.1 million/$12,203.0 million).

Therefore, the product of Year +1 residual ROCE and the cumulative growth factor is 40.2 percent, which we discount to present value using the 8.50 percent cost of equity capital. Exhibit 14.3 presents these computations for PepsiCo for Year +1 through Year +5. The sum of the present value of residual ROCE times growth in Year +1 through Year +5 is 1.921.[6]

We use the same steps to compute the Year +6 residual ROCE for purposes of computing continuing value. As described in the previous chapter, we project comprehensive income in Year +6 to grow by the 3.0 percent long-run growth rate. We compute book value as of the start of Year +6 (the end of Year +5), compute implied residual ROCE, and multiply by the cumulative growth factor in book value up to the beginning of Year +6. The projected ROCE in Year +6 is 52.8 percent [$= (NI_5 \times \{1+g\})/BV_5 =$ ($8,427.3 million × 1.03)/$16,453.6 million = $8,680.1 million/$16,453.6 million]. After subtracting the 8.50 percent cost of equity capital, the projected residual ROCE in Year +6 is 44.3 percent. Cumulative growth in book value from Year 0 to the beginning of Year +6 (the end of Year +5) is 1.348 ($= BV_5/BV_0 =$ $16,453.6 million/$12,203.0 million). Therefore, we project that in Year +6, the product of residual ROCE times cumulative growth is 59.7 percent (= 44.3 percent × 1.348).

EXHIBIT 14.3

Valuation of PepsiCo
Present Value of Residual ROCE in Year +1 through Year +5
(dollar amounts in millions)

	Year +1	Year +2	Year +3	Year +4	Year +5
Comprehensive Income Available for Common Shareholders	$ 5,941.9	$ 6,602.1	$ 7,272.7	$ 7,726.4	$ 8,427.3
Divide by Book Value of Common Shareholders' Equity (at *t*–1)	$12,203.0	$12,656.1	$13,467.4	$14,465.3	$15,323.5
Equals Implied ROCE	0.487	0.522	0.540	0.534	0.550
Residual ROCE (after subtracting 0.0850 percent required return on common equity)	0.402	0.437	0.455	0.449	0.465
Cumulative growth factor as of *t*–1	× 1.000	× 1.037	× 1.104	× 1.185	× 1.256
Residual ROCE times growth	0.402	0.453	0.502	0.532	0.584
Present Value Factors	× 0.922	× 0.849	× 0.783	× 0.722	× 0.665
PV Residual ROCE times growth	0.370	0.385	0.393	0.384	0.388
Sum of PV Residual ROCE times growth, Year +1 through Year +5	1.921				

[6] This amount should be interpreted as a component of the VB ratio because all of the computations in the model are scaled by BV_0. Thus, the amount 1.921 should be interpreted as an estimate of the amount of residual income PepsiCo will create in Years +1 through +5 that, in present value, is equal to 1.921 times the book value of common equity. To reconcile this computation with the residual income model computations in Chapter 13, recognize that 1.921 times book value of $12,203.0 million equals $23,438.7 (allow for rounding), which is the sum of the present value of residual income in Year +1 through Year +5 computed in Exhibit 13.2.

We use the Year +6 residual ROCE times growth (59.7 percent) in the computation of the present value of continuing value as follows (allowing for rounding):

Present Value of Continuing Value$_0$

$$= [\{NI_5 \times (1 + g)/BV_5\} - R_E] \times [BV_5 / BV_0] \times [1/(R_E - g)] \times [1/(1 + R_E)^5]$$
$$= [(\$8{,}427.3 \times 1.03)/\$16{,}453.6 - 0.085] \times [\$16{,}453.6/\$12{,}203.0]$$
$$\times [1/(0.085 - 0.03)] \times [1/(1 + 0.085)^5]$$
$$= 0.443 \times 1.348 \times 18.182 \times 0.665$$
$$= 7.215$$

The total present value of PepsiCo's expected residual ROCE with growth, expressed as components of the VB ratio, is the sum of these two parts (allow for rounding):

Present Value of Residual ROCE in Year +1 through Year +5	1.921
Present Value of Continuing Value of ROCE in Year +6 and beyond	7.215
Present Value of All Future Residual ROCE	9.136

To compute the VB ratio for common equity, we need to add PepsiCo's beginning book value of common equity expressed as a ratio of beginning book value of equity, which is, of course, equal to 1. Also, as described in prior chapters, our present value calculations overdiscount because they discount each year's residual ROCE for full periods when, in fact, the firm generates residual ROCE throughout each period and we should discount from the midpoint of each year to the present. Therefore, to make the correction, we multiply the present value sum by the midyear discounting adjustment factor of 1.0425 [$= 1 + (R_E/2) = 1 + (0.085/2)$]. Making these two adjustments produces the implied VB ratio as follows:

Present Value of All Future Residual ROCE	9.136
Add: Beginning Book Value	+ 1.000
Total	10.136
Multiply by the Midyear Correction Factor	× 1.0425
Implied VB Ratio	10.567

These computations suggest that PepsiCo common equity should be valued at 10.567 times the book value of equity at the start of the valuation horizon, which is the end of 2008. At the end of 2008, PepsiCo's market value was \$85,058.0 million (= \$54.77 per share × 1,553 million shares) and PepsiCo's 2008 book value of common shareholders' equity was \$12,203.0 million (Appendix A). Thus, PepsiCo was trading at an MB ratio equal to 6.970 (= \$85,058.0 million/\$12,203.0 million). The VB ratio of 10.567 is 52 percent greater than the MB ratio of 6.970, implying that PepsiCo shares were underpriced by 52 percent at that time.

Equivalently, we can convert the VB ratio into a share value estimate for purposes of comparing to market price per share. If we multiply book value equity by the VB ratio, we obtain the value estimate of PepsiCo common equity of \$128,945.0 million [= \$12,203.0 million × 10.567 VB ratio (allow for rounding)]. Dividing by 1,553 million shares outstanding indicates that PepsiCo's common equity shares have a value of \$83.03 per share, which is identical to the value estimates we obtained from the residual income model in Chapter 13, the free cash flows to common equity shareholders model in Chapter 12, and the dividend models in Chapter 11. Comparing the share value estimate of \$83.03 to market price per share of \$54.77 also indicates that PepsiCo's shares were underpriced by

52 percent at the end of 2008. We summarize the computations to arrive at PepsiCo's common equity share value using the value-to-book approach in Exhibit 14.4, where we present the value-to-book model for PepsiCo from FSAP.

FSAP

We can conduct a sensitivity analysis for the estimate of PepsiCo's VB ratio to assess a reasonable range of VB ratios for PepsiCo. We will find that the sensitivity of the VB ratio estimate is identical to the sensitivity of the residual income model value estimates demonstrated in Chapter 13. This is to be expected because both models use the same forecasts and valuation assumptions and the VB model is a scaled version of the residual income model.

Reasons Why VB Ratios and MB Ratios May Differ From 1

We described earlier that in long-run equilibrium, VB ratios and MB ratios should converge to 1. We also described a number of *economic* reasons why VB and MB ratios may differ from 1. For example, the firm may have competitive advantages that enable it to earn a ROCE that is greater than R_E. To the extent that the firm can create and sustain these competitive advantages, the firm will increase the magnitude and persistence over time of the degree to which ROCE exceeds R_E, thereby increasing the VB and MB ratios. In addition, if the firm is expected to generate future growth by investing in abnormally profitable projects, the VB and MB ratios will differ from 1.

A firm's VB and MB ratio may differ from 1 for *accounting* reasons in addition to economic reasons.[7] The firm may have investments in projects for which accounting methods and principles cause ROCE to differ from R_E. For example, firms may make substantial investments in successful R&D projects, brand equity, human capital, or other intangible resources. If these investments are internally generated through R&D activities, marketing and advertising activities, or human capital recruiting and training activities, firms are typically required to expense investments in these activities according to conservative accounting principles (as is common under GAAP and IFRS).[8] If these investments subsequently develop into successful and profitable resources, the firm will have substantial off-balance-sheet assets and off-balance-sheet common shareholders' equity. These off-balance-sheet assets generate net income, but by being off-balance-sheet, they cause common shareholders' equity to be understated; so ROCE is relatively high. These effects can be observed among certain firms in many industries, such as pharmaceuticals, biotechnology, software, and consumer goods.

Considering PepsiCo and Coca-Cola, these firms have created substantial off-balance-sheet brand equity over many years of successful product development, advertising, and brand-building activities. Following U.S. GAAP, these firms have expensed their investments in these activities. Thus, for these firms, the book value of common shareholders' equity does not recognize the off-balance-sheet value of brand equity. Relative to R_E, ROCE for PepsiCo and Coca-Cola is very high and likely will continue to be very high for many years in the future.

---

[7] Stephen Ryan (1995) found that book value changes lag market value changes in part because U.S. GAAP uses historical cost valuations for assets. The lag varies in part based on the degree of capital intensity of firms. See Stephen Ryan, "A Model of Accrual Measurement and Implications for the Evolution of the Book-to-Market Ratio," *Journal of Accounting Research* (Spring 1995), pp. 95–112.

[8] GAAP and IFRS typically require expensing (rather than capitalizing) expenditures on internally generated intangible resources such as R&D (except IFRS does permit capitalization of development costs), advertising, and human capital because the highly uncertain future cash flows associated with them are inherently difficult to measure reliably.

EXHIBIT 14.4

Valuation of PepsiCo
Value-to-Book Approach
(dollar amounts in millions except per share amounts)

RESIDUAL INCOME VALUATION Market-to-Book Approach		**Year +1**	**Year +2**	**Year +3**	**Year +4**	**Year +5**	**Continuing Value Year +6**
Comprehensive Income Available for Common Shareholders		$ 5,941.9	$ 6,602.1	$ 7,272.7	$ 7,726.4	$ 8,427.3	$ 8,680.1
Book Value of Common Shareholders' Equity (at *t*–1)		$ 12,203.0	$12,656.1	$13,467.4	$14,465.3	$15,323.5	$16,453.6
Implied ROCE		0.487	0.522	0.540	0.534	0.550	0.528
Residual ROCE		0.402	0.437	0.455	0.449	0.465	0.443
Cumulative Growth Factor in Common Equity as of *t*–1		1	1.037	1.104	1.185	1.256	1.348
Residual ROCE times Cumulative Growth		0.402	0.453	0.502	0.532	0.584	0.597
Present Value Factors		0.922	0.849	0.783	0.722	0.665	
Present Value Residual ROCE times Growth		0.370	0.385	0.393	0.384	0.388	
Sum of Present Value Residual ROCE times Growth		1.921					
Present Value of Continuing Value	+	7.215					
Total Present Value Residual ROCE		9.136					
Add One for Book Value of Equity at *t*–1	+	1.000					
Sum		10.136					
Adjust to Midyear Discounting	×	1.0425					
Implied Market-to-Book Ratio		10.567					
Times Beginning Book Value of Equity	×	$ 12,203.0					
Total PV of Equity		$128,945.0					
Shares Outstanding	÷	1,553.0					
Estimated Value per Share		$ 83.03					
Current Share Price		$ 54.77					
Percent Difference		52%					

Over a sufficiently long period of time, however, the impact of accounting principles on the VB and MB ratio will diminish because economics teaches us to expect that competitive equilibrium forces will drive ROCE to converge to R_E in the long run. Also, the self-correcting nature of accounting will eventually eliminate biases in ROCE and book value of equity. For example, consider a biotechnology company that for several years invests in R&D to develop a particular drug. During the initial years of research, the firm incurs research costs that the firm is required to expense under U.S. GAAP. Its ROCE and book value of equity will be "low" during these years. After successfully developing and marketing the drug, ROCE will be "high" because the firm generates revenues without matching expenses for research costs. The "high" ROCE will increase retained earnings, and over time, the initial conservative biases in ROCE and book value will be corrected.

Empirical Data on MB Ratios

Exhibit 14.5 presents descriptive statistics for MB ratios across 37 industries during the decade from 1998–2007 (the same industries and years for which Exhibit 11.3 in Chapter 11 provided data on median market betas).[9] The descriptive statistics include the 25th percentile, median, and 75th percentile MB ratios for the sample as a whole and for each industry, listed in ascending order of the median MB ratio. The median MB ratio for the 69,810 firm-years in this sample is 1.91. These data reveal substantial variation in MB ratios across industries and within industries during this period. The descriptive statistics on MB and other ratios across industries and years in Appendix D also reveal substantial variation in MB ratios.

The differences in industry median MB ratios in Exhibit 14.5 likely relate, in part, to differences in competitive conditions driving differences in growth and ROCE relative to R_E as well as differences in applicable accounting principles across firms and time. Economically, in an industry that can be characterized as mature and competitive, the median firm will likely generate ROCE that is close to R_E and will not likely generate unusually high rates of growth. Such firms tend to have median MB ratios closer to 1. For example, firms in mature competitive industries such as textiles, insurance, hotels, wholesalers of durables, primary metals, real estate, metal products, airlines, banks, and paper and wood products tend to have MB ratios that are lower than the sample average.

With respect to accounting, the assets of firms in some of these industries—particularly banks and insurers—are primarily investments in financial assets, some of which appear on the balance sheet at fair value; thus, MB ratios are closer to 1. In contrast, some of the industries with relatively high MB ratios are more likely to have off-balance-sheet assets and shareholders' equity. For example, the tobacco industry contains firms with significant off-balance-sheet brand equity and the chemical industry includes pharmaceutical firms, which expense R&D expenditures in the year incurred. The balance sheet understates the economic value of key resources in these industries. These industries have MB ratios considerably in excess of 1.

Empirical Research Results on the Predictive Power of MB Ratios

Several empirical studies have found that MB ratios are fairly stable, mean reverting slowly over time, and that MB ratios are reliable predictors of future growth in book value and

[9] To compute these descriptive statistics on market-to-book value ratios, we deleted firm-years with negative book value of equity. We also deleted firm-year observations in the top 1 percent of the distribution as potential outliers with undue influence on the descriptive statistics.

EXHIBIT 14.5

Descriptive Statistics on Market-to-Book Ratios, 1998–2007
Industries Sorted by Median Market-to-Book Ratio

Industry:	25th Percentile	Median	75th Percentile
Full Sample on Compustat (N = 69,810 firm-years)*	1.17	1.91	3.52
Industry:			
Textiles	0.49	0.88	1.33
Insurers	0.90	1.24	1.72
Hotels	0.77	1.24	2.10
Wholesalers—Durables	0.80	1.31	2.35
Primary Metals	0.77	1.35	2.16
Real Estate	0.81	1.36	2.80
Metal Products	0.91	1.43	2.35
Transportation by Air	1.04	1.54	2.96
Paper	1.07	1.54	2.33
Depository Institutions	1.15	1.55	2.09
Lumber and Wood Products	0.91	1.57	2.42
Personal Services	0.86	1.70	3.12
Wholesalers—Nondurables	0.99	1.71	3.06
Restaurants	0.93	1.72	3.16
Utilities	1.34	1.75	2.34
Retailers—Home Furniture, Furnishings and Equipment	0.86	1.76	3.32
Retailers—General Merchandise	0.86	1.80	3.31
Grocery Stores	0.98	1.82	3.07
Transportation Equipment	1.12	1.83	3.19
Forestry	1.28	1.91	2.69
Motion Pictures	1.08	1.98	3.93
Amusements and Recreation	1.04	1.99	3.49
Retailers—Apparel	1.23	2.00	3.53
Printing and Publishing	1.18	2.00	3.56
Electronic and Electrical Equipment	1.24	2.08	3.79
Food Products	1.26	2.11	3.95
Health Services	1.23	2.12	3.70
Industrial and Commercial Machinery and Computer Equipment	1.27	2.12	3.78
Oil and Gas Extraction	1.35	2.14	3.46
Petroleum Refining	1.52	2.16	3.01
Security and Commodity Brokers	1.28	2.20	4.75
Communications	1.37	2.40	4.77
Instruments and Related Products	1.46	2.54	4.49
Business Services	1.44	2.75	5.61
Metal Mining	1.47	2.84	4.95
Chemicals	1.88	3.43	6.53
Tobacco	2.69	5.52	14.43

* To compute these descriptive statistics on market-to-book value ratios, we deleted firm-years with negative book value of equity. We also deleted firm-year observations in the top 1 percent of the distribution as potential outliers with undue influence on the descriptive statistics.

expected future ROCE (implying that ROCE also mean reverts slowly).[10] For example, Victor Bernard grouped roughly 1,900 firms into ten portfolios each year between 1972 and 1981 based on their MB ratios. He then computed the mean ROCE for each portfolio in the formation year and for each of the ten subsequent years. Exhibit 14.6 summarizes a portion of Bernard's results, grouping firms in the lowest three MB portfolios, middle four MB portfolios, and highest three MB portfolios.[11]

The data in Exhibit 14.6 indicate that firms with the highest MB ratios tend to have the highest ROCEs through Year +10 and firms with the lowest MB ratios tend to have the lowest ROCEs through Year +10. The results from the Bernard study also indicate that firms with the highest MB ratios have the highest growth rates in book value of equity through Year +10 and firms with the lowest MB ratios have the lowest growth rates through Year +10. In addition, the results in the Bernard study indicate (although it is not apparent from the summary of results in Exhibit 14.6) that the predictive power of MB ratios for future ROCEs tends to diminish as the horizon lengthens. In Year +10, for example, there is relatively little difference in ROCEs across firms in the third through ninth MB portfolios, as these firms experience ROCEs that tended to converge to 14 percent during Bernard's sample period. These results are consistent with the steady mean reversion in ROCEs over time, consistent with movement toward competitive equilibrium.

EXHIBIT 14.6

The Relation between MB Ratios, Future ROCE, and Future Book Value Growth

		Median ROCE for Year:			
MB Portfolio	**Mean MB Ratio**	**0**	**+1**	**+5**	**+10**
Low	0.67	0.11	0.09	0.12	0.12
Medium	1.15	0.11	0.13	0.14	0.14
High	2.65	0.10	0.17	0.16	0.20

		Cumulative Percent Increase in Book Value through Year:			
MB Portfolio	**Mean MB Ratio**	**0**	**+1**	**+5**	**+10**
Low	0.67	0%	15%	54%	190%
Medium	1.15	0%	15%	69%	204%
High	2.65	0%	21%	139%	394%

[10] Victor L. Bernard, "Accounting-Based Valuation Methods, Determinants of Market-to-Book Ratios and Implications for Financial Statement Analysis," *Working Paper*, University of Michigan (1993); Jane A. Ou and Stephen H. Penman, "Financial Statement Analysis and the Evaluation of Market-to-Book Ratios," *Working Paper*, Columbia University (1995); Stephen H. Penman, "The Articulation of Price-Earnings Ratios and Market-to-Book Ratios and the Evaluation of Growth," *Journal of Accounting Research*, Vol. 34, No. 2 (Autumn 1996), pp. 235–259; William H. Beaver and Stephen G. Ryan, "Biases and Lags in Book Value and Their Effects on the Ability of the Book-to-Market Ratio to Predict Book Return on Equity," *Journal of Accounting Research*, Vol. 38, No. 1 (Spring 2000), pp. 127–149.

[11] To reduce the effects of survivorship bias, Bernard included firms that did not survive the entire ten-year future horizon and included any gain or loss on the cessation of the firm (from bankruptcy, takeover, or liquidation) in the final year ROCE.

PRICE-EARNINGS AND VALUE-EARNINGS RATIOS

As noted in Chapter 13, the capital markets devote enormous amounts of time and energy to forecasting and analyzing firms' earnings. Therefore, it is no surprise that the market multiple that receives most frequent use and attention is the PE ratio. Analysts' reports and the financial press make frequent references to PE ratios. *The Wall Street Journal* reports PE ratios as part of the daily coverage of stock prices and trading activity. The capital markets increasingly evaluate ratios that integrate the PE ratio with expected future earnings growth to capture explicitly the links between price, profitability, and growth.

This section begins by describing the theoretical model for computing VE ratios and then describes computing and using PE ratios from a practical perspective. It then discusses the strict assumptions implied by PE ratios and describes the conditions in which PE ratios may not capture appropriately the theoretical relation between value and earnings for most firms and the difficulties encountered in reconciling actual PE ratios with those indicated by the theoretical value-earnings model. This section also incorporates the role of earnings growth and examines PEG ratios. The section concludes by describing empirical data on PE ratios, the predictive power of PE ratios, and the empirical evidence on the articulation between PE ratios and MB ratios.

A Model for the Value-Earnings Ratio

The VE ratio is computed as the value of common shareholders' equity divided by earnings for a single period. The previous chapter described how to determine common equity value as a function of present value of expected *future* earnings and the residual income model. In the residual income model, we use clean surplus accounting and measure future earnings as expected future comprehensive income (that is, income that includes all of the income to common shareholders). Thus, in theory, the analyst should measure the VE ratio as the value of common equity divided by the next period's expected comprehensive income. This way, the VE ratio achieves consistent alignment of *perspective* (numerator and denominator both forward-looking) and *measurement* (numerator and denominator both based on comprehensive income).

If one has already computed firm value using the forecasting and valuation models developed in the last four chapters, computing the VE ratio is a simple matter of division. For example, in the preceding section and in prior chapters, we estimated PepsiCo's common shareholders' equity value to be \$128,945.0 million at the end of 2008. We also projected that Year +1 comprehensive income will equal net income available for common shareholders, which will equal \$5,941.9 million. Thus, we can compute the VE ratio for PepsiCo at the end of 2008 as follows:

$$V_0/E_1 = \$128{,}945.0 \text{ million}/\$5{,}941.9 \text{ million} = 21.7$$

Or equivalently, on a per-share basis as:

$$\begin{aligned} Vps_0/Eps_1 &= (\$128{,}945.0 \text{ million}/1{,}553 \text{ million shares})/(\$5{,}941.9 \text{ million}/1{,}553 \text{ million shares}) \\ &= \$83.03/\$3.83 = 21.7. \end{aligned}$$

We also can derive the VE ratio from the VB ratio determined using the residual income model in the previous section. For this derivation, we employ an algebraic step to derive the firm's VE ratio from the firm's VB ratio as follows:

$$V_0/E_1 = V_0/BV_0 \times BV_0/E_1 = V_0/BV_0 \times (1/ROCE_1)$$

This formula shows that the same factors that drive the VB ratio (V_0/BV_0) also drive the VE ratio. In fact, the model shows that the VE ratio should be a multiple of the VB ratio, where the multiple is the inverse of ROCE. However, the VE ratio also makes an additional simplifying and restrictive assumption: that value can be summarized by one-period-ahead ROCE. A consequence of this assumption is that VE ratios vary *inversely* with expected future ROCE. Holding VB ratios constant, a firm with a temporarily high level of expected ROCE next period will have a temporarily low VE ratio, and vice versa.

Using this approach, we can derive PepsiCo's VE ratio from the VB ratio we computed in the previous section, as follows:

$$
\begin{aligned}
V_0/E_1 &= V_0/BV_0 \times BV_0/E_1 = V_0/BV_0 \times (1/ROCE_1) \\
&= (\$128{,}945.0 \text{ million}/\$12{,}203.0 \text{ million}) \times (\$12{,}203.0 \text{ million}/\$5{,}941.9 \text{ million}) \\
&= 10.567 \times 2.054 \\
&= 10.567 \times (1/0.487) \\
&= 21.7
\end{aligned}
$$

Thus, PepsiCo's VE ratio should equal 21.7. We convert PepsiCo's VB ratio of 10.567 into the VE ratio by multiplying by $1/ROCE_1$, which we project will be the inverse of 48.7 percent.

Notice that we derived the VE ratio simply from the computation that PepsiCo's value is equal to $128,945.0 million, which is based on specific forecasts of PepsiCo's future earnings. Obviously, using value to compute a VE ratio will not provide any new information about PepsiCo's value. So what is the point of computing a VE ratio?

The VE ratio provides the analyst with a theoretically correct benchmark to evaluate the firm's PE ratio. We can compare PepsiCo's VE ratio of 21.7 to PepsiCo's PE ratio to assess the market value of PepsiCo shares. This comparison is equivalent to comparing V to P (that is, value to price). We compute the PE ratio for PepsiCo as of the end of 2008 using our forecast that Year +1 earnings (comprehensive income available to common shareholders) will be $5,941.9 million as follows:

$$
\begin{aligned}
P_0/E_{+1} &= \textit{Price per share}_0/\textit{Earnings per share}_{+1} \\
&= \$54.77 \text{ per share}/(\$5{,}941.9 \text{ million}/1{,}553 \text{ million shares}) \\
&= \$54.77/\$3.83 \\
&= 14.3
\end{aligned}
$$

Thus, at the end of 2008, PepsiCo shares traded at a multiple of 14.3 times the Year +1 earnings forecast. PepsiCo's VE ratio of 21.7 is 52 percent greater than PepsiCo's PE ratio of 14.3 at the end of 2008, consistent with our prior estimates of PepsiCo's value.

With the theoretically correct VE ratio, we also can project VE ratios for other firms after we have made any necessary adjustments to capture the other firms' fundamental characteristics of profitability, growth, and risk. In addition, with the theoretically correct VE ratio, we have a benchmark to gauge other firms' PE ratios to assess whether the market is under- or overpricing their shares. In the next section, we discuss the practical advantages and disadvantages in using PE ratios as shortcut valuation metrics.

Price-Earnings Ratios

As a practical matter, analysts, the financial press, and financial databases commonly measure PE ratios as current period share price divided by reported (historical) earnings per share for the most recent prior fiscal year or the most recent four quarters (sometimes referred to as the *lagged* or *trailing-twelve-months earnings per share*).[12] *The Wall Street Journal* and financial data websites such as Yahoo! Finance commonly compute PE ratios this way. With this approach, the PE ratio for PepsiCo as of the end of 2008 is equal to price per $\text{share}_{2008}/\text{earnings per share}_{2008} = \$54.77/\$3.26 = 16.8$. Thus, at the end of 2008, PepsiCo shares traded at a PE multiple of 16.8 times 2008 earnings per share.[13]

The common approach to compute the PE ratio by dividing market price per share by earnings per share for the most recent year is practical because analysts can readily observe price and earnings per share for most firms. This approach is efficient because it does not require the analyst to produce a computation of value or a forecast of earnings. However, this common approach creates a logical misalignment for valuation purposes because it divides *historical* earnings into share price, which reflects the present value of *future* earnings. If historical earnings contain unusual or nonrecurring gains or losses that are not expected to persist in future earnings, the analyst should normalize the reported historical earnings by removing these effects to compute a PE ratio that reflects earnings that are likely to persist in the future. Chapter 9 describes techniques to identify elements of income that are unusual and nonrecurring, adjust reported earnings to eliminate their effects, and thereby measure recurring, persistent earnings.

As an alternative approach to create a more logical alignment of price and earnings, the analyst can compute the "*forward PE ratio*" by dividing share price by a forecast of future earnings per share (for example, analysts' consensus forecast of expected earnings per share one year ahead). A PE ratio based on expected future earnings, however, requires the analyst to forecast future earnings (or have access to another analyst's forecast). Thus, the reliability of a forward PE ratio depends on the reliability of the earnings forecast. Earnings forecast errors will distort forward PE ratios. In addition, as discussed previously for VE ratios, PE ratios will vary inversely with transitory earnings components. If the analysts uses trailing or forward earnings that are temporarily increased by transitory gains or temporarily decreased by transitory losses, the PE ratio will be temporarily biased down or up, respectively.

Recall that in the preceding subsection, we computed the forward PE ratio for PepsiCo as of the end of 2008 using our forecast that Year +1 earnings (comprehensive income available to common shareholders) will be \$5,941.9 million as follows: price per $\text{share}_0/\text{earnings per share}_{+1} = \$54.77$ per share/(\$5,941.9 million/1,553 million shares) $= \$54.77/\$3.83 = 14.3$. Thus, at the end of 2008, PepsiCo shares traded at a forward PE multiple of 14.3 times the Year +1 earnings forecast. PepsiCo's VE ratio of 21.7 is 52 percent greater than PepsiCo's forward PE ratio of 14.3 at the end of 2008, consistent with our prior estimates of PepsiCo's value.[14]

Notice that we derived the PE ratio simply by dividing PepsiCo's market share price by earnings per share of the past year or by our forecasts of PepsiCo's future earnings per

---

[12] In theory, to be consistent with clean surplus accounting and residual income valuation, the denominator should be based on comprehensive income per share. However, analysts, the financial press, and financial databases rarely compute PE ratios based on comprehensive income per share, in part because (1) U.S. GAAP does not yet require reporting comprehensive income on a per-share basis and (2) the other comprehensive income items are usually unrealized gains and losses that are not likely to be a permanent component of income each period. We follow traditional practice in this chapter and compute PE ratios using reported earnings figures.

[13] The common approach to computing PE ratios also can be slightly distorted by differences in the number of shares outstanding at year-end that the market uses to compute share price versus the weighted average number of shares outstanding used to compute earnings per share under U.S. GAAP. If we compute PepsiCo's PE ratio using amounts in millions rather than per-share amounts, we obtain a PE ratio of 16.5 [= \$85,058.0 million/(net income of \$5,142 million − \$1 million preferred dividends)]. This PE ratio is slightly lower than the PE ratio of 16.8 based on per share amounts because PepsiCo reports earnings per share based on the weighted average number of common shares outstanding during the year (as required by U.S. GAAP) rather than the number of shares outstanding at year-end.

[14] In this case, our forecasts of net income and comprehensive income for PepsiCo in Year +1 are the same; so the PE ratio using earnings per share is equal to that using comprehensive income per share.

share. Obviously, using price to compute a PE ratio will not provide any new information about PepsiCo's share *value.* So what is the point of computing a PE ratio?

PE ratios are practical tools used by analysts interested in valuation shortcuts. In some circumstances, analysts need to react with timely ballpark estimates of valuation, and PE ratios provide a quick and efficient way to estimate firm value as a multiple of earnings. Analysts commonly assess benchmark PE ratios that they expect a firm to have based on past PE ratios for that firm, on industry-average PE ratios, or on comparable firms' PE ratios. Analysts use benchmarks such as these to project a firm's PE ratio quickly, using one-period earnings as a common denominator for relative valuations rather than engaging in the extensive computations necessary to determine the correct VE ratio to assess whether the market has priced the firm's shares appropriately.

Analysts also use PE ratios as potentially informative benchmarks to compare valuations across companies or to project the valuations of other companies. For example, we could compare PepsiCo's PE ratio to the PE ratios of Coca-Cola, Cadbury Schweppes, or other beverage companies. We also might use PepsiCo's PE ratio to project valuations for these beverage companies or to project valuations for privately held firms or divisions of companies. Investment bankers use comparable companies' PE ratios, for example, to benchmark reasonable ranges of share prices for IPOs (initial public offerings).

PE ratios have the advantage of speed and efficiency, but they are not necessarily precise valuation estimates. Therefore, when using PE ratios, the analyst must be careful to adjust them to match the fundamental characteristics of different companies. For example, PepsiCo's PE ratio should differ from Coca-Cola's insofar as the fundamental characteristics of profitability, growth, and risk differ across the two firms. Such differences might arise, for example, because PepsiCo derives a major portion of earnings from the snack food business and Coca-Cola does not. Coca-Cola derives more of its earnings from international beverage sales than does PepsiCo. These and other factors cause the profitability, growth, and risk of PepsiCo and Coca-Cola to differ and therefore cause their PE ratios to differ. We will describe PE ratio differences in more detail after we describe the conceptual basis for PE ratios.

PE Ratios Project Firm Value from Permanent Earnings

What should a firm's PE ratio be? What is an appropriate valuation multiple for a firm's earnings? We have seen that in theory, the firm's PE ratio should equal the firm's VE ratio. However, if the analyst has not computed value to determine the VE ratio and wants to use a shortcut PE ratio instead, what is the correct PE ratio to use?

In projecting firm value using a simple PE ratio (that is, one that uses only one period of earnings and ignores earnings growth), the analyst imposes a *very strong assumption* on the earnings for a single period: the analyst treats these earnings (whether trailing earnings or a one-period-ahead forecast) as the beginning amount of a permanent stream of earnings, valued as a perpetuity. In essence, the PE assumes that one year of earnings is sufficient information to value a firm and to determine share price. Conceptually, suppose the firm's common shareholders' equity value equals its market value, the firm's earnings will be constant in the future, and the firm's investors expect a rate of return R_E. Under these restrictive conditions, we can value the firm's common equity using the perpetuity model based on one-year-ahead earnings (denoted as E_1) as follows:

$$V_0 = P_0 = E_1/R_E$$

Rearranged slightly, under these assumptions, the firm's VE and PE ratios are:

$$V_0/E_1 = P_0/E_1 = 1/R_E$$

Thus, strictly speaking, the PE multiple assumes that firm value is the present value of a constant stream of expected future earnings, which is discounted at a constant expected future discount rate. Under these conditions, the analyst can value the firm using simply a multiple of one-period-ahead earnings and the PE ratio of the firm is simply the inverse of the discount rate.

To illustrate this model, assume that the market expects the firm to generate earnings of \$700 next period and requires a 14 percent return on equity capital. The market value of the firm at the beginning of the next period should be \$5,000 (= \$700/0.14). Note that the inverse of the 14 percent discount rate translates into a PE ratio of 7.14 (= 1/0.14). Thus, \$700 times 7.14 equals \$5,000.

The simple PE ratio assumes that future earnings will be permanent, which is not realistic for most firms. Most firms' earnings are not expected to remain constant; most firms' earnings grow. Not surprisingly, such strict assumptions match the fundamental characteristics of very few firms. We have already seen that such strict assumptions do not fit PepsiCo. Under the assumptions that PepsiCo's earnings will be constant in the future and that PepsiCo's constant future ROCE will equal the 8.50 percent cost of equity capital, PepsiCo's PE ratio should be 11.8 (= 1/0.085). This PE ratio is far below the theoretically derived VE ratio of 21.7 for PepsiCo.

Descriptive Data on PE Ratios

Exhibit 14.7 includes descriptive statistics on forward-looking PE ratios (share price to one-year-ahead earnings before extraordinary items: P_t/E_{t+1}) for the same 37 industries described in Exhibit 14.5 (MB ratios) and Exhibit 11.3 (market betas) during 1998–2007. These data represent a broad cross-sectional sample of 33,671 firm-years drawn from the Compustat database, excluding all firm-years with negative earnings.[15] Exhibit 14.7 lists the industries in ascending order of the median PE ratios. To describe the industry-wide variation in PE ratios, Exhibit 14.7 also includes the 25th percentile PE ratio and the 75th percentile PE ratio for each industry. Descriptive statistics on PE and other ratios across industries and years also appear in Appendix D.

These descriptive data indicate substantial differences in median PE ratios across industries during 1998–2007. The firms in the petroleum refining, metals, insurance, and oil and gas extraction industries experienced the lowest median PE ratios during the period, whereas firms in the business services, motion pictures, and instruments and related products industries experienced the highest median PE ratios. These data also depict wide variation in PE ratios across firms in each industry. For example, most of these 37 industries experienced wide differences between the 25th percentile and the 75th percentile PE ratio during 1998–2007. With only a few exceptions, in most industries, the 75th percentile PE ratio was more than double the 25th percentile PE ratio.[16]

What Factors Cause PE Ratios to Differ across Firms?

As noted earlier, the same set of economic factors that can cause firms' MB ratios to differ also can cause PE ratios to differ across firms. The primary drivers of differences in PE ratios across firms are the fundamental drivers of value: risk, profitability, and growth. In addition to economic factors, differences across firms in accounting methods and accounting principles and differences in earnings across time also can drive differences in PE ratios. We describe the effects of each of these determinants of PE ratios in the following sections,

[15] It does not make sense to compute PE ratios on the basis of negative earnings. PE ratios assume that earnings are permanent; negative earnings cannot be permanent.

[16] The analyst must be careful with PE ratios because they are sensitive to earnings that are near zero. Firms with earnings that are positive but temporarily very low will experience PE ratios that are temporarily very high.

EXHIBIT 14.7

Descriptive Statistics on Forward Price-Earnings Ratios (P_t/E_{t+1}), 1998–2007
Industries Sorted by Median Forward PE Ratio

Industry:	25th Percentile	Median	75th Percentile
Full Sample on Compustat (N = 33,671 firm-years)*	10.23	15.11	23.27
Industry:			
Petroleum Refining	6.36	8.87	14.23
Metals	5.89	10.66	17.35
Insurers	8.25	11.17	15.93
Oil and Gas Extraction	7.61	11.77	21.23
Tobacco	9.51	12.06	14.49
Transportation by Air	7.99	12.17	20.61
Textiles	6.58	12.42	18.56
Wholesalers—Durables	8.07	12.82	19.85
Forestry	6.85	12.95	43.53
Real Estate	7.16	13.05	24.71
Transportation Equipment	9.45	13.15	19.08
Metal Products	9.31	13.84	21.31
Depository Institutions	10.81	13.96	18.05
Wholesalers—Nondurables	8.24	14.06	21.14
Metal Mining	9.15	14.17	27.99
Utilities	11.41	14.58	19.10
Retailers—Apparel	11.32	14.59	20.43
Restaurants	11.08	15.82	24.57
Retailers—Home Furniture, Furnishings and Equipment	10.43	15.87	24.34
Health Services	10.67	16.03	24.10
Industrial and Commercial Machinery and Computer Equipment	10.93	16.23	27.98
Hotels	9.21	16.25	23.34
Paper	10.98	16.39	22.85
Amusements and Recreation	10.09	16.40	26.41
Grocery Stores	12.05	16.45	24.57
Lumber and Wood Products	10.20	16.64	26.41
Security and Commodity Brokers	10.79	16.76	23.97
Personal Services	12.32	16.85	25.14
Printing and Publishing	11.28	17.01	24.28
Food Products	11.64	17.07	25.23
Communications	10.98	17.19	30.86
Retailers—General Merchandise	12.42	18.31	25.58
Chemicals	12.69	18.50	29.00
Electronic and Electrical Equipment	11.53	18.57	32.01
Instruments and Related Products	12.69	19.82	31.22
Motion Pictures	11.76	20.64	36.49
Business Services	13.81	22.28	36.49

* To compute these descriptive statistics on price-earnings ratios, we divided firm value (computed as year-end closing price times number of shares outstanding) by one-year-ahead net income. We deleted firm-years with negative one-year-ahead net income.

saving growth for last because we will expand on the role of growth in determining PE ratios.

Risk and the Cost of Capital. As the previous discussion points out, firms with equivalent amounts of earnings but different levels of risk and therefore different costs of equity capital will experience different PE ratios (and different VE ratios). All else equal, a riskier firm will experience a lower market value and PE ratio.

Profitability. A firm with competitive advantages will be able to earn ROCE that exceeds R_E. To the extent that the firm can sustain these competitive advantages, the persistence over time of the degree to which ROCE exceeds R_E will increase, thereby increasing the PE ratio relative to similar firms that do not have sustainable competitive advantages. Thus, both the magnitude and persistence of the difference between ROCE and R_E will increase PE ratios across firms.

Accounting Differences. In addition to economic factors, firms' PE ratios may differ for a variety of accounting reasons, including the periodic nature of earnings measurement, and differences in accounting methods and principles. Some firms select accounting methods that are conservative with respect to income recognition and asset measurement (for example, LIFO for inventories during periods of rising input prices and accelerated depreciation of fixed assets). Some firms invest in projects for which accounting principles are conservative. For example, firms may make substantial expenditures on intangible activities that must be expensed under conservative accounting principles, leading to economic assets that are off-balance-sheet, such as successful R&D, brand equity, or human capital. The effects of accounting methods and principles on reported earnings and PE ratios will likely change over the life of the firm. All else equal, conservative accounting will reduce reported earnings early in the life of the firm (for example, when accelerated depreciation charges are high or R&D is being expensed), thereby increasing the PE ratio. Ironically, later in the life of the firm, after the investments have been completely expensed, reported earnings will be higher and PE ratios will be lower.

Accounting Measures Earnings in Annual Periods. Firms' PE ratios will be significantly different when one-period earnings are unusually high or low and therefore not representative of persistent earnings. For example, if earnings include an unusual loss that will not persist, the firm's PE ratio will be unusually high. The transitory nature of a single period of accounting earnings can cause PE ratios to be more volatile than the long-run expectations of earnings warrant. In particular, if the analyst uses PE ratios based on trailing-twelve-months earnings that include nonrecurring gains or losses that are not expected to persist, the PE ratios will be artificially volatile. The variability in PE ratios will be inverse to the unusual and nonrecurring items in income. (That is, nonrecurring gains will drive PE ratios down temporarily, whereas nonrecurring losses will drive PE ratios up temporarily.)

Continuing the simple example introduced earlier, assume that the analyst expects the firm to generate earnings of $600 next period instead of $700 because the firm will recognize a nonrecurring $100 restructuring charge. Because this charge is nonrecurring (not a permanent change in earnings), the market price should fall to roughly $4,900 (= $5,000 − $100) in the no-growth scenario and the PE ratio for that period will be 8.17 (= $4,900/$600) instead of 7.14 (= $5,000/$700). Conversely, if the current period's earnings exceed their expected permanent level, the PE ratio will be lower than normal.

The analyst must assess whether the lower or higher level of earnings for the period (and therefore higher or lower PE ratio) represents a transitory event or a change to a new level of permanent earnings. If the analyst expects that the decrease in earnings from $700 to $600 will be permanent, the market price (assuming no change in risk or growth) should decrease to $4,286 (= $600/0.14). Thus, the PE ratio remains the same at 7.14 (= 1/0.14).

To illustrate the effects of accounting differences on PE ratios across firms, consider the historical data in the following table, which includes PE ratios (computed as year-end share price over trailing earnings per share) for PepsiCo and Coca-Cola for 2000 and 2001.

		PE Ratio	Price per Share	Earnings per Share
2000:	PepsiCo	31.9	$46.25	$1.45
	Coca-Cola	69.3	$60.94	$0.88
2001:	PepsiCo	34.2	$46.18	$1.35
	Coca-Cola	29.5	$47.15	$1.60

Considered at face value, the PE ratios for PepsiCo and Coca-Cola in 2000 indicate that the market valued Coca-Cola's earnings at a multiple of 69.3, more than twice PepsiCo's earnings multiple of 31.9, implying that Coca-Cola had lower cost of capital, higher growth, and/or greater profitability than PepsiCo. To the contrary, however, Coca-Cola recognized a large restructuring charge in income in 2000, driving EPS down to only $0.88, thereby temporarily inflating Coca-Cola's PE ratio. Thus, the big jump in Coca-Cola's PE ratio occurred largely because earnings temporarily declined that year and did not reflect the market's expectations for Coca-Cola's long-term earnings. In 2001, both firms reported earnings closer to normal levels and their PE ratios were quite similar.

Growth. All else equal, market values and PE ratios will be greater for firms that the market expects will generate greater earnings growth with future investments in abnormally profitable projects. In the next section, we discuss techniques that analysts use to incorporate earnings growth into PE ratios.

Incorporating Earnings Growth into PE Ratios

Analysts commonly modify the PE ratio to incorporate earnings growth. In this section, we describe and apply two related approaches to include expected future earnings growth in the computation of the PE ratio: (1) the perpetuity-with-growth approach and (2) the price-earnings-growth approach.[17]

The Perpetuity-with-Growth Approach. The perpetuity-with-growth approach assumes that the firm's current period earnings will grow at a constant rate g. Therefore, the firm can be valued as the present value of a permanent stream of future earnings that will grow at constant rate g. In this case, we can express forward VE and forward PE ratios as perpetuity-with-growth models as follows:

$$V_0 = P_0 = \frac{E_0 \times (1 + g)}{(R_E - g)} = \frac{E_1}{(R_E - g)}, \quad so\ \frac{V_0}{E_1} = \frac{P_0}{E_1} = \frac{1}{(R_E - g)}$$

To continue the illustration, assume that the firm generated $666.67 in earnings in the current period. The market expects the firms' earnings to grow 5 percent next year and each year thereafter, so that Year +1 earnings will be $700. The model suggests that the forward PE ratio incorporating growth should be 11.11 [= 1.0/(0.14 − 0.05)] and market value should be $7,778 (= $700 × 11.11). The present value of the expected future growth in earnings adds $2,778 (= $7,778 − $5,000) to the value of the firm.

Note that the above expression describes forward VE and forward PE ratios because they use E_1 (one-year-ahead earnings). As mentioned earlier, PE ratios are commonly measured in practice using historical earnings. If current period (historical) earnings are expected to

[17] In recent research, James Ohlson and Beate Juettner-Nauroth develop a theoretical model for the price-earnings ratio that incorporates short-term and long-term earnings per share growth. The model is a promising addition to the earnings-based valuation literature, providing new insights into the relation between value, earnings, and growth. See James Ohlson and Beate Juettner-Nauroth, "Expected EPS and EPS Growth as Determinants of Value," *Review of Accounting Studies* (June–September 2005), pp. 349–365.

grow at the constant rate g and if the VE and PE ratios are expressed as multiples of current period (historical) earnings (E_0):

$$V_0 = P_0 = \frac{E_0 \times (1 + g)}{(R_E - g)} = \frac{E_1}{(R_E - g)}, \quad so \ \frac{V_0}{E_0} = \frac{P_0}{E_0} = \frac{1}{(R_E - g)}$$

Continuing with the illustration, the VE and PE ratios based on current period earnings would then be 11.667 [= $(1+g)/(R_E - g)$ = 1.05/(0.14 − 0.05)]. Note that using this VE and PE ratio will lead to market value for the firm of $7,778 (= $666.67 × 11.667). This is the same market value as we determined using the forward VE and PE ratios.

PE ratios are particularly sensitive to the growth rate. If the growth rate in our illustration becomes 6 percent instead of 5 percent, the forward PE ratio becomes 12.50 [= 1.0/(0.14 − 0.06)] and the market value becomes $8,750 (= $700 × 12.50). The sensitivity occurs because the model assumes that the firm will grow at the specified growth rate in perpetuity. Competition, new discoveries or technologies, or other factors eventually erode rapid growth rates in an industry. In using the constant growth version of the PE ratio, the analyst should select a long-run equilibrium growth rate in earnings.

This expression for the VE and PE ratio underscores the joint importance of risk and growth in valuation. Given the relation between expected return (R_E) and risk, the VE and PE ratio should be inversely related to risk. Holding earnings and growth constant, higher risk levels should translate into lower PE and VE ratios, and vice versa. Risk-averse investors will not pay as much for a higher risk security as for a lower risk security with identical expected earnings and growth. In contrast, VE and PE should relate positively to growth. Holding earnings and R_E constant, firms with higher expected long-run growth rates in earnings should experience higher VE and PE ratios.

With respect to our valuation of PepsiCo at the end of 2008, we assumed that PepsiCo would experience a long-run growth rate of 3.0 percent beginning in Year +6 and beyond. If we assume that PepsiCo will experience a 3.0 percent constant growth rate in earnings beginning in Year +1, using the perpetuity-with-growth approach, we calculate the forward PE ratio for PepsiCo as follows:

$$\frac{P_0}{E_0} = \frac{1}{(R_E - g)} = \frac{1}{(0.085 - 0.030)} = 18.182$$

Clearly, incorporating growth makes a big difference in PepsiCo's forward PE ratio [as compared to the PE ratio of 11.8 (= 1/0.085) that ignores growth]. Assuming that PepsiCo's earnings will grow at 3.0 percent per year beginning in Year +1, this PE with growth ratio would value PepsiCo shares at a multiple of 18.182 times the Year +1 earnings forecast. This PE ratio is still less than the theoretically correct VE ratio of 21.7, however, because it does not take into account our forecasts projecting that PepsiCo earnings will grow at an average rate of 10.4 percent during Year +1 to Year +5. Thus, this PE ratio understates the value of PepsiCo's expected earnings growth during those years.

The Price-Earnings-Growth Approach. An alternative ad hoc approach to incorporate growth into PE ratios has emerged from practice in recent years. Using this approach, analysts' divide the PE ratio by the expected medium-term earnings growth rate (expressed as a percent). (Some analysts use the expected earnings growth rate over a three- to five-year horizon.) This approach produces the so-called PEG ratio seen with increasing frequency in practice. Analysts compute the PEG ratio as follows:

$$PEG_0 = (Price\ per\ share_0 / Earnings\ per\ share_0)/(g \times 100)$$

Analysts and the financial press use the PEG ratio as a rule of thumb to assess share price relative to earnings and expected future earnings growth. Although there is little theoretical foundation for this rule of thumb (which tends to vary among analysts), proponents of PEG ratios generally assert that firms should have PEG ratios equal to 1.0, indicating that market price fairly reflects expected earnings and growth.

This rule of thumb implies the following value model for a VEG ratio under the following set of assumptions:

- The firm's earnings behave as a perpetuity with growth.
- The firm's earnings generate an ROCE equivalent to R_E.
- All of the firm's growth arises from reinvesting all of its earnings.
- All of the reinvested earnings generate an ROCE equivalent to R_E, so the firm's earnings growth rate is equivalent to R_E.

Under this set of restrictive assumptions, the VEG ratio follows. [For notation, assume that $(g \times 100) = G = R_E$.]

$$\begin{aligned} VEG_0 &= (Value\ per\ share_0 / Earnings\ per\ share_0)/(g \times 100) \\ &= V_0/E_1/G = 1/R_E/R_E = 1 \end{aligned}$$

Alternatively, note that the VEG ratio is mathematically equivalent to a simple valuation model that values shares as next year's earnings per share multiplied by the growth rate times 100 (that is, $V_0 = E_1 \times G$).

Using the rule of thumb that VEG ratios should equal 1, proponents assert that market prices for firms with PEG ratios below 1 are underpriced given earnings and expected earnings growth and that market prices for firms with PEG ratios above 1 are overpriced relative to earnings and expected earnings growth. Proponents of PEG ratios argue that this heuristic provides a convenient means to rank stocks, taking into account one-year-ahead earnings and expected earnings growth.[18]

In Chapter 10, we assumed that PepsiCo would experience earnings growth of roughly 10.4 percent per year through Year +5. Using this growth rate assumption and the 2008 reported earnings per share, we compute PepsiCo's PEG ratio at the end of 2008 as follows:

$$\begin{aligned} PEG_{2008} &= (Price\ per\ share_{2008} / Earnings\ per\ share_{2008})/(g \times 100) \\ &= (\$54.77/\$3.26)/(0.104 \times 100) \\ &= 16.8/10.4 = 1.62 \end{aligned}$$

Thus, PepsiCo shares traded at the end of 2008 at a PEG ratio of 1.62. Based on the PEG heuristic, PepsiCo's PEG ratio of 1.62 suggests that the market price for PepsiCo shares reflect substantial *overpricing* of PepsiCo's earnings and expected earnings growth.

However, the PEG ratio heuristic does not take into account differences in risk and costs of equity capital across firms. For example, PepsiCo's PEG ratio seems high because it does not account for the fact that PepsiCo's expected future ROCE is significantly greater than PepsiCo's R_E because of PepsiCo's substantial off-balance-sheet brand equity. In addition, this heuristic does not take into account the fact that PepsiCo is likely to achieve this future earnings growth with relatively low risk. (PepsiCo's beta is 0.75.) The PEG ratio deserves considerable attention from researchers and practitioners so that its uses and limitations can be tested and understood.

---

[18] Mark Bradshaw (2002) demonstrates that sell-side analysts' target price estimates are highly correlated with valuation estimates based on the PEG model in "The Use of Target Prices to Justify Sell-Side Analysts' Stock Recommendations," *Accounting Horizons*, Vol. 16, No. 1 (March 2002), pp. 27–41.

PE Ratio Measurement Issues

Thus far, we have discussed a variety of different measurement issues for PE ratios. Forward-looking PE ratios divide share price by one-year-ahead earnings forecasts, which is theoretically more correct. However, at least two problems arise in using forward PE ratios. First, one-year-ahead earnings forecasts are not readily available for all firms. Second, the accuracy of the forecasts depends on the analysts' forecast assumptions, which can differ widely. Therefore, as noted earlier, in practice PE ratios are most commonly measured as share price divided by earnings per share for the most recent prior fiscal year or for the most recent four quarters. This is a sensible approach because historical earnings are observable and unique; however, computation of PE ratios using historic earnings introduces the potential for bias. To recap, the analyst should be aware of (at least) the following two types of measurement error:

1. *Growth.* Simple ratios of price over earnings do not explicitly consider firm-specific differences in long-term earnings growth. The price-earnings ratios described in prior sections provide mechanisms that incorporate growth into price-earnings multiples.
2. *Transitory earnings.* Past earnings are historical and may not be indicative of expected future "permanent" earnings levels. Insofar as historic earnings contain transitory gains or losses (or other elements that are not expected to recur), temporarily high or low earnings can cause the PE ratio to vary considerably. The analyst should cleanse the earnings figure of nonrecurring or unusual gains or losses.

In addition, the analyst must be aware of the potential bias in PE ratios because of differences in firms' dividend payouts. Dividends displace future earnings. A dividend paid in Year t reduces market price by the amount of the dividend, but the dividend is not subtracted from earnings. The dividend paid will cause future earnings to decline, all else equal, because the firm has paid out a portion of its resources to shareholders. Therefore, price should decline by the present value of the firm's forgone amount of expected future return on assets distributed as dividends. Thus, for dividend-paying firms, dividends cause a mismatch between current period price and lagged earnings. To eliminate this mismatch, the analyst should compute a PE ratio with growth for a dividend-paying firm as follows: $(P_t + D_t)/E_t = 1/(R_E - g)$.

Empirical Properties of PE Ratios

The theoretical models indicate that the PE ratio is related to R_E, the cost of equity capital, and g, the growth rate in future earnings. Several empirical studies have examined the relation between PE ratios, risk (measured using market beta), and growth (measured using realized prior growth rates or analysts' forecasts of future growth). These studies have found that approximately 50–70 percent of the variability in PE ratios across firms relates to risk and growth.[19]

PE Ratios as Predictors of Future Earnings Growth. Stephen Penman, a leading scholar in the relation between earnings, book values, and market values, studied the relation between PE ratios and changes in earnings per share for all firms on the Compustat database for 1968–1985.[20] For each year, Penman grouped firms into 20 portfolios based on the

[19] See William Beaver and Dale Morse, "What Determines Price-Earnings Ratios?," *Financial Analysts Journal* (July–August 1978), pp. 65–76; Paul Zarowin, "What Determines Earnings-Price Ratios: Revisited," *Journal of Accounting, Auditing and Finance* (Summer 1990), pp. 439–454.

[20] Stephen H. Penman, "The Articulation of Price-Earnings Ratios and Market-to-Book Ratios and the Evaluation of Growth," *Journal of Accounting Research* (Autumn 1996), pp. 235–259.

level of their PE ratios, computed using lagged earnings per share. He then computed the percentage change in earnings per share for the formation year and for each of the nine subsequent years. Penman then aggregated the results across years. The table below presents a subset of the aggregate results.

	Median Percentage Change in Earnings per Share in:				
PE Portfolio:	**Year 0**	**Year +1**	**Year +2**	**Year +3**	**Year +4**
High	3.9%	52.2%	17.5%	17.8%	15.0%
Medium	14.0%	11.8%	11.6%	13.7%	15.8%
Low	18.4%	4.8%	10.2%	12.3%	13.1%

The results for the portfolio formation year are consistent with transitory components in earnings in Year 0. Firms with high PE ratios experienced, on average, low percentage changes in earnings (and many experienced earnings declines) during the formation year relative to the preceding year. Firms with low PE ratios experienced high percentage changes in earnings during the formation year. The results for Year 1 after the formation year suggest a counterbalancing effect of the earnings change in the formation year. A low percentage increase (or decrease) in earnings is followed by a high percentage earnings increase for the high PE portfolios, and vice versa for the low PE portfolios.

The results for subsequent years reflect the tendency toward mean reversion in percentage earnings changes to a level in the midteens. This result is consistent with the data presented in Exhibit 14.6 for ROCE, where Victor Bernard observed a mean reversion in ROCE toward the midteens during his sample period. The mean reversion suggests systematic directional changes in earnings growth over time (that is, serial autocorrelation), but the reversion takes several years to occur.

Articulation of MB and PE Ratios. In the same research study, Penman also utilized the residual income valuation model and empirical data to examine the articulation between firms' PE and MB ratios.[21] Penman collected data from the CRSP and Compustat databases on roughly 2,574 firms during 1968–1985. For each sample year, Penman ranked and grouped these firms into 20 portfolios based on PE ratios. He also ranked and grouped the same firms each year into three MB ratio portfolios, classifying MB ratios below 0.90 as low, MB ratios above 1.10 as high, and MB ratios between 0.90 and 1.10 as normal.

Exhibit 14.8 presents a matrix summarizing a portion of the results from Penman's study. Exhibit 14.8 presents residual income figures after assuming a 10.0 percent cost of capital for all firm-years and after scaling by beginning-of-period book value of common equity (so that they are essentially residual ROCE figures). We denote current period residual income as CRI and future residual income one year ahead and six years ahead as FRI_1 and FRI_6, respectively.

Penman's research results generally support his predictions and shed light on the residual income conditions that cause MB ratios and PE ratios to covary. His results show that future residual income is substantially *higher* for *high* MB firms than for *low* MB firms. Examining future residual income across columns of the matrix, Penman's results show that MB ratios are positive predictors of future residual income, consistent with the results from Bernard in Exhibit 14.6. Examining the results across rows, high PE ratio firms tend to have current period residual income that is much *lower than* future residual income, suggesting that PE ratios for these firms are temporarily high because residual income is temporarily low. In contrast, firms with low PE ratios tend to have current residual income amounts that are *greater than* the future residual income amounts, suggesting that these

[21] Stephen H. Penman, *op. cit.*

EXHIBIT 14.8

The Articulation of Market-to-Book (MB) and Price-Earnings (PE) Ratios

	MB Ratio Portfolios:		
PE Ratio Portfolios:	**High**	**Normal**	**Low**
High (Portfolios 15–20)	CRI < FRI > 0 CRI: −0.50 to 0.07 FRI_1: −0.07 to 0.08 FRI_6: 0.01 to 0.11	CRI < FRI = 0 CRI: −0.36 to −0.04 FRI_1: −0.13 to −0.03 FRI_6: −0.06 to 0.07	CRI < FRI < 0 CRI: −0.24 to −0.06 FRI_1: −0.13 to −0.06 FRI_6: −0.01 to 0.02
Normal (Portfolios 7–14)	CRI = FRI > 0 CRI: 0.07 to 0.10 FRI_1: 0.08 to 0.10 FRI_6: 0.11 to 0.14	CRI = FRI = 0 CRI: −0.02 to 0.04 FRI_1: −0.02 to 0.04 FRI_6: 0.01 to 0.06	CRI = FRI < 0 CRI: −0.05 to 0.00 FRI_1: −0.04 to 0.00 FRI_6: −0.02 to 0.03
Low (Portfolios 1–6)	CRI > FRI > 0 CRI: 0.12 to 0.41 FRI_1: 0.12 to 0.25 FRI_6: 0.11 to 0.24	CRI > FRI = 0 CRI: 0.05 to 0.22 FRI_1: 0.05 to 0.15 FRI_6: 0.07 to 0.12	CRI > FRI < 0 CRI: 0.00 to 0.06 FRI_1: −0.01 to 0.04 FRI_6: 0.03 to 0.05

Source: We obtained these data from Table 4 in Stephen H. Penman, "The Articulation of Price-Earnings Ratios and Market-to-Book Ratios and the Evaluation of Growth," *Journal of Accounting Research* vol. 34, no. 2 (Autumn 1996), pp. 235–259.

firms are experiencing low PE ratios because residual income is temporarily high. Penman's results provide intuition about when MB ratios should be high, low, or normal and, concurrently, when PE ratios should be high, low, or normal.

Summary of Value-Earnings and Price-Earnings Ratios

Summarizing, the VE and PE ratios are determined by:

- Risk
- Growth
- Differences between current and expected future (permanent) earnings
- Alternative accounting methods and principles

The analyst must assess each of these elements when estimating VE ratios, particularly when comparing VE ratios to PE ratios to assess whether shares appear to be under- or overpriced and when projecting VE ratios to value non-traded firms. The analyst should be aware of the following considerations when using VE and PE ratios:

1. The VE ratio is particularly sensitive to the cost of equity capital and to the earnings growth rate because it assumes that a firm can grow earnings at that rate forever. The analyst should select a sustainable long-term growth rate when computing the VE model.
2. The VE model does not work when the growth rate in earnings exceeds the cost of equity capital. Firms are not likely to grow earnings forever at rates exceeding the cost of equity capital. Competition will eventually force growth rates to diminish.

3. The VE model should not be used when the cost of equity capital and the growth rate in earnings are similar in amount. The denominator of the VE model ($R_E - g$) approaches zero, and the VE ratio becomes exceeding large.
4. The VE and PE models should not be used when earnings are negative because the VE and PE models assume that earnings are permanent, and negative earnings cannot persist in perpetuity.
5. Before concluding that the market is undervaluing or overvaluing a firm because the actual PE ratio differs from the theoretically correct VE ratio, the analyst should assess whether earnings of the period include transitory elements. The analyst should adjust the current period's earnings to remove the effects of unusual, nonrecurring income items before measuring the PE ratio for the period.
6. When comparing PE ratios across firms, the analyst should consider the impact of the firms' use of different accounting methods and principles.

Using Market Multiples of Comparable Firms

The analyst can use the PE and MB ratios of comparable firms to assess the corresponding ratios of publicly traded firms. The analyst also can value firms whose common shares are not publicly traded by using PE ratios and MB ratios of comparable firms that are publicly traded. The theoretical models assist in this valuation task by identifying the variables the analyst should use in selecting comparable firms. Bhojraj and Lee (2002) demonstrate a technique for selecting comparable firms in multiples-based valuation by computing "warranted multiples" based on factors that drive cross-sectional differences in multiples, such as expected profitability, growth, and cost of capital.[22] Alford (1992) examined the accuracy of the PE valuation models using industry, risk, ROCE, and earnings growth as the bases for selecting comparable firms.[23] The results indicate that industry membership, particularly at a three-digit SIC code level, provides a useful basis for comparisons if firms in the same industry experience similar profitability, face similar risks, and grow at similar rates. Thus, in some circumstances, industry membership serves as an effective proxy for the variables in the PE valuation model. However, as the data in Exhibit 14.7 reveal, substantial differences commonly exist in PE ratios of firms in the same industry. The warranted-multiples approach of Bhojraj and Lee (2002) provides a mechanism to determine comparable companies within similar industries and across different industries.

PRICE DIFFERENTIALS[24]

In light of the critical role of risk and expected returns in valuation and in light of the uncertainty surrounding how to measure risk and expected returns, the analyst needs a variety of tools to assess the impact of risk on share prices and firm values. One such tool involves computing *price differentials.* Price differentials can be used to address questions such as these: To what extent has the market priced risk? What is the impact of risk on share price? Is the per-share price impact too large or too small relative to risk? We rely on an adaptation of the residual income model to address these questions by computing the price differential—the amount the market has discounted share price for risk.

[22] Sanjeev Bhojraj and Charles M.C. Lee, "Who Is My Peer? A Valuation-Based Approach to the Selection of Comparable Firms," *Journal of Accounting Research,* Vol. 40, No. 2 (May 2002), pp. 407–439.

[23] Andrew W. Alford, "The Effect of the Set of Comparable Firms on the Accuracy of the Price-Earnings Valuation Method," *Journal of Accounting Research* (Spring 1992), pp. 94–108.

[24] This section relies heavily on Stephen Baginski and James Wahlen, "Residual Income Risk, Intrinsic Values, and Share Prices," *The Accounting Review,* Vol. 78, No. 1 (January 2003), pp. 327–351.

As described in detail in the previous chapter, the residual income model determines the present value of common shareholders' equity as follows:

$$V_0 = BV_0 + \sum_{t=1}^{\infty} \frac{NI_t - (R_E \times BV_{t-1})}{(1 + R_E)^t}$$

To implement this model, the analyst must estimate the cost of equity capital (R_E) and then use it to compute residual income $[NI_t - (R_E \times BV_{t-1})]$ and discount residual income to present value at $1/(1 + R_E)^t$. But state-of-the-art in financial economics does not provide a clear picture of how R_E should be determined. Substantial controversy surrounds expected returns models such as the CAPM. What is the appropriate measure for market beta? In addition to market betas, do other risk factors belong in the expected returns model, such as firm size, MB ratios, or some other set of risk factors? Assuming that one can identify the appropriate risk factors that are priced in the market, what are the appropriate risk premia to use to determine expected returns for each of these factors? At an even more fundamental level, questions arise about whether risk and expected returns should be measured based on covariation between a firm's returns and a market index of returns. These questions arise in part because market-based models such as the CAPM are essentially circular—should stock returns be used to estimate risk to determine expected returns to evaluate stock prices? Or should risk and expected returns be based on covariation between a firm's returns and its fundamental risk characteristics (such as volatility in earnings)? Or should risk and expected returns derive from the covariation between a firm's stock returns and an economy-wide measure of consumption, on the theory that investors' risk aversion is driven by the need to diversify volatility in expected future consumption?

The procedure for computing price differential offers an alternative approach for evaluating the market's pricing of risk. To begin, substitute the prevailing risk-free rate of interest (denoted R_F; for example, the yield on five-year U.S. Treasury securities) for the cost of equity capital (R_E) and use the residual income model to estimate risk-neutral value (denoted as RNV_0), which is an estimate of the hypothetical value of the firm in a risk-neutral market:

$$RNV_0 = BV_0 + \sum_{t=1}^{\infty} \frac{NI_t - (R_F \times BV_{t-1})}{(1 + R_F)^t}$$

Risk-neutral value represents the value of the firm, based on book value of equity and forecasts of expected future earnings, in the absence of discounting for risk. Dividing risk-neutral value by the number of shares outstanding gives risk-neutral value per share, which represents the hypothetical value at which shares would trade in a risk-neutral market. Market price per share of common equity reflects the risk-discounted value in the real-world, which is risk-averse. Therefore, market price per share can be subtracted from risk-neutral value per share to determine the total amount by which share price has been discounted for risk. We refer to this difference as the *price differential* (denoted as PDIFF), computed as follows:

$$PDIFF_0 = RNV\ per\ share_0 - Price\ per\ share_0$$

The analyst can also divide $PDIFF_0$ by RNV_0 to determine the *percentage PDIFF*. The analyst can evaluate the PDIFF or the percentage PDIFF to assess whether the market discount for risk is sufficient to compensate the investor to hold the firm's shares and bear risk. The analyst can also compare percentage PDIFF across time for a given firm or across firms to evaluate the extent to which the market is discounting share prices for risk. If the analyst assesses that $PDIFF_0$ is large relative to the risk of the firm, the firm's shares may be overdiscounted for risk (undervalued). On the other hand, if the analyst assesses that $PDIFF_0$ is small relative to firm risk, perhaps the firm's shares are underdiscounted for risk (overvalued). In the next section, we illustrate how to compute the PDIFF for PepsiCo. In the following section that discusses reverse engineering, we describe and apply more formal methods to gauge the relative magnitude of PDIFF.

Computing PDIFF for PepsiCo

To compute the price differential of PepsiCo as of the end of 2008, we rely on the forecast assumptions developed in Chapter 10 and the residual income model developed in the previous chapter. However, instead of using an 8.5 percent cost of equity capital for PepsiCo for purposes of computing residual income and discounting it to present value, we use the risk-free interest rate at the time of the valuation. At the end of 2008, U.S. Treasury bills with one to five years to maturity yielded roughly 4.0 percent. Exhibit 14.9 reports the present value of PepsiCo's expected future residual income in Year +1 through Year +5 amounts to $29,399.3 million, computed using the 4.0 percent risk-free discount rate.

To compute continuing value, we use the now-familiar perpetuity-with-growth model $[= 1/(R_F - g)]$ assuming that long-term growth for PepsiCo will be 3.0 percent and that the risk-free discount rate is 4.0 percent. The present value of continuing value under this approach is $659,346.6 million. After adding book value of common equity at the end of 2008, adjusting for midyear discounting, and dividing by the number of shares outstanding, we estimate that PepsiCo shares have a risk-neutral value of $460.38. Subtracting the market price at 2008 of $54.77 per share, we estimate the PDIFF to be $405.61. These computations suggest that PepsiCo shares have been discounted by the risk-averse market by roughly $405.61 per share below the value at which they would trade in a hypothetical risk-neutral market, conditional on the forecast assumptions made in Chapter 10. These computations indicate that PepsiCo shares traded at the end of 2008 at a price equal to roughly 12 percent of risk-neutral value (= $54.77/$460.38). Alternately stated, at a price of $54.77,

EXHIBIT 14.9

Price Differential of PepsiCo:
Present Value of Residual Income in Year +1 through Year +5 after Discounting at the Risk-Free Rate of Interest (4.0 percent)
(dollar amounts in millions)

	Year +1	Year +2	Year +3	Year +4	Year +5
Lagged Book Value of Common Shareholders' Equity (at t–1)	$12,203.0	$12,656.1	$13,467.4	$14,465.3	$15,323.5
Comprehensive Income Available for Common Shareholders	$ 5,941.9	$ 6,602.1	$ 7,272.7	$ 7,726.4	$ 8,427.3
Required Earnings	$ 488.1	$ 506.2	$ 538.7	$ 578.6	$ 612.9
Residual Income	$ 5,453.8	$ 6,095.8	$ 6,734.0	$ 7,147.8	$ 7,814.3
Present Value Factors	× 0.962	× 0.925	× 0.889	× 0.855	× 0.822
Present Value of Residual Income	$ 5,244.0	$ 5,635.9	$ 5,986.5	$ 6,110.0	$ 6,422.8
Sum of Present Value of Residual Income, Year +1 through Year +5	$29,399.3				

EXHIBIT 14.10

Price Differential of PepsiCo
(dollar amounts in millions except per share amounts)

Valuation Steps:	Computations:	Amounts:
Sum of Present Value Residual Income in Year +1 through Year +5	Discounted at the risk-free rate of interest of 4.0 percent. See Exhibit 14.9.	$ 29,399.3
Add continuing value in present value	Year +6 residual income assumed to grow at 3.0% in perpetuity; discounted at 4.0%. Computations not shown.	+ $659,346.6
Total Present Value Residual Income		$688,745.9
Add: Beginning Book Value of Equity	Book Value of Equity from 2008 Balance Sheet	+ $ 12,203.0
		$700,948.9
Adjust to Midyear Discounting	Multiply by $1 + (R_F / 2)$	× 1.020
Present Value of Common Equity		$714,967.8
Shares Outstanding		÷ 1,553.0
Estimated Risk-Neutral Value per Share		$ 460.38
Current Price per Share		− $ 54.77
Price Differential		$ 405.61
Price Differential as a Percent of Risk-Neutral Value		88.1%

PepsiCo's shares have been discounted 88 percent relative to the risk-neutral value. Exhibit 14.10 presents these computations.

In Chapters 11−13, we estimated that PepsiCo shares may have been underpriced at the end of 2008 by roughly 52 percent, conditional on our forecast assumptions and valuation models. The price differential computation indicates that the market imposed a substantial discount to PepsiCo's expected future residual income relative to the risk of PepsiCo. To more formally evaluate the relative magnitude of the price differential, we turn to the method of reverse-engineering market values.

REVERSE ENGINEERING

Reverse engineering is an analytical approach through which the analyst can deduce and evaluate the assumptions implicit in a stock price. Throughout this text, we have emphasized the process of using a firm's fundamental characteristics to estimate firm value. The valuation process can be characterized essentially as a puzzle with four pieces, or as an equation with four variables, as follows:

1. Value
2. Expected future profitability
3. Expected long-run future growth
4. Expected risk-adjusted discount rates

Thus far, we have developed forecasts and expectations about three of the variables—expected future profitability, long-run growth, and risk-adjusted discount rates—and have used them to solve for the fourth variable, firm value. In fact, we can make assumptions about any three of the four variables and then solve for the fourth variable.

For example, we can treat the market value of common equity as one of the "known" variables. We can assume that V_0 equals market value. (That is, we can assume that the market is correct; hence, price equals value.) We can then develop forecast assumptions for any two other variables and solve for the missing fourth variable. We refer to this process as *reverse-engineering* stock prices because it takes the valuation process and reverses it. It is a process in which the analyst assumes that shareholders' equity value equals market price and then solves for the assumptions the market appears to be making to value the firm's shares. For example, if we assume that a firm's share value equals the market's share price and use the consensus analysts' forecasts for future earnings and growth as reasonable proxies for the market's expectations, we can solve for the implied expected risk-adjusted rate of return on common equity that is consistent with the observed market price, conditional on the analysts' assumptions about earnings and growth. This is essentially equivalent to solving for the internal rate of return on the stock.

As another example, suppose we assume that share value equals market price, that the market's risk-adjusted expected return on a stock can be determined by an asset pricing model such as the CAPM, and that analysts' consensus earnings forecasts through Year +5 are reasonable proxies for the market's earnings expectations. We can then solve for the long-run growth rate implicit in the firm's stock price, conditional on the other assumptions.

The process of reverse-engineering stock prices allows the analyst to infer a set of assumptions that the market appears to have impounded into a share price. The analyst can then assess whether the assumptions the market appears to be making are realistic, optimistic, or pessimistic. If the analyst determines that the market's assumptions seem optimistic, it suggests that the market has overpriced the stock (or perhaps the analyst will question whether he or she is more pessimistic than the market). Alternatively, if the analyst determines that the market's assumptions seem pessimistic, it suggests that the market has underpriced the stock (or again, the analyst may be less pessimistic than the market).

Reverse-Engineering PepsiCo's Stock Price

To illustrate the process of reverse engineering, we apply the approach to PepsiCo using the end of 2008 market price of $54.77 per share. To reverse-engineer PepsiCo's share price, we again rely on the residual income model in the previous chapter and the forecasts developed in Chapter 10.

Assume that we want to solve for the expected rate of return (that is, the risk-adjusted discount rate) implied by PepsiCo's 2008 share price of $54.77. Also assume that our forecasts of earnings and book value of common equity for PepsiCo through Year +5 and our forecast of 3.0 percent long-run growth are realistic proxies for the market's expectations. Armed with share price, earnings and growth forecasts through Year +5, and a constant long-run growth assumption beyond Year +5, we can use the residual income value model to solve for the discount rate that reduces future earnings and book value to a present value equal to the $54.77 market price per share.

Procedurally, one way to solve for the implied expected return on PepsiCo stock, conditional on the price, earnings, and growth assumptions, is to estimate the value of common equity using the risk-free discount rate, as in the price differential illustration above. The risk-neutral value will likely far exceed the market price because the future residual income has not been discounted for risk. In applying the price differential model to PepsiCo in the previous section, we determined that PepsiCo's risk-neutral value was $460.38 per share. We then steadily increase the discount rate as necessary until the residual income model value exactly agrees with the market price of $54.77 per share. Following this approach, the implied expected rate of return on PepsiCo stock is 11.32 percent. At this discount rate, conditional on our residual income and growth assumptions, the present value of PepsiCo shares is \$54.77 per share, exactly equal to market price. Recall that we assumed that PepsiCo common equity had a required rate of return of 8.50 percent based on the CAPM. However, this reverse-engineering approach indicates that if we buy a share of PepsiCo stock at the market price of \$54.77, it will yield an 11.32 percent rate of return, conditional on our other assumptions. The Valuation spreadsheet in FSAP allows the analyst to make these iterative computations easily by varying the discount rate for equity capital.

FSAP

To demonstrate another example, we can reverse-engineer PepsiCo's 2008 stock price to solve for the implicit long-run growth assumption. To illustrate, we again take the market price of \$54.77 per share as given and our earnings and book value forecasts through Year +5 as reasonable proxies for the market's expectations. We return to our original assumption that based on the CAPM the risk-adjusted discount rate for PepsiCo stock is 8.50 percent. With this, we have established three assumptions—value, earnings through Year +5, and the risk-adjusted discount rate—and can solve for the missing piece of the puzzle: long-run implied growth. We begin with the long-run growth assumption set at zero. We compute our first estimate of firm value using a zero growth assumption and compare that estimate to market price. The first estimate is normally substantially lower than market price because market price probably includes the present value of the market's expectations for long-run growth. For PepsiCo, however, the initial value estimate assuming zero growth is \$60.84 per share—*above* current share price. This suggests that conditional on our other valuation assumptions, the market is pricing *negative* long-run growth in PepsiCo shares. To determine the implied negative growth rate, we steadily decrease the long-run growth parameter assumption as necessary until the present value from the residual income model equals market price. In the case of PepsiCo at the end of 2008, market price of \$54.77 reflects *long-run negative growth* of −1.5 percent (significantly lower than our expectation of 3.0 percent long-run growth). That is, conditional on our assumptions for residual income through Year +5 and on our assumption that PepsiCo's cost of equity capital is 8.5 percent, if the market expects long-run growth to be −1.5 percent per year, the present value of PepsiCo shares exactly agrees with the market price of \$54.77. Given that PepsiCo will not likely experience negative long-run growth, it further confirms our assessment that PepsiCo shares are underpriced at the end of 2008. Again, note that the valuation spreadsheet in FSAP is a useful tool that allows the analyst to establish assumptions for earnings and cost of capital and then vary the long-run growth assumption for reverse engineering.

THE RELEVANCE OF ACADEMIC RESEARCH FOR THE WORK OF THE SECURITY ANALYST

Throughout this text, we have referred to relevant examples of empirical accounting research, including the classic study by Ball and Brown (1968) that helped set the stage for future research by being the first to show that changes in earnings correlate with unexpected changes in stock prices.[25] As demonstrated in Exhibit 1.21 in Chapter 1, the Nichols and Wahlen (2004) replication of the Ball and Brown results indicate that during their sample period 1988−2002, merely the difference in the sign of the change in annual earnings (whether positive or negative) was associated with nearly a 35 percent difference in annual market-adjusted stock returns.[26] The average sample firm that reported an earnings

---

[25] Ray Ball and Philip Brown, "An Empirical Evaluation of Accounting Income Numbers," *Journal of Accounting Research* (Autumn 1968), pp. 159–178.

[26] D. Craig Nichols and James Wahlen, "How Do Earnings Numbers Relate to Stock Returns? A Review of Classic Accounting Research with Updated Evidence," *Accounting Horizons* (December 2004), pp. 263–286.

increase in a given year experienced stock returns that, on average, "beat" the market average returns by 19 percent, while the average sample firm that reported an earnings decrease in a given year experienced stock returns that, on average, fell 16 percent short of the market average returns.

The results of academic research in accounting have provided many insights into multifaceted dimensions of the relations between accounting numbers and a variety of capital market variables such as stock prices, stock price reactions around earnings announcements, stock returns cumulated over long periods of time, trading volume, analysts' and managements' earnings forecasts, equity costs of capital, implied market risk premia, market betas and other risk factors, bankruptcy, and earnings management. Despite the existence of academic accounting research, the natural question for the security analyst is whether the academic research models and empirical findings are relevant to the task of making buy, sell, or hold recommendations on individual firms. This concluding section offers some thoughts on this important question. This section also summarizes the role of market efficiency and describes some striking empirical evidence on the relative degree of market efficiency with respect to earnings. In addition, this section describes an empirical study that used the residual income valuation models demonstrated in this chapter and in Chapter 13 to pick stocks and form portfolios. We consider the results to date to be very encouraging for analysts.

Creating Relevant Academic Research Results[27]

Accounting academics and the research process itself provide important elements that should lead to relevant and reliable insights into the relation between accounting numbers and stock market variables. Some of the elements of the research process that help academic researchers are as follows:

- **Rigor and Objectivity:** Academic accounting researchers develop and test theories to explain the observed relation between accounting information and stock prices. Academics are trained to base their predictions and hypotheses as much as possible on formal theory integrating economics, finance, and accounting (rather than ad hoc or ex post reasoning). Academics commonly test these predictions with rigorous statistical methods on large empirical samples of real data. Academics usually have no commercial interest in the results, so the findings should not be biased by the need to obtain a particular conclusion or the need to sell. Furthermore, academic research is not published in a leading scholarly research journal unless it survives the stringent peer review process. Few research studies pass the "publish" test; most "perish."
- **Level of Aggregation:** Both academic and professional analyst communities must recognize that their interests share common ground but involve different levels of aggregation. The academic seeks big picture explanations of general phenomena. Academic research in accounting seeks to develop conclusions and results that predict and explain the relation between accounting information and stock market variables in general. The analyst is concerned with specific assessments of the value of individual firms at particular points in time. Academic research results provide a basis for the analyst to assess the link between accounting numbers and a firm's value and to identify deviations from the average for individual firms. Professional analysts create value by acting on the deviations, that is, identifying and taking positions in under- or overpriced stocks.

[27] This section draws heavily from Clyde P. Stickney, "The Academic's Approach to Securities Research: Is It Relevant to the Analyst?" *Journal of Financial Statement Analysis* (Summer 1997), pp. 52–60.

- **Theory and Practice Feed Each Other:** The previous section identified the common ground that the academic and professional analyst communities share. Both communities want to better understand how accounting information relates to stock prices. Academics predict and explain analysts' earnings forecasts and price targets and, more generally, the actions of market participants on the whole. Analysts, directly or indirectly, rely on theories and results from academic research to inform their analysis. Much of what analysts learn in their academic training (such as in undergraduate and MBA programs) and in professional development training is developed and validated by academic work, including textbooks such as this one that seek to link practice, theory, and research.

What Does "Capital Market Efficiency" Really Mean?

Academics generally perceive market efficiency from the perspective of the big picture, with a view of large samples and market movements in general. In contrast, many analysts view their task as the constant pursuit of market inefficiencies—temporarily mispriced securities. Analysts see market efficiency from the front lines, experiencing daily swings in market prices that are sometimes hard to explain in the context of an efficient market. Thus, it is not surprising that the perspective on the degree of market efficiency (or the lack thereof) differs substantially between academics and professional analysts. This section seeks to reach a common understanding, and the next section provides some striking evidence on the degree of market efficiency with respect to earnings and accounting information.

Capital markets may be described as "efficient" with regard to accounting information based on the degree to which market prices react *completely* and *quickly* to available accounting information. Notice that efficiency should be described as a matter of *degree*, not as an absolute. The issue is not whether the capital markets are or are not efficient. Rather, the issue is the degree to which the capital markets impound in prices all the available value-relevant information.

The term *completely* in this description implies the degree to which share prices reflect the value-relevant implications of all available accounting information without systematic bias. A capital market that is relatively efficient will impound in stock prices the economic implications of all value-relevant financial statement information, even including accounting items that may be disclosed in the notes.

The term *quickly* in this description suggests that market participants cannot consistently earn abnormal returns using accounting information for a long period of time after the information has been made public. If capital markets exhibit a high degree of efficiency, market prices should react quickly (within a matter of days) to capture any value-relevant signals in the accounting information.

The degree of efficiency, or the completeness and speed of price reactions, in an information-efficient capital market depends on analysts and financial statement analysis. Analysts study accounting information to assess appropriate values for stocks and to take positions in under- or overpriced securities, thereby driving stock market prices to efficient levels. Share prices move to new efficient levels based on the speed with which analysts can forecast and anticipate accounting information before it is released and on the speed with which they can analyze and react quickly to surprises in accounting information when it is released.

Also consider what a high degree of market efficiency *does not imply*. A capital market with a high degree of information efficiency does not necessarily price all stocks correctly every day. As a practical matter, relatively efficient markets experience valuation errors at the level of the individual firm, but these random inefficiencies cancel out at an aggregated market level and do not persist for long periods of time.[28] Analysts are driving forces involved in identifying and correcting security mispricings. A capital market with a high degree of information efficiency does not necessarily have perfect foresight—surprises happen. Firms frequently surprise the market by announcing earnings that are higher or lower than the market's expectations. Again, analysts drive market prices to react quickly and completely to new information.

Striking Evidence on the Degree of Market Efficiency and Inefficiency with Respect to Earnings

Two studies by Victor Bernard and Jacob Thomas (1989 and 1990) provide the most striking evidence to date on the degree of market efficiency and inefficiency with respect to accounting earnings.[29] The Bernard and Thomas results during the post-earnings-announcement period suggest that the market's reaction to quarterly earnings news is highly, but not completely, efficient. Nichols and Wahlen (2004) used data from 1988–2002 to replicate the seminal results in Bernard and Thomas (which were based on data from 1974–1986). Nichols and Wahlen collected a sample of 90,470 quarterly earnings announcements for firms on the CRSP and Compustat databases. They ranked all sample firms each quarter into ten portfolios on the basis of each firm's unexpected earnings. (Unexpected earnings equals actual earnings per share minus analysts' consensus forecast of earnings per share, scaled by price per share as of 60 trading days prior to the earnings announcement for cross-sectional comparability.) They studied the average abnormal (market-adjusted) stock returns to each portfolio over the 60 trading days leading up to the quarterly earnings announcement and over the 60 trading days following the announcement. Exhibit 14.11 depicts a portion of the Nichols and Wahlen results, which mirror the Bernard and Thomas results.

The results in Exhibit 14.11 during the pre-announcement period indicate that the market is highly efficient in anticipating and reacting to quarterly earnings surprises. Firms with quarterly earnings surprises in the "good news" portfolios—portfolios 7 through 10—experience positive cumulative abnormal returns during the 60 days prior to and including the release of earnings. Firms with quarterly earnings surprises in the "bad news" portfolios—portfolios 1 through 4—experience negative cumulative abnormal returns during the 60 days prior to and including the release of earnings. The average difference in cumulative abnormal returns between portfolio 10 (roughly +6.7 percent) and portfolio 1 (roughly −6.8 percent) was roughly 13.5 percent *per quarter.* These results suggest that the market anticipates and reacts quickly to quarterly earnings information.

The results in Exhibit 14.11 during the post-announcement period suggest that the market's reaction to quarterly earnings news is highly, but not completely, efficient. In the post-announcement period, Nichols and Wahlen measured the cumulative abnormal returns to the exact same portfolios over the 60 trading days *after* the earnings announcements. If the market's reactions to quarterly earnings were, on average, quick and complete, these portfolios should exhibit no systematic abnormal returns in the post-announcement period. Upon the announcement of earnings, market prices should adjust efficiently within a few

---

[28] For a discussion of these issues, see Ray Ball, "The Earnings-Price Anomaly," *Journal of Accounting and Economics* (1992), pp. 319–345.

[29] Victor Bernard and Jacob Thomas, "Post-Earnings Announcement Drift: Delayed Price Response or Risk Premium?" *Journal of Accounting Research* Vol. 27, (Supplement, 1989), pp. 1–36; and "Evidence that Stock Prices Do Not Fully Reflect the Implications of Current Earnings for Future Earnings," *Journal of Accounting and Economics* Vol. 13, No. 4 (1990), pp. 305–340.

EXHIBIT 14.11

Evidence from Nichols and Wahlen (2004) Replication of Bernard and Thomas (1989) on Market Efficiency with Respect to Quarterly Earnings

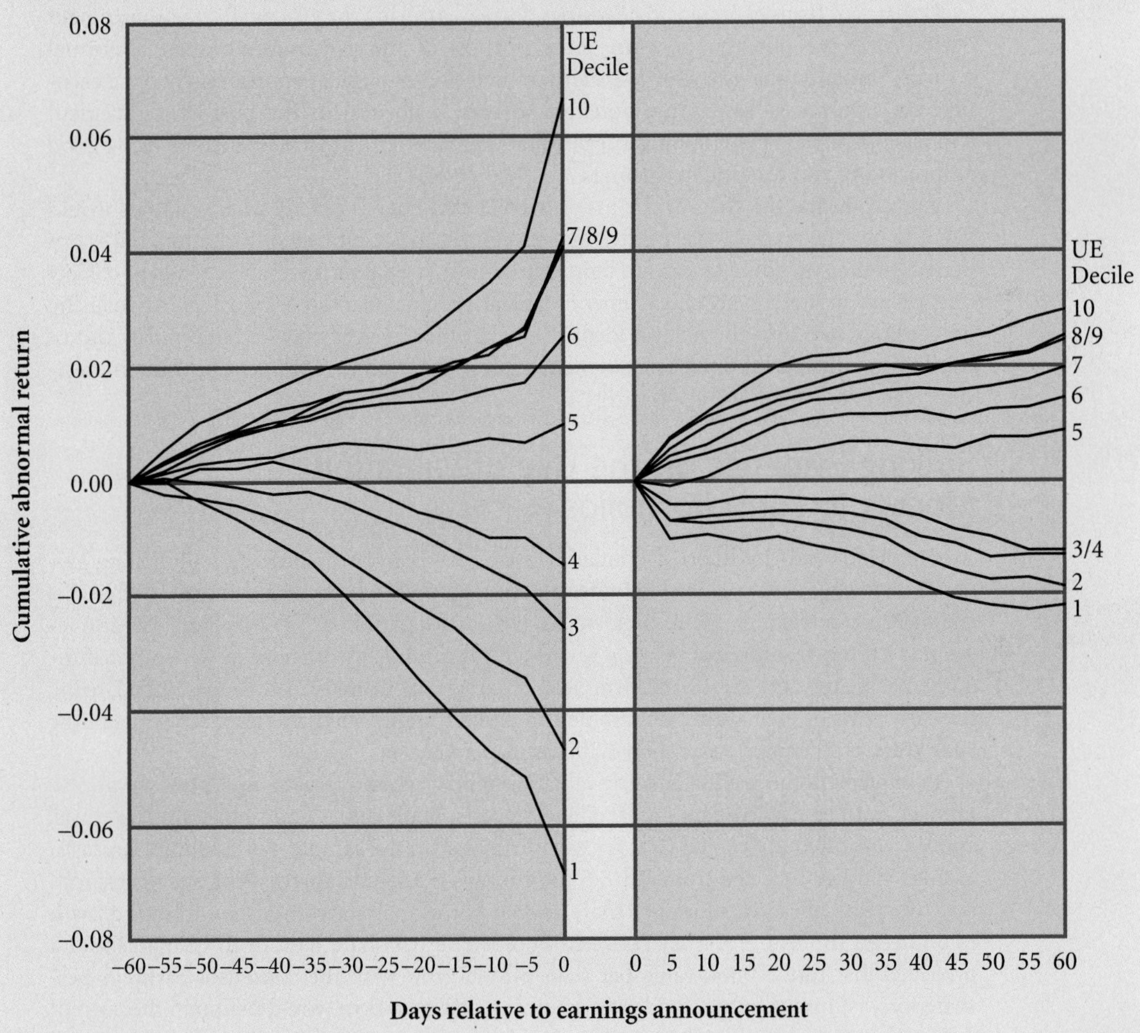

days of the announcement. Post-announcement abnormal returns should arise only from new information that arrives during those 60 days, and the post-announcement abnormal returns should not be associated with the prior quarter's earnings news.

The results for the post-announcement period clearly indicate significant cumulative abnormal returns for the firms in portfolio 10 (best news) and portfolio 1 (worst news). Mean cumulative abnormal returns amount to roughly +3.0 percent and −2.2 percent for the best and worst news portfolios, respectively. In a follow-up study, Bernard and Thomas (1990) show that, in part, the market seems to underreact to the persistence in current period earnings for future period earnings, failing to fully anticipate the momentum in quarterly earnings changes.

Taken together, the Bernard and Thomas studies reveal that the market is highly, but not completely, efficient with respect to quarterly earnings. The results from the Nichols and Wahlen study using current data suggest that the Bernard and Thomas findings still hold. We consider these results to be very encouraging for analysts. We interpret the results to suggest that analysts who can sharpen their ability to forecast future earnings and take long positions in (buy) shares of firms experiencing earnings increases and short positions in (sell) shares of firms experiencing earnings decreases during the 60-day pre-announcement period have the potential to earn some portion of the pre-announcement abnormal returns. Similarly, analysts who can sharpen their ability to react appropriately once earnings are announced have some potential to earn a portion of the post-announcement abnormal returns. These findings suggest that there are returns to be earned by being good at forecasting and reacting to earnings.

We believe that the state-of-the-art of market efficiency is exactly where analysts would like it to be. The market is very efficient with respect to accounting information, but is not perfectly efficient. Some stocks are temporarily mispriced, but the market tends to correct mispricings in a relatively short time. Financial statements analysis, particularly focusing on earnings, can help the analyst identify stocks whose prices may be temporarily out of equilibrium. Insightful financial statement analysis can lead to intelligent investment decisions and better-than-average returns.

Striking Evidence on the Use of Valuation Models to Form Portfolios

An empirical study by Richard Frankel and Charles Lee (1998) provides compelling evidence on the use of the residual income valuation models (which were demonstrated in this chapter and in Chapter 13) to pick stocks and form portfolios.[30] Frankel and Lee implemented a three-year forecast horizon version of the residual income model to compute fundamental share value for 18,162 firm-year observations from 1976 through 1993. During the early years of their study, the sample contained roughly 500 firms per year, while in the later years, it contained more than 1,300 firms per year.

To implement the residual income valuation model across a large sample of observations, Frankel and Lee needed data on earnings forecasts, book values and book value forecasts, and the cost of equity capital (R_E) for each firm-year in the sample. For earnings forecasts, Frankel and Lee collected from I/B/E/S the consensus analysts' forecasts of one-year-ahead and two-years-ahead earnings per share as well as the analysts' consensus earnings growth rate forecast for Year +3. They collected book-value-per-share data from Compustat and projected that future book value per share would grow with the consensus earnings-per-share forecast minus future dividends, assuming that each firm would maintain the current dividend payout policy. Finally, to determine the cost of equity capital, Frankel and Lee used an industry-average three-factor (beta, size, and market-to-book) expected returns model. They also assumed a constant cost of capital (11 percent, 12 percent, or 13 percent) across time and firms. Their results were not very sensitive to the R_E estimate.

Applying the three-year-horizon residual income model enabled Frankel and Lee to compute value per share (denoted as V) for each sample observation. They then scaled each firm's V by market share price (P) to compute a V/P ratio. If a firm's V/P ratio is exactly 1, it suggests that the market price per share is exactly equal to value per share. If a V/P ratio is greater than 1, it suggests that the share price is underpriced, whereas a V/P ratio of less

[30] Richard Frankel and Charles M.C. Lee, "Accounting Valuation, Market Expectation, and Cross-Sectional Stock Returns," *Journal of Accounting and Economics*, Vol. 25 (1998), pp. 283–319.

than 1 suggests that the share is overpriced. During each year of the study, Frankel and Lee ranked all of the sample firms from highest to lowest V/P. They then formed five portfolios, from the quintile of firms with the highest V/P ratios that year (the top 20 percent) down to the quintile of firms with the lowest V/P ratios that year (the bottom 20 percent). They held these portfolios for 36 months and cumulated the average returns.

Exhibit 14.12 presents the Frankel and Lee results averaged across all of the years of their study. Judging by the bars in the graph and the axis on the left-hand side of the exhibit, the bottom quintile portfolio had an average V/P ratio of roughly 0.40, implying that these firms tended to be significantly overpriced. The top quintile portfolio had an average V/P ratio of roughly 1.5, indicating that these firms tended to be underpriced. The square dots and the right-hand axis of the graph indicate the average buy-and-hold returns cumulated by each portfolio over the 36 months after portfolio formation. Notice that the lowest quintile V/P firms generated, on average, cumulative three-year returns of only 35 percent, whereas the highest quintile V/P firms generated average cumulative three-year returns of nearly 65 percent. Frankel and Lee's study also included various sensitivity analyses and control tests indicating that their results were robust. The V/P ratio seemingly distinguished under- and overpriced stocks.

EXHIBIT 14.12

Evidence from Frankel and Lee (1998) on Using Residual Income Valuation Models to Pick Stocks and Form Portfolios

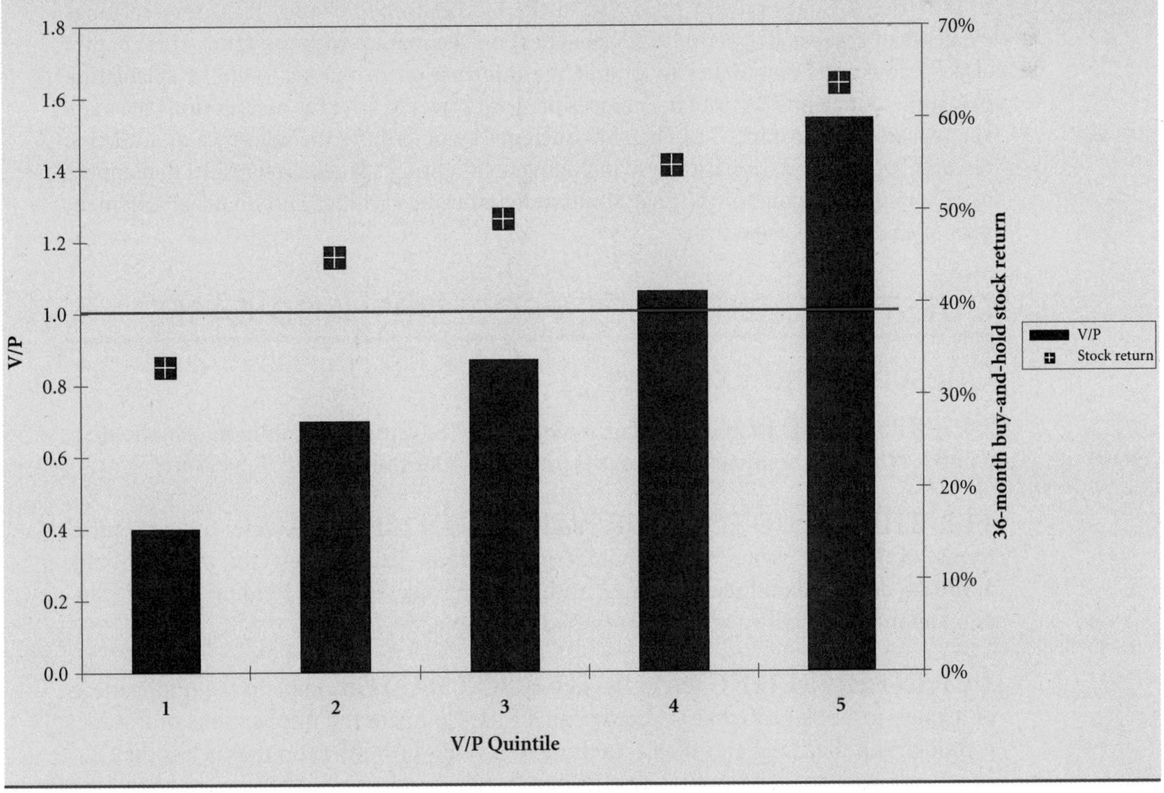

These results suggest that the valuation models we have discussed and demonstrated are useful in estimating share values and in evaluating which stocks are more likely to be under- or overpriced. Although these results are very encouraging for analysts, the results do not imply that the valuation process is simple or easy or error-proof. Indeed, we strongly encourage analysts to carefully follow the six steps of the analysis framework demonstrated throughout this book to conduct thorough financial statement analysis, develop accurate forecasts, and determine reliable estimates of value to increase the likelihood of making good investment decisions and decrease the likelihood of making poor decisions.

SUMMARY

This chapter examines the use of market multiples in valuation by relying on the residual income model to develop the theoretical rationale relating market prices to economic drivers of value and to accounting fundamentals. This chapter describes the conceptual bases and practical applications of market multiples such as the market-to-book value ratio, the price-earnings ratio, and the price-earnings-growth ratio. The chapter focuses on four factors that affect these market multiples: (1) risk and the cost of equity capital, (2) the expected future growth rate in earnings, (3) the presence of permanent and transitory components in the earnings of a particular year, and (4) the effects of accounting methods and principles on reported earnings and the book value of common shareholders' equity. For decades, analysts have relied heavily on price-earnings ratios to relate market prices to earnings. However, in recent years, analysts and academics alike increasingly recognize that transitory elements in earnings and earnings growth can cloud the interpretation of the price-earnings ratio as an indicator of value. Analysts and academics are shifting emphasis to the price-earnings-growth ratio and to the market-to-book ratio. Transitory earnings elements of a particular period have less effect on the market-to-book ratio. This chapter also demonstrates techniques to exploit the information in market value by calculating price differentials and by reverse-engineering stock prices to infer the assumptions the market appears to be making. The chapter concludes by describing the relevance of academic research for the professional analyst, including highlighting key research results that appear to be very encouraging for the analyst interested in using earnings and financial statement data to analyze and value firms.

QUESTIONS, EXERCISES, PROBLEMS, AND CASES

Questions and Exercises

14.1 RESIDUAL ROCE. Explain *residual* ROCE (return on common shareholders' equity). What does residual ROCE represent? What does residual ROCE measure?

14.2 THE VALUE-TO-BOOK VALUATION APPROACH. In conceptual terms, explain the value-to-book valuation approach. Explain how the value-to-book approach described and demonstrated in this chapter relates to the residual income valuation approach described and demonstrated in Chapter 13.

14.3 INTERPRETING VALUE-TO-BOOK RATIOS. Explain the implications of a value-to-book ratio that is exactly equal to 1. Compare the implications of a value-to-book ratio that is greater than 1 to those of a value-to-book ratio that is less than 1.

14.4 INTERPRETING VALUE-TO-BOOK RATIOS. Explain the implications of a value-to-book ratio that is greater than the market-to-book ratio. Explain the implications of a value-to-book ratio that is less than the market-to-book ratio.

14.5 VALUE-TO-BOOK RATIO DRIVERS. Identify three economic factors that will drive a firm's value-to-book ratio to be higher than that of other firms in the same industry. Identify three accounting factors that will drive a firm's value-to-book ratio to be higher than that of other firms in the same industry.

14.6 VALUE-TO-BOOK RATIO DRIVERS. Identify three economic factors that will drive a firm's value-to-book ratio to decrease over time. Identify three accounting factors that will drive a firm's value-to-book ratio to decrease over time.

14.7 THE VALUE-EARNINGS RATIO. In conceptual terms, explain the value-earnings ratio. Explain the difference between the value-earnings ratio and the price-earnings ratio. What is the critical assumption about future earnings in both the value-earnings and price-earnings ratio?

14.8 THE PRICE-EARNINGS RATIO. In practice, it is common to observe price-earnings ratios measured as current period price divided by trailing twelve months (or most recent annual) earnings per share. Identify and explain three potential flaws inherent in this measurement of the price-earnings ratio as a valuation multiple.

14.9 PRICE-EARNINGS RATIO DRIVERS. Identify three economic factors that will drive a firm's price-earnings ratio to be higher than that of other firms in the same industry. Identify three accounting factors that will drive a firm's price-earnings ratio in a given period to be higher than that of other firms in the same industry.

14.10 PRICE-EARNINGS RATIO DRIVERS. Identify three economic factors that will drive a firm's price-earnings ratio to decrease over time. Identify three accounting factors that will drive a firm's price-earnings ratio down in a given period.

14.11 MARKET-TO-BOOK VERSUS PRICE-EARNINGS RATIOS. Explain why market-to-book multiples demonstrate less variance over time and across firms than do price-earnings multiples.

14.12 PRICE DIFFERENTIALS. EXPLAIN PRICE DIFFERENTIALS IN CONCEPTUAL TERMS. What does a price differential measure? How does a price differential relate to risk?

14.13 REVERSE-ENGINEERING SHARE PRICES. Explain reverse-engineering of share prices in conceptual terms. How does reverse-engineering of share prices enable an analyst to infer (or deduce) the assumptions that the capital markets appear to impound in share price?

14.14 MARKET EFFICIENCY. What does market efficiency mean? What does market efficiency not mean? Explain how market efficiency relates to the *amount* of information that affects share prices and the *speed* with which information affects share prices.

14.15 ANALYSTS' ROLE IN MARKET EFFICIENCY. Explain the analysts' role in making the capital markets efficient.

14.16 MARKET EFFICIENCY WITH RESPECT TO QUARTERLY EARNINGS SURPRISES. Using the evidence presented in Exhibit 14.11, describe the extent to which the market is efficient with respect to quarterly earnings surprises during the 60 trading days *prior to* quarterly earnings announcements. Using the evidence presented in Exhibit 14.11, describe the extent to which the market is efficient with respect to quarterly earnings surprises during the 60 trading days *following* quarterly earnings announcements.

Problems and Cases

14.17 USING MARKET MULTIPLES TO ASSESS VALUES AND MARKET PRICES. Problem 13.18 and Exhibit 13.7 in Chapter 13 present selected data from projected financial statements for Steak 'n Shake for Year +1 to Year +11. The amounts for Year +11 reflect a long-term growth assumption of 3 percent. The cost of equity capital is 9.34 percent. The market value of common shareholders' equity in Steak 'n Shake on January 1, Year +1, is $309.98 million.

Required

a. Compute the value-to-book ratio as of January 1, Year +1, using the residual ROCE valuation method.

b. Using the analyses developed in Part a, prepare an exhibit summarizing the following ratios for Steak 'n Shake as of January 1, Year +1:

1. Value-to-book ratio (using the amounts from Part a)
2. Market-to-book ratio
3. Value-earnings ratio, using reported earnings for Year 0 of $21.8 million
4. Price-earnings ratio, using reported earnings for Year 0 of $21.8 million
5. Value-earnings ratio, using projected earnings for Year +1 of $24.5 million
6. Price-earnings ratio, using projected earnings for Year +1 of $24.5 million

c. Compute the risk-neutral value of Steak 'n Shake as of January 1, Year +1, using a risk-free rate of 4.2 percent. Use the projected earnings for Year +1 to Year +10 and the projected earnings for Year +11 given in Exhibit 13.7. Maintain the continuing value growth assumption of 3 percent. Compute the price differential for Steak 'n Shake as of January 1, Year +1. Compute the ratio of market value to risk-neutral value for Steak 'n Shake as of January 1, Year +1.

d. Use reverse engineering to solve for the long-run growth rate in continuing residual income in Year +11 and beyond that is implicitly impounded in the market value of Steak 'n Shake on January 1, Year +1. Use the 9.34 percent cost of equity capital and the projected earnings amounts for Year +1 to Year +10 in Exhibit 13.7 before solving for the long-run growth rate in continuing residual income.

e. Using the analyses in Parts a–d, evaluate the extent of the market's mispricing (if any) of Steak 'n Shake.

14.18 INTERPRETING MARKET-TO-BOOK RATIOS. Exhibit 14.13 presents data on market-to-book ratios, ROCE, the cost of equity capital, and price-earnings ratios for seven pharmaceutical companies. (Note that price-earnings ratios for these firms typically fall in the 30–35 range.) Exhibit 14.13 also provides historical data on the five-year average rate of growth in earnings and dividend payout ratios for each firm. The data on excess earnings years represent the number of years that each firm would need to earn a rate of return on common shareholders' equity (ROCE) equal to that in Exhibit 14.13 in order to produce value-to-book ratios that equal the market-to-book ratios shown. For example, Bristol-Myers Squibb would need to earn a ROCE of 48.9 percent for 58.3 years in order

EXHIBIT 14.13

Selected Data for Pharmaceutical Companies
(Problem 14.18)

Company	MB	ROCE	Cost of Equity Capital	Dividend Payout Ratio	PE	Growth in Earnings	Excess Earnings Years
Bristol-Myers Squibb	13.9	0.489	0.134	0.77	32.4	0.068	58.3
Warner-Lambert	13.0	0.350	0.133	0.48	42.7	0.051	32.2
Eli Lilly	12.4	0.281	0.155	0.42	49.3	0.110	89.8
Pfizer	11.2	0.350	0.143	0.43	40.4	0.152	27.8
Abbott Laboratories	10.4	0.428	0.113	0.39	26.9	0.116	13.5
Merck	10.3	0.331	0.154	0.46	31.8	0.130	41.9
Wyeth	6.9	0.340	0.138	0.51	25.0	0.065	24.6

for the present value of the excess earnings over the cost of equity capital to produce a value-to-book ratio that matches the market-to-book ratio of 13.9.

Required

Assume that market share prices for each firm are reasonably efficient. That is, do not simply assume that the market has over- or undervalued these firms. Considering the theoretical determinants of the market-to-book ratio, discuss the likely reasons for the relative ordering of these seven companies on their market-to-book ratios.

14.19 SENSITIVITY OF THE THEORETICAL MODELS OF VALUE-EARNINGS AND VALUE-TO-BOOK TO CHANGES IN ASSUMPTIONS.

This problem explores the sensitivity of the value-earnings and value-to-book models to changes in underlying assumptions. We recommend that you design a computer spreadsheet to perform the calculations, particularly for the value-to-book ratio.

Required

a. Assume that current period earnings per share were $1.00 for each of the following scenarios. Compute the value-earnings ratio based on projected one-year-ahead earnings under each of the following sets of assumptions:

Scenario	Cost of Equity Capital	Growth Rate in Earnings
A	0.15	0.06
B	0.15	0.08
C	0.15	0.10
D	0.13	0.06
E	0.13	0.08
F	0.13	0.10
G	0.11	0.06
H	0.11	0.08
I	0.11	0.10

b. Assess the sensitivity of the value-earnings ratio to changes in the cost of equity capital and changes in the growth rate.

c. Compute the value-to-book ratio under each of the following sets of assumptions. Assume zero abnormal ROCE in the periods following the number of years of excess earnings.

Scenario	ROCE	Cost of Equity Capital	Dividend Payout Percentage	Years of Excess Earnings
A	0.20	0.13	0.30	10
B	0.18	0.13	0.30	10
C	0.14	0.13	0.30	10
D	0.18	0.15	0.30	10
E	0.18	0.11	0.30	10
F	0.18	0.13	0.40	10
G	0.18	0.13	0.20	10
H	0.18	0.13	0.30	15
I	0.18	0.13	0.30	20

d. Assess the sensitivity of the value-to-book ratio to changes in the assumptions made about the various underlying variables.

14.20 MARKET MULTIPLES AND REVERSE-ENGINEERING SHARE PRICES. In 2000, Enron enjoyed remarkable success in the capital markets. During that year, Enron's shares increased in value by 89 percent, while the S&P 500 index fell by 9 percent. At the end of 2000, Enron's shares were trading at roughly $83 per share and all of the sell-side analysts following Enron recommended the shares as a "buy" or a "strong buy." With 752.2 million shares outstanding, Enron had a market capitalization of $62,530 million and was one of the largest firms (in terms of market capital) in the United States. At year-end 2000, Enron's book value of common shareholders' equity was $11,470 million.

At year-end 2000, Enron posted earnings per share of $1.19. Among sell-side analysts following Enron, the consensus forecast for earnings per share was $1.31 per share for 2001 and $1.44 per share for 2002, with 10 percent earnings growth expected from 2003–2005. At the time, Enron was paying dividends equivalent to roughly 40 percent of earnings and was expected to maintain that payout policy.

At year-end 2000, Enron had a market beta of 1.7. The risk-free rate of return was 4.3 percent, and the market risk premium was 5.0 percent.

[Note: The data provided in this problem, and the inferences you draw from them, do not depend on foresight of Enron's declaring bankruptcy by the end of 2001.]

Required

a. Use the CAPM to compute the required rate of return on common equity capital for Enron.

b. Use year-end 2000 data to compute the following ratios for Enron:
- **i.** Market-to-book
- **ii.** Price-earnings (using 2000 earnings per share)
- **iii.** Forward price-earnings (using consensus forecast earnings per share for 2001).

c. Reverse-engineer Enron's $83 share price to solve for the implied expected return on Enron shares at year-end 2000. Do the reverse engineering under the following assumptions:
- **i.** Enron's market price equals value.
- **ii.** The consensus analysts' earnings-per-share forecasts through 2005 are reliable proxies for market expectations.
- **iii.** Enron will maintain a 40 percent dividend payout rate.
- **iv.** Beyond 2005, Enron's long-run earnings growth rate will be 3.0 percent.

d. What do these analyses suggest about investing in Enron's shares at a price of $83?

14.21 VALUATION OF COCA-COLA USING MARKET MULTIPLES. The Coca-Cola Company is a global soft-drink beverage company (ticker symbol = KO) that is a primary and direct competitor with PepsiCo. The data in Chapter 12's Exhibits 12.13–12.15 include the actual amounts for 2008 and projected amounts for Year +1 to Year +6 for the income statements, balance sheets, and statements of cash flows for Coca-Cola (in millions).

The market equity beta for Coca-Cola at the end of 2008 is 0.61. Assume that the risk-free interest rate is 4.0 percent and the market risk premium is 6.0 percent. Coca-Cola has 2,312 million shares outstanding at the end of 2008, when Coca-Cola's share price was $44.42.

In this problem, we use these actual and projected financial statement data to apply the techniques in Chapter 14 to compute Coca-Cola's required rate of return on equity and share value based on the value-to-book valuation model. We also compare our value-to-book ratio estimate to Coca-Cola's market-to-book ratio at the end of 2008 to determine an investment recommendation. In addition, we compute the value-earnings and price-earnings ratios and the price differential and we reverse-engineer Coca-Cola's share price as of the end of 2008.

Required

Part I—Computing Coca-Cola's Value-to-Book Ratio Using the Value-to-Book Valuation Approach.

a. Use the CAPM to compute the required rate of return on common equity capital for Coca-Cola.

b. Using the projected financial statements in Chapter 12's Exhibits 12.13–12.15, derive the projected residual ROCE (return on common shareholders' equity) for Coca-Cola for Years +1 through +5.

c. Assume that the steady-state long-run growth rate will be 3 percent in Year +6 and beyond. Project that the Year +5 income statement and balance sheet amounts will grow by 3 percent in Year +6; then derive the projected residual ROCE for Year +6 for Coca-Cola.

d. Using the required rate of return on common equity from Part a as a discount rate, compute the sum of the present value of residual ROCE for Coca-Cola for Years +1 through +5.

e. Using the required rate of return on common equity from Part a as a discount rate and the long-run growth rate from Part c, compute the continuing value of Coca-Cola as of the start of Year +6 based on Coca-Cola's continuing residual ROCE in Year +6 and beyond. After computing continuing value as of the start of Year +6, discount it to present value at the start of Year +1.

f. Compute Coca-Cola's value-to-book ratio as of the end of 2008 with the following three steps: (1) Compute the total sum of the present value of all future residual ROCE (from Parts d and e). (2) To the total from (1), add 1 (representing the book value of equity as of the beginning of the valuation as of the end of 2008). (3) Adjust the total sum from (2) using the midyear discounting adjustment factor.

g. Compute Coca-Cola's market-to-book ratio as of the end of 2008. Compare the value-to-book ratio to the market-to-book ratio. What investment decision does the comparison suggest? What does the comparison suggest regarding the pricing of Coca-Cola shares in the market: underpriced, overpriced, or fairly priced?

h. Use the value-to-book ratio to project the value of a share of common equity in Coca-Cola.

i. If you computed Coca-Cola's common equity share value using the free cash flows to common equity valuation approach in Problem 12.16 in Chapter 12 and/or the residual income valuation approach in Problem 13.19 in Chapter 13, compare the value estimate you obtained in those problems with the estimate you obtained in this case. You should obtain the same value estimates under all three approaches. If you have not yet worked those problems, you would benefit from doing so now.

Part II—Analyzing Coca-Cola's Share Price Using the Value-Earnings Ratio, the Price-Earnings Ratio, Price Differentials, and Reverse Engineering

j. Use the forecast data for Year +1 to project Year +1 earnings per share. To do so, divide the projection of Coca-Cola's comprehensive income available for common shareholders in Year +1 by the number of common shares outstanding at the end of 2008. Using this Year +1 earnings-per-share forecast and using the share value computed in Part h, compute Coca-Cola's value-earnings ratio.

k. Using the Year +1 earnings-per-share forecast from Part j and using the share price at the end of 2008, compute Coca-Cola's price-earnings ratio. Compare Coca-Cola's value-earnings ratio with its price-earnings ratio. What investment decision does the comparison suggest? What does the comparison suggest regarding the pricing of Coca-Cola shares in the market: underpriced, overpriced, or fairly priced? Does this comparison lead to the same conclusions you reached when comparing value-to-book ratios with market-to-book ratios in Part g?

l. Compute Coca-Cola's price differential at the end of 2008. Compute Coca-Cola's price differential as a percentage of Coca-Cola's risk-neutral value. What dollar amount and what percentage amount has the market discounted Coca-Cola shares for risk?

m. Reverse-engineer Coca-Cola's share price at the end of 2008 to solve for the implied expected rate of return. First, assume that value equals price and that the earnings and growth forecasts through Year +6 and beyond are reliable proxies for the market's expectations for Coca-Cola. Then solve for the implied expected rate of return (the discount rate) the market has impounded in Coca-Cola's share price. (Hint: Begin with the forecast and valuation spreadsheet you developed to value Coca-Cola shares. Vary the discount rate until you solve for the discount rate that makes your value estimate exactly equal the end of 2008 market price of $44.42 per share.)

n. Reverse-engineer Coca-Cola's share price at the end of 2008 to solve for the implied expected long-run growth. First, assume that value equals price and that the earnings forecasts through Year +5 are reliable proxies for the market's expectations for Coca-Cola. Also assume that the discount rate implied by the CAPM (computed in Part a) is a reliable proxy for the market's expected rate of return. Then solve for the implied expected long-run growth rate the market has impounded in Coca-Cola's share price. (Hint: Begin with the forecast and valuation spreadsheet you developed to value Coca-Cola shares and use the CAPM discount rate. Set the long-run growth parameter initially to zero. Increase the long-run growth rate until you solve for the growth rate that makes your value estimate exactly equal the end of 2008 market price of $44.42 per share.)

14.22 ANALYSIS OF COMPARABLE COMPANIES USING MARKET MULTIPLES. In this chapter, we evaluated shares of common equity in PepsiCo using the value-to-book approach, market multiples, price differentials, and reverse engineering. The Coca-Cola Company is a direct competitor with PepsiCo. The data in Chapter 12's Exhibits 12.13–12.15 include the actual amounts for 2008 and projected amounts for Year +1 to Year +6 for the income statements, balance sheets, and statements of cash flows for Coca-Cola (in millions). In Problem 14.21, we evaluated shares of common equity in Coca-Cola using the value-to-book approach, market multiples, price differentials, and reverse engineering.

Required

a. Prepare an exhibit using the data and analyses for PepsiCo from this chapter and the data and analyses for Coca-Cola from the previous problem that will allow you to compare these two competitors on the following dimensions:

1. Cost of equity capital (R_E)
2. ROCE for 2008
3. Projected ROCE for Year +1
4. Book value of common shareholders' equity
5. Market value of common shareholders' equity
6. Intrinsic value of common shareholders' equity

7. Value-to-book ratio
8. Market-to-book ratio
9. Value-earnings ratio (using Year +1 projected comprehensive income)
10. Price-earnings ratio (using Year +1 projected comprehensive income)
11. Value-earnings ratio (using 2008 reported earnings per share)
12. Price-earnings ratio (using 2008 reported earnings per share)
13. Price differential (on a per-share basis)
14. Price as a percentage of risk-neutral value
15. Reverse engineer share price to solve for implied expected rate of return (assuming 3 percent long-run growth)
16. Reverse engineer share price to solve for implied long-run growth (assuming the cost of equity capital as the discount rate)

b. What inferences can you draw from these comparisons about the valuation of PepsiCo versus Coca-Cola? In the chapter, we concluded that PepsiCo shares were underpriced by roughly 52 percent in the market at the end of 2008. In the previous problem, we concluded that Coca-Cola shares also were underpriced in the market at the end of 2008, by roughly 47 percent. Are these comparisons consistent with the conclusion that both PepsiCo and Coca-Cola shares could be underpriced at the end of 2008? Explain.

14.23 VALUATION OF WALMART USING MARKET MULTIPLES. In Problem 10.16, we projected financial statements for Walmart Stores for Years +1 through +5. The data in Chapter 12's Exhibits 12.16–12.18 include the actual amounts for 2008 and the projected amounts for Year +1 to Year +5 for the income statements, balance sheets, and statements of cash flows for Walmart (in millions).

The market equity beta for Walmart at the end of 2008 was 0.80. Assume that the risk-free interest rate was 3.5 percent and the market risk premium was 5.0 percent. Walmart had 3,925 million shares outstanding at the end of 2008. At the end of 2008, Walmart's share price was $46.06.

In this problem, we use these actual and projected financial statement data to apply the techniques in Chapter 14 to compute Walmart's required rate of return on equity and share value based on the value-to-book valuation model. We also compare our value-to-book ratio estimate to Walmart's market-to-book ratio at the end of 2008 to determine an investment recommendation. In addition, we compute the value-earnings and price-earnings ratios and the price differential and we reverse-engineer Walmart's share price as of the end of 2008.

Required

Part I—Computing Walmart's Value-to-Book Ratio Using the Value-to-Book Valuation Approach.

a. Use the CAPM to compute the required rate of return on common equity capital for Walmart.

b. Using the projected financial statements in Chapter 12's Exhibits 12.16–12.18, derive the projected residual ROCE (return on common shareholders' equity) for Walmart for Years +1 through +5.

c. Assume that the steady-state long-run growth rate will be 3 percent in Year +6 and beyond. Project that the Year +5 income statement and balance sheet amounts will grow by 3 percent in Year +6; then derive the projected residual ROCE for Year +6 for Walmart.

d. Using the required rate of return on common equity from Part a as a discount rate, compute the sum of the present value of residual ROCE for Walmart for Years +1 through +5.

e. Using the required rate of return on common equity from Part a as a discount rate and the long-run growth rate from Part c, compute the continuing value of Walmart as of the start of Year +6 based on Walmart's continuing residual ROCE in Year +6 and beyond. After computing continuing value as of the start of Year +6, discount it to present value at the start of Year +1.

f. Compute Walmart's value-to-book ratio as of the end of 2008 with the following three steps: (1) Compute the total sum of the present value of all future residual ROCE (from Parts d and e). (2) To the total from (1), add 1 (representing the book value of equity as of the beginning of the valuation as of the end of 2008). (3) Adjust the total sum from (2) using the midyear discounting adjustment factor.

g. Compute Walmart's market-to-book ratio as of the end of 2008. Compare the value-to-book ratio to the market-to-book ratio. What investment decision does the comparison suggest? What does the comparison suggest regarding the pricing of Walmart shares in the market: underpriced, overpriced, or fairly priced?

h. Use the value-to-book ratio to project the value of a share of common equity in Walmart.

i. If you computed Walmart's common equity share value using the dividends valuation approach in Problem 11.14 in Chapter 11, and/or the free cash flows to common equity valuation approach in Problem 12.17 in Chapter 12, and/or the residual income valuation approach in Problem 13.20 in Chapter 13, compare the value estimate you obtained in those problems with the estimate you obtained in this case. You should obtain the same value estimates under all four approaches. If you have not yet worked those problems, you would benefit from doing so now.

Part II—Analyzing Walmart's Share Price Using the Value-Earnings Ratio, the Price-Earnings Ratio, Price Differentials, and Reverse Engineering

j. Use the forecast data for Year +1 to project Year +1 earnings per share. To do so, divide the projection of Walmart's comprehensive income available for common shareholders in Year +1 by the number of common shares outstanding at the end of 2008. Using this Year +1 earnings-per-share forecast and the share value computed in Part h, compute Walmart's value-earnings ratio.

k. Using the Year +1 earnings-per-share forecast from Part j and using the share price at the end of 2008, compute Walmart's price-earnings ratio. Compare Walmart's value-earnings ratio with its price-earnings ratio. What investment decision does the comparison suggest? What does the comparison suggest regarding the pricing of Walmart shares in the market: underpriced, overpriced, or fairly priced? Does this comparison lead to the same conclusions you reached when comparing value-to-book ratios with market-to-book ratios in Part g?

l. Compute Walmart's price differential at the end of 2008. Compute Walmart's price differential as a percentage of Walmart's risk-neutral value. What dollar amount and what percentage amount has the market discounted Walmart shares for risk?

m. Reverse-engineer Walmart's share price at the end of 2008 to solve for the implied expected rate of return. First, assume that value equals price and that the earnings and growth forecasts through Year +6 and beyond are reliable proxies for the market's expectations for Walmart. Then solve for the implied expected rate of return (the discount rate) the market has impounded in Walmart's share price. (Hint: Begin with the forecast and valuation spreadsheet you developed to value Walmart shares. Vary the discount rate until you solve for the discount rate that makes your value estimate exactly equal the end-of-2008 market price of $46.06 per share.)

n. Reverse-engineer Walmart's share price at the end of 2008 to solve for the implied expected long-run growth. First, assume that value equals price and that the earnings forecasts through Year +5 are reliable proxies for the market's expectations for Walmart. Also assume that the discount rate implied by the CAPM (computed in Part a) is a reliable proxy for the market's expected rate of return. Then solve for the implied expected long-run growth rate the market has impounded in Walmart's share price. (Hint: Begin with the forecast and valuation spreadsheet you developed to value Walmart shares and use the CAPM discount rate. Set the long-run growth parameter initially to zero. Increase the long-run growth rate until you solve for the growth rate that makes your value estimate exactly equal the end-of-2008 market price of $46.06 per share.)

INTEGRATIVE CASE 14.1

STARBUCKS

Valuation of Starbucks' Common Equity Using Market Multiples

In Integrative Case 10.1, we projected financial statements for Starbucks for Years +1 through +5. In this portion of the Starbucks Integrative Case, we use the projected financial statements from Integrative Case 10.1 and apply the techniques in Chapter 14 to compute Starbucks' required rate of return on equity and share value based on the value-to-book valuation model. We also compare our value-to-book ratio estimate to Starbucks' market-to-book ratio at the time of the case to determine an investment recommendation. In addition, we compute the value-earnings and price-earnings ratios and the price differential and we reverse-engineer Starbucks' share price as of the end of 2008.

The market equity beta for Starbucks at the end of 2008 is 0.58. Assume that the risk-free interest rate is 4.0 percent and the market risk premium is 6.0 percent. Starbucks has 735.5 million shares outstanding at the end of 2008. At the start of Year +1, Starbucks' share price was $14.17.

Required

Part I—Computing Starbucks' Value-to-Book Ratio Using the Value-to-Book Valuation Approach

a. Use the CAPM to compute the required rate of return on common equity capital for Starbucks.

b. Using your projected financial statements from Integrative Case 10.1 for Starbucks, derive the projected residual ROCE (return on common shareholders' equity) for Starbucks for Years +1 through +5.

c. Assume that the steady-state long-run growth rate will be 3 percent in Year +6 and beyond. Project that the Year +5 income statement and balance sheet amounts will grow by 3 percent in Year +6; then derive the projected residual ROCE for Year +6.

d. Using the required rate of return on common equity from Part a as a discount rate, compute the sum of the present value of residual ROCE for Starbucks for Years +1 through +5.

e. Using the required rate of return on common equity from Part a as a discount rate and the long-run growth rate from Part c, compute the continuing value of Starbucks as of the start of Year +6 based on Starbucks' continuing residual ROCE in Year +6 and beyond. After computing continuing value as of the start of Year +6, discount it to present value at the start of Year +1.

f. Compute Starbucks' value-to-book ratio as of the end of 2008 with the following three steps: (1) Compute the total sum of the present value of all future residual ROCE (from Parts d and e). (2) To the total from (1), add 1 (representing the book value of equity as of the beginning of the valuation as of the end of 2008). (3) Adjust the total sum from (2) using the midyear discounting adjustment factor.

g. Compute Starbucks' market-to-book ratio as of the end of 2008. Compare the value-to-book ratio to the market-to-book ratio. What investment decision does the comparison suggest? What does the comparison suggest regarding the pricing of Starbucks' shares in the market: underpriced, overpriced, or fairly priced?

h. Use the value-to-book ratio to project the value of a share of common equity in Starbucks.

i. If you computed Starbucks' common equity share value using the dividends valuation approach in Integrative Case 11.1 in Chapter 11, and/or the free cash flows to common equity valuation approach in Integrative Case 12.1 in Chapter 12, and/or the residual income valuation approach in Integrative Case 13.1 in Chapter 13, compare the value estimate you obtained in those cases with the estimate you obtained in this case. You should obtain the same value estimates under all four approaches. If you have not yet worked those prior cases, you would benefit from doing so now.

Part II—Analyzing Starbucks' Share Price Using the Value-Earnings Ratio, the Price-Earnings Ratio, Price Differentials, and Reverse Engineering

j. Use your forecast data for Year +1 to project Year +1 earnings per share. To do so, divide your projection of Starbucks' comprehensive income available for common shareholders in Year +1 by the number of common shares outstanding at the end of 2008. Using this Year +1 earnings-per-share forecast and using the share value computed in Part h, compute Starbucks' value-earnings ratio.

k. Using the Year +1 earnings–per-share forecast from Part j and using the share price at the end of 2008, compute Starbucks' price-earnings ratio. Compare Starbucks' value-earnings ratio with its price-earnings ratio. What investment decision does the comparison suggest? What does the comparison suggest regarding the pricing of Starbucks' shares in the market: underpriced, overpriced, or fairly priced? Does this comparison lead to the same conclusions you reached when comparing value-to-book ratios with market-to-book ratios in Part g?

l. Compute Starbucks' price differential at the end of 2008. Compute Starbucks' price differential as a percentage of Starbucks' risk-neutral value. What dollar amount and what percentage amount has the market discounted Starbucks' shares for risk?

m. Reverse-engineer Starbucks' share price at the end of 2008 to solve for the implied expected rate of return. First, assume that value equals price and that your earnings and growth forecasts through Year +6 and beyond are reliable proxies for the market's expectations for Starbucks. Then solve for the implied expected rate of return (the discount rate) the market has impounded in Starbucks' share price. (Hint: Begin with the forecast and valuation spreadsheet you developed to value Starbucks' shares. Vary the discount rate until you solve for the discount rate that makes your value estimate exactly equal the end-of-2008 market price of $14.17 per share.)

n. Reverse-engineer Starbucks' share price at the end of 2008 to solve for the implied expected long-run growth. First, assume that value equals price and that your earnings forecasts through Year +5 are reliable proxies for the market's expectations for Starbucks. Also assume that the discount rate implied by the CAPM (computed in Part a) is a reliable proxy for the market's expected rate of return. Then solve for the implied expected long-run growth rate the market has impounded in Starbucks' share price. (Hint: Begin with the forecast and valuation spreadsheet you developed to value Starbucks' shares and use the CAPM discount rate. Set the long-run growth parameter initially to zero. Increase the long-run growth rate until you solve for the growth rate that makes your value estimate exactly equal the end-of-2008 market price of $14.17 per share.)

Appendix A

Financial Statements and Notes for PepsiCo, Inc. and Subsidiaries

Consolidated Statement of Income

PepsiCo, Inc. and Subsidiaries
(in millions except per share amounts)

Fiscal years ended December 27, 2008, December 29, 2007 and December 30, 2006	**2008**	2007	2006
Net Revenue	**$43,251**	$39,474	$35,137
Cost of sales	**20,351**	18,038	15,762
Selling, general and administrative expenses	**15,901**	14,208	12,711
Amortization of intangible assets	**64**	58	162
Operating Profit	**6,935**	7,170	6,502
Bottling equity income	**374**	560	553
Interest expense	**(329)**	(224)	(239)
Interest income	**41**	125	173
Income before Income Taxes	**7,021**	7,631	6,989
Provision for Income Taxes	**1,879**	1,973	1,347
Net Income	**$ 5,142**	$ 5,658	$ 5,642
Net Income per Common Share			
Basic	**$ 3.26**	$ 3.48	$ 3.42
Diluted	**$ 3.21**	$ 3.41	$ 3.34

See accompanying notes to consolidated financial statements.

Consolidated Statement of Cash Flows

PepsiCo, Inc. and Subsidiaries
(in millions)

Fiscal years ended December 27, 2008, December 29, 2007 and December 30, 2006	2008	2007	2006
Operating Activities			
Net income	**$ 5,142**	$ 5,658	$ 5,642
Depreciation and amortization	**1,543**	1,426	1,406
Stock-based compensation expense	**238**	260	270
Restructuring and impairment charges	**543**	102	67
Excess tax benefits from share-based payment arrangements	**(107)**	(208)	(134)
Cash payments for restructuring charges	**(180)**	(22)	(56)
Pension and retiree medical plan contributions	**(219)**	(310)	(131)
Pension and retiree medical plan expenses	**459**	535	544
Bottling equity income, net of dividends	**(202)**	(441)	(442)
Deferred income taxes and other tax charges and credits	**573**	118	(510)
Change in accounts and notes receivable	**(549)**	(405)	(330)
Change in inventories	**(345)**	(204)	(186)
Change in prepaid expenses and other current assets	**(68)**	(16)	(37)
Change in accounts payable and other current liabilities	**718**	522	279
Change in income taxes payable	**(180)**	128	(295)
Other, net	**(367)**	(209)	(3)
Net Cash Provided by Operating Activities	**6,999**	6,934	6,084
Investing Activities			
Capital spending	**(2,446)**	(2,430)	(2,068)
Sales of property, plant and equipment	**98**	47	49
Proceeds from (Investment in) finance assets	**–**	27	(25)
Acquisitions and investments in noncontrolled affiliates	**(1,925)**	(1,320)	(522)
Cash restricted for pending acquisitions	**(40)**	–	–
Cash proceeds from sale of PBG and PAS stock	**358**	315	318
Divestitures	**6**	–	37
Short-term investments, by original maturity			
More than three months – purchases	**(156)**	(83)	(29)
More than three months – maturities	**62**	113	25
Three months or less, net	**1,376**	(413)	2,021
Net Cash Used for Investing Activities	**(2,667)**	(3,744)	(194)
Financing Activities			
Proceeds from issuances of long-term debt	**3,719**	2,168	51
Payments of long-term debt	**(649)**	(579)	(157)
Short-term borrowings, by original maturity			
More than three months – proceeds	**89**	83	185
More than three months – payments	**(269)**	(133)	(358)
Three months or less, net	**625**	(345)	(2,168)
Cash dividends paid	**(2,541)**	(2,204)	(1,854)
Share repurchases – common	**(4,720)**	(4,300)	(3,000)
Share repurchases – preferred	**(6)**	(12)	(10)
Proceeds from exercises of stock options	**620**	1,108	1,194
Excess tax benefits from share-based payment arrangements	**107**	208	134
Net Cash Used for Financing Activities	**(3,025)**	(4,006)	(5,983)
Effect of exchange rate changes on cash and cash equivalents	**(153)**	75	28
Net Increase/(Decrease) in Cash and Cash Equivalents	**1,154**	(741)	(65)
Cash and Cash Equivalents, Beginning of Year	**910**	1,651	1,716
Cash and Cash Equivalents, End of Year	**$ 2,064**	$ 910	$ 1,651

See accompanying notes to consolidated financial statements.

Consolidated Balance Sheet

PepsiCo, Inc. and Subsidiaries
(in millions except per share amounts)

December 27, 2008 and December 29, 2007	2008	2007
ASSETS		
Current Assets		
Cash and cash equivalents	$ 2,064	$ 910
Short-term investments	213	1,571
Accounts and notes receivable, net	4,683	4,389
Inventories	2,522	2,290
Prepaid expenses and other current assets	1,324	991
Total Current Assets	10,806	10,151
Property, Plant and Equipment, net	11,663	11,228
Amortizable Intangible Assets, net	732	796
Goodwill	5,124	5,169
Other nonamortizable intangible assets	1,128	1,248
Nonamortizable Intangible Assets	6,252	6,417
Investments in Noncontrolled Affiliates	3,883	4,354
Other Assets	2,658	1,682
Total Assets	$ 35,994	$ 34,628
LIABILITIES AND SHAREHOLDERS' EQUITY		
Current Liabilities		
Short-term obligations	$ 369	$ –
Accounts payable and other current liabilities	8,273	7,602
Income taxes payable	145	151
Total Current Liabilities	8,787	7,753
Long-Term Debt Obligations	7,858	4,203
Other Liabilities	7,017	4,792
Deferred Income Taxes	226	646
Total Liabilities	23,888	17,394
Commitments and Contingencies		
Preferred Stock, no par value	41	41
Repurchased Preferred Stock	(138)	(132)
Common Shareholders' Equity		
Common stock, par value 1 2/3¢ per share (authorized 3,600 shares, issued 1,782 shares)	30	30
Capital in excess of par value	351	450
Retained earnings	30,638	28,184
Accumulated other comprehensive loss	(4,694)	(952)
Repurchased common stock, at cost (229 and 177 shares, respectively)	(14,122)	(10,387)
Total Common Shareholders' Equity	12,203	17,325
Total Liabilities and Shareholders' Equity	$ 35,994	$ 34,628

See accompanying notes to consolidated financial statements.

Consolidated Statement of Common Shareholders' Equity

PepsiCo, Inc. and Subsidiaries
(in millions)

	2008		2007		2006	
Fiscal years ended December 27, 2008, December 29, 2007 and December 30, 2006	Shares	Amount	Shares	Amount	Shares	Amount
Common Stock	1,782	$ 30	1,782	$ 30	1,782	$ 30
Capital in Excess of Par Value						
Balance, beginning of year		450		584		614
Stock-based compensation expense		238		260		270
Stock option exercises/RSUs converted (a)		(280)		(347)		(300)
Withholding tax on RSUs converted		(57)		(47)		–
Balance, end of year		351		450		584
Retained Earnings						
Balance, beginning of year		28,184		24,837		21,116
Adoption of FIN 48				7		
SFAS 158 measurement date change		(89)				
Adjusted balance, beginning of year		28,095		24,844		
Net income		5,142		5,658		5,642
Cash dividends declared – common		(2,589)		(2,306)		(1,912)
Cash dividends declared – preferred		(2)		(2)		(1)
Cash dividends declared – RSUs		(8)		(10)		(8)
Balance, end of year		30,638		28,184		24,837
Accumulated Other Comprehensive Loss						
Balance, beginning of year		(952)		(2,246)		(1,053)
SFAS 158 measurement date change		51				
Adjusted balance, beginning of year		(901)				
Currency translation adjustment		(2,484)		719		465
Cash flow hedges, net of tax:						
Net derivative gains/(losses)		16		(60)		(18)
Reclassification of losses/(gains) to net income		5		21		(5)
Adoption of SFAS 158		–		–		(1,782)
Pension and retiree medical, net of tax:						
Net pension and retiree medical (losses)/gains		(1,376)		464		–
Reclassification of net losses to net income		73		135		–
Minimum pension liability adjustment, net of tax		–		–		138
Unrealized (losses)/gains on securities, net of tax		(21)		9		9
Other		(6)		6		–
Balance, end of year		(4,694)		(952)		(2,246)
Repurchased Common Stock						
Balance, beginning of year	(177)	(10,387)	(144)	(7,758)	(126)	(6,387)
Share repurchases	(68)	(4,720)	(64)	(4,300)	(49)	(3,000)
Stock option exercises	15	883	28	1,582	31	1,619
Other, primarily RSUs converted	1	102	3	89	–	10
Balance, end of year	(229)	(14,122)	(177)	(10,387)	(144)	(7,758)
Total Common Shareholders' Equity		$ 12,203		$ 17,325		$15,447

	2008	2007	2006
Comprehensive Income			
Net income	$ 5,142	$ 5,658	$ 5,642
Currency translation adjustment	(2,484)	719	465
Cash flow hedges, net of tax	21	(39)	(23)
Minimum pension liability adjustment, net of tax	–	–	5
Pension and retiree medical, net of tax			
Net prior service cost	55	(105)	–
Net (losses)/gains	(1,358)	704	–
Unrealized (losses)/gains on securities, net of tax	(21)	9	9
Other	(6)	6	–
Total Comprehensive Income	$ 1,349	$ 6,952	$ 6,098

(a) *Includes total tax benefits of $95 million in 2008, $216 million in 2007 and $130 million in 2006.*

See accompanying notes to consolidated financial statements.

Notes to Consolidated Financial Statements

Note 1 Basis of Presentation and Our Divisions

BASIS OF PRESENTATION

Our financial statements include the consolidated accounts of PepsiCo, Inc. and the affiliates that we control. In addition, we include our share of the results of certain other affiliates based on our economic ownership interest. We do not control these other affiliates, as our ownership in these other affiliates is generally less than 50%. Equity income or loss from our anchor bottlers is recorded as bottling equity income in our income statement. Bottling equity income also includes any changes in our ownership interests of our anchor bottlers. Bottling equity income includes $147 million of pre-tax gains on our sales of PBG and PAS stock in 2008 and $174 million and $186 million of pre-tax gains on our sales of PBG stock in 2007 and 2006, respectively. See Note 8 for additional information on our significant noncontrolled bottling affiliates. Income or loss from other noncontrolled affiliates is recorded as a component of selling, general and administrative expenses. Intercompany balances and transactions are eliminated. Our fiscal year ends on the last Saturday of each December, resulting in an additional week of results every five or six years.

Raw materials, direct labor and plant overhead, as well as purchasing and receiving costs, costs directly related to production planning, inspection costs and raw material handling facilities, are included in cost of sales. The costs of moving, storing and delivering finished product are included in selling, general and administrative expenses.

The preparation of our consolidated financial statements in conformity with generally accepted accounting principles requires us to make estimates and assumptions that affect reported amounts of assets, liabilities, revenues, expenses and disclosure of contingent assets and liabilities. Estimates are used in determining, among other items, sales incentives accruals, tax reserves, stock-based compensation, pension and retiree medical accruals, useful lives for intangible assets, and future cash flows associated with impairment testing for perpetual brands, goodwill and other long-lived assets. We evaluate our estimates on an on-going basis using our historical experience, as well as other factors we believe appropriate under the circumstances, such as current economic conditions, and adjust or revise our estimates as circumstances change. As future events and their effect cannot be determined with precision, actual results could differ significantly from these estimates.

See "Our Divisions" below and for additional unaudited information on items affecting the comparability of our consolidated results, see "Items Affecting Comparability" in Management's Discussion and Analysis.

Tabular dollars are in millions, except per share amounts. All per share amounts reflect common per share amounts, assume dilution unless noted, and are based on unrounded amounts. Certain reclassifications were made to prior years' amounts to conform to the 2008 presentation.

OUR DIVISIONS

We manufacture or use contract manufacturers, market and sell a variety of salty, convenient, sweet and grain-based snacks, carbonated and non-carbonated beverages, and foods in approximately 200 countries with our largest operations in North America (United States and Canada), Mexico and the United Kingdom. Division results are based on how our Chief Executive Officer assesses the performance of and allocates resources to our divisions. For additional unaudited information on our divisions, see "Our Operations" in Management's Discussion and Analysis. The accounting policies for the divisions are the same as those described in Note 2, except for the following allocation methodologies:

- stock-based compensation expense,
- pension and retiree medical expense, and
- derivatives.

Stock-Based Compensation Expense

Our divisions are held accountable for stock-based compensation expense and, therefore, this expense is allocated to our divisions as an incremental employee compensation cost. The allocation of stock-based compensation expense in 2008 was approximately 29% to FLNA, 4% to QFNA, 7% to LAF, 23% to PAB, 13% to UKEU, 13% to MEAA and 11% to corporate unallocated expenses. We had similar allocations of stock-based compensation expense to our divisions in 2007 and 2006. The expense allocated to our divisions excludes any impact of changes in our assumptions during the year which reflect market conditions over which division management has no control. Therefore, any variances between allocated expense and our actual expense are recognized in corporate unallocated expenses.

Pension and Retiree Medical Expense

Pension and retiree medical service costs measured at a fixed discount rate, as well as amortization of gains and losses due to demographics, including salary experience, are reflected in division results for North American employees. Division results also include interest costs, measured at a fixed discount rate, for retiree medical plans. Interest costs for the pension plans, pension asset returns and the impact of pension funding, and gains and losses other than those due to demographics, are all reflected in corporate unallocated expenses. In addition, corporate unallocated expenses include the difference between the service costs measured at a fixed discount rate (included in division results as noted above) and the total service costs determined using the Plans' discount rates as disclosed in Note 7.

Derivatives

We centrally manage commodity derivatives on behalf of our divisions. These commodity derivatives include energy, fruit and other raw materials. Certain of these commodity derivatives do not qualify for hedge accounting treatment and are marked to market with the resulting gains and losses reflected in corporate unallocated expenses. These derivatives hedge underlying commodity price risk and were not entered into for speculative purposes. These gains and losses are subsequently reflected in division results when the divisions take delivery of the underlying commodity. Therefore, division results reflect the contract purchase price of these commodities.

In 2007, we expanded our commodity hedging program to include derivative contracts used to mitigate our exposure to price changes associated with our purchases of fruit. In addition, in 2008, we entered into additional contracts to further reduce our exposure to price fluctuations in our raw material and energy costs. The majority of these contracts do not qualify for hedge accounting treatment and are marked to market with the resulting gains and losses recognized in corporate unallocated expenses within selling, general and administrative expenses. These gains and losses are subsequently reflected in divisional results.

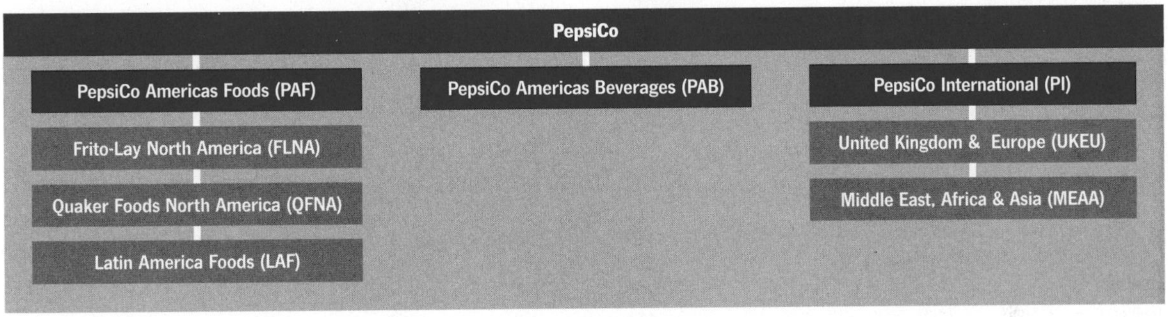

	2008	2007	2006	2008	2007	2006
	Net Revenue			Operating Profit(a)		
FLNA	**$12,507**	$11,586	$10,844	**$2,959**	$2,845	$2,615
QFNA	**1,902**	1,860	1,769	**582**	568	554
LAF	**5,895**	4,872	3,972	**897**	714	655
PAB	**10,937**	11,090	10,362	**2,026**	2,487	2,315
UKEU	**6,435**	5,492	4,750	**811**	774	700
MEAA	**5,575**	4,574	3,440	**667**	535	401
Total division	**43,251**	39,474	35,137	**7,942**	7,923	7,240
Corporate – net impact of mark-to-market on commodity hedges	**–**	–	–	**(346)**	19	(18)
Corporate – other	**–**	–	–	**(661)**	(772)	(720)
	$43,251	$39,474	$35,137	**$6,935**	$7,170	$6,502

(a) *For information on the impact of restructuring and impairment charges on our divisions, see Note 3.*

Net Revenue

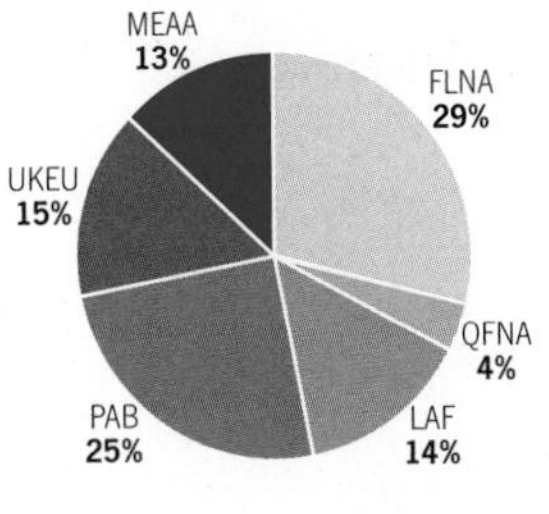

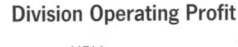

Division Operating Profit

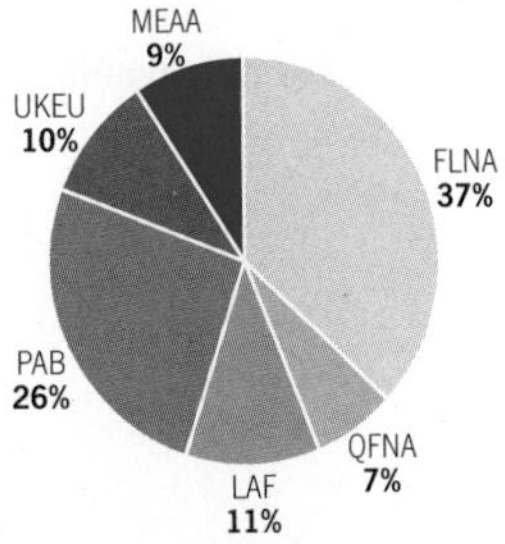

Notes to Consolidated Financial Statements

CORPORATE

Corporate includes costs of our corporate headquarters, centrally managed initiatives, such as our ongoing business transformation initiative and research and development projects, unallocated insurance and benefit programs, foreign exchange transaction gains and losses, certain commodity derivative gains and losses and certain other items.

OTHER DIVISION INFORMATION

	2008	2007	2006	2008	2007	2006
	Total Assets			Capital Spending		
FLNA	**$ 6,284**	$ 6,270	$ 5,969	**$ 553**	$ 624	$ 499
QFNA	**1,035**	1,002	1,003	**43**	41	31
LAF	**3,023**	3,084	2,169	**351**	326	235
PAB	**7,673**	7,780	7,129	**344**	450	516
UKEU	**8,635**	7,102	5,865	**377**	349	277
MEAA	**3,961**	3,911	2,975	**503**	413	299
Total division	**30,611**	29,149	25,110	**2,171**	2,203	1,857
Corporate [(a)]	**2,729**	2,124	1,739	**275**	227	211
Investments in bottling affiliates	**2,654**	3,355	3,081	**–**	–	–
	$35,994	$34,628	$29,930	**$2,446**	$2,430	$2,068

(a) *Corporate assets consist principally of cash and cash equivalents, short-term investments, derivative instruments and property, plant and equipment.*

	2008	2007	2006	2008	2007	2006
	Amortization of Intangible Assets			Depreciation and Other Amortization		
FLNA	**$ 9**	$ 9	$ 9	**$ 441**	$ 437	$ 432
QFNA	**–**	–	–	**34**	34	33
LAF	**6**	4	1	**194**	166	140
PAB	**16**	16	83	**334**	321	298
UKEU	**22**	18	17	**199**	181	167
MEAA	**11**	11	52	**224**	198	155
Total division	**64**	58	162	**1,426**	1,337	1,225
Corporate	**–**	–	–	**53**	31	19
	$64	$58	$162	**$1,479**	$1,368	$1,244

	2008	2007	2006	2008	2007	2006
	Net Revenue [(a)]			Long-Lived Assets [(b)]		
U.S.	**$22,525**	$21,978	$20,788	**$12,095**	$12,498	$11,515
Mexico	**3,714**	3,498	3,228	**904**	1,067	996
Canada	**2,107**	1,961	1,702	**556**	699	589
United Kingdom	**2,099**	1,987	1,839	**1,509**	2,090	1,995
All other countries	**12,806**	10,050	7,580	**7,466**	6,441	4,725
	$43,251	$39,474	$35,137	**$22,530**	$22,795	$19,820

(a) *Represents net revenue from businesses operating in these countries.*

(b) *Long-lived assets represent property, plant and equipment, nonamortizable intangible assets, amortizable intangible assets, and investments in noncontrolled affiliates. These assets are reported in the country where they are primarily used.*

Total Assets

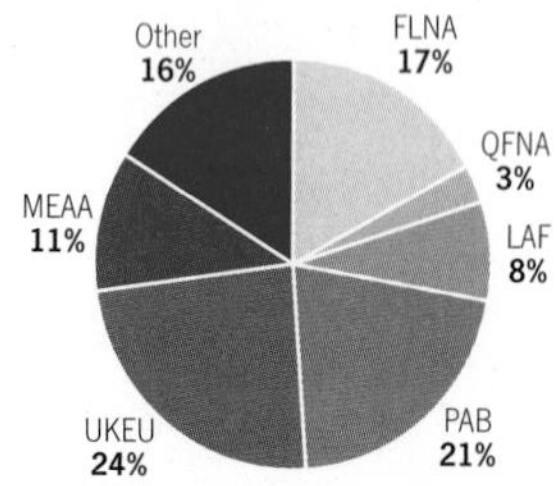

Capital Spending

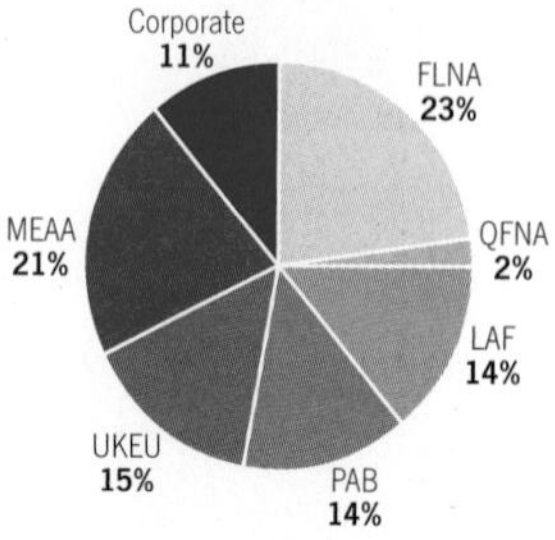

Net Revenue

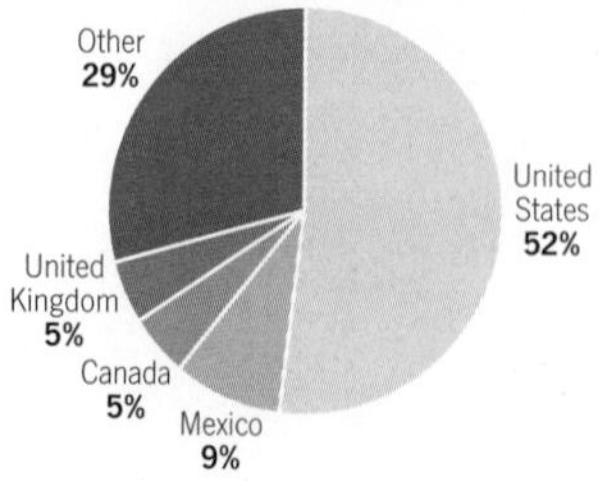

Long-Lived Assets

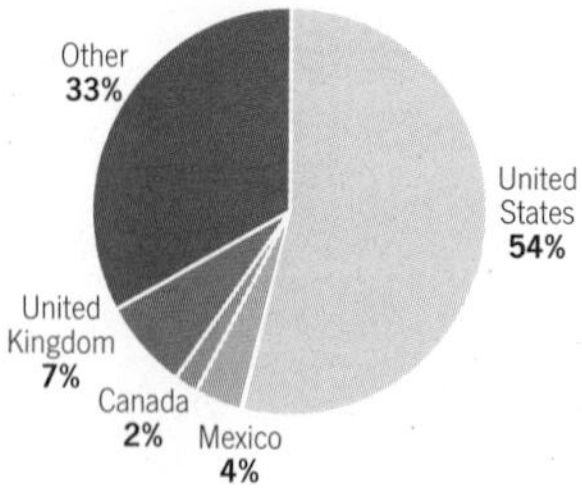

Note 2 Our Significant Accounting Policies

REVENUE RECOGNITION

We recognize revenue upon shipment or delivery to our customers based on written sales terms that do not allow for a right of return. However, our policy for DSD and chilled products is to remove and replace damaged and out-of-date products from store shelves to ensure that our consumers receive the product quality and freshness that they expect. Similarly, our policy for certain warehouse-distributed products is to replace damaged and out-of-date products. Based on our experience with this practice, we have reserved for anticipated damaged and out-of-date products. For additional unaudited information on our revenue recognition and related policies, including our policy on bad debts, see "Our Critical Accounting Policies" in Management's Discussion and Analysis. We are exposed to concentration of credit risk by our customers, Wal-Mart and PBG. In 2008, Wal-Mart (including Sam's) represented approximately 12% of our total net revenue, including concentrate sales to our bottlers which are used in finished goods sold by them to Wal-Mart; and PBG represented approximately 8%. We have not experienced credit issues with these customers.

SALES INCENTIVES AND OTHER MARKETPLACE SPENDING

We offer sales incentives and discounts through various programs to our customers and consumers. Sales incentives and discounts are accounted for as a reduction of revenue and totaled $12.5 billion in 2008, $11.3 billion in 2007 and $10.1 billion in 2006. While most of these incentive arrangements have terms of no more than one year, certain arrangements, such as fountain pouring rights, may extend beyond one year. Costs incurred to obtain these arrangements are recognized over the shorter of the economic or contractual life, as a reduction of revenue, and the remaining balances of $333 million at December 27, 2008 and $314 million at December 29, 2007 are included in current assets and other assets on our balance sheet. For additional unaudited information on our sales incentives, see "Our Critical Accounting Policies" in Management's Discussion and Analysis.

Other marketplace spending, which includes the costs of advertising and other marketing activities, totaled $2.9 billion in 2008, $2.9 billion in 2007 and $2.7 billion in 2006 and is reported as selling, general and administrative expenses. Included in these amounts were advertising expenses of $1.8 billion in both 2008 and 2007 and $1.6 billion in 2006. Deferred advertising costs are not expensed until the year first used and consist of:

- media and personal service prepayments,
- promotional materials in inventory, and
- production costs of future media advertising.

Deferred advertising costs of $172 million and $160 million at year-end 2008 and 2007, respectively, are classified as prepaid expenses on our balance sheet.

DISTRIBUTION COSTS

Distribution costs, including the costs of shipping and handling activities, are reported as selling, general and administrative expenses. Shipping and handling expenses were $5.3 billion in 2008, $5.1 billion in 2007 and $4.6 billion in 2006.

CASH EQUIVALENTS

Cash equivalents are investments with original maturities of three months or less which we do not intend to rollover beyond three months.

SOFTWARE COSTS

We capitalize certain computer software and software development costs incurred in connection with developing or obtaining computer software for internal use when both the preliminary project stage is completed and it is probable that the software will be used as intended. Capitalized software costs include only (i) external direct costs of materials and services utilized in developing or obtaining computer software, (ii) compensation and related benefits for employees who are directly associated with the software project and (iii) interest costs incurred while developing internal-use computer software. Capitalized software costs are included in property, plant and equipment on our balance sheet and amortized on a straight-line basis when placed into service over the estimated useful lives of the software, which approximate five to ten years. Net capitalized software and development costs were $940 million at December 27, 2008 and $761 million at December 29, 2007.

COMMITMENTS AND CONTINGENCIES

We are subject to various claims and contingencies related to lawsuits, certain taxes and environmental matters, as well as commitments under contractual and other commercial obligations. We recognize liabilities for contingencies and commitments when a loss is probable and estimable. For additional information on our commitments, see Note 9.

Notes to Consolidated Financial Statements

RESEARCH AND DEVELOPMENT

We engage in a variety of research and development activities. These activities principally involve the development of new products, improvement in the quality of existing products, improvement and modernization of production processes, and the development and implementation of new technologies to enhance the quality and value of both current and proposed product lines. Consumer research is excluded from research and development costs and included in other marketing costs. Research and development costs were $388 million in 2008, $364 million in 2007 and $282 million in 2006 and are reported within selling, general and administrative expenses.

OTHER SIGNIFICANT ACCOUNTING POLICIES

Our other significant accounting policies are disclosed as follows:

- *Property, Plant and Equipment and Intangible Assets* – Note 4, and for additional unaudited information on brands and goodwill, see "Our Critical Accounting Policies" in Management's Discussion and Analysis.
- *Income Taxes* – Note 5, and for additional unaudited information, see "Our Critical Accounting Policies" in Management's Discussion and Analysis.
- *Stock-Based Compensation* – Note 6.
- *Pension, Retiree Medical and Savings Plans* – Note 7, and for additional unaudited information, see "Our Critical Accounting Policies" in Management's Discussion and Analysis.
- *Financial Instruments* – Note 10, and for additional unaudited information, see "Our Business Risks" in Management's Discussion and Analysis.

RECENT ACCOUNTING PRONOUNCEMENTS

In February 2007, the FASB issued SFAS 159 which permits entities to choose to measure many financial instruments and certain other items at fair value. We adopted SFAS 159 as of the beginning of our 2008 fiscal year and our adoption did not impact our financial statements.

In December 2007, the FASB issued SFAS 141R, to improve, simplify and converge internationally the accounting for business combinations. SFAS 141R continues the movement toward the greater use of fair value in financial reporting and increased transparency through expanded disclosures. It changes how business acquisitions are accounted for and will impact financial statements both on the acquisition date and in subsequent periods. The provisions of SFAS 141R are effective as of the beginning of our 2009 fiscal year, with the exception of adjustments made to valuation allowances on deferred taxes and acquired tax contingencies. Adjustments made to valuation allowances on deferred taxes and acquired tax contingencies associated with acquisitions that closed prior to the beginning of our 2009 fiscal year would apply the provisions of SFAS 141R. Future adjustments made to valuation allowances on deferred taxes and acquired tax contingencies associated with acquisitions that closed prior to the beginning of our 2009 fiscal year would apply the provisions of SFAS 141R and will be evaluated based on the outcome of these matters. We do not expect the adoption of SFAS 141R to have a material impact on our financial statements.

In December 2007, the FASB issued SFAS 160. SFAS 160 amends ARB 51 to establish new standards that will govern the accounting for and reporting of (1) noncontrolling interests in partially owned consolidated subsidiaries and (2) the loss of control of subsidiaries. The provisions of SFAS 160 are effective as of the beginning of our 2009 fiscal year on a prospective basis. We do not expect our adoption of SFAS 160 to have a significant impact on our financial statements. In the first quarter of 2009, we will include the required disclosures for all periods presented.

In March 2008, the FASB issued SFAS 161 which amends and expands the disclosure requirements of SFAS 133 to provide an enhanced understanding of the use of derivative instruments, how they are accounted for under SFAS 133 and their effect on financial position, financial performance and cash flows. The disclosure provisions of SFAS 161 are effective as of the beginning of our 2009 fiscal year.

Note 3 Restructuring and Impairment Charges

2008 RESTRUCTURING AND IMPAIRMENT CHARGE

In 2008, we incurred a charge of $543 million ($408 million after-tax or $0.25 per share) in conjunction with our Productivity for Growth program. The program includes actions in all divisions of the business that we believe will increase cost competitiveness across the supply chain, upgrade and streamline our product portfolio, and simplify the organization for more effective and timely decision-making. Approximately $455 million of the charge was recorded in selling, general and administrative expenses, with the remainder recorded in cost of sales. Substantially all cash payments related to this charge are expected to be paid by the end of 2009.

A summary of the restructuring and impairment charge is as follows:

	Severance and Other Employee Costs	Asset Impairments	Other Costs	Total
FLNA	$ 48	$ 38	$ 22	$108
QFNA	14	3	14	31
LAF	30	8	2	40
PAB	68	92	129	289
UKEU	39	6	5	50
MEAA	11	2	2	15
Corporate	2	–	8	10
	$212	$149	$182	$543

Severance and other employee costs primarily reflect termination costs for approximately 3,500 employees. Asset impairments relate to the closure of 6 plants and changes to our beverage product portfolio. Other costs include contract exit costs and third-party incremental costs associated with upgrading our product portfolio and our supply chain.

A summary of our Productivity for Growth program activity is as follows:

	Severance and Other Employee Costs	Asset Impairments	Other Costs	Total
2008 restructuring and impairment charge	$212	$ 149	$ 182	$ 543
Cash payments	(50)	–	(109)	(159)
Non-cash charge	(27)	(149)	(9)	(185)
Currency translation	(1)	–	–	(1)
Liability at December 27, 2008	$134	$ –	$ 64	$ 198

2007 RESTRUCTURING AND IMPAIRMENT CHARGE

In 2007, we incurred a charge of $102 million ($70 million after-tax or $0.04 per share) in conjunction with restructuring actions primarily to close certain plants and rationalize other production lines across FLNA, LAF, PAB, UKEU and MEAA. The charge was recorded in selling, general and administrative expenses. All cash payments related to this charge were paid by the end of 2008.

A summary of the restructuring and impairment charge is as follows:

	Severance and Other Employee Costs	Asset Impairments	Other Costs	Total
FLNA	$ –	$19	$ 9	$ 28
LAF	14	25	–	39
PAB	12	–	–	12
UKEU	2	4	3	9
MEAA	5	9	–	14
	$33	$57	$12	$102

Severance and other employee costs primarily reflect termination costs for approximately 1,100 employees.

2006 RESTRUCTURING AND IMPAIRMENT CHARGE

In 2006, we incurred a charge of $67 million ($43 million after-tax or $0.03 per share) in conjunction with consolidating the manufacturing network at FLNA by closing two plants in the U.S., and rationalizing other assets, to increase manufacturing productivity and supply chain efficiencies. The charge was comprised of $43 million of asset impairments, $14 million of severance and other employee costs and $10 million of other costs. Severance and other employee costs primarily reflect the termination costs for approximately 380 employees. All cash payments related to this charge were paid by the end of 2007.

Note 4 Property, Plant and Equipment and Intangible Assets

	Average Useful Life	2008	2007	2006
Property, plant and equipment, net				
Land and improvements	10–34 yrs.	**$ 868**	$ 864	
Buildings and improvements	20–44	**4,738**	4,577	
Machinery and equipment, including fleet and software	5–14	**15,173**	14,471	
Construction in progress		**1,773**	1,984	
		22,552	21,896	
Accumulated depreciation		**(10,889)**	(10,668)	
		$ 11,663	$ 11,228	
Depreciation expense		**$ 1,422**	$ 1,304	$1,182
Amortizable intangible assets, net				
Brands	5–40	**$ 1,411**	$ 1,476	
Other identifiable intangibles	10–24	**360**	344	
		1,771	1,820	
Accumulated amortization		**(1,039)**	(1,024)	
		$ 732	$ 796	
Amortization expense		**$ 64**	$ 58	$ 162

Property, plant and equipment is recorded at historical cost. Depreciation and amortization are recognized on a straight-line basis over an asset's estimated useful life. Land is not depreciated and construction in progress is not depreciated until ready for service. Amortization of intangible assets for each of the next five years, based on average 2008 foreign exchange rates, is expected to be $64 million in 2009, $63 million in 2010, $62 million in 2011, $60 million in 2012 and $56 million in 2013.

Notes to Consolidated Financial Statements

Depreciable and amortizable assets are only evaluated for impairment upon a significant change in the operating or macroeconomic environment. In these circumstances, if an evaluation of the undiscounted cash flows indicates impairment, the asset is written down to its estimated fair value, which is based on discounted future cash flows. Useful lives are periodically evaluated to determine whether events or circumstances have occurred which indicate the need for revision. For additional unaudited information on our amortizable brand policies, see "Our Critical Accounting Policies" in Management's Discussion and Analysis.

NONAMORTIZABLE INTANGIBLE ASSETS

Perpetual brands and goodwill are assessed for impairment at least annually. If the carrying amount of a perpetual brand exceeds its fair value, as determined by its discounted cash flows, an impairment loss is recognized in an amount equal to that excess. No impairment charges resulted from the required impairment evaluations. The change in the book value of nonamortizable intangible assets is as follows:

	Balance, Beginning 2007	Acquisitions	Translation and Other	Balance, End of 2007	Acquisitions	Translation and Other	**Balance, End of 2008**
FLNA							
Goodwill	$ 284	$ –	$ 27	$ 311	$ –	$ (34)	**$ 277**
QFNA							
Goodwill	175	–	–	175	–	–	**175**
LAF							
Goodwill	144	–	3	147	338	(61)	**424**
Brands	22	–	–	22	118	(13)	**127**
	166	–	3	169	456	(74)	**551**
PAB							
Goodwill	2,203	146	20	2,369	–	(14)	**2,355**
Brands	59	–	–	59	–	–	**59**
	2,262	146	20	2,428	–	(14)	**2,414**
UKEU							
Goodwill	1,412	122	92	1,626	45	(215)	**1,456**
Brands	1,018	–	23	1,041	14	(211)	**844**
	2,430	122	115	2,667	59	(426)	**2,300**
MEAA							
Goodwill	376	114	51	541	1	(105)	**437**
Brands	113	–	13	126	–	(28)	**98**
	489	114	64	667	1	(133)	**535**
Total goodwill	4,594	382	193	5,169	384	(429)	**5,124**
Total brands	1,212	–	36	1,248	132	(252)	**1,128**
	$5,806	$382	$229	$6,417	$516	$(681)	**$6,252**

Note 5 Income Taxes

	2008	2007	2006
Income before income taxes			
U.S.	$3,274	$4,085	$3,844
Foreign	3,747	3,546	3,145
	$7,021	$7,631	$6,989
Provision for income taxes			
Current: U.S. Federal	$ 815	$1,422	$ 776
Foreign	732	489	569
State	87	104	56
	1,634	2,015	1,401
Deferred: U.S. Federal	313	22	(31)
Foreign	(69)	(66)	(16)
State	1	2	(7)
	245	(42)	(54)
	$1,879	$1,973	$1,347
Tax rate reconciliation			
U.S. Federal statutory tax rate	35.0%	35.0%	35.0%
State income tax, net of U.S. Federal tax benefit	0.8	0.9	0.5
Lower taxes on foreign results	(7.9)	(6.5)	(6.5)
Tax settlements	–	(1.7)	(8.6)
Other, net	(1.1)	(1.8)	(1.1)
Annual tax rate	26.8%	25.9%	19.3%
Deferred tax liabilities			
Investments in noncontrolled affiliates	$1,193	$1,163	
Property, plant and equipment	881	828	
Intangible assets other than nondeductible goodwill	295	280	
Pension benefits	–	148	
Other	73	136	
Gross deferred tax liabilities	2,442	2,555	
Deferred tax assets			
Net carryforwards	682	722	
Stock-based compensation	410	425	
Retiree medical benefits	495	528	
Other employee-related benefits	428	447	
Pension benefits	345	–	
Deductible state tax and interest benefits	230	189	
Other	677	618	
Gross deferred tax assets	3,267	2,929	
Valuation allowances	(657)	(695)	
Deferred tax assets, net	2,610	2,234	
Net deferred tax (assets)/liabilities	$ (168)	$ 321	

	2008	2007	2006
Deferred taxes included within:			
Assets:			
Prepaid expenses and other current assets	$372	$325	$223
Other assets	$ 22	–	–
Liabilities:			
Deferred income taxes	$226	$646	$528
Analysis of valuation allowances			
Balance, beginning of year	$695	$624	$532
(Benefit)/provision	(5)	39	71
Other (deductions)/additions	(33)	32	21
Balance, end of year	$657	$695	$624

For additional unaudited information on our income tax policies, including our reserves for income taxes, see "Our Critical Accounting Policies" in Management's Discussion and Analysis.

In 2007, we recognized $129 million of non-cash tax benefits related to the favorable resolution of certain foreign tax matters. In 2006, we recognized non-cash tax benefits of $602 million, substantially all of which related to the IRS's examination of our consolidated income tax returns for the years 1998 through 2002.

RESERVES

A number of years may elapse before a particular matter, for which we have established a reserve, is audited and finally resolved. The number of years with open tax audits varies depending on the tax jurisdiction. Our major taxing jurisdictions and the related open tax audits are as follows:

- U.S. – continue to dispute one matter related to tax years 1998 through 2002. Our U.S. tax returns for the years 2003 through 2005 are currently under audit. In 2008, the IRS initiated its audit of our U.S. tax returns for the years 2006 through 2007;
- Mexico – audits have been substantially completed for all taxable years through 2005;
- United Kingdom – audits have been completed for all taxable years prior to 2004; and
- Canada – audits have been completed for all taxable years through 2005. We are in agreement with the conclusions, except for one matter which we continue to dispute. The Canadian tax return for 2006 is currently under audit.

Notes to Consolidated Financial Statements

While it is often difficult to predict the final outcome or the timing of resolution of any particular tax matter, we believe that our reserves reflect the probable outcome of known tax contingencies. We adjust these reserves, as well as the related interest, in light of changing facts and circumstances. Settlement of any particular issue would usually require the use of cash. Favorable resolution would be recognized as a reduction to our annual tax rate in the year of resolution.

For further unaudited information on the impact of the resolution of open tax issues, see "Other Consolidated Results."

In 2006, the FASB issued FASB Interpretation No. 48, *Accounting for Uncertainty in Income Taxes – an interpretation of FASB Statement No. 109,* (FIN 48), which clarifies the accounting for uncertainty in tax positions. FIN 48 requires that we recognize in our financial statements the impact of a tax position, if that position is more likely than not of being sustained on audit, based on the technical merits of the position. We adopted the provisions of FIN 48 as of the beginning of our 2007 fiscal year.

As of December 27, 2008, the total gross amount of reserves for income taxes, reported in other liabilities, was $1.7 billion. Any prospective adjustments to these reserves will be recorded as an increase or decrease to our provision for income taxes and would impact our effective tax rate. In addition, we accrue interest related to reserves for income taxes in our provision for income taxes and any associated penalties are recorded in selling, general and administrative expenses. The gross amount of interest accrued, reported in other liabilities, was $427 million as of December 27, 2008, of which $95 million was recognized in 2008. The gross amount of interest accrued was $338 million as of December 29, 2007, of which $34 million was recognized in 2007.

A rollforward of our reserves for all federal, state and foreign tax jurisdictions, is as follows:

	2008	2007
Balance, beginning of year	**$1,461**	$1,435
FIN 48 adoption adjustment to retained earnings	–	(7)
Reclassification of deductible state tax and interest benefits to other balance sheet accounts	–	(144)
Adjusted balance, beginning of year	**1,461**	1,284
Additions for tax positions related to the current year	**272**	264
Additions for tax positions from prior years	**76**	151
Reductions for tax positions from prior years	**(14)**	(73)
Settlement payments	**(30)**	(174)
Statute of limitations expiration	**(20)**	(7)
Translation and other	**(34)**	16
Balance, end of year	**$1,711**	$1,461

CARRYFORWARDS AND ALLOWANCES

Operating loss carryforwards totaling $7.2 billion at year-end 2008 are being carried forward in a number of foreign and state jurisdictions where we are permitted to use tax operating losses from prior periods to reduce future taxable income. These operating losses will expire as follows: $0.3 billion in 2009, $6.2 billion between 2010 and 2028 and $0.7 billion may be carried forward indefinitely. We establish valuation allowances for our deferred tax assets if, based on the available evidence, it is more likely than not that some portion or all of the deferred tax assets will not be realized.

UNDISTRIBUTED INTERNATIONAL EARNINGS

At December 27, 2008, we had approximately $17.1 billion of undistributed international earnings. We intend to continue to reinvest earnings outside the U.S. for the foreseeable future and, therefore, have not recognized any U.S. tax expense on these earnings.

Note 6 Stock-Based Compensation

Our stock-based compensation program is a broad-based program designed to attract and retain employees while also aligning employees' interests with the interests of our shareholders. A majority of our employees participate in our stock-based compensation program. This program includes both our broad-based SharePower program which was established in 1989 to grant an annual award of stock options to eligible employees, based upon job level or classification and tenure (internationally), as well as our executive long-term awards program. Stock options and restricted stock units (RSU) are granted to employees under the shareholder-approved 2007 Long-Term Incentive Plan (LTIP), our only active stock-based plan. Stock-based compensation expense was $238 million in 2008, $260 million in 2007 and $270 million in 2006. Related income tax benefits recognized in earnings were $71 million in 2008, $77 million in 2007 and $80 million in 2006. Stock-based compensation cost capitalized in connection with our ongoing business transformation initiative was $4 million in 2008, $3 million in 2007 and $3 million in 2006. At year-end 2008, 57 million shares were available for future stock-based compensation grants.

METHOD OF ACCOUNTING AND OUR ASSUMPTIONS

We account for our employee stock options, which include grants under our executive program and our broad-based SharePower program, under the fair value method of accounting using a Black-Scholes valuation model to measure stock option expense at the date of grant. All stock option grants have an exercise price equal to the fair market value of our common stock on the date of grant and generally have a 10-year term. We do not backdate, reprice or grant stock-based compensation awards retroactively. Repricing of awards would require shareholder approval under the LTIP.

The fair value of stock option grants is amortized to expense over the vesting period, generally three years. Executives who are awarded long-term incentives based on their performance are offered the choice of stock options or RSUs. Executives who elect RSUs receive one RSU for every four stock options that would have otherwise been granted. Senior officers do not have a choice and are granted 50% stock options and 50% performance-based RSUs. Vesting of RSU awards for senior officers is contingent upon the achievement of pre-established performance targets approved by the Compensation Committee of the Board of Directors. RSU expense is based on the fair value of PepsiCo stock on the date of grant and is amortized over the vesting period, generally three years. Each RSU is settled in a share of our stock after the vesting period.

Our weighted-average Black-Scholes fair value assumptions are as follows:

	2008	2007	2006
Expected life	**6 yrs.**	6 yrs.	6 yrs.
Risk free interest rate	**3.0%**	4.8%	4.5%
Expected volatility	**16%**	15%	18%
Expected dividend yield	**1.9%**	1.9%	1.9%

The expected life is the period over which our employee groups are expected to hold their options. It is based on our historical experience with similar grants. The risk free interest rate is based on the expected U.S. Treasury rate over the expected life. Volatility reflects movements in our stock price over the most recent historical period equivalent to the expected life. Dividend yield is estimated over the expected life based on our stated dividend policy and forecasts of net income, share repurchases and stock price.

A summary of our stock-based compensation activity for the year ended December 27, 2008 is presented below:

Our Stock Option Activity

	Options[(a)]	Average Price[(b)]	Average Life (years)[(c)]	Aggregate Intrinsic Value[(d)]
Outstanding at December 29, 2007	108,808	$47.47		
Granted	12,512	68.74		
Exercised	(14,651)	42.19		
Forfeited/expired	(2,997)	60.13		
Outstanding at December 27, 2008	103,672	$50.42	4.93	$736,438
Exercisable at December 27, 2008	61,085	$43.41	3.16	$683,983

(a) *Options are in thousands and include options previously granted under Quaker plans. No additional options or shares may be granted under the Quaker plans.*
(b) *Weighted-average exercise price.*
(c) *Weighted-average contractual life remaining.*
(d) *In thousands.*

Our RSU Activity

	RSUs[(a)]	Average Intrinsic Value[(b)]	Average Life (years)[(c)]	Aggregate Intrinsic Value[(d)]
Outstanding at December 29, 2007	7,370	$58.63		
Granted	2,135	68.73		
Converted	(2,500)	54.59		
Forfeited/expired	(854)	62.90		
Outstanding at December 27, 2008	6,151	$63.18	1.20	$335,583

(a) *RSUs are in thousands.*
(b) *Weighted-average intrinsic value at grant date.*
(c) *Weighted-average contractual life remaining.*
(d) *In thousands.*

OTHER STOCK-BASED COMPENSATION DATA

	2008	2007	2006
Stock Options			
Weighted-average fair value of options granted	**$ 11.24**	$ 13.56	$ 12.81
Total intrinsic value of options exercised[(a)]	**$410,152**	$826,913	$686,242
RSUs			
Total number of RSUs granted[(a)]	**2,135**	2,342	2,992
Weighted-average intrinsic value of RSUs granted	**$ 68.73**	$ 65.21	$ 58.22
Total intrinsic value of RSUs converted[(a)]	**$180,563**	$125,514	$ 10,934

(a) *In thousands.*

At December 27, 2008, there was $243 million of total unrecognized compensation cost related to nonvested share-based compensation grants. This unrecognized compensation is expected to be recognized over a weighted-average period of 1.7 years.

Notes to Consolidated Financial Statements

Note 7 Pension, Retiree Medical and Savings Plans

Our pension plans cover full-time employees in the U.S. and certain international employees. Benefits are determined based on either years of service or a combination of years of service and earnings. U.S. and Canada retirees are also eligible for medical and life insurance benefits (retiree medical) if they meet age and service requirements. Generally, our share of retiree medical costs is capped at specified dollar amounts, which vary based upon years of service, with retirees contributing the remainder of the costs.

Gains and losses resulting from actual experience differing from our assumptions, including the difference between the actual return on plan assets and the expected return on plan assets, and from changes in our assumptions are also determined at each measurement date. If this net accumulated gain or loss exceeds 10% of the greater of the market-related value of plan assets or plan liabilities, a portion of the net gain or loss is included in expense for the following year. The cost or benefit of plan changes that increase or decrease benefits for prior employee service (prior service cost/(credit)) is included in earnings on a straight-line basis over the average remaining service period of active plan participants, which is approximately 10 years for pension expense and approximately 12 years for retiree medical expense.

On December 30, 2006, we adopted SFAS 158. In connection with our adoption, we recognized the funded status of our Plans on our balance sheet as of December 30, 2006 with subsequent changes in the funded status recognized in comprehensive income in the years in which they occur. In accordance with SFAS 158, amounts prior to the year of adoption have not been adjusted. SFAS 158 also required that, no later than 2008, our assumptions used to measure our annual pension and retiree medical expense be determined as of the balance sheet date, and all plan assets and liabilities be reported as of that date. Accordingly, as of the beginning of our 2008 fiscal year, we changed the measurement date for our annual pension and retiree medical expense and all plan assets and liabilities from September 30 to our year-end balance sheet date. As a result of this change in measurement date, we recorded an after-tax $39 million decrease to 2008 opening shareholders' equity, as follows:

	Pension	Retiree Medical	Total
Retained earnings	$(63)	$(20)	$(83)
Accumulated other comprehensive loss	12	32	44
Total	$(51)	$ 12	$(39)

Selected financial information for our pension and retiree medical plans is as follows:

	Pension				Retiree Medical	
	2008	2007	2008	2007	2008	2007
	U.S.		International			
Change in projected benefit liability						
Liability at beginning of year	$ 6,048	$5,947	$1,595	$1,511	$ 1,354	$ 1,370
SFAS 158 measurement date change	(199)	–	113	–	(37)	–
Service cost	244	244	61	59	45	48
Interest cost	371	338	88	81	82	77
Plan amendments	(20)	147	2	4	(47)	–
Participant contributions	–	–	17	14	–	–
Experience loss/(gain)	28	(309)	(165)	(155)	58	(80)
Benefit payments	(277)	(319)	(51)	(46)	(70)	(77)
Settlement/curtailment loss	(9)	–	(15)	–	(2)	–
Special termination benefits	31	–	2	–	3	–
Foreign currency adjustment	–	–	(376)	96	(10)	9
Other	–	–	(1)	31	(6)	7
Liability at end of year	$ 6,217	$6,048	$1,270	$1,595	$ 1,370	$ 1,354
Change in fair value of plan assets						
Fair value at beginning of year	$ 5,782	$5,378	$1,595	$1,330	$ –	$ –
SFAS 158 measurement date change	(136)	–	97	–	–	–
Actual return on plan assets	(1,434)	654	(241)	122	–	–
Employer contributions/funding	48	69	101	58	70	77
Participant contributions	–	–	17	14	–	–
Benefit payments	(277)	(319)	(51)	(46)	(70)	(77)
Settlement/curtailment loss	(9)	–	(11)	–	–	–
Foreign currency adjustment	–	–	(341)	91	–	–
Other	–	–	(1)	26	–	–
Fair value at end of year	$ 3,974	$5,782	$1,165	$1,595	$ –	$ –
Reconciliation of funded status						
Funded status	$(2,243)	$ (266)	$ (105)	$ –	$(1,370)	$(1,354)
Adjustment for fourth quarter contributions	–	15	–	107	–	19
Adjustment for fourth quarter special termination benefits	–	(5)	–	–	–	–
Net amount recognized	$(2,243)	$ (256)	$ (105)	$ 107	$(1,370)	$(1,335)
Amounts recognized						
Other assets	$ –	$ 440	$ 28	$ 187	$ –	$ –
Other current liabilities	(60)	(24)	(1)	(3)	(102)	(88)
Other liabilities	(2,183)	(672)	(132)	(77)	(1,268)	(1,247)
Net amount recognized	$(2,243)	$ (256)	$ (105)	$ 107	$(1,370)	$(1,335)
Amounts included in accumulated other comprehensive loss/(credit) (pre-tax)						
Net loss	$ 2,826	$1,136	$ 421	$ 287	$ 266	$ 276
Prior service cost/(credit)	112	156	20	28	(119)	(88)
Total	$ 2,938	$1,292	$ 441	$ 315	$ 147	$ 188
Components of the increase/(decrease) in net loss						
SFAS 158 measurement date change	$ (130)	$ –	$ 105	$ –	$ (53)	$ –
Change in discount rate	247	(292)	(219)	(224)	36	(50)
Employee-related assumption changes	(194)	–	52	61	6	(9)
Liability-related experience different from assumptions	(25)	(17)	(4)	7	10	(21)
Actual asset return different from expected return	1,850	(255)	354	(25)	–	–
Amortization of losses	(58)	(136)	(19)	(30)	(8)	(18)
Other, including foreign currency adjustments and 2003 Medicare Act	–	–	(135)	23	(1)	10
Total	$ 1,690	$ (700)	$ 134	$ (188)	$ (10)	$ (88)
Liability at end of year for service to date	$ 5,413	$5,026	$1,013	$1,324		

Notes to Consolidated Financial Statements

Components of benefit expense are as follows:

	Pension						Retiree Medical		
	2008	2007	2006	2008	2007	2006	2008	2007	2006
	U.S.			International					
Components of benefit expense									
Service cost	**$ 244**	$ 244	$ 245	**$ 61**	$ 59	$ 52	**$ 45**	$ 48	$ 46
Interest cost	**371**	338	319	**88**	81	68	**82**	77	72
Expected return on plan assets	**(416)**	(399)	(391)	**(112)**	(97)	(81)	**–**	–	–
Amortization of prior service cost/(credit)	**19**	5	3	**3**	3	2	**(13)**	(13)	(13)
Amortization of net loss	**55**	136	164	**19**	30	29	**7**	18	21
	273	324	340	**59**	76	70	**121**	130	126
Settlement/curtailment loss	**3**	–	3	**3**	–	–	**–**	–	–
Special termination benefits	**31**	5	4	**2**	–	–	**3**	–	1
Total	**$ 307**	$ 329	$ 347	**$ 64**	$ 76	$ 70	**$124**	$130	$127

The estimated amounts to be amortized from accumulated other comprehensive loss into benefit expense in 2009 for our pension and retiree medical plans are as follows:

	Pension		Retiree Medical
	U.S.	International	
Net loss	$ 98	$10	$ 11
Prior service cost/(credit)	11	2	(17)
Total	$109	$12	$ (6)

The following table provides the weighted-average assumptions used to determine projected benefit liability and benefit expense for our pension and retiree medical plans:

	Pension						Retiree Medical		
	2008	2007	2006	2008	2007	2006	2008	2007	2006
	U.S.			International					
Weighted average assumptions									
Liability discount rate	**6.2%**	6.2%	5.8%	**6.3%**	5.8%	5.2%	**6.2%**	6.1%	5.8%
Expense discount rate	**6.5%**	5.8%	5.7%	**5.6%**	5.2%	5.1%	**6.5%**	5.8%	5.7%
Expected return on plan assets	**7.8%**	7.8%	7.8%	**7.2%**	7.3%	7.3%			
Rate of salary increases	**4.6%**	4.7%	4.5%	**3.9%**	3.9%	3.9%			

The following table provides selected information about plans with liability for service to date and total benefit liability in excess of plan assets:

	Pension				Retiree Medical	
	2008	2007	2008	2007	2008	2007
	U.S.		International			
Selected information for plans with liability for service to date in excess of plan assets						
Liability for service to date	**$(5,411)**	$(364)	**$ (49)**	$ (72)		
Fair value of plan assets	**$ 3,971**	$ –	**$ 30**	$ 13		
Selected information for plans with benefit liability in excess of plan assets						
Benefit liability	**$(6,217)**	$(707)	**$(1,049)**	$(384)	**$(1,370)**	$(1,354)
Fair value of plan assets	**$ 3,974**	$ –	**$ 916**	$ 278		

Of the total projected pension benefit liability at year-end 2008, $587 million relates to plans that we do not fund because the funding of such plans does not receive favorable tax treatment.

FUTURE BENEFIT PAYMENTS AND FUNDING

Our estimated future benefit payments are as follows:

	2009	2010	2011	2012	2013	2014-18
Pension	$350	$335	$370	$400	$425	$2,645
Retiree medical (a)	$110	$115	$120	$125	$130	$ 580

(a) *Expected future benefit payments for our retiree medical plans do not reflect any estimated subsidies expected to be received under the 2003 Medicare Act. Subsidies are expected to be approximately $10 million for each of the years from 2009 through 2013 and approximately $70 million in total for 2014 through 2018.*

These future benefits to beneficiaries include payments from both funded and unfunded pension plans.

In 2009, we will make pension contributions of up to $1.1 billion, with up to $1 billion being discretionary. Our net cash payments for retiree medical are estimated to be approximately $100 million in 2009.

PENSION ASSETS

Our pension plan investment strategy includes the use of actively-managed securities and is reviewed annually based upon plan liabilities, an evaluation of market conditions, tolerance for risk and cash requirements for benefit payments. Our investment objective is to ensure that funds are available to meet the plans' benefit obligations when they become due. Our overall investment strategy is to prudently invest plan assets in high-quality and diversified equity and debt securities to achieve our long-term return expectations. We employ certain equity strategies which, in addition to investments in U.S. and international common and preferred stock, include investments in certain equity- and debt-based securities used collectively to generate returns in excess of certain equity-based indices. Debt-based securities represent approximately 3% and 30% of our equity strategy portfolio as of year-end 2008 and 2007, respectively. Our investment policy also permits the use of derivative instruments which are primarily used to reduce risk. Our expected long-term rate of return on U.S. plan assets is 7.8%, reflecting estimated long-term rates of return of 8.9% from our equity strategies, and 6.3% from our fixed income strategies. Our target investment allocation is 60% for equity strategies and 40% for fixed income strategies. Actual investment allocations may vary from our target investment allocations due to prevailing market conditions. We regularly review our actual investment allocations and periodically rebalance our investments to our target allocations. Our actual pension plan asset allocations are as follows:

	Actual Allocation	
Asset Category	**2008**	2007
Equity strategies	**38%**	61%
Fixed income strategies	**61%**	38%
Other, primarily cash	**1%**	1%
Total	**100%**	100%

The expected return on pension plan assets is based on our pension plan investment strategy, our expectations for long-term rates of return and our historical experience. We also review current levels of interest rates and inflation to assess the reasonableness of the long-term rates. To calculate the expected return on pension plan assets, we use a market-related valuation method that recognizes investment gains or losses (the difference between the expected and actual return based on the market-related value of assets) for securities included in our equity strategies over a five-year period. This has the effect of reducing year-to-year volatility. For all other asset categories, the actual fair value is used for the market-related value of assets.

Pension assets include 5.5 million shares of PepsiCo common stock with a market value of $302 million in 2008, and 5.5 million shares with a market value of $401 million in 2007. Our investment policy limits the investment in PepsiCo stock at the time of investment to 10% of the fair value of plan assets.

RETIREE MEDICAL COST TREND RATES

An average increase of 8.0% in the cost of covered retiree medical benefits is assumed for 2009. This average increase is then projected to decline gradually to 5% in 2014 and thereafter. These assumed health care cost trend rates have an impact on the retiree medical plan expense and liability. However, the cap on our share of retiree medical costs limits the impact. A 1-percentage-point change in the assumed health care trend rate would have the following effects:

	1% Increase	1% Decrease
2008 service and interest cost components	$ 6	$ (5)
2008 benefit liability	$33	$(29)

SAVINGS PLAN

Our U.S. employees are eligible to participate in 401(k) savings plans, which are voluntary defined contribution plans. The plans are designed to help employees accumulate additional savings for retirement. We make matching contributions on a portion of eligible pay based on years of service. In 2008 and 2007, our matching contributions were $70 million and $62 million, respectively.

For additional unaudited information on our pension and retiree medical plans and related accounting policies and assumptions, see "Our Critical Accounting Policies" in Management's Discussion and Analysis.

Notes to Consolidated Financial Statements

Note 8 Noncontrolled Bottling Affiliates

Our most significant noncontrolled bottling affiliates are PBG and PAS. Sales to PBG reflected approximately 8%, 9% and 10% of our total net revenue in 2008, 2007 and 2006, respectively.

THE PEPSI BOTTLING GROUP

In addition to approximately 33% and 35% of PBG's outstanding common stock that we owned at year-end 2008 and 2007, respectively, we owned 100% of PBG's class B common stock and approximately 7% of the equity of Bottling Group, LLC, PBG's principal operating subsidiary.

PBG's summarized financial information is as follows:

	2008	2007	2006
Current assets	$ 3,141	$ 3,086	
Noncurrent assets	9,841	10,029	
Total assets	$12,982	$13,115	
Current liabilities	$ 3,083	$ 2,215	
Noncurrent liabilities	7,408	7,312	
Minority interest	1,148	973	
Total liabilities	$11,639	$10,500	
Our investment	$ 1,457	$ 2,022	
Net revenue	$13,796	$13,591	$12,730
Gross profit	$ 6,210	$ 6,221	$ 5,830
Operating profit	$ 649	$ 1,071	$ 1,017
Net income	$ 162	$ 532	$ 522

Our investment in PBG, which includes the related goodwill, was $536 million and $507 million higher than our ownership interest in their net assets at year-end 2008 and 2007, respectively. Based upon the quoted closing price of PBG shares at year-end 2008, the calculated market value of our shares in PBG exceeded our investment balance, excluding our investment in Bottling Group, LLC, by approximately $567 million.

Additionally, in 2007, we formed a joint venture with PBG, comprising our concentrate and PBG's bottling businesses in Russia. PBG holds a 60% majority interest in the joint venture and consolidates the entity. We account for our interest of 40% under the equity method of accounting.

During 2008, together with PBG, we jointly acquired Russia's leading branded juice company, Lebedyansky. Lebedyansky is owned 25% and 75% by PBG and us, respectively. See Note 14 for further information on this acquisition.

PEPSIAMERICAS

At year-end 2008 and 2007, we owned approximately 43% and 44%, respectively, of the outstanding common stock of PAS.

PAS summarized financial information is as follows:

	2008	2007	2006
Current assets	$ 906	$ 922	
Noncurrent assets	4,148	4,386	
Total assets	$5,054	$5,308	
Current liabilities	$1,048	$ 903	
Noncurrent liabilities	2,175	2,274	
Minority interest	307	273	
Total liabilities	$3,530	$3,450	
Our investment	$ 972	$1,118	
Net revenue	$4,937	$4,480	$3,972
Gross profit	$1,982	$1,823	$1,608
Operating profit	$ 473	$ 436	$ 356
Net income	$ 226	$ 212	$ 158

Our investment in PAS, which includes the related goodwill, was $318 million and $303 million higher than our ownership interest in their net assets at year-end 2008 and 2007, respectively. Based upon the quoted closing price of PAS shares at year-end 2008, the calculated market value of our shares in PAS exceeded our investment balance by approximately $143 million.

Additionally, in 2007, we completed the joint purchase of Sandora, LLC, a juice company in the Ukraine, with PAS. PAS holds a 60% majority interest in the joint venture and consolidates the entity. We account for our interest of 40% under the equity method of accounting.

RELATED PARTY TRANSACTIONS

Our significant related party transactions include our noncontrolled bottling affiliates. We sell concentrate to these affiliates, which they use in the production of CSDs and non-carbonated beverages. We also sell certain finished goods to these affiliates, and we receive royalties for the use of our trademarks for certain products. Sales of concentrate and finished goods are reported net of bottler funding. For further unaudited information on these bottlers, see "Our Customers" in Management's Discussion and Analysis. These transactions with our bottling affiliates are reflected in our consolidated financial statements as follows:

	2008	2007	2006
Net revenue	$4,919	$4,874	$4,837
Selling, general and administrative expenses	$ 131	$ 91	$ 87
Accounts and notes receivable	$ 153	$ 163	
Accounts payable and other current liabilities	$ 104	$ 106	

Such amounts are settled on terms consistent with other trade receivables and payables. See Note 9 regarding our guarantee of certain PBG debt.

In addition, we coordinate, on an aggregate basis, the contract negotiations of sweeteners and other raw material requirements for certain of our bottlers. Once we have negotiated the contracts, the bottlers order and take delivery directly from the supplier and pay the suppliers directly. Consequently, these transactions are not reflected in our consolidated financial statements. As the contracting party, we could be liable to these suppliers in the event of any nonpayment by our bottlers, but we consider this exposure to be remote.

Note 9 Debt Obligations and Commitments

	2008	2007
Short-term debt obligations		
Current maturities of long-term debt	**$ 273**	$ 526
Commercial paper (0.7% and 4.3%)	**846**	361
Other borrowings (10.0% and 7.2%)	**509**	489
Amounts reclassified to long-term debt	**(1,259)**	(1,376)
	$ 369	$ –
Long-term debt obligations		
Short-term borrowings, reclassified	**$ 1,259**	$ 1,376
Notes due 2009-2026 (5.8% and 5.3%)	**6,382**	2,673
Zero coupon notes, $300 million due 2009-2012 (13.3%)	**242**	285
Other, due 2009-2016 (5.3% and 6.1%)	**248**	395
	8,131	4,729
Less: current maturities of long-term debt obligations	**(273)**	(526)
	$ 7,858	$ 4,203

The interest rates in the above table reflect weighted-average rates at year-end.

In the second quarter of 2008, we issued $1.75 billion of senior unsecured notes, maturing in 2018. We entered into an interest rate swap, maturing in 2018, to effectively convert the interest rate from a fixed rate of 5% to a variable rate based on LIBOR. The proceeds from the issuance of these notes were used for general corporate purposes, including the repayment of outstanding short-term indebtedness.

In the third quarter of 2008, we updated our U.S. $2.5 billion euro medium term note program following the expiration of the existing program. Under the program, we may issue unsecured notes under mutually agreed upon terms with the purchasers of the notes. Proceeds from any issuance of notes may be used for general corporate purposes, except as otherwise specified in the related prospectus. As of December 27, 2008, we had no outstanding notes under the program.

In the fourth quarter of 2008, we issued $2 billion of senior unsecured notes, bearing interest at 7.90% per year and maturing in 2018. We used the proceeds from the issuance of these notes for general corporate purposes, including the repayment of outstanding short-term indebtedness.

Additionally, in the fourth quarter of 2008, we entered into a new 364-day unsecured revolving credit agreement which enables us to borrow up to $1.8 billion, subject to customary terms and conditions, and expires in December 2009. This agreement replaced a $1 billion 364-day unsecured revolving credit agreement we entered into during the third quarter of 2008. Funds borrowed under this agreement may be used to repay outstanding commercial paper issued by us or our subsidiaries and for other general corporate purposes, including working capital, capital investments and acquisitions. This line of credit remained unused as of December 27, 2008.

This 364-day credit agreement is in addition to our $2 billion unsecured revolving credit agreement. Funds borrowed under this agreement may be used for general corporate purposes, including supporting our outstanding commercial paper issuances. This agreement expires in 2012. This line of credit remains unused as of December 27, 2008.

As of December 27, 2008, we have reclassified $1.3 billion of short-term debt to long-term based on our intent and ability to refinance on a long-term basis.

In addition, as of December 27, 2008, $844 million of our debt related to borrowings from various lines of credit that are maintained for our international divisions. These lines of credit are subject to normal banking terms and conditions and are fully committed to the extent of our borrowings.

INTEREST RATE SWAPS

In connection with the issuance of the $1.75 billion notes in the second quarter of 2008, we entered into an interest rate swap, maturing in 2018, to effectively convert the interest rate from a fixed rate of 5% to a variable rate based on LIBOR. In addition, in connection with the issuance of the $1 billion senior unsecured notes in the second quarter of 2007, we entered into an interest rate swap, maturing in 2012, to effectively convert the interest rate from a fixed rate of 5.15% to a variable rate based on LIBOR. The terms of the swaps match the terms of the debt they modify. The notional amounts of the interest rate swaps outstanding at December 27, 2008 and December 29, 2007 were $2.75 billion and $1 billion, respectively.

Notes to Consolidated Financial Statements

At December 27, 2008, approximately 58% of total debt, after the impact of the related interest rate swaps, was exposed to variable interest rates, compared to 56% at December 29, 2007. In addition to variable rate long-term debt, all debt with maturities of less than one year is categorized as variable for purposes of this measure.

LONG-TERM CONTRACTUAL COMMITMENTS[(a)]

	Payments Due by Period				
	Total	2009	2010–2011	2012–2013	2014 and beyond
Long-term debt obligations[(b)]	$ 6,599	$ –	$ 184	$2,198	$4,217
Interest on debt obligations[(c)]	2,647	388	605	522	1,132
Operating leases	1,088	262	359	199	268
Purchasing commitments	3,273	1,441	1,325	431	76
Marketing commitments	975	252	462	119	142
Other commitments	46	46	–	–	–
	$14,628	$2,389	$2,935	$3,469	$5,835

(a) *Reflects non-cancelable commitments as of December 27, 2008 based on year-end foreign exchange rates and excludes any reserves for income taxes under FIN 48 as we are unable to reasonably predict the ultimate amount or timing of settlement of our reserves for income taxes.*

(b) *Excludes short-term obligations of $369 million and short-term borrowings reclassified as long-term debt of $1,259 million. Includes $197 million of principal and accrued interest related to our zero coupon notes.*

(c) *Interest payments on floating-rate debt are estimated using interest rates effective as of December 27, 2008.*

Most long-term contractual commitments, except for our long-term debt obligations, are not recorded on our balance sheet. Non-cancelable operating leases primarily represent building leases. Non-cancelable purchasing commitments are primarily for oranges and orange juice, cooking oil and packaging materials. Non-cancelable marketing commitments are primarily for sports marketing. Bottler funding is not reflected in our long-term contractual commitments as it is negotiated on an annual basis. See Note 7 regarding our pension and retiree medical obligations and discussion below regarding our commitments to noncontrolled bottling affiliates.

OFF-BALANCE-SHEET ARRANGEMENTS

It is not our business practice to enter into off-balance-sheet arrangements, other than in the normal course of business. However, at the time of the separation of our bottling operations from us various guarantees were necessary to facilitate the transactions. We have guaranteed an aggregate of $2.3 billion of Bottling Group, LLC's long-term debt ($1.0 billion of which matures in 2012 and $1.3 billion of which matures in 2014). In the fourth quarter of 2008, we extended our guarantee of $1.3 billion of Bottling Group, LLC's long-term debt in connection with the refinancing of a corresponding portion of the underlying debt. The terms of our Bottling Group, LLC debt guarantee are intended to preserve the structure of PBG's separation from us and our payment obligation would be triggered if Bottling Group, LLC failed to perform under these debt obligations or the structure significantly changed. At December 27, 2008, we believe it is remote that these guarantees would require any cash payment. See Note 8 regarding contracts related to certain of our bottlers.

See "Our Liquidity and Capital Resources" in Management's Discussion and Analysis for further unaudited information on our borrowings.

Note 10 Financial Instruments

We are exposed to market risks arising from adverse changes in:

- commodity prices, affecting the cost of our raw materials and energy,
- foreign exchange risks, and
- interest rates.

In the normal course of business, we manage these risks through a variety of strategies, including the use of derivatives. Certain derivatives are designated as either cash flow or fair value hedges and qualify for hedge accounting treatment, while others do not qualify and are marked to market through earnings. Cash flows from derivatives used to manage commodity, foreign exchange or interest risks are classified as operating activities. See "Our Business Risks" in Management's Discussion and Analysis for further unaudited information on our business risks.

For cash flow hedges, changes in fair value are deferred in accumulated other comprehensive loss within shareholders' equity until the underlying hedged item is recognized in net income. For fair value hedges, changes in fair value are recognized immediately in earnings, consistent with the underlying hedged item. Hedging transactions are limited to an underlying exposure. As a result, any change in the value of our derivative instruments would be substantially offset by an opposite change in the value of the underlying hedged items. Hedging ineffectiveness and a net earnings impact occur when the change in the value of the hedge does not offset the change in the value of the underlying hedged item. If the derivative instrument is terminated, we continue to defer the related gain or loss and include it as a component of the cost of the underlying hedged item. Upon determination that the underlying hedged item will not be part of an actual transaction, we recognize the related gain or loss in net income in that period.

We also use derivatives that do not qualify for hedge accounting treatment. We account for such derivatives at market value with the resulting gains and losses reflected in our income statement. We do not use derivative instruments for trading or speculative purposes. We perform a quarterly assessment of our counterparty credit risk, including a review of credit ratings, credit default swap rates and potential nonperformance of the counterparty. We consider this risk to be low, because we limit our exposure to individual, strong creditworthy counterparties and generally settle on a net basis.

COMMODITY PRICES

We are subject to commodity price risk because our ability to recover increased costs through higher pricing may be limited in the competitive environment in which we operate. This risk is managed through the use of fixed-price purchase orders, pricing agreements, geographic diversity and derivatives. We use derivatives, with terms of no more than three years, to economically hedge price fluctuations related to a portion of our anticipated commodity purchases, primarily for natural gas and diesel fuel. For those derivatives that qualify for hedge accounting, any ineffectiveness is recorded immediately. However, such commodity cash flow hedges have not had any significant ineffectiveness for all periods presented. We classify both the earnings and cash flow impact from these derivatives consistent with the underlying hedged item. During the next 12 months, we expect to reclassify net losses of $64 million related to cash flow hedges from accumulated other comprehensive loss into net income. Derivatives used to hedge commodity price risks that do not qualify for hedge accounting are marked to market each period and reflected in our income statement.

In 2007, we expanded our commodity hedging program to include derivative contracts used to mitigate our exposure to price changes associated with our purchases of fruit. In addition, in 2008, we entered into additional contracts to further reduce our exposure to price fluctuations in our raw material and energy costs. The majority of these contracts do not qualify for hedge accounting treatment and are marked to market with the resulting gains and losses recognized in corporate unallocated expenses. These gains and losses are then subsequently reflected in divisional results.

Our open commodity derivative contracts that qualify for hedge accounting had a face value of $303 million at December 27, 2008 and $5 million at December 29, 2007. These contracts resulted in net unrealized losses of $117 million at December 27, 2008 and net unrealized gains of less than $1 million at December 29, 2007.

Our open commodity derivative contracts that do not qualify for hedge accounting had a face value of $626 million at December 27, 2008 and $105 million at December 29, 2007. These contracts resulted in net losses of $343 million in 2008 and net gains of $3 million in 2007.

FOREIGN EXCHANGE

Our operations outside of the U.S. generate 48% of our net revenue, with Mexico, Canada and the United Kingdom comprising 19% of our net revenue. As a result, we are exposed to foreign currency risks. On occasion, we enter into hedges, primarily forward contracts with terms of no more than two years, to reduce the effect of foreign exchange rates. Ineffectiveness of these hedges has not been material.

INTEREST RATES

We centrally manage our debt and investment portfolios considering investment opportunities and risks, tax consequences and overall financing strategies. We may use interest rate and cross currency interest rate swaps to manage our overall interest expense and foreign exchange risk. These instruments effectively change the interest rate and currency of specific debt issuances. Our 2008 and 2007 interest rate swaps were entered into concurrently with the issuance of the debt that they modified. The notional amount, interest payment and maturity date of the swaps match the principal, interest payment and maturity date of the related debt.

FAIR VALUE

In September 2006, the FASB issued SFAS 157, *Fair Value Measurements* (SFAS 157), which defines fair value, establishes a framework for measuring fair value, and expands disclosures about fair value measurements. The provisions of SFAS 157 were effective as of the beginning of our 2008 fiscal year. However, the FASB deferred the effective date of SFAS 157, until the beginning of our 2009 fiscal year, as it relates to fair value measurement requirements for nonfinancial assets and liabilities that are not remeasured at fair value on a recurring basis. These include goodwill, other nonamortizable intangible assets and unallocated purchase price for recent acquisitions which are included within other assets. We adopted SFAS 157 at the beginning of our 2008 fiscal year and our adoption did not have a material impact on our financial statements.

The fair value framework requires the categorization of assets and liabilities into three levels based upon the assumptions (inputs) used to price the assets or liabilities. Level 1 provides

Notes to Consolidated Financial Statements

the most reliable measure of fair value, whereas Level 3 generally requires significant management judgment. The three levels are defined as follows:

- *Level 1*: Unadjusted quoted prices in active markets for identical assets and liabilities.
- *Level 2*: Observable inputs other than those included in Level 1. For example, quoted prices for similar assets or liabilities in active markets or quoted prices for identical assets or liabilities in inactive markets.
- *Level 3*: Unobservable inputs reflecting management's own assumptions about the inputs used in pricing the asset or liability.

The fair values of our financial assets and liabilities are categorized as follows:

	2008				2007
	Total	Level 1	Level 2	Level 3	Total
Assets					
Short-term investments – index funds (a)	**$ 98**	$ 98	$ –	$–	$189
Available-for-sale securities (b)	**41**	41	–	–	74
Forward exchange contracts (c)	**139**	–	139	–	32
Commodity contracts – other (d)	**–**	–	–	–	10
Interest rate swaps (e)	**372**	–	372	–	36
Prepaid forward contracts (f)	**41**	–	41	–	74
Total assets at fair value	**$691**	$139	$552	$–	$415
Liabilities					
Forward exchange contracts (c)	**$ 56**	$ –	$ 56	$–	$ 61
Commodity contracts – futures (g)	**115**	115	–	–	–
Commodity contracts – other (d)	**345**	–	345	–	7
Cross currency interest rate swaps (h)	**–**	–	–	–	8
Deferred compensation (i)	**447**	99	348	–	564
Total liabilities at fair value	**$963**	$214	$749	$–	$640

The above items are included on our balance sheet under the captions noted or as indicated below. In addition, derivatives qualify for hedge accounting unless otherwise noted below.

(a) *Based on price changes in index funds used to manage a portion of market risk arising from our deferred compensation liability.*

(b) *Based on the price of common stock.*

(c) *Based on observable market transactions of spot and forward rates. The 2008 asset includes $27 million related to derivatives that do not qualify for hedge accounting and the 2008 liability includes $55 million related to derivatives that do not qualify for hedge accounting. The 2007 asset includes $20 million related to derivatives that do not qualify for hedge accounting and the 2007 liability includes $5 million related to derivatives that do not qualify for hedge accounting.*

(d) *Based on recently reported transactions in the marketplace, primarily swap arrangements. The 2008 liability includes $292 million related to derivatives that do not qualify for hedge accounting. Our commodity contracts in 2007 did not qualify for hedge accounting.*

(e) *Based on the LIBOR index.*

(f) *Based primarily on the price of our common stock.*

(g) *Based on average prices on futures exchanges. The 2008 liability includes $51 million related to derivatives that do not qualify for hedge accounting.*

(h) *Based on observable local benchmarks for currency and interest rates. Our cross currency interest rate swaps matured in 2008.*

(i) *Based on the fair value of investments corresponding to employees' investment elections.*

Derivative instruments are recognized on our balance sheet in current assets, current liabilities, other assets or other liabilities at fair value. The carrying amounts of our cash and cash equivalents and short-term investments approximate fair value due to the short term maturity. Short-term investments consist principally of short-term time deposits and index funds of $98 million at December 27, 2008 and $189 million at December 29, 2007 used to manage a portion of market risk arising from our deferred compensation liability.

Under SFAS 157, the fair value of our debt obligations as of December 27, 2008 was $8.8 billion, based upon prices of similar instruments in the market place. The fair value of our debt obligations as of December 29, 2007 was $4.4 billion.

The table above excludes guarantees, including our guarantee aggregating $2.3 billion of Bottling Group, LLC's long-term debt. The guarantee had a fair value of $117 million at December 27, 2008 and $35 million at December 29, 2007 based on our estimate of the cost to us of transferring the liability to an independent financial institution. See Note 9 for additional information on our guarantees.

Note 11 Net Income per Common Share

Basic net income per common share is net income available to common shareholders divided by the weighted average of common shares outstanding during the period. Diluted net income per common share is calculated using the weighted average of common shares outstanding adjusted to include the effect that would occur if in-the-money employee stock options were exercised and RSUs and preferred shares were converted into common shares. Options to purchase 9.8 million shares in 2008, 2.7 million shares in 2007 and 0.1 million shares in 2006 were not included in the calculation of diluted earnings per common share because these options were out-of-the-money. Out-of-the-money options had average exercise prices of $67.59 in 2008, $65.18 in 2007 and $65.24 in 2006.

The computations of basic and diluted net income per common share are as follows:

	2008		2007		2006	
	Income	Shares[a]	Income	Shares[a]	Income	Shares[a]
Net income	$5,142		$5,658		$5,642	
Preferred shares:						
Dividends	(2)		(2)		(2)	
Redemption premium	(6)		(10)		(9)	
Net income available for common shareholders	$5,134	1,573	$5,646	1,621	$5,631	1,649
Basic net income per common share	$ 3.26		$ 3.48		$ 3.42	
Net income available for common shareholders	$5,134	1,573	$5,646	1,621	$5,631	1,649
Dilutive securities:						
Stock options and RSUs	–	27	–	35	–	36
ESOP convertible preferred stock	8	2	12	2	11	2
Diluted	$5,142	1,602	$5,658	1,658	$5,642	1,687
Diluted net income per common share	$ 3.21		$ 3.41		$ 3.34	

(a) *Weighted-average common shares outstanding.*

Note 12 Preferred Stock

As of December 27, 2008 and December 29, 2007, there were 3 million shares of convertible preferred stock authorized. The preferred stock was issued only for an ESOP established by Quaker and these shares are redeemable for common stock by the ESOP participants. The preferred stock accrues dividends at an annual rate of $5.46 per share. At year-end 2008 and 2007, there were 803,953 preferred shares issued and 266,253 and 287,553 shares outstanding, respectively. The outstanding preferred shares had a fair value of $72 million as of December 27, 2008 and $108 million as of December 29, 2007. Each share is convertible at the option of the holder into 4.9625 shares of common stock. The preferred shares may be called by us upon written notice at $78 per share plus accrued and unpaid dividends. Quaker made the final award to its ESOP plan in June 2001.

	2008		2007		2006	
	Shares	Amount	Shares	Amount	Shares	Amount
Preferred stock	0.8	$ 41	0.8	$ 41	0.8	$ 41
Repurchased preferred stock						
Balance, beginning of year	0.5	$132	0.5	$120	0.5	$110
Redemptions	–	6	–	12	–	10
Balance, end of year	0.5	$138	0.5	$132	0.5	$120

Notes to Consolidated Financial Statements

Note 13 Accumulated Other Comprehensive Loss

Comprehensive income is a measure of income which includes both net income and other comprehensive income or loss. Other comprehensive income or loss results from items deferred from recognition into our income statement. Accumulated other comprehensive loss is separately presented on our balance sheet as part of common shareholders' equity. Other comprehensive (loss)/income was $(3,793) million in 2008, $1,294 million in 2007 and $456 million in 2006. The accumulated balances for each component of other comprehensive loss were as follows:

	2008	2007	2006
Currency translation adjustment	**$(2,271)**	$ 213	$ (506)
Cash flow hedges, net of tax (a)	**(14)**	(35)	4
Unamortized pension and retiree medical, net of tax (b)	**(2,435)**	(1,183)	(1,782)
Unrealized gain on securities, net of tax	**28**	49	40
Other	**(2)**	4	(2)
Accumulated other comprehensive loss	**$(4,694)**	$ (952)	$(2,246)

(a) *Includes $17 million after-tax loss in 2008 and $3 million after-tax gain in 2007 and 2006 for our share of our equity investees' accumulated derivative activity.*

(b) *Net of taxes of $1,288 million in 2008, $645 million in 2007 and $919 million in 2006. Includes $51 million decrease to the opening balance of accumulated other comprehensive loss in 2008 due to the change in measurement date. See Note 7.*

Note 14 Supplemental Financial Information

	2008	2007	2006
Accounts receivable			
Trade receivables	**$3,784**	$3,670	
Other receivables	**969**	788	
	4,753	4,458	
Allowance, beginning of year	**69**	64	$ 75
Net amounts charged to expense	**21**	5	10
Deductions (a)	**(16)**	(7)	(27)
Other (b)	**(4)**	7	6
Allowance, end of year	**70**	69	$ 64
Net receivables	**$4,683**	$4,389	
Inventories (c)			
Raw materials	**$1,228**	$1,056	
Work-in-process	**169**	157	
Finished goods	**1,125**	1,077	
	$2,522	$2,290	

(a) *Includes accounts written off.*

(b) *Includes currency translation effects and other adjustments.*

(c) *Inventories are valued at the lower of cost or market. Cost is determined using the average, first-in, first-out (FIFO) or last-in, first-out (LIFO) methods. Approximately 14% in 2008 and 2007 of the inventory cost was computed using the LIFO method. The differences between LIFO and FIFO methods of valuing these inventories were not material.*

	2008	2007
Other assets		
Noncurrent notes and accounts receivable	**$ 115**	$ 121
Deferred marketplace spending	**219**	205
Unallocated purchase price for recent acquisitions	**1,594**	451
Pension plans	**28**	635
Other	**702**	270
	$2,658	$1,682
Accounts payable and other current liabilities		
Accounts payable	**$2,846**	$2,562
Accrued marketplace spending	**1,574**	1,607
Accrued compensation and benefits	**1,269**	1,287
Dividends payable	**660**	602
Other current liabilities	**1,924**	1,544
	$8,273	$7,602

	2008	2007	2006
Other supplemental information			
Rent expense	**$ 357**	$ 303	$ 291
Interest paid	**$ 359**	$ 251	$ 215
Income taxes paid, net of refunds	**$ 1,477**	$ 1,731	$2,155
Acquisitions (a)			
Fair value of assets acquired	**$ 2,907**	$ 1,611	$ 678
Cash paid and debt issued	**(1,925)**	(1,320)	(522)
Liabilities assumed	**$ 982**	$ 291	$ 156

(a) *During 2008, together with PBG, we jointly acquired Lebedyansky, for a total purchase price of $1.8 billion. Lebedyansky is owned 25% and 75% by PBG and us, respectively. The unallocated purchase price is included in other assets on our balance sheet and Lebedyansky's financial results subsequent to the acquisition are reflected in our income statement.*

Management's Responsibility for Financial Reporting

To Our Shareholders:

At PepsiCo, our actions – the actions of all our associates – are governed by our Worldwide Code of Conduct. This Code is clearly aligned with our stated values – a commitment to sustained growth, through empowered people, operating with responsibility and building trust. Both the Code and our core values enable us to operate with integrity – both within the letter and the spirit of the law. Our Code of Conduct is reinforced consistently at all levels and in all countries. We have maintained strong governance policies and practices for many years.

The management of PepsiCo is responsible for the objectivity and integrity of our consolidated financial statements. The Audit Committee of the Board of Directors has engaged independent registered public accounting firm, KPMG LLP, to audit our consolidated financial statements and they have expressed an unqualified opinion.

We are committed to providing timely, accurate and understandable information to investors. Our commitment encompasses the following:

Maintaining strong controls over financial reporting. Our system of internal control is based on the control criteria framework of the Committee of Sponsoring Organizations of the Treadway Commission published in their report titled *Internal Control – Integrated Framework.* The system is designed to provide reasonable assurance that transactions are executed as authorized and accurately recorded; that assets are safeguarded; and that accounting records are sufficiently reliable to permit the preparation of financial statements that conform in all material respects with accounting principles generally accepted in the U.S. We maintain disclosure controls and procedures designed to ensure that information required to be disclosed in reports under the Securities Exchange Act of 1934 is recorded, processed, summarized and reported within the specified time periods. We monitor these internal controls through self-assessments and an ongoing program of internal audits. Our internal controls are reinforced through our Worldwide Code of Conduct, which sets forth our commitment to conduct business with integrity, and within both the letter and the spirit of the law.

Exerting rigorous oversight of the business. We continuously review our business results and strategies. This encompasses financial discipline in our strategic and daily business decisions. Our Executive Committee is actively involved – from understanding strategies and alternatives to reviewing key initiatives and financial performance. The intent is to ensure we remain objective in our assessments, constructively challenge our approach to potential business opportunities and issues, and monitor results and controls.

Engaging strong and effective Corporate Governance from our Board of Directors. We have an active, capable and diligent Board that meets the required standards for independence, and we welcome the Board's oversight as a representative of our shareholders. Our Audit Committee is comprised of independent directors with the financial literacy, knowledge and experience to provide appropriate oversight. We review our critical accounting policies, financial reporting and internal control matters with them and encourage their direct communication with KPMG LLP, with our General Auditor, and with our General Counsel. We also have a compliance team to coordinate our compliance policies and practices.

Providing investors with financial results that are complete, transparent and understandable. The consolidated financial statements and financial information included in this report are the responsibility of management. This includes preparing the financial statements in accordance with accounting principles generally accepted in the U.S., which require estimates based on management's best judgment.

PepsiCo has a strong history of doing what's right. We realize that great companies are built on trust, strong ethical standards and principles. Our financial results are delivered from that culture of accountability, and we take responsibility for the quality and accuracy of our financial reporting.

Peter A. Bridgman
Senior Vice President and Controller

Richard Goodman
Chief Financial Officer

Indra K. Nooyi
Chairman of the Board of Directors and Chief Executive Officer

Management's Report on Internal Control over Financial Reporting

To Our Shareholders:

Our management is responsible for establishing and maintaining adequate internal control over financial reporting, as such term is defined in Rule 13a-15(f) of the Exchange Act. Under the supervision and with the participation of our management, including our Chief Executive Officer and Chief Financial Officer, we conducted an evaluation of the effectiveness of our internal control over financial reporting based upon the framework in *Internal Control – Integrated Framework* issued by the Committee of Sponsoring Organizations of the Treadway Commission. Based on that evaluation, our management concluded that our internal control over financial reporting is effective as of December 27, 2008.

KPMG LLP, an independent registered public accounting firm, has audited the consolidated financial statements included in this Annual Report and, as part of their audit, has issued their report, included herein, on the effectiveness of our internal control over financial reporting.

During our fourth fiscal quarter of 2008, we continued migrating certain of our financial processing systems to SAP software. This software implementation is part of our ongoing global business transformation initiative, and we plan to continue implementing such software throughout other parts of our businesses over the course of the next few years. In connection with the SAP implementation and resulting business process changes, we continue to enhance the design and documentation of our internal control processes to ensure suitable controls over our financial reporting.

Except as described above, there were no changes in our internal control over financial reporting during our fourth fiscal quarter of 2008 that have materially affected, or are reasonably likely to materially affect, our internal control over financial reporting.

Peter A. Bridgman
Senior Vice President and Controller

Richard Goodman
Chief Financial Officer

Indra K. Nooyi
Chairman of the Board of Directors and Chief Executive Officer

Report of Independent Registered Public Accounting Firm

The Board of Directors and Shareholders
PepsiCo, Inc.:

We have audited the accompanying Consolidated Balance Sheets of PepsiCo, Inc. and subsidiaries ("PepsiCo, Inc." or "the Company") as of December 27, 2008 and December 29, 2007, and the related Consolidated Statements of Income, Cash Flows, and Common Shareholders' Equity for each of the fiscal years in the three-year period ended December 27, 2008. We also have audited PepsiCo, Inc.'s internal control over financial reporting as of December 27, 2008, based on criteria established in *Internal Control – Integrated Framework* issued by the Committee of Sponsoring Organizations of the Treadway Commission (COSO). PepsiCo, Inc.'s management is responsible for these consolidated financial statements, for maintaining effective internal control over financial reporting, and for its assessment of the effectiveness of internal control over financial reporting, included in the accompanying Management's Report on Internal Control over Financial Reporting. Our responsibility is to express an opinion on these consolidated financial statements and an opinion on the Company's internal control over financial reporting based on our audits.

We conducted our audits in accordance with the standards of the Public Company Accounting Oversight Board (United States). Those standards require that we plan and perform the audits to obtain reasonable assurance about whether the financial statements are free of material misstatement and whether effective internal control over financial reporting was maintained in all material respects. Our audits of the consolidated financial statements included examining, on a test basis, evidence supporting the amounts and disclosures in the financial statements, assessing the accounting principles used and significant estimates made by management, and evaluating the overall financial statement presentation. Our audit of internal control over financial reporting included obtaining an understanding of internal control over financial reporting, assessing the risk that a material weakness exists, and testing and evaluating the design and operating effectiveness of internal control based on the assessed risk. Our audits also included performing such other procedures as we considered necessary in the circumstances. We believe that our audits provide a reasonable basis for our opinions.

A company's internal control over financial reporting is a process designed to provide reasonable assurance regarding the reliability of financial reporting and the preparation of financial statements for external purposes in accordance with generally accepted accounting principles. A company's internal control over financial reporting includes those policies and procedures that (1) pertain to the maintenance of records that, in reasonable detail, accurately and fairly reflect the transactions and dispositions of the assets of the company; (2) provide reasonable assurance that transactions are recorded as necessary to permit preparation of financial statements in accordance with generally accepted accounting principles, and that receipts and expenditures of the company are being made only in accordance with authorizations of management and directors of the company; and (3) provide reasonable assurance regarding prevention or timely detection of unauthorized acquisition, use, or disposition of the company's assets that could have a material effect on the financial statements.

Because of its inherent limitations, internal control over financial reporting may not prevent or detect misstatements. Also, projections of any evaluation of effectiveness to future periods are subject to the risk that controls may become inadequate because of changes in conditions, or that the degree of compliance with the policies or procedures may deteriorate.

In our opinion, the consolidated financial statements referred to above present fairly, in all material respects, the financial position of PepsiCo, Inc. as of December 27, 2008 and December 29, 2007, and the results of its operations and its cash flows for each of the fiscal years in the three-year period ended December 27, 2008, in conformity with U.S. generally accepted accounting principles. Also in our opinion, PepsiCo, Inc. maintained, in all material respects, effective internal control over financial reporting as of December 27, 2008, based on criteria established in *Internal Control – Integrated Framework* issued by COSO.

KPMG LLP

New York, New York
February 19, 2009

Selected Financial Data

(in millions except per share amounts, unaudited)

Quarterly	First Quarter	Second Quarter	Third Quarter	Fourth Quarter
Net revenue				
2008	$8,333	$10,945	$11,244	$12,729
2007	$7,350	$ 9,607	$10,171	$12,346
Gross profit				
2008	$4,499	$ 5,867	$ 5,976	$ 6,558
2007	$4,065	$ 5,265	$ 5,544	$ 6,562
Restructuring and impairment charges (a)				
2008	–	–	–	$ 543
2007	–	–	–	$ 102
Tax benefits (b)				
2007	–	–	$ (115)	$ (14)
Mark-to-market net impact (c)				
2008	$ 4	$ (61)	$ 176	$ 227
2007	$ (17)	$ (13)	$ 29	$ (18)
PepsiCo portion of PBG restructuring and impairment charge (d)				
2008	–	–	–	$ 138
Net income				
2008	$1,148	$ 1,699	$ 1,576	$ 719
2007	$1,096	$ 1,557	$ 1,743	$ 1,262
Net income per common share – basic				
2008	$ 0.72	$ 1.07	$ 1.01	$ 0.46
2007	$ 0.67	$ 0.96	$ 1.08	$ 0.78
Net income per common share – diluted				
2008	$ 0.70	$ 1.05	$ 0.99	$ 0.46
2007	$ 0.65	$ 0.94	$ 1.06	$ 0.77
Cash dividends declared per common share				
2008	$0.375	$ 0.425	$ 0.425	$ 0.425
2007	$ 0.30	$ 0.375	$ 0.375	$ 0.375
2008 stock price per share (e)				
High	$79.79	$ 72.35	$ 70.83	$ 75.25
Low	$66.30	$ 64.69	$ 63.28	$ 49.74
Close	$71.19	$ 67.54	$ 68.92	$ 54.56
2007 stock price per share (e)				
High	$65.54	$ 69.64	$ 70.25	$ 79.00
Low	$61.89	$ 62.57	$ 64.25	$ 68.02
Close	$64.09	$ 66.68	$ 67.98	$ 77.03

2008 results reflect our change in reporting calendars of Spain and Portugal.

(a) *The restructuring and impairment charge in 2008 was $543 million ($408 million after-tax or $0.25 per share). The restructuring and impairment charge in 2007 was $102 million ($70 million after-tax or $0.04 per share). See Note 3.*

(b) *The non-cash tax benefits in 2007 of $129 million ($0.08 per share) relate to the favorable resolution of certain foreign tax matters. See Note 5.*

(c) *In 2008, we recognized $346 million ($223 million after-tax or $0.14 per share) of mark-to-market net losses on commodity hedges in corporate unallocated expenses. In 2007, we recognized $19 million ($12 million after-tax or $0.01 per share) of mark-to-market net gains on commodity hedges in corporate unallocated expenses.*

(d) *In 2008, we recognized a non-cash charge of $138 million ($114 million after-tax or $0.07 per share) included in bottling equity income as part of recording our share of PBG's financial results.*

(e) *Represents the composite high and low sales price and quarterly closing prices for one share of PepsiCo common stock.*

Five–Year Summary	2008	2007	2006
Net revenue	**$43,251**	$39,474	$35,137
Net income	**$ 5,142**	$ 5,658	$ 5,642
Income per common share – basic	**$ 3.26**	$ 3.48	$ 3.42
Income per common share – diluted	**$ 3.21**	$ 3.41	$ 3.34
Cash dividends declared per common share	**$ 1.65**	$ 1.425	$ 1.16
Total assets	**$35,994**	$34,628	$29,930
Long-term debt	**$ 7,858**	$ 4,203	$ 2,550
Return on invested capital (a)	**25.5%**	28.9%	30.4%

Five–Year Summary *(continued)*	2005	2004
Net revenue	$32,562	$29,261
Income from continuing operations	$ 4,078	$ 4,174
Net income	$ 4,078	$ 4,212
Income per common share – basic, continuing operations	$ 2.43	$ 2.45
Income per common share – diluted, continuing operations	$ 2.39	$ 2.41
Cash dividends declared per common share	$ 1.01	$ 0.85
Total assets	$31,727	$27,987
Long-term debt	$ 2,313	$ 2,397
Return on invested capital (a)	22.7%	27.4%

(a) *Return on invested capital is defined as adjusted net income divided by the sum of average shareholders' equity and average total debt. Adjusted net income is defined as net income plus net interest expense after-tax. Net interest expense after-tax was $184 million in 2008, $63 million in 2007, $72 million in 2006, $62 million in 2005 and $60 million in 2004.*

- Includes restructuring and impairment charges of:

	2008	2007	2006	2005	2004
Pre-tax	**$ 543**	$ 102	$ 67	$ 83	$ 150
After-tax	**$ 408**	$ 70	$ 43	$ 55	$ 96
Per share	**$0.25**	$0.04	$0.03	$0.03	$0.06

- Includes mark-to-market net expense (income) of:

	2008	2007	2006
Pre-tax	**$ 346**	$ (19)	$ 18
After-tax	**$ 223**	$ (12)	$ 12
Per share	**$0.14**	$(0.01)	$0.01

- In 2008, we recognized $138 million ($114 million after-tax or $0.07 per share) of our share of PBG's restructuring and impairment charges.
- In 2007, we recognized $129 million ($0.08 per share) of non-cash tax benefits related to the favorable resolution of certain foreign tax matters. In 2006, we recognized non-cash tax benefits of $602 million ($0.36 per share) primarily in connection with the IRS's examination of our consolidated income tax returns for the years 1998 through 2002. In 2005, we recorded income tax expense of $460 million ($0.27 per share) related to our repatriation of earnings in connection with the American Job Creation Act of 2004. In 2004, we reached agreement with the IRS for an open issue related to our discontinued restaurant operations which resulted in a tax benefit of $38 million ($0.02 per share).
- On December 30, 2006, we adopted SFAS 158 which reduced total assets by $2,016 million, total common shareholders' equity by $1,643 million and total liabilities by $373 million.
- The 2005 fiscal year consisted of 53 weeks compared to 52 weeks in our normal fiscal year. The 53rd week increased 2005 net revenue by an estimated $418 million and net income by an estimated $57 million ($0.03 per share).

Reconciliation of GAAP and Non-GAAP Information

The financial measures listed below are not measures defined by generally accepted accounting principles. However, we believe investors should consider these measures as they are more indicative of our ongoing performance and with how management evaluates our operational results and trends. Specifically, investors should consider the following:

- Our 2008 and 2007 division operating profit and total operating profit excluding the impact of restructuring and impairment charges (including, for 2008, charges associated with our Productivity for Growth initiatives); 2008 and 2007 total operating profit excluding the mark-to-market net impact on commodity hedges; and our 2008 division operating growth and total operating profit growth excluding the impact of the aforementioned items;
- Our 2008 net income and diluted EPS excluding the impact of restructuring and impairment charges (including, for 2008, charges associated with our Productivity for Growth initiatives), mark-to-market net losses on commodity hedges, and our share of PBG's restructuring and impairment charges; our 2007 net income and diluted EPS excluding the impact of restructuring and impairment charges, mark-to-market net gains on commodity hedges and certain tax benefits; our 2008 net income and diluted EPS growth excluding the impact of the aforementioned items; and our 2006 diluted EPS excluding the impact of restructuring and impairment charges, mark-to-market net losses on commodity hedges and certain tax benefits; and
- Our 2008 return on invested capital (ROIC) excluding the impact of restructuring and impairment charges (including, for 2008, charges associated with our Productivity for Growth initiatives), mark-to-market net impact on commodity hedges, our share of PBG's restructuring and impairment charges and certain tax benefits.

Operating Profit Reconciliation

	2008	2007	Growth
Total PepsiCo Reported Operating Profit	$6,935	$7,170	(3)%
Impact of Mark-to-Market Net Losses/(Gains) on Commodity Hedges	346	(19)	
Impact of Restructuring and Impairment Charges	543	102	
Total Operating Profit Excluding above Items	7,824	7,253	8%
Impact of Other Corporate Unallocated	651	772	
PepsiCo Total Division Operating Profit Excluding above Items	$8,475	$8,025	6%

Net Income Reconciliation

	2008	2007	Growth
Reported Net Income	$5,142	$5,658	(9)%
Impact of Mark-to-Market Net Losses/(Gains) on Commodity Hedges	223	(12)	
Impact of Restructuring and Impairment Charges	408	70	
Impact of PBG Restructuring and Impairment Charges	114	–	
Impact of Tax Benefits	–	(129)	
Net Income Excluding above Items	$5,887	$5,587	5%

Diluted EPS Reconciliation

	2008	2007	2008 Growth	2006
Reported Diluted EPS	$3.21	$ 3.41	(6)%	$ 3.34
Impact of Mark-to-Market Net Losses/(Gains) on Commodity Hedges	0.14	(0.01)		0.01
Impact of Restructuring and Impairment Charges	0.25	0.04		0.03
Impact of PBG's Restructuring and Impairment Charges	0.07	–		–
Impact of Tax Benefits	–	(0.08)		(0.37)
Diluted EPS Excluding above Items	$3.68*	$ 3.37*	9%	$ 3.01

* Does not sum due to rounding

2008 Operating Profit Growth Reconciliation

	PepsiCo Americas Foods	PepsiCo Americas Beverages	PepsiCo International
Reported Operating Profit Growth	8%	(19)%	13%
Impact of Restructuring and Impairment Charges	3	11	3
Operating Profit Growth Excluding above Items	10%*	(7)%*	16%

* Does not sum due to rounding

ROIC Reconciliation

	2008
Reported ROIC	26%
Impact of Mark-to-Market Net Impact on Commodity Hedges	1
Impact of Restructuring and Impairment Charges	2
Impact of PBG's Restructuring and Impairment Charges	1
Impact of Tax Benefits	(0.5)
ROIC Excluding above Items	29%*

* Does not sum due to rounding

Glossary

Acquisitions: reflect all mergers and acquisitions activity, including the impact of acquisitions, divestitures and changes in ownership or control in consolidated subsidiaries. The impact of acquisitions related to our non-consolidated equity investees is reflected in our volume and, excluding our anchor bottlers, in our operating profit.

Anchor bottlers: The Pepsi Bottling Group (PBG), PepsiAmericas (PAS) and Pepsi Bottling Ventures (PBV).

Bottlers: customers to whom we have granted exclusive contracts to sell and manufacture certain beverage products bearing our trademarks within a specific geographical area.

Bottler Case Sales (BCS): measure of physical beverage volume shipped to retailers and independent distributors from both PepsiCo and our bottlers.

Bottler funding: financial incentives we give to our bottlers to assist in the distribution and promotion of our beverage products.

Concentrate Shipments and Equivalents (CSE): measure of our physical beverage volume shipments to bottlers, retailers and independent distributors. This measure is reported on our fiscal year basis.

Consumers: people who eat and drink our products.

CSD: carbonated soft drinks.

Customers: authorized bottlers and independent distributors and retailers.

Derivatives: financial instruments that we use to manage our risk arising from changes in commodity prices, interest rates, foreign exchange rates and stock prices.

Direct-Store-Delivery (DSD): delivery system used by us and our bottlers to deliver snacks and beverages directly to retail stores where our products are merchandised.

Effective net pricing: reflects the year-over-year impact of discrete pricing actions, sales incentive activities and mix resulting from selling varying products in different package sizes and in different countries.

Management operating cash flow: net cash provided by operating activities less capital spending plus sales of property, plant and equipment. It is our primary measure used to monitor cash flow performance.

Mark-to-market net gain or loss or impact: the change in market value for commodity contracts, that we purchase to mitigate the volatility in costs of energy and raw materials that we consume. The market value is determined based on average prices on national exchanges and recently reported transactions in the market place.

Marketplace spending: sales incentives offered through various programs to our customers and consumers (trade spending), as well as advertising and other marketing activities.

Servings: common metric reflecting our consolidated physical unit volume. Our divisions' physical unit measures are converted into servings based on U.S. Food and Drug Administration guidelines for single-serving sizes of our products.

Transaction gains and losses: the impact on our consolidated financial statements of exchange rate changes arising from specific transactions.

Translation adjustment: the impact of converting our foreign affiliates' financial statements into U.S. dollars for the purpose of consolidating our financial statements.

Appendix B

Management's Discussion and Analysis for PepsiCo, Inc. and Subsidiaries

Indra K. Nooyi
Chairman and Chief Executive Officer

Dear Fellow Shareholders,

It is now two years since we introduced a new strategic mission to try to capture the heart and soul of PepsiCo. The simple but powerful idea of Performance with Purpose combines the two things that define what we do—growing the business, and acting as ethical and responsible citizens of the world.

As I look back on 2008, I'm proud to report that Performance with Purpose is woven into the fabric of our company. Wherever we see success, we see both parts of our mission in action.

All over the world, whether it's Cedar Rapids or Calgary, Shanghai or São Paulo, Mexico City, Moscow or Mumbai, our associates draw strength and inspiration from this shared mission. This year's annual report brings some of their stories to life. It shows how performance and purpose combine to great effect in everything we do.

When times are tough it is especially important to be clear about your mission. By any measure, 2008 was a year of extremes, an incredibly volatile year.

Easy credit turned into a credit crunch that left many businesses and consumers strapped for cash. The global economy lurched rapidly into recession. Oil prices approached $150 a barrel before returning back below $40. Corn, sugar, oats and other key commodities saw significant price swings throughout the year. Global business was made harder by foreign exchange rates that fluctuated, at times wildly. The Dow Jones Index began 2008 above 13,000 and ended the year below 9,000. That dragged down even the strongest companies' stock—including PepsiCo shares.

All told, I can't recall a more eventful or trying year. Not that I think pessimism is in order. The ingenuity of our company showed through again. All our teams of extraordinary people applied their can-do spirit and must-do sense of responsibility to meet the economic and market challenges head on.

As a result, PepsiCo performed slightly better for the year than both the Dow Jones Industrial Average and the S&P 500. I believe that's because, while we can't control market volatility, we remained focused on our strategies for growth, and that is why our underlying businesses continued to perform very well in 2008.

We increased our dividend, continued our share repurchase program and positioned ourselves for even stronger performance as economic conditions improve.

- Net revenue grew 10%.
- Core division operating profit grew 6%.*
- Cash flow from operations was $7 billion.
- Core return on invested capital was 29%.
- Core EPS grew 9%.*

In **PepsiCo Americas Foods** we had another year of strong growth to both the top and the bottom lines. That is testament to our strong brands and our efficient go-to-market systems. This year brought unprecedented cost inflation, but we carefully adjusted our pricing and the weights and package formats across our brands to find the right solution for each channel, each market, each customer and each consumer. The year presented some other unexpected problems that we coped with well. Our flagship Quaker plant in Cedar Rapids, Iowa, experienced a major flood but returned to normal production levels by year-end. In Latin America, our Brazil snacks business overcame a fire at one of our major plants to perform really well. We also refreshed the product portfolio. Frito-Lay North America introduced TrueNorth nut snacks and entered a joint venture that offers Sabra refrigerated dips. Some of our established products powered on. The Quaker business and our market-leading Sabritas and Gamesa brands helped us generate tremendous growth. On these strengths, PepsiCo Americas Foods increased revenues by 11 percent and core operating profit by 10 percent.*

PepsiCo Americas Beverages had a difficult year. In North America, our beverage volume was not immune to the overall category weakness triggered by the weak U.S. economy. As a result, PepsiCo Americas Beverages revenues declined by 1 percent and core operating profit fell by 7 percent.* But PepsiCo has proved time and again our skill in anticipating and responding to market changes and consumer preferences. Liquid refreshment beverages in the United States declined in 2008 for the first time in more than 50 years. We acted quickly and decisively to refresh the category. We refreshed the look of our iconic brands Pepsi-Cola, Mtn Dew, Sierra Mist and Gatorade. In Latin America, where we achieved strong results, we introduced SoBe Life, the world's first beverage made with PureVia™, an all-natural, zero-calorie sweetener; and early in 2009, we launched SoBe Lifewater with PureVia in the United States.

*For a reconciliation to the most directly comparable financial measure in accordance with GAAP, see page 1127.

We are investing aggressively to keep our total beverage portfolio relevant to consumers of all ages. In non-carbonated beverages, we are working to deliver the right value for the money, to identify untapped thirst occasions and to deliver even more health benefits. We added vitamins to our Gatorade sublines; and this year we will introduce a new Trop50 orange juice beverage, with half the calories of orange juice, great nutritional benefits and the natural sweetness of PureVia.

We have a great portfolio that gives us all confidence. And we have reexamined how that portfolio connects with today's world. We have brought two things together—the fun and bubbles of our carbonated beverages that people really love, and the symbols and experiences of today's online world.

Our re-branding strategy sets an irresistible tone of joy, optimism and energy. Those are three words that I always want to be associated with PepsiCo.

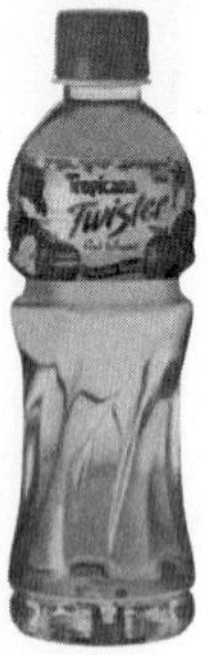

PepsiCo International's balanced and diverse snack and beverage portfolio had a good year. It delivered strong growth from treats to healthy eats. This thriving business spans Europe, the Middle East, Asia, Africa and Australia, serving 86 percent of the world's population. With per-capita consumption still relatively low in many of these markets, we have a strong opportunity to drive sales ahead of GDP growth.

This year we broadened our beverage portfolio by partnering with The Pepsi Bottling Group to acquire Russia's leading juice company, Lebedyansky, by acquiring V Water in the United Kingdom and by expanding our successful Lipton Tea partnership with Unilever. In the snack business, we acquired Bulgaria's leading nuts and seeds producer, and we introduced a variety of local flavors, including Lay's Shashlyk in Russia and Lay's Cool Blueberry in China. In India, we introduced Kurkure Naughty Tomato and Lay's Balsamic Blast and Spunky Pimento flavors; and our Doritos brand helped drive volume in the Middle East and South Africa. Together, these initiatives helped PepsiCo International revenues grow by 19 percent and core operating profit by 16 percent.*

To sustain our worldwide growth, we announced significant investments in key countries like Brazil, India, Mexico and China. In India and Brazil, we are combining capacity expansion and research and development (R&D) with sustainability efforts as we grow in those regions. Building on a brand history of more than 100 years in Mexico, we are investing over the next five years in R&D, manufacturing and distribution, marketing and advertising. And in China—one of our fastest-growing markets—we are funding capacity expansion, R&D, increased distribution, brand building, agricultural sustainability and resource conservation.

All over the company, we have Performance with Purpose as our mission. And the way we achieve it, all over the world, is always to encourage new ways of working. Innovation is our lifeblood—it drives success in all our businesses.

That is why we implemented a Productivity for Growth initiative across all sections of our business. Over the next three years, our productivity measures are expected to cumulatively free up more than $1.2 billion. That money will allow us to step up investments in long-term product development, innovation and brand building. Our productivity savings will also enhance our operating agility and create some breathing room to respond to the changing economic environment. And, as long as that innovation is driven through the company, we will deliver the demands of Performance with Purpose.

2008 was a year in which our mission could easily have been abandoned. The extraordinary circumstances would have resulted in it being abandoned if it were not already embedded into our culture. So, during 2008 we stayed true to our beliefs, even as the backdrop got tougher.

For example, we never took our eyes off the sustainability agenda that underpins our commercial success. We have now driven sustainability all the way through the business. It is a *part* of what we do, not an *addition* to what we do.

To promote human sustainability, we worked within World Health Organization policies to teach

**For a reconciliation to the most directly comparable financial measure in accordance with GAAP, see page 1127.*

children the benefits of nutrition and inspire them to be more active. This work complements and extends our success in transforming our broad portfolio of beverages, snacks and foods, to ensure it delivers everything from treats to healthy eats.

To sustain the environment for future generations, we stepped up our global efforts to conserve water and energy and worked on lightweighting our packages, starting with new packaging for Aquafina that contains 35 percent less plastic.

To sustain our world-class talent, we're developing "PepsiCo University," a new learning management system that brings together functional and leadership training for associates around the world.

Our Performance with Purpose mission is not confined to PepsiCo associates alone. Even retired members of the PepsiCo family have joined our purpose movement, banding together as the PepsiCo Service Corps to further our goals and ideals in the communities we serve.

Such a resolute performance and such a focus on our purpose is why I have such confidence in this company for the future. Nobody can predict exactly how the global economic slowdown will affect specific markets in 2009, or how consumers will respond to the pressures they face. But we've shown we have the competitive strengths, the right strategies and the tenacity to maintain our competitive edge.

We have to remember the deep brand value we have. In good times and bad, people view our products as simple, affordable pleasures that keep them nourished and refreshed. Worldwide, our retail partners consider us a strategic partner whose powerful go-to-market systems deliver strong brands and fast-selling products that help them generate healthy cash flow.

We're led by an experienced management team that has proven it can address hyperinflation, currency devaluation and political turmoil as it keeps us growing. We're sustained by the associates, customers and business partners who help us deliver fun, nourishment and refreshment each day.

And we are always facing the future, looking for new ways of working, new ways of making good on the promise of Performance with Purpose.

What you see in these pages is an account of the immediate past with some sense of how it brought us to the present. But the essential point about our company, the thing that makes us successful year in, year out, is that we are always thinking about the future.

To celebrate the future generation, we asked the children of our associates around the world to draw their favorite PepsiCo products. Some of these drawings are featured on this annual report's cover, demonstrating that we're growing in ways that nurture, sustain and inspire people.

A great company is a place where people come together, with a purpose in common. By defining that purpose, by trying to bottle it, we are bound together. That is the message you see on every page of this report. It is full of stories and portraits that truly demonstrate the deeply personal, emotional connection our associates have made to Performance with Purpose. In any language, our associates will tell you, "We are Performance with Purpose." Please join us on this trip around the globe, and see for yourself why I'm so inspired by the great things we've accomplished together—and so excited about the many opportunities that still lie ahead.

Indra K. Nooyi
Chairman and Chief Executive Officer

Financial Contents

Management's Discussion and Analysis

OUR BUSINESS

Our discussion and analysis is an integral part of understanding our financial results. Definitions of key terms can be found in the glossary on page 1128. Tabular dollars are presented in millions, except per share amounts. All per share amounts reflect common per share amounts, assume dilution unless noted, and are based on unrounded amounts. Percentage changes are based on unrounded amounts.

EXECUTIVE OVERVIEW

We are a leading global beverage, snack and food company. We manufacture or use contract manufacturers, market and sell a variety of salty, convenient, sweet and grain-based snacks, carbonated and non-carbonated beverages and foods in approximately 200 countries, with our largest operations in North America (United States and Canada), Mexico and the United Kingdom. Additional information concerning our divisions and geographic areas is presented in Note 1.

Our commitment to sustainable growth, defined as Performance with Purpose, is focused on generating healthy financial returns while giving back to the communities we serve. This includes meeting consumer needs for a spectrum of convenient foods and beverages, reducing our impact on the environment through water, energy and packaging initiatives, and supporting our employees through a diverse and inclusive culture that recruits and retains world-class talent. In September 2008, we were again included on the Dow Jones Sustainability North America Index and the Dow Jones Sustainability World Index. These indices are compiled annually.

We were again included on the Dow Jones Sustainability North America Index and the Dow Jones Sustainability World Index.

Our management monitors a variety of key indicators to evaluate our business results and financial conditions. These indicators include market share, volume, net revenue, operating profit, management operating cash flow, earnings per share and return on invested capital.

Key Challenges and Strategies for Growth

To achieve our financial objectives, we consistently focus on initiatives to improve our results and increase returns for our shareholders. For 2009, we have identified the following key challenges and related competitive strategies for growth that we believe will enable us to achieve our financial objectives:

Revitalizing our North American Beverage Business

In 2008, the U.S. liquid refreshment beverage category declined on a year-over-year basis. During 2009, we intend to invest to keep our total beverage portfolio relevant to consumers of all ages. We plan to capitalize on our new "Refresh Everything" campaign, which features new brand identities for trademarks Gatorade, Pepsi, Sierra Mist and Mountain Dew, as well as key product innovations like new SoBe Lifewater, sweetened with PureVia™, an all-natural, zero-calorie sweetener recently approved by the U.S. Food and Drug Administration. In non-carbonated beverages, we will work to identify untapped thirst occasions and to deliver even more functional benefits.

Broadening our Diverse Portfolio of Global Products

Consumer tastes and preferences are constantly changing. The increasingly on-the-go lifestyles of consumers and their desire for healthier choices means that it is more important than ever for us to continue to broaden our diverse portfolio of global products. We remain committed to offering consumers a broad range of choices to satisfy their diverse lifestyles and desires. For example, in 2008, we broadened the beverage portfolio by partnering with The Pepsi Bottling Group (PBG) to acquire JSC Lebedyansky (Lebedyansky), Russia's leading juice company, by acquiring V Water in the United Kingdom and by expanding our successful Lipton Tea partnership with Unilever. We expanded into adjacent snack categories by introducing TrueNorth nut snacks and forming a joint venture that offers Sabra refrigerated dips. During 2009, through a combination of tuck-in acquisitions and innovation, we plan to continue to broaden the range of products we offer in our existing categories and expand into adjacent ones. We are also committed to securing our innovation pipeline, and have coordinated our research and development departments across the Company into one global innovation team.

Successfully Navigating the Global Economic Crisis

We and our customers, suppliers and distributors have all been impacted by the continuing global economic crisis. Global economic conditions have resulted in decreased consumer purchasing power, volatile fluctuations in the prices of key commodities such as oil, corn, sugar and oats and adverse foreign currency exchange rates. To navigate through these conditions we plan to continue to focus on fundamentals, such as ensuring that we offer products with the right price to value proposition and managing cash flow, interest expense and commodity costs. We have also implemented our Productivity for Growth program which is expected to cumulatively generate more than $1.2 billion in pretax savings over the next three years and that will also allow us to increase investments in long-term research and development, innovation, brand building and market-specific growth initiatives.

We have also implemented our Productivity for Growth program which is expected to cumulatively generate more than $1.2 billion in pre-tax savings over the next three years.

Expanding in International Markets
Our operations outside of the United States contribute significantly to our revenue and profitability. Because per capita consumption of our products is still relatively low in many of these markets, we believe there is a significant opportunity to grow internationally by expanding our existing businesses and through acquisitions, particularly in emerging markets. During 2008, we announced significant capital investments in Brazil, India, Mexico and China. We also strengthened our international presence through acquisitions such as Marbo, a snacks company in Serbia, by expanding our successful Lipton Tea partnership with Unilever, and by partnering with PBG to acquire Russia's largest juice company. We plan to seek opportunities to make similar investments to drive international growth in 2009 and beyond. We also plan to continue developing products that leverage our existing brands but appeal to local tastes.

Maintaining our Commitment to Sustainable Growth
Consumers and government officials are increasingly focused on the impact companies have on the environment. We are committed to maintaining high standards for product quality, safety and integrity and to reducing our impact on the environment through water, energy and packaging initiatives. We plan to continue to invest in programs that help us reduce energy costs, conserve more energy and use clean energy sources, such as our wind turbine project in India which supplies more than two-thirds of the power used by our Mamandur beverage plant each year. We are also actively working on new packaging initiatives to further reduce the amount of plastic used in our beverage containers, and we continue to partner with community organizations to increase recycling efforts.

We are committed to maintaining high standards for product quality, safety and integrity and to reducing our impact on the environment through water, energy and packaging initiatives.

OUR OPERATIONS

We are organized into three business units, as follows:

(1) PepsiCo Americas Foods (PAF), which includes Frito-Lay North America (FLNA), Quaker Foods North America (QFNA) and all of our Latin American food and snack businesses (LAF), including our Sabritas and Gamesa businesses in Mexico;
(2) PepsiCo Americas Beverages (PAB), which includes PepsiCo Beverages North America and all of our Latin American beverage businesses; and
(3) PepsiCo International (PI), which includes all PepsiCo businesses in the United Kingdom, Europe, Asia, Middle East and Africa.

Our three business units are comprised of six reportable segments (referred to as divisions), as follows:

- FLNA,
- QFNA,
- LAF,
- PAB,
- United Kingdom & Europe (UKEU), and
- Middle East, Africa & Asia (MEAA).

Frito-Lay North America

FLNA manufactures or uses contract manufacturers, markets, sells and distributes branded snacks. These snacks include Lay's potato chips, Doritos tortilla chips, Cheetos cheese flavored snacks, Tostitos tortilla chips, branded dips, Fritos corn chips, Ruffles potato chips, Quaker Chewy granola bars, SunChips multigrain snacks, Rold Gold pretzels, Santitas tortilla chips, Frito-Lay nuts, Grandma's cookies, Gamesa cookies, Munchies snack mix, Funyuns onion flavored rings, Quaker Quakes corn and rice snacks, Miss Vickie's potato chips, Stacy's pita chips, Smartfood popcorn, Chester's fries and branded crackers. FLNA branded products are sold to independent distributors and retailers. In addition, FLNA's joint venture with Strauss Group manufactures, markets, sells and distributes Sabra refrigerated dips.

Quaker Foods North America

QFNA manufactures or uses contract manufacturers, markets and sells cereals, rice, pasta and other branded products. QFNA's products include Quaker oatmeal, Aunt Jemima mixes and syrups, Quaker grits, Cap'n Crunch cereal, Life cereal, Rice-A-Roni, Pasta Roni and Near East side dishes. These branded products are sold to independent distributors and retailers.

Management's Discussion and Analysis

Latin America Foods

LAF manufactures, markets and sells a number of leading salty and sweet snack brands including Gamesa, Doritos, Cheetos, Ruffles, Sabritas and Lay's. Further, LAF manufactures or uses contract manufacturers, markets and sells many Quaker brand cereals and snacks. These branded products are sold to independent distributors and retailers.

PepsiCo Americas Beverages

PAB manufactures or uses contract manufacturers, markets and sells beverage concentrates, fountain syrups and finished goods, under various beverage brands including Pepsi, Mountain Dew, Gatorade, 7UP (outside the U.S.), Tropicana Pure Premium, Sierra Mist, Mirinda, Tropicana juice drinks, Propel, Dole, Amp Energy, SoBe Lifewater, Naked juice and Izze. PAB also manufactures or uses contract manufacturers, markets and sells ready-to-drink tea, coffee and water products through joint ventures with Unilever (under the Lipton brand name) and Starbucks. In addition, PAB licenses the Aquafina water brand to its bottlers and markets this brand. PAB sells concentrate and finished goods for some of these brands to authorized bottlers, and some of these branded finished goods are sold directly by us to independent distributors and retailers. The bottlers sell our brands as finished goods to independent distributors and retailers. PAB's volume reflects sales to its independent distributors and retailers, as well as the sales of beverages bearing our trademarks that bottlers have reported as sold to independent distributors and retailers. Bottler case sales (BCS) and concentrate shipments and equivalents (CSE) are not necessarily equal during any given period due to seasonality, timing of product launches, product mix, bottler inventory practices and other factors. While our revenues are not based on BCS volume, we believe that BCS is a valuable measure as it quantifies the sell-through of our products at the consumer level.

United Kingdom & Europe

UKEU manufactures, markets and sells through consolidated businesses as well as through noncontrolled affiliates, a number of leading salty and sweet snack brands including Lay's, Walkers, Doritos, Cheetos and Ruffles. Further, UKEU manufactures or uses contract manufacturers, markets and sells many Quaker brand cereals and snacks. UKEU also manufactures, markets and sells beverage concentrates, fountain syrups and finished goods, under various beverage brands including Pepsi, 7UP and Tropicana. In addition, through our acquisition of Lebedyansky, we acquired Russia's leading juice brands. These brands are sold to authorized bottlers, independent distributors and retailers. However, in certain markets, UKEU operates its own bottling plants and distribution facilities. In addition, UKEU licenses the Aquafina water brand to certain of its authorized bottlers. UKEU also manufactures or uses contract manufacturers, markets and sells ready-to-drink tea products through an international joint venture with Unilever (under the Lipton brand name).

UKEU reports two measures of volume. Snack volume is reported on a system-wide basis, which includes our own sales and the sales by our noncontrolled affiliates of snacks bearing Company-owned or licensed trademarks. Beverage volume reflects Company-owned or authorized bottler sales of beverages bearing Company-owned or licensed trademarks to independent distributors and retailers (see PepsiCo Americas Beverages above).

Middle East, Africa & Asia

MEAA manufactures, markets and sells through consolidated businesses as well as through noncontrolled affiliates, a number of leading salty and sweet snack brands including Lay's, Doritos, Cheetos, Smith's and Ruffles. Further, MEAA manufactures or uses contract manufacturers, markets and sells many Quaker brand cereals and snacks. MEAA also manufactures, markets and sells beverage concentrates, fountain syrups and finished goods, under various beverage brands including Pepsi, Mirinda, 7UP and Mountain Dew. These brands are sold to authorized bottlers, independent distributors and retailers. However, in certain markets, MEAA operates its own bottling plants and distribution facilities. In addition, MEAA licenses the Aquafina water brand to certain of its authorized bottlers. MEAA also manufactures or uses contract manufacturers, markets and sells ready-to-drink tea products through an international joint venture with Unilever. MEAA reports two measures of volume (see United Kingdom & Europe above).

New Organizational Structure

Beginning in the first quarter of 2009, we realigned certain countries within PI to be consistent with changes in geographic responsibility. As a result, our businesses in Turkey and certain Central Asia markets will become part of UKEU, which was renamed the Europe division. These countries were formerly part of MEAA, which was renamed the Asia, Middle East & Africa division. The changes did not impact the other existing reportable segments. Our historical segment reporting will be restated in 2009 to reflect the new structure. The division amounts and discussions reflected in this Annual Report reflect the management reporting that existed through 2008.

OUR CUSTOMERS

Our customers include authorized bottlers and independent distributors, including foodservice distributors and retailers. We normally grant our bottlers exclusive contracts to sell and manufacture certain beverage products bearing our trademarks within a specific geographic area. These arrangements provide us with the right to charge our bottlers for concentrate, finished goods and Aquafina royalties and specify the manufacturing process required for product quality.

Since we do not sell directly to the consumer, we rely on and provide financial incentives to our customers to assist in the distribution and promotion of our products. For our independent distributors and retailers, these incentives include volume-based rebates, product placement fees, promotions and displays. For our bottlers, these incentives are referred to as bottler funding and are negotiated annually with each bottler to support a variety of trade and consumer programs, such as consumer incentives, advertising support, new product support, and vending and cooler equipment placement. Consumer incentives include coupons, pricing discounts and promotions, and other promotional offers. Advertising support is directed at advertising programs and supporting bottler media. New product support includes targeted consumer and retailer incentives and direct marketplace support, such as point-of-purchase materials, product placement fees, media and advertising. Vending and cooler equipment placement programs support the acquisition and placement of vending machines and cooler equipment. The nature and type of programs vary annually.

Retail consolidation and the current economic environment continue to increase the importance of major customers. In 2008, sales to Wal-Mart Stores, Inc. (Wal-Mart), including Sam's Club (Sam's), represented approximately 12% of our total net revenue. Our top five retail customers represented approximately 32% of our 2008 North American net revenue, with Wal-Mart (including Sam's) representing approximately 18%. These percentages include concentrate sales to our bottlers which are used in finished goods sold by them to these retailers. In addition, sales to PBG represented approximately 8% of our total net revenue in 2008. See "Our Related Party Bottlers" and Note 8 for more information on our anchor bottlers.

Retail consolidation and the current economic environment continue to increase the importance of major customers.

Our Related Party Bottlers

We have ownership interests in certain of our bottlers. Our ownership is less than 50%, and since we do not control these bottlers, we do not consolidate their results. We have designated three related party bottlers, PBG, PepsiAmericas, Inc. (PAS) and Pepsi Bottling Ventures LLC (PBV), as our anchor bottlers. We include our share of their net income based on our percentage of economic ownership in our income statement as bottling equity income. Our anchor bottlers distribute approximately 60% of our North American beverage volume and approximately 17% of our beverage volume outside of North America. Our anchor bottlers participate in the bottler funding programs described above. Approximately 6% of our total 2008 sales incentives were related to these bottlers. See Note 8 for additional information on these related parties and related party commitments and guarantees. Our share of net income from other noncontrolled affiliates is recorded as a component of selling, general and administrative expenses.

OUR DISTRIBUTION NETWORK

Our products are brought to market through direct-store-delivery (DSD), customer warehouse and foodservice and vending distribution networks. The distribution system used depends on customer needs, product characteristics and local trade practices.

Direct-Store-Delivery

We, our bottlers and our distributors operate DSD systems that deliver snacks and beverages directly to retail stores where the products are merchandised by our employees or our bottlers. DSD enables us to merchandise with maximum visibility and appeal. DSD is especially well-suited to products that are restocked often and respond to in-store promotion and merchandising.

Customer Warehouse

Some of our products are delivered from our manufacturing plants and warehouses to customer warehouses and retail stores. These less costly systems generally work best for products that are less fragile and perishable, have lower turnover, and are less likely to be impulse purchases.

Foodservice and Vending

Our foodservice and vending sales force distributes snacks, foods and beverages to third-party foodservice and vending distributors and operators. Our foodservice and vending sales force also distributes certain beverages through our bottlers. This distribution system supplies our products to schools, businesses, stadiums, restaurants and similar locations.

Management's Discussion and Analysis

OUR COMPETITION

Our businesses operate in highly competitive markets. We compete against global, regional, local and private label manufacturers on the basis of price, quality, product variety and distribution. In U.S. measured channels, our chief beverage competitor, The Coca-Cola Company, has a larger share of carbonated soft drinks (CSD) consumption, while we have a larger share of liquid refreshment beverages consumption. In addition, The Coca-Cola Company has a significant CSD share advantage in many markets outside the United States. Further, our snack brands hold significant leadership positions in the snack industry worldwide. Our snack brands face local and regional competitors, as well as national and global snack competitors, and compete on the basis of price, quality, product variety and distribution. Success in this competitive environment is dependent on effective promotion of existing products and the introduction of new products. We believe that the strength of our brands, innovation and marketing, coupled with the quality of our products and flexibility of our distribution network, allow us to compete effectively.

OTHER RELATIONSHIPS

Certain members of our Board of Directors also serve on the boards of certain vendors and customers. Those Board members do not participate in our vendor selection and negotiations nor in our customer negotiations. Our transactions with these vendors and customers are in the normal course of business and are consistent with terms negotiated with other vendors and customers. In addition, certain of our employees serve on the boards of our anchor bottlers and other affiliated companies and do not receive incremental compensation for their Board services.

OUR BUSINESS RISKS

Demand for our products may be adversely affected by changes in consumer preferences and tastes or if we are unable to innovate or market our products effectively.

We are a consumer products company operating in highly competitive markets and rely on continued demand for our products. To generate revenues and profits, we must sell products that appeal to our customers and to consumers. Any significant changes in consumer preferences or any inability on our part to anticipate or react to such changes could result in reduced demand for our products and erosion of our competitive and financial position. Our success depends on our ability to respond to consumer trends, including concerns of consumers regarding obesity, product attributes and ingredients. In addition, changes in product category consumption or consumer demographics could result in reduced demand for our products. Consumer preferences may shift due to a variety of factors, including the aging of the general population, changes in social trends, changes in travel, vacation or leisure activity patterns, weather, negative publicity resulting from regulatory action or litigation against companies in our industry, a downturn in economic conditions or taxes specifically targeting the consumption of our products. Any of these changes may reduce consumers' willingness to purchase our products. See also the discussions under "The global economic crisis has resulted in unfavorable economic conditions and increased volatility in foreign exchange rates and may have an adverse impact on our business results or financial condition." and "Changes in the legal and regulatory environment could limit our business activities, increase our operating costs, reduce demand for our products or result in litigation."

Our continued success is also dependent on our product innovation, including maintaining a robust pipeline of new products, and the effectiveness of our advertising campaigns and marketing programs. Although we devote significant resources to meet this goal, there can be no assurance as to our continued ability either to develop and launch successful new products or variants of existing products, or to effectively execute advertising campaigns and marketing programs. In addition, both the launch and ongoing success of new products and advertising campaigns are inherently uncertain, especially as to their appeal to consumers. Our failure to successfully launch new products could decrease demand for our existing products by negatively affecting consumer perception of existing brands, as well as result in inventory write-offs and other costs.

Our continued success is also dependent on our product innovation, including maintaining a robust pipeline of new products, and the effectiveness of our advertising campaigns and marketing programs.

Our operating results may be adversely affected by increased costs, disruption of supply or shortages of raw materials and other supplies.

We and our business partners use various raw materials and other supplies in our business, including aspartame, cocoa, corn, corn sweeteners, flavorings, flour, grapefruits and other fruits, juice and juice concentrates, oats, oranges, potatoes, rice, seasonings, sucralose, sugar, vegetable and essential oils, and wheat. Our key packaging materials include polyethylene terephthalate (PET) resin used for plastic bottles, film packaging used for snack foods, aluminum used for cans, glass bottles and cardboard. Fuel and natural gas are also important commodities due to their use in our plants and in the trucks delivering our products. Some of these raw materials and supplies are available from a limited number of suppliers. We are exposed to the market risks arising from adverse changes in commodity prices, affecting the cost of our raw materials and energy. The raw materials and energy which we use for the production of our products are largely commodities that are subject to price volatility and fluctuations in availability caused by changes in global supply and demand, weather conditions, agricultural uncertainty or governmental controls. We purchase these materials and energy mainly in the open market. If commodity price changes result in unexpected increases in raw materials and energy costs, we may not be able to increase our prices to offset these increased costs without suffering reduced volume, revenue and operating income. See also the discussion under "The global economic crisis has resulted in unfavorable economic conditions and increased volatility in foreign exchange rates and may have an adverse impact on our business results or financial condition."

The global economic crisis has resulted in unfavorable economic conditions and increased volatility in foreign exchange rates and may have an adverse impact on our business results or financial condition.

The global economic crisis has resulted in unfavorable economic conditions in many of the countries in which we operate. Our business or financial results may be adversely impacted by these unfavorable economic conditions, including: adverse changes in interest rates or tax rates; volatile commodity markets; contraction in the availability of credit in the marketplace potentially impairing our ability to access the capital markets on terms commercially acceptable to us, or at all; the effects of government initiatives to manage economic conditions; reduced demand for our products resulting from a slow-down in the general global economy or a shift in consumer preferences to private label products for economic reasons; or a further decrease in the fair value of pension assets that could increase future employee benefit costs and/or funding requirements of our pension plans. The global economic crisis has also resulted in increased foreign exchange rate volatility. We hold assets and incur liabilities, earn revenues and pay expenses in a variety of currencies other than the U.S. dollar. The financial statements of our foreign subsidiaries are translated into U.S. dollars. As a result, our profitability may be adversely impacted by an adverse change in foreign currency exchange rates. In addition, we cannot predict how current or worsening economic conditions will affect our critical customers, suppliers and distributors and any negative impact on our critical customers, suppliers or distributors may also have an adverse impact on our business results or financial condition.

If we are not able to build and sustain proper information technology infrastructure, successfully implement our ongoing business transformation initiative or outsource certain functions effectively our business could suffer.

We depend on information technology as an enabler to improve the effectiveness of our operations and to interface with our customers, as well as to maintain financial accuracy and efficiency. If we do not allocate and effectively manage the resources necessary to build and sustain the proper technology infrastructure, we could be subject to transaction errors, processing inefficiencies, the loss of customers, business disruptions, or the loss of or damage to intellectual property through security breach.

We have embarked on a multi-year business transformation initiative that includes the delivery of an SAP enterprise resource planning application, as well as the migration to common business processes across our operations. There can be no certainty that these programs will deliver the expected benefits. The failure to deliver our goals may impact our ability to (1) process transactions accurately and efficiently and (2) remain in step with the changing needs of the trade, which could result in the loss of customers. In addition, the failure to either deliver the application on time, or anticipate the necessary readiness and training needs, could lead to business disruption and loss of customers and revenue.

In addition, we have outsourced certain information technology support services and administrative functions, such as payroll processing and benefit plan administration, to third-party service providers and may outsource other functions in the future to achieve cost savings and efficiencies. If the service providers that we outsource these functions to do not perform effectively, we may not be able to achieve the expected cost savings and may have to incur additional costs to correct errors made by such service providers. Depending on the function involved, such errors may also lead to business disruption, processing inefficiencies or the loss of or damage to intellectual property through security breach, or harm employee morale.

Our information systems could also be penetrated by outside parties intent on extracting information, corrupting information or disrupting business processes. Such unauthorized access could disrupt our business and could result in the loss of assets.

Management's Discussion and Analysis

Any damage to our reputation could have an adverse effect on our business, financial condition and results of operations.

Maintaining a good reputation globally is critical to selling our branded products. If we fail to maintain high standards for product quality, safety and integrity, our reputation could be jeopardized. Adverse publicity about these types of concerns or the incidence of product contamination or tampering, whether or not valid, may reduce demand for our products or cause production and delivery disruptions. If any of our products becomes unfit for consumption, misbranded or causes injury, we may have to engage in a product recall and/or be subject to liability. A widespread product recall or a significant product liability judgment could cause our products to be unavailable for a period of time, which could further reduce consumer demand and brand equity. Failure to maintain high ethical, social and environmental standards for all of our operations and activities or adverse publicity regarding our responses to health concerns, our environmental impacts, including agricultural materials, packaging, energy use and waste management, or other sustainability issues, could jeopardize our reputation. In addition, water is a limited resource in many parts of the world. Our reputation could be damaged if we do not act responsibly with respect to water use. Failure to comply with local laws and regulations, to maintain an effective system of internal controls or to provide accurate and timely financial statement information could also hurt our reputation. Damage to our reputation or loss of consumer confidence in our products for any of these reasons could result in decreased demand for our products and could have a material adverse effect on our business, financial condition and results of operations, as well as require additional resources to rebuild our reputation.

Trade consolidation, the loss of any key customer, or failure to maintain good relationships with our bottling partners could adversely affect our financial performance.

We must maintain mutually beneficial relationships with our key customers, including our retailers and bottling partners, to effectively compete. There is a greater concentration of our customer base around the world generally due to the continued consolidation of retail trade. As retail ownership becomes more concentrated, retailers demand lower pricing and increased promotional programs. Further, as larger retailers increase utilization of their own distribution networks and private label brands, the competitive advantages we derive from our go-to-market systems and brand equity may be eroded. Failure to appropriately respond to these trends or to offer effective sales incentives and marketing programs to our customers could reduce our ability to secure adequate shelf space at our retailers and adversely affect our financial performance.

Retail consolidation and the current economic environment continue to increase the importance of major customers. Loss of any of our key customers could have an adverse effect on our business, financial condition and results of operations.

Furthermore, if we are unable to provide an appropriate mix of incentives to our bottlers through a combination of advertising and marketing support, they may take actions that, while maximizing their own short-term profit, may be detrimental to us or our brands. Such actions could have an adverse effect on our profitability. In addition, any deterioration of our relationships with our bottlers could adversely affect our business or financial performance. See "Our Customers," "Our Related Party Bottlers" and Note 8 to our consolidated financial statements for more information on our customers, including our anchor bottlers.

If we are unable to hire or retain key employees or a highly skilled and diverse workforce, it could have a negative impact on our business.

Our continued growth requires us to hire, retain and develop our leadership bench and a highly skilled and diverse workforce. We compete to hire new employees and then must train them and develop their skills and competencies. Any unplanned turnover or our failure to develop an adequate succession plan to backfill current leadership positions or to hire and retain a diverse workforce could deplete our institutional knowledge base and erode our competitive advantage. In addition, our operating results could be adversely affected by increased costs due to increased competition for employees, higher employee turnover or increased employee benefit costs.

Our continued growth requires us to hire, retain and develop our leadership bench and a highly skilled and diverse workforce.

Changes in the legal and regulatory environment could limit our business activities, increase our operating costs, reduce demand for our products or result in litigation.

The conduct of our businesses, and the production, distribution, sale, advertising, labeling, safety, transportation and use of many of our products, are subject to various laws and regulations administered by federal, state and local governmental agencies in the United States, as well as to foreign laws and regulations administered by government entities and agencies in markets in which we operate. These laws and regulations may change, sometimes dramatically, as a result of political, economic or social events. Such regulatory environment changes may include changes in: food and drug laws; laws related to advertising and deceptive marketing practices; accounting standards; taxation requirements, including taxes specifically targeting the consumption of our products; competition laws; and environmental laws, including laws relating to the regulation of water rights and treatment. Changes in laws, regulations or governmental policy and the related interpretations may alter the environment in which we do business and, therefore, may impact our results or increase our costs or liabilities.

In particular, governmental entities or agencies in jurisdictions where we operate may impose new labeling, product or production requirements, or other restrictions. For example, studies are underway by various regulatory authorities and others to assess the effect on humans due to acrylamide in the diet. Acrylamide is a chemical compound naturally formed in a wide variety of foods when they are cooked (whether commercially or at home), including french fries, potato chips, cereal, bread and coffee. It is believed that acrylamide may cause cancer in laboratory animals when consumed in significant amounts. If consumer concerns about acrylamide increase as a result of these studies, other new scientific evidence, or for any other reason, whether or not valid, demand for our products could decline and we could be subject to lawsuits or new regulations that could affect sales of our products, any of which could have an adverse effect on our business, financial condition or results of operations.

We are also subject to Proposition 65 in California, a law which requires that a specific warning appear on any product sold in California that contains a substance listed by that State as having been found to cause cancer or birth defects. If we were required to add warning labels to any of our products or place warnings in certain locations where our products are sold, sales of those products could suffer not only in those locations but elsewhere.

In many jurisdictions, compliance with competition laws is of special importance to us due to our competitive position in those jurisdictions. Regulatory authorities under whose laws we operate may also have enforcement powers that can subject us to actions such as product recall, seizure of products or other sanctions, which could have an adverse effect on our sales or damage our reputation. See also "Regulatory Environment and Environmental Compliance."

Disruption of our supply chain could have an adverse impact on our business, financial condition and results of operations.

Our ability and that of our suppliers, business partners, including bottlers, contract manufacturers, independent distributors and retailers, to make, move and sell products is critical to our success. Damage or disruption to our or their manufacturing or distribution capabilities due to adverse weather conditions, natural disaster, fire, terrorism, the outbreak or escalation of armed hostilities, pandemic, strikes and other labor disputes or other reasons beyond our or their control, could impair our ability to manufacture or sell our products. Failure to take adequate steps to mitigate the likelihood or potential impact of such events, or to effectively manage such events if they occur, could adversely affect our business, financial condition and results of operations, as well as require additional resources to restore our supply chain.

Unstable political conditions, civil unrest or other developments and risks in the countries where we operate may adversely impact our business.

Our operations outside of the United States contribute significantly to our revenue and profitability. Unstable political conditions, civil unrest or other developments and risks in the countries where we operate could have an adverse impact on our business results or financial condition. Factors that could adversely affect our business results in these countries include: import and export restrictions; foreign ownership restrictions; nationalization of our assets; regulations on the repatriation of funds; and currency hyperinflation or devaluation. In addition, disruption in these markets due to political instability or civil unrest could result in a decline in consumer purchasing power, thereby reducing demand for our products.

Risk Management Framework

The achievement of our strategic and operating objectives will necessarily involve taking risks. Our risk management process is intended to ensure that risks are taken knowingly and purposefully. As such, we leverage an integrated risk management framework to identify, assess, prioritize, manage, monitor and communicate risks across the Company. This framework includes:

- The PepsiCo Executive Committee (PEC), comprised of a cross-functional, geographically diverse, senior management group which meets regularly to identify, assess, prioritize and address strategic and reputational risks;

Management's Discussion and Analysis

- Division Risk Committees (DRCs), comprised of cross-functional senior management teams which meet regularly each year to identify, assess, prioritize and address division-specific operating risks;
- PepsiCo's Risk Management Office, which manages the overall risk management process, provides ongoing guidance, tools and analytical support to the PEC and the DRCs, identifies and assesses potential risks, and facilitates ongoing communication between the parties, as well as to PepsiCo's Audit Committee and Board of Directors;
- PepsiCo Corporate Audit, which evaluates the ongoing effectiveness of our key internal controls through periodic audit and review procedures; and
- PepsiCo's Compliance Office, which leads and coordinates our compliance policies and practices.

Market Risks

We are exposed to market risks arising from adverse changes in:

- commodity prices, affecting the cost of our raw materials and energy,
- foreign exchange rates, and
- interest rates.

In the normal course of business, we manage these risks through a variety of strategies, including productivity initiatives, global purchasing programs and hedging strategies.

In the normal course of business, we manage these risks through a variety of strategies, including productivity initiatives, global purchasing programs and hedging strategies. Ongoing productivity initiatives involve the identification and effective implementation of meaningful cost saving opportunities or efficiencies. Our global purchasing programs include fixed-price purchase orders and pricing agreements. See Note 9 for further information on our noncancelable purchasing commitments. Our hedging strategies include the use of derivatives. Certain derivatives are designated as either cash flow or fair value hedges and qualify for hedge accounting treatment, while others do not qualify and are marked to market through earnings. We do not use derivative instruments for trading or speculative purposes. We perform a quarterly assessment of our counterparty credit risk, including a review of credit ratings, credit default swap rates and potential nonperformance of the counterparty. We consider this risk to be low, because we limit our exposure to individual, strong creditworthy counterparties and generally settle on a net basis.

The fair value of our derivatives fluctuates based on market rates and prices. The sensitivity of our derivatives to these market fluctuations is discussed below. See Note 10 for further discussion of these derivatives and our hedging policies. See "Our Critical Accounting Policies" for a discussion of the exposure of our pension plan assets and pension and retiree medical liabilities to risks related to stock prices and discount rates.

Inflationary, deflationary and recessionary conditions impacting these market risks also impact the demand for and pricing of our products.

Commodity Prices

We expect to be able to reduce the impact of volatility in our raw material and energy costs through our hedging strategies and ongoing sourcing initiatives.

Our open commodity derivative contracts that qualify for hedge accounting had a face value of $303 million at December 27, 2008 and $5 million at December 29, 2007. These contracts resulted in net unrealized losses of $117 million at December 27, 2008 and net unrealized gains of less than $1 million at December 29, 2007. At the end of 2008, the potential change in fair value of commodity derivative instruments, assuming a 10% decrease in the underlying commodity price, would have increased our net unrealized losses in 2008 by $19 million.

Our open commodity derivative contracts that do not qualify for hedge accounting had a face value of $626 million at December 27, 2008 and $105 million at December 29, 2007. These contracts resulted in net losses of $343 million in 2008 and net gains of $3 million in 2007. At the end of 2008, the potential change in fair value of commodity derivative instruments, assuming a 10% decrease in the underlying commodity price, would have increased our net losses in 2008 by $34 million.

Foreign Exchange

Financial statements of foreign subsidiaries are translated into U.S. dollars using period-end exchange rates for assets and liabilities and weighted-average exchange rates for revenues and expenses. Adjustments resulting from translating net assets are reported as a separate component of accumulated other comprehensive loss within shareholders' equity under the caption currency translation adjustment.

Our operations outside of the U.S. generate 48% of our net revenue, with Mexico, Canada and the United Kingdom comprising 19% of our net revenue. As a result, we are exposed to foreign currency risks. During 2008, net favorable foreign currency, primarily due to appreciation in the euro and Chinese yuan, partially offset by depreciation in the British pound, contributed 1 percentage point to net revenue growth. Currency declines against the U.S. dollar which are not offset could adversely impact our future results.

Exchange rate gains or losses related to foreign currency transactions are recognized as transaction gains or losses in our income statement as incurred. We may enter into derivatives to manage our exposure to foreign currency transaction risk. Our foreign currency derivatives had a total face value of $1.4 billion at December 27, 2008 and $1.6 billion at December 29, 2007. The contracts that qualify for hedge accounting resulted in net unrealized gains of $111 million at December 27, 2008 and net unrealized losses of $44 million at December 29, 2007. At the end of 2008, we estimate that an unfavorable 10% change in the exchange rates would have decreased our net unrealized gains by $70 million. The contracts that do not qualify for hedge accounting resulted in a net loss of $28 million in 2008 and a net gain of $15 million in 2007. All losses and gains were offset by changes in the underlying hedged items, resulting in no net material impact on earnings.

Interest Rates

We centrally manage our debt and investment portfolios considering investment opportunities and risks, tax consequences and overall financing strategies. We may use interest rate and cross currency interest rate swaps to manage our overall interest expense and foreign exchange risk. These instruments effectively change the interest rate and currency of specific debt issuances. Our 2008 and 2007 interest rate swaps were entered into concurrently with the issuance of the debt that they modified. The notional amount, interest payment and maturity date of the swaps match the principal, interest payment and maturity date of the related debt.

Assuming year-end 2008 variable rate debt and investment levels, a 1-percentage-point increase in interest rates would have increased net interest expense by $21 million in 2008.

OUR CRITICAL ACCOUNTING POLICIES

An appreciation of our critical accounting policies is necessary to understand our financial results. These policies may require management to make difficult and subjective judgments regarding uncertainties, and as a result, such estimates may significantly impact our financial results. The precision of these estimates and the likelihood of future changes depend on a number of underlying variables and a range of possible outcomes. Other than our accounting for pension plans, our critical accounting policies do not involve the choice between alternative methods of accounting. We applied our critical accounting policies and estimation methods consistently in all material respects, and for all periods presented, and have discussed these policies with our Audit Committee.

Our critical accounting policies arise in conjunction with the following:

- **revenue recognition,**
- **brand and goodwill valuations,**
- **income tax expense and accruals, and**
- **pension and retiree medical plans.**

REVENUE RECOGNITION

Our products are sold for cash or on credit terms. Our credit terms, which are established in accordance with local and industry practices, typically require payment within 30 days of delivery in the U.S., and generally within 30 to 90 days internationally, and may allow discounts for early payment. We recognize revenue upon shipment or delivery to our customers based on written sales terms that do not allow for a right of return. However, our policy for DSD and chilled products is to remove and replace damaged and out-of-date products from store shelves to ensure that consumers receive the product quality and freshness they expect. Similarly, our policy for certain warehouse-distributed products is to replace damaged and out-of-date products. Based on our experience with this practice, we have reserved for anticipated damaged and out-of-date products. Our bottlers have a similar replacement policy and are responsible for the products they distribute.

Management's Discussion and Analysis

Our policy is to provide customers with product when needed. In fact, our commitment to freshness and product dating serves to regulate the quantity of product shipped or delivered. In addition, DSD products are placed on the shelf by our employees with customer shelf space limiting the quantity of product. For product delivered through our other distribution networks, we monitor customer inventory levels.

As discussed in "Our Customers," we offer sales incentives and discounts through various programs to customers and consumers. Sales incentives and discounts are accounted for as a reduction of revenue and totaled $12.5 billion in 2008, $11.3 billion in 2007 and $10.1 billion in 2006. Sales incentives include payments to customers for performing merchandising activities on our behalf, such as payments for in-store displays, payments to gain distribution of new products, payments for shelf space and discounts to promote lower retail prices. A number of our sales incentives, such as bottler funding and customer volume rebates, are based on annual targets, and accruals are established during the year for the expected payout. These accruals are based on contract terms and our historical experience with similar programs and require management judgment with respect to estimating customer participation and performance levels. Differences between estimated expense and actual incentive costs are normally insignificant and are recognized in earnings in the period such differences are determined. The terms of most of our incentive arrangements do not exceed a year, and therefore do not require highly uncertain long-term estimates. For interim reporting, we estimate total annual sales incentives for most of our programs and record a pro rata share in proportion to revenue. Certain arrangements, such as fountain pouring rights, may extend beyond one year. The costs incurred to obtain these incentive arrangements are recognized over the shorter of the economic or contractual life, as a reduction of revenue, and the remaining balances of $333 million at year-end 2008 and $314 million at year-end 2007 are included in current assets and other assets on our balance sheet.

We estimate and reserve for our bad debt exposure based on our experience with past due accounts and collectibility, the aging of accounts receivable and our analysis of customer data. Bad debt expense is classified within selling, general and administrative expenses in our income statement.

BRAND AND GOODWILL VALUATIONS

We sell products under a number of brand names, many of which were developed by us. The brand development costs are expensed as incurred. We also purchase brands in acquisitions. Upon acquisition, the purchase price is first allocated to identifiable assets and liabilities, including brands, based on estimated fair value, with any remaining purchase price recorded as goodwill. Determining fair value requires significant estimates and assumptions based on an evaluation of a number of factors, such as marketplace participants, product life cycles, market share, consumer awareness, brand history and future expansion expectations, amount and timing of future cash flows and the discount rate applied to the cash flows.

We believe that a brand has an indefinite life if it has a history of strong revenue and cash flow performance, and we have the intent and ability to support the brand with marketplace spending for the foreseeable future. If these perpetual brand criteria are not met, brands are amortized over their expected useful lives, which generally range from five to 40 years. Determining the expected life of a brand requires management judgment and is based on an evaluation of a number of factors, including market share, consumer awareness, brand history and future expansion expectations, as well as the macroeconomic environment of the countries in which the brand is sold.

Perpetual brands and goodwill, including the goodwill that is part of our noncontrolled bottling investment balances, are not amortized. Perpetual brands and goodwill are assessed for impairment at least annually. If the carrying amount of a perpetual brand exceeds its fair value, as determined by its discounted cash flows, an impairment loss is recognized in an amount equal to that excess. Goodwill is evaluated using a two-step impairment test at the reporting unit level. A reporting unit can be a division or business within a division. The first step compares the book value of a reporting unit, including goodwill, with its fair value, as determined by its discounted cash flows. If the book value of a reporting unit exceeds its fair value, we complete the second step to determine the amount of goodwill impairment loss that we should record. In the second step, we determine an implied fair value of the reporting unit's goodwill by allocating the fair value of the reporting unit to all of the assets and liabilities other than goodwill (including any unrecognized intangible assets). The amount of impairment loss is equal to the excess of the book value of the goodwill over the implied fair value of that goodwill.

Amortizable brands are only evaluated for impairment upon a significant change in the operating or macroeconomic environment. If an evaluation of the undiscounted future cash flows indicates impairment, the asset is written down to its estimated fair value, which is based on its discounted future cash flows.

Management judgment is necessary to evaluate the impact of operating and macroeconomic changes and to estimate future cash flows. Assumptions used in our impairment evaluations, such as forecasted growth rates and our cost of capital, are based on the best available market information and are consistent with our internal forecasts and operating plans. These assumptions could be adversely impacted by certain of the risks discussed in "Our Business Risks."

We did not recognize any impairment charges for perpetual brands or goodwill in the years presented.

We did not recognize any impairment charges for perpetual brands or goodwill in the years presented. As of December 27, 2008, we had $6.3 billion of perpetual brands and goodwill, of which approximately 55% related to Tropicana and Walkers.

INCOME TAX EXPENSE AND ACCRUALS

Our annual tax rate is based on our income, statutory tax rates and tax planning opportunities available to us in the various jurisdictions in which we operate. Significant judgment is required in determining our annual tax rate and in evaluating our tax positions. We establish reserves when, despite our belief that our tax return positions are fully supportable, we believe that certain positions are subject to challenge and that we may not succeed. We adjust these reserves, as well as the related interest, in light of changing facts and circumstances, such as the progress of a tax audit.

An estimated effective tax rate for a year is applied to our quarterly operating results. In the event there is a significant or unusual item recognized in our quarterly operating results, the tax attributable to that item is separately calculated and recorded at the same time as that item. We consider the tax adjustments from the resolution of prior year tax matters to be such items.

Tax law requires items to be included in our tax returns at different times than the items are reflected in our financial statements. As a result, our annual tax rate reflected in our financial statements is different than that reported in our tax returns (our cash tax rate). Some of these differences are permanent, such as expenses that are not deductible in our tax return, and some differences reverse over time, such as depreciation expense. These temporary differences create deferred tax assets and liabilities. Deferred tax assets generally represent items that can be used as a tax deduction or credit in our tax returns in future years for which we have already recorded the tax benefit in our income statement. We establish valuation allowances for our deferred tax assets if, based on the available evidence, it is more likely than not that some portion or all of the deferred tax assets will not be realized. Deferred tax liabilities generally represent tax expense recognized in our financial statements for which payment has been deferred, or expense for which we have already taken a deduction in our tax return but have not yet recognized as expense in our financial statements.

In 2008, our annual tax rate was 26.8% compared to 25.9% in 2007 as discussed in "Other Consolidated Results." The tax rate in 2008 increased 0.9 percentage points primarily due to the absence of the tax benefits recognized in the prior year related to the favorable resolution of certain foreign tax matters, partially offset by lower taxes on foreign results in the current year. In 2009, our annual tax rate is expected to be approximately the same as 2008.

PENSION AND RETIREE MEDICAL PLANS

Our pension plans cover full-time employees in the U.S. and certain international employees. Benefits are determined based on either years of service or a combination of years of service and earnings. U.S. and Canada retirees are also eligible for medical and life insurance benefits (retiree medical) if they meet age and service requirements. Generally, our share of retiree medical costs is capped at specified dollar amounts which vary based upon years of service, with retirees contributing the remainder of the cost.

Our Assumptions

The determination of pension and retiree medical plan obligations and related expenses requires the use of assumptions to estimate the amount of the benefits that employees earn while working, as well as the present value of those benefits. Annual pension and retiree medical expense amounts are principally based on four components: (1) the value of benefits earned by employees for working during the year (service cost), (2) increase in the liability due to the passage of time (interest cost), and (3) other gains and losses as discussed below, reduced by (4) expected return on plan assets for our funded plans.

Management's Discussion and Analysis

Significant assumptions used to measure our annual pension and retiree medical expense include:

- the interest rate used to determine the present value of liabilities (discount rate);
- certain employee-related factors, such as turnover, retirement age and mortality;
- for pension expense, the expected return on assets in our funded plans and the rate of salary increases for plans where benefits are based on earnings; and
- for retiree medical expense, health care cost trend rates.

Our assumptions reflect our experience and management's best judgment regarding future expectations. Due to the significant management judgment involved, our assumptions could have a material impact on the measurement of our pension and retiree medical benefit expenses and obligations.

At each measurement date, the discount rate is based on interest rates for high-quality, long-term corporate debt securities with maturities comparable to those of our liabilities. Prior to 2008, we used the Moody's Aa Corporate Bond Index yield (Moody's Aa Index) in the U.S. and adjusted for differences between the average duration of the bonds in this Index and the average duration of our benefit liabilities, based upon a published index. As of the beginning of our 2008 fiscal year, our U.S. discount rate is determined using the Mercer Pension Discount Yield Curve (Mercer Yield Curve). The Mercer Yield Curve uses a portfolio of high-quality bonds rated Aa or higher by Moody's. We believe the Mercer Yield Curve includes bonds that provide a better match to the timing and amount of our expected benefit payments than the Moody's Aa Index.

The expected return on pension plan assets is based on our pension plan investment strategy, our expectations for long-term rates of return and our historical experience. We also review current levels of interest rates and inflation to assess the reasonableness of the long-term rates. Our pension plan investment strategy includes the use of actively-managed securities and is reviewed annually based upon plan liabilities, an evaluation of market conditions, tolerance for risk and cash requirements for benefit payments. Our investment objective is to ensure that funds are available to meet the plans' benefit obligations when they become due. Our overall investment strategy is to prudently invest plan assets in high-quality and diversified equity and debt securities to achieve our long-term return expectations. We employ certain equity strategies which, in addition to investments in U.S. and international common and preferred stock, include investments in certain equity- and debt-based securities used collectively to generate returns in excess of certain equity-based indices. Debt-based securities represent approximately 3% and 30% of our equity strategy portfolio as of year-end 2008 and 2007, respectively. Our investment policy also permits the use of derivative instruments which are primarily used to reduce risk. Our expected long-term rate of return on U.S. plan assets is 7.8%, reflecting estimated long-term rates of return of 8.9% from our equity strategies, and 6.3% from our fixed income strategies. Our target investment allocation is 60% for equity strategies and 40% for fixed income strategies. Actual investment allocations may vary from our target investment allocations due to prevailing market conditions. We regularly review our actual investment allocations and periodically rebalance our investments to our target allocations. To calculate the expected return on pension plan assets, we use a market-related valuation method that recognizes investment gains or losses (the difference between the expected and actual return based on the market-related value of assets) for securities included in our equity strategies over a five-year period. This has the effect of reducing year-to-year volatility. For all other asset categories, the actual fair value is used for the market-related value of assets.

The difference between the actual return on plan assets and the expected return on plan assets is added to, or subtracted from, other gains and losses resulting from actual experience differing from our assumptions and from changes in our assumptions determined at each measurement date. If this net accumulated gain or loss exceeds 10% of the greater of the market-related value of plan assets or plan liabilities, a portion of the net gain or loss is included in expense for the following year. The cost or benefit of plan changes that increase or decrease benefits for prior employee service (prior service cost/(credit)) is included in earnings on a straight-line basis over the average remaining service period of active plan participants, which is approximately 10 years for pension expense and approximately 12 years for retiree medical expense.

Effective as of the beginning of our 2008 fiscal year, we amended our U.S. hourly pension plan to increase the amount of participant earnings recognized in determining pension benefits. Additional pension plan amendments were also made as of the beginning of our 2008 fiscal year to comply with legislative and regulatory changes.

The health care trend rate used to determine our retiree medical plan's liability and expense is reviewed annually. Our review is based on our claim experience, information provided by our health plans and actuaries, and our knowledge of the health care industry. Our review of the trend rate considers factors such as demographics, plan design, new medical technologies and changes in medical carriers.

Weighted-average assumptions for pension and retiree medical expense are as follows:

	2009	2008	2007
Pension			
Expense discount rate	6.2%	6.3%	5.7%
Expected rate of return on plan assets	7.6%	7.6%	7.7%
Expected rate of salary increases	4.4%	4.4%	4.5%
Retiree medical			
Expense discount rate	6.2%	6.4%	5.8%
Current health care cost trend rate	8.0%	8.5%	9.0%

Based on our assumptions, we expect our pension expense to decrease in 2009, as expected asset returns on 2009 contributions and costs associated with our Productivity for Growth program recognized in 2008 are partially offset by an increase in experience loss amortization. The increase in experience loss amortization is due primarily to pension plan asset losses in 2008 and a slight decline in discount rates.

Sensitivity of Assumptions

A decrease in the discount rate or in the expected rate of return assumptions would increase pension expense. The estimated impact of a 25-basis-point decrease in the discount rate on 2009 pension expense is an increase of approximately $31 million. The estimated impact on 2009 pension expense of a 25-basis-point decrease in the expected rate of return is an increase of approximately $18 million.

See Note 7 regarding the sensitivity of our retiree medical cost assumptions.

Future Funding

We make contributions to pension trusts maintained to provide plan benefits for certain pension plans. These contributions are made in accordance with applicable tax regulations that provide for current tax deductions for our contributions, and taxation to the employee only upon receipt of plan benefits. Generally, we do not fund our pension plans when our contributions would not be currently tax deductible.

Our pension contributions for 2008 were $149 million, of which $23 million was discretionary. In 2009, we will make contributions of $1.1 billion with up to $1 billion being discretionary. Our cash payments for retiree medical benefits are estimated to be approximately $100 million in 2009. As our retiree medical plans are not subject to regulatory funding requirements, we fund these plans on a pay-as-you-go basis. Our pension and retiree medical contributions are subject to change as a result of many factors, such as changes in interest rates, deviations between actual and expected asset returns, and changes in tax or other benefit laws. For estimated future benefit payments, including our pay-as-you-go payments as well as those from trusts, see Note 7.

In 2009, we will make pension contributions of $1.1 billion with up to $1 billion being discretionary.

RECENT ACCOUNTING PRONOUNCEMENTS

In February 2007, the Financial Accounting Standards Board (FASB) issued Statement of Financial Accounting Standards (SFAS) 159, *The Fair Value Option for Financial Assets and Financial Liabilities including an amendment of FASB Statement No. 115* (SFAS 159), which permits entities to choose to measure many financial instruments and certain other items at fair value. We adopted SFAS 159 as of the beginning of our 2008 fiscal year and our adoption did not impact our financial statements.

In December 2007, the FASB issued SFAS 141 (revised 2007), *Business Combinations* (SFAS 141R), to improve, simplify and converge internationally the accounting for business combinations. SFAS 141R continues the movement toward the greater use of fair value in financial reporting and increased transparency through expanded disclosures. It changes how business acquisitions are accounted for and will impact financial statements both

Management's Discussion and Analysis

on the acquisition date and in subsequent periods. The provisions of SFAS 141R are effective as of the beginning of our 2009 fiscal year, with the exception of adjustments made to valuation allowances on deferred taxes and acquired tax contingencies. Future adjustments made to valuation allowances on deferred taxes and acquired tax contingencies associated with acquisitions that closed prior to the beginning of our 2009 fiscal year would apply the provisions of SFAS 141R and will be evaluated based on the outcome of these matters. We do not expect the adoption of SFAS 141R to have a material impact on our financial statements.

In December 2007, the FASB issued SFAS 160, *Noncontrolling Interests in Consolidated Financial Statements, an Amendment of ARB 51* (SFAS 160). SFAS 160 amends Accounting Research Bulletin (ARB) 51 to establish new standards that will govern the accounting for and reporting of (1) noncontrolling interests in partially owned consolidated subsidiaries and (2) the loss of control of subsidiaries. The provisions of SFAS 160 are effective as of the beginning of our 2009 fiscal year on a prospective basis. We do not expect our adoption of SFAS 160 to have a significant impact on our financial statements. In the first quarter of 2009, we will include the required disclosures for all periods presented.

In March 2008, the FASB issued SFAS 161, *Disclosures about Derivative Instruments and Hedging Activities* (SFAS 161), which amends and expands the disclosure requirements of SFAS 133, *Accounting for Derivative Instruments and Hedging Activities* (SFAS 133), to provide an enhanced understanding of the use of derivative instruments, how they are accounted for under SFAS 133 and their effect on financial position, financial performance and cash flows. The disclosure provisions of SFAS 161 are effective as of the beginning of our 2009 fiscal year.

OUR FINANCIAL RESULTS

ITEMS AFFECTING COMPARABILITY

The year-over-year comparisons of our financial results are affected by the following items:

	2008	2007	2006
Operating profit			
Mark-to-market net impact	$(346)	$ 19	$ (18)
Restructuring and impairment charges	$(543)	$ (102)	$ (67)
Net income			
Mark-to-market net impact	$(223)	$ 12	$ (12)
Restructuring and impairment charges	$(408)	$ (70)	$ (43)
Tax benefits	–	$ 129	$ 602
PepsiCo share of PBG restructuring and impairment charges	$(114)	–	–
PepsiCo share of PBG tax settlement	–	–	$ 18
Net income per common share – diluted			
Mark-to-market net impact	$(0.14)	$ 0.01	$(0.01)
Restructuring and impairment charges	$(0.25)	$(0.04)	$(0.03)
Tax benefits	–	$ 0.08	$ 0.36
PepsiCo share of PBG restructuring and impairment charges	$(0.07)	–	–
PepsiCo share of PBG tax settlement	–	–	$ 0.01

Mark-to-Market Net Impact

We centrally manage commodity derivatives on behalf of our divisions. These commodity derivatives include energy, fruit and other raw materials. Certain of these commodity derivatives do not qualify for hedge accounting treatment and are marked to market with the resulting gains and losses recognized in corporate unallocated expenses. These gains and losses are subsequently reflected in division results when the divisions take delivery of the underlying commodity.

In 2008, we recognized $346 million ($223 million after-tax or $0.14 per share) of mark-to-market net losses on commodity hedges in corporate unallocated expenses.

In 2007, we recognized $19 million ($12 million after-tax or $0.01 per share) of mark-to-market net gains on commodity hedges in corporate unallocated expenses.

In 2006, we recognized $18 million ($12 million after-tax or $0.01 per share) of mark-to-market net losses on commodity hedges in corporate unallocated expenses.

Restructuring and Impairment Charges

In 2008, we incurred a charge of $543 million ($408 million after-tax or $0.25 per share) in conjunction with our Productivity for Growth program. The program includes actions in all divisions of the business, including the closure of six plants that we believe will increase cost competitiveness across the supply chain, upgrade and streamline our product portfolio, and simplify the organization for more effective and timely decision-making. In connection with this program, we expect to incur an additional pre-tax charge of approximately $30 million to $60 million in 2009.

In 2007, we incurred a charge of $102 million ($70 million after-tax or $0.04 per share) in conjunction with restructuring actions primarily to close certain plants and rationalize other production lines.

In 2006, we incurred a charge of $67 million ($43 million after-tax or $0.03 per share) in conjunction with consolidating the manufacturing network at FLNA by closing two plants in the U.S., and rationalizing other assets, to increase manufacturing productivity and supply chain efficiencies.

Tax Benefits

In 2007, we recognized $129 million ($0.08 per share) of non-cash tax benefits related to the favorable resolution of certain foreign tax matters.

In 2006, we recognized non-cash tax benefits of $602 million ($0.36 per share), substantially all of which related to the Internal Revenue Service's (IRS) examination of our consolidated tax returns for the years 1998 through 2002.

PepsiCo Share of PBG's Restructuring and Impairment Charges

In 2008, PBG implemented a restructuring initiative across all of its geographic segments. In addition, PBG recognized an asset impairment charge related to its business in Mexico. Consequently, a non-cash charge of $138 million was included in bottling equity income ($114 million after-tax or $0.07 per share) as part of recording our share of PBG's financial results.

PepsiCo Share of PBG Tax Settlement

In 2006, the IRS concluded its examination of PBG's consolidated income tax returns for the years 1999 through 2000. Consequently, a non-cash benefit of $21 million was included in bottling equity income ($18 million after-tax or $0.01 per share) as part of recording our share of PBG's financial results.

RESULTS OF OPERATIONS – CONSOLIDATED REVIEW

In the discussions of net revenue and operating profit below, *effective net pricing* reflects the year-over-year impact of discrete pricing actions, sales incentive activities and mix resulting from selling varying products in different package sizes and in different countries. Additionally, *acquisitions* reflect all mergers and acquisitions activity, including the impact of acquisitions, divestitures and changes in ownership or control in consolidated subsidiaries. The impact of acquisitions related to our non-consolidated equity investees is reflected in our volume and, excluding our anchor bottlers, in our operating profit.

Servings

Since our divisions each use different measures of physical unit volume (i.e., kilos, gallons, pounds and case sales), a common servings metric is necessary to reflect our consolidated physical unit volume. Our divisions' physical volume measures are converted into servings based on U.S. Food and Drug Administration guidelines for single-serving sizes of our products.

In 2008, total servings increased 3% compared to 2007, as servings for both beverages and snacks worldwide grew 3%. In 2007, total servings increased over 4% compared to 2006, as servings for beverages worldwide grew 4% and servings for snacks worldwide grew 6%.

Net Revenue and Operating Profit

				Change	
	2008	2007	2006	**2008**	2007
Total net revenue	**$43,251**	$39,474	$35,137	**10%**	12%
Operating profit					
FLNA	**$ 2,959**	$ 2,845	$ 2,615	**4%**	9%
QFNA	**582**	568	554	**2.5%**	2.5%
LAF	**897**	714	655	**26%**	9%
PAB	**2,026**	2,487	2,315	**(19)%**	7%
UKEU	**811**	774	700	**5%**	11%
MEAA	**667**	535	401	**25%**	34%
Corporate – net impact of mark-to-market on commodity hedges	**(346)**	19	(18)	**n/m**	n/m
Corporate – other	**(661)**	(772)	(720)	**(14)%**	7%
Total operating profit	**$ 6,935**	$ 7,170	$ 6,502	**(3)%**	10%
Total operating profit margin	**16.0%**	18.2%	18.5%	**(2.2)**	(0.3)

n/m represents year-over-year changes that are not meaningful.

2008

Total operating profit decreased 3% and margin decreased 2.2 percentage points. The unfavorable net mark-to-market impact of our commodity hedges and increased restructuring and impairment charges contributed 11 percentage points to the operating profit decline and 1.9 percentage points to the margin decline. Leverage from the revenue growth was offset by the impact of higher commodity costs. Acquisitions and foreign currency each positively contributed 1 percentage point to operating profit performance.

Management's Discussion and Analysis

Other corporate unallocated expenses decreased 14%. The favorable impact of certain employee-related items, including lower deferred compensation and pension costs were partially offset by higher costs associated with our global SAP implementation and increased research and development costs. The decrease in deferred compensation costs are offset by a decrease in interest income from losses on investments used to economically hedge these costs.

2007

Total operating profit increased 10% and margin decreased 0.3 percentage points. The operating profit growth reflects leverage from the revenue growth, offset by increased cost of sales, largely due to higher raw material costs. The impact of foreign currency contributed 2 percentage points to operating profit growth. There was no net impact of acquisitions on operating profit growth.

Other corporate unallocated expenses increased 7%, primarily reflecting increased research and development costs and the absence of certain other favorable corporate items in 2006, partially offset by lower pension costs.

Other Consolidated Results

				Change	
	2008	2007	2006	**2008**	2007
Bottling equity income	**$ 374**	$ 560	$ 553	**(33)%**	1%
Interest expense, net	**$ (288)**	$ (99)	$ (66)	**$(189)**	$(33)
Annual tax rate	**26.8%**	25.9%	19.3%		
Net income	**$5,142**	$5,658	$5,642	**(9)%**	–
Net income per common share – diluted	**$ 3.21**	$ 3.41	$ 3.34	**(6)%**	2%

Bottling equity income includes our share of the net income or loss of our anchor bottlers as described in "Our Customers." Our interest in these bottling investments may change from time to time. Any gains or losses from these changes, as well as other transactions related to our bottling investments, are also included on a pre-tax basis. In November 2007, our Board of Directors approved the sale of additional PBG stock to an economic ownership level of 35%, as well as the sale of PAS stock to the ownership level at the time of the merger with Whitman Corporation in 2000 of about 37%. We sold 8.8 million and 9.5 million shares of PBG stock in 2008 and 2007, respectively. In addition, in 2008, we sold 3.3 million shares of PAS stock. The resulting lower ownership percentages reduce the equity income from PBG and PAS that we recognize. See "Our Liquidity and Capital Resources – Investing Activities" for further information with respect to planned sales of PBG and PAS stock in 2009.

2008

Bottling equity income decreased 33%, primarily reflecting a non-cash charge of $138 million related to our share of PBG's restructuring and impairment charges. Additionally, lower pre-tax gains on our sales of PBG stock contributed to the decline.

Net interest expense increased $189 million, primarily reflecting higher average debt balances and losses on investments used to economically hedge our deferred compensation costs, partially offset by lower average rates on our borrowings.

The tax rate increased 0.9 percentage points compared to the prior year, primarily due to $129 million of tax benefits recognized in the prior year related to the favorable resolution of certain foreign tax matters, partially offset by lower taxes on foreign results in the current year.

Net income decreased 9% and the related net income per share decreased 6%. The unfavorable net mark-to-market impact of our commodity hedges, the absence of the tax benefits recognized in the prior year, our increased restructuring and impairment charges and our share of PBG's restructuring and impairment charges collectively contributed 15 percentage points to both the decline in net income and net income per share. Additionally, net income per share was favorably impacted by our share repurchases.

2007

Bottling equity income increased 1%, reflecting higher earnings from our anchor bottlers, partially offset by the impact of our reduced ownership level in 2007 and lower pre-tax gains on our sale of PBG stock.

Net interest expense increased $33 million, primarily reflecting the impact of lower investment balances and higher average rates on our debt, partially offset by higher average interest rates on our investments and lower average debt balances.

The tax rate increased 6.6 percentage points compared to the prior year, primarily reflecting an unfavorable comparison to the prior year's non-cash tax benefits.

Net income remained flat and the related net income per share increased 2%. Our solid operating profit growth and favorable net mark-to-market impact were offset by unfavorable comparisons to the non-cash tax benefits and restructuring and impairment charges in the prior year. These items affecting comparability reduced both net income performance and related net income per share growth by 10 percentage points. Additionally, net income per share was favorably impacted by our share repurchases.

RESULTS OF OPERATIONS – DIVISION REVIEW

The results and discussions below are based on how our Chief Executive Officer monitors the performance of our divisions. In addition, our operating profit and growth, excluding the impact of restructuring and impairment charges, are not measures defined by accounting principles generally accepted in the U.S. However, we believe investors should consider these measures as they are more indicative of our ongoing performance and with how management evaluates our operating results and trends. For additional information on our divisions, see Note 1 and for additional information on our restructuring and impairment charges, see Note 3.

	FLNA	QFNA	LAF	PAB	UKEU	MEAA	Total
Net Revenue, 2008	**$12,507**	**$1,902**	**$5,895**	**$10,937**	**$6,435**	**$5,575**	**$43,251**
Net Revenue, 2007	$11,586	$1,860	$4,872	$11,090	$5,492	$4,574	$39,474
% Impact of:							
Volume (a)	–%	(1.5)%	–%	(4.5)%	4%	13%	1%
Effective net pricing (b)	7	4	11	3	4	6	6
Foreign exchange	–	–	–	–	2	1	1
Acquisitions	–	–	9	–	8	2	2
% Change (c)	8%	2%	21%	(1)%	17%	22%	10%
Net Revenue, 2007	$11,586	$1,860	$4,872	$11,090	$5,492	$4,574	$39,474
Net Revenue, 2006	$10,844	$1,769	$3,972	$10,362	$4,750	$3,440	$35,137
% Impact of:							
Volume (a)	3%	2%	5%	(1)%	4%	12%	3%
Effective net pricing (b)	4	3	5	5	3	5	4
Foreign exchange	0.5	1	2	0.5	9	5.5	2
Acquisitions	–	–	11	2	–	11	3
% Change (c)	7%	5%	23%	7%	16%	33%	12%

(a) *Excludes the impact of acquisitions. In certain instances, volume growth varies from the amounts disclosed in the following divisional discussions due to non-consolidated joint venture volume, and, for our beverage businesses, temporary timing differences between BCS and CSE. Our net revenue excludes non-consolidated joint venture volume, and, for our beverage businesses, is based on CSE.*

(b) *Includes the year-over-year impact of discrete pricing actions, sales incentive activities and mix resulting from selling varying products in different package sizes and in different countries.*

(c) *Amounts may not sum due to rounding.*

Frito-Lay North America

				% Change	
	2008	2007	2006	2008	2007
Net revenue	**$12,507**	$11,586	$10,844	8	7
Operating profit	**$ 2,959**	$ 2,845	$ 2,615	4	9
Impact of restructuring and impairment charges	**108**	28	67		
Operating profit, excluding restructuring and impairment charges	**$ 3,067**	$ 2,873	$ 2,682	7	7

2008

Net revenue grew 8% and pound volume grew 1%. The volume growth reflects our 2008 Sabra joint venture and mid-single-digit growth in trademark Cheetos, Ruffles and dips. These volume gains were largely offset by mid-single-digit declines in trademark Lay's and Doritos. Net revenue growth benefited from pricing actions. Foreign currency had a nominal impact on net revenue growth.

FLNA's net revenue grew 8% and 7% in 2008 and 2007, respectively.

Operating profit grew 4%, reflecting the net revenue growth. This growth was partially offset by higher commodity costs, primarily cooking oil and fuel. Operating profit growth was negatively impacted by 3 percentage points, resulting from higher fourth quarter restructuring and impairment charges in 2008 related to the Productivity for Growth program. Foreign currency and acquisitions each had a nominal impact on operating profit growth. Operating profit, excluding restructuring and impairment charges, grew 7%.

2007

Net revenue grew 7%, reflecting volume growth of 3% and positive effective net pricing due to pricing actions and favorable mix. Pound volume grew primarily due to high-single-digit growth in trademark Doritos and double-digit growth in dips, SunChips and multipack. These volume gains were partially offset by a mid-single-digit decline in trademark Lay's.

Management's Discussion and Analysis

Operating profit grew 9%, primarily reflecting the net revenue growth, as well as a favorable casualty insurance actuarial adjustment reflecting improved safety performance. This growth was partially offset by higher commodity costs, as well as increased advertising and marketing expenses. Operating profit benefited almost 2 percentage points from the impact of lower restructuring and impairment charges in 2007 related to the continued consolidation of the manufacturing network. Operating profit, excluding restructuring and impairment charges, grew 7%.

Quaker Foods North America

				% Change	
	2008	2007	2006	**2008**	2007
Net revenue	**$1,902**	$1,860	$1,769	**2**	5
Operating profit	**$ 582**	$ 568	$ 554	**2.5**	2.5
Impact of restructuring and impairment charges	**31**	–	–		
Operating profit, excluding restructuring and impairment charges	**$ 613**	$ 568	$ 554	**8**	2.5

2008

Net revenue increased 2% and volume declined 1.5%, partially reflecting the negative impact of the Cedar Rapids flood that occurred at the end of the second quarter. The volume decrease reflects a low-single-digit decline in Quaker Oatmeal and ready-to-eat cereals. The net revenue growth reflects favorable effective net pricing, due primarily to price increases, partially offset by the volume decline. Foreign currency had a nominal impact on net revenue growth.

In 2008, QFNA's net revenue grew 2% and volume declined 1.5%, partially reflecting the impact of the Cedar Rapids flood.

Operating profit increased 2.5%, reflecting the net revenue growth and lower advertising and marketing costs, partially offset by increased commodity costs. The negative impact of the flood was mitigated by related business disruption insurance recoveries, which contributed 5 percentage points to operating profit. The fourth quarter restructuring and impairment charges related to the Productivity for Growth program reduced operating profit growth by 5 percentage points. Foreign currency had a nominal impact on operating profit growth. Operating profit, excluding restructuring and impairment charges, grew 8%.

2007

Net revenue increased 5% and volume increased 2%. The volume increase reflects mid-single-digit growth in Oatmeal and Life cereal, as well as low-single-digit growth in Cap'n Crunch cereal. These increases were partially offset by a double-digit decline in Rice-A-Roni. The increase in net revenue primarily reflects price increases taken earlier in 2007, as well as the volume growth. Favorable Canadian exchange rates contributed nearly 1 percentage point to net revenue growth.

Operating profit increased 2.5%, primarily reflecting the net revenue growth partially offset by increased raw material costs.

Latin America Foods

				% Change	
	2008	2007	2006	**2008**	2007
Net revenue	**$5,895**	$4,872	$3,972	**21**	23
Operating profit	**$ 897**	$ 714	$ 655	**26**	9
Impact of restructuring and impairment charges	**40**	39	–		
Operating profit, excluding restructuring and impairment charges	**$ 937**	$ 753	$ 655	**24**	15

2008

Snacks volume grew 3%, primarily reflecting the acquisition in Brazil, which contributed nearly 3 percentage points to the volume growth. A mid-single-digit decline at Sabritas in Mexico, largely resulting from weight-outs, was offset by mid-single digit growth at Gamesa in Mexico and double-digit growth in certain other markets.

In 2008, LAF's net revenue and operating profit grew 21% and 26%, respectively.

Net revenue grew 21%, primarily reflecting favorable effective net pricing. Gamesa experienced double-digit growth due to favorable pricing actions. Acquisitions contributed 9 percentage points to the net revenue growth, while foreign currency had a nominal impact on net revenue growth.

Operating profit grew 26%, driven by the net revenue growth, partially offset by increased commodity costs. An insurance recovery contributed 3 percentage points to the operating profit growth. The impact of the fourth quarter restructuring and impairment charges in 2008 related to the Productivity for Growth program was offset by the prior year restructuring charges. Acquisitions contributed 4 percentage points and foreign currency contributed 1 percentage point to the operating profit growth. Operating profit, excluding restructuring and impairment charges, grew 24%.

2007

Snacks volume grew 6%, reflecting double-digit growth at Gamesa and in Argentina and high-single-digit growth in Brazil, partially offset by a low-single-digit decline at Sabritas. An acquisition in Brazil in the third quarter of 2007 contributed 0.5 percentage points to the reported volume growth rate.

Net revenue grew 23%, reflecting favorable effective net pricing and volume growth. Acquisitions contributed 11 percentage points to the net revenue growth. Foreign currency contributed 2 percentage points of growth, primarily reflecting the favorable Brazilian real.

Operating profit grew 9%, driven by the favorable effective net pricing and volume growth, partially offset by increased raw material costs. Acquisitions contributed 3 percentage points to the operating profit growth. Foreign currency contributed 2 percentage points of growth, primarily reflecting the favorable Brazilian real. The impact of restructuring actions taken in the fourth quarter to reduce costs in our operations, rationalize capacity and realign our organizational structure reduced operating profit growth by 6 percentage points. Operating profit, excluding restructuring and impairment charges, grew 15%.

PepsiCo Americas Beverages

				% Change	
	2008	2007	2006	2008	2007
Net revenue	$10,937	$11,090	$10,362	(1)	7
Operating profit	$ 2,026	$ 2,487	$ 2,315	(19)	7
Impact of restructuring and impairment charges	289	12	–		
Operating profit, excluding restructuring and impairment charges	$ 2,315	$ 2,499	$ 2,315	(7)	8

2008

BCS volume declined 3%, reflecting a 5% decline in North America, partially offset by a 4% increase in Latin America.

Our North American business navigated a challenging year in the U.S., where the liquid refreshment beverage category declined on a year-over-year basis. In North America, CSD volume declined 4%, driven by a mid-single-digit decline in trademark Pepsi and a low-single-digit decline in trademark Sierra Mist, offset in part by a slight increase in trademark Mountain Dew. Non-carbonated beverage volume declined 6%.

Our North American business navigated a challenging year in the U.S., where the liquid refreshment beverage category declined on a year-over-year basis.

Net revenue declined 1 percent, reflecting the volume declines in North America, partially offset by favorable effective net pricing. The effective net pricing reflects positive mix and price increases taken primarily on concentrate and fountain products this year. Foreign currency had a nominal impact on the net revenue decline.

Operating profit declined 19%, primarily reflecting higher fourth quarter restructuring and impairment charges in 2008 related to the Productivity for Growth program, which contributed 11 percentage points to the operating profit decline. In addition, higher product costs and higher selling and delivery costs, primarily due to higher fuel costs, contributed to the decline. Foreign currency had a nominal impact on the operating profit decline. Operating profit, excluding restructuring and impairment charges, declined 7%.

2007

BCS volume grew 1%, driven by a 4% increase in our Latin America businesses. BCS volume was flat in North America.

In North America, BCS volume was flat due to a 3% decline in CSDs, entirely offset by a 5% increase in non-carbonated beverages. The decline in the CSD portfolio reflects a mid-single-digit decline in trademark Pepsi offset slightly by a low-single-digit increase in trademark Sierra Mist. Trademark Mountain Dew volume was flat. Across the brands, regular CSDs experienced a mid-single-digit decline and diet CSDs experienced a low-single-digit decline. The non-carbonated portfolio performance was driven by double-digit growth in Lipton ready-to-drink teas, double-digit growth in waters and enhanced waters under the Aquafina, Propel and SoBe Lifewater trademarks and low-single-digit growth in Gatorade, partially offset by a mid-single-digit decline in our juice and juice drinks portfolio as a result of previous price increases.

In our Latin America businesses, volume growth reflected double-digit increases in Brazil, Argentina and Venezuela, partially offset by a low-single-digit decline in Mexico. Both CSDs and non-carbonated beverages grew at mid-single-digit rates.

Net revenue grew 7%, driven by effective net pricing, primarily reflecting price increases on Tropicana Pure Premium and CSD concentrate and growth in finished goods beverages. Acquisitions contributed 2 percentage points to net revenue growth.

Management's Discussion and Analysis

Operating profit increased 7%, reflecting the net revenue growth, partially offset by higher cost of sales, mainly due to increased fruit costs, as well as higher general and administrative costs. The impact of restructuring actions taken in the fourth quarter was fully offset by the favorable impact of foreign exchange rates during the year. Operating profit was also positively impacted by the absence of amortization expense related to a prior acquisition, partially offset by the absence of a $29 million favorable insurance settlement, both recorded in 2006. The impact of acquisitions reduced operating profit by less than 1 percentage point. Operating profit, excluding restructuring and impairment charges, increased 8%.

United Kingdom & Europe

				% Change	
	2008	2007	2006	**2008**	2007
Net revenue	**$6,435**	$5,492	$4,750	**17**	16
Operating profit	**$ 811**	$ 774	$ 700	**5**	11
Impact of restructuring and impairment charges	**50**	9	–		
Operating profit, excluding restructuring and impairment charges	**$ 861**	$ 783	$ 700	**10**	12

2008

Snacks volume grew 6%, reflecting broad-based increases led by double-digit growth in Russia. Additionally, Walkers in the United Kingdom, as well as the Netherlands, grew at low-single-digit rates and Spain increased slightly. Acquisitions contributed 2 percentage points to the volume growth.

Beverage volume grew 17%, primarily reflecting the expansion of the Pepsi Lipton Joint Venture and the Sandora and Lebedyansky acquisitions, which contributed 16 percentage points to the growth. CSDs increased at a low-single-digit rate and non-carbonated beverages grew at a double-digit rate.

In 2008, UKEU net revenue grew 17%, reflecting favorable effective net pricing and volume growth.

Net revenue grew 17%, reflecting favorable effective net pricing and volume growth. Acquisitions contributed 8 percentage points and foreign currency contributed 2 percentage points to the net revenue growth.

Operating profit grew 5%, driven by the net revenue growth, partially offset by increased commodity costs. Acquisitions contributed 5.5 percentage points and foreign currency contributed 3.5 percentage points to the operating profit growth. Operating profit growth was negatively impacted by 5 percentage points, resulting from higher fourth quarter restructuring and impairment charges in 2008 related to the Productivity for Growth program. Operating profit, excluding restructuring and impairment charges, grew 10%.

2007

Snacks volume grew 6%, reflecting broad-based increases led by double-digit growth in Russia and Romania, partially offset by low-single-digit declines at Walkers in the United Kingdom and in France. The acquisition of a business in Europe in the third quarter of 2006 contributed nearly 2 percentage points to the reported volume growth rate.

Beverage volume grew 8%, reflecting broad-based increases led by double-digit growth in Russia and Poland, partially offset by a high-single-digit decline in Spain. The acquisition of a noncontrolling interest in a business in the Ukraine in the fourth quarter of 2007 contributed 3 percentage points to the reported volume growth rate. CSDs grew at a low-single-digit rate while non-carbonated beverages grew at a double-digit rate.

Net revenue grew 16%, primarily reflecting volume growth and favorable effective net pricing. Foreign currency contributed 9 percentage points to net revenue growth, primarily reflecting the favorable euro and British pound. The net impact of acquisitions reduced net revenue growth slightly.

Operating profit grew 11%, driven by the net revenue growth, partially offset by increased raw material costs and less-favorable settlements of promotional spending accruals in 2007. Foreign currency contributed 10 percentage points of growth, primarily reflecting the favorable British pound and euro. The net impact of acquisitions reduced operating profit growth by 4 percentage points. Operating profit, excluding restructuring and impairment charges, grew 12%.

Middle East, Africa & Asia

				% Change	
	2008	2007	2006	**2008**	2007
Net revenue	**$5,575**	$4,574	$3,440	**22**	33
Operating profit	**$ 667**	$ 535	$ 401	**25**	34
Impact of restructuring and impairment charges	**15**	14	–		
Operating profit, excluding restructuring and impairment charges	**$ 682**	$ 549	$ 401	**24**	37

2008

Snacks volume grew 10%, reflecting broad-based increases led by double-digit growth in China, the Middle East and South Africa. Additionally, Australia experienced low-single-digit growth and India grew at mid-single-digit rates.

Beverage volume grew 11%, reflecting broad-based increases driven by double-digit growth in China, the Middle East and India, partially offset by low-single-digit declines in Thailand and the Philippines. Acquisitions had a nominal impact on beverage volume growth. CSDs grew at a high-single-digit rate and non-carbonated beverages grew at a double-digit rate.

MEAA experienced double-digit volume growth in both 2008 and 2007.

Net revenue grew 22%, reflecting volume growth and favorable effective net pricing. Acquisitions contributed 2 percentage points and foreign currency contributed 1 percentage point to the net revenue growth.

Operating profit grew 25%, driven by the net revenue growth, partially offset by increased commodity costs. Foreign currency contributed 2 percentage points and acquisitions contributed 1 percentage point to the operating profit growth. The impact of the fourth quarter restructuring and impairment charges in 2008 related to the Productivity for Growth program was offset by the prior year restructuring charges. Operating profit, excluding restructuring and impairment charges, grew 24%.

2007

Snacks volume grew 19%, reflecting broad-based growth. The Middle East, Turkey, India, South Africa and China all grew at double-digit rates, and Australia grew at a high-single-digit rate. Acquisitions contributed 4 percentage points to volume growth.

Beverage volume grew 11%, reflecting broad-based growth led by double-digit growth in the Middle East, Pakistan and China, partially offset by a high-single-digit decline in Thailand and a low-single-digit-decline in Turkey. Acquisitions had no impact on the growth rates. Both CSDs and non-carbonated beverages grew at double-digit rates.

Net revenue grew 33%, reflecting volume growth and favorable effective net pricing. Foreign currency contributed 5.5 percentage points to net revenue growth. Acquisitions contributed 11 percentage points to net revenue growth.

Operating profit grew 34%, driven by volume growth and favorable effective net pricing, partially offset by increased raw material costs. Foreign currency contributed 7 percentage points to operating profit growth. Acquisitions contributed 1 percentage point to the operating profit growth rate. The absence of amortization expense recorded in 2006 related to prior acquisitions contributed 11 percentage points to operating profit growth. The impact of restructuring actions taken in the fourth quarter of 2007 to reduce costs in our operations, rationalize capacity and realign our organizational structure reduced operating profit growth by 3.5 percentage points. Operating profit, excluding restructuring and impairment charges, grew 37%.

OUR LIQUIDITY AND CAPITAL RESOURCES

Global capital and credit markets, including the commercial paper markets, experienced in 2008 and continue to experience considerable volatility. Despite this volatility, we continue to have access to the capital and credit markets. In addition, we have revolving credit facilities that are discussed in Note 9. We believe that our cash generating capability and financial condition, together with our revolving credit facilities and other available methods of debt financing (including long-term debt financing which, depending upon market conditions, we intend to use to replace a portion of our commercial paper borrowings), will be adequate to meet our operating, investing and financing needs. However, there can be no assurance that continued or increased volatility in the global capital and credit markets will not impair our ability to access these markets on terms commercially acceptable to us or at all.

In addition, our cash provided from operating activities is somewhat impacted by seasonality. Working capital needs are impacted by weekly sales, which are generally highest in the third quarter due to seasonal and holiday-related sales patterns, and generally lowest in the first quarter.

Management's Discussion and Analysis

Operating Activities

In 2008, our operations provided $7.0 billion of cash, compared to $6.9 billion in the prior year, primarily reflecting our solid business results. Our operating cash flow in 2008 reflects restructuring payments of $180 million, including $159 million related to our Productivity for Growth program, and pension and retiree medical contributions of $219 million, of which $23 million were discretionary.

In 2007, our operations provided $6.9 billion of cash, compared to $6.1 billion in 2006, primarily reflecting solid business results.

Substantially all cash payments related to the Productivity for Growth program are expected to be paid by the end of 2009. In addition, in 2009, we will make a $640 million after-tax discretionary contribution to our U.S. pension plans.

Investing Activities

In 2008, we used $2.7 billion for our investing activities, primarily reflecting $2.4 billion for capital spending and $1.9 billion for acquisitions. Significant acquisitions included our joint acquisition with PBG of Lebedyansky in Russia and the acquisition of a snacks company in Serbia. The use of cash was partially offset by net proceeds from sales of short-term investments of $1.3 billion and proceeds from sales of PBG and PAS stock of $358 million.

In 2007, we used $3.7 billion for our investing activities, reflecting capital spending of $2.4 billion and acquisitions of $1.3 billion. Acquisitions included the remaining interest in a snacks joint venture in Latin America, Naked Juice Company and Bluebird Foods, and the acquisition of a minority interest in a juice company in the Ukraine through a joint venture with PAS. Proceeds from our sale of PBG stock of $315 million were offset by net purchases of short-term investments of $383 million.

We expect a high-single-digit decrease in net capital spending in 2009. In addition, we do not anticipate cash proceeds in 2009 from sales of PBG and PAS stock due to the current capital market conditions.

Financing Activities

In 2008, we used $3.0 billion for our financing activities, primarily reflecting the return of operating cash flow to our shareholders through common share repurchases of $4.7 billion and dividend payments of $2.5 billion. The use of cash was partially offset by proceeds from issuances of long-term debt, net of payments, of $3.1 billion, stock option proceeds of $620 million and net proceeds from short-term borrowings of $445 million.

2008 Cash Utilization

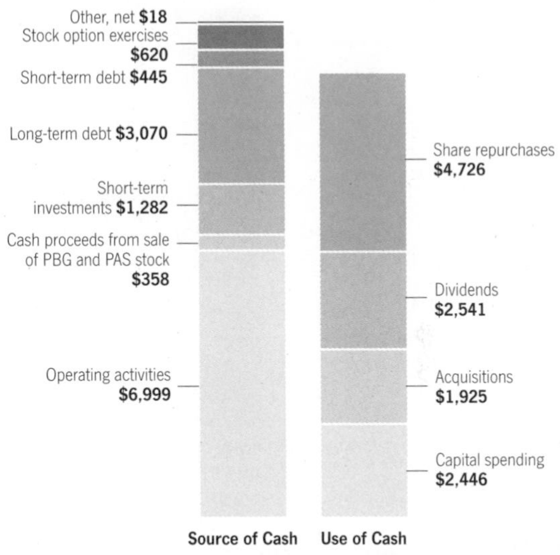

In 2007, we used $4.0 billion for our financing activities, primarily reflecting the return of operating cash flow to our shareholders through common share repurchases of $4.3 billion and dividend payments of $2.2 billion, as well as net repayments of short-term borrowings of $395 million. The use of cash was partially offset by stock option proceeds of $1.1 billion and net proceeds from issuances of long-term debt of $1.6 billion.

We annually review our capital structure with our Board, including our dividend policy and share repurchase activity. In the second quarter of 2008, our Board of Directors approved a 13% dividend increase from $1.50 to $1.70 per share. During the third quarter of 2008, we completed our $8.5 billion repurchase program publicly announced on May 3, 2006 and expiring on June 30, 2009 and began repurchasing shares under our $8.0 billion repurchase program authorized by the Board of Directors in the second quarter of 2007 and expiring on June 30, 2010. The current $8.0 billion authorization has approximately $6.4 billion remaining for repurchase. We have historically repurchased significantly more shares each year than we have issued under our stock-based compensation plans, with average net annual repurchases of 1.8% of outstanding shares for the last five years. In 2009, we intend, subject to market conditions, to spend up to $2.5 billion repurchasing shares.

2007 Cash Utilization

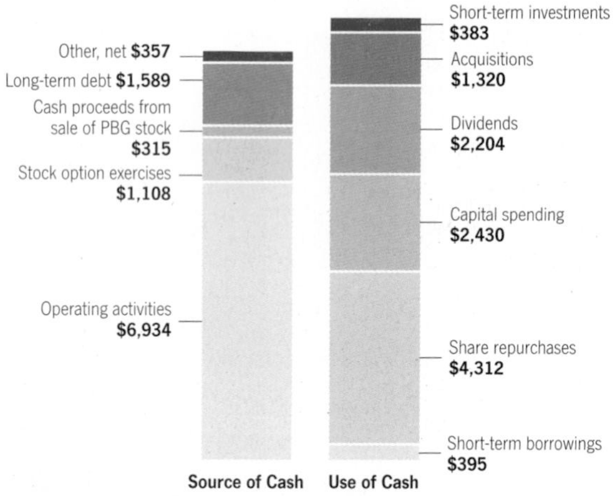

2006 Cash Utilization

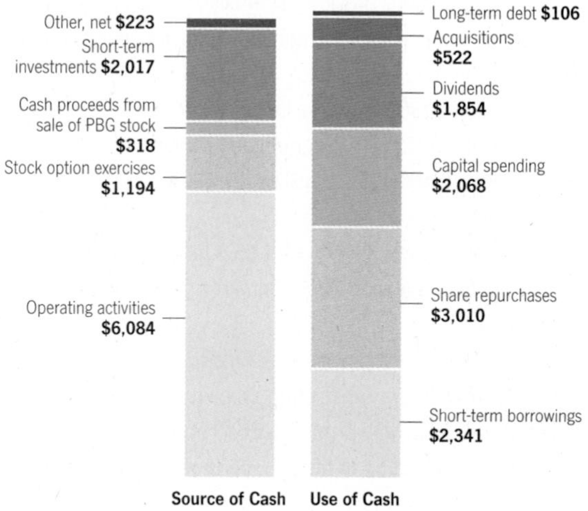

Management Operating Cash Flow

We focus on management operating cash flow as a key element in achieving maximum shareholder value, and it is the primary measure we use to monitor cash flow performance. However, it is not a measure provided by accounting principles generally accepted in the U.S. Since net capital spending is essential to our product innovation initiatives and maintaining our operational capabilities, we believe that it is a recurring and necessary use of cash. As such, we believe investors should also consider net capital spending when evaluating our cash from operating activities. The table below reconciles the net cash provided by operating activities, as reflected in our cash flow statement, to our management operating cash flow.

	2008	2007	2006
Net cash provided by operating activities (a)	$ 6,999	$ 6,934	$ 6,084
Capital spending	(2,446)	(2,430)	(2,068)
Sales of property, plant and equipment	98	47	49
Management operating cash flow	$ 4,651	$ 4,551	$ 4,065

(a) *Includes restructuring payments of $180 million in 2008, $22 million in 2007 and $56 million in 2006.*

Management operating cash flow was used primarily to repurchase shares and pay dividends. We expect to continue to return approximately all of our management operating cash flow to our shareholders through dividends and share repurchases. However, see "Our Business Risks" for certain factors that may impact our operating cash flows.

Credit Ratings

Our debt ratings of Aa2 from Moody's and A+ from Standard & Poor's contribute to our ability to access global capital and credit markets. We have maintained strong investment grade ratings for over a decade. Each rating is considered strong investment grade and is in the first quartile of its respective ranking system. These ratings also reflect the impact of our anchor bottlers' cash flows and debt.

Credit Facilities and Long-Term Contractual Commitments

See Note 9 for a description of our credit facilities and long-term contractual commitments.

Off-Balance-Sheet Arrangements

It is not our business practice to enter into off-balance-sheet arrangements, other than in the normal course of business. However, at the time of the separation of our bottling operations from us various guarantees were necessary to facilitate the transactions. In 2008, we extended our guarantee of a portion of Bottling Group LLC's long-term debt in connection with the refinancing of a corresponding portion of the underlying debt. At December 27, 2008, we believe it is remote that these guarantees would require any cash payment. We do not enter into off-balance-sheet transactions specifically structured to provide income or tax benefits or to avoid recognizing or disclosing assets or liabilities. See Note 9 for a description of our off-balance-sheet arrangements.

Appendix C

Financial Statement Analysis Package (FSAP)

Output from FSAP for PepsiCo Inc. and Subsidiaries

FSAP

The Financial Statement Analysis Package (**FSAP**) that accompanies this text is a user-friendly, adaptable series of Excel®-based spreadsheet templates. FSAP enables the user to manually input financial statement data for a firm and then perform financial statement analysis, forecasting, and valuation. FSAP contains five spreadsheets: Data, Analysis, Forecasts, Forecast Development, and Valuation.

Appendix C presents the output of these spreadsheets using the data for PepsiCo. The output includes the financial statement data for the years 2003–2008, the profitability and risk ratios for the years 2004–2008, financial statement forecasts, and a variety of valuation models applied to the forecasted data for PepsiCo.

FSAP contains a series of User Guides that provide line-by-line instructions on how to use FSAP. You can download a blank FSAP template as well as the FSAP output for PepsiCo from the website for this book: www.cengage.com/accounting/wahlen. FSAP data files also are available for various problems and cases in the book. The FSAP icon has been used throughout the book to denote potential applications for FSAP.

Data Spreadsheet

Analyst Name:	**Wahlen, Baginski, and Bradshaw**					
Company Name:	**PepsiCo**					
Year (Most recent in far right column.)	**2003**	**2004**	**2005**	**2006**	**2007**	**2008**
BALANCE SHEET DATA						
Assets:						
Cash and cash equivalents	820	1,280	1,716	1,651	910	2,064
Marketable securities	1,181	2,165	3,166	1,171	1,571	213
Accounts receivable—Net	2,830	2,999	3,261	3,725	4,389	4,683
Inventories	1,412	1,541	1,693	1,926	2,290	2,522
Prepaid expenses and other current assets	687	654	618	657	991	1,324
Deferred tax assets—Current						
Other current assets (1)						
Other current assets (2)						
Current Assets	**6,930**	**8,639**	**10,454**	**9,130**	**10,151**	**10,806**
Long-term investments	2,920	3,284	3,485	3,690	4,354	3,883
Property, plant, and equipment—At cost	14,755	15,930	17,145	19,058	21,896	22,552
<Accumulated depreciation>	–6,927	–7,781	–8,464	–9,371	–10,668	–10,889
Amortizable intangible assets (net)	718	598	530	637	796	732
Goodwill and nonamortizable intangibles	4,665	4,842	5,174	5,806	6,417	6,252
Deferred tax assets—Noncurrent						
Other noncurrent assets (1)	2,266	2,475	3,403	980	1,682	2,658
Other noncurrent assets (2)						
Total Assets	**25,327**	**27,987**	**31,727**	**29,930**	**34,628**	**35,994**
Liabilities and Equities:						
Accounts payable—Trade	1,638	1,731	1,799	2,102	2,562	2,846
Current accrued liabilities	3,575	3,868	4,172	4,394	5,040	5,427
Notes payable and short-term debt	145	894	2,746	274	0	369
Current maturities of long-term debt	446	160	143	0	0	0
Deferred tax liabilities—Current						
Income taxes payable	611	99	546	90	151	145
Other current liabilities (1)						
Other current liabilities (2)						
Current Liabilities	**6,415**	**6,752**	**9,406**	**6,860**	**7,753**	**8,787**
Long-term debt	1,702	2,397	2,313	2,550	4,203	7,858
Long-term accrued liabilities	4,075	4,099	4,323	4,624	4,792	7,017
Deferred tax liabilities—Noncurrent	1,261	1,216	1,434	528	646	226
Other noncurrent liabilities (1)						
Other noncurrent liabilities (2)						
Total Liabilities	**13,453**	**14,464**	**17,476**	**14,562**	**17,394**	**23,888**

Data Spreadsheet (Continued)

Year (Most recent in far right column.)	**2003**	**2004**	**2005**	**2006**	**2007**	**2008**
Minority interest						
Preferred stock	–22	–49	–69	–79	–91	–97
Common stock + Additional paid-in capital	578	648	644	614	480	381
Retained earnings <deficit>	15,961	18,730	21,116	24,837	28,184	30,638
Accum. other comprehensive income <loss>	–1,267	–886	–1,053	–2,246	–952	–4,694
Other equity adjustments						
<Treasury stock>	–3,376	–4,920	–6,387	–7,758	–10,387	–14,122
Common Shareholders' Equity	**11,896**	**13,572**	**14,320**	**15,447**	**17,325**	**12,203**
Total Liabilities and Equities	**25,327**	**27,987**	**31,727**	**29,930**	**34,628**	**35,994**

INCOME STATEMENT DATA	**2003**	**2004**	**2005**	**2006**	**2007**	**2008**
Revenues	26,971	29,261	32,562	35,137	39,474	43,251
<Cost of goods sold>	–11,691	–12,674	–14,176	–15,762	–18,038	–20,351
Gross Profit	**15,280**	**16,587**	**18,386**	**19,375**	**21,436**	**22,900**
<Selling, general, and administrative expenses>	–10,148	–11,031	–12,252	–12,711	–14,208	–15,901
<Research and development expenses>						
<Amortization of intangible assets>	–145	–147	–150	–162	–58	–64
<Other operating expenses (1)>						
<Other operating expenses (2)>						
Other operating income (1)						
Other operating income (2)						
Nonrecurring operating gains						
<Nonrecurring operating losses>	–206	–150				
Operating Profit	**4,781**	**5,259**	**5,984**	**6,502**	**7,170**	**6,935**
Interest income	51	74	159	173	125	41
<Interest expense>	–163	–167	–256	–239	–224	–329
Income <Loss> from equity affiliates	323	380	495	553	560	374
Other income or gains						
<Other expenses or losses>						
Income before Tax	**4,992**	**5,546**	**6,382**	**6,989**	**7,631**	**7,021**
<Income tax expense>	–1,424	–1,372	–2,304	–1,347	–1,973	–1,879
<Minority interest in earnings>						
Income <Loss> from discontinued operations		38				
Extraordinary gains <losses>						
Changes in accounting principles						
Net Income (computed)	**3,568**	**4,212**	**4,078**	**5,642**	**5,658**	**5,142**
Net Income (enter reported amount as a check)	3,568	4,212	4,078	5,642	5,658	5,142
Other comprehensive income items	405	381	–167	456	1,294	–3,793
Comprehensive Income	**3,973**	**4,593**	**3,911**	**6,098**	**6,952**	**1,349**

(Continued)

Data Spreadsheet (Continued)

Year (Most recent in far right column.)	2003	2004	2005	2006	2007	2008
STATEMENT OF CASH FLOWS DATA						
Net Income	**3,568**	**4,212**	**4,078**	**5,642**	**5,658**	**5,142**
Add back depreciation and amortization expenses	1,221	1,264	1,308	1,406	1,426	1,543
Add back stock-based compensation expense	407	368	311	270	260	238
Deferred income taxes	–323	17	440	–510	118	573
<Income from equity affiliates, net of dividends>	–276	–297	–414	–442	–441	–202
<Increase> Decrease in accounts receivable	–220	–130	–272	–330	–405	–549
<Increase> Decrease in inventories	–49	–100	–132	–186	–204	–345
<Increase> Decrease in prepaid expenses	23	–31	–56	–37	–16	–68
<Increase> Decrease in other current assets (1)						
<Increase> Decrease in other current assets (2)						
Increase <Decrease> in accounts payable	–11	216	188	223	500	718
Increase <Decrease> in other current liabilities (1)						
Increase <Decrease> in other current liabilities (2)						
Increase <Decrease> in other noncurrent liabilities (1)	182	–268	609	–295	128	–180
Increase <Decrease> in other noncurrent liabilities (2)	–171	–100	227	64	–107	–367
Other add backs to net income	621	491	464	544	535	1,002
<Other subtractions from net income>	–644	–588	–899	–265	–518	–506
Other operating cash flows						
Net Cash Flow from Operations	**4,328**	**5,054**	**5,852**	**6,084**	**6,934**	**6,999**
Proceeds from sales of property, plant, and equipment	49	38	88	49	47	98
<Property, plant, and equipment acquired>	–1,345	–1,387	–1,736	–2,068	–2,430	–2,446
<Increase> Decrease in marketable securities	–950	–969	–991	2,017	–383	1,282
Investments sold	46	52	3	37	27	364
<Investments acquired>	–71	–64	–1,095	–547	–1,320	–1,925
Other investment transactions (1)			214	318	315	–40
Other investment transactions (2)						
Net Cash Flow from Investing Activities	**–2,271**	**–2,330**	**–3,517**	**–194**	**–3,744**	**–2,667**
Increase in short-term borrowing	128	1,272	1,933	185	83	714
<Decrease in short-term borrowing>	–115	–160	–85	–2,526	–478	–269
Increase in long-term borrowing	52	504	25	51	2,168	3,719
<Decrease in long-term borrowing>	–641	–512	–177	–157	–579	–649
Issue of capital stock						
Proceeds from stock option exercises	689	965	1,099	1,194	1,108	620
<Share repurchases—Treasury stock>	–1,945	–3,055	–3,031	–3,010	–4,312	–4,726
<Dividend payments>	–1,070	–1,329	–1,642	–1,854	–2,204	–2,541
Other financing transactions (1)				134	208	107
Other financing transactions (2)						
Net Cash Flow from Financing Activities	**–2,902**	**–2,315**	**–1,878**	**–5,983**	**–4,006**	**–3,025**

Data Spreadsheet (Continued)

Year (Most recent in far right column.)	**2003**	**2004**	**2005**	**2006**	**2007**	**2008**
Effects of exchange rate changes on cash	27	51	–21	28	75	–153
Net Change in Cash	**–818**	**460**	**436**	**–65**	**–741**	**1,154**
Cash and cash equivalents, beginning of year		820	1,280	1,716	1,651	910
Cash and cash equivalents, end of year		1,280	1,716	1,651	910	2,064

SUPPLEMENTAL DATA	**2003**	**2004**	**2005**	**2006**	**2007**	**2008**
Statutory tax rate	35.0%	35.0%	35.0%	35.0%	35.0%	35.0%
Average tax rate implied from income statement data	28.5%	24.7%	36.1%	19.3%	25.9%	26.8%
After-tax effects of nonrecurring and unusual items on net income	–206	–112	0	0	0	0
Total deferred tax assets (from above)	0	0	0	0	0	0
Deferred tax asset valuation allowance	438	564	532	624	695	657
Allowance for uncollectible accounts receivable	105	97	75	64	69	70
Depreciation expense	1,020	1,062	1,103	1,182	1,304	1,422
Preferred stock dividends (total, if any)	3	3	3	1	2	1
Common shares outstanding	1,705	1,679	1,656	1,638	1,605	1,553
Earnings per share (basic)	2.07	2.45	2.43	3.42	3.48	3.26
Common dividends per share	0.63	0.79	0.99	1.13	1.37	1.64
Market price per share at fiscal year-end	46.47	51.94	55.80	60.18	75.67	54.77

FINANCIAL DATA CHECKS						
Assets – Liabilities – Equities	0	0	0	0	0	0
Net Income (computed) – Net Income (reported)	0	0	0	0	0	0
Cash Changes	0	0	0	0	0	0

Analysis Spreadsheet

Analyst Name: Wahlen, Baginski, and Bradshaw
Company Name: PepsiCo

PROFITABILITY FACTORS:

Year	2004	2005	2006	2007	2008
RETURN ON ASSETS (based on reported amounts):					
Profit Margin for ROA	14.8%	13.0%	16.5%	14.7%	12.4%
× Asset Turnover	1.1	1.1	1.1	1.2	1.2
= Return on Assets	16.2%	14.2%	18.8%	18.0%	15.2%
RETURN ON ASSETS (excluding the effects of nonrecurring items):					
Profit Margin for ROA	15.1%	13.0%	16.5%	14.7%	12.4%
× Asset Turnover	1.1	1.1	1.1	1.2	1.2
= Return on Assets	16.6%	14.2%	18.8%	18.0%	15.2%
RETURN ON COMMON EQUITY (based on reported amounts):					
Profit Margin for ROCE	14.4%	12.5%	16.1%	14.3%	11.9%
× Asset Turnover	1.1	1.1	1.1	1.2	1.2
× Capital Structure Leverage	2.1	2.1	2.1	2.0	2.4
= Return on Common Equity	33.1%	29.2%	37.9%	34.5%	34.8%
RETURN ON COMMON EQUITY (excluding the effects of nonrecurring items):					
Profit Margin for ROCE	14.8%	12.5%	16.1%	14.3%	11.9%
× Asset Turnover	1.1	1.1	1.1	1.2	1.2
× Capital Structure Leverage	2.1	2.1	2.1	2.0	2.4
= Return on Common Equity	33.9%	29.2%	37.9%	34.5%	34.8%
OPERATING PERFORMANCE:					
Gross Profit/Revenues	56.7%	56.5%	55.1%	54.3%	52.9%
Operating Profit/Revenues	18.0%	18.4%	18.5%	18.2%	16.0%
Net Income/Revenues	14.4%	12.5%	16.1%	14.3%	11.9%
Comprehensive Income/Revenues	15.7%	12.0%	17.4%	17.6%	3.1%
PERSISTENT OPERATING PERFORMANCE (excluding the effects of nonrecurring items):					
Persistent Operating Profit/Revenues	18.5%	18.4%	18.5%	18.2%	16.0%
Persistent Net Income/Revenues	14.8%	12.5%	16.1%	14.3%	11.9%
GROWTH:					
Revenue Growth	8.5%	11.3%	7.9%	12.3%	9.6%
Net Income Growth	18.0%	–3.2%	38.4%	0.3%	–9.1%
Persistent Net Income Growth	14.6%	–5.7%	38.4%	0.3%	–9.1%
OPERATING CONTROL:					
Gross Profit Control Index	100.1%	99.6%	97.7%	98.5%	97.5%
Operating Profit Control Index	101.4%	102.3%	100.7%	98.2%	88.3%
Profit Margin Decomposition:					
Gross Profit Margin	56.7%	56.5%	55.1%	54.3%	52.9%
Operating Profit Index	31.7%	32.5%	33.6%	33.4%	30.3%
Leverage Index	105.5%	106.7%	107.5%	106.4%	101.2%
Tax Index	75.9%	63.9%	80.7%	74.1%	73.2%
Net Profit Margin	14.4%	12.5%	16.1%	14.3%	11.9%
Comprehensive Income Performance:					
Comprehensive Income Index	109.0%	95.9%	108.1%	122.9%	26.2%
Comprehensive Income Margin	15.7%	12.0%	17.4%	17.6%	3.1%

Analysis Spreadsheet (Continued)

RISK FACTORS:					
Year	**2004**	**2005**	**2006**	**2007**	**2008**
LIQUIDITY:					
Current Ratio	1.28	1.11	1.33	1.31	1.23
Quick Ratio	0.95	0.87	0.95	0.89	0.79
Operating Cash Flow to Current Liabilities	76.8%	72.4%	74.8%	94.9%	84.6%
ASSET TURNOVER:					
Accounts Receivable Turnover	10.0	10.4	10.1	9.7	9.5
Days Receivables Held	36	35	36	38	38
Inventory Turnover	8.6	8.8	8.7	8.6	8.5
Days Inventory Held	43	42	42	43	43
Accounts Payable Turnover	7.6	8.1	8.2	7.9	7.6
Days Payables Held	48	45	45	46	48
Net Working Capital Days	31	32	34	34	33
Revenues/Average Net Fixed Assets	3.7	3.9	3.8	3.8	3.8
Cash Turnover	27.9	21.7	20.9	30.8	29.1
Days Sales Held in Cash	13.1	16.8	17.5	11.8	12.5
SOLVENCY:					
Total Liabilities/Total Assets	51.7%	55.1%	48.7%	50.2%	66.4%
Total Liabilities/Shareholders' Equity	106.6%	122.0%	94.3%	100.4%	195.8%
LT Debt/LT Capital	15.0%	13.9%	14.2%	19.5%	39.2%
LT Debt/Shareholders' Equity	17.7%	16.2%	16.5%	24.3%	64.4%
Operating Cash Flow to Total Liabilities	36.2%	36.6%	38.0%	43.4%	33.9%
Interest Coverage Ratio (reported amounts)	34.4	25.9	30.2	35.1	22.3
Interest Coverage Ratio (recurring amounts)	35.1	25.9	30.2	35.1	22.3
RISK FACTORS:					
Bankruptcy Predictors:					
Altman Z-Score	6.35	5.86	7.29	7.30	5.27
Bankruptcy Probability	0.00%	0.00%	0.00%	0.00%	0.00%
Earnings Manipulation Predictors:					
Beneish Earnings Manipulation Score	−2.60	−2.69	−2.41	−2.49	−2.75
Earnings Manipulation Probability	0.46%	0.35%	0.80%	0.64%	0.30%
STOCK MARKET-BASED RATIOS:					
Stock Returns	13.5%	9.3%	9.9%	28.0%	−25.5%
Price-Earnings Ratio (reported amounts)	21.2	23.0	17.6	21.7	16.8
Price-Earnings Ratio (recurring amounts)	20.6	23.0	17.6	21.7	16.8
Market Value to Book Value Ratio	6.4	6.5	6.4	7.0	7.0

(Continued)

Analysis Spreadsheet (Continued)

INCOME STATEMENT ITEMS AS A PERCENT OF REVENUES:

Year	2004	2005	2006	2007	2008
Revenues	**100.0%**	**100.0%**	**100.0%**	**100.0%**	**100.0%**
<Cost of goods sold>	–43.3%	–43.5%	–44.9%	–45.7%	–47.1%
Gross Profit	**56.7%**	**56.5%**	**55.1%**	**54.3%**	**52.9%**
<Selling, general, and administrative expenses>	–37.7%	–37.6%	–36.2%	–36.0%	–36.8%
<Research and development expenses>					
<Amortization of intangible assets>	–0.5%	–0.5%	–0.5%	–0.1%	–0.1%
<Other operating expenses (1)>					
<Other operating expenses (2)>					
Other operating income (1)					
Other operating income (2)					
Nonrecurring operating gains					
<Nonrecurring operating losses>	–0.5%				
Operating Profit	**18.0%**	**18.4%**	**18.5%**	**18.2%**	**16.0%**
Interest income	0.3%	0.5%	0.5%	0.3%	0.1%
<Interest expense>	–0.6%	–0.8%	–0.7%	–0.6%	–0.8%
Income <Loss> from equity affiliates	1.3%	1.5%	1.6%	1.4%	0.9%
Other income or gains					
<Other expenses or losses>					
Income before Tax	**19.0%**	**19.6%**	**19.9%**	**19.3%**	**16.2%**
<Income tax expense>	–4.7%	–7.1%	–3.8%	–5.0%	–4.3%
<Minority interest in earnings>					
Income <Loss> from discontinued operations	0.1%				
Extraordinary gains <losses>					
Changes in accounting principles					
Net Income (computed)	**14.4%**	**12.5%**	**16.1%**	**14.3%**	**11.9%**
Other comprehensive income items	1.3%	–0.5%	1.3%	3.3%	–8.8%
Comprehensive Income	**15.7%**	**12.0%**	**17.4%**	**17.6%**	**3.1%**

Analysis Spreadsheet (Continued)

INCOME STATEMENT ITEMS: GROWTH RATES

Year	2004	2005	2006	2007	2008	
	Year–to–Year Growth Rates					Compound Growth Rates
Revenues	**8.5%**	**11.3%**	**7.9%**	**12.3%**	**9.6%**	**9.9%**
<Cost of goods sold>	8.4%	11.9%	11.2%	14.4%	12.8%	11.7%
Gross Profit	**8.6%**	**10.8%**	**5.4%**	**10.6%**	**6.8%**	**8.4%**
<Selling, general and administrative expenses>	8.7%	11.1%	3.7%	11.8%	11.9%	9.4%
<Research and development expenses>						
<Amortization of intangible assets>	1.4%	2.0%	8.0%	–64.2%	10.3%	–15.1%
<Other operating expenses (1)>						
<Other operating expenses (2)>						
Other operating income (1)						
Other operating income (2)						
Nonrecurring operating gains						
<Nonrecurring operating losses>	–27.2%	–100.0%				
Operating Profit	**10.0%**	**13.8%**	**8.7%**	**10.3%**	**–3.3%**	**7.7%**
Interest income	45.1%	114.9%	8.8%	–27.7%	–67.2%	–4.3%
<Interest expense>	2.5%	53.3%	–6.6%	–6.3%	46.9%	15.1%
Income <Loss> from equity affiliates	17.6%	30.3%	11.7%	1.3%	–33.2%	3.0%
Other income or gains						
<Other expenses or losses>						
Income before Tax	**11.1%**	**15.1%**	**9.5%**	**9.2%**	**–8.0%**	**7.1%**
<Income tax expense>	–3.7%	67.9%	–41.5%	46.5%	–4.8%	5.7%
<Minority interest in earnings>						
Income <Loss> from discontinued operations						
Extraordinary gains <losses>						
Changes in accounting principles						
Net Income (computed)	**18.0%**	**–3.2%**	**38.4%**	**0.3%**	**–9.1%**	**7.6%**
Other comprehensive income items	–5.9%	–143.8%	–373.1%	183.8%	–393.1%	–256.4%
Comprehensive Income	**15.6%**	**–14.8%**	**55.9%**	**14.0%**	**–80.6%**	**–19.4%**

(Continued)

Analysis Spreadsheet (Continued)

COMMON SIZE BALANCE SHEET—AS A PERCENT OF TOTAL ASSETS

Year	2004	2005	2006	2007	2008
Assets:					
Cash and cash equivalents	4.6%	5.4%	5.5%	2.6%	5.7%
Marketable securities	7.7%	10.0%	3.9%	4.5%	0.6%
Accounts receivable—Net	10.7%	10.3%	12.4%	12.7%	13.0%
Inventories	5.5%	5.3%	6.4%	6.6%	7.0%
Prepaid expenses and other current assets	2.3%	1.9%	2.2%	2.9%	3.7%
Deferred tax assets—Current					
Other current assets (1)					
Other current assets (2)					
Current Assets	**30.9%**	**32.9%**	**30.5%**	**29.3%**	**30.0%**
Long-term investments	11.7%	11.0%	12.3%	12.6%	10.8%
Property, plant, and equipment—At cost	56.9%	54.0%	63.7%	63.2%	62.7%
<Accumulated depreciation>	–27.8%	–26.7%	–31.3%	–30.8%	–30.3%
Amortizable intangible assets (net)	2.1%	1.7%	2.1%	2.3%	2.0%
Goodwill and nonamortizable intangibles	17.3%	16.3%	19.4%	18.5%	17.4%
Deferred tax assets—Noncurrent					
Other noncurrent assets (1)	8.8%	10.7%	3.3%	4.9%	7.4%
Other noncurrent assets (2)					
Total Assets	**100.0%**	**100.0%**	**100.0%**	**100.0%**	**100.0%**
Liabilities and Equities:					
Accounts payable—Trade	6.2%	5.7%	7.0%	7.4%	7.9%
Current accrued liabilities	13.8%	13.1%	14.7%	14.6%	15.1%
Notes payable and short-term debt	3.2%	8.7%	0.9%	0.0%	1.0%
Current maturities of long-term debt	0.6%	0.5%	0.0%	0.0%	0.0%
Deferred tax liabilities—Current					
Income taxes payable	0.4%	1.7%	0.3%	0.4%	0.4%
Other current liabilities (1)					
Other current liabilities (2)					
Current Liabilities	**24.1%**	**29.6%**	**22.9%**	**22.4%**	**24.4%**
Long-term debt	8.6%	7.3%	8.5%	12.1%	21.8%
Long-term accrued liabilities	14.6%	13.6%	15.4%	13.8%	19.5%
Deferred tax liabilities—Noncurrent	4.3%	4.5%	1.8%	1.9%	0.6%
Other noncurrent liabilities (1)					
Other noncurrent liabilities (2)					
Total Liabilities	**51.7%**	**55.1%**	**48.7%**	**50.2%**	**66.4%**

Analysis Spreadsheet (Continued)

COMMON SIZE BALANCE SHEET—AS A PERCENT OF TOTAL ASSETS

Year	2004	2005	2006	2007	2008
Minority interest					
Preferred stock	-0.2%	-0.2%	-0.3%	-0.3%	-0.3%
Common stock + Additional paid-in capital	2.3%	2.0%	2.1%	1.4%	1.1%
Retained earnings <deficit>	66.9%	66.6%	83.0%	81.4%	85.1%
Accum. other comprehensive income <loss>	-3.2%	-3.3%	-7.5%	-2.7%	-13.0%
Other equity adjustments					
<Treasury stock>	-17.6%	-20.1%	-25.9%	-30.0%	-39.2%
Common Shareholders' Equity	**48.5%**	**45.1%**	**51.6%**	**50.0%**	**33.9%**
Total Liabilities and Equities	**100.0%**	**100.0%**	**100.0%**	**100.0%**	**100.0%**

BALANCE SHEET ITEMS: GROWTH RATES

Year	2004	2005	2006	2007	2008	
	Year-to-Year Growth Rates					Compound Growth Rates
Assets:						
Cash and cash equivalents	56.1%	34.1%	-3.8%	-44.9%	126.8%	20.3%
Marketable securities	83.3%	46.2%	-63.0%	34.2%	-86.4%	-29.0%
Accounts receivable—Net	6.0%	8.7%	14.2%	17.8%	6.7%	10.6%
Inventories	9.1%	9.9%	13.8%	18.9%	10.1%	12.3%
Prepaid expenses and other current assets	-4.8%	-5.5%	6.3%	50.8%	33.6%	14.0%
Deferred tax assets—Current						
Other current assets (1)						
Other current assets (2)						
Current Assets	**24.7%**	**21.0%**	**-12.7%**	**11.2%**	**6.5%**	**9.3%**
Long-term investments	12.5%	6.1%	5.9%	18.0%	-10.8%	5.9%
Property, plant, and equipment—At cost	8.0%	7.6%	11.2%	14.9%	3.0%	8.9%
<Accumulated depreciation>	12.3%	8.8%	10.7%	13.8%	2.1%	9.5%
Amortizable intangible assets (net)	-16.7%	-11.4%	20.2%	25.0%	-8.0%	0.4%
Goodwill and nonamortizable intangibles	3.8%	6.9%	12.2%	10.5%	-2.6%	6.0%
Deferred tax assets—Noncurrent						
Other noncurrent assets (1)	9.2%	37.5%	-71.2%	71.6%	58.0%	3.2%
Other noncurrent assets (2)						
Total Assets	**10.5%**	**13.4%**	**-5.7%**	**15.7%**	**3.9%**	**7.3%**

(Continued)

Analysis Spreadsheet (Continued)

BALANCE SHEET ITEMS: GROWTH RATES

Year	2004	2005	2006	2007	2008	
			Year–to–Year Growth Rates			Compound Growth Rates
Liabilities and Equities:						
Accounts payable—Trade	5.7%	3.9%	16.8%	21.9%	11.1%	11.7%
Current accrued liabilities	8.2%	7.9%	5.3%	14.7%	7.7%	8.7%
Notes payable and short-term debt	516.6%	207.2%	−90.0%	−100.0%		20.5%
Current maturities of long-term debt	−64.1%	−10.6%	−100.0%			−100.0%
Deferred tax liabilities—Current						
Income taxes payable	−83.8%	451.5%	−83.5%	67.8%	−4.0%	−25.0%
Other current liabilities (1)						
Other current liabilities (2)						
Current Liabilities	**5.3%**	**39.3%**	**−27.1%**	**13.0%**	**13.3%**	**6.5%**
Long-term debt	40.8%	−3.5%	10.2%	64.8%	87.0%	35.8%
Long-term accrued liabilities	0.6%	5.5%	7.0%	3.6%	46.4%	11.5%
Deferred tax liabilities—Noncurrent	−3.6%	17.9%	−63.2%	22.3%	−65.0%	−29.1%
Other noncurrent liabilities (1)						
Other noncurrent liabilities (2)						
Total Liabilities	**7.5%**	**20.8%**	**−16.7%**	**19.4%**	**37.3%**	**12.2%**
Minority interest						
Preferred stock	122.7%	40.8%	14.5%	15.2%	6.6%	34.5%
Common stock + Additional paid-in capital	12.1%	−0.6%	−4.7%	−21.8%	−20.6%	−8.0%
Retained earnings <deficit>	17.3%	12.7%	17.6%	13.5%	8.7%	13.9%
Accum. other comprehensive income <loss>	−30.1%	18.8%	113.3%	−57.6%	393.1%	29.9%
Other equity adjustments						
<Treasury stock>	45.7%	29.8%	21.5%	33.9%	36.0%	33.1%
Common Shareholders' Equity	**14.1%**	**5.5%**	**7.9%**	**12.2%**	**−29.6%**	**0.5%**
Total Liabilities and Equities	**10.5%**	**13.4%**	**−5.7%**	**15.7%**	**3.9%**	**7.3%**

Analysis Spreadsheet (Continued)

RETURN ON ASSETS ANALYSIS (excluding the effects of nonrecurring items)

Level 1	**RETURN ON ASSETS**		
	2006	**2007**	**2008**
	18.8%	18.0%	15.2%

Level 2	**PROFIT MARGIN FOR ROA**			**ASSET TURNOVER**		
	2006	**2007**	**2008**	**2006**	**2007**	**2008**
	16.5%	14.7%	12.4%	1.1	1.2	1.2

Level 3	**2006**	**2007**	**2008**	**2006**	**2007**	**2008**	**Turnovers:**
Revenues	100.0%	100.0%	100.0%	10.1	9.7	9.5	**Receivables**
<Cost of goods sold>	–44.9%	–45.7%	–47.1%	8.7	8.6	8.5	**Inventory**
Gross Profit	55.1%	54.3%	52.9%	3.8	3.8	3.8	**Fixed Assets**
<Selling, general, and administrative expenses>	–36.2%	–36.0%	–36.8%				
Operating Profit	18.5%	18.2%	16.0%				
Income before Tax	19.9%	19.3%	16.2%				
<Income tax expense>	–3.8%	–5.0%	–4.3%				
Profit Margin for ROA*	16.5%	14.7%	12.4%				

*Amounts do not sum.

RETURN ON COMMON EQUITY ANALYSIS (excluding the effects of nonrecurring items)

	2006	**2007**	**2008**
Return on Common Equity	37.9%	34.5%	34.8%

	2006	**2007**	**2008**
Profit Margin for ROCE	16.1%	14.3%	11.9%
Asset Turnover	1.1	1.2	1.2
Capital Structure Leverage	2.1	2.0	2.4

(Continued)

Analysis Spreadsheet (Continued)

STATEMENT OF CASH FLOWS: SUMMARY

Year	2004	2005	2006	2007	2008
Operating Activities:					
Net Income	**4,212**	**4,078**	**5,642**	**5,658**	**5,142**
Add back depreciation and amortization expenses	1,264	1,308	1,406	1,426	1,543
Net cash flows for working capital	–413	564	–561	–104	–791
Other net add backs/subtractions	–9	–98	–403	–46	1,105
Net Cash Flow from Operations	**5,054**	**5,852**	**6,084**	**6,934**	**6,999**
Investing Activities:					
Capital expenditures (net)	–1,349	–1,648	–2,019	–2,383	–2,348
Investments	–981	–2,083	1,507	–1,676	–279
Other investing transactions	0	214	318	315	–40
Net Cash Flow from Investing Activities	**–2,330**	**–3,517**	**–194**	**–3,744**	**–2,667**
Financing Activities:					
Net proceeds from short-term borrowing	1,112	1,848	–2,341	–395	445
Net proceeds from long-term borrowing	–8	–152	–106	1,589	3,070
Net proceeds from share issues and repurchases	–2,090	–1,932	–1,816	–3,204	–4,106
Dividends	–1,329	–1,642	–1,854	–2,204	–2,541
Other financing transactions	0	0	134	208	107
Net Cash Flow from Financing Activities	**–2,315**	**–1,878**	**–5,983**	**–4,006**	**–3,025**
Effects of exchange rate changes on cash	51	–21	28	75	–153
Net Change in Cash	**460**	**436**	**–65**	**–741**	**1,154**

Forecasts Spreadsheet

FSAP OUTPUT: **FINANCIAL STATEMENT FORECASTS**

Analyst Name: **Wahlen, Baginski, and Bradshaw**
Company Name: **PepsiCo**

Row Format:	Row Format:	Year +6 and beyond:	
Actual Amounts	**Forecast Amounts**		
Common-Size Percentage	Forecast assumption	Long-Run Growth Rate:	3.0%
Rate of Change Percentage	Forecast assumption explanation	Long-Run Growth Factor:	103.0%

	Actuals			Forecasts					
Year	**2006**	**2007**	**2008**	**Year +1**	**Year +2**	**Year +3**	**Year +4**	**Year +5**	**Year +6**
INCOME STATEMENT									
Revenues	**35,137**	**39,474**	**43,251**	**47,191**	**51,562**	**57,502**	**61,820**	**67,839**	**69,875**
common size	100.0%	100.0%	100.0%	9.1%	9.3%	11.5%	7.5%	9.7%	
rate of change		12.3%	9.6%	See Forecast Development worksheet for details of revenues forecasts.					
<Cost of goods sold>	**–15,762**	**–18,038**	**–20,351**	**–22,321**	**–24,492**	**–27,429**	**–29,612**	**–32,563**	**–33,540**
common size	–44.9%	–45.7%	–47.1%	–47.3%	–47.5%	–47.7%	–47.9%	–48.0%	
rate of change		14.4%	12.8%	Assume slowly increasing cost of goods sold as a percent of sales.					
Gross Profit	**19,375**	**21,436**	**22,900**	**24,870**	**27,070**	**30,074**	**32,208**	**35,277**	**36,335**
common size	55.1%	54.3%	52.9%	52.7%	52.5%	52.3%	52.1%	52.0%	52.0%
rate of change		10.6%	6.8%	8.6%	8.8%	11.1%	7.1%	9.5%	3.0%
<Selling, general, and administrative expenses>	**–12,711**	**–14,208**	**–15,901**	**–16,517**	**–18,047**	**–20,126**	**–21,637**	**–23,744**	**–24,456**
common size	–36.2%	–36.0%	–36.8%	–35.0%	–35.0%	–35.0%	–35.0%	–35.0%	
rate of change		11.8%	11.9%	Assume steady SG&A expense as a percent of sales.					
<Research and development expenses>	**0**	**0**	**0**	**0**	**0**	**0**	**0**	**0**	**0**
common size	0.0%	0.0%	0.0%	0.0%	0.0%	0.0%	0.0%	0.0%	
rate of change				Explain assumptions.					
<Amortization of intangible assets>	**–162**	**–58**	**–64**	**–64**	**–63**	**–62**	**–60**	**–56**	**–58**
common size	–0.5%	–0.1%	–0.1%	–64.0	–63.0	–62.0	–60.0	–56.0	
rate of change		–64.2%	10.3%	Amounts based on PepsiCo disclosures in Note 4.					

(Continued)

Forecasts Spreadsheet (Continued)

	Actuals			Forecasts					
Year	**2006**	**2007**	**2008**	**Year +1**	**Year +2**	**Year +3**	**Year +4**	**Year +5**	**Year +6**
<Other operating expenses (1)>	**0**	**0**	**0**	**0**	**0**	**0**	**0**	**0**	**0**
common size	0.0%	0.0%	0.0%	0.0%	0.0%	0.0%	0.0%	0.0%	
rate of change				Explain assumptions.					
<Other operating expenses (2)>	**0**	**0**	**0**	**0**	**0**	**0**	**0**	**0**	**0**
common size	0.0%	0.0%	0.0%	0.0%	0.0%	0.0%	0.0%	0.0%	
rate of change				Explain assumptions.					
Other operating income (1)	**0**	**0**	**0**	**0**	**0**	**0**	**0**	**0**	**0**
common size	0.0%	0.0%	0.0%	0.0%	0.0%	0.0%	0.0%	0.0%	
rate of change				Explain assumptions.					
Other operating income (2)	**0**	**0**	**0**	**0**	**0**	**0**	**0**	**0**	**0**
common size	0.0%	0.0%	0.0%	0.0%	0.0%	0.0%	0.0%	0.0%	
rate of change				Explain assumptions.					
Nonrecurring operating gains	**0**	**0**	**0**	**0**	**0**	**0**	**0**	**0**	**0**
common size	0.0%	0.0%	0.0%	0.0	0.0	0.0	0.0	0.0	
rate of change				Explain assumptions.					
<Nonrecurring operating losses>	**0**	**0**	**0**	**0**	**0**	**0**	**0**	**0**	**0**
common size	0.0%	0.0%	0.0%	0.0	0.0	0.0	0.0	0.0	
rate of change				Explain assumptions.					
Operating Profit	**6,502**	**7,170**	**6,935**	**8,289**	**8,960**	**9,886**	**10,511**	**11,477**	**11,821**
common size	18.5%	18.2%	16.0%	17.6%	17.4%	17.2%	17.0%	16.9%	16.9%
rate of change		10.3%	–3.3%	19.5%	8.1%	10.3%	6.3%	9.2%	3.0%
Interest income	**173**	**125**	**41**	**73**	**81**	**90**	**98**	**107**	**110**
common size	0.5%	0.3%	0.1%	3.0%	3.0%	3.0%	3.0%	3.0%	
rate of change		–27.7%	–67.2%	Interest rate earned on average balance in cash and marketable securities					
<Interest expense>	**–239**	**–224**	**–329**	**–493**	**–531**	**–579**	**–626**	**–677**	**–697**
common size	–0.7%	–0.6%	–0.8%	–5.8%	–5.8%	–5.8%	–5.8%	–5.8%	
rate of change		–6.3%	46.9%	Interest rate paid on average balance in financial liabilities					
Income <Loss> from equity affiliates	**553**	**560**	**374**	**480**	**509**	**539**	**572**	**606**	**624**
common size	1.6%	1.4%	0.9%	12.0%	12.0%	12.0%	12.0%	12.0%	
rate of change		1.3%	–33.2%	Assume expected return of 12% on investments in noncontrolled affiliates.					

Other income or gains	**0**	**0**	**0**	**0**	**0**	**0**	**0**	**0**	**0**
common size	0.0%	0.0%	0.0%	0.0	0.0	0.0	0.0	0.0	
rate of change				Explain assumptions.					
<Other expenses or losses>	**0**	**0**	**0**	**0**	**0**	**0**	**0**	**0**	**0**
common size	0.0%	0.0%	0.0%	0.0	0.0	0.0	0.0	0.0	
rate of change				Explain assumptions.					
Income before Tax	**6,989**	**7,631**	**7,021**	**8,348**	**9,019**	**9,935**	**10,555**	**11,513**	**11,858**
common size	19.9%	19.3%	16.2%	17.7%	17.5%	17.3%	17.1%	17.0%	17.0%
rate of change		9.2%	−8.0%	18.9%	8.0%	10.2%	6.2%	9.1%	3.0%
<Income tax expense>	**−1,347**	**−1,973**	**−1,879**	**−2,237**	**−2,417**	**−2,663**	**−2,829**	**−3,085**	**−3,178**
common size	−3.8%	−5.0%	−4.3%	−26.8%	−26.8%	−26.8%	−26.8%	−26.8%	
rate of change		46.5%	−4.8%	Effective income tax rate assumptions					
<Minority interest in earnings>	**0**	**0**	**0**	**0**	**0**	**0**	**0**	**0**	**0**
common size	0.0%	0.0%	0.0%	0.0	0.0	0.0	0.0	0.0	
rate of change				Explain assumptions.					
Income <Loss> from discontinued operations	**0**	**0**	**0**	**0**	**0**	**0**	**0**	**0**	**0**
common size	0.0%	0.0%	0.0%	0.0	0.0	0.0	0.0	0.0	
rate of change				Explain assumptions.					
Extraordinary gains <losses>	**0**	**0**	**0**	**0**	**0**	**0**	**0**	**0**	**0**
common size	0.0%	0.0%	0.0%	0.0	0.0	0.0	0.0	0.0	
rate of change				Explain assumptions.					
Changes in accounting principles	**0**	**0**	**0**	**0**	**0**	**0**	**0**	**0**	**0**
common size	0.0%	0.0%	0.0%	0.0	0.0	0.0	0.0	0.0	
rate of change				Explain assumptions.					
Net Income (computed)	**5,642**	**5,658**	**5,142**	**6,111**	**6,602**	**7,273**	**7,726**	**8,427**	**8,680**
common size	16.1%	14.3%	11.9%	12.9%	12.8%	12.6%	12.5%	12.4%	12.4%
rate of change		0.3%	−9.1%	18.8%	8.0%	10.2%	6.2%	9.1%	3.0%
Other comprehensive income items	**456**	**1,294**	**−3,793**	**0**	**0**	**0**	**0**	**0**	**0**
common size	1.3%	3.3%	−8.8%	0.0	0.0	0.0	0.0	0.0	
rate of change		183.8%	−393.1%	Assume random walk.					
Comprehensive Income	**6,098**	**6,952**	**1,349**	**6,111**	**6,602**	**7,273**	**7,726**	**8,427**	**8,680**
common size	17.4%	17.6%	3.1%	12.9%	12.8%	12.6%	12.5%	12.4%	12.4%
rate of change		14.0%	−80.6%	353.0%	8.0%	10.2%	6.2%	9.1%	3.0%

(Continued)

Forecasts Spreadsheet (Continued)

FSAP OUTPUT: FINANCIAL STATEMENT FORECASTS

Analyst Name: **Wahlen, Baginski, and Bradshaw**
Company Name: **PepsiCo**

Row Format:	**Row Format:**	
Actual Amounts	**Forecast Amounts**	**Year +6 and beyond:**
Common-Size Percentage	Forecast assumption	Long-Run Growth Rate: 3.0%
Rate of Change Percentage	Forecast assumption explanation	Long-Run Growth Factor: 103.0%

	Actuals			**Forecasts**					
Year	**2006**	**2007**	**2008**	**Year +1**	**Year +2**	**Year +3**	**Year +4**	**Year +5**	**Year +6**
BALANCE SHEET									
ASSETS:									
Cash and cash equivalents	**1,651**	**910**	**2,064**	**1,551**	**1,695**	**1,890**	**2,032**	**2,230**	**2,297**
common size	5.5%	2.6%	5.7%	12.0	12.0	12.0	12.0	12.0	
rate of change		–44.9%	126.8%	Assume ending cash balances equal to 12 days sales.					
Marketable securities	**1,171**	**1,571**	**213**	**1,034**	**1,130**	**1,260**	**1,355**	**1,487**	**1,531**
common size	3.9%	4.5%	0.6%	8.0	8.0	8.0	8.0	8.0	
rate of change		34.2%	–86.4%	Assume ending balances equal to 8 days sales.					
Accounts receivable—Net	**3,725**	**4,389**	**4,683**	**5,143**	**5,593**	**6,380**	**6,492**	**7,633**	**7,862**
common size	12.4%	12.7%	13.0%	38.0	38.0	38.0	38.0	38.0	
rate of change		17.8%	6.7%	Assume 38 days to collect sales in accounts receivable.					
Inventories	**1,926**	**2,290**	**2,522**	**2,730**	**3,033**	**3,421**	**3,546**	**4,116**	**4,239**
common size	6.4%	6.6%	7.0%	8.5	8.5	8.5	8.5	8.5	
rate of change		18.9%	10.1%	Assume average inventory turnover of roughly 8.5 times per year.					
Prepaid expenses and other current assets	**657**	**991**	**1,324**	**1,445**	**1,578**	**1,760**	**1,892**	**2,077**	**2,139**
common size	2.2%	2.9%	3.7%	9.1%	9.3%	11.5%	7.5%	9.7%	
rate of change		50.8%	33.6%	Assume growth with sales.					
Deferred tax assets—Current	**0**	**0**	**0**	**0**	**0**	**0**	**0**	**0**	**0**
common size	0.0%	0.0%	0.0%	0%	0%	0%	0%	0%	
rate of change				Assume steady growth.					
Other current assets (1)	**0**	**0**	**0**	**0**	**0**	**0**	**0**	**0**	**0**
common size	0.0%	0.0%	0.0%	0%	0%	0%	0%	0%	
rate of change				Assume steady growth.					

Other current assets (2)	**0**	**0**	**0**	**0**	**0**	**0**	**0**	**0**	**0**
common size	0.0%	0.0%	0.0%	0%	0%	0%	0%	0%	
rate of change				Assume steady growth.					
Current Assets	**9,130**	**10,151**	**10,806**	**11,904**	**13,029**	**14,712**	**15,318**	**17,543**	**18,069**
common size	30.5%	29.3%	30.0%	30.9%	31.3%	32.1%	31.5%	32.8%	32.8%
rate of change	11.2%	6.5%	10.2%	9.5%	12.9%	4.1%	14.5%	3.0%	
Long-term investments	**3,690**	**4,354**	**3,883**	**4,116**	**4,363**	**4,625**	**4,902**	**5,196**	**5,352**
common size	12.3%	12.6%	10.8%	6%	6%	6%	6%	6%	
rate of change		18.0%	−10.8%	Assume steady growth.					
Property, plant, and equipment—At cost	**19,058**	**21,896**	**22,552**	**24,723**	**27,662**	**30,939**	**34,463**	**38,330**	**39,480**
common size	63.7%	63.2%	62.7%						
rate of change		14.9%	3.0%	PP&E assumptions—see schedule in forecast development.					
<Accumulated depreciation>	**−9,371**	**−10,668**	**−10,889**	**−12,471**	**−14,241**	**−16,220**	**−18,426**	**−20,878**	**−21,504**
common size	−31.3%	−30.8%	−30.3%						
rate of change		13.8%	2.1%	See depreciation schedule in forecast development worksheet.					
Amortizable intangible assets (net)	**637**	**796**	**732**	**668**	**605**	**543**	**483**	**427**	**440**
common size	2.1%	2.3%	2.0%	−64.0	−63.0	−62.0	−60.0	−56.0	
rate of change		25.0%	−8.0%	Assume amortization per PepsiCo disclosures in Note 4; assume no new investments.					
Goodwill and nonamortizable intangibles	**5,806**	**6,417**	**6,252**	**6,822**	**7,453**	**8,312**	**8,936**	**9,806**	**10,100**
common size	19.4%	18.5%	17.4%	9.1%	9.3%	11.5%	7.5%	9.7%	
rate of change		10.5%	−2.6%	Assume growth with sales.					
Deferred tax assets—Noncurrent	**0**	**0**	**0**	**0**	**0**	**0**	**0**	**0**	**0**
common size	0.0%	0.0%	0.0%	0.0%	0.0%	0.0%	0.0%	0.0%	
rate of change				Assume steady state growth.					
Other noncurrent assets (1)	**980**	**1,682**	**2,658**	**2,738**	**2,820**	**2,904**	**2,992**	**3,081**	**3,174**
common size	3.3%	4.9%		7.4%	3.0%	3.0%	3.0%	3.0%	3.0%
rate of change		71.6%	58.0%	Assume steady growth.					
Other noncurrent assets (2)	**0**	**0**	**0**	**0**	**0**	**0**	**0**	**0**	**0**
common size	0.0%	0.0%	0.0%	0.0%	0.0%	0.0%	0.0%	0.0%	
rate of change				Assume steady state growth.					
Total Assets	**29,930**	**34,628**	**35,994**	**38,499**	**41,692**	**45,815**	**48,669**	**53,506**	**55,111**
common size	100.0%	100.0%	100.0%	100.0%	100.0%	100.0%	100.0%	100.0%	100.0%
rate of change	15.7%	3.9%	7.0%	8.3%	9.9%	6.2%	9.9%	3.0%	

(Continued)

Forecasts Spreadsheet (Continued)

	Actuals			Forecasts					
Year	**2006**	**2007**	**2008**	**Year +1**	**Year +2**	**Year +3**	**Year +4**	**Year +5**	**Year +6**
LIABILITIES:									
Accounts payable—Trade	**2,102**	**2,562**	**2,846**	**3,080**	**3,442**	**3,875**	**3,947**	**4,768**	**4,911**
common size	7.0%	7.4%	7.9%	48.0	48.0	48.0	48.0	48.0	
rate of change		21.9%	11.1%	Assume a steady payment period consistent with recent years.					
Current accrued liabilities	**4,394**	**5,040**	**5,427**	**5,921**	**6,470**	**7,215**	**7,757**	**8,512**	**8,768**
common size	14.7%	14.6%	15.1%	9.1%	9.3%	11.5%	7.5%	9.7%	
rate of change		14.7%	7.7%	Assume growth with SG&A expenses, which grow with sales.					
Notes payable and short-term debt	**274**	**0**	**369**	**385**	**417**	**458**	**487**	**535**	**551**
common size	0.9%	0.0%	1.0%	1.0%	1.0%	1.0%	1.0%	1.0%	
rate of change		−100.0%		Assume 1.0 percent of total assets.					
Current maturities of long-term debt	**0**	**0**	**0**	**0**	**0**	**0**	**0**	**0**	**0**
common size	0.0%	0.0%	0.0%	0.0	0.0	0.0	0.0	0.0	
rate of change				Current maturities of long-term debt per long-term debt note					
Deferred tax liabilities—Current	**0**	**0**	**0**	**0**	**0**	**0**	**0**	**0**	**0**
common size	0.0%	0.0%	0.0%	0.0%	0.0%	0.0%	0.0%	0.0%	
rate of change				Assume steady state growth.					
Income taxes payable	**90**	**151**	**145**	**154**	**167**	**183**	**195**	**214**	**220**
common size	0.3%	0.4%	0.4%	0.4%	0.4%	0.4%	0.4%	0.4%	
rate of change		67.8%	−4.0%	Assume a steady percentage of total assets.					
Other current liabilities (1)	**0**	**0**	**0**	**0**	**0**	**0**	**0**	**0**	**0**
common size	0.0%	0.0%	0.0%	0.0%	0.0%	0.0%	0.0%	0.0%	
rate of change				Assume steady state growth.					
Other current liabilities (2)	**0**	**0**	**0**	**0**	**0**	**0**	**0**	**0**	**0**
common size	0.0%	0.0%	0.0%	0.0%	0.0%	0.0%	0.0%	0.0%	
rate of change				Assume steady state growth.					
Current Liabilities	**6,860**	**7,753**	**8,787**	**9,540**	**10,495**	**11,731**	**12,385**	**14,029**	**14,450**
common size	22.9%	22.4%	24.4%	24.8%	25.2%	25.6%	25.4%	26.2%	26.2%
rate of change		13.0%	13.3%	8.6%	10.0%	11.8%	5.6%	13.3%	3.0%

Long-term debt	**2,550**	**4,203**	**7,858**	**8,405**	**9,102**	**10,002**	**10,625**	**11,681**	**12,031**
common size	8.5%	12.1%	21.8%	21.8%	21.8%	21.8%	21.8%	21.8%	
rate of change		64.8%	87.0%	Assume steady percent of total assets.					
Long-term accrued liabilities	**4,624**	**4,792**	**7,017**	**7,656**	**8,365**	**9,329**	**10,030**	**11,006**	**11,336**
common size	15.4%	13.8%	19.5%	9.1%	9.3%	11.5%	7.5%	9.7%	
rate of change		3.6%	46.4%	Assume growth with SG&A expenses, which grow with sales.					
Deferred tax liabilities—Noncurrent	**528**	**646**	**226**	**242**	**262**	**288**	**306**	**336**	**346**
common size	1.8%	1.9%	0.6%	0.6%	0.6%	0.6%	0.6%	0.6%	
rate of change		22.3%	−65.0%	Assume steady percent of total assets.					
Other noncurrent liabilities (1)	**0**	**0**	**0**	**0**	**0**	**0**	**0**	**0**	**0**
common size	0.0%	0.0%	0.0%	0.0%	0.0%	0.0%	0.0%	0.0%	
rate of change				Assume steady state growth.					
Other noncurrent liabilities (2)	**0**	**0**	**0**	**0**	**0**	**0**	**0**	**0**	**0**
common size	0.0%	0.0%	0.0%	0.0%	0.0%	0.0%	0.0%	0.0%	
rate of change				Assume steady state growth.					
Total Liabilities	**14,562**	**17,394**	**23,888**	**25,843**	**28,224**	**31,350**	**33,345**	**37,052**	**38,164**
common size	48.7%	50.2%	66.4%	67.1%	67.7%	68.4%	68.5%	69.2%	69.2%
rate of change		19.4%	37.3%	8.2%	9.2%	11.1%	6.4%	11.1%	3.0%
SHAREHOLDERS' EQUITY:									
Minority interest	**0**	**0**	**0**	**0**	**0**	**0**	**0**	**0**	**0**
common size	0.0%	0.0%	0.0%	0.0	0.0	0.0	0.0	0.0	
rate of change				Minority interest assumptions					
Preferred stock	**−79**	**−91**	**−97**	**0**	**0**	**0**	**0**	**0**	**0**
common size	−0.3%	−0.3%	−0.3%	0.0	0.0	0.0	0.0	0.0	
rate of change		15.2%	6.6%	Preferred stock assumptions					
Common stock + Additional paid–in capital	**614**	**480**	**381**	**408**	**441**	**485**	**515**	**566**	**583**
common size	2.1%	1.4%	1.1%	1.1%	1.1%	1.1%	1.1%	1.1%	
rate of change		−21.8%	−20.6%	Assume steady percent of total assets.					
Retained earnings <deficit>	**24,837**	**28,184**	**30,638**	**33,565**	**36,842**	**40,296**	**43,624**	**47,203**	**48,479**
common size	83.0%	81.4%	85.1%						
rate of change		13.5%	8.7%	Add net income and subtract dividends; see dividends forecast box below.					
Accum. other comprehensive income <loss>	**−2,246**	**−952**	**−4,694**	**−4,694**	**−4,694**	**−4,694**	**−4,694**	**−4,694**	**−4,694**
common size	−7.5%	−2.7%	−13.0%	0.0	0.0	0.0	0.0	0.0	
rate of change		−57.6%	393.1%	Add accumulated other comprehensive income items from income statement.					

(Continued)

Forecasts Spreadsheet (Continued)

	Actuals			Forecasts					
Year	**2006**	**2007**	**2008**	**Year +1**	**Year +2**	**Year +3**	**Year +4**	**Year +5**	**Year +6**
Other equity adjustments	**0**	**0**	**0**	**0**	**0**	**0**	**0**	**0**	**0**
common size	0.0%	0.0%	0.0%	0.0	0.0	0.0	0.0	0.0	
rate of change				Other equity adjustments assumptions					
<Treasury stock>	**−7,758**	**−10,387**	**−14,122**	**−16,622**	**−19,122**	**−21,622**	**−24,122**	**−26,622**	**−27,421**
common size	−25.9%	−30.0%	−39.2%	−2,500	−2,500	−2,500	−2,500	−2,500	
rate of change		33.9%	36.0%	Treasury stock repurchases, net of treasury stock reissues					
Common Shareholders' Equity	**15,447**	**17,325**	**12,203.0**	**12,656.1**	**13,467.4**	**14,465.3**	**15,323.5**	**16,453.6**	**16,947**
common size	51.6%	50.0%	33.9%	32.9%	32.3%	31.6%	31.5%	30.8%	30.8%
rate of change		12.2%	−29.6%	3.7%	6.4%	7.4%	5.9%	7.4%	3.0%
Total Liabilities and Equities	**29,930**	**34,628**	**35,994**	**38,499**	**41,692**	**45,815**	**48,669**	**53,506**	**55,111**
common size	100.0%	100.0%	100.0%	100.0%	100.0%	100.0%	100.0%	100.0%	100.0%
rate of change		15.7%	3.9%	7.0%	8.3%	9.9%	6.2%	9.9%	3.0%
Check figures:									
Balance Sheet A = L + OE?	0	0	0	0	0	0	0	0	0
				Account adjusted:		**Dividends**			
				Dividends forecasts:					
Common dividends:				**2,571**	**3,055**	**3,301**	**3,636**	**3,863**	**3,979**
				50.0%	50.0%	50.0%	50.0%	50.0%	
				Assume dividend payout of lagged net income from continuing operations.					
Preferred dividends:				**169**	**0**	**0**	**0**	**0**	**0**
				169.0	0.0	0.0	0.0	0.0	
				Enter preferred stock dividend payments, if any.					
Implied dividends:				**444**	**269**	**517**	**762**	**985**	**3,426**
				Implied dividend amount to balance the balance sheet					
Total dividends:				**3,184**	**3,325**	**3,818**	**4,398**	**4,848**	**7,405**
				Total dividend forecast amounts					

Forecasts Spreadsheet (Continued)

FSAP OUTPUT: FINANCIAL STATEMENT FORECASTS

Analyst Name: Wahlen, Baginski, and Bradshaw
Company Name: PepsiCo

	Actuals		Forecasts					
IMPLIED STATEMENT OF CASH FLOWS	**2007**	**2008**	**Year +1**	**Year +2**	**Year +3**	**Year +4**	**Year +5**	**Year +6**
Net Income	**5,658**	**5,142**	**6,111**	**6,602**	**7,273**	**7,726**	**8,427**	**8,680**
Add back depreciation expense (net)	1,297	221	1,582	1,770	1,980	2,205	2,453	626
Add back amortization expense (net)	58	64	64	63	62	60	56	58
<Increase> Decrease in receivables—Net	–664	–294	–460	–450	–787	–112	–1,141	–229
<Increase> Decrease in inventories	–364	–232	–208	–303	–388	–125	–569	–123
<Increase> Decrease in prepaid expenses	–334	–333	–121	–134	–182	–132	–184	–62
<Increase> Decrease in other current assets (1)	0	0	0	0	0	0	0	0
<Increase> Decrease in other current assets (2)	0	0	0	0	0	0	0	0
Increase <Decrease> in accounts payable—Trade	460	284	234	362	433	72	821	143
Increase <Decrease> in current accrued liabilities	646	387	494	548	745	542	755	255
Increase <Decrease> in income taxes payable	61	–6	9	13	16	11	19	6
Increase <Decrease> in other current liabilities (1)	0	0	0	0	0	0	0	0
Increase <Decrease> in other current liabilities (2)	0	0	0	0	0	0	0	0
Net change in deferred tax assets and liabilities	118	–420	16	20	26	18	30	10
Increase <Decrease> in long-term accrued liabilities	168	2,225	639	709	964	700	977	330
Increase <Decrease> in other noncurrent liabilities (1)	0	0	0	0	0	0	0	0
Increase <Decrease> in other noncurrent liabilities (2)	0	0	0	0	0	0	0	0
Net Cash Flows from Operations	**7,104**	**7,038**	**8,360**	**9,201**	**10,142**	**10,966**	**11,644**	**9,694**

(Continued)

Forecasts Spreadsheet (Continued)

FSAP OUTPUT: **FINANCIAL STATEMENT FORECASTS**

Analyst Name: **Wahlen, Baginski, and Bradshaw**
Company Name: **PepsiCo**

	Actuals		**Forecasts**					
Year	**2007**	**2008**	**Year +1**	**Year +2**	**Year +3**	**Year +4**	**Year +5**	**Year +6**
IMPLIED STATEMENT OF CASH FLOWS (*Continued*)								
<Increase> Decrease in property, plant, & equip. at cost	–2,838	–656	–2,171	–2,939	–3,278	–3,524	–3,867	–1,150
<Increase> Decrease in marketable securities	–400	1,358	–821	–96	–130	–95	–132	–45
<Increase> Decrease in investment securities	–664	471	–233	–247	–262	–277	–294	–156
<Increase> Decrease in amortizable intangible assets (net)	–217	0	0	0	0	0	0	–70
<Increase> Decrease in goodwill and nonamort. intangibles	–611	165	–570	–632	–859	–624	–870	–294
<Increase> Decrease in other noncurrent assets (1)	–702	–976	–80	–82	–85	–87	–90	–92
<Increase> Decrease in other noncurrent assets (2)	0	0	0	0	0	0	0	0
Net Cash Flows from Investing Activities	**–5,432**	**362**	**–3,874**	**–3,996**	**–4,613**	**–4,607**	**–5,253**	**–1,808**
Increase <Decrease> in short-term debt	–274	369	16	32	41	29	48	16
Increase <Decrease> in long-term debt	1,653	3,655	547	697	900	623	1,056	350
Increase <Decrease> in minority interest and preferred stock	–12	–6	97	0	0	0	0	0
Increase <Decrease> in common stock + paid–in capital	–134	–99	27	34	44	30	51	17
Increase <Decrease> in accum. OCI and other equity adjs.	1,294	–3,742	0	0	0	0	0	0
Increase <Decrease> in treasury stock	–2,629	–3,735	–2,500	–2,500	–2,500	–2,500	–2,500	–799
Dividends	–2,311	–2,688	–3,184	–3,325	–3,818	–4,398	–4,848	–7,405
Net Cash Flows from Financing Activities	**–2,413**	**–6,246**	**–4,998**	**–5,062**	**–5,333**	**–6,217**	**–6,193**	**–7,820**
Net Change in Cash	**–741**	**1,154**	**–513**	**144**	**195**	**142**	**198**	**67**
Check Figure:								
Net change in cash – Change in cash balance =	0	0	0	0	0	0	0	0

FSAP OUTPUT: **FINANCIAL STATEMENT FORECASTS**

Analyst Name: **Wahlen, Baginski, and Bradshaw**
Company Name: **PepsiCo**

	Actuals			Forecasts					
Year	**2006**	**2007**	**2008**	**Year +1**	**Year +2**	**Year +3**	**Year +4**	**Year +5**	**Year +6**
FORECAST VALIDITY CHECK DATA:									
GROWTH:									
Revenue Growth Rates	7.9%	12.3%	9.6%	9.1%	9.3%	11.5%	7.5%	9.7%	3.0%
Net Income Growth Rates	38.4%	0.3%	–9.1%	18.8%	8.0%	10.2%	6.2%	9.1%	3.0%
Total Asset Growth Rates	–5.7%	15.7%	3.9%	7.0%	8.3%	9.9%	6.2%	9.9%	3.0%
RETURN ON ASSETS (based on reported amounts):									
Profit Margin for ROA	16.5%	14.7%	12.4%	13.7%	13.6%	13.4%	13.2%	13.2%	13.2%
× Asset Turnover	1.1	1.2	1.2	1.3	1.3	1.3	1.3	1.3	1.3
= Return on Assets	18.8%	18.0%	15.2%	17.4%	17.4%	17.6%	17.3%	17.5%	16.9%
RETURN ON ASSETS (excluding the effects of nonrecurring items):									
Profit Margin for ROA	16.5%	14.7%	12.4%	13.7%	13.6%	13.4%	13.2%	13.2%	13.2%
× Asset Turnover	1.1	1.2	1.2	1.3	1.3	1.3	1.3	1.3	1.3
= Return on Assets	18.8%	18.0%	15.2%	17.4%	17.4%	17.6%	17.3%	17.5%	16.9%
RETURN ON COMMON EQUITY (based on reported amounts):									
Profit Margin for ROCE	16.1%	14.3%	11.9%	12.6%	12.8%	12.6%	12.5%	12.4%	12.4%
× Asset Turnover	1.1	1.2	1.2	1.3	1.3	1.3	1.3	1.3	1.3
× Capital Structure Leverage	2.1	2.0	2.4	3.0	3.1	3.1	3.2	3.2	3.3
= Return on Common Equity	37.9%	34.5%	34.8%	47.8%	50.5%	52.1%	51.9%	53.0%	52.0%
RETURN ON COMMON EQUITY (excluding the effects of nonrecurring items):									
Profit Margin for ROCE	16.1%	14.3%	11.9%	12.6%	12.8%	12.6%	12.5%	12.4%	12.4%
× Asset Turnover	1.1	1.2	1.2	1.3	1.3	1.3	1.3	1.3	1.3
× Capital Structure Leverage	2.1	2.0	2.4	3.0	3.1	3.1	3.2	3.2	3.3
= Return on Common Equity	37.9%	34.5%	34.8%	47.8%	50.5%	52.1%	51.9%	53.0%	52.0%

(Continued)

Forecasts Spreadsheet (Continued)

FSAP OUTPUT: FINANCIAL STATEMENT FORECASTS

Analyst Name: **Wahlen, Baginski, and Bradshaw**
Company Name: **PepsiCo**

	Actuals			Forecasts					
Year	**2006**	**2007**	**2008**	**Year +1**	**Year +2**	**Year +3**	**Year +4**	**Year +5**	**Year +6**
OPERATING PERFORMANCE:									
Gross Profit/Revenues	55.1%	54.3%	52.9%	52.7%	52.5%	52.3%	52.1%	52.0%	52.0%
Operating Profit before Taxes/Revenues	18.5%	18.2%	16.0%	17.6%	17.4%	17.2%	17.0%	16.9%	16.9%
ASSETS TURNOVER:									
Revenues/Average Accounts Receivable	10.1	9.7	9.5	9.6	9.6	9.6	9.6	9.6	9.0
COGS/Average Inventory	8.7	8.6	8.5	8.5	8.5	8.5	8.5	8.5	8.0
Revenues/Average Fixed Assets	3.8	3.8	3.8	3.9	4.0	4.1	4.0	4.1	3.9
LIQUIDITY:									
Current Ratio	1.3	1.3	1.2	1.2	1.2	1.3	1.2	1.3	1.3
Quick Ratio	1.0	0.9	0.8	0.8	0.8	0.8	0.8	0.8	0.8
SOLVENCY:									
Total Liabilities/Total Assets	48.7%	50.2%	66.4%	67.1%	67.7%	68.4%	68.5%	69.2%	69.2%
Total Liabilities/Total Equity	94.3%	100.4%	195.8%	204.2%	209.6%	216.7%	217.6%	225.2%	225.2%
Interest Coverage Ratio	30.2	35.1	22.3	17.9	18.0	18.1	17.9	18.0	18.0

Forecasts Development Spreadsheet

This Forecast Development spreadsheet provides work space in which the analyst can:

- **build detailed sales revenue forecasts**
- **build forecasts of capital expenditures; property, plant, and equipment; depreciation expense; and accumulated depreciation**
- **build detailed forecasts of other financial statement amounts**

It is not necessary to use this spreadsheet to build financial statement forecasts in the FSAP Forecasts spreadsheet. If you use this spreadsheet to build more detailed forecasts, you must link these forecast amounts to the appropriate cells in the financial statements in the FSAP Forecasts spreadsheet.

Analyst Name:	**Wahlen, Baginski, and Bradshaw**
Company Name:	**PepsiCo**

Sales Revenue Forecast Development

	Actuals			Forecasts				
Year	**2006**	**2007**	**2008**	**Year +1**	**Year +2**	**Year +3**	**Year +4**	**Year +5**
Revenues	**35,137**	**39,474**	**43,251**	**47,191**	**51,562**	**57,502**	**61,820**	**67,839**
growth rates		12.3%	9.6%	9.1%	9.3%	11.5%	7.5%	9.7%
				Sales growth rate assumptions				
Sales Forecasts Combined by Segments:								
Frito-Lay North America	10,844	11,586	12,507	13,269	14,077	15,221	15,843	16,808
Quaker Foods North America	1,769	1,860	1,902	1,979	2,058	2,183	2,228	2,317
Latin America Foods	3,972	4,872	5,895	6,660	7,524	8,663	9,602	10,848
PepsiCo Americas Foods	**16,585**	**18,318**	**20,304**	**21,907**	**23,659**	**26,067**	**27,673**	**29,974**
PepsiCo Americas Beverages	**10,362**	**11,090**	**10,937**	**11,603**	**12,310**	**13,310**	**13,855**	**14,698**
United Kingdom & Europe	4,750	5,492	6,435	7,168	7,984	9,063	9,905	11,032
Middle East, Africa & Asia	3,440	4,574	5,575	6,513	7,610	9,061	10,387	12,135
PepsiCo International	**8,190**	**10,066**	**12,010**	**13,681**	**15,593**	**18,125**	**20,291**	**23,167**
PepsiCo Total Net Revenues	**35,137**	**39,474**	**43,251**	**47,191**	**51,562**	**57,502**	**61,820**	**67,839**
growth rates		12.3%	9.6%	9.1%	9.3%	11.5%	7.5%	9.7%

(Continued)

Forecasts Development Spreadsheet (Continued)

Sales Forecasts for PepsiCo:

Year	2006	2007	2008	Year +1	Year +2	Year +3	Year +4	Year +5
PepsiCo Americas Foods	**16,585**	**18,318**	**20,304**	**21,907**	**23,659**	**26,067**	**27,673**	**29,974**
growth rates		10.4%	10.8%	7.9%	8.0%	10.2%	6.2%	8.3%
compound growth rate			10.6%					
Frito-Lay North America	**10,844**	**11,586**	**12,507**	**13,269**	**14,077**	**15,221**	**15,843**	**16,808**
growth rates		6.8%	7.9%	6.1%	6.1%	8.1%	4.1%	6.1%
compound growth rate			7.4%					
compound growth in volume			1.5%	3.0%	3.0%	3.0%	3.0%	3.0%
compound growth in prices			5.6%	3.0%	3.0%	3.0%	3.0%	3.0%
foreign exchange and acquisitions			0.2%	0.0%	0.0%	0.0%	0.0%	0.0%
53rd-week effect				0.0%	0.0%	1.9%	–1.9%	0.0%
Quaker Foods North America	**1,769**	**1,860**	**1,902**	**1,979**	**2,058**	**2,183**	**2,228**	**2,317**
growth rates		5.1%	2.3%	4.0%	4.0%	6.0%	2.1%	4.0%
compound growth rate			3.7%					
compound growth in volume			0.2%	1.0%	1.0%	1.0%	1.0%	1.0%
compound growth in prices			2.9%	3.0%	3.0%	3.0%	3.0%	3.0%
foreign exchange and acquisitions			0.5%	0.0%	0.0%	0.0%	0.0%	0.0%
53rd-week effect				0.0%	0.0%	1.9%	–1.9%	0.0%
Latin America Foods	**3,972**	**4,872**	**5,895**	**6,660**	**7,524**	**8,663**	**9,602**	**10,848**
growth rates		22.7%	21.0%	13.0%	13.0%	15.1%	10.8%	13.0%
compound growth rate			21.8%					
compound growth in volume			2.5%	2.5%	2.5%	2.5%	2.5%	2.5%
compound growth in prices			7.0%	5.0%	5.0%	5.0%	5.0%	5.0%
foreign exchange and acquisitions			11.1%	5.0%	5.0%	5.0%	5.0%	5.0%
53rd-week effect				0.0%	0.0%	1.9%	–1.9%	0.0%
PepsiCo Americas Beverages	**10,362**	**11,090**	**10,937**	**11,603**	**12,310**	**13,310**	**13,855**	**14,698**
growth rates		7.0%	–1.4%	6.1%	6.1%	8.1%	4.1%	6.1%
compound growth rate			2.7%					
compound growth in volume			–2.8%	3.0%	3.0%	3.0%	3.0%	3.0%
compound growth in prices			4.4%	3.0%	3.0%	3.0%	3.0%	3.0%
foreign exchange and acquisitions			1.2%	0.0%	0.0%	0.0%	0.0%	0.0%
53rd-week effect				0.0%	0.0%	1.9%	–1.9%	0.0%

PepsiCo International	**8,190**	**10,066**	**12,010**	**13,681**	**15,593**	**18,125**	**20,291**	**23,167**
growth rates		22.9%	19.3%	13.9%	14.0%	16.2%	12.0%	14.2%
compound growth rate			21.1%					
United Kingdom & Europe	**4,750**	**5,492**	**6,435**	**7,168**	**7,984**	**9,063**	**9,905**	**11,032**
growth rates		15.6%	17.2%	11.4%	11.4%	13.5%	9.3%	11.4%
compound growth rate			16.4%					
compound growth in volume			4.0%	4.0%	4.0%	4.0%	4.0%	4.0%
compound growth in prices			2.1%	2.0%	2.0%	2.0%	2.0%	2.0%
foreign exchange and acquisitions			9.6%	5.0%	5.0%	5.0%	5.0%	5.0%
53rd-week effect				0.0%	0.0%	1.9%	–1.9%	0.0%
Middle East, Africa & Asia	**3,440**	**4,574**	**5,575**	**6,513**	**7,610**	**9,061**	**10,387**	**12,135**
growth rates		33.0%	21.9%	16.8%	16.8%	19.1%	14.6%	16.8%
compound growth rate			27.3%					
compound growth in volume			12.5%	8.0%	8.0%	8.0%	8.0%	8.0%
compound growth in prices			3.0%	3.0%	3.0%	3.0%	3.0%	3.0%
foreign exchange and acquisitions			9.8%	5.0%	5.0%	5.0%	5.0%	5.0%
53rd-week effect				0.0%	0.0%	1.9%	–1.9%	0.0%

Forecast Development: Capital Expenditures; Property, Plant, and Equipment; and Depreciation

Capital Expenditures				**CAPEX Forecasts**				
	2006	**2007**	**2008**	**Year +1**	**Year +2**	**Year +3**	**Year +4**	**Year +5**
CAPEX:								
PP&E Acquired	2,068	2,430	2,446					
PP&E Sold	–49	–47	–98					
Net CAPEX	**2,019**	**2,383**	**2,348**	**2,171**	**2,939**	**3,278**	**3,524**	**3,867**
Net CAPEX as a percent of:								
Gross PP&E	10.6%	10.9%	10.4%					
Revenues	5.7%	6.0%	5.4%	4.6%	5.7%	5.7%	5.7%	5.7%

(Continued)

Forecasts Development Spreadsheet (Continued)

Property, Plant, and Equipment and Depreciation				**Property, Plant, and Equipment and Depreciation Forecasts**				
PP&E at cost:	**2006**	**2007**	**2008**	**Year +1**	**Year +2**	**Year +3**	**Year +4**	**Year +5**
Beginning balance at cost:				22,552	24,723	27,662	30,939	34,463
Add: CAPEX forecasts from above:				2,171	2,939	3,278	3,524	3,867
Ending balance at cost:	**19,058**	**21,896**	**22,552**	**24,723**	**27,662**	**30,939**	**34,463**	**38,330**
Accumulated Depreciation:								
Beginning Balance:				−10,889	−12,471	−14,241	−16,220	−18,426
Subtract: Depreciation expense forecasts from below:				−1,582	−1,770	−1,980	−2,205	−2,453
Ending Balance:	**−9,371**	**−10,668**	**−10,889**	**−12,471**	**−14,241**	**−16,220**	**−18,426**	**−20,878**
PP&E—Net	**9,687**	**11,228**	**11,663**	**12,252**	**13,421**	**14,719**	**16,038**	**17,452**

Depreciation Expense Forecast Development:				**Depreciation expense forecast on existing PP&E:**				
Existing PP&E at cost:			22,552	1,443	1,443	1,443	1,443	1,443
PP&E Purchases:				**Depreciation expense forecasts on new PP&E:**				
CAPEX Year +1			2,171	139	139	139	139	139
CAPEX Year +2			2,939		188	188	188	188
CAPEX Year +3			3,278			210	210	210
CAPEX Year +4			3,524				225	225
CAPEX Year +5			3,867					247
Total Depreciation Expense				**1,582**	**1,770**	**1,980**	**2,205**	**2,453**

Depreciation methods:	**2006**	**2007**	**2008**
PP&E at Cost	19,058	21,896	22,552
Average Depreciable PP&E		20,477	22,224
Depreciation Expense	1,182	1,304	1,422
Implied Average Useful Life in Years		15.7	15.6
Useful Life Forecast Assumption:			15.6 (years)

Valuation Spreadsheet

DATA CHECKS – Estimated Value per Share

Dividend-Based Valuation	$83.03
Free Cash Flow Valuation	$83.03
Residual Income Valuation	$83.03
Residual Income Market-to-Book Valuation	$83.03
Free Cash Flow for All Debt and Equity Valuation	$83.99

Check: All Estimated Value per Share amounts should be the same, with the possible exception of the share value from the Free Cash Flow for All Debt and Equity model.

FSAP OUTPUT:	**VALUATION MODELS**
Analyst Name:	**Wahlen, Baginski, and Bradshaw**
Company Name:	**PepsiCo**

VALUATION PARAMETER ASSUMPTIONS

Current share price	$ 54.77	**COST OF DEBT CAPITAL**	
Number of shares outstanding	1,553.0	Debt capital	$ 8,227
Current market value	$85,058	Cost of debt capital, before tax	5.8%
Long-run growth assumption used in forecasts	3.0%	Effective tax rate	–26.8%
		After-tax cost of debt capital	4.25%
Long-run growth assumption used in valuation	3.0%	**COST OF PREFERRED STOCK**	
(Both long-run growth assumptions should be the same.)		Preferred stock capital	$ —
		Preferred dividends	$ —
		Implied yield	0.00%
COST OF EQUITY CAPITAL		**WEIGHTED AVERAGE COST OF CAPITAL**	
Equity risk factor (market beta)	0.75	Weight of equity in capital structure	0.912
Risk-free rate	4.0%	Weight of debt in capital structure	0.088
Market risk premium	6.0%	Weight of preferred in capital structure	0.00
Required rate of return on common equity	8.50%	Weighted average cost of capital	8.12%

(Continued)

Valuation Spreadsheet (Continued)

FSAP OUTPUT:	**VALUATION MODELS**					
Analyst Name:	**Wahlen, Baginski, and Bradshaw**					
Company Name:	**PepsiCo**					
	1	**2**	**3**	**4**	**5**	**Continuing Value**
DIVIDENDS-BASED VALUATION	**Year +1**	**Year +2**	**Year +3**	**Year +4**	**Year +5**	**Year +6**
Dividends Paid to Common Shareholders	3,015.3	3,324.5	3,818.5	4,398.5	4,848.3	
Less: Common Stock Issues	−26.5	−33.8	−43.7	−30.2	−51.2	
Plus: Common Stock Repurchases	2,500.0	2,500.0	2,500.0	2,500.0	2,500.0	
Dividends to Common Equity	**5,488.8**	**5,790.7**	**6,274.8**	**6,868.3**	**7,297.1**	**8,186.5**
Present Value Factors	0.922	0.849	0.783	0.722	0.665	
Present Value Net Dividends	5,058.8	4,919.0	4,912.6	4,956.0	4,852.9	
Sum of Present Value Net Dividends	24,699.3					
Present Value of Continuing Value	98,988.9					
Total	123,688.2					
Adjust to Midyear Discounting	1.0425					
Total Present Value Dividends	128,945.0					
Shares Outstanding	1,553.0					
Estimated Value per Share	$83.03					
Current share price	$54.77					
Percent difference	52%					

Valuation Spreadsheet (Continued)

FSAP OUTPUT: **VALUATION MODELS**

Analyst Name: **Wahlen, Baginski, and Bradshaw**
Company Name: **PepsiCo**

	1	2	3	4	5	Continuing Value
FREE CASH FLOWS FOR COMMON EQUITY	**Year +1**	**Year +2**	**Year +3**	**Year +4**	**Year +5**	**Year +6**
Net Cash Flow from Operations	8,359.9	9,201.1	10,141.5	10,965.8	11,643.5	9,694.4
Decrease (Increase) in Cash Required for Operations	512.5	–143.7	–195.3	–141.9	–197.9	–66.9
Net Cash Flow from Investing	–3,874.4	–3,995.7	–4,612.9	–4,607.1	–5,252.9	–1,807.5
Net CFs from Debt Financing	562.8	729.0	941.5	651.5	1,104.4	366.5
Net CFs into Financial Assets	0.0	0.0	0.0	0.0	0.0	0.0
Net CFs—Pref. Stock and Minority Int.	–72.0	0.0	0.0	0.0	0.0	0.0
Free Cash Flow for Common Equity	**5,488.8**	**5,790.7**	**6,274.8**	**6,868.3**	**7,297.1**	**8,186.5**
Present Value Factors	0.922	0.849	0.783	0.722	0.665	
Present Value Free Cash Flows	5,058.8	4,919.0	4,912.6	4,956.0	4,852.9	
Sum of Present Value Free Cash Flows	24,699.3					
Present Value of Continuing Value	98,988.9					
Total	123,688.2					
Adjust to Midyear Discounting	1.0425					
Total Present Value Free Cash Flows to Equity	128,945.0					
Shares Outstanding	1,553.0					
Estimated Value per Share	$83.03					
Current share price	$54.77					
Percent difference	52%					

(Continued)

Valuation Spreadsheet (Continued)

FSAP OUTPUT: **VALUATION MODELS**

Analyst Name: **Wahlen, Baginski, and Bradshaw**
Company Name: **PepsiCo**

FREE CASH FLOW VALUATION SENSITIVITY ANALYSIS:

		Long-Run Growth Assumptions							
		0%	2%	3%	4%	5%	6%	8%	10%
Discount	5%	105.16	160.50	229.67	437.20				
Rates:	6%	87.18	120.00	152.81	218.45	415.34			
	7%	74.37	95.73	114.41	145.56	207.85	394.72		
	8.50%	60.84	73.36	**83.03**	97.00	118.95	158.47	711.69	
	9%	57.34	68.04	76.06	87.30	104.14	132.22	356.87	
	10%	51.41	59.41	65.13	72.75	83.42	99.42	179.45	
	11%	46.57	52.71	56.94	62.37	69.61	79.75	120.30	323.07
	12%	42.55	47.37	50.58	54.59	59.76	66.64	90.73	163.00
	13%	39.16	43.00	45.50	48.55	52.37	57.28	72.98	109.63
	14%	36.26	39.37	41.35	43.73	46.63	50.26	61.15	82.93
	15%	33.76	36.30	37.90	39.78	42.04	44.80	52.70	66.90
	16%	31.57	33.68	34.98	36.50	38.29	40.44	46.35	56.21
	18%	27.95	29.44	30.33	31.35	32.53	33.90	37.47	42.83
	20%	25.08	26.16	26.79	27.51	28.31	29.24	31.55	34.79

Valuation Spreadsheet (Continued)

FSAP OUTPUT:	**VALUATION MODELS**					
Analyst Name:	**Wahlen, Baginski, and Bradshaw**					
Company Name:	**PepsiCo**					

	1	**2**	**3**	**4**	**5**	**Continuing Value**
RESIDUAL INCOME VALUATION	**Year +1**	**Year +2**	**Year +3**	**Year +4**	**Year +5**	**Year +6**
Comprehensive Income Available for Common Shareholders	5,941.9	6,602.1	7,272.7	7,726.4	8,427.3	8,680.1
Lagged Book Value of Common Shareholders' Equity (at t-1)	12,203.0	12,656.1	13,467.4	14,465.3	15,323.5	16,453.6
Required Earnings	1,037.3	1,075.8	1,144.7	1,229.5	1,302.5	1,398.6
Residual Income	**4,904.6**	**5,526.3**	**6,128.0**	**6,496.9**	**7,124.8**	**7,281.5**
Present Value Factors	0.922	0.849	0.783	0.722	0.665	
Present Value Residual Income	4,520.4	4,694.4	4,797.6	4,688.0	4,738.3	
Sum of Present Value Residual Income	23,438.7					
Present Value of Continuing Value	88,046.5					
Total	111,485.2					
Add: Beginning Book Value of Equity	12,203.0					
Present Value of Equity	123,688.2					
Adjust to Midyear Discounting	1.0425					
Total Present Value of Equity	128,945.0					
Shares Outstanding	1,553.0					
Estimated Value per Share	$83.03					
Current share price	$54.77					
Percent difference	52%					

(Continued)

Valuation Spreadsheet (Continued)

FSAP OUTPUT: **VALUATION MODELS**

Analyst Name: **Wahlen, Baginski, and Bradshaw**
Company Name: **PepsiCo**

RESIDUAL INCOME VALUATION SENSITIVITY ANALYSIS:

		Long-Run Growth Assumptions							
		0%	2%	3%	4%	5%	6%	8%	10%
Discount	5%	105.16	160.50	229.67	437.20				
Rates:	6%	87.18	120.00	152.81	218.45	415.34			
	7%	74.37	95.73	114.41	145.56	207.85	394.72		
	8.50%	60.84	73.36	**83.03**	97.00	118.95	158.47	711.69	
	9%	57.34	68.04	76.06	87.30	104.14	132.22	356.87	
	10%	51.41	59.41	65.13	72.75	83.42	99.42	179.45	
	11%	46.57	52.71	56.94	62.37	69.61	79.75	120.30	323.07
	12%	42.55	47.37	50.58	54.59	59.76	66.64	90.73	163.00
	13%	39.16	43.00	45.50	48.55	52.37	57.28	72.98	109.63
	14%	36.26	39.37	41.35	43.73	46.63	50.26	61.15	82.93
	15%	33.76	36.30	37.90	39.78	42.04	44.80	52.70	66.90
	16%	31.57	33.68	34.98	36.50	38.29	40.44	46.35	56.21
	18%	27.95	29.44	30.33	31.35	32.53	33.90	37.47	42.83
	20%	25.08	26.16	26.79	27.51	28.31	29.24	31.55	34.79

Valuation Spreadsheet (Continued)

FSAP OUTPUT: **VALUATION MODELS**

Analyst Name: **Wahlen, Baginski, and Bradshaw**
Company Name: **PepsiCo**

	1	2	3	4	5	Continuing Value
Market-to-Book Approach	**Year +1**	**Year +2**	**Year +3**	**Year +4**	**Year +5**	**Year +6**
Comprehensive Income Available for Common Shareholders	5,941.9	6,602.1	7,272.7	7,726.4	8,427.3	8,680.1
Book Value of Common Shareholders' Equity (at t-1)	12,203.0	12,656.1	13,467.4	14,465.3	15,323.5	16,453.6
Implied ROCE	48.7%	52.2%	54.0%	53.4%	55.0%	52.8%
Residual ROCE	40.2%	43.7%	45.5%	44.9%	46.5%	44.3%
Cumulative growth factor in common equity as of t-1	100.0%	103.7%	110.4%	118.5%	125.6%	134.8%
Residual ROCE times cumulative growth	**40.2%**	**45.3%**	**50.2%**	**53.2%**	**58.4%**	**59.7%**
Present Value Factors	0.922	0.849	0.783	0.722	0.665	
Present Value Residual ROCE times growth	0.370	0.385	0.393	0.384	0.388	
Sum of Present Value Residual ROCE times growth	1.92					
Present Value of Continuing Value	7.22					
Total Present Value Residual ROCE	9.14					
Add one for book value of equity at t-1	1.00					
Sum	10.14					
Adjust to Midyear Discounting	1.0425					
Implied Market-to-Book Ratio	10.567					
Times Beginning Book Value of Equity	12,203.0					
Total Present Value of Equity	128,945.0					
Shares Outstanding	1,553.0					
Estimated Value per Share	$83.03					
Current share price	$54.77					
Percent difference	52%					

Sensitivity analysis for the market-to-book approach should be identical to that of the residual income approach.

(Continued)

Valuation Spreadsheet (Continued)

FSAP OUTPUT:	**VALUATION MODELS**
Analyst Name:	**Wahlen, Baginski, and Bradshaw**
Company Name:	**PepsiCo**

	1	2	3	4	5	Continuing Value
FREE CASH FLOWS FOR ALL DEBT AND EQUITY	**Year +1**	**Year +2**	**Year +3**	**Year +4**	**Year +5**	**Year +6**
Net Cash Flow from Operations	8,359.9	9,201.1	10,141.5	10,965.8	11,643.5	9,694.4
Add back: Interest Expense after tax	361.2	388.7	424.1	457.9	495.2	510.1
Subtract: Interest Income after tax	0.0	0.0	0.0	0.0	0.0	0.0
Decrease (Increase) in Cash Required for Operations	512.5	−143.7	−195.3	−141.9	−197.9	−66.9
Free Cash Flow from Operations	9,233.6	9,446.1	10,370.3	11,281.8	11,940.8	10,137.6
Net Cash Flow from Investing	−3,874.4	−3,995.7	−4,612.9	−4,607.1	−5,252.9	−1,807.5
Add back: Net Cash Flows into Financial Assets	0.0	0.0	0.0	0.0	0.0	0.0
Free Cash Flows—All Debt and Equity	**5,359.3**	**5,450.4**	**5,757.4**	**6,674.7**	**6,688.0**	**8,330.1**
Present Value Factors	0.925	0.855	0.791	0.732	0.677	
Present Value Free Cash Flows	4,956.5	4,662.1	4,554.6	4,883.5	4,525.5	
Sum of Present Value Free Cash Flows	23,582.3					
Present Value of Continuing Value	109,988.1					
Total Present Value Free Cash Flows to Equity and Debt	133,570.4					
Less: Value of Outstanding Debt	−8,227.0					
Less: Value of Preferred Stock	0.0					
Plus: Value of Financial Assets	0.0					
Present Value of Equity	125,343.4					
Adjust to Midyear Discounting	1.0406					
Total Present Value of Equity	130,435.3					
Shares Outstanding	1,553.0					
Estimated Value per Share	$83.99					
Current share price	$54.77					
Percent difference	53%					

Appendix D

Financial Statement Ratios: Descriptive Statistics by Industry and by Year

This appendix contains descriptive statistics on 24 financial statement ratios, which are defined and explained in Chapters 4 and 5 and used throughout this book. The formulae to compute the ratios also are presented on the inside back cover of the book. The descriptive statistics include the 25th percentile, median, and 75th percentile for each industry over the period 1998–2008. In addition, the statistics report the industry median for each ratio in 2008, 2007, and 2006. The appendix contains descriptive statistics for 48 individual industries (listed alphabetically) and aggregated across all industries. These data are helpful for benchmarking financial statement ratios of companies you are analyzing, as well as for developing forecast assumptions and projections.

The website for this book (www.cengage.com/accounting/wahlen) contains an Excel file with these descriptive statistics data, the formulae used to compute the ratios (specified with variable names from the Compustat database), and the specific Standard Industrial Classification (SIC) codes included in each of the 48 industries.

		1998–2008					
		25th Percentile	Median	75th Percentile	2008 Median	2007 Median	2006 Median
All Industries	Stock Return	–0.333	0.018	0.428	–0.455	–0.046	0.130
	Market-to-Book	1.065	1.798	3.302	1.103	1.931	2.212
	Price-Earnings	11.152	16.667	26.784	12.963	17.498	18.470
	Profit Margin for ROA	–0.127	0.035	0.111	0.028	0.048	0.054
	Total Asset Turnover	0.256	0.705	1.296	0.664	0.659	0.687
	ROA	–0.140	0.029	0.077	0.012	0.034	0.041
	Profit Margin for ROCE	–0.132	0.026	0.097	0.016	0.039	0.045
	Capital Structure Leverage	1.458	2.169	3.989	2.104	2.059	2.105
	ROCE	–0.134	0.073	0.171	0.039	0.078	0.095
	Gross Profit Margin	0.198	0.364	0.564	0.352	0.375	0.382
	SG&A Percentage	0.149	0.271	0.475	0.262	0.261	0.264
	Operating Income Margin	–0.061	0.064	0.175	0.066	0.081	0.083
	Days Receivable	33.392	52.871	76.473	49.130	51.840	51.012
	Days Inventory	20.671	58.191	113.093	54.511	54.443	54.420
	Days Payables	29.828	51.414	115.666	48.977	51.717	50.970
	Days Revenues in Cash	9.799	37.625	120.649	42.829	44.162	42.692
	Revenue Growth	–0.042	0.085	0.270	0.054	0.097	0.126
	Earnings Growth	–0.599	0.067	0.602	–0.166	0.020	0.097
	Assets Growth	–0.064	0.056	0.232	0.006	0.078	0.094
	Current Ratio	1.001	1.701	3.070	1.709	1.816	1.776
	Long-Term Debt to Common Equity	0.139	0.484	1.145	0.544	0.469	0.447
	Interest Coverage Ratio	–4.073	1.763	6.962	1.377	2.178	2.618
	Liabilities to Equity	0.414	1.100	2.802	1.103	1.016	1.014
	Operating Cash Flow to Current Liabilities	–0.099	0.074	0.236	0.075	0.075	0.076

		1998–2008					
		25th Percentile	Median	75th Percentile	2008 Median	2007 Median	2006 Median
Agriculture	Stock Return	–0.327	0.011	0.347	–0.312	0.221	0.139
	Market-to-Book	0.517	1.062	2.365	1.095	2.187	2.168
	Price-Earnings	8.292	16.827	29.923	10.833	25.381	29.659
	Profit Margin for ROA	–0.092	0.039	0.105	0.028	0.034	0.041
	Total Asset Turnover	0.400	0.760	1.261	1.050	0.803	0.793
	ROA	–0.054	0.032	0.076	0.042	0.060	0.036
	Profit Margin for ROCE	–0.082	0.024	0.077	0.021	0.024	0.023
	Capital Structure Leverage	1.685	2.283	3.286	2.155	2.091	2.425
	ROCE	–0.103	0.060	0.153	0.110	0.060	0.045
	Gross Profit Margin	0.173	0.298	0.394	0.255	0.269	0.286
	SG&A Percentage	0.101	0.206	0.315	0.124	0.141	0.206
	Operating Income Margin	–0.032	0.049	0.118	0.034	0.052	0.040
	Days Receivable	23.803	34.641	69.335	30.235	33.707	34.483
	Days Inventory	37.532	74.519	260.355	45.801	49.878	57.530
	Days Payables	21.025	32.690	49.661	28.402	26.677	33.525
	Days Revenues in Cash	4.459	13.164	42.724	15.211	14.818	16.137
	Revenue Growth	–0.026	0.086	0.208	0.158	0.148	0.124
	Earnings Growth	–0.836	0.053	1.126	0.099	0.354	–0.052
	Assets Growth	–0.057	0.039	0.145	0.062	0.050	0.066
	Current Ratio	1.286	1.643	2.448	1.439	1.653	1.702
	Long-Term Debt to Common Equity	0.171	0.574	1.118	0.387	0.349	0.457
	Interest Coverage Ratio	–1.351	1.909	5.185	1.429	4.354	3.990
	Liabilities to Equity	0.582	1.152	2.152	1.056	1.037	1.152
	Operating Cash Flow to Current Liabilities	–0.009	0.113	0.232	0.089	0.061	0.088

(Continued)

		1998–2008					
		25th Percentile	Median	75th Percentile	2008 Median	2007 Median	2006 Median
Aircraft	Stock Return	–0.264	0.066	0.415	–0.444	0.220	0.287
	Market-to-Book	1.104	1.754	3.170	1.327	2.904	2.890
	Price-Earnings	10.458	16.317	21.749	9.285	18.731	19.798
	Profit Margin for ROA	0.012	0.069	0.105	0.072	0.081	0.073
	Total Asset Turnover	0.760	0.907	1.147	1.040	0.988	0.965
	ROA	0.007	0.061	0.094	0.068	0.074	0.064
	Profit Margin for ROCE	0.003	0.050	0.077	0.063	0.069	0.055
	Capital Structure Leverage	1.783	2.505	3.992	2.672	2.354	2.578
	ROCE	0.012	0.118	0.218	0.134	0.164	0.137
	Gross Profit Margin	0.183	0.266	0.350	0.248	0.272	0.275
	SG&A Percentage	0.104	0.135	0.180	0.131	0.131	0.133
	Operating Income Margin	0.045	0.101	0.138	0.107	0.111	0.095
	Days Receivable	42.502	55.337	66.582	52.792	52.652	54.151
	Days Inventory	73.560	110.106	149.471	110.015	106.594	108.293
	Days Payables	30.420	40.362	53.546	43.066	42.824	41.202
	Days Revenues in Cash	5.749	16.652	37.030	19.584	21.347	16.154
	Revenue Growth	–0.006	0.103	0.213	0.127	0.151	0.134
	Earnings Growth	–0.412	0.133	0.645	0.110	0.254	0.398
	Assets Growth	–0.016	0.063	0.183	0.072	0.151	0.066
	Current Ratio	1.372	1.894	2.721	1.992	2.113	1.951
	Long-Term Debt to Common Equity	0.238	0.481	1.189	0.448	0.457	0.444
	Interest Coverage Ratio	0.826	3.575	10.586	7.062	6.630	3.613
	Liabilities to Equity	0.769	1.501	2.770	1.449	1.335	1.601
	Operating Cash Flow to Current Liabilities	0.026	0.098	0.182	0.119	0.086	0.067

		1998–2008					
		25th Percentile	Median	75th Percentile	2008 Median	2007 Median	2006 Median
Apparel	Stock Return	–0.335	–0.005	0.414	–0.448	–0.212	0.158
	Market-to-Book	0.824	1.441	2.668	1.013	1.627	2.577
	Price-Earnings	10.319	15.006	20.620	12.124	16.440	19.105
	Profit Margin for ROA	0.009	0.046	0.074	0.045	0.054	0.057
	Total Asset Turnover	1.252	1.532	1.973	1.476	1.461	1.526
	ROA	0.011	0.066	0.117	0.053	0.069	0.085
	Profit Margin for ROCE	–0.008	0.033	0.067	0.041	0.039	0.050
	Capital Structure Leverage	1.379	1.712	2.326	1.600	1.696	1.662
	ROCE	0.000	0.101	0.182	0.085	0.108	0.123
	Gross Profit Margin	0.283	0.386	0.453	0.424	0.418	0.418
	SG&A Percentage	0.230	0.293	0.353	0.325	0.309	0.295
	Operating Income Margin	0.024	0.071	0.111	0.072	0.078	0.087
	Days Receivable	33.430	47.173	60.139	43.381	48.574	47.174
	Days Inventory	76.383	99.367	133.000	98.562	96.093	95.354
	Days Payables	24.539	34.548	47.059	39.804	40.341	38.954
	Days Revenues in Cash	4.188	14.817	40.468	26.449	16.909	13.630
	Revenue Growth	–0.038	0.051	0.161	0.014	0.051	0.087
	Earnings Growth	–0.537	0.079	0.656	–0.325	0.111	0.115
	Assets Growth	–0.052	0.048	0.177	–0.011	0.067	0.062
	Current Ratio	1.844	2.617	3.828	2.662	2.467	2.665
	Long-Term Debt to Common Equity	0.052	0.222	0.512	0.153	0.145	0.176
	Interest Coverage Ratio	0.792	5.296	21.589	5.678	6.476	6.848
	Liabilities to Equity	0.356	0.685	1.305	0.582	0.680	0.647
	Operating Cash Flow to Current Liabilities	0.040	0.187	0.441	0.207	0.231	0.175

(Continued)

		1998–2008					
		25th Percentile	Median	75th Percentile	2008 Median	2007 Median	2006 Median
Automobiles and Trucks	Stock Return	–0.347	–0.035	0.327	–0.605	–0.048	0.133
	Market-to-Book	0.957	1.518	2.615	0.892	1.656	1.902
	Price-Earnings	9.398	13.197	18.808	10.251	14.997	15.433
	Profit Margin for ROA	–0.041	0.027	0.056	–0.003	0.030	0.029
	Total Asset Turnover	0.883	1.223	1.650	1.235	1.234	1.209
	ROA	–0.054	0.033	0.079	–0.009	0.042	0.037
	Profit Margin for ROCE	–0.049	0.013	0.047	–0.012	0.014	0.018
	Capital Structure Leverage	1.728	2.735	4.427	2.618	2.640	2.646
	ROCE	–0.082	0.097	0.211	–0.013	0.126	0.120
	Gross Profit Margin	0.145	0.214	0.287	0.202	0.210	0.201
	SG&A Percentage	0.084	0.132	0.202	0.135	0.132	0.132
	Operating Income Margin	0.001	0.046	0.082	0.030	0.046	0.038
	Days Receivable	35.044	51.292	65.578	52.991	53.263	52.271
	Days Inventory	36.593	54.276	80.452	58.774	54.900	53.899
	Days Payables	33.155	45.704	61.345	49.220	49.276	50.007
	Days Revenues in Cash	5.748	17.201	34.151	24.768	21.945	17.037
	Revenue Growth	–0.058	0.048	0.167	–0.048	0.047	0.068
	Earnings Growth	–0.764	–0.006	0.512	–0.559	0.051	0.038
	Assets Growth	–0.071	0.031	0.149	–0.089	0.038	0.041
	Current Ratio	1.113	1.478	2.326	1.724	1.675	1.518
	Long-Term Debt to Common Equity	0.208	0.585	1.501	0.749	0.559	0.445
	Interest Coverage Ratio	–1.309	1.886	8.027	–0.265	3.007	2.898
	Liabilities to Equity	0.678	1.647	3.604	1.506	1.588	1.366
	Operating Cash Flow to Current Liabilities	–0.007	0.092	0.196	0.081	0.111	0.093

		1998–2008					
		25th Percentile	Median	75th Percentile	2008 Median	2007 Median	2006 Median
Banking	Stock Return	–0.144	0.065	0.304	–0.356	–0.186	0.110
	Market-to-Book	1.030	1.458	2.013	0.782	1.204	1.687
	Price-Earnings	11.635	14.836	19.224	14.958	14.611	16.429
	Profit Margin for ROA	0.040	0.216	0.391	0.066	0.229	0.275
	Total Asset Turnover	0.063	0.073	0.085	0.064	0.074	0.073
	ROA	0.007	0.032	0.056	0.009	0.032	0.042
	Profit Margin for ROCE	0.075	0.124	0.169	0.047	0.104	0.132
	Capital Structure Leverage	8.647	11.038	13.519	10.951	10.513	10.795
	ROCE	0.056	0.106	0.149	0.030	0.081	0.110
	Gross Profit Margin	0.475	0.578	0.679	0.502	0.535	0.584
	SG&A Percentage	0.214	0.270	0.324	0.301	0.267	0.273
	Operating Income Margin	0.213	0.286	0.361	0.198	0.253	0.292
	Days Receivable	72.404	1,096.444	2,722.238	944.495	1,099.943	1,073.813
	Days Inventory	10.261	41.329	152.451	44.592	31.777	33.893
	Days Payables	5,260.518	7,958.902	11,797.255	7,157.698	7,482.045	8,651.434
	Days Revenues in Cash	74.230	123.271	177.434	103.709	102.030	114.833
	Revenue Growth	–0.015	0.082	0.203	–0.043	0.103	0.200
	Earnings Growth	–0.133	0.087	0.300	–0.435	–0.064	0.064
	Assets Growth	0.025	0.090	0.186	0.053	0.066	0.094
	Current Ratio	0.848	1.434	2.838	1.444	1.668	1.704
	Long-Term Debt to Common Equity	0.407	0.917	1.775	1.095	0.834	0.772
	Interest Coverage Ratio	0.871	1.664	3.633	0.831	1.521	2.174
	Liabilities to Equity	7.560	10.002	12.445	9.633	9.428	9.505
	Operating Cash Flow to Current Liabilities	0.008	0.015	0.024	0.013	0.013	0.014

(Continued)

		1998–2008					
		25th Percentile	Median	75th Percentile	2008 Median	2007 Median	2006 Median
Beer & Liquor	Stock Return	–0.150	0.047	0.288	–0.240	0.058	0.154
	Market-to-Book	1.113	1.878	3.811	1.572	2.621	2.890
	Price-Earnings	14.216	18.462	24.040	16.063	18.721	19.610
	Profit Margin for ROA	0.031	0.085	0.132	0.098	0.101	0.094
	Total Asset Turnover	0.532	0.736	0.993	0.693	0.742	0.651
	ROA	0.016	0.060	0.092	0.050	0.061	0.060
	Profit Margin for ROCE	0.024	0.065	0.120	0.082	0.116	0.087
	Capital Structure Leverage	1.631	2.058	2.510	1.924	1.946	1.969
	ROCE	0.044	0.119	0.227	0.079	0.155	0.175
	Gross Profit Margin	0.354	0.470	0.591	0.522	0.504	0.493
	SG&A Percentage	0.233	0.296	0.382	0.302	0.303	0.296
	Operating Income Margin	0.074	0.126	0.191	0.152	0.161	0.152
	Days Receivable	27.138	42.729	62.793	40.361	37.339	38.883
	Days Inventory	47.950	120.629	223.673	122.028	85.129	109.577
	Days Payables	37.589	52.151	81.319	51.582	52.338	54.774
	Days Revenues in Cash	5.228	16.986	42.578	16.529	22.229	25.847
	Revenue Growth	–0.004	0.064	0.178	0.045	0.118	0.078
	Earnings Growth	–0.182	0.092	0.396	–0.134	0.168	0.117
	Assets Growth	–0.026	0.047	0.147	0.034	0.087	0.042
	Current Ratio	1.028	1.602	2.431	1.325	1.394	1.450
	Long-Term Debt to Common Equity	0.177	0.360	0.749	0.306	0.316	0.337
	Interest Coverage Ratio	1.354	3.931	6.701	5.819	5.064	5.295
	Liabilities to Equity	0.601	0.989	1.510	0.937	0.968	0.919
	Operating Cash Flow to Current Liabilities	0.080	0.146	0.296	0.128	0.147	0.186

		1998–2008					
		25th Percentile	Median	75th Percentile	2008 Median	2007 Median	2006 Median
Broker Dealers	Stock Return	–0.187	0.109	0.429	–0.408	–0.040	0.309
	Market-to-Book	0.937	1.514	2.799	0.996	1.616	2.015
	Price-Earnings	10.608	17.143	29.462	16.927	20.640	21.725
	Profit Margin for ROA	0.073	0.292	0.526	0.182	0.281	0.320
	Total Asset Turnover	0.118	0.176	0.498	0.156	0.161	0.170
	ROA	0.014	0.052	0.085	0.032	0.050	0.057
	Profit Margin for ROCE	–0.011	0.129	0.308	0.060	0.107	0.146
	Capital Structure Leverage	1.442	2.373	4.139	2.390	2.308	2.383
	ROCE	–0.009	0.085	0.183	0.034	0.075	0.107
	Gross Profit Margin	0.220	0.425	0.670	0.347	0.381	0.416
	SG&A Percentage	0.086	0.236	0.568	0.190	0.185	0.223
	Operating Income Margin	0.117	0.347	0.572	0.287	0.325	0.338
	Days Receivable	25.480	58.290	207.120	62.111	62.604	62.004
	Days Inventory	17.260	69.441	324.476	56.731	90.388	118.043
	Days Payables	35.684	72.779	153.876	68.234	71.453	74.842
	Days Revenues in Cash	14.143	51.200	141.918	65.799	59.401	67.844
	Revenue Growth	–0.053	0.094	0.310	0.015	0.132	0.181
	Earnings Growth	–0.429	0.096	0.630	–0.281	0.044	0.226
	Assets Growth	–0.063	0.052	0.245	–0.027	0.082	0.125
	Current Ratio	0.979	1.851	4.566	1.898	2.020	1.842
	Long-Term Debt to Common Equity	0.413	1.110	2.146	1.180	1.269	1.217
	Interest Coverage Ratio	0.941	1.937	3.669	1.286	1.851	2.028
	Liabilities to Equity	0.365	1.161	2.657	1.235	1.158	1.196
	Operating Cash Flow to Current Liabilities	0.005	0.087	0.195	0.072	0.076	0.083

(Continued)

		1998–2008					
		25th Percentile	Median	75th Percentile	2008 Median	2007 Median	2006 Median
Business Services	Stock Return	–0.491	–0.078	0.473	–0.497	–0.005	0.104
	Market-to-Book	1.239	2.355	4.856	1.415	2.556	2.741
	Price-Earnings	13.429	22.950	39.972	14.479	22.950	25.709
	Profit Margin for ROA	–0.523	–0.020	0.069	0.007	0.029	0.035
	Total Asset Turnover	0.476	0.862	1.384	0.872	0.849	0.874
	ROA	–0.388	–0.027	0.066	0.002	0.025	0.036
	Profit Margin for ROCE	–0.580	–0.043	0.056	–0.004	0.020	0.016
	Capital Structure Leverage	1.334	1.691	2.552	1.790	1.745	1.726
	ROCE	–0.405	0.022	0.181	0.061	0.073	0.079
	Gross Profit Margin	0.249	0.471	0.705	0.490	0.524	0.503
	SG&A Percentage	0.269	0.534	0.855	0.444	0.458	0.478
	Operating Income Margin	–0.432	–0.006	0.090	0.043	0.040	0.037
	Days Receivable	45.198	64.117	87.279	62.021	62.665	61.986
	Days Inventory	7.308	22.901	55.543	17.962	19.243	18.828
	Days Payables	24.584	49.309	105.819	40.537	42.295	45.913
	Days Revenues in Cash	21.134	68.492	178.292	59.089	67.994	68.074
	Revenue Growth	–0.062	0.112	0.410	0.084	0.143	0.136
	Earnings Growth	–0.992	0.047	0.692	–0.084	0.098	0.074
	Assets Growth	–0.142	0.053	0.364	–0.009	0.098	0.097
	Current Ratio	1.003	1.699	3.004	1.535	1.671	1.624
	Long-Term Debt to Common Equity	0.014	0.152	0.635	0.228	0.220	0.204
	Interest Coverage Ratio	–22.833	–0.632	7.216	0.325	1.561	2.094
	Liabilities to Equity	0.304	0.654	1.499	0.815	0.692	0.725
	Operating Cash Flow to Current Liabilities	–0.363	0.056	0.284	0.148	0.139	0.130

		1998–2008					
		25th Percentile	Median	75th Percentile	2008 Median	2007 Median	2006 Median
Business Supplies	Stock Return	–0.288	–0.044	0.236	–0.529	–0.138	0.154
	Market-to-Book	0.774	1.351	1.993	0.729	1.263	1.495
	Price-Earnings	10.483	15.299	23.132	11.624	14.793	19.207
	Profit Margin for ROA	0.003	0.040	0.075	0.008	0.042	0.039
	Total Asset Turnover	0.726	1.047	1.468	1.096	1.029	1.027
	ROA	0.002	0.043	0.078	0.010	0.055	0.041
	Profit Margin for ROCE	–0.022	0.023	0.056	–0.013	0.022	0.019
	Capital Structure Leverage	1.917	2.612	3.548	2.624	2.551	2.637
	ROCE	–0.062	0.067	0.157	–0.025	0.084	0.049
	Gross Profit Margin	0.184	0.263	0.350	0.205	0.211	0.203
	SG&A Percentage	0.079	0.141	0.234	0.106	0.108	0.123
	Operating Income Margin	0.023	0.060	0.105	0.042	0.057	0.047
	Days Receivable	37.739	46.093	57.996	41.319	43.690	46.209
	Days Inventory	42.805	58.228	75.202	57.331	56.303	57.006
	Days Payables	29.928	39.232	55.922	37.185	41.405	39.327
	Days Revenues in Cash	3.340	9.256	24.913	9.477	11.683	7.980
	Revenue Growth	–0.044	0.040	0.133	0.022	0.044	0.041
	Earnings Growth	–0.683	0.037	0.738	–0.739	0.218	0.425
	Assets Growth	–0.066	0.001	0.100	–0.038	0.050	0.000
	Current Ratio	1.238	1.622	2.231	1.696	1.735	1.850
	Long-Term Debt to Common Equity	0.312	0.664	1.349	0.778	0.622	0.589
	Interest Coverage Ratio	0.265	2.252	5.771	0.696	2.439	2.773
	Liabilities to Equity	0.876	1.528	2.530	1.597	1.436	1.577
	Operating Cash Flow to Current Liabilities	0.046	0.116	0.224	0.083	0.121	0.116

(Continued)

		1998–2008					
		25th Percentile	Median	75th Percentile	2008 Median	2007 Median	2006 Median
Candy & Soda	Stock Return	–0.288	0.018	0.400	–0.375	0.113	0.191
	Market-to-Book	1.627	2.290	4.163	1.690	2.429	3.713
	Price-Earnings	15.276	19.716	28.615	18.157	17.190	23.481
	Profit Margin for ROA	–0.069	0.040	0.076	0.028	0.050	0.041
	Total Asset Turnover	0.815	1.035	1.583	1.094	1.081	1.086
	ROA	–0.201	0.044	0.086	0.029	0.056	0.025
	Profit Margin for ROCE	–0.076	0.026	0.054	–0.010	0.033	0.028
	Capital Structure Leverage	1.856	2.392	3.996	2.155	2.403	2.381
	ROCE	–0.034	0.122	0.217	0.082	0.121	0.129
	Gross Profit Margin	0.305	0.455	0.508	0.449	0.459	0.450
	SG&A Percentage	0.296	0.327	0.425	0.360	0.362	0.322
	Operating Income Margin	–0.035	0.067	0.101	0.066	0.069	0.073
	Days Receivable	21.724	30.734	37.155	32.887	32.618	29.923
	Days Inventory	29.231	36.583	60.710	42.348	38.758	38.834
	Days Payables	31.597	43.086	63.387	42.463	36.520	46.617
	Days Revenues in Cash	4.697	11.226	27.322	18.855	16.123	18.035
	Revenue Growth	–0.001	0.066	0.183	0.030	0.098	0.066
	Earnings Growth	–0.536	0.042	0.586	–0.335	0.099	0.048
	Assets Growth	–0.073	0.030	0.165	–0.098	0.113	0.038
	Current Ratio	0.850	1.143	1.805	1.187	1.269	1.255
	Long-Term Debt to Common Equity	0.360	0.632	1.956	0.666	0.558	0.563
	Interest Coverage Ratio	–1.740	2.046	4.665	1.502	2.044	1.684
	Liabilities to Equity	0.816	1.288	3.041	1.289	1.097	1.312
	Operating Cash Flow to Current Liabilities	–0.032	0.120	0.217	0.101	0.131	0.131

		1998–2008					
		25th Percentile	**Median**	**75th Percentile**	**2008 Median**	**2007 Median**	**2006 Median**
Chemicals	Stock Return	–0.303	0.020	0.373	–0.501	0.091	0.213
	Market-to-Book	1.194	2.056	3.539	1.438	2.637	2.536
	Price-Earnings	11.460	17.076	25.311	10.213	18.539	20.494
	Profit Margin for ROA	–0.079	0.037	0.082	0.041	0.059	0.048
	Total Asset Turnover	0.637	0.903	1.277	0.960	0.914	0.939
	ROA	–0.094	0.037	0.078	0.030	0.054	0.051
	Profit Margin for ROCE	–0.116	0.017	0.063	0.024	0.036	0.030
	Capital Structure Leverage	1.622	2.393	3.418	2.296	2.145	2.318
	ROCE	–0.118	0.088	0.211	0.089	0.122	0.116
	Gross Profit Margin	0.176	0.293	0.404	0.298	0.292	0.282
	SG&A Percentage	0.095	0.189	0.334	0.155	0.158	0.172
	Operating Income Margin	–0.028	0.063	0.114	0.067	0.075	0.072
	Days Receivable	38.595	52.411	64.391	46.145	51.433	48.844
	Days Inventory	45.387	66.675	107.683	61.250	62.964	65.079
	Days Payables	33.632	46.147	66.050	38.777	44.960	42.945
	Days Revenues in Cash	5.756	17.184	51.354	22.868	21.487	19.876
	Revenue Growth	–0.032	0.075	0.209	0.073	0.091	0.091
	Earnings Growth	–0.660	0.024	0.657	–0.097	0.160	0.130
	Assets Growth	–0.072	0.024	0.144	–0.016	0.075	0.080
	Current Ratio	1.166	1.697	2.552	1.855	1.859	1.866
	Long-Term Debt to Common Equity	0.239	0.560	1.118	0.544	0.534	0.507
	Interest Coverage Ratio	–2.076	1.937	6.216	3.082	2.784	2.880
	Liabilities to Equity	0.588	1.316	2.339	1.282	1.131	1.313
	Operating Cash Flow to Current Liabilities	–0.058	0.085	0.191	0.079	0.093	0.084

(Continued)

		1998–2008					
		25th Percentile	Median	75th Percentile	2008 Median	2007 Median	2006 Median
Coal	Stock Return	–0.264	0.237	0.749	–0.568	0.525	–0.241
	Market-to-Book	1.442	2.777	5.612	1.137	4.009	2.701
	Price-Earnings	8.319	13.813	32.518	6.383	21.569	13.120
	Profit Margin for ROA	–0.026	0.056	0.128	0.069	0.054	0.046
	Total Asset Turnover	0.482	0.662	0.978	0.832	0.727	0.738
	ROA	–0.061	0.034	0.094	0.047	0.035	0.034
	Profit Margin for ROCE	–0.105	0.017	0.088	0.065	0.022	0.020
	Capital Structure Leverage	1.551	2.796	5.498	2.327	2.387	2.888
	ROCE	–0.147	0.063	0.294	0.227	0.106	0.062
	Gross Profit Margin	0.130	0.199	0.287	0.249	0.201	0.207
	SG&A Percentage	0.032	0.060	0.152	0.058	0.052	0.042
	Operating Income Margin	–0.078	0.043	0.119	0.103	0.052	0.058
	Days Receivable	23.372	29.658	42.508	25.119	32.039	29.688
	Days Inventory	14.726	29.586	59.141	19.525	20.526	25.350
	Days Payables	28.103	35.959	61.871	32.590	33.418	36.796
	Days Revenues in Cash	5.224	18.456	82.268	47.511	10.903	15.884
	Revenue Growth	–0.015	0.131	0.326	0.329	0.064	0.124
	Earnings Growth	–1.183	–0.111	1.114	0.452	–0.498	–0.296
	Assets Growth	–0.027	0.083	0.382	0.304	0.031	0.163
	Current Ratio	0.881	1.319	2.723	1.252	1.386	1.279
	Long-Term Debt to Common Equity	0.230	0.821	1.783	0.652	0.709	0.691
	Interest Coverage Ratio	–1.229	1.463	6.618	4.235	1.862	1.049
	Liabilities to Equity	0.423	1.552	3.929	1.369	1.347	1.492
	Operating Cash Flow to Current Liabilities	–0.043	0.084	0.262	0.118	0.121	0.081

		1998–2008					
		25th Percentile	Median	75th Percentile	2008 Median	2007 Median	2006 Median
Communications	Stock Return	–0.413	–0.027	0.480	–0.422	0.001	0.196
	Market-to-Book	1.174	2.058	3.941	1.371	2.079	2.219
	Price-Earnings	12.325	19.215	34.978	13.115	19.248	19.423
	Profit Margin for ROA	–0.256	0.047	0.150	0.047	0.090	0.088
	Total Asset Turnover	0.289	0.478	0.715	0.563	0.587	0.580
	ROA	–0.133	0.021	0.075	0.030	0.048	0.046
	Profit Margin for ROCE	–0.384	–0.009	0.100	0.010	0.038	0.033
	Capital Structure Leverage	1.833	2.601	4.021	2.567	2.432	2.469
	ROCE	–0.245	0.058	0.245	0.062	0.109	0.094
	Gross Profit Margin	0.304	0.450	0.602	0.525	0.513	0.487
	SG&A Percentage	0.208	0.306	0.485	0.271	0.271	0.287
	Operating Income Margin	–0.171	0.080	0.195	0.147	0.134	0.127
	Days Receivable	33.724	50.543	69.254	43.641	44.047	42.574
	Days Inventory	7.590	14.908	28.180	16.529	14.025	13.040
	Days Payables	40.766	69.230	118.743	54.270	59.163	55.461
	Days Revenues in Cash	11.722	34.522	95.453	35.244	35.470	35.409
	Revenue Growth	–0.015	0.106	0.326	0.059	0.114	0.118
	Earnings Growth	–0.914	–0.032	0.658	–0.134	0.162	0.084
	Assets Growth	–0.082	0.033	0.251	–0.030	0.043	0.043
	Current Ratio	0.672	1.119	1.822	1.124	1.160	1.240
	Long-Term Debt to Common Equity	0.320	0.755	1.726	0.953	0.727	0.750
	Interest Coverage Ratio	–2.036	1.029	4.328	1.536	2.408	1.916
	Liabilities to Equity	0.726	1.419	2.697	1.713	1.374	1.302
	Operating Cash Flow to Current Liabilities	–0.033	0.096	0.244	0.148	0.136	0.133

(Continued)

		1998–2008					
		25th Percentile	Median	75th Percentile	2008 Median	2007 Median	2006 Median
Computers	Stock Return	–0.472	–0.080	0.518	–0.471	–0.147	0.081
	Market-to-Book	1.369	2.386	4.575	1.469	2.461	2.515
	Price-Earnings	15.128	23.938	40.600	17.433	22.911	22.812
	Profit Margin for ROA	–0.374	–0.034	0.057	–0.005	0.003	0.004
	Total Asset Turnover	0.604	0.972	1.462	0.914	0.906	1.000
	ROA	–0.349	–0.037	0.065	–0.010	0.000	–0.003
	Profit Margin for ROCE	–0.380	–0.037	0.053	–0.005	–0.007	0.002
	Capital Structure Leverage	1.314	1.647	2.309	1.693	1.719	1.697
	ROCE	–0.365	0.012	0.165	0.026	0.057	0.059
	Gross Profit Margin	0.273	0.427	0.589	0.475	0.457	0.449
	SG&A Percentage	0.271	0.444	0.716	0.434	0.453	0.456
	Operating Income Margin	–0.298	–0.016	0.072	0.016	0.010	0.003
	Days Receivable	48.445	64.594	86.599	63.586	65.706	64.309
	Days Inventory	27.096	64.044	108.331	51.522	54.841	58.682
	Days Payables	37.709	57.041	90.021	55.662	58.466	56.167
	Days Revenues in Cash	23.616	60.521	141.117	71.730	67.021	57.830
	Revenue Growth	–0.109	0.081	0.310	0.085	0.111	0.146
	Earnings Growth	–0.934	0.077	0.770	0.000	0.094	0.028
	Assets Growth	–0.147	0.041	0.294	–0.013	0.093	0.103
	Current Ratio	1.220	2.029	3.512	1.913	1.976	1.842
	Long-Term Debt to Common Equity	0.019	0.137	0.489	0.215	0.201	0.155
	Interest Coverage Ratio	–20.947	–1.888	7.927	–0.286	–0.448	–0.318
	Liabilities to Equity	0.298	0.621	1.347	0.668	0.678	0.686
	Operating Cash Flow to Current Liabilities	–0.327	0.040	0.302	0.116	0.106	0.072

		1998–2008					
		25th Percentile	Median	75th Percentile	2008 Median	2007 Median	2006 Median
Construction	Stock Return	–0.314	0.076	0.552	–0.447	–0.244	0.054
	Market-to-Book	0.778	1.306	2.117	1.198	1.577	1.873
	Price-Earnings	6.194	9.675	19.555	10.000	26.778	15.960
	Profit Margin for ROA	–0.019	0.034	0.069	0.026	0.021	0.035
	Total Asset Turnover	0.854	1.327	1.908	1.083	1.054	1.308
	ROA	–0.033	0.051	0.094	0.029	0.013	0.050
	Profit Margin for ROCE	–0.042	0.024	0.055	0.009	–0.005	0.027
	Capital Structure Leverage	1.982	2.533	3.539	2.458	2.534	2.497
	ROCE	–0.068	0.116	0.232	0.052	–0.008	0.106
	Gross Profit Margin	0.105	0.167	0.231	0.140	0.119	0.173
	SG&A Percentage	0.074	0.104	0.147	0.120	0.117	0.093
	Operating Income Margin	0.001	0.046	0.093	0.040	0.027	0.051
	Days Receivable	37.705	63.414	84.683	63.038	67.795	62.450
	Days Inventory	17.592	61.853	262.784	41.332	44.513	42.165
	Days Payables	21.828	34.113	53.496	32.682	33.547	30.773
	Days Revenues in Cash	6.526	18.255	43.290	37.249	26.809	25.238
	Revenue Growth	–0.050	0.132	0.314	0.067	0.050	0.120
	Earnings Growth	–0.658	0.187	0.657	0.098	–0.479	0.016
	Assets Growth	–0.043	0.100	0.284	–0.014	–0.013	0.150
	Current Ratio	1.174	1.516	2.046	1.666	1.600	1.558
	Long-Term Debt to Common Equity	0.190	0.578	1.053	0.492	0.409	0.447
	Interest Coverage Ratio	–0.657	3.256	8.260	2.643	1.811	5.692
	Liabilities to Equity	0.950	1.501	2.504	1.489	1.374	1.471
	Operating Cash Flow to Current Liabilities	–0.059	0.055	0.180	0.154	0.155	0.075

(Continued)

		1998–2008					
		25th Percentile	**Median**	**75th Percentile**	**2008 Median**	**2007 Median**	**2006 Median**
Construction Materials	Stock Return	–0.280	–0.004	0.314	–0.493	–0.153	0.077
	Market-to-Book	0.845	1.331	2.254	0.839	1.581	1.917
	Price-Earnings	8.718	14.395	21.593	11.561	18.672	14.505
	Profit Margin for ROA	0.001	0.044	0.084	0.023	0.039	0.062
	Total Asset Turnover	0.795	1.103	1.531	1.046	1.043	1.165
	ROA	–0.002	0.054	0.093	0.015	0.038	0.079
	Profit Margin for ROCE	–0.016	0.032	0.071	0.012	0.030	0.052
	Capital Structure Leverage	1.511	1.981	2.665	1.890	1.856	1.868
	ROCE	–0.019	0.088	0.175	0.013	0.062	0.130
	Gross Profit Margin	0.192	0.275	0.359	0.265	0.262	0.271
	SG&A Percentage	0.100	0.164	0.237	0.159	0.159	0.142
	Operating Income Margin	0.012	0.068	0.119	0.050	0.065	0.082
	Days Receivable	28.325	43.590	58.147	40.240	40.728	41.275
	Days Inventory	44.099	65.916	96.248	66.818	62.800	59.739
	Days Payables	22.884	34.118	51.549	33.045	34.182	32.472
	Days Revenues in Cash	5.035	14.678	33.401	24.767	16.061	13.716
	Revenue Growth	–0.067	0.048	0.167	–0.057	–0.012	0.090
	Earnings Growth	–0.672	0.038	0.636	–0.510	–0.241	0.219
	Assets Growth	–0.054	0.030	0.131	–0.020	0.018	0.091
	Current Ratio	1.406	1.990	2.873	2.265	2.204	2.060
	Long-Term Debt to Common Equity	0.177	0.424	0.827	0.400	0.393	0.352
	Interest Coverage Ratio	0.113	3.238	7.998	1.543	3.346	4.866
	Liabilities to Equity	0.482	0.954	1.633	0.798	0.816	0.872
	Operating Cash Flow to Current Liabilities	0.034	0.148	0.281	0.120	0.150	0.157

		1998–2008					
		25th Percentile	**Median**	**75th Percentile**	**2008 Median**	**2007 Median**	**2006 Median**
Consumer Goods	Stock Return	–0.351	–0.041	0.278	–0.489	–0.095	0.087
	Market-to-Book	0.867	1.535	2.872	0.827	1.552	1.823
	Price-Earnings	10.427	15.574	23.293	15.786	15.565	18.404
	Profit Margin for ROA	–0.044	0.034	0.072	0.013	0.037	0.033
	Total Asset Turnover	0.929	1.228	1.667	1.127	1.176	1.204
	ROA	–0.055	0.043	0.092	0.017	0.053	0.038
	Profit Margin for ROCE	–0.066	0.022	0.061	0.007	0.024	0.022
	Capital Structure Leverage	1.518	2.039	3.227	2.006	1.975	1.997
	ROCE	–0.056	0.089	0.189	0.032	0.079	0.092
	Gross Profit Margin	0.265	0.394	0.516	0.427	0.423	0.399
	SG&A Percentage	0.197	0.311	0.435	0.330	0.326	0.324
	Operating Income Margin	–0.002	0.059	0.104	0.043	0.062	0.047
	Days Receivable	41.220	53.733	68.537	51.091	54.269	54.106
	Days Inventory	59.113	89.660	139.540	90.977	92.227	93.286
	Days Payables	32.121	46.314	67.675	58.235	55.466	49.927
	Days Revenues in Cash	4.968	14.813	39.690	21.472	19.515	19.226
	Revenue Growth	–0.062	0.045	0.149	–0.025	0.067	0.061
	Earnings Growth	–0.648	0.061	0.520	–0.301	0.191	0.021
	Assets Growth	–0.072	0.019	0.124	–0.051	0.022	0.045
	Current Ratio	1.255	1.866	2.884	1.898	1.972	1.939
	Long-Term Debt to Common Equity	0.135	0.396	0.949	0.453	0.382	0.404
	Interest Coverage Ratio	–0.863	2.507	10.175	1.813	3.383	2.550
	Liabilities to Equity	0.484	1.028	2.302	1.069	0.934	0.993
	Operating Cash Flow to Current Liabilities	–0.016	0.126	0.261	0.076	0.129	0.127

(Continued)

		1998–2008					
		25th Percentile	Median	75th Percentile	2008 Median	2007 Median	2006 Median
Defense	Stock Return	–0.330	0.017	0.377	–0.343	–0.056	0.093
	Market-to-Book	1.291	2.290	4.533	2.558	3.620	4.585
	Price-Earnings	10.732	17.404	27.459	14.007	18.000	20.920
	Profit Margin for ROA	–0.057	0.056	0.085	0.035	0.053	–0.010
	Total Asset Turnover	0.669	0.960	1.241	1.160	1.169	0.934
	ROA	–0.048	0.054	0.090	0.039	0.066	–0.013
	Profit Margin for ROCE	–0.069	0.039	0.075	0.037	0.053	–0.048
	Capital Structure Leverage	1.291	1.966	4.264	2.577	1.648	2.169
	ROCE	–0.080	0.090	0.235	0.130	0.137	0.102
	Gross Profit Margin	0.168	0.250	0.333	0.215	0.221	0.216
	SG&A Percentage	0.113	0.184	0.239	0.149	0.184	0.218
	Operating Income Margin	0.001	0.073	0.117	0.086	0.080	0.000
	Days Receivable	41.780	55.993	75.915	60.376	62.137	59.918
	Days Inventory	26.851	65.353	110.626	38.766	37.445	46.285
	Days Payables	21.478	36.879	58.228	26.133	23.366	28.213
	Days Revenues in Cash	11.648	30.851	86.483	40.559	45.197	35.965
	Revenue Growth	–0.027	0.065	0.298	0.043	0.200	0.108
	Earnings Growth	–0.658	0.045	0.634	–0.050	0.381	0.197
	Assets Growth	–0.085	0.012	0.121	–0.006	0.059	0.073
	Current Ratio	1.143	1.947	3.963	1.862	1.978	1.582
	Long-Term Debt to Common Equity	0.076	0.515	1.249	0.315	0.333	0.106
	Interest Coverage Ratio	–2.160	3.012	6.766	1.087	1.609	–2.160
	Liabilities to Equity	0.279	0.883	3.114	0.808	0.689	1.462
	Operating Cash Flow to Current Liabilities	–0.029	0.105	0.285	0.231	0.187	0.047

		1998–2008					
		25th Percentile	**Median**	**75th Percentile**	**2008 Median**	**2007 Median**	**2006 Median**
Electrical Equipment	Stock Return	–0.364	–0.003	0.466	–0.485	0.140	0.062
	Market-to-Book	1.135	1.928	3.432	1.528	2.610	2.309
	Price-Earnings	10.900	16.971	25.000	11.048	19.456	17.877
	Profit Margin for ROA	–0.261	0.019	0.070	0.003	0.012	0.027
	Total Asset Turnover	0.673	1.030	1.385	1.084	1.013	1.094
	ROA	–0.218	0.020	0.083	–0.003	0.006	0.040
	Profit Margin for ROCE	–0.279	0.010	0.059	0.013	0.008	0.023
	Capital Structure Leverage	1.365	1.772	2.555	1.678	1.700	1.755
	ROCE	–0.247	0.053	0.165	0.063	0.065	0.081
	Gross Profit Margin	0.221	0.306	0.385	0.314	0.300	0.295
	SG&A Percentage	0.180	0.255	0.430	0.253	0.251	0.259
	Operating Income Margin	–0.188	0.042	0.100	0.034	0.034	0.046
	Days Receivable	50.101	62.694	79.587	56.542	62.769	60.078
	Days Inventory	67.152	91.661	132.100	80.659	82.190	87.386
	Days Payables	30.893	47.492	72.659	44.158	47.611	48.538
	Days Revenues in Cash	8.582	26.213	75.385	36.619	33.866	35.760
	Revenue Growth	–0.084	0.066	0.238	0.141	0.174	0.112
	Earnings Growth	–0.636	0.058	0.588	0.059	0.130	0.152
	Assets Growth	–0.117	0.031	0.194	–0.019	0.126	0.084
	Current Ratio	1.465	2.075	3.423	2.149	2.240	1.986
	Long-Term Debt to Common Equity	0.056	0.249	0.581	0.192	0.182	0.287
	Interest Coverage Ratio	–7.678	1.595	8.695	1.945	1.051	3.134
	Liabilities to Equity	0.331	0.760	1.520	0.661	0.597	0.815
	Operating Cash Flow to Current Liabilities	–0.315	0.055	0.219	0.039	0.023	0.062

(Continued)

		1998–2008					
		25th Percentile	Median	75th Percentile	2008 Median	2007 Median	2006 Median
Electronic Equipment	Stock Return	–0.437	–0.073	0.504	–0.522	–0.068	0.001
	Market-to-Book	1.146	1.971	3.629	0.987	1.911	2.105
	Price-Earnings	14.572	23.202	43.210	13.713	20.545	23.077
	Profit Margin for ROA	–0.277	–0.003	0.075	–0.022	0.019	0.023
	Total Asset Turnover	0.553	0.861	1.261	0.852	0.857	0.887
	ROA	–0.204	–0.004	0.074	–0.032	0.017	0.023
	Profit Margin for ROCE	–0.292	–0.012	0.068	–0.029	0.010	0.016
	Capital Structure Leverage	1.245	1.529	2.129	1.515	1.538	1.516
	ROCE	–0.232	0.024	0.152	0.000	0.054	0.055
	Gross Profit Margin	0.259	0.386	0.534	0.391	0.405	0.403
	SG&A Percentage	0.209	0.346	0.554	0.342	0.324	0.346
	Operating Income Margin	–0.193	0.012	0.092	0.013	0.024	0.025
	Days Receivable	44.601	56.053	72.728	54.630	54.417	53.889
	Days Inventory	55.646	86.902	128.963	86.062	86.204	82.807
	Days Payables	37.144	54.963	83.869	52.846	54.756	53.214
	Days Revenues in Cash	24.765	68.139	147.096	71.837	72.060	70.515
	Revenue Growth	–0.079	0.098	0.341	0.049	0.083	0.145
	Earnings Growth	–0.845	0.118	0.823	–0.174	0.067	0.221
	Assets Growth	–0.115	0.044	0.287	–0.038	0.065	0.082
	Current Ratio	1.629	2.674	4.629	2.735	2.695	2.697
	Long-Term Debt to Common Equity	0.024	0.174	0.497	0.248	0.204	0.183
	Interest Coverage Ratio	–13.308	–0.141	11.208	–1.193	1.107	2.008
	Liabilities to Equity	0.221	0.490	1.074	0.481	0.492	0.495
	Operating Cash Flow to Current Liabilities	–0.212	0.089	0.394	0.138	0.131	0.114

		1998–2008					
		25th Percentile	Median	75th Percentile	2008 Median	2007 Median	2006 Median
Entertainment	Stock Return	–0.414	–0.008	0.478	–0.606	–0.100	0.148
	Market-to-Book	0.964	1.937	3.669	1.070	2.327	2.546
	Price-Earnings	11.822	19.518	32.292	17.871	26.620	27.684
	Profit Margin for ROA	–0.134	0.040	0.106	0.003	0.046	0.060
	Total Asset Turnover	0.427	0.655	1.053	0.580	0.627	0.600
	ROA	–0.129	0.023	0.070	–0.004	0.018	0.037
	Profit Margin for ROCE	–0.211	–0.005	0.064	–0.028	0.013	0.019
	Capital Structure Leverage	1.656	2.445	4.308	2.476	2.352	2.657
	ROCE	–0.153	0.064	0.230	0.029	0.059	0.085
	Gross Profit Margin	0.220	0.369	0.490	0.368	0.365	0.375
	SG&A Percentage	0.135	0.208	0.347	0.218	0.214	0.212
	Operating Income Margin	–0.071	0.063	0.146	0.062	0.064	0.073
	Days Receivable	6.055	14.819	42.755	12.485	15.735	14.245
	Days Inventory	3.200	7.664	23.086	5.421	5.129	5.446
	Days Payables	18.177	33.970	77.630	29.183	30.890	31.784
	Days Revenues in Cash	14.353	31.591	72.071	35.266	44.323	42.370
	Revenue Growth	–0.044	0.059	0.237	0.018	0.072	0.106
	Earnings Growth	–0.976	0.055	0.736	–0.208	–0.161	0.158
	Assets Growth	–0.101	0.019	0.186	–0.042	0.029	0.058
	Current Ratio	0.476	0.945	1.516	0.874	1.024	1.106
	Long-Term Debt to Common Equity	0.299	0.945	2.277	0.905	0.869	0.972
	Interest Coverage Ratio	–1.917	0.904	2.734	0.383	0.875	1.167
	Liabilities to Equity	0.627	1.398	3.119	1.523	1.334	1.389
	Operating Cash Flow to Current Liabilities	–0.051	0.081	0.198	0.075	0.081	0.089

(Continued)

		1998–2008					
		25th Percentile	Median	75th Percentile	2008 Median	2007 Median	2006 Median
Fabricated Products	Stock Return	–0.441	–0.041	0.391	–0.499	0.108	0.195
	Market-to-Book	0.671	1.040	1.741	0.714	1.271	1.438
	Price-Earnings	8.373	14.145	22.943	8.562	13.283	19.925
	Profit Margin for ROA	–0.017	0.027	0.056	0.032	0.035	0.024
	Total Asset Turnover	0.884	1.162	1.452	1.311	1.434	1.356
	ROA	–0.027	0.032	0.066	0.042	0.063	0.036
	Profit Margin for ROCE	–0.034	0.011	0.044	0.029	0.030	0.023
	Capital Structure Leverage	1.693	2.186	3.033	1.962	2.017	2.014
	ROCE	–0.108	0.046	0.123	0.071	0.098	0.074
	Gross Profit Margin	0.165	0.219	0.289	0.267	0.194	0.194
	SG&A Percentage	0.097	0.141	0.187	0.135	0.139	0.109
	Operating Income Margin	0.006	0.049	0.085	0.114	0.051	0.050
	Days Receivable	45.241	53.514	66.776	52.595	56.645	54.974
	Days Inventory	42.090	61.945	84.794	67.997	62.220	59.659
	Days Payables	33.591	42.805	57.957	44.160	52.498	45.056
	Days Revenues in Cash	2.598	8.910	26.335	19.701	10.583	12.985
	Revenue Growth	–0.074	0.050	0.174	0.005	0.090	0.179
	Earnings Growth	–1.036	0.023	1.000	–0.286	0.444	0.259
	Assets Growth	–0.091	0.009	0.132	–0.037	0.060	0.101
	Current Ratio	1.215	1.746	2.482	2.126	1.851	1.687
	Long-Term Debt to Common Equity	0.084	0.428	1.158	0.304	0.114	0.281
	Interest Coverage Ratio	–0.571	2.148	5.501	5.787	3.914	3.491
	Liabilities to Equity	0.649	1.207	2.178	1.103	0.948	0.926
	Operating Cash Flow to Current Liabilities	0.036	0.116	0.193	0.195	0.165	0.156

		1998–2008					
		25th Percentile	Median	75th Percentile	2008 Median	2007 Median	2006 Median
Food Products	Stock Return	–0.214	0.051	0.318	–0.253	0.060	0.127
	Market-to-Book	1.031	1.708	3.002	1.444	1.970	1.957
	Price-Earnings	12.151	17.614	26.370	14.261	20.539	21.429
	Profit Margin for ROA	0.007	0.037	0.066	0.030	0.048	0.042
	Total Asset Turnover	1.025	1.489	1.971	1.608	1.488	1.402
	ROA	0.009	0.054	0.092	0.046	0.065	0.056
	Profit Margin for ROCE	–0.006	0.025	0.057	0.021	0.044	0.031
	Capital Structure Leverage	1.483	2.194	3.316	2.059	1.933	1.985
	ROCE	0.010	0.095	0.186	0.081	0.117	0.098
	Gross Profit Margin	0.154	0.281	0.398	0.259	0.274	0.266
	SG&A Percentage	0.106	0.201	0.292	0.175	0.181	0.192
	Operating Income Margin	0.018	0.056	0.101	0.056	0.071	0.061
	Days Receivable	23.174	29.778	38.769	26.875	27.406	30.116
	Days Inventory	34.846	56.171	82.242	56.279	58.516	59.802
	Days Payables	21.189	31.449	47.283	30.033	30.588	33.447
	Days Revenues in Cash	2.423	8.411	24.610	7.387	9.548	11.099
	Revenue Growth	–0.018	0.059	0.172	0.091	0.112	0.075
	Earnings Growth	–0.417	0.093	0.657	–0.131	0.144	0.131
	Assets Growth	–0.037	0.038	0.141	0.034	0.090	0.045
	Current Ratio	1.130	1.700	2.495	1.637	1.777	1.825
	Long-Term Debt to Common Equity	0.180	0.502	1.050	0.477	0.458	0.419
	Interest Coverage Ratio	0.662	3.144	9.346	3.815	4.306	3.534
	Liabilities to Equity	0.470	1.134	2.189	1.178	0.892	0.937
	Operating Cash Flow to Current Liabilities	0.036	0.150	0.304	0.149	0.153	0.153

(Continued)

		1998–2008					
		25th Percentile	Median	75th Percentile	2008 Median	2007 Median	2006 Median
Healthcare	Stock Return	–0.371	0.014	0.550	–0.363	0.006	0.122
	Market-to-Book	1.144	2.063	3.696	1.754	2.775	2.645
	Price-Earnings	12.493	18.263	27.756	13.532	19.917	20.325
	Profit Margin for ROA	–0.042	0.041	0.083	0.056	0.044	0.046
	Total Asset Turnover	0.814	1.196	1.827	1.083	1.237	1.182
	ROA	–0.055	0.053	0.098	0.061	0.059	0.057
	Profit Margin for ROCE	–0.063	0.021	0.058	0.029	0.024	0.026
	Capital Structure Leverage	1.526	2.121	3.031	2.269	2.050	1.895
	ROCE	–0.092	0.085	0.189	0.086	0.097	0.092
	Gross Profit Margin	0.154	0.304	0.446	0.333	0.315	0.321
	SG&A Percentage	0.115	0.236	0.373	0.224	0.249	0.224
	Operating Income Margin	0.002	0.063	0.120	0.073	0.067	0.062
	Days Receivable	41.803	53.764	68.254	49.024	51.385	52.166
	Days Inventory	6.452	10.721	20.217	11.081	10.690	10.147
	Days Payables	13.698	23.032	38.123	21.170	21.809	23.544
	Days Revenues in Cash	6.368	17.449	43.924	19.297	17.499	18.957
	Revenue Growth	0.007	0.112	0.263	0.107	0.131	0.114
	Earnings Growth	–0.594	0.142	0.758	0.145	0.083	0.038
	Assets Growth	–0.038	0.066	0.229	0.049	0.135	0.118
	Current Ratio	1.068	1.662	2.565	1.720	1.617	1.697
	Long-Term Debt to Common Equity	0.137	0.505	1.180	0.583	0.503	0.476
	Interest Coverage Ratio	–1.165	2.311	8.285	3.598	2.707	3.551
	Liabilities to Equity	0.482	1.048	1.922	1.236	1.051	0.925
	Operating Cash Flow to Current Liabilities	0.016	0.139	0.309	0.148	0.161	0.136

		1998–2008					
		25th Percentile	**Median**	**75th Percentile**	**2008 Median**	**2007 Median**	**2006 Median**
Insurance	Stock Return	–0.197	0.042	0.305	–0.324	–0.044	0.126
	Market-to-Book	0.886	1.286	1.880	0.973	1.244	1.431
	Price-Earnings	9.513	13.119	19.459	14.359	10.986	11.797
	Profit Margin for ROA	0.022	0.073	0.130	0.031	0.115	0.116
	Total Asset Turnover	0.177	0.287	0.566	0.255	0.286	0.284
	ROA	0.004	0.021	0.050	0.009	0.035	0.039
	Profit Margin for ROCE	0.012	0.059	0.114	0.022	0.095	0.102
	Capital Structure Leverage	2.716	4.349	7.808	4.184	3.939	4.197
	ROCE	0.029	0.104	0.164	0.034	0.135	0.148
	Gross Profit Margin	0.079	0.153	0.249	0.106	0.199	0.201
	SG&A Percentage	0.103	0.167	0.299	0.143	0.126	0.146
	Operating Income Margin	0.032	0.101	0.171	0.059	0.147	0.151
	Days Receivable	55.429	159.102	358.112	166.879	150.407	157.844
	Days Inventory	1.696	6.780	24.040	8.588	3.934	3.555
	Days Payables	23.337	53.609	111.231	46.636	45.924	51.433
	Days Revenues in Cash	12.464	33.209	80.609	46.983	35.867	39.425
	Revenue Growth	–0.022	0.075	0.214	–0.070	0.048	0.073
	Earnings Growth	–0.416	0.100	0.580	–0.645	0.061	0.260
	Assets Growth	–0.006	0.072	0.183	–0.031	0.051	0.084
	Current Ratio	0.895	1.227	1.776	1.040	1.274	1.254
	Long-Term Debt to Common Equity	0.160	0.268	0.475	0.337	0.253	0.248
	Interest Coverage Ratio	1.622	7.700	16.885	3.176	9.902	13.070
	Liabilities to Equity	1.686	3.266	6.738	3.258	2.849	2.958
	Operating Cash Flow to Current Liabilities	0.013	0.050	0.134	0.042	0.057	0.064

(Continued)

		1998–2008					
		25th Percentile	**Median**	**75th Percentile**	**2008 Median**	**2007 Median**	**2006 Median**
Machinery	Stock Return	−0.310	0.012	0.411	−0.501	0.071	0.138
	Market-to-Book	1.150	1.889	3.171	1.228	2.546	2.354
	Price-Earnings	11.506	17.163	25.946	10.423	17.478	17.161
	Profit Margin for ROA	−0.072	0.036	0.075	0.045	0.062	0.055
	Total Asset Turnover	0.729	1.026	1.337	1.008	1.041	1.077
	ROA	−0.101	0.035	0.084	0.043	0.059	0.065
	Profit Margin for ROCE	−0.078	0.024	0.066	0.041	0.054	0.045
	Capital Structure Leverage	1.488	1.982	2.801	1.836	1.819	1.887
	ROCE	−0.064	0.086	0.189	0.111	0.145	0.141
	Gross Profit Margin	0.244	0.320	0.408	0.314	0.322	0.325
	SG&A Percentage	0.160	0.231	0.351	0.215	0.215	0.226
	Operating Income Margin	−0.024	0.058	0.110	0.082	0.081	0.076
	Days Receivable	51.550	64.592	81.122	61.211	62.725	60.980
	Days Inventory	67.767	96.801	143.782	93.304	95.031	88.883
	Days Payables	34.353	46.202	67.969	45.217	46.199	43.207
	Days Revenues in Cash	7.495	23.404	72.467	24.227	31.575	24.713
	Revenue Growth	−0.068	0.071	0.238	0.081	0.109	0.153
	Earnings Growth	−0.613	0.095	0.738	−0.034	0.125	0.295
	Assets Growth	−0.070	0.044	0.198	0.019	0.093	0.106
	Current Ratio	1.419	2.018	2.991	2.083	2.032	2.077
	Long-Term Debt to Common Equity	0.094	0.323	0.690	0.319	0.230	0.282
	Interest Coverage Ratio	−3.428	2.243	9.649	3.312	5.777	5.834
	Liabilities to Equity	0.468	0.937	1.747	0.853	0.787	0.860
	Operating Cash Flow to Current Liabilities	−0.067	0.097	0.238	0.121	0.126	0.130

		1998–2008					
		25th Percentile	**Median**	**75th Percentile**	**2008 Median**	**2007 Median**	**2006 Median**
Measuring and Control Equipment	Stock Return	–0.361	–0.034	0.448	–0.432	0.052	0.101
	Market-to-Book	1.277	2.038	3.565	1.234	2.076	2.227
	Price-Earnings	14.310	22.236	37.973	15.639	23.057	22.671
	Profit Margin for ROA	–0.264	0.021	0.089	0.028	0.035	0.058
	Total Asset Turnover	0.572	0.844	1.181	0.832	0.810	0.862
	ROA	–0.204	0.020	0.085	0.027	0.026	0.056
	Profit Margin for ROCE	–0.268	0.013	0.079	0.018	0.032	0.053
	Capital Structure Leverage	1.212	1.402	1.876	1.432	1.392	1.391
	ROCE	–0.161	0.048	0.158	0.043	0.067	0.092
	Gross Profit Margin	0.379	0.479	0.577	0.463	0.467	0.498
	SG&A Percentage	0.330	0.425	0.592	0.429	0.413	0.393
	Operating Income Margin	–0.173	0.032	0.111	0.042	0.054	0.077
	Days Receivable	55.329	67.300	84.843	65.568	67.300	61.532
	Days Inventory	88.123	129.822	179.752	128.684	112.713	114.002
	Days Payables	33.052	45.849	71.860	45.090	44.722	40.322
	Days Revenues in Cash	23.925	58.354	131.792	62.516	66.643	48.972
	Revenue Growth	–0.081	0.079	0.279	0.065	0.101	0.169
	Earnings Growth	–0.654	0.078	0.744	–0.043	0.076	0.225
	Assets Growth	–0.102	0.045	0.200	–0.012	0.060	0.108
	Current Ratio	1.786	3.002	4.879	2.966	2.950	2.834
	Long-Term Debt to Common Equity	0.015	0.100	0.416	0.166	0.055	0.088
	Interest Coverage Ratio	–16.144	1.398	15.242	3.454	3.209	7.578
	Liabilities to Equity	0.200	0.381	0.861	0.459	0.365	0.376
	Operating Cash Flow to Current Liabilities	–0.251	0.109	0.367	0.159	0.185	0.189

(Continued)

		1998–2008					
		25th Percentile	Median	75th Percentile	2008 Median	2007 Median	2006 Median
Medical Equipment	Stock Return	–0.369	0.008	0.526	–0.479	0.022	0.010
	Market-to-Book	1.602	2.839	5.229	1.699	3.027	3.256
	Price-Earnings	15.471	23.842	39.603	17.146	28.768	26.974
	Profit Margin for ROA	–0.726	–0.017	0.085	–0.079	–0.017	–0.019
	Total Asset Turnover	0.491	0.823	1.123	0.718	0.773	0.815
	ROA	–0.473	–0.044	0.081	–0.106	–0.050	–0.059
	Profit Margin for ROCE	–0.768	–0.032	0.076	–0.080	–0.020	–0.025
	Capital Structure Leverage	1.222	1.464	2.001	1.523	1.455	1.394
	ROCE	–0.494	0.021	0.165	0.003	0.026	0.042
	Gross Profit Margin	0.345	0.532	0.678	0.582	0.580	0.549
	SG&A Percentage	0.376	0.542	1.050	0.601	0.590	0.575
	Operating Income Margin	–0.717	–0.019	0.119	–0.025	–0.010	–0.047
	Days Receivable	46.847	60.144	78.924	57.756	57.681	58.122
	Days Inventory	91.522	141.533	205.313	146.249	142.970	129.169
	Days Payables	34.409	54.142	97.259	55.131	55.520	58.458
	Days Revenues in Cash	19.087	62.929	169.272	69.477	75.803	64.341
	Revenue Growth	–0.012	0.123	0.341	0.101	0.144	0.127
	Earnings Growth	–0.538	0.056	0.535	–0.007	–0.047	–0.044
	Assets Growth	–0.105	0.065	0.293	–0.044	0.106	0.158
	Current Ratio	1.729	2.881	4.953	2.701	3.063	3.086
	Long-Term Debt to Common Equity	0.025	0.137	0.409	0.254	0.156	0.130
	Interest Coverage Ratio	–23.852	–0.624	11.100	–2.359	–0.844	–1.496
	Liabilities to Equity	0.202	0.420	0.937	0.568	0.418	0.369
	Operating Cash Flow to Current Liabilities	–0.914	–0.037	0.294	–0.042	–0.029	–0.053

		1998–2008					
		25th Percentile	Median	75th Percentile	2008 Median	2007 Median	2006 Median
Non-Metallic and Industrial Metal Mining	Stock Return	–0.424	0.084	0.821	–0.712	0.149	0.524
	Market-to-Book	1.046	2.206	4.071	0.770	2.436	3.178
	Price-Earnings	9.309	16.242	26.706	6.337	16.818	13.497
	Profit Margin for ROA	–1.532	–0.006	0.163	–0.229	–0.016	0.041
	Total Asset Turnover	0.093	0.422	0.700	0.322	0.350	0.444
	ROA	–0.381	–0.120	–0.010	–0.134	–0.091	–0.120
	Profit Margin for ROCE	–1.862	–0.038	0.130	–0.334	–0.029	0.005
	Capital Structure Leverage	1.050	1.187	1.711	1.177	1.133	1.142
	ROCE	–0.384	–0.111	0.042	–0.143	–0.101	–0.115
	Gross Profit Margin	–0.361	0.239	0.393	0.178	0.329	0.236
	SG&A Percentage	0.070	0.168	0.702	0.201	0.264	0.226
	Operating Income Margin	–2.490	–0.033	0.164	–0.342	–0.032	–0.113
	Days Receivable	30.551	50.755	88.257	38.526	45.286	46.092
	Days Inventory	37.723	63.817	108.923	48.268	74.124	68.667
	Days Payables	40.717	83.332	233.739	93.179	128.918	115.118
	Days Revenues in Cash	17.705	74.153	362.242	62.668	124.198	234.143
	Revenue Growth	–0.157	0.105	0.431	0.062	0.181	0.208
	Earnings Growth	–1.429	–0.171	0.476	–0.497	–0.283	–0.145
	Assets Growth	–0.078	0.133	0.804	0.021	0.449	0.689
	Current Ratio	1.059	2.940	10.344	2.709	4.910	5.053
	Long-Term Debt to Common Equity	0.038	0.214	0.516	0.195	0.175	0.130
	Interest Coverage Ratio	–125.988	–8.347	1.797	–12.272	–10.276	–17.285
	Liabilities to Equity	0.044	0.164	0.625	0.165	0.151	0.113
	Operating Cash Flow to Current Liabilities	–2.559	–0.427	0.017	–0.350	–0.508	–0.702

(Continued)

		1998–2008					
		25th Percentile	Median	75th Percentile	2008 Median	2007 Median	2006 Median
Others	Stock Return	–0.328	0.077	0.541	–0.422	0.100	0.212
	Market-to-Book	0.982	1.645	2.980	1.099	2.590	2.426
	Price-Earnings	10.714	17.290	28.661	12.959	21.944	24.441
	Profit Margin for ROA	–0.199	0.045	0.139	0.015	0.005	0.067
	Total Asset Turnover	0.258	0.571	0.951	0.387	0.466	0.488
	ROA	–0.123	0.026	0.065	–0.012	0.006	0.032
	Profit Margin for ROCE	–0.282	0.006	0.081	–0.062	–0.017	0.013
	Capital Structure Leverage	1.705	2.648	4.739	2.635	2.674	2.597
	ROCE	–0.204	0.039	0.172	0.018	–0.038	0.063
	Gross Profit Margin	0.198	0.333	0.436	0.338	0.337	0.349
	SG&A Percentage	0.096	0.160	0.371	0.178	0.158	0.165
	Operating Income Margin	–0.156	0.070	0.173	0.068	0.036	0.073
	Days Receivable	43.090	61.632	89.176	48.129	54.439	55.492
	Days Inventory	5.131	16.413	37.694	21.821	17.462	14.241
	Days Payables	34.320	53.127	107.426	61.488	67.048	50.714
	Days Revenues in Cash	6.154	27.704	85.200	51.223	40.861	50.826
	Revenue Growth	–0.058	0.088	0.310	0.130	0.130	0.139
	Earnings Growth	–0.714	0.028	0.664	–0.065	–0.061	0.017
	Assets Growth	–0.072	0.030	0.294	0.022	0.080	0.064
	Current Ratio	0.824	1.239	1.931	1.262	1.404	1.379
	Long-Term Debt to Common Equity	0.245	0.866	1.965	1.192	1.167	0.915
	Interest Coverage Ratio	–2.967	1.211	3.092	0.615	0.862	1.281
	Liabilities to Equity	0.649	1.528	3.139	1.736	1.709	1.365
	Operating Cash Flow to Current Liabilities	–0.076	0.064	0.170	0.011	0.061	0.080

		1998–2008 25th Percentile	1998–2008 Median	1998–2008 75th Percentile	2008 Median	2007 Median	2006 Median
Personal Services	Stock Return	–0.390	–0.061	0.409	–0.386	0.112	0.003
	Market-to-Book	0.943	1.798	3.956	1.565	2.541	2.286
	Price-Earnings	14.323	20.552	30.672	17.582	24.257	22.095
	Profit Margin for ROA	–0.040	0.038	0.082	0.057	0.052	0.057
	Total Asset Turnover	0.614	1.121	1.673	1.051	1.099	1.145
	ROA	–0.052	0.038	0.079	0.057	0.055	0.057
	Profit Margin for ROCE	–0.071	0.020	0.064	0.038	0.039	0.033
	Capital Structure Leverage	1.639	2.196	3.597	2.056	1.929	2.150
	ROCE	–0.103	0.069	0.193	0.070	0.095	0.072
	Gross Profit Margin	0.224	0.368	0.560	0.460	0.443	0.427
	SG&A Percentage	0.116	0.272	0.477	0.322	0.306	0.267
	Operating Income Margin	–0.008	0.064	0.122	0.091	0.085	0.082
	Days Receivable	11.154	26.377	47.415	22.644	24.180	23.468
	Days Inventory	8.776	21.174	47.926	16.160	22.567	20.659
	Days Payables	15.488	24.692	50.120	27.212	24.596	23.246
	Days Revenues in Cash	8.685	25.251	59.654	50.146	35.168	30.552
	Revenue Growth	–0.006	0.101	0.254	0.120	0.087	0.077
	Earnings Growth	–0.731	0.140	0.701	0.027	0.241	0.102
	Assets Growth	–0.060	0.043	0.227	0.047	0.075	0.034
	Current Ratio	0.796	1.219	1.837	1.351	1.339	1.193
	Long-Term Debt to Common Equity	0.144	0.545	1.250	0.536	0.563	0.357
	Interest Coverage Ratio	–1.680	1.713	7.415	4.608	4.290	4.596
	Liabilities to Equity	0.580	1.095	2.362	0.887	0.948	0.960
	Operating Cash Flow to Current Liabilities	0.012	0.121	0.313	0.208	0.199	0.153

(Continued)

		1998–2008					
		25th Percentile	Median	75th Percentile	2008 Median	2007 Median	2006 Median
Petroleum and Natural Gas	Stock Return	–0.263	0.175	0.728	–0.521	0.048	0.046
	Market-to-Book	1.181	1.946	3.056	0.890	1.993	2.284
	Price-Earnings	9.099	14.435	25.830	7.056	16.090	14.269
	Profit Margin for ROA	–0.070	0.101	0.233	0.044	0.076	0.115
	Total Asset Turnover	0.237	0.385	0.689	0.400	0.317	0.367
	ROA	–0.054	0.047	0.107	0.013	0.029	0.060
	Profit Margin for ROCE	–0.142	0.069	0.197	0.021	0.051	0.091
	Capital Structure Leverage	1.435	1.880	2.510	1.812	1.736	1.737
	ROCE	–0.073	0.083	0.217	0.035	0.043	0.103
	Gross Profit Margin	0.248	0.522	0.730	0.428	0.524	0.521
	SG&A Percentage	0.055	0.104	0.235	0.092	0.113	0.101
	Operating Income Margin	–0.098	0.125	0.296	0.095	0.101	0.137
	Days Receivable	42.512	61.259	85.164	50.982	65.556	64.689
	Days Inventory	9.735	20.896	38.242	16.619	19.637	19.748
	Days Payables	48.930	119.059	376.679	87.201	135.564	123.941
	Days Revenues in Cash	8.019	28.144	104.300	23.734	28.394	24.236
	Revenue Growth	0.020	0.267	0.653	0.355	0.162	0.244
	Earnings Growth	–0.590	0.251	1.123	0.057	–0.117	0.120
	Assets Growth	0.000	0.172	0.514	0.099	0.183	0.286
	Current Ratio	0.652	1.086	1.943	1.230	1.067	1.173
	Long-Term Debt to Common Equity	0.210	0.470	0.873	0.449	0.459	0.411
	Interest Coverage Ratio	–1.239	3.403	10.897	1.992	2.029	4.535
	Liabilities to Equity	0.403	0.846	1.445	0.800	0.746	0.720
	Operating Cash Flow to Current Liabilities	0.029	0.256	0.474	0.272	0.248	0.318

		1998–2008					
		25th Percentile	Median	75th Percentile	2008 Median	2007 Median	2006 Median
Pharmaceutical Products	Stock Return	–0.422	–0.022	0.568	–0.469	–0.126	0.104
	Market-to-Book	2.110	3.769	7.000	2.369	3.615	3.971
	Price-Earnings	15.612	23.567	39.897	13.705	20.686	22.786
	Profit Margin for ROA	–5.593	–0.870	0.034	–0.627	–0.766	–1.122
	Total Asset Turnover	0.090	0.340	0.744	0.400	0.327	0.302
	ROA	–0.686	–0.310	–0.006	–0.390	–0.361	–0.365
	Profit Margin for ROCE	–6.264	–0.976	0.020	–0.771	–0.927	–1.262
	Capital Structure Leverage	1.197	1.451	2.069	1.565	1.510	1.522
	ROCE	–0.823	–0.262	0.161	–0.263	–0.365	–0.281
	Gross Profit Margin	–3.316	0.270	0.632	0.389	0.350	0.314
	SG&A Percentage	0.380	0.592	1.434	0.645	0.651	0.681
	Operating Income Margin	–6.098	–0.906	0.046	–0.729	–0.930	–1.310
	Days Receivable	35.352	55.603	80.567	50.809	53.385	53.940
	Days Inventory	43.181	114.955	194.906	121.466	124.238	129.420
	Days Payables	22.795	49.258	104.549	45.590	47.583	47.621
	Days Revenues in Cash	57.148	242.690	1,215.684	220.266	314.843	315.518
	Revenue Growth	–0.167	0.120	0.501	0.095	0.134	0.115
	Earnings Growth	–0.618	–0.054	0.370	0.025	–0.075	–0.113
	Assets Growth	–0.207	0.038	0.420	–0.126	0.070	0.095
	Current Ratio	1.720	3.472	6.948	2.659	3.572	3.533
	Long-Term Debt to Common Equity	0.027	0.133	0.498	0.192	0.136	0.144
	Interest Coverage Ratio	–71.629	–10.808	1.317	–8.689	–9.224	–8.697
	Liabilities to Equity	0.173	0.401	0.976	0.598	0.474	0.458
	Operating Cash Flow to Current Liabilities	–2.014	–0.559	0.087	–0.435	–0.566	–0.554

(Continued)

		1998–2008					
		25th Percentile	Median	75th Percentile	2008 Median	2007 Median	2006 Median
Precious Metals	Stock Return	–0.362	0.098	0.906	–0.568	0.171	0.682
	Market-to-Book	1.080	2.171	4.058	1.024	2.612	3.330
	Price-Earnings	12.837	24.915	51.447	21.678	30.667	23.739
	Profit Margin for ROA	–0.742	–0.102	0.143	–0.034	–0.243	–0.061
	Total Asset Turnover	0.167	0.338	0.512	0.343	0.265	0.308
	ROA	–0.293	–0.088	–0.005	–0.093	–0.091	–0.095
	Profit Margin for ROCE	–0.873	–0.149	0.114	–0.045	–0.248	–0.138
	Capital Structure Leverage	1.060	1.258	1.633	1.213	1.243	1.219
	ROCE	–0.330	–0.099	0.006	–0.108	–0.115	–0.120
	Gross Profit Margin	–0.092	0.239	0.413	0.274	0.282	0.347
	SG&A Percentage	0.084	0.145	0.384	0.190	0.171	0.170
	Operating Income Margin	–0.938	–0.097	0.116	–0.071	–0.170	–0.055
	Days Receivable	11.794	24.271	52.075	18.991	23.672	20.965
	Days Inventory	39.323	71.950	108.608	64.323	81.797	77.772
	Days Payables	42.327	83.706	245.545	79.708	95.809	100.857
	Days Revenues in Cash	36.590	104.065	280.200	53.258	148.047	179.061
	Revenue Growth	–0.179	0.071	0.425	0.298	0.149	0.391
	Earnings Growth	–1.393	–0.091	0.591	–0.190	–0.316	–0.016
	Assets Growth	–0.106	0.074	0.464	0.045	0.266	0.473
	Current Ratio	0.915	2.496	7.955	2.337	3.812	3.959
	Long-Term Debt to Common Equity	0.047	0.156	0.412	0.120	0.157	0.112
	Interest Coverage Ratio	–51.813	–5.454	1.396	–4.571	–9.333	–6.462
	Liabilities to Equity	0.050	0.226	0.566	0.223	0.208	0.194
	Operating Cash Flow to Current Liabilities	–1.572	–0.277	0.089	–0.295	–0.441	–0.459

		1998–2008 25th Percentile	1998–2008 Median	1998–2008 75th Percentile	2008 Median	2007 Median	2006 Median
Printing & Publishing	Stock Return	–0.290	–0.014	0.228	–0.522	–0.155	0.002
	Market-to-Book	1.257	2.265	3.999	1.140	1.779	1.827
	Price-Earnings	12.343	17.868	25.002	9.166	14.555	17.446
	Profit Margin for ROA	–0.040	0.066	0.124	0.002	0.070	0.070
	Total Asset Turnover	0.503	0.779	1.100	0.675	0.672	0.696
	ROA	–0.030	0.046	0.087	0.013	0.048	0.051
	Profit Margin for ROCE	–0.073	0.046	0.096	–0.005	0.052	0.045
	Capital Structure Leverage	1.692	2.274	3.817	2.275	2.287	2.206
	ROCE	–0.067	0.103	0.214	–0.002	0.020	0.091
	Gross Profit Margin	0.379	0.509	0.603	0.510	0.519	0.503
	SG&A Percentage	0.270	0.369	0.474	0.382	0.378	0.358
	Operating Income Margin	0.036	0.116	0.167	0.098	0.128	0.123
	Days Receivable	39.271	50.226	68.112	52.119	52.477	48.380
	Days Inventory	9.013	20.522	76.070	25.829	17.736	15.473
	Days Payables	29.694	49.156	79.630	49.512	51.105	43.330
	Days Revenues in Cash	4.170	10.506	35.441	11.011	11.657	8.976
	Revenue Growth	–0.050	0.024	0.121	–0.049	0.012	0.034
	Earnings Growth	–0.691	–0.019	0.442	–0.667	0.078	–0.079
	Assets Growth	–0.081	0.008	0.118	–0.087	0.017	0.024
	Current Ratio	0.826	1.167	1.816	1.235	1.302	1.169
	Long-Term Debt to Common Equity	0.310	0.607	1.469	0.964	0.837	0.735
	Interest Coverage Ratio	–0.241	2.594	6.895	1.100	2.286	1.838
	Liabilities to Equity	0.667	1.317	3.124	1.636	1.508	1.274
	Operating Cash Flow to Current Liabilities	0.030	0.123	0.238	0.142	0.127	0.119

(Continued)

		1998–2008					
		25th Percentile	Median	75th Percentile	2008 Median	2007 Median	2006 Median
Real Estate	Stock Return	–0.224	0.045	0.391	–0.473	–0.044	0.151
	Market-to-Book	0.789	1.277	2.435	0.892	1.887	2.200
	Price-Earnings	8.180	14.544	26.547	12.463	22.587	19.993
	Profit Margin for ROA	0.025	0.163	0.332	0.101	0.187	0.196
	Total Asset Turnover	0.143	0.237	0.505	0.214	0.211	0.236
	ROA	0.002	0.044	0.075	0.022	0.045	0.054
	Profit Margin for ROCE	–0.068	0.059	0.177	0.025	0.084	0.089
	Capital Structure Leverage	1.690	2.720	4.503	2.596	2.574	2.665
	ROCE	–0.019	0.072	0.169	0.041	0.058	0.094
	Gross Profit Margin	0.199	0.413	0.598	0.394	0.419	0.416
	SG&A Percentage	0.082	0.185	0.465	0.224	0.188	0.156
	Operating Income Margin	–0.002	0.148	0.328	0.099	0.156	0.168
	Days Receivable	11.810	37.481	89.480	44.794	46.327	30.955
	Days Inventory	33.723	178.956	503.248	166.287	164.274	169.537
	Days Payables	27.416	65.936	143.407	67.433	64.286	59.168
	Days Revenues in Cash	16.357	44.188	162.060	62.843	60.796	56.154
	Revenue Growth	–0.102	0.066	0.312	0.017	0.050	0.113
	Earnings Growth	–0.670	0.018	0.845	–0.457	–0.038	–0.035
	Assets Growth	–0.058	0.041	0.195	–0.022	0.108	0.110
	Current Ratio	0.701	1.311	2.648	1.630	1.784	1.621
	Long-Term Debt to Common Equity	0.388	1.083	2.531	0.809	0.893	0.916
	Interest Coverage Ratio	0.634	1.672	4.305	1.033	1.911	3.164
	Liabilities to Equity	0.581	1.545	3.195	1.537	1.513	1.540
	Operating Cash Flow to Current Liabilities	–0.050	0.043	0.131	0.009	0.034	0.041

		1998–2008					
		25th Percentile	Median	75th Percentile	2008 Median	2007 Median	2006 Median
Recreation	Stock Return	–0.449	–0.098	0.333	–0.579	–0.212	0.102
	Market-to-Book	0.858	1.593	2.851	1.025	1.437	2.050
	Price-Earnings	9.516	15.244	24.469	13.237	13.414	21.053
	Profit Margin for ROA	–0.092	0.024	0.071	–0.042	0.012	0.042
	Total Asset Turnover	0.844	1.175	1.598	1.140	1.088	0.996
	ROA	–0.196	0.024	0.089	–0.059	0.010	0.044
	Profit Margin for ROCE	–0.111	0.013	0.064	–0.037	0.019	0.027
	Capital Structure Leverage	1.344	1.850	3.068	1.807	1.618	1.677
	ROCE	–0.137	0.076	0.207	–0.061	0.081	0.088
	Gross Profit Margin	0.272	0.372	0.466	0.357	0.360	0.378
	SG&A Percentage	0.213	0.302	0.436	0.346	0.299	0.295
	Operating Income Margin	–0.063	0.040	0.098	0.005	0.048	0.056
	Days Receivable	37.572	58.356	75.283	57.139	58.671	55.525
	Days Inventory	59.949	91.227	133.425	99.000	94.782	95.589
	Days Payables	29.661	44.674	68.009	45.394	44.022	45.259
	Days Revenues in Cash	6.721	26.388	65.844	29.003	33.183	39.084
	Revenue Growth	–0.105	0.032	0.218	–0.012	0.051	0.091
	Earnings Growth	–0.848	–0.058	0.642	–0.469	–0.145	0.007
	Assets Growth	–0.131	0.021	0.196	–0.047	0.045	0.111
	Current Ratio	1.231	2.014	3.384	1.946	2.042	2.133
	Long-Term Debt to Common Equity	0.087	0.322	0.920	0.360	0.297	0.309
	Interest Coverage Ratio	–6.288	1.003	6.532	–10.652	0.574	1.634
	Liabilities to Equity	0.323	0.841	1.931	0.957	0.634	0.607
	Operating Cash Flow to Current Liabilities	–0.124	0.084	0.285	0.043	0.103	0.072

(Continued)

		1998–2008					
		25th Percentile	Median	75th Percentile	2008 Median	2007 Median	2006 Median
Restaurants, Hotels, Motels	Stock Return	–0.304	–0.003	0.338	–0.463	–0.189	0.095
	Market-to-Book	0.905	1.616	2.979	1.271	2.031	2.738
	Price-Earnings	11.690	17.012	25.926	13.571	20.800	21.423
	Profit Margin for ROA	–0.006	0.036	0.065	0.012	0.037	0.042
	Total Asset Turnover	0.792	1.421	1.887	1.425	1.472	1.518
	ROA	–0.009	0.046	0.086	0.012	0.044	0.064
	Profit Margin for ROCE	–0.032	0.019	0.054	0.003	0.024	0.031
	Capital Structure Leverage	1.639	2.130	3.492	2.489	2.149	2.105
	ROCE	–0.063	0.075	0.169	0.014	0.067	0.087
	Gross Profit Margin	0.154	0.201	0.289	0.202	0.202	0.204
	SG&A Percentage	0.072	0.100	0.167	0.105	0.104	0.103
	Operating Income Margin	0.016	0.055	0.094	0.049	0.060	0.065
	Days Receivable	2.566	5.888	15.353	7.189	7.019	6.518
	Days Inventory	3.902	6.611	11.884	6.146	6.673	6.621
	Days Payables	13.380	18.555	29.912	17.985	17.654	18.763
	Days Revenues in Cash	4.746	11.065	25.887	11.178	12.164	14.288
	Revenue Growth	–0.024	0.060	0.154	0.037	0.067	0.066
	Earnings Growth	–0.606	0.068	0.593	–0.414	–0.066	0.026
	Assets Growth	–0.052	0.032	0.140	0.008	0.062	0.057
	Current Ratio	0.479	0.765	1.150	0.791	0.788	0.846
	Long-Term Debt to Common Equity	0.270	0.583	1.471	0.774	0.675	0.480
	Interest Coverage Ratio	0.045	1.716	5.790	0.600	1.787	2.726
	Liabilities to Equity	0.618	1.114	2.544	1.642	1.332	1.028
	Operating Cash Flow to Current Liabilities	0.051	0.156	0.349	0.126	0.163	0.203

		1998–2008					
		25th Percentile	Median	75th Percentile	2008 Median	2007 Median	2006 Median
Retail	Stock Return	−0.343	−0.001	0.385	−0.446	−0.221	0.092
	Market-to-Book	0.927	1.696	3.093	1.073	1.831	2.309
	Price-Earnings	11.334	16.513	24.552	12.110	15.424	18.775
	Profit Margin for ROA	0.001	0.024	0.046	0.017	0.029	0.029
	Total Asset Turnover	1.515	2.056	2.727	1.888	1.906	2.084
	ROA	0.003	0.053	0.091	0.041	0.055	0.060
	Profit Margin for ROCE	−0.010	0.017	0.040	0.013	0.021	0.022
	Capital Structure Leverage	1.630	2.121	3.055	2.179	2.155	2.028
	ROCE	−0.031	0.097	0.182	0.071	0.103	0.111
	Gross Profit Margin	0.239	0.321	0.403	0.318	0.324	0.330
	SG&A Percentage	0.208	0.266	0.353	0.270	0.270	0.263
	Operating Income Margin	0.010	0.039	0.070	0.035	0.041	0.044
	Days Receivable	3.620	8.307	23.314	7.314	8.238	7.703
	Days Inventory	41.391	73.299	118.215	68.606	70.461	69.759
	Days Payables	24.224	35.219	51.892	34.365	36.110	34.715
	Days Revenues in Cash	3.514	8.791	23.763	10.597	8.925	9.307
	Revenue Growth	0.007	0.082	0.185	0.019	0.062	0.105
	Earnings Growth	−0.500	0.106	0.543	−0.208	0.031	0.092
	Assets Growth	−0.027	0.062	0.182	−0.001	0.049	0.067
	Current Ratio	1.189	1.651	2.449	1.665	1.634	1.616
	Long-Term Debt to Common Equity	0.123	0.395	0.928	0.454	0.420	0.359
	Interest Coverage Ratio	0.312	3.106	11.562	2.269	3.477	4.510
	Liabilities to Equity	0.622	1.111	2.066	1.223	1.197	1.072
	Operating Cash Flow to Current Liabilities	0.045	0.147	0.294	0.158	0.162	0.162

(Continued)

		1998–2008					
		25th Percentile	Median	75th Percentile	2008 Median	2007 Median	2006 Median
Rubber and Plastic Products	Stock Return	–0.385	–0.056	0.338	–0.430	–0.066	0.150
	Market-to-Book	0.888	1.563	2.637	1.087	1.793	2.013
	Price-Earnings	9.959	14.961	21.619	12.500	17.260	17.228
	Profit Margin for ROA	–0.015	0.031	0.069	0.024	0.034	0.036
	Total Asset Turnover	0.916	1.169	1.493	1.217	1.161	1.161
	ROA	–0.035	0.038	0.078	0.022	0.046	0.050
	Profit Margin for ROCE	–0.050	0.010	0.051	0.012	0.022	0.015
	Capital Structure Leverage	1.689	2.441	4.032	2.221	2.206	2.293
	ROCE	–0.066	0.082	0.192	0.104	0.137	0.123
	Gross Profit Margin	0.186	0.265	0.332	0.263	0.273	0.276
	SG&A Percentage	0.105	0.176	0.248	0.171	0.171	0.171
	Operating Income Margin	0.015	0.056	0.095	0.056	0.064	0.065
	Days Receivable	40.741	51.020	64.032	44.420	49.571	50.117
	Days Inventory	42.207	61.112	84.221	61.712	56.333	61.856
	Days Payables	31.046	39.399	53.031	35.734	37.274	38.689
	Days Revenues in Cash	2.755	9.796	31.020	15.535	15.834	13.370
	Revenue Growth	–0.045	0.041	0.167	0.064	0.032	0.046
	Earnings Growth	–0.837	0.074	0.723	–0.104	0.053	0.422
	Assets Growth	–0.081	0.006	0.119	0.000	0.030	0.021
	Current Ratio	1.130	1.651	2.348	1.733	1.692	1.868
	Long-Term Debt to Common Equity	0.245	0.646	1.364	0.448	0.369	0.460
	Interest Coverage Ratio	–0.085	1.393	4.406	1.236	2.418	2.188
	Liabilities to Equity	0.618	1.399	2.818	1.275	1.075	1.043
	Operating Cash Flow to Current Liabilities	0.010	0.094	0.205	0.086	0.105	0.115

		1998–2008					
		25th Percentile	Median	75th Percentile	2008 Median	2007 Median	2006 Median
Shipbuilding, Railroad Equipment	Stock Return	–0.288	0.037	0.338	–0.400	–0.190	0.070
	Market-to-Book	1.195	1.958	3.056	1.249	2.019	2.886
	Price-Earnings	11.017	16.845	21.653	11.934	16.055	16.907
	Profit Margin for ROA	0.004	0.036	0.070	0.062	0.048	0.055
	Total Asset Turnover	1.006	1.202	1.506	1.197	1.287	1.232
	ROA	0.003	0.052	0.085	0.074	0.068	0.087
	Profit Margin for ROCE	0.007	0.039	0.068	0.043	0.053	0.054
	Capital Structure Leverage	1.873	2.371	3.897	2.341	2.228	2.210
	ROCE	0.035	0.116	0.197	0.093	0.132	0.200
	Gross Profit Margin	0.127	0.187	0.267	0.183	0.185	0.191
	SG&A Percentage	0.071	0.110	0.158	0.083	0.103	0.094
	Operating Income Margin	0.029	0.075	0.103	0.065	0.088	0.089
	Days Receivable	20.868	34.939	50.656	38.725	26.521	32.689
	Days Inventory	43.891	61.952	81.941	71.657	61.121	61.952
	Days Payables	27.310	36.180	50.789	34.647	36.928	34.869
	Days Revenues in Cash	8.493	20.600	38.762	17.983	27.579	24.330
	Revenue Growth	–0.062	0.104	0.228	0.004	0.108	0.093
	Earnings Growth	–0.411	0.116	0.727	–0.135	0.059	0.328
	Assets Growth	–0.019	0.063	0.176	0.068	0.025	0.146
	Current Ratio	1.177	1.674	2.380	1.953	2.154	1.996
	Long-Term Debt to Common Equity	0.180	0.470	1.012	0.713	0.243	0.282
	Interest Coverage Ratio	0.647	3.146	6.907	4.350	5.622	6.574
	Liabilities to Equity	0.882	1.342	2.496	1.510	1.218	1.277
	Operating Cash Flow to Current Liabilities	0.041	0.136	0.221	0.138	0.215	0.121

(Continued)

		1998–2008					
		25th Percentile	Median	75th Percentile	2008 Median	2007 Median	2006 Median
Shipping Containers	Stock Return	–0.208	0.074	0.333	–0.347	0.208	0.325
	Market-to-Book	1.021	1.762	3.282	2.001	2.724	3.139
	Price-Earnings	11.995	15.343	21.340	13.650	15.933	15.799
	Profit Margin for ROA	0.018	0.045	0.070	0.050	0.050	0.042
	Total Asset Turnover	0.849	1.037	1.224	1.171	1.134	1.093
	ROA	0.004	0.040	0.069	0.048	0.047	0.036
	Profit Margin for ROCE	–0.006	0.021	0.044	0.029	0.038	0.017
	Capital Structure Leverage	2.729	3.823	5.593	4.200	4.070	4.124
	ROCE	–0.022	0.083	0.239	0.130	0.159	0.059
	Gross Profit Margin	0.166	0.223	0.272	0.212	0.212	0.212
	SG&A Percentage	0.050	0.098	0.132	0.090	0.095	0.097
	Operating Income Margin	0.056	0.080	0.096	0.085	0.085	0.073
	Days Receivable	32.350	39.482	46.797	35.780	39.007	39.749
	Days Inventory	43.547	53.392	77.320	53.392	45.798	45.384
	Days Payables	33.285	44.027	53.909	47.793	45.507	43.809
	Days Revenues in Cash	2.665	6.767	16.390	17.568	16.337	13.528
	Revenue Growth	–0.004	0.046	0.108	0.042	0.096	0.097
	Earnings Growth	–0.550	0.054	0.716	0.027	0.140	0.260
	Assets Growth	–0.040	0.016	0.096	0.011	0.048	0.080
	Current Ratio	1.119	1.369	1.664	1.220	1.303	1.429
	Long-Term Debt to Common Equity	0.836	1.430	2.535	1.363	1.681	1.679
	Interest Coverage Ratio	0.531	1.592	2.938	2.350	1.370	1.329
	Liabilities to Equity	1.661	2.741	4.196	3.401	3.109	2.666
	Operating Cash Flow to Current Liabilities	0.052	0.104	0.162	0.095	0.084	0.090

		1998–2008					
		25th Percentile	Median	75th Percentile	2008 Median	2007 Median	2006 Median
Steel Works	Stock Return	–0.382	0.036	0.581	–0.577	0.284	0.511
	Market-to-Book	0.728	1.294	2.136	1.034	2.143	1.986
	Price-Earnings	7.220	11.145	18.886	7.100	12.538	10.516
	Profit Margin for ROA	–0.028	0.038	0.082	0.044	0.061	0.070
	Total Asset Turnover	0.786	1.078	1.442	1.179	1.139	1.318
	ROA	–0.033	0.042	0.096	0.074	0.094	0.100
	Profit Margin for ROCE	–0.050	0.021	0.066	0.036	0.056	0.060
	Capital Structure Leverage	1.796	2.328	3.180	1.993	2.089	2.124
	ROCE	–0.078	0.087	0.220	0.115	0.180	0.206
	Gross Profit Margin	0.117	0.179	0.269	0.195	0.204	0.214
	SG&A Percentage	0.052	0.079	0.134	0.065	0.071	0.066
	Operating Income Margin	–0.001	0.054	0.108	0.088	0.091	0.103
	Days Receivable	37.211	46.716	57.551	38.805	44.096	41.238
	Days Inventory	54.214	76.134	102.631	66.102	71.154	67.981
	Days Payables	28.035	37.960	53.565	32.198	35.560	33.263
	Days Revenues in Cash	3.535	10.566	28.178	21.129	19.987	12.964
	Revenue Growth	–0.063	0.077	0.267	0.143	0.109	0.220
	Earnings Growth	–0.825	0.033	0.763	–0.088	0.019	0.472
	Assets Growth	–0.076	0.034	0.193	0.029	0.177	0.178
	Current Ratio	1.293	1.882	2.700	2.068	2.224	2.162
	Long-Term Debt to Common Equity	0.212	0.491	0.994	0.287	0.364	0.305
	Interest Coverage Ratio	–0.608	2.426	8.008	4.983	7.583	7.628
	Liabilities to Equity	0.718	1.263	2.099	1.037	0.929	0.893
	Operating Cash Flow to Current Liabilities	0.000	0.091	0.217	0.175	0.151	0.128

(Continued)

		1998–2008					
		25th Percentile	**Median**	**75th Percentile**	**2008 Median**	**2007 Median**	**2006 Median**
Textiles	Stock Return	–0.495	–0.142	0.235	–0.588	–0.214	0.019
	Market-to-Book	0.438	0.840	1.298	0.924	1.031	1.294
	Price-Earnings	7.175	12.860	19.556	20.370	17.000	18.632
	Profit Margin for ROA	–0.029	0.022	0.058	–0.097	0.021	0.005
	Total Asset Turnover	0.985	1.194	1.481	1.282	1.242	1.217
	ROA	–0.032	0.025	0.062	–0.101	0.021	0.007
	Profit Margin for ROCE	–0.061	0.001	0.037	–0.090	0.008	0.002
	Capital Structure Leverage	1.749	2.242	3.518	2.092	2.021	2.063
	ROCE	–0.167	0.019	0.113	–0.155	0.014	–0.017
	Gross Profit Margin	0.146	0.221	0.309	0.245	0.233	0.209
	SG&A Percentage	0.094	0.137	0.221	0.165	0.153	0.152
	Operating Income Margin	0.006	0.052	0.086	0.060	0.056	0.039
	Days Receivable	40.463	50.826	61.968	43.570	44.804	44.400
	Days Inventory	59.508	76.863	104.998	70.197	70.764	68.329
	Days Payables	24.183	29.067	37.779	32.705	32.158	26.784
	Days Revenues in Cash	2.021	8.851	23.021	14.050	17.106	14.815
	Revenue Growth	–0.113	–0.017	0.073	–0.011	0.010	0.039
	Earnings Growth	–1.404	–0.177	0.545	–2.922	–0.514	–0.192
	Assets Growth	–0.144	–0.043	0.045	–0.182	0.008	0.016
	Current Ratio	1.718	2.354	3.061	2.673	2.539	2.770
	Long-Term Debt to Common Equity	0.247	0.638	1.235	0.790	0.562	0.521
	Interest Coverage Ratio	–0.861	1.373	3.393	–2.449	2.054	0.273
	Liabilities to Equity	0.740	1.222	2.384	1.435	0.951	0.968
	Operating Cash Flow to Current Liabilities	0.042	0.115	0.204	0.102	0.114	0.108

		1998–2008					
		25th Percentile	Median	75th Percentile	2008 Median	2007 Median	2006 Median
Tobacco Products	Stock Return	–0.039	0.210	0.409	–0.170	0.174	0.251
	Market-to-Book	3.072	5.748	13.540	10.977	10.836	10.420
	Price-Earnings	11.067	14.271	17.245	13.066	17.022	15.297
	Profit Margin for ROA	0.082	0.186	0.270	0.209	0.274	0.254
	Total Asset Turnover	0.491	0.699	1.204	0.496	0.546	0.553
	ROA	0.065	0.116	0.258	0.098	0.143	0.134
	Profit Margin for ROCE	0.042	0.147	0.224	0.177	0.234	0.171
	Capital Structure Leverage	2.526	3.381	4.475	3.817	2.776	3.293
	ROCE	–0.295	0.297	0.563	0.531	0.371	0.324
	Gross Profit Margin	0.423	0.494	0.603	0.481	0.549	0.493
	SG&A Percentage	0.213	0.266	0.336	0.222	0.233	0.246
	Operating Income Margin	0.160	0.261	0.388	0.308	0.381	0.305
	Days Receivable	11.554	22.723	56.117	40.866	27.844	15.502
	Days Inventory	96.535	173.412	238.855	128.747	223.261	169.047
	Days Payables	26.991	37.954	58.444	33.816	57.588	31.432
	Days Revenues in Cash	22.693	39.155	88.091	115.437	59.941	48.020
	Revenue Growth	–0.019	0.046	0.105	0.014	0.067	0.026
	Earnings Growth	–0.151	0.076	0.289	–0.064	0.103	0.157
	Assets Growth	–0.056	0.055	0.177	–0.056	0.050	0.060
	Current Ratio	1.140	1.558	2.178	1.279	1.938	1.664
	Long-Term Debt to Common Equity	0.609	1.023	2.008	1.518	0.737	0.960
	Interest Coverage Ratio	3.772	7.011	13.753	8.312	8.097	7.858
	Liabilities to Equity	1.653	2.509	5.676	3.396	2.168	2.107
	Operating Cash Flow to Current Liabilities	0.081	0.144	0.263	0.142	0.219	0.199

(Continued)

		1998–2008					
		25th Percentile	Median	75th Percentile	2008 Median	2007 Median	2006 Median
Transportation	Stock Return	–0.256	0.058	0.421	–0.455	0.070	0.153
	Market-to-Book	0.985	1.530	2.565	1.016	1.770	1.943
	Price-Earnings	9.225	15.000	23.631	9.368	16.107	14.122
	Profit Margin for ROA	0.012	0.052	0.134	0.051	0.081	0.078
	Total Asset Turnover	0.416	0.860	1.615	0.724	0.722	0.770
	ROA	0.013	0.053	0.088	0.050	0.062	0.067
	Profit Margin for ROCE	–0.001	0.036	0.103	0.032	0.047	0.057
	Capital Structure Leverage	1.838	2.522	3.609	2.571	2.415	2.335
	ROCE	0.011	0.105	0.190	0.091	0.128	0.131
	Gross Profit Margin	0.127	0.236	0.390	0.260	0.269	0.271
	SG&A Percentage	0.067	0.106	0.165	0.096	0.102	0.095
	Operating Income Margin	0.024	0.075	0.171	0.085	0.100	0.097
	Days Receivable	18.860	36.367	49.885	28.220	30.785	33.759
	Days Inventory	4.516	10.061	18.089	9.636	10.673	9.572
	Days Payables	16.188	28.941	48.712	25.649	28.436	29.356
	Days Revenues in Cash	5.454	18.891	50.961	22.139	21.843	20.475
	Revenue Growth	0.013	0.100	0.231	0.119	0.117	0.127
	Earnings Growth	–0.500	0.097	0.678	–0.225	0.103	0.182
	Assets Growth	–0.019	0.068	0.229	0.037	0.120	0.113
	Current Ratio	0.838	1.206	1.818	1.192	1.269	1.306
	Long-Term Debt to Common Equity	0.341	0.779	1.542	0.973	0.805	0.643
	Interest Coverage Ratio	0.894	2.922	7.433	2.485	3.564	3.693
	Liabilities to Equity	0.812	1.523	2.600	1.622	1.531	1.331
	Operating Cash Flow to Current Liabilities	0.057	0.142	0.272	0.151	0.144	0.174

		1998–2008					
		25th Percentile	Median	75th Percentile	2008 Median	2007 Median	2006 Median
Utilities	Stock Return	–0.059	0.114	0.319	–0.185	0.103	0.204
	Market-to-Book	1.293	1.643	2.153	1.356	1.890	1.941
	Price-Earnings	12.826	15.818	20.299	12.900	17.710	17.579
	Profit Margin for ROA	0.070	0.108	0.159	0.100	0.107	0.104
	Total Asset Turnover	0.324	0.434	0.572	0.433	0.435	0.434
	ROA	0.038	0.049	0.061	0.045	0.047	0.047
	Profit Margin for ROCE	0.039	0.070	0.106	0.071	0.070	0.070
	Capital Structure Leverage	2.866	3.358	4.132	3.319	3.246	3.330
	ROCE	0.076	0.110	0.142	0.101	0.109	0.106
	Gross Profit Margin	0.173	0.246	0.342	0.224	0.233	0.234
	SG&A Percentage	0.045	0.101	0.181	0.086	0.090	0.085
	Operating Income Margin	0.103	0.154	0.224	0.140	0.148	0.142
	Days Receivable	31.745	42.836	56.016	41.349	42.352	43.870
	Days Inventory	12.297	22.904	36.118	23.664	25.142	24.581
	Days Payables	31.085	42.596	61.584	41.346	42.088	44.294
	Days Revenues in Cash	1.834	5.438	17.989	5.633	4.701	5.010
	Revenue Growth	–0.008	0.063	0.167	0.080	0.058	0.051
	Earnings Growth	–0.145	0.055	0.331	0.034	0.081	0.078
	Assets Growth	–0.002	0.051	0.121	0.088	0.056	0.047
	Current Ratio	0.665	0.887	1.151	0.957	0.901	0.952
	Long-Term Debt to Common Equity	0.743	1.015	1.388	0.992	0.958	0.959
	Interest Coverage Ratio	2.215	3.132	4.169	3.274	3.336	3.188
	Liabilities to Equity	1.750	2.287	2.990	2.321	2.175	2.259
	Operating Cash Flow to Current Liabilities	0.069	0.101	0.139	0.095	0.103	0.104

(Continued)

		1998–2008					
		25th Percentile	Median	75th Percentile	2008 Median	2007 Median	2006 Median
Wholesale	Stock Return	–0.338	0.009	0.434	–0.482	0.030	0.105
	Market-to-Book	0.810	1.392	2.488	0.992	1.774	1.896
	Price-Earnings	9.000	14.175	21.446	10.118	14.967	16.811
	Profit Margin for ROA	–0.004	0.020	0.046	0.020	0.029	0.031
	Total Asset Turnover	1.320	2.041	3.019	2.155	2.094	2.110
	ROA	–0.017	0.046	0.083	0.051	0.059	0.061
	Profit Margin for ROCE	–0.013	0.012	0.035	0.014	0.022	0.024
	Capital Structure Leverage	1.819	2.489	3.570	2.260	2.291	2.296
	ROCE	–0.038	0.096	0.180	0.106	0.125	0.133
	Gross Profit Margin	0.117	0.203	0.305	0.193	0.187	0.192
	SG&A Percentage	0.089	0.161	0.250	0.142	0.140	0.144
	Operating Income Margin	0.005	0.029	0.065	0.032	0.041	0.040
	Days Receivable	29.745	43.500	56.904	41.527	41.224	41.543
	Days Inventory	26.816	52.592	88.476	43.058	48.238	49.354
	Days Payables	26.470	39.168	57.219	36.733	41.556	40.153
	Days Revenues in Cash	2.139	5.842	20.494	7.380	6.134	6.714
	Revenue Growth	–0.044	0.075	0.211	0.064	0.079	0.095
	Earnings Growth	–0.596	0.106	0.656	–0.126	0.123	0.232
	Assets Growth	–0.061	0.055	0.192	0.011	0.072	0.089
	Current Ratio	1.236	1.687	2.481	1.763	1.824	1.764
	Long-Term Debt to Common Equity	0.159	0.450	1.056	0.438	0.345	0.333
	Interest Coverage Ratio	–0.028	2.782	8.564	3.208	4.675	4.757
	Liabilities to Equity	0.753	1.426	2.565	1.245	1.241	1.228
	Operating Cash Flow to Current Liabilities	–0.028	0.082	0.196	0.113	0.100	0.094

Index

A

B

C

D

E

G

Q

R

S

T